Explanation of Terms (continued)

OAS-L	OAS's definition of Latin America (*see* SALA, 24-1000)		PTP	percent of total population
OECD	Organization for Economic Cooperation and Development		R-GAP	relative gap
			SDRs	Special Drawing Rights (IMF's currency)
OECS	Organization of Eastern Caribbean States (*see* SALA, 24-1000)		SNA	system of national accounts
			T	thousand (i.e., 000 omitted)
OPEC	Organization of Petroleum Exporting Countries		T1 (T2, etc.)	territory and its number among listed territories
p (pp)	page(s)			
PC	percentage change		TJ	Terajoules
PHI	per hundred inhabitants		U	unit
PHTI	per hundred thousand inhabitants		UN	United Nations
PI	per inhabitant		US	U.S. currency
PIB	*producto interno bruto* (English = GDP)		U.S. or USA	United States of America
PTI	per thousand inhabitants		WDC	Washington, D.C.
P10I	per ten thousand inhabitants		YA	yearly arithmetic m
			YE	year end

Sources

Sources frequently cited. (Abbreviation generally shows agency followed by title of publication or se
Other sources appear in tables throughout.

ADEMA	*See* ECLA		IBRD	International Bank for Reconstruction and Development (*see* WB)
AE	Anuario Estadístico			
AR	Annual Report		ICAO	International Civil Aviation Organization
BDM	Banco de México		ICAO-DS-B	Digest of Statistics, *Bulletin*
BID	Banco Interamericano de Desarrollo (*see* IDB)		ICAO-DS-T	Digest of Statistics, *Traffic: Commercial Air Carriers*
C/CAA	Caribbean/Central American Action, *Caribbean Data Book*		ICAO-DS-AT	Digest of Statistics, *Airport Traffic*
CELADE	Centro Latinoamericano de Demografía (Santiago)		IDB	Inter-American Development Bank (WDC)
			IDB-AR	*Annual Report*
CELADE-BD	*Boletín Demográfico*		IDB-SPTF	Social Progress Trust Fund, *Socio-Economic Progress in Latin America* (1961–71) and *Economic and Social Progress in Latin America* (1972-)
CEPAL	Comisión Económica para América Latina (*see* ECLA)			
COHA	Council on Hemispheric Affairs, *Washington Report on the Hemisphere*		ILO	International Labour Office (Geneva)
Colombia-DANE	Departamento Administrativo Nacional		ILO-YLS	*Yearbook of Labor Statistics*
Cuba-CEE	Comité Estatal de Estadística		IMF	International Monetary Fund (WDC)
DGE	Dirección General de Estadística		IMF-BPS	*Balance of Payment Statistics*
DGEC	Dirección General de Estadística y Censos		IMF-BPS-Y	*Balance of Payment Statistics Yearbook*
ECLA	Economic Commission for Latin America (Santiago)		IMF-DOT	*Direction of Trade Statistics*
ECLA-ADEMA	*Agua, Desarrollo y Medio Ambiente* (1977)		IMF-DOT-Y	*Yearbook*
ECLA-AE	*Anuario Estadístico de América Latina*		IMF-GFSY	*Government Finance Statistics Yearbook*
ECLA-BPAL	*Balance de Pagos 1950-77*		IMF-IFS	*International Financial Statistics*
ECLA-CC	Cuadernos de la CEPAL		IMF-IFS-S	*IFS Supplement* (No. 1, 1981–). (*See also* IFS-Y)
ECLA-CEC	Cuadernos Estadísticos de la CEPAL		IMF-IFS-Y	*Yearbook* (entitled IFS-S from 1961 through 1978)
ECLA-D	Document			
ECLA-EIC	*Estudios e Informes de la CEPAL*		INE	Instituto Nacional de Estadística
ECLA-N	*Notas sobre la Economía y el Desarrollo*		INEC	Instituto Nacional de Estadística y Censos
ECLA-S	*Economic Survey of Latin America*		JLP	José López Portillo (Mexico City)
ECLA-SHCAL	*Series Históricas del Crecimiento 1900-76* (1978)		JLP-AE-H	*Anexo Estadístico Histórico*
ECLA-SP	Preliminary version of ECLA-S		JLP-AP-E	*Anexo de Política Económica*
ECLA-SY	*Statistical Yearbook* (*see* ECLA-AE)		Mexico-BNCE	Banco Nacional de Comercio Exterior
EYB	*Europa Year Book*		BNCE-CE	*Comercio Exterior*
FAO	UN, Food and Agriculture Organization (Rome)		Mexico-NAFINSA	Nacional Financiera, S.A.
FAO-FY	*Fertilizer Yearbook*		NAFINSA-EMC	*La Economía Mexicana en Cifras*
FAO-PY	*Production Yearbook* (1958–)		NAFINSA-MV	*Mercado de Valores*
FAO-SFA	*State of Food and Agriculture*		OAS	Organization of American States (WDC)
FAO-TY	*Trade Yearbook* (1958-)		OAS-A	*Latin America's Development and the Alliance for Progress* (1973)
FAO-YFP	*Yearbook of Forestry Products*			
FAO-YFS	*Yearbook of Fishery Statistics*		OAS-DB	*Datos Básicos de Población*
FAO-YFSCL	*Catches and Landings*		OASL	OAS's definition of L. (*see* SALA, 24–1000)
FAO-YFSFC	*Fishery Commodities*		OAS-SB	*Statistical Bulletin*
IASI	OAS, Inter-American Statistical Institute		PAHO	Pan American Health Organization (WDC)
IASI-AC	*América en Cifras*		PAHO-F	*Facts on Health Progress*
IASI-BE	*Boletín Estadístico*		PAHO-HC	*Health Conditions in the Americas*
IASI-C	*Características de la Estructura Demográfica*		PC	Population Council (NYC)

STATISTICAL ABSTRACT OF LATIN AMERICA

Series editor

JAMES W. WILKIE

SALA PUBLICATION HISTORY

Edition	Editors	Year of Publication
1 (1955)	[Robert N. Burr and Russell H. Fitzgibbon], 8 tables	1956
2 (1956)	[John D. Rees], 10 tables	1957
3 (1957)	[Berl Golomb], 18 tables	1959
4 (1960)	[Berl Golomb], 20 tables	1960
5 (1961)	[Berl Golomb], 23 tables	1961
6 (1962)	Berl Golomb and Ronald H. Dolkart, 51 tables	1963
7 (1963)	Donald S. Castro, Berl Golomb, and C. Breyer, 59 tables	1963
8 (1964)	Juan Gómez-Quiñones, 78 tables	1965
9 (1965)	Norris B. Lyle and Richard A. Calman, 102 tables	1966
10 (1966)	C. Paul Roberts and Takako Kohda, 81 tables	1967
11 (1967)	C. Paul Roberts and Takako Kohda, 95 tables	1968
12 (1968)	C. Paul Roberts and Takako Kohda Karplus, 102 tables	1969
13 (1969)	Kenneth Ruddle and Mukhtar Hamour, 131 tables	1970
14 (1970)	Kenneth Ruddle and Mukhtar Hamour, 200 tables	1971
15 (1971)	Kenneth Ruddle and Donald Odermann, 195 tables	1973
16 (1972)	Kenneth Ruddle and Kathleen Barrows, 282 tables	1974
17*	James W. Wilkie and Paul Turovsky, 303 tables	1976
18	James W. Wilkie and Peter Reich, 415 tables	1977
19	James W. Wilkie and Peter Reich, 439 tables	1978
20	James W. Wilkie and Peter Reich, 684 tables	1980
21	James W. Wilkie and Stephen Haber, 666 tables	1981
22	James W. Wilkie and Stephen Haber, 752 tables	1983
23	James W. Wilkie and Adam Perkal, 892 tables	1984
24	James W. Wilkie and Adam Perkal, 982 tables	1985

*Beginning with volume 17, designation by volume number rather than year of edition.

STATISTICAL ABSTRACT OF LATIN AMERICA

volume 24

JAMES W. WILKIE
Editor

ADAM PERKAL
Co-Editor

UCLA Latin American Center Publications
University of California • Los Angeles

Citation

James W. Wilkie and Adam Perkal, eds., *Statistical Abstract of Latin America*, Volume 24 (Los Angeles: UCLA Latin American Center Publications, University of California, 1985).

Other Library Entries

1. Statistical Abstract of Latin America.

2. California. University, Los Angeles. Latin American Center. Statistical Abstract of Latin America.

3. [Earlier name]. California. Univeristy, Los Angeles. Committee on Latin American Studies. Statistical Abstract of Latin America.

4. University of California. Los Angeles. Latin American Center. *Statistical Abstract of Latin America*.

Statistical Abstract of Latin America Volume 24
UCLA Latin American Center Publications
Los Angeles, California 90024

Copyright © 1986 by The Regents of the University of California

ISBN (cloth): 0-87903-245-6

Library of Congress Card Number: 56-63569

Printed In the United States of America

CONTENTS

Preface ix

Tables xii

Figures xxxiii

Editor's Note on Methodology xxxv

Population Cartogram of Latin America, 1980 xxxvii

Explanation of Terms xxxviii

PART I. GEOGRAPHY AND LAND TENURE

1. Geography 1
2. Land Use 21
3. Land Tenure 29

PART II. TRANSPORTATION AND COMMUNICATION

4. Transportation Patterns 41
5. Communication Flows 55

PART III. POPULATION, HEALTH, AND EDUCATION

6. Demography 65
7. Vital Statistics and Disease 107
8. Health, Nutrition, Family Planning, and Welfare 121
9. Education and Science 143

PART IV. POLITICS, RELIGION, AND THE MILITARY

10. Political Statistics 165
11. Religion 183
12. The Military 193

PART V. WORKING CONDITIONS, MIGRATION, AND HOUSING

13. Labor Force, EAP, Unemployment, Class Structure, and Crime 209
14. Wages and Income Distribution 237
15. Migration and Tourism 251
16. Construction, Housing, and Utilities 269

PART VI. INDUSTRY, MINING, AND ENERGY

17. Industrial Production 289
18. Mining Production 301
19. Energy Resources: Production, Consumption, and Reserves 313

PART VII. SEA AND LAND HARVESTS

20. Fisheries Production 349
21. Agricultural Production 357
22. Ranch Production 369
23. Forestry Production 375

PART VIII. FOREIGN TRADE

24. Selected Commodities in Foreign Trade 383
25. Structure and Terms of Trade 431
26. Direction of Trade and Major Trading Partners 481

viii   **Contents**

PART IX. FINANCIAL FLOWS

27. Balance of Payments and International Liquidity   557
28. Loans, Grants, Assistance, and Peace Corps   615
29. Investments and Corporate Business Activity   663

PART X. NATIONAL ACCOUNTS, GOVERNMENT POLICY AND FINANCE, AND PRICES

30. Government Plans, Revenue and Expenditure, and Money Supply   695
31. Exchange Rates   739
32. Price Changes, Commodity Prices, and Interest Rates   779
33. Gross Product   811

PART XI. DEVELOPMENT OF DATA

34. Changes in Mexico Since 1895: Central Government Revenue,
     Public Sector Expenditure, and National Economic Growth,
     by James W. Wilkie   861
Index   881

PREFACE

Goals of the Statistical Abstract

The goals of the *Statistical Abstract of Latin America* (SALA) are ten:

1. To provide a yearly one-volume selection of important statistics culled from nearly 150 sources.
2. To offer the latest figures available on a timely basis.
3. To provide a context for present and future-oriented statistics by presenting whenever possible the data in series covering several decades or years.
4. To generate through research new data not published elsewhere.
5. To develop new types of data and/or to provide new analytical treatment of statistical series through SALA-sponsored research.
6. To guide the user of this volume to the wide variety of statistical material and sources available.
7. To suggest kinds of data that may be found in other sources as well as where to look for more complete coverage than can be abstracted here.
8. To present maps and graphs so that statistics take on greater meaning than would otherwise be possible to achieve.
9. To provide a SALA Supplement Series which offers interpretation, longitudinal data, and cartographic analysis of statistics on Latin America.
10. To coordinate presentation of statistics in SALA with the theory and model presented in James W. Wilkie, *Statistics and National Policy*, Statistical Abstract of Latin America, Supplement 3 (1974).

Organization

In order to accomplish these goals, SALA is organized in the following ways:

1. Historical statistics are presented across time. As new statistics become available, they can be traced back in time from volume to volume generating a long-term profile of Latin America's past and present as well as providing baselines for projecting into the future.
2. Explicit sources and qualifying notes are given for all data presented. Sources are given at the end of each table, not at the end of chapters where difficulty of use would be increased manyfold.
3. Source abbreviations and symbols are standardized. A key to sources is included for convenient reference.
4. A section on "Explanation of Terms" lists the abbreviations used. This information is repeated in the front endsheets for easy use.

5. The "Editor's Note on Methodology" defines "Latin America," itemizes regional groupings, and explains alternative methods for calculating rate of change over time.
6. Data are cross-referenced from one table to another throughout the volume.
7. Each volume is fully indexed to help readers find topics and related subjects.
8. A "Guide to Data" section in some volumes leads the user to additional sources and supplemental bibliographic aids.
9. The "Development of Data" section contains analysis of concepts, problems, and methods in organizing new topics or chapters included in SALA.
10. A carefully selected international advisory board guides the research and compilation for SALA and its Supplements.

Thus, SALA is intended to be the standard source for statistical information on Latin America and to encourage the use of data by scholars, researchers, business, and governments.

Cautions in Use of Statistics

Readers are cautioned that all data for any topic vary according to definition, parameters, methods of compilation and calculation, and completeness of coverage as well as date gathered, and/or date adjusted. Indeed, readers are reminded that statistics do not reveal "truth," but rather serve as proxy to interpret reality, and alternative statistics are available for most data series. Although such data as import statistics are often suspect because they do not take into account the extensive smuggling of goods, such figures are important because national and international policy decisions are made on the basis of the data recorded, data which interact with events to help change the course of "history." In this manner, "statistical reality" becomes quite as important as "reality" itself.

Revised Presentation

To help make the SALA series more useful to readers, beginning with this twenty-fourth issue (and the eighth for which I have served as editor), we have included here alternative data in the form of partial tables from previous issues going back to volume 17. Previously we included in a cumulative index references to tables not reprinted from volume to volume. Such an index, however, created a problem for investigators who had to consult each back issue in order to determine whether or not (regardless of title) the table format carried the information (or additional data) actually sought.

For example, the method of presenting here a partial table showing subheadings and data for one country among the twenty permits the reader to see at a glance the relevance of the type of information given, hence eliminating searches in earlier issues.

Elimination of the cumulative index also has two added advantages:

1. Data and references (to full data in the partial tables) on similar topics are now grouped together and not separated between the chapters and the index.
2. No cumulative index is necessary—the cumulative index often led readers to the same table (with no new information) reprinted in more than one volume for persons who might not have a complete set of SALA.

We hope that this change in presentation of partial tables integrated at the appropriate place in the chapters will aid researchers.

Readers will note also that SALA has been reorganized and chapters shifted and/or divided to facilitate access to topical materials.

Analysis of New Trends in Latin America or in Availability of Statistical Data

In addition to explaining the goals, organization, and presentation of the data, the Preface to SALA often seeks to assess new trends in the Latin American situation as well as types of data becoming available (or decreasing in availability). Previous issues of SALA contain discussion of the following topics in the preface:

"On the Accuracy of Statistics and Development of Time-Series Data" (vol. 19)

"Mexico's 'New' Financial Crisis of 1982 in Historical Perspective" (vol. 22)

"On Defining the Concepts of Latin America, the Caribbean, and Economically Questionable Nations (EQNs)" (vol. 23)

In a recent new trend, political cartoons have dealt with the topic of statistics and those who generate them. The drawings below, from *The New Yorker*, *San Juan Star* (Puerto Rico), and *La Nación* (Buenos Aires), illustrate an increasing popular awareness of statistics, their meaning, and their use.

"What's the latest with our 'arbitrary or unlawful deprivation of life' stats?"

The San Juan Star, March 10, 1984, p. 24.

"Frankly, Harold, you're beginning to bore everyone with your statistics."

Drawing by Levin; © 1983, The New Yorker Magazine, Inc., October 31, 1983, p. 58.

"Have you heard? They've reduced the military budget by ten percent."

(Carlos Basurto in La Nación, Buenos Aires)

Reprinted in *Times of the Americas*, Washington, D.C., May 26, 1982.

Marina del Rey, California
June 1985

J.W.W.

TABLES

Detailed data in tables may not equal totals because of rounding

PART I. GEOGRAPHY AND LAND TENURE

Chapter 1   Geography

100   Economic Regions: Area Population, and Density, 20 LRC
101   Argentina Major Civil Divisions: Area and Percentage
102   Bolivia Major Civl Divisions: Area and Percentage
103   Brazil Major Civil Divisons: Area and Percentage
104   Chile Major Civil Divisions: Area and Percentage
105   Colombia Major Civil Divisions: Area and Percentage
106   Costa Rica Major Civil Divisions: Area and Percentage
107   Cuba Major Civil Divisions: Area and Percentage
108   Dominican Republic Major Civil Divisions: Area and Percentage
109   Ecuador Major Civil Divisions: Area and Percentage
110   El Salvador Major Civil Divisions: Area and Percentage
111   Guatemala Major Civil Divisions: Area and Percentage
112   Haiti Major Civil Divisions: Area and Percentage
113   Honduras Major Civil Divisions: Area and Percentage
114   Mexico Major Civil Divisions: Area and Percentage
115   Nicaragua Major Civil Divisions: Area and Percentage
116   Panama Major Civil Divisions: Area and Percentage
117   Paraguay Major Civil Divisions: Area and Percentage
118   Peru Major Civil Divisions: Area and Percentage
119   Uruguay Major Civil Divisions: Area and Percentage
120   Venezuela Major Civil Divisions: Area and Percentage
121   Altitude of Principal Mountains, 20 L
122   High Peaks of Latin America
123   Volcanoes of Latin America
124   Major Earthquakes in Latin America, 1797-1983
125   Rivers
126   Principal Natural Lakes of Latin America
127   Principal Deserts
128   Temperature and Rainfall by Geographic Location, 20 L
129   High and Low Temperature—Monthly Averages in Capital City, 20 L
130   Average Number of Days Without Rain Each Month, 20 L

Chapter 2   Land Use

200   FAO Land Use Data, 20 LRC
201   IDB Land Use Data by Region
202   IDB Agricultural Land Use Data by Region
203   Cultivated Land, 20 LR, 1959–74
204   FAO Irrigated Land Data, 20 LRC, 1961–80
205   IDB Arable and Irrigated Land Data
206   U.N. Arable Land and Cropland, 20 LC
207   Humid Tropical Land Resources of South America, 8 LR
208   Projected New Land Development and Investments in South America, 7 LR, 1962–85
209   Fertilizer Consumption, 20 LRC, 1970–81
210   Fertilizer Consumption per Hectare of Arable Land and per Inhabitant, 20 LC, 1970–80
211   Tractors in Use, 20 LRC, 1961–80

Chapter 3   Land Tenure
300   Systems of Land Tenure, Absolute Data, 18 LC
301   Systems of Land Tenure, Percentage Data, 18 LC
302   Agricultural Landholdings: Number and Area by Size and Class, 20 L
303   Size of Agricultural Holdings, 15 LC, 1950–70
304   Cumulative Land Reform Data, 15 L

PART II: TRANSPORTATION AND COMMUNICATION

Chapter 4   Transportation Patterns
400   City to City Distances by Nonstop Air Service
401   Air Passenger Kilometers of Scheduled Service, 20 LC, 1970–82
402   Kilometers Flown of Scheduled Service, 20 LC, 1970–82
403   Air Passengers Transported, 18 LRC, 1970–82
404   Utilization of Airline Capacity, Passenger Load Factor, 20 LC, 1970–82
405   Air Transport in Ton Kilometers, 19 LC, 1970–82
406   Length of Railway Network, 16 LR, 1970–81
407   Railway Rolling Stock, 20 LC
408   Railroad Passenger Kilometers, 17 LC, 1965–81
409   Railroad Freight in Ton Kilometers, 17 LC, 1965–81
410   Length of Roads, 19 LR
411   Commercial Motor Vehicle Registration, 20 LC, 1960–80
412   Passenger Motor Vehicle Registration, 20 LC, 1960–80
413   Merchant Fleets, 16 L, 1982
414   International Seaborne Shipping, 20 LC, 1965–82
415   International Seaborne Goods Loaded and Unloaded, 18 LC, 1976–77

Chapter 5   Communication Flows
500   Daily Newspapers, Circulation, and Newsprint Consumption per Inhabitant, 20 LC, 1965–80
501   Newsprint: Volume of Imports, 20 LC, 1965–82
502   Newsprint: Value of Imports, 20 LC, 1965–82
503   Book Production: Copies by Subject Classification, 16 LR
504   Book Production: Titles by Subject Classification, 15 LRC
505   Mail Traffic, 16 LC, 1970–78
506   Telegraph Service, by Number of Telegrams, 12 L, 1970–80
507   U.N. Data on Telephones, 19 L, 1975–80
508   American Telephone and Telegraph Data on Telephones, 20 LC, 1960–81
509   Telephones by Continental Area, 1960–81
510   Radio and Television Transmitters, 19 LC
511   Radio Receivers, 20 LC, 1965–81
512   Television Sets, 20 LC, 1965–81
513   Cinema Attendance, 20 LC, 1955–80
514   Motion Picture Theaters, 20 LC, 1926–80

PART III: POPULATION, HEALTH, AND EDUCATION

Chapter 6   Demography
600   World Population (Mid 1979) and Average Annual Growth Rates and Ranks, 20 LRC, 1960–79
601   Argentina Population Estimate and Index, 1900–83
602   Bolivia Population Estimate and Index, 1900–83
603   Brazil Population Estimate and Index, 1900–83
604   Chile Population Estimate and Index, 1900–83
605   Colombia Population Estimate and Index, 1900–82
606   Costa Rica Population Estimate and Index, 1900–83
607   Cuba Population Estimate and Index, 1900–83
608   Dominican Republic Population Estimate and Index, 1900–83

609   Ecuador Population Estimate and Index, 1900–83
610   El Salvador Population Estimate and Index, 1900–82
611   Guatemala Population Estimate and Index, 1900–82
612   Haiti Population Estimate and Index, 1900–82
613   Honduras Population Estimate and Index, 1900–83
614   Mexico Population Estimate and Index, 1900–82
615   Nicaragua Population Estimate and Index, 1900–83
616   Panama Population Estimate and Index, 1900–83
617   Paraguay Population Estimate and Index, 1900–83
618   Peru Population Estimate and Index, 1900–83
619   Uruguay Population Estimate and Index, 1900–83
620   Venezuela Population Estimate and Index, 1900–83
621   United States Population Estimate and Index, 1900–83
622   Index of Estimated Population, 20 LRC, 1900–80
623   Population Estimates by Decade, 20 LRC, 1900–80
624   CELADE Population Estimates and Projections by Decade, 20 LRC, 1920–2020
625   National Population Census Series, 20 L, 1774–1982
626   Argentina Population Census and Density of Major Civil Divisions
627   Bolivia Population Census and Density of Major Civil Divisions
628   Brazil Population Census and Density of Major Civil Divisions
629   Chile Population Census and Density of Major Civil Divisions
630   Colombia Population Census and Density of Major Civil Divisions
631   Costa Rica Population Census and Density of Major Civil Divisions
632   Cuba Population Census and Density of Major Civil Divisions
633   Dominican Republic Population Census and Density of Major Civil Divisions
634   Ecuador Population Census and Density of Major Civil Divisions
635   El Salvador Population Census and Density of Major Civil Divisions
636   Guatemala Population Census and Density of Major Civil Divisions
637   Haiti Population Census and Density of Major Civil Divisions
638   Honduras Population Census and Density of Major Civil Divisions
639   Mexico Population Census and Density of Major Civil Divisions
640   Nicaragua Population Census and Density of Major Civil Divisions
641   Panama Population Census and Density of Major Civil Divisions
642   Paraguay Population Census and Density of Major Civil Divisions
643   Peru Population Census and Density of Major Civil Divisions
644   Uruguay Population Census and Density of Major Civil Divisions
645   Venezuela Population Census and Density of Major Civil Divisions
646   Extended Caribbean Region (ECR) Population, 28 CSOR, 6 CA, and 3 Tangential Countries,
        1960–79
647   Population of Largest City, 20 L, 1900–80
648   Percentage of Population in Largest City, 20 L, 1900–70
649   Population of Principal Cities, According to Recent Censuses, 20 L
650   Population of Capital City Urban Areas, According to Recent Censuses, 20 LC
651   SALA Rural Population Percentages According to National Self-Perception, 20 LRC, 1940–80
652   SALA Urban Population Percentages According to National Self-Perception, 20 LRC, 1940–80
653   CELADE Urban Population Percentages, Non-Standard Terms, 20 LR, 1970–2025
654   CELADE Urban and Rural Population Estimates, Non-Standard Terms, 20 LR, 1970–2020
655   ECLA Urban and Rural Population Estimates, by Age Group, Non-Standard Definition, 20 L,
        1975–2025
656   Urban Population in Non-Standard and Standard Terms, 20 LR, 1960–80
657   Vanhanen Urban and Rural Population Percentage Estimates, 20 LRC, 1900–70
658   Number and Population of Places with 20,000 Inhabitants and Over, According to Censuses, 20 L,
        ca. 1950, 1960, 1970
659   Indices of Urbanization and Urban Concentration, 20 LR, 1950 and 1975

660   Male and Female Total Population Projections, 20 LR, 1975-90
661   Age Structure, 20 LC, 1960-80
662   Distribution of Population by Sex and Age, 18 LC
663   Estimates of Female Population 15-49 Years of Age, 20 LRC, 1950-2010
664   Population Percentage Under 15 Years, 20 LRC, 1950-2010
665   Persons by Age Up to 15 Years, 20 LC
666   CELADE Rates of Demographic Growth, 20 LR, 1920-2000
667   CELADE Growth Rates for Total, Urban, and Rural Population, 20 LR, 1970-2000
668   Estimated Amerind Population, 16 L, Mid-1950s
669   Amerind Population Estimates, 16 LC, Late 1970s
670   U.S. Population Census Data On Hispanics

Chapter 7   Vital Statistics and Disease
700   Life Expectancy, 20 LC
701   Live Births by Age of Mother, 19 L
702   Crude Birth Rates, 20 LC, 1960-81
703   Age-Specific Fertility Rates, Crude Birth Rate, Total Fertility Rate, and Gross Reproduction Rate,
           20 LC, 1975-80
704   Fetal Mortality Rates, 16 LC, 1960-81
705   Infant Mortality Rates, 19 LC, 1960-81
706   Deaths of Children Under 5 Years Old by Principal Cause, 20 LC
707   Maternal Death Rates, 11 LC, 1970-80
708   First Five Principal Causes of Death and Rate by Sex, 18 LC
709   Reported Cases and Deaths From Diphtheria, 20 LC, 1973-76
710   Reported Cases and Rates of Amebiasis and Bacillary Dysentery, 17 LC, 1973-76
711   Marriages, 19 LC, 1965-81
712   Divorces, 19 LC, 1965-81

Chapter 8   Health, Nutrition, Family Planning, and Welfare
800   Summary of Health, Education, and Communication (HEC) Indicators, 1940-80
801   HEC Total Index by Country, 20 LRC, 1940-70
802   Adjusted Physical Quality of Life Index (PQLI), 20 LRC, 1950 to Mid-1970s
803   Physicians, Nurses, and Nursing Auxiliaries, 20 LRC
804   Population per Physician, 20 L, 1960-80
805   Professional and Auxiliary Health Personnel, 20 LC
806   Dentists and Dental Auxiliaries, 20 LC
807   Nurses by Major Function, 18 LC
808   Hospitals by Type, 20 LRC
809   Hospitals: Number, Percentage, and Ownership, 20 LRC
810   Short-Stay Hospitals: Indices of Utilization by All Types of Ownership, 19 LRC
811   Hospital Beds and Rate, in the Capital and Rest of Country, 20 LC
812   Hospital Beds: Number, Percentage, and Ownership, 20 LRC
813   Health Establishments With Outpatient Services, 15 L
814   Urban and Rural Health Establishments with Outpatient Services, 8 L
815   Mental Health Clinics, Rehabilitation Centers, and Dental Clinics, 11 LC
816   Child Health Services, 8 L
817   Children Under One Year Receiving BCG, DEPT, Measles, and Poliomyelitis Vaccines, 20 L
818   Total Food Production Index, 20 LC, 1966-81
819   Per Capita Food Production Index, 20 LC, 1966-81
820   Daily Caloric Intake, 20 LRC, 1965-80
821   Percent of Minimum Daily Caloric Requirements, 19 LR, 1961-77
822   Fish Consumption, 11 LC, 1949-74
823   Fats Consumed Daily, 19 LRC, 1966-80
824   Per Capital Private Food Consumption Change, 19 LR, 1960-75
825   Protein Consumption, 20 LRC, 1965-80

826   Average Yearly PC in Food/C Production by Period, 20 LRC, 1953-81
827   Acceptors of Government Family Planning Services by Method and Year of Acceptance, 12 L,
           1971 and 1975
828   Acceptors of Government Family Planning Services by Method and Age of Wife, 7 L
829   Acceptors of Government Family Planning Services by Method and Number of Living Children, 7 L
830   Users of Birth Control Methods by Public and Private Source, 6 L
831   Relative Age Distribution of Family Planning Participants at Entry into Program, 14 L
832   Women Participating in Family Planning Programs, by Birth Control Method, 19 LR, 1970-73
833   Social Security: Percentage Served of Economically Active Population, 20 LR, 1960 and 1970
834   Insured Population in Relation to Total and Economically Active Population in Argentina, 1960-70
835   Insured Population in Relation to Total and Economically Active Population in Chile, 1960-71
836   Insured Population in Relation to Total and Economically Active Population in Mexico, 1960-70
837   Insured Population in Relation to Total and Economically Active Population in Peru, 1961-69
838   Insured Population in Relation to Total and Economically Active Population in Uruguay, 1960-69

Chapter 9 Education and Science
900   Illiteracy, Age 15 and Over, by Urban and Rural Areas and by Sex, 20 LC
901   Students Enrolled as Share of Eligible Ages, 20 LR, 1960 and 1980
902   Enrollment Ratios for the First, Second, and Third Levels of Education, 20 LC
903   Compulsory Education, Entrance Ages, and Duration of Schooling at First and Second Levels, 20 LC
904   Educational Attainment, by Urban and Rural Areas, Age, and Sex, 19 LC
905   Teachers per 10,000 Persons Ages 7-14, 20 LR, 1960-75
906   Teachers and School Enrollment, by Level and Type, 20 L
907   Pre-Primary Schools, Teachers, and Pupils, 19 LC
908   Primary Schools, Teachers, and Pupils, 20 LC
909   Higher Education: Teachers and Students, by Type of Institution, 20 LC
910   Higher Education: Distribution of Students, by Sex and Field of Study, 19 L
911   Higher Education: Graduates, by Field of Study, 18 LC
912   Higher Education: Graduates, by Level of Degree and Field of Study, 17 LC
913   Percentage of "Leftist" Students in Sample by Father's Religion and University, 4 L
914   Academic Students Studying in Communist Countries, 10 L
915   School Enrollment, 20 L, 1880-1929
916   Adult Education: Teachers and Student Enrollment, 20 L
917   Special Education: Establishments, Teachers, and Student Enrollment, 20 L
918   University Library Collections, Borrowers, Works Loaned, Current Expenditure, and Personnel,
           13 LC
919   Libraries by Category, 13 LC
920   School and Financial Years, 20 LC
921   Total Public Educational Expenditure, 20 LC
922   Public Current Educational Expenditure, According to Purpose, 20 L
923   Public Current Educational Expenditure, by Level, 20 LC
924   Scientists and Engineers Engaged in Research and Development, by Field of Science, 14 L
925   Research and Development Personnel, by Sector of Performance, 14 LC
926   Indicators of Scientific and Technological Development, 17 LC

PART IV: POLITICS, RELIGION, AND THE MILITARY

Chapter 10 Political Statistics
1000   Political Dependence, Independence, and International Memberships of Countries and Territories,
           20 L, and 45 ELA
1001   Share of Adult Population Voting, 12 LC
1002   Political and Civil Rights, 20 LC, 1972-83
1003   Revised Fitzgibbon-Johnson Index Rankings: U.S. View of Political Democracy, Five Key Criteria,
           20 L, 1945-80
1004   Argentina Presidential and Congressional Final Election Results, by Political Party
1005   Argentina Presidential Election Results, by Political Party and Province

1006   Chile Electoral Intentions in Santiago Plebiscite
1007   Chile Comparison of Gallup Predictions with Actual Vote in Santiago Plebiscite
1008   Costa Rica Presidential Winning Percentages, 1953–82
1009   Colombian Presidential Election Results, 1978 and 1982
1010   Ecuador Presidential Elections, Final Results, by Province and Political Party
1011   Ecuador Absenteeism in Elections, by Province, 1978 and 1984
1012   Ecuador Elections for Provincial Deputies, by Political Party
1013   El Salvador First Round Provisional Election Results, by Department and Political Party
1014   El Salvador Second Round Provisional Election Results, by Department and Political Party
1015   El Salvador Election for the Constituent Assembly
1016   Honduras Presidential Election Results
1017   Mexico Presidential Election Results, by Party and State
1018   Nicaragua Election Results
1019   Panama Presidential Election Results, by Political Party
1020   Venezuelan Presidential Election Results, 1947–78
1021   Population Voting in Total Population Age 20 and Over, by Type of Election, 12 LC

Chapter 11 Religion
1100   Catholic Church Hierarchy and Institutions, 20 L, 1983–84
1101   Inhabitants per Catholic Priest, 20 L, 1912–80
1102   Jehovah's Witnesses Publishers and Members, 20 LC
1103   Estimated Jewish Population, 20 LC, 1968–79
1104   World Christian Encyclopedia Scheme for Categorizing Religious (Including Protestant) and Non-Religious Persons, 1900–80
1105   Religious (Including Protestant) and Non-Religious Persons, 20 LC, 1900–80
1106   Practicing and Non-Practicing Christians, 20 LC, 1900–80
1107   Organized Bible Distribution per Year, 20 LC, 1900–75
1108   Catholic Baptisms per 1,000 Catholics, 20 L, 1972–75
1109   Protestant Sects and Missionaries, 20 LC

Chapter 12 The Military
1200   U.S. Data on Military Expenditures, Armed Forces, GNP, and Central Government Expenditures, 20 LRC, 1972–82
1201   U.S. Data on Value of Arms Transfers and Total Imports and Exports, by Region, Organization, and Country, 20 LRC, 1972–82
1202   U.S. Data on World Arms Trade: Recipient Countries by Major Suppliers, 20 L, Cumulative, 1978–82
1203   IISA Data on Armed Forces Expenditure, Personnel, Vessels, and Aircraft, 20 L, 1982
1204   IISS Data on Defense Expenditure per Military Man and as Percentage of Total Government Spending per Military Man, 7 LC, 1975–82
1205   Military Expenditure as Percentage of GDP, 20 LC, 1956–81
1206   USDOD Data on U.S. Military Sales Agreements, 20 LR, 1950–83
1207   USDOD Data on U.S. Military Sales Deliveries, 20 LR, 1950–83
1208   USDOD Data on Students Trained Under U.S. International Military Education and Training Program, 20 LR, 1950–83
1209   USDOD Data on U.S. Expenditure for International Military Education and Program, 20 LR, 1950–83
1210   USDOD Data on Total Value of U.S. Arms Transfers, 20 L, FY 1970–83
1211   Argentina and Great Britain (GB) Human Losses in the 1982 Falklands War

PART V: WORKING CONDITIONS, MIGRATION, AND HOUSING

Chapter 13 Labor Force, EAP, Unemployment, Class Structure, and Crime
1300   Labor Force Participation by Sex, 17 L, 1950–80
1301   Alternative Labor Force Participation by Sex, 20 L

1302   Estimated Growth of Labor Force by Sex, 19 L, 1975–2000
1303   Children in the Labor Force, 20 LC, 1960–2000
1304   Labor Force Structure, 20 LC, 1960–2000
1305   Agricultural Labor Force, 26 ECLA:L, 1950–75
1306   Agricultural Population as Share of Total Population, 26 ECLA:L, 1950–75
1307   Agricultural Population and Economically Active Population in Agriculture, 20 LRC, 1965 and 1981
1308   Economically Active Population (EAP), 20 LC
1309   EAP by Industry, 20 LC
1310   EAP by Major Occupations, 20 LC
1311   Occupational Categories, by Sex, 20 LC
1312   Occupational Strata, 9 L, 1960–70
1313   Economically Active Population Estimated by Age Group, 20 L, 1970–2000
1314   EAP by Activity, 14 L, 1950–80
1315   Population Employed by Sector, 13 L, 1960 and 1970
1316   Employment in Manufacturing, 15 LC, 1971–81
1317   Hours of Work in Manufacturing, 9 LC, 1964–81
1318   Government Employees by Level, 6 LC
1319   Central Government Employees by Functional Sector, 6 LC
1320   Central Government Employees by Functional Sector as a Share of Total Central Government Employment, 5 LC
1321   Underutilization of Labor, 6 L
1322   Underdevelopment Topics Covered in Household Surveys, 13 L
1323   Unemployment Topics Covered in Household Surveys, 13 L
1324   Minimum Age from Which Economic Characteristics Were Investigated in Population Censuses and National Household Surveys in the 1970s, 20 L
1325   Declaration Period and Minimum Time of Employment for Determining Activity Status, Population Census 1970, 20 L
1326   Unemployment, 13 LC, 1963–82
1327   Unemployment According to Previous Job Experience, 8 LC, 1971–82
1328   Unemployment by Sex and Age Group, 5 LC, 1976–82
1329   Urban Open Unemployment, 12 LR, 1970–82
1330   Middle and Upper Classes, 18 L, 1950–70
1331   Mexico Social Modernization Index (SMI), 1930–70
1332   Absolute Poverty Estimates, 10 LR
1333   Availability of Criminal Statistics for Latin America and the English-Speaking Caribbean
1334   Persons Arrested, 5 L, 1965–70
1335   Prison Population, 4 L, 1965–70

Chapter 14 Wages and Income Distribution
1400   Compensation of Employees and National Income, 15 LC, 1962–75
1401   Wages in Nonagricultural Activities, 8 LC, 1965–82
1402   Wages in Manufacturing, 18 LC, 1965–82
1403   Wages in Construction, 15 LC, 1965–82
1404   Wages in Transport, Storage, and Communication, 13 LC, 1965–82
1405   Wages in Agriculture, 15 LC, 1965–82
1406   Evolution of Real Wages, 10 LR, 1978–82
1407   Real Wage Indexes, 18 L, 1965–80
1408   Real Industrial Wage Index for Mexico City, 1934–76
1409   Real Industrial Wage Index, 18 LC, 1940–73
1410   Minimum Urban Wages and Agricultural, Industrial, and Construction Wages, 18 L, 1965–80
1411   Metropolitan Legal Minimum Wages, 18 LC, 1965–80
1412   Industrial Disputes, 14 LC, 1965–82
1413   Income Distribution, 8 LC
1414   Income Distribution: Latin America Average, 1960 and 1970
1415   Distribution of Income: Chronological Series, 3 LC, 1953–62
1416   Distribution of Average per Inhabitant Income, by Income Groups, 5 L, 1965

1417   Income Groups, Percentage Shares, 5 L, 1965
1418   National Distribution of Total Household Income, by Income Groups, 10 L
1419   Urban Distribution of Household Income, by Income Groups, 11 L
1420   Number of Cooperatives and Membership, 20 L, 1962 and 1969

Chapter 15 Migration and Tourism
1500   Population in United States Reporting Latin American Ancestry
1501   Immigrants Admitted to the United States, 20 LC, 1951–80
1502   Immigrants Admitted to the United States, by Occupation, 16 L, 1973–78
1503   Immigrants Admitted to the United States, by Classification, 20 L
1504   U.S. Naturalization, by Country of Origin and Year of Entry, 20 L, 1965–80
1505   "Deportable Aliens" Located in the United States, FY 1966–80
1506   Aliens Deported, by Country and Cause, 19 L
1507   Temporary Workers Admitted to the United States, 18 L, 1977 and 1978
1508   "Legal" Mexican Immigration to the United States, 1900–80
1509   Mexican Illegal Aliens Reported, 1924–78
1510   U.S. Immigration and Naturalization Service Man-Hours per Deportable Undocumenteds Located, 1978–82
1511   Mexican Undocumenteds Counted in the 1980 U.S. Census, by Period of Entry, 1960–80
1512   Known Excludable Haitian Arrivals, Miami, Florida, 1979–82
1513   Immigrants to and Emigrants from Cuba, 1959–77
1514   Immigrants Admitted to Recipient Country, by Sex and Educational Level, 4 L
1515   Immigrants Admitted to Recipient Country, by Educational Level and Occupation, 4 L
1516   Immigrants Admitted to Recipient Country, by Occupation, 4 L
1517   Refugees "In Need"
1518   Entry of Tourists, 19 LC, 1970–82
1519   Tourist Entry, by Means of Transportation, 18 LC, 1970–82
1520   Lodging Establishments Capacity, 17 LC
1521   Exit of National Tourists, 14 LC, 1970–76
1522   Receipts from Tourism, 19 LC, 1965–82
1523   Tourist Arrivals to Cuba, 1950–76

Chapter 16 Construction, Housing, and Utilities
1600   New Building Construction Authorized and New Buildings Completed, 15 LC, 1973–81
1601   Argentina New Building Construction Authorized, 1973–81
1602   Brazil New Building Construction Authorized and New Buildings Completed, 1973–81
1603   Chile New Building Construction Authorized and New Buildings Completed, 1973–81
1604   Colombia New Building Construction Authorized, 1973–81
1605   Costa Rica New Building Construction Authorized, 1973–81
1606   Dominican Republic New Building Construction Authorized, 1973–81
1607   Ecuador New Building Construction Authorized, 1973–81
1608   El Salvador New Building Construction Authorized and New Buildings Completed, 1973–81
1609   Guatemala New Building Construction Authorized and New Buildings Completed, 1973–81
1610   Haiti New Building Construction Authorized and New Buildings Completed, 1973–81
1611   Honduras New Building Construction Authorized and New Buildings Completed, 1973–81
1612   Nicaragua New Building Construction Authorized, 1973–81
1613   Panama New Building Construction Authorized, 1973–81
1614   Uruguay New Building Construction Authorized and New Buildings Completed, 1973–81
1615   Venezuela New Building Construction Authorized, 1973–81
1616   Index of Construction Activity, 20 LC, 1974–81
1617   Population with Water Supply and Sewerage Services, 19 L
1618   Water Services in 26 Cities, 13 L, 1975
1619   Housing Access to Water Supply, 18 L
1620   Housing Sanitary Facilities, 18 LC
1621   Electrically Lighted Occupied Housing Units, 13 LC
1622   Population with Electric Lighting, 20 LR, 1960–73

1623   Housing Deficit, 20 L, 1960–69
1624   Occupied Housing Units by Number of Rooms, 15 LC
1625   Tenancy of Occupied Housing Units, 19 LC, 1970–76
1626   Inhabitants by Size of Household, 20 LC
1627   Status of Persons Residing in Private Households, 14 L
1628   Mexico: Geographic Distribution of Construction According to the Internal Consumption of Cement, 1970–79

PART VI: INDUSTRY, MINING, AND ENERGY

Chapter 17 Industrial Production
1700   Industrial Production Index, 18 LC, 1970–83
1701   Automobile Production, ALADI Countries, 10 LR, 1977–82
1702   Butter Production, 20 LC, 1959–81
1703   Cement Production, 20 LRC, 1953–82
1704   Cheese Production, 20 LC, 1959–81
1705   Cigarette Production, 20 LC, 1953–80
1706   Copper (Refined) Production, 4 LC, 1970–80
1707   Cotton (Woven) Fabric Production, 16 LC, 1953–80
1708   Cotton (Yarn) Production, 13 LC, 1953–80
1709   Fertilizer (Nitrogenous) Production, 19 LC, 1948–81
1710   Iron (Pig and Ferroalloy) Production, 7 LC, 1967–80
1711   Meat Production, 19 LC, 1961–81
1712   Metal (Sheet) Production, ALADI Countries, 9 LR, 1977–82
1713   Ships (Merchant Vessels) Under Construction in Argentina, 1975–83
1714   Steel (Crude) Production, 11 LR, 1950–82
1715   Sugar (Raw) Production, 20 LC, 1850–1981
1716   Wheat Flour Production, 19 LC, 1953–80

Chapter 18 Mining Production
1800   Antimony Mine Production, 7 LC, 1977–83
1801   Bauxite Mine Production, 3 LC, 1977–83
1802   Chromite Mine Production, 3 L, 1977–83
1803   Copper Mine Production, 12 LC, 1977–83
1804   Fluorspar Mine Production, 5 LC, 1977–83
1805   Gold Mine Production, 14 LC, 1977–83
1806   Gypsum Mine Production, 16 LC, 1977–83
1807   Iron Ore Production, 8 LC, 1977–83
1808   Lead Mine Production, 11 LC, 1977–83
1809   Manganese Ore Production, 4 L, 1977–83
1810   Mercury Mine Production, 3 LC, 1977–83
1811   Molybdenum Mine Production, 3 LC, 1977–83
1812   Nickel Mine Production, 5 LC, 1977–83
1813   Phosphate Rock Mine Production, 4 LC, 1977–81
1814   Salt Mine Production, 15 LC, 1977–83
1815   Silver Mine Production, 14 LC, 1977–83
1816   Sulfur Mine Production, 11 LC, 1977–81
1817   Tin Mine Production, 5 LC, 1977–83
1818   Tungsten Concentrate Production, 5 LC, 1977–83
1819   Zinc Mine Production, 11 LC, 1977–83
1820   Indicators of the Economic Contribution of Mining
1821   Production and Reserves of Non-Fuel Minerals, by Major Producers

Chapter 19 Energy Resources: Production, Consumption, and Reserves
1900   Total Energy Reserves and Production Potential, 19 LR
1901   Biomass Participation in the Total Energy Supply, 13 L
1902   Total Commercial Energy Production, 20 LC, 1950–81

1903   PC of Total Commercial Energy Production, 20 LC, 1955–81
1904   Index of Total Production of Commercial Energy, 20 LC, 1970–81
1905   Total Commercial Energy Production, by Resource Classification, 20 LC
1906   Total Commercial Energy Consumption, 20 LC, 1929–81
1907   Index of Total Consumption of Commercial Energy, 17 LC, 1970–81
1908   Crude Oil Production, 10 LC and 10 L, 1955–82
1909   PC of Crude Oil Production, 10 LC, 1971–81
1910   Off-Shore Production of Crude Petroleum, 5 LC, 1970–81
1911   Refined Oil Production, 18 LC, 1960–82
1912   PC of Refined Oil Production, 18 LC, 1960–82
1913   Petroleum Refinery Distillation Capacity, 19 LC, 1970–81
1914   Index of Total Production of Crude Petroleum, 9 LC, 1970–81
1915   Index of Total Consumption of Crude Petroleum, 18 LC, 1970–81
1916   Refined Petroleum Products Production, 20 LC, 1950–81
1917   Consumption of Petroleum and Derivatives, 19 L, 1960–82
1918   Actual and Potential Proven Reserves and Production of Crude Petroleum and Natural Gas, 19 L,
            1960–82
1919   Natural Gas Production, 20 LC, 1970–81
1920   Hard Coal Production, 20 LC, 1970–81
1921   Bituminous Coal/Anthracite Resources, 6 LC
1922   Sub-Bituminous Coal/Lignite Resources, 10 LC
1923   Geothermal Energy Installed Capacity, 5 LC, 1980–2000
1924   Production of Fuelwood and Bagasse, 20 LRC, 1976–81
1925   Electrical Energy Production, 20 LC, 1975–81
1926   Electricity Consumption, 20 LC, 1929–81
1927   Index of Total Production of Electricity, 20 LC, 1970–81
1928   Index of Total Consumption of Electricity, 20 LC, 1970–81
1929   Electrical Energy Installed Capacity, 20 LC, 1975–81
1930   Argentina: Electrical Energy Installed Capacity and Projections, 1979 and 2000
1931   Bolivia: Electrical Energy Installed Capacity and Projections, 1979 and 2000
1932   Brazil: Electrical Energy Installed Capacity and Projections, 1979 and 2000
1933   Chile: Electrical Energy Installed Capacity and Projections, 1979 and 2000
1934   Colombia: Electrical Energy Installed Capacity and Projections, 1979 and 2000
1935   Ecuador: Electrical Energy Installed Capacity and Projections, 1979 and 2000
1936   Mexico: Electrical Energy Installed Capacity and Projections, 1979 and 2000
1937   Paraguay: Electrical Energy Installed Capacity and Projections, 1979 and 2000
1938   Peru: Electrical Energy Installed Capacity and Projections, 1979 and 2000
1939   Uruguay: Electrical Energy Installed Capacity and Projections, 1979 and 2000
1940   Venezuela: Electrical Energy Installed Capacity and Projections, 1979 and 2000
1941   Uranium Production, 3 LC, 1970–81

PART VII: SEA AND LAND HARVESTS

Chapter 20 Fisheries Production

2000   Total Nominal Catches by Major Fishing Area, 20 LC, 1970–81
2001   Nominal Catches, Marine Areas, 18 LRC, 1971–81
2002   Distribution of Marine Area Nominal Catches, 18 LR, 1971–81
2003   PC of Nominal Catches in Marine Areas, 18 LRC, 1971–81
2004   Nominal Catches, Inland Waters, 18 LRC, 1971–81
2005   Distribution of Nominal Catches in Inland Waters, 18 LR, 1971–81
2006   PC of Nominal Catches in Inland Waters, 18 LRC, 1971–81
2007   Production of Seaweeds, 5 LC, 1970–81

Chapter 21 Agricultural Production

2100   Index of Total Agricultural Production, 20 LC, 1966–81
2101   Index of Per Capita Agricultural Production, 20 LC, 1966–81

2102   Barley Crops, 10 LC, 1975–81
2103   Banana Production, 17 LC, 1970–81
2104   Bean Production, 20 LC, 1975–81
2105   Cassava Production, 18 L, 1975–81
2106   Cocoa Bean Production, 16 L, 1975–81
2107   Coffee Production, 17 LC, 1975–81
2108   Copra Production, 11 L, 1970–81
2109   Cotton Lint Production, 18 LC, 1970–81
2110   Cottonseed Production, 18 LC, 1970–81
2111   Maize Production, 20 LC, 1975–81
2112   Orange and Tangerine Production, 20 LC, 1970–81
2113   Potato Production, 20 LC, 1975–81
2114   Rice Paddy Production, 20 LC, 1975–81
2115   Sugar Cane Production, 19 LC, 1975–81
2116   Tobacco Leaf Production, 20 LC, 1975–81
2117   Wheat Production, 13 LC, 1975–81
2118   Sweet Potato and Yam Production, 17 LC, 1975–81

Chapter 22 Ranch Production
2200   Cattle Population, 20 LRC, 1947–81
2201   Horse Population, 20 LRC, 1947–81
2202   Sheep Population, 19 LRC, 1947–81
2203   Swine Population, 20 LRC, 1947–81
2204   Cow Milk Production, 20 LRC, 1948–81
2205   Milk Yield per Milking Cow per Annum, 20 LC, 1948–81
2206   Wood Production, 9 LRC, 1948–81

Chapter 23 Forestry Production
2300   Estimated Forest Area, Natural Forests, and Industrial Plantations
2301   Total Roundwood Production, 20 LRC, 1970–82
2302   Industrial Roundwood Production, 20 LC, 1970–82
2303   Industrial Wood as a Percentage of Total Roundwood Production, 20 LC, 1970–82
2304   Total Sawnwood and Sleeper Production, 19 LC, 1970–82
2305   Total Wood-Based Panel Production, 17 LC, 1970–82
2306   Fiberboard Production, 8 LC, 1970–82
2307   Particle Board Production, 14 LC, 1970–82
2308   Plywood Production, 17 LC, 1970–82
2309   Veneer Sheet Production, 11 LC, 1970–82
2310   Total Wood Pulp Production, 9 L, 1970–82
2311   Total Paper and Paperboard Production, 17 LC, 1970–82
2312   Printing and Writing Paper Production, 12 LC, 1970–82
2313   Newsprint Production, 6 LC, 1970–82

PART VIII: FOREIGN TRADE

Chapter 24 Selected Commodities in Foreign Trade
2400   Principal Export Commodities, 19 LC, 1973
2401   Principal Export Commodities, 19 LC, 1975
2402   Two Leading Exports as Share of Total Export Value, 20 LC, 1955–73
2403   Contribution of the Thirteen Main Latin American Primary Export Products to Each Country's
        Total Value of Merchandise Exports, 19 LR, 1971–81
2404   Food Trade by Category, 19 LC, 1981–82
2405   Food Trade Balances, 20 L, 1961–75
2406   Fish Exports, 9 LC, 1978–82
2407   Fishery Exports, 11 OASL, 1970–80
2408   Meat Import Volume, 16 L, 1975–82

2409   Meat Export Volume, 17 LC, 1975–82
2410   Meat Exports, 15 LC, 1978–82
2411   Meat (Fresh) Export Volume, 15 LRC, 1960–75
2412   Comparison of Argentina and Australia Beef Cattle Exports, 1938–77
2413   Banana Export Volume, 14 LC, 1975–82
2414   Banana Exports, 12 LC, 1978–82
2415   Barley Import Volume, 17 LC, 1975–82
2416   Barley Export Volume, 4 LC, 1975–82
2417   Butter Import Volume, 18 LC, 1975–82
2418   Cacao Bean Export Volume, 9 LC, 1975–82
2419   Cocoa Exports, 13 LC, 1978–82
2420   Coffee Bean Export Volume, 17 LC, 1975–82
2421   Coffee Exports, 16 LC, 1978–82
2422   Maize Import Volume, 17 L, 1975–82
2423   Maize Export Volume, 15 LC, 1975–82
2424   Milk (Dry) Import Volume, 19 L, 1975–82
2425   Oat Import Volume, 13 L, 1975–82
2426   Oat Export Volume, 4 L, 1975-82
2427   Rice Import Volume, 20 L, 1975–82
2428   Soybean Exports, 11 LC, 1978–82
2429   Soybean Oil Import Volume, 19 L, 1975–82
2430   Soybean Oilcake Exports, 8 LC, 1978–82
2431   Sugar Export Volume, 19 L, 1975–82
2432   Sugar Exports, 15 LC, 1978–82
2433   Cuba Sugar Exports as Share of Cuba's Total Export Value, 1900–80
2434   U.S. Sugar Import Quotas, 17 LC, 1983–84
2435   Wheat Import Volume, 20 L, 1975–82
2436   Wheat Export Volume, 5 L, 1975–82
2437   Wheat Exports, 6 LC, 1978–82
2438   Wool (Clean) Export Volume, 5 LC, 1975–82
2439   Wool Exports, 7 LC, 1978–82
2440   Forest Product Exports, 10 OASL, 1970–80
2441   Roundwood Trade, 17 LC, 1975–82
2442   Sawnwood and Sleepers Trade, 18 LC, 1975–82
2443   Wood Pulp Trade, 15 LC, 1975–82
2444   Paper and Paperboard Trade, 20 LC, 1975–82
2445   Wood-Based Panel Trade, 18 LC, 1975–82
2446   Fuel as Share of Total Country Imports, 20 LC, 1975–80
2447   Fuelwood and Charcoal Trade, 7 LC, 1975–82
2448   Crude Oil Trade, 19 L, 1960–82
2449   Refined Oil Trade, 19 L, 1960–82
2450   Petroleum and Derivatives Trade, 19 L, 1973–82
2451   Lead Exports, 8 LC, 1978–82
2452   Copper Exports, 9 LC, 1978–82
2453   Tin Exports, 9 LC, 1978–82
2454   Zinc Exports, 7 LC, 1978–82
2455   Structure of Total Merchandise Imports, 20 LC, 1960–73
2456   Manufactured Goods as Share of Total Value of Country Trade, 20 LC, 1970–80
2457   Total Merchandise Exports as Share of Country GDP, 1970–82
2458   Cotton Exports, 11 LC, 1978–82
2459   Fertilizer Imports, 20 LRC, 1970–81
2460   Fertilizer Exports, 9 LC, 1970–81
2461   Cotton Lint Export Volume, 13 LC, 1975–82

Chapter 25 Structure and Terms of Trade

2500	Argentina Percentage Value of Trade, 1970-80
2501	Bolivia Percentage Value of Trade, 1971-81
2502	Brazil Percentage Value of Trade, 1970-81
2503	Chile Percentage Value of Trade, 1970-80
2504	Colombia Percentage Value of Trade, 1970-80
2505	Costa Rica Percentage Value of Trade, 1970-80
2506	Cuba Total Trade Value, 1950-80, and Percentages According to Origin, 1970-80
2507	Dominican Republic Percentage Value of Trade, 1970-80
2508	Ecuador Percentage Value of Trade, 1972-80
2509	El Salvador Percentage Value of Trade, 1970-80
2510	Guatemala Percentage Value of Trade, 1970-80
2511	Haiti Percentage Value of Trade, 1970-78
2512	Honduras Percentage Value of Trade, 1970-80
2513	Mexico Percentage Value of Trade, 1970-78
2514	Nicaragua Percentage Value of Trade, 1970-80
2515	Panama Percentage Value of Trade, 1970-80
2516	Paraguay Percentage Value of Trade, 1970-81
2517	Peru Percentage Value of Trade, 1970-81
2518	Uruguay Percentage Value of Trade, 1970-80
2519	Venezuela Percentage Value of Trade, 1970-80
2520	United States Percentage Value of Trade, 1970-81
2521	Argentina Absolute Value of Trade, 1970-81
2522	Bolivia Absolute Value of Trade, 1970-81
2523	Brazil Absolute Value of Trade, 1970-81
2524	Chile Absolute Value of Trade, 1970-81
2525	Colombia Absolute Value of Trade, 1970-81
2526	Costa Rica Absolute Value of Trade, 1970-81
2527	Cuba Absolute Value of Trade, 1975-81
2528	Dominican Republic Absolute Value of Trade, 1970-81
2529	Ecuador Absolute Value of Trade, 1970-81
2530	El Salvador Absolute Value of Trade, 1970-81
2531	Guatemala Absolute Value of Trade, 1970-81
2532	Haiti Absolute Value of Trade, 1975-81
2533	Honduras Absolute Value of Trade, 1970-81
2534	Mexico Absolute Value of Trade, 1970-81
2535	Nicaragua Absolute Value of Trade, 1970-81
2536	Panama Absolute Value of Trade, 1970-81
2537	Paraguay Absolute Value of Trade, 1975-81
2538	Peru Absolute Value of Trade, 1970-81
2539	Uruguay Absolute Value of Trade, 1975-81
2540	Venezuela Absolute Value of Trade, 1970-81
2541	United States Absolute Value of Trade, 1970-81
2542	IMF Import Unit Value Index, 4 LC, 1953-83
2543	IMF Export Unit Value Index, 11 LC, 1953-83
2544	IMF Terms of Trade Index, 7 LC, 1952-81
2545	IMF Terms of Trade Index, 4 L, 1955-83
2546	ECLA Import Unit Values (FOB), 19 L, 1960-80
2547	ECLA Export Unit Values, 19 L, 1960-80
2548	ECLA Total Import, Export, and Terms of Trade Indexes for Latin America, 1930-60
2549	ECLA Merchandise Terms of Trade Index (FOB/CIF), 19 L, 1960-80
2550	Value, Indexes, and Purchasing Power of Foreign Trade, 19 LR, 1928-76

Chapter 26 Direction of Trade and Major Trading Partners

2600	Share in Value of World Exports, 20 LRC and Regional Groupings, 1950-80
2601	Imports as a Percentage of World Imports, 20 LRC, 1950-75

2602   Major Trading Partners, 20 L, 1973–82

2603   Intra-Regional Merchandise Exports, 19 LR, 1970–82

2604   Intra-Regional Exports as a Share of Country GDP, 19 LR, 1970–82

2605   Latin American Intra-Regional Exports as a Percentage of Total Exports, by Product Group, 1965–79

2606   ALADI, CACM, and ECLA:L Intrazonal Imports as Share of Each Country's Total Imports, 25 ECLA:L, 1960–78

2607   ALADI Intrazonal Imports as Share of Each Country's Total Imports, 1962–80

2608   Origin of Andean Group Imports, 1961–77

2609   Intra-Regional Exports as a Percentage of Total Exports, 19 LR, 1962–79

2610   Geographic Concentration Indexes of Intra-Regional Exports, 19 LR, 1962–82

2611   CACM Trade with 18 ECR Countries, 1970–80

2612   Value of Imports from Countries with Centrally Planned Economies, 9 L, 1965–82

2613   Value of Exports to Countries with Centrally Planned Economies, 9 L, 1965–82

2614   Argentina Absolute Value of Goods Traded with Selected Regions and Countries, 1975–82

2615   Bolivia Absolute Value of Goods Traded with Selected Regions and Countries, 1975–82

2616   Brazil Absolute Value of Goods Traded with Selected Regions and Countries, 1975–82

2617   Chile Absolute Value of Goods Traded with Selected Regions and Countries, 1975–82

2618   Colombia Absolute Value of Goods Traded with Selected Regions and Countries, 1975–82

2619   Costa Rica Absolute Value of Goods Traded with Selected Regions and Countries, 1975–82

2620   Cuba Absolute Value of Goods Traded with Selected Regions and Countries, 1975–82

2621   Cuba's Most Important Trading Partners, 1900–80

2622   Cross References to Cuba Data in SALA 20

2623   Dominican Republic Absolute Value of Goods Traded with Selected Regions and Countries, 1975–82

2624   Ecuador Absolute Value of Goods Traded with Selected Regions and Countries, 1975–82

2625   El Salvador Absolute Value of Goods Traded with Selected Regions and Countries, 1975–82

2626   Guatemala Absolute Value of Goods Traded with Selected Regions and Countries, 1975–82

2627   Haiti Absolute Value of Goods Traded with Selected Regions and Countries, 1975–82

2628   Honduras Absolute Value of Goods Traded with Selected Regions and Countries, 1975–82

2629   Mexico Absolute Value of Goods Traded with Selected Regions and Countries, 1975–82

2630   Nicaragua Absolute Value of Goods Traded with Selected Regions and Countries, 1975–82

2631   Panama Absolute Value of Goods Traded with Selected Regions and Countries, 1975–82

2632   Paraguay Absolute Value of Goods Traded with Selected Regions and Countries, 1975–82

2633   Peru Absolute Value of Goods Traded with Selected Regions and Countries, 1975–82

2634   Uruguay Absolute Value of Goods Traded with Selected Regions and Countries, 1975–82

2635   Venezuela Absolute Value of Goods Traded with Selected Regions and Countries, 1975–82

2636   United States Value of Goods Traded with Each Latin American Country, 19 LC, 1975–82

PART IX: FINANCIAL FLOWS

Chapter 27 Balance of Payments and International Liquidity

2700   Guide to Balance of Payments Analysis

2701   Argentina: IMF Balance of Payments, 1976–83

2702   Bolivia: IMF Balance of Payments, 1976–83

2703   Brazil: IMF Balance of Payments, 1976–83

2704   Chile: IMF Balance of Payments, 1976–83

2705   Colombia: IMF Balance of Payments, 1976–83

2706   Costa Rica: IMF Balance of Payments, 1976–83

2707   Dominican Republic: IMF Balance of Payments, 1975–82

2708   Ecuador: IMF Balance of Payments, 1976–83

2709   El Salvador: IMF Balance of Payments, 1975–82

2710   Guatemala: IMF Balance of Payments, 1976–83

2711   Haiti: IMF Balance of Payments, 1976–83

2712   Honduras: IMF Balance of Payments, 1976–83

2713   Mexico: IMF Balance of Payments, 1976–83

2714   Nicaragua: IMF Balance of Payments, 1976–83

2715   Panama: IMF Balance of Payments, 1976–83
2716   Paraguay: IMF Balance of Payments, 1976–83
2717   Peru: IMF Balance of Payments, 1976–83
2718   Uruguay: IMF Balance of Payments, 1976–83
2719   Venezuela: IMF Balance of Payments, 1976–83
2720   United States: IMF Balance of Payments, 1976–83
2721   IMF Value of Merchandise Imports, 19 LC, 1951–83
2722   IMF Value of Merchandise Exports, 19 LC, 1951–83
2723   IMF Trade Balances, 19 LC, 1951–83
2724   Physical Holdings of Gold, 18 LC, 1950–82
2725   IMF Total Reserves, 19 LC, 1950–82
2726   IMF Foreign Exchange Reserves, 19 LC, 1950–82
2727   IMF Total Change in Reserves, 19 LC, 1951–83
2728   Argentina: ECLA Balance of Payments, 1977–82
2729   Bolivia: ECLA Balance of Payments, 1977–82
2730   Brazil: ECLA Balance of Payments, 1977–82
2731   Chile: ECLA Balance of Payments, 1976–82
2732   Colombia: ECLA Balance of Payments, 1977–82
2733   Costa Rica: ECLA Balance of Payments, 1977–82
2734   Dominican Republic: ECLA Balance of Payments, 1977–82
2735   Ecuador: ECLA Balance of Payments, 1977–82
2736   El Salvador: ECLA Balance of Payments, 1977–82
2737   Guatemala: ECLA Balance of Payments, 1977–82
2738   Haiti: ECLA Balance of Payments, 1977–82
2739   Honduras: ECLA Balance of Payments, 1977–82
2740   Mexico: ECLA Balance of Payments, 1977–82
2741   Nicaragua: ECLA Balance of Payments, 1977–82
2742   Panama: ECLA Balance of Payments, 1977–82
2743   Paraguay: ECLA Balance of Payments, 1972–82
2744   Peru: ECLA Balance of Payments, 1977–82
2745   Uruguay: ECLA Balance of Payments, 1977–82
2746   Venezuela: ECLA Balance of Payments, 1977–82
2747   Latin America: ECLA Balance of Payments, 1950–77
2748   LAFTA: ECLA Balance of Payments, 1950–77
2749   AG: ECLA Balance of Payments, 1950–77
2750   CACM: ECLA Balance of Payments, 1950–77
2751   ECLA Balance on Current Account, in Dollars of 1970, 19 LR, 1950–77

Chapter 28 Loans, Grants, Assistance, and Peace Corps

2800   Total External Public and Private Debt, 20 LR, 1977–83
2801   Relationship Between Total Public and Private Interest Payments and the Exportation of Goods and Services, 20 LC, 1977–83
2802   External Public Sector Debt Outstanding, 19 L, 1960–82
2803   Disbursed Portion of the External Public Sector Debt Outstanding, 19 L, 1960–82
2804   Structure of the Latin American External Public Sector Debt, by Type of Creditor, 1960–82
2805   Interest Payments on the External Public Sector Debt, 19 L, 1960–82
2806   Amortization Payments on the External Public Sector Debt, 19 L, 1960–82
2807   Service Payments on the External Public Sector Debt, 19 L, 1960–82
2808   External Public Sector Debt Service as Share of Exports of Goods and Services, 19 L, 1960–80
2809   Three Views of the Cumulative Foreign Loans Disbursed to Mexico's Public Sector, 1970–82
2810   Assistance from International Organizations, 20 LRC, 1946–84
2811   IMF Definitions for Fund Account Data
2812   Argentina IMF Fund Account, 1960–83
2813   Bolivia IMF Fund Account, 1960–83
2814   Brazil IMF Fund Account, 1960–83
2815   Chile IMF Fund Account, 1960–83

2816   Colombia IMF Fund Account, 1960–83

2817   Costa Rica IMF Fund Account, 1960–83

2818   Dominican Republic IMF Fund Account, 1960–83

2819   Ecuador IMF Fund Account, 1960–83

2820   El Salvador IMF Fund Account, 1960–83

2821   Guatemala IMF Fund Account, 1960–83

2822   Haiti IMF Fund Account, 1960–83

2823   Honduras IMF Fund Account, 1960–83

2824   Mexico IMF Fund Account, 1960–83

2825   Nicaragua IMF Fund Account, 1960–83

2826   Panama IMF Fund Account, 1960–83

2827   Paraguay IMF Fund Account, 1960–83

2828   Peru IMF Fund Account, 1960–83

2829   Uruguay IMF Fund Account, 1960–83

2830   Venezuela IMF Fund Account, 1960–83

2831   Inter-American Development Bank Loans, Yearly Lending, 19 L, 1974–84

2832   World Bank (International Bank for Reconstruction and Development) Actual Loans, 20 LR, FY 1949–76

2833   Average Financing Terms of Loans to Latin America Authorized by the U.S. Government and Multilateral Institutions, 1961–79

2834   U.S. Voting Power in Multilateral Agencies

2835   Gross Projected U.S. Assistance for Grants and Loans, 19 L, 1970–83

2836   Yearly U.S. Projected Assistance to Latin America, 1946–83

2837   U.S. Peace Corps Budget, 1962–80

2838   U.S. Peace Corps Volunteers in Full-Time Equivalents (FTE), 12 L, 1975–81

2839   U.S. Peace Corps Volunteer Characteristics

2840   U.S. Peace Corps Volunteers, by Skill Classification, 9 L

2841   Gross Projected AID Assistance During Three Periods, 20 L, 1949–74

2842   AID Commitments to Individual Latin American Countries, 20 L, 1949–74

2843   AID Actual Disbursement, 20 LR, 1979–81

2844   Ex-Im Bank Actual Loans, 20 L, 1973–81

2845   Exposure of U.S. Bank Holding Companies, 4 L

2846   U.S. Claims on Foreign Countries Held by U.S. Offices and Foreign Branches of U.S.-Chartered Banks, 9 L, 1979–84

2847   U.S. Claims on Unaffiliated Foreigners as Reported by Nonbanking Business Enterprises to the Federal Reserve, 3 L, 1980–84

2848   U.S. Banks' Own Claims on Foreigners as Reported to the Federal Reserve, 12 L, 1981–85

2849   U.S. Liabilities Due to Foreigners as Reported to the Federal Reserve, 12 L, 1981–85

Chapter 29 Investments and Corporate Business Activity

2900   Direct Investment Flow, 19 L, 1975–83

2901   U.S. Direct Investment in Latin America, 19 LRC, 1960–82

2902   U.S. Direct Investment Abroad, 1977–83

2903   Accumulated Direct Investment in Latin America by Origin, 5 L, 1969–76

2904   Accumulated Foreign Direct Investment by Major Industrial Sector, 5 L, 1969–76

2905   Accumulated Direct Investment by DAC/OECD Countries, 8 LRC, 1967–78

2906   British Direct Investment Flows, 9 L, 1969–75

2907   Portfolio Investment Flow, 19 L, 1976–83

2908   Capital Expenditures by U.S. Majority-Owned Foreign Affiliates, 9 LR, 1981–84

2909   Gross Product of U.S. Majority-Owned Foreign Affiliates, 9 LR

2910   Gross Product of U.S. Majority-Owned Foreign Affiliates in Latin America

2911   Argentina Corporate Business Activity

2912   Bolivia Corporate Business Activity

2913   Brazil Corporate Business Activity

2914   Chile Corporate Business Activity

2915   Colombia Corporate Business Activity

2916   Costa Rica Corporate Business Activity

2917   Dominican Republic Corporate Business Activity

2918   Ecuador Corporate Business Activity
2919   El Salvador Corporate Business Activity
2920   Guatemala Corporate Business Activity
2921   Haiti Corporate Business Activity
2922   Honduras Corporate Business Activity
2923   Mexico Corporate Business Activity
2924   Nicaragua Corporate Business Activity
2925   Panama Corporate Business Activity
2926   Paraguay Corporate Business Activity
2927   Uruguay Corporate Business Activity
2928   Venezuela Corporate Business Activity

PART X: NATIONAL ACCOUNTS, GOVERNMENT POLICY AND FINANCE, AND PRICES

Chapter 30 Government Plans, Revenue and Expenditure, and Money Supply

3000   Current Development Plans, 17 L
3001   Central Government Current Revenues, 19 L, 1970, 1975, 1980–83
3002   Central Government Tax Revenues, 19 L, 1970–83
3003   Central Government Direct Taxes, 19 L, 1970–83
3004   Central Government Income Taxes, 19 L, 1970–83
3005   Central Government Property Taxes, 18 L, 1970–83
3006   Central Government Production and Sales Taxes, 19 L, 1970–83
3007   Central Government International Trade Taxes, 19 L, 1970–83
3008   Central Government Total Expenditure, 19 L, 1970, 1975, 1980–83
3009   Total Expenditure and Deficit of Central Governments, 19 L, 1975–81
3010   Functional Analysis of Central Government Expenditure, 18 LC
3011   Defense and Social Expenditures, 20 L, 1972 and 1981
3012   Central Government Expenditures, Lending Repayments, and Deficits, 19 LC
3013   Central Government Current Savings, 19 L, 1970, 1975, 1980–83
3014   Central Government Overall Surplus or Deficit, 19 L, 1970, 1975, 1980–83
3015   Central Government Net Domestic Borrowing, 19 L, 1970–1975, 1980–83
3016   Central Government Net Foreign Borrowing, 19 L, 1970, 1975, 1980–83
3017   Central Government Interest Payments, 19 L, 1970–83
3018   Argentina Central Government Revenue, Expenditure, and Financing the Deficit, 1975–81
3019   Bolivia Central Government Revenue, Expenditure, and Financing the Deficit, 1975–81
3020   Brazil Central Government Revenue, Expenditure, and Financing the Deficit, 1975–81
3021   Chile Central Government Revenue, Expenditure, and Financing the Deficit, 1975–81
3022   Colombia Central Government Revenue, Expenditure, and Financing the Deficit, 1975–81
3023   Costa Rica Central Government Revenue, Expenditure, and Financing the Deficit, 1975–81
3024   Dominican Republic Central Government Revenue, Expenditure, and Financing the Deficit, 1975–81
3025   Ecuador Central Government Revenue, Expenditure, and Financing the Deficit, 1975–81
3026   El Salvador Central Government Revenue, Expenditure, and Financing the Deficit, 1975–80
3027   Guatemala Central Government Revenue, Expenditure, and Financing the Deficit, 1975–81
3028   Haiti Central Government Revenue, Expenditure, and Financing the Deficit, 1975–81
3029   Honduras Central Government Revenue, Expenditure, and Financing the Deficit, 1975–81
3030   Mexico Central Government Revenue, Expenditure, and Financing the Deficit, 1975–81
3031   Nicaragua Central Government Revenue, Expenditure, and Financing the Deficit, 1975–81
3032   Panama Central Government Revenue, Expenditure, and Financing the Deficit, 1975–81
3033   Paraguay Central Government Revenue, Expenditure, and Financing the Deficit, 1975–81
3034   Peru Central Government Revenue, Expenditure, and Financing the Deficit, 1975–81
3035   Uruguay Central Government Revenue, Expenditure, and Financing the Deficit, 1975–81
3036   Venezuela Central Government Revenue, Expenditure, and Financing the Deficit, 1975–81
3037   United States Central Government Revenue, Expenditure, and Financing the Deficit, 1970–83
3038   Argentina Money Supply, 1048–83
3039   Bolivia Money Supply, 1952–83
3040   Brazil Money Supply, 1948–83

3041   Chile Money Supply, 1955–83
3042   Colombia Money Supply, 1952–83
3043   Costa Rica Money Supply, 1952–80
3044   Dominican Republic Money Supply, 1952–83
3045   Ecuador Money Supply, 1952–83
3046   El Salvador Money Supply, 1952–82
3047   Guatemala Money Supply, 1952–83
3048   Haiti Money Supply, 1952–83
3049   Honduras Money Supply, 1952–83
3050   Mexico Money Supply, Inflation, and GDP, 1952–84
3051   Nicaragua Money Supply, 1952–83
3052   Panama Money Supply, 1952–83
3053   Paraguay Money Supply, 1952–83
3054   Peru Money Supply, 1952–83
3055   Uruguay Money Supply, 1952–83
3056   Venezuela Money Supply, 1952–83
3057   Money Supply Changes, 19 LC, 1955–83
3058   Income Velocity of Money, 18 L, 1951–82
3059   Income Velocity of Money Plus Quasi-Money, 19 L, 1951–83
3060   Ratio of Currency to Money, 18 LC, 1951–82

Chapter 31 Exchange Rates
3100   IMF Dollar Year-End Exchange Rates, 20 L, 1948–84
3101   IMF Dollar Average Exchange Rates, 19 L, 1965–84
3102   IMF SDR Year-End Exchange Rates, 19 LC, 1970–84
3103   IMF SDR Average Exchange Rates, 19 LC, 1970–84
3104   IMF Dollar Value of SDR, 1969–84
3105   IMF U.S. Dollar Effective Exchange Rate Index, 1970–84
3106   Exchange Rate Agreements, 19 L
3107   Parallel or Black Market Exchange Rates of U.S. Dollars, 12 L, 1968–82
3108   Dollar Exchange Rates on the U.S. Market, 18 L, 1977–85
3109   Exchange Rate History, 13 L, 1937–74
3110   Bolivia Official and Parallel Market Exchange Rates, 1982–85
3111   Central America Official, Financial, and Black Market Exchange Rates, 7 L, 1983 and 1985
3112   Official and Real Mexican Peso Values Compared to Mexico's Real Trade Deficits, 1952–82
3113   ECLA Real Exchange Rate Index, 10 L, 1970–82
3114   Argentina Evolution of Real Exchange Rates and Price Indexes, 1970–82
3115   Bolivia Evolution of Real Exchange Rates and Price Indexes, 1970–81
3116   Brazil Evolution of Real Exchange Rates and Price Indexes, 1970–82
3117   Chile Evolution of Real Exchange Rates and Price Indexes, 1970–82
3118   Colombia Evolution of Real Exchange Rates and Price Indexes, 1970–82
3119   Costa Rica Evolution of Real Exchange Rates and Price Indexes, 1970–82
3120   Ecuador Evolution of Real Exchange Rates and Price Indexes, 1970–82
3121   Nicaragua Evolution of Real Exchange Rates and Price Indexes, 1978–79
3122   Mexico Evolution of Real Exchange Rates and Price Indexes, 1970–82
3123   Paraguay Evolution of Real Exchange Rates and Price Indexes, 1970–82
3124   Peru Evolution of Real Exchange Rates and Price Indexes, 1970–82
3125   Uruguay Evolution of Real Exchange Rates and Price Indexes, 1970–82
3126   Venezuela Evolution of Real Exchange Rates and Price Indexes, 1970–81

Chapter 32 Price Changes, Commodity Prices, and Interest Rates
3200   Guide to Tables 3201–3221: Consumer Price Changes
3201   Argentina Comparative PC of Prices, 1914–83
3202   Bolivia Comparative PC of Prices, 1932–83
3203   Brazil Comparative PC of Prices, 1913–83
3204   Chile Comparative PC of Prices, 1899–1983

3205   Colombia Comparative PC of Prices, 1929–83

3206   Costa Rica Comparative PC of Prices, 1937–83

3207   Cuba Prices, 1938–83

3208   Dominican Republic Comparative PC of Prices, 1942–82

3209   Ecuador Comparative PC of Prices, 1922–83

3210   El Salvador Comparative PC of Prices, 1938–83

3211   Guatemala Comparative PC of Prices, 1939–83

3212   Haiti Comparative PC of Prices, 1949–83

3213   Honduras Comparative PC of Prices, 1926–83

3214   Mexico Comparative PC of Prices, 1901–83

3215   Nicaragua Comparative PC of Prices, 1938–83

3216   Panama Comparative PC of Prices, 1941–83

3217   Paraguay Comparative PC of Prices, 1939–83

3218   Peru Comparative PC of Prices, 1914–83

3219   Uruguay Comparative PC of Prices, 1930–83

3220   Venezuela Comparative PC of Prices, 1929–83

3221   United States Comparative PC of Prices, 1901–83

3222   Retail Price Index Relating to Living Expenditures of U.N. Officials in Latin American Capitals, 20 L, 1966–83

3223   IMF Wholesale Price Index, 13 LC, 1970–83

3224   U.N. Wholesale Price Index, 15 LC, 1971–81

3225   ECLA Import and Export Price Changes, 19 LR, 1976–80

3226   Commodity Prices, 1970–84

3227   OPEC Crude Oil Prices, 1973–83

3228   Prime Rate of Interest Charged by U.S. Banks, 1960–85

3229   Interest on U.S. Commercial Paper, 1900–84

3230   U.S. Federal Funds Interest Rate, 1955–85

3231   Ninety-Day Interest Rates, 11 LC, 1978–82

Chapter 33 Gross Product

3300   General Sources and Methods for Comparative PC of Real GDP Series Presented in Tables 3301 through 3322

3301   Argentina Comparative PC of Real GDP, 1901–84

3302   Bolivia Comparative PC of Real GDP, 1946–84

3303   Brazil Comparative PC of Real GDP, 1921–84

3304   Chile Comparative PC of Real GDP, 1940–84

3305   Colombia Comparative PC of Real GDP, 1926–84

3306   Costa Rica Comparative PC of Real GDP, 1946–84

3307   Cuba Comparative PC of Real Product, 1947–81

3308   Dominican Republic Comparative PC of Real GDP, 1946–84

3309   Ecuador Comparative PC of Real GDP, 1940–84

3310   El Salvador Comparative PC of Real GDP, 1946–84

3311   Guatemala Comparative PC of Real GDP, 1946–84

3312   Haiti Comparative PC of Real GDP, 1946–84

3313   Honduras Comparative PC of Real GDP, 1926–84

3314   Mexico Comparative PC of Real GDP, 1896–1984

3315   Nicaragua Comparative PC of Real GDP, 1946–84

3316   Panama Comparative PC of Real GDP, 1946–84

3317   Paraguay Comparative PC of Real GDP, 1939–84

3318   Peru Comparative PC of Real GDP, 1946–84

3319   Uruguay Comparative PC of Real GDP, 1936–84

3320   Venezuela Comparative PC of Real GDP, 1937–84

3321   Latin America Comparative PC of Real GDP, 1940–84

3322   United States Comparative PC of Real GNP, 1910–84

3323   IMF GDP Annual Percentage Change, 19 LRC, 1955–83

3324   GDP in Constant Dollars of 1970, 19 LR, 1940–79

3325   Structure and Growth of Gross Domestic Product, by Sector, 1961-83
3326   Agricultural Sector: Value Added, Distribution, and Growth, 19 LR, 1961-83
3327   Manufacturing Sector: Value Added, Distribution, and Growth, 19 LR, 1961-83
3328   Shares of Agricultural GDP in Total GDP, 19 LR, 1950-75
3329   Agriculture Share in GDP, 19 LR, 1920-81
3330   Mining and Quarrying Share in GDP, 19 LR, 1920-81
3331   Manufacturing Share in GDP, 19 LR, 1920-81
3332   Construction Share in GDP, 19 LR, 1920-81
3333   Utilities Share in GDP, 19 LR, 1920-81
3334   Transport and Communication Share in GDP, 19 LR, 1920-81
3335   Manufacturing Real Rates of Growth, 18 LC, 1962-83
3336   Agriculture, Forestry, and Fishing Real Rates of Growth, 19 LC, 1962-83
3337   Housing, Defense, Government, and Other Services Share in GDP, 1920-79
3338   Expenditure on GDP, 19 LC, 1960-73
3339   GDP, National Currency, and Current Prices, 18 LC, 1935-66
3340   Argentina Expenditure on GDP and GNP, 1976-82
3341   Bolivia Expenditure on GDP and GNP, 1976-83
3342   Brazil Expenditure on GDP and GNP, 1976-83
3343   Chile Expenditure on GDP and GNP, 1976-83
3344   Colombia Expenditure on GDP and GNP, 1976-83
3345   Costa Rica Expenditure on GDP and GNP, 1976-82
3346   Cuba Gross Material Product, by Economic Sector, 1970-81
3347   Dominican Republic Expenditure on GDP and GNP, 1976-82
3348   Ecuador Expenditure on GDP and GNP, 1976-83
3349   El Salvador Expenditure on GDP and GNP, 1976-83
3350   Guatemala Expenditure on GDP and GNP, 1976-83
3351   Haiti Expenditure on GDP and GNP, 1976-83
3352   Honduras Expenditure on GDP and GNP, 1976-83
3353   Mexico Expenditure on GDP and GNP, 1976-83
3354   Nicaragua Expenditure on GDP and GNP, 1976-83
3355   Panama Expenditure on GDP and GNP, 1976-82
3356   Paraguay Expenditure on GDP and GNP, 1976-83
3357   Peru Expenditure on GDP and GNP, 1976-83
3358   Uruguay Expenditure on GDP and GNP, 1976-83
3359   Venequela Expenditure on GDP and GNP, 1976-83
3360   United States Expenditure on GDP and GNP, 1976-83
3361   Provincial Level GDP and GDP/C in Mexico, 1970 and 1980
3362   GDP and Per Capita GDP at Market Prices, 19 LR, 1960-83
3363   Growth of GDP and of Per Capita GDP, 19 LR, 1961-83
3364   Total Consumption, 19 LR, 1960-83
3365   Gross Domestic Investment, 19 LR, 1960-83
3366   Gross Capital Formation as a Percentage of GDP, 18 L, 1962-83
3367   Estimates of National Income, 18 LRC, 1960-80
3368   Estimates of National Disposable Income, 15 LRC, 1960-80

PART XI: DEVELOPMENT OF DATA

Chapter 34 Changes in Mexico Since 1895: Central Government Revenue, Public Sector Expenditure, and National Economic Growth, by James W. Wilkie
3400   Comparative Price Indexes for Mexico, 1900-82
3401   DGE-BDM Composite Index of Prices for Mexico, 1900-82
3402   Projected and Actual Gross Central Government Expenditure in Mexico, Current and Deflated Terms, 1900-82
3403   Average Per Capita Real Amount of Mexican Central Government Gross Budgetary Expenditure, by Presidential Term, 1900-82

3404   Projected and Actual Parastate Gross Expenditure in Mexico, Current and Deflated Terms, 1940–82
3405   Central Government Gross Expenditure as Share of Mexico's GDP, 1900–82
3406   Parastate Actual Gross Expenditure as Share of Mexico's GDP, 1940–82
3407   Mexico's Real GDP, Average by Period, 1895–1982
3408   Gross Income in Mexico: Central, State, and Local Government Shares in Selected Years, 1900–82
3409   Actual Mexican Central Government Revenue and Selected Shares, 1935–82
3410   Apparent and True Shares of Income Tax Compared to Borrowing as Share of Mexican Central
            Government Revenues, 1935–82
34-A   Mexico's Estimated Population, 1895–1982

FIGURES

Chapter 1 Geography
1:1   Political Map of Extended Latin America (ELA)
1:2   Political Map of Extended Caribbean Region (ECR)
1:3   Central America and the Caribbean: Hydrographic Regions
1:4   South America: Hydrographic Regions

Chapter 4 Transportation Patterns
4:1   Principal Ports and Airports
4:2   Pan American Highway System

Chapter 6 Demography
6:1   Urban Population, Non-Standard Terms, 20 L, 1970-2000

Chapter 8 Health, Nutrition, Family Planning, and Welfare
8:1   Argentina 1955-Based Index of Food/C Production, 20 LRC, 1952-81
8:2   Argentina PC in Food/C Production, 20 LRC, 1953-81

Chapter 10 Political Statistics
10:1   Approximation of Guatemalan Political Violence, May 1983-December 1984

Chapter 13 Labor Force, EAP, Unemployment, Class Structure, and Crime

Chapter 15 Migration and Tourism
15:1   Migratory Currents of Latin American Countries

Chapter 19 Energy Resources: Production, Consumption, and Reserves
19:1   Total Commercial Energy Production
19:2   Electric Plant Location, Mexico, Central America, and the Caribbean
19:3   Electric Plant Location, South America

Chapter 20 Fisheries Production
20:1   FAO Fishing Area Codes

Chapter 24 Selected Commodities in Foreign Trade
24:1   Share of Fourteen Major Commodity Exports in Latin America's Total Export Earnings, 1960-81
24:2   OPEC Oil Production, 1960-83

Chapter 26 Direction of Trade and Major Trading Partners
26:1   Western Hemisphere Declining Share in World Exports, 1950-80
26:2   Regional Imports as Share of Each Country's Total Imports, 1960-80

Chapter 27 Balance of Payments and International Liquidity
27:1   Balance of Payments: Current Account Deficit, 19 L, 1981-83

Chapter 28 Loans, Grants, Assistance, and Peace Corps
28:1   External Public Debt, 19 L, 1981-83

Chapter 30 Government Plans, Revenue and Expenditure, and Money Supply
30:1   Government Deficit as Share of GDP, 19 L, 1981-83
30:2   Mexico Money Supply and Inflation Indexes, 1952-82

Chapter 32 Price Changes, Commodity Prices, and Interest Rates
32:1   Twelve-Month Variations in Consumer Price Indexes, 5 LC, 1981–84
32:2   Twelve-Month Variations in Consumer Price Indexes, 6 LC, 1981–84

Chapter 33 Gross Product
33:1   GDP Shares of Important Activities for Total Latin America and the United States, Ten-Year
         Intervals, 1950–80
33:2   Growth of GDP, 19 L, 1981–83
33:3   PC of GDP for Total Latin America and GNP for the United States, 1940–82

**Chapter 34 Changes in Mexico Since 1895: Central Government Revenue, Public Sector Expenditure, and
         National Economic Growth**
34:1   Mexican Central Government Actual Expenditure Per Capita, in Real Terms, Average by President,
         1900–82
34:2   Actual Gross Expenditure Compared to Projected Gross Expenditure in Mexico, by President,
         1900–82
34:3   Real GDP and GDP/C in Mexico, by Presidential Period, 1895–1982
34:4   Mexican Central Government Gross Income as Share of Central, State, and Municipal Gross Income,
         1900–80
34:5   Mexican Central Government Gross Revenue Shares, 1935–82

EDITOR'S NOTE ON METHODOLOGY

Countries of Latin America

Latin America's self-identification includes twenty republics traditionally united by core language, religion, culture, bureaucratic outlook, and timing of the post-independence experience based upon nineteenth-century liberalism and free trade. Countries are coded A through T:

A. ARGENTINA
B. BOLIVIA
C. BRAZIL
D. CHILE
E. COLOMBIA
F. COSTA RICA
G. CUBA
H. DOMINICAN REPUBLIC
I. ECUADOR
J. EL SALVADOR
K. GUATEMALA
L. HAITI
M. HONDURAS
N. MEXICO
O. NICARAGUA
P. PANAMA
Q. PARAGUAY
R. PERU
S. URUGUAY
T. VENEZUELA

Haiti is included not because of its Latin-based French language but because of its interaction with the Dominican Republic (which it ruled between 1822 and 1844) and its historic identification with Latin American affairs. Former non-Spanish colonies of the Caribbean and South America are excluded because they have had little or no interaction in dialogue and events in Latin America—this region's population is less than 2% of that of Latin America and occupies less than 1% of the geographic area. Puerto Rico is excluded from Latin America, of course, because it has never been independent, belonging until 1898 to Spain and subsequently to the United States.

Problems in the definition of Latin America have come from several directions. After 1910 the twenty traditional Latin American republics (plus the United States) made up the Pan American Union, known since 1948 as the Organization of American States (OAS). Cuba was expelled from the OAS in 1962, reducing the number of Latin American members to nineteen. In 1967 the former English colonies of Barbados and Trinidad-Tobago joined the OAS as did Jamaica in 1969; and thus, in the minds of those who equate the Latin American region with the OAS, the number of countries south of the U.S. border rose to twenty-two. Statistical publications of the OAS in the 1970s began to compare total figures for the twenty-two countries with data for the United States. Further problems of definition come from some geographically minded observers who have sought to delimit the world neatly into physical regions regardless of cultural ties and other historical patterns. For those observers "Latin America" includes all of the islands of the Caribbean and the three South American mainland Guianas even though they are oriented toward Europe.

For further discussion, see SALA, 23, pp. vii–xxv, and SALA, 24-1000.

Regional Groupings in Latin America

LAIA *Latin American Integration Association* (Latin American Free Trade Association [LAFTA] from 1960–80)

Member	Date of Entry
ARGENTINA	Jan. 1981
BOLIVIA	Mar. 1982
BRAZIL	Nov. 1981
CHILE	May 1981
COLOMBIA	May 1981
ECUADOR	Mar. 1982
MEXICO	Feb. 1981
PARAGUAY	Dec. 1980
PERU	Nov. 1981
URUGUAY	Mar. 1981
VENEZUELA	Mar. 1982

AG *Cartagena Agreement, Andean Group*

Member	Date of Entry
BOLIVIA	Nov. 1969
CHILE	Sept. 1969[a]
COLOMBIA	Sept. 1969
ECUADOR	Nov. 1969
PERU	Oct. 1969
VENEZUELA	Nov. 1973

CACM *Central American Common Market*

Member	Date of Entry
COSTA RICA	Sept. 1963
EL SALVADOR	May 1961
GUATEMALA	May 1961
HONDURAS	Apr. 1962[b]
NICARAGUA	May 1961

a. Withdrew Oct. 1976.
b. Withdrew Jan. 1971.

Mathematical Calculation of "Average" Rates
of Change Over Time

*Example data for calculating rate of change in a country
according to four methods*

Elapsed Time	Date	Absolute Data
0.00	March 26, 1937	15,920,694
10.00	March 26, 1947	18,966,767
13.49	Sept. 20, 1960	26,085,326

Methods of Calculating Average Annual (AA) Change[1] in Example Data

Category	Linear	Non-Linear		
	1. APGR Average of Percent Change	2. AA-EC Exponential Change	3. AA-GA Geometric Approximation	4. Geometric Change
Formula[2]	$r = \dfrac{\left(\dfrac{P_n}{P_o}\right) - 1}{n}$	$r = \dfrac{\log \dfrac{P_n}{P_o}}{n \log e}$	$r = \dfrac{2(P_n - P_o)}{n(P_n + P_o)}$	$r = \dfrac{\log\left(\dfrac{P_n}{P_o}\right)}{n}$
Rate 1937-47	1.91	1.75	1.75	1.77
Rate 1947-60	2.78	2.36	2.34	2.39
Analysis	$\dfrac{PC}{n}$	Continuous compounding	Annual compounding; adequate for periods of 5 years or longer	Annual compounding
Short-cut Method	**	Calculate P_n/P_o and look up corresponding value of x in U.S. National Bureau of Standards, *Tables of the Exponential Function e^x*, Applied Mathematics Series 14 (1951), "values of the ascending exponential," pp. 18 and 32. Divide result by elapsed time in example data (10.00 and 13.49).	**	**

---

[1] For further analysis of methodology, see U.S. Bureau of the Census, *The Methods and Materials of Demography*, 2 vols. (Washington, D.C.: Government Printing Office, 1971), II, pp. 377-380, from which the presentation of methods 2, 3, and 4 is adapted. Cf. *SNP*, p. 184.

[2] P_o the initial population

P_n the population at the end of period (in years)
n, the time in years
b, the annual amount of change
e, a mathematical constant (logarithm to the base 10 = .4342945)
PC, percentage change

POPULATION CARTOGRAM OF LATIN AMERICA, 1980

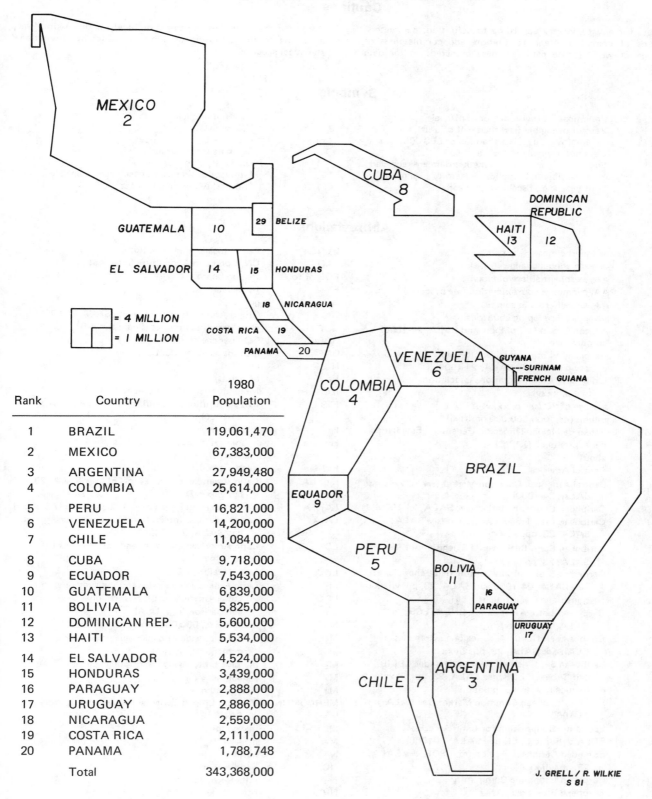

Rank	Country	1980 Population
1	BRAZIL	119,061,470
2	MEXICO	67,383,000
3	ARGENTINA	27,949,480
4	COLOMBIA	25,614,000
5	PERU	16,821,000
6	VENEZUELA	14,200,000
7	CHILE	11,084,000
8	CUBA	9,718,000
9	ECUADOR	7,543,000
10	GUATEMALA	6,839,000
11	BOLIVIA	5,825,000
12	DOMINICAN REP.	5,600,000
13	HAITI	5,534,000
14	EL SALVADOR	4,524,000
15	HONDURAS	3,439,000
16	PARAGUAY	2,888,000
17	URUGUAY	2,886,000
18	NICARAGUA	2,559,000
19	COSTA RICA	2,111,000
20	PANAMA	1,788,748
	Total	343,368,000

SOURCE: SALA LAPUA, pp. 30, 33.

EXPLANATION OF TERMS

Cautions

1. All data for any topic vary according to definition, parameters, methods of compilation and calculation, and completeness of coverage as well as date gathered, date prepared, and/or date adjusted.

2. Totals for the "Latin American region" and for the "world" vary according to the definition used by the different international statistical agencies.

Symbols

‡	Preliminary, provisional, or unofficial	**	Data not applicable
0 or #	Zero or negligible (less than half of unit employed, e.g., less than .05 or 500,000)	$	U.S. dollars
		† or x	Estimate by or in source
~	Data not available in source	@	Estimate made herein
--	Source does not specify whether data are recorded separately, not applicable, zero or negligible	***	Obviously erroneous data
		*	Link (splice) in series or technical change
1965/66	Split year, e.g., fiscal or crop year	( )	Subtotal within tabular data

Abbreviations

A	arithmetic mean
AA	average annual change
AA-EC	AA, exponential (see p. xxxvi)
AA-GA	AA, geometric approximation (see p. xxxvi)
AA-GR	AA, Growth rate in source
ADCs	advanced developing countries
AG	Andean Group (see p. xxxv and SALA, 24-1000)
A-GAP	absolute gap
ALALC	Asociación Latinoamericano de Libre Comercio (see p. xxxv and SALA, 24-1000)
ALADI	Latin American Integration Association (see p. xxxv)
APGR	average of PC (see p. xxxvi)
B	billion (i.e., 000,000,000 omitted)
BDM-DGE	Banco de México-Dirección General de Estadística
C	per capita (e.g., GDP/C)
ca.	about
CA	Central America
CACM	Central American Common Market (see p. xxxv and SALA, 24-1000)
CARICOM	Caribbean Common Market (see SALA, 24-1000)
CARIFTA	Caribbean Free Trade Association (see SALA, SALA, 23, pp. vii-xxv)
CBI	Caribbean Basin Initiative (U.S. legislation) (see SALA, 23, pp. vii-xxv)
CBI-IB	Caribbean Basin Initiative—Intended Beneficiaries (see SALA, 24-1000 and SALA, 23, pp. vii-xxv)
CIF or cif	cost, insurance, and freight
CLA	Caribbean Latin America (cf. CNLA, ECR; see SALA, 23, vii-xxv)
CNLA	Caribbean Not Latin America (e.g., Grenada; cf. CLA). See SALA, 23, pp. vii-xxv
CSOR	Caribbean Sea Oriented Region (includes CBI-IB and Cuba; cf. ECR; see SALA, 23, pp. vii-xxv)
EAP	economically active population
ECCM	Eastern Caribbean Common Market (see SALA 24-1000)
ECLA	Economic Commission for Latin America
ECLA-L	ECLA definition of L (see SALA 24-1000)
ECR	Extended Caribbean Region (cf. CSOR; see SALA, 23, pp. vii-xxv)
EEC	European Economic Community
EFTA	European Free Trade Area
EL or ELA	Extended Latin America (cf. L; see SALA, 23, pp. vii-xxv)
EQN	Economically Questionable Nation

EVN	Economically Viable Nation
FAO	UN, Food and Agriculture Organization
FOB or fob	free on board
FY	fiscal year
G	grams
GA	Grupo Andino (see p. xxxv and SALA 24-1000)
GDP	gross domestic product (Spanish = PIB)
GDP/C	GDP per capita
GNP	gross national product
H	hundred
Ha	hectare(s)
IDB	Inter-American Development Bank
IDB-L	IDB's definition of Latin America (see SALA, 24-1000)
kg	kilogram(s)
km, km^2	kilometer(s), square kilometers
Kw	kilowatt(s)
KWH	kilowatt hours
L or LA	Latin American countries (cf. EL; see SALA, 23, pp. vii-xxv)
LAFTA	Latin American Free Trade Association (see p. xxxv)
LAIA	Latin American Integration Association (see p. xxxv and SALA, 24-1000)
LC	Latin American countries and comparisons (e.g., to USA)
LDCs	Less Developed Countries
LR	Latin American countries and their regional totals
LRC	20 Latin American countries, regional total, and comparison (e.g., USA)
M	million (i.e., 000,000 omitted)
M$_1$	currency outside of banks plus private sector demand deposits
M$_2$	M$_1$ plus time, savings, and foreign currency deposits
Me^2	square meters
Me^3	cubic meters
MERCOMUN	Mercado Común Centroamericano (see p. xxxv and SALA, 24-1000)
MET	metric tons
Mw	megawatts
N	number
NC	national currency
nes	not elsewhere shown
NIC	newly industrializing country
nie	not included elsewhere
NYC	New York City
OAS	Organization of American States (see SALA, 24-1000)

OAS-L	OAS's definition of Latin America (*see* SALA, 24-1000)	PTP	percent of total population
OECD	Organization for Economic Cooperation and Development	R-GAP	relative gap
		SDRs	Special Drawing Rights (IMF's currency)
OECS	Organization of Eastern Caribbean States (*see* SALA, 24-1000)	SNA	system of national accounts
		T	thousand (i.e., 000 omitted)
OPEC	Organization of Petroleum Exporting Countries	T1 (T2, etc.)	territory and its number among listed territories
p (pp)	page(s)	TJ	Terajoules
PC	percentage change	U	unit
PHI	per hundred inhabitants	UN	United Nations
PHTI	per hundred thousand inhabitants	US	U.S. currency
PI	per inhabitant	U.S. or USA	United States of America
PIB	*producto interno bruto* (English = GDP)	WDC	Washington, D.C.
PTI	per thousand inhabitants	YA	yearly arithmetic mean
P10I	per ten thousand inhabitants	YE	year end

Sources

Sources frequently cited. (Abbreviation generally shows agency followed by title of publication or series). Other sources appear in tables throughout.

ADEMA	*See* ECLA	IBRD	International Bank for Reconstruction and Development (*see* WB)
AE	Anuario Estadístico		
AR	Annual Report	ICAO	International Civil Aviation Organization
BDM	Banco de México	ICAO-DS-B	Digest of Statistics, *Bulletin*
BID	Banco Interamericano de Desarrollo (*see* IDB)	ICAO-DS-T	Digest of Statistics, *Traffic: Commercial Air Carriers*
C/CAA	Caribbean/Central American Action, *Caribbean Data Book*	ICAO-DS-AT	Digest of Statistics, *Airport Traffic*
CELADE	Centro Latinoamericano de Demografía (Santiago)	IDB	Inter-American Development Bank (WDC)
		IDB-AR	*Annual Report*
CELADE-BD	*Boletín Demográfico*	IDB-SPTF	Social Progress Trust Fund, *Socio-Economic Progress in Latin America* (1961-71) and *Economic and Social Progress in Latin America* (1972-)
CEPAL	Comisión Económica para América Latina (*see* ECLA)		
COHA	Council on Hemispheric Affairs, *Washington Report on the Hemisphere*		
		ILO	International Labour Office (Geneva)
Colombia-DANE	Departamento Administrativo Nacional	ILO-YLS	*Yearbook of Labor Statistics*
Cuba-CEE	Comité Estatal de Estadística	IMF	International Monetary Fund (WDC)
DGE	Dirección General de Estadística	IMF-BPS	*Balance of Payment Statistics*
DGEC	Dirección General de Estadística y Censos	IMF-BPS-Y	*Balance of Payment Statistics Yearbook*
ECLA	Economic Commission for Latin America (Santiago)	IMF-DOT	*Direction of Trade Statistics*
ECLA-ADEMA	*Agua, Desarrollo y Medio Ambiente* (1977)	IMF-DOT-Y	*Yearbook*
ECLA-AE	*Anuario Estadístico de América Latina*	IMF-GFSY	*Government Finance Statistics Yearbook*
ECLA-BPAL	*Balance de Pagos 1950-77*	IMF-IFS	*International Financial Statistics*
ECLA-CC	Cuadernos de la CEPAL	IMF-IFS-S	*IFS Supplement* (No. 1, 1981-). (See also IFS-Y)
ECLA-CEC	Cuadernos Estadísticos de la CEPAL	IMF-IFS-Y	*Yearbook* (entitled IFS-S from 1961 through 1978)
ECLA-D	Document		
ECLA-EIC	*Estudios e Informes de la CEPAL*	INE	Instituto Nacional de Estadística
ECLA-N	*Notas sobre la Economía y el Desarrollo*	INEC	Instituto Nacional de Estadística y Censos
ECLA-S	*Economic Survey of Latin America*	JLP	José López Portillo (Mexico City)
ECLA-SHCAL	*Series Históricas del Crecimiento 1900-76* (1978)	JLP-AE-H	*Anexo Estadístico Histórico*
ECLA-SP	Preliminary version of ECLA-S	JLP-AP-E	*Anexo de Política Económica*
ECLA-SY	*Statistical Yearbook* (see ECLA-AE)	Mexico-BNCE	Banco Nacional de Comercio Exterior
EYB	*Europa Year Book*	BNCE-CE	*Comercio Exterior*
FAO	UN, Food and Agriculture Organization (Rome)	Mexico-NAFINSA	Nacional Financiera, S.A.
FAO-FY	*Fertilizer Yearbook*	NAFINSA-EMC	*La Economía Mexicana en Cifras*
FAO-PY	*Production Yearbook* (1958-)	NAFINSA-MV	*Mercado de Valores*
FAO-SFA	*State of Food and Agriculture*	OAS	Organization of American States (WDC)
FAO-TY	*Trade Yearbook* (1958-)	OAS-A	*Latin America's Development and the Alliance for Progress* (1973)
FAO-YFP	*Yearbook of Forestry Products*		
FAO-YFS	*Yearbook of Fishery Statistics*	OAS-DB	*Datos Básicos de Población*
FAO-YFSCL	*Catches and Landings*	OASL	OAS's definition of L (*see* SALA, 24-1000)
FAO-YFSFC	*Fishery Commodities*	OAS-SB	*Statistical Bulletin*
IASI	OAS, Inter-American Statistical Institute	PAHO	Pan American Health Organization (WDC)
IASI-AC	*América en Cifras*	PAHO-F	*Facts on Health Progress*
IASI-BE	*Boletín Estadístico*	PAHO-HC	*Health Conditions in the Americas*
IASI-C	*Características de la Estructura Demográfica*	PC	Population Council (NYC)

PC-PFP	*Population and Family Planning*
PC-RPFP	*Report on Population/Family Planning*
SA	*South American Handbook*
SALA	*Statistical Abstract of Latin America*
SALA, 23:1	Volume 23, figure 1 (sample reference)
SALA, 23-100	Volume 23, table 100 (sample reference)
SALA-Cuba	Supplement 1: *Cuba 1968*
SALA LAPUA	Supplement 8: *Latin American Population and Urbanization Analysis*
SALA-MB	Supplement 9: *Statistical Abstract of the United States—Mexico Borderlands*
SALA-MLR	Supplement 5: *Measuring Land Reform*
SALA-SNP	Supplement 3: *Statistics and National Policy*
SALA-TNG	Supplement forthcoming: *The Narrowing Gap*
Schroeder	Susan Schroeder, *Cuba: A Handbook of Historical Statistics* (Boston: G. K. Hall, 1982)
SIPRI-Y	Stockholm International Peace Research Institute, *Yearbook*
SY	Statistical Yearbook
UN	United Nations (NYC)
UN-CSS	*Compendium of Social Statistics*
UN-DY	*Demographic Yearbook*
UN-MB	*Monthly Bulletin of Statistics*
UN-SP	*Statistical Papers*
UN-SP-A	*Series A, Population and Vital Statistics*
UN-SP-J	*Series J, World Energy Supplies*
UN-SP:T	*Series T, Direction of International Trade*
UN-SY	*Statistical Yearbook*
UN-YCS	*Yearbook of Construction Statistics*
UN-YIS	*Yearbook of Industrial Statistics*
UN-YITS	*Yearbook of International Trade Statistics*
UN-YNAS	*Yearbook of National Account Statistics*
UN-YWES	*Yearbook of World Energy Statistics*
UNESCO	UN Educational and Scientific Organization (NYC)
UNESCO-SY	*Statistical Yearbook*
U.S.	United States (WDC)
USAID	U.S. Agency for International Development
USAID-OLG	*U.S. Overseas Loans and Grants Assistance from International Organizations*
USBC	U.S. Bureau of the Census
USBC-HS	*Historical Statistics of the United States*
USBC-SA	*Statistical Abstract of the United States*
USBG	U.S. Board of Governors, Federal Reserve System
USBG-FRB	*Federal Reserve Bulletin*
USBOM	U.S. Bureau of the Mines
USBOM-MCP	*Mineral Commodity Profiles*
USBOM-MIS	*Mineral Industry Surveys*
USBOM-MY	*Minerals Yearbook*
USCIA	U.S. Central Intelligence Agency
USDA	U.S. Department of Agriculture
USDA-AT	*Agricultural Trade of the Western Hemisphere*
USDA-ERS	Economic Research Service
USDA-FAT	*Foreign Agricultural Trade*
USDC-SCB	U.S. Dept. of Commerce, *Survey of Current Business*
USDOD	U.S. Department of Defense
USDOD-FMSA	*Foreign Military Sales Assistance*
USEX-IM	U.S. Export-Import Bank
USINS	U.S. Immigration and Naturalization Service
USINS-AR	*Annual Report*
USINS-SY	*Statistical Yearbook*
USNCC	U.S. National Climatic Center
USNCC-MCDW	*Monthly Climatic Data of the World*
WA	*World Almanac*
WB	World Bank (formerly IBRD)
WB-EDC	*Energy in Developing Countries*
WB-WDR	*World Development Report*
WB-WT	*World Bank Tables*, published by Johns Hopkins Univeristy Press, 1976, 1980
WCE	*World Christian Encyclopedia*
WHO	World Health Organization
WHO-WHSA	*World Health Statistics Annual*
Wilkie	*See SALA*
WTO	World Tourism Organization (Madrid)
WTO-WTS	*World Tourism Statistics*
YC	Yearbook Compendium

Weights and Measures

Length		
	1 kilometer	.6213712 mile
	1.609344 kilometers	1 mile
	1 yard	.914 meter
	1 meter	1.093 yard
	1 foot	.3048 meters
	1 meter	3.2808 feet
	1 inch	25.4 millimeter
	1 inch	2.54 centimeter
	1 millimeter	.03937 inch
	1 centimeter	.3937 inch

Area		
	1 Hectare (10,000 sq. meters)	2.471054 acres
	.4046856 hectares	1 acre
	1 square kilometer	.3861022 square mile
	2.589988 square kilometers	1 square mile

Volume		
	1 cubic meter	35.31467 cubic feet
		1.307951 cubic yards
	.02831685 cubic meter	1 cubic foot

Liquid measure		
	1 liter	1.056688 U.S. quarts
		.26417200 U.S. gallon
	1 U.S. quart	.9463529 liter
	1 U.S. gallon	3.785412 liters

Weight		
	1 kilogram	35.27396 avoirdupois ounces
		32.15075 troy ounces
	.45359237 kilogram	1 avoirdupois pound
	1 metric ton	1.1023113 short tons
		.9842065 long ton
	.9071847 metric ton	1 short ton (2,000 pounds)
	1.0160469 metric tons	1 long ton (2,240 pounds)

Ship tonnage		
	1 register ton (110 cubic feet)	2.83 cubic meters
	1 deadweight ton (1 long ton)	1.016047 metric tons

Rail traffic		
	1 metric ton-kilometer	.684945 short ton-mile
		.611558 long ton-mile
	1 short ton-mile	1.459972 ton-kilometers
	1 long ton-mile	1.635169 ton-kilometers

Lumber		
	1 cubic meter	220.75 board feet
	1,000 board feet	4.53 cubic meters

Agricultural products

		Bales per metric ton
Wheat, pulses, and root crops	Bushel (60 lbs.)	36.744
Maize	Bushel (56 lbs.)	39.638
Coffee	Bags (132.28 lbs.)	16.67
Coffee (El Salvador)	Bags (152.12 lbs.)	14.493
Cotton	Gross Bales (500 lbs.)	4.409
	Net Bales (480 lbs.)	4.593

Coal equivalence

	Metric tons of coal equivalent
Bituminous coal briquettes (1 metric ton)	1.00
Lignite briquettes (1 metric ton)	.67
Pitch coal and black lignite (1 metric ton)	.67
Lignite and brown coal (1 metric ton)	.33
Coke (1 metric ton)	.90
Crude petroleum and shale oil (1 metric ton)	1.30
Gasoline and fuel oil (1 metric ton)	1.50
Natural gas (1,000 cubic meters)	1.33
Manufactured gas (1,000 cubic meters)	.60
Refinery gas (1,000 cubic meters)	1.67
Electric energy (1,000 kilowatt hours)	.125

Energy equivalence

Terajoule $1 \text{ TJ} = 7 \times 10^{6} / .0293076$ Kilo. calories

Temperature Equivalence

See table 305

Other conversions

For other conversions used to obtain standard measures of international comparability, see appendices to U.N., *Statistical Yearbook*; F.A.O., *Production Yearbook*; F.A.O., *World Forestry Inventory 1963*; and especially, U.N., Statistical Papers, Series M, No. 21, *World Weights and Measures*, 1955.

Part I: Geography and Land Tenure

CHAPTER 1

GEOGRAPHY

Figure 1:1

POLITICAL MAP OF EXTENDED LATIN AMERICA (ELA)

NOTE: See SALA 23, pp. vii-xxv, for additional maps and analysis.

Figure 1:2

POLITICAL MAP OF EXTENDED CARIBBEAN REGION (ECR)

NOTE: See SALA 23, pp. vii-xxv, for additional maps and analysis.

Figure 1:3

CENTRAL AMERICA AND THE CARIBBEAN: HYDROGRAPHIC REGIONS

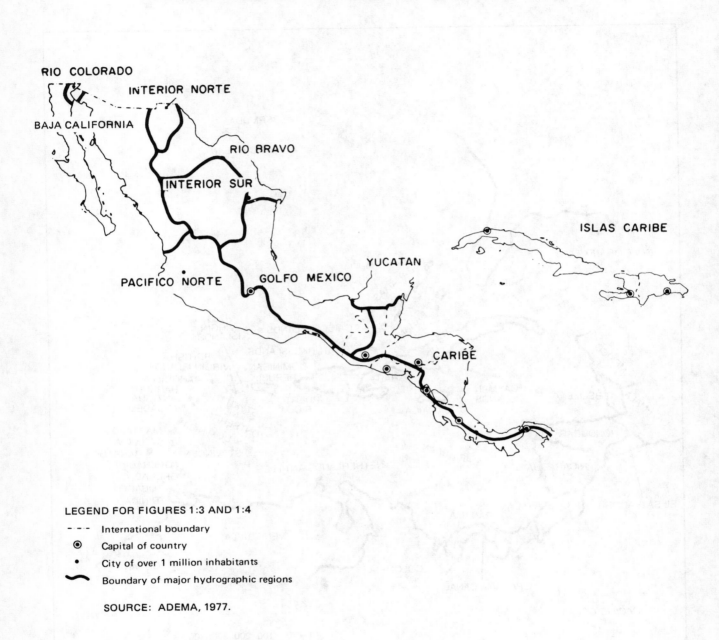

LEGEND FOR FIGURES 1:3 AND 1:4

- – – International boundary
- ◉ Capital of country
- • City of over 1 million inhabitants
- 〰 Boundary of major hydrographic regions

SOURCE: ADEMA, 1977.

Figure 1:4

SOUTH AMERICA: HYDROGRAPHIC REGIONS

NOTE: See SALA 19, pp. 6-10, for maps of River Usage, Reservoir Capacity, and Major Irrigated Areas.

Table 100

ECONOMIC REGIONS: AREA, POPULATION, AND DENSITY, 20 LRC

Country	Area (km^2)	Population 1981		
		M	%	Density[a]
A. World				
Total	135,830,000	4,508	100.0	32.5
Africa	30,319,000	484	10.6	15.5
Asia	27,580,000	2,625	58.0	92.7
Europe	4,937,000	486	11.0	98.2
Oceania	8,510,000	23	.5	2.7
USSR	22,402,000	267	6.0	11.9
Americas	42,082,000	622	13.9	14.6
B. Americas				
Total	42,082,000	622	100.0	14.6
United States[1]	9,363,123	230	37.1	24.4
Latin America	20,003,443	368	59.0	18.1
Canada	9,976,139	24	3.9	2.4
Other	2,739,295	#	#	#
C. Latin American Economic Regional Groupings				
CACM	425,718	21	100.0	39.9
Costa Rica	50,700	2	9.5	39.4
El Salvador	21,041	5	23.8	237.6
Guatemala	108,889	7	33.3	64.3
Honduras	112,088	4	19.0	36.7
Nicaragua	133,000	3	14.3	22.6
ALADI	13,834,368	312	100.0	22.6
Argentina	2,766,889	28	8.7	9.8
Bolivia	1,098,581	6	1.9	5.5
Brazil	8,511,965	123[b]	39.4	14.5
Chile‡	756,945	11	3.5	14.5
Colombia	1,138,914	27	8.6	23.7
Ecuador	283,561	8	2.5	28.2
Mexico	1,972,547	72	23.1	36.5
Paraguay	406,742	3	1.0	7.4
Peru‡	1,285,216	18	5.8	14.0
Uruguay	176,215	3	1.0	17.0
Venezuela	912,050	14	4.5	15.4
AG	5,475,267	73	100.0	13.3
Bolivia	1,098,581	6	8.2	5.5
Colombia	1,138,914	27	37.0	23.7
Ecuador	283,561	8	11.0	28.2
Peru‡	1,285,216	18	24.6	14.0
Venezuela	912,050	14	19.2	15.4
Other				
Total	268,090	22	100.0	82.1
Cuba	114,524	10	45.5	87.3
Dominican Rep.	48,734	5	22.7	102.6
Haiti	27,750	5	22.7	180.2
Panama	75,650	2	9.1	26.4
Panama Canal Zone‡	1,432	~	~	~

1. De jure population, but excluding civilian citizens absent from the country for an extended period of time estimated at 764,701 at the time of the 1960 census.

a. Population divided by area.
b. 1980 data.

SOURCE: Area data from IASI-AC, 1974, table 201-01; population data from UNESCO-SY, 1983, table 1.1; density calculated.

Table 101

ARGENTINA MAJOR CIVIL DIVISIONS: AREA
AND PERCENTAGE
(1980)

| Division[1] | Area[2] | |
	km^2	%
Total	2,794,948	100.0
Capital Federal	200	#
Provinces		
Buenos Aires	310,440	11.1
Catamarca	103,859	3.7
Córdoba	171,982	6.2
Corrientes	94,493	3.4
Chaco	100,199	3.6
Chubut	263,116	9.4
Entre Ríos	75,693	2.7
Formosa	73,972	2.6
Jujuy	51,251	1.8
La Pampa	208,260	7.4
La Rioja	82,109	2.9
Mendoza	149,529	5.3
Misiones	29,449	1.1
Neuquén	81,283	2.9
Río Negro	191,677	6.9
Salta	165,718	5.9
San Juan	93,195	3.3
San Luis	71,472	2.6
Santa Cruz	229,882	8.2
Santa Fé	129,766	4.6
Santiago del Estero	148,730	5.3
Tucumán	22,620	.8
Tierra del Fuego and territories	29,392	1.1

1. For number of civil subdivisions during previous years, see SALA, 23-310.
2. Totals may not add up due to rounding.

SOURCE: Calculated from census data included in SALA, 23-626.

Table 102

BOLIVIA MAJOR CIVIL DIVISIONS: AREA
AND PERCENTAGE
(1976)[‡]

| Division[1] | Area[2] | |
	km^2	%
Total	1,161,954	100.0
Departments		
Bení	167,969	14.4
Chuquisaca	59,541	5.1
Cochabamba	56,181	4.8
La Paz	134,923	11.6
Oruro	51,874	4.5
Pando	34,409	3.0
Potosí	109,786	9.4
Santa Cruz	357,536	30.8
Tarija	37,731	3.2

1. For number of civil subdivisions during previous years, see SALA, 23-301.
2. Totals may not add up due to rounding.

SOURCE: Calculated from census data included in SALA, 23-627.

Table 103

BRAZIL MAJOR CIVIL DIVISIONS: AREA
AND PERCENTAGE
(1980)[‡]

| Division[1] | Area[2] | |
	km[2]	%
Total	8,650,935	100.0
Distrito Federal	5,810	.1
States		
Acre	153,458	1.8
Alagoas	27,561	.3
Amapá	180,078	2.1
Amazonas	1,447,373	16.7
Bahía	564,334	6.5
Ceará	149,442	1.7
Espírito Santo	45,858	.5
Fernando de Noronha	26	#
Goiás	661,217	7.6
Maranhão	315,178	3.6
Mato Grosso[3]	1,169,287	13.5
Mato Grosso do Sul[3]	349,867	4.0
Minas Gerais	593,212	6.9
Pará	1,168,864	13.5
Paraíba	56,200	.6
Paraná	198,706	2.3
Pernambuco	97,513	1.1
Piauí	243,128	2.8
Rio de Janeiro[4]	44,194	.5
Rio Grande do Norte	52,247	.6
Rio Grande do Sul	1,985,512	23.0
Randônia	251,530	2.9
Roraima	20,474	.2
Santa Catarina	97,044	1.1
São Paulo	248,610	2.9
Sergipe	21,834	.3

1. For number of civil subdivisions during previous years, see SALA, 23-301.
2. Totals may not add up due to rounding.
3. Mato Grosso and Mato Grosso do Sul are new states created by dividing the old state of Mato Grosso.
4. Guanabara and Rio de Janeiro states were combined to create the new state of Rio de Janeiro.

SOURCE: Calculated from census data included in SALA, 23-628.

Table 104

CHILE MAJOR CIVIL DIVISIONS: AREA
AND PERCENTAGE
(1982)

| Division[1] | Area[2] | |
	km[2]	%
Total	751,696	100.0
Regions		
Antofagasta	113,734	15.1
Araucanía	31,497	4.2
Atacama	91,536	12.2
Aysén del General Carlos Ibáñez del Campo	109,130	14.5
Bío Bío	36,989	4.9
Coquimbo	41,918	5.6
Libertador General Bernardo O'Higgins	16,250	2.2
Los Lagos	64,879	8.6
Magallanes y la Antártica Chilena	132,333	17.6
Maule	30,134	4.0
Metropolitana de Santiago	15,505	2.1
Tarapacá	54,685	7.3
Valparaíso	16,063	2.1

1. For number of civil subdivisions during previous years, see SALA, 23-301.
2. Totals may not add up due to rounding.

SOURCE: Calculated from census data included in SALA, 23-629.

Table 105

COLOMBIA MAJOR CIVIL DIVISIONS: AREA AND PERCENTAGE

(1973)

Division[1]	Area[2]	
	km[2]	%
Total	1,170,562	100.0
Bogotá, D.E.	1,587	.1
Departments		
Antioquia	63,322	5.4
Atlántico	3,272	.3
Bolívar	29,719	2.5
Boyacá	67,798	5.8
Caldas	7,302	.6
Cauca	30,195	2.6
César	24,275	2.1
Córdobo	24,826	2.1
Cundinamarca (excludes Bogotá, D.E.)	22,133	1.9
Chocó	50,479	4.3
Huila	19,576	1.7
La Guajira	20,058	1.7
Magdalena	23,310	2.0
Meta	81,725	7.0
Nariño	31,043	2.7
Norte de Santander	21,009	1.8
Quindío	1,828	.2
Risaralda	3,970	.3
Santander	30,567	2.6
Sucre	10,424	.9
Tolima	23,167	1.9
Valle del Cauca	21,199	1.8
Intendencias[3]		
Aracuca	23,196	1.9
Caquetá	83,343	7.1
Putumayo	27,584	2.4
San Andrés y Providencia	44	#
Comisarías[3]		
Amazonas	112,025	9.6
Guainía	70,160	6.0
Vaupés[4]	82,610	7.1
Vichada	107,800	9.2

1. For number of civil subdivisions during previous years, see SALA, 23-301.
2. Totals may not add up due to rounding.
3. Four *intendencias* and four *comisarías* have been estimated from the known total for all growth between 1964 and 1968 published in the *Diccionario Geográfico de Colombia* (1970), p. 334.
4. In 1982 a new political unit, Guaviare, was created by dividing Vaupés. The capital is San José del Guaviare.

SOURCE: Calculated from census data included in SALA, 23-630.

Table 106

COSTA RICA MAJOR CIVIL DIVISIONS: AREA AND PERCENTAGE

(1973)

Division[1]	Area[2]	
	km[2]	%
Total	50,589	100.0
Provinces		
Alajuela	9,589	18.9
Cartago	2,591	5.1
Guanacaste	10,511	20.7
Heredia	2,910	5.7
Limón	9,595	18.9
Puntarenas	10,910	21.5
San José	5,188	10.3

1. For number of civil subdivisions during previous years, see SALA, 23-301.
2. Totals may not add up due to rounding.

SOURCE: Calculated from census data included in SALA, 23-631.

Table 107

CUBA MAJOR CIVIL DIVISIONS: AREA
AND PERCENTAGE
(1981)[‡]

Division[1]	Area[2]	
	km[2]	%
Total	110,300	100.0
Ciudad de la Habana	741	.7
Provinces		
Camagüey	14,140	12.8
Ciego de Avila	6,550	5.9
Cienfuegos	4,132	3.7
Granma	8,498	7.7
Guantánamo	6,392	5.8
Holquín	8,932	8.1
Isla de la Juventud	2,226	2.0
La Habana	741	.7
Las Tunas	6,417	5.8
Matanzas	11,617	10.5
Pinar del Río	10,860	9.8
Sancti Spíritus	6,775	6.1
Santiago de Cuba	6,360	5.8
Villa Clara	8,050	7.3

1. For number of civil subdivisions during previous years, see SALA, 23-301.
2. Totals may not add up due to rounding.

SOURCE: Calculated from census data included in SALA, 23-632.

Table 108

DOMINICAN REPUBLIC MAJOR CIVIL DIVISIONS: AREA
AND PERCENTAGE
(1980)[‡]

Division[1]	Area[2]	
	km[2]	%
Total	48.465	100.0
Distrito Nacional	1,477	3.0
Provinces		
Azúa	2,434	5.0
Bahoruco	1,377	2.8
Barahona	2,540	5.2
Dajabón	902	1.8
Duarte	1,294	2.6
El Seibo	3,033	6.2
Espaillat	974	2.0
Independencia	1,903	3.9
La Altagracia	2,781	5.7
La Estrelleta	3,871	7.9
La Romana	3,785	7.8
La Vega	3,455	7.1
María Trinidad Sánchez	1,324	2.7
Montecristi	2,034	4.2
Pedernales	1,032	2.1
Peravia	1,631	3.3
Puerto Plata	1,895	3.9
Salcedo	493	1.0
Samaná	983	2.0
San Cristóbal	3,739	7.7
San Juan	3,582	7.4
San Pedro de Macorís	1,162	2.4
Sánchez Ramírez	1,170	2.4
Santiago	3,100	6.4
Santiago Rodríguez	1,026	2.1
Valverde	580	1.2

1. For number of civil subdivisions during previous years, see SALA, 23-301.
2. Totals may not add up due to rounding.

SOURCE: Calculated from census data included in SALA, 23-633.

Table 109

ECUADOR MAJOR CIVIL DIVISIONS: AREA AND PERCENTAGE
(1982)[‡]

Division[1]	Area[2]	
	km[2]	%
Total	277,699	100.0
Provinces		
Archipiélago de Colón	6,201	2.2
Azuay	9,374	3.3
Bolívar	4,004	1.4
Cañar	4,507	1.6
Carchi	4,418	1.6
Cotopaxi	5,825	2.1
Chimborazo	6,469	2.3
El Oro	6,581	2.3
Esmeraldas	17,705	6.3
Guayas	18,674	6.7
Imbabura	5,684	2.0
Loja	12,364	4.4
Los Ríos	6,633	2.4
Manabí	20,829	7.5
Morona/Santiago	22,365	8.1
Napo	56,521	20.3
Pastaza	32,536	11.7
Pichincha	17,113	6.2
Tungurahua	3,490	1.3
Zamora Chinchipe	22,421	8.1

1. For number of civil subdivisions during previous years, see SALA, 23-301.
2. Totals may not add up due to rounding.

SOURCE: Calculated from census data included in SALA, 23-634.

Table 110

EL SALVADOR MAJOR CIVIL DIVISIONS: AREA AND PERCENTAGE
(1971)[‡]

Division[1]	Area[2]	
	km[2]	%
Total	20,878	100.0
Departments		
Ahuachapán	1,175	5.6
Cabañas	1,025	4.9
Cuscatlán	739	3.5
Chalatenango	1,509	7.2
La Libertad	1,644	7.8
La Paz	1,205	5.7
La Unión	2,472	11.8
Morazán	1,386	6.6
San Miguel	2,139	10.2
San Salvador	868	4.1
San Vicente	1,202	5.7
Santa Ana	2,043	9.7
Sonsonate	1,391	6.6
Usulután	2,125	10.1

1. For number of civil subdivisions during previous years, see SALA, 23-301.
2. Totals may not add up due to rounding.

SOURCE: Calculated from census data included in SALA, 23-635.

Table 111

GUATEMALA MAJOR CIVIL DIVISIONS: AREA AND PERCENTAGE
(1981)

Division[1]	Area[2] km^2	%
Total	107,921	100.0
Departments		
Alta Verapaz	8,706	8.0
Baja Verapaz	3,114	2.8
Chimaltenango	1,972	1.8
Chiquimula	2,386	2.2
El Progreso	1,931	1.7
Escuintla	4,376	4.0
Guatemala	2,125	1.9
Huehuetenango	7,404	6.8
Izabal	9,236	8.5
Jalapa	2,051	1.9
Jutiapa	3,226	2.9
Petén	32,771	30.3
Quezaltenango	1,949	1.8
Quiché	8,363	7.7
Retalhuleu	1,853	1.7
Sacatepéquez	465	.4
San Marcos	3,798	3.5
Santa Rosa	2,953	2.7
Sololá	1,061	.9
Suchitepéquez	2,500	2.3
Totonicapán	1,060	.9
Zacapa	2,693	2.4

1. For number of civil subdivisions during previous years, see SALA, 23-301.
2. Totals may not add up due to rounding.

SOURCE: Calculated from census data included in SALA, 23-636.

Table 112

HAITI MAJOR CIVIL DIVISIONS: AREA AND PERCENTAGE
(1971)

Division[1]	Area[2] km^2	%
Total	27,756	100.0
Departments		
Artibonite	6,171	22.2
Nord	4,221	15.2
Nord-Ouest	2,364	8.5
Ouest	8,435	30.3
Sud	6,642	23.9

1. For number of civil subdivisions during previous years, see SALA, 23-301.
2. Totals may not add up due to rounding.

SOURCE: Calculated from census data included in SALA, 23-637.

Table 113

HONDURAS MAJOR CIVIL DIVISIONS: AREA AND PERCENTAGE

(1974)

Division[1]	Area[2]	
	km²	%
Total	110,577	100.0
Departments		
Atlántida	4,241	3.8
Colón	8,582	7.7
Comayagua	5,209	4.7
Copán	3,219	2.9
Cortes	3,932	3.5
Choluteca	4,177	3.7
El Paraíso	7,042	6.3
Francisco Morazán	7,925	7.1
Gracias a Dios	21,079	19.0
Intibucá	3,025	2.7
Islas de la Bahía	259	.2
La Paz	2,335	2.1
Lempira	4,248	3.8
Ocotepeque	1,650	1.4
Olancho	25,320	22.8
Santa Bárbara	5,143	4.6
Valle	1,568	1.4
Yoro	7,798	7.0

1. For number of civil subdivisions during previous years, see SALA, 23-301.
2. Totals may not add up due to rounding.

SOURCE: Calculated from census data included in SALA, 23-638.

Table 114

MEXICO MAJOR CIVIL DIVISIONS: AREA AND PERCENTAGE

(1980)[‡]

Division[1]	Area[2]	
	km²	%
Total	1,981,853	100.0
Federal District	1,479	.1
States		
Aguascalientes	5,471	.2
Baja California	68,079	3.4
Baja California Sur	73,796	3.7
Campeche	53,175	2.6
Chiapas	74,886	3.7
Chihuahua	241,732	12.1
Coahuila	155,840	7.8
Colima	5,218	.2
Durango	128,910	6.5
Guanajuato	30,444	1.5
Guerrero	63,945	3.2
Hidalgo	20,774	1.0
Jalisco	81,010	4.0
México	21,375	1.1
Michoacán	59,778	3.0
Morelos	4,955	.2
Nayarit	27,037	1.3
Nuevo León	64,823	3.2
Oaxaca	93,265	4.7
Puebla	33,814	1.7
Querétaro	11,524	.6
Quintana Roo	52,464	2.6
San Luis Potosí	64,255	3.2
Sinaloa	58,753	3.0
Sonora	187,366	9.4
Tabasco	24,994	1.3
Tamaulipas	80,205	4.0
Tlaxcala	4,024	.2
Veracruz	72,117	3.6
Yucatán	38,320	1.9
Zacatecas	71,582	3.6

1. For number of civil subdivisions during previous years, see SALA, 23-301.
2. Totals may not add up due to rounding.

SOURCE: Calculated from census data included in SALA, 23-639.

Table 115

NICARAGUA MAJOR CIVIL DIVISIONS: AREA
AND PERCENTAGE

(1971)

Division[1]	Area[2]	
	km^2	%
Total	135,335	100.0
Departments		
Boaco	5,060	3.7
Carazo	1,025	.7
Chinandega	4,653	3.4
Chontales	4,966	3.7
Estelí	4,966	3.6
Granada	962	.7
Jinotega	9,234	6.8
León	5,196	3.8
Madriz	1,727	1.2
Managua	3,628	2.6
Masaya	541	.4
Matagalpa	6,887	5.0
Nueva Segovia	3,332	2.4
Río San Juan	6,750	4.9
Rivas	2,160	1.6
Zelaya	49,610	3.6

1. For number of civil subdivisions during previous years, see SALA, 23-301.
2. Totals may not add up due to rounding.

SOURCE: Calculated from census data included in SALA, 23-640.

Table 116

PANAMA MAJOR CIVIL DIVISIONS: AREA
AND PERCENTAGE

(1980)

Division[1]	Area[2]	
	km^2	%
Total	77,772	100.0
Provinces		
Bocas del Toro	8,736	11.2
Chiriquí	8,679	11.1
Coclé	5,018	6.4
Colón[3]	7,506	9.6
Darién	13,123	16.8
Herrera	2,408	3.1
Los Santos	3,904	5.0
Panamá	11,274	14.4
Veraguas	10,804	13.8

1. For number of civil subdivisions during previous years, see SALA, 23-301.
2. Totals may not add up due to rounding.
3. Includes San Blas territory.

SOURCE: Calculated from census data included in SALA, 23-641.

Table 117

PARAGUAY MAJOR CIVIL DIVISIONS: AREA AND PERCENTAGE
(1972)

Division[1]	Area[2] km^2	%
Total	392,345	100.0
Departments		
Alto Paraná	15,607	4.0
Amambay	13,105	3.3
Boquerón	130,710	33.3
Caaguazú	23,706	6.0
Caazapá	9,364	2.4
Asunción	200	#
Central	2,650	.7
Concepción	18,033	4.6
De la Cordillera	4,984	1.3
Guairá	3,201	.8
Itapuá	16,815	4.3
Misiones	7,702	2.0
Ñeembucú	145,956	3.7
Olimpo	17,893	4.6
Paraguarí	8,142	2.1
Presidente Hayes	38,515	9.8
San Pedro	19,727	5.0

1. For number of civil subdivisions during previous years, see SALA, 23-301.
2. Totals may not add up due to rounding.

SOURCE: Calculated from census data included in SALA, 23-642.

Table 118

PERU MAJOR CIVIL DIVISIONS: AREA AND PERCENTAGE
(1981)

Division[1]	Area[2] km^2	%
Total	1,288,274	100.0
Departments		
Amazonas	41,058	3.2
Ancash	36,368	2.8
Apurimac	20,595	1.6
Arequipa	63,656	4.9
Ayacucho	44,157	3.4
Cajamarca	35,443	2.8
Callao (Provincia Constitucional)	148	#
Cuzco	76,377	5.9
Huancavelica	21.146	1.6
Huánuco	35,385	2.7
ICA	21,269	1.7
Junín	43,482	3.4
La Libertad	23,260	1.8
Lambayeque	13,250	1.0
Lima	33,827	2.6
Loreto	342,591	26.6
Madre de Dios	85,518	6.4
Moquegua	16,129	1.3
Pasco	21,747	1.7
Piura	36,435	2.8
Puno	72,379	5.6
San Martín	53,292	4.1
Tacna	14,751	1.1
Tumbes	4,742	.4
Ucayali[3]	167,224	12.9

1. For number of civil subdivisions during previous years, see SALA, 23-301.
2. Totals may not add up due to rounding.
3. The department of Ucayali was created on June 18, 1980, and is formed by the provinces of Ucayali and Coronel Portillo.

SOURCE: Calculated from census data included in SALA, 23-643.

Table 119

URUGUAY MAJOR CIVIL DIVISIONS: AREA
AND PERCENTAGE
(1975)

Division[1]	Area[2]	
	km^2	%
Total	173,111	100.0
Departments		
Artigas	11,486	6.6
Canelones	4,595	2.7
Cerro Largo	14,739	8.5
Colonia	6,104	3.5
Durazno	10,939	6.3
Flores	4,937	2.9
Florida	11,046	6.4
Lavalleja	10,870	6.3
Maldonado	4,727	2.7
Montevideo	543	.3
Paysandú	14,128	8.2
Río Negro	9,993	5.8
Rivera	9,108	5.3
Rocha	9,893	5.7
Salto	14,700	8.5
San José	4,967	2.9
Soriano	10,038	5.8
Tacuarembó	16,966	9.8
Treinta y Tres	9,136	5.3

1. For number of civil subdivisions during previous years, see SALA, 23-301.
2. Totals may not add up due to rounding.

SOURCE: Calculated from census data included in SALA, 23-644.

Table 120

VENEZUELA MAJOR CIVIL DIVISIONS: AREA
AND PERCENTAGE
(1981)[‡]

Division[1]	Area[2]	
	km^2	%
Total	912,655	100.0
Distrito Federal	1,929	.2
States		
Anzoátegui	43,097	4.7
Apure	65,602	7.2
Aragua	6,944	.8
Barinas	35,378	3.9
Bolívar	222,121	24.3
Carabobo	43,736	.5
Cojedes	15,064	1.7
Falcón	25,395	2.8
Guárico	61,903	6.8
Lara	19,767	2.2
Mérida	11,314	1.2
Miranda	7,934	.9
Monagas	30,009	3.3
Nueva Esparta	1,152	.1
Portuguesa	14,947	1.6
Sucre	11,834	1.3
Táchira	11,126	1.2
Trujillo	7,370	.8
Yaracuy	7,115	.8
Zulia	50,936	5.6
Territories		
Amazonas	152,000	1.7
Delta Amacuro	34,629	3.8

1. For number of civil subdivisions during previous years, see SALA, 23-301.
2. Totals may not add up due to rounding.

SOURCE: Calculated from census data included in SALA, 23-645.

Table 121

ALTITUDE OF PRINCIPAL MOUNTAINS, 20 L

Country	Peak or Volcano	Cordillera	Major Political Division	Altitude Above Sea Level	
				Meters	Feet
A. ARGENTINA	Aconcagua	Andes	Mendoza	6,960[a]	22,835

Continued in SALA, 23-302.

Table 122

HIGH PEAKS OF LATIN AMERICA
(In Descending Order of Altitude)

Peak	Mountain Range	Country	Meters	Peak	Mountain Range	Country	Meters
Aconcagua	Andes	Argentina-Chile	7,040[a]	Huila	Andes	Colombia	5,750

Continued in SALA, 23-303.

Table 123

VOLCANOES OF LATIN AMERICA
(In Descending Order of Altitude)

Volcano (Last Eruption)	Place	Meters
North America		
Colima (1982)	Mexico	4,268

Continued in SALA, 23-304.

Table 124

MAJOR EARTHQUAKES IN LATIN AMERICA, 1797–1983

Date	Place	Deaths	Magnitude[a]
1797 Feb 4	Quito, Ecuador	41,000	~
1868 Aug 13-15	Peru and Ecuador	40,000	~
1875 May 16	Venezuela and Colombia	16,000	~
1906 Aug 16	Valparaiso, Chile	20,000	8.6
1939 Jan 24	Chillan, Chile	28,000	8.3
1949 Aug 5	Pelileo, Ecuador	6,000	6.8
1960 May 21-30	Southern Chile	5,000	8.3
1970 May 31	Northern Peru	66,794	7.7
1972 Dec 23	Nicaragua	5,000	6.2
1976 Feb 4	Guatemala	22,778	7.5
1979 Dec 12	Colombia and Ecuador	800	7.9
1983 Mar 31	Southern Colombia	250	5.5
1983 Apr 3	Southwest Costa Rica	~	7.2
1983 June 7	Southern Mexico	~	7.0, 6.7
1983 June 19	El Salvador	~	7.0
1983 Nov 19	Central Peru	~	6.5
1983 Dec 16	Western Cuba	~	4.4

a. Each higher number represents a tenfold increase in energy measured in ground motion.

SOURCE: WA, 1984, pp. 593, 698.

Table 125

RIVERS

Part I: Principal Rivers of the World

River	Continent	Length (Miles)	Drainage Area (T Sq. Mi.)	Flow[1]
Nile	Africa	4,132	1,293	110
Amazon	South America	3,915	2,722	4,200
Mississippi-Missouri	North America	3,892	1,243.7	620
Yangtze	Asia	3,434	756.5	770
Congo	Africa	2,900	1,425	2,000
Amur	Asia	2,900	711	390
Lena	Asia	2,650	963	530
Yenisei	Asia	2,566	1,003	614
La Plata-Paraná	South America	2,450	1,198	2,800
Ob	Asia	2,287	1,431	441

Part II: Principal Rivers of Latin America

River	Continent	Length (Miles)	Drainage Area (T Sq. Mi.)	Flow[1]
Amazon	South America	3,915	2,722	4,200
Araguaia	South America	1,367	~	~
La Plata-Paraná	South America	2,450	1,198	2,800
Madeira	South America	2,013	~	600
Orinoco	South America	1,700	350	600
Paraguay	South America	1,584	~	160
Paraná	South America	2,796	1,198	550
Purus	South America	1,995	~	~
Río Grande	North America	1,885	172	3
São Francisco	South America	1,811	252	120
Tocantins	South America	1,677	~	~

1. Thousands of cubic feet per second.

SOURCE: U. S. National Oceanic and Atmospheric Administration, *Principal Rivers and Lakes of the World* (Rockville, Md.: U.S. Department of Commerce, 1971).

Table 126

PRINCIPAL NATURAL LAKES OF LATIN AMERICA

Lake	Continent	Depth (Feet)	Sq. Mile Area	Length (Miles)
Maracaibo	South America	115	5,127	96
Nicaragua	North America	230	3,100	102
Titicaca	South America	922	3,200	122

SOURCE: See table 125.

Table 127

PRINCIPAL DESERTS

Desert	Place	Sq. Mile Area
Atacama	Northern Chile	70,000
Bolsón de Mapimi	North Central Mexico	50,000
Olmos	Northwestern Peru	1,000
Morrope	Northwestern Peru	1,500
Sechura	Northwestern Peru	2,000
Vizcaino	Northwestern Mexico	6,000

SOURCE: See table 125.

Table 128

TEMPERATURE AND RAINFALL BY GEOGRAPHIC LOCATION, 20 L

$$\left(\frac{\text{Temp., }°\text{F}}{\text{Rain, inches}}\right)$$

Station	Years Covered	Elev.	Lat.	Long.	Jan.	Feb.	Mar.	Apr.	May	June	July	Aug.	Sept.	Oct.	Nov.	Dec.	Annual
A. ARGENTINA					58.5	57.2	53.1	48.0	42.1	38.1	36.7	37.0	41.0	46.4	50.4	54.3	46.9
SAN CARLOS DE BARILOCHE	30	2,798	41.09	71.18	1.16	1.42	2.40	2.97	5.66	7.95	6.65	5.17	3.08	1.75	1.82	1.75	41.78

Continued in SALA, 23-309 to 23-328. For centigrade conversions, see SALA, 22-305.

Table 129

HIGH AND LOW TEMPERATURE — MONTHLY AVERAGES IN CAPITAL CITY,[1] 20 L

(Fahrenheit)[2]

Country		Jan.	Feb.	March	Apr.	May	June	July	Aug.	Sept.	Oct.	Nov.	Dec.
A. ARGENTINA	high	83	83	79	72	64	57	57	60	64	69	76	82
	low	63	63	60	53	47	41	42	43	46	50	56	61

Continued in SALA, 23-329. For centigrade conversions, see SALA, 22-305.

Table 130

AVERAGE NUMBER OF DAYS WITHOUT RAIN EACH MONTH, 20 L

(Capital Cities)

Country	Jan.	Feb.	March	April	May	June	July	Aug.	Sept.	Oct.	Nov.	Dec.
A. ARGENTINA	24	22	24	22	24	23	23	22	22	22	21	23

Continued in SALA, 23-330.

CHAPTER 2

LAND USE

Table 200

FAO LAND USE DATA, 20 LRC

(T Ha., 1980[a])

		Surface		Agricultural			Nonagricultural	
	Country	Total Area[1]	Land Area[2]	Arable Land[3]	Land under Permanent Crops[4]	Permanent Meadows and Pastures[5]	Forests and Woodlands[6]	Other Uses
A.	ARGENTINA[7]	276,689	273,669	25,150†	10,050†	143,200†	60,050†	35,219
B.	BOLIVIA	109,858	108,439	3,250†	120	27,050†	56,200†	21,819
C.	BRAZIL	851,197	845,651	53,500†	8,450†	159,000†	575,000‡	49,701
D.	CHILE	75,695	74,880	5,332†	198†	11,880†	15,460‡	42,010
E.	COLOMBIA	113,891	103,870	4,050†	1,600†	30,000†	53,300‡	14,920
F.	COSTA RICA	5,070	5,066	283†	207†	1,558‡	1,830‡	1,188
G.	CUBA	11,452	11,452	2,525†	675†	2,523‡	1,900†	3,829
H.	DOMINICAN REP.	4,873	4,838	880†	350†	1,510†	635‡	1,463
I.	ECUADOR	28,356	27,684	1,755†	865†	2,560†	14,550†	7,954
J.	EL SALVADOR	2,104	2,072	560	165	610	140‡	597
K.	GUATEMALA	10,889	10,843	1,480†	354†	870†	4,550‡	3,589
L.	HAITI	2,775	2,756	545†	345†	508†	102‡	1,256
M.	HONDURAS	11,209	11,189	1,560†	197†	3,400†	4,060‡	1,972
N.	MEXICO	197,255	192,304	21,800†	1,530†	74,499	48,500‡	45,975
O.	NICARAGUA	13,000	11,875	1,340†	176‡	3,420†	4,480‡	2,459
P.	PANAMA[8]	7,708	7,599	458†	116†	1,161†	4,170‡	1,694
Q.	PARAGUAY	40,675	39,730	1,620†	300†	15,600†	20,600†	1,610
R.	PERU	128,522	128,000	3,100†	300†	27,120‡	70,900‡	26,580
S.	URUGUAY	17,662	17,362	1,850†	60†	13,819	560‡	1,073
T.	VENEZUELA	91,205	88,205	3,080†	675†	17,200†	34,990‡	32,260
	LATIN AMERICA	2,000,045	1,967,484	134,118	26,733	537,488	971,977	297,168
	UNITED STATES	936,312	912,680	188,755	1,869	237,539	284,464	200,053

1. Refers to total area of country, including area under inland water bodies. Definition of such bodies usually embraces major rivers and lakes.
2. Refers to total area excluding that beneath water bodies.
3. Land under temporary crops, temporary meadows for mowing or pasture, truck gardens or temporarily fallow or idle. Areas double cropped are counted only once.
4. Refers to long-lived perennial crops. Trees for timber production are excluded.
5. Land under permanent (5 or more years) herbaceous forage crops, both cultivated and natural.
6. Land under natural or planted stand of trees, whether productive or not.
7. Continental sector only.
8. Excludes Canal Zone.

a. For previous years see SALA, 18-400; SALA, 19-400; SALA, 20-400; SALA, 21-400; SALA, 22-400; SALA, 23-400.

SOURCE: FAO-PY, 1980-81, table 1.

Table 201

IDB LAND USE DATA BY REGION
(km^2 1970)

Region	Arable Land		Pastures		Forests		Other	
	Area	%	Area	%	Area	%	Area	%
Mexico	232,200	12.1	744,990	38.7	707,000	36.8	238.850	12.4
Central America[1]	60,580	11.9	96.140	18.9	271,130	53.3	80,850	15.0
Caribbean[2]	60,620	25.9	54,030	23.1	47,220	20.2	71,700	30.7
South America								
Andean[3]	226,690	5.0	908,000	19.9	2,700,100	59.2	728,270	15.9
Atlantic[4]	740,369	7.9	1,821,140	19.6	5,373,382	57.8	1,358,550	14.6
Southern Cone[5]	427,380	11.6	1,700,500	46.3	809,068	22.0	734,340	20.0
Latin America and the Caribbean	1,747,839	8.5	5,324,800	26.3	9,907,900	49.1	3,212,560	15.9

1. Belize, Costa Rica, El Salvador, Guatemala, Honduras, Nicaragua, and Panama.
2. Cuba, Haiti, and the Dominican Republic plus thirteen smaller island republics and possessions.
3. Bolivia, Colombia, Ecuador, Peru, and Venezuela.
4. Brazil, French Guiana, Guyana, Paraguay, and Suriname.
5. Argentina, Chile, and Uruguay.

SOURCE: IDB-SPTF, 1983, table II-1.

Table 202

IDB AGRICULTURAL LAND USE DATA BY REGION
(km^2 1977)

Region	Arable	Cultivated	Irrigated	
			Area	% of Cultivated Land
Mexico	232,200	151,900	50,000	32.9
Central America	60,580	43,979	3,210	7.3
Caribbean	60,620	55,175	10,070	18.3
South America				
Andean	226,690	108,850	24,500	22.5
Atlantic	740,369	471,590	12,070	2.6
Southern Cone	427,380	310.360	28,700	9.2
Latin America and the Caribbean	1,747,839	1,141,854	128,550	11.3

SOURCE: IDB-SPTF, 1983, table II-2.

Table 203

CULTIVATED LAND, 20 LR, 1959–74

		T Ha.					Indexes (1959-61 = 100)			
Country		1959-1961	1964-1966	1970	1973	1974	1964-1966	1970	1973	1974
A.	ARGENTINA	14,498	14,745	15,232	15,687	15,655	101.7	106.1	108.2	108.0
B.	BOLIVIA	613	680	771	771	888	110.9	125.8	125.8	144.9
C.	BRAZIL	25,152	29,441	33,906	36,662	40,971	117.1	134.8	145.8	162.9
D.	CHILE	1,544	1,424	1,425	1,200	1,312	92.2	92.3	77.7	85.0
E.	COLOMBIA	3,192	3,546	3,580	3,804	3,997	111.1	112.2	119.2	125.2
F.	COSTA RICA	321	401	352	351	358	124.9	109.7	109.3	111.5
G.	CUBA	1,710	1,679	2,026	1,810	1,817	98.2	118.5	105.8	106.3
H.	DOMINICAN REP.	625	618	667	671	676	98.9	106.7	107.4	108.2
I.	ECUADOR	1,024	1,425	1,678	1,662	1,644	139.2	163.9	162.3	160.5
J.	EL SALVADOR	585	708	614	709	689	121.0	105.0	121.2	117.8
K.	GUATEMALA	1,257	1,523	1,491	1,759	1,809	121.2	118.6	139.9	143.9
L.	HAITI	867	917	931	956	957	105.8	107.4	110.3	110.4
M.	HONDURAS	618	617	599	660	682	99.8	96.9	106.8	110.4
N.	MEXICO	11,458	14,225	13,971	14,570	14,632	124.1	121.9	127.2	127.7
O.	NICARAGUA	518	819	705	708	715	158.1	136.1	136.7	138.0
P.	PANAMA	371	332	449	458	478	89.5	121.0	123.5	128.8
Q.	PARAGUAY	336	497	622	618	742	147.9	185.1	183.9	220.8
R.	PERU	1,612	1,727	1,894	1,749	1,809	107.1	117.5	108.5	112.2
S.	URUGUAY	1,415	1,231	1,035	989	1,073	87.0	73.1	69.9	75.8
T.	VENEZUELA	1,250	1,332	1,727	1,534	1,659	106.6	138.2	122.7	132.7
	LATIN AMERICA[1]	69,257	78,292	84,023	87,677	92,913	111.9	121.3	126.6	134.2

1. Includes Barbados, Guyana, Jamaica, Trinidad and Tobago.

SOURCE: ECLA, *El Desarrollo Latinoamericano y la Coyuntura Económica Internacional, Tercera Parte*, 1975, p. 253.

Table 204

FAO IRRIGATED LAND DATA, 20 LRC, 1961–80

(T Ha.)

Country		1961-65	1966	1970	1975	1976	1977	1978	1979[†]	1980
A.	ARGENTINA	1,046[†]	1,650[†]	1,700[†]	1,800[†]	1,477[†]	1,510[†]	1,540[†]	1,560	1,580
B.	BOLIVIA	74[†]	75[†]	80[‡]	120[†]	120[†]	120[†]	125[†]	125	140
C.	BRAZIL	546[†]	640[†]	796	950[†]	1,400[†]	1,000[†]	1,050[†]	1,700	1,800[†]
D.	CHILE	1,084	1,100[†]	1,180[†]	1,260[†]	1,245[†]	1,300[†]	1,320[†]	1,252	1,255[†]
E.	COLOMBIA	231	240[†]	250[†]	280[†]	285[†]	290[†]	295[†]	305	310[†]
F.	COSTA RICA	26	26[‡]	26[‡]	26[‡]	26[‡]	26[‡]	26[‡]	26	26[‡]
G.	CUBA	280	500[†]	520[†]	535[†]	650[†]	700	720[†]	900	962
H.	DOMINICAN REP.	113	120[†]	125	135	135[†]	140[†]	140[†]	145	145[†]
I.	ECUADOR	446[†]	463[‡]	470[†]	500[†]	510[†]	510[†]	520[†]	520	520[†]
J.	EL SALVADOR	18	20[†]	20[‡]	33	30	50	50	102	110[†]
K.	GUATEMALA	38	45[†]	56	60[‡]	62[†]	64[†]	64[†]	66	68[†]
L.	HAITI	38[†]	42	60[†]	70	70[‡]	70[‡]	70[‡]	70	70[‡]
M.	HONDURAS	60	66[‡]	70[†]	80[†]	80[†]	80[†]	80[†]	80	82[†]
N.	MEXICO	2,900[†]	3,750[†]	3,950[†]	4,479	4,816	5,000[†]	5,000[†]	5,100	5,100[†]
O.	NICARAGUA	18	18[‡]	29[‡]	32	70	74	76[†]	78	80[†]
P.	PANAMA	15	18[†]	20[†]	23[†]	23[†]	25[†]	26[†]	28	28[†]
Q.	PARAGUAY	30[†]	40[†]	40[†]	55[†]	55[†]	55[†]	55[†]	55	60[†]
R.	PERU	1,041	1,078	1,106	1,130[†]	1,150[†]	1,180[†]	1,180[†]	1,180	1,190[†]
S.	URUGUAY	32	42	52	57[†]	58[†]	60[†]	64[†]	70	80[†]
T.	VENEZUELA	218	255[‡]	284[‡]	314[‡]	303[†]	350[†]	360[†]	310	315[†]
	LATIN AMERICA	8,254	9,725[@]	10,364[@]	11,439[@]	12,565[@]	12,604[@]	12,761[@]	13,672[@]	13,921[@]
	UNITED STATES	14,659	15,300[†]	15,900[†]	16,500[†]	16,694[†]	17,200[†]	16,700[†]	16,697	20,517

SOURCE: FAO-PY, 1976-81, table 2.

Table 205

IDB ARABLE AND IRRIGATED LAND DATA

(T Ha., ca. 1978)

	Country	Land		Under Irrigation/Arable (%)
		Arable[1]	Under Irrigation[2]	
A.	ARGENTINA	34,420	1,400	4.1
B.	BOLIVIA	1,100	100	9.1
C.	BRAZIL	38,803	851	2.2
D.	CHILE	5,742	1,244	21.7
E.	COLOMBIA	5,090	270	5.3
F.	COSTA RICA	622	66	10.6
H.	DOMINICAN REP.	995	130	13.1
I.	ECUADOR	4,324	190	4.4
J.	EL SALVADOR	733	26	3.5
K.	GUATEMALA	1,700	60	3.5
L.	HAITI	908	70	7.7
M.	HONDURAS	870	44	5.1
N.	MEXICO	27,390	5,000	18.3
O.	NICARAGUA	960	29	3.0
P.	PANAMA	555	30	5.4
Q.	PARAGUAY	970	50	5.2
R.	PERU	2,880	1,120	38.9
S.	URUGUAY	2,252	45	2.0
T.	VENEZUELA	5,214	235	4.5
	LATIN AMERICA[3]	135,528	10,960	8.1

1. Includes annual and perennial crops, cultivated prairies, and fallow lands.
2. Includes all land irrigated by means of canals, deposits, common and artesian wells, and machinery for drip irrigation, whether it is subject to irrigation all year or only during the dry season.
3. Includes Guyana, Jamaica, Trinidad and Tobago.

SOURCE: IDB-SPTF, 1983, table III-4.

Table 206

U.N. ARABLE LAND AND CROPLAND, 20 LC

(Ha. per Capita and per Person Agriculturally Employed, 1970)

	Country	Arable Land PI	Cropland	
			PI	Agricultural Population
A.	ARGENTINA	1.43	1.07	7.03
B.	BOLIVIA	.47	.63	1.08
C.	BRAZIL	.36	.32	.73
D.	CHILE	.55	.47	1.86
E.	COLOMBIA	.23	.25	.55
F.	COSTA RICA	.28	~	~
G.	CUBA	.42	.43	1.30
H.	DOMINICAN REP.	.23	~	~
I.	ECUADOR	.63	~	~
J.	EL SALVADOR	.18	~	~
K.	GUATEMALA	.30	.29	.46
L.	HAITI	.21	.08	.10
M.	HONDURAS	.33	~	~
N.	MEXICO	.55	.47	1.01
O.	NICARAGUA	.46	~	~
P.	PANAMA	.37	~	~
Q.	PARAGUAY	.43	~	~
R.	PERU	.21	.21	.46
S.	URUGUAY	.63	.67	4.04
T.	VENEZUELA	.48	.47	1.81
	UNITED STATES	.94	.86	21.48

SOURCE: UN-CSS, 1977, pp. 150-152, 1157.

Table 207

HUMID TROPICAL LAND RESOURCES OF SOUTH AMERICA, 8 LR

(M Ha.)

	Country	Soil Areas According to Suitability								
		Cropping						Pasture or Plantations[6]	Forestry or Reserve	Total
		Alluvial[1]	Hydromorphic[2]	Good Upland[3]	Marginal-low Fertility[4]	Marginal-shallow or Steep[5]	Total			
A.	ARGENTINA	2.7	2.3	3.1	5.7	1.7	15.5	15.2	6.5	37.2
B.	BOLIVIA	.7	10.8	.6	12.3	2.2	26.6	52.2 ←		78.8
C.	BRAZIL	3.2	25.4	21.8	174.4	18.5	243.3	333.3	170.1	746.7
E.	COLOMBIA	3.6	6.3	1.5	20.2	.4	32.0	69.4 ←		101.4
I.	ECUADOR	.1	.6	.4	4.8	.1	6.0	15.3 ←		21.3
Q.	PARAGUAY	.7	2.8	4.2	7.1	.7	15.5	14.8	10.4	40.7
R.	PERU	.1	2.7	1.6	17.2	.4	22.0	55.1 ←		77.1
T.	VENEZUELA	.2	5.7	2.3	17.1	5.0	30.3	6.1	18.7	55.1
	Total	11.3	56.6	35.5	258.8	29.0	391.2	767.1 ←		1,158.3

1. Soils developed from recent deposits and located in floodplains or deltas. Characteristics of the soils depend on their parent material.
2. These soils are found on flat or depressed landscapes with little or no runoff where drainage presents a problem.
3. These soils occur on undulating or level topography, are well drained, are not susceptible to serious erosion, and have medium-high natural fertility.
4. These soils are of the upland type but with very low natural fertility. With appropriate crops and fertilizer, reasonable yields may be expected.
5. These soils pose special problems for agricultural use due to shallowness or slope, heavy texture or sandiness. They occur primarily in highland areas and are susceptible to severe erosion.
6. These soils are unsuited to normal crop production because of major limiting factors such as steep topography, poor drainage, low fertility, sandiness, heavy texture, and rock outcrops or stones.

SOURCE: Adapted from Michael Nelson, *The Development of Tropical Lowlands: Policy Issues in Latin America* (Baltimore: John Hopkins University Press, 1973), table 2.

Table 208

PROJECTED NEW LAND DEVELOPMENT AND INVESTMENTS IN SOUTH AMERICA, 7 LR, 1962–85
(M Ha.)

| Country | Irrigated | Dry Land | Dry and Irrigated Cropland[1] | | | Pasture From Forest | Total Forest Clearing | Total Investment[3] |
			From Pasture[2]	From Forest	Total			
B. BOLIVIA	.3	#	.15	.15	.3[a]	4.15	4.3	120
C. BRAZIL	.4	9.4	4.9	4.9	9.8	12.2	17.1	2,120
E. COLOMBIA	.3	1.7	1.0	1.0	2.0[a]	6.6	7.6	440
I. ECUADOR	.1	.6	.35	.35	.7	.85	1.2	93
Q. PARAGUAY	#	.4	.2	.2	.4	3.7	3.9	147
R. PERU	.3[b]	.8	.4	.4	.8	.7	1.1	70
T. VENEZUELA	.3	.1	.2	.2	.4[a]	3.8	4.0	270
TOTAL	1.7	13.0	7.2	7.2	14.4	31.7	39.2[c]	3,260

1. Irrigated land derived 50 percent from pasture and 50 percent from dryland crop area. For table on humid land tropical resources, see SALA, 18-403.
2. Assumption that 50 percent of new cropland will be derived from existing pasture.
3. Investment in development of new lands not associated with irrigation, drainage, or flood control, at 1962 prices.

a. Total area in nonirrigated crops in Colombia is projected to increase by 1.7 million ha. The additional .3 million compensate for projected irrigation of currently nonirrigated pasture and croplands. Increases of .3 million ha. are made for both Bolivia and Venezuela in similar compensation.
b. Irrigated land derived from desert.
c. Annual rate of forest clearing would be 1.75 million ha.

SOURCE: FAO, *Indicative World Plan for Agricultural Development to 1975 and 1985, South America*, vol. 1 (Rome, 1968). Cf. table 2300.

Table 209

FERTILIZER CONSUMPTION,[1] 20 LRC, 1970–81[a]
(T MET)

Country	1970/71	1971/72	1972/73	1973/74	1974/75	1975/76	1976/77	1977/78	1978/79	1979/80	1980/81
A. ARGENTINA	87	77[‡]	86[‡]	83	75[‡]	60[‡]	78	74	107	130	113
B. BOLIVIA	2	4[‡]	5	5	6[‡]	3[‡]	3[‡]	4	5	3	5[‡]
C. BRAZIL	1,002	1,123	1,624	1,673	1,825	1,978	2,528	3,209	3,216	3,563	4,198[‡]
D. CHILE	153	161	157	201	167	99	121	103	129	121	116
E. COLOMBIA	144	184	206	256	250	215	246	282[‡]	276	294	304[‡]
F. COSTA RICA	49	57	48[‡]	64	73[‡]	66[‡]	56	67[‡]	80[‡]	79[‡]	74[‡]
G. CUBA	396	292	229	277	302	331	356	418[‡]	451	464	529[‡]
H. DOMINICAN REP.	38	53	76	76	98	73[‡]	76[‡]	50[‡]	57	72	52[‡]
I. ECUADOR	34	18[‡]	42	52	41	33	81	86	71	79	73
J. EL SALVADOR	65	81[‡]	95[‡]	110[‡]	99[‡]	94[‡]	102	106	112	75[‡]	65
K. GUATEMALA	46	25	43	50	65	55[‡]	95	103	95	100[‡]	93[‡]
L. HAITI	~	~	1	1[‡]	2	2[‡]	~	3[‡]	4[‡]	4[‡]	~
M. HONDURAS	24[‡]	28[‡]	24[‡]	24[‡]	19[‡]	20[‡]	25[‡]	28[‡]	23[‡]	20[‡]	25[‡]
N. MEXICO	538	615	679	780	864	1,073	1,120	1,068	1,067	1,134	1,206[‡]
O. NICARAGUA	26	26	29[‡]	55[‡]	35[‡]	19[‡]	48	48	48	23[‡]	54[‡]
P. PANAMA	21	24	26	22	28	25	23[‡]	23	23[‡]	30[‡]	31[‡]
Q. PARAGUAY	9	5	5	3	2	1	1[‡]	1[‡]	3[‡]	6	6
R. PERU	84[‡]	82	122	98	142	94	117	131	126	110	110
S. URUGUAY	69	88	78	77	68	47	74	63	58	92	81
T. VENEZUELA	59	67	85	91	129	140	161	176	197	222	241
LATIN AMERICA	2,846[@]	3,010[@]	3,660[@]	3,998[@]	4,290[@]	4,428[@]	5,311[@]	6,046[@]	6,144[@]	6,621[@]	7,376[@]
UNITED STATES	15,535	15,580	16,322	17,516	15,941	18,914	20,059	18,676	20,471	20,941	21,274
WORLD	69,068	72,799	77,962	84,369	82,365	90,404	96,658	101,217	108,832	112,403	116,089

1. Includes nitrogenous, phosphate, and potash fertilizers.

a. For 1961-70 data, see SALA, 23-1519.

SOURCE: FAO-FY, 1979 and 1981, table 33.

Table 210

FERTILIZER CONSUMPTION[1] PER HECTARE OF ARABLE LAND AND PER INHABITANT, 20 LC, 1970–80[a]

(H G)

Country	Per Ha. Arable Land and Permanent Crops				PI			
	1970	1975	1979	1980	1970	1975	1979	1980
A. ARGENTINA	26	16	37	32	37	22	49	42
B. BOLIVIA	7	10	12	16	3	6	7	10
C. BRAZIL	283	523	576	678	101	174	288	343
D. CHILE	285	162	246	210	158	92	125	105
E. COLOMBIA	284	421	525	537	65	83	112	118
F. COSTA RICA	1,001	1,353	1,614	1,500	284	344	366	332
G. CUBA	1,517	1,071	1,557	1,653	463	351	505	543
H. DOMINICAN REP.	393	843	585	421	87	164	124	87
I. ECUADOR	89	91	358	277	57	55	120	90
J. SALVADOR	1,043	1,442	1,052	892	185	229	160	135
K. GUATEMALA	300	285	587	507	87	81	151	128
L. HAITI	4	24	44	4	1	5	7	1
M. HONDURAS	286	226	111	139	94	66	55	66
N. MEXICO	216	393	481	517	118	186	169	173
O. NICARAGUA	283	200	152	358	131	83	86	198
P. PANAMA	387	455	523	533	144	152	157	159
Q. PARAGUAY	95	11	29	33	39	4	11	20
R. PERU	300	297	321	325	64	63	64	63
S. URUGUAY	273	231	481	424	171	139	316	277
T. VENEZUELA	113	262	599	642	56	114	154	154
UNITED STATES	809	900	1,106	1,116	758	881	945	934
WORLD	217	287	~	799	88	109	~	262

1. Includes nitrogenous, phosphate, and potash fertilizers.

a. For 1961-65 data, see SALA, 23-1520.

SOURCE: FAO, *Annual Fertilizer Review*, 1976, table 12; FAO-FY, 1979-81, table 11.

Table 211

TRACTORS IN USE, 20 LRC, 1961–80

(N)

Country	1961-65	1969-71	1974	1975	1976	1977	1978	1979[†]	1980[†]
A. ARGENTINA	139,000	171,450	184,000	188,000[†]	190,000[†]	195,000[†]	173,000	171,400	166,700
B. BOLIVIA	220	355	720[†]	759	676	665	726	750	750
C. BRAZIL	97,200	168,257	236,000[†]	254,000	270,000[†]	280,000[†]	300,000[†]	320,000	330,000
D. CHILE	21,061	21,523	28,000[†]	28,000[†]	20,750[†]	20,700[†]	34,500[†]	34,550	34,600
E. COLOMBIA	24,290	22,780	31,000[†]	24,187	24,621	25,594	26,500[†]	27,500	28,423
F. COSTA RICA	4,311	5,100	5,500[†]	5,650[†]	5,700[†]	5,750[†]	5,850[†]	5,900	5,950
G. CUBA	19,800	48,434	52,700	54,851	49,033	64,423	66,349	70,374	68,300
H. DOMINIAN REP.	2,330	2,510	5,500[†]	2,800[†]	2,870[†]	2,930[†]	3,000[†]	3,050	3,150
I. ECUADOR	1,689	3,133	3,400[†]	3,550[†]	5,208	5,440	5,564	5,650	5,750
J. EL SALVADOR	1,800	2,514	2,850[†]	2,900[†]	3,000[†]	3,050[†]	3,150[†]	3,250	3,300
K. GUATEMALA	2,250	3,167	3,600[†]	3,700[†]	3,750[†]	3,800[†]	3,900[†]	3,950	4,000
L. HAITI	271	363	420[†]	440[†]	450[†]	460[†]	480[†]	500	520
M. HONDURAS	331	1,693	950[†]	1,000[†]	3,000[†]	3,100[†]	3,080	3,160	3,250
N. MEXICO	72,000	91,318	135,000[†]	130,000[†]	140,000[†]	101,611	108,259	114,000	120,000
O. NICARAGUA	450	500	768	1,058	1,316	1,636	1,900[†]	2,100	2,200
P. PANAMA	789	2,414	3,500[†]	3,700[†]	3,800[†]	3,850[†]	3,900[†]	3,950	4,000
Q. PARAGUAY	1,500	2,200	2,600[†]	2,700[†]	2,800[†]	2,900[†]	3,000[†]	3,100	3,200
R. PERU	7,707	10,902	12,000[†]	12,500[†]	12,700	13,000[†]	13,300[†]	13,600	13,900
S. URUGUAY	23,812	26,659	27,400[†]	27,500[†]	27,550[†]	27,700[†]	27,900[†]	28,000	28,200
T. VENEZUELA	13,086	19,200	23,460	26,600[‡]	31,164	33,888	35,000[†]	37,000	38,000
LATIN AMERICA	433,447	604,472	765,200[@]	773,895[@]	798,388[@]	795,497[@]	819,358[@]	851,784[@]	864,193[@]
UNITED STATES	4,751,600	4,584,000	4,273,000	4,434,000	4,402,000	4,370,000	4,839,000	4,810,000	4,775,000

SOURCE: FAO-PY, 1976-81, table 109.

CHAPTER 3

LAND TENURE

Table 300

SYSTEMS OF LAND TENURE, ABSOLUTE DATA, 18 LC
(N and Ha.)

Column groups in the original:
- **Operated Under Single Tenurial Systems** spans: *Total, Operated by Owner, Rented from Others (Total, Payment in Cash/Kind, Partnerships or Similar Forms, Payment by Services, Other Arrangements), Occupied Without Title, Operated Under Collective System, Operated Under Other Simple Systems.*
- **Rented from Others** spans: *Total, Payment in Cash/Kind, Partnerships or Similar Forms, Payment by Services, Other Arrangements.*
- **Operated Under Mixed Systems** is a separate column.

Country	Year		Total	Single: Total	Operated by Owner	Rented: Total	Rented: Payment in Cash/Kind	Rented: Partnerships or Similar Forms	Rented: Payment by Services	Rented: Other Arrangements	Occupied Without Title	Operated Under Collective System	Operated Under Other Simple Systems	Operated Under Mixed Systems
A. ARGENTINA[1,2]	1960	N	457,173	457,173	~	~	~	~	#	~	#	#	~	#
		Ha.	175,142,497	175,142,497	103,219,103	29,592,386	22,679,273	2,095,770[a]	#	4,817,343[b]	#	#	42,331,008[c]	#
B. BOLIVIA[3]	1950[v]	N	86,377	86,377	64,396[d]	17,248	13,598	3,033	617[e]	#	#	3,779[f]	954[g]	#
		Ha.	32,749,850	32,749,850	22,227,498[d]	2,471,306	1,983,765	382,115	105,426[e]	#	#	7,178,448[f]	872,598[g]	#
C. BRAZIL	1970	N	4,924,019	4,793,215	2,975,572	1,006,505	?	?	?	?	811,338	?	?	130,804
		Ha.	294,145,466	252,020,808	242,873,710	17,949,833	?	?	?	?	21,197,265	?	?	12,124,658
D. CHILE[6]	1965	N	253,532	225,572	119,704	99,746	12,312	18,009	53,922	15,503[n]	6,122	#	#	27,960
		Ha.	30,644,131	27,513,587	22,669,238	4,354,313	3,523,319	261,673	94,607	474,714[n]	490,037	#	#	3,130,543
E. COLOMBIA[4]	1960	N	1,209,672	1,110,316	755,318	282,347	?	?	?	?	46,961	#	25,690	99,356
		Ha.	27,337,826	25,660,351	19,779,585	2,009,274	?	?	?	?	3,314,076	#	557,416	1,677,475
F. COSTA RICA	1973	N	81,562	81,562	69,660	3,821[b]	1,474	359	?	244	–[l]	7,909	172	··
		Ha.	3,122,457	3,122,457	2,836,060	37,993[b]	24,926	3,563	?	2,712	–[l]	243,495	4,909	··
H. DOMINICAN REP.	1960	N	447,098		262,979	137,865	16,474	30,782	8,716[f]	81,893[pp]	39,596[j]	?	6,658	30,652
		Ha.	2,069,156[t]		1,512,375	427,241	92,549	86,561	35,840[f]	212,291[pp]	109,281[j]	?	20,259	330,900
I. ECUADOR	1954	N	344,234	313,582	233,900	50,121	17,038	13,336[o]	19,747[p]	#	#	5,778[f]	23,783[q]	29,805[i]
		Ha.	5,999,700	5,668,800	4,889,400	551,700	426,200	64,700[o]	60,800[p]	#	#	25,700[f]	202,000[q]	123,900[i]
J. EL SALVADOR	1961	N	226,896	197,091	89,918	99,226	43,457	?	55,769[f]	?	#	#	7,947	7,947
		Ha.	1,581,428	1,458,110	1,225,221	122,954	78,877	?	44,077[f]	?	#	#	109,935	109,935
EL SALVADOR	1971	N	272,432	233,999	107,450	126,549	80,547	?	?	?	#	#	46,002[s]	38,433[i]
		Ha.	1,463,859	1,326,162	1,118,080	208,082	108,841	?	?	?	#	#	99,241[s]	137,697[i]
K. GUATEMALA	1964	N	417,344	371,039	241,541	95,631	47,026	~[w]	48,605[f]	~[q]	~[q]	20,593[f]	13,274[v]	46,305
		Ha.	3,448,736	2,983,292	2,670,962	195,380	106,712	~[w]	88,668[f]	~[q]	~[q]	59,328[f]	57,622[v]	465,445
M. HONDURAS	1966	N	178,361	148,564	39,991	60,142	40,053	~	~	20,089[z]	4,308	44,123[aa]	#	29,797
		Ha.	2,417,053	1,869,402	1,106,907	363,710	122,760	~	~	240,950[z]	30,114	368,671[aa]	#	547,651
N. MEXICO[7]	1970	N	1,020,016	997,324	931,476	52,433	27,277	25,156[bb]	~[cc]	~[cc]	20,375[dd]	~[ee]	38,324	22,692
		Ha.	139,868,191	70,144,089	62,243,958	3,669,841	3,047,110	622,731[bb]	~[cc]	~[cc]	1,747,805[dd]	~[ee]	2,482,486	69,724,102
O. NICARAGUA	1963	N	102,201	88,223	39,445	12,872	4,799	2,906	1,215	3,952	16,049	8,170[aa]	11,687[ff]	13,978
		Ha.	3,822,813	3,822,813	2,550,113	98,300	53,135	13,542	4,354	27,269	735,846	311,343[aa]	127,211[ff]	~99
P. PANAMA	1971	N	105,272	92,971	12,906	4,671	?	?	?	?	75,394	··	··	12,301
		Ha.	2,098,062	1,552,489	545,414	73,961	?	?	?	?	933,144	··	··	545,573

Table 300 (Continued)

SYSTEMS OF LAND TENURE, ABSOLUTE DATA, 18 LC

(N and Ha.)

Country	Year	Total	Operated Under Single Tenurial Systems									Operated Under Mixed Systems
			Operated by Owner	Rented from Others					Occupied Without Title	Operated Under Collective System	Operated Under Other Simple Systems	
				Total	Payment in Cash/Kind	Partnerships or Similar Forms	Payment by Services	Other Arrangements				
q. PARAGUAY[5]	1961											
N		160,777	59,994	12,000	12,000	#	#	#	66,653	#	#	22,130
Ha.		17,473,474	14,200,935	726,799	726,799	#	#	#	1,235,656	#	#	1,310,084
R. PERU	1961											
N		869,945[hh]	574,560	132,647	84,139	48,508[ii]	#	#	#	45,235[ii]	28,678	88,825
Ha.		17,722,044	11,875,859	2,465,253	2,256,939	2,208,314[ii]	#	#	#	1,933,939[ii]	540,887	906,106
S. URUGUAY[8]	1966											
N		79,193	43,656	22,068	19,201	2,867[k]	#	#	4,147	#	2,090	7,232
Ha.		16,533,556	8,198,667	3,845,625	3,688,187	157,438[k]	#	#	167,936	#	503,314	3,818,014
URUGUAY[8]	1970											
N		77,163	45,205	17,398	15,086	2,312[k]	#	#	4,233	#	2,662	7,665
Ha.		16,517,730	8,700,215	3,081,084	2,933,699	147,385[k]	#	#	174,984	#	606,670	3,954,777
T. VENEZUELA	1961[n]											
N		320,094[m]	125,627	41,189	25,966	15,223	#	#	124,119	#	#	24,542
Ha.		26,004,862[x]	21,187,669	613,631	494,950	118,681	#	#	2,832,834	#	#	1,370,728
UNITED STATES	1969											
N		2,730,250	1,705,720	352,923	?	~[u]	?	?	..	?	~[h]	671,607[i]
Ha.		430,336,324	151,799,714	55,688,760	?	~[u]	?	?	..	?	~[h]	222,847,850[i]

1. Details on the number of holdings were not obtained.
2. Excluding 14,583 holdings, the area of which is unknown.
3. For data on Bolivian and Venezuelan land reform, see James W. Wilkie, *Measuring Land Reform*, Supplement 5 (1974).
4. Excluding *Intendencias* and *Comisarías*.
5. Data obtained by sampling.
6. Excluding 5,125 properties without lands.
7. The data refer to the type of producer for 997,324 of total number.
8. Excluding holdings with an area of less than 1 ha.

a. "*Medieros y Tanteros.*"
b. Free occupancy.
c. Comprises 29,477,389 ha. operated in the *Tierras Fiscales* and 12,883,619 ha. operated under "Other Forms of Tenancy."
d. Comprises holdings worked by proprietors alone, properties with settlers, day laborers, etc.
e. "*Tolerados.*"
f. Communal lands.
g. Comprises 818 properties (439,264 ha.) operated by possessors of *Tierras Fiscales* and 136 properties (433,334 ha.) operated by *Granjas Cooperativas y Sociedades Agrícolas.*
h. Holdings operated by administrators.
i. Holdings operated by proprietors lessees.
j. Concessionaire.
k. Holdings operated by "*Medianeros.*"
l. Holdings operated illegally.
m. Including 4,617 holdings without agricultural land.

n. For data on Venezuelan land reform, see Wilkie, *Measuring Land Reform.*
o. Holdings operated by "*Partidarios.*"
p. Holdings operated by "*Huasipungueros.*"
q. Data obtained by sampling.
r. Properties operated by settlers.
s. Holdings operated by "*Colonos.*"
t. Excluding 185,544 ha. in sugar cane.
u. Holdings operated by sharecroppers and livestock sharers.
v. See note 3.
w. Excluding 14,583 holdings, the area of which is unknown.
x. See note 3.
y. Comprises those lands not included in preceding categories. Such lands include those in legal usufruct at time of census; those continuously and pacifically occupied without owners' permission by squatters who do not pay rent; lands in judicial process of transfer.
z. Agricultural holdings in National Lands.
aa. Agricultural holdings in Ejidal Lands.
bb. "*Aparcero*" only.
cc. "*Arrendatario.*"
dd. "*Ocupantes.*"
ee. Property overseen by ejidal president.
ff. Including 7,543 properties (93,716 ha.) operated by usufructuaries.
gg. Farms operated under mixed tenure systems are included in the category of those operated under single systems.
hh. Including 26,663 holdings without land.
ii. Comprises partnership and bound-service by Amerinds (*Yanaconaje*).
jj. Including communal lands.

SOURCE: IASI-AC, 1974, table 311-03; IASI-AC, 1977, table 311-03.

Table 301

SYSTEMS OF LAND TENURE, PERCENTAGE DATA, 18 LC

(N and Ha.)

Country	Year	Total	Operated Under Single Tenurial Systems								Operated Under Collective System	Operated Under Other Simple Systems	Operated Under Mixed Systems
			Total	Operated by Owner	Rented from Others					Occupied Without Title			
					Total	Payment in Cash/Kind	Partnerships or Similar Forms	Payment by Services	Other Arrangements				
A. ARGENTINA[1,2]	1960												
N		100.0	100.0	~	~	~	~	#	~	#	#	~	#
Ha.		100.0	100.0	58.9	16.9	12.9	1.2[a]	#	2.8[b]	#	#	24.2[c]	#
B. BOLIVIA[3]	1950[u]												
N		100.0	100.0	74.6[d]	20.0	15.8	3.5	.7[e]	#	#	4.4[f]	1.1[g]	#
Ha.		100.0	100.0	67.9[d]	7.5	6.0	1.2	.3[e]	#	#	21.9[f]	2.7[g]	#
C. BRAZIL	1970												
N		100.0	97.3	60.4	20.4	~	~	~	~	16.5	~	~	2.7
Ha.		100.0	95.9	82.6	6.1	~	~	~	~	7.2	~	~	4.1
D. CHILE[6]	1965												
N		100.0	89.0	47.2	41.8	4.9	7.1	21.3	6.1	2.4	#	#	11.0
Ha.		100.0	89.8	74.0	14.2	11.5	.9	.3	1.5	1.6	#	#	10.2
E. COLOMBIA[4]	1960												
N		100.0	91.8	62.4	23.3	~	~	~	~	3.9	#	2.1	8.2
Ha.		100.0	93.9	72.4	7.3	~	~	~	~	12.1	#	2.0	6.1
F. COSTA RICA[5]	1973												
N		100.0	90.1	85.4	4.7[b]	1.8	.4[j]	--	.3[k]	-.[l]	9.7	.2	--
Ha.		100.0	92.0	90.8	1.2[b]	.8	.1[j]	--	.1[k]	-.[l]	7.8	.2	--
H. DOMINICAN REP.	1960												
N		100.0	~	58.8	30.8	3.7	6.9	1.9[r]	18.3[jj]	8.9[jj]	~	1.5	~
Ha.		100.0[ii]	~	73.1	20.6	4.5	4.2	1.7[r]	10.3[jj]	5.3[jj]	~	1.0	~
I. ECUADOR	1954												
N		100.0	91.1	67.9	14.6	5.0	3.9[n]	5.7[o]	#	#	1.7[f]	6.9[p]	8.9
Ha.		100.0	94.5	81.5	9.2	7.1	1.1[n]	1.0[o]	#	#	.4[f]	3.4[p]	5.5
J. EL SALVADOR	1961												
N		100.0	86.9	39.6	43.7	19.2	~	24.6[q]	~	#	#	3.5	13.1[i]
Ha.		100.0	92.2	77.5	7.8	5.0	~	2.8[q]	~	#	#	7.0	7.8[i]
EL SALVADOR	1971												
N		100.0	85.9	39.4	46.5	29.6	~	~	~	#	#	16.9[r]	14.1[i]
Ha.		100.0	90.6	76.4	14.2	7.4	~	~	~	#	#	6.8[r]	9.4[i]
K. GUATEMALA	1964												
N		100.0	88.9	57.9	22.9	11.3	~[v]	11.6[q]	#	~	4.9[f]	3.2[x]	11.1
Ha.		100.0	86.5	77.4	5.7	3.1	~[v]	2.6[q]	#	~	1.7[f]	1.7[x]	13.5
M. HONDURAS	1966												
N		100.0	83.3	22.4	33.8	22.5	~	~	11.3[y]	2.4	24.7[aa]	#	16.7
Ha.		100.0	77.3	45.8	15.0	5.1	~	~	10.0[y]	1.2	15.3[aa]	#	22.7
N. MEXICO	1970												
N[7]		100.0	97.8	~	~	~	~[bb]	~	~[cc]	~[dd]	~	~	2.2
Ha.		100.0	50.2	44.5	2.6	2.2	.4[bb]	~	~[cc]	1.2[dd]	~	1.8	49.8
O. NICARAGUA	1963												
N		100.0	86.3	38.6	12.6	4.7	2.8	1.2	3.9	15.7	8.0[aa]	11.4[ee]	13.7
Ha.		100.0	100.0	66.7	2.6	1.4	.4	.1	.7	19.2	8.1[aa]	3.3[ee]	~[ff]
P. PANAMA[8]	1971												
N		100.0	88.3	12.3	4.4	~	~	~	~	71.6	--	--	11.7
Ha.		100.0	74.0	26.0	3.5	~	~	~	~	44.5	--	--	26.0
Q. PARAGUAY[9]	1961												
N		100.0	86.2	37.3	7.5	7.5	#	#	#	41.5	#	#	13.8
Ha.		100.0	92.5	81.3	4.2	4.2	#	#	#	7.1	#	#	7.5
R. PERU	1961												
N		100.0[jj]	89.8	66.0	15.2	9.7	5.6[gg]	#	#	#	5.2[hh]	3.3	10.2
Ha.		100.0	94.9	67.0	13.9	12.7	1.2[gg]	#	#	#	10.9[hh]	3.1	5.1
S. URUGUAY[8]	1966												
N		100.0	90.9	55.1	27.9	24.2	3.6[z]	#	#	5.2	#	2.6	9.1
Ha.		100.0	76.9	49.6	23.3	22.3	1.0[z]	#	#	1.0	#	3.0	23.1
URUGUAY[8]	1970												
N		100.0	90.1	58.6	22.6	19.6	3.0[z]	#	#	5.5	#	3.4	9.9
Ha.		100.0	76.1	52.7	18.6	17.7	.9[z]	#	#	1.1	#	3.7	23.9
T. VENEZUELA	1961[w]												
N		100.0[s]	90.9	39.2	12.9	8.1	4.8	#	#	38.8	#	#	7.7
Ha.		100.0[m]	94.7	81.5	2.4	1.9	.5	#	#	10.9	#	#	5.3
UNITED STATES	1969												
N		100.0	75.4	62.5	12.9	~	~[t]	~	~	--	--	--[h]	24.6[i]
Ha.		100.0	48.2	35.3	12.9	~	~[t]	~	~	--	--	--[h]	51.8[i]

Table 301 (Continued)

SYSTEMS OF LAND TENURE, PERCENTAGE DATA, 18 LC

(N and Ha.)

1. Details on the number of holdings were not obtained.
2. Excluding 14,583 holdings, the area of which is unknown.
3. For data on Bolivian and Venezuelan land reform, see James W. Wilkie, *Measuring Land Reform*, Supplement 5 (1974).
4. Excluding *Intendencias and Comisarías*.
5. Data obtained by sampling.
6. Excluding 5,125 properties without lands.
7. The data refer to the type of producer.
8. Excluding holdings with an area of less than 1 ha.

a. *"Medieros y Tanteros."*
b. Free occupancy.
c. Comprises 29,477,389 ha. operated in the *Tierras Fiscales* and 12,833,619 ha. operated under "Other Forms of Tenancy."
d. Comprises holdings worked by proprietors alone, properties with settlers, day laborers, etc.
e. *"Tolerados."*
f. Communal lands.
g. Comprises 818 properties (439,264 ha.) operated by possessors of *Tierras Fiscales* and 136 properties (433,334 ha.) operated by *Granjas Cooperativas y Sociedades Agrícolas*.
h. Holdings operated by administrators.
i. Holdings operated by proprietors lessees.
j. Product-sharing arrangements.
k. Holdings operated without payment.
l. Holdings operated illegally.
m. For data on Venezuelan land reform, see Wilkie, *Measuring Land Reform*.
n. Holdings operated by *"Partidarios."*
o. Holdings operated by *"Huasipungueros."*

p. Data obtained by sampling.
q. Properties operated by settlers.
r. Holdings operated by *"Colonos."*
s. Including 4,617 holdings without agricultural land.
t. Holdings operated by sharecroppers and livestock-sharers.
u. See note 3.
v. Excluding 14,583 holdings, the area of which is unknown.
w. See note 3.
x. Comprises those lands not included in preceding categories. Such lands include those in legal usufruct at time of census; those continuously and pacifically occupied without owner's permission by squatters who do not pay rent; lands in judicial process of transfer.
y. Agricultural holdings in National Lands.
z. Holdings operated by *"Medianeros."*
aa. Agricultural holdings in Ejidal Lands.
bb. *"Aparcero"* only.
cc. *"Arrendatario."*
dd. *"Ocupantes."*
ee. Including 7,543 properties (93,716 ha.) operated by usufructuaries.
ff. Farms operated under mixed tenure systems are included in the category of those operated under single systems.
gg. Comprises partnership and bound-service by Amerinds (*Yanaconaje*).
hh. Including communal lands.
ii. Excluding 188,544 ha. in sugar cane.
jj. Concessionaire.

SOURCE: IASI-AC, 1974, table 311-03; IASI-AC, 1977, table 311-03.

Table 302

AGRICULTURAL LANDHOLDINGS:[1] NUMBER AND AREA BY SIZE AND CLASS, 20 L

(T Ha.)

In each country block the first data line is **N** (number of holdings, with its %) and the second is **Ha.** (area, with its %). An arrow "→" marks a value that is combined across the spanned size classes.

Country	Measure	Total	Under 1 Ha.	1 to 5 Ha.	5 to 10 Ha.	10 to 20 Ha.	20 to 50 Ha.	50 to 100 Ha.	100 to 200 Ha.	200 to 500 Ha.	500 to 1,000 Ha.	1,000 to 2,500 Ha.	Over 2,500 Ha.
A. ARGENTINA (1960)[2,3]	N	457,173	71,814 (15.7)	109,590 (24.0)	→	→	127,463 (27.9)	→	58,795 (12.9)	38,277 (8.4)	24,876 (5.4)	14,899 (3.3)	11,459 (2.5)
	Ha.	175,142	201 (.1)	1,559 (.9)	→	→	7,710 (4.4)	→	8,778 (5.0)	10,290 (6.2)	15,625 (8.9)	25,774 (14.7)	104,576 (59.7)
B. BOLIVIA (1950)[4]	N	86,377	24,756 (28.7)	26,472 (30.6)	8,760 (10.1)	5,881 (6.8)	4,837 (5.6)	2,776 (3.2)	2,239 (2.6)	2,443 (2.8)	1,540 (1.8)	2,140 (2.5)	3,272 (3.8)
	Ha.	32,750	11 (#)	63 (.2)	63 (.2)	82 (.3)	142 (.4)	183 (.6)	295 (.9)	756 (2.3)	1,051 (3.2)	3,295 (10.1)	26,803 (81.8)
C. BRAZIL (1970)[5]	N	4,912,499	2,524,982 (51.4)	1,935,130 (39.0)	→	→	→	→	415,224 (8.5)	→	→	37,163 (.8)	→
	Ha.	293,012	9,111 (3.1)	60,163 (20.1)	→	→	→	→	108,910 (37.2)	→	→	114,829 (39.2)	→
D. CHILE (1965)[6,7]	N	253,532	45,233 (17.8)	78,460 (30.9)	33,076 (13.0)	29,976 (11.8)	29,360 (11.6)	14,785 (5.8)	9,164 (3.6)	6,998 (2.8)	3,156 (1.2)	3,324 (1.3)	→
	Ha.	30,644	22 (.1)	184 (.6)	230 (.8)	414 (1.4)	912 (3.0)	1,023 (3.3)	1,262 (4.1)	2,168 (7.1)	2,144 (7.0)	22,285 (72.7)	→
E. COLOMBIA (1960)	N	1,209,672	298,071 (24.6)	458,534 (37.9)	169,145 (14.0)	114,231 (9.4)	86,789 (7.2)	32,990 (3.3)	22,317 (1.8)	13,693 (1.1)	4,141 (.3)	1,975 (.2)	786 (.1)
	Ha.	27,338	132 (.5)	1,107 (4.0)	1,165 (4.3)	1,572 (5.8)	2,639 (9.7)	2,680 (9.8)	2,996 (11.0)	3,994 (14.6)	2,731 (10.0)	2,808 (10.2)	5,513 (20.2)
F. COSTA RICA (1963)[8,9,10]	N	64,621	3,661 (5.7)	19,572 (30.3)	10,805 (16.7)	9,161 (14.2)	17,197 (26.6)	→	2,237 (3.5)	1,746 (2.7)	→	183 (.3)	59 (.1)
	Ha.	2,671	3 (.1)	49 (1.8)	77 (2.9)	135 (5.1)	742 (27.8)	→	309 (11.6)	667 (25.0)	→	258 (9.7)	431 (16.1)
G. CUBA (1952)	N	100,965	2,912 (2.9)	11,146 (11.0)	12,480 (12.4)	30,045 (29.8)	20,427 (20.2)	11,282 (11.2)	10,158 (10.1)	→	1,638 (1.6)	877 (.9)	→
	Ha.	7,790	?	?	?	?	?	?	?	→	?	?	→
H. DOMINICAN REP. (1960)	N	447,098	19,201 (4.3)	184,220 (41.2)	48,985 (11.0)	→	12,359 (2.8)	2,450 (.5)	→	676 (.2)		207 (#)	→
	Ha.	2,258	85 (3.8)	373 (16.5)	408 (18.1)	→	366 (16.2)	240 (10.6)	→	224 (9.9)		561 (24.8)	→
I. ECUADOR (1954)	N	344,234	92,387 (26.8)	159,299 (46.3)	36,250 (10.5)	21,400 (6.2)	19,415 (5.6)	8,327 (2.4)	3,452 (1.0)	2,335 (.7)	664 (.2)	464 (.1)	241 (.1)
	Ha.	6,000	46 (.8)	386 (6.4)	272 (4.5)	294 (4.9)	592 (9.9)	547 (9.1)	463 (7.7)	693 (11.6)	465 (7.8)	685 (11.4)	1,557 (26.0)
J. EL SALVADOR (1971)	N	272,432	132,907 (48.8)	103,844 (38.1)	15,730 (5.8)	8,977 (3.3)	6,772 (2.5)	2,241 (.8)	1,115 (.4)	640 (.2)	141 (.1)	65 (#)	→
	Ha.	1,464	71 (4.8)	217 (14.8)	113 (7.7)	127 (8.7)	213 (14.5)	155 (10.6)	154 (10.5)	192 (13.1)	97 (6.6)	127 (8.7)	→
K. GUATEMALA (1964)[8]	N	417,344	364,879 (87.4)	→	→	37,025 (8.9)	6,631 (1.6)	7,859 (1.9)	→	561 (.1)		294 (.1)	95 (#)
	Ha.	3,449	642 (18.7)	→	→	447 (13.0)	204 (5.9)	915 (26.5)	→	346 (10.0)		387 (11.2)	509 (14.8)
L. HAITI (1970)[11]	N	616,710	293,725 (47.6)	231,340 (37.5)	18,550 (3.0)	3,945 (.6)	890 (.1)	→	→	→	→	→	→
	Ha.	864	185 (21.4)	485 (56.1)	121 (14.0)	49 (5.7)	24 (2.8)	→	→	→	→	→	→
M. HONDURAS (1966)[8]	N	178,361	120,441 (67.5)	→	27,112 (15.2)	26,406 (14.8)	→	2,449 (1.4)	1,286 (.7)	398 (.2)		196 (.1)	#
	Ha.	2,417	300 (12.4)	→	252 (10.4)	710 (29.4)	→	226 (9.4)	265 (11.0)	190 (7.9)		202 (8.4)	(11.3)
N. MEXICO (1960)	N	1,365,141	899,108 (65.9)	94,319 (6.9)	132,355 (9.7)	→	70,250 (5.1)	59,091 (4.3)	42,264 (3.1)	30,382 (2.2)	14,792 (1.1)	22,600 (1.7)	→
	Ha.	169,084	1,328 (.8)	679 (.4)	2,185 (1.3)	→	2,490 (1.5)	4,169 (2.5)	5,846 (3.5)	9,492 (5.6)	10,436 (6.2)	132,540 (78.4)	→
O. NICARAGUA (1963)[8,12]	N	102,201	51,936 (50.8)	13,273 (13.0)	25,652 (25.1)	→	6,291 (6.2)	3,554 (3.5)	→	→	920 (.9)	405 (.4)	170 (.2)
	Ha.	3,823	133 (3.5)	122 (3.2)	783 (20.5)	→	538 (14.1)	673 (17.6)	→	→	409 (10.7)	394 (10.3)	771 (20.2)

Table 302 (Continued)

AGRICULTURAL LANDHOLDINGS:[1] NUMBER AND AREA BY SIZE AND CLASS, 20 L

(T Ha.)

Country		Total	Under 1 Ha. N	%	1 to 5 Ha. N	%	5 to 10 Ha. N	%	10 to 20 Ha. N	%	20 to 50 Ha. N	%	50 to 100 Ha. N	%	100 to 200 Ha. N	%	200 to 500 Ha. N	%	500 to 1,000 Ha. N	%	1,000 to 2,500 Ha. N	%	Over 2,500 Ha. N	%
P. PANAMA (1971)[13]	N	90,942	6,665	7.3	34,642	38.1	14,116	15.5	13,641	15.0	13,388	14.7	5,497	6.0	1,887	2.1	816	.9	188	.2	102	→	→	.1
	Ha.	2,019	2	.1	73	3.6	91	4.5	174	8.6	396	19.6	362	17.9	248	12.3	229	11.3	124	6.1	320	→	→	15.8
Q. PARAGUAY (1961)[14]	N	160,777	7,937	4.9	66,622	41.4	37,735	23.5	26,451	16.5	13,700	8.5	3,053	1.9	1,699	1.1	1,310	.8	641	.4	720	.4	909	.6
	Ha.	17,473	~	~	~	~	~	~	~	~	~	~	~	~	~	~	~	~	~	~	~	~	~	~
R. PERU (1972)	N	157,842	46,465	29.4	67,868	43.0	42,531	26.9	→	→	→	→	→	→	→	→	→	→	388	.2	299	.2	214	.1
	Ha.	3,949,191	16,668	.4	167,636	4.2	1,085,180	27.5	→	→	→	→	→	→	→	→	→	→	257,975	6.5	440,802	11.2	1,970,938	49.9
S. URUGUAY (1970)[15]	N	77,163	22,982	29.8	→	→	→	→	12,259	15.9	13,071	16.9	7,927	10.3	6,603	8.6	6,734	8.7	3,626	4.7	2,784	3.6	1,177	1.5
	Ha.	16,518	110	.7	→	→	→	→	169	1.0	411	2.5	559	3.4	931	5.6	2,133	12.9	2,561	15.5	4,305	26.1	5,339	32.3
T. VENEZUELA (1961)[16]	N	320,094	17,734	5.5	137,883	43.0	57,802	18.1	41,387	12.9	28,600	8.9	11,567	3.6	7,332	2.3	6,147	1.9	2,802	.9	2,335	.7	1,888	.6
	Ha.	26,005	9	=	343	1.3	396	1.5	507	1.9	618	2.4	719	2.8	943	3.6	1,766	6.8	1,844	7.1	3,456	13.3	15,199	58.4

1. Economic units of land used for the production of agricultural crops or of livestock. These units are worked or administered by one person, with or without the aid of others; they may consist of either one or of several parcels of land separated one from another so long as they form part of the same economic or management unit.
2. Excluding 14,583 holdings for unknown areas.
3. Actual sizes are: 5-25; 200-400; 400-1,000.
4. Including 1,127 (1.4%) holdings (8,747 equals .03% ha.) not distributed for extension.
5. Including 4,023 (.1%) holdings, not distributed for extension.
6. Excluding 5,162 holdings without area.
7. Actual sizes are: 1,000-2,000; 2,000 and over.
8. Original figures presented in manzanas. A manzana is equal to .7 ha. Sixty-four manzanas equal one caballeria.
9. Actual sizes are: 0-14; 1.05-4.89; 4.90-10.49; 10.50-20.99; 21.00-101.49; 101.50-199.49; 199.50-1,000.99; 1,001.00-2,449.99; 2,450.00 and over

10. Excluding holdings less than .7 ha. (1 manzana).
11. Actual sizes are: 0-.10; .11-.20; .21-.32; .33-.49; .50-.64; .65-1.00; 1.01-1.29; 1.30-1.99; 2.00-2.58; 2.59-3.00; 3.01-3.87; 3.88-4.99; 5.00-5.16; 5.17-6.45; 6.46-9.99; 10.00-12.90; 12.91-19.99; 20.00-25.80; 25.81 and over.
12. Actual sizes are: 0-6.99; 7.00-13.99; 14.00-69.99; 70.00-139.99; 140.00-349.99; 350.00-699.99; 700.00-1,749.99; 1,750.00 and over.
13. Excluding holdings less than .5 ha.
14. Data obtained by sampling.
15. Excluding holdings less than 1 ha.
16. Including 4,617 (1.4%) holdings without area.

SOURCE: Adapted from IASI-AC, 1972, table 311-04. FAO Preliminary Results of the 1960 World Census of Agriculture, 5th, 19th and 21st Issues. IASI-AC, 1974, table 311-04; Peru from 1972 Peru agricultural census.

Table 303

SIZE OF AGRICULTURAL HOLDINGS, 15 LC, 1950-70

(Area in T Ha.)

Size of Holding	Number 1970	Number 1960	Number 1950	Area 1970	Area 1960	Area 1950
A. ARGENTINA[1]						
Total	527,314‡	457,173	441,431	142,445‡	175,142	173,448
To 5.0	~	71,814	59,616	~	201	~
5.1-25.0	~	109,590	101,836	~	1,559	~
25.1-100.0	~	127,463	128,285	~	7,710	~
100.1-200.0	~	58,795	63,025	~	8,778	~
200.1-400.0	~	38,277	62,976	~	10,920	~
400.1-1,000.0	~	24,876		~	15,625	~
1,000.1-2,500.0	~	14,899	20,151	~	25,774	~
2,500.1-5,000.0	~	5,798		~	22,240	~
5,000.1-10,000.0	~	3,110	3,393	~	23,929	~
10,000.1 +	~	2,551	2,149	~	58,407	~
C. BRAZIL[2]						
Total	4,912,499	3,333,746	2,064,278	293,012	249,862	232,211
To 10	2,524,982	1,495,020	710,934	9,111	5,952	3,025
10 to less than 100	1,935,130	1,491,415	1,052,557	60,163	47,566	35,563
100 to less than 1,000	415,224	314,831	268,159	108,910	86,029	75,521
1,000 to less than 10,000	35,772	30,883	31,017	80,399	71,421	73,093
10,000 +	1,391	1,597	1,611	34,430	38,893	45,009
D. CHILE[3]						
Total	258,657	253,532	159,959	30,644	30,644	27,712
Less than 1.0	~	45,233	28,246	~	22	8
1.0-4.9	~	78,460	27,515	~	184	70
5.0-9.9	~	33,076	19,866	~	230	139
10.0-19.9	~	29,976	19,225	~	414	272
50.0-99.9	~	14,785	12,346	~	1,023	857
100.0-199.9	~	9,164	8,474	~	1,262	1,164
200.0-499.9	~	6,998	6,766	~	2,168	2,100
500.0-999.9	~	3,156	3,076	~	2,144	2,101
1,000.0-1,999.9	~	1,533	1,555	~	2,115	2,112
2,000.0-4,999.9	~	1,061	999	~	3,315	3,020
5,000.0 +	~	730	696	~	16,855	15,165
E. COLOMBIA[4]						
Total	~	1,209,672	919,000	~	27,338	27,748
Less than .5	~	165,652	161,778	~	38	84
.5 to less than 1	~	132,419		~	94	
1 to less than 2	~	191,347	342,788[a]	~	270	843[a]
2 to less than 3	~	117,005		~	276	
3 to less than 4	~	92,001		~	309	
4 to less than 5	~	58,181		~	252	
5 to less than 10	~	169,145	143,549	~	1,165	983
10 to less than 20	~	114,231	101,275	~	1,572	1,376
20 to less than 30	~	44,049	85,371[b]	~	1,044	2,594[b]
30 to less than 40	~	26,500		~	890	
40 to less than 50	~	16,240		~	705	
50 to less than 100	~	39,990	37,814	~	2,680	2,586
100 to less than 200	~	22,317	22,969	~	2,996	3,432
200 to less than 500	~	13,693	15,366	~	3,994	4,686
500 to less than 1,000	~	4,141	4,912	~	2,731	3,749
1,000 to less than 2,500	~	1,975	2,541	~	2,808	4,037
2,500 +	~	786	637	~	5,513	3,378

Size of Holding	Number 1970	Number 1960	Number 1950	Area 1970	Area 1960	Area 1950
F. COSTA RICA[5]						
Total	81,562	64,621	47,286	3,122	2,671	1,854
0.70-1.04	~	3,661	2,940	~	3	2
1.05-4.89	~	19,572	10,693	~	49	21
4.90-6.99	~	4,692	7,362	~	26	35
7.00-10.49	~	6,113	4,580	~	51	38
10.50-13.99	~	3,429	2,468	~	40	29
14.00-20.99	~	5,732	4,231	~	95	70
21.00-34.99	~	7,435	5,614	~	195	147
35.00-69.99	~	7,240	5,061	~	342	238
70.00-101.49	~	2,522	1,725	~	205	139
101.50-121.49	~	745	480	~	82	52
122.50-174.99	~	1,174	704	~	169	101
175.00-199.49	~	318	183	~	58	34
199.50-349.99	~	973	634	~	247	160
350.00-699.99	~	596	359	~	276	164
700.00-1,000.99	~	177	92	~	144	74
1,001.00-1,049.99	~	14	13	~	14	14
1,050.00-2,449.99	~	169	97	~	244	147
2,450.00 +	~	59	50	~	431	388
J. EL SALVADOR[6]						
Total	272,432	226,896	174,204	1,464	1,581	1,530
To .99	132,907	107,054	70,416	71	61	35
1.00-1.99	59,842	48,501	35,189	83	68	48
2.00-2.99	44,002	22,038	19,882	134	54	48
3.00-3.99		8,527	7,760		31	27
4.00-4.99		7,178	7,226		33	32
5.00-9.99	15,730	14,001	14,064	113	99	99
10.00-19.99	8,977	8,824	8,874	127	117	122
20.00-49.99	6,772	6,711	6,660	213	209	206
50.00-99.99	2,241	2,214	2,107	155	155	148
100.00-199.99	1,115	1,121	1,059	154	158	146
200.00-499.99	640	713	654	192	219	198
500.00-999.99	141	189	168	97	128	115
1,000.00-2,499.99	65	91	110	127	132	172
2,500.00 +		34	35		117	133
K. GUATEMALA[7]						
Total	~	417,344	348,687	~	3,449	3,721
To .69	~	85,083	74,269	~	33	29
0.70-1.39	~	98,658	91,581	~	95	95
1.40-3.49	~	129,116	99,779	~	271	212
3.50-6.99	~	52,023	42,444	~	243	198
7.00-22.39	~	37,025	26,916	~	447	311
22.40-44.71	~	6,631	6,125	~	204	190
44.72-447.19	~	7,859	6,488	~	915	813
447.20-894.39	~	561	569	~	346	354
894.40-2,235.99	~	293	358	~	387	496
2,236.00-4,471.99	~	56	104	~	170	328
4,472.00-8,943.99	~	30	32	~	178	196
8,944.00 +	~	9	22	~	161	500

Table 303 (Continued)

SIZE OF AGRICULTURAL HOLDINGS, 15 LC, 1950-70

(Area in T Ha.)

Size of Holding	Number 1970	Number 1960	Number 1950	Area 1970	Area 1960	Area 1950
L. HAITI[8]						
Total	616,710	~	~	864	~	~
To .10	16,820	~	~	1	~	~
.11-.20	36,050	~	~	6	~	~
.21-.32	107,480	~	~	35	~	~
.33-.49	28,485	~	~	13	~	~
.50-.64	104,890	~	~	66	~	~
.65-1.00	68,260	~	~	64	~	~
1.01-1.29	76,010	~	~	96	~	~
1.30-1.99	65,920	~	~	116	~	~
2.00-2.58	44,340	~	~	110	~	~
2.59-3.00	9,260	~	~	27	~	~
3.01-3.87	27,370	~	~	97	~	~
3.88-4.99	8,440	~	~	39	~	~
5.00-5.16	4,300	~	~	22	~	~
5.17-6.45	7,810	~	~	48	~	~
6.46-9.99	6,440	~	~	51	~	~
10.00-12.90	2,660	~	~	29	~	~
12.91-19.99	1,285	~	~	20	~	~
20.00-25.80	590	~	~	13	~	~
25.81+	300	~	~	11	~	~
M. HONDURAS[9]						
Total	~	178,361	156,135	~	2,417	2,507
.69	~	26,719	~	~	19	~
.70-3.49	~	57,409	~	~	113	~
3.50-6.99	~	36,313	~	~	168	~
7.00-13.99	~	27,112	~	~	252	~
14.00-34.99	~	19,977	~	~	412	~
35.00-69.99	~	6,429	~	~	298	~
70.00-139.99	~	2,449	~	~	226	~
140.00-349.99	~	1,286	~	~	265	~
350.00-699.99	~	398	~	~	190	~
700.00-1,749.99	~	196	~	~	202	~
1,750.00+	~	73	~	~	272	~
N. MEXICO[10]						
Total	1,016,569	1,365,141	1,383,212	144,637	169,084	145,517
Less than 1	~	899,108	498,399 }	~	1,328	182 }
1-5	~	94,319	506,440	~	679	1,180
5-10	~	132,335	90,216	~	2,105	703
10-25	~	70,250	101,143	~	2,490	1,708
25-50	~	59,091	59,605	~	4,169	2,237
50-100	~	42,264	43,568	~	5,846	3,304
100-200	~	30,382	28,585	~	9,492	4,212
200-500	~	14,749	24,247	~	10,436	8,057
500-1,000	~	17,036	11,469	~	39,905	8,359
1,000-5,000	~	5,564	14,802	~	92,635	33,757
5,000-10,000	~	~	2,564 }	~	~	18,110 }
10,000+	~	~	2,174	~	~	63,706
O. NICARAGUA[11]						
Total	~	102,201	51,581	~	3,823	2,372
To .69	~	2,258	~	~	1	~
.70-3.49	~	33,948	10,214	~	58	18
3.50-6.99	~	15,730	7,729	~	74	36
7.00-13.99	~	13,273	8,621	~	122	79
14.00-34.99	~	14,703	10,687	~	308	224
35.00-69.99	~	10,949	7,829	~	475	344
70.00-139.99	~	6,291	3,782	~	538	321
140.00-349.99	~	3,554	1,874	~	673	356
350.00-699.99	~	920	483	~	409	215
700.00-1,749.99	~	405	256	~	394	249
1,750.00+	~	170	106	~	771	529
P. PANAMA[12]						
Total	90,942	95,505	85,473	2,019	1,806	1,159
.5 to less than 1	6,665	4,959	~	2	3 }	~
1-5	34,642	38,733	44,442	73	93	96
5-10	14,116	18,086	16,847	91	118	106
10-20	13,641	14,897	12,235	174	192	153
20-50	13,388	12,038	8,231	396	355	237
50-100	5,497	4,329	2,407	362	284	156
100-200	1,887	1,574	809	248	201	103
200-500	816	665	348	229	189	100
500-1,000	188	133	96	124	87	67
1,000+	102	91	58	320	284	141
Q. PARAGUAY[13]						
Total	~	160,777	149,614	~	17,473	16,817
.1-.4	~	2,192	1,593	~	~	~
.5-.9	~	5,745	4,829	~	~	3
1.0-1.9	~	18,870	17,549	~	~	22
2.0-2.9	~	18,977	17,793	~	~	40
3.0-3.9	~	15,575	15,253	~	~	49
4.0-4.9	~	13,200	11,697	~	~	49
5.0-9.9	~	37,735	34,949	~	~	230
10.0-19.9	~	26,451	25,192	~	~	317
20.0-49.9	~	13,700	12,982	~	~	341
50.0-99.9	~	3,053	2,837	~	~	183
100.0-199.9	~	1,699	1,568	~	~	224
200.0-499.9	~	1,310	1,234	~	~	375
500.0-999.9	~	641	589	~	~	399
1,000-1,999.9	~	720 }	1,015 }	~	~	2,220
2,000-4,999.9	~	361	259	~	~	1,795
5,000-9,999.9	~	270	130	~	~	1,787
10,000-19,999.9	~	132	145	~	~	8,783
20,000+	~	146	~	~	~	~

Table 303 (Continued)
SIZE OF AGRICULTURAL HOLDINGS, 15 LC, 1950-70
(Area in T Ha.)

Size of Holding	Number 1970	Number 1960	Number 1950	Area 1970	Area 1960	Area 1950
S. URUGUAY[14]						
Total	77,163	86,928	85,258	16,518	16,988	16,974
1-4	11,085	12,769	10,953	30	34	29
5-9	11,897	13,028	11,117	80	89	77
10-19	12,259	14,032	13,771	169	197	193
20-49	13,071	15,715	16,910	411	495	535
50-99	7,927	9,490	10,375	559	674	732
100-199	6,603	7,387	7,814	931	1,042	1,104
200-499	6,734	6,986	7,241	2,133	2,174	2,272
500-999	3,626	3,712	3,475	2,561	2,609	2,444
1,000-2,499	2,784	2,587	2,452	4,305	3,994	3,810
2,500-4,999	869	891	763	2,963	3,043	2,584
5,000-9,999	253	280	316	1,644	1,857	2,065
10,000 +	55	51	71	732	780	1,130
T. VENEZUELA[15]						
Total	?	315,477	234,730	?	26,005	22,127
Less than .5	?	5,068	} 14,274	?	1	} 7
.5-.9	?	12,666		?	8	
1.0-1.9	?	40,920	} 111,716	?	49	} 260
2.0-2.9	?	42,449		?	94	
3.0-3.9	?	29,899		?	98	
4.0-4.9	?	24,615		?	107	
5.0-5.9	?	19,083		?	103	
6.0-6.9	?	14,703	} 42,014	?	95	} 276
7.0-7.9	?	8,874		?	65	
8.0-8.9	?	10,392		?	88	
9.0-9.9	?	4,750		?	45	

Size of Holding	Number 1970	Number 1960	Number 1950	Area 1970	Area 1960	Area 1950
T. VENEZUELA (Cont'd)						
10.0-14.9	?	29,535	} 27,551	?	316	} 363
15.0-19.9	?	11,852		?	191	
20.0-29.9	?	15,920	} 18,900	?	345	} 546
30.0-39.9	?	7,646		?	251	
40.0-49.9	?	5,034	7,123	?	220	464
50.0-99.9	?	11,567	4,284	?	719	541
100.0-199.9	?	7,332	3,582	?	943	1,044
200.0-499.9	?	6,147	1,864	?	1,766	1,221
500.0-999.9	?	2,802	1,669	?	1,844	2,468
1,000-2,499.9	?	2,335	1,753	?	3,456	
2,500.0 +	?	1,888		?	15,199	14,936
UNITED STATES[16]						
Total	2,730,250	3,157,857	3,710,503	430,321	449,293	454,631
to 4.04	?	182,581	244,328	?	315	431
4.05-20.23	?	637,434	813,216	?	7,012	8,896
20.24-40.46	?	542,430	657,990	?	16,022	19,397
40.47-56.65	?	324,652	394,505	?	15,333	18,624
56.66-72.84	?	308,288	378,003	?	19,711	24,155
72.85-89.02	?	191,254	225,576	?	15,299	18,035
89.03-105.21	?	164,188	188,899	?	15,805	18,166
105.22-202.34	?	451,301	471,547	?	64,589	67,051
202.35-404.69	?	210,437	200,012	?	58,519	55,444
404.70 +	?	145,292	136,427	?	236,688	224,432

1. 1960 = Census of September, 1960; 1950 = Census of April, 1947.
2. 1970 = Census of December, 1970; 1960 = Census of September, 1960; 1950 = Census of December, 1950.
3. 1960 = Census of April, 1965; 1950 = Census of July, 1950.
4. 1960 = Census of 1960; 1950 = Census of June, 1954.
5. 1960 = Census of April, 1963; 1950 = Census of March, 1955.
6. 1970 = Census of July 1971; 1960 = Census of June, 1961; 1950 = Census of October, 1950.
7. 1960 = Census of April, 1964; 1950 = Census of April, 1950.
8. 1970 = Census of September, 1971.
9. 1960 = Census of March, 1966; 1950 = Census of March, 1952.
10. 1960 = Census of May, 1960; 1950 = Census of May, 1950.

11. 1960 = Census of May, 1963; 1950 = Census of May, 1952.
12. 1970 = Census of May, 1971; 1960 = Census of April, 1961; 1950 = Census of December, 1950.
13. 1960 = Census of August, 1961; 1950 = Census of September, 1956.
14. 1970 = Census of 1970; 1960 = Census of May, 1961; 1950 = Census of May, 1951.
15. 1960 = Census of February, 1961; 1950 = Census of November, 1950.
16. 1960 = Census of October, 1964; 1950 = Census of October, 1959.

a. 1-5 Ha.
b. 21-50 Ha.

SOURCE: IASI-AC, 1974, table 311-04; FAO-PY, 1975, table 3.

Table 304

CUMULATIVE LAND REFORM DATA[1], 15 L

(Through 1969)

	Country	Initiation of Program	Number of Families Benefitted	Number of Hectares Distributed or Confirmed
B.	BOLIVIA	1955	208,181	9,740,681
C.	BRAZIL	1964	46,457	957,106
D.	CHILE	1965	15,800	2,093,300
E.	COLOMBIA	1961	91,937	2,832,312
F.	COSTA RICA	1963	3,889	60,055
H.	DOMINICAN REP.	1963	9,717	46,082
I.	ECUADOR	1964	27,857	152,115
K.	GUATEMALA	1955	26,500	166,734
M.	HONDURAS	1963	5,843	90,642
N.	MEXICO	1916	2,525,811	59,413,656
O.	NICARAGUA	1964	8,117	357,989
P.	PANAMA	1963	2,594	37,339
Q.	PARAGUAY	1963	#	#
R.	PERU	1961	31,600	850,522
T.	VENEZUELA	1959	117,286	4,605,594

1. Excludes colonization and land settlement.

SOURCE: James W. Wilkie, *Measuring Land Reform*, Statistical Abstract of Latin America, Supplement 5 (Los Angeles: UCLA Latin American Center Publications, University of California, 1974), p. 3, from which this table is adapted.

Part II: Transportation and Communication

CHAPTER 4

TRANSPORTATION

Table 400

CITY TO CITY DISTANCES BY NONSTOP AIR SERVICE
(Miles)

From/To	Country[1]	City Code/Miles	From/To	Country[1]	City Code/Miles	From/To	Country[1]	City Code/Miles
ACAPULCO	**MEX**	**ACA**	SANTA MARTA	COL	42	MANAUS	BRAZ	1,119
ATLANTA GA	USA	1,507	SANTO DOMINGO	D R	619	MANIZALES	COL	109
CHICAGO ILL	USA	1,879	VALLEDUPAR	COL	109	MARACAIBO	VEN	447
DALLAS TEX	USA	1,124	**BELEM**	**BRAZ**	**BEL**	MEDELLIN	COL	145
GUADALAJARA	MEX	346	BELO HORIZONTE	BRAZ	1,382	MEXICO CITY	MEX	1,961
HOUSTON TEX	USA	934	BRASILIA	BRAZ	1,001	MIAMI FLA	USA	1,513
LIMA	PERU	2,527	CAMPO GRANDE	BRAZ	1,545	NEIVA	COL	145
LOS ANGELES CAL	USA	1,654	CAYENNE	F GU	506	NEW YORK NY	USA	2,487
MEXICO CITY	MEX	191	CONCEICAO	BRAZ	480	OCANA	COL	250
MONTREAL QUE	CAN	1,487	CUIABA	BRAZ	1,567	PANAMA CITY	PAN	470
NEW YORK NY	USA	2,260	CURITIBA	BRAZ	1,674	PEREIRA	COL	112
OAXACA	MEX	204	FLORIANOPOLIS	BRAZ	1,828	POINTE A PITRE	GUAD	1,171
PAPEETE	F POL	4,138	FORTALEZA	BRAZ	710	QUITO	ECUA	450
PUERTO VALLARTA	MEX	448	GOIANIA	BRAZ	1,102	RIO DE JANEIRO	BRAZ	2,827
SAN ANTONIO TEX	USA	886	IMPERATRIZ	BRAZ	400	SAN ANDRES	COL	749
TORONTO ONT	CAN	2,202	LISBON	PORT	3,733	SAN JUAN	P R	1,096
						SANTA MARTA	COL	444

Continued in SALA, 23-308

Table 401

AIR PASSENGER KILOMETERS OF SCHEDULED SERVICE,[1] 20 LC, 1970–82[d]
(M)

	Country	Total[3]					International Flights[4]				
		1970	1975	1980	1981	1982[a]	1970	1975	1980	1981	1982
A.	ARGENTINA	2,395	4,373	8,031	7,019	6,083	1,420	2.128	4.413	3.651	2.758
B.	BOLIVIA	109	331	944	963	780[b]	45[†]	163	570	626	449[b]
C.	BRAZIL	4,385	9,787	15,573	10.762	17,229	2,278	4,503	6,008	6,149	6,368
D.	CHILE	839	1,276	1,875	2,220	1,824	426	892	1,364	1,554	1,109
E.	COLOMBIA	2,063	2,778	4,161	4,289	5,050	882	1,384	2,203	2,383	2,353
F.	COSTA RICA	168	306	647[c]	568	618[b]	145	279	438[c]	568	618[b]
G.	CUBA	502	517	694[c]	517[c]	1,100	185	264	380[c]	416[c]	830
H.	DOMINICAN REP.	68[†]	319	460[c]	271[c]	481[b]	68[†]	319	460[c]	271[c]	481[b]
I.	ECUADOR	256[‡]	301	851	~	862	177	220	851	~	732
J.	EL SALVADOR	144	~	289	300	335[b]	144[†]	~	289	300	335[b]
K.	GUATEMALA	104[†]	139	159	174	159[b]	85[†]	139	159	174	159[b]
L.	HAITI[‡]	1[†]	~	~	~	~	~	~	~	~	~
M.	HONDURAS	167	240	387	341	271[b,c]	143	225	369	327	256[b,c]
N.	MEXICO	2,939	6,710	11,560[c]	14,638	13,363	1,446[†]	2,889	5,557[c]	7,600	6,019
O.	NICARAGUA	77[†]	83	~	~	~	71[†]	376	395	~	~
P.	PANAMA	134	405	409	377	329[b,c]	100[†]	376	395	377	329[b,c]
Q.	PARAGUAY	81[†]	76	~	~	~	71[†]	~	~	~	~
R.	PERU	789[†]	1,222	1,974	1,954	1,685	682	387	822	739	690
S.	URUGUAY	63	79	5[c]	82[c]	151[c]	60	60	5[c]	77[c]	142[c]
T.	VENEZUELA	1,033	2,269	4,367	4,332[c]	5,165	827	1,558	2,670	2,246[c]	3,291
	UNITED STATES[2]	210,327	262,013	404,978[c]	399,521[c]	409,397	38,507	43,404	81,187[c]	84,790[c]	83,387

1. Regularly scheduled domestic and international services of the registered airlines, including flights occasioned by excess traffic.
2. Since 1965 flights to U.S. territories have been considered domestic.
3. Includes scheduled domestic and international services of the registered domestic and international airlines.
4. Includes international flights from international scheduled, registered airlines.

a. Unless otherwise stated data taken from ICAO Bulletin, 1984.
b. Data from ICAO-DS-T, 1978–82; see source.
c. Data for one or more months missing.
d. For earlier years, see SALA, 23-2200.

SOURCE: Calculated from ICAO-DS-T, 1969–73, no. 33, vol. 2, tables 9 and 14; ICAO-DS-T, 1975–79, no 39, parts B and C; ICAO-DS-T, 1978–82, parts A, B, and C; ICAO Bulletin, July 1984.

Table 402

KILOMETERS[1] FLOWN OF SCHEDULED SERVICE,[2] 20 LC, 1970–82[a]

(T)

Country	1970	1975	1980	1981	1982
A. ARGENTINA	47,400	63,700	93,800	90,300	75,900
B. BOLIVIA	3,600	6,000	13,500	12,600	10,500
C. BRAZIL	95,400	170,200	203,400	116,900	169,400
D. CHILE	20,900	21,000	24,700	28,800	26,300
E. COLOMBIA	54,800	43,300	42,900	48,900	61,300
F. COSTA RICA	6,000	6,000	7,300[b]	7,600	7,500
G. CUBA	7,200	8,400	6,700[b]	6,800[b]	~
H. DOMINICAN REP.	3,100[†]	4,000	4,800[b]	3,200[b]	5,500
I. ECUADOR	12,300	3,000	10,800[b]	~	~
J. EL SALVADOR	5,800[†]	~	6,100	6,200	6,400
K. GUATEMALA	4,900[†]	3,800	3,700	3,500	3,500
L. HAITI	500[†]	~	~	~	~
M. HONDURAS	6,000	5,700	7,300	5,900	4,300[b]
N. MEXICO	57,700	89,200	125,300[b]	160,200	72,200
O. NICARAGUA	2,200[†]	~	~	~	~
P. PANAMA	5,000[†]	8,700	6,600	6,800	5,000[b]
Q. PARAGUAY	2,300[†]	~	~	~	~
R. PERU	20,000	21,800	24,600	24,400	12,900[b]
S. URUGUAY	2,300	2,700	100[b]	2,000[b]	3,100[b]
T. VENEZUELA	21,300	37,200	61,000	41,800[b]	24,000[b]
UNITED STATES	3,887,600	3,605,400	4,413,400	4,331,300[b]	4,252,700[b]

1. Some figures may be rounded.
2. Regularly scheduled domestic and international services of the registered airlines, including flights occasioned by excess traffic.

a. For previous years, see SALA, 23-2201.
b. Data for one or more months missing.

SOURCE: ICAO-DS-T, 1969-73, no. 33, vol. 2, table 4; ICAO-DS-T, 1975-79, no. 39, parts B and C; ICAO-DS-T, 1978-82, parts A, B, and C.

Table 403

AIR PASSENGERS TRANSPORTED,[1] 18 LRC, 1970–82

(T)

Country	1970 Total	1970 Domestic	1970 International	1975 Total	1975 Domestic	1975 International	1980 Total	1980 Domestic	1980 International	1981 Total	1981 Domestic	1981 International	1982 Total	1982 Domestic	1982 International
A. ARGENTINA	2,332	1,201†	1,131	3,299	2,623	676	5,589	4,289	1,300	5,199	3,899	1,300	5,735	3,752	1,983
B. BOLIVIA	244	204†	40	653	547	106	1,342	1,074	268	1,221	962	259	1,160	944	216
C. BRAZIL	3,340	2,811	529	7,773	6,772	1,001	13,008	11,678	1,330	6,866	5,579	1,287	13,168	11,867	1,301
D. CHILE	575	430	145	510	288	222	669	370	299	885	559	326	822	551	271
E. COLOMBIA	3,011	2,726	285	3,376	2,882	494	4,728	3,976	752	4,570	3,819	751	6,702	5,948	754
F. COSTA RICA	256	159	97	372	185	187	393	99	294a	327a	~	327a	357	~	357
G. CUBA	874	844†	30†	711	653	58	296a	232	64a	67a	~	67a	~	~	~
H. DOMINICAN REP.	129†	1†	128†	296	~	296	764a	372a	392a	315a	~	315a	414	~	414
I. ECUADOR	419	347†	72	108	~	108	255	~	255	242	~	242	255	~	255
J. EL SALVADOR	138†	~	138	~	~	~	4	~	4	124	~	124	115	~	115
K. GUATEMALA	113†	47†	66	114	#	114	119	#	119	411	84	327	282	57a	225a
M. HONDURAS	296	160	136	299	92	207	508	139	369						
N. MEXICO	2,966	2,282†	684	6,523	5,278	1,245	11,189	8,396	2,793	13,639	9,133	4,506	7,352	5,849	1,503
P. PANAMA	307†	194†	113	357	103	254	355	48	307	309	~	309	218	~	218a
Q. PARAGUAY	81†	14†	67	~	~	~	1,098	877	221	1,777	1,572	205	846	752a	94a
R. PERU	391	230†	161	1,335	1,226	109				177a	17	160a	193	23a	170a
S. URUGUAY	219	6	213	334	47	287	89	~	89						
T. VENEZUELA	757	501	226	2,355	1,810	545	5,133	4,173	960	4,922a	4,143	779a	2,749	2,686	63a
LATIN AMERICA	16,448	12,157	4,291	28,415	22,506	5,909	45,539	35,723	9,816	41,051	29,767	11,284	40,368	32,429	7,939
UNITED STATES	163,449	148,174	15,275	205,825	189,326	16,499	294,186	268,463	25,723	257,334	230,913	26,421	260,003	235,076	24,927

1. Regularly scheduled domestic and international services of the airlines registered in each country, including flights occasioned by excess traffic.

a. Data for one or more months missing.

SOURCE: 1970-82 calculated from ICAO-DS-T, 1969-73, no. 33, vol. 2, tables 4, 9, and 14; ICAO-DS-T, 1975-79, no. 39, parts B and C; ICAO-DS-T, 1978-82, parts A, B, and C.

Table 404

UTILIZATION OF AIRLINE CAPACITY, PASSENGER LOAD FACTOR,[1] 20 LC, 1970–82[a]

(%)

Country	1970	1974	1975	1976	1977	1978	1979	1980	1981	1982
A. ARGENTINA	53	66	64	56	58	59	62	60	50	48
B. BOLIVIA	43[†]	72	64	60	61	59	55	61	60	59
C. BRAZIL	59	56	57	57	86	58	68	63	60	63
D. CHILE	55	58	57	55	58	62	61	64	63	57
E. COLOMBIA	54	58	61	58	58	59	61	63	59	66
F. COSTA RICA	61	61	64	66	67	69	72	69[b]	64	59
G. CUBA	86	76	73	68	72	75	74	69[b]	69[b]	~
H. DOMINICAN REP.	48[†]	66	72	79	74	73	74	78[b]	68[b]	68
I. ECUADOR	57	51	52	54	60	53	58	62	~	~
J. EL SALVADOR	52[†]	55	56	53	66	64	68	70	65	57
K. GUATEMALA	53[†]	48	48	41	39	46	47	41	43	42
L. HAITI	54[†]	~	~	~	~	~	~	~	~	~
M. HONDURAS	49	56	50	53	54	57	58	57	59	57[b]
N. MEXICO	51	57	57	61	77	68	70	66[b]	65	60
O. NICARAGUA	49[†]	38	38	40	40	40	51	~	~	~
P. PANAMA	52[†]	54	47	49	49	52	54	57	58	57[b]
Q. PARAGUAY	54[†]	52	53	55	53	48	50	~	~	~
R. PERU	52	63	58	56	58	59	62	61	55	57[b]
S. URUGUAY	39	66	70	57	53	50	51	~	52[b]	48[b]
T. VENEZUELA	44	49	51	52	59	52	54	46	63[b]	60[b]
UNITED STATES	49	55	54	55	57	62	63	59[b]	58[b]	58[b]

1. Obtained by dividing actual passengers/km by available seats/km of the regularly
scheduled domestic and international services of the registered airlines, including
flights occasioned by excess traffic.

a. Data for the years 1972-77 are from SALA, 22-2103.
b. Data for one or more months missing.

SOURCE: ICAO-DS-T, 1969-73, no. 33, vol. 2, table 4; ICAO-DS-T, 1975-79, vol. 39;
1980-82 calculated from ICAO-DS-T, 1978-82, parts B and C.

Table 405

AIR TRANSPORT IN TON KILOMETERS,[1] 19 LC, 1970–82

(M)

Country	Total[3]					International Flights[4]				
	1970	1975	1980	1981[c]	1982[b]	1970	1975	1980	1981[c]	1982[b]
A. ARGENTINA										
Freight	47.9	74.6	195.4	195.5	171	35.9	52.3	165.9	170.7	148
Mail	6.0	7.2	20.5	20.1	~	4.5	5.2	8.5	7.9	~
Total[2]	277	482	939	849.1	722	177	260	600	529.5	419
B. BOLIVIA										
Freight	1.5	2.6	37.6	43.7	28	.6	1.3	35.3	41.8	26
Mail	~	.1	.2	.5	~	~	.1	.1	.4	~
Total[2]	12	31	121	125.7	~	5	16	89	96.9	~
C. BRAZIL										
Freight	164.1	460.5	588.2	511.8	735	129.8	331.2	370.7	386.2	408
Mail	9.3	14.2	23.3	16.8	~	6.2	10.9	15.5	14.9	~
Total[2]	538	1,274	1,956	1,483.0	2,229	340	744	945	978.4	1,023
D. CHILE										
Freight	41.1	57.2	144.9	153.3	142	18.6	43.2	134.2	139.6	124
Mail	1.1	1.8	3.7	4.5	~	.8	1.5	3.5	4.3	~
Total[2]	117	176	324	367.6	315	59	128	267	292.6	231
E. COLOMBIA										
Freight	74.7	121.9	147.4	203.9	307	31.0	76.4	125.3	179.7	270
Mail	4.1	4.4	5	5.0	~	3.2	3.9	4.3	4.4	~
Total[2]	260	371	532	608.5	773	116	206	339	410.6	499
F. COSTA RICA										
Freight	9.3	8.9	22.4	20.8	~	7.8	8.5	22.3	20.8	~
Mail	.2	.2	.4	.7	~	.2	.2	.4	.7	~
Total[2]	25	35	68	77.8	~	21	33	67	77.8	~
G. CUBA										
Freight	9.1	13.6	10.4	5.1[a]	~	5.7	10.9	8.4	4.4[a]	~
Mail	2.1	1.9	1.9	1.3[a]	~	1.8	1.8	1.8	1.2[a]	~
Total[2]	53	61	95	53.7[a]	112	24	38	72	45.1[a]	88
H. DOMINICAN REP.										
Freight	~	~	~	#	~	~	~	~	#	~
Mail	~	~	~	#	~	~	~	~	#	~
Total[2]	~	~	~	.3[a]	~	~	~	~	.3[a]	~
I. ECUADOR										
Freight	9.3	6.4	~	~	37	1.7	2.8	~	~	31
Mail	.3	.3	~	~	~	.3	.3	~	~	~
Total[2]	34	35	~	~	118	19	24	~	~	100
J. EL SALVADOR										
Freight	11.4	14.0	12.7	12.8	~	11.4	14.0	12.7	12.8	~
Mail	#	#	#	#	~	#	#	#	#	~
Total[2]	26	31	29	37.3	~	26	31	29	37.3	~
K. GUATEMALA										
Freight	6.3	4.7	6.4	4.9	~	5.5	4.7	6.4	4.9	~
Mail	.2	~	.1	.1	~	.1	~	.1	.1	~
Total[2]	16	17	21	20.6	~	14	17	21	20.6	~
M. HONDURAS‡										
Freight	3.6	3.0	3.8	2.9	~	2.7	2.7	3.7	2.9	~
Mail	~	.1	.6	.6	~	~	.1	.5	.6	~
Total[2]	18	26	43	35.9	~	15	25	41	34.5	~
N. MEXICO										
Freight	36.7	76.2	131.5	136.8	111	17.1	42.7	69	78.9	57
Mail	3.7	3.4	6.6	4.4	~	1.9	1.9	4.1	2.7	~
Total[2]	288	622	1,319	1,505.0	1,343	138	274	644	811.1	625
O. NICARAGUA‡										
Freight	.8	1.9	~	~	~	.5	1.7	~	~	~
Mail	.1	.1	~	~	~	.1	.1	~	~	~
Total[2]	8	9	~	~	~	7	8	~	~	~
P. PANAMA										
Freight	4.2	5.4	2.7	15.1	~	3.9	4.9	2.5	15.1	~
Mail	~	.3	.4	.4	~	~	.2	.4	.4	~
Total[2]	16	42	40	49.5	~	13	39	38	49.5	~
Q. PARAGUAY										
Freight	.7	1.0	2.6	~	~	.1	.3	1.8	~	~
Mail	#	#	#	~	~	#	#	#	~	~
Total[2]	8	8	26	~	~	6	6	24	~	~
R. PERU										
Freight	22.4	22.3	40.1	47.6	83	16.1	10.9	23.9	32.6	63
Mail	2.2	.4	.7	.5	~	2.1	.3	.4	.4	~
Total[2]	99	127	217	205.0	236	83	46	98	99.5	126

Table 405 (Continued)

AIR TRANSPORT IN TON KILOMETERS,[1] 19 LC, 1970-82

(M)

Country	Total[3]					International Flights[4]				
	1970	1975	1980	1981[c]	1982[b]	1970	1975	1980	1981[c]	1982[b]
S. URUGUAY										
Freight	.3	.1	.7	.9[a]	~	.3	.1	.7	.3[a]	~
Mail	~	~	.1	.1[a]	~	~	~	.1	.1[a]	~
Total[2]	5	7	17	7.0[a]	~	5	5	15	6.7[a]	~
T. VENEZUELA										
Freight	58.6	71.4	149.3	106.9[a]	136	54.1	68.0	145.8	104.9[a]	134
Mail	2.1	2.2	2.7	1.9[a]	~	2.0	2.2	2.7	1.9[a]	~
Total[2]	166	272	504	438.2[a]	579	132	212	395	312.2[a]	433
UNITED STATES										
Freight	5,151.2	7,001.3	8,371.2	8,305.9	7,972	7,714.3	2,432.2	3,378.6	3,988.3	3,500
Mail	2,154.8	1,619.2	1,954.1	2,015.7	~	990.1	533.5	516.8	515.8	~
Total[2]	26,537	32,391	47,358	46,561	47,144	6,198	6,903	11,316	11,629	11,619

1. To convert to long ton miles, multiply by coefficient of .6611558.
2. Includes freight, mail, and passengers.
3. Includes domestic and international scheduled, registered airlines.
4. International flights from international scheduled, registered airlines.

a. Data for one or more months missing.
b. Data calculated from ICAO Bulletin, July 1984.
c. Data calculated from ICAO-DS-T, 1978-82.

SOURCE: UN-SY, 1981, table 193; 1981-82: Calculated from ICAO-DS-T, 1978-82,
    parts B and C; ICAO Bulletin, July 1984.

Table 406

LENGTH OF RAILWAY NETWORK, 16 LR, 1970-81

(km)

Country	1970	1975	1976	1977	1978	1979	1980	1981
A. ARGENTINA	39,905	39,787	39,779	36,996	34,393	34,350	34,077	34,172
B. BOLIVIA	3,284	3,269	3,269	3,373	3,473	3,473	3,328	3,628
C. BRAZIL	30,445	29,788	29,277	28,756	28,972	29,061	28,671	28,310
D. CHILE	6,475[a]	6,606	6,378	6,372	6,366	6,365	6,302	6,300
E. COLOMBIA	3,436	3,431	3,403	3,403	2,884	3,403	3,403	3,403
G. CUBA	5,286	5,342	5,342	4,214	4,382	4,382	4,382	4,382
I. ECUADOR	~	1,008	990	990	965	965	965	965
J. EL SALVADOR	620	161***	602	602	602	602	602	602
K. GUATEMALA	~	775	775	775	775	927	927	927
M. HONDURAS	~	~	~	205	205	205	205	205
N. MEXICO	19,868	19,960	19,441	19,999	20,000	20,031	20,058	19,953
O. NICARAGUA	318	320	320	345	345	345	345	345
Q. PARAGUAY[1]	441	441	441	441	441	441	441	441
R. PERU	2,242	1,875	1,875	1,875	1,875	1,882	2,099	2,159
S. URUGUAY	2,975	2,975	2,988	2,988	2,998	3,005	3,005	3,005
T. VENEZUELA[2]	226	226	264	284	264	268	268	268
LATIN AMERICA[3]	115,521	115,964	115,144	111,618	108,940	109,705	109,496	109,183

1. President Carlos A. López railway only.
2. Excluding the 145 km Orinoco Mining Company railway.
3. Does not include Costa Rica, Dominican Republic, Haiti, and Panama.

a. 1969.

SOURCE: ECLA-AE, 1983, table 348.

Table 407

RAILWAY ROLLING STOCK, 20 LC

	Country	Year	Rolling Stock		
			Locomotives	Coaches	Cars
A.	ARGENTINA	1976‡	3,104	3,837	60,275
B.	BOLIVIA	1972	156	236	2,005
C.	BRAZIL	1976‡	1,970	3,042	63,770
D.	CHILE	1976‡	672	709	10,046
E.	COLOMBIA	1975‡	208	316	5,719
F.	COSTA RICA	1975‡	94	225	2,821
G.	CUBA		~	~	~
H.	DOMINICAN REP.	1973‡	2	2	15
I.	ECUADOR[1]	1971	60	50	518
J.	EL SALVADOR	1971	55	96	747
K.	GUATEMALA	1972	92	106	2,121
L.	HAITI	~		~	~	~
M.	HONDURAS	1972	66	90	2,846
N.	MEXICO	1976‡	1,293	1,634	39,240
O.	NICARAGUA	1972	8	35	231
P.	PANAMA	1972	42	70	1,473
Q.	PARAGUAY[2]	1973	17	9	151
R.	PERU[3]	1972	158	233	4,806
S.	URUGUAY[4]	1976‡	157	117	2,438
T.	VENEZUELA[5]	1972	13	19	265
	UNITED STATES	1976‡	27,573	5,478	1,269,602

1. Data for Empresa de Ferrocarriles del Estado.
2. Data for Ferrocarril Central del Paraguay.
3. Including 286 km of lines used exclusively for industrial and agricultural purposes.
4. Data for Los Ferrocarriles del Estado only.
5. Data for El Instituto Autónomo de Administración de Ferrocarriles del Estado only.

a. Only government railroads.

SOURCE: IASI-AC, 1970, 1972 and 1974, tables 333-01-03; UN-SY, 1977,
   table 158.

Table 408

RAILROAD PASSENGER KILOMETERS,[1] 17 LC, 1965–81

(M)

	Country	1965	1970	1974	1975	1976	1977	1978	1979	1980	1981
A.	ARGENTINA	12,829	12,684	13,572	14,367	14,598	13,333	12,284	12,894	13,510	12,025
B.	BOLIVIA	220	266	248	310	367	396	397	363	529	482
C.	BRAZIL	16,684	12,070	10,282	10,622	11,281	11,271	12,875	12,347	13,390	14,419
D.	CHILE	2,411	2,256	2,875	2,096	2,356	2,350	2,004	1,727	1,421	1,558
E.	COLOMBIA	513	235	483	523	511	392	345	322	315	235
F.	COSTA RICA[5]	~	55	81	~	99	~	~	~	~	~
G.	CUBA	822	1,130	635	695	767	1,076	1,571	1,571	1,571	1,571
I.	ECUADOR	52[a]	85	69	65	69	63	65	65	65	65
J.	EL SALVADOR	~	~	53	23	24	31	31	31	27	14
K.	GUATEMALA	~	~	~	~	~	2	2	~	~	~
N.	MEXICO	3,882	4,534	4,614	4,123	4,058	5,040	5,326	5,253	5,296	5,287
O.	NICARAGUA	51	30	22	18	20	19	19	15	15	15
P.	PANAMA	470	544	~	~	~	~	~	~	38	38
Q.	PARAGUAY[2]	35[b]	24	27	24	16	18	17	21	22	22
R.	PERU	236[c]	248	291	354	528	651	354	402	496	495
S.	URUGUAY	522[d]	473	343	337	374	389	494	455	418	337
T.	VENEZUELA[3]	44[e]	36	43	40	42	39	41	25	28	10
	UNITED STATES[4]	28,090	17,284	16,635	15,715	15,688	16,565	16,452	18,025	17,695	~

1. To convert to passenger miles, multiply by coefficient of .62137.
2. Presidente Carlos A. López railway only.
3. Excluding the 145 km Orinoco Mining Company railway.
4. Beginning 1967, Class 1 railway only.
5. Incomplete coverage.

a. Data for Empresa de Ferrocarriles del Estado.
b. Data for Ferrocarril Central del Paraguay.
c. Including 286 km of lines used exclusively for industrial and agricultural purposes.
d. Data for Los Ferrocarriles del Estado only.
e. Data for El Instituto Autónomo de Administración de Ferrocarriles del Estado only.

SOURCE: IASI-AC, 1970 and 1972, tables 333-01-03; ECLA-AE, 1983, table 349.
   U.S. data; UN-SY, 1981, table 189.

Table 409

RAILROAD FREIGHT IN TON KILOMETERS,[1] 17 LC, 1965–81

(M)

Country	1965	1970	1974	1975	1976	1977	1978	1979	1980	1981
A. ARGENTINA	14,027	13,274	12,412	10,729	11,107	11,636	9,909	10,978	9,492	9,260
B. BOLIVIA	301	456	394	470	523	595	592	602	658	632
C. BRAZIL	18,815[a]	15,495	22,174	23,669	27,744	29,588	29,707	33,642	40,603	37,981
D. CHILE	2,621	2,022	1,942	1,478	1,657	1,516	1,424	1,345	1,445	1,300
E. COLOMBIA	934[a]	1,173	1,329	1,139	1,157	1,215	1,228	1,105	862	625
F. COSTA RICA[4]	31	18	14	~	16	~	~	~	~	~
G. CUBA	1,326	1,625	1,654	1,825	1,848	2,024	1,904	1,904	1,904	1,904
I. ECUADOR	84[b]	56	49	46	35	35	32	32	32	32
J. EL SALVADOR	72	64	54	52	48	56	76	78	55	31
K. GUATEMALA	129	106	143	127	117	139	139	91	91	91
N. MEXICO	18,332	23,083	31,094	33,400	33,666	36,375	36,713	37,275	41,831	43,802
O. NICARAGUA	13	16	11	8	12	11	11	6	6	6
P. PANAMA	19,070	15,889	~	~	~	~	~	~	10	10
Q. PARAGUAY[2]	19[c]	31	33	21	13	24	23	28	29	23
R. PERU	464[d]	592	665	621	621	621	621	571	742	687
S. URUGUAY	332[e]	301	270	276	311	285	303	296	253	221
T. VENEZUELA[3]	32[f]	13	10	14	14	20	20	18	21	14
UNITED STATES[5]	1,029,585	1,116,602	1,242,381	1,101,667	1,112,689	1,206,366	1,252,812	1,334,417	1,341,717	~

1. To convert to long ton miles, multiply by coefficient of .6611558.
2. Presidente Carlos A. López railway only.
3. Excluding the 145 km Orinoco Mining Company railway.
4. Incomplete coverage.
5. Class 1 railways only.

a. Including service traffic.
b. Data for Empresa de Ferrocarriles del Estado.
c. Data for Ferrocarril Central del Paraguay.
d. Including 286 km of lines used exclusively for industrial and agricultural purposes.
e. Data for Los Ferrocarriles del Estado only.
f. Data for El Instituto Autónomo de Administración de Ferrocarriles del Estado only.

SOURCE: IASI-AC, 1970 and 1972, tables 333-01-03; ECLA-AE, 1983, table 349; U.S. data; UN-SY, 1981, table 189.

Table 410

LENGTH OF ROADS, 19 LR

(ca. 1980)

Country	Year	Total (km)	Percentage Paved
A. ARGENTINA	1978	208,087	23
B. BOLIVIA	1980	39,651	3
C. BRAZIL	1981	1,399,443	6
D. CHILE	1981	78,025	12
E. COLOMBIA	1981	74,735	~
F. COSTA RICA	1981	28,525	9
H. DOMINICAN REP.	1981	12,227	83
I. ECUADOR	1980	33,006	13
J. EL SALVADOR	1981	12,269	14
K. GUATEMALA	1980	26,429	11
L. HAITI	1981	3,443	17
M. HONDURAS	1981	9,020	27
N. MEXICO	1981	213,316	45
O. NICARAGUA[1]	1981	6,712	10
P. PANAMA	1980	11,110	37
Q. PARAGUAY[2]	1979	31,460	~
R. PERU	1979	56,642	~
S. URUGUAY	1980	50,024	14
T. VENEZUELA	1981	62,448	38
LATIN AMERICA	1980[a]	2,356,572	27

1. Excluding urban roads.
2. National only.

a. Ca. 1980.

SOURCE: ECLA-AE, 1983, table 347.

Table 411

COMMERCIAL MOTOR VEHICLE REGISTRATION,[1] 20 LC, 1960–80

(T)

Country	1960	1965	1970	1975	1976	1977	1978	1979	1980
A. ARGENTINA	389.7	571.2	754.8	~	~	~	~	~	~
B. BOLIVIA	~	16.4	28.8‡	21.3	24.5	27.8	29.4	20.7	32.5
C. BRAZIL	~	516.9	696.2	1,150.2	1,397.2	905.2	1,574.6	~	~
D. CHILE[2,3]	68.8	105.4	149.8	168.7	171.5	181.2	191.2	203.3	226.5
E. COLOMBIA[3,4]	82.9	109.2	83.5	88.4	93.4	104.5	~	~	~
F. COSTA RICA[2,3]	9.7	12.1	27.1	40.7	42.4	49.3	~	~	~
G. CUBA	65.3‡	103.7	32.0‡	~	~	~	~	~	~
H. DOMINICAN REP.[5]	6.3	9.7	20.5	35.6	39.4	41.1	46.2	50.9	45.0
I. ECUADOR	19.0	20.6	36.4	77.2	87	114.9	114.9	~	~
J. EL SALVADOR	9.0	12.0	19.0	~	~	37	46.4	58.2	~
K. GUATEMALA	14.7	17.2	24.4	40.1	40.9	41.3	43.9	~	~
L. HAITI	3.7	1.4	1.4	2.5	2.4	3.8	6.5	8.3	5.2
M. HONDURAS[2,3]	5.2	8.2	15.8	25.7	30.2	~	~	~	~
N. MEXICO	315.0	388.6	588.9	887.9	988.0	1,057.1	1,352.2	1,513.8	1.572.9
O. NICARAGUA[5]	5.5	9.5	~	22.7	29.8	27.3	25.5	~	27.7
P. PANAMA[5]	6.6	10.5	14.5	19.6	20.8	21.8	24.7	30.3	32.5
Q. PARAGUAY[2]	2.5	5.2	~	13.0	24.0	28.4	30.8	30.8	36.6
R. PERU	65.2	98.7	117.5	145	156.3	166.2	~	~	~
S. URUGUAY	76.0	82.0	88.0	~	104.2	~	~	~	~
T. VENEZUELA	100.7	151.8	198.2	369.4	428.2	498.0	~	~	~
UNITED STATES[6]	11,466.9	14,190.4	17,978.4	26,242.8	28,257.8	30,092.9	32,203	31,841.2	33,410.6

1. Including trucks, buses, tractor and semitractor combinations; but excluding trailers
   and farm tractors.
2. Including vehicles operated by police and government security organizations.
3. Including special-purpose vehicles.
4. Excluding diplomatic corps vehicles.
5. Excluding government vehicles.
6. Excluding Alaska and Hawaii.

a. 1973.

SOURCE: UN-SY, 1972, table 150; UN-SY, 1974, table 153; UN-SY, 1981, table 190.

Table 412

PASSENGER MOTOR VEHICLE REGISTRATION,[1,6] 20 LC, 1960–80

(T)

Country	1960	1965	1970	1975	1976	1977	1978	1979	1980
A. ARGENTINA	473.5	914.6	1,439.6‡	~	~	~	~	~	~
B. BOLIVIA	9.7	9.9	19.2‡	29.6	33.5	36.1	38.6	43.1	50.2
C. BRAZIL	~	1,289.3	2,324.3	4,833.6	5,916.3	6,850.0	7,123.9	~	~
D. CHILE	57.6	97.3	176.1	255.7	262.8	294.6	335.8	386.0	466.0
E. COLOMBIA[2,3]	89.6	123.7	238.5	376.1	401.3	453.6	~	~	~
F. COSTA RICA[3,4]	16.0	22.7	39.3	59.8	64.9	73.4	~	~	~
G. CUBA	179.6‡	162.0	72.0†	~	~	157.6	160.4	152.6	~
H. DOMINICAN REP.[5]	11.0	30.2	39.3	71.5	77.3	84.4	90.6	89.8	84.8
I. ECUADOR	9.3	17.1	27.0	51.3	48.6	61	61	~	~
J. EL SALVADOR	20.2	26.2	34.2	~	~	72.9	69.9	78.8	~
K. GUATEMALA	26.1	29.0	42.6	76.1	82.7	83.7	90.5	~	~
L. HAITI	8.2	8.7	11.6	17.9	18.7	22.7	24.3	24.9	23.3
M. HONDURAS[2,4]	5.5	10.3	12.6	18.2	20.5	~	~	~	~
N. MEXICO	476.4	761.1	1,233.8	2,400.9	2,580.4	2,829.1	3,359.9	3,762.7	4,254.9
O. NICARAGUA[5]	8.6	13.0	34.4	36.5	36.1	42.9	41	~	37.8
P. PANAMA[5]	17.6	30.1	45.5	66.2	67.9	71.0	75.4	90.2	98.0
Q. PARAGUAY	3.8	5.0	~	11.6	18	22.1	24.8	33.2	39.2
R. PERU	79.4	155.0	230.4	256.7	278.3	300.4	~	~	~
S. URUGUAY	99.8	114.0	121.0	~	127.1	~	~	~	~
T. VENEZUELA	268.7	383.2	565.8	955.2	1,073.2	1,186.7	~	~	~
UNITED STATES	61,430.9	74,903.2	88,840.5	106,075.9	110,188.6	112,287.5	116,575	116,573.4	118,458.7

1. Motor cars seating less than eight persons, including taxis, jeeps, and station-wagons.
2. Including special-purpose vehicles.
3. Excluding diplomatic corps vehicles.
4. Including vehicles operated by police and government security organizations.
5. Excluding government vehicles.
6. Official estimates of vehicles in use. Unless otherwise stated, special-purpose vehicles
   are not included.

a. 1973.

SOURCE: UN-SY, 1972, table 150; UN-SY, 1974, table 153; UN-SY, 1981, table 190.

Table 413
MERCHANT FLEETS,[1] 16 L, 1982
(Tons)

Country	Overseas					Coastal				Inland Waterways
	Cargo Vessels	Bulk Carriers	Refrigerated Vessels	Tankers	Others	Cargo Vessels	Refrigerated Vessels	Tankers	Others	
A. ARGENTINA	634,381	350,157	34,742	~	~	33,195	~	628,665	29,607	166,972
B. BOLIVIA	15,129	~	~	~	~	~	~	~	~	~
C. BRAZIL	927,026	916,394	17,709	2,377,710	~	199,582	~	550,061	190,649	58,250
D. CHILE[2]	32,262	95,915	16,186	104,935	~	318	~	38,783	13,610	~
E. COLOMBIA	214,715	18,028	~	24,136	~	1,544	~	1,135	11,234	~
F. COSTA RICA	11,792	~	~	~	~	~	~	~	2,509	~
G. CUBA	476,831	48,921	96,135	3,600	14,182	10,772	~	59,519	21,658	~
H. DOMINICAN REP.	15,469	10,403	~	~	~	~	~	~	~	~
I. ECUADOR	102,757	~	66,544	55,614	~	1,132	~	82,116	3,845	~
K. GUATEMALA	22,374	5,631	~	~	~	~	~	~	~	~
N. MEXICO	162,811	128,228	~	471,698	182,436	18,732	~	19,985	60,997	~
O. NICARAGUA	12,003	~	~	~	~	~	~	~	~	~
Q. PARAGUAY	9,065	~	~	~	~	~	~	~	~	15,713
R. PERU	272,001	184,887	1,544	126,462	~	~	~	73,245	~	10,955
S. URUGUAY	68,215	13,203	4,172	88,617	~	2,992	~	3,548	~	3,749
T. VENEZUELA	201,535	36,237	6,682	19,600	~	3,541	~	370,677	69,762	1,325

1. Gross registered tons for vessels of 1,000 tons and over.
2. Ca. 1978.

SOURCE: ECLA-AE, 1983, table 350.

Table 414

INTERNATIONAL SEABORNE SHIPPING,[1] 20 LC, 1965–82

(Vessels in T Net Registered Tons; Goods in T MET)

Country		1965	1970	1975	1976	1977	1978	1979	1980	1981	1982
A. ARGENTINA[14]											
Vessels:[2]	entered	13,078	12,863	12,859	13,178	15,394	~	~	~	~	~
	cleared	~	~	~	~	~	~	~	~	~	~
Goods:[3]	loaded	15,217	15,237	980	1,275	1,984	1,946	2,052	1,721	2,504	2,208
	unloaded	11,145	10,867	1,018	763	885	698	962	878	735	550
B. BOLIVIA		**	**	**	**	**	**	**	**	**	**
C. BRAZIL											
Vessels:[2,4]	entered	59,311	~	143,172	165,681	146,249	141,471	~	~	~	~
	cleared	~	~	~	~	~	~	~	~	~	~
Goods:[5,6]	loaded	19,679	39,970	7,749	7,474	6,821	7,293	8,257	9,092	10,333	~
	unloaded	16,633	28,073	4,421	5,138	5,172	5,816	6,277	5,959	5,339	~
D. CHILE											
Vessels:	entered	3,426	~	~	~	~	~	~	~	~	~
	cleared	6,281	~	~	~	~	~	~	~	~	~
Goods:[3,7]	loaded	12,781	12,293	~	~	~	~	~	~	1,532	995
	unloaded	3,312	5,429	~	~	~	~	~	~	1,267	434
E. COLOMBIA											
Vessels:[2]	entered	11,265	12,362	10,943	10,731	11,302	10,942	11,230	11,200	~	~
	cleared	11,184	~	~	~	~	~	~	~	~	~
Goods:[5]	loaded	7,529	5,364	281	195	163	223	551	670	451	451
	unloaded	1,073	2,461	175	182	305	334	590	606	596	592
F. COSTA RICA											
Vessels:[2]	entered	2,773	2,902	3,736	~	~	~	~	~	~	~
	cleared	~	~	~	~	~	~	~	~	~	~
Goods:	loaded	475	1,129	~	~	~	~	~	~	~	~
	unloaded	682	1,005	~	~	~	~	~	~	~	~
G. CUBA											
Vessels:	entered	~	~	~	~	~	~	~	~	~	~
	cleared	~	~	~	~	~	~	~	~	~	~
Goods:	loaded	6,041	7,838	495	508	604	711	795	180	193	229
	unloaded	7,956	10,797	1,108	1,094	1,196	1,204	1,290	219	200	154
H. DOMINICAN REP.											
Vessels:[2]	entered	1,383	5,106	~	~	~	~	~	~	~	~
	cleared	1,902	3,638	~	~	~	~	~	~	~	~
Goods:	loaded	2,169	2,219	~	~	~	~	~	~	~	~
	unloaded	1,289	2,643	3,065	~	~	~	~	~	~	~
I. ECUADOR											
Vessels:	entered	~	8,887	13,244	13,256	12,894	12,994	13,036	~	~	~
	cleared	~	~	~	~	~	~	~	~	~	~
Goods:[8]	loaded	1,500	1,768	~	~	~	~	~	~	~	~
	unloaded	684	1,521	~	~	~	~	~	~	~	~
J. EL SALVADOR											
Vessels:	entered	1,653	1,633	2,291	2,390	3,308	3,172	3,226	2,741	~	~
	cleared	1,277	~	~	~	~	~	~	~	~	~
Goods:	loaded	486	357	41	43	46	45	42	30	29	26
	unloaded	904	1,090	107	100	172	154	117	123	116	94
K. GUATEMALA											
Vessels:[2]	entered	3,602	~	~	~	~	~	~	~	~	~
	cleared	3,585	~	~	~	~	~	~	~	~	~
Goods:	loaded	309	528	~	~	~	~	~	~	~	~
	unloaded	1,215	436	~	~	~	~	~	~	~	~
L. HAITI											
Vessels:[2]	entered	2,286	~	~	~	~	~	~	~	~	~
	cleared	~	~	~	~	~	~	~	~	~	~
Goods:	loaded	557	752	~	~	~	~	~	~	~	~
	unloaded	233	250	~	~	~	~	~	~	~	~
M. HONDURAS											
Vessels:[2]	entered	2,825	~	~	~	~	~	~	~	~	~
	cleared	~	~	~	~	~	~	~	~	~	~
Goods:[5]	loaded	843	1,660	~	~	~	~	~	~	~	~
	unloaded	382	1,050	~	~	~	~	~	~	~	~
N. MEXICO											
Vessels:	entered	2,868	4,252	10,102	9,300	~	~	~	~	~	~
	cleared	6,644	6,715	12,058	11,480	~	~	~	~	~	~
Goods:	loaded	9,221	9,705	1,165	1,190	1,704	2,516	3,079	4,202	5,226	6,134
	unloaded	1,427	3,376	775	597	696	897	991	1,213	1,586	1,068

Table 414 (Continued)

INTERNATIONAL SEABORNE SHIPPING,[1] 20 LC, 1965–82

(Vessels in T Net Registered Tons; Goods in T MET)

Country		1965	1970	1975	1976	1977	1978	1979	1980	1981	1982
O. NICARAGUA											
Vessels:[2]	entered	~	~	~	~	~	~	~	~	~	~
	cleared	~	~	~	~	~	~	~	~	~	~
Goods:[5]	loaded	434	400	~	~	~	~	~	~	~	~
	unloaded	540	745	~	~	~	~	~	~	~	~
P. PANAMA											
Vessels:[15]	entered	~	~	~	~	~	~	~	~	~	~
	cleared	~	~	~	~	~	~	~	~	~	~
Goods:	loaded	1,584	1,563	7,120[a]	5,587[a]	5,887[a]	5,766[a]	6,689[a]	~	7,563	7,436
	unloaded	2,732	4,193	4,742[b]	4,337[b]	4,525[b]	6,300[b]	6,365[b]	~	~	4,891
Q. PARAGUAY		**	**	**	**	**	**	**	**	**	**
R. PERU											
Vessels:[2]	entered	26,361	21,320	19,982	17,783	19,012	19,601	~	~	~	~
	cleared	~	~			~	~	~	~	~	~
Goods:[9,10]	loaded	10,904	14,410	~	~	~	~	~	~	~	~
	unloaded	2,598	2,693	~	~	~	~	~	~	~	~
S. URUGUAY											
Vessels:	entered	~	~	~	~	~	~	~	~	~	~
	cleared	~	~	~	~	~	~	~	~	~	~
Goods:	loaded	~	1,631	~	~	~	~	~	~	~	~
	unloaded	2,235	2,412	~	~	~	~	~	~	~	~
T. VENEZUELA											
Vessels:[5,11]	entered	90,813	~	~	~	~	~	~	~	~	~
	cleared	~	~	~	~	~	~	~	~	~	~
Goods:[16]	loaded	187,851	204,487	10,885	10,943	~	~	~	~	~	~
	unloaded	2,934	4,343	559	543	723	714	~	~	~	~
UNITED STATES[12]											
Vessels:	entered	153,513	186,053	254,346	296,910	338,300	346,535	360,572	320,684	~	~
	cleared	122,114	152,383	188,845	196,876	199,737	215,162	249,833	269,660	~	~
Goods:[13]	loaded	157,752	218,256	20,478	21,514	20,855	24,588	27,165	30,328	30,161	35,225
	unloaded	244,790	292,786	34,104	44,412	55,923	51,481	45,630	36,887	30,304	28,458

1. Vessels: Unless otherwise stated, the data for vessels entered and cleared represent the sum of the net registered tonnage of sea-going foreign and domestic merchant vessels entered with cargo, from or cleared with cargo to a foreign port. They refer to only one entrance of clearance for each foreign voyage. Where possible the data exclude vessels "in ballast."
   Goods: The data for goods loaded and unloaded represent the weight of goods (including packaging) in external trade loaded onto and unloaded from sea-going vessels of all flags at the ports of the country in question. Goods excluded are: bunker, ships' stores, ballast, and transshipment.
2. Includes vessels in ballast. (Costa Rica prior to 1966).
3. Excluding transit traffic, packing, and reexports except for 1981 and 1982.
4. All entrances counted.
5. Excluding transit traffic and packing.
6. Including mail, passengers' baggage, and a small amount of goods imported and exported other than by sea.
7. Including mail, passengers' baggage, bullion, and bunkers except for 1981 and 1982.
8. Excluding transit traffic, packing and certain government goods; including goods imported and exported other than by sea.
9. Excluding transit traffic, packing, reexports, and certain government goods.

10. Including bunkers.
11. Including mail, passengers' baggage, and bullion.
12. Including Great Lakes International traffic.
13. Including transshipments.
14. Thousand manifest tons.
15. Data are for former Canal Zone only. Prior to 1977, 12 months ending June 30. From 1977, 12 months beginning October 1.
16. Excludes packaging.

a. Traffic from Atlantic to Pacific.
b. Traffic from Pacific to Atlantic.

SOURCE: UN-SY, 1972, table 153; UN-MB, Nov., 1982, table 55; Mar., 1984, table 55.

Table 415

INTERNATIONAL SEABORNE GOODS LOADED AND UNLOADED, 18 LC, 1976–77

(T MET)

			Goods Loaded				Goods Unloaded		
				Petroleum				Petroleum	
Country	Year	Total	Crude	Products	Dry Cargo	Total	Crude	Products	Dry Cargo
A. ARGENTINA	1976	15,299	#	120	15,179	9,154	1,412	2,066	5,676
	1977	23,807	#	198	23,609	10,619	781	2,777	7,061

Continued in SALA, 22-2213.

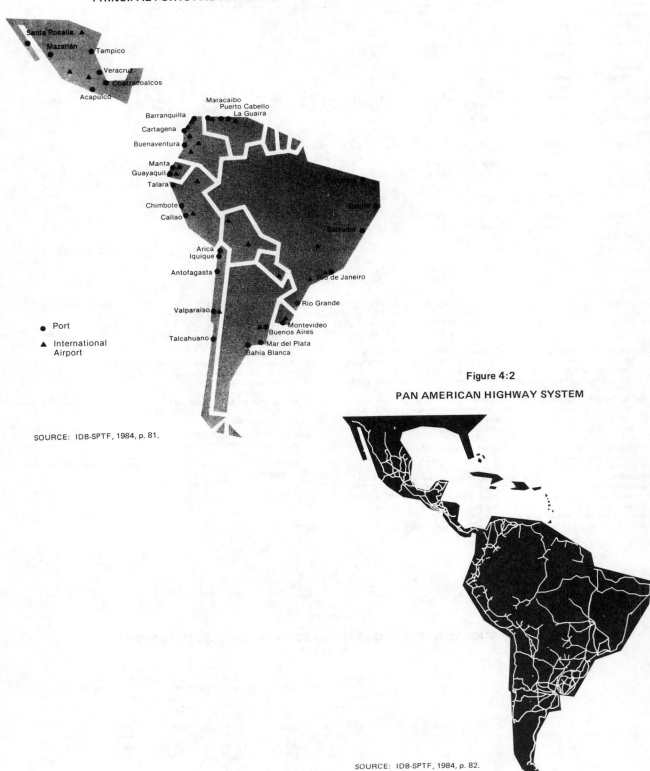

Figure 4:1

PRINCIPAL PORTS AND AIRPORTS

- ● Port
- ▲ International Airport

SOURCE: IDB-SPTF, 1984, p. 81.

Figure 4:2

PAN AMERICAN HIGHWAY SYSTEM

SOURCE: IDB-SPTF, 1984, p. 82.

CHAPTER 5

COMMUNICATION FLOWS

Table 500

DAILY NEWSPAPERS, CIRCULATION, AND NEWSPRINT CONSUMPTION PER INHABITANT, 20 LC, 1965–80

Country	Newspapers Published[1] (N)							Circulation (PTI)							Newsprint, Consumption[2] (kg/PI)							
	1965	1970	1975	1976	1977	1978	1979	1965	1970	1975	1976	1977	1978	1979	1965	1970	1975	1976	1977	1978	1979	1980
A. ARGENTINA	171	179	164	142	~	141	133	148	~	~	~	~	~	~	10.1	11.7	5.7	5.6	4.6	7.5	7.4	7.8
B. BOLIVIA	9	21	14	13	~	14	14	26	~	35	26	~	37	39	.7	1.0	.9	.8	.9	1.5	1.4	1.3
C. BRAZIL	~	~	~	299	318	328	~	~	~	~	45	45	44	~	2.1	2.6	2.2	2.1	1.5	2.2	1.9	1.6
D. CHILE	~	~	47	48	47	37	37	~	~	~	~	~	84	87	4.8	5.0	4.1	4.3	4.1	5.2	5.4	6.0
E. COLOMBIA	39	~	40	42	~	39	38	~	~	~	~	~	48[b]	48[b]	2.4	2.7	1.7	1.7	1.7	2.4	2.6	2.5
F. COSTA RICA	~	8	6	6	~	4	4	~	101	88	104	~	72	70	4.1	6.4	5.6	5.5	5.4	7.1	6.9	6.7
G. CUBA	~	16	15	16	~	9	9	~	~	~	~	~	93	91	2.4	2.7	2.5	2.5	2.4	2.8	2.7	3.2
H. DOMINICAN REP.	7	~	10	10	~	7	7	27	~	42	~	~	49	42	.2	1.0	.5	.5	.5	1.7	1.6	2.1
I. ECUADOR	23	25	29	29	37	37	38	47	41	49	45	46	45	49	2.6	2.3	1.5	1.5	1.5	3.9	3.9	4.0
J. EL SALVADOR	~	13	12	12	~	12	12	~	~	~	~	~	~	~	3.0	3.7	2.9	2.8	2.3	3.1	3.0	3.0
K. GUATEMALA	~	8	11	9	~	9	9	~	28	~	20	~	~	~	1.2	1.6	1.3	1.2	1.2	1.0	1.7	2.4
L. HAITI	6	7	7	6	~	7	4	5	~	20	20	~	~	7	.1	.2	.2	.2	.2	.1	.1	.1
M. HONDURAS	~	~	8	8	~	7	7	~	~	~	~	~	~	63	.7	1.1	.7	.7	.7	1.3	1.6	1.3
N. MEXICO	220	200	256	268	352	~	~	116	~	~	51	~	49	69	2.6	3.2	3.6	4.0	3.9	2.7	3.0	4.5
O. NICARAGUA	6	~	7	6	~	6	8	49	92	79	79	~	81	79	1.7	1.9	1.7	1.7	1.6	1.1	1.0	1.0
P. PANAMA	10	7	6	6	~	6	6	81	~	~	~	~	~	~	2.8	4.0	2.0	2.0	1.9	2.8	2.7	2.4
Q. PARAGUAY	~	11	8	4	~	5	5	~	~	~	39	~	~	~	.7	1.8	1.2	1.1	1.1	2.2	2.2	2.0
R. PERU	69	85	35	36	30	57	59	~	~	~	56	51	~	~	3.5	3.7	3.3	1.8	1.7	2.2	2.1	.1
S. URUGUAY	~	~	30	30	26	29	28	~	~	~	~	~	~	~	6.4	7.0	3.7	4.0	4.0	4.4	4.3	6.0
T. VENEZUELA	33	~	49	54	54	55	69	70	~	~	150	178	101	176	4.8	8.0	8.2	7.9	7.7	9.4	9.4	9.0
UNITED STATES	1,751[a]	1,773[a]	1,812[a]	1,781[a]	1,829[a]	1,774[a]	1,787[a]	310	302	287	287	287	284	282	39.3	43.5	38.8	41.5	41.6	45.4	46.1	49.5

1. A daily newspaper is defined as a publication devoted primarily to recording news of current events in public affairs, international affairs, politics, etc., and which is published at least four times a week.
2. Newsprint consumption represents apparent consumption (i.e., domestic production plus imports, minus exports, or simply annual imports). For a few countries, where information is available, fluctuation in stocks has been taken into account, and this is indicated in a footnote. Data cover newsprint for both daily and non-daily newspapers.

a. English-language papers only.
b. Circulation figures refer to 33 dailies only.

SOURCE: UNESCO-SY, 1977, tables 12.1, 13.1; UNESCO-SY, 1981, tables 8.16, 8.19; UNESCO-SY, 1982, tables 8.6, 8.19.

Table 501

NEWSPRINT: VOLUME OF IMPORTS, 20 LC, 1965–82

(T MET)

Country	1965	1970	1975	1976	1977	1978	1979	1980	1981	1982
A. ARGENTINA	220	274	140	110	160	161	117	174	137	49
B. BOLIVIA	3‡	5	5†	5†	6	8	7†	7†	7†	7†
C. BRAZIL	54	149	30	73	234	225	203	221	218	206
D. CHILE	5	1	#	#	#	#	#	#	#	#
E. COLOMBIA	45	59	44	36‡	44‡	60‡	67‡	52	96†	95
F. COSTA RICA	6	11	11	11	12	16	12	16	11	7
G. CUBA	19	23‡	27†	27†	28†	32	32	33	33†	33†
H. DOMINICAN REP.	1	4	7	7	9	9	10	12	15	15†
I. ECUADOR	13	14	11	22‡	28	29	31	33	32	32†
J. EL SALVADOR	9	13	10	10	14	14†	8	15	15	130
K. GUATEMALA	6	8	8	7	7	7	12	17	10	11
L. HAITI	~	1†	1†	1‡	1	1†	1‡	1†	1†	1†
M. HONDURAS	2	3	2	3	2	5	5	6	6†	6†
N. MEXICO	91	119	186	191	297	97	110	200	351	351†
O. NICARAGUA	3	4	4	3	3†	6	2	4	4†	4†
P. PANAMA	4	6	3	3†	4	5	5	3	5	3
Q. PARAGUAY	1	4	3†	4	7	7	6	8	5	3
R. PERU	40	49	51	29	56	41	7	8	32	39
S. URUGUAY	18	21	11	11	12	13	14	17	22	22†
T. VENEZUELA	44	84	86	91	107‡	133	135‡	140†	140†	140
UNITED STATES	5,736	6,019	5,305	5,959	5,950	6,787	6,552	6,594	6,330	5,924

SOURCE: FAO-YFP, 1973, p. 275; FAO-YFP, 1975, p. 264; FAO-YFP, 1976, p. 264; FAO-YFP, 1980, p. 324; FAO—YFP, 1981, p. 317; FAO-YFP, 1982, p. 317.

Table 502

NEWSPRINT: VALUE OF IMPORTS, 20 LC, 1965–82

(T US)

Country	1965	1970	1975	1976	1977	1978	1979	1980	1981	1982
A. ARGENTINA	36,345	47,870	73,990	54,491	74,427	76,291	59,552	98,724	83,637	30,843
B. BOLIVIA	319‡	950	950†	950†	2,373	2,790	2,600†	2,600†	3,000†	3,000†
C. BRAZIL	10,259	27,950	10,515	29,669	86,833	85,379	82,926	129,837	136,245	126,399
D. CHILE	872	88	#	#	#	#	#	#	#	#
E. COLOMBIA	7,349	9,947	16,608	13,650‡	16,700‡	22,700‡	27,600	26,379	48,567	47,342
F. COSTA RICA	843	1,918	4,262	4,534	4,967	6,294	4,898	7,060	6,028	4,294
G. CUBA	3,015	3,370‡	4,500†	4,800†	6,000	8,249	9,058	11,679	11,679†	11,679†
H. DOMINICAN REP.	100	607	2,100‡	2,600‡	3,551‡	4,634‡	4,023	4,957	7,260	7,260†
I. ECUADOR	1,867	2,306	7,600	15,000‡	12,139	10,214	12,146	17,227	16,144	16,144†
J. EL SALVADOR	1,360	2,171	4,000	4,130	5,933	5,933†	3,032	6,900	7,200	6,800
K. GUATEMALA	888	1,352	2,722	2,800	2,631	2,701	5,065	9,016	5,609	6,447
L. HAITI	80‡	123†	190†	210†	312	312†	267†	267†	267†	267†
M. HONDURAS	280	472	801	1,345	1,001	1,950	2,025	2,595	2,595†	2,595†
N. MEXICO	13,644	19,016	59,687	78,077	121,800†	40,000†	46,000†	84,000†	146,600†	146,600†
O. NICARAGUA	443	635	1,607†	1,607†	1,607†	2,707	1,087	2,148	2,148†	2,148†
P. PANAMA	457	818	1,130	1,130†	1,511	1,990	1,914	1,079	2,388	1,385
Q. PARAGUAY	199	636	1,366†	1,412	2,513	2,513	2,790	3,877	2,624	2,624†
R. PERU	5,940	7,171	18,182	8,653	20,186	12,188	2,597	3,450	20,281	18,625
S. URUGUAY	3,213	3,347	4,805	4,803	5,380	5,488	6,502	9,416	11,686	11,686†
T. VENEZUELA	6,008	12,180	25,284†	26,973†	31,565†	51,088	40,600†	54,000†	54,000†	54,000†
UNITED STATES	789,604	929,626	1,456,914	1,779,063	1,913,894	2,140,814	2,379,109	2,637,857	2,824,777	3,748,652

SOURCE: FAO-YFP, 1973, p. 277; FAO-YFP, 1977; FAO-YFP, 1980, p. 326; FAO-YFP, 1981, p. 319; FAO-YFP, 1982, p. 319.

Table 503

BOOK PRODUCTION: COPIES BY SUBJECT CLASSIFICATION, 16 LR

(N)

		Year	Total	General	Philosophy	Religion	Social Sciences	Pure Sciences	Applied Sciences	Arts	Literature	Geography/ History
A.	ARGENTINA	1981	14,190	1,415	2,568	- -	4,390	272	664	1,237	3,478	166
B.	BOLIVIA	1975	399	15	3	13	88	14	37	4	108	57
C.	BRAZIL	1978	319,336	38,781	3,906	40,682	98,102	22,920	17,819	19,874	58,289	18,963
D.	CHILE	1981	4,095	#	105	405	1,125	180	300	210	1,110	660
E.	COLOMBIA	1980	22,646	1,200	105	515	6,639	2,880	1,607	1,011	7,480	1,209
F.	COSTA RICA	1981	110	#	6	#	48	15	24	#	11	6
G.	CUBA	1980	48,327	4,093	24	#	36,568	233	1,259	539	5,413	198
H.	DOMINICAN REP.	1981	4,337	121	177	125	7,763	203	423	367	44	114
I.	ECUADOR	1974	31	1	#	#	9	#	#	1	17	2
K.	GUATEMALA	1979	68	19	2	#	21	11	10	#	5	#
M.	HONDURAS	1974	30	#	#	3	17	#	2	1	6	1
N.	MEXICO	1976	4,851	43	85	35	498	297	2,882	166	583	262
P.	PANAMA	1979	146	19	2	1	70	2	24	5	17	6
R.	PERU	1977	910	26	30	31	354	25	130	40	205	69
S.	URUGUAY	1975	481	99	12	14	102	19	61	23	77	74
T.	VENEZUELA	1978	1,194	40	29	20	409	59	226	43	235	133
	LATIN AMERICA	**a	421,151	45,872	7,054	41,844	156,203	27,130	25,468	23,521	77,078	21,920

a. Total of the 16 countries, for years given.

SOURCE: UNESCO–SY, 1981, table 8.6; UNESCO-SY, 1983, table 7.8.

Table 504

BOOK PRODUCTION: TITLES BY SUBJECT CLASSIFICATION,[1] 15 LRC[2]

(N)

	Country	Year	Total	General	Philosophy	Religion	Social Sciences	Pure Sciences	Applied Sciences	Arts	Literature	Geography/ History
A.	ARGENTINA	1980	4,698	231	715	- -	1,008	141	731	630	1,104	138
B.	BOLIVIA	1979	596	36	8	17	222	14	74	23	129	73
C.	BRAZIL	1978	18,102	1,358	678	1,513	4,670	1,659	1,531	1,025	3,840	1,828
D.	CHILE	1981	918	24	26	69	416	29	114	62	84	94
E.	COLOMBIA	1980	5,492	700	70	155	1,408	430	671	441	1,277	340
F.	COSTA RICA	1981	71	#	2	#	35	10	14	#	6	4
G.	CUBA	1981	1,438	150	2	#	770	24	180	31	263	18
H.	DOMINICAN REP.	1980	2,219	46	82	70	1,360	98	227	250	23	63
J.	EL SALVADOR	1978	144	0	1	1	25	4	64	5	37	7
K.	GUATEMALA	1981	574	55	#	1	203	11	38	155	41	70
N.	MEXICO	1981	2,954	112	194	53	857	136	414	133	852	203
P.	PANAMA	1981	171	34	2	4	62	7	14	13	19	16
R.	PERU	1981	767	12	17	16	344	40	109	12	144	73
S.	URUGUAY	1981	837	#	34	35	238	80	189	32	163	66
T.	VENEZUELA	1981	4,200	151	90	92	1,241	233	636	307	807	643
	LATIN AMERICA	**a	43,181	2,909	1,921	2,026	12,859	2,916	5,006	3,119	8,789	3,636
	UNITED STATES	1981	76,976	1,448	1,193	2,086	8,760	2,850	7,638	2,793	3,044	2,673

1. Unless otherwise stated, the data are assumed to cover non-periodical publications
    (books and pamphlets), whether first editions or original works or translations.
2. For earlier years, see SALA, 22-1204.

a. Total of the 13 countries, for years given.

SOURCE: UNESCO–SY, 1982, table 8.2; UNESCO-SY, 1983, table 7.4.

Table 505

MAIL TRAFFIC,[1] 16 LC, 1970–78

(M items sent or received)

Country	Code[2]	1970	1971	1972	1973	1974	1975	1976	1977	1978
A. ARGENTINA	A	833	903	885	960	870	737	620	~	~
	B	124	103	87	88	89	79	70	~	~
	C	55	61	55	54	58	56	50	~	~

Continued in SALA, 23-1205.

1. The figure covers letters (airmail, ordinary mail, and registered), postcards, printed
   matter, merchandise samples, small packets, and phonopost packets. Includes mail
   carried without charge, but excludes ordinary parcels, and insured letters and boxes.
2. Code: A = Domestic: items mailed for distribution within the national territory.
   B = Foreign-received: items received from or mail from places outside the
       national territory. Mail in transit is not included.
   C = Foreign-sent: items sent or mailed for distribution outside the national
       territory. Mail in transit is not included.

Table 506

TELEGRAPH SERVICE, BY NUMBER OF TELEGRAMS, 12 L, 1970–80[a]

(T)

Country		1970	1973	1974	1975	1976	1977	1978	1979	1980
A. ARGENTINA	Domestic	14,645	17,409	16,831	14,340	12,400	12,710	11,193	12,255	13,435
	Foreign	689	564	605	515	342	364	376	382	421
C. BRAZIL	Domestic	16,430	20,840	19,710	18,064	18,027	17,396	16,420	15,614	15,327
	Foreign	118	586	691	522	410	364	357	349	340
D. CHILE	Domestic	5,116	7,338	4,135	4,292	4,551	4,984	4,404	3,966	4,064
	Foreign	199	164	94	89	103	89	78	85	118
E. COLOMBIA	Domestic	16,140	18,945	18,976	20,537	19,406	19,570	21,567	22,400	23,952
	Foreign	434	298	268	241	220	192	189	204	245
F. COSTA RICA	Domestic	1,212	~	~	~	209	~	244	271	270
	Foreign	128	155	147	~	196	115	106	97	85
G. CUBA	Domestic	~	17,716	16,413	~	15,454	15,372	15,442	15,592	~
	Foreign	~	395	328	~	282	128	278	394	~
I. ECUADOR	Domestic	~	~	~	~	~	~	~	~	~
	Foreign	76	212	210	200	173	167	143	163	182
J. EL SALVADOR	Domestic	1,367	1,278	1,417	1,185	1,194	1,189	1,230	1,267	1,282
	Foreign	141	78	124	110	107	89	78	58	49
N. MEXICO	Domestic	47,286	53,301	54,571	44,464	43,800	44,634	46,761	50,142	52,000
	Foreign	778	688	677	580	553	454	478	498	670
Q. PARAGUAY	Domestic	187	197	222	202	180	179	184	199	175
	Foreign	69	75	89	66	58	59	57	58	55
R. PERU	Domestic	3,526	5,178	~	~	11,267	10,898	11,289	8,460	8,739
	Foreign	~	~	~	~	169	139	129	106	107
S. URUGUAY	Domestic	~	~	~	941	979	1,154	1,242	1,363	1,517
	Foreign	~	~	~	57	57	67	77	88	99

a. For pre-1970 data see SALA, 21-1206.

SOURCE: UN-SY, 1977, p. 616; UN-SY, 1978, p. 624; UN-SY, 1979, table 153; UN-SY, 1981,
    table 187.

Table 507

U.N. DATA ON TELEPHONES, 19 L, 1975–80[a]

	Country	T						PHI					
		1975	1976	1977	1978	1979	1980	1975	1976	1977	1978	1979	1980
A.	ARGENTINA	1,996	2,302	2,342	2,404	2,491	2,588	7.8	9.0	9.0	9.1	9.2	9.3
C.	BRAZIL	3,372	4,036	4,836	5,525	6,494	7,496	3.0	3.5	4.1	4.5	5.1	6.3
D.	CHILE	434	451	467	514	536	551	4.1	4.6	4.8	4.8	4.8	5.0
E.	COLOMBIA	1,227	1,296	1,396	1,493	1,587	1,718	5.2	5.2	5.6	5.8	6.0	6.4
F.	COSTA RICA	122	127	151	185	200	236	6.3	6.2	7.2	8.8	9.3	10.7
G.	CUBA	~	311	321	341	362	~	~	3.3	3.3	3.5	3.7	~
H.	DOMINICAN REP.	108	127	139	~	155	165	2.4	2.6	2.8	~	2.9	2.9
I.	ECUADOR	182	202	221	240	260	272	2.7	2.9	2.9	3.0	3.2	3.3
J.	EL SALVADOR	60	60	72	80	83	86	1.5	1.4	1.9	1.8	1.9	1.9
K.	GUATEMALA	~	~	71	~	~	~	~	~	1.2	~	~	~
L.	HAITI	~	18	~	~	~	~	~	.4	~	~	~	~
M.	HONDURAS	20	19	~	21	27	~	.7	.7	~	.7	.8	~
N.	MEXICO	2,915	3,309	3,712	4,140	4,533	4,992	5.0	5.4	5.9	6.4	6.8	7.2
O.	NICARAGUA	36	40	43	~	58	~	1.6	1.8	1.9	~	2.2	~
P.	PANAMA	142	155	155	152	164	173	8.4	8.8	8.6	8.3	8.7	9.5
Q.	PARAGUAY	37	40	43	48	55	59	1.4	1.4	1.5	1.6	1.8	1.8
R.	PERU	369	389	403	420	437	475	2.5	2.6	2.6	2.5	2.5	2.7
S.	URUGUAY	250	258	268	270	279	287	9.0	9.2	9.5	9.6	9.9	9.9
T.	VENEZUELA	650	742	843	678	789	~	5.3	6.0	6.5	5.1	5.8	~

a. For pre-1975 data see SALA, 21-1207.

SOURCE: UN-SY, 1977, p. 620; UN-SY, 1978, p. 628; UN-SY, 1979, table 154; UN-SY, 1981, table 188.

Table 508

AMERICAN TELEPHONE AND TELEGRAPH DATA ON TELEPHONES, 20 LC, 1960–81

	Country	T Telephones[1]						PHI[1]					
		1960	1970	1975	1979	1980	1981	1960	1970	1975	1979	1980	1981
A.	ARGENTINA	1,244	1,668	2,374	2,660	2,760	2,881	6.0	6.9	9.4	10.1	10.3[†]	10.4
B.	BOLIVIA	21	38	~	126	~	135	.6	.8	~	2.6	~	2.6
C.	BRAZIL	964	1,787	2,652	5,733	6,494	7,496	1.5	1.9	4.3	4.6	5.1	6.3
D.	CHILE	184	348	445	531	554	570	2.4	3.6	2.5	4.8	4.9	5.0
E.	COLOMBIA	266	546	1,186	1,445	1,524	1,623	1.9	2.6	4.7	5.7	5.8	5.9
F.	COSTA RICA	15	56	98	175	195	236	1.3	3.3	5.0	8.3	8.9	10.4
G.	CUBA	191	263	~	~	~	~	2.8	3.2	~	~	~	~
H.	DOMINICAN REP.	19	40	95	~	~	~	.7	1.0	2.1	~	~	~
I.	ECUADOR	27[†]	94	168	240	260	~	.6[†]	1.6	2.6	3.1	3.3	~
J.	EL SALVADOR	16	35	50	60	~	76	.6	1.0	1.2	1.3	~	1.6
K.	GUATEMALA	22	38	~	77	82	82	.6	.8	~	1.5	1.6	1.6
L.	HAITI	4	~	~	23	35	~	.1	.1[a,†]	~	.5	.7	~
M.	HONDURAS	6	13	15	21	27	~	.3	.5	.5	.7	1.0[c]	~
N.	MEXICO	492	1,328	2,546	4,140	4,533	5,083	1.5	2.7	4.4	6.0	6.4[†]	7.5[†]
O.	NICARAGUA	.8	~	20	~	58	~	.6	1.3[a]	.9	~	2.2	~
P.	PANAMA	26	75[b]	140[b]	164	176	192	2.5	4.9[b]	8.6[b]	8.9	9.3	9.9
Q.	PARAGUAY	10	21	35	55	~	59	.6	.9	1.3	1.8	~	1.8
R.	PERU	102	192	333	~	87[d]	487	1.0	1.4	2.1	~	.7[†]	2.8
S.	URUGUAY	137	206	248	270	272	287	5.0	7.2	9.0	9.6	~	~
T.	VENEZUELA	180[†]	377	554	920	930	~	2.7[†]	3.7	4.6	6.2	8.5	9.9
	UNITED STATES	70,597[e]	114,798[e]	143,427[e]	168,994[e]	170,500	191,595	39.5	56.4	67.7	77.0	79.1	83.7

1. January 1st each year.

a. 1969.

b. Includes Canal Zone.

c. 1974.

d. ENTEL Peru only.

e. Excludes Hawaii.

SOURCE: American Telephone and Telegraph Overseas Administration, *World's Telephones*, 1960, 1965, 1969, 1970, 1971, 1974, 1975, 1977, 1978, 1979, 1980, and 1981.

Table 509

TELEPHONES BY CONTINENTAL AREA, 1960–81

Category	1960	1965	1970	1975	1979	1980	1981
Absolute Total (Million)	133.6	182.5	255.2	358.6	448.3	472.1	508.3
Percentage Total	100.0	100.0	100.0	100.0	100.0	100.0	100.0
Latin America[1]	3.1	3.0	3.1	3.5	5.0	4.0	3.9
North America	56.9	52.3	48.6	43.5	41.1	40.5	41.0
Europe	30.2	31.5	32.8	34.6	37.2	37.6	37.4
Africa	1.4	1.3	1.2	1.2	1.1	1.0	1.0
Asia	6.1	9.7	12.2	15.2	14.8	14.9	14.7
Oceania	2.3	2.2	2.1	2.0	1.8	2.0	2.0

1. Includes non-Latin American Caribbean and mainland countries and dependencies.

SOURCE: American Telephone and Telegraph Overseas Administration, *World's Telephones*, 1960, 1965, 1969, 1970, 1971, 1974, 1977, 1978, 1979, 1980, and 1981.

Table 510

RADIO AND TELEVISION TRANSMITTERS, 19 LC

(N)

Country	Radio[1] Year	Total	Governmental	Public	Commercial	Television[2] Year	Total	Governmental	Public	Commercial
A. ARGENTINA	1979	202	42	16	144	1977	75	8	2	65
B. BOLIVIA	1981	184	5	25	154	~	~	~	~	~
C. BRAZIL	1977	962	57	~	905	~	~	~	~	~
D. CHILE	1979	109	24	12	73	~	~	~	~	~
E. COLOMBIA	~	~	~	~	~	1977	71	~	71	~
F. COSTA RICA	1981	123	3	17	103	~	~	~	~	~
G. CUBA	1979	143	143	~	~	1981	58	58	~	~
H. DOMINICAN REP.	1979	188	~	~	188	~	~	~	~	~
J. EL SALVADOR	1979	75	~	7	68	~	~	~	~	~
K. GUATEMALA	1979	115	~	~	115	~	~	~	~	~
L. HAITI	1979	48	~	~	48	~	~	~	~	~
M. HONDURAS	1979	153	~	~	153	~	~	~	~	~
N. MEXICO	1981	680	36	~	644	1979	115	4	~	111
O. NICARAGUA	1979	87	~	5	82	~	~	~	~	~
P. PANAMA	1977	93	10	~	83	1977	10	~	~	10
Q. PARAGUAY	1979	56	3	~	53	~	~	~	~	~
R. PERU	1977	189	35	~	154	~	~	~	~	~
S. URUGUAY	1981	94	4	~	90	1981	21	2	~	19
T. VENEZUELA	1977	210	11	3	196	1977	42	19	~	23
UNITED STATES	1977	8,359	414	531	7,414	1977	972[a]	184	71	717

1. Figures relate to low, medium, high, and super high frequency transmitters in service used for domestic radio broadcasts to the general public.
2. Figures relate to very-high and ultra-high frequency transmitters operating on a regular basis and used for broadcasting to the general public.

a. The total does not include relay transmitters.

SOURCE: UNESCO-SY, 1983, tables 9.1 and 9.3.

Table 511

RADIO RECEIVERS,[1] 20 LC, 1965–81

	Country	T					PTI				
		1965	1970	1975	1980	1981	1965	1970	1975	1980	1981
A.	ARGENTINA	6,600	9,000	~	~	21,000	298	379	~	~	748
B.	BOLIVIA	~	402	1,150	2,800	3,150	~	82	204	500	547
C.	BRAZIL	~	11,800	16,980	35,000	40,000	~	128	160	284	308
D.	CHILE	~	1,400	1,700	3,250	3,350	~	149	166	293	297
E.	COLOMBIA	1,600	2,217	2,808	3,250	3,450	104	108	119	120	120
F.	COSTA RICA	~	130	151	180	186	~	75	77	80	82
G.	CUBA	~	1,330	1,805	2,914	3,000	~	156	193	299	309
H.	DOMNICAN REP.	~	164	190	220	229	~	40	40	41	42
I.	ECUADOR	540	1,700	~	2,650	2,750	107	285	~	317	318
J.	EL SALVADOR	396	583	1,400	1,550	1,600	135	165	350	322	324
K.	GUATEMALA	~	220	262	310	320	~	42	43	43	43
L.	HAITI	63	76	87	101	105	16	18	19	20	21
M.	HONDURAS	135	147	160	176	180	59	56	52	48	47
N.	MEXICO	8,593	14,005	~	20,500	20,510	208	276	~	304	288
O.	NICARAGUA	100	137	~	700	750	62	75	~	259	266
P.	PANAMA	~	215	250	285	305	~	149	150	155	157
Q.	PARAGUAY	~	~	180	224	240	~	~	68	73	73
R.	PERU	~	1,748	2,050	2,750	2,900	~	130	133	155	159
S.	URUGUAY	900	1,000	1,500	1,630	1,650	331	347	533	562	564
T.	VENEZUELA	~	~	4,775	5,600	5,800	~	~	398	403	405
	UNITED STATES	240,000	290,000	413,100	477,800	485,000	1,235	1,415	1,934	2,099	2,110

1. Estimated number of receivers in use.

SOURCE: UNESCO-SY, 1983, table 9.2.

Table 512

TELEVISION SETS,[1] 20 LC, 1965–81

	Country	T					PTI				
		1965	1970	1975	1980	1981	1965	1970	1975	1980	1981
A.	ARGENTINA	1,600	3,500	~	5,140	5,540	72	147	~	190	197
B.	BOLIVIA	~	~	45	300	341	~	~	8	54	59
C.	BRAZIL	~	6,100	~	15,000	15,500	~	66	~	122	122
D.	CHILE	~	500	700	1,225	1,250	~	53	68	110	111
E.	COLOMBIA	350	810	1,600	2,250	2,500	19	39	68	83	87
F.	COSTA RICA	50	100	155	162	164	34	58	79	72	72
G.	CUBA	~	~	595	1,273	1,500	~	~	64	129	154
H.	DOMINICAN REP.	50	100	158	385	396	14	25	34	71	71
I.	ECUADOR	42	150	252	500	530	8	25	36	60	61
J.	EL SALVADOR	35	92	135	300	310	12	26	34	62	63
K.	GUATEMALA	55	72	110	175	180	12	14	18	24	24
L.	HAITI	~	11	13	16	17	~	3	3	3	3
M.	HONDURAS	2	22	47	49	49	1	8	12	13	13
N.	MEXICO	1,218	2,993	~	7,500	7,900	30	59	~	111	111
O.	NICARAGUA	16	55	83	175	185	10	30	39	65	66
P.	PANAMA	70	~	185	220	233	57	~	111	120	120
Q.	PARAGUAY	~	~	54	68	75	~	~	20	22	23
R.	PERU	210	395	610	850	900	18	29	39	48	49
S.	URUGUAY	200	~	351	363	366	74	~	125	125	125
T.	VENEZUELA	650	~	1,284	1,710	1,800	75	~	107	123	126
	UNITED STATES	70,350	84,600	125,060	142,000	145,000	362	413	586	624	631

1. Estimated number of television sets in use.

SOURCE: UNESCO-SY, 1983, table 9.4.

Table 513

CINEMA ATTENDANCE, 20 LC, 1955–80

Country	1955 Attendance (M)	1955 Per Capita Visits	1960 Attendance (M)	1960 Per Capita Visits	1965 Attendance (M)	1965 Per Capita Visits	1970 Attendance (M)	1970 Per Capita Visits	1975 Attendance (M)	1975 Per Capita Visits	1980 Attendance (M)	1980 Per Capita Visits
A. ARGENTINA	120[a]	6.3[a]	145	7.0	344[b]	15.5[b]	53	2.2	82	3.2	44[m]	.2[m]
B. BOLIVIA	~	~	~	~	3[c]	.7[c]	~	~	~	~	31[n]	5.7[n]
C. BRAZIL	312[d]	5.0[d]	316	4.5	314[e]	3.8[e]	234[b]	2.5[b]	276	2.6	209[o]	1.9[o]
D. CHILE	28	4.2	~	~	61	7.1	47[f]	4.8[f]	23	2.3	15[m]	1.3[m]
E. COLOMBIA	56[g]	4.19	67[h]	5.8[h]	80	4.3	92[i]	4.2[i]	96	4.1	68[m]	2.4[m]
F. COSTA RICA	~	~	~	~	~	~	~	~	~	~	~	~
G. CUBA	~	~	49[j]	8.4[j]	~	~	~	~	124[q]	14.2[q]	89[m]	9.2[m]
H. DOMINICAN REP.	4	1.5	~	~	~	~	~	~	~	~	~	~
I. ECUADOR	8	2.2	15	~	15	2.9	22	3.7	39	5.6	16[o]	~
J. EL SALVADOR	9	4.1	15	8.1	~	~	10[f]	2.9[f]	14[r]	3.5[r]	10[n]	1.4[n]
K. GUATEMALA	9	2.6	10	3.6	~	~	9[f]	1.7[f]	15[s]	2.8[†,s]	6[o]	1.3[o]
L. HAITI	1	··	1[k]	1.3[k]	1[c]	··	~	~	6[o]	1.3[o]	~	~
M. HONDURAS	2	1.2	~	~	~	~	~	~	~	~	~	~
N. MEXICO	362	11.7	374[j]	10.7[j]	346	8.0	251	4.9	251	4.2	264[p]	3.7[m]
O. NICARAGUA	5[l]	3.9[l]	6	5.7	7	4.1	5[i]	3.6[i]	~	~	5[m]	1.9[m]
P. PANAMA	~	~	~	~	~	~	~	~	.3[r]	6.5[r]	~	~
Q. PARAGUAY	~	~	~	~	~	~	~	~	~	~	~	~
R. PERU	~	~	67[j]	6.7[j]	~	~	~	~	~	~	33[p]	1.9[p]
S. URUGUAY	~	~	25[h]	9.8[h]	16[e]	5.7[e]	~	~	~	~	6[m]	2.1[m]
T. VENEZUELA	42	7.0	60[h]	7.8[h]	~	~	37[f]	3.5[f]	33[o]	2.6[o]	67[m]	4.7[m]
UNITED STATES	2,000	12.1	2,165[j]	12.0[j]	2,288	11.8	920	4.5	1,565[†,o]	7.2[o]	1,067[m]	4.6[m]

a. 1953.
b. 1967.
c. 1964.
d. 1954.
e. 1963.
f. 1971.
g. 1956.
h. 1959.
i. 1968.
j. 1961
k. 1958.
l. 1952.
m. 1981.
n. 1979.
o. 1977.
p. 1980.
q. 1972.
r. 1974.
s. 1973.

SOURCE: For years 1955-70, Daniel I. Geffner, "Alternative Interpretations of Time-Series Data on the Growth of Latin American Film Industry, 1926-1970," SALA, 19-3601. For previous years see UNESCO-SY, 1977, table 14.3; UNESCO-SY, 1980, table 9.3; UNESCO-SY, 1983, table 8.3.

Table 514

MOTION PICUTRE THEATERS, 20 LC, 1926–80

(N)

Country	1926	1930	1940	1950	1955	1960	1965	1970	1975	1980
A. ARGENTINA	200	975	1,208	1,881	2,063	2,228	1,587[a,b]	1,637[c]	1,420	1,018[n]
B. BOLIVIA	16	20	38	60	47	82	120[d]	~	~	226[o]
C. BRAZIL	200	1,600	1,300	1,736	3,301	3,284	3,261[e]	3,194[a]	2,910	3,195[p]
D. CHILE	200	221	263	300	410	336	336	368[f]	291	172[n]
E. COLOMBIA	200	218	274	500	641	819[g]	895	726[h]	700	393[n]
F. COSTA RICA	8	21	42	100	100	136[i]	~	~	~	~
G. CUBA	350	457	375	516	555	481[i,k]	~	439[l,c]	888[s]	1,322[n]
H. DOMINICAN REP.	~	31	28	55	74	84	~	80[f,c]	~	~
I. ECUADOR	25	25	37	71	240	122	164	164	255[t]	~
J. EL SALVADOR	33	~	41	32	34	55[i]	~	57[f]	72[t]	~
K. GUATEMALA	20	39	28	25	99	105	~	105[f,c]	131[u]	126[q]
L. HAITI	6	9	7	24	21	26[m,i]	20[d,b]	~	~	23[p]
M. HONDURAS	6	27	23	28	30	60[i]	~	~	~	2,831[o]
N. MEXICO	700	701	829	1,726	2,062	2,000[i,k]	1,555[b]	1,765[c]	2,505	2,831[o]
O. NICARAGUA	11	24	27	~	50	98	104[e,i]	~	~	128[n]
P. PANAMA	30	38	54	60	60	62	~	23[h,c]	6[t]	~
Q. PARAGUAY	~	9	8	~	30	55	~	~	~	~
R. PERU	60	70	212	~	243	319[j]	~	276[l,c]	388[p]	425[o]
S. URUGUAY	101	125	181	177	220	223[i,k]	386[e]	180[a]	~	120[n]
T. VENEZUELA	18	123	177	350	575	744[g,k]	~	436[f,c]	588[p]	555[n]
LATIN AMERICA	~	~	5,162	~	10,855	11,319	~	~	~	11,000[r]
UNITED STATES	~	23,000	17,003	20,239	19,000	15,105[i,k]	9,805[b]	10,520[c]	15,000	18,040[n]

a. 1967.
b. Does not include drive-in cinemas or their capacity (in parentheses) for cars:
Argentina 1; Haiti, 1 (450); Mexico, 5 (3,200); United States, 3,600.
c. Does not include drive-in cinemas or their capacity (in parentheses) for cars:
Argentina, 8 (5,150); Cuba, 1 (550); Dominican Republic, 2 (420);
Guatemala, 1 (544); Mexico, 3 (1,970); Panama, 1 (330); Peru, 1 (100);
Venezuela, 20 (4,030); United States, 3,900.
d. 1964.
e. 1963.
f. 1971.
g. 1959.
h. 1968.
i. It was not indicated if the cinemas concerned were equipped to exhibit 35 mm or
16 mm films.

SOURCE: For years 1926-70, same as table 513. For previous years see UNESCO-SY,
1977, table 14.3; UNESCO-SY, 1978-79, table 17.3; UNESCO-SY, 1983, table 8.3.

j. 1961.
k. Does not include drive-in cinemas or their capacity (in parentheses) for cars:
Cuba, 2 (1,366); Mexico, 5 (2,500); Venezuela, 3 (900); United States, 6,000
(2,400,000).
l. 1972.
m. 1958.
n. 1981.
o. 1980.
p. 1977.
q. 1979.
r. Indicates the number of fixed cinemas for 1981.
s. 1972.
t. 1974.
u. 1976.

Part III: Population, Health, and Education

CHAPTER 6

DEMOGRAPHY

Table 600

WORLD POPULATION (MID 1979) AND AVERAGE ANNUAL GROWTH RATES AND RANKS, 20 LRC, 1960-79

(125 Countries with Populations of 1 Million or More)[1]

Population Rank	Country	Population (T)	AA-GR 1960-73	AA-GR 1970-79
1	China[1]	981,812	1.7	1.9
2	India	659,590	2.3	2.1
3	USSR	264,115	1.0	.9
4	United States[2]	223,631	1.0	.9
5	Indonesia	142,870	2.1	2.3
6	**Brazil**	**116,539**	**2.9**	**2.3**
7	Japan	115,692	1.2	1.2
8	Bangladesh	87,668	2.4	3.0
9	Nigeria	82,603	2.5	2.5
10	Pakistan	79,705	2.9	3.1
11	**Mexico**	**65,509**	**3.5**	**3.0**
12	Germany, Federal Republic of	61,159	.6	.0
13	Italy	56,764	.7	.7
14	United Kingdom[3]	55,940	.4	.1
15	France[4]	53,380	.8	.6
16	Viet Nam	52,943	2.6	2.9
17	Philippines	46,748	3.0	2.7
18	Thailand	45,475	3.0	2.5
19	Turkey	44,237	2.4	2.5
20	Egypt, Arab Republic of	38,868	2.5	2.0
21	Korea, Republic of	37,814	1.9	1.9
22	Spain	37,033	1.1	1.1
23	Iran	36,971	3.2	3.0
24	Poland	35,436	.8	.9
25	Burma	32,573	2.2	2.2
26	Ethiopia	30,861	2.4	2.2
27	South Africa	28,469	3.2	2.7
28	Zaire	27,509	2.7	2.7
29	**Argentina**	**27,313**	**1.5**	**1.6**
30	**Colombia**	**26,122**	**1.8**	**2.3**
31	Canada	23,690	1.4	1.1
32	Yugoslavia	22,139	.9	.9
33	Romania	22,068	1.2	.9
34	Morocco	19,538	2.4	3.0
35	Algeria	18,260	3.4	3.4
36	Sudan	17,862	2.8	2.7
37	Tanzania[5]	17,538	2.8	3.4
38	Korea, Dem. People's Rep. of	17,474	2.8	2.6
39	**Peru**	**17,149**	**2.9**	**2.7**
40	German Democratic Republic	16,846	.0	-.2
41	Afghanistan	15,542	2.2	2.6
42	Kenya	15,274	3.2	3.5
43	Czechoslovakia	15,236	.3	.7
44	Sri Lanka	14,542	2.3	1.7
45	**Venezuela**	**14,453**	**3.4**	**3.4**
46	Australia	14,321	1.9	1.5
47	Netherlands, The[6]	14,007	1.1	.8
48	Nepal	13,963	1.9	2.4
49	Malaysia	13,137	2.6	2.3
50	Uganda	12,797	2.8	3.0
51	Iraq	12,631	3.2	3.4
52	Ghana	11,313	2.6	3.1
53	**Chile**	**10,917**	**2.2**	**1.7**
54	Hungary	10,716	.3	.4
55	Mozambique	10,199	2.0	2.5
56	Belgium	9,829	.5	.2
57	Portugal[7]	9,771	.0	1.4
58	**Cuba**	**9,760**	**2.0**	**1.4**
59	Greece	9,272	.5	.6
60	Bulgaria	8,951	.7	.6
61	Syrian Arab Republic	8,639	3.3	3.6
62	Saudi Arabia	8,606	1.7	4.6
63	Madagascar	8,480	2.7	2.5
64	Sweden	8,264	.7	.3
65	Cameroon	8,245	2.0	2.2
66	Ivory Coast	8,227	3.8	5.7
67	**Ecuador**	**8,081**	**3.4**	**3.3**
68	Austria	7,491	.5	.1
69	Zimbabwe	7,146	3.3	3.3
70	Angola	6,901	1.3	2.4
71	**Guatemala**	**6,811**	**2.4**	**2.9**
72	Mali	6,750	2.1	2.6
73	Switzerland	6,458	1.3	.3
74	Tunisia	6,194	2.1	2.1
75	Malawi	5,817	2.6	2.9
76	Yemen Arab Republic	5,718	2.4	1.8
77	Upper Volta	5,642	2.1	1.6
78	Zambia	5,580	2.9	3.1
79	Senegal	5,518	2.1	2.6
80	**Bolivia**	**5,428**	**2.6**	**2.6**
81	**Dominican Republic**	**5,280**	**2.9**	**3.0**
82	Guinea	5,275	2.8	2.9
83	Niger	5,163	2.7	2.8
84	Denmark[8]	5,112	.7	.4
85	Hong Kong	4,965	3.3	2.6
86	Rwanda	4,947	3.4	2.8
87	**Haiti**	**4,921**	**1.7**	**1.7**
88	Finland	4,835	.3	.6
89	**El Salvador**	**4,410**	**3.5**	**2.9**
90	Chad	4,365	1.8	2.0
91	Norway	4,066	.8	.5
92	Burundi	4,022	2.0	2.2
93	Somalia	3,828	2.4	2.3
94	Israel	3,783	3.1	2.7
95	**Honduras**	**3,563**	**3.2**	**3.4**
96	Puerto Rico	3,547	1.0	3.0
97	Benin	3,425	2.7	2.9
98	Sierra Leone	3,381	2.2	2.6
99	Lao People's Dem. Rep.	3,349	2.4	1.3
100	Ireland	3,272	.5	1.2
101	New Zealand[9]	3,234	1.6	1.6
102	Jordan	3,126	3.3	3.5
103	**Paraguay**	**2,974**	**2.6**	**2.9**
104	Papua New Guinea	2,939	2.4	2.3
105	**Uruguay**	**2,904**	**1.3**	**.3**
106	Libya	2,862	3.7	4.2
107	Albania	2,670	2.8	2.5
108	Lebanon	2,662	2.6	-1.0
109	**Nicaragua**	**2,584**	**2.6**	**3.3**
110	Togo	2,420	2.7	2.4
111	Singapore	2,361	2.1	1.4
112	Central African Rep.	2,245	2.2	2.3
113	**Costa Rica**	**2,162**	**3.1**	**2.5**
114	Jamaica	2,159	1.6	1.6
115	Yemen, People's Dem. Rep. of	1,855	3.1	2.4
116	Liberia	1,797	3.3	3.4
117	**Panama**	**1,794**	**3.1**	**2.3**
118	Mongolia	1,622	2.7	3.0
119	Mauritania	1,588	2.1	2.7
120	Congo, People's Rep. of the	1,497	2.6	2.5
121	Lesotho	1,309	2.2	2.4
122	Kuwait	1,279	~	6.2
123	Bhutan	1,267	2.3	2.2
124	Trinidad and Tobago	1,150	1.7	1.2
125	Kampuchea, Dem.	~	~	~
	Latin American 20-Country Average[10]	**16,934**	**2.7**	**2.3**

1. Includes data for Taiwan, China, which are as follows: Population, mid-1979—17,307,000; growth rate, 1970-79—2.0%.
2. Excludes Puerto Rico, the Trust Territory of the Pacific Islands, and its unorganized and unincorporated territories.
3. Excludes colonies, dependencies, and associated states.
4. Excludes overseas departments and territories.
5. Mainland Tanzania.
6. Excludes overseas portion of the Netherlands realm.

7. Excludes overseas administered territory.
8. Excludes overseas integral parts with home rule of the Danish realm.
9. Excludes overseas territory and self-governing associated states.
10. Regardless of size.

SOURCE: Adapted from World Bank, *Atlas*, 1975; World Bank, *Atlas*, 1980; World Bank, *Atlas*, 1981.

Table 601

ARGENTINA POPULATION ESTIMATE AND INDEX, 1900–83[a]

Year	M	1970 = 100	Year	M	1970 = 100
1900	4.61	19	1950	17.07	72
1901	4.74	20	1951	17.48	74
1902	4.87	21	1952*	17.70	75
1903	4.98	21	1953	17.96	76
1904	5.10	22	1954	18.24	77
1905	5.29	22	1955	18.53	78
1906	5.52	23	1956	18.80	79
1907	5.82	25	1957	19.10	80
1908	6.15	26	1958	19.38	82
1909	6.43	27	1959	19.66	83
1910	6.80	29	1960	19.92	84
1911	7.07	30	1961	20.24	85
1912	7.47	31	1962	20.54	86
1913	7.84	33	1963	20.85	88
1914	8.00	34	1964	21.17	89
1915	8.15	34	1965	22.18	93
1916	8.30	35	1966	22.49	95
1917	8.45	36	1967	22.80	96
1918	8.60	36	1968	23.11	97
1919	8.75	37	1969	23.43	99
1920	8.97	38	1970	23.75	100
1921	9.22	39	1971	24.07	101
1922	9.52	40	1972	24.39	103
1923	9.89	42	1973	24.82	105
1924	10.22	43	1974	25.22	106
1925	10.50	44	1975	26.05	110
1926	10.80	45	1976	26.48	112
1927	11.13	47	1977	26.91	113
1928	11.44	48	1978	27.35	115
1929	11.75	49	1979	27.79	117
1930	12.05	51	1980	28.24	119
1931	12.29	52	1981	28.69	121
1932	12.52	53	1982	29.16	123
1933	12.73	54	1983	29.63	125
1934	12.94	54			
1935	13.15	55			
1936	13.37	56			
1937	13.61	57			
1938	13.84	58			
1939	14.06	59			
1940	14.17	60			
1941	14.40	62			
1942	14.64	62			
1943	14.88	63			
1944	15.13	64			
1945	15.40	65			
1946	15.65	66			
1947	15.93	67			
1948	16.27	69			
1949	16.66	70			

a. Mid-year estimates.

SOURCE: 1900-51 data from SALA-SNP, pp. 173–183; since 1952, data from IMF-IFS-Y, 1984; cf. SALA, 24-600, 624, 625.

Table 602

BOLIVIA POPULATION ESTIMATE AND INDEX, 1900–83[a]

Year	M	1970 = 100	Year	M	1970 = 100
1900	1.77	39	1950	3.01	66
1901	1.79	39	1951	3.07	67
1902	1.80	39	1952*	3.13	68
1903	1.82	40	1953	3.19	70
1904	1.84	40	1954	3.26	71
1905	1.86	41	1955	3.34	73
1906	1.88	41	1956	3.42	75
1907	1.90	41	1957	3.50	76
1908	1.91	42	1958	3.59	78
1909	1.93	42	1959	3.70	81
1910	1.95	43	1960	3.82	83
1911	1.97	43	1961	3.92	86
1912	1.98	43	1962	4.02	88
1913	2.01	44	1963	4.12	90
1914	2.03	44	1964	4.23	92
1915	2.04	45	1965	4.33	95
1916	2.06	45	1966	4.45	97
1917	2.08	45	1967	4.48†	98
1918	2.10	46	1968	4.51†	98
1919	2.12	46	1969	4.55†	99
1920	2.14	47	1970	4.58†	100
1921	2.16	47	1971	4.62†	101
1922	2.19	48	1972	4.64†	101
1923	2.21	48	1973	4.67†	102
1924	2.24	49	1974	4.75†	104
1925	2.26	49	1975*	4.89	107
1926	2.29	50	1976	5.03	110
1927	2.32	51	1977	5.16	113
1928	2.34	51	1978	5.30	116
1929	2.37	52	1979	5.45	119
1930	2.40	52	1980	5.60	122
1931	2.43	53	1981	5.76	126
1932	2.45	53	1982	5.92	129
1933	2.48	54	1983	6.08	133
1934	2.51	55			
1935	2.54	55			
1936	2.57	56			
1937	2.60	57			
1938	2.63	57			
1939	2.66	58			
1940	2.70	59			
1941	2.72	59			
1942	2.75	60			
1943	2.79	61			
1944	2.82	62			
1945	2.85	62			
1946	2.88	63			
1947	2.92	64			
1948	2.95	64			
1949	2.96	65			

a. Mid-year estimates.

SOURCE: 1900-51 data from SALA-SNP, pp. 173–183; since 1952, data from IMF–IFS-Y, 1984; cf. SALA, 24-600, 624, 625.

Table 603

BRAZIL POPULATION ESTIMATE AND INDEX, 1900-83[a]

Year	M	1970 = 100	Year	M	1970 = 100
1900	17.98	19	1950	52.18	56
1901	18.39	20	1951	53.68	58
1902	18.78	22	1952	55.10	60
1903	19.18	21	1953	56.74	61
1904	19.58	21	1954	58.44	63
1905	20.00	22	1955	60.18	65
1906	20.43	22	1956	61.98	67
1907	20.86	23	1957	63.83	69
1908	21.30	23	1958	65.74	71
1909	21.75	24	1959	67.70	73
1910	22.22	24	1960*	69.72	75
1911	22.69	25	1961	71.94	78
1912	23.17	25	1962	74.17	80
1913	23.66	26	1963	76.53	83
1914	24.16	26	1964	78.73	85
1915	24.67	27	1965	81.01	88
1916	25.20	27	1966	82.93	90
1917	25.73	28	1967	85.24	92
1918	26.28	28	1968	87.62	95
1919	26.84	29	1969	90.07	97
1920	27.40	30	1970	92.52	100
1921	27.97	30	1971	95.17	103
1922	28.54	31	1972	97.85	106
1923	29.13	31	1973	99.92	108
1924	29.72	32	1974	102.40	111
1925	30.33	33	1975	104.94	113
1926	30.95	33	1976	107.54	116
1927	31.59	34	1977	110.21	119
1928	32.23	35	1978	112.94	122
1929	32.90	36	1979*	115.74	125
1930	33.57	36	1980	121.27	131
1931	34.26	37	1981	124.02	134
1932	34.96	38	1982	126.81	137
1933	35.67	39	1983	129.66	140
1934	36.40	39			
1935	37.15	40			
1936	37.91	41			
1937	38.69	42			
1938	39.48	43			
1939	40.29	44			
1940	41.11	44			
1941	42.07	45			
1942	43.06	47			
1943	43.99	48			
1944	44.84	48			
1945	45.86	50			
1946	46.97	51			
1947	48.16	52			
1948	49.42	53			
1949	50.76	55			

a. Mid-year estimates.

SOURCE: 1900-51 data from SALA-SNP, pp. 173-183; since 1952, data from IMF-IFS-Y, 1984; cf. SALA, 24-600, 624, 625.

Table 604

CHILE POPULATION ESTIMATE AND INDEX, 1900–83[a]

Year	M	1970 = 100	Year	M	1970 = 100
1900	2.96	32	1950	6.07	65
1901	2.99	32	1951	6.21	65
1902	3.03	32	1952*	6.30	67
1903	3.07	33	1953	6.46	69
1904	3.10	33	1954	6.62	71
1905	3.14	34	1955	6.79	72
1906	3.18	34	1956	6.96	74
1907	3.21	34	1957	7.14	76
1908	3.25	35	1958	7.32	78
1909	3.29	35	1959	7.49	80
1910	3.34	36	1960	7.58	81
1911	3.38	36	1961	7.76	83
1912	3.42	36	1962	7.95	85
1913	3.47	37	1963	8.14	87
1914	3.51	37	1964	8.33	89
1915	3.55	38	1965	8.51	91
1916	3.60	38	1966	8.68	93
1917	3.64	39	1967	8.85	94
1918	3.69	39	1968	9.03	96
1919	3.74	40	1969	9.20	98
1920	3.79	40	1970	9.37	100
1921	3.85	41	1971	9.53	102
1922	3.91	42	1972	9.70	104
1923	3.96	42	1973	9.86	105
1924	4.02	43	1974	10.03	107
1925	4.07	43	1975	10.20	109
1926	4.13	44	1976	10.37	111
1927	4.19	45	1977	10.55	113
1928	4.25	45	1978	10.73	115
1929	4.31	46	1979	10.92	117
1930	4.37	47	1980	11.10	118
1931	4.43	47	1981	11.29	120
1932	4.50	48	1982	11.49	123
1933	4.56	49	1983	11.68	125
1934	4.63	49			
1935	4.70	50			
1936	4.77	51			
1937	4.84	52			
1938	4.91	52			
1939	4.99	53			
1940	5.06	54			
1941	5.15	55			
1942	5.24	56			
1943	5.34	57			
1944	5.44	58			
1945	5.54	59			
1946	5.64	60			
1947	5.75	61			
1948	5.85	62			
1949	5.96	64			

a. Mid-year estimates.

SOURCE: 1900-51 data from SALA-SNP, pp. 173-183; since 1952, data from IMF-IFS-Y, 1984; cf. SALA, 24-600, 624, 625.

Table 605

COLOMBIA POPULATION ESTIMATE AND INDEX, 1900–82[a]

Year	M	1970 = 100	Year	M	1970 = 100
1900	3.89	19	1950	11.33	56
1901	3.94	19	1951	11.62	57
1902	3.99	19	1952*	11.81	58
1903	4.04	20	1953	12.07	59
1904	4.09	20	1954	12.34	61
1905	4.14	20	1955	12.97	64
1906	4.28	21	1956	13.59	67
1907	4.41	21	1957	14.03	69
1908	4.54	22	1958	14.48	71
1909	4.67	23	1959	14.94	73
1910	4.81	23	1960	15.42	76
1911	4.94	24	1961	15.91	78
1912	5.07	25	1962	16.42	80
1913	5.19	25	1963	16.94	83
1914	5.32	26	1964	17.48	86
1915	5.45	27	1965	18.04	88
1916	5.58	27	1966	18.47	90
1917	5.72	28	1967	18.96	93
1918	5.86	29	1968	19.46	95
1919	6.03	29	1969	19.98	98
1920	6.09	30	1970	20.53	100
1921	6.21	30	1971	21.09	103
1922	6.37	31	1972	21.67	106
1923	6.46	31	1973	22.34	109
1924	6.59	32	1974	22.98	112
1925	6.72	33	1975	23.64	115
1926	6.86	33	1965	24.33	119
1927	7.00	34	1977	25.05	122
1928	7.14	35	1978	25.64	125
1929	7.28	35	1979	26.36	128
1930	7.43	36	1980	27.09	132
1931	7.57	37	1981	26.73	130
1932	7.73	38	1982	27.19	132
1933	7.88	38			
1934	8.03	39			
1935	8.20	40			
1936	8.36	41			
1937	8.53	42			
1938	8.70	42			
1939	8.90	43			
1940	9.10	44			
1941	9.32	45			
1942	9.54	47			
1943	9.77	48			
1944	10.02	49			
1945	10.27	50			
1946	10.53	52			
1947	10.80	53			
1948*	10.85	53			
1949	11.09	54			

a. Mid-year estimates.

SOURCE: 1900-51 data from SALA-SNP, pp. 173-183; since 1952, data from IMF–IFS-Y, 1984; cf. SALA, 24-600, 624, 625.

Table 606

COSTA RICA POPULATION ESTIMATE AND INDEX, 1900–83[a]

Year	M	1970 = 100	Year	M	1970 = 100
1900	.31	18	1950	.80	47
1901	.31	18	1951	.83	48
1902	.32	19	1952*	.92	54
1903	.32	19	1953	.95	55
1904	.33	19	1954	.99	58
1905	.34	20	1955	1.03	60
1906	.34	20	1956	1.07	62
1907	.35	21	1957	1.11	65
1908	.35	21	1958	1.15	67
1909	.36	21	1959	1.19	69
1910	.36	21	1960	1.25	75
1911	.37	22	1961	1.30	76
1912	.38	22	1962	1.35	78
1913	.38	22	1963	1.39	81
1914	.39	23	1964	1.44	84
1915	.39	23	1965	1.49	87
1916	.40	24	1966	1.54	89
1917	.40	24	1967	1.59	92
1918	.41	24	1968	1.63	95
1919	.42	25	1969	1.69	98
1920	.42	25	1970	1.73	100
1921	.43	25	1971	1.80	104
1922	.43	25	1972	1.84	107
1923	.44	26	1973	1.87	108
1924	.45	26	1974	1.92	111
1925	.46	27	1975	1.96	113
1926	.47	28	1976	2.01	116
1927	.47	28	1977	2.07	120
1928	.48	28	1978	2.12	123
1929	.49	29	1979	2.17	125
1930	.50	29	1980	2.25	130
1931	.51	30	1981	2.27	131
1932	.52	30	1982	2.32	134
1933	.53	31	1983	2.44	141
1934	.54	32			
1935	.55	32			
1936	.56	33			
1937	.58	34			
1938	.59	35			
1939	.61	36			
1940	.62	36			
1941	.63	36			
1942	.65	37			
1943	.66	39			
1944	.68	40			
1945	.70	41			
1946	.71	41			
1947	.73	43			
1948	.75	44			
1949	.77	45			

a. Mid-year estimates.

SOURCE: 1900-51 data from SALA-SNP, pp. 173-183; since 1952, data from IMF–IFS-Y, 1984; cf. SALA, 24-600, 624, 625.

Table 607

CUBA POPULATION ESTIMATE AND INDEX, 1900–83

Year	M	1970 = 100	Year	M	1970 = 100
1900	1.60	19	1950	5.51	65
1901	1.68	20	1951	5.62	66
1902	1.76	21	1952	5.73	67
1903	1.84	22	1953*	6.04	71
1904	1.88	22	1954	6.16	72
1905	1.93	23	1955	6.28	73
1906	1.98	24	1956	6.41	75
1907	2.03	24	1957	6.54	76
1908	2.09	25	1958	6.76	79
1909	2.15	20	1959	6.90	81
1910	2.22	20	1960	7.03	83
1911	2.29	27	1961	7.13	84
1912	2.36	40	1962	7.25	85
1913	2.41	29	1963	7.41	87
1914	2.51	30	1964	7.61	89
1915	2.59	31	1965	7.81	92
1916	2.66	32	1966	7.99	94
1917	2.75	33	1967	8.14	96
1918	2.83	45	1968	8.28	97
1919	2.91	34	1969	8.42	99
1920	3.00	35	1970	8.55	100
1921	3.08	36	1971	8.69	102
1922	3.17	37	1972	8.86	104
1923	3.26	39	1973	9.04	106
1924	3.35	40	1974	9.19	108
1925	3.43	41	1975*	9.29	109
1926	3.52	42	1976	9.42	110
1927	3.61	43	1977	9.54	111
1928	3.51	41	1978	9.64	113
1929	3.58	42	1979	9.71	114
1930	3.65	43	1980	9.72	114
1931	3.96	47	1981	9.72	114
1932	3.96	47	1982	9.78	114
1933	3.96	47	1983	9.88	116
1934	4.04	48			
1935	4.07	48			
1936	4.11	48			
1937	4.17	49			
1938	4.23	50			
1939	4.25	50			
1940	4.29	51			
1941	4.33	51			
1942	4.37	52			
1943	4.78	56			
1944	4.85	57			
1945	4.93	58			
1946	5.04	59			
1947	5.15	61			
1948	5.27	62			
1949	5.39	63			

SOURCE: 1900-52 data from SALA–SNP, p. 176; 1953-74 data from Cuba, JUCEPLAN, AE, 1972, 1974, and 1975; since 1975, data from UN–MB, Jan. 1985. Cf. SALA, 23–103, 622, 623.

Table 608

DOMINICAN REPUBLIC POPULATION ESTIMATE AND INDEX, 1900–83[a]

Year	M	1970 = 100	Year	M	1970 = 100
1900	.60	15	1950	2.24	55
1901	.61	15	1951	2.27	57
1902	.63	16	1952*	2.29	56
1903	.64	16	1953	2.37	58
1904	.66	17	1954	2.45	60
1905	.67	17	1955	2.54	63
1906	.68	17	1956	2.63	65
1907	.70	18	1957	2.73	67
1908	.71	18	1958	2.83	70
1909	.73	18	1959	2.93	72
1910	.74	19	1960	3.04	75
1911	.75	19	1961	3.12	77
1912	.77	19	1962	3.21	79
1913	.78	20	1963	3.31	82
1914	.80	20	1964	3.41	84
1915	.81	20	1965	3.51	87
1916	.82	21	1966	3.62	90
1917	.84	21	1967	3.72	92
1918	.85	21	1968	3.83	95
1919	.87	22	1969	3.95	98
1920	.88	22	1970	4.06	100
1921	.91	23	1971	4.18	103
1922	.95	24	1972	4.30	106
1923	.98	25	1973	4.43	110
1924	1.02	26	1974	4.56	113
1925	1.05	26	1975	4.70	116
1926	1.09	27	1976	4.89	120
1927	1.13	28	1977	5.03	124
1928	1.17	29	1978	5.17	127
1929	1.21	30	1979	5.30	131
1930	1.26	31	1980	5.44	134
1931	1.30	32	1981	5.58	137
1932	1.35	34	1982	5.74	141
1933	1.39	35	1983	5.96	147
1934	1.44	36			
1935	1.48	37			
1936	1.52	38			
1937	1.56	39			
1938	1.60	40			
1939	1.63	41			
1940	1.76	44			
1941	1.80	45			
1942	1.84	46			
1943	1.89	47			
1944	1.93	48			
1945	1.98	49			
1946	2.03	50			
1947	2.08	52			
1948	2.13	53			
1949	2.19	54			

a. Mid-year estimates.

SOURCE: 1900-51 data from SALA–SNP, pp. 173-183; since 1952, data from IMF–IFS-Y, 1984; cf. SALA, 24-600, 624, 625.

Table 609

ECUADOR POPULATION ESTIMATE AND INDEX, 1900–83[a]

Year	M	1970 = 100	Year	M	1970 = 100
1900	1.30	22	1950	3.20	54
1901	1.31	22	1951	3.25	55
1902	1.32	22	1952*	3.43	58
1903	1.34	22	1953	3.53	59
1904	1.35	23	1954	3.64	61
1905	1.36	23	1955	3.75	63
1906	1.37	23	1956	3.87	65
1907	1.38	23	1957	3.98	67
1908	1.40	23	1958	4.11	69
1909	1.41	24	1959	4.23	71
1910	1.42	24	1960	4.36	73
1911	1.43	24	1961	4.50	76
1912	1.45	24	1962*	4.65	78
1913	1.46	24	1963	4.78	80
1914	1.47	25	1964	4.93	83
1915	1.48	25	1965	5.07	85
1916	1.49	25	1966	5.22	88
1917	1.51	25	1967	5.40	91
1918	1.52	26	1968	5.58	94
1919	1.53	26	1969	5.77	97
1920	1.54	26	1970	5.96	100
1921	1.57	26	1971	6.17	104
1922	1.61	27	1972	6.38	107
1923	1.65	28	1973	6.60	111
1924	1.69	28	1974	6.83	115
1925	1.72	29	1975	7.06	118
1926	1.76	30	1976	7.31	123
1927	1.80	30	1977	7.56	127
1928	1.84	31	1978	7.81	131
1929	1.90	32	1979	8.08	136
1930	1.94	33	1980	8.35	140
1931	2.00	34	1981	8.64	145
1932	2.05	34	1982	8.95	150
1933	2.10	35	1983	9.25	155
1934	2.14	36			
1935	2.20	37			
1936	2.25	38			
1937	2.30	39			
1938	2.36	40			
1939	2.41	40			
1940	2.47	41			
1941	2.52	42			
1942	2.58	43			
1943	2.64	44			
1944	2.71	45			
1945	2.78	47			
1946	2.85	48			
1947	2.94	49			
1948	3.02	51			
1949	3.10	52			

a. Mid-year estimates.

SOURCE: 1900-51 data from SALA-SNP, pp. 173-183; since 1952, data from IMF–IFS-Y, 1984; cf. SALA, 24-600, 624, 625.

Table 610

EL SALVADOR POPULATION ESTIMATE AND INDEX, 1900–82[a]

Year	M	1970 = 100	Year	M	1970 = 100
1900	.80	24	1950	1.86	54
1901	.82	24	1951	1.90	56
1902	.84	25	1952*	1.97*	58
1903	.86	25	1953	2.02	59
1904	.87	26	1954	2.08	61
1905	.89	26	1955	2.14	63
1906	.91	27	1956	2.20	64
1907	.93	27	1957	2.26	66
1908	.95	28	1958	2.32	68
1909	.97	29	1959	2.39	70
1910	.99	29	1960	2.45	72
1911	1.00	29	1961*	2.51	73
1912	1.02	30	1962[†]	2.63	77
1913	1.04	31	1963[†]	2.72	79
1914	1.06	31	1964[†]	2.82	82
1915	1.07	32	1965[†]	2.93	86
1916	1.10	32	1966[†]	3.04	89
1917	1.11	33	1967[†]	3.15	92
1918	1.13	33	1968[†]	3.27	95
1919	1.15	34	1969[†]	3.36	98
1920	1.17	34	1970[†]	3.44	100
1921	1.19	35	1971[†]	3.55	104
1922	1.22	36	1972*	3.67	107
1923	1.24	36	1973	3.77	107
1924	1.27	37	1974	3.89	113
1925	1.30	38	1975	4.01	117
1926	1.33	39	1976	4.12	120
1927	1.35	40	1977	4.26	124
1928	1.39	41	1978	4.35	126
1929	1.41	41	1979	4.44	129
1930	1.44	42	1980	4.75	138
1931	1.46	43	1981	4.87	142
1932	1.47	43	1982	5.00	145
1933	1.49	44			
1934	1.51	44			
1935	1.53	45			
1936	1.55	45			
1937	1.57	46			
1938	1.59	47			
1939	1.61	47			
1940	1.63	48			
1941	1.65	48			
1942	1.68	48			
1943	1.69	50			
1944	1.72	50			
1945	1.74	51			
1946	1.76	52			
1947	1.78	52			
1948	1.81	53			
1949	1.84	54			

a. Mid-year estimates.

SOURCE: 1900-51 data from SALA-SNP, pp. 173-183; since 1952, data from IMF–IFS-Y, 1984; cf. SALA, 24-600, 624, 625.

Table 611

GUATEMALA POPULATION ESTIMATE AND INDEX, 1900–82[a]

Year	M	1970 = 100	Year	M	1970 = 100
1900	.89	19	1950*	2.81	58
1901	.91	19	1951	2.89	60
1902	.94	20	1952	2.98	61
1903	.96	21	1953	3.07	63
1904	.99	21	1954	3.18	66
1905	1.01	21	1955	3.29	68
1906	1.03	22	1956	3.39	70
1907	1.05	22	1957	3.49	72
1908	1.06	22	1958	3.61	74
1909	1.08	23	1959	3.72	77
1910	1.10	23	1960	3.83	79
1911	1.12	23	1961	3.95	81
1912	1.14	24	1962	4.06	84
1913	1.17	24	1963	4.19	86
1914	1.18	25	1964*	4.31	89
1915	1.20	25	1965[†]	4.41	91
1916	1.21	25	1966[†]	4.50	93
1917	1.23	26	1967[†]	4.70	95
1918	1.24	26	1968[†]	4.84	97
1919	1.26	26	1969	5.02	99
1920	1.27	26	1970	5.27	100
1921	1.32	27	1971	5.42	102
1922	1.37	28	1972	5.58	114
1923	1.42	29	1973	5.74	118
1924	1.47	31	1974*	6.05	124
1925	1.51	31	1975	6.24	128
1926	1.56	32	1976	6.43	132
1927	1.60	33	1977	6.63	136
1928	1.66	34	1978	6.84	140
1929	1.71	35	1979	7.05	144
1930	1.76	36	1980	7.26	149
1931	1.81	37	1981	7.48	153
1932	1.86	39	1982	7.70	158
1933	1.91	40			
1934	1.94	40			
1935	1.98	40			
1936	2.02	42			
1937	2.07	43			
1938	2.11	44			
1939	2.15	44			
1940	2.20	45			
1941	2.25	47			
1942	2.30	47			
1943	2.34	48			
1944	2.39	49			
1945	2.44	50			
1946	2.50	52			
1947	2.57	53			
1948	2.64	54			
1949	2.72	56			

a. Mid-year estimates.

SOURCE: 1900-51 data from SALA-SNP, pp. 173-183; since 1952, data from IMF–IFS-Y, 1984; cf. SALA, 24-600, 624, 625.

Table 612

HAITI POPULATION ESTIMATE AND INDEX, 1900–82[a]

Year	M	1970 = 100	Year	M	1970 = 100
1900	1.25	30	1950	3.39	80
1901	1.29	31	1951	3.44	82
1902	1.34	32	1952	3.51	83
1903	1.38	33	1953	3.58	84
1904	1.43	34	1954	3.65	86
1905	1.47	35	1955	3.72	88
1906	1.51	36	1956	3.80	90
1907	1.56	37	1957*,[a]	3.75	88
1908	1.56	37	1958[a]	3.70	87
1909	1.64	39	1959[a]	3.67	87
1910	1.69	40	1960*	3.62	85
1911	1.73	41	1961	3.68	87
1912	1.77	42	1962	3.74	88
1913	1.82	43	1963	3.79	89
1914	1.86	44	1964*	3.85	91
1915	1.91	45	1965	3.91	92
1916	1.95	46	1966	3.97	94
1917	1.99	47	1967	4.03	95
1918	2.04	49	1968	4.10	97
1919	2.08	49	1969	4.16	99
1920	2.12	50	1970	4.24	100
1921	2.15	51	1971	4.31	103
1922	2.18	52	1972	4.37	103
1923	2.21	53	1973	4.44	105
1924	2.23	53	1974	4.51	107
1925	2.26	54	1975	4.58	108
1926	2.29	54	1976	4.67	110
1927	2.33	55	1977	4.75	112
1928	2.36	56	1978	4.83	114
1929	2.39	57	1979	4.92	116
1930	2.42	58	1980	5.01	118
1931	2.46	58	1981	5.10	120
1932	2.50	59	1982	5.20	123
1933	2.54	60			
1934	2.57	61			
1935	2.61	62			
1936	2.65	63			
1937	2.70	64			
1938	2.74	65			
1939	2.79	66			
1940	2.83	67			
1941	2.88	68			
1942	2.94	70			
1943	2.98	71			
1944	3.03	72			
1945	3.09	73			
1946	3.14	74			
1947	3.20	76			
1948	3.26	77			
1949	3.32	79			

a. Mid-year estimates.

SOURCE: 1900–56 data from SALA-SNP, p. 179; 1957–59, estimated by SALA with assumed impact of Duvalier's rise to power; since 1960, data from IMF–IFS-Y, 1984; cf. SALA, 24-600, 624, 625.

Table 613
HONDURAS POPULATION ESTIMATE AND INDEX, 1900–83[a]

Year	M	1970 = 100	Year	M	1970 = 100
1900	.42	16	1950	1.43	54
1901	.44	17	1951	1.47	56
1902	.45	17	1952*	1.53*	58
1903	.47	18	1953	1.57	59
1904	.48	18	1954	1.62	61
1905	.50	19	1955	1.65	63
1906	.51	19	1956	1.68	64
1907	.52	20	1957	1.71	65
1908	.53	20	1958	1.75	66
1909	.54	20	1959	1.80	68
1910	.55	21	1960	1.85	70
1911	.56	21	1961	1.91	72
1912	.57	22	1962	1.97	75
1913	.58	22	1963	2.04	77
1914	.59	22	1964	2.11	80
1915	.60	23	1965	2.18	83
1916	.61	23	1966	2.26	86
1917	.63	24	1967	2.28	86
1918	.66	25	1968	2.31	88
1919	.69	26	1969	2.45	93
1920	.72	27	1970	2.64	100
1921	.74	28	1971	2.72	103
1922	.77	29	1972	2.81	106
1923	.80	30	1973	2.90	110
1924	.82	31	1974	2.99	113
1925	.85	32	1975	3.09	117
1926	.88	33	1976	3.20	121
1927	.89	34	1977	3.32	126
1928	.91	34	1978	3.44	130
1929	.93	35	1979	3.56	135
1930	.95	36	1980	3.69	140
1931	.97	37	1981	3.83	145
1932	.99	38	1982	3.96	150
1933	1.01	38	1983	4.09	155
1934	1.02	39			
1935	1.04	39			
1936	1.06	40			
1937	1.08	41			
1938	1.10	42			
1939	1.12	42			
1940	1.15	44			
1941	1.17	44			
1942	1.20	45			
1943	1.21	46			
1944	1.24	47			
1945	1.26	48			
1946	1.29	49			
1947	1.32	50			
1948	1.35	51			
1949	1.39	53			

a. Mid-year estimates.

SOURCE: 1900-51 data from SALA-SNP, pp. 173-183; since 1952, data from IMF–IFS-Y, 1984; cf. SALA, 24-600, 624, 625.

Table 614
MEXICO POPULATION ESTIMATE AND INDEX, 1900–82[a]

Year	M	1970 = 100	Year	M	1970 = 100
1900	13.61	27	1950	25.79	51
1901	13.76	27	1951	25.59	50
1902	13.91	27	1952*	27.85	55
1903	14.07	28	1953	28.70	57
1904	14.21	28	1954	29.61	58
1905	14.36	28	1955	30.56	60
1906	14.52	29	1956	31.56	62
1907	14.68	29	1957	32.61	64
1908	14.84	29	1958	33.70	66
1909	15.00	30	1959	34.86	69
1910	15.16	30	1960	36.05	71
1911	15.33	30	1961	37.27	74
1912	15.51	31	1962	38.54	76
1913	15.37	30	1963	39.87	79
1914	15.09	30	1964	41.25	81
1915	14.64	29	1965	42.69	84
1916	14.03	28	1966	44.14	87
1917	13.90	27	1967	45.67	90
1918	14.00	28	1968	47.27	93
1919	14.15	28	1969	48.93	97
1920	14.15	28	1970	50.69	100
1921	14.34	28	1971	52.45	103
1922	14.44	28	1972	54.27	107
1923	14.69	29	1973	56.16	111
1924	14.95	29	1974	58.12	115
1925	15.20	30	1975	60.15	119
1926	15.47	31	1976	62.33	123
1927	15.74	31	1977	64.59	127
1928	16.01	32	1978*	65.43	129
1929	16.93	33	1979	67.42	133
1930	16.55	33	1980	69.35	137
1931	16.88	33	1981	71.19	140
1932	17.17	34	1982	73.01	144
1933	17.47	34			
1934	17.78	35			
1935	18.09	36			
1936	18.41	36			
1937	18.76	37			
1938	19.07	38			
1939	19.41	38			
1940	19.65	39			
1941	20.21	40			
1942	20.66	41			
1943	21.17	42			
1944	21.67	43			
1945	22.23	44			
1946	22.78	45			
1947	23.44	46			
1948	24.13	48			
1949	24.83	49			

a. Mid-year estimates.

SOURCE: 1900-51 data from SALA-SNP, pp. 173-183; since 1952, data from IMF–IFS-Y, 1984; cf. SALA, 24-600, 624, 625.

Table 615

NICARAGUA POPULATION ESTIMATE AND INDEX, 1900–83[a]

Year	M	1970 = 100	Year	M	1970 = 100
1900	.42	23	1950	1.06	58
1901	.43	24	1951	1.09	60
1902	.45	25	1952*	1.12*	62
1903	.46	26	1953	1.15	63
1904	.48	27	1954	1.18	65
1905	.49	27	1955	1.22	67
1906	.51	28	1956	1.26	69
1907	.52	29	1957	1.29	71
1908	.52	29	1958	1.33	73
1909	.53	29	1959	1.37	75
1910	.54	30	1960	1.41	77
1911	.55	30	1961	1.45	80
1912	.56	31	1962	1.50	82
1913	.57	32	1963	1.54	85
1914	.58	32	1964	1.58	87
1915	.59	33	1965	1.62	89
1916	.60	33	1966	1.66	91
1917	.61	34	1967	1.70	93
1918	.62	34	1968	1.74	95
1919	.63	35	1969	1.79	98
1920	.64	35	1970	1.83	100
1921	.64	35	1971	1.89	104
1922	.65	36	1972	1.95	107
1923	.65	36	1973	2.01	110
1924	66	36	1974	2.08	114
1925	.66	36	1975	2.16	118
1926	.67	37	1976	2.24	122
1927	.67	37	1977	2.32	127
1928	.67	37	1978	2.41	132
1929	.68	38	1979	2.54	144
1930	.68	38	1980	2.73	149
1931	.69	38	1981	2.86	156
1932	.69	38	1982	2.96	162
1933	.70	39	1983	3.06	167
1934	.71	39			
1935	.73	40			
1936	.75	41			
1937	.77	42			
1938	.78	43			
1939	.81	45			
1940	.83	46			
1941	.84	46			
1942	.86	47			
1943	.88	48			
1944	.90	50			
1945	.92	51			
1946	.95	52			
1947	.98	54			
1948	1.00	55			
1949	1.03	57			

a. Mid-year estimates.

SOURCE: 1900-51 data from SALA-SNP, pp. 173-183; since 1952, data from IMF–IFS-Y, 1984; cf. SALA, 24-600, 624, 625.

Table 616

PANAMA POPULATION ESTIMATE AND INDEX, 1900–83[a]

Year	M	1970 = 100	Year	M	1970 = 100
1900	.26	19	1950	.80	56
1901	.27	19	1951	.82	58
1902	.28	20	1952*	.84*	59
1903	.28	20	1953	.87	61
1904	.29	21	1954	.89	63
1905	.30	21	1955	.92	65
1906	.30	21	1956	.95	67
1907	.31	22	1957	.97	68
1908	.32	23	1958	1.00	70
1909	.33	23	1959	1.03	72
1910	.33	23	1960	1.06	75
1911	.34	24	1961	1.09	77
1912	.35	25	1962	1.13	79
1913	.36	26	1963	1.17	82
1914	.38	27	1964	1.20	84
1915	.39	28	1965	1.24	87
1916	.40	28	1966	1.27	89
1917	.41	29	1967	1.31	92
1918	.43	30	1968	1.35	95
1919	.44	31	1969	1.39	98
1920	.45	32	1970	1.43	100
1921	.45	32	1971	1.48	104
1922	.45	32	1972	1.52	107
1923	.45	32	1973	1.57	110
1924	.46	33	1974	1.62	114
1925	.46	33	1975	1.68	117
1926	.46	33	1976	1.72	120
1927	.46	33	1977	1.77	124
1928	.46	33	1978	1.81	127
1929	.47	33	1979	1.85	129
1930	.47	33	1980	1.90	133
1931	.49	35	1981	1.94	136
1932	.50	35	1982	2.04	143
1933	.52	37	1983	2.09	146
1934	.53	37			
1935	.55	39			
1936	.56	40			
1937	.58	41			
1938	.59	42			
1939	.61	43			
1940	.62	44			
1941	.64	45			
1942	.65	46			
1943	.67	47			
1944	.69	49			
1945	.70	49			
1946	.72	51			
1947	.74	52			
1948	.76	54			
1949	.78	55			

a. Mid-year estimates.

SOURCE: 1900-51 data from SALA-SNP, pp. 173-183; since 1952, data from IMF–IFS-Y, 1984; cf. SALA, 24-600, 624, 625.

Table 617

PARAGUAY POPULATION ESTIMATE AND INDEX, 1900–83[a]

Year	M	1970 = 100	Year	M	1970 = 100
1900	.49	22	1950	1.40	61
1901	.51	23	1951	1.43	63
1902	.52	23	1952*	1.46	64
1903	.54	24	1953	1.50	66
1904	.56	25	1954	1.53	67
1905	.57	25	1955	1.57	69
1906	.58	26	1956	1.61	70
1907	.59	26	1957	1.68	73
1908	.60	26	1958	1.68	73
1909	.61	27	1959	1.71	74
1910	.62	27	1960	1.75	76
1911	.63	28	1961	1.80	78
1912	.64	28	1962	1.85	80
1913	.65	29	1963	1.91	83
1914	.66	29	1964	1.97	86
1915	.66	29	1965	2.03	88
1916	.67	30	1966	2.07	90
1917	.68	30	1967	2.13	93
1918	.69	30	1968	2.18	95
1919	.69	30	1969	2.24	97
1920	.70	31	1970	2.30	100
1921	.72	32	1971	2.36	103
1922	.73	32	1972	2.43	106
1923	.75	33	1973*	2.50	109
1924	.77	34	1974	2.57	112
1925	.79	35	1975	2.65	115
1926	.80	35	1976	2.78	121
1927	.82	36	1977	2.87	125
1928	.84	37	1978	2.97	129
1929	.86	38	1979	3.07	133
1930	.88	39	1980	3.17	138
1931	.90	40	1981	3.27	142
1932	.92	40	1982	3.37	147
1933	.94	41	1983	3.47	151
1934	.97	43			
1935	.99	43			
1936	1.01	44			
1937	1.04	46			
1938	1.06	46			
1939	1.09	48			
1940	1.11	49			
1941	1.14	50			
1942	1.16	51			
1943	1.19	52			
1944	1.22	53			
1945	1.25	55			
1946	1.28	56			
1947	1.31	57			
1948	1.34	59			
1949	1.37	60			

a. Mid-year estimates.

SOURCE : 1900-51 data from SALA-SNP, pp. 173-183; since 1952, data from IMF-IFS, Oct., 1984; cf. SALA, 24-600, 624, 625.

Table 618

PERU POPULATION ESTIMATE AND INDEX, 1900–83[a]

Year	M	1970 = 100	Year	M	1970 = 100
1900	3.00	23	1950	7.97	60
1901	3.10	23	1951	8.12	61
1902	3.20	24	1952*	8.27	62
1903	3.30	25	1953	8.43	63
1904	3.40	26	1954	8.60	64
1905	3.50	26	1955	8.80	66
1906	3.60	27	1956	9.00	67
1907	3.70	28	1957	9.23	69
1908	3.80	29	1958	9.48	70
1909	3.90	29	1959	9.75	72
1910	4.00	30	1960	10.02	74
1911	4.10	31	1961	10.32	77
1912	4.19	32	1962	10.63	79
1913	4.27	32	1963	10.96	82
1914	4.35	33	1964	11.30	84
1915	4.43	33	1965	11.65	87
1916	4.51	34	1966	12.01	90
1917	4.59	35	1967	12.31	92
1918	4.67	35	1968	12.67	94
1919	4.75	36	1969	13.05	97
1920	4.83	36	1970	13.45	100
1921	4.91	37	1971	13.83	103
1922	4.99	38	1972	14.22	106
1923	5.07	38	1973	14.63	109
1924	5.15	39	1974	15.04	112
1925	5.23	39	1976	15.91	118
1926	5.31	40	1977	15.99	119
1927	5.40	41	1978	16.41	122
1928	5.48	41	1979	16.85	125
1929	5.57	42	1980	17.30	129
1930	5.65	42	1981	17.75	132
1931	5.74	43	1982	18.23	136
1932	5.84	44	1983	18.71	139
1933	5.94	45			
1934	6.04	45			
1935	6.13	46			
1936	6.24	47			
1937	6.35	48			
1938	6.46	48			
1939	6.57	49			
1940	6.68	50			
1941	6.80	51			
1942	6.92	52			
1943	7.04	53			
1944	7.16	54			
1945	7.29	55			
1946	7.42	56			
1947	7.55	57			
1948	7.68	58			
1949	7.82	59			

a. Mid-year estimates.

SOURCE : 1900-51 data from SALA-SNP, pp. 173-183; since 1952, data from IMF-IFS, Oct., 1984; cf. SALA, 24-600, 624, 625.

Table 619

URUGUAY POPULATION ESTIMATE AND INDEX, 1900–83[a]

Year	M	1970 = 100	Year	M	1970 = 100
1900	.96	35	1950	2.20	81
1901	.97	36	1951	2.22	81
1902	.90	33	1952*	2.26*	83
1903	1.02	37	1953	2.30	84
1904	1.04	38	1954	2.33	85
1905	1.07	39	1955	2.36	86
1906	1.10	40	1956	2.40	88
1907	1.14	42	1957	2.43	89
1908	1.05	38	1958	2.46	90
1909	1.10	40	1959	2.50	92
1910	1.13	41	1960	2.54	93
1911	1.18	43	1961	2.58	95
1912	1.23	45	1962	2.61	96
1913	1.28	47	1963	2.65	97
1914	1.32	48	1964	2.68	98
1915	1.35	49	1965	2.71	99
1916	1.38	51	1966	2.75	101
1917	1.41	52	1967	2.69	99
1918	1.43	52	1968	2.70	99
1919	1.46	53	1969	2.71	99
1920	1.48	54	1970	2.73	100
1921	1.50	55	1971	2.74	100
1922	1.52	56	1972	2.75	101
1923	1.54	56	1973	2.76	101
1924	1.55	57	1974*	2.77	101
1925	1.57	58	1975	2.83	104
1926	1.60	59	1976	2.85	104
1927	1.63	60	1977	2.86	105
1928	1.67	61	1978	2.88	105
1929	1.70	62	1979	2.89	106
1930	1.73	63	1980	2.91	107
1931	1.76	64	1981	2.93	107
1932	1.79	66	1982	2.95	108
1933	1.82	67	1983	2.97	109
1934	1.84	67			
1935	1.87	68			
1936	1.89	69			
1937	1.91	70			
1938	1.93	71			
1939	1.95	71			
1940	1.97	72			
1941	1.99	73			
1942	2.01	74			
1943	2.03	74			
1944	2.06	75			
1945	2.08	76			
1946	2.10	77			
1947	2.12	78			
1948	2.14	78			
1949	2.17	79			

a. Mid-year estimates.

SOURCE : 1900-51 data from SALA-SNP, pp. 173-183; since 1952, data from IMF-IFS, Oct., 1984; cf. SALA, 24-600, 624, 625.

Table 620

VENEZUELA POPULATION ESTIMATE AND INDEX, 1900–83[a]

Year	M	1970 = 100	Year	M	1970 = 100
1900	2.45	24	1950	4.97	48
1901	2.45	24	1951	5.14	50
1902	2.46	24	1952*	5.39	52
1903	2.47	24	1953	5.62	55
1904	2.47	24	1954	5.85	57
1905	2.49	24	1955	6.09	59
1906	2.51	24	1956	6.33	62
1907	2.53	25	1957	6.57	64
1908	2.55	25	1958	6.83	66
1909	2.57	25	1959	7.09	69
1910	2.60	25	1960	7.35	71
1911	2.61	25	1961	7.61	74
1912	2.64	26	1962	7.86	76
1913	2.66	26	1963	8.12	79
1914	2.68	26	1964	8.40	82
1915	2.71	26	1965	8.71	85
1916	2.73	27	1966	9.03	88
1917	2.75	27	1967	9.31	91
1918	2.77	27	1968	9.62	94
1919	2.79	27	1969	9.94	97
1920	2.82	27	1970	10.28	100
1921	2.84	28	1971	10.61	103
1922	2.87	28	1972	10.94	106
1923	2.90	28	1973	11.28	110
1924	2.93	29	1974	11.63	113
1925	2.95	29	1975	11.99	117
1926	2.98	29	1976	12.36	120
1927	3.01	29	1977	13.59	132
1928	3.04	30	1978	14.07	137
1929	3.08	30	1979	14.55	142
1930	3.12	30	1980	15.02	146
1931	3.15	31	1981	15.48	151
1932	3.19	31	1982	15.94	155
1933	3.23	31	1983	16.39	159
1934	3.26	32			
1935	3.30	32			
1936	3.38	33			
1937	3.46	34			
1938	3.55	35			
1939	3.63	35			
1940	3.71	36			
1941	3.80	37			
1942	3.91	38			
1943	4.03	39			
1944	4.15	40			
1945	4.27	42			
1946	4.39	43			
1947	4.55	44			
1948	4.69	46			
1949	4.83	47			

a. Mid-year estimates.

SOURCE : 1900-51 data from SALA-SNP, pp. 173-183; since 1952, data from IMF-IFS, Oct., 1984; cf. SALA, 24-600, 624, 625.

Table 621

UNITED STATES POPULATION ESTIMATE
AND INDEX, 1900-83[a]

Year	M	1970 = 100	Year	M	1970 = 100
1900	76.09	37	1941	133.89	65
1901	77.59	38	1942	135.36	66
1902	79.16	39	1943	137.25	67
1903	80.63	39	1944	138.92	68
1904	82.17	40	1945	140.47	69
1905	83.82	41	1946	141.94	69
1906	84.44	41	1947	144.70	71
1907	87.00	42	1948	147.21	72
1908	88.71	43	1949	149.77	73
1909	90.49	44	1950	152.27	74
1910	92.40	45	1951	154.88	76
1911	93.87	46	1952	157.55	77
1912	95.33	46	1953	160.18	78
1913	97.23	47	1954	163.03	80
1914	99.12	48	1955	165.93	81
1915	100.55	49	1956	168.90	82
1916	101.97	50	1957	171.98	84
1917	103.27	50	1958	174.88	85
1918	103.20	50	1959	177.83	87
1919	104.51	51	1960*	180.68	88
1920	106.47	52	1961	183.69	90
1921	108.54	53	1962	186.54	91
1922	110.95	54	1963	189.24	92
1923	111.95	55	1964	191.89	94
1924	114.11	56	1965	194.30	95
1925	115.83	56	1966	196.56	96
1926	117.40	57	1967	198.71	97
1927	119.04	58	1968	200.71	98
1928	120.50	59	1969	202.68	99
1929	121.77	59	1970	205.05	100
1930	123.07	60	1971	207.66	101
1931	124.84	61	1972	209.90	102
1932	124.84	61	1973	211.91	103
1933	125.58	61	1974	213.85	104
1934	126.37	62	1975	215.97	105
1935	127.25	62	1976	218.04	106
1936	128.05	62	1977	220.24	107
1937	128.83	63	1978	222.59	109
1938	129.83	63	1979	225.06	110
1939	130.88	64	1980	227.66	111
1940	132.59	65	1981	229.81	112
			1982	232.06	113
			1983	233.7	114

a. Mid-year estimates.

SOURCE: 1900-51 data from SALA-SNP, pp. 173-183; since 1952, data from IMF–IFS-Y, 1984; cf. SALA, 24-600, 624, 625.

Table 622

INDEX OF ESTIMATED POPULATION, 20 LRC, 1900–80

(1970 = 100)

	Country	1900	1910	1920	1930	1940	1950	1960	1970	1980
A.	ARGENTINA	19	29	38	51	60	72	84	100	119
B.	BOLIVIA	39	43	47	52	59	66	83	100	122
C.	BRAZIL	19	24	30	36	44	56	75	100	131
D.	CHILE	32	36	40	47	54	65	81	100	118
E.	COLOMBIA	19	23	30	36	44	56	76	100	132
F.	COSTA RICA	18	21	25	29	36	47	75	100	130
G.	CUBA	19	20	35	43	51	65	83	100	114
H.	DOMINICAN REP.	15	19	22	31	44	56	75	100	134
I.	ECUADOR	22	24	26	33	41	54	73	100	140
J.	EL SALVADOR	24	29	34	42	48	54	72	100	138
K.	GUATEMALA	19	23	26	36	45	58	79	100	149
L.	HAITI	30	40	50	58	67	80	85	100	118
M.	HONDURAS	16	21	27	36	44	54	70	100	140
N.	MEXICO	27	30	28	33	39	51	71	100	137
O.	NICARAGUA	23	30	35	38	46	58	77	100	149
P.	PANAMA	19	23	32	33	44	56	75	100	133
Q.	PARAGUAY	22	27	31	39	49	61	76	100	138
R.	PERU	23	30	36	42	50	60	74	100	129
S.	URUGUAY	35	41	54	63	72	81	93	100	107
T.	VENEZUELA	24	25	27	30	36	48	71	100	146
	LATIN AMERICA	24	28	34	40	49	60	77	100	131
	UNITED STATES	37	45	52	60	65	74	88	100	111

SOURCE: 1900-51 data from SALA-SNP, pp. 173-183; since 1952, data from IMF–IFS-Y, 1984; cf. SALA, 24-600, 624, 625.

Table 623

POPULATION ESTIMATES BY DECADE, 20 LRC, 1900–80

(M)

	Country	1900	1910	1920	1930	1940	1950	1960	1970	1980
A.	ARGENTINA	4.61	6.80	8.97	12.05	14.17	17.07	19.92	23.75	28.24
B.	BOLIVIA	1.77	1.95	2.14	2.40	2.70	3.01	3.82	4.58	5.60
C.	BRAZIL	17.98	22.22	27.40	33.57	41.11	52.18	69.72	92.52	121.27
D.	CHILE	2.96	3.34	3.79	4.37	5.06	6.07	7.58	9.37	11.10
E.	COLOMBIA	3.89	4.81	6.09	7.43	9.10	11.33	15.42	20.53	27.09
F.	COSTA RICA	.31	.36	.42	.50	.62	.80	1.25	1.73	2.25
G.	CUBA	1.60	2.22	3.00	3.65	4.29	5.51	7.03	8.55	9.72
H.	DOMINICAN REP.	.60	.74	.88	1.26	1.76	2.24	3.04	4.06	5.44
I.	ECUADOR	1.30	1.42	1.54	1.94	2.47	3.20	4.36	5.96	8.35
J.	EL SALVADOR	.80	.99	1.17	1.44	1.63	1.86	2.45	3.44	4.75
K.	GUATEMALA	.89	1.10	1.27	1.76	2.20	2.81	3.83	4.88	7.26
L.	HAITI	1.25	1.69	2.12	2.42	2.83	3.39	3.62	4.24	5.01
M.	HONDURAS	.42	.55	.72	.95	1.15	1.43	1.85	2.64	3.69
N.	MEXICO	13.61	15.16	14.15	16.55	19.65	25.79	36.05	50.69	69.35
O.	NICARAGUA	.42	.54	.64	.68	.83	1.06	1.41	1.83	2.73
P.	PANAMA	.26	.33	.45	.47	.62	.80	1.06	1.43	1.90
Q.	PARAGUAY	.49	.62	.70	.88	1.11	1.40	1.75	2.30	3.17
R.	PERU	3.00	4.00	4.83	5.65	6.68	7.97	10.02	13.45	17.30
S.	URUGUAY	.96	1.13	1.48	1.73	1.97	2.20	2.54	2.73	2.91
T.	VENEZUELA	2.45	2.60	2.82	3.12	3.71	4.97	7.35	10.28	15.02
	LATIN AMERICA	59.56	72.56	84.58	102.82	123.66	155.09	204.07	268.96	352.15
	UNITED STATES	76.09	92.40	106.47	123.07	132.59	152.27	180.68	205.05	227.66

SOURCE: SALA, 24-601 through 24-621.

Table 624

CELADE POPULATION ESTIMATES AND PROJECTIONS BY DECADE, 20 LRC, 1920–2020

(M)

	Country	1920	1930	1940	1950	1960	1970	1980	1990	2000	2010	2020
A.	ARGENTINA	8,861	11,896	14,169	17,150	20,611	23,962	28,237	32,879	37,196	41,507	45,564
B.	BOLIVIA	1,918	2,153	2,508	2,766	3,428	4,324	5,570	7,314	9,724	12,820	16,401
C.	BRAZIL	27,404	33,568	41,233	53,443	72,593	95,846	121,286	150,367	179,486	207,453	233,816
D.	CHILE	3,783	4,424	5,147	6,091	7,585	9,368	11,104	13,061	14,934	16,647	18,141
E.	COLOMBIA	6,057	7,350	9,077	11,597	15,536	20,803	25,794	31,820	37,999	43,840	49,259
F.	COSTA RICA	421	499	619	858	1,236	1,732	2,278	2,937	3,596	4,239	4,837
G.	CUBA	2,950	3,837	4,566	5,858	7,029	8,572	9,732	10,540	11,718	12,584	13,307
H.	DOMINICAN REP.	1,140	1,400	1,759	2,409	3,224	4,289	5,558	6,971	8,407	9,945	11,465
I.	ECUADOR	1,898	2,160	2,586	3,307	4,422	5,958	8,021	10,949	14,596	18,740	23,327
J.	EL SALVADOR	1,168	1,443	1,633	1,940	2,574	3,582	4,797	6,484	8,708	11,188	13,769
K.	GUATEMALA	1,450	1,771	2,201	2,962	3,966	5,353	7,262	9,676	12,739	16,125	19,818
L.	HAITI	2,124	2,422	2,825	3,097	3,723	4,605	5,809	7,509	9,860	12,868	16,438
M.	HONDURAS	783	948	1,119	1,401	1,943	2,639	3,691	5,105	6,978	9,394	11,972
N.	MEXICO	14,500	16,589	19,815	27,376	37,073	51,176	69,393	89,012	109,180	128,241	145,956
O.	NICARAGUA	639	742	893	1,098	1,492	2,052	2,771	3,871	5,261	6,824	8,435
P.	PANAMA	429	502	595	839	1,105	1,487	1,956	2,418	2,893	3,324	3,701
Q.	PARAGUAY	699	880	1,111	1,371	1,778	2,290	3,168	4,231	5,405	6,653	7,930
R.	PERU	4,862	5,651	6,681	7,632	9,931	13,193	17,295	22,332	27,952	33,479	38,647
S.	URUGUAY	1,391	1,704	1,947	2,239	2,537	2,808	2,908	3,128	3,364	3,581	3,782
T.	VENEZUELA	2,408	2,950	3,710	5,139	7,550	10,962	15,620	21,284	27,207	33,432	39,755
	LATIN AMERICA	84,885	102,889	124,194	158,573	209,336	275,001	352,250	441,888	537,203	632,884	726,320
	UNITED STATES	106,470	123,070	132,590	152,270	180,680	205,050	227,660	244,000	260,000	275,000	290,000

SOURCE: CELADE-BD, 23 (1979); CELADE-BD, 30 (1982); CELADE-BD, 32 (1983).
For higher range estimates, see CELADE data quoted in SALA, 22-625. U.S. data
are from SALA, 23-621 through 1980, then from USBC-SA, 1978, p. 7.

Table 625

NATIONAL POPULATION CENSUS SERIES, 20 L, 1774–1982[a]

A. ARGENTINA		G. CUBA		N. MEXICO	
1869	1,737,076	1774	171,620	1895	12,632,427
1895	3,954,911	1792	272,300	1900	13,607,259
1914	7,885,237	1817	572,363	1910	15,160,369
1947	15,897,127	1827	704,487	1921	14,334,780
1960	20,010,539	1841	1,007,624	1930	16,552,722
1970	23,364,431	1861	1,396,530	1940	19,653,552
1980	27,947,446	1877	1,509,291	1950	25,791,017
		1887	1,631,687	1960	34,923,129
B. BOLIVIA[1]		1899	1,572,797	1970	48,225,238
1831	1,018,900	1907	2,048,980	1980	66,846,833
1835	992,700	1919	2,889,004		
1845	1,031,500	1931	3,962,344	O. NICARAGUA	
1854	1,544,300	1943	4,778,583	1778	106,926
1882	1,097,600	1953	5,829,029	1867	257,000
1900	1,696,400	1970	8,553,395	1906	505,377
1950	3,019,031	1981	9,706,369	1920	638,119
1976	4,613,486			1940	983,000
		H. DOMINICAN REP.		1950	1,057,023
C. BRAZIL		1920	894,665	1963	1,535,588
1872	10,112,061	1935	1,479,417	1971	1,877,952
1890	14,333,915	1950	2,135,872		
1900	17,318,556	1960	3,047,070	P. PANAMA[2]	
1920	30,635,605	1970	4,011,589	1911	336,742
1940	41,236,315	1981	5,647,977	1920	446,098
1950	51,944,397			1930	467,459
1960	70,119,071	I. ECUADOR		1940	622,576
1970	93,215,311	1950	3,202,757	1950	805,285
1980	118,674,604	1962	4,476,000	1960	1,075,541
		1974	6,521,110	1970	1,428,082
D. CHILE		1982	8,053,280[‡]	1980	1,824,796[d],[‡]
1835	1,010,336				
1843	1,083,801	J. EL SALVADOR		Q. PARAGUAY	
1854	1,439,120	1930	1,434,361	1936	931,799
1865	1,819,223	1950	1,855,917	1950	1,328,452
1875	2,075,971	1961	2,510,984	1962	1,819,103
1885	2,507,005	1971	3,554,648	1972	2,354,071
1895	2,695,625			1982	3,026,165[‡]
1907	3,231,022	K. GUATEMALA			
1920	3,730,235	1880	1,224,602	R. PERU	
1930	4,287,445	1893	1,364,678	1836	1,373,736
1940	5,023,539	1921	2,004,900***	1850	2,001,203
1952	5,932,995	1930	1,771,000	1862	2,460,684[c]
1960	7,374,115	1935	1,996,000	1876	2,651,840[c]
1970	8,884,768	1940	2,222,000	1940	6,208,000
1982	11,275,440	1950	2,790,686	1961	9,906,746
		1964	4,284,473	1972	13,567,939
E. COLOMBIA		1973	5,211,929	1981	17,031,221[‡]
1825	1,223,598	1981	6,043,559		
1835	1,686,038			S. URUGUAY	
1843	1,955,264	L. HAITI		1852	131,969
1851	2,243,730	1918	1,631,260	1860	229,480
1864	2,694,487	1950	3,097,220	1908	1,042,686
1870	2,391,984	1971	4,329,991	1963	2,595,510
1905	4,143,632			1975	2,788,429
1912	5,072,604	M. HONDURAS			
1918	5,855,077	1791	93,505	T. VENEZUELA	
1928	7,851,000[b]	1801	130,000	1873	1,784,194
1938	8,701,816	1881	307,289	1881	2,075,545
1951	11,548,172	1887	331,917	1891	2,323,527
1964	17,484,508	1905	500,136	1920	2,365,098
1973	22,551,811	1910	553,446	1926	2,890,631
		1916	605,997	1936	3,491,159
F. COSTA RICA		1926	700,811	1941	3,850,771
1864	120,499	1930	854,184	1950	5,034,838
1883	182,073	1935	962,000	1961	7,523,999
1892	243,205	1940	1,107,859	1971	10,721,522
1927	471,524	1945	1,200,542	1981	14,602,480[‡]
1950	800,875	1950	1,368,605		
1963	1,336,274	1961	1,884,765		
1973	1,871,780	1974	2,656,948		

1. Territorial variations have been taken into account — the figures refer to the population within the present boundaries of the country.
2. Includes the indigenous population.

a. Territorial changes have not necessarily been taken into account.
b. This census was not accepted by the National Congress because it was believed that the figures for certain civil divisions were inflated.
c. Excludes the population of the province of Arica and the department of Tarapaca.
d. Includes former U.S. Canal Zone.

SOURCE: Since 1900, SALA-SNP, table VIII-1; BE, 96, 109, 114, 122; IASI-AC, 1974; Cuban, El Salvadoran, Guatemalan, Mexican, and Venezuelan statistical agencies. Before 1900, IASI, *Noticiero*, January 3, 1965. Data for the 1970s and 1980s revised with figures from UN-DY, 1982, pp. 135-136, except Chile and Venezuela from SALA-LAPUA, p. 178 and p. 430; Mexico data from Instituto Nacional de Estadística, *Resumen General Abreviado* (1984); and Peru data from SALA, 24-643.

Table 626
ARGENTINA POPULATION CENSUS AND DENSITY OF MAJOR CIVIL DIVISIONS
(1980)

Division	Population	%	Density Per km^2
Total	27,949,480	100.0	10
Capital Federal	2,922,829	10.4	14,614
Provinces			
Buenos Aires	10,865,408	38.9	35
Catamarca	207,717	.7	2

Continued in SALA, 23-626.

Table 627
BOLIVIA POPULATION CENSUS AND DENSITY OF MAJOR CIVIL DIVISIONS
(1976[‡])

Division	Population	%	Density Per km^2
Total	4,647,816	100.0	4
Departments			
Beni	167,969	3.6	1
Chuquisaca	357,244	7.7	6

Continued in SALA, 23-627.

Table 628
BRAZIL POPULATION CENSUS AND DENSITY OF MAJOR CIVIL DIVISIONS[1]
(1980[‡])

Division	Population	%	Density Per km^2
Total	121,113,084	100.0	14
Distrito Federal	1,202,683	1.0	207
States			
Acre	306,916	.2	2
Alagoas	2,011,956	1.7	73
Amapá	180,078	.1	1
Amazonas	1,447,373	1.2	1
Bahia	9,593,687	7.9	17
Ceará	5,379,927	4.4	36
Espíritu Santo	2,063,610	1.7	45
Fernando de Noronha	1,342	#	52
Goiás	3,967,300	3.3	6
Maranhao	4,097,311	3.4	13
Mato Grosso[2]	1,169,287	1.0	1
Mato Grosso do Sul[2]	1,399,468	1.1	4
Minas Gerais	13,643,886	11.3	23
Pará	3,506,592	2.9	3
Paraíba	2,810,003	2.3	50
Paraná	7,749,523	6.4	39
Pernambuco	6,240,836	5.2	64
Piauí	2,188,148	1.8	9
Rio de Janeiro[3]	11,490,471	9.5	260
Rio Grande do Norte	1,933,131	1.6	37
Rio Grande do Sul	7,942,047	6.6	4
Rondônia	503,059	.4	2
Roraima	81,896	.1	.4
Santa Catarina	3,687,659	3.0	38
São Paulo	25,358,245	20.9	102
Sergipe	1,157,176	1.0	53

1. Unless otherwise indicated the data refer to the de facto population. For the size of each political unit see SALA, 23-301. Population density is calculated by dividing the population figure by km^2.
2. Mato Grosso and Mato Grosso do Sul are new states created by dividing the old state of Mato Grosso.
3. Guanabara and Rio de Janeiro states were combined to create the new state of Rio de Janeiro.

SOURCE: SALA-LAPUA, table 7-1.

Table 629

CHILE POPULATION CENSUS AND DENSITY OF MAJOR CIVIL DIVISIONS
(1982)

Division	Population	%	Density Per km^2
Total	11,275,440	100.0	15
Regions			
Antofagasta	341,203	3.0	3
Araucanía	692,924	6.1	22

Continued in SALA, 23-629.

Table 630

COLOMBIA POPULATION CENSUS AND DENSITY OF MAJOR CIVIL DIVISIONS
(1973)

Division	Population	%	Density Per km^2
Total	21,070,115	100.0	18
Bogotá, D.E.	2,855,065	13.6	1,799
Departments			
Antioquia	2,976,153	14.1	47

Continued in SALA, 23-630.

Table 631

COSTA RICA POPULATION CENSUS AND DENSITY OF MAJOR CIVIL DIVISIONS
(1973)

Division	Population	%	Density Per km^2
Total	1,871,780	100.0	37
Provinces			
Alajuela	326,032	17.4	34

Continued in SALA, 23-631.

Table 632

CUBA POPULATION CENSUS AND DENSITY OF MAJOR CIVIL DIVISIONS
(1981[‡])

Division	Population	%	Density Per km^2
Total	9,706,369	100.0	88
Ciudad de la Habana	1,924,886	19.8	2,598
Provinces			
Camagüey	664,566	6.9	47

Continued in SALA, 23-632. For projections to 1985 by province, see SALA, 22-627.

Table 633

DOMINICAN REPUBLIC POPULATION CENSUS AND DENSITY OF MAJOR CIVIL DIVISIONS
(1980[‡])

Division	Population	%	Density Per km^2
Total	5,621,985	100.0	116
Distrito Nacional	1,555,739	27.7	1,053
Provinces			
Azúa	143,628	2.6	59
Baoruco	78,508	1.4	57

Continued in SALA, 23-633.

Table 634

ECUADOR POPULATION CENSUS AND DENSITY OF MAJOR CIVIL DIVISIONS
(1982[‡])

Division	Population	%	Density Per km^2
Total	8,053,280	100.0	29
Provinces			
Archipiélago de Colón	6,201	.1	1
Azuay	440,571	5.5	47

Continued in SALA, 23-634.

Table 635

EL SALVADOR POPULATION CENSUS AND DENSITY OF MAJOR CIVIL DIVISIONS
(1971[‡])

Division	Population	%	Density Per km^2
Total	3,549,260	100.0	170
Departments			
Ahuachapán	179,820	5.1	153
Cabañas	129,199	3.6	126

Continued in SALA, 23-635.

Table 636

GUATEMALA POPULATION CENSUS AND DENSITY OF MAJOR CIVIL DIVISIONS
(1981)

Division	Population	%	Density Per km^2
Total	6,043,559	100.0	56
Departments			
Alta Verapaz	322,132	5.3	37
Baja Verapaz	115,206	1.9	37

Continued in SALA, 23-636.

Table 637

HAITI POPULATION CENSUS AND DENSITY
OF MAJOR CIVIL DIVISIONS[1]
(1971)

Division	Population	%	Density Per km^2
Total	4,329,991	100.0	156
Departments			
Artibonite	765,228	17.7	124
Nord	700,725	16.2	166
Nord-Ouest	217,489	5.0	92
Ouest	1,670,140	38.6	198
Sud	976,409	22.5	147

1. Unless otherwise indicated the data refer to the de facto population. For the size of each political unit see SALA, 23-301. Population density is calculated by dividing the population figure by km^2.

SOURCE: SALA-LAPUA, table 16-1.

Table 638

HONDURAS POPULATION CENSUS AND DENSITY
OF MAJOR CIVIL DIVISIONS[1]
(1974)

Division	Population	%	Density Per km^2
Total	2,653,857	100.0	24
Departments			
Atlántida	148,440	5.6	35
Colón	77,239	2.9	9
Comayagua	135,455	5.1	26
Copán	151,331	5.7	47
Cortes	373,629	14.1	95
Choluteca	192,145	7.2	46
El Paraíso	140,840	5.3	20
Francisco Morazan	451,778	17.0	57
Gracias a Dios	21,079	.4	1
Intibucá	81,685	3.1	27
Islas de la Bahía	13,227	.5	51
La Paz	65,390	2.5	28
Lempira	127,465	4.8	30
Ocotepeque	51,161	1.9	31
Olancho	151,923	5.7	6
Santa Bárbara	185,163	7.0	36
Valle	90,954	3.4	58
Yoro	194,953	7.3	25

1. Unless otherwise indicated the data refer to the de facto population. For the size of each political unit see SALA, 23-301. Population density is calculated by dividing the population figure by km^2.

SOURCE: SALA-LAPUA, table 17-1.

Table 639

MEXICO POPULATION CENSUS AND DENSITY OF MAJOR CIVIL DIVISIONS

(1980[‡])

Division	Population	%	Density Per km[2]
Total	67,383,000	100.0	34
Distrito Federal	9,373,958	13.9	6,337
States			
Aguascalientes	503,410	.7	92
Baja California	1,225,436	1.8	18

Continued in SALA, 23-639.

Table 640

NICARAGUA POPULATION CENSUS AND DENSITY OF MAJOR CIVIL DIVISIONS

(1971)

Division	Population	%	Density Per km[2]
Total	1,894,690	100.0	14
Departments			
Boaco	70,850	3.7	14
Carazo	71,810	3.8	70
Chinandega	158,210	8.4	34
Chontales	69,530	3.7	14
Estelí	78,630	4.2	36
Granada	73,150	3.9	76
Jinotega	92,340	4.9	10
León	166,270	8.8	32
Madriz	53,560	2.8	31
Managua	482,600	25.5	133
Masaya	94,200	5.0	174
Matagalpa	172,180	9.1	25
Nueva Segovia	66,650	3.5	20
Río San Juan	20,250	1.1	3
Rivas	75,630	4.0	35
Zelaya	148,830	7.9	3

1. Unless otherwise indicated the data refer to the de facto population. For the size of each political unit see SALA, 23-301. Population density is calculated by dividing the population figure by km[2].

SOURCE: SALA-LAPUA, table 19-1.

Table 641

PANAMA POPULATION CENSUS AND DENSITY OF MAJOR CIVIL DIVISIONS

(1980)

Division	Population	%	Density Per km[2]
Total	1,788,748	100.0	23
Provinces			
Bocas del Toro	52,416	2.9	6
Chiriquí	286,416	16.0	33
Coclé	140,524	7.8	28
Colón[2]	157,627	8.8	21
Darién	26,247	1.5	2
Herrera	81,876	4.6	34
Los Santos	70,272	3.9	18
Panamá	800,500	44.8	71
Veraguas	172,868	9.7	16
Canal Zone	44,198	~	~

1. Unless otherwise indicated the data refer to the de facto population. For the size of each political unit see SALA, 23-301. Population density is calculated by dividing the population figure by km[2].
2. Includes San Blas territory.

SOURCE: SALA-LAPUA, table 20-1.

Table 642

PARAGUAY POPULATION CENSUS AND DENSITY OF MAJOR CIVIL DIVISIONS

(1972)

Division	Population	%	Density Per km[2]
Total	2,354,071	100.0	6.0
Departments			
Alto Paraná	78,037	3.3	5.0
Amambay	65,527	2.7	5.0

Continued in SALA, 23-642.

Table 643

PERU POPULATION CENSUS AND DENSITY OF MAJOR CIVIL DIVISIONS

(1981)

Division	Population	%	Density Per km[2]
Total	17,005,210	100.0	13.2
Departments			
Amazonas	254,560	1.5	6.2
Ancash	818,289	4.8	22.5

Continued in SALA, 23-643.

Table 644

URUGUAY POPULATION CENSUS AND DENSITY OF MAJOR CIVIL DIVISIONS

(1975)

Division	Population	%	Density Per km[2]
Total	2,769,781	100.0	16
Departments			
Artigas	57,432	2.1	5
Canelones	321,662	11.6	70

Continued in SALA, 23-644.

Table 645

VENEZUELA POPULATION CENSUS AND DENSITY OF MAJOR CIVIL DIVISIONS

(1981[‡])

Division	Population	%	Density Per km[2]
Total	14,602,480	100.0	16
Distrito Federal	2,074,203	14.2	1075
Dependencias Federales[2]	~	~	~
States			
Anzoátegui	689,555	4.7	16
Apure	196,808	1.3	3
Aragua	854,121	5.8	123
Barinas	318,401	2.2	9

Continued in SALA, 23-645.

Table 646

EXTENDED CARIBBEAN REGION (ECR) POPULATION, 28 CSOR, 6 CA, AND 3 TANGENTIAL COUNTRIES, 1960–79

Category	T			PC
	1960	1979	Change	
I. Caribbean Sea Oriented Region (CSOR)				
Anguilla	6@	6@	0	0
Antigua-Barbuda[1]	55	74	19	34.5
Bahamas[1]	112	236	124	110.7
Barbados[1]	232	279	47	20.3
Belize[1]	92	152	60	65.2
Bermuda	45	72	27	60.0
British Virgin Islands[1]	7	12	5	71.4
Cayman Islands[1]	8	17	9	112.5
G. Cuba	7,027	9,824	2,797	39.6
Dominica[1]	60	78	18	30.0
H. Dominican Republic[1]	3,159	5,551	2,392	75.7
French Guiana	32	63	31	96.9
Grenada[1]	90	106	16	17.8
Guadeloupe	273	312	39	14.3
Guyana[1]	571	832	261	45.7
L. Haiti[1]	3,723	5,670	1,947	52.3
Jamaica[1]	1,632	2,215	583	35.7
Martinique	283	310	27	9.5
Montserrat[1]	12	11	–1	–.8
Netherlands Antilles[1]	194	240	46	23.7
Puerto Rico	2,358	3,395	1,037	44.0
St. Kitts-Nevis[1]	51	51	0	0
St. Lucia[1]	88	121	33	37.5
St. Vincent and Grenadines[1]	81	111	30	37.0
Suriname[1]	285	404	119	41.8
Trinidad and Tobago[1]	840	1,150	310	36.9
Turks and Caicos[1]	6	7	1	16.7
U.S. Virgin Islands	33	99	66	200.0
Total CSOR	(21,355)	(31,398)	(10,043)	(47.0)
II. Central America (CA)				
F. Costa Rica[1]	1,248	2,184	936	75.0
J. El Salvador[1]	2,574	4,662	2,088	81.1
K. Guatemala[1]	3,969	6,849	2,880	72.5
M. Honduras[1]	1,952	3,645	1,693	86.7
O. Nicaragua[1]	1,438	2,365	927	64.5
P. Panama[1]	1,112	1,876	764	68.7
Total CA	(12,293)	(21,581)	(9,288)	75.6
III. Mainland Tangential Countries				
E. Colombia	15,953	26,205	10,252	64.3
N. Mexico	36,182	65,770	29,588	81.8
T. Venezuela	7,632	14,539	6,907	90.5
Total Tangential	(59,767)	(106,514)	(46,747)	78.2
Total ECR	93,415	159,493	66,078	70.7
Subtotal CBI-IB[2]	(23,591)	(38,898)	(15,307)	(64.9)

1. CBI-IB.
2. CBI-IB includes CA and CSOR, except Anguilla, Bermuda, Cuba, French Guiana, Guadeloupe, Martinique, Puerto Rico, U.S. Virgin Islands.

SOURCE: SALA, 23-3.

Table 647

POPULATION OF LARGEST CITY, 20 L, 1900–80

(T)

Country/Largest City	1900	1920	1930	1940	1950	1960	1970	1980
A. ARGENTINA (Buenos Aires)[1]	756	1,576	~	2,410	5,213	7,000	9,400	9,927
B. BOLIVIA (La Paz)[1]	54	~	~	~	300	400	500	635[u]
C. BRAZIL (Rio de Janeiro except São Paulo in 1970 and 1980)[1]	683	1,158	~	1,519	3,025	4,692	8,213	7,033[l]
D. CHILE (Santiago)[1]	307	507	713	952	1,275	1,907	2,600	4,039[m]
E. COLOMBIA (Bogotá)	101	144[a]	260	356[b]	607	1,241	2,500	~
F. COSTA RICA (San José)[1]	28	39	89[c]	~	140	257	435	1,925[‡,l,n]
G. CUBA (Havana)[1]	209	466[d]	721[e]	936[f]	1,081	1,549	1,700	~
H. DOMINICAN REP. (Santo Domingo)	15	31	~	71[g]	182	367	650	1,279[m,o]
I. ECUADOR (Guayaquil)	79	~	~	~	259	450	800	~
J. EL SALVADOR (San Salvador)[1]	49	81	89	103	162	239	375	~
K. GUATEMALA (Guatemala City)[1]	41	112[h]	~	186	294	474	770	494[o,p]
L. HAITI (Port-au-Prince)	56	~	~	~	134	240	400	485[n,o]
M. HONDURAS (Tegucigalpa)[1]	12	~	~	56[i]	72	159	281	~
N. MEXICO (Mexico City)[2]	381	615	1,049	1,560	2,872	4,910	8,567	~
O. NICARAGUA (Managua)[1]	24	28	~	63	109	197	350	386[q]
P. PANAMA (Panama City)[1]	- -	~	74	112	128	273	440	463[t]
Q. PARAGUAY (Asunción)[1]	42	~	~	~	219	311	445	463[t]
R. PERU (Lima-Callao)[1]	78	255	~	~	947	1,519	2,500	4,601[‡,r]
S. URUGUAY (Montevideo)	290	393	482	537	609	962	1,530	~
T. VENEZUELA (Caracas)[1]	80	92	259[j]	354[k]	694	1,280	2,147	2,944[o,s]

1. Beginning in 1950, figures are for city proper and adjacent urban area.
2. All figures are for city proper and adjacent urban area.

a. 1918.
b. 1938.
c. 1927.
d. 1919, Greater Havana.
e. 1931, Greater Havana.
f. 1943.
g. 1935.
h. 1921.
i. 1945.
j. 1936, metropolitan area.
k. 1941, metropolitan area.
l. For city proper area only.
m. As of 1982.
n. As of 1981.
o. Estimate of questionable reliability.
p. De jure population.
q. Including corregimientos of Bella Vista, Betania, Calidonia, El Chorillo, Juan Diaz, Parque Lefevre, Pedregal, Pueblo Nuevo, Río Abajo, San Felipe, San Francisco, and Santa Ana.
r. "Metropolitan Area" (Gran Lima).
s. "Metropolitan Area" comprising Caracas proper (the urban parishes of Department of Libertador) and a part of district of Sucre in state of Miranda.
t. 1978.
u. 1976.

SOURCE: 1900-1970: Marshall C. Eakin, "Determining the Population in the Largest City of Each Latin American Country, 1920-1970," SALA, 19-3500 and 19-3503; UN-DY, 1982, table 8.

Table 648

PERCENTAGE OF POPULATION OF LARGEST CITY, 20 L, 1900–80

Country/Largest City	1900	1920	1930	1940	1950	1960	1970	1980
A. ARGENTINA (Buenos Aires)	16.4	17.6	~	17.0	30.5	35.1	39.6	35.2
B. BOLIVIA (La Paz)	3.1	~	~	8.5	10.0	10.8	10.7	12.6[o]
C. BRAZIL (Rio de Janeiro except São Paulo for 1970)	3.8	4.2	~	3.7	5.8	6.7	8.9	5.8
D. CHILE (Santiago)	10.4	13.4	16.3	18.8	21.0	25.2	27.7	36.4
E. COLOMBIA (Bogotá)	2.6	2.5[a]	3.5	4.1[b]	5.4	8.0	12.2	~
F. COSTA RICA (San José)	9.3	9.3	18.9[c]	10.6	17.5	20.6	25.1	~
G. CUBA (Havana)	13.1	16.0[d]	18.2[e]	19.6[f]	19.6	22.0	19.9	19.8[m]
H. DOMINICAN REP. (Santo Domingo)	2.5	3.5	~	4.8[g]	8.1	12.1	16.0	~
I. ECUADOR (Quito, except Guayaquil since 1940)	6.1	~	~	5.2	8.1	10.3	13.7	15.3
J. EL SALVADOR (San Salvador)	6.2	6.9	6.2	6.3	8.7	9.8	10.9	~
K. GUATEMALA (Guatemala City)	4.7	8.5[h]	~	8.5	10.5	12.4	15.8	~
L. HAITI (Port-au-Prince)	4.5	~	~	4.0	4.0	6.2	9.4	9.9
M. HONDURAS (Tegucigalpa)	3.0	~	~	4.4[i]	5.0	8.6	11.2	13.1
N. MEXICO (Mexico City)	2.8	4.3	6.3	7.9	11.1	14.1	17.8	~
O. NICARAGUA (Managua)	5.9	4.4	~	7.6	10.3	14.0	19.1	~
P. PANAMA (Panama City)	~	14.4[j]	15.7	18.1	16.0	25.8	30.8	20.3
Q. PARAGUAY (Asunción)	8.7	~	~	8.7	15.6	17.6	19.3	15.6[n]
R. PERU (Lima-Callao)	2.6	5.3	~	7.4	11.9	15.1	18.6	26.6
S. URUGUAY (Montevideo)	30.3	26.6	27.9	27.3	27.7	37.9	52.9	~
T. VENEZUELA (Caracas)	3.3	3.3	7.7[k]	9.3[l]	14.0	17.4	20.6	19.6

a. 1918. f. 1943. k. 1936.
b. 1938. g. 1935. l. 1941.
c. 1927. h. 1921. m. 1981.
d. 1919. i. 1945. n. 1978.
e. 1931. j. 1919. o. 1976.

SOURCE: SALA, 19-3501; 1980 data calculated from SALA, 24-647 and 24-601 through 24-620.

Table 649

POPULATION OF PRINCIPAL CITIES, ACCORDING TO RECENT CENSUSES,[1] 20 L

A. ARGENTINA (Census X-22-1980)	
Buenos Aires	9,927,404[a]
Rosario, Santa Fé	954,608[a]
Córdoba, Córdoba	982,018[a]
La Plata, Buenos Aires	560,341[a]
La Matanza,Buenos Aires (1960)	402,642
Mendoza, Mendoza	596,796[a]
Lanús, Buenos Aires (1960)	381,561[‡]
San Miguel de Tucumán, Tucumán	496,914[a]
Morón, Buenos Aires (1960)	344,041[‡]
Avellaneda, Buenos Aires (1960)	329,626[‡]
Quilmes, Buenos Aires (1960)	318,144[‡]
Mar del Plata, Buenos Aires	299,700
General San Martín, Buenos Aires (1960)	279,213[‡]
Lomas de Zamora, Buenos Aires (1960)	275,219[‡]
Vincente López, Buenos Aires (1960)	250,823[‡]
Santa Fé, Santa Fé (1970)	244,579
San Juan, San Juan	290,479
San Isidro, Buenos Aires (1960)	196,188
Bahía Blanca	220,765
Salta (1970)	176,130
Corrientes	131,392
Paraná (1970)	127,836
Santiago del Estero (1970)	105,209
San Fernando, Buenos Aires (1960)	103,815
B. BOLIVIA (Census XI-29-1976)[f]	
La Paz, La Paz[2]	654,713
Santa Cruz, Santa Cruz	237,128
Cochabamba, Cochabamba	194,156
Oruro, Oruro	124,091
Sucre, Chuquisaca[2]	106,590
Potosí, Potosí	77,253
C. BRAZIL (Census VII-1-1980)[f]	
São Paulo, São Paulo	7,033,529
Rio de Janeiro, Guanabara	5,093,232
Belo Horizonte, Minas Gerais	1,442,483
Recife, Pernambuco	1,184,215
Salvador, Bahia	1,496,276
Porto Alegre, Rio Grande do Sul	1,108,883
Belém, Pará	758,117
Fortaleza, Ceará	648,815
Curitiba, Paraná	843,733
Santo André, São Paulo	549,278
Gioania, Goiás	703,263
Nova Iguacú, Rio de Janeiro	491,802
Campinas, São Paulo	566,517
Santos, São Paulo	411,023
Niterói, Rio de Janeiro	386,185
Manaus, Amazonas	613,068
Osasco, São Paulo	473,856
Brasília, Distrito Federal	411,305
Duque de Caxias, Rio de Janeiro	306,057
Natal, Rio Grande do Notre	376,552
Maceló, Alagoas	376,479
Guarulhos, São Paulo	395,117
Juiz de Fora, Minas Gerais	299,728
João Pessoa, Paraíba	290,424
Ribeirão Prêto, São Paulo	300,704
Olinda, Pernambuco	266,392
Teresina, Pisuí	339,264
Aracaju, Sergipe	288,106
São Luis, Maranhão	182,466
Sorocaba, São Paulo	254,718
São João de Meriti, Rio de Janeiro	210,548
Campina Grande, Paraíba	222,229
São Gonçalo, Rio de Janeiro	221,278
Londrina, Paraná	258,054
Campos, Rio de Janeiro	282,844
Ponta Grossa, Paraná	171,111
Pelotas, Rio Grande do Sul	197,092
São Caetano do Sul	163,030
Canoas, Rio Grande do Sul	214,115
Jundiaí, São Paulo	210,015

C. BRAZIL (Continued)	
Colatina, Espírito Santo	111,600
Teófilo Otoni, Minas Gerais	155,800
Campo Grande, Mato Grosso	282,844
Nilópolis, Rio de Janeiro	103,033
Feira de Santana, Bahia	225,003
Guarapauva, Paraná	156,500
Piracicaba, São Paulo	179,395
Governado Valadares, Espírito Santo	173,699
Caratinga, Minas Gerais	114,200
Vitória, Espírito Santo	144,143
Montes Claros, Minas Gerais	151,881
Santa María, Rio Grande do Sul	151,202
Volta Redonda, Rio de Janeiro	177,772
Bauru, São Paulo	178,861
Rio Grande, Rio Grande do Sul	124,706
Petrópolis, Rio de Janeiro	149,427
Florianópolis, Santa Catarina	153,547
Jaboatão, Pernambuco	320,900
Maringá, Paraná	158,047
Bacabal, Maranhão (1968)	111,753
Santarém, Pará	101,534
Mogi das Cruzes, São Paulo	122,265
Caxias do Sul, Rio Grande do Sul	198,824
Marília, São Paulo	111,500
Caruaru, Pernambuco	137,636

D. CHILE (Estimate of VI-30-1978)[g]	
Santiago, Santiago[3]	4,039,287
Valparaíso, Valparaíso	266,577
Concepción, Concepción	206,107
Vina del Mar Valparaíso	290,014
Talcahuano	208,941
Antofagasta	166,964
Temuco	162,058
Talca	134,721
Arica	120,846
Rancagua	137,773
Chillán	120,941
Valdivia	113,565

E. COLOMBIA	Census X-24-1973[f]	Estimated 1979
Bogotá D.E., Cundinamarca	2,836,361	4,584,000
Medellín, Antioquia	1,112,390	1,664,000
Cali, Valle de Cauca	967,908	1,450,000
Barranquilla, Atlántico	690,471	924,000
Bucaramanga, Santander	315,565	441,000
Cartagena, Bolívar	309,428	470,000
Cúcuta, Norte de Santander	223,868	420,000
Pereira, Risaralda	186,615	270,000
Manizales, Coldas	205,780	252,000
Ibagué, Tolima	193,879	360,000
Bello, Antioquia	115,743	~
Ciénega, Magdalena (1972)	168,100	
Montería, Córdoba	98,897	226,000
Armenia, Quinidio	147,635	184,000
Valledupar, Magdalena	97,066	301,000
Itagüi, (1972)	144,100	~
Palmirá Valle del Cauca	140,338	~
Pasto, Narino	127,811	219,000
Tunja (1972)	118,600	
Buenaventura, Valle del Cauca	108,710	~
Barrancabermeja	106,100	~
Neiva, Huila	112,479	~
Papayán (1972)	103,900	~
Santa Marta, Magdalena	108,007	234,000

F. COSTA RICA (Estimate of V-1973)	
San José, San José (1977)[c]	395,401[j]
Limón, Limón	35,000
Puntarenas, Puntarenas	30,000
Alajuela, Alajuela	28,000
Heredia, Heredia	22,000
Cartago, Cartago	21,000

Table 649 (Continued)

POPULATION OF PRINCIPAL CITIES, ACCORDING TO RECENT CENSUSES,[1] 20 L

G. CUBA (Census of IX-11-1981)[‡]		
Gran Habana, Habana (1975)		1,861,442
La Habana, Habana		1,924,886[f]
Santiago de Cuba, Oriente		345,289[f]
Camagüey, Camagüey		345,235[f]
Santa Clara, Las Villas		171,914[f]
Guantánamo, Oriente		167,405[f]
Matanzas, Matanzas (1970)		81,000
Holguín		186,613[f]
H. DOMINICAN REP. (Census of I-9-1970)		
Santo Domingo, Distrito Nacional (1970)		817,645
Santiago de los Caballeros, Santiago (1970)		245,165
San Francisco de Macorís, Duarte (1960)		27,000
La Romana, La Romana (1960)		22,000
San Pedro de Macorís, San Pedro de Macorís (1960)		22,000
San Juan de la Maguana, San Juan		22,000
I. ECUADOR (Estimate of VI-30-1982)[f]		
Guayaquil, Guayas		1,278,908[a]
Quito, Pichincha		880,971[a]
Cuenca		150,987[a]
J. EL SALVADOR (Census of VI-28-1971)		
San Salvador, San Salvador		335,930[f]
Santa Ana, Santa Ana (1969)		168,047
San Miguel, San Miguel (1969)		107,658
Nueva San Salvador, La Libertad (1961)		36,000
Villa Delgado, San Salvador (1961)		30,000
K. GUATEMALA (Estimate of VII 1979)		
Ciudad de Guatemala, Guatemala		793,336[f]
Quetzaltenago, Quetzaltenango (1970)		54,000
Escuintla, Escuintla (1970)		32,000
Puerto Barrios, Izabel (1970)		29,000
Mazantenango, Suchitepéquez		24,000
L. HAITI (Census of VIII-31-1971)[c]		
Port-au-Prince, Ouest (1980)		493,932[a]
Cap-Haitien, Nord		46,000
Gonaives, Artibonite		29,000
Les Cayes, Sud		22,000
M. HONDURAS (Estimate of VI-30-1981)		
Tegucigalpa, D.C., Francisco Morazán (1981)		485,049[a]
San Pedro Sula, Cortés (1981)		318,777[a]
La Ceiba, Atlántida (1961)		25,000
Puerto Cortés, Cortés (1961)		17,000
El Progreso, Yoro (1961 Census)		14,000
N. MEXICO (Estimate VI-30-1978)[a,g]		
Ciudad de México, Distrito Federal		14,750,182
Guadalajara, Jalisco		2,467,657
Monterrey, Nuevo León		2,018,625
León, Guanajuato		624,816[f]
Puebla, Puebla		710,833[f]
Ciudad Juárez, Chihuahua		625,040[f]
Mexicali, Baja California		348,528[f]
Chihuahua, Chihuahua		385,953[f]
Culiacán, Sinaloa		324,292[f]
Tijuana, Baja California		566,344[f]

N. MEXICO (Continued)	
San Luis Potosí, San Luis Potosí	327,333[f]
Torreón, Coahuila	407,271
Mérida, Yucatán	269,582[f]
Veracruz, Veracruz	306,843[f]
Aguascalientes, Aguascalientes	257,179[f]
Morelia, Michoacán	251,011[f]
Hermosillo, Sonora	319,257[f]
Tampico, Tamaulipas	389,940[f]
Durango, Durango	228,686[f]
Saltillo, Coahuila	258,492[f]
Matamoros, Tamaulipas	193305[f]
Villa de Guadalupe, Hidalgo (part of Federal District)	124,573[b]
Nuevo Laredo, Tamaulipas	223,606[f]
O. NICARAGUA (Estimate of VII-1-1979)	
Managua, D.N., Managua (1979)	608,020[f]
León, León (1967)	58,000
Granada, Granada (1967)	36,000
Masaya, Masaya (1967)	30,000
Chinandega, Chinandega	30,000
P. PANAMA (Census of V-11-1980)	
Panamá, Panamá	386,393[i]
Colón, Colón (1970)	68,000
David, Chiriquí (1970)	36,000
La Chorrería, Panamá (1970)	26,000
Puerto Armuelles, Chiriquí (1970)	12,000
Q. PARAGUAY (Census of VII-9, 1972)	
Asunción (1978)	601,646[a,d]
Encarnación, Itapuá	23,343
Concepción, Concepción	19,392
Villarrica, Guarirá	17,687
R. PERU (Census of VII-12-1981)[‡,h]	
Lima, Lima	4,600,891
Callao, Provincia Constitucional de Callao	441,374
Arequipa, Arequipa	447,431
Trujillo, La Libertad	386,900[g]
Chiclayo, Lemayeque	280,244
Cuzco, Cuzco	181,604
Chimbote	280,244
Huancayo	165,132
Piura	186,354
Iquitos	173,629
S. URUGUAY (Census of V-21-1975)	
Montevideo	1,173,254[f]
T. VENEZUELA (Estimate of VI-30-1980)[a]	
Caracas, Distrito Federal	2,944,000[e]
Maracaibo, Zulia	901,000
Valencia, Carabobo	506,000
Barquisimeto, Lara	489,000
Maracay, Araqua	344,000
San Cristóbal, Táchira	272,000
Cabimas, Zulia	178,000
Ciudad Bolívar, Bolívar	147,000

1. Unless otherwise indicated, data refer to "Urban Agglomeration." Each city is followed by the name of the major territorial division (department, state, province, etc.) to which it belongs.
2. La Paz is the actual capital and seat of government, but Sucre is the legal capital and seat of the judiciary.
3. "Metropolitan Area" (Gran Santiago).

a. Estimate of questionable reliability.
b. Villa de Guadalupe, 1973.
c. De jure population.
d. The metropolitan area, comprising Asunción proper and the localities of Trinidad, Zeballos, Cué, Campo Grande, and Lambaré.
e. "Metropolitan Area," comprising Caracas proper (the urban parishes of the department of Libertador) and a part of the district of Sucre in the state of Miranda.
f. Data refer to city proper.

g. Data refer to city proper with the exception of Mexico City, Guadalajara, Monterrey, Tampico, and Torreón.
h. Data refer to city proper with the exception of Lima, where the data refer to "Metropolitan Area" (Gran Lima).
i. Data refer to city proper and include the *corregimientos* of Bella Vista, Betania, Calidonia, El Chorillo, Juan Diaz, Parque Lefevre, Pedregal, Pueblo Nuevo, Río Abajo, San Felipe, San Francisco, and Santa Ana.
j. "Metropolitan area" comprising *cantón central* of San José (including San José city), cantones Curridabat, Escazú, Montes de Oca, and Tibá, and parts of cantones of Alajuelita, Desamparados, Goicoechea, and Moravia.

SOURCE: IASI-AC, 1970 and 1973, table 201-07; UN-DY, 1979; UN-DY, 1980, table 8. Colombia estimates from *Colombia Today*, 18:1 (1983); UN-DY, 1982, table 8.

Table 650

POPULATION OF CAPITAL CITY URBAN AREAS, ACCORDING TO RECENT CENSUSES,[1] 20 LC

	Country	Date of Estimate	Date of Census[2]	Capital City	City Proper	Urban Agglomeration
A.	ARGENTINA	**	X-22-1980	Buenos Aires	2,908,001	9,927,404
B.	BOLIVIA	**	XI-29-1976	La Paz[6]	635,283	~
C.	BRAZIL	**	XI-I-1980	Brasilia, D.F.	411,305	~
D.	CHILE	VI-30-1982	**	Santiago[7]	4,039,287	~
E.	COLOMBIA	**	X-24-1973	Bogota	2,836,361	2,855,065
F.	COSTA RICA	VII-1-1977	**	San José	236,747	395,401[a,i]
G.	CUBA	**	IX-II-1981‡	La Habana	1,924,886	1,861,442[b,j]
H.	DOMINICAN REP.	**	I-9-1970	Santo Domingo	673,470	817,645
I.	ECUADOR	VI-30-1982	**	Quito	808,971[c]	~
J.	EL SALVADOR	**	VI-28-1971	San Salvador	335,930	~
K.	GUATEMALA	VII-1979	**	Guatemala, Ciudad de	793,336	~
L.	HAITI[3]	VII-1-1979	**	Port-Au-Prince	862,900[c]	493,932[k]
M.	HONDURAS	**	III-6-1974	Tegucigalpa	273,894	302,483[c,d]
N.	MEXICO	VI-30-1978	**	México, Ciudad de	9,191,295[c]	14,750,182[c]
O.	NICARAGUA	**	IV-20-1971	Managua	608,020	~
P.	PANAMA	**	V-II-1980	Panamá	386,393[e]	~
Q.	PARAGUAY	XII-1978	**	Asunción	463,735[c]	601,645[c,f]
R.	PERU	**	VII-12-1981‡	Lima	3,968,972	4,600,891[g]
S.	URUGUAY	**	V-21-1975	Montevideo	1,173,254	~
T.	VENEZUELA	VI-30-1977	**	Caracas	1,662,627[l]	2,849,191[c,h]
	UNITED STATES[4,5]	**	IV-I-1980	Washington, D.C.	638,333	3,060,922

1. Definition of cities varies from country to country. Urban agglomeration includes the suburban fringe or thickly settled territory lying outside of, but adjacent to, the city boundaries.
2. Data are the result of a national or municipal census.
3. Based on de jure population.
4. De jure population, but excluding armed forces overseas and civilian citizens absent from the country for an extended period of time.
5. Urban agglomeration data refer to "Standard Metropolitan Statistical Area."
6. La Paz is the actual capital and seat of government, but Sucre is the legal capital and the seat of the judiciary.
7. "Metropolitan Area" (Gran Santiago).

a. "Metropolitan Area," comprising *canto central* of San José (including San José city), *cantones* Curridabat, Escazú, Montes de Oca, and Tibás, and parts of *cantones* of Alajuelita, Desamparados, Goicoechea, and Moravia.
b. Comprising municipios of La Habana, Marianao, and Regla, the urban zones of Cojimar and San Miguel de Padrón (municipio of Guanabocoa). The population of "Gran Habana" which comprises the urban agglomeration plus the municipios of Santa María del Rosario and Santiago de las Vegas was 1,700,300 on 30 June 1967.
c. Estimate of questionable reliability.
d. For VI-30-1973.
e. Including *corregimientos* of Bellavista, Betania, Calidonia, El Chorillo, Juan Díaz, Parque Levevre, Pedregal, Pueblo Nuevo, Río Abajo, San Felipe, San Francisco, and Santa Ana.
f. "Metropolitan Area," comprising Asunción proper and localities of Trinidad, Zeballos, Cué, Campo Grande, and Lambaré.
g. "Metropolitan Area" (Gran Lima).
h. "Metropolitan Area," comprising Caracas proper and part of the district of Sucre in the State of Miranda.
i. For VII-1-1970.
j. For VII-I-1975.
k. For IX-9-1971.
l. For XI-2-1971.

SOURCE: UN-DY, 1978, table 8, and 1979, table 8; UN-DY, 1980, table 8; UN-DY, 1982, table 8.

Table 651

SALA RURAL POPULATION PERCENTAGES ACCORDING TO NATIONAL SELF-PERCEPTION, 20 LRC, 1940–80[a]

(Non-Standard Definition)

	Country	Data Years	ca. 1940	ca. 1950	ca. 1960	ca. 1970	ca. 1980	Rural Defined as Population Clusters Which Are:
A.	ARGENTINA	1947, 1960, 1970, 1980	~	38	26	21	17	Less than 2,000 persons
B.	BOLIVIA	1950, 1960, 1970, 1980	~	74	76	72	67	Less than 2,000 persons
C.	BRAZIL	1940, 1950, 1960, 1970, 1980	69	64	54	44	36	Non-administrative centers
D.	CHILE	1940, 1952, 1960, 1970, 1980	48	40	32	24	19	Lack of certain public services
E.	COLOMBIA	1938, 1951, 1964, 1973, 1980	71	61	47	40	32	Less than 1,500 persons
F.	COSTA RICA	1950, 1963, 1973, 1980	~	67	65	59	54	Non-administrative centers
G.	CUBA	1943, 1953, 1960, 1970, 1980	54	49	45	40	35	Less than 2,000 persons (adjusted by source)
H.	DOMINICAN REP.	1935, 1950, 1960, 1970, 1980	82	76	70	60	53	Non-administrative centers
I.	ECUADOR	1950, 1962, 1974, 1980	~	72	64	59	56	Non-administrative centers
J.	EL SALVADOR	1930, 1950, 1961, 1971, 1980	62	64	61	60	56	Lightly populated
K.	GUATEMALA	1940, 1950, 1964, 1973, 1980	74	75	66	66	62	Varies[1]
L.	HAITI	1950, 1960, 1971, 1980	~	88	85[†]	80	75	Non-administrative centers
M.	HONDURAS	1950, 1960, 1974, 1980	~	82[†]	77	69	51	Less than 1,000–2,000 persons
N.	MEXICO	1940, 1950, 1960, 1970, 1980	65	57	49	42	34	Less than 2,500 persons
O.	NICARAGUA	1950, 1963, 1971, 1980	~	65	59	52	46	Non-administrative centers
P.	PANAMA	1940, 1950, 1960, 1970, 1980	63	64	58	52	46	Less than 1,500 persons
Q.	PARAGUAY	1950, 1962, 1972, 1980	~	65	64	62	58	Non-administrative centers
R.	PERU	1940, 1950, 1961, 1972, 1980	65	59[†]	53	40	35	Non-administrative centers and/or lack of certain public services
S.	URUGUAY	1950, 1960, 1970, 1980	~	43[†]	28[†]	16[†]	15	Not cities[2]
T.	VENEZUELA	1941, 1950, 1961, 1971, 1980	69	52	37	25	21	Less than 2,500 persons
	LATIN AMERICA	20 countries	67[b]	63	56	42	36	Average of above, weighted by population
	UNITED STATES	1940, 1950, 1960, 1970, 1980	39	36	30	27	23	"Current Definition"[3]

1. In 1940: hamlets, small settlements, and farms; since 1950: less than 2,000 except 1,500 if running water.
2. In 1963 census definition gave 19%.
3. Less than 2,500 persons except for urbanized unincorporated areas; data for 1940 adjusted for consistency.

a. Self-definitions vary according to national circumstances.
b. Calculated from population-weighted data for 11 countries which had 80% of Latin America's population.

SOURCE: See SALA, 23-651.

Table 652

SALA URBAN POPULATION PERCENTAGES ACCORDING TO
NATIONAL SELF-PERCEPTION, 20 LRC, 1940–80
(Non-Standard Definition)[1]

				%		
	Country	Ca. 1940	Ca. 1950	Ca. 1960	Ca. 1970	Ca. 1980
A.	ARGENTINA	~	62	74	79	83
B.	BOLIVIA	~	26	24	28	33
C.	BRAZIL	31	36	46	56	64
D.	CHILE	52	60	68	76	81
E.	COLOMBIA	29	39	53	60	68
F.	COSTA RICA	~	33	35	41	46
G.	CUBA	46	51	55	60	65
H.	DOMINICAN REP.	18	24	30	40	47
I.	ECUADOR	~	28	36	41	44
J.	EL SALVADOR	38	36	39	40	44
K.	GUATEMALA	26	25	34	34	38
L.	HAITI	~	12	15	20	25
M.	HONDURAS	~	18	23	31	49
N.	MEXICO	35	43	51	58	66
O.	NICARAGUA	~	35	41	48	54
P.	PANAMA	37	36	42	48	54
Q.	PARAGUAY	~	35	36	38	42
R.	PERU	35	41	47	60	65
S.	URUGUAY	~	57	72	84	85
T.	VENEZUELA	31	48	63	75	79
	LATIN AMERICA	33	37	44	58	64
	UNITED STATES	61	64	70	73	77

1. For national definitions, see SALA, 23-652.

SOURCE:
   1940: U.N., *Demographic Yearbook* (1948), pp. 213-216.
   1950: SALA, 3-2.
   1960: IASI-AC, 1970, table 201-08.
   1970: IASI-AC, 1977, table 201-08.
   1980: ECLA, *Latin American Development Projections for the 1980s* (Santiago, 1982) p. 19. Exceptions: Data for Haiti in 1960, Peru for 1950, and Uruguay for 1950-1960 are from Kingsley Davis, *World Urbanization, 1950-1970*; 2 vols. (Berkeley: Population Monograph Series, University of California, 1969), 1, pp. 54-68. Figure for Colombia in 1950 is from AC, 1977, table 201-08. Bolivian data for 1950 are from *Human Resources in Bolivia* (Columbus: Center for Human Resource Research, Ohio State University, 1971), p. 55 and for 1960 and 1970 from WB-WBT, 1980, p. 439. Mexican data are from the Mexican Statistical Agency. Cuban data for 1943 and 1953 are from UCLA-Cuba, p. 24 and 1960 from WB-BDR, 1982, p. 149. Venezuelan data are from DGE, *Censo de Población*, 1961, A, p. 11; and *idem, Censo General de Población y Vivienda*, 1971: *Resultados Comparativos*, table 2. U.S. Data are from USBC-SA, p. 17, the figure for 1940 being adjusted here (splice of "previous" and "current" series). Bolivia, Cuba, and United States for 1980 are from WB-WDR, 1982, pp. 148-149. Cf. SALA-SNP, p. 483.

Table 653

CELADE URBAN POPULATION PERCENTAGES, NON-STANDARD TERMS,[1] 20 LR, 1970–2025
(%)

	Country	1970	1975	1980	1985	1990	1995	2000	2005	2010	2015	2020	2025
A.	ARGENTINA	78.48	80.16	81.62	82.96	84.10	85.15	86.05	86.85	87.55	88.20	88.70	89.14
B.	BOLIVIA	38.19	41.30	44.68	50.54	51.45	54.28	56.58	58.15	60.53	62.85	65.30	67.65
C.	BRAZIL	55.84	59.26	62.78	66.09	69.27	72.20	74.80	77.19	79.15	80.95	82.40	83.70
D.	CHILE	75.18	76.99	78.73	80.31	81.70	82.89	83.99	84.98	85.81	86.53	87.16	87.70
E.	COLOMBIA	59.26	62.79	66.33	69.50	72.42	75.02	77.38	79.44	81.14	82.62	83.85	84.87
F.	COSTA RICA	38.78	42.13	45.69	49.20	52.65	56.06	59.39	62.52	65.36	67.88	70.04	71.99
G.	CUBA	59.62	63.21	66.95	70.39	73.65	76.47	78.86	80.91	82.60	84.08	85.24	86.24
H.	DOMINICAN REP.	39.36	42.83	46.81	50.83	54.83	58.55	61.99	65.12	67.79	70.05	71.97	73.52
I.	ECUADOR	39.58	42.07	44.74	47.49	50.34	53.18	55.99	58.69	61.21	63.56	65.64	67.52
J.	EL SALVADOR	39.46	41.75	44.18	46.66	49.22	51.86	54.44	57.01	59.51	61.92	64.11	66.17
K.	GUATEMALA	34.37	35.56	36.51	37.78	39.33	41.11	43.11	45.51	47.91	50.19	52.57	54.89
L.	HAITI	19.76	21.32	23.06	25.03	27.14	29.44	31.88	34.49	37.15	39.81	42.44	44.97
M.	HONDURAS	33.24	35.88	38.81	42.17	45.74	49.37	53.01	56.53	59.91	63.10	65.95	68.42
N.	MEXICO	58.87	62.23	65.48	68.54	71.39	73.93	76.28	78.31	80.12	81.62	82.92	84.01
O.	NICARAGUA	47.00	50.41	53.84	57.24	60.41	63.34	65.97	68.25	70.25	72.00	73.46	74.68
P.	PANAMA	47.76	51.51	55.29	58.89	62.24	65.16	67.75	70.00	71.91	73.53	74.87	75.90
Q.	PARAGUAY	37.02	37.70	38.61	40.04	41.79	43.20	44.52	45.95	47.83	50.01	52.35	54.95
R.	PERU	58.04	60.74	63.42	65.88	68.24	70.45	72.60	74.57	76.37	78.02	79.45	80.69
S.	URUGUAY	81.96	82.92	83.80	84.63	85.35	86.01	86.58	87.09	87.54	87.94	88.30	88.67
T.	VENEZUELA	72.09	74.14	76.22	78.04	79.70	81.22	82.59	83.75	84.83	85.74	86.50	87.15
	LATIN AMERICA	57.69	60.50	63.34	66.05	68.57	70.89	72.99	74.90	76.58	78.10	79.40	80.57

1. For each of the countries involved, the definition adopted for an urban population is the
   one appearing in the last population census of the corresponding country. See SALA, 23-652.

SOURCE: CELADE-BD, 28 (1981), table 28; CELADE-BD, 30 (1982).

Figure 6:1

URBAN POPULATION, NON–STANDARD TERMS, 20 L, 1970–2000
(%)

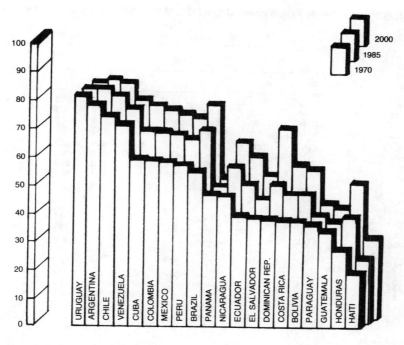

Source: CELADE-BD, No. 34, July 1984, cover.

Table 654

CELADE URBAN AND RURAL POPULATION ESTIMATES, NON-STANDARD TERMS,[1] 20 LR, 1970–2020

(T)

Country	1970	1980	1990	2000	2010	2020
A. ARGENTINA						
Total	23,748	27,036	30,277	33,222	35,843	38,101
Urban	18,637	22,066	25,463	28,586	31,380	33,795
Rural	5,111	4,970	4,814	4,636	4,463	4,306

1. For each of the countries involved, the definition adopted for an urban population is the one appearing in the last population census of the corresponding country. Cf. SALA, 23-652.

Continued in SALA, 23-654.

Table 655

ECLA URBAN AND RURAL POPULATION ESTIMATES, BY AGE GROUP, NON-STANDARD DEFINITION,[1] 20 L, 1975–2025

(% and T)

Country/Age Group	1975 Urban	1975 Rural	1980 Urban	1980 Rural	2000 Urban	2000 Rural	2025 Urban	2025 Rural
A. ARGENTINA								
0-14 (%)	26.38	36.42	26.05	36.12	24.07	33.95	20.96	30.46
15-59	60.85	54.87	60.45	54.67	60.65	55.52	61.02	56.74
60-	12.77	8.71	13.50	9.21	15.28	10.53	18.02	12.80
Total (T)	20,343	5,035	22,066	4,970	28,586	4,636	34,816	4,241

1. Rural and urban defined according to national self-perception as defined in SALA, 23-652.

Continued in SALA, 23-656.

Table 656

URBAN POPULATION IN NON-STANDARD AND STANDARD TERMS, 20 LR, 1960–80

| | | | | Non-Standard Terms[1] | | | | | | Standard Terms | | | | | |
| | | Density Per km[2] | | | T | | | % | | | % over 20,000 | | | % over 100,000 | | |
Country	1960	1970	1980	1960	1970	1980	1960	1970	1980	1960	1970	1980	1960	1970	1980
A. ARGENTINA	7.4	8.6	10.2	15,112	18,810	23,041	73.3	78.5	81.6	59.0	66.3	70.2	50.6	55.6	57.7
B. BOLIVIA	3.1	3.9	5.1	1,035	1,652	2,490	30.2	38.2	44.7	22.9	27.2	34.0	15.3	20.9	29.2
C. BRAZIL	8.6	11.3	14.3	33,538	53,483	76,168	46.2	55.8	62.8	27.0	36.2	45.7	25.2	32.5	38.0
D. CHILE	10.1	12.5	14.7	5,144	7,111	8,756	67.6	75.2	78.7	50.6	60.6	67.9	32.9	41.7	52.0
E. COLOMBIA	13.6	18.3	22.6	7,551	12,336	17,101	48.6	59.3	66.3	33.5	43.9	54.3	27.5	35.7	42.5
F. COSTA RICA	24.3	34.0	44.8	421	672	1,042	34.1	38.8	45.7	18.5	26.0	30.1	18.5	20.9	22.2
G. CUBA	63.4	77.2	87.7	3,803	5,109	6,520	54.1	59.6	67.0	38.9	43.4	47.5	24.5	30.8	33.2
H. DOMINICAN REP.	66.6	89.4	114.7	935	1,690	2,601	29.0	19.4	45.8	18.7	30.2	40.8	12.1	20.7	27.5
I. ECUADOR	17.0	22.9	30.8	1,406	2,359	3,585	31.8	39.6	44.7	26.5	33.0	39.5	18.6	22.0	28.7
J. EL SALVADOR	123.0	170.6	229.1	808	1,415	2,120	31.4	39.5	44.2	17.7	20.5	24.9	13.3	15.7	17.8
K. GUATEMALA	36.4	49.1	66.7	1,214	1,841	2,651	30.6	34.4	36.5	14.5	15.9	18.9	13.2	13.7	14.3
L. HAITI	134.6	164.5	209.9	484	912	1,342	13.0	19.8	23.1	9.5	13.4	16.5	7.9	11.1	14.7
M. HONDURAS	17.3	23.6	32.9	464	876	1,432	23.9	33.2	38.8	11.1	17.7	23.8	6.9	13.3	17.9
N. MEXICO	18.8	26.0	35.3	19,204	30,143	45,452	51.8	58.9	65.5	29.6	34.8	42.5	13.6	23.3	29.8
O. NICARAGUA	12.6	17.4	23.4	596	965	1,491	39.9	47.0	53.8	20.3	30.5	36.9	14.1	20.5	24.4
P. PANAMA	14.6	19.6	25.9	454	711	1,082	41.1	47.8	55.3	33.1	39.4	40.9	25.4	30.3	30.6
Q. PARAGUAY	4.4	5.6	7.8	558	847	1,223	31.4	37.0	38.6	22.1	27.3	32.2	22.1	24.2	25.9
R. PERU	7.7	10.3	13.5	4,419	7,652	10,965	44.5	58.0	63.4	27.4	38.5	47.2	18.3	28.0	38.0
S. URUGUAY	13.6	15.0	15.6	1,972	2,303	2,437	77.7	82.0	83.8	60.0	63.3	66.1	40.4	44.7	41.5
T. VENEZUELA	8.4	11.8	16.7	4,719	7,645	11,448	62.9	72.1	76.2	47.0	59.4	67.0	25.8	38.0	52.7
LATIN AMERICA	10.5	13.8	17.6	103,837	158,532	222,947	49.6	57.7	63.3	32.4	39.9	47.3	25.3	31.5	36.4

1. Urban defined according to national definitions (see SALA, 24).

SOURCE: ECLA-N, No. 397/8 (July, 1984), p. 5.

Table 657

VANHANEN URBAN AND RURAL POPULATION PERCENTAGE ESTIMATES, 20 LRC, 1900–70
(Urban = Clusters of Population 20,000 and Over)

PART I. URBAN

(%)

Country	1900	1910	1920	1930	1940	1950	1960	1970
A. ARGENTINA	24.9	28.4	37.0	38.0	41.0	49.91	58.98	66.25
B. BOLIVIA	6.6	9.2	9.4[a]	13.1[b]	18.7[c]	19.36	22.93	27.22
C. BRAZIL	8.7	9.8	13.0	14.0	16.0	20.26	28.08	39.51
D. CHILE	19.9	24.2[d]	27.6	32.0	37.0	42.57	50.61	60.58
E. COLOMBIA	6.2	7.3	8.9[e]	10.0	14.0	23.00	36.57	46.21
F. COSTA RICA	8.5	7.9	12.2	13.2	15.4	17.71	24.38	26.96
G. CUBA	25.0	28.0	23.2	27.3	32.2	36.07	38.92[†]	43.37
H. DOMINICAN REP.	3.6	3.1	4.0	~	7.0[g]	11.15	18.66	30.17
I. ECUADOR	9.3	12.0	13.6	14.0[b]	17.0[h]	17.80	27.94	35.26
J. EL SALVADOR	6.0[†]	8.8	~	10.4	12.4	12.95	17.66	20.46
K. GUATEMALA	~	8.9	9.2	10.3	9.8	11.18	15.49	16.09
L. HAITI	8.2	8.2	6.3	5.9	5.3	15.12	7.47[†]	12.66
M. HONDURAS	~	6.3	6.3	4.7	6.1	6.83	11.54	20.20
N. MEXICO	9.2	10.8	12.6	15.6	18.0	23.57	28.87	35.19
O. NICARAGUA	~	~	10.9	17.9[i]	21.8	15.22	23.05	30.97
P. PANAMA	6.8[j]	13.4	21.9	24.6	25.0	22.36	33.10	39.39
Q. PARAGUAY	13.0[h]	17.7	18.0	12.9	15.7	15.25	15.88	21.48
R. PERU	6.0[j]	5.4[l]	5.0	9.6	12.9	18.13[†]	28.50	40.34
S. URUGUAY	~	26.0	27.8[m]	37.6[b]	36.8[f]	53.13[†]	61.44	64.68
T. VENEZUELA	8.5	9.0	11.7	19.4	28.5	31.01	47.00	59.36
LATIN AMERICA[1]	10.9	13.2	15.5	18.0	20.5	28.8	33.0	41.5
UNITED STATES	25.9	30.8	42.0	47.0	47.0	51.1	58.5	64.0[†]

1. Weighted by population in each country.

a. 1923.	h. 1938.
b. 1932.	i. 1933.
c. 1942.	j. 1903.
d. 1912.	k. 1895.
e. 1918.	l. 1908.
f. 1937.	m. 1922.
g. 1935.	

PART II. RURAL

(%)

Country	1900	1910	1920	1930	1940	1950	1960	1970
A. ARGENTINA	75.1	71.6	63.0	62.0	59.0	50.1	41.0	33.8
B. BOLIVIA	93.4	90.8	90.6[a]	86.9[b]	81.3[c]	80.1	77.1	72.8
C. BRAZIL	91.3	90.2	87.0	86.0	84.0	79.7	71.9	60.5
D. CHILE	80.1	75.8[d]	72.4	68.0	63.0	57.4	49.4	39.4
E. COLOMBIA	93.8	92.7	91.1[e]	90.0	86.0	77.0	63.4	53.8
F. COSTA RICA	91.5	92.1	87.2	86.8	84.6	82.3	75.6	73.0
G. CUBA	75.0	72.0	76.8	72.7	67.8	63.9	61.1[l]	56.6
H. DOMINICAN REP.	96.4	96.9	96.0	94.0[@]	93.0[g]	88.9	81.3	69.8
I. ECUADOR	90.7	88.0	86.4	86.0[b]	83.0[h]	82.2	72.1	64.7
J. EL SALVADOR	94.0[@]	91.2	90.4[@]	89.6	87.6	87.1	82.3	79.5
K. GUATEMALA	90.9[@]	91.1	90.8	89.7	90.2	88.8	84.5	83.9
L. HAITI	91.8	91.8	93.7	94.1	94.7	84.9	92.5[‡]	87.3
M. HONDURAS	95.7[@]	93.7	93.7	95.3	93.9	93.2	88.5	79.8
N. MEXICO	90.8	89.2	87.4	84.4	82.0	76.4	71.1	64.9
O. NICARAGUA	92.2[@]	90.7[@]	89.1	82.1[i]	78.2	84.8	77.0	69.0
P. PANAMA	93.2[m]	86.6	78.1	75.4	75.0	77.6	66.9	60.6
Q. PARAGUAY	87.0[k]	82.3	82.0	87.1	84.3	84.7	84.1	78.5
R. PERU	94.0[j]	94.6[l]	95.0	90.4	87.1	81.9[‡]	71.5	59.7
S. URUGUAY	74.0	74.0	72.2[m]	62.4[b]	63.2[f]	46.9[‡]	38.6	35.3
T. VENEZUELA	91.5	91.0	88.3	80.6	71.5	69.0	53.0	40.6
LATIN AMERICA[1]	89.1	86.8	84.5	82.0	79.5	71.2	67.0	58.5
UNITED STATES	74.1	69.2	58.0	53.0	53.0	48.9	41.5	36.0

1. Weighted by population in each country.

a. 1923.	h. 1938.
b. 1932.	i. 1933.
c. 1942.	j. 1903.
d. 1912.	k. 1895.
e. 1918.	l. 1906.
f. 1937.	m. 1922.
g. 1935.	

SOURCE: Adapted from Tata Vanhanen, *Political and Social Structures; Part I: American Countries, 1850-1973* (Tampere, Finland: University of Tampere, 1975); republished as *Power and the Means of Power . . . , 1850-1975* (Ann Arbor: University Microfilms, 1979), pp. 221-237; and CELADE-BD, Jan. 1977, which gives data to two decimal places.

Table 658

NUMBER AND POPULATION OF PLACES WITH 20,000 INHABITANTS AND OVER, ACCORDING TO CENSUSES, 20 L, ca. 1950, 1960, 1970

Country	Number of Inhabitants	1950		1960		1970	
		Number of Localities	Population	Number of Localities	Population	Number of Localities	Population
A. ARGENTINA	Total 20,000+	42	7,934,082	57	11,804,276	79	15,479,372
	1,000,000 and more	1	4,927,919	1	6,807,236	1	8,435,840
	500,000 – 999,999	#	≈	2	1,260,736	2	1,597,450
	100,000 – 499,999	7	1,694,032	10	2,059,161	12	2,951,313
	50,000 – 99,999	8	552,643	7	475,009	16	1,057,550
	20,000 – 49,999	26	759,488	37	1,202,134	48	1,437,219
B. BOLIVIA[1]	Total 20,000+	6	523,556	7	847,621	8	1,267,917
	1,000,000 and more	#	≈	#	≈	#	#
	500,000 – 999,999	#	≈	#	≈	1	675,100
	100,000 – 499,999	1	267,008	2	566,489	2	299,800
	50,000 – 99,999	2	133,377	4	257,979	3	229,117
	20,000 – 49,999	3	123,171	1	23,153	2	63,900
C. BRAZIL[2]	Total 20,000+	101	10,525,939	190	19,924,752	343	36,801,063
	1,000,000 and more	2	4,352,956	2	6,388,212	5	12,707,187
	500,000 – 999,999	1	512,370	4	2,679,988	3	1,989,925
	100,000 – 499,999	8	2,040,777	25	4,241,263	61	11,201,404
	50,000 – 99,999	22	1,613,409	42	2,951,388	68	4,617,919
	20,000 – 49,999	68	2,006,427	117	3,663,901	206	6,284,628
D. CHILE	Total 20,000+	24	2,525,491	35	3,732,005	44	5,382,600
	1,000,000 and more	1	1,350,409	1	1,907,378	1	2,730,895
	500,000 – 999,999	#	≈	#	≈	#	≈
	100,000 – 499,999	2	338,928	3	516,410	6	974,350
	50,000 – 99,999	6	361,467	9	597,259	12	869,772
	20,000 – 49,999	15	474,687	22	710,958	25	907,583
E. COLOMBIA[3]	Total 20,000+	27	2,656,119	47	6,393,632	70	9,737,000
	1,000,000 and more	#	≈	1	1,697,311	2	3,767,194
	500,000 – 999,999	1	715,250	2	1,336,080	2	1,559,262
	100,000 – 499,999	5	1,060,028	9	1,769,221	13	2,202,440
	50,000 – 99,999	6	401,268	13	896,880	15	1,122,455
	20,000 – 49,999	15	479,573	22	694,140	38	1,085,649
F. COSTA RICA	Total 20,000+	1	141,857	4	325,785	6	504,672
	1,000,000 and more	#	≈	≈	≈	#	#
	500,000 – 999,999	#	≈	≈	≈	≈	≈
	100,000 – 499,999	1	141,857	1	246,440	1	359,327
	50,000 – 99,999	≈	≈	#	≈	≈	≈
	20,000 – 49,999	#	≈	3	79,345	5	145,345
G. CUBA	Total 20,000+	22	2,102,309	26	2,642,166	31	3,684,707
	1,000,000 and more	1	1,098,587	1	1,322,440	1	1,751,216
	500,000 – 999,999	#	≈	#	≈	#	≈
	100,000 – 499,999	2	273,625	2	340,806	5	866,222
	50,000 – 99,999	5	321,549	7	502,774	9	612,961
	20,000 – 49,999	14	408,548	16	476,146	16	454,308
H. DOMINICAN REP.	Total 20,000+	2	238,111	7	568,700	14	1,208,545
	1,000,000 and more	#	≈	#	≈	#	#
	500,000 – 999,999	#	≈	#	≈	1	673,470
	100,000 – 499,999	1	181,553	1	369,980	1	155,000
	50,000 – 99,999	1	56,558	1	85,640	#	#
	20,000 – 49,999	#	≈	5	113,080	12	380,075
I. ECUADOR[4]	Total 20,000+	5	570,023	13	1,250,608	21	2,285,355
	1,000,000 and more	#	≈	#	≈	≈	#
	500,000 – 999,999	#	≈	1	510,804	2	1,411,197
	100,000 – 499,999	2	468,898	1	354,746	1	104,667
	50,000 – 99,999	#	≈	2	113,774	7	439,568
	20,000 – 49,999	3	101,125	9	271,284	11	329,923
J. EL SALVADOR	Total 20,000+	3	240,355	6	443,397	10	726,074
	1,000,000 and more	#	≈	#	≈	#	#
	500,000 – 999,999	#	≈	#	≈	#	#
	100,000 – 499,999	1	161,951	1	255,744	1	337,171
	50,000 – 99,999	1	51,702	1	72,839	3	210,526
	20,000 – 49,999	1	26,702	4	114,814	6	178,377
K. GUATEMALA[5]	Total 20,000+	2	311,948	4	664,232	5	832,613
	1,000,000 and more	#	≈	#	≈	#	#
	500,000 – 999,999	#	≈	1	572,671	1	700,504
	100,000 – 499,999	1	284,276	#	≈	#	#
	50,000 – 99,999	#	≈	#	≈	1	53,021
	20,000 – 49,999	1	27,672	3	91,561	3	79,088
L. HAITI[6]	Total 20,000+	2	158,540	2	271,056	4	546,350
	1,000,000 and more	#	≈	#	≈	#	#
	500,000 – 999,999	#	≈	#	≈	#	#
	100,000 – 499,999	1	134,117	1	237,994	1	448,807
	50,000 – 99,999	#	≈	#	≈	#	#
	20,000 – 49,999	1	24,423	1	33,062	3	97,543

Table 658 (Continued)

NUMBER AND POPULATION OF PLACES WITH 20,000 INHABITANTS AND MORE, ACCORDING TO CENSUSES, 20 L, ca. 1950, 1960, 1970

Country	Number of Inhabitants	1950 Number of Localities	1950 Population	1960 Number of Localities	1960 Population	1970 Number of Localities	1970 Population
M. HONDURAS[3]	Total 20,000+	2	93,524	3	217,570	6	536,104
	1,000,000 and more	=	=	=	=	=	=
	500,000 – 999,999	=	=	=	=	=	=
	100,000 – 499,999	=	=	1	134,075	2	418,727
	50,000 – 99,999	1	72,385	1	58,632	=	=
	20,000 – 49,999	1	21,139	1	24,863	4	117,377
N. MEXICO	Total 20,000+	64	6,078,876	104	10,083,633	181	16,969,547
	1,000,000 and more	1	2,233,914	1	2,832,133	2	4,096,570
	500,000 – 999,999	=	=	2	1,333,739	2	1,438,543
	100,000 – 499,999	9	1,676,787	13	2,243,758	30	5,707,130
	50,000 – 99,999	13	867,868	23	1,667,076	34	2,356,569
	20,000 – 49,999	41	1,300,307	65	2,006,927	113	3,370,735
O. NICARAGUA[4]	Total 20,000+	3	160,931	5	353,946	7	591,916
	1,000,000 and more	=	=	=	=	=	=
	500,000 – 999,999	=	=	=	=	=	=
	100,000 – 499,999	1	109,352	1	234,580	1	398,514
	50,000 – 99,999	=	=	=	=	1	55,625
	20,000 – 49,999	2	51,579	4	119,366	5	137,777
P. PANAMA[7]	Total 20,000+	2	180,073	3	355,962	4	562,489
	1,000,000 and more	=	=	=	=	=	=
	500,000 – 999,999	=	=	=	=	=	=
	100,000 – 499,999	1	127,874	1	273,440	1	433,241
	50,000 – 99,999	1	52,204	1	59,598	1	67,695
	20,000 – 49,999	=	=	1	22,924	2	61,553
Q. PARAGUAY	Total 20,000+	1	202,540	1	288,882	5	505,619
	1,000,000 and more	=	=	=	=	=	=
	500,000 – 999,999	=	=	=	=	=	=
	100,000 – 499,999	1	202,540	1	288,882	1	392,753
	50,000 – 99,999	=	=	=	=	=	=
	20,000 – 49,999	=	=	=	=	4	112,866
R. PERU[8]	Total 20,000+	11	1,412,579	29	2,822,985	43	5,472,870
	1,000,000 and more	=	=	1	1,524,450	1	2,941,473
	500,000 – 999,999	1	872,643	=	=	=	=
	100,000 – 499,999	2	202,504	3	391,441	7	1,122,393
	50,000 – 99,999	3	168,760	5	357,444	8	538,445
	20,000 – 49,999	5	168,672	20	549,650	27	870,559
S. URUGUAY[8]	Total 20,000+	10	1,196,542	14	1,594,562	16	1,787,663
	1,000,000 and more	=	=	1	1,159,685	1	1,229,748
	500,000 – 999,999	1	909,619	=	=	=	=
	100,000 – 499,999	=	=	=	=	=	=
	50,000 – 99,999	=	=	2	110,430	3	188,276
	20,000 – 49,999	9	286,923	11	325,047	12	369,639
T. VENEZUELA	Total 20,000+	22	1,561,109	43	3,536,306	64	6,363,994
	1,000,000 and more	=	=	=	=	1	1,035,499
	500,000 – 999,999	=	=	1	786,863	1	651,574
	100,000 – 499,999	3	835,922	6	1,133,181	15	2,645,258
	50,000 – 99,999	4	263,152	12	823,151	15	1,034,841
	20,000 – 49,999	15	462,035	24	793,111	32	996,822

1. Estimated figures for 1960 and 1970.
2. For 1970 census, population in "Vilas" of 50,000 inhabitants and over and all places with 20,000 to 49,999 inhabitants is de jure population.
3. Places are equivalent to capital of municipalities.
4. Places are equivalent to urban part of capital of cantons.
5. The places correspond to the urban part of leading municipalities by department.
6. Estimated figure for 1960.
7. Does not include Canal Zone, which does not have any place of 20,000 inhabitants and over for these periods.
8. Estimated figure for 1950.

SOURCE: CELADE-BD, Jan. 1977, table 6.

Table 659

INDICES OF URBANIZATION AND URBAN CONCENTRATION,[1] 20 LR,
1950 AND 1975

Country	Year	% Total Population in Urban Areas of			% Urban Population in Urban Areas of	
		20,000 Inhabitants or More	100,000 Inhabitants or More	Most Populated City[2]	100,000 Inhabitants or More	Most Populated City[3]
A. ARGENTINA	1950	52.4	44.0	32.0	84.0	61.1
	1975	69.8	57.9	37.0	83.0	53.0

Continued in SALA, 21-635.

Table 660

MALE AND FEMALE TOTAL POPULATION PROJECTIONS, 20 LR, 1975–90
(T)

PART I. TOTALS

Country	1975			1980			1985			1990		
	Total	Male	Female	Total	Male	Female	Total	Male	Female	Total	Male	Female
A. ARGENTINA	26,501	13,006	13,045	28,237	14,045	14,192	30,564	15,164	15,400	32,879	16,285	16,594
B. BOLIVIA	4,894	2,412	2,482	5,570	2,744	2,826	6,371	3,138	3,232	7,314	3,605	3,709
C. BRAZIL	108,032	54,029	54,002	121,286	60,607	60,679	135,564	67,677	67,887	150,368	74,992	75,376
D. CHILE	10,196	5,051	5,145	11,104	5,499	5,605	12,074	5,979	6,096	13,061	6,466	6,594
E. COLOMBIA	23,177	11,591	11,586	25,794	12,924	12,869	28,714	14,407	14,307	31,820	15,979	15,840
F. COSTA RICA	1,965	991	974	2,278	1,151	1,127	2,599	1,312	1,287	2,937	1,482	1,455
G. CUBA	9,332	4,767	4,565	9,732	4,962	4,769	10,038	5,113	4,925	10,540	5,358	5,181
H. DOMINICAN REP.	4,945	2,502	2,443	5,557	2,803	2,754	6,242	3,141	3,101	6,971	3,501	3,470
I. ECUADOR	6,891	3,447	3,444	8,021	4,015	4,006	9,380	4,697	4,682	10,949	5,486	5,463
J. EL SALVADOR	4,143	2,084	2,059	4,797	2,410	2,387	5,552	2,788	2,764	6,484	3,260	3,225
K. GUATEMALA	6,243	3,164	3,078	7,262	3,682	3,581	8,403	4,260	4,143	9,676	4,905	4,771
L. HAITI	5,157	2,532	2,625	5,809	2,859	2,950	6,585	3,248	3,337	7,509	3,711	3,797
M. HONDURAS	3,093	1,551	1,542	3,691	1,851	1,840	4,372	2,192	2,181	5,105	2,559	2,546
N. MEXICO	60,153	30,124	30,029	69,393	34,748	34,645	78,995	39,555	39,440	89,012	44,569	44,443
O. NICARAGUA	2,409	1,204	1,205	2,771	1,382	1,389	3,272	1,636	1,636	3,871	1,940	1,931
P. PANAMA	1,704	868	835	1,956	999	957	2,180	1,111	1,069	2,418	1,230	1,188
Q. PARAGUAY	2,686	1,337	1,349	3,168	1,580	1,588	3,681	1,838	1,843	4,231	2,114	2,117
R. PERU	15,161	7,640	7,521	17,295	8,714	8,581	19,697	9,923	9,794	22,332	11,249	11,083
S. URUGUAY	2,828	1,401	1,427	2,908	1,435	1,473	3,012	1,482	1,530	3,128	1,538	1,590
T. VENEZUELA	13,109	6,590	6,518	15,620	7,826	7,794	18,386	9,192	9,194	21,284	10,626	10,658
LATIN AMERICA	312,170	156,293	155,877	352,251	176,239	176,012	395,685	197,856	197,829	441,888	220,856	221,032

SOURCE: CELADE-BD, 32 (1983).

PART II. URBAN AND RURAL NON-STANDARD TERMS
(1985) [1]

Country	Urban		Rural	
	Male	Female	Male	Female
A. ARGENTINA	11,651,447	12,149,302	2,644,068	2,244,382
B. BOLIVIA	1,497,863	1,721,842	1,640,551	1,510,323
C. BRAZIL	44,660,418	46,035,015	24,384,877	22,153,073
D. CHILE	4,700,713	4,996,456	1,278,075	1,099,231
E. COLOMBIA	9,690,290	10,265,508	4,716,850	4,041,056
F. COSTA RICA	585,592	636,824	665,544	596,560
G. CUBA	3,502,656	3,563,097	1,609,876	1,362,152
H. DOMINICAN REP.	1,649,418	1,763,714	1,744,234	1,557,157
I. ECUADOR	2,166,195	2,288,188	2,531,278	2,393,883
J. EL SALVADOR	1,246,733	1,343,765	1,541,669	1,420,249
K. GUATEMALA	1,544,685	1,630,105	2,715,356	2,512,879
L. HAITI	744,497	904,095	2,503,576	2,433,132
M. HONDURAS	893,592	950,395	1,298,393	1,230,109
N. MEXICO	27,298,934	27,860,769	13,127,748	12,196,423
O. NICARAGUA	887,258	954,568	714,315	661,541
P. PANAMA	610,602	635,969	466,952	403,253
Q. PARAGUAY	705,129	768,987	1,132,926	1,074,417
R. PERU	6,671,002	6,684,033	3,498,433	3,419,325
S. URUGUAY	1,216,609	1,318,417	257,485	203,039
T. VENEZUELA	7,071,394	7,277,590	2,120,740	1,916,514
LATIN AMERICA	128,995,027	133,748,639	70,592,946	64,428,698

1. For each of the countries involved, the definition adopted for an urban population is the one appearing in the last population census of the corresponding country. Cf. SALA 23-652.

SOURCE: CELADE-BD, 28 (1981).

Table 661

AGE STRUCTURE, 20 LC, 1960–80
(%)

Country	0-14 Years			15-64 Years			65 Years and Over		
	1960	1970	1980	1960	1970	1980	1960	1970	1980
A. ARGENTINA	31.0	29.0	28.1	63.0	63.0	63.2	6.0	8.0	8.6
B. BOLIVIA	42.0	42.0	43.9	54.0	55.0	52.7	4.0	3.0	3.4
C. BRAZIL	42.7	42.0	41.4	54.4	55.0	55.0	2.9	3.0	3.5
D. CHILE	40.0	39.0	45.2	56.0	55.0	52.5	4.0	6.0	2.8
E. COLOMBIA	47.0	47.0	37.7	50.0	50.0	56.6	3.0	3.0	3.0
F. COSTA RICA	48.0	44.0	37.7	49.0	52.0	58.3	3.0	4.0	3.7
G. CUBA	~	~	32.0	~	~	61.3	~	~	7.1
H. DOMINICAN REP.	47.0	48.0	44.8	50.0	49.0	52.1	3.0	3.0	2.8
I. ECUADOR	45.0	47.0	44.4	52.0	50.0	52.1	3.0	3.0	3.6
J. EL SALVADOR	45.0	47.0	45.2	52.0	50.0	51.3	3.0	3.0	3.4
K. GUATEMALA	45.0	46.0	~	52.0	51.0	~	3.0	3.0	~
L. HAITI	42.0	42.0	43.6	55.0	53.0	52.8	3.0	5.0	3.5
M. HONDURAS	48.0	47.0	47.9	50.0	51.0	49.4	2.0	2.0	2.7
N. MEXICO	44.0	46.0	45.4	52.0	50.0	51.1	4.0	4.0	3.6
O. NICARAGUA	47.0	47.0	48.1	50.0	50.0	49.5	3.0	3.0	2.4
P. PANAMA	43.0	43.0	39.9	53.0	53.0	56.0	4.0	4.0	4.2
Q. PARAGUAY	45.0	46.0	44.5	51.0	51.0	52.2	4.0	3.0	3.4
R. PERU	44.0	45.0	~	52.0	52.0	~	4.0	3.0	~
S. URUGUAY	28.0	28.0	27.2	64.0	63.0	62.5	8.0	9.0	10.3
T. VENEZUELA	46.0	47.0	39.5	51.0	50.5	57.0	3.0	2.5	3.3
UNITED STATES	31.1	28.5	22.5	59.7	61.6	66.3	9.2	9.9	9.7

SOURCE: Adapted from WB-WT76, Series IV, table 2; 1980 data calculated from PAHO-HC, table 1-3.

Table 662

DISTRIBUTION OF POPULATION BY SEX AND AGE, 18 LC
(%, 1980)

Country	All Ages		Under 5 Years		5-14 Years		15-24 Years		25-44 Years		45-64 Years		65 Years and Over	
	M	F	M	F	M	F	M	F	M	F	M	F	M	F
A. ARGENTINA	49.9	50.1	5.1	4.9	9.2	8.9	8.5	8.2	13.5	13.2	9.7	10.1	3.8	4.8
B. BOLIVIA	49.3	50.7	8.5	8.4	13.5	13.5	9.4	9.6	11.0	11.5	5.3	5.9	1.5	1.9
C. BRAZIL	49.9	50.1	8.0	7.8	12.9	12.7	9.8	9.7	11.8	12.0	5.8	5.9	1.6	1.9
D. CHILE	49.5	50.5	9.1	9.9	13.0	13.2	9.4	9.5	11.3	11.4	5.3	5.6	1.3	1.5
E. COLOMBIA	50.2	49.8	4.9	7.3	12.9	12.6	11.4	11.0	11.8	11.8	5.1	5.5	1.3	1.7
F. COSTA RICA	50.4	49.6	6.6	6.4	12.6	12.1	11.6	11.3	12.2	12.1	5.5	5.6	1.8	1.9
G. CUBA	50.9	49.1	4.6	4.5	11.7	11.2	10.0	10.0	13.3	13.0	7.6	7.4	3.7	3.4
H. DOMINICAN REP.	50.5	49.5	8.0	7.8	14.7	14.3	11.0	11.0	11.0	11.0	3.5	4.6	1.4	1.4
I. ECUADOR	50.1	49.9	8.8	8.6	13.6	13.4	9.9	9.9	11.0	10.9	5.2	5.2	1.7	1.9
J. EL SALVADOR	50.2	49.8	9.0	8.7	14.0	13.5	10.1	9.8	10.7	10.5	5.0	5.2	1.5	1.9
L. HAITI	49.2	50.8	8.5	8.4	13.4	13.3	9.6	9.7	10.8	11.6	5.2	5.9	1.6	1.9
M. HONDURAS	50.1	49.9	9.7	9.6	14.4	14.2	9.6	9.5	10.3	10.2	4.9	4.9	1.3	1.4
N. MEXICO	50.3	49.7	9.1	8.8	14.0	13.5	10.1	9.8	10.8	10.8	4.7	4.9	1.6	1.9
O. NICARAGUA	49.7	50.3	9.7	9.4	14.7	14.3	10.1	10.0	10.3	10.6	3.9	4.6	1.0	1.4
P. PANAMA	51.0	49.0	7.2	7.0	13.1	12.6	10.3	9.8	12.4	11.7	6.0	5.8	2.0	2.2
Q. PARAGUAY	50.0	50.0	8.7	8.4	13.9	13.5	10.2	10.0	10.6	11.0	5.1	5.3	1.6	1.8
S. URUGUAY	49.2	50.8	4.8	4.6	9.0	8.8	8.2	8.1	12.2	12.4	10.5	11.1	4.5	5.8
T. VENEZUELA	50.3	49.7	8.1	7.8	13.0	10.6	10.6	12.6	11.3	11.4	5.6	5.5	1.6	1.7
UNITED STATES	48.7	51.3	3.7	3.5	7.8	7.5	9.4	9.2	13.8	14.1	9.5	10.3	4.6	5.1

SOURCE: PAHO-HC, table 1-3.

Table 663

ESTIMATES OF FEMALE POPULATION 15–49 YEARS OF AGE, 20 LRC, 1950–2010

(%)

Country	1950	1960	1970	1980	1990	2000	2010
A. ARGENTINA	54.1	51.2	49.8	48.3	48.4	49.6	49.2
B. BOLIVIA	46.8	47.4	45.8	45.4	46.4	47.6	47.7
C. BRAZIL	47.9	46.2	46.5	47.1	48.2	49.7	52.9
D. CHILE	48.1	47.0	47.5	51.7	52.5	52.4	51.3
E. COLOMBIA	46.1	44.1	44.7	49.3	50.7	52.4	53.8
F. COSTA RICA	46.1	42.8	44.0	50.9	53.3	53.5	52.6
G. CUBA	50.0	50.0	46.7	50.4	54.7	52.7	52.0
H. DOMINICAN REP.	44.6	43.1	42.4	46.2	51.2	53.0	54.9
I. ECUADOR	45.7	43.8	43.8	45.1	45.9	48.4	50.8
J. EL SALVADOR	48.1	44.8	43.6	44.3	46.2	48.6	50.5
K. GUATEMALA	46.1	44.6	45.2	46.1	47.7	49.1	50.3
L. HAITI	47.7	47.0	45.6	45.6	46.2	46.9	48.2
M. HONDURAS	47.3	45.6	43.3	42.8	45.3	48.2	48.5
N. MEXICO	46.0	43.6	43.5	44.7	45.4	47.6	54.9
O. NICARAGUA	46.6	43.4	43.2	44.0	45.6	47.7	50.7
P. PANAMA	44.9	44.4	44.8	47.7	51.6	53.0	53.9
Q. PARAGUAY	46.3	43.4	43.6	45.1	47.0	49.4	52.2
R. PERU	44.9	44.1	44.5	46.6	48.3	50.4	53.3
S. URUGUAY	51.5	50.5	48.7	46.4	46.2	47.6	48.8
T. VENEZUELA	46.5	43.8	43.6	47.9	49.0	51.8	52.9
LATIN AMERICA[1]	47.8	45.8	45.6	47.0	48.1	49.7	52.7
Caribbean	48.2	46.7	44.8	48.4	51.8	52.0	54.2[a]
Continental Middle America	46.2	43.8	43.7	44.9	45.9	48.0	50.5[b]
Temperate South America	52.4	50.1	49.1	49.1	49.4	50.3	52.3[c]
Tropical South America	47.2	45.4	45.7	47.2	48.4	50.2	52.4[d]
UNITED STATES	50.9	45.6	46.7	50.5	50.8	49.4	~

1. Includes Barbados, Guadeloupe, Jamaica, Martinique, Puerto Rico, Suriname, Trinidad and Tobago, and the Windward Islands for decades 1950 to 2000.

a. Includes Mexico, Cuba, Dominican Republic, and Haiti.
b. Includes Costa Rica, El Salvador, Guatemala, Honduras, Nicaragua, and Panama.
c. Includes Argentina, Brazil, Paraguay, and Uruguay.
d. Includes Bolivia, Chile, Colombia, Ecuador, Peru, and Venezuela.

SOURCE: PAHO-HC, table 1-4; 2010 data calculated from CELADE-BD, 32 (1983).

Table 664

POPULATION PERCENTAGE UNDER 15 YEARS, 20 LRC, 1950–2010
(%)

Country	1950	1960	1970	1980	1990	2000	2010
A. ARGENTINA	30.6	30.7	29.2	28.2	27.3	25.0	27.2
B. BOLIVIA	42.5	41.9	43.7	43.8	42.5	41.2	42.6
C. BRAZIL	42.4	43.5	42.7	41.5	39.9	37.3	28.7
D. CHILE	38.2	39.1	38.1	32.5	30.6	28.1	26.0
E. COLOMBIA	43.3	46.8	46.1	40.4	38.4	35.2	28.9
F. COSTA RICA	43.5	47.5	46.1	37.9	34.1	31.7	28.1
G. CUBA	36.2	34.4	37.1	32.0	25.9	25.1	21.3
H. DOMINICAN REP.	44.8	47.8	49.0	44.8	38.8	35.5	28.9
I. ECUADOR	41.7	44.4	45.3	44.4	43.9	41.3	37.8
J. EL SALVADOR	42.2	45.1	46.1	45.1	43.4	40.6	37.3
K. GUATEMALA	44.3	46.2	45.7	44.1	41.8	39.5	36.6
L. HAITI	39.5	40.9	42.9	43.6	43.6	43.4	42.4
M. HONDURAS	44.7	45.7	47.5	47.8	45.2	42.3	41.4
N. MEXICO	42.9	45.6	46.5	45.3	44.8	42.3	30.0
O. NICARAGUA	44.1	47.8	48.5	48.0	46.5	44.0	38.4
P. PANAMA	41.6	44.0	43.3	39.8	34.7	31.5	27.8
Q. PARAGUAY	42.4	45.9	46.0	44.3	42.7	39.7	34.2
R. PERU	41.1	43.6	44.3	42.5	40.8	38.0	31.1
S. URUGUAY	28.2	28.5	28.2	27.2	26.7	26.1	24.5
T. VENEZUELA	42.3	46.2	46.4	41.6	39.9	35.6	32.4
LATIN AMERICA[1]	40.6	42.5	42.7	40.9	39.5	37.1	30.5
Caribbean	39.1	40.2	41.7	37.5	33.3	31.7	30.3[a]
Continental Middle America	43.0	45.8	46.4	45.2	44.1	41.7	36.7[b]
Temperate South America	32.2	32.7	31.4	29.4	28.1	26.0	28.5[c]
Tropical South America	42.4	44.3	43.7	41.7	40.1	37.3	31.9[d]
UNITED STATES	26.9	31.1	28.3	22.5	22.7	21.9	~

1. Includes Barbados, Guadeloupe, Guyana, Jamaica, Martinique, Puerto Rico, Suriname, Trinidad and Tobago, and the Windward Islands for decades 1950 to 2010.

a. Includes Mexico, Cuba, Dominican Republic, and Haiti.
b. Includes Costa Rica, El Salvador, Guatemala, Honduras, Nicaragua, and Panama.
c. Includes Argentina, Brazil, Paraguay, and Uruguay.
d. Includes Bolivia, Chile, Colombia, Ecuador, Peru, and Venezuela.

SOURCE: PAHO-HC, table 1-5; 2010 data calculated from CELADE-BD, 32 (1983).

Table 665

PERSONS BY AGE UP TO 15 YEARS, 20 LC

(N)

Country	Year	Code	Age			
			Under 1 Year	1-4 Years	5-9 Years	10-14 Years
A. ARGENTINA	1980	C	3,240,844[a]	~[a]	2,783,755	2,456,168
B. BOLIVIA[1,13]	1981	E	983,489[a]	~[a]	804,348	690,164
C. BRAZIL[2,3]	1980	C	16,649,135[a]	~[a]	14,271,782	13,549,664
D. CHILE[4]	1982	E	274,414	1,029,473	1,191,985	1,166,894
E. COLOMBIA[5]	1973	C	716,643	2,815,649	3,452,201	3,194,164
F. COSTA RICA[2]	1973	C	50,133	208,802	289,013	276,514
G. CUBA[2]	1981	E	573,456[a]	~[a]	1,016,117	1,172,897
H. DOMINICAN REP.[5]	1980	E	183,719	736,468	890,819	774,522
I. ECUADOR[6,7,13]	1982	E	1,637,000[a]	~[a]	1,341,000	1,109,000
J. EL SALVADOR[8]	1971	C	129,516	467,798	575,313	465,975
K. GUATEMALA[2]	1980	E	1,243,600[a]	~[a]	1,059,100	898,300
L. HAITI[2,13]	1981	E	170,523	616,221	671,892	609,829
M. HONDURAS[13]	1981	E	159,037	570,104	395,851	497,427
N. MEXICO[2]	1979	E	12,826,415[a]	~[a]	10,416,694	8,800,246
O. NICARAGUA	1980	E	466,640	~[a]	455,852	387,061
P. PANAMA[9,13]	1981	E	54,979	218,267	260,581	238,421
Q. PARAGUAY[13]	1980	E	512,665[a]	~[a]	440,895	399,241
R. PERU[6,10,13]	1981	E	2,953,600[a]	~[a]	2,546,200	2,283,000
S. URUGUAY[8,13]	1980	E	274,427[a]	~[a]	267,110	245,206
T. VENEZUELA[5,11,13]	1980	E	2,207,763[a]	~[a]	1,941,566	1,663,873
UNITED STATES[6,12]	1981	E	3,691,000	13,348,000	16,045,000	18,241,000

Code: C = census data; E = estimate.

1. Data have not been adjusted for underenumeration.
2. De jure population.
3. Excluding Indian jungle population.
4. Data have been adjusted for underenumeration at largest census.
5. Provisional data.
6. Because of rounding, totals are not in all cases the sum of the parts.
7. Excluding nomadic Indian tribes.
8. Based on a sample of census returns.
9. Excluding the former Canal Zone.
10. Excluding Indian jungle population estimated at 39,800 in 1972.
11. Excluding Indian jungle population estimated at 31,800 in 1961.
12. De jure population, but excluding civilian citizens absent from country for extended period of time.
13. Estimates are unreliable.

a. Figures for under one year category include 1-4 years population.

SOURCE: UN-DY, 1980, table 7; UN-DY, 1982, table 7.

Table 666

CELADE RATES OF DEMOGRAPHIC GROWTH, 20 LR, 1920–2000[a]

(AA–GR)

Country	1920-25	1925-30	1930-35	1935-40	1940-45	1945-50	1950-55	1955-60	1960-65	1965-70
A. ARGENTINA	3.17	2.81	1.86	1.67	1.67	2.11	2.05	1.98	1.58	1.56
B. BOLIVIA	1.06	1.26	1.45	1.62	1.78	1.92	1.97	2.16	2.29	2.41
C. BRAZIL	2.05	2.05	2.05	2.11	2.27	2.55	2.97	3.03	2.86	2.87
D. CHILE	1.54	1.61	1.55	1.50	1.54	1.74	2.41	2.40	2.50	2.26
E. COLOMBIA	1.94	1.96	2.03	2.19	2.36	2.65	3.05	3.27	3.32	3.46
F. COSTA RICA	1.61	1.82	2.00	2.35	2.98	3.44	3.74	4.13	3.65	3.05
G. CUBA	2.66	2.67	1.93	1.58	1.55	2.28	2.13	2.14	2.07	2.00
H. DOMINICAN REP.	1.99	2.16	2.28	2.34	2.62	2.84	3.02	3.20	3.25	3.44
I. ECUADOR	1.14	1.46	1.71	1.91	2.06	2.41	2.83	3.11	3.35	3.41
J. EL SALVADOR	2.18	2.09	1.19	1.30	1.23	2.05	2.51	2.90	3.04	3.36
K. GUATEMALA	1.11	2.94	2.42	1.97	3.36	3.10	2.67	2.82	2.98	2.89
L. HAITI	1.25	1.39	1.51	1.60	1.78	1.84	1.95	2.15	2.28	2.45
M. HONDURAS	1.94	1.92	1.61	1.73	2.01	2.36	2.62	3.18	3.37	3.43
N. MEXICO	.95	1.76	1.75	1.84	2.88	3.12	2.94	3.20	3.45	3.50
O. NICARAGUA	1.46	1.55	1.74	2.00	2.27	2.55	2.66	3.04	3.06	2.98
P. PANAMA	1.58	1.59	.86	2.57	2.55	2.53	2.89	2.97	3.23	3.27
Q. PARAGUAY	2.35	2.31	2.34	2.37	1.82	2.01	2.60	2.78	3.24	3.46
R. PERU	1.47	1.56	1.65	1.72	1.75	1.81	1.98	2.66	3.05	3.12
S. URUGUAY	2.06	2.04	1.50	1.18	1.13	1.30	1.48	1.44	1.35	1.23
T. VENEZUELA	1.93	2.17	2.27	2.37	2.84	3.11	3.99	3.92	3.31	3.37
LATIN AMERICA	1.86	2.03	1.89	1.91	2.22	2.54	2.73	2.85	2.85	2.91

Country	1970-75	1975-80	1980-85	1985-90	1990-95	1995-2000
A. ARGENTINA	1.3	1.3	1.2	1.1	9.7***	8.8***
B. BOLIVIA	2.5	2.6	2.7	2.8	2.8	2.9
C. BRAZIL	2.6	2.4	2.3	2.2	2.1	2.0
D. CHILE	1.7	1.7	1.7	1.6	1.4	1.3
E. COLOMBIA	2.2	2.1	2.1	2.1	1.9	1.7
F. COSTA RICA	2.5	2.4	2.3	2.2	2.1	1.9
G. CUBA	1.7	.8	.6	1.0	1.1	1.0
H. DOMINICAN REP.	2.9	2.6	2.4	2.3	2.2	2.1
I. ECUADOR	2.9	3.0	3.1	3.1	3.0	2.8
J. EL SALVADOR	2.9	2.9	2.9	3.1	3.0	2.9
K. GUATEMALA	3.1	3.0	2.9	2.8	2.8	2.7
L. HAITI	2.3	2.4	2.5	2.6	2.7	2.7
M. HONDURAS	3.2	3.5	3.4	3.1	3.1	3.2
N. MEXICO	3.2	3.0	2.9	2.7	2.4	2.2
O. NICARAGUA	3.3	3.3	3.3	3.2	3.1	3.1
P. PANAMA	2.7	2.5	2.2	2.1	1.9	1.8
Q. PARAGUAY	3.2	3.3	3.0	2.8	2.6	2.3
R. PERU	2.7	2.7	2.8	2.8	2.8	2.7
S. URUGUAY	.1	.5	.7	.7	.7	.7
T. VENEZUELA	3.6	3.5	3.3	2.9	2.6	2.3
LATIN AMERICA	2.6	2.5	2.4	2.3	2.2	2.0

a. 1920-70 estimated in 1972; 1970-80 estimated in 1981.

SOURCE: CELADE-BD 10 (1972); CELADE-BD, 28 (1981); CELADE-BD, 30 (1982).

Table 667

CELADE GROWTH RATES FOR TOTAL, URBAN, AND RURAL POPULATION, 20 LR, 1970–2000

(AA-GR for Non-Standard Definition)[1]

Country	Period					
	1970-75	1975-80	1980-85	1985-90	1990-95	1995-2000
A. ARGENTINA						
Total	1.3	1.3	1.2	1.1	9.7	8.8
Urban	1.8	1.6	1.5	1.4	1.2	1.1
Rural	−.3	−.3	−.3	−.3	−.4	−.4

Continued in SALA, 23-655 (based upon CELADE-BD, 30 [1982]).

Table 668

ESTIMATED AMERIND POPULATION, 16 L, MID–1950s

Country	Date	Total Population	Amerind Population	%	Geographic Distribution of Principal Amerind Groups
A. ARGENTINA	1960	20,956,039	130,000	.6	a. Northern or Chaqueña region (30,000). Chulupíes, Chorotes, Matacos, Tobas, Pilagas.
					b. Northwest or Andean regions and Central (18,000). Coyas, Tobas, Mocobies.
					c. Pampeana region and South (18,000). Araucanos, Onas, Yaganes, Alacalufes.

Continued in SALA, 17-610.

Table 669

AMERIND POPULATION ESTIMATES,[1] 16 LC, LATE 1970s
(1978)

Category	Indigenous Population (T)	% of National Population
Countries with High Percentage of Indigenous Peasant Population		
B. BOLIVIA	3,526	59.2
I. ECUADOR	2,564	33.9
K. GUATEMALA	3,739	59.7
N. MEXICO	8,042	12.4
R. PERU	6,025	36.8
Countries with Principally Tribal Indigenous Population		
C. BRAZIL	243	.2
E. COLOMBIA	547	2.2
P. PANAMA	121	6.8
Q. PARAGUAY	67	2.3
T. VENEZUELA	202	1.5
Countries with Indigenous Minorities		
A. ARGENTINA	398	1.5
D. CHILE	616	5.7
F. COSTA RICA	10	.6
J. EL SALVADOR[2]	100	2.3
M. HONDURAS[2]	107	3.2
O. NICARAGUA[2]	43	1.8
UNITED STATES[3]	1,568	.7
TOTAL	27,927	

1. Indigenous peoples are those who still maintain specific social ties that give them an identity of their own as indigenous in the local context and are, in turn, recognized as such by the nonindigenous people of the countries, although they might have undergone substantial changes since their first contacts with the European colonizers.

2. Unreliable information.

3. The 1980 census gave a total of 1,418,195 who identified themselves as Indian, including American Indians, Eskimos, and Aleuts.

SOURCE: Inter-American Indian Institute, "La Población Indígena en América en 1978," *América Indígena* 39:2 (1979), quoted in *Intercom*, The International Population News Magazine of the Population Reference Bureau 9:6(1981), 4.

Table 670

U. S. POPULATION CENSUS DATA ON HISPANICS
(1980)

PART I. STATE

Rank	State	Hispanic Population	Hispanic Percentage of Population	Percentage of U.S. Hispanic State Population	Hispanics in State Elected Offices
1	California	4,543,770	19.2	31.1	10/120[a]
2	Texas	2,985,643	21.0	20.4	22/181[b]
3	New York	1,659,245	9.5	11.4	7/210
4	Florida	857,898	8.8	5.9	1/170
5	Illinois	635,525	5.6	4.4	0/236
6	New Jersey	491,867	6.7	3.4	0/120
7	New Mexico	476,089	36.6	3.3	33/112**
8	Arizona	440,915	16.2	3.0	12/90
9	Colorado	339,300	11.7	2.3	9/100
10	Michigan	162,388	1.8	1.1	2/148
11	Pennsylvania	154,004	1.3	1.1	0/252
12	Massachusetts	141,043	2.5	1.0	0/199
13	Connecticut	124,499	4.0	.9	0/187
14	Washington	119,986	2.9	.8	0/147
15	Ohio	119,880	1.1	.8	0/132

PART II. CITY

Rank	City	Hispanic Population	Percentage of Total Population	Hispanics on Elected Council[1]
1	New York City	1,405,957	19.9	3/43
2	Los Angeles	815,989	27.5	0/15
3	Chicago	422,061	14.0	1/50
4	San Antonio[2]	421,774	53.7	4/9
5	Houston	281,224	17.6	1/14
6	El Paso	265,819	62.5	2/6
7	Miami[2]	194,087	55.8	2/4
8	San Jose	140,574	22.1	1/6
9	San Diego	130,610	14.9	1/8
10	Phoenix	115,572	15.1	0/6
11	Albuquerque	112,084	33.8	3/9
12	Dallas	111,082	12.3	1/10
13	Corpus Christi	108,175	46.6	0/6
14	Hialeah[2]	107,908	74.3	2/7
15	Denver	91,937	18.7	2/13
16	Santa Ana	90,646	39.3	2/7
17	Laredo[2]	85,076	93.0	8/8
18	San Francisco	83,373	12.3	0/11
19	Tucson	82,189	24.9	2/6
20	Brownsville[2]	71,139	83.7	3/4

1. Column shows the number of Hispanics and the total membership of the city council or comparable elected body. For example, of New York City's 43 council members, 3 are Hispanic.
2. City has a Hispanic mayor.

a. These figures include both houses of state legislatures.
b. Figures adjusted after November 1982 elections.

SOURCE: *Los Angeles Herald Examiner,* Nov. 21, 1982.

CHAPTER 7
VITAL STATISTICS AND DISEASE

Table 700

LIFE EXPECTANCY,[1] 20 LC

PART I. AGES 0–80

Country	Years[2]	0 Male	0 Female	1 Male	1 Female	5 Male	5 Female	10 Male	10 Female	15 Male	15 Female	20 Male	20 Female	25 Male	25 Female	30 Male	30 Female
A. ARGENTINA	1975-80	65.4	72.1	67.5	73.9	64.0	70.4	59.2	65.6	54.3	60.7	49.6	55.9	45.1	51.2	40.5	46.5
B. BOLIVIA	1975-80	46.5	50.9	53.5	57.3	55.7	58.6	52.0	54.7	47.7	50.3	43.6	46.1	39.8	42.1	36.0	38.1
C. BRAZIL	1975-80	59.5	64.3	64.5	67.7	62.9	65.4	58.5	60.8	53.8	56.1	49.3	51.4	44.9	46.9	40.7	42.5
D. CHILE	1975-80	64.6	70.8	66.7	72.8	63.2	69.2	58.4	64.4	53.6	59.5	48.9	54.7	44.4	50.0	39.9	45.3
E. COLOMBIA	1975-80	60.0	64.5	63.2	67.0	61.8	65.1	57.4	60.7	52.9	56.1	48.4	51.6	44.2	47.2	39.8	43.8
F. COSTA RICA	1975-80	69.0	74.0	70.4	74.9	66.8	71.4	62.0	66.5	57.2	61.6	52.5	56.8	48.0	52.0	43.4	47.2
G. CUBA	1975-80	71.2	74.5	72.4	75.1	69.0	71.6	64.2	66.7	59.3	61.9	54.6	57.0	49.9	52.2	45.2	47.4
H. DOMINICAN REP.	1975-80	58.4	62.2	62.3	65.4	60.7	63.7	56.4	59.4	51.9	54.8	47.5	50.5	43.3	46.2	39.1	42.0
I. ECUADOR	1975-80	58.0	62.0	62.9	65.8	61.7	64.0	57.3	59.5	52.8	54.8	48.5	50.4	44.4	46.1	40.2	41.8
J. EL SALVADOR	1975-80	60.0	64.5	64.7	68.8	63.2	67.0	59.2	63.0	54.5	58.2	50.0	53.7	45.6	49.1	41.3	44.8
K. GUATEMALA	1975-80	56.9	58.8	61.2	62.2	60.9	62.3	57.0	58.3	52.5	53.9	48.0	49.4	43.8	45.1	39.7	40.9
L. HAITI	1975-80	49.2	52.2	55.5	57.7	55.4	57.0	51.3	52.8	47.0	48.4	43.0	44.3	39.2	40.4	35.4	36.5
M. HONDURAS	1975-80	55.4	58.9	61.2	62.9	61.0	62.5	57.0	58.3	52.5	53.8	48.1	49.3	43.9	45.0	39.8	40.7
N. MEXICO	1975-80	61.9	66.3	65.3	69.2	63.2	67.1	58.7	62.6	54.0	57.8	49.5	53.2	45.0	48.6	40.7	44.2
O. NICARAGUA	1975-80	55.3	57.3	60.3	61.7	59.7	60.8	55.4	56.6	50.0	52.1	46.9	47.8	42.9	43.8	38.9	39.8
P. PANAMA	1975-80	67.6	70.9	69.0	72.0	66.1	69.1	61.5	64.5	56.8	59.7	52.3	55.0	47.8	50.3	43.4	45.7
Q. PARAGUAY	1975-80	61.9	66.4	64.5	68.3	62.5	65.9	58.0	61.3	53.3	56.5	48.9	51.8	44.6	47.4	40.3	42.9
R. PERU	1975-80	55.2	58.7	61.0	64.2	60.7	63.8	56.4	59.5	51.9	55.0	47.4	50.5	43.2	46.2	39.0	41.9
S. URUGUAY	1975-80	66.4	73.0	68.7	74.7	65.0	71.0	60.2	66.1	55.3	61.2	50.6	56.4	45.9	51.6	41.3	46.8
T. VENEZUELA	1975-80	64.9	70.7	67.1	72.5	64.0	69.5	59.3	64.7	54.6	59.8	50.0	55.1	45.5	50.3	41.1	45.6
UNITED STATES	1979	70.0	77.8	70.1	77.7	66.3	73.9	61.4	69.0	56.5	64.1	51.9	59.2	47.3	54.4	42.8	49.6

Country	Years[2]	35 Male	35 Female	40 Male	40 Female	45 Male	45 Female	50 Male	50 Female	55 Male	55 Female	60 Male	60 Female	65 Male	65 Female	70 Male	70 Female	75 Male	75 Female	80 Male	80 Female
A. ARGENTINA	1975-80	35.9	41.8	31.5	37.3	27.3	32.8	23.3	28.4	19.6	24.2	16.2	20.0	13.1	16.1	10.3	12.6	7.8	9.3	5.4	6.6
B. BOLIVIA	1975-80	32.1	34.1	28.3	30.1	24.5	26.1	20.8	22.3	17.2	18.5	13.9	15.0	10.9	11.8	8.3	9.0	6.2	6.7	4.7	5.0
C. BRAZIL	1975-80	36.5	38.1	32.5	33.9	28.5	29.8	24.7	25.8	21.0	22.0	17.5	18.3	14.3	14.9	11.3	11.8	8.6	9.0	6.3	6.6
D. CHILE	1975-80	35.5	40.6	31.2	36.0	27.0	31.6	23.1	27.3	19.5	23.2	16.2	19.4	13.2	15.9	10.6	12.7	8.4	10.0	6.8	7.7
E. COLOMBIA	1975-80	35.5	38.5	31.3	34.1	27.1	29.8	23.1	25.6	19.3	21.4	15.7	17.4	12.3	13.8	9.4	10.5	6.9	7.7	5.0	5.7
F. COSTA RICA	1975-80	38.8	42.4	34.3	37.7	29.9	33.1	25.6	28.6	21.5	24.2	17.5	19.9	14.0	16.0	10.8	12.4	8.9	9.2	6.6	6.5
G. CUBA	1975-80	40.6	42.7	36.0	38.0	31.5	33.4	27.1	28.9	22.9	24.6	18.9	20.4	15.2	16.5	11.8	12.9	8.9	9.5	6.3	7.0
H. DOMINICAN REP.	1975-80	35.0	37.8	30.9	33.7	27.0	29.6	23.2	25.6	19.6	21.8	16.3	18.2	13.4	14.9	10.6	11.8	8.5	9.3	6.3	6.9
I. ECUADOR	1975-80	36.0	37.5	31.9	33.3	27.9	29.1	24.0	25.1	20.2	21.2	16.7	17.5	13.4	14.0	10.4	10.9	7.9	8.2	5.8	6.0
J. EL SALVADOR	1975-80	37.1	40.5	32.8	36.2	28.7	32.0	24.7	27.8	21.0	23.8	17.4	19.9	14.2	16.0	11.3	12.4	8.9	9.5	6.9	7.0
K. GUATEMALA	1975-80	35.6	36.8	31.6	32.7	27.6	28.7	23.8	24.7	20.2	20.9	16.8	17.2	13.6	14.0	10.7	11.0	8.3	8.5	6.1	6.3
L. HAITI	1975-80	31.6	32.5	27.9	28.7	24.2	24.9	20.7	21.3	17.4	17.9	14.3	14.7	11.5	11.8	9.0	9.2	7.0	7.1	5.5	5.5
M. HONDURAS	1975-80	35.7	36.6	31.7	32.5	27.7	28.5	23.8	24.5	20.0	20.6	16.5	17.0	13.4	13.8	10.5	10.6	7.9	8.1	5.3	5.5
N. MEXICO	1975-80	36.5	39.8	32.4	35.4	28.4	31.2	24.6	27.0	21.0	23.0	17.6	19.2	14.4	15.7	11.6	12.6	9.1	9.9	6.8	7.4
O. NICARAGUA	1975-80	34.9	35.7	30.9	31.6	26.9	27.5	23.1	23.6	19.4	19.8	15.9	16.2	12.7	13.0	9.8	10.0	7.5	7.7	5.7	5.8
P. PANAMA	1975-80	38.9	41.1	34.4	36.6	30.1	32.2	25.9	27.8	21.9	23.6	18.1	19.6	14.7	15.9	11.7	12.6	8.9	9.7	6.7	7.2
Q. PARAGUAY	1975-80	36.0	38.4	31.8	34.1	27.7	29.9	23.7	25.7	19.9	21.7	16.2	17.9	13.0	14.3	10.0	11.1	7.7	8.4	5.9	6.4
R. PERU	1975-80	34.7	37.6	30.5	33.3	26.4	29.0	22.5	24.8	18.7	21.1	15.2	16.7	11.9	13.1	9.0	9.9	6.6	7.3	4.8	5.2
S. URUGUAY	1975-80	36.6	42.0	32.1	37.4	27.7	32.8	23.6	28.4	19.7	24.1	16.2	20.1	13.0	16.3	10.3	12.8	7.9	9.8	6.0	7.3
T. VENEZUELA	1975-80	36.7	41.0	32.4	36.4	28.2	31.9	24.3	27.6	20.5	23.5	16.9	19.7	13.8	16.2	10.4	13.1	8.9	10.4	7.1	8.1
UNITED STATES	1979	38.2	44.8	33.7	40.0	29.2	35.4	25.0	30.9	21.0	26.7	17.5	22.6	14.3	18.7	11.5	15.1	9.1	11.9	7.0	9.0

1. The life expectancy represents average number of years of life remaining to persons surviving to exact age specified if subject to mortality conditions of period indicated, i.e., the average number of years a person of the age specified may be expected to live if the age specific mortality rates of the indicated period do not change in the future.

2. For previous years, see SALA, 23-700.

SOURCE: CELADE-BD, 33, 1984, tables 2-21, except data for U.S. from UN-DY, 1981, table 16.

Table 700 (Continued)

LIFE EXPECTANCY,[1] 20 LC

PART II. ESTIMATES AND PROJECTIONS, 1950-2000

Country	1950-55			1980-85			1995-2000			2020-25		
	M	F	T	M	F	T	M	F	T	M	F	T
A. ARGENTINA	60.4	65.1	62.7	66.7	73.3	69.9	68.1	74.5	71.2	68.6	75.5	72.0
B. BOLIVIA	38.5	42.5	40.4	48.6	53.0	50.7	57.0	62.0	59.4	64.5	70.0	67.2
C. BRAZIL	49.8	52.2	51.0	61.6	65.4	63.5	65.2	69.7	67.4	69.1	74.8	71.9
D. CHILE	52.3	56.0	54.1	63.8	70.4	67.0	67.4	73.9	70.6	68.5	75.5	71.9
E. COLOMBIA	48.8	52.6	50.6	61.4	66.0	63.6	64.7	69.3	66.9	69.0	73.8	71.3
F. COSTA RICA	56.0	58.6	57.3	68.7	73.3	70.9	70.4	75.4	72.8	71.4	76.6	73.9
G. CUBA	56.7	61.0	58.8	71.8	75.2	73.4	72.7	76.7	74.7	73.0	77.4	75.1
H. DOMINICAN REP.	43.6	46.7	45.1	60.7	64.6	62.6	66.1	70.2	68.1	70.4	74.6	72.4
I. ECUADOR	46.0	47.9	46.9	60.6	64.7	62.6	67.0	71.0	69.0	69.3	73.8	71.5
J. EL SALVADOR	44.1	46.5	45.3	62.6	67.1	64.8	69.4	73.3	71.3	71.1	75.1	73.1
K. GUATEMALA	42.1	43.3	42.7	59.7	61.8	60.7	66.8	69.3	68.0	70.2	74.3	72.2
L. HAITI	36.3	38.9	37.6	51.2	54.4	52.7	56.7	60.2	58.4	63.8	68.4	66.0
M. HONDURAS	40.9	43.5	42.2	58.2	61.7	59.9	66.0	69.7	67.8	70.2	74.3	72.2
N. MEXICO	50.3	53.3	51.8	63.9	68.2	66.0	68.0	72.3	70.1	70.6	75.0	72.7
O. NICARAGUA	41.5	44.6	43.0	55.8	59.5	57.6	62.8	66.8	64.7	67.8	72.5	70.1
P. PANAMA	57.6	60.1	58.8	68.5	73.0	70.7	70.4	75.4	72.8	70.5	76.6	73.5
Q. PARAGUAY	50.0	54.0	51.9	62.8	67.5	65.1	65.3	70.5	67.8	69.0	74.5	71.7
R. PERU	42.6	44.8	43.7	57.6	60.7	59.1	62.7	66.1	64.4	69.5	73.0	71.2
S. URUGUAY	63.3	69.4	66.3	67.1	73.7	70.3	69.5	76.0	72.7	70.1	77.1	73.6
T. VENEZUELA	50.3	54.4	52.3	65.1	70.6	67.8	68.1	73.8	70.9	71.0	77.0	73.9

SOURCE: CEPAL, *Informe de la Reunión Regional Latinoamericana Preparatoria de la Asamblea Mundial sobre el Envejecimiento*, San José, March 31, 1982, pp. 30-31.

Table 701

LIVE BIRTHS BY AGE OF MOTHER, 19 L

(N)

Country	Year	Total	Under Age 15	15-19	20-24	25-29	30-34	35-39	40-44	45 +	Unknown
A. ARGENTINA	1970	544,521	1,892	64,525	146,594	138,633	89,441	51,342	19,420	4,991	27,683
B. BOLIVIA	1966	106,889	56	8,859	26,960	25,180	18,968	15,025	6,138	3,741	1,962
D. CHILE	1979	223,098	610	36,833	75,905	55,361	32,537	15,900	5,186	676	~
E. COLOMBIA[5]	1969	691,000	382	66,073	170,675	152,191	99,638	75,909	23,292	6,206	96,634
F. COSTA RICA	1978	67,659	239	13,477	22,669	15,663	8,655	4,554	1,611	215	576
G. CUBA[1,2]	1971	256,014	~	55,984	87,681	56,071	33,402	16,751	5,493	632	~
H. DOMINICAN REP.[1]	1976	169,161	388	17,685	42,314	34,607	25,388	19,336	10,728	10,887	7,828
I. ECUADOR[6]	1977	233,653	213	27,569	64,621	51,238	34,465	23,554	9,864	1,983	10,146
J. EL SALVADOR	1978	172,897	129	35,172	52,864	37,586	22,777	16,039	5,669	1,420	1,241
K. GUATEMALA	1977	284,747	765	49,606	84,435	66,157	42,520	28,179	10,336	2,376	373
L. HAITI[4]	1972	137,621	--	12,659	32,519	33,873	23,917	23,493	7,703	3,457	--
M. HONDURAS[1,4]	1976	132,793	274	24,426	37,703	27,956	18,620	12,836	5,121	1,010	4,847
N. MEXICO[1]	1976	1,555,963	1,829	237,838	475,372	372,666	226,495	160,409	56,760	10,896	13,698
O. NICARAGUA[1]	1967	78,141	51	10,521	19,780	17,338	9,581	6,634	1,982	533	11,721
P. PANAMA[3]	1979	52,919	270	10,468	16,983	12,522	7,083	3,456	1,140	174	823
Q. PARAGUAY[1,4]	1971	21,317	30	2,376	5,530	4,795	3,415	2,068	1,018	343	1,742
R. PERU[1,8]	1972	413,531	559	52,094	117,089	101,300	65,738	49,019	16,527	3,760	7,445
S. URUGUAY[1]	1977	57,976	166	8,286	16,706	14,590	9,684	5,522	1,823	175	1,024
T. VENEZUELA[1,7]	1979	481,349	3,515	80,676	153,366	122,144	69,045	36,394	13,431	2,487	291

1. Data tabulated by year of registration, not of occurrences.
2. Data are births recorded in National Register of Consumers.
3. Excluding the Canal Zone.
4. Data incomplete.
5. Data based on baptismal records of the Roman Catholic Church.
6. Excluding nomadic Indian tribes.
7. Excluding Indian jungle population, estimated at 31,800 in 1961.
8. Excluding Indian jungle population, estimated at 100,830 in 1961.

SOURCE: UN-DY, 1975, table 23; 1976, table 10; 1978, table 10; 1979, table 10; and 1980, table 10; UN-DY, 1981, table 23.

Table 702

CRUDE BIRTH RATES, 20 LC, 1960–81[a]
(PTI)[1]

Country	Code	1960	1965	1970	1975	1977	1978	1979	1980	1981
A. ARGENTINA	C	22.8‡	21.7	22.9	~	25.4	25.2	~	~	~
B. BOLIVIA[9,10]	U	25.6‡,c	46.1	45.6	46.6	44.8	44.8	44.8	44.8	~
C. BRAZIL[10]	U	~	42.1	38.8	35.8	33.3	33.3	33.3	33.3	~
D. CHILE[8]	C	35.7	33.2	27.0	24.6	21.6	21.4	21.5	22.2	~
E. COLOMBIA[10]	U	42.4c,d	44.6	39.6	33.3	32.1	32.1	32.1	32.1	~
F. COSTA RICA	C	48.4	42.3	33.4	29.5	31.1	29.9	30.2	29.4	~
G. CUBA[2,4]	C	29.8	33.8	27.6	20.7	17.6	15.3	14.7	~	13.9‡
H. DOMINICAN REP.[2]	C	36.8c	42.7	~	~	21.8	21.3	~	~	~
I. ECUADOR[3,10]	U	47.7c	46.1	44.2	42.2	41.6	41.6	41.6	41.6	~
J. EL SALVADOR	C	46.5	46.9	40.0	39.9	41.7	39.7	39.3	35.8	~
K. GUATEMALA	C	49.5	45.3	40.2	39.9	42.9	41.5	41.9	41.8	~
L. HAITI[10]	U	~	44.4	43.7	42.7	41.8	41.8	41.8	41.8	~
M. HONDURAS[10]	U	44.7c,d	50.9	50.0	48.6	47.1	47.1	47.1	47.1	~
N. MEXICO[10]	U	46.0b,d	44.6	43.9	41.8	38.3	38.3	38.3	38.3	~
O. NICARAGUA[10]	U	45.2c,d	50.0	48.6	48.3	46.6	46.6	46.6	46.6	~
P. PANAMA[6]	C	40.8	38.4	36.4	33.2	30.9	30.3	29.5	27.7	~
Q. PARAGUAY[3,10]	U	~	42.2	40.4	37.5	36.7	36.7	36.7	36.7	~
R. PERU[2,7,10]	U	38.9c,d	46.4	44.5	40.0	39.7	39.7	39.3	39.0	38.6
S. URUGUAY	C	21.4‡,c,d	22.4	19.5	20.9	20.3	20.0	19.8	18.6	18.3
T. VENEZUELA[5,10]	U	45.9c,d	45.2	40.9	37.5	36.9	36.9	36.9	36.9	~
UNITED STATES	C	23.7	19.4	18.2	14.6	15.3	15.3	15.9	15.8	15.9

Code: C = Data estimated to be virtually complete, representing at least 90% of the events occurring each year.

U = Data estimated to be incomplete, representing less than 90% of the events occurring each year.

1. Crude birth rates are determined by the number of live births per thousand, mid-year population.
2. Data tabulated by year of registration rather than year of occurrence.
3. Excluding nomadic Amerind tribes.
4. For 1960, data estimates based on analysis of 1943 and 1953 census returns plus an assumed rate of growth.
5. Excluding Indian jungle population estimated at 31,800 in 1961.
6. Excluding Canal Zone.
7. Excluding Indian jungle population estimated at 100,830 in 1961.
8. For 1960, data are births tabulated by year of occurrence.
9. Data for 1975 were based on a national sample survey.
10. U.N. Population Division estimate for years 1965-81.

a. For 1930-59 data, see SALA, 21-705.
b. Data considered complete.
c. Data considered incomplete.
d. Data tabulated by year of registration.

SOURCE: UN-DY, 1964, table 16; 1981, special topic table 21.

Table 703

AGE-SPECIFIC FERTILITY RATES, CRUDE BIRTH RATE (CBR), TOTAL FERTILITY RATE (TFR), AND GROSS REPRODUCTION RATE (GRR), 20 LC, 1975–80

	Age of Mother									
Country	15-19	20-24	25-29	30-34	35-39	40-44	45-49	CBR	TFR	GRR
A. ARGENTINA	57.2	149.1	158.5	115.4	66.8	21.9	5.4	21.24	2.87	1.40

Continued in SALA, 23-702.

Table 704

FETAL MORTALITY RATES,[1] 16 LC, 1960–81[a]
(Deaths per 1,000 Live Births)

	Country	1960	1965	1970	1975	1977	1978	1979	1980	1981
A.	ARGENTINA	24.3	23.9	20.6	~	~	~	~	~	~
C.	BRAZIL[2]	28.5	~	~	~	29.4	26.6	25.8	24.3	~
D.	CHILE[3,4]	26.5	24.2	18.6	15.5	12.7	11.0	10.1	9.1	7.7
E.	COLOMBIA[3,5]	11.3	15.6	~	12.3	~	~	~	~	~
F.	COSTA RICA[3,8]	17.2	17.2	15.7	~	~	~	~	~	~
G.	CUBA[3,6]	26.8	20.5	15.0	11.3[b]	11.7	11.5	~	~	~
H.	DOMINICAN REP.[3]	27.7	23.2	25.4	19.7[b]	~	~	~	~	~
I.	ECUADOR[7]	22.4	21.0	19.6	22.2	24.9	25.6	~	~	~
J.	EL SALVADOR	8.5	9.5	10.2	8.0	7.5	6.6	6.6	6.2	~
K.	GUATEMALA	30.1	29.5	28.7	27.1	21.8	23.8	23.2	~	~
N.	MEXICO[3]	17.2	17.3	16.6	~	13.8	11.8	12.2	~	~
O.	NICARAGUA	2.0	8.5	~	~	~	~	~	~	~
P.	PANAMA[10]	24.1	24.8	21.0	~	~	~	~	~	~
R.	PERU[3,7,9]	11.2	10.8	~	~	~	~	~	~	~
S.	URUGUAY	~	14.9	13.2	~	~	~	~	~	~
T.	VENEZUELA[3,7]	19.9	17.8	15.9	16.2	15.6	14.6	14.7	15.5	~
	UNITED STATES	12.7	12.6	14.2	8.3	8.1	7.7	6.5	~	~

1. Deaths after more than 20-28 weeks gestation. Reliability and comparability of data known to be greatly affected by incomplete or irregular registration of fetal deaths, and/or live births, and by variations in definitions.
2. 1960 data for state of Guanabara only.
3. Data tabulated by year of registration rather than of occurrence.
4. Rates for 1960 computed on live births which have been adjusted or under-registration.
5. Based on burial permits but computed on number of baptisms recorded in Roman Catholic Church registers.
6. 1960 data computed on births which are estimated based on analysis of 1943 and 1953 census returns and application of an assumed rate of growth.
7. Excluding tropical forest Amerinds.
8. Ratios for 1951-65 computed on live births registered during the period 1951-65 tabulated by year of occurrence.
9. Ratios are based on burial permits, estimated to be 50% complete.
10. Excluding Canal Zone and tribal Amerind population.

a. Includes fetuses of less than 5 months gestation; for 1950-59 data, see SALA, 23-704.
b. Data tabulated by year of occurrence.

SOURCE: UN-DY, 1966, table 10; 1974, table 17; 1981 Special topic table 38; 1982, table 12.

Table 705

INFANT MORTALITY RATES, 19 LC, 1960–81[a]
(Deaths per 1,000 Live Births)[1]

	Country	Code	1960	1965	1970	1975	1977	1978	1979	1980	1981
A.	ARGENTINA[11]	~	62.4	56.9	58.9	~	47.2	47.2	47.2	47.2	~
B.	BOLIVIA[11]	U	~	76.5	~	~	138.2	138.2	138.2	138.2	~
C.	BRAZIL[2,11]	~	~	~	~	~	82.4	82.4	82.4	82.4	~
D.	CHILE[6,11]	C	125.1	107.1	78.8	56.4	50.1	40.1	37.9	33.0	~
E.	COLOMBIA[2,3,7,11]	U	99.8	82.4	~	46.7	59.4	59.4	59.4	59.4	~
F.	COSTA RICA[12]	C	70.8	71.8	61.5	38.2	27.9	23.8	23.4	20.2	~
G.	CUBA[2,5,9]	C	35.4[c]	38.4	35.9	27.3[‡]	23.5	22.4	19.3	~	18.5[‡]
H.	DOMINICAN REP.[11]	U	100.6[d]	72.7	50.1	43.5	73.1	73.1	73.1	73.1	~
I.	ECUADOR[8,11,12]	U	100.0	93.0	76.6	65.8	86.0	86.0	86.0	86.0	~
J.	EL SALVADOR	C	76.3	70.6	66.6	58.1	59.3	50.8	53.0	42.0	~
K.	GUATEMALA	C	91.9	92.6	87.1	81.4	69.8	69.2	70.4	65.9	~
M.	HONDURAS[2,11]	U	52.0	41.2	33.2	33.7	95.4	95.4	95.4	95.4	~
N.	MEXICO[2,11,13]	U	74.2[b]	60.7	68.5	52.8	59.8	59.8	59.8	59.8	~
O.	NICARAGUA[2,11]	U	70.2	51.6[d]	~	~	96.5	96.5	96.5	96.5	~
P.	PANAMA[4,11]	U	56.9	44.7	40.5	31.6	36.2	36.2	36.2	36.2	~
Q.	PARAGUAY[2,11]	U	~	41.5	33.3	~	48.6	48.6	48.6	48.6	~
R.	PERU[10,11]	U	92.1	74.0	65.1	~	39.2	39.2	39.2	39.2	~
S.	URUGUAY[2]	C	47.4[‡,c]	49.8	42.6	48.8[d]	48.5	43.8	38.6	37.5	34.1[‡]
T.	VENEZUELA[8,11]	U	53.9	47.7	49.3	43.7[d]	44.8	44.8	44.8	44.8	~
	UNITED STATES	C	26.0	24.7	20.0	16.1	14.1	13.8	12.9	12.5	11.7[‡]

Code: C = Data estimated to be virtually complete, representing at least 90% of the events occurring each year.

U = Data estimated to be virtually incomplete, representing less than 90% of the events occurring each year.

1. Number of deaths of infants of less than 1 year, per 1,000 live births.
2. Data tabulated by year of registration rather than of occurrence.
3. Prior to 1951 tabulated by year of registration rather than of occurrence.
4. Excluding the former Canal Zone.
5. Prior to 1957 rates excluded those dying within 24 hours of birth. Beginning in 1957 rates computed on births which are in turn estimates based on analysis of 1943 and 1953 census and the application of an assumed rate of growth.
6. Prior to 1968 rates computed on live births with an upward adjustment for undernumeration.
7. Rates computed on number of baptisms recorded in Roman Catholic Church registers, for years 1960, 1965, and 1970 while years 1975-81 are based on burial permits.
8. Excluding tropical forest Amerinds.
9. Rates for 1965-80 computed on live births recorded in the National Register of Consumers established December 31, 1964.
10. Excluding Indian jungle population estimated at 100,830 in 1961.
11. Estimate for 1975-80 prepared by the Population Division of the United Nations.
12. Rates for 1960 and 1965 were computed on live births registered during the period 1951-65 tabulated by year of occurrence.
13. Rates computed by date of occurrence for years 1975-80.

a. For 1930-59, see SALS, 23-705.
b. Data considered complete.
c. Data considered incomplete.
d. Data tabulated by year of occurrence.

SOURCE: UN-DY, 1966, table 14; 1974, table 20; 1979, table 15; 1981, table 9.

Table 706

DEATHS OF CHILDREN UNDER 5 YEARS OLD BY PRINCIPAL CAUSE,[1] 20 LC
(N, PHTI, and %)

	Country	Date	Total		Childhood Diseases			Gastritis, Enteritis, etc.			Influenza, and Pneumonia		
			Number	Rate	Number	Rate	%	Number	Rate	%	Number	Rate	%
A.	ARGENTINA	1967	26,358	1,145.2	10,175	442.1	38.6	3,408	148.1	12.9	3,016	131.0	11.4
B.	BOLIVIA	1965	14,706	~	4,451	~	30.3	798	~	5.4	315	~	2.1
C.	BRAZIL	1962	45,134	2,219.0	12,344	606.9	27.3	7,885	387.6	17.5	5,351	263.1	11.9
D.	CHILE[2]	1969	24,433	1,824.4	2,078	155.2	8.5	~	~	~	8,470	632.5	34.6
E.	COLOMBIA[6]	1967	83,935	2,398.2	17,752	507.2	21.1	18,930	540.9	22.6	9,177	262.2	10.9
F.	COSTA RICA[2]	1971	4,027	1,257.2	5,220	436.4	45.1	1,579	132.0	13.6	1,566	130.9	13.5
G.	CUBA	1965	11,575	967.8	5,220	436.4	45.1	1,579	132.0	13.6	1,566	130.9	13.5
H.	DOMINICAN REP.[2]	1970	11,433	1,679.8	2,054	301.8	18.0	2,238	328.8	19.6	398	58.5	3.5
I.	ECUADOR[2,7]	1970	30,622	2,648.8	~	~	~	4,030	348.6	13.2	3,353	290.0	11.0
J.	EL SALVADOR[2,3]	1970	15,350	2,585.4	~	~	~	~	~	~	~	~	~
K.	GUATEMALA[2]	1969	40,897	4,760.3	1,853	215.7	4.5	10,427	1,213.7	25.5	7,894	918.8	19.3
L.	HAITI	~	~	~	~	~	~	~	~	~	~	~	~
M.	HONDURAS[4]	1970	7,420	1,561.1	206	43.3	2.8	1,561	328.4	21.0	628	132.1	8.5
N.	MEXICO[2]	1971	200,308	2,318.1	~	~	~	50,429	583.6	25.2	49,219	569.6	24.6
O.	NICARAGUA[2]	1966	5,405	1,753.9	1,370	444.6	25.3	1,267	411.1	23.4	318	103.2	5.9
P.	PANAMA[2,5]	1971	3,401	1,423.3	234	97.9	6.9	409	171.2	12.0	431	180.4	12.7
Q.	PARAGUAY	1967	3,271	2,340.3	1,195	751.6	32.1	721	453.5	19.4	457	287.4	12.3
R.	PERU	1967	44,547	2,176.5	10,457	510.9	23.5	5,309	259.4	11.9	9,354	457.0	21.0
S.	URUGUAY	1967	3,339	1,186.1	1,753	622.7	52.5	308	109.4	9.2	250	88.8	7.5
T.	VENEZUELA[7]	1967	23,727	1,307.8	6,340	349.4	26.7	3,441	189.6	14.5	1,952	107.6	8.2
	UNITED STATES	1967	92,534	482.2	48,293	251.6	52.2	1,326	6.9	1.4	7,159	37.3	7.7

1. Unless otherwise stated, the causes of death have been classified according to the seventh revision of the International Classification of Diseases. The data refer to the number of deaths of children under 5 years of age with the national boundaries indicated. Fetal deaths are excluded as, in some cases, are those which occurred before the respective births or within 24 hours of birth.
2. Causes of death classified according to the eighth revision of the International Classification of Diseases.

3. Includes deaths of residents living abroad.
4. Data tabulated by year of record and not of death.
5. Excluding Canal Zone.
6. Data based on burial permits.
7. Excluding Selvatic Amerinds.

SOURCE: AC, 1974, table 202-28.

Table 707

MATERNAL DEATH RATES,[1] 11 LC, 1970–80
(Deaths PHT Live Births)

	Country	1970	1975	1977	1978	1979	1980
A.	ARGENTINA[2]	~	~	91.5	84.5	~	~
D.	CHILE[2]	125.7	122.2	107.8	94.7	74.9	~
F.	COSTA RICA[9,10]	105.6	70.5	54.6	38.3[a]	15.3[a]	24.2[a]
G.	CUBA[4,2]	48.0	68.4	49.1	45.2	~	~
I.	ECUADOR[4,5,9]	220.3	231.9	198.5	216.3	~	~
K.	GUATEMALA[2]	142.8	~	83.9	120.8	~	~
N.	MEXICO[2]	135.3	113.5	~	~	~	~
P.	PANAMA[4,6,9,10]	118.2	94.7	68.3	90.5	69.9	~
R.	PERU[3,4,7,9]	198.5	~	171.5	103.4	~	~
S.	URUGUAY[2]	44.8[a]	69.3	58.6	55.9	~	~
T.	VENEZUELA[3,4,8,9]	~	68.4	74.8	65.1	~	~
	UNITED STATES[2]	18.1	12.9	11.2	9.6	~	~

1. Deaths due to complications of pregnancy, childbirth, and the puerperium. For an alternative series, 1965-75, see SALA, 21-711.
2. All data classified by 1965 Revision.
3. Data tabulated by date of registration rather than date of occurrence.
4. Data from incomplete civil registers.
5. Excluding nomadic Indian tribes.
6. Excluding former Canal Zone.
7. Excluding Indian jungle population estimated at 100,831 in 1961.
8. Excluding Indian jungle population estimated at 31,800 in 1961.
9. Data for 1970 was classified by 1965 revision.
10. Separates data classified by the 8th and 9th Revisions of the Abbreviated List of Causes for Tabulation of Mortality in the International Classification of Diseases from 1979 on.

a. Rates based on 30 or fewer maternal deaths.

SOURCE: UN-DY, 1979, table 17; 1981, table 11.

Table 708

FIRST FIVE PRINCIPAL CAUSES OF DEATH AND RATE BY SEX, 18 LC

(All Ages)

Principal Cause of Death	Total				Male				Female			
	Rank Order	N	Rate PHTI	%	Rank Order	N	Rate PHTI	%	Rank Order	N	Rate PHTI	%
A. ARGENTINA (1979)												
All causes	**	234,926	860.2	100.0	~	134,813	988.7	100.0	~	100,113	732.1	100.0
Diseases of the heart[2]	1	75,836	277.7	32.3	1	42,453	311.3	31.5	1	33,383	244.1	33.3
Malignant neoplasms	2	40,411	148.0	17.2	2	23,404	171.6	17.4	2	17,007	124.4	17.0
Cerebrovascular disease	3	21,820	79.9	9.3	3	11,346	83.2	8.4	3	10,474	~	10.5
Accidents and adverse effects	4	11,812	43.3	5.0	4	8,446	61.9	6.3	5	3,366	24.6	3.4
Causes of perinatal mortality	5	10,881	39.8	4.6	5	6,397	46.9	4.7	4	4,484	37.8	4.5
C. BRAZIL (1979)[3]												
All causes	**	710,702	577.7	100.0	~	409,211	668.0	100.0	~	301,491	488.1	100.0
Diseases of the heart[2]	1	104,677	85.1	14.7	1	57,580	94.0	14.1	1	47,097	76.2	15.6
Infectious, parasitic, and intestinal diseases	2	72,990	59.3	10.3	2	41,965	68.5	10.3	2	31,025	50.2	10.3
Cerebrovascular disease	3	58,162	47.3	8.2	4	30,116	49.2	7.4	3	28,046	45.4	9.3
Malignant neoplasms	4	56,296	45.8	7.9	3	30,920	50.5	7.6	4	25,376	41.1	8.4
Causes of perinatal mortality	5	50,113	40.7	7.1	5	28,783	47.0	7.0	5	21,330	34.5	7.1
D. CHILE (1980)												
All causes	**	73,710	663.8	100.0	~	40,647	739.2	100.0	~	33,063	589.9	100.0
Malignant neoplasms	1	11,321	102.0	15.4	2	5,627	102.3	13.8	1	5,694	101.6	17.2
Diseases of the heart[2]	2	11,613	104.6	15.8	1	6,002	109.1	14.8	2	5,631	100.5	17.0
Cerebrovascular disease	3	6,743	60.7	9.1	3	3,165	57.6	7.9	3	3,578	63.8	10.8
Influenza and pneumonia	4	4,774	43.0	6.5	5	2,361	42.9	5.8	4	2,413	43.1	7.3
Accidents and adverse effects	5	3,681	33.2	5.0	4	2,648	48.2	6.5	~	1,033	18.4	3.1
Causes of perinatal mortality	~	3,064	27.6	4.2	~	1,763	32.1	4.3	5	1,301	23.2	3.9
E. COLOMBIA (1977)												
All causes	**	145,426	580.6	100.0	~	78,948	640.7	100.0	~	33,059	599.9	100.0
Diseases of the heart	1	23,739	94.8	16.3	1	12,293	99.8	15.6	1	11,446	89.9	17.2
Malignant neoplasms	2	13,020	52.0	9.0	4	5,996	48.7	7.6	2	7,024	55.2	10.6
Enteritis and other diarrheal diseases	4	11,375	45.4	7.8	3	6,010	48.8	7.6	3	5,365	42.2	8.1
Accidents	3	11,400	45.5	7.8	2	8,440	68.5	10.7	~	2,960	23.3	4.5
Influenza and pneumonia	5	10,308	41.2	7.1	5	5,343	43.4	6.8	4	4,965	39.0	7.5
Cerebrovascular disease	~	8,625	34.4	5.9	~	3,935	31.9	5.0	5	4,690	36.9	7.1
F. COSTA RICA (1980)												
All causes	**	9,273	413.1	100.0	~	5,481	486.3	100.0	~	3,792	339.2	100.0
Malignant neoplasms	2	1,503	66.9	16.2	2	850	75.4	15.5	2	653	58.4	17.2
Diseases of the heart[2]	1	1,608	71.6	17.3	1	901	80.0	16.4	1	707	63.2	18.6
Accidents and adverse effects	3	957	42.6	10.3	3	796	70.6	14.5	5	188	16.8	5.0
Cerebrovascular disease	4	583	26.0	6.3	5	296	26.3	5.4	3	287	25.7	7.6
Causes of perinatal mortality	5	517	23.0	5.6	4	304	27.0	5.5	4	213	19.1	5.6
G. CUBA (1978)												
All causes	**	54,949	567.1	100.0	~	31,393	634.5	100.0	~	23,556	496.8	100.0
Diseases of the heart	1	16,394	169.2	29.8	1	9,400	190.0	29.9	1	6,994	147.5	29.7
Malignant neoplasms	2	9,623	99.3	17.5	2	5,798	117.2	18.5	2	3,825	80.7	16.2
Accidents	3	6,190	63.9	11.3	3	4,051	81.9	12.9	4	2,139	45.1	9.1
Cerebrovascular disease	4	5,194	53.6	9.5	4	2,610	52.7	8.3	3	2,584	54.5	11.0
Influenza and pneumonia	5	4,343	44.8	7.9	5	2,425	49.0	7.7	5	1,918	40.4	8.1
H. DOMINICAN REP. (1977)												
All causes	**	23,127	451.3	100.0	~	12,547	494.6	100.0	~	10,480	408.2	100.0
Diseases of the heart	1	2,138	41.7	9.2	1	1,181	46.2	9.3	1	957	37.3	9.1
Enteritis and other diarrheal diseases	3	1,492	29.1	6.5	4	776	30.4	6.1	3	716	27.9	6.8
Causes of perinatal mortality	2	1,697	33.1	7.3	3	890	34.8	7.0	2	807	31.4	7.7
Malignant neoplasms	5	1,121	21.9	4.8	5	570	22.3	4.5	4	551	21.5	5.3
Cerebrovascular disease	~	939	18.3	4.1	~	485	19.0	3.8	5	454	17.7	4.3
Accidents	4	1,345	26.2	5.8	2	1,007	39.4	8.0	~	338	13.2	3.2
I. ECUADOR (1978)												
All causes	**	56,601	716.5	100.0	~	30,147	757.6	100.0	~	26,454	674.7	100.0
Enteritis and other diarrheal diseases	1	6,892	87.2	12.2	1	3,571	89.7	11.8	1	3,321	84.7	12.6
Influenza and pneumonia	4	4,602	58.3	8.1	4	2,381	59.8	7.9	3	2,221	56.6	8.4
Diseases of the heart	2	4,881	61.8	8.6	3	2,407	60.5	8.0	2	2,474	63.1	9.4
Accidents	3	4,614	58.4	8.2	2	3,458	86.9	11.5	~	1,156	29.5	4.4
Bronchitis, emphysema, and asthma	5	3,575	45.3	6.3	5	1,849	46.5	6.1	4	1,726	44.0	6.5
Malignant neoplasms	~	2,815	35.6	5.0	~	1,283	32.2	4.3	5	1,532	39.1	5.8

Table 708 (Continued)
FIRST FIVE PRINCIPAL CAUSES OF DEATH AND RATE BY SEX, 18 LC
(All Ages)

Principal Cause of Death	Total				Male				Female			
	Rank Order	N	Rate PHTI	%	Rank Order	N	Rate PHTI	%	Rank Order	N	Rate PHTI	%
J. EL SALVADOR (1974)												
All causes	**	30,533	784.9	100.0	**	17,132	888.4	100.0	**	13,401	683.2	100.0
Enteritis and other diarrheal diseases	1	4,072	104.7	13.3	1	2,191	113.6	12.8	1	1,881	95.9	14.0
Accidents	2	1,835	47.2	6.0	2	1,414	73.3	8.3	~	421	21.5	3.1
Causes of perinatal mortality	3	1,366	35.1	4.5	4	784	40.7	4.6	3	582	29.7	4.3
Homicide, legal intervention, and operations of war	4	1,283	33.0	4.2	3	1,206	62.5	7.0	~	77	3.9	.6
Influenza and pneumonia	5	1,257	32.3	4.1	5	629	32.6	3.7	2	628	32.0	4.7
Bronchitis, emphysema, asthma	~	1,089	28.0	3.6	~	553	28.7	3.2	4	536	27.3	4.0
Diseases of the heart	~	1,008	25.9	3.3	~	519	26.9	3.0	5	489	24.9	3.6
K. GUATEMALA (1980)												
All causes	**	71,360	982.9	100.0	~	40,156	1,155.9	100.0	~	31,204	824.2	100.0
Infectious, parasitic, and intestinal diseases	1	20,739	285.7	29.1	1	10,654	306.7	26.5	1	10,085	266.4	32.3
Influenza, pneumonia	2	9,961	137.2	14.0	2	5,315	153.0	13.2	2	4,640	122.6	14.9
Causes of perinatal mortality	3	9,103	125.4	12.8	3	5,191	149.4	12.9	3	3,912	103.3	12.5
Homicide	4	4,572	63.0	6.4	4	4,218	121.4	10.5	~	354	9.4	1.1
Diseases of the heart[2]	5	2,648	36.5	3.7	~	1,394	40.1	3.5	4	1,077	28.4	3.5
Malignant neoplasms	~	1,893	26.1	2.7	~	818	23.5	2.0	5	1,075	28.4	3.4
Accidents and adverse effects	~	2,111	29.1	3.0	5	1,670	48.1	4.2	~	441	11.6	1.4
M. HONDURAS (1979)												
All causes	**	18,556	520.7	100.0	~	10,255	573.9	100.0	~	8,301	467.2	100.0
Infectious, parasitic and intestinal diseases	1	3,157	88.6	17.0	1	1,718	96.1	16.8	1	1,439	81.0	17.3
Diseases of the heart[2]	3	1,483	41.6	8.0	3	790	44.2	7.7	2	693	39.0	8.3
Accidents and adverse effects	2	1,808	50.7	9.7	2	1510	84.5	14.7	5	298	16.8	3.6
Influenza, pneumonia	4	644	18.1	3.5	4	336	18.8	3.3	4	308	17.3	3.7
Malignant neoplasms	5	556	15.6	3.0	5	244	13.7	2.4	3	332	18.7	4.0
N. MEXICO (1976)												
All causes	**	455,660	731.1	100.0	~	252,563	802.6	100.0	~	201,549	653.0	100.0
Influenza, pneumonia	1	61,096	98.0	13.4	2	32,563	103.5	12.0	1	28,379	92.0	14.1
Enteritis and other diarrheal diseases	2	51,235	82.2	11.2	3	26,931	85.6	10.7	2	24,172	78.3	12.0
Diseases of the heart	3	48,084	77.2	10.6	4	24,198	76.9	9.6	3	23,973	77.7	11.9
Accidents	4	42,307	67.9	9.3	1	32,584	103.6	12.9	5	9,507	30.8	4.7
Malignant neoplasms	5	22,635	36.3	5.0	~	9,845	31.3	3.9	4	12,756	41.3	6.3
Causes of perinatal mortality	~	22,578	36.2	5.0	5	13,300	42.3	5.3	~	9,181	29.7	4.6
O. NICARAGUA (1979)												
All causes	**	12,492	504.3	100.0	~	7,012	618.2	100.0	~	5,480	465.1	100.0
Diseases of the heart	2	1,404	60.7	11.2	3	681	60.1	9.7	2	723	61.4	13.2
Enteritis and other diarrheal diseases	1	1,702	73.6	13.6	1	973	85.8	13.9	1	729	61.9	13.3
Accidents	3	932	40.3	7.5	2	755	66.6	10.8	~	177	15.0	3.2
Malignant neoplasms	~	395	17.1	3.2	~	133	11.7	1.9	3	262	22.2	4.8
Homicide, legal intervention, and operations of war	4	693	30.0	5.5	4	606	53.5	8.6	~	87	7.4	1.6
Influenza, pneumonia	5	506	21.9	4.1	5	279	24.6	4.0	4	227	19.3	4.1
Cerebrovascular disease	~	441	19.1	3.5	~	214	18.9	3.1	4	227	19.3	4.1
P. PANAMA (1980)												
All causes	**	7,959	432.6	100.0	**	4,573	489.6	100.0	**	3,386	373.7	100.0
Diseases of the heart[2]	1	1,278	69.5	16.1	1	722	77.3	15.8	1	556	61.4	16.4
Accidents	3	724	39.3	9.1	2	546	58.5	11.9	5	178	19.6	5.3
Malignant neoplasms	2	1,000	54.3	12.6	3	528	56.5	11.5	2	472	52.1	13.9
Cerebrovascular disease	5	550	29.9	6.9	5	303	32.4	6.6	4	247	27.3	7.3
Infectious, parasitic and intestinal diseases	4	634	34.5	8.0	4	348	37.3	7.6	3	286	31.6	8.4

Table 708 (Continued)

FIRST FIVE PRINCIPAL CAUSES OF DEATH AND RATE BY SEX, 18 LC[1]

(All Ages)

Principal Cause of Death	Total				Male				Female			
	Rank Order	N	Rate PHTI	%	Rank Order	N	Rate PHTI	%	Rank Order	N	Rate PHTI	%
Q. PARAGUAY (1980)												
All causes	**	13,059	743.7	100.0	~	6,812	786.6	100.0	~	6,247	701.9	100.0
Diseases of the heart[2]	2	1,943	110.6	14.8	3	974	112.5	14.3	2	969	108.9	15.5
Infectious, parasitic, and intestinal diseases	3	1,838	104.7	14.1	2	1,007	116.3	14.8	3	831	93.4	13.3
Cerebrovascular disease	4	1,066	60.7	8.2	4	549	63.4	8.1	5	517	58.1	8.3
Malignant neoplasms	5	948	54.0	7.3	5	413	47.7	6.1	4	535	60.1	8.6
Influenza, pneumonia	~	915	~	~	~	~	~	~	~	~	~	~
Accidents	1	2,333	132.9	17.9	1	1,177	135.9	17.3	1	1,156	129.9	18.5
R. PERU (1977)												
All causes	**	81,806	486.4	100.0	~	42,439	503.4	100.0	~	39,367	469.3	100.0
Influenza and pneumonia	1	12,912	76.8	15.8	1	6,646	78.3	15.7	1	6,266	74.7	15.9
Enteritis and other diarrheal diseases	2	9,340	55.5	11.4	2	4,776	56.6	11.3	2	4,564	54.4	11.6
Malignant neoplasms	3	5,722	34.0	7.0	5	2,585	30.7	6.1	3	3,137	37.4	8.0
Diseases of the heart	4	5,336	31.7	6.5	4	2,628	31.2	6.2	4	2,708	32.3	6.9
Accidents	5	4,190	24.9	5.1	3	3,037	36.0	7.2	~	1,153	13.7	2.9
Bronchitis, emphysema, tuberculosis	~	4,053	24.1	5.0	~	2,255	26.7	8.3	5	1,798	21.4	4.6
S. URUGUAY (1978)												
All causes	**	28,041	979.1	100.0	~	15,608	1,112.1	100.0	~	12,425	850.7	100.0
Disease of the heart	1	6,802	237.5	24.3	1	3,872	275.9	24.8	1	2,930	200.6	23.6
Malignant neoplasms	2	5,993	209.3	21.4	2	3,522	250.9	22.6	2	2,471	169.2	19.9
Cerebrovascular disease	3	3,430	119.8	12.2	3	1,500	106.9	9.6	3	1,930	132.1	15.5
Accidents	4	1,262	44.1	4.5	4	836	59.6	5.4	5	423	29.0	3.4
Causes of perinatal mortality	5	1,075	37.5	3.8	5	627	44.7	4.0	4	445	30.5	3.6
T. VENEZUELA (1978)												
All causes	**	72,470	552.3	100.0	~	41,197	627.0	100.0	~	31,273	477.3	100.0
Diseases of the heart	1	10,827	82.5	14.9	2	6,020	91.6	14.6	1	4,807	73.4	15.4
Accidents	2	8,573	65.3	11.8	1	6,717	102.2	16.3	~	1,856	28.3	5.9
Malignant neoplasms	3	7,009	53.4	9.7	3	3,314	50.4	8.0	2	3,695	56.4	11.8
Causes of perinatal mortality	4	5,308	40.5	7.3	4	3,097	47.1	7.5	3	2,211	33.7	7.1
Cerebrovascular disease	5	4,223	32.2	5.8	~	2,051	31.2	5.0	4	2,172	33.2	6.9
Influenza and pneumonia	~	4,170	31.8	5.8	5	2,183	33.2	5.3	5	1,987	30.3	6.4
UNITED STATES (1979)												
All causes	**	1,913,841	852.2	100.0	~	1,044,959	957.1	100.0	~	868,882	753.0	100.0
Diseases of the heart[2]	1	737,281	328.3	38.5	1	397,332	363.9	38.0	1	339,949	294.6	39.1
Malignant neoplasms	2	403,395	179.6	21.1	2	220,015	201.5	21.1	2	183,380	158.9	21.1
Cerebrovascular disease	3	169,488	75.5	8.9	4	70,439	64.5	6.7	3	99,049	85.8	11.4
Accidents and adverse effects	4	105,312	46.9	5.5	3	74,403	68.1	7.1	4	30,909	26.8	3.6
Influenza, pneumonia	5	45,030	20.1	2.4	5	23,725	21.7	2.3	5	21,305	18.5	2.5

1. For deaths by all causes in previous years, see SALA, 23-707.
2. Includes chronic rheumatic heart disease, acute myocardial infarction, other ischaemic heart diseases, diseases of pulmonary circulation, and other forms of heart disease and atherosclerosis.
3. Rates based on 1980 population figures.

SOURCE: PAHO-HC, 1977-80, p. 270; adapted from WHO-WHSA, 1982, table 7A; 1983, tables 8, 9A.

Table 709

REPORTED CASES AND DEATHS FROM DIPHTHERIA, 20 LC, 1973-76

	Country	Cases N 1973	1974	1975	1976	Cases PHTI 1973	1974	1975	1976	Deaths N 1973	1974	1975	1976	Deaths PHTI 1973	1974	1975	1976
A.	ARGENTINA	325	290	148	183	1.3	1.2	.6	.7	~	~	~	~	~	~	~	~
B.	BOLIVIA	413	125	229	117	7.7	2.3	4.1	2.0	~	~	~	~	~	~	~	~
C.	BRAZIL	5,380	3,636	4,004	5,009	5.4	3.6	3.8	4.6	~	~	~	~	~	~	~	~
D.	CHILE	544	412	428	491	5.5	4.1	4.2	4.7	59	43	37	38	.6	.4	.4	.4
E.	COLOMBIA	461	303	260	280	2.1	1.3	1.1	1.2	143	90	77	~	.6	.4	.3	~
F.	COSTA RICA	25	9	6	#	1.3	.5	.3	#	5	#	#	#	.3	#	#	#
G.	CUBA	#	#	1	1	#	#	#	#	#	#	#	#	.3	#	#	#
H.	DOMINICAN REP.	291	359	299	433	6.6	7.9	6.4	9.0	88	72	46	~	2.0	1.6	1.0	~
I.	ECUADOR	148	107	40	33	2.2	1.6	.6	.5	23	19	~	~	.3	.3	~	~
J.	EL SALVADOR[a]	38	14	4	#	1.0	.4	.1	#	49	26	~	18	1.3	.7	~	.4
K.	GUATEMALA	50	17	7	4	.9	.3	.1	.1	~	~	17	~	~	~	~	~
L.	HAITI	34	15	31	25	.8	.3	.7	.5	~	~	~	~	~	~	.3	~
M.	HONDURAS	1	2	2	3	#	.1	.1	.1	1	#	#	~	#	#	#	~
N.	MEXICO	119	64	37	33	.2	.1	.1	.1	109	108	~	~	.2	.2	~	~
O.	NICARAGUA	1	6	#	#	#	.3	#	#	#	#	~	~	#	.2	~	~
P.	PANAMA	3	2	#	#	.2	.1	#	#	#	4	~	~	#	.2	~	~
Q.	PARAGUAY[a,b]	47	29	13	11	3.5	2.1	.9	.7	15	10	6	7	1.1	.7	.4	.5
R.	PERU[a]	86	118	138	109	1.1	1.5	1.8	1.1	~	~	~	~	~	~	~	~
S.	URUGUAY	#	3	1	#	#	.1	#	#	#	1	#	#	#	#	#	#
T.	VENEZUELA[a]	98	92	205	230	1.1	1.0	2.1	1.9	10	11	18	~	.1	.1	.2	~
	UNITED STATES	228	272	307	128	.1	.1	.1	.1	10	5	5	~	#	#	#	~

a. Reporting area, for case data, except El Salvador, 1975-76, and Venezuela, 1976.
b. Area of information, for death data.

SOURCE: PAHO-HC, 1973-1976, table III-3.

Table 710

REPORTED CASES AND RATES OF AMEBIASIS AND BACILLARY DYSENTERY, 17 LC, 1973-76

	Country	Amebiasis N 1973	1974	1975	1976	Amebiasis PHTI 1973	1974	1975	1976	Bacillary Dysentery N 1973	1974	1975	1976	Bacillary Dysentery PHTI 1973	1974	1975	1976
A.	ARGENTINA[a]	~	~	~	~	~	~	~	~	139,439	144,811	~	~	564.1	578.1	~	~
B.	BOLIVIA	852	1,093	831	927	16.0	20.0	14.8	16.0	859	628	681	882	16.1	11.5	12.1	15.2
D.	CHILE	237	200	192	633	2.4	2.0	1.9	6.1	22	~	31	5	.2	~	.3	#
F.	COSTA RICA	#	78	35	53	#	4.1	1.8	2.6	928[b]	21	16	16	49.6[b]	1.1	.8	.8
G.	CUBA	1,528	1,328	1,223	1,552	16.9	14.5	13.1	16.4	3	3	1	2	#	#	#	#
H.	DOMINICAN REP.	~	~	~	~	~	~	~	~	7,017	~	~	~	158.3	~	~	~
J.	EL SALVADOR[c]	4,539[d]	4,327[d]	3,662	3,223	122.4[d]	112.4[d]	91.4	78.2	4,539[e]	~	~	~	122.4[e]	~	~	~
K.	GUATEMALA	4,122	5,569	9,158	8,897	71.8	94.2	150.6	142.2	2,157	1,532	1,991	2,194	37.6	25.9	32.7	35.1
L.	HAITI	3,138	2,643	2,930	1,963	70.7	58.6	68.9	42.1	213	220	378	356	4.8	4.9	8.2	7.6
M.	HONDURAS	9,333	12,720	17,874	18,046	359.0	474.6	649.4	637.4	8,644	5,265	4,006	2,276	332.5	196.5	145.5	80.4
N.	MEXICO	58,926	67,198	86,556	100,306	104.9	115.6	143.9	160.9	8,320	6,331	4,793	4,199	14.8	10.9	8.0	6.7
O.	NICARAGUA	7,422	10,936	5,801	4,403	368.3	524.8	269.2	197.2	1,782	2,171	2,386	1,788	88.4	104.2	110.7	80.1
P.	PANAMA	442	350	495	704	28.2	21.6	29.7	41.0	36	36	102	73	2.3	2.2	6.1	4.2
Q.	PARAGUAY[c]	#	4	18	13	#	.3	1.2	.9	162	184	192	137	12.1	13.1	13.2	9.1
R.	PERU[c]	561	438	1,546	1,006	6.9	5.4	19.8	9.9	2,938	2,324	3,818	3,553	36.2	28.8	48.9	35.1
S.	URUGUAY	#	#	#	#	#	#	#	#	#	1	#	#	#	#	#	#
T.	VENEZUELA[c]	13,737	15,717	13,079	10,314	156.1	171.8	137.1	83.4	467	474	296	11	5.3	5.2	3.1	.1
	UNITED STATES	2,235	2,743	2,775	2,906	1.1	1.3	1.3	1.4	22,642	22,600	16,584	13,140	10.8	10.7	7.8	6.1

a. Includes dysentery, all forms.
b. Includes dysentery, unspecified.
c. Reporting area, except El Salvador, 1975-1976, and Venezuela, 1976.
d. Includes dysentery.
e. Includes amebiasis.

SOURCE: PAHO-HC, 1973-1976, table III-1.

Table 711

MARRIAGES, 19 LC, 1965–81

Country	Code	N 1965	N 1970	N 1975	N 1977	N 1978	N 1979	N 1980	N 1981	Rate PTI 1965	1970	1975	1977	1978	1979	1980	1981
A. ARGENTINA	C	152,625	174,137	~	182,497	~	~	~	~	6.8	7.3	~	7.0	~	~	~	~
B. BOLIVIA	U	20,838	~	24,315	28,233	29,851	~	~	~	4.8	1.2	4.3	5.5	5.6	~	~	~
C. BRAZIL[6]	U	~	109,027	840,614	882,360	126,801	936,986	948,164	~	~	7.7	7.4	7.0	7.2	7.3	7.7	~
D. CHILE[1]	C	64,922	71,631	76,205	74,302	77,499	80,072	86,001	~	7.5	~	7.4	7.0	7.8	~	7.8	7.5‡
E. COLOMBIA[1,4]	U	86,722	110,704	72,370	88,401	~	~	~	~	4.8	5.2	3.1	3.5	~	~	~	~
F. COSTA RICA	C	8,562	11,024	14,683	15,422	16,453	~	17,527	~	5.7	6.4	7.5	6.5	6.0	6.7	5.3	~
G. CUBA	C	67,323	110,982	65,416‡	62,113	58,361	62,256	~	72,853‡	8.8	13.1	7.0‡	4.4	4.3	4.5	4.8	7.5‡
H. DOMINICAN REP.[1]	C	12,712	16,987	20,411	22,000	22,000	24,000	29,000	~	3.5	4.2	4.4	~	5.9	5.7	~	~
I. ECUADOR[5,7]	U	30,362	35,558	37,858	47,228	46,600	46,278	~	~	5.9	5.8	5.4	6.2	4.1	4.3	~	~
J. EL SALVADOR	C	10,315	11,763	16,628	17,766	17,833	19,280	22,763	~	3.5	3.3	4.2	4.2	4.2	4.2	4.1	~
K. GUATEMALA	C	15,112	18,150	24,354	28,894	28,493	29,290	29,519	~	3.4	3.6	4.0	4.4	4.1	~	~	~
M. HONDURAS[1]	C	7,611	9,704	11,254	14,039	14,056	~	17,174	~	3.5	3.9	3.6	4.2	7.0	6.5	~	~
N. MEXICO[1]	C	293,227	356,658	472,091	466,788	463,157	444,528	~	~	6.9	7.0	7.8	7.3	5.3	3.9	6.3	~
O. NICARAGUA[1]	C	6,224	~	~	12,290	12,742	10,373	10,252	~	3.8	~	4.8	5.3	5.2	5.6	5.4	~
P. PANAMA[2]	C	4,710	7,324	8,042	8,804	9,132	9,949	17,259	~	4.0	5.1	5.4	5.2	5.9	5.8	5.4	~
Q. PARAGUAY[1]	U	8,065	13,103	14,313	18,354	17,618	17,786	~	~	4.0	5.7	~	6.4	~	~	~	~
R. PERU[1,7]	C	45,160	50,810	~	37,114	~	~	~	~	3.9	3.7	~	2.3	~	~	~	~
S. URUGUAY[3]	C	20,976	23,668	24,404	22,368	22,728	22,929	22,337	22,671‡	7.7	8.2	8.7	7.8	7.9	7.0	7.7	7.7‡
T. VENEZUELA	~	49,523	60,128	85,662	90,063	92,870	95,000	~	~	5.7	5.9	10.0‡	10.0	10.5	10.6	10.4‡	10.6‡
UNITED STATES	C	1,800,207	2,158,802	2,127,000‡	2,178,367	2,282,272	2,331,337	2,359,000‡	2,438,000‡	9.3	10.5	10.0‡	10.0	~	~	~	~

Code: C = Data estimated to be virtually complete, representing at least 90% of the events
occurring each year.

U = Data estimated to be incomplete, representing less than 90% of the events
occurring each year.

1. Data tabulated according to year of registration rather than year of marriage.
2. Excludes marriages in Canal Zone and indigenous villages.
3. Data for years 1965 and 1970 are considered incomplete.
4. Except for Bogotá, data are only for marriages recorded in Roman Catholic Church
   registers.
5. Excludes marriages in indigenous jungle population.
6. For state capitals only except for the 1965 data.
7. Includes marriages in indigenous jungle population; estimated in 1961 at 31,800.

SOURCE: UN-DY, 1969, table 47; 1974, table 11; 1979, table 23; 1981, table 17.

Table 712

DIVORCES, 19 LC, 1965–81

N

	Country	Code	1965	1970	1975	1977	1978	1979	1980	1981
A.	ARGENTINA[1]	~	**	**	**	**	**	**	**	
B.	BOLIVIA[1]	~	**	**	**	**	**	**	**	**
C.	BRAZIL[1]	~	**	**	**	**	**	**	**	**
D.	CHILE[1]	~	**	**	**	**	**	**	**	**
E.	COLOMBIA[1]	~	**	**	**	**	**	**	**	**
F.	COSTA RICA	C	181	226	318	969	~	~	~	
G.	CUBA[7]	C	8,937	24,813	22,819‡	23,078	25,397	24,892	~	28,259‡
H.	DOMINICAN REP.[2]	C	1,199	3,754	9,292	~	8,000	9,000	~	~
I.	ECUADOR[6]	~	1,300	1,291	1,679	2,269	2,096	2,279	≈	~
J.	EL SALVADOR	C	671	847	1,286	1,452	1,528	1,576	1,549	~
K.	GUATEMALA[2]	C	436	674	912	909	951	1,086	~	~
M.	HONDURAS[2]	C	363	454	672	771	727	~	~	~
N.	MEXICO[2]	C	24,705	28,779	16,791	21,269	21,394	~	~	~
O.	NICARAGUA[1]	~	292	~	~	601	639	~	~	~
P.	PANAMA[3]	C	579	574	949	1,030	863	966	759	~
Q.	PARAGUAY[1]	~	**	**	**	**	**	**	**	**
R.	PERU[4]	~	1,803	~	~	~	~	~	~	~
S.	URUGUAY[2,8,9]	C	2,500	2,927	3,430	5,044	3,676	3,121	3,120	4,392‡
T.	VENEZUELA[4]	~	2,292	2,467	4,377	5,050	4,765	4,852	~	~
	UNITED STATES[5]	U	479,000	708,000	1,026,000	1,191,000	1,130,000	1,181,000	1,182,000	1,219,000

Rate PTI

	Country	Code	1965	1970	1975	1977	1978	1979	1980	1981
A.	ARGENTINA[1]	~	**	**	**	**	**	**	**	**
B.	BOLIVIA[1]	~	**	**	**	**	**	**	**	**
C.	BRAZIL[1]	~	**	**	**	**	**	**	**	**
D.	CHILE[1]	~	**	**	**	**	**	**	**	**
E.	COLOMBIA[1]	~	**	**	**	**	**	**	**	**
F.	COSTA RICA	C	.12	.13	.16	.47	~	~	~	
G.	CUBA[7]	C	1.17	2.92	2.45‡	2.40	2.62	2.55	~	2.89‡
H.	DOMINICAN REP.[2]	C	.33	.92	1.98	~	1.56	1.71	~	~
I.	ECUADOR[6]	~	.25	.21	.24	.30	.26	.28	~	~
J.	EL SALVADOR	C	.23	.24	.32	.34	.35	.35	.33	~
K.	GUATEMALA[2]	C	.10	.13	.15	.14	.14	.15	~	~
M.	HONDURAS[2]	C	.17	.18	.24	.23	.21	~	~	~
N.	MEXICO[2]	C	.58	.57	.28	.33	.32	~	~	~
O.	NICARAGUA[1]	~	.18	**	**	.26	.26	~	~	~
P.	PANAMA[3]	C	.49	.40	.57	.60	.49	.54	.28	~
Q.	PARAGUAY[1]	~	**	**	**	**	**	**	**	**
R.	PERU[4]	~	.15	~	~	~	~	~	~	~
S.	URUGUAY[2,8,9]	C	.92	1.01	1.22	1.17	1.28	1.08	1.08	1.50‡
T.	VENEZUELA[4]	~	.26	.24	.37	.40	.36	.36	~	~
	UNITED STATES[5]	U	2.47	3.47	4.82	5.03	5.18	5.36	5.19	5.30

Code: C = Data estimated to be virtually complete, representing at least 90% of the events occurring each year.

U = Data estimated to be incomplete, representing less than 90% of the events occurring each year.

1. There are no legal provisions for "divorce."
2. Data tabulated according to year of registration and not year of divorce.
3. Excludes divorces in the Canal Zone and among indigenous tribal Indian population numbering 62,187 in 1960.
4. Excludes indigenous jungle population.
5. Estimates based on incomplete data for some states; includes annulments.
6. Excludes nomadic Indian tribes.
7. Data for years 1965 and 1970 are considered incomplete.
8. Includes annulments since 1970.
9. Data for 1965 are considered incomplete.

SOURCE: UN-DY, 1969, table 49; 1974, table 13; 1979, table 25; 1981, table 19.

CHAPTER 8

HEALTH, NUTRITION, FAMILY PLANNING, AND WELFARE

Figure 8:1

A. ARGENTINA 1955-BASED INDEX OF FOOD/C PRODUCTION, 20 LRC, 1952–81

(1955 = 100)

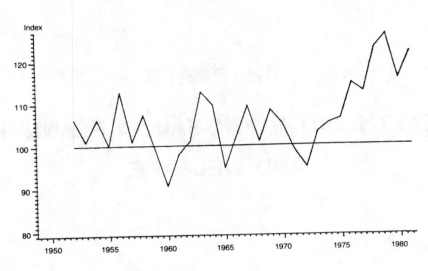

Continued in SALA, 23-35:23 through 35:44.

Figure 8:2

A. ARGENTINA PC IN FOOD/C PRODUCTION, 20 LRC, 1953–81

(0 = Equilibrium between Food Production and Population)

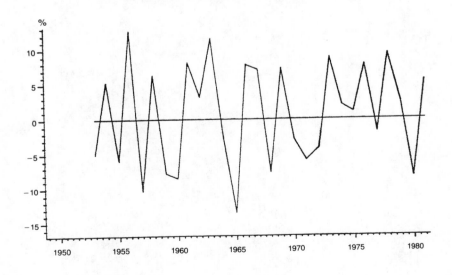

Continued in SALA, 23-35:1 through 35:22.

Table 800

SUMMARY OF HEALTH, EDUCATION, AND COMMUNICATION (HEC) INDICATORS, 1940-80

PART I: HEC COMPONENTS

Health (H), 5 items

> Life expectancy at birth—LIFE
> Infant mortality rate (deaths under one year of age per 1,000 live births)—INFANT
> Persons per hospital bed—BEDS
> Population per physician—DOCTORS
> Persons per dentist—DENTISTS

Education (E), 4 items

> Literacy percentage for population age 15 and over—Literate
> Percentage of school-age population 7-14 enrolled in primary school—Primary
> Students enrolled in secondary school as a percentage of school-age population 13-18—Secondary
> College enrollment (including, professional, technical, and vocational schools) as a percentage of primary school enrollment—College

Communication (C), 3 items

> Newspaper circulation, copies per 1,000 persons—News
> Number of telephones per 100 persons—Telephone
> Number of persons per motor vehicle (autos, buses, trucks) in use—Motor

PART II: HEC INDEXES[1] AND INDEX REDUCTION RATES (IRR) FOR LATIN AMERICA
(0% = EQUALITY)

Health Indexes

Year	LIFE	INFANT	BEDS	DOCTORS	DENTISTS	Subtotals and Total Indexes[2]	IRR[3]
1940	39.5	67.8	81.5	73.0	81.9	68.7	- -
1950	26.5	73.6	82.8	77.4	82.7	68.6	−.1
1960	18.6	70.5	79.1	73.5	80.6	64.5	−6.0
1970	14.1	74.4	70.7	69.6	69.9	59.7	−7.4
1980	12.2	80.3	64.3	64.1	64.0	57.0	−4.5

Education Indexes

Year	LITERATE	PRIMARY	SECONDARY	COLLEGE		
1940	48.5	44.4	89.0	90.7	68.2	- -
1950	43.3	49.0	90.4	85.0	66.9	−1.9
1960	32.7	36.0	83.3	80.9	58.2	−13.0
1970	26.3	22.2	69.9	82.2	50.2	−13.7
1980	19.2	16.2	58.8	82.5	44.2	−12.0

Communication Indexes

Year	NEWS	TELEPHONE	MOTOR		
1940	78.4	93.7	98.4	90.2	- -
1950	82.2	95.0	97.9	91.7	1.7
1960	76.4	95.0	97.1	89.5	−2.4
1970	74.3	94.9	95.6	88.3	−1.3
1980	70.2	92.7	91.7	84.9	-3.6

Total Index

Year		IRR
1940	73.9	- -
1950	73.8	−.1
1960	68.6	−7.0
1970	63.7	−7.1
1980	59.7	−6.3

1. The indexes (weighted by population in each Latin American country) presented here are calculated as the scaled percentage decrease necessary in each year to bring the United States and Latin America to equality. (The scale occurs in the process of calculating the percentage decrease between high and low absolute numbers because there is a ceiling of 100% on possible changes.) At .0 equality will exist. In 1940 the total index was 73.9, closing to 63.7 in 1970. If during the 1970s to 1990s the Index Reduction Rate (IRR) closes linearly at the same rate as during the 1950s and 1960s, the index will stand at about 59.2 by 1980 and 51.1 by the year 2000.
2. Arithmetic mean for 5 Health items, 4 Education items, 3 Communication items, and 12 HEC items in each decade. Each item is equally weighted, thus giving Health an implicit weight of 42% in the total index, Education 33%, and Communication 25%.
3. The IRR is calculated here as the rate of change in the subtotals and totals, summary index scores from decade to decade. A minus sign (−) indicates that the index is improving, i.e., the gap is narrowing between Latin America and United States.

SOURCE: James W. Wilkie, *The Narrowing Gap: Primary Social Change in the Americas since 1940*. Statistical Abstract of Latin America Supplement Series (Los Angeles: UCLA Latin American Center Publications, forthcoming).

Table 801

HEC TOTAL INDEX BY COUNTRY,[1] 20 LRC, 1940–80

(Average for 12 indicators; 0 = U.S. Equality with Latin America)

	Country	1940	1950	1960	1970	1980
A.	ARGENTINA	46.1	46.4	39.9	34.0	38.2
B.	BOLIVIA	83.9	79.8	76.1	70.6	67.8
C.	BRAZIL	74.7	73.9	68.5	61.5	56.4
D.	CHILE	63.5	61.8	57.9	54.1	55.1
E.	COLOMBIA	77.3	73.8	69.7	65.6	61.7
F.	COSTA RICA	69.3	65.8	60.9	57.2	49.9
G.	CUBA	58.7	57.5	55.2	54.3	40.3
H.	DOMINICAN REP.	80.4	77.5	70.2	66.7	67.2
I.	ECUADOR	80.2	76.3	71.2	67.7	60.6
J.	EL SALVADOR	79.9	78.8	74.1	69.7	69.9
K.	GUATEMALA	83.8	81.2	79.1	77.0	76.1
L.	HAITI	88.3	89.7	86.7	86.2	83.9
M.	HONDURAS	82.9	81.0	77.2	71.7	73.1
N.	MEXICO	74.1	75.5	70.1	63.8	54.9
O.	NICARAGUA	80.3	76.9	73.3	68.9	66.8
P.	PANAMA	66.9	61.9	60.3	56.6	48.0
Q.	PARAGUAY	77.0	71.8	67.9	67.3	63.8
R.	PERU	77.5	75.5	67.6	61.2	56.8
S.	URUGUAY	44.2	42.3	40.6	40.4	34.9
T.	VENEZUELA	75.2	69.9	61.2	55.8	49.2
	LATIN AMERICA[2]	73.9	73.8	68.6	63.7	59.7

1. The index presented here is calculated as the scaled percentage decrease necessary to bring the United States and Latin America to equality. (The scale occurs in the process of calculating the percentage decrease between high and low absolute numbers because there is a ceiling of 100% on possible changes.) At .0 no index gap will exist. In 1940 the 12-item average was 73.9 closing to 63.7 in 1970.
2. Data are weighted by the population of each Latin American country.

SOURCE: See table 800.

Table 802

ADJUSTED PHYSICAL QUALITY OF LIFE INDEX (PQLI),[1] 20 LRC, 1950 TO MID 1970s

(Zero = No Gap with U.S. Best Performance Expected by the Year 2000 for Arithmetic Average of Three Equally Weighted Items)[2]

	Country	1950	1960	1970[a]	Mid-1970s
A.	ARGENTINA	12	9	8	10
B.	BOLIVIA	~	~	~	56
C.	BRAZIL	36	28	27	29
D.	CHILE	27	26	16	16
E.	COLOMBIA	42	27[g]	20	23
F.	COSTA RICA	22	13[f]	7[j]	10
G.	CUBA	~	~	~	10
H.	DOMINICAN REP.	42[k]	29	30	31
I.	ECUADOR	41[b]	31[c]	26	26
J.	EL SALVADOR	38	30[e]	29[j]	31
K.	GUATEMALA	53	47[e]	41	41
L.	HAITI	~	68	56	55
M.	HONDURAS	~	~	~	42
N.	MEXICO	34[k]	26[d]	22	20
O.	NICARAGUA	47	38[f]	~	40
P.	PANAMA	21	18	12[i]	16
Q.	PARAGUAY	~	~	~	20
R.	PERU	~	33[e]	27	30
S.	URUGUAY	~	6[h]	~	9
T.	VENEZUELA	31	22[e]	14[i]	16
	LATIN AMERICA[3]	~	~	~	25

1. Converted here from "100 = no gap" to "0 = no gap" according to the following formula: (100) minus (unadjusted PQLI) minus (U.S. figure).
2. The PQLI includes 3 items: life expectancy at age 1, infant mortality, literacy of persons age 15 and over.

   a. Compared to United States in 1971.

b. 1952.	d. 1959.	f. 1963.	h. 1966.	j. 1973.
c. 1962.	e. 1961.	g. 1964.	i. 1971.	k. 1951.

3. Data are weighted by the population of each Latin American country.

SOURCE: 1950-70 data adapted from Morris David Morris, *Measuring the Condition of the World's Poor: The Physical Quality of Life Index* (New York: Pergamon, 1979), pp. 150-152; and *The United States and World Development: Agenda 1979* (New York: Praeger, 1979), pp. 169-171. Mid-1970s data adapted from *Agenda 1979*, pp. 158-166, except total here calculated with population weights for each country.

Table 803

PHYSICIANS, NURSES, AND NURSING AUXILIARIES, 20 LRC

| | Country | Year | Physicians | | Year | Nursing Personnel | | | |
| | | | N | PTI | | Nurses | | Nursing Auxiliaries | |
						N	PTI	N	PTI
A.	ARGENTINA	1979	71,253	26.7	1977	18,658	7.2	22,153	8.5
B.	BOLIVIA	1974	2,583	4.7	1980	955	1.7	2,498	4.5
C.	BRAZIL	1980	106,479	8.7	1980	22,895	1.9	153,214	12.6
D.	CHILE	1979	5,671	5.2	1980	3,596	3.2	22,961	20.7
E.	COLOMBIA	1977	12,720	5.1	1980	3,010	1.1	27,760	10.2
F.	COSTA RICA	1979	1,506	6.9	1980	1,226	5.5	4,884	21.9
G.	CUBA[1]	1979	13,531	13.8	1980	14,156	14.3	13,037	13.2
H.	DOMINICAN REP.[1]	1976	1,203	2.5	1980	500	.9	3,981	7.3
I.	ECUADOR‡	1977	4,660	6.2	1980	2,200	2.6	10,000	12.0
J.	EL SALVADOR	1980	1,491	3.1	1980	1,715	3.8	3,521	7.7
K.	GUATEMALA[1]	1979	819	1.2	1980	811	1.1	4,088	5.6
L.	HAITI[1]	1979	600	1.2	1980	771	1.5	1,128	2.3
M.	HONDURAS	1979	1,141	3.2	1980	545	1.5	3,000	8.1
N.	MEXICO	1974	46,473	8.0	1980	39,189	5.4	58,877	8.2
O.	NICARAGUA[1]	1980	1,212	4.5	1980	1,017	3.7	4,306	15.7
P.	PANAMA	1978	1,550	8.5	1980	2,132	11.0	3,524	18.2
Q.	PARAGUAY	1979	1,700	5.7	1980	521	1.7	1,421	4.6
R.	PERU	1979	11,682	6.8	1980	8,350	4.6	3,524	1.9
S.	URUGUAY	1979	5,400	18.8	1979	15,200	52.8	~	~
T.	VENEZUELA	1978	14,771	11.3	1978	9,077	6.9	28,984	22.1
	LATIN AMERICA	**a	306,455	9.2	**a	146,524	6.0	372,861	15.3
	UNITED STATES	1980	414,916	18.2	1980	1,164,000	51.1	~	~

1. Physicians in government services.

a. Total for the 20 countries for years given.

SOURCE: PAHO-HC, 1977-80, table IV-5; WHO-WHSA, 1983, table 18.

Table 804

POPULATION PER PHYSICIAN 20 L, 1960–80

	Country	1960	1969	1970	1971	1972	1973	1974	1975	1976	1977	1978	1979	1980
A.	ARGENTINA	680	518	~	~	495	~	~	521	~	~	~	383	~
B.	BOLIVIA	5,756	~	2,231	~	2,342	~	2,117	~	~	~	~	~	~
C.	BRAZIL	2,181	1,958	~	~	2,025	2,025	1,648	~	~	~	~	~	~
D.	CHILE	1,661	1,842	~	~	~	1,836	~	~	2,117	1,636	2,069b	1,935	~
E.	COLOMBIA	2,632	~	2,331	~	2,282	2,184	~	1,818	~	1,969	~	~	~
F.	COSTA RICA	2,729	1,805	~	~	2,663	1,413	~	1,524	~	1,396d	2,044	1,441	~
G.	CUBA	1,021a	1,395	1,392	1,408	1,360	~	1,121	~	~	~	673b	722	~
H.	DOMINICAN REP.	7,149	~	2,244	2,189	2,088	1,866	~	~	402b	~	~	~	~
I.	ECUADOR	2,609	2,930	2,900	~	~	2,165	~	2,017	~	1,622	~	~	~
J.	EL SALVADOR	5,232	5,218	4,065	4,477	3,934	4,063	~	3,592	3,745	3,685	3,640	3,491	3,179
K.	GUATEMALA	4,644	~	~	4,515	~	4,338	~	~	~	~	~	8,608b	~
L.	HAITI	34,325	14,055	15,666	~	13,264	~	~	~	5,936b	~	8,198b	~	~
M.	HONDURAS	5,132	4,046	3,668	~	3,503	~	3,352	2,992	~	3,297	3,176	3,120	~
N.	MEXICO	1,798	~	1,480	~	1,385	~	1,251	~	~	~	~	~	~
O.	NICARAGUA	2,809	1,963	1,727	~	1,516	1,437	1,713	1,543	1,592	~	~	2,579c	2,228b
P.	PANAMA	2,701	1,787	1,701	1,491	1,441	1,339	1,234	1,335	~	1,262	1,129	~	~
Q.	PARAGUAY	1,996	1,800	2,529	~	2,270	~	1,875	1,189	2,196	~	~	1,747	~
R.	PERU	1,975	1,872	~	~	1,751	~	~	~	~	1,556	1,525	1,480	~
S.	URUGUAY	821	~	~	921	911	~	~	700	~	~	~	533	~
T.	VENEZUELA	1,513	1,100	1,053	1,065	997	866	~	915	870	875	888	~	~

a. 1958.

b. Physicians in government services.

c. Physicians in hospitals and other health establishments.

d. Registered physicians.

SOURCE: SALA, 19–800; WHO-WHSA, 1983, table 18.

Table 805

PROFESSIONAL AND AUXILIARY HEALTH PERSONNEL, 20 LC
(Ca. 1979)

PART I.

		Pharmacy		Radiology		Midwifery			Community Health	
Country	Year	Pharmacists	Auxiliaries	Radiologists	X-Ray Technicians[1]	Nurse Midwives	Assistant Midwives	Traditional Birth Attendants	Health Educators	Health Promoters
A. ARGENTINA	1979	919	692	~	3,447	~	~	~	25	1,789
B. BOLIVIA	1979	115	~	~	~	~	~	2,557	~	3,181
C. BRAZIL	1974	2,394	~	~	7,332	~	~	1,962	~	~
D. CHILE	1979	290	~	~	~	2,372	~	~	~	~
E. COLOMBIA	1978	98	322	117	158	~	~	~	~	~
F. COSTA RICA	1976	638	421	48[a]	96	1,600	~	~	~	~
G. CUBA	1979	773	3,203	~	1,375	~	~	~	88	3,873
H. DOMINICAN REP.	1978	48	~	~	65	~	~	~	81	~
I. ECUADOR	1973	146[b]	79	75	234	166	~	~	18	228[d]
J. EL SALVADOR	1979	597	179	~	90	~	~	1,174	~	~
K. GUATEMALA	1976	7	35	4	78	100	#	2,325	.9	~
L. HAITI	1979	6	14	7	20	~	~	3,791	10	~
M. HONDURAS	1979	392	~	13	116	~	~	~	64	~
N. MEXICO	1979	~	~	~	186	~	~	~	~	~
O. NICARAGUA	1979	26	~	~	65	~	~	~	~	~
P. PANAMA	1978	157	~	17	200	~	~	~	~	~
Q. PARAGUAY	1979	860	~	~	44	224	396	163	26	~
R. PERU	1979	3,309	166	150	309	~	~	2,194	#	~
S. URUGUAY	1979	~	125	75	157	~	1,206	~	4	~
T. VENEZUELA	1978	3,187	~	~	~	~	~	1,200[c]	~	~
UNITED STATES	1978	135,000	~	12,062[c]	100,000	~	~	~	~	~

1. Includes radiographers, technicians, auxiliaries, and hygienists.

a. 1975.
b. Includes biochemists.
c. 1977.
d. 1978.

SOURCE: PAHO-HC, 1977-80, table IV-20; WHO-WHSA, 1983, table 18.

PART II.

		Environmental Health		Nutrition	Data Management		Rehabilitation	Health Institution Support Personnel		Animal Health
Country	Year	Sanitary Engineers	Sanitary Inspectors	Nutritionists and Dieticians	Statistical Personnel	Medical Record Personnel	Therapy Personnel	Health Administrators[1]	Laboratory Personnel	Veterinarians
A. ARGENTINA	1979	~	61	508	1,283	~	~	~	3,142	~
B. BOLIVIA	1976	~	~	~	~	~	~	~	4,674	310
C. BRAZIL	1974	~	~	1,522	~	~	~	~	~	~
D. CHILE	1979	20	~	1,300	~	~	~	~	~	97
E. COLOMBIA	1978	51	32	141	217	~	181	52	142	102
F. COSTA RICA	1976	15	74	69	124	~	6	~	4,921	1,168[a]
G. CUBA	1979	21[a]	~	~	~	~	4	55	440	150
H. DOMINICAN REP.	1976	27	312	20	111	~	18	331	456	240
I. ECUADOR	1973	42	415	12	29	798	49	46[a]	259	87
J. EL SALVADOR	1979	10	266	29	29	8	~	~	243	~
K. GUATEMALA	1976	~	122	~	8	17	~	11	95	~
L. HAITI	1979	2	137	8	17	~	~	18	235	2
M. HONDURAS	1979	2	112	17	173	~	15	401	303	279
N. MEXICO	1979	114	1,353	116	180	~	379	~	92	~
O. NICARAGUA	1979	~	~	6	~	~	32	~	543	~
P. PANAMA	1978	~	151	~	~	~	27	4	84	545
Q. PARAGUAY	1979	18	123	24	98	~	393	~	687	1,514
R. PERU	1979	308	575	273	290	~	~	15	80	1,200
S. URUGUAY	1979	~	~	~	~	~	~	~	~	144
T. VENEZUELA	1978	369	1,332	250	~	313[a]	~	~	~	~
UNITED STATES	1978	~	~	35,000	~	50,000	149,500	180,000[a]	219,000	33,500

1. Non-physician public health and hospital administrators.

a. 1978.

SOURCE: PAHO-HC, 1977-80, table IV-21; WHO-WHSA, 1983, table 18.

Table 806

DENTISTS AND DENTAL AUXILIARIES, 20 LC
(Ca. 1979)

	Country	Year	Dentists N	Dentists PTI	Dental Auxiliaries[1] N
A.	ARGENTINA	1979	7,415	2.8	1,068
B.	BOLIVIA‡	1979	118	.2	~
C.	BRAZIL‡	1979	55,784	4.7	~
D.	CHILE	1979	1,477	1.4	~
E.	COLOMBIA‡	1978	1,396	.5	300
F.	COSTA RICA	1979	239	1.4	~
G.	CUBA	1979	3,356	3.5	1,094
H.	DOMINICAN REP.‡	1978	90	.2	22
I.	ECUADOR	1973	579	.9	762
J.	EL SALVADOR	1978	393	.9	83
K.	GUATEMALA‡	1976	62	1.0	7
L.	HAITI	1979	73	.2	~
M.	HONDURAS	1979	183	.1	~
N.	MEXICO‡	1981	24,000	3.2	~
O.	NICARAGUA	1980	190	.7	~
P.	PANAMA	1978	250	1.4	~
Q.	PARAGUAY	1979	855	2.9	~
R.	PERU	1979	3,477	2.0	~
S.	URUGUAY	1979	2,300	8.0	110
T.	VENEZUELA	1978	4,342	3.3	~
	UNITES STATES	1979	126,420	5.6	~

1. Includes technicians, auxiliaries, and hygienists.

SOURCE: PAHO-HC, 1977-80, table 80; WHO-WHSA, 1983, table 18.

Table 807

NURSES BY MAJOR FUNCTION, 18 LC
(Ca. 1980)

	Country	Practicing Nurses	Hospital Nurses	Nursing Faculty	Providers of Direct Community Care	Community Health Supervisors	Trainers of Community Health Workers	Private Sector	Other
A.	ARGENTINA	18,658	12,607	310	~	~	380	5,361	#

Continued in SALA, 23–809.

Table 808

HOSPITALS BY TYPE, 20 LRC

	Country	Year	Total	Short-Stay Hospitals				Other Hospitals					
				Total	General[2]	Maternity	Pediatrics	Total	Tuberculosis	Mental Diseases	Leprosy	Cancer	Other[3]
A.	ARGENTINA	1973	2,864	2,733	2,486	216	31	131	31	57	7	6	30
B.	BOLIVIA	1975	345	229	227	~	2	116	~	~	~	~	116
C.	BRAZIL[1]	1973	4,067	3,463	3,144	195	124	604	109	281	34	~	180
D.	CHILE	1980	300	256	230	17	9	44	4	19	~	1	20
E.	COLOMBIA	1978	809	751	712	20	19	58	11	30	2	1	14
F.	COSTA RICA	1980	39	27	25	1	1	12	~	2	~	~	10
G.	CUBA	1979	305	262	184	57	21	43	1	25	1	3	13
H.	DOMINICAN REP.	1973	339	330	316	6	8	9	2	1	1	1	4
I.	ECUADOR	1973	221	185	149	30	6	36	11	8	3	2	12
J.	EL SALVADOR	1979	82	74	68	3	3	8	2	4	~	1	1
K.	GUATEMALA	1973	159	122	118	2	2	37	5	1	1	~	30
L.	HAITI	1979	58	54	51	2	1	4	3	1	~	~	1
M.	HONDURAS	1980	35	32	31	1	~	3	1	2	~	~	~
N.	MEXICO	1974	1,575	1,530	1,409	100	21	45	2	27	1	2	13
O.	NICARAGUA	1976	67	33	33	~	~	34	3	1	1	~	29
P.	PANAMA	1978	67	~	~	~	~	~	~	~	~	~	~
Q.	PARAGUAY	1975	143	137	136	1	~	6	1	1	1	1	2
R.	PERU	1977	437	419	397	17	5[a]	18	~	11	1	1	5
S.	URUGUAY	1978	66	57	54	1	2[a]	9	1	2	1	1	4
T.	VENEZUELA	1978	444	~	~	~	~	~	~	~	~	~	~
	LATIN AMERICA	**[b]	12,722	10,707	9,770	682	255	1,217	186	473	54	20	484
	UNITED STATES	1980	7,051	6,222	6,176	14	32[a]	829	11	504	~	~	314

1. Data on distribution by type of hospitals refer to 1971.
2. Includes medical centers
3. Includes alcohol centers and nursing homes.

a. Includes orthopediatric hospitals.
b. Totals of the 20 countries for years given.

SOURCE: PAHO-HC, 1977-80, table IV-1; WHO-WHSA, 1983, table 20.

Table 809

HOSPITALS: NUMBER, PERCENTAGE, AND OWNERSHIP, 20 LRC

	Country	Year	Total	Government		Private Non-Profit		Private Profit	
				N	%	N	%	N	%
A.	ARGENTINA	1969	2,864	1.294[c]	45.2[c]	~	~	1,570	54.8
B.	BOLIVIA	1975	345	264	76.5	11	3.2	70	20.3
C.	BRAZIL	1976	5,426	~	~	~	~	~	~
D.	CHILE	1980	300	234	78.0	#	#	66	22.0
E.	COLOMBIA	1980	849	697	79.7	172[d]	20.3[d]	~	~
F.	COSTA RICA	1980	39	36	92.3	#	#	3	7.7
G.	CUBA	1979	305	305	100.0	#	#	#	#
H.	DOMINICAN REP.	1973	339	138	40.7	1	.3	200	59.0
I.	ECUADOR	1973	221	109	49.3	10	4.5	102	46.2
J.	EL SALVADOR	1979	82	57	69.5	1	1.2	24	29.3
K.	GUATEMALA	1973	159	122	76.7	#	#	37	23.3
L.	HAITI	1980	52	29	55.8	19	36.5	4	7.7
M.	HONDURAS	1980	35	21	60.0	#	#	14	40.0
N.	MEXICO	1974	1,575	~	~	~	~	~	~
O.	NICARAGUA	1976	67	31	46.3	#	#	36	53.7
P.	PANAMA	1978	67	53	79.1	#	#	14	20.9
Q.	PARAGUAY	1975	143	131	91.6	12	8.4	#	#
R.	PERU	1977	437	264	60.4	68	15.6	105	24.0
S.	URUGUAY	1978	66	66	100.0	#	#	#	#
T.	VENEZUELA	1978	444	~	~	~	~	~	~
	LATIN AMERICA	**[e]	13,815	2,537[a]	18.4[a]	122[b]	.9[b]	675	4.9
	UNITED STATES	1980	7,051	2,562	36.3	3,547	50.3	942	13.4

a. Excludes Argentina.
b. Excludes Colombia.
c. Includes private non-profit figures.
d. Includes private profit figures.
e. Totals of the 20 countries for years given.

SOURCE: WHO-WHSA, 1983, table 20.

Table 810

SHORT-STAY HOSPITALS[1]: INDICES OF UTILIZATION
BY ALL TYPES OF OWNERSHIP, 19 LRC
(Ca. 1978)

	Country	Year	Beds	Discharges	Patient Days	Turnover Rate	Average Days of Stay	Occupancy Rate (%)
A.	ARGENTINA	1973	72,221	1,174,415	18,314,265	16.3	15.6	69.5
B.	BOLIVIA	1975	5,947	81,782	849,331	13.8	10.4	39.1
D.	CHILE	1980	31,340	1,018,590	7,731,242	32.5	7.6	~
E.	COLOMBIA	1978	35,413	1,243,116	7,421,215	35.1	6.0	~
F.	COSTA RICA	1980	5,204	244,424	1,465,139	47.0	6.0	~
G.	CUBA	1979	29,411	1,222,219	8,473,203	38.2	7.6	~
H.	DOMINICAN REP.	1973	7,977	266,433	1,665,327	33.4	6.3	~
I.	ECUADOR	1973	10,424	281,867	2,341,877	27.0	8.3	61.6
J.	EL SALVADOR	1978	5,406	257,564	1,512,591	47.6	5.9	76.7
K.	GUATEMALA	1978	6,287	167,627	1,345,617	26.7	8.0	58.6
L.	HAITI	1976	3,218	47,102	~	14.6	~	~
M.	HONDURAS	1980	4,353	156,765	1,085,903	36.0	6.9	~
N.	MEXICO	1976	42,959	1,749,797	8,096,685	40.7	4.6	~
O.	NICARAGUA	1976	2,881	99,285	746,490	34.5	7.5	70.8
P.	PANAMA	1977	5,359	140,490	1,508,834	26.2	10.7	77.1
Q.	PARAGUAY	1976	2,241	58,764	465,380	26.2	7.9	56.7
R.	PERU	1977	28,360	671,599	9,090,772	23.7	13.5	~
S.	URUGUAY	1978	5,818	129,421	1,211,043	22.2	9.4	~
T.	VENEZUELA	1976	13,823	530,505	4,085,382	38.4	7.7	80.8
	LATIN AMERICA		318,642	9,441,765	77,410,296	29.6	8.2	~
	UNITED STATES	1979	1,080,168	37,033,757	291,148,605	34.3	7.9	~

1. Includes general, maternity, pediatric, rural or local hospitals, and medical centers.

SOURCE: PAHO-HC, 1977-80, table V-2; WHO-WHSA, 1983, table 20.

Table 811

HOSPITAL BEDS AND RATE, IN THE CAPITAL
AND REST OF COUNTRY, 20 LC

	Country	Year	Total Hospital/Beds	Capital and Major Cities		Rest of Country	
				Beds	Rate PTI	Beds	Rate PTI
A.	ARGENTINA	1971	46,149	32,129[g]	2.5[g]	14,020	1.3

Continued in SALA, 20-810.

Table 812

HOSPITAL BEDS: NUMBER, PERCENTAGE, AND OWNERSHIP, 20 LRC

(Ca. 1978)

Country	Year	Total	Government		Private Non-Profit		Private Profit	
			N	%	N	%	N	%
A. ARGENTINA	1969	133,847	103,752[a]	77.5[a]	~	~	30,095	22.5
B. BOLIVIA	1975	10,722	9,040	84.3	478	4.5	1,204	11.2
C. BRAZIL	1976	445,818	~	~	~	~	~	~
D. CHILE	1980	37,971	35,334	93.1	#	#	2,637	6.9
E. COLOMBIA	1980	44,495	37,077	83.3	7,418[b]	16.7[b]	~	~
F. COSTA RICA	1980	7,570	7,429	98.1	#	#	141	1.9
G. CUBA	1979	39,809	39,809	100.0	#	#	#	#
H. DOMINICAN REP.	1973	12,618	9,698	76.8	150	1.2	2,770	22.0
I. ECUADOR	1973	13,594	11,439	84.1	648	4.8	1,507	11.1
J. EL SALVADOR	1979	7,848	7,136	90.9	70	.9	642	8.2
K. GUATEMALA	1973	12,115	11,315	93.4	#	#	800	6.6
L. HAITI	1980	3,964	2,789	70.4	1,011	25.5	164	4.1
M. HONDURAS	1980	4,723	3,890	82.4	#	#	833	17.6
N. MEXICO	1973	67.363	~	~	~	~	~	~
O. NICARAGUA	1976	4,697	3,930	83.4	#	#	767	16.3
P. PANAMA	1978	6,954	6,314	90.8	#	#	640	9.2
Q. PARAGUAY	1975	3,816	3,659	95.9	157	4.1	#	#
R. PERU	1977	29,934	24,200	80.8	2,052	6.9	3,682	12.3
S. URUGUAY	1978	11,559	11,559	100.0	#	#	#	#
T. VENEZUELA	1978	41,386	~	~	~	~	~	~
LATIN AMERICA		940,803	224,618[d]	23.9[d]	4,566[c]	.5[c]	45,882	4.9
UNITED STATES	1980	1,333,360	511,311	38.3	718,663	53.9	103,386	7.8

a. Includes private non-profit figures.
b. Includes private profit figures.
c. Excludes Colombia.
d. Excludes Argentina.

SOURCE: WHO-WHSA, 1983, table 20.

Table 813

HEALTH ESTABLISHMENTS WITH
OUTPATIENT SERVICES, 15 L

(Ca. 1979)

Country	Year	Total	Health Centers	Clinics and Dispensaries	Other
C. BRAZIL	1980	8,646	4,370	4,276	#

Continued in SALA, 23-804.

Table 814

URBAN AND RURAL HEALTH ESTABLISHMENTS
WITH OUTPATIENT SERVICES, 8 L

(Ca. 1979)

Country	Year	Total	Localities of 20,000 or More				Localities of 19,999 or Less			
			Total				Total			
			N	%	Hospitals	Other	N	%	Hospitals	Other
J. EL SALVADOR	1979	330	125	37.9	25	100	205	62.1	7	198

Continued in SALA, 23-805.

Table 815

MENTAL HEALTH CLINICS, REHABILITATION
CENTERS, AND DENTAL CLINICS, 11 LC
(Ca. 1972 and 1978)

Country	Mental Health Clinics		Rehabilitation Centers		Dental Clinics	
	1972	1978	1972	1978	1972	1978
D. CHILE	2	4	24	~	1	50

Continued in SALA, 23-806.

Table 816

CHILD HEALTH SERVICES, 8 L
(Ca. 1979)

Country	Year	Children Attended					Visits		
		Centers with Information	Under 1 Year	Per 100 Live Births	1-4 Years	Ratio[1]	Centers with Information	Under 1 Year	1-4 Years
E. COLOMBIA	1976	~	502,431	68.7	703,915	20.6	~	1,011,195	1,373,960

Continued in SALA, 23-812.

Table 817

CHILDREN UNDER ONE YEAR RECEIVING BCG, DPT, MEASLES,
AND POLIOMYELITIS VACCINES, 20 L
(%)

Country	BCG	DPT		Measles	Polio	
		First Dose	Third Dose		First Dose	Third Dose
A. ARGENTINA	64	67	42	60	100	96

Continued in SALA, 23-813.

Table 818

TOTAL FOOD PRODUCTION INDEX,[1] 20 LC, 1966–81

(1969–71 = 100)

Year	A. ARGENTINA	B. BOLIVIA	C. BRAZIL	D. CHILE	E. COLOMBIA	F. COSTA RICA	G. CUBA	H. DOMINICAN REP.	I. ECUADOR	J. EL SALVADOR	K. GUATEMALA
1966	92	87	82	97	86	80	74	81	91	87	83
1967	101	89	88	97	88	80	85	81	96	85	87
1968	94	97	91	101	92	89	83	83	100	92	93
1969	102	95	94	96	95	93	81	93	97	91	96
1970	101	101	102	104	99	100	124	100	101	102	101
1971	96	104	104	100	106	107	95	107	101	105	103
1972	94	112	107	97	108	111	87	109	98	98	109
1973	103	117	112	88	108	115	92	110	100	112	116
1974	106	121	124	100	115	114	95	115	111	112	119
1975	109	131	129	106	124	131	96	110	114	124	125
1976	119	136	142	104	131	134	99	118	117	126	134
1977	118	130	147	113	131	138	106	122	121	127	138
1978	131	131	141	104	143	138	119	124	118	147	139
1979	135	131	150	112	149	142	128	125	121	150	149
1980	127	134	165	112	148	139	116	132	132	142	156
1981	136	137	172	120	158	142	123	137	139	136	164

Year	L. HAITI	M. HONDURAS	N. MEXICO	O. NICARAGUA	P. PANAMA	Q. PARAGUAY	R. PERU	S. URUGUAY	T. VENEZUELA	UNITED STATES
1966	94	78	92	81	81	90	87	91	81	92
1967	96	91	93	87	86	93	92	80	85	98
1968	93	94	95	92	96	92	83	91	89	98
1969	98	99	95	96	103	93	94	100	97	98
1970	100	97	100	101	94	103	102	107	101	97
1971	103	105	105	103	103	105	104	93	102	105
1972	106	109	107	102	102	102	104	91	102	103
1973	105	106	111	104	107	103	107	96	107	105
1974	108	97	114	111	111	112	112	105	109	107
1975	108	83	117	123	116	112	108	103	122	114
1976	111	95	118	129	116	119	111	117	115	118
1977	107	104	128	130	125	132	111	99	125	122
1978	113	112	140	144	128	130	106	98	135	121
1979	115	108	133	140	125	147	109	96	145	127
1980	109	112	145	104	129	155	100	104	151	123
1981	110	116	155	110	132	158	112	119	147	135

1. Food Production Index is included in index of total agricultural production, table 1517.

SOURCE: FAO-PY, 1977, table 4; FAO-PY, 1979, table 4; FAO-PY, 1980, table 4; FAO-PY, 1981, table 4.

Table 819

PER CAPITA FOOD PRODUCTION INDEX,[1] 20 LC, 1966-81

(1969-71 = 100)[a]

Year	A. ARGENTINA	B. BOLIVIA	C. BRAZIL	D. CHILE	E. COLOMBIA	F. COSTA RICA	G. CUBA	H. DOMINICAN REP.	I. ECUADOR	J. EL SALVADOR	K. GUATEMALA
1966	98	96	92	104	99	90	80	92	105	100	93
1967	105	96	96	103	97	87	90	90	106	95	95
1968	97	102	97	105	97	95	86	89	106	98	98
1969	104	98	97	98	97	95	83	96	100	94	99
1970	101	101	102	104	99	100	124	101	101	102	101
1971	95	101	101	99	104	105	94	104	99	102	100
1972	91	104	102	93	103	105	84	103	92	93	103
1973	98	111	104	84	101	106	88	101	92	103	106
1974	101	110	111	94	105	103	89	102	99	100	105
1975	102	116	114	97	111	115	88	95	98	107	107
1976	110	117	122	94	115	116	90	99	98	106	111
1977	107	109	123	100	113	116	96	100	99	104	111
1978	118	108	115	91	120	114	106	100	93	116	109
1979	120	105	120	96	123	114	113	98	93	115	113
1980	111	104	129	94	119	109	103	101	98	106	115
1981	117	104	131	99	125	109	108	102	100	99	117

Year	L. HAITI	M. HONDURAS	N. MEXICO	O. NICARAGUA	P. PANAMA	Q. PARAGUAY	R. PERU	S. URUGUAY	T. VENEZUELA	UNITED STATES
1966	99	88	104	91	91	100	98	94	91	96
1967	100	99	103	95	94	101	100	83	92	101
1968	98	100	101	98	102	97	88	93	95	100
1969	100	102	99	100	106	95	97	101	100	99
1970	100	97	100	101	94	103	102	107	101	97
1971	100	102	101	100	100	102	101	93	98	104
1972	101	103	101	96	97	96	99	90	95	101
1973	98	97	101	95	99	94	99	96	96	102
1974	99	86	100	97	99	99	100	105	94	103
1975	97	71	100	105	102	96	94	102	102	109
1976	97	79	98	106	99	99	94	115	93	111
1977	92	83	103	104	103	106	92	97	98	114
1978	94	86	109	111	105	101	86	96	102	111
1979	94	80	101	105	100	110	86	93	105	116
1980	87	80	107	75	101	112	76	100	106	111
1981	85	80	111	76	101	111	83	113	100	120

1. Per Capita Food Production Index is included in index of per capita agricultural production, table 2100. For long-term data, cf. SALA, 23, Ch. 35.

a. These index numbers are calculated by FAO on a uniform basis employing regionally constant weights. They differ from national index numbers produced by the countries themselves because of differences in concepts of production, coverage, weights, time reference of the production data, and method of calculation. They are not substitutes for National Index numbers. Whenever revised basic data are reported, the index numbers previously published are revised accordingly.

SOURCE: FAO-PY, 1977, table 6; FAO-PY, 1979, table 6; FAO-PY, 1980, table 79; FAO-PY, 1981, table 6.

Table 820

DAILY CALORIC INTAKE, 20 LRC, 1965–80

(PI)

	Country		YA				PC
		1965	1966-68	1969-71	1975-77	1978-80	1965-80
A.	ARGENTINA	2,868	3,252	3,358	3,362	3,386	7.0
B.	BOLIVIA	1,731	1,915	1,976	2,041	2,086	22.6
C.	BRAZIL	2,541	2,487	2,493	2,493	2,517	7.5
D.	CHILE	2,523	2,742	2,696	2,616	2,738	5.2
E.	COLOMBIA	2,220	~	~	~	2,473	.6
F.	COSTA RICA	2,223	2,313	2,415	2,480	2,635	11.2
G.	CUBA	2,665	2,381	2,579	2,678	2,717	3.6
H.	DOMINICAN REP.	2,004	1,919	1,952	2,117	2,133	10.9
I.	ECUADOR	1,848	1.924	1.987	2,087	2,092	9.0
J.	EL SALVADOR	1,877	1,840	1,840	2,076	2,163	6.7
K.	GUATEMALA	1,952	1,971	2,049	2,035	2,064	9.9
L.	HAITI	1,904	1,855	1,873	1,793	1,882	.1
M.	HONDURAS	1,930	2,059	2,115	2,081	2,175	14.1
N.	MEXICO	2,623	2,685	2,701	2,756	2,803	2.9
O.	NICARAGUA	2,253	2,523	2,470	2,445	2,284	7.7
P.	PANAMA	2,317	2,425	2,500	2,398	2,290	14.8
Q.	PARAGUAY	2,732	2,658	2,752	2,774	2,902	3.8
R.	PERU	2,255	2,225	2,254	2,209	2,166	7.7
S.	URUGUAY	3,039	2,837	3,027	2,918	2,868	4.2
T.	VENEZUELA	2,392	2,316	2,389	2,538	2,649	10.4
	LATIN AMERICA[1]	2,295	2,333	2,391	2,416	2,449	7.6
	UNITED STATES	3,393[a]	3,380	3,462	3,552	3,652	4.2[b]

1. Unweighted average.

a. 1966-68.
b. 1966-77.

SOURCE: Derived from Mexico — BNCE — CE, March 1981; FAO-PY, 1982, table 103.

Table 821

PERCENT OF MINIMUM DAILY CALORIC REQUIREMENTS,
19 LR, 1961–77

Country	1961–63	1975–77
A. ARGENTINA	137.9	143.1

Continued in SALA, 23-108.

TABLE 822

FISH CONSUMPTION,[1] 11 LC, 1949–74

(kg PI)

Country	1949-51	1970	1974
A. ARGENTINA	4.0	4.8	6.9

Continued in SALA, 23-3510.

Table 823

FATS CONSUMED DAILY,[1] 19 LRC, 1966-80
(PI)

	Country	YA (G)			
		1966-68	1969-71	1975-77	1978-80
A.	ARGENTINA	111.7	114.0	117.2	119.1
B.	BOLIVIA	36.8	38.0	42.1	44.6
C.	BRAZIL	48.4	48.9	50.9	51.5
D.	CHILE	58.4	59.5	51.7	55.7
F.	COSTA RICA	53.7	55.1	62.1	65.8
G.	CUBA	52.6	55.8	56.3	58.8
H.	DOMINICAN REP.	45.9	47.5	50.3	49.9
I.	ECUADOR	43.5	45.6	50.3	54.1
J.	EL SALVADOR	40.0	38.5	46.0	46.7
K.	GUATEMALA	35.5	36.0	37.6	39.3
L.	HAITI	28.1	28.6	28.0	30.2
M.	HONDURAS	38.4	39.2	39.3	41.6
N.	MEXICO	55.6	56.8	59.7	62.7
O.	NICARAGUA	51.6	53.4	56.2	51.5
P.	PANAMA	51.1	53.9	55.5	55.7
Q.	PARAGUAY	72.8	75.0	73.5	78.9
R.	PERU	45.8	46.2	44.3	44.0
S.	URUGUAY	104.7	111.9	108.4	104.7
T.	VENEZUELA	57.6	59.4	66.5	69.4
	LATIN AMERICA	54.3	56.0	57.7	59.1
	UNITED STATES	154.8	160.8	161.5	169.2

1. Total grams per day includes vegetable and animal products.

SOURCE: FAO-PY, 1982, table 105.

Table 824

PER CAPITA PRIVATE FOOD CONSUMPTION CHANGE, 19 LR, 1960-75
(AAGR)

Country	Previous Decade		1970	1971	1972	1973	1974	1975
	Decade	Second Half of Decade						
A. ARGENTINA	3.1	2.4	2.8	2.0	1.4	2.8	6.3	1.9

Continued in SALA, 21-107.

Table 825

PROTEIN CONSUMPTION, 20 LRC, 1965-80

Country	Animal Proteins						Vegetable Proteins						Total Proteins					
	Daily G PI					PC	Daily G PI					PC	Daily G PI					PC
	1965	1966-68	1969-71	1975-77	1978-80	1965-80	1965	1966-68	1969-71	1975-77	1978-80	1965-80	1965	1966-68	1969-71	1975-77	1978-80	1965-80
A. ARGENTINA	51.7	66.8	66.7	72.2	74.3	17.2	36.8	38.2	39.4	37.5	37.6	2.7	88.5	104.9	106.1	109.8	111.9	11.2
B. BOLIVIA	12.1	13.3	13.7	15.8	16.7	38.0	33.0	36.6	36.5	36.7	36.1	17.9	45.1	50.0	50.1	52.5	52.8	23.3
C. BRAZIL	22.4	20.9	21.1	22.8	22.7	14.3	41.5	43.0	41.3	37.1	36.8	3.4	63.9	63.6	62.3	60.0	59.4	7.2
D. CHILE	25.1	26.2	25.9	23.5	27.3	23.5	40.2	47.3	45.0	46.3	47.7	-1.5	65.3	73.5	70.9	70.0	75.0	8.1
E. COLOMBIA	22.7	22.3	22.5	22.4	23.7	10.1	30.5	26.5	26.4	28.6	31.3	8.2	53.2	48.9	48.9	51.1	55.0	9.0
F. COSTA RICA	24.6	21.0	23.9	26.6	30.7	23.6	32.1	34.9	34.2	30.7	30.1	12.1	56.7	55.9	57.9	57.4	60.8	17.1
G. CUBA	27.3	29.2	33.6	33.9	32.8	8.4	35.2	33.2	35.9	37.4	38.3	2.6	62.5	62.4	69.5	71.2	71.1	5.1
H. DOMINICAN REP.	17.3	15.5	16.1	15.3	18.2	18.5	27.5	25.8	25.8	28.7	28.3	8.7	44.8	41.4	41.9	44.0	46.6	12.5
I. ECUADOR	16.2	19.1	19.8	20.7	24.4	12.3	30.5	31.1	30.2	27.5	24.3	8.2	46.7	50.2	50.0	48.1	48.7	9.6
J. EL SALVADOR	30.0	15.4	14.7	16.8	18.2	-.3	32.9	35.2	35.0	37.6	39.4	4.6	62.9	50.5	49.8	54.3	57.6	2.2
K. GUATEMALA	11.9	12.3	12.6	12.4	13.7	20.2	37.3	42.0	44.0	41.3	42.2	7.5	49.2	54.4	56.6	53.7	55.9	10.6
L. HAITI	4.7	6.5	7.0	7.9	8.5	17.0	42.1	38.1	38.0	34.0	36.0	-1.4	46.8	44.6	45.1	41.8	44.5	.4
M. HONDURAS	13.1	12.9	13.4	12.3	13.9	42.7	35.5	40.6	40.4	38.0	37.5	9.0	48.6	53.4	53.8	50.3	51.5	18.1
N. MEXICO	14.2	17.9	18.5	20.7	23.9	28.9	52.3	50.7	50.8	49.0	48.3	-6.1	66.5	68.6	69.3	69.7	72.2	1.4
O. NICARAGUA	19.8	25.4	27.6	30.1	28.3	6.1	40.9	47.5	46.0	39.7	36.4	7.1	60.7	72.9	73.5	69.9	64.7	6.8
P. PANAMA	24.9	22.3	24.8	26.6	26.5	34.1	37.6	37.2	36.2	31.9	29.6	6.6	62.5	59.2	60.9	58.6	56.1	17.6
Q. PARAGUAY	29.8	35.1	33.8	30.1	33.0	4.4	38.3	38.6	40.5	46.0	48.2	5.7	68.1	73.7	74.3	76.1	81.3	5.1
R. PERU	20.2	21.1	20.2	19.5	19.4	18.3	38.3	39.8	39.9	37.2	37.0	7.0	58.5	61.0	60.1	56.7	56.3	10.9
S. URUGUAY	71.7	55.0	59.2	55.4	55.4	3.9	33.7	30.2	31.8	31.3	31.3	4.2	105.4	85.2	91.0	86.7	86.8	4.0
T. VENEZUELA	26.6	25.5	27.2	32.3	37.0	7.9	34.5	33.4	33.6	34.4	33.8	11.3	61.1	58.9	60.8	66.7	70.8	15.9
LATIN AMERICA[1]	24.3	24.2	25.2	26.1	27.5	14.4	36.5	38.1	38.1	37.0	36.8	5.5	60.8	62.3	63.4	63.0	64.3	9.0
UNITED STATES	71.1[a]	70.7	71.9	72.2	72.0	2.3[b]	33.0[a]	33.0	32.8	34.5	34.7	1.5[b]	104.1[a]	103.7	104.8	106.7	106.7	2.0[b]

1. Unweighted average.

a. 1966-68.

b. 1966-77.

SOURCE: Derived from Mexico-BNCE-CE, March 1981; FAO-PY, 1982, table 104.

Table 826

AVERAGE YEARLY PC IN FOOD/C PRODUCTION BY PERIOD, 20 LRC, 1953–81

Country	1953–59 (7 years)	1960–69 (10 years)	1970–79 (10 years)	1980–81 (2 years)	Total (29 years)
A. ARGENTINA	-.7	1.3	1.7	-1.5	.7
B. BOLIVIA	4.8	1.1	.7	-1.9	1.7
C. BRAZIL	2.0	1.3	2.2	3.8	1.9
D. CHILE	.4	-.4	.1	1.1	.1
E. COLOMBIA	-.8	-.4	2.5	.5	.6
F. COSTA RICA	-1.5	.8	1.9	-3.1	.4
G. CUBA	-2.8	-1.1	4.6	-3.8	.3
H. DOMINICAN REP.	-.1	-1.5	.2	1.0	-.4
I. ECUADOR	6.9	-.1	-.7	3.8	1.6
J. EL SALVADOR	-3.7[a]	-.4	1.2	-6.9	-.6[b]
K. GUATEMALA	-.1	.8	1.7	0	.8
L. HAITI	-2.0[a]	0	-.9	-3.8	-1.0[b]
M. HONDURAS	-.3	1.7	-2.0	0	-.2
N. MEXICO	3.4	1.0	.4	3.4	1.5
O. NICARAGUA	1.1[a]	1.7	.7	-12.9	-.1[b]
P. PANAMA	1.7	2.0	-.5	2.5	1.1
Q. PARAGUAY	-.1	-.4	1.6	.2	.4
R. PERU	.1	.8	-1.2	1.1	0
S. URUGUAY	-3.7	2.6	-.4	11.2	.6
T. VENEZUELA	1.3	3.1	1.0	-5.2	1.4
LATIN AMERICA[1]	.2	.2	.9	1.0	.5
UNITED STATES	.2	.5	1.7	1.9	.9

1. ELA.

a. 1955-59.

b. 27 years.

SOURCE: SALA, 23-3502.

Table 827

ACCEPTORS OF GOVERNMENT FAMILY PLANNING SERVICES BY METHOD AND YEAR OF ACCEPTANCE,[1] 12 L, 1971 AND 1975

(T)

Country	All Program Methods		IUD		Oral Contraceptives		Sterilization		Other Program Methods	
	1971	1975	1971	1975	1971	1975	1971	1975	1971	1975
B. BOLIVIA	~	7.6	~	5.6	~	1.2	~	- -	~	.8

Continued in SALA, 20-802.

Table 828

ACCEPTORS OF GOVERNMENT FAMILY PLANNING SERVICES BY METHOD AND AGE OF WIFE,[1] 7 L

Country	Year	Method	N (T)	% in Wife's Age Group							Wife's Median Age
				Under 20	20-24	25-29	30-34	35-39	40+	Unknown	
C. BRAZIL	1974	All	15.4	13.1	32.0	25.6	15.6	9.1	4.1	.5	25.9
		IUD	1.0	3.6	22.5	31.5	22.5	12.6	6.8	.5	28.7
		Oral	13.6	14.0	32.8	25.3	15.0	8.8	3.7	.4	25.5

Continued in SALA, 20-803.

Table 829

ACCEPTORS OF GOVERNMENT FAMILY PLANNING SERVICES BY METHOD AND NUMBER OF LIVING CHILDREN,[1] 7 L

Country	Year	Method	N (T)	% by Number of Living Children							Median Number of Living Children
				0-1	2	3	4	5	6+	Unknown	
C. BRAZIL	1974	All	15.4	33.5	21.3	13.4	27.2 ←——————————→			4.6	2.2
		IUD	1.0	19.7	23.3	17.9	37.2 ←——————————→			1.9	2.8
		Oral	13.6	34.4	21.5	13.2	26.5 ←——————————→			4.4	2.1

Continued in SALA, 20-804.

Table 830

USERS OF BIRTH CONTROL METHODS BY PUBLIC AND PRIVATE SOURCE,[1] 6 L

Country	Year[2]	Method	All Sources		National Program Supplies and Services		Private Sector Supplies and Services	
			N (T)	Users as % of Married Women Age 15-44	N (T)	Users as % of Married Women Age 15-44	N (T)	Users as % of Married Women Age 15-44
F. COSTA RICA	1976	All	78.8	33.7	~	~	~	~
		IUD	8.1	3.5	~	~	~	~
		Oral	53.7	23.0	~	~	~	~
		Condoms	9.0	3.8	~	~	~	~
		Other	8.1	3.4	~	~	~	~

Continued in SALA, 20-805.

Table 831

RELATIVE AGE DISTRIBUTION OF FAMILY PLANNING PARTICIPANTS AT ENTRY INTO PROGRAM, 14 L

Country	Year	Relative Age Distribution						Median Age
		15-19	20-24	25-29	30-34	35-39	40+	
B. BOLIVIA	1973	5.5	26.5	32.0	23.1	11.6	1.3	28.1

Continued in SALA, 20-807.

Table 832

WOMEN PARTICIPATING IN FAMILY PLANNING PROGRAMS, BY BIRTH CONTROL METHOD, 19 LR, 1970–73

Country and Years	Total		IUD		Oral		Sterilization		Other		Not Specified	
	N	%	N	%	N	%	N	%	N	%	N	%
A. ARGENTINA	27,003	100.0	7,627	28.2	18,187	67.4	–	–	1,189	4.4	–	–
1970	11,162	100.0	2,582	23.1	8,209	73.6	–	–	371	3.3	–	–

Continued in SALA, 20-808.

Table 833

SOCIAL SECURITY: PERCENT SERVED
OF ECONOMICALLY ACTIVE POPULATION,
20 LR, 1960 and 1970

Country	1960	1970
A. ARGENTINA	53.8	67.4

Continued in SALA, 17-810.

Table 834

INSURED POPULATION IN RELATION TO TOTAL AND ECONOMICALLY ACTIVE
POPULATION IN ARGENTINA, 1960–70

Year	Total Population[1] (T) (1)	Economically Active Population[1,2] (T) (2)	Insured Population[3] Active[4] (3)	Passive[5] (4)	Dependents (5)	Total (6)	Percent of EAP Insured (3)/(2)	Percent of Total Population Insured (6)/(1)	Ratio of Active to Passive (3)/(4)
1960	20,850	7,270	4,011	745	4,412	9,168	55.2	44.0	5.4
1961	21,203	7,334	4,031	812	4,407	9,250	55.0	43.6	5.0
1962	21,540	7,447	4,101	889	4,479	9,469	55.1	44.0	4.6
1963	21,870	7,563	4,137	970	4,520	9,627	54.7	44.0	4.3
1964	22,202	7,684	4,235	1,013	4,628	9,876	55.1	44.5	4.2
1965	22,545	7,809	4,322	1,086	4,723	10,131	55.3	44.9	4.0
1966	22,897	7,939	4,305	1,131	4,698	10,134	54.2	44.3	3.8
1967	23,255	8,073	4,303	1,150	4,684	10,137	53.3	43.6	3.7
1968	23,617	8,211	4,297	1,256	4,677	10,230	52.3	43.3	3.4
1969	23,983	8,353	4,044	1,302	4,141	9,760	48.4	40.7	3.1
1970	24,350	8,500	5,781	1,389	6,328	13,498	68.0	55.4	4.2

1. Estimates at mid-year.
2. Eighteen years and older. Other sources give a higher EAP.
3. Estimates as of December 31.
4. Basically in pension funds. For coverage of other risks, see source.
5. Retired and disabled workers and survivors under pensions.

SOURCE: Carmelo Mesa-Lago, *Social Security in Latin America* (Pittsburgh: University
of Pittsburgh Press, 1978), p. 180.

Table 835

INSURED POPULATION IN RELATION TO TOTAL AND ECONOMICALLY ACTIVE POPULATION IN CHILE, 1960-71

Year	Total Population (T) (1)	Economically Active Population[1] (T) (2)	Insured Population[4] (T)				Percent of EAP Insured (3)/(2)	Percent of Total Population Insured (6)/(1)	Ratio of Active to Passive (3)/(4)
			Active (3)	Passive[2] (4)	Dependents[3] (5)	Total (6)			
1960	7,689.0	2,521.0	1,691.3	269.4	2,875.0	4,835.7	67.1	63.0	6.3
1961	7,858.0	2,577.0	1,741.8	287.6	2,961.0	4,990.4	67.6	63.5	6.1
1962	8,029.0	2,634.0	1,797.1	311.4	3,055.0	5,163.5	68.2	64.3	5.8
1963	8,217.0	2,695.0	1,835.2	348.7	3,170.0	5,353.9	68.1	65.1	5.3
1964	8,391.0	2,752.0	1,891.8	384.4	3,360.0	5,636.2	68.7	67.1	4.9
1965	8,584.0	2,815.0	1,946.6	441.1	3,584.0	5,971.7	69.1	69.5	4.4
1966	8,850.0	2,903.0	2,026.8	501.1	3,648.0	6,175.9	69.8	69.8	4.0
1967	9,136.6	2,978.0	2,093.2	524.6	3,768.0	6,385.8	70.3	69.9	4.0
1968	9,351.2	3,048.0	2,158.3	552.0	3,885.0	6,595.3	70.8	70.5	3.9
1969	9,555.6	3,107.4	2,143.2	580.7	3,858.0	6,581.9	69.0	68.8	3.7
1970	9,780.1	3,189.2	2,217.3	603.1	3,991.0	6,811.4	69.5	69.6	3.7
1971	10,001.3	3,278.1	2.294.9	643.7	4,253.0	7,191.0	70.0	71.9	3.6

1. Includes unemployed, unpaid family workers, and employers.
2. Retired and disabled workers and survivors under pensions.
3. Wives of active insured covered by maternity insurance, and relatives with right to health services under Servicio de Seguro Social (SSS) and other funds.
4. Coverage is in pension funds; it also includes preventive medicine, maternity, family allowances, and unemployment compensation when the insured and his dependents have such coverage. For coverage of health and occupational accidents and diseases, see source. Estimates are for mid-year.

SOURCE: Carmelo Mesa-Lago, *Social Security in Latin America* (Pittsburgh: University of Pittsburgh Press, 1978), p. 41.

Table 836

INSURED POPULATION IN RELATION TO TOTAL AND ECONOMICALLY ACTIVE POPULATION IN MEXICO, 1960-70

Year	Total Population (T) (1)	Economically Active Population (T) (2)	Insured Population (T)				Percent of EAP Insured (3)/(2)	Percent of Total Population Insured (6)/(1)	Ratio of Active to Passive (3)/(4)
			Active[1] (3)	Passive[2] (4)	Dependents[3] (5)	Total (6)			
1960	36,046.0	11,332.0	1,360.2	58.2	2,459.7	3,878.1	12.0	10.8	23.4
1961	37,268.0	11,721.5	1,595.0	67.8	2,947.8	4,610.6	13.6	12.4	23.5
1962	38,543.0	12,125.7	1,785.7	80.2	3,478.6	5,344.5	14.8	13.9	22.3
1963	39,871.0	12,544.8	1,928.7	88.2	3,845.0	5,861.9	15.4	14.7	21.9
1964	41,253.0	12,978.5	2,311.9	103.4	4,653.5	7,068.8	17.9	17.2	22.4
1965	42,689.0	13,427.0	2,601.3	118.1	5,701.9	8,421.3	19.4	19.8	22.0
1966	44,145.0	13,890.4	2,753.5	135.2	5,593.4	8,482.1	19.9	19.3	20.4
1967	45,671.0	14,368.4	2,960.8	158.8	6,042.7	9,162.3	20.6	20.1	18.6
1968	47,267.0	14,861.2	3,178.1	183.9	6,441.5	9,803.5	21.4	20.8	17.3
1969	48,933.0	15,366.5[b]	3,571.6	205.5	7,356.0	11,133.1	23.3	22.8	17.4
1970	49,788.0[a]	15,888.9[b]	3,912.0	257.2	8,209.1	12,378.3	24.7	24.9	15.2

1. Includes Instituto Mexicano del Seguro Social (IMSS), the Instituto de Seguridad y Servicios Sociales de los Trabajadores y del Estado (ISSSTE), and railroads in 1960-70, plus armed forces in 1965-70, plus petroleum in 1969.
2. Includes IMSS, ISSSTE, in 1960-70, plus petroleum in 1969 and railroads in 1970.
3. Includes IMSS, ISSSTE, in 1960-70, plus railroads in 1965-70, plus all armed forces in 1970 (navy only in 1966-69,) plus petroleum in 1969.

a. Census population (January 1970) plus 3 percent adjustment used by United Nations.
b. Extrapolation of series of Secretaria de Industria y Comercio, using their assumed annual rate of growth: 3.4 percent.

SOURCE: Carmelo Mesa-Lago, *Social Security in Latin America* (Pittsburgh: University of Pittsburgh Press, 1978), p. 231.

Table 837

INSURED POPULATION IN RELATION TO TOTAL AND ECONOMICALLY ACTIVE POPULATION IN PERU, 1961–69

Year	Total Population[1] (T) (1)	Economically Active Population[2] (T) (2)	Insured Population (T)				Percent of EAP Insured (3)/(2)	Percent of Total Population Insured (6)/(1)	Ratio of Active to Passive (3)/(4)
			Active[3] (3)	Passive[4] (4)	Dependents[5] (5)	Total (6)			
1961	10,320.0	3,250.5	807.9	12.6	61.4	881.9	24.8	8.5	64.1
1962	10,630.0	3,344.3	920.3	14.0	67.0	1,001.3	27.5	9.4	65.7
1963	10,960.0	3,442.9	1,023.9	16.4	73.3	1,113.6	29.7	10.1	62.4
1964	11,300.0	3,546.4	1,087.7	19.8	79.2	1,186.7	30.6	10.5	54.9
1965	11,650.0	3,654.7	1,155.7	22.8	85.5	1,264.0	31.6	10.8	50.7
1966	12,011.5	3,767.8	1,216.7	25.5	91.5	1,333.7	32.2	11.1	47.7
1967	12,385.2	3,885.8	1,245.8	29.2	97.8	1,372.8	32.0	11.0	42.7
1968	12,771.8	4,008.6	1,347.3	32.9	104.5	1,484.7	33.6	11.6	40.9
1969	13,171.8	4,136.2	1,474.4	39.5	111.2	1,625.1	35.6	12.3	37.3

1. Estimate of mid-year. The year 1961 has been adjusted for undernumeration of 1961 census which excluded Indian jungle population.
2. Period not specified. The year 1961 has been adjusted for undernumeration.
3. At the end of the year. Excludes fishermen, jockeys, and possibly longshoremen.
4. At the end of the year. Retired and disabled workers and survivors under pensions of Seguro Social Obligatorio (SSO) and Seguro Social del Empleado (SSE) in 1961–68, plus retired from Fondo Especial de Jubilación de Empleados Particulares (FEJEP).
5. At the end of the year. Only wives of active insured for maternity care in SSE.

SOURCE: Carmelo Mesa-Lago, *Social Security in Latin America* (Pittsburgh: University of Pittsburgh Press, 1978), p. 134.

Table 838

INSURED POPULATION IN RELATION TO TOTAL AND ECONOMICALLY ACTIVE POPULATION IN URUGUAY, 1960–69

Year	Total Population (T) (1)	Economically Active Population (T) (2)	Insured Population (T)				Percent of EAP Insured (3)/(2)	Percent of Total Population Insured (6)/(1)	Ratio of Active to Passive (3)/(4)
			Active (3)	Passive (4)	Dependents[1] (5)	Total (6)			
1960	2,540	988[a]	1,077	276	251	1,604	109	63	3.9
1961	2,580	998[a]	1,101	302	288	1,691	110	59	3.6
1962	2,610	1,008[a]	1,109	322	303	1,734	110	66	3.4
1963	2,650	1,016	1,095	337	296	1,728	108	65	3.2
1964	2,680	1,027[a]	1,083	353	284	1,720	106	64	3.1
1965	2,710	1,038[a]	1,230	366	275	1,871	119	69	3.4
1966	2,750	1,050	1,058	394	295	1,747	101	64	2.7
1967	2,780	1,061	1,049	422	305	1,776	99	64	2.5
1968	2,820	1,072	1,042	435	342	1,819	97	65	2.4
1969	2,850	1,084	1,035	451	340	1,826	95	64	2.3

1. *Beneficiarios*, which are minors receiving payments through the family allowance system in the private sector: hence, only blue- and white-collar and rural beneficiaries are here included.
a. Interpolated estimates by source.

SOURCE: Carmelo Mesa-Lago, *Social Security in Latin America* (Pittsburgh: University of Pittsburgh Press, 1978), p. 90.

CHAPTER 9

EDUCATION AND SCIENCE

Table 900

ILLITERACY, AGE 15 AND OVER, BY URBAN AND RURAL AREAS AND BY SEX, 20 LC

Country	Year	Category	Illiterate Population			% of Total Population		
			Total (N)	Male (N)	Female (N)	Total	Male	Female
A. ARGENTINA	1971	Total[4]	1,177,400	~	~	8.4	~	~
B. BOLIVIA	1976	Total	993,437	315,460	677,977	36.8	24.2	48.6
		Urban	176,748	34,393	142,355	15.2	6.2	23.2
		Rural	816,689	281,067	535,622	53.2	37.3	68.5
C. BRAZIL	1978	Total	16,223,404	7,308,439	8,914,965	23.9	22.0	25.7
		Urban	7,308,975	2,870,786	4,438,189	15.6	12.8	18.1
		Rural	8,914,429	4,437,653	4,476,776	42.4	40.9	43.9
D. CHILE	1970	Total	594,749	262,937	331,812	11.0	10.1	11.8
		Urban	276,270	103,183	173,087	6.6	5.4	7.7
		Rural	318,479	159,754	158,725	25.6	23.6	27.9
E. COLOMBIA	1973	Total	2,110,850	933,027	1,177,823	19.2	18.0	20.2
		Urban	814,945	288,686	526,259	11.2	9.0	13.0
		Rural	1,295,905	644,341	651,564	34.7	32.8	36.8
F. COSTA RICA	1973	Total	121,312	59,084	62,228	11.6	11.4	11.8
		Urban	23,177	8,522	14,655	4.9	4.0	5.7
		Rural	98,135	50,562	47,573	17.0	16.6	17.5
G. CUBA	1979	Total	218,358	101,119	117,239	4.6	4.3	4.9
H. DOMINICAN REP.[2]	1970	Total	678,910	319,825	359,085	32.8	31.2	34.3
		Urban	165,841	~	~	19.0	~	~
		Rural	517,796	~	~	43.4	~	~
I. ECUADOR	1974	Total	932,723	390,435	542,288	25.8	21.8	29.6
		Urban	153,280	50,615	102,665	9.7	6.9	12.2
		Rural	779,443	339,820	439,623	38.2	32.3	44.4
J. EL SALVADOR	1975	Total[1]	1,064,159	462,705	601,454	38.0	34.5	41.1
		Urban	216,593	67,830	148,763	18.0	12.7	22.2
		Rural	847,566	394,875	452,691	53.0	48.9	57.2
K. GUATEMALA	1973	Total	1,528,732	651,915	876,817	54.0	46.4	61.5
		Urban	291,380	97,460	193,920	28.2	20.0	35.5
		Rural	1,235,220	549,980	685,240	68.6	59.9	77.6
L. HAITI	1971	Total	2,005,052	884,678	1,120,374	78.7	73.8	83.1
M. HONDURAS	1974	Total	594,194	274,815	319,379	43.1	41.1	44.9
		Urban	99,015	37,523	61,492	21.1	17.6	24.0
		Rural	495,179	237,292	257,887	54.4	52.1	56.8
N. MEXICO	1980	Total	9,400,000	4,100,000	5,300,000	19.0	16.7	21.2
O. NICARAGUA[5]	1971	Total	410,755	193,475[a]	217,277	42.5	42.0	42.9
		Urban	94,319	33,873	60,446	19.5	16.1	22.1
		Rural	316,436	159,605	156,831	65.4	63.8	67.0
P. PANAMA	1980	Total	166,669[a]	80,163[a]	86,506[a]	15.4	14.7	16.0
		Urban	26,221	10,985	15,236	6.3	5.6	7.0
		Rural	149,162	75,687	93,475	38.1	35.5	41.1
Q. PARAGUAY	1972	Total	256,690	93,150	163,540	19.9	14.9	24.5
		Urban	61,570	18,240	43,330	11.4	7.4	14.7
		Rural	195,120	74,910	120,210	25.9	19.7	32.3
R. PERU	1972	Total	2,062,870[a]	624,018	1,438,852	27.5	16.7	38.2
		Urban	586,191	137,018	444,176	12.6	5.9	19.1
		Rural	1,454,676	487,000	994,676	50.9	32.9	69.2
S. URUGUAY	1975	Total	124,664[a]	65,007[a]	59,657[a]	6.1	6.6	5.7
		Urban	87,500	40,200	47,300	5.2	5.1	5.2
		Rural	37,000	24,900	12,100	11.0	12.6	8.6
T. VENEZUELA	1971	Total	1,373,561	585,928	787,633	23.5	20.3	26.6
UNITED STATES[3]	1969	Total	1,435,000	708,000	727,000	1.0	1.1	1.0

1. Data refer to age 10 and over.
2. Excluding 8% of the population unspecified as to literacy or illiteracy.
3. Data refer to age 14 and over.
4. Data refer to age 18 and over.
5. In 1980, after the National Literacy Campaign, the Ministry of Education estimated that of the 722,431 illiterates identified in the census of October, 1979, 130,372 were "analfabetos inaptos" and 406,056 were made literate, leaving only 186,003 "analfabetos aptos" (or 12.96% of the population of 10 years and over).

a. Urban and rural do not equal the total.

SOURCE: UNESCO-SY, 1980-83, table 1.3.

Table 901

STUDENTS ENROLLED AS SHARE OF ELIGIBLE AGES, 20 LR, 1960 AND 1980
(%)

	Country	6 to 11 Years		12 to 17 Years		18 to 23 Years	
		1960	1980	1960	1980	1960	1980
A.	ARGENTINA	91.2	99.9	48.1	72.7	13.2	36.7
B.	BOLIVIA	45.1	76.6	29.0	54.2	5.0	17.1
C.	BRAZIL	47.7	76.2	29.6	58.6	4.7	32.0
D.	CHILE	76.4	100.0	54.7	86.5	7.2	22.2
E.	COLOMBIA	47.9	70.0	28.8	63.8	4.4	32.9
F.	COSTA RICA	74.4	97.5	35.7	54.7	8.0	21.4
G.	CUBA	77.7	100.0	43.0	83.4	6.6	29.9
H.	DOMINICAN REP.	66.8	82.2	39.4	64.4	3.7	20.6
I.	ECUADOR	66.3	80.0	30.3	60.8	5.1	28.5
J.	EL SALVADOR	48.7	69.2	40.3	58.1	8.5	18.9
K.	GUATEMALA	32.0	53.3	17.7	33.8	3.6	10.1
L.	HAITI	33.6	41.4	16.4	21.9	1.9	4.3
M.	HONDURAS	49.5	71.3	24.6	44.7	3.2	14.8
N.	MEXICO	58.4	94.2	37.4	67.3	4.7	18.2
O.	NICARAGUA	42.9	60.8	29.7	53.7	3.6	18.6
P.	PANAMA	68.3	95.7	50.3	83.2	12.7	43.3
Q.	PARAGUAY	69.7	80.0	44.8	51.9	5.8	13.3
R.	PERU	56.7	83.9	43.2	84.0	13.0	32.6
S.	URUGUAY	89.9	~	53.2	67.2	14.1	24.3
T.	VENEZUELA	68.8	83.2	49.0	60.9	8.6	24.0
	LATIN AMERICA[1]	57.3	82.3	35.4	63.3	6.3	26.1

1. Includes Barbados, Guyana, Jamaica, and Trinidad and Tobago.

SOURCE: ECLA-D, "Informe del Secretario Ejecutivo al Décimonoveno Período de Sesiones de la Comisión," July 27, 1981.

Table 902

ENROLLMENT RATIOS FOR THE FIRST, SECOND, AND THIRD LEVELS OF EDUCATION, 20 LC

Country	School Year Beginning	Sex	First Level Gross	First Level Net	Second Level Gross	Second Level Net	First and Second Levels Gross	Third Level Gross
A. ARGENTINA[2]	1982	MF	119	~	~	~	~	24.5
		F	119	~	~	~	~	23.4
B. BOLIVIA[3]	1981	MF	86	~	34	~	70	~
		F	78	~	31	~	64	~
C. BRAZIL[4]	1978	MF	92	~	32	13	77	11.5
		F	91	~	35	~	77	~
D. CHILE[3]	1981	MF	115	~	57	~	95	12.8
		F	114	~	62	~	96	10.4
E. COLOMBIA[5]	1981	MF	130	~	48	~	85	12.0
		F	132	~	51	~	87	10.7
F. COSTA RICA[6]	1981	MF	108	92	48	40	80	~
		F	107	93	51	42	81	~
G. CUBA[7]	1981	MF	107	97	75	~	90	~
		F	104	97	77	~	90	~
H. DOMINICAN REP.[8]	1981	MF	109	~	41	~	77	~
I. ECUADOR[9]	1980	MF	107	~	40	~	77	35.0
		F	105	~	42	~	76	25.1
J. EL SALVADOR[10]	1981	MF	61	56	20	~	52	~
		F	61	57	21	~	53	~
K. GUATEMALA[8]	1980	MF	69	56	16	~	45	9.2
		F	63	~	15	~	41	5.1
L. HAITI[8]	1981	MF	69	40	13	~	44	~
		F	64	38	12	~	41	~
M. HONDURAS[11]	1980	MF	95	76	30	~	69	8.2
		F	95	75	30	~	69	6.2
N. MEXICO[9]	1981	MF	121	~	51	~	89	14.6
		F	120	~	49	~	88	10.1
Q. NICARAGUA[11]	1981	MF	104	75	41	23	77	14.1
		F	107	76	45	26	80	~
P. PANAMA[7]	1981	MF	111	93	65	49	89	27.4
		F	108	93	69	53	90	27.7
Q. PARAGUAY[8]	1979	MF	102	86	26	21	67	~
		F	98	84	~	~	~	~
R. PERU[6]	1980	MF	112	85	57	~	88	19.0
		F	108	~	52	~	84	13.6
S. URUGUAY[9]	1981	MF	122	~	70	~	97	15.8
		F	120	~	~	~	~	~
T. VENEZUELA[8]	1981	MF	105	83	40	33	74	~
		F	104	~	38	36	73	~
UNITED STATES[12]	1980	MF	~	~	~	~	99	57.1
		F	~	~	~	~	99	59.3

1. The gross enrollment ratio is the total enrollment of all ages divided by the population of the specific age groups which correspond to the age groups of primary and secondary schooling. The net enrollment ratio has been calculated by using only that part of the enrollment which corresponds to the age groups of primary and secondary schooling.

   These ratios have been calculated taking into account the differing national systems of education and the duration of schooling at the first and second levels. At the third level, the figures for the population age 20-24 have been used throughout.

   First level = primary school; second level = high school, teacher training, or vocational school; third level = university and other institutions of higher learning. See table 1005.
2. The age brackets are: 1st level 6-12, 2nd level 13-17, combined 1st and 2nd levels 6-17, and 3rd level 20-24.
3. The age brackets are: 1st level 6-13, 2nd level 14-17, combined 1st and 2nd levels 6-17, and 3rd level 20-24.
4. The age brackets are: 1st level 7-14, 2nd level 15-17, combined 1st and 2nd levels 7-17, and 3rd level 20-24.
5. The age brackets are: 1st level 6-10, 2nd level 11-16, combined 1st and 2nd levels 6-16, and 3rd level 20-24.
6. The age brackets are: 1st level 6-11, 2nd level 12-16, combined 1st and 2nd levels 6-16, and 3rd level 20-24.
7. The age brackets are: 1st level 6-11, 2nd level 12-17, combined 1st and 2nd levels 6-17, and 3rd level 20-24.
8. The age brackets are: 1st level 7-12, 2nd level 13-18, combined 1st and 2nd levels 7-18, and 3rd level 20-24.
9. The age brackets are: 1st level 6-11, 2nd level 12-17, combined 1st and 2nd levels 6-17, and 3rd level 20-24.
10. The age brackets are: 1st level 7-15, 2nd level 16-18, combined 1st and 2nd levels 7-18, and 3rd level 20-24.
11. The age brackets are: 1st level 7-12, 2nd level 13-17, combined 1st and 2nd levels 7-17, and 3rd level 20-24.
12. The age brackets are: 1st level 6-12, 2nd level 13-17, combined 1st and 2nd levels 6-17 and 3rd level 20-24.

SOURCE: UNESCO-SY, 1983, table 3.2.

Table 903

COMPULSORY EDUCATION, ENTRANCE AGES, AND DURATION OF SCHOOLING AT FIRST AND SECOND LEVELS, 20 LC

Country	Compulsory Education		Pre-Primary Entrance Age	First Level		Second Level	
	Age Limits	Duration (Years)		Entrance Age	Duration (Years)	Entrance Age	Duration (Years)
A. ARGENTINA	6-14	7	3	6	7	13	3 + 2
B. BOLIVIA	6-14	8	4	6	8	14	4
C. BRAZIL	7-14	8	4	7	8	15	3
D. CHILE	6-13	8	2	6	8	14	4
E. COLOMBIA	6-12	5	5	6	5	11	4 + 2
F. COSTA RICA	6-15	9	5	6	6	12	3 + 2
G. CUBA	6-11	6	4	6	6	12	3 + 3
H. DOMINICAN REP.	7-14	7	3	7	6	13	2 + 4
I. ECUADOR	6-14	6	4	6	6	12	3 + 3
J. EL SALVADOR	7-15	9	4	7	9	16	3
K. GUATEMALA	7-14	6	4	7	6	13	3 + 3
L. HAITI	6-14	6	2	7	6	13	3 + 3
M. HONDURAS	6-13	6	4	7	6	13	3 + 2
N. MEXICO	6-12	6	3	6	6	12	3 + 3
O. NICARAGUA	7-12	6	5	7	6	13	3 + 2
P. PANAMA	6-15	9	4	6	6	12	3 + 3
Q. PARAGUAY	7-14	6	5	7	6	13	3 + 3
R. PERU	6-15	9	4	6	6	12	3 + 2
S. URUGUAY	6-15	9	3	6	6	12	3 + 3
T. VENEZUELA	7-14	6	4	7	6	13	3 + 3
UNITED STATES	7-16	10	3	6	8	14	4

SOURCE: UNESCO–SY, 1983, table 3.1.

Table 904

EDUCATIONAL ATTAINMENT, BY URBAN AND RURAL AREAS, AGE, AND SEX, 19 LC

Country and Category	Year	Sex	Age Group	Total Population	No Schooling	Highest Level Attained[1] (%)				
						First Level		Entered Second Level		Post-Secondary
						Incompleted	Completed	First Cycle	Second Cycle	
A. ARGENTINA										
Total Population	1970	MF	25+	12,366,850	8.3	41.8	30.6	15.3	7.5	4.0
		F	25+	6,304,250	9.5	41.8	31.5	6.1	8.5	2.5
B. BOLIVIA										
Total Population	1976	MF	25+	1,759,432	48.6	28.5 →		10.8	7.1	5.0
		F	25+	918,709	62.2	20.7 →		8.2	5.6	3.3
C. BRAZIL										
Total Population	1976	MF	25+	42,096,300	32.7	53.0	4.3	5.7 →		4.3
		F	25+	21,419,800	36.0	50.8	4.0	6.0 →		3.2
D. CHILE										
Total Population	1970	MF	25+	3,721,125	12.4	57.2 →		26.6 →		3.8
		F	25+	1,945,921	13.3	57.7 →		26.5 →		2.5
Urban Population		MF	25+	2,712,020	8.3	34.1	26.0	27.0 →		4.8
Rural Population		MF	25+	792,400	29.8	54.2	10.0	5.4 →		.6
E. COLOMBIA										
Total Population	1973	MF	20+	8,478,100	22.4	55.9 →		18.4 →		3.3
		F	20+	4,483,086	23.7	56.0 →		18.5 →		1.8
Urban Population		MF	20+	5,593,002	14.2	54.8 →		26.1 →		4.9
		F	20+	3,108,408	16.1	56.2 →		25.1 →		2.6
Rural Population		MF	20+	2,885,098	38.4	58.0 →		3.5 →		.2
		F	20+	1,374,677	40.8	55.6 →		3.5 →		.1
F. COSTA RICA										
Total Population	1973	MF	25+	657,543	16.1	49.1	17.8	6.3	4.9	5.8
		F	25+	331,240	16.0	49.8	17.7	6.5	4.5	5.4
Urban Population		MF	25+	297,887	7.2	37.4	24.8	10.9	9.0	10.6
		F	25+	161,996	8.1	39.3	24.4	10.9	8.1	9.3
Rural Population		MF	25+	359,656	23.6	58.8	12.1	2.4	1.4	1.8
		F	25+	169,244	23.6	59.8	11.4	2.3	1.1	1.7
H. DOMINICAN REP.										
Total Population	1970	MF	25+	1,145,090	40.1	41.6	4.3	9.6	2.5	1.9
		F	25+	563,150	42.8	40.9	3.9	8.7	2.4	1.3
Urban Population		MF	25+	487,675	22.9	42.1	7.4	18.3	5.2	4.1
Rural Population		MF	25+	657,415	52.8	41.2	2.0	3.2	.5	.3
I. ECUADOR										
Total Population	1974	MF	25+	2,296,282	31.9	53.7 →		5.9	5.3	3.2
		F	25+	1,160,896	36.8	49.8 →		6.0	5.8	1.7
Urban Population		MF	25+	958,110	13.0	56.7 →		12.1	11.2	7.0
		F	25+	508,630	16.4	56.3 →		11.9	11.9	3.5
Rural Population		MF	25+	1,338,172	45.4	51.5 →		1.5	1.1	.4
		F	25+	652,265	52.8	44.7 →		1.3	1.1	.2
J. EL SALVADOR	1971	MF	25+	1,252,939	54.7	37.9 →		6.0 →		1.9
K. GUATEMALA										
Total Population	1973	MF	25+	1,785,720	93.9 →	→	4.9 →		1.2
		F	25+	897,960	94.7 →	→	4.8 →		.5
Urban Population		MF	25+	639,780	85.2 →	→	11.8 →		2.9
Rural Population		MF	25+	1,145,940	98.7 →	→	1.1 →		.2
L. HAITI[2]										
Total Population	1971	MF	25+	1,726,108	83.5	10.6	1.8	1.8	2.0	.3
		F	25+	915,644	88.0	7.6	1.5	1.4	1.3	.2
M. HONDURAS										
Total Population	1974	MF	25+	858,459	53.1	34.5	6.0	1.5	3.8	1.0
		F	25+	440,453	56.3	32.1	6.0	1.4	3.8	.4
Urban Population		MF	25+	279,554	29.5	41.1	12.5	3.9	10.0	3.0
		F	25+	152,135	33.7	40.2	12.0	3.5	9.5	1.1
Rural Population		MF	25+	578,905	64.5	31.4	2.9	.4	.8	.1
		F	25+	288,318	68.3	27.8	2.8	.3	.8	#
N. MEXICO										
Total Population	1970	MF	20+	20,797,757	35.0	39.4	15.3	4.1	3.7	2.6
O. NICARAGUA										
Total Population	1971	MF	25+	593,100	53.9	41.8 →	→	4.4 →	
P. PANAMA	1970	MF	25+	537,394	24.9	53.5 →		9.0	8.4	4.2

Table 904 (Continued)

EDUCATIONAL ATTAINMENT, BY URBAN AND RURAL AREAS, AGE, AND SEX, 19 LC

Country and Category	Year	Sex	Age Group	Total Population	No Schooling	First Level — Incompleted	First Level — Completed	Entered Second Level — First Cycle	Entered Second Level — Second Cycle	Post-Secondary
Q. PARAGUAY										
Total Population	1972	MF	25+	842,223	19.6	57.7	10.3	5.9	4.6	2.0
		F	25+	438,419	25.4	53.8	10.6	5.1	4.0	1.2
Urban Population		MF	25+	346,870	11.3	46.8	16.5	11.0	9.8	4.6
		F	25+	192,086	15.4	47.0	17.5	9.5	8.0	2.5
Rural Population		MF	25+	495,353	25.5	65.3	5.9	2.2	.9	.2
		F	25+	246,333	33.2	59.1	5.1	1.6	.8	.1
R. PERU[3]										
Total Population	1972	MF	25+	5,008,980	35.0	31.1	16.1	6.3	7.1	4.5
		F	25+	2,539,525	47.5	25.0	13.7	4.9	6.1	3.0
Urban Population		MF	5+	7,073,800	23.7	31.1	17.6	12.8	10.1	4.8
		F	5+	3,545,100	28.4	31.2	16.8	11.0	9.0	3.6
Rural Population		MF	5+	4,689,400	57.7	32.8	6.3	2.0	.9	.3
		F	5+	2,334,600	70.3	24.3	3.6	1.1	.5	.2
S. URUGUAY										
Total Population	1975	MF	25+	1,590,200	9.9	36.7	29.6	17.4 ⟶		6.3
		F	25+	824,700	10.4	34.9	31.2	16.6 ⟶		6.8
T. VENEZUELA[4]										
Total Population	1971	MF	25+	3,714,362	47.1	39.2 ⟶		11.1 ⟶		2.6
		F	25+	1,872,317	50.6	37.6 ⟶		10.4 ⟶		1.3
UNITED STATES										
Total Population	1979	MF	25+	125,295,000	3.5 ⟶		65.4	⟶		31.1
		F	25+	66,309,000	3.2 ⟶		69.9	⟶		26.9

Highest Level Attained[1] (%)

1. For definition of levels, see table 1003, above.
2. "No Schooling" includes illiteracy data.
3. "No Schooling" includes persons who did not state their level of education.
4. The number and percentage within the total population of persons whose educational level is unknown was: MF 25+ 426,614 (15.3%); F 25+ 194,484 (14.2%).

SOURCE: UNESCO-SY, 1983, table 1.4.

Table 905

TEACHERS PER 10,000 PERSONS AGES 7-14, 20 LR, 1960-75

Country	1960	1965	1970	1975
A. ARGENTINA	343.4	388.4	470.1	525.3
B. BOLIVIA	145.8	164.8	187.7	239.9
C. BRAZIL	125.8	170.3	220.4	288.4
D. CHILE	170.0	173.8	188.0[a]	248.7
E. COLOMBIA	124.2	137.0	152.0	197.1
F. COSTA RICA	223.4	222.2	228.0	250.7
G. CUBA	143.7	199.1	275.2	365.5
H. DOMINICAN REP.	98.2	104.4	113.8	121.4
I. ECUADOR	138.8	159.9	187.8	230.7
J. EL SALVADOR	144.6	139.7	128.1	152.6
K. GUATEMALA	103.7	101.9	100.5	107.6
L. HAITI	46.2	44.7	46.1[b]	~
M. HONDURAS	109.1	119.1	149.2[b]	~
N. MEXICO	113.3	129.3	153.5[a]	169.5
O. NICARAGUA	104.7	111.6	122.9	119.7
P. PANAMA	193.5	221.7	240.0	296.8
Q. PARAGUAY	210.0	204.5	209.7	225.8
R. PERU	166.2	180.0	204.6	221.5
S. URUGUAY	288.1	270.3	328.1[b]	~
T. VENEZUELA	177.2	176.0	188.4	223.8
LATIN AMERICA	150.7	176.8	208.2	253.5

a. 1969.
b. 1968.

SOURCE: ECLA: *Indicators of Social and Economic Development in Latin America*, (Santiago), p. 32.

Table 906

TEACHERS AND SCHOOL ENROLLMENT, BY LEVEL AND TYPE, 20 L

Country	Level and Type of Education[1]	Year	Teaching Staff		Students Enrolled	
			Total	Females	Total	Females
A. ARGENTINA	Pre-primary	1982	27,454	27,377	570,353	287,100
	Primary	1982	206,535	189,438	4,197,372	2,061,532
	Intermediate	1981	178,681[c]	~	1,366,444	725,620
	Higher	1982	53,166	29,972	550,556	258,160
B. BOLIVIA	Pre-primary	1981	~	~	65,951	36,262
	Primary	1981	45,024	~	1,022,624	468,604
	Intermediate	1981	7,143[a]	~[a]	166,325	75,961
	Higher	1976	~		51,585[‡]	~
C. BRAZIL	Pre-primary	1979	52,038	50,038	1,198,104	595,747
	Primary	1979	863,335	750,450	22,025,449	10,887,324
	Intermediate	1978	180,782	96,426	2,537,949	1,358,213
	Higher	1978	~		1,251,116	~
D. CHILE	Pre-primary	1981	~	~	127,836	64,151
	Primary	1981	~	~	4,217,800	2,109,081
	Intermediate	1981	27,207[d]	14,220[d]	554,749	296,324
	Higher	1981	11,419[a,b]	~[a,b]	145,497	62,804
E. COLOMBIA	Pre-primary	1981	8,407	~	204,541	~
	Primary	1981	137,721	108,815	4,217,800	2,109,081
	Intermediate	1981	88,103	39,380	1,891,530	993,875
	Higher	1981	34,844	7,136	318,293	141,506
F. COSTA RICA	Pre-primary	1981	739	727	23,969	11,857
	Primary	1981	10,556	8,316	348,616	169,052
	Intermediate	1981	6,955	3,784	133,909	70,405
	Higher	1980	~	~	60,990	~
G. CUBA	Pre-primary	1981	5,248	5,094	123,302	60,156
	Primary	1981	83,113	63,761	1,409,765	670,946
	Intermediate	1981	86,578	40,898	1,056,763	531,667
	Higher	1980	10,680	~	151,733	73,413
H. DOMINICAN REP.	Pre-primary	1981	~	~	27,983	~
	Primary	1981	~	~	1,149,805	~
	Intermediate	1981	4,668[f]	2,644[f]	379,377	~
	Higher	1978	~	~	42,412	19,196
I. ECUADOR	Pre-primary	1979	1,390	1,332	42,856	21,855
	Primary	1979[g]	39,825[‡]	26,273[‡]	1,427,627[‡]	692,309[‡]
	Intermediate	1979[g]	31,489[‡]	11,753[‡]	535,445[‡]	263,382[‡]
	Higher	1978	10,706	~	235,274	83,401
J. EL SALVADOR	Pre-primary	1981	1,055	927	44,834	23,414
	Primary	1981	17,441	11,732	709,567	352,291
	Intermediate	1981	3,080[e]	844[e]	64,702	33,320
	Higher	1980	893	208	16,838	5,202
K. GUATEMALA	Pre-primary	1980	1,700	~	48,869	24,464
	Primary	1980	23,770	~	803,404	362,083
	Intermediate	1980	7,575[c]	~	156,612	70,809
	Higher	1979	2,845[d]	~	47,555	~
L. HAITI	Pre-primary	~	~	~	~	~
	Primary	1981	14,927	~	658,102	304,103
	Intermediate	1981	4,392[e]	~	101,519	~
	Higher	1978	493	50	4,186	979
M. HONDURAS	Pre-primary	1980	833	~	33,034	~
	Primary	1980	16,385	12,187	601,337	298,163
	Intermediate	1980	4,489	2,152	127,293	64,182
	Higher	1980	1,653	42	25,825	9,736
N. MEXICO	Pre-primary	1981	43,531	43,531	1,411,316	703,561
	Primary	1981	400,417	~	14,981,028	7,301,482
	Intermediate	1981	301,939	~	5,332,131	2,508,918
	Higher	1981	82,967	~	966,228	330,897
O. NICARAGUA	Pre-primary	1981	1,212	1,203	38,534	20,219
	Primary	1981	14,105	10,391	472,167	239,968
	Intermediate	1981	2,720[d]	~	136,629	73,494
	Higher	1982	1,369	~	32,838	15,374
P. PANAMA	Pre-primary	1981	851	848	22,616	11,373
	Primary	1981	12,598	10,112	335,239	161,272
	Intermediate	1981	8,610	4,594	174,078	90,775
	Higher	1981	3,378	997	50,185	24,708

Table 906 (Continued)

TEACHERS AND SCHOOL ENROLLMENT, BY LEVEL AND TYPE, 20 L

Country	Level and Type of Education[1]	Year	Teaching Staff		Students Enrolled	
			Total	Females	Total	Females
Q. PARAGUAY	Pre-primary	1978	~	~	8,680	4,332
	Primary	1979[g]			504,377	239,554
	Intermediate	1979	5,938[f]	3,455[f]	110,095	~
	Higher	1978	~	~	20,812	9,037
R. PERU	Pre-primary	1980	6,778	6,689	228,168	114,940
	Primary	1980	84,360	50,676	3,161,375	1,514,621
	Intermediate	1980	37,383	~	1,203,116	547,393
	Higher	1978	13,468[h]	~[h]	210,083	~
S. URUGUAY	Pre-primary	1981	~	~	44,415	~
	Primary	1981	18,017	~	387,150	187,510
	Intermediate	1981	~	~	188,123	78,487
	Higher	1982	3,847[e]	1,141[e]	48,234	26,782[e]
T. VENEZUELA	Pre-primary	1981	16,683	16,393	461,017	230,274
	Primary	1981	97,045	80,241	2,591,051	1,274,791
	Intermediate	1981	45,888[c]	22,808[c]	884,233	421,402
	Higher	1980	28,052	~	307,133	~

1. For definition of levels, see table 903 above; intermediate is defined as "Secondary" level.

a. 1975 data.
b. Full-time teachers only.
c. 1979 data.
d. 1978 data.
e. 1980 data.
f. 1970 data.
g. Includes evening schools.
h. 1977 data.

SOURCE: UNESCO-SY, 1983, tables 3.3, 3.4, 3.7, and 3.11.

Table 907

PRE-PRIMARY SCHOOLS, TEACHERS, AND PUPILS, 19 LC

Country	School Year Beginning	Number of Institutions	Teaching Staff			Pupils Enrolled			% Private
			Total	Female	%	Total	Female	%	
A. ARGENTINA	1982	7,345	27,454	27,377	100	570,353	287,100	51	31
B. BOLIVIA	1981	~	~	~	~	65,951	36,262	5	~
C. BRAZIL	1979	13,130	52,038	50,838	98	1,198,104	595,747	50	46
D. CHILE	1981	~	~	~	~	127,836	164,151	50	29
E. COLOMBIA	1981	3,756	8,407	~	~	204,541	~	~	63
F. COSTA RICA	1981	424	739	727	98	23,969	11,857	50	9
G. CUBA	1981	~	5,248	5,094	97	123,302	60,156	49	#
H. DOMINICAN REP.	1981	292	~	~	~	27,983	~	~	87
I. ECUADOR	1979	539	1,390	1,322	96	42,856	21,855	51	36
J. EL SALVADOR	1981	347	1,055	927	88	44,834	23,414	52	17
K. GUATEMALA	1980	564	1,700	~	~	48,869	24,464	50	38
M. HONDURAS	1980	441	833	~	~	33,034	~	~	16
N. MEXICO	1981	17,798	43,531	43,531	100	1,411,316	703,561	50	12
O. NICARAGUA	1981	646	1,212	1,203	99	38,534	20,219	53	30
P. PANAMA	1981	498	851	848	100	22,616	11,373	50	32
Q. PARAGUAY	1978	~	~	~	~	8,680	4,332	50	65
R. PERU	1980	3,271	6,778	6,689	99	228,168	114,940	50	27
S. URUGUAY	1981	772	~	~	~	44,415	~	~	24
T. VENEZUELA	1981	~	16,683	16,393	98	461,017	230,274	50	17
UNITED STATES	1980	~	~	~	~	5,163,000	2,449,000	47	36

SOURCE: UNESCO-SY, 1983, table 3.3.

Table 908

PRIMARY SCHOOLS,[1] TEACHERS, AND PUPILS, 20 LC

	Country	School Year Beginning	Number of Institutions (A)	Teaching Staff			Pupils Enrolled			Pupil/Teacher Ratio (H)
				Total (B)	Female (C)	% Female (D)	Total (E)	Female (F)	% Female (G)	
A.	ARGENTINA	1982	20,201	206,535	189,438	92	4,197,372	2,061,532	49	19
B.	BOLIVIA	1981	~	45,024	~	~	1,022,624	468,604	46	23
C.	BRAZIL	1979	192,723	863,335	750,450	87	22,025,449	10,887,324	49	26
D.	CHILE	1981	8,658	66,354[a]	48,972[a]	74[a]	2,139,319	1,046,326	49	~
E.	COLOMBIA	1981	34,641	137,721	108,815	79	4,217,800	2,109,081	50	31
F.	COSTA RICA	1981	2,944	10,556	8,316	79	348,616	169,052	49	33
G.	CUBA	1981	11,771	83,113	63,761	77	1,409,765	670,946	48	17
H.	DOMINICAN REP.[2]	1980	4,606	~	~	~	1,149,805	~	~	~
I.	ECUADOR[3]	1979	11,036‡	39,825‡	26,273‡	66‡	1,427,627‡	692,309	49‡	36‡
J.	EL SALVADOR[4]	1981	2,311	17,441	11,732	67	709,567	352,291	50	41
K.	GUATEMALA	1980	6,959	23,770	~	~	803,404	362,083	45	34
L.	HAITI	1981	3,321	14,927	~	~	658,102	304,103	46	44
M.	HONDURAS	1980	5,524	16,385	12,187	74	601,337	298,163	50	37
N.	MEXICO	1981	76,286	400,417	~	~	14,981,028	7,301,482	49	37
O.	NICARAGUA[6]	1981	4,056	14,105	11,153	79	509,240	258,245	51	36
P.	PANAMA	1981	2,316	12,598	10,112	80	335,239	161,272	48	27
Q.	PARAGUAY[4]	1979	~	~	~	~	504,377	239,554	48	~
R.	PERU	1980	20,776	84,360	50,676	60	3,161,375	1,514,621	48	37
S.	URUGUAY	1981	2,543	18,017	~	~	387,150	187,510	48	21
T.	VENEZUELA	1981	12,788	97,045	80,241	83	2,591,051	1,274,791	49	27
	UNITED STATES[5]	1980	80,500[a]	1,351,000‡,a	~	~	27,448,000	13,361,000	49	~

1. For primary levels see table 903.
2. Columns F and G refer to public education only.
3. Except for column E, includes evening schools.
4. Includes evening schools.
5. Includes special education.
6. Data in columns A, B, C, D, and H include pre-school.

a. 1979 data.

SOURCE: UNESCO-SY, 1983, table 3.4.

Table 909

HIGHER EDUCATION: [1] TEACHERS AND STUDENTS, BY TYPE OF INSTITUTION, 20 LC

Country	School Year Beginning	All Institutions		Universities and Equivalent Institutions		Other Non-University Institutions	
		Total	Female	Total	Female	Total	Female
A. ARGENTINA							
Teachers	1981	47,637	20,951	30,120	8,876	17,517	12,075
Students	1979	527,596	280,972	403,978	175,392	123,618	105,580
B. BOLIVIA							
Teachers	1978	~	~	2,797	~	~	~
Students	1978	~	~	44,946	~	~	~
C. BRAZIL							
Teachers	1978	~	~	104,231	~	~	~
Students	1978	1,251,116	~	1,225,557	~	25,559	~
D. CHILE[2]							
Teachers	1981	~	~	14,386	~	~	~
Students	1981	145,497[b]	62,804[b]	120,101	48,437	25,329	14,342
E. COLOMBIA							
Teachers	1981	34,844	7,136	30,384	6,106	4,460	1,030
Students	1981	318,293	141,506	283,242	121,715	35,051	19,790
F. COSTA RICA							
Teachers	1980	~	~	4,382	~	~	~
Students	1980	60,990	~	50,812	~	10,178	~
G. CUBA							
Teachers	1980	10,680	~	10,680	~	#	#
Students	1980	151,733	73,413	151,733	73,413	#	#
H. DOMINICAN REP.							
Teachers	1975	~	~	1,435	~	~	~
Students	1978	~	~	42,412	~	~	~
I. ECUADOR							
Teachers	1981	~	~	11,679	~	~	~
Students	1981	~	~	258,054	93,623	~	~
J. EL SALVADOR							
Teachers	1980	893	208	445	72	448	136
Students	1980	16,838	5,202	12,740	3,999	4,098	1,203
K. GUATEMALA[3]							
Teachers	1978	2,845	~	2,845	~	#	#
Students	1979	47,555	~	44,253	~	3,302	~
L. HAITI							
Teachers	1980	~	~	559	~	~	~
Students	1980	~	~	4,099	1,292	~	~
M. HONDURAS							
Teachers	1980	1,653	42	1,439	#	214	42
Students	1980	25,825	9,736	24,021	9,025	1,804	711
N. MEXICO							
Teachers	1981	82,967	~	77,209	~	5,758	~
Students	1981	966,228	330,897	840,368	266,904	125,860	63,993
O. NICARAGUA							
Teachers	1982	1,369	~	1,181	~	188	~
Students	1982	32,838	15,374	29,849	14,376	2,989	998
P. PANAMA							
Teachers	1981	3,378	997	3,378	3,378	#	#
Students	1981	50,185	24,708	50,185	24,708	#	#
Q. PARAGUAY							
Teachers	1978	~	~	~	441	~	~
Students	1978	20,812	9,037	20,496	8,791	316	246
R. PERU							
Teachers	1980	17,853	~	14,727	2,343	3,126	~
Students	1980	306,353	107,980	246,510	83,791	59,843	24,189
S. URUGUAY							
Teachers	1981	4,149	~	4,149	~	#	#
Students	1982	48,234	26,782	48,234	26,782	#	#
T. VENEZUELA							
Teachers	1980	28,052	~	23,984	~	4,068	~
Students	1980	307,133	~	271,583	~	35,550	~
UNITED STATES							
Teachers	1980	395,992	104,663	305,982	71,980	90,010	32,683
Students	1980	12,096,895	6,396,616	7,572,657	3,745,958	4,524,238	2,476,563

1. For pre-higher education levels, see table 903.
2. 1975 teachers data refer to full-time teachers only.
3. University of San Carlos only.

a. 1979 data.
b. 1980 data.

SOURCE: UNESCO-SY, 1983, table 3.11.

Table 910

HIGHER EDUCATION:[1] DISTRIBUTION OF STUDENTS, BY SEX AND FIELD OF STUDY, 19 L

Country	School Year Beginning	Sex	Total	Humanities	Education	Fine Arts	Law	Social Sciences	Natural Sciences	Engineering	Medical Sciences	Agriculture	Not Specified
A. ARGENTINA	1981	MF	527,596	26,178	7,681	4,194	59,165	10,075	22,969	69,323	51,112	23,466	123,618
		F	280,972	19,487	6,622	2,940	27,296	7,245	13,495	7,730	26,683	6,460	105,580
B. BOLIVIA[6]	1978	MF	44,946	800	401	122	3,452	5,844	687	8,970	9,662	504	#
C. BRAZIL	1978	MF	1,251,116	23,132	393,431	8,848	133,529	93,579	14,731	151,146	104,298	33,324	26,340
D. CHILE[3,6]	1981	MF	120,101	11,284	12,239	4,797	2,247	1,281	8,929	34,213	12,945	3,146	4,578
		F	48,437	6,970	9,792	2,580	698	698	4,271	4,077	7,638	1,176	2,545
E. COLOMBIA[5]	1981	MF	318,293	2,698	53,166	6,272	30,090	15,284	5,211	59,300	33,331	11,141	#
		F	141,506	1,328	32,961	4,303	12,904	11,801	2,006	12,373	17,906	2,002	#
F. COSTA RICA[6]	1980	MF	50,812	7,947	6,838	924	2,428	4,622	1,952	4,319	2,824	3,169	6,149
G. CUBA	1980	MF	151,733	2,795	60,942	902	3,175	1,727	3,791	18,893	15,559	14,538	4,511
H. DOMINICAN REP.[2,4]	1978	MF	42,412	222	6,710	388	1,356	2,645	911	7,305	10,054	1,119	498
I. ECUADOR[6]	1981	MF	258,054	10,252	48,837	1,239	13,396	23,148	2,667	52,942	32,686	14,799	6,512
		F	93,623	7,414	26,495	688	4,006	9,888	607	6,379	13,993	2,695	2,614
J. EL SALVADOR[3]	1980	MF	16,838	158	698	339	592	1,959	29	6,308	479	#	#
K. GUATEMALA[7]	1979	MF	47,555	4,838	4,056	107	6,177	1,968	1,189	5,197	5,496	2,978	1,350
		F	~	~	~	~	~	~	~	~	~	~	~
L. HAITI	1979	MF	3,801	#	328	#	838	620	#	548	1,022	152	#
		F	1,086	#	30	#	244	241	#	71	382	15	#
M. HONDURAS	1980	MF	25,825	204	491	16	2,222	3,345	232	6,389	4,432	707	1,193
		F	9,736	114	343	3	766	1,575	126	1,009	2,300	#	656
N. MEXICO[4]	1981	MF	840,368	10,739	9,789	6,937	69,803	59,517	22,212	177,083	147,948	82,905	1,745
		F	266,904	5,937	6,874	3,465	22,274	31,375	7,602	18,604	65,731	8,544	160
P. PANAMA	1981	MF	50,185	3,644	4,205	645	1,917	2,840	1,369	16,060	3,417	936	#
		F	19,061	1,526	1,748	355	687	1,534	495	3,282	2,178	84	#
Q. PARAGUAY[2]	1978	MF	20,812	354	404	311	3,208	633	938	1,593	1,915	1,108	5,968
		F	9,037	195	322	227	1,350	459	583	203	978	219	2,487
R. PERU[6]	1980	MF	306,353	3,513	23,314	441	14,534	37,388	8,373	53,338	23,781	24,081	14,356
S. URUGUAY	1981	MF	36,706	545	215	234	12,441	1,565	1,522	1,551	7,511	3,322	427
		F	~	394	181	118	8,537	1,249	843	165	4,658	953	401
T. VENEZUELA	1980	MF	307,133	3,478	44,875	410	18,975	21,699	5,912	51,306	35,650	12,813	51,389

1. Includes awards not equivalent to a first university degree, first university degrees, and post-graduate university degrees.
2. The figures shown under "Not Specified" refer mainly to students enrolled either in the first year or in the preparatory year (general studies).
3. Social Sciences include commercial and business administration, mass communication and documentation, home economics, and service trades. Natural Sciences include mathematics and computer science. Engineering includes architecture and town planning, trade, craft and industrial programs, and transport and communications.
4. Data refer to universities and equivalent institutions only.
5. Fine and applied arts and architecture are combined. Natural Sciences include mathematics and computer science. Engineering includes trade, craft and industrial programs, and transport and communications.
6. Data refer to universities only.
7. University of San Carlos only.

a. Data refer to 1978.

SOURCE: UNESCO-SY, 1983, table 3.12.

Table 911

HIGHER EDUCATION: GRADUATES, BY FIELD OF STUDY,[1] 18 LC

Country	School Year Beginning	Sex	Total	Humanities	Education	Fine Arts	Law	Social Sciences	Natural Sciences	Engineering	Medical Sciences	Agriculture	Not Specified
B. BOLIVIA[2]	1978	MF	1,542	35	3	2	172	187	24	107	505	46	#
C. BRAZIL	1978	MF	198,716	3,872	77,143	2,162	16,574	13,230	2,740	18,140	19,380	5,931	3,759
D. CHILE[6]	1981	MF	20,037	423	9,147	308	272	180	373	2,912	3,043	536	374
		F	10,849	286	6,462	176	101	98	168	351	1,907	132	322
E. COLOMBIA	1981	MF	28,573	306	6,672	596	2,029	1,333	450	4,627	3,825	868	#
		F	13,800	186	4,168	420	852	1,097	203	944	2,382	131	#
F. COSTA RICA[3]	1978	MF	4,146	383	1,273	71	112	541	154	234	699	177	#
G. CUBA	1980	MF	25,898	533	13,691	152	650	383	623	2,905	1,409	1,739	431
H. DOMINICAN REP.[4]	1978	MF	2,452	13	523	28	79	86	118	406	823	76	#
		F	1,320	2	397	18	26	54	90	63	492	6	#
I. ECUADOR	1981	MF	15,441	179	6,892	86	858	1,445	#	1,074	2,077	1,252	36
		F	6,262	92	3,603	43	225	603	#	100	883	187	12
J. EL SALVADOR	1978	MF	1,487	1	150	#	46	28	12	691	164	205	#
K. GUATEMALA[5]	1979	MF	1,340	23	425	#	74	19	29	142	354	71	25
L. HAITI[6]	1978	MF	344	7	11	#	#	10	31	83	151	38	#
M. HONDURAS[7]	1980	MF	918	11	14	#	131	164	14	146	132	167	12
		F	288	7	10	#	38	70	12	22	68	#	7
N. MEXICO[6]	1981	MF	78,644	757	626	570	6,877	6,208	1,925	15,032	20,744	7,688	221
O. NICARAGUA	1981	MF	4,173	243	54	#	63	751	201	682	496	52	84
P. PANAMA	1981	MF	2,900	37	935	58	117	158	101	433	310	178	#
		F	1,595	22	634	36	37	123	48	106	191	30	#
R. PERU[6]	1980	MF	18,530	16	3,034	19	685	547	153	1,943	2,340	1,077	612
S. URUGUAY	1981	MF	2,932	44	1	3	827	66	113	127	901	224	68
		F	1,016	38	#	2	304	49	57	6	275	36	63
T. VENEZUELA[4]	1980	MF	15,819	217	3,582	#	1,197	1,589	315	2,878	2,307	827	#
U. UNITED STATES[8]	1980	MF	1,752,995	102,915	193,566	60,258	39,110	167,605	91,237	95,041	162,679	35,885	276,460
		F	870,601	51,352	144,719	37,279	12,493	81,766	31,894	9,201	120,918	10,518	152,390

1. Includes awards not equivalent to a first university degree, first university degrees, and post-graduate university degrees.
2. Excludes higher teacher training at non-university institutions.
3. University of Costa Rica only.
4. Universities and equivalent institutions only.
5. University of San Carlos only.
6. Universities only.
7. University of Honduras only.
8. The figures under "Not Specified" include associate degrees.

SOURCE: UNESCO-SY, 1982, table 3.14; UNESCO-SY, 1983, table 3.4.

Table 912

HIGHER EDUCATION: GRADUATES, BY LEVEL OF DEGREE AND FIELD OF STUDY, 17 LC

Country	School Year Beginning	Stage or Degree of Diploma[1]	Total	Humanities, Education Fine Arts	Law, Social Sciences	Natural Sciences	Engineering	Medical Sciences	Agriculture	Not Specified
B. BOLIVIA[2]	1978	A	96	1	#	1	1	22	35	#
		B	1,446	1	359	23	106	483	11	#
		C	#	#	#	#	#	#	#	#
C. BRAZIL	1978	A	#	#	#	#	#	#	#	#
		B	187,973	81,050	27,991	1,776	16,593	17,645	5,042	3,534
		C	10,743	2,127	1,813	964	1,547	1,735	889	225
D. CHILE[6]	1981	A	961	#	69	#[a]	592	#	66	#
		B	18,953	9,824	381	342	2,314	3,042	461	374
		C	123	54	2	31	6		9	#
E. COLOMBIA	1981	A	5,218	1,109	2,320	150[a]	1,275	206	152	#
		B	23,355	6,441	8,032	300[a]	3,352	3,619	716	#
		C	#	#	#	#	#[b]	#	#	#
F. COSTA RICA[3]	1978	A	#	#	#	#	#	#	#	#
		B	4,146	1,727	653	154	234	699	177	#
		C	#	#	#	#	#	#	#	#
G. CUBA	1980	A	#	#	#	#	#	#	#	#
		B	25,898	14,376	1,033	623	2,905	1,409	1,739	431
		C	#	#	#	#	#	#	#	#
H. DOMINICAN REP.[2]	1978	A	252	55	9	#	62	3	#	#
		B	2,200	509	156	118	344	820	76	#
		C	#	#	#	#	#	#	#	#
I. ECUADOR	1970	A	132	19	36	#	36	41	#	#
		B	2,242	891	532	44	279	254	242	#
		C	26	23	3	#	#	#	#	#
J. EL SALVADOR	1978	A	966	92	#	#	546	64	146	#
		B	500	38	74	12	145	100	59	#
		C	21	21	#	#	#	#	#	#
K. GUATEMALA[4]	1979	A	#	#	#	#	#	#	#	#
		B	1,340	448	93	29	142	354	71	#
		C	#	#	#	#	#	#	#	#
L. HAITI[6]	1978	A	13	#	#	#	#	#	#	#
		B	331	#	10	31	83	151	38	#
		C	#	#	#	#	#	#	#	#
N. MEXICO[6]	1981	A	#	#	#	#	#	#	#	#
		B	78,644	1,953	13,085	1,925	15,032	20,744	7,688	221
		C	#	#	#	#	#	#	#	#
O. NICARAGUA	1980	A	1,026	#	#	8	33	290	30	#
		B	3,113	297	814	159	649	206	22	84
		C	34	1	#	34	#	#	#	#
P. PANAMA[5]	1981	A	1,131	494	29	32	338	75	27	#
		B	1,266	33	246	69	95	235	151	#
		C	503	- -	- -	- -	- -	- -	- -	- -
R. PERU[6]	1979	A	#	#	#	#	#	#	#	#
		B	6,108	1,106	1,006	137	796	1,378	609	286
		C	#	#	#	#	#	#	#	#
S. URUGUAY	1981	A	1,103	42	395	80	#	328	#	68
		B	1,819	6	498	33	127	563	224	#
		C	10					10		
T. VENEZUELA[2]	1980	A	3,098	530	351	#	738	39	389	#
		B	12,721	3,269	2,435	315	2,049	2,268	438	#
		C	#	#	57	#	#	#	#	#
UNITED STATES[7]	1980	A	416,377	14,736	#	1,725	#	60,049	6,810	175,659
		B	935,468	224,711	137,333	71,110	74,689	61,193	21,873	69,873
		C	401,150	117,292	69,382	18,402	20,355	41,437	7,202	30,928

1. Code:
   A = Diploma and certificates not equivalent to a first university degree. These correspond to higher studies of reduced duration (generally less than three years). They include, for instance, certificates awarded to certain types of technicians, nursing diplomas, land-surveying diplomas, associate degrees, certificates of competence in law, etc.

   B = First university degrees or equivalent qualifications. These represent higher studies of normal duration (generally three to five years and, in certain cases, seven years). These are the most numerous. They include typical first degrees such as the bachelor's degree, the *license*, etc., as well as in certain countries first professional degrees such as doctorates awarded after completion of studies in medicine, engineering, law, etc.

   C = Post-graduate university degrees or equivalent qualifications. These are those which persons who already possess a first university degree (or equivalent qualification) can obtain by continuing their studies. For example, the post-graduate diploma, the *diplôme d'études supérieures*, the master's degree, the doctor's degree (Ph.D.), the *doctorat de spécialité ou d'état*, etc.

2. Excludes higher teacher training at non-university institutions.
3. University of Costa Rica only.
4. University of San Carlos only.
5. Programs of Level C are included with Level B.
6. Universities only.
7. The figures under "Not Specified" include associate degrees for which the distribution by field of study is not available; these numbered 503,598 in 1976.

a. Includes mathematics and computer science.
b. Includes trade, craft and industrial programs, transport, and communications.

SOURCE: UNESCO-SY, 1981-83, table 3.14.

Table 913

PERCENTAGE OF "LEFTIST" STUDENTS IN SAMPLE[1] BY FATHER'S RELIGION AND UNIVERSITY, 4 L

	Father's Religion		
Country	Practicing Catholic	Non-practicing Catholic	Non-Catholic, Atheist, Agnostic
E. COLOMBIA			
Los Andes[2]	9	21	13
Javeriana[3]	7	15	0
Nacional[4]	31	55	56
Libre[2]	73	85	93
Cauca[4]	27	36	60
N. MEXICO			
UNAM[4]	21	36	47
Guanajuato[4]	11	7	62
Q. PARAGUAY[4]	6	9	20
S. URUGUAY[4]	38	33	46

1. Percentage of students in sample with high scores in Leftist ideology, based on answers to questionnaire in survey of 4,815 Latin American students conducted by Seymour Martin Lipset in 1964 and 1965. Questions used to determine political ideology on a Left/Right scale dealt with attitudes toward the Cuban Revolution, government control of the economy, effect of foreign capital, living conditions in various world nations, and students' perception of their own political ideology.
2. Private, secular universities.
3. Private, Catholic university.
4. Public universities.

SOURCE: Arthur Liebman, Kenneth N. Walker, and Myron Glazer, *Latin American University Students: A Six Nation Study* (Cambridge, Mass.: Harvard University Press, 1972), p. 104.

Table 914

ACADEMIC STUDENTS STUDYING IN COMMUNIST COUNTRIES, 10 L
(December 1978)

Country	Total	USSR	Eastern Europe
B. BOLIVIA	170	110	60
C. BRAZIL	70	35	35
E. COLOMBIA	1,020	490	530
F. COSTA RICA	550	350	200
I. ECUADOR	825	315	510
J. EL SALVADOR	135	30	105
K. GUATEMALA	25	25	~
O. NICARAGUA	125	110	15
R. PERU	595	575	20
T. VENEZUELA	105	50	55

SOURCE: CIA, *Communist Aid Activities in Non-Communist Less Developed Countries, 1978* (Washington, D. C., Sept. 1979), p. 17.

Table 915

SCHOOL ENROLLMENT, 20 L, 1880–1929

A. ARGENTINA

Year	Total	Primary	Secondary	Higher	Year	Total	Primary	Secondary	Higher
1880	~	~	~	~	1905	~	543,881	~	~
1881	~	~	1,616	~	1906	~	659,460[t]	16,852[t,i]	~
1882	101,027	97,756[a]	2,270	1,001	1907	~	~	~	~
1883	~	107,961	~	~	1908	~	~	~	~
1884	~	~	5,198[t,b]	904[c]	1909	~	668,534	~	10,289

Continued in SALA, 18-1024 through 1043.

Table 916

ADULT EDUCATION: TEACHERS AND STUDENT ENROLLMENT, 20 L

Country	Number of Teachers				Number of Students Enrolled				Ratio of Students to Teachers
	Year	Total	Male	Female	Year	Total	Male	Female	
A. ARGENTINA[1]	1973[‡]	19,204	~	~	1973[‡]	518,752	~	~	27.0

Continued in SALA, 18-1022.

Table 917

SPECIAL EDUCATION: ESTABLISHMENTS, TEACHERS, AND STUDENT ENROLLMENT, 20 L

Country	Year	Type of Establishment (N)					Teachers	Students Enrolled		
		Total	Blind	Deaf and Dumb	Mentally Retarded	Others		Total	Male	Female
A. ARGENTINA	1971	316	17	16	283	- -	5,675	22,668	14,043	8,625

Continued in SALA, 18-1023.

Table 918

UNIVERSITY LIBRARY COLLECTIONS, BORROWERS, WORKS LOANED, CURRENT EXPENDITURE,
AND PERSONNEL, 13 LC

Country	Year	Number of Administrative Units	Number of Service Points	Collections		Annual Additions (Volumes)	Number of Registered Borrowers	Works Loaned (Volumes)	Current Expenditures		Library Employees		
				Meters of Shelving	Number of Volumes (T)				Amount (T)	Staff (%)	Total	Holding a Diploma	Trained on the Job
A. ARGENTINA	1974	29[‡]	35	43,805[‡]	2,136	14,875[‡]	212,892[‡]	841,284	~	~	454	103	151

Continued in SALA, 22-1018.

Table 919

LIBRARIES BY CATEGORY, 13 LC

Country			National	Higher Education	School	Special	Public
A.	ARGENTINA[1]	1979	1	29	~	699	1,528[a]
C.	BRAZIL	1974	1	613	~	572	2,332
D.	CHILE[2]	1980	1	182[a]	296	~	161
E.	COLOMBIA[3]	1980	1	~	~	~	~
F.	COSTA RICA	1977	1	~	~	~	
J.	EL SALVADOR	1980	1	~	~	~	~
K.	GUATEMALA	1980	1	1[b]		1[a]	[a]
M.	HONDURAS[4]	1977	~	1	~	~	
N.	MEXICO	1979	2	250	1,604	112	485[b]
P.	PANAMA	1980	~	2[a]	54[a]	1[a]	18
R.	PERU[1]	1980	1	1	81	~	520
S.	URUGUAY	1980	1	~	~	~	~
T.	VENEZUELA[5]	1980	1	131	46[b]	35	23
	UNITED STATES	1978	3	3,122	70,854	1,143	8,456

1. Data on libraries of institutions of higher education refer to 1974.
2. Data on school libraries refer to 1976 and those on public libraries to 1978.
3. Data on special libraries refer to 1975.
4. Data on special libraries refer to 1974.
5. Data on libraries of institutions of higher education and on special libraries refer to 1977.

a. 1977 data.
b. 1978 data.

SOURCE: UNESCO-SY, 1983, table 7.1.

Table 920

SCHOOL AND FINANCIAL YEARS, 20 LC

Country		School Year		Financial Year
		Beginning	End	Beginning
A.	ARGENTINA	March	November	January
B.	BOLIVIA	February	November	January
C.	BRAZIL	February	December	January
D.	CHILE	March	December	January
E.	COLOMBIA	February	November	January
F.	COSTA RICA	March	November	January
G.	CUBA	September	June	January
H.	DOMINICAN REP.	September	June	January
I.	ECUADOR	October	July	January
J.	EL SALVADOR	February	November	January
K.	GUATEMALA	January	October	January
L.	HAITI	October	June	October
M.	HONDURAS	February	November	January
N.	MEXICO	September	June	January
O.	NICARAGUA	February	November	January
P.	PANAMA	April	December	January
Q.	PARAGUAY	February	November	January
R.	PERU	April	December	January
S.	URUGUAY	March	December	January
T.	VENEZUELA	October	July	January
	UNITED STATES	September	June	October

SOURCE: UNESCO-SY, 1983, Appendix B.

Table 921

TOTAL PUBLIC EDUCATIONAL EXPENDITURE, 20 LC
(Current and Capital Funds)

	Country	Year	Total Educational Expenditure			Current Educational Expenditure				Capital Expenditure (T NC)
			Amount (T NC)	As % of Gross National Product	As % of Total Government Expenditure	Amount (T NC)	As % of Total	As % of Gross National Product	As % of Current Government Expenditure	
A.	ARGENTINA	1980	10,176,746	3.9	15.1	8,598,918	84.5	3.3	18.8	1,577,828
B.	BOLIVIA	1980	5,122,191	3.6	25.3	4,919,122	96.0	3.4	27.0	203,069
C.	BRAZIL	1979	201,519,339	3.3	~	~	~	~	~	~
D.	CHILE	1981	66,140,828	5.4	~	62,609,745	94.7	5.1	~	3,531,083
E.	COLOMBIA	1981	51,777,416	2.6	~	49,004,771	94.6	2.5	~	2,772,645
F.	COSTA RICA	1981	4,101,727	7.8	~	3,836,001	93.5	7.3	~	265,726
G.	CUBA	1981	1,397,200	~	~	1,275,300	91.3	~	~	121,900
H.	DOMINICAN REP.	1980	138,500	2.0	16.0	104,896		1.5	17.2	9,899
I.	ECUADOR	1980	15,579,992	5.8	33.3	14,649,139	94.0	5.4	36.0	930,853
J.	EL SALVADOR	1980	340,136	4.0	17.1	320,009	94.1	3.7	22.9	20,127
K.	GUATEMALA	1981	156,706	1.8	10.7	149,714	95.5	1.7	22.5	6,992
L.	HAITI	1980	107,136	1.5	10.7	85,781	80.1	1.2	15.3	21,355
M.	HONDURAS	1981	183,661	3.5	9.8	163,615	89.1	3.1	10.5	20,046
N.	MEXICO	1981	196,492,000	3.9	13.6	181,262,144	92.2	3.6	~	15,229,856
O.	NICARAGUA	1980	662,132	3.2	10.4	579,693	87.5	2.8	~	82,434
P.	PANAMA	1981	178,019	4.9	18.4	162,341	91.2	4.4	18.7	15,678
Q.	PARAGUAY	1979	5,627,500	1.3	12.4	~	~	~	~	~
R.	PERU	1981	326,128,000	3.7	16.8	310,790,000	95.3	3.5	20.6	15,338,000
S.	URUGUAY	1980	2,035,103	2.3	10.0	1,926,769	94.7	2.2	~	108,334
T.	VENEZUELA	1980	13,162,451	5.2	14.7	12,523,608	95.1	4.9	24.3	638,843
	UNITED STATES	1981	199,800	6.9	~	~	~	~	~	~

SOURCE: UNESCO-SY, 1983, table 4.1.

Table 922

PUBLIC CURRENT EDUCATIONAL EXPENDITURE, ACCORDING TO PURPOSE, 20 L

	Country	Year	Total = 100%					
			Administration	Teachers' Salaries	Scholarships and Grants	Other Instructional Expenditure	Welfare Services	Other
A.	ARGENTINA[1]	1980	~	86.7	5.0	7.9	~	.3
B.	BOLIVIA[2]	1980	6.5	89.5	.2	#	2.9	.9
C.	BRAZIL	~	~	~	~	~	~	~
D.	CHILE[6]	1981	2.8	83.8	5.9	6.0		1.6
E.	COLOMBIA[3]	1981	1.8	93.4	~	~	~	4.9
F.	COSTA RICA[1,6]	1980	~	74.3	2.0	.2	~	23.5
G.	CUBA	1980	3.8	38.8	2.5	6.6	45.1	3.1
H.	DOMINICAN REP.[2]	1980	7.7	84.9	2.0	~	~	5.3
I.	ECUADOR[6]	1980	2.2	77.4	.2	.8	- -	19.3
J.	EL SALVADOR	1975	4.5	82.5	1.7	7.8	.4	3.1
K.	GUATEMALA[2]	1979	6.2	69.1	.6	.5	22.2	1.3
L.	HAITI	1980	11.8	70.4	1.3	2.3	.2	14.0
M.	HONDURAS[1,2]	1980	6.5	88.6	1.6	2.6	.6	.1
N.	MEXICO[2,3]	1980	7.5	67.3	.2	- -	- -	25.1
O.	NICARAGUA[4]	1980	10.8	69.7	.7	2.2	10.7	5.9
P.	PANAMA[2]	1981	13.7	81.3	3.7	1.3	~	#
Q.	PARAGUAY[2]	1973	7.4	90.0	1.0	.7	.3	.6
R.	PERU[5]	1980	8.4	59.4	~	.9	~	31.3
S.	URUGUAY[6]	1980	20.5	56.9	7.5	5.1	~	10.1
T.	VENEZUELA[2]	1980	13.7	60.7	7.4	1.0	3.2	14.0

1. Administration is included under Teachers' Salaries.
2. The totality of transfers to universities, used for all purposes (salaries, etc.), is included under Teachers' Salaries.
3. Expenditure of the Ministry of Education only.
4. Other Instructional Expenditure is included under Other.
5. Transfers to universities and some other institutions as well as various types of pensions and other benefits are shown under Other.
6. Welfare Services are included in Scholarships and Grants.

SOURCE: UNESCO-SY, 1983, table 4.2.

Table 923

PUBLIC CURRENT EDUCATIONAL EXPENDITURE,[1] BY LEVEL, 20 LC

Country	Year	Total Expenditure (T NC)	Total = 100%					
			Pre-school	First Level	Second Level	Third Level	Other Types of Education	Expenditure Not Allocated by Level
A. ARGENTINA	1970[a]	1,620[e]	1.4	29.0	30.3	21.0	2.2	16.2
	1980	8,598,918	- -[b]	40.1	25.6	22.7	1.9	9.7
B. BOLIVIA	1970	396,056	1.9	60.2	12.8	10.9	2.0	12.3
	1980	4,919,122	#	58.9	11.4	17.1	5.0	7.6
C. BRAZIL[2]	1975	25,194,300	- -	62.7[c]	- -	26.1	2.3	9.0
	1978	97,382,980	- -	34.2	12.7	30.4	4.0	18.6
D. CHILE	1975	1,321,482	- -[b]	34.9	13.5	25.2	4.1	22.4
	1981	62,609,745	- -[b]	47.7	15.5	33.5	#	3.2
E. COLOMBIA	1970[a]	1,545,185	.1[b]	36.5	16.9	23.9	1.4	21.2
	1981	49,004,771	- -[b]	47.4	26.9	23.2	.6	2.0
F. COSTA RICA	1970	318,500	- -[b]	51.2	18.9	10.5	#	19.4
	1980	2,802,162	- -[b]	28.0	21.5	26.1	1.0	23.4
G. CUBA	1980	1,134,500	5.1	24.4	40.8	6.9	5.9	16.9
H. DOMINICAN REP.	1970	39,306	#	41.1	18.3	20.7	7.6	12.5
	1980	104,896	#	36.6	26.8	23.8	7.0	5.9
I. ECUADOR	1970	1,133,523	- -[b]	45.9	41.0	9.9	1.1	2.0
	1980	14,649,139	- -[b]	20.6	18.5	15.6	2.5	42.7
J. EL SALVADOR	1970	69,621	#	57.9	11.8	21.4	2.5	6.4
	1980	320,009	#	61.9	6.2	14.2	1.9	15.9
K. GUATEMALA	1970	32,566	2.8	55.2	16.9	13.1	4.5	7.4
	1979	109,089	1.6	35.7	12.4	18.4	2.4	29.4
L. HAITI	1970	25,098	#	65.1	17.8	9.1	- -[d]	8.0
	1980	85,781	#	61.6	18.1	10.7	5.9	3.7
M. HONDURAS	1970	41,660	#	64.2	15.4	12.2	1.7	6.5
	1980	141,705	#	61.6	17.8	19.2	.9	#
N. MEXICO	1970[a]	7,148,000	3.1	47.7	27.2	10.4	#	11.5
	1980	114,913,003	2.3	39.7	18.8	26.5	4.2	8.5
O. NICARAGUA	1970	120,901	#	57.9	17.6	10.0	9.7	4.8
	1980	579,693	.4	44.7	25.1	10.5	7.7	11.5
P. PANAMA[3]	1970	50,824	#	38.9	18.7	10.8	18.4	13.2
	1981	162,341	#	43.0	23.0	15.6	3.0	15.4
Q. PARAGUAY	~	~	~	~	~	~	~	~
R. PERU	1970	8,730,500	1.1	39.8	20.8	- -[e]	4.8	33.5
	1980	166,040,000	2.8	45.1	19.9	3.1	3.8	25.2
S. URUGUAY	1980	1,926,769	#	48.4	33.2	16.1	2.3	#
T. VENEZUELA	1970	2,220,651	- -[b]	38.3	20.6	25.5	8.5	7.0
	1980	12,523,608	3.2	15.4	13.2	34.6	15.8	17.8
UNITED STATES	1970	56,000[e]	- -[b]	70.5	- -[b]	29.5	#	#
	1979	158,149	- -[b]	63.7	- -[b]	14.3	#	#

1. Current expenditure includes expenditure on administration, emoluments of teachers and supporting teaching staff, school books and other teaching materials, scholarships, welfare services and maintenance of school buildings. It differs from capital expenditure which includes expenditure on land, buildings, construction, equipment, and loan transactions.
2. Data refer to current and capital expenditure incurred by the Federal Government and by the Federal States. Expenditure of municipalities is not included.
3. Does not include Canal Zone.
a. Expenditure of the Ministry of Education only.
b. Included in First Level.
c. Includes pre-primary, first and second levels and also special education and ensino supletivo.
d. Included in Expenditure Not Allocated by Level.
e. In millions.

SOURCE: UNESCO-SY, 1983, table 4.3.

Table 924

SCIENTISTS AND ENGINEERS ENGAGED IN RESEARCH AND DEVELOPMENT (R AND D), BY FIELD OF SCIENCE, 14 L

| | Country | Year | Code[1] | Total | Scientists and Engineers Field of Science | | | | |
					Natural Sciences	Engineering and Technology	Medical Sciences	Agriculture	Social Sciences and Humanities
A.	ARGENTINA[2]	1980	FTE	9,500‡	3,500‡	1,370‡	2,100‡	1,330‡	1,200‡
			FPT	19,900‡	6,100‡	2,400‡	5,800‡	2,300‡	3,300‡
C.	BRAZIL[3]	1977	FTE	13,678	4,363	2,581	1,817	2,693	2,224
D.	CHILE	1975	FTE	5,948	1,885	1,367	1,562	411	723
E.	COLOMBIA[4]	1971	FPT	1,140	188	154	127	348	323
G.	CUBA	1978	FTE	4,972	668	1,441	1,112	1,257	494
I.	ECUADOR[5]	1976	FT	378	88	33	#	242	15
			PT	239	26	26	#	180	7
			FTE	469	100	45	#	304	20
J.	EL SALVADOR[6]	1974	FT	674	190	71	153	78	182
			PT	255	#	98	60	14	83
			FTE	802	190	120	183	85	224
K.	GUATEMALA	1974	FT	250	34	79	16	49	72
			PT	134	18	42	9	27	38
			FTE	310	43	98	20	61	88
M.	HONDURAS[7]	1974	FT	5	#	5	#	#	#
N.	MEXICO[8]	1974	FT	2,227	631	422	216	375	519
			PT	6,219	1,379	1,232	919	594	1,772
			FTE	5,896	1,523	1,170	648	765	1,535
P.	PANAMA[8]	1975	FT	193	39	41	31	33	28
			PT	34	1	2	21	#	#
			FTE	204	39	41	40	33	28
R.	PERU[8,9]	1970	FT	1,522	445	76	267	494	151
			PT	318	100	13	125	24	54
			FTE	1,686	496	83	330	507	180
S.	URUGUAY[8,10]	1971	FPT	1,537‡	184‡	356‡	359‡	253‡	160‡
			FTE	1,150‡	142‡	285‡	239‡	253‡	109‡
T.	VENEZUELA[8]	1977	FPT	4,060	1,033	730	944	774	560

1. FT = Full-Time; PT = Part-time; FPT = Full-time plus part-time; FTE = Full-time equivalent.
2. Data are for net man-years.
3. Data refer to post-graduate fundamental research and post-graduate teaching in the higher education sector only.
4. Excludes data for law, humanities, and education.
5. Data refer to research and development in the agricultural sciences only.
6. Data refer to 28 institutions out of a total of 41 which perform research and development.
7. Data relate to one research institute only.
8. Total data include scientists and engineers for whom a distribution by field of science is unknown.
9. Excludes humanities and education.
10. Data refer to the year 1971/72.

SOURCE: UNESCO-SY, 1977, table 7.3; UNESCO-SY, 1978, table 7.3; UNESCO-SY, 1980, table 5.3; UNESCO-SY, 1983, table 5.3.

Table 925

RESEARCH AND DEVELOPMENT (R AND D) PERSONNEL, BY SECTOR OF PERFORMANCE, 14 LC

Country	Year	Type of Personnel [1]	(A) All Sectors	(B) Integrated R&D	(C) Non-integrated R&D	(D) Higher Education	(E) General Service
A. ARGENTINA[2,9]	1980	Total in R&D	22,800‡	950‡	4,050‡	9,200‡	8,600‡
		% by Sector	**	4.2‡	17.8‡	40.3‡	37.7‡
		Scientists & Engineers	9,500‡	350‡	1,350‡	5,200‡	2,600‡
		Technicians	13,300‡	600‡	2,700‡	4,000‡	6,000‡
C. BRAZIL	1978	Total in R&D	~	43,056	⟶	~	~
		Scientists & Engineers	~	8,497	⟶	15,518	~
		Technicians	~	5,392	⟶	~	~
		Auxiliary	~	29,167	⟶	~	~
D. CHILE	1980	% by Sector	100	.9	⟶	80.3	18.8
		Total in R&D	3,985	34	⟶	3,201	756
E. COLOMBIA[3,4]	1978	Total in R&D	4,571	21	33	2,710	1,807
		% by Sector	100	.5	.7	59.3	39.5
		Scientists & Engineers	3,404	21	29	2,004	1,350
		Technicians	704	#	3	462	239
		Auxiliary	463	#	1	244	218
G. CUBA	1979	Total in R&D	21,786	384	12,553	1,205	7,644
		% by Sector	100	1.8	57.6	5.5	35.1
		Scientists & Engineers	5,680	160	2,778	624	2,118
		Technicians	6,593	137	3,563	248	2,645
		Auxiliary	9,513	87	6,212	333	2,881
I. ECUADOR[5]	1976	Total in R&D	1,038	4	787	247	#
		% by Sector	**	.4	75.8	23.8	#
		Scientists & Engineers	469	2	376	91	#
		Technicians	411	1	328	82	#
		Auxiliary	158	1	83	74	#
K. GUATEMALA[9]	1974	Total in R&D	749	#	290	113	346
		% by Sector	**	#	38.7	15.1	46.2
		Scientists & Engineers	310	#	166	43	101
		Technicians	439	#	124	70	245
M. HONDURAS[6]	1974	Total in R&D	7	#	#	#	7
		% by Sector	**	#	#	#	100
		Scientists & Engineers	5	#	#	#	5
		Technicians	1	#	#	#	1
		Auxiliary	1	#	#	#	1
N. MEXICO	1974	% by Sector	**	11.9	21.6	33.4	33.2
		Scientists & Engineers	5,896	701	1,272	1,968	1,955
P. PANAMA	1975	Total in R&D	982	#	600	249	133
		% by Sector	100	#	61.1	25.4	13.5
		Scientists & Engineers	204	#	116	62	26
		Technicians	301	#	194	80	27
		Auxiliary	477	#	290	107	80
Q. PARAGUAY	1971	% by Sector	**	28.4	⟶	36.6	35.1
		Scientists & Engineers	134	38	⟶	49	47
R. PERU	1976	Total in R&D	8,984‡	992‡	2,793‡	1,609‡	3,590‡
		% by Sector	100	11‡	31.1‡	17.9‡	40‡
		Scientists & Engineers	3,932‡	416	879‡	1,544	1,093‡
		Technicians	2,235‡	276‡	587‡	6‡	1,366‡
		Auxiliary	2,817‡	300‡	1,327‡	59‡	1,131‡
S. URUGUAY[7]	1971	Total in R&D	3,033‡	385‡	758‡	1,068‡	822‡
		% by Sector	**	12.7‡	25.0‡	35.2‡	27.1‡
		Scientists & Engineers	1,150‡	114‡	280‡	537‡	219‡
		Technicians	1,087‡	138‡	241‡	336‡	372‡
		Auxiliary	796‡	133‡	237‡	195‡	231‡
T. VENEZUELA[3,10]	1977	Total in R&D	9,951	256	3,412	5,604	679
		% by Sector	100	2.6	34.3	56.3	6.8
		Scientists & Engineers	4,060	56	910	2,881	213
		Technicians	2,500	141	1,089	1,033	237
		Auxiliary	3,391	59	1,413	1,690	229
UNITED STATES[4,8]	1981	% by Sector	100	71.2	⟶	14.5	14.3
		Scientists & Engineers	660,700	470,200	⟶	96,000	94,500

1. Scientists and engineers engaged in research and development are given in full-time equivalent (FTE).
2. Data are in net man-years.
3. Data for scientists and engineers refer to full-time plus part-time.
4. Excludes law, humanities, and education.
5. Data refer to research and development in the agricultural sciences only.
6. Data relate to one research institute only.
7. Data refer to 1971-72.
8. The general service sector includes data referring to private non-profit organizations.
9. Excludes auxiliary personnel.
10. Data concern 167 institutes out of a total of 406 which perform R&D.

SOURCE: UNESCO-SY, 1981, table 5.3; UNESCO-SY, 1982, table 5.4; UNESCO-SY, 1983, table 5.4.

Table 926

INDICATORS OF SCIENTIFIC AND TECHNOLOGICAL DEVELOPMENT, 17 LC

Country	Year	Qualified Manpower		Personnel Engaged in R&D			Expenditure for R&D		
		Scientists and Engineers P10TI	Technicians P10TI	Scientists and Engineers (FTE)[1] P10TI	Technicians P10TI	Number of Technicians per Scientists and Engineers	% of GNP	Per Capita (NC)	Annual Average per R&D Scientists and Engineers (NC)
A. ARGENTINA[2]	1980	141.7	482.1	3.5	4.9	1.4‡	.5	46,508.3‡	132,494,700‡
B. BOLIVIA	1976	100.4	~	~	~	~	~	~	~
C. BRAZIL[3]	1978	58.5	127.3	2.1	3.0	1.4	.6	180.1	865,300
D. CHILE[3,7]	1978	74.7	~	5.8	~	~	.5‡	222.6‡	~
E. COLOMBIA	1978	~	~	5.7	2.7	.5	.1	28.7	507,800
G. CUBA[4]	1979	62.7	~	5.8	6.7	1.2	.5	9.3	16,000
I. ECUADOR[5]	1979	~	~	1.88‡	1.56‡	.8	.3	92.5	499,000
J. EL SALVADOR	1974	14.1	4.6	2.1	1.3	.6	.8	8.0	39,000
K. GUATEMALA[5]	1978	9.5	12.2	.8	.7	.8	.2‡	2.0‡	24,600‡
M. HONDURAS	1974	22.5	10.6	.02	~	.2	~	~	~
N. MEXICO[6]	1974	69.1‡	150.0	1.0	~	~	.2	22.7	216,700‡
O. NICARAGUA	1971	~	~	~	~	~	.1‡	4.2	~
P. PANAMA[7,8]	1976	47.0	80.6	1.2	1.8	1.5	.2	1.8	14,300‡
Q. PARAGUAY	1971	~	~	.6	~	~	.2	70.7	1,248,200
R. PERU[5,10]	1976	56.5‡	39.9‡	2.5‡	1.4‡	.6‡	.3‡	145.5‡	588,700‡
S. URUGUAY[9,11]	1975	200.4	104.9	3.9‡	3.7‡	.9‡	.2	.6	1,620‡
T. VENEZUELA	1977	~	~	1.3	2.0	1.5	.6	69.4	543,100
UNITED STATES	1981	137.81	~	28.75	~	~	2.5	303.9	105,700

1. Code: FTE = Full-time equivalent.
2. Data under Qualified Manpower refer to 1976.
3. Data under Qualified Manpower refer to 1970.
4. Data under Qualified Manpower refer to 1977.
5. Data under Qualified Manpower refer to 1974.
6. Data under Qualified Manpower refer to 1969; Expenditure for R & D refers to 1973.
7. Data under Personnel Engaged in R & D refer to 1975.
8. Data under Expenditure for R & D refer to 1974.
9. Data under Personnel Engaged in R & D refer to 1971.
10. Data under Personnel Engaged in R & D refer to 1976.
11. Data under Expenditure for R & D refer to 1972.

SOURCE: UNESCO-SY, 1981, table 5.9; UNESCO-SY, 1982, table 5.14: UNESCO-SY, 1983, table 5.14.

Part IV: Politics, Religion, and the Military

CHAPTER 10

POLITICAL STATISTICS

Note: This volume contains statistics from numerous sources. Alternative data on many topics are presented. Variations in statistics can be attributed to differences in definition, parameters, coverage, methodology, as well as date gathered, prepared, or adjusted. See also Editor's Note on Methodology.

Table 1000

POLITICAL DEPENDENCE, INDEPENDENCE, AND INTERNATIONAL MEMBERSHIPS OF COUNTRIES AND TERRITORIES, 20 L AND 45 ELA

(1983)

PART I. TRADITIONALLY DEFINED LATIN AMERICA

Independent Countries[1]	As Result of			Memberships						
	War[2]		Special Circumstances	OAS	IDB:L	ECLA:L	ALADI	AG	CACM	CBI-IB
	Declared	Won								
A. ARGENTINA	1810	1816[a]		A	A	A	A			
B. BOLIVIA	1809	1825[a]		B	B	B	B	B		
C. BRAZIL			1822[b]	C	C	C	C			
D. CHILE	1810	1818[a]		D	D	D	D	D[5]		
E. COLOMBIA	1810	1824[a]	1830[e]	E	E	E	E	E		
F. COSTA RICA		1821[c]	1838[d]	F	F	F			F	F
G. CUBA		1898[a]	1902[i]	G[4]		G				
H. DOMINICAN REP.[3]		1821[a]	1844[h]	H	H	H				H
I. ECUADOR[7]	1809	1822[a]	1830[e]	I	I	I	I	I		
J. EL SALVADOR		1821[c]	1841[d]	J	J	J			J	J
K. GUATEMALA		1821[c]	1839[d]	K	K	K			K	K
L. HAITI	1791	1804[k]		L	L	L				L
M. HONDURAS		1821[c]	1838[d]	M	M	M			M[6]	M
N. MEXICO	1810	1821[a]		N	N	N	N			
O. NICARAGUA		1821[c]	1838[d]	O	O	O			O	O
P. PANAMA			1903[j]	P	P	P				P
Q. PARAGUAY			1811[a]	Q	Q	Q	Q			
R. PERU	1821	1824[a,f]		R	R	R	R	I		
S. URUGUAY	1811	1814[a]	1828[l]	S	S	S	S			
T. VENEZUELA[7]	1810	1821[a,g]	1829[e]	T	T	T	T	T		

1. The three events that provided the immediate stimulation for independence were the U.S. War for Independence (1776-81); the French Revolution of 1789 proclaiming the Rights of Man and abolishing slavery for France but not its colonies—the most prosperous of which was Saint Domingue (the future Haiti); and the capture of the Spanish monarch by Napoleon Bonaparte, Spain's "ally," who placed his brother Joseph on the throne of Spain in 1808, thus breaking strong allegiances between Spain and its colonies. (The latter event occurred after France had passed through Spain, driving the monarchy of Portugal to Brazil in 1807, laying the basis for Brazil's independence once the monarchy returned to Portugal in 1821.)
2. Excludes precursor movements such as that by Tiradentes in 1788 (Brazil) or by Miranda in 1806 (Venezuela).
3. France ceded to Spain in 1795.
4. Cuba suspended from OAS in 1962.
5. Chile withdrew from AG in 1976.
6. Honduras partially withdrew from CACM in 1971.
7. Member of OPEC.

a. Won from Spain.
b. Won from Portugal.
c. Won from Spain and became part of Mexico in 1822-23.
d. Breakup of United Provinces of Central America, which existed to unite Costa Rica, El Salvador, Guatemala, Honduras, and Nicaragua from 1823 to 1841. For all practical purposes the breakup came by 1838 and attempts to revive union were militarily defeated by 1842.
e. Breakup of Gran Colombia, which existed to unite Colombia, Ecuador, and Venezuela from 1819 to 1830.
f. Last Spanish troops left Peru in 1826.
g. Last Spanish troops left Venezuela in 1823.
h. Won from Haiti, which governed Hispaniola or Santo Domingo (future Dominican Republic) from 1822 to 1844. Spain reoccupied from 1861 to 1865.
i. Won from the United States.
j. Won from Colombia.
k. Won from France.
l. Won from Brazil.

SOURCE: SALA, 23-1.

Table 1000 (Continued)

POLITICAL DEPENDENCE, INDEPENDENCE, AND INTERNATIONAL MEMBERSHIPS
OF COUNTRIES AND TERRITORIES, 20 L AND 45 ELA
(1983)

PART II. NON-TRADITIONALLY DEFINED LATIN AMERICA ADDS:

	Independent Countries	Year of Independence	From	OAS	IDB:L	ECLA:L	CARICOM[1]	ECCM	OECS	CBI-IB	FAO[4]
1.	Antigua-Barbuda	1981	Gr. Britain				1	1	1	1	1
2.	Bahamas	1973	Gr. Britain		2	2				2	2
3.	Barbados	1966	Gr. Britain	3	3	3	3			3	3
4.	Belize	1981	Gr. Britain				4			4	4
5.	Dominica	1978	Gr. Britain	5			5	5	5	5	5
6.	Grenada	1974	Gr. Britain	6		6	6	6	6	6	6
7.	Guyana	1966	Gr. Britain	7	7	7	7			7	7
8.	Jamaica	1962	Gr. Britain	8	8	8	8			8	8
9.	St. Kitts-Nevis[2]	1983	Gr. Britain				9	9	9	9	9
10.	St. Lucia	1977	Gr. Britain	10			10	10	10	10	10
11.	St. Vincent-Grenadines	1979	Gr. Britain				11	11	11	11	11
12.	Suriname	1975	Netherlands	12	12	12				12	12
13.	Trinidad and Tobago	1962	Gr. Britain	13	13	13	13				

	Dependent Countries	Belonging to	OAS	IDB:L	ICLA:L	CARICOM[1]	ECCM	OECS	CBI-IB	FAO
T1.	Anguilla	Great Britain					T1			T1
T2.	Bermuda	Great Britain[3]								
T3.	British Virgin Islands	Great Britain							T3	T3
T4.	Cayman Islands	Great Britain							T4	T4
T5.	French Guiana	France								T5
T6.	Guadeloupe	France								T6
T7.	Martinique	France								T7
T8.	Montserrat	Great Britain				T8	T8	T8	T8	T8
T9.	Netherlands Antilles	Netherlands							T9	T9
T10.	Puerto Rico	United States								T10
T11.	Turks and Caicos	Great Britain							T11	T11
T12.	U.S. Virgin Islands	United States								T12

1. The Caribbean Community and Common Market (CARICOM) was established in 1973 to replace the Caribbean Free Trade Association (CARIFTA), founded in 1967.
2. St. Kitts is officially known as St. Christopher.
3. Bermuda has been self-governing since 1968. Although under Great Britain, it claims Bermudian nationality.
4. Includes Falkland Islands.

SOURCE: SALA 23–1.

Table 1001

SHARE OF ADULT POPULATION VOTING, 12 LC

	Country	Year	Type of Election[1]	Total Vote (T)	% Adult Population Voting[2]
A.	ARGENTINA	1983	P, L	15,180	89
C.	BRAZIL	1982	L	48,440	81
E.	COLOMBIA	1982	P	6,816	68
F.	COSTA RICA	1982	P, L	992	87
I.	ECUADOR	1984	L	2,204	53
J.	EL SALVADOR	1984	P	1,524	69
K.	GUATEMALA	1984	CA	1,856	57
M.	HONDURAS	1981	P, L	1,171	79
N.	MEXICO	1982	P, L	22,523	75
O.	NICARAGUA	1984	P, CA	1,170	91
R.	PERU	1980	P, L	4,030	49
T.	VENEZUELA	1983	P, L	6,741	90
	UNITED STATES	1984	P, L	92,000	53

1. P = Presidential, L = Legislative, CA = Constituent Assembly.
2. Estimates based on votes cast as a percentage of total population age 20 or over.

SOURCE: *LASA Forum* (Latin American Studies Association), Winter, 1985, p. 25.

Figure 10:1

APPROXIMATION OF GUATEMALAN POLITICAL VIOLENCE, MAY 1983–DECEMBER 1984[a]

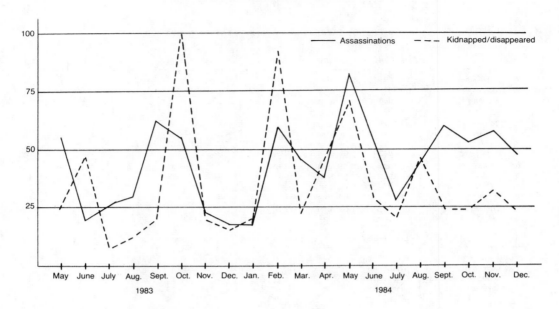

a. These cases have been selected exclusively from the local press for their probable political links. All cases that appeared to be common crime, or which were directly related to military-guerrilla encounters or guerrilla actions, were excluded. Apparent political motivations were determined on the basis of the victim's personal data (university student or professor, police officer, political leader, union activist) combined with the circumstances (abduction by "heavily armed men," signs of torture, machine-gun wounds, decapitation). When a kidnapped or missing person was later found dead in the same calendar month he or she was abducted, it was counted only as an assassination. Of course, there may be some cases in which a victim of a common crime was mistakenly included, or in which a non-obvious political killing or abduction was mistakenly excluded.

SOURCE: *Central American Report*, Feb. 1, 1985.

Table 1002

POLITICAL AND CIVIL RIGHTS,[1] 20 LC, 1972–83

(1+ = Best Score; 7– = Worst Score)

Country	Year	Political Rights[2]	Civil Rights[3]	Country	Year	Political Rights[2]	Civil Rights[3]
A. ARGENTINA	1972	6	3	H. DOMINICAN REP.	1972	3	2
	1973	2	2		1973	3	2
	1974	2	4–		1974	4	2
	1975	2	4		1975	4	2
	1976	6–	5–		1976	4	3[a]
	1977	6	6–[a]		1977	4	2+[a]
	1978	6	5+		1978	2+	2
	1979	6	5		1979	2	3–
	1980	6	5		1980	2	3
	1981	6	5		1981	2	3
	1982	6	5		1982	1+	2+
	1983	3+	3+		1983	1	2
B. BOLIVIA	1972	5	4	I. ECUADOR	1972	7	3
	1973	5	4		1973	7	4[a]
	1974	6–	5–		1974	7	4
	1975	6	5		1975	7	4
	1976	6	4[a]		1976	6[a]	4
	1977	6	4		1977	6	4
	1978	5+	3+		1978	5+	3+
	1979	3+	3		1979	2+	2+
	1980	7–	5–		1980	2	2
	1981	7	5		1981	2	2
	1982	2+	3+		1982	2	2
	1983	2	3		1983	2	2
C. BRAZIL	1972	5	5	J. EL SALVADOR	1972	2	3
	1973	5	5		1973	2	3
	1974	4+	4+		1974	2	3
	1975	4	5–		1975	2	3
	1976	4	5		1976	3–	3
	1977	4	5		1977	3	3
	1978	4	4+		1978	4–	4–
	1979	4	3+		1979	5[a]	3+
	1980	4	3		1980	6–	4–
	1981	4	3		1981	5	5–
	1982	3+	3		1982	4+	5
	1983	3	3		1983	4 .	5
D. CHILE	1972	1	2	K. GUATEMALA	1972	2	3
	1973	7[b]	5[b]		1973	2	2
	1974	7	5		1974	4	3
	1975	7	5		1975	4	3
	1976	7	5		1976	4	3
	1977	7	5		1977	4	4[a]
	1978	6+	5		1978	3+	4
	1979	6	5		1979	3	5[a]
	1980	6	5		1980	5–	6–
	1981	6	5		1981	6–	6
	1982	6	5		1982	6	6
	1983	6	5		1983	6	6
E. COLOMBIA	1972	2	2	L. HAITI	1972	7	6
	1973	2	2		1973	6	6
	1974	2	2		1974	6	6
	1975	2	3–		1975	6	6
	1976	2	3		1976	6	6
	1977	2	3		1977	7[a]	6
	1978	2	3		1978	7	6
	1979	2	3		1979	6+	5+
	1980	2	3		1980	6	6–
	1981	2	3		1981	7–	6
	1982	2	3		1982	7	6
	1983	2	3		1983	7	6
F. COSTA RICA	1972	1	1	M. HONDURAS	1972	7	3
	1973	1	2		1973	6	3
	1974	1	1		1974	6	3
	1975	1	1		1975	6	3
	1976	1	1		1976	6	3
	1977	1	1		1977	6	3
	1978	1	1		1978	6	3
	1979	1	1		1979	6	3
	1980	1	1		1980	4+	3
	1981	1	1		1981	3+	3
	1982	1	1		1982	2+	3
	1983	1	1		1983	3–	3
G. CUBA	1972	7	7	N. MEXICO	1972	5	3
	1973	7	7		1973	4[b]	3
	1974	7	7		1974	4	3
	1975	7	7		1975	4	3
	1976	7	6[a]		1976	4	4–
	1977	7	6		1977	4	4
	1978	6[a]	6		1978	4	4
	1979	6	6		1979	3+	3+
	1980	6	6		1980	3	4
	1981	6	6		1981	3	4
	1982	6	6		1982	3	4
	1983	6	6		1983	3	4

a

Table 1002 (Continued)

POLITICAL AND CIVIL RIGHTS,[1] 20 LC, 1972-83

(1+ = Best Score; 7- = Worst Score)

Country	Year	Political Rights[2]	Civil Rights[3]	Country	Year	Political Rights[2]	Civil Rights[3]
O. NICARAGUA	1972	4	3	S. URUGUAY	1972	3	4
	1973	5	4[b]		1973	5[b]	5[b]
	1974	5	4		1974	5	5
	1975	5	4		1975	5	5
	1976	5	5[a]		1976	6-	6-[a]
	1977	5	5		1977	6	6
	1978	5	5		1978	6	6
	1979	5	5		1979	6	6
	1980	5	5		1980	5+	5+
	1981	6-	5		1981	5	5
	1982	6	5		1982	5	4+
	1983	6	5		1983	5	4
P. PANAMA	1972	7	6	T. VENEZUELA	1972	2	2
	1973	7	6		1973	2	2
	1974	7	6		1974	2	2
	1975	7	6		1975	2	2
	1976	7	6		1976	1[a]	2
	1977	6+	5+		1977	1	2
	1978	5+	5		1978	1	2
	1979	5	5		1979	1	2
	1980	4+	4+		1980	1	2
	1981	4	4		1981	1	2
	1982	5-	5-		1982	1	2
	1983	5	4+		1983	1	2
Q. PARAGUAY	1972	4	6	UNITED STATES	1972	1	1
	1973	5	5		1973	1	1
	1974	5	5		1974	1	1
	1975	5	5		1975	1	1
	1976	5	6-		1976	1	1
	1977	5	6		1977	1	1
	1978	5+	5		1978	1	1
	1979	5	5		1979	1	1
	1980	5	5		1980	1	1
	1981	5	5		1981	1	1
	1982	5	5		1982	1	1
	1983	5	5		1983	1	1
R. PERU	1972	7	5				
	1973	7	5				
	1974	6[a]	6-				
	1975	6	4+				
	1976	6	4				
	1977	6	4				
	1978	5+	4				
	1979	5	4				
	1980	2+	3+				
	1981	2	3				
	1982	2	3				
	1983	2	3				

1. This "freedom" survey, conducted annually by Freedom House, defines freedom in terms of both civil and political freedoms as these have been traditionally understood in the constitutional democratic states.
2. The score for *political rights* is determined by the degree to which a given country satisfies the following requirements: (a) that leaders are chosen in decisions made on the basis of an open voting process, (b) that significant opposition is allowed to compete in this process, (c) that there are multiple political parties and candidates not selected by the government, (d) that polling and counting of votes is conducted without coercion or fraud, (e) that a significant share of political power is exercised by elected representatives, (f) that all regions, even the most remote, are included in the political process, and (g) that the country is free of foreign or military control or influence. Countries assigned a rank of 1 most closely satisfy these requirements and those assigned a rank of 7 most seriously violate them.
3. The score for *civil rights* is determined by the degree of liberty a given country grants its news media and individual citizens, primarily as it applies to political expression. The survey looks at censorship applied to the press or radio. It also assesses the rights granted any individual to openly express ideas, to belong to an organization free of government supervision, and the individual's right to a free trial, i.e., the degree to which the judiciary is independent of administrative control. Also important is the number of political prisoners held in a country, the use of torture or brutality, and the degree to which the state security forces respect individual rights. Countries assigned the rank of 1 grant the greatest degree of civil liberties and those assigned the rank of 7 most seriously violate them.

a. Change in status since the previous year owing to reevaluation by the author. This does not imply any change in the country.
b. Change in status since the previous year owing to events in the country.

SOURCE: Freedom House — *Freedom at Issue*, Jan.-Feb., 1973, 1974, 1975, 1976, 1977, 1978, 1979, 1980, 1981, 1982, 1983, and 1984.

Table 1003

REVISED FITZGIBBON-JOHNSON INDEX RANKINGS: U.S. VIEW OF POLITICAL DEMOCRACY, FIVE KEY CRITERIA,[1] 20 L, 1945-80
(Most Democratic = #1)

Country	1945	1950	1955	1960	1965	1970	1975	1980
A. ARGENTINA	9	15[a]	15	4	7	14	5	15

Continued in SALA, 23-3401.

Table 1004

ARGENTINA PRESIDENTIAL AND CONGRESSIONAL FINAL ELECTION RESULTS, BY POLITICAL PARTY
(Oct. 30, 1983)

Party	Presidential/Vice Presidential			Congressional		
	Votes	As % of Total Votes Received	Electoral Votes	Votes	As % of Total Votes Received	Electoral Votes
Alianza Demócrata Socialista	47,736	.32	0	121,889	.82	0
Demócrata Progresista	2,183	.01	0	2,907	.02	0
Socialista Democrático	269	.00	0	293	#	0
Alianza Federal	57,027	.38	0	91,283	.62	0
Federal	10,153	.07	0	9,965	.07	0
Movimiento Linea Popular	14,409	.10	0	19,198	.13	0
Comunista	#	#	0	181,847	1.23	0
Confederación Nacional de Centro	7,745	.05	0	12,126	.08	0
Conservador Popular	13	#	0	13	#	0
Demócrata Cristiano	46,547	.31	0	139,875	.94	1
Frente Izquierda Popular	14,201	.09	0	18,748	.13	0
Intransigente	347,648	2.33	0	411,872	2.78	3
Justicialista	5,994,406	40.15	259	5,696,348	38.47	112
Movimiento al Socialismo	42,499	.28	0	56,378	.38	0
Movimiento de Integración y Desarrollo	177,426	1.19	2	223,598	1.51	0
Obrero	13,056	.09	0	17,721	.12	0
Socialista Popular	21,314	.14	0	35,630	.24	0
Unión Cívica Radical	7,725,173	51.74	317	7,104,237	47.98	128
Other Parties	411,703	2.76	20	663,329	4.48	10
Positive Votes	14,929,508	97.10	* *	14,807,257	96.31	* *
Null Votes	85,304	.55	* *	72,944	.47	* *
Blank Votes	359,957	2.34	* *	494,568	3.22	* *
Total Votes	15,374,769	100.00	* *	15,374,769[a]	100.00	* *

a. 85.79% of total eligible voters (17,920,435).

SOURCE: U.S. Embassy, Argentina.

Table 1005

ARGENTINA PRESIDENTIAL ELECTION RESULTS, BY POLITICAL PARTY AND PROVINCE

Political Party
(% of Total Vote)

Province	Alianza Demócrata Socialista	Alianza Federal	Comunista	Demócrata Cristiano	Frente de Izquierda Popular	Intransigente	Justicialista	Movimiento al Socialismo	Movimiento de Integración y Desarrollo	Obrero	Socialista Popular	Unión Cívica Radical	Unión del Centro Democrático	Positive Votes	Null Votes	Blank Votes	Participation as % of Eligible Voters
Federal Capital	.32	.72	#	.18	.05	4.48	27.36	.40	.73	.13	.09	64.26	1.28	98.34	.62	1.05	85.78
Buenos Aires	.25	.59	#	.23	.07	3.24	42.23	.44	.84	.11	.09	51.41	.44	97.23	.38	2.39	87.69
Catamarca	**	**	#	.47	.11	.58	43.50	.09	.77	~	.13	46.73	**	95.00	.95	4.06	82.90
Córdoba	.19	**	#	.37	.08	.87	39.92	.17	.93	.05	.18	56.22	**	97.68	.33	1.99	88.35
Corrientes	**	.65	#	.76	.08	.74	23.38	**	3.52	**	.05	33.84	**	98.13	.89	.97	77.02
Chaco	.13	**	**	.51	.15	.42	47.98	.08	2.16	**	**	46.55	**	96.88	.42	2.70	75.90
Chubut	.12	.37	#	.44	**	1.75	**	.27	2.11	.03	.23	50.85	**	95.61	1.28	3.11	80.61
Entre Ríos	.07	**	#	.94	.11	1.49	44.21	**	1.56	**	.31	49.53	**	96.30	.62	3.08	85.06
Formosa	.09	**	#	.48	**	.46	**	.29	**	**	.14	37.20	**	95.91	.84	3.25	75.80
Jujuy	**	**	#	**	.04	.51	48.73	.29	.83	.18	.21	35.46	**	95.23	1.30	3.47	84.29
La Pampa	**	**	#	.39	#	1.57	40.87	.10	2.68	**	.09	41.38	**	96.04	1.10	2.86	90.15
La Rioja	**	.25	#	.36	.35	.53	55.52	.12	1.83	**	**	41.04	**	81.52	18.48	#	98.15
Mendoza	.9	**	#	.23	.13	.95	36.56	.14	1.13	.02	.07	57.81	**	96.67	1.10	2.24	88.00
Misiones	**	**	#	**	.16	.31	47.80	**	1.62	.03	**	49.55	.22	95.68	.61	3.71	80.68
Neuquén	**	**	#	**	.13	1.98	22.20	**	.85	.23	**	45.31	**	94.66	2.07	3.26	86.81
Río Negro	**	**	#	.94	.16	1.82	39.94	.44	1.66	.14	**	53.57	**	93.90	.81	5.29	87.81
Salta	.12	**	#	.37	.15	.44	45.27	#	.58	.16	**	44.62	**	97.57	1.03	1.40	80.03
San Juan	**	.03	#	.20	.12	.88	30.65	.19	1.20	**	.25	40.23	**	98.14	.88	.99	86.33
San Luis	**	5.33	#	.14	.15	.45	41.44	**	3.67	**	.09	48.58	**	96.99	.27	2.74	84.73
Santa Cruz	.10	**	#	**	.20	1.50	50.83	.33	1.91	.28	.09	44.76	**	97.81	.21	1.97	81.24
Santa Fe	1.52	**	#	.38	.13	1.87	42.94	.21	1.43	.09	.47	50.22	**	96.80	.30	2.90	83.30
Sgo. del Estero	**	.25	#	**	.19	.43	48.54	**	.41	**	.26	40.56	**	96.45	1.70	1.85	70.16
Tucumán	.26	**	#	.57	.24	.56	51.46	.20	.69	.13	.15	41.46	.35	98.64	.69	.67	81.23

SOURCE: Information provided by U.S. Embassy, Argentina.

Table 1006

CHILE ELECTORAL INTENTIONS IN SANTIAGO PLEBISCITE
(%, September 1980)

Response	Aug. 25	Aug. 29	Sept. 3	Sept. 5	Sept. 7	Sept. 9
Yes	50.0	45.3	51.0	52.4	58.7	58.4
No	32.1	31.4	32.5	28.4	19.5	19.4
No answer	18.9	23.3	16.5	19.2	21.8	22.2
	(483)	(468)	(433)	(487)	(491)	(448)

SOURCE: SALA, 23-3701.

Table 1007

CHILE COMPARISON OF GALLUP PREDICTIONS WITH ACTUAL
VOTE IN SANTIAGO PLEBISCITE
(%, September 1980)

Response	Gallup Forecast	Official Vote in Santiago	Difference
Yes	61.5	62.1	-.6
No	34.8	35.6	-.8
Null	3.6	2.2	+1.4

SOURCE: SALA, 23-3702.

Table 1008

COSTA RICA PRESIDENTIAL WINNING
PERCENTAGES, 1953-82[a]

Year	President	%
1953	José Figueres	64.70
1958	Mario Echandi	46.42
1962	Francisco J. Orlich	50.29
1966	José Joaquín Trejos	50.47
1970	José Figueres	54.78
1974	Daniel Oduber	43.44
1978	Rodrigo Carazo	50.51
1982	Luis Alberto Monge	58.60

a. For related tables, see SALA, 23-3404 through 3407.

SOURCE: SALA, 23-3406.

Table 1009

COLOMBIAN PRESIDENTIAL ELECTION RESULTS, 1978 AND 1982[a]

(T)

Regions and Departments	Conservatives		Liberals		"New Liberalism"
	1978	1982	1978	1982	1982
Total	2,357	3,155	2,504	2,749	751
Eastern Region[1]	590	703	564	582	144
Northwestern Region[2]	535	738	442	575	93
Atlantic Region[3]	330	451	493	546	90
Pacific Region[4]	464	602	528	551	61
Bogotá, D. E.	231	388	215	220	283
Central Region[5]	197	241	250	238	54
Abroad	8	32	11	30	26

1. Includes Santander, Cundinarmarca, Boyacá, Norte de Santander, Meta, Arauca and Casanare.
2. Includes Antioquia, Caldas, Risaralda, and Quindio.
3. Includes Atlántico Córdoba, Bolívar, Magdalena, Sucre, Cesar, Guagira, and San Andrés.
4. Includes Valle, Nariño, Cauca, and Chocó.
5. Includes Tolima, Huila, Caquetá and Amazonas, and Putumayo.

a. For related tables, see SALA, 23-3409 and 3410.

SOURCE: SALA, 23-3408.

Table 1010

ECUADOR PRESIDENTIAL ELECTIONS, FINAL RESULTS, BY PROVINCE AND POLITICAL PARTY

(June 1984)

Province	FRN[1]		CID[2]		Null Votes		Blank Votes		Total		
	Votes	%	Votes	%	Votes	%	Votes	%	Votes	Voters	%
Azuay	47,662	31.97	87,596	58.76	10,809	7.25	2,998	2.01	149,065	191,995	77.64
Bolívar	23,070	47.04	19,101	38.95	5,247	10.69	1,621	3.30	49,039	67,436	72.71
Cañar	17,484	31.68	31,746	57.54	4,653	8.43	1,289	2.33	55,172	73,699	74.86
Carchi	20,491	40.39	25,120	49.51	4,263	8.40	854	1.68	50,728	60,675	83.60
Cotopaxi	39,235	40.35	43,468	44.70	11,446	11.77	3,078	3.16	97,227	121,204	80.21
Chimborazo	34,954	27.62	71,016	56.12	15,907	12.57	4,648	3.67	126,525	161,784	78.20
El Oro	48,771	37.69	70,963	54.84	7,877	6.08	1,789	1.38	129,400	165,175	78.34
Esmeraldas	28,180	37.04	39,262	51.60	6,881	9.04	1,754	2.30	76,077	100,019	76.06
Guayas	493,581	62.85	232,410	29.59	50,653	6.44	8,679	1.10	783,323	983,838	79.82
Imbabura	31,721	33.44	50,468	53.20	10,293	10.85	2,371	2.49	94,853	121,743	77.91
Loja	51,253	39.53	65,462	50.49	10,262	7.91	2,668	2.05	129,645	166,366	77.92
Los Ríos	68,309	49.46	56,231	40.71	11,403	8.25	2,162	1.56	138,105	177,759	77.69
Manabí	129,622	51.33	104,730	41.47	14,815	5.86	3,342	1.32	252,509	346,144	72.94
Morona Santiago	5,502	28.71	11,941	62.31	1,370	7.14	349	1.82	19,162	25,937	73.87
Napo	10,031	30.74	18,682	57.26	3,115	9.54	794	2.43	32,622	44,604	73.13
Pastaza	4,053	37.74	5,698	53.06	794	7.39	192	1.78	10,737	14,317	74.99
Pichincha	258,639	42.39	295,125	48.37	47,930	7.85	8,378	1.37	610,072	748,584	81.49
Tungurahua	63,156	44.55	61,466	43.36	13,588	9.58	3,527	2.48	141,737	170,161	83.29
Zamora Chinchipe	4,999	35.69	7,365	53.31	1,233	8.80	306	2.18	14,003	18,469	75.81
Galápagos	996	43.39	1,138	49.58	137	5.96	24	1.04	2,295	3,083	74.44
National Total	1,381,709	46.61	1,299,088	43.82	232,676	7.84	50,823	1.71	2,964,295	3,762,992	78.77

1. Frente de Reconstrucción Nacional, led by León Febres Cordero and Blasco Peñaherrera Padilla, coalition integrated by the Partido Conservador, Partido Liberal, Partido Social Cristiano, Partido Velazquista, Partido Nacionalista Revolucionario, and Partido Cidista.
2. Coalición de Izquierda Democrática, led by Rodrigo Borja Cevallos and Aquiles Rigail Santistevan.

SOURCE: *El Comercio* (Quito), June 20, 1984.

Table 1011

ECUADOR ABSENTEEISM IN ELECTIONS, BY PROVINCE, 1978 AND 1984

Province	1978				1984			
	Registered N	Participated N	Absentee		Registered[1] N	Participated N	Absentee	
			N	%			N	%
Carchi	43,117	36,501	6,616	15.34	63,981	47,748	16,233	25.37
Imbabura	64,108	47,660	16,448	25.66	122,453	72,672	49,781	40.65
Pichincha	472,393	370,354	102,039	21.60	747,302	580,010	167,292	22.39
Cotopaxi	56,973	43,632	13,341	23.42	123,805	92,288	31,517	25.46
Tungurahua	99,619	84,230	15,389	15.45	172,913	137,601	35,312	20.42
Bolívar	33,409	26,490	6,919	20.71	64,460	36,977	27,483	42.64
Chimborazo	79,354	59,439	19,915	25.10	164,189	111,633	52,556	32.01
Cañar	37,731	27,631	10,100	26.77	72,943	46,129	26,814	36.76
Azuay	111,670	85,831	25,839	23.14	192,721	146,734	45,987	23.86
Loja	111,526	85,325	26,201	23.49	174,386	82,860	91,526	52.48
Esmeraldas	41,023	28,480	12,543	30.58	98,973	57,539	41,434	41.86
Manabí[2]	176,270	137,208	38,662	21.93	356,595	216,230	140,365	39.36
Los Ríos[2]	79,329	64,609	14,720	18.56	174,818	28,512	146,306	83.69
Guayas	536,424	316,579	219,845	40.98	933,432	625,005	308,427	33.04
El Oro	99,987	74,014	25,973	25.98	169,192	121,506	47,686	28.18
Napo	13,190	8,942	4,248	32.21	43.304	24.562	18,742	43.28
Pastaza	7,152	6,055	1,097	15.34	13,168	8,591	4,577	34.76
Morona Santiago	11,601	8,693	2,908	25.07	25.623	15,054	10,569	41.25
Zamora Chinchipe	10,306	7,394	2,912	28.26	16,710	4,896	11,814	70.70
Galápagos	1,519	1,140	379	24.95	3,098	2,503	595	19.21
Total	2,086,701	1,521,449	565,252	27.09	3,734,066	2,459,050	1,275,016	34.15

1. Unofficial.
2. Takes into account suspension of elections in some departments within Los Ríos province.

SOURCE: *El Comercio* (Quito), February 4, 1984.

Table 1012

ECUADOR ELECTIONS FOR PROVINCIAL DEPUTIES, BY POLITICAL PARTY

(June 1984)

Province	PCE[1]	LRE[2]	PD[3]	CFP[4]	DP[5]	SC[6]	PCD[7]	CID[8]	FADI[9]	PRE[10]	PNR[11]	ID[12]	APRE[13]	FRA[14]	MPD[15]	Nacional Velazquista	Socialista Ecuatoriano	Valid Votes	Null Votes	Blank Votes	Total
Pichincha	14,158	44,809	70,661	10,127	20,221	71,820	6,521	5,588	27,869	11,333	3,958	108,950	210	24,166	30,576	1,611	5,133	457,521	45,700	48,963	530,184
Cotopaxi	2,618	#	4,645	5,248	7,822	9,438	#	#	2,755	2,202	#	13,053	#	10,369	7,434	#	#	65,566	9,465	19,584	94,615
Carchi	8,624	2,592	#	818	6,276	#	1,256	488	#	#	#	14,969	#	#	2,236	#	2,395	38,608	3,643	6,172	48,430
Imbabura	#	#	10,146	#	5,230	8,932	3,190	1,236	3,810	#	#	24,952	517	1,971	9,530	#	#	67,497	7,137	14,678	89,322
Tungurahua	6,272	2,333	11,999	2,907	4,767	16,336	#	#	8,575	#	771	24,705	146	5,739	14,882	434	1,368	104,501	12,486	19,506	136,493
Bolívar	1,380	5,052	1,703	540	2,732	2,406	#	#	1,559	#	#	6,511	#	#	707	76	#	23,352	5,026	7,410	35,788
Chimborazo	4,852	2,959	#	8,060	6,482	#	2,453	2,024	12,862	#	#	23,247	#	5,222	9,638	#	9,960	87,759	10,127	23,098	121,074
Cañar	3,724	#	2,231	#	#	3,144	1,559	#	2,519	2,173	#	12,929	212	2,311	2,529	#	#	33,331	4,679	8,244	46,234
Azuay	3,407	2,790	14,595	5,313	10,840	12,609	2,481	563	4,411	#	#	26,628	#	4,083	7,697	#	9,894	103,902	11,027	17,597	132,526
Loja	18,055	9,902	11,400	7,182	14,047	#	#	#	6,040	#	#	19,381	#	5,524	9,250	#	#	98,781	10,340	16,375	125,496
Esmeraldas	#	2,457	1,785	10,671	6,725	#	3,699	488	5,519	630	591	6,111	115	1,435	2,183	156	#	42,389	6,942	8,192	57,523
Manabí	1,879	13,962	11,773	24,653	22,881	5,818	1,237	5,794	2,553	2,553	417	30,324	572	17,810	5,583	8,470	1,593	177,994	24,393	33,677	236,066
Los Ríos	#	1,656	2,077	6,975	7,284	13,448	5,638	668	3,745	2,876	2,503	11,301	245	10,139	3,823	468	454	71,222	10,673	#	102,032
Guayas	3,135	30,674	19,710	92,490	17,293	64,899	16,356	15,577	13,111	79,292	365	45,274	2,148	78,748	15,333	6,676	4,492	529,792	57,450	102,894	692,136
El Oro	3,703	677	#	11,473	7,165	6,107	1,234	#	4,283	1,722	24,584	26,173	343	9,392	10,351	390	278	96,133	10,083	13,152	119,367
Napo	#	#	3,981	#	1,644	2,073	3,449	#	#	#	#	7,391	#	2,141	1,331	#	297	22,203	2,407	3,472	28,186
Pastaza	#	2,622	#	#	#	#	1,452	#	2,569	486	12,892	#	#	#	#	#	#	7,129	506	1,253	~
Morona Santiago	#	#	#	#	5,443	868	#	#	#	#	#	6,197	#	2,577	#	#	#	15,085	1,278	2,472	18,835
Zamora Chinchipe	716	#	2,110	184	1,431	#	#	#	#	#	#	2,083	#	709	1,013	#	#	8,246	918	1,990	11,155
Galápagos	#	#	#	#	337	136	291	#	#	#	#	753	#	560	#	#	#	2,097	198	211	2,506
Totals	72,523	122,485	164,835	190,622	148,620	218,634	50,816	32,426	102,180	103,267	46,081	410,932	4,508	182,896	134,036	18,381	35,864	2,053,118	234,478	348,895	2,627,968

1. Partido Conservador Ecuatoriano.
2. Liberal Radical Ecuatoriano.
3. Partido Demócrata.
4. Concentración de Fuerzas Populares.
5. Democracia Popular.
6. Social Cristiano.
7. Pueblo, Cambio y Democracia.
8. Coalición Institucionalista Democrática.
9. Frente Amplio de Izquierda.
10. Partido Roldocista Ecuatoriano.
11. Partido Nacionalista Revolucionario.
12. Izquierda Democrática.
13. Acción Popular Revolucionaria Ecuatoriana.
14. Frente Radical Alfarista.
15. Movimiento Popular Democrático.

SOURCE: El Comercio (Quito), June 19, 1984, p. A2.

Table 1013

EL SALVADOR FIRST ROUND PROVISIONAL ELECTION RESULTS, BY DEPARTMENT AND POLITICAL PARTY

(March 25, 1984)

Department	Party								Valid Votes	Null Votes	Factors				
	Arena[1]	PDC[2]	PCN[3]	Merecen[4]	PAISA[5]	PPS[6]	AD[7]	POP[8]			Abstentions	Contested Votes	Not Used	Lost Ballots	Total
San Salvador	101,834	205,381	44,701	3,066	4,239	6,237	19,196	1,677	386,331	29,606	3,261	1,506	363,536	1,760	791,000
Santa Ana	41,781	66,832	26,368	644	1,201	2,827	3,986	521	144,160	10,999	5,070	906	141,152	213	302,500
San Miguel	18,770	27,048	19,142	235	817	1,916	2,898	277	71,103	5,124	1,689	319	119,910	355	198,500
La Libertad	48,792	65,024	23,797	720	1,318	2,586	5,219	546	148,002	14,584	6,028	1,020	112,631	335	282,500
Usulutan	19,184	20,708	19,932	269	1,369	2,472	1,933	302	66,169	6,328	2,141	200	85,925	237	161,000
Sonsonate	35,448	47,921	20,517	583	1,319	2,356	3,187	357	111,688	9,189	4,261	544	87,666	152	213,500
La Unión	7,129	13,465	13,900	57	296	861	700	91	36,499	2,755	1,190	375	82,502	679	124,000
La Paz	22,050	26,306	15,530	445	1,063	1,021	2,362	241	69,018	6,501	2,993	463	74,481	2,044	155,500
Chalatenango	8,963	12,741	7,979	37	638	368	468	78	31,322	2,969	1,477	86	34,514	2,132	72,500
Cuscatlan	13,544	11,509	11,158	133	738	598	1,150	148	44,028	3,766	2,100	381	84,601	124	135,000
Ahuachapan	23,765	24,299	18,954	136	937	1,354	1,011	188	68,642	5,322	2,939	232	75,647	718	153,500
Morazan	5,939	9,059	8,077	30	363	687	424	73	24,652	2,592	888	223	61,434	211	90,000
San Vicente	11,590	11,853	3,032	135	375	688	797	101	33,571	2,749	1,545	98	104,365	172	142,500
Cabañas	13,130	7,581	8,439	55	757	424	598	77	31,091	2,073	1,154	571	62,042	69	97,000
National Total	376,917	549,727	244,556	6,645	15,430	24,395	43,929	4,677	1,266,276	104,557	41,736	6,924	1,490,306	9,201	2,919,000
As % of Total	29.76	43.41	19.31	.52	1.21	1.92	3.46	.36							
As % of Counted Ballots	8.84														

1. Alianza Republicana Nacional, led by Roberto D'Aubuisson.
2. Partido Demócrata Cristiano, led by Napoleón Duarte.
3. Partido de Coalición Nacional, former military party, which controlled the country for 17 years.
4. A minor splinter party.
5. A minor splinter party.
6. Partido Popular Salvadoreño.
7. Acción Demócrata.
8. Partido de Orientación Popular.

SOURCE: Information provided by the U.S. Embassy, El Salvador.

Table 1014

EL SALVADOR SECOND ROUND PROVISIONAL ELECTION RESULTS, BY DEPARTMENT AND POLITICAL PARTY

(May 6, 1984)

Department	Arena[1]	PDC[2]	Valid Votes	Null Votes	Abstentions	Contested Votes	Not Used	Lost Ballots	Total
San Salvador	156,460	278,786	435,246	25,678	6,840	1,917	319,312	1,513	790,506
Santa Ana	66,663	87,015	153,678	8,318	3,576	480	100,828	121	267,001
San Miguel	42,611	41,786	84,697	4,583	1,714	299	96,930	77	188,000
La Libertad	71,279	82,756	154,035	9,990	3,619	868	102,834	154	271,500
Usulutan	42,147	34,842	76,989	4,646	1,973	329	101,437	126	185,500
Sonsonate	57,019	61,597	118,616	6,174	2,708	363	64,546	101	192,508
La Unión	28,236	26,087	54,323	2,998	1,466	266	84,757	190	144,000
La Paz	39,269	35,093	74,362	3,538	2,187	287	57,081	44	137,499
Chalatenango	20,019	18,183	38,202	2,770	1,436	182	36,358	52	79,000
Cuscatlan	32,580	15,913	48,493	3,287	1,851	286	57,076	39	111,032
Ahuachapan	39,051	32,264	71,315	4,166	2,263	175	45,029	52	123,000
Morazan	15,988	13,044	29,032	1,729	887	147	32,655	50	64,500
San Vicente	19,428	15,317	34,745	1,906	1,097	189	58,504	59	96,500
Cabañas	20,991	9,942	30,953	1,234	965	326	40,007	35	73,500
National Total	651,741	752,625	1,404,366	81,017	32,582	6,114	1,197,354	2,613	2,724,046
As % of Total	46.40	53.59							
% of Counted Ballots	96.08								

1. Alianza Republicana Nacional, led by Roberto D'Aubuisson.
2. Partido Demócrata Cristiano, led by Napoleón Duarte.

SOURCE: Information provided by the U.S. Embassy, El Salvador.

Table 1015

EL SALVADOR ELECTION FOR THE CONSTITUENT ASSEMBLY

(March 28, 1982)[a]

Party	Valid Votes	%	Seats	Political Orientation
PDC[1]	526,890	40.7	24	Centrist

Continued in SALA, 23-3403.

Table 1016

HONDURAS PRESIDENTIAL ELECTION RESULTS

(1981)

Department	PDCH[1]	PINU[2]	PL[3]	PN[4]	Total Valid Votes	Blank Votes	Null Votes	Total Votes
Atlántida	701	2,031	33,900	21,879	58,511	885	1,102	60,498

Continued in SALA, 23-3411.

Table 1017

MEXICO PRESIDENTIAL ELECTION RESULTS, BY PARTY AND STATE

(July 4, 1982)

State	PAN[1]	PRI[2]	PPS[3]	PARM[4]	PDM[5]	PSUM[6]	PST[7]	PRT[8]	PSD[9]	Other[10]	Total[11]	Null
Aguascalientes	31,576	137,847	1,379	770	3,112	1,879	4,809	1,306	345	38	200,023	16,967
Baja California Norte	147,092	271,899	12,264	3,510	6,298	16,456	11,047	12,403	1,149	385	533,499	50,996
Baja California Sur	13,852	64,573	996	479	537	2,336	763	3,444	124	23	90,744	3,617
Campeche	8,052	103,193	993	230	401	898	419	333	52	29	124,231	9,631
Coahuila	86,155	224,753	2,499	1,435	996	4,770	6,581	2,334	351	292	334,972	4,805
Colima	7,126	136,139	965	267	2,009	1,331	1,788	737	82	15	153,993	3,534
Chiapas	21,103	679,429	6,691	5,863	1,463	7,745	8,848	4,998	1,109	762	753,144	15,200
Chihuahua	153,709	362,027	7,184	3,062	4,729	13,139	5,683	2,811	739	67	600,770	47,620
Distrito Federal	906,753	1,796,431	71,798	33,097	86,929	284,796	72,639	195,348	17,369	2,836	3,759,299	291,303
Durango	67,159	280,606	4,620	3,584	2,732	7,619	2,453	2,080	413	13	379,331	8,052
Guanajuato	178,468	518,412	8,232	6,039	61,135	10,755	12,194	3,053	1,154	76	887,274	27,756
Guerrero	22,392	422,905	3,516	6,419	5,667	20,798	15,583	6,522	594	17	517,568	15,155
Hidalgo	50,641	487,739	8,977	2,407	2,998	8,876	10,289	4,806	537	107	595,775	18,398
Jalisco	360,192	814,470	15,354	11,863	49,243	89,842	12,208	8,694	2,301	115	1,438,001	75,519
Mexico	606,871	1,490,682	58,957	25,067	67,432	140,745	40,001	91,490	7,669	383	2,710,762	180,965
Michoacán	88,330	599,259	7,563	4,280	35,121	16,771	7,825	5,078	692	63	794,567	29,585
Morelos	33,673	249,769	3,968	2,326	4,754	8,587	6,514	15,142	644	44	337,447	12,026
Nayarit	6,883	157,242	3,184	1,135	2,013	22,577	1,106	708	160	48	205,159	10,103
Nuevo León	213,919	635,010	4,128	4,696	2,460	4,447	3,633	3,975	843	12	888,019	14,896
Oaxaca	46,185	638,965	27,896	14,549	2,296	20,908	4,467	4,948	580	64	766,915	11,057
Puebla	135,372	1,050,921	13,346	5,837	8,443	25,393	9,061	10,714	1,172	98	1,303,271	42,919
Querétaro	40,518	197,152	1,350	1,616	4,543	3,439	1,429	1,267	467	18	263,021	11,222
Quintana Roo	3,513	87,798	1,344	221	247	896	845	300	65	15	96,587	1,343
San Luis Potosí	41,171	411,796	2,020	2,035	21,249	3,909	4,139	2,391	710	49	499,790	10,321
Sinaloa	65,035	475,275	9,267	4,739	2,713	31,947	4,596	5,374	827	142	615,027	15,112
Sonora	113,166	422,712	2,686	1,250	1,688	6,759	1,215	4,759	742	152	576,464	21,335
Tabasco	11,706	309,194	5,186	960	645	2,129	2,921	1,045	207	9	339,082	5,080
Tamaulipas	60,620	463,612	5,011	45,579	6,234	8,255	3,986	3,319	961	2,695	620,648	20,376
Tlaxcala	23,890	187,790	2,001	963	10,035	3,897	836	1,028	139	35	236,372	5,758
Veracruz	70,630	1,705,902	71,740	45,103	29,185	43,783	73,689	13,995	4,565	14,217	2,116,943	44,564
Yucatán	59,275	270,002	1,352	490	389	3,022	411	536	141	19	347,499	11,862
Zacatecas	39,859	347,836	1,958	1,192	2,707	6,903	1,587	1,435	176	25	412,196	8,518
Total	3,714,886	16,061,340	363,025	239,063	430,376	825,607	333,565	414,333	47,079	23,388	23,498,393	1,045,731

1. Partido Acción National (Pablo Emilio Madero).
2. Partido Revolucionario Institucional (Miguel de la Madrid).
3. Partido Popular Socialista (Miguel de la Madrid).
4. Partido Auténtico de la Revolución Mexicana (Miguel de la Madrid).
5. Partido Demócrata Mexicano (Ignacio González Góllaz).
6. Partido Socialista Unificado de México (Arnoldo Martínez Verdugo).
7. Partido Socialista de los Trabajadores (Cándido Díaz Cenecedo).
8. Partido Revolucionario de los Trabajadores (Rosario Ibarra de la Piedra).
9. Partido Social Demócrata (Manuel Moreno Sánchez).
10. Unregistered.
11. Includes null votes.

SOURCE: Secretaría General y Presidencia del Comité Técnico y de Vigilancia del Registro Nacional de Electores. México, D.F., August 18, 1982.

Table 1018

NICARAGUA ELECTION RESULTS

(1984)

Party	Presidential Votes	% of Valid Votes Cast	Seats Won in Assembly
FSLN[1]	735,967	67.0	61
PCD[2]	154,327	14.0	14
PLI[3]	105,560	9.6	9
PPSC[4]	61,199	5.6	6
PCdeN[5]	16,034	1.5	2
PSN[6]	14,494	1.3	2
MAP–ML[7]	11,352	1.0	2
Null	71,209	- -	- -
Total	1,170,142	100.0	96

1. Frente Sandinista de Liberación Nacional.
2. Partido Conservador Demócrata de Nicaragua.
3. Partido Liberal Independiente.
4. Partido Popular Social Cristiano.
5. Partido Comunista de Nicaragua.
6. Partido Socialista Nicaragüense.
7. Movimiento de Acción Popular Marxista Leninista.

SOURCE: *LASA Forum* (Latin American Studies Association), Winter, 1985, p. 24.

Table 1019

PANAMA PRESIDENTIAL ELECTION RESULTS,
BY POLITICAL PARTY

(May 20, 1984)

Party	Votes
Unión Nacional Democrática[1]	266,533
Alianza de Oposición[2]	299,035
Partido del Pueblo	4,598
Acción Popular	13,782
Partido Nacionalista Popular	15,976
Partido Socialista de los Trabajadores	2,085
Partido Revolucionario de los Trabajadores	3,969

1. Formed by the Partido Liberal (28,568 votes), Partido Revolucionario Democrático
    (175,722 votes), Frampo (5,280 votes), Partido Laborista (45,384 votes), and Partido
    Panameñista (11,579 votes), led by Nicolás Ardito Barletta.
2. Formed by Partido Demócrata Cristiano (46,963 votes), Molinena (30,737 votes), and
    Partido Panameñista Auténtico (221,335 votes), led by Arnulfo Arias.

SOURCE: Information provided by the U.S. Embassy, Panama.

Table 1020

VENEZUELAN PRESIDENTIAL ELECTION RESULTS, 1947–78

Year	Candidate	Votes	%
1947	Rómulo Gallegos	871,752	74.34

Continued in SALA, 23-3402.

Table 1021

POPULATION VOTING IN TOTAL POPULATION AGE 20 AND OVER, BY TYPE OF ELECTION, 12 LC

	Country	Year	Type of Election[1]	Total Vote (T)	Estimated % of Adult Population Voting
A.	ARGENTINA	1983	P, L	15,180	89
C.	BRAZIL	1982	L	48,440	81
E.	COLOMBIA	1982	P	6,816	68
F.	COSTA RICA	1982	P, L	992	87
I.	ECUADOR	1984	L	2,204	53
J.	EL SALVADOR	1984	P	1,524	69
K.	GUATEMALA	1984	CA	1,856	57
M.	HONDURAS	1981	P, L	1,171	79
N.	MEXICO	1982	P, L	22,523	75
O.	NICARAGUA	1984	P, CA	1,170	91
R.	PERU	1980	P, L	4,030	49
S.	VENEZUELA	1983	P, L	6,741	90
	UNITED STATES	1984	P, L	92,000	53

1. P = Presidential, L = Legislative, CA = Constituent Assembly.

SOURCE: *LASA Forum* (Latin American Studies Association), Winter, 1985, p. 25.

CHAPTER 11

RELIGION

Table 1100

CATHOLIC CHURCH HIERARCHY AND INSTITUTIONS, 20 L, 1983–84[a]

Country	Year	Cardinals	Archbishops	Bishops	Priests	Seminarians	Brothers	Sisters	Schools	Charitable Institutions	Catholic % of Total Population
A. ARGENTINA	1983	3	10	66	5,450	1,373	1,179	12,446	~	~	92.1
	1984	3	10	65	5,482	1,655	1,188	12,552	~	~	92.8
B. BOLIVIA	1983	1	4	19	929	167	233	1,682	~	~	93.7
	1984	1	5	17	872	165	232	1,680	~	~	94
C. BRAZIL	1983	7	37	239	13,169	4,283	2,701	37,024	~	~	90.1
	1984	6	35	237	13,443	4,606	2,638	36,983	~	~	90.1
D. CHILE	1983	1	4	24	2,020	663	467	5,088	~	~	85.5
	1984	1	3	24	2,046	895	445	5,091	~	~	85.5
E. COLOMBIA	1983	1	11	49	5,254	1,857	1,025	17,654	~	~	95.5
	1984	2	12	49	5,196	2,174	939	18,304	~	~	95.5
F. COSTA RICA	1983	0	1	5	434	189	31	867	~	~	93.5
	1984	0	1	5	452	226	29	1,001	~	~	92.7
G. CUBA	1983	0	2	5	200	50	22	214	~	~	41.2
	1984	0	2	5	221	47	20	218	~	~	41.2
H. DOMINICAN REP.	1983	1	2	8	505	286	90	1,496	~	~	94.8
	1984	1	2	8	550	283	82	1,320	~	~	94.8
I. ECUADOR	1983	1	3	19	1,513	185	367	4,151	~	~	90.2
	1984	1	3	18	1,524	180	367	4,133	~	~	91
J. EL SALVADOR	1983	0	0	5	361	105	88	836	~	~	90.4
	1984	0	1	6	347	110	76	852	~	~	90.9
K. GUATEMALA	1983	1	0	14	699	244	136	1,191	~	~	83.6
	1984	0	0	13	652	251	124	1,181	~	~	83.3
L. HAITI	1983	0	1	6	405	139	239	900	~	~	83.4
	1984	0	1	6	420	149	218	917	~	~	86.5
M. HONDURAS	1983	0	1	6	236	26	22	359	~	~	95.8
	1984	0	1	7	249	29	16	341	~	~	96
N. MEXICO	1983	3	10	74	10,087	2,947	1,127	25,598	~	~	92.8
	1984	3	10	74	10,235	3,385	1,155	25,468	~	~	96.4
O. NICARAGUA	1983	0	1	7	340	49	100	692	~	~	91.6
	1984	0	1	7	341	52	95	701	~	~	90.7
P. PANAMA	1983	0	1	6	290	52	46	457	~	~	88.8
	1984	0	1	6	302	105	39	490	~	~	89
Q. PARAGUAY	1983	0	1	15	543	151	106	932	~	~	91.2
	1984	0	1	14	554	172	96	977	~	~	91.4
R. PERU	1983	1	6	42	2,233	693	443	4,732	~	~	92.1
	1984	1	5	44	2,198	787	427	4,944	~	~	92.4
S. URUGUAY	1983	0	1	10	587	67	149	1,621	~	~	78.6
	1984	0	1	11	586	89	148	1,595	~	~	78.6
T. VENEZUELA	1983	1	6	29	1,995	371	326	4,345	~	~	92.2
	1984	2	5	31	2,022	383	229	4,270	~	~	92.4

a. For years 1956-80, see SALA, 23-1109.

SOURCE: *Catholic Almanac*, 1984.

Table 1101

INHABITANTS PER CATHOLIC PRIEST, 20 L, 1912–80

(T)

	Country	1912	1945	1950	1955	1960	1966	1970	1975	1980
A.	ARGENTINA	4.5	5.1	4.3	4.3	4.3	4.3	4.2	5.0	5.5
B.	BOLIVIA	2.8	5.8	6.1	5.1	4.9	4.8	4.3	6.9	6.8
C.	BRAZIL	5.7	6.8	6.9	6.8	6.4	7.1	7.8	8.6	8.5
D.	CHILE	2.1	3.2	3.3	3.5	3.1	3.6	3.6	4.7	5.7
E.	COLOMBIA	3.8	3.8	3.7	3.7	3.6	3.3	3.6	5.0	5.4
F.	COSTA RICA	2.5	4.7	4.8	4.1	4.6	4.2	3.7	5.4	5.7
G.	CUBA	6.1	9.5	10.8	8.8	9.4	34.4	39.8	48.4	50.1
H.	DOMINICAN REP.	10.0	17.3	13.5	10.5	11.0	9.7	9.0	10.7	11.4
I.	ECUADOR	2.2	3.1	3.2	3.3	3.3	3.4	4.2	5.3	6.2
J.	EL SALVADOR	7.0	8.7	8.7	9.1	9.2	8.4	9.0	10.2	13.8
K.	GUATEMALA	9.4	20.7	21.2	13.5	12.3	9.5	10.2	9.3	10.8
L.	HAITI	10.5	12.5	9.3	8.4	7.8	10.7	10.5	15.0	13.1
M.	HONDURAS	5.0	12.3	11.9	13.0	11.5	12.0	10.6	14.9	9.7
N.	MEXICO	2.6	5.3	5.8	5.3	5.3	5.8	5.7	6.4	6.9
O.	NICARAGUA	~	~	~	~	~	~	6.3	7.2	8.5
P.	PANAMA	6.4	7.8	6.7	6.2	6.2	6.0	5.6	6.0	6.5
Q.	PARAGUAY	7.2	6.1	6.3	5.7	4.9	4.5	6.6	5.7	6.2
R.	PERU	3.6	5.8	6.0	5.9	5.7	5.3	5.9	6.8	7.8
S.	URUGUAY	4.8	3.6	3.7	4.3	4.1	4.2	4.1	5.0	5.2
T.	VENEZUELA	4.4	6.4	6.4	5.3	5.2	5.1	5.5	5.7	7.0

SOURCE: Data to 1960 from Yvan Labelle and Adriana Estrada (Comp.), *Latin America in Maps, Charts, Tables; No. 2: Socio-Religious Data (Catholicism)* (Mexico, D.F.: Center of Intercultural Formation, 1964); data for 1966 from *Atlas Hierarchicus*, 1968; and data for 1960 to 1980 calculated from number of priests in *Catholic Almanac* and SALA, 23–601 through 620.

Table 1102

JEHOVAH'S WITNESSES PUBLISHERS AND MEMBERS, 20 LC

(1983)[a]

	Country	Publishers[1] (N)	Population per Publisher	Persons Baptized (N)	Congregations (N)	Memorial Attendance (N)
A.	ARGENTINA	43,815	605	4,149	638	102,839
B.	BOLIVIA	3,228	1,589	369	76	14,783
C.	BRAZIL	133,765	883	11,649	2,498	392,844
D.	CHILE	19,323	547	1,842	288	70,522
E.	COLOMBIA	18,827	1,395	1,533	289	80,786
F.	COSTA RICA	6,946	320	690	148	20,351
G.	CUBA	~	~	~	~	~
H.	DOMINICAN REP.	7,432	733	589	131	28,072
I.	ECUADOR	6,892	1,177	579	119	36,827
J.	EL SALVADOR	11,085	429	1,457	200	44,967
K.	GUATEMALA	6,325	1,056	522	104	24,189
L.	HAITI	3,248	1,700	216	76	18,713
M.	HONDURAS	3,162	1,192	218	68	16,542
N.	MEXICO	122,327	561	13,070	4,474	619,564
O.	NICARAGUA	~	~	~	~	~
P.	PANAMA	3,462	572	265	76	12,678
Q.	PARAGUAY	1,734	1,666	77	44	4,391
R.	PERU	15,788	1,100	1,574	321	67,192
S.	URUGUAY	4,458	594	297	90	14,516
T.	VENEZUELA	20,392	766	1,752	212	81,098
	UNITED STATES	616,058	361	35,303	7,837	1,574,212

1. Local printers or distributors who are Jehovah's Witnesses.

a. Average for year.

SOURCE: *Yearbook of Jehovah's Witnesses*, 1983.

Table 1103

ESTIMATED JEWISH POPULATION,[1] 20 LC, 1968-79

(N)

	Country	1968	1970	1974	1976	1978	1979
A.	ARGENTINA[2]	500,000	500,000	475,000	300,000	300,000	300,000
B.	BOLIVIA	4,000	2,000	2,000	2,000	2,000	750
C.	BRAZIL	140,000	150,000	155,000	165,000	150,000[b]	150,000[c]
D.	CHILE	35,000	35,000	30,000	27,000	28,000	30,000[c]
E.	COLOMBIA	10,000	10,000	12,000	12,000	14,000	12,000
F.	COSTA RICA	1,500	1,500	1,500	1,500	2,500[b]	2,500
G.	CUBA	1,700	1,700	1,500	1,500	1,500	1,500
H.	DOMINICAN REP.	350	350	110	200	250	200
I.	ECUADOR	2,000	2,000	1,000	1,000	1,000	1,000
J.	EL SALVADOR	300	300	300	310	350[b]	350
K.	GUATEMALA	1,500	1,900	1,900	1,900	2,000	2,000
L.	HAITI	150	150	150	150	150	150
M.	HONDURAS	150	150	200	200	200	200[c]
N.	MEXICO	30,000	35,000[a]	40,000	37,500	37,500	37,500
O.	NICARAGUA	200	200	200	200	200	200
P.	PANAMA	2,000	2,000	2,000	2,000	2,000	2,000
Q.	PARAGUAY	1,200	1,200	1,200	1,200	1,200	1,200
R.	PERU	4,000	5,300	5,300	6,000	5,200[b]	5,200
S.	URUGUAY	54,000	50,000	50,000	50,000	50,000	50,000[c]
T.	VENEZUELA	12,000	12,000	15,000	15,000	17,000	15,000
	UNITED STATES	5,870,000	5,870,000	5,800,000	5,840,000	5,860,900	5,920,890

1. Prepared by AJY staff from questionnaires sent to local Jewish community leaders.
2. Decline after 1972 reflects revision of estimate rather than mass exodus.

a. 49,181 according to 1970 Mexican census.
b. Reply to 1977 inquiry.
c. Reply to 1980 inquiry.

SOURCE: *American Jewish Yearbook* since 1969.

Table 1104

WORLD CHRISTIAN ENCYCLOPEDIA (WCE) SCHEME[1] FOR CATEGORIZING RELIGIOUS (INCLUDING PROTESTANT) AND NON-RELIGIOUS PERSONS, 1900–80

(Guide to table 1105)

Category[2] (A + G = 100.0%)	Definition
A. Christians	Total of all Christian adherents of all kinds (professing and crypto-Christians, which is by definition equal to nominal plus affiliated).
B. Professing (C + D)	Those publicly professing (declaring, stating, confessing, self-identifying) their preference or adherence in a government census or public opinion poll, hence known to the state or society or the public.
(Crypto-Christians)	Secret believers in Christ not professing publicly nor enumerated or known in government census or public opinion poll, hence known to the state or the public or society (but usually affiliated and known to churches), of the following seven varieties: (1) unorganized individuals in legal churches, (2) political prisoners or exiles, (3) organized believers in unregistered denominations or congregations, (4) members of deliberately clandestine illegal underground churches, (5) members of anti-state minority churches or sects, (6) organized believers in Christ rejecting the label Christian (anti-church believers), and (7) isolated radio or radiophonic or correspondence-course believers in small groups or cells in non-Christian or anti-Christian areas.
C. Roman Catholics	All in communion with the Church of Rome (affiliated Roman Catholics are here defined as baptized Roman Catholics plus catechumens).
(Catholic Pentecostals)	Roman Catholics regularly active or involved in the organized Catholic Charismatic Renewal; active Catholic charismatics (healings, tongues, prophesying).
(Christo-pagans)	Amerindian Roman Catholics syncretizing folk-Catholicism with organized traditional Amerindian pagan religion.
(Evangelical Catholics)	In Latin countries, professing Roman Catholics (counted in a government census of Roman Catholics) who also regard themselves as Evangélicos or Evangéliques and are affiliated to churches which the state terms Evangelical (Protestant, Anglican, indigenous or marginal Protestant).
(Spiritist Catholics)	Roman Catholics active in organized high or low spiritism, including syncretistic spirit-possession cults.
D. Other Christians Protestants	Followers of churches originating in, or reformulated at the time of, or in communion with, the Western World's sixteenth-century Protestant Reformation; called Evangelicals in French, German, Italian, Portuguese, and Spanish, although usually more extensive than Evangelicals properly so called.
(Evangelicals)	Conservative Evangelicals (in denominations outside the Ecumenical Movement), Conciliar Evangelicals (in denominations within the Ecumenical Movement), and Fundamentalists.
(Neo-pentecostals)	Charismatics regularly active in organized groups within non-Pentecostal Protestant denominations (excluding any who secede and form new Pentecostal or indigenous pentecostal denominations). (Note: this category is not distinct from the previous one, Evangelicals, and usually overlaps somewhat with it.)
Non-White Indigenous	Black/Third World Indigenous (all categories with "indigenous") Christians in denominations, churches, or movements indigenous to Black or Non-White races originating in the Third World (i.e., to all races except the White peoples; locally founded, Black-founded, Black-led, Non-White founded, Non-White led; begun since A.D. 1500; forming autonomous bodies independent of White origin or control, often separatist, schismatic, anti-establishment, in reaction to Western influences.
(Black Evangelicals)	Black Evangelicals: Conservative Evangelicals, Conciliar Evangelicals, and Fundamentalists, in the Black churches of the United States.
(Black Neo-pentecostals)	Regularly active Black charismatics (more traditionally, "sanctified") in the non-pentecostal-Black denominations in the United States.
Orthodox	Eastern (Chalcedonian), Oriental (Pre-Chalcedonian, Non-Chalcedonian, Monophysite), Nestorian (Assyrian), and non-historical Orthodox.
Orthodox Pentecostals	Orthodox active in the organized charismatic renewal (healings, tongues, prophesying).
Marginal Protestants	Followers of para-Christian or quasi-Christian Western movements or deviations out of mainline Protestantism (including pseudo-Christian "New Age" cults), not pro-

Category[2] (A + G = 100.0%)	Definition
	fessing mainstream Protestant christocentric doctrine but claiming a second or supplementary or ongoing source of divine revelation in addition to the Bible (a new Book, angels, visions), yet nevertheless centered on Jesus, Christ, and the Cross.
Catholics (non-Roman)	Old Catholics and others in secessions from the Church of Rome since 1700 in the Western world, and other Catholic-type sacramentalist or hierarchical secessions from Protestantism or Anglicanism.
Anglicans	Those related to the Anglican Communion, Episcopalians, including dissident Anglicans in the Western world.
(Evangelicals)	Anglican Evangelicals (Conciliar Evangelicals, Conservative Evangelicals, Low Churchmen, and other Evangelicals).
(Anglican Pentecostals)	Anglicans regularly active in the organized charismatic renewal (healings, tongues, prophesying).
E. Nominal	Unaffiliated, unchurched; non-church members; those professing to be Christians but not affiliated to churches (residual Christians, latent Christians, anonymous Christians, sometimes called post-Christians in industrialized countries); Christians not, or not yet, or no longer, attached to organized Christianity, or who have rejected the institutional churches while retaining Christian beliefs and values, who may be Christians individually but are not part of the churches' corporate life, community, or fellowship.
F. Affiliated (B minus E)[3]	Church members; all persons belonging to or connected with organized churches; those on the churches' books or records, or with whom the churches are in touch, usually known by name and address to the churches at grass-roots or local parish level, i.e., those attached to or claimed by or known to the institutional churches or organized Christianity and hence part of their corporate life, community, and fellowship, including children, infants, adherents, catechumens, and members under discipline; total church membership, or total Christian community or inclusive membership; minus any doubly-affiliated, minus any disaffiliated.
1. Disaffiliated	Dechristianized persons; baptized Roman Catholics (or other Christians) enumerated as affiliated by a majority or state-linked Catholic Church (or other majority or state church) but who have recently formally-withdrawn or disaffiliated themselves completely from Christianity and now profess to be non-religious (agnostics) or atheists; i.e., recent withdrawals from state or majority churches still, however, regarded as members by those churches, although in fact now backsliders, lapsed, or apostates; sometimes termed post-Christians; because a duplication, they are shown as a negative quantity (with a minus sign).
2. Doubly-affiliated	Persons affiliated to or claimed by two denominations at once; because a duplication, they are shown as a negative quantity (with a minus sign).
3. 4. 5. etc.	Religions listed under C and D above.
G. Non-Christian Groups (including Atheists and non-religious)	
Neo-Christians	All persons who are not Christian adherents of any kind, including non-believers.
Afro-American Spiritists	Low spiritists syncretizing Catholicism with African and/or Amerindian animism, also Afro-American syncretistic cults with Christian elements (see, e.g., SALA, 23-1116).
Atheists	Those professing atheism, skepticism, disbelief or irreligion or other anti-religious quasi-religions, including Marxist-Leninist Communism regarded as a quasi-religion; dialectical materialists and militant non-believers opposed to all religion; skeptics.
Baha'is	Followers of the Bah'i World Faith founded by Baha'u'llah (Baha' Allah, Glory of God).
Buddhists	Followers of Mahayana (Northern), Theravada (Hinayana or Southern), or Vajrayana (Tantrayana, Tantrism, Lamaism); traditional sects but not neo-Buddhist new religions or religious movements.

Table 1104 (Continued)

WORLD CHRISTIAN ENCYCLOPEDIA (WCE) SCHEME[1] FOR CATEGORIZING RELIGIOUS (INCLUDING PROTESTANT)
AND NON-RELIGIOUS PERSONS, 1900–80

(Guide to table 1105)

Category[2] (A + G = 100.0%)	Definition
Religious Buddhists	Buddhists who profess Buddhism as both a family religion and also a personal religion.
Non-religious Buddhists	Persons whose family religion is Buddhism but who as individuals profess to have no personal religion.
Chinese folk-religionists	Followers of traditional Chinese religion; with six elements: Taoism and local deities, Confucianism, Buddhist elements, ancestor worship, Chinese universism, divination, and magic.
Confucians	Non-Chinese followers of Confucius and Confucianism.
Hindus	Followers of the main Hindu traditions: (a) Vaishnavites, (b) Saivites, (c) Saktists, (d) Arya Samaj and other reform sectarians, and (e) followers of modern neo-Hindu sects.
Jains	Followers of the Svetambara and Digambara sects.
Jews	Followers of the Orthodox, Reformed, or Liberal schools of Judaism; Ashkenazis, Sefardis (Sephardis); crypto-Jews.
(Karaites)	Readers of the Scriptures, followers of Jewish sect Qaraism.
(Samaritans)	Children of Israel (Bene-Yisrael) or Shamerim (Observant Ones), a small Jewish sect.
Mandaeans	Gnostics (Christians of St. John, followers of John the Baptist, Sabaeans).
Muslims	Followers of Islam, in its two main branches (Sunnis, Shias) and all other orthodox and heterodox sects and reform movements.
(Ahmadis, Druzes, Yazidis)	Followers of heterodox Muslim sects (enumerated both here and also in total statistics of Muslims in line above).
New-Religionists	Followers of the so-called twentieth-century New Religions or radical new crisis religions (new Far Eastern or Asiatic indigenous non-Christian syncretistic mass religions embodying major innovations and new religious systems), including Japanese neo-Buddhist and neo-Shinto new religious movements.
Non-religious	Those professing no religion, or professing unbelief or non-belief; non-believers, doubters, agnostics, free-thinkers, non-religious humanists, non-religious quasi-religionists, post-religious; indifferent to both religion and atheism; secularists, materialists; also post-Christian, dechristianized or de-religionized populations.
Parsis (Parsees)	Descendants of Zoroastrians.
Shintoists	Japanese who profess, or still profess, Shinto as their first or major religion.
Sikhs	Followers of the Sikh reform movement out of Hindusim.
Spiritists	Non-Christian high (as opposed to low) spiritists, spiritualists, thaumaturgicalists, medium-religionists.
Tribal religionists	Primal or primitive religionists, animists, spirit-worshippers, shamanists, ancestor-venerators, polytheists, pantheists, traditionalists, local or tribal folk-religionists, including adherents of local or tribal syncretistic or nativistic movements, neo-paganism, cargo cults, witchcraft eradication cults, possession healing movements, tribal messianic movements, etc.
Other religionists	Term used for (a) adherents of remaining non-Christian religions listed above but too few in a particular country for their religions to be individually listed (excluding non-religious and atheists), and (b) adherents of all other smaller non-Christian religions, faiths, quasi-religions, brotherhoods, or other religious systems not included in the above listing.

1. Includes children.
2. All categories may not be used by WCE for Latin American countries or may not be abstracted for presentation here in SALA, 23-1114 through 1134.
3. B less E = F.

SOURCE: David B. Barrett, ed., *World Christian Encyclopedia* (Oxford: Oxford University Press, 1982).

Table 1105

RELIGIOUS (INCLUDING PROTESTANT)
AND NON-RELIGIOUS PERSONS, 20 LC, 1900–80
(A + G = 100.0%)

A. ARGENTINA Category	1900 N	1900 %	1970 N	1970 %	AA–GR 1970-80	1980 N	1980 %
A. Christians	4,126,500	98.3	22,757,300	95.8	1.28	25,871,100	95.6
B. Professing (C + D)	4,126,500	98.3	22,757,300	95.8	1.28	25,871,100	95.6
C. Roman Catholics	4,092,100	97.4	21,962,300	92.5	1.21	24,802,600	91.6
Christo-pagans	50,000	(1.2)	200,000	(.8)	(1.31)	228,000	(.8)
D. Protestants	29,000	.7	500,000	2.1	3.03	676,600	2.5
Argentinian indigenous	0	.0	120,000	.5	4.56	189,500	.7
Orthodox	3,000	.1	100,000	.4	1.31	114,000	.4
Marginal Protestants	1,000	.0	45,000	.2	1.84	54,000	.2
Catholics (non-Roman)	0	.0	20,000	.1	1.40	23,000	.1
Anglicans	1,000	.0	10,000	.0	1.31	11,400	.0
E. Nominal	21,000	.5	337,000	1.4	2.46	430,940	1.6
F. Affiliated (B – E) = (1 to 8)	4,105,000	97.8	22,419,000	94.4	1.26	25,440,160	94.0
1. Doubly-affiliated	–72,000	–1.7	–975,000	–4.1	2.86	–1,291,380	–4.8
2. Roman Catholics	4,132,000	98.4	22,301,530	93.9	1.26	25,304,840	93.5
3. Protestants	40,000	1.0	593,007	2.5	2.80	784,900	2.9
4. Argentinian Indigenous	0	.0	251,400	.9	3.60	351,800	1.3
5. Orthodox	3,000	.1	122,000	.5	1.23	138,000	.5
6. Marginal Protestants	1,000	.0	63,774	.3	2.25	80,000	.4
7. Catholics (non-Roman)	0	.0	50,000	.2	1.32	57,000	.2
8. Anglicans	1,000	.0	13,200	.1	1.28	15,000	.1
G. Jews	6,500	.2	475,000	2.0	1.28	540,000	2.0
Non-religious	5,000	.1	210,000	.9	3.20	290,000	1.1
Atheists	5,000	.1	140,000	.6	1.94	170,000	.6
Muslims	4,000	.1	50,000	.2	1.31	57,000	.2
Spiritists[1]	1,000	.0	50,000	.2	1.48	58,000	.2
Tribal religionists[2]	50,000	1.2	30,000	.1	–4.00	20,000	.1
Buddhists	1,000	.0	10,000	.0	.95	11,000	.0
Baha'is	0	.0	5,700	.0	1.90	6,900	.0
Other religionists	1,000	.0	20,000	.1	6.67	40,000	.1
Country Population	4,200,000	100.0	23,748,000	100.0	1.31	27,064,000	100.0

1. Spiritists: Organized under the Confederación Espiritista Argentina. A number of lapsed Catholics and Protestants become spiritists each year, and by 1976 spiritism was recognized as a growing phenomenon.
2. Tribal Religionists: Of the 170,000 tribal lowland Amerindians (or Aborigines) in 1970, mostly along the Paraguayan border, a proportion are still shamanists or animists, including a majority of the 20,000 Chiriguano (Guarani) and the other 8 Aboriginal groups: Chane (Guana), Chorote, Chulupi, Mataco (population 12,000), Mbya, Mocovi, Pilaca and some Toba (17,060). Guarani shamans in particular occupy a respected healing role in society, and Guarani mysticism remains the main agent for social cohesion.

DEFINITIONS: See table 1104.

Continued in SALA, 23-1115 through 1134.

Table 1106

PRACTICING AND NON-PRACTICING CHRISTIANS, 20 LC, 1900–80
(Total = 100.0%)

	Country	Practicing[1]			Non-Practicing[2]		
		1900	1970	1980	1900	1970	1980
A.	ARGENTINA	90	70	70	10	30	30
B.	BOLIVIA	85	71	69	15	29	31
C.	BRAZIL	80	62	60	20	38	40
D.	CHILE	80	75	65	20	25	35
E.	COLOMBIA	96	92	92	4	8	8
F.	COSTA RICA	95	85	85	5	15	15
G.	CUBA	90	40	60	10	60	40
H.	DOMINICAN REP.	90	70	70	10	30	30
I.	ECUADOR	90	80	80	10	20	20
J.	EL SALVADOR	95	85	85	5	15	15
K.	GUATEMALA	90	75	75	10	25	25
I.	HAITI	95	85	85	5	15	15
M.	HONDURAS	90	80	80	10	20	20
N.	MEXICO	80	65	65	20	35	35
O.	NICARAGUA	95	85	85	5	15	15
P.	PANAMA	90	80	80	10	20	20
Q.	PARAGUAY	70	45	45	30	55	55
R.	PERU	95	80	80	5	20	20
S.	URUGUAY	80	70	70	20	30	30
T.	VENEZUELA	85	70	70	15	30	30
	UNITED STATES	95	90	88	5	10	12

1. Practicing: Total affiliated of all denominations who attend public worship at least once a year, or who fulfill their churches' minimum annual attendance requirements, or who are radio/TV-service listeners (% here = % of affiliated, not % of total population); church attenders (daily, weekly, fortnightly, monthly, occasional, on festivals only, or annual), excluding civic attenders, private attenders, attending non-members, and attending non-Christians; active Christians, committed Christians, militant Christians.

2. Non-Practicing: Affiliated but inactive, non-attending (dominant Christians) (% = % of affiliated).

SOURCE: See table 1104.

Table 1107

ORGANIZED BIBLE DISTRIBUTION PER YEAR, 20 LC, 1900-75

(N)

	Country	Free					Subsidized					Commercial
		1900	1950	1960	1970	1975	1900	1950	1960	1970	1975	1975
A.	ARGENTINA	0	0	0	0	0	13,000	37,579	73,640	67,191	44,159	60.000
B.	BOLIVIA	0	0	0	0	0	0	8,016	10,434	15,894	39,401	10,000
C.	BRAZIL	0	0	0	260	0	17,782	77,387	297,546	204,943	189,005	486,975
D.	CHILE	0	0	0	0	0	500	13,934	31,338	34,964	28,736	4,000
E.	COLOMBIA	0	0	0	0	0	0	2,721	25,736	47,660	37,964	50,000
F.	COSTA RICA	0	0	0	0	0	400	832	3,695	8,886	14,222	20,000
G.	CUBA	0	0	0	0	0	1,360	12,206	40,532	0	2,000	0
H.	DOMINICAN REPUBLIC	0	0	0	60	200	300	5,510	5,396	17,302	22,124	10,000
I.	ECUADOR	0	0	0	0	0	10	2,868	4,052	15,972	21,878	30,000
J.	EL SALVADOR	0	0	0	0	0	400	2,274	6,103	9,328	16,513	20,000
K.	GUATEMALA	0	0	0	0	0	100	4,661	11,096	24,944	31,925	50,000
L.	HAITI	0	0	0	0	0	200	7,944	3,846	24,776	35,475	5,000
M.	HONDURAS	0	0	0	0	1,000	50	1,606	3,666	9,054	21,807	30,000
N.	MEXICO	0	0	0	0	10,000	6,544	27,130	38,579	93,501	149,164	100,000
O.	NICARAGUA	0	0	0	0		400	992	3,540	6,761	13,709	2,000
P.	PANAMA	0	0	0	200	0	200	2,174	3,218	10,627	11,419	5,000
	Panama Canal Zone	0	0	0	0	0	200	1,710	1,100	2,000	3,000	500
Q.	PARAGUAY	0	0	0	0	0	50	3,177	3,676	3,117	7,027	5,000
R.	PERU	0	0	0	0	0	49	13,344	22,117	46,557	79,390	60,000
S.	URUGUAY	0	0	0	0	0	50	4,547	8,736	14,974	10,490	5,000
T.	VENEZUELA	0	0	0	0	0	0	5,835	20,998	45,663	45,233	60,000

SOURCE: See table 1104.

Table 1108

CATHOLIC BAPTISMS PER 1,000 CATHOLICS, 20 L, 1972-75

	Country	1972	1973	1974	1975
A.	ARGENTINA	21.7	21.2	22.0	21.7

Continued in SALA, 21-1107.

Table 1109

PROTESTANT SECTS AND MISSIONARIES,[1] 20 LC

(1968)

	Country	Places of Worship	Protestant Population	Native Personnel		Foreign Missionaries		Seminaries and Bible Schools
				Ordained	Laymen	Ordained	Laymen	
A.	ARGENTINA	2,412	529,657	695	506	401	112	15

Continued in SALA, 21-1108.

CHAPTER 12

THE MILITARY

Table 1200

U.S. DATA ON MILITARY EXPENDITURES, ARMED FORCES, GNP, AND CENTRAL GOVERNMENT EXPENDITURES,
20 LRC, 1972-82[a]

Country	Year	Military Expenditures (ME) (M US) Current	Constant 1981	Armed Forces (T)	GNP (M US) Current	Constant 1981	Central Government Expenditures (CGE) (M US) Constant 1981	ME GNP (%)	ME CGE (%)	ME Per Capita (Constant 1981 Dollars)	Armed Forces (PTI)	GNP Per Capita (Constant 1981 Dollars)
A. ARGENTINA	1972	792	1,541	140	56,158	109,242	18,065	1.4	8.5	62	5.7	4,458
	1973	932	1,716	160	61,520	113,279	19,653	1.5	8.7	69	6.5	4,567
	1974	1,173	1,986	150	71,179	120,522	25,362	1.6	7.8	78	6.0	4,782
	1975	1,658	2,575	160	77,010	119,572	25,754	2.2	10.0	101	6.3	4,689
	1976	1,948	2,863	155	80,748	118,622	23,361	2.4	12.3	110	6.0	4,580
	1977	2,259	3,134	155	90,884	126103	21,664	2.5	14.5	118	5.9	4,776
	1978	2,617	3,381	155	93,933	121,353	23,866	2.8	14.2	126	5.8	4,528
	1979	2,758	3,285	155	109,261	130,140	25,732	2.5	12.8	120	5.7	4,784
	1980	2,739	2,995	155	119,578	130,734	27,704	2.3	10.8	108	5.6	4,719
	1981	3,186	3,186	155	120,403	120,403	30,987	2.6	10.3	111	5.4	4,195
	1982	~	~	175	120,344	113,516	~	~	~	~	6.0	3,887
B. BOLIVIA	1972	39	75	17	2,600	5,058	468	1.5	16.2	17	3.9	1,149
	1973	53	99	18	2,947	5,426	522	1.8	19.0	22	4.0	1,205
	1974	55	93	18	3,385	5,732	619	1.6	15.1	20	3.9	1,246
	1975	78	121	20	3,895	6,048	690	2.0	17.6	25	4.3	1,287
	1976	88	129	22	4,398	6,462	805	2.0	16.1	27	4.6	1,346
	1977	89	123	20	4,772	6,622	836	1.9	14.7	24	4.0	1,324
	1978	108	140	20	5,262	6,798	870	2.1	16.1	27	3.9	1,333
	1979	114	136	20	5,776	6,879	820	2.0	16.6	26	3.8	1,323
	1980	140	153	24	6,298	6,885	853	2.2	18.0	29	4.5	1,299
	1981	196	196	26	6,818	6,818	865	2.9	22.7	35	4.6	1,217
	1982	100	95	26	6,566	6,193	~	1.5	~	16	4.6	1,086
C. BRAZIL	1972	1,116	2,172	410	81,542	158,621	29,283	1.4	7.4	21	4.1	1,573
	1973	1,304	2,402	420	98,202	180,823	33,347	1.3	7.2	23	4.1	1,750
	1974	1,385	2,346	435	116,975	198,064	35,037	1.2	6.7	22	4.1	1,870
	1975	1,446	2,245	455	134,046	208,132	40,341	1.1	5.6	20	4.2	1,918
	1976	1,780	2,616	450	155,152	227,925	44,747	1.1	5.8	23	4.1	2,051
	1977	1.623	2,252	450	173,016	240,061	49,938	.9	4.5	19	4.0	2,111
	1978	1,639	2,117	450	193,434	249,901	53,894	.8	3.9	18	3.9	2,146
	1979	1,629	1,940	450	223,020	265,638	61,208	.7	3.2	16	3.8	2,228
	1980	1,796	1,964	450	260,812	285,145	69,570	.7	2.8	16	3.7	2,337
	1981	1,837	1,837	450	274,214	274,214	71,652	.7	2.6	14	3.6	2,188
	1982	~	~	460	295,648	278,875	~	~	~	~	3.6	2,173
D. CHILE	1972	384	747	75	13,482	26,225	11,437	2.8	6.5	77	7.7	2,703
	1973	495	912	75	13,381	24,639	8,903	3.7	10.2	92	7.6	2,488
	1974	712	1,205	90	14,622	24,759	8,481	4.9	14.2	120	9.0	2,475
	1975	649	1,007	110	13,555	21,047	7,674	4.8	13.1	98	10.8	2,063
	1976	607	892	111	14,931	21,934	6,924	4.1	12.9	85	10.7	2,109
	1977	705	978	111	17,479	24,252	8,200	4.0	11.9	93	10.6	2,309
	1978	853	1,102	111	20,295	26,220	8,732	4.2	12.6	103	10.4	2,450
	1979	861	1,026	111	23,721	28,254	8,552	3.6	12.0	95	10.3	2,616
	1980	996	1,088	116	27,756	30,346	8,963	3.6	12.1	99	10.5	2,758
	1981	1,175	1,175	116	31,620	31,620	10,245	3.7	11.5	104	10.4	2,823
	1982	1,391	1,312	116	28,801	27,167	10,813	4.8	12.1	116	10.3	2,404
E. COLOMBIA	1972	149	290	50	11,908	23,165	3,155	1.3	9.2	12	2.2	1,029
	1973	159	292	50	13,514	24,885	3,216	1.2	9.1	12	2.2	1,077
	1974	155	262	50	15,671	26,535	3,132	1.0	8.4	11	2.1	1,124
	1975	210	326	50	17,709	27,496	3,543	1.2	9.2	13	2.1	1,141
	1976	181	267	60	19,547	28,716	3,194	.9	8.4	10	2.4	1,167
	1977	157	219	60	21,780	30,219	3,393	.7	6.5	8	2.4	1,204
	1978	185	239	60	25,525	32,976	3,816	.7	6.3	9	2.3	1,283
	1979	281	334	60	29,191	34,770	4,200	1.0	8.0	12	2.3	1,327
	1980	351	384	60	33,129	36,220	4,973	1.1	7.7	15	2.4	1,460
	1981	366	366	65	36,897	36,897	4,822	1.0	7.6	13	2.4	1,387
	1982	327	309	70	39,460	37,222	3,971	.8	7.8	11	2.6	1,373
F. COSTA RICA	1972	4	9	2	883	1,718	348	.5	2.6	5	1.1	954
	1973	5	10	2	1,008	1,856	376	.5	2.7	5	1.1	977
	1974	6	11	2	1,167	1,976	389	.6	2.8	5	1.1	1,040
	1975	8	12	2	1,287	1,998	417	.6	3.0	6	1.0	999
	1976	10	14	3	1,429	2,100	455	.7	3.2	7	1.5	1,050
	1977	13	18	3	1,653	2,294	465	.8	3.9	8	1.4	1,092
	1978	12	16	3	1,874	2,421	600	.7	2.8	7	1.4	1,153
	1979	14	17	3	2,120	2,526	656	.7	2.7	8	1.4	1,148
	1980	15	17	3	2,333	2,551	675	.7	2.5	7	1.3	1,109
	1981	14	14	3	2,342	2,342	544	.6	2.7	5	1.2	937
	1982	~	~	4	2,205	2,079	~	~	~	~	1.5	800

Table 1200 (Continued)

U.S. DATA ON MILITARY EXPENDITURES, ARMED FORCES, GNP, AND CENTRAL GOVERNMENT EXPENDITURES, 20 LRC, 1972-82[a]

Country	Year	Military Expenditures (ME) (M US) Current	Constant 1981	Armed Forces (T)	GNP (M US) Current	Constant 1981	Central Government Expenditures (CGE) (M US) Constant 1981	ME GNP (%)	ME CGE (%)	ME Per Capita (Constant 1981 Dollars)	Armed Forces (PTI)	GNP Per Capita (Constant 1981 Dollars)
G. CUBA[1,2]	1972	249	484	140	7,174	13,955	~	3.5	~	54	15.7	1,568
	1973	291	535	140	8,014	14,756	~	3.6	~	59	15.6	1,639
	1974	340	575	140	9,239	15,643	~	3.7	~	62	15.2	1,700
	1975	393	610	120	10,595	16,450	~	3.7	~	65	12.9	1,768
	1976	~	~	125	11,515	16,916	~	~	~	~	13.2	1,780
	1977	~	~	200	12,745	17,683	~	~	~	~	20.8	1,842
	1978	1,040	1,343	210	14,520	18,758	~	7.2	~	138	21.6	1,933
	1979	1,160	1,381	210	16,218	19,317	~	7.2	~	141	21.4	1,971
	1980	1,140	1,246	220	17,440	19,067	~	6.5	~	129	22.9	1,986
	1981	1,199	1,199	225	20,429	20,429	~	5.9	~	123	23.2	2,106
	1982	1,109	1,046	230	21,971	20,724	~	5.0	~	106	23.5	2,114
H. DOMINICAN REP.	1972	36	70	16	2,167	4,215	792	1.7	8.9	15	3.5	916
	1973	39	73	16	2,572	4,736	873	1.5	8.4	15	3.4	1,007
	1974	50	85	18	2,974	5,036	985	1.7	8.7	17	3.7	1,027
	1975	53	83	18	3,408	5,292	969	1.6	8.6	16	3.6	1,058
	1976	64	94	19	3,843	5,646	936	1.7	10.0	18	3.7	1,107
	1977	69	96	19	4,285	5,946	906	1.6	10.6	18	3.6	1,121
	1978	88	114	19	4,710	6,085	1,017	1.9	11.2	21	3.5	1,127
	1979	100	120	19	5,320	6,337	1,272	1.9	9.4	21	3.4	1,131
	1980	84	92	24	6,151	6,725	1,195	1.4	7.7	16	4.2	1,179
	1981	104	104	24	6,933	6,933	1,186	1.5	8.8	17	4.1	1,175
	1982	107[†]	101[†]	25	7,443	7,021	~	1.4	~	16	4.1	1,151
I. ECUADOR[1]	1972	83	162	20	3,511	6,829	1,041	2.4	15.6	25	3.2	1,084
	1973	95	176	20	4,564	8,404	10,826	2.1	1.6	27	3.1	1,293
	1974	112	189	20	5,221	8,840	1,515	2.1	12.5	28	3.0	1,319
	1975	151	235	20	6,272	9,739	1,618	2.4	14.5	34	2.9	1,411
	1976	174	256	24	7,159	10,518	1,769	2.4	14.5	36	3.4	1,481
	1977	182	253	30	8,089	11,224	1,914	2.3	13.2	34	4.1	1,537
	1978	263	340	35	9,265	11,970	1,932	2.8	17.6	45	4.7	1,596
	1979	246	294	35	10,397	12,384	2,018	2.4	14.6	37	4.5	1,587
	1980	262	287	35	11,709	12,802	2,211	2.2	13.0	35	4.4	1,600
	1981	296	296	34	13,146	13,146	2,500	2.3	11.8	35	4.1	1,584
	1982	~	~	36	13,779	12,997	2,228	~	~	~	4.2	1,529
J. EL SALVADOR	1972	20	38	8	1,578	3,071	398	1.3	9.7	10	2.1	808
	1973	20	37	8	1,748	3,220	402	1.2	9.4	9	2.1	825
	1974	25	42	8	2,026	3,430	450	1.2	9.4	10	2.0	857
	1975	27	42	8	2,329	3,617	519	1.2	8.2	10	2.0	882
	1976	30	44	8	2,579	3,789	556	1.2	8.0	10	1.9	881
	1977	33	46	8	2,885	4,003	611	1.2	7.7	10	1.8	909
	1978	47	61	10	3,284	4,242	626	1.5	9.8	13	2.3	942
	1979	53	63	11	3,533	4,208	626	1.5	10.1	13	2.3	895
	1980	83	90	12	3,489	3,814	661	2.4	13.7	18	2.5	794
	1981	116	116	13	3,491	3,491	693	3.3	16.7	25	2.8	759
	1982	142	134	25	3,496	3,298	641	4.1	20.9	29	5.4	717
K. GUATEMALA	1972	30	60	14	2,823	5,492	609	1.1	9.9	10	2.5	980
	1973	27	50	13	3,195	5,884	583	.9	8.6	8	2.3	1,032
	1974	32	54	13	3,708	6,279	655	.9	8.3	9	2.2	1,064
	1975	50	78	13	4,104	6,373	637	1.2	12.3	12	2.1	1,044
	1976	49	72	14	4,709	6,918	833	1.0	8.6	11	2.2	1,098
	1977	67	93	14	5,395	7,486	881	1.2	10.6	14	2.2	1,169
	1978	73	95	14	6,111	7,894	954	1.2	10.0	14	2.1	1,196
	1979	82	98	14	6,952	8,281	978	1.2	10.1	14	2.1	1,217
	1980	100	110	15	7,800	8,528	1,299	1.3	8.5	15	2.1	1,218
	1981	114	114	16	8,577	8,577	1,433	1.3	8.0	15	2.2	1,159
	1982	146	138	17	8,752	8,255	1,220	1.7	11.3	18	2.3	1,100
L. HAITI	1972	12	23	12	579	1,126	163	2.1	14.6	5	2.5	234
	1973	10	19	12	620	1,142	139	1.7	14.2	4	2.4	233
	1974	9	16	6	717	1,215	158	1.4	10.4	3	1.2	243
	1975	11	17	6	767	1,191	211	1.5	8.2	3	1.2	229
	1976	11	16	6	880	1,294	242	1.3	6.7	3	1.1	244
	1977	11	16	7	937	1,300	276	1.2	5.9	3	1.3	240
	1978	13	17	7	1,046	1,351	256	1.3	6.8	3	1.3	245
	1979	15	17	7	1,221	1,455	272	1.2	6.6	3	1.2	255
	1980	24	26	7	1,413	1,545	284	1.7	9.3	4	1.2	266
	1981	27	27	8	1,502	1,502	292	1.9	9.6	5	1.5	273
	1982	26	24	8	1,584	1,495	249	1.6	9.9	4	1.4	267

Table 1200 (Continued)

U.S. DATA ON MILITARY EXPENDITURES, ARMED FORCES, GNP, AND CENTRAL GOVERNMENT EXPENDITURES, 20 LRC, 1972-82[a]

Country	Year	Military Expenditures (ME) (M US) Current	Constant 1981	Armed Forces (T)	GNP (M US) Current	Constant 1981	Central Government Expenditures (CGE) (M US) Constant 1981	ME GNP (%)	ME CGE (%)	ME Per Capita (Constant 1981 Dollars)	Armed Forces (PTI)	GNP Per Capita (Constant 1981 Dollars)
M. HONDURAS	1972	17	33	12	902	1,756	270	1.9	12.3	11	4.1	605
	1973	17	31	12	987	1,818	254	1.7	12.4	10	4.0	606
	1974	17	30	10	1,096	1,857	286	1.6	10.5	9	3.2	599
	1975	22	35	12	1,164	1,807	348	2.0	10.1	11	3.8	565
	1976	24	36	12	1,313	1,928	388	1.9	9.3	11	3.6	584
	1977	30	41	12	1,505	2,089	411	2.0	10.1	12	3.5	614
	1978	40	52	13	1,720	2,222	467	2.4	11.2	14	3.9	635
	1979	46	55	14	1,968	2,345	472	2.4	11.8	15	3.9	651
	1980	~	~	14	2,261	2,472	601	~	~	~	3.7	650
	1981	~	~	15	2,497	2,497	671	~	~	~	3.8	624
	1982	~	~	16	2,587	2,440	725	~	~	~	3.9	595
N. MEXICO	1972	448	872	80	67,664	131,624	17,799	.7	4.9	16	1.5	2,469
	1973	488	898	80	77,383	142,488	20,341	.6	4.4	16	1.5	2,586
	1974	557	943	85	89,091	150,851	22,094	.6	4.3	16	1.5	2,655
	1975	788	1,223	95	102,565	159,250	27,534	.8	4.4	20	1.6	2,713
	1976	765	1,125	100	112,543	165,330	28,660	.7	3.9	18	1.7	2,732
	1977	795	1,103	100	123,483	171,334	28,602	.6	3.9	17	1.6	2,750
	1978	688	889	145	143,529	185,428	31,256	.5	2.8	13	2.3	2,892
	1979	817	973	145	169,277	201,625	36,413	.5	2.7	14	2.2	3,064
	1980	827	904	145	198,679	217,215	42,183	.4	2.1	13	2.1	3,199
	1981	1,196	1,196	145	231,759	231,759	52,502	.5	2.3	16	2.0	3,223
	1982	1,261[†]	1,190[†]	145	243,677	229,852	~	.5	~	16	2.0	3,114
O. NICARAGUA	1972	22	43	6	1,161	2,258	378	1.9	11.4	21	3.0	1,129
	1973	18	34	6	1,262	2,323	380	1.5	9.0	16	2.9	1,106
	1974	23	40	6	1,574	2,665	548	1.5	7.4	19	2.9	1,269
	1975	31	49	5	1,786	2,773	557	1.8	8.9	22	2.3	1,260
	1976	41	60	5	1,965	2,887	523	2.1	11.5	26	2.2	1,255
	1977	53	74	6	2,095	2,907	624	2.5	11.9	32	2.6	1,264
	1978	70	91	~	2,062	2,665	543	3.4	16.8	38	~	1,110
	1979	55	65	~	1,649	1,965	450	3.3	14.6	27	~	818
	1980	119[†]	130[†]	15	2,082	2,276	693	5.7	18.8	52	6.0	910
	1981	169[†]	169[†]	40	2,461	2,461	875	6.9	19.3	65	15.4	946
	1982	~	~	75	2,515	2,372	~	~	~	~	27.8	878
P. PANAMA	1972	10	19	7	1,249	2,429	680[†]	.8	2.9	12	4.4	1,518
	1973	10	20	7	1,390	2,560	723	.8	2.8	12	4.4	1,600
	1974	12	21	8	1,548	2,621	837	.8	2.5	12	4.7	1,542
	1975	14	22	8	1,747	2,712	896	.8	2.5	13	4.7	1,595
	1976	14	21	8	1,854	2,724	920	.8	2.3	11	4.4	1,513
	1977	14	20	8	1,983	2,752	911	.7	2.3	11	4.4	1,529
	1978	16	21	8	2,357	3,046	959	.7	2.2	12	4.4	1,692
	1979	18	22	8	2,659	3,168	1,243	.7	1.8	11	4.2	1,667
	1980	23	25	8	3,247	3,550	1,235	.7	2.1	13	4.2	1,868
	1981	27	27	9	3,659	3,659	1,364	.7	2.0	13	4.5	1,829
	1982	31	29	10	4,035	3,806	~	.8	~	14	5.0	1,903
Q. PARAGUAY	1972	23	45	15	1,286	2,502	333	1.8	13.5	17	5.8	962
	1973	22	41	15	1,460	2,689	295	1.5	13.9	15	5.6	996
	1974	22	38	15	1,731	2,931	295	1.3	13.1	13	5.4	1,046
	1975	31	49	15	2,027	3,148	362	1.6	13.6	17	5.4	1,124
	1976	33	49	15	2,264	3,326	412	1.5	12.0	17	5.2	1,146
	1977	38	53	15	2,698	3,743	429	1.4	12.5	17	5.0	1,247
	1978	43	55	15	3,191	4,123	494	1.4	11.3	18	5.0	1,374
	1979	48	57	15	3,924	4,674	512	1.2	11.3	18	4.8	1,507
	1980	60	66	15	4,721	5,162	563	1.3	11.7	20	4.7	1,613
	1981	78	78	15	5,593	5,593	662	1.4	11.9	23	4.5	1,695
	1982	96[†]	91[†]	16	5,780	5,452	857[†]	1.7	10.6	26	4.7	1,603
R. PERU	1972	246	478	75	8,367	16,276	2,785	2.9	17.2	33	5.2	1,138
	1973	310	571	75	9,185	16,913	2,810	3.4	20.3	38	5.1	1,150
	1974	345	584	90	10,792	18,273	2,884	3.2	20.3	38	6.0	1,210
	1975	506	786	95	12,305	19,106	3,295	4.1	23.9	50	6.1	1,232
	1976	626	919	100	13,171	19,348	3,495	4.8	26.3	57	6.3	1,216
	1977	968	1,344	125	13,904	19,292	3,417	7.0	39.3	82	7.7	1,183
	1978	779	1,006	125	14,775	19,089	3,143	5.3	32.0	60	7.5	1,143
	1979	539	642	125	16,482	19,632	3,001	3.3	21.4	37	7.3	1,141
	1980	994[†]	1,087[†]	151	18,868	20,629	4,021	5.3	27.0	61	8.6	1,172
	1981	1,026[†]	1,026[†]	157	21,432	21,432	4,329	4.8	23.7	56	8.7	1,184
	1982	1,078[†]	1,017[†]	164	22,783	21,490	3,945	4.7	25.8	54	8.8	1,155

Table 1200 (Continued)

U.S. DATA ON MILITARY EXPENDITURES, ARMED FORCES, GNP, AND CENTRAL GOVERNMENT EXPENDITURES, 20 LRC, 1972-82[a]

Country	Year	Military Expenditures (ME) (M US) Current	Military Expenditures (ME) (M US) Constant 1981	Armed Forces (T)	GNP (M US) Current	GNP (M US) Constant 1981	Central Government Expenditures (CGE) (M US) Constant 1981	ME GNP (%)	ME CGE (%)	ME Per Capita (Constant 1981 Dollars)	Armed Forces (PTI)	GNP Per Capita (Constant 1981 Dollars)
S. URUGUAY	1972	103	202	20	4,395	8,549	2,161	2.4	9.4	72	7.1	3,053
	1973	111	204	20	4,694	8,643	1,985	2.4	10.3	73	7.1	3,087
	1974	149	252	25	5,222	8,842	2,149	2.9	11.8	90	8.9	3,158
	1975	164	254	25	6,005	9,324	2,195	2.7	11.6	91	8.9	3,330
	1976	146	215	28	6,628	9,737	2,405	2.2	8.9	74	9.7	3,357
	1977	168	234	28	7,122	9,882	2,421	2.4	9.7	80	9.7	3,407
	1978	184	238	28	8,062	10,416	2,462	2.3	9.7	82	9.7	3,591
	1979	222	264	28	9,336	11,120	2,370	2.4	11.2	91	9.7	3,834
	1980	271	296	28	10,711	11,710	2,612	2.5	11.4	102	9.7	4,038
	1981	363	363	28	11,526	11,526	2,845	3.2	12.8	125	9.7	3,974
	1982	409	386	29	10,998	10,374	3,159	3.7	12.2	133	10.0	3,577
T. VENEZUELA	1972	474	922	45	23,816	46,328	10,731	2.0	8.6	80	3.9	4,028
	1973	515	950	50	26,615	49,008	11,063	1.9	8.6	79	4.2	4,118
	1974	610	1,033	50	31,022	52,527	20,008	2.0	5.2	84	4.1	4,270
	1975	723	1,123	55	36,752	57,065	20,210	2.0	5.6	88	4.3	4,493
	1976	738	1,085	55	42,056	61,783	20,859	1.8	5.2	82	4.2	4,680
	1977	833	1,156	55	47,421	65,797	22,437	1.8	5.2	85	4.0	4,838
	1978	852	1,101	55	52,402	67,700	21,852	1.6	5.0	78	3.9	4,801
	1979	750	893	55	57,272	68,217	16,496	1.3	5.4	61	3.8	4,704
	1980	780	853	55	61,822	67,589	18,513	1.3	4.6	49	3.2	3,906
	1981	1,059[†]	1,059[†]	55	68,120	68,120	24,571	1.6	4.3	62	3.3	4,030
	1982	1,638[†]	1,545[†]	56	70,469	66,471	22,904	2.3	6.7	88	3.2	3,820
LATIN AMERICA[3]	1972	4.3	8.3	1,173	297	579	106.6	1.4	7.8	28	4.0	1,979
	1973	5.0	9.1	1,208	339	625	122.8	1.5	7.4	30	4.0	2,082
	1974	5.8	9.9	1,248	394	667	132.6	1.5	7.5	32	4.1	2,167
	1975	7.1	11.0	1,297	446	692	145.4	1.6	7.6	34	4.1	2,192
	1976	8.1	11.9	1,328	496	728	150.5	1.6	7.9	36	4.1	2,249
	1977	9.1	12.6	1,436	552	766	158.0	1.6	8.0	37	4.3	2,310
	1978	9.7	12.5	1,509	616	796	168.5	1.6	7.4	36	4.4	2,348
	1979	9.9	11.8	1,513	709	845	179.0	1.4	6.6	34	4.4	2,431
	1980	11.0	12.0	1,564	811	886	201.3	1.4	6.0	33	4.4	2,490
	1981	12.8	12.8	1,612	885	885	226.8	1.4	5.6	34	4.4	2,406
	1982	16.6	15.7	1,717	926	873	198.5	1.8	7.9	41	4.6	2,322
UNITED STATES	1972	77,639	151,027	2,323	1,190,900	2,316,602	452,796	6.5	33.4	722	11.1	11,084
	1973	78,358	144,283	2,252	1,331,300	2,451,375	479,871	5.9	30.1	687	10.7	11,673
	1974	85,906	145,457	2,162	1,440,700	2,439,420	479,909	6.0	30.3	686	10.2	11,506
	1975	90,948	141,213	2,128	1,556,100	2,416,129	538,206	5.8	26.2	659	9.9	11,290
	1976	91,013	133,702	2,081	1,726,400	2,536,152	567,299	5.3	23.6	621	9.7	11,796
	1977	100,925	140,034	2,074	1,926,100	2,672,477	587,956	5.2	23.8	645	9.6	12,315
	1978	109,247	141,137	2,062	2,162,000	2,793,121	614,525	5.1	23.0	644	9.4	12,754
	1979	122,279	145,646	2,027	2,421,000	2,883,642	624,979	5.1	23.3	659	9.2	13,048
	1980	143,981	157,413	2,050	2,637,000	2,883,021	680,314	5.5	23.1	691	9.0	12,661
	1981	169,888	169,888	2,082	2,948,700	2,948,700	718,600	5.8	23.6	739	9.1	12,831
	1982	196,345	185,205	2,108	3,071,400	2,897,151	741,040	6.4	25.0	798	9.1	12,482
WORLD[3]	1972	290.9	565.0	25,341	4,828	9,391	2,282.6	6.0	24.8	147	6.6	2,446
	1973	313.8	577.9	25,580	5,453	10,041	2,427.7	5.8	23.8	147	6.5	2,564
	1974	358.7	607.3	26,884	6,131	10,381	2,631.8	5.8	23.1	152	6.7	2,600
	1975	405.9	630.2	25,996	6,784	10,534	2,932.3	6.0	21.5	154	6.4	2,580
	1976	438.6	644.4	25,944	7,506	11,027	3,094.1	5.8	20.8	155	6.2	2,652
	1977	472.4	655.5	25,741	8,284	11,494	3,235.7	5.7	20.3	155	6.1	2,717
	1978	517.5	668.5	26,158	9,243	11,942	3,377.0	5.6	19.8	155	6.1	2,775
	1979	572.7	682.2	26,383	10,400	12,388	3,536.6	5.5	19.3	155	6.0	2,830
	1980	647.3	707.6	26,294	11,605	12,688	3,787.0	5.6	18.7	158	5.9	2,842
	1981	733.6	733.6	26,818	12,844	12,844	3,957.8	5.7	18.5	161	5.9	2,828
	1982	817.5	771.1	27,510	13,632	12,858	4,071.0	6.0	18.9	166	6.0	2,781

1. This series probably excludes most capital expenditures or arms acquisitions.
2. For years 1972-82 GNP is an estimate based on partial or uncertain data.
3. Latin America and World totals are expressed in billions of dollars instead of millions of dollars. In order to reduce distortions in trends caused by data gaps, the totals for World and Latin America include rough approximations for those countries and years in which data or estimates are unavailable.

a. For 1963-73, see SALA, 17-2302.

SOURCE: U.S. Arms Control and Disarmament Agency, *World Military Expenditures and Arms Transfers, 1972-82* (Washington D.C., 1984), table I.

Table 1201

U.S. DATA ON VALUE OF ARMS TRANSFERS AND TOTAL IMPORTS AND EXPORTS, BY REGION, ORGANIZATION, AND COUNTRY, 20 LRC, 1972–82

Country	Year	Arms Imports[1] (MUS)		Arms Exports[1] (MUS)		Total Imports[2] (MUS)		Total Exports[2] (MUS)		Arms Imports / Total Imports (%)	Arms Exports / Total Exports (%)
		Current	Constant 1981	Current	Constant 1981	Current	Constant 1981	Current	Constant 1981		
A. ARGENTINA	1972	60	116	10	19	1,905	3,705	1,941	3,775	3.1	.5
	1973	50	92	10	18	2,230	4,106	3,266	6,013	2.2	.3
	1974	40	67	0	0	3,635	6,154	3,931	6,656	1.1	.0
	1975	30	46	0	0	3,947	6,128	2,961	4,597	.7	.0
	1976	50	73	0	0	3,033	4,455	3,916	5,752	1.6	.0
	1977	40	55	5	6	4,162	5,774	5,652	7,842	.9	.1
	1978	370	478	0	0	3,834	4,953	6,400	8,268	9.6	.0
	1979	490	583	10	11	6,600	7,861	7,810	9,302	7.4	.1
	1980	200	218	5	5	10,541	11,524	8,021	8,769	1.8	.1
	1981	430	430	10	10	9,430	9,430	9,143	9,143	4.5	.1
	1982	300	282	0	0	5,338	5,035	7,623	7,190	5.6	.0
B. BOLIVIA	1972	0	0	0	0	185	359	201	391	.0	.0
	1973	10	18	0	0	230	423	261	480	4.3	.0
	1974	5	8	0	0	366	619	556	941	1.3	.0
	1975	10	15	0	0	575	892	445	690	1.7	.0
	1976	5	7	0	0	594	872	566	831	.8	.0
	1977	5	6	0	0	591	820	634	879	.8	.0
	1978	20	25	0	0	777	1,003	627	810	2.5	.0
	1979	80	95	0	0	894	1,064	762	907	8.9	.0
	1980	60	65	0	0	814	889	942	1,029	7.3	.0
	1981	60	60	0	0	825	825	909	909	7.2	.0
	1982	0	0	0	0	536	505	823	776	.0	.0
C. BRAZIL	1972	60	116	0	0	4,783	9,304	3,991	7,763	1.2	.0
	1973	120	220	0	0	6,999	12,887	6,199	11,414	1.7	.0
	1974	60	101	0	0	14,168	23,989	7,951	13,462	.4	.0
	1975	100	155	30	46	13,592	21,104	8,670	13,461	.7	.3
	1976	140	205	80	117	13,726	20,164	10,128	14,878	1.0	.8
	1977	100	138	20	27	13,257	18,394	12,120	16,816	.7	.2
	1978	210	271	110	142	15,054	19,448	12,659	16,354	1.3	.9
	1979	240	285	120	142	19,804	23,588	15,244	18,157	1.2	.8
	1980	130	142	150	164	24,961	27,289	20,132	22,010	.5	.7
	1981	60	60	150	150	24,079	24,079	23,293	23,293	.2	.6
	1982	30	28	625	589	21,069	19,873	20,175	19,030	.1	.3.1
D. CHILE	1972	10	19	0	0	941	1,830	855	1,663	1.0	.0
	1973	70	128	0	0	1,098	2,021	1,231	2,266	6.3	.0
	1974	70	118	0	0	1,911	3,235	2,481	4,200	3.6	.0
	1975	20	31	0	0	1,338	2,077	1,552	2,409	1.4	.0
	1976	130	190	0	0	1,643	2,413	2,083	3,060	7.9	.0
	1977	60	83	0	0	2,259	3,134	2,190	3,038	2.6	.0
	1978	60	77	0	0	3,002	3,878	2,478	3,201	1.9	.0
	1979	190	226	0	0	4,218	5,024	2,894	3,447	4.5	.0
	1980	250	273	0	0	5,824	6,367	4,671	5,106	4.2	.0
	1981	260	260	5	5	6,364	6,364	3,906	3,906	4.0	.1
	1982	280	264	0	0	3,528	3,327	3,822	3,605	7.9	.0
E. COLOMBIA	1972	30	58	0	0	859	1,671	866	1,684	3.4	.0
	1973	40	73	0	0	1,062	1,955	1,177	2,167	3.7	.0
	1974	10	16	0	0	1,597	2,704	1,417	2,399	.6	.0
	1975	40	62	0	0	1,495	2,321	1,465	2,274	2.6	.0
	1976	0	0	0	0	1,708	2,509	1,745	2,563	.0	.0
	1977	10	13	0	0	2,028	2,813	2,443	3,389	.4	.0
	1978	10	12	0	0	2,836	3,663	3,003	3,879	.3	.0
	1979	20	23	0	0	3,233	3,850	3,300	3,930	.6	.0
	1980	70	76	0	0	4,663	5,098	3,945	4,313	1.5	.0
	1981	40	40	0	0	5,201	5,201	2,956	2,956	.7	.0
	1982	30	28	0	0	5,480	5,169	3,097	2,921	.5	.0
F. COSTA RICA	1972	0	0	0	0	373	725	281	546	.0	.0
	1973	0	0	0	0	455	837	345	635	.0	.0
	1974	0	0	0	0	720	1,219	440	745	.0	.0
	1975	0	0	0	0	694	1,077	493	765	.0	.0
	1976	0	0	0	0	770	1,131	593	871	.0	.0
	1977	0	0	0	0	1,021	1,416	828	1,148	.0	.0
	1978	0	0	0	0	1,185	1,530	844	1,090	.0	.0
	1979	0	0	0	0	1,397	1,664	934	1,112	.0	.0
	1980	~	~	0	0	1,508	1,648	1,018	1,113	~	.0
	1981	0	0	0	0	1,211	1,211	964	964	.0	.0
	1982	0	0	0	0	866	816	872	822	.0	.0

Table 1201 (Continued)

U.S. DATA ON VALUE OF ARMS TRANSFERS AND TOTAL IMPORTS AND EXPORTS, BY REGION, ORGANIZATION, AND COUNTRY, 20 LRC, 1972-82

Country	Year	Arms Imports[1] (MUS) Current	Constant 1981	Arms Exports[1] (MUS) Current	Constant 1981	Total Imports[2] (MUS) Current	Constant 1981	Total Exports[2] (MUS) Current	Constant 1981	Arms Imports Total Imports (%)	Arms Exports Total Exports (%)
G. CUBA	1972	70	136	0	0	1,300	2,528	840	1,634	5.4	.0
	1973	70	128	0	0	1,780	3,277	1,400	2,577	3.9	.0
	1974	60	101	0	0	2,690	4,554	2,690	4,554	2.2	.0
	1975	70	108	30	46	3,767	5,849	3,572	5,546	1.9	.8
	1976	130	191	120	176	3,879	5,698	3,284	4,824	3.4	3.7
	1977	100	138	10	13	4,362	6,052	3,669	5,090	2.3	.3
	1978	350	452	0	0	4,751	6,137	4,575	5,910	7.4	.0
	1979	260	309	0	0	5,089	6,061	4,829	5,751	5.1	.0
	1980	260	284	0	0	6,409	7,006	5,593	6,114	4.1	.0
	1981	800	800	10	10	6,602	6,602	5,389	5,389	12.1	.2
	1982	975	919	20	18	6,916	6,523	6,498	6,129	14.1	.3
H. DOMINICAN REP.	1972	0	0	0	0	388	754	348	676	.0	.0
	1973	0	0	0	0	489	900	442	813	.0	.0
	1974	0	0	0	0	808	1,368	637	1,078	.0	.0
	1975	0	0	0	0	889	1,380	894	1,388	.0	.0
	1976	0	0	0	0	878	1,289	716	1,051	.0	.0
	1977	0	0	0	0	975	1,352	780	1,082	.0	.0
	1978	0	0	0	0	987	1,275	676	873	.0	.0
	1979	0	0	0	0	1,213	1,444	875	1,042	.0	.0
	1980	10	10	0	0	1,640	1,793	962	1,051	.6	.0
	1981	0	0	0	0	1,668	1,668	1,188	1,188	.0	.0
	1982	5	4	0	0	1,444	1,362	768	724	.3	.0
I. ECUADOR	1972	10	19	0	0	319	620	343	667	3.1	.0
	1973	20	36	0	0	397	731	548	1,009	5.0	.0
	1974	5	8	0	0	678	1,148	1,135	1,921	.7	.0
	1975	60	93	0	0	987	1,532	989	1,535	6.0	.0
	1976	90	132	0	0	958	1,407	1,267	1,861	9.3	.0
	1977	160	222	0	0	1,508	2,092	1,216	1,687	10.6	.0
	1978	90	116	0	0	1,630	2,105	1,502	1,940	5.5	.0
	1979	180	214	0	0	1,986	2,365	2,067	2,462	9.0	.0
	1980	180	196	0	0	2,250	2,459	2,506	2,739	8.0	.0
	1981	60	60	0	0	2,246	2,246	2,542	2,542	2.6	.0
	1982	230	216	0	0	1,989	1,876	2,139	2,017	11.5	.0
J. EL SALVADOR	1972	0	0	0	0	278	540	302	587	.0	.0
	1973	0	0	0	0	374	688	358	659	.0	.0
	1974	10	16	0	0	563	953	462	782	1.7	.0
	1975	5	7	0	0	598	928	531	824	.8	.0
	1976	0	0	0	0	735	1,079	743	1,091	.0	.0
	1977	0	0	0	0	929	1,289	972	1,348	.0	.0
	1978	5	6	0	0	1,027	1,326	801	1,034	.4	.0
	1979	30	35	0	0	1,039	1,237	1,131	1,347	2.8	.0
	1980	0	0	0	0	962	1,051	1,074	1,174	.0	.0
	1981	10	10	0	0	985	985	797	797	1.0	.0
	1982	50	47	0	0	883	832	704	664	5.6	.0
K. GUATEMALA	1972	10	19	0	0	324	630	338	657	3.0	.0
	1973	5	9	0	0	431	793	445	819	1.1	.0
	1974	0	0	0	0	700	1,185	582	985	.0	.0
	1975	10	15	0	0	733	1,138	641	995	1.3	.0
	1976	20	29	0	0	839	1,232	782	1,148	2.3	.0
	1977	5	6	0	0	1,053	1,461	1,225	1,699	.4	.0
	1978	10	12	0	0	1,286	1,661	1,113	1,437	.7	.0
	1979	10	11	0	0	1,504	1,791	1,270	1,512	.6	.0
	1980	10	10	0	0	1,598	1,747	1,557	1,702	.6	.0
	1981	0	0	0	0	1,674	1,674	1,253	1,253	.0	.0
	1982	40	37	0	0	1,399	1,319	1,173	1,106	2.8	.0
L. HAITI	1972	0	0	0	0	69	134	44	85	.0	.0
	1973	0	0	0	0	83	152	54	99	.0	.0
	1974	0	0	0	0	125	211	80	135	.0	.0
	1975	0	0	0	0	149	231	80	124	.0	.0
	1976	0	0	0	0	207	304	125	183	.0	.0
	1977	0	0	0	0	213	295	149	206	.0	.0
	1978	0	0	0	0	233	301	155	200	.0	.0
	1979	0	0	0	0	272	324	185	220	.0	.0
	1980	0	0	0	0	375	410	195	213	.0	.0
	1981	10	10	0	0	461	461	154	154	2.1	.0
	1982	0	0	0	0	~	~	164	154	~	.0

Table 1201 (Continued)

U.S. DATA ON VALUE OF ARMS TRANSFERS AND TOTAL IMPORTS AND EXPORTS, BY REGION, ORGANIZATION, AND COUNTRY, 20 LRC, 1972–82

Country	Year	Arms Imports[1] (MUS)		Arms Exports[1] (MUS)		Total Imports[2] (MUS)		Total Exports[2] (MUS)		Arms Imports / Total Imports (%)	Arms Exports / Total Exports (%)
		Current	Constant 1981	Current	Constant 1981	Current	Constant 1981	Current	Constant 1981		
M. HONDURAS	1972	0	0	0	0	193	375	210	408	.0	.0
	1973	0	0	0	0	262	482	261	480	.0	.0
	1974	0	0	0	0	380	643	294	497	.0	.0
	1975	0	0	0	0	404	627	303	470	.0	.0
	1976	40	58	0	0	453	665	397	583	8.8	.0
	1977	5	6	0	0	579	803	519	720	.8	.0
	1978	5	6	0	0	699	903	613	791	.7	.0
	1979	10	11	0	0	826	983	734	874	1.2	.0
	1980	0	0	0	0	1,009	1,103	829	906	.0	.0
	1981	10	10	0	0	949	949	760	760	1.0	.0
	1982	0	0	0	0	~	~	~	~	~	~
N. MEXICO	1972	0	0	0	0	2,719	5,289	1,699	3,305	.0	.0
	1973	5	9	0	0	3,814	7,022	2,261	4,163	.1	.0
	1974	10	16	0	0	6,057	10,255	2,987	5,057	.1	.0
	1975	20	31	0	0	6,571	10,202	2,904	4,509	.3	.0
	1976	20	29	0	0	6,028	8,855	3,418	5,021	.3	.0
	1977	10	13	0	0	5,883	8,162	4,518	6,268	.1	.0
	1978	5	6	0	0	7,555	9,760	5,958	7,697	.0	.0
	1979	10	11	0	0	12,086	14,395	8,982	10,698	.0	.0
	1980	20	21	0	0	19,460	21,275	15,570	17,022	.1	.0
	1981	50	50	0	0	24,068	24,068	19,383	19,383	.2	.0
	1982	190	179	0	0	14,559	13,733	21,580	20,355	1.3	.0
O. NICARAGUA	1972	0	0	0	0	218	424	249	484	.0	.0
	1973	0	0	0	0	327	602	278	511	.0	.0
	1974	0	0	0	0	562	951	381	645	.0	.0
	1975	0	0	0	0	517	802	375	582	.0	.0
	1976	0	0	0	0	532	781	542	796	.0	.0
	1977	10	13	0	0	762	1,057	637	883	1.3	.0
	1978	10	12	0	0	596	770	646	834	1.6	.0
	1979	5	5	0	0	360	428	448	533	1.3	.0
	1980	5	5	0	0	887	969	566	618	.5	.0
	1981	30	30	0	0	999	999	508	508	3.0	.0
	1982	100	94	0	0	776	732	408	384	12.8	.0
P. PANAMA	1972	0	0	0	0	440	855	123	239	.0	.0
	1973	0	0	0	0	502	924	138	254	.0	.0
	1974	0	0	0	0	822	1,391	211	357	.0	.0
	1975	5	7	0	0	892	1,385	286	444	.5	.0
	1976	0	0	0	0	848	1,245	238	349	.0	.0
	1977	5	6	0	0	861	1,194	251	348	.5	.0
	1978	0	0	0	0	942	1,217	256	330	.0	.0
	1979	0	0	0	0	1,184	1,410	303	360	.0	.0
	1980	30	32	0	0	1,449	1,584	360	393	2.0	.0
	1981	5	5	0	0	1,540	1,540	328	328	.3	.0
	1982	10	9	0	0	1,570	1,480	372	350	.6	.0
Q. PARAGUAY	1972	0	0	0	0	83	161	86	167	.0	.0
	1973	0	0	0	0	122	224	127	233	.0	.0
	1974	0	0	0	0	198	335	170	287	.0	.0
	1975	0	0	0	0	206	319	177	274	.0	.0
	1976	5	7	0	0	220	323	182	267	2.2	.0
	1977	0	0	0	0	308	427	279	387	.0	.0
	1978	10	12	0	0	383	494	257	332	2.6	.0
	1979	10	11	0	0	521	520	305	363	1.9	.0
	1980	40	43	0	0	615	672	310	338	6.5	.0
	1981	5	5	0	0	600	600	296	296	.8	.0
	1982	0	0	0	0	672	633	330	311	.0	.0
R. PERU	1972	80	155	0	0	797	1,550	945	1,838	10.0	.0
	1973	80	147	0	0	1,019	1,876	1,112	2,047	7.8	.0
	1974	80	135	0	0	1,531	2,592	1,503	2,544	5.2	.0
	1975	120	186	0	0	2,551	3,960	1,291	2,004	4.7	.0
	1976	260	381	0	0	2,037	2,992	1,360	1,997	12.7	.0
	1977	420	582	0	0	1,911	2,651	1,726	2,394	21.9	.0
	1978	310	400	0	0	1,959	2,530	1,941	2,507	15.8	.0
	1979	90	107	0	0	1,820	2,167	3,491	4,158	4.9	.0
	1980	260	284	0	0	2,500	2,733	3,898	4,261	10.4	.0
	1981	290	290	0	0	3,447	3,447	3,255	3,255	8.4	.0
	1982	280	264	60	56	3,601	3,396	3,230	3,046	7.7	1.9

Table 1201 (Continued)

U.S. DATA ON VALUE OF ARMS TRANSFERS AND TOTAL IMPORTS AND EXPORTS, BY REGION, ORGANIZATION, AND COUNTRY, 20 LRC, 1972–82

Country	Year	Arms Imports[1] (MUS)		Arms Exports[1] (MUS)		Total Imports[2] (MUS)		Total Exports[2] (MUS)		Arms Imports Total Imports (%)	Arms Exports Total Exports (%)
		Current	Constant 1981	Current	Constant 1981	Current	Constant 1981	Current	Constant 1981		
S. URUGUAY	1972	0	0	0	0	212	412	224	416	.0	.0
	1973	0	0	0	0	285	524	322	592	.0	.0
	1974	0	0	0	0	487	824	382	646	.0	.0
	1975	5	7	0	0	557	864	384	596	.8	.0
	1976	5	7	0	0	587	862	547	803	.8	.0
	1977	20	27	0	0	730	1,012	608	843	2.7	.0
	1978	0	0	0	0	774	999	686	886	.0	.0
	1979	5	5	0	0	1,206	1,436	788	938	.4	.0
	1980	40	43	0	0	1,625	1,776	1,059	1,157	2.4	.0
	1981	60	60	0	0	1,641	1,641	1,215	1,215	3.6	.0
	1982	20	18	0	0	1,052	992	1,027	968	1.9	.0
T. VENEZUELA	1972	60	116	0	0	2,434	4,734	3,151	6,129	2.4	.0
	1973	90	165	0	0	2,799	5,153	4,727	8,704	3.2	.0
	1974	100	169	0	0	4,141	7,011	11,071	18,745	2.4	.0
	1975	90	139	0	0	6,004	9,322	8,800	13,663	1.4	.0
	1976	60	88	0	0	7,663	11,257	9,299	13,660	.7	.0
	1977	100	138	0	0	10,938	15,176	9,551	13,252	.9	.0
	1978	30	38	0	0	11,766	15,200	9,188	11,870	.2	.0
	1979	30	35	0	0	10,670	12,709	14,317	17,052	.2	.0
	1980	130	142	0	0	11,827	12,930	19,221	21,014	1.0	.0
	1981	290	290	0	0	13,106	13,106	20,125	20,125	2.2	.0
	1982	240	226	0	0	12,623	11,906	18,692	17,631	1.9	.0
UNITED STATES	1972	160	311	4,000	7,781	59,328	115,408	49,783	96,840	.2	8.0
	1973	170	313	4,900	9,022	74,280	136,774	71,404	131,479	.2	6.9
	1974	120	203	4,600	7,788	110,875	187,735	98,552	166,870	.1	4.7
	1975	140	217	4,800	7,452	105,880	164,398	108,112	167,863	.1	4.4
	1976	110	161	5,900	8,667	132,493	194,637	115,413	169,546	.0	5.1
	1977	120	166	6,800	9,435	160,411	222,571	121,232	168,210	.0	5.6
	1978	120	155	6,400	8,268	186,045	240,354	143,766	185,733	.0	4.5
	1979	130	154	6,300	7,503	222,228	264,694	182,025	216,809	.0	3.5
	1980	140	153	6,500	7,106	256,984	280,959	220,786	241,384	.0	2.9
	1981	210	210	8,300	8,300	273,352	273,352	233,739	233,739	.0	3.6
	1982	430	405	9,500	8,961	254,884	240,423	212,276	200,233	.1	4.5

1. To avoid the appearance of excessive accuracy, arms transfer data have been independently rounded, with greater severity for large numbers. Because of this rounding and the fact that they are obtained from different sources, world arms exports do not equal world arms imports.

2. Total imports and exports are total trade figures as reported by individual countries. The extent to which arms are included may differ from country to country. Country imports are reported "cif" (includes the costs of shipping, insurance, and freight) and country exports are reported "fob" (excludes these costs). For these reasons and because of divergent sources, world totals for imports and exports are not equal.

SOURCE: U.S. Arms Control and Disarmament Agency, *World Military Expenditures and Arms Transfers, 1972–1982* (Washington, D.C., 1984), table II.

Table 1202

U.S. DATA ON WORLD ARMS TRADE: RECIPIENT COUNTRIES BY MAJOR SUPPLIERS, 20 L, CUMULATIVE 1978–82[a]

Recipient	Total	Soviet Union	United States	France	United Kingdom	West Germany	Italy	Czechoslovakia	Poland	Romania	China	Others
A. ARGENTINA	1,800	#	100	575	160	120	170	#	#	10	#	650
B. BOLIVIA	220	#	10	#	#	5	#	#	#	#	#	200
C. BRAZIL	675	#	70	60	410	#	70	#	#	#	#	#
D. CHILE	1,100	#	20	500	40	30	#	#	#	5	#	#
E. COLOMBIA	170	#	50	#	10	20	#	#	#	5	#	#
F. COSTA RICA	5	#	#	#	#	#	#	#	#	#	#	10
G. CUBA	2,700	2,600	#	#	#	#	#	#	40	#	#	10
H. DOMINICAN REP.	10	#	10	#	#	#	#	#	#	#	#	#
I. ECUADOR	725	#	50	340	70	40	10	#	#	#	#	220
J. EL SALVADOR	100	#	60	30	#	#	#	#	#	#	#	10
K. GUATEMALA	70	#	10	5	#	#	#	#	#	#	#	50
L. HAITI	10	#	#	#	#	#	#	#	#	#	#	10
M. HONDURAS	30	#	10	#	10	#	#	#	#	#	#	10
N. MEXICO	270	#	90	20	#	#	#	#	#	#	#	160
O. NICARAGUA	150	70	#	#	#	#	#	#	#	#	#	80
P. PANAMA	40	#	30	#	#	#	#	#	#	#	#	10
Q. PARAGUAY	60	#	#	#	#	5	#	#	#	#	#	50
R. PERU	1,200	525	60	260	#	180	150	#	#	#	#	60
S. URUGUAY	120	#	5	60	#	#	#	#	#	#	#	50
T. VENEZUELA	725	#	90	30	20	5	550	#	#	#	#	50
LATIN AMERICA	10,200	3,200	650	1,900	750	400	950	40	#	20	#	2,300

a. For previous years, see SALA, 18-2802.

SOURCE: Same as table 1201.

Table 1203

IISA DATA ON ARMED FORCES EXPENDITURE, PERSONNEL, VESSELS, AND AIRCRAFT, 20 L, 1982

Country	Defense Expenditure (MUS)	Total Armed Forces (N)	Army (N)	Army Reserves (N)	Navy (N)	Naval Vessels (N)	Air Force (N)	Combat Aircraft (N)	Para-Military (N)
A. ARGENTINA	2,145@[d]	153,000	100,000	250,000	36,000[a]	44	75,000	164	21,000
B. BOLIVIA	186[b]	27,600	20,000	~	3,600	47	4,000	22	185,000
C. BRAZIL	1,838	277,100	182,800	1,115,000	49,000	74	45,300	187	185,000
D. CHILE	2,103[b]	96,000	53,000	240,000	28,000[a]	60	15,000	84	27,000
E. COLOMBIA	420[b]	70,200	57,000	70,000	9,000[c]	32	4,200	28	50,000
F. COSTA RICA	11.2	7,000	~	~	~	10	~	8	2,500
G. CUBA	1,271[b]	153,000	125,000	190,000	12,000	122	16,000	250	~
H. DOMINICAN REP.	102[b]	23,000	14,000	~	4,500	24	4,500	19	10,000
I. ECUADOR	177	36,800	27,500	~	4,500[c]	25	4,800	54	~
J. EL SALVADOR	157	24,650	22,000	~	300	10	2,350	36	~
K. GUATEMALA	9,862	21,560	20,000	~	960[c]	38	600	16	~
L. HAITI	15.4	6,800	6,300	~	300	15	200	~	14,900
M. HONDURAS	60[b]	15,200	13,500	~	500	8	1,200	26	4,500
N. MEXICO	695@[e]	120,000	94,500	~	20,000[a]	97	5,500	85	~
O. NICARAGUA	126@[b][f]	48,800	47,000	25,000	300	14	1,500	10	34,000
P. PANAMA	440	9,500	1,500	~	300	14	200	~	7,500
Q. PARAGUAY	87[b]	16,070	12,500	25,000	2,500[a]	27	1,070	20	1,500
R. PERU	716@[g]	135,500	75,000	~	20,500[a]	63	40,000	106	31,500
S. URUGUAY	386[b]	30,000	22,300	~	4,700	13	3,000	24	1,500
T. VENEZUELA	1,142[b]	40,500	27,500	~	8,500[c]	27	4,500	79	20,000

a. Includes naval air force and marines.
b. 1981.
c. Includes marines.
d. Calculated by SALA; source reports range from 1,010 to 3,279 (M US).
e. Calculated by SALA; source reports range from 595.9 to 794.8 (M US).
f. Calculated by SALA; source reports range from 94 to 159 (M US).
g. Calculated by SALA; source reports range from 501.7 to 931.8 (M US).

SOURCE: International Institute for Strategic Studies (IISS), The Military Balance, 1983-84, pp. 104-115.

Table 1204

IISS DATA ON DEFENSE EXPENDITURE PER MILITARY MAN AND AS PERCENTAGE OF TOTAL GOVERNMENT SPENDING PER MILITARY MAN, 7 LC, 1975–82

Country	Per Military Man (US)						% of Government Spending					
	1975	1976	1978	1980	1981	1982	1975	1976	1978	1980	1981	1982
A. ARGENTINA	41	49	56	113	~	~	9.7	11.6	11.8	15.1	~	~
C. BRAZIL	12	16	16	16	12	15	9.3	9.7	10.0	8.7	6.7	13.3
E. COLOMBIA	--	5	7	128	14	16	--	9.2	6.2	16.6	8.2	8.5
G. CUBA	--	--	~	111	130	~	--	--	~	--	~	~
N. MEXICO	10	9	9	150	20	~	2.4	4.4	3.4	2.4	~	~
R. PERU	24	--	34	33	50	~	5.3	--	~	15.8	20.6	~
T. VENEZUELA	41	34	47	52	63	78	5.4	5.5	5.7	8.6	~	~
UNITED STATES	417	423	491	644	759	938	23.8	23.8	23.8	28.8	24.6	29.2

SOURCE: International Institute for Strategic Studies (IISS), *The Military Balance,*
1978–79, pp. 88–89; 1980–81, p. 96; 1981–82, pp. 124–125; 1983–84, pp. 126–127.

Table 1205

MILITARY EXPENDITURE AS PERCENTAGE OF GDP, 20 LC, 1956-81

Country	1956	1957	1958	1959	1960	1961	1962	1963	1964	1965	1966	1967	1968	1969	1970	1971	1972	1973	1974	1975	1976	1977	1978	1979	1980	1981
A. ARGENTINA	2.5	2.6	2.5	2.3	2.3	2.2	2.2	2.1	1.7	1.8	2.1	2.3	1.9	1.9	1.9	1.6	1.6	1.3	1.6	2.8	2.5	2.5	2.2†	2.6	2.6	2.8
B. BOLIVIA	.4	.8	.8†	.9†	1.1†	1.2	1.1	2.4	2.3	2.5	2.2	2.0	1.6	1.3	1.6	1.4	1.8	1.9	2.1	2.4	2.3	2.1	2.0	2.2	1.9	2.3
C. BRAZIL	2.6	2.9	2.8	2.2	2.0	1.7	1.7	1.6	1.7	2.5	2.2	2.9	2.6	2.6	2.5	2.4	2.2	2.3	1.2	1.2	1.2	1.1	1.0†	.8	.5	.6
D. CHILE	3.1	3.2	2.7	2.2	2.6	2.5	2.4	2.1	1.9	1.9	2.1	2.0	2.0	2.0	2.0	2.3	2.6	3.7	2.7	2.2	3.5	3.4†	4.1	6.5	7.3	6.0
E. COLOMBIA	1.9	1.6	1.5	1.2	1.2	1.3	1.9	2.2	2.0	2.0	2.0	2.0	2.3	1.3	1.4	2.5	1.2	1.0	.9	1.0	.9	.8	.8†	.8†	.9	.8†
F. COSTA RICA	1.3	1.4	1.3	1.2	1.2	1.1	1.1	1.0	.9	.9	1.0	.9	1.1	1.1	.5	.6	.5	.5	.5	.6	.7	.6	.6	.7	.6	.6
G. CUBA	~	~	~	~	~	~	6.6	6.2	5.3	5.1	5.3	6.1	6.9	6.0	6.9	6.0	4.4	4.0	3.8	~	~	1.3	7.6	7.9	7.5	~
H. DOMINICAN REP.	~	~	4.8	6.1	4.6	4.5	3.7	3.4	3.4	3.7	3.1	2.8	2.8	2.3	2.1	1.9	1.7	1.6	1.6	1.6	1.7	1.7	1.9	2.0	~	~
I. ECUADOR	2.6	2.4	2.3	1.9	2.4	2.2	2.0	1.8	1.9	1.9	1.7	1.7	1.8	2.2	2.3	1.8	2.0	2.0	2.0	2.3	2.0†	3.1	2.0	2.0	1.9	1.9†
J. EL SALVADOR	~	~	1.4	1.2	1.1	1.1	1.4	1.4	1.2	1.2	1.1	1.1	1.3	3.0	1.0	1.1	1.1	1.1	1.7	1.6	1.7	1.8	1.9	2.0	2.1	3.3
K. GUATEMALA	1.0	1.0	.9	.9	.9	.9	.8	.8	1.0	1.1	1.1	1.1	1.0	.9	1.5	.9	.9	.8	.8	1.1	1.1	1.4	1.2	1.5	1.6	1.7
L. HAITI	~	~	~	~	2.4	2.6	2.6	2.4	2.3	2.1	1.9	1.9	1.9	1.8	1.7	1.6	1.6	1.2	1.1	1.2	1.0	.9	~	2.0	1.6	1.7
M. HONDURAS	1.4	1.3	1.3†	1.2	1.2	2.0	1.9	1.9	1.3	1.2	1.3	1.3	1.0	2.2	1.2	1.5	1.9	1.7	1.7	1.6	1.0	1.7	1.7	2.3	3.5†	4.1†
N. MEXICO	.6	.7	.7	.6	.7	.7	.7	.7	.7	.7	.7	.9	.7	.7	.8	.7	.7	.7	.7	.7	.8	.9	.6	.5	.4	.6
O. NICARAGUA	~	~	~	~	~	1.9	1.9	1.8	1.5	1.4	1.6	1.6	1.5	1.4	1.6	1.5	1.8	1.4	1.5	1.8	2.0	1.8†	~	3.4	6.7	~
P. PANAMA	~	~	~	~	~	~	.5	.5	.4	.5	.4	.5	.5	.7	.8	1.2	.7	.7	.7	.8	.8	~	~	~	~	~
Q. PARAGUAY	~	~	~	~	~	1.8†	1.7†	1.8†	1.6†	1.7†	1.9	2.0	2.0	2.0	2.0	1.3	2.2	1.7	1.5	1.7	1.4†	1.5	1.5	1.3	~	~
R. PERU	3.2	2.9	3.1	2.7	2.4	2.6†	2.4†	3.2	2.9	2.9	2.6	3.2	3.2	3.2	3.7	3.7	3.3	3.6	3.5	4.7	5.7†	4.7	5.5	3.9	5.7†	5.1†
S. URUGUAY	1.9	2.1	2.4	2.4	2.1	1.1	1.2	1.6	1.6	1.7	1.5	1.9	1.5	1.8	1.9	2.6	2.5	2.2	1.9	2.7	1.9	2.1	1.7	3.0†	2.6	3.4
T. VENEZUELA	1.9	2.1	2.4	~	2.1	2.0	1.7	1.9	1.8	2.0	2.0	2.1	2.0	1.9	1.7	1.9	2.0	1.7	1.5	2.0	1.4	1.7	1.7	1.4	1.5	1.6
UNITED STATES	9.8	9.9	10.0	9.4	8.9	9.0	9.2	8.7	8.0	7.5	8.4	9.4	9.3	8.7	7.9	7.1	6.6	6.0	6.1	6.0	5.4	5.4	5.1	5.1	5.6	5.9

SOURCE: SIPRI-Y, 1977, pp. 222-225, 242-245; SIPRI-Y, 1978, pp. 144, 145, 162-165; SIPRI-Y, 1980, table 1A.4; SIPRI-Y, 1983, pp. 171-174.

Table 1206

USDOD DATA ON U.S. MILITARY SALES AGREEMENTS, 20 LR, 1950–83
(T US)

Country	1975	1976[a]	1977	1978	1979	1980	1981	1982	1983	1950–83
A. ARGENTINA	12,779	18,962	19,516	5,569	--	--	--	--	--	194,754
B. BOLIVIA	651	70	142	--	78	19	--	--	--	2,093
C. BRAZIL	21,789	10,495	14,718	13,243	311	2,771	4,143	13,522	35,761	337,409
D. CHILE	37,900	8,794	235	--	--	--	--	--	--	184,009
E. COLOMBIA	829	1,800	3,500	7,358	4,482	10,342	8,455	13,178	17,155	87,721
F. COSTA RICA	110	124	7	--	--	--	--	--	4,515	5,995
G. CUBA	--	--	--	--	316	--	--	--	--	4,510
H. DOMINICAN REP.	1	117	--	--	112	--	3	3,906	1,068	7,268
I. ECUADOR	15,183	2,680	23,186	32,468	14,772	2,454	11,572	831	2,803	110,539
J. EL SALVADOR	393	726	146	9	--	2,421	10,841	18,840	68,255	103,531
K. GUATEMALA	935	3,518	5,731	3,261	1,942	10	4	--	69	32,325
L. HAITI	79	253	190	--	241	12	--	--	--	1,305
M. HONDURAS	303	597	766	657	269	5,076	4,319	9,402	32,279	60,704
N. MEXICO	141	2,056	156	1,973	88	15	102,940	5,509	2,046	132,039
O. NICARAGUA	536	543	666	2	--	1	--	--	--	5,219
P. PANAMA	222	1,288	173	121	134	246	415	515	195	6,471
Q. PARAGUAY	36	7	248	40	9	90	23	121	7	971
R. PERU	16,510	23,962	10,743	12,084	5,652	3,794	5,339	2,677	1,884	182,216
S. URUGUAY	6,664	2,099	626	44	17	932	692	1,664	859	22,371
T. VENEZUELA	47,022	6,210	1,975	4,143	1,884	3,398	71,881	618,274	3,851	937,394
LATIN AMERICA	162,162	84,305	82,726	80,972	30,303	31,580	220,703	688,438	176,004	2,424,417

a. Includes transitional quarter.

SOURCE: USDOD–FMSA, September 1983, pp. 5–7.

Table 1207

USDOD DATA ON U.S. MILITARY SALES DELIVERIES, 20 LR, 1950–83
(T US)

Country	1975	1976[a]	1977	1978	1979	1980	1981	1982	1983	1950–83
A. ARGENTINA	7,985	8,299	6,815	9,439	6,859	14,595	6,430	4,284	2,009	188,426
B. BOLIVIA	377	305	24	90	23	161	--	--	--	2,030
C. BRAZIL	42,141	45,687	8,531	7,551	7,593	7,322	--	--	--	282,127
D. CHILE	12,256	39,154	56,026	10,993	7,794	5,507	5,321	4,269	9,060	178,145
E. COLOMBIA	797	1,161	944	1,917	5,018	3,695	9,133	15,069	7,024	64,218
F. COSTA RICA	--	138	--	21	266	123	--	9	814	2,294
G. CUBA	--	--	--	--	--	--	--	--	--	4,510
H. DOMINICAN REP.	30	31	2	71	8	137	--	3,477	329	6,093
I. ECUADOR	1,353	3,999	9,051	7,798	8,134	10,605	6,353	11,942	29,374	93,162
J. EL SALVADOR	259	327	257	594	21	1,227	1,953	16,715	28,113	51,098
K. GUATEMALA	3,378	3,041	2,169	2,410	3,408	1,926	462	655	734	31,323
L. HAITI	50	20	102	314	251	79	12	--	5	1,305
M. HONDURAS	588	4,705	384	461	899	581	1,724	1,427	12,176	25,014
N. MEXICO	212	763	3,612	467	362	2,291	1,325	73,263	20,821	116,458
O. NICARAGUA	219	615	354	781	43	18	--	--	--	5,218
P. PANAMA	1,631	1,526	243	165	246	187	154	360	482	5,918
Q. PARAGUAY	22	14	219	43	2	48	41	182	12	971
R. PERU	9,142	29,865	25,990	13,473	12,977	14,165	6,565	5,601	3,626	166,397
S. URUGUAY	2,008	1,223	5,320	1,171	650	717	689	445	764	19,924
T. VENEZUELA	34,765	8,621	43,566	3,895	4,776	5,935	13,809	19,263	33,037	299,924
LATIN AMERICA	117,229	149,563	153,608	61,661	59,331	69,320	53,985	156,984	148,667	1,545,117

a. Includes transitional quarter.

SOURCE: USDOD–FMSA, September 1983, pp. 13–15.

Table 1208

USDOD DATA ON STUDENTS TRAINED UNDER U.S. INTERNATIONAL MILITARY EDUCATION AND TRAINING PROGRAM, 20 LR, 1950-83
(N)

Country	1975	1976[a]	1977	1978	1979	1980	1981	1982	1983	1950-83
A. ARGENTINA	19	139	140	#	--	--	--	--	--	4,082
B. BOLIVIA	323	241	183	227	211	36	--	--	--	4,917
C. BRAZIL	273	220	--	--	--	--	--	--	--	8,726
D. CHILE	565	--	--	--	--	--	--	--	--	6.917
E. COLOMBIA	310	688	350	257	408	444	539	642	914	10,456
F. COSTA RICA	--	--	--	--	--	--	37	55	79	882
G. CUBA	--	--	--	--	--	--	--	--	--	523
H. DOMINICAN REP.	201	235	73	90	113	47	163	129	154	4,711
I. ECUADOR	153	220	288	421	451	385	217	252	384	7,251
J. EL SALVADOR	158	233	47	--	--	125	256	736	1,212	4,317
K. GUATEMALA	139	134	127	--	--	--	--	--	--	3,360
L. HAITI	3	13	12	14	17	28	75	99	191	725
M. HONDURAS	240	256	116	219	226	166	261	328	332	4,530
N. MEXICO	83	98	37	39	54	43	107	63	28	1,263
O. NICARAGUA	260	246	234	275	6	--	--	--	--	5,740
P. PANAMA	354	316	234	83	219	202	293	219	301	5,974
Q. PARAGUAY	102	196	99	145	--	--	--	8	14	2,077
R. PERU	247	411	677	56	72	195	178	369	284	9,067
S. URUGUAY	136	192	--	--	--	--	--	1	15	2,845
T. VENEZUELA	142	150	13	30	--	--	18	22	52	5,676
LATIN AMERICA	3,708	3,988	2,630	1,856	1,778	1,671	2,144	2,923	3,960	94,351

a. Includes transitional quarter.

SOURCE: USDOD-FMSA, September 1983, pp. 92-93.

Table 1209

USDOD DATA ON U.S. EXPENDITURE FOR INTERNATIONAL MILITARY EDUCATION AND PROGRAM, 20 LR, 1950-83
(T US)

Country	1975	1976[a]	1977	1978	1979	1980	1981	1982	1983	1950-83
A. ARGENTINA	116	425	716	5	--	--	--	--	--	12,796
B. BOLIVIA	598	736	589	648	374	145	--	--	75	14,226
C. BRAZIL	644	562	62	11	--	--	--	--	--	16,363
D. CHILE	624	--	--	--	--	--	--	--	--	16,847
E. COLOMBIA	647	1,078	706	1,056	499	277	207	465	725	16,882
F. COSTA RICA	--	--	--	--	--	--	31	49	125	1,106
G. CUBA	--	--	--	--	--	--	--	--	--	2,023
H. DOMINICAN REP.	504	630	495	641	461	255	355	433	591	12,145
I. ECUADOR	381	468	393	703	452	222	298	482	613	14,182
J. EL SALVADOR	482	801	565	#	5	253	1,196	5,245	5,001	17,531
K. GUATEMALA	420	484	509	--	--	--	--	#	8	7,502
L. HAITI	14	100	94	130	177	120	120	212	377	2,095
M. HONDURAS	792	771	602	695	224	493	511	1,239	797	11,452
N. MEXICO	110	100	118	115	190	121	101	82	66	3,040
O. NICARAGUA	656	709	621	421	7	#	--	--	--	11,583
P. PANAMA	320	561	399	507	393	245	358	367	433	6,166
Q. PARAGUAY	290	528	389	585	--	--	--	11	54	6,756
R. PERU	800	1,011	914	852	413	289	283	452	537	20,968
S. URUGUAY	357	391	35	16	6	#	--	7	58	6,666
T. VENEZUELA	668	679	73	97	1	1	8	24	48	13,945
LATIN AMERICA	8,422	10,034	7,280	6,480	3,208	2,504	3,611	9,261	9,932	215,139

a. Includes transitional quarter.

SOURCE: USDOD-FMSA, September 1983, pp. 86-87.

Table 1210

USDOD DATA ON TOTAL VALUE OF U.S. ARMS TRANSFERS, 20 L, FY 1970–83

(T US)

	Country	1970[a]	1975	1976[b]	1977	1978	1979	1980	1981	1982	1983
A.	ARGENTINA	10,730	10,287	12,028	13,129	23,625	36,408	22,378	10,983	9,284	7,009
B.	BOLIVIA	345	779	1,014	732	884	1,427	360	9	700	--
C.	BRAZIL	2,458	46,478	89,675	14,586	12,545	15,817	15,385	15,222	14,269	29,060
D.	CHILE	6,982	12,824	40,581	57,383	10,993	7,794	5,507	--	--	--
E.	COLOMBIA	1,317	1,842	2,324	8,015	4,500	7,099	5,113	11,838	20,069	12,024
F.	COSTA RICA	#	123	231	132	187	470	325	57	159	964
G.	CUBA	#	--	--	--	--	--	--	--	--	--
H.	DOMINICAN REP.	222	283	73	841	891	204	443	101	4,477	1,329
I.	ECUADOR	770	2,485	6,468	9,694	24,356	8,664	10,930	7,763	12,942	31,374
J.	EL SALVADOR	35	1,727	611	486	864	172	1,434	1,990	17,513	28,313
K.	GUATEMALA	701	3,849	3,386	3,189	2,960	4,276	2,647	469	1,405	834
L.	HAITI	#	270	245	553	710	268	79	18	200	55
M.	HONDURAS	26	916	4,910	486	1,563	2,758	1,247	2,674	1,927	12,676
N.	MEXICO	12	963	1,780	5,998	3,077	1,746	4,032	4,928	75,463	25,821
O.	NICARAGUA	423	724	1,581	1,966	1,378	44	15	5	50	50
P.	PANAMA	206	1,903	2,069	2,823	1,141	1,074	29,432	908	1,360	1,482
Q.	PARAGUAY	151	342	1,792	672	255	279	688	218	482	312
R.	PERU	2,185	9,288	32,616	31,279	17,865	15,409	15,053	9,917	10,601	8,626
S.	URUGUAY	2,375	2,159	1,751	5,716	1,238	1,033	985	1,280	695	2,764
T.	VENEZUELA	738	42,360	12,647	51,652	9,944	13,496	19,948	21,809	29,263	43,037

1. Includes foreign military sales deliveries, commercial exports licensed under arms export control act, and military assistance program excess defense articles program acquisition act.

a. Data on commercial export licensed under arms control act not available prior to 1971.

b. Fiscal year 1976 includes transitional quarter.

SOURCE: USDOD–FMSA, Dec. 1979, pp. 2, 3, 16, 22; USDOD–FMSA, Dec. 1980, pp. 12, 34, 46; USDOD–FMSA, Sept. 1981, pp. 9–12, 35–36, 51–52; USDOD–FMSA, Sept. 1982, pp. 10–12, 37–38, 55–56; USDOD–FMSA, Sept. 1983, pp. 12–13, 42–43, 66–67.

Table 1211

ARGENTINA AND GREAT BRITAIN (GB) HUMAN LOSSES IN THE 1982 FALKLANDS WAR

PART I. ARGENTINA

Category	Freedman			GB Official	Gaceta Marinera			Press[1]	
	Engaged	Killed	Injured	Prisoners	Engaged	Killed	Injured	Killed	Prisoners
Navy									
Regular	~	~	~	~	~	244[a]	~	**	~
Conscripted	~	~	~	~	~	124[a]	~	**	~
Total	~	~	~	~	~	368[a]	~	**	~
Air Force	~	~	~	~	~	~	~	**	~
Army	~	50	~	~	~	~	~	**	~
Belgrano Incident	~	360	~	~	1,042	321	~	**	~
Total	12,000	800-1,000	~	11,400	~	~	~	1,000	11,845

PART II. GREAT BRITAIN

Category	Freedman			GB Official			Gaceta Marinera			Press[1]	
	Engaged	Killed	Injured	Engaged	Killed	Injured	Engaged	Killed	Injured	Killed	Injured
Marines	3,000	~	~	~	~	~	~	~	~	**	**
Air Force	~	~	~	~	~	~	~	~	~	**	**
Army	6,000	~	~	~	~	~	~	~	~	**	**
Total	~	~	~	28,000	255	777	~	~	~	250+	**
Remaining Garrison	~	**	**	3,000-4,000[b]	**	**	~	**	**	**	**

1. Ongoing casualty reports by the press are not considered applicable since they were often drastically inaccurate. The totals cited are from "Surrender in the Falklands," *Newsweek*, June 28, 1982, pp. 33-37.

a. To date there have been no official reports on Argentine war losses. The data presented are for those men given distinction and honors by the Argentine navy for death in combat. It appears that none of these medals were given to victims of the *General Belgrano* sinking.

b. Based upon press reports outlined by the British Consul General (letter to the author, January 14, 1983).

SOURCE: Adam Perkal, "Losses and Lessons of the 1982 War for the Falklands," SALA, 23, Chapter 38.

Part V: Working Conditions, Migration, and Housing

CHAPTER 13

LABOR FORCE, EAP, UNEMPLOYMENT, CLASS STRUCTURE, AND CRIME

Note: This volume contains statistics from numerous sources. Alternative data on many topics are presented. Variations in statistics can be attributed to differences in definition, parameters, coverage, methodology, as well as date gathered, prepared, or adjusted. See also Editor's Note on Methodology.

Table 1300

LABOR FORCE PARTICIPATION BY SEX, 17 L, 1950–80

(%)

	Country	1950 Total	1950 M	1950 F	1960 Total	1960 M	1960 F	1970 Total	1970 M	1970 F	1980 Total	1980 M	1980 F
A.	ARGENTINA	51.36	79.14	21.71	50.18	77.69	21.78	48.36	72.59	23.98	48.16	71.28	25.30
B.	BOLIVIA	71.94	84.78	59.33	50.42	79.08	22.56	47.29	75.09	20.59	46.75	73.17	21.61
C.	BRAZIL	48.41	81.23	15.12	46.96	77.05	16.32	45.53	72.34	18.31	45.56	70.85	19.93
D.	COLOMBIA	48.81	81.05	17.50	45.93	74.49	17.29	44.89	68.49	21.69	46.01	68.36	23.87
E.	COSTA RICA	49.08	83.85	14.28	47.12	78.74	15.33	44.87	73.21	16.28	46.46	73.77	18.84
F.	CHILE	49.19	77.19	20.06	45.73	72.73	19.56	41.66	66.03	18.07	42.97	66.92	19.80
H.	DOMINICAN REP.	50.09	80.35	17.65	48.97	76.39	20.54	47.12	69.63	24.09	46.49	68.10	24.52
I.	ECUADOR	49.49	85.21	15.58	48.64	82.38	15.70	47.84	77.77	18.20	47.71	75.88	20.05
J.	EL SALVADOR	50.57	85.19	16.08	49.15	81.77	16.56	47.23	77.12	17.16	47.15	75.20	18.82
K.	GUATEMALA	49.37	85.69	12.33	47.36	81.99	12.03	45.36	78.11	11.84	45.76	77.43	13.27
M.	HONDURAS	49.42	86.72	11.64	48.18	84.19	11.93	45.88	78.72	12.98	45.45	75.36	15.46
N.	MEXICO	47.09	82.30	12.13	45.55	77.83	13.80	43.29	71.78	15.05	43.97	71.41	16.46
O.	NICARAGUA	49.58	85.82	13.83	48.17	80.79	16.19	46.29	75.69	18.30	47.04	74.56	20.36
P.	PANAMA	49.31	77.81	19.48	48.37	74.51	20.98	49.76	72.19	26.27	50.30	71.04	28.74
R.	PERU	56.82	80.16	34.65	51.54	73.91	29.72	47.21	68.14	26.47	46.72	66.69	26.80
S.	URUGUAY	47.80	73.39	21.74	47.96	73.39	22.67	48.21	71.69	25.28	47.65	69.73	26.39
T.	VENEZUELA	49.10	80.17	17.09	47.35	75.73	17.46	43.39	67.88	18.46	44.65	68.15	21.26
	LATIN AMERICA	49.74	81.02	18.23	47.49	77.04	17.84	45.44	71.65	19.20	45.58	70.53	20.59

SOURCE: ILO, *Mercado de Trabajo en Cifras, 1950-1980*, 1982, table I-1.

Table 1301

ALTERNATIVE LABOR FORCE PARTICIPATION BY SEX, 20 L

(%, 1975)

	Country	Total	M	F
A.	ARGENTINA	38.57	57.29	19.79
B.	BOLIVIA	33.02	52.66	13.44
C.	BRAZIL	31.54	49.52	13.62
D.	CHILE	31.79	49.35	14.69
E.	COLOMBIA	29.65	44.65	14.62
F.	COSTA RICA	32.21	51.50	12.60
H.	DOMINICAN REP.	26.47	46.28	6.33
I.	ECUADOR	31.63	50.19	12.82
J.	EL SALVADOR	30.92	49.68	11.92
K.	GUATEMALA	30.56	52.15	8.37
L.	HAITI	50.50	55.01	46.24
M.	HONDURAS	29.81	51.83	7.91
N.	MEXICO	28.83	46.76	10.71
O.	NICARAGUA	29.81	47.34	12.60
P.	PANAMA	33.80	49.13	17.84
Q.	PARAGUAY	31.90	49.58	14.32
R.	PERU	29.18	45.34	12.84
S.	URUGUAY	38.48	55.53	21.75
T.	VENEZUELA	29.40	45.14	13.42

SOURCE: ILO, *Labor Force Estimates and Projections, 1950-2000*, 1977.

Table 1302

ESTIMATED GROWTH OF LABOR FORCE BY SEX, 19 L, 1975–2000

(AA-GR)

	Country	1975-80			1980-85			1985-90			1990-95			1995-2000		
		Total	M	F	Total	M	F	Total	M	F	Total	M	F	Total	M	F
A.	ARGENTINA	1.10	.87	1.76	1.09	.89	1.65	1.08	.87	1.66	1.12	.95	1.54	1.08	.94	1.42
B.	BOLIVIA	2.40	2.19	3.20	2.54	2.25	3.60	2.63	2.32	3.69	2.84	2.42	4.16	2.84	2.42	4.06
C.	BRAZIL	2.81	2.50	3.91	2.93	2.54	4.20	2.92	2.52	4.13	3.03	2.59	4.26	2.96	2.55	4.03
D.	CHILE	2.66	2.28	3.84	2.48	2.19	3.34	2.13	1.89	2.81	1.93	1.73	2.46	1.88	1.67	2.41
E.	COLOMBIA	3.25	3.25	3.24	3.40	3.31	3.67	3.28	3.20	3.52	3.33	3.17	3.80	3.17	3.01	3.61
F.	COSTA RICA	3.59	3.26	4.91	3.27	2.92	4.55	2.86	2.56	3.91	2.79	2.44	3.93	2.67	2.32	3.73
H.	DOMINICAN REP.	3.27	3.12	4.35	3.42	3.24	4.68	3.50	3.32	4.67	3.61	3.38	5.00	3.62	3.39	4.89
I.	ECUADOR	3.34	3.07	4.37	3.46	3.12	4.67	3.38	3.05	4.52	3.39	3.00	4.63	3.28	2.88	4.43
J.	EL SALVADOR	3.38	3.12	4.44	3.36	3.06	4.53	3.25	2.96	4.30	3.33	2.95	4.60	3.31	2.93	4.52
K.	GUATEMALA	2.87	2.74	3.73	2.90	2.72	3.95	2.90	2.71	3.98	2.95	2.71	4.24	2.91	2.66	4.13
L.	HAITI	1.49	1.62	1.34	1.51	1.71	1.27	1.54	1.77	1.28	1.72	1.98	1.40	1.80	2.08	1.46
M.	HONDURAS	3.19	3.07	3.91	3.36	3.20	4.37	3.42	3.24	4.47	3.40	3.19	4.54	3.34	3.14	4.35
N.	MEXICO	3.39	3.13	4.49	3.49	3.18	4.71	3.43	3.12	4.59	3.58	3.21	4.86	3.59	3.21	4.78
O.	NICARAGUA	3.26	3.00	4.23	3.44	3.10	4.61	3.54	3.18	4.65	3.72	3.27	5.02	3.67	3.24	4.83
P.	PANAMA	2.78	2.77	2.82	2.82	2.75	3.03	2.66	2.62	2.78	2.78	2.61	3.26	2.73	2.55	3.21
Q.	PARAGUAY	3.12	2.86	4.01	3.18	2.83	4.28	3.15	2.79	4.22	3.23	2.78	4.45	3.91	2.76	4.30
R.	PERU	3.12	2.82	4.14	3.28	2.91	4.48	3.31	2.94	4.42	3.35	2.96	4.44	3.27	2.89	4.26
S.	URUGUAY	1.00	.75	1.61	1.19	.97	1.73	1.03	.81	1.54	1.05	.88	1.42	.97	.80	1.32
T.	VENEZUELA	3.73	3.34	5.02	3.59	3.24	4.67	3.25	2.93	4.17	3.08	2.84	3.72	3.02	2.78	3.63

SOURCE: ILO, *Labor Force Estimates and Projections, 1950-2000*, 1977.

Table 1303

CHILDREN IN THE LABOR FORCE,[1] 20 LC, 1960–2000

	Country	T				PT I			
		1960	1970	1975	2000	1960	1970	1975	2000
A.	ARGENTINA	211	192	167	107	10.2	8.1	6.6	3.3

Continued in SALA, 21-1310.

Table 1304

LABOR FORCE STRUCTURE, 20 LC, 1960–2000

Country	% of Population of Working Age (15-64 Years)		% Agriculture		% Industry		% Services		AA-GR		
	1960	1982	1960	1980	1960	1980	1960	1980	1960–70	1970–82	1980–2000
A. ARGENTINA	64	63	44	28	29	35	27	37	.4	.6	.9
B. BOLIVIA	55	53	61	50	18	24	21	26	1.7	2.3	2.9
C. BRAZIL	54	55	52	30	15	24	33	46	2.7	1.0	3.0
D. CHILE	57	62	31	19	20	19	50	61	1.4	2.0	2.2
E. COLOMBIA	50	60	51	26	19	21	29	53	3.0	3.3	2.5
F. COSTA RICA	50	59	51	29	19	23	30	48	3.5	3.9	2.8
G. CUBA	61	61	39	23	22	31	39	46	.8	1.7	1.9
H. DOMINICAN REP.	49	53	67	49	12	18	21	33	2.2	3.6	3.3
I. ECUADOR	52	52	57	52	19	17	23	31	2.9	3.3	3.5
J. EL SALVADOR	52	52	62	50	17	22	21	27	2.6	2.8	3.5
K. GUATEMALA	51	54	67	55	14	21	19	25	2.8	3.2	2.9
L. HAITI	55	53	80	74	6	7	14	19	.6	1.3	2.1
M. HONDURAS	52	50	70	63	11	15	19	23	2.5	3.1	3.5
N. MEXICO	51	52	55	36	20	26	25	39	2.8	3.2	3.5
O. NICARAGUA	50	50	62	43	16	20	22	37	2.3	3.8	3.9
P. PANAMA	52	56	51	27	14	18	35	55	3.4	2.4	2.6
Q. PARAGUAY	51	53	56	44	19	20	25	36	2.3	2.9	3.0
R. PERU	52	54	52	39	20	18	28	43	2.1	2.9	3.0
S. URUGUAY	64	63	21	11	30	32	50	57	.8	.2	1.1
T. VENEZUELA	51	55	35	18	22	27	43	55	2.8	4.0	3.1
UNITES STATES	60	66	7	2	36	32	57	66	1.8	1.9	.9

SOURCE: WB-WDR, 1984, table 21.

Table 1305

AGRICULTURAL LABOR FORCE,[1] 26 ECLA:L,[2] 1950–75

Country	1950	1955	1960	1965	1970	1975*	1950–60	1960–70	1970–75	1950–75
	T						AA-GR			
A. ARGENTINA	4,318	4,270	4,118	4,023	3,883	3,142	−.5	−.6	−.7	−.6
Bahamas	23	26	30	33	35	34	2.7	1.6	−.6	1.5
Barbados	61	62	62	54	47	41	.2	−2.7	−2.7	−1.5
B. BOLIVIA	1,855	2,067	2,307	2,470	2,655	2,869	2.2	1.4	1.6	1.8
C. BRAZIL	31,598	34,514	37,100	40,247	43,423	46,811	1.6	1.6	1.5	1.6
D. CHILE	1,984	2,111	2,274	2,287	2,224	2,150	1.4	−.2	−.7	.3
E. COLOMBIA	6,637	7,362	8,180	8,319	8,355	8,334	2.1	.2	−.1	.9
F. COSTA RICA	494	562	642	697	730	756	2.7	1.3	.7	1.7
G. CUBA	2,468	2,603	2,749	2,717	2,620	2,548	1.1	−.5	−.6	.1
H. DOMINICAN REP.	1,636	1,840	2,100	2,367	2,660	3,004	2.5	2.4	2.4	2.4
I. ECUADOR	1,853	2,125	2,484	2,757	3,069	3,392	3.0	2.1	2.0	2.5
J. EL SALVADOR	1,265	1,391	1,553	1,739	1,975	2,201	2.1	2.4	2.2	2.2
Grenada	22	23	24	22	21	19	.9	−1.3	−2.0	−.6
K. GUATEMALA	2,096	2,355	2,655	2,924	3,215	3,542	2.4	2.0	2.0	2.1
Guyana	184	196	205	206	198	189	1.1	−.4	−.9	.1
L. HAITI	2,892	3,125	3,404	3,681	4,007	4,373	1.6	1.6	1.7	1.6
M. HONDURAS	991	1,136	1,316	1,509	1,695	1,960	2.9	2.6	2.9	2.8
Jamaica	726	701	634	603	555	515	−1.4	−1.3	−1.5	−1.4
N. MEXICO	16,275	17,988	20,039	21,541	22,747	24,078	2.1	1.3	1.1	1.6
O. NICARAGUA	732	815	905	940	966	1,009	2.1	.7	.9	1.3
P. PANAMA	451	499	551	584	606	625	2.0	1.0	.6	1.3
Q. PARAGUAY	768	880	1,002	1,099	1,212	1,348	2.7	1.9	2.2	2.3
R. PERU	4,476	4,861	5,340	5,704	6,067	6,512	1.8	1.3	1.4	1.5
Trinidad and Tabago	155	167	183	182	179	177	1.7	−.2	−.2	.5
S. URUGUAY	532	535	537	500	448	401	.1	−1.8	−2.2	−1.1
T. VENEZUELA	2,358	2,449	2,665	2,761	2,699	2,632	1.2	.1	.5	.4
Total	86,850	94,663	103,059	109,966	116,291	123,262	1.7	1.2	1.2	1.4

1. For EAP in agriculture, see SALA, 24-1307; for rural population, see SALA, 24-651 through 657.
2. Excluding Suriname.

SOURCE: *25 Años en la Agricultura: Rasgos Principales, 1950–75* (Santiago: ECLA, 1979), Anexo 3.

Table 1306

AGRICULTURAL POPULATION AS SHARE
OF TOTAL POPULATION,[1]
26 ECLA:L,[2] 1950–75

(%)

Country	1950	1960	1970	1975*
A. ARGENTINA	25.2	20.0	16.4	14.7
Bahamas	28.9	26.8	19.7	16.7
Barbados	28.9	26.8	19.7	16.7
B. BOLIVIA	61.4	61.0	55.5	53.0
C. BRAZIL	59.7	51.9	45.6	42.7
D. CHILE	32.6	30.0	23.7	21.0
E. COLOMBIA	56.8	51.4	37.9	32.2
F. COSTA RICA	57.0	51.4	42.0	37.9
G. CUBA	42.9	39.2	30.6	26.9
H. DOMINICAN REP.	70.7	66.5	61.3	58.7
I. ECUADOR	57.5	57.4	50.9	47.8
J. EL SALVADOR	65.5	61.5	56.2	53.6
Grenada	28.9	26.8	19.7	16.7
K. GUATEMALA	68.6	66.6	61.0	58.3
Guyana	43.5	36.6	27.9	23.9
L. HAITI	85.6	82.6	77.1	74.3
M. HONDURAS	71.3	70.3	66.4	64.5
Jamaica	51.8	38.9	29.5	25.4
N. MEXICO	61.2	55.1	45.2	40.6
O. NICARAGUA	66.0	61.5	49.0	43.5
P. PANAMA	56.4	50.9	41.6	37.3
Q. PARAGUAY	56.0	56.5	52.7	50.9
R. PERU	57.2	52.5	44.8	41.3
Trinidad and Tabago	24.5	21.7	18.7	17.5
S. URUGUAY	24.3	20.5	15.2	12.9
T. VENEZUELA	45.8	34.9	25.6	21.6
Total	54.0	48.5	41.6	38.4

1. For EAP in agriculture, see SALA, 24-1307; for rural population, see SALA, 24-651 through 657.
2. Excluding Suriname.

SOURCE: *25 Años en la Agricultura: Rasgos Principales, 1950–75* (Santiago: ECLA, 1979), Anexo 4.

Table 1307

AGRICULTURAL POPULATION AND ECONOMICALLY ACTIVE POPULATION IN AGRICULTURE, 20 LRC, 1965 AND 1981

	Country	1965					1981				
		Total Population (T)	Agricultural Population (T)	EAP			Total Population (T)	Agricultural Population (T)	EAP		
				Total (T)	In Agriculture (T)	% Agriculture			Total (T)	In Agriculture (T)	% Agriculture
A.	ARGENTINA	22,179	4,025	8,659	1,572	18.2	27,369	3,464	10,453	1,323	12.7
B.	BOLIVIA	4,246	2,472	1,425	829	58.2	5,720	2,827	1,866	922	49.4
C.	BRAZIL	82,541	40,255	26,116	12,737	48.8	125,220	46,824	39,442	14,749	37.4
D.	CHILE	8,510	2,286	2,687	732	26.9	11,294	2,079	3,760	676	18.0
E.	COLOMBIA	18,691	8,317	5,587	2,486	44.5	26,355	6,986	7,888	2,091	26.5
F.	COSTA RICA	1,495	697	447	208	46.7	2,266	779	764	262	34.4
G.	CUBA	7,802	2,707	2,510	871	34.7	9,791	2,215	3,008	680	22.6
H.	DOMINICAN REP.	3,703	2,364	1,021	651	63.8	6,095	3,386	1,602	890	55.6
I.	ECUADOR	5,095	2,758	1,630	882	54.1	8,275	3,624	2,642	1,157	43.8
J.	EL SALVADOR	2,954	1,738	925	544	58.9	4,938	2,508	1,541	768	49.8
K.	GUATEMALA	4,583	2,924	1,416	903	63.8	7,481	4,058	2,272	1,233	54.2
L.	HAITI	3,950	3,048	2,146	1,656	77.2	5,954	3,916	2,963	1,949	65.8
M.	HONDURAS	2,209	1,510	684	468	68.4	3,822	2,376	1,126	700	62.2
N.	MEXICO	42,859	21,541	12,519	6,292	50.3	71,814	25,243	20,708	7,279	35.2
O.	NICARAGUA	1,701	950	516	294	56.9	2,824	1,155	839	352	41.9
P.	PANAMA	1,261	581	420	194	46.1	1,970	665	662	224	33.8
Q.	PARAGUAY	2,016	1,099	644	351	54.5	3,269	1,586	1,054	511	48.5
R.	PERU	11,440	5,567	3,453	1,680	48.7	18,119	7,035	5,354	1,960	36.6
S.	URUGUAY	2,802	500	1,099	196	17.8	2,945	340	1,135	131	11.6
T.	VENEZUELA	9,105	2,761	2,681	813	30.3	16,156	2,798	4,961	859	17.3
	LATIN AMERICA	239,142	108,100	76,585	34,359	44.9	361,677	123,864	114,040	38,716	37.9
	UNITED STATES	184,303	9,909	79,412	4,050	5.1	230,049	4,730	104,910	2,157	2.1

SOURCE: FAO-PY, 1977–81, table 3.

Table 1308

ECONOMICALLY ACTIVE POPULATION (EAP),[1] 20 LC

	Country	Year[4]	Total Population	Economically Active Population		Males	Active Males As % of Total Male Population	Females	Active Females As % of Total Female Population
				N	%				
A.	ARGENTINA[6]	1983	28,237,149	10,815,220	38.3	7,955,672	56.6	2,859,548	20.1
B.	BOLIVIA[6]	1982	5,915,844	1,871,600	31.6	1,437,570	49.2	434,030	14.5
C.	BRAZIL[15]	1980	119,070,865	43,796,763	36.8	31,757,833	53.7	12,038,930	20.1
D.	CHILE[16]	1981	11,368,800	3,687,900	32.4	2,627,000	46.7	1,060,900	18.5
E.	COLOMBIA[2]	1980	26,806,866	8,467,000	31.6	6,247,000	50.0	2,220,000	15.5
F.	COSTA RICA[5]	1982	2,324,257	838,456	36.1	618,979	53.1	219,477	18.9
G.	CUBA[2,8]	1970	8,553,395	2,633,309	30.8	2,151,052	49.2	482,257	11.5
H.	DOMINICAN REP.	1979	5,275,410	1,592,072	30.2	1,177,656	44.7	414,416	15.7
I.	ECUADOR[6]	1981	8,644,000	2,808,159	32.5	2,057,889	47.2	750,270	17.5
J.	EL SALVADOR[5]	1980	4,497,257	1,593,353	35.4	1,039,446	47.5	553,907	24.0
K.	GUATEMALA[2,13]	1981	6,053,344	1,695,911	28.0	1,448,872	48.0	247,039	8.1
L.	HAITI[2,6,14]	1980	4,796,700	2,541,400	53.0	1,343,300	58.1	1,198,100	48.3
M.	HONDURAS[6]	1982	3,955,116	1,166,506	29.5	975,830	49.2	190,676	9.7
N.	MEXICO[2]	1980	67,382,581	23,987,684	35.6	~	~	~	~
O.	NICARAGUA[6,9]	1980	2,703,147	863,925	32.0	681,089	51.4	182,836	13.3
P.	PANAMA[7]	1980	1,788,748	548,460	30.7	396,315	43.8	152,145	17.2
Q.	PARAGUAY[3,6]	1980	3,167,985	1,111,117	35.1	874,472	55.3	236,645	14.9
R.	PERU[6]	1982	18,790,300	5,977,600	31.8	4,270,300	45.4	1,707,300	18.2
S.	URUGUAY[11]	1975	2,788,429	1,094,400	39.2	782,100	57.1	312,300	22.0
T.	VENEZUELA[5]	1982	14,632,626	4,684,689	32.0	3,423,711	46.7	1,260,978	17.3
	UNITED STATES[10,12]	1982	231,534,000	112,384,000	48.5	64,440,000	57.3	47,944.000	40.3

1. "Economically active" includes all persons engaged or seeking to be engaged in productive work in some branch of economic activity. Comparability of data is limited by the various differing minimum age limits, seasonal fluctuations in some economies, and international differences in the concepts and definitions of the term "labor force."
2. Provisional figures.
3. Economically active population data relate to persons 12 to 65 years of age.
4. May or may not coincide with year of population census.
5. Estimates based on the findings of a households-sample survey.
6. Official estimates.
7. Figures based on a 20% sample tabulation of census returns. Includes 16,380 Canal Zone workers.

8. Excludes domestic servants.
9. Excludes unemployed.
10. Estimates based on results of labor force sample surveys.
11. Based on a 12% sample tabulation of census returns.
12. Economically active population figures relate to persons 16 years of age and over. Figures rounded to the nearest thousand.
13. Excludes institutional households.
14. Includes persons 5 years of age and over.
15. Based on a 1% sample tabulation of census returns.
16. Figures rounded to the nearest hundred.

SOURCE: ILO-YLS, 1983, table 1.

Table 1309

EAP BY INDUSTRY, 20 LC

Country	Year	EAP	Agriculture Forestry, Hunting, and Fishing		Mining and Quarrying		Manufacturing		Construction		Electricity Gas, and Water		Wholesale/Retail Trade, Restaurants, and Hotels	
			N	%	N	%	N	%	N	%	N	%	N	%
A. ARGENTINA[1]	1970	9,011,450	1,331,100	14.8	44,600	.5	1,771,250	19.7	711,300	7.9	96,550	1.1	1,324,800	14.7
B. BOLIVIA[1]	1976	1,501,391	693,049	46.2	60,599	4.0	145,404	9.7	82,447	5.5	2,143	~k	106,862	7.1
C. BRAZIL[2],‡	1980	43,796,763	13,109,415	29.9	7,523,883[a]	17.2	~k	~k	3,151,094	7.2	~k	~k	4,111,307	9.4
D. CHILE[9]	1981	3,687,900	541,700	14.7	70,600	1.9	585,000	15.9	228,300	6.2	29,500	.8	670,300	18.1
E. COLOMBIA[3],‡	1980	8,467,000	2,412,413	28.5	49,740	.6	1,136,735	13.4	242,191	2.9	44,233	.5	1,261,633	14.9
F. COSTA RICA[3],‡	1980	770,272	206,913	26.9	124,819[f]	16.2[f]	~k	~k	60,722	7.9	~[l]	~?	139,098[g]	18.0[g]
G. CUBA[6],‡	1970	2,633,309	790,356	30.0	~[a]	~[a]	583,258[o]	20.3[o]	157,182	6.0	~[a]	~[a]	305,958[s]	11.6[s]
H. DOMINICAN REP.[4]	1970	1,241,000	549,315	44.3	840	.1	100,989	8.1	28,508	2.3	1,728	.1	77,064	6.2
I. ECUADOR[8]	1981	2,808,159	1,336,894	47.6	9,350	.3	297,555	10.6	133,529	4.7	14,655	.6	296,851	10.6
J. EL SALVADOR[3]	1980	1,593,353	636,617	40.0	4,394	.2	247,621	15.6	80,089	5.0	9,681	.6	256,086	16.1
K. GUATEMALA‡	1981	1,695,911	908,513	53.6	2,348	.1	177,494	10.5	86,191	5.1	7,714	.4	147,120	8.7
L. HAITI[8]	1980	2,317,800	1,319,600	56.9	1,200	.1	132,100	5.7	22,200	.9	1,600	.1	321,200	13.9
M. HONDURAS[8]	1981	1,124,216	594,928	52.9	3,139	.3	128,786	11.5	34,323	3.0	3,847	.3	84,541	7.6
N. MEXICO[8]	1979	19,650,695	7,885,824	40.1	288,865	1.5	3,574,461	18.2	909,827	4.6	82,533[b]	.4[b]	1,974,895[g]	10.1[g]
O. NICARAGUA[5],[8]	1980	863,925	391,963	45.4	6,566	.7	91,403	10.6	37,322	4.3	6,652	.8	105,053	12.2
P. PANAMA	1980	548,460	144,590	26.4	965	.1	52,720	9.7	29,825	5.4	7,965	1.4	67,920	12.4
Q. PARAGUAY[8],‡	1981	1,290,947	571,456	44.3	9,435	.7	191,901	14.9	57,984	4.5	3,944	.3	114,538	8.8
R. PERU[8]	1982	5,977,600	2,296,100	38.4	68,100	1.2	745,800	12.4	246,300	4.2	12,900	.2	976,000	16.3
S. URUGUAY[3]	1975	1,094,599	174,871	16.0	2,159	.2	205,943	18.8	59,428	5.4	16,206	1.5	134,509	12.3
T. VENEZUELA[3]	1981	4,561,043	647,732	14.2	56,447	1.2	729,381	16.0	432,003	9.5	50,453	1.1	840,200	18.4
UNITED STATES[7],[10]	1982	112,384,000	3,870,000	3.4	1,182,000	1.1	23,073,000	20.5	6,890,000	6.2	1,480,000	1.3	22,878,000	20.3

Table 1309 (Continued)

EAP BY INDUSTRY, 20 LC

	Country	Year	Transport, Storage, and Communication N	%	Financing, Insurance, Real Estate, and Business Services N	%	Community, Social, and Personal Services N	%	Activities Not Adequately Defined N	%	Other N	%
A.	ARGENTINA[1]	1970	593,250	6.6	252,650	2.8	2,098,750	23.2	787,200	8.7	~	~
B.	BOLIVIA[1]	1976	55,972	3.8	12,941	.8	281,911	18.8	53,600	3.6	6,463[d]	.4[d]
C.	BRAZIL[2],‡	1980	1,815,541	4.1	7,089,709	16.2	4,857,061	11.1	1,255,815	2.9	882,938	2.0
D.	CHILE[9]	1981	238,600	6.5	125,400	3.4	1,096,500	29.7	6,300	.2	95,700[d]	2.6[d]
E.	COLOMBIA[3],‡	1980	352,623	4.2	278,210	3.2	1,998,460	23.6	690,762	8.2	~	~
F.	COSTA RICA[3],‡	1980	49,645	6.5	~[q]	~[q]	176,690[m,r]	22.9[m,r]	2,171	.3	10,214[d]	1.3[d]
G.	CUBA[6],‡	1970	161,378[e]	6.1[e]	~[i]	~[i]	647,738[i,j]	24.6[i,j]	37,439	1.4	~	~
H.	DOMINICAN REP.[4]	1970	43,297	3.5	20,080	1.6	153,883	12.4	236,000	19.0	29,296[d]	2.4[d]
I.	ECUADOR[8]	1981	68,470	2.4	31,506	1.1	438,336	15.7	128,876	4.5	52,137[d]	1.9[d]
J.	EL SALVADOR[3]	1980	65,593	4.1	15,863	1.0	250,158	15.7	224	#	27,027[d]	1.7[d]
K.	GUATEMALA‡	1981	43,255	2.5	21,159	1.3	214,980	12.7	74,501	4.4	12,636	.7
L.	HAITI[8]	1980	15,400	.6	3,700	.2	136,600	5.9	5,400[c]	.2[c]	358,800[h]	15.5[h]
M.	HONDURAS[8]	1981	29,665	2.6	9,315	.8	123,927	11.1	~	~	111,745[h]	9.9[h]
N.	MEXICO[8]	1979	1,581,661	2.9	~[q]	~[q]	4,352,629[f]	22.2[f]	~	~	~	~
O.	NICARAGUA[5,8]	1980	30,064	3.4	16,761	2.0	158,789	18.4	19,352	2.2	~	~
P.	PANAMA	1980	28,840	5.3	19,290	3.5	128,815	23.5	22,610[p]	4.1[p]	44,920	8.2
Q.	PARAGUAY[8],‡	1981	31,305	2.5	~[i]	~[i]	232,993[h]	18.0[h]	50,758	3.9	26,633[d]	2.1[d]
R.	PERU[8]	1982	282,000	4.7	104,900	1.8	1,245,500	20.8	~	~	~	~
S.	URUGUAY	1975	53,728	4.9	29,461	2.7	316,078	28.9	85,085	7.7	17,131[d]	1.6[d]
T.	VENEZUELA[3]	1981	329,564	7.3	212,696	4.6	1,205,405	26.4	16,994	.4	40,168[d]	.9[d]
	UNITED STATES[7,10]	1982	5,524,000	4.9	9,641,000	8.6	34,478,000	30.7	2,179,000[c]	1.9[c]	1,190,000[d]	1.1[d]

1. Figures based on a sample tabulation of census returns.
2. Figures based on 1% sample of census returns.
3. Estimates based on the results of a households-sample survey.
4. Figures based on a 10% sample tabulation of census returns.
5. Economically active population figures do not include unemployed.
6. Excludes domestic servants.
7. Economically active population figures refer to persons 16 years of age and over.
8. Official estimates.
9. Estimates based on results of labor force sample surveys. Rounded to nearest hundred.
10. Estimates based on results of labor force sample surveys. Rounded to nearest thousand.

a. Electricity and gas and mining and quarrying industries included in manufacturing.
b. Water included in community, social, and personal services. Includes sanitary services.
c. Data refer to members of the armed forces.
d. Data refer to persons seeking first job.
e. Storage included in wholesale and retail trade category.
f. Includes manufacturing.
g. Data refer to general commerce category.
h. Data refer to the unemployed.
i. Includes water, financing, insurance, real estate, and business services.
j. Personal services included in wholesale and retail trade category.
k. Included in mining and quarrying industries.
l. Included in community, social, and personal services.
m. Includes electricity, gas, and water.
n. Includes financing, insurance, real estate, and business services.
o. Includes electricity and gas and mining and quarrying industries.
p. Includes 16,380 Canal Zone workers.
q. Not recorded separately.
r. Data refer to general services category.
s. Includes storage and personal services.

SOURCE: ILP-YLS, 1977; 1980; 1982, table 2A; 1983, table 2A.

Table 1310

EAP BY MAJOR OCCUPATIONS, 20 LC

Country	Year	Code[1]	Total EAP	Professional, Technical, and Related Workers (0-1) N	%	Administrative and Managerial Workers (2) N	%	Clerical and Related Workers (3) N	%	Sales Workers (4) N	%	Service Workers (5) N	%	Agriculture, Animal Husbandry, and Forestry Workers, Fishermen and Hunters (6) N	%	Production and Related Workers, Transport Equipment Operators, and Laborers (7-9) N	%	Workers Not Classifiable by Occupation (X) N	%	Person Seeking First Job N	%
A. ARGENTINA	1970	B	9,011,450	677,500	7.5	137,850	1.5	1,025,400	11.4	1,072,800	11.9	1,136,550b	12.6b	1,296,100	14.4	3,091,350	34.3	573,900	6.4	~	~
B. BOLIVIA	1976	A	1,501,391	85,500	5.7	9,092	.6	59,609	4.0	91,385	6.1	128,595h	8.5h	1,067,675c	71.1c			53,072	3.6	6,463	.4
C. BRAZIL[4]	1970	C	29,557,224	1,410,746	4.8	497,079	1.7	1,561,678	5.3	2,193,661	7.4	3,404,014h	11.6h	13,039,149	44.0	6,263,571	21.2	1,187,308	4.0	~	~
D. CHILE[6]	1981	D	3,687,900	237,000	6.4	88,400	2.4	472,900	12.8	468,700	12.8	438,900	11.9	544,900	14.7	1,291,700	35.1	49,700	1.3	95,700	2.6
E. COLOMBIA[5,7]	1980	E	8,467,000	138,813	1.6	87,590	1.1	501,582	5.9	1,044,854	12.3	1,619,334	19.2	2,405,538	28.4	1,978,527	23.3	690,762	8.2	~d	~d
F. COSTA RICA[7]	1980	E	770,272	65,032	8.4	105,165f	13.7f	~f	~f	107,061	13.9	113,320	14.7	367,532g	47.7g	~g	~g	1,948	.3	10,214	1.3
G. CUBA[10,7]	1970	~	2,633,309	220,298	8.4	112,745	4.3	136,185	5.2	564,403e	21.4e	~e	~e	708,165	26.9	857,089	32.5	34,424	1.3	~	~
H. DOMINICAN REP.	1970	B	1,241,000	34,060	2.7	3,797	.3	81,193	6.5	61,705	5.0	63,171	5.1	551,617	44.4	241,500	19.5	174,661b	14.1b	29,296	2.4
I. ECUADOR[2]	1974	~	1,940,628	100,510	5.2	19,344	1.0	73,482	3.8	151,616	7.8	135,790	7.0	892,013	45.9	435,677	22.5	101,448	5.2	30,748	1.6
J. EL SALVADOR	1980	E	1,593,353	67,411	4.2	8,476	.6	85,929	5.4	225,438	14.1	128,413	8.1	629,345	39.5	421,090	26.4	224	#	27,027	1.7
K. GUATEMALA[7]	1981	A	1,695,911	81,037	4.8	20,005	1.2	56,566	3.3	99,515	5.9	109,847	6.4	911,257	53.8	349,943	20.6	55,105	3.3	12,636	.7
L. HAITI[8]	1971	A	2,272,082	22,733	1.0	253	#	11,788	.5	194,138	8.6	123,833b	5.4b	1,430,984	63.0	163,421	7.2	1,850	.1	323,082a	14.2a
M. HONDURAS	1974	~	762,795	30,982	4.1	7,012	.9	31,784	4.2	43,907	5.8	49,674	6.5	453,113	59.4	131,408	17.2	7,744	1.0	7,171	.9
N. MEXICO	1977	F	18,042,729	1,118,649	6.2	469,111	2.6	1,463,265	8.1	1,468,678	8.1	2,376,227	13.2	7,092,597	39.3	4,054,202	22.5			~	~
O. NICARAGUA	1971	~	504,240	26,040	5.2	4,750	.9	21,080	4.2	35,840	7.1	55,130	10.9	235,120	46.7	110,500	21.9	15,780	3.1	~	~
P. PANAMA[3,12]	1980	C	548,460	55,095	10.0	24,245	4.5	51,495	9.4	33,825	6.1	73,520	13.4	139,400	25.4	117,710	21.5	8,250	1.5	44,920a	8.2a
Q. PARAGUAY[2]	1972	C	754,710	31,370	4.2	4,640	.6	27,420	3.6	50,190	6.6	72,120	9.6	367,570	48.7	161,310	21.4	13,700	1.8	26,390a	3.5a
R. PERU[7]	1981	A	5,281,734	392,593	7.4	24,329	.5	514,363	9.7	523,921	10.0	375,804	7.1	1,817,407	34.4	992,653	18.8	284,963	5.4	355,701	6.7
S. URUGUAY	1975	A	1,094,599	79,699	7.3	14,237	1.3	118,270	10.8	105,209	9.6	185,842b	17.0b	172,214	15.7	316,023	28.9	85,913	7.8	17,131	1.6
T. VENEZUELA[9]	1981	E	4,561,043	434,449	9.5	179,124	4.0	536,270	11.7	573,662	12.6	603,437	13.2	648,900	14.2	1,513,378	33.2	31,655	.7	40,168	.9
UNITED STATES[11]	1982	D	112,384,000	17,530,000	15.6	11,910,000	10.6	19,830,000	17.6	6,968,000	6.2	15,363,000	13.7	2,914,000	2.6	34,501,000	30.7	2,179,000b	1.9b	1,190,000	1.1

1. Code: A, Complete count, final data; B, Sample tabulation, size not specified; C, Sample tabulation, size specified; D, Labor force sample survey; E, Household survey; F, Official estimates.

2. All figures based on a 10% sample tabulation of census returns.

3. Includes 16,380 persons working in the Canal Zone.

4. De jure population. EAP figures based on a 25% sample tabulation of census returns.

5. Figures include persons seeking work for the first time.

6. Figures rounded to nearest hundred.

7. Provisional data.

8. Includes persons 10 years of age and over.

9. The group not classifiable by status refers to unemployed.

10. Does not include domestic servants.

11. Includes persons 16 years of age and over.

12. Figures based on a 20% sample tabulation of census returns.

a. Figures relate to unemployed or other unemployed.

b. Figures include members of the armed forces.

c. Figures include miners and quarrymen.

d. Not recorded separately.

e. Figures for service workers are included under sales workers.

f. Administrative and managerial workers includes clerical and related workers.

g. Figures in category 6 include workers from categories 7-9.

h. Service workers includes sport and recreation workers.

SOURCE: ILO-YLS, 1977; ILO-YLS, 1980; ILO-YLS, 1982, table 2B; and ILO-YLS, 1983, table 2B.

Table 1311

OCCUPATIONAL CATEGORIES, BY SEX, 20 LC
(%)

	Country	Year	Code[1]	N (M) M	N (M) F	Professional, Technical, and Related Workers (0-1) M	F	Administrative and Managerial Workers (2) M	F	Clerical and Related Workers (3) M	F	Sales Workers (4) M	F	Service Workers (5) M	F	Agriculture, Animal Husbandry, and Forestry Workers, Fishermen and Hunters (6) M	F	Production and Related Workers, Transport Equipment Operators and Laborers (7-9) M	F	Workers Not Classifiable by Occupation (X) M	F	Other (Y) M	F
A.	ARGENTINA	1970	~	6.7	2.3	4.5	1.6	1.9	.4	9.8	15.9	12.1	11.2	6.7	30.0	18.1	3.4	41.0	15.2	5.9	7.6	~	~
B.	BOLIVIA	1976	E	1.2	.3	4.3	10.5	.6	.4	3.5	3.5	3.5	14.9	4.9[a]	21.2[a]	52.2	26.5	26.6[b]	18.0[b]	3.8	2.6	.6	.4
C.	BRAZIL	1970	~	23.4	6.2	2.5	13.5	1.9	1.0	4.4	8.5	8.0	5.2	3.7	35.6	50.4	20.4	23.7	11.4	3.9	4.4	1.5[a]	#
D.	CHILE[2]	1970	~	2.0	.6	4.7	15.6	2.0	1.4	8.5	13.1	7.5	10.3	4.6	34.8	26.6	2.6	38.4	17.3	7.7	5.0	~	~
E.	COLOMBIA[8]	1973	~	6.0	↓	4.5	↓	.7	↓	5.9	↓	7.4	↓	10.0	↓	26.8	↓	20.6	↓	9.8	↓	14.3[c]	↓
F.	COSTA RICA[8]	1973	~	.5	.1	5.2	19.2	1.8	1.0	4.6	10.6	7.5	8.6	5.1	39.0	43.3	2.9	26.4	14.6	2.2	1.9	3.8[d]	2.1[d]
G.	CUBA[8]	1970	~	2.2	↓	8.4	↓	4.3	↓	5.2	↓	21.4[e]	↓	–[e]	↓	26.9	↓	32.5	↓	1.3	↓	~	↓
H.	DOMINICAN REP.	1970	~	.9	.3	1.9	5.1	.3	.2	6.1	7.8	5.3	3.9	2.6	12.4	49.7	29.2	20.5	16.3	10.7	24.0	2.7[d]	1.2[d]
I.	ECUADOR[8]	1974	~	1.9	↓	5.0	↓	.8	↓	3.6	↓	7.5	↓	6.8	↓	46.4	↓	22.6	↓	5.7	↓	1.6[d]	↓
J.	EL SALVADOR	1980	B	1.0	.6	3.6	5.4	.7	.2	4.8	6.5	6.3	28.9	3.6	16.5	49.5	20.8	30.7	18.4	.0	.0	.8	.3
K.	GUATEMALA‡,[3]	1981	E	1.4	.2	3.4	12.8	1.2	1.3	2.3	9.5	4.6	13.4	2.6	29.1	61.5	8.4	21.2	17.5	2.6	7.2	.7	.9
L.	HAITI	1971	E	1.2	1.1	1.2	.8	#	#	.7	.3	1.6	16.3	3.0	7.8	73.7	51.1	7.8	6.5	.1	.1	11.9[c,d]	17.1[c,d]
M.	HONDURAS	1974	~	.6	.1	2.6	12.2	.8	1.3	3.5	7.8	4.3	13.5	2.1	30.3	69.6	5.0	15.2	28.0	1.0	1.0	.9[d]	.9[d]
N.	MEXICO	1977	~	13.8	4.1	4.9	10.6	2.7	2.3	5.5	16.7	6.9	12.2	8.4	29.3	47.3	12.4	24.3	16.5	#	#	~	~
O.	NICARAGUA	1971	~	.4	.1	3.7	10.2	1.0	.5	3.4	7.0	4.5	16.3	3.0	39.1	57.8	6.4	23.6	15.7	2.7	4.6	~	~
P.	PANAMA[4]	1980	D[7]	.4	.2	6.9	18.4	4.9	3.2	4.2	22.8	5.6	7.6	8.4	26.3	34.3	2.4	27.2	6.5	1.7	1.0	6.8[c]	11.9[c]
Q.	PARAGUAY	1972	~	.6	.2	2.3	10.6	.7	.4	3.4	4.5	4.9	12.9	4.7	27.2	58.6	12.9	19.8	27.7	1.9	1.3	3.7[c]	2.5[c]
R.	PERU	1981	~	3.9	1.3	6.3	10.8	.6	.1	8.5	13.4	8.7	13.6	4.6	14.5	39.6	19.1	22.4	8.3	4.0	9.5	5.4	10.7
S.	URUGUAY	1975	E	.8	.3	4.3	14.8	1.6	.6	10.0	12.9	9.7	9.3	7.4	31.5	21.0	2.4	33.3	17.8	7.9	7.7	4.8[d]	3.0[d]
T.	VENEZUELA	1981	B	3.3	1.2	5.9	19.2	4.8	1.5	7.4	23.4	12.3	13.3	8.0	27.2	19.0	1.6	41.0	12.2	.9[c]	.2[c]	.7[d]	1.4[d]
	UNITED STATES[5,6]	1982	A	64.4	47.9	14.9	16.6	13.2	7.0	5.9	33.4	5.9	6.7	9.2	19.7	3.7	1.1	43.3	13.8	.9[c]	1.3[c]	3.1[a]	.4[a]

a. Includes members of the armed forces.

b. Figures include miners, quarrymen, and related workers.

c. Figures refer to the unemployed.

d. Figures refer to persons seeking work for the first time.

e. Figures for service workers are included in sales workers.

SOURCE: ILO-YLS, 1976; ILO-YLS, 1977; ILO-YLS, 1979; ILO-YLS, 1980; ILO-YLS, 1981, table 2B; and ILO-YLS, 1982, table 2B.

1. Code: A, Labor force sample survey; B, Household survey; C, Official estimate; D, Census sample tabulation; E, Complete census count, final data.
2. Adaptation of categories.
3. Excludes institutional households.
4. Includes 16,380 persons working in the Canal Zone (13,330 males and 3,050 females).
5. Economically active population figures relate to persons 16 years of age and over.
6. All figures are rounded to the nearest thousand; consequently, the totals shown may differ from the sum of the component parts.
7. Based on a 20% sample tabulation.
8. Figures for female workers are included in the male cateogy.

Table 1312

OCCUPATIONAL STRATA, 1 9 L, 1960-70

(%)

Category	A. ARGENTINA 1960	A. ARGENTINA 1970	C. BRAZIL 1960	C. BRAZIL 1972	D. CHILE 1960	D. CHILE 1970	F. COSTA RICA 1963	F. COSTA RICA 1970	J. ECUADOR 1962	J. ECUADOR 1968	P. PANAMA 1960	P. PANAMA 1970	Q. PARAGUAY 1962	Q. PARAGUAY 1972	S. URUGUAY 1963	S. URUGUAY 1970	T. VENEZUELA 1960	T. VENEZUELA 1973
I. Medium and High Strata (except the occupations of the primary sector)	31.4	32.2	15.0	23.3	20.3	27.8	33.6	46.2	25.0	39.8	16.4	21.8	11.8	13.9	50.9	45.8	23.9	36.8
a. Employees	8.2	4.3	1.9	4.1	1.5	2.4	3.0	6.0	1.7	4.1	1.3	1.0	1.2	1.4	8.4	5.6	1.8	3.6
b. Self-Employed, Owners of Commercial Establishments	2.4	4.4	.2	1.6	3.7	4.9	4.4	3.1	9.1	12.1	.9	1.3	2.7	3.1	3.0	3.8	5.4	7.0

Continued in SALA, 21-1304.

Table 1313

ECONOMICALLY ACTIVE POPULATION ESTIMATED BY AGE GROUP, 20 L, 1970-2000

(T)

Age Groups	1970	1975	1980	1985	1990	1995	2000
A. ARGENTINA							
Total	9,305,481	9,928,234	10,535,362	11,131,300	11,764,237	12,445,898	13,131,540
10-14	196,560	202,571	208,884	224,398	237,828	242,375	242,962
15-19	1,009,796	1,053,107	1,085,327	1,119,087	1,202,110	1,273,972	1,298,427
20-24	1,276,212	1,405,232	1,465,509	1,510,270	1,557,122	1,672,389	1,772,278
25-29	1,136,718	1,287,531	1,417,897	1,478,737	1,523,415	1,570,155	1,686,260
30-34	1,029,669	1,100,823	1,247,121	1,373,304	1,432,311	1,475,437	1,520,797
35-39	1,010,869	1,003,876	1,073,459	1,216,284	1,339,525	1,397,262	1,439,563
40-44	982,748	972,691	966,441	1,033,742	1,171,678	1,290,807	1,346,909
45-49	865,789	927,443	918,624	913,089	977,190	1,108,390	1,221,836
50-54	697,479	778,873	835,102	827,819	823,523	882,161	1,001,861
55-59	520,153	552,815	618,267	663,678	658,613	655,955	703,574
60-64	303,972	327,353	348,411	390,287	419,643	417,056	415,957
65-69	158,449	176,855	190,801	203,568	228,493	246,248	245,232
70-74	73,990	86,980	97,215	105,300	112,766	127,004	137,374
75-79	29,869	35,395	41,856	47,057	51,247	55,159	62,397
80 +	13,208	16,689	20,448	24,680	28,773	32,528	36,113

Continued in SALA, 17-1301.

Table 1314

EAP BY ACTIVITY,[1] 14 L, 1950–80

(%)

| Country | Year | Urban | | | Agricultural | | | Mining (7) | Coverage of the Underemployed (2+5) (8) |
		Formal (1)	Informal[a] (2)	Total (3)	Modern (4)	Traditional (5)	Total (6)		
A. ARGENTINA	1950	56.8	15.2	72.0	19.9	7.6	27.5	.5	22.8
	1970	66.0	15.6	81.6	11.2	6.7	17.9	.5	22.3
	1980[b]	65.0	19.4	84.4	8.8	6.3	15.1	.5	25.7
B. BOLIVIA	1950	9.1	15.0	24.1	19.0	53.7	72.7	3.2	68.7
	1970	15.4	19.6	35.0	8.3	53.5	61.8	3.2	73.1
	1980[b]	17.9	23.2	41.1	5.2	50.9	56.1	2.8	74.1
C. BRAZIL	1950	28.5	10.7	39.2	22.5	37.6	60.1	.7	48.3
	1970	38.6	14.9	53.5	12.5	33.4	45.9	.6	48.3
	1980[b]	45.2	16.9	62.1	9.8	27.6	37.4	.5	44.5
D. CHILE	1950	40.8	22.1	62.9	23.1	8.9	32.0	5.1	31.0
	1970	53.1	16.7	69.8	17.9	9.3	27.2	3.0	26.0
	1980[b]	54.1	20.1	74.2	14.0	8.8	22.8	3.0	28.9
E. COLOMBIA	1950	23.9	15.3	39.2	26.2	33.0	59.2	1.6	48.3
	1970	38.7	17.7	56.4	20.4	22.3	42.7	.9	40.0
	1980[b]	42.6	22.3	64.9	15.8	18.7	34.5	.6	41.0
F. COSTA RICA	1950	29.7	12.3	42.0	37.3	20.4	57.7	.3	32.7
	1970	44.1	12.9	57.0	24.1	18.6	42.7	.3	31.5
	1980[b]	52.9	12.4	65.3	19.6	14.8	34.4	.3	27.2
I. ECUADOR	1950	21.5	11.7	33.2	27.4	39.0	66.4	.4	50.7
	1970	17.2	23.7	40.9	17.6	41.2	58.8	.3	64.9
	1980[b]	22.7	25.4	48.1	13.7	37.9	51.6	.3	63.3
J. EL SALVADOR	1950	18.5	13.7	32.2	32.5	35.0	67.5	.3	48.7
	1970	25.4	16.6	42.0	29.9	28.0	57.9	.1	44.6
	1980[b]	28.6	18.9	47.5	22.3	30.1	52.4	.1	49.0
K. GUATEMALA	1950	15.2	16.2	31.4	23.7	44.8	68.5	.1	61.0
	1970	22.5	17.3	39.8	23.1	37.0	60.1	.1	54.3
	1980[b]	26.7	17.8	44.5	22.3	33.1	55.4	.1	50.9
N. MEXICO	1950	21.6	12.9	34.5	20.4	44.0	64.4	1.1	56.9
	1970	33.9	18.2	52.1	21.9	24.9	46.8	1.1	43.1
	1980[b]	39.5	22.0	61.5	19.2	18.4	37.6	.9	40.4
P. PANAMA	1950	34.9	11.8	46.7	6.2	47.0	53.2	.1	58.8
	1970	43.8	15.8	59.6	8.5	31.7	40.2	.2	47.5
	1980[b]	45.3	20.9	66.2	9.1	24.6	33.7	.1	45.5
R. PERU	1950	19.1	16.9	36.0	21.9	39.4	61.3	2.7	56.3
	1970	29.8	20.7	50.5	10.3	37.7	48.0	1.5	58.4
	1980[b]	35.0	23.8	58.8	8.0	32.0	40.0	1.2	55.8
S. URUGUAY	1950	63.3	14.5	77.8	17.2	4.8	22.0	.2	19.3
	1970	64.2	16.8	81.0	11.9	6.9	18.8	.2	23.7
	1980[b]	63.3	19.0	82.3	9.5	8.0	17.5	.2	27.0
T. VENEZUELA	1950	34.7	16.4	51.1	23.3	22.5	45.8	3.1	38.9
	1970	48.9	22.4	71.3	7.2	19.9	27.1	1.6	42.3
	1980[b]	62.6	16.4	79.0	4.4	15.1	19.5	1.5	31.5

1. Estimates are based on national census and survey information.

a. Includes domestic labor.
b. The estimates for 1950 and 1970 are based on population census information; estimates for 1980 are based on the most recent surveys.

SOURCE: ECLA-EIC, E/CEPAL/G. 1189, 1981, p. 16.

Table 1315

POPULATION EMPLOYED BY SECTOR, 13 L, 1960 and 1970

(N)

| Country | Agricultural Sector | | Basic Services | | And Other Services | |
	1960	1970	1960	1970	1960	1970
A. ARGENTINA	19.1	15.2	38.0	37.0	42.9	47.8

Continued in SALA, 21-1305.

Table 1316

EMPLOYMENT IN MANUFACTURING, 15 LC, 1971–81[a]

(T)

Country	Code[1]	1971	1972	1973	1974	1975	1976	1977	1978	1979	1980	1981	1982
B. BOLIVIA[2]	D	108.2	112.6	117.1	121.8	126.6	131.7	137.2	141.5	146.9	~	~	155.5
C. BRAZIL[3]	C	2,599	2,830	3,230	3,720	3,953	4,053[b]	~	~	~	~	~	~
E. COLOMBIA[4]	C	102.3	106.2	111.7	116.4	117.9	120.6	122.3	124.3	127.2	126.1	~	~
F. COSTA RICA[5]	A	**	**	**	**	**	72.94	83.24	82.55	89.47	95.86[‡]	88.05	89.48
G. CUBA[6]	D	440.5	438.5	453.2	466.7	472.2	477.4	563.7[‡]	~	~	~	~	~
H. DOMINICAN REP.	C	113.98	124.21	137.74	139.43	122.31	110.78	112.56	113.33	~	~	~	~
I. ECUADOR[7]	C	123.4	125.4	132.1	139.2	147.6	158.7	154.1	165.3	173.2	174.5	177.4	~
J. EL SALVADOR	C	**	**	**	**	49.49	54.16	56.37	57.70	58.84	60.28[‡]	~	~
K. GUATEMALA	C	37.68	40.93	41.56		32.83	32.38	36.81	38.55	~	~	~	~
L. HAITI[2,8]	D	119.41	121.57	120.85	121.51	122.30	115.93	116.60	117.18	117.77	~	134.2	136.3
N. MEXICO[2,9]	C	~	346.70	361.86	403.21[e]	413.51	468.73[f]	464.88	487.49	524.61	563.33	592.85[‡]	606.17
O. NICARAGUA[10]	B	18.77	23.32	22.27	25.49	26.57	28.17	30.51	29.17	24.83	27.95	~	~
P. PANAMA[11,14]	A	29.30	29.10	~	37.40[c]	33.71[d]	34.16	37.89[c]	39.97[‡]	42.69	~	~	~
R. PERU[2]	D	~	627.4	658.4	694.7	727.9	744.0	741.2	772.3[‡]	803.9	812.5	~	~
T. VENEZUELA[12,13]	C	62.10	62.90	65.45	70.10	75.0	82.30	85.85	89.91[‡]	~	~	~	75.66
UNITED STATES[12]	C	18,263	19,151	20,154	20,077	18,323	18,997	19,682	20,505	21,040	20,285	20,173	18,853

1. The series refer, in general, to salaried employees and wage earners in manufacturing (excluding public utilities, building, and other construction). Workers on paid or unpaid holiday or vacation are generally included, but employers, self-employed, and workers on strike, or temporary military leave or temporarily laid off are generally excluded. Code: A, Labor force sample surveys; B, Social insurance statistics; C, Statistics of establishments; D, Official estimates.
2. Civilian labor force employed.
3. December of each year; registered establishments on 31 December of each year.
4. Base: July 1970, June 1971 = 100.
5. July of each year.
6. Includes mining and quarrying, electricity, gas, and water; state sector.
7. Base: 1965 = 100.
8. Year beginning in July of each year indicated.
9. Figures include 57 industrial groups of the national classification; June of each year.

10. Eight main cities of the country; insured persons.
11. August of each year.
12. Employees.
13. Second semester of each year.
14. Wage earners and salaried employees.
a. For employment indices data, 1964-79, see SALA, 22-1304.
b. Beginning 1978 revised questionnaire.
c. October.
d. November.
e. Not strictly comparable.
f. Prior to 1976: 54 industrial groups.

SOURCE: ILO-YLS, 1981; ILO-YLS, 1983, table 5A.

Table 1317

HOURS OF WORK IN MANUFACTURING, 9 LC, 1964–81

(Actual Hours of Work per Week per Worker)[1]

Country	1964	1970	1974	1975	1976	1977	1978	1979	1980	1981	1982
B. BOLIVIA[7]	~	~	42.6	43.1	46.1	46.9	47.7	~	46.8	46.3	~
E. COLOMBIA	50.0	50.0[a]	~	~	~	~	~	~	~	~	~
I. ECUADOR	45.0	48.0	51.0	51.0	50.0	51.0	53.0	47.0	45.0	45.0	~
J. EL SALVADOR[2,3]	49.5	48.0	48.2	44.3	44.3	44.3	44.6	44.6	44.6	44.1	~
K. GUATEMALA[4]	45.7	45.9	48.2	47.2	47.3	48.5	47.5	~	~	~	~
N. MEXICO[5]	45.6	45.1	45.5	45.6	45.6	45.5	46.4	46.5	46.6	~	~
P. PANAMA	44.6	42.3	45.7	45.5	45.9	45.9	45.4	46.0	~	~	~
R. PERU[5,6]	47.3	~	47.2	46.1	48.1	45.4	45.8	45.7	45.6	45.0	45.4
T. VENEZUELA	~	44.4	43.7	42.3	43.1	43.7	43.9	44.9	44.2	44.2	~
UNITED STATES	40.7	39.8	40.0	39.5	40.1	40.3	40.4	40.2	39.7	39.8	38.9

1. The series generally represent the average hours actually worked by wage earners. In a few cases the data refer to hours paid for, or to normal hours, rather than to actual hours worked. Where possible, annual data are averages of twelve monthly figures.
2. San Salvador.
3. Males only.
4. Prior to 1974, Guatemala City.
5. October of each year.
6. Lima, May of each year; prior to 1980, June of each year.
7. Employees.

a. January-June.

SOURCE: ILO-YLS, 1974; 1983, table 12A.

Table 1318

GOVERNMENT EMPLOYEES BY LEVEL, 6 LC

	Country	Year	Central Government		State and Local Government		Nonfinancial Public Enterprises		General Government		Public Sector	
			T	PHI	T	PHI	T	PHI	T	PHI	T	PHI
A.	ARGENTINA	1981	573.5	2.12	703.0	2.60	313.8	1.16	1,276.5	4.72	1,590.3	5.88
I.	ECUADOR	1980	163.3	1.96	~	~	~	~	~	~	~	~
J.	EL SALVADOR	1982	111.5	2.32	~	~	13.9	.29	~	1.71	13.1	1.81
K.	GUATEMALA	1981	105.0	1.45	18.8	.26	7.3	.10	123.8	~	~	~
M.	HONDURAS	1981	27.0	.73	4.1	.22	~	~	~	~	~	~
P.	PANAMA	1979	63.7	3.39	~	~	38.5	2.05	71.7	3.81	110.2	5.86

SOURCE: IMF, Occasional Paper 24, October 1983, tables 20 and 21.

Table 1319

CENTRAL GOVERNMENT EMPLOYEES BY FUNCTIONAL SECTOR[1], 6 LC
(PHI)

	Country	Year	Administration	Education	Health	Defense	Police	Finance and Planning	Agriculture	Mining, Manufacturing and Construction	Utilities	Transport and Communication	Posts	Labor and Social Security	Other
A.	ARGENTINA	1981	.09	1.83	.36	.43	.72	.07	.03	.07	.01	.07	~	.05	.11
I.	ECUADOR	1980	.06	.74	.19	.43	.20	.06	.10	.01	.01	.11	~	.03	~
J.	EL SALVADOR	1982	.11	.64	.34	.23	.07	.09	.11	.03	~	.50	~	.16	.01
K.	GUATEMALA	1981	.08	.54	.17	.19	.15	.07	.05	.08	~	~	~	.09	.01
P.	PANAMA	1979	.26	1.38	.50	~	.60	.14	.18	.31	~	.08	.08	.07	.09
S.	URUGUAY	1979	~	~	~	1.03	~	~	~	~	+	.27	~	~	~
	UNITED STATES	1981	.07	2.33	.67	1.38	.36	.06	.05	.01	.01	.27	~	.21	.18

1. The number of employees in the police, health, and education sectors has been augmented by the number of such employees at the state and local government levels.

SOURCE: IMF, Occasional Paper 24, October 1983, table 30.

Table 1320

CENTRAL GOVERNMENT EMPLOYEES BY FUNCTIONAL SECTOR AS A SHARE OF TOTAL
CENTRAL GOVERNMENT EMPLOYMENT,[1] 5 LC

(%)

Country	Year	Administration	Education	Health	Defense	Police	Finance and Planning	Agriculture	Mining, Manufacturing, and Construction	Utilities	Transport and Communication	Posts	Labor and Social Security	Other
A. ARGENTINA	1981	2.40	47.80	9.32	11.25	18.74	1.75	.80	1.72	.38	1.75	~	1.31	2.80
I. ECUADOR	1980	3.18	37.66	9.74	22.23	10.29	3.00	5.27	.61	.73	5.88	~	1.35	~
J. EL SALVADOR	1982	4.75	27.44	14.80	9.87	3.14	4.04	4.84	1.43	~	21.61	~	6.82	.36
K. GUATEMALA	1981	5.71	37.52	11.81	13.33	10.57	4.86	3.62	5.62	~	~	~	6.10	.67
P. PANAMA	1979	7.69	40.66	14.76	~	17.74	4.24	5.18	9.11	~	2.35	2.35	2.04	2.51
UNITED STATES	1981	1.26	41.58	12.01	24.72	6.48	1.03	.89	.14	.06	4.81	~	3.75	3.27

SOURCE: IMF, Occasional Paper 24, October 1983, table 31.

Table 1321

UNDERUTILIZATION OF LABOR, 6 L

(Ca. 1970)

Country	EAP			Open Unemployment		Equivalent Unemployment in Agriculture[1]		Nonagricultural Underemployment[2]		Equivalent Nonagricultural Employment		Total Underutilization of Labor	
	N	Agricultural	Nonagricultural	Thousands	Rate[3]	Thousands	Rate[3]	Thousands	Rate[3]	Thousands	Rate[3]	Thousands	Rate[3]
A. ARGENTINA	8,823	1,318	7,505	168	1.9	132	10	2,086	27.8	901	12.0	1,201	13.6

Continued in SALA, 21-1309.

Table 1322

UNDEREMPLOYMENT TOPICS COVERED IN HOUSEHOLD SURVEYS, 13 L

Country	Hours Worked	Average Workday	Reasons for Not Working Longer Hours	Desire to Work Longer Hours	Job Stability	Method of Payment	Reasons for Not Having Worked	Job Search	Reasons for Search
A. ARGENTINA	Yes	No	No	Yes	Yes	No	Yes	Yes	Yes

Continued in SALA, 23-1310.

Table 1323

UNEMPLOYMENT TOPICS COVERED IN HOUSEHOLD SURVEYS, 13 L

Country	Length of Search for Employment	Means of Search	Part-time or Full-time Search	Type of Employment Sought	Characteristics of Last Employment					
					Date of Last Employment	Occupation	Economic Activity	Employment Category	Size of Establishment	Reasons for Leaving
A. ARGENTINA	Yes	No	No	Yes	Yes	Yes	Yes	Yes	Yes	Yes

Continued in SALA, 23-1311.

Table 1324

MINIMUM AGE FROM WHICH ECONOMIC CHARACTERISTICS WERE INVESTIGATED IN POPULATION CENSUSES AND NATIONAL HOUSEHOLD SURVEYS IN THE 1970s, 20 L

	Country	Population Censuses	Household Surveys
A.	ARGENTINA	10 years and over	--
B.	BOLIVIA	7 years and over	--
C.	BRAZIL	10 years and over	10 years and over
D.	CHILE	12 years and over	12 years and over
E.	COLOMBIA	10 years and over	12 years and over
F.	COSTA RICA	12 years and over	12 years and over
G.	CUBA	10 years and over	--
H.	DOMINICAN REP.	10 years and over	--
I.	ECUADOR	12 years and over	--
J.	EL SALVADOR	10 years and over	10 years and over
K.	GUATEMALA	10 years and over	--
L.	HAITI	5 years and over	--
M.	HONDURAS	10 years and over	--
N.	MEXICO	12 years and over	12 years and over
O.	NICARAGUA	10 years and over	--
P.	PANAMA	10 years and over	15 years and over
Q.	PARAGUAY	12 years and over	--
R.	PERU	6 years and over	14 years and over
S.	URUGUAY	12 years and over	14 years and over
T.	VENEZUELA	15 years and over	10 years and over

SOURCE: ECLA-CC, Nov. 1983, table III.3, p. 157.

Table 1325

DECLARATION PERIOD AND MINIMUM TIME OF EMPLOYMENT FOR DETERMINING ACTIVITY STATUS, POPULATION CENSUS 1970, 20 L

	Country	Period of Declaration	Minimum Time Employed	Work	Unpaid Family Worker
A.	ARGENTINA	Preceding week	Majority of week, i.e. 4 normal working days	Not specified	Not specified
B.	BOLIVIA	Preceding week	Majority of week	Not specified	Not specified
C.	BRAZIL	Time of the census	Not specified	Not specified	Not specified
D.	CHILE	Preceding week	More than half of the week	1 day	1/3 normal working day
E.	COLOMBIA	Preceding week	Not specified	1 hour	15 hours
F.	COSTA RICA	Preceding week	Not specified	1 hour	Not Specified
G.	CUBA	Preceding week	Not specified	1 day	1/3 normal working day
H.	DOMINICAN REP.	Preceding week	More than half of the week	Not specified	Not specified
I.	ECUADOR	Preceding week	More than half of the week	Not specified	Not specified
J.	EL SALVADOR	Preceding week	Not specified	Not specified	Not specified
K.	GUATEMALA	Preceding week	Not specified	1 day	15 hours
L.	HAITI	Preceding six months	More than half of time covered	Not specified	1/3 normal working day
M.	HONDURAS	Preceding week	Not specified	1 day	15 hours
N.	MEXICO	Preceding week	Not specified	1 hour	15 hours
O.	NICARAGUA	Preceding week	More than half of the week	Not specified	1/3 normal working day
P.	PANAMA	Preceding week	Not specified	Not specified	1/3 normal working day
Q.	PARAGUAY	Preceding week	More than half of the week	Not specified	2 days
R.	PERU	Preceding week	Not specified	Not specified	15 hours
S.	URUGUAY	Preceding week	Not specified	Not specified	Not specified
T.	VENEZUELA	Preceding week	More than half of the week	Not specified	15 hours

SOURCE: ECLA-CC, 1983, table III.4, p. 158.

Table 1326

UNEMPLOYMENT,[1] 13 LC, 1963-82[a]

Country	Code[2]	1963 T	1963 %	1968 T	1968 %	1970 T	1970 %	1971 T	1971 %	1972 T	1972 %	1973 T	1973 %	1974 T	1974 %	1982 T	1982 %
A. ARGENTINA[3]	A	~	~	153.3	5.0	158.0	4.8	196.5[b]	6.0[b]	221.5[c]	6.6[c]	173.0	5.6	121.2	3.4	220.3	5.7
B. BOLIVIA	C	~	~	~	~	121.3	~	122.7	9.0	112.1	8.1	100.9	7.1	89.1	6.1	~	~
C. BRAZIL[4]	A	~	~	710.0	~	725.0[d]	~	723.0	~[e]	1,033.9[f]	~	968.0	~	-.-	~	272.1	20.0
D. CHILE[5]	A	39.6	5.1	57.1	6.0	42.8	4.1	43.7	4.2	34.0	3.3	47.6	4.8	83.9	8.3	~	~
E. COLOMBIA[6]	A	~	~	~	~	~	~	~	~	~	~	~	~	~	~	~	~
F. COSTA RICA	A	~	~	~	~	~	~	~	~	~	~	~	~	~	~	78.6	9.4
K. GUATEMALA[7]	B	.1	~	.6	~	.6	~	.6	~	.6	~	.6	~	.4	~	1.3	~
M. HONDURAS	C	~	~	47.1	~	49.4	~	51.1	~	51.7	~	53.1	~	52.3	~	128.3	~
O. NICARAGUA	~	21.0	5.8[j]	~	~	20.3	3.7	20.5	3.6	35.4	6.0	54.5	9.1	45.9	7.3	~	~
P. PANAMA	A	~	~	31.0	7.0	33.3	7.1	36.3	7.6	32.2	6.8	34.9	7.0	30.0[k]	5.8[k]	417.1	7.0
R. PERU[8]	A	~	~	~	~	201.2	~	195.7	4.4	194.0	4.2	191.5	4.2	186.9	4.0	~	~
S. URUGUAY[9]	A	~	~	43.3[n]	8.4[n]	39.3	7.5	41.2	7.6	41.7[o]	7.7[o]	49.4[p]	8.9[p]	38.2[i]	8.1[i]	333.3	7.1
T. VENEZUELA	A	~	~	181.6[o]	6.3[o]	198.8[a]	6.3[a]	195.2[b]	6.0	~	~	~	~	219.5	~	~	~
UNITED STATES	A	4,070.0	5.7	2,817.0	3.6	4,088.0	4.9	4,993.0	5.9	4,882.0	5.6	4,365.0	4.9	5,156.0	5.6	10,678	9.7

Country	Code[2]	1975 T	1975 %	1976 T	1976 %	1977 T	1977 %	1978 T	1978 %	1979 T	1979 %	1980 T	1980 %	1981 T	1981 %
A. ARGENTINA[3]	A	97.0	2.3	159.1	4.5	103.3	2.8	101.6	2.8	69.5	2.0[h]	82.2	2.3	174.8	4.5
B. BOLIVIA	C	76.6	5.2	63.4	4.2	62.1	4.0	54.1	3.4	~	~	~	~	2,023	~
C. BRAZIL[4]	A	-.-	~	721.7	~	~	~	~	~	~	~	~	~	~	~
D. CHILE[5]	A	157.7	15.0	192.9	17.1	158.2	13.9	169.4	13.7	169.4	13.4	152.4	12.0	121.3	9.0
E. COLOMBIA[6]	A	253.1[j]	10.5	276.0	10.8	266.7	9.8	261.7	8.9	289.6	9.0	349.8	9.9	374.3	8.1
F. COSTA RICA	A	.9	~	40.9	6.2	31.4	4.6	32.7	4.5	36.2	4.9	45.6	5.9	69.6	8.7
K. GUATEMALA[7]	B	.9	~	.4	~	.2	~	.2	~	.2	~	.2	~	3.1	~
M. HONDURAS	C	78.6	~	101.1	~	104.8	~	108.7	~	112.8	~	117.0	~	113.5	~
O. NICARAGUA	~	31.6[l]	6.4[l]	33.7[n]	6.7[m]	45.0[k]	8.7[k]	43.8[m]	8.1[m]	50.7[m]	8.8[m]	~	~	~	~
P. PANAMA	A	236.9	4.9	258.3	5.2	298.2	5.8	341.5	6.5	387.6	7.0	394.5	7.0	392.0	6.8
R. PERU[8]	A	~	~	68.2	12.8	64.1	11.8	53.0	10.2	43.2	8.4	43.6	8.4	37.0	6.6
S. URUGUAY[9]	A	268.7	7.6	233.8	6.0	192.6	6.0	193.3	4.8	231.4	5.4	263.4	6.0	287.7	6.2
T. VENEZUELA	A	~	~	~	~	~	~	~	~	~	~	~	~	~	~
UNITED STATES	A	7,929.0	8.5	7,406.0	7.7	6,991.0	7.1	6,202.0	6.1	6,137.0	5.8	7,637.0	7.1	8,273.0	7.6

1. The series generally represent the total number of persons wholly unemployed and temporarily laid off. The nature of Latin American economies makes gathering, reporting, and interpretation of unemployment somewhat difficult. Thus cautious use of the few data available is recommended.
2. Code: A, Labor force sample surveys and general household sample surveys; B, Employment office statistics; C, Official estimates.
3. Greater Buenos Aires.
4. Data relate to Rio de Janeiro, São Paulo, and other areas varying according to the surveys. Date exclude rural areas of Rondânia, Acre, Amazonas, Roraima, Pará, Amapá, Mato Grosso, and Goiás.
5. Greater Santiago.
6. Bogotá, Barranquilla, Bucaramanga, Cali, Manizales, Medellín, and Pasto.
7. Guatemala City, Quetzaltenango, Escuintla, and Puerto Barrios; prior to 1973 Guatemala City only.
8. Urban areas.
9. Montevideo.

a. April and Dec.
b. April and July.
c. April and Oct.
d. First quarter.
e. Fourth quarter.
f. Aug. and Dec.
g. Sept.
h. April.
i. Aug. 1974 - Feb. 1975.
j. July.
k. Oct.
l. Nov.
m. Oct.-Dec.
n. Aug.
o. Jan.-May.
p. Feb.-June.

SOURCE: ILO-YLS, 1970; 1983, table 9A.

Table 1327

UNEMPLOYMENT ACCORDING TO PREVIOUS JOB EXPERIENCE, 8 LC, 1971–82

(T)

Country	Category[1]	1971	1972	1973	1974	1975	1976	1977	1978	1979	1980	1981	1982
A. ARGENTINA[2,3]	A. Total	~	~	~	84.0	75.8	125.4	89.9	82.3	57.9	68.4	145.4	188.7
	B. Total	~	~	~	29.8	21.2	33.7	13.4	19.3	11.5	10.3	22.3	31.6
D. CHILE[3]	A. Total	~	~	~	~	308.2	264.9	259.9	343.5	336.1	273.9	321.3	~
	B. Total	~	~	~	~	159.4	140.9	118.6	151.8	138.1	104.4	95.7	~
E. COLOMBIA[3,4]	A. Total	~	~	~	~	161.95	175.70	164.52	157.59	194.33	217.78	233.02	~
	Male	~	~	~	~	95.09	112.86	93.37	89.35	106.24	122.76	~	~
	Female	~	~	~	~	66.86	62.83	71.15	68.24	88.09	95.01	~	~
	B. Total	~	~	~	~	91.17	93.34	96.48	86.05	98.56	103.02	108.17	~
	Male	~	~	~	~	41.97	42.43	39.58	37.10	38.53	39.01	~	~
	Female	~	~	~	~	49.21	50.91	56.89	48.95	60.03	64.01	~	~
F. COSTA RICA[3,5]	A. Total	~	~	~	~	~	23.18	22.33	23.27	25.17	35.35	~	62.66
	B. Total	~	~	~	~	~	17.74	9.11	9.40	11.08	10.21	~	15.91
P. PANAMA[3]	A. Total	27.70	18.00	~	21.50[a]	24.40[b]	24.60[c]	24.47[a]	21.17[c]	30.12[c]	~	~	~
	Male	~	~	~	14.90[a]	13.70[b]	15.49[c]	15.75[a]	12.21[c]	17.36[c]	~	~	~
	Female	~	~	~	6.60[a]	10.70[b]	9.11[c]	8.72[a]	8.96[c]	12.76[c]	~	~	~
	B. Total	8.60	15.20	~	8.50[a]	7.20[b]	9.10[c]	20.53[a]	22.61[c]	20.61[c]	~	~	~
	Male	~	~	~	4.80[a]	3.50[b]	3.55[c]	10.72[a]	11.20[c]	9.56[c]	~	~	~
	Female	~	~	~	3.70[a]	3.70[b]	5.55[c]	9.81[a]	11.41[c]	11.50[c]	~	~	~
R. PERU[3]	A. Total	149.5	144.5	139.5	132.3	~	~	~	~	~	~	~	~
	B. Total	46.2	49.5	52.0	54.6	~	~	~	~	~	~	~	~
S. URUGUAY[3,6]	A. Total	29.5	30.4[d]	35.5[d]	22.6[e]	~	46.1	425.0	32.2	29.0	28.0[d]	~	~
	B. Total	11.7	11.3[d]	13.9[d]	15.6[e]	~	22.1	21.6	17.8	13.4	15.6[d]	~	~
T. VENEZUELA[3,7]	A. Total	99.21	~	~	183.68	207.84	192.03	157.21	151.57	207.85	239.56[d]	244.88[d]	~
	Male	~	~	~	~	~	154.92	122.65	125.78	170.34	196.74[d]	203.89[d]	~
	Female	~	~	~	~	~	37.11	34.56	25.78	37.51	42.81[d]	44.99[d]	~
	B. Total	95.95	~	~	35.79	33.91	29.55	28.20	28.79	36.79	32.80[d]	40.17[d]	~
	Male	~	~	~	~	~	14.79	15.84	16.09	20.42	19.29[d]	22.49[d]	~
	Female	~	~	~	~	~	14.76	12.36	12.70	16.38	13.51[d]	17.67[d]	~
UNITED STATES[3]	A. Total	4,363	4,200	3,713	4,471	7,101	6,508	6,036	5,316	5,319	6,764	7,291	9,488
	Male	2,486	2,350	1,972	2,418	4,063	3,609	3,225	2,748	2,767	3,861	4,105	5,612
	Female	1,877	1,849	1,740	2,052	3,037	2,898	2,811	2,569	2,553	2,903	3,186	3,876
	B. Total	630	682	652	685	828	898	955	886	818	873	982	1,190
	Male	290	309	303	296	379	427	442	394	353	406	472	567
	Female	340	373	349	389	449	471	513	492	465	467	510	623

1. Category A refers to those with previous job experience. Category B refers to those seeking their first job.
2. Greater Buenos Aires.
3. Labor force sample survey or general household sample survey.
4. Seven main cities.
5. July of each year.
6. Montevideo.
7. Second semester.

a. Oct.
b. Nov.
c. Aug.
d. First semester.
e. Mean of the observation: Aug. 1974-Feb. 1975.

SOURCE: ILO-YLS, 1981; 1983, table 10A.

Table 1328

UNEMPLOYMENT BY SEX AND AGE GROUP, 5 LC, 1976-82

(T)

Country	Age Group	Male							Female						
		1976	1977	1978	1979	1980	1981	1982	1976	1977	1978	1979	1980	1981	1982
A. ARGENTINA[1,2]	-20	27.9	14.9	13.4	13.8	12.9	18.7	23.8	29.8	18.3	14.8	2.6	9.1	17.0	26.4
	20-24	9.1	8.5	13.5	10.8	9.2	23.1	19.3	16.2	15.0	9.7	12.9	9.9	14.8	17.2
	25-39	11.6	5.1	10.7	3.8	11.2	30.7	32.3	30.3	15.5	14.0	8.3	10.4	17.7	24.3
	40-49	6.4	7.3	7.5	.9	4.4	13.0	14.1	7.9	6.3	6.6	2.7	3.8	10.4	7.8
	50-59	13.8	5.5	4.5	4.3	6.1	17.3	17.6	3.0	5.2	3.1	5.1	2.0	6.1	4.8
	60+	1.3	1.7	2.5	4.2	2.0	5.1	5.1	.7	#	.4	#	1.2	.7	.7
	Unspecified	1.2	#	.4	#	#	#	#	#	#	.3	#	#	#	#
	Total	71.2	43.1	52.6	37.9	45.7	108.0	112.3	87.9	60.3	49.0	31.6	36.4	66.8	81.3
E. COLOMBIA[2,3,4]	-20	49.46	45.01	41.58	49.20	53.54	~	~	40.02	47.01	39.55	49.80	54.34	~	~
	20-29	62.08	53.22	57.12	62.11	73.70	~	~	52.65	57.78	58.90	71.82	78.56	~	~
	30-39	17.38	13.57	11.49	13.71	18.50	~	~	13.33	13.36	11.85	18.25	18.11	~	~
	40-49	12.72	9.77	7.52	8.85	6.48	~	~	6.01	6.90	4.81	6.84	5.75	~	~
	50-59	9.51	7.88	4.55	8.42	6.15	~	~	1.42	2.55	1.64	1.21	2.27	~	~
	60+	4.14	3.50	4.19	2.49	3.40	~	~	.30	.43	.43	.21	#	~	~
	Total	155.30	132.95	126.46	144.78	161.77	~	~	113.74	128.03	117.18	148.12	159.03	~	~
F. COSTA RICA[2,5]	-20	~	~	~	~	14.92	~	19.33	~	~	~	~	6.78	8.4	8.58
	20-29	~	~	~	~	9.70	~	19.65	~	~	~	~	5.97	8.7	11.62
	30-39	~	~	~	~	2.55	~	6.84	~	~	~	~	1.24	2.89	2.84
	40-49	~	~	~	~	1.34	~	4.12	~	~	~	~	.50	1.34	1.42
	50-59	~	~	~	~	1.27	~	2.10	~	~	~	~	.29	.45	.49
	60+	~	~	~	~		~		~	~	~	~			.04
	Unspecified	~	~	~	~	.89	~	.17	~	~	~	~	.12	.08	.07
	Total	~	~	~	~	30.67	~	53.51	~	~	~	~	14.90	21.83	25.06
P. PANAMA[2]	15-19	3.82	6.38	6.41	8.16	~	~	7.07	3.53	4.19	5.24	6.15	~	~	~
	20-29	8.76	11.98	10.82	11.84	~	~	13.95	7.52	10.30	10.94	11.64	~	~	~
	30-39	3.25	3.75	3.40	3.29	~	~	2.71	2.36	2.84	3.02	4.00	~	~	~
	40-49	1.69	2.25	1.48	1.58	~	~	1.44	1.04	.85	1.02	1.62	~	~	~
	50-59	.80	1.38	.75	1.41	~	~	.77	.17	.27	.11	.20	~	~	~
	60+	.72	.73	.55	.64	~	~	.74	.04	.08	.04	.20	~	~	~
	Total	19.04	26.47	23.41	26.92	~	~	26.68	14.66	18.53	20.37	23.81	~	~	~
T. VENEZUELA[2,6]	-20	52.16	42.36	46.49	55.39	63.79	62.71	69.64	16.32	15.18	12.17	15.27	14.14	16.34	12.23
	20-24	47.27	39.08	38.78	53.94	60.78	66.56	80.14	16.84	15.04	15.08	17.83	19.82	23.65	24.49
	25-34	35.40	29.15	29.53	44.76	50.71	56.63	68.45	12.43	11.25	8.54	16.17	17.52	17.28	21.94
	35-44	17.48	13.27	13.11	18.30	21.34	21.65	26.11	4.84	3.74	1.62	3.83	3.74	4.22	4.55
	45-54	9.98	8.86	8.42	10.69	10.60	10.92	14.12	1.08	1.20	.80	.32	1.00	.77	1.26
	55+	7.43	5.77	5.53	7.70	8.82	7.92	9.69	.36	.50	.28	.45	.10	.41	.69
	Total	169.71	138.49	141.87	190.76	216.04	226.39	268.15	51.87	46.91	38.49	53.88	56.33	62.66	65.16
UNITED STATES[2]	16-19	928.00	874.00	813.00	811.00	913.00	962.00	1,090	773.00	789.00	769.00	743.00	755.00	800.00	886.00
	20-24	924.00	877.00	768.00	744.00	1,076.00	1,144.00	1,407	746.00	752.00	714.00	697.00	760.00	833.00	985.00
	25-44	1,314.00	1,242.00	1,005.00	1,028.00	1,619.00	1,765.00	2,670	1,192.00	1,194.00	1,112.00	1,123.00	1,345.00	1,511.00	1,919.00
	45-54	414.00	326.00	277.00	272.00	357.00	390.00	550	345.00	340.00	275.00	268.00	318.00	325.00	416.00
	55-59	169.00	143.00	125.00	120.00	145.00	161.00	262	133.00	122.00	89.00	96.00	101.00	120.00	157.00
	60+	219.00	206.00	155.00	145.00	158.00	155.00	200	130.00	128.00	102.00	94.00	92.00	107.00	135.00
	Total	3,968.00	3,667.00	3,142.00	3,120.00	4,267.00	4,577.00	6,179	3,320.00	3,324.00	3,061.00	3,018.00	3,370.00	3,696.00	4,499

1. Greater Buenos Aires.
2. Labor force sample survey or general household sample survey.
3. Total of seven cities.
4. September of each year.
5. July.
6. Second semester.

SOURCE: ILO-YLS, 1983, table 9B.

Table 1329

URBAN OPEN UNEMPLOYMENT, 12 LR, 1970-82

(%)

Country	1970	1978	1979	1980	1981	1982
A. ARGENTINA	4.9	2.8	2.0	2.3	4.5	5.7

Continued in SALA, 23-1315.

Table 1330

MIDDLE AND UPPER CLASSES, 18 L, 1950-70

(%)

Country	1950	1960	1970
A. ARGENTINA	35.9	36.6	38.2
B. BOLIVIA	~	~	~
C. BRAZIL	15.2	15.3	18.6
D. CHILE	21.4	22.1	29.0
E. COLOMBIA	21.9	23.6	26.8
F. COSTA RICA	22.3	22.1	24.1
H. DOMINICAN REP.	~	13.6	18.2
I. EQUADOR	10.5	15.0	18.7
J. EL SALVADOR	10.5	12.2	13.6
K. GUATEMALA	7.7	12.3	11.8
M. HONDURAS	5.1	10.9	20.6
N. MEXICO	~	21.1	24.4
O. NICARAGUA	~	14.7	19.2
P. PANAMA	15.2	20.4	23.4
Q. PARAGUAY	14.2	14.3	15.7
R. PERU	~	18.1	23.2
S. URUGUAY	~	35.8	35.0
T. VENEZUELA	18.2	24.8	31.3

SOURCE: Carlos Filgueira and Carlo Genelitti, *Estratificación y Movilidad Ocupacional en América Latina*, ECLA–CC, E/CEPAL/G. 1122, Oct. 1981, p. 53.

Figure 13:1

THE MIDDLE CLASS, 17 L, 1950-70

(% of EAP)

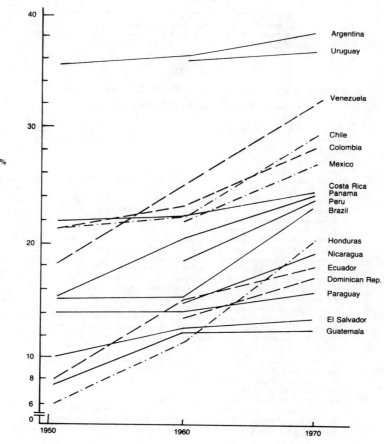

SOURCE: Table 1330, above.

Figure 13:2

MEXICO NEW SERIES ON THE CLASS STRUCTURE, 1895–1970, WITH ESTIMATION TO 1990

(%)

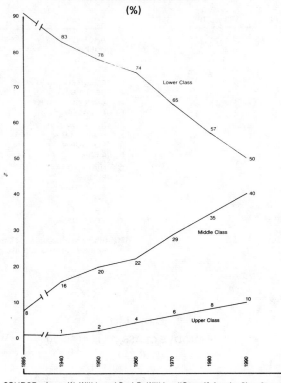

SOURCE: James W. Wilkie and Paul D. Wilkins, "Quantifying the Class Structure of
Mexico, 1895–1970," SALA, 22, ch. 36, p. 585; and estimation here for 1980
and 1990.

Table 1331

MEXICO SOCIAL MODERNIZATION INDEX (SMI)[1], 1930–70

(Zero Indicates Complete Modernization)[2]

Category[3]	1930[e]	1940	1950	1960	1970
Selected Rural[a]	69.1	67.7	61.1	54.6	46.2
Selected Semiurban[b]	34.0	30.8	25.6	20.7	16.5
Selected Urban[c]	10.5	7.2	5.9	6.1	5.2
National Average[d]	52.6	48.6	40.7	33.5	24.1

1. Nonmodern persons live in social isolation (are [1] illiterate, [2] speak Indian and
   Spanish, or [3] do not speak Spanish) and geographic isolation (definition as
   [4] living in localities of less than 2,500 persons), eat a nonmodern diet (measured
   by [5] share of persons who habitually consume tortillas instead of wheat bread),
   and have traditional dress patterns (those who [6] go barefoot or who [7] wear
   sandals instead of shoes). These seven items in the SMI are averaged with equal
   weight because there is no theoretical reason to assume that any one component is
   more important than the others as a measure of modernization.
2. The SMI divides the total of seven components by five values instead of seven
   because non-Spanish speakers and bilingual persons are both part of a larger category
   of Indian speakers, and barefoot persons and sandal-wearers are subcategories of the
   larger category of shoeless persons.
3. Represents 103 sample municipios from the 2,367 Mexican municipios including
   the municipio in each state which had the highest percentage of illiterates in 1940,
   the capital of each of the 32 Mexican states, and 40 municipios represented in the
   community-study literature.

a. Municipios which in 1930 had more than 50% of the population living in localities of
   less than 2,500 persons.
b. Municipios not included in "Rural" or "Urban."
c. Mexico City, Guadalajara, and Monterrey.
d. Includes all of Mexico's population in 2,367 municipios.
e. Variance between seven-item average (seven items, five values) and four-item average
   (four items, three values) in 1940 is used to link the 1930 index to make it comparable
   to the post-1940 index.

SOURCE: Stephen Haber, "Modernization and Change in Mexican Communities, 1930–
1970," SALA, 22, ch. 40.

Figure 13:3

SMI FOR RURAL, SEMIURBAN, AND URBAN CATEGORIES, 1930–70

(100 = Nonmodern Characteristics)

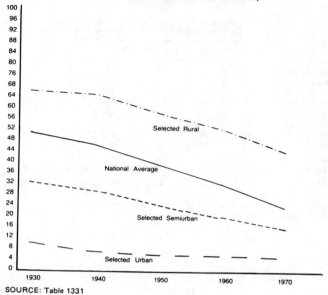

SOURCE: Table 1331

Figure 13:4

SOCIAL POVERTY INDEX FOR MEXICO, 1910–70

(%)

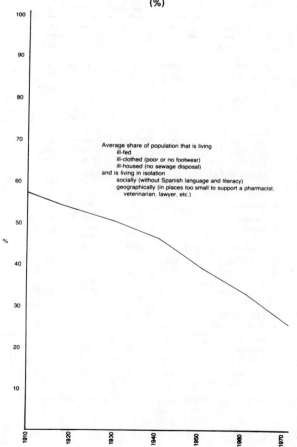

Average share of population that is living
    ill-fed
    ill-clothed (poor or no footwear)
    ill-housed (no sewage disposal)
and is living in isolation
    socially (without Spanish language and literacy)
    geographically (in places too small to support a pharmacist,
        veterinarian, lawyer, etc.)

SOURCE: James W. Wilkie, *La Revolución Mexicana (1910-1976): Gasto Público y Cambio Social* (México, D.F.: Fondo de Cultura Económica, 1978), p. 384.

Table 1332

ABSOLUTE POVERTY ESTIMATES, 10 LR
(%, Ca. 1970)

Country	Households Below the Poverty Line			Households Below the Extreme Poverty Line		
	Urban	Rural	National	Urban	Rural	National
A. ARGENTINA	5	19	8	1	1	1
C. BRAZIL	35	73	49	15	42	25
D. CHILE	12	25	17	3	11	6
E. COLOMBIA	38	54	45	14	23	18
F. COSTA RICA	15	30	24	5	7	6
M. HONDURAS	40	75	65	15	57	45
N. MEXICO	20	49	34	6	18	12
R. PERU	28	68	50	8	39	25
S. URUGUAY	10	~	~	4	~	~
T. VENEZUELA	20	36	25	6	19	10
LATIN AMERICA	26	62	40	10	34	19

SOURCE: Oscar Altimir, *La Dimensión de la Pobreza en América Latina,* ECLA-CC, No. 27 (Santiago, Chile, 1979), p. 63.

Table 1333

AVAILABILITY OF CRIMINAL STATISTICS FOR LATIN AMERICA AND THE ENGLISH-SPEAKING CARIBBEAN

Country	Data Year Utilized in 1978 Survey			
	Crimes	Arrests	Sentenced	Inmates
A. ARGENTINA	~	1975	1976	1975
Bahamas	1973	~	1973	1973
Barbados	1973	~	1973	1973
B. BOLIVIA	1977	1977	~	1977
C. BRAZIL	~	1973	~	1973
E. COLOMBIA	1975	1975	1974	1975
F. COSTA RICA	1974	~	1977	1978
D. CHILE	~	1975	1975	1975
G. CUBA	1977	1977	1977	~
Dominica	1974	~	1973	1973
I. ECUADOR	~	~	~	1976
J. EL SALVADOR	~	1975	1975	1971
K. GUATEMALA	~	1974	1969	~
Guyana	1973	~	~	1973
L. HAITI	~	~	~	~
M. HONDURAS	~	1957	1957	~
Jamaica	1976	1971	1976	1976
N. MEXICO	~	~	1972	~
O. NICARAGUA	~	~	1974	~
P. PANAMA	~	1976	1976	1977
Q. PARAGUAY	1977	~	~	1977
R. PERU	1976	1976	~	1976
H. DOMINICAN REP.	~	~	1978	~
Trinidad and Tobago	1974	~	1974	1975
S. URUGUAY	~	1975	~	~
T. VENEZUELA	1973	~	~	1972
Number of Countries				
With Data	13	13	17	18
Without Data	13	13	9	8
Mean Delay for Reporting Countries	3.23	4.46	5.00	3.29

SOURCE: SALA, 23-3603. See SALA, 23, Chap. 36 for other data.

Table 1334

PERSONS ARRESTED, 5 L, 1965-70

	Country	1965	1966	1967	1968	1969	1970
C.	BRAZIL	47,094	49,606	50,323	62,721	69,809	~
D.	CHILE	548,944	610,729	614,049	647,048	~	~
J.	EL SALVADOR	47,599	55,999	54,875	50,817	46,892	43,550
K.	GUATEMALA	85,609	69,566	~	~	~	~
P.	PANAMA	27,584	28,440	33,671	35,926	36,320	36,206

SOURCE: IASI-AC, 1967 and 1972, table 603-01.

Table 1335

PRISON POPULATION, 4 L, 1965-70

	Country	1965	1966	1967	1968	1969	1970
C.	BRAZIL	23,385	24,219	22,534	24,767	27,521	28,538
E.	COLOMBIA	32,088	31,816	~	~	~	~
J.	EL SALVADOR	11,043	5,148	5,541	5,745	5,729	5,425
T.	VENEZUELA	9,025	10,519	10,858	11,492	11,278	11,144

SOURCE: IASI-AC, 1967 and 1972, table 603-01.

CHAPTER 14

WAGES AND INCOME DISTRIBUTION

Table 1400

COMPENSATION OF EMPLOYEES AND NATIONAL INCOME,[1] 15 LC, 1962–75

(M of NC)

	Country	Code[2]	1962	1965	1967	1968	1969	1970	1971	1972	1973	1974	1975
A.	ARGENTINA	A	~	~	58,700	67,900	79,600	93,800	124,451	209,460	350,376	469,022	1,289,312
		B	~	~	24,200	27,300	31,500	38,500	55,928	85,813	156,638	208,963	579,370
		C	~	~	41.2	40.2	39.6	41.0	44.9	41.0	44.7	44.6	44.9

Continued in SALA, 21-1404.

Table 1401

WAGES IN NONAGRICULTURAL ACTIVITIES,[1] 8 LC, 1965–82

	Country	1965	1970	1975	1976	1977	1978	1979	1980	1981	1982
B.	BOLIVIA[2,3]	~	1,015.05	1,750	1,750	2,518	2,716	3,979	4,380	4,390	~
F.	COSTA RICA[4]	~	~	1,338	1,487	1,639	1,854	2,104	2,411[a]	2,977	4,513
G.	CUBA	~	~	140	143	145	148	151	154	~	~
M.	HONDURAS[3,5,6]	~	~	43.21	58.54	53.09	68.47	77.54	93.52	130.28	197.84
O.	NICARAGUA[3,7,8]	~	~	5.92	6.33	6.60	6.96	8.73	11.23	~	~
R.	PERU[9,10]	73	115	260	314	379	516	753	1,432[b]	2,428	3,979
S.	URUGUAY[11,12,13]	~	100	1,593	2,226	3,067	4,242	6,378	9,860	14,424	17,054
T.	VENEZUELA[4,14]	~	1,201	1,523	1,547	2,284	2,548	2,265	2,733	3,102	~
	UNITED STATES[7]	2.45	3.22	4.53	4.86	5.25	5.69	6.16	6.66	7.25	7.67

1. The wage series shown in this table cover the following divisions of economic activity: mining and quarrying; manufacturing; electricity, gas, and water; construction; wholesale and retail trade, restaurants, and hotels; transports, storage, and communication; financing, insurance, real estate, and business services; community, social, and personal services. In some cases, however, these divisions are only represented by certain of the groups composing them.
2. Rates per month.
3. Includes salaried employees.
4. Earnings per month.
5. Establishments with ten or more persons employed.
6. Earnings per week.
7. Earnings per hour.
8. Excluding electricity, gas, water, wholesale and retail trade, restaurants, hotels, financing, insurance, real estate, business services, and community, social, and personal services.
9. Excluding mining, quarrying, electricity, gas and water.
10. Earnings per day for Lima only during May of each year.
11. For Montevideo only.
12. Excluding mining and quarrying.
13. For private sector employees with an index of average monthly earnings (1968 = 100).
14. Excluding construction and transport.

a. Includes only an eleven-month average.
b. Prior to 1980, data were taken at June of each year.

SOURCE: ILO-YLS, 1975, table 18; 1983, table 16.

Table 1402
WAGES IN MANUFACTURING,[1] 18 LC, 1965–82
(NC)

Total	Specification	1965	1970	1975	1976	1977	1978	1979	1980	1981	1982
A. ARGENTINA[2]	Pesos/hour	69.30	1.65[a]	20	62	134	237	604	1,476	~	~
B. BOLIVIA[3]	Pesos/month	~	902.22	1,709	1,709	2,339	1,898	3,926	4,279	4,301	~
C. BRAZIL[3,4]	Cruzeiros/month	~	442.36	1,938	2,844	~	~	~	~	~	~
D. CHILE[10,11]	Pesos/month	212.14	1,041.63	206	805	2,258	3,886	5,721	8,774	11,781	13,005
E. COLOMBIA	Pesos/hour	3.65	6.47	13.18	16.34	20.54	26.56	35.69	47.30	~	~
F. COSTA RICA[14]	Colones/month	~	~	1,123	1,290	1,445	1,642	1,889	2,334[b]	2,763	4,335
G. CUBA[3,15]	Pesos/month	~	~	141	141	150	~	~	~	~	~
H. DOMINICAN REP.[3]	Pesos/month	76.59	72.06	120.25	136.28	132.93	145.75	149.72	~	~	~
I. ECUADOR	Sucres/hour	3.22	6.10	13.20	16.30	18.20	19.90	25.3	35.8	39.9	~
J. EL SALVADOR[5]	Colones/hour	.81	.94	1.14	1.45	1.56	1.69	1.90	2.61	2.76	~
K. GUATEMALA	Centavos/hour	37.3	43.30	.46	.49	.53	.60	.63	~	~	~
M. HONDURAS[3,16]	Lempiras/week	~	~	41.30	50.13	48.54	55.71	87.24	70.35	83.94	124.42
N. MEXICO	Pesos/month	1,324	1,703	3,412	4,292	5,618	6,465	7,552	9,103	12,006	~
O. NICARAGUA[3]	Córdobas/hour	2.08	~	5.54	5.96	6.31	6.65	8.62	10.90	~	~
P. PANAMA	Balboas/hour	.65	.80	1.07	1.12	1.19	1.19	1.25	~	~	~
R. PERU[6,7,12,13]	Soles/day	75.54	120.50	255	325	394	539	786	1,477	2,470	4,115
S. URUGUAY[8,9]	Index: 1968 = 100	~	100	1,492	2,031	2,758	3,788	5,688	8,844	12,653	~
T. VENEZUELA	Bolívares/month	793.0	959.90	1,473	1,514	1,653	1,870	2,177	2,621	2,955	~
UNITED STATES	Dollars/hours	2.61	3.36	4.83	5.22	5.68	6.17	6.70	7.27	7.99	8.50

1. The figures generally relate to average earnings of all wage-earners. They normally include bonuses, cost of living allowances, taxes, social insurance contributions payable by the employed person and, in some cases, payment in kind. They normally exclude social insurance contributions payable by the employers, family allowances, and other social security benefits. Unless otherwise indicated, figures relate to earnings of both male and female wage-earners.
2. Minimum earnings; unskilled workers.
3. Including salaried employees.
4. 1964-65, production workers.
5. Metropolitan area. Figures are for male wage-earners only. Data for female wage-earners are as follows: 1965 — .57; 1970 — .77; 1975 — 1.03; 1976 — 1.25; 1977 — 1.26; 1978 — 1.39; 1979 — 1.50; 1980 — 2.12; 1981 — 2.37.
6. Lima and Callao.
7. May of each year.

8. Montevideo only.
9. Private sector; employees; index of average monthly earnings.
10. Including the value of payments in kind.
11. April of each year.
12. Lima only after 1975.
13. Prior to 1980; June of each year.
14. Insured persons since 1975.
15. Including mining and quarrying, electricity, gas, and water for the years 1975-77.
16. Includes establishments with ten or more persons employed.

a. New currency introduced in January 1970: 1 new peso = 100 old pesos.
b. An eleven-month average.

SOURCE: ILO-YLS, 1975, table 19; 1983, table 17A.

Table 1403
WAGES IN CONSTRUCTION,[1] 15 LC, 1965–82
(NC)

Country	Specification	1965	1970	1975	1976	1977	1978	1979	1980	1981	1982
A. ARGENTINA[2,3,4]	Pesos/hour	76.44	1.79	~	~	~	~	~	~	~	~
B. BOLIVIA[6]	Pesos/month	~	775	1,609	1,609	2,053	1,687	~	4,377	4,412	~
C. BRAZIL	Cruzeiros/hour	~	~	~	~	~	~	~	~	~	~
F. COSTA RICA	Colones/month	~	~	883	1,008	1,166	1,360	1,561	1,851[a]	~	3,370
G. CUBA[6]	Pesos/month	~	~	157	153	145	154	160	164	~	~
J. EL SALVADOR[7]	Colones/hour	.70	.69	~	~	~	~	~	~	~	~
K. GUATEMALA	Quetzales/week	~	~	~	~	~	~	~	~	~	~
M. HONDURAS[5,6]	Lempiras/week	~	~	36.52	54.12	56.47	74.52	45.36	77.59	168.54	241.50
N. MEXICO[8]	Pesos/hour	3.40	5.31	11.51	15.56	18.23	20.73	22.21	29.13	34.92	~
O. NICARAGUA[6]	Córdobas/hour	~	~	5.40	5.81	5.98	6.54	7.94	9.94	~	~
P. PANAMA	Balboas/week	~	~	~	~	~	~	~	~	~	~
Q. PARAGUAY	Guaraníes/month	~	~	~	~	~	~	~	~	~	~
R. PERU[9]	Soles/day	81.16	117.25	289	337	384	516	808	1,414	2,300	4,211
S. URUGUAY[10]	1970 = 100	~	100.0	2,064	2,815	3,856	5,279	7,912	12,320	18,707	~
T. VENEZUELA[11]	Bolívares/day	~	~	~	~	~	~	~	~	~	~
UNITED STATES	Dollars/hour	3.55	5.08	7.31	7.71	8.10	8.66	9.27	9.94	10.80	11.62

1. Unless otherwise indicated the data pertain to the average nominal gross wages (i.e., before tax deductions and the workers' social security contribution) of construction workers.
2. Minimum earnings.
3. Unskilled workers.
4. To make the series uniform, wages to 1969 were converted to new pesos which equal 100 of the former pesos.
5. Establishments with ten or more persons employed.
6. Including salaried employees.
7. Males only: metropolitan area of San Salvador.

8. October of each year.
9. Lima; mean of the observation: May of each year; prior to 1980, June of each year.
10. Montevideo; private sector only and including salaried employees; index of average monthly wage rates.
11. The data refer to the average nominal wages of electricians in Caracas during the fourth trimester of the year indicated.

a. Mean of the observation: eleven-month average.

SOURCE: ILO-YLS , 1975, table 21; 1983, table 19.

Table 1404

WAGES IN TRANSPORT, STORAGE, AND COMMUNICATION,[1] 13 LC, 1965-82

(NC)

Country	Specification	1965	1970	1975	1976	1977	1978	1979	1980	1981	1982
A. ARGENTINA[2,3]	Road Haulage/hour	58.88	1.67[b]	~	~	~	~	~	~	~	~
B. BOLIVIA[5]	Transports/month	~	982	1,717	1,717	2,577	2,026	~	5,074	5,183	~
C. BRAZIL[4]	Per month	~	~	~	~	~	~	~	~	~	~
F. COSTA RICA[10]	Per month	~	~	1,289	1,433	1,591	1,788	2,042	2,305[a]	2,683	4,790
G. CUBA[5]	Transports/month	~	~	162	168	172	173	177	180	~	~
M. HONDURAS[5,9]	Per week	~	~	109.10	49.72	58.01	81.56	82.98	74.30	172.80	253.26
N. MEXICO[6]	Transports/hour	8.00	8.09	~	~	~	~	~	~	~	~
O. NICARAGUA[5]	Per hour	~	~	5.60	6.17	6.71	6.71	7.48	11.17	~	~
P. PANAMA	Per week	~	~	~	~	~	~	~	~	~	~
Q. PARAGUAY	Per month	~	~	299	335	403	514	834	1,787	3,087	5,062
R. PERU[7]	Transport/day	95.34	115.76	1,333	1,830	2,481	3,397	5,092	8,030	11,655	~
S. URUGUAY[5,8]	Index: 1970 = 100	~	100	~	~	~	~	~	~	~	~
T. VENEZUELA	Bus Drivers/day	~	~	~	~	~	~	~	~	~	~
UNITED STATES	Principal Railways/hour	3.00	3.89	6.05	6.88	7.39	7.87	8.94	9.92	10.65	11.50

1. Unless otherwise indicated, the data pertain to the average nominal gross wages (i.e., before income tax deduction and the workers' social security contribution) in national currency of workers in transport, storage, and communications. Details concerning the type of work and earnings are included under the column "specifications." Due to the use of different data sources, not all specifications are equally detailed for every country.
2. Minimum earnings: unskilled workers.
3. To make the series uniform wages for 1963 to 1969 were converted to new pesos which equal 100 of the former pesos.
4. Includes workers in maritime transport.
5. Data include salaried employees.
6. October of each year.
7. Lima area; May of each year; prior to 1980, June of each year.
8. Montevideo; private sector only.
9. Establishments with ten or more persons employed.
10. Insured persons.

a. Eleven-month average.
b. New currency Jan. 1970: 1 new peso = 100 old pesos.

SOURCE: ILO-YLS, 1975, table 22; 1983, table 20.

Table 1405

WAGES IN AGRICULTURE,[1] 15 LC, 1965-82
(NC)

Country/Specification	Code	1965	1970	1975	1976	1977	1978	1979	1980	1981	1982
A. ARGENTINA[2]											
Unskilled Workers	M-I-H	43.99	1.14[c]	16.83	50.29	106.32	?	?	?	?	?
C. BRAZIL[3]											
Workers in Rice Production	H	?	?	?	?	?	?	?	?	?	?
D. CHILE[3,4]	M-I-D	3.26	12.00	4.35[b]	17.81	41.44	60.45	79.97	108.25	155.44	172.86
E. COLOMBIA	M-I-D	11.95	19.30								
	F-I-D	9.55	14.75								
	MF-I-D	?	?	61.75	61.75	92.13	119.13	147.63	181.50	?	?
F. COSTA RICA[3]											
General Farm Hands:											
Coffee Plantations	MF-III-H	1.28	1.34	2.52	3.00	3.39	4.00	4.50	5.30	6.50	12.00
Agriculture and Livestock	MF-III-H	1.15	1.21	2.52	3.00	3.39	?	?	?	?	?
G. CUBA[5,7]	MF-I-Mo	?	?	129	133	113	116	121	129	?	?
J. EL SALVADOR[6]											
Permanent Workers	M-I-D	?	2.25	3.10	3.75	3.75	4.25	5.20	5.20	?	?
	F-I-D	?	1.75	2.50	3.15	3.15	3.65	4.60	4.60	?	?
M. HONDURAS[7]											
Establishments with Ten or More Persons Employed	W	?	?	**	**	30.69	28.90	39.92	108.82	183.72	91.83
N. MEXICO[3]											
Regular Day Laborers	M-II-D	13.47	21.20	46.10	?	76.48	88.50	106.81	134.16	178.87	?
O. NICARAGUA	W	?	?	238	266	310	330	402	593	?	?
P. PANAMA											
Agriculture, Silviculture, Hunting and Fishing	W	?	19.49	?	?	?	?	?	?	?	?
Q. PARAGUAY	Mo	?	5,603	?	?	?	?	?	?	?	?
R. PERU											
General Farm Hands	MF-I-D	?	?	?	?	?	?	?	?	?	?
S. URUGUAY[8]											
General Farm Hands	MF-I-Mo	920	17,315	206[a]	262	460	662	1,049	1,500	1,832	?
	MF-II-Mo	530	12,070	140[a]	178	260	374	412	848	1,035	?
T. VENEZUELA											
Agricultural Workers	D	?	?	?	?	?	?	?	?	?	?
General Farm Hands	D	?	?	?	?	?	?	?	?	?	?
UNITED STATES	MF-I-H	?	?	2.60	2.81	3.06	3.22	3.58	3.82	?	?
	MF-I-II-III-H	?	?	2.43	2.66	2.87	3.09	3.39	3.66	?	?

1. The statistics of agricultural wages presented in this table refer in most cases to wages paid in national currency to general farm laborers. A distinction is made between permanent workers, seasonal workers, and day workers; in the last mentioned group, regular day laborers and casual day laborers are distinguished. These distinctions as well as any further details are included under Specifications. The methods of payment and the types of labor contracts and arrangements in agriculture are often quite different from those in other activities. To indicate the sex of the laborer and the nature of the wage statistics, special notations have been adopted under Code. The key to this Code is as follows:

M — Male laborer
F — Female laborer
MF — Both male and female
I — Complete Wage — workers remunerated wholly in cash
II — Cash part only of remuneration — where received partly in cash and partly in kind.
III — Cash part of remuneration — where received partly in cash and partly in kind — as well as the estimated value of payments in kind for board and lodging.
H — Hourly earnings
D — Daily earnings
W — Weekly earnings
Mo — Monthly earnings

Owing to the use of different data sources, not all details of labor arrangements are available in every country.

2. To make the series uniform, wages from 1963 to 1969 were converted to new pesos which equal 100 of the former pesos.
3. Minimum wages.
4. Adults only.
5. Includes forestry and fishing.
6. Department of San Salvador.
7. Includes salaried employees.
8. December of each year.

a. New currency July 1975: 1 peso = 1,000 old pesos.
b. New currency Sept. 1975: 1 peso = 1,000 old escudos.
c. New currency Jan. 1970: 1 new peso = 100 old pesos.

SOURCE: ILO-YLS, 1975, table 23; 1983, table 21.

Table 1406

EVOLUTION OF REAL WAGES, 10 LR, 1978-82

(1970 = 100)

Country	Minimum Real Salaries					Real Industrial Salaries					Real Construction Salaries				
	1978	1979	1980	1981	1982	1978	1979	1980	1981	1982	1978	1979	1980	1981	1982
A. ARGENTINA[1]	50.5	46.8	55.0	53.6	49.1	72.3	83.1	92.9	82.9	73.8	60.6	59.2	63.7	58.7	~
C. BRAZIL[2]	99.4	99.4	101.7	100.6	100.0	126.7	126.4	128.4	135.1	139.4	102.9	96.6	93.7	96.0	~
D. CHILE[3]	76.5	75.8	76.0	75.3	75.0	84.0	92.5	103.8	115.9	102.9	85.1	101.0	102.3	108.1	95.6
E. COLOMBIA[4]	105.8	96.0	127.3	124.4	~	90.9	107.2	97.6	97.4	~	102.5	109.3	117.2	120.6	~
F. COSTA RICA[5]	110.6	113.1	112.6	101.4	92.6	125.5	128.7	126.4	110.2	89.0	126.9	133.3	128.7	125.1	98.4
I. ECUADOR[6]	95.2	115.2	203.7	201.2	~	134.7	142.8	171.1	168.0	~	120.9	109.2	97.5	91.4	~
M. HONDURAS[7]	78.3	85.5	78.3	73.5	~	108.8	135.3	105.9	100.0	~	133.8	134.7	131.5	136.0	~
N. MEXICO[8]	120.9	117.7	110.0	110.7	109.6	122.4	121.0	115.4	119.0	119.0					
R. PERU[9]	66.1	67.3	83.3	70.3	~	84.9	73.8	87.7	86.2	86.2	83.5	78.0	87.4	86.5	93.8
T. VENEZUELA[10]	72.9	64.9	105.6	92.0	85.9	118.7	123.3	122.1	117.5	116.0	109.9	116.1	111.3	104.1	~
LATIN AMERICA[11]	90.6	88.6	92.3	90.8	88.9	110.1	111.9	114.6	116.4	115.5	98.7	96.9	96.5	97.2	**
Relation of Minimum Salary to Industrial Salary	82.3	79.2	80.5	78.0	77.0	**	**	**	**	**	**	**	**	**	**
Relation of Construction Salary to Industrial Salary	**	**	**	**	**	**	**	**	**	**	90.4	86.2	84.6	83.7	~

1. Minimum Salary figures for 1982 are based on a January to September average. Industrial Salary figures refer to salaries paid to national laborers.
2. Minimum Salary figures for 1982 are based on a January to August average. Industrial Salary figures refer to the national average of individual employee monthly salaries and for 1982 are based on a January to June average. Construction Salaries refer to day laborers.
3. All figures are based on a January to October average.
4. National Industrial Salaries. For Construction Salaries the index is 1971 = 100.
5. Minimum Salary figures for 1982 are based on a January to August average. National 1982 Industrial Salary and Construction Salary data are based on a January to March average.
6. National Industrial Salaries.
7. Industrial Salary data since 1973.
8. Minimum Salary figures for 1982 are based on a January to July average. Industrial Salary figures are national, refer to salaries paid to laborers, and for 1982 are based on a January to April average. Construction Salary figures are national. Cf. SALA, 21-1405.
9. Industrial Salary figures for 1982 refer to Metropolitan Lima and are based on a January to April average. Construction Salary figures are national.
10. Minimum Salary figures for 1982 are based on a January to August average. Industrial Salary figures for 1982 are based on a January to June average. Construction Salary figures are national.
11. Figures are averages only of those countries with continuous information.

SOURCE: ECLA-N, No. 372, 1982, table 2.

Table 1407

REAL WAGE INDEXES,[1] 18 L, 1965–80

(1970 = 100)

Country	Code	1965	1966	1967	1968	1969	1970	1971	1972	1973	1974	1975	1976	1977	1978	1979	1980
A. ARGENTINA	Sm	128.6	130.5	102.7	87.7	103.2	100.0	106.8	95.0	111.8	136.4	101.8	52.7	50.9	50.5	46.8	55.0
	Si(1)	102.7	104.2	106.1	93.9	96.4	100.0	101.8	94.2	103.0	106.7	104.8	60.3	54.5	47.3	47.9	56.7
	Si(2)	#	#	#	#	#	100.0	103.4	98.3	104.4	117.9	111.7	74.2	81.4	79.7	90.4	~
	Sc(m)	104.2	102.0	104.5	95.3	97.2	100.0	101.1	93.0	103.1	110.1	137.4	73.2	72.1	60.6	~	~
	Sa(m)	94.3	93.4	96.1	87.3	90.8	100.0	113.6	103.1	115.4	132.5	122.8	67.5	61.8	54.4	~	~
B. BOLIVIA	Sm	#	#	#	#	#	100.0	96.3	90.7	76.0	130.0	131.3	148.3	174.0	157.7	182.3	~
	Si	113.2	99.2	86.7	100.1	101.3	100.0	112.8	110.8	118.4	95.7	92.7	110.1	105.7	107.0	97.4	81.5
	Sc	#	#	#	#	#	100.0	118.0	116.4	108.7	99.1	89.6	109.3	102.1	115.0	104.5	97.0
	Sa	#	#	#	#	#	#	#	#	#	#	#	#	#	#	#	#
C. BRAZIL	Sm	117.5	109.0	105.6	106.8	101.7	100.0	100.0	102.8	98.3	91.5	96.0	97.2	97.7	99.4	99.4	101.7
	Si(1)	90.5	93.7	94.3	98.6	105.2	100.0	98.9	115.5	109.8	116.4	#	#	#	#	#	#
	Si(2)	#	#	#	94.6	98.1	100.0	104.1	113.5	114.4	117.0	128.2	132.7	138.3	145.2	147.5	155.3
	Sc	#	#	#	#	102.3	100.0	105.1	102.9	98.3	100.0	105.1	108.6	114.3	117.7	113.1	113.7
	Sa	#	109.3	109.3	104.7	100.9	100.0	105.6	109.3	121.5	138.3	143.9	140.2	144.9	150.5	~	~
D. COLOMBIA	Sm	130.7	108.9	100.7	95.1	88.0	100.0	91.8	82.0	83.1	93.6	96.7	84.4	97.6	105.8	96.0	127.3
	Si	87.9	83.4	85.1	88.6	88.1	100.0	98.6	87.9	87.2	83.2	80.2	83.9	82.1	90.9	97.4	97.6
	Sc(1)	125.8	109.8	107.7	108.9	101.7	100.0	104.0	#	#	#	#.	#	#	#	#	#
	Sc(2)	#	#	#	#	#	100.0	96.5	90.9	89.6	97.5	94.2	89.5	102.5	109.3	117.2
	Sa	100.0	99.6	95.2	94.8	105.2	100.0	#	#	#	#	#	121.3	140.8	150.4	146.8	148.2
	Sa(m)	145.4	121.2	111.9	105.8	96.8	100.0	91.9	82.3	85.0	125.8	142.3	124.2	143.5	157.3	143.1	205.8
E. CHILE	Sm	107.9	108.7	109.7	103.4	102.6	100.0	105.7	77.6	49.8	62.9	62.9	65.5	69.4	81.8	81.1	81.3
	Si	68.3	78.2	85.3	89.4	93.6	100.0	117.8	98.3	60.2	69.4	62.2	70.1	80.3	89.8	99.0	111.0
	Sc	#	#	95.8	96.5	95.5	100.0	128.7	140.4	89.0	85.6	87.4	91.9	95.4	91.0	108.0	109.5
	Sa	78.1	84.2	87.8	84.4	82.8	100.0	131.7	121.1	84.2	78.6	86.7	106.7	116.1	112.8	111.9	111.9
	PEM	#	#	#	#	#	#	#	#	#	#	100.0	90.9	64.8	51.4	45.6	43.4
F. COSTA RICA	Sm	100.3	100.3	99.4	97.7	102.0	100.0	104.0	102.0	95.4	88.6	88.3	96.3	102.6	110.6	113.1	112.6
	Si(ss)	#	81.4	87.5	94.7	96.4	100.0	110.9	107.6	105.1	99.2	95.6	108.2	117.6	125.5	128.7	126.4
	Sc(ss)	#	#	#	#	#	100.0	102.4	105.9	110.2	90.5	94.1	103.8	115.2	126.9	133.3	128.7
	Sa(ss)	#	#	#	#	#	100.0	98.7	95.2	87.8	88.3	101.6	125.3	137.2	149.5	149.7
	Sa(m)	100.8	100.4	99.2	98.1	102.3	100.0	104.2	103.1	99.6	100.8	102.7	118.1	128.2	142.5	146.7	~
H. DOMINICAN REP.	Sm	98.5	99.8	98.0	96.4	98.1	100.0	108.3	108.6	94.4	83.4	104.7	97.1	86.1	83.2	~	~
	Si	86.4	92.2	85.0	90.8	107.7	100.0	101.9	102.4	93.8	95.8	95.3	~	~	~	~	~
	Sc(m)	100.1	107.0	105.0	103.2	105.1	100.0	97.1	90.1	78.2	69.1	90.4	83.7	74.2	71.8	~	~
	Sa	#	#	#	#	#	#	#	#	#	#	#	#	#	#	#	#
I. ECUADOR	Sm	#	#	#	111.7	105.0	100.0	115.3	106.8	94.7	102.3	103.5	120.2	106.3	95.2	115.2	203.7
	Si	79.0	79.8	82.0	86.2	98.2	100.0	104.2	114.0	113.7	114.1	122.0	133.2	133.7	132.2	140.2	163.3
	Sc	#	#	#	#	#	100.0	#	#	#	#	#	#	#	#	#	#
	Sa(m)	#	#	#	111.8	105.1	100.0	92.2	85.6	75.8	95.3	88.7	102.4	90.7	81.3	103.6	169.8
J. EL SALVADOR	Sm	99.0	100.0	105.2	102.1	103.1	100.0	100.0	97.9	117.7	126.0	128.1	119.8	107.3	107.3	#	#
	Si	85.5	93.3	96.4	98.4	99.5	100.0	101.0	99.5	100.0	95.9	74.1	88.6	75.1	81.9	81.9	93.3
	Sc	106.1	100.8	94.7	98.5	91.7	100.0	103.8	109.8	114.4	101.5	#	#	#	#	#	#
	Sa(m)	105.9	107.4	105.9	102.9	102.9	100.0	100.0	98.5	100.0	100.0	91.2	98.5	92.6	92.6	100.0	85.3
K. GUATEMALA	Sm	107.7	107.0	106.6	104.7	102.3	100.0	100.4	100.0	89.4	91.5	80.9	73.0	64.9	60.0	53.8	84.3
	Si	93.3	95.8	98.3	99.6	102.3	100.0	100.5	100.9	88.3	76.8	70.5	68.9	65.3	68.6	70.5	63.1
	Sc(1)(ss)	#	#	#	#	#	#	#	#	100.0	77.3	105.1	116.2	87.5	106.4	120.3	110.7
	Sc(2)	100.2	107.3	112.9	112.3	113.2	100.0	98.3	94.0	83.0	79.1	102.5	~	~	~	~	~
	Sa(ss)	#	#	#	#	#	#	#	#	100.0	101.4	102.3	93.5	84.3	87.6	85.3	74.2
	Sa(m)	#	#	#	#	#	#	#	#	#	100.0	88.7	80.1	71.1	65.6	59.0	117.2
M. HONDURAS	Sm	#	#	#	#	#	#	#	#	#	100.0	92.8	88.0	81.9	78.3	85.5	78.3
	Si	#	#	#	#	#	#	#	#	#	100.0	87.5	97.1	111.8	100.0	108.8	135.3	105.9
	Sc	#	#	#	#	#	#	#	#	100.0	86.5	68.1	100.6	96.9	120.9	102.0	97.5
	Sa(m)	#	#	#	#	#	#	#	#	#	100.0	107.1	109.5	100.0	97.6	104.8	107.1
N. MEXICO	Sm	79.9	89.1	86.5	96.0	92.8	100.0	94.8	107.3	95.8	111.7	112.0	120.1	126.0	120.9	117.7	110.0
	Si(1)	92.4	92.7	95.5	98.5	100.0	100.0	103.1	103.8	104.3	107.3	113.3	123.1	125.0	122.4	121.0	115.4
	Si(2)	90.0	93.2	93.7	96.9	100.9	100.0	104.0	109.8	116.6	123.7	121.6	150.1	134.3	125.9	120.6	~
	Sc	76.2	86.0	90.9	85.0	86.3	100.0	109.8	96.6	115.9	128.6	122.6	148.0	134.5	~	~	~
	Sa(m)	74.9	84.8	82.3	93.1	90.0	100.0	94.9	106.7	101.0	110.8	111.1	124.6	123.4	123.0	126.9	126.4
O. NICARAGUA	Sm	113.9	109.5	108.2	103.5	102.2	100.0	98.4	97.8	82.3	84.2	89.3	92.1	93.7	95.0	89.3	76.0
	Si(ss)	84.4	88.5	95.2	101.3	100.0	100.0	99.5	100.8	85.2	86.9	82.9	86.9	85.2	85.9	73.6	~
	Sc(ss)	94.8	98.2	100.5	96.1	100.8	100.0	104.0	93.9	66.8	81.4	83.4	73.7	71.8	73.4	62.2	~
	Sa(m)	113.6	109.5	108.2	103.7	102.5	100.0	98.4	105.3	90.1	89.7	89.7	90.1	95.1	97.9	83.5	74.9
P. PANAMA	Sm	108.3	108.1	106.7	104.9	103.1	100.0	98.2	116.6	109.2	99.6	97.1	93.4	89.3	85.7	84.2	87.5
	Si(1)	88.6	92.7	95.2	96.6	99.4	100.0	97.7	98.4	97.6	93.2	97.2	98.9	98.4	~	~	~
	Si(2)	87.7	91.8	95.0	98.3	100.1	100.0	103.4	96.4	94.7	99.1	98.5	103.4	107.6	~	~	~
	Sc(m)	81.4	81.3	80.2	83.9	103.1	100.0	98.2	93.1	87.2	83.0	82.6	79.4	76.0	72.9	71.2	71.1
	Sa(m)	108.2	107.9	106.7	104.9	103.1	100.0	98.2	155.1	145.4	143.3	141.5	135.9	130.0	124.9	125.9	135.4

Table 1407 (Continued)

REAL WAGE INDEXES,[1] 18 L, 1965–80

(1970 = 100)

Country	Code	1965	1966	1967	1968	1969	1970	1971	1972	1973	1974	1975	1976	1977	1978	1979	1980
Q. PARAGUAY	Sm	106.5	103.4	102.0	101.4	99.1	100.0	101.6	95.8	107.7	95.6	92.4	88.5	80.9	84.1	65.6	66.3
	Si	#	#	95.2	95.3	95.2	100.0	99.5	95.3	94.8	96.5	91.8	96.3	91.0	94.2	86.6	88.0
	Sc	#	#	96.0	96.1	96.0	100.0	98.8	94.2	88.0	83.6	79.1	79.7	79.0	84.0	74.6	71.8
	Sa	#	96.0	96.0	96.1	96.0	100.0	98.8	94.2	95.2	89.3	84.7	89.2	81.5	99.2	90.6	98.3
R. PERU	Sm	80.1	94.0	91.0	90.0	84.7	100.0	99.7	104.5	102.9	104.6	97.0	89.4	78.5	66.1	67.3	75.2
	Si	99.5	99.2	#	93.1	98.1	100.0	100.0	115.5	129.4	137.1	117.0	111.5	98.0	84.9	73.8	87.1
	Sc	109.9	109.5	#	109.5	118.5	100.0	108.4	110.8	119.7	116.5	136.0	118.7	98.2	83.5	78.0	85.7
	Sa(m)	109.9	100.9	94.5	91.4	97.8	100.0	111.2	109.1	112.1	102.0	105.5	101.6	88.6	69.9	92.3	92.8
S. URUGUAY	Sm	#	#	#	#	111.5	100.0	127.9	114.4	118.3	120.2	114.4	105.8	91.3	95.2	84.6	80.8
	Si[(1)]	#	#	107.9	98.5	104.8	100.0	103.2	86.8	84.0	83.5	75.8	68.5	58.8	55.9	50.3	47.5
	Si[(2)]	#	#	#	#	#	#	#	#	#	#	#	#	100.0	100.5	~	~
	Sc	#	#	117.5	97.1	105.9	100.0	127.4	111.0	115.3	117.6	102.9	93.1	80.6	76.3	68.6	65.3
	Sa	#	58.3	67.3	73.1	95.5	100.0	101.3	78.8	65.4	74.4	75.6	71.8	69.9	75.6	69.2	62.8
	Sa	#	#	#	90.0	96.3	100.0	106.9	86.8	81.2	87.8	86.1	79.1	70.5	84.6	65.4	~
T. VENEZUELA	Sm	#	#	#	#	#	#	#	#	#	100.0	90.7	84.3	78.2	72.9	71.5	70.7
	Si	89.4	89.5	93.6	100.0	95.0	100.0	103.0	107.3	102.9	112.2	116.4	111.0	112.5	118.8	105.7	~
	Sc	88.2	86.7	88.3	98.6	100.0	#	#	#	#	#	#	#	#	#	#	#
	Sr	#	#	#	#	#	#	#	#	#	#	100.0	111.5	115.0	119.3	~	~

1. Calculated from consumer prices in each country.

Code: Sm,   minimum non-agricultural wage
  Si,   average manufacturing wage
  Sc   construction wage
  Sa   agricultural wage
  PEM   Plan del Empleo Mínimo
  (m)   average minimum rate unless otherwise specified
  (ss)   Social Security records
  (1) }
  (2) }   alternative series

SOURCE: ILO, *Mercado de Trabajo en Cifras, 1950-1980*, table III-3.

Table 1408

REAL INDUSTRIAL WAGE INDEX (RIWI) FOR MEXICO CITY, 1934–76

Year	(A) Worker Cost of Living[1] Index (WCL)	(B) Annual Average Percentage Change	(C) New WCL (BXC)[2]	(D) Industrial Wage Index (IWI)	(E) Annual Average Percentage Change	(F) New IWI (EXF)[2]	(G) RIWI (F/C)	(H) Annual Average Percentage Change
1934	100	**	63.7	.28	**	44.5	70	**
1935	108	8.0	68.8	.30[a]	7.1	47.6	69	−1.4
1936	114	5.6	72.6	.33	10.0	52.4	72	4.3

Continued in SALA, 21-1405.

Table 1409

REAL INDUSTRIAL WAGE INDEX, 18 LC, 1940–73

A. ARGENTINA

Year	(A) Consumer Price Index (CPI)	(B) Percentage Change	(C) New CPI (A x B)	(D) Industrial Wage Index (IWI)	(E) Percentage Change	(F) New IWI (D x E)	(G) RIWI (F/C)	(H) Percentage Change
1940	91.2	~	100	88	~	100	100	~
1941	93.6	2.6	103	91	3.4	103	101	1.0
1942	98.9	5.7	108	96	5.5	109	101	=

Continued in SALA, 18-1411 through 1429.

Table 1410

MINIMUM URBAN WAGES AND AGRICULTURAL, INDUSTRIAL, AND CONSTRUCTION WAGES, 18 L, 1965–80

(NC, Monthly)

A. ARGENTINA

| | Nominal Wages | | | | | | Real Wages (1970 Prices) | | | | |
| | Manufacturing | | Construction (Laborer) MA | Agriculture (Laborer) NA | Urban Minimum MA | Consumer Price Index (1970=100) MA | Manufacturing | | Construction (Laborer) MA | Agriculture (Laborer) NA | Urban Minimum MA |
Year	Base MA[1]	Paid NA[2]					Base MA[1]	Paid NA[2]			
1965	139	#	153	88	116	41	339	#	373	215	283
1966	189	#	201	117	158	55	344	#	365	213	287
1967	245	#	262	153	158	70	350	#	374	219	226

Continued in SALA, 23-1406 through 1423.

Table 1411

METROPOLITAN LEGAL MINIMUM WAGES, 18 L, 1965–80

(NC, Monthly)

Year	A. ARGENTINA	B. BOLIVIA	C. BRAZIL	D. COLOMBIA	E. CHILE	F. COSTA RICA	H. DOMINICAN REP.	I. ECUADOR	J. EL SALVADOR
1965	116	#	62	364	.21	310	55.1	#	~
1966	158	#	81	364	.26	310	55.1	#	~
1967	158	#	102	364	.31	310	55.1	#	~
1968	158	#	126	364	.31	318	55.1	#	96
1969	200	#	147	371	.48	341	55.1	600	96
1970	220	300	177	450	.62	350	59.0	600	96
1971	317	300	213	450	.83	375	65.8	600	96
1972	446	300	254	460	1.27	385	71.2	750	96
1973	842	331	298	572	4.52	415	71.2	750	96
1974	1,275	922	355	802	34.06	501	71.2	750	123
1975	2,692	1,006	481	1,040	163.41	585	102.3	1,000	154
1976	7,608	1,187	690	1,066	564.87	661	102.3	1,167	186
1977	20,125	1,505	994	1,601	1,278.96	734	102.3	1,500	186
1978	55,000	1,505	1,409	2,045	2,265.09	838	102.3	1,500	186
1979	133,000	2,088	2,143	2,298	2,996.29	937	~	1,500	210
1980	313,000	~	4,024	3,900	4,056.00	1,100	~	2,000	~
								4,000	~

Year	K. GUATEMALA	M. HONDURAS	N. MEXICO	O. NICARAGUA	P. PANAMA	Q. PARAGUAY	R. PERU	S. URUGUAY	T. VENEZUELA
1965	47	#	559	317	83	5,850	938	#	#
1966	47	#	650	317	83	5,850	1,200	#	#
1967	47	#	650	317	83	5,850	1,275	#	#
1968	47	#	735	317	83	5,850	1,500	#	#
1969	47	#	735	317	83	5,850	1,500	#	#
1970	47	#	832	317	83	5,850	1,860	10.0	#
1971	47	#	832	317	83	6,240	1,980	10.4	#
1972	47	#	988	325	104	6,430	2,225	16.5	#
1973	48	#	988	347	104	8,150	2,400	26.0	#
1974	57	104	1,426	402	111	9,057	2,850	53.0	#
1975	57	104	1,648	459	114	9,340	3,270	95.2	450
1976	57	104	2,044	487	114	9,340	4,020	165.2	450
1977	57	104	2,766	552	114	9,340	4,875	229.0	450
1978	57	106	3,120	584	114	10,740	6,475	312.2	450
1979	57	125	3,588	815	121	10,740	11,063	472.7	450
1980	99	137	4,238	940	~	13,275	19,675	697.0	495
								1,087.7	600

SOURCE: ILO, *Mercado de Trabajo en Cifras, 1950-1980*, table III-2.

Table 1412

INDUSTRIAL DISPUTES,[1] 14 LC, 1965–82

Country	Code[2]	1965	1970	1975	1976	1977	1978	1979	1980	1981	1982
A. ARGENTINA[6]	A[4,5]	32	5	~	~	~	~	~	~	~	~
	B[3]	203,596	2,912	~	~	~	~	~	~	~	~
	C	590,511	32,849	~	~	~	~	~	~	~	~
D. CHILE	A[4]	723	1,819	~	~	~	~	~	89[b]	~	2,400[b]
	B	182,359	656,170	~	~	~	~	~	29,400[b]	25,000[b]	51,400[b]
	C	~	2,814,517	~	~	~	~	~	428,400[b]	676,200[b]	
E. COLOMBIA	A	~	~	~	~	~	266	137	261	219	149
	B	~	~	~	~	~	22,628	29,712	30,915	22,560	60,119
	C	~	~	~	~	~	~	~	~	~	
F. COSTA RICA	A	~	~	18	14	10	14	20	61	6	14
	B	~	~	11,500	~	10,592	20,168	25,671	24,750	7,380	13,387
	C	~	~	47,252	~	74,121	176,780	275,130	427,350	166,580	285,930
I. ECUADOR	A	~	~	61	58	9	7	37	75	99	~
	B	~	~	11,913	7,016	802	538	2,387	16,065	13,094	~
	C	~	~	418,226	265,107	43,282	17,394	60,012	508,170	373,210	~
J. EL SALVADOR	A	~	~	14	2	19	29	103	42	15[c]	~
	B	~	~	2,902	25,300	84,879	7,169	29,432	12,110	5,324[c]	~
	C	~	~	39,059	601,800	154,792	72,962	292,276	44,217	138,490[c]	~
K. GUATEMALA	A	~	36	7	16	9	229	7	51	3	~
	B[3]	~	27,067	8,336	5,757	8,670	144,956	42,170	68,683	1,350	~
	C	~	50,934	53,476	167,831	60,641	1,479,246	41,120	817,300	37,070	~
L. HAITI	A	~	~	~	~	2,647	1,337	1,751	2,946	~	~
	B	~	~	~	~	792	1,615	2,141	3,688	~	~
	C	~	~	~	~	~	9,139	19,883	21,954	~	~
M. HONDURAS	A	1	~	~	~	~	~	19	37	49	~
	B	135	~	~	~	~	~	27,354	34,431	9,273	13,387
	C	13,770	~	~	~	~	~	~	~	~	~
N. MEXICO	A[4]	67	206	236	547	476	758	795	1,339	~	~
	B[3]	610	14,329	9,680	23,684	13,411	14,976	17,264	42,774	~	~
P. PANAMA	A	~	6	6	15	4	3	10	18	16	7
	B	~	17,510	~	2,080	205	867	1,161	2,438	7,835	1,333
	C[7]	~	13,148	~	18,939	915	3,003	44,292	158,740	248,280	~
Q. PARAGUAY	A	3	~	~	~	~	~	~	~	~	~
	B	780	~	~	~	~	~	~	~	~	~
	C	540	~	~	~	~	~	~	~	~	~
R. PERU	A	397	345	779	440	234	364	653	739	871	809
	B	135,582	110,990	617,120	258,101	406,461	1,398,387	841,140	481,480	856,910	572,260
	C[7]	802,576	722,732	2,533,676	852,778	817,919	4,518,092	1,676,300	2,239,900	2,496,700	2,843,900
T. VENEZUELA	A	24	64	100	171	214	140	145	195	129	102
	B	4,690	23,934	25,752	33,932	63,920	25,340	23,270	67,960	29,560	14,870
	C[7]	17,800	234,349	100,662	91,267	86,000	39,840	50,020	315,310	255,920	329,600
UNITED STATES[5]	A	3,963	5,716	5,031	5,649	5,506	4,230	4,827	3,873	2,568	~
	B	1,550,000	3,305,200	1,746,000	2,412,300	2,040,100	1,623,600	1,727,100	1,365,500	1,080,800	~
	C	23,300,000	66,413,800	31,237,000	37,960,300	35,821,800	36,921,500	34,754,000	33,389,000	24,730,000	~

1. This table shows the total number of industrial disputes which resulted in a stoppage of work, and the numbers of workers involved and working days lost. No differentiation between strikes and lockouts has been possible, since in most countries the distinction is not observed in the compilations. In a few cases, however, the data relate to strikes only. Disputes of small importance and political strikes are frequently not included in the statistics. In some cases the data do not cover workers "indirectly affected," i.e., workers who, though not parties in the dispute, are thrown out of work within the establishment directly affected by the stoppage of work. As far as possible such cases are indicated by footnotes. Various methods are used for calculating the number of working days lost, and these data, as well as the statistics of workers involved, are often approximations only. Nevertheless, the statistics indicate in a general way the extent of industrial disputes in the different countries.

2. Code: A — number of disputes;
    B — number of workers involved;
    C — number of working days lost.

3. Excluding workers indirectly affected.
4. Strikes only.
5. Excluding disputes involving less than six workers and those lasting less than a full day or shift.
6. Buenos Aires.
7. Computed on the basis of eight-hour working days.

a. Includes 57 disputes for which data relating to workers involved and working days lost are not available.
b. Includes data from Sept. 1979 to Dec. 1980.
c. Includes data from Jan. to June.

SOURCE: ILO-YLS, 1975, table 27; 1983, table 29A.

Table 1413

INCOME DISTRIBUTION,[1] 8 LC

(% Share of Household Income by Percentile Groups of Households[2])

	Country	Year	Lowest 20%	Second Quintile	Third Quintile	Fourth Quintile	Highest 20%	Highest 10%
A.	ARGENTINA	1970	4.4	9.7	14.1	21.5	50.3	35.2
C.	BRAZIL	1972	2.0	5.0	9.4	17.0	66.6	50.6
D.	CHILE	1968	4.4	9.0	13.8	21.4	51.4	34.8
F.	COSTA RICA	1971	3.3	8.7	13.3	19.9	54.8	39.5
N.	MEXICO	1977	2.9	7.0	12.0	20.4	57.7	40.6
P.	PANAMA	1970	2.0	5.2	11.0	20.0	61.8	44.2
R.	PERU	1972	1.9	5.1	11.0	21.0	61.0	42.9
T.	VENEZUELA	1970	3.0	7.3	12.9	22.8	54.0	35.7
	UNITED STATES	1972	4.5	10.7	17.3	24.7	42.8	26.6

1. These estimates should be treated with caution because the collection of data on income distribution has not been systematically organized and integrated with the official statistical system in many countries; estimates were typically derived from surveys designed for other purposes, most often consumer expenditure surveys, which also collect some information on income. These surveys use a variety of income concepts and sample designs. Furthermore, the coverage of many of these surveys is too limited to provide reliable nationwide estimates of income distribution. Thus, although the estimates shown are considered the best available, they do not avoid all these problems and should be interpreted with extreme caution.

   The scope of the indicator is similarly limited. Because households vary in size, a distribution in which households are ranked according to per capita household income, not according to their total household income, is superior for many purposes. The distinction is important because households with low per capita incomes frequently are large households, whose total income may be relatively high.

2. Data refer to distribution of total disposable household income accruing to percentile groups of households ranked by total household income. The distributions cover rural and urban areas.

SOURCE: WB-WDR, 1983, table 27.

Table 1414

INCOME DISTRIBUTION: LATIN AMERICA AVERAGE,[1] 1960 AND 1970

Stratum	Share of Each Stratum in the Total Income		Per Capita Income in 1960 Dollars[a]		Increase in Per Capita Income		Total Increase	Percentage of the Total Increase Represented by the Increase in Each Stratum
	1960	1970	1960	1970	Percentage	1960 Dollars		
20% poorest	3.1	2.5	53	55	3.8	2	107.6	.4
30% following	10.3	11.4	118	167	41.5	49	3,919	15.4
20% following	14.1	13.9	243	306	25.9	63	3,359	13.2
20% before the highest 10%	24.6	28.0	424	616	45.3	192	10,237	40.3
10% highest	47.9	44.2	1,643	1,945	17.7	292	7,785	30.7
(5% highest)[b]	(33.4)	(29.9)	(2,305)	(2,630)	(14.1)	(325)	(4,332)	(17.1)
Total	100.0	100.0	345	440	27.5	95	25,406	100.0

1. The average distribution in Latin America in 1970 has been estimated on the basis of information provided by Argentina, Brazil, Chile, Colombia, Mexico, Paraguay, Honduras, and Venezuela.

a. Corresponds to the concept of personal per capita income.
b. Subtotal within 10% highest.

SOURCE: ECLA, *Long-Term Trends and Projections of Economic Development of Latin America*, Spanish edition, 1977, table 1.

Table 1415

DISTRIBUTION OF INCOME: CHRONOLOGICAL
SERIES, 3 LC, 1953-62

	Country	Year	Unit[1]	Income PI, (US)[2]	Coefficients Gini	Coefficients Variation	D.S. Log
A.	ARGENTINA	1953	H	786	.41	1.09	.64
		1959	H	832	.45	1.29	.70
		1961	H	927	.42	1.18	.67
C.	BRAZIL	1960A	E	289	.52	1.24	1.17
		1970A	E	383	.64	1.32	2.37
		1960B	E	289	.49	1.18	.94
		1970B	E	383	.56	1.49	.99
N.	MEXICO	1950	H	397	.526	2.50	.72
		1957	H	488	.551	1.65	.88
		1963	H	542	.55	~	~
		1963	H	~	.54	1.26	.97
	UNITED STATES	1955-57	C	2,397	.36	.78	.68
		1960-62	C	2,837	.36	.72	.70

1.   H, home; E, Economically Active; C, Consumption Unit.
2.   Constant 1960 terms.

SOURCE: Adolfo Figueroa and Richard Weiskoff, "Visión de las Pirámides Sociales:
       Distribución del Ingreso en América Latina," *Ensayos ECIEL,* 1 (November 1974),
       p. 121.

Table 1416

DISTRIBUTION OF AVERAGE PER INHABITANT INCOME,
BY INCOME GROUPS, 5 L, 1965

	Country	Average PI Personal Income[1]	Average Income by Group Poorest 20%	30% Below the Median	30% Above the Median	15% Below the Top	Top 5%
C.	BRAZIL	260	45	100	200	380	2,055
	Rio de Janeiro	805	200	405	780	1,425	3,880
	São Paulo	775	225	390	675	1,280	4,340
D.	CHILE	480	85	200	410	890	2,930
	Greater Santiago	660	140	315	640	1,285	3,035
F.	COSTA RICA	385	115	155	280	640	2,695
	San José	500	125	240	425	965	2,600
N.	MEXICO	475	85	185	415	935	2,755
	Federal District	1,050	280	495	935	1,940	5,460
T.	VENEZUELA	530	80	200	490	1,115	2,810
	Metropolitan Area of Caracas	870	250	500	850	1,610	3,480

1.   In constant US of 1960.

SOURCE: SALA, 16-15 (p. 26).

Table 1417

INCOME GROUPS, PERCENTAGE SHARES, 5 L, 1965

	Country	Lowest 20%	30% Below the Median	30% Above the Median	15% Below the Median	Top 5%
A.	ARGENTINA	5.2	15.3	25.4	22.9	31.2
F.	COSTA RICA	5.5	12.5	22.0	25.0	35.0
J.	EL SALVADOR	5.5	10.5	22.2	28.4	32.9
N.	MEXICO	3.6	11.8	26.1	29.5	29.0
T.	VENEZUELA	3.0	11.3	27.7	31.5	26.5

SOURCE: SALA, 16-16 (p. 26).

Table 1418

NATIONAL DISTRIBUTION OF TOTAL HOUSEHOLD INCOME, BY INCOME GROUPS, 10 L

	Country	Year	Per Capita GDP (Dollars at 1970 Prices)	Household Percentile Groups (Percentage Shares in Total Income)						Coefficients of Concentration	
				0-20	21-40	41-60	61-80	81-90	91-100	Gini	Theil
A.	ARGENTINA	1970	1,208	4.4	9.7	14.1	21.5	15.1	35.2	.44	.15
C.	BRAZIL	1972	539	1.6	4.0	7.1	14.2	14.4	58.7	.66	.38
D.	CHILE	1968	823	3.7	8.3	13.1	20.4	16.2	38.3	.48	.18
E.	COLOMBIA	1972	575	2.0	4.5	9.5	17.9	16.0	50.1	.61	.30
F.	COSTA RICA	1971	684	3.3	8.7	13.3	19.9	15.3	39.5	.49	.19
M.	HONDURAS	1967	275	2.0	4.6	7.5	16.2	17.5	52.2	.63	.32
N.	MEXICO	1967	800	2.6	5.8	9.2	16.9	16.2	49.3	.59	.28
P.	PANAMA	1970	868	1.7	5.3	11.2	20.4	17.8	43.5	.57	.25
R.	PERU	1972	555	1.5	4.2	9.6	20.0	18.5	46.2	.60	.29
T.	VENEZUELA	1971	1,163	2.8	7.0	12.6	22.7	18.6	36.3	.50	.19

SOURCE: ECLA, *Economic and Social Development and External Relations of Latin America*, 1979, p. 125.

Table 1419

URBAN DISTRIBUTION OF HOUSEHOLD INCOME, BY INCOME GROUPS, 11 L

	Country	Year	Non-Agricultural GDP (Dollars at 1970 Prices)	Household Percentile Groups (Percentage Shares in Total Income)						Coefficients of Concentration	
				0-20	21-40	41-60	61-80	81-90	91-100	Gini	Theil
A.	ARGENTINA	1970	1,254	4.3	9.3	14.2	21.3	15.1	35.8	.45	.15
C.	BRAZIL	1972	878	1.7	4.6	6.3	15.9	14.7	54.8	.63	.34
D.	CHILE	1968	1,000	4.3	8.9	13.7	20.4	16.3	36.4	.46	.16
E.	COLOMBIA	1975	721	2.1	6.0	10.2	18.7	17.8	45.2	.57	.26
F.	COSTA RICA	1971	880	4.1	8.6	13.0	20.6	16.1	37.6	.47	.17
M.	HONDURAS	1967	496	3.3	7.2	12.2	19.5	16.2	41.6	.52	.21
N.	MEXICO	1967	1,340	3.1	6.2	10.3	19.2	15.8	45.4	.55	.24
P.	PANAMA	1970	1,179	3.5	7.0	13.0	21.0	25.0	30.5	.49	.18
R.	PERU	1972	823	3.4	8.2	13.1	20.8	15.7	38.8	.49	.18
S.	URUGUAY	1967	926	4.0	9.3	14.0	21.4	15.6	35.7	.45	.15
T.	VENEZUELA	1970	1,439	3.1	7.5	12.0	19.5	15.6	42.3	.52	.21

SOURCE: ECLA, *Economic and Social Development and External Relations of Latin America*, 1979, p. 130.

Table 1420

NUMBER OF COOPERATIVES AND MEMBERSHIP, 20 L, 1962 AND 1969

	Country	Cooperatives			Membership		
		1962	1969	PC	1962	1969	PC
A.	ARGENTINA	3,220	3,654	13	2,088,000	3,453,947	65
B.	BOLIVIA	217	904	316	17,100	143,219	737
C.	BRAZIL	4,625	7,513	62	1,859,000	3,100,000	67
D.	CHILE	995	1,572	58	447,000	563,808	26
E.	COLOMBIA	525	1,845	251	263,100	904,803	244
F.	COSTA RICA	54	240	186	13,200	54,547	313
G.	CUBA	~	~	~	~	~	~
H.	DOMINICAN REP.	87	246	183	5,000	34,840	597
I.	ECUADOR	700	1,817	159	35,000	96,028	174
J.	EL SALVADOR	73	120	64	13,200	17,809	35
K.	GUATEMALA	50	403	706	3,500	35,782	922
L.	HAITI	86	236	174	11,000	35,529	223
M.	HONDURAS	100	162	62	6,200	20,298	227
N.	MEXICO	4,775	4,862	2	604,400	618,580	2
O.	NICARAGUA	45	140	211	8,600	15,701	82
P.	PANAMA	60	161	168	5,600	15,515	177
Q.	PARAGUAY	80	185	131	9,300	25,447	174
R.	PERU	375	1,437	283	97,800	416,100	325
S.	URUGUAY	130	267	105	98,900	154,826	56
T.	VENEZUELA	130	221	70	14,300	46,113	222

SOURCE: OAS-A, table A-62.

CHAPTER 15

MIGRATION AND TOURISM

Table 1500

POPULATION IN UNITED STATES REPORTING LATIN AMERICAN ANCESTRY[1]
(Number of Persons Reporting in 1980)

PART I. TOTAL NUMBER OF PERSONS REPORTING

Nation of Ancestry	Type of Ancestry				Location in the U.S.			
	Single[2] Ancestry	Multiple[3] Ancestry	Reported[4] Ancestry	Percent of[5] Total	Northeast	North Central	South	West
A. ARGENTINA	28,109	9,800	37,909	.02	15,357	2,439	7,915	12,198
B. BOLIVIA	12,585	3,463	16,048	.01	3,516	1,853	5,402	5,277
C. BRAZIL	18,750	8,890	27,640	.01	12,035	3,128	6,387	6,090
D. CHILE	24,410	7,433	31,843	.02	10,711	2,829	7,678	10,625
E. COLOMBIA	137,162	19,114	156,276	.08	84,307	10,793	40,214	20,962
F. COSTA RICA	21,121	5,871	26,992	.01	9,623	1,828	5,009	10,532
G. CUBA	500,564	97,138	597,702	.32	143,036	24,625	373,695	56,346
H. DOMINICAN REP.	155,930	14,768	170,698	.09	156,053	2,054	9,939	2,652
I. ECUADOR	77,247	10,726	87,973	.05	56,392	5,961	9,804	15,816
J. EL SALVADOR	77,384	7,373	84,757	.05	10,992	2,286	7,917	63,562
K. GUATEMALA	54,674	7,424	62,098	.03	10,508	7,507	7,897	36,186
L. HAITI	81,509	8,714	90,223	.05	65,246	3,505	19,346	2,126
M. HONDURAS	45,294	10,271	55,565	.03	19,986	4,297	18,568	12,714
N. MEXICO	6,992,476	700,143	7,692,619	4.09	62,116	705,349	2,663,868	4,261,286
O. NICARAGUA	37,845	7,232	45,077	.02	6,239	1,543	12,257	25,038
P. PANAMA	33,546	11,208	44,754	.02	21,557	3,376	10,669	9,152
R. PERU	44,884	13,054	57,938	.03	24,360	4,538	11,237	17,803
S. URUGUAY	7,240	1,350	8,590	#	4,876	543	1,842	1,329
T. VENEZUELA	25,548	7,481	33,029	.02	10,355	3,536	14,031	5,107
PUERTO RICO	1,270,420	173,442	1,443,862	.77	1,057,461	157,857	120,394	108,150
SPANISH/HISPANIC[6]	1,685,151	1,001,529	2,686,680	1.43	613,844	205,758	705,594	1,161,484
OTHER SPANISH[7]	52,774	12,421	65,195	.03	14,992	4,887	27,199	18,117

1. The source provides "ethnic data on persons regardless of the number of generations removed from their country of origin." The ancestry question was based on self-identification. About 83% of the population reported at least one specific ancestry.
2. Persons reporting only one ancestry group.
3. Persons reporting more than one ancestry group. Double origin ancestry reports were coded; 17 triple-origin ancestries expected to be frequently reported were also coded. A person reporting double origin will appear twice in the table.
4. Reported at least one specific ancestry. Sum of single and multiple ancestry. The total of the column will add to more than the total reporting a Latin American ancestry due to double counting (see note 3 above).
5. Percent of total population reporting at least one specific ancestry. Numbers and percents by ancestry group do not add to totals due to persons with multiple ancestry being included in more than one group.
6. This category represents a general type of response, which may encompass several ancestry groups.
7. Other Spanish not elsewhere considered. Since the "Spaniard" entry excludes Basques they may appear here. However, Latin America appears under the general heading "Spanish" so a clear distinction is lacking.

SOURCE: US–BOC, 1980 Supplementary Report, PC 80-SI-10, April 1983, table 3.

Table 1500 (Continued)

POPULATION IN UNITED STATES REPORTING LATIN AMERICAN ANCESTRY[1]
(Number of Persons Reporting in 1980)

PART II. NUMBER OF PERSONS REPORTING AT LEAST ONE SPECIFIC ANCESTRY GROUP

Nation of Ancestry	New England	Middle Atlantic	East North Central	West North Central	South Atlantic	East South Central	West South Central	Mountain	Pacific
A. ARGENTINA	1,629	13,728	1,990	449	6,254	242	1,419	1,027	11,171
B. BOLIVIA	412	3,104	1,442	411	4,041	152	1,209	630	4,647
C. BRAZIL	2,683	9,352	2,549	579	4,677	426	1,284	1,020	5,070
D. CHILE	1,306	9,405	2,209	620	6,171	213	1,294	1,186	9,439
E. COLOMBIA	7,961	76,346	9,104	1,689	33,072	635	6,507	1,732	19,230
F. COSTA RICA	1,829	7,794	1,600	228	3,189	197	1,623	533	9,999
G. CUBA	10,603	132,433	21,965	2,660	355,950	2,123	15,622	5,972	50,374
H. DOMINICAN REP.	7,360	148,493	1,861	193	8,747	172	1,020	590	2,062
I. ECUADOR	2,102	54,290	5,336	625	7,899	154	1,751	668	15,148
J. EL SALVADOR	874	10,118	1,948	338	5,371	253	2,293	947	62,615
K. GUATEMALA	2,028	8,480	7,127	380	4,984	217	2,696	862	35,324
L. HAITI	6,004	59,242	3,132	373	18,446	184	716	198	1,928
M. HONDURAS	1,919	18,067	3,638	659	8,499	775	9,294	690	12,024
N. MEXICO	10,849	51,267	579,234	126,115	98,860	17,891	2,547,117	781,190	3,480,096
O. NICARAGUA	312	5,927	1,150	393	8,945	252	3,060	421	24,617
P. PANAMA	1,129	20,428	2,570	806	6,886	670	3,113	1,102	8,050
R. PERU	2,538	21,822	3,904	634	8,349	342	2,546	1,274	16,529
S. URUGUAY	469	4,407	471	72	1,452	48	342	109	1,220
T. VENEZUELA	2,209	8,146	2,574	962	9,131	823	4,077	1,020	4,087
PUERTO RICO	118,833	938,628	151,896	5,961	92,515	5,493	22,386	11,018	97,132
SPANISH/HISPANIC[2]	81,976	531,868	158,219	47,539	352,533	32,078	320,983	548,787	612,697
OTHER SPANISH[3]	1,065	13,927	4,382	505	6,245	456	20,498	1,272	16,845

1. The source provides "ethnic data on persons regardless of the number of generations removed from their country of origin." The ancestry question was based on self-identification. About 83% of the population reported at least one specific ancestry. Some individuals reported a single ancestry group; others reported more than one group. All single- and double-ancestry responses were coded. In addition, 17 triple-origin ancestries expected to be frequently reported were coded; only the first two ancestries were coded for all other responses of three or more ancestries. Since persons who reported multiple ancestries were included in more than one group, the sum of persons reporting the ancestry group is greater than the total.
2. This category represents a general type of response, which may encompass several ancestry groups.
3. Other Spanish not elsewhere considered. Since the "Spaniard" entry excludes Basques they may appear here. However, Latin America appears under the general heading "Spanish" so a clear distinction is lacking.

SOURCE: US-BOC, 1980 Supplementary Report, PC 80-SI-10, April 1983, table 3.

Table 1501

IMMIGRANTS ADMITTED TO THE UNITED STATES,[1] 20 LC, 1951–80

(N)

	Country	Total			1970	1975	1976	1977	1978	1979	1980
		1951–60	1961–70	1971–80							
A.	ARGENTINA	14,300	42,100	25,100	3,400	2,227	2,267	2,787	3,732	2,856	2,815
B.	BOLIVIA	~	~	~	~	451	522	130	699	1,030	751
C.	BRAZIL	8,900	20,500	13,700	1,900	1,070	1,038	1,513	1,923	1,450	1,570
D.	CHILE	~	~	~	800	1,111	1,266	2,596	3,122	2,289	2,569
E.	COLOMBIA	17,600	70,300	77,600	6,800	6,434	5,742	8,272	11,032	10,637	11,289
F.	COSTA RICA	~	~	~	1,500	889	1,137	1,664	1,575	1,467	1,535
G.	CUBA	78,300	256,800	276,800	16,300	25,955	29,233	69,708	29,754	15,585	15,054
H.	DOMINICAN REP.	9,800	94,100	148,000	10,800	14,066	12,526	11,655	19,458	17,519	17,245
I.	ECUADOR	9,500	37,000	50,200	4,400	4,727	4,504	5,302	5,732	4,383	6,133
J.	EL SALVADOR	4,800	15,000	34,400	1,700	2,416	2,363	4,426	5,826	4,479	6,101
K.	GUATEMALA	4,100	15,400	25,600	2,100	1,859	1,970	3,599	3,996	2,583	3,751
L.	HAITI	4,000	37,500	58,700	6,900	5,145	5,410	5,441	6,470	6,433	6,540
M.	HONDURAS	~	~	~	1,300	1,357	1,310	1,626	2,727	2,545	2,552
N.	MEXICO	319,300	443,300	637,200	44,500	62,205	57,863	44,079	92,367	52,096	56,680
O.	NICARAGUA	~	~	~	700	947	934	1,850	1,888	1,938	2,337
P.	PANAMA[4]	9,700	18,400	22,700	1,600	1,694	1,699	2,390	3,108	3,472	3,572
Q.	PARAGUAY	~	~	~	~	119	110	216	202	175	181
R.	PERU	5,700	18,600	29,100	900	2,256	2,640	3,903	5,243	4,135	4,021
S.	URUGUAY	~	~	~	800	781	676	1,156	1,052	754	887
T.	VENEZUELA	~	~	~	500	527	191	736	990	841	1,010
	LATIN AMERICA[2]	486,000	1,069,000	~	106,900	135,600	133,000	172,900	200,000	125,700	~
	ALL COUNTRIES[3]	2,515,500	3,321,700	4,493,300	373,300	386,194	398,613	462,315	601,442	460,348	530,639

1. Countries indicated are those of birth rather than those of last permanent residence.
2. Excludes Bolivia and Paraguay. In addition, the total figures for 1951–60, 1961–70, and 1971–80 exclude Chile, Costa Rica, Honduras, Nicaragua, Uruguay, and Venezuela.
3. Includes Latin America.
4. Historical data for the Canal Zone are included in Panama.

SOURCE: USBC-SA, 1984, table 126; USINS-SY, 1979/80, table 13.

Table 1502

IMMIGRANTS ADMITTED TO THE UNITED STATES, BY OCCUPATION, 16 L, 1973–78

(N)

Country of Origin	Year	Total Admitted	Professionals, Technicians	Farmers, Farm Managers	Managers, Officials, Proprietors	Clerical Workers	Sales Workers	Craftsmen	Operatives[1]	Private Household Workers	Service Workers	Farm Laborers	Laborers	Housewives, Children, No Occupation
A. ARGENTINA	1973	2,034	179	--	72	52	14	191	127	15	122	1	21	1,240
	1974	2,077	158	8	74	77	18	241	159	12	147	8	20	1,163
	1975	2,227	202	1	68	67	20	253	177	22	119	4	18	706
	1976	2,267	256	6	96	55	32	245	162	30	135	--	19	1,231
	1977	2,787	289	2	140	93	35	271	210	22	128	2	25	1,570
	1978	3,732	361	6	257	118	57	297	285	30	197	8	36	2,080

Continued in SALA, 23-3301.

Table 1503

IMMIGRANTS ADMITTED TO THE UNITED STATES, BY CLASSIFICATION, 20 L

(1980)

Country	Total Admitted (1+2)	Immigrants Subject to Numerical Limitation (1)	Immigrants Admitted Without Numerical Limitation (2=3+4+5+6+7+8+9+10)	Parents of U.S. Citizens (3)	Spouses of U.S. Citizens (4)	Children of U.S. Citizens[1] (5)	Special Immigrants (6)	Spouse Child[2] (7)	Children Born Abroad to Aliens[3] (8)	Refugee and Exile (9)	Other (10)
A. ARGENTINA	2,815	1,824	891	150	566	74	33	28	14	25	1
B. BOLIVIA	730	436	294	52	193	39	1	1	7	1	~
C. BRAZIL	1,570	751	819	56	522	135	38	55	12	1	~
D. CHILE	2,659	1,443	1,126	120	480	155	6	42	11	312	~
E. COLOMBIA	11,289	7,853	3,436	405	1,874	962	36	83	60	16	~
F. COSTA RICA	1,535	944	591	45	352	153	4	12	17	7	1
G. CUBA	15,054	7,659	7,395	931	262	85	80	7	2	6,024	4
H. DOMINICAN REP.	17,255	14,244	3,011	159	2,069	528	15	25	195	10	~
I. ECUADOR	6,133	4,787	1,346	191	815	245	9	15	66	5	~
J. EL SALVADOR	6,101	4,443	1,669	171	923	490	18	49	12	4	1
K. GUATEMALA	3,751	2,539	1,212	113	730	308	13	26	14	8	~
L. HAITI	6,540	5,131	1,419	127	1,060	106	12	9	32	~	~
M. HONDURAS	2,552	1,579	973	69	601	255	~	15	3	30	~
N. MEXICO	66,680	24,831	31,849	1,639	19,190	4,272	92	638	2,427	25	110
O. NICARAGUA	2,237	1,360	977	229	482	236	23	5	1	1	~
P. PANAMA	3,572	1,806	1,765	259	831	386	232	18	21	17	~
Q. PARAGUAY	181	102	79	5	57	9	~	3	2	3	~
R. PERU	4,021	2,515	1,506	268	998	168	2	47	13	10	~
S. URUGUAY	887	683	204	47	128	15	~	7	2	~	~
T. VENEZUELA	1,010	496	514	25	381	88	3	3	10	~	~

1. Includes legitimate children of U.S. Citizens, orphans adopted abroad, and orphans to be adopted.
2. Act of April 7, 1970, refers to alien fiancé(e)s and children of the fiancé(e)s.
3. Includes children born abroad to U.S. lawful permanent resident aliens and those born after the issuances of visas.

SOURCE: USINS-SY, 1979/80, table 7.

Table 1504

U.S. NATURALIZATION, BY COUNTRY OF ORIGIN AND YEAR OF ENTRY, 20 L 1965–80

(N)

Country	1965	1970	1971	1972	1973	1974	1975	1976	1977	1978	1979	1980[a]
A. ARGENTINA	151	85	51	91	103	117	28	26	8	3	3	~
B. BOLIVIA	~	8	28	14	29	33	8	19	8	6	7	1
C. BRAZIL	45	18	15	26	40	37	16	27	14	10	4	~
D. CHILE	49	21	28	38	40	61	86	43	13	21	11	~
E. COLOMBIA	257	154	120	157	214	299	153	216	178	155	35	1
F. COSTA RICA	~	22	15	18	16	30	16	33	21	14	13	~
G. CUBA	3,613	1,165	1,323	1,275	1,075	1,603	268	27	10	2	2	1
H. DOMINICAN REP.	243	285	225	271	309	326	61	33	11	6	3	1
I. ECUADOR	74	96	99	89	122	146	30	32	12	10	5	2
J. EL SALVADOR	28	53	69	83	93	100	43	48	24	20	16	1
K. GUATEMALA	37	55	34	51	67	60	22	31	29	19	13	1
L. HAITI	134	259	169	164	199	265	35	32	6	2	~	~
M. HONDURAS	73	47	37	40	67	76	29	19	9	4	8	~
N. MEXICO	284	374	463	572	603	448	203	115	64	26	26	~
O. NICARAGUA	41	32	40	31	38	79	23	46	17	12	6	1
P. PANAMA	42	52	45	43	73	74	38	53	35	8	7	9
Q. PARAGUAY	~	3	5	4	7	11	2	3	1	~	1	~
R. PERU	62	37	54	95	135	193	74	92	31	15	25	2
S. URUGUAY	16	24	17	37	53	89	11	13	3	~	~	~
T. VENEZUELA	14	8	5	10	8	21	4	4	2	3	4	~

a. Jan-Sept.

SOURCE: USINS-SY, 1977/78, table 44; USINS-SY, 1979/80, table 29.

Table 1505

"DEPORTABLE ALIENS" LOCATED IN THE UNITED STATES, FY 1966–80
(N)

Year	Total	Mexican	Mexicans as % of Total
1966	138,520[a]	89,751	65
1967	161,608[a]	108,327	67
1968	212,057[a]	151,705	72
1969	283,557[a]	201,636	71
1970	231,116*	219,254*	94*
1971	302,517	290,152	95
1972	369,495	355,099	96
1973	498,123	480,588	96
1974	634,777	616,630	97
1975	596,796	579,448	97
1976	871,189	848,130	97
1977	812,541	792,613	97
1978	862,217	841,525	97
1979	888,729	866,761	97
1980[b]	910,361	817,479	90

a. Includes "involuntary" deportation given in table 1509.
b. Year ended Sept. 30, 1980.

SOURCE: USINS-AR, 1966-79, yearly.

Figure 15:1

MIGRATORY CURRENTS OF LATIN AMERICAN COUNTRIES

Note: An extremely important transfer involves Cubans to the U.S. This is probably the most significant of all relative to the sending society, but has been excluded here as Cuba is not an active member of the OAS system.

SOURCE: IDB-SPTF, 1984, p. 141.

Table 1506

ALIENS DEPORTED, BY COUNTRY AND CAUSE, 19 L

(1980)

	Country to which Deported	Total	Subversive or Anarchistic	Criminal	Immoral	Violation of Narcotic Laws	Mental or Physical Defect	Previously Excluded or Deported	Entered without Proper Documents	Failed to Maintain or Comply with Conditions of Nonimmigrant Status	Entered without Inspection or by False Statements	Miscellaneous
A.	ARGENTINA	32	~	~	~	~	~	~	2	23	7	~
B.	BOLIVIA	7	~	~	~	~	~	~	~	6	1	~
C.	BRAZIL	11	~	~	~	2	~	~	1	4	4	~
D.	CHILE	59	~	~	~	1	~	~	~	32	26	~
E.	COLOMBIA	373	~	~	~	20	~	5	7	88	253	~
F.	COSTA RICA	25	~	~	~	3	~	~	~	12	10	~
G.	CUBA	5	~	~	~	~	~	~	1	2	2	~
H.	DOMINICAN REP.	261	~	4	~	3	~	5	14	38	197	~
I.	ECUADOR	182	~	~	~	2	~	~	3	47	130	~
J.	EL SALVADOR	2,378	~	4	~	2	~	7	15	43	2,305	1
K.	GUATEMALA	644	~	2	2	~	~	2	7	32	598	1
L.	HAITI	37	~	1	~	~	~	~	2	20	13	1
M.	HONDURAS	141	~	~	~	2	~	1	1	17	120	~
N.	MEXICO	11,144	~	81	1	70	~	81	330	167	10,147	7
O.	NICARAGUA	20	~	2	~	1	~	~	~	3	14	~
P.	PANAMA	42	~	1	~	3	~	1	2	11	24	~
R.	PERU	99	~	2	~	3	~	~	1	45	48	~
S.	URUGUAY	19	~	~	~	~	~	~	~	10	9	~
T.	VENEZUELA	17	~	1	~	2	~	1	~	10	3	~

SOURCE: USINS-SY, 1979-80, table 42.

Table 1507

TEMPORARY WORKERS ADMITTED TO THE UNITED STATES,[1] 18 L, 1977 AND 1978

(N)

	Country	1977				1978			
		Total	Workers of Distinguished Merit and Ability	Other Temporary Workers	Industrial Trainees	Total	Workers of Distinguished Merit and Ability	Other Temporary Workers	Industrial Trainees
A.	ARGENTINA	206	150	17	39	258	200	34	24
B.	BOLIVIA	12	11	- -	1	15	8	5	2
C.	BRAZIL	255	172	39	44	331	252	21	58
D.	CHILE	101	72	9	20	76	57	10	9
E.	COLOMBIA	256	144	88	24	290	83	164	43
F.	COSTA RICA	56	15	27	14	47	7	32	8
H.	DOMINICAN REP.	653	275	335	43	862	581	230	51
I.	ECUADOR	89	32	44	13	44	10	19	15
J.	EL SALVADOR	88	9	75	4	100	37	53	10
K.	GUATEMALA	38	13	18	7	113	61	36	16
L.	HAITI	40	12	28	~	60	33	24	3
M.	HONDURAS	8	3	4	1	45	20	23	2
N.	MEXICO	2,011	904	977	130	2,271	975	1,189	2,011
O.	NICARAGUA	44	8	32	4	53	14	36	3
P.	PANAMA	79	25	45	9	88	36	48	4
R.	PERU	136	88	37	11	98	32	48	18
S.	URUGUAY	22	12	5	5	21	11	3	7
T.	VENEZUELA	276	136	95	45	217	117	79	21

1. Under Immigration and Nationality Act of 1952.

SOURCE: USINS-SY, 1977/78, table 16A.

Table 1508
"LEGAL" MEXICAN IMMIGRATION TO THE UNITED STATES,[1] 1900–80
(N)

Year	N	Year	N	Year	N	Western Hemisphere Ceiling	Eastern Hemisphere Ceiling	Numerically Exempt
1900	237	1927	67,721	1954	30,645	~	~	~
1901	347	1928	59,016	1955	43,702	~	~	~
1902	709	1929	40,154	1956	61,320	~	~	~
1903	528	1930	12,703	1957	49,321	~	~	~
1904	1,009	1931	3,333	1958	26,791	~	~	~
1905	2,637	1932	2,171	1959	22,909	~	~	~
1906	1,997	1933	1,936	1960	32,708	~	~	~
1907	1,406	1934	1,801	1961	41,476	~	~	~
1908	6,067	1935	1,560	1962	55,805	~	~	~
1909	16,251	1936	1,716	1963	55,986	~	~	~
1910	18,691	1937	2,347	1964	34,448	~	~	~
1911	19,889	1938	2,502	1965*	37,969	~	~	~
1912	23,238	1939	2,640	1966	45,163	~	~	~
1913	11,926	1940	2,313	1967	42,371	~	~	~
1914	14,614	1941	2,824	1968	43,563	~	~	~
1915	12,340	1942	2,378	1969	44,623	31,933	18	12,672
1916	18,425	1943	4,172	1970	44,469	27,044	20	17,405
1917	17,869	1944	6,598	1971	50,103	31,695	15	18,393
1918	18,524	1945	6,702	1972	64,040	41,694	13	22,333
1919	29,818	1946	7,146	1973	70,141	43,510	71	26,560
1920	52,361	1947	7,558	1974	71,586	45,156	91	26,339
1921	30,758	1948	8,384	1975	62,205	41,894	83	20,228
1922	19,551	1949	8,083	1976	57,863	39,314	145	18,903
1923	63,768	1950	6,744	1977	44,079	23,847	278	20,521
1924	89,336	1951	6,153	1978	92,400	66,885	77	25,405
1925	32,964	1952	9,079	1979	52,100	~	~	~
1926	43,316	1953	17,183	1980[a]	56,680	~	~	31,849

1. Immigration data to 1907 refer only to seaport arrivals.

a. Year ended Sept. 30, 1980.

SOURCE: 1900-64: USBC-HS, 1976; 1965-77: USINS-AR, 1965-77, yearly. USINS-AR, 1966-77, yearly: USINS-SY, 1977/80.

Table 1509
MEXICAN ILLEGAL ALIENS REPORTED,[1] 1924–78
(N)

Year	Total	Year	Total	Year	Total
1924	4,614	1942	~	1960	29,651
1925	2,961	1943	8,189	1961	29,817
1926	4,047	1944	26,689	1962	30,272
1927	4,495	1945	63,602	1963	39,124
1928	5,529	1946	91,456	1964	43,844
1929	8,538	1947	182,986	1965	55,349
1930	18,319	1948	179,385	1966	89,751
1931	8,409	1949	278,538	1967	108,327
1932	7,116	1950	458,215	1968	151,705
1933	15,875	1951	500,000	1969	201,636
1934	8,910	1952	543,538	1970	277,377
1935	9,139	1953	865,318	1971	348,178
1936	9,534	1954	1,075,168	1972	430,213
1937	9,535	1955	242,608	1973	576,823
1938	8,684	1956	72,442	1974	709,959
1939	9,376	1957	44,451	1975	680,392
1940	8,051	1958	37,242	1976	781,474
1941	6,082	1959	30,196	1977	954,778
				1978	976,667

1. Includes deportations, voluntary departures, and forced departures.

SOURCE: Julian Samora, *Los Mojados: The Wetbacks* (South Bend, Ind.: University of Notre Dame Press, 1971); USINS-AR, 1966-78, yearly.

Table 1510

U.S. IMMIGRATION AND NATURALIZATION SERVICE MAN-HOURS PER DEPORTABLE UNDOCUMENTEDS LOCATED, 1978–82[a]

(N)

Year	Border Patrol[1]		Investigations[2]	
	Mexican Undocumenteds	All Undocumenteds	Mexican Undocumenteds	All Undocumenteds
1978	7.03	6.86	21.38	15.58
1979	7.22	7.04	22.17	16.20
1980	8.26	7.99	33.70	19.53
1981	7.94	7.68	34.62	20.60
1982	8.12	7.88	25.48	16.44

1. Includes line watch, patrol, farm-ranch check, traffic check, city patrol, boat patrol, crewman-stowaway, aircraft operations, liaison, intelligence, litigation, identification, special programs, and headquarters staff sections.
2. Includes subversive, criminal, fraud, general, and area control sections.

a. Productive and support hours divided by number of undocumenteds located inside the United States.

SOURCE: SALA-MB, table 404.

Table 1511

MEXICAN UNDOCUMENTEDS COUNTED[†] IN THE 1980 U.S. CENSUS, BY PERIOD OF ENTRY, 1960–80[a]

Period of Entry	Mexican Undocumenteds (T)	As % of Western Hemisphere Undocumenteds in U.S.	As % of Total Undocumenteds in U.S.
Total Entered Since 1960[1]	931	64.1	45.5
Entered 1960-69	138	42.3	24.2
Entered 1970-74	280	64.7	50.8
Entered 1975-80	292	72.3	53.5

1. Includes 36,000 Mexican undocumenteds who entered before 1960 (only figure available for pre-1960 undocumenteds).

a. Estimates based on differences between 1980 census alien population as modified and 1980 alien registration (I-53) data adjusted for underregistration.

SOURCE: SALA-MB, table 405.

Table 1512

KNOWN EXCLUDABLE HAITIAN ARRIVALS, MIAMI, FLORIDA,[1] 1979–82

(N)

Month	1979	1980	1981	1982
January	8	577	769	41
February	12	308	262	12
March	38	1,401	530	14
April	44	1,174	475	20
May	75	1,266	803	2
June	171	1,456	1,507	6
July	219	1,462	1,717	~
August	223	1,731	978	~
September	185	1,874	629	~
October	637	2,280	306	~
November	330	1,021	47	~
December	580	543	46	~
Total	2,522	15,093	8,069	~

1. Low illegal entry figures for the period beginning October 1981 and ending June 1982 are the result of an Interdiction Program jointly conducted by the INS and the Coast Guard. Initiated in October 1981, after a joint U.S.—Haitian deportation agreement was signed, the program proved to be a deterrent to unauthorized traffic to U.S. shores.

SOURCE: USINS-AR, 1982, p. 8.

Table 1513

IMMIGRANTS TO AND EMIGRANTS FROM CUBA, 1959–77

(N)

Year	Immigrants	Emigrants	Balance	Year	Immigrants	Emigrants	Balance
1959	86,069	73,724	12,345	1968	2,353	59,108	−56,755
1960	56,557	118,936	−62,379	1969	2,648	52,424	−49,776
1961	19,137	86,605	−67,468	1970	2,445	58,849	−56,404
1962	9,434	75,698	−66,264	1971	2,441	52,072	−49,631
1963	7,214	19,415	−12,201	1972	3,297	20,153	−16,856
1964	6,923	19,714	−12,791	1973	1,733	8,806	−7,073
1965	2,886	20,889	−18,003	1974	2,095	5,988	−3,893
1966	2,999	56,408	−53,409	1975	2,686	5,577	−2,891
1967	2,624	54,596	−51,972	1976	3,071	5,962	−2,891
				1977	3,083	4,051	−968
				Total	219,695	798,975	−579,280

SOURCE: Cuba, CEE, *Estadísticas de Migraciones Externas y Turismo*, 1982, p. 101.

Table 1514

IMMIGRANTS ADMITTED TO RECIPIENT COUNTRY, BY SEX AND
EDUCATIONAL LEVEL,[1] 4 L

(%)

Recipient Country	Code[2]	Years of Education					
		Men			Women		
		Less than 4	4 to 9	10 or More	Less than 4	4 to 9	10 or More
A. ARGENTINA	A	53.7	40.4	5.9	52.4	40.5	7.1
	B	59.6	31.2	9.2	69.0	23.6	7.3
	C	47.8	4.1	8.6	50.2	43.6	6.2
	D	66.8	27.0	6.3	64.7	28.8	6.5
	E	27.5	48.3	24.2	26.8	53.5	19.7
F. COSTA RICA	H	67.8	24.1	8.2	60.8	31.3	8.0
Q. PARAGUAY	D	72.3	24.9	2.8	77.3	19.8	2.9
	F	39.0	45.2	15.8	44.0	44.0	12.0
T. VENEZUELA	G	64.3	27.7	8.0	63.3	31.2	5.5

1. Statistics derived from national census data. The dates of the censuses are as follows:
   Argentina, 1970; Bolivia, 1976; Brazil, 1970; Colombia, 1973; Costa Rica, 1973;
   Chile, 1970; Nicaragua, 1971; Paraguay, 1972; Uruguay, 1975; Venezuela, 1971.
2. Code: A, Chileans; B, Bolivians; C, Paraguayans; D, Brazilians; E, Uruguayans;
   F, Argentines; G, Colombians; H, Nicaraguans.

SOURCE: ECLA-N, no. 346, Aug. 1981.

Table 1515

IMMIGRANTS ADMITTED TO RECIPIENT COUNTRY, BY EDUCATIONAL
LEVEL AND OCCUPATION,[1] 4 L

(%)

Recipient Country	Code[2]	Population with More than 10 Years of Schooling	Agricultural and Service Workers		Nonagricultural Workers	
			Observed	Estimated	Observed	Estimated
A. ARGENTINA	A	7	31	53	52	22
	B	9	28	49	57	24
	C	7	30	53	53	22
	D	6	54	55	27	21
	E	22	19	21	39	36
F. COSTA RICA	H	8	57	51	22	23
Q. PARAGUAY	D	3	82	62	10	18
	F	14	54	38	22	28
T. VENEZUELA	G	7	50	53	21	22

1. Statistics derived from national census data. The dates of the censuses are as follows:
   Argentina, 1970; Bolivia, 1976; Brazil, 1970; Colombia, 1973; Costa Rica, 1973;
   Chile, 1970; Nicaragua, 1971; Paraguay, 1972; Uruguay, 1975; Venezuela, 1971.
2. Code: A, Chileans; B, Bolivians; C, Paraguayans; D, Brazilians; E, Uruguayans;
   F, Argentines; G, Colombians; H, Nicaraguans.

SOURCE: ECLA-N, no. 346, Aug. 1981.

Table 1516

IMMIGRANTS ADMITTED TO RECIPIENT COUNTRY, BY OCCUPATION,[1] 4 L
(%)

Recipient Country	Code[2]	Structure of the Labor Force in Home Country		Structure of Migratory Labor Force	
		Agricultural and Service Workers	Nonagricultural Workers	Agricultural and Service Workers	Nonagricultural Workers
A. ARGENTINA	**	27	34	**	**
	A	31	52	31	52
	B	54	25	28	57
	C	60	22	30	53
	D	60	18	54	27
	E	30	31	19	39
F. COSTA RICA	**	48	24	**	**
	H	58	22	57	22
Q. PARAGUAY	**	60	22	**	**
	D	60	18	82	10
	F	27	34	54	22
T. VENEZUELA	**	33	26	*	**
	G	43	24	50	21

1. Statistics derived from national census data. The dates of the censuses are as follows: Argentina, 1970; Bolivia, 1976; Brazil, 1970; Colombia, 1973; Costa Rica, 1973; Chile, 1970; Nicaragua, 1971; Paraguay, 1972; Uruguay, 1975; Venezuela, 1971.
2. Code: A, Chileans; B, Bolivians; C, Paraguayans; D, Brazilians; E, Uruguayans; F, Argentines; G, Colombians; H, Nicaraguans.

SOURCE: ECLA-N, no. 346, Aug. 1981.

Table 1517

REFUGEES "IN NEED"
(N 1983)

	Country of Asylum	Source Country/Area	Total
A.	ARGENTINA	Europe, Latin America, SE Asia	12,300
C.	BRAZIL	Europe, Latin America	5,400
D.	CHILE	Europe	1,500
F.	COSTA RICA	Latin America	15,000[a]
H.	DOMINICAN REP.	Haiti	5,000
K.	GUATEMALA	El Salvador	70,000
M.	HONDURAS	Latin America	33,300[b]
N.	MEXICO	Latin America	140,000[c]
P.	PANAMA	Latin America	1,500[d]
R.	PERU	Europe, Latin America	500
T.	VENEZUELA	Europe, Latin America	500

a. 10,000 from El Salvador.
b. 20,000 from El Salvador; 12,000 from Nicaragua.
c. 120,000 from El Salvador; 20,000 from Guatemala.
d. 1,000 from El Salvador.

SOURCE: U.S. Committee for Refugees, New York, *World Refugee Survey 1983*, p. 61.

Table 1518

ENTRY OF TOURISTS,[1] 19 LC, 1970-82

(N)

Country Entered	1970	1975	1976	1977	1978	1979	1980	1981	1982
A. ARGENTINA	694,940	1,200,000†	~	1,104,923	1,198,407	1,019,439	~	1,357,879	1,146,881
B. BOLIVIA	22,248[b]	156,600[d]	171,200[d]	101,637	202,903	159,417	155,412	405,000	263,250
C. BRAZIL	194,186	517,967	555,967	634,595	784,316	1,081,799†	913,878	1,059,630	1,127,662
D. CHILE	198,824	250,000†	235,371	296,964	267,239	285,000†	320,000	~	~
E. COLOMBIA	161,668	443,264	462,044	~	826,276	1,151,284	~	~	~
F. COSTA RICA	154,867	297,207	299,039	327,548	340,442	317,724	345,470	333,102	341,166
H. DOMINICAN REP.[4]	67,566[a]	221,795	361,198	309,459	257,107[a]	286,573[a]	301,070	451,209	371,582
I. ECUADOR	57,548	172,945	171,841	201,897	228,917	239,802	243,485	~	~
J. EL SALVADOR	137,804	266,016	277,896	278,761	293,080	230,889	124,353	81,847	98,981
K. GUATEMALA[3]	173,652	454,436	407,937	444,843	415,580	503,908	466,041	328,878	233,881
L. HAITI	62,304	77,322	85,918	95,036	112,018	134,118	~	158,484	~
M. HONDURAS	45,800	167,100	176,500	~	~	134,507	~	~	~
N. MEXICO[2]	2,250,159	3,217,878	3,107,193	3,247,246	3,754,348	4,141,801	4,144,576	4,031,432	3,767,600
O. NICARAGUA	132,000	189,070	195,400	~	~	~	~	~	~
P. PANAMA	125,237	282,728	281,036	362,666	388,045	389,877	390,435	376,217	352,570
Q. PARAGUAY	119,239	93,113	97,600	~	201,919[c]	301,906[c]	302,056	267,089	184,914
R. PERU	133,546[c]	256,210	264,015	265,191	269,659	338,468	372,790	~	~
S. URUGUAY	615,000‡	602,506[c]	618,800[c]	690,143[c]	713,653[c]	1,103,857[c]	1,066,692	927,666	621,732
T. VENEZUELA	116,962[c]	436,182	534,797	652,845	783,670	269,569	215,042	~	~
UNITED STATES	13,264,380[c]	15,698,118	17,523,239	18,609,794	19,816,380	20,310,000	22,500,000	~	~

1. Unless otherwise indicated refers to foreign nationals staying for more than 24 hours and less than 90 days. Not included are day visitors at border points or from cruise ships; also excludes passengers in transit.

2. Excludes Mexican nationals residing in other countries and who entered as tourists.

3. Includes visitors from neighboring countries entering with a "local pass."

4. Includes tourists from the Dominican Republic residing abroad.

a. Excludes Dominican Republic tourists residing abroad.

b. Arrivals to La Paz only.

c. Refers to visitors.

d. Arrival of passengers.

SOURCE: IASI-AC, 1977, table 334-01; WTO-WTS, 1975, 1976, 1977, 1978/79, 1979/80, 1981/82.

Table 1519

TOURIST ENTRY,[1] BY MEANS OF TRANSPORTATION, 18 LC, 1970–82

(%)

Recipient Country	Code[2]	1970	1975	1976	1977	1978	1979	1980	1981	1982
A. ARGENTINA	A	45.0	40.9†	~	69.0†	68.3†	69.8	~	~	40.4
	B	15.4	17.3†	~	~†	~	~	~	~	38.8
	C	1.3	.7†	~	24.9†	25.4	24.1	~	~	20.8
	D	38.4ᵇ	41.1ᵇ,†	~	6.1	6.3†	6.1	~	~	#
B. BOLIVIA	A	67.9	~	~	47.2	47.8	~	~	~	~
	B	15.4	~	~	~	~	~	~	~	~
	C	**	**	**	**	**	**	**	**	**
	D	16.8ᶜ	~	~	52.8ᵈ	52.2ᵈ	~	~	~	~
C. BRAZIL	A	62.7	82.4	75.1	73.2	65.8	57.6	~	57.7	59.2
	B	33.3	15.9	23.3	25.8	33.6	40.7	~	1.2	1.5
	C	4.0	1.7	1.6	1.1	.7	1.7	~	41.0	39.3
	D	#	#	#	#	#	#	~	#	#
D. CHILE	A	43.9	41.6	41.1	42.8	50.1†	~	~	47.1	51.4
	B	55.0	57.3	57.3	55.6	48.7†	~	~	50.9	45.7
	C	1.1	1.1	1.5	1.4	1.2†	~	~	.5	.7
	D	#	#	#	#	#	~	~	1.5	2.2
E. COLOMBIA	A	74.8	61.5	53.5	~	37.9	27.9	~	24.3	~
	B	24.2	37.1	46.2	~	61.2	71.9	~	75.3	~
	C	1.0	1.4	.3	~	.9	.2	~	~	~
	D	#	#	.1	~	#	#	~	.4	~
F. COSTA RICA	A	47.1	43.2	42.5	42.6	45.0	~	~	46.8	48.3
	B	52.6	56.6	56.8	57.0	55.4	~	~	52.0	51.0
	C	.3	.2	.6	.4	.7	~	~	1.2	.7
	D	#	#	#	#	#	#	~	#	#
H. DOMINICAN REP.	A	93.3	79.9	71.9	69.9	66.1	63.7	67.7	73.5	70.5
	B	#	#	#	#	#	#	#	#	#
	C	6.7	20.1	28.1	30.1	33.9	36.3	32.3	26.5	29.5
	D	#	#	#	#	#	#	#	#	#
I. ECUADOR	A	~	70.7	71.4	64.3	68.3	63.9	68.3	~	~
	B	~	26.8	27.1	33.9	30.0	35.0	30.0	~	~
	C	~	2.5	1.5	1.8	1.7	1.1	1.7	~	~
	D	~	#	#	#	#	#	#	~	~
J. EL SALVADOR	A	~	23.4	24.9	26.8	27.8	27.1	15.4	18.3	27.5
	B	~	75.6	72.5	72.6	71.5	70.9	83.8	81.3	71.8
	C	~	1.0	2.5	.6	.7	2.0	.8	.5	.8
	D	~	#	#	#	#	#	#	~	~
K. GUATEMALA	A	37.8	35.1	33.4	39.3	44.9	43.7	41.3	44.0	41.0
	B	61.4	64.1	66.2	59.7	54.8	56.0	58.0	55.3	58.6
	C	.8	.8	.4	1.0	.3	.3	.7	.6	.4
	D	#	#	#	#	#	#	#	#	#
L. HAITI	A	54.1	27.8	29.9ᵃ	100	100	~	~	~	~
	B	#	#	~	#	#	~	~	~	~
	C	45.9	72.2	70.1	#	#	~	~	~	~
	D	#	#	#	#	#	~	~	~	~
N. MEXICO	A	39.4	48.5	49.3	53.1	57.7	60.3	59.5	~	~
	B	60.1	47.6	50.6	46.8	42.1	39.6	40.4	~	~
	C	.3	.4	.1	.1	.2	.1	.1	~	~
	D	.2	3.5	#	#	#	#	#	~	~
O. NICARAGUA	A	~	25.8	24.4†	~	~	~	~	~	~
	B	~	63.4	64.4†	~	~	~	~	~	~
	C	~	10.9	11.2†	~	~	~	~	~	~
	D	~	#	#	~	~	~	~	~	~
P. PANAMA	A	85.0	35.8	38.6	41.5	44.9	82.1	82.4	88.2	87.3
	B	12.8	10.4	13.8	17.1	16.3	17.9	17.6	11.8	12.7
	C	2.2	53.1	47.6	41.4	38.8	~	~	#	#
	D	#	.7	#	#	#	#	#	#	#
Q. PARAGUAY	A	26.0	~	~	~	27.8	26.0	24.3	21.4	26.1
	B	72.0	~	~	~	69.9	72.1	73.6	77.1	73.3
	C	2.0	~	~	~	2.3	1.9	2.1	1.5	.6
	D	#	~	~	~	#	#	#	#	#
R. PERU	A	85.0	82.4	81.9	80.1	81.0	84.6	75.1	~	~
	B	11.7	17.6ᵃ	18.1ᵃ	16.1	17.9	13.4	23.7	~	~
	C	.4	~	~	.8	.5	1.6	.7	~	~
	D	2.8	~	~	3.0	.6	.4	.5	~	~
S. URUGUAY	A	31.1‡	29.3	29.7	32.2	31.5	28.8	30.8	28.8	32.5
	B	11.1‡	18.3	19.1	32.8	35.0	41.6	45.0	47.0	46.1
	C	~	#	#	#	33.5	29.6	24.2	24.2	21.4
	D	57.9ᵇ,‡	52.3ᵇ	51.2ᵇ	34.9ᵇ	#	#	#	#	#

Table 1519 (Continued)

TOURIST ENTRY,[1] BY MEANS OF TRANSPORTATION, 18 LC, 1970–82

(%)

Recipient Country	Code[2]	1970	1975	1976	1977	1978	1979	1980	1981	1982
T. VENEZUELA	A	~	50.1	50.9	50.6	~	96.6	97.5	~	~
	B	~	9.4	9.3	9.9	~	2.1	.9	~	~
	C	~	40.0	38.6	38.7	~	1.3	1.6	~	~
	D	~	.6	1.2	.9	~	~	~	~	~
UNITED STATES	A	25.5	35.1	38.1	37.7	43.3[†]	49.9[†]	~	53.2	52.2
	B	73.1	62.8	60.1	60.3	54.8[†]	48.1[†]	~	~	~
	C	1.5	2.0	1.8	2.0	1.9[†]	2.0[†]	~	~	~
	D	#	~	~	~	~	#	~	46.8[e]	47.8[e]

1. For absolute data see table 1518 above. Note that totals may not balance due to rounding.
2. Code: A, air; B, terrestrial; C, maritime; D, other.

a. Includes land arrivals.
b. Arrivals via river travel.
c. Arrivals via boat to Lake Titicaca.
d. Includes all arrivals except those by air.
e. Includes arrivals by sea and railroad.

SOURCE: Derived from IASI-AC, 1977, table 335-03; WTO-WTS, 1973, 1974, 1975, 1976, 1977, 1978, 1978/79, 1979/80, 1981/82.

Table 1520

LODGING ESTABLISHMENTS CAPACITY,[1]
17 LC

(N 1982)

Country	Rooms	Beds
A. ARGENTINA	~	~
B. BOLIVIA	~	~
C. BRAZIL	99,854	199,708
D. CHILE	14,293	31,903
E. COLOMBIA[2]	15,439	41,840
F. COSTA RICA	3,804	7,608
H. DOMINICAN REP.	~	~
I. ECUADOR	~	~
J. EL SALVADOR	1,740	2,585
K. GUATEMALA[2]	7,514	15,028
L. HAITI	~	~
N. MEXICO	~	~
P. PANAMA[2]	2,916	5,213
Q. PARAGUAY	2,786	6,135
R. PERU	~	~
S. URUGUAY[2]	11,293	25,104
T. VENEZUELA	~	~
UNITED STATES	~	~

1. Unless otherwise indicated figures refer to lodging establishments called hotels and motels.
2. Hotels only.

SOURCE: WTO-WTS, 1981/82.

Table 1521

EXIT OF NATIONAL TOURISTS, 14 LC, 1970-76

(N)

Country	1970	1971	1972	1973	1974	1975	1976
B. BOLIVIA	42,948	55,022	68,261	76,859	87,220	~	~

Continued in SALA, 20-3209.

Table 1522

RECEIPTS FROM TOURISM,[1] 19 LC, 1965-82

(M US)

Country	1965	1970	1975	1976	1977	1978	1979	1980	1981	1982
A. ARGENTINA	~	74.0	154	180	213	266[†]	279	344	~	~
B. BOLIVIA	2	2.6	19	25	29	35	37	40	~	~
C. BRAZIL	30	30.0	72	56	55	108	132	182	1,798[a]	1,608[a]
D. CHILE	45	50.0	83	96	97	109	127	161	192[b]	123[b]
E. COLOMBIA	28	54.0	164	146	201	329	358	357	763[c]	624[c]
F. COSTA RICA	~	22.1	52	49	54	71	71	87	94	131
H. DOMINICAN REP.	3	16.4	61	91	93[‡]	108	131	168	~	~
I. ECUADOR	7	8.5	29	31	36	50	80	91	~	~
J. EL SALVADOR	~	8.5	18	32	23	37	14	7	~	~
K. GUATEMALA	6	12.1	78	85	105	107	201	183	131	87
L. HAITI[3]	1	8.7	22	28	37	47	63	65	~	~
M. HONDURAS	~	4.1	11	12	14	~	29	27[†]	~	~
N. MEXICO	782	1,454.0	2,171	822	781	3,485	1,443	1,670	1,760	1,406
O. NICARAGUA	~	13.2	26	28	~	~	18	~	~	~
P. PANAMA	~	78.1	133	124	145	146	164	163	171	169
Q. PARAGUAY	~	14.2	10	14	35	46	69	91	80	54
R. PERU	25	52.0	91	118	113	169	202	334	~	~
S. URUGUAY	~	40.8	57	68	180	129	223	298	283[d]	149[d]
T. VENEZUELA	15	50.0	180	214	261	~	265	246	~	~
UNITED STATES[2]	1,380	2,330.0	4,842	5,808	6,164	7,186	8,335	10,100	12,163	11,293

1. Travel receipts are defined by the International Monetary Fund to include receipts for goods and services provided to foreigners visiting the reporting country, including transportation within that country. Includes funds spent by tourists, business travelers, students, patients undergoing medical treatment, military personnel on leave, and traveling government officials. In many cases, comparable data for a national series are not available throughout the period covered by the table, and also close comparisons between countries are often rendered difficult by the lack of uniformity in definitions and scope.

2. For all countries figures cover the following categories of travelers who are formally admitted into the United States as non-immigrant aliens: temporary visitors for pleasure, students, temporary visitors for business, foreign government officials and their employees and families, treaty traders and investors, representatives to international organizations, and miscellaneous minor groups. These figures do not include less formally admitted visitors arriving from Mexico for less than three days.

3. Fiscal year ending September 30.

a. International tourism receipts for 1981-82 have been estimated by EMBRATUR through sample survey based parameters.

b. Latest data received as estimates of receipts are $116.6 million (U.S.)

c. Receipts do not include earnings of retired persons and annuitants.

d. Calculated on the basis of the average rate of the dollar in Dec. 1982.

SOURCE: UN-SY, 1972 and 1973, table 153; UN-SY, 1975, table 164; UN-SY, 1976, table 161; UN-SY, 1977, table 163; UN-SY, 1978, table 162; WTO-WTS, 1978/79, table 20; WTO-WTS, 1979/80, payments section. WTO-WTS, 1981/82, table 15.

Table 1523

TOURIST ARRIVALS TO CUBA, 1950-76[a]

(T)

Year	N	Year	N	Year	N	Year	N
1950	168.0	1957	272.3	1964	--	1971	--

Continued in SALA, 23-3315.

CHAPTER 16

CONSTRUCTION, HOUSING, AND UTILITIES

DEFINITIONS OF TERMS

STAGES OF CONSTRUCTION

Construction Authorized. Building projects for the carrying out of which a permit has been issued.

Construction Completed. It is considered that the work is completed when the building or other structure is physically ready to be occupied or to be put into use.

TYPE OF BUILDING ACTIVITY

Building. A building is any independent structure comprising one or more rooms or other spaces, covered by a roof, enclosed with external walls or dividing walls, which extend from the foundation to the roof and intended for residential, industrial, commercial, educational, or other purposes.

Residential building. A building should be regarded as residential when the major part of the building (i.e., more than half of its floor area) is used for dwelling purposes.

One- or two-dwelling buildings. Detached, semi-detached, row, and terraced buildings with one or two dwellings on one or more floors.

Multi-dwelling buildings. All residential buildings other than one- or two-dwelling buildings.

Non-residential buildings. A building should be regarded as non-residential when less than half of its floor area is used for dwelling purposes.

Industrial buildings. All buildings which are used to house the production, assembly, and warehousing activities of industrial establishments, i.e., factories, plants, workshops, etc.

Commercial buildings. Office buildings and all buildings which are intended for use primarily in wholesale, retail, and service trades, i.e., hotels, restaurants, shops, warehouses, public garages, etc.

Educational buildings. All buildings which are intended for use directly in instructional activities, furnishing academic and technical courses, i.e., schools, universities, etc., as well as museums, art galleries, libraries, etc.

Health buildings. All buildings which are primarily engaged in providing hospital and institutional care, i.e., hospitals, infirmaries, sanitariums, etc.

Other Buildings. Buildings which are not included in any of the above classifications, i.e., non-residential farm buildings, stadiums, recreational buildings, etc.

FLOOR AREA OF BUILDINGS

The sum of the area of each floor of the building measured to the outer surface of the outer walls including the area of lobbies, cellars, elevator shafts, and in multi-dwelling buildings all the common spaces. Areas of balconies are excluded.

DWELLING

A dwelling is a room or a suite of rooms and its accessories in a permanent building or a structurally separated part which is intended for private habitation. It should have a separate access to a street or to a common space within the buildings. Detached rooms for habitation which are clearly built to be used as a part of the dwelling should be counted as part of the dwelling.

Table 1600

NEW BUILDING CONSTRUCTION AUTHORIZED AND NEW BUILDINGS COMPLETED, 15 LC, 1973–81

(N)

Country	Code[1]	1973	1974	1975	1976	1977	1978	1979	1980	1981
A. ARGENTINA	I[a]	101,593	140,068	143,483	107,943	54,198	35,095	33,863	33,335	27,115
	II	~	~	~	~	~	~	~	~	~
C. BRAZIL	I[b,c]	108,154	106,396	112,169	135,535	116,555	139,048	137,615	162,217	132,222
	II[b]	60,019	68,885	63,086	70,178	64,479	87,296	89,567	90,026	88,910
D. CHILE	I[i,q,u]	1,350.9	1,619	1,353.9	1,243	1,244.6	1,932.8	2,975.3	4,031.7	4,935.2
	II[v]	1,247.7	285.2	363.4	1,354.9	953	484.5	198.6	311.9	279.4
E. COLOMBIA	I[c]	17,706	16,583	13,768	14,167	16,040	17,052	14,984	15,194	15,800
	II	~	~	~	~	~	~	~	~	~
F. COSTA RICA	I[d,e]	11,027	15,353	14,316	16,421	13,878	14,852	15,269	15,958	11,385
	II	~	~	~	~	~	~	~	~	~
H. DOMINICAN REP.	I[f]	3,059	5,016	5,331	3,625	4,656	7,065	4,594	5,456	3,532
	II	~	~	~	~	~	~	~	~	~
I. ECUADOR	I[c,g]	5,869	8,340	7,699	8,072	8,824	12,181	9,726	9,612	10,494
	II	~	~	~	~	~	~	~	~	~
J. EL SALVADOR	I[c,h]	2,016	2,819	2,463	1,976	1,521	2,058	4,124	4,762	10,957
	II[l]	2,851	2,217	2,744	2,299	4,203	3,014	5,073	2,977	2,976
K. GUATEMALA	I[e]	1,618	1,623	1,701	2,683	2,432	2,269	1,904	1,529	~
	II[e]	975	811	1,034	1,091	950	~	428	364	310
L. HAITI	I[c,j]	369	325	320	304	445	462	553	620	597
	II[e,j]	408	438	398	370	527	571			
M. HONDURAS[2]	I[k]	1,143	1,516	1,683	1,948	1,727	1,515	1,593	2,271	1,298
	II[k]	1,219	1,516	1,683	1,948	1,727	1,515	1,593	~	
O. NICARAGUA	I[t]	478	1,472	1,789	2,333	1,162	747	168	356	1,017
	II	~	~	~	~	~				
P. PANAMA	I[l,s]	1,621	1,064	506	618	872	871	1,184	952	878
	II	~	~	~	~	~	~	~	~	~
S. URUGUAY	I[m]	514	444	515	429	1,120	~	~	~	~
	II	~	~	~	~	~	~	~	~	~
T. VENEZUELA	I[c,n]	5,229	5,605	5,512	6,653	5,778	5,428	4,495	5,661	4,532
	II	~	~	~	~	~	~	~	~	~
UNITED STATES	I[o,p,q]	1,402.4[r]	1,069.7[r]	1,052.9[r]	1,333.6[r]	1,602.1[r]	1,719.5[r]	1,494.4[r]	1,137.3[r]	986.5[r]
	II	~	~	~	~	~	~	~	~	~

1. Code: I = New building construction authorized.
    II = New buildings completed.
2. Data on construction authorized and completed refer to private construction in Tegucigalpa, San Pedro Sola, and La Ceiba.

a. Beginning 1977 data refer to the capital and Greater Buenos Aires.
b. Including reconstruction and alterations.
c. Data refer to buildings for which a building permit has been issued.
d. Data based on building permits issued by the municipalities.
e. Number of works.
f. Data cover only the urban areas of the country.
g. Including reconstructions.
h. Permits issued by the municipalities to private enterprises and individuals. Construction work done by the Instituto de Vivienda Urbana and the Instituto de Colonización Rural are excluded.
i. Data provided by the Dirección General de Servicios Eléctricos.
j. Data relating to construction authorized and completed cover the municipalities of Port-au-Prince and Petion Ville.
k. Year ending 30 September of the year stated.
l. New construction excluding extensions.

m. Data obtained from the Intendencia Municipal de Montevideo and refer to new construction, restoration, and conversion in the capital.
n. Data refer to private building construction.
o. Data do not include buildings constructed in areas not requiring building permits and represent, therefore, only about 85% of the actual number of all buildings stated. Prior to 1978, construction authorized in building permit–issuing places were based on a universe of 14,000 places. Beginning 1978, the universe was increased to 16,000, accounting for an increase of about 7% in total new building construction authorized.
p. Excluding publicly owned structures.
q. Excluding extensions.
r. Thousands.
s. Data based on permits supplied by the Oficina de Seguridad and refer to new private construction in Panama City.
t. Data on construction authorized refer to building activity in Managua only.
u. Data refer to private holding projects in 80 communes, approved by the Dirección de Obras Municipales. Prior to 1975, data refer to 60 communes.
v. New construction started by the public sector, excluding extensions.

SOURCE: UN-YCS, 1973-80; 1974-81. For previous years, see SALA, 20-900.

Table 1601

ARGENTINA NEW BUILDING CONSTRUCTION AUTHORIZED, 1973–81

Category	Unit	1973	1974	1975	1976	1977	1978	1979	1980	1981
					I. New Building Construction Authorized[1]					
All Buildings										
Number	N	101,593	140,068	143,483	107,943	54,198	35,095	33,863	33,335	27,115
Floor Area	T Me[2]	13,177	17,611	18,251	15,063	12,093	8,055	4,115	4,308	3,812

1. Beginning in 1977 data refer to the capital and Greater Buenos Aires.

SOURCE: UN-YCS, 1973-80; 1974-81.

Table 1602

BRAZIL NEW BUILDING CONSTRUCTION AUTHORIZED AND NEW BUILDINGS COMPLETED, 1973–81

Category	Unit	1973	1974	1975	1976	1977	1978	1979	1980	1981
I. New Building Construction Authorized [1,2]										
All Buildings										
Number	N	108,154	106,396	112,169	135,535	116,555	139,048	137,615	162,217	132,222
Floor Area	T Me^2	30,813	27,735	26,683	31,487	27,199	28,510	30,327	43,592	34,145
Tender Value	T NC	15,639	17,473	19,291	25,622	25,649	~	~	~	~
Residential										
Number	N	~	~	~	~	~	~	129,272	153,444	125,234
Floor Area	T Me^2	21,163	18,292	17,757	22,792	20,338	21,345	23,251	35,369	28,973
Non-Residential										
Number	N	~	~	~	~	~	~	8,343	8,773	6,988
Floor Area	T Me^2	9,650	9,443	8,926	8,695	6,861	7,165	7,076	8,223	5,192
Industrial										
Number	N	~	~	~	~	~	~	1,244	1,261	815
Floor Area	T Me^2	3,596	3,388	3,022	2,352	1,735	2,004	1,978	2,460	1,205
Commercial										
Number	N	~	~	~	~	~	~	5,734	6,102	4,962
Floor Area	T Me^2	4,722	4,777	4,303	4,499	3,646	3,635	3,801	4,320	2,886
Educational										
Number	N	~	~	~	~	~	~	204	169	144
Floor Area	T Me^2	~	~	~	~	~	~	314	294	253
Health										
Number	N	~	~	~	~	~	~	75	100	60
Floor Area	T Me^2	~	~	~	~	~	~	182	151	163
Other[3]										
Number	N	~	~	~	~	~	~	1,086	1,141	1,007
Floor Area	T Me^2	1,332	1,278	1,601	1,844	1,480	1,526	801	998	665
II. New Buildings Completed [1,4]										
All Buildings										
Number	N	60,019	68,885	63,086	70,178	64,479	87,296	89,567	90,026	88,910
Floor Area	T Me^2	16,539	16,241	15,297	17,671	18,627	18,394	19,451	19,432	19,590
Value	T NC	7,180	9,699	10,819	14,846	17,626	~	~	~	~
Residential										
Number	N	~	~	~	~	~	~	84,118	85,127	84,674
Floor Area	T Me^2	12,298	12,217	11,253	12,388	13,082	13,710	14,573	15,500	16,111
Non-Residential										
Number	N	~	~	~	~	~	~	5,449	4,899	4,236
Floor Area	T Me^2	4,241	4,024	4,044	5,283	5,545	4,684	4,879	3,932	3,479
Industrial										
Number	N	~	~	~	~	~	~	872	717	566
Floor Area	T Me^2	1,609	1,553	1,498	1,907	1,883	1,245	1,317	992	885
Commercial										
Number	N	~	~	~	~	~	~	3,831	3,577	3,129
Floor Area	T Me^2	1,924	1,859	2,065	2,513	2,749	2,564	2,487	2,151	2,036
Educational										
Number	N	~	~	~	~	~	~	95	100	77
Floor Area	T Me^2	~	~	~	~	~	~	234	179	94
Health										
Number	N	~	~	~	~	~	~	40	31	21
Floor Area	T Me^2	~	~	~	~	~	~	102	109	33
Other[3]										
Number	N	~	~	~	~	~	~	611	474	443
Floor Area	T Me^2	708	612	481	863	913	875	741	501	431

1. Including reconstruction and alterations.
2. Data for construction authorized refer to buildings for which a building permit has been issued.
3. Prior to 1979 including educational and health buildings.
4. Information covers buildings for which occupancy permits have been issued, although in some cities occupancy permits are not required after completion.

SOURCE: UN—YCS, 1973-80; 1974-81.

Table 1603

CHILE NEW BUILDING CONSTRUCTION AUTHORIZED AND NEW BUILDINGS COMPLETED, 1973–81

Category	Unit	1973	1974	1975	1976	1977	1978	1979	1980	1981
				I. New Building Construction Authorized[1,2]						
All Buildings										
Floor Area	T Me[2]	1,350.9	1,619	1,353.9	1,243	1,244.6	1,932.8	2,975.3	4,031.7	4,935.2
Tender Value	M NC	11.4	140.5	258.7	930.7	2,817.8	6,412.1	13,155.5	26,697	42,079.1
Residential										
Floor Area	T Me[2]	1,098.9	1,384.5	1,050.7	868	776.1	1,276.7	2,173.2	2,932.8	3,660.8
Tender Value	M NC	10	127.2	209.9	638.9	1,799.4	4,470.9	9,841.9	19,573.9	31,956.7
Non-Residential										
Floor Area	T Me[2]	252	234.5	303.2	375	468.5	656.1	802.1	1,093.9	1,294.4
Tender Value	M NC	1.4	13.3	48.8	291.8	1,018.4	1,941.2	3,313.6	7,123.1	10,122.4
Industrial[3]										
Floor Area	T Me[2]	206.7	208	261.9	316.8	414.4	584.9	699.6	929.4	1,064.6
Tender Value	M NC	1	10.8	43	235.9	902.8	1,699.7	2,818.6	5,960.4	8,278.7
Other[4]										
Floor Area	T Me[2]	45.3	26.5	41.3	58.2	54.1	71.2	102.5	169.5	209.8
Tender Value	M NC	.4	2.5	5.8	55.9	115.6	241.5	495	1,162.7	1,843.7
				II. New Buildings Completed[5]						
All Buildings										
Floor Area	T Me[2]	1,247.7	285.2	363.4	1,354.9	953	484.5	198.6	311.9	279.4
Value	M NC	12.5	39	110.3	1,207.4	1,764.1	2,054.7	1,426.8	2,697.7	4,068.2
Residential										
Floor Area	T Me[2]	1,057.5	201.8	239	1,220.6	823.4	259.3	23.5	134.8	46.4
Value	M NC	11.1	32.5	81.7	1,051.5	1,408.4	998	101.1	883.1	471.3
Non-Residential										
Floor Area	T Me[2]	190.2	83.4	124.4	134.3	129.6	225.2	175.1	177.1	233.0
Value	M NC	1.4	6.5	28.6	155.9	355.7	1,056.7	1,325.7	1,814.6	3,656.9
Industrial[3]										
Floor Area	T Me[2]	2.4	12.8	38.3	12.5	35	31	11.9	5.3	1.7
Value	M NC	~	1	5.2	11.1	61.2	82	55.6	37.3	12.9
Other[4]										
Floor Area	T Me[2]	187.8	70.6	86.1	121.8	94.6	194.2	163.2	171.8	231.3
Value	M NC	1.4	5.5	23.4	144.8	294.5	974.7	1,270.1	1,777.3	3,644.0

1. Private new construction projects, excluding extensions.
2. Data refer to private holding projects in 80 communes, approved by the Dirección de Obras Municipales. Prior to 1975, data refer to 60 communes.
3. Including commercial buildings.
4. Including educational and health buildings.
5. New construction started by the public sector, excluding extensions.

SOURCE: UN—YCS, 1973-80; 1974-81.

Table 1604

COLOMBIA NEW BUILDING CONSTRUCTION AUTHORIZED, 1973–81

Category	Unit	1973	1974	1975	1976	1977	1978	1979	1980	1981
					I. New Building Construction Authorized					
All Buildings										
Number of Permits	N	17,706	16,583	13,768	14,167	16,040	17,052	14,984	15,194	15,800
Floor Area	T Me^2	6,072.8	6,725.7	4,842.5	5,127.9	6,404.5	7,126.6	6,093.7	5,942.9	6,173.9
Tender Value	M NC	4,361.7	5,748.5	5,478.5	7,634.1	12,940.2	17,364.8	17,930.8	27,870.1	37,101.6
Residential										
Number of Permits	N	16,740	15,442	12,600	12,985	14,737	15,817	13,813	14,086	14,730
Floor Area	T Me^2	4,948.6	5,074.1	3,637	3,928.2	5,011.4	5,941.3	4,717.7	4,633.6	5,051.7
Tender Value	M NC	3,362.3	4,198.7	3,975.5	5,748.6	9,775.3	14,447.4	13,201.7	20,726.2	28,888
One, Two-Dwelling										
Number of Permits	N	13,572	12,183	9,615	10,889	12,784	12,222	10,057	10,644	10,091
Multi-Dwelling										
Number of Permits	N	3,168	3,259	2,985	2,096	1,953	3,595	3,756	3,442	4,639
Non-Residential										
Number of Permits	N	966	1,141	1,168	1,182	1,303	1,235	1,171	1,108	1,070
Floor Area	T Me^2	1,124.2	1,651.6	1,205.5	1,199.7	1,393.1	1,185.3	1,376	1,308.3	1,122.2
Tender Value	M NC	999.4	1,549.8	1,503	1,885.5	3,164.9	2,917.4	4,729.1	7,144.1	8,213.6
Industrial										
Number of Permits	N	140	186	182	160	173	169	140	121	81
Floor Area	T Me^2	181.8	297.2	290.5	260	223.3	210.8	246.2	175.1	97.9
Tender Value	M NC	126.9	244.3	347.3	355.9	389.4	372	893.9	950.7	650.4
Commercial										
Number of Permits	N	650	740	765	783	877	772	797	744	762
Floor Area	T Me^2	718.8	1,032.2	696.1	714.5	934.6	755.5	919.7	744	762
Tender Value	M NC	647.6	978.1	832.7	1,195.5	2,256.8	2,064.5	3,136.8	4,567.3	6,323.5
Educational										
Number of Permits	N	44	54	64	65	60	63	51	42	42
Floor Area	T Me^2	78	64.7	61.9	87.7	68.5	85.3	70.7	132.8	67.6
Tender Value	M NC	61.9	64.9	73.6	144.1	137.6	153.6	240.8	250.5	379.0
Health										
Number of Permits	N	22	37	30	18	24	19	23	19	21
Floor Area	T Me^2	21.7	65.8	32.6	15.2	59.1	32.3	43.4	29.6	21.2
Tender Value	M NC	20.7	81.8	33.6	17.9	173.5	85.7	110.6	294.2	135.6
Other										
Number of Permits	N	110	124	127	156	169	212	160	182	164
Floor Area	T Me^2	123.9	191.7	124.4	122.3	107.6	101.4	96	189.8	173.2
Tender Value	M NC	142.3	180.7	215.8	172.1	207.6	241.6	347	1,081.4	725.1

SOURCE: UN-YCS, 1973-80; 1974-81.

Table 1605

COSTA RICA NEW BUILDING CONSTRUCTION AUTHORIZED, 1973–81

Category	Unit	1973	1974	1975	1976	1977	1978	1979	1980	1981
				I. New Building Construction Authorized[1]						
All Buildings										
Number of Permits	N	11,027	15,353	14,316	16,421	13,878	14,852	15,269	15,958	11,385
Floor Area	T Me^2	1,160	2,058	2,221	3,246	2,079	2,902	1,793	3,291	1,854
Tender Value	M NC	423.2	804.8	806.2	820.8	877.9	1,134.7	1,480.7	1,533.9	1,506.8
Residential										
Number of Permits	N	9,921	12,784	11,918	13,273	11,163	12,208	12,229	12,439	10,473
Floor Area	T Me^2	832	880	736	751	853	986	1,075	1,016	805
Tender Value	M NC	301.1	420.9	535	507.6	639.9	834.9	1,101.9	1,151	1,207.9
Non-Residential										
Number of Permits	N	1,106	2,569	2,398	3,142	2,715	2,644	3,040	3,519	912
Floor Area	T Me^2	328	1,178	1,485	2,495	1,220	1,915	718	2,275	1,049
Tender Value	M NC	122.1	383.9	271.2	313.2	238	299.8	378.8	382.9	298.9
Industrial										
Number of Permits	N	134	179	157	156	115	120	85	82	42
Floor Area	T Me^2	83	87	66	73	48	69	49	44	20
Tender Value	M NC	26.6	42.3	51	57.5	45.5	56	51.1	42.1	24.3
Commercial										
Number of Permits	N	773	1,405	1,278	795	478	478	533	469	372
Floor Area	T Me^2	195	350	236	122	110	113	146	97	96
Tender Value	M NC	71.8	265.4	179.3	105	108.7	99.1	123.3	145.7	169.6
Educational										
Number of Permits	N	11	16	23	16	12	12	16	27	15
Floor Area	T Me^2	4	7	6	8	7	5	5	7	4
Tender Value	M NC	1.6	4.7	4.6	7.1	8.5	5.3	5.8	6.7	6.4
Health										
Number of Permits	N	6	6	5	1	2	1	~	1	2
Floor Area	T Me^2	3	45	1	#	1	#	#	2	#
Tender Value	M NC	2.1	30.1	.6	.2	.4	#	#	2	.1
Other										
Number of Permits	N	182	963	935	2,174	2,108	2,033	2,406	2,940	481
Floor Area	T Me^2	43	689	1,176	2,292	1,055	1,728	518	2,125	929
Tender Value	M NC	20	41.4	35.7	143.4	74.9	139.4	198.6	186.4	98.5

1. Data based on building permits issued by the municipalities.

SOURCE: UN—YCS, 1973-80; 1974-81.

Table 1606

DOMINICAN REPUBLIC NEW BUILDING CONSTRUCTION AUTHORIZED, 1973–81

Category	Unit	1973	1974	1975	1976	1977	1978	1979	1980	1981
I. New Building Construction Authorized[1]										
All Buildings										
Number of Permits	N	3,059	5,016	5,331	3,625	4,656	7,065	4,594	5,456	3,532
Floor Area	T Me^2	964	1,179	1,191	1,172	1,156	1,385	1,048	1,177	869
Tender Value	M NC	72.3	102.8	132.3	140	150.5	171.5	155.7	195	167.5
Residential										
Number of Permits	N	2,547	4,466	4,861	3,173	4,041	6,388	3,873	4,816	3,026
Floor Area	T Me^2	540	780	879	799	781	980	798	881	659
Tender Value	M NC	40.9	65.3	99.3	94.7	100.5	121.5	115.2	150.2	130.1
One, Two-Dwelling										
Number of Permits	N	2,539	4,297	4,199	2,777	3,820	6,201	3,582	4,594	2,812
Multi-Dwelling										
Number	N	8	169	662	396	221	187	291	222	214
Non-Residential										
Number of Permits	N	512	550	470	452	615	677	721	640	506
Floor Area	T Me^2	424	399	312	373	375	405	250	296	210
Tender Value	M NC	31.4	37.5	33	45.3	50	50	40.5	44.8	37.4
Industrial										
Number of Permits	N	21	26	19	25	15	20	13	21	20
Floor Area	T Me^2	41	86	64	110	24	25	17	31	22
Tender Value	M NC	2.5	4.5	6.5	11.9	1.9	2.8	2.1	3.4	3.2
Commercial										
Number of Permits	N	102	94	84	73	108	81	88	130	112
Floor Area	T Me^2	57	47	34	36	77	62	28	50	37
Tender Value	M NC	3.7	4.2	3.3	4.1	9.6	7.3	3.5	7.1	6.1
Educational										
Number of Permits	N	30	65	35	32	51	104	136	30	16
Floor Area	T Me^2	37	45	37	41	55	71	40	21	11
Tender Value	M NC	2.7	3.1	3.3	4.8	5.2	7.7	5.2	2.9	1.9
Health										
Number of Permits	N	8	2	3	3	24	5	33	8	8
Floor Area	T Me^2	10	2	6	14	10	2	14	12	3
Tender Value	M NC	.8	.3	.9	2	1.1	.2	2.5	2.3	.6
Other										
Number of Permits	N	351	363	329	319	417	467	451	451	350
Floor Area	T Me^2	279	219	171	172	209	245	151	185	137
Tender Value	M NC	21.7	25.4	19	22.5	32.2	32	27.2	29.1	25.6

1. Data cover only the urban areas of the country.

SOURCE: UN-YCS, 1973-80; 1974-81.

Table 1607

ECUADOR NEW BUILDING CONSTRUCTION AUTHORIZED, 1973–81

Category	Unit	1973	1974	1975	1976	1977	1978	1979	1980	1981
				I. New Building Construction Authorized[1]						
All Buildings										
Number of Permits	N	5,869	8,340	7,699	8,072	8,824	12,181	9,726	9,612	10,494
Floor Area	T Me^2	1,401.9	1,888.3	1,931.5	2,172.6	2,326.4	2,763	2,398.7	2,320.4	4,702.8
Tender Value	M NC	1,567.9	2,734.5	3,256.1	4,510.8	5,521.5	6,947.8	6,965.4	7,545.8	9,152
Residential										
Number of Permits	N	5,530	7,920	7,240	7,564	8,268	11,580	9,149	9,009	9,880
Floor Area	T Me^2	~	~	~	~	~	1,865.8	1,656.4	1,529.8	1,659.3
Tender Value	M NC	1,276.2	2,172	2,586	3,531.2	4,125.4	5,417.5	4,918	5,715.9	6,645.1
One, Two-Dwelling										
Number of Permits	N	4,219	6,489	5,196	5,480	6,015	9,030	6,764	6,083	7,395
Multi-Dwelling										
Number of Permits	N	1,311	1,431	2,044	2,084	2,253	2,550	7,385	2,926	2,485
Non-Residential										
Number of Permits	N	339	420	459	508	556	601	577	603	614
Floor Area	T Me^2	~	~	~	~	~	897.2	742.3	790.6	757.1
Tender Value	M NC	291.7	562.5	670.1	979.6	1,396.1	1,530.3	2,047.4	1,829.9	2,506.7
Industrial										
Number of Permits	N	~	~	~	152	165	143	119	119	111
Tender Value	M NC	~	~	~	~	~	382.9	384.4	314.5	321.3
Commercial										
Number of Permits	N	~	~	~	249	295	320	333	344	363
Tender Value	M NC	~	~	~	~	~	915.5	1,194.1	1,055.4	1,838
Educational										
Number of Permits	N	~	~	~	26	33	30	23	35	24
Tender Value	M NC	~	~	~	~	~	80.9	63.2	131.3	100.7
Health										
Number of Permits	N	~	~	~	4	12	9	7	13	8
Tender Value	M NC	~	~	~	~	~	15.9	17.5	65	20.8
Other										
Number of Permits	N	~	~	~	77	51	99	95	92	108
Tender Value	M NC	~	~	~	~	~	135.1	388.2	263.7	226.1

1. Includes reconstructions.

SOURCE: UN-YCS, 1973-80; 1974-81.

Table 1608

EL SALVADOR NEW BUILDING CONSTRUCTION AUTHORIZED AND NEW BUILDINGS COMPLETED, 1973–81

Category	Unit	1973	1974	1975	1976	1977	1978	1979	1980	1981
I. New Building Construction Authorized[1]										
All Buildings										
Number of Permits	N	2,016	2,819	2,463	1,976	1,521	2,058	4,124	4,762	10,957
Floor Area	T Me²	412.8	603.4	383	~	440.9	572.8	567.2	427.2	504.3
Tender Value	M NC	63.4	98.7	86.9	100	177.8	224.9	215.9	156.3	167.1
Residential										
Number of Permits	N	1,864	2,679	2,357	1,805	1,375	1,738	3,879	4,646	10,922
Floor Area	T Me²	297.4	405.2	241.7	291.2	295.2	378.9	379.4	332.9	483.5
Tender Value	M NC	43.4	63.2	47	65.3	132.8	147.3	132.8	115.1	158.7
One, Two-Dwelling										
Number of Permits	N	1,848	2,673	2,355	1,799	1,364	1,475	3,845	4,616	10,840
Multi-Dwelling										
Number of Permits	N	16	6	2	6	11	263	34	30	82
Non-Residential										
Number of Permits	N	152	140	106	171	146	320	245	116	35
Floor Area	T Me²	115.4	198.2	141.3	~	145.7	193.9	187.8	94.2	20.8
Tender Value	M NC	20	35.4	39.9	34.7	45	77.6	83.1	41.2	8.4
Industrial										
Number of Permits	N	24	37	18	44	10	22	14	14	3
Floor Area	T Me²	31	71.2	19.3	~	13.8	10.6	33.2	31.3	3
Tender Value	M NC	2.7	7.5	3.2	8.3	2.6	1.9	8.3	9.4	1.1
Commercial[2]										
Number of Permits	N	128	103	88	127	136	298	231	102	32
Floor Area	T Me²	84.4	127	122	89.8	131.9	183.3	154.6	62.9	17.8
Tender Value	M NC	17.3	27.9	36.7	26.4	42.4	75.7	74.8	31.8	7.3
II. New Buildings Completed[3]										
All Buildings										
Number	N	2,851	2,217	2,744	2,299	4,203	3,014	5,073	2,977	2,976
Floor Area	T Me²	291.7	279.8	256.8	181.6	371.2	300.7	364.8	174.4	181.6
Value	M NC	40	45.3	50.7	37.2	93.3	96.9	124.5	59.9	69
Residential										
Number	N	2,776	2,155	2,730	2,272	4,131	2,925	5,025	2,972	2,973
Floor Area	T Me²	263.9	245.6	245.5	173	340	274.1	342.6	169.9	180
Value	M NC	36.3	41.3	48.9	35.6	86	87.4	115.8	56.9	67.5
One, Two-Dwelling										
Number	N	2,775	2,151	2,728	2,271	4,131	2,925	5,016	2,972	2,901
Multi-Dwelling										
Number	N	1	4	2	1	#	#	9	~	72
Non-Residential										
Number	N	75	62	14	27	72	89	48	5	3
Floor Area	T Me²	27.9	34.3	11.3	8.7	31.2	26.6	22.2	4.5	1.6
Value	M NC	3.7	4	1.8	1.6	7.3	9.5	8.7	3	1.5
Industrial										
Number	N	11	7	1	#	3	1	3	1	#
Floor Area	T Me²	6.2	4.2	1.2	#	1.8	2.4	2.3	#	#
Value	M NC	.5	.6	.1	#	.3	.3	.3	#	#
Commercial[2]										
Number	N	64	55	13	27	69	88	45	4	3
Floor Area	T Me²	21.7	30.1	10.1	8.7	29.4	24.2	19.9	4.5	1.6
Value	M NC	3.2	3.4	1.7	1.6	7	9.2	8.4	3	1.5

1. Permits issued by the municipalities to private enterprises and individuals. Construction work done by the Instituto de Vivienda Urbana and the Instituto de Colonización Rural is excluded.
2. Including educational, health, and other buildings.
3. Data provided by the Dirección General de Servicios Eléctricos.

SOURCE: UN-YCS, 1973-80; 1974-81.

Table 1609

GUATEMALA NEW BUILDING CONSTRUCTION AUTHORIZED AND NEW BUILDINGS COMPLETED,[1] 1973–81

Category	Unit	1973	1974	1975	1976	1977	1978	1979	1980	1981
I. New Building Construction Authorized										
All Buildings										
Number of Construction Works	N	1,618	1,623	1,701	2,683	2,432	2,269	1,904	1,529	~
Floor Area[2]	T Me^2	365.5	353	423.2	451.3	519.4	633.4	997.2	228.2	~
Tender Value	M NC	20.7	21.3	27.7	29.4	36.8	46.7	40.4	23	~
Residential										
Floor Area[2]	T Me^2	211	196.6	208.4	270.2	281.3	278.5	229.4	128.5	~
Tender Value	M NC	11.9	11.6	13.5	18.4	20.4	18	20.2	13.9	~
Non-Residential										
Floor Area[2]	T Me^2	154.5	156.4	214.8	181.1	238.1	354.9	767.8	99.7	~
Tender Value	M NC	8.8	9.7	14.2	11	16.4	28.7	20.2	9.1	~
Industrial										
Floor Area[2]	T Me^2	25.8	21.5	17.8	8.6	21.3	16.2	112.9	6	~
Tender Value	M NC	1	1.1	.7	.4	1.5	.9	1.8	.4	~
Commercial										
Floor Area[2]	T Me^2	60.6	70.1	142.9	87.8	103.6	227	530.1	64.5	~
Tender Value	M NC	3.5	4.5	10.6	5.7	7.6	24.7	16.2	7.1	~
Other[3]										
Floor Area[2]	T Me^2	68.1	64.8	54.1	84.7	113.2	111.7	124.8	29.2	~
Tender Value	M NC	4.3	4.1	2.9	4.9	7.3	3.1	2.2	1.6	~
II. New Buildings Completed										
All Buildings										
Number of Construction Works	N	975	811	1,034	1,091	950	818	1,008	~	~
Floor Area[2]	T Me^2	176.9	165.1	173.1	184.2	139.6	124	248.2	~	~
Value	M NC	9.5	9.5	10.4	11.3	8.9	~	~	~	~

1. Data on authorized and completed construction refer to private building activity in Guatemala City.
2. Area covered by the building.
3. Including educational and health buildings.

SOURCE: UN-YCS, 1973-80; 1974-81.

Table 1610

HAITI NEW BUILDING CONSTRUCTION AUTHORIZED AND NEW BUILDINGS COMPLETED,[1] 1973–81

Category	Unit	1973	1974	1975	1976	1977	1978	1979	1980	1981
I. New Building Construction Authorized										
Residential										
Number of Permits	N	369	325	320	304	445	462	428	364	310
II. New Buildings Completed										
All Buildings										
Number of Works	N	408	438	398	370	527	571	553	620	597

1. Data relating to construction authorized and completed cover the municipalities of Port-au-Prince and Petion-Ville.

SOURCE: UN-YCS, 1973-80; 1974-81.

Table 1611

HONDURAS NEW BUILDING CONSTRUCTION AUTHORIZED AND NEW BUILDINGS COMPLETED,[1] 1973–81

Category	Unit	1973	1974	1975	1976	1977	1978	1979	1980	1981
I. New Building Construction Authorized[2]										
All Buildings										
Number	N	1,143	1,686	1,683	1,948	1,727	1,515	~	~	~
Floor Area	T Me²	223	235.1	224.6	297.5	263.8	287.0	~	~	~
Tender Value	M NC	27.2	31.6	31.8	41.3	39.4	50.9	~	~	~
Residential[3]										
Number	N	985	1,504	1,452	1,741	1,513	~	~	~	~
Floor Area	T Me²	131.6	154.4	123.3	199.2	174	~	~	~	~
Tender Value	M NC	18.3	19.6	17.6	28.6	30.2	32.6	~	~	~
Non-Residential										
Number	N	158	182	231	207	214	~	~	~	~
Floor Area	T Me²	91.4	80.7	101.3	98.3	89.8	~	~	~	~
Tender Value	M NC	8.9	12	14.3	14.2	11.2	21.2	~	~	~
Industrial										
Number	N	25	22	16	28	7	~	~	~	~
Floor Area	T Me²	27.3	14.9	14.6	27	7.9	~	~	~	~
Tender Value	M NC	2	1.5	1.5	1.9	.8	5.5	~	~	~
Commercial										
Number	N	114	146	202	156	161	~	~	~	~
Floor Area	T Me²	57.6	63.2	82	62	66.6	~	~	~	~
Tender Value	M NC	6.2	8.9	12.3	11.1	9.1	13.8	~	~	~
Other[4]										
Number	N	19	14	13	23	46	~	~	~	~
Floor Area	T Me²	6.5	2.6	4.7	9.3	15.3	~	~	~	~
Tender Value	M NC	.7	1.6	.4	1.2	1.3	1.9	~	~	~
II. New Buildings Completed[2]										
All Buildings										
Number	N	1,219	1,516	1,683	1,948	1,727	1,515	1,593	2,271	1,298
Floor Area	T Me²	243.1	227.8	224.6	297.6	263.8	287	354.9	304.6	218.1
Value	M NC	26.3	32.3	31.8	41.3	39.4	50.9	85.5	70.3	61.6
Residential[3]										
Number	N	1,061	1,352	1,443	1,739	1,513	1,314	1,381	2,090	1,177
Floor Area	T Me²	136.5	146.8	129.7	186	178.9	169.6	222.8	220.2	156.1
Value	M NC	16.8	22.5	17.6	27	28.1	29.7	52.9	52.4	44.2
Non-Residential										
Number	N	158	164	240	209	208	201	212	181	121
Floor Area	T Me²	106.6	81	94.9	111.6	84.9	117.4	132.1	84.4	62
Value	M NC	9.5	9.8	14.2	14.3	11.3	21.2	32.6	84.4	17.4
Industrial										
Number	N	25	19	16	31	7	23	29	15	14
Floor Area	T Me²	35.3	14.3	13.1	29.9	7.5	43.6	37.6	20.3	10.3
Value	M NC	2.6	1.4	1.5	1.9	.8	5.5	8.6	3.3	2.1
Commercial										
Number	N	115	126	209	155	162	146	156	150	79
Floor Area	T Me²	67.8	60.9	78.5	72.5	63.7	64.3	86.2	57.7	38.8
Value	M NC	6.5	7.8	12.2	11.2	9.2	13.8	22.2	13	11.9
Other[4]										
Number	N	18	19	15	23	39	32	27	16	28
Floor Area	T Me²	3.5	5.8	3.3	9.2	13.7	9.5	8.3	6.4	12.9
Value	M NC	.4	.6	.5	1.2	1.3	1.9	1.8	1.6	3.4

1. Data on construction authorized and completed refer to private construction in
   Tegucigalpa, San Pedro Sala, and La Ceiba.
2. Year ending September 30th of the year stated.
3. Dwellings or one-family houses.
4. Includes educational and health buildings.

SOURCE: UN-YCS, 1973-80; 1974-81.

Table 1612

NICARAGUA NEW BUILDING CONSTRUCTION AUTHORIZED, 1973–81

Category	Unit	1973	1974	1975	1976	1977	1978	1979	1980	1981
					I. New Building Construction Authorized					
All Buildings										
Number	N	478	1,472	1,789	2,333	1,162	747	168	356	1,017
Floor Area	T Me^2	79.6	322.5	270.2	251.6	217.8	90.2	17.1	19.6	54.7
Tender Value	M NC	32.2	221.6	236.5	213.9	204.3	81.5	13.8	12.5	42.9
Residential										
Number	N	404	1,314	1,694	2,236	1,068	708	153	339	987
Floor Area	T Me^2	50	164.7	176.5	140.5	128.9	58.8	8.5	16.6	45.4
Tender Value	M NC	18.1	110.9	145.2	110.7	118.1	53.6	5.5	10.4	30.8
Non-Residential										
Number	N	74	158	95	97	94	39	15	17	30
Floor Area	T Me^2	29.6	157.8	93.7	111.1	88.9	31.4	8.6	3	9.2
Tender Value	M NC	14.1	110.7	91.3	103.2	86.2	27.9	8.4	2.1	12.1
Industrial[1]										
Number	N	4	7	2	4	2	1	4	3	6
Floor Area	T Me^2	.6	9.6	6.3	8.1	4.7	.1	2.7	.4	1.8
Tender Value	M NC	.2	5.9	3.2	4	3.3	.1	1.5	.2	1.8
Commercial[1]										
Number	N	17	30	16	6	12	3	2	5	10
Floor Area	T Me^2	7.1	52.6	13.4	11	13.2	3.5	2	.6	3
Tender Value	M NC	2.4	38.7	15.1	12.3	17.3	3.4	1	.2	2.7
Educational[1]										
Number	N	11	10	10	8	6	2	2	#	1
Floor Area	T Me^2	7.2	19.6	15.3	17.2	5.8	2	.5	#	.1
Tender Value	M NC	3.1	9.6	8.4	17	4.6	2.2	.3	#	.1
Other[1,2]										
Number	N	42	111	67	79	74	33	7	9	13
Floor Area	T Me^2	14.7	76	58.7	74.8	65.2	25.8	3.4	2	4.3
Tender Value	M NC	8.4	56.5	64.6	69.9	61	22.2	5.6	1.7	7.5

1. Extensions to all non-residential buildings are included in other buildings.
2. Includes health buildings.

SOURCE: UN-YCS, 1973-80; 1974-81.

Table 1613
PANAMA NEW BUILDING CONSTRUCTION AUTHORIZED,[1] 1973–81

Category	Unit	1973	1974	1975	1976	1977	1978	1979	1980	1981
I. New Building Construction Authorized[2]										
All Buildings										
Number	N	1,621	1,064	506	618	872	871	1,184	952	878
Floor Area	T Me2	807.7	429.9	175.8	172.1	131.9	205.5	411.3	400.9	369.5
Tender Value	M NC	77.5	35.9	20.2	20.2	16.7	27.5	57.9	68.3	73.5
Residential										
Number	N	1,530	998	449	571	835	824	1,121	886	807
Floor Area	T Me2	593	253.3	94	101.2	99.1	131.6	203	208.2	259.6
Tender Value	M NC	60.5	27.1	9.9	12	13.3	18.4	29.2	39.4	52.7
One, Two-Dwelling[3]										
Number	N	1,281	884	414	519	810	809	1,068	815	934
Multi-Dwelling[3]										
Number	N	249	114	35	52	25	15	53	71	73
Non-Residential										
Number	N	91	66	57	47	37	47	63	66	71
Floor Area	T Me2	214.7	176.6	81.8	70.9	32.8	73.9	208.3	192.7	136.9
Tender Value	M NC	17	8.8	10.3	8.2	3.4	9.1	28.7	28.9	20.7
Industrial										
Number	N	23	24	6	11	13	7	15	14	6
Floor Area	T Me2	25.4	22	3.5	17.9	7.5	26.9	40.5	22	136.9
Tender Value	M NC	1.1	1.5	.4	1.6	1	3.5	3	3.3	20.7
Commercial										
Number	N	55	33	45	27	20	38	40	37	53
Floor Area	T Me2	158.6	145.5	56.9	42.1	23.2	45.5	161.6	136.6	90.3
Tender Value	M NC	14.1	6.2	5.8	4.2	2.1	5.3	24.8	22.9	14.3
Educational										
Number	N	~	~	1	1	1	#	2	3	5
Floor Area	T Me2	~	~	.2	.1	.1	.1	1.4	6.1	10.2
Tender Value	M NC	~	~	.3	.1	.2	#	.2	.7	2.6
Other[4]										
Number	N	13	9	5	8	3	2	6	12	7
Floor Area	T Me2	30.7	9.1	21.2	10.8	2	1.4	4.8	28	27.3
Tender Value	M NC	1.8	1.1	3.8	2.3	.1	.3	.7	2	2.8

1. Data based on permits supplied by the Oficina de Seguridad and refer to new private construction in Panama City.
2. New construction excluding extensions.
3. Buildings with two dwellings are included with multi-dwelling buildings.
4. Including health buildings.

SOURCE: UN-YCS, 1973-80; 1974-81.

Table 1614
URUGUAY NEW BUILDING CONSTRUCTION AUTHORIZED AND NEW BUILDINGS COMPLETED, 1973–81

Category	Unit	1973	1974	1975	1976	1977	1978	1979	1980	1981
I. New Building Construction Authorized[1]										
All Buildings										
Number	N	514	444	515	429	1,120	~	~	~	~
Floor Area	T Me2	120.6	396.6	303.8	333	482.9	649.1	~	~	~
Tender Value	M NC	144.7	160	182.5	229.4	569.4	517.9	913.2	1,237.2	862.8
Residential										
Floor Area[2]	T Me2	84	316	194.9	229	353.3	471.2	667.7	911.9	626.2
Non-Residential										
Floor Area[3]	T Me2	36.6	80.6	108.9	104	129.6	177.9	245.5	325.8	236.6
II. New Buildings Completed[4]										
All Buildings										
Floor Area	T Me2	335.5	337.3	375.4	380.5	353.7	415.2	667.1	909.3	1,055
Value	M NC	39	76.3	131.7	183.8	238.8	390.4	1,044.4	~	~
Residential										
Floor Area	T Me2	280.6	290.5	318.5	303.8	257.3	310	437.6	~	~
Non-Residential										
Floor Area	T Me2	54.9	46.8	56.9	76.7	96.4	105.2	229.5	~	~

1. Data obtained from the Intendencia Municipal de Montevideo and refer to new construction, restoration and conversion in the capital.
2. Residential area of all buildings.
3. Non-residential area of all buildings.
4. Data obtained from the Banco Central del Uruguay and refer to new construction in Montevideo.

SOURCE: UN-YCS, 1973-80; 1974-81.

Table 1615

VENEZUELA NEW BUILDING CONSTRUCTION AUTHORIZED, 1973–81

Category	Unit	1973	1974	1975	1976	1977	1978	1979	1980	1981
				I. New Building Construction Authorized[1]						
All Buildings										
Number of Permits	N	5,229	5,605	5,512	6,653	5,778	5,428	4,495	5,661	4,532
Floor Area	T Me^2	5,194.1	4,862.1	6,403.4	8,053.8	8,572	8,652	8,609	7,254	5,670.3
Tender Value	M NC	1,778.7	1,970.3	2,990.1	4,714.7	5,959.7	8,315	8,180	9,541	7,824.6
Residential										
Number of Permits	N	4,549	4,959	4,726	5,829	4,854	4,683	3,752	4,690	3,763
Floor Area	T Me^2	3,548.1	3,760.8	4,462.4	5,697.3	5,913	6,694	6,897	5,015	4,346.1
Tender Value	M NC	1,337.8	1,497.9	2,122.3	3,449.9	4,336.7	6,482	6,492	6,605	6,267.9
One, Two-Dwelling[3]										
Number of Permits	N	3,446	3,825	3,673	4,635	3,658	3,563	2,675	4,000	3,204
Multi-Dwelling[2,3]										
Number of Permits	N	1,103	1,134	1,053	1,194	1,196	1,120	1,077	690	559
Non-Residential										
Number of Permits	N	680	646	786	824	924	745	743	971	769
Floor Area	T Me^2	1,646	1,101.3	1,941	2,356.5	2,659	1,958	1,712	2,239	1,323.5
Tender Value	M NC	440.9	472.9	867.8	1,264.8	1,623	1,833	1,688	2,936	1,556.5
Industrial[4]										
Number of Permits	N	525	512	664	649	694	644	693	~	176
Floor Area	T Me^2	1,394.2	912.6	1,663.1	1,846.8	2,032	1,717	1,311	~	497.9
Tender Value	M NC	341.1	347.6	675.7	843.2	1,254	1,611	1,298	~	367.1
Commercial										
Number	N	~	~	~	~	~	~	~	~	524
Floor Area	T Me^2	~	~	~	~	~	~	~	~	709.3
Tender Value	M NC	~	~	~	~	~	~	~	~	1,009.5
Educational										
Number	N	~	~	~	~	~	~	~	~	20
Floor Area	T Me^2	~	~	~	~	~	~	~	~	32
Tender Value	M NC	~	~	~	~	~	~	~	~	40.1
Health										
Number	N	~	~	~	~	~	~	~	~	10
Floor Area	T Me^2	~	~	~	~	~	~	~	~	26.9
Tender Value	M NC	~	~	~	~	~	~	~	~	32.8
Other[4]										
Number	N	155	134	122	175	230	101	150	~	39
Floor Area	T Me^2	251.8	188.7	277.9	509.7	627	241	401	~	57.4
Tender Value	M NC	99.8	124.8	192.1	421.6	369	222	390	~	107

1. Data refer to private building construction.
2. Two-dwelling buildings are included in multi-dwelling buildings.
3. Including commercial buildings.
4. Including educational and health buildings.

SOURCE: UN-YCS, 1973-80; 1974-81.

Table 1616

INDEX OF CONSTRUCTION ACTIVITY, 20 LC, 1974–81[a]
(1975 = 100)

	Country	1974	1975	1976	1977	1978	1979	1980	1981
A.	ARGENTINA	96	100	113	128	127	130	148	~
B.	BOLIVIA	89	100	105	116	120	118	112	~
C.	BRAZIL	88	100	113	123	135	~	~	~
D.	CHILE	135	100	83	83	89	111	139	162
E.	COLOMBIA	105	100	86	91	94	93	102	112
F.	COSTA RICA	95	100	121	126	133	158	158	~
G.	CUBA	84	100	106	116	126	126	126	141
H.	DOMINICAN REP.	92	100	100	111	114	120	130	130
I.	ECUADOR	93	100	107	110	115	114	116	117
J.	EL SALVADOR	67	100	91	125	129	110	73	~
K.	GUATEMALA	87	100	174	195	202	215	225	259
L.	HAITI	96	100	110	114	124	134	137	146
M.	HONDURAS	98	100	104	110	121	131	127	115
N.	MEXICO	94	100	105	99	111	126	141	~
O.	NICARAGUA	101	100	100	105	112	173	229	262
P.	PANAMA	91	100	105	76	106	106	130	146
Q.	PARAGUAY	82	100	118	155	204	266	333	391
R.	PERU	98	100	100	89	80	85	99	110
S.	URUGUAY	75	100	113	116	151	170	176	169
T.	VENEZUELA	85	100	121	150	167	151	128	~
	UNITED STATES	92	100	104	112	126	144	160	171

a. For previous years, see SALA, 21-901

SOURCE: UN-YCS, 1974-81, pp. 234-36.

Table 1617

POPULATION WITH WATER SUPPLY AND SEWERAGE SERVICES, 19 L
(As of December 31, 1980)

	Country	Total					Urban					Rural				
		Total	With Water (T)	(%)	With Sewerage (T)	(%)	Total	With Water (T)	(%)	With Sewerage (T)	(%)	Total	With Water (T)	(%)	With Sewerage (T)	(%)
A.	ARGENTINA	27,863	16,141	58	12,560	45	22,359	14,636	65	8,060	36	5,504	1,505	27	4,500[b]	82
B.	BOLIVIA	5,370	1,842	34	1,022	19	2,430	1,577	65	892	37	2,940	265	9	130	4
C.	BRAZIL	119,099	66,531	56	25,386	21	80,479	64,600	80	25,000	31	38,620	1,931	5	386	1
D.	CHILE	11,260	8,745	78	6,406	57	9,095	8,408	92	6,195	68	2,165	337	16	211	10
E.	COLOMBIA	28,276	15,944	56	11,441	40	17,804	13,910	78	10,850	61	10,472	2,034	19	591	6
F.	COSTA RICA	2,600	2,095	81	973	37	1,466	1,404	96	372	25	1,134	691	61	601[b]	53
H.	DOMINICAN REP.	5,485	2,220	40	691	13	2,806	1,232	47	691	25	2,679	897	34	#	#
I.	ECUADOR	8,354	3,456	41	2,848	34	3,647	2,892	79	2,344	64	4,707	564	12	504	11
J.	EL SALVADOR	4,540	2,477	55	1,602	35	1,903	1,428	75	914	48	2,637	1,049	40	688	26
K.	GUATEMALA	7,260	3,234	45	2,068	28	2,650	2,308	87[d]	1,192	45	4,610	926	20	876[e]	19
L.	HAITI	5,011	338	7	117	2	1,274	271	21	117	9	3,737	67	2	#	#
M.	HONDURAS	3,691	883	24	571	15	1,324	668	50	569	43	2,367	215	9	2	#
N.	MEXICO	67,383	33,539	50	30,217	45	38,767	25,586	66	26,211	68	28,616	7,953	28	4,606	14
O.	NICARAGUA	2,636	1,013	38	735	28	1,344	924	69	503	37	1,292	89	7	232[b]	18
P.	PANAMA	1,830	1,246	68	1,363	74	900	852	95	614	68	930	394	42	749[b]	81
Q.	PARAGUAY	3,000	629	21	1,931	64	1,087	503	46	309	28	1,913	126	7	1,622[c]	85
R.	PERU	17,780	9,011	51	6,676	38	11,480	7,814	68	6,613	58	6,300	1,197	19	63	1
S.	URUGUAY	2,912	2,244	77	1,359	47	2,368	2,229	94	1,359	57	544	15	3	#	#
T.	VENEZUELA	14,033	11,241	80	7,268	52	10,897	9,117	84	7,091	65	3,136	2,124	68	177	6
	LATIN AMERICA[a]	338,383	182,829	54	115,234	34	214,080	160,450	75	99,896	47	124,303	22,393	18	15,338	12

a. Excludes Cuba.
b. Including other sources of supply.
c. Not including public sewerage.
d. 50 percent household connections and 37 percent easy access.
e. Latrines only.

SOURCE: IDB-SPTF, 1983, p. 41.

Table 1618

WATER SERVICES IN 26 CITIES, 13 L, 1975

	City	Drinking Water		Sewerage	Recipient Water Body			Flow Me[3]/sec.		Estimated Outflow of Sewage Me[3]/sec.
		Coverage[1] (%)	Quantity[1] (L/I/D)[2]	Coverage[1] (%)	Name (R = Rio)	Type[3]	Annual minimum	Annual average	
A.	ARGENTINA									
	Buenos Aires	885-91	852[a]	52.4	R. de la Plata and Affluents	II	~	20,425	96
	Córdova	65	460	~	R. Primero	I	2.52	9.44	4

Continued in SALA, 20-910.

Table 1619

HOUSING ACCESS TO WATER SUPPLY, 18 L
(%)

Country	Area	Year	Piped System					Self-Supply				
			Inside House	Within Lot but Outside House	Less than 100 Meters from House	More than 100 Meters from House	Subtotal[a]	Well	Rainwater	River	Other Means	Subtotal[a]
A. ARGENTINA	Total	1960	43.5	3.6	4.4	~	51.5	41.8	~	~	6.7	48.5
	Urban	1960	54.5	3.9	4.5	←——|	62.9	33.5	~	~	3.6	37.1
	Rural	1960	7.4	2.3	4.4	←——|	14.1	68.9	~	~	16.9	85.9
B. BOLIVIA	Total	1976	~	~	~	~	36.8	23.5	.5	33.5	5.8	63.2
	Urban	1976	~	~	~	~	78.9	6.7	.2	4.0	10.1	21.1
	Rural	1976	~	~	~	~	7.9	34.9	.7	53.7	2.8	92.1
C. BRAZIL	Total	1970	~	~	~	~	32.8	24.7	~	~	42.4	67.1
	Urgan	1970	~	~	~	~	55.0	23.6	~	~	21.4	45.0
	Rural	1970	~	~	~	~	2.5	26.3	~	~	71.2	97.5
D. CHILE	Total	1970	57.7	~	13.3	~	71.0	18.9	~	~	10.1	29.0
	Urban	1970	73.4	~	16.1	~	89.5	5.8	~	~	4.7	10.5
	Rural	1970	4.9	~	4.1	~	9.0	62.8	~	~	28.2	91.0
E. COLOMBIA	Total	1973	67.8	←——|	2.1	←——|	69.9	11.8	2.0	12.9	3.4	30.1
	Urban	1973	88.9	←——|	2.5	←——|	91.4	2.7	1.4 ·	1.4	3.1	8.6
	Rural	1973	28.8	←——|	1.4	←——|	30.2	28.4	3.2	34.2	3.9	69.8
F. COSTA RICA	Total	1973	~	~	~	~	69.8	8.0	~	~	22.2	30.2
	Urban	1973	~	~	~	~	~	~	~	~	~	~
	Rural	1973	~	~	~	~	~	~	~	~	~	~
G. CUBA	Total	1970	40.9	~	15.4	~	56.3	33.2	←——|	7.9	2.6	43.7
	Urban	1970	60.8	~	21.8	~	82.6	14.3	←——|	.9	2.2	17.4
	Rural	1970	3.8	~	3.6	~	7.4	68.2	←——|	21.1	3.3	92.6
I. ECUADOR	Total	1970	20.0	13.4	9.5	←——|	42.9	26.1	.8	22.8	7.3	57.1
	Urban	1970	44.8	28.2	10.4	←——|	83.4	3.8	.4	1.8	10.6	16.6
	Rural	1970	3.0	3.2	8.9	←——|	15.1	41.5	1.1	37.3	5.0	84.9
J. EL SALVADOR	Total	1971	26.4	~	20.7	~	47.2	15.3	2.6	33.6	1.3	52.8
	Urban	1971	59.9	~	27.9	~	87.8	6.2	.2	4.9	.9	12.2
	Rural	1971	2.8	~	15.7	~	18.5	21.7	4.3	53.9	1.6	81.5
K. GUATEMALA	Total	1973	16.7	8.7	16.9	←——|	42.3	27.3	~	27.2	3.2	57.7
	Urban	1973	38.1	20.0	24.3	←——|	82.3	9.3	~	3.5	4.9	17.7
	Rural	1973	4.2	2.1	12.6	←——|	18.9	37.8	~	41.1	2.2	81.1
M. HONDURAS	Total	1974	15.4	17.2	10.5	←——|	43.1	29.7	~	26.0	1.1	56.9
	Urban	1974	39.3	36.0	15.2	←——|	90.5	5.7	~	2.2	1.6	9.5
	Rural	1974	4.4	8.5	8.4	←——|	21.2	40.8	~	37.0	.9	78.8
N. MEXICO	Total	1970	38.8	10.6	11.6	←——|	61.0	~	~	~	~	39.0
	Urban	1970	54.0	15.8	10.4	←——|	80.2	~	~	~	~	19.8
	Rural	1970	17.1	3.4	13.3	←——|	33.8	~	~	~	~	66.2
O. NICARAGUA	Total	1971	26.3	6.0	5.2	←——|	37.5	31.2	~	25.4	6.0	62.6
	Urban	1971	52.0	11.9	8.0	←——|	71.8	18.6	~	2.7	6.0	28.1
	Rural	1971	1.6	.2	2.5	←——|	4.4	43.3	~	47.3	5.1	95.6
P. PANAMA	Total	1970	24.2	~	26.9	~	51.1	12.2	.6	13.3	22.8	48.9
	Urban	1970	~	~	~	~	90.7	4.0	~	~	5.3	9.3
	Rural	1970	~	~	~	~	11.9	20.2	~	~	67.9	88.1
Q. PARAGUAY	Total	1972	~	~	~	~	11.1	80.6	←——|	6.7	1.6	88.9
	Urban	1972	~	~	~	~	27.6	67.7	←——|	3.2	1.6	72.4
	Rural	1972	~	~	~	~	#	89.2	←——|	9.1	1.7	100.0
R. PERU	Total	1972	25.3	4.3	11.8	←——|	41.4	9.1	~	39.8	9.7	58.6
	Urban	1972	43.5	7.5	18.1	←——|	69.1	5.7	~	9.7	15.5	30.9
	Rural	1972	1.3	#	3.5	←——|	4.8	13.6	~	79.6	2.0	95.2
S. URUGUAY	Total	1975	~	~	~	~	72.8	17.0	8.1	~	2.1	27.2
	Urban	1975	~	~	~	~	73.2	17.3	7.1	~	2.4	26.8
	Rural	1975	~	~	~	~	3.6	58.4	32.3	~	5.8	96.4
T. VENEZUELA	Total	1971	72.4	~	6.2	~	78.6	~	5.5	7.6	8.3	21.4
	Urban	1971	~	~	~	~	~	~	~	~	~	~
	Rural	1971	~	~	~	~	~	~	~	~	~	~

a. Subtotal for "piped system" plus subtotal for "self-supply" equals 100%.

SOURCE: UN, ECLA, "The Financial Demands of the International Drinking Water Supply and Sanitation Decade in Latin America,"E/CEPAL/6.1165, February 1981.

Table 1620

HOUSING SANITARY FACILITIES, 18 LC

(%)

County	Area	Year	Water Closet			Latrine[a]	None or Unknown[a]
			Sewerage	Septic Tank	Subtotal[a]		
A. ARGENTINA	Total	1960	~	~	61.5	25.2	13.3
	Urban	1960	~	~	73.8	19.3	6.9
	Rural	1960	~	~	21.1	44.7	34.2
B. BOLIVIA	Total	1976	12.7	1.7	14.5	6.8	78.7
	Urban	1976	30.7	3.6	34.4	12.2	53.4
	Rural	1976	.4	.4	.8	3.1	96.1
C. BRAZIL	Total	1970	17.5	9.5	26.9	33.3	39.7
	Urban	1970	29.8	15.2	45.1	40.9	14.0
	Rural	1970	.5	1.6	2.1	22.8	75.1
D. CHILE	Total	1970	45.7	5.9	51.5	45.7	2.7
	Urban	1970	58.3	6.2	64.5	35.2	.3
	Rural	1970	3.3	4.8	8.1	81.2	10.7
E. COLOMBIA	Total	1973	51.4	6.2	57.6	10.5	31.9
	Urban	1973	75.7	6.5	82.2	9.4	8.4
	Rural	1973	6.8	5.6	12.3	12.7	75.0
F. COSTA RICA	Total	1973	14.8	29.4	44.3	44.7	11.1
	Urban	1973	~	~	~	~	~
	Rural	1973	~	~	~	~	~
G. CUBA	Total	1970	~	~	43.8	38.2	18.0
	Urban	1970	~	~	64.1	29.0	6.9
	Rural	1970	~	~	6.0	55.1	38.8
I. ECUADOR	Total	1974	28.1	~	28.1	9.9	62.0
	Urban	1974	64.4	~	64.4	15.8	19.8
	Rural	1974	3.2	~	3.2	5.9	90.9
J. EL SALVADOR	Total	1971	16.1	6.3	22.4	18.8	58.8
	Urban	1971	39.0	12.8	51.8	30.5	17.8
	Rural	1971	.0	1.7	1.7	10.6	87.8
K. GUATEMALA	Total	1973	14.9	3.0	17.9	22.8	59.2
	Urban	1973	39.5	6.0	45.5	36.9	17.6
	Rural	1973	.6	1.3	1.8	14.6	83.6
M. HONDURAS	Total	1974	13.0	1.3	14.4	17.8	67.8
	Urban	1974	38.6	3.3	41.9	36.9	21.2
	Rural	1974	1.2	.4	1.6	9.0	89.4
N. MEXICO	Total	1970	~	~	~	58.5	←——|
	Urban	1970	~	~	~	39.0	←——|
	Rural	1970	~	~	~	86.2	←——|
O. NICARAGUA	Total	1971	15.3	4.0	19.3	34.0	46.7
	Urban	1971	31.0	6.9	37.9	52.7	9.4
	Rural	1971	.2	1.1	1.3	16.1	82.6
P. PANAMA	Total	1970	31.7	8.4	40.1	31.6	28.3
	Urban	1970	62.2	11.7	74.0	23.1	2.9
	Rural	1970	1.5	5.2	6.6	40.1	53.3
Q. PARAGUAY	Total	1972	4.3	10.0	14.3	79.4	6.2
	Urban	1972	10.8	22.8	33.6	63.9	2.5
	Rural	1972	.0	1.3	1.3	89.9	8.8
R. PERU	Total	1972	22.1	.1	22.2	4.8	73.0
	Urban	1972	38.4	.2	38.6	7.7	53.7
	Rural	1972	.5	.0	.5	.8	98.6
S. URUGUAY	Total	1975	43.8	~	43.8	48.3[a]	7.9
	Urban	1975	25.4	~	25.4	67.4[a]	7.3
	Rural	1975	.9	~	.9	74.7[a]	24.5
T. VENEZUELA	Total	1971	40.3	13.2	53.5	23.9	22.6
	Urban	1971	~	~	~	~	~
	Rural	1971	~	~	~	~	~

a. "Water closet" subtotal plus "latrine" plus "None or unknown" equals 100%.

SOURCE: UN, ECLA, "The Financial Demands of the International Drinking Water
Supply and Sanitation Decade in Latin America," E/CEPAL/6.1165, Februrary 1981.

Table 1621

ELECTRICALLY LIGHTED OCCUPIED HOUSING UNITS, 13 LC

			Number of Occupied Housing Units				
					Lacking Electric Lighting		
Country	Year	Area	Total	With Electric Lighting	Total	Kerosene	Other
B. BOLIVIA[1]	1976[†]	Total	989,055	326,287	662,768	~	~

Continued in SALA, 20-907.

Table 1622

POPULATION WITH ELECTRIC LIGHTING, 20 LR, 1960-73

(%)

Country	1960	1970	1973
A. ARGENTINA	69.0	76.0	78.5

Continued in SALA, 21-902.

Table 1623

HOUSING DEFICIT, 20 L, 1960-69

(N)

	Housing Unit Deficit			Housing Units Constructed by Public Sector			
Country	Ca. 1960	Ca. 1965	Ca. 1969	1960-69	Annual Average 1960-65	Annual Average 1960-69	% Increase in Average
A. ARGENTINA	1,500,000	2,000,000	2,630,000	240,323	21,187	28,300	33.6

Continued in SALA, 18-903.

Table 1624

OCCUPIED HOUSING UNITS BY NUMBER OF ROOMS, 15 LC

				Room					
Country	Year	Area	Total	1	2	3	4	5	6 and Over
B. BOLIVIA	1976[1,2]	Total	989,055[a]	441,388	115,458	41,066	12,425	4,414	2,132

Continued in SALA, 20-904.

Table 1625

TENANCY OF OCCUPIED HOUSING UNITS, 19 LC, 1970-76

Country	Year	Code	Total		Urban Areas		Rural Areas	
			N	%	N	%	N	%
A. ARGENTINA	1970	A[1]	6,056,100	100.0	~	~	~	~
		B	3,553,250	58.7	~	~	~	~
		C	1,380,950	22.8	~	~	~	~
		D	1,121,900	18.5	~	~	~	~

Continued in SALA, 20-905.

Table 1626

INHABITANTS BY SIZE OF HOUSEHOLD,[1] 20 LC

Country	Year	Total	Size of Household				
			1 Person	2 Persons	3-4 Persons	5-8 Persons	9 and Over
A. ARGENTINA[2,‡]	1970	22,961,500	615,900	2,250,500	8,711,800	9,661,100	1,722,200

Continued in SALA, 20-903.

Table 1627

STATUS OF PERSONS RESIDING IN PRIVATE HOUSEHOLDS, 14 L

Country	Year of Census	Total	Heads of Household	Spouses	Children	Other Relatives	Guests	Servants	Other Persons
A. ARGENTINA	1960	19,227,447	4,418,791	3,252,791	7,820,735	2,325,279	772,271	239,576	398,776

Continued in SALA, 18-902.

Table 1628

MEXICO: GEOGRAPHIC DISTRIBUTION OF CONSTRUCTION ACCORDING
TO THE INTERNAL CONSUMPTION OF CEMENT, 1970–79

(Each Year = 100.0%)

State	1970	1971	1972	1973	1974	1975	1976	1977	1978	1979
Aguascalientes	1.0	1.0	.8	.8	.9	.9	.9	.9	1.0	.9

Continued in SALA, 23-904.

Part VI: Industry, Mining, and Energy

CHAPTER 17

INDUSTRIAL PRODUCTION

Note: This volume contains statistics from numerous sources. Alternative data on many topics are presented. Variations in statistics can be attributed to differences in definition, parameters, coverage, methodology, as well as date gathered, prepared, or adjusted. See also Editor's Note on Methodology.

Table 1700

INDUSTRIAL PRODUCTION INDEX, 18 LC, 1970–83

(1975 = 100)

Country	1970	1975	1976	1977	1978	1979	1980	1981	1982	1983
A. ARGENTINA										
General[†]	79	100	96	100	91	100	97	83	79	87
Mining	100	100	102	111	114	121	125	126	128	130
Manufacturing	78	100	96	100	89	98	94	79	76	83
Electricity, gas, and water	67	100	103	109	114	130	141	138	142	153
Construction	~	100	112	128	128	131	139	128	86	80
B. BOLIVIA										
Manufacturing	72	100	108	115	~	~	~	~	~	~
C. BRAZIL										
General[†]	61	100	113	116	124	133	142	115	130	108
Mining	92	100	101	96	102	112	127	129	141	157
Manufacturing[10]	61	100	113	116	125	133	143	115	129	107
Electricity	~	100	~	~	~	~	~	~	~	~
D. CHILE										
Mining[1]	90	100	114	116	113	118	124	133	147	146
Manufacturing[9]	128	100	105	116	124	134	142	142	120	126
E. COLOMBIA										
General[†]	78	100	107	110	120	125	129	~	~	~
Mining	114	100	98	95	99	99	104	~	~	~
Manufacturing	73	100	107	112	121	127	130	~	~	~
Electricity, gas, and water	66	100	110	113	123	134	141	~	~	~
E. COSTA RICA[14]										
General	66	100	106	119	128	132	136	~	~	~
Mining	65	100	106	120	129	133	135	~	~	~
Manufacturing	65	100	106	119	129	132	135	~	~	~
Electricity, gas, and water	68	100	109	116	123	129	144	~	~	~
H. DOMINICAN REP.										
Manufacturing[2]	67	100	108	119	123	~	~	~	~	~
I. ECUADOR										
Manufacturing	62	100	110	123	134	147	157	~	~	~
J. EL SALVADOR[4]										
General	76	100	111	118	115	108	~	~	~	~
Mining	68	100	75	75	57	75	~	~	~	~
Manufacturing	77	100	111	117	113	104	~	~	~	~
Electricity, gas, and water	63	100	110	124	135	146	~	~	~	~
K. GUATEMALA[3]										
General	78	100	110	123	132	140	~	~	~	~
Mining	81	100	129	148	229	429	~	~	~	~
Manufacturing	79	100	110	122	130	137	~	~	~	~
Electricity, gas, and water	66	100	108	135	149	159	~	~	~	~
M. HONDURAS										
Manufacturing	87	100	110	121	133	138	~	~	~	~
N. MEXICO										
General[5]	72	100	105	108	119	133	146	159	156	142
Mining[13]	76	100	106	114	130	150	183	211	234	226
Manufacturing[6]	73	100	105	108	119	131	141	152	146	133
Electricity	64	100	112	123	134	147	157	170	183	187
Construction	~	100	104	101	115	130	147	163	160	136
Q. NICARAGUA										
Manufacturing	69	100	113	~	~	~	~	~	~	~
P. PANAMA										
Mining[7]	~	100	115	~	~	~	~	~	~	~
Manufacturing[11]	84	100	102	96	103	114	118	~	~	~
Q. PARAGUAY										
General[12]	79	100	104	122	138	149	160	~	~	~
Manufacturing	81	100	104	130	139	150	161	~	~	~
Electricity	44	100	101	106	120	134	145	~	~	~
R. PERU										
Manufacturing	67	100	105	98	104	110	129	~	~	~
S. URUGUAY										
Manufacturing	93	100	104	110	117	129	132	~	~	~
Electricity, gas, and water	89	100	105	110	121	122	135	~	~	~
T. VENEZUELA										
General[†]	122	100	104	~	~	~	~	~	~	~
Mining	151	100	98	~	~	~	~	~	~	~
Manufacturing[8]	78	100	118	134	156	174	201	~	~	~
Electricity	56	100	105	~	~	~	~	~	~	~

Table 1700 (Continued)

INDUSTRIAL PRODUCTION INDEX, 18 LC, 1970–83

(1975 = 100)

Country	1970	1975	1976	1977	1978	1979	1980	1981	1982	1983
UNITED STATES[15]										
General	92	100	111	117	124	129	125	128	118	125
Mining	99	100	101	105	110	111	118	126	112	103
Manufacturing	91	100	112	119	126	132	126	129	118	127
Electricity and gas	85	100	104	107	111	114	115	116	116	118
Construction	~	100	108	114	119	118	107	104	~	~

1. Including smelting and refining of copper; excluding natural gas.
2. Excluding products of petroleum and coal, pottery, transport equipment, and musical instruments.
3. Index numbers of gross domestic product (at constant prices of 1958).
4. Index numbers of gross domestic product (at constant prices of 1966).
5. Including construction.
6. Excluding petroleum refineries and furniture.
7. Nonmetallic mineral products.
8. Excluding footwear, including cold storage and motion picture production.
9. Excluding slaughtering, sawmills, and smelting and refining of copper.
10. Excluding leather and leather products, wood products, furniture, printing and publishing, and miscellaneous manufacturing industries.
11. Excluding textiles, machinery, and transport equipment.
12. Including mining.
13. Including petroleum refineries.
14. Index numbers of gross domestic product (at constant prices of 1966).
15. Adjusted for seasonal variations.

SOURCE: UN-SY, 1981, table 107; UN-MB, 38:6 (1984) table 10.

Table 1701

AUTOMOBILE PRODUCTION, ALADI COUNTRIES,[1] 10 LR, 1977-82

(N)

	Country	1977	1978	1979	1980	1981	1982[‡]
A.	ARGENTINA	235,350	179,160	253,217	281,793	172,363	132,116
B.	BOLIVIA	~	~	~	416	683	747
C.	BRAZIL	919,239	1,063,194	1,127,966	1,165,206	780,852	860,593
D.	CHILE	13,089	20,048	20,151	29,259	25,893	10,234
E.	COLOMBIA	36,966	44,468	48,677	42,727	35,558	35,567
I.	ECUADOR	~	839	1,132	3,136	2,200	2,500
N.	MEXICO	280,820	384,127	444,426	489,812	597,118	485,500
R.	PERU	25,222	11,243	10,745	18,699	22,034	21,696
S.	URUGUAY	6,937	9,462	12,941	13,264	12,586	6,292
T.	VENEZUELA	163,297	182,678	157,895	155,087	154,472	~
	LATIN AMERICA	1,680,926	1,895,219	2,077,150	2,199,399	1,803,788	1,555,245

1. Except for Argentina, Brazil, and Mexico, data represent assembly plant production.

SOURCE: Mexico-NAFINSA-MV, May 9, 1983.

Table 1702

BUTTER PRODUCTION, 20 LC, 1959–81

(T MET)

	Country	1959	1970	1975	1976	1977	1978	1979	1980	1981
A.	ARGENTINA	61	28	40	40	30	29	33	29	29‡
B.	BOLIVIA	~	#	#	#	#	1	#	1†	1†
C.	BRAZIL	29	45†	63‡	66‡	69‡	90‡	90‡	90‡	95‡
D.	CHILE[1]	7	8‡	7	5	5	4	4	4‡	5‡
E.	COLOMBIA	~	11†	11†	11†	11†	12†	12†	12†	13†
F.	COSTA RICA	~	3†	3†	3†	3†	3†	3†	3†	3†
G.	CUBA	~	#	8	5	6	11	11	10	10†
H.	DOMINICAN REP.	~	#	1	1	1	1	1	1	1†
I.	ECUADOR	~	4†	5†	6†	6†	6†	4†	4†	4†
J.	EL SALVADOR	~	5†	5†	5†	5†	5†	6†	6†	6†
K.	GUATEMALA	~	4†	4†	4†	4†	4†	4†	4†	5†
L.	HAITI	~	~	~	~	~	~	~	~	~
M.	HONDURAS	~	4†	4†	4†	4†	4†	4†	4†	4†
N.	MEXICO	~	18†	23†	23†	24†	25†	25†	26†	27†
O.	NICARAGUA	~	3†	4†	4†	4†	4†	4†	2†	2†
P.	PANAMA	~	#†	#†	#†	#†	#†	#†	#†	#†
Q.	PARAGUAY	~	~	~	~	~	~	~	~	~
R.	PERU	3	5	6	6	5‡	4†	5‡	5‡	4‡
S.	URUGUAY	5	7	6‡	6†	6†	6†	6	8‡	8‡
T.	VENEZUELA	4	5	6	8	7	7	10‡	10‡	10‡
	UNITED STATES	640	518	446	444	493	451	447	519	561

1.   Twelve months beginning in April of year stated.

SOURCE: SALA, 22-1904; UN-SY, 1981, table 125.

Table 1703

CEMENT PRODUCTION,[1] 20 LRC, 1953–82

(T MET)

PART I. UN-SY SERIES

	Country	1953	1968	1970	1975	1976	1977	1978	1979	1980
A.	ARGENTINA	1,655	4,213	4,770	5,361	5,707	6,030	6,322	6,698	7,263
B.	BOLIVIA	34	71	116	226	220	267	254	251	260
C.	BRAZIL	1,655	7,281	9,002	16,391	18,675	20,545	22,348	23,683	25,879
C.	CHILE	762	1,251	1,349	1.026	968	1,140	1,203	1,357	1,583
E.	COLOMBIA	875	2,367	1,757	3,091	3,612	3,298	4,153	4,257‡	4,336‡
F.	COSTA RICA	~	128	187	330	362	406	425	438‡	440‡
G.	CUBA	405	780	742	2,083	2,501	2,656	2,712	2,613	2,831
H.	DOMINICAN REP.	130	328	493	555	654	862	839	862	928
I.	ECUADOR	91	434	458	604	608	623	834	1,099	1,397
J.	EL SALVADOR	30	158	167	340	322	334	520	490	550
K.	GUATEMALA	67[a]	200	231	341	445	491	515	573	576‡
L.	HAITI	26[b]	44	65	144	246	268	247	195	243
M.	HONDURAS	~	129	161	271	234	247	274	625‡	635‡
N.	MEXICO	1,754	6,126	7,267	11,200	12,691	13,328	14,150	15,352	16,398
O.	NICARAGUA	24	90	98	177	226	226	199	340	349
P.	PANAMA	80	165	181	277	282	271	300‡	466‡	499‡
Q.	PARAGUAY	3	24	63	138	155	200	166	155	177
R.	PERU	449	1,098	1,144	1,949	1,966	1,970	2,019	2,500	2,994
S.	URUGUAY	297	506	497	632	676	682	674	680	684
T.	VENEZUELA	982	2,384	2,318	3,455	3,538	3.136	3,426	3,979	4,100
	UNITED STATES	45,001	68,792	67,682	62,130	66,665	71,200	74,828	73,648	67,675

1.   The figures cover, as far as possible, all hydraulic cements used for construction
     (portland, metallurgic, aluminous, natural, etc.).
a.   Refers to volume of sales only.
b.   1954.

SOURCE: UN-SY, 1967, table 125; UN-SY, 1978, table 124; UN-SY, 1979/80, table 112;
     UN-SY, 1981, table 152.

Table 1703 (Continued)

CEMENT PRODUCTION,[1] 20 LRC, 1953–82
(T MET)

PART II. MV SERIES

	Country	1977	1978	1979	1980	1981	1982[‡]
A.	ARGENTINA	6,002	6,316	6,667	7,073	6,651	5,595
B.	BOLIVIA	267	275	270	277	372	342
C.	BRAZIL	21,123	23,239	24,871	27,194	26,052	25,718
D.	CHILE	1,140	1,203	1,357	1,584	1,863	1,011
E.	COLOMBIA	3,298	4,152	4,257	4,351	4,633	5,126
I.	ECUADOR	645	1,058	1,035	1,200	1,700	1,800
N.	MEXICO	13,097	13,928	15,127	16,263	17,972	19,029
Q.	PARAGUAY	200	166	154	182	156	107
R.	PERU	2,100	2,063	2,351	2,810	2,729	2,567
S.	URUGUAY	683	687	702	700	611	573
T.	VENEZUELA	3,472	4,107	3,973	4,842	4,877	4,304
	LATIN AMERICA	49,927	57,194	60,784	66,476	67,616	66,112

SOURCE: Mexico-NAFINSA-MV, May 9, 1983.

Table 1704

CHEESE PRODUCTION, 20 LC, 1959–81
(T MET)

	Country	1959	1970	1975	1976	1977	1978	1979	1980	1981
A.	ARGENTINA	116	167	226	240	236	245	248	248	240[‡]
B.	BOLIVIA[1]	~	6[†]	7[†]	7[†]	7[†]	7[†]	7[†]	7[†]	7[†]
C.	BRAZIL[2,3]	31	50[†]	53[†]	54[†]	55[†]	56[†]	58[†]	58[†]	58[†]
D.	CHILE[1]	~	23	14	15	19	17	18	19	21
E.	COLOMBIA[1]	~	39[†]	38[†]	39[†]	42[†]	43[†]	44[†]	44[†]	45[†]
F.	COSTA RICA[1]	~	4	5[†]	5[†]	5[†]	5[†]	6[†]	6	5
G.	CUBA[1]	~	1	7	7	10	9	10	11	12[†]
H.	DOMINICAN REP.[1]	1	1	1	1	1	2	2	2	1[†]
I.	ECUADOR[1,2]	~	10[†]	13[†]	14[†]	14[†]	15[†]	13[†]	12[†]	12[†]
J.	EL SALVADOR[1]	~	15[†]	16[†]	16[†]	17[†]	17[†]	18[†]	18[†]	18[†]
K.	GUATEMALA[1]	~	12[†]	13[†]	13[†]	13[†]	14[†]	14[†]	14[†]	15[†]
L.	HAITI[3]	~	1[†]	2[†]	2[†]	2[†]	2[†]	2[†]	2[†]	2[†]
M.	HONDURAS[1]	~	7[†]	8[†]	8[†]	8[†]	8[†]	8[†]	8[†]	8[†]
N.	MEXICO[1,3]	~	78[†]	89	91	93	96	96[†]	97[†]	99[†]
O.	NICARAGUA[1]	~	14[†]	16[†]	16[†]	17[†]	16[†]	15[†]	7[†]	8[†]
P.	PANAMA	~	1	#	#[†]	#[†]	#[†]	#[†]	#[†]	#[†]
Q.	PARAGUAY	~	~	~	~	~	~	~	~	~
R.	PERU[1,3]	9	35	37	37	38[†]	37	34	34	33
S.	URUGUAY[1]	7	9	8[†]	8[†]	8[†]	8[†]	11[†]	12[†]	12[†]
T.	VENEZUELA[1]	15	27	39	44	43	29	28[‡]	28[‡]	28[‡]
	UNITED STATES[1]	~	1,330	1,593	1,829	1,834	1,909	1,989	2,108	2,212

1. Cheese from whole and partly skimmed milk of cows or buffalo.
2. Cheese from sheep milk.
3. Cheese from goat milk.

SOURCE: SALA, 22-1904; UN-SY, 1981, table 126.

Table 1705

CIGARETTE PRODUCTION, 20 LC, 1953–80

(M)[1]

	Country	1953	1963	1970	1975	1976	1977	1978	1979	1980
A.	ARGENTINA	21,675	24,619	30,220	38,621	37,526	35,926	33,558	33,368	34,680
B.	BOLIVIA	443	496	730	1,500	1,650	1,336	1,400	1,260	1,300
C.	BRAZIL[3]	41,599	59,964	70,703	101,741	112,101	129,000	137,000	137,000	142,300
D.	CHILE	5,382	6,315	6,590	8,149	8,850	9,502	9,860	9,988	10,510
E.	COLOMBIA	12,089	17,753	19,080	16,972	18,344	18,520	18,500	20,600	21,200
F.	COSTA RICA	~	1,265	1,420	2,154	2,270	2,381	2,322	2,403	2,452
G.	CUBA	7,743	15,346	19,806	15,366	14,760	15,881	16,908	17,377	15,109
H.	DOMINICAN REP.	896	1,722	2,125	3,023	3,227	3,128	3,230	3,364	3,375
I.	ECUADOR	743	729	1,295	2,085	3,736	4,224	3,931	4,090	3,858
J.	EL SALVADOR	799	1,076	1,441	1,779	1,912	2,154	2,320‡	2,500‡	2,500‡
K.	GUATEMALA	1,550	1,997	2,986	2,360	3,187	3,307	3,462	3,615	2,699
L.	HAITI	259	336	421	674	746	782	919	988	1,094
M.	HONDURAS	801	1,214	1,266	1,804	1,965	2,151	2,170	2,311	2,475
N.	MEXICO	26,434	33,659	40,633	46,763	46,653	49,933	50,580	52,791	54,520
O.	NICARAGUA	654	891	1,260	1,588	1,695	1,838	1,831	1,904	2,228
P.	PANAMA	~	742	1,011	1,045	1,077	983	1,081	1,057	1,083
Q.	PARAGUAY	660	528	458	834	681	787	818	808	648
R.	PERU	2,280	1,938	2,904	3,722	3,750	3,657	3,378	3,650	4,034
S.	URUGUAY	~	2,455	3,121	3,349‡	3,453‡	3,377‡	3,548‡	3,863‡	3,914
T.	VENEZUELA	2,725	8,256	10,463	16,486	18,755	19,880	21,073	22,000	21,500
	UNITED STATES[2]	423,070	543,687	562,153	626,760	688,171	672,639	687,988	706,974	697,000

1. Where production of cigarettes was reported by weight, a conversion rate of one million
   cigarettes per metric ton has been used.
2. Twelve months ending June 30 of year stated.
3. Production by main establishments only.

SOURCE: UN-SY, 1968, table 95; UN-SY, 1978, table 92; UN-SY, 1979/80, table 86;
   UN-SY, 1981, table 132.

Table 1706

COPPER (REFINED) PRODUCTION, 4 LC, 1970–80

(T MET)

	Country	1970	1975	1976	1977	1978	1979	1980
C.	BRAZIL	18.6[a]	74.8	31.1	28.6	70.9	83.9	72.9‡
D.	CHILE	461.3	535.2	632.0	614.0	749.1	781.8	810.7
N.	MEXICO	53.9	73.6	82.9	79.0	79.3	87.0	84.3
R.	PERU	36.2	53.8	131.7	182.4	185.4	230.8	230.6
	UNITED STATES	2,065.7	1,621.9	1,736.8	1,707.0	1,869.2	2,013.8	1,745.4

a. Primary metal only.

SOURCE: UN-SY, 1977, table 129.

Table 1707

COTTON (WOVEN) FABRIC PRODUCTION,[1] 16 LC, 1953–80

(Measure Varies)[3,4,7]

	Country	Code[2]	1953	1963	1970	1975	1976	1977	1978	1979	1980
A.	ARGENTINA[3]	A + B	72	63	76	70	73	~	~	~	~
B.	BOLIVIA[4]	A	6	10	12	10	6	4	~	12	~
C.	BRAZIL[4]	A + B	~	231	784[a]	864[a]	901	~	~	~	~
D.	CHILE[4,5]	A + B	81	89	100	53	50	59	69	67	~
E.	COLOMBIA[4,6]	A	181	299	~	~	~	~	~	~	~
G.	CUBA[7]	A	~	91	76	138	134	149	154	149	157
H.	DOMINICAN REP.[4,8]	A + B	2	8	7	8	10	9	12	~	~
I.	ECUADOR[4,9]	A + B	17	31	29	28	29	34	35	~	~
J.	EL SALVADOR[4,6]	A	13	36	37	23	13	16	~	~	~
L.	HAITI[4]	A	2	3	3	1	2	1	1	1	1
M.	HONDURAS[4,6]	A	1	2	11	15	14	14	14	8	8
N.	MEXICO[3]	A + B	36	99	119	123	73	70	67	68	67
O.	NICARAGUA[4]	A	4	11	16	~	~	~	~	4.8	7.4
Q.	PARAGUAY[4]	A	2	15	20	16	15	20	21	20	17
R.	PERU[4]	A	~	85	~	126	~	~	~	~	~
T.	VENEZUELA[4,6]	A + B	18	59	80	~	~	~	~	~	~
	UNITED STATES[4]	A + B	9,330	8,009	5,711	3,744	4,314	3,983	3,664	3,527	4,355

1. The data refer, in general, to the total production of woven cotton fabrics (including mixed fabrics where indicated) before undergoing finishing processes such as bleaching, dyeing, printing, mercerizing, glazing, etc.
2. Code: A = pure; B = mixed.
3. Thousand metric tons.
4. Million meters.
5. Incomplete coverage.
6. Including finished fabrics.

7. Million square meters.
8. Including a small amount of rayon fabrics.
9. After undergoing finishing processes.

a. Incomplete coverage.

SOURCE: UN-SY, 1968, table 99; UN-SY, 1978, table 94; UN-SY, 1979/80, table 88; UN-SY, 1981, table 133.

Table 1708

COTTON (YARN) PRODUCTION,[1] 13 LC, 1953–80

(T MET)

	Country	Code[4]	1953	1963	1970	1975	1976	1977	1978	1979	1980
A.	ARGENTINA	A	76.2	72.8	89.6	89.2	91.7	95.0	83.6	92.4	74.6
B.	BOLIVIA	A	.2	.3	1.2	.3	.6	2	1	1.8	~
C.	BRAZIL[2]	A + B	71.1	110.9	118.0	60.4	69.7	~	~	~	~
D.	CHILE[3]	A	3.9	23.4	26.8	~	~	~	~	~	~
E.	COLOMBIA	A + B	.6	5.4	1.3	22.8	53.7	54	47.8	55.5	~
G.	CUBA	A	~	14.2	11.8	21.0	22.2	24.0	24.3	21.7	25
H.	DOMINICAN REP.	B	.2	~	#	.5	.5	.2	1.0	~	~
I.	ECUADOR	A + B	.3	.9	1.7	1.2	1.7	1.1	~	~	~
J.	EL SALVADOR	A	.7	3.1	3.7	5.7	4.5	6.4	~	~	~
N.	MEXICO	A	~	103.7	132.0	158.3	~	~	~	~	~
Q.	PARAGUAY	A	12.0	12.9	11.6	32.2	33.8	72.8	90.7	73.3	74.9
R.	PERU	A + B	~	17.5	~	~	~	~	~	~	~
T.	VENEZUELA	A + B	4.2	13.6	13.0	~	~	~	~	~	~
	UNITED STATES	A + B	1,695.0	1,761.4	1,525	1,101.0	1,222	1,141	1,096	1,112‡	1,119‡

1. The data refer to the total weight of pure cotton yarn spun (including mixed yarns where indicated), whether for sale, on commission, or for further processing. Yarn spun from cotton waste is included. Unless otherwise stated, tire cord yarn is excluded.
2. Production in São Paulo only.
3. Estimated on the basis of mill consumption data supplied by the international Cotton Advisory Committee, allowing an average waste rate of about 8%.
4. Code: A = pure; B = mixed.

SOURCE: UN-SY, 1968, table 98; UN-SY, 1978, table 93; UN-SY, 1979/80, table 87; UN-SY, 1981, table 134.

Table 1709

FERTILIZER (NITROGENOUS) PRODUCTION, 19 LC, 1948–81[a]

(T MET)

Country	1948/49-1952/53	1952/53-1956/57	1965/66	1969/70	1973/74	1974/75	1975/76	1976/77	1977/78	1978/79	1979/80	1980/81
A. ARGENTINA	2.3[b]	1.1	4.0‡	20.4	28.6	25.0‡	18.0‡	20.7‡	27.2	27.9	25.4	25.4
B. BOLIVIA	#	#	#	#	#	#	#	#	#	~	~	~
C. BRAZIL[1]	.5	1.4	14.4	6.5	114.3	150.2	160.8	200.3	231.4	273.1	288.0	384.5‡
D. CHILE[1]	237.3	215.0	183.0‡	120.3‡	106.7	113.3	115.6	99.8	96.0	89.2	93.9	100.7
E. COLOMBIA[1]	~	~	39.0‡	49.5‡	81.3	86.7	65.5	66.4	71.6‡	59.4	56.7	41.9‡
F. COSTA RICA	~	~	10.0‡	12.4	27.0‡	30.0‡	30.0‡	30.8	32.4‡	33.1‡	36.0‡	40‡
G. CUBA[1]	~	~	~	~	20.0‡	45.9‡	82.0‡	68.7	49.6	34.3‡	131.5	111.9
H. DOMINICAN REP.	#	#	#	#	#	#	#	#	#	#	#	#
I. ECUADOR	~	~	~	2.8	1.5‡	2.0‡	1.7	1.9	1.6	1.6‡	2.5	2.4‡
J. EL SALVADOR	~	~	4.0‡	8.0‡	7.0‡	7.0‡	5.3	4.5	12.4‡	24.4	15.0‡	~
K. GUATEMALA	~	~	~	~	~	~	3.0‡	6.0‡	6.4‡	6.6	2.0‡	~
L. HAITI	#	#	#	#	#	#	#	#	#	#	#	~
M. HONDURAS	#	#	#	#	#	#	#	#	#	#	#	~
N. MEXICO	8.8	13.7	155.0‡	362.3	542.5	564	606.7	604.5	611.2	593.4	642.0	753.2‡
O. NICARAGUA	#	#	#	#	#	#	#	#	#	#	#	~
P. PANAMA	#	#	#	#	#	#	#	#	#	#	#	~
Q. PARAGUAY	#	#	#	#	#	#	#	#	#	#	#	~
R. PERU[1]	33.3[d]	39.5[d]	43.4[d]	32.9[c]	21.1	20.0	33.6	55.0	68.8	70.7	66.9	73.8
T. VENEZUELA	~	~	24.2‡	14.0	6.1‡	47.7‡	49.8‡	74.7‡	75.0‡	61.7	102.6	144.7‡
UNITED STATES[2,3]	~	~	~	7,562.0	9,158.0	8,474.0	9,591.0	9,787.9	9,495.0	10,076.0	11,180.0	11,788.0

1. Calendar year referring to the first part of the split year.
2. Excluding sodium nitrate.
3. Including data for Puerto Rico.

a. Cf. SALA, 22-1521.
b. 1952/53.
c. Production of guano only.
d. Includes guano.

SOURCE: SALA, 16-224; UN-SY, 1974, table 117; UN-SY, 1978, table 117; UN-SY, 1979/80, table 105; UN-SY, 1981, table 148.

Table 1710

IRON (PIG AND FERROALLOY) PRODUCTION, 7 LC, 1970–80

(T MET)

Country	1970	1975	1976	1977	1978	1979	1980
A. ARGENTINA[1]	847	1,094	1,280	1,100	1,480	1,195	1,100
C. BRAZIL	4,339	7,393	8,581	9,879	10,571	12,203	13,379
D. CHILE[1]	481	432	403	427	590	668	659
E. COLOMBIA	229	293	286	223	297	240	279
N. MEXICO	2,353	3,082	3,548	4,206	5,058	5,026	5,330
R. PERU[1]	86	307	223	244	246	257	261
T. VENEZUELA[1]	510	535	427	497	693	1,332	1,695
UNITED STATES	85,303	74,253	80,541	73,780	81,054	80,630	63,746

1. Excluding ferro-alloys.

SOURCE: UN-SY, 1977, table 125; UN-SY, 1978, table 125; UN-SY, 1979/80, table 113; UN-SY, 1981, table 153.

Table 1711

MEAT PRODUCTION,[1] 19 LC, 1961–81
(T MET)

	Country	1961-65	1970	1975	1976	1977	1978	1979	1980	1981[‡]
A.	ARGENTINA	2,569	3,021	2,825	3,204	3,295	3,544	3,486	3,267	3,377
B.	BOLIVIA	70	90	113	121	127	131	139	141	145
C.	BRAZIL	2,026	2,669	2,981	3,025	3,336	3,218	3,066	3,135	3,282
D.	CHILE	202	249	273	277	228	219	232	232	250
E.	COLOMBIA	447	495	577	558	646	685	703	648	702
F.	COSTA RICA	36	52	74	72	72	85	93	86	90
G.	CUBA	190	237	171	195	200	206	207	206	207
H.	DOMINICAN REP.	33	43	57	63	59	68	69	61	47
I.	ECUADOR	81	99	115	112	128	145	154	164	174
K.	GUATEMALA	55	72	75	81	83	85	96	99	115
L.	HAITI	33	47	56	47	55	60	59	51	43
M.	HONDURAS	27	40	48	57	50	65	74	65	62
N.	MEXICO	705	708	923	944	1,028	1,057	1,015	1,127	1,127
O.	NICARAGUA	40	76	82	92	101	100	98	66	49
P.	PANAMA	29	39	50	53	54	58	44	53	48
Q.	PARAGUAY	139	172	156	162	186	184	190	198	202
R.	PERU	175	190	188	189	190	191	189	185	168
S.	URUGUAY	381	488	407	459	405	377	318	384	453
T.	VENEZUELA	182	253	357	369	363	400	432	447	450
	UNITED STATES	13,826	16,448	16,675	17,966	18,013	17,498	17,066	17,680	17,703

1. Beef, veal, pork, mutton, and lamb.

SOURCE: UN-SY, 1976, table 80; UN-SY, 1978, table 80; UN-SY, 1979/80, table 75;
UN-SY, 1981, table 124.

Table 1712

METAL (SHEET) PRODUCTION, ALADI COUNTRIES,
9 LR, 1977–82
(T MET)

	Country	1977	1978	1979	1980	1981	1982[‡]
A.	ARGENTINA	2,282	2,167	2,554	2,127	1,937	2,345
C.	BRAZIL	8,815	10,005	11,189	12,850	11,052	11,357
D.	CHILE	383	454	503	571	512	390
E.	COLOMBIA	295	332	307	320	321	314
I.	ECUADOR	74	85	118	116	111	127
N.	MEXICO	4,151	5,157	5,642	5,876	6,119	5,565
R.	PERU	312	304	295	285	279	218
S.	URUGUAY	15	15	25	34	49	40
T.	VENEZUELA	1,140	1,087	1,224	1,698	1,699	2,061
	LATIN AMERICA	17,467	19,606	21,856	23,877	22,079	22,417

SOURCE: Mexico-NAFINSA-MV, May 9, 1983.

Table 1713

SHIPS (MERCHANT VESSELS) UNDER
CONSTRUCTION IN ARGENTINA,
1975–83

(T Gross Tons Registered)

Year	Amount
1975	97
1976	136
1977	117
1978	170
1979	143
1980	127
1981	155
1982	78
1983	82

SOURCE: UN-MB, Jan. 1983, special table A, p. xv; Oct. 1984,
special table A, p. xiv.

Table 1714

STEEL (CRUDE) PRODUCTION, 11 LR, 1950–82

(T MET)

PART I. MV SERIES

	Country	1950	1965	1977	1978	1979	1980	1981	1982[‡]
A.	ARGENTINA	100	1,300	2,684	2,783	3,203	2,702	2,517	2,897
C.	BRAZIL	800	3,000	11,166	12,112	13,866	15,186	13,232	12,999
D.	CHILE	100	500	509	574	642	695	625	484
E.	COLOMBIA	#	200	327	391	361	402	395	408
I.	ECUADOR	~	~	~	~	8	15	26	27
N.	MEXICO	400	2,500	5,513	6,694	7,002	6,982	7,480	7,055
R.	PERU	~	~	379	373	420	470	357	275
S.	URUGUAY	~	~	17	7	16	16	13	19
T.	VENEZUELA	#	600	855	859	1,480	1,975	2,080	2,501
	LATIN AMERICA[1]	1,400	8,100	21,450	23,793	26,998	28,443	26,675	26,665

1. Total from above.

SOURCE: Mexico-NAFINSA-MV, May 9, 1983; for 1950 and 1965 data, Jan. 7, 1985.

PART II. UN-SY SERIES

	Country	1969	1970	1975	1976	1977	1978	1979	1980
A.	ARGENTINA	1,720	1,859	2,043	2,244	2,676	2,647	3,090	2,556
C.	BRAZIL	4,925	5,390	7,829	9,169	11,164	9,032	10,039	10,232
D.	CHILE	601	547	458	448	506	574	642	695
E.	COLOMBIA	206	239	266	252	210	265	234	263
G.	CUBA	119	140	298	261	341	324	328	304
N.	MEXICO	3,470	3,846	5,196	5,243	5,529	6,712	7,023	7,003
R.	PERU	194	94	432	349	379	377	426	471
T.	VENEZUELA	840	927	919	752	676	860	1,480	2,077
	UNITED STATES	128,152	119,309	105,817	116,121	113,701	124,314	123,695	101,456

SOURCE: UN-SY, 1979/80, table 114; UN-SY, 1981, table 153.

Table 1715

SUGAR (RAW) PRODUCTION, 20 LC, 1850–1981

PART I. WORLD AND CUBA

(BASE = 96°)

1850-1949 (T MET)									1950-81 (M MET)		Cuba	
Year	World[1]	Cuba	Year	World[1]	Cuba	Year	World[1]	Cuba	Year	World[1]	Plan	Actual
1850	1,202	223	1884	4,775	559	1917	16,863	3,063	1950	29.2		5.6
1851	1,349	263	1885	4,472	631	1918	15,880	3,473	1951	33.6		5.8
1852	1,369	251	1886	5,087	732	1919	15,213	4,012	1952	36.1		7.3
1853	1,478	322	1887	4,908	647	1920	16,831	3,742	1953	35.0		5.2
1854	1,477	374	1888	5,915	657	1921	17,870	3,983	1954	38.8		5.0
1855	1,489	392	1889	5,675	~	1922	17,857	4,035	1955	38.4		4.6
1856	1,471	348	1890	6,277	632	1923	19,579	3,646	1956	39.7		4.8
1857	1,590	355	1891	6,983	817	1924	23,201	4,113	1957	41.6		5.7
1858	1,767	385	1892	6,421	976	1925	23,759	5,189	1958	44.4		5.9
1859	1,825	536	1893	7,394	816	1926	23,211	4,932	1959	49.6		6.0
1860	1,727	447	1894	8,257	1,054	1927	25,118	4,509	1960	52.1		5.9
1861	1,879	446	1895	7,061	1,004	1928	26,801	4,042	1961	54.7		6.9
1862	1,857	525	1896	7,644	225	1929	26,730	5,156	1962	51.6		4.9
1863	1,791	507	1897	7,564	212	1930	27,853	4,671	1963	52.6		3.9
1864	1,837	575	1898	7,685	306	1931	24,997	3,121	1964	60.1		4.5
1865	2,195	620	1899	8,292	336	1932	22,736	2,604	1965	65.1	6.0[b]	6.2
1866	2,215	612	1900	11,259[a]	300	1933	24,272	1,994	1966	64.2	6.5	4.5
1867	2,186	597	1901	12,643	636	1934	24,634	2,256	1967	66.7	7.5	6.2
1868	2,519	749	1902	11,544	850	1935	27,029	2,538	1968	66.9	8.0	5.2
1869	2,549	726	1903	12,101	1,000	1936	28,649	2,557	1969	70.0	9.0	4.5
1870	2,601	726	1904	11,185	1,045	1937	29,975	2,975	1970	71.1	10.0	7.6
1871	2,673	547	1905	14,003	1,173	1938	28,676	2,976	1971	74.0	7.0	5.9
1872	2,933	690	1906	14,349	1,231	1939	30,511	2,724	1972	75.7	- -	4.3
1873	3,046	775	1907	13,706	1,431	1940	30,499	2,779	1973	75.8	5.5	5.3
1874	3,167	681	1908	14,358	970	1941	28,598	2,407	1974	76.4	- -	5.9
1875	3,193	718	1909	14,690	1,536	1942	24,340	3,345	1975	78.8	- -	6.3
1876	2,877	590	1910	16,824	1,843	1943	23,037	2,842	1976	82.4	- -	6.2
1877	3,128	520	1911	15,518	1,465	1944	22,132	4,171	1977	90.4	- -	6.5
1878	3,488	533	1912	18,008	1,913	1945	19,362	3,454	1978	90.6	7.3	7.4
1879	3,367	670	1913	18,715	2,442	1946	18,185	3,940	1979	89.2	- -	8.0
1880	3,740	530	1914	18,213	2,615	1947	22,733	5,677	1980	84.6	- -	6.7
1881	3,638	493	1915	16,721	2,609	1948	24,594	5,877	1981[‡]	91.9	- -	7.4
1882	4,252	595	1916	17,038	3,034	1949	28,110	5,074				
1883	4,533	460										

1. Cane and beet.

a. Excludes India and some Far Eastern production prior to 1900.

b. No plan prior to 1965.

SOURCE: 1850-1949, adapted from Hugh Thomas, *Cuba: The Pursuit of Freedom*
(New York: Harper and Row, 1971), pp. 1561-1564; and from Noel Deere,
The History of Sugar, 2 vols. (London: Chapman and Hall, 1949), I. p. 133
and II, pp. 490-491.

1950-69, compiled from *Los Angeles Times, New York Times, Wall Street
Journal*, USDA, FAO, and ECLA sources. World data are from Deere,
History of Sugar.

1970-81, UN-SY, 1981, table 128, and Cuba, CEE, *Anuario Estadístico*, 1983,
p. 109.

Table 1715 (Continued)

SUGAR (RAW) PRODUCTION, 20 LC, 1850–1981

PART II. 19 LC[1]

Country		1953	1970	1975	1976	1977	1978	1979	1980	1981[‡]
A.	ARGENTINA	740	976	1,353	1,559	1,666	1,397	1,411	1,716	1,624
B.	BOLIVIA	3	131	213	282	281	285	288	262	260
C.	BRAZIL[2]	2,002	5,019[a]	6,299	7,236	8,759	7,913	7,362	8,270	8,726
D.	CHILE	~	228	219	319	315	131	92	65	200
E.	COLOMBIA	190	676	970	935	854	1,014	1,107	1,247	1,212
F.	COSTA RICA	31	150	205	210	200	227	204	220	190
H.	DOMINICAN REP.	552	1,014	1,170	1,287	1,258	1,199	1,200	1,013	1,108
I.	ECUADOR[3]	61	235[‡]	292	309	266	347	355	368	330
J.	EL SALVADOR	30	117	244	261	318	279	274	217	182
K.	GUATEMALA	37	185	384	517[‡]	487	446	415	452	474
L.	HAITI	55	66	69	60	50	57	60	65	50
M.	HONDURAS	8	53[‡]	75[‡]	81	115	131	164	191	172
N.	MEXICO	868	2,402	2,636	2,710	2,790	3,131	3,095	2,719	2,642
O.	NICARAGUA	33	141	210[‡]	242[‡]	226	222	202	190	214
P.	PANAMA	17	76	135[‡]	161	181	187	226	200	186
Q.	PARAGUAY	14	52	59	56	53	69	76	89	77
R.	PERU	602	771	964[a]	930	900	856	695	537	478
S.	URUGUAY	21	53	95[‡]	120[‡]	120	91	84	102	98
T.	VENEZUELA	78	455	508	536	443	403	347	358	303
	UNITED STATES	3,148	5,327	5,680	6,163	5,523	5,133	5,435	5,313	5,634

1. Covers the production of centrifugal sugar from both beet and cane, and the figures
   are expressed, as far as possible, in terms of raw sugar. Where exact information
   about polarization or grades is lacking, qualities are expressed in terms of sugar
   "Tel quel".
2. "Tel quel" sugar indicates lack of exact information about polarization of grades.
3. Crop year, except 1967.

a. "Tel quel" (see note 2).

SOURCE: UN-SY, 1968, table 89; UN-SY, 1978, table 86; UN-SY, 1979/80, table 81;
   UN-SY, 1981, table 128.

Table 1716

WHEAT FLOUR PRODUCTION,[1] 19 LC, 1953–80

(T MET)

Country		1953	1963	1967	1970	1975	1976	1977	1978	1979	1980
A.	ARGENTINA	2,013	2,163	2,161	2,347	2,483	2,529	2,530	2,523	2,482	2,438
B.	BOLIVIA	~	10	20	39	60	~	~	151	~	~
C.	BRAZIL	1,475	1,607	1,865	2,393	2,053[a]	2,288[a]	~	4,345	4,698	5,154
D.	CHILE	585	653	762	808	479	1,384	494	455	~	~
E.	COLOMBIA	56	170	180	231	215	~	~	278	300	~
G.	CUBA	~	133	131	160	176	166	176	175	170	271
H.	DOMINICAN REP.	~	44	53	55	85	91	92	92	107	115
I.	ECUADOR[3,4]	31	64	68	91	156	~	~	207	~	~
J.	EL SALVADOR	~	27	41	43	56	65	76	~	~	~
K.	GUATEMALA	15	58	71	72	86	87	73	133	~	~
L.	HAITI	~	44	42	28	67	48	41	63	75	117
M.	HONDURAS	5	15	23	33	35	35	43	42	43	47
N.	MEXICO	368	1,040	1,142	1,331	1,580	1,714	1,753	1,814	1,951	2,147
O.	NICARAGUA	~	~	24	29	~	~	~	~	33	43
P.	PANAMA[5]	~	~	~	32	38	39	~	~	43	~
Q.	PARAGUAY	34	85	60	70	38	50	59	85	82	82
R.	PERU[2]	265	364	417	500	587	~	~	~	~	~
S.	URUGUAY	~	239	249	251	~	~	~	~	~	~
T.	VENEZUELA	~	257	322	388	157	~	~	~	~	~
	UNITED STATES	10,078	11,794	11,124	11,504	11,747	11,770	11,860	12,606	12,884	12,821

1. Sifted (bolted) flours from soft and hard wheat and from spelt. Bran and offal, wheat
   groats, meal, and flour obtained by milling cereals other than wheat are excluded.
2. Incomplete coverage. Data for main establishments only.
3. Twelve months ending June 30.
4. Including flour from other grains.
5. Including groats.

a. Incomplete coverage. Data for main establishments only.

SOURCE: IASI-AC, 1970, table 323-05; UN-SY, 1968, table 88; UN-SY, 1978, table 85;
   UN-SY, 1979/80, table 80; UN-SY, 1981, table 127.

CHAPTER 18

MINING PRODUCTION

Table 1800

ANTIMONY MINE PRODUCTION, 7 LC, 1977–83

(Short Tons)

	Country	1977	1978	1979	1980[‡]	1981	1982	1983[†]
B.	BOLIVIA	18,012	14,702	14,351	17,047	16,861	16,000[†]	12,000
C.	BRAZIL	289	216	74	72	72[†]	~	~
K.	GUATEMALA	1,010	254	728	613	441[†]	~	~
M.	HONDURAS	77[a]	86[a]	51	25	22[†]	~	~
N.	MEXICO[1]	2,974	2,708	3,166	2,399	1,984	2,000[†]	2,000
R.	PERU[3]	903	821	840	1,157	1,213[†]	~	~
	UNITED STATES[2]	610	798	722	343	646	550[†]	850

1. Antimony content of ores for export plus antimony content of antimonial lead and other smelter products produced.
2. Production from antimony mines; excludes a small amount produced as a byproduct of domestic lead ores.
3. Recoverable.

a. Revised.

SOURCE: USBOM-MY, 1981, Volume I; USBOM-MIS, *Antimony in 1982*, p. 3; 1983, p. 3.

Table 1801

BAUXITE MINE PRODUCTION, 3 LC, 1977–83

(T MET)

	Country	1977	1978	1979	1980[‡]	1981	1982[†]	1983[†]
C.	BRAZIL[3]	1,120[†]	1,160[†]	2,388[†]	4,152	5,300	5,400	~
H.	DOMINICAN REP.[1,4]	576	568	524	510	405[†a]	~	~
L.	HAITI[2]	588	580	584	477	400[†]	~	~
	UNITED STATES	2,013	1,669	1,821	1,559	1,510	700	3,640

1. Dry bauxite equivalent of crude ore.
2. Dry bauxite equivalent of ore processed by drying plant.
3. Estimate dry bauxite equivalent of crude ore, calculated from reported crude ore, assuming a moisture content of 17.2%.
4. Shipments.

a. Reported figure.

SOURCE: USBOM-MY, 1981, Volume I; USBOM-MIS, *Bauxite in 1982*, p. 5; 1983, p.3.

Table 1802

CHROMITE MINE PRODUCTION, 3 L, 1977–83

(T Short Tons)

	Country	1977	1978	1979	1980[‡]	1981[†]	1982	1983
C.	BRAZIL	342	297	375	316	450	1,050	1,000
E.	COLOMBIA[†]	6	6	6	6	6	~	~
G.	CUBA	22	32	31	35	32	~	~

SOURCE: USBOM-MY, 1981, Volume I; 1983, p. 3.

Table 1803

COPPER MINE PRODUCTION, 12 LC, 1977–83
(T MET)

	Country	1977	1978	1979	1980[‡]	1981	1982[†]	1983[†]
A.	ARGENTINA	.2	.3	.1	.2	.2[†]	~	~
B.	BOLIVIA	3.2	2.9	1.8	1.9	2.6[†,a]	~	~
C.	BRAZIL	#	#	5.3	1.4	18[†]	~	~
D.	CHILE	1,056.2	1,035.5	1,060.6	1,067.7	1,080	1,190	1,250
E.	COLOMBIA	#[b]	.1[b]	.1	.1	.1[†,a]	~	~
G.	CUBA	2.6	2.8	2.8	3.3	3.6[†]	~	~
I.	ECUADOR	1.0	.8	1.2	1.2	1.2[†]	~	~
K.	GUATEMALA	2.5	2.1	1.8	.8	.5[†]	~	~
M.	HONDURAS	.5	.6	1.4	.3	.3[†]	~	~
N.	MEXICO	89.7	87.2	107.1	175.4	230.5[†,a]	~	~
O.	NICARAGUA[1]	3	.1[†]	- -	- -	- -	~	~
R.	PERU	338.1[b]	366.4	390.7	366.8	327.6[†,a]	350	330
	UNITED STATES[2]	1,364.4	1,357.6	1,443.6	1,181.1	1,538	1,100	1,050

1. Copper content of concentrates produced.
2. Recoverable.

a. Reported figure.
b. Revised.

SOURCE: USBOM-MY, 1981, Volume I; USBOM-MIS, *Copper in 1982*, p. 3; 1983, p. 3.

Table 1804

FLUORSPAR MINE PRODUCTION,[1] 5 LC, 1977–83
(Short Tons)

	Country	1977	1978	1979	1980[‡]	1981	1982	1983[†]
A.	ARGENTINA	48,272	29,482	41,972	17,050	21,000	~	~
B.	BOLIVIA	75,598[a]	68,123	57,866	61,144	66,000	~	~
C.	BRAZIL	127,824	139,147	179,874	179,897	~	~	~
N.	MEXICO	727,621[a]	1,057,980[a]	1,084,514	1,219,755	1,231,000	800,000	1,000,000
S.	URUGUAY	83	125	85[†]	95[†]	90[†]	~	~
	UNITED STATES[2]	169,489	129,428	109,299	92,635[b]	115,000[b]	~	~

1. Total for all grades.
2. Shipments.

a. Revised.
b. Reported figure.

SOURCE: USBOM-MY, 1981, Volume I; USBOM-MIS, *Fluorspar in 1982*, p. 3;
USBOM-MCP, *Fluorspar, 1982*, p. 5; 1983, p. 3.

Table 1805

GOLD MINE PRODUCTION, 14 LC, 1977–83

(Troy Ounces)

	Country	1977	1978	1979	1980[‡]	1981	1982[†]	1983[†]
A.	ARGENTINA	5,509	5,600[a]	10,140	10,956	10,900[†]	~	~
B.	BOLIVIA	24,293	24,660	30,319	52,075	66,372[†]	~	~
C.	BRAZIL[1]	279,520	300,898	319,258	1,300,000	1,200,000	~	~
D.	CHILE	116,376	102,287[a]	111,405	219,773	297,000[†]	~	~
E.	COLOMBIA	257,070[a]	246,446[a]	269,369	510,439	535,000[†]	~	~
F.	COSTA RICA[†]	12,200	15,900	16,718	16,000	16,000	~	~
H.	DOMINICAN REP.	342,755	342,830	352,982	369,603	412,982[†]	~	~
I.	ECUADOR	8,124	2,734	3,215	3,537	3,700[†]	~	~
J.	EL SALVADOR	2,156	3,619	2,720	2,492	1,000[†]	~	~
M.	HONDURAS	2,481	2,500[†]	1,501	2,027	3,000[†]	~	~
N.	MEXICO	212,709	202,003	190,364	195,991	185,000[†]	~	~
O.	NICARAGUA	65,764	73,947[a]	61,086	60,000[†]	50,000[†]	~	~
R.	PERU	104,393	103,069	141,656	148,890	220,000[†]	~	~
T.	VENEZUELA	17,403	13,384	14,989	16,519	17,500[†]	~	~
	UNITED STATES	1,100,347	998,832	964,390	969,782	1,380,000	1,400,000[†]	1,600,000

1. All figures except those for 1978 differ substantially from those appearing in latest
    available official Brazilian sources owing to the inclusion here of estimates for
    unreported production by small mines (garimpos).

a. Revised.

SOURCE: USBOM-MY, 1981, Volume III; USBOM-MIS, *Gold in 1982*, p. 3;
    USBOM-MCP, *Gold*, 1982, p. 4; 1983, p. 3.

Table 1806

GYPSUM MINE PRODUCTION, 16 LC, 1977–83

(T Short Tons)

	Country	1977	1978	1979	1980[‡]	1981	1982[†]	1983[†]
A.	ARGENTINA	603	674	648	1,028	748[†,a]	~	~
B.	BOLIVIA	1[†,b]	1[†]	1[†]	1	1[†,a]	~	~
C.	BRAZIL[1]	599[b]	523[b]	512	668	695[†]	~	~
D.	CHILE	162[b]	192[b]	179	218	293[†,a]	~	~
E.	COLOMBIA	231	281	283	289	300[†]	~	~
G.	CUBA	100[†]	105[†]	100[†]	134[†]	145[†]	~	~
H.	DOMINICAN REP.	249	190	193	206	200[†]	~	~
I.	ECUADOR	46	38	40[†]	39	40[†]	~	~
J.	EL SALVADOR	8	8	8	10	7[†]	~	~
K.	GUATEMALA	35	42	28	37	30[†]	~	~
M.	HONDURAS	20	25[†]	25[†]	25	20	~	~
N.	MEXICO	1,649	1,938	2,228	1,884	2,076	1,900	1,900
O.	NICARAGUA	40[†]	40[†]	40[†]	44[†]	35[†]	~	~
Q.	PARAGUAY	15	10	12	13	15[†]	~	~
R.	PERU	157[b]	186[b]	239	309	385[†]	~	~
T.	VENEZUELA	184[b]	206[b]	287	129	240[†,a]	~	~
	UNITED STATES[2]	13,390	14,891	14,630	12,376	11,497	11,200	12,200

1. Series revised to represent sum of (1) mine product sold without benefication and (2)
    output of concentrates.
2. Excludes byproduct gypsum.

a. Reported figure.
b. Revised.

SOURCE: USBOM-MY, 1981, Volume I; USBOM-MIS, *Gypsum in 1982*, p. 3; 1983, p. 3.

Table 1807

IRON ORE PRODUCTION,[1] 8 LC, 1977–83
(T Long Tons)

	Country	1977	1978	1979	1980[‡]	1981	1982[†]	1983[†]
A.	ARGENTINA	1,014	895	601	430	487[†]	~	~
B.	BOLIVIA	7[a]	55	25	6	6[†,a]	~	~
C.	BRAZIL	80,706	83,643	94,594	112,920	98,400	96,000	98,000
D.	CHILE	7,535[b]	6,695[b]	7,006	8,138	7,873[†]	~	~
E.	COLOMBIA	497[b]	489[b]	391	498	412[†,a]	~	~
N.	MEXICO[2]	5,296[b]	5,249[b]	5,965	7,510	7,893[†,b]	~	~
R.	PERU	6,184[b]	4,844	5,358	5,614	5,973[†]	~	~
T.	VENEZUELA	13,467	13,302	15,019	15,848	15,300	13,000	10,000
	UNITED STATES[3]	55,750	81,583	85,716	69,613	73,200	35,000	38,000

1. Gross weight: insofar as availability of sources permits, gross weight data represent the nonduplicative sum of marketable direct-shipping iron ores, iron ore concentrates, and iron ore agglomerates produced by each of the listed countries. Concentrates and agglomerates produced from imported iron ores have been excluded, under the assumption that the ore from which such materials are produced has been credited as marketable ore in the country where it was mined.
2. Gross weight calculated from reported iron content based on grade of 63% Fe.
3. Includes byproduct ore.

a. Reported figure.
b. Revised.

SOURCE: USBOM-MY, 1981, Volume I; USBOM-MIS, *Iron in 1982*, p. 3; 1983, p. 3.

Table 1808

LEAD MINE PRODUCTION, 11 LC, 1977–83
(T MET)

	Country	1977	1978	1979	1980[‡]	1981	1982[†]	1983[†]
A.	ARGENTINA	33.6	30.3	31.7	34.0	32.0[†]	~	~
B.	BOLIVIA	18.9[a]	18.0	15.4	17.7	16.7[†]	~	~
C.	BRAZIL	24.0[a]	31.2	27.9	27.5	29.6[†]	~	~
D.	CHILE	.1[a]	.4	.3	.5	.5[†]	~	~
E.	COLOMBIA	.2[a]	.1	.2	.2	.1[†]	~	~
I.	ECUADOR	.2	.2	.2	.2	.2[†]	~	~
K.	GUATEMALA	.1	.1[†]	.1[†]	.1	.1[†]	~	~
M.	HONDURAS	20.6	21.8	16.4	15.1	14.0[†]	~	~
N.	MEXICO[1]	163.5	170.6	173.5	145.5	158	155	160
O.	NICARAGUA	1.0	.4	- -	- -	- -	- -	~
R.	PERU[2]	175.7[a]	182.7	174.0	189.1	187	210	110
	UNITED STATES[3]	537.5	529.7	525.6	550.4	446	510	450

1. Recoverable metal content of lead in concentrates for export plus lead content of domestic smelter products (refined lead, antimonial lead, mixed bars, and other unspecified items).
2. Recoverable metal content of lead in concentrates for export plus lead content of domestic smelter products (refined lead, antimonial lead, and bizmuth-lead bars).
3. Recoverable.

a. Revised.

SOURCE: USBOM-MY, 1981, Volume I; USBOM-MIS, *Lead in 1982*, p. 3; 1983, p. 3.

Table 1809

MANGANESE ORE PRODUCTION, 4 L, 1977–83

(Short Tons, Gross Weight)

	Country	1977	1978	1979	1980[‡]	1981	1982[†]	1983[†]
B.	BOLIVIA[1,2]	9,464	1,364	11,574	4,960	- -[†]	~	~
C.	BRAZIL[2]	1,670,741	2,113,261[a]	2,490,483	2,601,452	2,090,000	1,700,000	1,400
D.	CHILE	19,843	25,621	27,524	30,535	29,800[†]	~	~
N.	MEXICO	536,409	576,692	543,068	492,874	637,500[†,b]	~	~

1. Estimated on the basis of reported contained manganese.
2. Exports.

a. Revised.
b. Reported figure.

SOURCE: USBOM-MY, 1981, Volume I; USBOM-MIS, *Manganese Ore in 1982*, p. 3; 1983, p. 3.

Table 1810

MERCURY MINE PRODUCTION, 3 LC, 1977–83

(Flasks)

	Country	1977	1978	1979	1980[‡]	1981	1982[†]	1983[†]
D.	CHILE	20	- -	- -	- -	- -[†]	~	~
H.	DOMINICAN REP.	495	500	500	500[†]	500[†]	~	~
N.	MEXICO	9,660	2,205	1,973	4,206	4,000	4,000	6,000
	UNITED STATES	28,244	24,163	29,519	30,657	27,904	25,000	25,000

SOURCE: USBOM-MY, 1981, Volume I; USBOM-MIS, *Mercury in 1982*, p. 3; 1983, p. 3.

Table 1811

MOLYBDENUM MINE PRODUCTION, 3 LC, 1977–83

(T Pounds Contained Molybdenum)

	Country	1977	1978	1979	1980[‡]	1981	1982[†]	1983[†]
D.	CHILE	24,112[a]	29,092	29,895	30,133	33,300[†]	46,000	32,000
N.	MEXICO	2	24	105	225	770[†]	~	~
R.	PERU	1,005[a]	1,607	2,606	5,860	5,485[†]	6,000	6,000
	UNITED STATES	122,408	131,843	143,967	150,686	139,900	75,000	30,000

a. Revised.

SOURCE: USBOM-MY, 1981, Volume I; USBOM-MIS, *Molybdenum in 1982*, p. 3; 1983, p. 3.

Table 1812

NICKEL MINE PRODUCTION, 5 LC, 1977–83

(Short Tons)

	Country	1977	1978	1979	1980[‡]	1981	1982[†]	1983[†]
C.	BRAZIL[1]	4,675	3,968	3,267	2,800	2,600[†]	~	~
G.	CUBA[2]	40,510[a]	38,346[a]	35,631	42,108	44,600[†]	35,000[†]	40,000
H.	DOMINICAN REP.	27,446[a]	15,765[a]	27,680	18,019	21,500[†]	~	~
K.	GUATEMALA	328	1,189[a]	6,833	7,434	~	~	~
N.	MEXICO[1]	37	24	1	- -	- -	~	~
	UNITED STATES[3]	14,347	13,509	15,065	14,653	12,100	3,200	400

1. Content of ore.
2. Content of oxide and sulfide.
3. Content of ore shipped.

a. Revised.

SOURCE: USBOM-MY, 1981, Volume I; USBOM-MIS, *Nickel in 1982*, p. 3; USBOM-MCP,
Nickel, 1982, p. 6; 1983, p. 6.

Table 1813

PHOSPHATE ROCK MINE PRODUCTION, 4 LC, 1977–81

(T MET)

	Country	1977	1978	1979	1980[‡]	1981[†]
C.	BRAZIL[1]	676[a]	1,096[a]	1,628	2,472	2,637[b]
E.	COLOMBIA	6[a]	1[a]	7	8	9
N.	MEXICO	285	322	171	283	355
T.	VENEZUELA	139	109	- -	- -	- -
	UNITED STATES	47,256	50,037	51,611	54,415	53,624[b]

1. Figure represents total of direct sales of run-of-mine product plus output of marketable
   concentrate. Direct sales of run-of-mine product were as follows, in thousand metric
   tons: 1977, 26; 1978, 27; 1979, 39; 1980, 40; 1981, 40 (estimated). Total output of
   crude ore reported in Brazilian sources is far higher than figures presented here, but
   such figures are not equivalent to data shown for other countries.

a. Revised.
b. Reported figure.

SOURCE: USBOM-MY, 1981, Volume I.

Table 1814

SALT MINE PRODUCTION, 15 LC, 1977–83

(T Short Tons)

	Country	1977	1978	1979	1980[‡]	1981	1982[†]	1983[†]
A.	ARGENTINA[1]	2	1	1	1	1[†]	~	~
C.	BRAZIL[1]	323	631	759	877	885[†]	~	~
D.	CHILE	467	434	650	486	440[†]	~	~
E.	COLOMBIA	383[a]	416[a]	422	383	348[†]	~	~
F.	COSTA RICA	30	38	51	44	45[†]	~	~
G.	CUBA	142	144	134	137	140[†]	~	~
H.	DOMINICAN REP.	38	42	42	61	70[†]	~	~
J.	EL SALVADOR	30[†]	30[†]	30[†]	30[†]	25[†]	~	~
K.	GUATEMALA	12	12	16	11	10[†]	~	~
M.	HONDURAS	35[†]	35[†]	35[†]	35[†]	35[†]	~	~
N.	MEXICO	5,400	6,212	6,800	7,248	7,720	7,700	8,900
O.	NICARAGUA	18[†]	20[†]	20[†]	22[†]	20[†]	~	~
P.	PANAMA	23	17	21	21	25[†]	~	~
R.	PERU	350[a]	384[a]	440	504	550[†]	~	~
T.	VENEZUELA	266	174	170[†]	268	270[†]	~	~
	UNITED STATES[2]	43,412	42,869	45,793	40,351	38,907	38,700	31,500

1. Rock salt figures only.
2. Includes Puerto Rico with regard to rock salt.

a. Revised.

SOURCE: USBOM-MY, 1981, Volume I; USBOM-MIS, *Salt in 1982*, p. 3; 1983, p. 3.

Table 1815

SILVER MINE PRODUCTION, 14 LC, 1977–83

(T Troy Ounces)

	Country	1977	1978	1979	1980[‡]	1981	1982[†]	1983[†]
A.	ARGENTINA	2,450[b]	2,164[b]	2,209	2,305	2,300[†]	~	~
B.	BOLIVIA	5,813	6,285	5,742	6,099	6,602[†]	~	~
C.	BRAZIL	372	506	1,065	837	800[†]	~	~
D.	CHILE	8,461	8,210	8,740	9,598	10,000[†]	~	~
E.	COLOMBIA[1]	91	77[b]	99	152	143[†,a]	~	~
F.	COSTA RICA	1[†]	2[†]	2[†]	2[†]	2[†]	~	~
H.	DOMINICAN REP.	1,852	1,848	2,276	1,623	2,062[†]	~	~
I.	ECUADOR	57	29	44[a]	45	44[†]	~	~
J.	EL SALVADOR	112	185	152	146	110[†]	~	~
K.	GUATEMALA	~	10	10	10	8[†]	~	~
M.	HONDURAS	2,819	2,788	2,434	1,766	2,400[†,a]	~	~
N.	MEXICO	47,030	50,779	49,408	47,344	53,200	55,000	55,000
O.	NICARAGUA	167	482	389	164	150[†]	~	~
R.	PERU	39,731[b]	37,022[b]	39,248	42,989	46,900	48,000	54,000
	UNITED STATES	38,166	39,385	37,896	32,329	40,700	36,000	42,000

1. Smelter and/or refinery production.

a. Reported figure.
b. Revised.

SOURCE: USBOM-MY, 1981, Volume I; USBOM-MIS, *Gold and Silver in 1982*, p. 5; 1983, p. 5.

Table 1816

SULFUR MINE PRODUCTION,[1] 11 LC, 1977–81
(T MET)

Country	1977	1978	1979	1980‡	1981†
A. ARGENTINA	47	38	20	~	~
B. BOLIVIA[2]	6[a]	14[a]	15[a]	11	11
C. BRAZIL[3]	44	57	92	131	150
D. CHILE[2]	61	52	104	121	125
E. COLOMBIA	29[b]	38[b]	18	27	32
G. CUBA	42†	31†	20†	30†	10†
I. ECUADOR	13†	15†	15†	15†	14†
N. MEXICO	1,936†,b	1,918†,b	2,125†	2,252†	2,202†
R. PERU	20	28	20	20	20
S. URUGUAY	2	2	2	2†	2†
T. VENEZUELA	95	95	85	85	85
UNITED STATES	10,727	11,175	12,101	11,866	12,145

1. In all forms.
2. Data are for native sulfur. May, however, produce limited quantities of byproduct sulfur from crude oil and natural gas and/or from petroleum refining.
3. May also produce limited quantities of byproduct sulfur from metallurgical operations and/or coal processing.

a. Exports regarded as tantamount to production, owing to minimal domestic consumption levels.
b. Revised.

SOURCE: USBOM-MY, 1981, Volume I.

Table 1817

TIN MINE PRODUCTION,[1] 5 LC, 1977–83
(MET)

Country	1977	1978	1979	1980‡	1981	1982†	1983†
A. ARGENTINA	537[a]	362[a]	386	351	340†	~	~
B. BOLIVIA	33,740[b]	30,881	27,648	27,272	29,800	26,000	25,000
C. BRAZIL	6,287[b]	6,341[b]	7,005	6,930	9,000	10,000	11,000
N. MEXICO	220	73	23	60	100†	~	~
R. PERU	329[b]	458[b]	870	1,077	1,519†	~	~
UNITED STATES	~c	~c	~c	~c	#	#	#

1. Contained-tin basis.

a. Estimate by the International Tin Council.
b. Revised.
c. Withheld to avoid disclosing company proprietary data.

SOURCE: USBOM-MY, 1981, Volume I; USBOM-MIS, *Tin in 1982*, p. 3; 1983, p. 3.

Table 1818

TUNGSTEN CONCENTRATE PRODUCTION, 5 LC, 1977–83

(T Pounds of Contained Tungsten)

	Country	1977	1978	1979	1980[‡]	1981	1982[†]	1983[†]
A.	ARGENTINA	154	214	130	77	111[†]	~	~
B.	BOLIVIA	5,355[a]	5,373[a]	5,445	5,873	6,031	5,100	3,000
C.	BRAZIL	2,672	2,568	2,595	2,504	2,690	2,600	1,000
N.	MEXICO	421	516	556	586	370	400	100
R.	PERU	1,160	1,283	1,243	1,210	1,149[†,b]	~	~
	UNITED STATES	6,008	6,896	6,643	6,072	7,815[c]	3,200[c]	1,100

a.   Revised.
b.   Reported figure.
c.   Mine shipments.

SOURCE: USBOM-MY, 1981, Volume I; USBOM-MIS, *Tungsten in 1982*, p. 3; 1983, p. 3.

Table 1819

ZINC MINE PRODUCTION, 11 LC, 1977–83

(T MET)

	Country	1977	1978	1979	1980[‡]	1981	1982[†]	1983[†]
A.	ARGENTINA	39.2	36.6	37.5	33.7	30.0	~	~
B.	BOLIVIA	61.4	53.9	51.6	50.3	47.0[a]	~	~
C.	BRAZIL	57.6[b]	58.7[b]	89.9	101	103	~	~
D.	CHILE[1]	3.9	1.8	1.8	1.1	1.1	~	~
E.	COLOMBIA	- -	- -	- -	- -	.1	~	~
I.	ECUADOR	2.0	1.3	1.6[†]	1.6[†]	1.6	~	~
K.	GUATEMALA	1.0	1.0	1.0[†]	1.0[†]	.5	~	~
M.	HONDURAS	26.5	24.3	22.0	19.6	18.0	~	~
N.	MEXICO[1]	265.5	244.9	245.5	238.2	212	230	245
O.	NICARAGUA	11.2	3.6	- -	- -	- -	~	~
R.	PERU[1]	405.3[b]	402.6[b]	432	487.6	497	535	575
	UNITED STATES[1]	407.9	302.7	267.3	317.1	312	300	280

1.   Recoverable content of concentrates.

a.   Reported figure.
b.   Revised.

SOURCE: USBOM-MY, 1981, Volume I; USBOM-MIS, *Zinc in 1982*, p. 3; 1983, p. 3.

Table 1820

INDICATORS FOR THE ECONOMIC CONTRIBUTION OF MINING
(%)

| | | | | Share of the Mining Sector in: | | |
| | | | | | Exports | | |
	Country	GDP	Employment	Non-Fuel Minerals[1]	Petroleum[2]	Public Revenues
		1981	Various, 1970-76	Average, 1978-80		Year Varies
	Mining Economies					
B.	BOLIVIA	6.8	3.9	41.2	3.4	90.0
D.	CHILE	7.1	3.2	47.7	.1	54.0
H.	DOMINICAN REP.	4.4	.1	2.6	#	~
I.	ECUADOR	10.4	.4	.0	50.4	43.0
N.	MEXICO	3.5	~	2.7	50.1	~
R.	PERU	7.5	~	33.6	11.9	36.0
T.	VENEZUELA	7.7	1.7	.9	60.8	73.0
	Semi-Mining Economies					
A.	ARGENTINA	2.6	.5	.2	#	~
C.	BRAZIL	.6	.8	8.7	#	~
E.	COLOMBIA	1.1	1.6	#	#	~
J.	EL SALVADOR	.1	~	#	#	~
K.	GUATEMALA	.3	~	.2	#	~
L.	HAITI	1.1	~	8.6	#	~
M.	HONDURAS	2.2	.3	1.9	#	~
O.	NICARAGUA	1.1	.6	.1	#	~
	LATIN AMERICA	3.0	~	26.3	22.4	~

1. Includes only iron ore, bauxite, copper, lead, zinc, tin and manganese in unprocessed form.
2. Refers to crude oil.

SOURCE: IDB-SPTF, 1983, p. 106.

Table 1821

PRODUCTION AND RESERVES OF NON-FUEL MINERALS, BY MAJOR PRODUCERS
(%, 1982)

Mineral and Major Producer	Share of Major Producers In	
	World Production	World Reserves[1]
Ferrous Metals		
Colombium (Brazil)	85.8[a]	93.4[a]
Tantalum (Brazil)	29.6[a]	4.2[a]
Molybdenum (Chile, Peru)	28.0	27.2
Iron-ore (Brazil, Venezuela)	14.0	21.3
Tungsten (Bolivia, Brazil, Mexico)	8.6	2.7
Manganese (Brazil)	7.4	1.8
Nickel (Brazil, Dominican Republic, Guatemala)	5.0[b]	5.8
Vanadium (Chile)	2.1[b]	1.5
Non-Ferrous Base Metals		
Bauxite (Brazil, Guyana, Jamaica, Suriname)	23.7	25.0
Copper (Chile, Peru)	19.8	25.2
Tin (Bolivia, Brazil)	15.4	13.8
Zinc (Mexico, Peru)	12.4	4.2
Lead (Mexico, Peru)	10.6	6.2
Industrial Metals		
Strontium (Argentina, Mexico)	41.1	~
Bismuth (Bolivia, Mexico, Peru)	37.3	25.2
Arsenic (Chile, Mexico, Peru)	33.9	~
Antimony (Bolivia, Mexico)	28.8	13.2
Rhenium (Chile, Peru)	24.5	37.1
Beryllium (Argentina, Brazil)	23.3	~
Indium (Peru)	9.4	4.0
Tellurium (Peru)	7.3[b]	7.0
Ytrium (Brazil)	7.0[b]	6.5
Selenium (Chile, Mexico, Peru)	4.8	25.3
Cadmium (Mexico)	4.7	2.5
Lithium (Argentina, Brazil, Chile)	3.2	52.0
Mercury (Mexico)	2.1	5.7
Rutile (Brazil)	~	71.5
Precious Metals		
Silver (Mexico, Peru)	28.3	20.2
Non-Metallic Minerals		
Quartz Crystal (Brazil)	69.6	~
Iodine (Chile)	22.3	~
Fluorspar (Mexico)	18.9	11.0
Sodium Sulfate (Argentina, Chile, Mexico)	18.0	~
Barite (Mexico, Peru)	9.2	7.4
Graphite (Mexico)	6.2	~
Lime (Brazil, Chile)	4.7	~
Sulfur (Mexico)	4.2	3.9
Feldspar (Mexico)	4.1	~
Boron (Argentina, Chile, Peru)	3.8	~
Gypsum (Mexico)	2.3	~
Diatomite (Mexico, Peru)	1.6	~

1. Measured and indicated reserves that meet minimum physical and chemical requirements for current mining and production practices (grade, quality, thickness and depth).

a. World excludes centrally planned economies.
b. Refers to 1979.

SOURCE: IDB-SPTF, 1983, p. 96.

CHAPTER 19

ENERGY RESOURCES: PRODUCTION, CONSUMPTION, AND RESERVES

Chapter Outline

Subsistence	
Biomass	1900–1901
Commercial	
Totals	1902–1907
Liquids (Petroleum Products)	1908–1918
Solids (Coal)	1920–1922, 1929
Gas (Natural Gas)	1919
Electrical	1925–1941
Hydroelectric	1930–1940
Geothermal	1923, 1930–1940
Nuclear	1941

Table 1900

TOTAL ENERGY RESERVES AND PRODUCTION POTENTIAL, 19 LR

(M Tons of Oil Equivalent, 1982)

	Country	Petroleum	R/P[1]	Natural Gas	R/P[1]	Coal[2]	R/P	Hydroelectric	R/P[3]	Geothermal	Uranium	Bituminous Coal	Unrefined Petroleum	Biomass	Solar
A.	ARGENTINA	362	15	518	45	2,359	100ᵃ	493	6.6	#ᵇ	74	#ᵇ	--	--	--
B.	BOLIVIA	22	15	93	45	--	~	--	--	~	--	--	--	--	--
C.	BRAZIL	167	21	31	21	8,129	100ᵃ	232	1.3	~	1	--	--	--	--
D.	CHILE	55	--	~	--	2,984	100ᵃ	3,083	9.5	~	284	84	--	--	--
E.	COLOMBIA	97	16	112	30	5,778	100ᵃ	229	5.6	#ᵇ	10	--	--	--	--
F.	COSTA RICA	--	--	--	--	#ᵇ		774	5.3	~	102	--	#ᵇ	--	--
H.	DOMINICAN REP.	--	--	--	--	#ᵇ	~	~	~	~	~	~	~	~	~
I.	ECUADOR	151	13	31	--	98	100ᵃ	98	4.7	#ᵇ	--	--	--	--	--
J.	EL SALVADOR	--	--	--	--	--	~	388	.6	#ᵇ	--	--	#ᵇ	--	--
K.	GUATEMALA	2	--	--	--	--	~	12	18.9	#ᵇ	--	--	--	--	--
L.	HAITI	--	--	--	--	#ᵇ	~	186	--	--	--	--	--	--	--
M.	HONDURAS	--	--	--	--	--	~	10	2.9	~	--	--	--	--	--
N.	MEXICO	3,900	59	1,480	64	2,108	100ᵃ	6	5.1	~	--	--	--	--	--
O.	NICARAGUA	--	--	--	--	--	~	444	25	#ᵇ	21	--	--	--	--
P.	PANAMA	--	--	--	--	--	~	46	2.3	#ᵇ	--	--	--	--	--
Q.	PARAGUAY	--	--	--	--	--	~	31	10.7	#ᵇ	--	--	--	--	--
R.	PERU	90	12	29	15	573	100ᵃ	77	2.3	~	--	--	--	--	--
S.	URUGUAY	--	--	--	--	--	~	25	16.5	--	--	--	--	--	--
T.	VENEZUELA	2,448	23	1,065	34	5,394	100ᵃ	784	4.8	~	--	--	20,000	--	--
	LATIN AMERICA	7,294	~	3,359	~	27,423	~	6,918	~	~	492	84	20,000	~	~

1. Reserves in relation to production. Indicates number of years reserves will last at present rate of production or generation of energy.
2. Includes "turba," lignite and anthracite.
3. Percentage of utilization of the existent capacity.

a. More than 100 years.
b. It is known to exist.

SOURCE: Mexico-NAFINSA-MV, Oct. 11, 1982, table 5.

Table 1901

BIOMASS PARTICIPATION IN THE TOTAL ENERGY SUPPLY, 13L

(T Tons of Oil Equivalent, 1980)

	Country	Biomass[1]	Total Consumption	% Participation
B.	BOLIVIA	20,403	88,039	23
E.	COLOMBIA	3,280	13,358	25
F.	COSTA RICA	558	1,406	40
H.	DOMINICAN REP.	1,130	2,999	38
J.	EL SALVADOR	1,407	2,031	69
K.	GUATEMALA	2,078	3,312	63
L.	HAITI	1,249	1,718	73
M.	HONDURAS	1,211	1,822	67
N.	MEXICO	12,830	67,080	19
O.	NICARAGUA	692	1,224	57
P.	PANAMA	421	1,114	38
R.	PERU	3,061	9,197	33
S.	URUGUAY	575	2,144	27

1. Plant and animal material that can be converted into energy. Includes trees, shrubs, other woody vegetation, grasses, other herbaceous plants, energy crops, algae, aquatic plants, agricultural and animal residues.

SOURCE: IDB-SPTF, 1983, table IV-7.

Figure 19:1

TOTAL COMMERCIAL ENERGY PRODUCTION
(M MET Coal Equivalent, 1975)

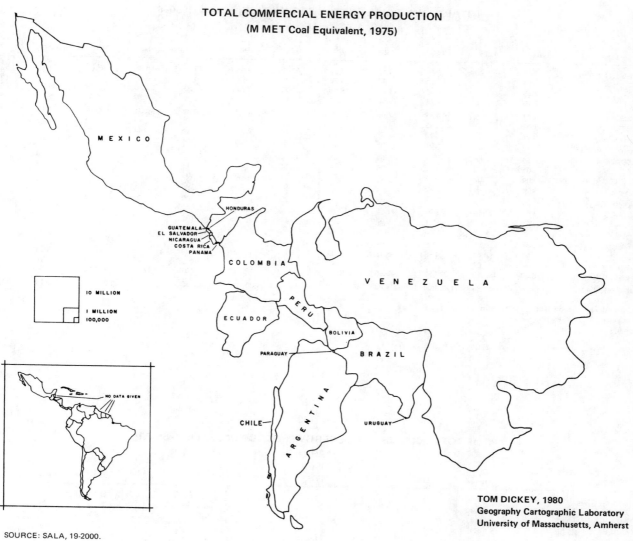

SOURCE: SALA, 19-2000.

TOM DICKEY, 1980
Geography Cartographic Laboratory
University of Massachusetts, Amherst

Table 1902

TOTAL COMMERCIAL ENERGY PRODUCTION,[1] 20 LC, 1950–81

(M MET Coal Equivalent)

Country	1950	1955	1960	1965	1970	1975	1976	1977	1978	1979	1980	1981
A. ARGENTINA	5.00	7.00	15.60	24.10	37.29	41.13	41.35	43.31	44.88	48.61	51.13	52.41
B. BOLIVIA	.14	.49	.74	.73	1.76	4.87	4.97	4.70	4.54	4.64	4.91	5.12
C. BRAZIL	2.95	4.04	9.36	11.70	18.69	24.47	25.42	27.27	28.65	30.90	34.37	36.84
D. CHILE	2.10	2.99	4.26	6.60	6.11	5.94	5.65	6.00	5.79	5.34	5.77	6.54
E. COLOMBIA	8.02	9.36	14.74	17.99	21.81	19.32	18.79	19.07	20.31	20.19	21.14	22.02
F. COSTA RICA	.02	.03	.05	.07	.12	.16	.18	.17	.18	.20	.26	.26
G. CUBA	.03	.07	.02	.08	.24	.36	.38	.38	.44	.46	.43	.42
H. DOMINICAN REP.	~	~	.01	.01	.01	.01	.01	.01	.01	.01	.01	.01
I. ECUADOR	.54	.64	.57	.54	.38	12.02	13.95	13.67	15.11	16.09	15.43	15.88
J. EL SALVADOR	.01	.02	.03	.05	.06	.06	.09	.11	.16	.18	.18	.18
K. GUATEMALA	.01	.02	.02	.01	.04	.05	.05	.04	.08	.15	.34	.34
L. HAITI	~	- -	~	- -	~	.02	.02	.02	.02	.03	.03	.03
M. HONDURAS	#	~	#	.01	.02	.05	.05	.06	.07	.07	.08	.08
N. MEXICO	17.58	21.50	30.97	41.97	53.81	82.05	88.99	103.02	127.01	151.76	787.36	218.56
O. NICARAGUA	#	~	#	.03	.04	.05	.05	.02	.02	.05	.06	.06
P. PANAMA	#	~	#	~	.01	.01	.02	.04	.09	.10	.15	.15
Q. PARAGUAY	~	~	~	~	.02	.07	.07	.07	.08	.09	.11	.11
R. PERU	3.93	3.44	4.86	5.18	6.43	6.89	7.29	8.34	12.73	15.68	16.08	15.97
S. URUGUAY	.07	.08	.08	.08	.15	.14	.15	.19	.20	.13	.28	.31
T. VENEZUELA	116.02	153.92	226.59	246.60	298.49	199.39	196.94	193.01	187.25	206.06	193.83	186.00
UNITED STATES	1,165.06	1,269.88	1,434.90	1,633.26	2,103.70	1,963.02	1,958.27	1,960.58	1,983.01	2,074.01	2,105.21	2,087.75

1. Based on the production of coal, lignite, crude petroleum, natural gas, and hydro and nuclear electricity. Where peat used as fuel is important, it is included with coal and lignite.

SOURCE: UN-SP: J, 19 (1976), tables 1 and 2; UN-YWES, 1979-81, table 1.

Table 1903

PC OF TOTAL COMMERCIAL ENERGY PRODUCTION, 20 LC, 1955–81

(APGR)

Country	1955	1960	1965	1970	1975	1976	1977	1978	1979	1980	1981
A. ARGENTINA	80	24.56	10.8	10.9	2.1	.5	4.7	3.6	8.3	5.2	2.5
B. BOLIVIA	50	10.2	−.3	28.2	35.3	2.1	−5.4	−3.4	2.2	5.8	4.3
C. BRAZIL	7.4	26.3	5	11.9	6.2	3.9	7.2	5.0	7.9	11.2	7.2
D. CHILE	8.5	8.5	11	−1.5	−.6	−4.9	6.2	−3.5	−7.8	8.1	13.3
E. COLOMBIA	3.3	11.5	4.4	4.2	−2.3	−2.7	1.5	6.5	−.6	4.7	4.2
F. COSTA RICA	10	13.3	8	14.3	6.7	12.5	−5.6	5.9	11.1	30.0	0
G. CUBA	26.7	−14.3	60	40	10	5.6	0	15.8	4.5	−6.5	−2.3
H. DOMINICAN REP.	~	~	0	0	0	0	0	0	0	0	0
I. ECUADOR	3.7	−2.2	−1.1	−5.9	612.6	16.1	−2.0	10.5	6.5	−4.1	2.9
J. EL SALVADOR	20	10	13.3	4	0	50.0	22.2	45.5	12.5	0	0
K. GUATEMALA	20	0	−10	60	5	0	−20.0	100.0	87.5	126.7	0
L. HAITI	~	~	~	~	~	0	0	0	0	50	0
M. HONDURAS	~	~	#	20	30	0	20.0	16.7	0	14.3	0
N. MEXICO	4.5	8.8	7.1	5.6	10.5	8.4	15.8	23.3	19.4	23.5	16.7
O. NICARAGUA	~	~	#	6.7	5	0	−60	0	150.0	20	0
P. PANAMA	~	~	~	~	0	100.0	100.0	125.0	11.1	50	0
Q. PARAGUAY	~	~	~	~	50	0	0	14.3	12.5	22.2	0
R. PERU	−2.5	8.3	1.3	4.8	1.4	5.8	14.4	52.6	23.2	2.6	−.68
S. URUGUAY	2.9	0	0	17.5	−1.3	7.1	26.7	5.3	−35.0	115.4	10.7
T. VENEZUELA	6.5	9.4	1.8	4.2	−6.6	−1.2	−2.0	−3.0	10	−5.9	−4.0
UNITED STATES	1.8	2.6	2.8	5.8	−1.3	−.24	.1	1.1	4.6	1.5	−.83

SOURCE: SALA calculations from table 1902.

Table 1904

INDEX OF TOTAL PRODUCTION OF COMMERCIAL ENERGY,[1] 20 LC, 1970–81

(1975 = 100)

	Country	1970	1971	1972	1973	1974	1976	1977	1978	1979	1980	1981
A.	ARGENTINA	91	98	100	99	100	101	105	109	118	124	127
B.	BOLIVIA	36	54	89	108	107	102	97	93	95	101	105
C.	BRAZIL	76	80	84	89	98	106	111	117	126	141	151
D.	CHILE	103	108	111	105	103	95	101	97	90	97	110
E.	COLOMBIA	113	114	110	108	103	97	99	105	105	109	114
F.	COSTA RICA	72	80	85	87	96	112	103	114	125	164	164
G.	CUBA	68	53	50	63	78	104	106	124	127	121	118
H.	DOMINICAN REP.	157	~	~	109	~	~	~	100	96	89	69
I.	ECUADOR	3	3	49	129	110	116	114	126	134	128	132
J.	EL SALVADOR	100	~	~	92	~	~	~	265	309	302	304
K.	GUATEMALA	86	96	78	83	85	129	91	176	322	723	723
L.	HAITI	~	~	~	89	~	~	~	152	175	179	183
M.	HONDURAS	47	58	73	86	95	103	112	129	144	152	153
N.	MEXICO	66	65	68	73	86	108	126	155	185	228	266
O.	NICARAGUA	86	51	88	86	99	106	37	52	104	139	140
P.	PANAMA	84	86	85	93	107	141	348	732	819	1,265	1,270
Q.	PARAGUAY	29	32	36	56	82	102	107	115	133	161	168
R.	PERU	93	83	87	91	99	106	121	185	228	233	232
S.	URUGUAY	110	130	88	137	121	108	138	144	94	201	225
T.	VENEZUELA	150	144	132	139	125	99	97	94	103	97	93
	UNITED STATES	107	105	107	106	102	100	100	101	106	107	106

1. Includes all types of solid, liquid, and gaseous fuels, plus electricity production.

SOURCE: UN-YWES, 1979, table 7; UN-YWES, 1981, table 2.

Table 1905

TOTAL COMMERCIAL ENERGY PRODUCTION, BY RESOURCE CLASSIFICATION, 20 LC

(1981)

	Country	T MET Coal Equivalent					%				
		Total	Solids[1]	Liquids[2]	Gas[3]	Electricity[4]	Total[5]	Solids	Liquids	Gas	Electricity
A.	ARGENTINA	52,406	420	38,229	11,606	2,151	100	1.0	72.9	22.1	4.1
B.	BOLIVIA	5,122	**	1,707	3,273	142	100	0	33.3	63.9	2.8
C.	BRAZIL	36,844	3,929	15,299	1,543	16,074	100	10.6	41.5	4.2	43.6
D.	CHILE	6,537	1,126	3,400	1,077	933	100	17.2	52.0	16.5	14.3
E.	COLOMBIA	22,023	5,300	10,408	4,308	2,007	100	24.1	47.3	19.6	9.1
F.	COSTA RICA	263	**	**	**	263	100	0	0	0	100
G.	CUBA	424	**	404	12	7	100	0	95.3	2.8	1.7
H.	DOMINICAN REP.	5	**	**	**	5	100	0	0	0	100
I.	ECUADOR	15,877	**	15,706	55	117	100	0	98.9	#	#
J.	EL SALVADOR	178	**	**	**	178	100	0	0	0	100
K.	GUATEMALA	339	**	300	**	40	100	0	88.5	0	11.8
L.	HAITI	28	**	**	**	28	100	0	0	0	100
M.	HONDURAS	79	**	**	**	79	100	0	0	0	100
N.	MEXICO	216,559	5,776	177,382	32,255	3,147	100	2.6	81.2	14.8	1.4
O.	NICARAGUA	64	**	**	**	64	100	0	0	0	100
P.	PANAMA	153	**	**	**	153	100	0	0	0	100
Q.	PARAGUAY	111	**	**	**	111	100	0	0	0	100
R.	PERU	15,970	50	13,958	1,002	959	100	#	85.2	6.3	6.0
S.	URUGUAY	313	**	**	**	313	100	0	0	0	100
T.	VENEZUELA	185,999	46	164,611	19,486	1,856	100	#	88.5	10.5	1.0
	UNITED STATES	2,087,754	614,779	692,974	713,483	66,518	100	29.4	33.2	34.1	3.2

1. Comprised of hard coal, lignite-brown coal, peat and oil shale.
2. Comprised of crude petroleum and natural gas liquids.
3. Comprised of natural gas.
4. Comprised of electricity generation from hydro, nuclear and geothermal sources.
5. May not total due to rounding.

SOURCE: UN-YWES, 1981, table 1; percentages calculated by SALA.

Table 1906

TOTAL COMMERCIAL ENERGY CONSUMPTION,[1] 20 LC, 1929-81[a],[b]
(M MET Coal Equivalent and Kg PI)

Year	A. ARGENTINA Total	Per Capita	B. BOLIVIA Total	Per Capita	C. BRAZIL Total	Per Capita	D. CHILE Total	Per Capita	E. COLOMBIA Total	Per Capita	F. COSTA RICA Total	Per Capita	G. CUBA Total	Per Capita	H. DOMINICAN REP. Total	Per Capita	I. ECUADOR Total	Per Capita	J. EL SALVADOR Total	Per Capita	K. GUATEMALA Total	Per Capita
1929	7.58	680	.10	30	4.13	100	3.09	740	.60	70	.08	150	2.11	590	.10	40	.04	20	.08	40	.13	60
1937	9.22	650	.13	40	5.02	130	3.21	670	1.18	140	.09	150	1.49	340	.07	40	.11	40	.06	40	.12	60
1949	11.92	710	.32	80	10.06	200	4.35	760	2.84	260	.18	260	2.49	470	.19	80	.36	120	.14	60	.40	150
1950	13.08	760	.36	90	11.52	220	4.43	760	3.04	270	.19	270	2.56	480	.19	90	.37	120	.16	90	.45	160
1951	16.08	919	.34	110	15.51	289	5.49	884	3.67	306	.24	288	2.98	533	.15	65	.43	132	.19	100	.41	142
1952	16.85	943	.36	115	17.57	318	5.33	839	3.52	285	.31	357	3.41	505	.26	110	.45	134	.20	103	.41	138
1953	15.98	878	.37	116	18.14	319	5.72	877	4.24	334	.33	364	3.59	476	.27	111	.45	130	.23	114	.40	131
1954	17.24	930	.52	160	20.20	344	6.42	960	5.84	447	.29	307	3.78	457	.30	120	.52	146	.26	125	.43	136
1955	18.79	982	.47	145	16.92	289	5.33	788	5.26	415	.20	214	3.95	512	.40	159	.50	134	.23	104	.43	131
1956	19.84	1,017	.54	165	18.72	312	5.92	852	5.44	420	.26	263	4.21	517	.43	163	.51	135	.26	113	.45	134
1957	21.56	1,085	.52	156	18.57	303	5.75	840	6.15	464	.25	240	4.71	819	.44	163	.59	150	.29	122	.45	131
1958	21.85	1,078	.47	140	20.68	329	5.81	829	6.14	454	.25	229	4.70	1,043	.46	164	.63	155	.29	120	.52	146
1959	21.85	1,070	.50	145	21.27	314	6.04	808	6.64	480	.23	200	5.34	924	.49	169	.65	156	.30	120	.58	158
1960	22.3	1,088	.5	152	23.5	337	6.5	839	7.3	516	.3	215	5.8	912	.5	158	.8	186	.3	128	.6	170
1961	24.8	1,225	.6	144	24.4	340	7.3	928	8.2	516	.3	228	6.2	799	.5	146	.9	193	.3	120	.7	173
1962	26.0	1,267	.6	164	26.9	363	8.7	1,087	8.8	538	.3	241	6.9	934	.6	173	.8	176	.4	132	.7	166
1963	24.8	1,192	.6	162	28.2	368	9.1	1,110	9.2	544	.3	251	6.6	869	.6	175	.9	188	.4	152	.7	169
1964	27.8	1,313	.7	173	29.2	471	9.1	1,069	8.8	501	.4	258	7.1	926	.8	237	1.0	201	.5	186	.8	183
1965	30.1	1,399	.8	181	29.9	367	9.1	1,048	9.7	539	.4	296	7.7	930	.6	170	1.1	214	.5	171	.9	201
1966	31.3	1,436	.8	199	32.7	389	9.7	1,088	9.8	528	.5	303	7.7	951	.8	214	1.1	214	.6	191	.9	184
1967	32.2	1,452	.9	208	34.0	393	10.1	1,107	11.3	586	.5	291	8.5	978	.7	194	1.2	224	.5	171	1.0	192
1968	33.3	1,480	1.0	218	39.9	446	10.8	1,151	11.8	600	.5	324	8.4	959	1.1	2.88	1.5	261	.6	194	1.2	208
1969	34.3	1,625	1.1	231	43.4	479	11.5	1,204	12.1	586	.5	356	8.9	1,023	1.2	314	1.5	270	.5	168	1.1	214
1970	37.9	1,595	1.0	227	41.7	450	10.8	1,152	12.0	586	.7	387	8.5	997	1.4	335	1.7	282	.7	194	1.0	194
1971	40.4	1,678	.01	230	46.4	488	11.8	1,239	13.0	617	.8	437	9.1	1,046	1.7	396	1.9	301	.7	197	1.1	204
1972	41.4	1,698	.2	251	52.0	532	11.5	1,187	13.3	615	.9	469	9.4	1,059	2.2	509	1.9	299	.7	199	1.2	217
1973	44.3	1,793	1.2	259	59.5	591	11.6	1,177	14.6	655	1.0	534	10.0	1,102	2.5	566	2.1	313	.9	241	1.3	228
1974	44.0	1,756	.4	298	66.7	649	11.3	1,124	15.2	660	1.0	500	10.1	1,096	2.8	622	2.4	355	.9	234	1.4	233
1975	43.1	1,698	1.6	333	71.2	670	9.9	974	15.6	660	1.0	524	11.8	1,261	2.7	578	2.8	399	1.0	238	1.5	239
1976	44.2	1,720	1.8	357	77.7	712	9.6	933	16.6	684	1.0	483	10.7	1,126	2.6	537	3.2	433	1.0	251	1.4	217
1977	46.1	1,769	2.1	410	82.0	731	10.1	956	17.9	713	1.2	582	12.4	1,297	2.6	520	3.2	418	1.1	259	1.6	226
1978	44.9	1,746	2.2	427	87.8	777	10.4	972	19.3	754	1.4	645	12.7	1,312	2.4	465	4.3	543	1.1	260	1.8	263
1979	48.6	1,831	2.3	430	91.2	788	10.9	1,002	19.8	749	1.2	572	13.2	1,346	2.2	410	5.0	621	1.2	261	2.1	291
1980	51.1	1,824	2.1	382	94	793	11.5	1,035	20.8	768	1.2	552	13.8	1,404	2.6	484	5.6	669	1.0	206	1.9	267
1981	52.4	1,718	2.2	365	92	757	10.4	925	20.9	752	1.3	591	13.5	1,382	2.5	454	5.4	630	1.0	210	1.7	224

Table 1906 (Continued)

TOTAL COMMERCIAL ENERGY CONSUMPTION, [1] 20 LC, 1929–81 [a,b]
(M MET Coal Equivalent and Kg PI)

Year	L. HAITI Total	Per Capita	M. HONDURAS Total	Per Capita	N. MEXICO Total	Per Capita	O. NICARAGUA Total	Per Capita	P. PANAMA Total	Per Capita	Q. PARAGUAY Total	Per Capita	R. PERU Total	Per Capita	S. URUGUAY Total	Per Capita	T. VENEZUELA Total	Per Capita	UNITED STATES Total	Per Capita	WORLD Total	Per Capita
1929	.02	10	.22	236	4.82	300	0.3	40	--	--	--	--	.86	140	.82	440	.70	230	803.40	6,570	1,857.4	975
1937	.02	10	.18	167	8.19	440	.05	60	--	--	.01	10	.85	130	.83	400	1.04	300	759.30	5,890	2,002.2	1,001
1949	.06	20	.20	144	14.97	610	.08	70	.23	310	.03	20	1.69	210	1.45	610	3.01	640	1,032.05	6,920	~	~
1950	.06	20	.23	161	14.9	567	.09	90	.24	300	.03	20	1.62	190	1.52	640	3.89	770	1,139.85	7,510	2,492.7	1,004
1951	.06	17	.23	156	16.8	620	.10	92	.27	330	.03	21	2.52	311	1.99	905	4.8	622	1,252.58	8,087	2,718.9	1,077
1952	.08	23	.24	159	18.0	648	.13	116	.35	417	.05	34	2.64	318	2.34	1,017	5.5	1,660	1,247.00	7,912	2,784.4	1,085
1953	.08	22	.24	154	17.7	619	.14	120	.35	405	~	~	2.80	333	2.19	952	6.1	1,655	1,287.88	8,039	2,873.9	1,100
1954	.10	27	.19	118	17.7	5.99	.16	133	.32	360	~	~	3.06	356	2.37	1,030	6.5	2,033	1,257.34	7,713	2,951.7	1,109
1955	.12	36	.21	126	19.3	632	.19	151	.35	386	.09	60	2.58	274	1.72	655	7.1	2,123	1,285.09	7,768	3,243.2	1,196
1956	.12	34	.23	135	20.4	648	.18	139	.31	333	.09	59	2.72	281	1.85	696	9.1	2,256	1,334.25	7,928	3,431.3	1,242
1957	.12	34	.28	158	23.5	722	.20	149	.38	392	.10	62	2.95	297	1.99	741	10.0	2,593	1,336.00	7,771	3,553.8	1,263
1958	.13	38	.29	157	25.3	749	.25	211	.47	467	.12	71	3.30	323	1.85	683	11.5	2,500	1,334.07	7,632	3,744.3	1,305
1959	.14	35	.29	160	25.9	742	.25	163	.49	470	.13	75	3.34	317	2.16	770	12.4	2,503	1,390.25	7,817	3,954.4	1,352
1960	.2	38	.3	160	27.8	770	.3	174	.5	493	.2	87	4.9	494	2.1	851	14.8	2,623	1,454.0	8,047	4,242.8	1,423
1961	.1	31	.4	184	28.5	789	.4	192	.5	724	.2	97	5.0	508	2.0	776	13.1	2,667	1,481.8	8,068	4,204.2	1,383
1962	.1	31	.3	168	27.8	746	.3	199	.5	811	.2	97	5.7	539	2.0	772	14.0	2,914	1,545.7	8,288	4,429.7	1,429
1963	.1	30	.3	164	29.4	760	.4	278	.5	892	.2	103	6.3	575	2.1	794	15.5	2,731	1,632.5	8,628	4,709.6	1,490
1964	.1	35	.3	163	31.8	796	.4	265	.5	875	.2	104	6.2	551	2.2	826	16.5	2,288	1,712.5	8,927	4,970.9	1,543
1965	.1	36	.4	164	32.8	795	.4	244	.6	1,031	.3	129	6.4	536	2.4	882	18.2	2,658	1,790.8	9,219	5,212.4	1,587
1966	.1	36	.4	194	35.7	836	.5	277	.7	1,223	.3	121	7.4	646	2.3	843	19.0	2,525	1,894.1	9,640	5,525.2	1,651
1967	.1	30	.4	175	39.7	898	.5	313	.7	1,249	.3	138	7.7	634	2.3	817	20.2	2,288	1,962.6	9,881	5,614.8	1,647
1968	.1	30	.5	217	42.7	935	.6	366	.8	1,301	.3	142	8.2	625	2.2	784	21.1	2,595	2,080.3	10,398	6,032.2	1,736
1969	.1	35	.4	190	47.4	1,003	.6	358	.9	676	.2	117	8.1	611	2.6	916	21.8	2,024	2,188.0	10,795	6,437.7	1,819
1970	.2	40	.6	227	53.1	1,048	.7	358	.9	629	.3	142	8.0	596	2.5	907	24.6	2,392	2,216.9	10,811	6,446.3	1,762
1971	.2	42	.6	207	57.6	1,098	.7	366	1.1	768	.3	130	8.3	600	2.6	889	25.1	2,369	2,258.8	10,909	6,770.8	1,817
1972	.2	41	.6	226	61.2	1,128	.8	397	1.2	818	.3	134	8.3	583	2.8	944	27.1	2,478	2,376.6	11,380	7,078.1	1,868
1973	.2	42	.7	230	65.9	1,174	.8	415	1.3	846	.4	154	8.6	589	2.7	955	31.8	2,817	2,437.7	11,504	7,438.1	1,923
1974	.2	36	.7	223	71.9	1,238	.9	429	1.3	799	.4	162	9.0	596	2.6	947	32.1	2,760	2,345.6	11,070	7,471.3	1,899
1975	.2	45	.7	232	73.1	1,217	.9	419	1.4	856	.4	149	10.2	660	2.6	935	33.5	2,796	2,260.8	10,468	7,447.0	1,842
1976	.2	40	.8	247	77.6	1,247	1.0	442	1.4	842	.5	169	10.1	634	2.9	1,030	35.8	2,975	2,378.3	11,054	7,872.2	1,930
1977	.2	48	.9	275	84.3	1,290	1.2	505	1.4	809	.6	198	10.1	619	2.8	946	37.9	2,952	2,406.2	11,095	8,075.5	1,946
1978	.3	67	.8	229	93.5	1,397	1.1	456	1.4	760	.7	233	10.2	612	2.7	931	40.0	3,046	2,489.8	11,186	8,369.7	1,967
1979	.3	67	.8	231	106.6	1,536	.8	296	1.5	817	.6	210	10.8	626	2.8	981	45.6	3,372	2,502.5	11,120	8,653.5	2,000
1980	.3	65	.8	225	117.1	1,629	.9	319	1.9	1,004	.6	186	11.1	624	2.8	957	49.0	3,520	2,419.5	10,628	8,566.2	1,946
1981	.3	66	.9	237	125.7	1,687	.9	319	1.8	923	.5	159	10.9	595	2.6	895	45.1	3,153	2,344.8	10,204	8,493.4	1,893

1. Includes solid and liquid fuels; natural and imported gas; hydro, nuclear, and imported electricity.

a. Change in terminology: "gross commercial consumption" through 1950; "gross consumption" through 1954; "aggregate consumption" since 1955.

b. Prior to 1960 total data given to two decimal places, and per capita data for 1951-54 calculated with population statistics in SALA-SNP, chapter VIII. Per capita data for 1929 and 1937 calculated with population statistics in WA, 1929 and 1937.

SOURCE: SALA-SNP, XI-1; UN-SP: J, 1 (1952); J, 17 (1974); J, 19 (1976), table 2; WA 1929 and 1937; UN-SP: J, 20 (1977); table J, 21 (1978), table 2; UN-YWES, yearly, 1979-81, table 1.

Table 1907

INDEX OF TOTAL CONSUMPTION OF COMMERCIAL ENERGY,[1] 17 LC, 1970–81

(1975 = 100)

	Country	1970	1971	1972	1973	1974	1976	1977	1978	1979	1980	1981
A.	ARGENTINA	88	94	96	103	102	103	107	107	114	115	112
B.	BOLIVIA	60	62	70	74	87	110	130	139	143	131	133
C.	BRAZIL	59	65	73	84	94	110	116	123	128	132	129
D.	CHILE	109	121	118	117	116	99	103	105	110	116	105
E.	COLOMBIA	77	84	86	94	98	107	114	124	127	133	134
F.	COSTA RICA	65	80	88	97	98	99	123	132	120	120	130
G.	CUBA	73	86	89	85	96	101	118	108	112	117	115
I.	ECUADOR	60	66	67	73	86	112	112	152	178	198	193
K.	GUATEMALA	69	73	80	88	91	95	109	120	137	130	112
M.	HONDURAS	83	79	88	93	93	110	127	110	115	116	126
N.	MEXICO	73	78	83	90	97	105	113	128	146	160	172
O.	NICARAGUA	73	76	86	93	99	110	130	122	87	97	100
P.	PANAMA	64	79	87	94	90	101	100	96	105	132	125
Q.	PARAGUAY	81	77	82	97	104	115	139	103	161	148	130
R.	PERU	78	81	81	84	88	99	99	101	106	109	106
S.	URUGUAY	95	95	102	101	96	107	99	101	107	105	99
T.	VENEZUELA	73	77	83	95	99	110	116	119	136	146	134
	UNITED STATES	98	99	104	108	103	105	107	110	111	107	104

1. Includes all types of solid, liquid, and gaseous fuels, plus electricity production.

SOURCE: UN-YWES, 1979, table 7; UN-YWES, 1981, table 2.

Table 1908

CRUDE OIL PRODUCTION, 10 LC AND 10 L, 1955–82

PART I: M MET

Country	1955	1960	1965	1966	1967	1968	1969	1970	1971	1972	1973	1974	1975	1976	1977	1978	1979	1980	1981
A. ARGENTINA	4.37	9.17	13.81	14.67	16.02	17.53	18.16	20.02	21.57	22.13	21.48	21.14	20.77	20.81	22.17	23.24	24.28	25.28	25.53
B. BOLIVIA	.35	.41	.44	.78	1.84	1.90	1.87	1.12	1.70	2.03	2.20	2.11	1.87	1.89	1.61	1.51	1.29	1.11	1.03
C. BRAZIL	.28	3.87	4.49	5.55	7.08	7.82	8.36	7.98	8.39	8.14	8.28	8.62	8.35	8.12	7.81	7.79	8.04	8.84	10.37
D. CHILE	.35	.96	1.71	1.68	1.68	1.84	1.71	1.47	1.65	1.42	1.28	1.11	.99	.94	.93	.78	1.01	1.60	1.87
E. COLOMBIA	5.49	7.71	10.17	9.99	9.66	9.10	10.93	11.33	11.12	10.13	9.49	8.69	8.10	7.55	7.11	6.76	6.41	6.50	6.93
G. CUBA	.05	.01	.06	.07	.12	.12	.20	.16	.11	.11	.14	.17†	.23	.23	.24†	.29	.29	.27	.28
I. ECUADOR	.48	.38	.39	.36	.30	.25	.20	.19	.17	4.01	10.62	9.00	8.16	9.49	9.28	10.22	10.87	10.42	10.73
N. MEXICO	13.02	15.75	18.54	18.95	20.69	22.15	21.05	21.51	21.41	22.16	23.26	29.59	36.89	41.34	49.28	63.33	75.48	96.85	115.41
R. PERU	2.41	2.64	3.19	3.17	3.53	3.72	3.51	3.55	3.05	3.19	3.48	3.82	3.55	3.78	4.50	7.44	9.45	9.65	9.55
T. VENEZUELA	115.54	152.86	182.84	176.83	185.92	189.64	187.91	194.31	185.28	168.06	175.78	156.17	122.40	120.15	117.01	113.63	124.03	115.16	111.58
UNITED STATES	352.12	364.34	405.36	430.32	456.67	473.30	455.60	475.29	466.70	466.95	454.19	432.79	413.09	401.25	405.71	428.49	420.82	421.82	421.80
WORLD	791.65	1,076.29	1,539.04	1,670.59	1,791.63	1,955.53	2,071.05	2,275.0	2,413.43	2,547.85	2,779.94	2,789.03	2,643.66	2,870.19	2,984.87	3,010.12	3,126.08	2,974.50	2,788.92

SOURCE: SALA-SNP, p. 223; UN-SP: J, 17 (1974); UN-SP: J, 19 (1976); J, 20 (1977), p. 64; J, 21 (1978l), table 6; J, 22 (1979), table 10; UN-YWES, yearly, 1978-81, table 16.

PART II: T BARRELS

Country	1960	1973	1974	1975	1976	1977	1978	1979	1980	1981	1982‡
A. ARGENTINA	63,860	153,537	151,094	144,465	145,591	157,528	165,119	172,354	179,680	181,316	179,071
B. BOLIVIA	3,111	17,261	16,602	14,732	14,856	12,695	11,845	10,200	8,704	8,091	8,918
C. BRAZIL	29,614	62,397	64,800	62,700	62,934	58,685	58,528	60,434	66,435	80,321	97,682
D. CHILE	7,231	11,430	10,061	8,946	8,371	7,120	6,291	7,572	12,140	15,104	14,965
E. COLOMBIA	55,770	67,089	61,387	57,318	53,376	50,221	47,741	45,297	45,944	48,852	51,725
I. ECUADOR	2,807	76,221	64,616	58,753	68,362	67,002	73,668	78,800	74,797	77,062	77,400
K. GUATEMALA	#	#	#	#	#	#	221	571	1,513	1,494	2,292
N. MEXICO	99,049	164,909	238,271	294,254	326,390	358,090	442,607	536,926	708,593	844,241	984,200
R. PERU	19,272	25,769	28,142	26,294	28,101	33,271	55,071	69,972	71,175	70,445	72,270
T. VENEZUELA	1,041,675	1,228,594	1,086,332	856,364	839,738	816,870	790,590	863,590	793,488	769,055	690,945

SOURCE: IDB-SPTF, yearly, 1978-83, p. 395.

Table 1909

PC OF CRUDE OIL PRODUCTION, 10 LC, 1971–81

Country	1971	1973	1974	1975	1976	1977	1978	1979	1980	1981
A. ARGENTINA	7.7	−2.9	−1.6	−1.8	.2	6.5	4.8	4.5	4.1	1.0
B. BOLIVIA	51.8	8.4	−4.1	−11.4	1.1	−14.8	−6.2	−14.6	−14.0	−7.2
C. BRAZIL	5.1	1.7	4.1	−3.1	−2.8	−3.8	−.3	3.2	9.9	17.3
D. CHILE	12.2	−9.9	−13.3	−10.8	−5.1	889.4	−16.1	38.4	58.4	16.9
E. COLOMBIA	−1.9	−6.3	−8.4	−6.8	−6.8	−5.8	−4.9	−5.1	1.4	6.6
G. CUBA	−31.3	27.3	21.4	35.3	0	4.3	20.8	0	−6.9	3.7
I. ECUADOR	−10.5	164.8	−15.3	−9.3	16.3	−2.2	10.1	6.4	−4.1	3.0
N. MEXICO	−.5	5.0	27.2	24.7	12.1	19.2	28.5	19.2	28.3	19.2
R. PERU	−14.1	9.1	9.8	−7.1	6.5	19.0	65.3	27.0	2.1	−1.0
T. VENEZUELA	−4.6	4.6	−11.2	−21.6	−1.8	−2.6	−2.9	9.2	−7.2	−3.1
UNITED STATES	−1.8	−2.7	−4.7	−4.6	−2.9	1.1	5.6	−1.8	.2	#
WORLD	6.1	9.1	.3	−5.2	8.6	4.0	.8	3.9	−4.8	−6.2

SOURCE: SALA calculations from table 1908, part I.

Table 1910

OFF-SHORE PRODUCTION OF CRUDE PETROLEUM, 5 LC, 1970–81
(T MET)

Country	1970	1972	1973	1974	1975	1976	1977	1978	1979	1980	1981
A. ARGENTINA	95[†]	98	90[†]	94	90[†]	90[†]	90[†]	90[†]	90[†]	95[†]	95[†]
C. BRAZIL	396	462	661	1,190	1,340	1,584	1,864	2,104	2,763	3,638	4,864
N. MEXICO	1,991	1,538	1,777	2,341	2,665	2,242	2,283	2,199	4,914	34,669	53,987
R. PERU	1,000[†]	1,177	1,544	1,676	1,500[†]	1,600[†]	1,900[†]	1,400[†]	1,425[†]	1,400[†]	1,500[†]
T. VENEZUELA	128,050	130,489	140,543	108,437	85,000[†]	85,000[†]	85,000[†]	83,000[†]	87,000[†]	80,500[†]	78,100[†]
UNITED STATES	77,786	82,333	79,690	73,466	67,200	62,351	57,848	55,914	52,500	51,033	50,895

SOURCE: UN-YWES, yearly, 1979-81, table 16.

Table 1911

REFINED OIL PRODUCTION, 18 L, 1960–82
(T Barrels)

Country	1960	1973	1974	1975	1976	1977	1978	1979	1980	1981	1982[‡]
A. ARGENTINA	85,702	162,548	156,453	157,931	165,768	175,224	177,283	182,400	189,624	189,771	183,217
B. BOLIVIA	2,263	5,533	5,932	7,365	8,568	9,283	9,816	7,261	9,777	8,867	9,623
C. BRAZIL	64,276	205,100	307,400	336,150	344,157	343,950	385,577	401,931	405,101	397,922	~
D. CHILE	9,855	36,559	38,313	31,783	34,212	35,180	34,442	37,278	35,805	35,455	~
E. COLOMBIA	26,573	59,713	60,592	57,685	59,127	60,174	57,461	59,247	58,699	62,343	63,291
F. COSTA RICA	#	3,358	2,736	1,941	1,902	2,535	3,054	2,981	3,690	~	~
H. DOMINICAN REP.	#	5,465	6,617	8,545	8,885	9,009	9,422	9,147	9,384	9,447	8,804
I. ECUADOR	4,234	11,023	12,758	14,643	15,571	31,724	29,047	32,000	33,937	32,182	~
J. EL SALVADOR	#	4,199	4,012	4,491	4,680	4,962	5,254	5,288	4,588	4,304	~
K. GUATEMALA	#	7,132	6,536	4,855	4,443	4,615	5,959	5,767	5,381	5,345	4,508
M. HONDURAS	#	3,439	3,310	3,459	3,004	3,090	3,107	3,383	3,639	~	~
N. MEXICO	102,389	206,108	223,336	232,839	258,282	300,635	320,220	349,920	417,114	459,990	~
O. NICARAGUA	#	3,869	4,430	4,728	5,006	5,376	4,459	1,364	4,709	~	~
P. PANAMA	#	25,974	~	~	18,207	20,451	17,013	15,731	13,653	10,543	23,450
Q. PARAGUAY	#	1,480	1,680	1,662	2,121	1,863	2,278	2,186	1,960	1,913	1,611
R. PERU	16,524	36,624	39,735	41,157	41,511	43,328	44,399	53,282	62,980[†]	~	~
S. URUGUAY	9,490	11,667	11,614	12,465	12,452	12,767	13,490	12,964	12,377	11,603	~
T. VENEZUELA	323,125	376,836	436,538	317,044	360,885	353,065	358,940	360,255	377,452	313,535	316,090

SOURCE: IDB-SPTF, 1978, p. 470; IDB-SPTF, 1979, p. 455; IDB-SPTF, 1980, p. 451;
    IDB-SPTF, 1983, p. 395.

Table 1912

PC OF REFINED OIL PRODUCTION, 18 L, 1960–82

Country	1960-73	1974	1975	1976	1977	1978	1979	1980	1981	1982
A. ARGENTINA	89.7	-3.7	.9	5.0	5.7	1.2	2.8	4.0	.1	-3.5
B. BOLIVIA	144.5	7.2	24.2	16.3	8.3	5.7	-26.0	28.2	-9.3	8.5
C. BRAZIL	219.0	49.9	9.4	2.4	.1	12.1	4.2	.8	-1.8	~
D. CHILE	271.0	4.8	-17.0	7.6	2.8	-2.1	8.2	-4.0	-1.0	~
E. COLOMBIA	124.7	1.5	-4.8	2.5	1.8	-4.5	3.1	-9.2	6.2	1.5
F. COSTA RICA	~	-18.5	-29.1	-2.0	33.3	20.4	-2.4	23.8	~	~
H. DOMINICAN REP.	~	21.1	29.1	4.0	1.4	4.6	-2.9	2.6	.7	-6.8
I. ECUADOR	160.3	15.7	14.8	6.3	103.7	-8.4	10.2	6.0	-5.2	~
J. EL SALVADOR	~	-4.5	11.9	4.2	6.0	5.9	.6	-13.2	-6.2	~
K. GUATEMALA	~	-8.4	-25.7	-8.5	3.9	29.1	-3.2	-6.7	-.7	-15.7
M. HONDURAS	~	-3.8	4.5	-13.2	2.9	.6	8.9	7.6	~	~
N. MEXICO	101.2	8.4	4.3	10.9	16.4	6.5	9.3	19.2	10.3	~
O. NICARAGUA	~	14.5	6.7	5.9	7.4	-17.1	-69.4	245.2	~	~
P. PANAMA	~	~	~	~	12.3	-16.8	-7.5	-13.2	-22.8	122.4
Q. PARAGUAY	~	13.5	-1.1	27.6	-12.2	22.3	-4.0	-10.3	-2.4	-15.8
R. PERU	121.6	8.5	3.6	.9	4.4	2.5	20.0	18.2	~	~
S. URUGUAY	22.9	-2.5	7.3	-.1	2.5	5.7	-3.9	-4.5	-6.2	~
T. VENEZUELA	16.6	15.8	-27.4	13.8	-2.2	1.7	.4	4.8	-16.9	.8

SOURCE: SALA calculations from table 1911.

Table 1913

PETROLEUM REFINERY DISTILLATION CAPACITY, 19 LC, 1970–81
(T MET)

Country	1970	1972	1973	1974	1975	1976	1977	1978	1979	1980	1981
A. ARGENTINA	23,980	31,310	31,310	31,310	31,310	31,310	33,205	33,786	34,235	34,500[†]	34,604
B. BOLIVIA	1,180	1,290	1,290	1,290	1,290	1,290	1,930	1,955	3,715[†]	3,725	2,800[†]
C. BRAZIL	27,300	39,200	42,600	51,000	51,700	51,300	57,500	62,300	62,300[†]	72,200	72,260
D. CHILE	3,850	5,450	5,450	6,000	6,000	6,000	6,000	6,000	6,000[†]	6,000[†]	6,000[†]
E. COLOMBIA	7,000[†]	8,100[†]	8,100	8,670	8,670	8,670	8,670	8,670	8,670[†]	9,680	10,250
F. COSTA RICA	470	470	470	470	470	470[†]	470[†]	470[†]	470[†]	550[†]	550[†]
G. CUBA	4,340	5,700	5,700[†]	5,700[†]	6,000[†]	6,450[†]	6,450[†]	6,450[†]	6,450[†]	6,450[†]	6,450[†]
H. DOMINICAN REP.	~	~	1,500	1,500	1,500	1,500	1,550	2,350[†]	2,350[†]	2,350[†]	2,350[†]
I. ECUADOR	1,740	1,770	1,770	2,190	2,190	2,190	5,040	5,040	4,800	4,800[†]	4,800[†]
J. EL SALVADOR	650	650	650	650	750	750[†]	750[†]	800[†]	800[†]	800[†]	800[†]
K. GUATEMALA	1,250	1,250	1,250	1,250	1,250	1,250	1,250[†]	1,250[†]	1,250[†]	1,250[†]	1,250[†]
M. HONDURAS	700	700	700	700	700	700	700	700[†]	700[†]	700[†]	700[†]
N. MEXICO	29,600	31,250	38,000	38,000	39,250	48,400	48,650	49,322	66,910	73,646	76,016
O. NICARAGUA	650	650	650	650	750	750	750	750[†]	750[†]	750[†]	750[†]
P. PANAMA	4,000	4,000[†]	4,000[†]	5,000	5,000	10,000	10,000	10,000[†]	10,000[†]	5,000[†]	5,000[†]
Q. PARAGUAY	500[†]	500[†]	500[†]	500[†]	500[†]	500[†]	500[†]	500[†]	500[†]	500[†]	500[†]
R. PERU	4,680	5,180	5,540	5,540	5,540	9,060	9,060	9,060	9,060[†]	8,900	8,000[†]
S. URUGUAY	2,250	2,250	2,350	2,450	2,450	2,450	2,450	2,232	2,232	2,232	2,408
T. VENEZUELA	68,200	77,750	77,750	77,750	77,750	77,750	80,220	80,225	80,225[†]	80,225[†]	68,547
UNITED STATES	643,000	683,550	718,100	748,100	760,000	819,920	793,100	839,700	885,200	890,730	792,450

SOURCE: UN-YWES, 1979, table 26; UN-YWES, 1981, table 21.

Table 1914

INDEX OF TOTAL PRODUCTION OF CRUDE PETROLEUM, 9 LC, 1970–81

(1975 = 100)

	Country	1970	1971	1972	1973	1974	1976	1977	1978	1979	1980	1981
A.	ARGENTINA	96	104	107	103	102	100	107	112	117	122	123
B.	BOLIVIA	60	91	108	117	113	101	86	80	69	59	55
C.	BRAZIL	96	99	97	99	103	97	94	93	96	106	124
D.	CHILE	148	141	143	128	112	94	93	78	102	161	188
E.	COLOMBIA	140	137	125	117	107	93	88	83	79	80	85
G.	CUBA	70	53	50	61	74	104	104	127	127	121	123
N.	MEXICO	58	58	60	63	80	112	134	172	205	263	313
R.	PERU	100	86	90	98	107	106	127	209	266	271	269
T.	VENEZUELA	159	151	138	144	128	98	96	93	101	94	91
	UNITED STATES	115	113	113	110	105	97	98	104	102	102	102
	WORLD	86	91	96	105	105	109	113	114	118	113	105

SOURCE: UN-YWES, 1979, table 23; UN-YWES' 1981, table 18.

Table 1915

INDEX OF TOTAL CONSUMPTION OF CRUDE PETROLEUM, 18 LC, 1970–81

(1975 = 100)

	Country	1970	1971	1972	1973	1974	1976	1977	1978	1979	1980	1981
A.	ARGENTINA	96	104	104	104	105	104	112	113	115	120	119
B.	BOLIVIA	62	86	103	75	107	101	86	133	149	125	108
C.	BRAZIL	59	64	75	98	100	97	94	122	128	126	122
D.	CHILE	92	122	125	118	125	94	93	121	140	127	109
E.	COLOMBIA	88	137	125	101	107	93	88	98	96	93	99
F.	COSTA RICA	113	158	168	160	147	94	124	148	144	185	168
G.	CUBA	72	73	79	89	93	103	105	108	107	105	107
H.	DOMINICAN REP.	~	~	~	62	76	107	108	112	105	108	116
I.	ECUADOR	54	60	66	73	83	101	94	195	206	221	209
J.	EL SALVADOR	27	66	69	95	87	108	134	118	116	107	106
K.	GUATEMALA	78	83	92	97	98	78	76	87	89	90	93
M.	HONDURAS	112	86	98	98	97	82	85	65	78	78	81
N.	MEXICO	72	71	77	85	98	113	125	131	139	167	182
O.	NICARAGUA	70	74	76	91	92	106	113	99	75	93	88
P.	PANAMA	94	104	104	98	92	69	73	61	54	50	50
Q.	PARAGUAY	91	82	98	117	112	112	111	156	139	96	122
S.	URUGUAY	97	92	86	93	93	99	99	100	98	99	92
T.	VENEZUELA	149	142	127	145	141	109	106	109	110	104	100
	UNITED STATES	88	90	94	100	98	108	117	119	118	108	100
	WORLD	86	90	96	105	104	107	113	115	118	113	107

SOURCE: UN-YWES,1979, table 23; UN-YWES, 1981, table 18.

Table 1916

REFINED PETROLEUM PRODUCTS PRODUCTION,[1] 20 LC, 1950-81

(T MET)

Country / Product	1950	1955	1960	1965	1968	1970	1974	1975	1976	1977	1978	1979	1980	1981
A. ARGENTINA														
Liquefied Petrol. Gas	30	51	74	323	408	548	383	677	730	779	715	718	765	883
Motor Spirit	1,525	1,681	1,951	32,000	3,458	3,978	4,158	3,841	4,013	4,318	4,475	4,621	5,157	5,087
Kerosene	586	844	1,124	1,057	859	886	853	786	796	755	654	524	591	423
Jet Fuel	3†	4	19	122	220	301	425	463	469	516	578	625	782	784
Distillate Fuel Oils	763	1,170	1,623	3,092	3,999	4,829	5,796	5,512	6,035	6,318	6,418	6,775	7,736	7,595
Residual Fuel Oils	2,573	3,716	6,264	7,990	8,184	8,502	8,615	7,749	7,911	8,584	8,277	8,421	8,134	7,985
Lubricating Oils	85	109	145	140	128	144	257	244	237	294	243	307	277	297
Bitumen (Asphalt)	~	~	263	374	612	695	487	429	431	545	572	677	640†	623
Petroleum Coke	~	~	84	356	436	663	721	666	681	746	896	810	710†	869
B. BOLIVIA														
Liquefied Petrol. Gas	~	6	6	~	2	3	21	27	39	47	66	84	103	95
Motor Spirit	39	108	106	139	195	220	274	377	399	502	497	526	433	392
Kerosene	9	19	52	66	90	103	137	143	139	135	151	133	132	93
Jet Fuel	~	~	~	2	8	13	29	43	52	62	78	70	92	91
Distillate Fuel Oils	6	32	48	73	86	89	127	159	189	232	255	253	220	175
Residual Fuel Oils	25	113	82	124	154	143	170	191	204	226	230	210	15	15
Lubricating Oils	~	~	~	~	~	7	9†	14	15	16	14	22	25	21
C. BRAZIL														
Liquefied Petrol. Gas	~	47	242	562	652	972	1,604	1,940	1,981	2,100	2,259	2,274	2,553	2,300
Motor Spirit	19	1,323	2,514	4,310	5,511	7,067	9,822	10,472	10,573	10,077	10,781	9,959	8,178	10,179
Kerosene	7	12	519	531	691	629	860	830	828	591	646	700	514	500
Jet Fuel	~	~	~	~	309	663	1,204	1,413	1,481	1,448	1,700	1,911	2,098	1,950
Distillate Fuel Oils	24	298	1,378	3,831	4,855	5,766	9,472	10,316	11,932	13,495	14,869	15,350	16,322	15,500
Residual Fuel Oils	14	1,560	3,561	5,282	6,944	8,439	13,892	14,762	14,540	15,207	16,896	17,100	16,810	15,800
Lubricating Oils	~	~	~	5	5	11	142	218	315	331	288	485	556	525†
Bitumen (Asphalt)	3†	40†	207	300	688	702	831	807	909	974	1,269	1,316	1,020	950†
D. CHILE														
Liquefied Petrol. Gas	~	7	29	46	145	226	224	457	470	471	509	481	479	471
Motor Spirit	~	213	527	751	1,008	1,137	1,067	899	932	926	1,003	1,010	990	1,052
Kerosene	~	15	142	240	319	354	428	322	367	344	311	260	227	208
Jet Fuel	~	~	~	~	~	62	113	95	120	135	164	165	158	195
Distillate Fuel Oils	~	99	264	418	651	607	886	824	840	876	1,053	1,207	1,211	1,062
Residual Fuel Oils	~	251	378	679[a]	1,289[a]	1,090	1,871	1,332	1,503	1,575	1,649	1,645	1,629	1,375
Bitumen (Asphalt)	~	~	~	1	7	7	11	6	9	12	15	15†	6†	21
E. COLOMBIA														
Liquefied Petrol. Gas	~	~	46	95	156	292	160	320	332	309	290	285	310	300
Motor Spirit	227	556	1,022	1,410	1,577	1,810	2,362	2,311	2,215	2,426	1,963	1,797	1,700	2,320
Kerosene	50	145	232	250	381	457	429	432	424	403	395	413	352	340
Jet Fuel	~	6	6	31	108	167	269	315	351	371	406	453	453	490
Distillate Fuel Oils	76	201	460	636	1,067	920	1,148	916	1,036	1,039	1,101	1,074	1,187	1,320
Residual Fuel Oils	926	834	1,450	1,515	2,408	2,470	2,707	2,643	2,786	2,783	2,862	2,304	2,571	2,400
Lubricating Oils	11	9	10	60	56	68	8	9	8		7	10†	10†	6†
Bitumen (Asphalt)	~	~	28	30	28	116	127	92	94	76	99	117	156†	190†
Petroleum Coke	~	~	98	109	162	158	163	148	149	151	155†	175†	150†	140†
F. COSTA RICA														
Liquefied Petrol. Gas	~	~	~	~	~	1	~	5	5	7	9	8	8	9
Motor Spirit	~	~	~	~	7	57	71	60	48	65	74	70	87	85
Kerosene	~	~	~	~	16	18	17	22	19	22	24	24	20	18
Distillate Fuel Oils	~	~	~	~	119	116	182	63	63	75	96	85	151	150
Residual Fuel Oils	~	~	~	~	69[a]	112	127	113	112	162	172	181	216	180

Table 1916 (Continued)

REFINED PETROLEUM PRODUCTS PRODUCTION,[1] 20 LC, 1950–81
(T MET)

Country	1950	1955	1960	1965	1968	1970	1974	1975	1976	1977	1978	1979	1980	1981
G. CUBA														
Liquefied Petrol. Gas	~	~	~	52	61	57	70	83	91	96	102	92	106	103
Motor Spirit	84	118	710	810	843‡	745	868	947	909	828	885	872	816	982
Kerosene	59	107	130	202	294	401	424	447	454	436	427	415	440	428
Distillate Fuel Oils	54	129	606	643	809‡	583	974	1,084	966	1,020	1,083	1,094	1,088	1,107
Residual Fuel Oils	38	81	1,654	1,899	2,017‡	2,367	2,769	2,821	3,033	3,209	3,101	3,213	3,018	3,091
Lubricating Oils	~	~	~	67	~a	95	137	151	165†	170†	126	133	137	119
Bitumen (Asphalt)	~	~	~	10	41	63	149	148	150†	157†	202	173	196	210
H. DOMINICAN REP.														
Liquefied Petrol. Gas	~	~	~	~	~	~	40	47	49	53	62	67	53	47
Motor Spirit	~	~	~	~	~	~	279	322	321	322	321	301	289	267
Kerosene	~	~	~	~	~	~	21‡	17	16	14	19	27	29	30
Jet Fuel	~	~	~	~	~	~	31	34	32	32	36	40	42	45
Distillate Fuel Oils	~	~	~	~	~	~	260	370	357	369	357	347	393	374
Residual Fuel Oils	~	~	~	~	~	~	246	369	406	399	427	353	528	493
I. ECUADOR														
Liquefied Petrol. Gas	1	1	1	1	2	5	3	5	3	14	46	70	72	60
Motor Spirit	62	78	204	254	327	365	569	668	715	581	858	958	968	918
Kerosene	16	25	39	57	73	65	76	184	245	245	350	322	292	284
Jet Fuel	~	~	4	23	52	79	124	60	60	48	127	146	139	148
Distillate Fuel Oils	33	47	96	133	206	255	431	436	399	285	625	711	785	694
Residual Fuel Oils	104	117	194	224	287	352	495	541	570	748	1,966	2,096	2,260	2,163
Lubricating Oils	1	1	13	16	24	9	19	19	24	28	33	37	42	43
J. EL SALVADOR														
Liquefied Petrol. Gas	~	~	~	3	13	4	16	18	22	23	26	28	25	28
Motor Spirit	~	~	~	104	111	36	103	115	133	142	155	153	128	135
Kerosene	~	~	~	52	48	15	32	32	47	47	40	42	35	45
Jet Fuel	~	~	~	27	11	6	13	14	11	11	9	9	8	9
Distillate Fuel Oils	~	~	~	140	147	43	167	206	198	219	232	240	199	205
Residual Fuel Oils	~	~	~	105	170	68	252	220	246	251	227	213	201	215
Bitumen (Asphalt)	~	~	~	~	~	~	22	21	25	22	22	18	16	20†
K. GUATEMALA														
Liquefied Petrol. Gas	~	~	~	3	7	9	8	6	5	4	4	3	2	2
Motor Spirit	~	~	~	105	155	163	208	209	136	131	144	132	108	108
Kerosene	~	~	~	27	44	49	47	51	30	30	31	35	37	35
Jet Fuel	~	~	~	16	26	31	38	39	30	34	41	46	32	27
Distillate Fuel Oils	~	~	~	98	207	215	286	225	216	204	261	259	242	222
Residual Fuel Oils	~	~	~	155	233	257	352	360	298	303	326	307	313	334
L. HAITI	~	~	~	~	~	~	~	~	~	~	~	~	~	~
M. HONDURAS														
Liquefied Petrol. Gas	~	~	~	~	~	4	7	8	8	7	4	3	3	4
Motor Spirit	~	~	~	~	~	106	83	84	106	104	90	86	81	85
Kerosene	~	~	~	~	~	30	32	32	40†	40†	37	40	38	40
Jet Fuel	~	~	~	~	~	6	9	11	17	17	15	19	22	24
Distillate Fuel Oils	~	~	~	~	90	214	171	172	199	235	171	190	202	210
Residual Fuel Oils	~	~	~	~	130	348	289	313	148	130	99	118	141	145

Table 1916 (Continued)

REFINED PETROLEUM PRODUCTS PRODUCTION,[1] 20 LC, 1950–81
(T MET)

Country / Product	1950	1955	1960	1965	1968	1970	1974	1975	1976	1977	1978	1979	1980	1981
N. MEXICO[2]														
Liquefied Petrol. Gas	50	101	334	503	401	1,134	1,998	1,620	2,309	2,650	2,320	2,838	3,763	4,297
Motor Spirit	1,298	1,831	3,090	4,514	5,317	5,913	7,608	7,839	8,114	8,513	10,233	11,878	13,722	15,069
Kerosene	547	888	1,413	1,567	1,574	1,461	1,659	1,666	1,745	1,715	1,783	1,893	2,411	2,422
Jet Fuel	~	~	23	138	289	397	739	718	797	973	952	1,179	1,299	1,319
Distillate Fuel Oils	735	680	1,649	2,908	3,731	4,206	6,947	7,626	8,032	9,113	9,792	10,619	12,080	13,315
Residual Fuel Oils	4,883	7,221	6,354	6,325	6,788	7,195	9,409	9,853	11,079	12,283	13,143	13,355	17,488	19,104
Lubricating Oils	27	81	151	195	179	276	383	423	362	391	413	400	404	500
Bitumen (Asphalt)	32	178	299	249	847	1,076	443	342	300	298	440	351	467	490
Petroleum Coke	~	~	~	~	36	54	70	71	78	20	100	89	108	92
O. NICARAGUA														
Liquefied Petrol. Gas	~	~	~	2	5	9	14	13	16	16	16	13	14	17
Motor Spirit	~	~	~	79	104	109	137	141	161	167	136	121	130	135
Kerosene[3]	~	~	~	25	28	27	31	17	15	15	16	13	14	15
Distillate Fuel Oils	~	~	~	65	102	129	159	159	170	172	181	131	174	175
Residual Fuel Oils	~	~	~	47	103	158	214	243	233	284†	184	117	146	150
Bitumen (Asphalt)	~	~	~	~	~	~	22	31	35†	32†	16	15†	15†	17†
P. PANAMA														
Liquefied Petrol. Gas	~	~	~	~	~	19	29	35	31	31	27	23	22	20
Motor Spirit	~	~	~	314	357‡	386	336	342	281	289	305	277	240	245
Kerosene	~	~	~	95	52‡	54	22	16	19	25	11	10	10	12
Jet Fuel	~	~	~	44	104‡	318	374	337	220	238	148	135	125	120
Distillate Fuel Oils	~	~	~	702	671‡	725	612	662	400	607	632	576	462	475
Residual Fuel Oils	~	~	~	1,210	1,967‡	2,048	2,214	2,366	1,650†	1,590	1,191	1,021	1,001	1,000
Bitumen (Asphalt)	~	~	~	~	~	90	15	10†	15†	15†	20†	20†	18†	20†
Q. PARAGUAY														
Liquefied Petrol. Gas	~	~	~	~	2	3	6	4	4	4	4	4	5	6
Motor Spirit	~	~	~	~	66	77	68	51	56	76	94	85	70	85
Kerosene	~	~	~	~	19	19	12	14	16	19	17	20	15	20
Jet Fuel	~	~	~	~	9	5	8	6	7	9	10	10	7	7
Distillate Fuel Oils	~	~	~	~	56	34	33	80	80	70	110	95	50	75
Residual Fuel Oils	~	~	~	~	30	33	70	41	43	50	56	50	40	45
Bitumen (Asphalt)	~	~	~	~	2	3	4†	4†	5†	5†	2	2†	2†	2†
R. PERU														
Liquefied Petrol. Gas	4	6	7	22[d]	44[d]	27	46	167	101	112	110	122	106	100
Motor Spirit	454	551	576	711	1,206	1,116	1,390	1,525	1,451	1,410	1,306	1,540	1,507	1,400
Kerosene	153	327	470	423	500	510	592	605	643	646	713	793	868	800
Jet Fuel	~	~	32	102	170	198	247	238	210	171	233	342	387	350
Distillate Fuel Oils	194	547	705	865	905	929	1,013	1,006	1,066	1,009	1,348	1,653	1,707	1,600
Residual Fuel Oils	832	473	372	820	1,230	1,231	1,974	1,931	2,007	2,333	2,194	2,335	2,511	2,450
Lubricating Oils	11	12	10	12[c]	9[c]	11	12	12	15	19†	20	20	12	15†
Bitumen (Asphalt)	11	30	9	33	27	47	36	38	49	40†	35	30	30	25†
S. URUGUAY														
Liquefied Petrol. Gas	~	~	~	17	18	31	25	29	26	26	38	37	40	36
Motor Spirit	173	239	243	268	238	244	202	268	253	227	238	225	207	185
Kerosene	153	327	470	166	134	168	184	160	180	154†	149	133	116	96
Jet Fuel	63	~	7	14	19	23	18	23	24	35	28	41	30	26
Distillate Fuel Oils	376	167	205	307	242	361	405	423	400	464	513	460	473	468
Residual Fuel Oils	~	581	651	751	616	785	764	816	930	815†	763	788	845	788
Lubricating Oils	~	~	2	1	~	#†	~	#	~	5†	1	8	9	7†
Bitumen (Asphalt)	~	~	11	19	27	41†	25†	39†	33	35	48	59	51	44

Table 1916 (Continued)

REFINED PETROLEUM PRODUCTS PRODUCTION,[1] 20 LC, 1950–81

(T MET)

Country	1950	1955	1960	1965	1968	1970	1974	1975	1976	1977	1978	1979	1980	1981
T. VENEZUELA														
Liquefied Petrol. Gas	111	316	640	489	454	1,295	265	1,842	1,928	2,125	1,667	1,957	1,647	1,251
Motor Spirit[4]	620†	1,215†	1,755†	2,247	2,858	3,138	4,266	4,674	5,586	5,560	6,095	6,774	7,037	7,009
Kerosene	282	984	1,223	1,038	618	554	462	421	680	845	492	482	594	560
Jet Fuel	~	~	473	2,206	3,232	3,494	1,612	1,062	1,173	1,379	1,441	1,391	1,580	1,180
Distillate Fuel Oils	2,378	5,727	7,671	9,584	9,002	7,628	6,681	6,908	6,245	6,922	7,129	7,737	9,294	7,396
Residual Fuel Oils	7,879	15,832	28,613	40,917	39,507	44,939	42,304	26,953	32,352	30,242	31,139	30,764	25,484	22,217
Lubricating Oils	523	143	209	527	595	551	520	497	462	400	411	439	492	344
Bitumen (Asphalt)	109	163	1,047	912	853	849	628	564	617	709	917	1,219	1,135	1,404
UNITED STATES														
Liquefied Petrol. Gas	7,530	13,015	20,045	26,433	34,057	45,123	10,587	47,859	48,242	49,073	48,169	48,765	48,229	50,090
Motor Spirit	108,835	143,554	166,192	193,554	223,801	245,377	273,000	279,999	294,556	302,009	307,850	294,223	280,194	275,017
Kerosene	15,262	15,085	13,504†	11,996	12,948	12,321	7,295	7,170	7,178	8,064	7,254	8,601	6,447	5,609
Jet Fuel	~	7,169	15,150†	27,516	40,653	38,883	39,286	40,950	43,250	45,722	45,580	47,548	47,081	45,524
Distillate Fuel Oils	55,177	83,344	92,266	105,824	116,102	124,085	134,691	133,983	148,030	165,470	159,910	159,173	134,743	132,080
Residual Fuel Oils	64,224	63,486	50,167	40,564	41,659	38,894	58,980	68,113	76,116	96,685	91,927	92,976	87,364	72,545
Lubricating Oils	7,403	7,990	8,498	9,004	9,399	9,470	10,116	8,045	8,843	9,227	9,940	10,157	9,318	8,668
Bitumen (Asphalt)	10,698	15,051	17,236	21,449	23,451	24,190	27,089	23,744	23,043	28,588	28,588	27,908	23,339	20,528
Petroleum Coke	3,122	5,141	10,877	15,594	17,252	19,551	22,452	23,449	23,614	24,447	24,418	24,907	24,580	25,670
WORLD														
Liquefied Petrol. Gas	8,072	15,321	26,182	45,029	60,563	81,477	42,789	99,925	100,421	105,568	111,322	119,926	118,764	121,211
Motor Spirit	148,543	213,861	273,626	365,848	431,554	478,095	568,270	585,457	614,914	635,270	657,426	655,723	641,370	636,193
Kerosene	30,937	41,421	55,921	64,546	86,137	91,796	102,936	104,865	114,897	124,672	122,599	129,077	123,762	120,290
Jet Fuel	472	12,414	25,338	50,700	77,595	81,373	88,994	89,900	93,165	96,651	99,362	105,789	106,128	102,204
Distillate Fuel Oils	94,942	157,588	219,722	322,560	404,395	482,643	603,954	589,398	637,248	681,875	699,278	727,867	694,242	669,009
Residual Fuel Oils	175,429	235,150	330,798	513,241	648,391	798,319	946,356	880,417	934,776	957,639	956,250	974,154	920,254	848,275
Lubricating Oils	10,016	12,181	14,631	18,335	20,582	20,721	34,046	31,228	33,085	35,120	36,788	39,469	39,117	37,557
Bitumen (Asphalt)	13,654	21,833	30,668	42,688	52,433	75,457	88,046	85,721	86,904	92,372	98,485	102,009	97,263	92,111
Petroleum Coke	3,142	5,535	12,017	17,186	19,247	22,534	25,862	27,052	27,786	29,152	30,647	31,449	30,569	32,129

1. The figures in this table refer to the liquid fuels, lubricant oils, and solid and semisolid products obtained by distillation of domestic and imported crude petroleum, shale oil, or unfinished petroleum products. So far as possible, the figures include fuels consumed in refining but exclude oils obtained from natural gas, coal, lignite, and their derivatives.

Liquefied petroleum gas. A hydrocarbon fraction of the paraffin series lighter than gasoline derived from the distillation of crude petroleum only (excluding LPG from natural gas or liquefied natural gas and also unliquefied gases). It is presented in the liquid state by compression or absorption process to facilitate storage, transport, and handling. It mainly consists of butanes (normal butane and isobutane) and propane or a mixture of them, and is used in domestic heating, as fuel and as solvent.

Motor spirit. Blended light petroleum fuel. Commonly known as petrol or gasoline, suitable as a fuel in spark-ignition internal-combustion engines.

Aviation gasoline. Any of the specially blended grades of gasoline, with high antiknock value, high stability, a high volatility, and low freezing point, intended for use in aviation piston power unit only.

Kerosene. A refined crude petroleum fuel, in volatility between motor spirit and gas oil, free of gasolines and heavy hydrocarbons such as gas oil and lubricating oil. It is used as an illuminant and as a fuel in certain types of spark-ignition engines such as those used for agricultural tractors and stationary engines. The data cover those products commonly termed as burning oil, vaporizing oil, power kerosene illuminating oil, and also white spirit (used commonly as a paint thinner).

Jet fuels. Fuel meeting the required properties for use in jet engines and aircraft turbine engines, mainly refined from kerosene; gasoline-type jet fuel is included.

Distillate fuel oils. A fuel oil which is a crude petroleum distillate, having a viscosity and distillation range between those of kerosene and lubricating oil; used as a fuel for internal combustion in diesel engines, as a burner fuel in heating installations such as furnaces, and for enriching water gas to increase its luminosity. The data cover those products commonly termed as diesel fuel (diesel oil or gas oil, solar oil, etc.

Residual fuel oil. A fuel oil which is crude petroleum residues, such as viscous residuum, obtained by the refinery opeations of crude petroleum after gasoline, kerosene, and sometimes heavier distillates (such as gas oil or diesel oil) have been removed. It is commonly used by ships and industrial, large-scale heating installations as a fuel in furnace or boilers firing to produce heat and power (known as mazoul).

Lubricating oils. A heavy liquid distillate obtained by refining crude petroleum, used for lubricating purposes. It may be produced either from petroleum distillates or residues at refineries. Solid lubricants (e.g. grease) are excluded.

Bitumen. Brown or black solid or semisolid material, obtained as a residue in the distillation of crude petroleum; used mainly for asphalt paving in road construction. Excluding that which may be obtained from natural occurrence.

Petroleum coke. A solid residue consisting mainly of carbon, obtained by the distillation of heavier petroleum oils, used mainly in metallurgical processes (excluding those solid residues obtained from carbonization of coal).

2. Including aviation spirit.
3. Including jet fuel.
4. Including naphtha prior to 1968.

a. Excluding quantities used at refineries and lost.
b. Data not strictly comparable with those of previous years.
c. Including grease.
d. Including liquefied petroleum gas made from natural gas.
e. Including aviation spirit.

SOURCE: SALA, 16-226; UN-SP: J, 14-16 (1970-1973), tables 9, 11, 12, 13, 14, J, 19 (1976), tables 9, 11, 12, 13, 14; J, 20 (1977), tables 9, 11, 12, 13, 14; J, 21 (1978), tables 9, 11, 12, 13, 14; J, 22 (1979), tables 13, 15, 16, 17, 18; UN-YWES, 1979, tables 28 and 30; UN-SP: J, 19 (1950-74), tables 9, 11, 12, 13 and 14; UN-YWES, 1981, tables 22 through 28 and 30.

Table 1917

CONSUMPTION OF PETROLEUM AND DERIVATIVES, 19 L, 1960–82
(T Barrels)

	Country	1960	1973	1976	1977	1978	1979	1980	1981	1982[‡]
A.	ARGENTINA	95,285	167,766	158,848	141,352	138,113	177,285	168,266	173,777	168,240
B.	BOLIVIA	1,819	4,526	2,014	7,323	7,625	7,261	8,690	8,689	8,720
C.	BRAZIL	96,106	281,654	343,075	351,343	385,368	411,237	413,882	367,965	340,000 [†]
D.	CHILE	16,179	37,376	32,970	34,809	36,736	37,258	36,941	39,057	~
E.	COLOMBIA	21,179	47,270	53,747	54,632	53,206	59,814	60,375	56,420	56,474
F.	COSTA RICA	1,304	3,797	4,235	5,103	6,927	5,957	5,343	~	~
H.	DOMINICAN REP.	2,835	12,331	13,978	14,193	14,879	15,879	15,123	14,892	14,277
I.	ECUADOR	3,806	10,853	17,820	23,415	24,676	27,990	32,325	~	~
J.	EL SALVADOR	1,588	3,972	4,362	4,320	5,067	4,761	3,909	3,572	~
K.	GUATEMALA	3,523	7,014	7,891	8,383	10,702	11,575	11,422	10,177	9,199
L.	HAITI	620	971	1,035	1,553	1,697	1,775	1,674	1,670	1,528
M.	HONDURAS	1,495	3,283	3,784	3,706	3,792	4,711[†]	5,019[†]	~	~
N.	MEXICO	104,100	221,500	266,346	306,800	331,700	358,300	404,800	420,000[†]	430,000 [†]
O.	NICARAGUA	1,418	4,107	5,395	6,491	6,226	4,302	5,000	~	~
P.	PANAMA	2,845	6,405	6,874	7,756	7,266	7,098	7,224[†]	~	~
Q.	PARAGUAY	673	1,750	2,237	1,805	3,100	3,032	3,215	3,114	3,147
R.	PERU	18,514	39,085	43,721	44,720	43,300	44,700	48,253	48,180	~
S.	URUGUAY	9,888	12,509	12,761	12,152	12,850	12,052	13,597	12,245	~
T.	VENEZUELA	46,683	92,548	93,870	103,000	103,185	107,300	122,244	127,389	131,400

SOURCE: IDB-SPTF, yearly, 1978-83, p. 398.

Table 1918

ACTUAL AND POTENTIAL PROVEN RESERVES AND PRODUCTION OF CRUDE PETROLEUM
AND NATURAL GAS, 19 L, 1960–1982

PART I: 1960 AND 1975

	Crude Petroleum						Natural Gas					
	Reserves (M Barrels)		Production (M Barrels)		Production Potential[1] (Years)		Reserves (B Cubic Feet)		Production (B Cubic Feet)		Production Potential[1] (Years)	
Country	1960	1975	1960	1975	1960	1975	1961	1975	1961	1975	1961	1975
A. ARGENTINA	1,550	2,465	63.9	144.4	24.2	17.1	6,004	7,200	156.3	276.0	38.4	26.1
B. BOLIVIA	125	235	3.1	14.7	40.1	16.0	250	10,800	5.8	137.4	53.1	78.6
C. BRAZIL	375	780	29.6	62.7	12.7	12.4	350	927	17.4	53.3	20.1	17.4
D. CHILE	60	190	7.2	8.9	8.3	21.3	1,800	2,300	44.6	--	40.4	--
E. COLOMBIA	625	526	55.8	57.3	11.2	9.2	1,400	1,452	73.9	120.0	18.9	12.1
F. COSTA RICA	--	--	--	--	--	--	--	--	--	--	#	#
H. DOMINICAN REP.	--	--	--	--	--	--	--	--	--	--	--	--
I. ECUADOR	25	2,450	2.8	58.8	8.9	41.7	--	5,000	--	--	#	#
J. EL SALVADOR	--	--	--	--	--	--	--	--	--	--	--	--
K. GUATEMALA	--	--	--	--	--	--	--	--	--	--	#	#
L. HAITI	--	--	--	--	--	--	--	--	--	--	#	#
M. HONDURAS	--	--	--	--	--	--	--	--	--	--	--	--
N. MEXICO	2,458	6,338	108.8	294.3	22.6	21.5	--	11,923	227.1	786.5	--	15.2
O. NICARAGUA	--	--	--	--	--	--	--	--	--	--	#	#
P. PANAMA	--	--	--	--	--	--	--	--	--	--	#	#
Q. PARAGUAY	--	--	--	--	--	--	--	--	--	--	#	#
R. PERU	300	770	19.3	26.9	15.6	28.6	725	2,260	32.2	--	22.5	#
S. URUGUAY	--	--	--	--	--	--	--	--	--	--		
T. VENEZUELA	17,402	18,410	1,041.7	856.4	16.7	21.5	32.469	42,284	709.0	1,342.3	45.8	31.5

PART II: 1982

	Crude Petroleum			Natural Gas		
Country	Reserves (M Barrels)	Production (M Barrels)	Production Potential[1] (Years)	Reserves (B Cubic Feet)	Production (B Cubic Feet)	Production Potential[1] (Years)
A. ARGENTINA	2,590	173	15	25,200	529 †	48
B. BOLIVIA	180	8.6	21	5,700	107 †	53
C. BRAZIL	1,750	90.7	19	2,300	~	~
D. CHILE	760	14.8	51	2,515	~	~
E. COLOMBIA	536	50.4	11	4,580	176	26
F. COSTA RICA	#	#	#	#	#	#
H. DOMINICAN REP.	#	#	#	#	#	#
I. ECUADOR	1,400	77.4	18	410	1.3	315
J. EL SALVADOR	#	#	#	35	~	~
K. GUATEMALA	50	2.3	22	#	#	#
L. HAITI	#	#	#	#	#	#
M. HONDURAS	#	#	#	#	#	#
N. MEXICO	48,300	984.2	49	75,850	1,630	47
O. NICARAGUA	#	#	#	#	#	#
P. PANAMA	#	#	#	#	#	#
Q. PARAGUAY	#	#	#	#	#	#
R. PERU	835	71.3	12	1,201	27	44
S. URUGUAY	#	#	#	54,079	#	#
T. VENEZUELA	21,500	657.3	33	54,079	1,348	40

1. Derived by dividing proven reserves by actual production in each given year.

SOURCE: IDB-SPTF, 1976, p. 446; IDB-SPTF, 1979, p. 458; IDB-SPTF, 1980, p. 455; IDB-SPTF, 1983, p. 97.

Table 1919

NATURAL GAS PRODUCTION,[1] 20 LC, 1970–81
(T TJ)

	Country	1970	1973	1975	1978	1979	1980	1981
A.	ARGENTINA	209.0	233.8	265.5	255.5	302.9	326.9	340.2
B.	BOLIVIA	1.3	56.9	59.1	63.2	74.1	87.9	95.9
C.	BRAZIL	3.3	10.0	24.6	39.2	38.1	48.5	45.2
D.	CHILE	48.1	46.1	45.8	59.1	40.7	27.1	31.6
E.	COLOMBIA	55.2	74.9	73.2	113.2	117.1	125.4	126.3
F.	COSTA RICA	#	#	#	#	#	#	#
G.	CUBA	~	.6	.7	.4	.7	.7	.4
H.	DOMINICAN REP.	#	#	#	#	#	#	#
I.	ECUADOR	.7	1.4	1.5	1.9	1.7	1.5	1.6
J.	EL SALVADOR	#	#	#	#	#	#	#
K.	GUATEMALA	#	#	#	#	#	#	#
L.	HAITI	#	#	#	#	#	#	#
M.	HONDURAS	#	#	#	#	#	#	#
N.	MEXICO	450.9	502.1	523.5	668.7	802.5	893.4	945.3
O.	NICARAGUA	#	#	#	#	#	#	#
P.	PANAMA	#	#	#	#	#	#	#
Q.	PARAGUAY	#	#	#	#	#	#	#
R.	PERU	16.0	15.3	27.4	29.0	29.4	29.6	29.4
S.	URUGUAY	#	#	#	#	#	#	#
T.	VENEZUELA	381.9	480.1	480.4	509.2	600.2	630.2	571.1
	UNITED STATES	22,860	23,410	20,723	20,654	21,275	21,102	20,910
	WORLD	38,440	45,284	46,232	51,742	59,376	54,921	55,758

1. Natural gas comprises any combustible gas of natural origin from underground sources consisting primarily of hydrocarbons.

SOURCE: UN-YWES, 1981, table 35.

Table 1920

HARD COAL PRODUCTION,[1] 20 LC, 1970–81
(T MET)

	Country	1970	1973	1975	1978	1979	1980	1981
A.	ARGENTINA	616	451	502	434	727	390	498
B.	BOLIVIA	#	#	#	#	#	#	#
C.	BRAZIL	2,361	2,427	2,817	4,283	4,643[†]	5,240	5,550[†]
D.	CHILE	1,351	1,374	1,461	1,129	926	968	1,121
E.	COLOMBIA	2,268	3,048	3,447	4,754	4,885	5,260	5,300[†]
F.	COSTA RICA	#	#	#	#	#	#	#
G.	CUBA	#	#	#	#	#	#	#
H.	DOMINICAN REP.	#	#	#	#	#	#	#
I.	ECUADOR	#	#	#	#	#	#	#
J.	EL SALVADOR	#	#	#	#	#	#	#
K.	GUATEMALA	#	#	#	#	#	#	#
L.	HAITI	#	#	#	#	#	#	#
M.	HONDURAS	#	#	#	#	#	#	#
N.	MEXICO	2,959	4,263	5,193	6,756	7,357	7,010	8,086
O.	NICARAGUA	#	#	#	#	#	#	#
P.	PANAMA	#	#	#	#	#	#	#
Q.	PARAGUAY	#	#	#	#	#	#	#
R.	PERU	156	10	23	66	51	47	50[†]
S.	URUGUAY	#	#	#	#	#	#	#
T.	VENEZUELA	40	50	60	81	55	44	46
	UNITED STATES	550,388	530,163	575,901	566,646	670,483	710,384	697,608
	WORLD	824,911	971,772	992,116	1,110,367	1,166,881	1,178,589	1,196,563

1. Hard coal comprises all grades of anthracite and bituminous coal with a gross calorific value over 5,700 calories per gram. Includes lignite, brown coal, and peat.

SOURCE: UN-YWES, 1981, table 7.

Table 1921

BITUMINOUS COAL/ANTHRACITE RESOURCES, 6 LC

(M MET in Oil Equivalents)

| | Country | Year | Total | Proven Reserves | | Additional Resources |
				In Place	Recoverable	
C.	BRAZIL	1978	1,717	270	189	1,447
D.	CHILE	1979	522	231	27	291
E.	COLOMBIA	1979	9,225	2,025	1,010	7,200
N.	MEXICO	1979	2,800	1,500	1,200	1,300
R.	PERU	1979	960	125	~	835
T.	VENEZUELA	1979	4,861	161	134	4,700
	UNITED STATES	1974	1,286,366	214,366	107,183	1,072,000

SOURCE: UN-YWES, 1979, table 56; UN-YWES, 1980, table 56.

Table 1922

SUB-BITUMINOUS COAL/LIGNITE RESOURCES, 10 LC

(M MET in Oil Equivalents)

| | Country | Year | Total | Proven Reserves | | Additional Resources |
				In Place	Recoverable	
A.	ARGENTINA	1978	9,900	150	150	9,750
C.	BRAZIL	1978	14,090	1,320	924	12,770
D.	CHILE	1979	5,285	1,150	1,150	4,135
E.	COLOMBIA	1979	~	48	25	790
I.	ECUADOR	1979	36	#	#	36
L.	HAITI	1979	40	13	~	27
M.	HONDURAS	1979	21	~	~	~
N.	MEXICO	1979	980	480	384	500
R.	PERU	1979	~	~	~	100
T.	VENEZUELA	1979	4,317	17	6	4,300
	UNITED STATES	1974	2,313,291	183,291	116,076	2,130,000

SOURCE: UN-YWES, 1979, table 56; UN-YWES, 1980, table 56.

Table 1923

GEOTHERMAL ENERGY INSTALLED
CAPACITY, 5 LC, 1980–2000

(T Kw)

	Country	1980	1985	1990	1995	2000
D.	CHILE	#	#	15	15[a]	15[a]
F.	COSTA RICA	#	#	80	380	380
J.	EL SALVADOR	95	150	260	425	535
N.	MEXICO	150	620	1,000	2,000	4,000
O.	NICARAGUA	#	#	35	35	100
	UNITED STATES	923	1,674	4,374	4,974	5,284

a. Minimum estimate.

SOURCE: Mexico-NAFINSA-MV, August 17, 1981, p. 863.

Table 1924

PRODUCTION OF FUELWOOD AND BAGASSE,[1] 20 LRC, 1976-81
(T MET of Coal Equivalent)

Country	1976 Fuelwood	1976 Bagasse	1977 Fuelwood	1977 Bagasse	1978 Fuelwood	1978 Bagasse	1979 Fuelwood	1979 Bagasse	1980 Fuelwood	1980 Bagasse	1981 Fuelwood	1981 Bagasse
A. ARGENTINA	2,110†	1,339	2,137†	1,431	2,166†	1,200	1,841†	1,212	1,932†	1,395	1,886†	1,395
B. BOLIVIA	1,201†	242	1,351	241	1,357†	245	1,359†	247	1,399†	225	1,456†	223
C. BRAZIL	51,874†	**	53,367†	**	54,900†	6,797	56,640†	6,324	58,29†	7,104	59,406†	7,495
D. CHILE	1,240	**	1,148	**	1,127†	**	1,073	**	1,088†	**	1,103†	**
E. COLOMBIA	12,030†	803	12,321†	733	12,625†	871	12,936†	951	13,258†	1,071	13,546†	1,041
F. COSTA RICA	639†	180	654†	172	491†	195	492†	175	492†	189	492†	163
G. CUBA	500†	5,283	500†	5,972	767	6,581	829†	6,700	809†	5,845	465†	6,808
H. DOMINICAN REP.	54†	1,106	55†	1,081	57†	1,030	58†	1,031	60†	870	61†	952
I. ECUADOR	1,367	265	1,410	228	1,453†	298	1,498†	305	1,543†	316	1,592†	284
J. EL SALVADOR	910†	224	937†	273	965†	240	994†	235	1,023†	186	1,023†	156
K. GUATEMALA	3,346†	444	3,441†	418	3,537†	383	3,633†	356	3,690†	388	3,745†	407
L. HAITI	1,455†	52	1,489†	43	1,524†	49	1,558†	52	1,593†	56	1,630†	43
M. HONDURAS	1,265†	70	1,298†	99	1,333†	113	1,370†	141	1,407†	164	1,445†	148
N. MEXICO	1,708†	2,328	1,723†	2,396	1,740†	2,689	1,888†	2,659	1,951†	2,336	2,008†	2,269
O. NICARAGUA	679†	208	699†	194	720†	191	741†	174	763†	163	786†	184
P. PANAMA	500†	138	514†	155	529†	161	544†	194	557†	172	569†	160
Q. PARAGUAY	1,060	48	1,131	46	1,379†	59	1,410†	65	1,436†	76	1,310†	66
R. PERU	879†	799	903†	773	930†	735	1,010†	597	1,037†	461	1,066†	412
S. URUGUAY	529	34	572	43	591†	41	624†	29	624†	37	624†	36
T. VENEZUELA	2,515†	460	2,589†	380	2,666†	346	2,745†	298	2,836†	307	2,933†	260
LATIN AMERICA	85,361	13,885	87,695	14,523	90,857	22,224	93,243	21,745	95,327	21,361	97,146	22,502
UNITED STATES	4,956	2,158	4,716†	2,057	6,419†	1,845	7,079†	2,116	7,079†	2,067	7,079†	2,190
WORLD	502,508	43,947	511,001	46,919	524,239	47,090	537,258	46,950	549,748	44,171	559,414	48,502

1. Bagasse is a residue of the sugarcane industry which is often used as a fuel within the sugar milling industry.

SOURCE: UN-YWES, 1980, table 55; UN-YWES, 1981, table 15.

Table 1925

ELECTRICAL ENERGY PRODUCTION,[1] 20 LC, 1975–81[a]
(M KWH)

Country	1975 Total	1975 Hydro-Electric	1976 Total	1976 Hydro-Electric	1977 Total	1977 Hydro-Electric	1978 Total	1978 Hydro-Electric	1979 Total	1979 Hydro-Electric	1980 Total	1980 Hydro-Electric	1981 Total	1981 Hydro-Electric
A. ARGENTINA	29,468	5,197	30,328	5,000	32,477	5,771	33,434	7,751	37,640	10,660	39,676	15,148	39,288	14,670
B. BOLIVIA	1,057	800	1,132	836	1,260	908	1,354	964	1,432	1,013	1,564	1,080	1,677	1,155
C. BRAZIL[2]	78,936	72,287	100,032	82,913	100,804	93,480	112,492	102,676	126,079	116,194	139,347	128,664	142,430	130,680
D. CHILE	8,732	6,135	9,276	6,234	9,776	6,502	10,360	6,822	11,133	6,938	11,751	7,343	11,978	7,588
E. COLOMBIA	14,025	9,851	15,467	10,374	16,099	10,618	18,108	12,225	19,859	13,460	21,508	14,692	23,690	16,320
F. COSTA RICA	1,531	1,301	1,646	1,456	1,760	1,344	1,927	1,485	1,987	1,621	2,227	2,130	2,300	2,140
G. CUBA	6,583	62	7,198	53	7,700	73	8,481	83	9,403	104	9,896	97	10,572	60
H. DOMINICAN REP.[2]	2,556	54	2,580	77	3,063	57	3,221	54	3,113	52	3,420	48	3,350	37
I. ECUADOR	1,650	647	1,885	628	2,260	721	2,569	791	2,665	825	2,845	890	2,950	950
J. EL SALVADOR	1,059	404	1,199	436	1,354	528	1,488	869	1,587	1,079	1,544	1,047	1,565	1,050
K. GUATEMALA	1,167	382	1,275	341	1,564	263	1,726	318	1,914	309	1,970	315	1,995	325
L. HAITI	158	123	209	159	215	164†	246	187	280	215	315	220	325	225
M. HONDURAS	545	419	607	431	701†	469	777	540	859	604	942	637	955	640
N. MEXICO	43,329	15,140	46,372	17,189	50,632	19,076	57,257	16,217	62,860	18,008	66,954	16,910	73,559	24,618
O. NICARAGUA	932	371	1,057	395	1,188	137	1,180	193	985	386	1,099	517	1,110	520
P. PANAMA	1,447	98	1,546	138	1,630	341	1,564	717	1,893	803	2,550	1,240	2,565	1,245
Q. PARAGUAY	598	538	605	550	666	575	670	620	772	717	930	865	975	905
R. PERU	7,486	5,470	7,911	5,798	8,627	6,027	8,765	6,199	9,252	6,543	9,805	7,622	10,100	7,800
S. URUGUAY	2,444	1,132	2,637	1,221	2,834	1,567	3,046	1,630	2,724	1,064	3,355	2,273	3,603	2,546
T. VENEZUELA	19,591	8,898	21,052	10,558	23,051	11,934	25,625	12,148	28,409	13,390	32,100	14,600	37,542	15,090
UNITED STATES[2]	2,003,002	303,153	2,123,406	286,883	2,211,031	223,934	2,285,880	283,986	2,318,783	281,587	2,356,139	277,721	2,365,062	262,434
WORLD	6,518,535	1,456,368	6,983,391	1,463,068	7,298,955	1,504,200	7,688,247	1,629,407	7,998,650	1,713,201	8,223,775	1,759,066	8,357,061	1,783,772

1. Unless otherwise indicated, the data refer to the production of generating centers and therefore include station use and transmission loss. "Total" refers to all. "Total" minus "Hydroelectric" production generally equals "Thermal" (not given), except for data on the United States. Unless stated otherwise, production includes electrical energy produced for both public and industrial purposes.

2. Production of industrial establishments nil or negligible.

a. For data prior to 1975 see SALA, 21-2008.

SOURCE: UN-YWES, 1979, tables 49 and 50; UN-YWES, 1981, table 42.

Table 1926

ELECTRICITY CONSUMPTION,[1] 20 LC, 1929–81
(Total = B Kw, Per Capita = KWH)

	A. ARGENTINA		B. BOLIVIA		C. BRAZIL		D. CHILE		E. COLOMBIA		F. COSTA RICA		G. CUBA		H. DOMINICAN REP.		I. ECUADOR		J. EL SALVADOR		K. GUATEMALA	
Year	Total	Per Capita	Total	Per Capita	Total	Per Capita	Total	Per Capita	Total	Per Capita	Total	Per Capita	Total	Per Capita	Total	Per Capita	Total	Per Capita	Total	Per Capita	Total	Per Capita
1929	1.67	143	.02	8	.74	22	.68	158	.15	21	.03	61	.20	56	.01	8	.04	21	.02	14	.02	12
1937	2.20	162	.05	19	2.03	52	1.45	302	.29	34	.06	104	.26	62	.02	13	.05	22	.03	19	.03	14
1949	4.12	247	.18	60	4.60	91	2.90	483	.63	55	.10	130	.69	128	.07	32	.13	42	.07	39	.07	26
1950	4.43	259	.20	67	4.70	90	3.00	492	.71	61	.10	125	.76	138	.08	36	.13	41	.08	42	.07	25
1951	4.72	270	.18	58	8.76	163	3.14	506	1.05	88	.18	216	.84	150	.10	43	.11	33	.07	37	.08	28
1952	4.70	263	.20	65	10.03	181	3.30	524	1.19	97	.19	219	.92	161	.11	46	.12	36	.09	46	.08	30
1953	4.93	271	.21	66	10.34	182	3.26	502	1.30	102	.20	222	1.01	171	.17	71	.13	37	.13	65	.09	29
1954	5.37	290	.23	70	10.70	182	3.54	528	1.40	107	.22	244	1.09	182	.19	76	.17	47	.15	71	.09	28
1955	6.00	317	.22	67	13.65	226	4.10	594	2.23	164	.27	270	1.90	311	.19	73	.24	65	.15	71	.22	67
1956	7.00	363	.23	68	15.45	248	4.20	592	2.40	174	.30	300	2.00	317	.23	85	.28	74	.18	82	.24	73
1957	8.80	449	.40	114	16.96	265	4.19	566	2.79	197	.35	318	2.36	369	.26	94	.29	74	.18	78	.19	55
1958	9.42	471	.40	114	19.77	299	4.16	562	3.03	205	.36	327	2.59	398	.28	100	.32	80	.21	91	.22	63
1959	9.54	470	.43	119	21.11	309	4.60	605	3.41	227	.38	317	2.81	420	.32	110	.35	83	.23	96	.24	65
1960	10.5	510	.5	135	22.9	328	4.6	597	3.8	265	.4	374	2.7	399	.4	116	.4	90	.3	103	.3	75
1961	11.5	571	.5	118	24.4	340	4.9	621	3.8	237	.5	376	3.0	437	.4	120	.4	92	.3	106	.3	75
1962	11.9	579	.5	123	27.2	367	5.3	658	4.3	261	.5	385	3.0	424	.4	136	.5	98	.3	114	.3	81
1963	12.4	597	.5	129	27.9	365	5.6	684	5.3	311	.5	385	3.1	422	.5	134	.5	103	.3	125	.4	87
1964	13.9	658	.5	126	29.1	369	5.9	698	5.9	338	.6	398	3.3	437	.5	152	.6	111	.4	134	.4	101
1965	15.4	716	.5	125	30.1	371	6.1	704	5.8	323	.7	443	3.4	449	.5	138	.6	111	.4	143	.4	101
1966	15.9	730	.6	132	32.7	389	6.7	747	6.1	327	.7	452	4.1	522	.6	166	.6	114	.5	157	.5	108
1967	16.7	753	.6	133	34.2	395	6.9	754	6.6	342	.8	476	4.5	565	.7	179	.7	122	.5	166	.5	113
1968	18.0	798	.7	149	38.2	427	6.9	740	7.0	353	.8	510	4.7	582	.7	173	.7	132	.6	174	.6	121
1969	20.0	876	.7	152	41.6	459	7.2	754	8.1	399	.9	535	4.2	512	.8	219	.8	144	.6	182	.7	144
1970	21.7	915	.8	184	45.4	491	7.6	806	8.8	426	1.0	595	4.9	570	1.0	247	.9	159	.7	190	.8	144
1971	23.6	981	.8	189	51.0	535	8.5	893	9.5	450	1.1	638	5.0	578	1.0	253	1.0	170	.7	204	.8	158
1972	25.3	1,037	.9	193	64.7	582	8.9	919	11.0	508	1.3	687	5.3	594	1.2	279	1.1	175	.8	228	.9	169
1973	26.7	1,081	.9	198	64.8	644	8.8	889	12.6	564	1.3	719	5.7	631	2.3	509	1.3	190	.9	242	1.0	178
1974	28.0	1,119	1.0	208	80.3	701	9.3	923	13.2	575	1.4	764	6.0	655	2.4	527	1.4	209	1.0	254	1.1	187
1975	29.5	1,164	1.1	216	79.0	744	8.7	857	14.0	594	1.5	778	6.6	705	2.6	544	1.7	234	1.1	264	1.2	187
1976	30.4	1,184	1.1	225	90.1	812	9.3	888	15.5	637	1.6	818	7.2	761	2.6	534	1.9	258	1.2	291	1.3	198
1977	32.6	1,249	1.3	244	100.9	890	9.8	918	16.1	643	1.7	850	7.7	802	3.1	615	2.2	299	1.4	318	1.6	236
1978	33.5	1,270	1.4	256	112.4	995	10.4	965	18.1	707	1.9	911	8.5	875	3.2	629	2.6	326	1.5	342	1.7	252
1979	37.7	1,410	1.4	264	126.0	1,089	11.1	1,020	19.9	754	2.0	917	9.4	962	3.1	590	2.7	331	1.6	358	1.9	272
1980	39.7	1,467	1.6	279	139.2	1,174	11.8	1,058	21.5	795	2.2	992	9.9	1,006	3.4	630	2.9	342	1.5	325	2.0	271
1981	39.3	1,400	1.7	283	142.2	1,170	12.0	1,061	23.7	853	2.3	1,015	10.6	1,080	3.4	599	3.0	342	1.6	317	2.0	267

Table 1926 (Continued)

ELECTRICITY CONSUMPTION,[1] 20 LC, 1929-81

(Total = B Kw, Per Capita = KWH)

Year	L. HAITI Total	L. HAITI Per Capita	M. HONDURAS Total	M. HONDURAS Per Capita	N. MEXICO Total	N. MEXICO Per Capita	O. NICARAGUA Total	O. NICARAGUA Per Capita	P. PANAMA Total	P. PANAMA Per Capita	Q. PARAGUAY Total	Q. PARAGUAY Per Capita	R. PERU Total	R. PERU Per Capita	S. URUGUAY Total	S. URUGUAY Per Capita	T. VENEZUELA Total	T. VENEZUELA Per Capita	UNITED STATES Total	UNITED STATES Per Capita	WORLD Total	WORLD Per Capita
1929	.01	4	.01	11	1.46	86	.01	15	.02	43	.01	1	.20	36	.13	76	.10	32	92.18	756	255.9	134
1937	.01	4	.02	18	2.48	132	.01	13	.03	52	.01	10	.32	50	.20	105	.07	20	118.91	922	411.4	205
1949	.01	3	.04	29	4.33	173	.03	29	.08	103	.03	22	.75	96	.57	259	.41	85	291.10	1,940	839.9	371
1950	.02	6	.05	36	4.42	171	.03	27	.09	113	.03	21	.80	100	.60	273	.52	104	329.14	2,164	959.2	386
1951	.02	6	.06	41	5.07	198	.08	73	.09	113	.05	36	?	?	.68	309	.62	122	435.54	2,813	1,072.4	425
1952	.02	6	.06	40	5.53	201	.09	82	.10	119	.05	34	?	?	.75	326	.72	136	465.32	2,943	1,156.8	451
1953	.02	6	.07	45	5.92	209	.10	86	.10	116	.06	40	?	?	.85	370	.84	150	516.28	3,225	1,265.0	484
1954	.02	6	.08	50	6.50	223	.11	92	.11	124	.06	40	?	?	.93	404	.98	169	546.74	3,356	1,369.4	515
1955	.06	16	.06	35	7.17	240	.11	92	.14	156	.07	45	1.48	168	1.02	426	1.60	265	633.42	3,813	1,543.2	569
1956	.07	18	.07	41	8.13	266	.12	92	.15	160	.08	50	1.55	172	1.06	442	2.00	317	689.99	4,083	1,691.1	612
1957	.08	21	.07	39	8.87	276	.13	100	.17	176	.07	44	1.67	182	1.15	479	3.10	470	722.27	4,198	1,802.4	640
1958	.09	24	.07	39	9.58	291	.14	102	.21	211	.08	47	2.01	211	1.24	517	3.79	559	730.25	4,171	1,909.8	666
1959	.09	23	.08	42	10.24	301	.17	121	.23	230	.09	53	2.22	229	1.18	480	4.31	506	801.15	4,500	2,099.2	718
1960	.1	23	.1	48	11.2	320	.2	131	.2	223	.1	55	2.7	268	1.2	512	4.7	632	848.8	4,698	2,300.9	772
1961	.1	24	.1	52	12.2	338	.2	134	.3	258	.1	59	2.9	297	1.3	516	5.2	685	883.8	4,812	2,453.4	807
1962	.1	23	.1	55	13.1	353	.2	142	.3	290	.1	58	3.1	288	1.7	639	5.9	752	947.2	5,079	2,662.3	859
1963	.1	24	.1	56	14.2	357	.3	163	.3	298	.1	65	3.4	312	1.6	619	6.8	831	1,011.6	5,347	2,879.9	911
1964	.1	25	.1	61	15.9	385	.3	176	.4	342	.1	66	3.7	327	1.8	678	7.6	902	1,084.8	5,655	3,135.4	973
1965	.2	25	.2	80	17.4	407	.3	188	.5	364	.1	67	3.8	330	1.7	642	8.2	945	1,157.5	5,959	3,380.8	1,029
1966	.2	26	.2	90	19.0	429	.4	213	.5	391	.2	72	4.3	361	1.9	698	8.7	967	1,250.6	6,365	3,642.8	1,088
1967	.2	25	.2	99	20.8	455	.4	231	.6	433	.2	76	4.8	385	1.9	699	9.5	1,014	1,317.0	6,630	3,863.1	1,133
1968	.3	24	.3	111	22.9	485	.5	263	.7	477	.2	80	5.0	392	1.9	688	10.8	1,116	1,435.4	7,175	4,206.9	1,211
1969	.2	24	.2	116	25.7	544	.5	288	.8	604	.2	88	5.2	401	2.0	733	11.6	1,164	1,553.9	7,667	4,570.5	1,291
1970	.3	28	.3	119	28.9	569	.6	342	.8	573	.2	95	5.5	411	2.2	811	12.7	1,237	1,642.0	8,008	4,953.8	1,393
1971	.3	28	.3	136	31.5	600	.7	348	1.0	669	.2	104	5.9	430	2.4	820	13.4	1,261	1,721.1	8,312	5,269.2	1,413
1972	.3	30	.3	146	34.7	640	.8	386	1.1	724	.3	112	6.3	442	2.4	825	14.8	1,356	1,861.1	8,911	5,398.7	1,501
1973	.4	32	.4	151	37.4	667	.7	354	1.3	811	.3	120	6.7	455	2.5	913	16.1	1,425	1,979.1	9,339	6,127.7	1,584
1974	.5	32	.5	183	41.1	707	.9	419	1.4	877	.3	133	7.3	484	2.4	860	18.2	1,567	1,980.0	9,344	6,313.8	1,604
1975	.5	34	.5	176	43.6	725	.9	432	1.5	868	.4	163	7.5	484	2.5	875	19.6	1,632	2,009.2	9,303	6,516.7	1,612
1976	.6	45	.6	187	46.5	747	1.1	476	1.5	898	.4	143	7.9	497	2.6	973	21.0	1,701	2,417.4	9,901	6,983.4	1,711
1977	.7	45	.7	209	50.7	784	1.2	516	1.5	864	.5	170	8.6	527	2.8	1,001	23.0	1,808	2,528.2	10,299	7,296.0	1,759
1978	.8	51	.8	226	57.3	855	1.2	489	1.6	876	.5	178	8.8	521	3.1	1,074	25.6	1,951	2,305.2	10,357	7,686.8	1,806
1979	.9	57	.9	240	62.9	906	1.0	373	1.8	961	.6	211	9.3	535	2.7	955	28.4	2,100	2,348.4	10,435	7,998.0	1,848
1980	.9	63	.9	254	67.5	938	1.1	404	2.6	1,345	.9	268	9.8	551	3.4	1,169	32.1	2,305	2,382.9	10,467	8,219.8	1,868
1981	1.0	64	1.0	249	73.8	991	1.1	394	2.6	1,322	.9	289	10.1	553	3.6	1,243	37.5	2,623	2,398.6	10,438	8,357.1	1,862

1. Prior to 1950 data are for production, in Latin America essentially the same as consumption. For further notes and methods, see SALA-SNP, especially with regard to calculation of per capita data through 1954 and rounding of data after 1960.

SOURCE: SALA-SNP, XI-9, updated with WA, 1929, 1937, and 1949; UN-SP: J, 17 (1974); J, 19 (1976), table 21; J, 20 (1977), table 21; J, 21 (1978), table 21; J, 22 (1979), table 25; UN-YWES, 1979, table 50; UN-YWES, 1981, table 43.

Table 1927

INDEX OF TOTAL PRODUCTION OF ELECTRICITY, 20 LC, 1970–81

(1975 = 100)

	Country	1970	1971	1972	1973	1974	1976	1977	1978	1979	1980	1981
A.	ARGENTINA	74	80	86	90	95	103	110	113	128	135	133
B.	BOLIVIA	74	79	82	87	94	107	119	128	135	148	159
C.	BRAZIL	58	64	71	82	90	114	128	143	160	177	180
D.	CHILE	86	98	102	100	106	106	112	119	127	135	137
E.	COLOMBIA	62	68	78	90	94	110	115	129	142	153	169
F.	COSTA RICA	67	75	83	88	96	108	115	126	130	145	150
G.	CUBA	74	76	80	87	91	109	117	129	143	150	161
H.	DOMINICAN REP.	39	42	66	88	94	101	120	126	122	134	131
I.	ECUADOR	58	64	68	76	87	114	137	156	162	172	179
J.	EL SALVADOR	63	70	79	86	93	113	128	141	150	146	148
K.	GUATEMALA	65	73	80	87	95	109	134	148	164	169	171
L.	HAITI	75	76	84	89	92	132	136	156	177	199	206
M.	HONDURAS	58	64	71	80	90	110	127	143	158	173	175
N.	MEXICO	66	72	80	86	94	107	116	132	145	155	170
O.	NICARAGUA	67	70	81	77	94	114	128	127	106	118	119
P.	PANAMA	66	72	80	94	99	106	105	108	131	176	177
Q.	PARAGUAY	36	41	46	63	84	89	109	112	129	156	163
R.	PERU	74	79	84	89	97	106	115	117	124	131	135
S.	URUGUAY	90	97	98	103	96	108	116	125	111	137	147
T.	VENEZUELA	65	68	70	82	93	107	118	131	145	164	192
	UNITED STATES	82	86	93	98	98	106	110	114	116	118	118
	WORLD	76	81	87	94	97	107	112	118	123	126	128

SOURCE: UN-YWES, 1979, table 51; UN-YWES, 1981, table 44.

Table 1928

INDEX OF TOTAL CONSUMPTION OF ELECTRICITY, 20 LC, 1970–81

(1975 = 100)

	Country	1970	1971	1972	1973	1974	1976	1977	1978	1979	1980	1981
A.	ARGENTINA	74	80	86	90	95	103	110	113	128	134	133
B.	BOLIVIA	74	79	82	87	94	107	119	128	135	148	159
C.	BRAZIL	58	63	71	82	90	114	128	142	160	176	180
D.	CHILE	86	98	102	100	106	106	112	119	127	135	137
E.	COLOMBIA	62	68	78	90	94	110	115	129	142	153	169
F.	COSTA RICA	67	75	83	88	96	108	115	126	130	145	150
G.	CUBA	74	76	80	87	91	109	117	129	143	150	161
H.	DOMINICAN REP.	39	42	66	88	94	101	120	126	122	134	131
I.	ECUADOR	58	64	68	76	87	114	137	156	162	173	179
J.	EL SALVADOR	63	70	79	86	93	113	128	141	150	146	148
K.	GUATEMALA	65	73	80	87	95	109	134	148	164	169	171
L.	HAITI	75	76	84	89	92	132	136	156	177	199	206
M.	HONDURAS	58	64	71	80	90	110	127	143	157	172	174
N.	MEXICO	66	72	80	86	94	107	116	131	144	155	169
O.	NICARAGUA	67	70	81	77	94	114	128	127	106	118	120
P.	PANAMA	58	68	76	89	97	106	105	109	122	175	176
Q.	PARAGUAY	50	56	62	69	78	89	109	121	148	194	216
R.	PERU	74	79	84	89	97	106	115	117	124	131	135
S.	URUGUAY	90	97	99	103	96	108	116	125	111	137	148
T.	VENEZUELA	65	68	76	82	93	107	118	131	145	164	192
	UNITED STATES	82	86	93	99	99	106	111	115	117	119	119
	WORLD	76	81	87	94	97	107	112	118	123	126	128

SOURCE: UN-YWES, 1979, table 51; UN-YWES, 1981, table 44.

Table 1929

ELECTRICAL ENERGY INSTALLED CAPACITY,[1] 20 LC, 1975–81[a]

(Mw)

	1975		1976		1977		1978		1979		1980		1981	
Country	Total	Hydro-Electric	Total	Hydro-Electric	Total	Hydro-Electric	Total	Hydro-Electric	Total	Hydro-Electric	Total	Hydro-Electric	Total	Hydro-Electric
A. ARGENTINA	9,260	1,531	9,856	1,745	10,073	1,945	11,187	2,944	11,498	3,169	11,988	3,626	12,220	3,800
B. BOLIVIA	376	242	399	241	406	242	428	242	421	238	489	265	508	283
C. BRAZIL	19,569	16,184	21,060	17,675	22,637	19,038	26,970	21,823	30,272	24,406	33,917	27,557	37,832	31,324
D. CHILE	2,620	1,462	2,661	1,462	2,905	1,474	2,939	1,474	2,931	1,471	3,771	2,306	3,210	1,771
E. COLOMBIA	3,504	2,297	3,850	2,305	4,334	2,801	4,600	3,049	4,612	2,938	4,960	3,225	5,370	3,480
F. COSTA RICA	404	239	406	239	440	239	508	305	570	364	637	445	632	437
G. CUBA[2]	1,677	44	1,705†	44	858	46	2,288	46	2,561	46	2,673	46	2,704	46
H. DOMINICAN REP.	732	150	852	150	900	150	930	163	950	172	970	180	960	165
I. ECUADOR	525	139	633	145	799	120	923	224	992	227	1,055	240	1,100	250
J. EL SALVADOR	314	109	346	109	491	243	495	244	495	244	495	244	502	246
K. GUATEMALA	327	121	380†	119	504	121	551	121	566	123	564	119	575	120
L. HAITI	89	47	89†	47†	102	47†	121	50	121	50	121	50	126	50
M. HONDURAS	159	69	159	69	162	69	202	109	203	109	234	109	240	110
N. MEXICO	11,328	4,120	12,847	4,616	13,955	4,796	16,032	5,296	16,380	5,290	16,985	6,063	19,895	6,621
O. NICARAGUA	252	107	308	103	361	103	362	103	358	103	361	103	370	105
P. PANAMA	346	16	519	166	529	166†	525	187	575	256	748	298	755	300
Q. PARAGUAY[3]	191	122	334	265	334	265†	355	285	360	290	375	300	395	320
R. PERU	2,357	1,396	2,516	1,406	2,540	1,413	2,570	1,409	2,913	1,633	3,192	1,861	3,300	1,900
S. URUGUAY	705	252	697	236	699	236	700	236	745	281	835	371	948	484
T. VENEZUELA	4,570	1,735	5,176	2,245	5,427	2,353	6,727	2,460	8,356	2,680	9,113	2,920	9,224	2,950
UNITED STATES	527,346	66,553	550,369	68,422	576,206	68,933	599,058	71,636	615,686	75,626	630,746	76,651	652,108	77,445
WORLD	1,606,428	371,495	1,685,997	388,190	1,773,507	404,117	1,862,451	423,601	1,936,176	443,836	2,010,330	466,938	2,087,790	483,938

1. Unless otherwise indicated, the data refer to production of generating centers and therefore station losses. "Total" refers to all. "Total" minus "Hydraulic" production generally equals "Thermal" (not given), except for data from the United States. Unless otherwise stated, production is for both public and industrial purposes.

2. On June 30 of year.

3. Beginning 1960 Asunción only.

a. For data prior to 1975 see SALA, 21-2009.

SOURCE: UN-YWES, 1979, table 46; UN-YWES, 1981, table 40.

Table 1930

ARGENTINA: ELECTRICAL ENERGY INSTALLED CAPACITY AND PROJECTIONS, 1979 AND 2000

(Mw)

Firm	Capacity in Place, 1979			Projected Increases, 1980–2000		
	Hydro-Electric	Thermo-Electric	Total	Hydro-Electric	Thermo-Electric	Total
Public Service[5]						
AyE[1]	1,237.1	2,071.6	3,308.7	14,098.0	780.0	14,878.0
SEGBA	#	2,224.1	2,224.1	#	660.0	660.0
ASE Ex-CIAE	#	579.0	579.0	#	#	#
DEBA	#	452.6	452.6	1,200.0	620.0	1,820.0
EPEC	6.5	411.1	417.6	15.0	203.0	218.0
HIDRONOR	1,650.0	#	1,650.0	4,730.0	#	4.730.0
CNEA	#	370.0	370.0	#	2,622.0	2,622.0
CTMSG[2]	225.0	#	225.0	#	#	#
EMSA[3]	#	#	#	120.0	#	120.0
Cooperatives	0.5	160.6	161.1	#	#	#
Binationals	#	#	#	5,252.0	#	5,252.0
Other	25.9	157.0	182.9[a]	31.0	#	31.0[b]
Total Public Service	3,145.0	6,426.0	9,571.0	25,446.0	4,885.0	30,331.0
Self-Production[4]	24.0	1,903.0	1,927.0	~	~	~
Total	3,169.0	8,329.0	11,498.0	~	~	~

1. For "Projected Additions," joint projects with the province of Santa Cruz are included.
2. Appropriation of capacity according to 1947 resolution.
3. See "Other"and footnote a.
4. Refers to firms producing energy for their own use. Data on projects for expansion are unknown.
5. Code: AyE Agua y Energía Eléctrica, Sociedad Anónima del Estado. Coordinated by Secretería de Estado de Energía.

SEGBA   Servicios Eléctricos del Gran Buenos Aires, Sociedad Anónima. State owned. Coordinated directly by Secretaría de Estado de Energía.

CTMSG   Comisión Técnica Mixta de Salto Grande. Binational entity Argentina-Uruguay.

HIDRONOR   Hidroeléctrica Nor Patagónica, Sociedad Anónima. State owned. Coordinated directly by Secretaría de Estado de Energía.

EBY   Ente Binacional Yacireta. Binational entity Argentina-Paraguay.

CNEA   Comisión Nacional de Energía Atómica. Controlled directly by Presidencia de la República.

EPEC   Impresa Provincial de Energía de la Provincia de Buenos Aires. Property of the provincial government.

EMSA   Electricidad de Misiones Sociedad Anónima. Property of the provincial government.

ASE Ex-CIAE   Administración Servicios Eléctricos, Ex-Compañía Italo-Argentina de Electricidad. State owned. Coordinated directly by the Secretaría de Estado de Energía.

a. Includes EMSA and other provincial and municipal firms.
b. Corresponds to project Uruguay I, firm owner of project is unknown.

SOURCE: ECLA-CC, E/CEPAL/G. 1241, June 1983, pp. 30–32.

Table 1931

BOLIVIA: ELECTRICAL ENERGY INSTALLED CAPACITY AND PROJECTIONS, 1979 AND 2000

(Mw)

Firm[2]	Capacity in Place, 1979			Projected Increases, 1980–2000		
	Hydro-Electric	Thermo-Electric	Total	Hydro-Electric	Thermo-Electric	Total
Public Service						
ENDE	63.30	90.13	153.43	922.00	~	922.00
COBEE	142.22	#	142.22	#	~	~
ELFEC	5.81	#	5.81	#	~	~
CESSA	1.85	#	1.85	#	~	~
COSERELEC	#	1.52	1.52	#	~	~
SETAR	#	0.70	0.70	#	~	~
OTHER	0.90	20.84	21.74	#	~	~
Total Public Service[1]	214.08	113.19	327.27	922.00	~	~
Self-Production	24.36	69.69	94.05	~	~	~
Total	238.44	182.88	421.32	~	~	~

1. Refers to firms producing energy for their own use. Data on projects for expansion unknown.
2. Code: ENDE Empresa Nacional de Electricidad S.A. State owned. Source does not specify full titles for the other firms.

SOURCE: ECLA-CC, E/CEPAL/G. 1241, June 1983, pp. 38–39.

Table 1932

BRAZIL: ELECTRICAL ENERGY INSTALLED CAPACITY AND PROJECTIONS, 1979 AND 2000
(Mw)

Firm[3]	Capacity in Place, 1979			Projected Increases, 1980–2000		
	Hydro-Electric	Thermo-Electric	Total	Hydro-Electric	Thermo-Electric	Total
Public Service						
CEM	#	178.0	178.0	#	#	#
CHESF	2,712.0	589.0	3,301.0	10,277.0	#	10,277.0
ESCELSA	160.0	#	160.0	#	#	#
FURNAS	4,721.0	662.0	5,383.0	5,184.0	3,135.0	8,319.0
ELECTRONORTE	39.0	33.0	72.0	8,014.0	#	8,014.0
ELECTROSVL	921.0	517.0	1,438.0	12,152.0	125.0	12,277.0
LIGHT	1,688.0	450.0	2,138.0	1,250.0	#	1,250.0
Binational[1]	**	**	**	9,170.5	#	9,170.5
Total ELECTROBRAS	10,241.0	2,429.0	12,670.0	46,047.5	3,260.0	49,307.5
CEEE	850.0	213.0	1,063.0	124.0	320.0	444.0
CEMIG	3,121.0	134.0	3,255.0	5,297.0	#	5,297.0
CESP	8,125.0	20.0	8,145.0	3,558.0	1,245.0	4,803.0
COPEL	390.0	31.0	421.0	4,978.0	#	4,978.0
CELG	#	#	#	.350.0	#	350.0
CELPA	#	#	#	20.0	#	20.0
Other	934.0	625.0	1,559.0	#	1,500.0[a]	1,500.0
Total Public Service	23,661.0	3,452.0	27,113.0	60,374.5	6,325.0	66,699.5
Self-Production	476.0	797.0	1,273.0	~	~	~
Total	24,137.0	4,249.0	28,386.0	~	~	~

1. Included here are binational projects. ELECTROBRAS is the Brazilian counterpart of binational entities. Data refer to capacity allocated to BRAZIL in project.
2. Data refer to firms producing electricity for their own use. Data for projects of expansion are unknown.
3. Code: CEEE   Companhia Estadual de Energia Eléctrica. State owned.
      CELG   Centrais Elétricas de Goicés. State owned.
      CELPA   Centrais Elétricas de Pará. State owned.
      CEMIG   Centrais Elétricas de Minas Gerais. State owned.
      CESP   Companhia Energética de São Paulo. State owned.
      COPEL   Companhia Paranense de Energia Eléctrica. State owned.
      ELECTROBRAS   Centrais Elétricas Brasileiras S.A. Property of the Federal Union.
   Firms controlled by ELECTROBRAS:
      CEM   Companhia de Electricidade de Manaus.
      CHESF   Companhia Hidro-Elétrica de São Francisco.
      ESCELSA   Espirito Santo Centrais Eléctricas S.A.
      FURNAS   Furnus Centrais Elétricas S.A.
      ELECTRONORTE   Centrais Elétricas do Norte do Brasil S.A.
      ELECTROSUL   Centrais Elétricas do Sul do Brasil S.A.
      LIGHT   Light Servicios de Electricidade S.A.

a. Refers to a project for which the firm owner of the project is unknown.

SOURCE: ECLA-CC, E/CEPAL/G. 1241, June 1983, pp. 44–47.

Table 1933

CHILE: ELECTRICAL ENERGY INSTALLED CAPACITY AND PROJECTIONS, 1979 AND 2000
(Mw)

Firm[2]	Capacity in Place, 1979			Projected Increases, 1980–2000		
	Hydro-Electric	Thermo-Electrical	Total	Hydro-Electric	Thermo-Electric	Total
Public Service						
ENDESA	1,254.5	348.1	1,602.6	5,425.0	300.0	5,725.0
CHILECTRA	104.7	484.7	589.4	#	#	#
Other[1]	1.0	2.1	3.1	#	#	#
Total Public Service	1,360.2	834.9	2,195.1	5,425.0	300.0	5,725.0
Self-Production	110.8	625.0	735.8	~	~	~
Total	1,471.0	1,459.9	2,930.9	~	~	~

1. Includes minor regional electrical firms. (CGEI, SAE and others).
2. Code: CHILECTRA Compañía Chilena de Electricidad. State owned.
         ENDESA Empresa Nacional de Electricidad Sociedad Anónima. State owned.

SOURCE: ECLA-CC, E/CEPAL/G. 1241, June 1983, pp. 54-55.

Table 1934

COLOMBIA: ELECTRICAL ENERGY INSTALLED CAPACITY AND PROJECTIONS, 1979 AND 2000
(Mw)

Firm[2]	Capacity in Place, 1979			Projected Increases, 1980–2000		
	Hydro-Electric	Thermo-Electric	Total	Hydro-Electric	Thermo-Electric	Total
Public Service						
EPM	979	#	979	811	#	811
EEEB	551	136	687	3,408	216	3,624
CORELCA	#	602	602	1,180	664	1,844
ISA	500	#	500	2,239	166	2,405
CHIDRAL	453	#	453	#	#	#
ICEL	51	165	216	1,801	216	2,017
CHEC	180	#	180	324	#	324
EDAT	#	134	134	#	#	#
CVC	120	#	120	3,140	#	3,140
ESSA	14	57	71	#	#	#
EDBOL	#	60	60	#	#	#
Other[1]	145	102	247	#	#	#
Total Public Service	2,993	1,256	4,249	12,903	1,262	14,165
Self-Production	70	280	350	~	~	~
Total	3,063	1,536	4,599	~	~	~

1. Includes minor regional electrical firms.
2. Code: ICEL Instituto Colombiano de Energía Eléctrica. State owned. In charge of executing government policy on electrical energy.
         CORELCA Corporación Eléctrica de la Costa Atlántica. State owned, dependent upon Ministerio de Minas y Energía.
         CVC Corporación Autónoma Regional del Cauca. State owned, dependent upon Departamento Nacional de Planeación.
         EEEB Empresa de Energía Eléctrica de Bogotá. Owned by Municipio de Bogotá.
         EPM Empresa Públicas de Medellín. Owned by Municipio de Medellín.
         ISA Interconexión Eléctrica Sociedad Anónima. Owned by ICEL, CHEC, EEEB, EPM, CVC.
         CHEC Central Hidroeléctrica de Caldas. A subsidiary of ICEL.

SOURCE: ECLA-CC, E/CEPAL/G. 1241, June 1983, pp. 62-64.

Table 1935

ECUADOR: ELECTRICAL ENERGY INSTALLED CAPACITY AND PROJECTIONS, 1979 AND 2000
(Mw)

Firm[2]	Capacity in Place, 1979[1]			Projected Increases, 1980–2000		
	Hydro-Electric	Thermo-Electric	Total	Hydro-Electric	Thermo-Electric	Total
Public Service						
INECEL	73.6	139.5	213.1	1,633.1	355.8	1,988.9
EMELEC	#	183.5	183.5	#	#	#
EEQSA	85.4	56.1	141.5	#	#	#
CEDEGE	#	#	#	130.0	#	130.0
Other	134.7	226.7	401.4[a]	#	300.0	300.0[b]
Total Public Service	293.7	645.8	939.5	1,763.1	655.8	2,418.9
Self-Production	15.9	122.9	138.8	~	~	~
Total	309.6	768.9	1,078.3	~	~	~

1. Estimate in source, based on capacity in place of 1977 and plants starting operating in 1978 and 1979.
2. Code: CEDEGE Comisión de Estudios para el Desarrollo del Rio Guayas. State entity.
   EEQSA Empresa Eléctrica de Quito S.A. Data on ownership of firm unavailable.
   EMELEC Empresa Eléctrica del Ecuador Inc. Data on ownership of firm unavailable.
   INECEL Instituto Ecuatoriano de Electrificación. State entity.
a. Includes many minor municipal and regional firms.
b. Refers to project Santo Domingo, the firm owner of the project is not known.

SOURCE: ECLA-CC, E/CEPAL/G. 1241, June 1983, pp. 70-71.

Table 1936

MEXICO: ELECTRICAL ENERGY INSTALLED CAPACITY AND PROJECTIONS, 1979 AND 2000
(Mw)

Firm[1]	Capacity in Place, 1979			Projected Increases, 1980–2000		
	Hydro-Electric	Thermo-Electric	Total	Hydro-Electric	Thermo-Electric	Total
Public Service						
CFE	5,721.0	8,063.0	13,784.0	4,466.0	23,751.0	28,217.0
CLFC	271.0	570.0	841.0	#	#	#
Total Public Service	5,992.0	8,663.0	14,625.9	4,466.0	23,751.0	28,217.0
Self-Production	71.0	1,799.0	1,870.0	~	~	~
Total	6,063.0	10,432.0	16,495.0	~	~	~

1. Code CLFC Companía Luz y Fuerza del Centro, in liquidation.
   CFE Comisión Federal de Electricidad. State owned.

SOURCE: ECLA-CC, E/CEPAL/G. 1241, June 1983, pp. 84, 87.

Table 1937

PARAGUAY: ELECTRICAL ENERGY INSTALLED CAPACITY AND PROJECTIONS, 1979 AND 2000

(Mw)

Firm[1]	Capacity in Place, 1979			Projected Increases, 1980–2000		
	Hydro-Electric	Thermo-Electric	Total	Hydro-Electric	Thermo-Electric	Total
Public Service						
ANDE	190.0	80.3	270.3	7,650.0	#	7,650.0
Self-Production	#	57.0	57.0	~	~	~
Total	190.0	137.3	327.3	~	~	~

1. Code: ANDE Administración Nacional de Electricidad. State owned.

SOURCE: ECLA-CC, E/CEPAL/G. 1241, June 1983, pp. 92-93.

Table 1938

PERU: ELECTRICAL ENERGY INSTALLED CAPACITY AND PROJECTIONS, 1979 AND 2000

(Mw)

Firm[2]	Capacity in Place, 1979			Projected Increases, 1980–2000		
	Hydro-Electric	Thermo-Electric	Total	Hydro-Electric	Thermo-Electric	Total
Public Service						
ELECTROPERU	745.4	202.4	947.8	5,742.0	433.0	6,175
ELECTROLIMA	447.0	52.0	499.0	#	100.0	100.0
HIDRANDINA	134.0	#	134.0	#	#	#
SEAL	30.2	12.0	42.2	#	40.0	40.0
COSERELEC	#	25.0	25.0	#	20.0	20.0
Other[1]	25.1	83.4	108.5	150.0	275.0	425.0
Total Public Service	1,381.7	374.8	1,756.5	5,892.0	868.0	6,760.0
Self-Production	262.9	813.9	1,076.8	~	~	~
Total	1,644.6	1,188.7	2,833.3	~	~	~

1. Small isolated centers. Data for 'Projected Increases' include firms that own or are responsible for small isolated centers.
2. Code: COSERELEC Compañía de Servicios Eléctricos S.A. State owned (2.9% private ownership).
   ELECTROLIMA Electricidad de Lima. State owned (1.7% private ownership).
   ELECTROPERU Electricidad del Perú. State owned.
   HIDRANDINA Energía Hidro-Eléctrica Andina S.A. State owned (6.5% private ownership).
   SEAL Sociedad Eléctrica de Arequipa Ltda. State owned (4.9% private ownership).
   SPCC Siderurgia de Chimbote, CENTROMIN, Cooperativa Azucarera (Self-Production).

SOURCE: ECLA-CC, E/CEPAL/G. 1241, June 1983, pp. 98-100.

Table 1939

URUGUAY: ELECTRICAL ENERGY INSTALLED CAPACITY AND PROJECTIONS, 1979 AND 2000
(Mw)

Firm[1]	Capacity in Place, 1979			Projected Increases, 1980–2000		
	Hydro-Electric	Thermo-Electric	Total	Hydro-Electric	Thermo-Electric	Total
Public Service						
VTE	236	424	660	1,641	270	1,911
CTMSG	45	#	45	#	#	#
Total Public Service	281	424	705	1,641	270	1,911
Self-Production	#	40	40	~	~	~
Total	281	464	745	~	~	~

1. Code: COMIPAL Comisión Mixta del Palmar. Created by executive order of 15/5/73, to be in charge of project Central Hidraúlica del Palmar.
   CTMSG Comisión Técnica Mixta de Salto Grande. Binational entity Uruguay-Argentina.
   UTE Administración Nacional de Usinas y Transmisiones Eléctricas. State owned.

SOURCE: ECLA-CC, E/CEPAL/G. 1241, June 1983, pp. 106-107.

Table 1940

VENEZUELA: ELECTRICAL ENERGY INSTALLED CAPACITY AND PROJECTIONS, 1979 AND 2000
(Mw)

Firm[1]	Capacity in Place, 1979			Projected Increases, 1980–2000		
	Hydro-Electric	Thermo-Electric	Total	Hydro-Electric	Thermo-Electric	Total
Public Service						
CADAFE	240.0	2,414.5	2,654.5	5,657.0	1,200.0	6,857.0
CALEY	#	6.4	6.4	#	#	#
CAPEC	#	25.1	25.1	#	#	#
EDELCA	2,435.0	#	2,435.0	10,445.0	#	10,445.0
ELECAR	2.7	1,595.0	1,597.7	#	#	#
ELEGUA	1.8	#	1.8	#	#	#
ELEVAL	#	92.3	92.3	#	#	#
ENELBAR	#	73.6	73.6	#	#	#
ENELVEN	#	726.2	726.2	#	3,360.0	3,360.0
Total Public Service	2,679.5	4,933.1	7,612.6	16,102.0	4,560	20,662.0
Self-Production	#	602.0	602.0	~	~	~
Total	2,679.5	5,535.1	8,214.6	~	~	~

1. Code: CADAFE C.A. de Administración y Fomento Eléctrico. State owned.
   CALEY C.A. Luz Eléctrica de Yaracuy. Private firm.
   CAPEC C.A. Planta Eléctrica de Corora. State owned.
   EDELCA Electrificación del Caroní. State owned.
   ELECAR Electricidad de Caracas. Private firm.
   ELEGUA Electricidad de Guarenas. Private firm.
   ELEVAL Electricidad de Valencia. Private firm.
   ENELBAR Energía Eléctrica de Barquirimeto. State owned.
   ENELVEN Energía Eléctrica de Venezuela. State owned.

SOURCE: ECLA-CC, E/CEPAL/G. 1241, June 1983, pp. 114, 116.

Table 1941

URANIUM PRODUCTION,[1] 3 LC, 1970–81
(MET)

	Country	1970	1973	1975	1978	1979	1980	1981
A.	ARGENTINA	45	24	22	126	134	187	180[†]
C.	BRAZIL	#	#	#	#	103	#	100[†]
N.	MEXICO	~	~	#	#	90[†]	~	~
	UNITED STATES	9,900	10,200	8,900	14,200	14,400	16,800	13,500[†]
	WORLD	18,289	19,773	19,068	33,891	38,303	43,964	44,033

1. Uranium content.

SOURCE: UN-YWES, 1981, table 46.

Figure 19:2

ELECTRIC PLANT LOCATION, CENTRAL AMERICA AND THE CARIBBEAN
(ca. 1977)

LEGEND

- ●   Thermal plants
- ▲   Hydroelectric plants
- - - -   International boundary
- ◉   Capital of country
- ⏜   Navigable rivers for ocean-going vessels
- ⏜   Navigable rivers except for ocean-going vessels
- R   River

SOURCE: SALA, 19, map 10.

Figure 19:3

ELECTRIC PLANT LOCATION, SOUTH AMERICA

(ca. 1977)

SOURCE: SALA, 19, map. 11.

Part VII: Sea and Land Harvests

CHAPTER 20

FISHERIES PRODUCTION

STATISTICAL NOTES

This chapter presents annual time-series statistics on Latin American fisheries production. The data include statistics on the nominal catches of fish, crustaceans, molluscs, and other types of acquatic animals and plants which have been killed, caught, trapped, collected, bred, or cultivated for all kinds of commercial, industrial, and subsistence purposes. The nominal catch data include quantities taken by all types and classes of fishing units operating in both fresh and marine fishing areas, with the exception of quantities taken in recreational facilities by sports fishermen.

The statistical category *nominal catches* refers to the landings converted to a live weight basis. The term *landings* refers to the weight of fish and fish products brought ashore, i.e., the actual weight of the quantities landed. The nominal catch data include quantities caught during the calendar year (January–December) although landed in the subsequent year. Nominal catch data for Argentina, Chile, Mexico, Peru, Uruguay, and the United States exclude the production of acquatic plants.

For a related discussion of Latin American fisheries resources and fishery statistics between 1938 and 1970 see M. Moreno Ibáñez, "Latin American Fisheries: Natural Resources and Expanded Jurisdiction, 1938–1978," SALA, 21.

Note: This volume contains statistics from numerous sources. Alternative data on many topics are presented. Variations in statistics can be attributed to differences in definition, parameters, coverage, methodology, as well as date gathered, prepared, or adjusted. See also Editor's Note on Methodology.

Table 2000

TOTAL NOMINAL CATCHES BY MAJOR FISHING AREA,[1] 20 LC, 1970–81[a]

(MET)

Country	Code[2]	1970	1973	1974	1975	1976	1977	1978	1979	1980	1981
A. ARGENTINA	03	5,400	7,600	10,181	15,068	9,846	10,436	15,077	16,082	8,407	9,653
	34	600	400	#	#	#	#	#	#	#	#
	41	208,800	294,100	286,180	213,830	255,931	359,281	504,138	550,266	376,792	349,981
	Total	214,800	302,100	296,361	228,898	265,777	369,281	519,215	566,348	385,199	359,634
B. BOLIVIA	03	1,600	2,200	1,800	1,800	2,000	2,300	1,550	3,650	4,379	5,617
	Total	1,600	2,200	1,800	1,800	2,000	2,300	1,550	3,650	4,379	5,617
C. BRAZIL	03	93,500	84,100[†]	168,145	173,455	144,829	168,444	170,645	126,701	170,000[†]	180,000[†]
	41	434,800	619,400[†]	572,177	598,691	508,202	580,031	631,983	728,418	680,000[†]	720,000[†]
	Total	528,300	703,500[†]	740,322	772,146	653,031	748,475	802,628	855,119	850,000[†]	900,000[†]
D. CHILE	03	#	#	#	#	#	#	#	35	92	52
	87	1,181,400	691,000	1,157,053	929,464	1,378,600	1,318,950	1,929,091	2,632,216	2,816,614	3,393,347
	Total	1,181,400	691,000	1,157,053	929,464	1,378,600	1,318,950	1,929,091	2,632,251	2,816,706	3,393,399
E. COLOMBIA	03	33,200	73,100	37,234	42,075	51,437	42,174	56,612	48,535	46,903	47,719
	31	13,600	14,700	12,758	11,600	5,880	7,621	5,837	5,320	5,155	8,530
	77	7,700	17,500	12,426	12,900	17,790	14,170	17,129	9,538	13,263	37,005
	Total	54,500	105,300	62,418	66,575	75,107	63,965	79,578	63,393	65,321	93,254
F. COSTA RICA	02	#	#	40	50	60	61	61	100	350	400
	31	100	#	134	423	456	254	342	110	132	141
	77	7,000	10,700	13,316	13,591	12,376	12,781	16,919	20,649	14,405	12,016
	Total	7,100	10,700	13,490	14,064	12,892	13,096	17,322	20,859	14,887	12,557
G. CUBA	02	500	1,000	2,200	1,700	1,800	1,900	3,200	5,400	6,339	10,314
	21	#	1,300	#	7,495	29,871	18,282	13,124	12,482	9,255	6,668
	31	61,800	72,800	73,000	58,900	79,200	72,300	71,077	66,100	68,424	59,846
	34	22,100	10,600	10,700	6,600	6,400	20,700	7,200	7,500	9,258	8,729
	47	21,400	54,000	53,579	44,630	33,219	29,300	63,569	42,917	4,555	#
	87	#	10,300	25,500	24,000	43,600	42,700	55,000	19,400	88,650	78,791
	Total	105,800	150,000	164,979	143,325	194,090	185,182	213,170	153,799	186,481	164,528
H. DOMINICAN REP.	02	200	300	367	585	618	359	513	1,040	2,459	2,836
	31	5,000	8,900	8,025	6,467	6,435	4,235	4,573	6,845	8,199	9,167
	Total	5,200	9,200	8,392	7,052	7,053	4,594	5,086	7,885	10,658	12,003
I. ECUADOR	03	#	#	#	#	#	#	#	#	671,310[†]	685,657
	77	91,400	153,900	174,400	263,400	298,268	433,950	616,550	607,835	671,310[†]	685,657
	Total	91,400	153,900	174,400	263,400	298,268	433,950	616,550	607,835		
J. EL SALVADOR	02	800	900	1,552	2,689	3,072	1,624	1,512	1,719	1,818	983
	77	10,300	11,000	8,110	7,861	6,058	4,744	8,028	11,019	12,140	19,271
	Total	11,100	11,900	9,662	10,550	9,130	6,368	9,540	12,738	13,958	20,254
K. GUATEMALA	02	1,400	500	528	550	574	600	580	615	400	410
	31	100	100[†]	100	100	100	100	100	100	50	50
	77	3,500	3,100	3,253	3,880	2,979	2,374	4,824	4,183	3,057	3,805
	Total	5,000	3,700	3,881	4,530	3,653	3,074	5,504	4,898	3,507	4,265
L. HAITI	02	300[†]	300[†]	300[†]	300[†]	300[†]	300[†]	300[†]	300[†]	300[†]	300[†]
	31	2,200[†]	2,200[†]	2,200[†]	3,700[†]	3,700[†]	3,700[†]	3,700[†]	3,700[†]	3,700[†]	3,700[†]
	Total	2,500[†]	2,500[†]	2,500[†]	4,000[†]	4,000[†]	4,000[†]	4,000[†]	4,000[†]	4,000[†]	4,000[†]
M. HONDURAS	02	100	100	172	170	170	97	114	110	83	238
	31	3,700	1,100[†]	2,674	3,066	2,928	4,953	5,478	6,333	5,031	4,550
	77	#	300[†]	21	26	56	782	783	859	1,295	1,512
	Total	3,800	3,500	2,867	3,262	3,154	5,832	6,375	7,302	6,409	6,300
N. MEXICO	02	7,500	15,000	14,176	17,826	18,023	18,971	18,865	28,653	37,747	95,861
	21	1,400	700	#	#	#	#	3,954	8,085	4,697	#
	31	114,200	130,300	124,770	117,454	122,944	124,886	147,499	163,687	213,546	269,448
	77	267,700	333,400[†]	303,096	364,064	385,364	466,909	532,315	676,554	987,575	1,199,510
	Total	390,800	479,400[†]	442,042	499,344	526,331	610,766	702,633	876,979	1,243,565	1,564,819
O. NICARAGUA	02	1,300	2,600	3,100	3,500	4,467	4,043	178	126	79	193
	31	6,200	7,900[†]	9,000	9,900	10,062	12,889	7,676	5,637	5,025	3,385
	77	2,300	3,400[†]	4,600	5,000	3,352	5,429	2,306	1,478	1,892	2,366
	Total	9,800	13,900	16,700	18,400	17,881	22,361	10,160	7,241	6,996	5,944
P. PANAMA	02	#	#	#	#	#	#	#	#	#	#
	31	~	8,600	7,346	~	~	~	~	~	~	~
	77	53,200	100,100	81,045	81,085	152,368	207,798	109,958	147.072	194,701	132,152
	Total	53,200	108,700	88,391	81,085	152,368	207,798	109,958	147.072	194,701	132,152

Table 2000 (Continued)

TOTAL NOMINAL CATCHES BY MAJOR FISHING AREA,[1] 20 LC, 1970–81[a]
(MET)

Country	Code[2]	1970	1973	1974	1975	1976	1977	1978	1979	1980	1981
Q. PARAGUAY	03	1,800†	2,700†	2,700†	2,700†	2,700†	2,700†	2,700†	2,700†	2,700†	2,700†
	Total	1,800†	2,700†	2,700†	2,700†	2,700†	2,700†	2,700†	2,700†	2,700†	2,700†
R. PERU	03	2,000†	5,400	5,514	6,777	6,280	9,015	14,064	15,217	12,537	15,440
	87	12,532,900	2,323,100	4,139,344	3,440,713	4,338,005	2,525,388	3,458,341	3,666,969	2,738,088	2,735,065
	Total	12,534,900	2,328,500	4,144,858	3,447,490	4,344,285	2,534,403	3,472,405	3,682,186	2,750,625	2,750,505
S. URUGUAY	03	#	#	300	245	179	321	472	578	312	92
	41	13,200	17,500	15,700	26,088	33,425	47,953	73,751	107,555	120,087	144,839
	Total	13,200	17,500	16,000	26,333	33,604	48,274	74,223	108,133	120,399	144,931
T. VENEZUELA	03	12,300	8,600	9,198	7,657	6,626	8,021	11,260	12,456	15,863	13,346
	31	114,100	153,800	140,887	145,750	139,105	137,898	154,858	113,573	158,822	167,497
	Total	126,400	162,400	150,085	153,407	145,731	145,919	166,118	126,029	174,685	180,843
UNITED STATES	02	78,000	83,800	84,516	77,267	76,368	71,831	80,416	65,684	69,572	65,197
	21	972,500	1,040,200	992,437	930,879	979,955	1,076,037	1,117,140	1,196,504	1,298,798	1,236,253
	31	1,016,300	908,500	1,041,819	1,024,947	1,080,706	940,874	1,332,572	1,281,468	1,216,251	1,259,193
	34	~	~	~	~	3,402	10,616	5,789	2,764	2,650	3,904
	67	397,200	367,000	360,829	352,602	442,890	477,662	516,175	593,307	653,674	806,594
	77	312,400	318,500	449,198	533,071	458,777	398,536	364,107	367,883	369,493	353,945
	87	0	800	0	1,172	8,380	4,740	1,360	3,244	13,111	11,584
	Total	2,776,400	2,718,800	2,928,799	2,919,938	3,050,478	2,980,296	3,417,559	3,510,854	3,634,526	3,767,425

1. Includes marine and inland catches.
2. Code: 02, America, North–Inland Waters; 03, American, South–Inland Waters; 21, Atlantic, Northwest; 31, Atlantic, Western Central; 34, Atlantic, Eastern Central; 41, Atlantic, Southwest; 47, Atlantic Southeast; 67, Pacific, Northeast; 77, Pacific, Eastern Central; 87, Pacific, Southeast. See map of FAO fishing areas on following page.

a. For 1964–1970 data see SALA, 21-3815.

SOURCE: FAO-YFSCL, 1976–81, tables A-2, D-2, and D-3.

Figure 20:1

FAO FISHING AREA CODES

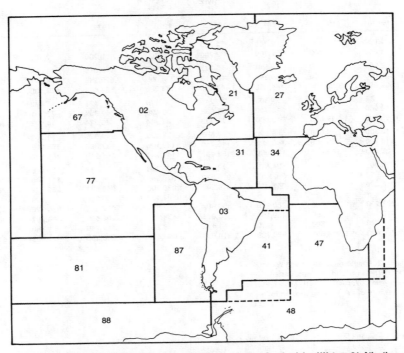

FAO fishing areas. 02, America, North—Inland Waters; 03, America, South—Inland Waters; 21, Atlantic, Northwest; 27, Atlantic, Northeast; 31, Atlantic, Western Central; 34, Atlantic, Eastern Central; 41, Atlantic, Southwest; 47, Atlantic, Southeast; 48, Atlantic, Antarctic; 67, Pacific, Northeast; 77, Pacific, Eastern Central; 81, Pacific Southwest; 87, Pacific, Southeast; 88, Pacific, Antarctic.
SOURCE: Adapted from FAO map of major fishing areas for statistical purposes.

Table 2001

NOMINAL CATCHES, MARINE AREAS, 18 LRC, 1971–81
(MET)

	Country	1971	1972	1973	1974	1975	1976	1977	1978	1979	1980	1981
A.	ARGENTINA	201,400	211,100	270,000	266,380	195,820	255,931	359,281	504,138	550,266	376,792	349,981
C.	BRAZIL	493,800	523,800	614,600	557,775	579,536	508,202	580,031	631,983	728,418	680,000[†]	720,000[†]
D.	CHILE	1,491,600	795,300	667,700	1,127,772	899,464	1,378,600	1,318,953	1,929,090	2,632,615	2,816,614	3,393,347
E.	COLOMBIA	18,400	27,900	32,200	25,184	24,500	23,670	21,791	22,966	14,858	18,418	45,535
F.	COSTA RICA	7,200	10,800	10,700	13,450	14,052	12,832	13,035	17,261	20,759	14,537	12,157
G.	CUBA	125,400	138,600	148,900	162,779	141,625	192,290	183,282	209,970	148,399	180,142	154,214
H.	DOMINICAN REP.	4,100	4,600	8,900	8,025	6,467	6,435	4,235	4,573	6,845	8,199	9,167
I.	ECUADOR	106,700	108,200	153,900	174,400	222,038	298,268	433,950	616,550	607,835	671,310[†]	685,657
J.	EL SALVADOR	9,900	9,600	11,000	8,110	7,861	6,058	4,744	8,028	11,019	12,140	19,271
K.	GUATEMALA	2,800	2,700	3,200	3,353	3,980	3,079	2,474	4,924	4,283	3,107	3,855
L.	HAITI	2,500[†]	2,900[†]	3,300[†]	3,700[†]	3,700[†]	3,700[†]	3,700[†]	3,700[†]	3,700[†]	3,700[†]	3,700[†]
M.	HONDURAS	6,600	5,100	3,700	3,403	4,484	4,290	5,735	6,261	7,192	6,326	6,062
N.	MEXICO	390,200	414,900	433,400	387,506	449,677	508,308	591,795	683,768	848,326	1,205,818	1,468,958
O.	NICARAGUA	8,100	10,000	11,300	8,229	10,419	9,205	10,161	9,982	7,115	6,917	5,751
P.	PANAMA	72,500	63,400	92,300	68,560	80,606	152,368	207,798	109,958	147,072	194,701	132,152
R.	PERU	10,526,100	4,722,300	2,323,200	4,139,395	3,440,861	4,338,005	2,525,388	3,458,341	3,666,969	2,738,088	2,735,065
S.	URUGUAY	14,400	20,600	17,500	15,700	26,003	33,425	47,953	73,751	107,555	120,087	144,839
T.	VENEZUELA	133,400	145,700	153,700	135,774	145,078	139,184	137,898	154,858	113,573	158,822	167,497
	LATIN AMERICA	13,615,100	7,217,500	4,959,500	7,109,495	6,256,171	7,873,850	6,452,204	8,450,102	9,626,799	9,215,718	10,057,208
	UNITED STATES	2,797,700	2,686,300	2,712,200	2,762,078	2,764,803	2,974,110	2,908,465	3,337,143	3,445,170	3,564,954	3,702,228
	WORLD	59,678,800	55,451,400	55,891,800	59,504,200	59,143,200	62,680,800	61,524,700	63,320,000	64,019,500	64,788,900	66,706,700

SOURCE: FAO-YFSCL, 1979–81, table A-4.

Table 2002

DISTRIBUTION OF MARINE AREA NOMINAL CATCHES, 18 LR, 1971–81

(%)

	Country	1971	1972	1973	1974	1975	1976	1977	1978	1979	1980	1981
A.	ARGENTINA	1.5	3.0	5.4	3.7	3.1	3.2	5.5	5.9	5.7	4.0	3.4
C.	BRAZIL	3.6	7.3	12.4	7.8	9.2	6.4	8.9	7.4	7.5	7.3	7.1
D.	CHILE	11.0	11.0	13.5	15.9	14.3	17.5	20.4	22.8	27.3	30.5	33.7
E.	COLOMBIA	.1	.4	.6	.3	.3	.3	.3	.2	.1	.1	.4
F.	COSTA RICA	.1	.2	.2	.1	.2	.1	.2	.2	.2	.1	.1
G.	CUBA	.9	1.9	3.0	2.2	2.2	2.4	2.8	2.4	1.5	1.9	1.5
H.	DOMINICAN REP.	0	.1	.2	.1	.1	0	0	0	0	0	0
I.	ECUADOR	.8	1.5	3.1	2.4	3.5	3.7	6.7	7.2	6.3	7.2	6.8
J.	EL SALVADOR	.1	.1	.2	.1	.1	0	0	0	.1	.1	.1
K.	GUATEMALA	0	0	.1	0	0	0	0	0	0	0	0
L.	HAITI	0	0	.1	0	0	0	.1	0	0	0	0
M.	HONDURAS	0	.1	.1	0	0	0	0	0	0	0	0
N.	MEXICO	2.9	5.7	8.7	5.5	7.1	6.4	9.2	8.0	8.8	13.0	14.6
O.	NICARAGUA	.1	.1	.2	.1	.1	.1	.1	.1	0	0	0
P.	PANAMA	.5	.9	1.9	1.3	1.2	1.9	3.2	1.3	1.5	2.1	1.3
R.	PERU	77.8	66.0	46.8	58.2	54.9	55.0	39.1	40.9	38.0	29.7	27.1
S.	URUGUAY	.1	.3	.4	.2	.4	.4	.7	.8	1.1	1.3	1.4
T.	VENEZUELA	1.0	2.0	3.2	1.9	2.3	1.7	2.1	1.8	1.1	1.7	0
	LATIN AMERICA	100.0	100.0	100.0	100.0	100.0	100.0	100.0	100.0	100.0	100.0	100.0

SOURCE: Calculated from table 2001.

Table 2003

PC OF NOMINAL CATCHES IN MARINE AREAS, 18 LRC, 1971–81

	Country	1971	1972	1973	1974	1975	1976	1977	1978	1979	1980	1981
A.	ARGENTINA	8.2	4.8	27.9	−1.3	−26.5	30.7	40.4	40.3	9.1	−31.5	−7.1
C.	BRAZIL	14.1	6.1	17.3	−9.2	3.9	−12.3	14.1	9.0	15.3	−6.6[†]	5.9[†]
D.	CHILE	24.3	−46.7	−16.0	68.9	−20.2	53.3	−4.3	46.3	36.5	7.0	20.5
E.	COLOMBIA	−13.6	51.6	15.4	−21.8	−2.7	−3.4	−7.9	5.4	−35.3	24.0	147.2
F.	COSTA RICA	2.9	50.0	−.9	25.7	4.5	−8.7	1.6	32.4	20.3	−30.0	−16.4
G.	CUBA	19.1	10.5	7.4	9.3	−13.0	35.8	−4.7	14.6	−29.3	21.4	−14.4
H.	DOMINICAN REP.	−18.0	12.2	93.5	−9.8	−19.4	−.5	−34.2	8.0	49.7	19.8	11.8
I.	ECUADOR	16.7	1.4	42.2	13.3	27.3	34.3	45.5	42.1	−1.4	10.4	2.1
J.	EL SALVADOR	−3.9	−3.0	14.6	−26.3	−3.1	−22.9	−21.7	69.2	37.3	10.2	58.7
K.	GUATEMALA	−6.7	−3.6	18.5	4.8	18.7	−22.6	−19.6	99.0	−13.0	−27.5	24.1
L.	HAITI	13.6	16.0	13.8	12.1	0	0	0	0	0	0[†]	0[†]
M.	HONDURAS	78.4	−22.7	−27.5	−8.0	31.8	−4.3	33.7	9.2	14.9	−12.0	−4.2
N.	MEXICO	13.4	6.3	4.5	−10.6	16.0	13.0	16.4	15.5	24.1	42.1	21.8
O.	NICARAGUA	−4.7	23.5	13.0	−27.2	26.6	−11.7	10.4	−1.8	−28.7	−2.8	−16.9
P.	PANAMA	0	−12.6	45.6	−25.7	17.6	89.0	36.4	−47.1	33.8	32.4	−32.1
R.	PERU	−16.0	−55.1	−50.8	78.2	−16.9	26.1	−41.8	36.9	6.0	−25.3	−.1
S.	URUGUAY	9.1	43.1	−15.0	−10.3	65.6	28.5	43.5	53.8	45.8	11.7	20.6
T.	VENEZUELA	8.8	9.2	5.5	−11.7	6.9	−4.1	−.9	12.3	−26.7	39.8	5.5
	LATIN AMERICA	90.2	22.1	−15.0	43.4	−12.0	25.9	−18.0	31.0	13.9	−4.3	9.1
	UNITED STATES	2.5	−4.0	1.0	1.8	.1	7.6	−2.2	14.7	3.2	−4.3	3.9
	WORLD	.3	−7.1	.8	6.5	−.6	6.0	−1.8	2.9	1.1	1.2	3.0

SOURCE: Calculated from table 2001.

Table 2004

NOMINAL CATCHES, INLAND WATERS, 18 LRC, 1971–81

(MET)

	Country	1971	1972	1973	1974	1975	1976	1977	1978	1979	1980	1981
A.	ARGENTINA	5,700	6,300	7,600	10,181	15,068	9,846	10,436	15,077	16,082	8,407	9,653
B.	BOLIVIA	1,900	1,500	1,500	1,050	1,050	1,250	1,550	1,550	3,650	4,379	5,617
C.	BRAZIL	87,900	77,800	84,100	168,145	173,455	144,829	168,444	170,645	126,701	170,000[†]	180,000[†]
D.	CHILE	#	#	#	#	#	#	#	#	35	92	52
E.	COLOMBIA	19,300	82,800	73,100	37,234	42,075	51,437	42,174	56,612	48,535	46,903	47,719
F.	COSTA RICA	--	--	--	40	50	60	61	61	100	350	400
G.	CUBA	600	1,000	1,000	2,200	1,700	1,800	1,900	3,200	5,400	6,339	10,314
H.	DOMINICAN REP.	500	1,000	300	367	585	618	359	513	1,040	2,459	2,836
J.	EL SALVADOR	800	800	900	1,514	869	1,143	1,624	1,512	1,719	1,818	983
K.	GUATEMALA	500	400	500	528	550	574	600	580	615	400	410
L.	HAITI	300[†]	300[†]	300[†]	300[†]	300[†]	300[†]	300[†]	300[†]	300[†]	300[†]	300[†]
M.	HONDURAS	100	--	100	172	170	170	97	114	110	83	238
N.	MEXICO	7,900	11,100	15,000	14,164	17,826	18,023	18,971	18,865	28,653	37,747	95,861
O.	NICARAGUA	1,300	1,200	2,600	460	359	458	393	178	126	79	193
Q.	PARAGUAY	2,200[†]	2,500[†]	2,700	2,700[†]	2,700[†]	2,700[†]	2,700[†]	2,700[†]	2,700[†]	2,700[†]	2,700[†]
R.	PERU	2,500	3,000	5,400	5,514	6,777	6,280	9,015	14,064	15,217	12,537	15,440
S.	URUGUAY	--	--	--	300	245	179	321	472	578	312	92
T.	VENEZUELA	5,700	6,500	8,600	9,198	7,657	6,626	8,021	11,260	12,456	15,863	13,346
	LATIN AMERICA	137,200	196,200	203,700	254,067	271,436	246,293	266,966	297,703	264,017	310,768	386,154
	UNITED STATES	77,500	73,400	83,800	84,516	77,267	76,368	71,831	80,416	65,684	69,572	65,197
	WORLD	6,382,000	6,536,600	6,770,900	6,846,600	6,992,400	6,909,400	7,153,000	7,079,400	7,294,700	7,587,900	8,053,700

SOURCE: FAO-YFSCL, 1979–81, table A-3.

Table 2005

DISTRIBUTION OF NOMINAL CATCHES IN INLAND WATERS, 18 LR, 1971–81

(%)

	Country	1971	1972	1973	1974	1975	1976	1977	1978	1979	1980	1981
A.	ARGENTINA	4.2	3.2	3.7	4.0	5.6	4.0	3.9	5.0	6.1	2.7	2.5
B.	BOLIVIA	1.4	.8	.7	.4	.4	.5	.6	.5	1.4	1.4	1.5
C.	BRAZIL	64.1	39.7	41.3	66.2	63.9	58.8	63.1	57.3	48.0	54.7	46.6
D.	CHILE	0	0	0	0	0	0	0	0	0	0	0
E.	COLOMBIA	14.1	42.2	35.9	14.7	15.5	20.9	15.8	19.0	18.4	15.1	12.4
F.	COSTA RICA	0	0	0	0	0	0	0	0	0	.1	.1
G.	CUBA	.4	.5	.5	.9	.6	.7	.7	1.1	2.0	2.0	2.7
H.	DOMINICAN REP.	.4	.5	.1	.1	.2	.2	.1	.2	.4	.8	.7
J.	EL SALVADOR	.6	.4	.4	.6	1.0	1.2	1.1	.5	.7	.6	.3
K.	GUATEMALA	.4	.2	.2	.2	.2	.2	.2	.2	.1	.1	.1
L.	HAITI	.2	.2	.1	.1	.1	.1	.1	.1	.1	0	0
M.	HONDURAS	.1	0	0	.1	.1	.1	0	0	0	0	0
N.	MEXICO	5.8	5.7	7.3	5.6	6.6	7.3	7.1	6.3	10.9	12.1	24.8
O.	NICARAGUA	.9	.6	1.3	.2	.1	.2	.1	.1	0	0	0
Q.	PARAGUAY	1.6	1.3	1.3	1.0	1.0	1.1	1.0	.9	1.0	.9	.7
R.	PERU	1.8	1.5	2.7	2.2	2.4	2.5	3.4	4.7	5.8	4.0	4.0
S.	URUGUAY	0	0	0	.1	.1	.1	.1	.2	.2	.1	0
T.	VENEZUELA	4.2	3.3	4.2	3.6	2.8	2.6	2.9	3.8	4.7	5.1	3.5
	LATIN AMERICA	100.0	100.0	100.0	100.0	100.0	100.0	100.0	100.0	100.0	100.0	100.0

SOURCE: Calculated from table 2004.

Table 2006

PC OF NOMINAL CATCHES IN INLAND WATERS, 18 LRC, 1971–81

	Country	1971	1972	1973	1974	1975	1976	1977	1978	1979	1980	1981
A.	ARGENTINA	5.6	10.5	20.6	34.0	48.0	-34.7	6.0	44.5	6.7	-47.7	14.8
B.	BOLIVIA	18.8	-21.1	0	-30.0	0	19.0	24.0	0	135.5	20.0	28.3
C.	BRAZIL	-6.0	-11.5	8.1	99.9	3.2	-16.5	16.3	1.3	-25.8	34.2	5.9
D.	CHILE	0	0	0	0	0	0	0	0	**	162.9	-43.5
E.	COLOMBIA	-41.9	329.0	-11.7	-49.1	13.0	22.3	-18.0	34.2	-14.3	-3.7	1.7
F.	COSTA RICA	~	~	~	~	25.0	20.0	1.7	0	63.9	25.0	14.3
G.	CUBA	50.0	66.7	0	120.0	-22.7	5.9	5.6	68.4	68.8	17.3	62.7
H.	DOMINICAN REP.	150.0	100.0	-70.0	22.3	59.4	5.6	-41.9	42.9	102.7	136.4	15.3
J.	EL SALVADOR	0	0	12.5	68.2	-42.6	31.5	42.1	-6.9	13.7	5.8	-45.9
K.	GUATEMALA	25.0	-20.0	25.0	5.6	4.2	4.4	4.5	-3.3	6.0	-35.0	2.5
L.	HAITI	0†	0†	0†	0†	0†	0†	0†	0†	0†	0†	0†
M.	HONDURAS	0	-100	~	72.0	-1.2	0	-42.9	17.5	-3.5	-24.5	186.7
N.	MEXICO	9.7	40.5	35.1	-5.6	25.9	1.1	5.3	-.6	51.9	31.7	154.0
O.	NICARAGUA	0	-7.7	116.7	-82.3	-22.0	27.6	-14.2	-54.7	-29.2	-37.3	144.3
Q.	PARAGUAY	22.2	13.6	8.0	0†	0†	0†	0†	0†	0†	0†	0†
R.	PERU	25.0	20.0	80.0	2.1	22.9	-7.3	43.6	56.0	8.2	-17.6	23.2
S.	URUGUAY	~	~	~	~	-18.3	-26.9	79.3	47.0	22.5	-46.0	-70.5
T.	VENEZUELA	50.0	14.0	32.3	7.0	-16.8	-13.5	21.1	40.4	10.6	27.4	-15.9
	LATIN AMERICA	-9.7	43.0	3.8	24.7	6.8	9.3	8.4	11.5	-11.3	17.7	24.3
	UNITED STATES	-4.0	-5.3	14.2	.9	-8.6	-1.2	-5.9	12.0	-18.3	5.9	-6.3
	WORLD	4.8	2.4	3.6	1.1	2.1	1.2	3.5	-1.0	3.0	4.0	6.1

SOURCE: Calculated from table 2004.

Table 2007

PRODUCTION OF SEAWEEDS,[1] 5 LC, 1970–81
(MET)

	Country	1970	1973	1974	1975	1976	1977	1978	1979	1980	1981
A.	ARGENTINA	23,300	24,300	19,400	18,010	15,670	22,754	23,161	15,305	14,734	14.734
D.	CHILE	28,000	26,800	30,000	30,000	30,000	30,000	30,000	65,000	74,523	109,631
N.	MEXICO	35,200	30,300	40,372	31,841	45,954	59,330	36,739	48,039	34.698	29,571
R.	PERU	#	200	228	193	292	265	326	286	361	323
S.	URUGUAY	#	#	#	85	200	100	76	37	#	#
	UNITED STATES	117,100	139,900	156,907	157,853	158,468	160,810	160,761	160,624	162,809	48,703
	WORLD	1,633,400	2,305,700	2,614,600	2,480,400	2,492,400	3,093,900	3,224,400	3,187,100	3,348,700	3,061,900

1. Includes production of seaweeds and other aquatic plants through both culture and harvesting of wild stocks.

SOURCE: FAO-YFSCL, 1979–81, table A-6.

CHAPTER 21

AGRICULTURAL PRODUCTION

Table 2100

INDEX OF TOTAL AGRICULTURAL PRODUCTION[1], 20 LC, 1966–81

(1969–71 = 100)[a]

Country	1968	1969	1970	1971	1972	1973	1974	1975	1976	1977	1978	1979	1980	1981
A. ARGENTINA	94	102	102	95	96	102	106	109	118	119	130	134	126	132
B. BOLIVIA	95	95	100	105	114	126	126	134	137	132	135	134	135	138
C. BRAZIL	91	97	98	105	109	108	123	124	126	136	134	142	152	165
D. CHILE	101	96	104	100	96	88	100	106	104	112	103	111	111	119
E. COLOMBIA	94	96	100	104	105	108	112	121	126	132	140	146	146	156
F. COSTA RICA	91	95	98	108	107	115	112	124	127	133	135	137	138	143
G. CUBA	85	82	123	95	88	93	96	97	101	107	119	127	114	123
H. DOMINICAN REP.	84	94	100	106	109	115	117	112	122	124	130	126	136	138
I. ECUADOR	100	96	102	102	99	103	113	115	119	123	119	123	132	140
J. EL SALVADOR	89	96	98	106	105	107	116	125	118	121	136	142	133	122
K. GUATEMALA	93	97	101	102	111	119	125	129	131	138	141	150	155	160
L. HAITI	94	97	100	103	106	105	108	109	111	107	112	112	109	109
M. HONDURAS	96	99	97	104	109	105	99	88	99	108	121	119	123	131
N. MEXICO	98	96	100	105	108	110	115	114	115	126	137	131	141	150
O. NICARAGUA	97	99	98	103	106	109	124	130	133	135	148	140	95	113
P. PANAMA	97	103	94	103	102	106	110	116	116	124	128	125	129	132
Q. PARAGUAY	93	93	102	105	104	106	116	116	126	141	137	152	158	161
R. PERU	86	95	102	104	102	106	110	105	108	109	106	111	102	112
S. URUGUAY	92	100	106	94	88	93	101	99	111	96	95	93	102	114
T. VENEZUELA	89	97	101	102	101	108	108	122	113	124	133	142	149	144
UNITED STATES	98	98	97	104	104	106	107	113	117	122	120	126	122	135

1. The index numbers of total agricultural production cover all of the items included in food production (cereals, starchy roots, sugar, pulses, edible oil crops, nuts, fruit, vegetables, wine, cocoa, livestock and livestock products) and, in addition, industrial oilseeds, tobacco, fibres (vegetable and animal), rubber, coffee and tea. Agricultural commodities used in the agricultural production process are deducted from total production. The deduction items include amounts used for seed (or, in the case of eggs, used for hatching), and for livestock feed, i.e., agricultural products fed as such and semi-processed feed such as oilcakes and grain as well as imported feed, to the extent that adequate estimates are possible.

a. For subindex of food production, see SALA, 24-818, above.

SOURCE: FAO-PY, 1978, and 1980–81, table 5.

Table 2101

INDEX OF PER CAPITA AGRICULTURAL PRODUCTION[1], 20 LC, 1966–81

(1969–71 = 100)[a]

Country	1968	1969	1970	1971	1972	1973	1974	1975	1976	1977	1978	1979	1980	1981
A. ARGENTINA	97	104	102	94	91	98	101	102	109	108	117	119	110	115
B. BOLIVIA	100	97	101	102	106	120	115	119	118	111	110	107	105	104
C. BRAZIL	97	100	98	103	104	100	111	109	108	114	109	114	118	126
D. CHILE	105	98	104	98	93	83	93	97	94	100	90	95	94	99
E. COLOMBIA	100	98	100	101	100	101	103	108	110	113	118	120	117	123
F. COSTA RICA	97	98	98	105	102	107	101	109	110	112	111	110	108	110
G. CUBA	88	84	123	93	85	89	90	89	91	96	106	112	101	107
H. DOMINICAN REP.	89	97	100	103	103	106	104	97	103	102	104	98	103	103
I. ECUADOR	107	99	102	99	94	94	100	99	100	100	94	94	98	101
J. EL SALVADOR	95	99	98	102	99	98	104	108	99	98	108	109	99	88
K. GUATEMALA	99	100	101	99	105	108	111	110	109	112	111	114	114	115
L. HAITI	97	99	100	101	101	98	99	97	97	91	94	91	87	85
M. HONDURAS	102	102	97	101	102	96	87	75	81	86	93	89	88	91
N. MEXICO	104	99	100	101	101	100	101	97	95	101	106	99	103	107
O. NICARAGUA	104	102	98	100	99	99	109	110	109	108	114	104	68	79
P. PANAMA	102	106	94	100	97	98	99	101	99	103	105	100	101	101
Q. PARAGUAY	98	96	103	102	98	96	102	99	104	112	106	113	114	113
R. PERU	92	97	102	101	97	98	99	92	92	90	86	87	78	83
S. URUGUAY	94	101	106	93	88	92	100	98	110	95	93	90	98	109
T. VENEZUELA	94	100	101	99	94	97	93	102	91	97	100	104	105	98
UNITED STATES	100	99	97	103	102	102	103	108	110	114	111	115	110	120

1. For alternative data from 1971 to 1977, see SALA, 21-1517.

a. For subindex of per capita food production, see SALA, 24-819, above.

SOURCE: FAO-PY, 1978 and 1980–81, table 7.

Table 2102

BARLEY PRODUCTION, 10 LC, 1975–81[a]
(Area = T Ha.; Production = T MET; Yield = kg/Ha.)

	Country	1975 Production	1978 Production	1979 Production	1980 Production	1981 Area[1]	1981 Production	1981 Yield[2]
A.	ARGENTINA	523	554	339	217	162[‡]	215[‡]	1,327
B.	BOLIVIA	80	63	52	49	80[†]	55[†]	688
C.	BRAZIL	25	144	98	75	91	101	1,108
D.	CHILE	121	126	112	105	46	91	1,988
E.	COLOMBIA	122	119	137	109	36	56	1,567
I.	ECUADOR	63	22	21	24	29	27	942
K.	GUATEMALA	~	1	~	1[†]	~	1[†]	1,486
N.	MEXICO	440	505	368	610	274	559	2,038
R.	PERU	149	144	131	150[‡]	170[‡]	160[‡]	941
S.	URUGUAY	38	57	71	55	50[‡]	100[‡]	2,000
	UNITED STATES	8,153	9,901	8,334	7,859	3,703	10,414	2,812

1. Area harvested.
2. Yield may not equal kg/Ha. due to rounding of area and production data.
a. For 1948–52 data see SALA, 23-1501.

SOURCE: FAO-PY, 1977 and 1980–81, table 12.

Table 2103

BANANA PRODUCTION, 17 LC, 1970–81[a]
(T MET)

	Country	1970	1975	1977	1978	1979	1980	1981
A.	ARGENTINA	223	374	220	129	144	146	180[†]
B.	BOLIVIA	212	252	250	152	203	216	220[†]
C.	BRAZIL	6,408[†]	5,311	6,415	6,240	6,133	6,736	6,696
E.	COLOMBIA	780	1,050[†]	1,100[†]	1,100[†]	1,040[†]	1,030[‡]	1,155[‡]
F.	COSTA RICA	1,146[‡]	1,121	1,125	1,149	1,078	1,092	1,144
G.	CUBA	47	92[‡]	140[†]	150	147	145	155[†]
H.	DOMINICAN REP.	275	318	314	315[‡]	275	301	320[‡]
I.	ECUADOR	2,700[‡]	2,544	2,451	2,152	2,032	2,269	2,275[‡]
J.	EL SALVADOR	45	53[†]	53[†]	53[†]	52[†]	52[†]	53[†]
K.	GUATEMALA	487	520[†]	550[†]	550[†]	556[†]	650[†]	650[†]
L.	HAITI	176[†]	51[†]	51[†]	195[‡]	210	200[†]	210[†]
M.	HONDURAS	1,200[†]	852	1,235	1,267	1,300[‡]	1,330[†]	1,330[†]
N.	MEXICO	1,136	1,194	1,276	1,384	1,553	1,515	1,562[†]
O.	NICARAGUA[1]	217	153	154	157[†]	170[†]	171[†]	170[†]
P.	PANAMA	947	989	1,028	1,056	1,000[†]	1,050[†]	1,082[†]
Q.	PARAGUAY	249	260[†]	252	254	306	300[†]	305[†]
T.	VENEZUELA	968	860	875	900	961	983	980[†]
	UNITED STATES	3	3	3	3	3	2	3

1. Refers to exports.
a. For 1948 data see SALA, 23-1512.

SOURCE: FAO-PY, 1971, table 71; 1972, table 76; 1976-77 and 1979-81, table 65.

Table 2104

BEAN PRODUCTION,[1] 20 LC, 1975–81[a]

(Area = T Ha.; Production = T MET; Yield = kg/Ha.)

	Country	1975 Production	1978 Production	1979 Production	1980 Production	1981 Area[2]	1981 Production	1981 Yield[3]
A.	ARGENTINA	109	133	232	156	210	221	1,052
B.	BOLIVIA	2[†]	2	4	4	4[†]	4[†]	1,053
C.	BRAZIL	2,271	2,194	2,186	1,969	5,030	2,339	465
D.	CHILE	74	112	116	84	118	138	1,174
E.	COLOMBIA	74	75	75	84	115	87	757
F.	COSTA RICA	16	9	11	12	24	12	519
G.	CUBA	24[†]	25[†]	26[†]	26[†]	35[†]	26[†]	749
H.	DOMINICAN REP.	36[‡]	38	36	49	55[‡]	42[‡]	764
I.	ECUADOR	26	19	23	26	51[†]	29[‡]	569
J.	EL SALVADOR	40	43	47	40	50[‡]	37[‡]	753
K.	GUATEMALA	65	81[‡]	85[‡]	80	119	81	682
L.	HAITI	44[†]	46	52	45[‡]	92[†]	50[†]	543
M.	HONDURAS	43	44[‡]	38[‡]	36[‡]	73[‡]	42[‡]	578
N.	MEXICO	1,027	949	601	971	2,150	1,469	683
O.	NICARAGUA	44	55	39[‡]	60[‡]	77[‡]	60[‡]	779
P.	PANAMA	4	4	3	5	11[‡]	5[‡]	455
Q.	PARAGUAY	45[†]	65	58	65	85[†]	68[†]	800
R.	PERU	42[‡]	56[†]	55	39	39	42[‡]	1,074
S.	URUGUAY	2[†]	3[†]	3[†]	3[†]	5[†]	3[†]	578
T.	VENEZUELA	37	34	39	46	79[‡]	54[‡]	684
	UNITED STATES	790	859	929	1,197	891	1,443	1,620

1. Includes *Phaseolus vulgaris, P. lunatus, P. aureus,* and *P. mungo.*
2. Area harvested.
3. Yield may not equal kg/Ha. due to rounding of area and production data.

SOURCE: FAO-PY, 1977 and 1980-81, table 23.

Table 2105

CASSAVA PRODUCTION, 18 L, 1975–81[a]

(Area = T Ha.; Production = T MET; Yield = kg/Ha.)

	Country	1975 Production	1978 Production	1979 Production	1980 Production	1981 Area[1]	1981 Production	1981 Yield[2]
A.	ARGENTINA	300	182	183	222	23[†]	230[†]	10,000
B.	BOLIVIA	285	210	201	219	19[†]	230[†]	12,432
C.	BRAZIL	25,812	25,459	24,962	23,411	2,093	25,050	11,968
E.	COLOMBIA	1,900[‡]	2,044	1,909	2,150	207	2,150	10,386
F.	COSTA RICA	11	14[†]	15	18	3[†]	18[†]	6,667
G.	CUBA	246[†]	312[‡]	325[‡]	325[‡]	48[†]	328[†]	6,899
H.	DOMINICAN REP.	160	185[‡]	119	115	18[†]	180[‡]	10,000
I.	ECUADOR	597	168	183	229	26[‡]	236[‡]	9,100
J.	EL SALVADOR	16	15	20	20	2	25	11,840
K.	GUATEMALA	7[†]	8[†]	8[†]	8[†]	3[†]	8	2,567
L.	HAITI	145[†]	261	254	250[†]	63[†]	255[†]	4,048
M.	HONDURAS	10[†]	8	9	7	2[†]	7[†]	3,273
N.	MEXICO	- -	39	33	20	2[†]	22[†]	10,000
O.	NICARAGUA	18[†]	26[†]	24[†]	26[†]	7[†]	27[†]	4,077
P.	PANAMA	40	40	40	40[†]	5[†]	43[†]	8,212
Q.	PARAGUAY	1,420[†]	1,838	1,888	2,031	135[†]	2,000[†]	14,815
R.	PERU	470	396	403	400[†]	36[‡]	410[‡]	11,389
T.	VENEZUELA	317	304	350	361	37[†]	360[†]	9,730

1. Area harvested.
2. Yield may not equal kg/Ha. due to rounding of area and production data.

a. For 1948-52 data see SALA, 23-1509.

SOURCE: FAO-PY, 1977 and 1980–81, table 21.

Table 2106

COCOA BEAN PRODUCTION, 16 L, 1975–81[a]

(Area = T Ha.; Production = T MET; Yield = kg/Ha.)

	Country	1975 Production	1978 Production	1979 Production	1980 Production	1981 Area[1]	1981 Production	1981 Yield[2]
B.	BOLIVIA	3	3	2	2	4†	2†	545
C.	BRAZIL	290‡	279	309	296	500	345‡	690
E.	COLOMBIA	26‡	31	32	34	70‡	41	580
F.	COSTA RICA	7	10	10	1	9‡	3	318
G.	CUBA	2‡	2‡	3	1†	3†	2‡	667
H.	DOMINICAN REP.	33‡	33	36	32‡	97†	35‡	361
i.	ECUADOR	74	72	77	91	283‡	96‡	339
J.	EL SALVADOR	~	~	~	~	~	~	892
K.	GUATEMALA	1‡	5	2	4‡	7†	4‡	500
L.	HAITI	4‡	3‡	3‡	3‡	2†	3‡	1,733
M.	HONDURAS	~	1‡	1‡	1‡	~	~	1,000
N.	MEXICO	37	42	38	38	74	32	435
O.	NICARAGUA	1‡	1‡	1‡	1‡	4†	~	100
P.	PANAMA	1‡	1	1‡	1‡	4†	1†	250
R.	PERU	2‡	5‡	4	4‡	9†	4‡	471
T.	VENEZUELA	19	15	15	13	67†	14‡	209

1. Area harvested.
2. Yield may not equal kg/Ha. due to rounding of area and production data.

a. For 1961–65 data see SALA, 23-1507.

SOURCE: FAO-PY, 1975, table 90; 1976–81, table 70.

Table 2107

COFFEE PRODUCTION, 17 LC, 1975–81[a]

(Area = T Ha.; Production = T MET; Yield = kg/Ha.)

	Country	1975 Production	1978 Production	1979 Production	1980 Production	1981 Area[1]	1981 Production	1981 Yield[2]
B.	BOLIVIA	15	16	20	21	24†	22†	917
C.	BRAZIL	1,228	1,268	1,333	998	2,337	1,878	803
E.	COLOMBIA	540‡	652	713	724	1,075‡	808	752
F.	COSTA RICA	79	96	99	109	85	120	1,407
G.	CUBA	25‡	27‡	26	24	50†	24†	476
H.	DOMINICAN REP.	55	61‡	38	54‡	160†	51‡	319
I.	ECUADOR	76	75	90	69	261†	88‡	338
J.	EL SALVADOR	193	162	180	165	170†	150†	882
K.	GUATEMALA	129	151	156	156‡	253	173	682
L.	HAITI	40‡	32‡	25‡	38‡	32‡	33‡	1,031
M.	HONDURAS	50‡	68‡	75‡	76‡	150†	90‡	600
N.	MEXICO	214	242	223	208	508	217	427
O.	NICARAGUA	48	65	51‡	55‡	110‡	63‡	573
P.	PANAMA	5	6	6	6‡	24†	6†	247
Q.	PARAGUAY	9†	7	8	9	20†	11†	525
R.	PERU	59	83	105	95‡	140†	95†	679
T.	VENEZUELA	65	59	61	61	253†	62‡	245
	UNITED STATES	1	1	1	1	1	1	1,178

1. Area harvested.
2. Yield may not equal kg/Ha. due to rounding of area and production data.

a. For 1948–52 data see SALA, 23-1506.

SOURCE: FAO-PY, 1976–81, table 69.

Table 2108

COPRA PRODUCTION, 11 L, 1970-81[a]

(T MET)

Country	1970	1975	1976	1977	1978	1979	1980	1981
C. BRAZIL	2.2	2[†]	2[†]	2[†]	2[†]	2[†]	2[†]	2[†]
E. COLOMBIA	2.2[†]	~	~	~	~	~	~	~
F. COSTA RICA	1.2	2[†]	2[†]	2[†]	2[†]	2[†]	2[†]	2[†]
H. DOMINICAN REP.	7.5	9[†]	4	4[‡]	13[†]	9	12	9[†]
I. ECUADOR	2.2[†]	4[†]	5[†]	8[†]	11[†]	11[†]	14[†]	17[†]
J. EL SALVADOR	3.0[†]	5[‡]	5[†]	3	4	4	3[‡]	3[†]
M. HONDURAS	2.4[†]	3[†]	3[†]	3[†]	3[†]	3[†]	3[†]	3[†]
N. MEXICO	137.4	145[‡]	160	150	161	130	140[‡]	143[‡]
O. NICARAGUA	.2[†]	~	~	~	~	~	~	~
P. PANAMA	.6	1[†]	2	1[†]	1[†]	1[†]	1[†]	1[†]
T. VENEZUELA	16.9	18	18[‡]	19[‡]	19[‡]	12	12	12[‡]

a. For 1948-52 data see SALA, 23-1516.

SOURCE: FAO-PY, 1971, table 90; 1974, table 57; 1977-81, table 38.

Table 2109

COTTON LINT PRODUCTION, 18 LC, 1970-81[a]

(T MET)

Country	1970	1975	1977	1978	1979	1980	1981
A. ARGENTINA	145	171	160	220	174	146	82
B. BOLIVIA	5	22	15	18	16	7	5[‡]
C. BRAZIL	672	515	555	477	549	572[‡]	613
E. COLOMBIA	128	121	162	111	95	116[‡]	87[‡]
F. COSTA RICA	1[†]	1	7	3	4	4[‡]	5
G. CUBA	1[†]	1[‡]	1[‡]	1[‡]	1[‡]	1[‡]	1[‡]
H. DOMINICAN REP.	1[†]	1[†]	1	1[‡]	1[‡]	2[‡]	2[†]
I. ECUADOR	4[‡]	11	10[‡]	10[‡]	9[‡]	15[‡]	15[‡]
J. EL SALVADOR	46	78	66	79	72	65	41
K. GUATEMALA	57	105[‡]	137	149	161	156	126
L. HAITI	1[†]	1[†]	1[†]	2[†]	2[†]	1[†]	1[†]
M. HONDURAS	3	5[‡]	6	11	9[‡]	7[‡]	7[‡]
N. MEXICO	312	197	418	366	384	329[‡]	344
O. NICARAGUA	67	123	118	123	113	21[‡]	75[‡]
Q. PARAGUAY	13	33[‡]	73	91	73	75	103[‡]
R. PERU	92	60[‡]	72[‡]	87[‡]	100[‡]	90[‡]	87[‡]
S. URUGUAY	..	1	~	~	~	~	~
T. VENEZUELA	13	31	20[‡]	19	14	18	15[‡]
UNITED STATES	2,213	1,807	3,133	2,364	3,185	2,422	3,425

a. For 1948-52 data see SALA, 23-1504.

SOURCE: FAO-PY, 1971, table 96; 1974, table 106; 1976-81, table 78.

Table 2110

COTTONSEED PRODUCTION, 18 LC, 1970–81[a]

(T MET)

Country	1970	1975	1977	1978	1979	1980	1981
A. ARGENTINA	249	541	324	414	330	276	153
B. BOLIVIA	10	61‡	32	36	25	12	10‡
C. BRAZIL	1,227	1,751	1,008‡	975‡	1,085‡	1,125‡	1,206‡
E. COLOMBIA	231	385	277	186	161	216‡	160†
F. COSTA RICA	2	2‡	14	5	7	8†	9
G. CUBA	2†	3†	2†	2†	2‡	2‡	9
H. DOMINICAN REP.	3	2†	3	2‡	3‡	4‡	2‡
I. ECUADOR	10‡	30	16‡	16†	15‡	24‡	4‡
J. EL SALVADOR	76	210	119	134	119	109	24‡
K. GUATEMALA	92	280‡	230	249	268	251	68
L. HAITI	1†	3†	2†	3†	3†	2†	249
M. HONDURAS	6	15‡	12‡	21‡	15‡	15‡	3†
N. MEXICO	550	544	659	576	605	538	11‡
O. NICARAGUA	112	330‡	191	201	186	37‡	530
Q. PARAGUAY	25	94‡	143‡	178‡	145‡	37‡	115‡
R. PERU	153	180‡	122‡	166‡	191‡	146‡	208†
S. URUGUAY	#	2‡	~	~	~	172‡	165‡
T. VENEZUELA	23	88	34‡	31	24‡	~	~
UNITED STATES	3,690	4,556	5,009	3,873	5,242	4,056	5,673

a. For 1948–52 data see SALA, 23-1505.

SOURCE: FAO-PY, 1971, table 80; 1974, table 53; 1976–81, table 37.

Table 2111

MAIZE PRODUCTION, 20 LC, 1975–81[a]

(Area = T Ha.; Production = T MET; Yield = kg/Ha.)

Country	1975 Production	1978 Production	1979 Production	1980 Production	1981 Area[1]	1981 Production	1981 Yield[2]
A. ARGENTINA	7,700	9,500	8,700	6,400	3,500	13,500	3,857
B. BOLIVIA	305	331	378	383	190‡	250‡	1,316
C. BRAZIL	16,354	13,569	16,306	20,374	11,491	21,098	1,836
D. CHILE	329	257	489	405	126	518	4,128
E. COLOMBIA	723	862	870	813	629	880	1,399
F. COSTA RICA	92	64	73	75	47	88	1,876
G. CUBA	21	95†	95†	95†	77†	95†	1,234
H. DOMINICAN REP.	32	49	38	49	24‡	50‡	2,083
I. ECUADOR	275	176	218	242	225‡	246‡	1,094
J. EL SALVADOR	439	507	523	527	259‡	487‡	1,882
K. GUATEMALA	683	906	941	1,041‡	680	1,052	1,547
L. HAITI	180‡	161	183	175†	250†	180†	720
M. HONDURAS	363	455	354	337‡	340‡	338‡	994
N. MEXICO	8,459	10,930	8,124	12,383	8,150	14,766	1,812
O. NICARAGUA	192	254	168‡	229‡	250‡	250‡	1,000
P. PANAMA	65	64	63	63‡	70‡	68‡	971
Q. PARAGUAY	301	355	550	585	400†	600†	1,500
R. PERU	635	623	631	443	316	628‡	1,986
S. URUGUAY	157	172	71	119	146	196	1,338
T. VENEZUELA	653	804	848	662	335‡	486‡	1,451
UNITED STATES	148,061	184,614	201,665	168,787	30,200	208,314	6,898

1. Area harvested.
2. Yield may not equal kg/Ha. due to rounding of area and production data.

a. For 1948–52 data see SALA, 23-1502.

SOURCE: FAO-PY, 1977 and 1980–81, table 13.

Table 2112

ORANGE AND TANGERINE PRODUCTION, 18 LC, 1970–81[a]

(T MET)

	Country	1970	1975	1977	1978	1979	1980	1981
A.	ARGENTINA	1,092	959	990	925	930	918	862[†]
B.	BOLIVIA	68	87	96	101	108	109	111[†]
C.	BRAZIL	3,343	6,643[†]	7,489[†]	6,676	7,224	9,327[‡]	9,785[‡]
D.	CHILE[1]	42[‡]	43	49	51	51	49[‡]	54[‡]
E.	COLOMBIA[1]	- -	- -	- -	192	221[‡]	225[‡]	253[‡]
F.	COSTA RICA[1]	59	68[†]	73[†]	74[†]	74[†]	75[†]	76[†]
G.	CUBA	138	142	158[‡]	204	203	328	390
H.	DOMINICAN REP.[1]	60[†]	68[†]	70[†]	70[†]	69	71	72[†]
I.	ECUADOR	197[†]	303	548	526	532	564	563[†]
J.	EL SALVADOR[1]	41	45[†]	51	99	99[†]	101[†]	100[†]
K.	GUATEMALA	~	~	~	~	~	~	~
L.	HAITI	6[†,b]	32[†]	34[†]	36[†]	37[†]	38[†]	39[†]
M.	HONDURAS[1]	48	25[†]	26[†]	27[†]	27[†]	27[†]	28[†]
N.	MEXICO	1,555[b]	2,478[‡]	1,915	2,007[‡]	1,835[‡]	1,810[‡]	1,720[‡]
O.	NICARAGUA[1]	45	50[†]	53[†]	54[†]	53[‡]	52[†]	53[†]
P.	PANAMA[1]	42	62	62	62	65	66	69[†]
Q.	PARAGUAY	225[†]	154[†]	235[†]	229	267	272[†]	272[†]
R.	PERU	261	241[†]	160[†]	187[†]	164	170[†]	173[†]
S.	URUGUAY	59[b]	77[†]	76[†]	62	72	85[‡]	89[‡]
T.	VENEZUELA[1]	184	245	252[†]	314	369	433	430[†]
	UNITED STATES	7,761	9,913	10,144	9,268	8,889	11,490	10,111

1. Oranges only.

a. For 1948–65 data, see SALA, 23-1513.

SOURCE: FAO-PY, 1971, table 65; 1972, table 73; 1976–77 and 1979–81, table 62.

Table 2113

POTATO PRODUCTION, 20 LC, 1975–81[a]

(Area = T Ha.; Production = T MET; Yield = kg/Ha.)

	Country	1975 Production	1978 Production	1979 Production	1980 Production	1981 Area[1]	1981 Production	1981 Yield[2]
A.	ARGENTINA	1,349	1,593	1,694	1,568	117[†]	2,247[†]	19,255
B.	BOLIVIA	834	716	730	787	150[†]	950[‡]	6,333
C.	BRAZIL	1,669	2,015	2,154	1,948	171	1,911	11,175
D.	CHILE	738	981	770	903	90	1,007	11,202
E.	COLOMBIA	1,120	1,996	1,966	1,727	160	2,100	13,169
F.	COSTA RICA	24	26	27	27	3	28	9,333
G.	CUBA	90	198	201	239	13[†]	239[†]	18,850
H.	DOMINICAN REP.	28	23	11	15	2[†]	27[‡]	12,857
I.	ECUADOR	499	343	255	323	31[‡]	349[‡]	11,271
J.	EL SALVADOR	13	4	4	6	~	6[†]	19,677
K.	GUATEMALA	28	61	51	38[‡]	9[†]	37[†]	4,353
L.	HAITI	7[†]	9[†]	9[†]	9[†]	1[†]	9[†]	15,000
M.	HONDURAS	5[†]	5[†]	5[†]	5[†]	1[†]	5[†]	5,667
N.	MEXICO	693	837[†]	727	892[‡]	67	868	12,945
O.	NICARAGUA	1	2[†]	2[†]	2[†]	~	2[†]	4,250
P.	PANAMA	9	9	10[‡]	12[‡]	2[†]	13[†]	8,667
Q.	PARAGUAY	4	7	9	9	1[†]	9[†]	9,000
R.	PERU	1,870	1,713	1,695	1,380	189	1,627[‡]	8,596
S.	URUGUAY	121	102	135	110	20[‡]	130[‡]	6,500
T.	VENEZUELA	152	171	225	247	19[‡]	200[‡]	10,526
	UNITED STATES	14,512	16,616	15,535	13,737	498	15,135	30,368

1. Area harvested.
2. Yield may not equal kg/Ha. due to rounding of area and production data.

a. For 1948–52 data see SALA, 23-1510.

SOURCE: FAO-PY, 1977 and 1980–81, table 19.

Table 2114

RICE PADDY PRODUCTION, 20 LC, 1975–81[a]
(Area = T Ha.; Production = T MET; Yield = kg/Ha.)

	Country	1975 Production	1978 Production	1979 Production	1980 Production	1981 Area[1]	1981 Production	1981 Yield[2]
A.	ARGENTINA	351	310	312	266	82	286	3,496
B.	BOLIVIA	127	93	76	95	65[†]	100[‡]	1,538
C.	BRAZIL	7,538	7,296	7,595	9,748	6,066	8,261	1,362
D.	CHILE	76	105	181	95	31	100	3,176
E.	COLOMBIA	1,614	1,715	1,932	1,798	413	1,799	4,354
F.	COSTA RICA	196	196	208	180	80	210	2,630
G.	CUBA	420[‡]	458	425	478	163[†]	518[†]	3,186
H.	DOMINICAN REP.	278[‡]	351	377	398	110[‡]	430[‡]	3,909
I.	ECUADOR	378	233	318	381	130	402	3,090
J.	EL SALVADOR	61	51	58	61	14[‡]	52[‡]	3,705
K.	GUATEMALA	33	26	37	39[‡]	16	46	2,880
L.	HAITI	110[†]	114	122	91[‡]	50[†]	90[‡]	1,800
M.	HONDURAS	29	27	31	29	23[‡]	40[‡]	1,764
N.	MEXICO	510	402	500	456	180	644	3,583
O.	NICARAGUA	89	85	37	58[‡]	30[‡]	65[‡]	2,167
P.	PANAMA	185	162	170	156[‡]	96[‡]	192[‡]	1,999
Q.	PARAGUAY	45	58	57	73	30	60	2,000
R.	PERU	547	468	560	420	146	684[‡]	4,680
S.	URUGUAY	193	226	248	290	62	326[‡]	5,236
T.	VENEZUELA	363	502	653	712	264[‡]	708[‡]	2,682
	UNITED STATES	5,805	6,040	5,985	6,629	1,539	8,408	5,462

1. Area harvested.
2. Yield may not equal kg/Ha. due to rounding of area and production data.

a. For 1948-52 data see SALA, 23-1503.

SOURCE: FAO-PY, 1977 and 1980-81, table 11.

Table 2115

SUGAR CANE PRODUCTION, 19 LC, 1975–81[a]
(Area = T Ha.; Production = T MET; Yield = kg/Ha.)

	Country	1975 Production	1978 Production	1979 Production	1980 Production	1981 Area[1]	1981 Production	1981 Yield[2]
A.	ARGENTINA	15,600	13,600	14,120	17,200	323[‡]	15,260	47,201
B.	BOLIVIA	2,367	3,049	3,120	3,080	65[‡]	3,259[‡]	50,039
C.	BRAZIL	91,386	129,145	138,899	146,065	2,803	153,858	54,888
E.	COLOMBIA	19,411[†]	22,900[†]	24,700[†]	26,100[†]	300[†]	25,900[†]	86,333
F.	COSTA RICA	2,324	2,579	2,615	2,516	51[‡]	2,522	49,448
G.	CUBA	56,000[†]	69,653	77,311	62,374	1,400[†]	67,000[†]	47,857
H.	DOMINICAN REP.	10,157[†]	11,094	10,304	9,056	185[†]	11,600[†]	62,703
I.	ECUADOR	7,723	6,928	6,599	6,615	108[†]	6,650[†]	61,574
J.	EL SALVADOR	3,204	3,692	3,214	2,207	28	1,916	68,501
K.	GUATEMALA	4,900	5,500[†]	5,100[†]	5,409[‡]	83[‡]	5,680[‡]	68,811
L.	HAITI	2,969[†]	2,844	2,900[†]	3,000[†]	80[†]	3,000[†]	37,500
M.	HONDURAS	1,570	2,164	2,600[†]	2,820[†]	90[†]	3,000[†]	33,333
N.	MEXICO	35,581	35,475	34,587	36,480	545	35,461	65,076
O.	NICARAGUA	2,604	2,706	2,699	2,431[‡]	37[‡]	2,800[‡]	76,072
P.	PANAMA	1,722	2,757	2,624	2,386	48[†]	2,556[†]	53,250
Q.	PARAGUAY	1,400[†]	1,260	1,287	1,373	41[‡]	1,550[‡]	37,805
R.	PERU	9,000[‡]	7,970	7,034	5,598	40[‡]	4,160	104,680
S.	URUGUAY	325	475	323	448	10[‡]	445[‡]	44,500
T.	VENEZUELA	5,482	4,939	4,400	5,500	80[‡]	4,000[‡]	50,000
	UNITED STATES	28,875	23,584	24,069	24,460	305	27,076	88,802

1. Area harvested.
2. Yield may not equal kg/Ha. due to rounding of area and production data.

a. For 1961-65 data see SALA, 23-1514.

SOURCE: FAO-PY, 1975, table 76; 1976-81, table 58.

Table 2116

TOBACCO LEAF PRODUCTION, 20 LC, 1975–81[a]

(Area = T Ha.; Production = T MET; Yield = kg/Ha.)

		1975	1978	1979	1980	1981		
	Country	Production	Production	Production	Production	Area[1]	Production	Yield[2]
A.	ARGENTINA	98	63	70	62	47	52	1,120
B.	BOLIVIA	3	2	2	2	2[†]	2[†].	947
C.	BRAZIL	287	405	422	406	287	362	1,264
D.	CHILE	8	9	8[‡]	5	2	6	2,624
E.	COLOMBIA	46[‡]	47	60	47	30	49	1,653
F.	COSTA RICA	3	3	2	2	2	2	952
G.	CUBA	50[‡]	41	33	8	58[†]	34[‡]	586
H.	DOMINICAN REP.	17[‡]	54	45	52	27[‡]	45[‡]	1,659
I.	ECUADOR	1	3	3	3	2[‡]	3[‡]	1,999
J.	EL SALVADOR	2[‡]	2[†]	4	4	2[‡]	3[‡]	1,515
K.	GUATEMALA	7[‡]	10	11	8[‡]	5[†]	9[†]	1,809
L.	HAITI	3[†]	2[†]	~	~	~	~	739
M.	HONDURAS	6[‡]	7[†]	8[‡]	7	6[‡]	8[‡]	1,326
N.	MEXICO	68	70	74	77	43	66	1,519
O.	NICARAGUA	3	3[‡]	3[‡]	3[‡]	2[‡]	4[‡]	2,020
P.	PANAMA	1	1	2	1	1[‡]	1[‡]	1,600
Q.	PARAGUAY	33	27	26	21	9	9	1,047
R.	PERU	5[‡]	3[‡]	2	4[‡]	4[‡]	5[‡]	1,205
S.	URUGUAY	1[‡]	2[‡]	2	1[‡]	1[‡]	1[‡]	1,673
T.	VENEZUELA	16	15	22[‡]	23[‡]	14[‡]	16[‡]	1,142
	UNITED STATES	990	918	692	810	391	929	2,377

1. Area harvested.
2. Yield may not equal kg/Ha. due to rounding of area and production data.

a. For 1948-52 data see SALA, 23-1515.

SOURCE: FAO-PY, 1977 and 1980-81, table 73.

Table 2117

WHEAT PRODUCTION, 13 LC, 1975–81[a]

(Area = T Ha.; Production = T MET; Yield = kg/Ha.)

		1975	1978	1979	1980	1981		
	Country	Production	Production	Production	Production	Area[1]	Production	Yield[2]
A.	ARGENTINA	8,570	8,100	8,100	7,780	5,757[†]	8,100	1,407
B.	BOLIVIA	62	56	68	60[‡]	77[†]	50[‡]	649
C.	BRAZIL	1,788	2,691	2,927	2,708	1,921	2,207	1,148
D.	CHILE	1,002	893	995	966	432	686	1,587
E.	COLOMBIA	39	38	42	46	39	62	1,597
I.	ECUADOR	65	29	31	31	37	41	1,120
K.	GUATEMALA	45	60	57	42[‡]	64	45	712
M.	HONDURAS	1[‡]	1[‡]	1[‡]	1[‡]	1[†]	1[†]	1,000
N.	MEXICO	2,789	2,785	2,339	2,785	861	3,189	3,704
Q.	PARAGUAY	18	38	58	47	70[†]	80[†]	1,143
R.	PERU	126	113	102	77	100	117[‡]	1,172
S.	URUGUAY	456	174	430	307	350[‡]	400[‡]	1,143
T.	VENEZUELA	1	1	1	1[‡]	2[‡]	1[‡]	375
	UNITED STATES	57,765	48,322	58,081	64,619	32,759	76,026	2,321

1. Area harvested.
2. Yield may not equal kg/Ha. due to rounding of area and production data.

a. For 1948-52 data see SALA, 23-1500.

SOURCE: FAO-PY, 1977 and 1980-81, table 10.

Table 2118

SWEET POTATO AND YAM PRODUCTION, 17 LC, 1975–81[a]

(Area = T Ha.; Production = T MET; Yield = kg/Ha.)

Country	1975 Production	1978 Production	1979 Production	1980 Production	1981 Area[1]	1981 Production	1981 Yield[2]
A. ARGENTINA	418	320	322	302	24	247	10,107
B. BOLIVIA	16	30	14	15	3†	15†	5,000
C. BRAZIL	1,669	882	819	800†	90†	800†	8,889
D. CHILE	8‡	7‡	7‡	7‡	1†	7†	7,000
E. COLOMBIA	178†	~‡	~‡	~	~	~	~
G. CUBA	248†	305‡	316‡	325‡	80†	327†	4,070
H. DOMINICAN REP.[3]	88	61	59	68	13†	85‡	6,800
I. ECUADOR	14	4	4	3	1†	3†	4,615
J. EL SALVADOR	. .	. .	~	~	~	~	5,000
L. HAITI[3]	91†	306	265	260†	64†	270†	4,219
M. HONDURAS	1†	1†	1†	1†	~	1†	3,750
N. MEXICO	134	56	58	33	2†	33†	14,130
P. PANAMA[4]	~	~	~	~	~	~	~
Q. PARAGUAY	97†	117	106	112	15†	115†	7,667
R. PERU	185	154	149	150‡	15†	151†	9,941
S. URUGUAY	79	85†	60‡	60‡	15‡	60‡	4,000
T. VENEZUELA[4]	27	5	4	4†	1†	4†	3,583
UNITED STATES	615	596	606	497	44	573	12,944

1. Area harvested.
2. Yield may not equal kg/Ha. due to rounding of area and production data.
3. Combined figures for sweet potatoes and yams. All other countries produce sweet potatoes only.
4. Yams only.

a. For 1948-52 data see SALA, 23-1511.

SOURCE: FAO-PY, 1977 and 1980-81, table 20.

CHAPTER 22

RANCH PRODUCTION

Table 2200

CATTLE POPULATION, 20 LRC, 1947–81

(T)

	Country	Average 1947/48– 1951/52	Average 1961-65	1975	1977	1978	1979	1980	1981
A.	ARGENTINA	42,320[†]	43,096	59,600[‡]	61,054	57,791	56,864	55,761	54,235
B.	BOLIVIA	1,450[b]	1,930	2,877	3,578	3,772	3,990	4,000[‡]	4,100[†]
C.	BRAZIL	51,305	59,770	92,480[‡]	91,000[‡]	89,000[‡]	90,000[‡]	91,000[‡]	93,000[‡]
D.	CHILE	2,293	2,850	3,606	3,427	3,487	3,575	3,664	3,745
E.	COLOMBIA	13,750	16,281	23,888[‡]	24,335	24,342	24,132	23,945	24,251
F.	COSTA RICA	601	1,074	1,843	1,920	2,002[‡]	2,093	2,181	2,275
G.	CUBA	4,333[‡]	5,951	5,450[†]	5,644	5,700[‡]	5,800[†]	5,900[†]	5,900[†]
H.	DOMINICAN REP.	711	899	1,900	2,000[‡]	2,050[‡]	2,150[‡]	2,153[‡]	2,155[‡]
I.	ECUADOR	1,467[d]	1,816	2,800	2,860	2,767[‡]	2,846	2,916	3,032
J.	EL SALVADOR	795	1,158	1,031	1,283	1,350	1,387	1,440	1,211
K.	GUATEMALA	977[c]	1,216	2,148[‡]	1,431	1,500	1,575	1,653	1,730
L.	HAITI	582[a]	685	742[†]	900[‡]	900[‡]	1,000[‡]	1,100[‡]	1,200[‡]
M.	HONDURAS	884	1,447	1,689[†]	1,862	1,900[‡]	2,234	2,262	2,336
N.	MEXICO	12,980	20,658	27,863	28,935	29,333	29,920	31,094	31,784[†]
O.	NICARAGUA	1,068	1,672	2,500[‡]	2,768	2,782[‡]	2,737[‡]	2,401[‡]	2,301[‡]
P.	PANAMA	567	860	1,348	1,374	1,395	1,437	1,525[‡]	1,604[‡]
Q.	PARAGUAY	4,600[‡]	5,348	4,836	5,800	5,810	5,203	5,300[†]	5,400[†]
R.	PERU	2,830	3,358	4,200[‡]	4,106	4,150	4,006	3,837	3,895
S.	URUGUAY	7,981	8,630	11,362[†]	10,128	10,007	10,301	10,952	10,971[‡]
T.	VENEZUELA	5,768	6,769	9,089	9,546	9,919	10,373	10,607	10,840
	LATIN AMERICA	157,262	185,468	261,252	263,951	259,957	261,603	263,691	265,965
	UNITED STATES	80,569	103,785	131,826	122,810	116,375	110,864	111,192	114,321

a. 1950/51.
b. 1949/50.
c. Four-year average.
d. Three-year average.

SOURCE: FAO-PY, 1971, table 107; 1976-81, table 80.

Table 2201

HORSE POPULATION, 20 LRC, 1947–81

(T)

	Country	Average 1947/48– 1951/52	Average 1961-65	1975	1977	1978	1979	1980	1981
A.	ARGENTINA	7,265[b]	3,696	3,400[‡]	3,073	3,050[‡]	3,000[‡]	3,000[‡]	3,000[‡]
B.	BOLIVIA	158[c]	197	340[†]	370[‡]	380[‡]	390[†]	400[†]	410[†]
C.	BRAZIL	6,942[d]	8,693	5,215	6,000[‡]	6,000[‡]	4,928	6,300[‡]	6,300[‡]
D.	CHILE	523[c]	503	450[‡]	450[‡]	450[‡]	450[†]	450[‡]	450[†]
E.	COLOMBIA	1,208[a]	937	1,435	1,535	1,588	1,644	1,696	1,710[‡]
F.	COSTA RICA	76[a]	100	112[‡]	190[‡]	111[‡]	112[‡]	113	113
G.	CUBA	410[c]	488	804	815	807	814	812	829[†]
H.	DOMINICAN REP.	137	213	201[‡]	202[‡]	203[‡]	203[‡]	204[‡]	204[‡]
I.	ECUADOR	111[c]	218	285[†]	291	297	309	314	299[‡]
J.	EL SALVADOR	130[c]	73	81[†]	87[‡]	88[‡]	89[‡]	88[‡]	88[‡]
K.	GUATEMALA	166[a]	159	125[†]	100	100[†]	100[†]	100[†]	100
L.	HAITI	253[d]	282	379[†]	392[‡]	400[‡]	407[†]	410[†]	415[†]
M.	HONDURAS	178[a]	262	278[†]	152[‡]	150	149[†]	150[†]	151[†]
N.	MEXICO	3,181[d]	4,323	6,376	6,551	5,479	6,447	6,300	6,502[†]
O.	NICARAGUA	150[c]	172	164[†]	270[‡]	275[‡]	280[†]	275[‡]	270[†]
P.	PANAMA	138[c]	162	164[†]	164[‡]	164[†]	165[†]	165[†]	166[†]
Q.	PARAGUAY	302[d]	555	325	326	328	329	330[†]	330[†]
R.	PERU	496	579	637[‡]	643[‡]	645[‡]	648[‡]	650[‡]	653[‡]
S.	URUGUAY	667[b]	473	470[†]	491	520[‡]	525[‡]	530[‡]	530[‡]
T.	VENEZUELA	344[b]	402	454	463[‡]	470[‡]	474[‡]	478[‡]	482[‡]
	LATIN AMERICA	22,835	22,490	21,695	22,565	21,505	21,463	22,765	23,002
	UNITED STATES	7,757	4,579	8,600[†]	9,075[‡]	9,106[‡]	9,397[†]	9,662[†]	9,928[†]

a. Three-year average.
b. 1950/51.
c. Two-year average.
d. Four-year average.

SOURCE: FAO-PY, 1971, table 106; 1976-81, table 79.

Table 2202

SHEEP POPULATION, 19 LRC, 1947–81

(T)

	Country	Average 1947/48– 1951/52	Average 1961-65	1975	1977	1978	1979	1980	1981
A.	ARGENTINA	52,940[t]	48,023	34,000[‡]	35,220	34,200	35,220	33,000	30,000[‡]
B.	BOLIVIA	7,224[b]	6,136	7,694	8,229	8,462	8,722[‡]	8,750[‡]	8,900[t]
C.	BRAZIL	14,427	19,996	17,400[‡]	17,200[‡]	17,200[‡]	17,806	18,000[‡]	18,000[‡]
D.	CHILE	5,789	6,356	5,644	5,699	6,692	5,928	6,064	6,185
E.	COLOMBIA	1,153[c]	1,506	1,921	2,138	2,255	2,357[t]	2,413	2,427
F.	COSTA RICA	1[t]	1	2[t]	2[‡]	2[‡]	2[t]	2[t]	2[t]
G.	CUBA	177[t]	229	330[t]	346[‡]	350[‡]	352[t]	355[t]	365[t]
H.	DOMINICAN REP.	27	38	50[t]	52[‡]	52[‡]	53[t]	54[t]	55[t]
I.	ECUADOR	1,720[d]	1,699	2,105	2,174	2,198	2,318[‡]	2,980	3,034
J.	EL SALVADOR	5[e]	3	4[‡]	4[‡]	4[‡]	4[‡]	4[‡]	4[‡]
K.	GUATEMALA	735[c]	743	540[t]	612	600	685	679	734
L.	HAITI	52[a]	58	79[t]	83[‡]	85[‡]	87[t]	89[t]	90[t]
M.	HONDURAS	8	8	5[‡]	3[‡]	3[‡]	5[‡]	5[‡]	5[‡]
N.	MEXICO	5,041[t]	5,886	7,825	7,860	7,856	7,850	7,318	7,990[‡]
O.	NICARAGUA	1[t]	1	2[‡]	2[‡]	2[‡]	3[‡]	3[‡]	3[‡]
Q.	PARAGUAY	207	413	366	374	403	423	430[t]	430[t]
R.	PERU	17,515	14,311	15,400	14,473	14,473	14,473	14,473	14,671[‡]
S.	URUGUAY	21,935	21,818	15,062[‡]	16,030	16,161	17,234	20,034	20,429[‡]
T.	VENEZUELA	101[a]	88	101	275[‡]	298	320	306[‡]	321[‡]
	LATIN AMERICA	46,545	54,166	67,977	71,690	73,868	72,361	73,868	71,980
	UNITED STATES	31,565	29,144	14,515	12,766	12,421	12,365	12,687	12,936

a. 1950/51.
b. 1949/50.
c. Four-year average.
d. Three-year average.
e. Two-year average.

SOURCE: FAO-PY, 1971, table 110; 1976-82, table 81.

Table 2203

SWINE POPULATION, 20 LRC, 1947–81

(T)

	Country	Average 1947/48– 1951/52	Average 1961-65	1975	1977	1978	1979	1980	1981
A.	ARGENTINA	3,250	3,476	4,200[‡]	3,332	3,600[‡]	3,552	3,800	3,900[‡]
B.	BOLIVIA	509[b]	650	1,158	1,292	1,351	1,412	1,450[‡]	1,500[t]
C.	BRAZIL	24,879	26,500	34,192	36,800[‡]	37,600[‡]	35,695	36,500[‡]	35,000[‡]
D.	CHILE	710	945	701	924	979	1,036	1,068	1,150
E.	COLOMBIA	2,368[c]	1,649	1,877	1,876	1,884	1,916	2,078	2,245
F.	COSTA RICA	111[a]	146	225[‡]	215[‡]	215[‡]	207[‡]	223[‡]	240[‡]
G.	CUBA	1,315[t]	1,296	1,450[t]	1,506	1,800[‡]	1,900[t]	1,950[t]	1,950[t]
H.	DOMINICAN REP.	739	706	700[‡]	753[‡]	718	600[‡]	250[‡]	50[‡]
I.	ECUADOR	547[b]	1,461	2,543	2,935	3,150	3,385	3,549	3,721
J.	EL SALVADOR	335[t]	392	420[‡]	515	503	560	421	386
K.	GUATEMALA	408[c]	595	659	667	704	747	792	835
L.	HAITI	1,137[a]	1,264	1,735[t]	1,900[‡]	2,000[‡]	1,500[‡]	1,100[‡]	600[‡]
M.	HONDURAS	445	748	511[‡]	525[‡]	530[‡]	531	534	580[‡]
N.	MEXICO	6,340[b]	9,168	11,466	11,986	12,321	12,578	13,222	12,900[‡]
O.	NICARAGUA	243[b]	423	650[‡]	690[‡]	710[‡]	725[‡]	500[‡]	510[‡]
P.	PANAMA	196[a]	201	166	202	204	190	195[‡]	202[‡]
Q.	PARAGUAY	340[c]	635	975	1,174	1,201	1,273	1,300[t]	1,310[t]
R.	PERU	960	1,813	2,135	2,021	1,960	1,960	2,150	2,100[t]
S.	URUGUAY	259[a]	414	418[‡]	461	398	412	450[‡]	450[‡]
T.	VENEZUELA	1,454[a]	1,696	1,795	1,916	2,040	2,165	2,230	2,351[‡]
	LATIN AMERICA	46,545	54,172	67,977	71,690	73,868	72,341	73,768	71,980
	UNITED STATES	58,895	55,610	54,693	54,934	56,539	60,356	67,353	64,512

a. 1950/51.
b. Two-year average.
c. Four-year average.

SOURCE: FAO-PY, 1971, table 109; 1976-81, table 81.

Table 2204

COW MILK PRODUCTION,[1] 20 LRC, 1948–81

(T MET)

	Country	Average 1948-52	Average 1961-65	1970	1975	1977	1978	1979	1980	1981
A.	ARGENTINA	3,758	4,294	4,189	5,650	5,309	5,213‡	5,349‡	5,307‡	5,155†
B.	BOLIVIA	18†	23	25†	53	56‡	57‡	55‡	57‡	60†
C.	BRAZIL	2,581	5,870	7,300‡	9,971	10,783	10,500‡	10,503	10,265‡	10,500‡
D.	CHILE	683	779	950‡	986	1,035	1,008	983	1,080	1,163‡
E.	COLOMBIA	1,540†	1,843	2,250	2,096	2,303	2,360	2,395	2,419	2,600‡
F.	COSTA RICA	138ᵃ	131	242‡	259	279	294	316	318	308
G.	CUBA	180†	394	300†	612	1,080‡	1,150‡	1,180†	1,188†	1,224†
H.	DOMINICAN REP.	140†	186	283	320	325‡	340‡	409	431	360‡
I.	ECUADOR	174ᵇ	376	530†	773	849	866	754‡	758‡	765‡
J.	EL SALVADOR	107ᵇ	156	177†	235	244	253	264	291	293†
K.	GUATEMALA	78ᵇ	194	262‡	310†	314	310†	315†	320†	325
L.	HAITI	15†	23	20†	40†	42‡	23	20	19†	20†
M.	HONDURAS	99	128	175‡	180†	192‡	202‡	202‡	205†	209†
N.	MEXICO	1,539	2,305ᵃ	3,053	4,980	5,731	6,426	6,848	6,750‡	6,885‡
O.	NICARAGUA	92†	158	200‡	246‡	292‡	465	386	165†	153†
P.	PANAMA	34ᵇ	56	73	73	86	98	95	95†	95†
Q.	PARAGUAY	80ᵃ	81	92†	121	136	149	162	165†	168†
R.	PERU	229ᶜ	515	825	814†	828	822	824	780	790
S.	URUGUAY	449	764	763	745	730	753	784	838	855‡
T.	VENEZUELA	203ᵃ	548	830	1,224	1,236	1,270	1,302	1,318	1,385‡
	LATIN AMERICA	12,137	18,824	22,539	29,688	31,850	32,559	33,146	32,769	33,313
	UNITED STATES	52,349	56,998	53,268	52,314	55,655	55,093	55,978	58,298	60,161

1. Intended to represent the total production for consumption fresh or for conversion
into dairy products. The figures generally exclude milk sucked by young animals, but
include milk fed to them.

a. Three-year average.
b. Two-year average.
c. Four-year average.

SOURCE: FAO-PY, 1971, table 123; 1973, table 111; 1976-81, table 90.

Table 2205

MILK YIELD PER MILKING COW PER ANNUM, 20 LC, 1948–81

(kg)

	Country	Average 1948-52	Average 1961-65	1970	1975	1977	1978	1979	1980	1981
A.	ARGENTINA	1,624†	1,836	1,920†	1,883	1,930	1,993	1,837	1,698	1,856
B.	BOLIVIA	1,760ᵇ	1,200	~	1,403	1,383	1,289	1,310	1,295	1,304
C.	BRAZIL	502†	746	800†	767	805	750	705	752	739
D.	CHILE	2,360†	1,787	2,720†	1,340	1,439	1,294	1,392	1,470	1,550
E.	COLOMBIA	462	707	1,090†	937	976	985	985	985	981
F.	COSTA RICA	~	920	1,175‡	1,043	978	1,033	1,040	1,077	1,045
G.	CUBA	524ᶜ	733	840†	986	1,317	1,386	1,405	1,398	1,440
H.	DOMINICAN REP.	950	917	~	1,391	1,354	1,429	1,670	1,760	1,469
I.	ECUADOR	1,129ᵈ	1,301	1,300†	1,311	1,415	1,443	1,371	1,217	1,214
J.	EL SALVADOR	795ᵉ	769	850‡	925	960	960	960	960	961
K.	GUATEMALA	980	866	900‡	912	871	886	904	913	905
L.	HAITI	382	232	~	357	362	229	197	190	200
M.	HONDURAS	380ᵃ	480	543‡	545	549	580	590	606	607
N.	MEXICO	933†	948	1,100†	1,360	705	775	778	763	782
O.	NICARAGUA	700‡	549	550‡	654	654	884	859	825	850
P.	PANAMA	610†	872	747†	910	981	1,000	1,001	1,001	1,001
Q.	PARAGUAY	180†	188	220†	201	1,892	1,913	1,908	1,919	1,909
R.	PERU	509†	1,019	1,320†	1,291	1,150	1,121	1,117	1,068	1,075
S.	URUGUAY	1,332†	1,397	1,550†	1,702	1,584	1,673	1,632	1,612	1,629
T.	VENEZUELA	400ᶜ	540	720†	1,106	1,199	1,222	1,243	1,097	1,152
	UNITED STATES	2,389	3,519	4,258	4,695	5,071	5,100	5,211	5,393	5,510

a. Four-year average.
b. 1950.
c. 1949.
d. Two-year average.
e. 1952.

SOURCE: FAO-PY, 1971, table 123; 1973, table 111; 1976-81, table 90.

Table 2206

WOOL OUTPUT, 9 LRC, 1948–81

(H MET)

Country	Code[1]	Average 1948-52	Average 1961-65	1970	1975	1977	1978	1979	1980	1981
A. ARGENTINA	I	1,859	1,842	1,720	1,600	1,640	1,710	1,680	1,676	1,651
	II	1,082	995	980	864	869	855	907	905	892
B. BOLIVIA	I	42[b]	61	40†	77†	80‡	85‡	87†	88†	89†
	II	22[c]	33	21†	41†	44‡	45‡	45†	45†	46†
C. BRAZIL	I	194	267	299‡	345‡	270‡	257‡	306‡	305‡	305‡
	II	122	168	188‡	218‡	170‡	190‡	192‡	192‡	192‡
D. CHILE	I	198	225	260†	188	188	191	196	206	216‡
	II	99	113	130†	94	94	96	99‡	96‡	96†
E. COLOMBIA	I	9[a]	8	11	11	12‡	13	14	28	15†
	II	5[a]	5	7	7	7	8	8	9	9†
I. ECUADOR	I	3†	11	16†	17†	17	18‡	30‡	31‡	31†
	II	2†	5	8†	9†	10‡	9‡	15†	15†	15†
N. MEXICO	I	57†	71	80	74	73	86	86†	85	86
	II	29†	35	36	37	39	43	42	42†	42†
R. PERU	I	87	110	122‡	110†	120‡	120‡	120‡	130†	130†
	II	44	55	61‡	59†	60‡	60‡	60†	65†	65†
S. URUGUAY	I	754	815	790	542	625	630	626	673	711
	II	453	489	474	325	350	378	400	480†	500†
LATIN AMERICA	I	3,203	3,410	3,338	2,964	3,025	3,110	3,145	3,222	3,234
	II	1,858	1,898	1,905	1,654	1,643	1,684	2,578	1,849	1,857
UNITED STATES	I	1,287	1,263	848	585	499	467	483	486	503
	II	567	576	399	277	241	222	254	256	256†

1. Wool Code: I = greasy; II = clean.

a. Three-year average.
b. 1950.
c. Two-year average.

SOURCE: FAO-PY, 1971, table 133; 1973, table 117; 1976-81, table 95.

CHAPTER 23

FORESTRY PRODUCTION

Table 2300

ESTIMATED FOREST AREA, NATURAL FORESTS, AND INDUSTRIAL PLANTATIONS
(T Ha. 1980)

| Subregion | Total Land Area | Total Forest Area | % of Land Area | Natural Forest | | | Forest Plantations | | | |
| | | | | Productive Coniferous | Share Broadleaf | Annual Deforestation | Total Forest Plantation | Industrial Plantations | | Annual Planting Area |
								Coniferous	Broadleaf	
Latin America	2,014,786	719,735	35.7	15,794	531,147	3,983	5,913.6	2,367.5	1,327.3	297.8[a]
MEXICO	197,255	46,250	23.5	11,720	12,580	530	159.0	37.0	35.0	7.8
Central America	50,862	18,679	36.7	2,512	11,682	382	25.4	15.8	9.6	3.9
Caribbean[1]	56,435	44,511	78.9	277	34,960	21	48.8	26.1	16.0	8.1
BRAZIL	851,196	357,480	42.0	280	300,910	1,360	3,855.0	1,232.0	741.0	158.0
Andean	446,311	206,210	46.2	185	142,975	1,535	372.4	181.8	115.6	26.8
Southern Cone	412,727	46,605	11.3	820	28,040	155	1,453.0	874.8	410.1	93.2

1. Includes Suriname, French Guiana, and Guyana. They account for the large share of forest area in this category.

a. Of which 211.0 are softwoods and 86.8 are hardwoods.

SOURCE: IDB-SPTF, 1983, table IV-5.

Table 2301

TOTAL ROUNDWOOD PRODUCTION,[1,2] 20 LRC, 1970–82
(T Me[3])

	Country	1970*	1975	1976	1977	1978	1979	1980	1981	1982
A.	ARGENTINA	8,915	8,770	9,440	9,434	10,144	10,311	9,866	8,889	10,478[†]
B.	BOLIVIA	4,279	1,175	1,209[†]	1,166	1,326	1,490	1,474	1,451	1,401[†]
C.	BRAZIL	155,073	164,753	171,464	178,444[†]	189,194[†]	200,380[†]	209,292[†]	213,002[†]	216,463[†]
D.	CHILE	8,269	10,331	11,053	11,351	12,079	13,855	20,052	13,849	12,751
E.	COLOMBIA	34,295	14,726	14,983	15,246	15,521	16,094	16,132	16,316	16,312
F.	COSTA RICA	2,362	2,863	2,948	2,960	2,968	2,970	2,732	2,614	2,627[†]
G.	CUBA	2,064	2,490	2,354	2,070	2,367	3,216	3,151	3,179	3,193[†]
H.	DOMINICAN REP.	136	479	490	501[†]	514	526	539[†]	552	566[†]
I.	ECUADOR	4,944	5,641[†]	5,773[†]	6,107[†]	6,080	7,364	7,547	7,711	7,729
J.	EL SALVADOR	2,374	3,576	3,674	3,782[†]	3,888[†]	4,010[†]	4,132[†]	4,448	4,397[†]
K.	GUATEMALA	8,937	5,780	5,752	6,049	6,200	6,141	6,247	6,474	6,652
L.	HAITI	4,056[†]	4,678[†]	4,784[†]	4,893[†]	5,006[†]	5,115[†]	5,230[†]	5,355[†]	5,494[†]
M.	HONDURAS	4,752	4,080[†]	4,410	4,620	4,716	4,764	4,945	5,035	5,071
N.	MEXICO	10,115	17,147	17,741	18,190	16,620	17,912	18,579	18,849	19,462[†]
O.	NICARAGUA	2,123	2,795	2,859[†]	2,925[†]	2,994[†]	3,064[†]	3,138[†]	3,213[†]	3,291[†]
P.	PANAMA	1,366	1,577	1,684	1,629	1,632	1,677	2,010	2,047[†]	2,047[†]
Q.	PARAGUAY	3,969	4,935	4,945	5,180	5,660	6,219	6,720	6,744[†]	6,792[†]
R.	PERU	3,326	6,862	7,635	7,418	7,358	7,635	8,152	7,833	7,769
S.	URUGUAY	1,406	1,750	1,897	2,063	2,117	2,299	1,564	1,666	1,678
T.	VENEZUELA	6,893	1,140	1,158[†]	1,177[†]	1,196[†]	1,216[†]	1,236[†]	1,257[†]	1,278[†]
	LATIN AMERICA	169,654	265,548	276,253	285,205	297,580	316,258	332,738	330,484	335,461
	UNITED STATES	327,945	304,723	336,867	349,438	391,381	419,134	415,453	416,016	393,896

1. Wood in the rough. Wood in its natural state as felled, or otherwise harvested, with or without bark, round, split, roughly squared or other forms (e.g., roots, stumps, burls, etc.). It may also be impregnated (e.g., telegraph poles) or roughly shaped or pointed. It comprises all wood obtained from removals, i.e., the quantities removed from forests and from trees outside the forest, including wood recovered from natural, felling and logging losses during the period—calendar year or forest year. Commodities included are saw-logs and veneer logs, pitprops, pulpwood, other industrial roundwood, and fuelwood.
2. For coniferous and non-coniferous, see SALA, 23-1800 and 1801.

SOURCE: FAO-YFP, 1981, p. 64; 1982, p. 64.

Table 2302

INDUSTRIAL ROUNDWOOD PRODUCTION,[1] 20 LC, 1970–82

$(T\ Me^3)$

Country	1970*	1975	1976	1977	1978	1979	1980	1981	1982
A. ARGENTINA	3,072	3,628	4,188	4,029	3,644	4,787	4,070	3,894	3,864
B. BOLIVIA	231‡	300	300†	229	355	488	433	323	323†
C. BRAZIL	23,823	30,597	33,854	37,327†	44,511†	52,080†	57,318†	57,427†	57,499†
D. CHILE	4,625	5,178	5,816	6,022	6,656	8,342	14,449	8,154	6,951
E. COLOMBIA	2,851	3,002	3,002	3,002	3,002	3,301	3,054	2,954	2,673
F. COSTA RICA	838	1,335	1,412	1,491	1,495†	1,495†	1,257	1,139	1,146†
G. CUBA	382	385†	385†	385†	385†	385†	385†	385†	385†
H. DOMINICAN REP.	1	13	11	10†	10	9	9†	9	9†
I. ECUADOR	1,506	1,659	1,672†	1,878†	1,720†	1,868†	2,029†	2,161	2,149
J. EL SALVADOR	79	78	75	79†	78†	91†	100†	127†	120†
K. GUATEMALA	530	546	356	486	466	231	159	202	194
L. HAITI	232†	239†	239†	239†	239†	239†	239†	239†	239†
M. HONDURAS	800	868†	1,085	1,175	1,146	1,064	1,112	1,066	962
N. MEXICO	5,302	6,613	6,879	6,995	5,082	6,030	6,345	6,253	6,498
O. NICARAGUA	445	880	880†	880†	880†	880†	880†	880†	880†
P. PANAMA	98	117	184	86	44	44	339	339†	339†
Q. PARAGUAY	806	1,155	948	1,128	1,522	1,989	2,412	2,412†	2,412†
R. PERU	1,087	1,475	2,104	1,738	1,518	1,636	1,988	1,498	1,256
S. URUGUAY	148	290	311	347	345	427	242	244	244
T. VENEZUELA	558	636	636†	636†	636†	636†	636†	636†	636†
UNITED STATES	312,653	288,581	319,875	320,441	346,919	354,707	327,095	317,094	294,974
WORLD	1,277,638	1,285,956	1,359,818	1,375,008	1,415,419	1,443,840	1,439,928	1,404,962	1,357,857

1. All wood as defined in "Total Roundwood" with the exception of fuelwood and charcoal.

SOURCE: FAO-YFP, 1981, p. 96; 1982, p. 96.

Table 2303

INDUSTRIAL WOOD AS A PERCENTAGE OF TOTAL ROUNDWOOD PRODUCTION,[1] 20 LC, 1970–82

(%)

Country	1970*	1975	1976	1977	1978	1979	1980	1981	1982
A. ARGENTINA	34.5	41.4	44.4	42.7	35.9	46.4	41.3	43.8	36.9
B. BOLIVIA	5.4‡	25.5	24.8†	19.6	26.8	32.8	29.4	22.3	23.1†
C. BRAZIL	15.4	18.6	19.7	21.8†	23.5†	25.9†	27.4†	26.9†	26.6†
D. CHILE	55.7	50.1	52.6	53.1	55.1	60.2	72.1	58.9	54.5
E. COLOMBIA	8.3	20.4	20.0	19.7	19.3	20.5	18.9	18.1	16.4
F. COSTA RICA	35.5	46.6	47.9	50.4	50.4†	50.3†	46.0	43.6	43.6†
G. CUBA	18.5	15.5†	16.4†	18.6†	16.3†	11.9†	12.2†	12.1†	12.1†
H. DOMINICAN REP.	.7	2.7	2.2	1.9‡	1.9	1.7	1.7‡	1.6	1.6‡
I. ECUADOR	30.5	29.4†	28.9†	30.8†	28.3†	25.4†	26.9†	28.0	27.8
J. EL SALVADOR	3.3	2.2	2.0	2.1†	2.0†	2.3‡	2.4‡	2.9‡	2.7‡
K. GUATEMALA	5.9	9.5	6.2‡	8.0	7.5	3.8	2.5	3.1	2.9
L. HAITI	5.7‡	5.1‡	4.9‡	4.8‡	4.8‡	4.7‡	4.6‡	4.5‡	4.4‡
M. HONDURAS	16.8	21.3†	24.6	25.4	24.3	22.3	22.5	21.2	18.9
N. MEXICO	52.4	38.6	38.8	38.5	30.6	33.7	34.2	33.2	33.4
O. NICARAGUA	20.9	31.5	30.8‡	30.1‡	29.4‡	28.7‡	28.0‡	27.4‡	26.7‡
P. PANAMA	7.2	7.4	10.9	5.3	2.7	2.7	16.9	16.6‡	16.6‡
Q. PARAGUAY	20.3	23.4	19.2	21.8	26.9	31.9	35.9	35.8‡	35.5‡
R. PERU	32.7	21.5	27.6	23.4	20.6	21.4	24.4	19.1	16.2
S. URUGUAY	10.5	16.6	16.4	16.8	16.3	18.8	15.5	14.6	14.5
T. VENEZUELA	8.1	55.8	54.9	54.0	53.2	52.3	51.5	50.6	49.8
UNITED STATES	95.3	94.7	94.9	91.7	88.6	84.6	78.7	76.2	74.9
WORLD	48.4	49.1	49.9	50.0	49.9	49.5	48.5	47.2	45.9

1. Industrial roundwood is comprised of all of those woods included in table 2301, above, with the exception of fuelwoods and charcoal. This table thus demonstrates the amount of wood produced for industry rather than fuel. For fuelwood, coal, and bagasse production see Chapter 19, above.

SOURCE: Calculated from tables 2301 and 2302 above.

Table 2304

TOTAL SAWNWOOD AND SLEEPER PRODUCTION,[1,2] 19 LC, 1970–82

(T Me^3)

	Country	1970	1975	1976	1977	1978	1979	1980	1981	1982
A.	ARGENTINA	736	480	631	859	640	908	883	1,047	947
B.	BOLIVIA	72	140	143	109	167	233	220	172	172[†]
C.	BRAZIL	8,035	10,129	11,243	12,643	13,337	14,070	14,881	15,852	15,852[†]
D.	CHILE	1,075	1,320	1,278	1,267	1,717	2,371	2,186	1,735	1,003
E.	COLOMBIA	1,100	954	934[†]	934[†]	934[†]	983	970	1,006	721
F.	COSTA RICA	369	612	513[†]	689	689[†]	364	524	534	378
G.	CUBA	96[†]	105[†]	105[†]	105[†]	105[†]	101	112	108	108[†]
I.	ECUADOR	704	755	761	852	762	830	906	987	981
J.	EL SALVADOR	20	38	31	34	33[†]	37	37	47	45
K.	GUATEMALA	204	222	326	353	346	138	93	136	130
L.	HAITI	13	14[†]	14[†]	14[†]	14[†]	14[†]	14[†]	14[†]	14[†]
M.	HONDURAS	457	551	598	628	633	624	546[†]	546[†]	546[†]
N.	MEXICO	1,572	1,986	2,147	2,259	2,299	2,109	1,991	1,928	1,669
O.	NICARAGUA	197	402	402[†]	402[†]	402[†]	402[†]	402[†]	402[†]	402[†]
P.	PANAMA	44	50	81	33	12	12[†]	53	53[†]	53
Q.	PARAGUAY	214	340	345	314	380	524	655	655[†]	655[†]
R.	PERU	351	516	786	476	486	546	611	653	577
S.	URUGUAY	73	105	117	107	104	99	99[†]	99[†]	99[†]
T.	VENEZUELA	328	349	349[†]	349[†]	349[†]	349[†]	349[†]	349[†]	349[†]
	UNITED STATES	81,854	75,903	86,148	88,593	88,932	87,678	74,955	70,048	61,110
	WORLD	415,009	405,288	436,243	445,465	450,235	450,679	438,997	419,163	399,843

1. Sawnwood, unplaned, planed, grooved, tongued, etc., sawn lengthwise, or produced
    by a profile-chipping process (e.g., planks, beams, joists, boards, rafters, scantlings,
    laths, boxboards, "lumber," etc.) and planed wood which may also be finger jointed,
    tongued or grooved, chamfered, rabbeted, V-jointed, beaded, etc. Wood flooring is
    excluded. With few exceptions, sawnwood exceeds 5 mm in thickness. Pieces of
    wood of more or less rectangular section laid transversely on the railway road-bed to
    support the rails. Sleepers may be sawn or hewn.
2. For coniferous and non-coniferous, see SALA, 23-1802 and 1803.

SOURCE: FAO-YFP, 1982, p. 172.

Table 2305

TOTAL WOOD-BASED PANEL PRODUCTION,[1] 17 LC, 1970–82[a]

(T Me^3)

	Country	1970	1975	1976	1977	1978	1979	1980	1981	1982
A.	ARGENTINA	193	331	343	280	302	367	414	357	341
B.	BOLIVIA	1	2	5	21	17	23	28	28	28[†]
C.	BRAZIL	819	1,725	1,956	2,139	2,218[†]	2,236	2,545	2,639	2,639[†]
D.	CHILE	57	44	60	74	95	113	115	142	122
E.	COLOMBIA	77	80	109	112	112[†]	103	111	106	123
F.	COSTA RICA	25	45	51	73	61	67	98	57	52
G.	CUBA	70	19[†]	19	19	19[†]	19[†]	19[†]	19[†]	19[†]
I.	ECUADOR	20	39	41	51	66	75	87	95	117
K.	GUATEMALA	5	21	10	11	9	11	9[†]	6[†]	5
M.	HONDURAS	6	10	11	13	9	8	8[†]	8[†]	8
N.	MEXICO	174	253	270[†]	362	404	442	604	683	761
O.	NICARAGUA	16	10	10[†]	10[†]	10[†]	16	14	14[†]	14
P.	PANAMA	4	9	10	14	14[†]	14[†]	14[†]	14[†]	14[†]
Q.	PARAGUAY	15	17	13	19	27[†]	43[†]	69[†]	69[†]	69[†]
R.	PERU	54	60	87	64	48	66	84	78	57
S.	URUGUAY	18	15	13	14	15	17	16	15	15
T.	VENEZUELA	59	81	83[†]	74	69	101	136	151	136
	UNITED STATES	23,026	25,005	29,255	32,464	32,023	31,519	26,224	27,498	23,000
	WORLD	69,591	84,484	95,357	101,613	104,336	106,135	101,279	99,428	94,118

1. Includes veneer sheets, plywood, particle board, and fiberboard.

a. For 1962-69 data see SALA, 21-1704.

SOURCE: FAO-YFP, 1981; 1982, p. 206.

Table 2306

FIBERBOARD PRODUCTION,[1] 8 LC, 1970–82

(T Me^3)

	Country	1970	1975	1976	1977	1978	1979	1980	1981	1982
A.	ARGENTINA	24	51	51	52	68	59	90	86	80
C.	BRAZIL	269	504	631	710[†]	765[†]	724[‡]	843[†]	843[†]	843[†]
D.	CHILE	20	14	22	28	33	44	45	44	46
E.	COLOMBIA	11	15	13	13	13[†]	17	19	17	18
G.	CUBA	64[†]	13[†]	13[†]	13[†]	13[†]	13[†]	13[†]	13[†]	13[†]
N.	MEXICO	21	14	25	30	26	26	26	26	26
S.	URUGUAY	4	3	3	3	3	3	2	1	1
T.	VENEZUELA	2	6[†]	8[†]	10[†]	12[†]	16[‡]	16[‡]	16[†]	16[†]
	UNITED STATES	5,821	6,236	7,219	7,343	7,170	7,187	5,098	5,098	4,500
	WORLD	1,277,638	1,286,027	1,359,842	1,375,995	1,414,724	1,444,998	1,441,716	1,383,970	14,881

1. A panel manufacture from fibers of wood or other ligno-cellulosic materials with the primary bond deriving from the felting of the fibers and their inherent adhesive properties. Bonding materials and/or additives may be added. It is usually flat pressed but may be moulded.

SOURCE: FAO-YFP, 1982, p. 242.

Table 2307

PARTICLE BOARD PRODUCTION,[1] 14 LC, 1970–82

(T Me^3)

	Country	1970	1975	1976	1977	1978	1979	1980	1981	1982
A.	ARGENTINA	117	209	225	176	185	248	268	217	212
C.	BRAZIL	112[‡]	407	461	541	541[†]	550	660	660[†]	660[†]
D.	CHILE	22	16	29	32	42	46	43	72	56
E.	COLOMBIA	9	12[†]	17[‡]	20[‡]	20[†]	30[‡]	31	42	50
F.	COSTA RICA	#	#	6	24	28	31	32	23	11
G.	CUBA	4	4[†]	4[†]	4[†]	4[†]	4[†]	4[†]	4[†]	4[†]
I.	ECUADOR	#	#	#	8	14	19	26	28	49
K.	GUATEMALA	4	16[†]	4	6	3	4	3	3	3
N.	MEXICO	56	125	99	155	162	194	316	339	412
P.	PANAMA	#	2[†]	2[†]	2[†]	2[†]	2[†]	2[†]	2[†]	2[†]
Q.	PARAGUAY	1[†]	2[†]	2	2	2[†]	2[†]	2[†]	2[†]	2[†]
R.	PERU	7	8	5	1	#	#	#	#	#
S.	URUGUAY	2	6	7	6	6	7	7[†]	7[†]	7[†]
T.	VENEZUELA	24	35	35[†]	35[†]	35[†]	35[†]	65	66	70
	UNITED STATES	3,127	4,190	5,310	7,140	7,797	7,204	6,269	6,100	5,200
	WORLD	19,144	30,739	34,886	38,235	40,277	41,303	41,512	40,097	38,470

1. A sheet material manufactured from small pieces of wood or other ligno-cellulosic materials (e.g., chip, flakes, splinters, strands, shreds, shives, etc.) agglomerated by use of an organic binder together with one or more of the following agents: heat, pressure, humidity, a catalyst, etc. (Flaxboard is included. Wood wool and other particle boards, with inorganic binders, are excluded.)

SOURCE: FAO-YFP, 1981; 1982, p. 234.

Table 2308

PLYWOOD PRODUCTION,[1] 17 LC, 1970–82

(T Me^3)

	Country	1970	1975	1976	1977	1978	1979	1980	1981	1982
A.	ARGENTINA	48	61	58	50	47	53	53	50	45
B.	BOLIVIA	1‡	2	2	3	1	4	6	6	6†
C.	BRAZIL	342‡	660	695	698†	722†	762	826	902	902†
D.	CHILE	13	13	7	9	13	16	20	18	10
E.	COLOMBIA	52	50†	75	75	75†	52	52	40	48
F.	COSTA RICA	22	40	40†	44	30	31	31	26	33
G.	CUBA	2	2†	2	2	2†	2†	2†	2†	2†
I.	ECUADOR	20	38	38	40	50	55	59	65	65
K.	GUATEMALA	1	4	4	4	4	4	4	3	1
M.	HONDURAS	6	10	11	13	9	8	8†	8†	8
N.	MEXICO	96	110	139	171	188	206	254	304	313
O.	NICARAGUA	16	10	10†	10†	10†	16	14	14†	14†
P.	PANAMA	4	7	8	12	12†	12†	12†	12†	12†
Q.	PARAGUAY	7	8	2	3†	3†	4†	4†	4†	4†
R.	PERU	33	49	76	39	24	38	49	40	37
S.	URUGUAY	12	6	4	5	6	7	7†	7†	7†
T.	VENEZUELA	33	40	40†	29‡	22‡	50	55	69	50
	UNITED STATES	14,078	14,579	16,726	17,981	17,056	17,128	14,857	16,300	13,300
	WORLD	33,174	34,292	38,795	41,283	41,788	42,279	39,202	39,573	36,900

1. Plywood, veneer plywood, core plywood including veneered wood, blockboard, laminboard, and battenboard. Other plywood such as cellular board and composite plywood.

SOURCE: FAO-YFP, 1981–82, p. 224.

Table 2309

VENEER SHEET PRODUCTION,[1] 11 LC, 1970–82

(T Me^3)

	Country	1970	1975	1976	1977	1978	1979	1980	1981	1982
A.	ARGENTINA	4	10	9	2	2	7	3	4	4
B.	BOLIVIA	#	#	3	18†	16†	19†	22†	22†	22†
C.	BRAZIL	96‡	154	169	190‡	190†	200	216	234	234†
D.	CHILE	2†	2	3	5	6	7	7	8	10
E.	COLOMBIA	5†	4†	4	4	4†	4	9	7	7
F.	COSTA RICA	3	5	5†	5	3	5	35	8	8†
I.	ECUADOR	#	1	3	3	2	2	2†	2	3
K.	GUATEMALA	#	2†	2†	1†	2†	2	2	2	1
N.	MEXICO	1	4†	7	6	28	16	8	14	10
Q.	PARAGUAY	8	8†	9	14	22†	37†	63†	63†	63†
R.	PERU	14	3†	6†	24	24	28	35	38	20
	WORLD	3,049	3,717	4,105	4,306	4,301	4,395	4,472	3,964	3,866

1. Thin sheets of wood of uniform thickness, rotary cut, sliced or sawn, for use in plywood, laminated construction, furniture, veneer containers, etc. In production the quantity given excludes veneer sheets used for plywood production within the country.

SOURCE: FAO-YFP, 1981; 1982, p. 216.

Table 2310

TOTAL WOOD PULP PRODUCTION,[1] 9 LC, 1970–82[a]
(T MET)

	Country	1970	1975	1976	1977	1978	1979	1980	1981	1982
A.	ARGENTINA	166	259	275	265	287	387	309	254	308
C.	BRAZIL	811	1,208	1,415	1,649	1,976	1,992	2,911[†]	2,833[†]	2,929[†]
D.	CHILE	356	405	515	599	665	700	763	743	667
E.	COLOMBIA	42	82	103	110	105	119	123	126	115
F.	COSTA RICA	#	#	#	#	#	5	5	3	3
N.	MEXICO	319	366	415[†]	437[†]	476[†]	461[†]	447[†]	462[†]	457[†]
R.	PERU	#	#[‡]	12[‡]	13[‡]	15[‡]	15[‡]	15[‡]	15[‡]	15[‡]
S.	URUGUAY	6	15	14	14	19	23	24	24	24[†]
T.	VENEZUELA	#	29	36	46[‡]	44[‡]	56[‡]	56[†]	56[†]	56[†]
	UNITED STATES	37,318	36,808	43,292	44,482	45,699	45,318	46,179	47,263	44,833
	WORLD	102,118	102,932	115,189	116,695	121,502	123,504	126,031	126,609	120,517

1. Wood pulp obtained by grinding or milling into their fibers, coniferous or non-coniferous rounds, quarters, billets, etc. of through refining coniferous or non-coniferous chips. Also called groundwood pulp and refiner pulp. It can be bleached or unbleached. It excludes exploded and defibrated pulp.

a. For 1962-69 data, see SALA, 21-1705.

SOURCE: FAO-YFP, 1981; 1982, p. 261.

Table 2311

TOTAL PAPER AND PAPERBOARD PRODUCTION,[1] 17 LC, 1970–82
(T MET)

	Country	1970	1975	1976	1977	1978	1979	1980	1981	1982
A.	ARGENTINA	644	650	529	539	645	789	713	669	745
B.	BOLIVIA	1[‡]	1	1[†]	1[†]	1[†]	1[†]	1[†]	1[†]	1[†]
C.	BRAZIL	1,219	1,688	2,012	2,253	2,530	2,965	2,965[†]	2,965[†]	3,228
D.	CHILE	234	266	279	296	294	276	374	327	317
E.	COLOMBIA	220	258	283	281	307	325	351	407	366
F.	COSTA RICA	5[†]	7	7	8	8[†]	11	12	15	18
G.	CUBA	80	123	123[†]	70	73	73[†]	73[†]	73[†]	73[†]
H.	DOMINICAN REP.	8	9[†]	9[†]	9[†]	9[†]	9[†]	9[†]	9[†]	9[†]
I.	ECUADOR	8	34	34	34	36	21	26	31	34
J.	EL SALVADOR	1[†]	5	5	5[†]	5	16	16	16	16[†]
K.	GUATEMALA	14	19	18	23	27	29	32	29	30
N.	MEXICO	897	1,184	1,346	1,463	1,596	1,684	1,979	1,893	1,914
P.	PANAMA	15	9	20	20[†]	20[†]	20[†]	20[†]	43	43[†]
Q.	PARAGUAY	#	1	1	1	8	12	13	13	13[†]
R.	PERU	124[†]	142	152	149	159	207	205	272[†]	357[†]
S.	URUGUAY	40[‡]	29	35	35[†]	41	52	52	44	44[†]
T.	VENEZUELA	250	395[‡]	423[‡]	464[‡]	476	479	479[†]	479[†]	479[†]
	UNITED STATES	46,117	44,896[‡]	51,122	52,795	53,396	58,907	59,457	60,463	55,064

1. Includes printing and writing paper, newsprint, other paper and paperboard products, household and sanitary paper, wrapping and packaging paper, and paperboard.

SOURCE: FAO-YFP, 1981; 1982, p. 306.

Table 2312

PRINTING AND WRITING PAPER PRODUCTION, 12 LC, 1970–82[a]

(T MET)

	Country	1970	1975	1976	1977	1978	1979	1980	1981	1982
A.	ARGENTINA	123	94	129	142	142	236	152	139	155
C.	BRAZIL	254	417	445	476	627	755	860	864	898
D.	CHILE	#	41	48	44	56	34	48	48[†]	48[†]
E.	COLOMBIA	44	44	58	61	65	66	71	84	70
G.	CUBA	20	30	30[†]	31	31[†]	31[†]	31[†]	31[†]	31[†]
I.	ECUADOR	#	3	3	3	4	4	4	5	5
K.	GUATEMALA	7	9	7	12	13	15	15	15	16
N.	MEXICO	122	256	297	304	350	360	526	427	452
P.	PANAMA	#	#	3	3[†]	3[†]	3[†]	3[†]	5	5[†]
R.	PERU	22	38[‡]	46[‡]	41[‡]	36	41	42[†]	68[†]	68[†]
S.	URUGUAY	15[‡]	11	11	11[†]	18	25	25	20	20[†]
T.	VENEZUELA	26	56[‡]	59[‡]	69[‡]	81[‡]	84[‡]	84[†]	84[†]	84[†]
	UNITED STATES	10,046	10,142[‡]	12,176	12,702	13,374	14,023	13,716	13,850	13,910
	WORLD	27,290	28,686	33,356	35,197	38,287	40,686	41,158	41,703	42,103

a. For 1962-69 data, see SALA, 21-1707.

SOURCE: FAO-YFP, 1981; 1982, p. 323.

Table 2313

NEWSPRINT PRODUCTION, 6 LC, 1970–82[a]

(T MET)

	Country	1970	1975	1976	1977	1978	1979	1980	1981	1982
A.	ARGENTINA	3	#	3	16	38	94	97	110	90
C.	BRAZIL	103	124	127	107	127	119	116	118	106
D.	CHILE	124	120	133	132	132	134	131	131	124
K.	GUATEMALA	#	1	#	#	#	#	#	#	#
N.	MEXICO	40	29	56	90	84	95	116	129	125
S.	URUGUAY	#	1	#	#	#	#	#	#	#
	UNITED STATES	3,035	3,153	3,084	3,198	3,207	3,446	4,135	4,753	4,574
	WORLD	21,563	20,648	22,095	22,473	23,725	24,931	26,181	27,385	25,966

a. For 1962-69 data see SALA, 21-1707.

SOURCE: FAO-YFP, 1981; 1982, p. 316.

Part VIII: Foreign Trade

CHAPTER 24

SELECTED COMMODITIES IN FOREIGN TRADE

Chapter Outline

Exports of Major Commodities	2400–2403	Forestry		2440
Food Trade	2404–2405	Roundwood		2441
Fish	2406–2407	Sawnwood and Sleepers		2442
Meat	2408–2412	Wood Pulp		2443
Banana	2413–2414	Paper		2444
Barley	2415–2416	Wood-Based Panel		2445
Butter	2417	Fuel		2446
Cacao Bean	2418	Fuelwood and Charcoal		2447
Cocoa	2419	Crude Oil		2448
Coffee Bean	2420–2421	Refined Oil		2449
Maize	2422–2423	Petroleum and Derivatives		2450
Milk	2424	Minerals		
Oat	2425–2426	Lead		2451
Rice	2427	Copper		2452
Soybean	2428–2430	Tin		2453
Sugar	2431–2434	Zinc		2454
Wheat	2435–2437	Manufacturing and Merchandise	2455–2457	
Wool	2438–2439	Cotton		2458
		Fertilizer	2459–2460	
		Cotton Lint		2461

Note: This volume contains statistics from numerous sources. Alternative data on many topics are presented. Variations in statistics can be attributed to differences in definition, parameters, coverage, methodology, as well as date gathered, prepared, or adjusted. See also Editor's Note on Methodology.

Table 2400

PRINCIPAL EXPORT COMMODITIES,[1] 19 LC, 1973

Country and Commodity	Value (M US)	% of Total Exports	Country and Commodity	Value (M US)	% of Total Exports
A. ARGENTINA			N. MEXICO		
Total Exports	3,268.3	100.0	Total Exports	2,633.4	100.0
Wheat	276.3	8.5	Cotton	166.1	6.3
Corn	366.1	11.2	Coffee	157.2	6.8
Meat	780.2	23.9	Lead	23.9	.9
Wool	176.8	5.4	Zinc	27.6	1.0
Hides and Skin	120.3	3.7	Sugar	122.8	4.7
B. BOLIVIA			Shrimp	100.9	3.8
Total Exports	280.0	100.0	Copper	38.3	1.5
Tin	130.1	46.5	O. NICARAGUA		
Tungsten	11.0	3.9	Total Exports	271.7	100.0
Lead	8.3	3.0	Cotton	63.2	23.3
Zinc	25.7	9.8	Coffee	44.3	16.3
Silver	12.6	4.5	Sugar	13.5	5.0
Antimony	17.2	6.1	Meat	44.5	16.4
Crude Petroleum	48.9	17.5	Cotton Seed	2.9	1.1
C. BRAZIL			P. PANAMA		
Total Exports	6,199.0	100.0	Total Exports	132.66	100.0
Coffee	1,244.0	20.1	Bananas	63.43	47.8
Cotton	218.0	3.5	Refined Petroleum	24.27	18.3
Cacao	89.0	1.4	Shrimp	16.72	12.6
Iron Ore	363.0	5.9	Q. PARAGUAY		
Sugar	455.0	7.3	Total Exports	126 93	100.0
D. CHILE			Timber	11.78	9.3
Total Exports	855.4	100.0	Cotton	11.62	9.2
Copper	630.8	73.7	Quebracho Extract	2.41	1.9
Nitrates	18.7	2.2	Hides	3.91	3.1
Iron Ore	44.5	5.2	Oilseeds	6.60	5.2
E. COLOMBIA			Meat	40.41	31.8
Total Exports	1,084.2	100.0	Tobacco	7.46	5.9
Coffee	597.0	55.1	R. PERU		
Petroleum	25.7	2.4	Total Exports	1,047.5	100.0
F. COSTA RICA			Fishmeal	135.9	13.0
Total Exports	339.30	100.0	Cotton	64.7	6.2
Bananas	93.36	27.5	Sugar	88.1	8.4
Coffee	94.01	27.7	Copper	284.3	27.1
H. DOMINICAN REP.			Silver	68.8	6.6
Total Exports	442.1	100.0	Iron Ore	60.7	5.8
Sugar	197.9	44.8	Zinc	93.3	11.2
Coffee	45.5	10.3	Lead	42.7	4.1
Cacao	24.2	5.5	Coffee	64.3	6.1
Tobacco	29.8	6.7	S. URUGUAY		
Bauxite	14.8	3.3	Total Exports	321.5	100.0
I. ECUADOR			Wool	97.5	30.3
Total Exports	541.1	100.0	Meat	127.4	39.6
Bananas	125.9	23.3	Hides	25.8	8.2
Coffee	66.7	12.3	T. VENEZUELA		
Cacao	27.1	5.0	Total Exports	4,744.9	100.0
Crude Petroleum	249.6	46.1	Petroleum	4,369.1	92.1
J. EL SALVADOR			Iron Ore	~	3.5
Total Exports	352.0	100.0	UNITED STATES		
Coffee	156.8	44.5	Total Exports	70,223	100.0
Cotton	36.4	10.3	Food and Live Animals	11,931	17.0
K. GUATEMALA			Crude Metals, Inedibles		
Total Exports	436.2	100.0	Except Fuels	8,394	11.9
Coffee	145.6	33.4	Minerals, Fuel and Related		
Bananas	18.8	4.3	Materials	1,671	2.4
Cotton	47.8	11.0	Chemicals	5,748	8.2
Sugar	21.9	5.0	Machinery and Transport		
L. HAITI			Equipment	27,842	39.6
Total Exports	51.6	100.0	Other Manufactured Goods	11,112	15.8
Coffee	20.9	40.5			
Sisal	1.6	3.1			
Sugar	3.9	7.6			
Bauxite	6.3	12.2			
M. HONDURAS					
Total Exports	236.8	100.0			
Bananas	79.7	33.7			
Coffee	46.9	19.8			
Silver	3.8	1.6			
Wood	39.1	16.5			

1. Selected exports do not add to 100.0%.

SOURCE: IMF-IFS, Jan. 1975, and U.S. *Bureau of the Census, Statistical Abstract of the United States*, 1974, table 1328. Cf. SALA, 18–2700.

Table 2401

PRINCIPAL EXPORT COMMODITIES,[1] 19 LC, 1975

Country and Commodity	Value (M US)	% of Total Exports	Country and Commodity	Value (M US)	% of Total Exports
A. ARGENTINA			N. MEXICO		
Total Exports	2,961.3	100.0	Total Exports	2,908.6	100.0
Wheat	300.7	10.2	Cotton	174.0	5.9
Corn	517.8	17.5	Coffee	184.1	6.3
Meat	281.5	9.5	Lead	~	~
Wool	104.2	3.5	Zinc	85.9	2.9
Hides and Skin	71.1	2.4	Sugar	162.1	5.5
B. BOLIVIA			Shrimp	118.5	4.0
Total Exports	443.2	100.0	Copper	~	~
Tin	182.3	41.1	O. NICARAGUA		
Tungsten	22.3	5.0	Total Exports	376.5	100.0
Lead	7.4	1.7	Cotton	95.9	25.4
Zinc	39.6	8.9	Coffee	48.2	12.8
Silver	28.5	6.4	Sugar	42.7	11.3
Antimony	17.1	3.8	Meat	27.0	7.1
Crude Petroleum	114.5	25.8	Cotton Seed	~	~
C. BRAZIL			P. PANAMA		
Total Exports	8,670.0	100.0	Total Exports	282.5	100.0
Coffee	855	9.8	Bananas	59.5	21.0
Cotton	98	1.1	Refined Petroleum	128.6	45.5
Cacao	220	2.5	Shrimp	19.0	6.7
Iron Ore	921	10.6	Q. PARAGUAY		
Sugar	974	11.2	Total Exports	173.0	100.0
D. CHILE[2]			Timber	27.7	16.0
Total Exports	2,480.5	100.0	Cotton	19.7	11.3
Copper	1,653.6	66.6	Quebracho Extract	2.5	1.4
Nitrates	496.6	20.0	Hides	1.9	1.0
Iron Ore	72.7	2.9	Oilseeds (Vegetable Oils)	10.4	6.0
E. COLOMBIA[2]			Meat	31.6	18.2
Total Exports	1,508.8	100.0	Tobacco	11.8	6.8
Coffee	624.8	41.4	R. PERU[2]		
Petroleum	4.5	.2	Total Exports	1,499.2	100.0
F. COSTA RICA			Fishmeal	195.8	13.0
Total Exports	488.5	100.0	Cotton	93.8	6.2
Bananas	132.8	27.1	Sugar	155.9	10.3
Coffee	97.0	19.8	Copper	347.9	23.2
H. DOMINICAN REP.			Silver	165.0	11.0
Total Exports	893.8	100.0	Iron Ore	60.1	4.0
Sugar	577.2	64.5	Zinc	160.0	10.6
Coffee	43.2	4.8	Lead	25.8	1.7
Cacao	29.0	3.2	Coffee	34.8	2.3
Tobacco	34.5	3.8	S. URUGUAY		
Bauxite	16.7	1.8	Total Exports	383.8	100.0
I. ECUADOR			Wool	86.6	22.5
Total Exports	910.3	100.0	Meat	73.4	19.1
Bananas	155.6	17.0	Hides	16.6	4.3
Coffee	64.3	7.0	T. VENEZUELA		
Cacao	42.3	4.6	Total Exports	10,134.4	100.0
Crude Petroleum	515.9	56.6	Petroleum	9,653.9	95.2
J. EL SALVADOR			Iron Ore	~	~
Total Exports	514.7	100.0	UNITED STATES[2]		
Coffee	168.7	32.7	Total Exports	97,143	100.0
Cotton	76.3	14.8	Food and Live Animals	13,983	14.4
K. GUATEMALA			Crude Metals, Inedibles Except Fuels	10,934	11.3
Total Exports	646.8	100.0	Minerals, Fuel and Related Materials	3,442	3.5
Coffee	161.7	25.0	Chemicals	8,822	9.1
Bananas	26.9	4.1	Machinery and Transport Equipment	38,189	39.3
Cotton	74.0	11.4	Other Manufactured Goods	16,516	17.0
Sugar	115.6	17.8			
L. HAITI[2]					
Total Exports	71.6	100.0			
Coffee	23.8	33.2			
Sisal	3.2	4.4			
Sugar	6.4	8.9			
Bauxite	5.9	8.2			
M. HONDURAS					
Total Exports	283.3	100.0			
Bananas	45.3	15.9			
Coffee	57.1	20.1			
Silver	13.7	4.8			
Wood	39.1	13.8			

1. Principal exports do not add to 100.0%.
2. 1974.

SOURCE: IMF-IFS, Jan. 1975, Sept. 1976; and U.S. Bureau of the Census, *Statistical Abstract of the United States*, 1974, table 1328. Cf. SALA, 18-2709.

Table 2402

TWO LEADING EXPORTS AS SHARE OF TOTAL EXPORT VALUE, 20 LC, 1955-73

Country	1955 Exports	% of Total	1960 Exports	% of Total	1965 Exports	% of Total	1970 Exports	% of Total	1973 Exports	% of Total
A. ARGENTINA	Cereals	27.4	Meats	30.5	Wheat	24.9	Meat	24.7	Meat	23.9
	Meats	26.3	Cereals	29.4	Meat	22.0	Corn	14.9	Corn	11.2
B. BOLIVIA	Tin	54.9	Tin	64.8	Tin	67.0	Tin	56.8	Tin	50.3
	Wolframite	13.4	Lead	7.3	Silver	4.7	Antimony	16.3	Petroleum	18.8
C. BRAZIL	Coffee	60.8	Coffee	56.2	Coffee	43.9	Coffee	34.3	Coffee	20.1
	Cacao	5.0	Cacao	7.4	Cotton	6.4	Iron Ore	12.0	Sugar	7.3
D. CHILE	Metal and Ores	85.6	Copper	70.1	Copper	70.1	Copper	75.8	Copper	73.7
	Iron	3.8	Iron Ore	6.4	Iron Ore	11.4	Iron Ore	6.6	Iron Ore	5.2
E. COLOMBIA	Coffee	76.7	Coffee	71.7	Coffee	64.8	Coffee	56.6	Coffee	55.1
	Petroleum	14.9	Petroleum	17.2	Petroleum	13.9	Petroleum	9.3	Petroleum	2.4
F. COSTA RICA	Coffee	48.6	Coffee	49.3	Coffee	37.9	Coffee	31.8	Coffee	27.7
	Bananas	38.7	Bananas	28.0	Bananas	24.0	Bananas	29.0	Bananas	27.5
G. CUBA	Sugar	81.2	Sugar	75.7	Sugar	74.4	Sugar	76.9	Sugar	64.6a
	Tobacco	5.9	Tobacco	10.2	Nickel, Cobalt	.4	Nickel, Cobalt	16.5	Nickel, Cobalt	14.7a
H. DOMINICAN REP.	Sugar	58.6	Sugar	49.6	Sugar	55.8	Sugar	51.8	Sugar	44.8
	Coffee	15.6	Coffee	12.6	Coffee	15.3	Coffee	13.5	Coffee	10.3
I. ECUADOR	Bananas	35.6	Bananas	61.5	Bananas	57.0	Bananas	50.9	Petroleum	46.1
	Coffee	30.4	Coffee	15.0	Coffee	14.7	Coffee	23.1	Bananas	23.3
J. EL SALVADOR	Coffee	78.2	Coffee	69.3	Coffee	46.3	Coffee	49.6	Coffee	44.5
	Cotton	15.6	Cotton	13.5	Cotton	14.2	Cotton	10.1	Cotton	10.3
K. GUATEMALA	Coffee	79.0	Coffee	65.8	Coffee	49.1	Coffee	34.4	Coffee	33.4
	Bananas	8.0	Bananas	16.7	Cotton	18.4	Cotton	9.1	Cotton	11.0
L. HAITI	Coffee	71.9	Coffee	55.6	Coffee	54.8	Coffee	38.1	Coffee	40.5
	Sisal	13.6	Sisal	12.2	Sisal	7.2	Bauxite	16.4	Bauxite	12.2
M. HONDURAS	Bananas	61.1	Bananas	46.1	Bananas	49.8	Bananas	40.6	Bananas	33.6
	Coffee	19.0	Coffee	18.9	Coffee	13.6	Coffee	14.7	Coffee	19.8
N. MEXICO	Cotton	14.5	Cotton	20.7	Cotton	19.7	Cotton	8.8	Cotton	6.3
	Coffee	13.2	Coffee	9.4	Coffee	7.4	Sugar	7.0	Coffee	6.0
O. NICARAGUA	Coffee	40.0	Coffee	34.4	Cotton	41.3	Cotton	29.4	Cotton	23.3
	Cotton	30.6	Cotton	26.3	Coffee	15.8	Meat	13.5	Meat	16.4
P. PANAMA	Bananas	64.0	Bananas	72.9	Bananas	49.8	Bananas	57.4	Bananas	47.8
	Shrimp	25.8	Refined Petroleum	3.8	Refined Petroleum	29.0	Refined Petroleum	18.8	Refined Petroleum	18.3
Q. PARAGUAY	Woods	37.2	Meat	26.5	Meat	28.6	Meat	23.9	Meat	31.8
	Quebracho Extract	20.4	Wood	18.6	Timber	21.7	Timber	19.7	Timber	9.3
R. PERU	Cotton	25.1	Cotton	16.9	Fishmeal	24.4	Fishmeal	27.6	Copper	27.1
	Lead	11.9	Sugar	11.0	Copper	23.8	Copper	25.0	Fishmeal	13.0
S. URUGUAY	Wool	51.0	Wool	34.8	Wool	45.4	Meat	37.7	Meat	39.6
	Meat	19.7	Meat	23.8	Meat	24.3	Wool	31.5	Wool	30.3
T. VENEZUELA	Petroleum	91.9	Petroleum	90.6	Petroleum	93.6	Petroleum	90.2	Petroleum	92.1
	Iron Ore	4.8	Iron Ore	6.8	Iron Ore	5.0	Iron Ore	5.7	Iron Ore	3.5
UNITED STATES	Manufactured Goods	54.8	Machinery	34.3	Machinery	20.4	Machinery	43.7	Machinery	39.6
	Semi-Manufactured Goods	15.6	Vegetable Food Products	8.6	Motor Vehicles	7.2	Other Manufactured Goods	18.7	Food, Live Animals	17.0

a. 1972.

SOURCE: IMF-IFS, Jan. 1975, Dec. 1969, Aug. 1967, Aug. 1961, Sept. 1958, Mar. 1976, and Jan. 1971. Cuban data beginning 1960 are from UCLA, 6 (1962) and 10 (1966), UCLA-Cuba, and Cuba, DGE, AE, 1973. Cf. SALA, 18-2801.

Table 2403

CONTRIBUTION OF THE THIRTEEN MAIN LATIN AMERICAN PRIMARY EXPORT PRODUCTS TO EACH COUNTRY'S TOTAL VALUE OF MERCHANDISE EXPORTS, 19 LR, 1971-81

(%)

Country	Beef 1971-75	Beef 1976-80	Beef 1981‡	Maize 1971-75	Maize 1976-80	Maize 1981‡	Bananas 1971-75	Bananas 1976-80	Bananas 1981‡	Sugar 1971-75	Sugar 1976-80	Sugar 1981‡	Coffee 1971-75	Coffee 1976-80	Coffee 1981‡
A. ARGENTINA	11.0	7.6	5.7	14.2	8.1	14.3	#	#	#	2.4	1.7	2.9	#	#	#
B. BOLIVIA	.4	#	#	#	#	#	.3	.1	#	3.1	4.3	.3	1.5	2.2	1.8
C. BRAZIL	1.5	.1	.5	1.3	.4	#	.3	.1	.1	11.3	3.0	2.9	15.9	15.4	6.5
D. CHILE	#	#	#	#	#	#	#	#	#	#	#	#	#	#	#
E. COLOMBIA	2.3	.9	1.3	#	#	#	1.8	2.3	3.7	4.3	2.1	2.6	48.5	61.2	50.0
F. COSTA RICA	8.2	7.0	7.9	#	#	#	25.2	17.7	26.5	6.4	2.8	4.6	25.3	31.4	25.9
H. DOMINICAN REP.	1.3	.5	.7	#	#	#	.2	.1	.2	52.7	27.8	43.5	6.3	14.4	5.2
I. ECUADOR	#	#	#	#	#	#	17.3	10.3	8.2	2.3	.9	.6	8.7	12.1	4.2
J. EL SALVADOR	.7	.8	.1	.3	.2	.5	#	#	#	8.8	3.2	1.9	37.7	48.6	18.5
K. GUATEMALA	4.2	1.6	2.4	#	#	#	4.0	2.1	4.4	9.3	6.0	6.2	29.8	35.6	22.6
L. HAITI	1.5	1.0	2.2	#	#	#	#	#	#	6.8	1.7	.7	32.0	43.6	21.5
M. HONDURAS	6.8	6.6	5.7	.1	.1	.2	29.1	24.1	29.0	1.2	1.7	4.5	15.3	28.0	13.8
N. MEXICO	1.6	.4	#	.4	#	#	#	#	#	5.4	.1	#	6.0	7.1	1.8
O. NICARAGUA	10.9	10.4	8.2	.3	#	#	1.3	1.0	1.8	6.5	5.0	10.4	13.7	28.6	27.3
P. PANAMA	1.1	.8	1.6	#	#	#	34.5	24.2	21.8	11.1	11.9	16.1	1.2	2.8	4.3
Q. PARAGUAY	9.3	1.1	.3	.2	.3	#	#	#	#	3.0	.3	#	2.4	2.2	#
R. PERU	#	#	#	#	#	#	#	#	#	12.0	2.2	#	4.1	7.0	2.9
S. URUGUAY	31.8	14.8	17.6	#	.1	#	#	#	#	.1	#	#	#	#	#
T. VENEZUELA	#	#	#	#	#	#	#	#	#	#	#	#	.3	.2	#
LATIN AMERICA¹	2.4	1.3	1.1	1.7	.9	1.3	1.5	1.0	.9	6.1	2.1	2.0	8.1	10.2	4.5

Country	Cocoa 1971-75	Cocoa 1976-80	Cocoa 1981‡	Fishmeal 1971-75	Fishmeal 1976-80	Fishmeal 1981‡	Soybeans 1971-75	Soybeans 1976-80	Soybeans 1981‡	Cotton 1971-75	Cotton 1976-80	Cotton 1981‡	Iron Ore 1971-75	Iron Ore 1976-80	Iron Ore 1981‡
A. ARGENTINA	#	#	#	.1	.2	#	.1	7.1	7.8	.4	1.7	.3	#	#	#
B. BOLIVIA	#	#	#	#	#	#	#	#	#	3.8	1.2	#	#	#	#
C. BRAZIL	3.2	4.9	1.7	--	#	#	7.9	11.1	10.9	2.5	.2	.2	7.8	7.3	4.9
D. CHILE	#	#	#	1.5	4.1	5.1	#	#	#	#	#	#	5.6	4.6	4.2
E. COLOMBIA	1.4	.6	#	#	#	#	#	#	#	4.2	2.4	3.1	#	#	#
F. COSTA RICA	5.0	2.1	.4	#	#	#	#	#	#	#	.3	#	#	#	#
H. DOMINICAN REP.	9.0	9.0	3.9	#	#	#	#	#	#	#	.1	#	#	#	#
I. ECUADOR	8.0	9.9	5.2	#	#	#	#	#	#	#	#	#	#	#	#
J. EL SALVADOR	.1	.6	.3	#	#	#	#	#	#	11.7	11.4	6.8	#	#	#
K. GUATEMALA	.1	.6	.3	#	#	#	#	#	#	11.1	12.2	11.1	#	#	#
L. HAITI	1.0	3.0	2.1	#	#	#	#	#	#	#	#	#	#	#	#
M. HONDURAS	#	.1	.1	#	#	#	#	#	#	.8	1.6	1.6	#	#	#
N. MEXICO	.4	.4	#	#	#	#	#	#	#	6.0	3.3	1.6	#	#	#
O. NICARAGUA	.1	.1	.3	#	#	#	#	#	#	27.1	20.7	26.7	#	#	#
P. PANAMA	.2	.9	#	1.0	2.0	#	#	#	#	#	#	#	#	#	#
Q. PARAGUAY	#	#	#	#	#	#	6.9	19.2	4.2	6.1	28.5	4.0	#	#	#
R. PERU	#	.2	#	17.7	23.1	19.8	#	#	#	5.4	2.3	1.8	7.0	5.2	5.8
S. URUGUAY	.2	.2	#	#	#	#	#	#	#	#	.2	.5	#	#	#
T. VENEZUELA	.2	.2	.1	#	#	#	#	#	#	#	#	#	3.4	1.7	#
LATIN AMERICA¹	1.1	1.6	.6	.8	1.2	1.4	2.4	3.2	3.3	2.2	1.5	1.0	3.0	2.3	1.5

Table 2403 (Continued)

CONTRIBUTION OF THE THIRTEEN MAIN LATIN AMERICAN PRIMARY EXPORT PRODUCTS TO EACH COUNTRY'S TOTAL VALUE OF MERCHANDISE EXPORTS, 19 LR, 1971-81

(%)

Country	Bauxite			Copper			Petroleum			Total 13 Products			Total Merchandise Exports
	1971-75	1976-80	1981‡	1971-75	1976-80	1981‡	1971-75	1976-80	1981‡	1971-75	1976-80	1981‡	
A. ARGENTINA	#	#	#	#	#	#	.1	#	.2	28.3	26.4	31.2	100.0
B. BOLIVIA	#	#	#	#	#	#	24.3	5.3	#	33.1	13.0	2.1	100.0
C. BRAZIL	#	.1	.5	#	#	#	.5	.1	.8	52.2	42.8	29.1	100.0
D. CHILE	#	#	#	72.2	38.9	36.1	#	#	#	79.3	47.6	45.4	100.0
E. COLOMBIA	#	#	#	#	#	#	1.9	#	#	61.1	69.5	60.7	100.0
F. COSTA RICA	#	#	#	#	#	#	#	#	#	66.5	61.3	65.3	100.0
H. DOMINICAN REP.	3.1	2.5	1.3	#	#	#	#	#	#	68.6	54.3	54.8	100.0
I. ECUADOR	#	#	#	#	#	#	47.9	45.4	61.4	84.2	78.7	79.6	100.0
J. EL SALVADOR	#	#	#	#	#	#	#	#	#	59.2	64.2	27.8	100.0
K. GUATEMALA	#	#	#	#	#	#	#	#	#	58.5	58.1	47.0	100.0
L. HAITI	12.2	10.2	11.6	#	#	#	#	#	#	53.5	59.5	38.1	100.0
M. HONDURAS	#	#	#	#	#	#	#	#	#	53.3	62.2	54.9	100.0
N. MEXICO	#	#	#	.8	.1	#	4.2	46.0	73.1	24.8	57.8	76.5	100.0
O. NICARAGUA	#	#	#	.5	#	#	#	#	#	60.4	65.8	74.4	100.0
P. PANAMA	#	#	#	#	#	#	#	#	#	49.1	42.6	43.8	100.0
Q. PARAGUAY	#	#	#	#	#	#	#	#	#	27.9	51.6	8.5	100.0
R. PERU	#	#	#	16.1	42.5	43.9	.5	.3	#	62.8	82.8	74.2	100.0
S. URUGUAY	#	#	#	#	#	#	#	#	#	31.8	15.1	18.1	100.0
T. VENEZUELA	#	#	#	#	#	#	61.6	55.5	69.1	65.6	57.6	69.2	100.0
LATIN AMERICA¹	.9	.7	.6	4.5	3.5	2.8	16.6	59.7	30.6	51.3	89.2	51.6	100.0

1. Excludes Bahamas, Barbados, Guyana, Suriname, and Trinidad and Tobago.

SOURCE: IDB-SPTF, 1983, pp. 390-392.

Figure 24:1

SHARE OF FOURTEEN MAJOR COMMODITY EXPORTS IN LATIN AMERICA'S TOTAL EXPORT EARNINGS,[1] 1960–81

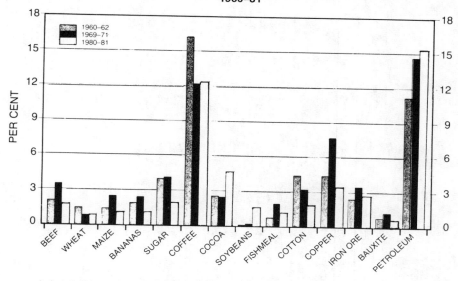

1. Includes Bahamas, Barbados, Guyana, Jamaica, and Trinidad and Tobago.

SOURCE: IDB-SPTF, 1983, p. 13.

Table 2404

FOOD TRADE BY CATEGORY,[1] 19 LC, 1981-82 (M US)[2]

Country	Cereals and Preparations		Meat and Preparations		Dairy Products and Eggs		Fruits and Vegetables		Sugar and Honey		Animal and Vegetable Oils		Subtotal		Coffee, Tea, and Cocoa		Total	
	Exports	Imports	Exports	Imports	Exports	Imports	Exports	Imports	Exports	Imports	Exports	Imports	Exports	Imports	Exports	Imports	Exports	Imports
A. ARGENTINA	2,340.6	6.2	995.9	21.0	38.0	17.0	398.2	104.4	204.2	10.6	406.1	7.6	4,383.0	166.6	36.7	126.9	4,419.7	293.7
B. BOLIVIA	.1	54.8	~	.8	~	15.0	3.4	4.4	15.8	1.5	~	8.5	19.3	85.0	25.3	2.5	44.6	87.5
C. BRAZIL	61.6	1,186.1	837.8	48.6	14.8	23.1	814.8	224.2	873.9	3.6	710.7	43.1	3,313.6	1,528.7	2,575.2	6.3	5,888.8	1,535.0
D. CHILE	14.9	263.1	6.3	30.3		38.3	279.7	32.8	6.9	55.0	1.4	52.2	309.2	471.7	~	55.0	309.2	526.7
E. COLOMBIA	10.6	150.1	49.6	2.5	13.4	34.2	156.0	59.1	78.8	5.3	~	121.4	308.4	372.6	1,527.4	11.7	1,835.8	384.3
F. COSTA RICA	19.1	46.5	73.3	3.5	.1	7.1	234.0	17.6	29.1	2.5	.2[a]	6.7	360.8	83.9	248.3	2.5	609.1	86.4
H. DOMINICAN REP.	1.3	78.6	8.7	13.5	.1[b]	11.2	30.0	5.3	410.8	2.7	.8	53.2	451.7	164.5	141.1	.5	592.8	165.0
I. ECUADOR	.2[a]	76.1	.7[b]	.3	~	5.5	212.4	4.5	12.9	2.1	2.9	34.0	229.1	122.5	279.0	.7	508.1	123.2
J. EL SALVADOR	6.1	40.5	2.6	2.3	.5	19.4	5.3	47.2	25.8	14.8	.6	18.9	40.9	143.1	436.3	3.5	477.2	146.6
K. GUATEMALA	6.7	43.7	51.3	2.1	2.7	11.5	89.3	11.6	73.8	2.8	~	14.3	233.8	86.0	241.5	2.7	465.3	88.7
L. HAITI	~	57.8	3.1	2.7	~	12.2	2.0	2.9	1.6	8.2	~	21.5	6.7	105.3	52.0	1.2	58.7	106.5
M. HONDURAS	1.3	31.2	41.1	2.7	~	12.9	244.5	6.3	40.8	1.2	.3[b]	5.9	328.0	60.2	164.2	1.5	492.2	61.7
N. MEXICO	4.8	753.8	25.0	85.0	~	216.1	433.0	269.1	21.7	254.2	2.4	111.4	496.9	1,689.6	378.6	21.4	875.5	1,711.0
O. NICARAGUA	4.9	38.9	34.2	6.1	~	15.2	20.7	21.8	43.7	2.7	1.1	14.6	104.6	99.3	131.9	1.4	236.5	100.7
P. PANAMA	3.3[a]	31.3	4.8	13.8	7.6	12.9	76.3	27.4	39.2	2.1	~	15.8	131.2	103.3	13.4	4.8	144.6	108.1
Q. PARAGUAY	.4	13.2	1.0	.8	~	2.6	8.2	2.2	2.0	.7	~	20.7	11.6	40.2	~	1.0	11.6	41.2
R. PERU	2.4	263.8	2.1	45.4	.2	47.6	7.8	7.5	45.0	53.4	1.7	37.6	59.2	455.3	109.3	3.5	168.5	458.8
S. URUGUAY	147.5	18.3	238.1	4.8	20.4	1.3	13.3	22.7	5.3	12.7	6.4	3.3	431.0	63.1	1.8	30.8	432.8	93.9
T. VENEZUELA	4.6	569.5	.6[a]	94.9	.1[a]	202.3	28.2	169.3	~	265.7	~	143.9	33.5	1,445.6	26.3	8.6	59.8	1,454.2
LATIN AMERICA	2,707.0	3,965.5	2,383.3	502.1	100.0	835.1	3,101.4	1,138.7	2,141.3	737.9	1,156.4	781.0	11,590.0	7,960.3	6,420.2	308.7	18,010.2	8,269.0

1. Category by FAO classification.
2. Exports are valued fob and imports cif.

a. 1981 only.
b. 1982 only.

SOURCE: IDB-SPTF, 1984, table 8.

Table 2405

FOOD TRADE BALANCES, 20 L, 1961–75

(M US)

Division	Exports (FOB)			Imports (CIF)			Balance		
	1961	1971	1975	1961	1971	1975	1961	1971	1975
LAFTA	3,284	5,290	10,496	871	1,454	3,835	2,413	3,836	6,661
Andean Pact	650	974	2,102	472	741	1,610	178	233	492
B. BOLIVIA	3	13	73	22	38	57	−19	−25	16
D. CHILE	36	43	120	123	232	455	−32	−189	−335
E. COLOMBIA	343	534	1,132	64	106	153	279	428	979
I. ECUADOR	135	188	352	13	23	96	122	165	256
R. PERU	100	162	358	63	136	321	37	26	37
T. VENEZUELA	33	34	67	187	206	528	−154	−172	−461
Other LAFTA	2,634	4,316	8,394	399	713	2,225	(2,725)	3,603	6,169
A. ARGENTINA	938	1,452	2,169	85	129	217	853	1,323	1,952
C. BRAZIL	1,145	1,941	4,845	211	325	881	934	1,616	3,964
N. MEXICO	364	700	960	62	193	985	302	507	−25
Q. PARAGUAY	22	51	129	8	25	69	14	26	60
S. URUGUAY	165	172	291	33	41	73	132	131	218
CACM	397	813	1,555	67	148	270	330	665	1,285
F. COSTA RICA	76	169	373	13	43	78	63	126	295
J. EL SALVADOR	110	160	348	20	32	48	90	128	300
K. GUATEMALA	106	198	417	17	31	58	89	167	359
M. HONDURAS	51	145	145	9	19	43	42	126	102
O. NICARAGUA	54	141	272	8	23	43	46	118	229
Other Latin America	177	1,031	4,380	35	410	824	142	621	3,556
G. CUBA	~	721	3,503	~	313	601	~	408	2,902
H. DOMINICAN REP.	126	211	712	6	40	127	120	171	585
L. HAITI	23	26	37	11	16	46	12	10	−9
P. PANAMA	28	73	128	18	41	50	10	32	78
Total Latin America	3,858	7,134	16,431	973	2,012	4,929	2,885	5,122	11,502

SOURCE: *25 Años en la Agricultura: Rasgos Principales, 1950–75*
(Santiago: ECLA, 1979), Anexo 14.

Table 2406

FISH EXPORTS,[1] 9 LC, 1978–82

	Country	Value of Exports (T US)					Value as % of World Exports				
		1978	1979	1980	1981	1982	1978	1979	1980	1981	1982
A.	ARGENTINA	106,014	144,340	126,908	196,882[†]	161,748[†]	2.8	3.1	2.7	3.8[†]	3.2[†]
C.	BRAZIL	25,434	26,054	36,605	43,089	34,452	#	#	#	#	#
D.	CHILE	6,865	26,800	37,909	41,586[†]	40,423[†]	#	#	#	#[†]	#[†]
E.	COLOMBIA	7,128	8,818	13,591	15,451	9,175	#	#	#	#	#
G.	CUBA	18,099	25,136	30,984	62,274[†]	53,279[†]	#	#	#	#[†]	#[†]
I.	ECUADOR	10,707	19,185	23,319[†]	23,893[†]	21,487[†]	#	#	#[†]	#[†]	#[†]
N.	MEXICO	26,120	18,386	2,459[†]	2,647[†]	13,639[†]	#	#	#[†]	#[†]	#[†]
R.	PERU	29,725	35,127	36,013	15,961	10,438	#	#	#	#	#
S.	URUGUAY	21,277	33,140	47,399	55,734	43,872	#	#	#	#	#
	LAIA	233,521	312,084	324,532	395,343[†]	352,612[†]	6.2	6.7	6.8	7.7[†]	6.9[†]
	CACM	3,726	5,077	2,645	2,570	627[†]	.1	.1	.1	#	#[†]
	UNITED STATES	366,435	460,207	363,324	545,055	588,079	9.7	9.9	7.6	10.6	11.6

1. Fresh, chilled, and frozen.

SOURCE: UN-YITS, 1982, vol. 2, p. 21.

Table 2407

FISHERY EXPORTS, 11 OASL, 1970-80

(% and M US)

Category	1970		%[a]	1975		%[a]	1980		%[a]
Total fishery commodities	R.	PERU	65	R.	PERU	33	N.	MEXICO	30
	N.	MEXICO	14	N.	MEXICO	25	D.	CHILE	19
	D.	CHILE	5	C.	BRAZIL	7	R.	PERU	16
				D.	CHILE	6	I.	ECUADOR	9
				I.	ECUADOR	6	A.	ARGENTINA	7
							B.	BRAZIL	7
		Rest of OASL	16		Rest of OASL	23		Rest of OASL	12
Total Value		$518.7	100		$640.7	100		$1,942.7	100
Fish, fresh, chilled, or frozen	R.	PERU	21	A.	ARGENTINA	26	A.	ARGENTINA	38
	N.	MEXICO	17	C.	BRAZIL	17	S.	URUGUAY	14
	I.	ECUADOR	15	I.	ECUADOR	15	D.	CHILE	13
	C.	BRAZIL	15	R.	PERU	14	C.	BRAZIL	11
	A.	ARGENTINA	14	N.	MEXICO	9	R.	PERU	10
	D.	CHILE	5	T.	VENEZUELA	6	I.	ECUADOR	5
				S.	URUGUAY	5	N.	MEXICO	5
		Rest of OASL	13		Rest of OASL	8		Rest of OASL	4
Total Value		$14.9	100		$65.7	100		$327.8	100
Fish, dried, salted or smoked	A.	ARGENTINA	61	A.	ARGENTINA	43	R.	PERU	40
	T.	VENEZUELA	18	T.	VENEZUELA	30	A.	ARGENTINA	28
	R.	PERU	5	N.	MEXICO	8	N.	MEXICO	16
				R.	PERU	5	C.	BRAZIL	10
		Rest of OASL	16		Rest of OASL	14		Rest of OASL	6
Total Value		$.8	100		$4.1	100		$17.5	100
Crustaceans and mollusks, fresh, frozen, dried, salted, etc.	N.	MEXICO	47	N.	MEXICO	48	N.	MEXICO	60
	C.	BRAZIL	12	C.	BRAZIL	10	C.	BRAZIL	10
	P.	PANAMA	7	P.	PANAMA	6	D.	ECUADOR	7
	T.	VENEZUELA	7	I.	ECUADOR	5	P.	PANAMA	5
				O.	NICARAGUA	5			
		Rest of OASL	27		Rest of OASL	26		Rest of OASL	18
Total Value		$138.7	100		$305.5	100		$898.6	100
Fish products and preparations, whether or not in airtight containers	R.	PERU	56	I.	ECUADOR	43	R.	PERU	38
	I.	ECUADOR	29	R.	PERU	26	I.	ECUADOR	33
	F.	COSTA RICA	8	N.	MEXICO	7	D.	CHILE	17
	T.	VENEZUELA	5	F.	COSTA RICA	7	N.	MEXICO	5
				C.	BRAZIL	6			
		Rest of OASL	2		Rest of OASL	11		Rest of OASL	7
Total Value		$4.9	100		$15.5	100		$144.6	100
Crustacean and mollusk products and preparations, whether or not in airtight containers	N.	MEXICO	54	D.	CHILE	47	N.	MEXICO	62
	D.	CHILE	40	N.	MEXICO	38	D.	CHILE	29
				T.	VENEZUELA	8	F.	COSTA RICA	6
		Rest of OASL	6		Rest of OASL	7		Rest of OASL	3
Total Value		$6.9	100		$18.2	100		$24.8	100
Oils and fats, crude or refined, of aquatic animal origin	R.	PERU	92	R.	PERU	89	D.	CHILE	85
	D.	CHILE	7	D.	CHILE	8	R.	PERU	8
		Rest of OASL	1		Rest of OASL	3		Rest of OASL	7
Total Value		$40.9	100		$41.9	100		$41.4	100
Meals, solubles, and similar animal feed-ingstuffs, of aquatic animal origin	R.	PERU	94	R.	PERU	85	D.	CHILE	48
	D.	CHILE	5	D.	CHILE	11	R.	PERU	43
							I.	ECUADOR	7
		Rest of OASL	1		Rest of OASL	4		Rest of OASL	2
Total Value		$311.5	100		$189.8	100		$488.0	100

a. Percentage of total fishery exports for Latin America.

SOURCE: IDB-SPTF, 1983, p. 86.

Table 2408

MEAT IMPORT VOLUME,[1] 16 L, 1975–82[a]

(T MET)

	Country	1975	1976	1977	1978	1979	1980	1981	1982
A.	ARGENTINA	~	~	#	#	9	20	11	13
B.	BOLIVIA	~	~	#	~	~	~	~	~
C.	BRAZIL	244	242	27	122	122	70	66	22
D.	CHILE	11	1	4	14	6	11	17	11
E.	COLOMBIA	~	~	#	#	#	#	.5	1
F.	COSTA RICA	9	7	1	3	2	2	#	#
G.	CUBA	~	~	6	11	16	20	22	23
H.	DOMINICAN REP.[3]	14	14	#	#	2	12	11	10
J.	EL SALVADOR	3	3	#	#	#	.5	#	#
K.	GUATEMALA	~	~	#	1	.5	#	.6	#
M.	HONDURAS	~	~	#	#	#	#	#	#
N.	MEXICO[4,3]	147	29	19	11	45	47	94	90
O.	NICARAGUA[3]	3	4	#	#	#	3	3	3
P.	PANAMA[2]	1	1	#	#	#	#	1	2
R.	PERU	157	167	8	4	1	7	25	39
T.	VENEZUELA[3]	102	102	40	75	56	27	47	52[‡]

1. Includes meat fresh, chilled, and frozen. Figures refer to "special trade" except where otherwise noted. "Special" imports include goods for domestic consumption and withdrawals from bonded warehouses or free zones for purposes of domestic consumption.
2. Data exclude the free zone of Colón and the Canal Zone.
3. Figures refer to "general trade," i.e., total imports.
4. Imports through free zones are included.

a. For 1934–74, see SALA, 20-2927.

SOURCE: FAO-TY, 1978; FAO-TY, 1980, table 10; FAO-TY, 1981, table 10; FAO-TY, 1982, table 10.

Table 2409

MEAT EXPORT VOLUME,[1] 17 LC, 1975–82[a]

(T MET)

	Country	1975	1976	1977	1978	1979	1980	1981	1982
A.	ARGENTINA	79	3,831	389	481	489	313	342	363
B.	BOLIVIA	2	~	.1	~	~	~	~	~
C.	BRAZIL	5	91	116	110	120	213	383	428
D.	CHILE	- -	3	3	2	4	5	4	4
E.	COLOMBIA	18	3	14	30	16	12	22	16
F.	COSTA RICA	29	31	32	35	32	26	33	29
H.	DOMINICAN REP.[2]	4	6	1	1	1	1	4	4
J.	EL SALVADOR	2	6	3	5	5	2	.6	2
K.	GUATEMALA	15	10	19	15	16	11	15	14
L.	HAITI[2]	~	1	1	1	2	.7	2[‡]	2
M.	HONDURAS	23	21	18	23	30	29	23	16
N.	MEXICO[2]	5	22	36	55	26	19	14	11
O.	NICARAGUA[2]	22	28	28	37	38	21	15	15
P.	PANAMA[4]	1	3	1	.3	.6	1	2	2
Q.	PARAGUAY	8	20	4	4	4	1	1	1
R.	PERU	2[†]	2[‡]	2[†]	2[‡]	2	1	1	1
S.	URUGUAY[2]	79	155	120	103	69	113	167	143
	UNITED STATES[2,3]	370	572	574	578	597	731	800	674
	WORLD	2,394	6,163	6,744	7,070	7,838	8,115	8,889	8,638

1. Includes meat fresh, chilled or frozen. Figures refer to "special trade" except where otherwise indicated. "Special" exports comprise exports of goods wholly or partly produced or manufactured in the country, together with exports of "nationalized" goods, but not of goods held in bonded warehouses or free zones.
2. Figures refer to "general trade," i.e., total exports including re-exports.
3. The customs area includes the Commonwealth of Puerto Rico.
4. Data exclude the free zone of Colón and the Canal Zone.

a. For 1934–74, see SALA, 20-2925. See SALA, 20-2926 for comparison of Argentina and Australia beef cattle exports.

SOURCE: FAO-TY, 1978; FAO-TY, 1980, table 10; FAO-TY, 1981, table 10.

Table 2410

MEAT EXPORTS,[1] 15 LC, 1978–82

	Country	Value of Exports (T US)					Value as % of World Exports				
		1978	1979	1980	1981	1982	1978	1979	1980	1981	1982
A.	ARGENTINA	381,695	678,741	519,738	522,209	455,819	6.5	8.8	6.4	6.9	6.1
C.	BRAZIL	16,945	7,996	18,399	123,568	188,288	#	#	#	#	#
D.	CHILE	~	1,355[†]	36	2,026[†]	1,970[†]	~	#[†]	#	#[†]	#[†]
E.	COLOMBIA	33,723	28,083	26,917	53,217	45,386	#	#	#	#	#
F.	COSTA RICA	60,339	81,667	70,722	73,948	~	#	#	#	#	~
H.	DOMINICAN REP.	2,339	3,503	2,883	8,435	8,829	#	#	#	#	#
J.	EL SALVADOR	12,494	13,530	4,146	961	4,643[†]	#	#	#	#	#[†]
K.	GUATEMALA	30,772	4,238	34,735	30,572	17,988[†]	#	#	#	#	#[†]
L.	HAITI	1,207	616[†]	941[†]	654[†]	675[†]	#	#[†]	#[†]	#[†]	#[†]
M.	HONDURAS	38,818	60,733	60,739	46,471	44,328[†]	#	#	#	#	#[†]
N.	MEXICO	60,310	2,513	3,006[†]	2,839[†]	4,689[†]	#	#	#[†]	#[†]	#[†]
O.	NICARAGUA	88,228	105,609	58,551	21,232	31,404	#	#	#	#	#
P.	PANAMA	462	1,526	3,148	5,066	9,392	#	#	#	#	#
Q.	PARAGUAY	3,403	4,330	32	259[†]	788[†]	#	#	#	#[†]	#[†]
S.	URUGUAY	80,019	95,359	155,777	214,476	171,174	#	#	#	#	#
	LAIA	576,132	818,379	723,962	918,649	868,160	9.8	10.6	9.0	12.2	11.7
	CACM	230,651	265,778	228,893	173,186	98,363[†]	3.9	3.5	2.8	2.3	1.3[†]
	UNITED STATES	187,614	228,224	235,436	280,732	352,286	3.2	3.0	2.9	3.7	4.7

1. Bovine, fresh and frozen.

SOURCE: UN-YITS, 1982, Vol. 2, p. 256.

Table 2411

MEAT (FRESH) EXPORT VOLUME, 15 LRC, 1960–75

(T MET)

Country	1960	1961	1962	1963	1964	1965	1966	1967	1968	1969	1970	1971	1972	1973	1974	1975
A. ARGENTINA	280	271	389	532	421	349	401	380	255	405	352	231	385	294	110	79
B. BOLIVIA	~	~	~	~	~	~	21	12	39	78	98	89	156	99	19	2
C. BRAZIL	6	15	13	13	19	36	3	3	2	6	8	17	28	34	24	18
E. COLOMBIA	~	~	~	~	~	5	~	~	~	~	~	~	3	5	19	5
F. COSTA RICA	7	5	4	7	9	5	7	10	15	17	18	19	23	20	28	29
H. DOMINICAN REP.	3	2	~	~	~	~	~	1	5	5	3	3	7	4	7	4
J. EL SALVADOR	~	~	~	~	~	~	~	~	~	~	~	~	4	4	6	2
K. GUATEMALA	1	1	5	6	5	6	6	9	9	12	12	16	15	17	13	15
L. HAITI	~	~	~	~	~	~	~	1	1	1	1	1	1	1	1	~
M. HONDURAS	~	~	~	5	4	5	6	6	7	11	12	15	18	26	13	23
N. MEXICO	19	26	28	34	24	22	28	21	33	35	37	35	42	28	14	5
O. NICARAGUA	~	~	~	13	11	9	13	15	17	20	24	25	30	26	16	22
P. PANAMA	~	~	~	~	~	~	1	1	2	2	2	1	2	1	1	1
Q. PARAGUAY	~	~	~	~	2	5	1	~	~	2	10	12	19	20	7	8
S. URUGUAY	52	43	55	65	122	65	55	58	96	107	131	80	104	99	100	79
LATIN AMERICA	368	363	494	675	617	507	542	517	481	700	708	546	837	678	361	292
WORLD	972	979	1,342	1,161	1,450	1,450	1,472	1,833	1,825	2,001	2,085	1,974	2,348	2,556	2,286	2,394

SOURCE: Marchán, table 30.

Table 2412

COMPARISON OF ARGENTINA AND AUSTRALIA
BEEF CATTLE EXPORTS, 1938–77
(T MET)

Year	(1) Argentina Exports	(2) Australia Exports	(2/1) Australia % Argentina
1938–43	472.2	110.7	23.4
1955	411.4	224.5	54.6
1956	575.3	241.4	42.0
1957	672.4	236.3	35.1
1958	782.6	221.8	28.3
1959	582.5	358.5	61.5
1960	436.9	303.4	69.4
1961	475.4	211.9	44.6
1962	601.1	333.1	55.4
1963	793.6	398.7	50.2
1964	578.3	449.1	77.7
1965	471.0	467.2	99.2
1966	609.6	434.4	71.2
1967	682.0	380.7	55.8
1968	580.0	394.6	68.0
1969	775.0	404.8	52.2
1970	715.0	500.1	69.9
1971	477.0	508.3	106.6
1972	703.0	626.2	89.1
1973	551.0	884.4	160.5
1974	289.0	738.8	255.6
1975	262.0	648.1	247.4
1976	527.0	846.0	160.5
1977[†]	570.0	1,000.0	175.4

SOURCE: *El Economista* (Buenos Aires), July 29, 1977, p. 8.

Table 2413

BANANA EXPORT VOLUME,[1] 14 LC, 1975–82[a]
(T MET)

	Country	1975	1976	1977	1978	1979	1980	1981	1982
B.	BOLIVIA	~	~	20	~	#	#	#	#
C.	BRAZIL	147	92	112	132	128	67	67	59
E.	COLOMBIA	486	465	455	592	626	692	795[‡]	733[‡]
F.	COSTA RICA	1,077	1,076	1,013	1,007	1,007	1,027	950	1,010[‡]
H.	DOMINICAN REP.[2]	26	30	18	11	6	11	28	18
I.	ECUADOR[2]	1,450	1,231	1,318	1,425	1,386	1,437	1,230	1,261
K.	GUATEMALA	260	328	320	316	299	336	370	404
L.	HAITI[2]	~	25	#	#	#	#	#	#
M.	HONDURAS	420	658	777	760	897	987	820	914
N.	MEXICO[2]	3	10	16	18	17	16	6[‡]	7[‡]
O.	NICARAGUA[2]	135	128	112	123	119	121	100	147
P.	PANAMA[3]	558	524	547	628	565	505	573	524[‡]
R.	PERU	~	~	~	~	#	#	#	#
T.	VENEZUELA[2]	7	7	5	6	5	6	7[‡]	7[†]
	WORLD	6,641	6,644	6,668	7,149	7,097	6,956	6,929	7,028

1. Figures refer to "special trade" except where otherwise indicated. For explanation of "Special" exports, see table 2409, n. 1.
2. Figures refer to "general trade," i.e., total exports including re-exports.
3. Data exclude the free zone of Colón and the Canal Zone.

a. For 1934–74, see SALA, 20-2916.

SOURCE: FAO-TY, 1978; FAO-TY, 1980; FAO-TY, 1981, table 55; FAO, TY, 1982, table 55.

Table 2414

BANANA EXPORTS,[1] 12 LC, 1978–82

Country	Value of Exports (T US)					Value as % of World Exports				
	1978	1979	1980	1981	1982	1978	1979	1980	1981	1982
C. BRAZIL	~	~	11,164	12,741	10,520	~	~	#	#	#
D. CHILE	2	189†	330	215†	209†	#	#†	#	#†	#†
E. COLOMBIA	80,522	79,612	94,141	122,430	151,119	7.7	7.3	6.0	7.5	10.4
F. COSTA RICA	172,314	194,329	214,501	229,128	~	16.6	17.8	13.6	14.0	~
H. DOMINICAN REP.	1,201	552	1,605	4,572	2,836	#	#	#	#	#
I. ECUADOR	150,935	156,539	467,340†	478,831†	430,609†	14.5	14.4	29.7†	29.2†	29.7†
K. GUATEMALA	25,266	~	52,418	58,476	66,989†	2.4	~	3.3	3.6	4.6†
M. HONDURAS	139,582	191,144	233,143	201,457	214,842†	13.4	17.5	14.8	12.3	14.8†
N. MEXICO	1,309	1,878	~	~	~	#	#	~	~	~
O. NICARAGUA	6,257	7,196	8,386	20,904	9,794	#	#	#	#	#
P. PANAMA	71,703	65,702	61,714	69,683	66,546	6.9	6.0	3.9	4.3	4.6
T. VENEZUELA	1,252	1,209	1,649	2,633	888†	#	#	#	#	#†
LAIA	234,103	239,786	574,652†	616,862†	593,361†	22.5	22.0	36.5†	37.7†	40.9†
CACM	343,496	392,757	508,448	510,026	291,634†	33.0	36.1	32.3	31.1	20.1†
UNITED STATES	57,120	63,479	71,505	75,896	72,988	5.5	5.8	4.5	4.6	5.0

1. Including fresh and dry plantain.

SOURCE: UN-YITS, 1982, vol. 2, p. 292.

Table 2415

BARLEY IMPORT VOLUME,[1] 17 LC, 1975–82[a]
(T MET)

Country	1975	1976	1977	1978	1979	1980	1981	1982
A. ARGENTINA	~	~	~	~	#	#	#	#
C. BRAZIL	22	14	11	32	41	93	119	102
D. CHILE	~	~	~	~	70	38	6	#
E. COLOMBIA	12	85	88	108	49	39	80	86‡
F. COSTA RICA	#	6	#	#	32	17	#	#‡
G. CUBA	31	~	42	44	23	57	60‡	50‡
H. DOMINICAN REP.	~	~	~	~	#	#	#	#
I. ECUADOR[3]	10‡	11	12	28	22	23	36	26
J. EL SALVADOR	#	~	~	~	#	#	#	#
K. GUATEMALA	~	~	~	~	#	#	#	#
M. HONDURAS	~	~	~	~	#	#	#	#
N. MEXICO[2,3]	150	2	.1	88	44	176	91	20
O. NICARAGUA	~	~	~	~	#	#	#	#
P. PANAMA	#	#	#	#	#	#	#	1‡
R. PERU	33‡	32	20	21‡	34	36	36	37‡
S. URUGUAY[3]	4	8	#	#	19	7	22	25‡
T. VENEZUELA[3]	#	~	#	#	#	#	#	#‡
UNITED STATES	~	~	~	~	157	140	127	198
WORLD	~	~	~	~	14,824	14,997	18,599	18,121

1. Figures refer to "special trade" except where otherwise indicated. For explanation of "Special" imports, see table 2408, n. 1.
2. Imports through free zones included.
3. Figures refer to "general trade," i.e., total imports.

a. For 1934–74, see SALA, 20-2918.

SOURCE: FAO-TY, 1978; FAO-TY, 1980; FAO-TY, 1981; FAO-TY, 1982, table 40.

Table 2416

BARLEY EXPORT VOLUME,[1] 4 LC, 1975–82[a]

(T MET)

	Country	1975	1976	1977	1978	1979	1980	1981	1982
A.	ARGENTINA	18	35	75	15	58	43	6	1
D.	CHILE	7	30	4	#	#	9‡	#	8
N.	MEXICO[3]	1	1	50	--	#	#	#	#
S.	URUGUAY[3]	3	7	1	3	#	22	26	12‡
	UNITED STATES[2,3]	651	1,103	1,553	649	721	1,463	2,067	1,375
	WORLD	12,412	13,795	13,109	14,596	14,111	16,215	19,299	18,263

1. Figures refer to "special trade" except where otherwise indicated. See table 2409, n. 1, for explanation of "special" exports.
2. The customs area includes the Commonwealth of Puerto Rico.
3. Figures refer to "general trade," i.e., total exports including re-exports.

a. For 1934–74, see SALA, 20-2917.

SOURCE: FAO-TY, 1978; FAO-TY, 1980; FAO-TY, 1981, table 40; FAO-TY, 1982, table 40.

Table 2417

BUTTER IMPORT VOLUME,[1] 18 LC, 1975–82[a]

(T MET)

	Country	1975	1976	1977	1978	1979	1980	1981	1982
A.	ARGENTINA	4	~	.3	2	3	1	2‡	.5‡
B.	BOLIVIA	~	~	~	~	#	#	#	#
C.	BRAZIL	4	4	2	#	1	6	#	#
D.	CHILE	50	30	4	6	9	7	4	5
E.	COLOMBIA	~	~	~	~	3	3	#	2‡
F.	COSTA RICA	2	3	.4	.5	1	1	#	#
G.	CUBA	~	~	18	17	17	21	20‡	35‡
H.	DOMINICAN REP.[3]	#	1	#	#	#	#	#	#
J.	EL SALVADOR	1	10	#	#	#	#	#†	#†
K.	GUATEMALA	~	--	#	.1‡	#	#‡	#‡	#‡
L.	HAITI[3]	#	--	#	.4‡	#	#‡	#‡	#‡
M.	HONDURAS	1	1	.1	1‡	#	#	1‡	.8‡
N.	MEXICO[2,3]	31	76	14	23‡	19‡	25	24	18
O.	NICARAGUA	~	~	~	~	#	#	1‡	.8‡
P.	PANAMA[4]	1	11	2	2	2	2	1	1‡
R.	PERU	110	100‡	12	12	13	8	7	8
S.	URUGUAY	~	~	~	~	#	#	#	#
T.	VENEZUELA[3]	1	3‡	4	4	2	2	3‡	2‡
	UNITED STATES	#	~	~	~	#	#	1	1
	WORLD	1,014	~	~	~	1,221	1,380	1,478	1,337

1. Figures refer to "special trade" except where otherwise indicated. See table 2408, n.1, for explanation of "special" imports.
2. Imports through free zones are included.
3. Figures refer to "general trade," i.e., total imports.
4. Data exclude the free zone of Colón and the Canal Zone.

a. For 1934-76, see SALA, 20-2919.

SOURCE: FAO-TY, 1976; FAO-TY, 1978; FAO-TY, 1980; FAO-TY, 1981, table 30; FAO, TY, 1982, table 30.

Table 2418

CACAO BEAN EXPORT VOLUME,[1] 9 LC, 1975–82[a]

(T MET)

Country	1975	1976	1977	1978	1979	1980	1981	1982
C. BRAZIL	177	129	108	134	157	124	125 2‡	143 2‡
F. COSTA RICA	5	4	6	6	4	2		
H. DOMINICAN REP.[2]	22	24	26	28	26	23	27	39
I. ECUADOR[2]	38	22	19	16	15	14	24	42
K. GUATEMALA	1	1	4	3	2[†]	1	#	#
L. HAITI[2]	1	1	2	2‡	3	2	3	2‡
N. MEXICO[2]	4	8	5	4	2	1	#	#
P. PANAMA[3]	~	1	1	1	1	1	#	#
T. VENEZUELA[2]	16	7	9	7	7	8	8‡	7‡
WORLD	1,169	1,144	962	108	1,017	1,090	1,171	2,328

1. Figures refer to "special trade" except where otherwise indicated. See table 2409, n.1,
   for explanation of "special" imports.
2. Figures refer to "general trade," i.e., total exports including re-exports.
3. Data exclude the free zone of Colón and the Canal Zone.

a. For 1934-74, see SALA, 20-2920.

SOURCE: FAO-TY, 1978; FAO-TY, 1980; FAO-TY, 1981; table 71; FAO-TY, 1982,
   table 71.

Table 2419

COCOA EXPORTS, 13 LC, 1978–82

	Value of Exports (T US)					Value as % of World Exports				
Country	1978	1979	1980	1981	1982	1978	1979	1980	1981	1982
B. BOLIVIA	1,859	1,730	1,663[†]	1,597[†]	1,335[†]	#	#	#[†]	#[†]	#[†]
C. BRAZIL	828,293	945,008	696,586	596,757	428,991	15.6	18.6	15.0	14.5	12.0
E. COLOMBIA	3,462	4,744	4,557	5,697	3,723	#	#	#	#	#
F. COSTA RICA	24,685	21,318	13,979	8,058	~	#	#	#	#	~
G. CUBA	~	~	11,687[†]	9,606[†]	8,218[†]	~	~	#[†]	#[†]	#[†]
H. DOMINICAN REP.	86,143	75,172	53,790	48,203	57,480	#	#	#	#	#
I. ECUADOR	259,356	273,308	222,608[†]	228,082[†]	205,112[†]	4.9	5.4	4.8[†]	5.5[†]	5.7[†]
K. GUATEMALA	7,964	9,249	3,394	758	2,768[†]	#	#	#[†]	#[†]	#[†]
L. HAITI	7,145	6,793	4,023[†]	2,795[†]	2,884[†]	#	#	#[†]	#[†]	#[†]
N. MEXICO	29,611	33,715	29,794	8,142	35,373[†]	#	#	#	#	#
P. PANAMA	3,122	3,875	2,118	1,192	2,309	#	#	#	#	#
R. PERU	9,666	13,644	16,742	15,936	17,731	#	#	#	#	#[†]
T. VENEZUELA	27,895	32,676	28,626	20,634	36,736[†]	#	#	#	#	#
LAIA	1,160,182	1,304,886	1,000,793[†]	876,912[†]	729,056[†]	21.8	25.7	21.5[†]	21.3[†]	20.4[†]
CACM	34,100	31,659	18,349	9,620	3,346[†]	.6	.6	.4	.2	.1[†]
UNITED STATES	49,980	43,202	35,829	46,068	42,192	#	#	#	#	#

SOURCE: UN-YITS, 1982, vol. 2, p. 40.

Table 2420

COFFEE BEAN EXPORT VOLUME,[1] 17 LC, 1975–82
(T MET)

Country	1975	1976	1977	1978	1979	1980	1981	1982
B. BOLIVIA	5	5	4.5	6	7.5	5	5	7
C. BRAZIL	774	805	512	621	562	785	825	887
E. COLOMBIA	489	317	307	509	657	660	544	532
F. COSTA RICA	75	68	71	87	97	72	106	95[‡]
G. CUBA	8	~	9.0	9[‡]	7	9	6	9[†]
H. DOMINICAN REP.[2]	32	40	43	27	43	26	32	36
I. ECUADOR[2]	64	92	54	103	82	54	56	79
J. EL SALVADOR	141	153	134	121	185	147	212[‡]	115
K. GUATEMALA	125	119	133	132	147	125	132[‡]	82
L. HAITI	18	27	16	15[‡]	14	25	14	14[‡]
M. HONDURAS	49	44	36	58	66	60	70[‡]	58[‡]
N. MEXICO	142	167	107	115	175	130	122	126
O. NICARAGUA[2]	41	53	50	55	55	46	49[‡]	57
P. PANAMA[4]	2	2	1	3	3	3	5	4
Q. PARAGUAY	6	4	2	#	1	.6	#	#
R. PERU	43	47	44	55	70	43	40	44
T. VENEZUELA[2]	14	18	11	14	8	2	2	1
UNITED STATES[2,3]	55	69	106	58	79	79	70	61
WORLD	3,550	3,671	2,931	3,391	3,800	3,717	3,763	3,863

1. Figures refer to "special trade" except where otherwise indicated. See table 2409, n.1,
   for explanation of "special" imports.
2. Figures refer to "general trade," i.e., total exports including re-exports.
3. The customs area includes the Commonwealth of Puerto Rico.
4. Data exclude the free zone of Colón and the Canal Zone.

a. For 1934–75, see SALA, 20-2921.

SOURCE: FAO-TY, 1978; FAO-TY, 1980; FAO-TY, 1981; table 70; FAO-TY, 1982,
   table 70.

Table 2421

COFFEE EXPORTS,[1] 16 LC, 1978–82

Country	Value of Exports (T US)					Value as % of World Exports				
	1978	1979	1980	1981	1982	1978	1979	1980	1981	1982
B. BOLIVIA	16,698	19,698	19,569[†]	18,796[†]	15,712[†]	#	#	#[†]	#[†]	#[†]
C. BRAZIL	2,294,711	2,326,177	2,773,093	1,760,612	2,130,199	19.5	18.1	21.0	19.0	21.7
E. COLOMBIA	1,991,213	2,022,631	2,371,838	1,462,188	1,579,527	16.9	15.7	17.9	15.8	16.1
F. COSTA RICA	314,216	315,406	247,827	240,059	~	#	#	#	#	~
G. CUBA	~	~	137,058[†]	112,650[†]	96,378[†]	~	~	#[†]	#[†]	#[†]
H. DOMINICAN REP.	96,655	156,997	77,214	75,510	96,877	#	#	#	#	#
I. ECUADOR	270,469	276,444	219,083[†]	224,469[†]	201,864[†]	#	#	#[†]	#[†]	#[†]
J. EL SALVADOR	223,250	585,153	270,604	152,028	414,553[†]	1.9	4.5	2.0	1.6	4.2[†]
K. GUATEMALA	478,211	431,946	470,304	269,737	356,771[†]	4.1	3.4	3.6	2.9	3.6[†]
L. HAITI	62,277	39,305	50,778[†]	35,275[†]	36,398[†]	#	#	#[†]	#[†]	#[†]
M. HONDURAS	208,446	195,394	207,458	170,623	140,015[†]	#	#	#	#	#[†]
N. MEXICO	382,954	603,136	437,109	343,403	371,113	3.3	4.7	3.3	3.7	3.8
O. NICARAGUA	261,119	180,186	169,603	141,509	128,087	#	#	#	#	#
P. PANAMA	8,981	9,975	10,441	13,633	12,394	#	#	#	#	#
R. PERU	168,992	241,711	139,760	99,272	104,362	#	#	#	#	#
T. VENEZUELA	42,195	24,597	7,931	3,330	10,029[†]	#	#	#	#	#[†]
LAIA	5,167,479	5,518,742	5,971,275	3,918,577	4,484,400	44.0	42.9	45.1	42.4	45.7
CACM	1,485,243	1,708,085	1,365,796	973,956	1,039,426[†]	12.6	13.3	10.3	10.5	10.6[†]
UNITED STATES	289,133	408,200	391,047	317,381	282,253	2.5	3.2	3.0	3.4	2.9

1. Including substitutes.

SOURCE: UN-YITS, 1982, vol. 2, p. 39.

Table 2422

MAIZE IMPORT VOLUME,[1] 17 L, 1975–82[a]

(T MET)

Country	1975	1976	1977	1978	1979	1980	1981	1982
B. BOLIVIA	~	~	~	~	#	#	#	#
C. BRAZIL	2	1	.6	1,262	1,526	1,594	902	#
D. CHILE	86	89	84	253	200	357	309	397
E. COLOMBIA	18	203	101	83‡	60	193	80	90‡
F. COSTA RICA	13	4	5	6	4	61	25	68‡
G. CUBA	~	~	325	481	350	610	580‡	410‡
H. DOMINICAN REP.[3]	54	78	117	87	102	171	162	172
J. EL SALVADOR	27	#	23	76	12	14	11	29
K. GUATEMALA	68	27	13	84	55‡	81‡	52‡	6
L. HAITI[3]	~		20	5‡	25‡	5‡	10‡	5†
M. HONDURAS	44	#	15	40	7	64	23‡	6
N. MEXICO[4,3]	2,636	912	1,755	1,418	744	3,777	3,065	233
O. NICARAGUA[3]	21	10	5	17	2	48	40	25
P. PANAMA[2]	6	2	4	1	25	39	26	52‡
R. PERU	236	281	209	150‡	101	261	336	498
S. URUGUAY[3]	#	#	.4	.6	44	10‡	14‡	10‡
T. VENEZUELA[3]	508	537	623	339	448	1,227	1,008	980‡

1. Figures refer to "special trade" except where otherwise noted. See table 2408, n. 1,
     for explanation of "special" imports.
2. Data exclude the free zone of Colón and the Canal Zone.
3. Figures refer to "general trade," i.e., total imports.
4. Imports through free zones are included.

a. For 1934–74, see SALA, 20-2924.

SOURCE: FAO-TY, 1978; FAO-TY, 1980; FAO-TY, 1981, table 47; FAO-TY, 1982,
     table 44.

Table 2423

MAIZE EXPORT VOLUME,[1] 15 LC, 1975–82[a]

(T MET)

Country	1975	1976	1977	1978	1979	1980	1981	1982
A. ARGENTINA	4,001	3,080	5,431	5,895	5,960	3,481	9,163	5,226
C. BRAZIL	1,200	1,417	1,420	14	10	6	7	544
D. CHILE	~	~	.4	#	#	#	#	#
E. COLOMBIA	~	~	~	~	#	#	#	#
F. COSTA RICA	~	~	3	~	#	#	#	#
H. DOMINICAN REP.[2]	~	~	~	~	#	#	#	#
I. ECUADOR[2]	~	~	~	~	#	#	1	#
J. EL SALVADOR	~	4	~	~	2	20	10	#
K. GUATEMALA	~	~	~	.1‡	#	#	#	#
M. HONDURAS	~	~	.5	#	#	#	#	6
N. MEXICO[2]	4	1	.1	~	#	1	#	#
O. NICARAGUA[2]	~	2	.2	.1	3	#	#	#
Q. PARAGUAY	6	12	~	~	#	25	2	7
R. PERU	7	1	~	4†	2	3	2‡	3‡
S. URUGUAY[2]	~	23	2	10	4	2	6	#
WORLD	49,638	61,993	57,487	68,626	76,087	80,280	78,930	69,993

1. Figures refer to "special trade" except where otherwise indicated. See table 2409, n. 1,
     for explanation of "special" imports.
2. Figures refer to "general trade," i.e., total exports including re-exports.

a. For 1934–74, see SALA, 20-2923.

SOURCE: FAO-TY, 1978; FAO-TY, 1980; FAO-TY, 1981, table 41; FAO-TY, 1982,
     table 41.

Table 2424

MILK (DRY) IMPORT VOLUME,[1] 19 L, 1975–82[a]
(T MET)

Country	1975	1976	1977[b]	1978[b]	1979[b]	1980	1981	1982
A. ARGENTINA	~	1	9	13	18	18	4	#
B. BOLIVIA	5	5	2	8‡	7	8‡	7‡	3
C. BRAZIL	14	14	46	12	10	62	8	8
D. CHILE	9	9	14‡	14	18	16	14	11
E. COLOMBIA[6]	4	4	15	19‡	7	19	36	9‡
F. COSTA RICA	3	3	5	3	2	2	2	2‡
G. CUBA	~	~	38	35‡	40	39	43	38†
H. DOMINICAN REP.[2,5]	2	2	5	6	7	9	7	3
I. ECUADOR[5]	3	3	5	4	7	7	3	2‡
J. EL SALVADOR[2]	8	8	9	11	11	12	12	8
K. GUATEMALA	3	3	5	5‡	6	8	7	7‡
L. HAITI[6,5]	5	5	1	5‡	2‡	4‡	2‡	5‡
M. HONDURAS	5	5	3	4	5	6	6	4
N. MEXICO[3,5]	38	38	58	60	85	185	91	70
O. NICARAGUA[5]	1	1	1	1	4	2	5‡	10
P. PANAMA[4]	3	3	3	2	2	2	3	3‡
Q. PARAGUAY[6]	#	#	#	#	#	.6	1	1‡
R. PERU	18	18	26	18‡	16	27	18	30‡
T. VENEZUELA[5]	28	28	130	103	73	89	103	90‡

1. Figures refer to "special trade" except where otherwise indicated. See table 2408, n. 1, for explanation of "special" imports.
2. Includes condensed and powdered milk.
3. Imports through free zones included.
4. Data exclude the free zone of Colón and the Canal Zone.
5. Figures refer to "general trade," i.e., total imports.
6. Includes fresh, condensed, and powdered milk.

a. For 1934–74, see SALA, 20-2928.
b. Powdered milk only.

SOURCE: FAO-TY, 1978; FAO-TY, 1980; FAO-TY, 1982, table 28.

Table 2425

OAT IMPORT VOLUME,[1] 13 L, 1975–82[a]
(T MET)

Country	1975	1976	1977	1978	1979	1980	1981	1982
B. BOLIVIA	~	~	~	~	~	~	~	.5‡
C. BRAZIL	254	254	23	33	40	24	18	4
E. COLOMBIA	75	76	9	9‡	13	10	10	9‡
F. COSTA RICA	1	1	#	#	#	#	#	#
G. CUBA	~	~	22	27	26	13	10	23‡
H. DOMINICAN REP.[3]	65	70	2	1	2	2	2	1
I. ECUADOR[3]	191	199	18	18	22	11	12	26‡
N. MEXICO[4,3]	1	1	#	#	#	.7	21	3‡
O. NICARAGUA[3]	22	22	4	2	3	6	6†	1
P. PANAMA[2]	4	4	.6	.9	#	#‡	#‡	#‡
R. PERU	5	5	9‡	4‡	4	#	5	12‡
S. URUGUAY[3]	1	1	2	1	19	2	3	6‡
T. VENEZUELA[3]	60	60	8	6	4	3	7	5‡

1. Figures refer to "special trade" except where otherwise indicated. See table 2408, n. 1, for explanation of "special" imports.
2. Data exclude the free zone of Colón and the Canal Zone.
3. Figures refer to "general trade," i.e., total imports.
4. Imports through free zones included.

a. For 1934–74, see SALA, 20-2930.

SOURCE: FAO-TY, 1978; FAO-TY, 1980; FAO-TY, 1982, table 43.

Table 2426

OAT EXPORT VOLUME,[1] 4 L, 1975–82[a]
(T MET)

	Country	1975	1976	1977	1978	1979	1980	1981	1982
A.	ARGENTINA	204	105	179	337	83	62	123	54
D.	CHILE	6	7	#	1	#	2‡	1‡	#
N.	MEXICO[2]	1	~	~	~	#	#	#	#
S.	URUGUAY	2	1	1	1	#	2	1	2‡

1. Figures refer to "special trade" except where otherwise noted. See table 2409, n. 1, for explanation of "special" imports.
2. Figures refer to "general trade," i.e., total exports including re-exports.

a. For 1934–74, see SALA, 20-2929.

SOURCE: FAO-TY, 1978; FAO-TY, 1980; FAO-TY, 1982, table 43.

Table 2427

RICE IMPORT VOLUME,[1] 20 L, 1975–82[a]
(T MET)

	Country	1975	1976	1977	1978	1979	1980	1981	1982
A.	ARGENTINA	~	~	5	2	10	3	5‡	#
B.	BOLIVIA	2	~	~	~	~	~	~	3
C.	BRAZIL	44	17	#	30	711	239	143	137
D.	CHILE	21	20	32	11	9	48	16	21
E.	COLOMBIA	~	~	21	~	14	4	#	1
F.	COSTA RICA	1	#	#	#	#	#	#	#
G.	CUBA	~	~	144	171	161	224	200‡	200‡
H.	DOMINICAN REP.[3]	50	32	58	18	#	33	65	#
I.	ECUADOR[3]	20	~	~	#	25	22	10	9
J.	EL SALVADOR	8	8	#	1	5	5	5	3‡
K.	GUATEMALA	6	6	4	12	10	4	4	4
L.	HAITI[3]	2	14	45	15‡	17‡	23‡	24‡	25‡
M.	HONDURAS	11	1	5	10	5	4	4	3
N.	MEXICO[4,3]	~	#	#	#	36	93	74	22
O.	NICARAGUA[3]	~	~	#	1	10	37	22	4‡
P.	PANAMA[2]	#	~	#	#	#	#	#	#
Q.	PARAGUAY	~	~	~	~	#	#	#	#
R.	PERU	78	71	~	80	202	211	111	59
S.	URUGUAY[3]	~	~	~	~	#	#	#	#
T.	VENEZUELA[3]	~	90	#	~	1	#	#	#

1. Figures refer to "special trade" except where otherwise noted. See table 2408, n. 1, for explanation of "special" imports.
2. Data exclude the free zone of Colón and the Canal Zone.
3. Figures refer to "general trade," i.e., total imports.
4. Imports through free zones included.

a. For 1934–74, see SALA, 20-2931.

SOURCE: FAO-TY, 1978; FAO-TY, 1980; FAO-TY, 1982, table 39.

Table 2428

SOYBEAN EXPORTS, 11 LC, 1978–82

Country	Value of Exports (T US)					Value as % of World Exports				
	1978	1979	1980	1981	1982	1978	1979	1980	1981	1982
A. ARGENTINA	454,766	702,937	604,539	380,950	425,786	7.6	10.3	8.6	7.9	6.1
B. BOLIVIA	751	172	~	~	~	#	#	~	~	~
C. BRAZIL	169,886	179,506	393,930	403,672	123,457	2.8	2.6	5.6	3.3	1.8
E. COLOMBIA	194	~	98	62[†]	~	#	~	#	#[†]	~
F. COSTA RICA	#	~	32	8[†]	~	#	~	#	#[†]	~
K. GUATEMALA	26	29	#	1	85[†]	#	#	#	#	#[†]
M. HONDURAS	5[†]	7[†]	7[†]	3[†]	6[†]	#[†]	#[†]	#[†]	#[†]	#[†]
N. MEXICO	2[†]	#	3[†]	3[†]	2[†]	#[†]	#	#[†]	#[†]	#[†]
O. NICARAGUA	450[†]	350[†]	3	799[†]	570[†]	#[†]	#[†]	#	#[†]	#[†]
Q. PARAGUAY	38,349	78,617	42,098	47,533	62,562[†]	.6	1.2	.6	.6	.9[†]
S. URUGUAY	2,164	1,815	1,895	6,066	4,911	#	#	#	.1	.1
LAIA	666,111	963,046	1,042,564	1,038,286	616,718	11.2	14.2	14.8	14.1	8.9
CACM	481[†]	386[†]	42[†]	811[†]	661[†]	#[†]	#[†]	#[†]	#[†]	#[†]
UNITED STATES	5,210,443	5,708,063	5,882,911	6,199,640	6,239,881	87.2	84.0	83.4	84.5	89.7

SOURCE: UN-YITS, 1982, vol. 2, p. 329.

Table 2429

SOYBEAN OIL IMPORT VOLUME,[1] 19 L, 1975–82[a]
(T MET)

Country	1975	1976	1977	1978	1979	1980	1981	1982
A. ARGENTINA	~	~	~	~	#	#	#	#
B. BOLIVIA	3	45	13[‡]	8[‡]	4	13[‡]	15[‡]	7
C. BRAZIL	2	2	~	~	77	50	#	22
D. CHILE	74	20	38	54	53	59	65	74[‡]
E. COLOMBIA	60	376	40	48	76	79	109	135[‡]
F. COSTA RICA	3	3	1	1	2	7	4[‡]	2[‡]
H. DOMINICAN REP.[3]	170	130	8	13	19	22	20	39
I. ECUADOR[3]	156	222	10	24	20	30	26	33
J. EL SALVADOR	1	22	#	#	2	.6	3	2
K. GUATEMALA	#	#	1	1[‡]	1	#	#	2
L. HAITI[3]	53	156	15	15[‡]	17	25[‡]	19[‡]	17[‡]
M. HONDURAS	1	3	#	#	1	#	.9[‡]	1[‡]
N. MEXICO[4,3]	18	39	15	34	#	42	5[‡]	104
O. NICARAGUA[3]	1	~	#	~	1	1	.6[‡]	#
P. PANAMA[2]	108	175	18	14	20	32	18	24[‡]
Q. PARAGUAY	~	~	~	~	#	#	#	#
R. PERU	548	557	72	82	14	35	70	64
S. URUGUAY[3]	#	~	2	2[‡]	.9	#[‡]	#	#[‡]
T. VENEZUELA[3]	~	160	#	15	36	20	56[‡]	43[‡]

1. Figures refer to "special trade" except where otherwise indicated. See table 2408, n. 1, for explanation of "special" imports.
2. Data exclude the free zone of Colón and the Canal Zone.
3. Figures refer to "general trade," i.e., total imports.
4. Imports through free zones included.

a. For 1934–74, see SALA, 20-2932.

SOURCE: FAO-TY, 1978; FAO-TY, 1980; FAO-TY, 1982, table 116.

Table 2430

SOYBEAN OILCAKE EXPORTS, 8 LC, 1978–82

	Country	Value of Exports (T US)					Value as % of World Exports				
		1978	1979	1980	1981	1982	1978	1979	1980	1981	1982
A.	ARGENTINA	44,961[†]	51,848[†]	~	53,132[†]	63,328[†]	1.5[†]	1.5[†]	~	1.1[†]	1.5[†]
B	BOLIVIA	~	2,253	347[†]	333[†]	278[†]	~	#	#	#	#
C.	BRAZIL	970,812[†]	1,064,135[†]	1,361,905[†]	1,977,433[†]	1,522,183[†]	32.3[†]	31.4[†]	33.7[†]	41.3[†]	36.7[†]
I.	ECUADOR	~	~	467[†]	478[†]	430[†]	~	~	#	#	#
P.	PANAMA	5[†]	38[†]	118[†]	23[†]	9[†]	#	#	#	#	#
Q.	PARAGUAY	3,285[†]	4,559[†]	7,062[†]	4,599[†]	4,179[†]	#	#	#	#	#
R.	PERU	~	~	~	11[†]	11[†]	~	~	~	#	#
S.	URUGUAY	3,365[†]	2,508[†]	3,538[†]	1,710[†]	~	#	#	#	#	~
	LAIA	1,022,422[†]	1,125,303[†]	1,373,318[†]	2,037,696[†]	1,590,409[†]	35.0[†]	33.2[†]	34.0[†]	42.6[†]	38.3[†]
	UNITED STATES	1,295,794	1,416,472	1,654,233	1,588,551	1,411,441	42.6	41.8	41.0	33.2	34.0

SOURCE: UN-YITS, 1982, vol. 2, p. 311.

Table 2431

SUGAR EXPORT VOLUME,[1] 19 L, 1975–82[a]
(T MET)

	Country	1975	1976	1977	1978	1979	1980	1981	1982
A.	ARGENTINA	197	291	933	362	361	487	726	255
B.	BOLIVIA	62	148	107	78	125	107	20	77
C.	BRAZIL	1,750	1,198	2,509	2,015	1,867	2,626	2,781	2,677
D.	CHILE	56	~	39	17	18	39	13	#
E.	COLOMBIA	198	84	13	132	241	278	177	250
F.	COSTA RICA	102	69	68	70	69	72	83	53[†]
G.	CUBA	~	~	6,238[‡]	7,231[‡]	7,199[‡]	6,170[‡]	7,071[‡]	7,735[†]
H.	DOMINICAN REP.[2]	950	977	1,101	901	986	794	855	827
I.	ECUADOR[2]	21	33	55	39	69	67	47	#
J.	EL SALVADOR	128	130	133	133	138	37	34	54
K.	GUATEMALA	204	314	305	153	157	199	228	75
L.	HAITI[2]	25	~	6	5[‡]	#	19	#	6[†]
M.	HONDURAS	10	7	20	23	55	78	95	96
N.	MEXICO[2]	178	1	~	71	101	#	#	#
O.	NICARAGUA[2]	89	154	100	98	91	62	89	79
P.	PANAMA[3]	82	84	114	119	135	130	94	107
Q.	PARAGUAY	14	4	~	~	#	6	#	15
R.	PERU	422	299	436	266	181	54	#	59
T.	VENEZUELA[2]	~	~	1	#	#	#	#	#

1. Figures refer to "special trade" except where otherwise indicated. See table 2409, n. 1, for explanation of "special" imports.
2. Figures refer to "general" trade.
3. Data exclude the free zone of Colón and the Canal Zone.

a. For 1934–74, see SALA, 20-2933.

SOURCE: FAO-TY, 1978; FAO-TY, 1980; FAO-TY, 1982, table 66.

Table 2432

SUGAR EXPORTS,[1] 15 LC, 1978–82

	Country	Value of Exports (T US)					Value as % of World Exports				
		1978	1979	1980	1981	1982	1978	1979	1980	1981	1982
A.	ARGENTINA	30,639	36,425	260,053	260,478	41,506	.5	.5	2.6	3.7	.9
B.	BOLIVIA	~	750[†]	674[†]	647[†]	541[†]	~	#[†]	#[†]	#[†]	#[†]
C.	BRAZIL	228,693	269,977	941,936	665,806	327,075	3.6	3.9	9.4	9.3	7.0
E.	COLOMBIA	19,536	42,789	164,685	76,881	54,720	#	#	#	#	#
F.	COSTA RICA	15,909	17,499	40,746	42,007	~	#	#	#	#	~
G.	CUBA	3,854,825	4,098,862	4,581,429	1,966,544[†]	1,682,487[†]	60.0	59.5	45.5	28.1[†]	36.2[†]
H.	DOMINICAN REP.	171,540	190,608	286,904	516,650	201,487	2.7	2.8	2.9	7.4	5.6
I.	ECUADOR	5,453	8,842	4[†]	4[†]	3[†]	#	#	#[†]	#[†]	#[†]
J.	EL SALVADOR	18,915	26,828	13,367	14,832	~	#	#	#	#	~
K.	GUATEMALA	45,753	53,008	80,379	84,094	~	#	#	#	#	~
M.	HONDURAS	5,501	13,301	27,975	37,890	~	#	#	#	#	~
N.	MEXICO	~	23,642	~	~	~	~	#	~	~	~
O.	NICARAGUA	25,549	22,080	20,458	39,708	14,333	#	#	#	#	#
P.	PANAMA	19,957	25,893	65,809	52,608	23,676	#	#	#	#	#
R.	PERU	43,641	61,014	13,440	144[†]	16,870	#	#	#	#[†]	#
	LAIA	327,973	443,444	1,380,959	1,003,963	441,458	5.1	6.4	13.7	14.3	9.5
	CACM	111,627	132,716	182,925	218,531	14,333	1.7	1.9	1.8	3.1	.3

1. Raw beet and cane sugar.

SOURCE: UN-YITS, 1982, vol. 2, p. 300.

Table 2433

CUBA SUGAR EXPORTS AS SHARE OF CUBA'S TOTAL
EXPORT VALUE,[1] 1900–80

Year	%	Year	%	Year	%
1900	37	1928	81	1956	79
1901	51	1929	80	1957	81
1902	48	1930	71	1958	81
1903	54	1931	70	1959	77
1904	62	1932	77	1960	79
1905	66	1933	73	1961	85
1906	57	1934	74	1962	83
1907	63	1935	80	1963	87
1908	56	1936	82	1964	88
1909	65	1937	80	1965	86
1910	73	1938	79	1966	85
1911	65	1939	79	1967	82
1912	72	1940	75	1968	77
1913	72	1941	79	1969	77
1914	77	1942	79	1970	77
1915	84	1943	80	1971	77
1916	85	1944	75	1972	75
1917	86	1945	72	1973	79
1918	85	1946	74	1974	89
1919	89	1947	89	1975	89
1920	92	1948	90	1976	86
1921	85	1949	88	1977	83
1922	86	1950	89	1978	86
1923	89	1951	88	1979	87
1924	88	1952	86	1980	83
1925	84	1953	83		
1926	83	1954	80		
1927	85	1955	80		

1. Raw Sugar, 96° base.

SOURCE: For most years data are from Cuban Economic Research Project, *A Study on Cuba: The Colonial and Republic Periods; the Socialist Experiment* (Coral Gables: University of Miami Press, 1965), pp. 280, 403, 616; and Cuba, JUCEPLAN, AE, 1973, pp. 193-194. Data for scattered years are from SALA-Cuba, pp. 169 and 174; IBRD (WB), *Report on Cuba* (Baltimore: Johns Hopkins, 1951), p. 801; FAO-TY, 1971, p. 225; K. S. Karol, *Guerrillas in Power: The Course of the Cuban Revolution* (New York: Hill and Wang, 1970), p. 587. Data for 1973-74 are from U.S. Central Intelligence Agency, *Cuba: Foreign Trade,* Intelligence Handbook A(ER) 75-69 (July 1975), tables 1, 4, and 9; and CIA, *Cuban Economy . . . 1968-76*, p. 9. Since 1975, data are from Cuba-CEE, AE, 1981, pp. 189, 195.

Table 2434

U.S. SUGAR IMPORT QUOTAS, 17 LC, 1983–84

	Country	%	Annual Quota — Short Tons Raw Value[1]	Imported as of September 28	% of Quota
A.	ARGENTINA	4.3	130,806	130,806	100
B.	BOLIVIA	.8	24,336	23,669	97.3
C.	BRAZIL	14.5	441,090	438,149	99.3
E.	COLOMBIA	2.4	73,008	73,008	100
F.	COSTA RICA[2]	1.5	62,415	62,418	100
H.	DOMINICAN REP.	17.6	535,392	527,810	98.6
I.	ECUADOR	1.1	33,462	32,776	97.6
J.	EL SALVADOR[2]	2.6	89,163	88,830	99.6
K.	GUATEMALA	4.8	146,016	146,016	100
L.	HAITI	. .[b]	16,776	16,490	98.3
M.	HONDURAS[2]	1.0	59,514	59,682	100.3[a]
N.	MEXICO	. .[b]	16,776	16,495	98.3
O.	NICARAGUA[2]	2.1	6,000	6,049	100.8[a]
P.	PANAMA	2.9	88,218	88,239	100 [a]
Q.	PARAGUAY	. .[b]	16,776	16,260	96.9
R.	PERU	4.1	124,722	120,659	96.7
S.	URUGUAY	. .[b]	16,776	16,789	100.1[a]

1. Value of sugar ranging from 94° – 98° polarization.
2. Nicaragua's quota was decreased to 6,000 short tons. The balance was alloted to:
   Honduras (52%), Costa Rica (30%), and El Salvador (18%).

a. Overfilled—will be deducted from 1985 quota.
b. Minimum quota.

SOURCE: Amerop Sugar Corporation/Westway Trading Company (New Jersey),
  Newsletter, various monthly, 1984, 1985.

Table 2435

WHEAT IMPORT VOLUME,[1] 20 L, 1975–82[a]
(T MET)

	Country	1975	1976	1977	1978	1979	1980	1981	1982
A.	ARGENTINA	~	#	#	#	#	#	#	#
B.	BOLIVIA	194	167	238	281	371	282	252	290
C.	BRAZIL	2,106	3,435	2,626	4,335	3,658	4,759	4,363	4,225
D.	CHILE	6,844	1,117	474	926	739	1,069	1,054	1,006
E.	COLOMBIA	302	304	216	295	338	641	507[‡]	566[†]
F.	COSTA RICA	83	88	76	85	88	104	96	250[†]
G.	CUBA	~	~	1,208	1,124	1,294	1,228	1,244[‡]	1,558
H.	DOMINICAN REP.	125	164	111	159	144	158	198	128
I.	ECUADOR	210	205	241	222	168	200	249	250
J.	EL SALVADOR	34	85	105	68	105	116	106	148
K.	GUATEMALA	72	83	111	65	96	108	108[‡]	93[†]
L.	HAITI	82	87	122	126[‡]	149[‡]	149[‡]	199[‡]	167[†]
M.	HONDURAS	52	57	60	63	69	71	78	80
N.	MEXICO[2]	864	2	477	506	1,148	823	1,028	398
O.	NICARAGUA	50	41	51	56	27	52	37[‡]	39
P.	PANAMA[3]	55	52	68	57	47	47	62	57
Q.	PARAGUAY	27	59	44	49	65	75	68	38
R.	PERU	833	761	833	732[‡]	781	800	756	918[†]
S.	URUGUAY[4]	~	~	#	112[‡]	92	55	4	80[†]
T.	VENEZUELA	620	686	705	506	719	785	890	890

1. Wheat and wheat flour in wheat equivalent. Figures refer to "special trade" unless
   otherwise indicated. See table 2408, n. 1, for explanation of "special" imports.
2. Imports through free zones included.
3. Data exclude the free zone of Colón and the Canal Zone.
4. Figures refer to "general trade," i.e., total exports.

a. For 1934–74, see SALA, 20-2936.

SOURCE: FAO-TY, 1978; FAO-TY, 1980; FAO-TY, 1982, table 37.

Table 2436

WHEAT EXPORT VOLUME,[1] 5 L, 1975–82[a]

(T MET)

Country	1975	1976	1977	1978	1979	1980	1981	1982
A. ARGENTINA	1,920	3,264	5,970	1,776	4,364	4,538	3,788	3,837
D. CHILE	~	- -	- -	- -	#	#	#	#
M. HONDURAS	~	- -	#	#	2	1	1	1
N. MEXICO[2]	31	13	23	17	14	23	23	#
S. URUGUAY[2]	68	36	71	~	#	#	112	127

1. Includes wheat and wheat flour in wheat equivalent. Figures refer to "special trade" except where otherwise indicated. See table 2409, n. 1, for explanation of "special" exports.
2. Figures refer to "general trade," i.e., total exports including re-exports.

a. For 1934–74, see SALA, 20-2934.

SOURCE: FAO-TY, 1978; FAO-TY, 1980; FAO-TY, 1980, table 347.

Table 2437

WHEAT EXPORTS,[1] 6 LC, 1978–82

	Country	Value of Exports (T US)					Value as % of World Exports				
		1978	1979	1980	1981	1982	1978	1979	1980	1981	1982
A.	ARGENTINA	174,202	605,994	816,137	394,749[†]	324,306[†]	1.9	5.2	5.2	2.4[†]	2.1[†]
C.	BRAZIL	~	1	39	36	247	~	#	#	#	#
D.	CHILE	#	1,825[†]	#	2,729[†]	2,652[†]	#	#[†]	#	#[†]	#[†]
N.	MEXICO	2,619	4,449	666[†]	717[†]	3,695[†]	#	#	#[†]	#[†]	#[†]
O.	NICARAGUA	~	~	#	1,065	1,192	~	~	#	#	#
S.	URUGUAY	~	~	~	16,094	21,887	~	~	~	#	#
	LAIA	176,820	612,269	816,843	414,326[†]	352,787[†]	1.9	5.2	5.2	2.5[†]	2.3[†]
	CACM	~	5	~	1,068	1,196	~	#	~	#	#
	UNITED STATES	4,334,828	5,264,906	6,375,556	7,843,960	6,675,575	47.4	44.8	40.3	47.6	43.3

1. Unmilled.

SOURCE: UN-YITS, 1982, vol. 2, p. 25.

Table 2438

WOOL (CLEAN) EXPORT VOLUME,[1] 5 LC, 1975–82[a]

(T MET)

	Country	1975	1976	1977	1978	1979	1980	1981	1982
A.	ARGENTINA	27	40	26	29	22	27	34 ‡	24
C.	BRAZIL	1	#	#	#	#	.4	.6	.7‡
D.	CHILE	1	1	~	1	#	.2	.06	.7
R.	PERU	1	1	#	2 [b]	#	.2‡	.5 ‡	.2‡
S.	URUGUAY[2]	6	6	5	6	5	6	7	5
	UNITED STATES	~	.6	.2	.4	.4	.4	.3	.9
	WORLD	~	~	279	278	299	323	346	316

1. Figures refer to "special trade" unless otherwise indicated. See table 2409, n. 1, for explanation of "special" exports.
2. Figures refer to "general trade," i.e., total exports including re-exports.

a. For 1934–74, see SALA, 20-2937.
b. Greasy wool.

SOURCE: FAO-TY, 1978; FAO-TY, 1980; FAO-TY, 1982, table 114.

Table 2439

WOOL EXPORTS, 7 LC, 1978–82

	Country	Value of Exports (T US)					Value as % of World Exports				
		1978	1979	1980	1981	1982	1978	1979	1980	1981	1982
A.	ARGENTINA	200,708	201,937	247,618	238,822†	196,204†	5.6	5.0	5.7	5.4†	5.0†
B.	BOLIVIA	412	336	609†	643†	537†	#	#	#†	#†	#†
C.	BRAZIL	12,997	8,688	69,714	82,502	52,864	.4	.2	1.6	1.9	1.4
D.	CHILE	17,888	22,200	22,811	28,716†	27,913†	#	#	#	#†	#†
Q.	PARAGUAY	251	239	266†	285†	867†	#	#	#†	#†	#†
R.	PERU	27,888	39,989	30,169	9,465	7,086	#	#	#	#	#
S.	URUGUAY	86,949	51,924	134,031	144,216	132,398	2.4	1.3	3.1	3.2	3.4
	LAIA	347,290	325,595	505,501	504,845†	418,423†	9.7	8.0	11.5	11.3†	10.8†
	CACM	68	2	90	380†	86†	#	#	#	#†	#†
	UNITED STATES	40,527	49,027	40,004	48,155	43,900	#	#	#	#	#

SOURCE: UN-YITS, 1982, vol. 2, p. 69.

Table 2440

FOREST PRODUCT EXPORTS, 10 OASL, 1970–80
(% and M US)

Category	1970	%[a]	1975	%[a]	1980	%[a]
All Forest Products	C. BRAZIL	51	C. BRAZIL	39	C. BRAZIL	53
	D. CHILE	18	D. CHILE	26	D. CHILE	30
	M. HONDURAS	6	M. HONDURAS	10		
	Q. PARAGUAY	6	Q. PARAGUAY	5		
			B. BOLIVIA	5		
	Rest of OASL	19	Rest of OASL	15	Rest of OASL	17
Total Value	$220.7	100	$460.6	100	$1,541.1	100
Roundwood	Q. PARAGUAY	35	M. HONDURAS	13	D. CHILE	81
	C. BRAZIL	16	C. BRAZIL	10		
			F. COSTA RICA	9		
	Rest of OASL	49	Rest of OASL	68	Rest of OASL	19
Total Value	$19.1	100	$11.7	100	$70.1	100
Sawnwood and Sleepers	C. BRAZIL	65	C. BRAZIL	39	C. BRAZIL	43
	M. HONDURAS	10	M. HONDURAS	19	D. CHILE	30
	D. CHILE	7	D. CHILE	10	Q. PARAGUAY	10
	Q. PARAGUAY	4	Q. PARAGUAY	10	M. HONDURAS	8
			B. BOLIVIA	10		
	Rest of OASL	13	Rest of OASL	12	Rest of OASL	9
Total Value	$122.3	100	$229.6	100	$492.4	100
Wood-based Panels	C. BRAZIL	76	C. BRAZIL	79	C. BRAZIL	62
					I. ECUADOR	13
					Q. PARAGUAY	7
	Rest of OASL	24	Rest of OASL	21	Rest of OASL	18
Total Value	$33.2	100	$64.3	100	$181.6	100
Wood Pulp	D. CHILE	75	D. CHILE	66	C. BRAZIL	63
	C. BRAZIL	25	C. BRAZIL	34	D. CHILE	35
Total Value	$22.0	100	$90.5	100	$561.5	100
Paper and Paperboard	D. CHILE	62	D. CHILE	57	C. BRAZIL	53
	K. GUATEMALA	9	K. GUATEMALA	10	D. CHILE	21
	A. ARGENTINA	7	C. BRAZIL	9	K. GUATEMALA	8
	R. PERU	7			A. ARGENTINA	7
	E. COLOMBIA	5				
	Rest of OASL	10	Rest of OASL	17	Rest of OASL	7
Total	$24.1	100	$64.5	100	$235.5	100

a. Percentage of total forest product exports for Latin America.

SOURCE: IDB-SPTF, 1983, p. 59.

Table 2441

ROUNDWOOD TRADE, 17 LC, 1975–82
(T US)

PART I. VALUE OF IMPORTS

	Country	1975	1976	1977	1978	1979	1980	1981	1982
A.	ARGENTINA	3,477	982	495	1,379	2,457	4,613	2,659	2,216
C.	BRAZIL	5,009	4,401	3,911	5,848	6,239	6,912	6,485	3,976
D.	CHILE	#	#	#	#	#	#	#	#
E.	COLOMBIA	#	#	#	#	#	#	#	#
F.	COSTA RICA	834	836	726	926	602	891	577	374
G.	CUBA	200[†]	200[†]	200[†]	200[†]	#	#	#	#
H.	DOMINICAN REP.	#	#	#	#	#	7,256	7,256[†]	7,256[†]
J.	EL SALVADOR	70	32	49	49	60	102	102	102
K.	GUATEMALA	#	#	#	#	149	149[†]	972	972[†]
L.	HAITI	156[†]	180[†]	234	234[†]	234[†]	#	#	#
M.	HONDURAS	#	#	#	#	#	#	#	#
N.	MEXICO	3,056	4,094	1,021	1,021	8,895	16,310	15,145	15,145
O.	NICARAGUA	306	510[†]	720[†]	936[†]	1,171	1,171[†]	1,171[†]	1,171[†]
P.	PANAMA	576	576[†]	581	1,063	1,055	900[†]	2,269	2,269[†]
R.	PERU	1,157	399	288	18	24	411	54	252
S.	URUGUAY	1,096	521	790	384	1,034	1,070	388	388
T.	VENEZUELA	188[†]	2,165	2,498	2,896	2,447	2,355	2,355	2,355
	UNITED STATES	52,226	52,123	74,805	80,859	83,562	93,867	96,907	90,685

PART II. VALUE OF EXPORTS

	Country	1975	1976	1977	1978	1979	1980	1981	1982
A.	ARGENTINA	~	~	43	176	346	410	302	234
B.	BOLIVIA	~	~	925	~	~	~	~	~
C.	BRAZIL	1,236	1,708	1,465	2,410	3,951	3,072	2,370	10,770
D.	CHILE	603	726	4,302	20,595	31,235	56,835	17,672	36,891
E.	COLOMBIA	234	234[†]	234[†]	234[†]	~	~	~	~
F.	COSTA RICA	1,088	908	1,269	1,105	942	17	17	46
H.	DOMINICAN REP.	31[†]	31[†]	~	~	~	~	17	17[†]
K.	GUATEMALA	123	~	~	11	11	11	78	16
L.	HAITI	~	~	~	~	~	~	~	~
M.	HONDURAS	1,470	2,261	2,678	2,882	2,353	4,414	4,414[†]	4,414[†]
N.	MEXICO	160	360	145	119	769	613	746	746
O.	NICARAGUA	308	319[†]	322[†]	567	1,008	1,511[†]	1,511[†]	1,511[†]
P.	PANAMA	~	~	3	3[†]	~	~	~	~
Q.	PARAGUAY	162	17	148	19	15	23	23	23
R.	PERU	~	~	23	~	~	~	~	~
T.	VENEZUELA	~	~	~	~	~	~	~	~
	UNITED STATES	871,286	1,105,636	1,167,383	1,382,083	1,998,552	2,006,672	1,584,554	1,529,598

1. For definitions of roundwood, fuelwood, etc., see SALA, 24-2301.

SOURCE: FAO-YFP, 1982, pp. 68, 72.

Table 2442

SAWNWOOD AND SLEEPERS TRADE,[1] 18 LC, 1975–82
(T US)

PART I. VALUE OF IMPORTS

	Country	1975	1976	1977	1978	1979	1980	1981	1982
A.	ARGENTINA	85,274	24,836	43,235	44,829	103,028	139,409	90,217	51,714
C.	BRAZIL	3,626	8,782	13,154	19,646	16,084	24,297	17,663	12,871
D.	CHILE	#	#	#	#	#	#	#	#
E.	COLOMBIA	31	31[†]	31[†]	31[†]	31[†]	1,365	1,008	1,008[†]
F.	COSTA RICA	209	254	425	425	220	142	239	238
G.	CUBA	50,500[†]	50,500[†]	50,500[†]	66,758	53,900	87,885	87,885[†]	87,885[†]
H.	DOMINICAN REP.	14,100[†]	21,500[‡]	30,244[‡]	49,600[‡]	9,961	21,361	16,388	16,388[†]
J.	EL SALVADOR	2,326	2,780	5,058	5,058[†]	2,783	680	3,600	800
K.	GUATEMALA	389	487	421	421	240	74	166	99
L.	HAITI	1,400[†]	1,700[†]	1,906	1,906[†]	1,906[†]	1,906[†]	1,906[†]	1,906[†]
M.	HONDURAS	#	#	#	521	#	#	#	#
N.	MEXICO	22,061	20,353	4,905	4,872	24,000	66,547	66,547	66,547
O.	NICARAGUA	#	#	#	#	#	#	#	#
P.	PANAMA	1,091	1,091[†]	627	1,163	1,414	1,707	1,204	536
Q.	PARAGUAY	#	#	#	#	#	#	#	#
R.	PERU	7,115	1,838	862	906	1,567	2,827	3,182	2,940
S.	URUGUAY	3,393	3,358	4,917	5,110	10,682	9,171	8,542	8,542
T.	VENEZUELA	1,242	32,491	30,087	25,775	35,623	35,623[†]	35,623[†]	35,623[†]
	UNITED STATES	919,931	1,299,567	1,882,975	2,857,217	2,644,010	1,915,294	1,850,925	1,676,504

PART II. VALUE OF EXPORTS

	Country	1975	1976	1977	1978	1979	1980	1981	1982
A.	ARGENTINA	10	16	23	185	112	198	471	383
B.	BOLIVIA	22,000	22,000[†]	9,325	9,667	18,000[†]	19,000[†]	9,800[†]	9,800[†]
C.	BRAZIL	90,225	70,546	121,268	104,440	207,987	211,471	210,404	139,855
D.	CHILE	23,938	22,580	43,176	51,223	92,683	149,027	95,879	63,524
E.	COLOMBIA	3,002	3,002	3,002	3,002	4,273	2,597	4,807	3,830
F.	COSTA RICA	189	425	189[†]	76	17	20	505	521
I.	ECUADOR	8,898	8.997	9,200	2,000	2,000	4,078	12,969	10,173
J.	EL SALVADOR	#	#	#	#	#	#	#	#
K.	GUATEMALA	2,129	3,112	3,427	3,718	3,854	3,971	4,448	2,950
L.	HAITI	#	#	#	#	#	#	#	#
M.	HONDURAS	42,952[†]	40,005	39,126	39,314	39,522	20,208[†]	20,208[†]	20,208[†]
N.	MEXICO	4,855	71	149	30	563	246	359	359
O.	NICARAGUA	5,567	5,866[†]	5,886[†]	7,129	3,257	539	539	539
P.	PANAMA	29	29[†]	47	#	#	#	#	#
Q.	PARAGUAY	22,022[†]	9,989	16,672	16,719	32,152	52,195	26,556[†]	26,556[†]
R.	PERU	167	1,107	1,677	2,606	3,293	3,032	2,741	2,741
S.	URUGUAY	34	33	44	44[†]	#	#	#	#
	UNITED STATES	413,187	566,114	548,988	568,430	1,009,775	1,053,683	925,864	805,025

1. Cf. SALA, 23-2904 and 2905 for coniferous and nonconiferous sawnwood trade.

SOURCE: FAO-YFP, 1982, pp. 176, 180.

Table 2443

WOOD PULP TRADE, 15 LC, 1975–82
(T US)

PART I. VALUE OF IMPORTS

	Country	1975	1976	1977	1978	1979	1980	1981	1982
A.	ARGENTINA	57,713	45,819	36,900	41,808	65,291	68,391	73,314	73,350
C.	BRAZIL	44,397	29,477	29,000	31,840	35,300	37,755	21,483	9,349
D.	CHILE	1,050	1,250	950	1,000	#	#	#	#
E.	COLOMBIA	9,921	9,921†	9,921†	9,921†	22,548	29,661	38,547	26,232
F.	COSTA RICA	1,401	886	886†	636	1,772	4,542	2,995	2,775
G.	CUBA	6,800†	8,000†	9,000†	10,955	13,523	22,734	22,734†	22,734†
H.	DOMINICAN REP.	1,000†	1,000†	1,000†	298	1,362	969	969†	969†
I.	ECUADOR	886	916	857	1,593	3,426	5,248	32,857	30,745
J.	EL SALVADOR	375	340	1,003	1,003†	463	284	284†	284†
K.	GUATEMALA	2,112	5,022	3,493	2,989	6,038	17,038	7,112	868
N.	MEXICO	56,638	69,714	28,899	52,315†	62,815+	107,000	114,900	111,000
P.	PANAMA	24	24†	456	283	828	642	683	344
R.	PERU	14,524	8,464	12,221	8,942	16,451	14,469	13,770	13,770
S.	URUGUAY	3,947	2,397	3,035	3,119	5,260	5,174	4,182	4,182
T.	VENEZUELA	27,507†	32,823†	38,040†	50,736	42,700†	44,700†	44,700†	44,700†
	UNITED STATES	1,037,051	1,190,827	1,169,303	1,135,108	1,452,468	1,673,405	1,753,467	1,484,974

PART II. VALUE OF EXPORTS

	Country	1975	1976	1977	1978	1979	1980	1981	1982
C.	BRAZIL	30,503	26,656	19,487	57,468	181,266	364,211	365,531	278,504
D.	CHILE	59,593	68,896	82,393	107,896	166,615	197,276	183,415	172,639
R.	PERU	#	#	#	#	#	#	#	#
	LATIN AMERICA	90,096	95,552	101,880	165,364	347,881	561,487	548,946	451,143
	UNITED STATES	896,516	848,751	880,275	806,572	1,092,702	1,628,666	1,655,709	1,407,655

SOURCE: FAO-YFP, 1982, pp. 264, 267.

Table 2444

PAPER AND PAPERBOARD TRADE, 20 LC, 1975–82[a]

(T US)

PART I. VALUE OF IMPORTS

	Country	1975	1976	1977	1978	1979	1980	1981	1982
A.	ARGENTINA	104,627	74,022	100,544	110,585	111,167	183,304	162,262	83,392
B.	BOLIVIA	3,460[†]	3,460[†]	8,731	9,555	10,200[†]	12,100[†]	12,500[†]	12,500[†]
C.	BRAZIL	109,215	147,914	137,766	123,854	160,892	181,915	188,358	170,902
D.	CHILE	#	#	#	#	#	#	#	#
E.	COLOMBIA	41,458	39,900[‡]	35,900[‡]	40,950[‡]	66,977	82,441	118,273	98,020
F.	COSTA RICA	32,063	39,659	35,298	22,321	52,164	54,470	76,599	61,943
G.	CUBA	18,900[†]	20,300[†]	22,200[†]	30,790	38,608	75,654	75,654[†]	75,654[†]
H.	DOMINICAN REP.	7,873	8,373	20,551[‡]	21,634	25,366	26,427	37,142	37,142[†]
I.	ECUADOR	40,062	50,420	27,624	23,915	27,541	50,038	50,939	50,939[†]
J.	EL SALVADOR	21,768	21,870	25,288	25,288[†]	21,403	26,287	27,450	38,800
K.	GUATEMALA	10,411	14,080	15,262	30,740	30,065	74,055	55,309	54,599
L.	HAITI	945[†]	1,845[†]	3,076	3,076[†]	2,031[†]	2,031[†]	3,031[†]	3,031[†]
M.	HONDURAS	13,787	31,194	33,116	37,567	25,874	27,470	27,470[†]	27,470[†]
N.	MEXICO	90,673	158,604	297,909[†]	130,500[†]	161,600[†]	414,300[†]	379,900[†]	379,900[†]
O.	NICARAGUA	10,008	12,927	12,927[†]	10,800	8,428	12,562	12,562[†]	12,562[†]
P.	PANAMA	15,018	15,018[†]	19,303	26,740	24,772	29,911	30,522	29,559
Q.	PARAGUAY	4,747[†]	4,268	5,692	6,534	8,611	11,524	8,902	8,902[†]
R.	PERU	34,249	17,768	28,513	15,064	8,572	20,120	40,026	38,370
S.	URUGUAY	6,527	6,307	7,044	7,193	8,814	15,270	16,977	16,977[†]
T.	VENEZUELA	48,322[†]	57,012[†]	66,223[†]	118,091	118,903[†]	121,003[†]	121,003[†]	121,003[†]
	UNITED STATES	1,613,910	2,013,097	2,279,547	2,773,293	3,153,597	3,313,973	3,346,918	4,338,482

PART II. VALUE OF EXPORTS

	Country	1975	1976	1977	1978	1979	1980	1981	1982
A.	ARGENTINA	4,284	6,818	11,399	11,343	17,636	11,649	7,690	5,577
C.	BRAZIL	6,022	14,403	18,981	52,153	90,786	155,543	219,629	174,187
D.	CHILE	36,472	39,382	38,900	36,625	46,941	49,849	41,857	43,856
E.	COLOMBIA	541	541[†]	541[†]	541[†]	36,598	23,588	55,078	45,509
F.	COSTA RICA	594	285	552	239	3,412	13,217	12,475	10,679
J.	EL SALVADOR	1,171	973	771	771	771	771	771	771
K.	GUATEMALA	6,163	7,692	8,839	5,823	12,695	17,992	18,840	11,991
M.	HONDURAS	754[†]	845	599	2,494	2,375	4,999	4,999	4,999
N.	MEXICO	919[†]	919[†]	1,033	1,033[†]	1,100[†]	2,700[†]	4,000[†]	4,000[†]
P.	PANAMA	122	122[†]	270	124	191	635	670	947
R.	PERU	1,285	3,416	3,489	3,489	3,489	1,427	1,165	1,165
S.	URUGUAY	793	648	2,711	4,165	6,535	10,381	8,090	8,090[†]
T.	VENEZUELA	2,545	2,440	~	~	~	~	~	~
	UNITED STATES	1,100,742	1,252,434	1,121,609	1,104,708	1,340,141	2,016,959	2,013,112	1,714,085

a. For 1962-74 data see SALA, 21-2805.

SOURCE: FAO-YFP, 1982, pp. 314 and 310.

Table 2445

WOOD-BASED PANEL TRADE,[1] 18 LC, 1975–82[a]

(T US)

PART I. VALUE OF IMPORTS

	Country	1975	1976	1977	1978	1979	1980	1981	1982
A.	ARGENTINA	3,075	1,120	1,229	1,480	8,102	15,906	9,465	3,668
B.	BOLIVIA	#	#	229	105	105	105	105	105
C.	BRAZIL	1,248	1,728	2,949	5,937	7,807	14,174	12,633	11,010
D.	CHILE	#	#	#	#	#	#	#	#
E.	COLOMBIA	#	#	#	#	4,274	4,215	8,579	5,151
F.	COSTA RICA	924	1,297	1,339	836	628	1,160	245	245
G.	CUBA	2,086	2,086[†]	2,086[†]	8,841	5,587	11,439	11,439[†]	11,439[†]
H.	DOMINICAN REP.	713[†]	713[†]	3,699	6,955	10,143	919	821	821[†]
I.	ECUADOR	46	46	#	#	#	#	#	#
J.	EL SALVADOR	1,790	2,810	3,173	3,173	1,721	2,498	3,241	2,441
K.	GUATEMALA	#	#	#	756	2,712	2,616	1,912	2,279
M.	HONDURAS	222	407	507	1,036	842	99	99	99
N.	MEXICO	4,304	5,546	3,636	3,150	11,261	20,825	18,919	18,419
O.	NICARAGUA	467	467	467	627	117	136	136	136
P.	PANAMA	740	740	660	577	1,086	1,104	878	1,439
R.	PERU	448	142	19	2	2	2	2	69
S.	URUGUAY	295	244	491	524	723	1,423	765	765[†]
T.	VENEZUELA	1,972	6,696	10,726	17.075	18,628	18,628	18,628	18,628
	UNITED STATES	333,518	489,254	611,849	816,463	792,641	585,526	660,463	504,468

PART II. VALUE OF EXPORTS

	Country	1975	1976	1977	1978	1979	1980	1981	1982
A.	ARGENTINA	932	1,538	2,169	2,737	1,563	4,144	3,993	4,898
B.	BOLIVIA	#	409	3,727	3,268	1,150[†]	1,450[†]	1,510[†]	1,510[†]
C.	BRAZIL	50,568	56,763	63,049	84,114	104,035	124,976	141,179	104,942
D.	CHILE	54	2,800	2,161	3,605	4,759	6,919	5,895	9,252
E.	COLOMBIA	416	472	572	577	471	541	1,073	2,205
F.	COSTA RICA	1,697	2,584	3,275	4,416	4,177	7,647	8,229	7,400[†]
I′	ECUADOR	450	3,320	3,400	5,744	7,278	23,256	22,187	23,228
K.	GUATEMALA	822	800	712	990	1,530	480	251	352
M.	HONDURAS	922	1,450	1,755	2,293	2,243	1,718	1,718[†]	1,718[†]
N.	MEXICO	473	1,600	2,633	3,295[‡]	2,081	1,877	1,877	1,877
O.	NICARAGUA	1,412	1,412[†]	1,412[†]	3,320	3,125	2,220	2,220[†]	2,220[†]
Q.	PARAGUAY	1,869[†]	2,129	3,092	4,414	7,310	14,233	10,430	10,430[†]
R.	PERU	373	905	3,123	4,914	3,842	2,371	3,227	3,206[†]
	UNITED STATES	222,018	241,358	168,705	188,769	246,832	283,990	349,142	251,198

1. Includes veneer sheets, plywood, particle board, and fiberboard.

a. For 1962-74 data see SALA, 21-2802.

SOURCE: FAO-YFP, 1982, pp. 214 and 210.

Table 2446

FUEL[1] AS SHARE OF TOTAL COUNTRY IMPORTS, 20 LC, 1970-80

(% VALUE)

Year	A. ARGENTINA	B. BOLIVIA	C. BRAZIL	D. CHILE	E. COLOMBIA	F. COSTA RICA	G. CUBA	H. DOMINICAN REP.	I. ECUADOR	J. EL SALVADOR	K. GUATEMALA
1970	4.7	1.2	12.3	6.2	1.1	3.9	8.7	6.9	6.2	2.5	2.2
1975	13.2	2.2	26.2	19.8	1.0	10.6	10.0	~	2.1	8.4	14.1
1980	10.3	1.0	50.5[a]	~[a]	12.2	15.4	~	32.9[a]	1.3	17.7	~

Year	L. HAITI	M. HONDURAS	N. MEXICO	O. NICARAGUA	P. PANAMA	Q. PARAGUAY	R. PERU	S. URUGUAY	T. VENEZUELA	UNITED STATES
1970	5.6	6.7	3.2	6.1	18.8	14.5	2.3	14.1	1.4	7.7
1975	9.0	17.0	5.5	14.3	40.4	21.0	12.1	31.2	.7	27.2
1980	~	15.9	1.5	20.6	~[a]	~[a]	2.4	~[a]	1.6	31.1[a]

1. Includes coal, petroleum, and natural gas.

a. 1981.

SOURCE: UN-YITS, vol. 1, special table M, 1981.

Table 2447

FUELWOOD AND CHARCOAL TRADE, 7 LC, 1975–82
(T US)

PART I. VALUE OF IMPORTS

	Country	1975	1976	1977	1978	1979	1980	1981	1982
C.	BRAZIL	14	2	#	#	#	#	#	#
D.	CHILE	#	#	#	#	#	#	#	#
F.	COSTA RICA	184	224	308	82	#	#	#	#
J.	EL SALVADOR	#	#	#	#	#	#	#	#
N.	MEXICO	118	151	102	102	146	194	768	768[†]
S.	URUGUAY	#	#	#	#	#	#	#	#
T.	VENEZUELA	26[†]	26[†]	246	26[†]	26[†]	26[†]	26[†]	26[†]
	UNITED STATES	1,030	727	1,381	4,844	3,837	5,967	3,093	1,561

PART II. VALUE OF EXPORTS

	Country	1975	1976	1977	1978	1979	1980	1981	1982
C.	BRAZIL	#	#	570	808	2,000	1,582	1,010	9,400[†]
F.	COSTA RICA	1,088	908	1,269	905	905[†]	#	#	#
N.	MEXICO	158	259	145	119[†]	769	613	746	746[†]
	UNITED STATES	4,881	4,548	5,707	5,672	7,003	4,566	9,225	5,609

SOURCE: FAO-YFP, 1982, pp. 81, 83.

Table 2448

CRUDE OIL TRADE, 19 L, 1960-82
(T Barrels)

PART I. VALUE OF IMPORTS

	Country	1960	1975	1976	1977	1978	1979	1980	1981	1982[‡]
A.	ARGENTINA	23,172	15,637	22,165	21,950	16,012	12,635	15,907	9,104	3,887
B.	BOLIVIA	#	#	#	#	#	#	#	#	#
C.	BRAZIL	42,166	261,773	300,662	297,517	328,967	366,078	304,395	295,820	268,795
D.	CHILE	#	19,788	25,260	26,902	27,117	33,421	23,867	19,810	~
E.	COLOMBIA	#	#	6,726	9,405	8,833	8,995	7,339	7,714	7,327
F.	COSTA RICA	#	1,995	1,845	2,377	3,377	2,927	3,483	~	~
H.	DOMINICAN REP.	#	12,284	12,174	12,056	11,582	12,563	10,914	11,828	9,944
I.	ECUADOR	1,566	8,265	8,165	5,175	178	2,700[a]	#	#	~
J.	EL SALVADOR	#	4,980	5,094	5,255	5,472	5,142	4,563	4,123	~
K.	GUATEMALA	#	5,538	5,213	5,291	5,829	5,723	5,443	5,324	4,341
L.	HAITI	#	#	#	#	#	#	#	#	#
M.	HONDURAS	#	4,561	3,395	3,462	3,270	3,509	3,626	1,710	~
N.	MEXICO	#	#	#	#	#	#	#	#	#
O.	NICARAGUA	#	4,759	4,257	5,413	3,928	3,124	4,457	~	~
P.	PANAMA	#	29,880	18,928	20,111	16,161	16,940	13,841	10,685	11,752
Q.	PARAGUAY	#	1,501	1,488	1,860	2,334	2,198	2,030	1,839	1,741
R.	PERU	#	17,138	16,452	14,659	#	#	#	#	#
S.	URUGUAY	9,147	13,201	12,775	13,500	15,063	11,716	13,389	12,300	~
T.	VENEZUELA	#	#	#	#	#	#	#	#	#

PART II. VALUE OF EXPORTS

	Country	1960	1975	1976	1977	1978	1979	1980	1981	1982[‡]
A.	ARGENTINA	233	113	#	#	#	#	#	#	#
B.	BOLIVIA	1,093	8,282	8,057	4,480	2,863	165	#	#	#
C.	BRAZIL	4,294	7,894	#	9,471	1,694	#	420	5,166	~
D.	CHILE	#	#	#	#	#	#	#	#	#
E.	COLOMBIA	31,332	#	#	#	#	#	#	#	#
F.	COSTA RICA	#	#	#	#	#	#	#	#	#
H.	DOMINICAN REP.	#	#	#	#	#	#	#	#	#
I.	ECUADOR	#	52,094	61,509	50,453	42,000	46,000	39,636	46,449	~
J.	EL SALVADOR	#	#	#	#	#	#	#	#	#
K.	GUATEMALA	#	#	#	#	#	#	782	662	1,546
L.	HAITI	#	#	#	#	#	#	#	#	#
M.	HONDURAS	#	#	#	#	#	#	#	#	#
N.	MEXICO	1,100	34,382	34,420	73,736	133,247	194,485	302,957	400,778	544,614
O.	NICARAGUA	#	#	#	#	#	#	#	#	#
P.	PANAMA	#	#	#	#	#	#	#	#	#
Q.	PARAGUAY	#	#	#	#	#	#	#	#	#
R.	PERU	2,931	1,482	1,992	586	1,225	11,521	17,744	20,586	~
S.	URUGUAY	#	#	#	#	#	#	#	#	#
T.	VENEZUELA	730,962	537,345	501,500	482,165	454,425	511,730	469,578	462,455	387,630

a. Includes refined oil.

SOURCE: IDB-SPTF, 1978, pp. 471-472; IDB-SPTF, 1983, pp. 396-397.

Table 2449

REFINED OIL TRADE, 19 L, 1960–82
(T Barrels)

PART I. VOLUME OF IMPORTS

	Country	1960	1975	1976	1977	1978	1979	1980	1981	1982[‡]
A.	ARGENTINA	12,469	4,925	4,070	3,855	1,390	1,266	2,450	3,887	736
B.	BOLIVIA	95	133	92	199	180	127	#	#	#
C.	BRAZIL	31,857	4,372	800	10,064	7,088	8,560	13,244	8,043	7,300[†]
D.	CHILE	3,699	#	#	#	2,294	3,837	371	5,064	~
E.	COLOMBIA	1,030	2,080	2,604	3,764	7,784	10,341	12,997	11,025	11,033
F.	COSTA RICA	1,530	2,286	2,538	2,493	3,117	2,821	3,460	3,486	~
H.	DOMINICAN REP.	2,490	1,499	1,804	2,137	3,297	3,317	4,200	3,064	4,333
I.	ECUADOR	#	739	1,200	3,915	1,900	2,700	4,591	4,875	~
J.	EL SALVADOR	1,590	#	#	#	#	#	#	#	#
K.	GUATEMALA	2,930	2,175	3,533	4,356	4,522	5,679	5,369	4,054	~
L.	HAITI	620	1,093	1,494	1,493	1,643	1,704	1,625[†]	1,628	~
M.	HONDURAS	1,490	360	417	764	1,058	884	758	1,411	~
N.	MEXICO	7,804	18,150	9,285	3,807	1,138	1,264	1,719	2,146	4,516
O.	NICARAGUA	1,380	410	318	957	1,448	324	612	~	~
P.	PANAMA	2,770	704	2,667	469	181	221	560	1,492	607
Q.	PARAGUAY	799	116	333	818	932	996	1,470	1,459	1,531
R.	PERU	4,150	4,316	3,060	4,508	1,722	284	403	~	~
S.	URUGUAY	1,782	668	1,150	956	654	2,066	899	1,260	~
T.	VENEZUELA	#	#	#	#	#	#	#	#	#

PART II. VOLUME OF EXPORTS

	Country	1960	1975	1976	1977	1978	1979	1980	1981	1982[‡]
A.	ARGENTINA	220	296	836	1,184	2,428	2,078	9,430	19,881	15,713
B.	BOLIVIA	#	5	10	#	102	1,181	727	312	592
C.	BRAZIL	#	13,081	21,006	9,436	14,476	9,317	12,775	27,013	33,000[†]
D.	CHILE	112	805	967	371	#	#	#	#	#
E.	COLOMBIA	4,080	8,760	8,959	8,758	11,152	8,967	9,469	10,369	11,900
F.	COSTA RICA	#	#	#	#	#	#	#	#	#
H.	DOMINICAN REP.	#	#	#	#	#	#	#	#	#
I.	ECUADOR	#	104	123	1,037	7,900	7,400	7,957	5,846	~
J.	EL SALVADOR	#	#	#	#	#	#	#	#	#
K.	GUATEMALA	#	#	#	#	#	#	#	#	#
L.	HAITI	#	#	#	#	#	#	#	#	#
M.	HONDURAS	#	1,200	107	119	490	383	48	28	~
N.	MEXICO	6,447	2,568	1,221	1,652	673	3,701	17,062	23,645	14,704
O.	NICARAGUA	#	188	197	106	93	186	119	~	~
P.	PANAMA	#	10,197	14,000	12,173	10,493	7,345	7,723	6,118	5,661
Q.	PARAGUAY	#	#	#	#	#	#	#	#	#
R.	PERU	3,317	2,257	1,465	3,535	3,266	6,308	4,511	~	~
S.	URUGUAY	#	#	#	#	#	#	#	#	#
T.	VENEZUELA	251,747	224,099	286,890	243,090	262,070	254,405	212,646	179,580	179,580

a. Includes crude oil.

SOURCE: IDB-SPTF, 1978, pp. 471-472; IDB-SPTF, 1983, pp. 396-397.

Figure 24:2

OPEC[1] OIL PRODUCTION, 1960-83

(M Barrels Daily)

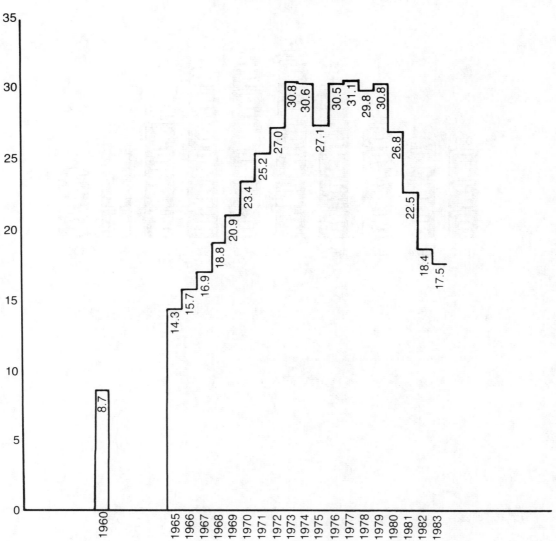

1. The thirteen OPEC countries include Ecuador and Venezuela.

SOURCE: *Los Angeles Times,* Aug. 28 and Dec. 8, 1983.

Figure 24:3

U.S. IMPORTS OF OPEC OIL,[1] 1973–83

(M Barrels Daily)

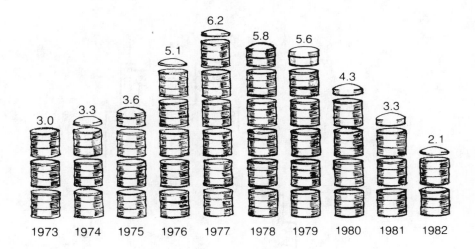

1973	1974	1975	1976	1977	1978	1979	1980	1981	1982
3.0	3.3	3.6	5.1	6.2	5.8	5.6	4.3	3.3	2.1

 1 million barrels

1. The thirteen OPEC countries include Ecuador and Venezuela.

SOURCE: *Los Angeles Times,* Aug. 18, 1983.

Table 2450

PETROLEUM AND DERIVATIVES TRADE, 19 L, 1973–82
(M US)

PART I. VALUE OF NET IMPORTS

	Country	1973	1975	1977	1979	1981	1982[‡]
A.	ARGENTINA	172.4	357.6	413.4	941.7	281.4	~
C.	BRAZIL	710.8	2,932.5	4,010.8	6,410.3	9,672.0	8,600.0
D.	CHILE	78.9	251.6	418.0	846.9	983.2	~
E.	COLOMBIA	**	**	82.4	420.5	412.2	371.6
F.	COSTA RICA	31.5	73.8	102.2	168.4	180.5	~
H.	DOMINICAN REP.	42.3	168.5	187.8	314.9	472.3	449.5
I.	ECUADOR	**	**	**	**	**	**
J.	EL SALVADOR	16.1	62.1	73.0	113.3	167.9	~
K.	GUATEMALA	33.2	106.2	166.5	254.9	344.3	265.0
L.	HAITI	6.6	12.7	28.0	45.0	62.0[‡]	61.7
M.	HONDURAS	26.0	63.1	72.0	112.8	148.0[‡]	~
N.	MEXICO	262.0	**	**	**	**	**
O.	NICARAGUA	23.6	73.8	105.1	76.6	191.9	~
P.	PANAMA	91.5	334.5	268.2	319.4	379.7	223.0
Q.	PARAGUAY	12.5	44.6	60.9	123.9	139.4	~
R.	PERU	46.3	202.2	234.0	**	**	**
S.	URUGUAY	54.7	160.2	240.2	303.2	493.5	~
T.	VENEZUELA	**	**	**	**	**	**

PART II. VALUE OF NET EXPORTS

	Country	1973	1975	1977	1979	1981	1982[‡]
A.	ARGENTINA	**	**	**	**	**	**
B.	BOLIVIA	48.9	114.5	67.4	40.1	9.8	12.3
C.	BRAZIL	**	**	**	**	**	**
D.	CHILE	**	**	**	**	**	**
E.	COLOMBIA	61.4	58.2	**	**	**	**
F.	COSTA RICA	**	**	**	**	**	**
H.	DOMINICAN REP.	**	**	**	**	**	**
I.	ECUADOR	207.1	515.9	484.1	909.1	1,344.0	~
J.	EL SALVADOR	**	**	**	**	**	**
K.	GUATEMALA	**	**	**	**	**	**
L.	HAITI	**	**	**	**	**	**
M.	HONDURAS	**	**	**	**	**	**
N.	MEXICO	**	186.5	987.3	3,789.3	13,548.7	15,473.5
O.	NICARAGUA	**	**	**	**	**	**
P.	PANAMA	**	**	**	**	**	**
Q.	PARAGUAY	**	**	**	**	**	**
R.	PERU	**	**	**	645.7	701.4	~
S.	URUGUAY	**	**	**	**	**	**
T.	VENEZUELA	4,458.3	9,984.6	11,649.7	20,269.5	36,345.6	34,000

SOURCE: IDB-SPTF, 1983, p. 126.

Table 2451

LEAD EXPORTS, 8 LC, 1978–82

	Country	Value of Exports (T US)					Value as % of World Exports				
		1978	1979	1980	1981	1982	1978	1979	1980	1981	1982
A.	ARGENTINA	693	673	3	200[†]	165[†]	#	#	#	#[†]	#[†]
B.	BOLIVIA	698	1,949	121[†]	116[†]	97[†]	#	#	#[†]	#[†]	#[†]
C.	BRAZIL	#	400	898	186	29	#	#	#	#	#
E.	COLOMBIA	24	94	131	107	30	#	#	#	#	#
N.	MEXICO	53,541	79,671	55,462	29,620	22,047	5.7	4.8	3.2	2.8	2.2
P.	PANAMA	385	502	632	690	581	#	#	#	#	#
R.	PERU	46,486	85,038	58,510	46,934	36,786	5.0	5.2	3.3	4.4	3.7
T.	VENEZUELA	~	13	2	433	~	~	#	#	#	~
	LAIA	101,442	167,838	115,127	77,598	59,154	10.8	10.2	6.6	7.2	6.0
	CACM	32	75	40	170	19[†]	#	#	#	#	#[†]
	UNITED STATES	9,271	13,947	163,680	26,050	49,102	1.0	.8	9.4	2.4	4.9

SOURCE: UN-YITS, 1982, vol. 2, p. 159.

Table 2452

COPPER EXPORTS,[1] 9 LC, 1978–82

	Country	Value of Exports (T US)					Value as % of World Exports				
		1978	1979	1980	1981	1982	1978	1979	1980	1981	1982
A.	ARGENTINA	330	504	411	1,928[†]	1,584[†]	#	#	#	#[†]	#[†]
B.	BOLIVIA	~	198[†]	772[†]	742[†]	620[†]	~	#[†]	#[†]	#[†]	#[†]
C.	BRAZIL	5,806	11,856	10,606	23,932	21,867	#	#	#	#	#
D.	CHILE	1,184,664	1,799,600	2,009,061	1,624,943[†]	1,579,485[†]	15.2	16.4	15.5	16.3[†]	17.4[†]
E.	COLOMBIA	99	222	145	105	209	#	#	#	#	#
K.	GUATEMALA	50	228	335	91	8[†]	#	#	#	#	#[†]
N.	MEXICO	20,024	14,109	6,631[†]	7,138[†]	36,781[†]	#	#	#[†]	#[†]	#[†]
R.	PERU	348,541	667,147	609,927	317,932	382,923	4.5	6.1	4.7	3.2	4.2
T.	VENEZUELA	920	~	53	484	9[†]	#	~	#	#	#[†]
	LAIA	1,560,387	2,493,636	2,637,648	1,977,308[†]	2,023,014[†]	20.0	22.7	20.3	19.9[†]	22.3[†]
	CACM	50	367	344	131	117[†]	#	#	#	#	#[†]
	UNITED STATES	321,572	437,119	457,223	452,943	330,584	4.1	4.0	3.5	4.6	3.6

1. Except cement copper.

SOURCE: UN-YITS, 1982, vol. 2, p. 156.

Table 2453

TIN EXPORTS,[1] 9 LC, 1978–82

	Country	Value of Exports (T US)					Value as % of World Exports				
		1978	1979	1980	1981	1982	1978	1979	1980	1981	1982
A.	ARGENTINA	~	~	1	5	~	~	~	~	~	~
B.	BOLIVIA	~	~	230,355[†]	221,265[†]	184,962[†]	~	~	7.4[†]	8.1[†]	8.2[†]
C.	BRAZIL	21,058	23,293	46,547	64,517	55,920	1.1	.9	1.5	2.4	2.5
D.	CHILE	~	3,195[†]	5,154[†]	4,778[†]	4,644[†]	~	#	#	#	#
F.	COSTA RICA	~	~	~	9	~	~	~	~	#	~
J.	EL SALVADOR	~	8	1	~	~	~	#	#	~	~
K.	GUATEMALA	~	~	~	16	~	~	~	~	#	~
N.	MEXICO	13	23	7[†]	8[†]	39[†]	#	#	#	#	#
R.	PERU	60	22	25	36	33	#	#	#	#	#
	LAIA	21,131	26,533	282,088[†]	290,608[†]	245,599[†]	1.1	1.1	9.1[†]	10.6[†]	10.9[†]
	CACM	~	~	10	25	~	~	~	#	#	~
	UNITED STATES	57,827	50,857	72,576	86,558	135,788	2.9	2.1	2.3	3.2	6.0

1. Unwrought alloys.

SOURCE: UN-YITS, 1982, vol. 2, p. 584.

Table 2454

ZINC EXPORTS, 7 LC, 1978–82

	Country	Value of Exports (T US)					Value as % of World Exports				
		1978	1979	1980	1981	1982	1978	1979	1980	1981	1982
A.	ARGENTINA	3,765	452	185	79[†]	65[†]	#	#	#	#[†]	#[†]
C.	BRAZIL	79	146	106	2,508	2,043	#	#	#	#	#
D.	CHILE	14	47[†]	#	71[†]	69[†]	#	#[†]	#	#[†]	#[†]
H.	DOMINICAN REP.	2	11	~	104	~	#	#	~	#	~
K.	GUATEMALA	6	154	120	68	~	#	#	#	#	~
N.	MEXICO	65,308	56,697	46,588	18,588	10,853	#	#	#	#	#
R.	PERU	28,113	39,435	32,759	90,207	113,959	2.3	2.8	2.2	5.4	7.0
	LAIA	97,291	96,856	79,638	111,525	127,022	8.1	6.9	5.3	6.6	7.8
	CACM	17	163	125	149	~	#	#	#	#	~
	UNITED STATES	7,931	7,967	14,123	15,000	9,530	#	#	#	#	#

SOURCE: UN-YITS, 1982, vol. 2, p. 160.

Table 2455

STRUCTURE OF TOTAL MERCHANDISE IMPORTS, 20 LC, 1960–73

Country	Food and Raw Materials (%)				Fuels and Lubricants (%)				Machinery and Equipment (%)				Other Manufactured Products (%)				Total Merchandise Imports (M US)			
	1960	1965	1970	1973	1960	1965	1970	1973	1960	1965	1970	1973	1960	1965	1970	1973	1960	1965	1970	1973
A. ARGENTINA	26.7	42.2	36.5	~	12.5	9.6	4.7	~	43.9	25.1	30.7	~	16.9	23.1	28.1	~	1,249.3	1,198.6	1,688.6	1,905.0^a
B. BOLIVIA	~	~	16.5^b	~	~	~	.7^b	~	~	~	14.9^b	~	~	~	67.9^b	~	69.4	134.0	166.2	249.5
C. BRAZIL	26.9	33.3	23.7	19.0^a	19.2	20.5	12.3	13.5^a	35.7	22.3	35.3	39.8^a	18.2	23.9	28.7	27.7^a	1,462.1	1,096.4	2,844.6	7,211.0
D. CHILE	~	~	31.1	~	~	~	7.3	~	~	~	37.5	~	~	~	24.1	27.7^a	499.7	603.6	930.6	941.1
E. COLOMBIA	23.1	25.4	23.3	~	2.7	1.3	1.1	~	42.8	45.4	46.5	~	31.4	27.9	29.1	~	518.6	453.5	844.0	836.5
F. COSTA RICA	19.6	16.8	19.9	16.9	5.6	4.9	3.9	6.2	26.1	29.2	28.7	27.1	48.7	49.1	47.5	49.8	110.4	178.2	316.7	455.4
G. CUBA	~	~	~	~	~	~	~	~	~	~	~	~	~	~	~	~	~	~	~	~
H. DOMINICAN REP.	~	~	19.8	~	~	~	6.9	~	~	~	33.7	~	~	~	39.6	~	87.0	86.7	278.0	422.6
I. ECUADOR	22.3	~	7.1	~	2.7	~	6.8	~	33.8	~	38.1	~	41.2	~	48.0	~	100.0	169.0	247.6	326.5
J. EL SALVADOR	22.1	23.0	22.1	~	6.0	5.1	2.5	~	25.5	27.5	23.0	~	46.4	44.4	52.4	~	122.4	200.6	213.6	276.6
K. GUATEMALA	19.2	18.1	20.6	~	10.1	6.9	2.2	~	26.3	28.7	27.0	~	44.4	46.3	50.2	~	137.9	229.0	284.3	403.9
L. HAITI	~	~	27.6	~	~	~	5.6	~	~	~	20.6	~	~	~	46.2	~	40.4	37.1	53.4	73.9
M. HONDURAS	15.8	16.7	17.3	13.9	8.6	5.6	6.7	10.0	24.0	25.4	29.5	28.9	51.6	52.3	46.5	47.2	71.8	121.9	220.7	262.2
N. MEXICO	17.1	18.8	21.8	20.8^a	2.4	2.4	3.2	4.8^a	51.6	49.6	50.1	48.4^a	28.9	29.2	24.9	25.8^a	1,186.5	1,559.7	2,460.7	4,144.8
O. NICARAGUA	14.4	16.9	18.9	11.9	9.6	4.8	6.1	7.2	22.0	30.1	27.7	25.7	54.0	48.2	47.3	55.2	71.7	160.0	197.9	327.0
P. PANAMA	19.8	16.7	14.5	10.6^a	10.0	20.7	18.7	17.1^a	22.2	20.6	27.6	28.3^a	48.0	42.0	39.1	44.0^a	108.6	208.4	352.7	488.5
Q. PARAGUAY	~	~	27.7	~	~	~	6.7	~	37.1	~	38.1	~	30.8	~	27.5	~	33.0	47.0	70.8	122.2
R. PERU	27.1	~	31.5^b	~	5.0	~	2.0	5.6	37.1	~	36.0	37.4	30.8	~	32.2^b	~	372.9	718.8	622.1	768.5
S. URUGUAY	~	~	28.2	23.1^a	~	~	14.1	32.3^a	~	~	28.2	17.7^a	~	~	29.5	26.9^a	244.0	150.0	233.1	186.7^a
T. VENEZUELA	27.8	25.1	21.7	16.9	1.1	.7	1.4	~	36.0	42.6	43.3	50.0	35.1	31.6	33.6	33.1	1,060.3	1,297.5	1,739.0	3,242.0
UNITED STATES	52.4	45.2	33.5	28.8	10.5	10.4	7.7	11.7	9.7	13.8	28.0	30.3	27.4	30.6	30.8	29.2	15.1^c	21.3^c	40.0^c	69.1^c

a. 1972.
b. 1969.
c. Total imports in billions.

SOURCE: WB-WT, 1976, Series 3, table 9.

Table 2456

MANUFACTURED GOODS[1] AS SHARE OF TOTAL VALUE OF COUNTRY TRADE, 20 LC, 1970–80

(%)

Country	Year	Imports CIF	Exports FOB	Country	Year	Imports CIF	Exports FOB
A. ARGENTINA	1970	78.2	14.0	L. HAITI	1970	69.0	23.8
	1975	71.6	24.4		1975	54.0	38.0
	1980	78.9	24.9		1978	~	55.3
B. BOLIVIA	1970	76.8	43.4	M. HONDURAS	1970	80.8	8.6
	1975	79.3	35.4		1975	68.6	11.0
	1980	71.5	38.3		1980	72.7	12.5
C. BRAZIL	1970	73.3	13.5	N. MEXICO[2,3]	1970	81.5	40.1
	1975	64.9	25.6		1975	74.9	40.5
	1981	38.4	39.6		1980	74.5	11.9
D. CHILE[2]	1970	73.2	82.0	O. NICARAGUA	1970	82.3	16.2
	1975	57.1	71.6		1975	76.1	17.0
	1978	~	55.6		1980	62.6	13.7
E. COLOMBIA	1970	85.5	8.7	P. PANAMA	1970	71.2	1.6
	1975	83.6	21.0		1975	50.2	5.0
	1980	71.6	19.7		1978	65.2	12.2
F. COSTA RICA	1970	83.4	18.7	Q. PARAGUAY[4]	1970	64.2	8.5
	1975	77.1	24.0		1975	62.9	10.4
	1980	69.7	28.4		1979	58.6	6.9
G. CUBA	1970	~	.6	R. PERU[2]	1970	73.4	30.4
	1975	48.0	.1		1975	68.8	26.6
	1980	~	.3		1980	74.0	40.8
H. DOMINICAN REP.	1970	72.2	3.4	S. URUGUAY	1970	65.1	23.9
	1975	~	17.3		1975	51.3	30.0
	1981	47.5	18.8		1979	56.3	32.8
I. ECUADOR	1970	84.6	1.7	T. VENEZUELA[4]	1970	83.3	1.6
	1975	87.3	2.2		1975	83.9	1.2
	1980	88.0	~		1980	80.6	3.8
J. EL SALVADOR	1970	81.3	29.5	UNITED STATES[5]	1970	64.8	68.8
	1975	76.9	27.8		1975	53.8	67.0
	1980	62.1	37.4		1981	55.4	68.6
K. GUATEMALA	1970	84.7	28.0				
	1975	74.8	24.8				
	1980	~	28.8				

1. Includes machinery, transportation equipment, chemicals, rubber, wool, textiles, iron, steel, nonferrous metals, metal equipment, etc. Cf. SALA, 23-2909.
2. Consists mainly of the exports of nonferrous base materials.
3. Exports include revaluation, but exclude goods from customs bonded warehouses.
4. Imports FOB.
5. Prior to 1974, imports FOB.

SOURCE: UN-YITS, vol. 1, special table M, 1981.

Table 2457

TOTAL MERCHANDISE EXPORTS AS SHARE
OF COUNTRY GDP, 1970–82

(%)

Country	1970	1975	1978	1979	1980	1981	1982
LAIA							
A. ARGENTINA	4.2	6.1	12.9	14.7	15.0	18.1	16.0
C. BRAZIL	3.2	6.0	7.4	8.4	10.3	12.1	10.5
D. CHILE	8.9	13.3	16.1	~	25.7	~	~
N. MEXICO	1.7	3.7	5.7	7.3	~	~	~
Q. PARAGUAY	4.0	7.9	8.7	9.4	~	~	~
S. URUGUAY	5.2	7.7	12.7	13.8	17.6	20.5	~
Andean Group							
B. BOLIVIA	11.0	19.6	23.2	25.6	~	~	~
E. COLOMBIA	5.3	7.9	13.8	14.2	16.4	11.9	12.3
I. ECUADOR	5.3	20.3	20.6	26.5	~	~	~
R. PERU	7.6	6.8	10.5	19.0	17.8	12.2	14.3
T. VENEZUELA	13.0	28.8	24.9	38.0	52.2	47.2	~
CACM							
F. COSTA RICA	11.7	18.7	28.5	27.6	30.2	31.0	~
J. EL SALVADOR	9.4	16.1	16.8	28.1	21.5	16.2	~
K. GUATEMALA	5.9	9.7	14.3	14.2	17.6	13.1	~
M. HONDURAS	11.2	17.2	27.3	30.6	33.6	29.3	~
O. NICARAGUA	8.6	15.6	30.4	31.4	18.6	19.8	15.6
Non-associated countries							
H. DOMINICAN REP.	~	19.2	11.7	13.9	12.3	16.8	10.5
L. HAITI	4.5	7.4	12.6	11.4	~	~	~
P. PANAMA	5.5	9.6	8.7	9.9	10.6	9.2	8.8

SOURCE: IDB-SPTF, 1984, p. 97.

Table 2458

COTTON EXPORTS, 11 LC, 1978–82

Country	Value of Exports (T US)					Value as % of World Exports				
	1978	1979	1980	1981	1982	1978	1979	1980	1981	1982
A. ARGENTINA	152,241	74,198	126,791	193,515[†]	158,982[†]	3.1	1.3	1.9	3.2[†]	3.0[†]
B. BOLIVIA	14,786	10,579	3,395[†]	3,261[†]	2,726[†]	#	#	#[†]	#[†]	#[†]
C. BRAZIL	54,185	4,239	17,452	45,050	64,593	#	#	#	#	#
E. COLOMBIA	57,417	38,044	82,359	93,812	26,707	#	#	#	#	#[†]
J. EL SALVADOR	100,469	87,003	87,142	55,213	41,808[†]	2.9	3.4	2.5	1.8	1.9[†]
K. GUATEMALA	141,679	187,573	172,330	111,434	103,232[†]	#	#	#	#	#[†]
M. HONDURAS	15,741	11,510	13,649	12,577	4,421[†]	#	#	#	#	#
N. MEXICO	292,045	313,515	324,173	306,490	183,825	5.9	5.7	4.7	5.1	3.5
O. NICARAGUA	188,644	157,144	30,922	123,639	85,941	#	#	#	#	#[†]
Q. PARAGUAY	100,024	98,596	105,833	129,288	70,809[†]	#	#	#	#	#
R. PERU	37,861	43,989	62,565	59,657	74,691	#	#	#	#	#
LAIA	708,679	588,627	723,417	833,816[†]	583,381[†]	14.4	10.6	10.6	13.8[†]	11.0[†]
LACM	456,085	443,753	305,503	302,875	233,402[†]	9.3	8.0	4.5	5.0	4.4[†]
UNITED STATES	1,767,513	2,230,302	2,907,170	2,299,164	2,004,918	35.9	40.3	42.4	38.2	37.7

SOURCE: UN-YITS, 1982, vol. 2, p. 64.

Table 2459

FERTILIZER IMPORTS,[1] 20 LRC, 1970–81[a]

(T MET)

	Country	1970/71	1971/72	1972/73	1973/74	1974/75	1975/76	1976/77	1977/78	1978/79	1979/80	1980/81
A.	ARGENTINA	64	34	52‡	41	52	36	48	43	80	119	64
B.	BOLIVIA	2	4‡	5‡	6	6‡	3‡	3‡	4	5	3	5‡
C.	BRAZIL	777	777	1,214	1,164	1,197	1,223	1,402	1,855	1,763	1,977	2,194‡
D.	CHILE	98	105	80	142	125	86	35	82	93	112	142
E.	COLOMBIA	61	77	110	182	172	31	112	195‡	225	186	210‡
F.	COSTA RICA	60	80	65‡	67	80	53	61	65	85	64‡	60‡
G.	CUBA	400	252	198	287	282	352	315	359	413	324	412
H.	DOMINICAN REP.	43	58	68	76	98	84‡	66‡	56	65	90‡	87
I.	ECUADOR	30	18	36	49	35	26	74	86	70	75	73
J.	EL SALVADOR	72	89‡	106	116	103‡	95	111	106	104	67	64
K.	GUATEMALA	46	25	43	50	65	52‡	84	107	70	102‡	89‡
L.	HAITI	~	~	1	1‡	2	2‡	~	3‡	4‡	4‡	~
M.	HONDURAS	24‡	32‡	24‡	25‡	18‡	20‡	25‡	28‡	23‡	20‡	31‡
N.	MEXICO	35	75	89	95	81	210	308	229	313	331	351‡
O.	NICARAGUA	26	30	27‡	55‡	45‡	10‡	48	58	39	23‡	65‡
P.	PANAMA	21	24	26	22	28	25	23‡	23‡	23‡	30‡	31‡
Q.	PARAGUAY	9	5	5	3	2	1	1‡	1‡	3‡	6	6
R.	PERU	58‡	53	95	69	134	84	30	63	61	54	44
S.	URUGUAY	25	54	44	33	24	37	58	49	45	67	60
T.	VENEZUELA	40	47	65	68	92	63	176‡	165	136‡	155	175
	LATIN AMERICA	1,891@	1,839@	2,353@	2,551@	2,641@	2,493@	2,980@	3,578@	3,620@	3,809@	4,163@
	UNITED STATES	3,377	3,865	3,984	4,989	4,827	4,852	6,389	6,408	6,808	7,491	7,448
	WORLD	18,512	19,842	22,168	25,125	24,985	24,291	26,151	29,586	32,864	33,978	36,365

1. Includes nitrogenous, phosphate, and potash fertilizers.

a. For 1961–70 data see SALA, 23-1522.

SOURCE: FAO-FY, 1979 and 1981, table 31.

Table 2460

FERTILIZER EXPORTS,[1] 9 LC, 1970–81[a]

(T MET)

	Country	1970/71	1971/72	1972/73	1973/74	1974/75	1975/76	1976/77	1977/78	1978/79	1979/80	1980/81
A.	ARGENTINA	#	#	#	#	#	#	#	#	1	2	1
C.	BRAZIL	#	#	3	7	2	#	#	#	5	8	4‡
D.	CHILE	82	102	81	76	87	66	73	77	82	89	96
E.	COLOMBIA	2	2	1	#	14‡	23‡	9	2‡	5‡	5‡	8‡
F.	COSTA RICA	9	17‡	16‡	19‡	15‡	13‡	17	19	18	13‡	11‡
J.	EL SALVADOR	5	10‡	15‡	13‡	10	8	16	20	15	12‡	~
N.	MEXICO	78	88	111	99	40	1	30	75	51	48	30
S.	URUGUAY	#	#	#	#	#	#	#	#	4	5	8‡
T.	VENEZUELA	#	#	#	#	5‡	3‡	54‡	33‡	9	75	71‡
	UNITED STATES	2,355	2,530	3,357	3,444	3,472	3,924	4,305	5,511	6,641	6,908	7,590
	WORLD	19,142	20,912	23,301	24,934	25,540	22,834	26,630	30,806	34,191	34,371	37,337

1. Includes nitrogenous, phosphate, and potash fertilizers.

a. For 1961–70 data see SALA, 23-1523.

SOURCE: FAO-FY, 1979 and 1981, table 32.

Table 2461

COTTON LINT EXPORT VOLUME,[1] 13 LC, 1975–82
(T MET)

	Country	1975	1976	1977	1978	1979	1980	1981	1982
A.	ARGENTINA	6	50	64	147	62	86	24[‡]	69
B.	BOLIVIA	15	9	9	8	10	.6	#	#
C.	BRAZIL	83	5	35	45	#	9	30	56
E.	COLOMBIA	86	53	71	54	26	48	52[‡]	25[‡]
F.	COSTA RICA	~	2	2	9	#	1	#	#
H.	DOMINICAN REP.[3]	~	~	#	~	#	#	#	#
J.	EL SALVADOR	53	52	51	58	56	53	30	33
K.	GUATEMALA	107	100	124	130	147	137	110[‡]	66
M.	HONDURAS	4	4	5	13	9	9	7[‡]	6
N.	MEXICO[3]	166	143	131	200	212	172	183	126
O.	NICARAGUA[3]	132	112	116	129	114	20	73[‡]	60
Q.	PARAGUAY	17	33	59	84	77	75	91	112
R.	PERU	46	39	21	21[‡]	20	30	32[‡]	60
	UNITED STATES[2,3]	871	748	973	1,279	1,527	1,823	1,269	1,392
	WORLD	3,879	4,002	3,892	4,387	4,374	4,815	4,296	4,448

1. Figures refer to "special trade" except where otherwise indicated. See table 2409, n. 1, for explanation of "special" exports.
2. The customs area includes the Commonwealth of Puerto Rico.
3. Figures refer to "general trade," i.e., total exports including re-exports.

a. For 1934–75 see SALA, 20-2922.

SOURCE: FAO-TY, 1958; FAO-TY, 1980; FAO-TY, 1981, table 109; FAO-TY, 1982, table 109.

CHAPTER 25

STRUCTURE AND TERMS OF TRADE

Table 2500

ARGENTINA PERCENTAGE VALUE OF TRADE, 1970–80

Category	Imports by Broad Economic Category						
	1970	1975	1976	1977	1978	1979	1980
Total Imports	100.0	100.0	100.0	100.0	100.0	100.0	100.0
1. Food and Beverages	5.5	4.4	4.7	5.2	5.5	7.0	5.4
Primary	4.2	3.6	4.0	4.0	3.7	3.9	3.1
For Industry	2.6	2.1	2.9	2.9	2.2	1.7	1.1
For Hshold Consm	1.6	1.5	1.2	1.1	1.5	2.2	2.0
Processed	1.3	.8	.7	1.1	1.8	3.1	2.3
For Industry	.3	.3	.3	.6	.8	1.0	.5
For Hshold Consm	1.0	.5	.4	.5	1.0	2.1	1.8
2. Ind. Supplies Nes	53.2	58.3	49.6	39.1	37.9	37.1	32.7
Primary	5.0	6.4	6.0	5.0	4.2	3.9	2.6
Processed	48.1	51.9	43.7	34.1	33.6	33.2	30.1
3. Fuels Lubricants	4.6	13.1	17.4	16.2	12.2	16.3	10.1
Primary	2.8	11.2	14.9	14.2	11.1	9.1	8.9
Processed	1.8	1.9	2.5	2.1	1.1	7.2	1.2
4. Machinery	25.8	16.7	20.6	26.5	30.1	22.1	27.3
Machines Capt. Eqp	21.0	13.3	16.3	21.9	25.4	19.0	23.5
Parts Accessories	4.8	3.4	4.3	4.6	4.6	3.2	3.8
5. Transport	6.1	4.4	5.6	10.1	9.4	10.7	10.6
Passenger Cars	.1	0	.1	.1	.1	1.2	2.3
Other	.7	1.3	1.5	5.8	4.8	5.9	4.3
Parts Accessories	5.3	3.1	4.1	4.3	4.5	3.6	4.0
6. Consumer Goods	4.7	3.0	2.0	2.9	4.9	6.9	13.8
Durable	1.6	1.3	.4	1.1	1.9	2.4	6.1
Semi-Durable	1.3	.5	.4	.6	1.3	2.8	5.4
Non-Durable	1.8	1.2	1.2	1.2	1.8	1.7	2.3
7. Other	.1	.1	0	0	0	0	0

Origin	Exports by Industrial Origin						
	1970	1975	1976	1977	1978	1979	1980
Total Exports (1 + 2 + 3)	100.0	100.0	100.0	100.0	100.0	100.0	100.0
1. Agriculture	39.4	47.1	41.7	41.4	41.4	40.7	38.7
2. Mining Quarrying	.3	.4	.2	.2	.3	.3	.4
3. Manufacturing	60.2	52.6	58.1	58.4	58.2	59.1	60.9
31. Food, Bev., Tobac.	43.3	25.8	30.9	32.0	29.0	32.1	30.6
32. Textiles	5.5	4.9	7.5	8.6	9.9	10.4	8.9
33. Wood, Wood Prod.	#	0	0	0	0	0	0
34. Paper and Prod.	.9	.9	.8	2.3	.9	.8	.9
35. Chemicals	4.0	4.7	4.3	3.9	4.7	4.5	8.8
36. Non-Metal Minrl	.1	.2	.3	.4	.6	.4	.4
37. Basic Metal Ind.	1.7	.8	2.4	1.5	3.7	3.3	3.5
38. Metal Manufact.	4.5	15.1	11.7	9.6	9.3	7.6	7.6
39. Oth. Manf. Ind.	.1	.1	.1	.1	.1	.1	.2

SOURCE: UN-YITS, 1976, 1981.

Table 2501

BOLIVIA PERCENTAGE VALUE OF TRADE, 1971–78

Category	Imports by Broad Economic Category						
	1971	1972	1974	1975	1976	1977	1978
Total Imports	100.0	100.0	100.0	100.0	100.0	100.0	100.0
1. Food and Beverages	20.2	18.2	20.9	16.7	14.2	13.2	13.1
Primary	3.3	2.6	3.5	3.2	3.4	4.4	5.1
For Industry	2.4	1.7	2.6	2.5	2.8	3.8	4.2
For Hshold Consm	.9	.9	.9	.6	.6	.7	.9
Processed	17.0	15.6	17.4	13.5	10.8	8.8	8.0
For Industry	10.5	6.7	10.4	8.8	6.7	3.8	2.9
For Hshold Consm	6.4	8.9	7.0	4.8	4.1	5.0	5.2
2. Ind. Supplies Nes.	32.0	30.4	28.3	28.8	29.9	26.7	23.4
Primary	.8	1.0	.7	.7	.5	.3	.5
Processed	31.2	29.4	27.6	28.1	29.4	26.4	22.9
3. Fuels Lubricants	.7	.6	.7	1.7	1.6	1.2	.9
Primary	0	0	0	0	0	0	0
Processed	.7	.6	.7	1.6	1.6	1.2	.9
Motor Spirit	.5	.5	.6	.6	.5	.7	.5
Other	.2	0	.1	1.0	1.1	.5	.4
4. Machinery	21.7	19.4	17.9	19.8	24.4	28.8	31.3
Machines Capt. Eqp	18.5	17.4	15.8	18.1	22.0	26.4	29.0
Parts Accessories	3.2	2.1	2.1	1.7	2.4	2.5	2.3
5. Transport	13.0	15.8	19.3	21.7	18.7	15.8	17.4
Passenger Cars	.6	1.2	2.5	4.3	2.0	1.6	3.0
Other	6.4	8.5	11.4	11.9	11.6	8.9	9.1
Industrial	6.1	8.2	11.0	11.3	11.1	8.0	8.5
Non-Industrial	.2	.3	.4	.6	.5	.9	.7
Pars Accessories	6.0	6.1	5.4	5.5	5.1	5.2	5.3
6. Consumer Goods	12.2	11.7	12.5	11.2	11.2	12.8	12.7
Durable	3.2	3.2	4.9	4.4	4.8	5.1	4.4
Semi-Durable	3.0	3.0	2.5	2.4	2.1	2.5	3.0
Non-Durable	6.0	5.6	5.0	4.4	4.3	5.2	5.3
7. Other	.2	3.9	.5	.1	0	1.4	1.2

Origin	Exports by Industrial Origin							
	1971	1972	1973	1974	1975	1976	1977	1978
Total Exports (1 + 2 + 3)	100.0	100.0	100.0	100.0	100.0	100.0	100.0	100.0
1. Agriculture	5.4	8.4	4.8	4.5	5.7	4.9	5.2	6.4
2. Mining Quarrying	39.3	41.4	44.4	49.8	48.9	46.4	37.9	58.1
3. Manufacturing	55.3	50.2	50.8	45.7	45.3	48.6	56.9	35.5
31. Food, Bev., Tobac.	1.5	1.0	3.1	3.6	3.5	6.9	4.3	2.6
32. Textiles	.3	.4	.1	.1	.2	.3	.5	.3
33. Wood, Wood Prod.	1.4	.3	.8	1.8	1.6	1.6	1.5	1.7
34. Paper and Prod.	0	0	0	~	0	0	0	0
35. Chemicals	2.3	.1	2.1	2.1	3.2	1.9	2.3	.3
36. Non-Metal Minrl	0	0	.6	.1	0	0	0	0
37. Basic Metal Ind.	49.5	48.1	43.8	37.9	36.5	37.7	47.9	29.9
38. Metal Manufact.	.3	.2	.4	1.	.1	.1	.3	.6
39. Oth. Manf. Ind.	0	0	0	.1	.2	.1	.2	.1

SOURCE: UN-YITS, 1976, 1977, 1978.

Table 2502

BRAZIL PERCENTAGE VALUE OF TRADE, 1970–81

	Imports by Broad Economic Category							
Category	1970	1975	1976	1977	1978	1979	1980	1981
Total Imports	100.0	100.0	100.0	100.0	100.0	100.0	100.0	100.0
1. Food and Beverages	10.4	5.9	7.6	6.6	8.7	10.3	8.2	7.9
Primary	8.3	4.7	6.5	5.2	7.4	7.9	6.7	6.8
For Industry	5.2	3.2	4.6	2.9	4.8	5.4	5.1	5.6
For Hshold Consm	3.1	1.5	1.9	2.3	2.6	2.5	1.6	1.3
Processed	2.1	1.1	1.2	1.4	1.3	2.5	1.5	1.1
For Industry	.8	.6	.6	.7	.7	.8	.5	.5
For Hshold Consm	1.3	.5	.6	.7	.6	1.6	1.0	.6
2. Ind. Supplies Nes.	36.5	33.9	30.0	31.1	29.4	28.5	27.0	21.1
Primary	2.0	2.0	2.2	2.4	3.5	3.7	3.4	2.6
Processed	34.5	31.9	27.7	28.7	25.9	24.8	23.6	18.6
3. Fuels Lubricants	12.2	25.3	30.4	33.4	32.5	36.9	43.0	50.4
Primary	10.6	24.3	29.3	32.1	31.4	35.8	40.7	48.6
Processed	1.6	.9	1.1	1.2	1.1	1.1	2.2	1.8
Motor Spirit	.1	.1	.1	.2	.1	.2	.2	.2
Other	1.5	.8	1.0	1.1	.9	.9	2.0	1.6
4. Machinery	27.5	27.8	24.8	22.2	23.3	19.2	15.7	15.6
Machines Capt. Eqp	23.6	24.0	20.7	17.7	18.9	15.0	11.9	11.7
Parts Accessories	3.9	3.8	4.1	4.5	4.5	4.2	3.7	3.9
5. Transport	9.0	4.8	4.9	4.6	3.6	2.9	4.5	3.6
Passenger Cars	.1	.1	0	0	0	0	0	0
Other	5.5	1.9	1.8	1.5	.9	.7	2.0	.9
Industrial	5.4	1.8	1.8	1.5	.9	.7	1.9	.9
Non-Industrial	#	0	0	0	0	0	0	0
Parts Accessories	3.5	2.8	3.1	3.1	2.7	2.3	2.6	2.6
6. Consumer Goods	3.7	2.3	2.1	2.0	2.3	2.0	1.6	1.4
Durable	1.6	1.1	1.0	.8	1.0	.8	.6	.4
Semi-Durable	.9	.5	.4	.4	.4	.4	.3	.2
Non-Durable	1.2	.7	.8	.8	.9	.8	.7	.7
7. Other	.6	.1	.1	.1	.2	.1	.1	0

	Exports by Industrial Origin							
Origin	1970	1975	1976	1977	1978	1979	1980	1981
Total Exports (1 + 2 + 3)	100.0	100.0	100.0	100.0	100.0	100.0	100.0	100.0
1. Agriculture	53.6	28.4	37.4	34.2	25.8	22.1	19.9	13.5
2. Mining Quarrying	10.2	13.5	13.3	9.6	9.5	9.7	9.2	10.0
3. Manufacturing	36.2	58.1	49.3	56.2	64.7	68.2	70.9	76.6
31. Food, Bev., Tobac.	18.1	27.6	23.0	28.4	27.3	25.2	26.9	28.5
32. Textiles	2.6	7.6	7.1	6.9	8.1	8.9	7.1	7.0
33. Wood, Wood Prod.	3.9	1.6	1.3	1.3	1.5	1.8	1.9	1.7
34. Paper and Prod.	.3	.9	.7	.7	1.2	2.1	2.7	2.6
35. Chemicals	2.1	3.7	2.1	2.6	3.9	5.1	6.4	9.4
36. Non-Metal Minrl	.4	.5	.4	.4	.6	.7	.8	.8
37. Basic Metal Ind.	3.8	2.3	2.4	2.4	4.0	5.6	4.9	4.9
38. Metal Manufact.	4.0	11.5	10.4	12.5	16.8	17.6	18.6	19.9
39. Oth. Manf. Ind.	1.0	2.4	1.8	1.0	1.2	1.2	1.6	1.8

SOURCE: UN-YITS, 1977, 1978, 1979, 1980.

Table 2503

CHILE PERCENTAGE VALUE OF TRADE, 1970–80

Category	Imports by Broad Economic Category				
	1970	1975	1976	1977	1978
Total Imports	100.0	100.0	100.0	100.0	100.0
1. Food and Beverages	12.5	16.3	24.3	10.8	14.6
Primary	8.4	9.8	18.0	5.9	8.1
For Industry	5.2	8.2	16.5	4.1	6.1
For Hshold Consm	3.2	1.6	1.5	1.9	2.0
Processed	4.0	6.5	6.4	4.8	6.4
For Industry	1.9	5.7	5.2	2.3	3.2
For Hshold Consm	2.2	.8	1.2	2.6	3.3
2. Ind. Supplies Nes.	31.1	25.7	22.4	24.2	24.6
Primary	5.6	4.4	5.5	4.2	4.3
Processed	25.5	21.3	16.9	20.0	20.3
3. Fuels Lubricants	6.0	19.6	11.6	19.8	16.6
Primary	4.1	19.1	10.7	18.7	15.6
Processed	1.9	.6	.9	1.1	1.0
Motor Spirit	.3	0	.2	0	0
Other	1.7	.6	.8	1.1	1.0
4. Machinery	27.7	22.6	21.9	23.1	19.9
Machines Capt. Eqp	23.7	18.7	17.6	19.9	16.9
Parts Accessories	4.0	3.9	4.3	3.2	2.9
5. Transport	16.6	11.5	13.2	12.2	11.4
Passenger Cars	2.5	.8	.8	3.5	2.6
Other	9.0	7.3	7.5	5.6	5.2
Industrial	8.9	7.2	7.3	5.0	4.6
Non-Industrial	#	.1	.1	.6	.6
Parts Accessories	5.1	3.5	4.9	3.1	3.5
6. Consumer Goods	5.8	3.7	5.7	8.1	10.5
Durable	1.5	.9	.9	3.5	5.0
Semi-Durable	1.7	1.0	1.1	2.9	3.4
Non-Durable	2.7	1.7	3.7	1.8	2.0
7. Other	.3	.5	.9	1.8	2.5

Origin	Exports by Industrial Origin						
	1970	1975	1976	1977	1978	1979	1980
Total Exports (1 + 2 + 3)	100.0	100.0	100.0	100.0	100.0	100.0	100.0
1. Agriculture	3.2	5.7	5.5	8.4	9.9	7.8	8.4
2. Mining Quarrying	10.0	9.9	10.7	8.7	11.4	9.4	9.5
3. Manufacturing	86.8	84.5	83.8	82.9	78.6	82.8	82.2
31. Food, Bev., Tobac.	2.2	6.1	5.9	7.7	8.2	6.3	7.7
32. Textiles	#	.4	1.0	.4	.4	.1	0
33. Wood, Wood Prod.	.7	1.5	1.6	2.6	2.7	2.7	3.4
34. Paper and Prod.	2.7	6.0	6.0	6.0	7.0	6.5	7.0
35. Chemicals	1.3	4.3	3.6	8.7	4.7	11.2	9.0
36. Non-Metal Minrl	#	.3	.2	.3	.2	~	~
37. Basic Metal Ind.	78.3	64.2	63.2	54.3	52.5	51.2	50.7
38. Metal Manufact.	1.3	1.6	2.3	2.5	2.2	3.1	3.3
39. Oth. Manf. Ind.	.1	0	0	.4	.7	1.7	1.1

SOURCE: UN-YITS, 1976, 1980.

Table 2504

COLOMBIA PERCENTAGE VALUE OF TRADE, 1970–80

Category	Imports by Broad Economic Category						
	1970	1975	1976	1977	1978	1979	1980
Total Imports	100.0	100.0	100.0	100.0	100.0	100.0	100.0
1. Food and Beverages	5.6	8.2	10.8	10.2	8.9	8.2	9.2
Primary	3.6	5.2	5.7	4.3	3.6	3.3	5.1
For Industry	3.2	4.3	4.6	3.2	2.7	2.3	3.9
For Hshold Consm	.5	.9	1.1	1.1	.9	1.0	1.1
Processed	1.9	3.1	5.2	5.9	5.3	4.9	4.2
For Industry	.9	1.4	3.0	2.8	3.0	3.1	1.9
For Hshold Consm	1.0	1.6	2.2	3.1	2.3	1.9	2.3
2. Ind. Supplies Nes.	39.8	45.2	39.2	39.3	37.2	37.0	35.1
Primary	3.3	3.1	3.2	3.6	2.5	2.9	2.9
Processed	36.5	42.1	36.0	35.7	34.7	34.2	32.2
3. Fuels Lubricants	.4	1.0	2.3	6.7	7.2	10.0	12.1
Primary	#	0	1.9	4.4	3.9	4.2	3.2
Processed	.4	1.0	.4	2.3	3.3	5.8	8.9
Motor Spirit	#	.7	.1	2.0	2.8	5.1	6.6
Other	.4	.2	.3	.4	.4	.7	2.4
4. Machinery	27.6	23.1	23.6	23.2	22.1	21.7	23.4
Machines Capt. Eqp	23.8	19.1	19.9	19.9	19.2	18.7	20.6
Parts Accessories	3.8	3.9	3.7	3.4	3.0	3.0	2.8
5. Transport	20.0	17.1	16.6	14.9	14.9	16.1	15.0
Passenger Cars	3.5	1.4	1.6	1.4	1.1	3.9	3.9
Other	8.0	9.5	8.4	7.0	7.4	5.1	5.1
Industrial	7.9	9.5	8.3	6.6	6.7	4.5	4.4
Non-Industrial	#	.1	.2	.5	.7	.5	.7
Parts Accessories	8.5	6.2	6.6	6.5	6.4	7.1	5.9
6. Consumer Goods	6.1	4.8	4.3	5.1	4.3	4.5	4.4
Durable	1.2	.8	.9	1.4	1.1	1.1	1.0
Semi-Durable	.8	1.3	1.2	1.4	1.2	1.3	1.1
Non-Durable	4.1	2.7	2.2	2.3	2.0	2.2	2.3
7. Other	.6	.6	3.2	.6	5.3	2.3	.8

Origin	Exports by Industrial Origin						
	1970	1975	1976	1977	1978	1979	1980
Total Exports (1 + 2 + 3)	100.0	100.0	100.0	100.0	100.0	100.0	100.0
1. Agriculture	76.6	60.1	67.6	72.7	74.2	66.9	69.1
2. Mining Quarrying	8.6	1.1	.9	1.2	.6	.4	2.0
3. Manufacturing	14.8	38.8	31.6	26.1	25.2	32.7	28.9
31. Food, Bev., Tobac.	3.8	11.2	5.6	3.9	3.8	4.8	7.4
32. Textiles	2.8	8.1	9.1	6.9	6.4	6.6	7.4
33. Wood, Wood Prod.	.6	.4	.7	.4	.2	.1	.3
34. Paper and Prod.	.5	1.1	2.0	2.1	2.4	1.3	1.8
35. Chemicals	3.9	11.7	7.5	6.1	6.2	4.7	5.3
36. Non-Metal Minrl	1.2	1.8	2.3	1.6	1.5	1.5	1.8
37. Basic Metal Ind.	.7	.4	.4	.2	.2	.2	.1
38. Metal Manufact.	1.3	3.6	3.6	4.0	3.5	1.3	3.7
39. Oth. Manf. Ind.	.1	.6	.4	.7	1.0	12.2	1.1

SOURCE: YN-YITS, 1976, 1981.

Table 2505

COSTA RICA PERCENTAGE VALUE OF TRADE, 1970–80

Category	Imports by Broad Economic Category						
	1970	1975	1976	1977	1978	1979	1980
Total Imports	100.0	100.0	100.0	100.0	100.0	100.0	100.0
1. Food and Beverages	8.8	8.5	7.1	6.3	6.2	6.2	7.1
Primary	4.8	4.9	3.2	2.4	2.4	2.5	3.3
For Industry	2.6	4.0	2.9	2.0	1.8	1.8	2.0
For Hshold Consm	2.3	.9	.4	.4	.6	.8	1.3
Processed	4.0	3.6	3.8	3.9	3.8	3.7	3.8
For Industry	1.3	1.2	1.2	1.0	.9	.8	1.0
For Hshold Consm	2.7	2.4	2.7	2.9	2.9	2.9	2.8
2. Ind. Supplies Nes.	44.1	43.0	38.8	37.7	37.0	35.3	38.4
Primary	2.6	1.7	1.6	1.4	1.3	1.5	2.3
Processed	41.5	41.3	37.2	36.3	35.7	33.8	36.1
3. Fuels Lubricants	3.6	10.3	8.9	9.3	9.3	12.7	14.7
Primary	1.8	3.8	3.2	3.6	3.9	4.5	8.0
Processed	1.8	6.5	5.7	5.7	5.4	8.2	6.7
Motor Spirit	.4	1.5	1.5	1.3	1.2	1.5	1.7
Other	.4	5.0	4.3	4.4	4.2	6.6	4.9
4. Machinery	16.8	16.8	19.4	17.7	17.3	19.2	15.2
Machines Capt. Eqp	15.9	15.7	18.3	16.7	16.3	18.2	14.2
Parts Accessories	.9	1.1	1.0	1.1	1.0	1.0	1.0
5. Transport	10.9	10.4	10.4	12.8	12.5	11.2	8.7
Passenger Cars	2.2	1.9	1.9	2.7	2.5	2.4	2.1
Other	3.8	4.0	3.5	4.7	4.9	4.3	2.1
Industrial	3.0	3.8	3.3	4.4	4.6	4.0	1.7
Non-Industrial	.3	.2	.3	.3	.3	.3	.4
Parts Accessories	5.4	4.5	5.0	5.3	5.0	4.5	4.4
6. Consumer Goods	15.6	10.4	10.9	11.4	12.7	11.8	11.7
Durable	2.6	1.1	1.3	1.7	2.4	2.1	1.8
Semi-Durable	7.0	4.3	4.4	4.6	5.1	4.6	4.7
Non-Durable	6.0	5.0	5.1	5.1	5.2	5.2	5.2
7. Other	.2	.7	4.5	4.9	5.0	3.6	4.2

Origin	Exports by Industrial Origin						
	1970	1975	1976	1977	1978	1979	1980
Total Exports (1 + 2 + 3)	100.0	100.0	100.0	100.0	100.0	100.0	100.0
1. Agriculture	63.4	53.3	56.7	63.9	58.1	58.6	48.1
2. Mining Quarrying	0	0	0	0	0	0	.1
3. Manufacturing	36.6	46.7	43.2	36.1	41.9	41.4	51.8
31. Food, Bev., Tobac.	16.4	20.2	14.4	11.5	13.1	16.7	16.8
32. Textiles	4.4	4.6	5.6	4.2	3.8	4.5	6.8
33. Wood, Wood Prod.	.6	.6	.7	.8	.7	.6	.9
34. Paper and Prod.	1.1	1.3	.9	.8	.7	1.0	1.9
35. Chemicals	6.9	11.2	10.6	8.4	8.2	8.3	10.2
36. Non-Metal Minrl	.1	.1	.2	.2	.3	.9	.9
37. Basic Metal Ind.	.7	.9	1.7	1.5	1.2	1.2	1.7
38. Metal Manufact.	4.7	5.1	5.5	5.3	5.2	5.4	6.3
39. Oth. Manf. Ind.	1.6	2.8	3.6	3.5	8.7	2.7	6.4

SOURCE: UN-YITS, 1976, 1981.

Table 2506

CUBA TOTAL TRADE VALUE, 1950–80, AND PERCENTAGES
ACCORDING TO ORIGIN, 1970–80

Historical Series, 1950-80, Special Trade, Imports CIF, Exports FOB.
(M Pesos)

Year	Imports	Exports
1950	515.4	642.0
1951	640.2	766.1
1952	618.2	675.3
1953	489.7	640.3
1954	487.9	539.0
1955	575.1	594.2
1956	649.0	666.2
1957	772.8	807.7
1958	777.0	733.5
1959	673.5	637.4
1960	579.9	618.2
1961	638.7	624.7
1962	759.3	520.7
1963	867.3	543.8
1964	1,018.8	713.8
1965	866.2	690.6
1966	925.5	597.8
1967	999.1	705.0
1968	1,102.3	651.4
1969	1,221.6	666.7
1970	1,311.0	1,049.5
1971	1,386.6	861.2
1972	1,189.8	770.9
1973	1,467.0	1,153.0
1974	2,225.9	2,236.5
1975	3,113.0	2,952.2
1976	3,179.7	2,692.3
1977	3,461.6	2,918.4
1978	3,573.8	3,440.1
1979	3,687.0	3,500.4
1980	4,509.3	3,967.0

Exports by Industrial Origin
(Percentage of Total Value) [1]

Origin	1970	1975	1976	1977	1978	1979	1980
Total Exports (1 + 2 + 3)	100.0	100.0	100.0	100.0	100.0	100.0	100.0
1. Agriculture	5.2	3.5	4.3	4.4	4.4	5.4	4.3
2. Mining Quarrying	16.4	4.6	5.9	6.3	4.5	4.4	4.6
3. Manufacturing	78.4	91.9	89.8	89.3	91.1	90.2	91.1
31. Food, Bev., Tobac.	78.4	91.9	89.2	86.1	88.9	87.7	85.6
32. Textiles	~	0	0	~	~	~	~
33. Wood, Wood Prod.	~	~	~	~	~	~	~
34. Paper and Prod.	~	~	~	~	~	~	~
35. Chemicals	~	4.6	5.9	~	0	0	0
36. Non-Metal Minrl	~	~	~	~	~	~	~
37. Basic Metal Ind.	~	~	~	~	~	~	~
38. Metal Manufact.	~	~	~	~	~	~	~
39. Oth. Manf. Ind.	~	~	.6	3.1	2.1	2.5	5.4

1. No percentages on imports available in source.

SOURCE: UN-YITS, 1976, 1981.

Table 2507

DOMINICAN REPUBLIC PERCENTAGE VALUE OF TRADE, 1970–80

Category	Imports by Broad Economic Category						
	1970	1975	1976	1977	1978	1979	1980
Total Imports	100.0	~	~	100.0	100.0	100.0	100.0
1. Food and Beverages	12.7	~	~	13.1	13.1	13.7	13.5
Primary	3.9	~	~	7.0	6.1	4.8	6.7
For Industry	1.4	~	~	5.4	4.3	2.2	4.0
For Hshold Consm	2.5	~	~	1.6	1.8	2.5	2.7
Processed	8.8	~	~	6.1	7.0	8.9	6.8
For Industry	.9	~	~	2.7	3.4	5.2	3.3
For Hshold Consm	7.9	~	~	3.4	3.6	3.7	3.5
2. Ind. Supplies Nes.	28.7	~	~	32.8	32.4	32.2	31.4
Primary	2.0	~	~	4.0	3.8	3.7	3.8
Processed	26.7	~	~	28.7	28.6	28.5	27.6
3. Fuels Lubricants	6.9	~	~	20.3	22.0	25.9	24.9
Primary	2.4	~	~	19.0	20.8	23.7	23.7
Processed	4.5	~	~	1.3	1.2	2.2	1.2
Motor Spirit	2.5	~	~	.1	.1	.5	.2
Other	1.9	~	~	1.2	1.1	1.7	1.0
4. Machinery	22.7	~	~	15.2	14.6	12.9	14.9
Machines Capt. Eqp	~	~	~	13.8	13.2	11.3	13.4
Parts Accessories	~	~	~	1.4	1.3	1.6	1.5
5. Transport	13.3	~	~	10.6	9.5	8.1	8.6
Passenger Cars	~	~	~	2.2	1.9	1.6	1.4
Other	~	~	~	3.7	3.6	3.1	3.8
Industrial	~	~	~	3.5	3.3	2.7	2.8
Non-Industrial	~	~	~	.2	.2	.4	1.0
Parts Accessories	~	~	~	4.7	4.1	3.4	3.4
6. Consumer Goods	12.5	~	~	8.0	8.2	7.0	6.5
Durable	.4	~	~	1.4	1.4	1.2	1.2
Semi-Durable	4.3	~	~	2.4	2.3	1.9	1.7
Non-Durable	7.9	~	~	4.3	4.6	3.9	3.6
7. Other	3.0	~	~	0	.1	.1	.1

Origin	Exports by Industrial Origin						
	1970	1975	1976	1977	1978	1979	1980
Total Exports (1 + 2 + 3)	100.0	~	~	100.0	100.0	100.0	100.0
1. Agriculture	32.0	~	~	45.2	41.3	40.2	26.2
2. Mining Quarrying	7.3	~	~	3.2	4.2	3.1	3.0
3. Manufacturing	60.7	~	~	51.6	54.5	56.7	70.8
31. Food, Bev., Tobac.	55.6	~	~	34.0	33.3	30.8	47.1
32. Textiles	.1	~	~	.4	1.4	1.3	1.1
33. Wood, Wood Prod.	0	~	~	0	0	0	0
34. Paper and Prod.	.1	~	~	.1	.1	.1	.1
35. Chemicals	3.2	~	~	2.8	5.9	5.4	6.0
36. Non-Metal Minrl	.1	~	~	0	.1	.3	.7
37. Basic Metal Ind.	.1	~	~	12.7	12.3	16.5	14.5
38. Metal Manufact.	.2	~	~	1.5	1.3	2.4	1.2
39. Oth. Manf. Ind.	1.4	~	~	.1	0	0	.1

SOURCE: UN-YITS, 1976, 1981.

Table 2508

ECUADOR PERCENTAGE VALUE OF TRADE, 1972–80

Category	Imports by Broad Economic Category						
	1972	1975	1976	1977	1978	1979	1980
Total Imports	100.0	100.0	100.0	100.0	100.0	~	100.0
1. Food and Beverages	7.8	7.1	6.8	5.4	6.3	~	7.6
Primary	3.5	4.2	3.2	2.3	2.5	~	3.8
For Industry	3.4	4.0	2.9	2.1	2.1	~	3.5
For Hshold Consm	.2	.2	.3	.2	.4	~	.3
Processed	4.3	2.9	3.6	3.1	3.8	~	3.8
For Industry	2.6	1.0	1.7	1.2	1.2	~	1.1
For Hshold Consm	1.7	1.9	1.9	1.9	2.6	~	2.6
2. Ind. Supplies Nes.	33.5	34.7	36.0	35.5	31.9	~	34.6
Primary	2.0	1.5	2.0	2.3	1.9	~	1.2
Processed	31.5	33.2	34.0	33.2	30.0	~	33.4
3. Fuels Lubricants	6.3	1.9	1.0	.6	.7	~	1.0
Primary	1.7	.2	.1	0	0	~	0
Processed	4.6	1.6	.9	.6	.7	~	1.0
Motor Spirit	.2	0	~	0	0	~	0
Other	4.4	1.6	.9	.6	.7	~	1.0
4. Machinery	25.3	29.9	30.4	28.9	30.4	~	28.2
Machines Capt. Eqp	22.8	27.9	27.9	26.7	28.0	~	25.8
Parts Accessories	2.5	2.0	2.4	2.2	2.3	~	2.4
5. Transport	15.2	17.1	15.6	20.8	20.0	~	21.2
Passenger Cars	1.9	.6	.4	.5	2.9	~	2.6
Other	7.3	11.5	10.1	14.6	11.2	~	11.9
Industrial	7.3	11.3	9.9	14.5	11.1	~	11.8
Non-Industrial	0	.2	.1	.1	.1	~	0
Parts Accessories	5.9	5.1	5.2	5.7	5.9	~	6.8
6. Consumer Goods	11.5	8.6	8.5	7.9	8.7	~	6.5
Durable	2.9	2.2	2.3	2.2	3.0	~	2.1
Semi-Durable	1.5	1.8	1.8	1.8	1.8	~	1.9
Non-Durable	7.1	4.5	4.4	3.8	3.8	~	2.5
7. Other	.3	.7	1.7	1.0	2.1	~	.8

Origin	Exports by Industrial Origin							
	1972	1973	1974	1975	1976	1977	1978	1979
Total Exports (1 + 2 + 3)	100.0	100.0	100.0	100.0	100.0	100.0	100.0	100.0
1. Agriculture	70.8	37.7	29.6	29.1	29.6	30.4	33.0	25.2
2. Mining Quarrying	18.6	53.3	61.8	60.3	58.9	49.0	40.0	49.3
3. Manufacturing	10.7	9.1	8.6	10.6	11.5	20.6	26.9	25.5
31. Food, Bev., Tobac.	8.0	6.3	5.7	7.3	8.3	17.1	17.7	15.4
32. Textiles	.8	1.1	.7	1.0	1.1	.6	.6	.8
33. Wood, Wood Prod.	.4	.2	.7	1.0	.9	.9	1.0	1.0
34. Paper and Prod.	.2	.1	.1	.1	.1	.1	.1	.1
35. Chemicals	.8	.9	.7	.4	.4	1.0	6.4	6.9
36. Non-Metal Minrl	0	0	0	0	0	0	0	0
37. Basic Metal Ind.	0	0	0	0	0	0	0	.1
38. Metal Manufact.	.4	.3	.4	.5	.5	.7	1.0	1.2
39. Oth. Manf. Ind.	.1	.2	.2	.2	.1	.1	.1	0

SOURCE: UN-YITS, 1977, 1981.

Table 2509

EL SALVADOR PERCENTAGE VALUE OF TRADE, 1970–80

	Imports by Broad Economic Category						
Category	1970	1975	1976	1977	1978	1979	1980
Total Imports	100.0	100.0	100.0	100.0	100.0	100.0	100.0
1. Food and Beverages	11.4	9.9	9.6	8.1	8.7	10.1	15.3
Primary	4.9	4.8	4.4	3.5	3.3	4.2	7.9
For Industry	2.4	2.9	2.8	2.2	2.0	2.1	2.9
For Hshold Consm	2.5	1.9	1.6	1.3	1.3	2.1	5.0
Processed	6.5	5.1	5.2	4.6	5.4	5.9	7.3
For Industry	1.2	.6	1.1	.6	.6	.8	1.2
For Hshold Consm	5.3	4.5	4.1	4.0	4.8	5.1	6.1
2. Ind. Supplies Nes.	45.0	41.6	40.6	40.2	39.9	41.1	37.4
Primary	1.5	2.2	1.4	1.5	2.9	2.2	1.7
Processed	43.6	39.4	39.2	38.7	37.0	38.9	35.7
3. Fuels Lubricants	2.2	8.3	7.2	9.7	7.7	9.3	17.6
Primary	1.4	7.7	6.7	9.1	7.1	8.7	17.0
Processed	.8	.6	.5	.5	.5	.6	.6
Motor Spirit	.1	.1	.1	.1	.1	.1	.1
Other	.6	.5	.5	.4	.4	.5	.5
4. Machinery	14.1	19.1	20.1	17.6	17.6	14.7	9.3
Machines Capt. Eqp	13.2	18.2	19.2	16.7	16.5	13.5	8.5
Parts Accessories	.9	.9	.9	.9	1.1	1.1	.8
5. Transport	9.8	8.0	9.2	10.8	12.6	9.7	4.5
Passenger Cars	3.0	1.2	1.7	1.9	1.8	1.3	.6
Other	3.0	3.9	4.6	5.7	7.5	5.1	1.6
Industrial	3.0	3.7	4.4	5.6	7.3	4.8	1.4
Non-Industrial	.1	.1	.2	.2	.2	.3	.2
Parts Accessories	3.8	2.9	2.9	3.2	3.3	3.3	2.4
6. Consumer Goods	17.3	13.1	13.1	13.5	13.3	14.9	15.8
Durable	2.4	1.7	1.8	2.3	2.2	2.3	1.3
Semi-Durable	5.3	4.6	4.7	4.7	4.7	5.0	5.9
Non-Durable	9.6	6.8	6.7	6.5	6.4	7.7	8.7
7. Other	.2	.1	.2	.1	.3	.2	.1

	Exports by Industrial Origin									
Origin	1970	1972	1973	1974	1975	1976	1977	1978	1979	1980
Total Exports (1 + 2 + 3)	100.0	100.0	100.0	100.0	100.0	100.0	100.0	100.0	100.0	100.0
1. Agriculture	62.8	55.9	57.3	54.6	50.5	64.5	72.0	53.4	66.8	53.5
2. Mining Quarrying	.2	.3	.3	.2	.3	.3	.2	.1	.1	.4
3. Manufacturing	37.0	43.8	42.4	45.1	49.2	35.2	27.9	46.4	33.1	46.1
31. Food, Bev., Tobac.	6.7	12.1	10.1	12.4	19.9	9.3	5.7	9.4	6.6	5.4
32. Textiles	13.8	14.7	14.0	13.2	10.9	10.3	9.3	15.2	10.4	16.1
33. Wood, Wod Prod.	0	0	0	0	0	0	0	.1	.1	.1
34. Paper and Prod.	1.9	2.6	2.8	3.6	2.9	2.8	2.4	4.2	3.0	4.8
35. Chemicals	7.1	7.5	7.1	7.2	8.4	7.1	5.3	8.6	6.2	10.1
36. Non-Metal Minrl	.2	.1	.2	.2	.2	.2	1.	.7	.8	.9
37. Basic Metal Ind.	2.0	1.7	2.2	2.5	1.6	1.3	1.1	2.1	2.0	2.5
38. Metal Manufact.	4.6	4.6	5.2	5.3	4.5	3.5	3.3	5.2	3.4	5.2
39. Oth. Manf. Ind.	.5	.6	.7	.7	.8	.7	.6	1.0	.6	.9

SOURCE: UN-YITS, 1976, 1981.

Table 2510

GUATEMALA PERCENTAGE VALUE OF TRADE, 1970–80

	Imports by Broad Economic Category					
Category	1970	1975	1976	1977	1978	1979
Total Imports	100.0	100.0	100.0	100.0	100.0	100.0
1. Food and Beverages	8.7	7.1	4.5	5.1	5.1	5.4
Primary	3.5	3.7	1.9	1.9	1.7	2.0
For Industry	2.9	2.6	1.6	1.6	1.2	1.6
For Hshold Consm	.6	1.0	.3	3	.5	.4
Processed	5.1	3.4	2.7	3.2	3.5	3.4
For Industry	1.0	.6	.7	.8	.9	.8
For Hshold Consm	4.2	2.8	2.0	2.5	2.6	2.6
2. Ind. Supplies Nes.	46.7	40.9	37.9	36.1	40.0	40.3
Primary	1.7	2.4	1.8	1.5	2.0	1.9
Processed	45.0	38.6	36.1	34.7	38.0	38.5
3. Fuels Lubricants	1.4	13.7	12.3	13.7	12.4	10.2
Primary	.4	10.1	7.7	8.2	7.0	1.3
Processed	1.1	3.6	4.7	5.5	5.4	8.9
Motor Spirit	.2	1.9	2.0	2.0	1.8	3.2
Other	.9	1.7	2.7	3.6	3.5	5.7
4. Machinery	16.9	16.2	21.6	18.5	18.1	18.6
Machines Cap. Eqp	15.8	15.2	20.1	17.2	16.8	17.4
Parts Accessories	1.1	1.1	1.4	1.3	1.3	1.2
5. Transport	9.9	10.9	12.4	15.1	11.8	12.4
Passenger Cars	2.3	1.6	2.0	3.0	2.6	3.2
Other	3.6	5.5	6.4	7.9	5.3	5.5
Industrial	3.5	5.4	6.4	7.8	5.3	5.4
Non-Industrial	.1	0	0	.1	.1	0
Parts Accessories	4.0	3.9	4.0	4.2	3.9	3.7
6. Consumer Goods	16.2	11.0	11.2	10.9	12.3	12.7
Durable	2.6	2.0	2.1	2.8	2.9	2.8
Semi-Durable	6.8	4.6	4.8	4.2	5.0	4.8
Non-Durable	6.8	4.5	4.4	3.9	4.4	5.0
7. Other	.2	.1	.1	.4	.3	.3

	Exports by Industrial Origin						
Origin	1970	1975	1976	1977	1978	1979	1980
Total Exports (1 + 2 + 3)	100.0	100.0	100.0	100.0	100.0	100.0	100.0
1. Agriculture	55.4	47.6	53.9	68.1	66.4	65.8	57.6
2. Mining Quarrying	.3	.7	.6	.4	.3	.4	1.4
3. Manufacturing	44.3	51.7	45.6	31.5	33.3	33.8	41.0
31. Food, Bev., Tobac.	15.2	26.0	21.5	13.7	11.4	9.4	11.9
32. Textiles	10.6	7.7	7.2	5.1	5.6	6.7	7.0
33. Wood, Wood Prod.	.8	.6	.3	.2	.5	.3	.2
34. Paper and Prod.	1.7	1.6	1.5	1.0	1.2	1.4	1.5
35. Chemicals	8.7	8.7	8.9	7.0	8.4	8.9	10.6
36. Non-Metal Minrl	2.1	2.7	2.2	1.7	2.2	1.8	1.6
37. Basic Metal Ind.	1.3	.8	.6	.4	1.1	2.4	5.3
38. Metal Manufact.	3.5	3.1	3.0	2.1	2.5	2.6	2.6
39. Oth. Manf. Ind.	.3	.5	.4	.3	.3	.3	.4

SOURCE: UN-YITS, 1976, 1981.

Table 2511

HAITI PERCENTAGE VALUE OF TRADE, 1970–78

Imports by Broad Economic Category

Category	1970	1972	1973	1974	1975	1976	1977	1978
Total Imports	100.0	100.0	100.0	100.0	100.0	100.0	100.0	100.0
1. Food and Beverages	16.5	22.2	22.2	19.7	25.1	27.0	23.7	21.9
Primary	3.0	7.0	6.8	6.3	13.1	11.1	9.3	7.8
For Industry	1.9	5.8	5.7	5.2	12.0	10.0	8.0	6.3
For Hshold Consm	1.2	1.2	1.1	1.1	1.1	1.2	1.3	1.5
Processed	13.4	15.2	15.4	13.4	11.9	15.9	14.4	14.1
For Industry	6.2	6.8	5.2	5.2	4.7	6.4	7.8	4.3
For Hshold Consm	7.2	8.4	10.2	8.2	7.3	9.4	6.6	9.8
2. Ind. Supplies Nes.	32.1	32.0	33.7	33.1	29.0	29.5	29.2	30.3
Primary	2.0	2.2	3.4	3.5	4.0	3.3	3.1	3.5
Processed	30.1	29.9	30.3	29.6	25.0	26.3	26.1	26.8
3. Fuels Lubricants	5.5	6.0	5.7	11.2	9.1	8.2	11.0	11.0
Primary	~	.2	.2	.3	.3	.2	.2	.2
Processed	~	5.8	5.5	10.8	8.8	8.0	10.7	10.7
Motor Spirit	~	1.5	2.0	3.8	2.6	2.2	3.0	3.2
Other	~	4.3	3.5	7.1	6.2	5.8	7.7	7.6
4. Machinery	12.7	10.0	8.5	7.6	10.7	10.1	11.3	7.5
Machines Capt. Eqp	~	~	~	7.1	10.2	9.8	10.9	7.2
Parts Accessories	~	~	~	.5	.5	.3	.4	.3
5. Transport	10.3	9.2	10.1	8.6	9.3	8.0	8.9	12.8
Passenger Cars	~	2.7	1.8	1.6	1.7	1.9	2.1	2.7
Other	~	.4	.4	3.9	4.3	3.2	3.7	6.6
Industrial	~	.4	.4	3.9	4.2	3.2	3.6	6.4
Non-Industrial	~	~	~	0	.1	.1	.1	.2
Parts Accessories	~	6.1	8.0	3.1	3.4	2.8	3.2	3.4
6. Consumer Goods	20.2	17.0	17.3	15.9	12.9	13.6	15.4	16.0
Durable	2.1	2.0	3.5	4.2	3.1	2.7	2.6	2.9
Semi-Durable	9.7	8.1	6.5	5.4	4.6	6.2	8.2	7.9
Non-Durable	8.4	6.8	7.3	6.3	5.2	4.7	4.6	5.2
7. Other	2.7	3.7	2.6	3.9	3.9	3.6	.6	.5

Export by Industrial Origin

Origin	1970	1972	1973	1974	1975	1976	1977	1978
Total Exports (1 + 2 + 3)	100.0	100.0	100.0	100.0	100.0	100.0	100.0	100.0
1. Agriculture	47.0	40.7	45.5	43.0	28.2	41.4	49.8	45.2
2. Mining Quarrying	16.9	16.6	12.0	9.6	12.9	15.6	12.1	10.8
3. Manufacturing	36.1	42.7	41.7	47.4	58.9	43.0	38.1	44.0
31. Food, Bev., Tobac.	10.4	13.7	11.2	10.0	19.0	5.3	2.5	4.9
32. Textiles	8.9	8.3	11.2	13.5	14.5	9.2	9.3	6.8
33. Wood, Wood Prod.	1.7	1.8	1.5	1.3	.9	.7	.5	~
34. Paper and Prod.	~	~	0	0	0	0	0	0
35. Chemicals	9.2	9.6	7.8	9.2	6.1	7.2	4.7	6.4
36. Non-Metal Minrl	~	0	~	0	.1	2.1	2.2	1.8
37. Basic Metal Ind.	~	~	~	0	~	~	~	~
38. Metal Manufact.	2.3	5.9	1.7	9.5	14.8	14.2	13.3	15.5
39. Oth. Manf. Ind.	3.5	3.4	8.3	3.8	3.5	4.2	5.6	8.5

SOURCE: UN-YITS, 1976, 1981.

Table 2512

HONDURAS PERCENTAGE VALUE OF TRADE, 1970–80

Category	1970	1975	1976	1977	1978	1979	1980
				Imports by Broad Economic Category			
Total Imports	100.0	100.0	100.0	100.0	100.0	100.0	100.0
1. Food and Beverages	10.0	10.1	8.8	7.2	7.1	7.1	7.7
Primary	2.4	3.4	2.5	2.1	2.2	2.1	2.2
For Industry	1.7	3.1	2.1	1.7	1.9	1.7	1.7
For Hshold Consm	.7	.3	.4	.4	.3	.4	.6
Processed	7.5	6.6	6.3	5.0	4.9	5.0	5.4
For Industry	1.6	1.4	1.8	1.0	1.0	.7	1.1
For Hshold Consm	5.9	5.2	4.5	4.0	3.9	4.3	4.3
2. Ind. Supplies Nes.	36.1	34.0	37.3	36.0	34.9	36.1	33.7
Primary	.8	3.1	1.7	1.8	2.1	1.2	2.4
Processed	35.4	31.0	35.7	34.1	32.8	34.9	31.3
3. Fuels Lubricants	6.3	16.7	10.2	11.6	10.5	12.6	15.6
Primary	4.9	15.0	8.8	8.9	7.4	9.7	11.8
Processed	1.4	1.7	1.4	2.6	3.1	2.9	3.8
Motor Spirit	.3	.2	.2	.5	.5	.7	.7
Other	1.1	1.5	1.2	2.2	2.6	2.2	3.0
4. Machinery	16.8	17.0	16.5	18.8	19.9	19.3	18.6
Machines Capt. Eqp	16.2	16.3	15.8	18.1	19.2	18.8	18.0
Parts Accessories	.6	.7	.7	.8	.7	.5	.6
5. Transport	12.8	10.6	13.1	11.9	13.1	12.2	11.1
Passenger Cars	2.1	1.0	1.1	1.5	1.7	1.4	1.3
Other	6.3	5.7	7.3	6.3	7.2	.8	5.9
Industrial	6.1	5.5	7.1	6.1	7.0	.8	5.8
Non-Industrial	.2	.1	.2	.2	.2	.1	.2
Parts Accessories	4.4	3.9	4.7	4.1	4.2	9.9	3.9
6. Consumer Goods	17.7	11.3	13.8	14.5	14.1	12.5	13.2
Durable	2.6	2.2	2.7	3.1	3.0	2.1	2.6
Semi-Durable	7.8	3.5	4.4	4.8	4.9	4.7	4.7
Non-Durable	7.3	5.7	6.7	6.6	6.2	5.8	5.9
7. Other	.3	.4	.3	.1	.4	.3	.2

Origin	1970	1975	1976	1977	1978	1979	1980
				Exports by Industrial Origin			
Total Exports (1 + 2 + 3)	100.0	100.0	100.0	100.0	100.0	100.0	100.0
1. Agriculture	64.0	49.9	62.1	67.5	68.2	63.5	63.7
2. Mining Quarrying	5.2	10.8	8.2	6.3	5.2	6.2	6.5
3. Manufacturing	30.8	39.3	29.7	26.2	26.6	30.3	29.8
31. Food, Bev., Tobac.	9.3	11.5	9.9	7.7	10.2	13.6	14.3
32. Textiles	2.8	2.3	2.5	1.8	1.6	2.2	2.8
33. Wood, Wood Prod.	9.6	13.7	10.6	10.3	8.8	8.4	4.9
34. Paper and Prod.	.7	.4	.3	.2	.5	.5	.6
35. Chemicals	7.6	8.4	4.1	4.3	3.8	3.9	5.1
36. Non-Metal Minrl	.1	1.1	.3	0	0	0	.1
37. Basic Metal Ind.	.5	.4	.3	.2	.2	.2	.2
38. Metal Manufact.	.2	1.4	1.5	1.5	1.4	1.4	1.5
39. Oth. Manf. Ind.	0	.1	.1	.1	.1	1.1	.1

SOURCE: UN-YITS, 1976, 1981.

Table 2513

MEXICO PERCENTAGE VALUE OF TRADE, 1970–78

Imports by Broad Economic Category

Category	1970	1972	1973	1974	1975	1976	1977	1978
Total Imports	100.0	100.0	100.0	100.0	100.0	100.0	100.0	100.0
1. Food and Beverages	3.8	6.3	7.2	12.0	5.9	5.2	8.9	8.2
Primary	1.9	3.3	3.8	8.0	4.5	3.3	6.6	6.3
For Industry	1.3	2.8	3.3	7.1	3.2	2.9	5.9	5.7
For Hshold Consm	.6	.5	.4	1.0	1.4	.4	.7	.6
Processed	2.0	2.9	3.4	4.0	1.4	1.9	2.4	1.9
For Industry	.5	.4	1.2	1.2	.2	.3	.7	.6
For Hshold Consm	1.4	2.6	2.2	2.8	1.2	1.6	1.7	1.4
2. Ind. Supplies Nes.	35.5	31.3	33.6	38.8	38.8	34.0	37.9	40.0
Primary	8.6	5.2	8.1	9.0	11.4	6.2	8.2	7.3
Processed	26.8	26.1	25.5	29.8	27.4	27.8	29.7	32.8
3. Fuels Lubricants	2.8	4.3	6.6	6.7	5.0	5.3	2.3	2.7
Primary	1.3	2.8	3.7	3.5	2.1	1.8	1.5	1.3
Processed	1.5	1.5	2.9	3.2	2.9	3.4	.8	1.4
Motor Spirit	.4	.8	1.7	2.0	1.0	1.1	.2	0
Other	1.1	.7	1.1	1.2	1.9	2.3	.6	1.4
4. Machinery	33.4	35.1	31.5	23.4	27.0	33.2	29.1	27.1
Machines Capt. Eqp	28.1	29.2	25.6	20.4	23.6	28.9	24.6	22.7
Parts Accessories	5.3	6.0	5.9	3.0	3.4	4.3	4.5	4.5
5. Transport	17.6	14.6	14.1	14.9	19.4	18.1	17.4	17.7
Passenger Cars	4.6	4.5	3.6	4.2	.1	.1	.1	.1
Other	6.7	4.5	5.5	6.3	6.6	4.1	5.0	5.0
Industrial	6.7	4.5	5.4	6.3	6.5	4.1	5.0	5.0
Non-Industrial	0	0	0	0	0	0	0	0
Parts Accessories	6.2	5.6	5.0	4.3	12.7	13.8	12.4	12.6
6. Consumer Goods	6.8	8.3	6.9	4.1	3.8	4.3	4.2	4.1
Durable	1.5	2.0	1.7	1.2	1.2	1.2	1.2	1.2
Semi-Durable	3.1	3.5	3.0	1.3	1.3	1.5	1.4	1.4
Non-Durable	2.2	2.8	2.2	1.6	1.4	1.7	1.6	1.5
7. Other	.1	.1	.1	.2	0	0	0	.1

Exports by Industrial Origin

Origin	1970	1972	1973	1974	1975	1976	1977	1978
Total Exports (1 + 2 + 3)	100.0	100.0	100.0	100.0	100.0	100.0	100.0	100.0
1. Agriculture	34.1	39.1	31.9	27.3	28.9	36.2	33.0	30.1
2. Mining Quarrying	8.7	6.2	4.6	7.5	20.3	20.7	25.6	31.9
3. Manufacturing	57.2	54.6	63.5	65.2	50.8	43.1	41.4	38.0
31. Food, Bev., Tobac.	14.2	12.8	10.4	13.3	9.1	5.7	5.9	6.0
32. Textiles	3.8	5.0	8.2	8.9	5.5	5.1	4.1	2.8
33. Wood, Wood Prod.	.6	.8	.7	.7	.6	.8	.9	.8
34. Paper and Prod.	2.1	1.3	1.3	1.2	1.3	1.3	1.3	1.1
35. Chemicals	11.1	8.2	8.2	13.9	9.0	8.8	8.0	6.7
36. Non-Metal Minrl	1.4	2.1	1.8	1.9	2.0	2.3	3.3	2.4
37. Basic Metal Ind.	10.1	8.7	11.1	12.2	11.2	9.3	8.5	5.9
38. Metal Manufact.	12.7	14.8	19.8	12.0	11.2	9.1	8.5	11.7
39. Oth. Manf. Ind.	1.3	.9	1.9	1.2	.9	.8	.9	.6

SOURCE: UN-YITS, 1976, 1981.

Table 2514

NICARAGUA PERCENTAGE VALUE OF TRADE, 1970–80

Category	Imports by Broad Economic Category									
	1970	1972	1973	1974	1975	1976	1977	1978	1979	1980
Total Imports	100.0	100.0	100.0	100.0	100.0	100.0	100.0	100.0	100.0	100.0
1. Food and Beverages	8.2	8.4	9.9	6.6	7.3	7.3	6.5	8.3	11.9	13.2
Primary	3.4	2.4	4.4	2.9	3.6	3.1	2.6	3.6	3.5	6.0
For Industry	2.0	1.9	2.8	2.0	2.6	2.1	1.5	2.2	1.4	2.1
For Hshold Consm	1.4	1.5	1.7	1.0	1.0	1.0	1.1	1.4	2.1	3.9
Processed	4.8	5.0	5.4	3.7	3.7	4.2	3.9	4.7	8.4	6.9
For Industry	.7	.7	1.1	.7	.6	.5	.7	.9	1.9	1.9
For Hshold Consm	4.1	4.3	4.4	3.0	3.1	3.7	3.2	3.8	6.6	5.0
2. Ind. Supplies Nes.	40.3	40.0	41.5	44.7	36.7	37.2	35.4	38.7	35.1	37.2
Primary	2.2	2.7	3.0	1.6	1.2	1.8	1.2	1.9	1.5	2.5
Processed	38.1	37.3	38.5	43.2	35.5	35.4	34.1	36.8	33.6	34.7
3. Fuels Lubricants	5.8	.2	7.1	10.7	14.2	12.9	13.6	15.1	21.1	19.8
Primary	4.0	5.5	5.4	9.1	12.3	10.7	10.2	9.7	18.2	16.8
Processed	1.8	1.7	1.7	1.5	1.9	2.3	3.4	5.3	2.9	3.0
Motor Spirit	.3	.3	.1	.3	.4	.7	.7	1.4	.8	.6
Other	1.5	1.4	1.6	1.2	1.5	1.6	2.7	4.0	2.1	2.4
4. Machinery	16.3	14.4	14.0	13.8	17.4	15.4	17.3	13.7	8.8	7.9
Machines Capt. Eqp	15.3	13.4	13.1	13.0	16.5	14.6	16.4	12.8	8.2	7.2
Parts Accessories	1.0	1.0	.9	.9	.9	.8	.9	.9	.6	.7
5. Transport	11.4	11.7	12.3	10.8	10.4	11.4	14.1	11.0	7.2	7.0
Passenger Cars	2.4	3.1	2.2	2.2	2.6	3.4	3.3	2.2	.9	.9
Other	4.3	3.7	5.5	5.0	3.9	4.0	6.5	4.1	2.6	2.8
Industrial	4.2	3.6	5.3	4.8	3.7	3.8	6.3	3.9	2.5	2.7
Non-Industrial	.1	.1	.1	.2	.2	.2	.2	.1	.1	.1
Parts Accessories	4.7	4.9	4.5	3.7	3.9	4.0	4.3	4.7	3.6	3.3
6. Consumer Goods	17.8	18.1	14.9	13.1	13.5	15.6	12.9	13.0	15.6	15.1
Durable	2.1	2.2	1.7	1.9	1.6	1.7	1.6	1.3	.7	.9
Semi-Durable	6.5	6.5	6.0	5.3	4.9	5.9	4.8	4.4	5.9	6.6
Non-Durable	9.2	9.5	7.2	6.0	7.1	8.0	6.5	7.3	9.0	7.6
7. Other	.2	.2	.4	.2	.4	.2	.2	.2	.3	.1

Origin	Exports by Industrial Origin									
	1970	1972	1973	1974	1975	1976	1977	1978	1979	1980
Total Exports (1 + 2 + 3)	100.0	100.0	100.0	100.0	100.0	100.0	100.0	100.0	100.0	100.0
1. Agriculture	48.2	51.0	48.0	57.3	49.6	55.0	62.7	58.9	59.6	58.7
2. Mining Quarrying	3.0	1.6	2.0	2.7	1.5	.9	.8	.4	.1	.1
3. Manufacturing	48.7	47.3	50.0	40.0	48.8	44.0	36.5	40.7	40.3	41.3
31. Food, Bev., Tobac.	29.7	29.1	29.3	16.9	28.3	24.2	16.6	21.3	26.5	23.8
32. Textiles	6.3	5.0	4.8	5.6	5.3	4.9	4.9	3.6	2.7	2.5
33. Wood, Wood Prod.	2.2	3.1	3.4	2.1	2.0	2.5	1.8	1.6	1.2	.7
34. Paper and Prod.	.3	.2	.4	.4	.1	.2	.2	.2	.1	.1
35. Chemicals	6.0	6.2	8.1	10.3	8.9	8.4	8.7	9.0	6.9	10.6
36. Non-Metal Minrl	1.0	.8	1.0	1.0	.8	.9	.9	1.0	.7	.7
37. Basic Metal Ind.	.9	.7	.6	.6	1.0	.7	.8	1.3	.6	1.4
38. Metal Manufact.	2.3	2.1	2.2	3.1	2.2	2.2	2.4	2.6	1.7	1.5
39. Oth. Manf. Ind.	.1	0	.1	.1	.2	.1	.1	0	0	0

SOURCE: UN-YITS, 1976, 1981.

Table 2515

PANAMA PERCENTAGE VALUE OF TRADE, 1970–80

Category	Imports by Broad Economic Category						
	1970	1975	1976	1977	1978	1979	1980
Total Imports	100.0	100.0	100.0	100.0	100.0	100.0	100.0
1. Food and Beverages	7.9	7.9	8.4	9.0	8.5	8.5	8.6
Primary	2.4	2.2	2.3	2.7	2.4	2.2	2.0
For Industry	1.0	1.3	1.1	1.4	1.0	.9	.9
For Hshold Consm	1.4	.9	1.2	1.3	1.3	1.3	1.2
Processed	5.5	5.7	6.1	6.3	6.1	6.3	6.6
For Industry	.7	2.0	2.0	2.0	1.7	2.0	2.0
For Hshold Consm	4.8	3.7	4.1	4.2	4.3	4.3	4.6
2. Ind. Supplies Nes.	27.8	21.4	23.3	24.3	27.6	26.9	25.4
Primary	.7	.7	.7	.7	.6	1.0	1.2
Processed	27.1	20.7	22.6	23.6	26.9	25.9	24.2
3. Fuels Lubricants	18.7	40.3	33.1	32.9	24.3	28.4	30.2
Primary	18.0	39.0	29.1	31.4	23.3	27.2	28.6
Processed	.7	1.4	4.0	1.4	1.0	1.2	1.5
Motor Spirit	0	0	.4	.8	.2	.5	.5
Other	.7	1.4	3.6	.7	.8	.7	1.0
4. Machinery	15.4	12.2	14.9	12.3	13.3	11.3	11.3
Machines Capt. Eqp	14.8	11.2	13.6	11.1	12.1	10.1	10.5
Parts Accessories	.5	1.1	1.2	1.1	1.2	1.2	.9
5. Transport	12.1	7.2	7.3	6.9	9.0	9.1	9.7
Passenger Cars	3.5	1.4	1.7	1.8	2.4	3.2	3.4
Other	4.0	2.7	2.5	1.8	2.6	2.2	2.9
Industrial	3.8	2.6	2.4	1.6	2.4	2.0	2.5
Non-Industrial	.2	.1	.1	.1	.2	.2	.4
Parts Accessories	4.6	3.1	3.1	3.3	3.9	3.7	3.3
6. Consumer Goods	17.8	10.9	13.0	14.6	17.2	15.7	14.7
Durable	4.0	2.4	3.2	3.6	4.5	4.2	3.6
Semi-Durable	8.7	4.3	5.3	6.0	7.4	6.5	6.3
Non-Durable	5.1	4.1	4.5	5.0	5.3	5.1	4.8
7. Other	.3	.1	.1	.1	.1	.1	.2

Origin	Exports by Industrial Origin						
	1970	1975	1976	1977	1978	1979	1980
Total Exports (1 + 2 + 3)	100.0	100.0	100.0	100.0	100.0	100.0	100.0
1. Agriculture	68.6	29.4	43.3	43.4	48.1	44.2	36.4
2. Mining Quarrying	0	~	~	0	0	~	0
3. Manufacturing	31.3	70.6	56.7	56.6	51.9	55.8	63.6
31. Food, Bev., Tobac.	8.2	21.0	19.0	19.5	17.9	19.6	30.3
32. Textiles	.2	1.9	3.4	4.3	4.8	5.6	4.3
33. Wood, Wood Prod.	0	0	0	.1	.2	.1	.1
34. Paper and Prod.	.5	.4	1.1	1.0	1.0	1.2	1.7
35. Chemicals	20.4	45.6	29.2	28.4	25.8	26.4	25.2
36. Non-Metal Minrl	0	.1	.1	.1	.3	1.1	0
37. Basic Metal Ind.	.5	.4	.6	.6	.7	.8	.6
38. Metal Manufact.	1.4	1.1	3.2	2.5	.9	.8	1.0
39. Oth. Manf. Ind.	~	.1	.1	.3	.2	.3	.4

SOURCE: UN-YITS, 1976, 1981.

Table 2516

PARAGUAY PERCENTAGE VALUE OF TRADE, 1970–81

	Imports by Broad Economic Category					
Category	1970	1975	1976	1977	1978	1979
Total Imports	~	100.0	100.0	100.0	100.0	100.0
1. Food and Beverages	~	11.9	12.9	9.1	9.7	9.4
Primary	~	1.8	3.1	2.5	2.4	2.2
For Industry	~	1.6	2.8	2.1	2.1	1.9
For Hshold Consm	~	.2	.3	.4	.3	.3
Processed	~	10.1	9.8	6.7	7.3	7.2
For Industry	~	1.3	2.4	.7	.4	.4
For Hshold Consm	~	8.8	7.5	6.0	6.9	6.8
2. Ind. Supplies Nes.	~	22.2	21.2	19.5	18.4	20.6
Primary	~	.9	1.1	1.1	.9	.8
Processed	~	21.3	20.1	18.5	17.5	19.8
3. Fuels Lubricants	~	20.3	23.8	19.6	22.4	24.0
Primary	~	16.8	16.7	12.0	14.3	14.2
Processed	~	3.5	7.0	7.6	8.2	9.9
Motor Spirit	~	1.4	3.2	2.2	2.7	2.6
Other	~	2.1	3.8	5.3	5.5	7.2
4. Machinery	~	20.1	18.4	24.3	18.5	19.1
Machines Capt. Eqp	~	18.6	17.3	23.1	17.4	18.0
Parts Accessories	~	1.4	1.1	1.1	1.2	1.1
5. Transport	~	15.9	15.1	17.5	20.1	16.5
Passenger Cars	~	2.8	3.2	3.5	3.4	4.0
Other	~	9.3	8.8	9.8	12.2	9.3
Industrial	~	8.9	8.3	8.9	11.0	8.5
Non-Industrial	~	.4	.5	.8	1.1	.8
Parts Accessories	~	3.8	3.1	4.2	4.5	3.2
6. Consumer Goods	~	9.1	8.2	9.7	10.8	10.3
Durable	~	1.7	1.8	2.2	2.0	1.7
Semi-Durable	~	2.0	1.5	2.0	2.3	1.8
Non-Durable	~	5.5	4.9	5.5	6.5	6.8
7. Other	~	.5	.3	.3	.1	.1

	Exports by Industrial Origin							
Origin	1970	1975	1976	1977	1978	1979	1980	1981
Total Exports (1 + 2 + 3)	100.0	100.0	100.0	100.0	100.0	100.0	100.0	100.0
1. Agriculture	32.7	39.6	53.1	59.9	60.8	64.9	65.5	62.1
2. Mining Quarrying	0	0	~	~	~	0	~	~
3. Manufacturing	67.2	60.4	46.9	40.1	39.2	35.1	34.5	37.9
31. Food, Bev., Tobac.	50.6	35.6	28.4	24.0	21.5	13.7	14.9	14.5
32. Textiles	.5	1.2	2.0	2.0	3.7	2.6	1.2	2.2
33. Wood, Wood Prod.	9.0	15.9	6.7	7.1	7.9	13.8	13.5	14.1
34. Paper and Prod.	0	0	0	0	0	0	~	~
35. Chemicals	6.4	6.1	8.5	6.4	5.7	4.5	4.5	4.1
36. Non-Metal Minrl	.5	.4	0	0	0	0	~	~
37. Basic Metal Ind.	~	~	~	~	~	0	~	~
38. Metal Manufact.	.1	0	~	~	0	0	~	~
39. Oth. Manf. Ind.	.1	1.2	1.2	.5	.5	.4	.4	2.9

SOURCE: UN-YITS, 1976, 1981.

Table 2517

PERU PERCENTAGE VALUE OF TRADE, 1970–80

Category	Imports by Broad Economic Category						
	1970	1975	1976	1977	1978	1979	1980
Total Imports	100.0	100.0	100.0	100.0	100.0	100.0	100.0
1. Food and Beverages	19.5	13.7	11.5	13.0	15.9	18.9	17.5
Primary	14.1	7.5	5.7	7.5	8.2	10.8	9.0
For Industry	11.1	7.1	5.3	7.0	8.0	10.7	7.9
For Hshold Consm	3.0	.4	.4	.6	.2	.1	1.1
Processed	5.4	6.2	5.9	5.5	7.7	8.1	8.5
For Industry	1.5	2.4	2.3	3.1	4.9	1.5	1.9
For Hshold Consm	3.9	3.8	3.5	2.4	2.8	6.6	6.5
2. Ind. Supplies Nes.	35.5	37.0	29.3	29.0	36.8	35.3	34.8
Primary	1.7	3.6	3.2	3.0	3.0	3.0	3.2
Processed	33.8	33.4	26.0	26.0	33.8	32.4	31.6
3. Fuels Lubricants	1.7	11.8	16.6	19.7	5.3	2.9	2.0
Primary	.3	8.3	13.3	13.7	.7	.2	.2
Processed	1.5	3.5	3.3	6.0	4.6	2.8	1.8
Motor Spirit	.1	.4	.4	.2	.3	.2	0
Other	1.3	3.0	2.9	5.8	4.3	2.5	1.8
4. Machinery	23.6	24.5	27.2	22.4	27.8	29.0	27.2
Machines Capt. Eqp	19.4	21.9	23.9	19.5	23.4	24.7	23.7
Parts Accessories	4.2	2.6	3.3	2.9	4.4	4.4	3.5
5. Transport	12.5	9.1	10.7	11.2	9.1	10.1	13.3
Passenger Cars	3.9	1.3	2.1	3.1	1.3	1.1	2.2
Other	1.1	4.1	3.8	4.3	3.2	4.1	6.0
Industrial	1.1	3.9	3.6	4.1	3.0	4.0	5.8
Non-Industrial	0	.2	.2	.3	.2	.1	.2
Parts Accessories	7.5	3.7	4.8	3.7	4.6	4.9	5.1
6. Consumer Goods	7.0	3.8	4.6	4.5	4.6	3.6	4.8
Durable	1.4	1.2	2.3	2.2	2.0	1.5	2.1
Semi-Durable	1.5	.9	.7	.7	.7	.7	1.2
Non-Durable	4.1	1.7	1.6	1.7	1.9	1.4	1.4
7. Other	.1	.1	.2	.1	.6	.2	.5

Origin	Exports by Industrial Origin						
	1970	1975	1976	1977	1978	1979	1980
Total Exports (1 + 2 + 3)	100.0	100.0	100.0	100.0	100.0	100.0	100.0
1. Agriculture	10.5	10.3	17.8	17.4	15.2	11.1	8.5
2. Mining Quarrying	19.6	19.8	18.6	12.5	22.0	28.1	35.9
3. Manufacturing	69.9	69.9	63.6	70.1	62.9	60.8	55.6
31. Food, Bev., Tobac.	38.8	39.2	21.3	17.7	15.5	10.6	9.5
32. Textiles	.3	1.1	2.2	3.3	5.3	7.6	7.5
33. Wood, Wood Prod.	.1	0	.2	.3	.3	.4	.4
34. Paper and Prod.	.3	.1	.3	.2	.3	.4	.2
35. Chemicals	.4	4.0	5.8	9.6	8.1	6.0	9.1
36. Non-Metal Minrl	.1	.1	.1	.2	.9	1.3	1.2
37. Basic Metal Ind.	29.6	23.8	31.9	36.1	29.6	30.5	24.6
38. Metal Manufact.	.1	1.4	1.4	2.4	2.4	2.5	2.3
39. Oth. Manf. Ind.	.1	.2	.4	.3	.4	1.5	.8

SOURCE: UN-YITS, 1976, 1981.

Table 2518

URUGUAY PERCENTAGE VALUE OF TRADE, 1970–80

Category	Imports by Broad Economic Category						
	1970	1975	1976	1977	1978	1979	1980
Total Imports	100.0	100.0	100.0	100.0	100.0	100.0	100.0
1. Food and Beverages	9.0	6.6	5.2	4.9	5.2	7.5	6.6
Primary	3.8	3.9	4.2	3.7	3.9	5.3	4.2
For Industry	1.5	1.1	1.4	1.2	1.4	2.9	1.4
For Hshold Consm	2.3	2.8	2.8	2.6	2.5	2.4	2.9
Processed	5.2	2.7	1.0	1.1	1.3	2.2	2.4
For Industry	3.7	2.3	.6	.6	.3	.6	.6
For Hshold Consm	1.5	.3	.4	.6	1.0	1.6	1.8
2. Ind. Supplies Nes.	40.8	41.4	31.4	37.2	34.5	38.3	29.6
Primary	8.3	7.1	5.5	7.0	6.1	6.2	3.9
Processed	32.5	34.3	25.8	30.2	28.4	32.1	25.6
3. Fuels Lubricants	14.1	31.0	34.6	25.5	32.1	23.9	28.4
Primary	~	28.6	31.9	22.3	29.5	18.5	25.6
Processed	~	2.5	2.7	3.1	2.7	5.4	2.8
Motor Spirit	~	.2	.2	.2	.1	.1	.2
Other	~	2.3	2.5	2.9	2.5	5.3	2.6
4. Machinery	12.4	12.0	17.5	20.3	16.4	16.0	15.8
Machines Capt. Eqp	~	10.4	15.9	18.7	15.0	14.6	14.2
Parts Accessories	~	1.6	1.6	1.6	1.4	1.4	1.6
5. Transport	16.4	6.7	8.6	8.7	7.8	10.1	14.0
Passenger Cars	~	1.7	2.2	3.2	3.0	4.9	6.2
Other	~	3.2	4.5	3.2	3.2	3.5	5.6
Industrial	~	2.9	4.1	2.7	2.8	3.0	4.6
Non-Industrial	~	.3	.4	.5	.4	.5	1.0
Parts Accessories	~	1.9	2.0	2.3	1.6	1.7	2.2
6. Consumer Goods	6.5	2.3	2.7	3.4	3.8	4.2	5.5
Durable	.3	.8	1.1	1.5	1.5	1.7	2.5
Semi-Durable	2.0	.4	.5	.7	1.0	1.0	1.6
Non-Durable	4.2	1.1	1.1	1.1	1.3	1.4	1.4
7. Other	.7	0	0	0	0	0	.2

Origin	Exports by Industrial Origin						
	1970	1975	1976	1977	1978	1979	1980
Total Exports (1 + 2 + 3)	100.0	100.0	100.0	100.0	100.0	100.0	100.0
1. Agriculture	22.8	30.6	20.7	23.5	23.9	16.1	21.5
2. Mining Quarrying	1.9	.3	.3	.5	.5	.8	.7
3. Manufacturing	75.3	69.1	79.0	75.9	75.6	83.1	77.8
31. Food, Bev., Tobac.	51.4	29.7	34.3	27.6	24.3	26.9	30.7
32. Textiles	21.1	28.3	35.3	37.9	39.5	39.2	32.3
33. Wood, Wood Prod.	0	0	0	0	0	0	0
34. Paper and Prod.	.1	.6	.2	.6	.7	1.2	1.3
35. Chemicals	.4	3.4	2.4	3.3	4.4	5.8	4.9
36. Non-Metal Minrl	.5	3.8	3.4	3.0	3.0	3.1	2.6
37. Basic Metal Ind.	.1	.5	.5	.7	.7	.8	.7
38. Metal Manufact.	1.3	2.8	2.7	2.7	2.9	5.6	5.0
39. Oth. Manf. Ind.	.3	.1	.1	.2	.2	.4	.4

SOURCE: UN-YITS, 1976, 1981.

Table 2519

VENEZUELA PERCENTAGE VALUE OF TRADE, 1970–80

Category	Imports by Broad Economic Category						
	1970	1975	1976	1977	1978	1979	1980
Total Imports	100.0	100.0	100.0	100.0	100.0	100.0	100.0
1. Food and Beverages	9.2	11.4	10.2	10.3	10.5	10.7	11.2
Primary	5.3	6.3	4.9	4.3	4.0	4.6	3.9
For Industry	3.8	5.2	3.7	2.7	2.3	2.9	2.5
For Hshold Consm	1.5	1.0	1.1	1.6	1.7	1.8	1.4
Processed	3.9	5.2	5.3	5.9	6.4	6.0	7.3
For Industry	1.3	2.3	2.0	1.8	2.4	1.7	2.5
For Hshold Consm	2.7	2.9	3.3	4.1	4.1	4.3	4.8
2. Ind. Supplies	34.3	31.4	30.6	32.8	28.1	32.1	33.7
Primary	2.7	1.4	2.4	2.7	1.7	2.9	4.0
Processed	31.6	30.0	28.2	30.1	26.4	29.2	29.7
3. Fuels Lubricants	1.3	.5	.3	.4	.2	.7	1.0
Primary	.1	0	.1	.1	0	.2	.5
Processed	1.2	.5	.3	.3	.2	.5	.4
Motor Spirit	.3	0	0	0	0	.2	.1
Other	.9	.5	.3	.3	.1	.3	.4
4. Machinery	28.6	31.8	33.4	35.1	32.2	30.0	28.0
Machines Capt. Eqp	25.4	28.7	30.3	32.8	29.3	26.7	24.5
Parts Accessories	3.2	3.1	3.1	2.3	2.9	3.3	3.5
5. Transport	15.6	16.8	17.6	14.3	20.0	16.6	14.3
Passenger Cars	5.6	6.5	5.7	4.4	5.5	5.7	5.4
Other	4.0	5.6	7.4	6.0	9.8	6.8	4.2
Industrial	3.8	5.4	7.1	5.8	9.5	6.4	3.8
Non-Industrial	.2	.3	.3	.2	.3	.3	.3
Parts Accessories	5.9	4.7	4.5	3.9	4.7	4.1	4.7
6. Consumer Goods	10.1	7.7	7.7	7.0	8.9	9.8	11.6
Durable	3.8	3.3	3.2	2.9	3.3	3.3	4.7
Semi-Durable	3.7	3.0	3.2	2.9	4.2	4.7	5.0
Non-Durable	2.6	1.4	1.2	1.2	1.5	1.8	1.9
7. Other	.9	.3	.2	.1	.1	.1	.2

Origin	Exports by Industrial Origin						
	1970	1975	1976	1977	1978	1979	1980
Total Exports (1 + 2 + 3)	100.0	100.0	100.0	100.0	100.0	100.0	100.0
1. Agriculture	1.4	.7	.9	.9	.9	.5	.3
2. Mining Quarrying	68.4	71.0	65.7	67.3	64.2	64.2	66.3
3. Manufacturing	30.2	28.3	33.4	31.8	34.9	35.3	33.5
31. Food, Bev., Tobac.	.2	.3	.1	.1	.2	.1	.1
32. Textiles	0	0	.1	0	0	0	0
33. Wood, Wood Prod.	0	0	0	0	0	0	0
34. Paper and Prod.	0	.1	.1	.1	.1	.1	.1
35. Chemicals	28.5	27.5	32.7	31.1	33.7	33.2	30.1
36. Non-Metal Minrl	.1	0	0	0	0	0	0
37. Basic Metal Ind.	.7	.1	.2	.2	.5	1.6	2.7
38. Metal Manufact.	.5	.2	0	.2	.4	.2	.5
39. Oth. Manf. Ind.	.1	0	0	0	0	0	0

SOURCE: UN-YITS, 1976, 1981.

Table 2520

UNITED STATES PERCENTAGE VALUE OF TRADE,[1] 1970–81

Category	Imports by Broad Economic Category							
	1970	1975	1976	1977	1978	1979	1980	1981
Total Imports	100.0	100.0	100.0	100.0	100.0	100.0	100.0	100.0
1. Food and Beverages	15.5	10.2	9.6	9.5	9.2	8.8	7.9	7.3
Primary	8.8	4.9	5.5	5.8	5.5	5.2	4.4	3.9
For Industry	4.0	2.2	2.7	3.2	2.8	2.3	2.0	1.5
For Hshold Consm	4.8	2.7	2.8	2.6	2.8	2.9	2.5	2.4
Processed	6.7	5.3	4.1	3.7	3.7	3.6	3.4	3.4
For Industry	1.3	.9	.9	1.0	.6	.6	.4	.4
For Hshold Consm	5.4	4.4	3.3	2.7	3.1	3.0	3.0	3.1
2. Ind. Supplies Nes.	32.5	24.6	24.0	23.7	24.3	22.8	21.0	21.7
Primary	7.0	4.8	4.7	4.3	4.3	3.9	3.7	3.6
Processed	25.5	19.8	19.3	19.4	20.1	18.9	17.2	18.1
3. Fuels Lubricants	7.6	27.0	27.6	29.1	24.4	29.1	32.7	30.9
Primary	3.9	20.4	22.6	24.4	20.2	24.3	27.9	25.8
Processed	3.6	6.6	5.1	4.7	4.2	4.9	4.8	5.1
Motor Spirit	0	.3	.1	.3	.6	1.0	.9	1.0
Other	3.6	6.2	5.0	4.5	3.5	3.8	3.9	4.1
4. Machinery	8.7	9.2	9.1	8.9	10.0	10.3	10.5	11.2
Machines Capt. Eqp	7.0	7.2	7.1	6.8	7.8	7.8	7.8	8.4
Parts Accessories	1.6	2.0	2.0	2.1	2.3	2.5	2.7	2.8
5. Transport	17.2	14.9	15.0	14.8	15.9	14.6	14.1	14.2
Passenger Cars	9.8	7.8	7.8	7.6	8.2	7.4	7.2	7.0
Other	2.0	1.8	1.4	1.7	2.1	1.9	2.2	2.9
Industrial	1.1	.9	.9	1.2	1.5	1.4	1.6	2.3
Non-Industrial	.9	.8	.5	.5	.6	.5	.5	.6
Parts Accessories	5.4	5.4	5.8	5.5	5.7	5.3	4.7	4.3
6. Consumer Goods	15.4	11.4	12.5	12.2	14.3	12.7	12.1	12.8
Durable	5.6	4.2	4.7	4.8	5.5	4.7	4.6	4.8
Semi-Durable	8.8	6.5	7.2	6.8	8.0	7.3	6.8	7.1
Non-Durable	.9	.6	.6	.6	.8	.7	.7	.8
7. Other	3.3	2.6	2.1	1.9	1.8	1.6	1.7	1.9

Origin	Exports by Industrial Origin							
	1970	1975	1976	1977	1978	1979	1980	1981
Total Exports (1 + 2 + 3)	100.0	100.0	100.0	100.0	100.0	100.0	100.0	100.0
1. Agriculture	12.6	17.1	16.4	15.7	16.8	16.3	15.5	15.3
2. Mining Quarrying	4.3	4.7	4.1	4.0	3.3	4.0	4.3	4.4
3. Manufacturing	83.1	78.2	79.4	80.3	79.9	79.7	80.2	80.3
31. Food, Bev., Tobac.	5.9	4.9	5.5	6.2	6.2	5.9	5.6	5.4
32. Textiles	2.3	2.3	2.6	2.6	2.5	2.8	2.7	2.5
33. Wood, Wood Prod.	.8	.8	1.0	.9	.8	1.0	.9	.8
34. Paper and Prod.	3.4	2.8	2.8	2.7	2.4	2.5	2.8	2.8
35. Chemicals	12.0	10.8	11.5	12.0	12.6	13.8	13.8	13.8
36. Non-Metal Minrl	.9	.7	.8	.8	.9	.8	.8	.8
37. Basic Metal Ind.	5.3	3.6	2.8	2.4	2.3	2.8	4.0	2.7
38. Metal Manufact.	49.7	49.6	50.2	50.1	49.6	47.4	46.3	48.9
39. Oth. Manf. Ind.	2.9	2.6	2.3	2.4	2.6	2.7	3.2	2.5

1. Includes Puerto Rico

SOURCE: UN-YITS, 1977, 1978, 1979, 1980, 1981.

Table 2521

ARGENTINA ABSOLUTE VALUE OF TRADE, 1970–81

(T US)

Imports

Category	1970	1975	1976	1977	1978	1979	1980	1981
Total Merchandise Trade	1,684,639	3,946,501	3,033,004	4,161,539	3,833,655	6,100,055	10,540,603	9,485,000
Agricultural Products, Total	120,070	238,534	190,844	269,220	258,791	526,699	680,092	542,975
Food and Animals	84,502	155,765	130,411	199,398	184,377	382,863	506,653	379,994
Live Animals	1,409	7,762	524	7,420	2,580	745	7,435	5,816
Meat and Meat Prep	3	255	81	213	449	14,548	49,476	25,007
Dairy Products Eggs	6,207	1,652	1,672	9,903	16,291	35,574	47,110	29,443
Cereals and Prep	651	84	414	2,079	2,975	8,444	18,025	12,060
Fruits and Vegetables	24,885	53,263	33,666	37,342	48,306	146,342	185,633	134,768
Sugar and Honey	419	795	570	1,085	1,259	7,004	14,779	10,138
Coffee, Tea, Cocoa Sp	47,038	89,267	92,818	139,384	108,512	165,224	164,437	130,211
Feeding Stuff	1,040	362	221	642	572	1,013	3,995	2,643
Miscellaneous Food	2,850	2,323	445	1,330	3,433	3,969	15,763	29,918
Beverages Tobacco	7,113	10,875	9,104	7,890	15,338	45,044	56,368	46,256
Beverages	6,118	10,308	8,765	6,846	12,967	41,274	44,821	34,234
Tobacco	995	567	339	1,044	2,371	3,770	11,547	12,022
Crude Materials	26,719	64,323	46,355	55,955	53,132	91,675	108,683	108,920
Hides and Skins	666	515	1	187	332	524	2,961	3,000
Oilseeds	204	292	261	846	2,956	4,080	2,593	5,495
Natural Rubber	12,406	20,489	26,095	28,047	27,505	40,577	38,540	30,000†
Textile Fibers	11,304	27,057	11,133	14,084	10,149	25,803	23,956	49,184
Crude Mat Nes	2,139	15,970	8,865	12,791	12,190	20,691	40,633	21,241
Animal Vegetable Oil	1,736	7,571	4,974	5,977	5,944	7,117	8,388	7,805
Animal Fats	75	126	154	167	202	569	498	349
Fixed Vegetable Oils	1,298	4,703	2,852	3,595	3,445	3,997	4,372	3,007
Processed Oils	363	2,742	1,968	2,215	2,297	2,551	3,518	4,449
Agricultural Requisites	24,289	52,619	38,743	75,510	74,269	139,092	196,157	188,900
Crude Fertilizers	858	1,934	1,954	1,308	785	826	584	600
Manuf Fertilizers	5,259	16,104	8,447	9,308	12,920	31,326	38,539	28,700†
Pesticides	5,713	15,364	17,145	20,717	18,847	36,171	43,643	47,000†
Agriculture Machines	12,459	19,217	11,197	44,177	41,717	70,769	113,391	112,600†

Exports

Category	1970	1975	1976	1977	1978	1979	1980	1981
Total Merchandise Trade	1,773,167	2,961,264	3,916,058	5,651,842	6,399,540	7,809,924	8,021,418	9,151,000
Agricultural Products, Total	1,490,606	2,180,259	2,846,091	4,121,927	4,437,774	5,552,530	5,557,001	6,455,087
Food and Animals	1,207,026	1,891,051	2,414,652	3,190,728	3,035,967	3,883,880	3,874,549	4,989,789
Live Animals	22,673	2,942	7,279	12,583	24,768	11,075	5,697	6,989
Meat and Meat Prep	441,313	287,548	522,859	639,716	794,751	1,226,421	981,521	951,053
Dairy Products Eggs	1,908	22,080	56,436	50,881	41,957	17,922	21,096	27,057
Cereals and Prep	518,523	1,106,315	1,215,518	1,563,480	1,263,198	1,649,257	1,656,781	2,840,601
Fruits and Vegetables	75,683	175,934	248,602	326,800	423,807	425,884	393,409	402,308
Sugar and Honey	17,608	132,587	106,457	189,216	94,787	98,832	339,357	315,474
Coffee, Tea, Cocoa Sp	10,344	16,919	19,318	39,078	29,082	27,288	38,971	33,052
Feeding Stuff	114,016	141,660	227,236	353,611	347,502	407,749	412,558	395,695
Miscellaneous Food	4,958	5,066	10,947	15,363	16,115	19,452	25,159	17,560
Beverages Tobacco	7,128	36,844	30,605	43,245	54,019	48,726	42,358	42,602
Beverages	793	4,738	10,075	19,281	26,528	17,237	15,494	13,996
Tobacco	6,335	32,106	20,530	23,964	27,491	31,489	26,864	28,606
Crude Materials	177,042	163,468	233,192	529,979	968,076	1,091,890	1,133,971	1,042,042
Hides and Skins	62,681	10,047	21,365	27,406	31,069	37,915	69,803	46,231
Oilseeds	282	1,877	16,621	201,885	561,248	751,778	662,194	639,334
Natural Rubber	- -	#	#	#	#	2	21	#
Textile Fibers	113,689	139,234	181,836	280,195	353,109	276,124	374,410	334,457
Crude Mat Nes	390	12,310	13,370	20,493	22,650	26,071	27,543	22,020
Animal Vegetable Oils	99,410	88,896	167,642	357,975	379,712	528,034	506,123	380,654
Animal Fats	21,192	41	8,386	12,437	36,947	49,830	28,894	35,379
Fixed Vegetable Oils	73,800	87,938	155,476	341,404	336,775	472,534	471,885	339,910
Processed Oils	4,418	917	3,780	4,134	5,990	5,670	5,344	5,365
Agricultural Requisites	5,717	43,040	29,410	36,993	38,995	47,213	49,550	54,900
Crude Fertilizers	4	579	4	3	6	15	#	#
Manuf Fertilizers	239	94	7	41	215	246	#	#
Pesticides	214	1,118	1,088	2,821	2,570	3,147	3,200†	3,200†
Agricultural Machines	5,260	41,249	28,311	34,128	36,204	43,805	46,350†	51,600†

SOURCE: FAO-TY, 1975, Section IV; FAO-TY, 1980, Section IV; FAO-TY, 1981, Section IV.

Table 2522

BOLIVIA ABSOLUTE VALUE OF TRADE, 1970–81

(T US)

				Imports				
Category	1970	1975	1976	1977	1978	1979	1980	1981
Total Merchandise Trade	~	557,900	587,600	665,900	848,200	1,011,000	813,800	820,600
Agricultural Products, Total	~	88,687	85,586	78,626	107,065	111,931	101,971	118,372
Food and Animals	~	85,590	74,887	70,149	94,784	99,956	86,246	101,187
Live Animals	#	1,900	1,494	1,287	1,047	447	114	#
Meat and Meat Prep	#	75	80	95	80	81	690	900
Dairy Products Eggs	#	9,702	8,012	10,941	16,122	11,954	13,400	14,345
Cereals and Prep	#	60,020	48,823	38,527	51,385	62,339	49,906	53,548
Fruits and Vegetables	#	1,876	2,621	2,543	3,458	4,137	5,266	4,351
Sugar and Honey	10[†]	#	545	1,090	1,026	2,054	1,780	1,700
Coffee, Tea, Cocoa Sp	34[†]	1,555	1,740	2,097	3,820	2,570	3,940	4,561
Feeding Stuff	#	#	#	#	1,027	234	250	1,639
Miscellaneous Food	#	10,862	11,572	13,569	16,819	16,140	10,900	20,143
Beverages Tobacco		2,897	2,307	2,665	3,502	4,728	4,470	4,131
Beverages	#	#	#	#	678	916	370	504
Tobacco	#	2,897	2,307	2,665	2,824	3,812	4,100	3,627
Crude Materials	~	#	#	#	1,220	917	265	1,712
Hides and Skins	~	#	#	#	#	#	#	#
Oilseeds	#	#	#	#	250	172	#	1,378
Natural Rubber	~	#	#	#	67	40	#	32
Textile Fibers	~	#	#	#	263	705	265	302
Crude Mat Nes	#	#	#	#	640	#	#	#
Animal Vegetable Oil	#	200	5,392	5,812	7,559	6,330	10,990	11,162
Animal Fats	#	#	250	75	311	117	90	114
Fixed Vegetable Oils	#	200	5,052	4,977	5,559	3,091	8,900	9,600
Processed Oils	#	#	90	760	1,679	3,122	2,000	1,448
Agricultural Requisites	#	16,107	14,439	15,969	26,907	23,807	8,801	36,262
Crude Fertilizers	#	#	#	#	9	27	2	7
Manuf Fertilizers	#	3,203	2,328	1,407	1,942	2,987	966	5,029
Pesticides	#	1,200[†]	1,500[†]	2,000[†]	5,388	4,670	2,445	7,231
Agriculture Machines	#	11,704	10,611	12,562	19,568	16,123	5,388	24,001

				Exports			
Category	1975	1976	1977	1978	1979	1980	1981
Total Merchandise Trade	444,700	566,100	634,300	627,300	761,800	941,900	908,900
Agricultural Products, Total	67,998	86,838	73,754	77,009	93,844	106,635	46,749
Food and Animals	49,273	70,935	56,130	53,958	72,552	97,887	39,926
Live Animals	17,000	14,000[†]	11,500[†]	12,500[†]	16,000[†]	11,420[‡]	9,975[‡]
Meat and Meat Prep	#	#	182	37	#	#	#
Dairy Products Eggs	#	#	#	#	#	#	#
Cereals and Prep	30	339	353	4,333	855	#	40
Fruits and Vegetables	1,611	2,664	2,790	3,262	2,961	2,898	3,539
Sugar and Honey	23,553	39,758	23,369	14,204	29,676	52,475	5,851
Coffee, Tea, Cocoa Sp	7,070	13,860	17,806	19,622	21,254	22,094	16,920
Feeding Stuff	9	314	130	#	1,806	9,000	3,601
Miscellaneous Food	#	#	#	#	#	#	#
Beverages Tobacco	774	444	784	1,018	1,293	1,065	838
Beverages	724	444	756	996	1,280	1,065	838
Tobacco	50	#	28	22	13	#	#
Crude Materials	17,951	15,449	16,840	22,033	19,999	7,683	5,985
Hides and Skins	600	600	686	4,700	6,663	2,000	2,200
Oilseeds	#	#	#	778	840	#	#
Natural Rubber	2,012	2,354	2,239	2,091	1,904	4,700	3,405
Textile Fibers	15,339	12,505	13,915	14,258	10,592	983	308
Crude Mat Nes	#	#	#	206	#	#	#
Animal Vegetable Oils	#	#	#	#	#	#	#
Animal Fats	#	#	#	#	#	#	#
Fixed Vegetable Oils	#	#	#	#	#	#	#
Processed Oils	#	#	#	#	#	#	#
Agricultural Requisites	#	#	#	#	#	#	#
Crude Fertilizers	#	#	#	#	#	#	#
Manuf Fertilizers	#	#	#	#	#	#	#
Pesticides	#	#	#	#	#	#	#
Agricultural Machines	#	#	#	#	#	#	#

SOURCE: FAO-TY, 1980, Section IV; FAO-TY, 1981, Section IV.

Table 2523

BRAZIL ABSOLUTE VALUE OF TRADE, 1970–81
(T US)

Imports

Category	1970	1975	1976	1977	1978	1979	1980	1981
Total Merchandise Trade	2,849,243	13,592,463	13,622,687	13,229,107	15,054,270	19,804,320	24,960,550	24,079,008
Agricultural Products, Total	300,618	867,719	1,112,538	924,989	1,546,033	2,361,048	2,470,568	2,186,543
Food and Animals	253,999	728,968	971,309	790,337	1,333,976	1,974,465	2,050,629	1,708,333
Live Animals	11,188	34,033	32,301	22,655	40,022	73,939	33,616	22,607
Meat and Meat Prep	895	16,804	19,331	23,407	98,856	166,724	95,715	76,594
Dairy Products Eggs	14,351	16,777	25,356	46,489	27,011	15,614	90,784	22,100
Cereals and Prep	155,130	479,168	644,270	382,695	870,021	1,212,704	1,537,363	1,355,944
Fruits and Vegetables	68,974	169,977	231,197	292,444	284,379	287,077	274,764	212,475
Sugar and Honey	168	1,868	3,114	2,492	3,071	3,235	4,147	4,445
Coffee, Tea, Cocoa Sp	1,675	4,344	10,307	15,628	5,172	205,177	6,184	6,359
Feeding Stuff	1,411	4,425	4,215	2,943	4,326	9,083	7,213	6,282
Miscellaneous Food	207	1,572	1,218	1,584	1,118	912	843	1,527
Beverages Tobacco	6,859	21,906	22,099	16,634	26,101	25,667	19,500	15,179
Beverages	6,782	21,025	19,315	15,860	25,308	24,015	17,801	14,510
Tobacco	77	881	2,784	774	793	1,652	1,699	669
Crude Materials	18,080	77,988	89,114	87,984	127,581	219,610	295,474	419,927
Hides and Skins	1,174	5,466	4,320	4,202	5,189	6,181	6,511	8,089
Oilseeds	65	466	1,860	4,414	29,332	91,580	131,002	278,964
Natural Rubber	6,519	30,361	44,903	52,312	63,764	81,917	97,306	80,122
Textile Fibers	4,378	18,352	11,002	2,568	2,894	3,281	24,487	21,687
Crude Mat Nes	5,944	23,343	27,029	24,488	26,402	36,651	36,168	31,065
Animal Vegetable Oil	21,680	38,857	30,016	30,034	58,375	141,306	104,965	43,104
Animal Fats	8,220	18,304	10,496	7,977	34,276	50,485	42,567	18,234
Fixed Vegetable Oils	13,327	20,194	19,107	21,844	23,796	90,424	61,880	24,649
Processed Oils	133	359	413	213	303	397	518	221
Agricultural Requisites	185,272	775,237	562,564	604,448	594,313	658,622	909,995	511,649
Crude Fertilizers	8,149	65,355	77,312	67,779	52,420	43,719	57,830	37,650
Manuf Fertilizers	70,637	349,672	247,752	360,241	368,984	522,511	777,850	436,403
Pesticides	18,771	100,653	109,372	107,892	125,098	52,999	30,991	7,855
Agriculture Machines	87,715	259,557	128,128	68,536	47,811	39,393	43,324	29,741

Exports

Category	1970	1975	1976	1977	1978	1979	1980	1981
Total Merchandise Trade	2,738,922	8,669,944	10,128,303	12,120,175	12,658,944	15,244,377	20,132,400	23,293,040
Agricultural Products, Total	1,972,459	4,896,894	6,142,598	7,554,797	6,716,053	7,096,358	9,420,975	9,652,323
Food and Animals	1,589,558	3,545,149	4,678,220	6,030,553	5,569,114	5,893,683	7,812,530	7,823,309
Live Animals	20,320	39,130	37,832	39,357	41,606	44,845	46,409	47,959
Meat and Meat Prep	101,208	147,424	234,052	258,296	234,476	292,260	539,999	869,567
Dairy Products Eggs	435	230	1,093	432	5,916	2,676	12,769	23,307
Cereals and Prep	88,034	162,452	190,508	230,436	51,115	12,896	20,243	48,191
Fruits and Vegetables	59,868	214,805	182,304	279,270	465,182	455,864	543,510	871,738
Sugar and Honey	134,492	1,157,461	359,252	520,063	398,664	434,342	1,398,202	1,161,426
Coffee, Tea, Cocoa Sp	1,107,567	1,305,103	2,805,653	3,460,009	3,216,733	3,354,741	3,592,827	2,486,050
Feeding Stuff	77,541	507,056	852,409	1,223,647	1,136,492	1,269,710	1,609,672	2,272,135
Miscellaneous Food	93	11,488	15,117	19,043	18,930	26,349	48,899	42,936
Beverages Tobacco	34,440	152,814	174,290	199,491	254,170	305,211	308,328	305,731
Beverages	1,471	3,825	5,420	5,444	4,849	10,794	13,067	17,067
Tobacco	32,969	148,989	168,870	194,047	249,321	294,417	295,261	368,664
Crude Materials	280,597	931,727	929,923	874,891	378,764	306,674	609,265	643,584
Hides and Skins	25,539	8,684	9,180	4,129	2,284	1,496	470	1,369
Oilseeds	40,758	717,815	802,169	730,170	181,512	195,464	415,681	436,262
Natural Rubber	4,424	1,749	2,075	1,476	2,163	497	91	104
Textile Fibers	203,009	180,029	96,096	108,992	154,991	66,707	154,027	169,572
Crude Mat Nes	6,867	23,450	20,403	30,124	37,814	42,510	38,996	36,277
Animal Vegetable Oils	67,864	267,204	360,165	449,862	514,005	590,790	690,852	879,699
Animal Fats	22	111	45	5	1	7	56	89
Fixed Vegetable Oils	57,769	250,873	341,739	433,152	493,402	569,154	670,790	858,680
Processed Oils	10,073	16,220	18,381	16,705	20,602	21,629	20,006	20,930
Agricultural Requisites	2,214	42,348	28,215	77,373	110,450	264,850	231,863	269,021
Crude Fertilizers	108	114	#	#	#	#	412	294
Manuf Fertilizers	11	3,006	1,152	490	1,660	3,737	2,760	4,197
Pesticides	376	6,064	5,046	5,393	10,376	22,406	27,320	31,794
Agricultural Machines	1,719	33,164	22,017	71,490	98,414	138,707	201,371	232,736

SOURCE: FAO–TY, 1975, Section IV; FAO–TY, 1980, Section IV; FAO–TY, 1981, Section IV.

Table 2524

CHILE ABSOLUTE VALUE OF TRADE, 1970–81

(T US)

Imports

Category	1970	1975	1976	1977	1978	1979	1980	1981
Total Merchandise Trade	960,820	1,876,200	1,642,991	1,906,265	2,553,630	4,217,600	5,124,000	6,364,000
Agricultural Products, Total	175,477	323,487	456,871	302,186	479,007	550,286	810,442	738,733
Food and Animals	121,104	248,047	389,839	204,391	360,640	418,255	684,692	601,472
Live Animals	24,747	1,732	2,466	5,579	4,815	2,400	4,500	4,610
Meat and Meat Prep	8,765	396	1,383	6,198	19,019	10,650	25,250	36,170
Dairy Products Eggs	6,548	1,233	3,767	10,375	21,654	34,920	40,070	42,895
Cereals and Prep	37,508	142,413	263,869	78,488	169,904	186,777	282,370	280,016
Fruits and Vegetables	13,435	14,947	10,485	9,773	18,725	30,215	45,128	43,066
Sugar and Honey	4,598	62,431	69,529	36,286	61,734	70,350	218,390	121,330
Coffee, Tea, Cocoa Sp	19,224	19,323	29,209	46,012	46,139	72,993	56,084	54,785
Feeding Stuff	1,695	4,000	7,422	6,356	8,326	6,600	9,200	12,800
Miscellaneous Food	4,584	1,572	1,709	5,324	10,324	3,350	3,700	5,800
Beverages Tobacco	4,197	1,604	4,828	18,269	21,068	23,032	26,600	32,900
Beverages	308	315	2,124	9,006	11,404	14,232	13,600	16,800
Tobacco	3,889	1,289	2,704	9,263	9,664	8,800	13,000	16,100
Crude Materials	34,798	30,773	38,947	44,264	56,460	61,964	51,560	50,086
Hides and Skins	3,663	4,812	2,729	2,550	2,761	3,600	6,200	7,300
Oilseeds	214	94	202	475	506	950	740	1,200
Natural Rubber	3,441	2,954	3,880	5,368	8,305	7,500	9,600	5,700
Textile Fibers	25,388	17,913	30,990	33,233	40,468	44,314	29,720	30,586
Crude Mat Nes	2,092	5,000†	1,146	2,638	4,420	2,600	5,300	5,300†
Animal Vegetable Oil	15,378	43,063	23,257	35,262	40,839	47,035	47,590	54,275
Animal Fats	1,512	1,105	704	2,786	2,565	3,000	2,900†	3,200‡
Fixed Vegetable Oils	13,428	40,976	21,968	31,038	36,316	42,255	43,390	49,595
Processed Oils	438	982	585	1,438	1,958	1,480	1,400	1,480
Agricultural Requisites	40,797	70,837	38,540	41,535	55,740	75,000	112,400	86,250
Crude Fertilizers	1,200†	1,969	2,603	286	125	#	#	#
Manuf Fertilizers	20,526	32,170	14,309	21,372	22,017	42,500	77,800	49,200
Pesticides	4,751	5,151	4,881	7,469	9,045	9,500†	10,000†	11,000†
Agriculture Machines	14,320	31,547	16,747	12,408	24,553	23,000	24,600	26,060

Exports

Category	1970	1975	1976	1977	1978	1979	1980	1981
Total Merchandise Trade	1,253,390	1,661,329	2,208,459	2,138,421	2,462,112	3,763,400	4,818,100	3,931,000
Agricultural Products, Total	40,221	154,282	148,626	211,713	254,908	299,219	385,974	377,560
Food and Animals	26,331	123,245	108,017	165,362	199,349	229,412	315,385	316,995
Live Animals	110	763	1,065	1,340	1,810	1,900	3,000	2,700
Meat and Meat Prep	- -	1,210	2,500	1,829	1,985	6,400	7,800	7,400
Dairy Products Eggs	- -	1,705	746	582	287	192	180	#
Cereals and Prep	1,686	10,435	6,013	13,326	10,162	20,525	22,510	15,770
Fruits and Vegetables	24,230	64,140	79,910	116,952	157,582	183,175	240,145	270,925
Sugar and Honey	45	40,395	1,465	10,014	11,684	7,590	28,439	12,800
Coffee, Tea, Cocoa Sp	28	119	68	405	165	#	#	#
Feeding Stuff	330	4,471	16,230	20,889	15,578	9,630	15,200	7,400
Miscellaneous Food	- -	7	20	25	96	#	#	#
Beverages Tobacco	1,840	3,971	7,919	7,689	9,760	20,901	19,600	15,000
Beverages	1,840	3,971	7,919	7,689	9,760	20,901	19,600	15,000
Tobacco	- -	#	#	#	#	#	#	#
Crude Materials	11,654	26,341	31,895	37,763	43,849	46,995	47,600	44,265
Hides and Skins	1,026	1,696	3,913	4,635	6,175	6,400	4,200	3,040
Oilseeds	788	791	407	2,808	669	570	#	#
Natural Rubber	- -	#	#	#	#	#	#	#
Textile Fibers	6,477	11,748	14,693	15,693	20,596	22,925	23,500	19,925
Crude Mat Nes	3,363	12,106	12,882	14,627	16,409	17,100	19,900	21,300†
Animal Vegetable Oils	396	725	795	899	1,950	1,911	1,500	1,300
Animal Fats	- -	6	35	5	43	#	#	#
Fixed Vegetable Oils	- -	#	#	#	208	268‡	#	#
Processed Oils	396	719	760	894	1,699	1,643	1,500	1,300
Agricultural Requisites	17,644	45,360	44,854	42,205	50,479	44,905	59,278	64,260
Crude Fertilizers	17,519	43,707	42,505	40,978	47,995	42,300	58,100	63,000†
Manuf Fertilizers	- -	773	1,790	#	1,367	1,500	#	#
Pesticides	125	499	171	541	986	1,000†	1,050†	1,100†
Agricultural Machines	- -	381	388	686	131	105	128	160

SOURCE: FAO–TY, 1975, Section IV; FAO–TY, 1980, Section IV; FAO–TY, 1981, Section IV.

Table 2525

COLOMBIA ABSOLUTE VALUE OF TRADE, 1970–81
(T US)

Imports

Category	1970	1975	1976	1977	1978	1979	1980	1981
Total Merchandise Trade	754,600	1,494,794	1,708,119	2,028,277	2,835,952	3,233,194	4,662,604	5,199,149
Agricultural Products, Total	81,137	151,756	212,010	251,712	292,005	322,726	536,361	496,041
Food and Animals	40,566	106,586	140,564	162,278	189,934	164,521	335,093	269,743
Live Animals	616	1,213	1,653	2,788	4,587	5,797	6,742	4,229
Meat and Meat Prep	230	104	192	338	748	353	1,049	2,115
Dairy Products Eggs	4,565	5,141	8,364	21,142	11,899	11,969	36,581	53,986
Cereals and Prep	21,055	60,034	80,451	79,672	89,530	82,078	202,635	121,934
Fruits and Vegetables	3,651	12,337	17,620	21,803	24,221	31,414	56,627	50,640
Sugar and Honey	587	1,552	2,094	2,658	12,269	3,933	5,399	5,594
Coffee, Tea, Cocoa Sp	9,366	15,631	17,102	18,940	28,375	15,654	10,019	10,044
Feeding Stuff	255	1,736	2,605	2,452	5,754	6,059	5,244	6,997
Miscellaneous Food	241	8,838	10,483	12,485	12,551	7,264	10,797	14,204
Beverages Tobacco	13,009	8,308	8,694	15,896	21,775	28,191	49,199	46,335
Beverages	4,007	6,889	7,237	9,854	11,923	13,866	23,456	23,351
Tobacco	9,002	1,419	1,457	6,042	9,852	14,325	25,743	22,984
Crude Materials	17,926	21,149	28,729	31,161	30,511	49,093	63,017	49,296
Hides and Skins	43	1,173	335	639	1,766	586	15	86
Oilseeds	613	166	793	1,581	817	3,000	11,124	1,153
Natural Rubber	4,256	7,660	13,367	11,365	12,782	17,105	19,316	19,685
Textile Fibers	9,675	6,696	8,143	10,449	7,546	17,893	20,156	17,864
Crude Mat Nes	3,339	5,454	6,091	7,127	7,600	10,509	12,406	10,508
Animal Vegetable Oil	14,636	15,713	34,023	42,377	49,785	80,921	89,052	130,667
Animal Fats	5,369	9,430	11,708	14,644	14,783	19,405	23,161	21,141
Fixed Vegetable Oils	8,650	5,050	20,928	26,115	33,004	54,542	60,114	107,107
Processed Oils	617	1,233	1,387	1,618	1,998	6,974	5,777	2,419
Agricultural Requisites	35,573	77,093	43,381	88,943	133,451	95,359	151,198	153,487
Crude Fertilizers	138	3,014	515	2,658	3,120	2,483	2,535	2,752
Manuf Fertilizers	20,418	38,111	4,110	27,843	50,529	39,385	74,798	66,575
Pesticides	1,355	6,903	8,057	14,545	24,478	16,244	19,403	21,406
Agriculture Machines	13,662	29,065	30,699	43,897	55,324	37,247	54,462	62,754

Exports

Category	1970	1975	1976	1977	1978	1979	1980	1981
Total Merchandise Trade	735,657	1,465,187	1,744,634	2,443,026	3,038,066	3,300,443	3,945,048	2,955,476
Agricultural Products, Total	597,394	1,089,814	1,317,560	1,908,963	2,396,033	2,489,924	3,045,230	2,101,822
Food and Animals	551,115	980,917	1,209,871	1,739,630	2,256,270	2,345,012	2,822,673	1,866,582
Live Animals	36,253	93,550	92,731	77,570	62,037	78,322	63,247	70,152
Meat and Meat Prep	4,734	23,216	22,373	24,077	33,985	28,587	27,289	53,637
Dairy Products Eggs	417	1,188	2,840	6,823	16,107	17,088	20,315	16,745
Cereals and Prep	1,546	26,267	24,519	22,932	3,873	17,900	22,836	14,374
Fruits and Vegetables	19,927	46,592	52,386	67,923	102,060	104,943	107,471	142,448
Sugar and Honey	15,119	101,493	32,257	6,050	30,251	60,861	195,990	93,046
Coffee, Tea, Cocoa Sp	466,765	678,454	977,810	1,530,521	1,998,061	2,030,069	2,380,803	1,470,213
Feeding Stuff	6,252	9,396	3,590	1,691	1,154	861	1,546	1,541
Miscellaneous Food	102	761	1,365	2,043	8,742	6,381	3,176	4,426
Beverages Tobacco	7,217	13,015	25,580	19,628	27,597	22,330	26,862	21,901
Beverages	32	108	100	126	105	333	550	960
Tobacco	7,185	12,907	25,480	19,502	27,492	21,997	26,312	20,941
Crude Materials	39,038	95,878	82,096	149,685	112,157	122,494	195,611	213,292
Hides and Skins	1,671	#	#	#	#	#	#	#
Oilseeds	1,182	434	48	140	2,449	10,137	11,317	6,750
Natural Rubber	226	74	67	53	34	65	160	5
Textile Fibers	34,640	75,072	59,383	114,416	57,433	38,072	82,603	93,866
Crude Mat Nes	1,319	20,298	22,598	35,076	52,241	74,220	101,531	112,671
Animal Vegetable Oils	24	4	13	20	9	88	84	47
Animal Fats	- -	#	#	#	#	#	#	#
Fixed Vegetable Oils	- -	#	#	#	3	82	26	3
Processed Oils	24	4	13	20	6	6	58	44
Agricultural Requisites	719	21,724	15,024	8,100	15,296	18,496	32,415	28,038
Crude Fertilizers	- -	#	#	#	#	#	6	2
Manuf Fertilizers	6	8,342	3,769	157	622	440	7,893	2,357
Pesticides	424	11,879	9,124	5,058	11,320	13,567	21,042	21,274
Agricultural Machines	289	1,503	2,131	2,885	3,354	4,489	3,474	4,405

SOURCE: FAO-TY, 1975, Section IV; FAO-TY, 1980, Section IV; FAO-TY, 1981, Section IV.

Table 2526

COSTA RICA ABSOLUTE VALUE OF TRADE, 1970–81

(T US)

				Imports				
Country	1970	1975	1976	1977	1978	1979	1980	1981
Total Merchandise Trade	316.687	693,969	770,412	1,021,430	1,091,729	1,396,812	1,540,390	1,208,529
Agricultural Products, Total	35,079	71,031	70,866	84,979	90,749	110,697	143,097	115,861
Food and Animals	28,037	57,653	54,495	64,946	69,089	85,528	108,324	92,788
Live Animals	1,885	4,930	5,749	6,632	5,222	3,646	1,198	476
Meat and Meat Prep	1,011	2,885	2,513	3,573	5,594	6,721	7,858	3,259
Dairy Products Eggs	1,696	3,095	3,784	8,814	6,714	9,513	9,672	7,139
Cereals and Prep	10,775	30,942	25,178	22,792	24,261	29,140	45,407	43,351
Fruits and Vegetables	6,665	6,100	4,130	7,006	8,445	13,978	20,316	15,872
Sugar and Honey	1,053	1,784	3,050	2,285	2,580	2,865	3,067	1,770
Coffee, Tea, Cocoa Sp	562	922	1,006	1,589	1,937	1,735	3,538	2,608
Feeding Stuff	2,612	5,103	6,691	9,560	10,533	13,350	11,374	15,616
Miscellaneous Food	1,677	1,892	2,394	2,695	3,803	4,580	5,894	2,697
Beverages Tobacco	1,644	2,487	3,027	5,600	7,037	8,384	10,157	7,697
Beverages	1,113	2,079	2,507	4,909	6,587	7,537	9,611	7,508
Tobacco	531	408	520	691	450	847	546	189
Crude Materials	2,075	4,897	6,167	7,128	5,708	8,349	13,096	4,701
Hides and Skins	32	4	59	19	27	8	1,780	134
Oilseeds	630	1,034	439	506	569	707	3,244	479
Natural Rubber	490	1,140	1,680	1,471	1,922	3,110	2,171	4,319
Textile Fibers	419	1,483	1,957	2,648	609	509	1,485	860
Crude Mat Nes	504	1,236	2,032	2,484	2,581	4,015	4,416	2,079
Animal Vegetable Oil	3,323	5,994	7,177	7,305	8,915	8,436	11,520	7,505
Animal Fats	63	384	301	805	747	817	871	579
Fixed Vegetable Oils	3,126	5,423	6,644	6,192	7,788	7,105	10,073	5,894
Processed Oils	134	187	232	308	380	514	516	1,032
Agricultural Requisites	17,236	69,392	56,885	70,046	65,966	72,879	82,679	61,642
Crude Fertilizers	9	#	3	24	26	285	141	407
Manuf Fertilizers	7,497	37,905	20,585	26,500	19,152	17,191	29,724	15,841
Pesticides	5,432	14,644	16,493	23,017	25,679	31,734	35,287	38,000[†]
Agricultural Machines	4,298	16,843	19,804	20,505	21,109	23,669	17,527	7,394

				Exports				
Category	1970	1975	1976	1977	1978	1979	1980	1981
Total Merchandise Trade	231,163	493,305	592,941	828,164	814,465	934,391	1,001,742	1,011,175
Agricultural Products, Total	182,315	361,164	421,741	626,884	646,107	690,583	659,967	691,360
Food and Animals	179,984	357,176	415,777	615,466	623,978	675,010	645,613	680,614
Live Animals	101	5,952	4,970	7,215	1,139	852	1,155	1,870
Meat and Meat Prep	18,467	33,069	41,701	45,805	62,642	84,164	75,447	79,665
Dairy Products Eggs	538	1,994	600	892	524	526	363	233
Cereals and Prep	1,174	5,024	3,051	12,640	11,544	17,243	18,910	27,775
Fruits and Vegetables	68,943	149,891	158,014	160,372	182,614	205,558	229,885	240,818
Sugar and Honey	10,868	49,308	25,983	16,949	16,980	18,896	42,701	43,782
Coffee, Tea, Cocoa Sp	75,773	106,354	175,034	363,902	340,129	338,650	265,598	277,360
Feeding Stuff	308	957	962	941	1,797	1,385	1,337	1,611
Miscellaneous Food	3,852	4,627	5,462	6,750	6,609	7,736	10,114	7,500
Beverages Tobacco	228	859	1,022	2,160	2,350	3,503	1,058	1,068
Beverages	65	166	66	58	504	2,442	249	402
Tobacco	163	693	956	2,102	1,846	1,061	809	666
Crude Materials	1,874	2,976	4,701	9,029	19,659	12,051	13,206	9,479
Hides and Skins	269	#	321	#	#	4	12	#
Oilseeds	292	696	335	553	2,127	2,410	1,032	168
Natural Rubber	- -	#	2	#	#	#	#	#
Textile Fibers	403	205	171	2,395	9,548	523	1,460	14
Crude Mat Nes	910	2,075	3,872	6,081	7,984	9,115	10,702	9,297
Animal Vegetable Oil	229	153	241	229	120	18	90	199
Animal Fats	124	#	#	21	#	#	#	#
Fixed Vegetable Oils	92	153	223	205	114	10	9	27
Processed Oils	13	#	18	3	6	8	81	172
Agricultural Requisites	3,092	23,741	25,517	25,040	25,924	21,297	20,931	35,211
Crude Fertilizers	- -	#	#	#	#	#	#	#
Manuf Fertilizers	2,410	18,305	16,656	13,712	10,994	9,331	10,057	15,631
Pesticides	581	5,399	8,790	10,601	14,035	11,861	10,709	19,383
Agricultural Machines	101	37	71	727	895	105	165	197

SOURCE: FAO-TY, 1975, Section IV; FAO-TY, 1980, Section IV; FAO-TY, 1981, Section IV.

Table 2527

CUBA ABSOLUTE VALUE OF TRADE, 1975–81
(T US)

Category	| Imports						
	1975	1976	1977	1978	1979	1980	1981
Total Merchandise Trade	3,883,000	4,217,500	4,223,000	4,709,000	5,300,000[†]	6,223,000[†]	6,300,000[†]
Agricultural Products, Total	748,869	793,107	751,736	840,665	817,213	1,086,546	1,101,019
Food and Animals	658,876	702,619	639,477	728,431	689,936	919,071	951,450
Live Animals	2,600	2,600	#	#	#	#	#
Meat and Meat Prep	53,745	51,635	41,940	61,690	75,722	84,585	96,011
Dairy Products Eggs	79,445	78,334	65,221	66,145	82,350	93,995	82,154
Cereals and Prep	364,428	395,140	347,392	392,003	360,385	501,994	527,831
Fruits and Vegetables	56,605	68,596	70,782	79,505	69,067	92,320	108,714
Sugar and Honey	#	#	#	#	#	#	#
Coffee, Tea, Cocoa Sp	33,504	35,487	31,574	42,867	24,528	22,844	25,228
Feeding Stuff	20,509	25,929	43,406	31,580	31,756	56,397	57,580
Miscellaneous Food	48,040	44,898	39,162	54,641	46,128	61,196	53,932
Beverages Tobacco	110	1,380	1,433	3,544	3,421	22,894	14,117
Beverages	110	1,380	1,433	3,544	3,421	5,882	9,445
Tobacco	#	#	#	#	#	16,962	4,672
Crude Materials	37,561	30,733	51,344	43,960	48,893	67,968	68,221
Hides and Skins	#	#	#	#	#	#	#
Oilseeds	4,600	4,400[†]	3,087	1,420	#	165	455
Natural Rubber	#	1,600[†]	1,598	2,489	3,165	4,871	3,420
Textile Fibers	32,961	24,733	46,659	40,051	45,228	62,932	64,346
Crude Mat Nes	~	~	~	~	~	~	~
Animal Vegetable Oil	52,322	58,375	59,482	64,730	75,463	76,663	67,231
Animal Fats	10,555	11,583	13,443	16,842	18,000[†]	16,028	15,718
Fixed Vegetable Oils	41,767	46,792	46,039	47,888	57,463	60,635	51,513
Processed Oils	#	#	#	#	#	#	#
Agricultural Requisites	221,797	259,042	198,410	252,587	244,600[†]	233,974	250,270
Crude Fertilizers	1,700[†]	1,000[†]	450[†]	700[†]	300[†]	1,075	1,032
Manuf Fertilizers	101,121	100,007	92,457	119,123	98,300[†]	112,690	99,351
Pesticides	65,758	63,785	37,236	43,788	40,000[†]	30,463	38,544
Agriculture Machines	53,218	94,250	68,267	88,976	106,000[†]	89,746	111,343

Category	| Exports						
	1975	1976	1977	1978	1979	1980	1981
Total Merchandise Trade	3,684,000	3,571,000	3,544,600	4,486,500	4,841,600	5,540,800	5,000,000[†]
Agricultural Products, Total	3,432,455	3,249,935	3,141,718	4,107,344	4,346,779	4,839,175	4,418,818
Food and Animals	3,347,144	3,149,206	3,043,122	3,999,046	4,239,998	4,752,907	4,325,950
Live Animals	#	#	#	#	#	343	4
Meat and Meat Prep	#	#	#	#	#	#	#
Dairy Products Eggs	#	#	#	#	164	116	388
Cereals and Prep	#	#	#	#	#	#	#
Fruits and Vegetables	17,958	21,849	24,902	50,503	59,319	71,732	111,577
Sugar and Honey	3,312,904	3,109,840	2,973,485	3,917,843	4,146,636	4,648,206	4,176,084
Coffee, Tea, Cocoa Sp	16,282	17,517	44,735	30,700	33,879	32,510	37,897
Feeding Stuff	#	#	#	#	#	#	#
Miscellaneous Food	#	#	#	#	#	#	#
Beverages Tobacco	85,311	100,729	98,596	108,298	106,178	86,268	91,016
Beverages	19,474	20,455	16,648	17,282	26,152	35,136	20,478
Tobacco	65,837	80,274	81,948	91,016	80,026	51,132	70,538
Crude Materials	#	#	#	#	#	#	1,852
Hides and Skins	#	#	#	#	#	#	#
Oilseeds	#	#	#	#	#	#	#
Natural Rubber	#	#	#	#	#	#	#
Textile Fibers	#	#	#	#	#	#	1,852
Crude Mat Nes	#	#	#	#	#	#	#
Animal Vegetable Oils	#	#	#	#	#	#	#
Animal Fats	#	#	#	#	#	#	#
Fixed Vegetable Oils	#	#	#	#	#	#	#
Processed Oils	#	#	#	#	#	#	#
Agricultural Requisites	#	#	#	#	#	#	#
Crude Fertilizers	#	#	#	#	#	#	#
Manuf Fertilizers	#	#	#	#	#	#	#
Pesticides	#	#	#	#	#	#	#
Agricultural Machines	#	#	#	#	#	#	#

SOURCE: FAO-TY, 1980, Section IV; FAO-TY, 1981, Section IV.

Table 2528

DOMINICAN REPUBLIC ABSOLUTE VALUE OF TRADE, 1970–81
(T US)

Imports

Country	1970	1975	1976	1977	1978	1979	1980	1981
Total Merchandise Trade	278,034	717,752	763,586	847,803	860,861	1,080,433	1,498,397	1,450,169
Agricultural Products, Total	35,978	136,362	164,900	137,979	134,068	164,666	217,015	240,294
Food and Animals	25,146	99,040	119,543	88,884	84,888	92,830	148,909	174,707
Live Animals	1,197	1,273	1,040	1,023	957	1,531	2,049	1,558
Meat and Meat Prep	835	1,135	1,412	500	516	4,129	17,781	15,038
Dairy Products Eggs	6,926	3,204	3,457	6,083	7,713	10,436	15,370	13,740
Cereals and Prep	6,148	75,001	89,618	59,873	48,152	44,625	75,157	104,551
Fruits and Vegetables	4,579	8,634	10,343	5,538	6,424	10,208	9,836	5,225
Sugar and Honey	343	1,220	1,530	2,046	2,484	2,228	2,895	3,042
Coffee, Tea, Cocoa Sp	526	793	1,293	963	1,289	952	591	410
Feeding Stuff	2,168	4,150	6,910	6,800	8,620	8,208	10,714	14,147
Miscellaneous Food	2,424	3,630	3,940	6,058	8,733	10,513	14,516	16,496
Beverages Tobacco	2,670	6,366	7,000	9,585	8,817	11,054	6,366	7,539
Beverages	854	2,766[†]	3,000[†]	3,838	3,978	3,692	2,298	2,428
Tobacco	1,816	3,600	4,000	5,747	4,839	7,362	4,068	5,111
Crude Materials	803	4,058	7,817	10,850	10,407	6,551	16,222	14,660
Hides and Skins	--	#	#	1,177	1,332	1,747	1,331	454
Oilseeds	--	3,528	7,317	5,538	5,837	401	10,327	9,890
Natural Rubber	--	#	#	135	108	207	129	266
Textile Fibers	613	530	500	1,470	1,074	1,430	1,287	1,173
Crude Mat Nes	190[‡]	#	#	2,530	2,056	2,766	3,148	2,877
Animal Vegetable Oil	7,359	26,898	30,540	28,660	29,956	54,231	45,518	43,388
Animal Fats	1,105	5,000	5,000	6,163	10,162	10,470	9,988	10,963
Fixed Vegetable Oils	6,248	21,898	25,540	20,637	16,892	40,549	30,290	26,032
Processed Oils	6	#	#	1,860	2,902	3,212	5,240	6,393
Agricultural Requisites	8,248	19,936	25,450	30,303	32,968	38,015	71,495	56,621
Crude Fertilizers	--	#	#	929	876	2	12	1,113
Manuf Fertilizers	2,300	7,600[†]	13,650[†]	14,771	16,601	21,111	37,401	25,865
Pesticides	1,750[‡]	4,718	4,000[†]	7,208	7,665	9,076	13,693	16,265
Agriculture Machines	4,198	7,618	7,800	7,395	7,826	7,826	20,389	13,378

Exports

Category	1970	1975	1976	1977	1978	1979	1980	1981
Total Merchandise Trade	213,957	890,007	707,959	782,144	676,369	876,797	963,309	1,198,738
Agricultural Products, Total	186,876	711,800	481,935	512,599	449,379	530,475	515,137	784,777
Food and Animals	171,598	675,182	440,626	541,433	397,750	472,150	478,827	714,299
Live Animals	--	6	6	27	30	32	35	40
Meat and Meat Prep	3,390	4,733	8,234	1,209	2,360	3,502	2,886	8,564
Dairy Products Eggs	2	20	153	170	205	178	20	#
Cereals and Prep	214	833	642	829	2,399	629	889	1,510
Fruits and Vegetables	6,243	17,831	21,053	22,317	23,472	20,758	26,648	30,032
Sugar and Honey	111,248	576,771	264,020	231,971	181,433	206,603	307,540	538,028
Coffee, Tea, Cocoa Sp	48,955	72,620	144,446	281,732	183,732	234,753	133,485	126,061
Feeding Stuff	1,380	333	306	27	33	1,035	1,642	1,876
Miscellaneous Food	166	2,035	1,766	3,151	4,086	4,660	5,682	8,188
Beverages Tobacco	14,648	35,624	39,919	29,501	46,590	53,973	34,374	67,943
Beverages	--	83	114	104	391	100	275	366
Tobacco	14,648	35,541	39,805	29,397	46,199	53,873	34,099	67,577
Crude Materials	324	556	959	977	993	1,007	1,243	1,655
Hides and Skins	35	26	12	29	119	81	74	89
Oilseeds	252	1	1	1	7	4	23	45
Natural Rubber	--	#	#	10	#	#	#	#
Textile Fibers	37	6	2	154	1	#	#	#
Crude Mat Nes	--	523	944	783	866	922	1,146	1,521
Animal Vegetable Oils	306	438	431	688	4,046	3,345	693	880
Animal Fats	--	#	#	#	#	#	#	#
Fixed Vegetable Oils	--	#	#	#	3,296	2,559	#	#
Processed Oils	306	438	431	688	750	786	693	880
Agricultural Requisites	--	18	20,726	1,670	3,328	10,973	19,701	15,750
Crude Fertilizers	--	#	#	57	138	#	7	#
Manuf Fertilizers	--	#	20,711	1,600	3,159	10,891	19,638	15,705
Pesticides	--	18	15[†]	3	31	65	55	36
Agricultural Machines	--	#	#	10	#	17	1	9

SOURCE: FAO-TY, 1975, Section IV; FAO-TY, 1980, Section IV; FAO-TY, 1981, Section IV.

Table 2529

ECUADOR ABSOLUTE VALUE OF TRADE, 1970–81
(T US)

Imports

Category	1970	1975	1976	1977	1978	1979	1980	1981
Total Merchandise Trade	238,317	863,778	958,332	1,188,524	1,505,056	1,599,714	2,253,305	2,246,100
Agricultural Products, Total	19,376	83,548	83,026	87,723	117,397	134,402	180,034	170,705
Food and Animals	9,839	51,486	40,925	40,126	55,950	71,288	112,847	101,929
Live Animals	317	3,380	1,048	696	1,536	2,051	4,237	4,532
Meat and Meat Prep	40	#	3	51	45	50	130	400
Dairy Products Eggs	934	1,449	2,929	4,332	6,350	7,842	11,056	6,131
Cereals and Prep	6,503	41,810	30,016	26,855	36,725	49,761	84,354	80,469
Fruits and Vegetables	533	1,534	2,823	2,832	5,591	4,490	7,940	5,100
Sugar and Honey	116	227	609	793	686	10	64	120
Coffee, Tea, Cocoa Sp	340	827	856	925	1,053	1,084	766	677
Feeding Stuff	16	103	362	417	#	1,900	#	#
Miscellaneous Food	1,040	2,156	2,279	3,225	3,964	4,000	4,300	4,500
Beverages Tobacco	1,923	14,512	14,742	22,280	27,993	22,599	21,770	11,196
Beverages	364	7,161	8,248	7,485	13,551	9,997	9,561	2,804
Tobacco	1,559	7,351	6,494	14,795	14,442	12,602	12,209	8,392
Crude Materials	939	2,595	3,476	3,650	4,938	7,291	7,946	16,399
Hides and Skins	- -	8	#	#	#	#	#	#
Oilseeds	- -	80	19	12	362	385	136	6,135
Natural Rubber	310	1,426	1,537	1,585	1,367	1,230	3,853	6,697
Textile Fibers	461	524	528	496	528	3,748	1,190	767
Crude Mat Nes	168	557	1,392	1,557	2,681	1,928	2,767	2,800[†]
Animal Vegetable Oil	6,675	14,955	23,883	21,667	28,516	33,224	37,471	41,281
Animal Fats	3,520	7,314	5,293	7,801	10,909	11,914	13,945	10,522
Fixed Vegetable Oils	2,924	7,501	18,429	13,608	17,380	20,708	23,509	30,737
Processed Oils	231	140	161	258	227	602	17	22
Agricultural Requisites	10,430	86,696	49,997	52,791	71,578	53,632	89,202	103,653
Crude Fertilizers	- -	497	605	207	644	296	743	194
Manuf Fertilizers	4,092	29,438	8,602	7,644	16,304	9,714	32,921	28,795
Pesticides	2,605	13,379	11,711	8,918	10,833	14,884	17,966	30,178
Agriculture Machines	3,733	43,382	29,079	36,022	43,797	28,738	37,572	44,486

Exports

Category	1970	1975	1976	1977	1978	1979	1980	1981
Total Merchandise Trade	210,300	973,882	1,257,548	1,436,274	1,557,491	2,104,233	2,480,804	2,541,600
Agricultural Products, Total	175,760	322,732	430,877	610,588	710,256	788,411	624,230	523,415
Food and Animals	170,998	310,050	412,764	595,678	695,027	765,493	606,223	497,658
Live Animals	2,579	#	#	2	#	#	#	#
Meat and Meat Prep	- -	79	#	277	213	138	#	#
Dairy Products Eggs	- -	32	#	#	3	4	#	#
Cereals and Prep	- -	5,479	2,547	2,412	5	8	4	235
Fruits and Vegetables	84,481	141,890	105,758	150,653	153,040	203,966	198,321	208,593
Sugar and Honey	8,739	25,165	12,755	12,974	6,866	11,740	50,274	19,616
Coffee, Tea, Cocoa Sp	75,112	137,007	291,297	426,992	532,760	548,335	356,836	268,374
Feeding Stuff	87	398	407	2,113	1,918	1,302	788	840
Miscellaneous Food	- -	#	#	255	222	#	#	#
Beverages Tobacco	525	411	626	515	774	2,872	1,283	1,134
Beverages	5	10	#	#	61	1,362	#	#
Tobacco	520	401	626	515	713	1,510	1,283	1,134
Crude Materials	4,237	12,270	16,798	11,721	11,412	16,233	13,063	20,010
Hides and Skins	155	#	170	575	452	429	236	331
Oilseeds	1,659	3,462	2,260	572	48	96	#	#
Natural Rubber	- -	#	13	#	#	#	#	#
Textile Fibers	421	5,774	11,792	6,850	6,053	12,107	9,377	16,079
Crude Mat Nes	2,002	3,034	2,563	3,724	4,859	3,601	3,450	3,600[†]
Animal Vegetable Oils	- -	1	689	2,674	3,043	3,813	3,661	4,613
Animal Fats	- -	#	#	#	#	#	#	#
Fixed Vegetable Oils	- -	1	689	2,674	3,043	3,813	3,661	4,613
Processed Oils	- -	#	#	#	#	#	#	#
Agricultural Requisites	13	56	462	629	559	457	350	250
Crude Fertilizers	- -	#	#	#	#	#	#	#
Manuf Fertilizers	- -	#	#	#	#	#	#	#
Pesticides	13	56	462	629	559	420	209	250[†]
Agriculture Machines	- -	#	#	#	#	31	141	#

SOURCE: FAO-TY, 1975, Section IV; FAO-TY, 1980, Section IV; FAO–TY, 1981, Section IV.

Table 2530

EL SALVADOR ABSOLUTE VALUE OF TRADE, 1970–81

(T US)

				Imports				
Category	1970	1975	1976	1977	1978	1979	1980	1981
Total Merchandise Trade	213,600	598,037	717,880	972,762	1,023,915	1,011,972	1,106,880	985,000
Agricultural Products, Total	30,837	74,646	82,297	98,605	120,367	134,532	172,719	165,168
Food and Animals	23,833	62,924	65,445	78,736	100,960	102,752	143,914	133,451
Live Animals	1,015	1,440	1,293	1,128	1,175	944	876	885
Meat and Meat Prep	812	2,823	2,948	3,489	3,902	4,584	7,096	1,990
Dairy Products Eggs	4,458	9,194	10,518	12,805	16,770	14,339	21,938	25,128
Cereals and Prep	5,808	27,680	24,374	27,444	40,955	31,399	42,951	35,301
Fruits and Vegetables	6,421	12,507	14,004	16,601	18,534	28,270	46,473	46,177
Sugar and Honey	1,650	2,301	2,551	3,743	4,134	5,521	4,650	4,750
Coffee, Tea, Cocoa Sp	757	1,073	1,485	2,375	2,704	3,155	4,140	2,202
Feeding Stuff	1,605	2,949	4,426	6,229	6,329	7,251	7,198	8,180
Miscellaneous Food	1,307	2,957	3,846	4,922	6,457	7,289	8,592	8,838
Beverages Tobacco	1,810	2,120	2,596	3,119	3,415	3,897	4,538	3,941
Beverages	474	927	1,193	1,782	2,207	2,514	2,075	2,258[†]
Tobacco	1,336	1,193	1,403	1,337	1,208	1,383	2,463	1,683
Crude Materials	2,049	4,251	4,514	5,058	6,676	8,574	7,107	7,218
Hides and Skins	417	881	727	1,479	1,432	713	795	830[†]
Oilseeds	255	79	211	426	556	259	295	88
Natural Rubber	384	729	1,168	1,335	1,397	1,781	1,868	#
Textile Fibers	696	2,023	1,626	810	2,251	4,466	1,542	3,600
Crude Mat Nes	297	539	782	1,008	1,040	1,355	2,607	2,700[†]
Animal Vegetable Oil	3,145	5,351	9,742	11,692	9,316	19,309	17,166	20,558
Animal Fats	2,269	5,092	5,106	10,845	6,995	16,260	12,022	14,000[†]
Fixed Vegetable Oils	850	184	4,540	714	2,169	2,180	5,034	6,481
Processed Oils	26	75	96	133	152	869	110	77
Agricultural Requisites	33,485	62,319	42,480	62,765	66,505	55,625	42,846	58,020
Crude Fertilizers	109	300	609	#	#	386	#	#
Manuf Fertilizers	10,287	45,256	26,594	33,711	36,841	28,305	27,634	39,400[†]
Pesticides	21,248	7,103	8,204	14,381	14,764	17,460	10,835	13,000[†]
Agriculture Machines	1,841	9,660	7,073	14,673	14,900	9,474	4,377	5,620[†]

				Exports				
Category	1970	1975	1976	1977	1978	1979	1980	1981
Total Merchandise Trade	228,320	513,378	720,727	942,452	848,440	1,031,720	1,080,100	791,920
Agricultural Products, Total	161,881	352,884	521,964	750,324	606,421	747,095	835,491	570,745
Food and Animals	136,536	272,107	452,804	663,866	498,390	650,758	737,249	505,706
Live Animals	914	246	634	935	1,170	1,328	1,472	1,590
Meat and Meat Prep	68	2,896	9,528	4,386	13,897	14,549	5,063	1,816
Dairy Products Eggs	824	312	792	277	445	1,090	530	500
Cereals and Prep	2,025	2,834	5,196	5,174	6,511	5,064	7,667	7,631
Fruits and Vegetables	130	1,265	2,522	3,588	5,536	7,447	7,551	7,053
Sugar and Honey	8,008	87,457	45,532	31,283	25,485	32,935	18,187	21,591
Coffee, Tea, Cocoa Sp	120,971	173,425	384,477	613,997	442,136	586,392	694,709	462,805
Feeding Stuff	1,931	1,703	2,064	1,524	408	532	804	1,420
Miscellaneous Food	1,665	1,969	2,059	2,702	2,802	1,421	1,266	1,300
Beverages Tobacco	204	844	981	1,406	1,848	2,202	3,430	2,959
Beverages	164	317	275	480	682	886	1,003	1,000
Tobacco	40	527	706	926	1,166	1,316	2,427	1,959
Crude Materials	24,360	79,355	67,596	84,088	105,816	93,349	94,032	61,510
Hides and Skins	- -	3	4	6	90	11	#	#
Oilseeds	338	1,697	1,335	1,229	3,424	3,930	4,063	3,560
Natural Rubber	- -	3	2	5	#	19	28	#
Textile Fibers	23,455	76,537	64,381	81,100	100,475	87,064	87,392	55,350
Crude Mat Nes	567	1,115	1,874	1,748	1,827	2,325	2,549	2,600[†]
Animal Vegetable Oils	781	578	583	964	367	786	780	570
Animal Fats	- -	#	#	#	#	#	#	#
Fixed Vegetable Oils	759	566	583	946	343	693	714	570
Processed Oils	22	12	#	18	24	93	66	#
Agricultural Requisites	5,188	9,367	19,554	12,494	13,036	14,587	8,458	8,535
Crude Fertilizers	2	#	#	#	#	2	#	#
Manuf Fertilizers	3,211	4,500	13,452	6,422	7,663	9,662	#	#
Pesticides	1,920	4,832	5,793	5,751	5,032	4,291	6,077	6,100[†]
Agricultural Machines	55	35	309	321	341	632	2,381	2,435

SOURCE: FAO-TY, 1975, Section IV; FAO-TY, 1980, Section IV; FAO-TY, 1981, Section IV.

Table 2531

GUATEMALA ABSOLUTE VALUE OF TRADE, 1970–81
(T US)

Imports

Category	1970	1975	1976	1977	1978	1979	1980	1981
Total Merchandise Trade	284,274	732,368	838,430	1,052,507	1,285,641	1,503,937	1,598,217	1,673,476
Agricultural Products, Total	32,129	69,668	52,347	62,455	116,013	139,895	146,294	155,447
Food and Animals	23,911	60,270	40,619	50,713	102,516	120,227	119,554	126,953
Live Animals	1,769	1,426	912	1,813	28,429	45,450	23,828	28,329
Meat and Meat Prep	724	976	844	1,063	1,605	1,603	1,980	2,967
Dairy Products Eggs	2,849	2,866	2,212	7,253	7,692	5,638	13,007	10,041
Cereals and Prep	10,123	37,525	24,056	26,716	42,431	46,031	55,146	53,943
Fruits and Vegetables	1,813	8,915	4,724	6,221	10,053	10,241	11,183	13,344
Sugar and Honey	659	1,362	1,651	1,113	2,098	2,566	2,132	2,958
Coffee, Tea, Cocoa Sp	746	1,054	1,213	1,108	2,033	2,211	3,149	2,947
Feeding Stuff	2,355	4,288	3,777	4,213	6,806	4,648	7,287	10,146
Miscellaneous Food	2,873	1,858	1,230	1,213	2,369	1,839	1,842	2,278
Beverages Tobacco	1,817	3,249	2,579	3,578	3,164	5,882	5,711	4,583
Beverages	1,258	2,556	1,754	2,656	2,057	3,800	3,128	3,136
Tobacco	559	693	825	922	1,107	2,082	2,583	1,447
Crude Materials	2,322	2,420	3,135	2,911	5,179	5,931	10,313	7,422
Hides and Skins	138	189	27	47	80	346	668	487
Oilseeds	295	274	529	572	1,779	1,821	2,228	1,789
Natural Rubber	567	168	182	134	220	285	88	#
Textile Fibers	727	999	1,433	968	1,202	1,469	4,802	2,498
Crude Mat Nes	595	790	964	1,190	1,898	2,010	2,527	2,648
Animal Vegetable Oil	4,079	3,729	6,024	5,253	5,154	7,855	10,716	16,489
Animal Fats	2,672	2,907	4,506	3,195	3,247	5,555	6,919	9,722
Fixed Vegetable Oils	1,328	672	1,351	1,757	1,516	1,881	3,418	5,773
Processed Oils	79	150	167	301	391	419	379	994
Agricultural Requisites	13,717	72,748	47,473	76,305	70,905	80,245	76,253	83,139
Crude Fertilizers	- -	53	28	35	68	77	47	40
Manuf Fertilizers	5,000	44,944	18,180	31,844	28,257	33,782	43,124	50,724
Pesticides	3,714	9,342	8,424	13,541	16,932	27,263	16,506	17,092
Agriculture Machines	5,003	18,409	20,841	30,885	25,648	19,123	16,576	15,283

Exports

Category	1970	1975	1976	1977	1978	1979	1980	1981
Total Merchandise Trade	290,182	623,621	760,333	1,160,218	1,111,602	1,217,076	1,472,796	1,226,113
Agricultural Products, Total	203,978	451,127	564,493	938,084	857,871	919,456	1,014,349	769,897
Food and Animals	163,843	346,913	433,621	726,296	650,055	636,785	751,288	564,744
Live Animals	523	369	352	218	7,044	9,759	17,441	13,793
Meat and Meat Prep	14,599	20,983	20,027	34,381	37,637	49,643	47,693	51,313
Dairy Products Eggs	1,162	1,028	1,323	1,120	1,453	2,251	3,025	3,135
Cereals and Prep	3,064	3,212	3,212	4,591	5,403	6,911	11,736	7,362
Fruits and Vegetables	22,025	24,868	32,062	38,434	42,185	60,624	84,255	96,155
Sugar and Honey	13,146	122,362	123,413	99,181	56,101	65,432	90,765	107,029
Coffee, Tea, Cocoa Sp	103,927	167,604	246,442	540,653	487,170	441,810	484,265	274,491
Feeding Stuff	2,212	3,158	1,982	2,642	5,457	4,199	4,799	3,257
Miscellaneous Food	3,185	3,329	4,808	5,076	6,645	6,598	7,339	8,209
Beverages Tobacco	3,084	7,492	8,394	10,857	13,640	14,994	17,887	17,257
Beverages	565	384	500	653	603	520	504	387
Tobacco	2,519	7,108	7,894	10,204	13,037	14,474	17,383	16,870
Crude Materials	36,345	96,701	122,400	201,045	192,295	267,536	244,860	187,802
Hides and Skins	107	14	211	134	27	133	83	27
Oilseeds	1,074	3,895	8,421	6,113	4,786	12,650	11,170	15,431
Natural Rubber	- -	#	#	#	#	#	#	#
Textile Fibers	27,215	75,925	87,830	154,958	141,679	187,096	172,336	135,751
Crude Mat Nes	7,949	16,867	25,938	39,840	40,803	67,657	61,271	36,593
Animal Vegetable Oils	706	21	78	321	1,881	141	314	94
Animal Fats	17	1	1	#	#	#	#	#
Fixed Vegetable Oils	633	8	63	280	1,837	104	222	79
Processed Oils	56	12	14	41	44	37	92	15
Agricultural Requisites	587	7,369	8,465	11,503	17,344	13,946	28,135	33,417
Crude Fertilizers	- -	1	1	144	#	17	#	1
Manuf Fertilizers	- -	240	796	1,127	71	157	4,873	5,175
Pesticides	587	7,128	7,668	10,207	17,218	13,566	23,052	27,992
Agricultural Machines	- -	#	#	25	55	206	210	249

SOURCE: FAO-TY, 1975, Section IV; FAO-TY, 1980, Section IV; FAO-TY, 1981, Section IV.

Table 2532

HAITI ABSOLUTE VALUE OF TRADE, 1975–81
(T US)

| | Imports | | | | | | |
Category	1975	1976	1977	1978	1979	1980	1981
Total Merchandise Trade	142,516	201,064	208,242	220,686	266,163	354,158	586,930
Agricultural Products, Total	41,335	64,861	80,204	63,205	91,473	122,217	121,197
Food and Animals	29,631	42,218	57,233	43,042	67,257	89,348	94,082
Live Animals	112	129	78[‡]	#	#	189	#
Meat and Meat Prep	570	860	635	835	1,300	1,504	2,683
Dairy Products Eggs	4,006	6,067	6,357	11,121	8,333	12,847	11,130
Cereals and Prep	20,918	29,391	38,486	22,972	46,012	56,000	65,320
Fruits and Vegetables	1,381	1,694	1,806	1,937	2,409	2,408	2,689
Sugar and Honey	505	476	5,814	1,931	4,200	11,769	7,720
Coffee, Tea, Cocoa Sp	209	850	751	689	1,023	1,052	1,355
Feeding Stuff	366	439	814	399	1,022	1,159	465
Miscellaneous Food	1,483	2,418	2,492	3,158	2,958	2,420	2,720[†]
Beverages Tobacco	2,635	3,567	3,295	4,050	4,477	7,066	5,690
Beverages	956	1,354	1,139	1,397	1,425	1,382	2,090[†]
Tobacco	1,679	2,213	2,156	2,653	3,052	5,684	3,600
Crude Materials	1,145	2,482	1,130	2,487	779	1,201	955
Hides and Skins	#	#	#	#	#	20	#
Oilseeds	#	#	#	#	#	#	#
Natural Rubber	171	388	371	597	#	10	#
Textile Fibers	719	1,102	149	1,285	129	491	255
Crude Mat Nes	255	992	610	605	650[†]	680[†]	700[†]
Animal Vegetable Oil	7,924	16,594	18,546	13,626	18,960	24,602	20,470
Animal Fats	2,217	4,881	5,583	5,071	5,900	8.125	7,300[‡]
Fixed Vegetable Oils	5,534	11,626	12,577	8,383	12,674	16,477	13,170
Processed Oils	173	85	386	172	386	#	#
Agricultural Requisites	2,372	4,233	3,833	4,095	4,305	3,719	5,435
Crude Fertilizers	19	17	96	328	26	#	#
Manuf Fertilizers	108	7	1	2	1,245	1,020	2,340[†]
Pesticides	430	1,096	977	1,439	913	1,283	1,300[†]
Agriculture Machines	1,815	3,113	2,759	2,326	2,121	1,416	1,795[†]

| | Exports | | | | | | |
Category	1975	1976	1977	1978	1979	1980	1981
Total Merchandise Trade	102,000	117,534	143,310	158,948	148,396	226,137	180,000[†]
Agricultural Products, Total	37,752	54,376	73,946	78,581	53,622	112,766	45,833
Food and Animals	33,633	51,613	71,570	75,512	51,865	108,889	44,358
Live Animals	#	#	#	#	#	#	#
Meat and Meat Prep	771	1,267	1,539	1,745	3,178	1,802	3,780
Dairy Products Eggs	#	#	#	#	#	#	#
Cereals and Prep	167	1	1	2	4	#	#
Fruits and Vegetables	499	601	1,239	1,447	1,795	2,108	1,800
Sugar and Honey	11,083	2,043	477	2,896	410[†]	7,079	578[†]
Coffee, Tea, Cocoa Sp	20,323	46,941	68,314	69,422	46,098	45,400	36,400
Feeding Stuff	790	760	#	#	380	2,500	1,800
Miscellaneous Food	#	#	#	#	#	#	#
Beverages Tobacco	138	136	148	216	226	267	350
Beverages	138	136	148	216	226	267	350
Tobacco	#	#	#	#	#	#	#
Crude Materials	3,920	2,542	2,154	2,724	1,438	3,481	1,125
Hides and Skins	469	807	989	960	497	1,852	490
Oilseeds	47	69	89	64	126	41	45[†]
Natural Rubber	#	#	#	#	#	#	#
Textile Fibers	3,221	1,441	1,039	1,634	745	1,508	500
Crude Mat Nes	183	225	37	66	70[†]	80[†]	90[†]
Animal Vegetable Oils	61	85	74	129	93	129	#
Animal Fats	#	#	#	#	#	#	#
Fixed Vegetable Oils	#	#	#	#	#	#	#
Processed Oils	61	85	74	129	93	129	#
Agricultural Requisites	#	#	#	#	#	#	#
Crude Fertilizers	#	#	#	#	#	#	#
Manuf Fertilizers	#	#	#	#	#	#	#
Pesticides	#	#	#	#	#	#	#
Agricultural Machines	#	#	#	#	#	#	#

SOURCE: FAO-TY, 1980, Section IV; FAO-TY, 1981, Section IV.

Table 2533

HONDURAS ABSOLUTE VALUE OF TRADE, 1970–81
(T US)

Category				Imports				
	1970	1975	1976	1977	1978	1979	1980	1981
Total Merchandise Trade	220,668	404,284	453,083	579,409	692,984	825,778	1,008,689	1,042,000
Agricultural Products, Total	25,740	53,691	47,954	53,030	78,795	178,979	135,556	117,826
Food and Animals	20,728	43,396	36,182	38,267	61,743	163,235	115,003	100,791
Live Animals	485	613	533	544	13,629	108,699	35,164	22,521
Meat and Meat Prep	653	1,079	1,395	1,879	2,008	2,728	3,404	3,460
Dairy Products Eggs	3,315	5,196	5,743	5,975	5,226	7,704	11,887	14,180
Cereals and Prep	8,123	27,707	17,337	15,811	24,198	23,512	39,466	37,935
Fruits and Vegetables	2,652	2,968	3,381	3,768	4,840	6,518	8,309	6,269
Sugar and Honey	744	383	525	593	900	1,142	1,153	1,174
Coffee, Tea, Cocoa Sp	510	758	938	1,368	1,676	1,944	1,863	1,397
Feeding Stuff	824	1,364	2,103	3,513	3,152	3,688	4,817	4,500
Miscellaneous Food	3,389	3,328	4,227	4,816	6,114	7,300	8,940	9,355[†]
Beverages Tobacco	1,684	1,396	2,249	4,292	4,859	5,159	4,414	5,044
Beverages	432	1,124	1,583	2,362	3,411	4,168	3,418	3,270
Tobacco	1,252	272	666	1,930	1,448	991	996	1,774
Crude Materials	469	4,456	3,921	3,388	4,878	3,678	4,502	4,491
Hides and Skins	105	18	5	#	#	#	7	#
Oilseeds	36	1,102	167	243	185	268	108	191
Natural Rubber	- -	115	198	300	179	198	105	#
Textile Fibers	74	2,442	2,535	1,067	2,216	1,294	1,943	1,900
Crude Mat Nes	254	779	1,016	1,778	2,298	1,918	2,339	2,400[†]
Animal Vegetable Oil	2,870	4,443	5,602	7,083	7,315	6,907	11,637	7,500
Animal Fats	1,615	2.411	2,231	3,665	4,439	4,290	5,001	3,400[‡]
Fixed Vegetable Oils	1,224	1,949	3,335	3,371	2,802	2,561	6,248	3,719
Processed Oils	31	83	36	47	74	56	388	381
Agricultural Requisites	13,206	28,752	30,214	46,137	46,781	61,582	57,681	53,955
Crude Fertilizers	12	#	#	#	5	9	148	140
Manuf Fertilizers	3,329	8,656	7,631	12,232	8,209	9,686	16,507	10,600[†]
Pesticides	3,086	7,360	10,323	13,235	19,032	24,579	21,321	22,000[†]
Agriculture Machines	6,779	12,736	12,260	20,670	19,535	27,308	19,705	21,215[†]

Country				Exports				
	1970	1975	1976	1977	1978	1979	1980	1981
Total Merchandise Trade	169,738	293,263	391,831	510,777	596,869	733,616	813,444	804,250
Agricultural Products, Total	123,766	166,670	267,125	364,231	471,542	574,969	625,425	575,910
Food and Animals	119,115	152,136	249,942	341,928	436,519	537,449	584,452	534,110
Live Animals	565	325	51	83	22,049	40,049	21,049	24,000
Meat and Meat Prep	9,719	18,571	25,737	21,721	38,856	61,146	61,017	47,900
Dairy Products Eggs	1	45	#	122	750	472	375	#
Cereals and Prep	1,038	338	2,860	617	1,172	1,346	2,279	630
Fruits and Vegetables	78,733	66,735	116,036	138,461	154,639	218,073	254,946	232,780
Sugar and Honey	1,675	7,826	3,489	5,620	7,563	17,794	34,081	53,580
Coffee, Tea, Cocoa Sp	26,061	57,340	101,010	173,927	209,705	196,674	208,678	173,890
Feeding Stuff	208	617	457	770	932	1,010	848	230
Miscellaneous Food	1,115	339	296	607	853	885	1,179	1,100
Beverages Tobacco	2,599	7,601	7,914	10,833	10,574	14,833	18,821	19,600
Beverages	6	68	#	#	#	3	12	#
Tobacco	2,593	7,533	7,914	10,833	10,574	14,830	17,720	19,600
Crude Materials	1,979	6,877	9,164	11,374	23,443	22,176	21,768	22,200
Hides and Skins	324	189	962	917	1,175	3,240	1,682	3,300
Oilseeds	276	338	1,548	554	2,127	3,102	2,814	2,100
Natural Rubber	57	121	171	113	185	265	82	#
Textile Fibers	1,232	4,572	4,372	6,956	15,751	11,512	13,648	13,000
Crude Mat Nes	90	1,657	2,111	2,834	4,205	4,057	3,542	3,800[†]
Animal Vegetable Oils	73	56	105	96	1,006	511	384	#
Animal Fats	23	9	#	#	200	8	93	#
Fixed Vegetable Oils	49	43	103	96	801	499	291	#
Processed Oils	1	4	2	#	5	4	#	#
Agricultural Requisites	52	74	33	223	88	1,038	369	360
Crude Fertilizers	2	#	#	#	6	13	8	10[†]
Manuf Fertilizers	- -	13	#	1	#	842	129	100
Pesticides	50	61	33	22	82	183	232	250[†]
Agricultural Machines	- -	#	#	#	#	#	#	#

SOURCE: FAO-TY, 1975, Section IV; FAO-TY, 1980, Section IV; FAO-TY, 1981, Section IV.

Table 2534

MEXICO ABSOLUTE VALUE OF TRADE, 1970-81
(T US)

Imports

Category	1970	1975	1976	1977	1978	1979	1980	1981
Total Merchandise Trade	2,319,520	6,570,490	6,029,589	5,487,500	8,053,874	12,502,626	19,516,960	23,929,584
Agricultural Products, Total	216,277	935,594	565,437	840,313	1,026,044	1,324,429	3,109,852	3,349,573
Food and Animals	123,497	782,525	270,628	490,171	547,248	793,349	2,398,003	2,414,412
Live Animals	9,144	24,817	24,336	22,133	29,689	37,439	32,727	68,420
Meat and Meat Prep	5,192	10,180	14,269	10,883	17,058	29,469	45,604	84,683
Dairy Products Eggs	18,166	35,268	54,923	58,842	62,789	88,664	238,115	223,229
Cereals and Prep	65,517	581,111	124,718	324,590	360,396	510,961	1,142,671	1,166,592
Fruits and Vegetables	10,685	81,215	14,875	26,194	22,620	34,266	275,575	393,493
Sugar and Honey	2,281	2,616	3,974	2,755	3,717	8,283	568,010	366,700
Coffee, Tea, Cocoa Sp	3,030	5,078	5,921	6,492	8,103	13,547	8,278	21,811
Feeding Stuff	1,945	29,729	16,322	24,064	27,307	39,275	80,940	78,128
Miscellaneous Food	7,537	12,151	11,290	14,218	15,569	31,445	6,083	11,356
Beverages Tobacco	4,926	24,812	27,762	20,572	22,201	43,712	73,388	98,668
Beverages	4,100	24,531	27,762	20,552	22,120	43,579	72,244	98,609
Tobacco	826	281	#	20	81	133	1,144	59
Crude Materials	76,323	93,460	236,032	297,125	388,642	435,161	521,104	760,085
Hides and Skins	18,248	26,016	26,677	33,327	47,269	85,923	66,186	75,182
Oilseeds	18,524	9,746	134,357	187,925	246,447	216,404	308,514	539,481
Natural Rubber	12,847	24,327	34,928	35,630	45,223	58,341	73,659	68,360
Textile Fibers	16,068	12,521	15,460	15,911	23,581	31,254	37,745	42,062
Crude Mat Nes	10,636	20,850	24,610	24,332	26,122	43,179	35,000[†]	35,000[†]
Animal Vegetable Oil	11,531	34,797	31,015	32,445	67,953	52,207	117,357	76,408
Animal Fats	3,290	10,746	12,296	15,724	25,472	35,950	49,938	38,884
Fixed Vegetable Oils	5,293	18,960	10,058	14,027	37,725	4,297	55,448	22,847
Processed Oils	2,948	5,091	8,661	2,694	4,756	11,960	11,971	14,677
Agricultural Requisites	76,879	306,824	261,212	198,318	400,153	417,780	390,355	506,764
Crude Fertilizers	7,077	42,844	52,737	60,010	52,698	41,666	73,276	67,294
Manuf Fertilizers	5,758	75,565	63,828	42,079	72,095	74,776	68,147	98,860
Pesticides	3,645	11,390	9,979	17,370	11,408	13,308	19,741	17,933
Agriculture Machines	60,399	177,025	134,668	78,859	263,952	288,030	229,191	372,677

Exports

Category	1970	1975	1976	1977	1978	1979	1980	1981
Total Merchandise Trade	1,282,000	2,861,031	3,264,186	4,064,800	6,172,210	8,798,245	15,307,480	19,419,616
Agricultural Products, Total	694,505	972,500	1,318,590	1,437,552	1,697,995	2,006,440	1,700,218	1,535,882
Food and Animals	521,228	697,796	913,927	1,148,167	1,250,885	1,409,018	1,140,710	1,003,587
Live Animals	79,184	29,052	84,501	76,914	168,071	120,594	98,350	64,340
Meat and Meat Prep	46,109	9,470	35,210	45,892	73,191	39,460	27,356	28,249
Dairy Products Eggs	27	176	870	856	127	81	35	11
Cereals and Prep	5,993	16,110	8,299	13,258	23,482	11,757	13,640	5,120
Fruits and Vegetables	187,148	257,411	287,626	440,908	507,222	506,927	433,450	495,955
Sugar and Honey	103,020	171,052	50,250	53,079	54,767	74,796	73,793	43,466
Coffee, Tea, Cocoa Sp	98,486	211,718	444,587	511,529	417,998	648,567	491,213	364,073
Feeding Stuff	505	175	610	573	1,458	810	1,838	973
Miscellaneous Food	756	2,632	1,974	5,158	4,569	6,026	1,035	1,400
Beverages Tobacco	15,838	53,394	65,158	61,333	86,440	100,117	126,254	121,810
Beverages	4,272	27,824	38,012	37,970	45,865	60,622	77,444	73,004
Tobacco	11,566	25,570	27,146	23,363	40,575	39,495	48,810	48,806
Crude Materials	155,619	219,034	335,886	222,464	356,816	493,940	428,240	407,872
Hides and Skins	16	31	23	628	531	65	1,256	1,611
Oilseeds	2,382	12,212	15,781	10,158	24,859	92,451	57,995	45,567
Natural Rubber	3,722	2,822	5,439	1,235	7,766	3,094	3,251	2,846
Textile Fibers	135,194	174,691	286,206	184,609	292,446	363,589	329,738	320,848
Crude Mat Nes	14,305	29,278	28,437	25,834	31,214	34,741	36,000[†]	37,000[†]
Animal Vegetable Oils	1,820	2,276	3,619	5,588	3,854	3,365	5,014	2,613
Animal Fats	- -	#	#	9	198	522	468	207
Fixed Vegetable Oils	- -	#	6	1,867	38	128	442	450
Processed Oils	1,820	2,276	3,613	3,712	3,618	2,715	4,104	1,956
Agricultural Requisites	9,724	7,700	7,965	17,398	16,578	26,083	27,688	17,612
Crude Fertilizers	344	4	26	60	#	#	#	1,127
Manuf Fertilizers	8,051	1,548	2,871	9,460	6,709	12,647	12,440	5,108
Pesticides	938	1,744	1,722	1,926	3,770	4,870	5,838	2,223
Agricultural Machines	391	4,404	3,346	5,952	6,099	8,566	9,410	9,154

SOURCE: FAO-TY, 1975, Section IV; FAO-TY, 1980, Section IV; FAO-TY, 1981, Section IV.

Table 2535

NICARAGUA ABSOLUTE VALUE OF TRADE, 1970–81

(T US)

Imports

Category	1970	1975	1976	1977	1978	1979	1980	1981
Total Merchandise Trade	198,748	516,864	532,136	761,927	593,930	360,196	887,211	897,000
Agricultural Products, Total	19,996	44,139	47,707	59,063	60,508	50,207	139,314	127,090
Food and Animals	15,870	37,805	39,739	48,809	51,145	40,789	109,750	103,853
Live Animals	737	1,271	1,506	998	613	651	2,708	5,060
Meat and Meat Prep	385	1,208	1,771	1,751	2,017	2,463	7,638	6,213
Dairy Products Eggs	1,055	1,719	1,212	2,269	2,361	4,148	6,811	12,210
Cereals and Prep	4,817	18,630	16,917	18,858	23,165	16,323	48,440	41,723
Fruits and Vegetables	3,494	6,850	7,493	10,883	10,485	9,581	31,983	27,130
Sugar and Honey	1,009	1,777	2,417	2,647	2,613	2,158	2,580	2,660
Coffee, Tea, Cocoa Sp	379	1,114	964	1,667	1,669	866	2,241	1,427
Feeding Stuff	429	1,033	1,236	2,179	2,004	724	453	230
Miscellaneous Food	3,565	4,203	6,223	7,557	6,218	3,875	6,896	7,300
Beverages Tobacco	1,304	1,524	2,128	2,383	2,091	1,643	1,086	1,181
Beverages	746	1,118	1,409	1,373	1,578	1,238	556	638
Tobacco	558	406	719	1,010	513	405	530	543
Crude Materials	1,185	1,405	2,786	2,573	2,809	2,528	9,994	7,564
Hides and Skins	39	188	137	56	1	#	#	#
Oilseeds	391	537	833	432	582	500	5,458	5,030
Natural Rubber	140	12	127	121	145	84	730	#
Textile Fibers	428	50	608	849	922	1,552	3,047	1,714
Crude Mat Nes	187	618	1,081	1,115	1,159	392	759	820[†]
Animal Vegetable Oil	1,637	3,405	3,054	5,298	4,463	5,247	18,484	14,392
Animal Fats	1,160	2,707	2,311	3,451	2,394	3,698	6,127	8,500[‡]
Fixed Vegetable Oils	381	603	644	1,656	1,955	1,490	12,202	5,849
Processed Oils	96	95	99	191	114	59	155	43
Agricultural Requisites	9,139	39,549	25,582	52,353	43,520	19,996	76,347	62,340
Crude Fertilizers	~	#	#	114	2	#	1	#
Manuf Fertilizers	4,112	22,002	7,445	18,768	16,593	6,768	35,455	22,700[†]
Pesticides	2,744	7,733	8,135	16,441	15,480	6,274	22,025	21,000[†]
Agriculture Machines	2,283	9,814	10,002	17,030	10,945	6,954	18,866	18,640[†]

Exports

Category	1970	1975	1976	1977	1978	1979	1980	1981
Total Merchandise Trade	178,623	375,172	541,901	636,805	645,969	566,555	450,442	500,000
Agricultural Products, Total	131,901	277,198	410,423	487,410	511,577	561,565	343,821	404,493
Food and Animals	82,914	154,921	253,026	307,921	342,012	407,148	301,590	269,367
Live Animals	581	2,444	3,785	8,116	14,311	100,135	30,041	20,000
Meat and Meat Prep	26,901	28,608	40,488	38,986	70,665	95,384	58,770	37,000
Dairy Products Eggs	2,356	6,794	7,243	6,845	6,663	2,554	2	#
Cereals and Prep	5,218	7,151	7,528	5,053	5,627	3,580	4,619	4,823
Fruits and Vegetables	1,633	5,785	6,291	5,416	7,256	8,327	9,825	9,330
Sugar and Honey	10,367	45,148	58,436	31,171	22,233	22,841	25,993	53,035
Coffee, Tea, Cocoa Sp	32,845	49,272	119,923	200,787	200,789	159,708	169,706	136,000
Feeding Stuff	2,983	9,691	9,320	11,533	14,445	14,576	2,506	9,100
Miscellaneous Food	30	28	12	14	23	43	128	79
Beverages Tobacco	2,442	5,825	7,372	7,470	6,006	4,374	2,657	3,146
Beverages	32	186	71	84	470	237	95	73
Tobacco	2,410	5,639	7,301	7,386	5,536	4,137	2,562	3,073
Crude Materials	42,505	107,930	143,912	166,569	154,865	145,867	39,566	130,280
Hides and Skins	265	482	537	1,079	2,707	2,282	586	630
Oilseeds	3,577	4,657	7,027	9,737	3,971	3,493	6,957	8,550
Natural Rubber	- -	#	#	#	#	#	#	#
Textile Fibers	35,262	98,524	132,517	153,091	144,822	139,166	30,922	120,000
Crude Mat Nes	3,401	4,267	3,831	2,662	3,365	926	1,101	1,100[†]
Animal Vegetable Oils	4,040	8,522	6,113	5,450	8,694	4,176	8	1,700
Animal Fats	- -	#	#	5	112	129	#	#
Fixed Vegetable Oils	4,035	8,515	6,113	5,445	8,582	4,039	8	1,700
Processed Oils	5	7	#	#	#	#	8	#
Agricultural Requisites	570	4,122	5,731	9,766	9,405	2,598	1,907	2,000
Crude Fertilizers	~	#	#	#	#	#	#	#
Manuf Fertilizers	30	201	84	514	374	91	#	#
Pesticides	540	3,827	5,541	9,139	11,745	2,507	1,907	2,000[†]
Agricultural Machines	- -	94	106	113	14	#	#	#

SOURCE: FAO-TY, 1975, Section IV; FAO-TY, 1980, Section IV; FAO-TY, 1981, Section IV.

Table 2536

PANAMA ABSOLUTE VALUE OF TRADE, 1970–81
(T US)

Imports

Category	1970	1975	1976	1977	1978	1979	1980	1981
Total Merchandise Trade	326,352	815,568	840,304	777,761	844,797	1,066,225	1,290,434	1,539,811
Agricultural Products, Total	28,227	65,890	67,065	71,791	73,004	95,559	120,014	139,451
Food and Animals	22,128	50,272	50,321	55,798	57,846	71,898	91,214	112,992
Live Animals	318	301	161	315	259	314	146	212
Meat and Meat Prep	4,106	6,633	8,113	7,719	8,026	10,170	12,247	14,245
Dairy Products Eggs	3,250	8,327	6,813	9,012	8,715	9,705	16,920	12,291
Cereals and Prep	4,863	17,037	14,738	15,691	14,234	18,941	23,800	32,931
Fruits and Vegetables	5,954	8,509	11,535	13,678	15,466	19,066	21,254	29,083
Sugar and Honey	423	3,516	1,410	1,212	1,423	1,595	2,011	2,240
Coffee, Tea, Cocoa Sp	1,109	1,959	2,715	2,845	3,226	3,770	4,560	5,421
Feeding Stuff	1,192	2,411	3,116	3,606	3,951	5,587	6,683	11,828
Miscellaneous Food	809	1,579	1,720	1,720	2,546	2,750	3,413	4,111
Beverages Tobacco	3,116	4,535	4,999	4,262	5,551	6,933	7,829	9,814
Beverages	1,883	2,704	2,883	2,580	3,552	4,439	5,359	7,274
Tobacco	1,233	1,831	2,116	1,682	1,999	2,494	2,470	2,540
Crude Materials	481	1,338	932	833	1,094	2,062	2,540	2,455
Hides and Skins	- -	#	#	#	#	102	22	37
Oilseeds	111	184	134	84	107	582	348	204
Natural Rubber	- -	3	#	62	136	235	595	560
Textile Fibers	121	163	149	87	86	99	332	188
Crude Mat Nes	249	988	649	600	765	1,044	1,243	1,466
Animal Vegetable Oil	2,606	9,745	10,813	10,898	8,513	14,666	18,531	14,190
Animal Fats	5	492	503	581	593	821	1,273	1,231
Fixed Vegetable Oils	2,594	9,191	10,238	10,209	7,836	13,741	17,016	12,780
Processed Oils	7	62	72	108	84	104	242	179
Agricultural Requisites	12,640	41,904	32,404	26,603	29,073	35,532	41,004	50,499
Crude Fertilizers	1	#	#	#	#	#	5	#
Manuf Fertilizers	2,948	13,314	8,213	7,908	8,204	14,959	17,715	18,431
Pesticides	2,617	10,037	8,292	8,933	8,988	12,052	14,706	19,140
Agriculture Machines	7,074	18,553	15,899	9,762	10,127	8,521	8,583	12,923

Exports

Category	1970	1975	1976	1977	1978	1979	1980	1981
Total Merchandise Trade	109,497	286,445	226,551	243,051	244,235	291,506	350,615	316,877
Agricultural Products, Total	71,592	120,439	103,060	108,414	122,288	128,753	168,714	164,726
Food and Animals	70,844	118,714	100,797	105,838	118,906	123,745	162,579	158,968
Live Animals	7	795	334	898	299	351	1,382	1,713
Meat and Meat Prep	2,448	1,569	3,807	1,471	490	1,564	3,125	5,094
Dairy Products Eggs	8	345	743	1,909	3,008	4,035	7,832	7,548
Cereals and Prep	5	40	26	107	4,448	3,419	115	271
Fruits and Vegetables	60,922	61,479	63,674	70,568	76,134	70,591	65,832	75,390
Sugar and Honey	5,689	50,885	26,670	21,956	20,331	26,982	67,409	52,650
Coffee, Tea, Cocoa Sp	1,717	3,101	4,713	7,605	11,981	13,928	13,024	14,282
Feeding Stuff	- -	9	8	68	23	189	584	115
Miscellaneous Food	48	491	822	1,256	2,192	2,686	3,276	1,905
Beverages Tobacco	20	1,103	1,276	2,136	2,659	3,998	5,289	5,140
Beverages	18	303	612	1,132	1,438	2,324	3,886	3,264
Tobacco	2	800	664	1,004	1,221	1,674	1,403	1,876
Crude Materials	728	622	753	439	577	997	846	617
Hides and Skins	537	325	388	213	307	417	396	432
Oilseeds	- -	#	#	#	#	#	#	#
Natural Rubber	34	#	#	#	#	#	#	#
Textile Fibers	- -	#	#	#	#	#	#	185
Crude Mat Nes	157	297	365	226	270	580	450	185
Animal Vegetable Oils	- -	#	234	1	146	13	#	7
Animal Fats	- -	#	234	#	#	#	#	1
Fixed Vegetable Oils	- -	#	#	1	146	13	#	#
Processed Oils	- -	#	#	#	#	#	#	#
Agricultural Requisites	- -	700	994	660	649	906	1,812	169
Crude Fertilizers	- -	#	#	#	#	#	#	#
Manuf Fertilizers	- -	#	#	#	#	#	#	17
Pesticides	- -	700[†]	994	660	649	906	2,218	152
Agricultural Machines	- -	#	#	#	#	#	1,224	#

SOURCE: FAO-TY, 1975, Section IV; FAO-TY, 1980, Section IV; FAO-TY, 1981, Section IV.

Table 2537

PARAGUAY ABSOLUTE VALUE OF TRADE, 1975–81

(T US)

Imports

Category	1975	1976	1977	1978	1979	1980	1981
Total Merchandise Trade	178,361	180,218	255,377	317,738	437,722	517,141	506,111
Agricultural Products, Total	70,657	75,078	82,025	98,382	116,337	127,321	129,638
Food and Animals	52,484	60,141	60,625	65,309	70,571	81,656	87,115
Live Animals	45,000	48,000	50,000	53,000	58,000	63,000	63,060
Meat and Meat Prep	#	#	#	#	#	850	600
Dairy Products Eggs	409	88	258	234	230	1,294	2,648
Cereals and Prep	5,526	10,105	7,303	7,455	10,362	14,406	17,148
Fruits and Vegetables	298	432	806	1,664	1,417	1,057	1,946
Sugar and Honey	65	87	97	324	325	304	423
Coffee, Tea, Cocoa Sp	#	#	7	527	6	#	#
Feeding Stuff	#	#	#	250	#	#	#
Miscellaneous Food	1,186	1,429	2,154	1,855	231	745	1,290[†]
Beverages Tobacco	18,173	14,937	21,400	31,074	45,766	45,665	41,223
Beverages	13,324	11,101	13,961	20,369	28,438	31,392	31,194
Tobacco	4,849	3,836	7,439	10,710	17,328	14,273	10,029
Crude Materials	#	#	#	1,924	#	#	1,300
Hides and Skins	#	#	#	#	#	#	#
Oilseeds	#	#	#	1,480	#	#	1,300
Natural Rubber	#	#	#	#	#	#	#
Textile Fibers	#	#	#	9	#	#	#
Crude Mat Nes	#	#	#	435	#	#	#
Animal Vegetable Oil	#	#	#	70	#	#	#
Animal Fats	#	#	#	#	#	#	#
Fixed Vegetable Oils	#	#	#	10	#	#	#
Processed Oils	#	#	#	60	#	#	#
Agricultural Requisites	10,590	8,795	13,430	23,716	21,520	25,200	25,055
Crude Fertilizers	131	#	#	2	#	#	#
Manuf Fertilizers	560	1,159	280	1,805	1,020[†]	2,500[†]	3,300
Pesticides	1,167	1,340	2,000[†]	3,012	2,800[†]	3,000[†]	2,900[†]
Agriculture Machines	8,732	6,296	11,150	18,897	17,700[†]	19,700[†]	18,855[†]

Exports

Category	1975	1976	1977	1978	1979	1980	1981
Total Merchandise Trade	176,711	181,834	278,891	256,984	305,176	310,176	295,541
Agricultural Products, Total	146,823	155,140	239,700	218,865	251,422	232,779	244,948
Food and Animals	80,849	51,454	53,687	45,640	40,726	46,033	24,602
Live Animals	12,000[†]	5,000[‡]	3,000[‡]	3,000[‡]	8,000[‡]	#	#
Meat and Meat Prep	32,050	20,865	21,823	23,927	5,400	1,054	3
Dairy Products Eggs	#	#	#	#	#	#	#
Cereals and Prep	635	1,495	182	116	24	2,493	295
Fruits and Vegetables	10,508	4,193	4,626	4,631	6,023	11,247	6,650
Sugar and Honey	7,523	1,180	#	31	27	3,112	101
Coffee, Tea, Cocoa Sp	8,987	8,313	10,915	1,006	5,325	4,233	1,609
Feeding Stuff	5,148	8,028	10,568	10,215	14,155	22,394	14,344
Miscellaneous Food	3,998	2,380	2,573	2,976	1,772	1,900[†]	1,600
Beverages Tobacco	12,017	14,797	13,754	9,394	8,564	10,197	6,489
Beverages	#	105	96	115	1	55	31
Tobacco	12,017	14,692	13,658	9,279	8,563	10,142	6,458
Crude Materials	43,345	71,678	142,872	147,013	183,021	159,568	191,436
Hides and Skins	2,776	860	2,246	3,391	1,218	786	406
Oilseeds	19,092	34,141	58,829	41,632	81,349	45,272	52,541
Natural Rubber	#	#	#	#	#	#	#
Textile Fibers	21,189	36,073	81,353	101,652	100,296	106,967	131,889
Crude Mat Nes	288	604	444	388	158	6,543	6,600[†]
Animal Vegetable Oils	10,612	17,211	29,387	16,818	19,111	16,981	22,421
Animal Fats	#	#	#	#	#	#	#
Fixed Vegetable Oils	10,612	17,211	29,387	16,818	19,111	16,981	22,421
Processed Oils	#	#	#	#	#	#	#
Agricultural Requisites	#	#	#	#	#	#	#
Crude Fertilizers	#	#	#	#	#	#	#
Manuf Fertilizers	#	#	#	#	#	#	#
Pesticides	#	#	#	#	#	#	#
Agricultural Machines	#	#	#	#	#	#	#

SOURCE: FAO-TY, 1980, Section IV; FAO-TY, 1981, Section IV.

Table 2538

PERU ABSOLUTE VALUE OF TRADE, 1970–81

(T US)

				Imports				
Category	1970	1975	1976	1977	1978	1979	1980	1981
Total Merchandise Trade	621,763	2,379,578	2,071,146	2,164,000	1,601,000	1,951,000	3,062,000	3,803,000
Agricultural Products, Total	125,526	389,991	290,932	271,367	271,367	249,463	430,059	566,036
Food and Animals	106,421	322,710	238,426	202,875	160,629	270,235	371,990	483,898
Live Animals	24,201	4,389	2,002	1,534	2,209	2,929	1,815	2,100
Meat and Meat Prep	13,007	8,794	7,652	8,603	2,482	1,476	12,416	34,413
Dairy Products Eggs	11,985	41,742	33,958	37,838	20,655	24,627	42,089	39,609
Cereals and Prep	43,668	252,337	187,199	144,619	129,453	234,300	232,356	269,253
Fruits and Vegetables	7,256	2,624	3,043	2,060	1,461	1,713	23,596	10,388
Sugar and Honey	71	660	205	257	310	218	34,894	106,345
Coffee, Tea, Cocoa Sp	2,376	5,607	1,634	3,873	1,315	2,966	6,419	3,089
Feeding Stuff	1,617	160	88	61	57	163	15,587	15,900
Miscellaneous Food	2,240	6,397	2,645	4,030	2,687	1,843	2,818	2,801
Beverages Tobacco	2,410	5,054	2,461	2,523	1,984	3,614	9,018	11,908
Beverages	1,948	1,832	398	1,040	408	1,334	5,559	8,390
Tobacco	462	3,222	2,063	1,483	1,576	2,280	3,459	3,518
Crude Materials	6,886	20,708	15,194	20,492	23,181	22,205	19,842	25,221
Hides and Skins	1,697	4,694	4,023	2,891	2,100	543	3,008	7,364
Oilseeds	788	4,359	1,436	5,032	4,672	8,520	239	2,773
Natural Rubber	2,001	5,004	4,425	5,887	7,344	9,828	10,196	8,700
Textile Fibers	627	1,771	1,326	791	105	290	386	1,384
Crude Mat Nes	1,773	4,880	3,984	5,891	3,960	3,024	6,013	5,000[†]
Animal Vegetable Oil	9,809	41,519	34,851	45,477	63,669	17,698	29,209	45,009
Animal Fats	720	2,549	2,097	2,937	2,517	2,028	1,730	1,319
Fixed Vegetable Oils	8,804	37,311	32,310	41,867	60,645	15,052	26,694	13,203
Processed Oils	285	1,659	444	673	507	618	785	487
Agricultural Requisites	16,386	99,837	39,285	42,310	51,294	51,079	77,020	103,394
Crude Fertilizers	111	400	300	700	#	#	735	27
Manuf Fertilizers	5,465	58,329	10,751	20,399	27,687	18,993	26,631	44,505
Pesticides	4,258	17,303	10,446	10,594	9,051	12,691	14,335	16,021
Agriculture Machines	6,552	23,805	17,788	10,617	15,186	19,395	35,319	42,841

				Exports				
Category	1970	1975	1976	1977	1978	1979	1980	1981
Total Merchandise Trade	1,047,858	1,314,599	1,296,091	1,647,410	1,819,768	3,389,905	3,308,989	3,197,480
Agricultural Products, Total	177,463	434,526	322,206	366,890	319,606	463,715	324,002	265,340
Food and Animals	114,797	353,681	210,059	291,308	244,181	359,489	216,200	200,455
Live Animals	247	249	386	1,013	1,210	2,784	1,136	1,250
Meat and Meat Prep	- -	621	500	553	1,756	1,951	2,450	1,700
Dairy Products Eggs	- -	40	61	408	2,098	3,841	1,435	171
Cereals and Prep	140	1,502	1,013	1,256	1,205	3,560	5,021	2,697
Fruits and Vegetables	2,900	4,582	6,794	6,812	9,282	22,258	23,635	8,893
Sugar and Honey	66,245	296,435	93,726	84,584	46,411	63,837	15,426	76,488
Coffee, Tea, Cocoa Sp	44,996	49,658	107,269	196,523	179,069	254,804	162,770	106,988
Feeding Stuff	243	16	48	125	2,032	1,816	1,680	161
Miscellaneous Food	26	578	262	34	1,118	4,638	2,647	2,107
Beverages Tobacco	285	1,365	935	961	801	2,427	1,145	557
Beverages	91	199	160	363	371	674	849	307
Tobacco	194	1,166	775	598	430	1,753	296	250
Crude Materials	61,387	77,929	110,017	72,526	72,021	92,802	101,601	62,954
Hides and Skins	2,274	610	601	583	1,323	1,158	201	24
Oilseeds	- -	#	#	#	#	40	52	34
Natural Rubber	- -	#	#	#	#	#	10	#
Textile Fibers	55,803	71,204	101,693	65,348	65,754	82,210	95,093	56,696
Crude Mat Nes	3,310	6,115	7,723	6,595	4,944	9,394	6,245	6,200
Animal Vegetable Oils	994	1,551	1,195	2,102	2,603	8,997	5,056	1,374
Animal Fats	- -	#	#	#	#	#	#	#
Fixed Vegetable Oils	- -	#	#	#	#	#	#	#
Processed Oils	994	1,551	1,195	2,102	2,603	8,997	5,056	1,374
Agricultural Requisites	454	1,432	1,357	1,023	1,759	1,441	3,980	1,646
Crude Fertilizers	410	1,016	1,057	600	600	200	33	388
Manuf Fertilizers	19	15	28	20	46	28	2,720	17
Pesticides	22	120	179	156	281	803	1,043	986
Agricultural Machines	3	281	93	247	614	410	184	255

SOURCE: FAO-TY, 1975, Section IV; FAO-TY, 1980, Section IV; FAO-TY, 1981, Section IV.

Table 2539

URUGUAY ABSOLUTE VALUE OF TRADE, 1975–81
(T US)

Imports

Category	1975	1976	1977	1978	1979	1980	1981
Total Merchandise Trade	516,198	587,177	720,970	757,320	1,206,290	1,680,350	1,598,950
Agricultural Products, Total	60,507	57,953	72,788	80,874	153,347	160,125	128,159
Food and Animals	22,627	27,584	29,114	39,118	82,896	94,704	84,768
Live Animals	302	245	341	124	738	1,876	1,569
Meats and Meat Prep	60	32	#	#	648	1,243	1,425
Dairy Products Eggs	761	326	1,022	1,492	969	2,333	1,463
Cereals and Prep	652	2,033	1,754	18,512	32,959	15,831	11,137
Fruits and Vegetables	5,926	6,516	5,710	18,512	16,324	22,864	23,416
Sugar and Honey	64	99	143	260	4,265	10,601	12,902
Coffee, Tea, Cocoa Sp	13,686	17,391	19,111	17,369	23,407	26,133	26,680
Feeding Stuff	1,094	753	813	1,107	3,027	2,739	4,190
Miscellaneous Food	82	189	220	254	559	1,084	1,986
Beverages Tobacco	6,206	7,460	7,351	8,293	14,986	20,509	17,380
Beverages	912	1,106	1,178	3,045	7,212	11,200	8,587
Tobacco	5,294	6,354	5,573	5,248	7,774	9,309	8,793
Crude Materials	17,890	19,377	31,978	28,622	37,981	34,665	23,328
Hides and Skins	3,885	2,714	13,422	8,640	11,397	7,903	4,340
Oilseeds	23	18	713	831	1,019	464	173
Natural Rubber	2,284	2,224	3,868	4,348	5,465	6,550	5,126
Textile Fibers	8,301	10,789	11,761	12,771	15,401	12,287	9,158
Crude Mat Nes	3,397	3,632	2,214	2,032	4,699	6,921	4,531
Animal Vegetable Oil	13,784	3,532	4,345	4,841	17,484	10,247	2,683
Animal Fats	224	67	1,421	1,279	6,763	3,877	648
Fixed Vegetable Oils	13,390	3,344	2,553	3,337	10,490	6,207	1,854
Processed Oils	170	121	371	195	231	163	181
Agricultural Requisites	40,148	41,249	33,261	29,088	75,986	84,000	54,315
Crude Fertilizers	6,743	2,415	3,872	3,200	7,100	6,800	3,057
Manuf Fertilizers	17,397	15,350	13,219	10,822	22,904	27,661	22,313
Pesticides	2,748	2,590	3,765	4,546	7,323	8,088	7,366
Agriculture Machines	13,260	20,894	12,405	10,520	38,659	41,451	21,579

Exports

Category	1975	1976	1977	1978	1979	1980	1981
Total Merchandise Trade	381,198	546,476	607,523	686,053	788,134	1,058,550	1,215,380
Agricultural Products, Total	260,116	350,150	352,692	362,675	368,142	596,772	768,821
Food and Animals	156,656	222,251	205,846	202,244	236,889	339,210	501,088
Live Animals	5,024	8,009	7,445	10,990	10,876	7,905	13,335
Meats and Meat Prep	85,692	129,393	116,698	101,862	111,990	188,955	263,917
Dairy Products Eggs	2,174	2,799	5,567	3,296	10,970	16,701	23,255
Cereals and Prep	50,184	43,222	49,147	58,427	74,315	88,070	166,746
Fruits and Vegetables	5,542	7,939	11,603	9,393	12,610	13,034	13,585
Sugar and Honey	708	15,804	863	2,869	1,496	2,435	3,060
Coffee, Tea, Cocoa Sp	109	298	228	468	1,113	1,961	1,490
Feeding Stuff	6,371	13,857	12,710	12,843	10,545	15,283	10,343
Miscellaneous Food	852	930	1,585	2,096	2,968	4,866	5,357
Beverages Tobacco	288	518	2,614	2,137	1,596	1,053	325
Beverages	279	473	2,518	2,061	1,489	952	288
Tobacco	9	45	96	76	80	101	37
Crude Materials	95,724	116,172	133,635	149,355	119,249	238,083	259,726
Hides and Skins	2,411	3,381	2,529	1,986	2,477	3,285	4,282
Oilseeds	#	1,820	#	2,240	2,440	6,316	6,400
Natural Rubber	#	37	278	22	60	124	3
Textile Fibers	90,524	106,500	126,436	139,674	110,302	221,209	239,335
Crude Mat Nes	2,789	4,434	4,392	5,433	3,970	7,149	9,706
Animal Vegetable Oil	7,488	11,209	10,597	8,939	10,435	18,426	7,682
Animal Fats	261	885	1,937	2,585	4,810	7,170	2,593
Fixed Vegetable Oils	7,089	9,531	7,398	5,909	5,283	10,722	9,099
Processed Oils	98	793	1,626	445	342	534	990
Agricultural Requisites	187	152	2,163	3,259	5,322	6,483	3,953
Crude Fertilizers	#	#	#	#	#	#	
Manuf Fertilizers	187	152	1,395	2,555	4,338	6,122	3,680
Pesticides	#	#	#	10	32	41	63
Agriculture Machines	#	#	768	694	952	320	210

SOURCE: FAO-TY, 1980, Section IV; FAO-TY, 1981, Section IV.

Table 2540

VENEZUELA ABSOLUTE VALUE OF TRADE, 1970–81
(T US)

Imports

Category	1970	1975	1976	1977	1978	1979	1980	1981
Total Merchandise Trade	1,665,031	5,807,319	6,023,615	9,777,557	10,622,754	9,626,832	9,256,861	11,810,909
Agricultural Products, Total	200,829	698,674	770,772	1,297,628	1,336,550	1,276,016	1,707,585	1,991,791
Food and Animals	151,369	482,918	571,776	1,004,650	952,116	930,263	1,339,296	1,626,570
Live Animals	23,510	60,449	82,111	98,374	74,764	63,686	67,439	74,412
Meat and Meat Prep	3,934	8,952	17,428	74,106	115,364	84,095	52,285	84,430
Dairy Products Eggs	13,079	55,566	55,812	170,792	117,574	88,316	132,261	212,226
Cereals and Prep	70,005	261,143	260,908	357,206	294,081	338,482	586,025	585,451
Fruits and Vegetables	28,303	60,496	66,018	121,100	113,802	128,010	133,195	178,973
Sugar and Honey	418	2,756	36,983	77,057	114,623	83,503	221,058	301,323
Coffee, Tea, Cocoa Sp	1,931	3,595	3,611	6,574	8,400	7,656	7,705	9,501
Feeding Stuff	3,198	19,816	31,779	67,351	68,819	91,924	103,977	119,053
Miscellaneous Food	6,469	10,145	17,125	32,090	44,679	44,591	35,351	61,201
Beverages Tobacco	16,550	61,238	68,473	90,247	135,404	113,378	152,668	127,729
Beverages	16,355	59,823	65,859	89,030	134,076	112,305	150,713	126,057
Tobacco	195	1,415	2,614	1,217	1,328	1,073	1,955	1,672
Crude Materials	22,233	71,549	48,925	64,527	68,914	63,951	62,733	75,800
Hides and Skins	473	1,690	1,140	1,715	2,002	617	3,013	2,848
Oilseeds	8,170	50,283	22,205	14,183	26,646	15,856	19,735	21,529
Natural Rubber	4,869	5,017	7,667	9,458	10,832	15,182	20,449	19,501
Textile Fibers	5,504	5,537	9,257	26,736	14,821	17,673	3,536	11,922
Crude Mat Nes	3,217	9,022	8,656	12,435	14,613	14,623	16,000[†]	20,000[†]
Animal Vegetable Oil	10,677	82,969	81,598	138,204	180,114	168,424	152,888	159,990
Animal Fats	1,570	4,256	6,551	6,108	15,195	10,960	15,716	11,422
Fixed Vegetable Oils	8,501	76,669	72,844	127,683	161,351	153,448	132,469	145,202
Processed Oils	606	2,044	2,203	4,413	3,568	4,016	4,703	3,366
Agricultural Requisites	36,833	178,606	161,837	246,860	196,001	150,688	223,753	230,632
Crude Fertilizers	..	4	14	4,977	3,105	4,937	4,741	2,907
Manuf Fertilizers	12,052	29,876	25,590	38,554	58,563	56,177	117,390	86,095
Pesticides	2,236	3,206	2,950	6,161	5,964	5,977	10,564	13,468
Agriculture Machines	22,545	145,520	133,283	197,168	128,369	83,597	91,058	128,162

Exports

Category	1970	1975	1976	1977	1978	1979	1980	1981
Total Merchandise Trade	3,147,702	9,009,643	9,465,947	9,626,548	9,270,321	14,158,466	19,292832	20,959,008
Agricultural Products, Total	43,337	64,904	71,248	86,383	95,424	90,700	77,444	77,014
Food and Animals	36,531	61,074	60,684	81,952	90,522	87,623	69,017	60,327
Live Animals	19	#	#	#	#	#	#	4
Meat and Meat Prep	213	533	709	416	518	666	747	642
Dairy Products Eggs	186	661	336	234	34	409	51	119
Cereals and Prep	7,600	12,606	1,205	553	574	3,492	6,756	264
Fruits and Vegetables	2,893	8,388	14,099	11,785	16,721	23,082	21,926	33,919
Sugar and Honey	5,690	298	419	326	266	50	15	6
Coffee, Tea, Cocoa Sp	19,607	36,503	41,778	66,385	70,155	57,545	36,688	23,998
Feeding Stuff	238	1	58	40	#	#	#	2
Miscellaneous Food	85	2,084	2,080	2,213	2,254	2,379	2,834	1,373
Beverages Tobacco	397	2,045	505	2,790	3,691	1,514	6,220	14,691
Beverages	50	1,041	505	2,216	3,565	703	499	537
Tobacco	347	1,004	#	574	126	811	5,721	14,154
Crude Materials	6,409	1,744	10,058	1,347	1,001	1,460	2,198	1,995
Hides and Skins	50	41	12	#	13	#	#	#
Oilseeds	5,850	#	#	#	#	#	#	#
Natural Rubber	69	18	15	2	3	2	6	10
Textile Fibers	..	693	8,761	120	64	31	187	106
Crude Mat Nes	440	992	1,270	1,225	921	1,427	2,005	1,879
Animal Vegetable Oils	..	41	1	294	210	103	9	1
Animal Fats	..	#	#	7	9	3	9	1
Fixed Vegetable Oils	..	39	1	287	201	100	#	#
Processed Oils	..	2	#	#	#	#	#	#
Agricultural Requisites	..	2,647	6,138	7,387	3,703	22,287	30,733	44,793
Crude Fertilizers	..	#	#	#	#	#	#	#
Manuf Fertilizers	..	2,124	4,772	6,684	2,318	18,526	26,657	43,351
Pesticides	..	523	1,137	699	638	393	646	700
Agricultural Machines	..	#	229	4	747	3,368	3,430	742

SOURCE: FAO-TY, 1975, Section IV; FAO-TY, 1980, Section IV; FAO-TY, 1981, Section IV.

Table 2541

UNITED STATES ABSOLUTE VALUE OF TRADE, 1970–81

(T US)

Category	Imports							
	1970	1975	1976	1977	1978	1979	1980	1981
Total Merchandise Trade	39,963,200	9,694,034	12,179,326	14,784,784	17,329,035	20,713,101	24,119,485	26,098,184
Agricultural Products, Total	6,306,490	1,016,017	1,181,090	14,121,166	1,574,783	1,783,778	1,818,170	1,833,852
Food and Animals	4,537,822	714,909	1,035,188	1,127,844	1,248,015	1,288,576	1,261,925	1,261,925
Live Animals	156,674	14,198	22,549	25,374	36,909	37,697	40,276	33,223
Meat and Meat Prep	1,015,480	114,039	144,533	127,162	185,270	253,483	234,220	199,427
Dairy Products Eggs	99,814	17,646	21,639	22,878	28,335	30,639	31,990	35,743
Cereals and Prep	69,612	17,970	14,900	15,058	15,684	17,931	21,663	24,170
Fruits and Vegetables	734,982	100,669	117,939	155,189	183,021	204,551	202,978	296,231
Sugar and Honey	806,463	207,622	137,759	122,139	91,631	123,000	221,081	240,271
Coffee, Tea, Cocoa Sp	1,602,590	232,794	365,334	554,016	570,378	562,940	516,018	407,496
Feeding Stuff	29,093	5,236	6,198	6,649	7,446	8,281	9,195	11,226
Miscellaneous Food	22,673	4,735	5,746	6,724	9,171	9,492	11,155	14,134
Beverages Tobacco	854,992	141,864	162,187	166,027	221,999	256,349	277,003	313,881
Beverages	726,519	103,597	117,636	128,724	176,775	206,897	224,789	243,254
Tobacco	128,473	38,267	44,551	37,303	45,224	49,452	52,214	70,627
Crude Materials	761,759	104,197	136,185	157,582	174,339	206,051	200,016	210,806
Hides and Skins	110,186	15,831	18,940	21,848	24,708	32,134	23,008	26,887
Oilseeds	52,163	3,786	5,012	4,770	4,858	5,763	5,972	9,885
Natural Rubber	240,818	36,789	52,165	65,336	68,846	90,324	82,099	78,059
Textile Fibers	154,504	12,315	18,674	15,693	18,496	18,215	19,600	20,711
Crude Mat Nes	204,088	35,476	41,394	49,935	57,432	59,616	69,337	70,263
Animal Vegetable Oil	152,358	55,048	46,122	53,369	50,602	73,362	52,575	47,240
Animal Fats	4,198	933	632	475	339	414	600	466
Fixed Vegetable Oils	140,510	52,952	44,074	51,427	48,250	71,108	49,918	44,683
Processed Oils	7,650	1,162	1,416	1,468	2,013	1,841	2,057	2,091
Fish and Fishery Products	~	138,127	189,092	208,585	222,817	267,417	263,316	298,820
Forest Products	~	395,664	504,487	601,848	766,294	812,628	758,454	770,868
Agricultural Requisites	466,106	155,797	158,246	175,045	203,296	253,872	272,656	629,440
Crude Fertilizers	8,744	2,772	1,274	2,295	4,457	3,635	3,669	2,848
Manuf Fertilizers	192,202	55,689	58,781	69,621	74,321	81,828	97,862	110,207
Pesticides	10,870	10,130	12,945	10,135	16,486	19,420	26,624	28,373
Agriculture Machines	254,290	87,205	85,246	92,994	108,031	148,989	144,500	128,012

Category	Exports							
	1970	1975	1976	1977	1978	1979	1980	1981
Total Merchandise Trade	42,593,300	10,765,183	11,499,704	12,016,315	14,120,000	17,857,800	21,659,222	22,888,782
Agricultural Products, Total	7,381,756	2,241,988	2,367,761	2,478,094	3,057,244	3,620,624	4,288,261	4,506,044
Food and Animals	4,226,991	1,530,650	1,559,044	1,403,677	1,778,557	2,161,472	2,722,321	2,959,357
Live Animals	60,115	13,978	16,551	13,902	19,148	20,073	21,596	27,101
Meat and Meat Prep	103,615	53,150	80,391	80,225	96,131	113,081	129,756	148,502
Dairy Products Eggs	137,348	13,428	12,909	18,362	19,162	16,155	25,559	43,642
Cereals and Prep	2,588,402	1,164,390	1,090,905	875,145	1,163,512	1,445,185	1,808,333	1,946,262
Fruits and Vegetables	581,117	133,788	159,519	167,056	196,151	221,322	302,266	342,072
Sugar and Honey	22,677	15,567	9,188	7,736	12,928	14,748	48,719	69,406
Coffee, Tea, Cocoa Sp	31,186	16,566	25,637	58,449	40,829	52,966	49,903	45,296
Feeding Stuff	496,171	95,549	131,984	150,308	190,751	231,273	284,297	272,195
Miscellaneous Food	143,437	24,234	31,076	32,782	40,052	46,653	51,242	64,882
Beverages Tobacco	701,657	133,981	154,560	187,275	231,898	236,081	269,106	294,031
Beverages	22,637	6,213	7,383	12,440	18,048	19,998	24,619	20,306
Tobacco	679,020	127,768	147,177	174,835	213,850	216,083	244,487	273,726
Crude Materials	1,967,353	483,214	558,639	750,378	896,959	1,041,111	1,104,963	1,080,240
Hides and Skins	193,660	41,521	79,246	79,584	92,339	133,383	105,095	103,060
Oilseeds	1,263,167	313,653	356,127	480,092	586,810	638,071	655,203	687,267
Natural Rubber	8,903	2,896	3,037	2,992	2,175	2,661	4,055	3,294
Textile Fibers	396,678	104,317	110,389	159,124	181,455	228,229	294,911	234,465
Crude Mat Nes	104,945	20,827	18,840	28,586	34,180	38,766	45,700	52,150
Animal Vegetable Oils	488,678	94,144	96,752	136,277	149,759	181,977	191,872	172,416
Animal Fats	198,731	33,181	40,448	54,928	55,088	69,892	72,871	70,231
Fixed Vegetable Oils	263,274	57,602	51,758	76,341	90,259	106,238	110,501	95,540
Processed Oils	26,673	3,361	4,546	5,008	4,413	5,847	8,500	6,644
Fish and Fishery Products	~	29,803	37,190	50,806	89,571	107,085	99,335	114,203
Forest Products	~	350,375	401,429	388,696	405,056	568,800	698,997	652,838
Agricultural Requisites	999,095	401,058	341,621	336,173	402,515	501,378	652,231	626,384
Crude Fertilizers	91,121	46,572	32,998	36,591	36,680	43,199	50,853	42,000
Manuf Fertilizers	177,659	108,386	61,340	70,275	103,694	140,550	226,810	173,633
Pesticides	102,142	35,491	35,063	39,947	44,794	51,885	55,454	54,712
Agricultural Machines	628,123	210,609	212,219	189,360	217,348	265,745	319,115	356,039

SOURCE: FAO-TY, 1975, Section IV; FAO-TY, 1980, Section IV; FAO-TY, 1981, Section IV.

Table 2542

IMF IMPORT UNIT VALUE INDEX, 4 LC, 1953-83

(YA, 1980 = 100)

Country	1953	1954	1955	1956	1957	1958	1959	1960	1961	1962	1963	1964	1965	1966	1967	1968
C. BRAZIL	~	~	~	~	~	~	~	~	23.7	23.9	24.5	23.7	24.1	24.6	25.1	25.9
E. COLOMBIA	40.3	40.3	41.1	42.0	45.1	41.0	41.3	40.8	41.3	40.1	39.2	38.8	35.5	36.3	37.4	37.0
J. EL SALVADOR	39.0	28.0	28.0	29.0	29.0	29.0	27.0	28.0	29.0	29.0	31.0	32.0	32.0	40.0	35.0	32.0
O. NICARAGUA	~	~	~	~	~	28.9	28.5	28.9	27.2	27.4	28.2	27.3	28.3	30.9	29.3	31.6
UNITED STATES	22.2	22.6	22.6	22.9	23.3	22.2	21.8	22.1	21.8	21.3	21.4	22.0	22.2	22.8	23.0	23.3

Country	1969	1970	1971	1972	1973	1974	1975	1976	1977	1978	1979	1980	1981	1982	1983
C. BRAZIL	25.4	25.9	26.9	26.5	35.9	52.5	57.1	58.7	61.0	65.2	78.1	100.0	111.1	107.1	101.2
E. COLOMBIA	37.6*	38.0	38.6	41.1	48.7	62.6	66.8	69.7	73.8	82.7	91.2	100.0	106.1	108.4	106.1
J. EL SALVADOR	32.0	33.0	33.0	35.0	41.0	59.0	65.0	63.0	63.0	70.0	79.0	100.0	~	~	~
O. NICARAGUA	33.0	34.5	36.1	38.0	42.6	56.1	68.5	67.4	70.9	74.8	80.3	100.0	~	~	~
UNITED STATES	24.0	25.7	27.0	28.9	34.4	50.9	55.5	57.2	62.0	66.9	80.4	100.0	105.5	103.8	99.8

SOURCE: IMF-IFS-Y, 1984, line 75d.

Table 2543

IMF EXPORT UNIT VALUE INDEX, 11 LC, 1953–83

(YA, 1980 = 100)

Country	1953	1954	1955	1956	1957	1958	1959	1960	1961	1962	1963	1964	1965	1966	1967	1968
B. BOLIVIA	10.8	10.8	10.8	11.3	10.0	9.6	10.0	10.0	10.8	10.8	11.3	14.6	16.7	15.9	15.0	15.0
C. BRAZIL	41.6	48.7	38.7	37.1	37.8	34.9	29.5	29.0	30.5	26.6	26.5	31.7	32.0	30.7	30.6	30.2
E. COLOMBIA	~	~	~	36.8	38.3	29.6	25.2	25.7	25.5	23.2	20.5	24.5	22.9	18.5	22.5	23.0
H. DOMINICAN REP.	27.1	32.9	27.8	26.7	34.0	29.4	25.4	25.6	26.3	29.7	32.6	34.5	30.6	33.3	33.2	36.0
I. ECUADOR	12.9	15.6	13.3	13.3	13.3	13.3	12.2	12.9	12.2	15.6	13.3	16.0	16.7	16.7	16.7	17.1
J. EL SALVADOR	35.0	44.0	39.0	39.0	39.0	32.0	26.0	26.0	25.0	23.0	26.0	29.0	31.0	30.0	28.0	27.0
M. HONDURAS	27.4	28.5	29.9	30.3	28.1	26.2	23.7	27.8	30.0	31.8	30.4	32.3	31.1	30.9	31.0	30.1
O. NICARAGUA	44.2	55.7	47.7	50.4	47.3	40.7	34.9	37.5	38.4	39.5	37.6	36.9	38.7	38.9	37.3	37.5
P. PANAMA	28.0	32.0	31.0	31.0	29.0	27.0	26.0	24.0	23.0	27.0	25.0	26.0	27.0	27.0	28.0	29.0
Q. PARAGUAY	29.9	39.7	38.8	35.0	34.9	34.0	32.9	26.2	25.9	26.4	30.9	35.8	36.3	37.1	33.7	36.3
R. PERU	~	~	~	~	~	~	~	20.0	19.0	19.0	20.0	23.0	24.0	28.0	25.0	27.0
UNITED STATES	29.4	28.9	29.3	30.4	31.4	31.1	31.1	31.3	31.9	31.7	31.7	32.0	33.0	34.0	34.7	35.2

Country	1969	1970	1971	1972	1973	1974	1975	1976	1977	1978	1979	1980	1981	1982	1983
B. BOLIVIA	16.3	21.1	17.1	17.8	23.3	40.6	38.8	43.8	54.4	61.5	74.0	100.0	97.1	92.3	~
C. BRAZIL	31.1	35.1	33.9	38.3	52.7	66.4	66.4	76.6	93.5	86.0	94.4	100.0	94.1	88.9	82.0
E. COLOMBIA	23.1*	28.5	27.1	30.3	38.2	51.2	50.6	74.1	108.9	91.0	89.7	100.0	89.5	88.8	89.0
H. DOMINICAN REP.	39.3	37.6	35.4	39.3	48.0	72.7	114.3	76.5	84.5	76.9	81.1	100.0	132.2	88.6	~
I. ECUADOR	15.2	17.1	18.2	15.2	20.9	43.2	39.8	44.8	57.4	52.2	77.3	100.0	89.9	83.6	73.4
J. EL SALVADOR	27.0	32.0	31.0	33.0	41.0	51.0	53.0	77.0	102.0	85.0	97.0	100.0	~	~	~
M. HONDURAS	30.0	33.6	32.6	34.2	40.3	47.0	56.2	66.4	91.2	90.7	85.6	100.0	92.2	~	~
O. NICARAGUA	38.2	39.0	39.4	42.8	47.4	60.7	57.0	74.8	92.6	87.2	89.9	100.0		~	~
P. PANAMA	28.0	28.0	28.0	29.0	49.0	69.0	80.0	73.0	66.0	64.0	78.0	100.0	105.0	84.0	92.3
Q. PARAGUAY	37.2	39.9	40.6	44.9	56.3	67.1	71.7	72.7	98.4	90.1	94.0	100.0	112.7	121.6	~
R. PERU	30.0	31.0	28.0	30.0	49.0	60.0	41.0	47.0	51.0	50.0	76.0	100.0	83.0	71.0	75.9
UNITED STATES	36.2	38.2	39.4	40.7	47.4	60.5	67.6	69.9	72.4	77.4	88.1	100.0	109.2	110.4	112.1

SOURCE: IMF-IFS-Y, 1984, line 74d.

Table 2544

IMF TERMS OF TRADE INDEX,[1] 7 LC, 1952–81

(YA, 1975 = 100)

Year	B. BOLIVIA	H. DOMINICAN REP.	I. ECUADOR	M. HONDURAS	Q. PARAGUAY	R. PERU	T. VENEZUELA	UNITED STATES
1952	~	~	~	~	~	~	~	105.3
1953	~	~	~	~	~	~	~	108.5
1954	~	~	~	~	~	~	~	104.9
1955	~	~	~	~	~	~	~	106.1
1956	~	~	~	~	~	~	~	109.0
1957	~	~	~	~	~	~	~	110.5
1958	~	~	~	~	~	~	~	115.3
1959	~	~	~	~	~	~	~	117.2
1960	52.9	54.9	76.6	145.4	86.2	69.4	33.6	116.3
1961	57.5	56.3	72.0	156.9	85.6	68.5	38.7	120.4
1962	58.0	63.9	92.8	167.0	88.2	71.0	38.8	122.5
1963	59.4	69.2	77.9	157.7	101.8	74.8	37.7	121.2
1964	74.8	71.7	91.7	164.1	114.3	82.0	36.8	119.4
1965	83.8	62.6	94.4	155.0	113.4	81.9	36.2	122.0
1966	77.8	66.6	92.2	150.6	113.7	92.1	35.4	122.4
1967	74.0	66.4	92.1	151.1	104.0	88.0	35.2	123.6
1968	74.2	72.5	94.8	147.7	112.1	93.9	35.4	124.1
1969	77.6	76.6	81.5	142.3	110.8	98.3	34.2	123.6
1970	96.4	70.0	87.5	152.7	114.1	103.1	32.6	122.1
1971	76.4	62.7	89.5	141.6	113.4	89.6	39.3	119.7
1972	73.5	64.0	68.4	136.8	116.8	82.7	38.6	115.4
1973	76.2	63.8	69.2	129.3	114.8	120.5	46.4	113.0
1974	120.1	68.8	120.6	106.3	105.4	116.5	102.9	97.4
1975	100.0	100.0	100.0	100.0	100.0	100.0	100.0	100.0
1976	104.6	65.8	109.6	133.5	106.2	103.4	102.8	100.2
1977	115.6	65.4	122.9	184.6	132.0	102.9	103.4	95.9
1978	114.0	54.3	102.7	155.4	114.2	90.8	91.5	95.0
1979	142.5	48.6	134.0	123.2	92.6	99.7	106.3	90.6
1980	146.9	50.0	161.3	114.8	78.3	107.9	154.3	81.9
1981	140.5	66.8	152.4	~	89.6	97.8	186.9	84.9

1. Export unit value divided by import unit value; 100.0 = base; numbers above 100.0 are
    favorable and those below 100.0 are unfavorable, relative to 1975.

SOURCE: IMF-IFS-S, No. 4, 1982.

Table 2545

IMF TERMS OF TRADE INDEX,[1] 4 L, 1955–83

(YA, 1980 = 100)

Year	C. BRAZIL	E. COLOMBIA	J. EL SALVADOR	O. NICARAGUA
1955	~	~	126.2	~
1956	~	87.6	132.4	~
1957	~	84.9	131.4	~
1958	~	72.2	110.7	97.2
1959	~	61.0	95.6	103.5
1960	~	63.0	91.6	85.5
1961	128.7	61.7	86.6	95.2
1962	111.3	58.9	79.0	96.4
1963	108.2	52.3	85.9	109.6
1964	133.8	63.1	92.1	131.1
1965	132.9	64.5	94.7	128.3
1966	124.8	51.0	75.0	120.1
1967	121.9	60.2	81.4	115.0
1968	116.6	62.2	85.3	114.9
1969	122.4	61.4	82.4	115.8[†]
1970	135.5	75.0*	97.6	113.0
1971	126.0	70.2	93.1	109.1
1972	144.5	73.7	93.8	112.6
1973	146.8	78.4	100.0	111.3
1974	126.5	81.8	87.6	108.2
1975	116.3	75.7	81.6	83.2
1976	130.5	106.3	122.6	111.0
1977	153.3	147.6	160.6	130.6
1978	131.9	110.0	120.9	116.6
1979	120.9	98.4	123.1	112.0
1980	100.0	100.0	100.0	100.0
1981	84.7	84.4	83.8	~
1982	82.3	81.9	74.2	~
1983	81.0	83.9	~	~

1. Export unit value divided by import unit value; 100.0 = base; numbers above
   100.0 are favorable and those below 100.0 are unfavorable, relative to 1980.

SOURCE: IMF-IFS-Y, 1984.

Table 2546

ECLA IMPORT UNIT VALUES (FOB), 19 L, 1960–80

(1970 = 100)

	Country	1960	1965	1971	1972	1973	1974	1975	1976	1977	1978	1979	1980
A.	ARGENTINA	89.5	86.2	109.6	106.3	127.8	188.9	216.1	225.4	238.2	266.8	327.3	328.8
B.	BOLIVIA	86.1	93.5	101.8	107.0	125.9	154.6	175.9	183.0	204.0	226.1	273.5	309.7
C.	BRAZIL	87.5	98.0	110.6	119.3	141.7	218.3	232.6	246.6	253.1	270.9	324.9	418.4
D.	CHILE	90.5	93.3	102.4	108.2	134.5	178.1	216.0	219.3	243.7	263.4	323.6	403.3
E.	COLOMBIA	90.9	94.0	101.7	105.2	128.6	164.7	175.6	183.4	194.0	217.9	240.4	263.8
F.	COSTA RICA	95.4	92.8	102.8	109.6	131.3	190.0	201.8	189.9	208.0	220.5	252.2	303.8
H.	DOMINICAN REP.	92.7	96.9	104.0	108.2	129.9	165.2	187.7	196.8	208.3	225.8	249.3	306.3
I.	ECUADOR	103.6	104.0	102.5	110.0	127.2	137.0	151.0	152.9	168.3	177.2	205.9	231.3
J.	EL SALVADOR	81.9	87.6	101.9	104.5	122.5	185.5	187.6	190.9	196.8	217.8	249.0	295.9
K.	GUATEMALA	73.6	83.6	103.6	114.4	131.3	188.8	219.0	197.0	200.1	213.7	253.5	302.3
L.	HAITI	91.8	96.2	103.0	106.9	127.2	164.7	185.0	198.8	214.9	230.8	257.3	293.2
M.	HONDURAS	73.0	77.1	102.1	109.6	127.6	163.0	184.5	200.0	222.6	233.4	249.9	295.0
N.	MEXICO	75.6	95.3	103.1	105.8	124.1	161.2	175.7	182.6	187.8	203.0	227.0	262.0
O.	NICARAGUA	80.1	82.5	101.2	103.2	123.1	162.3	187.1	193.2	205.2	226.4	259.4	311.5
P.	PANAMA	96.8	95.7	101.9	106.4	123.0	190.6	220.4	233.6	245.8	261.3	318.3	395.5
Q.	PARAGUAY	85.3	89.3	102.9	110.9	125.0	186.9	211.4	199.3	212.7	218.6	262.6	311.2
R.	PERU	83.7	99.5	102.7	109.5	137.9	141.8	167.1	170.8	188.6	217.1	241.4	270.6
S.	URUGUAY	82.7	96.2	101.3	112.4	120.6	173.4	210.9	214.7	215.1	219.5	270.5	344.3
T.	VENEZUELA	72.1	91.5	104.3	109.9	120.6	139.1	156.6	168.4	181.1	194.1	208.2	242.8
	LATIN AMERICA[1]	82.9	92.8	105.1	110.2	130.5	177.6	193.8	200.5	209.4	225.7	262.1	308.6

1. Includes Barbados, Guyana, Jamaica, Trinidad and Tobago.

SOURCE: ECLA-AE, 1981, pp. 508-509; except data for 1972 from ECLA-AE, 1980,
   and data for 1971 from ECLA-AE, 1978.

Table 2547

ECLA EXPORT UNIT VALUES, 19 L, 1960–80

(1970 = 100)

Country	1960	1965	1971	1972	1973	1974	1975	1976	1977	1978	1979	1980
A. ARGENTINA	91.9	94.2	114.0	131.7	186.3	238.8	214.8	198.7	203.9	211.0	260.7	306.2
B. BOLIVIA	50.0	92.4	83.6	86.6	109.9	218.0	195.6	208.0	244.1	271.6	322.7	407.9
C. BRAZIL	90.2	91.1	96.6	116.4	150.6	195.8	196.4	226.7	252.9	235.3	256.8	277.3
D. CHILE	56.0	63.1	80.1	78.5	111.3	155.9	113.2	124.0	123.4	129.5	169.5	190.5
E. COLOMBIA	88.0	90.0	92.2	103.7	132.7	159.1	143.3	220.7	368.7	311.2	280.4	345.1
F. COSTA RICA	94.0	99.3	92.3	96.3	115.8	133.3	155.4	176.9	252.5	246.1	268.0	295.0
H. DOMINICAN REP.	67.0	79.0	96.9	106.3	121.4	175.8	278.6	196.2	185.8	191.7	214.4	309.4
I. ECUADOR	98.0	85.0	95.9	93.2	117.2	267.6	244.5	280.3	335.0	311.2	437.4	549.4
J. EL SALVADOR	94.3	93.7	97.0	104.8	129.9	161.5	163.4	232.8	354.5	288.6	302.0	309.5
K. GUATEMALA	91.8	93.0	93.2	94.9	114.2	135.7	150.7	177.1	241.1	244.1	249.1	252.7
L. HAITI	83.9	89.6	94.0	96.6	112.7	144.4	171.2	191.9	265.3	260.4	249.5	287.7
M. HONDURAS	78.2	97.6	101.4	105.7	122.4	157.4	168.3	196.9	252.0	263.4	257.0	309.3
N. MEXICO	76.0	85.1	101.5	105.1	126.5	180.0	186.0	210.2	231.6	241.3	305.2	427.3
O. NICARAGUA	87.6	93.2	98.6	111.9	126.4	159.5	148.1	186.7	230.6	218.7	236.7	279.1
P. PANAMA	82.3	100.3	104.2	114.4	133.9	212.6	239.3	199.6	197.6	191.8	231.9	281.2
Q. PARAGUAY	85.2	100.0	105.0	117.1	168.6	219.5	220.1	219.5	295.8	269.6	287.8	299.0
R. PERU	58.5	71.3	93.0	92.2	131.8	193.4	174.5	186.0	192.3	188.1	282.4	367.3
S. URUGUAY	93.6	95.3	100.9	131.4	185.1	181.0	156.4	158.3	172.9	185.4	241.4	271.0
T. VENEZUELA	119.0	101.0	122.4	131.0	186.9	489.5	532.4	553.6	629.9	605.8	844.8	1,241.0
LATIN AMERICA[1]	88.1	88.7	102.3	112.2	147.1	234.3	224.6	240.8	266.8	257.2	310.8	381.4

1. Includes Barbados, Guyana, Jamaica, Trinidad and Tobago.

SOURCE: ECLA-AE, 1981, pp. 502-503; except data for 1972 from ECLA-AE, 1980, and data for 1971 from ECLA-AE, 1978.

Table 2548

ECLA TOTAL IMPORT, EXPORT, AND TERMS OF
TRADE INDEXES FOR LATIN AMERICA,[1]
1930–60[a]

(1970 = 100)

Year	Import Unit Value[2]	Export Unit Value[2]	Terms of Trade[3]
1930	53.6	54.9	102.4
1931	45.1	37.3	82.7
1932	37.3	33.4	89.5
1933	32.5	26.8	82.5
1934	27.0	25.2	93.3
1935	27.9	25.0	89.6
1936	27.8	26.6	95.7
1937	30.0	30.1	100.3
1938	29.0	27.3	94.1
1939	28.3	26.4	93.3
1940	30.3	27.5	90.8
1941	32.5	30.7	94.5
1942	38.6	36.6	94.8
1943	41.9	41.6	99.3
1944	42.2	44.8	106.2
1945	45.1	46.4	102.9
1946	51.5	60.8	118.1
1947	64.2	77.7	121.0
1948	69.9	85.3	122.0
1949	70.9	81.4	114.8
1950	68.8	94.0	136.6
1951	81.1	110.3	136.0
1952	85.0	103.9	122.2
1953	78.7	104.6	132.9
1954	81.0	108.4	133.8
1955	81.9	103.2	126.0
1956	82.1	102.7	125.1
1957	80.8	104.4	129.2
1958	80.2	96.0	119.7
1959	79.1	86.6	109.5
1960	82.2	88.2	107.3

1. Total for 19 countries — all years exclude Cuba.
2. Index — value divided by volume.
3. Calculated by dividing export unit value by import unit value; 100.0 = base; numbers above 100.0 are favorable and those below 100.0 are unfavorable, relative to 1970.

a. Cf. table 2549 below, for data after 1960.

Table 2549

ECLA MERCHANDISE TERMS OF TRADE INDEX[1] (FOB/CIF),[2] 19 L, 1960–80

(1970 = 100)

	Country	1960	1965	1971	1972	1973	1974	1975	1976	1977	1978	1979	1980
A.	ARGENTINA	104.9	109.2	109.0	123.2	146.2	127.6	100.7	88.9	86.3	79.9	81.1	94.2
B.	BOLIVIA	59.2	99.8	82.1	80.2	87.6	139.7	111.0	113.4	119.8	121.2	120.6	136.1
C.	BRAZIL	104.4	93.9	87.3	97.7	106.9	90.9	85.4	92.8	100.8	87.6	79.9	67.4
D.	CHILE	63.9	68.4	78.2	72.0	83.3	88.1	53.2	57.1	51.3	49.8	53.4	49.0
E.	COLOMBIA	97.7	96.3	90.7	97.9	103.6	96.6	81.5	120.2	189.8	143.0	116.8	131.1
F.	COSTA RICA	101.1	107.6	90.3	87.5	88.7	71.2	77.9	93.3	121.7	112.1	107.0	99.0
H.	DOMINICAN REP.	73.6	82.3	93.2	97.5	94.1	106.5	149.4	100.2	89.5	85.5	86.6	103.2
I.	ECUADOR	99.1	83.7	93.6	84.3	92.4	192.0	159.0	179.2	194.8	172.4	210.5	236.1
J.	EL SALVADOR	116.1	107.0	95.2	99.3	106.0	87.9	87.4	122.1	179.9	132.8	121.9	105.9
K.	GUATEMALA	124.6	110.8	90.0	82.9	87.6	73.0	70.2	90.3	120.4	114.3	98.8	85.0
L.	HAITI	93.2	94.2	91.3	89.4	89.2	87.8	92.8	97.4	124.8	114.4	98.2	100.6
M.	HONDURAS	106.8	125.3	99.3	96.0	96.2	96.6	91.4	98.9	114.2	113.8	103.4	106.4
N.	MEXICO	100.5	89.7	98.4	102.0	111.6	105.7	114.9	122.9	118.6	134.3	163.5
O.	NICARAGUA	110.2	112.3	97.4	107.6	102.7	98.2	79.4	96.8	112.5	97.0	91.6	90.4
P.	PANAMA	87.7	105.8	102.3	106.8	108.9	113.1	110.7	87.1	82.1	75.2	75.3	75.6
Q.	PARAGUAY	101.4	112.4	102.0	105.2	135.1	119.2	106.1	110.7	139.8	123.8	111.3	98.7
R.	PERU	70.9	72.9	90.6	83.8	96.6	135.3	104.0	108.3	101.6	86.8	117.2	136.4
S.	URUGUAY	114.6	100.3	99.6	116.5	153.1	105.1	75.4	74.5	80.8	84.7	90.1	80.4
T.	VENEZUELA	164.4	111.0	117.4	118.7	154.7	353.3	335.1	325.1	344.6	309.6	401.1	509.9
	LATIN AMERICA[3]	107.3	96.1	97.3	101.5	113.2	132.6	116.6	120.7	127.7	114.5	119.5	125.2

1. Export unit value divided by import unit value; 100.0 = base; numbers above 100.0 are favorable and those below 100.0 are unfavorable, relative to 1970.
2. ECLA uses the following procedures to calculate external trade indexes. Sample selection is made bearing in mind: (a) that the products considered were the most important in terms of their value; (b) that the products were homogeneous; (c) that the sample covered a large universe. Laspeyres indexes are used for quantities, Paasche for prices. For imports, indexes are calculated first for nine groupings of the "Foreign Trade Classification by Economic Use or Destination." For the period 1960–69 the year 1963 is used as the base; the data are then linked to the following period using 1970 as the base year; for imports this is done for each group of the "Foreign Trade Classification by Economic Use or Destination"; for exports, the total unit value indexes were linked together since similar groupings are not available.

   Global values of exports and imports are FOB values according to the balance of payments. The values of imports by groupings under the "Foreign Trade Classification" are CIF values and are based on customs declarations.
3. Includes Barbados, Guyana, Jamaica, Trinidad and Tobago.

SOURCE: ECLA-AE, 1981, pp. 504-506; except data for 1972 from ECLA-AE, 1980, and data for 1971 from ECLA-AE, 1978.

Table 2550

VALUE, INDEXES, AND PURCHASING POWER OF FOREIGN TRADE, 19 LR, 1928–76
(Value in Current and 1970 M US; Indexes 1970 = 100)

A. ARGENTINA

Year	Exports Value Current	Exports Value 1970	Exports Indexes Unit Value[1]	Exports Indexes Quantum[2]	Imports Value Current	Imports Value 1970	Imports Indexes Value[1]	Imports Indexes Quantum[3]	Indexes Terms of Trade	Indexes Exports Purchasing Power
	A	B	C(A/B)	D	E	F	G	H	I(C/G)	J(D x I)
1928	1,719.0	1,856.4	92.6	104.7	1,364.0	1,833.3	74.4	108.2	124.5	130.4
1929	1,537.0	1,865.3	82.4	105.2	1,388.0	1,906.6	72.8	112.6	113.2	119.1
1930	875.0	1,390.6	67.8	72.8	1,048.0	1,695.8	61.8	100.1	109.7	79.9
1931	724.0	1,770.2	40.9	99.8	591.0	1,184.4	49.9	69.9	82.0	81.8
1932	561.0	1,630.8	34.4	92.0	364.0	901.0	40.4	53.2	85.1	78.3
1933	470.0	1,535.9	30.6	86.6	378.0	994.7	38.0	58.7	80.5	69.7
1934	475.0	1,599.3	29.7	90.2	329.0	1,093.0	30.1	64.5	98.7	89.0
1935	501.0	1,686.9	29.7	95.1	340.0	1,129.6	30.1	66.6	98.7	93.9
1936	537.0	1,521.2	35.3	85.8	348.0	1,187.7	29.3	70.1	120.5	103.4
1937	758.0	1,775.2	42.7	100.1	482.0	1,559.9	30.9	92.0	138.2	138.3
1938	438.0	1,149.6	38.1	64.8	443.0	1,471.8	30.1	86.8	126.6	82.0
1939	466.0	1,474.7	31.6	83.2	353.0	1,238.6	28.5	73.1	110.9	92.3
1940	428.0	1,244.2	34.4	70.2	321.0	1,066.4	30.1	62.9	114.3	80.2
1941	455.0	1,112.5	40.9	62.7	272.0	836.9	32.5	49.4	125.8	78.9
1942	503.0	1,084.1	46.4	61.1	268.0	690.7	38.8	40.8	119.6	73.1
1943	610.0	1,113.1	54.8	62.8	204.0	460.5	44.3	27.2	123.7	77.7
1944	682.0	1,224.4	55.7	69.0	227.0	454.9	49.9	26.8	111.6	77.0
1945	739.0	1,244.1	59.4	70.2	300.0	505.1	59.4	29.8	100.0	70.2
1946	1,168.0	1,296.3	90.1	73.1	587.0	1,001.7	58.6	59.1	153.8	112.4
1947	1,612.0	1,411.6	114.2	79.6	1,342.0	1,823.4	73.6	107.6	155.2	123.5
1948	1,577.0	1,276.9	123.5	72.0	1,572.8	2,025.8	77.6	119.6	159.1	114.6
1949	1,011.1	851.1	118.8	48.0	1,171.1	1,394.8	84.0	82.3	141.4	67.9
1950	1,144.9	1,054.2	108.6	59.4	964.2	1,230.1	78.4	72.6	138.5	82.3
1951	1,169.4	834.1	140.2	47.0	1,480.2	1,386.1	106.8	81.8	131.3	61.7
1952	677.6	579.1	117.0	32.7	1,179.3	1,029.7	114.5	60.8	102.2	33.4
1953	1,101.6	941.5	117.0	53.1	795.1	797.0	99.8	47.0	117.2	62.2
1954	1,026.6	1,014.4	101.2	57.2	979.0	990.6	98.8	58.5	102.4	58.6
1955	928.6	892.9	104.0	50.4	1,172.6	1,151.4	101.8	68.0	102.2	51.5
1956	943.8	996.6	94.7	56.2	1,127.6	1,092.0	103.3	64.5	91.7	51.5
1957	974.8	1,060.7	91.9	59.8	1,310.4	1,261.6	103.9	74.5	88.5	52.9
1958	993.9	1,150.3	86.4	64.9	1,232.6	1,280.4	96.3	75.6	89.7	58.2
1959	1,009.0	1,167.8	86.4	65.9	993.0	1,095.3	90.7	64.7	95.3	62.8
1960	1,079.2	1,174.3	91.9	66.2	1,249.3	1,425.9	87.6	84.2	100.5	66.5
1961	964.1	1,059.5	91.0	59.7	1,460.4	1,721.2	85.3	101.1	106.7	63.7
1962	1,216.0	1,472.2	82.6	83.0	1,356.5	1,631.4	83.1	96.3	99.4	82.5
1963	1,365.1	1,469.4	92.9	82.9	980.7	1,244.0	78.8	73.4	117.9	97.7
1964	1,410.4	1,433.3	98.4	80.8	1,077.2	1,301.6	82.8	76.8	118.8	96.0
1965	1,492.8	1,584.7	94.2	89.4	1,198.6	1,388.4	86.3	81.9	109.2	97.6
1966	1,593.2	1,639.1	97.2	92.4	1,124.3	1,258.3	89.3	74.2	108.8	100.5
1967	1,464.5	1,535.1	95.4	86.6	1,095.5	1,275.4	85.9	75.2	111.1	96.2
1968	1,367.8	1,473.9	92.8	83.1	1,169.3	1,334.6	87.6	78.8	105.9	88.0
1969	1,612.1	1,658.5	97.2	93.5	1,576.0	1,756.0	89.6	103.7	108.4	101.4
1970	1,773.2	1,773.2	100.0	100.0	1,694.0	1,694.0	100.0	100.0	100.0	100.0
1971	1,740.4	1,526.6	114.0	86.1	1,867.8	1,785.1	104.6	105.4	109.0	93.8
1972	1,941.0	1,473.9	131.7	83.1	1,904.5	1,782.1	106.9	105.2	123.2	102.4
1973	3,266.0	1,747.5	186.9	98.6	2,235.2	1,755.1	127.4	103.6	146.7	144.6
1974	3,930.7	1,645.3	238.9	92.8	3,659.6	1,956.5	187.1	115.5	127.7	118.5
1975	3,000.0	1,363.6	220.0	76.9	4,000.0	1,861.3	214.9	109.9	102.4	78.7
1976	3,895.0	1,881.6	207.0	106.1	3,050.0	1,405.5	217.0	83.0	95.4	101.2

1. Index - value divided by volume.
2. Index for columb B.
3. Index for column F.

Continued in SALA, 20-2728 through 2749, including data on
LAFTA, CACM, and Total Latin America.

CHAPTER 26

DIRECTION OF TRADE AND
MAJOR TRADING PARTNERS

Table 2600

SHARE IN VALUE OF WORLD EXPORTS,[1] 20 LRC AND REGIONAL GROUPINGS, 1950–80

(%)

	Area	1950	1960	1970	1980
	World	100.00	100.00	100.00	100.00
A.	ARGENTINA	1.92	.84	.56	.40
B.	BOLIVIA	.12	.04	.06	.05
C.	BRAZIL	2.22	.99	.87	1.01
D.	CHILE	.47	.38	.39	.24
E.	COLOMBIA	.65	.36	.23	.21
F.	COSTA RICA	.09	.07	.07	.05
G.	CUBA	1.10	.48	.33	.20[a]
H.	DOMINICAN REP.	.14	.14	.07	.05
I.	ECUADOR	.12	.11	.06	.13
J.	EL SALVADOR	.11	.09	.07	.05
K.	GUATEMALA	.13	.09	.09	.08
L.	HAITI	.06	.02	.01	.01
M.	HONDURAS	.09	.05	.06	.04
N.	MEXICO	.86	59	.40	.81
O.	NICARAGUA	.04	.04	.06	.03
P.	PANAMA	.03	.02	.03	.02
Q.	PARAGUAY	.05	.02	.02	.02
R.	PERU	31	.34	.33	.19
S.	URUGUAY	.42	.10	.07	.05
T.	VENEZUELA	1.91	1.90	1.00	.96
	LATIN AMERICA	10.91	6.70	4.85	4.60
	ALADI	9.06	5.67	4.02	4.07
	Andean Group	3.13	2.74	1.70	1.54
	CACM	.48	.34	.36	.24
	UNITED STATES	16.91	15.91	13.60	10.87
	JAPAN	1.37	3.16	6.17	6.48
	WEST GERMANY	3.29	8.90	10.91	9.70

1. Excluding, through 1970, China and Mongolia and through 1980 North Korea and Vietnam. In 1980 the share for China and Mongolia combined was .93%.

a. Calculated from data in SALA, 23-2800 and Part II of 23-2829.

SOURCE: *CEPAL Review*, Aug. 1982, p. 53; UN-YITS, 1978, I, pp. 21, 23, 27; UN-MB, Oct. 1983, pp. 106, 112, 120.

Figure 26:1

WESTERN HEMISPHERE DECLINING SHARE IN
WORLD EXPORTS, 1950-80[a]

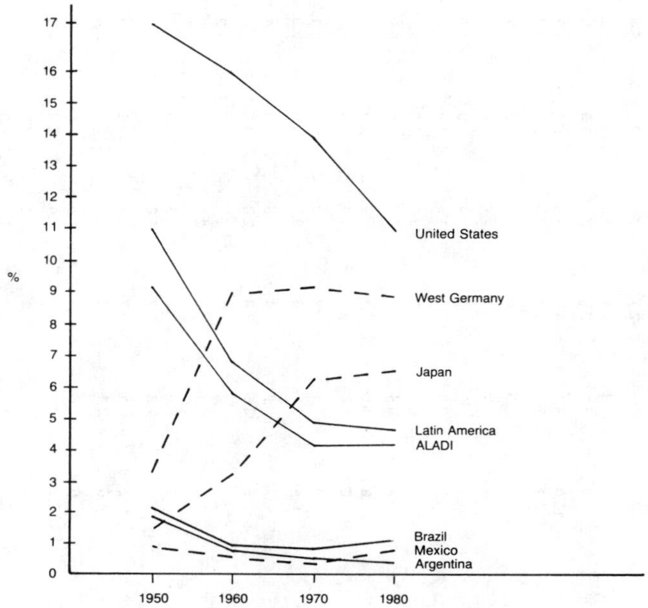

(%)

a. Trend line has been smoothed between the 5-year points sampled here.

SOURCE: SALA, 24-2600.

Table 2601

IMPORTS AS A PERCENTAGE OF WORLD IMPORTS,
20 LRC, 1950-75[a]

(Value, CIF)

	Country	1950	1955	1960	1965	1970	1975
A.	ARGENTINA	1.66	1.32	1.05	.68	.58	.48
B.	BOLIVIA	.10	.09	.06	.07	.05	.07
C.	BRAZIL	1.87	1.48	1.22	62	.97	1.66
D.	CHILE	.42	.42	.44	.34	.32	.19
E.	COLOMBIA	.63	.76	.42	.26	.29	.18
F.	COSTA RICA	.08	.10	.09	.10	.11	.09
G.	CUBA	.88	.65	.48	.49	.44	.38
H.	DOMINICAN REP.	.09	.13	.08	.06	.10	.11
I.	ECUADOR	.09	.13	.10	.10	.09	.12
J.	EL SALVADOR	.08	.10	.10	.11	.07	.07
K.	GUATEMALA	.12	.12	.10	.13	.10	.09
L.	HAITI	.06	.05	.03	.02	.02	.02
M.	HONDURAS	.08	.08	.06	.07	.07	.05
N.	MEXICO	.95	1.00	.99	.89	.84	.81
O.	NICARAGUA	.04	.08	.06	.09	.07	.06
P.	PANAMA	.12	.09	.10	.12	.12	.11
Q.	PARAGUAY	.04	.04	.03	.03	.03	.03
R.	PERU	.31	.34	.32	.42	.20	.31
S.	URUGUAY	.34	.26	.18	.09	.08	.07
T.	VENEZUELA	1.02	1.24	1.08	.86	.68	.74
	LATIN AMERICA	8.10	7.83	6.53	5.07	4.77	5.81
	UNITED STATES	16.53	14.10	13.70	13.21	14.44	12.68

a. For yearly data 1948-71, see SALA-SNP, pp. 295-296.

SOURCE: SALA-SNP, pp. 295-296; and IFS, March 1978, except Cuban data (problematic
    since the 1960s because of dollar exchange rate) calculated from Cuba, DGE, AE, 1957, and
    Cuba, JUCEPLAN, AE, 1972 and 1975.

Table 2602

MAJOR TRADING PARTNERS, 20 L, 1973-82[a]

(%)

Trade with Major Individual Countries

Country	Category	United States							United Kingdom						
		1973	1976	1978	1979	1980	1981	1982	1973	1976	1978	1979	1980	1981	1982
A. ARGENTINA	Export	8.2	7.3	8.6	7.5	8.9	9.4	13.4	6.5	3.1	3.1	3.0	2.5	2.4	1.0
	Import	21.4	17.9	18.6	21.1	22.6	22.2	22.0	4.7	4.2	4.4	3.3	3.3	3.4	1.3
B. BOLIVIA	Export	17.7	34.4	31.2	24.8	17.3	26.7	26.1	20.6	9.0	11.8	8.7	7.1	3.7	3.5
	Import	22.0	25.7	26.3	16.2	18.3	22.9	29.0	2.7	2.6	2.7	2.3	2.1	4.8	4.0
C. BRAZIL	Export	18.1	18.3	22.7	19.1	17.4	17.6	20.5	5.0	3.8	4.1	4.6	2.7	3.2	3.3
	Import	28.6	22.6	21.1	18.4	18.6	16.3	15.0	3.9	2.5	2.6	2.5	1.9	1.5	1.3
D. CHILE	Export	8.6	10.1	13.5	11.0	12.1	15.0	21.6	10.0	6.7	6.5	6.5	6.1	4.2	5.0
	Import	21.9	23.8	27.0	22.6	27.2	25.6	25.9	4.7	3.1	2.2	2.9	2.1	2.7	2.2
E. COLOMBIA	Export	37.4	31.2	29.8	29.6	30.1	23.4	23.4	1.7	2.0	1.4	.75	1.8	1.7	1.5
	Import	39.6	42.5	35.2	39.6	38.5	34.4	34.6	4.1	3.6	3.3	3.2	2.2	2.8	2.1
F. COSTA RICA	Export	33.4	39.7	33.0	37.1	33.8	32.5	33.5	.4	.2	.3	.4	.3	1.0	2.3
	Import	35.1	34.6	34.3	30.4	34.3	33.3	35.6	3.3	2.8	2.5	1.9	1.8	1.5	2.7
G. CUBA[1]	Export	~	~	#	#	#	#	.1†	7.1†	6.1†	2.3†	3.9†	5.0†	2.2†	2.4†
	Import	~	#	#	#	#	#	.1†	8.9†	5.4†	4.7†	6.6†	4.6†	4.0†	7.7†
H. DOMINICAN REP.	Export	66.4	69.6	60.0	59.0	46.3	67.0	54.0	1.8	1.0	.3	.7	.2	.4	.2
	Import	50.8	47.8	44.5	44.7	44.8	43.0	38.9	2.5	1.8	2.0	1.4	1.3	1.3	1.1
I. ECUADOR	Export	34.5	37.7	44.8	36.3	28.9	38.7	47.9	.9	.1	.3	.2	.3	.1	.1
	Import	38.5	39.1	34.9	34.6	38.3	33.7	37.3	6.4	3.7	3.8	3.5	2.6	2.9	3.0
J. EL SALVADOR	Export	33.2	32.7	23.0	28.4	39.7	17.1	34.6†	.2	.2	.4	.5	.6	.4	.4†
	Import	29.4	28.6	30.8	29.2	32.4	25.5	33.6†	2.5	2.5	2.3	2.0	1.3	.9	1.0†
K. GUATEMALA	Export	33.6	35.1	29.1	29.6	27.7	18.2	27.3	2.0	.4	.9	1.3	4.4	.6	1.7
	Import	31.5	36.4	30.0	32.2	34.5	33.8	31.1	3.5	3.1	2.5	2.1	2.3	1.8	1.2
L. HAITI	Export	72.6	66.8	58.8	74.6	69.5	79.4†	78.6†	.4	.4	.2	.8	.6	.8†	1.1†
	Import	56.2	56.4	44.6	57.9	57.2	56.3†	61.0†	2.6	2.3	2.7	1.6	1.2	.7†	1.3†
M. HONDURAS	Export	52.3	56.3	56.5	52.1	49.1	54.8	52.6	.2	.1	.7	.9	.9	.9	.8
	Import	43.5	43.7	44.4	41.6	40.4	41.5	41.0	1.6	2.1	2.6	2.5	2.9	1.4	2.1
N. MEXICO	Export	58.8	60.9	68.1	69.6	63.2	55.3	52.0	.6	.8	.9	.5	.5	1.2	4.2
	Import	62.2	62.5	60.4	62.6	65.6	63.8	59.9	2.2	3.1	2.5	2.4	2.2	1.8	1.8
O. NICARAGUA	Export	33.3	31.1	25.0	33.7	37.6	28.2†	24.4†	.3	.3	.3	.3	.6	.4†	1.4†
	Import	34.3	31.5	31.4	25.3	32.7	25.2†	18.9†	2.2	2.5	1.8	1.3	.8	.6†	1.4†
P. PANAMA	Export	44.7	48.3	44.3	46.5	49.3	52.7	41.5	.9	.1	~	.1	.1	.1	.2
	Import	34.3	32.1	32.6	32.8	33.8	34.8	35.0	2.1	1.6	1.6	1.2	1.1	1.1	1.2
Q. PARAGUAY	Export	13.0	11.9	8.8	5.9	5.5	5.6	2.8	6.8	6.0	5.8	.2	.6	1.0	1.2
	Import	16.5	10.3	11.1	11.7	9.9	9.9	9.0	7.4	7.6	9.6	5.6	5.6	4.9	5.8
R. PERU	Export	35.1	24.9	37.5	34.9	33.0	33.6	31.0†	2.9	5.9	2.9	3.7	4.1	4.1	4.4†
	Import	30.0	30.5	37.8	34.6	38.1	33.1	30.6†	3.5	3.4	3.7	2.4	3.5	2.7	1.9†
S. URUGUAY	Export	3.5	10.9	17.6	10.6	7.8	8.0	7.4	6.2	3.8	4.5	2.8	3.5	4.5	3.6
	Import	9.4	8.7	8.7	9.7	9.8	9.7	12.2	5.0	3.7	4.3	3.6	4.2	2.9	2.4
T. VENEZUELA	Export	46.5	38.4	39.8	37.3	27.8	25.6	26.3†	3.4	2.1	1.3	2.4	1.2	.3	1.3†
	Import	42.1	44.8	41.5	46.1	48.2	48.3	43.6†	3.6	3.2	3.7	2.9	2.9	2.8	2.2†

Table 2602 (Continued)

MAJOR TRADING PARTNERS, 20 L, 1973–82[a]

(%)

Trade with Major Individual Countries

Country	Category	Germany							Japan							Trade with EEC						
		1973	1976	1978	1979	1980	1981	1982	1973	1976	1978	1979	1980	1981	1982	1973	1976	1978	1979	1980	1981	1982
A. ARGENTINA	Export	8.1	5.2	6.4	5.6	5.1	3.9	4.4	4.1	5.3	5.9	5.1	2.6	3.2	3.7	40.2	33.2	34.4	33.3	27.6	23.1	21.3
	Import	10.9	11.2	10.6	9.2	9.4	9.6	9.0	11.4	8.2	7.0	5.3	9.3	10.3	8.0	30.1	27.4	30.0	26.6	25.9	26.1	22.1
B. BOLIVIA	Export	6.2	3.4	4.8	4.1	2.6	3.5	3.7	8.6	3.3	2.0	2.9	2.7	.9	1.8	28.8	18.8	23.5	22.9	21.4	20.1	15.0
	Import	8.6	7.7	9.0	7.2	4.3	8.1	7.3	2.7	11.1	15.4	7.7	7.0	11.9	11.0	18.1	15.4	15.3	20.1	12.4	18.6	16.3
C. BRAZIL	Export	8.9	8.9	8.4	7.2	6.6	5.6	5.9	6.9	6.3	5.1	5.8	6.1	5.2	6.5	37.0	30.7	30.0	29.8	27.2	25.4	26.9
	Import	12.6	8.7	8.1	7.5	7.0	4.9	4.4	7.8	7.3	8.9	6.0	4.8	5.7	4.6	27.6	20.0	18.7	17.9	15.4	13.6	12.6
D. CHILE	Export	14.0	14.8	14.2	15.9	12.2	11.5	11.5	17.7	10.7	11.7	11.0	10.3	10.8	11.9	40.3	35.7	34.6	37.7	36.8	31.7	31.4
	Import	9.4	5.7	7.4	6.4	5.4	5.6	6.1	3.5	11.1	7.5	7.6	10.4	10.6	6.5	25.1	13.8	15.9	17.8	15.2	16.8	16.8
E. COLOMBIA	Export	12.5	16.2	21.3	17.5	15.7	19.7	18.1	4.2	3.4	2.3	2.8	4.0	4.3	4.1	24.2	29.9	36.1	30.7	33.1	32.4	35.3
	Import	9.5	10.2	7.0	6.2	6.4	6.3	5.8	8.5	7.7	9.9	9.1	11.1	9.6	11.1	23.8	23.0	20.9	17.5	17.3	16.5	14.9
F. COSTA RICA	Export	13.1	10.5	14.4	11.8	11.3	12.2	14.3	.6	1.2	.8	1.1	.8	.5	.7	26.8	19.0	27.8	25.9	23.2	22.5	25.9
	Import	6.8	5.2	5.4	4.9	4.8	4.6	3.9	9.0	11.4	14.4	12.4	11.6	9.8	4.2	16.5	12.2	13.0	12.5	11.1	11.8	10.9
G. CUBA[1]	Export	.9†	2.5†	5.7†	3.7†	4.7†	1.8†	2.4†	39.3†	6.8†	16.0†	15.1†	15.4†	10.1	8.5	19.8	19.1	24.3	28.3	28.6	12.7	16.5
	Import	6.8†	6.2†	6.5†	8.9†	6.2†	5.0†	4.3†	22.4†	13.5†	19.0†	11.9†	13.6†	14.2	8.4	32.9	28.3	27.3	29.0	34.6	24.7	25.8
H. DOMINICAN REP.	Export	.6	.4	.5	#	.2	.1	.2	1.9	.6	1.5	3.2	.9	.8	.8	15.9	12.0	11.3	9.9	8.4	5.5	6.6
	Import	5.7	3.5	3.9	3.0	2.6	2.4	2.2	7.9	6.3	7.9	6.7	8.0	6.2	5.1	15.1	10.3	10.8	8.4	8.8	3.8	4.1
I. ECUADOR	Export	9.1	2.9	5.5	3.4	1.6	1.2	1.1	7.9	1.1	1.3	1.4	12.2	12.2	.8	16.9	8.2	14.1	9.4	7.6	4.0	4.1
	Import	10.3	8.6	9.8	8.3	7.3	7.4	8.0	11.3	16.5	14.4	13.0	13.7	11.7	12.4	25.9	18.2	22.1	22.4	18.2	17.5	18.9
J. EL SALVADOR	Export	13.2	14.3	18.2	21.0	19.4	21.8	15.7†	10.0	7.9	6.5	6.0	3.3	4.5	2.3†	17.9	25.2	31.4	33.9	28.8	24.3	19.8
	Import	7.7	5.9	5.2	4.8	2.8	3.1	3.2†	9.8	9.7	11.8	8.2	3.7	2.7	2.8†	19.6	16.2	13.5	15.0	10.0	13.7	8.1
K. GUATEMALA	Export	9.3	10.7	12.5	8.7	8.3	8.2	7.0	5.7	8.3	6.7	7.9	2.8	4.9	5.0	19.1	18.3	26.9	21.2	24.1	22.0	17.5
	Import	9.5	7.0	8.4	7.1	5.4	6.4	5.6	10.0	11.1	10.6	8.2	8.0	7.7	5.2	19.2	15.5	16.7	14.0	12.5	13.5	11.8
L. HAITI	Export	.9	.7	.7	2.0	2.6	2.7†	3.2†	.7	.6	.7	.4	.2	.3†	.7†	19.2	26.8	34.9	19.1	23.3	3.6	15.4
	Import	4.4	3.3	4.6	2.2	1.8	1.5†	2.3†	4.7	5.8	8.8	4.1	5.4	3.6†	5.2†	20.1	14.3	15.4	12.1	9.5	15.1	10.7
M. HONDURAS	Export	13.2	11.7	12.9	10.3	11.5	8.2	8.8	3.3	3.1	2.7	3.7	3.7	6.2	5.8	19.3	19.9	24.1	19.6	18.0	18.8	21.0
	Import	3.9	4.7	3.4	2.3	2.1	3.6	3.4	9.4	8.8	8.7	6.9	8.9	6.7	6.8	12.5	12.0	11.1	12.0	10.5	12.4	11.1
N. MEXICO	Export	2.6	2.6	1.9	2.4	1.7	4.6	4.3	6.6	5.1	3.4	2.8	3.7	6.0	6.7	6.7	8.6	5.8	5.8	6.6	8.5	12.0
	Import	8.1	7.0	7.1	6.4	5.2	4.9	6.1	4.6	5.1	8.1	6.5	5.3	5.0	5.7	17.4	16.3	18.5	16.2	13.8	12.6	14.8
O. NICARAGUA	Export	9.0	9.7	14.1	9.7	8.6	6.6†	9.3†	12.4	13.0	8.7	5.4	2.6	11.6†	12.0†	18.7	19.7	27.9	26.3	19.7	17.7	23.4
	Import	7.5	6.3	5.4	3.9	2.0	3.4†	2.2†	7.0	7.9	6.9	3.8	2.7	1.6†	1.4†	15.1	13.0	11.5	9.7	6.6	9.0	12.2
P. PANAMA	Export	14.8	8.5	11.7	7.9	5.1	7.6	5.9	.9	.3	.1	.2	.4	.1	.7	34.9	20.4	19.1	15.2	12.9	17.6	13.7
	Import	2.3	1.8	2.6	2.5	1.8	1.8	1.8	6.5	5.6	4.7	4.5	6.1	6.1	7.6	8.9	7.7	9.1	7.6	6.4	5.6	7.1
Q. PARAGUAY	Export	18.4	11.2	15.1	15.3	12.4	11.0	12.4	1.1	3.5	12.6	5.1	3.6	8.4	7.7	43.7	40.0	40.0	40.1	25.3	20.5	24.4
	Import	11.3	8.5	8.2	7.4	6.5	8.1	6.4	3.9	4.7	7.9	8.4	8.1	8.3	5.5	24.0	20.0	22.1	17.6	16.1	17.3	17.5
R. PERU	Export	8.1	7.2	4.7	3.9	3.9	3.1	3.6†	15.5	13.7	11.9	14.2	10.9	14.9	14.6†	22.2	26.7	16.9	16.2	16.6	15.9	18.4
	Import	12.1	7.2	8.1	7.8	6.3	6.6	6.6†	11.0	7.7	7.2	6.8	10.0	8.6	8.8†	25.4	20.6	24.6	31.9	21.7	16.4	17.3
S. URUGUAY	Export	13.9	12.3	11.8	16.3	12.9	10.4	8.9	3.4	1.7	1.7	1.1	.9	1.1	1.8	46.8	37.5	33.9	34.2	30.1	29.0	23.5
	Import	7.1	7.6	7.4	8.0	6.7	6.1	6.9	.7	1.8	2.0	2.5	4.1	4.9	2.7	18.8	18.3	20.5	18.1	17.9	15.7	15.3
T. VENEZUELA	Export	2.7	1.3	.7	.9	1.1	.9	2.6†	.7	.4	.4	1.0	3.5	3.9	3.8†	10.5	8.7	7.0	10.6	12.6	15.1	12.7
	Import	13.1	9.7	9.2	7.0	6.8	6.3	4.7†	8.3	8.7	9.6	8.2	8.1	8.0	9.8†	29.3	24.8	25.3	20.6	20.6	19.8	20.9

1. Cuban % trade total here excludes Cuba's trade with socialist countries.

a. For prior years from 1915, see SALA, SNP, table XV-3.

SOURCE: Calculated from IMF-DOT Annual, 1969-73; IMF-DOT Annual, 1969-75; IMF-DOT Annual, 1970-76; IMF-DOT Annual, 1971-77; IMF-DOT Yearbook, 1984.

Table 2603

INTRA-REGIONAL MERCHANDISE EXPORTS, 19 LR, 1970–82

(M US)

Country	1970	1975	1978	1979	1980	1981	1982
LAIA							
A. ARGENTINA	371.7	766.1	1,556.3	2,049.8	1,889.4	1,767.6	1,551.7
C. BRAZIL	316.5	1,350.3	1,772.2	2,608.1	3,636.3	4,455.0	3,025.9
D. CHILE	138.0	392.3	620.4	~	1,130.4	~	~
N. MEXICO	125.5	377.7	633.8	590.4	~	~	~
Q. PARAGUAY	24.7	62.7	67.3	105.0	~	~	~
S. URUGUAY	29.3	109.9	194.6	316.2	395.0	348.9	
Andean Group							
B. BOLIVIA	19.1	185.5	198.7	255.6	~	~	~
E. COLOMBIA	97.9	304.1	410.9	589.6	654.2	671.1	637.6
I. ECUADOR	21.1	367.9	450.2	507.1	~	~	~
R. PERU	67.4	221.9	258.9	719.9	708.3	473.0	429.8
T. VENEZUELA	399.5	1,106.0	1,168.8	1,666.4	2,721.5	2,964.4	~
CACM							
F. COSTA RICA	53.9	144.1	228.5	237.4	350.1	345.9	~
J. EL SALVADOR	74.6	149.0	235.3	373.9	305.7	217.0	~
K. GUATEMALA	106.4	185.6	269.0	313.0	436.7	425.6	~
M. HONDURAS	28.1	62.1	74.1	84.0	103.6	87.2	~
O. NICARAGUA	49.4	96.4	199.1	107.5	81.8	87.0	68.1
Non-Associated Countries							
H. DOMINICAN REP.	~	8.5	61.3	57.5	99.7	105.2	46.4
L. HAITI	.6	1.1	4.2	1.7	~	~	~
P. PANAMA	5.4	22.3	43.0	46.2	65.8	50.9	49.8

SOURCE: IDB-SPTF, 1984, p. 95.

Table 2604

INTRA-REGIONAL EXPORTS AS A SHARE OF COUNTRY GDP, 19 LR, 1970–82

(%)

Country	1970	1975	1978	1979	1980	1981	1982
LAIA							
A. ARGENTINA	.9	1.6	3.1	3.9	3.5	3.5	3.2
C. BRAZIL	.4	.9	1.0	1.4	1.9	2.3	1.6
D. CHILE	1.0	3.2	4.0	~	6.3	~	~
N. MEXICO	.2	.5	.6	.5	~	~	~
Q. PARAGUAY	1.5	2.8	2.3	3.2	~	~	~
S. URUGUAY	.6	2.2	3.6	5.5	6.6	5.9	~
Andean Group							
B. BOLIVIA	.9	6.9	6.4	8.0	~	~	~
E. COLOMBIA	.7	1.6	1.9	2.5	2.7	2.7	2.5
I. ECUADOR	.6	7.7	5.9	6.4	~	~	~
R. PERU	.5	1.1	1.5	4.0	3.9	2.5	2.2
T. VENEZUELA	1.6	3.5	3.1	4.4	7.4	8.0	~
CACM							
F. COSTA RICA	2.7	5.5	7.1	7.0	10.2	10.6	~
J. EL SALVADOR	3.1	4.7	6.3	7.5	9.1	7.2	~
K. GUATEMALA	2.2	2.9	3.5	3.8	5.2	5.0	~
M. HONDURAS	1.9	3.6	3.6	3.5	4.3	3.6	2.9
O. NICARAGUA	2.4	4.0	7.3	5.3	3.7	3.6	~
Non-Associated Countries							
H. DOMINICAN REP.	~	.2	1.2	1.1	1.7	1.8	.8
L. HAITI	.1	.1	.3	.1	~	~	~
P. PANAMA	.3	.7	1.5	1.6	2.0	1.5	1.4

SOURCE: IDB-SPTF, 1984, p. 96.

Table 2605

LATIN AMERICAN INTRA-REGIONAL EXPORTS AS A PERCENTAGE OF TOTAL EXPORTS, BY PRODUCT GROUP, 1965–79

Group	1965	1970	1975	1979
Basic Foodstuffs and Raw Materials				
Food and Live Animals	8.8	8.1	9.7	9.8
Beverages and Tobacco	7.6	12.8	8.7	8.5
Crude Materials, Inedible	9.4	9.7	7.9	8.8
Fuels and Mineral Fuels	13.9	13.7	15.7	11.5
Animal and Vegetable Oils and Fat	13.3	14.4	16.5	20.2
Manufactured Products				
Chemical Elements and Compounds	36.1	43.8	37.2	42.9
Manufactured Goods Classified by Material	15.6	18.1	27.1	30.1
Machinery and Transport Equipment	70.2	50.4	52.6	46.0
Miscellaneous Manufactured Articles	70.0	52.9	36.8	38.8
Other Products	27.4	38.3	16.4	12.1
Total	12.6	13.8	17.0	16.7

SOURCE: IDB-SPTF, 1984, p. 97.

Table 2606

ALADI, CACM, AND ECLA:L INTRAZONAL IMPORTS AS SHARE OF EACH COUNTRY'S TOTAL IMPORTS, 25 ECLA:L, 1960–78
(%)

Country	1960	1965	1970	1975	1976	1977	1978
A. ARGENTINA	13.6	22.3	21.1	25.8	27.4	22.3	18.8
B. BOLIVIA	12.5	11.0	20.4	36.1	37.2	38.2	34.9
C. BRAZIL	13.7	23.5	10.8	5.6	9.2	10.4	9.8
D. CHILE	17.1	21.1	19.4	29.3	29.4	29.6	24.8
E. COLOMBIA	1.9	8.3	8.6	11.0	15.2	18.1	16.1
I. ECUADOR	6.2	10.5	9.8	13.9	11.6	10.5	11.5
N. MEXICO	.2	1.4	2.8	5.6	4.2	3.9	3.7
Q. PARAGUAY	28.9	22.6	37.7	61.0	63.8	61.3	56.1
R. PERU	7.9	11.0	15.0	16.7	25.3	26.3	9.8
S. URUGUAY	26.9	33.3	35.2	36.1	49.1	47.3	37.2
T. VENEZUELA	1.9	2.8	3.7	6.9	8.1	9.2	9.6
Total ALADI	8.9	12.0	11.0	11.4	12.9	14.1	12.1
F. COSTA RICA	6.3	14.9	30.5	35.2	30.5	26.8	27.3
J. EL SALVADOR	15.1	28.9	32.0	37.5	34.6	32.6	31.8
K. GUATEMALA	10.3	22.5	33.1	35.0	31.5	33.6	34.2
M. HONDURAS	8.8	26.2	32.4	34.6	28.8	27.9	25.9
O. NICARAGUA	9.0	19.3	32.9	40.8	40.9	35.5	38.1
Total CACM	10.3	22.5	32.1	36.4	33.1	31.5	31.4
Barbados	6.7	20.0	28.0	31.7	29.4	29.1	21.2
Guyana	12.5	13.3	17.0	23.1	26.0	29.9	27.5
Jamaica	3.2	9.8	9.3	25.1	24.1	23.4	24.6
Trinidad and Tobago	32.4	33.1	28.8	3.4	4.8	4.1	6.0
Bahamas	5.4	16.7	6.7	7.2	5.2	2.8	2.0
L. HAITI	~	~	2.4	3.8	3.9	5.8	3.9
P. PANAMA	8.1	13.6	13.2	13.5	12.9	11.9	12.0
H. DOMINICAN REP.	~	3.0	5.4	18.8	21.5	21.8	21.0
Suriname	.7	1.2	3.1	17.4	19.0	20.6	19.1
Total ECLA:L	9.4	13.7	12.9	13.0	13.9	14.7	13.3

SOURCE: ECLA-AE, 1980, p. 164.

Figure 26:2

**REGIONAL IMPORTS AS SHARE OF EACH
COUNTRY'S TOTAL IMPORTS, 1960–80[a]**

(%)

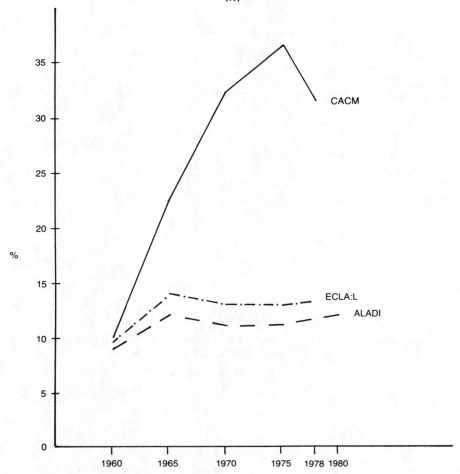

a. Trend line has been smoothed between the 5-year points sampled here.

SOURCE: SALA, 24-2606 and 24-2607.

Table 2607

**ALADI INTRAZONAL IMPORTS AS SHARE OF EACH
COUNTRY'S TOTAL IMPORTS, 1962–80**

(%)

	Country	1962/64	1970	1975	1980
A.	ARGENTINA	14.1	22.0	23.1	20.3
B.	BOLIVIA	10.9	17.0	30.4	27.5
C.	BRAZIL	18.0	10.9	5.7	11.8
D.	CHILE	4.4	20.3	27.6	22.6
E.	COLOMBIA	19.8	9.4	10.7	14.9
J.	ECUADOR	7.9	12.8	11.9	13.0
N.	MEXICO	.9	2.6	6.3	3.4
Q.	PARAGUAY	23.1	22.6	39.4	45.7
R.	PERU	10.5	17.5	18.4	15.0
S.	URUGUAY	23.8	31.7	29.6	36.3
T.	VENEZUELA	2.5	3.8	6.1	6.7
	Total	10.4	11.2	10.6	12.0

SOURCE: IDB-SPTF, 1978, p. 112; *Latin America Weekly Report*, WR-82-37,
Sept. 24, 1982, p. 10.

Table 2608

ORIGIN OF ANDEAN GROUP IMPORTS, 1961–77
(%)

Origin	1961-63	1975-77
United States	49.0	39.0
European Economic Community	29.0	25.5
Canada	3.0	3.5
Japan	4.0	9.5
Latin America		
(including Andean Group)	6.5	12.5
Rest of World	8.5	10.0
Total	100.0	100.0

SOURCE: *Colombia Today* 15:9 (1980)

Table 2609

INTRA-REGIONAL EXPORTS AS A PERCENTAGE OF TOTAL EXPORTS, 19 LR, 1962–79

Country	1962	1965	1970	1975	1979	Most Recent Year
LAIA						
A. ARGENTINA	13.0	16.8	21.0	25.9	26.3	20.3[a]
C. BRAZIL	6.4	12.8	11.6	15.6	17.1	15.0[a]
D. CHILE	8.5	8.3	11.2	23.8	~	24.7[c]
N. MEXICO	5.0	8.2	10.4	12.6	6.7	~
Q. PARAGUAY	32.6	30.7	38.5	36.0	34.4	~
S. URUGUAY	~	~	12.6	28.8	40.2	28.7[b]
Andean Group						
B. BOLIVIA	4.1	2.7	8.5	35.0	31.5	~
E. COLOMBIA	5.5	11.1	13.5	20.8	17.9	20.7[a]
I. ECUADOR	6.0	10.6	11.1	37.8	24.1	~
R. PERU	9.6	9.4	6.4	16.9	21.3	15.6[a]
T. VENEZUELA	10.1	12.6	12.5	12.3	11.7	16.9[b]
CACM						
F. COSTA RICA	~	19.8	23.3	29.2	25.4	34.2[b]
J. EL SALVADOR	~	23.5	32.7	29.0	26.6	44.2[b]
K. GUATEMALA	~	20.9	36.7	29.8	27.0	38.2[b]
M. HONDURAS	~	18.4	16.6	21.2	11.6	12.2[b]
O. NICARAGUA	~	9.2	28.3	25.9	17.0	18.4[a]
Non-Associated Countries						
H. DOMINICAN REP.	~	~	~	1.0	7.7	7.4[a]
L. HAITI	~	~	1.5	1.3	1.1	~
P. PANAMA	13.0	3.0	4.9	7.8	15.9	16.0[a]

a. 1982.
b. 1981.
c. 1980.

SOURCE: IDB-SPTF, 1984, p. 101.

Table 2610

GEOGRAPHIC CONCENTRATION INDEXES OF INTRA-REGIONAL EXPORTS, 19 LR, 1962-82

(%)

Country	1962	1963	1964	1965	1966	1967	1968	1969	1970	1971	1972	1973	1974	1975	1976	1977	1978	1979	1980	1981	1982
LAIA																					
A. ARGENTINA	51.2	47.9	47.7	50.6	48.6	48.0	47.9	45.5	47.0	47.3	51.5	49.2	43.9	42.1	46.1	41.2	43.9	47.9	46.0	41.9	42.6
C. BRAZIL	66.1	60.9	67.1	70.5	62.0	61.5	62.9	67.3	60.6	56.6	40.7	38.3	36.7	36.2	34.8	35.2	33.1	37.8	38.9	34.1	34.6
D. CHILE	53.3	58.0	55.0	53.7	50.6	54.0	57.4	62.9	60.7	52.1	56.1	58.3	55.1	50.5	52.4	54.5	51.5	?	49.3	?	?
N. MEXICO	33.9	32.6	30.4	31.0	32.0	30.1	30.3	30.7	31.4	31.5	32.6	30.8	31.3	34.0	44.7	37.4	34.9	35.1	?	?	?
Q. PARAGUAY	88.9	81.9	80.9	84.8	80.3	75.6	79.9	78.4	72.5	75.6	76.7	69.1	74.7	80.0	49.9	54.9	52.2	57.9	60.8	59.4	?
S. URUGUAY	?	?	?	?	?	?	?	?	50.2	58.2	51.5	?	70.1	64.9	56.7	66.6	68.7	65.6	?	?	?
Andean Group																					
B. BOLIVIA	67.2	73.3	57.8	52.8	54.7	59.1	63.1	64.6	66.1	55.7	58.3	73.9	58.4	74.9	65.7	69.0	65.9	58.4	47.8	53.9	59.5
E. COLOMBIA	53.6	71.7	60.1	50.3	44.2	43.1	31.8	37.0	40.5	39.7	35.7	33.3	31.7	37.5	45.4	54.3	61.1	60.9	?	?	?
I. ECUADOR	56.1	56.9	59.6	53.3	48.2	50.5	49.8	45.8	44.1	45.7	41.5	45.0	46.6	51.5	48.1	47.7	54.2	49.5	32.8	37.2	38.9
R. PERU	52.1	51.3	48.5	45.5	40.8	37.9	38.2	39.0	37.3	40.8	38.1	35.9	39.6	47.4	41.5	37.9	36.7	33.6	33.4	39.8	?
T. VENEZUELA	47.4	45.3	40.6	39.7	39.0	41.9	41.6	39.7	36.3	30.3	28.5	30.3	26.9	27.0	26.8	27.7	27.7	27.7	?	?	?
CACM																					
F. COSTA RICA	?	?	?	44.0	44.8	46.6	46.2	44.5	44.7	45.6	44.8	44.9	46.2	41.7	42.2	42.4	43.8	41.5	46.3	39.7	?
J. EL SALVADOR	?	61.9	61.2	57.0	53.9	53.7	52.0	56.1	62.5	63.0	65.1	63.7	62.4	61.2	58.3	63.8	67.6	69.2	63.6	68.3	?
K. GUATEMALA	?	?	?	58.7	61.2	55.9	54.0	52.1	51.1	53.7	53.3	50.1	48.3	50.3	50.5	51.3	53.8	55.3	51.5	50.1	?
M. HONDURAS	?	64.7	60.7	61.0	55.3	51.9	46.0	40.4	42.9	37.8	39.0	42.6	40.7	37.9	39.5	42.3	43.7	46.0	49.8	45.5	?
O. NICARAGUA	?	?	?	49.2	50.0	48.9	51.0	51.0	50.1	56.4	52.0	47.5	48.1	51.5	48.0	46.4	50.7	51.0	53.2	48.1	49.0
Non-Associated Countries																					
H. DOMINICAN REP.	?	?	?	?	?	?	?	?	?	41.2	46.1	47.0	59.9	46.7	51.0	68.4	88.8	85.7	85.1	72.3	62.8
L. HAITI	?	?	?	?	?	?	?	?	54.3	56.3	64.1	58.2	58.8	52.9	73.2	48.2	38.1	52.0	?	?	?
P. PANAMA	63.6	65.5	44.1	39.6	54.9	49.2	76.7	52.7	57.0	54.6	56.1	48.4	44.6	37.0	43.5	36.1	39.9	42.4	41.8	36.4	39.7

SOURCE: IDB-SPTF, 1984, p. 117.

Table 2611

CACM TRADE WITH 18 ECR COUNTRIES,[1] 1970–80
(%)

	Country	1970	1971	1972	1973	1974	1975	1976	1977	1978	1979	1980	Average 1970-1980
	Exports	1.2	1.4	1.6	1.8	2.2	1.7	1.1	1.0	1.1	1.0	1.0[a]	1.2[b]
F.	COSTA RICA	.2	.3	.2	.2	.4	.3	.3	1.0	1.8	1.8	1.5	1.0
J.	EL SALVADOR	.1	.1	.1	.1	.1	.2	.3	.2	.3	.2	~	.2[c]
K.	GUATEMALA	.7	.8	1.2	1.5	1.6	1.5	.8	.6	.5	.6	.6	.8
M.	HONDURAS	5.5	6.1	7.7	8.7	13.0	8.7	5.0	4.2	2.7	2.4	1.5	4.7
O.	NICARAGUA	.8	.7	.5	.4	.5	.5	.6	.3	.3	.2	.1	.4
	Imports	.8	1.1	.6	1.0	1.0	1.0	2.9	3.5	2.8	5.2	4.5[a]	2.9[b]
F.	COSTA RICA	.7	.8	.7	.9	1.1	1.3	2.5	6.1	2.2	8.8	2.0	3.3
J.	EL SALVADOR	.5	.3	.4	.1	.2	.3	.3	.2	.2	.2	~	.2[c]
K.	GUATEMALA	.5	.8	.5	1.0	.8	1.9	4.0	4.2	5.3	7.0	9.3	4.7
M.	HONDURAS	1.2	2.4	.4	2.4	2.7	.5	7.5	5.4	4.1	3.7	3.7	3.6
O.	NICARAGUA	1.5	1.4	1.0	.9	1.1	.9	1.2	1.7	1.8	1.1	1.4	1.3

1. Includes CARICOM countries (see SALA, 23-2) and Bahamas, Cuba, Dominican
   Republic, Haiti, Netherlands Antilles, and Suriname.

a. Excludes El Salvador.

b. Excludes El Salvador in 1980.

c. To 1979 only.

SOURCE: ECLA, *Economic Relations of Central America and Mexico with the Caribbean*
(Santiago: E/CEPAL/G.1197, April 1, 1982), p. 35.

Table 2612

VALUE OF IMPORTS FROM COUNTRIES WITH CENTRALLY PLANNED ECONOMIES, 9 L, 1965-82[a]
(M US)

Country	Year	Total[1]	Asia[2]	Europe,[3] USSR	China[2]	Bulgaria	Czechoslovakia	German Dem. Rep.[4]	Hungary[5]	Poland	Romania	USSR
A. ARGENTINA	1965	192	84	108	84	#	10	2	10	13	1	72
	1970	85	4	81	3	1	9	#	13	18	9	31
	1975	485	21	464	21	9	16	2	10	20	1	407
	1979	844	193	651	193	11	48	45	10	62	33	440
	1980	2,167	197	1,970	189	7	44	35	7	80	7	1,791
	1981	3,574	116	3,458	116	7	44	31	8	40	40	3,289
	1982	1,989	150	1,839	150	7	30	19	14	24	#	1,745
B. BOLIVIA	1965	#	#	#	#	#	#	#	#	#	#	#
	1970	4	#	4	#	#	1	#	#	#	#	3
	1975	28	#	28	#	#	6	#	1	7	#	13
	1979	66	#	66	#	#	13	#	2	1	#	49
	1980	51	#	51	#	#	18	#	2	#	#	31
	1981	17	#	17	#	#	#	#	1	#	#	16
	1982	26	#	26	#	#	#	#	#	#	#	26
C. BRAZIL	1965	81	#	81	#	#	14	14	8	7	5	33
	1970	120	11	109	1	3	15	29	15	19	5	23
	1975	801	67	734	67	29	62	51	75	64	33	420
	1979	1,298	121	1,177	118	20	142	93	205	429	43	244
	1980	1,553	74	1,479	72	19	164	85	212	509	100	390
	1981	2,052	117	1,935	117	8	204	140	252	478	112	740
	1982	1,418	132	1,286	132	14	121	187	171	219	#	573
E. COLOMBIA	1965	11	1	10	#	#	#	5	1	4	#	#
	1970	30	#	30	#	#	3	9	3	3	2	10
	1975	45	#	45	#	#	3	7	10	13	2	10
	1979	92	4	88	4	#	13	17	8	32	13	5
	1980	153	5	148	5	#	15	41	5	57	11	18
	1981	86	#	86	#	#	#	26	10	26	8	17
	1982	81	4	77	4	#	#	34	#	25	#	18
G. CUBA	1965	540	104	436	104	22	40	26	#	4	#	342
	1970	751	70	681	70	31	57	53	6	4	13	517
	1975	2,433	112	2,321	111	95	68	87	33	23	9	2,007
	1979	3,711	120	3,592	118	133	76	25	39	39	23	3,257
	1980	3,542	129	3,413	127	132	103	24	26	50	31	3,048
	1981	3,529	191	3,338	191	193	97	#	73	41	89	2,845
	1982	4,392	267	4,124	267	171	125	#	60	33	#	3,736
I. ECUADOR	1965	#	#	#	#	#	#	#	#	#	#	#
	1970	10	#	10	#	#	4	#	5	#	#	1
	1975	50	1	49	1	#	9	8	13	1	#	18
	1979	67	#	67	#	#	15	13	32	3	#	3
	1980	46	#	46	#	#	6	#	39	1	#	#
	1981	25	#	25	#	#	#	#	25	#	#	#
	1982	17	7	11	7	#	#	1	10	#	#	#
N. MEXICO	1965	72	2	70	2	#	#	#	#	69	#	#
	1970	4	#	4	#	#	1	1	2	#	#	#
	1975	46	34	12	34	#	2	2	3	2	#	2
	1979	41	8	33	#	#	7	2	6	2	9	6
	1980	51	#	51	#	17	12	#	3	9	7	3
	1981	171	138	33	138	#	#	#	2	#	4	26
	1982	93	54	39	54	7	#	#	#	3	#	29
R. PERU	1965	10	#	10	#	#	#	7	2	#	#	#
	1970	53	#	53	#	#	19	12	8	13	1	#
	1975	274	58	216	49	#	21	26	11	19	14	125
	1979	163	32	131	32	9	26	10	15	34	22	15
	1980	107	20	87	20	7	10	28	3	23	16	#
	1981	127	78	50	78	6	#	#	10	3	#	31
	1982	155	106	49	105	19	#	#	15	#	#	15
S. URUGUAY	1965	8	#	8	#	#	#	2	2	1	#	3
	1970	11	#	11	#	#	8	#	1	1	#	1
	1975	35	#	35	#	#	7	4	#	4	#	19
	1979	37	#	37	#	#	9	4	2	4	#	18
	1980	63	1	62	1	#	12	8	3	5	#	33
	1981	82	#	82	#	#	#	6	7	#	#	69
	1982	81	2	79	2	#	#	7	#	#	#	72

1. Figures for total imports of the centrally planned economies include unadjusted data for Albania, China, DPR Korea, Mongolia and Vietnam derived from the statistics of their trade partners.
2. Unofficial figures derived from the statistics of the trade partners of these countries which are not adjusted for freight and insurance, time lag, or other similar factors.
3. For Albania and beginning in 1975 for German Democratic Republic, trade data included in the totals of CPE Europe and USSR are unadjusted values as reported by trade partners or estimates based on other indicators.
4. Beginning in 1975 official data not available by country of origin and destination. Figures given are unadjusted data as reported by trade partners of German Democratic Republic.
5. Imports, CIF.
a. For 1960, see SALA, 22-2847.

SOURCE: UN-YITS, 1982, vol. 1, special table G.

Table 2613

VALUE OF EXPORTS TO COUNTRIES WITH CENTRALLY PLANNED ECONOMIES, 9 L, 1965–82[a]
(M US)

Country	Year	Total[1]	Asia[2]	Europe,[3] USSR	China[2]	Bulgaria	Czechoslovakia	German Dem. Rep.[4]	Hungary[5]	Poland	Romania	USSR
A. ARGENTINA	1965	30	#	30	#	#	4	1	1	3	1	20
	1970	19	1	18	1	#	5	#	1	10	#	2
	1975	95	1	94	1	#	9	#	2	33	34	15
	1979	129	11	118	11	4	20	#	7	20	24	38
	1980	151	32	119	32	6	19	15	10	14	8	47
	1981	153	24	128	24	4	40	12	12	11	7	42
	1982	74	5	69	5	2	9	4	3	12	#	38
B. BOLIVIA	1965	#	#	#	#	#	#	#	#	#	#	#
	1970	2	1	1	1	#	1	#	#	#	#	#
	1975	14	2	12	2	#	4	3	#	#	#	4
	1979	15	#	15	#	#	6	#	#	1	#	8
	1980	16	#	16	#	#	7	#	#	#	#	8
	1981	13	#	13	#	#	#	#	#	#	#	12
	1982	5	1	4	1	#	#	#	#	#	#	4
C. BRAZIL	1965	54	#	54	#	1	7	7	3	5	5	28
	1970	75	#	75	#	#	8	28	8	22	6	3
	1975	317	1	316	1	1	32	39	12	81	21	129
	1979	359	81	278	81	#	18	56	20	109	45	30
	1980	545	263	282	263	#	23	97	9	80	38	34
	1981	674	344	330	344	#	25	82	28	117	56	23
	1982	905	379	526	379	#	19	116	11	133	#	248
E. COLOMBIA	1965	8	#	8	#	#	#	6	#	2	#	#
	1970	22	#	22	#	#	2	5	1	9	3	2
	1975	16	#	16	#	#	3	4	1	3	3	3
	1979	94	1	93	#	#	6	15	1	14	3	13
	1980	77	1	76	#	#	7	34	1	15	5	14
	1981	63	#	63	#	#	#	33	1	15	10	5
	1982	76	2	74	2	#	#	27	#	37	#	9
G. CUBA	1965	578	112	466	112	16	34	24	8	5	2	375
	1970	851	71	780	71	24	27	62	5	3	15	644
	1975	1,912	85	1,827	85	113	54	#	41	20	17	1,582
	1979	3,681	94	3,587	94	150	92	#	38	65	17	3,226
	1980	4,109	93	4,016	93	181	123	#	46	83	60	3,523
	1981	4,514	77	4,437	77	190	146	#	51	59	180	3,811
	1982	4,968	117	4,851	117	204	214	#	71	52	#	4,311
I. ECUADOR	1965	#	#	#	#	#	#	#	#	#	#	#
	1970	5	#	5	#	#	1	#	2	2	#	#
	1975	5	1	4	1	#	#	1	#	2	#	1
	1979	34	#	34	#	#	7	1	#	25	#	1
	1980	15	1	14	1	#	6	4	#	1	#	1
	1981	6	#	6	#	#	#	#	3	3	#	#
	1982	14	6	8	6	#	#	#	8	3	#	#
N. MEXICO	1965	2	#	2	#	#	#	1	1	1	#	1
	1970	10	#	10	#	#	4	3	1	1	#	1
	1975	45	8	37	8	#	10	2	2	13	4	6
	1979	40	2	38	2	2	15	5	2	5	3	1
	1980	63	#	63	#	3	22	#	8	8	3	18
	1981	63	35	28	35	2	#	#	8	8	#	6
	1982	33	14	19	14	3	#	#	8	5	12	11
R. PERU	1965	#	#	#	#	#	#	#	#	#	#	#
	1970	2	#	2	#	#	1	#	#	#	#	#
	1975	71	2	69	1	#	6	#	8	1	#	39
	1979	84	#	84	#	1	3	#	7	2	14	4
	1980	40	#	40	#	2	8	#	6	68	#	5
	1981	49	11	38	10	1	#	#	3	19	1	17
	1982	36	9	26	9	1	#	#	6	7	9	20
S. URUGUAY	1965	1	#	1	#	#	#	#	#	1	#	#
	1970	4	#	4	#	1	2	#	#	1	#	#
	1975	8	#	8	#	#	1	1	1	#	#	1
	1979	19	1	18	1	1	4	#	1	4	#	1
	1980	28	3	25	3	1	12	1	3	9	#	2
	1981	5	#	5	#	#	#	1	2	7	#	4
	1982	3	1	1	1	#	#	#	1	#	#	1

1. Figures for total imports of the centrally planned economies include unadjusted data for Albania, China, DPR Korea, Mongolia and Vietnam derived from the statistics of their trade partners.

2. Unofficial figures derived from the statistics of the trade partners of these countries which are not adjusted for freight and insurance, time lag, or other similar factors.

3. For Albania and beginning in 1975 for German Democratic Republic, trade data included in the totals of CPE Europe and USSR are unadjusted values as reported by trade partners or estimates based on other indicators.

4. Beginning in 1975 official data not available by country of origin and destination. Figures given are unadjusted data as reported by trade partners of German Democratic Republic.

5. Imports, CIF.

a. For 1960, see SALA, 22-2848.

SOURCE: UN-YITS, 1982, vol. 1, special table G.

Table 2614

ARGENTINA ABSOLUTE VALUE OF GOODS TRADED WITH SELECTED REGIONS AND COUNTRIES,[1] 1975-82
(M US)[2]

Category	Exports FOB							Imports CIF						
	1975	1976	1977	1979	1980	1981	1982	1975	1976	1977	1979	1980	1981	1982
I. World	2,961.0	3,915.8	5,651.5	7,809.5	8,024.8	9,142.9	7,407.2	3,905.2	3,032.8	4,162.6	6,710.6	10,540.9	9,432.2	5,396.4
II. Industrial Countries	1,394.9	2,012.8	2,371.1	4,139.8	3,455.2	3,389.5	3,175.1	2,634.1	1,888.8	2,740.5	4,361.2	7,186.4	6,516.3	3,439.1
United States	196.8	283.9	396.8	582.3	717.6	863.5	974.6[a]	643.9	544.2	781.5	1,414.7	2,380.4	2,093.7	1,178.4[a]
Canada	10.0	15.4	17.2	62.7	42.5	9.9	39.7[a]	84.6	48.3	101.8	155.3	109.8	144.7	59.3[a]
Australia	1.9	3.0	3.2	5.3	6.2	9.9	3.0[a]	67.5	40.4	62.8	59.8	83.7	123.2	53.9[a]
Japan	136.1	209.2	308.4	395.4	210.9	166.5	271.3[a]	493.6	250.0	364.3	356.3	978.3	967.6	439.1[a]
New Zealand	~	.2	.2	.2	1.0	.6	.4[b]	~	~	~	10.7	9.9	1.3	.9[b]
Austria	.9	11.5	6.1	5.1	7.0	4.1	5.8[a]	30.1	19.6	34.1	54.6	45.9	44.2	29.9[a]
Belgium	45.6	71.1	84.4	91.1	59.4	86.9	71.5[a]	91.6	41.3	40.1	109.3	159.0	105.7	75.7[a]
Denmark	5.7	34.3	53.7	93.1	77.5	72.6	88.8[a]	7.1	13.7	9.2	25.1	42.8	31.7	29.0[a]
Finland	3.9	4.0	6.1	10.1	19.9	8.1	8.9[a]	49.2	16.2	20.5	37.0	75.4	61.7	23.0[a]
France	72.2	103.8	157.7	232.2	186.2	145.2	145.4[a]	145.2	105.8	200.5	266.3	374.2	353.2	197.2[a]
Germany	126.7	205.1	297.4	435.2	407.5	354.7	343.8[a]	423.8	341.0	427.5	618.9	984.8	904.8	521.3[a]
Iceland	~	.1	~	~	2.0	4.5	4.1[b]	1.4	.9	1.1	3.8	10.7	15.7	8.1[b]
Ireland	2.5	5.5	5.7	3.0	2.0	4.5	4.1[b]	~	~	~	~	~	~	~
Italy	299.5	372.0	457.7	617.1	520.3	376.4	311.5[a]	184.2	153.5	188.3	387.7	576.9	488.0	251.0[a]
Netherlands	224.4	355.8	572.0	813.8	716.3	696.8	551.4[a]	92.7	44.2	56.7	146.7	232.6	211.6	96.3[a]
Norway	5.5	10.6	15.8	16.5	13.3	8.6	9.1[a]	15.4	5.4	7.7	16.7	23.6	20.4	12.1[a]
Spain	161.0	171.6	301.5	453.2	187.6	209.8	210.0[a]	38.7	25.8	111.4	293.8	399.1	322.3	185.6[a]
Sweden	11.6	11.9	16.3	23.1	21.2	44.3	23.2[a]	48.8	40.8	54.0	76.2	139.9	131.5	77.3[a]
Switzerland	11.6	22.4	25.1	60.3	55.6	46.1	38.9[a]	79.2	68.8	109.7	107.6	216.2	173.0	132.0[a]
United Kingdom	78.7	121.3	145.9	235.2	203.4	217.8	73.7[a]	136.8	128.8	169.2	220.6	343.4	322.2	69.0[a]
III. Developing Countries														
Oil Exporting Countries	176.5	183.2	284.3	343.4	267.1	296.7	499.3	227.6	111.2	246.0	200.8	593.0	429.0	219.6
Algeria	33.2	30.4	46.9	57.2	56.3	41.0	128.1[b]	~	.9	~	1.4	6.0	7.3	.1[b]
Indonesia	3.0	2.5	8.0	12.2	5.6	1.5	12.0	~	~	~	~	~	.7	~
Iran, I.R. of	11.5	21.4	46.6	16.5	86.3	30.8	94.9[b]	6.0	~	23.1	6.5	127.5	9.7	~
Iraq	3.7	1.9	12.0	20.9	11.5	36.7	108.7[b]	~	6.5	57.8	23.7	5.7	~	~
Kuwait	1.1	4.5	1.9	21.5	2.2	20.8	1.9[b]	17.9	~	64.3	17.6	5.9	~	~
Libya	87.1	26.7	21.1	5.5	1.1	.3	.6[b]	142.4	28.7	~	11.4	37.4	66.7	15.2[b]
Nigeria	2.9	1.1	12.8	12.6	17.5	21.9	17.1[b]	~	~	~	~	~	~	~
Oman	.3	~	.2	~	~	1.4	.3[b]	~	~	~	~	~	~	~
Qatar	~	~	~	~	.1	.1	~	~	~	~	~	~	~	~
Saudi Arabia	~	1.4	4.0	36.0	21.5	39.3	22.2[b]	12.9	17.2	24.6	47.1	338.7	280.8	183.2[b]
United Arab Emirates	~	2.0	.1	.4	.1	1.2	.1[b]	~	~	4.1	~	~	~	~
T. VENEZUELA	33.7	91.4	130.6	160.6	65.1	101.7	113.5[b]	65.8	55.4	72.1	93.0	71.5	63.6	21.1[b]
Non-Oil Developing Countries	~	1,258.2	1,902.3	2,666.9	2,448.4	2,299.0	2,047.1	~	86.0	63.3	278.4	97.2	48.1	34.2
Africa	~	58.9	136.1	96.2	99.9	107.7	111.3	~	~	~	70.9	21.3	~	~
Angola	~	.8	.8	26.7	26.9	31.5	19.1[b]	~	~	~	~	~	~	~
Benin	~	.6	4.4	1.9	1.1	.5	.9[b]	~	~	~	.4	~	.2	.1[b]
Cameroon	~	~	.2	10.0	.1	.1	7.9[b]	~	~	~	~	.5	~	~
Cape Verde	~	1.6	.8	1.6	.7	~	~	~	~	~	~	.2	~	~
Central African Rep.	~	~	~	~	.3	~	.9[b]	~	~	~	92.0	20.0	1.6	.2[b]
Congo	~	~	~	3.8	~	1.9	3.6[b]	~	.1	~	~	~	~	.7[b]
Ethiopia	~	.9	1.6	2.3	2.5	3.5	.1[b]	~	66.6	41.1	77.8	~	~	~
Gabon	~	~	.4	~	.3	~	4.4[b]	~	~	~	~	~	~	~
Gambia, The	~	3.5	1.1	.7	.3	2.7	2[b]	~	5.0	~	~	~	~	~
Ghana	~	.3	1.6	~	1.9	~	3.6[b]	~	~	~	.6	~	.2	~
Guinea	~	5.5	3.9	6.7	3.6	3.4	3.1[b]	~	~	~	.5	~	.2	~
Ivory Coast	~	.3	.4	.2	.1	~	~	~	~	~	.3	~	.1	~
Kenya	~	.2	.2	2.9	11.6	16.9	2.0[b]	~	.2	1.1	1.1	~	~	~
Liberia	~	~	~	1.7	~	~	~	~	~	~	2.2	.1	~	.1[b]
Madagascar	~	~	~	~	~	~	~	~	~	~	~	~	~	.1[b]
Mali	~	2.1	.4	.1	.1	~	3.7[b]	~	~	~	~	~	~	~
Mauritania	~	~	~	~	~	~	~	~	~	~	~	~	~	~
Mauritius	~	.2	.3	~	.1	~	~	~	~	~	~	~	~	~

Table 2614 (Continued)

ARGENTINA ABSOLUTE VALUE OF GOODS TRADED WITH SELECTED REGIONS AND COUNTRIES,[1] 1975–82
(M US)[2]

Category	Exports FOB							Imports CIF						
	1975	1976	1977	1979	1980	1981	1982	1975	1976	1977	1979	1980	1981	1982
III. Developing Countries (Continued)														
Non-Oil Developing Countries														
Morocco	~	10.3	50.8	8.9	2.9	11.4	8.6b	~	.4	~	~	~	~	~
Mozambique	~	.1	2.6	.5	~	~	~	~	~	.3	.2	~	.1	~
Niger	~	~	~	3.8	~	~	.1b	~	~	~	~	~	~	~
Reunion	~	~	~	.1	~	~	~	~	~	~	~	~	~	~
Senegal	~	4.7	7.2	4.1	7.5	3.4	~	~	~	~	~	~	~	~
Sierra Leone	~	.1	.7	2.5	1.0	6.2	8.2b	~	~	~	~	~	~	~
Somalia	~	~	~	~	~	~	~	~	~	~	~	~	~	~
South Africa	~	4.7	5.9	9.9	15.6	18.1	20.0b	~	12.6	19.8	34.0	53.4	44.2	33.0b
Sudan	~	3.3	~	.5	3.7	.1	~	~	~	~	~	~	1.7	~
Swaziland	~	~	~	~	~	~	~	~	~	~	~	~	~	~
Tanzania	~	.1	~	~	~	~	1.9b	~	~	~	~	~	~	~
Togo	~	~	5.1	1.4	~	~	.3b	~	~	~	~	~	~	~
Tunisia	~	18.8	30.5	16.6	17.7	3.1	4.5a	~	~	~	~	~	~	~
Upper Volta	~	~	~	~	.1	~	~	~	~	.7	.4	1.4	~	~
Zaire	~	1.3	3.2	1.7	3.4	5.2	22.6b	~	.1	.1	.1	.2	~	~
Zimbabwe	~	~	~	~	~	~	~	~	~	~	~	~	~	.3b
Asia														
Bangladesh	~	41.2	196.9	296.4	267.4	252.9	266.3	~	40.8	42.9	98.5	259.3	249.1	76.7
Brunei	~	2.1	1.3	.1	~	2.6	2.1a	~	7.7	3.4	1.0	.8	1.8	.1a
China, People's Rep.	~	2.7	87.1	193.0	188.8	92.1	144.6a	~	.3	.9	11.7	32.7	21.4	10.4a
Guam	~	~	~	~	.1	.1	.1b	~	~	~	~	~	~	~
Hong Kong	~	24.2	21.7	20.4	21.9	19.4	3.3a	~	.6	3.8	28.1	110.9	95.8	17.4a
India	~	3.3	25.4	6.0	22.2	60.9	13.5b	~	4.7	4.7	1.5	6.5	5.4	1.2b
Korea	~	1.7	5.2	23.1	7.3	17.3	15.3b	~	.5	1.3	10.0	50.5	79.9	16.8b
Malaysia	~	.3	3.1	3.4	5.0	10.7	2.4b	~	9.0	9.5	6.7	2.8	1.1	1.8b
Nepal	~	~	~	.1	~	~	~	~	~	~	~	~	~	~
Pakistan	~	~	.1	23.9	8.4	4.9	5.4a	~	.1	.2	.2	.8	.5	.7a
Philippines	~	.3	1.2	1.0	.8	1.6	.8a	~	.4	.1	.5	.8	.7	.4a
Singapore	~	5.7	30.0	22.3	5.3	36.1	76.5a	~	~	~	~	~	~	~
Sri Lanka	~	17.4	19.0	37.3	50.7	40.6	.1a	~	17.4	19.0	37.3	50.7	40.6	26.9a
Thailand	~	.6	2.9	3.0	4.7	2.9	2.3b	~	.1	.2	1.6	1.6	1.7	1.0a
Viet Nam	~	.1	~	~	2.7	~	~	~	~	~	~	~	.1	~
Oceania not specified	.1	.1	17.7	.1	.1	~	~	~	~	~	~	~	~	~
Europe	~	130.8	183.7	181.9	134.6	106.2	76.5	~	40.6	23.9	45.7	31.3	61.5	21.1
Cyprus	~	7.0	5.9	5.2	3.6	1.7	3.3a	~	~	~	~	~	~	~
Gibraltar	~	~	~	~	~	.2	.1b	~	~	~	~	~	~	~
Greece	3.0	31.5	47.7	71.4	39.4	20.2	23.1a	~	1.2	2.2	5.4	1.9	31.8	.4a
Hungary	~	3.4	3.9	7.7	5.8	6.9	10.9b	~	2.2	2.2	2.5	6.0	11.6	7.1b
Malta	~	.5	4.4	6.5	1.0	4.1	6.6b	~	~	~	~	~	~	~
Portugal	11.3	57.2	46.6	46.1	42.3	34.5	29.4b	~	2.7	2.1	6.9	6.7	5.7	3.1b
Romania	.4	17.9	68.6	26.3	23.3	27.8	.5b	~	28.8	11.5	26.5	13.6	7.8	8.8b
Turkey	~	5.0	1.1	9.6	1.2	.1	.5b	~	.1	1.5	3.1	.3	1.1	.3b
Yugoslavia	4.6	8.4	5.4	8.9	18.0	10.7	2.1b	~	5.6	1.5	1.3	2.7	3.5	1.4b
Europe not specified	2.0	~	~	~	~	~	~	~	~	~	~	~	~	~
Middle East	~	57.4	73.7	199.4	98.8	134.1	168.6	~	4.9	3.4	18.2	17.7	14.7	11.2
Bahrain	~	~	~	~	~	~	~	~	~	~	~	~	~	~
Egypt	~	21.4	12.6	91.4	29.4	68.6	107.0b	~	1.4	~	~	~	~	~
Israel	17.4	30.9	31.9	73.2	39.9	51.7	44.4a	~	3.4	3.4	13.4	17.6	14.4	11.1a
Jordan	~	1.3	7.5	10.5	10.6	2.0	8.6b	~	~	~	~	~	~	~
Lebanon	~	.3	12.3	14.6	10.1	3.3	4.6b	~	~	~	~	~	~	~
Syrian Arab Rep.	3.1	3.5	8.5	2.6	8.4	8.2	3.9b	~	~	~	~	~	~	~
Yemen Arab Rep.	~	~	~	1.1	.3	~	~	~	~	~	~	~	~	~
Yemen P.D. Rep.	~	~	~	5.9	~	~	~	~	~	~	4.7	~	~	~
Middle East not specified	~	~	~	~	~	~	~	~	~	~	~	~	~	.1b

Table 2614 (Continued)

ARGENTINA ABSOLUTE VALUE OF GOODS TRADED WITH SELECTED REGIONS AND COUNTRIES,[1] 1975-82
(M US)[2]

Category	Exports FOB							Imports CIF						
	1975	1976	1977	1979	1980	1981	1982	1975	1976	1977	1979	1980	1981	1982
IV. Latin America[3]	729.5	969.9	1,311.9	1,892.9	1,847.7	1,698.1	1,424.5	879.9	807.6	971.4	1,586.0	2,182.9	1,923.9	1,506.8
Antigua and Barbuda	~	.2	.2	.7	1.1	.3	.1[b]	~	4.1	19.1	48.4	1.2	.3	.4[b]
Bahamas	~	1.4	1.9	2.4	2.0	1.3	.8[b]	~	~	~	~	~	.3	~
Barbados	~	~	~	.2	.2	.3	.1[b]	~	~	~	~	~	~	~
Belize	~	.1	.2	.4	1.1	.3	.1[b]	~	~	~	~	.9	.2	.2
Bermuda	~	~	~	~	~	~	.2[b]	~	.4	.9	30.5	.9	.2	~
B. BOLIVIA	63.8	67.0	112.9	120.2	133.4	125.9	112.9[b]	130.7	98.3	174.3	128.9	252.4	343.8	393.6[b]
C. BRAZIL	213.5	421.9	464.8	885.6	765.1	595.1	557.1[a]	358.9	371.5	372.5	657.2	1,072.4	893.2	610.8[a]
D. CHILE	130.6	178.6	274.9	159.6	217.6	189.0	151.5[a]	162.2	143.9	164.2	265.1	254.7	189.5	149.5[a]
E. COLOMBIA	16.3	26.3	64.8	52.4	39.0	51.2	71.5[b]	27.2	21.2	43.2	41.8	52.1	41.0	26.4[b]
F. COSTA RICA	1.7	1.8	11.2	6.1	5.5	5.2	1.6[b]	~	.1	.2	.2	2.1	1.3	.1[b]
Dominica	~	~	~	~	.2	~	~	~	~	~	~	.2	.2	~
H. DOMINICAN REP.	.5	3.4	17.7	1.0	1.4	.8	1.0[a]	11.1	7.9	24.8	37.9	61.1	50.1	34.7[b]
I. ECUADOR	11.4	12.2	21.1	16.0	17.5	16.9	20.9[b]	~	.1	.3	.3	.1	.1	.1[b]
J. EL SALVADOR	.6	1.7	1.4	1.9	1.9	.3	9.3[b]	~	.1	.3	.3	.1	.1	~
Grenada	~	~	~	~	.2	~	.1[b]	~	~	~	~	.1	.1	~
Guadeloupe	~	1.9	.2	3.1	3.2	3.7	3.2[b]	~	~	~	2.2	.2	.1	1.2[b]
K. GUATEMALA	1.3	1.9	4.4	3.1	3.2	3.7	3.2[b]	.3	4.0	2.6	2.2	.4	~	~
Guyana	~	.3	.3	.4	.4	.3	.3[b]	~	~	~	~	.3	.3	.1[b]
L. HAITI	.5	.4	.1	.1	.3	.3	.3[b]	~	~	~	~	~	~	~
M. HONDURAS	.5	1.0	3.5	2.0	4.2	3.0	4.0[b]	1.6	~	.1	.1	.5	~	.1[b]
Jamaica	~	.9	1.4	3.1	1.8	1.7	.2[b]	~	~	~	.1	.5	~	21.7[b]
Leeward Islands	~	~	.1	.1	.2	.1	.1[b]	~	~	~	~	~	~	~
Martinique	~	.1	.1	.1	.1	.1	.1[b]	~	~	~	~	~	~	54.5[b]
N. MEXICO	178.6	52.5	74.3	121.6	121.3	275.3	118.6[b]	58.1	33.1	36.7	45.4	71.7	66.6	10.9[b]
Netherlands Antilles	~	4.5	2.1	2.7	6.7	31.3	1.0[b]	32.0	32.0	30.3	107.4	11.9	41.1	23.5[a]
O. NICARAGUA	.6	1.0	.9	2.0	4.5	5.1	2.6[b]	.1	~	.1	.1	.1	.1	~
P. PANAMA	2.4	10.7	22.8	11.9	14.0	2.8	5.3[b]	15.9	8.1	16.0	26.9	90.9	56.7	46.4[a]
Q. PARAGUAY	37.3	56.4	84.7	184.0	189.4	169.3	147.2[a]	50.2	22.4	35.4	55.5	84.6	92.0	20.7[b]
R. PERU	29.6	61.9	46.5	72.7	116.8	89.1	99.9[b]	41.5	31.0	28.2	56.8	69.6	27.2	~
St. Kitts-Nevis	~	~	~	~	.2	.1	.1[b]	~	~	~	~	~	~	~
St. Lucia	~	~	~	~	.1	.1	.1[b]	~	~	~	~	~	~	~
St. Vincent	~	~	.7	.4	.1	.1	.1[b]	~	~	~	~	~	~	~
Suriname	~	~	~	~	.1	~	~	~	3.4	~	2.8	4.9	~	~
Trinidad and Tobago	~	1.0	1.6	2.2	2.0	1.6	8.9[b]	22.1	26.3	32.4	78.5	148.1	120.5	8.6[b]
S. URUGUAY	40.8	63.0	96.9	238.9	185.3	128.1	105.0[a]	~	~	~	~	4.9	1.4	103.6[a]
Windward Islands	~	~	~	.2	11.4	.4	~	~	~	~	~	1.4	.1	~
British West Indies	~	~	~	~	~	~	~	~	~	~	~	~	~	~
V. USSR, Eastern Europe, etc.	475.4	437.4	549.7	620.7	1,835.2	3,144.9	1,665.5	66.3	51.6	69.4	92.5	75.3	105.6	68.8
Albania	1.0	4.6	.6	.6	7.6	6.3	.4[b]	.4	.4	1.0	4.4	7.0	3.9	4.9[b]
Bulgaria	~	9.4	13.4	13.4	66.3	76.8	3.6[b]	~	.2	~	.2	.3	~	.2
G. CUBA	156.5	168.7	167.6	49.6	66.3	76.8	43.7[b]	8.1	4.8	11.0	28.6	16.6	33.1	15.3[b]
Czechoslovakia	8.5	11.9	22.2	30.9	25.1	24.8	21.0[b]	.5	~	.2	5.1	14.6	11.8	4.0[b]
Eastern Germany	1.9	12.4	38.2	44.6	35.4	31.0	19.2[b]	~	~	~	.2	~	~	~
Mongolia	~	~	~	~	~	~	~	~	~	~	.5	~	~	.5
North Korea	.1	.2	.2	1.8	4.7	~	~	~	.2	.6	.3	.2	.3	~
Poland	16.2	20.5	101.3	64.5	81.9	42.9	19.6[b]	31.6	33.6	36.9	23.1	22.2	24.5	12.6[b]
USSR	288.3	219.1	210.7	415.3	1,614.2	2,963.2	1,558.0[b]	22.0	12.8	20.3	30.7	14.6	32.4	32.0[b]
EEC	~	1,300.5	1,822.1	2,597.0	2,211.9	1,975.0	1,613.2	~	830.4	1,094.7	1,738.8	2,726.2	2,464.6	1,248.0
VI. Percent Distribution														
Industrial Countries	~	51.4	50.8	53.0	43.1	37.1	42.9	~	62.3	65.8	65.0	68.2	69.1	63.7
Oil Exporting Countries	~	4.7	5.0	4.4	3.3	3.2	6.7	~	3.7	5.9	3.0	5.6	4.5	4.1
Non-Oil Developing Countries	~	32.1	33.7	34.1	30.5	25.1	27.6	~	32.3	26.5	30.2	24.6	24.4	30.5
Africa	~	1.1	2.4	1.2	1.2	1.2	1.5	~	2.8	1.5	4.1	.9	.5	.6
Asia	~	3.3	3.5	3.8	3.3	2.8	3.6	~	1.3	1.0	1.5	2.5	2.6	1.4
Europe	~	1.5	1.3	2.3	1.7	1.2	1.0	~	1.3	.6	.6	.3	.7	.4
Middle East	~	~	1.3	2.6	1.2	1.5	2.3	~	.2	.6	.3	.2	.2	.2
Western Hemisphere	~	24.8	23.2	24.2	23.0	18.6	19.2	~	26.6	23.3	23.6	20.7	20.4	27.9
USSR, Eastern Europe, etc.	~	11.2	9.7	7.9	22.9	34.4	22.5	~	1.7	1.7	1.4	.7	1.1	1.3

Table 2614 (Continued)

ARGENTINA ABSOLUTE VALUE OF GOODS TRADED WITH SELECTED REGIONS AND COUNTRIES,[1] 1975-82
(M US)[2]

Category	Exports FOB							Imports CIF						
	1975	1976	1977	1979	1980	1981	1982	1975	1976	1977	1979	1980	1981	1982
VII. Annual Percent Change														
World	?	32.2	44.3	22.0	2.8	13.9	-19.0	?	-23.4	37.3	75.0	57.1	-10.5	-42.8
Industrial Countries	?	44.3	42.6	16.0	-16.5	-1.9	-6.3	?	-28.3	45.1	68.5	64.8	-9.3	-47.2
Oil Exporting Countries	?	3.9	55.2	19.4	-22.2	11.1	68.3	?	-51.2	121.2	115.7	195.3	-27.7	-48.8
Non-Oil Developing Countries	?	39.1	51.2	41.6	-8.2	-6.1	-11.0	?	-5.1	12.8	94.8	27.7	-11.3	-28.2
Africa	?	30.9	131.0	23.5	3.8	7.9	3.4	?	200.5	-26.4	78.2	-65.1	-50.6	-28.8
Asia	?	-14.6	377.9	104.9	-9.8	-5.4	5.3	?	-26.6	5.3	94.5	163.2	-4.0	-69.2
Europe	?	244.4	40.4	29.2	-26.0	-21.1	-28.0	?	-19.6	-41.2	93.4	-31.5	96.6	-65.8
Middle East	?	41.3	28.3	95.2	-50.4	35.7	25.7	?	-11.5	-29.3	284.5	-2.5	-17.2	-23.3
Western Hemisphere	?	32.3	35.3	33.5	-2.4	-8.1	-16.1	?	-9.5	20.3	96.9	37.6	-11.9	-21.7
USSR, Eastern Europe, etc.	?	-7.4	25.7	2.2	195.7	71.4	-47.0	?	-17.5	34.5	-13.3	-18.6	40.1	-34.8

1. DOT data may differ between countries and from IFS data because of the time it takes for an export to become an import, etc.
2. Data may be calculated from partner's reported data or estimated on basis of less than 12 months.
3. Cuba is included in category V; Venezuela is included in category III.
a. Eleven months of reported data, 1 month derived from partner.
b. Eleven months reported data, 1 month extrapolated.

SOURCE: IMF-DOT-Y, 1982; IMF-DOT-Y, 1983.

Table 2615

BOLIVIA ABSOLUTE VALUE OF GOODS TRADED WITH SELECTED REGIONS AND COUNTRIES,[1] 1975–82
(M US)[2]

Category	Exports FOB							Imports CIF						
	1975	1976	1977	1979	1980	1981	1982	1975	1976	1977	1979	1980	1981	1982
I. World	521.5	623.2	715.4	857.2	1,036.2	995.3	732.1	557.90	587.6	591.2	860.9	813.8	825.4	597.5
II. Industrial Countries	298.43	374.7	458.8	531.8	587.4	519.5	250.1	340.38	330.1	346.8	525.6	497.2	504.3	256.0
United States	160.70	214.1	252.4	271.0	266.6	266.2	103.1*	139.56	150.8	141.0	244.7	231.7	235.0	109.1*
Canada	~	.3	.2	.5	8.9	.4	6.5*	7.25	4.3	3.5	6.1	5.8	5.9	8.1*
Australia	~	~	~	~	~	~	.4	~	~	~	~	~	~	.4*
Japan	18.31	20.6	15.9	20.1	9.2	9.4	11.6*	88.28	65.2	78.5	83.3	78.8	79.9	45.9*
Austria	~	~	~	~	~	~	5.6*	~	~	~	~	~	~	1.0*
Belgium	9.75	9.8	8.4	17.4	36.2	28.1	10.9*	8.18	4.9	6.4	31.3	29.6	30.0	2.3*
Denmark	~	~	~	~	~	~	.9*	~	~	~	~	~	~	2.1*
Finland	2.73	8.7	11.1	12.1	44.4	24.7	.1*	~	~	~	~	~	~	.3*
France	17.60	21.1	27.9	45.0	54.8	34.6	33.8*	10.24	9.9	6.8	4.6	4.4	4.5	22.9*
Germany	~	~	~	~	~	~	30.1*	42.33	45.3	58.8	82.6	78.1	79.2	28.9*
Ireland	.76	.6	.8	1.7	1.3	1.9	2.5*	~	~	~	~	~	~	1.0[a]
Italy	12.65	20.5	36.8	48.8	45.4	72.3	4.3*	11.76	8.6	11.0	12.3	11.6	11.8	4.0*
Netherlands	~	~	~	~	~	~	.1*	5.21	6.1	8.6	10.1	9.5	9.7	5.3*
Norway	~	~	~	~	~	~	4.1*	~	~	~	~	~	~	.5*
Spain	~	~	~	.3	.1	.9	1.1*	~	~	~	~	~	~	4.4*
Sweden	21.6	22.9	26.9	32.0	49.3	42.5	1.1*	6.72	10.4	9.7	16.6	15.7	15.9	4.7*
Switzerland	~	~	~	~	~	~	1.1*	6.33	9.1	7.9	8.4	7.9	8.0	5.9*
United Kingdom	56.42	56.2	78.3	82.8	71.3	38.5	33.8*	13.62	15.5	14.7	25.5	24.1	24.4	9.6*
III. Developing Countries														
Oil Exporting Countries	.17	.2	1.4	3.5	4.8	3.8	3.6	.32	.3	.3	.6	.5	.5	.4[b]
T. VENEZUELA	.17	.2	1.4	3.5	4.8	3.8	3.6[b]	.32	.3	.3	.6	.5	.5	.4[b]
Non-Oil Developing Countries	~	218.5	189.1	250.1	376.9	438.1	449.3	214.3	212.5	285.9	265.5	269.3	296.0	
Africa							3.6							.4[a]
South Africa								2.1						.4[a]
Asia	~	~	.7	2.4	.2	12.3	33.6	~	2.1	10.6	22.1	16.8	17.0	17.7
China, People's Rep.	~	~	~	~	~	~	.3*	~	~	~	~	~	~	1.0*
Hong Kong	~	~	~	~	~	~	~	~	~	~	~	~	~	~
Korea	~	~	~	~	~	~	1.6[a]	~	~	~	~	~	~	1.8[a]
Malaysia	~	~	~	~	.2	~	20.9[a]	~	~	~	~	~	~	~
Sri Lanka	~	~	~	~	~	~	~	~	~	~	~	~	~	~
Thailand	~	~	.7	2.4	~	12.3	10.5[b]	~	2.1	10.6	22.1	21.2	21.2	17.2
Asia not specified	~	~	.7	~	~	~	.7*	~	~	13.2	~	~	~	.1*
Europe														
Greece	~	~	~	~	~	~	.4[a]	~	~	~	~	~	~	~
Portugal	~	6.0	9.7	~	~	~	2.0[a]	~	~	4.1	~	~	~	~
Yugoslavia	~	~	~	~	~	~	5.7[a]	~	6.9	13.2	21.2	19.5	19.7	16.8[b]
Europe not specified	~	6.0	9.7	.7	~	5.9	5.0[b]	~	6.0	6.9	~	~	~	~
Middle East	~	~	~	~	~	~	.2	~	~	~	~	~	~	~
Israel	~	~	~	~	~	~	.2*	~	~	~	~	~	~	.1*
IV. Latin America[3]	186.76	212.5	178.7	247.0	375.7	419.9	402.1	191.35	205.3	188.7	242.6	229.2	232.5	260.6
A. ARGENTINA	135.0	139.5	128.1	133.5	245.2	359.7	332.8[a]	80.32	87.8	78.9	94.8	89.6	90.9	115.0[a]
C. BRAZIL	18.48	20.3	20.4	43.5	36.3	12.7	27.7*	79.88	85.0	66.1	56.6	53.5	54.3	87.6*
D. CHILE	5.77	10.1	14.2	35.4	46.9	8.5	8.2*	10.57	11.3	16.7	32.8	30.9	31.4	12.3*
E. COLOMBIA	1.35	3.2	4.1	6.7	9.8	5.9	5.0[b]	9.83	10.1	3.1	3.5	3.3	3.4	2.9*
F. COSTA RICA	~	~	~	~	~	~	.6[a]	.43	.9	.4	1.0	1.0	1.0	.1[a]
I. ECUADOR	13.28	9.0	.4	.8	1.6	.8	.8[a]	.82	.9	2.4	2.8	2.6	2.6	.7[a]
N. MEXICO	.88	5.0	2.4	1.8	2.9	.9	.1[a]	~	~	~	~	~	~	~
P. PANAMA	~	~	~	~	~	~	~	~	~	~	~	~	~	~
Q. PARAGUAY	.51	.3	.1	~	~	~	.5	.35	4.1	4.1	.5	.5	.5	.4*
R. PERU	7.4	17.3	6.5	24.6	32.3	31.2	26.5[b]	8.68	9.0	13.8	46.9	44.4	45.0	38.2[b]
S. URUGUAY	4.09	7.9	2.5	.8	.6	.3	.1*	.47	.4	2.8	1.1	1.1	1.1	1.1*
Other Latin America not specified	~	~	~	~	~	~	.2[b]	~	.1	.6	2.5	2.4	2.4	2.0[b]

Table 2615 (Continued)

BOLIVIA ABSOLUTE VALUE OF GOODS TRADED WITH SELECTED REGIONS AND COUNTRIES,[1] 1975–82 (M US)[2]

Category	Exports FOB							Imports CIF						
	1975	1976	1977	1979	1980	1981	1982	1975	1976	1977	1979	1980	1981	1982
V. USSR, Eastern Europe, etc.	29.0	29.5	52.7	44.8	45.5	31.6	26.9	4.08	3.3	11.9	12.4	11.7	11.9	10.1
USSR, etc., not specified	~	29.5	52.7	44.8	45.5	31.6	26.9b	~	3.3	11.9	12.4	11.7	11.9	10.1b
Country or area not specified	~	.3	13.5	27.0	21.6	2.3	2.0b	~	6.6	19.8	36.4	38.9	39.5	33.5b
Special categories	~	~	~	~	~	~	~	~	33.0	~	~	~	~	~
EEC	~	116.9	163.3	207.7	253.3	200.2	117.0	~	90.3	106.2	166.5	157.4	159.6	76.2
VI. Percent Distribution														
Industrial Countries	~	60.1	64.1	62.0	56.7	52.2	34.2	~	56.2	58.7	61.0	61.1	61.1	42.8
Oil Exporting Countries	~	~	.2	.4	.5	.4	.5	~	.1	~	~	~	.1	.1
Non-Oil Developing Countries	~	35.1	26.4	29.2	36.4	44.0	61.4	~	36.5	35.9	33.2	32.6	32.6	49.5
Africa	~	~	~	~	~	~	~	~	~	~	~	~	~	.1
Asia	~	~	.1	.3	.1	1.2	4.6	~	.4	1.8	2.6	2.1	2.1	3.0
Europe	~	1.0	1.4	.1	.1	.6	1.8	~	1.2	2.2	2.5	2.4	2.4	2.9
Western Hemisphere	~	34.1	25.0	28.8	36.3	42.2	54.9	~	34.9	31.9	28.2	28.2	28.2	43.6
USSR, Eastern Europe, etc.	~	4.7	7.4	5.2	4.4	3.2	3.7	~	.6	2.0	1.4	1.4	1.4	1.7
VII. Annual Percent Change														
World	~	19.5	14.8	18.0	20.9	-3.9	-26.4	~	5.3	.6	10.8	-5.5	1.4	-27.6
Industrial Countries	~	25.5	22.5	19.6	10.5	-11.6	-51.9	~	-3.0	5.1	2.1	-5.4	1.4	-49.2
Oil Exporting Countries	~	17.6	575.0	43.6	38.3	-22.0	-5.0	~	-6.2	-16.0	-29.5	-19.1	1.4	-14.9
Non-Oil Developing Countries	~	12.8	-13.5	25.2	50.7	16.2	2.6	~	6.0	-.9	27.1	-7.1	1.4	9.9
Asia	~	~	~	-1.0	-90.4	~	173.4	~	-20.6	400.2	33.0	-24.2	1.4	4.0
Europe	~	-11.7	61.3	98.3	38.7	506.6	127.9	~	-14.7	90.1	-15.1	-8.2	1.4	-12.9
Western Hemisphere	~	13.7	-15.9	25.4	52.1	11.8	-4.2	~	7.2	-8.1	32.3	-5.5	1.4	12.1
USSR, Eastern Europe, etc.	~	1.9	78.3	-42.1	1.5	-30.5	-15.0	~	-20.3	265.8	-4.5	-5.5	1.4	-15.0

1. DOT data may differ between countries and from IFS data because of the time it takes for an export to become an import, etc.

2. Data may be calculated from partner's reported data or estimated on basis of less than 12 months.

3. No trade with Cuba; Venezuela is included in category III.

a. Five or fewer months of reported data; seven or more months derived or extrapolated.

b. Data extrapolated for the entire year.

SOURCE: IMF-DOT-Y, 1982; IMF-DOT-Y, 1983.

Table 2616

BRAZIL ABSOLUTE VALUE OF GOODS TRADED WITH SELECTED REGIONS AND COUNTRIES,[1] 1975-82 (M US)[2]

	Exports FOB							Imports CIF						
Category	1975	1976	1977	1979	1980	1981	1982	1975	1976	1977	1979	1980	1981	1982
I. World	8,668	10,100	12,152	15,248	20,132	23,329	20,168	13,592	13,761	13,254	19,804	24,961	24,075	21,069
II. Industrial Countries	5,219	6,637	7,864	9,437	11,539	12,513	12,048	9,144	8,006	7,082	9,690	11,626	10,058	8,122
United States	1,334	1,848	2,149	2,941	3,510	4,111	4,131	3,387	3,111	2,601	3,629	4,634	3,933	3,164
Canada	136	136	143	199	243	290	231	232	344	305	410	985	637	516
Australia	27	38	31	65	98	135	137	58	19	13	34	40	54	20
Japan	671	638	660	887	1,232	1,220	1,313	1,256	1,005	936	1,180	1,192	1,380	973
New Zealand	~	5	3	9	13	16	17	~	1	~	1	~	~	~
Austria	28	61	60	63	68	57	58	31	26	37	31	24	21	20
Belgium	116	124	155	237	356	413	401	256	148	124	174	175	146	155
Denmark	77	154	143	130	131	93	91	50	36	33	33	32	26	21
Finland	27	41	28	62	70	62	64	36	41	43	61	79	55	46
France	248	343	499	598	822	851	863	375	374	396	635	719	649	597
Germany	700	895	1,086	1,115	1,337	1,317	1,182	1,461	1,191	1,130	1,485	1,741	1,180	934
Iceland	~	5	6	6	5	3	2	6	3	1	3	13	9	8
Ireland	6	12	14	24	21	30	40	~	6	22	~	~	~	~
Italy	360	416	677	700	979	961	984	623	444	332	331	415	661	518
Netherlands	560	741	929	993	1,150	1,470	1,132	217	211	249	415	263	228	149
Norway	77	108	73	107	117	111	92	73	57	75	91	93	72	64
Spain	364	440	487	324	521	372	368	116	115	125	148	218	107	102
Sweden	83	186	151	176	197	157	171	338	258	181	144	166	237	286
Switzerland	61	60	145	93	120	109	97	264	268	193	369	349	295	278
United Kingdom	340	387	425	708	550	735	672	363	347	287	504	483	367	270
III. Developing Countries														
Oil Exporting Countries	660	554	787	800	1,461	2,350	1,795	3,069	3,849	4,002	6,551	9,087	9,962	8,825
Algeria	170	142	181	34	167	267	125	78	63	1	24	83	303	185
Indonesia	4	17	34	27	41	122	87	1	~	~	1	76	300	14
Iran, I.R. of	76	77	96	72	239	195	210	171	378	419	884	766	~	52
Iraq	179	50	94	240	289	298	318	915	1,197	1,153	2,824	3,948	2,031	2,765
Kuwait	20	16	20	17	42	79	24	370	534	489	296	797	607	229
Libya	30	18	19	15	35	11	11	214	152	159	27	140	369	350
Nigeria	57	87	115	137	272	770	244	~	82	95	34	90	756	237
Oman	~	1	1	2	8	3	2	37	~	~	~	~	~	~
Qatar	~	1	7	7	14	15	19	~	~	1	120	201	231	339
Saudi Arabia	14	15	17	41	96	161	267	1,128	1,231	1,430	1,947	2,177	4,038	3,196
United Arab Emirates	3	6	9	10	29	21	16	39	101	93	150	212	278	411
T. VENEZUELA	107	125	199	198	230	408	470	116	110	162	244	598	1,048	
Non-Oil Developing Countries	~	2,090	2,646	3,983	5,749	6,624	5,001	~	1,701	1,958	3,342	3,984	3,815	3,621
Africa	~	137	220	465	680	688	850	~	196	343	420	860	652	459
Angola	~	22	26	89	119	107	85	~	~	1	~	113	162	105
Benin	~	~	~	1	2	7	17	~	~	~	~	~	~	~
Cameroon	~	1	2	4	2	17	4	~	3	4	~	~	~	~
Comoros	~	1	~	~	~	~	~	~	~	~	~	~	~	~
Congo	~	~	5	12	36	73	65	~	~	~	43	85	116	~
Djibouti	~	1	1	~	1	~	2	~	~	~	~	~	~	~
Ethiopia	~	~	~	3	10	23	5	~	~	~	~	~	~	~
Gabon	~	1	1	3	3	~	~	~	105	153	115	311	217	226
Gambia, The	~	2	2	3	1	1	~	~	2	4	4	3	1	1
Ghana	~	9	9	3	1	6	16	~	~	~	~	~	~	~
Guinea	~	~	~	1	9	9	31	~	~	~	~	~	~	~
Guinea-Bissau	~	2	2	2	1	5	1	~	~	~	~	~	~	~
Ivory Coast	~	1	1	1	30	78	60	~	~	~	~	~	~	~
Kenya	~	14	14	10	44	28	62	~	~	~	~	~	~	~
Liberia	~	5	5	3	3	1	2	~	~	12	~	~	~	~
Madagascar	~	2	17	90	1	2	4	~	~	~	~	~	~	~
Mauritania	~	6	7	10	1	1	1	~	~	~	~	~	~	~
Mauritius	~	1	1	1	1	2	2	~	~	~	~	~	~	~

Table 2616 (Continued)

BRAZIL ABSOLUTE VALUE OF GOODS TRADED WITH SELECTED REGIONS AND COUNTRIES,[1] 1975-82

(M US)[2]

Category	Exports FOB							Imports CIF						
	1975	1976	1977	1979	1980	1981	1982	1975	1976	1977	1979	1980	1981	1982
III. Developing Countries (Continued)														
Non-Oil Developing Countries														
Morocco	~	21	30	29	86	36	56	~	36	38	48	55	14	2
Mozambique	~	4	10	17	72	37	99	~	~	~	~	~	1	14
Niger	~	~	1	~	2	2	1	~	~	~	~	~	~	~
Reunion	~	~	~	~	~	~	~	~	~	~	~	~	~	~
Senegal	~	6	4	10	4	3	7	~	1	~	~	~	~	~
Sierra Leone	~	~	~	~	2	1	1	~	~	~	~	~	~	~
Somalia	~	2	2	~	~	~	~	~	~	~	~	~	~	~
South Africa	~	33	27	53	103	132	103	~	38	122	170	227	104	85
Sudan	~	2	10	12	7	4	8	~	~	~	1	~	~	~
Tanzania	~	2	8	8	15	10	7	~	~	~	~	~	~	~
Togo	~	6	1	1	8	~	7	~	7	7	1	~	~	~
Tunisia	~	16	23	16	25	17	35	~	~	~	~	3	~	~
Uganda	~	~	~	~	~	~	~	~	~	~	~	~	~	~
Upper Volta	~	~	1	~	~	~	1	~	~	~	~	~	~	~
Zaire	~	5	5	90	106	78	147	~	3	1	37	58	25	15
Zambia	~	~	~	~	~	~	13	~	1	~	3	5	12	10
Zimbabwe	~	1	~	~	~	3	1	~	~	~	~	~	~	~
Asia	~	134	423	565	687	859	749	~	64	79	438	459	560	441
Bangladesh	~	3	7	~	6	5	1	~	5	~	~	10	6	2
Burma	~	~	~	~	~	~	~	~	~	~	16	26	20	2
China, People's Rep.	~	9	163	118	72	104	86	~	~	~	95	263	396	366
Fiji	~	~	1	3	3	~	2	~	~	~	~	~	~	~
Guam	~	~	~	1	~	~	~	~	~	~	~	~	~	~
Hong Kong	~	13	23	32	33	88	83	~	8	9	15	16	13	19
India	~	26	112	157	247	310	180	~	2	2	9	3	4	2
Korea	~	3	4	38	37	82	110	~	2	2	5	3	2	4
Malaysia	~	1	4	7	12	17	19	~	3	5	7	7	7	5
Pakistan	~	15	1	69	90	41	35	~	~	~	44	10	~	~
Papua New Guinea	~	~	~	~	3	2	5	~	~	~	~	~	~	~
Philippines	~	20	32	58	86	86	100	~	1	~	11	16	16	5
Singapore	~	34	50	59	50	69	72	~	42	54	134	92	60	39
Sri Lanka	~	~	7	2	26	~	1	~	~	~	~	~	~	~
Thailand	~	9	20	19	21	55	52	~	~	~	101	11	36	~
Europe	~	490	514	390	648	527	430	~	128	122	125	102	118	84
Cyprus	~	5	6	8	9	15	35	~	~	~	~	2	1	~
Greece	42	32	34	89	120	63	61	~	7	1	1	2	1	~
Hungary	~	106	76	78	114	160	138	~	7	4	19	10	11	11
Malta	~	1	5	2	9	6	11	~	~	~	~	~	~	~
Portugal	61	40	123	72	154	104	68	~	23	27	46	48	49	25
Romania	64	70	63	51	104	131	57	~	62	65	55	40	48	44
Turkey	~	48	41	8	24	48	23	~	~	~	1	1	6	2
Yugoslavia	60	188	167	82	115	~	38	~	36	25	2	2	2	1
Middle East	~	101	86	121	314	463	303	~	24	19	19	43	28	26
Bahrain	~	~	1	1	2	2	3	~	1	~	~	2	~	~
Egypt	54	46	35	42	159	258	154	~	14	3	1	1	1	~
Israel	~	10	13	24	28	59	55	16	9	15	18	40	27	26
Jordan	~	7	3	3	64	51	44	~	~	~	~	~	~	~
Lebanon	~	2	20	27	~	36	25	~	~	~	~	~	~	~
Syrian Arab Rep.	~	33	11	22	12	57	20	~	~	~	~	~	~	~
Yemen Arab Rep.	~	1	2	2	9	~	3	~	~	~	~	~	~	~
Middle East not specified	~	~	~	~	40	~	~	~	~	~	~	~	~	~

Table 2616 (Continued)

BRAZIL ABSOLUTE VALUE OF GOODS TRADED WITH SELECTED REGIONS AND COUNTRIES,[1] 1975-82 (M US)[2]

Category	Exports FOB							Imports CIF						
	1975	1976	1977	1979	1980	1981	1982	1975	1976	1977	1979	1980	1981	1982
IV. Latin America[3]	1,143	1,228	1,403	2,443	3,420	4,087	2,670	701	1,289	1,396	2,340	2,521	2,458	2,611
A. ARGENTINA	381	332	374	718	1,092	880	650	252	473	504	990	841	634	594
Bahamas	~	38	1	2	7	43	30	~	17	18	26	34	24	28
Barbados	~	2	3	4	7	7	5	~	~	1	1	2	2	3
Bermuda	~	~	~	~	~	~	~	~	1	1	1	2	2	3
B. BOLIVIA	122	101	144	127	180	255	80	17	16	21	89	47	27	30
D. CHILE	100	82	130	363	451	641	289	112	286	336	403	462	326	330
E. COLOMBIA	29	33	62	165	136	204	272	13	12	~	8	10	6	4
F. COSTA RICA	3	3	7	16	20	13	10	~	~	~	7	2	~	~
H. DOMINICAN REP.	7	21	23	10	17	23	17	2	~	~	~	~	11	~
I. ECUADOR	27	14	22	35	50	69	65	6	6	5	7	36	26	254
J. EL SALVADOR	3	6	5	7	3	2	2	~	~	~	~	7	~	~
Greenland	~	~	~	~	~	~	~	~	~	~	8	7	~	~
Grenada	~	~	1	1	1	1	1	~	~	~	~	~	~	2
Guadeloupe	~	~	~	~	~	~	~	~	~	~	~	~	~	~
K. GUATEMALA	4	5	8	14	12	15	10	2	2	2	3	3	4	~
Guiana, French	~	~	1	2	1	1	1	~	~	~	~	~	~	~
Guyana	~	~	~	~	7	~	~	~	~	~	3	3	~	~
L. HAITI	2	2	6	4	7	4	4	~	~	~	~	~	~	~
M. HONDURAS	7	4	8	18	16	13	5	1	~	~	~	1	1	2
Jamaica	~	7	9	1	2	16	18	~	~	~	~	~	6	~
Martinique	~	~	1	1	1	1	1	~	~	~	~	1	~	2
N. MEXICO	128	142	107	292	470	643	324	117	203	228	273	468	835	845
Netherlands Antilles	~	5	6	20	8	21	14	28	45	34	80	91	51	77
O. NICARAGUA	1	2	5	1	18	20	5	~	~	1	1	~	~	~
P. PANAMA	30	39	14	39	26	40	36	47	42	36	39	48	29	36
Panama Canal Zone	~	2	3	4	~	~	~	~	2	~	~	~	~	~
Q. PARAGUAY	118	132	185	324	409	450	324	~	28	33	72	99	213	170
R. PERU	93	80	56	44	130	285	222	67	64	69	107	130	63	75
Suriname	~	4	7	8	12	16	15	~	~	2	30	15	4	6
Trinidad and Tobago	~	5	6	11	24	39	30	~	~	2	~	22	10	~
S. URUGUAY	88	162	205	208	311	373	138	~	85	98	193	203	185	156
British West Indies	~	3	~	~	1	1	94	~	~	~	~	~	~	~
V. USSR, Eastern Europe, etc.	695	721	741	851	1,091	1,408	969	203	199	208	211	250	229	486
Albania	~	~	1	~	~	~	1	~	~	~	~	~	~	~
Bulgaria	23	32	42	18	15	7	21	2	2	2	1	6	6	10
Czechoslovakia	47	54	43	76	95	132	83	28	21	38	12	26	36	19
Eastern Germany	51	79	119	93	85	140	187	39	32	39	56	97	82	116
North Korea	~	~	~	3	2	~	~	~	~	~	~	~	~	~
Poland	135	155	239	434	523	507	168	91	124	120	100	84	89	127
USSR	397	400	288	226	370	621	509	25	22	9	42	37	22	213
USSR, etc., not specified	~	~	9	~	~	~	~	~	~	~	~	~	~	~
Country or area not specified	~	95	95	~	1	1	~	~	~	~	~	~	~	~
Special categories	~	~	~	143	259	355	261	~	~	~	~	~	~	~
EEC	~	3,103	3,963	4,594	5,466	5,933	5,426	~	2,758	2,573	3,591	3,844	3,265	2,651
VI. Percent Distribution														
Industrial Countries	~	65.7	64.7	61.9	57.3	53.6	59.7	~	58.2	53.4	48.9	46.6	41.8	38.6
Oil Exporting Countries	~	5.5	6.5	5.2	7.3	10.1	8.9	~	28.0	30.2	33.1	36.4	41.4	41.9
Non-Oil Developing Countries	~	20.7	21.8	26.1	28.6	28.4	24.8	~	12.4	14.8	16.9	15.8	17.2	17.2
Africa	~	1.4	1.8	3.0	3.4	2.9	4.2	~	1.4	2.6	2.1	3.4	2.7	2.2
Asia	~	1.3	3.5	3.7	3.4	3.7	3.7	~	.5	.6	2.2	1.8	2.3	2.1
Europe	~	4.9	4.2	2.6	3.2	2.3	2.1	~	.9	.6	.6	.4	.5	.4
Middle East	~	1.0	.7	.8	1.6	2.0	1.5	~	.2	.1	.1	.2	.1	.1
Western Hemisphere	~	12.2	11.5	16.0	17.0	17.5	13.2	~	9.4	10.5	11.8	10.1	10.2	12.4
USSR, Eastern Europe, etc.	~	7.1	6.1	5.6	5.4	6.0	4.8	~	1.4	1.6	1.1	1.0	1.0	2.3

Table 2616 (Continued)

BRAZIL ABSOLUTE VALUE OF GOODS TRADED WITH SELECTED REGIONS AND COUNTRIES,[1] 1975-82
(M US)[2]

Category	Exports FOB							Imports CIF						
	1975	1976	1977	1979	1980	1981	1982	1975	1976	1977	1979	1980	1981	1982
VII. Annual Percent Change														
World	?	16.5	20.3	20.5	32.0	15.9	-13.5	?	1.2	-3.7	31.6	26.0	-3.5	-12.5
Industrial Countries	?	27.2	18.5	14.3	22.3	8.4	-3.7	?	-12.4	-11.5	14.7	20.0	-13.5	-19.2
Oil Exporting Countries	?	-16.1	42.1	-11.7	82.6	60.9	-23.6	?	25.5	4.0	49.3	38.7	9.6	-11.4
Non-Oil Developing Countries	?	2.7	26.6	46.0	44.3	15.2	-24.5	?	43.2	15.2	66.0	19.2	-4.3	-5.1
Africa	?	-2.7	60.8	100.2	46.4	1.1	23.5	?	-19.6	74.9	36.2	104.5	-24.2	-29.6
Asia	?	-28.9	215.9	20.7	21.5	25.0	-12.8	?	-9.1	24.9	322.8	4.9	21.9	-21.2
Europe	?	66.9	4.9	6.0	66.3	-18.6	-18.5	?	55.0	-4.7	93.9	-18.8	15.5	-28.8
Middle East	?	-34.7	-14.6	30.7	159.3	47.6	-34.5	?	-40.5	-22.7	5.1	125.5	-34.8	-4.5
Western Hemisphere	?	-2.4	14.3	55.8	40.0	19.5	-34.7	?	71.8	8.3	54.1	7.8	-2.5	6.2
USSR, Eastern Europe, etc.	?	10.4	2.9	41.7	28.3	29.0	-31.2	?	8.3	4.0	4.9	18.5	-8.1	112.2

1. DOT data may differ between countries and from IFS data because of the time it takes for an export to become an import, etc.
2. Data may be calculated from partner's reported data or estimated on basis of less than 12 months.
3. No trade with Cuba; Venezuela is included in category III.

SOURCE: Adapted from the IMF-DOT Annual, 1970–74; IMF-DOT-Y, 1982; IMF-DOT-Y, 1983.

Table 2617

CHILE ABSOLUTE VALUE OF GOODS TRADED WITH SELECTED REGIONS AND COUNTRIES,[1] 1975-82 (M US)[2]

Category	Exports FOB 1975	1976	1977	1979	1980	1981	1982	Imports CIF 1975	1976	1977	1979	1980	1981	1982
World	1,660.8	2,094.8	2,189.2	3,885.3	4,687.5	3,949.3	3,835.6	1,534.5	1,683.7	2,259.5	4,217.6	5,123.7	6,363.8	3,536.1
I. Industrial Countries	1,136.5	1,309.8	1,335.6	2,393.1	2,959.4	2,530.0	2,688.5	929.3	903.0	1,205.9	2,285.9	3,079.8	3,860.0	2,015.5
United States	147.0	211.7	270.3	413.9	588.9	591.9	798.8	446.8	400.0	463.2	954.3	1,464.3	1,631.9	916.1
Canada	20.0	28.9	23.4	28.0	78.8	140.7	59.2	36.1	15.7	38.9	78.5	76.6	94.3	55.5
Japan	186.6	223.7	263.7	415.8	506.6	426.7	440.8	78.0	187.6	249.2	318.6	370.3	673.0	229.6
Belgium	56.2	64.7	63.6	138.4	147.3	85.4	100.9	20.1	7.8	13.3	35.3	35.2	47.6	36.7
Denmark	1.6	2.7	1.6	1.7	3.1	~	.5	10.6	4.6	6.7	11.5	16.0	32.7	27.3
France	70.3	70.2	62.1	120.9	215.2	191.5	152.6	34.6	30.1	36.0	172.8	195.6	219.4	124.6
Germany	239.2	310.2	298.9	596.9	612.9	453.5	432.4	127.6	96.3	183.7	269.5	308.7	354.5	214.3
Ireland	~	~	~	4.8	~	.7	2.6	.4	.2	.2	5.3	5.1	10.6	6.6
Italy	80.2	106.6	94.9	206.2	249.9	212.7	174.8	25.2	15.6	30.3	96.7	103.8	146.6	73.1
Netherlands	90.7	46.4	63.6	106.4	142.4	120.8	153.4	33.1	18.1	18.2	38.7	72.2	84.3	36.0
Spain	67.7	76.6	64.6	79.8	92.4	83.4	85.5	30.0	35.4	68.9	114.8	143.6	213.2	149.8
Sweden	34.4	22.4	16.1	32.2	50.3	50.9	40.5	13.1	13.0	14.0	31.4	28.6	36.3	26.1
Switzerland	1.2	4.4	4.2	3.8	23.5	5.8	41.4	6.1	27.0	28.9	36.2	118.1	144.6	43.7
United Kingdom	137.2	141.1	108.6	244.3	248.1	165.5	205.1	48.5	51.6	54.4	122.3	141.7	171.0	76.1
III. Developing Countries	32.0	46.2	92.3	124.7	186.1	182.9	97.3	200.2	134.1	310.2	535.6	268.2	484.1	272.0
Oil Exporting Countries	.2	3.3	19.8	3.3	10.3	31.7	5.5	63.0	49.6	161.5	325.1	11.1	~	5.5
Iran, I.R. of	~	~	~	~	~	~	~	~	~	~	~	~	~	~
Iraq	~	~	3.2	10.7	7.9	5.1	6.6	~	~	13.0	~	~	~	~
Kuwait	~	~	1.3	~	~	~	~	~	~	~	~	~	~	~
Libya	7.6	~	1.2	~	~	~	~	~	~	~	~	~	~	~
Qatar	~	.5	~	~	~	~	~	90.7	~	~	56.4	~	~	~
Saudi Arabia	~	~	4.1	27.4	30.2	23.5	28.4	.1	~	~	~	~	~	~
United Arab Emirates	~	~	11.3	12.1	59.3	50.6	18.9	45.7	84.5	135.7	154.1	257.1	359.5	260.4
T. VENEZUELA	23.9	42.4	51.4	71.2	78.4	72.0	43.4	~	503.3	719.5	1,217.7	1,584.8	1,653.7	772.3
Non-Oil Developing Countries	~	653.2	667.1	1,120.8	1,402.8	1,080.8	948.6	~	9.9	19.9	185.9	305.6	176.7	20.4
Africa	~	1.7	3.9	8.7	21.5	55.4	27.0	~	9.8	12.6	20.0	29.0	57.0	20.4
Gabon	~	~	~	~	~	~	~	~	~	~	~	~	~	~
South Africa	~	1.5	3.5	2.1	6.6	6.8	6.8	9.2	.1	.6	14.6	29.0	57.0	20.4
Africa not specified	~	.2	.4	6.6	14.9	48.6	27.0	~	.1	4.7	3.2	~	~	~
Asia	5.0	57.0	59.0	181.8	208.5	143.5	168.4	9.2	9.2	54.3	97.9	120.5	158.4	144.1
China, People's Rep.	~	32.5	19.4	96.6	105.3	60.7	61.9	1.6	1.6	10.1	26.3	21.1	35.0	21.7
Hong Kong	~	17.1	29.9	64.6	15.4	25.7	7.5	.9	.9	12.0	25.7	29.8	4.7	27.3
Korea	5.0	~	~	64.6	69.5	60.5	55.5	2.6	2.6	11.0	34.5	30.0	40.5	51.2
Malaysia	~	4.2	4.1	3.0	4.4	~	~	.2	.2	.6	5.0	11.4	9.2	~
Philippines	~	.3	~	~	~	~	~	~	.2	~	~	~	~	~
Singapore	~	1.4	~	~	~	~	~	~	1.4	4.7	~	~	~	~
Sri Lanka	~	1.3	~	~	~	~	~	~	1.3	3.2	~	~	~	~
Thailand	~	.3	2.4	15.0	13.0	17.5	35.8	~	.3	3.8	~	16.0	63.7	36.7
Asia not specified	~	.2	.3	.3	.9	2.7	7.7	~	.9	3.9	25.7	14.4	14.5	7.2
Oceania not specified	75.4	51.1	49.1	112.5	80.2	52.0	~	13.2	12.1	34.5	28.6	28.9	48.0	38.8
Europe	~	~	~	~	~	~	~	~	~	~	~	~	~	~
Cyprus	~	~	~	~	~	~	~	~	~	~	~	~	~	~
Greece	6.2	1.1	7.5	20.2	20.8	15.1	~	7.6	~	~	~	~	~	~
Portugal	~	13.7	13.7	5.8	17.4	6.3	~	~	~	~	~	~	~	~
Romania	4.5	1.3	~	31.2	27.6	15.8	~	~	.4	~	~	~	~	~
Yugoslavia	12.1	1.2	50.0	27.9	39.4	14.4	14.8	~	5.6	12.1	~	28.9	48.0	38.8
Europe not specified	~	66.7	~	~	15.9	26.1	~	~	.5	.7	~	~	~	~
Middle East	~	1.0	1.0	~	~	8.9	7.8	~	.5	~	~	~	~	~
Egypt	1.0	1.0	~	~	~	~	~	.5	.7	~	~	~	~	~
Israel	~	1.0	1.0	~	~	8.9	~	~	~	~	~	~	~	~
Middle East not specified	~	~	~	~	~	~	18.3	~	~	~	~	~	~	~

Table 2617 (Continued)

CHILE ABSOLUTE VALUE OF GOODS TRADED WITH SELECTED REGIONS AND COUNTRIES,[1] 1975-82 (M US)[2]

Category	Exports FOB 1975	1976	1977	1979	1980	1981	1982	Imports CIF 1975	1976	1977	1979	1980	1981	1982
IV. Latin America[3]	369.6	518.0	552.1	881.2	1,060.3	792.8	675.1	391.4	470.5	632.5	933.9	1,129.8	1,270.6	569.0
A. ARGENTINA	166.4	125.3	143.9	275.6	280.6	191.3	150.5	107.9	218.8	275.6	161.1	157.4	141.7	151.9
Barbados	~	~	~	~	~	~	~	~	~	~	~	~	~	~
B. BOLIVIA	13.4	20.7	20.5	19.8	26.4	23.8	11.2	10.9	14.1	10.8	28.4	26.3	9.0	9.0
C. BRAZIL	98.0	252.5	283.1	383.7	448.6	288.2	308.2	82.2	65.8	109.7	361.8	394.8	570.5	258.4
E. COLOMBIA	25.0	29.6	34.5	61.9	76.8	70.9	46.3	9.9	12.5	14.6	36.8	17.8	25.6	11.2
F. COSTA RICA	.7	.6	~	~	~	~	~	.1	~	~	~	~	~	~
H. DOMINICAN REP.	~	~	~	11.0	12.8	3.1	4.5	~	~	~	~	~	~	~
I. ECUADOR	19.1	20.8	24.9	28.8	21.6	14.2	51.3	91.3	90.7	107.2	173.5	210.2	99.5	32.8
J. EL SALVADOR	1.6	.4	6.4	44.1	~	~	~	~	~	~	~	~	~	~
N. MEXICO	10.0	15.7	~	~	67.9	86.8	22.3	23.2	21.7	42.8	55.7	28.2	42.6	11.0
Netherlands Antilles	~	~	~	~	~	~	~	~	~	~	22.8	81.0	152.0	~
P. PANAMA	1.0	.1	~	10.1	10.8	11.1	6.8	2.5	~	~	13.1	91.7	108.8	21.1
Q. PARAGUAY	1.4	2.0	3.3	5.1	7.7	7.2	7.5	1.9	10.8	21.4	15.2	7.3	11.9	14.0
R. PERU	25.0	29.0	12.3	19.8	70.7	70.3	49.0	4.6	17.4	35.8	52.6	40.6	66.9	33.4
S. URUGUAY	7.3	9.7	11.5	17.2	29.6	16.1	13.1	4.7	6.4	2.9	12.9	21.6	33.0	21.2
America not specified	~	4.3	6.1	4.1	6.8	9.8	4.4	~	11.3	10.5	~	52.9	9.1	5.0
Other Latin America not specified	~	7.2	5.6	~	~	~	~	~	1.0	1.2	~	~	~	~
V. USSR, Eastern Europe, etc.	3.8	42.8	38.2	17.5	20.8	23.3	21.4	9.3	5.2	3.3	~	2.3	7.5	7.2
Bulgaria	3.8	1.7	~	~	4.1	4.7	~	.2	~	~	~	~	~	~
Eastern Germany	~	~	2.9	6.1	14.7	18.6	18.4	~	~	~	~	~	~	~
North Korea	~	~	~	~	~	~	~	~	~	~	~	~	~	~
USSR, etc., not specified	~	41.1	35.3	11.4	2.0	~	3.0	~	5.2	3.3	~	~	~	7.2
Country or area not specified	~	29.0	25.5	171.6	90.1	72.8	60.8	~	133.8	.3	116.4	144.3	273.7	421.7
EEC	~	748.3	693.3	1,427.1	1,639.1	1,251.4	1,237.4	~	231.9	342.8	752.1	878.3	1,066.7	594.7
VI. Percent Distribution														
Industrial Countries	~	62.5	61.0	61.6	63.1	64.1	70.1	~	53.6	53.4	54.2	60.1	60.7	57.0
Oil Exporting Countries	~	2.2	4.2	3.2	4.0	4.6	2.5	~	8.0	13.7	12.7	5.2	7.6	7.7
Non-Oil Developing Countries	~	31.2	30.5	28.8	29.9	27.4	24.7	~	29.9	31.8	28.9	30.9	26.0	21.8
Africa	~	.1	.2	.5	.5	1.4	.7	~	.6	.9	~	6.0	2.8	.6
Asia	~	2.7	2.7	4.7	4.4	3.6	4.4	~	.5	2.4	2.3	2.4	2.5	4.1
Europe	~	3.6	2.3	1.3	2.4	2.0	1.4	~	.8	.5	~	.6	.8	1.1
Middle East	~	~	~	.2	.6	.2	.7	~	~	~	~	~	~	~
Western Hemisphere	~	24.7	25.2	22.7	22.6	20.1	17.6	~	27.9	28.0	22.1	22.1	20.0	16.1
USSR, Eastern Europe, etc.	~	2.0	1.7	.5	.4	.6	.6	~	.3	.1	~	~	.1	.2
VII. Annual Percentage Change														
World	~	26.1	4.5	58.3	20.6	-15.7	-2.9	~	9.7	34.2	40.5	21.5	24.2	-44.4
Industrial Countries	~	15.3	2.0	57.9	23.7	-14.5	6.3	~	-2.8	33.5	32.6	34.7	25.3	-47.8
Oil Exporting Countries	~	44.4	99.8	26.6	49.2	-1.7	-46.8	~	-33.0	131.3	72.9	-49.9	80.5	-43.8
Non-Oil Developing Countries	~	42.2	2.1	70.4	25.2	-23.0	-12.2	~	27.4	43.0	42.5	30.1	4.3	-53.3
Africa	~	-73.1	125.4	117.5	147.1	157.7	-51.3	~	746.2	491.0	145.6	64.4	-42.2	-88.5
Asia	~	165.9	3.5	156.1	14.7	-31.2	17.4	~	24.3	490.2	93.5	23.1	31.5	-9.0
Europe	~	55.6	-32.2	172.6	129.1	-28.7	-35.2	~	188.8	-8.3	~	64.4	66.1	-19.2
Middle East	~	-92.4	~	~	~	~	193.3	~	~	~	~	~	~	~
Western Hemisphere	~	40.1	6.6	56.0	20.3	-25.2	-14.8	~	23.2	40.0	28.3	21.0	12.5	-55.2
USSR, Eastern Europe, etc.	~	~	-10.7	37.8	18.9	12.0	-8.2	~	-41.3	-36.5	~	~	226.1	-4.0

1. DOT data may differ between countries and from IFS data because of the time it takes for an export to become an import, etc.
2. Data may be calculated from partner's reported data or estimated on basis of less than 12 months.
3. No trade with Cuba; Venezuela is included in category III.

SOURCE: IMF-DOT Annual, 1970-74; IMF-DOT-Y, 1982; IMF-DOT-Y, 1983.

Table 2618

COLOMBIA ABSOLUTE VALUE OF GOODS TRADED WITH SELECTED REGIONS AND COUNTRIES,[1] 1975-82
(M US)[2]

Category	Exports FOB							Imports CIF						
	1975	1976	1977	1979	1980	1981	1982	1975	1976	1977	1979	1980	1981	1982
I. World	1,470.2	1,745.1	2,432.7	3,325.4	3,945.0	2,956.4	2,991.9	1,494.8	1,708.1	2,027.8	3,233.1	4,662.6	5,199.1	5,350.2
II. Industrial Countries	1,101.2	1,320.2	1,870.6	2,521.7	2,978.0	2,073.8	2,358.7	1,274.4	1,420.0	1,546.0	2,438.1	3,511.5	3,676.4	4,041.1
United States	471.2	545.2	699.4	982.8	1,069.3	692.8	802.6*	644.8	725.1	713.4	1,278.8	1,839.8	1,787.4	2,093.2*
Canada	13.9	23.5	23.7	54.0	58.3	30.7	74.5*	42.9	50.7	65.4	74.2	109.5	179.8	199.6*
Australia	.5	.9	1.4	1.0	1.1	1.1	2.3*	4.7	1.6	.9	1.1	1.6	1.7	1.0*
Japan	27.1	61.6	82.8	92.2	147.6	126.5	129.6*	128.8	131.7	211.7	295.5	434.1	497.7	653.9*
New Zealand	.2	?	?	.6	.1	.2	.1[a]	?	?	?	.3	?	.2	.4*
Austria	.2	.5	.4	.6	3.2	2.3	25.7*	3.6	3.2	5.3	4.9	10.9	15.5	12.0*
Belgium	25.0	22.7	38.3	48.9	39.3	26.4	32.1*	12.5	13.6	17.5	23.4	26.2	40.3	35.9*
Denmark	12.6	12.1	25.5	27.9	35.4	26.6	30.8*	5.5	7.7	12.3	11.5	51.5	20.5	10.2*
Finland	29.0	41.0	79.2	79.5	79.9	57.8	62.0*	4.4	7.2	6.6	14.0	18.4	18.8	18.3*
France	32.0	48.1	59.6	87.9	91.5	54.9	67.2*	67.2	69.8	74.7	112.8	131.3	162.9	126.9*
Germany	217.9	282.7	490.5	583.6	741.0	582.5	553.3*	131.3	174.8	159.9	201.4	334.0	328.3	291.1*
Iceland	.6	.4	?	.1	.5	.2	.3*	.3	.1	.7	.2	.5	.2	.3*
Ireland	?	.8	.7	1.1	1.6	4.4	4.2[a]	.3	.3	.7	.8	1.5	2.4	4.5[a]
Italy	38.7	17.7	17.1	48.3	63.6	64.0	190.4*	37.8	38.0	51.2	80.8	120.9	129.5	140.4*
Netherlands	93.5	104.4	116.8	196.5	271.9	146.5	107.6*	23.7	27.2	25.1	28.7	29.4	29.2	30.9*
Norway	5.7	7.6	17.5	31.8	40.4	27.5	24.0*	.6	.7	1.1	1.1	13.1	24.9	14.6*
Spain	38.6	35.7	75.5	111.8	150.6	84.4	79.5*	50.3	47.0	63.5	105.9	143.9	136.4	155.3*
Sweden	46.4	72.7	88.1	134.1	118.2	85.7	89.1*	26.1	26.0	21.3	35.5	54.2	61.9	90.0*
Switzerland	7.1	9.5	9.1	14.5	23.1	9.8	29.1*	40.3	34.4	40.0	62.2	78.8	93.2	65.6*
United Kingdom	41.4	34.1	44.9	24.9	42.1	49.3	54.5*	53.0	60.8	73.9	104.9	111.9	145.8	96.7*
III. Developing Countries														
Oil Exporting Countries														
Algeria	91.7	127.2	221.3	383.7	332.1	370.8	352.2	18.9	33.6	94.1	107.4	197.2	409.7	348.8
Indonesia	.9	1.8	1.4	34.1	52.1	27.6	26.2[b]	?	?	?	?	?	?	?
Iran, I.R. of	.1	.1	.2	?	.5	?	?	?	?	.2	?	?	?	?
Iraq	.1	2.4	.2	?	?	?	?	.4	?	1.7	?	?	?	?
Kuwait	?	?	?	.1	.1	.1	.1[b]	?	?	?	?	?	?	?
Libya	1.0	.4	.3	1.3	.1	1.5	1.4[b]	?	?	?	?	?	?	?
Nigeria	.1	.2	?	.2	.1	.3	.3[b]	?	?	?	?	?	?	?
Qatar	?	?	?	?	?	?	?	?	?	?	?	?	?	?
Saudi Arabia	?	?	?	?	.1	?	?	?	?	?	?	?	?	?
United Arab Emirates	?	?	?	?	.1	?	?	?	?	?	.1	.1	?	.6[a]
T. VENEZUELA	89.6	122.3	219.2	347.9	279.2	341.2	324.2[b]	18.5	33.6	92.3	107.3	197.0	409.6	348.2[b]
Non-Oil Developing Countries	?	207.7	258.6	341.7	509.1	433.4	214.8	?	228.6	355.2	632.0	858.4	1,022.1	882.3
Africa	?	3.1	11.5	10.3	6.0	2.5	4.3	?	2.0	7.2	10.9	15.6	9.9	6.2
Cameroon	?	.1	?	?	.1	?	?	?	?	?	?	.1	?	?
Ethiopia	?	?	?	?	?	?	?	?	?	?	?	?	?	?
Gambia, The	?	?	?	?	?	?	?	?	.1	?	.1	?	?	?
Ghana	?	.1	.4	?	?	?	?	?	?	?	?	?	?	.1[b]
Guinea	?	?	?	?	?	?	?	?	?	?	?	?	?	?
Ivory Coast	?	.2	.2	?	.1	?	?	?	?	?	?	?	?	?
Liberia	?	?	?	?	?	?	?	?	.1	.1	.1	?	?	?
Madagascar	?	?	?	?	?	?	?	?	?	?	?	?	?	?
Mauritius	?	?	2.2	?	?	?	?	?	?	?	?	?	.5	?
Morocco	?	2.3	2.8	6.4	3.8	1.8	2.0[a]	?	?	?	?	.1	?	?
Mozambique	?	?	?	?	.7	?	?	?	?	?	?	?	?	?
Senegal	?	?	?	1.7	.5	.5	2.2[a]	?	?	?	?	?	?	?
South Africa	?	.3	?	.1	.1	.1	?	1.8	6.5	10.8	15.4	9.3	5.8[a]	
Sudan	?	?	?	.1	.3	.1	?	?	?	?	?	?	?	?
Tunisia	?	?	.2	2.0	?	?	?	?	?	?	?	?	?	?
Uganda	?	?	?	?	?	?	?	?	?	?	?	?	?	?
Zaire	?	.1	.1	?	?	.1	?	?	?	?	?	?	?	?
Zambia	?	?	?	?	?	?	?	?	?	?	?	.1	?	?
Zimbabwe	?	?	?	?	?	?	.1[b]	?	?	?	?	?	?	.3[a]
Spanish Africa	?	?	?	?	?	?	?	?	?	?	?	?	?	?

Table 2618 (Continued)

COLOMBIA ABSOLUTE VALUE OF GOODS TRADED WITH SELECTED REGIONS AND COUNTRIES,[1] 1975-82
(M US)[2]

Category	Exports FOB							Imports CIF						
	1975	1976	1977	1979	1980	1981	1982	1975	1976	1977	1979	1980	1981	1982
III. Developing Countries (Continued)														
Non-Oil Developing Countries														
Asia														
Bangladesh	~	4.0	2.4	9.4	12.6	7.4	9.0	~	11.1	28.7	26.8	27.9	33.1	46.7
China, People's Rep.	~	2.2	.2	3.7	.9	~	.2*	~	.2	.5	.3	~	.6	2.1*
French Polynesia	~	~	.2	~	5.2	.1	3.8*	~	~	.3	.3	.3	~	.1b
Hong Kong	~	.4	.8	.6	.7	1.9	.6*	~	1.2	1.6	3.4	3.7	4.9	9.4*
India	~	.6	.7	2.6	3.6	1.6	2.3a	~	.3	.6	.3	.4	.1	.1b
Korea	~	.1	~	.1	~	~	.2a	~	.3	6.0	2.9	7.1	9.6	16.0a
Malaysia	~	~	~	~	~	~	~	~	.6	6.6	2.1	2.6	1.5	2.9a
Pakistan	~	~	~	~	~	~	~	~	.1	~	3.6	.2	.1	.1*
Papua New Guinea	~	.2	.2	.7	.6	.7	.1*	~	~	.1	~	.2	.3	~
Philippines	~	.2	.4	1.6	1.1	.2	1.0*	~	.2	.1	.2	.2	.3	~
Singapore	~	.4	1.5	.2	.3	1.0	1.0*	~	.4	1.5	.2	.3	1.0	1.0*
Sri Lanka	~	.1	4.7	1.6	1.1	.2	1.6*	~	8.1	4.7	13.8	13.2	14.7	13.9*
Thailand	~	.2	.3	.1	.1	2.8	.2a	~	.4	.2	.8	.2	.2	1.1*
Asia not specified	~	~	7.0	~	~	~	~	~	~	7.0	~	~	~	.1b
Oceania not specified	~	~	~	~	.3	~	.1	~	~	~	~	~	~	.1b
Europe														
Gibraltar	~	7.9	19.0	45.1	66.9	56.9	13.8	~	5.5	12.4	18.0	53.4	21.4	19.1
Greece	~	~	1.8	1.5	9.1	1.9	.1*	~	.2	.2	.3	1.0	.3	.1b
Hungary	~	1.5	1.5	5.7	9.9	26.3	.2a	~	~	.1	.3	1.0	.1	.1*
Malta	~	.2	.2	~	~	~	.1*	~	.8	1.5	.7	.7	.8	.1*
Portugal	2.7	.2	1.2	11.0	13.9	9.2	5.2a	~	.9	.3	.6	1.2	.9	.1a
Romania	2.7	.3	1.2	8.5	13.5	8.0	6.8b	~	.9	4.6	.6	1.2	.9	.8b
Turkey	~	.3	10.4	8.5	13.5	8.0	6.8b	~	2.0	.3	8.2	39.9	9.9	8.4b
Yugoslavia	2.7	5.5	4.0	18.3	19.8	10.3	1.6a	2.8	1.4	.3	8.1	10.5	1.4	6.2a
Middle East														
Egypt	~	1.4	2.1	6.4	10.1	5.8	5.3	~	1.4	5.5	8.1	10.5	8.2	3.4a
Israel	.7	1.4	1.4	2.4	6.8	3.4	3.9*	.2	.2	1.0	1.0	5.0	8.0	14.6
Jordon	.7	~	~	.1	.7	.1	.1b	.2	.1	~	.4	.1	~	~
Lebanon	~	~	~	.1	~	~	.2b	~	~	~	~	~	~	~
Syrian Arab Rep.	~	~	.7	3.8	2.5	1.3	1.1b	~	.1	1.0	.6	4.9	8.0	14.6*
IV. Latin America[3]														
A. ARGENTINA	210.4	191.2	223.7	270.6	413.5	360.9	182.4	158.2	209.8	305.8	575.2	756.6	949.7	795.7
Antigua and Barbuda	27.8	17.1	40.9	46.5	68.7	51.4	22.8a	18.6	22.1	51.4	42.2	42.8	47.8	73.7a
Bahamas	~	15.6	10.7	.1	.4	.5	.5b	~	~	~	.2	.1	.1	.1b
Barbados	~	.4	.4	.3	.6	.4	.4a	~	~	.2	.2	3.2	8.9	7.5b
Belize	~	.2	.6	.5	.3	.5	.4b	~	.1	~	.1	.1	.1	~
Bermuda	~	~	~	~	~	~	~	~	~	.2	.2	.1	.1	~
B. BOLIVIA	6.5	3.2	2.9	2.3	2.2	3.8	3.2b	~	1.1	~	13.6	48.8	29.1	24.7b
C. BRAZIL	8.6	8.4	4.0	6.1	9.0	4.5	4.0*	1.1	2.2	3.5	5.7	7.4	12.0	10.2b
D. CHILE	23.9	10.7	12.0	29.3	64.3	28.3	10.2*	22.3	26.9	52.0	177.7	127.1	176.1	299.1*
F. COSTA RICA	5.6	3.7	5.6	5.6	5.5	4.6	3.0a	29.1	34.5	35.0	59.6	82.5	84.9	50.9*
Dominica	~	~	~	~	.1	.1	.1b	.5	.2	.6	.7	1.0	2.2	2.7a
H. DOMINICAN REP.	20.9	11.5	4.8	4.9	6.0	5.8	3.9*	.2	.2	.6	.1	.1	.1	~
I. ECUADOR	36.1	39.1	48.0	53.8	77.3	66.3	14.2a	.2	.2	.6	.6	1.2	2.1	2.6*
J. EL SALVADOR	3.8	3.2	3.1	3.3	1.2	1.7	1.4b	21.4	42.8	57.7	63.9	77.5	83.4	32.3b
Grenada	~	~	~	~	~	~	.6b	~	2.2	.2	.1	.2	.4	.3b
K. GUATEMALA	10.7	1.0	.8	.6	1.7	.7	.6b	~	.1	~	.1	.9	.7	.6b
Guiana, French	~	3.2	4.5	10.8	5.9	4.5	3.8b	~	.1	~	~	1.2	1.0	.8b
Guyana	~	.3	~	.1	.2	.4	.1b	.2	~	~	~	~	~	~
L. HAITI	1.3	2.0	1.2	1.0	1.4	1.1	.9b	.4	.3	1.4	1.0	1.4	1.2	1.1b
M. HONDURAS	1.1	2.7	3.2	4.0	5.8	5.2	4.4b	~	.6	~	~	.1	1.0	.9b
Jamaica	~	.5	.4	4.3	1.3	.4	.4b	~	~	~	~	~	~	~
Leeward Islands	~	.4	~	.6	.3	.1	.1b	~	~	~	~	~	~	~
Martinique	~	1.5	1.6	.3	.6	.3	.2b	~	~	~	~	~	~	~

Table 2618 (Continued)

COLOMBIA ABSOLUTE VALUE OF GOODS TRADED WITH SELECTED REGIONS AND COUNTRIES,[1] 1975-82
(M US)[2]

Category	Exports FOB 1975	1976	1977	1979	1980	1981	1982	Imports CIF 1975	1976	1977	1979	1980	1981	1982
IV. Latin America[3] (Continued)														
N. MEXICO	5.8	6.5	8.9	10.9	19.9	21.0	8.4[a]	28.1	28.7	34.2	51.1	61.7	67.9	40.2[a]
Montserrat	~	~	~	~	~	~	~	~	~	~	~	~	.1	~
Netherlands Antilles	~	12.2	13.0	26.4	33.5	28.0	26.6[b]	~	7.0	34.8	38.3	132.1	143.3	121.8[b]
O. NICARAGUA	2.3	1.9	2.3	.7	3.8	2.3	1.9[b]	.1	.1	.2	.1	~	~	~
P. PANAMA	21.4	20.3	20.2	36.0	59.2	61.3	6.5[a]	14.9	21.6	9.3	36.8	65.4	169.5	4.1[*]
Panama Canal Zone	~	.1	.1	.3	.6	.7	.4[*]	~	.2	.9	.5	.4	10.6	.2[*]
Q. PARAGUAY	.3	.1	.4	.3	.8	.9	.7[b]	.2	.6	~	~	~	~	~
R. PERU	33.7	19.8	28.5	13.7	29.2	45.4	38.6[b]	18.0	13.5	16.6	80.4	97.0	102.6	87.2[b]
St. Lucia	~	~	~	.2	.8	.1	~	~	~	~	~	~	~	~
St. Pierre-Miquelon	~	~	~	~	~	~	~	~	~	~	~	~	~	~
St. Vincent	~	~	~	.2	.4	.2	.2[b]	~	~	~	~	~	.1	.1[b]
Suriname	~	.6	1.5	.8	1.6	1.5	1.3[b]	~	~	~	~	~	~	~
Trinidad and Tobago	~	3.8	3.5	6.5	10.1	16.7	22.3[a]	~	.5	1.2	.4	.4	.5	30.9[a]
S. URUGUAY	.6	.7	.4	.6	.9	2.1	.5[*]	3.1	4.5	5.7	1.8	4.0	4.0	3.4[*]
Windward Islands	~	~	~	~	~	~	~	~	~	~	~	~	~	~
British West Indies	~	.1	.3	.1	.5	.2	.2[b]	~	~	~	.3	.2	.2	.2[b]
V. USSR, Eastern Europe, etc.	31.2	88.4	82.3	77.7	125.5	76.8	65.3	13.3	21.9	31.6	41.7	78.0	72.4	61.5
Bulgaria	.5	19.0	3.4	5.4	4.6	.7	.6[b]	.1	.3	.4	.4	2.0	2.9	2.5[b]
G. CUBA	2.3	4.7	9.5	2.0	5.6	3.5	2.9[b]	~	~	~	.8	.8	.7	.6[b]
Czechoslovakia	7.5	23.2	39.5	5.8	3.3	9.2	7.9[b]	3.3	4.1	6.1	5.5	7.9	8.3	7.0[b]
Eastern Germany	~	~	~	16.6	40.6	26.1	22.2[b]	3.9	8.6	9.3	15.3	33.7	32.7	27.8[b]
North Korea	~	~	~	~	~	~	~	~	~	1.7	.7	.7	.7	~
Poland	14.3	31.2	29.6	40.9	51.3	22.0	18.7[b]	3.9	5.6	11.1	11.4	17.9	18.1	15.4[b]
USSR	.1	10.3	.2	7.0	20.2	15.2	13.0[b]	1.3	3.2	2.9	7.7	15.0	9.4	8.0[b]
Country or area not specified	~	~	~	~	~	~	~	~	.1	.9	1.4	.4	.7	.7
Special categories	~	~	~	~	~	.8	.7[b]	~	~	~	1.4	~	.5	.4[b]
EEC	~	522.1	795.3	1,020.7	1,286.8	956.6	1,040.2	~	392.2	415.4	564.4	807.7	858.9	736.5
VI. Percent Distribution														
Industrial Countries	~	75.7	76.9	75.8	75.5	70.1	78.8	~	83.1	76.2	75.4	75.3	70.7	75.5
Oil Exporting Countries	~	7.3	9.1	11.5	8.4	12.5	11.8	~	2.0	4.6	3.3	4.2	7.9	6.5
Non-Oil Developing Countries	~	11.9	10.6	10.3	12.9	14.7	7.2	~	13.4	17.5	19.5	18.4	19.7	16.5
Africa	~	.2	.5	.3	.2	.1	.1	~	~	.4	.3	.3	.2	.1
Asia	~	.1	.1	.1	.2	.2	.3	~	.6	1.4	.8	.6	.6	.9
Europe	~	.5	.8	1.4	1.7	1.9	.5	~	.3	.6	.6	1.1	.4	.4
Middle East	~	.1	.1	.2	.3	.2	.2	~	~	~	~	.1	.2	.3
Western Hemisphere	~	11.0	9.2	8.1	10.5	12.2	6.1	~	12.3	15.1	17.8	16.2	18.3	14.9
USSR, Eastern Europe, etc.	~	5.1	3.4	2.3	3.2	2.6	2.2	~	1.3	1.6	1.3	1.7	1.4	1.1
VII. Annual Percent Change														
World	~	18.7	39.4	9.4	18.6	-25.1	1.2	~	14.3	18.7	14.0	44.2	11.5	2.9
Industrial Countries	~	19.9	41.7	3.2	18.1	-30.4	13.7	~	11.4	8.9	13.5	44.0	4.7	9.9
Oil Exporting Countries	~	38.8	74.0	34.6	-13.5	11.7	-5.0	~	77.5	180.3	-1.9	83.5	107.7	-14.9
Non-Oil Developing Countries	~	17.3	24.5	50.5	49.0	-14.9	-50.4	~	22.3	55.4	17.1	35.8	19.1	-13.7
Africa	~	-31.0	268.2	87.6	-41.6	-57.9	71.4	~	-46.4	268.9	148.6	42.8	-36.6	-37.1
Asia	~	73.6	-39.4	167.0	34.4	-41.7	22.3	~	79.6	158.6	28.7	4.1	18.6	41.0
Europe	~	-43.2	140.2	53.7	48.3	-15.0	-75.8	~	-35.4	126.7	-11.5	196.5	-60.0	-10.8
Middle East	~	98.6	44.1	30.4	57.6	-42.6	-8.1	~	-40.6	431.6	-49.5	386.3	61.5	82.8
Western Hemisphere	~	-16.7	17.0	47.2	52.8	-12.7	-49.5	~	24.7	45.8	16.9	31.5	25.5	-16.2
USSR, Eastern Eruope, etc.	~	258.3	-6.9	-6.6	61.5	-38.8	-15.0	~	73.8	44.2	46.8	87.0	-7.2	-15.0

1. DOT data may differ between countries and from IFS data because of the time it takes for an export to become an import, etc.
2. Data may be calculated from partner's reported data or estimated on basis of less than 12 months.
3. Cuba is included in category V; Venezuela is included in category III.

a. Five or fewer months of reported data; seven or more months derived or extrapolated.
b. Data extrapolated for the entire year.

SOURCE: Adapted from the IMF-DOT Annual, 1970-74; IMF-DOT-Y, 1982; IMF-DOT-Y, 1983.

Table 2619

COSTA RICA ABSOLUTE VALUE OF GOODS TRADED WITH SELECTED REGIONS AND COUNTRIES,[1] 1975-82
(M US)[2]

Category	Exports FOB							Imports CIF						
	1975	1976	1977	1979	1980	1981	1982	1975	1976	1977	1979	1980	1981	1982
I. World	493.3	592.5	828.1	934.0	980.9	966.6	897.7	694.0	770.4	1,021.5	1,397.6	1,470.8	1,208.9	870.0
II. Industrial Countries														
United States	339.1	401.3	548.7	668.4	616.9	596.9	606.1	443.8	502.5	670.5	872.0	936.2	735.9	503.9
Canada	207.3	235.4	257.1	346.9	331.4	313.1	307.3[a]	239.1	266.6	343.7	425.2	503.8	402.7	331.1[a]
Australia	1.2	.5	4.2	7.3	3.7	9.3	11.2[a]	15.6	16.0	16.1	24.3	34.5	26.4	14.3[a]
Japan	.4	.4	.2	.7	.7	.7	.8[a]	1.5	.7	2.1	1.3	1.3	.3	.5[a]
New Zealand	8.2	7.0	7.0	10.1	8.0	6.2	7.5[a]	61.2	88.2	136.4	172.9	171.3	118.3	37.5[a]
Austria	~	.2	.4	.5	.8	2.2	2.8[a]	~	1.5	5.5	.6	3.3	.2	~
Belgium	9.5	7.8	28.0	33.1	26.0	18.5	11.3[a]	1.4	4.1	4.7	2.7	2.1	2.9	1.2[a]
Denmark	1.1	3.5	.7	3.5	.8	1.2	1.5[a]	6.8	6.6	7.9	9.2	7.0	7.7	5.7[a]
Finland	11.4	24.1	36.1	30.4	25.6	18.6	18.6[a]	1.4	1.5	3.1	2.0	4.3	3.9	1.3[a]
France	4.1	5.2	8.6	16.2	18.9	11.3	14.0[a]	.3	.6	.5	.2	.4	.5	1.1[a]
Germany	55.8	62.3	106.8	110.1	110.5	125.0	118.1[a]	11.4	8.3	14.3	14.2	17.6	20.9	11.0[a]
Iceland	~	~	.3	~	.1	.1	.3[a]	39.4	39.9	55.6	69.1	70.9	55.4	31.9[a]
Ireland	~	~	~	2.3	.4	.3	.6[b]	.1	.4	.2	~	~	~	.1[a]
Italy	10.5	9.4	17.6	31.4	39.0	27.3	37.2[a]	9.4	8.7	13.3	36.5	23.4	24.9	18.3[a]
Netherlands	16.3	22.8	55.9	40.9	28.8	28.1	27.4[a]	8.7	6.8	6.7	13.0	11.1	7.0	4.0[a]
Norway	2.2	2.5	1.3	3.5	2.9	2.4	4.2[a]	1.7	2.5	1.1	.8	.8	.4	.5[a]
Spain	.1	2.0	.7	7.3	4.9	4.7	6.4[a]	8.6	10.7	17.5	50.5	33.2	24.5	16.0[a]
Sweden	9.5	16.2	20.0	15.4	9.2	14.4	11.8[a]	8.4	10.0	8.1	7.7	12.2	8.8	9.4[a]
Switzerland	.2	.5	1.7	5.4	2.4	4.3	4.3[a]	5.2	8.6	8.5	11.2	10.5	8.8	5.2[a]
United Kingdom	.7	1.4	2.0	3.5	2.7	9.0	21.1[a]	23.3	21.7	23.2	26.6	25.8	18.3	11.9[a]
III. Developing Countries														
Oil Exporting Countries	1.25	9.7	26.5	5.3	4.2	5.9	7.4	58.7	46.4	35.6	53.6	85.1	92.0	103.9
Algeria	~	~	~	~	~	~	~	~	~	~	~	~	~	.3[c]
Indonesia	~	~	.1	.1	.1	.1	~	~	~	~	~	~	~	~
Iran, I.R. of	.3	2.0	2.7	~	.1	.1	.1[c]	~	~	~	.4	.2	~	~
Iraq	.01	~	~	.1	~	~	~	~	~	~	~	~	~	~
Kuwait	~	.2	.9	~	~	.2	.5[c]	~	~	~	~	~	~	~
Libya	.9	.6	~	~	~	.7	.1[c]	~	~	~	~	~	~	~
Oman	~	~	~	~	~	~	1.4[c]	~	~	~	~	~	~	~
Qatar	~	~	~	.3	~	~	~	~	~	~	~	~	~	~
Saudi Arabia	~	1.0	2.6	.3	.3	.4	.4[b]	~	~	~	.1	~	~	~
T. VENEZUELA	~	6.0	20.2	1.3	2.4	2.3	4.3[c]	58.7	46.4	35.6	53.0	84.9	92.0	103.6[c]
Non-Oil Developing Countries	~	171.0	225.2	251.4	354.9	347.9	263.6		216.7	308.2	459.9	432.0	369.7	255.9
Africa	~	.5	1.4	.8	.3	.6	1.9		.1	.4	.2	.7	.3	.1[c]
Botswana														
Guinea		.3												.1[c]
Ivory Coast			.3											
Lesotho											.2			.2[c]
Liberia				.7		.1	1.4[c]							
Morocco	~	.4	1.1	.1	.1	.1	.4[b]				.1	.2	.1	
South Africa	~	.1	.1	.7	.3	.2	.1				.1	.4	.1	
Africa not specified				.3	.2	.2	.2[c]					.1		
Asia	~	.3	.4	1.2	1.4	2.8	2.4		2.2	3.7	11.7	8.2	14.3	5.8
China, People's Rep.				.2					.2	.5	.2	.7	.3	.3[a]
Hong Kong		.2	.2		.4	.2	.2[a]		.1	1.7	2.7	3.7	2.0	1.2[a]
India		.9	1.7	.2	.3		1.1[c]							.1[c]
Kampuchea, Dem.														
Kiribati, Rep. of														
Korea		.5	.5	.5	.1				1.5	2.5	2.3			
Malaysia		.5	1.5	.1			.2[b]		.5	3.3	2.3	11.5		3.9[b]
Pakistan											.1	.1	.1	
Philippines		.2	.1	.2	.2	.2	.2[a]							
Singapore		.2	.1	.1	.3	.9	.2[a]			.2	.2	.1	.4	.3[a]
Sri Lanka										1.9		1.2	2.0	
Thailand					.5	.7	.5[c]				.1	.1		
Tuvalu												.1		
Oceania not specified				.1							.2			

Table 2619 (Continued)

COSTA RICA ABSOLUTE VALUE OF GOODS TRADED WITH SELECTED REGIONS AND COUNTRIES,[1] 1975–82 (M US)[2]

Category	Exports FOB							Imports CIF						
	1975	1976	1977	1979	1980	1981	1982	1975	1976	1977	1979	1980	1981	1982
III. Developing Countries (Continued)														
Non-Oil Developing Countries														
Europe														
Cyprus	~	2.3	10.9	7.8	6.6	7.6	.6	~	3.2	4.5	3.3	4.2	1.0	.7
Greece	~	~	~	~	.2	4.0	~	~	~	~	~	~	~	~
Hungary	~	~	~	.6	.2	.1	.1[b]	~	1.1	.8	1.3	2.9	.1	.1[c]
Malta	~	~	~	~	~	.1	.1[c]	.3	.5	.2	.5	.6	.4	.2[b]
Portugal	1.4	2.0	9.3	5.6	~	2.8	.2[b]	.3	1.3	1.8	1.2	.2	.1	~
Romania	~	~	~	~	~	~	~	2.9	~	~	~	~	~	~
Turkey	1.3	.2	1.6	1.3	6.3	.5	.1[c]	.3	.3	1.6	.3	.5	.2	.3[c]
Yugoslavia	~	.4	2.0	3.5	5.4	3.4	5.2	.3	.2	.5	.6	.8	1.1	.7
Europe not specified	~	~	~	~	.3	.3	1.0[a]	~	~	~	~	~	~	~
Middle East														
Egypt	.1	.1	1.2	.7	2.9	.2	.2[a]	.3	.2	.5	.8	.8	1.1	.7[a]
Israel	.1	.1	~	.3	.7	.8	.7[c]	~	~	~	~	~	~	~
Jordan	~	~	~	~	.5	.5	2.8[c]	~	~	~	~	~	~	~
Lebanon	~	.2	.7	1.4	1.2	1.7	.4[c]	~	~	~	~	~	~	~
Syrian Arab Rep.	~	~	~	~	~	.4	~	~	~	~	~	~	~	~
Yemen Arab Rep.	~	~	~	.3	~	~	~	~	~	~	~	~	~	~
Yemen, P.D. Rep.	~	~	~	~	~	~	~	~	~	~	~	~	~	~
IV. Latin America[3]	141.0	167.5	210.4	238.1	341.1	333.6	253.5	161.8	210.9	299.1	444.2	418.2	353.1	248.5
A. ARGENTINA	~	.2	.2	.8	2.2	1.2	.1[b]	1.5	2.6	3.7	5.3	6.6	4.4	2.6[b]
Antigua and Barbuda	~	~	~	~	.1	.1	.1[c]	~	~	~	~	~	~	~
Bahamas	~	~	~	.3	.2	.4	.6[c]	~	~	~	~	~	~	~
Barbados	~	~	.4	.4	.2	.4	.8[c]	~	~	~	~	~	~	.1[c]
Belize	~	.3	.4	.4	.2	.5	.8[c]	~	~	~	~	~	~	~
Bermuda	.1	1.3	.7	.7	1.7	.5	.5[c]	~	~	~	~	~	~	.1[c]
B. BOLIVIA	.2	1.3	.1	4.5	2.9	.5	.5[c]	2.0	3.2	9.1	23.9	21.7	18.7	8.9[a]
C. BRAZIL	.2	.8	.1	.1	1.7	.1	2.0[a]	.7	2.8	3.8	1.8	7.5	5.0	4.4[a]
D. CHILE	.5	.5	.6	2.2	3.6	3.4	2.9[c]	7.0	4.5	6.7	6.5	5.7	4.3	4.0[c]
E. COLOMBIA	.5	~	~	~	.1	~	.1[c]	.1	~	~	.1	.1	.7	2.9[a]
Dominica	~	~	~	~	.1	.3	.2[c]	~	~	~	~	~	~	.7[c]
H. DOMINICAN REP.	.5	.8	4.0	5.3	3.1	3.1	2.2[a]	1.1	.3	.1	.4	.7	2.1	1.2
I. ECUADOR	6.3	2.0	1.2	2.6	1.4	12.1	3.3[c]	31.9	40.0	51.4	69.7	67.6	37.2	23.3[c]
J. EL SALVADOR	27.9	33.2	47.7	48.1	52.5	41.2	30.9[c]	~	~	~	~	~	~	~
Grenada	~	~	~	.1	.1	.2	.1[c]	~	~	~	~	~	~	~
Guadeloupe	~	~	~	.1	.1	.2	.1[c]	~	~	~	~	~	~	~
K. GUATEMALA	31.2	38.4	53.4	61.8	65.5	68.9	65.7[c]	39.2	44.1	58.6	85.3	100.6	64.9	51.6[c]
Guiana, French	~	~	~	.6	.4	.4	.2[c]	~	~	~	~	~	~	~
Guyana	~	~	1.3	.6	.7	.7	1.0[c]	.1	~	.1	.1	.1	~	.1[c]
L. HAITI	12.8	13.8	17.1	26.1	28.3	31.8	24.3[c]	12.9	7.3	9.4	14.8	18.8	16.4	12.5[c]
M. HONDURAS	.7	.7	.1	3.8	.4	.7	1.2[c]	.1	.1	.1	.4	.1	.1	~
Jamaica	~	~	~	~	~	~	~	~	~	~	~	~	~	~
Leeward Islands	~	~	~	~	~	~	~	~	~	~	~	~	~	~
Martinique	~	~	.1	~	~	~	~	~	~	~	~	~	~	~

Table 2619 (Continued)

COSTA RICA ABSOLUTE VALUE OF GOODS TRADED WITH SELECTED REGIONS AND COUNTRIES,[1] 1975-82
(M US)[2]

Exports FOB

Category	1975	1976	1977	1979	1980	1981	1982
IV. Latin America[3] (Continued)							
N. MEXICO	9.5	10.5	3.7	.4	1.1	18.1	16.5b
Netherlands Antilles	~	.1	1.1	.2	5.7	13.9	5.3c
O. NICARAGUA	35.3	45.2	55.6	39.5	124.1	84.8	51.1c
P. PANAMA	16.4	19.1	22.5	35.5	41.8	43.5	39.8a
Panama Canal Zone	~	~	~	~	~	~	~
R. PERU	.1	.1	~	2.4	.9	1.4	1.3c
St. Lucia	~	.1	~	~	.1	.2	.2c
St. Pierre-Miquelon	~	~	~	~	~	~	~
St. Vincent	~	~	.5	~	.1	.1	.3c
Suriname	~	~	~	.7	.3	~	.5c
Trinidad and Tobago	~	.1	~	~	1.5	.5	.5b
S. URUGUAY	~	~	.1	.5	.3	.1	
Windward Islands	~	~	~	~	~	.2	
British West Indies	.1	.6	.1	.5	.2	.2	1.1c
Other Latin America not specified	~	~	~	~	.1	~	~
V. USSR, Eastern Europe, etc.	1.5	9.6	27.1	8.8	4.4	15.4	19.6
Albania							
Bulgaria	.3	.1	~	.5	~	.8F	6.2c
G. CUBA	.3	2.3	.5	4.3	4.4	~	1.3c
Czechoslovakia	.1	.3	2.7	.7	~	5.9	4.6c
Eastern Germany	1.1	3.5	1.7	.3	~	6.6F	5.7c
North Korea	~	.1	.1	~	.1	~	.1c
Poland	~	.6	19.4	~	.1	~	.1c
USSR	.2	2.8	2.8	3.1	~	.8F	1.5c
Special categories	1.3	.8	.7	~	.5	1.3F	~
EEC	~	112.6	219.9	241.5	227.1	224.9	231.0
VI. Percent Distribution							
Industrial Countries	~	67.7	66.3	71.6	62.9	61.8	67.5
Oil Exporting Countries	~	1.6	3.2	.6	.4	.6	.8
Non-Oil Developing Countries	~	28.9	27.2	26.9	36.2	36.0	29.4
Africa	~	.1	.2	.1	~	.1	.2
Asia	~	.4	1.3	.7	.7	.8	.3
Europe	~	.1	.2	.8	.6	.3	.3
Middle East	~	~	~	~	.5	.3	.6
Western Hemisphere	~	28.3	25.4	25.5	34.8	34.5	28.2
USSR, Eastern Europe, etc.	~	1.6	3.3	.9	.4	1.6	2.2
VII. Annual Percent Change							
World	~	20.1	39.8	14.7	5.0	-1.5	-7.1
Industrial Countries	~	18.3	36.7	20.3	-7.7	-3.2	1.5
Oil Exporting Countries	~	268.8	171.8	-3.1	-21.2	41.7	25.2
Non-Oil Developing Countries	~	14.2	31.7	8.2	41.2	-2.0	24.2
Africa	~	-25.6	182.0	-17.8	-61.6	74.4	249.5
Asia	~	-88.3	44.9	-9.7	15.5	98.2	-14.3
Europe	~	-15.1	376.3	91.2	-15.1	14.8	-91.9
Middle East	~	-57.7	400.5	15.5	54.4	-37.6	54.0
Western Hemisphere	~	17.1	25.6	6.8	43.3	-2.2	-24.0
USSR, Eastern Europe, etc.	~	546.7	182.3	-55.7	-50.2	248.3	27.5

Imports CIF

Category	1975	1976	1977	1979	1980	1981	1982
N. MEXICO	39.6	20.4	23.4	44.4	75.5	110.7	77.2b
Netherlands Antilles	~	15.6	59.5	120.5	38.5	25.9	22.7c
O. NICARAGUA	37.1	44.2	48.5	41.8	32.8	33.8	22.2c
P. PANAMA	6.6	10.7	12.2	19.7	31.6	21.2	13.7a
Panama Canal Zone	~	1.1	~	~	~	~	~
R. PERU	~	1.2	5.1	5.2	5.9	5.0	3.3c
St. Lucia	.5						
St. Pierre-Miquelon	~	~	~	~	.2	~	~
St. Vincent	~	~	~	~	~	~	~
Suriname	~	~	~	~	~	~	~
Trinidad and Tobago	~	3.6	2.7	1.9	1.7	3.4	2.4b
S. URUGUAY	~	~	.1	.4	~	~	~
Windward Islands	~	~	~	~	~	~	~
British West Indies	~	~	~	~	~	~	~
Other Latin America not specified	.1	9.3	4.5	1.6	.7	~	1.1c
V. USSR, Eastern Europe, etc.							
Albania	3.0	2.8	4.5	4.0	5.3	3.4	1.5
Bulgaria	~	~	.9	.1	~	~	~
G. CUBA	~	~	~	~	~	~	~
Czechoslovakia	~	~	.2	.2	.1	.1	.9c
Eastern Germany	1.1	1.7	1.6	1.4	2.0	1.2	
North Korea	.1	.1	.1	~	~	~	~
Poland	~	.1	1.0	~	1.1	.3	.1c
USSR	~	.4	.3	1.1	.4	.5	.5c
Special categories	~	.5	.6	1.2	1.8	1.4	.1c
EEC	~	93.9	126.5	174.5	162.9	142.1	87.0
VI. Percent Distribution							
Industrial Countries	~	65.2	65.6	62.4	63.7	60.9	57.9
Oil Exporting Countries	~	6.0	3.5	3.8	5.8	7.6	11.9
Non-Oil Developing Countries	~	28.1	30.2	32.9	29.4	30.6	29.4
Africa	~	.3	.2	.2	.6	1.2	.7
Asia	~	.4	.4	.8	.3	.1	.1
Europe	~	.1	~	.2	~	~	~
Middle East	~	.3	.4	.8	.6	1.2	.7
Western Hemisphere	~	27.4	29.3	31.8	28.4	29.2	28.6
USSR, Eastern Europe, etc.	~	.4	.4	.3	.4	.3	.2
VII. Annual Percent Change							
World	~	11.0	32.6	28.0	5.2	-17.8	-28.0
Industrial Countries	~	13.2	33.4	17.4	7.4	-21.4	-31.5
Oil Exporting Countries	~	-21.0	-23.3	387.8	58.7	8.1	12.9
Non-Oil Developing Countries	~	15.7	42.2	39.4	-6.1	-14.4	-30.8
Africa	~	13.7	100.5	9.0	253.4	-60.7	-52.6
Asia	~	-18.3	73.2	87.8	-30.1	74.8	-59.2
Europe	~	-15.6	38.6	22.5	27.5	-77.2	-29.5
Middle East	~	-34.3	126.8	-34.4	42.6	39.3	-33.3
Western Hemisphere	~	16.9	41.8	38.8	-5.8	-15.6	-29.6
USSR, Eastern Europe, etc.	~	4.8	57.6	18.4	32.8	-35.4	-57.2

1. DOT may differ between countries and from IFS data because of the time it takes for an export to become an import, etc.
2. Data may be calculated from partner's reported data or estimated on basis of less than 12 months.
3. Cuba is included in category V; Venezuela is included in category III.

a. Nine months of reported data, three months derived from partner.
b. Data may be calculated from partner's reported data, three months derived or extrapolated.
c. Nine months of reported data, three months extrapolated.

SOURCE: Adapted from the IMF-DOT Annual, 1970-74; IMF-DOT-Y, 1982; IMF-DOT-Y, 1983.

Table 2620

CUBA ABSOLUTE VALUE OF GOODS TRADED WITH SELECTED REGIONS AND COUNTRIES,[1] 1975-82
(M US)[2]

PART I. NON-COMMUNIST TRADE

Category	Exports FOB							Imports CIF						
	1975	1976	1977	1979	1980	1981	1982	1975	1976	1977	1979	1980	1981	1982
I. World	1,134.3	671.1	581.6	883.6	1,313.6	1,423.0	1,207.1	1,956.6	1,633.0	1,636.7	1,399.9	2,172.4	2,096.2	1,565.2
II. Industrial Countries	863.1	399.8	393.5	549.0	766.3	619.8	521.3	1,647.3	1,288.0	1,284.3	1,061.8	1,637.3	1,530.6	1,021.5
United States	~	~	.1*	.3*	~	~	1.5*		.6	1.1*	.2*		.6*	1.0*
Canada	83.1	61.6*	42.6*	89.6*	34.2*	63.3*	77.1*	233.6	289.1	90.8*	242.4*	374.4*	414.1*	289.8*
Australia	29.9	1.3*	.4*	.2*	.5*	.4*	.5*		2.1	17.6*	1.9*	1.7*	2.0*	.5*
Japan	312.6	45.8*	57.8*	111.6*	170.7	139.8*	103.5*	483.6	219.8*	400.5*	153.6*	264.7*	293.1*	138.6*
New Zealand		14.3*	3.5*	9.8*	~	~	4.2[a]				~	~		7.1*
Austria	2.7	4.2	4.5*	4.8*	5.1*	2.8*	3.5*	33.7	22.1*	9.8*	6.2*	9.6*	9.1*	7.1*
Belgium	5.1	7.0	8.5*	13.4*	36.0*	6.9*	8.9*	56.0	24.4*	84.7*	21.5*	30.4*	36.9*	17.0*
Denmark	9.1	2.7	4.5*	10.2*	2.7*	2.4*	.5*	29.7	35.4*	90.7*	4.0*	8.1*	8.4*	6.7*
Finland	35.7	19.2*	13.8*	18.8*	48.7*	43.9*	24.0*	10.2	11.0*	62.2*	4.7*	7.2*	8.3*	3.0*
France	22.1	25.8*	29.6*	36.7*	59.7*	50.7*	50.5*	117.1	98.0*	82.4*	49.4*	291.6*	172.5*	62.1*
Germany	7.8	16.8*	14.3*	27.7*	51.9*	25.2*	29.0*	140.0	102.0*		115.0*	120.4*	102.1*	71.0*
Iceland	.4	~	~	.4*	2.7*	.8*	.3[a]		.8	~	1.3*	8.9*	.5*	27.9[a]
Ireland	17.8	3.5*	.3*	41.8*	42.8*	34.3*	39.5*	4.5	70.8*	35.5*	62.6*	59.7*	47.8*	42.3*
Italy	5.9	23.0*	17.9*	50.1*	64.6*	25.2*	42.9*	101.9	42.6*	20.6*	34.9*	49.9*	43.2*	65.6*
Netherlands		8.3*	23.3*	1.1*	.5*	~	.1*	63.1	2.3*	1.5*	1.8*	2.4*	2.1*	1.4*
Norway		.8*	.8*	~	~	~	~	10.7	~	~	~	~	~	~
Spain	285.4	82.7*	144.1*	94.2*	83.1*	55.3*	100.0*	193.9	230.9*	70.0*	218.5*	207.6*	192.9*	120.7*
Sweden	29.3	37.6*	5.2*	2.4*	1.2*	17.1*	.5*	48.6	37.7*	34.1*	30.3*	57.3*	63.2*	21.7*
Switzerland	3.7	4.5*	7.3*	7.0*	6.6*	5.8*	6.4*	29.9	10.6*	28.3*	29.2*	30.5*	36.1*	19.4*
United Kingdom	12.6	40.7*	15.6*	28.9*	55.4*	45.6*	28.5*	91.0	87.8*	52.7*	84.5*	90.2*	81.7*	125.7*
III. Developing Countries	51.1	29.4	46.3	66.0	147.3	20.3	10.5	1.9	~	~	57.6	108.5	85.6	69.0
Oil Exporting Countries	29.4	8.1*	26.6*	34.7*	69.4[b]	76.3[b]	72.5[b]	1.9	~	~	~	~	~	~
Algeria		~	~	6.5*	36.3*	5.3*	~				~	~	4.5*	~
Indonesia		4.4*	~	3.0[b]	~	~	~		~	~	~	~	~	~
Iran, I.R. of	19.8	13.6*	16.7*	~	~	~	~		~	~	~	~	~	~
Iraq	.4	.1*	2.8*	12.3*	31.9*	31.1*	29.5[b]		~	2*	~	~	~	~
Libya	1.5	2.9*	5.5*	5.5*	2.6*	3.9*	4.9[a]		~	~	~	~	~	~
Saudi Arabia		.3*	.2*	4.0*	.1*	.3*	.3[b]		~	~	~	~	~	~
United Arab Emirates		~	~	4.0*	7.0*	3.5*	3.3[b]		.7*	57.4*	57.4*	108.4*	81.2*	69.0[a]
T. VENEZUELA	241.9	241.9	141.7	268.7	400.1	682.9	575.4		345.0	352.5	280.4	426.6	480.0	474.7
Non-Oil Developing Countries	61.2	61.2	34.0	11.0	28.7	22.2	.9		.7	1.0		9.6	4.6	6.0
Africa							.1[b]							
Burundi				.1[b]	.1[b]	.1[b]	.1[b]							
Comoros			.1*	.1[b]	.2[b]	.2[b]	.2[b]							
Congo														
Gabon		.6*	.6*			.6*	.6*							
Ghana				3.0[b]			.5[a]							
Guinea-Bissau		4.8*							.7*	.3*		4.8*	4.8*	69.0[a]
Mali		55.6*	28.5*	10.7*	19.7*	21.2*			.7*	.3*	.3*	4.8*	81.2*	4.6*
Morocco		.6*	4.6*											
Somalia					8.6*	.6*	.6*			.7*	.7*	4.9*	4.6*	4.9*
Sudan			4.6*	.1*	8.6*									
Tunisia														

Table 2620 (Continued)

CUBA ABSOLUTE VALUE OF GOODS TRADED WITH SELECTED REGIONS AND COUNTRIES,[1] 1975–82
(M US)[2]

Part I. NON-COMMUNIST TRADE (Continued)

Category	Exports FOB							Imports CIF						
	1975	1976	1977	1979	1980	1981	1982	1975	1976	1977	1979	1980	1981	1982
III. Developing Countries (Continued)														
Non-Oil Developing Countries														
Asia														
China, People's Rep.	~	.2	7.1	120.2	125.9	236.9	261.4	~	2.5	6.3	109.7	126.0	127.2	137.1
Hong Kong	~	~	~	107.1*	115.7*	199.8*	240.0*	~	~	~	103.0*	102.1*	116.7*	126.4*
India	~	.1*	.3*	.5*	.4*	.3*	.3[a]	~	.5*	2.5*	2.2	4.1*	2.2*	1.0*
Malaysia	~	~	6.8*	12.6*	7.6*	36.7*	20.9[a]	~	.2*	1.8*	1.3*	1.9*	2.6*	.2[a]
Papua New Guinea	~	~	~	~	.1*	~	~	~	~	~	~	~	~	~
Philippines	~	~	~	~	~	~	~	~	~	~	~	.1*	~	~
Singapore	~	.1*	~	~	2.2*	.1*	.2*	~	1.7	2.0*	3.2*	5.3*	5.7*	2.6*
Sri Lanka	~	~	~	~	~	~	~	~	~	~	.1*	~	~	~
Thailand	~	~	~	~	~	~	~	~	~	~	~	~	~	~
Europe														
Cyprus	~	137.1	73.4	85.4	81.5	186.1	150.5	~	81.4	87.1	74.1	153.0	208.0	195.5
Greece	~	.1*	.1*	.1*	.4*	.3*	.1*	~	~	~	~	~	~	~
Hungary	~	32.8*	27.9*	35.1*	23.3*	67.1*	70.4[a]	~	54.6*	31.4*	41.6*	50.6*	56.0*	68.3[a]
Malta	~	1.0*	~	~	.1*	.1*	~	~	~	~	~	~	~	4.3*
Portugal	60.6	30.3*	14.6*	17.3*	20.5*	52.2*	29.1[a]	1.2	1.3*	.5*	4.7*	9.8*	10.2*	3.5[a]
Romania	8.6	15.0*	12.6*	22.8*	31.1*	59.7*	50.7[b]	18.7	19.1*	9.6*	18.8*	83.0*	34.8[b]	14.6[b]
Yugoslavia	~	57.9*	18.0*	10.0*	6.0*	6.7*	.1[a]	6.6	.1*	.5*	.6*	.6*	.5*	.2[a]
Middle East														
Bahrain	~	41.1	21.7	35.5	36.0	99.8	63.4	~	6.4*	45.7*	9.0*	9.1*	6.6*	4.6[a]
Egypt	~	3.8*	8.5*	11.3*	25.9	85.3	51.1*	~	3.7	4.6	5.1	5.8	5.8	4.9
Jordan	~	~	~	~	.1*	~	~	~	.1*	.9*	~	~	~	~
Lebanon	~	~	~	~	~	~	~	~	.6*	.9*	~	~	~	~
Syrian Arab Rep.	~	37.3*	11.9*	21.0*	7.5*	12.2[b]	10.4[b]	~	3.0[b]	3.7[b]	5.1[b]	5.8[b]	5.8[b]	4.9[b]
Yemen Arab Rep.	~	~	1.2*	3.2*	2.5*	2.3*	2.0[b]	~	~	~	~	~	~	~
IV. Latin America[3]														
A. ARGENTINA	1.6	2.3	5.5	16.6	28.0	37.9	99.3	229.1	256.7	253.6	91.5	132.3	134.4	131.2
Bahamas	.1	~	~	.2*	.3*	.2*	.2[b]	172.1	185.5*	184.4*	54.6*	73.0*	84.5*	48.1[a]
Barbados	~	~	.8*	2.2*	3.0*	4.0*	4.3[a]	~	~	~	~	~	~	~
Bermuda	~	~	.1*	.1*	.1[b]	.6*	.5[b]	~	~	~	~	~	~	~
E. COLOMBIA	~	.1*	.7*	.7*	.7*	.6*	.5*	.5	20.8*	3.8*	2.2*	6.1*	3.8*	3.2[b]
F. COSTA RICA	~	~	.1*	.2*	.1*	.1*	~	~	2.5*	.5*	4.7*	4.8*	~	~
H. DOMINICAN REP.	~	~	~	~	~	.1*	~	~	~	~	~	~	~	~
Guiana, French	~	~	.1*	.3*	.8[b]	.8[b]	.7[b]	~	~	~	~	~	~	~
Guyana	~	~	.1*	.4*	.5[b]	.5[b]	.4[b]	~	~	~	~	~	~	~
Jamaica	~	.7*	~	3.3*	.8[b]	.8[b]	.7[b]	32.7	.2*	1.2*	.7*	.8*	.8[b]	.7[b]
N. MEXICO	1.3	.9*	2.4*	4.0*	14.7*	23.1*	85.3[a]	~	24.5*	37.8*	8.2*	29.4*	21.0*	24.4[a]
P. PANAMA	~	~	1.1*	4.2*	5.7[b]	6.3[b]	6.0[b]	~	4.5*	3.8*	3.4[b]	3.1[b]	3.1[b]	2.7[b]
R. PERU	.1	.1*	.1*	.3*	.1*	.5*	.3[a]	.3	.4*	~	.1*	.5*	.9*	.5*
St. Vincent	.1	~	.1*	.2*	.3[b]	.3[b]	.3[b]	~	~	~	~	~	~	~
Suriname	~	.4*	.7*	.6[b]	.5[b]	.5[b]	.4[b]	23.4	18.0*	21.6*	14.8*	14.5*	20.3*	17.3[b]
Trinidad and Tobago	~	~	~	~	.2*	.1[a]	.2[a]	~	.1*	.4*	2.9*	~	~	~
EEC	~	127.9	114.2	209.1	316.2	191.1	200.2	~	461.9	428.8	373.0	673.2	508.7	422.6

Table 2620 (Continued)

CUBA ABSOLUTE VALUE OF GOODS TRADED WITH SELECTED REGIONS AND COUNTRIES,[1] 1975-82 (M US)[2]

PART I. NON-COMMUNIST TRADE (Continued)

| | Exports FOB | | | | | | | Imports CIF | | | | | | |
Category	1975	1976	1977	1979	1980	1981	1982	1975	1976	1977	1979	1980	1981	1982
V. Annual Percent Change														
Industrial Countries	?	-53.7	-1.6	29.3	39.6	-19.1	-15.9	?	-21.8	-.3	9.4	54.2	-6.5	-33.3
Oil Exporting Countries	?	-42.6	57.9	90.8	123.2	-18.3	-8.2	?	~	~	350.0	88.2	-21.0	-19.4
Non-Oil Developing Countries	?	9.9	-41.4	14.6	48.9	70.7	-15.7	?	11.8	2.2	-17.7	52.1	12.5	-1.1
Africa	?	-23.7	-44.4	-54.9	160.3	-22.6	-95.9	?	-85.6	34.2	-96.8	~	-52.2	29.6
Asia	?	-4.5	~	40.1	4.8	88.1	10.3	?	100.0	153.6	55.2	14.8	1.0	7.8
Europe	?	-28.7	-46.5	36.7	-4.6	128.5	-19.2	?	36.0	7.0	40.3	106.5	35.9	-6.0
Middle East	?	54.7	-47.3	-30.4	1.4	177.5	-36.5	?	-65.7	22.6	-20.4	13.6	~	-15.1
Western Hemisphere	?	-64.1	136.9	53.7	672.5	7.7	-28.0	?	10.8	-1.2	-56.4	44.6	1.6	-2.4

1. DOT data may differ between countries and from IFS data because of the time it takes for an export to become an import, etc.

2. Data may be calculated from partner's reported data or estimated on basis of less than 12 months.

3. Venezuela is included in category III.

a. Five or fewer months of reported data; seven or more months derived or extrapolated.

b. Data extrapolated for the entire year.

SOURCE: Adapted from the IMF-DOT Annual, 1970-74; IMF-DOT-Y, 1982.

PART II. ALL TRADE
(M Pesos)

Category	1970	1971	1972	1973	1974	1975	1976	1977	1978	1979‡	1980‡	1981[a]
Exports	1,050	861	771	1,153	2,237	2,952	2,962	2,912	3,440	3,500	3,967	4,259
USSR	529	304	224	477	811	1,662	1,638	2,066	2,496	2,370	2,253	2,455
Rest of Socialist Countries	248	261	197	268	472	341	452	378	420	514	533	823
Rest of World	273	296	350	408	954	949	602	468	524	616	1,181	981
Imports	1,311	1,387	1,190	1,463	2,226	3,113	3,180	3,433	3,574	3,687	4,509	5,081
USSR	691	731	714	811	1,025	1,250	1,490	1,858	2,328	2,524	2,811	3,223
Rest of Socialist Countries	226	239	200	224	328	437	374	467	521	534	699	877
Rest of World	394	417	276	428	873	1,456	1,316	1,108	725	629	999	981
Balance	-261	-526	-419	-310	11	-161	-488	-521	-134	-187	-542	-822
USSR	-162	-427	-490	-334	-214	412	148	208	168	-154	-558	-768
Rest of Socialist Countries	22	22	-3	44	144	-66	78	-89	-101	-20	-166	-54
Rest of World	-121	-121	74	-20	81	-507	-714	-640	-201	-13	182	~

a. Preliminary figures.

SOURCE: ECLA-S, 1981, p. 691.

Table 2620 (Continued)

CUBA ABSOLUTE VALUE OF GOODS TRADED WITH SELECTED REGIONS AND COUNTRIES,[1] 1975-82 (M US)[2]

PART III. TRADE WITH WORLD REGIONS, 1959-73

	1959-68ᵃ		1969		1970		1971		1972‡		1973‡	
	Export	Import	Export	Import	Export	Import	Export	Import	Export	Import	Export	Import
Absolute Total (M pesos)	630	843	667	1,222	1,049	1,312	861	1,388	771	1,190	1,151	1,391
Percentage Total	100	100	100	100	100	100	100	100	100	100	100	100
Socialist Eastern Europe	50	57	54	66	65	63	54	63	45	70	56	65
Other Eastern Europe	5	4	7	4	4	3	5	2	6	2	4	3
European Common Market	4	7	6	10	3	13	3	11	4	6	6	13
European Free Trade Area	4	4	4	8	3	7	3	7	4	6	2	1
Asia	16	12	24	9	22	10	25	12	28	11	24	13
Middle East	3	1	2	1	1	--	3	1	5	--	2	--
Africa	3	1	2	1	1	1	3	--	2	--	2	--
Americas	15	14	1	1	1	2	4	3	5	4	3	5

a. Yearly average.

SOURCE: Cuba: JUCEPLAN, AE, 1973, pp. 188-191.

PART IV. TRADE WITH LATIN AMERICAN COUNTRIES, 1959-73 (%)

	D. CHILE		N. MEXICO		R. PERU		OTHER	
Year	Exports	Imports	Exports	Imports	Exports	Imports	Exports	Imports
1959-68ᵃ	#	#	#	#	#	#	#	.2
1969	#	#	#	#	#	#	#	#
1970	#	#	#	#	#	#	#	#
1971	.2	.1	#	#	#	#	#	#
1972	.4	.1	#	.1	#	.1	#	#
1973	.2	.1	#	#	#	#	#	#

a. Yearly average.

SOURCE: Cuba, JUCEPLAN, AE, 1973, pp. 1980-191.

Table 2621

CUBA'S MOST IMPORTANT TRADING
PARTNERS, 1900–80
(% Value)

PART I. UNITED STATES, 1900-62				PART II. SOVIET UNION, 1960-80		
Year	Exports from Cuba	Imports to Cuba		Year	Exports from Cuba	Imports to Cuba
1900	71	43		1960	17	14
1905	87	45		1961	48	45
1910	86	53		1962	42	54
1915	83	64		1963	30	53
1919	77	76		1964	39	40
1925	75	63		1965	47	50
1929	77	59		1966	46	56
1937	81	69		1967	52	58
1942	90[a]	84[b]		1968	45	61
1945	79	79		1969	35	55
1950	59	79		1970	50	53
1955	67	74		1971	35	53
1959	73	73		1972	29	60
1960	59	39		1973	41	56
1961	6	2		1974	36	46
1962	1	2		1975	56	40
				1976	61	47
				1977	71	54
				1978	73[c]	65
				1979	68	68[c]
				1980	57	62

a. Highest U.S. figure.
b. Second highest U.S. figure; highest import figure, 87%, came in 1942.
c. Highest Soviet figure.

SOURCE: For U. S. trade, SALA-SNP, p. 284, revised with data in Schroeder, pp. 432-433, and William M. Leogrande, *Cuban Dependency* (Buffalo, N. Y.: Special Studies Series, Council on International Studies, 1978), p. 17. For Soviet data, Leogrande, *Cuban Dependency*, p. 18; SALA-Cuba, p. 168; ECLS-S, 1980, p. 201.

Table 2622

CROSS REFERENCES TO CUBA DATA IN SALA 20

Volume and Table Number	Table Title
20-2772	Cuba Total Exports and Exports to Europe, 1959–75
20-2773	Cuba Exports to EEC, 1959–75
20-2774	Cuba Exports to EFTA, 1959–75
20-2775	Cuba Exports to Rest of Western Europe, 1959–75
20-2776	Cuba Exports to Eastern Europe, 1959–75
20-2777	Cuba Exports to Asia, 1959–75
20-2778	Cuba Exports to Africa, 1959–75
20-2779	Cuba Exports to the Americas and North America, 1959–75
20-2780	Cuba Exports to Latin America and Oceania, 1959–75
20-2781	Cuba Total Imports and Imports from Europe, 1959–75
20-2782	Cuba Imports from EEC, 1959–75
20-2783	Cuba Imports from EFTA, 1959–75
20-2784	Cuba Imports from Rest of Western Europe, 1959–75
20-2785	Cuba Imports from Eastern Europe, 1959–75
20-2786	Cuba Imports from Asia, 1959–75
20-2787	Cuba Imports from Africa, 1959–75
20-2788	Cuba Imports from the Americas and North America, 1959–75
20-2789	Cuba Imports from Latin America and Oceania, 1959–75

Table 2623

DOMINICAN REPUBLIC ABSOLUTE VALUE OF GOODS TRADED WITH SELECTED REGIONS AND COUNTRIES,[1] 1975-82 (M US)[2]

Category	Exports FOB 1975	1976	1977	1979	1980	1981	1982	Imports CIF 1975	1976	1977	1979	1980	1981	1982
I. World	893.8	716.2	782.9	874.8	963.4	1,187.1	809.0	883.9	763.1	845.3	1,055.8	1,425.7	1,414.5	1,250.0
II. Industrial Countries	801.3	687.2	728.0	800.8	812.0	1,045.1	623.4	649.3	532.8	588.1	695.7	958.8	870.7	728.3
United States	596.5	498.6	579.3	516.1	502.6	795.4	437.2	452.8	364.4	373.7	471.8	539.1	608.3	486.1
Canada	9.7	19.3	1.2	2.7	2.9	15.0	10.0	27.4	19.0	19.7	25.9	34.9	37.0	32.5
Australia	~	~	~	~	~	.1	~	.1	.4	2.9	.1	.4	.8	.1
Japan	5.5	4.5	3.6	28.2	8.7	15.1	6.1	57.1	47.9	66.7	71.2	113.7	82.3	64.3
New Zealand	~	~	~	~	~	~	~	1.6	1.6	.5	1.6	2.6	5.0	.6
Austria	~	~	~	~	~	~	~	1.6	.6	.9	.9	2.4	1.5	.6
Belgium	19.0	20.4	12.6	22.6	21.1	25.2	24.2	7.5	7.9	5.8	7.7	10.9	9.7	9.8
Denmark	.3	.4	.7	.6	2.0	.2	.2	1.8	1.3	1.1	1.0	1.6	1.0	2.8
Finland	~	~	2.5	~	~	~	~	.5	.6	.5	.3	1.1	.6	.8
France	8.3	1.5	2.3	4.1	3.2	4.7	3.5	9.2	6.9	7.1	9.3	16.3	10.4	13.8
Germany	1.5	2.8	1.4	.4	1.6	1.5	1.3	23.9	26.8	33.7	31.3	37.6	33.5	28.1
Iceland	~	~	~	~	~	~	~	~	.2	.2	.7	.9	.7	.2
Ireland	~	~	~	~	~	~	~	~	~	~	~	~	~	~
Italy	27.8	2.5	2.8	5.4	2.0	2.4	2.4	14.4	12.5	13.2	12.9	24.9	15.3	10.5
Netherlands	62.0	51.0	44.2	47.0	48.1	26.9	20.6	6.6	9.0	8.2	11.5	14.8	12.9	8.7
Norway	1.0	1.3	~	1.3	~	~	1.9	4.2	4.3	5.4	7.0	5.4	4.8	2.4
Spain	17.0	22.5	16.6	39.9	14.0	47.4	13.1	13.6	11.2	27.0	18.1	22.7	21.2	46.5
Sweden	5.2	6.3	2.3	~	.1	3.4	1.0	4.2	1.3	1.6	2.8	2.2	1.0	1.8
Switzerland	34.4	49.0	55.3	126.2	204.5	102.9	100.5	5.6	2.7	5.1	7.0	8.3	6.7	4.3
United Kingdom	13.2	7.1	3.2	6.2	1.2	4.8	1.3	7.5	14.0	15.2	14.8	19.2	17.9	14.3
III. Developing Countries														
Oil Exporting Countries	8.0	2.9	14.2	52.1	91.3	82.1	31.2	108.5	46.7	127.6	190.1	301.5	275.6	221.1
Algeria	5.1	1.0	1.1	2.0	7.0	10.7	3.0	~	~	~	~	~	~	~
Iraq	~	~	~	~	~	~	~	~	~	~	~	~	~	~
Nigeria	~	~	~	1.0	~	~	~	~	~	~	~	~	~	~
T. VENEZUELA	2.9	2.0	13.1	49.1	84.3	71.4	28.2	108.5	46.7	127.6	190.0	301.5	275.6	221.0
Non-Oil Developing Countries	~	26.0	40.7	21.8	55.1	45.8	54.6	~	174.7	120.2	154.1	142.5	249.6	285.9
Africa	~	14.2	26.0	2.4	18.6	7.1	14.4	1.7	1.7	.7	1.5	4.9	1.7	2.6
Benin	~	~	~	~	.9	~	~	~	~	~	~	~	~	~
Ivory Coast	~	~	~	~	1.4	~	.3	~	~	~	~	~	~	~
Kenya	~	~	1.4	~	~	~	~	~	~	~	~	~	~	~
Liberia	~	~	~	~	~	~	~	~	~	~	~	~	~	~
Morocco	~	6.7	15.1	1.2	1.7	2.5	9.8	~	~	~	~	.2	~	~
Senegal	~	~	~	1.2	12.9	4.3	4.2	~	~	~	~	~	~	~
South Africa	~	1.7	.3	1.5	1.6	.3	.3	1.7	1.4	.7	1.5	4.6	1.2	2.5
Togo	~	~	~	~	1.6	~	~	~	~	~	~	~	~	~
Tunisia	~	4.2	5.3	~	~	~	~	~	~	~	~	~	~	~
Africa not specified	~	7.5	5.3	~	~	~	.1	~	~	~	~	~	~	~
Asia	~	~	~	~	~	~	~	~	2.8	3.8	6.5	10.7	7.3	7.4
China, People's Rep.	~	~	~	~	~	~	~	~	~	~	.1	.2	.5	.1
Hong Kong	~	~	~	~	~	~	~	~	1.4	1.7	2.3	3.3	2.7	2.1
India	~	~	~	~	~	~	~	1.8	.1	.8	.1	.3	.1	.1
Korea	~	~	~	~	~	~	~	.6	1.2	1.1	2.4	6.6	4.0	4.6
Pakistan	~	~	~	~	~	~	~	~	~	~	1.2	~	~	~
Philippines	~	~	~	~	~	~	~	~	~	~	~	.2	.2	.2
Singapore	~	~	~	~	~	~	~	~	~	.1	.1	~	.1	.3
Thailand	~	~	~	~	~	~	~	~	~	~	.1	.1	.1	.1
Oceania not specified	~	~	~	~	~	~	~	~	~	~	~	~	~	~
Europe	5.2	6.2	3.4	.9	8.5	.2	13.3	~	.8	.6	.8	1.1	.6	.5
Gibraltar	~	~	~	~	3.6	~	~	~	~	~	~	~	~	~
Hungary	~	~	~	~	~	~	~	~	.1	.1	.1	.1	.1	.1
Portugal	5.2	.3	3.4	.9	4.8	.2	13.3	~	.6	.4	.6	.8	.5	.3
Romania	~	~	~	~	~	~	~	~	~	~	~	~	~	~
Yugoslavia	~	5.9	~	~	~	~	~	~	~	~	.1	.2	.1	.2
Europe not specified	~	~	~	~	~	~	~	~	~	~	~	~	~	~

Table 2623 (Continued)

DOMINICAN REPUBLIC ABSOLUTE VALUE OF GOODS TRADED WITH SELECTED REGIONS AND COUNTRIES,[1] 1975-82 (M US)[2]

Category	Exports FOB							Imports CIF						
	1975	1976	1977	1979	1980	1981	1982	1975	1976	1977	1979	1980	1981	1982
III. Developing Countries (Continued)														
Non-Oil Developing Countries														
Middle East	~	~	~	~	~	~	~	~	.1	.3	.1	.3	.3	.2
Israel	~	~	~	~	~	~	~	~	.1	.3	.1	.3	.3	.2
IV. Latin America[3]														
A. ARGENTINA	4.5	5.5	11.4	18.4	28.0	38.5	26.9	54.9	169.2	114.9	145.2	125.5	239.7	275.3
Antigua and Barbuda	~	~	~	~	~	~	~	.5	.6	10.0	.7	1.2	.7	1.0
Bahamas	~	~	~	~	.3	.1	.3	~	.4	~	~	~	~	~
Barbados	~	~	.5	.7	.4	.1	.3	~	~	~	~	~	~	~
Belize	~	~	~	~	.1	.1	1.2	~	~	~	.3	~	.1	~
Bermuda	~	~	~	~	~	.1	.1	~	1.6	1.8	.3	~	~	.8
C. BRAZIL	1.9	~	~	~	~	6.2	~	6.6	7.1	15.6	11.6	11.7	21.6	15.0
D. CHILE	~	~	~	.1	.7	.7	~	.5	1.5	1.8	9.8	10.7	2.8	4.5
E. COLOMBIA	.2	.6	.1	.4	.9	.7	2.3	20.9	7.5	4.5	4.8	5.4	6.1	3.8
F. COSTA RICA	~	.2	~	.2	.9	.5	3.0	.5	.7	2.6	.9	2.4	2.9	1.9
Dominica	.5	~	~	~	.4	1.6	.7	~	~	~	.1	~	~	~
I. ECUADOR	.2	.2	~	~	~	~	.1	.4	.5	.6	1.1	1.3	1.5	1.6
J. EL SALVADOR	.4	~	~	.7	.7	.4	.2	~	~	~	.1	~	~	.1
Grenada	~	.1	~	~	.7	1.7	.9	~	~	~	~	~	~	~
Guadeloupe	~	~	~	1.0	2.8	~	.1	~	~	~	~	~	~	~
K. GUATEMALA	2.6	.1	.1	.1	.2	.4	.1	2.6	2.2	2.5	2.7	5.7	7.6	7.3
Guiana, French	~	~	~	.1	.2	~	~	~	~	~	~	~	~	~
Guyana	~	~	.6	~	.3	~	.1	~	~	~	~	~	~	~
L. HAITI	1.6	2.1	5.4	4.4	9.2	7.1	5.1	.5	1.0	1.0	1.1	3.2	.5	2.4
M. HONDURAS	.1	.2	.2	.3	.3	.6	.5	15.3	10.2	8.1	6.0	2.2	2.0	2.5
Jamaica	~	~	.5	.3	.7	4.9	1.3	~	1.4	1.1	2.1	1.4	2.1	1.7
Leeward Islands	~	~	~	.5	~	~	~	~	~	~	~	~	~	.4
Martinique	~	~	~	2.7	3.3	.1	.1	~	~	~	~	~	~	~
N. MEXICO	~	~	~	~	~	~	~	6.6	6.2	8.8	9.5	9.1	81.0	170.7
Montserrat	~	~	~	~	~	~	~	~	~	~	.1	~	~	.2
Netherlands Antilles	~	1.0	1.2	1.2	1.5	2.3	2.7	~	119.9	45.7	76.9	58.1	97.5	48.3
O. NICARAGUA	~	~	.1	.3	.7	.1	.8	~	.9	.9	.3	~	~	2.7
P. PANAMA	.5	.1	.1	.3	.7	.5	~	.2	5.8	7.6	9.4	9.6	9.7	11.4
Panama Canal Zone	~	~	~	~	~	~	~	~	~	.6	.3	~	~	~
Q. PARAGUAY	~	~	~	~	~	~	~	.2	.2	.2	~	~	~	.1
R. PERU	.2	.2	2.1	~	.2	.4	.5	.2	~	.2	4.4	.5	.1	.1
St. Kitts-Nevis	~	~	~	~	.1	~	~	~	~	~	~	~	~	~
St. Lucia	~	~	~	~	1.5	1.5	1.8	~	~	~	~	.5	.1	.1
St. Vincent	~	~	~	~	1.1	1.2	1.4	~	~	~	~	~	~	~
Suriname	~	.5	.4	.5	1.2	2.5	~	~	~	~	~	~	.2	~
Trinidad and Tobago	~	.2	.3	.1	.2	1.2	2.4	~	.3	.3	.2	.1	.3	.6
S. URUGUAY	~	.1	.1	.1	.2	.1	.5	~	1.0	1.0	3.0	2.6	2.5	1.0
Windward Islands	~	~	~	4.0	~	~	~	~	~	~	~	~	~	~
America not specified	~	.1	2.1	.1	.2	.4	~	~	~	~	.1	.5	.1	.1
British West Indies	~	~	.3	.1	~	.4	.5	~	~	~	~	~	~	~
French West Indies not specified	~	.1	~	~	~	~	~	~	~	~	~	~	~	~
V. USSR, Eastern Europe, etc.														
G. CUBA	~	~	~	~	5.0	14.1	99.8	~	.3	.6	.8	1.3	1.4	.2
Czechoslovakia	~	~	~	~	~	~	31.2	~	.2	.2	.2	.3	.4	.2
Eastern Germany	~	~	~	~	1.7	~	~	~	.2	.1	.1	.3	.9	.1
North Korea	~	~	~	~	~	~	~	~	~	~	~	~	~	~
Poland	~	~	~	4.0	~	~	~	~	.2	.2	.1	.1	.1	.1
USSR	~	~	~	~	~	~	~	~	~	~	.5	.9	.2	~
EEC	85.6	67.1	86.4	79.1	65.7	68.5	53.5	~	78.6	84.4	89.1	126.0	101.4	88.2

Table 2623 (Continued)

DOMINICAN REPUBLIC ABSOLUTE VALUE OF GOODS TRADED WITH SELECTED REGIONS AND COUNTRIES,[1] 1975–82 (M US)[2]

Category	Exports FOB							Imports CIF						
	1975	1976	1977	1979	1980	1981	1982	1975	1976	1977	1979	1980	1981	1982
VI. Percent Distribution														
Industrial Countries	~	96.0	93.0	91.5	84.3	88.0	77.1	~	69.8	69.6	65.9	67.3	61.6	58.3
Oil Exporting Countries	~	.4	1.8	6.0	9.5	6.9	3.9	~	6.1	15.1	18.0	21.1	19.5	17.7
Non-Oil Developing Countries	~	3.6	5.2	2.5	5.7	3.9	6.7	~	22.9	14.2	14.6	10.0	17.6	22.9
Africa	~	2.0	3.3	.3	1.9	.6	1.8	~	.2	.1	.1	.3	.1	.2
Asia	~	~	~	~	~	~	~	~	.4	.4	.6	.8	.5	.6
Europe	~	.9	.4	.1	.9	~	1.6	~	.1	.1	.1	.1	~	~
Middle East	~	~	~	~	~	~	~	~	~	~	~	~	~	~
Western Hemisphere	~	.8	1.5	2.1	2.9	3.2	3.3	~	22.2	13.6	13.8	8.8	16.9	22.0
USSR, Eastern Europe, etc.	~	~	~	~	.5	1.2	12.3	~	~	.1	.1	.1	.1	~
VII. Annual Percent Change														
World	~	-19.9	9.3	29.9	10.1	23.2	-31.9	~	-13.7	10.8	23.3	35.0	-8	-11.6
Industrial Countries	~	-14.2	5.9	35.6	1.4	28.7	-40.3	~	-17.9	10.4	17.5	37.8	-9.2	-16.4
Oil Exporting Countries	~	-63.4	381.0	-8.1	75.3	-10.1	-62.0	~	-57.0	173.5	43.9	58.6	-8.6	-19.8
Non-Oil Developing Countries	~	-69.2	56.4	-16.8	152.0	-16.7	19.1	~	47.7	-31.2	27.9	-7.6	75.2	14.5
Africa	~	-56.5	82.9	-62.2	666.3	-61.5	101.5	~	-34.2	-60.1	-28.3	218.7	-64.6	50.5
Asia	~	-99.2	-82.6	~	-96.2	~	-45.5	~	-43.9	32.7	28.2	65.3	-31.6	.6
Europe	~	-80.2	-46.0	-90.0	806.3	-97.8	~	~	-64.8	-26.3	-25.7	48.1	-42.8	-18.9
Middle East	~	~	~	~	~	~	~	~	120.0	150.8	-77.5	145.6	.4	-34.9
Western Hemisphere	~	-19.8	107.2	75.7	52.3	37.3	-30.1	~	56.4	-32.1	29.9	-13.6	91.0	14.8
USSR, Eastern Europe, etc.	~	~	~	~	~	180.2	608.5	~	-81.1	107.1	3.4	72.4	6.6	-84.9

1. DOT data may differ between countries and from IFS data because of the time it takes for an export to become an import, etc.
2. Data may be calculated from partner's reported data or estimated on basis of less than 12 months.
3. Venezuela is included in category III.

SOURCE: Adapted from the IMF-DOT Annual, 1970-74; IMF-DOT-Y, 1982; IMF-DOT-Y, 1983.

Table 2624

ECUADOR ABSOLUTE VALUE OF GOODS TRADED WITH SELECTED REGIONS AND COUNTRIES,[1] 1975–82 (M US)[2]

Category	Exports FOB							Imports CIF						
	1975	1976	1977	1979	1980	1981	1982	1975	1976	1977	1979	1980	1981	1982
I. World	935.9	1,262.5	1,200.5	2,067.3	2,496.4	2,540.3	2,671.0	995.6	969.1	1,508.1	1,985.7	2,249.8	2,246.3	2,360.5
II. Industrial Countries	552.6	619.4	694.6	1,031.4	1,336.6	1,413.0	1,301.3	828.3	795.8	1,245.2	1,594.5	1,812.5	1,650.1	1,785.6
United States	452.1	475.7	435.6	751.9	811.9	983.9	1,089.2[a]	386.1	378.5	579.1	686.9	862.4	757.3	903.9[a]
Canada	4.6	18.9	40.0	15.3	6.1	3.1	28.2[a]	14.5	15.7	36.0	39.7	42.3	82.2	52.0[a]
Australia	3.7	.1	.1	.9	1.5	1.6	3.4[a]	7.4	4.8	6.5	8.5	7.0	16.3	9.1[a]
Japan	10.2	14.0	20.0	28.1	302.2	310.7	21.6[a]	148.7	160.2	241.7	254.1	307.5	263.3	244.7[a]
New Zealand	3.7	2.6	3.5	5.6	2.4	5.1	10.0[a]	~	.5	1.0	3.6	1.2	.4	.3[a]
Austria	.1	.2	3.4	9.4	4.7	.8	2.9[a]	7.4	2.7	5.7	9.0	8.0	9.6	5.2[a]
Belgium	13.3	15.6	19.9	22.5	24.0	22.7	13.7[a]	9.9	5.2	7.9	12.1	11.6	14.3	11.6[a]
Denmark	.1	.1	.2	.1	~	~	.4[a]	3.8	5.1	3.1	5.9	7.8	9.0	13.4[a]
Finland	.8	1.4	.9	1.8	1.4	2.9	4.0[a]	.6	2.0	3.4	5.5	2.5	1.8	2.0[a]
France	4.4	5.4	31.4	20.0	17.5	4.2	12.0[a]	21.7	16.0	16.0	27.6	29.5	29.8	34.3[a]
Germany	26.5	36.7	53.6	71.1	40.4	29.3	41.1[a]	95.6	83.6	118.5	165.1	163.7	166.4	160.8[a]
Ireland	2.5	2.1	2.2	3.4	4.1	4.7	7.9[a]	.2	.4	1.0	.6	.6	1.0	1.7[a]
Italy	15.6	20.2	22.7	30.9	76.4	14.3	29.8[a]	32.5	20.1	36.7	148.2	114.6	83.4	102.8[a]
Netherlands	13.3	20.3	51.9	43.7	19.2	22.5	16.7[a]	17.0	10.1	16.6	16.1	23.3	24.3	25.1[a]
Norway	.2	.7	~	.1	~	~	.6[a]	1.5	1.4	3.0	3.0	42.2	18.6	8.8[a]
Spain	1.1	2.6	6.5	20.0	16.5	3.7	6.6[a]	21.3	12.8	25.9	42.2	40.1	35.5	51.2[a]
Sweden	1.5	.5	.2	1.0	.8	.1	.2[a]	12.1	18.4	36.6	14.8	18.3	10.9	27.0[a]
Switzerland	1.4	1.0	.7	2.1	.5	.4	4.2[a]	3.8	22.4	58.1	81.5	70.6	60.2	42.5[a]
United Kingdom	1.5	1.4	1.9	3.7	7.0	3.1	9.2[a]	40.5	36.1	48.5	70.0	59.3	65.8	89.3[a]
III. Developing Countries														
Oil Exporting Countries	10.4	14.5	8.9	33.9	42.1	53.0	60.7	14.5	4.1	5.7	18.1	22.7	23.6	22.3
Indonesia	.2	2.4	~	~	~	~	~	.6	.2	.4	~	.4	1.1	1.1[a]
Iran, I.R. of	8.1	6.6	.5	~	~	~	~	.3	.3	~	4.1	~	~	~
Libya	.7	.7	.5	~	~	~	4.0[a]	~	~	~	~	~	~	~
Saudi Arabia	~	.5	~	~	~	~	~	~	~	~	~	~	~	~
T. VENEZUELA	1.4	4.3	8.3	33.9	42.1	53.0	56.7[a]	13.6	3.6	5.3	14.1	22.4	22.6	21.2[a]
Non-Oil Developing Countries	~	601.6	468.7	974.8	1,100.0	1,045.9	1,204.0	~	150.2	232.6	308.6	355.2	501.8	483.4
Africa	~	2.1	1.0	.5	3.7	1.0	3.0	~	1.6	8.9	37.0	26.9	27.4	20.6
Morocco	3.7	1.0	.4	.5	3.1	.7	.5[a]	~	1.0	~	~	1.0	~	20.1[a]
South Africa	~	.3	.3	~	~	~	~	7.4	~	5.7	24.5	23.9	26.5	~
Tunisia	~	.2	.1	~	.6	.4	1.8[a]	~	.6	3.2	12.4	2.6	.7	.5[a]
Africa not specified	~	~	~	~	~	~	~	~	~	~	~	~	~	~
Asia	~	3.7	12.8	17.9	11.9	493.7	650.2	~	17.6	19.5	23.5	34.4	174.6	164.9
China, People's Rep.	~	~	~	~	~	~	~	.6	.6	1.5	.6	.5	.6	5.2[a]
Hong Kong	~	~	~	~	~	~	~	~	1.6	1.6	.3	~	~	7.1[a]
India	~	~	~	~	~	~	~	~	.6	.6	~	~	~	~
Korea	~	~	~	~	~	~	128.6[a]	.1	.8	6.8	1.5	3.6	1.3	5.0[a]
Malaysia	~	~	.3	.2	.4	.2	.2[a]	~	3.6	~	~	3.6	~	1.4[a]
Pakistan	~	~	~	~	~	~	~	~	.1	.1	~	~	~	~
Philippines	~	~	~	~	~	~	~	~	~	~	3.1	~	~	2.0[a]
Singapore	~	.1	~	~	~	2.0[a]	.2[a]	~	~	~	~	~	~	.2[a]
Sri Lanka	~	~	~	~	~	~	.2[a]	1.2	~	~	~	~	~	.5[a]
Western Samoa	~	~	~	~	~	~	~	~	.4	.4	.4	.5	.7	~
Asia not specified	~	~	12.6	17.7	11.6	493.5	514.7[a]	6.4	~	11.0	16.8	29.2	173.3	144.6[a]
Oceania not specified	~	.6	~	~	~	~	~	~	~	.2	5.0	1.0	~	~
Europe	~	36.3	34.3	84.4	42.8	26.8	19.1	~	5.5	10.5	7.6	11.8	20.5	10.9
Greece	8.6	1.4	~	~	~	~	.2[a]	~	~	~	.3	.3	~	2.9[a]
Hungary	~	13.9	15.9	31.2	17.2	11.8	8.2[a]	~	.3	.7	.3	~	12.2	4.4[a]
Malta	1.2	~	~	~	~	~	1.2[a]	~	~	~	~	~	~	~
Portugal	1.8	2.2	5.0	1.6	1.8	1.6	1.2[a]	.6	1.5	1.3	.9	2.7	2.4	2.2[a]
Romania	.2	7.2	.7	6.4	1.6	~	.5[a]	.2	.7	2.1	1.3	.2	.1	~
Turkey	~	~	~	~	~	~	~	~	.1	~	~	~	~	~
Yugoslavia	5.0	10.2	11.8	40.5	21.2	12.8	8.6[a]	4.0	2.8	5.6	4.9	5.6	5.7	1.3[a]
Europe not specified	~	1.4	.9	4.7	1.0	.6	.2[a]	~	.1	.8	.1	3.1	.2	.1[a]

Table 2624 (Continued)

ECUADOR ABSOLUTE VALUE OF GOODS TRADED WITH SELECTED REGIONS AND COUNTRIES,[1] 1975-82
(M US)[2]

Exports FOB

Category	1975	1976	1977	1979	1980	1981	1982
III. Developing Countries (Continued)							
Non-Oil Developing Countries							
Middle East							
Israel	~	2.4	~	~	~	~	15.8
Jordan	~	.1	~	~	~	~	15.8[a]
Syrian Arab Rep.	~	2.0	~	~	~	~	~
IV. Latin America[3]	314.0	557.1	421.1	872.1	1,041.6	524.3	515.9
A. ARGENTINA	9.3	6.8	13.8	30.3	48.0	31.8	28.8[a]
B. BOLIVIA	.3	.3	.3	.6	.6	.7	.6[a]
C. BRAZIL	5.8	5.8	5.0	6.2	34.4	65.5	207.8[a]
D. CHILE	78.0	75.8	87.9	151.2	214.8	73.7	28.5[a]
E. COLOMBIA	26.3	71.9	46.1	64.6	68.6	82.7	75.1[a]
F. COSTA RICA	1.0	.1	.1	1.5	1.9	1.2	.5[a]
H. DOMINICAN REP.	~	~	~	~	~	~	~
J. EL SALVADOR	.2	.2	.5	.2	.2	.4	.4[a]
K. GUATEMALA	.1	.3	.1	.3	.5	.7	~
L. HAITI	~	.1	~	~	~	~	~
M. HONDURAS	~	~	~	.2	~	~	~
Jamaica	~	.1	~	~	~	~	~
N. MEXICO	6.2	5.3	5.5	21.6	13.1	16.3	5.9[a]
Netherlands Antilles	~	52.7	~	~	~	~	~
O. NICARAGUA	~	~	~	~	~	~	~
P. PANAMA	83.3	155.2	122.6	190.2	57.6	17.3	57.7[a]
Panama Canal Zone	~	.1	.4	.4	.3	.3	~
Q. PARAGUAY	.1	.1	.4	.4	.3	.3	~
R. PERU	103.3	154.5	115.3	9.2	12.7	9.6	10.6[a]
Trinidad and Tobago	.1	27.5	.2	2.2	5.1	100.8	45.2[a]
S. URUGUAY	~	.4	.2	2.2	4.3	~	~
America not specified	~	~	~	~	~	~	31.7[a]
Other Latin America not specified	~	~	23.1	393.4	583.7	123.4	23.0[a]
V. USSR, Eastern Europe, etc.	33.7	24.8	28.2	24.5	12.6	13.9	10.8
Bulgaria	.2	.7	1.5	~	.4	1.3	1.2[a]
Czechoslovakia	3.0	3.9	6.4	10.9	4.7	4.8	3.9[a]
Eastern Germany	8.4	7.0	7.1	1.5	2.0	3.2	2.5[a]
Poland	.9	.4	1.6	5.7	.6	~	~
USSR	12.6	12.8	11.6	4.9	4.8	4.6	3.2[a]
USSR, etc., not specified	1.1	~	.1	1.6	1.6	~	~
Country or area not specified	~	~	~	2.5	4.3	.2	.3[a]
Special categories	~	~	~	~	1.8	.1	.1[a]
EEC	~	103.1	183.8	195.4	188.7	100.8	130.9
VI. Percent Distribution							
Industrial Countries	~	49.1	57.9	49.9	53.5	55.6	48.7
Oil Exporting Countries	~	1.1	.7	1.6	1.7	2.1	2.3
Non-Oil Developing Countries	~	47.7	39.0	47.2	44.1	41.2	45.1
Africa	~	.2	~	~	.1	~	.1
Asia	~	.3	1.1	.9	.5	19.4	24.3
Europe	~	2.9	2.9	4.1	1.7	~	.7
Middle East	~	.2	.7	~	~	~	.6
Western Hemisphere	~	44.1	35.1	42.2	41.7	20.6	19.3
USSR, Eastern Europe, etc.	~	2.0	2.3	1.2	.5	.5	.4

Imports CIF

Category	1975	1976	1977	1979	1980	1981	1982
III. Developing Countries (Continued)							
Non-Oil Developing Countries							
Middle East							
Israel	~	1.8	~	~	~	~	9.6
Jordan	.3	1.8	~	~	~	~	9.6[a]
Syrian Arab Rep.	~	~	~	~	~	~	~
IV. Latin America[3]	109.5	123.8	193.7	240.5	282.0	279.3	277.4
A. ARGENTINA	12.9	12.0	20.5	16.9	13.1	19.0	25.0[a]
B. BOLIVIA	~	.2	.4	1.2	1.7	1.3	1.7[a]
C. BRAZIL	24.8	16.4	25.7	40.2	55.1	83.1	28.1[a]
D. CHILE	12.0	22.7	25.0	32.2	17.7	16.7	66.1[a]
E. COLOMBIA	37.2	39.9	46.5	45.3	63.9	47.9	45.9[a]
F. COSTA RICA	3.0	1.6	1.5	2.1	1.0	14.6	5.3[a]
H. DOMINICAN REP.	~	~	~	4.7	2.3	.1	.1[a]
J. EL SALVADOR	.2	.1	.1	.9	1.6	1.9	~
K. GUATEMALA	.5	1.0	1.8	.9	1.6	~	7.0[a]
L. HAITI	~	~	~	~	~	~	~
M. HONDURAS	1.4	1.5	.9	~	~	~	~
Jamaica	~	~	~	~	~	~	~
N. MEXICO	11.0	9.7	33.4	23.4	22.2	23.7	17.1[a]
Netherlands Antilles	~	5.6	~	~	.1	~	~
O. NICARAGUA	~	~	~	~	~	~	~
P. PANAMA	.4	1.5	3.8	7.0	10.8	17.2	11.9[a]
Panama Canal Zone	~	.1	.1	.1	.1	~	~
Q. PARAGUAY	.1	.1	.3	~	.1	~	~
R. PERU	5.7	6.9	22.9	60.0	79.0	38.0	38.2[a]
Trinidad and Tobago	.1	.4	.1	1.5	1.0	.8	14.2[a]
S. URUGUAY	.3	.4	10.5	5.2	12.5	15.0	1.4[a]
America not specified	~	3.7	.1	~	~	~	~
Other Latin America not specified	~	~	.2	~	~	~	15.6[a]
V. USSR, Eastern Europe, etc.	8.3	6.9	9.1	37.5	24.7	38.3	35.1
Bulgaria	.2	.1	.7	.2	2.6	1.6	1.6[a]
Czechoslovakia	3.3	2.2	3.7	8.1	7.6	5.7	5.5[a]
Eastern Germany	.9	3.3	1.3	~	3.8	23.1	21.8[a]
Poland	1.5	.7	2.3	~	5.4	1.8	1.1[a]
USSR	1.1	.6	1.1	27.2	5.3	6.1	5.2[a]
USSR, etc., not specified	~	~	.1	1.3	~	~	~
Country or area not specified	~	5.6	~	1.6	1.8	.3	.3[a]
Special categories	~	~	~	~	~	~	~
EEC	~	176.6	248.2	445.6	410.5	394.0	441.8
VI. Percent Distribution							
Industrial Countries	~	82.1	82.6	80.3	80.6	73.5	75.6
Oil Exporting Countries	~	.4	.4	.9	1.0	1.1	.9
Non-Oil Developing Countries	~	15.5	15.4	15.5	15.8	22.3	20.5
Africa	~	.1	.6	1.9	1.2	1.2	.9
Asia	~	1.8	1.3	1.2	1.5	7.8	7.0
Europe	~	.6	.7	.4	.5	.9	.5
Middle East	~	.2	~	~	~	~	.4
Western Hemisphere	~	12.8	12.8	12.1	12.5	12.4	11.8
USSR, Eastern Europe, etc.	~	.7	.6	1.9	1.1	1.7	1.5

Table 2624 (Continued)

ECUADOR ABSOLUTE VALUE OF GOODS TRADED WITH SELECTED REGIONS AND COUNTRIES,[1] 1975-82
(M US)[2]

Category	Exports FOB							Imports CIF						
	1975	1976	1977	1979	1980	1981	1982	1975	1976	1977	1979	1980	1981	1982
VII. Annual Percent Change														
World	~	34.9	-4.9	38.4	20.8	1.8	5.1	~	-2.7	55.6	21.8	13.3	-.2	5.1
Industrial Countries	~	12.1	12.1	7.0	29.6	5.7	-7.9	~	-3.9	56.5	18.7	13.7	-9.0	8.2
Oil Exporting Countries	~	40.8	-38.9	119.5	24.0	25.9	14.6	~	-71.7	38.5	135.3	25.4	4.0	-5.8
Non-Oil Developing Countries	~	73.0	-22.1	104.3	12.8	-4.9	15.1	~	9.7	54.8	28.7	15.1	41.3	-3.7
Africa	~	-21.9	-78.5	-79.7	672.9	-72.0	189.4	~	-42.8	459.7	244.0	-27.1	1.8	-24.9
Asia	~	-70.6	246.9	-6.9	-33.3	~	31.7	~	168.4	11.1	79.4	46.3	407.5	-5.6
Europe	~	113.0	-5.4	105.9	-49.3	-37.4	-28.7	~	-11.8	91.9	23.6	56.6	73.0	-46.7
Middle East	~	208.8	~	~	~	~	~	~	389.2	~	~	~	~	~
Western Hemisphere	~	77.1	-24.4	110.3	19.4	-49.7	-1.6	~	2.2	56.5	14.7	17.2	-1.0	-.7
USSR, Eastern Europe, etc.	~	-.8	13.6	-5.0	-48.7	10.5	-22.0	~	-.7	32.8	60.9	-34.0	54.9	-8.3

1. DOT data may differ between countries and from IFS data because of the time it takes
   for an export to become an import, etc.

2. Data may be calculated from partner's reported data or estimated on basis of less than
   12 months.

3. No trade with Cuba; Venezuela is included in category III.

a. Five or fewer months of reported data; seven or more months derived or extrapolated.

SOURCE: Adapted from the IMF-DOT Annual, 1970-74; IMF-DOT-Y, 1982;
IMF-DOT-Y, 1983.

Table 2625

EL SALVADOR ABSOLUTE VALUE OF GOODS TRADED WITH SELECTED REGIONS AND COUNTRIES,[1] 1975–82
(M US)[2]

Category	Exports FOB							Imports CIF						
	1975	1976	1977	1979	1980	1981	1982	1975	1976	1977	1979	1980	1981	1982
I. **World**	514.2	720.7	974.4	1,223.4	1,070.3	796.5	879.2	598.7	717.9	945.4	1,039.5	971.4	981.4	929.0
II. **Industrial Countries**	340.8	493.1	726.2	910.9	710.1	376.6	536.7	365.3	437.6	569.4	570.0	348.3	460.3	473.4
United States	139.8	235.5	315.9	339.8	439.3	136.5	302.8*	188.3	205.1	277.2	295.0	194.2	249.8	320.9*
Canada	2.2	3.4	4.4	10.2	8.8	9.1	16.8*	9.6	10.1	11.7	13.2	11.5	17.2	12.5*
Australia	~	~	.2	.1	~	~	.1*	1.1	1.5	3.1	1.4	1.2	1.9	.1*
Japan	60.2	56.6	61.2	70.4	43.2	36.1	20.5*	41.4	69.6	104.4	82.5	37.5	33.5	26.6*
New Zealand	.8	.6	~	~	~	~	.1ᵃ	.3	.4	2.5	3.3		3.5	3.2ᵃ
Austria							13.7*	.3	.4	.8	1.0	.2	.9	2.5*
Belgium	8.3	10.0	14.5	13.2	6.2	.5	1.3*	15.8	7.3	9.9	12.9	6.6	9.4	5.1*
Denmark	.7	1.7	1.3	.9		.5	3.4*	1.4	1.8	2.6	3.4	3.3	2.6	2.1*
Finland	.7	3.6	3.9	.5			.5*	.7	~	~	.2	4.7	.2	1.5*
France	2.9	3.3	20.4	3.5	9.8	8.2	7.9*	5.5	5.7	10.0	15.2	8.1	30.8	5.9*
Germany	64.4	103.3	179.4	313.6	149.0	173.8	137.3*	35.7	42.0	54.3	48.7	24.4	36.8	30.1
Iceland	~	.1	~	.2			.1ᵃ							
Ireland								~	.1	.3	.2	.8	5.2	4.2ᵃ
Italy	5.2	4.0	7.6	18.7	12.2	2.6	13.0*	14.5	20.5	8.6	22.5	13.0	15.4	6.6*
Netherlands	31.0	57.6	91.6	122.0	28.8	5.2	7.6*	17.9	20.9	26.6	28.5	14.8	24.8	13.2*
Norway	1.4	5.9	9.7	2.6			.1*	1.4	1.1	2.1	.2	.1	.1	.3*
Spain	8.1	1.0	10.1	9.2	5.4		3.8*	5.3	23.4	17.2	11.6	9.8	12.0	11.5*
Sweden	.6	2.5	1.3	.1	.4		2.6*	4.5	4.3	3.4	5.1	3.3	3.5	10.5*
Switzerland	3.7	2.6	.5	1.2	3.3	1.5	1.9*	5.9	6.1	5.7	5.1	3.6	3.4	6.9*
United Kingdom	11.5	1.5	4.0	4.8	3.8	3.0	3.2*	16.1	17.8	28.9	20.5	11.1	9.2	10.0
III. **Developing Countries**														
Oil Exporting Countries	.1	.1	.5	.5	.4	.9	.8	46.4	48.2	87.5	115.3	244.5	40.4	34.4
Indonesia			.1	.4		.8	.8ᵃ							
Iran, I.R. of														
T. VENEZUELA	.1	.1	.3	.1	.4	~	~	46.4	48.2	87.5	115.3	244.5	40.4	34.4ᵇ
Non-Oil Developing Countries		201.4	237.3	282.7	307.5	229.3	188.0		224.3	279.6	342.2	366.9	396.7	351.7
Africa									5.1	.3	.7	.3	.3	.3
Morocco								.1	.1	.1	.2	.1	.2	.1ᵃ
South Africa								5.0	5.0	7.0	7.4	2.2	3.2	6.7
Asia														
China, People's Rep.	1.4	1.9	3.9	.1	.1	2.1		.1	.2	.4	.1	.2	.1	1.2*
Hong Kong	.3	.6		.1	1.5	.3*		3.2	7.0	2.3	2.6	1.6	1.1	1.1*
India	.4	.1	.7		.3	1.7*		.4	.1	.1	.3	.3		
Korea				1.1	.1			3.7	2.4		1.4			4.3ᵃ
Malaysia														
Pakistan								.5						
Philippines	.8	.7			1.1	.1*		1.6	.3	.4	.3		.6	
Singapore	.5				.1			.1	.2	.1	.3		.1	.2*
Sri Lanka								.4	1.0					
Thailand	.8	2.5	1.6	5.5	5.4									
Europe														
Hungary	8.2		10.8		1.6		1.5ᵃ	.2	.9	.6	.4	1.0	1.0	4.0
Portugal			.3	1.2	1.6	3.1	2.0ᵇ	.1	.2	.2	.1	.1	.1	.1ᵃ
Romania			10.6			2.4	1.8ᵃ	.2	.5	.4	.2	.3		3.4ᵃ
Yugoslavia								.6	.6	.5	.1	.3	.6	.5ᵃ
Middle East								.7	.7	.7			.2	1.2
Israel								.7	.7	.7			.2	1.2*

Table 2625 (Continued)

EL SALVADOR ABSOLUTE VALUE OF GOODS TRADED WITH SELECTED REGIONS AND COUNTRIES,[1] 1975-82

(M US)[2]

Category	Exports FOB							Imports CIF						
	1975	1976	1977	1979	1980	1981	1982	1975	1976	1977	1979	1980	1981	1982
IV. Latin America[3]	154.3	200.0	224.6	277.5	305.7	222.3	180.5	154.3	215.7	270.7	332.8	363.9	391.9	339.6
A. ARGENTINA	~	.1	~	~	.1	.1	~	1.5	1.5	1.7	1.9	2.2	.4	10.2[a]
Bahamas	~	~	~	~	~	~	~	~	~	~	~	~	.2	.2[b]
Belize	~	.7	.6	.4	.6	.7	.6[b]	~	~	~	~	.1	.1	.1[b]
C. BRAZIL	.2	7.2	~	~	.2	~	.2*	2.2	5.9	5.4	9.6	3.2	3.5	1.9*
D. CHILE	~	.2	~	.4	.2	.1	~	1.2	2.7	1.4	.2	.1	.3	.3
E. COLOMBIA	~	.4	~	~	.1	~	~	4.8	2.9	3.8	3.3	1.5	2.0	1.7[b]
F. COSTA RICA	32.9	40.0	50.6	66.8	67.5	34.4	21.2[a]	27.8	33.8	47.3	50.2	55.4	46.7	34.1[a]
H. DOMINICAN REP.	.4	.3	.3	.4	.4	.8	1.6*	.3	~	~	.5	.3	.2	.3[a]
I. ECUADOR	.1	.1	.1	4.8	.4	.1	~	.3	.3	.4	.5	.3	~	~
K. GUATEMALA	79.5	99.4	125.7	173.4	173.6	140.8	119.6[b]	84.4	106.0	127.6	180.7	253.6	247.5	210.3[b]
L. HAITI	~	.1	.1	~	~	~	~	~	~	~	~	~	~	~
M. HONDURAS	~	~	~	.2	~	1.4	1.2[b]	.3	~	.3	~	~	.3	.3[b]
Jamaica	~	.1	~	.1	~	~	~	~	~	.2	.2	~	~	~
N. MEXICO	6.1	10.2	2.2	.1	.5	1.1	.6[a]	13.2	13.2	18.3	27.2	11.8	50.6	64.5[a]
Netherlands Antilles	~	.1	.1	~	~	~	4.5[b]	~	1.2	1.3	1.2	1.6	1.4	1.2[b]
O. NICARAGUA	29.3	36.7	39.2	23.5	54.7	30.0	25.9[b]	24.6	30.7	35.5	26.0	11.4	10.2	8.7[b]
P. PANAMA	5.6	4.5	4.4	6.4	7.3	8.1	5.3[a]	13.1	16.6	21.6	24.6	20.6	25.7	3.8*
Panama Canal Zone	~	~	.4	.1	~	~	~	~	~	.5	~	~	~	~
Q. PARAGUAY	~	~	~	~	~	~	~	~	~	~	~	~	~	~
R. PERU	.1	~	.4	.4	~	~	~	1.3	1.0	1.8	6.5	1.8	2.6	2.2[b]
Suriname	~	~	.3	~	~	~	.1[a]	~	~	~	~	~	~	~
Trinidad and Tobago	~	~	.5	.5	~	~	~	~	.1	.1	.7	.3	.2	~
S. URUGUAY	~	~	~	~	~	~	~	.1	.1	3.7	.7	.3	~	~
Other Latin America not specified	~	~	~	~	~	~	~	~	~	~	~	~	~	~
V. USSR, Eastern Europe, etc.	.5	1.2	.6	.6	~	~	~	.3	.5	.5	.8	.4	.4	.4
Czechoslovakia	~	~	~	~	~	~	~	.3	.4	.5	.7	.4	.4	.3[b]
Poland	.5	1.2	.6	.6	~	~	~	~	.1	~	~	~	~	~
USSR	~	~	~	~	~	~	~	~	.1	.1	~	~	~	~
Country or area not specified	~	15.3	~	10.1	19.8	179.1	152.3[b]	~	4.9	3.7	3.3	6.3	77.0	64.6[b]
EEC	~	181.4	318.9	476.8	209.7	193.4	173.8	~	116.1	141.0	151.9	82.1	134.2	77.2
VI. Percent Distribution														
Industrial Countries	~	68.4	74.5	74.5	66.3	47.3	61.0	~	61.0	60.2	54.9	35.9	46.9	51.0
Oil Exporting Countries	~	.1	.1	.1	.1	.1	.1	~	6.7	9.3	11.1	25.2	4.1	3.7
Non-Oil Developing Countries	~	27.9	24.3	23.1	28.7	28.8	21.4	~	31.2	29.6	32.9	37.8	40.4	37.9
Africa	~	~	~	~	~	.2	.2	~	.7	.7	.7	.2	.3	.7
Asia	~	.2	.2	.3	.2	.2	.2	~	.5	.7	.7	.2	.1	.4
Europe	~	1.1	1.1	.1	.2	.7	.6	~	~	.1	.1	.1	.4	.1
Middle East	~	~	~	.1	~	~	~	~	~	.1	.1	.1	.1	.4
Western Hemisphere	~	27.7	23.0	22.7	28.6	27.9	20.5	~	30.0	28.6	32.0	37.5	39.9	36.6
USSR, Eastern Europe, etc.	~	.2	~	.1	~	~	~	~	.1	.1	.1	~	~	~

Table 2625 (Continued)

EL SALVADOR ABSOLUTE VALUE OF GOODS TRADED WITH SELECTED REGIONS AND COUNTRIES,[1] 1975-82
(M US)[2]

Category	Exports FOB							Imports CIF						
	1975	1976	1977	1979	1980	1981	1982	1975	1976	1977	1979	1980	1981	1982
VII. Annual Percent Change														
World	~	40.2	35.2	44.8	-12.5	-25.6	10.4	~	19.9	31.7	.8	-6.6	1.0	-5.3
Industrial Countries	~	44.7	47.3	65.3	-22.0	-47.0	42.5	~	19.8	30.1	-8.8	-38.9	32.1	2.9
Oil Exporting Countries	~	25.2	264.2	-4.3	-17.9	103.1	-4.9	~	4.0	81.5	48.0	112.0	-83.5	-15.0
Non-Oil Developing Countries	~	22.2	17.8	11.0	8.8	-25.4	-18.0	~	25.1	24.7	6.4	7.2	8.1	-11.3
Africa	~	-98.4	-52.0	-49.2	~	~	~	~	~	-93.7	78.8	-49.3	-1.8	-58.3
Asia	~	277.1	38.1	-45.2	-96.5	974.3	44.4	~	96.5	116.5	-40.0	-70.0	46.7	108.4
Europe	~	-99.6	~	-64.6	33.3	235.6	-.9	~	-86.9	272.8	23.9	-39.9	169.3	304.8
Middle East	~	~	~	~	~	~	~	~	~	~	73.1	~	~	387.9
Western Hemisphere	~	29.3	12.3	13.7	10.2	-27.3	-18.8	~	22.9	25.5	8.0	9.3	7.7	-13.3
USSR, Eastern Europe, etc.	~	116.5	~	~	~	~	~	~	68.4	4.8	-6.4	-47.7	4.6	-14.7

1. DOT data may differ between countries and from IFS data because of the time it takes for an export to become an import, etc.

2. Data may be calculated from partner's reported data or estimated on basis of less than 12 months.

3. No trade with Cuba; Venezuela is included in category III.

a. Five or fewer months of reported data; seven or more months derived or extrapolated.

b. Data extrapolated for the entire year.

SOURCE: Adapted from the IMF-DOT Annual, 1970-74; IMF-DOT-Y, 1982; IMF-DOT-Y, 1983.

Table 2626

GUATEMALA ABSOLUTE VALUE OF GOODS TRADED WITH SELECTED REGIONS AND COUNTRIES,[1] 1975–82
(M US)[2]

Category	Exports FOB							Imports CIF						
	1975	1976	1977	1979	1980	1981	1982	1975	1976	1977	1979	1980	1981	1982
I. World	623.5	760.3	1,187.3	1,243.4	1,517.5	1,226.1	1,244.6	732.7	838.9	1,064.9	1,503.9	1,597.7	1,673.5	1,340.5
II. Industrial Countries	402.4	511.2	821.7	773.6	882.8	566.7	676.2*	479.4	579.3	718.1	907.3	949.2	1,013.8	777.5
United States	142.8	267.2	383.6	368.6	419.9	223.3	331.5*	252.4	305.7	366.9	484.4	551.8	565.9	428.9*
Canada	15.1	5.0	6.0	~	6.0	4.2	18.6*	8.5	15.5	17.5	27.1	20.2	17.2	29.9*
Australia	~	.1	.1	~	.1	.1	1.4*	1.0	1.0	3.1	3.6	1.2	4.0	.8*
Japan	32.3	63.2	90.3	98.7	42.0	59.6	71.0*	65.0	93.2	120.9	122.9	128.5	129.2	51.4*
New Zealand	~	~	~	~	.1	~	~	.9	.2	.5	.5	.9	1.1	.6*
Austria	.2	~	~	.2	.3	.2	6.3*	1.7	1.6	1.6	2.1	1.9	2.2	3.6*
Belgium	10.0	7.8	16.9	21.9	21.6	12.1	5.5*	9.7	7.8	10.9	6.8	7.9	13.9	6.9*
Denmark	3.0	3.0	6.4	2.6	1.7	47.9	9.5*	1.5	1.7	2.7	4.9	4.3	4.2	4.1*
Finland	6.9	16.0	26.8	18.8	29.5	14.2	16.5*	.3	.3	.6	2.1	2.1	.5	2.6*
France	5.0	4.8	7.7	9.6	13.5	15.1	10.5*	11.1	11.2	15.3	23.3	27.3	30.4	23.3*
Germany	62.0	81.2	158.5	108.4	126.0	100.0	61.1*	51.1	58.9	79.2	107.2	86.7	107.8	61.5*
Iceland	~	~	~	~	~	~	~	~	~	~	~	~	~	~
Ireland	~	~	~	~	.1	~	.6[a]	3.3	.2	.8	1.0	1.9	1.5	3.5[a]
Italy	38.6	13.0	27.1	48.7	73.3	31.8	66.3*	13.2	15.6	18.0	22.2	21.5	24.1	12.5*
Netherlands	21.1	26.1	69.6	55.8	63.1	33.5	25.8*	11.2	8.4	13.9	13.7	13.8	13.4	8.9*
Norway	2.1	4.3	6.3	2.6	2.5	3.9	3.6*	~	4.7	2.0	1.0	.6	2.3	1.8*
Spain	7.8	11.1	8.6	10.3	7.2	2.1	1.6*	8.4	11.6	14.6	16.5	20.7	32.8	94.6*
Sweden	3.7	4.7	9.4	3.6	2.6	3.2	4.5*	5.2	4.2	3.9	5.4	4.5	5.6	11.2*
Switzerland	.1	.4	.4	4.9	6.7	1.1	19.7*	7.9	11.7	14.7	31.0	18.4	27.1	15.8*
United Kingdom	50.8	3.3	4.1	16.1	66.7	14.2	21.7*	23.8	25.8	31.2	31.4	36.9	30.5	15.7*
III. Developing Countries														
Oil Exporting Countries	3.5	3.6	14.7	11.3	11.6	14.6	45.3	77.2	64.4	87.2	110.3	159.0	113.4	96.4
Algeria	1.2	.5	.5	1.3	.9	2.0	2.2[a]	~	~	~	~	~	~	~
Indonesia	~	~	~	~	~	~	~	~	~	~	~	~	~	~
Kuwait	~	~	9.5	~	~	~	~	~	~	~	~	~	~	~
Oman	~	~	~	~	~	~	1.5*	~	~	~	~	~	~	~
Saudi Arabia	1.9	2.7	3.8	9.5	9.3	10.2	39.3[a]	~	~	.1	~	~	~	~
T. VENEZUELA	.4	.3	.5	.5	1.3	2.4	2.3[b]	77.2	64.4	87.1	110.3	159.0	113.4	96.4[b]
Non-Oil Developing Countries	~	231.2	291.7	450.7	613.7	613.1	514.9	~	181.7	236.8	437.7	462.8	508.1	438.9
Africa	8.4	.1	.1	~	.3	5.3	5.2	.3	.3	1.1	.9	.2	.3	.6[a]
Ethiopia	~	.1	.1	~	~	5.1	4.4[b]	~	.1	~	~	~	~	~
South Africa	8.3	~	~	~	.2	.2	.9[a]	.1	.2	1.0	.9	.2	.3	.6[a]
Africa not specified	~	~	~	~	~	~	~	~	~	~	~	~	~	~
Asia	~	5.6	23.0	70.3	82.8	61.4	47.7	6.7	6.7	9.5	13.6	17.1	16.7	11.0
China, People's Rep.	~	1.2	1.4	66.3	62.5	44.5	35.3*	~	1.2	.9	1.8	2.0	1.3	1.7*
Hong Kong	~	.7	.8	.8	1.0	1.1	.7*	2.7	2.7	3.4	4.7	4.5	5.2	2.7*
India	~	.7	17.0	.3	.1	.1	.1[b]	1.0	.1	.1	.4	.2	.1	.1[b]
Korea	~	.5	.2	.9	.1	2.5	1.1[a]	.4	1.0	3.8	3.0	7.6	7.8	5.8[a]
Malaysia	~	.5	.5	.2	.1	~	~	~	.4	.8	.1	.1	.1	~
Pakistan	~	~	.2	.2	~	.4	~	~	~	~	~	.1	.1	~
Philippines	~	1.2	.8	~	.2	.4	.5*	~	~	.5	.1	.1	.1	~
Singapore	~	~	.5	~	1.2	.6	~	~	.4	.5	~	.9	1.1	~
Sri Lanka	~	~	~	~	~	~	.1*	~	.4	.3	.2	.2	.5	.2*
Thailand	~	.5	2.3	1.8	.6	1.4	.7[a]	~	.7	.4	1.2	1.2	~	.7[a]
Asia not specified	~	.7	.1	.1	17.2	10.9	9.3[b]	.1	.9	~	1.2	1.5	.6	.5[b]
Europe	~	1.0	12.3	6.6	6.4	16.9	7.8	~	.6	7.2	1.8	6.7	4.3	4.7
Greece	~	~	~	~	~	~	~	~	.8	.8	~	~	~	~
Hungary	~	~	4.3	~	~	15.0	~	~	~	~	~	~	~	~
Portugal	9.6	1.0	5.6	3.5	6.0	1.0	4.2[a]	1.8	.4	1.9	1.7	1.4	4.3	4.6[a]
Romania	~	~	1.4	~	~	~	~	~	~	3.5	~	~	~	~
Turkey	~	~	~	~	.4	.3	3.0[a]	.1	.1	1.0	3.0	5.1	.1	~
Yugoslavia	~	~	.9	3.0	~	.6	.5[b]	~	~	~	~	5.1	.1	.1[b]
Europe not specified	~	~	~	~	~	~	~	~	~	~	~	.1	~	.1[b]

Table 2626 (Continued)

GUATEMALA ABSOLUTE VALUE OF GOODS TRADED WITH SELECTED REGIONS AND COUNTRIES,[1] 1975-82
(M US)[2]

Category	Exports FOB							Imports CIF						
	1975	1976	1977	1979	1980	1981	1982	1975	1976	1977	1979	1980	1981	1982
III. Developing Countries (Continued)														
Non-Oil Developing Countries														
Middle East	~	7.8	8.3	32.7	29.8	22.9	19.6	~	.9	2.5	.8	1.5	.6	4.2
Bahrain	~	~	~	~	~	~	~	~	~	~	~	~	~	.6
Egypt	~	~	4.4	.5	3.6	.2	.6*	~	~	~	~	~	~	~
Israel	~	~	3.0	~	.4	.5	.1*	.3	.9	1.7	.7	1.5	.5	4.2*
Jordan	~	~	.3	~	~	~	~	~	~	.8	~	~	~	~
Lebanon	~	~	.4	~	~	~	~	~	~	~	~	~	~	~
Syrian Arab Rep.	~	~	~	~	~	~	~	~	~	~	~	~	~	~
Middle East not specified	~	7.7	~	32.3	25.8	22.2	18.9[b]	~	~	~	.1	~	.1	.1[b]
IV. Latin America[3]	181.7	208.4	248.0	341.0	494.3	506.7	434.7	146.6	173.2	216.5	420.6	437.3	486.3	418.3
A. ARGENTINA	~	~	~	.1	.4	.2	1.1[a]	1.7	1.6	3.4	4.3	3.0	2.3	2.8[a]
Bahamas	~	~	~	~	~	~	~	~	~	4.7	~	~	~	~
Barbados	~	~	.1	~	~	~	.4[a]	~	~	~	~	~	~	.3[a]
Belize	~	1.1	.6	1.8	.6	3.0	2.6[b]	~	~	~	~	~	.1	.1[b]
B. BOLIVIA	.2	.4	.4	.3	.6	.5	.4[b]	~	~	~	~	~	.2	.2[b]
C. BRAZIL	.4	.3	.1	.2	2.1	.2	.2*	4.3	5.0	8.4	16.7	13.9	17.1	10.9*
D. CHILE	~	.3	.7	.1	.3	.5	~	.3	1.3	1.0	.6	.6	3.9	~
E. COLOMBIA	.1	.1	.1	.1	1.2	.8	.7[b]	11.1	2.8	4.7	6.6	4.3	4.7	4.0[b]
F. COSTA RICA	37.5	41.6	46.9	71.3	89.8	57.5	46.6[a]	16.5	18.4	25.4	61.9	65.3	57.3	66.5[a]
H. DOMINICAN REP.	2.6	2.7	3.1	4.5	6.0	7.7	7.3*	~	~	~	~	.2	.2	.2*
I. ECUADOR	.3	1.1	.8	.5	1.2	1.6	6.8[a]	~	.4	~	~	.3	.4	.2[a]
J. EL SALVADOR	74.9	84.4	105.9	153.3	194.0	230.9	196.3[b]	59.8	58.7	45.0	163.7	99.3	102.8	87.4[b]
Guadeloupe	~	~	.3	.4	.2	~	~	~	~	~	~	~	~	~
L. HAITI	.4	.5	2.4	.4	.4	.6	.5[b]	~	~	~	.1	.2	.1	.1[b]
M. HONDURAS	22.7	25.2	29.1	50.3	60.6	49.7	42.2[b]	12.5	14.5	19.1	29.8	36.9	18.8	16.0[b]
Jamaica	~	1.1	.3	.5	.9	.7	.6[b]	~	.8	1.2	1.0	.2	.1	.1[b]
Martinique	~	~	.7	~	~	~	~	~	~	~	~	~	~	~
N. MEXICO	3.6	4.6	5.9	11.7	23.3	65.1	53.7[a]	24.2	28.1	41.1	45.6	58.9	128.3	112.9[a]
Netherlands Antilles	~	.1	.1	.1	.2	.1	.1[b]	~	21.0	36.5	50.4	121.1	99.3	84.4[b]
O. NICARAGUA	33.9	37.9	40.5	31.6	96.4	69.1	58.7[b]	14.4	14.8	15.9	19.8	16.4	15.1	12.8[b]
P. PANAMA	5.1	6.7	8.9	14.1	15.9	16.9	15.8[a]	.8	1.2	3.7	5.6	6.6	5.7	2.7*
Panama Canal Zone	~	~	~	~	~	~	~	~	~	~	~	~	~	~
Q. PARAGUAY	~	.1	.8	.2	.2	.3	~	.4	.2	.6	1.0	.6	.7	~
R. PERU	.1	.1	.2	~	.2	.3	.3[b]	~	.2	.6	1.0	.6	.7	.6[b]
Suriname	~	~	.8	~	~	~	~	~	~	~	~	~	~	~
Trinidad and Tobago	~	.3	.2	.1	.2	1.2	.5[a]	~	4.3	5.6	13.1	9.4	29.3	16.3[a]
S. URUGUAY	4.3	3.5	5.8	2.2	.9	5.1	4.3	1.5	2.4	3.5	4.4	4.1	4.2	3.5
V. USSR, Eastern Europe, etc.	.5	.7	4.1	2.1	.8	3.7	3.1[b]	~	1.4	1.8	1.5	1.5	1.9	1.6[b]
Bulgaria	~	~	.1	~	~	~	~	~	~	~	~	~	~	~
Czechoslovakia	.5	.7	4.1	~	.8	3.7	3.1[b]	~	1.4	1.8	1.5	1.5	1.9	1.6[b]
Eastern Germany	~	~	1.4	~	~	~	~	~	~	.3	~	~	~	~
Poland	~	~	.3	~	~	~	~	~	~	.8	~	~	~	~
USSR	~	~	~	~	~	~	~	~	~	.4	~	~	~	~
USSR, etc., not specified	3.8	2.9	~	2.1	.1	1.4	1.2[b]	.5	1.0	~	2.9	2.6	2.3	1.9[b]
Country or area not specified	~	2.7	27.3	.2	1.8	2.4	2.0[b]	~	7.2	12.4	34.6	13.1	20.3	17.2[b]
EEC	~	139.1	290.3	263.3	365.9	269.7	201.1	129.1	129.8	172.0	210.6	200.3	225.9	136.3
VI. Percent Distribution														
Industrial Countries	~	67.2	69.2	62.2	58.2	46.2	54.3	~	69.1	67.4	60.3	59.4	60.6	58.0
Oil Exporting Countries	~	.5	1.2	.9	.8	1.2	3.6	~	7.7	8.2	7.3	9.9	6.8	7.2
Non-Oil Developing Countries	~	30.4	24.6	36.2	40.4	50.0	41.4	~	21.7	22.2	29.1	29.0	30.4	32.7
Africa	~	1.1	.4	~	.4	~	.4	~	.1	.1	.1	1.1	1.0	.8
Asia	~	.7	1.9	5.7	5.5	5.0	3.8	~	.8	.9	~	1.1	1.0	.4
Europe	~	.1	1.0	.5	.4	1.4	.6	~	.1	.7	.1	.4	.3	.3
Middle East	~	.1	.7	2.6	2.0	1.9	1.6	~	~	.2	.1	.1	~	~
Western Hemisphere	~	27.4	20.9	27.4	32.6	41.3	34.9	~	20.6	20.3	28.0	27.4	29.1	31.2
USSR, Eastern Europe, etc.	~	.5	.5	.2	.1	.4	.3	~	.3	.3	.3	.3	.2	.3

Table 2626 (Continued)

GUATEMALA ABSOLUTE VALUE OF GOODS TRADED WITH SELECTED REGIONS AND COUNTRIES,[1] 1975-82 (M US)[2]

Exports FOB

Category	1975	1976	1977	1979	1980	1981	1982
VII. Annual Percent Change							
World	~	21.9	56.2	14.1	22.0	-19.2	1.5
Industrial Countries	~	27.0	60.7	6.5	14.1	-35.8	19.3
Oil Exporting Countries	~	5.0	307.8	17.3	2.7	25.8	209.9
Non-Oil Developing Countries	~	10.4	26.2	47.5	36.2	-.1	-16.0
Africa	~	556.9	-99.1	-93.5	744.1	~	-1.5
Asia	~	116.2	314.7	797.6	17.8	-25.9	-22.3
Europe	~	-89.4	~	220.8	-3.1	162.9	-54.0
Middle East	~	-1.1	6.5	102.6	-8.9	-23.3	-14.4
Western Hemisphere	~	10.8	19.0	22.2	45.0	2.5	-14.2
USSR, Eastern Europe, etc.	~	-18.8	62.1	-59.2	-58.1	458.8	-15.0

Imports CIF

Category	1975	1976	1977	1979	1980	1981	1982
World	~	14.5	26.9	17.0	6.2	4.7	-19.9
Industrial Countries	~	20.9	23.9	11.5	4.6	6.8	-23.3
Oil Exporting Countries	~	-16.6	35.4	16.2	44.1	-28.6	-15.0
Non-Oil Developing Countries	~	5.9	30.3	22.1	5.7	9.8	-13.6
Africa	~	-59.5	333.1	-60.2	-77.0	45.3	106.8
Asia	~	83.1	42.1	31.8	25.6	-2.3	-34.1
Europe	~	-69.6	~	24.7	267.6	-35.7	9.6
Middle East	~	213.7	162.6	-9.2	101.1	-61.1	620.7
Western Hemisphere	~	5.0	25.0	22.4	4.0	11.2	-14.0
USSR, Eastern Europe, etc.	~	60.9	47.9	38.8	-7.3	1.0	-15.0

1. DOT data may differ between countries and from IFS data because of the time it takes for an export to become an import, etc.
2. Data may be calculated from partner's reported data or estimated on basis of less than 12 months.
3. No trade with Cuba; Venezuela is included in category III.

a. Five or fewer months of reported data, seven or more months derived or extrapolated.
b. Data extrapolated for the entire year.

SOURCE: Adapted from the IMF-DOT Annual, 1970-74; IMF-DOT-Y, 1982; IMF-DOT-Y, 1983.

Table 2627

HAITI ABSOLUTE VALUE OF GOODS TRADED WITH SELECTED REGIONS AND COUNTRIES,[1] 1975-82 (M US)[2]

Category	Exports FOB							Imports CIF						
	1975	1976	1977	1979	1980	1981	1982	1975	1976	1977	1979	1980	1981	1982
I. World	81.18	117.53	143.30	285.00	345.96	331.45	379.99	142.51	201.05	208.24	450.27	574.73	570.98	524.88
II. Industrial Countries														
United States	79.44	113.39	136.39	279.25	384.66	323.51	369.09	122.87	171.60	169.24	389.64	479.16	471.90	445.25
Canada	60.36	78.46	84.10	212.58*	240.17*	260.82*	296.00*	77.18	113.31	105.72	267.08*	341.99*	330.66*	328.46*
Australia	1.68	1.38	1.76	5.80*	5.48*	6.28*	6.97*	7.75	12.17	14.41	29.82*	25.17*	19.96*	20.96*
Japan	~	.71	.43	.13*	.26	.49	.49*	~	.05	.06	.02	.47	.30*	.01*
New Zealand	.18	~	~	1.04*	.62	1.12*	2.77*	9.68	11.71	14.61	18.68*	32.14*	21.42*	28.04[a]
Austria	~	~	~	.63*	.39*	.09	.14	.05	.06	.12	.06[a]	.18[a]	.05*	.92[a]
Belgium	3.92	6.78	11.67	8.97*	9.97*	6.87*	8.98*	.21	.30	2.56	.48*	2.81*	.69*	.96*
Denmark	.71	.86	1.51	1.12*	1.31*	1.53*	.81*	3.57	3.02	.79	5.69*	2.73*	2.90*	3.88*
Finland	.84	~	~	.02*	.02*	.04*	.97*	.84	.84	~	1.21*	1.84*	1.31*	.77*
France	6.40	12.24	18.24	22.43*	33.30*	15.79*	18.15[a]	6.63	7.04	6.68	15.34*	19.83*	25.73*	15.34*
Germany	.49	.79	2.75	5.60*	8.84*	8.72*	12.02*	4.91	6.57	8.26	10.35*	10.62*	9.10*	12.52*
Iceland	~	.05	.56	.09*	.01*	~	1.73[a]	~	~	~	.27	.47	.01*	.25*
Ireland	~	~	.90	~	~	1.41	~	1.58	.11	.09	~	~	.30*	.14[a]
Italy	3.61	7.33	8.87	12.02*	23.79*	11.24*	11.33*	1.58	1.90	2.46	6.08*	3.32*	32.95*	7.53*
Netherlands	1.28	3.08	3.83	2.05*	1.48*	2.30*	1.49*	3.96	4.75	4.46	9.33*	10.52*	12.26*	10.00*
Norway	.10	.32	.66	.74*	1.26*	.20*	.04*	.42	1.05	.83	1.92*	1.70*	1.76*	2.38*
Spain	.26	.11	.06	.31*	1.74*	2.21*	.99*	.75	.81	.88	12.36*	9.77*	2.83*	1.08*
Sweden	.04	.45	.30	1.38*	1.74*	.40*	.10*	.41	2.56	1.52	1.36*	3.42*	2.73*	1.68*
Switzerland	.14	.42	.33	2.16*	2.35*	1.41*	1.96*	.86	.81	.75	2.02*	5.23*	2.61*	3.14[b]
United Kingdom	.20	.43	.42	2.16*	1.93*	2.58*	4.14*	3.93	4.55	4.97	7.40*	7.20*	4.36*	7.22*
III. Developing Countries														
Oil Exporting Countries														
Nigeria	.04	.08	.42	.25	1.27	1.26	.68	.25	.05	.05	.26	.22	~	~
Saudi Arabia	~	~	~	.01[a]	.02[b]	.02[b]	.02[b]	~	~	~	~	~	~	~
T. VENEZUELA	.04	.08	.42	.23*	.55*	.54*	.67[b]	.24	.05	.05	.26*	.22*	~	~
Non-Oil Developing Countries	~	4.02	6.48	5.50	10.00	6.66	9.98	.24	28.32	37.81	49.35	84.19	89.34	70.21
Africa	~	.37	.29	.03	.72	.17	.25	~	.37	.29	.22	.16	.16	.35
Madagascar	~	~	~	~	~	~	~	~	.04	.01	~	~	~	.01*
Mauritius	~	~	~	~	~	~	~	~	~	~	~	~	~	~
Morocco	~	~	~	~	.69*	.17*	.25[a]	~	~	~	~	~	~	~
Mozambique	~	~	~	~	~	~	~	~	~	~	~	~	~	~
Senegal	~	~	~	~	~	~	~	~	.33	.27	.20[b]	.16[b]	.16[a]	.13[b]
Tanzania	~	~	~	~	~	~	~	~	~	~	.02*	~	~	~
Tunisia	~	~	~	.03*	.03*	.01*	.03*	~	~	~	.02*	.02*	.02*	~
Zambia	~	~	~	~	~	~	~	~	~	~	~	~	~	~
Zimbabwe	~	~	~	~	~	~	.13	~	~	~	~	~	~	.21[a]
Asia														
China, People's Rep.	~	~	~	~	~	~	~	~	2.46	5.39	5.34	11.76	8.62	8.79
Hong Kong	~	.01	.02	~	.07	.02	.09*	~	1.07	3.44	3.13	5.46[a]	5.24[b]	.08*
India	~	~	~	~	.07*	.02*	.09*	~	.84	1.20	3.13	.15[a]	.15[b]	3.90*
Korea	~	~	~	~	~	~	~	~	.05	.15	.09	5.73*	3.08*	.13[b]
Pakistan	~	~	~	.01*	.01*	.01*	.03*	~	.06	.04	1.83*	.28*	.04*	4.65[a]
Philippines	~	~	~	~	~	~	~	~	~	.02	.29	.11*	.11*	.03*
Singapore	~	~	~	~	~	~	~	~	~	.55	~	~	~	~
Thailand	~	~	~	~	~	~	~	.03	.43	~	.01*	.03*	.01*	~
Europe														
Gibraltar	~	~	.02	.04	.06	.05	1.85	.03	.05	.02	.01*	.03*	.05	.25
Greece	~	.01	.01	.03[b]	.04[b]	.04[b]	.03[b]	.11	.70	1.13	.14	.30	.04*	.02*
Hungary	~	~	~	.01*	.02*	.01*	.66*	~	.05	.02	.02*	.03*	.01*	.11[a]
Malta	~	~	~	~	~	~	1.15[a]	~	.19	.48	.02*	.03*	~	~
Portugal	~	~	~	.01*	.01*	.04*	.03*	.03	.05	.02	.02*	.27*	~	~
Romania	~	~	~	~	.27*	.01*	~	~	.37	.58	~	.30	~	~
Turkey	~	~	~	~	~	~	~	.11	.04	.02	.10*	~	~	~
Yugoslavia	~	~	~	.01[a]	~	~	~	~	~	~	~	~	~	.12[a]

Table 2627 (Continued)

HAITI ABSOLUTE VALUE OF GOODS TRADED WITH SELECTED REGIONS AND COUNTRIES,[1] 1975-82 (M US)[2]

Category	Exports FOB 1975	1976	1977	1979	1980	1981	1982	Imports CIF 1975	1976	1977	1979	1980	1981	1982
III. Developing Countries (Continued)														
Non-Oil Developing Countries														
Middle East														
Israel	~	.01	.18	.37	.51	.51	.44	~	.04	~	.11	2.09	.11	.11
Jordan	.01	.01	.02	~	~	~	~	~	.04	~	.11*	2.09*	.11*	.11*
Lebanon	~	~	.17	.34[a]	.51[b]	.51[b]	.44[b]	~	~	~	~	~	~	~
Yemen Arab Rep.	~	~	~	.03*	~	~	~	~	~	~	~	~	~	~
IV. Latin America[3]														
A. ARGENTINA	.51	4.00	6.28	5.06	8.63	5.91	7.32	3.69	24.75	31.01	43.54	69.88	80.41	60.72
Bahamas	~	~	~	.01*	.82[b]	.91[b]	.86[b]	.10	.03	.04	2.22*	.37*	.28*	.31[a]
Barbados	~	.24	.11	.59[b]	.09*	.23[b]	.23[b]	~	.06	.09	.14[b]	.17[b]	.17[b]	.14[b]
Belize	~	.21	.40	.08[b]	.07[b]	.07[b]	.06[b]	~	.01	.01	.22*	.47*	.27*	.26[a]
Bermuda	~	~	~	.05[b]	.05[b]	.05[b]	.04[b]	~	~	~	~	~	~	~
B. BOLIVIA	~	.03	.01	.02*	~	~	~	~	~	~	~	~	~	~
C. BRAZIL	.01	.01	.01	~	.01*	~	.01*	.45	2.02	2.05	4.30*	7.39*	4.13*	4.68*
D. CHILE	~	~	~	~	~	~	~	.02	.02	.16	~	~	~	~
E. COLOMBIA	.02	.04	.03	.06*	.04*	.01*	.01[b]	1.16	1.09	.61	1.14*	1.57*	1.17[a]	.99[b]
F. COSTA RICA	~	~	.04	.06*	~	~	~	~	.01	~	.63*	.83*	.77[a]	1.05[a]
H. DOMINICAN REP.	.48	2.07	.68	1.11*	3.25*	.54*	2.42*	1.00	1.77	2.39	4.85*	10.15*	7.80*	5.62[b]
I. ECUADOR	~	~	.29	~	~	~	~	.05	.01	.03	.06*	.05*	.02*	.02[b]
J. EL SALVADOR	~	.10	.14	.39*	.41[a]	.41[b]	.35[b]	~	.07	.10	.16*	.11*	.11[b]	.09[b]
Guadeloupe	~	~	.11	.12[a]	.19[a]	.07[a]	.06[b]	.42	.18	.07	.48*	.47*	.62*	.52[b]
K. GUATEMALA	~	.33	.05	.17[a]	.12[a]	.12[b]	.10[b]	~	.36	.19	.07*	~	~	~
Guiana, French	~	~	1.10	~	~	~	~	~	.01	~	~	~	~	~
Guyana	~	~	.14	.46[b]	.62[b]	.62[b]	.52[b]	~	~	~	~	.10*	.10[b]	.08[b]
M. HONDURAS	~	.08	1.96	.16*	.03*	.03[b]	.02[b]	.01	1.61	2.17	1.33*	1.04*	1.04[b]	.89[b]
Jamaica	~	.10	.10	.10	.19[b]	.19[b]	.16[b]	~	~	~	~	~	~	~
Leeward Islands	~	.11	.30	.29[b]	.28[b]	.28[b]	.24[b]	~	~	~	~	~	~	~
Martinique	~	.08	.09	.56*	1.01[b]	1.01[b]	.86[b]	~	.04	.04	.17*	.24[b]	.24[b]	.21[b]
N. MEXICO	.16	~	.01	~	.04*	.01*	.04[a]	.47	.77	.63	.83*	.79*	12.89*	.25[a]
Netherlands Antilles	~	.32	.18	.20*	.40*	.24*	.10[a]	11.37	14.88	20.91	22.41[b]	23.16[b]	23.16[b]	9.68[b]
O. NICARAGUA	~	.01	.02	.26[b]	.35[b]	.35[b]	.30[b]	~	.32	~	.24*	~	~	~
P. PANAMA	~	~	~	.02*	.01[b]	.05*	.04[b]	~	~	.90	.30*	.40*	.19*	.03*
Panama Canal Zone	~	.11	.08	.01*	.01[b]	.01[b]	.01[b]	~	1.04	~	.88[b]	.88[b]	.88[b]	.75[b]
R. PERU	~	~	~	.01*	.01*	.01*	.01[b]	~	~	~	.01*	.03*	.03*	.03[b]
St. Vincent	~	~	~	~	~	~	~	~	~	~	.37*	~	~	~
Suriname	~	~	.12	~	~	~	~	~	.25	.28	~	~	~	~
Trinidad and Tobago	~	.04	.05	.03*	.08*	.14[a]	.39[a]	~	.21	.27	.46*	21.68*	26.54[a]	25.11[a]
Windward Islands	~	.02	.03	.03[b]	.03[b]	.03[b]	.03[b]	~	~	~	~	~	~	~
British West Indies	~	.14	.23	.45[b]	.56[b]	.56[b]	.47[b]	~	~	~	~	~	~	~
V. USSR, Eastern Europe, etc.	.02	.04	~	~	~	~	~	1.19	1.09	1.14	1.74	2.03	2.03	1.73
Bulgaria	~	~	~	~	~	~	~	.09	.11	.20	.08[b]	.02[b]	.02[b]	.02[b]
Czechoslovakia	~	~	~	~	~	~	~	.53	.79	.53	.99[b]	1.22[b]	1.22[b]	1.03[b]
Poland	.02	.04	~	~	~	~	~	.47	.19	.40	.67[b]	.80[b]	.80[b]	.68[b]
EEC	~	31.50	48.18	54.45	80.64	50.45	59.31	~	28.71	30.31	55.69	56.55	88.93	57.41
VI. Percent Distribution														
Industrial Countries	~	96.5	95.2	98.0	96.7	97.6	97.1	~	85.4	81.3	86.5	83.4	82.6	84.8
Oil Exporting Countries	~	.1	.3	.1	.4	.4	.2	~	.1	~	.1	~	.1	~
Non-Oil Developing Countries	~	3.4	4.5	1.9	2.9	2.0	2.6	~	14.1	18.2	11.0	14.6	15.6	13.4
Africa	~	~	~	~	.2	.1	.1	~	.2	.1	~	.1	~	.1
Asia	~	~	~	.1	.1	.2	.1	~	1.2	2.6	1.2	2.0	1.5	1.7
Europe	~	~	~	~	~	~	.5	~	.3	.5	~	.1	~	~
Middle East	~	~	.1	~	~	~	.1	~	~	~	~	.4	~	~
Western Hemisphere	~	3.4	4.4	1.8	2.5	1.8	1.9	~	12.3	14.9	9.7	12.2	14.1	11.6
USSR, Eastern Europe, etc.	~	~	~	~	~	~	~	~	.5	.5	.4	.4	.4	.3

Table 2627 (Continued)

HAITI ABSOLUTE VALUE OF GOODS TRADED WITH SELECTED REGIONS AND COUNTRIES,[1] 1975-82 (M US)[2]

Category	Exports FOB							Imports CIF						
	1975	1976	1977	1979	1980	1981	1982	1975	1976	1977	1979	1980	1981	1982
VII. Annual Percent Change														
World	~	44.8	21.9	79.3	21.4	-4.2	14.6	~	41.1	3.6	104.0	27.6	-.7	-8.1
Industrial Countries	~	42.7	20.3	83.5	19.8	-3.3	14.1	~	39.7	-1.4	123.2	23.0	-1.5	-5.6
Oil Exporting Countries	~	130.6	406.0	-52.5	417.6	-.7	-45.7	~	-82.1	4.4	~	-14.1	~	~
Non-Oil Developing Countries	~	139.7	61.1	-12.1	81.8	-33.4	49.8	~	54.8	33.5	10.5	70.6	6.1	-21.4
Africa	~	-84.0	-25.0	316.7	~	-76.8	46.7	~	~	-23.8	-35.2	-27.6	~	122.3
Asia	~	400.0	~	-9.1	620.0	-69.4	468.2	~	62.6	119.1	-26.3	120.2	-26.7	1.9
Europe	~	~	~	41.4	56.1	-26.6	~	~	147.3	61.9	-87.4	118.4	-84.5	437.0
Middle East	~	-86.7	~	103.3	38.6	~	-15.0	~	270.0	-94.6	~	~	-94.7	~
Western Hemisphere	~	155.2	56.8	-16.1	70.8	-31.5	23.8	~	50.3	25.3	20.9	60.5	15.1	-24.5
USSR, Eastern Europe, etc.	~	90.0	~	~	~	~	~	~	-.5	4.4	20.8	17.2	~	-15.0

1. DOT data may differ between countries and from IFS data because of the time it takes for an export to become an import, etc.
2. Data may be calculated from partner's reported data or estimated on basis of less than 12 months.
3. No trade with Cuba; Venezuela is included in category III.
a. Five or fewer months of reported data, seven or more months derived or extrapolated.
b. Data extrapolated for the entire year.

SOURCE: Adapted from the IMF-DOT Annual, 1970-74; IMF-DOT-Y, 1982; IMF-DOT-Y, 1983.

Table 2628

HONDURAS ABSOLUTE VALUE OF GOODS TRADED WITH SELECTED REGIONS AND COUNTRIES,[1] 1975-82
(M US)[2]

Category	Exports FOB							Imports CIF						
	1975	1976	1977	1979	1980	1981	1982	1975	1976	1977	1979	1980	1981	1982
I. World	303.19	397.21	503.52	733.59	829.41	826.69	744.64	404.28	453.08	576.45	825.57	1,005.08	867.33	710.81
II. Industrial Countries	230.00	322.17	417.79	630.30	691.64	714.82	645.62	259.90	315.15	383.06	545.18	673.57	578.12	433.91
United States	156.57	223.73	245.66	425.21	437.85	448.28*	386.91*	170.88	198.17	248.49	358.13	426.04	384.23*	302.06*
Canada	.03	.80	.09	.14	.88	29.49*	22.86*	7.48	13.52	7.64	13.11	17.87	18.65*	13.53*
Australia	.03	~	~	~	8.48	.01*	.39*	.28	.12	~	1.03	1.90	.09*	.02*
Japan	11.86	12.31	28.04	30.05	34.00	43.54*	43.10*	26.62	39.91	63.21	64.01	99.37	50.88*	39.11*
New Zealand	~	~	~	~	~	.11*	.05[a]	~	.02	~	.08	~	~	~
Austria	~	.18	~	~	~	8.54*	11.23*	.65	.58	~	1.62	1.46	1.83*	1.74*
Belgium	7.19	13.37	7.34	8.48	15.39	10.84*	10.48*	6.09	7.23	7.13	8.00	9.57	9.88*	6.79*
Denmark	.08	.08	~	.27	.01	1.99*	2.17*	.90	.67	~	2.21	7.31	5.05*	1.42*
Finland	.08	.30	~	.36	.20	4.80*	4.07*	.06	.05	~	.08	.18	.26*	.18*
France	.45	2.25	1.68	8.18	3.93	6.73*	9.19*	3.81	3.69	4.24	12.49	15.88	18.50*	8.56*
Germany	33.31	46.58	93.25	71.35	102.28	66.07*	65.31*	13.77	21.22	21.41	23.34	28.71	21.95*	13.94*
Iceland	~	~	~	~	~	.48*	.53*	~	.12	~	.07	.01	.01*	.01*
Ireland	~	~	~	~	~	.12*	.07[a]	.05	.12	~	.07	.30	2.91*	.99[a]
Italy	3.46	5.74	9.30	14.27	12.84	13.95*	11.75*	3.95	4.37	5.35	10.62	10.00	16.11*	12.16*
Netherlands	12.51	10.55	23.91	43.85	37.86	16.57*	14.72*	5.45	7.53	6.75	12.12	15.96	11.95*	8.29*
Norway	.55	.94	~	3.21	4.04	4.77*	3.82*	.04	.31	~	.22	.12	.20*	.20*
Spain	3.10	3.57	6.87	11.31	8.65	18.44*	24.63*	2.36	4.14	4.45	6.72	8.49	7.52*	5.00*
Sweden	.14	1.07	~	3.14	2.54	11.40*	8.36*	1.54	.98	~	3.89	3.24	5.49*	1.80*
Switzerland	.09	.37	~	.84	.58	20.35*	18.52*	4.36	2.94	~	7.09	5.90	5.86*	9.11*
United Kingdom	.58	.34	1.65	9.66	22.09	9.33*	7.47*	11.77	9.62	14.39	20.36	21.27	16.82*	9.02*
III. Developing Countries														
Oil Exporting Countries	2.08	5.50	5.81	6.68	2.18	7.19	6.85	64.69	11.13	27.39	69.21	104.87	55.09	34.65
Indonesia	~	~	~	~	~	.04*	.04[a]	.02	.01	~	.07	.04	~	~
Iran, I.R. of	~	~	~	~	~	~	~	.08	.08	~	.11	.02	.02[b]	.01[b]
Libya	~	~	~	.49	~	.72*	.68[b]	~	~	~	~	~	~	~
Nigeria	~	~	~	~	~	~	~	~	~	~	.04	~	~	~
Oman	~	~	~	~	~	~	.08*	~	~	~	~	~	~	~
Saudi Arabia	~	.39	~	1.38	~	.84*	.74[a]	~	~	~	~	~	~	~
T. VENEZUELA	1.96	5.11	5.81	4.80	2.18	5.59*	5.31[b]	64.59	11.04	27.39	68.98	104.82	40.75*	34.63[b]
Non-Oil Developing Countries	~	68.04	76.98	96.14	127.22	101.30	91.78	~	123.40	152.72	200.84	214.33	221.95	232.98
Africa	~	~	~	~	~	.38	.32	~	.25	~	.22	1.20	.57	.51
Cameroon	~	~	~	~	~	~	~	~	~	~	~	~	.27*	.23[a]
Madagascar	~	~	~	~	~	~	~	~	.01	~	.01	~	~	~
Morocco	~	~	~	.20	~	~	~	~	~	~	~	.05	~	~
South Africa	~	~	~	~	~	.29*	.32[a]	~	.03	~	.10	1.15	.30*	.28[a]
Sudan	~	~	~	~	~	~	~	~	.21	~	~	~	~	~
Zambia	~	~	~	~	~	~	~	~	~	~	~	~	~	~
Africa not specified	~	~	~	~	~	~	~	~	.01	~	.01	~	~	~
Asia	~	~	~	~	~	~	~	~	~	~	~	~	~	~
China, People's Rep.	~	~	~	~	.03	2.30	1.00	~	4.10	~	11.46	12.75	6.12	7.58
Hong Kong	~	~	~	.05	~	~	~	~	1.09	~	3.82	4.58	2.11*	1.91*
India	~	~	~	~	~	.43*	.07*	~	.96	~	2.44	2.77	.21[b]	.17[b]
Korea	~	~	~	~	~	.26*	.14*	~	.97	~	4.47	4.38	3.24*	3.58[a]
Malaysia	~	~	~	~	~	.09*	~	~	.52	~	.12	.08	.35*	.01*
Pakistan	~	~	~	~	~	.01*	.01*	~	.05	~	.05	.04	.18*	.07*
Philippines	~	~	~	~	~	.03*	~	~	~	~	.04	.22	~	~
Singapore	~	~	~	~	~	~	.02*	~	~	~	.17	.23	.03*	.03*
Sri Lanka	~	~	~	.10	~	~	~	~	.05	~	.15	.22	.02*	~
Thailand	~	~	~	.06	.02	1.58*	.76[a]	~	~	~	~	.03	~	~

Table 2628 (Continued)

HONDURAS ABSOLUTE VALUE OF GOODS TRADED WITH SELECTED REGIONS AND COUNTRIES,[1] 1975-82
(M US)[2]

Ch. 26, Direction of Trade 533

Category	Exports FOB							Imports CIF						
	1975	1976	1977	1979	1980	1981	1982	1975	1976	1977	1979	1980	1981	1982
III. Developing Countries (Continued)														
Non-Oil Developing Countries														
Europe														
Gibraltar	~	1.06	5.58	2.49	10.55	5.01	3.82	~	1.31	14.91	2.42	1.68	.84	.96
Greece	~	~	~	~	~	.10*	.07*	~	.01	~	.01	.07	.07[b]	.06[b]
Hungary	~	~	~	~	~	~	~	~	.20	~	.44	.01	.05*	~
Malta	.31	~	~	~	~	~	~	~	~	~	~	.41	~	~
Portugal	~	~	~	.99	.57	.11*	.33[a]	~	.25	~	.59	.48	.50*	.74[a]
Romania	~	~	~	~	~	~	~	.21	.27	~	.86	.11	~	~
Turkey	~	~	~	~	~	~	~	~	~	~	~	~	.01*	~
Yugoslavia	~	1.06	5.58	1.50	9.98	4.80*	2.30[a]	.03	.59	~	.52	.43	.04*	.01[a]
Europe not specified	~	~	5.58	1.37	.53	.36	.27	~	.50	14.91	.20	.17	.17[b]	.14[b]
Middle East														
Egypt	~	~	~	~	~	~	~	~	.50	~	.03	.39	7.13	2.05
Israel	.04	~	~	1.37	.53	.36*	.27*	.02	.49	~	.17	.30	7.04*	1.98*
Syrian Arab Rep.	~	~	~	~	~	~	~	~	~	~	~	.08	.08[b]	.07[b]
Yemen, P.D. Rep.	~	~	~	~	~	~	~	~	~	~	~	~	~	~
IV. Latin America[3]	56.03	66.98	71.41	92.07	116.11	93.24	86.37	70.86	117.25	137.80	186.53	198.31	207.30	221.87
A. ARGENTINA	1.37	~	~	.18	.29	.02*	.06[a]	.70	.86	2.26	3.45	2.89	3.28*	4.43[a]
Antigua and Barbuda	~	~	~	.19	.23	.23[b]	.19[b]	~	~	~	~	~	.01[b]	.01[b]
Bahamas	~	.01	~	~	~	~	~	~	~	~	.02	.01	~	~
Barbados	~	1.80	~	1.77	.27	.50*	.90[a]	~	.01	~	.01	.07	.07[b]	.06[b]
Belize	~	1.19	~	2.19	2.80	2.80[b]	2.38[b]	~	~	~	~	.02	.02[b]	.02[b]
Bermuda	~	~	~	~	~	~	~	~	~	~	~	~	~	~
C. BRAZIL	.51	.06	.05	.45	.85	.68*	.16*	5.99	6.75	8.30	20.75	17.83	14.50[b]	5.93*
D. CHILE	~	~	~	.01	~	~	~	.01	.02	~	.30	.43	~	~
E. COLOMBIA	.96	.65	.78	1.95	1.06	1.12*	.95[b]	2.25	3.62	3.43	5.09	4.99	5.75*	4.89[b]
F. COSTA RICA	6.26	7.11	7.99	14.97	17.57	14.90*	11.36[a]	14.22	15.07	19.39	29.50	31.35	29.49[a]	22.00[a]
Dominica	~	~	~	.17	.09	.09[b]	.08[b]	~	~	~	~	~	.01[b]	.08[b]
H. DOMINICAN REP.	15.26	9.77	~	4.16	2.10	2.05*	2.49*	.09	.08	~	.20	.34	.67*	.50*
I. ECUADOR	1.34	.27	~	~	~	.01*	.01*	.01	.02	~	.04	.03	~	~
J. EL SALVADOR	~	~	~	~	~	.29*	.25[a]	~	~	~	~	~	1.50*	1.28[b]
Grenada	~	~	~	.08	.02	.02[b]	.01[b]	~	~	~	~	.03	~	~
Guadeloupe	~	1.57	~	1.52	1.88	1.88[b]	1.60[b]	~	~	~	~	~	~	~
K. GUATEMALA	12.16	17.15	21.64	33.61	41.20	17.06*	14.50[b]	23.69	26.62	32.94	50.92	57.73	54.65*	46.45[b]
Guyana	~	.09	~	2.07	.09	.09[b]	.07[b]	~	~	~	~	.03	.03[b]	.03[b]
L. HAITI	~	.09	~	3.27	.19	.19[b]	.16[b]	~	.68	~	1.05	1.41	1.41[b]	1.19[b]
Jamaica	~	3.98	~	.88	.37	.37[b]	.31[b]	~	~	~	~	~	~	~
Leeward Islands	~	.46	.03	~	~	~	~	~	~	~	~	~	~	~
Martinique	~	.58	~	~	.62	.86*	.56[a]	~	~	~	~	~	~	~
N. MEXICO	.78	1.83	.09	1.07	.62	.86*	.56[a]	8.26	9.81	14.18	20.01	22.59	22.30*	9.63[a]
Montserrat	~	~	~	~	~	~	~	~	~	~	~	~	~	~
Netherlands Antilles	~	.40	~	.20	.49	.49[b]	.42[b]	~	1.26	~	1.81	3.02	3.02[b]	2.56[b]
O. NICARAGUA	12.42	14.37	13.93	15.17	32.62	32.62[b]	27.73[b]	13.81	16.76	18.85	17.44	14.46	14.46[b]	12.29[b]
P. PANAMA	4.93	1.76	2.85	2.85	5.73	2.03*	2.14[a]	1.73	2.59	7.45	7.45	8.03	7.42*	10.07*
Panama Canal Zone	~	.40	~	.17	.09	.09[b]	.07[b]	~	.01	~	~	~	~	~
R. PERU	~	~	~	.02	.49	.09*	.08*	.07	1.37	~	.85	.73	.17*	.14[b]
St. Lucia	~	~	~	.48	.49	.49[b]	.42[b]	~	~	~	~	.03	.03[b]	.02[b]
St. Pierre-Miquelon	~	~	~	.09	.09	.09[b]	.07[b]	~	~	~	~	~	~	~
St. Vincent	~	~	~	.12	.12	.12[b]	.10[b]	~	~	~	~	.03	.03[b]	.02[b]
Suriname	~	~	~	~	1.13	1.13[b]	.96[b]	~	~	~	~	~	~	~
Trinidad and Tobago	1.60	2.65	5.67	4.46	5.77	13.01[a]	18.32[a]	.53	31.73	27.21	27.51	32.13	48.38[a]	100.27[a]
S. URUGUAY	.14	.01	~	~	.01	~	.08*	.03	~	~	~	.09	.02*	~
Windward Islands	~	1.18	~	.16	.53	.53[b]	.45[b]	~	~	~	~	~	~	~
America not specified	~	~	21.26	~	~	~	~	~	~	11.24	.05	~	~	~
British West Indies	~	~	~	~	~	~	~	~	~	~	~	.13	.13[b]	.11[b]
Other Latin America not specified	~	~	~	~	~	~	~	~	~	~	~	~	~	~

Table 2628 (Continued)

HONDURAS ABSOLUTE VALUE OF GOODS TRADED WITH SELECTED REGIONS AND COUNTRIES,[1] 1975-82 (M US)[2]

Category	Exports FOB							Imports CIF						
	1975	1976	1977	1979	1980	1981	1982	1975	1976	1977	1979	1980	1981	1982
V. USSR, Eastern Europe, etc.	.48	.23	~	.14	~	~	~	1.70	1.24	~	2.54	3.98	3.98	3.38
Albania	~	~	~	~	~	~	~	~	~	~	~	.01	.01[b]	.01[b]
Bulgaria	~	~	~	~	~	~	~	~	~	~	~	~	.17[b]	.15[b]
Czechoslovakia	.48	.23	~	~	~	~	~	.74	.89	~	1.62	1.87	1.87[b]	1.59[b]
East Germany	~	~	~	~	~	~	~	.11	.09	~	.36	.42	.42[b]	.36[b]
North Korea	~	~	~	~	~	~	~	~	~	~	.05	.07	.07[b]	.06[b]
Poland	~	~	~	.14	~	~	~	.48	.15	~	.22	.33	.33[b]	.28[b]
USSR	~	~	~	~	~	~	~	.06	.12	~	.16	1.10	1.10[b]	.94[b]
Country or area not specified	~	.17	2.94	.09	.17	.17[b]	.15[b]	~	.02	13.28	.01	.15	.15[b]	.13[b]
EEC	~	78.90	137.14	156.05	194.41	125.70	121.22	~	54.44	59.27	89.22	109.00	103.16	61.15
VI. Percent Distribution														
Industrial Countries	~	81.1	83.0	85.9	83.4	86.6	86.7	~	69.6	66.5	66.0	67.0	66.7	61.0
Oil Exporting Countries	~	1.4	1.2	.9	.3	.9	.9	~	2.5	4.8	8.4	10.4	6.4	4.9
Non-Oil Developing Countries	~	17.1	15.3	13.1	15.3	12.3	12.3	~	27.2	26.5	24.3	21.3	25.6	32.8
Africa	~	~	~	~	~	.3	.1	~	.1	~	.1	.1	.1	.1
Asia	~	.3	1.1	.3	1.3	.3	.1	~	.9	2.6	1.4	1.3	.7	1.1
Europe	~	~	~	.2	.1	.6	.5	~	.3	~	.3	.2	.1	.1
Middle East	~	~	~	~	~	~	~	~	.1	~	~	~	~	.3
Western Hemisphere	~	16.9	14.2	12.6	14.0	11.3	11.6	~	25.9	23.9	22.6	19.7	23.9	31.2
USSR, Eastern Europe, etc.	~	.1	~	~	.1	~	~	~	.3	~	.3	.4	.5	.5
VII. Annual Percent Change														
World	~	31.0	26.8	24.9	13.1	-.3	-9.9	~	12.1	27.2	22.2	21.7	-13.7	-18.0
Industrial Countries	~	40.1	29.7	25.2	9.7	3.5	-9.8	~	21.3	21.5	18.8	23.6	-14.2	-24.9
Oil Exporting Countries	~	164.6	5.6	22.3	-67.4	230.5	-4.7	~	-82.8	146.2	227.0	51.5	-47.5	-37.1
Non-Oil Developing Countries	~	-3.6	13.1	31.9	32.3	-20.4	-9.4	~	61.7	23.8	13.6	6.7	3.6	5.0
Africa	~	~	~	~	-85.3	~	-17.0	~	42.2	~	600.0	437.5	-52.6	-10.3
Asia	~	~	424.6	~	323.7	-52.5	-56.7	~	50.8	~	501.7	11.2	-52.0	23.8
Europe	~	-99.9	~	-67.6	-61.0	-31.8	-23.7	~	116.0	~	-88.0	-30.5	-50.1	14.3
Middle East	~	~	~	~	~	~	-25.0	~	~	~	~	92.6	~	-71.2
Western Hemisphere	~	-3.7	6.6	41.3	26.1	-19.7	-7.4	~	61.1	17.5	20.6	6.3	4.5	7.0
USSR, Eastern Europe, etc.	~	-52.9	~	~	~	~	~	~	-11.0	~	~	56.4	~	-15.0

1. DOT data may differ between countries and from IFS data because of the time it takes for an export to become an import, etc.
2. Data may be calculated from partner's reported data or estimated on basis of less than 12 months.
3. No trade with Cuba; Venezuela is included in category III.

a. Five or fewer months of reported data, seven or more months derived or extrapolated.
b. Data extrapolated for the entire year.

SOURCE: Adapted from the IMF-DOT Annual, 1970-74; IMF-DOT Y, 1982.

Table 2629

MEXICO ABSOLUTE VALUE OF GOODS TRADED WITH SELECTED REGIONS AND COUNTRIES,[1] 1975-82 (M US)[2]

Category	Exports FOB							Imports CIF						
	1975	1976	1977	1979	1980	1981	1982	1975	1976	1977	1979	1980	1981	1982
I. World	2,916	3,469	4,171	8,983	15,557	19,381	21,163	6,581	6,036	5,486	12,086	19,456	24,126	15,372
II. Industrial Countries	2,142	2,728	3,328	7,598	13,279	16,171	18,097	5,936	5,496	5,092	11,113	16,688	21,145	12,375
United States	1,668	2,111	2,738	6,252	10,072	10,716	11,887[a]	4,113	3,774	3,493	7,563	11,979	15,398	8,921[a]
Canada	43	48	45	75	117	661	579[a]	146	141	166	198	353	446	329[a]
Australia	~	5	5	6	9	14	15[a]	~	19	12	33	33	41	17[a]
Japan	109	177	129	248	671	1,157	1,241[a]	299	307	296	790	989	1,205	676[a]
New Zealand	~	~	~	~	1	2	2[b]	~	9	7	7	23	30	38[b]
Austria	1	1	2	1	1	3	81[a]	6	9	7	15	20	25	31[a]
Belgium	31	48	29	70	77	66	77[a]	56	35	47	119	155	120	67[a]
Denmark	3	3	2	9	2	5	2[a]	6	9	6	25	29	34	41[a]
Finland	1	4	1	1	4	12	10[a]	17	20	6	30	34	63	18[a]
France	21	35	37	72	567	900	882[a]	184	181	157	381	521	588	300[a]
Germany	87	89	92	213	256	212	178[a]	481	424	312	769	972	1,190	666[a]
Ireland	~	~	1	1	2	~	~	1	9	15	44	65	85	22[c]
Italy	40	62	38	56	101	112	384[a]	112	96	105	239	305	432	319[a]
Netherlands	48	30	28	46	76	89	91[a]	59	42	39	87	99	132	81[a]
Norway	~	3	9	2	1	3	~	3	5	35	21	21	21	17[a]
Spain	20	20	62	458	1,238	1,921	1,877[a]	58	50	87	223	348	472	300[a]
Sweden	9	10	7	17	19	46	12[a]	79	86	79	122	153	214	162[a]
Switzerland	28	55	60	27	23	13	19[a]	103	90	97	159	187	221	150[a]
United Kingdom	28	29	42	45	43	242	760[a]	193	190	128	287	405	429	222[a]
III. Developing Countries														
Oil Exporting Countries	70	66	102	133	81	91	74	67	33	14	48	41	37	34
Algeria	~	2	7	11	9	12	2[b]	~	1	1	5	12	15	18[b]
Indonesia	4	~	~	4	6	7	4[b]	1	~	~	~	1	2	1[b]
Iran, I.R. of	2	~	~	4	~	~	~	6	~	~	~	~	~	~
Iraq	~	~	~	11	~	~	3[b]	1	~	~	~	~	~	~
Kuwait	~	2	~	~	~	2	~	~	~	~	~	~	~	~
Libya	1	~	1	3	1	1	~	~	~	~	~	~	~	~
Nigeria	1	1	2	1	1	1	1[b]	~	~	~	1	~	~	1[b]
Saudi Arabia	5	1	1	4	1	1	3[b]	~	2	~	~	~	~	3[b]
T. VENEZUELA	57	61	89	95	62	69	60[b]	59	28	13	41	28	20	9[b]
Non-Oil Developing Countries	~	527	593	1,020	1,877	3,079	2,940	~	477	362	833	1,095	1,599	774
Africa	~	2	2	5	9	26	24	~	31	5	51	28	66	26
Ivory Coast	~	~	~	~	~	~	~	~	2	~	~	~	1	1[b]
Kenya	~	~	~	~	~	1	1[b]	~	8	5	7	7	12	6[b]
Liberia	~	~	~	2	4	16	15[b]	~	3	7	7	7	23	5[b]
Morocco	~	~	~	2	~	8	3[b]	~	2	1	22	1	~	3[b]
Mozambique	~	~	~	~	~	~	~	~	9	~	~	~	~	5[b]
Namibia	~	~	~	~	~	~	~	~	~	~	~	~	~	3[b]
South Africa	1	1	1	1	3	9	5[b]	7	7	3	15	14	6	5[b]
Zaire	~	~	~	~	2	9	3[b]	1	1	~	1	9	9	1[b]
Africa not specified	5	1	~	2	2	9	5[b]	~	1	7	7	6	16	5[b]
Asia	~	23	55	155	154	441	391	~	23	50	130	237	311	197
China, People's Rep.	~	10	33	114	94	170	82[a]	~	10	9	43	66	115	55[a]
Hong Kong	2	2	~	4	4	8	5[a]	~	2	4	18	44	83	65[a]
India	~	7	16	13	6	57	7[b]	~	7	4	6	10	15	18[b]
Korea	1	1	~	9	13	68	160[c]	10	4	10	6	38	24	25[c]
Malaysia	~	~	~	~	2	1	2[c]	6	3	6	7	11	17	6[c]
Pakistan	~	~	~	1	~	~	2[a]	~	3	~	7	11	17	1[a]
Philippines	2	2	1	2	6	90	107[a]	3	~	3	3	8	3	7[a]
Singapore	1	1	~	2	1	2	2[a]	14	14	15	39	35	21	11[a]
Sri Lanka	~	~	~	~	~	~	~	4	4	5	12	11	19	8[a]
Thailand	1	1	1	9	1	9	2[b]	5	~	~	1	~	~	~
Asia not specified	~	~	~	~	21	36	22[b]	~	~	~	~	2	9	2[b]
Oceania not specified	~	~	~	~	5	~	~	~	~	~	~	~	1	~

Table 2629 (Continued)

MEXICO ABSOLUTE VALUE OF GOODS TRADED WITH SELECTED REGIONS AND COUNTRIES,[1] 1975-82
(M US)[2]

Category	Exports FOB 1975	1976	1977	1979	1980	1981	1982	Imports CIF 1975	1976	1977	1979	1980	1981	1982
III. Developing Countries (Continued)														
Non-Oil Developing Countries														
Europe														
Greece	~	13	16	48	64	99	157	~	23	13	20	25	44	14
Hungary	~	4	2	10	10	18	11[a]	~	2	2	3	7	20	1[a]
Portugal	~	2	4	2	1	3	3[b]	~	2	2	5	6	6	3[b]
Romania	2	1	3	2	6	19	125[c]	1	2	9	3	3	2	2[c]
Turkey	2	~	~	15	11	11	7[b]	6	16	9	4	4	10	4[b]
Yugoslavia	6	~	~	~	1	16	9[c]	6	~	~	~	1	5	~
Europe not specified	3	6	7	18	43	26	3[b]	3	4	1	5	3	5	3[b]
Middle East	~	73	71	293	643	676	633	2	1	1	4	9	15	13
Egypt	44	73	70	287	641	672	627[a]	~	1	1	4	5	11	10[a]
Israel	~	4	2	4	2	3	2[a]	2	1	~	~	1	~	~
Lebanon	~	~	~	2	2	1	~	~	~	~	~	1	4	3[b]
Middle East not specified	~	~	1	1	~	~	4[b]	~	~	~	~	~	~	~
IV. Latin America[3]	317	416	450	520	1,007	1,836	1,736	388	383	294	628	796	1,164	523
A. ARGENTINA	36	22	38	38	44	35	47[c]	211	56	80	127	110	259	108[c]
Bahamas	~	9	9	5	1	59	56[b]	~	3	1	1	4	5	4[b]
Belize	~	2	2	1	7	6	4[b]	~	3	~	2	2	~	~
Bermuda	1	1	1	2	3	3	12[b]	1	2	3	3	3	2	1[b]
B. BOLIVIA	92	172	150	150	406	748	697[a]	96	119	108	293	464	609	253[a]
C. BRAZIL	15	14	27	38	27	40	10[a]	10	19	10	38	66	54	26[a]
D. CHILE	24	28	32	45	48	48	41[b]	7	6	9	13	16	17	12[b]
E. COLOMBIA	27	21	25	36	97	103	69[b]	8	7	1	1	1	17	16[b]
F. COSTA RICA	7	7	9	13	10	124	130[a]	~	2	~	1	15	18	6[b]
H. DOMINICAN REP.	10	10	26	24	39	77	39[b]	8	6	2	26	1	1	1[b]
I. ECUADOR	14	10	16	25	19	77	67[b]	2	4	3	1	1	1	1[b]
J. EL SALVADOR	25	28	43	53	59	129	97[b]	2	6	5	10	26	72	50[b]
K. GUATEMALA	~	1	~	1	1	~	~	9	1	1	4	6	4	1[b]
Guyana	~	~	~	~	~	12	~	1	~	~	~	~	~	~
L. HAITI	8	6	14	19	19	20	9[b]	~	3	~	1	~	4	1[b]
M. HONDURAS	2	2	3	3	4	88	65[b]	2	~	~	~	1	2	3[b]
Jamaica	41	40	16	16	29	86	1[b]	~	~	21	36	12	8	11[b]
Netherlands Antilles	8	9	14	4	54	127	116[b]	56	109	8	1	21	1	11[a]
O. NICARAGUA	14	12	14	20	22	2	164[b]	~	6	20	23	25	39	3[a]
P. PANAMA	1	1	2	1	1	31	2	14	11	3	3	7	16	8[b]
Q. PARAGUAY	29	18	12	12	26	~	31[b]	6	3	15	23	25	19	~
R. PERU	5	1	2	1	1	6	79[a]	9	3	5	17	7	11	5[a]
Trinidad and Tobago	~	2	3	10	8	~	6	5	5	~	4	7	7	~
S. URUGUAY	~	1	1	1	1	1	1[b]	5	1	~	3	8	~	5[b]
Windward Islands	~	~	~	1	1	~	~	~	1	~	~	~	~	~
America not specified	~	~	~	~	~	~	~	~	~	~	~	~	~	~
British West Indies	~	~	~	~	~	~	~	~	~	~	~	~	~	~
Other Latin America not specified	~	~	~	~	61	40	40	17	27	12	41	327	195	127
V. USSR, Eastern Europe, etc.	40	43	42	44	27	19	40	12	1	3	4	262	136	94[b]
G. CUBA	30	22	34	7	5	5	22[b]	6	7	5	22	20	19	12[b]
Czechoslovakia	1	1	2	2	21	10	7[b]	2	7	6	6	7	25	6[b]
Eastern Germany	2	3	1	30	9	~	3[b]	2	8	2	1	13	9	6[b]
Poland	3	4	4	5	~	~	8[b]	8	9	2	1	~	16	9[b]
USSR	4	14	3	3	~	~	~	4	~	2	~	~	~	~
USSR, etc., not specified	~	~	~	~	~	~	~	~	4	6	52	357	61	1,429[b]
Country or area not specified	~	4	~	~	~	~	~	~	~	~	~	949	1,089	627[b]
Special categories	~	105	102	184	259	~	~	~	~	~	~	~	~	~
EEC	~	299	271	522	1,134	1,644	2,385	809	985	809	1,955	2,557	3,029	1,717

Table 2629 (Continued)

MEXICO ABSOLUTE VALUE OF GOODS TRADED WITH SELECTED REGIONS AND COUNTRIES,[1] 1975-82
(M US)[2]

Category	Exports FOB							Imports CIF						
	1975	1976	1977	1979	1980	1981	1982	1975	1976	1977	1979	1980	1981	1982
VI. Percent Distribution														
Industrial Countries	~	78.6	79.8	84.6	85.4	83.4	85.5	~	91.1	92.8	92.0	85.8	87.6	80.5
Oil Exporting Countries	~	1.9	2.4	1.5	.5	.5	.3	~	.5	.3	.4	.2	.2	.2
Non-Oil Developing Countries	~	15.2	14.2	11.4	12.1	15.9	13.9	~	7.9	6.6	6.9	5.6	6.6	5.0
Africa	~	.1	.1	.1	.1	.1	.1	~	.5	.1	.4	.1	.3	.2
Asia	~	.7	1.3	1.7	1.0	2.3	1.8	~	.6	.9	1.1	1.2	1.3	1.3
Europe	~	.4	.4	.5	.4	.5	.7	~	.4	.2	.2	~	.2	.1
Middle East	~	2.1	1.7	3.3	4.1	3.5	3.0	~	~	~	~	~	.1	.1
Western Hemisphere	~	12.0	10.8	5.8	6.5	9.5	8.2	~	6.3	5.4	5.2	4.1	4.8	3.4
USSR, Eastern Europe, etc.	~	1.2	1.0	.5	.4	.2	.2	~	.4	.2	.3	1.7	.8	.8
VII. Annual Percent Change														
World	~	18.9	20.2	50.9	73.2	24.6	9.2	~	-8.3	-9.1	59.9	61.0	24.0	-36.3
Industrial Countries	~	27.4	22.0	56.1	74.8	21.8	11.9	~	-7.4	-7.3	57.9	50.2	26.7	-41.5
Oil Exporting Countries	~	-4.9	53.5	-12.0	-39.0	11.8	-18.9	~	-50.8	-57.3	69.6	-13.7	-9.0	-9.1
Non-Oil Developing Countries	~	13.5	12.6	36.8	84.0	64.1	-4.5	~	-14.0	-24.0	76.7	31.4	46.1	-51.6
Africa	~	37.5	-4.5	-69.3	76.5	192.2	-10.3	~	-36.4	-84.4	68.4	-44.0	133.1	-60.3
Asia	~	-51.8	141.2	6.2	-.6	186.6	-11.5	~	16.7	27.6	62.5	81.9	31.2	-36.5
Europe	~	92.6	21.4	111.6	34.7	54.9	58.2	~	100.0	-45.7	29.7	23.4	77.4	-68.2
Middle East	~	54.1	-3.6	158.3	119.8	5.1	-6.4	~	-68.4	-16.7	72.0	97.7	71.8	-10.3
Western Hemisphere	~	15.0	8.3	16.2	93.6	82.4	-5.4	~	-16.5	-23.2	82.9	26.8	46.2	-55.1
USSR, Eastern Europe, etc.	~	8.7	-2.1	21.6	36.7	-34.8	1.8	~	65.8	-56.9	116.0	704.2	-40.3	-34.8

1. DOT data may differ between countries and from IFS data because of the time it takes for an export to become an import, etc.

2. Data may be calculated from partner's reported data or estimated on basis of less than 12 months.

3. Cuba is included in category V; Venezuela is included in category III.

a. Ten months of reported data, two months derived from partner.

b. Ten months of reported data, two months extrapolated.

c. Ten months of reported data, one month derived and one month extrapolated.

SOURCE: Adapted from the IMF-DOT Annual, 1970-74; IMF-DOT-Y, 1982.

Table 2630

NICARAGUA ABSOLUTE VALUE OF GOODS TRADED WITH SELECTED REGIONS AND COUNTRIES,[1] 1975–82 (M US)[2]

Category	Exports FOB							Imports CIF						
	1975	1976	1977	1979	1980	1981	1982	1975	1976	1977	1979	1980	1981	1982
I. World	375.17	541.98	636.76	566.55	473.75	483.29	365.55	516.78	532.13	762.01	360.00	921.90	799.86	686.35
II. Industrial Countries														
United States	247.62	360.96	414.12	384.26	392.86	351.43	270.10	301.43	295.80	448.70	157.41	384.38	323.35	275.01
Canada	105.00	168.30	151.05	190.96	206.00*	138.28*	89.27*	167.73	164.63	219.73	91.00	274.4*	202.51*	130.46*
Australia	3.62	3.75	2.70	2.67	27.06*	43.56*	21.55*	3.45	3.73	5.51	3.80	14.19*	15.12*	13.80*
Japan	~	.02	.24	.16	.23*	.56*	.52*	~	.40	2.04	.84	.47*	.15*	.21*
New Zealand	48.68	70.32	69.81	30.42	14.26*	66.88*	44.04*	38.30	42.11	77.06	13.61	22.35*	13.01*	9.86*
Austria	~	.03	.06	~	.09*	.09*	.32[a]	.59	.8	.77	.21	.34*	1.11	3.26*
Belgium	10.34	19.71	31.92	18.05	8.53	8.55	5.46*	4.54	3.44	3.94	2.74	2.82	2.78	4.34*
Denmark	4.00	2.77	3.97	6.55	1.86*	3.69*	3.44*	1.67	2.02	3.24	2.06	3.26	2.26	3.16*
Finland	.39	1.89	1.02	.41	2.10*	2.12*	.83*	.27	.97	1.23	.07	.77	.22	2.20*
France	2.98	4.46	7.22	10.15	22.11*	19.43*	3.83*	4.05	3.57	4.91	1.45	11.17	6.80	19.09*
Germany	33.59	52.58	85.36	54.75	46.85*	32.38*	23.50*	30.16	33.71	51.36	14.01	17.03*	27.28*	15.14*
Ireland	~	.15	~	.16	.09*	.87*	.17[a]	~	.15	.11	2.74	1.15	3.71	4.93[a]
Italy	9.14	8.10	14.65	30.31	17.98*	18.14*	12.85*	13.57	8.94	8.13	2.15	6.39	10.31*	22.34*
Netherlands	9.48	17.67	35.68	27.11	7.10*	3.61*	6.28*	7.52	4.07	7.80	5.12	7.16	14.25*	5.03*
Norway	.68	.83	1.64	.40	.39*	1.25*	1.21*	.05	.19	.31	.05	.08*	.42	.62*
Spain	6.48	7.82	5.50	9.15	15.91*	8.64*	9.85*	7.36	5.59	37.48	10.37	5.42	7.40	22.92*
Sweden	.81	.68	1.35	1.06	1.02*	.05*	.03*	1.44	1.16	1.61	.22	2.18	3.57	2.59*
Switzerland	.11	.33	.12	.05	9.67*	4.80*	8.00*	6.84	6.71	7.10	2.45	8.15	7.59	5.61*
United Kingdom	12.00	1.56	1.85	1.93	3.19*	1.93*	5.14*	12.51	13.38	16.37	4.55	6.34	4.86*	9.45*
III. Developing Countries														
Oil Exporting Countries								64.27	57.29	86.57	66.46	93.28	91.49	77.76
Algeria	2.14	3.49	12.84	1.68	.41	1.04	1.05	.01	.01	.01	.06	.03*	.01*	~
Indonesia	1.45	.42	1.48	.15	.23*	.66*	~	~	~	~	~	~	~	~
Iran, I.R. of	~	.15	.79	~	~	~	.73[a]	~	.01	.01	.01	~	~	~
Nigeria	.02	~	1.74	.05	.10[b]	.11[b]	.10[b]	.02	~	~	~	~	~	~
Saudi Arabia	~	~	~	.20	.08*	.04*	.22[b]	~	~	~	~	~	~	~
T. VENEZUELA	.67	2.92	8.83	1.28	76.38	113.50	85.69	64.24	57.28	86.56	66.46	93.28	91.49	77.76
Non-Oil Developing Countries	~	151.21	203.61	164.79	76.38	113.50	85.69	~	175.48	222.91	135.06	442.76	83.37	329.18
Africa		2.51	2.04	~	.03	.07	~	~	.13	1.49	.06	.03	.01	~
Cape Verde	~	~	~	~	~	~	~	~	~	~	~	~	~	~
Ethiopia	~	~	~	~	~	~	~	~	.01	.01	.01	~	~	~
Morocco	~	2.51	.56	.10	~	.06*	~	~	~	.01	.01	~	.06*	~
Senegal	~	~	~	~	~	~	~	~	.05	.05	.01	~	~	~
South Africa	~	~	~	~	.03*	.02*	~	~	.06	.09	.04	.03*	.01*	~
Tunisia	~	~	1.48	~	~	~	~	~	.12	1.43	.04	.03*	.01*	~
Asia	~	20.04	48.61	69.97	1.80	35.32	21.36	~	1.59	7.83	2.63	3.56	10.00	6.23
Bangladesh	~	~	1.48	~	~	~	~	~	~	~	~	1.12	1.12[a]	~
China, People's Rep.	~	3.73	21.12	63.68	1.36*	20.64*	16.18*	~	.22	1.44	.56	.22*	.11[a]	.14*
Hong Kong	~	11.71	10.67	3.07	.02*	5.49*	.10*	~	.79	1.25	.19	.56*	.45[a]	.44*
India	~	~	8.03	~	~	~	~	~	.04	.79	1.50	.03[a]	.03[c]	.03[b]
Korea	~	.39	.95	~	~	5.73*	2.21[Y]	~	.13	3.62	.23	1.57*	1.65[a]	5.44[a]
Malaysia	~	.09	~	~	~	~	~	~	~	~	~	~	~	~
Pakistan	~	~	.50	~	~	~	~	~	.01	.01	.01	~	7.70[a]	~
Philippines	~	2.69	.17	~	~	.09*	~	~	.02	.04	.01	~	.01*	.09*
Singapore	~	.03	~	.10	.02*	~	~	~	.05	.05	.04	.05*	.05[a]	.08*
Sri Lanka	~	~	~	~	~	~	~	~	.06	.09	.11	.01*	.01[a]	.08*
Thailand	~	1.41	7.17	3.12	.40*	3.38*	2.87[a]	~	.27	.55	.73	.01*	.47	.62
Europe														
Greece	~	.63	7.34	.32	1.99	.33	.55	~	.10	.22	.03	.12	.47	.73
Hungary	~	~	~	~	.04*	.17*	.13*	~	~	.04	.03	~	.12[a]	.16
Portugal	2.40	.56	1.05	.25	.56*	.15*	.06[b]	.14	.99	1.32	.26	.09*	.11[a]	.06[a]
Romania	~	~	6.29	~	1.39*	.01*	.62	4.81	.05	.64	.29	.01*	.45[a]	.44*
Yugoslavia	.45	.07	~	~	~	.01*	.42[Y]	.01	~	~	~	.03*	.23[a]	.17[a]

Table 2630 (Continued)

NICARAGUA ABSOLUTE VALUE OF GOODS TRADED WITH SELECTED REGIONS AND COUNTRIES,[1] 1975-82
(M US)[2]

Exports FOB

Category	1975	1976	1977	1979	1980	1981	1982
III. Developing Countries (Continued)							
Non-Oil Developing Countries							
Middle East							
Israel	~	~	.03	~	~	~	.09
Lebanon	~	~	.03	~	~	~	.09*
IV. Latin America[3]	96.18	128.03	145.58	94.51	72.56	77.77	63.69
A. ARGENTINA	.20	.02	~	.19	.08*	~	~
Barbados	~	.11	.12	.04	~	~	~
Belize	~	.01	.05	.03	~	~	~
B. BOLIVIA	~	.02	.05	.03	~	~	~
C. BRAZIL	.23	.14	~	.93	~	~	~
D. CHILE	~	.01	~	~	.03*	~	~
E. COLOMBIA	.02	.06	.06	.29	.03*	~	~
F. COSTA RICA	37.27	43.95	48.31	37.46	29.82*	30.72*	20.14[a]
H. DOMINICAN REP.	.12	2.16	.13	.38	.06*	.01*	~
I. ECUADOR	.04	.10	.02	~	.06*	.01*	~
J. EL SALVADOR	27.29	27.75	33.67	17.90	10.38*	9.32*	7.92[b]
K. GUATEMALA	21.52	31.13	34.70	21.47	14.92*	13.70*	11.64[b]
L. HAITI	.22	.04	.36	.22	.43[b]	.43[b]	.37[b]
M. HONDURAS	12.49	14.99	17.31	13.31	13.15[a]	13.15[c]	11.18[b]
Jamaica	~	.40	.04	.03	~	~	~
N. MEXICO	.41	4.50	7.51	.53	.18[a]	6.87[b]	10.17[b]
Netherlands Antilles	.64	.31	.35	.45	~	~	~
P. PANAMA	1.02	1.95	2.21	.96	3.27[a]	3.29[a]	2.02[b]
R. PERU	.23	.11	.03	.16	.23[a]	.28[a]	.24[c]
Trinidad and Tobago	~	.30	.69	.16	~	~	.02[b]
S. URUGUAY	~	~	~	~	~	~	~
British West Indies	~	~	~	~	~	~	~
V. USSR, Eastern Europe, etc.	1.12	4.84	4.84	~	~	~	~
Czechoslovakia	~	~	~	~	~	~	~
Eastern Germany	~	~	~	~	~	~	~
Poland	1.12	4.84	4.84	~	~	~	~
USSR	~	~	~	~	~	~	~
EEC	~	107.00	180.64	149.06	107.64	86.82	86.15
VI. Percent Distribution							
Industrial Countries	~	66.6	65.0	67.8	82.9	72.7	73.9
Oil Exporting Countries	~	.6	2.0	.3	.1	.2	.3
Non-Oil Developing Countries	~	27.9	32.0	29.1	16.1	23.5	23.4
Africa	~	.5	.3	~	~	~	~
Asia	~	3.7	7.6	12.3	.4	7.3	5.8
Europe	~	.1	1.2	.1	.4	.1	.1
Middle East	~	~	~	~	~	~	~
Western Hemisphere	~	23.6	22.9	16.7	15.3	16.1	17.4
USSR, Eastern Europe, etc.	~	.9	~	~	~	~	~

Imports CIF

Category	1975	1976	1977	1979	1980	1981	1982
III. Developing Countries (Continued)							
Non-Oil Developing Countries							
Middle East							
Israel	~	.22	.22	.05	.11	.55	1.10
Lebanon	.57	.22	.22	.05	.11*	.55[a]	1.10*
IV. Latin America[3]	135.22	172.41	211.18	131.60	438.94	372.35	321.23
A. ARGENTINA	1.12	1.18	.89	1.05	4.94*	5.66[a]	2.81[a]
Barbados	~	~	~	~	~	~	~
Belize	~	~	.08	~	.01*	~	~
B. BOLIVIA	~	.07	~	.07	~	~	~
C. BRAZIL	1.92	1.91	5.08	1.40	19.69*	22.44*	5.79*
D. CHILE	.41	.56	1.28	.04	~	~	~
E. COLOMBIA	3.37	3.12	3.00	1.55	4.18*	2.47[a]	2.10[b]
F. COSTA RICA	36.52	47.89	58.30	39.15	136.52*	93.33[b]	56.18[a]
H. DOMINICAN REP.	.03	.16	.01	.07	.04*	.08[a]	~
I. ECUADOR	~	.08	.02	.01	~	~	~
J. EL SALVADOR	29.11	35.95	38.35	22.92	60.15*	32.97[a]	28.02*
K. GUATEMALA	36.50	41.72	52.31	36.28	106.07*	76.00[a]	64.60*
L. HAITI	~	.05	.03	.03	~	~	~
M. HONDURAS	10.55	14.78	15.49	12.82	35.88*	35.88[c]	30.50[c]
Jamaica	~	1.00	.98	.22	.03*	.03[c]	.02[c]
N. MEXICO	9.90	12.99	15.33	6.02	59.12*	94.94[a]	127.89[a]
Netherlands Antilles	3.05	4.92	11.44	3.79	~	~	~
P. PANAMA	5.51	5.67	8.02	6.19	11.78*	7.84[a]	2.76[a]
R. PERU	.25	.11	.06	.03	.51*	.66[a]	.56[b]
Trinidad and Tobago	~	.22	.44	.06	~	~	~
S. URUGUAY	.03	.03	.06	.06	.03*	.07[a]	.01*
British West Indies	~	~	~	~	~	~	~
V. USSR, Eastern Europe, etc.	1.60	1.30	.93	.12	~	~	~
Czechoslovakia	.34	.42	.39	.08	~	~	~
Eastern Germany	~	~	~	.01	~	~	~
Poland	1.13	.67	.34	.01	~	~	~
USSR	.13	.21	.20	.03	~	~	~
EEC	~	69.27	95.86	34.80	55.31	72.36	83.88
VI. Percent Distribution							
Industrial Countries	~	55.6	58.9	43.7	41.7	40.4	40.1
Oil Exporting Countries	~	10.8	11.4	18.5	10.1	11.4	11.3
Non-Oil Developing Countries	~	33.0	29.3	37.5	48.0	47.9	48.0
Africa	~	.3	.2	.7	.4	1.2	.9
Asia	~	.3	.3	.2	~	.1	.1
Europe	~	~	~	~	~	~	~
Middle East	~	~	~	~	~	~	~
Western Hemisphere	~	32.4	27.7	36.6	47.6	46.6	46.8
USSR, Eastern Europe, etc.	~	.2	.1	~	~	~	~

Table 2630 (Continued)

NICARAGUA ABSOLUTE VALUE OF GOODS TRADED WITH SELECTED REGIONS AND COUNTRIES,[1] 1975-82 (M US)[2]

Category	Exports FOB							Imports CIF						
	1975	1976	1977	1979	1980	1981	1982	1975	1976	1977	1979	1980	1981	1982
VII. Annual Percent Change														
World	~	44.5	17.5	-12.3	-16.4	2.0	-24.4	~	3.0	43.2	-39.3	156.1	-13.2	-14.2
Industrial Countries	~	45.8	14.7	-5.8	2.2	-10.5	-23.1	~	-1.9	51.7	-53.0	144.2	-15.9	-14.9
Oil Exporting Countries	~	63.4	267.9	-38.9	-75.6	154.4	.9	~	-10.9	51.1	-3.2	40.4	-1.9	-15.0
Non-Oil Developing Countries	~	29.7	34.6	-18.4	-53.7	48.6	-24.5	~	19.1	27.0	-27.4	227.8	-13.4	-14.1
Africa	~	-38.4	-18.8	~	~	125.0	~	~	13.4	~	-96.8	-40.4	-67.6	~
Asia	~	51.3	142.5	45.1	-97.4	~	-39.5	~	-8.9	393.1	-17.0	35.1	181.2	-37.7
Europe	~	-77.9	~	-81.5	527.4	-83.5	66.8	~	-77.2	91.3	-70.1	-83.5	289.2	32.5
Middle East	~	-93.8	~	~	~	~	~	~	-63.7	2.3	-84.5	144.4	400.0	100.0
Western Hemisphere	~	32.8	13.7	-37.8	-23.2	7.2	-18.1	~	23.3	22.5	-26.2	233.5	-15.2	-13.7
USSR, Eastern Europe, etc.	~	331.2	~	~	~	~	~	~	-19.2	-28.2	-86.8	~	~	~

1. DOT data may differ between countries and from IFS data because of the time it takes for an export to become an import, etc.

2. Data may be calculated from partner's reported data or estimated on basis of less than 12 months.

3. Cuba is included in category V; Venezuela is included in category III.

a. Five or fewer months of reported data, seven or more months derived or extrapolated.

b. Data extrapolated for the entire year.

SOURCE: Adapted from the IMF-DOT Annual, 1970–74; IMF-DOT-Y, 1982.

Table 2631

PANAMA ABSOLUTE VALUE OF GOODS TRADED WITH SELECTED REGIONS AND COUNTRIES,[1] 1975-82
(M US)[2]

Category	Exports FOB							Imports CIF						
	1975	1976	1977	1979	1980	1981	1982	1975	1976	1977	1979	1980	1981	1982
I. World	286.9	236.3	243.0	291.2	350.2	316.6	308.1	870.0	848.3	861.2	1,187.0	1,448.4	1,539.9	2,901.3
II. Industrial Countries	217.6	170.9	164.4	186.6	224.1	228.0	189.3	369.1	421.5	406.0	585.8	718.4	786.3	1,894.5
United States	168.0	114.1	113.0	135.5	172.6	167.0	127.9	232.4	272.7	264.1	389.6	489.1	535.6	639.6[a]
Canada	3.2	.9	4.2	5.2	1.0	1.2	13.2	11.4	10.1	10.6	14.9	12.6	17.0	19.1[a]
Australia	.3	.3	~	~	~	~	~	~	.9	2.0	.9	.7	1.3	.9[a]
Japan	.3	.8	1.4	.7	1.3	.3	.3	40.7	47.7	39.8	52.9	89.0	94.6	880.2[a]
New Zealand	~	~	~	~	~	~	~	.9	1.7	3.2	5.2	7.9	5.4	3.1[c]
Austria	~	~	~	~	~	~	~	.8	.8	1.1	1.7	1.3	.9	1.9[a]
Belgium	.2	.2	~	~	~	9.4	13.4	6.4	6.6	5.3	5.8	5.6	7.6	6.7[a]
Denmark	~	~	~	~	~	~	~	2.1	6.8	13.2	4.1	4.1	3.7	4.4[a]
Finland	.2	.7	~	~	.3	1.0	~	.4	.5	.2	.7	1.0	1.1	1.4[a]
France	.2	.1	.1	5.8	.3	24.2	.6	10.5	5.8	5.0	8.0	10.5	15.3	41.4[a]
Germany	15.3	20.2	19.6	23.0	17.7	24.2	18.2	15.4	15.3	14.2	30.1	25.8	27.8	39.9[a]
Iceland	~	~	~	~	~	~	~	.1	.4	.2	.7	.4	.3	.4[a]
Ireland	~	~	~	~	~	~	~	~	.3	.2	.8	2.7	1.5	1.6[b]
Italy	14.3	15.1	9.7	5.4	5.4	17.0	8.2	8.7	7.8	6.7	15.1	14.5	17.3	71.5[a]
Netherlands	7.6	12.6	12.0	9.5	21.2	3.9	1.2	10.2	8.5	8.0	12.3	14.3	11.9	12.5[a]
Norway	4.8	2.7	~	.5	3.6	2.8	3.0	.5	.4	.6	.7	1.2	1.6	11.2[a]
Spain	~	.2	.2	.7	.4	.1	.1	6.7	6.6	5.8	10.8	10.0	12.6	54.3[a]
Sweden	1.0	3.0	4.3	.1	.6	.3	2.6	4.3	10.4	10.0	12.1	7.2	9.1	31.3[a]
Switzerland	~	~	~	.1	.3	.1	.1	3.3	3.4	3.8	5.3	4.8	5.4	27.6[a]
United Kingdom	2.1	.3	.1	.2	.4	.3	.5	12.0	13.9	12.1	14.1	15.6	16.2	45.3[a]
III. Developing Countries														
Oil Exporting Countries	4.3	3.1	4.5	5.2	6.0	10.5	14.9	221.3	99.0	145.7	155.1	376.5	245.5	162.3
Indonesia	~	~	~	~	~	~	~	2.7	~	~	.3	~	.2	.1[c]
Iran, I.R. of	.2	.2	.8	~	~	~	~	~	~	5.7	~	~	~	~
Iraq	~	~	~	~	~	~	~	~	~	3.2	~	~	~	~
Kuwait	~	.3	.3	.3	~	.1	~	~	~	~	~	~	~	.1[c]
Libya	1.8	1.4	~	.3	.1	.1	.1	~	~	~	~	~	.1	~
Nigeria	1.5	~	.4	1.0	.8	2.0	.1	~	.1	~	.1	~	~	~
Saudi Arabia	~	~	~	~	~	~	2.3	144.9	33.6	64.4	90.6	266.6	118.5	~
United Arab Emirates	~	~	~	~	~	.1	~	~	~	~	~	~	~	~
T. VENEZUELA	1.0	1.5	2.7	3.7	5.1	8.2	12.5	73.7	65.2	72.4	64.5	109.9	126.7	162.1[c]
Non-Oil Developing Countries	~	61.4	74.1	99.2	67.1	59.7	45.8	~	318.5	298.9	423.5	198.6	345.6	624.3
Africa	~	~	~	5.4	.1	.1	2.0	~	.5	.3	.3	.2	.1	.2[c]
South Africa	~	~	~	~	~	~	~	~	~	~	~	~	~	~
Africa not specified	~	~	~	5.4	.4	.4	2.0	~	.5	.2	.3	.2	.1	.2[c]
Asia	~	1.5	1.0	1.0	.4	.4	.2	~	9.8	13.5	23.1	27.6	30.3	263.3
China, People's Rep.	1.5	~	.1	1.7	.1	.4	.2	~	.9	1.1	1.7	2.6	4.2	18.7[a]
Hong Kong	~	~	.1	~	.1	.2	.2	3.9	5.5	6.3	9.9	11.2	10.9	50.9[a]
India	~	~	~	~	.6	.5	~	~	.5	.5	.8	.6	.5	.4[c]
Korea	2.1	2.0	4.0	9.2	~	~	2.1	2.1	2.0	4.0	9.2	11.5	13.2	116.5[b]
Malaysia	~	~	~	~	~	~	~	~	.1	.2	.2	.2	.1	.6[b]
Pakistan	~	.1	.2	~	~	.2	.3	~	.1	.1	.1	.3	.2	.3[b]
Philippines	~	.1	.2	~	.1	.1	.2	~	.4	1.0	.6	.6	.4	5.7[a]
Singapore	~	~	~	~	~	~	~	~	.1	.2	.3	.2	.3	70.0[a]
Sri Lanka	~	~	~	~	~	~	~	~	.1	.1	.4	.1	.1	.1[a]
Thailand	~	1.4	.6	~	.3	.1	~	~	.2	.1	.4	.2	.2	.2[c]
Asia not specified	~	~	~	~	~	~	~	~	.2	.2	~	.1	.1	~

Table 2631 (Continued)

PANAMA ABSOLUTE VALUE OF GOODS TRADED WITH SELECTED REGIONS AND COUNTRIES,[1] 1975-82
(M US)[2]

Category	Exports FOB							Imports CIF						
	1975	1976	1977	1979	1980	1981	1982	1975	1976	1977	1979	1980	1981	1982
III. Developing Countries (Continued)														
Non-Oil Developing Countries														
Europe														
Greece	~	3.7	5.0	1.2	2.4	11.6	~	~	.8	1.0	1.6	1.3	1.1	1.6
Hungary	~	~	~	.3	~	~	~	~	.3	.2	.1	.1	.1	.1
Portugal	~	~	~	~	~	~	~	.4	.2	.2	.6	.2	.4	1.2[b]
Romania	~	~	~	~	~	~	~	.4	.1	.2	.4	.5	.2	.2[b]
Turkey	~	~	~	~	~	8.1	~	~	~	~	~	.3	~	~
Yugoslavia	2.3	3.7	5.0	.9	2.4	3.5	~	.2	.4	.4	.3	.2	.3	.1[c]
Middle East														
Egypt	~	1.0	.3	.2	~	.6	.7	~	.1	.1	.2	.2	.2	3.3
Israel	~	~	~	.1	~	.2	.3	~	.1	.1	.2	.2	.2	.2
Syrian Arab Rep.	~	1.0	.3	.1	~	.2	.2	.2	~	~	~	~	~	3.3[a]
Yemen Arab Rep.	~	~	~	~	~	.4	.2	~	~	~	~	~	~	~
IV. Latin America[3]	18.6	55.2	67.8	92.3	64.2	47.1	42.9	189.7	307.3	284.1	398.3	169.2	313.9	355.8
A. ARGENTINA	~	~	~	~	3.2	.3	.3	1.5	1.7	2.4	2.8	2.3	1.5	2.2[b]
Bahamas	~	~	~	.1	.5	.5	.1	~	~	~	~	~	~	~
Barbados	~	.2	~	.2	.1	~	~	~	~	~	~	~	~	~
Belize	~	~	~	~	.7	.5	~	.2	.2	~	~	.1	.1	.2[c]
B. BOLIVIA	~	.1	~	.1	.1	~	~	4.0	4.6	7.2	12.2	12.7	20.3	15.7[a]
C. BRAZIL	~	.1	~	.1	~	.6	.3	.9	1.7	2.2	3.2	3.2	2.9	6.0[a]
D. CHILE	~	.3	.1	.3	.6	.6	~	10.7	10.7	7.3	9.2	10.1	11.3	9.0[c]
E. COLOMBIA	1.0	3.9	4.6	3.9	3.7	2.0	3.7	16.7	17.6	20.8	34.2	36.8	42.8	37.7[c]
F. COSTA RICA	6.0	9.3	9.1	16.7	22.6	11.9	10.1	.4	.1	.1	.3	.7	.3	.4[a]
H. DOMINICAN REP.	.2	.3	7.6	3.6	1.4	1.6	.7	129.8	150.0	128.3	166.4	34.9	18.7	63.6[c]
I. ECUADOR	2.1	.4	.2	.4	1.8	1.1	2.3	5.4	4.5	4.8	6.5	6.3	5.5	5.7[c]
J. EL SALVADOR	1.8	1.8	3.0	4.2	4.6	4.3	3.4	6.3	7.2	9.2	14.7	15.9	18.0	16.7[c]
Guadeloupe	~	~	.1	~	~	~	~	~	~	~	~	~	~	~
K. GUATEMALA	3.3	.7	3.3	1.9	7.0	2.8	2.5	~	~	~	~	~	~	~
Guiana, French	~	~	~	.2	.3	.3	.4	~	~	~	~	~	~	~
Guyana	~	~	~	~	.5	1.6	~	~	~	~	~	~	~	~
L. HAITI	.1	~	.1	.3	.4	.2	~	.1	.2	.3	.2	.4	.3	.1[c]
M. HONDURAS	.6	.4	2.4	1.6	1.5	6.7	9.1	.9	1.6	.9	2.5	2.1	2.2	2.4[c]
Jamaica	~	.3	.6	.1	.2	~	.1	~	.9	1.0	1.4	.7	.2	.1[c]
Leeward Islands	~	~	~	~	~	.3	.5	~	~	~	~	~	~	~
N. MEXICO	.1	.2	~	3.4	3.1	.3	.9	9.7	9.4	10.9	14.1	14.4	118.5	164.6[b]
Netherlands Antilles	1.7	1.8	2.2	2.6	3.1	3.7	4.9	1.5	6.1	1.3	1.7	4.1	6.2	7.4[c]
O. NICARAGUA	3.0	4.4	6.5	5.1	10.7	7.1	2.5	2.6	3.5	3.5	3.5	3.6	3.6	2.2[c]
Panama Canal Zone	35.8	26.3	24.9	~	~	~	~	7.7	2.0	2.7	1.1	~	~	~
Q. PARAGUAY	~	~	~	~	.1	.1	~	~	~	~	~	.1	~	~
R. PERU	.4	.4	~	.2	.2	.3	.9	.6	.6	1.1	2.2	3.4	3.6	4.5[c]
St. Pierre-Miquelon	~	~	~	~	~	~	~	~	~	~	~	.1	.2	.4[c]
Suriname	~	1.9	.5	.3	.3	.2	.2	~	~	~	~	~	~	~
Trinidad and Tobago	~	~	1.2	.1	.1	.4	.2	~	22.9	3.9	9.4	17.1	57.5	14.0[b]
S. URUGUAY	~	~	~	~	.5	.1	.1	.1	.1	.1	.1	.1	.1	1.2[a]
Windward Islands	~	~	~	~	~	~	~	~	~	~	~	~	~	1.6[c]
French West Indies not specified	~	~	~	~	~	~	~	~	~	~	~	~	~	~
Other Latin America not specified	~	2.1	1.3	46.8	~	~	~	~	61.8	76.2	112.6	~	~	~

Table 2631 (Continued)

PANAMA ABSOLUTE VALUE OF GOODS TRADED WITH SELECTED REGIONS AND COUNTRIES,[1] 1975-82
(M US)[2]

Category	Exports FOB							Imports CIF						
	1975	1976	1977	1979	1980	1981	1982	1975	1976	1977	1979	1980	1981	1982
V. Developing Countries (Continued)														
Non-Oil Developing Countries														
USSR, Eastern Europe, etc.														
G. CUBA	.4	.5	.1	.2	.6	.8	.5	2.1	2.0	1.9	3.4	4.6	4.2	1.8
Czechoslovakia	.3	.4	~	.1	.5	.8	.5	~	.6	.2	.3	.1	.5	.3c
Eastern Germany	~	~	~	~	~	~	~	.5	.6	.5	1.2	1.3	1.3	.7c
Poland	.1	.1	.1	.1	.1	~	~	.1	.2	.1	~	~	.1	~
USSR	.1	~	~	~	~	~	~	1.1	1.2	1.2	.9	1.4	.9	.6c
Country or area not specified	~	~	~	~	~	~	~	~	~	~	.9	1.7	1.3	.6c
Special categories	~	~	~	~	52.4	17.6	57.7	~	1.3	1.5	3.4	134.4	140.8	147.1c
EEC	~	48.3	41.4	44.2	45.1	55.6	42.3	~	65.1	64.7	90.3	93.0	101.4	223.3
VI. Percent Distribution														
Industrial Countries	~	72.3	67.6	64.1	64.0	72.0	61.4	~	49.7	47.1	49.4	49.6	51.1	65.3
Oil Exporting Countries	~	1.3	1.8	1.8	1.7	3.3	4.8	~	11.7	16.9	13.1	26.0	15.9	5.6
Non-Oil Developing Countries	~	26.0	30.5	34.1	19.2	18.9	14.9	~	37.5	34.7	35.7	13.7	22.4	21.5
Africa	~	~	~	1.8	~	~	.6	~	.1	~	~	~	~	~
Asia	~	.6	.4	~	.1	.1	.1	~	1.2	1.6	1.9	1.9	2.0	9.1
Europe	~	1.6	2.1	.4	.7	3.7	.1	~	.1	.1	.1	.1	.1	.1
Middle East	~	.4	.1	.1	~	.2	.2	~	~	~	~	~	~	~
Western Hemisphere	~	23.4	27.9	31.7	18.3	14.9	13.9	~	36.2	33.0	33.6	11.7	20.4	12.3
USSR, Eastern Europe, etc.	~	.2	~	.1	.2	.2	.1	~	.2	.2	.3	.3	.3	.1
VII. Annual Percent Change														
World	~	-17.6	2.8	13.3	20.3	-9.6	-2.7	~	-2.5	1.5	26.0	22.0	6.3	88.4
Industrial Countries	~	-21.5	-3.8	12.1	20.1	1.7	-17.0	~	14.2	-3.7	21.6	22.6	9.5	140.9
Oil Exporting Countries	~	-27.7	43.4	-39.4	15.3	75.4	41.4	~	-55.3	47.1	91.2	142.2	-34.8	-33.9
Non-Oil Developing Countries	~	-4.9	20.7	22.1	-32.3	-11.1	-23.2	~	16.9	-6.1	23.5	-53.1	74.0	80.6
Africa	~	-99.8	~	~	~	~	~	~	-54.8	-61.2	80.7	-23.6	-36.0	42.4
Asia	~	10.1	-33.7	-94.4	~	-20.1	-38.3	~	25.0	38.2	23.2	19.7	9.6	769.5
Europe	~	64.1	35.0	-71.4	97.1	376.8	~	~	-30.2	22.0	-34.3	19.7	9.6	45.8
Middle East	~	-4.3	-67.2	~	-79.1	~	27.5	~	-39.5	-12.2	-39.7	-3.8	-11.4	~
Western Hemisphere	~	-6.6	22.7	20.8	-30.4	-26.7	-8.8	~	17.2	-7.5	24.0	-19.1	-15.7	13.4
USSR, Eastern Europe, etc.	~	34.4	-80.6	100.9	167.6	33.3	-41.5	~	10.9	-3.2	-10.6	-57.5	85.5	-55.9

1. DOT data may differ between countries and from IFS data because of the time it takes for an export to become an import, etc.

2. Data may be calculated from partner's reported data or estimated on basis of less than 12 months.

3. Cuba is included in category V; Venezuela is included in category III.

a. Nine months of reported data, three months derived from partner.

b. Nine months of reported data, three months derived or extrapolated.

c. Nine months of reported data, three months extrapolated.

SOURCE: Adapted from the IMF-DOT Annual, 1970-74; IMF-DOT-Y, 1982.

Table 2632

PARAGUAY ABSOLUTE VALUE OF GOODS TRADED WITH SELECTED REGIONS AND COUNTRIES,[1] 1975-82

(M US)[2]

Category	Exports FOB							Imports CIF						
	1975	1976	1977	1979	1980	1981	1982	1975	1976	1977	1979	1980	1981	1982
I. World	176.71	181.83	278.91	304.10	310.23	297.16	329.80	178.14	180.21	255.37	429.01	517.07	506.28	581.50
II. Industrial Countries	106.59	125.55	182.64	182.79	143.78	120.82	136.20	76.12	70.36	112.66	176.47	191.94	196.96	200.70
United States	15.81	21.58	39.90	17.91	17.10	16.60	9.10	21.96	18.59	31.10	50.15	51.37	50.32	52.30
Canada	.30	.64	.84	.04	.04	.01	~	.24	.22	.16	.52	.26	.62	.40
Australia	~	~	~	~	~	~	~	~	~	~	~	~	.01	~
Japan	3.68	6.40	6.40	15.41	11.30	24.90	25.50	8.81	8.46	22.85	36.08	42.03	42.05	32.00
Austria	.02	.01	~	.04	~	~	~	1.06	.72	1.14	2.03	2.13	2.25	1.10
Belgium	3.75	.78	1.08	1.81	5.74	3.74	6.10	1.81	1.44	1.60	1.82	1.64	2.37	2.10
Denmark	.70	.11	.41	.22	1.81	~	.30	.15	.17	.15	1.02	.36	.80	1.00
Finland	~	~	.35	.02	~	~	~	~	.03	.05	.28	.63	.10	.10
France	7.91	10.42	13.16	5.91	5.03	4.60	7.20	2.57	2.46	5.18	8.78	12.03	9.10	10.60
Germany	22.05	20.39	28.37	46.41	38.45	32.83	40.90	14.53	15.32	22.38	31.66	33.53	41.00	37.30
Ireland	~	~	~	.02	.01	~	.40	~	.01	.02	.01	.01	~	~
Italy	.84	2.99	5.55	21.69	6.05	3.38	5.70	2.11	2.06	2.23	5.37	4.71	6.08	6.60
Netherlands	15.10	27.12	42.98	45.34	19.75	13.30	16.00	1.00	.99	1.03	2.67	2.15	3.34	9.90
Norway	~	~	~	.02	.03	~	~	.24	.06	.12	.07	.27	.10	.10
Spain	4.61	2.79	3.78	5.57	4.80	3.80	6.90	1.29	2.81	5.94	5.36	5.50	6.51	6.10
Sweden	.03	.05	.03	~	.27	.01	~	3.14	2.37	3.69	4.14	3.56	4.39	2.20
Switzerland	13.43	21.37	26.33	21.79	31.61	14.70	14.20	1.01	.99	1.20	2.30	2.90	3.03	4.90
United Kingdom	18.35	10.91	13.46	.63	1.80	2.95	3.90	16.18	13.65	13.81	24.19	28.84	24.90	34.00
III. Developing Countries	1.24	.43	1.55	.13	1.27	4.60	12.80	19.86	23.87	23.72	50.10	37.09	37.37	75.70
Oil Exporting Countries	.43	.08	1.21	~	1.26	.10	.90	19.86	23.14	23.48	50.07	37.08	27.50	75.60
Algeria	~	~	~	~	~	.15	1.70	~	~	~	~	~	~	~
Indonesia	~	~	~	~	~	.10	.10	~	~	~	~	~	~	~
Iraq	~	~	~	~	~	3.80	.80	~	~	~	~	~	~	~
Nigeria	~	~	~	~	~	~	~	~	~	~	~	~	9.80	.10
Saudi Arabia	~	.35	.34	.13	.01	.55	9.30	~	.73	.24	.03	.01	.07	.07
T. VENEZUELA	.81	55.08	94.08	116.50	161.25	169.14	180.00	.81	83.58	115.64	199.39	284.42	263.45	298.30
Non-Oil Developing Countries	~	.45	1.99	.80	1.17	1.65	7.60	~	.05	.08	.43	1.93	.58	.90
Africa														
Cameroon	~	.03	.03	.06	.02	.02	.20	~	~	~	~	~	~	~
Congo	~	~	~	~	.04	.29	.20	~	~	~	~	~	~	~
Ivory Coast	~	~	~	~	~	.03	.10	~	~	~	~	~	~	~
Madagascar	~	~	~	~	~	~	.40	~	~	~	~	~	~	~
Mali	~	~	.40	.42	~	.16	.30	~	~	~	~	~	~	~
Morocco	~	.30	1.08	.18	.49	.58	6.20	~	.05	.06	.43	.65	.38	.90
Senegal	.05	.12	.48	.15	.65	.14	.20	~	~	~	~	~	.20	~
South Africa	~	~	~	~	~	.40	~	~	~	~	~	~	~	~
Tunisia	~	~	~	~	~	~	~	~	~	~	~	~	~	~
Upper Volta	~	~	~	~	~	~	~	~	.70	.02	~	1.28	1.12	~
Africa not specified	~	3.10	4.55	1.52	4.85	4.37	4.30	~	~	.77	5.77	8.42	3.04	2.80
Asia														
Burma	~	~	~	~	~	~	~	~	~	~	4.16	5.86	.03	~
China, People's Rep.	~	~	~	~	~	~	.80	~	.20	.36	.48	.91	.66	.80
Hong Kong	~	~	~	~	~	~	~	~	.10	.31	.55	.42	.47	.40
India	~	~	~	~	~	1.40	1.50	~	.02	.01	.53	1.12	1.70	1.60
Korea	~	~	~	~	~	.30	.50	~	.02	.01	.01	.01	.01	~
Malaysia	~	~	~	~	~	~	~	~	~	~	~	~	.03	~
Pakistan	~	~	~	.08	.19	1.00	.10	~	~	~	~	.01	~	~
Philippines	~	~	~	~	~	1.20	1.20	~	~	~	~	~	.11	~
Singapore	~	~	~	~	~	~	~	~	~	~	~	~	~	~
Sri Lanka	~	3.10	4.54	1.41	4.66	~	~	~	.02	.06	.10	.10	.03	.03
Asia not specified	~	~	.01	.02	~	.07	~	~	.34	.01	.03	~	~	~
Oceania not specified	~	~	~	~	~	~	~	~	~	~	~	~	~	~

Table 2632 (Continued)

PARAGUAY ABSOLUTE VALUE OF GOODS TRADED WITH SELECTED REGIONS AND COUNTRIES,[1] 1975-82 (M US)[2]

	Exports FOB							Imports CIF						
Category	1975	1976	1977	1979	1980	1981	1982	1975	1976	1977	1979	1980	1981	1982
III. Developing Countries (Continued)														
Non-Oil Developing Countries														
Europe														
Greece	~	3.58	10.72	9.34	13.25	14.52	9.40	~	.14	.14	.16	.13	.30	.70
Hungary	~	~	.02	~	~	~	~	~	~	~	.01	~	.02	.20
Portugal	.41	3.58	10.70	7.85	12.17	12.87	8.90	.07	.12	.13	.12	.11	.09	.40
Romania	~	~	~	~	~	~	~	~	~	~	~	.01	.11	.10
Turkey	~	~	~	~	~	~	~	~	.01	.01	.03	.01	.07	~
Yugoslavia	3.21	.01	.01	1.49	1.07	1.65	.50	~	~	~	~	~	.01	~
Middle East	~	.01	.01	.01	.02	~	.50	~	.03	.06	.10	1.80	.27	.40
Israel	~	.01	.01	.01	~	~	~	~	.03	.06	.10	~	~	~
Syrian Arab Rep.	~	~	~	~	~	~	~	~	~	~	~	~	~	~
Middle East not specified	~	~	~	~	.02	~	.50	~	~	~	~	1.80	.27	.40
IV. Latin America[3]	62.03	47.94	76.82	104.84	141.98	148.59	158.20	76.93	82.66	114.59	192.93	272.14	259.25	293.50
A. ARGENTINA	49.68	17.95	35.82	51.01	74.18	68.59	59.20	33.22	37.75	43.23	74.04	106.44	100.10	113.20
B. BOLIVIA	.04	.02	.03	.13	.58	1.18	.40	.33	.11	1.77	1.77	.57	.28	.20
C. BRAZIL	6.17	10.97	16.28	29.03	40.24	54.34	83.40	37.15	31.20	53.91	96.37	140.50	131.30	154.30
D. CHILE	1.02	7.42	8.66	7.15	11.31	11.10	6.90	1.27	1.62	2.68	2.93	4.30	3.92	7.30
E. COLOMBIA	.16	.10	.19	.38	.14	.07	.20	.31	.19	.21	.19	.20	.04	.40
F. COSTA RICA	~	~	~	~	~	~	~	~	~	~	~	~	~	~
H. DOMINICAN REP.	~	~	~	~	~	~	~	~	~	~	~	~	.01	~
I. ECUADOR	.11	.03	.02	~	~	~	~	.13	.13	.36	.47	.34	.42	.10
J. EL SALVADOR	~	~	~	~	~	~	~	~	~	~	~	~	.08	~
K. GUATEMALA	~	~	~	~	~	~	~	~	~	~	~	~	.02	~
Jamaica	~	~	~	~	~	~	~	~	~	~	~	~	~	2.80
N. MEXICO	2.16	2.24	.73	2.46	4.02	2.49	.90	.88	.29	.64	.50	.50	.64	.70
Netherlands Antilles	~	~	~	~	~	~	~	2.13	1.32	2.30	1.74	2.89	2.61	3.30
P. PANAMA	~	~	~	~	~	1.20	2.60	~	3.06	.03	.08	~	3.53	2.40
R. PERU	.41	.45	.12	.04	.02	.49	.20	.13	~	~	~	.13	.30	.20
Trinidad and Tobago	~	~	~	~	~	~	~	~	~	~	~	~	.17	.40
S. URUGUAY	2.28	8.75	12.89	13.61	10.16	9.13	4.40	3.51	6.94	8.50	14.27	14.95	15.50	8.20
America not specified	~	.01	2.08	1.03	~	~	~	.57	.05	.91	1.24	1.65	~	~
Other Latin America not specified	~	~	~	~	1.32	~	~	~	~	.04	.51	.15	~	~
V. USSR, Eastern Europe, etc.	.04	~	.02	3.64	.08	.90	~	~	.66	.84	2.44	2.13	2.68	1.60
Bulgaria	~	~	~	~	~	~	~	~	~	~	~	~	.10	.10
Czechoslovakia	~	~	~	~	~	~	~	~	~	~	~	~	.60	.90
North Korea	~	~	~	~	~	~	~	~	~	~	~	~	~	~
Poland	~	~	~	~	~	~	~	~	~	~	~	~	.01	.60
USSR	~	~	~	~	~	~	~	~	~	~	~	~	1.89	~
USSR, etc., not specified	.04	~	.02	3.64	.08	.90	~	~	.66	.84	2.44	2.13	.07	~
Country or area not specified	~	.78	.62	1.04	3.84	~	~	~	.70	.33	.61	1.49	~	~
EEC	~	72.71	105.03	122.00	78.64	60.79	80.50	~	36.11	46.41	75.54	83.29	87.61	101.50
VI. Percent Distribution														
Industrial Countries	~	69.0	65.5	60.1	46.3	40.7	41.3	~	39.0	44.1	41.1	37.1	38.9	34.5
Oil Exporting Countries	~	.2	.6	~	.4	1.5	3.9	~	13.2	9.3	11.7	7.2	7.4	13.0
Non-Oil Developing Countries	~	30.3	33.7	38.3	52.0	56.9	54.6	~	46.4	45.3	46.5	55.0	52.0	51.3
Africa	~	.2	.7	.3	.6	.6	2.3	~	.4	.3	.3	.4	.1	.2
Asia	~	1.7	1.6	.5	1.6	1.5	1.3	~	.1	.1	1.3	1.6	.6	.5
Europe	~	2.0	3.8	3.1	4.3	4.9	2.9	~	~	~	.1	.3	.1	.1
Middle East	~	~	~	~	~	~	~	~	~	~	~	~	~	~
Western Hemisphere	~	26.4	27.5	34.5	45.8	50.0	48.0	~	45.9	44.9	45.0	52.6	51.2	50.5
USSR, Eastern Europe, etc.	~	~	.2	1.2	~	.3	.2	~	.4	.3	.6	.4	.5	.3

Table 2632 (Continued)

PARAGUAY ABSOLUTE VALUE OF GOODS TRADED WITH SELECTED REGIONS AND COUNTRIES,[1] 1975-82
(M US)[2]

Category	Exports FOB							Imports CIF						
	1975	1976	1977	1979	1980	1981	1982	1975	1976	1977	1979	1980	1981	1982
VII. Annual Percent Change														
World	?	2.9	53.4	18.3	2.0	-4.2	11.0	?	1.0	41.7	35.0	20.5	-2.1	14.9
Industrial Countries	?	17.8	45.5	.9	-21.3	-16.0	12.7	?	-7.6	60.1	24.0	8.8	2.6	1.9
Oil Exporting Countries	?	-65.3	259.2	-87.3	887.6	261.1	178.3	?	20.2	-.6	44.6	-26.0	.7	102.6
Non-Oil Developing Countries	?	-19.2	70.8	61.7	38.4	4.9	6.4	?	3.8	38.4	45.6	42.6	-7.4	13.2
Africa	?	348.5	338.9	42.0	45.4	41.8	360.0	?	-87.1	54.4	4.4	347.3	-69.9	55.2
Asia	?	31.9	47.1	?	219.2	-9.7	-1.7	?	104.0	9.6	19.0	45.9	-63.8	-8.0
Europe	?	-1.2	?	94.1	41.9	9.6	-35.3	?	75.0	1.9	16.8	-19.3	127.4	131.9
Middle East	?	-79.5	199.7	-66.7	171.4	?	?	?	163.6	127.6	55.7	?	-85.2	50.2
Western Hemisphere	?	-22.8	60.2	57.3	35.4	4.7	6.5	?	3.8	38.6	46.7	41.1	-4.7	13.2
USSR, Eastern Europe, etc.	?	?	?	?	-97.8	?	?	?	14.9	27.9	61.3	-12.7	25.9	-40.2

1. DOT data may differ between countries and from IFS data because of the time it takes for an export to become an import, etc.

2. Data may be calculated from partner's reported data or estimated on basis of less than 12 months.

3. No trade with Cuba; Venezuela is included in category III.

SOURCE: Adapted from the IMF-DOT Annual, 1970-74; IMF-DOT-Y, 1982.

Table 2633

PERU ABSOLUTE VALUE OF GOODS TRADED WITH SELECTED REGIONS AND COUNTRIES,[1] 1975-82 (M US)[2]

Category	Exports FOB							Imports CIF						
	1975	1976	1977	1979	1980	1981	1982	1975	1976	1977	1979	1980	1981	1982
I. World	1,247.0	1,341.8	1,744.6	3,675.3	3,914.7	3,246.9	3,195.7	2,379.6	1,747.1	1,598.3	1,683.7	2,610.5	3,433.7	3,544.8
II. Industrial Countries	730.3	885.0	1,093.0	2,272.5	2,489.8	2,163.3	2,249.9	1,830.7	1,193.4	1,070.7	1,072.6	1,618.5	2,290.4	2,463.7
United States	301.5	335.9	499.4	1,126.1	1,257.7	1,089.8	1,045.6[a]	749.0	505.3	462.5	521.8	776.0	1,136.6	1,116.9
Canada	3.4	2.7	12.3	14.6	20.9	24.0	26.9[a]	71.9	38.1	38.6	27.9	26.0	48.1	88.8[a]
Australia	~	.3	.7	6.7	4.9	1.3	3.1[a]	.3	17.9	10.5	7.0	6.9	8.9	9.4[a]
Japan	143.3	176.7	200.1	493.5	371.2	484.1	491.3[a]	207.9	121.7	118.2	100.3	209.1	295.7	322.3[a]
New Zealand	~	.1	.5	11.6	.6	1.1	.3[b]	~	19.3	21.1	18.6	14.8	19.7	40.7[b]
Austria	.1	.4	.5	3.2	20.3	2.0	11.2[a]	5.2	6.2	10.9	5.8	5.8	14.0	17.7[a]
Belgium	33.0	61.9	31.8	58.4	99.3	68.5	80.5[a]	39.1	21.6	14.2	42.4	62.6	36.6	25.7[a]
Denmark	1.6	3.4	3.2	6.2	4.5	5.3	7.5[a]	7.6	3.9	2.8	5.5	5.1	9.0	6.9[a]
Finland	8.1	.6	.1	3.2	6.9	3.2	3.6[a]	5.8	13.2	13.5	3.6	4.3	10.3	6.4[a]
France	25.5	22.2	37.3	37.7	43.8	41.1	103.6[a]	55.1	41.4	45.6	31.6	38.0	69.8	78.6[a]
Germany	81.2	92.4	71.0	132.8	185.7	100.1	122.2[a]	254.4	158.8	118.2	126.2	178.1	228.2	242.6[a]
Iceland	~	~	~	.2	~	~	~	~	~	~	~	.4	~	~
Ireland	~	~	~	.6	~	.5	.5[b]	.4	2.0	2.2	3.9	3.0	2.9	4.1[b]
Italy	31.8	60.0	88.9	136.1	167.6	80.1	110.3[a]	55.5	55.2	24.3	34.0	59.2	83.3	155.6[a]
Netherlands	42.8	29.0	38.3	51.1	90.1	87.3	44.6[a]	84.3	31.1	25.7	18.3	22.3	39.4	47.3[a]
Norway	.4	.1	7.0	4.2	.7	1.0	2.6[a]	6.7	3.3	2.9	1.2	3.2	2.5	9.4[a]
Spain	9.2	13.6	25.3	14.0	23.9	13.4	13.9[a]	24.2	18.1	9.5	14.4	4.0	57.9	133.9[a]
Sweden	2.9	2.1	9.3	22.5	21.7	9.8	25.0[a]	53.4	41.4	51.5	31.8	79.0	79.2	38.3[a]
Switzerland	4.1	5.1	11.4	25.2	15.5	18.0	10.6[a]	51.6	34.7	30.3	37.1	33.8	56.3	49.7[a]
United Kingdom	41.2	78.7	63.3	124.7	154.4	132.9	146.8[a]	93.5	60.2	68.2	41.1	86.7	92.1	69.5[a]
III. Developing Countries														
Oil Exporting Countries	12.8	23.9	32.6	71.5	75.7	69.2	67.4	110.3	89.3	150.8	23.4	28.7	38.3	32.3
Algeria	2.6	2.8	5.0	~	4.0	~	.5[a]	~	~	~	~	~	~	~
Indonesia	~	~	~	~	.1	1.7	3.3[b]	.7	~	~	.6	.2	.3	~
Iran, I.R. of	1.1	5.4	7.0	.1	18.4	22.5	21.4[c]	.1	~	.2	.1	.1	~	~
Nigeria	~	~	.6	~	1.2	~	~	~	~	~	~	~	.4	.3[c]
Saudi Arabia	~	~	~	~	~	~	~	~	~	~	~	~	~	~
T. VENEZUELA	9.1	14.7	20.0	71.4	52.0	45.0	42.7[c]	109.5	89.3	150.7	22.7	28.4	37.6	32.0[c]
Non-Oil Developing Countries	~	253.9	395.1	802.1	1,055.5	595.4	519.6	~	405.4	367.1	211.3	332.4	521.9	557.4
Africa	~	.1	13.3	10.6	14.6	26.7	4.4	~	2.8	6.9	9.2	11.9	20.2	7.3
Angola	~	~	~	~	~	~	~	~	~	~	~	~	~	~
Madagascar	~	~	~	~	~	~	~	~	~	~	~	~	~	~
Mauritius	~	~	~	~	~	~	.5[a]	~	~	~	~	~	.1	.1[c]
Mozambique	~	~	~	~	~	~	~	~	~	~	2.4	~	~	~
South Africa	~	.1	13.3	10.5	14.2	26.2	3.5[b]	~	2.6	6.9	6.4	11.3	19.6	6.4[b]
Zimbabwe	~	~	~	~	~	~	~	~	~	~	~	~	~	.4[b]
Africa not specified	~	~	.5	.1	.3	.5	.4[c]	~	~	~	~	~	~	.4[c]
Asia	~	55.8	56.6	19.3	142.0	135.6	195.9	~	7.2	9.5	15.3	28.9	34.5	51.6
China, People's Rep.	~	46.4	35.7	10.0	88.2	70.7	93.1[a]	~	.4	.3	.2	.2	.8	10.9[a]
Fiji	~	~	~	~	~	~	.2[a]	~	~	~	~	~	~	~
Hong Kong	~	.6	.4	1.2	2.9	3.6	8.6[a]	~	1.1	1.1	.8	3.0	12.0	9.8[a]
India	~	1.0	1.9	.8	2.6	.6	.5[c]	~	1.5	1.4	.6	4.8	1.3	1.1[c]
Korea	~	4.5	13.6	.1	42.1	54.5	66.4[b]	~	.1	.1	.1	1.7	7.5	12.8[b]
Malaysia	~	~	~	.2	1.3	.2	3.4[b]	~	~	~	~	.2	~	.8[b]
Pakistan	~	~	~	~	1.2	1.4	.5[a]	~	3.8	6.0	~	~	~	.1[a]
Papua New Guinea	~	~	~	1.0	1.2	.4	1.3[a]	~	~	~	~	~	~	~
Philippines	~	3.0	1.5	.3	1.0	.4	14.6[a]	~	~	~	3.9	5.6	~	~[a]
Singapore	~	.4	3.3	6.2	1.6	2.3	6.9[a]	~	~	~	~	.1	.1	4.1[a]
Sri Lanka	~	~	.2	~	.7	1.5	.1[a]	~	~	~	9.1	8.5	8.0	6.1[a]
Thailand	~	~	~	~	~	~	.2[b]	~	~	~	~	~	~	1.9[a]
Asia not specified	~	~	~	.5	~	.4	.4[c]	~	.2	.4	.4	4.8	4.4	3.7[c]
Oceania not specified	~	~	~	~	~	~	~	~	~	~	.1	~	.3	.2[c]

Table 2633 (Continued)

PERU ABSOLUTE VALUE OF GOODS TRADED WITH SELECTED REGIONS AND COUNTRIES,[1] 1975-82 (M US)[2]

Category	Exports FOB							Imports CIF						
	1975	1976	1977	1979	1980	1981	1982	1975	1976	1977	1979	1980	1981	1982
III. Developing Countries (Continued)														
Non-Oil Developing Countries														
Europe														
Greece	~	44.7	91.1	79.6	115.7	60.9	65.2	~	13.0	16.0	4.3	11.6	11.7	8.4
Hungary	6.5	1.2	8.5	.3	1.8	.3	3.5[a]	~	~	~	.2	6.0	1.7	~
Malta	~	7.5	26.8	9.4	4.1	3.2	9.8[c]	3.9	9.2	4.9	2.8	3.5	2.2	1.9[b]
Portugal	.9	8.4	6.3	.1	.1	~	.1[c]	3.3	1.3	.6	.8	1.0	2.1	2.5[b]
Romania	14.2	17.8	13.6	1.3	9.8	6.1	9.8[c]	7.9	2.4	10.5	.2	.5	3.2	2.7[c]
Turkey	3.8	.3	~	18.5	14.2	~	~	.1	~	~	~	~	~	.2[b]
Yugoslavia	~	9.6	35.9	.1	.1	~	~	~	.2	~	.3	.6	1.7	.4[c]
Europe not specified	~	1.3	2.3	50.1	85.7	51.3	42.1[c]	~	~	.1	1.1	~	.8	.7[b]
Middle East														
Egypt	~	.1	.1	.1	5.7	1.3	3.0	~	.2	.1	~	1.7	.4	8.2
Israel	3.0	.2	1.0	~	2.5	.1	.3[a]	3.0	.2	.1	.9	1.6	.4	8.2[a]
Jordan	~	.2	.1	.1	1.1	.6	1.6[a]	~	~	~	~	~	~	~
Lebanon	~	~	~	~	~	.2	.5[c]	~	~	~	~	~	~	~
Syrian Arab Rep.	~	.5	~	~	~	~	.2[c]	~	~	~	.1	~	.1	~
Middle East not specified	~	1.1	.9	.1	2.1	.5	.4[c]	~	~	~	~	~	~	~
IV. Latin America[3]	200.6	151.9	231.7	692.5	777.6	370.9	251.0	322.5	382.2	334.5	181.4	278.3	455.0	481.8
A. ARGENTINA	34.9	21.4	21.2	52.4	59.4	19.7	15.6[b]	27.9	42.7	50.5	66.9	71.6	60.2	89.7[c]
Bahamas	~	.1	.9	14.2	126.6	14.1	13.4[c]	~	2.3	2.0	~	~	.1	.1[b]
Bermuda	~	~	~	~	~	~	~	~	~	~	~	~	~	~
B. BOLIVIA	5.5	6.5	12.1	102.0	69.2	24.5	20.8[c]	5.4	2.5	5.9	11.6	11.4	7.3	6.2[b]
C. BRAZIL	35.6	55.9	63.4	114.1	124.2	47.9	68.4[a]	76.3	74.7	52.6	39.4	81.3	194.0	222.3[a]
D. CHILE	82.8	18.6	37.3	64.8	45.0	58.9	30.4[a]	26.2	29.2	11.1	17.5	34.0	40.8	49.0[a]
E. COLOMBIA	15.9	12.0	18.6	69.8	55.9	91.9	78.1[c]	32.5	27.2	28.8	11.6	22.6	37.0	31.4[c]
F. COSTA RICA	.7	1.0	2.3	4.7	5.1	4.3	2.0[b]	~	.1	~	2.6	.3	1.6	1.0[b]
H. DOMINICAN REP.	.2	.2	.2	4.1	.1	.1	.1[a]	~	~	~	~	~	~	.5[a]
I. ECUADOR	10.1	17.2	21.7	106.9	83.8	11.5	9.3[c]	118.2	172.5	155.4	5.8	5.5	6.4	4.2[b]
J. EL SALVADOR	1.2	2.2	2.0	4.6	2.8	1.9	1.6[a]	.1	.1	.2	.5	~	~	.1[a]
K. GUATEMALA	.3	.1	.2	.6	.3	.5	.4[a]	~	~	~	.1	.3	.1	.1[b]
Guyana, French	~	~	~	.2	.3	.4	.3[a]	~	~	.2	.1	.1	.4	.3[c]
L. HAITI	~	~	~	.1	~	~	~	~	.1	.3	.1	~	.1	.1[c]
M. HONDURAS	~	1.4	.7	1.1	.1	.2	.1[c]	~	~	~	~	~	.1	.1[c]
Jamaica	~	~	.4	~	.1	.2	.2[c]	~	~	~	~	~	~	~
Martinique	~	~	~	~	~	~	~	~	~	~	~	~	~	~
N. MEXICO	9.9	9.3	34.0	59.1	90.7	43.0	4.5[b]	31.0	13.9	14.7	10.6	17.2	33.8	8.9[c]
Netherlands Antilles	~	.4	.5	33.3	.2	.3	.3[c]	14.4	11.8	8.1	8.6	13.1	25.2	21.5[b]
O. NICARAGUA	.1	.4	.5	~	.5	.6	.5[c]	.8	.3	.1	.6	~	~	21.4[c]
P. PANAMA	2.0	1.5	8.3	47.1	102.3	48.7	3.3[b]	2.0	.7	.3	4.7	13.0	28.7	.2[c]
Q. PARAGUAY	~	.1	.1	3.5	.5	.4	.2[a]	1.4	1.1	.8	.1	.2	.8	.9[a]
Trinidad and Tobago	~	2.1	.6	1.0	.4	.1	.6[b]	.5	~	~	~	~	~	.2[a]
S. URUGUAY	1.4	1.9	1.6	8.9	10.2	2.1	.9[a]	.7	2.8	3.4	.7	7.5	7.5	6.8[b]
America not specified	~	~	~	.1	~	~	~	~	~	~	~	~	~	16.6[a]
Other Latin America not specified	~	~	5.6	~	~	~	~	~	~	~	~	~	~	~
V. USSR, Eastern Europe, etc.	217.4	136.0	143.2	169.5	104.2	86.4	73.4	23.1	12.8	5.2	26.8	32.8	10.8	9.2
Bulgaria	2.5	6.0	6.0	8.2	7.3	10.8	9.2[c]	.5	1.5	.9	.3	1.3	.3	.3[c]
G. CUBA	21.2	16.4	19.6	13.4	13.2	18.5	15.7[c]	.1	.1	~	~	~	~	~
Czechoslovakia	8.2	15.8	18.8	18.7	6.8	4.1	3.4[c]	8.7	1.1	1.6	1.7	4.3	4.9	4.2[c]
Eastern Germany	23.0	25.7	42.1	57.1	24.2	28.6	24.3[c]	.4	~	.1	~	.2	~	~
North Korea	8.3	3.4	~	~	~	~	~	.8	~	~	~	~	.8	.7[c]
Poland	27.2	50.1	36.9	45.1	36.8	12.4	10.6[c]	2.7	1.3	.6	24.4	26.1	2.1	1.8[c]
USSR	120.4	24.7	19.8	27.0	16.0	12.1	10.2[c]	6.0	8.8	2.1	.3	.9	2.5	2.1[c]
Country or area not specified	~	40.9	63.6	356.3	178.6	312.2	265.4[c]	~	20.0	~	334.2	563.5	536.1	455.7[c]
EEC	~	348.7	342.2	547.9	747.3	516.0	619.3	~	374.3	301.2	303.3	461.1	563.0	630.3

Table 2633 (Continued)

PERU ABSOLUTE VALUE OF GOODS TRADED WITH SELECTED REGIONS AND COUNTRIES,[1] 1975-82
(M US)[2]

Category	Exports FOB							Imports CIF						
	1975	1976	1977	1979	1980	1981	1982	1975	1976	1977	1979	1980	1981	1982
VI. Percent Distribution														
Industrial Countries	~	66.0	62.6	61.8	63.6	66.6	70.4	~	68.3	67.0	63.7	62.0	66.7	69.5
Oil Exporting Countries	~	1.8	1.9	1.9	1.9	2.1	2.1	~	5.1	9.4	1.4	1.1	1.1	.9
Non-Oil Developing Countries	~	18.9	22.6	21.8	27.0	18.3	16.3	~	23.2	23.0	12.5	12.7	15.2	15.7
Africa	~	~	.8	.3	.4	.8	.1	~	.2	.4	.5	.5	.6	.2
Asia	~	4.2	3.2	.5	3.6	4.2	6.1	~	.4	.6	.9	1.1	1.0	1.5
Europe	~	3.3	5.2	2.2	3.0	1.9	2.0	~	.7	1.0	.3	.4	.3	.2
Middle East	~	.1	~	~	.1	~	.1	~	~	~	.1	.1	~	.1
Western Hemisphere	~	11.3	13.3	18.8	19.9	11.4	7.9	~	21.9	20.9	10.8	10.7	13.3	13.6
USSR, Eastern Europe, etc.	~	10.1	8.2	4.6	2.7	2.7	2.3	~	.7	.3	1.6	1.3	.3	.3
VII. Annual Percent Change														
World	~	.7	30.0	84.7	6.5	-17.1	-1.6	~	-20.5	-8.5	30.4	55.0	31.5	3.2
Industrial Countries	~	15.3	23.5	77.8	9.6	-13.1	4.0	~	-27.0	-10.3	11.0	50.9	41.5	7.6
Oil Exporting Countries	~	75.6	36.2	34.4	5.9	-8.6	-2.6	~	-19.4	69.0	-46.9	22.9	33.4	-15.7
Non-Oil Developing Countries	~	-16.7	55.6	117.4	31.6	-43.6	-12.7	~	6.0	-9.5	10.8	57.3	57.0	6.8
Africa	~	-94.6	~	-49.6	37.4	83.2	-83.5	~	-63.8	150.5	-13.0	29.6	68.7	-63.9
Asia	~	-6.6	1.4	-65.1	634.8	-4.5	44.5	~	-80.8	31.4	-21.0	89.2	19.4	49.5
Europe	~	60.9	103.6	37.8	45.3	-47.4	7.1	~	1.5	23.5	-61.5	168.2	1.2	-28.1
Middle East	~	-49.8	74.6	-96.1	~	-76.5	124.6	~	-91.9	-68.0	~	52.9	-74.2	~
Western Hemisphere	~	-28.4	52.6	197.9	12.3	-52.3	-32.3	~	18.8	-12.5	21.4	53.4	63.5	5.9
USSR, Eastern Europe, etc.	~	-39.3	5.3	40.9	-38.5	-17.1	-15.0	~	-21.4	-59.1	79.4	22.3	-67.0	-15.0

1. DOT data may differ between countries and from IFS data because of the time it takes for an export to become an import, etc.

2. Data may be calculated from partner's reported data or estimated on basis of less than 12 months.

3. Cuba is included in category V; Venezuela is included in category III.

a. Data derived from partner country for entire year.

b. Five or fewer months reported; balance of year derived or extrapolated.

c. Data extrapolated for entire year.

SOURCE: Adapted from the IMF-DOT Annual, 1970-74; IMF-DOT-Y, 1982; IMF-DOT-Y, 1983.

Table 2634

URUGUAY ABSOLUTE VALUE OF GOODS TRADED WITH SELECTED REGIONS AND COUNTRIES,[1] 1975-82 (M US)[2]

Category	Exports FOB							Imports CIF						
	1975	1976	1977	1979	1980	1981	1982	1975	1976	1977	1979	1980	1981	1982
I. World	383.9	545.0	607.5	788.9	1,059.0	1,182.6	1,032.3	559.5	588.6	729.9	1,194.4	1,649.3	1,626.5	1,057.7
II. Industrial Countries	181.0	293.6	305.7	393.7	425.7	487.8	375.6	228.0	204.2	281.0	416.3	592.7	581.7	357.0
United States	25.9	59.2	87.3	84.0	82.6	94.9	76.7	57.2	51.3	69.8	111.5	161.1	158.2	131.6
Canada	1.3	3.8	3.6	8.3	7.1	8.4	7.3	12.1	8.1	9.8	12.2	13.6	19.4	10.2
Australia	~	.2	.2	1.0	.4	.7	.6	~	1.6	.1	3.6	2.4	8.0	5.3
Japan	5.7	9.3	6.5	8.7	9.3	13.1	18.1	12.6	10.8	17.3	30.3	67.9	79.7	28.5
New Zealand								.2			.5		.3	.1
Austria	1.4	4.1	2.1	2.8	3.3	3.6	6.8	2.6	2.2	2.1	4.7	4.9	4.8	3.8
Belgium	7.7	8.7	10.5	10.7	18.2	23.6	15.5	8.5	5.4	4.6	6.6	7.5	8.2	4.1
Denmark	.9	1.1	.9	.8	2.6	.7	.7	.8	.6	1.9	1.8	15.2	4.0	2.8
Finland	.1	.2	.2	1.0	.6	5.0	4.5	2.7	.6	.4	1.5	1.3	1.7	.4
France	10.3	20.5	16.6	15.2	14.3	21.9	23.4	9.8	14.7	13.3	18.5	29.7	41.9	21.9
Germany	46.1	67.0	71.4	128.3	136.9	123.1	91.8	47.1	44.9	52.8	95.1	111.4	99.7	63.2
Ireland		.2	.2	.2		.1		.6	.2	.6	.5	.7	.8	.6
Italy	19.4	29.6	19.8	27.8	46.2	55.9	38.3	15.2	12.8	20.1	28.0	46.7	38.2	20.0
Netherlands	27.8	40.9	41.6	57.2	45.3	57.5	29.6	8.7	6.5	9.2	20.9	15.1	14.0	8.8
Norway	.1	.1	.2	.2	.3	.5	.2	1.8	.6	16.2	1.4	2.1	7.5	.6
Spain	11.8	22.9	13.0	18.9	10.3	16.2	11.0	7.4	6.4	13.3	13.8	19.1	23.3	12.3
Sweden	.5	1.6	.7	3.2	5.3	1.5	2.3	5.4	3.4	4.9	5.2	7.5	6.7	3.9
Switzerland	3.6	3.2	3.4	3.8	5.6	8.0	12.1	8.8	11.6	10.0	14.5	17.0	17.4	12.5
United Kingdom	18.1	20.9	27.4	21.7	37.4	53.0	36.7	24.3	21.8	34.4	46.1	69.1	47.8	26.4
III. Developing Countries														
Oil Exporting Countries	8.4	26.5	15.7	13.4	71.3	131.8	92.1	151.8	160.9	186.1	262.8	418.3	347.7	308.1
Algeria	~	~	~	~	1.0	7.1	.3	~	.1	~	~	~	~	~
Indonesia	~	~	~	~	~	~	.1	1.0	.6	~	~	.1	.1	~
Iran, I.R. of	7.1	8.9	8.2	1.1	37.5	47.3	55.0	18.6	57.5	68.7	93.2	211.1	~	89.2
Iraq	~	~	3.4	~	2.6	2.6	.2	99.9	40.4	12.5	33.7	~	~	~
Kuwait	.6	1.8	1.4	2.2	4.3	3.2	8.4	~	~	~	~	~	~	~
Libya	.2	.3	.7	1.4	.7	7.4	14.7	~	~	~	~	~	~	~
Nigeria	.2	.4	.8	5.1	15.1	47.7	14.7	17.1	38.8	51.0	47.3	134.4	210.1	127.8
Oman			.1	.4	10.2	12.6	11.2	~	~	~	~	~	~	~
Saudi Arabia								~	~	28.5	14.0	~	17.0	~
United Arab Emirates		.1	1.1	.6	3.0	1.9	2.1							
T. VENEZUELA	.5	14.9	1.1	2.6	3.0	1.8	2.1	15.1	23.6	25.4	74.5	72.8	120.5	91.1
Non-Oil Developing Countries	~	203.9	249.0	352.4	476.6	468.5	454.0	~	214.3	254.2	495.8	599.8	673.1	381.2
Africa	~	9.7	9.1	5.2	14.0	22.4	15.9	~	9.8	14.9	17.5	14.0	12.5	8.5
Angola	~	~	~	~	.7	1.1	.6	~	~	~	~	~	~	~
Benin	~	~	~	~	.1			~	~	~	~	~	~	~
Cameroon	~	.1	~	~	.1	~	.6	~	~	~	~	~	~	~
Cape Verde	~	~	.4	~	~	.2		~	~	~	.1	~	~	~
Congo	~	~	~	~	.1	.1	.3	~	~	~	~	.4	~	~
Gabon	~	~	~	~	.1			~	~	~	~	.1	~	~
Ghana	~	1.9	2.6	1.3	1.1	6.3	1.0	~	.3	.7	.5	.8	.1	~
Ivory Coast	~	.4	.5	.3	.5	.3		~	~	.7	2.7	~	~	~
Liberia														
Madagascar														
Mauritius								.3			.5	.1	~	~
Morocco	~	1.8	1.9	~	.1	.2	2.0	~	.3	1.8		.5	.4	.5
Niger	~	.2	~	~	.7	.2		~	~	~	~	~	~	~
Senegal	~	.2	~	~	~	~	~	~	.5	.5	~	~	.4	.6
South Africa	~	2.4	1.7	3.4	11.3	10.9	7.8	~	6.0	10.5	8.1	8.4	4.8	2.9
Togo	~	~	~	~	~	2.9		~	.5	1.2	1.6	2.0	1.9	.5
Tunisia	~	1.2	1.9	~	~	~	4.2	~	1.9	~	4.0	1.8	1.1	3.9
Zaire	~	1.8	1.9	~	~	~		~	~	~	~	~	~	~
Zimbabwe													.2	.3
British Africa not specified	~	~	~	~	~	~	~	~	.2	.2	~	~	~	~
Spanish Africa	~	~	~	~	~	~	~	~	.1	~	~	~	~	~

Table 2634 (Continued)

URUGUAY ABSOLUTE VALUE OF GOODS TRADED WITH SELECTED REGIONS AND COUNTRIES,[1] 1975-82 (M US)[2]

Category	Exports FOB							Imports CIF						
	1975	1976	1977	1979	1980	1981	1982	1975	1976	1977	1979	1980	1981	1982
III. Developing Countries (Continued)														
Non-Oil Developing Countries														
Asia														
Bangladesh	~	6.6	2.9	2.7	9.6	20.5	16.9	~	7.8	9.3	17.4	32.8	30.0	16.3
China, People's Rep.	~	.2	~	~	.6	.4	9.0	~	2.3	1.5	1.2	1.1	1.1	1.6
Hong Kong	~	5.5	1.9	2.2	6.6	8.4	5.8	~	.3	.4	1.2	3.2	4.0	2.3
India	~	~	.1	.1	.2	.8	.4	~	.8	1.4	3.5	5.8	6.3	4.0
Korea	~	.3	.3	.2	.2	2.3	1.0	~	.7	.5	1.6	6.4	3.5	1.7
Malaysia	~	~	~	~	.1	.5	.2	~	.6	.6	1.9	5.7	7.2	2.0
Pakistan	~	.5	.6	.2	.2	.1	.3	~	2.2	3.8	6.0	6.5	4.8	1.5
Philippines	~	~	~	~	.2	.1	.3	~	.3	.2	.1	.1	.1	.1
Singapore	~	~	~	~	~	.1	~	~	.3	.4	.1	~	.1	.2
Sri Lanka	~	~	~	~	~	~	~	~	.3	.4	1.5	3.2	2.0	2.1
Thailand	~	~	~	~	~	~	~	~	~	.6	.5	.6	.8	.7
French countries not specified	~	~	~	~	1.5	8.0	~	~	~	~	~	.2	.1	~
Europe														
Cyprus	~	33.7	43.0	15.6	30.3	33.8	30.8	~	2.8	14.5	3.1	3.0	5.4	4.0
Greece	~	15.5	.1	.3	.5	.4	.5	~	~	.1	.6	.2	.7	~
Hungary	~	.5	6.4	8.1	17.0	7.6	6.3	~	~	.5	.6	.2	.7	~
Malta	.1	~	2.7	2.0	3.0	5.0	6.7	.3	.9	12.1	1.0	1.2	1.1	1.1
Portugal	5.0	12.5	24.1	3.4	4.2	7.5	7.3	.3	1.0	.3	.3	.3	1.1	.4
Romania	.1	.3	1.0	~	.3	1.4	.4	.2	.5	1.6	1.2	1.2	1.7	1.1
Turkey	~	4.7	7.2	.4	5.2	2.4	1.5	~	~	~	~	~	.1	.1
Yugoslavia	1.2	.2	1.6	1.3	5.2	9.5	8.1	.2	.2	.2	~	.1	.2	.1
Europe not specified	~	~	~	~	~	~	~	~	~	~	~	.1	.6	.1
Middle East														
Egypt	~	28.2	34.7	15.4	30.8	78.5	74.3	~	.6	.8	2.0	2.4	2.9	1.2
Israel	7.9	19.8	23.0	6.7	27.2	55.7	46.6	~	~	~	~	~	~	1.7
Jordan	~	7.9	11.7	8.5	3.5	16.0	12.7	~	.6	.8	2.0	2.4	2.9	~
Lebanon	~	.1	.1	.1	~	.5	11.3	~	~	~	~	~	~	1.7
Syrian Arab Rep.	~	.3	.1	~	~	3.1	3.6	~	~	~	~	~	~	~
IV. Latin America[3]														
A. ARGENTINA	111.9	125.7	159.4	313.6	392.0	313.3	316.1	146.9	193.4	214.7	455.8	547.6	622.3	350.7
Bahamas	29.6	26.8	36.4	97.1	142.3	101.8	109.1	47.3	65.9	84.5	198.0	174.1	128.8	80.1
Barbados	~	.3	.2	.1	.2	.6	.2	~	~	~	.1	.1	~	~
B. BOLIVIA	2.8	1.4	.8	1.8	1.7	2.0	1.0	.2	.5	.1	~	~	.2	~
C. BRAZIL	65.5	73.1	96.4	182.4	191.0	152.7	145.8	71.9	89.4	92.6	192.1	284.0	322.0	124.9
D. CHILE	2.2	5.9	3.0	12.7	23.3	24.8	21.8	7.9	9.9	10.9	15.8	19.6	13.6	8.6
E. COLOMBIA	3.0	5.2	4.8	2.9	3.6	2.9	3.0	.5	.8	.4	.6	1.5	3.0	.5
F. COSTA RICA	~	~	~	~	~	~	~	~	~	~	.6	1.5	.2	.4
H. DOMINICAN REP.	~	.3	.5	.1	.8	.7	1.2	.7	~	~	~	~	~	~
I. ECUADOR	.4	.3	.5	~	.1	.2	~	.2	.6	.4	.4	.4	.4	.4
K. GUATEMALA	~	.5	.1	1.0	~	.7	~	~	.5	.2	4.0	6.3	105.0	34.3
L. HAITI	.1	.1	~	.1	.7	.1	~	~	~	~	~	~	~	~
M. HONDURAS	~	.3	.4	.1	~	.1	~	~	~	~	~	~	~	~
Jamaica	~	~	~	.1	~	.7	~	~	.7	.6	.4	.2	.7	.1
Leeward Islands	~	~	~	~	~	~	~	~	~	~	.4	1.8	~	.9
N. MEXICO	2.3	1.5	2.0	2.2	5.1	6.2	3.9	~	3.4	3.0	10.5	11.6	11.0	83.3
Netherlands Antilles	1.4	.1	~	~	~	.1	~	~	3.6	2.3	7.2	6.1	4.5	6.0
O. NICARAGUA	~	~	~	.4	.3	.2	.1	~	~	~	~	~	~	~
P. PANAMA	.1	2.2	1.5	~	~	~	~	~	3.5	1.2	1.9	7.1	8.7	2.3
Panama Canal Zone	~	~	~	~	~	~	~	~	.2	.1	~	~	~	~
Q. PARAGUAY	3.7	4.7	9.4	12.0	14.6	12.9	9.9	3.8	11.0	14.8	14.0	19.5	19.4	5.6
R. PERU	2.2	1.9	2.8	.7	8.0	7.5	16.6	2.0	2.1	2.1	7.3	10.8	2.6	.9
Trinidad and Tobago	~	1.4	.4	~	~	~	~	~	1.2	1.3	2.7	2.7	2.4	2.6
Windward Islands	~	~	.1	~	~	~	~	~	~	~	~	~	~	~
America not specified	~	~	~	~	~	~	~	~	~	~	~	~	~	.1

Table 2634 (Continued)

URUGUAY ABSOLUTE VALUE OF GOODS TRADED WITH SELECTED REGIONS AND COUNTRIES,[1] 1975–82
(M US)[2]

Category	Exports FOB							Imports CIF						
	1975	1976	1977	1979	1980	1981	1982	1975	1976	1977	1979	1980	1981	1982
V. USSR, Eastern Europe, etc.	28.7	17.1	34.6	28.4	77.0	86.6	94.4	8.2	8.7	7.4	15.2	27.2	13.5	5.5
Bulgaria	~	~	~	~	~	.1	.1	~	.4	.3	1.5	2.7	1.1	1.2
Czechoslovakia	7.1	3.9	8.5	6.6	14.3	9.6	6.4	1.2	1.7	1.8	2.4	10.6	4.4	1.2
Eastern Germany	4.3	5.8	10.5	3.9	8.0	6.2	7.4	.4	.4	.5	.2	1.5	.6	.6
Poland	3.6	2.0	1.1	4.2	6.5	3.9	1.8	4.5	3.5	3.1	8.2	9.2	4.2	.8
USSR	13.6	5.4	14.5	13.7	48.3	66.9	78.6	1.6	2.7	1.6	2.9	3.3	3.2	1.7
USSR, etc., not specified	~	~	~	~	~	~	~	~	~	~	~	~	~	~
Country or area not specified	~	~	~	~	.3	~	.7	~	~	~	~	.1	~	.2
Special categories	~	~	~	~	~	~	3.2	~	~	~	~	~	~	.2
EEC	~	204.5	194.9	269.9	318.0	343.5	242.2	~	107.5	137.4	218.1	295.6	255.4	148.0
VI. Percent Distribution														
Industrial Countries	~	53.9	50.3	49.9	40.2	41.3	36.4	~	34.7	38.5	34.9	35.9	35.8	33.8
Oil Exporting Countries	~	4.9	2.6	1.7	6.7	11.1	8.9	~	27.3	25.5	22.0	25.4	21.4	29.1
Non-Oil Developing Countries	~	37.4	41.0	44.7	45.0	39.6	44.0	~	36.4	34.8	41.5	36.4	41.4	36.0
Africa	~	1.8	1.5	.7	1.3	1.9	1.5	~	1.7	2.0	1.5	.9	.8	.8
Asia	~	1.2	.5	.3	.9	1.7	1.6	~	1.3	1.3	1.5	2.0	1.8	1.5
Europe	~	6.2	7.1	2.0	2.9	2.9	3.0	~	.5	2.0	.3	.2	.3	.4
Middle East	~	5.2	5.7	2.0	2.9	6.6	7.2	~	.1	.1	.2	.1	.2	.2
Western Hemisphere	~	23.1	26.2	39.8	37.0	26.5	30.6	~	32.9	29.4	38.2	33.2	38.3	33.2
USSR, Eastern Europe, etc.	~	3.1	5.7	3.6	7.3	7.3	9.1	~	1.5	1.0	1.3	1.7	.8	.5
VII. Annual Percent Change														
World	~	42.0	11.5	15.7	34.2	11.7	-12.7	~	5.2	24.0	66.9	38.1	-1.4	-35.0
Industrial Countries	~	62.2	4.1	4.4	8.1	14.6	-23.0	~	-10.4	37.6	58.0	42.4	-1.8	-38.6
Oil Exporting Countries	~	218.2	-40.6	-26.7	432.9	85.0	-30.2	~	6.0	15.7	41.2	59.2	-16.9	-11.4
Non-Oil Developing Countries	~	24.6	22.1	46.1	35.2	-1.7	-3.1	~	25.0	18.6	123.3	21.0	12.2	-43.4
Africa	~	90.2	-6.9	-30.4	170.3	60.5	-29.1	~	-18.3	53.1	220.7	-19.8	-11.2	-31.9
Asia	~	34.8	-56.2	-49.4	262.1	113.4	-17.5	~	-10.5	19.2	388.3	87.9	-8.6	-45.6
Europe	~	56.6	27.7	.9	94.0	11.6	-8.8	~	163.4	419.9	7.5	-1.0	76.2	-25.5
Middle East	~	39.0	23.1	-27.6	99.6	155.0	-5.3	~	210.1	44.1	200.9	19.2	23.4	-43.2
Western Hemisphere	~	12.4	26.7	63.5	25.0	-20.1	.9	~	29.3	11.0	117.6	20.1	13.6	-43.6
USSR, Eastern Europe, etc.	~	-40.6	102.0	-33.7	171.7	12.4	9.0	~	10.7	-15.5	125.1	79.1	-50.3	-59.6

1. DOT data may differ between countries and from IFS data because of the time it takes for an export to become an import, etc.
2. Data may be calculated from partner's reported data or estimated on basis of less than 12 months.
3. No trade with Cuba; Venezuela is included in category III.

SOURCE: Adapted from the IMF-DOT Annual, 1970-74; IMF-DOT-Y, 1982; IMF-DOT-Y, 1983.

Table 2635

VENEZUELA ABSOLUTE VALUE OF GOODS TRADED WITH SELECTED REGIONS AND COUNTRIES,[1] 1975-82
(M US)[2]

Category	Exports FOB 1975	1976	1977	1979	1980	1981	1982	Imports CIF 1975	1976	1977	1979	1980	1981	1982
I. World	8,800	9,300	9,548	14,310	19,261	20,002	17,047	5,327	6,460	9,003	9,613	11,183	12,098	11,695
II. Industrial Countries	5,590	5,852	6,079	9,017	11,220	11,642	9,404	4,797	5,631	7,695	8,198	9,650	10,416	10,094
United States	3,477	3,574	4,095	5,338	5,344	5,114	4,506*	2,559	2,897	3,570	4,431	5,350	5,844	5,206*
Canada	1,094	1,232	1,182	1,446	1,772	1,910	1,471*	176	181	265	399	533	564	552*
Australia	~	~	8	~	~	~	1*	~	~	22	~	14	14	29*
Japan	27	34	44	144	682	781	655*	428	560	994	793	896	969	1,174*
New Zealand	~	~	~	1	4	~	~	~	26	7	7	14	19	27[b]
Austria	~	~	~	~	~	~	~	9	26	15	6	8	11	37*
Belgium	22	34	30	114	208	215	164*	166	138	172	128	145	161	105*
Denmark	1	51	1	62	23	7	40*	20	25	38	52	48	49	45*
Finland	1	~	~	2	~	~	4*	11	7	20	26	37	39	14*
France	70	74	79	153	343	461	306*	159	158	193	246	334	364	459*
Germany	122	122	75	133	203	190	447*	429	625	1,076	672	758	766	566*
Iceland	~	~	~	~	~	4	~	~	~	~	10	10	20	22[b]
Ireland	~	~	~	~	~	~	~	304	363	538	395	471	487	854*
Italy	126	194	163	350	1,123	1,401	866*	110	90	142	194	196	208	179*
Netherlands	145	141	101	350	301	523	137*	6	11	26	30	20	23	18*
Norway	~	21	11	35	13	~	1*	125	149	242	332	340	358	348*
Spain	101	85	94	336	699	632	337*	35	91	55	75	62	78	78*
Sweden	66	88	82	193	281	215	243*	72	105	100	97	96	101	119*
Switzerland	2	10	2	2	~	~	4*	188	206	248	282	320	341	260*
United Kingdom	338	192	121	350	225	190	223*							
III. Developing Countries														
Oil Exporting Countries	~	~	~	8	26	21	4	2	3	3	3	40	9	1
Algeria	~	~	1	1	~	~	~	2	3	3	2	10	8	~
Indonesia	~	~	~	~	7	21	1[a]	2	~	~	~	~	1	1[b]
Iran, I.R. of	~	~	1	7	7	~	~	~	~	~	~	~	~	~
Iraq	~	~	~	5	3	~	~	~	~	~	~	~	~	~
Nigeria	~	~	~	3	16	~	3[a]	~	~	~	~	29	~	~
Saudi Arabia	~	~	~	~	~	~	~	~	~	~	~	~	~	~
Non-Oil Developing Countries	~	3,276	3,289	4,933	7,737	7,974	7,319	~	696	1,141	1,320	1,411	1,585	1,460
Africa	~	~	~	136	171	175	147	~	~	~	49	80	111	46
Congo	~	~	~	~	17	171	145[b]	~	~	~	~	~	~	~
Ivory Coast	~	~	~	21	149	~	~	~	~	~	1	13	~	~
Liberia	~	~	~	94	~	~	~	~	~	~	~	~	~	~
Malawi	~	~	~	~	~	~	~	~	~	~	1	~	1	~
Mauritius	~	~	~	3	2	2	1[a]	~	~	~	1	~	~	4[a]
Morocco	~	~	~	1	2	2	~	~	~	~	46	1	~	~
Mozambique	~	~	~	14	~	~	~	~	~	~	~	~	~	~
Namibia	~	~	~	~	~	~	~	~	~	~	~	~	~	~
Senegal	~	~	~	1	2	1	~	~	7	~	4	1	111	42[a]
South Africa	~	~	~	~	~	~	~	~	~	~	6	4	8	4*
Tunisia	~	~	~	~	21	1	1[b]	~	~	~	~	~	~	~
Africa not specified	~	12	17	15	134	240	186	~	86	146	128	155	175	181
Asia	~	~	1	1	19	14	1*	~	23	31	30	45	55	15*
China, People's Rep.	~	1	1	1	54	134	114[b]	~	~	~	48	62	60	80*
Hong Kong	~	~	~	11	24	89	42[a]	~	~	~	9	3	5	4[b]
India	~	~	~	~	~	~	3[a]	~	~	~	28	32	37	60[a]
Korea	~	~	~	~	~	~	~	~	~	~	3	8	5	1[a]
Malaysia	~	~	~	~	~	~	~	~	~	~	4	1	4	4*
Papua New Guinea	~	~	~	~	~	~	~	~	~	~	6	4	8	16*
Philippines	~	~	~	~	~	~	~	~	~	~	~	~	~	~
Singapore	~	~	~	~	~	3	25*	~	~	~	~	~	~	~
Thailand	~	11	17	3	16	3	~	~	55	115	~	~	~	~
Asia not specified	~	~	~	~	~	~	~	~	~	~	~	~	~	~
Oceania not specified	~	~	~	~	~	~	~	~	~	~	~	~	~	~

Table 2635 (Continued)

VENEZUELA ABSOLUTE VALUE OF GOODS TRADED WITH SELECTED REGIONS AND COUNTRIES,[1] 1975-82 (M US)[2]

Category	___ Exports FOB ___							___ Imports CIF ___						
	1975	1976	1977	1979	1980	1981	1982	1975	1976	1977	1979	1980	1981	1982
III. Developing Countries (Continued)														
Non-Oil Developing Countries														
Europe														
Gibraltar	~	30	13	50	232	232	128	~	39	90	21	23	43	26
Greece	~	~	~	2	8	~	~	~	~	~	~	~	~	2*
Hungary	~	~	~	7	76	34	~	~	~	~	1	1	2	~
Malta	~	~	~	~	3	~	~	~	~	~	1	1	2	1b
Portugal	6	4	~	3	142	150	96a	8	45	17	17	17	18	12a
Romania	~	~	~	36	3	17	7a	~	~	~	1	1	1	11b
Turkey	~	~	~	1	~	3	2a	~	~	~	2	4	11	1a
Yugoslavia	~	26	13	2	~	28	24b	31	44	~	~	~	~	1a
Europe not specified	~	~	~	~	~	~	10	~	~	~	~	~	~	~
Middle East														
Egypt	~	~	~	~	~	~	9*	~	~	~	5	7	6	21
Israel	~	~	~	~	~	~	1*	~	~	~	5	7	6	21*
IV. Latin America[3]														
A. ARGENTINA	866	3,234	3,258	4,732	7,201	7,327	6,849	358	572	905	1,118	1,146	1,249	1,186
Antigua and Barbuda	48	48	52	73	56	37	18a	37	76	176	164	85	97	95a
Bahamas	~	67	52	71	44	1	1b	~	~	~	1	2	1	1b
Barbados	~	13	16	23	29	31	11a	~	~	~	~	~	~	~
Bermuda	~	~	2	~	~	~	~	~	~	~	~	1	~	~
B. BOLIVIA	~	~	~	~	~	~	3b	~	4	3	3	3	3	3b
C. BRAZIL	95	103	139	229	678	933	953*	113	141	253	209	186	254	470*
D. CHILE	30	76	114	126	242	336	237*	22	49	50	67	81	71	43*
E. COLOMBIA	22	48	129	147	273	330	280b	83	102	138	171	183	195	185b
F. COSTA RICA	49	46	31	37	82	88	80a	1	4	22	22	1	2	4a
Dominica	~	~	~	~	~	~	~	~	~	~	3	~	~	~
H. DOMINICAN REP.	109	121	130	162	237	267	221*	3	3	14	52	136	67	28*
I. ECUADOR	8	4	8	9	17	20	6a	1	3	6	34	38	43	22a
J. EL SALVADOR	63	64	71	98	106	85	73b	~	1	1	1	~	~	1b
K. GUATEMALA	53	59	68	91	132	103	88b	~	1	1	1	1	1	1b
Guiana, French	~	~	~	48	~	~	~	~	~	~	~	~	~	~
Guyana	~	~	~	~	~	3	3b	~	~	~	~	~	1	1b
L. HAITI	56	12	30	51	86	37	31b	1	6	9	30	34	59	56b
M. HONDURAS	141	122	111	166	158	171	145b	~	~	~	7	3	6	1b
Jamaica	65	25	10	35	24	26	3a	1	6	9	7	3	6	5b
N. MEXICO	1,808	2,108	1,890	3,107	4,590	4,308	4,308b	55	62	94	112	84	91	49a
Netherlands Antilles	53	57	79	74	85	83	71b	22	38	26	70	94	86	86b
O. NICARAGUA	112	90	93	87	168	194	110a	1	6	7	99	121	160	12*
P. PANAMA	~	40	41	18	~	~	~	24	29	54	~	~	~	~
Panama Canal Zone	~	~	~	~	~	~	~	~	~	~	~	~	~	~
Q. PARAGUAY	4	~	~	~	~	~	9*	4	~	~	~	~	~	9*
R. PERU	87	88	154	15	26	28	23b	12	17	31	62	57	60	57b
St. Lucia	~	~	~	1	1	2	2b	~	~	~	1	1	~	~
St. Vincent	~	~	~	1	1	~	~	~	~	~	~	~	~	~
Suriname	~	~	~	1	1	1	1b	~	~	~	~	~	~	7b
Trinidad and Tobago	~	23	18	7	7	10	9a	~	4	5	4	11	8	12a
S. URUGUAY	16	21	21	52	80	125	83*	~	10	1	2	3	5	2*
French West Indies not specified	~	~	~	~	78	110	93b	~	~	~	~	~	~	~
V. USSR, Eastern Europe, etc.														
Bulgaria	1	3	4	65	129	96	82	7	7	10	23	32	28	27
G. Cuba	~	~	~	~	~	~	63b	~	1	~	1	1	4	3b
Czechoslovakia	1	3	4	52	99	74	1b	~	3	7	4	7	4	17b
Eastern Germany	~	~	~	4	3	1	18b	7	7	10	11	17	18	~
North Korea	~	~	~	~	~	~	~	~	~	~	~	~	~	~
Poland	~	~	~	9	19	21	~	~	~	~	7	7	6	6b
USSR	~	~	~	~	8	~	~	~	~	~	7	1	1	1b
Country or area not specified	~	169	177	285	137	261	222b	~	122	154	27	~	~	~
EEC	~	808	570	1,520	2,502	3,020	2,183	~	1,605	2,407	1,981	2,282	2,396	2,493

Table 2635 (Continued)

VENEZUELA ABSOLUTE VALUE OF GOODS TRADED WITH SELECTED REGIONS AND COUNTRIES,[1] 1975-82
(M US)[2]

Exports FOB

Category	1975	1976	1977	1979	1980	1981	1982
VI. Percent Distribution							
Industrial Countries	~	62.9	63.7	63.0	58.3	58.2	55.2
Oil Exporting Countries	~	.2	.1	.1	.1	.1	~
Non-Oil Developing Countries	~	35.2	34.4	34.5	40.2	39.9	42.9
Africa	~	.1	~	.9	.9	.9	.9
Asia	~	.1	.2	.1	.7	1.2	1.1
Europe	~	.3	.1	.3	1.2	1.2	.8
Middle East	~	~	~	~	~	~	.1
Western Hemisphere	~	34.8	34.1	33.1	37.4	36.6	40.2
USSR, Eastern Europe, etc.	~	~	~	.5	.7	.5	.5
VII. Annual Percent Change							
World	~	5.7	2.7	55.5	34.6	3.8	-14.8
Industrial Countries	~	4.7	3.9	61.8	24.4	3.8	-19.2
Oil Exporting Countries	~	~	~	100.0	220.0	-16.4	-81.8
Non-Oil Developing Countries	~	9.9	.4	42.1	56.9	3.1	-8.2
Africa	~	~	~	49.6	25.6	2.6	-16.2
Asia	~	552.6	37.1	539.1	808.8	79.3	-22.5
Europe	~	115.9	-55.7	55.1	366.5	-.1	-44.7
Middle East	~	~	~	~	~	~	~
Western Hemisphere	~	9.0	.8	41.4	52.2	1.8	-6.5
USSR, Eastern Europe, etc.	~	100.0	25.0	268.6	100.0	-25.6	-15.1

Imports CIF

Category	1975	1976	1977	1979	1980	1981	1982
VI. Percent Distribution							
Industrial Countries	~	87.2	85.5	85.3	86.3	86.1	86.3
Oil Exporting Countries	~	~	~	~	.4	.1	~
Non-Oil Developing Countries	~	10.8	12.7	13.7	12.6	13.1	12.5
Africa	~	~	.5	.5	.7	.9	.4
Asia	~	1.3	1.6	1.3	1.4	1.4	1.5
Europe	~	.6	1.0	.2	.2	.4	.2
Middle East	~	~	~	~	.1	~	.2
Western Hemisphere	~	8.9	10.1	11.6	10.2	10.3	10.1
USSR, Eastern Europe, etc.	~	.1	.1	.2	.3	.2	.2
VII. Annual Percent Change							
World	~	21.3	39.4	-9.3	16.3	8.2	-3.3
Industrial Countries	~	17.4	36.6	-10.3	17.7	7.9	-3.1
Oil Exporting Countries	~	83.3	-6.1	-56.7	~	-78.0	-88.5
Non-Oil Developing Countries	~	47.6	63.9	-2.3	6.9	12.3	-7.9
Africa	~	~	~	-33.5	63.9	39.8	-58.7
Asia	~	45.7	70.7	22.2	21.2	12.9	3.2
Europe	~	48.4	131.7	-78.4	12.2	83.7	-39.0
Middle East	~	~	~	4.1	47.1	-14.7	265.6
Western Hemisphere	~	47.8	58.3	4.3	2.5	9.1	-5.1
USSR, Eastern Europe, etc.	~	~	46.8	-16.3	40.9	-11.8	-4.8

1. DOT data may differ between countries and from IFS data because of the time it takes for an export to become an import, etc.
2. Data may be calculated from partner's reported data or estimated on basis of less than 12 months.
3. No trade with Cuba.
a. Five or fewer months of reported data; seven or more months derived or extrapolated.
b. Data extrapolated for the entire year.

SOURCE: Adapted from the IMF-DOT Annual, 1970-74; IMF-DOT-Y, 1982; IMF-DOT-Y, 1983.

Table 2636

UNITED STATES VALUE OF GOODS TRADED WITH EACH LATIN AMERICAN COUNTRY, 19 LC, 1975-82

(M US)

	Country	Exports							Imports, FOB						
		1975	1976	1977	1979	1980	1981	1982	1975	1976	1977	1979	1980	1981	1982
A.	ARGENTINA	629	544	731	1,890	2,630	2,192	1,294	235	337	431	639	792	1,214	1,222
B.	BOLIVIA	138	133	214	146	172	189	99	93	118	163	230	189	184	113
C.	BRAZIL	3,058	2,810	2,492	3,444	4,352	3,798	3,423	1,623	1,888	2,385	3,384	4,000	4,852	4,643
D.	CHILE	533	508	520	885	1,354	1,465	925	157	247	303	482	559	661	729
E.	COLOMBIA	643	703	782	1,409	1,736	1,771	1,903	636	705	861	1,289	1,327	900	883
F.	COSTA RICA	212	255	323	413	498	373	330	232	277	328	437	405	426	421
H.	DOMINICAN REP.	453	432	424	610	795	779	664	658	549	670	705	828	977	669
I.	ECUADOR	410	416	564	696	864	854	828	515	600	674	909	953	1,103	1,227
J.	EL SALVADOR	194	232	314	352	273	308	292	191	298	462	459	444	270	333
K.	GUATEMALA	255	334	377	467	553	559	390	189	317	431	437	465	384	365
L.	HAITI	144	150	203	243	311	301	299	112	156	176	234	264	287	326
M	HONDURAS	151	162	242	324	379	349	275	163	247	293	469	475	493	426
N.	MEXICO	5,141	4,990	4,821	9,858	15,146	17,789	11,817	3,112	3,655	4,770	8,997	12,835	14,013	15,770
O.	NICARAGUA	156	169	223	100	250	184	119	145	196	199	251	227	152	98
P.	PANAMA	317	358	346	527	699	884	845	212	155	179	223	353	329	289
Q.	PARAGUAY	33	38	51	128	109	108	78	21	22	26	172	85	52	41
R.	PERU	896	573	499	720	1,172	1,486	1,117	431	406	545	1,258	1,443	1,277	1,150
S.	URUGUAY	51	58	74	127	183	163	190	26	68	94	98	103	165	265
T.	VENEZUELA	2,243	2,632	3,171	3,937	4,577	5,445	5,206	3,982	3,782	4,320	5,502	5,571	5,800	4,957
	WORLD	108,112	115,413	121,306	182,007	220,781	233,738	212,274	105,880	132,498	160,432	222,335	256,959	273,351	254,881

SOURCE: IMF-DOT Annual, 1970-74; IMF-DOT Annual 1972-78; IMF-DOT Annual, 1973-79; IMF-DOT Annual, 1974-80; IMF-DOT Annual, 1975-81; IMF-DOT Annual, 1983.

Part IX: Financial Flows

CHAPTER 27

BALANCE OF PAYMENTS

AND

INTERNATIONAL LIQUIDITY

Note: This volume contains statistics from numerous sources. Alternative data on many topics are presented. Variations in statistics can be attributed to differences in definition, parameters, coverage, methodology, as well as date gathered, prepared, or adjusted. See also Editor's Note on Methodology.

Table 2700

GUIDE TO BALANCE OF PAYMENTS ANALYSIS

(IMF Focuses on Reserves; ECLA Focuses on the Balance of Current and Capital Accounts)

A. Current Account[1,7]
Merchandise: exports f.o.b.
Merchandise: imports f.o.b.
    Trade Balance
Other goods, services, and income:
    credit
Other goods, services, and income:
    debit

      Total goods, services and income
Private unrequited transfers[2,a]
    Total, excl. official unrequited transfers
Official unrequited transfers[2,b]

B. Direct Investment and Other Long-Term[3] Capital
Direct investment

Portfolio investment
Other long-term capital
    Resident official sector

    Deposit money banks

    Other sectors

      Total, Groups A plus B

C. Other Short-Term Capital[3]

Resident official sector

Deposit money banks

Other sectors

D. Net Errors and Omissions

    Total, Groups A through D

E. Counterpart Items
Monetization/demonetization of gold
Allocation/cancellation of SDRs
Valuation changes in reserves

    Total, Groups A through E

F. Exceptional Financing

    Total, Groups A through F

G. Liabilities Constituting Foreign[5] Authorities' Reserves

    Total, Groups A through G

H. Total Change in Reserves[4,6]
Monetary gold
SDRs
Reserve position in the Fund
Foreign exchange assets
Other claims
Use of Fund credit

---

1. ECLA inclusions are as follows (cf. table 2725):
   A. Goods, Services and Income
      Merchandise
      Shipment
      Other Transportation
         Passenger Services
         Port Services, etc.
      Travel
      Investment Income
         Direct Investment Income
            Reinvested Earnings
            Distributed Earnings
         Other
            Resident Official, Including Interofficial
            Foreign Official, Excluding Interofficial
            Private
      Other Goods, Services, and Income
         Official
            Interofficial
            Other, Resident Official
            Other, Foreign Official
         Private
            Labor Income, nie
            Property Income, nie
            Other
   B. Private Unrequited Transfers
      Migrants' Transfers
      Workers' Remittances
      Other
2. Required = payment for goods or services.
3. ECLA inclusions are as follows:
   A. Official Unrequited Transfers
      Interofficial
      Other, Resident Official
      Other, Foreign Official
   B. Capital Other Than Reserves
      Long-Term Capital
      Direct Investment
      Other Private Loans
      General Government Securities and Assets
      Short-Term Capital
      Deposit Money Banks
      Other Private
      Reserve Banks
   C. Net Errors and Omissions

D. Exceptional Financing
E. Counterpart Items
   Monetization/Demonetization of Gold
   Allocation of SDRs
4. Reserves (and related items) bring categories I and II into zero balance and include:
   A. Use of IMF Credit
   B. Other Liabilities
   C. Monetary Gold
   D. SDRs
   E. Reserve Position in IMF
   F. Foreign Exchange and Other Claims

According to Høst (cited in Source, below, pp. 50-51), "reserves and related items, as now defined, have always been considered to be the hard core of financing below the line of the balance of payments surpluses and deficits, as representing the response of monetary authorities at home or abroad to surplus or deficit situations. It was invariably so considered when the concept of compensatory official financing was used in the early days of the Fund's activities. For many years, a similar concept was used in the United States in its publication of balance of payments statistics as one measure of surplus or deficit, the so-called official settlements balance. Such a balance ceased to be published in the United States in 1976. For several reasons, reserves and related items have become less adequate for the assessment of the balance of payments. First, a build-up of reserves by the monetary authorities of a number of countries in a reserve center or other financial centers may not, in an environment of general floating of exchange rates, reflect surpluses or deficits in the countries holding the reserves. It may be the response to interest differentials between financial markets or confidence factors, inducing countries to adjust the currency composition of their foreign exchange portfolios. Moreover, after the sharp rise in the price of oil which began in 1973, part of the foreign assets held by the monetary authorities of some of the major oil exporting countries must be regarded to be in the nature of investments rather than balances held for the financing of balance of payments deficits. For all these reasons, it has become increasingly difficult to assess the surplus or deficit in the balance of payments calling for adjustment. But these difficulties do not apply to the great majority of developing countries."

5. Liabilities Constituting Foreign Authorities' Reserves.
6. Cf. ECLA's concept of compensatory financing in table 2725ff., the last three items of which equal change in reserves.
7. Because the Basic Balance (current account + official unrequited transfers) is not separately available prior to 1967 for most countries, IFS-Y standard format for all years precludes presentation for Basic Balance for any years.
a. One definition considers this item to belong to capital account.
b. ECLA's definition considers this item to belong to capital account.

SOURCE: Data are from IMF-IFS-Y, 1979. Analysis is also adapted from Poul Høst-Madsen, *Macroeconomic Accounts: An Overview*, Pamphlet Series No. 29 (Washington, D.C.: IMF, 1979), pp. 39, 49-51. Cf. table 2725ff.

Figure 27:1

BALANCE OF PAYMENTS: CURRENT ACCOUNT DEFICIT, 19 L, 1981–83

(B US)

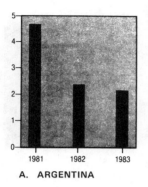

A. ARGENTINA

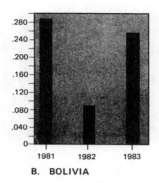

B. BOLIVIA

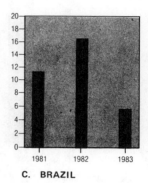

C. BRAZIL

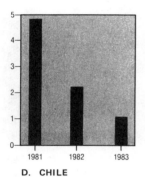

D. CHILE

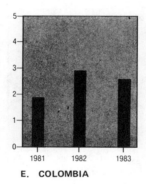

E. COLOMBIA

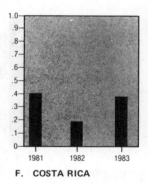

F. COSTA RICA

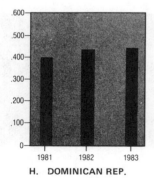

H. DOMINICAN REP.

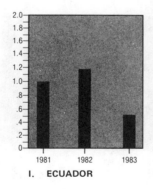

I. ECUADOR

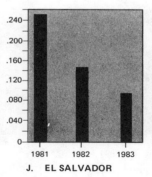

J. EL SALVADOR

Figure 27:1 (Continued)

BALANCE OF PAYMENTS: CURRENT ACCOUNT DEFICIT, 19 L, 1981–83

(B US)

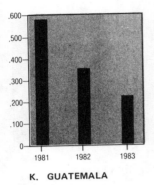

K. GUATEMALA

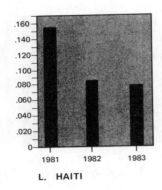

L. HAITI

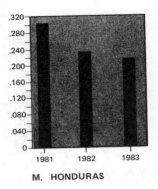

M. HONDURAS

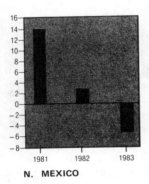

N. MEXICO

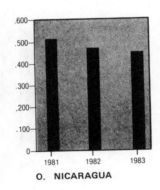

O. NICARAGUA

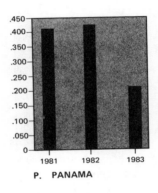

P. PANAMA

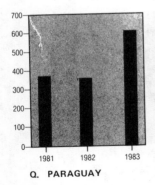

Q. PARAGUAY

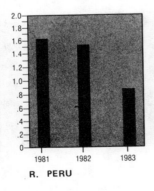

R. PERU

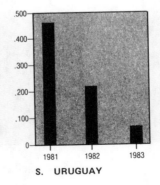

S. URUGUAY

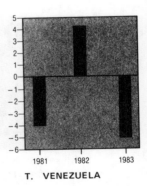

T. VENEZUELA

SOURCE: IDB-SPTF, 1984, Part Two.

Table 2701

ARGENTINA: IMF BALANCE OF PAYMENTS, 1976–83[a]
(M SDR)

Category	1976	1977	1978	1979	1980	1981	1982	1983
A. Current Account	566	969	1,494	−387	−3,675	−3,931	−2,155	−2,282
Merchandise: exports f.o.b.	3,397	4,843	5,118	6,049	6,162	7,776	6,881	7,328
Meat	443	509	587	932	743	772	712	552
Other	2,954	4,334	4,531	5,117	5,419	7,004	6,169	6,776
Merchandise: imports f.o.b.	2,396	−3,252	−2,781	−4,658	−7,221	−7,136	4,397	−3,857
Trade balance	1,001	1,591	2,337	1,390	−1,058	639	2,485	3,471
Other goods, services, and income: credit	670	931	1,146	1,629	2,444	2,252	1,928	1,805
Other goods, services, and income: debit	1,121	−1,579	−2,044	−3,450	−5,078	−6,803	−6,598	−7,573
Total: goods, services, and income	550	943	1,439	431	−3.693	−3.912	−2.186	−2.297
Private unrequited transfers	21	27	38	27	18	−18	31	15
Total, excl. official unrequited transfers	571	970	1,477	−404	−3.675	−3.931	−2.155	−2.282
Official unrequited transfers	−5	−1	16	17	#	#	#	#
B. Direct Investment and Other Long-Term Capital	−320	401	1,218	2,437	3,458	8,466	1,892	−579
Direct investment	#	124	219	204	607	790	231	170
Portfolio investment	−57	−1	81	173	118	957	267	612
Other long-term capital								
Resident official sector	−194	−173	−767	#	367	812	−210	−1.350
Loans received by general government	12	13	31	6	363	833	−14	−805
Loans received by Central Bank	−143	−107	−728	#	#	#	−151	−534
Other liabilities	−73	−70	#	−15	−3	−9	#	#
Assets	10	−9	−70	8	7	−12	−46	−11
Deposit money banks	36	52	81	153	−50	311	247	36
Other sectors	−104	398	1,603	1,907	2,416	5,597	1,358	−46
Loans received	−3	398	1,728	1,776	2,310	6,045	1,792	119
Other	−102	#	−125	131	106	−449	−434	−165
Total, Groups A plus B	246	1,370	2,711	2,049	−217	4,535	−263	−2,861
C. Other Short-Term Capital	−308	87	−973	989	−1,647	−7,016	−4,238	−1,335
Resident official sector	−254	−344	255	87	162	134	194	−219
Deposit money banks	−16	18	−22	−220	−279	30	311	298
Other sectors	−39	413	−1,206	1,122	−1,530	−7,180	4,355	−1,415
D. Net Errors and Omissions	−191	116	10	188	−238	−181	−364	−414
Total, Groups A through D	−254	1,573	1,748	3,226	−2,102	−2,661	−4,865	−4,610
E. Counterpart Items	−6	−102	−145	5	101	146	86	119
Monetization/demonetization of gold	#	#	#	#	#	#	#	#
Allocation/cancellation of SDRs	#	#	#	56	56	55	#	#
Valuation changes in reserves	−6	−102	−145	−50	45	92	86	119
Total, Groups A through E	−260	1,471	1,603	3,232	−2,001	−2,515	−4,779	−4,492
F. Exceptional Financing	1,052	#	#	#	#	#	4,273	2,438
Bonds issued to cancel external obligations	#	#	#	#	#	#	1,452	459
Loans received by Central Bank	1,052	#	#	#	#	#	167	1,676
Payments arrears	#	#	#	#	#	#	2,654	304
Total, Groups A through F	792	1,471	1,603	3,232	−2,001	−2,515	−506	−2,054
G. Liabilities Constituting Foreign Authorities' Reserves	#	#	3	50	83	69	−24	−141
Total, Groups A through G	792	1,471	1,606	3,282	−1,918	−2,446	−530	−2,194
H. Total Change in Reserves	−792	−1,471	−1,606	−3,282	1,918	2,446	530	2,194
Monetary gold	#	−7	−3	−2	−1	#	#	#
SDRs	−43	4	−88	−86	−9	−91	347	#
Reserve position in the Fund	#	#	−130	−24	−108	24	148	91
Foreign exchange assets	−954	−1,357	−1,040	−3,169	2,036	2,513	35	983
Other claims	#	#	#	#	#	#	#	#
Use of Fund credit	206	−111	−345	#	#	#	#	1,121
Conversion rates: pesos argentinos per SDR	.016	.048	.100	.170	.239	.519	2.862	11.257
Conversion rates: U.S. dollars per SDR	1.1545	1.1675	1.2520	1.2920	1.3015	1.1792	1.1040	1.0690

a. For 1951–81 data, see SALA, 23–2701.

SOURCE: IMF–BPS, Nov. 1984.

Table 2702

BOLIVIA: IMF BALANCE OF PAYMENTS, 1976–83[a]
(M SDR)

Category	1976	1977	1978	1979	1980	1981	1982	1983
A. Current Account	-46.3	-101.5	-263.4	-277.1	-91.3	-242.6	-84.5	-171.8
Merchandise: exports f.o.b.	487.6	542.6	500.4	589.5	723.6	774.5	749.7	708.0
Crude petroleum and gas	145.1	114.9	96.8	115.3	169.6	287.8	345.6	388.4
Metals	326.5	409.0	403.1	448.5	477.7	398.0	320.9	269.4
Other	16.0	18.7	.5	25.7	76.3	88.7	83.2	50.1
Merchandise: imports f.o.b.	-443.7	-495.9	-576.8	-630.9	-522.9	-578.2	-388.3	-450.7
Trade balance	43.9	46.7	-76.4	-41.4	200.7	196.4	361.4	257.2
Other goods, services, and income: credit	63.4	56.8	62.8	74.1	89.6	101.3	84.4	111.1
Other goods, services, and income: debit	-165.8	-217.9	-271.4	-350.0	-424.5	-572.8	-570.8	-639.1
Total: goods, services, and income	-58.5	-114.4	-285.0	-317.3	-134.3	-275.1	-125.0	-270.7
Private unrequited transfers	2.8	2.0	4.4	8.7	6.1	11.2	15.1	16.9
Total, excl. official unrequited transfers	-55.7	-112.4	-280.6	-308.6	-128.1	-263.9	-109.9	-253.8
Official unrequited transfers	9.4	10.9	17.2	31.5	36.8	21.3	25.4	82.0
B. Direct Investment and Other Long-Term Capital	186.4	278.3	218.8	199.6	40.2	286.5	164.7	408.0
Direct investment	-7.0	-1.0	9.2	13.9	31.9	50.9	33.4	40.1
Portfolio investment	#	#	#	#	-2.0	#	#	#
Other long-term capital								
Resident official sector	123.0	145.2	76.5	69.0	49.4	149.5	111.8	389.7
Loans received by general government	128.6	155.1	83.0	65.8	51.1	116.7	54.0	13.7
Loans received by Central Bank	-3.8	-1.5	.6	5.6	9.4	6.2	11.1	-5.9
Other	-1.8	-8.4	-7.0	-2.4	-11.1	26.5	46.6	381.9
Deposit money banks	#	#	#	60.1	-18.6	21.0	-10.6	-1.6
Other sectors	70.4	134.1	133.1	56.7	-20.5	65.1	30.1	-20.3
Total, Groups A plus B	140.1	176.7	-44.6	-77.4	-51.1	43.8	80.2	236.2
C. Other Short-Term Capital	-36.8	-56.6	39.3	29.3	14.2	-42.3	-151.7	.6
Resident official sector	-1.7	31.0	-33.3	63.7	7.5	-3.1	-38.5	83.4
Deposit money banks	-4.3	32.5	40.8	-8.5	-14.9	7.1	18.3	-15.2
Other sectors	-30.7	-120.1	31.9	-25.9	21.6	-46.3	-131.5	-67.7
D. Net Errors and Omissions	-54.9	-67.4	-67.7	-22.2	-200.9	-272.1	-46.4	55.2
Total, Groups A through D	48.4	52.7	-72.9	-70.3	-237.7	-270.6	-117.9	291.9
E. Counterpart Items	-2.9	-1.0	-7.6	3.3	10.9	14.8	7.8	30.4
Monetization/demonetization of gold	.3	6.5	1.2	1.0	1.5	2.5	1.7	.8
Allocation/cancellation of SDRs	#	#	#	4.7	4.7	4.6	#	#
Valuation changes in reserves	-3.1	-7.5	-8.7	-2.4	4.7	7.8	6.1	29.6
Total, Groups A through E	45.5	51.7	-80.5	-67.0	-226.8	-255.7	-110.1	322.3
F. Exceptional Financing	#	#	15.3	#	152.9	105.6	.8	.8
Grants from Subsidy Account	#	#	#	#	#	.9	.8	.8
IBRD structural adjustment loan	#	#	#	#	37.4	#	#	#
Loans from Argentine banks	#	#	#	#	96.0	100.6	#	#
Loans from U.S. commercial banks	#	#	#	#	#	4.0	#	#
Trust Fund loans	#	#	15.3	#	19.6	.2	#	#
Total, Groups A through F	45.5	51.7	-65.2	-67.0	-73.9	-150.1	-109.3	323.1
G. Liabilities Constituting Foreign Authorities' Reserves	-4.0	4.6	-10.1	85.0	-29.1	171.6	145.7	-310.6
Total, Groups A through G	41.5	56.3	-75.3	18.0	-103.0	21.5	36.4	12.5
H. Total Change in Reserves	-41.5	-56.3	75.3	-18.0	103.0	-21.5	-36.4	-12.5
Monetary gold	-3	-6.6	-1.4	-1.2	-1.8	-2.5	-1.7	-.8
SDRs	.2	1.2	-8.4	14.1	#	-.1	.1	-.1
Reserve position in the Fund	-6.4	-1.0	-1.6	9.0	#	#	#	#
Foreign exchange assets	1.2	-70.5	74.9	-28.9	52.2	-2.0	-56.1	-11.4
Other claims	-22.3	20.6	-3.1	-11.0	4.7	-14.9	4.4	-7.3
Use of Fund credit	-13.9	#	15.0	#	48.0	-1.9	16.9	7.2
Conversion rates: Bolivian pesos per SDR	23.09	23.35	25.04	26.35	31.90	28.90	70.79	245.63
Conversion rates: U.S. dollars per SDR	1.1545	1.1675	1.2520	1.2920	1.3015	1.1792	1.1040	1.0690

a. For 1951–81 data, see SALA, 23–2702.

SOURCE: IMF-BPS-Y, 1984.

Table 2703

BRAZIL: IMF BALANCE OF PAYMENTS, 1976–83[a]

(M SDR)

Category	1976	1977	1978	1979	1980	1981	1982	1983
A. Current Account	−5,674	−4,373	−5,616	−8,102	−9,829	−9,976	−14,793	−6,360
Merchandise: exports f.o.b.	8,635	10,214	9,944	11,792	15,474	19,795	18,287	20,508
Coffee	1,884	1,977	1,543	1,464	1,910	1,281	1,685	1,962
Iron ore	861	776	821	996	1,201	1,483	1,674	1,415
Other	5,890	7,461	7,581	9,333	12,363	17,031	14,927	17,131
Merchandise: imports f.o.b.	−10.699	−10.298	−10.867	−13,887	−17,634	−18,742	−17,572	−14,441
Trade balance	−2,064	−84	−923	−2,095	−2,160	1,054	715	6,068
Other goods, services, and income: credit	1,146	1,358	1,604	2,132	2,418	3,096	2,987	2,288
Other goods, services, and income: debit	−4,760	−5,647	−6,354	−8,151	−10,216	−14,293	−18,489	−14,816
Investment income	−2,499	−3,248	−3,893	−5,202	−6,466	−9,914	−13,585	−10,954
Other	−2,261	−2,400	−2,461	−2,950	−3,751	−4,378	−4,904	−3,862
Total: goods, services, and income	−5,678	−4,373	−5,673	−8,115	−9,958	−10,143	−14,787	−6,461
Private unrequited transfers	6	−3	55	9	97	158	−8	99
Total, excl. official unrequited transfers	−5,672	−4,376	−5,618	−8,105	−9,861	−9,985	−14,795	−6,362
Official unrequited transfers	−3	3	2	4	32	8	2	2
B. Direct Investment and Other Long-Term Capital	5,289	5,144	8,013	4,999	5,464	9,954	7,260	1,759
Direct investment	1,188	1,441	1,498	1,718	1,186	1,965	2,311	1,285
Portfolio investment	#	#	#	510	272	−1	−3	−270
Other long-term capital								
Resident official sector	1,308	2,041	3,142	2,592	−8	81	1,593	2,955
Loans received by general government	1,380	2,076	3,346	2,630	389	315	1,898	2,862
Loans received by Central Bank	−33	−32	−30	−24	−19	−5	−5	−6
Other	−40	−3	−174	−14	−377	−229	−300	98
Deposit money banks	787	383	1,475	384	1,615	3,433	1,498	−1,419
Other sectors	2,007	1,278	1,898	−205	2,398	4,476	1,861	−791
Loans received	2,211	1,513	2,232	370	2,072	5,016	2,186	−778
Other	−204	−235	−334	−575	327	−540	−324	−13
Total, Groups A plus B	−386	771	2,397	−3,103	−4,365	−23	−7,533	−4,601
C. Other Short-Term Capital	2,279	183	1,005	−9	1,790	884	−493	−1,076
Resident official sector	395	−276	393	298	−206	−59	−85	−78
Deposit money banks	939	204	713	−327	464	850	−147	−663
Other sectors	945	255	−101	20	1,532	94	−260	−335
D. Net Errors and Omissions	430	−529	239	950	−270	−331	−343	−573
Total, Groups A through D	2,324	424	3,641	−2,162	−2,845	531	−8,369	−6,250
E. Counterpart Items	−140	−81	−481	−21	282	515	1,288	747
Monetization/demonetization of gold	#	#	#	#	80	110	336	521
Allocation/cancellation of SDRs	#	#	#	69	69	68	#	#
Valuation changes in reserves	−140	−81	−481	−90	133	337	952	226
Total, Groups A through E	2,184	343	3,160	−2,183	−2,564	1,045	−7,081	−5,503
F. Exceptional Financing	#	#	#	#	#	#	#	~
Total, Groups A through F	2,184	343	3,160	−2,183	−2,564	1,045	−7,081	−5,503
G. Liabilities Constituting Foreign Authorities' Reserves	#	#	#	−88	185	42	3,609	4,502
Total, Groups A through G	2,184	343	3,160	−2,271	−2,378	1,087	−3,472	−1,001
H. Total Change in Reserves	−2,184	−343	−3,160	2,271	2,378	−1,087	3,472	1,001
Monetary gold	#	−7	−3	#	−80	−110	769	−147
SDRs	−8	−2	−11	−107	−10	−87	388	#
Reserve position in the Fund	−46	2	21	−44	−86	43	−33	260
Foreign exchange assets	−2,131	−336	−3,168	2,423	2,379	−1,105	1,758	−859
Other claims	#	#	#	#	175	173	92	−279
Use of Fund credit	#	#	#	#	#	#	499	2,027
Conversion rates: cruzeiros per SDR	12.32	16.51	22.62	34.81	68.61	109.81	198.19	616.86
Conversion rates: U.S. dollars per SDR	1.1545	1.1675	1.2520	1.2920	1.3015	1.1792	1.1040	1.0690

a. For 1951–81 data, see SALA, 23-2703.

SOURCE: IMF-BPS-Y, 1984.

Table 2704

CHILE: IMF BALANCE OF PAYMENTS, 1976–83[a]

(M SDR)

Category	1976	1977	1978	1979	1980	1981	1982	1983
A. Current Account	128	–472	–869	–920	–1,514	–4,014	–2,087	–999
Merchandise: exports f.o.b.	1,833	1,872	1,965	2,968	3,615	3,253	3,357	3,602
Copper	1,068	976	974	1,461	1,633	1,474	1,526	1,743
Other	765	897	991	1,507	1,982	1,779	1,831	1,860
Merchandise: imports f.o.b.	–1,276	–1,842	–2,305	–3,243	–4,202	–5,523	–3,300	–2,654
Trade balance	557	30	–340	–275	–587	–2,270	57	949
Other goods, services, and income: credit	268	373	419	705	1,207	1,508	1,312	912
Other goods, services, and income: debit	–738	–957	–1,025	–1,432	–2,221	–3,343	–3,554	–2,946
Investment income	–292	–328	–425	–621	–951	–1,755	–2,204	–1,781
Other	–446	–629	–600	–811	–1,270	–1,588	–1,351	–1,165
Total: goods, services, and income	87	–554	–946	–1,002	–1,601	–4,105	–2,186	–1,085
Private unrequited transfers	28	69	60	68	49	31	37	46
Total, excl. official unrequited transfers	114	–486	–887	–933	–1,552	–4,075	–2,149	–1,039
Official unrequited transfers	14	14	18	13	38	61	62	40
B. Direct Investment and Other Long-Term Capital	40	42	1,206	1,382	1,723	3,035	1,523	1,136
Direct investment	–1	14	141	180	131	307	348	142
Portfolio investment	–5	–6	#	39	#	#	#	#
Other long-term capital								
Resident official sector	22	–135	133	74	–148	–421	121	1,075
Loans received by general government	–54	–83	–99	–166	–43	–69	22	–108
Loans received by Central Bank	80	–36	232	240	–104	–344	100	1,182
Other	–4	–16	#	#	#	–9	–2	#
Deposit money banks	–16	6	232	406	1,105	2,117	296	–8
Other sectors	41	164	700	683	635	1,032	757	–73
Drawings on loans received	388	572	1,149	1,310	1,264	1,870	1,461	478
Repayments on loans received	–347	–409	–449	–627	–629	–815	–714	–551
Total, Groups A plus B	168	–430	337	462	208	–979	–564	137
C. Other Short-Term Capital	13	445	348	358	709	949	–422	–659
Resident official sector	–115	4	#	–4	18	47	178	94
Deposit money banks	–31	109	46	30	360	214	62	–384
Other sectors	159	331	302	331	331	688	–662	–370
D. Net Errors and Omissions	59	99	–102	–10	39	85	–63	28
Total, Groups A through D	240	113	583	810	956	55	–1,050	–495
E. Counterpart Items	–1	–20	–51	32	134	203	132	107
Monetization/demonetization of gold	#	#	#	33	61	#	#	22
Allocation/cancellation of SDRs	#	#	#	23	23	22	#	#
Valuation changes in reserves	–1	–20	–51	–24	50	181	132	85
Total, Groups A through E	239	94	532	842	1,090	258	–918	–387
F. Exceptional Financing	#	#	#	#	#	#	#	#
Total, Groups A through F	239	94	532	842	1,090	258	–918	–387
G. Liabilities Constituting Foreign Authorities' Reserves	46	33	11	7	58	59	–164	11
Total, Groups A through G	285	126	543	849	1,149	318	–1,082	–376
H. Total Change in Reserves	–285	–126	–543	–849	–1,149	–318	1,082	376
Monetary gold	–2	–1	–1	–34	–69	#	–2	43
SDRs	–27	–6	34	–1	19	–13	–1	12
Reserve position in the Fund	#	#	–38	1	–27	#	–6	71
Foreign exchange assets	–327	–17	–504	–684	–1,032	–250	1,127	–324
Other claims	#	#	#	#	#	#	#	#
Use of Fund credit	71	–102	–34	–131	–40	–55	–36	–573
Conversion rates: Chilean pesos per SDR	15.071	25.136	39.633	48.122	50.760	45.987	56.204	84.282
Conversion rates: U.S. dollars per SDR	1.1545	1.1675	1.2520	1.2920	1.3015	1.1792	1.1040	1.0690

a, For 1951–81 data, see SALA, 23–2704.

SOURCE: IMF-BPS-Y, 1984.

Table 2705

COLOMBIA: IMF BALANCE OF PAYMENTS, 1976-83[a]

(M SDR)

Category	1976	1977	1978	1979	1980	1981	1982	1983
A. Current Account	179	377	257	380	-122	-1,607	-2,622	-2,561
Merchandise: exports f.o.b.	1,943	2,324	2,561	2,714	3,121	2,730	2,912	2,808
Coffee	928	1,375	1,547	1,629	1,696	1,311	1,372	1,332
Other	1,015	949	1,014	1,085	1,425	1,419	1,540	1,476
Merchandise: imports f.o.b.	-1,442	-1,695	-2,048	-2,319	-3,304	-4,039	-4,895	-4,450
Trade balance	501	629	513	395	-183	-1,309	-1,983	-1,642
Other goods, services, and income: credit	547	686	738	1,041	1,383	1,522	1,591	1,164
Transportation	226	249	244	259	333	407	396	372
Other	321	437	494	782	1,050	1,115	1,195	792
Other goods, services, and income: debit	-921	-988	-1,052	-1,134	-1,449	-2,026	-2,383	-2,245
Transportation	-285	-328	-336	-334	-498	-617	-719	-731
Investment income	-332	-295	-346	-404	-531	-910	-1,174	-972
Other	-304	-365	-370	-396	-420	-499	-490	-542
Total: goods, services, and income	127	327	199	302	-249	-1,813	-2,775	-2,723
Private unrequited transfers	40	46	36	77	127	206	151	162
Total, excl. official unrequited transfers	167	373	235	379	-122	-1,607	-2,624	-2,561
Official unrequited transfers	12	4	12	1	#	#	2	#
B. Direct Investment and Other Long-Term Capital	90	197	76	561	613	1,376	1,458	1,245
Direct investment	12	37	54	81	37	180	306	267
Portfolio investment	-1	-2	-2	-9	-2	-1	-6	#
Other long-term capital								
Resident official sector	6	10	24	307	388	655	293	123
Loans received by general government	1	#	23	281	374	652	277	126
Loans received by Bank of the Republic	9	11	19	38	50	45	20	-3
Other	-4	-1	-18	-12	-36	-42	-4	#
Deposit money banks	#	#	#	#	#	#	#	#
Other sectors	73	152	#	182	190	542	865	855
Total, Groups A plus B	269	574	333	941	491	-231	-1,164	-1,316
C. Other Short-Term Capital	80	-220	-7	124	38	292	336	-227
Resident official sector	18	-3	-6	-29	-36	-8	56	81
Deposit money banks	52	-174	11	291	132	160	119	-4
Other sectors	10	-43	-12	-138	-58	140	161	-304
D. Net Errors and Omissions	183	136	15	53	288	268	58	-248
Total, Groups A through D	532	490	341	1,118	817	329	-770	-1,791
E. Counterpart Items	15	12	65	30	309	215	322	267
Monetization/demonetization of gold	10	12	51	57	238	203	153	166
Allocation/cancellation of SDRs	#	#	#	20	20	20	#	#
Valuation changes in reserves	5	#	14	-47	51	-8	169	101
Total, Groups A through E	547	502	405	1,147	1,126	544	-449	-1,524
F. Exceptional Financing	#	#	#	#	#	#	#	#
Total, Groups A through F	547	502	405	1,147	1,126	544	-449	-1,524
G. Liabilities Constituting Foreign Authorities' Reserves	6	#	18	12	-7	38	-22	5
Total, Groups A through G	553	502	423	1,159	1,119	582	-471	-1,519
H. Total Change in Reserves	-553	-502	-423	-1,159	-1,119	-582	471	1,519
Monetary gold	-11	-11	-45	-58	-249	-245	-153	-166
SDRs	-4	-1	-12	-34	-13	-34	-43	-26
Reserve position in the Fund	-6	-31	7	-4	-41	-37	-23	-87
Foreign exchange assets	-532	-458	-373	-1,064	-816	-265	690	1,798
Other claims	#	#	#	#	#	#	#	#
Use of Fund credit	#	#	#	#	#	#	#	#
Conversion rates: Colombian pesos per SDR	40.060	42.941	48.953	54.982	61.545	62.262	70.780	84.310
Conversion rates: U.S. dollars per SDR	1.1545	1.1675	1.2520	1.2920	1.3015	1.1792	1.1040	1.0690

a. For 1956-81 data, see SALA, 23-2705.

SOURCE: IMF-BPS-Y, 1984.

Table 2706

COSTA RICA: IMF BALANCE OF PAYMENTS, 1976–83[a]

(M SDR)

Category	1976	1977	1978	1979	1980	1981	1982	1983
A. Current Account	−174.5	−193.2	−290.1	−432.4	−509.5	−345.7	−270.4	−296.1
Merchandise: exports f.o.b.	513.1	709.0	690.0	728.7	769.5	850.1	786.2	815.0
Bananas	128.8	128.7	135.7	147.3	159.5	191.2	206.5	218.4
Coffee	133.3	273.4	250.6	243.9	190.8	203.3	214.3	215.1
Other	251.0	306.9	303.8	337.4	419.1	455.6	365.5	381.6
Merchandise: imports f.o.b.	−602.3	−792.4	−838.2	−972.9	−1,056.4	−923.6	−729.4	−835.9
Trade balance	−89.2	−83.3	−148.2	−244.2	−287.0	−73.4	56.8	−20.9
Other goods, services, and income: credit	102.4	121.0	128.7	131.0	167.3	166.8	248.5	286.5
Other goods, services, and income: debit	−199.1	−244.4	−283.9	−328.6	−400.9	−462.1	−608.2	−622.5
Total: goods, services, and income	−185.9	−206.8	−303.4	−441.8	−520.6	−368.7	−302.9	−356.8
Private unrequited transfers	9.7	13.2	12.7	12.8	15.2	23.1	26.8	21.6
Total, excl. official unrequited transfers	−176.2	−193.6	−290.7	−429.1	−505.4	−345.7	−276.1	−335.2
Official unrequited transfers	1.7	.3	.6	−3.3	−4.1	−.1	5.7	39.1
B. Direct Investment and Other Long-Term Capital	176.0	250.9	267.1	267.5	298.4	158.4	−170.1	253.2
Direct investment	54.8	53.5	37.5	32.8	37.0	56.1	24.0	46.5
Portfolio investment	#	3.0	16.7	#	95.9	.3	.4	#
Other long-term capital								
Resident official sector	45.9	63.8	76.7	165.3	50.9	72.6	−173.7	222.0
Loans received by general government	16.1	27.6	56.5	66.9	45.0	28.6	−10.4	44.9
Loans received by Central Bank	33.0	36.7	25.6	100.9	10.0	47.1	−151.5	178.2
Other	−3.2	−.4	−5.4	−2.5	−4.1	−3.1	−11.9	−1.1
Deposit money banks	23.4	31.9	−9.2	26.8	7.4	−15.7	−18.7	−6.3
Other sectors	66.4	98.7	145.4	42.5	107.2	45.0	−2.1	−9.0
Loans received by government enterprises	32.1	45.0	72.8	56.7	96.8	79.3	−10.8	14.4
Loans recieved by private enterprises	34.3	53.7	72.5	−14.2	10.4	−34.3	8.8	−23.4
Total, Groups A plus B	1.5	57.6	−23.0	−164.9	−211.0	−187.4	−440.5	−42.9
C. Other Short-Term Capital	46.2	51.2	27.1	32.3	30.2	−405.0	−162.1	−121.1
Resident official sector	3.4	−.3	2.3	29.2	143.1	−225.3	−8.2	−52.9
Deposit money banks	−.7	4.5	1.8	4.4	25.0	−28.0	4.2	−32.1
Other sectors	43.5	47.1	22.9	−1.3	−137.9	−151.7	−158.1	−36.1
D. Net Errors and Omissions	−17.4	−23.5	−40.5	62.2	−54.7	61.3	148.7	123.9
Total, Groups A through D	30.3	85.4	−36.4	−70.5	−235.6	−431.1	−453.9	−40.1
E. Counterpart Items	7.8	−8.1	−13.1	4.5	9.8	3.7	18.2	.5
Monetization/demonetization of gold	#	#	#	#	#	−22.7	5.8	.5
Allocation/cancellation of SDRs	#	#	#	4.3	4.3	4.2	#	#
Valuation changes in reserves	7.8	−8.1	−13.1	.2	5.5	22.2	12.4	#
Total, Groups A through E	38.2	77.3	−49.5	−66.0	−225.8	−527.4	−435.6	−39.6
F. Exceptional Financing	14.5	5.7	14.6	5.5	228.7	491.5	558.4	71.0
Loans received by Central Bank	#	5.7	14.6	5.5	11.3	23.8	39.0	1,057.3
Payments arrears	#	#	#	#	217.4	467.7	470.3	−986.3
Rescheduling of government enterprises' arrears	#	#	#	#	#	#	49.2	#
Total, Groups A through F	52.7	83.1	−34.9	−60.5	2.9	−35.8	122.8	31.3
G. Liabilities Constituting Foreign Authorities' Reserves	2.7	3.8	43.5	−27.6	77.4	−4.7	9.8	18.7
Total, Groups A through G	55.4	86.8	8.7	−88.1	80.2	−40.6	132.6	50.0
H. Total Change in Reserves	−55.4	−86.8	−8.7	88.1	−80.2	40.6	−132.6	−50.0
Monetary gold	#	−.4	−.2	−.2	#	22.7	−5.8	−.5
SDRs	2.6	−4.3	2.5	−1.5	4.5	#	−.1	−2.8
Reserve position in the Fund	#	#	−7.8	.2	7.5	#	#	#
Foreign exchange assets	−45.8	−69.9	10.4	60.8	−87.7	−7.3	−110.7	−159.5
Other claims	−14.5	−9.2	−8.6	9.3	−5.4	−18.4	−12.1	13.6
Use of Fund credit	2.3	−3.0	−5.0	19.5	.8	43.5	−4.0	99.1
Conversion rates: Costa Rican colones per SDR	9.894	10.006	10.730	11.072	11.154	25.662	41.297	43.930
Conversion rates: U.S. dollars per SDR	1.1545	1.1675	1.2520	1.2920	1.3015	1.1792	1.1040	1.0690

a. For 1951–81 data, see SALA, 23–2706.

SOURCE: IMF-BPS-Y, Jan. 1984.

Table 2707

DOMINICAN REPUBLIC: IMF BALANCE OF PAYMENTS, 1975–82[a]
(M SDR)

Category	1975	1976	1977	1978	1979	1980	1981	1982
A. Current Account	–60.0	–111.9	–110.1	–249.1	–256.4	–514.6	–344.2	–400.3
Merchandise: exports f.o.b.	736.2	620.5	668.5	539.5	672.3	739.1	1,007.5	695.4
Sugar	475.4	251.2	213.3	168.7	180.7	254.1	475.3	279.5
Other	260.8	369.3	455.2	370.8	491.6	485.0	532.2	415.8
Merchandise: imports f.o.b.	–636.4	–661.4	–727.4	–688.8	–880.4	–1,167.6	–1,231.1	–1,138.8
Trade balance	99.7	–40.9	–58.9	–149.3	–208.1	–428.6	–223.6	–443.5
Other goods, services, and income: credit	100.0	118.4	136.2	138.4	230.8	269.8	285.3	342.8
Other goods, services, and income: debit	–291.8	–298.4	–307.0	–357.9	–438.4	–500.2	–569.6	–485.3
Investment income	–97.2	–102.3	–94.8	–125.0	–170.0	–193.6	–258.6	–234.1
Other	–194.6	–196.1	–212.2	–232.9	–268.4	–306.6	–311.0	–251.2
Total: goods, services and income	–91.2	–220.9	–229.7	–368.8	–415.7	–658.9	–507.9	–586.0
Private unrequited transfers	28.2	106.5	116.6	116.9	137.0	140.7	155.1	172.1
Total, excl. official unrequited transfers	–63.9	–114.4	–113.1	–251.9	–278.7	–518.2	–352.8	–413.9
Official unrequited transfers	4.0	2.5	3.0	2.8	22.3	3.6	8.6	13.6
B. Direct Investment and Other Long-Term								
Capital	131.1	151.5	148.3	128.0	124.1	278.1	123.1	177.2
Direct investment	52.6	52.0	61.2	50.8	13.2	71.2	67.6	–1.3
Portfolio investment	#	#	#	#	#	#	#	#
Other long-term capital								
Resident official sector	45.0	41.9	48.7	94.9	127.8	159.0	119.0	202.3
Loans received by general government	40.4	~	~	~	~	~	~	~
Loans received by Central Bank	5.4	~	~	~	~	~	~	~
Other	–.8	~	~	~	~	~	~	~
Deposit money banks	#	1.3	–.7	–.6	5.5	#	–6.2	–.8
Other sectors	33.5	56.3	39.1	–17.0	–22.4	47.9	–57.3	–23.0
Total, Groups A plus B	71.2	39.6	38.2	–121.1	–132.4	–236.6	–221.2	–223.1
C. Other Short-Term Capital	–11.7	–14.0	11.9	–17.8	82.7	119.4	175.1	–147.6
Resident official sector	–.1	–1.1	17.7	–9.4	–25.9	–5.5	14.8	–31.6
Deposit money banks	–32.8	–8.2	8.1	15.5	–12.3	70.6	163.6	–41.1
Other sectors	21.2	–4.7	–14.0	–23.9	120.9	54.3	–3.2	–74.8
D. Net Errors and Omissions	–56.8	–61.4	–14.5	55.3	–56.3	23.0	13.0	–.6
Total, Groups A through D	2.7	–35.9	35.6	–83.6	–106.0	–94.2	–33.1	–371.3
E. Counterpart Items	2.3	.8	–4.2	–8.5	6.9	11.8	25.3	–3.6
Monetization/demonetization of gold	#	#	#	#	.3	4.5	4.3	–14.9
Allocation/cancellation of SDRs	#	#	#	#	5.7	5.7	5.6	#
Valuation changes in reserves	2.3	.8	–4.2	–8.5	.9	1.5	15.4	11.2
Total, Groups A through E	5.0	–35.1	31.4	–92.1	–99.1	–82.4	–7.7	–374.9
F. Exceptional Financing	–8.3	16.3	.8	54.6	72.1	60.2	59.1	147.2
Long-term borrowing by Central Bank	#	#	39.1	11.4	#	47.0	72.6	60.5
Short-term borrowing by Central Bank	8.2	5.2	–27.4	43.1	16.1	20.2	–13.0	–21.6
Commercial arrears	–16.5	11.1	–11.0	#	17.3	19.3	12.9	108.2
Deposits received for balance of payments support	#	#	#	#	38.7	–26.3	–13.4	#
Total, Groups A through F	–3.3	–18.8	32.2	–37.5	–27.0	–22.1	51.4	–227.7
G. Liabilities Constituting Foreign Authorities'								
Reserves	28.2	7.1	5.9	–2.1	32.0	59.7	6.5	91.9
Total, Groups A through G	24.9	–11.7	38.1	–39.6	5.0	37.6	57.9	–135.8
H. Total Change in Reserves	–24.9	11.7	–38.1	39.6	–5.0	–37.6	–57.9	135.8
Monetary gold	.2	#	–.7	#	#	–3.8	–4.3	14.9
SDRs	.7	.5	.8	.5	–2.5	7.2	–1.6	1.1
Reserve position in the Fund	#	#	#	#	#	#	#	#
Foreign exchange assets	–25.7	–10.6	–42.8	29.6	–60.4	15.7	–33.6	75.4
Other claims	#	.3	–10.4	9.6	.1	–.3	–.1	.1
Use of Fund credit	#	21.5	15.0	#	57.8	–56.3	–18.3	44.3
Conversion rates: Dominican pesos per SDR	1.2142	1.1545	1.1675	1.2520	1.2920	1.3015	1.1792	1.1040
Conversion rates: U.S. dollars per SDR	1.1545	1.1675	1.2520	1.2920	1.3015	1.1792	1.1040	1.0690

a. For 1951–81 data, see SALA, 23-2707.

SOURCE: IMF-BPS-Y, 1984.

Table 2708

ECUADOR: IMF BALANCE OF PAYMENTS, 1976–83[a]

(M SDR)

Category	1976	1977	1978	1979	1980	1981	1982	1983
A. Current Account	-5.8	-292.4	-560.1	-483.6	-493.0	-849.4	-1,082.4	-97.3
Merchandise: exports f.o.b.	1,132.2	1,199.8	1,221.4	1,664.5	1,954.8	2,157.6	2,122.3	2,212.3
Bananas	126.8	139.3	143.8	157.4	182.2	183.1	192.9	143.1
Coffee	177.9	149.9	223.6	204.2	101.6	89.8	125.9	139.4
Crude petroleum	637.0	557.7	445.9	798.7	1,070.8	1,323.1	1,257.2	1,537.9
Other	190.6	353.0	408.1	504.2	600.2	561.7	546.2	392.0
Merchandise: imports f.o.b.	-907.6	-1,165.3	-1,361.0	-1,622.9	-1,722.4	-2,002.7	-1,975.5	-1,317.1
Trade balance	224.6	34.5	-139.6	41.6	232.3	154.9	146.7	895.2
Other goods, services, and income: credit	107.9	186.0	168.7	253.8	331.5	386.9	354.2	302.2
Other goods, services, and income: debit	364.9	-544.0	-621.9	-802.0	-1,080.0	-1,412.4	-1,601.4	-1,317.1
Shipment	-124.4	-178.3	-174.1	-134.5	-156.1	-186.7	-148.5	-104.8
Investment income	-112.1	-167.0	-233.4	-327.7	-487.0	-686.3	-807.1	-732.5
Other	-128.4	-198.6	-214.4	-339.8	-436.9	-539.5	-645.8	-479.9
Total: goods, services, and income	-32.4	-323.4	-592.8	-506.7	-516.2	-870.6	-1,100.5	-119.7
Private unrequited transfers	6.8	.3	9.6	.3	#	#	#	#
Total, excl. official unrequited transfers	-25.5	-323.1	-583.2	-506.3	-516.2	-870.6	-1,100.5	-119.7
Official unrequited transfers	19.7	30.7	23.1	22.8	23.2	21.2	18.1	22.5
B. Direct Investment and Other Long-Term Capital	136.0	506.2	624.6	533.7	586.2	913.2	146.7	1,293.7
Direct investment	-17.2	29.5	38.8	49.1	53.8	50.9	36.2	46.8
Portfolio investment	4.9	44.5	#	#	#	#	#	#
Other long-term capital								
Resident official sector	142.1	377.0	280.8	266.6	468.1	761.3	-236.4	2,128.2
Loans received by general government	144.5	381.7	286.7	271.4	476.0	767.9	-221.9	2,140.3
Other	-2.4	-4.6	-5.8	-4.8	-7.9	-6.6	-14.5	-12.2
Deposit money banks	#	#	50.1	.9	3.7	1.5	#	-6.5
Other sectors	6.2	55.1	254.9	217.2	60.7	99.5	346.9	-874.6
Total, Groups A plus B	130.2	213.8	64.5	50.1	93.2	63.8	-935.7	1,196.4
C. Other Short-Term Capital	31.4	-67.2	-107.6	-57.0	128.0	-212.2	830.6	-978.5
Resident official sector	51.4	-78.5	-9.4	-32.2	-61.9	93.9	528.1	-461.2
Deposit money banks	-12.6	-22.0	2.2	-7.6	-13.1	-4.6	45.3	6.5
Other sectors	-7.4	33.4	-100.4	-17.3	203.1	-301.5	257.2	-523.9
D. Net Errors and Omissions	-11.4	-42.7	35.3	2.3	-52.5	-72.7	-204.9	-90.0
Total, Groups A through D	150.2	103.9	-7.8	-4.6	168.7	-221.1	-309.9	127.9
E. Counterpart Items	18.5	6.6	-29.0	26.1	38.6	63.3	40.6	33.6
Monetization/demonetization of gold	#	#	#	#	#	#	#	#
Allocation/cancellation of SDRs	#	#	#	7.3	7.3	7.1	#	#
Valuation changes in reserves	18.5	6.6	-29.0	18.8	31.3	56.1	40.6	33.6
Total, Groups A through E	168.7	110.4	-36.8	21.5	207.3	-157.9	-269.4	161.5
F. Exceptional Financing	#	#	#	#	#	#	#	#
Total, Groups A through F	168.7	110.4	-36.8	21.5	207.3	-157.9	-269.4	161.5
G. Liabilities Constituting Foreign Authorities' Reserves	25.8	-7.9	12.1	38.9	38.8	-93.0	1.8	-25.3
Total, Groups A through G	194.5	102.6	-24.7	60.3	246.1	-250.9	-267.6	136.3
H. Total Change in Reserves	-194.5	-102.6	24.7	-60.3	-246.1	250.9	267.6	-136.3
Monetary gold	#	-.5	-.2	-.2	#	#	#	#
SDRs	#	-1.9	-2.4	-8.6	.2	-9.9	28.9	-.1
Reserve position in the Fund	13.2	#	-8.0	-1.4	-12.4	-3.0	24.8	-11.4
Foreign exchange assets	-207.7	-100.1	35.4	-50.2	-233.9	263.8	213.9	-328.3
Other claims	#	#	#	#	#	#	#	#
Use of Fund credit	#	#	#	#	#	#	#	203.5
Conversion rates: sucres per SDR	28.863	29.188	31.300	32.300	32.538	29.479	33.149	47.159
Conversion rates: U.S. dollars per SDR	1.1545	1.1675	1.2520	1.2920	1.3015	1.1792	1.1040	1.0690

a. For 1951–81 data, see SALA, 23-2708.

SOURCE: IMF-BPS, Jan. 1985.

Table 2709

EL SALVADOR: IMF BALANCE OF PAYMENTS, 1975–82[a]

(M SDR)

Category	1975	1976	1977	1978	1979	1980	1981	1982
A. Current Account	-76.5	20.5	26.4	-228.3	16.6	23.5	-212.4	-138.0
Merchandise: exports f.o.b.	439.0	645.0	833.8	640.3	876.4	826.2	676.8	637.8
Coffee	142.3	350.3	518.7	308.0	522.6	472.7	383.8	364.7
Cotton	62.9	55.6	69.4	80.3	67.3	67.0	46.8	42.6
Other	233.8	239.1	245.7	252.0	286.5	286.6	246.1	230.5
Merchandise: imports f.o.b.	-453.6	-589.8	-737.5	-759.6	-738.9	-689.2	-761.9	-748.1
Trade balance	-14.6	55.2	96.4	-119.4	137.5	137.0	-85.1	-110.3
Other goods, services, and income: credit	55.2	134.3	130.9	126.2	172.9	150.2	146.0	152.4
Other goods, services, and income: debit	-139.7	-194.3	-234.8	-276.1	-333.6	-301.3	-324.5	-334.8
Total: goods, services, and income	-99.1	-4.9	-7.5	-269.3	-23.2	-14.1	-263.5	-292.7
Private unrequited transfers	20.7	21.2	26.0	35.8	34.8	13.3	33.2	46.8
Total, excl. official unrequited transfers	-78.4	16.3	18.5	-233.5	11.5	-.7	-230.3	-245.8
Official unrequited transfers	1.9	4.2	7.9	5.2	5.0	24.2	17.9	107.8
B. Direct Investment and Other Long-Term Capital	57.4	63.2	32.8	132.3	45.2	84.1	77.2	135.8
Direct investment	10.8	11.2	16.0	18.7	-7.7	4.5	-4.9	-.9
Portfolio investment	#	15.4	.6	3.2	-4.4	-.8	#	-.9
Other long-term capital								
Resident official sector	-1.2	13.2	21.0	84.2	48.7	78.7	82.0	132.3
Loans received by general government	16.0	21.3	17.7	41.5	43.3	59.7	139.4	129.3
Loans received by Central Reserve Bank	54.6	43.1	25.1	51.9	24.8	61.3	53.5	158.0
Other	-71.8	-51.2	-21.8	-9.2	-19.3	-42.3	-110.9	-155.1
Deposit money banks	#	#	#	#	#	2.5	-.2	-.1
Other sectors	47.8	23.3	-4.8	26.3	8.5	-.9	.3	5.5
Loans received	49.0	22.2	-20.0	18.4	8.5	-.9	.3	5.5
Other	-1.2	1.1	15.2	7.9	#	#	#	#
Total, Groups A plus B	-19.1	83.6	59.2	-95.9	61.7	107.6	-135.2	-2.2
C. Other Short-Term Capital	15.0	10.9	4.9	139.5	-83.1	-64.6	-16.2	20.6
Resident official sector	-3.7	.5	-.8	2.9	4.1	55.7	1.3	-5.5
Deposit money banks	-13.0	10.2	17.5	3.1	-1.7	-51.7	-9.3	26.2
Other sectors	31.7	.3	-11.8	133.5	-85.5	-68.7	-8.3	#
D. Net Errors and Omissions	8.0	-21.6	-29.0	-23.2	-82.2	-243.8	.2	-86.5
Total, Groups A through D	3.9	73.0	35.1	20.4	-103.5	-200.8	-151.3	-68.2
E. Counterpart Items	3.6	.3	-7.7	-12.4	6.2	4.9	10.1	3.5
Monetization/demonetization of gold	#	#	#	#	#	#	#	#
Allocation/cancellation of SDRs	#	#	#	#	4.5	4.5	4.4	#
Valuation changes in reserves	3.6	.3	-7.7	-12.4	1.7	.4	5.8	3.5
Total, Groups A through E	7.4	73.2	27.4	8.0	-97.3	-195.9	-141.1	-64.7
F. Exceptional Financing	20.6	#	#	24.0	#	139.4	79.0	74.1
Long-term loans received by the Central Reserve Bank	20.6	#	#	8.0	15.5	49.9	29.4	95.1
Short-term borrowing by the Central Reserve Bank	#	#	#	16.0	-15.5	89.5	49.6	-21.0
Total, Groups A through F	28.0	73.2	27.4	31.9	-97.3	-56.5	-62.1	9.4
G. Liabilities Constituting Foreign Authorities' Reserves	#	#	#	#	#	4.1	30.7	-32.6
Total, Groups A through G	28.0	73.2	27.4	31.9	-97.3	-52.5	-31.4	-23.1
H. Total Change in Reserves	-28.0	-73.2	-27.4	-31.9	97.3	52.5	31.4	23.1
Monetary gold	#	#	-.2	#	-.2	-.2	#	#
SDRs	-.4	-.1	-3.8	.2	-5.6	13.2	-.1	-1.6
Reserve position in the Fund	#	#	-5.1	-3.7	.3	8.5	#	#
Foreign exchange assets	-27.7	-68.1	-5.5	-28.4	102.9	25.6	-.8	-35.0
Other claims	#	#	#	#	#	#	#	#
Use of Fund credit	#	-5.1	-12.8	#	#	5.4	32.3	59.7
Conversion rates: Salvadoran colones per SDR	3.0354	2.8863	2.9188	3.1300	3.2300	3.2538	2.9479	2.7600
Conversion rates: U.S. dollars per SDR	1.1545	1.1675	1.2520	1.2920	1.3015	1.1792	1.1040	1.0690

a. For 1951–81 data, see SALA, 23-2709.

SOURCE: IMF-BPS-Y, 1984.

Table 2710

GUATEMALA: IMF BALANCE OF PAYMENTS, 1976-83[a]

(M SDR)

Category	1976	1977	1978	1979	1980	1981	1982	1983
A. Current Account	-67.1	-27.3	-211.3	-158.8	-125.8	-492.3	-343.5	-211.8
Merchandise: exports f.o.b.	658.6	995.4	876.6	945.7	1,167.0	1,094.1	1,085.5	1,020.4
Coffee	210.5	452.0	382.3	334.3	356.2	273.8	339.0	289.0
Other	448.2	543.4	494.3	611.4	810.9	820.3	746.5	731.4
Merchandise: imports f.o.b.	-823.5	-930.0	-1,024.3	-1,085.0	-1,130.9	-1,309.6	-1,164.4	-988.4
Trade balance	-164.8	65.4	-147.8	-139.4	36.1	-215.4	-78.9	32.1
Other goods, services, and income: credit	214.2	179.3	204.8	255.9	241.4	198.6	128.3	105.8
Other goods, services, and income: debit	-288.8	-354.0	-360.5	-373.3	-487.6	-552.6	-449.7	-378.3
Shipment and other transportation	-102.1	-146.8	-113.2	-124.4	-143.5	-159.5	-127.4	-92.6
Investment income	-62.0	-56.7	-66.4	-70.7	-104.3	-134.6	-132.1	-133.6
Other	-124.7	-150.5	-180.8	-178.2	-239.8	258.4	-190.2	-152.1
Total: goods, services, and income	-239.4	-109.3	-303.5	-256.8	-210.1	-569.4	-400.3	-240.4
Private unrequited transfers	171.2	80.4	91.7	95.4	83.4	75.9	56.1	27.9
Total, excl. official unrequited transfers	-68.1	-29.0	-211.8	-161.4	-126.7	-493.5	-344.2	-212.5
Official unrequited transfers	1.0	1.6	.5	2.6	.9	1.2	.7	.8
B. Direct Investment and Other Long-Term Capital	66.1	152.0	198.1	185.0	176.4	311.2	273.4	192.7
Direct investment	10.8	83.4	101.8	90.6	85.1	108.2	69.1	42.0
Portfolio investment	.1	4.5	9.4	4.2	3.0	.3	.4	.1
Other long-term capital								
Resident official sector	25.6	39.9	65.6	72.3	68.5	144.1	93.6	156.0
Loans received by general government	21.8	41.7	66.3	73.6	59.9	82.8	80.7	86.8
Loans received by Bank of Guatemala	-.7	-1.8	-.8	-1.3	6.5	61.4	12.9	69.2
Other	4.4	#	#	#	2.2	#	.1	#
Deposit money banks	#	#	#	#	#	#	#	#
Other sectors	29.6	24.2	21.4	17.9	19.8	58.5	110.3	-5.4
Loans received	16.2	16.5	13.4	9.8	11.4	48.6	96.8	-6.7
Other	13.4	7.7	8.1	8.1	8.5	9.9	13.5	1.2
Total, Groups A plus B	-1.0	124.7	-13.1	26.2	50.6	-181.2	-70.0	-19.1
C. Other Short-Term Capital	128.5	36.9	100.7	-25.8	-247.0	-108.6	30.5	108.3
Resident official sector	-3.6	.2	6.0	1.4	45.8	40.7	16.6	-23.3
Deposit money banks	9.4	2.9	.9	18.5	1.8	-5.8	12.6	66.9
Other sectors	122.7	33.8	93.8	-45.8	-294.5	-143.5	1.3	64.7
D. Net Errors and Omissions	42.4	-22.9	-47.1	-34.5	-14.2	-11.8	-29.9	-72.9
Total, Groups A through D	169.8	138.7	40.5	-34.2	-210.5	-301.5	-69.5	16.3
E. Counterpart Items	.6	-25.6	-41.8	-.8	17.9	36.4	13.0	13.3
Monetization/demonetization of gold	#	#	#	#	#	#	#	#
Allocation/cancellation of SDRs	#	#	#	5.3	5.3	5.2	#	#
Valuation changes in reserves	.6	-25.6	-41.8	-6.1	12.6	31.2	13.0	13.3
Total, Groups A through E	170.4	113.2	-1.3	-34.9	-192.6	-265.1	-56.5	29.7
F. Exceptional Financing	20.4	18.1	16.5	14.5	13.3	44.0	35.9	32.2
Loans received by Bank of Guatemala	20.4	18.1	16.5	14.5	13.3	44.0	35.9	32.2
Total, Groups A through F	190.8	131.3	15.2	-20.4	-179.3	-221.1	-20.6	61.8
G. Liabilities Constituting Foreign Authorities' Reserves	#	#	#	#	#	#	#	#
Total, Groups A through G	190.8	131.3	15.2	-20.4	-179.3	-221.1	-20.6	61.8
H. Total Change in Reserves	-190.8	-131.3	-15.2	20.4	179.3	221.1	20.6	-61.8
Monetary gold	#	-.6	-.2	-.3	#	#	#	#
SDRs	#	-.1	-.1	-6.8	.6	15.5	2.2	-.5
Reserve position in the Fund	-3.0	-.4	-.5	-1.2	-7.6	13.3	8.4	-7.9
Foreign exchange assets	-177.4	-127.4	-18.0	48.7	186.8	182.9	24.8	-90.6
Other claims	-10.3	-2.9	3.7	-20.0	-6	-86.2	-14.7	-1.1
Use of Fund credit	#	#	#	#	#	95.6	#	38.3
Conversion rates: quetzales per SDR	1.1545	1.1675	1.2520	1.2920	1.3015	1.1792	1.1040	1.0690
Conversion rates: U.S. dollars per SDR	1.1545	1.1675	1.2520	1.2920	1.3015	1.1792	1.1040	1.0690

a. For 1951-81 data, see SALA, 23-2710.

SOURCE: IMF-BPS, Jan. 1985.

Table 2711

HAITI: IMF BALANCE OF PAYMENTS, 1976–83[a]
(M SDR)

Category	1976	1977	1978	1979	1980	1981	1982	1983
A. Current Account	−16.4	−32.5	−36.7	−42.6	−79.6	−171.2	−120.4	−135.0
Merchandise: exports f.o.b.	85.9	118.7	122.5	106.9	165.3	124.8	157.4	166.9
Bauxite	15.8	14.9	14.1	13.9	15.0	13.7	19.0	~
Coffee	37.9	54.9	50.9	30.4	69.6	27.4	31.9	48.8
Other	32.3	48.8	57.5	62.5	80.7	83.7	106.6	118.1
Merchandise: imports f.o.b.	−141.6	−172.3	−169.5	−170.4	−244.4	−330.4	−304.7	−329.1
Trade balance	−55.6	−53.7	−47.0	−63.6	−79.1	−205.6	−147.3	−162.2
Other goods, services, and income: credit	36.2	32.6	51.7	60.1	71.2	78.1	90.1	89.8
Other goods, services, and income: debit	−53.0	−65.9	−96.7	−97.7	−139.6	−151.3	−181.2	−179.0
Shipment and other transportation	−32.4	−34.5	−40.1	−37.2	−63.4	−79.0	−82.8	−95.9
Distributed earnings on direct investment	−5.3	−7.8	−8.8	−7.2	−8.4	−8.9	−9.9	−9.5
Other	−15.2	−23.7	−47.7	−53.3	−67.8	−63.4	−88.5	−73.5
Total: goods, services, and income	−72.4	−87.1	−91.9	−101.2	−147.4	−278.9	−238.4	−251.4
Private unrequited transfers	28.6	26.7	23.5	26.4	39.9	53.5	73.4	56.9
Workers' remittances (net)	26.1	26.7	23.5	26.4	39.9	53.5	73.4	56.9
Other	2.5	~	~	~	~	~	~	~
Total, excl. official unrequited transfers	−43.8	−60.4	−68.5	−74.8	−107.5	−225.4	−165.0	−194.5
Official unrequited transfers	27.4	27.9	31.8	32.1	27.9	54.2	44.6	59.5
B. Direct Investment and Other Long-Term Capital	38.0	58.6	28.0	43.5	38.2	62.7	40.1	43.5
Direct investment	6.7	6.9	8.2	9.3	10.0	6.9	6.3	8.1
Portfolio investment	#	#	#	#	#	#	#	#
Other long-term capital								
Resident official sector	25.4	34.7	11.2	28.4	26.2	8.7	30.4	29.9
Deposit money banks	#	#	#	#	#	#	#	#
Other sectors	5.9	17.1	8.7	5.9	2.0	47.1	3.4	5.5
Total, Groups A plus B	21.6	26.1	−8.6	.9	−41.4	−108.6	−80.3	−91.5
C. Other Short-Term Capital	−6.4	−.6	−3.0	−.6	−.8	−4.9	−10.7	−2.0
Resident official sector	−2	.1	.2	1.1	1.2	−.3	~	~
Deposit money banks	−6.2	−.7	−3.3	−1.7	−2.0	−4.6	−10.7	−2.0
Other sectors	~	~	~	~	~	~	~	~
D. Net Errors and Omissions	−5.6	−17.2	17.2	1.3	8.4	51.5	49.9	62.8
Total, Groups A through D	9.6	8.3	5.5	1.6	−33.8	−62.0	−41.1	−30.7
E. Counterpart Items	#	#	#	2.4	2.4	2.3	#	#
Monetization/demonetization of gold	#	#	#	#	#	#	#	#
Counterpart to allocation/cancellation	#	#	#	2.4	2.4	2.3	#	#
Valuation changes in reserves	#	#	#	#	#	#	#	#
Total, Groups A through E	9.6	8.3	5.5	4.0	−31.4	−59.7	−41.1	−30.7
F. Exceptional Financing	.1	2.3	6.0	4.7	11.5	14.3	#	#
Subsidy Account grants	.1	.2	.2	.2	.2	#	#	#
Trust Fund loans	#	2.1	5.8	4.5	11.3	14.3	#	#
Total, Groups A through F	9.7	10.6	11.5	8.7	−19.9	−45.4	−41.1	−30.7
G. Liabilities Constituting Foreign Authorities' Reserves	#	#	#	#	#	#	#	#
Total, Groups A through G	9.7	10.6	11.5	8.7	−19.9	−45.4	−41.1	−30.7
H. Total Change in Reserves	−9.7	−10.6	−11.5	−8.7	19.9	45.4	41.1	30.7
Monetary gold	#	−.1	−.2	−4.1	−2.8	1.8	.8	#
SDRs	.7	−.2	−2.2	−1.7	3.4	2.3	−.2	−3.0
Reserve position in the Fund	#	#	−2.4	−2.2	4.6	#	−.1	#
Foreign exchange assets	−11.7	−6.3	−6.3	1.0	17.0	29.8	14.9	9.7
Other claims	#	#	#	#	#	#	#	#
Use of Fund credit	1.3	−4.0	−.5	−1.7	−2.3	11.5	25.7	24.0
Conversion rates: gourdes per SDR	5.7995	5.8000	6.1208	6.4561	6.5272	6.0551	5.6263	5.3771
Conversion rates: U.S. dollars per SDR	1.1545	1.1675	1.2520	1.2920	1.3015	1.1792	1.1040	1.0690

a. For 1951–81 data, see SALA, 23–2711.

SOURCE: IMF-BPS-Y, 1984.

Table 2712

HONDURAS: IMF BALANCE OF PAYMENTS, 1976–83[a]

(M SDR)

Category	1976	1977	1978	1979	1980	1981	1982	1983
A. Current Account	-90.7	-110.2	-125.6	-148.1	-243.4	-256.7	-206.7	-210.6
Merchandise: exports f.o.b.	356.6	453.8	500.1	585.9	653.3	664.7	612.8	649.4
Bananas	92.4	111.5	113.5	154.9	175.1	180.9	197.7	190.0
Coffee	86.9	144.1	168.5	152.7	156.8	146.6	138.7	141.4
Wood	35.3	40.4	33.8	32.6	27.8	36.6	40.4	37.8
Other	142.0	157.9	184.3	245.8	293.5	300.6	235.9	280.1
Merchandise: imports f.o.b.	-374.6	-471.2	-522.8	-606.2	-733.0	-762.1	-616.6	-711.6
Trade balance	-18.0	-17.3	-22.6	-20.3	-79.8	-97.4	-3.8	-62.2
Other goods, services, and income: credit	44.7	54.8	64.2	79.5	90.0	101.3	96.9	108.8
Other goods, services, and income: debit	-129.0	-159.8	-180.9	-223.1	-270.2	-283.9	-327.0	-298.8
Total: goods, services, and income	-102.2	-122.3	-139.4	-164.0	-259.9	-280.0	-233.9	-252.2
Private unrequited transfers	2.9	3.3	3.6	5.3	5.8	7.5	8.2	9.1
Total, excl. official unrequited transfers	-99.3	-119.0	-135.8	-158.6	-254.2	-272.5	-255.8	-243.2
Official unrequited transfers	8.6	8.8	10.3	10.5	10.8	15.8	19.0	32.6
B. Direct Investment and Other Long-Term Capital	82.4	113.2	126.2	121.7	173.2	160.0	152.4	151.8
Direct investment	4.5	7.6	10.5	21.8	4.5	-3.1	12.5	19.6
Portfolio investment	#	#	-.4	-.1	#	-.2	-.2	.1
Other long-term capital								
Resident official sector	39.6	14.6	26.0	25.9	9.9	1.5	69.7	32.1
Loans received by general government	39.9	24.0	31.2	20.2	25.2	21.4	28.8	44.7
Loans received by Central Bank	1.0	-3.3	-2.3	7.9	-7.3	-8.0	50.0	-4.4
Other	-1.3	-6.2	-2.9	-2.3	-7.9	-11.9	-9.0	-8.1
Deposit money banks	.9	10.9	.5	-11.3	1.2	4.0	-1.8	-2.3
Other sectors	37.4	80.1	89.7	85.5	157.7	157.7	72.2	102.2
Total, Groups A plus B	-8.3	3.0	.6	-26.4	-70.2	-96.7	-54.3	-58.8
C. Other Short-Term Capital	35.1	45.3	-17.1	39.2	9.1	21.4	9.5	-19.4
Resident official sector	1.1	9.1	-5.0	-1.1	-6.8	39.4	27.4	-31.6
Deposit money banks	12.6	8.5	-13.3	32.9	-6.3	-29.5	16.0	7.2
Other sectors	21.4	27.7	1.2	7.4	22.3	11.6	-33.9	5.0
D. Net Errors and Omissions	-1.4	-5.6	10.0	-15.1	-29.8	-5.7	-4.7	20.9
Total, Groups A through D	25.4	42.6	-6.5	-2.3	-90.9	-81.0	-49.5	-57.3
E. Counterpart Items	.4	-6.4	-9.7	2.1	7.6	11.8	-3.3	7.0
Monetization/demonetization of gold	#	#	#	#	#	#	#	#
Allocation/cancellation of SDRs	#	#	#	3.5	3.5	3.5	#	#
Valuation changes in reserves	.4	-6.4	-9.7	-1.4	4.1	8.3	-3.3	7.0
Total, Groups A through E	25.8	36.2	-16.2	-.2	-83.2	-69.3	-52.8	-50.3
F. Exceptional Financing	7.4	14.2	14.1	17.6	31.2	17.6	#	17.0
Loans from CAMSF	#	#	#	#	15.4	#	#	#
Loans from VIF	7.4	14.2	14.1	9.9	9.4	17.6	#	17.0
Trust Fund loans	#	#	#	7.6	6.4	.1	#	#
Total, Groups A through F	33.2	50.4	-2.1	17.4	-52.0	-51.6	-52.8	-33.4
G. Liabilities Constituting Foreign Authorities' Reserves	#	#	#	#	#	2.5	7.9	-3.9
Total, Groups A through G	33.2	50.4	-2.1	17.4	-52.0	-49.2	-44.8	-37.2
H. Total Change in Reserves	-33.2	-50.4	2.1	-17.4	52.0	49.2	44.8	37.2
Monetary gold	#	-.4	#	-.2	-.2	#	#	#
SDRs	1.3	-.9	.6	-4.7	7.7	-1.4	-.2	-.5
Reserve position in the Fund	#	#	-6.3	.2	6.1	#	#	-4.2
Foreign exchange assets	-31.1	-34.5	12.1	-12.7	27.6	32.1	-14.7	-2.1
Other claims	-3.5	-2.1	#	#	-.9	-2.2	-1.9	-1.9
Use of Fund credit	#	-12.5	-4.3	#	11.8	20.6	61.7	45.9
Conversion rates: lempiras per SDR	2.3090	2.3350	2.5040	2.5840	2.6031	2.3583	2.2080	2.1380
Conversion rates: U.S. dollars per SDR	1.1545	1.1675	1.2520	1.2920	1.3015	1.1792	1.1040	1.0690

a. For 1951–81 data, see SALA, 23–2712.

SOURCE: IMF-BPS-Y, 1984.

Table 2713

MEXICO: IMF BALANCE OF PAYMENTS, 1976–83[a]
(M SDR)

Category	1976	1977	1978	1979	1980	1981	1982	1983
A. Current Account	-2,954	-1,584	-2,526	-4,220	-6,271	-11,890	-5,053	4,886
Merchandise: exports f.o.b.	3,011	3,943	4,973	7,195	12,347	16,869	20,051	20,809
Merchandise: imports f.o.b.	-5,000	-4,814	-6,367	-9,382	-14,523	-20,396	-12,994	-7,236
Trade balance	-1,989	-871	-1,394	-2,188	-2,176	-3,528	7,057	13,573
Other goods, services, and income: credit	3,229	3,089	4,133	5,185	6,581	8,926	5,712	5,120
Travel	1,934	1,817	2,561	3,238	4,030	5,382	3,160	2,842
Other	1,295	1,272	1,572	1,947	2,551	3,543	2,552	2,279
Other goods, services, and income: debit	-4,329	-3,947	-5,418	-7,392	-10,887	-17,534	-18,058	-14,139
Travel	-1,401	-1,013	-1,715	-2,265	-3,206	-5,240	-2,891	-1,778
Investment income	-2,028	-2,037	-2,593	-3,602	-5,274	-8,753	-11,390	-9,502
Other	-900	-897	-1,110	-1,525	-2,407	-3,541	-3,778	-2,859
Total: goods, services, and income	-3,089	-1,729	-2,679	-4,394	-6,482	-12,136	-5,290	4,554
Private unrequited transfers	112	131	83	101	101	97	83	105
Total, excl. official unrequited transfers	-2,977	-1,598	-2,596	-4,293	-6,381	-12,040	-5,206	4,659
Official unrequited transfers	23	14	70	73	110	150	153	227
B. Direct Investment and Other Long-Term Capital	4,327	3,929	4,046	4,018	5,968	11,225	9,998	4,051
Direct investment	544	476	662	1,033	1,678	2,155	1,259	458
Portfolio investment	373	1,146	603	-306	-57	845	583	-505
Resident official sector	421	1,192	612	1	127	980	863	-187
Other	289	931	422	-151	-31	696	336	-317
Other long-term capital								
Resident official sector	943	908	279	-147	497	552	2,554	3,974
Deposit money banks and other institutions	1,603	768	780	987	872	2,596	1,943	-31
Public	1,556	804	701	987	872	2,596	1,943	-31
Private	47	-36	79	#	#	#	#	#
Other sectors	864	631	1,722	2,450	2,978	5,076	3,657	154
Public	786	467	1,671	1,838	1,690	3,791	3,057	-4
Private	78	164	51	613	1,288	1,285	600	158
Total, Groups A plus B	1,373	2,345	1,520	-203	-303	-665	4,945	8,937
C. Other Short-Term Capital	478	-1,816	-1,106	-35	3,941	8,649	-1,676	-4,768
Resident official sector	~	~	~	~	~	~	~	~
Deposit money banks and other institutions	829	-397	-676	828	1,790	5,275	-455	735
Other sectors	-351	-1,419	-430	-863	2,151	3,374	-1,221	-5,503
D. Net Errors and Omissions	-2,638	46	-69	457	-2,901	-7,362	-6,841	-2,290
Total, Groups A through D	-787	575	345	219	737	622	-3,573	1,879
E. Counterpart Items	-38	-80	-90	68	63	576	743	109
Monetization/demonetization of gold	-75	6	5	2	3	6	-6	~
Allocation/cancellation of SDRs	#	#	#	56	56	55	#	#
Valuation changes in reserves	37	-86	-95	10	5	515	749	109
Total, Groups A through E	-825	495	254	288	801	1,198	-2,829	1,988
F. Exceptional Financing	#	#	#	#	#	#	#	#
Total, Groups A through F	-825	495	254	288	801	1,198	-2,829	1,988
G. Liabilities Constituting Foreign Authorities' Reserves	272	-253	-2	#	53	-11	-122	~
Total, Groups A through G	-553	242	252	288	853	1,186	-2,952	1,988
H. Total Change in Reserves	553	-242	-252	-288	-853	-1,186	2,952	-1,988
Monetary gold	72	-5	-5	-2	-2	-7	7	-9
SDRs	85	-46	4	-110	39	-40	148	-17
Reserve position in the Fund	98	#	#	#	-100	-61	161	-91
Foreign exchange assets	-24	-289	-60	-49	-687	-1,079	2,436	-2,874
Other claims	3	-2	-1	#	#	#	#	#
Use of Fund credit	319	100	-190	-126	-103	#	201	1,003
Conversion rates: Mexican pesos per SDR	17.809	26.354	28.505	29.464	29.871	28.907	62.268	128.380
Conversion rates: U.S. dollars per SDR	1.1545	1.1675	1.2520	1.2920	1.3015	1.1792	1.1040	1.0690

a. For 1953–81 data, see SALA, 23–2713.

SOURCE: IMF-BPS-Y, 1984.

Table 2714

NICARAGUA: IMF BALANCE OF PAYMENTS, 1976–83[a]

(M SDR)

Category	1976	1977	1978	1979	1980	1981	1982	1983
A. Current Account	–34.0	–155.8	–19.9	139.5	–291.3	–429.0	–426.4	–414.6
Merchandise: exports f.o.b.	469.3	544.9	516.0	476.7	346.1	431.0	367.8	400.7
Coffee	103.5	170.3	159.4	122.7	127.3	116.0	112.3	139.0
Cotton	113.1	129.0	118.2	105.0	22.0	104.7	79.0	102.4
Other	252.7	245.6	238.3	249.0	196.8	210.3	176.4	159.3
Merchandise: imports f.o.b.	–420.1	–603.2	–441.9	–301.0	–616.9	–782.3	–655.3	–727.9
Trade balance	49.2	–58.2	74.0	175.7	–270.8	–251.3	–287.6	–327.1
Other goods, services, and income: credit	76.1	82.8	68.6	52.1	48.9	62.2	44.8	38.4
Other goods, services, and income: debit	–167.4	–190.0	–170.1	–159.2	–164.5	–199.6	–230.3	–200.1
Total: goods, services, and income	–42.1	–165.4	–27.5	68.6	–386.5	–488.7	–473.0	–488.8
Private unrequited transfers	.9	.6	.1	1.1	9.5	11.2	7.2	3.4
Total, excl. official unrequited transfers	–41.2	–164.8	–27.4	69.7	–376.9	–477.5	–465.8	–485.4
Official unrequited transfers	7.2	9.0	7.5	69.8	85.7	48.4	39.4	70.8
B. Direct Investment and Other Long-Term Capital	26.1	178.5	63.8	40.2	263.8	505.8	400.0	520.9
Direct investment	11.2	8.6	5.6	2.2	#	#	#	7.2
Portfolio investment	#	#	#	#	#	#	#	#
Other long-term capital								
Resident official sector	.3	117.6	53.9	–3.4	250.6	436.3	394.3	519.4
Deposit money banks	–6.2	–.4	–5.5	43.4	13.4	69.5	18.5	31.3
Other sectors	20.8	52.8	9.8	–1.9	–.2	#	–12.8	–37.0
Total, Groups A plus B	–7.9	22.7	43.9	179.7	–27.5	76.7	–26.4	106.3
C. Other Short-Term Capital	–8.4	–18.8	–138.3	–206.6	–105.5	–31.6	–44.4	–18.7
Resident official sector	–3.1	2.2	–1.5	#	#	#	#	#
Deposit money banks	–9.6	47.2	44.3	#	#	#	#	#
Other sectors	4.3	–68.2	–181.1	–206.6	–105.5	–31.6	–44.4	–18.7
D. Net Errors and Omissions	.7	–3.1	–7.7	–34.0	–15.9	–.3	130.2	–22.9
Total, Groups A through D	–15.6	.8	–102.1	–60.8	–148.9	44.8	59.5	64.6
E. Counterpart Items	–1.9	–5.3	–4.5	30.2	5.9	9.4	14.1	#
Monetization/demonetization of gold	#	–.1	#	#	#	#	#	#
Allocation/cancellation of SDRs	#	#	#	3.5	3.5	3.5	#	#
Valuation changes in reserves	–1.9	–5.2	–4.5	26.6	2.4	5.9	14.1	#
Total, Groups A through E	–17.5	–4.5	–106.6	–30.6	–142.9	54.1	73.5	64.6
F. Exceptional Financing	12.2	2.2	44.0	56.7	~	~	~	~
Loans from CAMSF	#	#	37.9	50.5	~	~	~	~
Loans from VIF	12.2	2.2	6.1	6.3	~	~	~	~
Total, Groups A through F	–5.3	–2.3	–62.5	26.1	–142.9	54.1	73.5	64.6
G. Liabilities Constituting Foreign Authorities' Reserves	8.3	4.8	–8.7	#	#	#	#	#
Total, Groups A through G	3.0	2.5	–71.2	26.1	–142.9	54.1	73.5	64.6
H. Total Change in Reserves	–3.0	–2.5	71.2	–26.1	142.9	–54.1	–73.5	–64.6
Monetary gold	#	–.3	–.1	–.4	#	#	#	#
SDRs	1.1	–.3	–.6	4.3	#	–.1	–.8	.9
Reserve position in the Fund	#	#	#	#	#	#	#	#
Foreign exchange assets	–22.9	3.9	83.7	–76.6	60.7	–45.1	–58.6	–61.3
Other claims	25.6	.9	–11.8	5.1	87.1	8.5	–10.4	~
Use of Fund credit	–6.8	–6.7	#	41.5	–4.8	–17.5	–3.7	–4.3
Conversion rates: córdobas per SDR	8.112	8.203	8.797	11.958	13.080	11.851	11.095	10.743
Conversion rates: U.S. dollars per SDR	1.1545	1.1675	1.2520	1.2920	1.3015	1.1792	1.1040	1.0690

a. For 1956–81 data, see SALA, 23-2714.

SOURCE: IMF-BPS-Y, 1984.

Table 2715

PANAMA: IMF BALANCE OF PAYMENTS, 1976–83[a]

(M SDR)

Category	1976	1977	1978	1979	1980	1981	1982	1983
A. Current Account	-152.6	-133.1	-165.9	-240.7	-238.8	53.6	-178.0	123.9
Merchandise: exports f.o.b.	233.0	247.1	243.1	275.2	1,741.9	2,163.8	2,134.1	1,583.8
To Canal Zone	43.1	44.0	50.6	65.7	#	#	#	#
To rest of world								
By enterprises in colón Free Zone	~	~	~	~	1,494.7	1,886.9	1,833.2	1,299.3
By others								
Bananas	53.3	56.9	57.4	50.9	47.3	58.7	59.7	70.2
Petroleum	57.4	58.5	48.0	56.0	62.8	49.5	63.5	34.0
Other	79.2	87.7	87.1	102.6	137.0	168.8	177.7	180.4
Merchandise: imports f.o.b.	-678.5	-677.0	-688.6	-840.3	-2,300.8	-2,815.4	-2,756.0	-2,162.5
By enterprises in Colón Free Zone	~	~'	~	~	-1,374.5	-1,690.4	-1,540.2	-1,074.6
By others	-674.7	-672.2	-683.4	-834.7	-926.2	-1,125.0	-1,215.7	-1,087.8
Trade balance	-445.5	-429.9	-445.4	-565.1	-558.9	-651.6	-621.8	-578.7
Other goods, services, and income: credit	833.0	941.8	1,149.5	1,724.3	4,202.2	6,259.5	6,064.9	6,836.3
Other goods, services, and income: debit	-536.7	-643.0	-868.3	-1,409.4	-3,893.3	-5,580.8	-5,652.8	-6,170.8
Total: goods, services, and income	-149.2	-131.0	-164.2	-250.2	-249.9	27.2	-209.8	86.8
Private unrequited transfers	-24.0	-25.6	-26.8	-30.4	-40.1	-40.4	-49.8	-56.2
Total, excl. official unrequited transfers	-173.2	-156.7	-191.0	-280.7	-290.0	-13.1	-259.6	30.6
Official unrequited transfers	20.6	23.6	25.1	39.9	51.2	66.7	81.6	93.3
B. Direct Investment and Other Long-Term Capital	626.4	-96.8	360.5	243.0	-553.6	479.8	1,254.5	162.3
Direct investment	-9.2	9.3	-2.0	38.5	-35.8	.3	251.3	46.0
Portfolio investment	.1	10.8	56.2	157.8	-680.3	172.2	236.9	59.6
Other long-term capital								
Resident official sector	72.3	77.0	272.6	88.5	165.2	71.5	333.4	150.8
Deposit money banks	385.3	-351.9	-26.7	33.2	31.9	114.0	231.9	-12.4
Other sectors	177.9	157.9	60.4	-75.0	-34.6	121.9	201.1	-81.7
Loans received by public enterprises	178.5	161.5	69.0	-75.5	-19.3	-7.2	73.2	60.0
Loans received by private enterprises	.9	-1.3	-14.0	.2	-15.6	126.4	127.1	-143.2
Other	-1.5	-2.2	5.4	.4	.3	2.7	.8	1.6
Total, Groups A plus B	473.8	-229.9	194.6	2.3	-792.4	533.4	1,076.5	286.2
C. Other Short-Term Capital	-326.7	283.7	-124.5	302.9	291.8	-388.2	-1,185.6	-36.8
Resident official sector	.7	2.9	4.1	-2.5	1.3	2.0	4.3	.8
Deposit money banks	-326.5	323.2	-129.4	335.1	-295.9	-73.8	-570.3	63.0
Other sectors	-.9	-42.5	.8	-29.7	586.4	-316.3	-619.6	-100.7
D. Net Errors and Omissions	-132.4	-60.0	-1.2	-326.2	509.2	-209.3	95.4	-261.5
Total, Groups A through D	14.7	-6.2	68.9	-21.0	8.7	-64.0	-13.7	-12.1
E. Counterpart Items	-1.3	-2.9	-10.0	4.6	6.6	12.6	6.5	10.0
Monetization/demonetization of gold	#	#	#	#	#	#	#	#
Allocation/cancellation of SDRs	#	#	#	4.7	4.7	4.6	#	#
Valuation changes in reserves	-1.3	-2.9	-10.0	-.1	1.9	8.1	6.5	10.0
Total, Groups A through E	13.4	-9.1	59.0	-16.5	15.3	-51.3	-7.2	-2.1
F. Exceptional Financing	#	#	#	#	#	#	#	#
Total, Groups A through F	13.4	-9.1	59.0	-16.5	15.3	-51.3	-7.2	-2.1
G. Liabilities Constituting Foreign Authorities' Reserves	#	#	#	#	#	#	#	#
Total, Groups A through G	13.4	-9.1	59.0	-16.5	15.3	-51.3	-7.2	-2.1
H. Total Change in Reserves	-13.4	9.1	-59.0	16.5	-15.3	51.3	7.2	2.1
Monetary gold	#	#	#	#	#	#	#	#
SDRs	1.2	.7	.5	#	2.9	-1.7	-1.0	3.4
Reserve position in the Fund	#	#	-3.7	1.3	-5.6	8.1	#	-8.7
Foreign exchange assets	-39.7	8.9	-53.9	24.0	.9	-17.4	12.5	-100.6
Other claims	#	#	#	#	#	#	#	#
Use of Fund credit	25.1	-.5	-1.8	-8.9	-13.4	62.4	-4.3	108.0
Conversion rates: balboas per SDR	1.1545	1.1675	1.2520	1.2920	1.3015	1.1792	1.1040	1.0690
Conversion rates: U.S. dollars per SDR	1.1545	1.1675	1.2520	1.2920	1.3015	1.1792	1.1040	1.0690

a. For 1955–81 data, see SALA, 23-2715.

SOURCE: IMF-BPS, Jan. 1985.

Table 2716

PARAGUAY: IMF BALANCE OF PAYMENTS, 1976–83[a]

(M SDR)

Category	1976	1977	1978	1979	1980	1981	1982	1983
A. Current Account	-59.3	-50.3	-90.2	-159.4	-216.7	-317.5	-351.2	-231.4
Merchandise: exports f.o.b.	175.1	280.2	284.4	297.6	307.6	338.0	258.9	305.0
Cotton	29.4	67.8	78.4	76.3	81.3	109.7	110.9	73.8
Soybeans	27.9	48.1	30.6	62.9	32.3	40.3	81.2	70.8
Other	117.7	164.3	175.4	158.4	193.9	188.0	166.8	160.3
Merchandise: imports f.o.b.	-204.8	-308.4	-345.0	-446.7	-518.9	-655.0	-644.3	-515.8
Trade balance	-29.7	-28.3	-60.6	-149.1	-211.3	-317.1	-285.4	-210.9
Other goods, services, and income: credit	48.2	79.2	106.2	161.9	224.6	281.3	347.6	229.8
Other goods, services, and income: debit	-81.5	-102.3	-140.4	-177.9	-233.5	-286.6	-417.9	-256.2
Total: goods, services, and income	-63.0	-51.3	-94.8	-165.1	-220.2	-322.4	-355.7	-237.2
Private unrequited transfers	.8	.6	.5	2.4	2.4	2.1	1.4	1.3
Total, excl. official unrequited transfers	-62.2	-50.7	-94.3	-162.7	-217.8	-320.3	-354.3	-235.9
Official unrequited transfers	2.9	.4	4.2	3.3	1.2	2.8	3.2	4.5
B. Direct Investment and Other Long-Term Capital	101.6	73.0	132.9	104.9	147.7	142.8	240.4	270.5
Direct investment	-2.6	18.6	15.7	38.9	24.4	33.1	40.3	7.7
Portfolio investment	#	#	#	#	#	#	#	#
Other long-term capital								
Resident official sector	31.1	26.3	44.8	7.7	65.5	33.3	54.8	129.7
Deposit money banks	-1.6	.1	.1	2.4	.6	9.1	9.7	6.7
Other sectors	74.7	28.0	72.4	56.0	57.2	67.3	135.6	126.4
Trade credits received	7.2	4.8	15.3	18.0	15.4	11.4	-1.8	-2.1
Other loans received	67.6	23.2	57.1	38.0	41.7	57.0	151.4	128.4
Other	#	#	#	#	#	-1.0	-13.9	#
Total, Groups A plus B	42.3	22.7	42.7	-54.5	-69.0	-174.7	-110.8	39.1
C. Other Short-Term Capital	-6.9	88.6	84.9	171.2	200.6	219.1	72.0	-37.9
Resident official sector	-2.5	.9	4.6	9.9	2.8	6.4	14.9	23.2
Deposit money banks	-10.2	3.2	6.9	-7.2	-10.8	-11.4	.5	6.9
Other sectors	5.8	84.5	73.4	168.5	208.6	224.1	56.6	-68.0
D. Net Errors and Omissions	-.1	-17.4	13.7	6.9	-15.4	-11.1	-12.5	5.5
Total, Groups A through D	35.2	93.9	141.3	123.6	116.2	33.3	-51.2	6.7
E. Counterpart Items	.5	-9.0	-19.7	-3.6	19.2	57.4	35.9	-20.8
Monetization/demonetization of gold	#	#	#	#	#	#	#	#
Allocation/cancellation of SDRs	#	#	#	2.4	2.4	2.4	#	#
Valuation changes in reserves	.5	-9.0	-19.7	-6.0	16.8	55.0	35.9	-20.8
Total, Groups A through E	35.8	84.8	121.6	120.0	135.4	90.7	-15.3	-14.1
F. Exceptional Financing	#	#	#	#	#	#	#	#
Total, Groups A through F	35.8	84.8	121.6	120.0	135.4	90.7	-15.3	-14.1
G. Liabilities Constituting Foreign Authorities' Reserves	1.6	1.9	1.2	1.5	-.3	3.6	-5.4	-2.5
Total, Groups A through G	37.3	86.7	122.8	121.6	135.1	94.3	-20.8	-16,6
H. Total Change in Reserves	-37.3	-86.7	-122.8	-121.6	-135.1	-94.3	20.8	16.6
Monetary gold	#	-.2	-.2	-3.0	-.2	.3	.2	.2
SDRs	#	#	-.1	-2.8	-1.6	-4.0	-8.6	-6.7
Reserve position in the Fund	-1.0	-.9	.1	-1.7	-6.7	-10.3	-2.4	-4.7
Foreign exchange assets	-36.3	-84.1	-124.0	-113.4	-126.6	-80.5	33.4	31.6
Other claims	#	-1.6	1.3	-.6	.2	.3	-1.8	-3.7
Use of Fund credit	#	#	#	#	#	#	#	#
Conversion rates: guaraníes per SDR	145.47	147.11	157.75	162.79	163.99	148.57	139.11	134.69
Conversion rates: U.S. dollars per SDR	1.1545	1.1675	1.2520	1.2920	1.3015	1.1792	1.1040	1.0690

a. For 1951–81 data, see SALA, 23-2716.

SOURCE: IMF-BPS-Y, 1984.

Table 2717

PERU: IMF BALANCE OF PAYMENTS, 1976-83[a]

(M SDR)

Category	1976	1977	1978	1979	1980	1981	1982	1983
A. Current Account	-1,033	-790	-158	565	47	-1,468	-1,457	-818
Merchandise: exports f.o.b.	1,179	1,478	1,544	2,702	2,996	2,755	2,986	2,824
Copper	197	336	325	522	577	448	417	415
Petroleum and petroleum products	46	45	144	500	609	580	653	509
Other	936	1,097	1,076	1,681	1,810	1,727	1,915	1,900
Merchandise: imports f.o.b.	-1,819	-1,854	-1,278	-1,510	-2,355	-3,226	-3,373	-2,548
Trade balance	-640	-376	265	1,192	641	-471	-387	275
Other goods, services, and income: credit	342	358	379	504	732	828	809	774
Other goods, services, and income: debit	-786	-821	-847	-1,225	-1,430	-1,963	-2,030	-2,072
Total: goods, services, and income	-1,084	-839	-202	471	-57	-1,606	-1,608	-1,023
Private unrequited transfers	3	2	2	~	~	~	~	~
Total, excl. official unrequited transfers	-1,081	-836	-200	471	-57	-1,606	-1,608	-1,023
Official unrequited transfers	48	46	43	94	103	138	152	206
B. Direct Investment and Other Long-Term Capital	556	577	11	86	-73	310	944	182
Direct investment	147	46	20	55	21	109	42	35
Portfolio investment	#	#	#	#	#	#	#	#
Other long-term capital								
Resident official sector	415	515	-21	56	-143	85	760	227
Deposit money banks	#	#	#	#	#	#	#	#
Other sectors	-6	15	11	-25	49	116	142	-80
Total, Groups A plus B	-477	-213	-147	651	-26	-1,158	-513	-636
C. Other Short-Term Capital	#	-24	-155	-181	375	65	-108	-7
Resident official sector	#	-26	-94	-183	56	4	-245	57
Deposit money banks	#	#	-63	-42	11	64	25	-1
Other sectors	#	1	2	44	308	-3	112	-62
D. Net Errors and Omissions	-284	-96	41	-10	-144	439	408	-404
Total, Groups A through D	-761	-334	-261	460	205	-655	-213	-1,047
E. Counterpart Items	5	-11	-15	-19	-2	223	59	66
Monetization/demonetization of gold	#	#	#	#	#	#	#	#
Allocation/cancellation of SDRs	#	#	#	17	17	17	#	#
Valuation changes in reserves	5	-11	-15	-36	-19	206	59	66
Total, Groups A through E	-756	-345	-277	441	203	-432	-154	-980
F. Exceptional Financing	450	371	282	431	297	72	99	983
Grants from Subsidy Account	#	#	#	#	#	5	3	3
Long-term financing received by								
Monetary authorities	143	241	39	#	#	#	#	#
Government (debt rescheduling)	#	#	161	417	286	67	97	980
Short-term financing received by								
Monetary authorities	252	98	69	14	11	#	#	#
Deposit money banks	55	33	12	#	#	#	#	#
Total, Groups A through F	-306	26	5	872	500	-360	-55	3
G. Liabilities Constituting Foreign Authorities' Reserves	40	19	-6	-62	#	-20	-8	#
Total, Groups A through G	-266	45	-1	810	500	-381	-63	3
H. Total Change in Reserves	266	-45	1	-810	-500	381	63	-3
Monetary gold	#	#	#	-49	-134	-102	#	#
SDRs	34	1	-2	-76	72	#	-20	29
Reserve position in the Fund	31	#	#	#	#	#	#	#
Foreign exchange assets	50	-45	-3	-779	-470	522	-173	-110
Other claims	-7	-10	-81	-22	33	~	~	~
Use of Fund credit	159	10	87	117	-2	-39	256	78
Conversion rates: soles per SDR	65.13	97.85	195.73	290.12	375.95	497.98	770.12	1,740.96
Conversion rates: U.S. dollars per SDR	1.1545	1.1675	1.2520	1.2920	1.3015	1.1792	1.1040	1.0690

a. For 1956-81 data, see SALA, 23-2717.

SOURCE: IMF-BPS-Y, 1984.

Table 2718

URUGUAY: IMF BALANCE OF PAYMENTS, 1976–83[a]

(M SDR)

Category	1976	1977	1978	1979	1980	1981	1982	1983
A. Current Account	-63.9	-143.1	-101.4	-276.4	-544.8	-391.3	-212.5	-55.9
Merchandise: exports f.o.b.	489.4	523.8	548.0	610.0	813.3	1,042.9	1,138.0	1,081.8
Hides	33.3	23.9	24.2	36.4	30.9	43.0	65.9	70.5
Meat	117.3	94.2	76.4	81.3	139.7	216.4	182.5	231.4
Wool	86.5	103.4	105.5	78.5	163.4	200.2	185.7	157.7
Manufactures: leather	52.1	38.2	79.3	78.6	79.7	74.2	60.5	59.6
Manufactures: wool	26.7	69.5	46.9	59.0	72.1	80.7	79.3	91.7
Other	173.5	194.6	215.7	276.2	327.5	428.4	564.2	470.8
Merchandise: imports f.o.b.	-464.8	-588.2	-566.9	-902.6	-1,281.7	-1,350.2	-940.6	-692.0
Trade balance	24.6	-64.4	-18.9	-292.6	-468.4	-307.3	197.5	389.8
Other goods, services, and income: credit	119.5	178.6	195.8	356.3	411.2	523.1	387.8	297.0
Other goods, services, and income: debit	-214.6	-263.0	-284.0	-345.5	-494.3	-615.3	-807.1	-753.0
Total: goods, services, and income	-70.5	-148.8	-107.1	-281.9	-551.5	-399.5	-221.9	-66.2
Private unrequited transfers	-.9	1.8	1.1	1.2	1.5	2.5	9.4	10.3
Total, excl. official unrequited transfers	-71.4	-147.0	-106.0	-280.7	-550.0	-397.1	212.5	-55.9
Official unrequited transfers	7.5	3.9	4.6	4.3	5.1	5.8	#	#
B. Direct Investment and Other Long-Term Capital	48.6	86.7	121.6	277.7	310.6	293.1	466.6	602.0
Direct investment	#	56.5	102.9	166.8	222.4	41.2	-12.4	5.2
Portfolio investment	28.2	17.8	-6.9	-24.1	-5.2	2.6	-6.2	14.6
Other long-term capital								
Resident official sector	-14.2	.6	30.7	119.2	82.7	93.0	382.8	308.0
Deposit money banks	3.2	.4	-1.9	-2.0	3.7	-2.5	-4.9	34.4
Other sectors	31.4	11.4	-3.1	17.8	7.1	158.7	107.2	268.8
Total, Groups A plus B	-15.3	-56.4	20.1	1.3	-234.2	-98.2	254.1	546.0
C. Other Short-Term Capital	89.7	163.9	-38.1	64.2	256.2	263.9	514.5	-336.0
Resident official sector	25.8	3.8	-1.1	-2.1	-.1	2.8	76.1	37.9
Deposit money banks	-31.3	63.6	-31.8	98.8	236.1	73.7	217.6	-62.3
Other sectors	95.2	96.5	-5.2	-32.6	20.2	187.4	220.8	-311.6
D. Net Errors and Omissions	-11.2	36.1	126.7	-8.4	68.8	-136.9	-1,144.9	-276.1
Total, Groups A through D	63.2	143.6	108.8	57.1	90.8	28.8	-376.4	-66.1
E. Counterpart Items	-.1	-11.2	2.4	25.0	26.7	36.6	-53.4	-41.5
Monetization/demonetization of gold	#	#	.6	19.7	16.7	-3.1	-76.6	48.6
Allocation/cancellation of SDRs	#	#	#	8.7	8.7	8.6	#	#
Valuation changes in reserves	.1	-11.2	1.8	-3.4	1.3	31.1	23.2	7.2
Total, Groups A through E	63.1	132.5	111.2	82.1	117.5	65.4	-429.8	-107.6
F. Exceptional Financing	18.5	-.3	#	#	#	#	#	#
Long-term loans	19.9	#	#	#	#	#	#	#
Commercial arrears	-1.4	-.3	#	#	#	#	#	#
Total, Groups A through F	81.6	132.2	111.2	82.1	117.5	65.4	-429.8	-107.6
G. Liabilities Constituting Foreign Authorities' Reserves	-18.4	10.2	-5.9	8.7	-17.5	-7.1	-1.0	.3
Total, Groups A through G	63.2	142.4	105.3	90.8	100.0	58.3	-430.8	-107.3
H. Total Change in Reserves	-63.2	-142.4	-105.3	-90.8	-100.0	-58.3	-430.8	107.3
Monetary gold	#	-1.0	-.6	-19.7	-16.7	3.1	76.6	48.6
SDRs	-2.1	-4.8	-2.9	-14.8	.2	-11.2	35.5	-1.9
Reserve position in the Fund	#	#	-16.7	.5	-10.5	-1.3	28.0	-9.5
Foreign exchange assets	-69.8	-86.0	31.9	-50.3	-50.6	-52.2	201.4	-80.7
Other claims	-16.5	-24.0	-18.8	-6.6	-22.4	3.4	2.5	10.8
Use of Fund credit	25.1	-26.6	-98.2	#	#	#	86.8	140.0
Conversion rates: new pesos per SDR	3.851	5.462	7.587	10.156	11.843	12.759	15.356	36.923
Conversion rates: U.S. dollars per SDR	1.1545	1.1675	1.2520	1.2920	1.3015	1.1792	1.1040	1.0690

a. For 1959–81 data, see SALA, 23-2718.

SOURCE: IMF-BPS, Oct. 1984.

Table 2719

VENEZUELA: IMF BALANCE OF PAYMENTS, 1976–83[a]
(M SDR)

Category	1976	1977	1978	1979	1980	1981	1982	1983
A. Current Account	220	–2,723	–4,581	271	3,633	3,392	–3,846	3,468
Merchandise: exports f.o.b.	8,015	8,185	7,256	10,959	14,637	16,930	14,793	13,708
Oil	7,547	7,802	6,881	10,431	13,889	16,008	14,017	12,713
Other	468	383	375	528	748	922	776	995
Merchandise: imports f.o.b.	–6,355	–8,731	–8,973	–7,743	–8,357	–10,281	–12,304	–6,341
Trade balance	1,660	–546	–1,717	3,216	6,280	6,649	2,489	7,368
Other goods, services, and income: credit	973	1,191	1,415	1,661	2,444	3,864	3,433	2,516
Other goods, services, and income: debit	–2,211	–3,125	–3,953	–4,291	–4,754	–6,773	–9,189	–6,235
Total: goods, services, and income	421	–2,480	–4,256	586	3,970	3,739	–3,267	3,649
Private unrequited transfers	–146	–198	–296	–300	–321	–325	–557	–181
Total, excl. official unrequited transfers	275	–2,678	–4,552	286	3,649	3,414	–3,824	3,468
Official unrequited transfers	–55	–45	–29	–15	–16	–22	–22	#
B. Direct Investment and Other Long-Term Capital	1,270	1,806	2,968	1,117	1,583	687	2,858	247
Direct investment	–770	–3	54	68	42	156	229	–58
In resident oil enterprises	–896	#	#	#	#	#	#	#
In other enterprises	126	–3	54	68	42	156	229	–58
Portfolio investment	626	–35	99	–57	1,007	70	1,433	497
Other long-term capital								
Resident official sector	771	1,071	1,481	794	–223	–222	1,193	76
Deposit money banks	207	355	549	–507	169	471	~	#
Other sectors	436	419	786	819	588	212	3	–268
Assets of Venezuelan Investment Fund	–226	–274	–166	–113	–124	–218	–209	–83
Other	662	693	952	932	711	430	212	–184
Total, Groups A plus B	1,490	–916	–1,613	1,388	5,215	4,079	–988	3,715
C. Other Short-Term Capital	–1,213	–349	–427	1,399	–1,457	–2,283	–4,451	–822
Resident official sector	10	38	–6	–2	79	28	–52	–16
Deposit money banks	31	2	–168	–50	–21	30	830	–529
Other sectors	–1,255	–388	–252	1,452	–1,515	–2,341	–5,229	–277
D. Net Errors and Omissions	1,753	1,951	1,189	385	–867	–1,814	–1,957	–2,747
Total, Groups A through D	2,029	686	–850	3,172	2,892	–18	–7,396	145
E. Counterpart Items	76	–418	–585	–54	494	1,464	868	316
Monetization/demonetization of gold	#	#	#	–1	#	#	#	#
Allocation/cancellation of SDRs	#	#	#	69	69	67	#	#
Valuation changes in reserves	76	–418	–585	–122	425	1,396	868	316
Total, Groups A through E	2,105	268	–1,435	3,118	3,386	1,446	–6,528	461
F. Exceptional Financing	#	#	#	#	#	#	#	#
Total, Groups A through F	2,105	268	–1,435	3,118	3,386	1,446	–6,528	461
G. Liabilities Constituting Foreign Authorities' Reserves	#	#	#	#	#	#	#	#
Total, Groups A through G	2,105	268	–1,435	3,118	3,386	1,446	–6,528	461
H. Total Change in Reserves	–2,105	–268	1,435	–3,118	–3,386	–1,446	6,528	–461
Monetary gold	#	#	#	#	#	#	#	#
SDRs	–2	–11	–30	–101	–2	–112	–17	62
Reserve position in the Fund	–121	93	245	180	–82	–59	–133	–195
Foreign exchange assets	309	542	1,522	–1,003	463	–1,666	1,200	–1,209
Other claims	–2,291	–892	–301	–2,194	–3,765	391	5,478	880
Use of Fund credit	#	#	#	#	#	#	#	#
Conversion rates: bolívares per SDR	4.9528	5.0116	5.3742	5.5459	5.5868	5.0615	4.7390	4.5940
Conversion rates: U.S. dollars per SDR	1.1545	1.1675	1.2520	1.2920	1.3015	1.1792	1.1040	1.0690

a. For 1956–81 data, see SALA, 23–2719.

SOURCE: IMF-BPS-Y, 1984.

Table 2720

UNITED STATES: IMF BALANCE OF PAYMENTS, 1976–83[a]

(M SDR)

Category	1976	1977	1978	1979	1980	1981	1982	1983
A. Current Account	3.59	–12.39	–12.52	–.72	1.49	5.17	–8.58	–39.21
Merchandise: exports f.o.b.	99.40	103.48	113.29	142.74	172.38	201.02	191.12	187.37
Merchandise: imports f.o.b.	–107.63	–130.09	–140.55	–164.04	–191.95	–224.89	–224.36	–244.74
Trade balance	–8.23	–26.61	–27.25	–21.31	–19.57	–23.87	–33.24	–57.37
Other goods, services, and income: credit	49.28	54.37	62.15	79.16	90.84	117.71	125.24	123.50
Reinvested earnings	6.67	5.49	9.02	14.68	13.06	11.39	5.72	8.49
Other investment income	18.70	22.08	24.63	34.93	42.66	61.98	70.25	63.60
Other	23.90	26.80	28.49	29.55	35.12	44.34	49.27	51.40
Other goods, services, and income: debit	–32.85	–35.87	–42.94	–53.85	–63.95	–82.35	–92.56	–96.62
Reinvested earnings	–1.44	–1.36	–2.06	–3.07	4.72	–3.19	1.18	–1.29
Other investment income	–10.10	–10.81	–15.20	–22.40	–27.60	–41.29	–51.96	–48.81
Other	–21.31	–23.69	–25.67	–28.38	–31.63	–37.88	–41.78	–46.52
Total: goods, services, and income	8.19	–8.11	–8.05	4.00	7.32	11.49	–.55	–30.49
Private unrequited transfers	–.79	–.70	–.69	–.70	–.79	–.78	–1.06	–.95
Total, excl. official unrequited transfers	7.41	–8.81	–8.74	3.30	6.53	10.70	–1.61	–31.44
Official unrequited transfers	–3.82	–3.57	–3.78	–4.02	–5.04	–5.54	–6.97	–7.77
Grants (excluding military)	–2.72	–2.39	–2.54	–2.74	–3.63	–3.80	–4.92	–5.70
Other	–1.09	–1.18	–1.24	–1.28	–1.41	–1.74	–2.05	–2.06
B. Direct Investment and Other Long-Term Capital	–13.10	–10.61	–9.37	–18.30	–6.55	–2.26	–3.54	–6.75
Direct investment	–6.57	–7.00	–6.53	–10.35	–1.83	11.74	17.92	5.97
In United States	3.76	3.19	6.31	9.18	12.97	19.81	13.51	10.58
Abroad	–10.33	–10.19	–12.84	–19.54	–14.80	–8.08	4.40	–4.61
Portfolio investment	–3.99	–.44	–2.9	–1.68	–2.20	–2.28	–.77	4.00
Other long-term capital								
Resident official sector	22	–2.45	–2.31	–2.57	–4.50	–4.31	–6.25	–4.72
Disbursements on loans extended	–5.05	–4.76	–5.28	–5.48	–6.69	–6.85	–7.81	–7.61
Repayments on loans extended	2.21	2.29	2.32	2.92	3.11	3.37	3.45	4.28
Other	3.06	.03	.64	–.01	–.92	–.83	–1.89	–1.39
Deposit money banks	–1.86	–.34	–.05	–4.44	–2.42	–11.97	–14.45	–12.00
Other sectors	–90	–.38	–.19	.75	#	#	#	#
Total, Groups A plus B	–9.51	–23.00	–21.89	–19.02	–5.06	2.90	–12.12	–45.95
C. Other Short-Term Capital	–8.72	–5.16	–14.77	7.18	–21.07	–22.32	–16.28	33.74
Resident official sector	–.02	–1.16	.22	–.27	1.35	1.00	6.50	5.23
Deposit money banks	–7.12	–3.64	–13.64	15.96	–21.02	–18.30	–23.87	29.25
Other sectors	–1.59	–.36	–1.36	–8.51	–1.41	–5.02	1.09	–.74
D. Net Errors and Omissions	9.14	–1.73	10.22	19.72	19.17	18.51	20.09	8.47
Total, Groups A through D	–9.10	–29.89	–26.44	7.87	–6.96	–.91	1.69	–3.75
E. Counterpart Items	–.02	–.12	–.66	–2.22	.80	.63	–.13	–.43
Monetization/demonetization of gold	#	#	–.40	–2.81	–.14	–.09	–.03	–.26
Allocation/cancellation of SDRs	#	#	#	.87	.87	.86	#	#
Valuation changes in reserves	–.02	–.12	–.26	–.29	.07	–.13	–.11	–.11
Total, Groups A through E	–9.11	–30.01	–27.10	5.65	–6.16	–.27	1.56	–4.18
F. Exceptional Financing	#	#	1.23	2.85	.90	#	#	#
Security issues in foreign currencies	#	#	1.23	2.85	.90	#	#	#
Total, Groups A through F	–9.11	–30.01	–25.87	8.50	–5.26	–.27	1.56	–4.18
G. Liabilities Constituting Foreign Authorities' Reserves	11.31	30.21	24.62	–10.70	11.45	4.20	2.84	4.86
Total, Groups A through G	2.20	.20	–1.25	–2.21	6.19	3.93	4.39	.68
H. Total Change in Reserves	–2.20	–.20	1.25	2.21	–6.19	–3.93	–4.39	–.68
Monetary gold	#	–.10	.35	2.76	.13	.10	.03	.25
SDRs	–.07	–.10	.97	–.87	.02	–1.47	–1.24	–.04
Reserve position in the Fund	–1.93	–.26	3.27	–.15	–1.29	–2.11	–2.32	–4.14
Foreign exchange assets	–.21	.26	–3.34	.47	–5.06	–.45	–.86	3.25
Other claims	#	#	#	#	#	#	#	#
Use of Fund credit	#	#	#	#	#	#	#	#
Conversion rates: U.S. dollars per SDR	1.1545	1.1675	1.2520	1.2920	1.3015	1.1792	1.1040	1.0690

a. For 1953–81 data, see SALA, 23-2720.

SOURCE: IMF-BPS, Nov. 1984.

Table 2721

IMF VALUE OF MERCHANDISE IMPORTS,[1] 19 LC, 1951-83

(M US)

Year	A. ARGENTINA	B. BOLIVIA	C. BRAZIL	D. CHILE	E. COLOMBIA	F. COSTA RICA	H. DOMINICAN REP.	I. ECUADOR	J. EL SALVADOR	K. GUATEMALA
1951	-1,311	90.3	1,703	-308	~	47.7	76.9	52.0	67.0	78.9
1952	-1,045	97.3	-1,702	-331	~	59.2	97.0	57.8	68.8	73.4
1953	-704	-71.4	-1,116	-304	~	-64.8	-8.60	-61.8	-74.4	-78.5
1954	-866	-71.6	-1,408	-298	~	-70.9	-83.1	-100.0	-86.7	-85.8
1955	-1,038	-77.6	-1,099	-327	~	-77.7	-100.2	-94.7	-91.9	-98.1
1956	-988	-79.1	-1,046	-332	-614	-81.6	-110.0	-95.9	-105.0	-126.9
1957	-1,160	-85.9	-1,285	-383	-451	-92.0	-117.5	-98.5	-115.2	-136.1
1958	-1,091	-74.1	-1,179	-363	-384	-88.9	-134.4	-102.2	-108.3	-138.1
1959	-879	-62.4	-1,210	-361	-402	-93.5	-111.5	-96.1	-99.7	124.3
1960	-1,106	-68.2	-1,293	-474	-496	-98.9	-90.3	-109.8	-122.6	-124.8
1961	-1,200	-74.7	-1,292	-532	-531	-96.0	-72.1	-108.7	-109.0	-120.6
1962	-1,200	-92.5	-1,304	-512	-537	-102.4	-132.3	-112.1	-124.9	-122.9
1963	-868	-98.1	-1,294	-490	-497	-112.7	-164.6	-118.7	-152.2	-150.4
1964	-953	-106.7	-1,086	-529	-582	-125.8	-202.4	-140.0	-191.8	-180.5
1965	-1,062	-126.6	-941	-530	-430	-160.9	-120.7	-151.8	-185.7	-206.1
1966	-995	-138.8	-1,303	-661	-639	-162.1	-166.9	-160.3	-201.0	-201.8
1967	-970	-151	-1,441	-651	-464	-173.7	-174.1	-195.7	-204.9	-224.9
1968	-1,035	-161.5	-1,855	-726	-615	-193.7	-196.8	-231.6	-198.2	-237.6
1969	-1,395	-173.4	-1,993	-786	-648	-221.5	-217.2	-218.7	-193.0	-240.9
1970	-1,499	-132.2	-2,507	-867	-802	-286.8	-278.0	-249.6	-194.7	-266.6
1971	-1,653	-144.3	-3,256	-927	-903	-317.2	-390.7	-306.8	-226.0	-290.0
1972	-1,685	-153.2	-4,193	-1,012	-849	-337.1	-337.7	-284.1	-249.7	-294.8
1973	-1,978	-193.2	-6,154	-1,329	-982	-412.1	-421.9	-397.5	-339.8	-391.4
1974	-3,510	-324.1	-12,562	-1,901	-1,511	-648.9	-673.0	-875.2	-522.2	-631.5
1975	-2,765	-469.9	-12,042	-1,597	-1,424	-627.2	-772.7	-1,006.3	-550.7	-672.4
1976	-3,799	-512.3	-12,347	-1,505	-1,665	-695.4	-763.6	-1,047.9	-618.0	-950.7
1977	-3,488	-579.0	-12,023	-2,152	-1,979	-925.0	-849.3	-1,360.5	-861.0	-1,087.2
1978	-6,028	-723.9	-13,631	-2,886	-2,564	-1,049.4	-862.4	-1,704.0	-951.1	-1,283.8
1979	-9,394	-815.0	-17,961	-4,190	-2,996	-1,257.2	-1,137.5	-2,096.8	-938.5	-1,401.7
1980	-8,421	-680.1	-22,955	-5,469	-4,300	-1,375.2	-1,519.7	-2,241.8	-897.0	-1,472.6
1981	712	-680.1	-22,091	-6,513	-4,763	-1,090.6	-1,451.7	-2,361.5	-898.4	-1,540.0
1982	2,726	-428.7	-19,395	-3,643	-5,404	-780.3	-1,257.5	-2,181.0	-825.9	-1,284.3
1983	~	~	~	-2,837	~	~	~	~	~	~

1. FOB.

SOURCE: IMF-IFS-Y, 1979, 1983, 1984.

Table 2721 (Continued)

IMF VALUE OF MERCHANDISE IMPORTS,[1] 19 LC, 1951–83

(M US)

Year	L. HAITI	M. HONDURAS	N. MEXICO	O. NICARAGUA	P. PANAMA	Q. PARAGUAY	R. PERU	S. URUGUAY	T. VENEZUELA	UNITED STATES
1951	~	47.6	~	~	~	26.9	~	~	~	~
1952	~	58.4	~	~	~	32.7	~	~	~	-10,963
1953	~	-54.6	-768	~	~	-30.9	~	~	~	-10,354
1954	~	-52.3	-760	~	~	-34.4	~	~	~	
1955	~	-55.3	-840	~	-975.5	-33.9	~	~	~	-11,516
1956	~	-57.7	-1,108	-57.6	-106.7	-37.1	-341	~	-1,170	-12,776
1957	~	-68.6	-1,102	-68.4	-121.7	-39.2	-397	~	-1,775	-13,291
1958	~	-65.7	-1,090	-65.3	-941.1	-44.3	-331	~	-1,512	-12,952
1959	~	-61.6	-964	-52.7	-97.2	-36.5	-273	-151.7	-1,520	-15,310
1960	~	-64.1	-1,132	-56.4	-108.7	-43.9	-327	-187.9	-1,145	-14,758
1961	~	-65.2	-1,086	-58.7	-123.8	-47.9	-408	-182.8	-1,055	-14,537
1962	~	-72.8	-1,097	-78.7	-144.5	-41.1	-468	-207.6	-1,161	-16,260
1963	-39.1	-88.3	-1,186	-91.0	-163.7	-41.4	-509	-151.6	-1,037	-17,048
1964	-37.1	-94.7	-1,424	-109.8	-168.2	-45.1	-511	-168.6	-1,192	-18,700
1965	-42.6	-113.2	-1,498	-133.9	-192.4	-56.7	-673	-123.1	-1,354	-21,510
1966	-43.7	-138.0	-1,581	-151.8	-217.7	-63.3	-803	-132.2	-1,316	-25,490
1967	-40.3	-152.0	-1,760	-172.2	-232.3	-65.7	-810	-146.4	-1,366	-26,870
1968	-38.7	-169.4	-1,892	-166.5	-246.1	-73.5	-673	-135.9	-1,510	-32,990
1969	-42.1	-169.7	-1,983	-159.3	-285.1	-81.2	-659	-170.0	-1,554	-35,810
1970	-47.8	-203.4	-2,236	-178.6	-331.0	-76.6	-699	-203.1	-1,713	-39,860
1971	-53.2	-178.0	-2,158	-190.2	-363.9	-82.9	-730	-203.0	-1,896	-45,580
1972	-57.3	-176.5	-2,610	-205.5	-408.7	-78.7	-812	-178.1	-2,222	-55,800
1973	-66.5	-243.4	-3,656	-327.5	-458.1	-127.3	-1,097	-248.6	-2,626	-70,500
1974	-96.5	-387.5	-5,791	-541.8	-760.7	-198.3	-1,909	-433.6	-3,876	-103,820
1975	-102.1	-372.4	-6,278	-482.1	-823.1	-227.3	-2,389	-494.0	-5,462	-98,180
1976	-164.2	-432.5	-5,771	-485.0	-783.3	-236.4	-2,099	-536.6	-7,337	-124,230
1977	-199.9	-550.1	-5,625	-704.2	-790.4	-360.1	-2,164	-686.7	-10,194	-151,910
1978	-207.4	-654.1	-7,992	-553.3	-862.1	-432.0	-1,601	-709.8	-11,234	-176,030
1979	-220.1	-783.5	-12,131	-388.9	-1,085.7	-577.1	-1,955	-1,166.2	-10,004	-212,030
1980	-319.0	-954.1	-18,896	-802.9	-2,995	-675.3	-3,062	-1,668.2	-10,877	-249,770
1981	-360.1	-898.1	-24,037	-922.4	-3,320	-772.4	-3,802	-1,592.1	-12,123	-265,080
1982	-301.9	-680.7	-14,489	-723.5	-3,043	-711.3	-3,787	-1,038.4	-13,584	-247,670
1983	-314.3	~	~	-760.9	-2,312	~	~	~	~	-261,320

1. FOB.

SOURCE: IMF-IFS-Y, 1979, 1983, 1984.

Table 2722

IMF VALUE OF MERCHANDISE EXPORTS,[1] 19 LC, 1951–83
(M US)

Year	A. ARGENTINA	B. BOLIVIA	C. BRAZIL	D. CHILE	E. COLOMBIA	F. COSTA RICA	H. DOMINICAN REP.	I. ECUADOR	J. EL SALVADOR	K. GUATEMALA
1951	1,169	124.5	1,770	378	~	60.9	119.5	70.5	83.6	82.5
1952	678	95.1	1,416	462	~	71.9	116.6	101.7	87.0	88.8
1953	1,102	64.0	1,539	339	~	79.3	104.3	92.3	93.6	99.5
1954	1,027	72.3	1,558	406	~	85.7	121.0	125.1	104.6	104.8
1955	929	81.0	1,419	487	~	80.7	115.0	114.9	106.5	106.3
1956	944	84.6	1,483	489	654	64.7	121.8	117.8	123.0	122.5
1957	974	76.9	1,392	402	590	82.7	161.5	137.1	127.1	115.9
1958	994	51.3	1,244	364	527	93.1	126.4	136.9	118.0	107.9
1959	1,009	61.6	1,282	451	514	76.0	131.8	144.2	111.8	103.7
1960	1,079	54.4	1,270	480	480	87.0	157.4	146.3	102.6	115.9
1961	964	63.8	1,405	444	462	83.3	138.9	132.0	118.8	114.0
1962	1,216	63.6	1,215	484	462	92.7	169.6	149.1	138.9	119.0
1963	1,365	71.9	1,406	493	474	94.9	174.3	150.9	150.2	153.4
1964	1,410	100.1	1,430	592	623	114.4	179.4	161.9	175.5	174.3
1965	1,493	115.1	1,596	692	581	111.7	125.5	181.0	190.0	192.1
1966	1,593	130.9	1,741	860	526	135.7	136.7	187.3	189.5	231.9
1967	1,464	153.2	1,654	883	552	143.3	156.2	198.9	207.9	203.9
1968	1,368	155.5	1,881	908	605	170.0	163.5	210.7	211.7	233.5
1969	1,612	177.8	2,311	1,172	672	189.6	183.4	193.4	202.1	262.5
1970	1,773	190.4	2,739	1,113	788	231.0	214.0	234.9	236.1	297.1
1971	1,740	181.6	2,891	1,000	754	225.3	240.7	238.0	243.9	286.9
1972	1,941	201.3	3,941	851	979	278.8	347.6	323.2	301.7	335.9
1973	3,266	260.8	6,092	1,316	1,262	344.8	442.1	584.7	358.4	442.0
1974	3,930	556.5	7,814	2,152	1,495	440.2	636.8	1,225.4	464.5	582.3
1975	2,961	444.7	8,492	1,591	1,717	493.1	893.8	1,012.8	533.0	640.9
1976	3,916	563.0	9,961	2,116	2,243	592.4	716.4	1,307.2	744.6	760.4
1977	5,651	634.3	11,923	2,186	2,713	827.8	780.5	1,400.8	973.5	1,160.2
1978	6,401	627.3	12,473	2,460	3,206	863.9	675.5	1,529.2	801.6	1,092.4
1979	7,810	761.8	15,244	3,835	3,506	942.0	868.5	2,150.5	1,132.3	1,221.4
1980	8,021	941.9	20,132	4,705	4,062	1,000.9	961.9	2,544.2	1,075.3	1,519.8
1981	9,143	909.1	23,276	3,836	3,219	1,002.6	1,188.0	2,544.2	798.0	1,299.0
1982	7,599	827.7	20,173	3,706	3,215	870.8	767.7	2,544.2	704.1	1,199.6
1983	~	~	~	3,851	~	~	~	2,343.0	~	~

1. FOB.

SOURCE: IMF-IFS-Y, 1979, 1983, 1984.

Table 2722 (Continued)

IMF VALUE OF MERCHANDISE EXPORTS,[1] 19 LC, 1951-83
(M US)

Year	L. HAITI	M HONDURAS	N. MEXICO	O. NICARAGUA	P. PANAMA	Q. PARAGUAY	R. PERU	S. URUGUAY	T. VENEZUELA	UNITED STATES
1951	?	67.7	?	?	?	38.3	?	?	?	?
1952	?	64.9	?	?	?	31.8	?	?	?	?
1953	?	69.9	-169	?	?	25.4	?	?	?	12,254
1954	?	56.4	668	?	?	34.8	?	?	?	12,814
1955	?	53.7	861	?	76	38.7	?	?	?	14,264
1956	?	72.9	844	65.5	73	36.8	-321	?	2,221	17,350
1957	?	64.8	740	70.6	70	36.9	332	?	2,764	19,390
1958	?	69.5	752	70.4	40	33.4	292	?	2,508	16,265
1959	?	68.5	744	75.0	43	35.4	323	108.3	2,326	16,298
1960	?	63.1	778	63.9	39	36.5	445	129.4	2,384	19,650
1961	?	73.0	826	69.9	41	43.1	510	174.7	2,453	20,180
1962	?	81.5	930	90.4	60	40.4	556	153.5	2,544	20,781
1963	43.2	84.4	985	106.6	73	39.5	555	166.2	2,464	22,272
1964	37.9	95.1	1,054	125.5	82	46.2	685	183.6	2,480	25,501
1965	37.8	128.2	1,146	149.2	93	60.8	685	196.3	2,482	26,461
1966	34.8	144.4	1,244	142.5	103	53.6	789	190.3	2,404	29,310
1967	32.3	155.9	1,152	147.9	109	50.4	742	159.8	2,495	20,670
1968	36.3	181.0	1,258	162.3	118	50.0	850	179.3	2,468	33,630
1969	36.7	170.9	1,454	158.7	133	55.2	881	199.2	2,409	36,410
1970	39.1	178.2	1,348	178.6	130	65.3	1,034	224.1	2,602	42,450
1971	45.3	194.6	1,409	187.3	138	66.5	890	196.8	3,103	43,310
1972	39.2	212.1	1,717	249.4	146	85.6	945	281.6	3,152	49,370
1973	49.6	266.6	2,141	278.4	162	128.0	1,112	327.6	4,721	71,420
1974	62.8	300.3	2,999	381.0	251	173.2	1,506	281.4	11,085	98,310
1975	71.2	309.7	3,007	374.9	331	188.0	1,291	384.9	8,853	107,120
1976	99.7	411.7	3,475	541.8	269	202.1	1,360	565.0	9,253	114,740
1977	137.6	529.9	4,604	636.2	289	327.1	1,726	611.5	9,545	120,810
1978	149.9	626.2	6,246	646.0	304	356.1	1,941	686.1	9,084	142,050
1979	138.0	756.5	9,301	615.9	356	384.5	3,520	788.1	14,164	184,470
1980	215.8	850.3	16,066	450.4	2,318	400.3	3,898	1,058.5	19,051	224,240
1981	151.1	783.8	19,838	499.8	2,567	398.5	3,249	1,229.7	19,963	237,020
1982	177.1	676.5	21,374	407.7	2,414	396.2	3,230	1,256.4	16,332	211,210
1983	186.6	?	?	411.4	1,726	?	?	?	?	200,250

1. FOB.

SOURCE: IMF-IFS-Y, 1979, 1983, 1984.

Table 2723

IMF TRADE BALANCES, 19 LC, 1951-83
(M US)

Year	A. ARGENTINA	B. BOLIVIA	C. BRAZIL	D. CHILE	E. COLOMBIA	F. COSTA RICA	H. DOMINICAN REP.	I. ECUADOR	J. EL SALVADOR	K. GUATEMALA
1951	-142	34.2	67	70	~	13.2	42.6	18.5	16.6	3.6
1952	-367	-2.2	-286	131	~	131.1	213.6	159.5	155.8	162.2
1953	398	-7.4	423	35	~	14.5	18.3	30.5	19.2	21.0
1954	161	.7	150	108	~	14.8	37.6	25.1	17.9	19.0
1955	-109	3.4	320	160	~	3.0	14.8	20.2	14.6	8.2
1956	-54	5.5	437	157	40	-16.9	11.8	21.9	18.0	-4.4
1957	-186	-9.0	107	19	139	-9.3	44.0	38.6	11.9	-20.2
1958	-97	-22.8	65	1	143	4.2	-8.0	34.7	9.7	-30.2
1959	130	-.8	72	90	112	-17.5	20.3	48.1	12.1	-20.6
1960	-27	-13.8	-23	6	-16	-11.9	67.1	36.5	-20.0	-8.9
1961	-328	-10.9	113	-88	-69	-12.7	66.8	23.3	9.8	-6.6
1962	16	-28.9	-89	-28	-75	-9.7	37.3	27.0	14.0	-3.9
1963	497	-26.2	112	3	-23	-17.8	9.7	32.2	-2.0	3.0
1964	457	-6.6	344	63	41	-11.4	-23.0	21.9	-16.3	-6.2
1965	431	-11.5	655	162	151	-49.2	4.8	29.2	4.3	-14.0
1966	598	-7.9	438	199	-113	-26.4	-30.2	27.0	-11.5	30.1
1967	494	1.4	213	232	88	-30.4	-18.5	3.2	3.0	-22.6
1968	333	-6.0	26	182	-10	-23.7	-33.3	-20.9	13.5	-4.1
1969	217	4.4	318	386	20	-31.9	-33.8	-25.3	9.1	21.6
1970	274	55.2	232	246	-14	-55	-64.0	-14.7	41.4	30.5
1971	87	37.3	-365	73	-148	-92.0	-69.0	-68.8	18.0	-3.1
1972	256	48.1	-252	-161	130	-58.3	9.9	39.1	52.0	41.1
1973	1,288	67.6	-61	-13	280	-67.4	20.2	187.2	18.6	50.7
1974	714	232.4	-4,748	251	-6	-208.8	-36.2	350.2	-57.7	49.2
1975	-549	-25	-3,550	-6	293	-134.2	121.1	6.6	-17.7	-31.4
1976	1,153	50.7	-2,386	611	578	-103.0	-47.2	259.3	63.7	-190.3
1977	1,852	55.3	-100	34	734	-97.3	-68.8	40.3	112.5	73.2
1978	2,913	-96.6	-1,158	-426	642	-185.5	-186.9	-174.8	-149.5	-191.4
1979	1,782	-53.2	-2,717	-355	510	-315.2	-268.9	53.7	177.6	-180.3
1980	-1,373	261.8	2,833	-764	-238	-374.3	-557.8	302.4	178.4	47.2
1981	712	229.0	1,185	-2,677	-1,544	-88.0	-263.7	182.7	-100.4	-241.0
1982	2,764	399.0	778	63	-2,189	90.5	-481.8	162.0	-121.8	-84.7
1983	3,716	~	~	1,014	~	~	~	~	~	~

SOURCE: IMF-IFS-Y, 1979, 1984.

Table 2723 (Continued)

IMF TRADE BALANCES, 19 LC, 1951–83

(M US)

Year	L. HAITI	M. HONDURAS	N. MEXICO	O. NICARAGUA	P. PANAMA	Q. PARAGUAY	R. PERU	S. URUGUAY	T. VENEZUELA	UNITED STATES
1951	5.7	20.1	?	?	?	11.4	?	?	?	?
1952	2.6	123.3	?	?	?	64.5	?	?	?	?
1953	-6.7	15.3	-16.9	?	?	-5.5	?	?	?	1,291
1954	8.0	4.1	-9.2	?	?	.4	?	?	?	2,460
1955	-17.1	-1.6	21	?	-21	4.8	?	?	?	2,748
1956	-6.1	15.2	-174	7.9	-34	-.3	-20	?	1,051	4,574
1957	-13.3	-3.8	-362	2.2	-52	-2.3	-65	?	989	6,099
1958	-5.4	3.8	-338	5.1	-54	-10.9	-39	?	996	3,313
1959	-9.5	6.9	-220	22.3	-54	-1.1	50	-43.4	806	988
1960	-5.3	-1.0	-354	7.5	-70	-7.4	118	-58.5	1,239	4,892
1961	-21.4	7.8	-260	11.2	-82	-4.8	102	-8.1	1,398	5,571
1962	-7.1	8.7	-167	11.7	-85	-.7	88	-54.1	1,383	4,521
1963	4.1	-3.9	-201	15.6	-91	-1.9	46	14.6	1,427	5,224
1964	.8	.4	-370	15.7	-86	1.1	174	15.0	1,288	6,801
1965	-4.8	15.0	-325	15.3	-100	4.1	32	73.2	1,128	4,951
1966	-8.9	6.4	-337	-9.3	-114	-9.7	-14	58.1	1,088	3,820
1967	-8.0	3.9	-608	-24.3	-123	-15.3	-68	13.4	1,129	3,800
1968	-2.4	11.6	-634	-4.2	-129	-23.5	177	43.4	958	640
1969	-5.4	1.2	-529	-.6	-153	-26.0	222	29.2	855	600
1970	-8.7	-25.2	-888	#	-201	-11.3	335	21.0	889	2,590
1971	-9.7	16.6	-749	-2.9	-226	-16.4	159	-6.2	1,207	-2,270
1972	-18.0	35.6	-894	43.9	-263	6.8	133	102.9	930	-6,420
1973	-16.9	23.2	-1,515	-49.1	-296	.7	15	79.0	2,095	950
1974	-33.7	-87.2	-2,791	-160.8	-509	-25.1	-403	-52.2	7,209	-5,510
1975	-50.9	-62.7	-3,272	-107.2	-492	-39.3	-1,099	-109.2	3,391	8,910
1976	-64.5	-20.8	-2,295	56.8	-514	-34.3	-740	28.4	1,916	-9,490
1977	-62.3	-20.2	-1,021	-68.0	-502	-33.0	-438	-75.2	-649	-31,100
1978	-57.5	-28.4	-1,745	92.7	-560	-75.9	340	-23.7	-2,150	-33,980
1979	-82.1	-26.9	-2,830	227.0	-730	-192.6	1,566	-378.1	4,160	-27,560
1980	-103.2	-103.8	-2,830	-352.5	-677	-275.0	837	-609.7	8,174	-25,530
1981	-209.0	-114.8	-4,099	422.6	-752	-373.9	-553	-362.4	7,804	-28,050
1982	-124.8	-4.2	6,885	-315.8	-631	-315.1	-557	218.0	2,748	-36,470
1983	-127.7	?	?	-349.5	-586	?	?	?	?	-61,070

SOURCE: IMF-IFS-Y, 1979, 1984.

Table 2724

PHYSICAL HOLDINGS OF GOLD, 18 LC, 1950-82

(M Ounces, YE)

	Country	1950	1951	1952	1953	1954	1955	1956	1957	1958	1959	1960	1961	1962	1963	1964	1965	1966	1967	1968	1969	1970
A.	ARGENTINA	2.36*	7.62	8.19	10.61	10.61	10.61	6.40	3.59	1.70	1.60	2.96	5.42	1.73	2.22	2.03	1.88	2.39	2.39	3.11	3.85	3.99
B.	BOLIVIA	.65	.65	.59	.63	.14	--	.03	.02	.03	.03	.03	.09	.09	.06	.13	.19	.21	.27	.31	.33	.36
C.	BRAZIL	9.09	9.11	9.14	9.17	9.20	9.23	9.26	9.26	9.29	9.33	8.20	8.14	7.87	8.15	2.61	1.80	1.30	1.30	1.29	1.29	1.29
D.	CHILE	1.15	1.29	1.19	1.20	1.21	1.27	1.31	1.15	1.15	1.19	1.29	1.37	1.22	1.23	1.23	1.25	1.29	1.29	1.32	1.35	1.33
E.	COLOMBIA	2.11	1.37	2.14	2.46	2.43	2.46	1.63	1.77	2.06	2.03	2.23	2.51	1.63	1.77	1.66	1.00	.71	.89	.89	.74	.49
F.	COSTA RICA	.06	.06	.06	.06	.06	.06	.06	.06	.06	.06	.06	.06	.06	.06	.06	.06	.06	.06	.06	.06	.06
H.	DOMINICAN REP.	.11	.35	.35	.35	.35	.35	.33	.33	.33	.30	.30	.09	.09	.09	.09	.06	.06	.06	.06	.06	.06
I.	ECUADOR	.54	.64	.65	.65	.65	.65	.62	.62	.62	.58	.57	.55	.55	.53	.32	.32	.31	.49	.75	.63	.55
J.	EL SALVADOR	.66	.73	.84	.83	.82	.81	.80	.90	.90	.87	.86	.51	.51	.51	.51	.52	.51	.51	.51	.49	.49
K.	GUATEMALA	.78	.78	.78	.78	.78	.78	.78	.78	.78	.67	.67	.67	.67	.66	.66	.62	.57	.57	.57	.57	.50
L.	HAITI	.07	.07	.07	.06	.06	.06	.06	.02	.02	.02	.02	.02	.02	.02	.02	.02	~	~	~	~	~
M.	HONDURAS	~	~	~	~	~	~	~	~	~	~	~	~	~	~	~	~	~	~	~	~	~
N.	MEXICO	5.94	5.94	4.11	4.51	1.77	4.06	4.77	5.14	4.09	4.06	3.89	3.20	2.69	3.97	4.83	4.51	3.11	4.74	4.71	4.83	5.03
O.	NICARAGUA	.08	.08	.08	.08	.08	.08	.04	.04	.04	.01	.01	.01	.02	.01	.01	.01	.03	.02	.02	.01	.02
Q.	PARAGUAY	.01	.01	.01	.01	.01	.01	.01	~	.55	.01	.01	.01	.01	.01	.01	.01	~	~	~	~	~
R.	PERU	.89	1.31	1.31	1.04	1.00	1.00	1.00	.79	.55	.80	1.21	1.35	1.35	1.64	1.93	1.92	1.85	.58	.57	.71	1.13
S.	URUGUAY	6.74	6.31	5.91	6.49	6.49	6.16	5.33	5.13	5.13	5.13	5.13	5.13	5.13	4.90	4.90	4.43	4.19	3.99	3.81	4.71	4.61
T.	VENEZUELA	10.66	10.66	10.66	10.66	11.51	11.54	17.29	20.57	20.57	18.71	11.46	11.46	11.46	11.46	11.46	11.46	11.46	11.46	11.51	11.51	10.97
	UNITED STATES	652.00	653.51	664.34	631.17	622.66	621.51	630.23	653.06	588.06	557.34	508.69	484.20	458.77	445.60	442.03	401.86	378.14	344.71	311.20	338.83	316.34

	Country	1971	1972	1973	1974	1975	1976	1977	1978	1979	1980	1981	1982
A.	ARGENTINA	2.56	3.99	4.00	4.00	4.00	4.00	4.18	4.28	4.37	4.37	4.37	4.37
B.	BOLIVIA	.38	.41	.41	.41	.41	.41	.60	.64	.68	.76	.83	.89
C.	BRAZIL	1.32	1.33	1.33	1.33	1.33	1.52	1.52	1.61	1.70	1.88	2.20	.15
D.	CHILE	1.35	1.36	1.38	1.44	1.30	1.34	1.36	1.39	1.52	1.70	1.70	1.71
E.	COLOMBIA	.40	.43	.43	.43	1.13	1.41	1.73	1.96	2.32	2.79	3.37	3.82
F.	COSTA RICA	.06	.06	.06	.06	.06	.06	.07	.08	.09	.09	.03	.05
H.	DOMINICAN REP.	.09	.09	.09	.09	.09	.09	.10	.10	.11	.13	.14	.09
I.	ECUADOR	.53	.36	.39	.39	.39	.39	.40	.41	.41	.41	.41	.41
J.	EL SALVADOR	.49	.49	.49	.49	.49	.49	.50	.50	.51	.52	.52	.52
K.	GUATEMALA	.50	.49	.49	.49	.49	.49	.51	.51	.52	.52	.52	.52
L.	HAITI	~	~	~	~	~	~	.01	.01	.02	.02	.02	.02
M.	HONDURAS	~	~	~	~	~	~	.01	.01	.01	.02	.02	.02
N.	MEXICO	5.26	4.94	4.63	3.66	3.66	1.60	1.76	1.89	1.98	2.06	2.26	2.07
O.	NICARAGUA	.02	.01	.02	.02	.02	.02	.03	.03	.04	.04	.04	.04
Q.	PARAGUAY	~	~	~	~	~	~	.01	.01	.04	.04	.02	.04
R.	PERU	1.13	1.09	1.00	1.00	1.00	1.00	1.00	1.00	1.16	1.40	1.40	1.40
S.	URUGUAY	4.23	3.54	3.54	3.54	3.54	3.54	3.58	3.64	3.31*	3.42	3.39	2.86
T.	VENEZUELA	11.17	11.17	11.17	11.18	11.18	11.18	11.25	11.39	11.46	11.46	11.46	11.46
	UNITED STATES	291.60	275.97	275.97	275.97	274.71	274.68	277.55	276.41	264.60	264.32	264.11	264.03

SOURCE: IMF-IFS-Y, 1982, pp. 45-47; IMF-IFS-S, 1983, no. 6. Cf. table 2725.

Table 2725

IMF TOTAL RESERVES, 19 LC, 1950–82

(M SDRs, YE)

PART I. INCLUDING GOLD (Valued at 35 SDRs per Ounce)

Country	1950	1951	1952	1953	1954	1955	1956	1957	1958	1959	1960	1961	1962	1963	1964	1965	1966	1967	1968	1969	1970
A. ARGENTINA	528	448	331	369	361	294	382	286	130	276*	525	386	115	270	153	236	216	727	759	538	672
B. BOLIVIA	29	35	29	25	11	4	4	4	3	7	3	7	4	10	23	37	41	38	40	42	46
C. BRAZIL	666	517	529	605	483	491	611	476	465	367*	345	470	335*	354	245	484	425	199	257	656	1,187
D. CHILE	55	60	74	68	55	86	83	51	63	128	111	74	79	77	89	137	172	126	208	343	389
E. COLOMBIA	114	138	167	203	257	136	131	145	161	216	170*	140	85	87	104	96	77	83	173	221	206
F. COSTA RICA	5	9	16	19	17	21	13	13	21	15	13	6	13	16	19	20	17	18	21	29	16
H. DOMINICAN REP.	21	31	33	30	37	37	40	48	47	42	26	9	20	42	41	51	44	32	36	40	32
I. ECUADOR	39	32	45	40	40	35	34	39	38	44	41	38	43	52	52	46	61	69	57	65	83
J. EL SALVADOR	42	43	44	44	45	39	39	42	40	38	33	25	26	44	53	57	57	55	62	64	63
K. GUATEMALA	39	41	44	43	40	56	71	75	49	44	54	55	46	57	60	68	61	65	66	74	78
L. HAITI	8	12	13	7	12	9	8	6	1	4	5	5	4	3	3	2	2	2	3	4	4
M. HONDURAS	11	21	23	23	24	20	18	16	10	12	13	12	13	12	20	23	27	25	32	31	20
N. MEXICO	297	297	282	250	209	441	512	476	391	458	442	413	427	548	587	538	564	586	657	662	744
O. NICARAGUA	4	9	15	17	14	14	7	11	8	12	12	14	17	32	39	57	58	32	48	44	49
P. PANAMA	4	2	3	5	7	6	8	4	9	9	7	7	5	7	5	6	6	7	11	14	16
Q. PARAGUAY	2	13	8	6	5	6	8	5	7	4*	1	3	2	3	5	10	12	12	12	10	18
R. PERU	57	63	62	55	62	58	73	40	31	59	76	110	117	135	160	175	155	126	111	167	336*
S. URUGUAY	312	267	320	368	333	218*	195	181	188	186	188	191	203	186	186	179	177	162	167	184	175
T. VENEZUELA	378	377	443	484	482	534	952	1,459	1,062	724	609	580	583	745	832	819	777	872	922	933	1,021
UNITED STATES	24,266	24,299	24,714	23,458	22,978	22,797	23,666	24,832	22,540	21,505	19,359	18,753	17,220	16,843	16,672	15,450	14,882	14,830	15,710	16,964	14,487

Country	1971	1972	1973	1974	1975	1976	1977	1978	1979	1980	1981	1982
A. ARGENTINA	267	428	1,092	1,074	386	1,383	2,743	3,962	7,280	5,421	2,961	2,425
B. BOLIVIA	50	55	60	158	134	145	195	153	159	110	115	172
C. BRAZIL	1,609	3,852	5,318	4,306	3,446	5,630	5,973	9,134	6,867	4,589	5,750	3,566
D. CHILE	204	137	149	84	93	396	399	885	1,525	2,508	2,820	1,705
E. COLOMBIA	187	300	443	367	445	997	1,499	1,886	2,999	3,886	4,242	3,634
F. COSTA RICA	27	39	42	36	44	84	159	152	93	117	114	207
H. DOMINICAN REP.	52	54	73	74	99	109	152	122	185	163	198	120
I. ECUADOR	60	132	200	286	230	424	527	502	563	809	558	290
J. EL SALVADOR	60	76	51	80	108	177	191	223	124	79	80	116
K. GUATEMALA	86	124	176	165	260	440	568	587	547	367	147	120
L. HAITI	10	17	14	16	11	24	28	30	42	13	21	4
M. HONDURAS	20	32	35	36	83	113	148	142	159	118	87	102
N. MEXICO	877	1,072	1,124	1,139	1,310	1,079	1,419	1,480	1,612	2,292	3,579	828
O. NICARAGUA	54	74	97	86	104	126	123	40	~	~	~	~
P. PANAMA	19	40	35	32	29	68	58	115	93	95	103	92
Q. PARAGUAY	19	29	47	71	98	136	221	345	464	599	693	620
R. PERU	390	446	471	791	399	284	329	334	1,195	1,600	1,087	1,271
S. URUGUAY	167	187	207	190	174	276	391	398	361*	421	488	205
T. VENEZUELA	1,401	1,594	2,000	5,319	7,568	7,384	6,762	5,031	5,958	5,579	7,415	6,365
UNITED STATES	12,148	12,112	11,919	13,115	13,567	15,767	15,965	15,031	15,170	21,479	25,502	29,918

SOURCE: IMF-IFS-Y, 1981, pp. 49-51; IMF-IFS-S, 1983, no. 6. Cf. table 2724.

Table 2725 (Continued)

IMF TOTAL RESERVES, 19 LC, 1950-82

(M SDRs, YE)

PART II. Minus Gold[1]

Country	1950	1951	1952	1953	1954	1955	1956	1957	1958	1959	1960	1961	1962	1963	1964	1965	1966	1967	1968	1969	1970
A. ARGENTINA	445	253	133	160	152	85	158	160	38	220*	422	196	54	192	82	170	132	643	651	403	533
B. BOLIVIA	6	12	8	3	6	6	3	6	2	6	6	6	1	8	18	30	34	29	29	30	33
C. BRAZIL	348	198	209	284	161	168	287	152	140	40*	58	185	60*	69	154	421	380	154	212	611	1,142
D. CHILE	15	14	26	26	13	42	38	11	23	86	66	26	36	34	46	94	127	81	162	296	342
E. COLOMBIA	40	90	92	117	172	50	74	83	89	145	92*	52	28	25	46	61	52	52	142	195	189
F. COSTA RICA	3	7	14	17	15	19	11	11	19	12	11	4	11	14	17	18	15	16	18	27	14
H. DOMINICAN REP.	17	19	21	17	25	25	28	37	36	31	15	6	17	39	38	48	41	29	33	27	29
I. ECUADOR	20	10	22	17	17	12	13	17	16	23	21	19	24	33	40	35	50	52	31	43	64
J. EL SALVADOR	19	17	15	15	16	11	11	10	11	7	3	7	9	27	36	38	39	37	44	47	45
K. GUATEMALA	11	14	17	15	13	28	44	48	22	21	31	31	22	34	37	46	41	45	45	54	61
L. HAITI	5	9	10	5	10	7	6	6	#	3	4	3	2	3	2	1	2	2	3	4	4
M. HONDURAS	11	20	22	23	24	20	18	16	10	12	13	12	13	12	20	23	27	25	31	31	20
N. MEXICO	89	89	138	92	147	299	345	296	248	316	306	301	333	409	418	380	455	420	492	493	568
O. NICARAGUA	1	6	13	14	11	12	10	6	9	12	11	13	17	32	39	57	57	31	48	44	49
P. PANAMA	4	2	3	5	7	6	8	4	9	4	7	5	5	7	5	6	6	7	11	14	16
Q. PARAGUAY	2	13	7	6	5	6	8	5	7	4*	1	2	2	3	5	10	11	12	12	10	18
R. PERU	26	18	16	19	27	23	38	12	12	31	34	63	69	78	93	108	90	106	91	142	296*
S. URUGUAY	76	46	113	141	106	2*	2	2	8	7	9	11	23	14	15	24	30	22	34	19	14
T. VENEZUELA	5	4	70	111	79	130	347	739	342	69	208	179	182	344	431	418	376	471	519	530	637
UNITED STATES	1,446	1,426	1,462	1,367	1,185	1,044	1,608	1,975	1,958	1,998	1,555	1,806	1,163	1,247	1,201	1,385	1,647	2,765	4,818	5,105	3,415

Country	1971	1972	1973	1974	1975	1976	1977	1978	1979	1980	1981	1982
A. ARGENTINA	177	289	952	935	246	1,244	2,596	3,812	7,127	5,268	2,808	2,272
B. BOLIVIA	37	41	46	144	119	130	174	130	135	83	86	141
C. BRAZIL	1,563	3,806	5,272	4,260	3,400	5,584	5,920	9,078	6,806	4,524	5,673	3,561
D. CHILE	157	89	101	34	48	349	351	837	1,471	2,449	2,761	1,645
E. COLOMBIA	173	285	428	352	406	948	1,438	1,817	2,918	3,788	4,124	3,500
F. COSTA RICA	25	37	40	34	42	82	157	149	90	114	113	205
H. DOMINICAN REP.	49	51	70	71	96	106	148	118	181	158	193	117
I. ECUADOR	41	120	186	272	216	411	513	488	548	794	543	276
J. EL SALVADOR	43	59	34	63	91	160	174	206	106	61	62	98
K. GUATEMALA	69	107	159	148	242	423	551	569	529	349	129	102
L. HAITI	10	17	14	16	11	24	28	30	42	13	21	4
M. HONDURAS	20	32	35	36	83	113	148	142	159	117	87	102
N. MEXICO	693	899	962	1,011	1,182	1,023	1,358	1,414	1,543	2,321	3,500	756
O. NICARAGUA	54	74	96	85	104	126	122	39	111	51	96	155
P. PANAMA	19	40	35	32	30	58	58	116	90	92	103	92
Q. PARAGUAY	19	29	47	71	98	136	221	344	462	597	692	619
R. PERU	351	408	436	756	363	249	294	299	1,154	1,551	1,038	1,222
S. URUGUAY	19	64	83	66	50	152	265	271	245*	301	369	105
T. VENEZUELA	1,010	1,203	1,609	4,928	7,177	6,993	6,368	4,632	5,557	5,178	7,014	5,964
UNITED STATES	1,942	2,453	2,260	3,456	3,952	6,153	6,251	5,357	5,909	12,228	16,258	20,677

1. Includes foreign exchange, SDR holdings, and reserve position in the fund. Gold is excluded here because its value fluctuates widely according to market and time. For physical holdings of gold, see table 2724. For IMF drawings and credits, see chapter 28. For SDR exchange rate, see chapter 31.

SOURCE: Adapted from IMF-IFS-Y, 1981, pp. 29-31; IMF-IFS-S, 1983, no. 6.

Table 2726

IMF FOREIGN EXCHANGE RESERVES[1], 19 LC, 1950-82

(M SDRs, YE)

Country	1950	1951	1952	1953	1954	1955	1956	1957	1958	1959	1960	1961	1962	1963	1964	1965	1966	1967	1968	1969	1970
A. ARGENTINA	445	253	133	160	152	85	158	160	38	220*	422	196	54	192	82	170	132	625	554	285	343
B. BOLIVIA	6	12	8	3	6	6	3	6	2	6	6	6	1	8	18	29	27	22	29	30	30
C. BRAZIL	348	198	209	284	161	168	287	152	140	40*	58	185	60*	69	154	421	368	142	200	599	962
D. CHILE	15	11	26	26	13	42	37	11	23	86	66	26	36	34	46	94	127	81	162	296	320
E. COLOMBIA	27	77	79	104	172	50	74	83	89	141	67*	52	28	25	46	61	52	52	142	195	189
F. COSTA RICA	2	6	13	16	14	17	17	10	17	11	10	6	10	14	17	18	15	16	18	25	8
H. DOMINICAN REP.	15	18	20	16	24	24	26	34	33	27	15	6	17	35	38	48	41	29	33	37	29
I. ECUADOR	19	9	21	16	16	11	10	17	14	20	17	19	24	33	37	35	50	52	31	43	64
J. EL SALVADOR	18	17	14	14	16	10	11	8	6	7	3	7	6	22	31	33	39	37	44	47	45
K. GUATEMALA	10	13	16	14	12	27	43	47	21	17	27	27	22	34	33	46	41	45	45	54	59
L. HAITI	5	9	10	5	9	7	6	5	-	3	4	3	2	3	2	1	2	2	1	4	4
M. HONDURAS	11	20	22	22	24	20	18	16	8	12	13	12	13	12	20	23	27	23	29	26	20
N. MEXICO	89	66	115	69	147	276	322	273	225	271	261	301	288	364	373	325	369	325	359	381	385
O. NICARAGUA	4	6	12	13	10	11	6	10	6	9	9	13	17	32	39	57	57	27	48	44	48
P. PANAMA	1	2	3	5	7	6	8	4	9	4	7	5	5	7	5	6	6	7	11	14	12
Q. PARAGUAY	1	12	7	6	4	5	8	5	7	4*	1	2	1	1	3	7	8	8	8	6	10
R. PERU	23	15	10	13	21	17	32	6	12	24	26	55	61	68	83	98	78	106	91	142	282*
S. URUGUAY	76	46	113	141	106	2*	9	2	8	7	9	4	23	14	15	24	30	20	34	19	14
T. VENEZUELA	1	~	66	107	75	126	343	735	338	65	170	141	144	306	393	380	313	398	438	441	472
UNITED STATES	~	~	~	~	~	~	~	~	~	~	~	116	99	212	432	781	1,321	2,345	3,528	2,781	629

Country	1971	1972	1973	1974	1975	1976	1977	1978	1979	1980	1981	1982
A. ARGENTINA	64	271	885	840	211	1,165	2,522	3,520	6,724	4,749	2,222	2,181
B. BOLIVIA	34	38	43	141	112	117	161	107	135	83	86	141
C. BRAZIL	1,336	3,533	4,999	3,981	3,120	5,251	5,587	8,755	6,333	3,953	5,059	3,301
D. CHILE	118	87	101	20	27	300	296	778	1,412	2,382	2,680	1,557
E. COLOMBIA	165	267	366	288	346	878	1,336	1,709	2,772	3,588	3,853	3,163
F. COSTA RICA	25	33	36	32	38	81	151	138	78	114	113	205
H. DOMINICAN REP.	49	44	52	64	90	100	143	114	174	158	192	116
I. ECUADOR	38	113	175	257	197	405	505	469	520	754	490	276
J. EL SALVADOR	40	55	30	60	88	156	161	189	85	61	62	97
K. GUATEMALA	58	90	138	128	222	399	527	545	496	309	118	102
L. HAITI	6	11	12	14	9	23	26	24	32	13	21	3
M. HONDURAS	17	27	23	31	79	110	144	132	145	117	85	100
N. MEXICO	507	673	736	784	998	1,022	1,311	1,371	1,420	2,108	3,187	751
O. NICARAGUA	50	68	91	80	99	122	118	35	111	51	96	154
P. PANAMA	12	29	24	30	23	63	54	108	84	83	100	88
Q. PARAGUAY	10	18	36	60	87	123	207	331	445	571	652	568
R. PERU	322	367	368	688	296	246	291	294	1,073	1,542	1,029	1,193
S. URUGUAY	19	56	73	54	48	148	257	242	203*	248	304	104
T. VENEZUELA	816	974	1,379	4,407	6,249	5,941	5,399	3,877	4,881	4,418	6,084	4,883
UNITED STATES	258	222	7	4	68	275	15	3,357	2,890	7,946	8,397	9,257

1. Included in table 2725.

SOURCE: IMF-IFS-Y, 1982, pp. 41-43; IMF-IFS-S, 1983, no. 6.

Table 2727

IMF TOTAL CHANGE IN RESERVES, 19 LC, 1951–83[a]
(M US)

Year	A. ARGENTINA	B. BOLIVIA	C. BRAZIL	D. CHILE	E. COLOMBIA	F. COSTA RICA	H. DOMINICAN REP.	I. ECUADOR	J. EL SALVADOR	K. GUATEMALA
1951	25	-5.5	137	-2	~	-4.7	-10.3	5.0	-1.6	-2.3
1952	49	4.0	-32	-19	~	-6.2	-2.5	-11.5	-1.0	-3.2
1953	-86	6.9	63	10	~	.2	4.0	2.9	.2	.1
1954	-30	12.1	38	15	~	-7.3	-7.6	2.3	-.8	2.5
1955	68	3.3	-15	-21	~	-3.9	-1.4	5.8	5.5	-15.5
1956	38	9.9	-148	3	8	7.8	-2.3	.2	2.6	-15.7
1957	175	-3.8	173	51	-7	#	-8.2	-2.4	-5.0	-3.9
1958	154	1.5	49	-1	-9	-7.8	.7	-1.2	2.0	26.0
1959	-178	-6.7	8	-73	-70	6.2	5.7	-5.9	4.7	5.1
1960	-258	3.9	24	4	41	1.2	21.1	2.8	10.4	-10.0
1961	232	-1.9	-101	92	69	10.9	16.8	12.7	5.0	-1.1
1962	297	4.7	114	-18	61	-10.0	-11.7	-7.1	-7.0	9.9
1963	-141	-5.1	39	42	47	6.4	-26.6	-11.7	-15.9	-12.0
1964	74	-16.5	-33	-2	-30	-4.0	9.3	-4.8	-10.9	-4.5
1965	-127	-14.0	-219	-50	-16	4.4	6.8	11.7	-5.2	-8.8
1966	-26	-4.6	14	-49	17	3.2	13.5	-10.1	14.5	12.4
1967	-541	3.3	193	30	28	-4.8	7.8	-8.8	2.1	5.6
1968	-33	3.5	-70	-73	-69	-10.4	-10.6	1.6	-4.2	-2.3
1969	222	.5	-399	-157	-56	-17.4	1.1	4.5	-4.5	-10.9
1970	-135	-5.5	-530	-100	-36	11.6	-.4	-7.7	-6.4	-15.3
1971	390	-6.5	-55.6	213	7	-13.1	-18.9	10.7	3.9	-13.7
1972	14	-4.1	-2,437	117	-180	-19.9	-10.1	-74.3	-18.0	-41.5
1973	-814	2.5	-2,227	-16	-207	-16.5	-33.4	-99.5	13.1	-75.1
1974	-127	-127.2	1,144	177	85	33.0	-2.8	-108.2	-14.4	10.1
1975	1,071	33.5	1,235	183	-73	16.6	-25.3	65.3	-30.4	-102.5
1976	-921	-47.1	-2,508	-271	-639	-64.1	14.1	-224.0	-84.5	-207.4
1977	-1,828	-75.8	-712	-156	-659	-109.5	38.1	-146.3	-41.0	-180.4
1978	-2,235	81.8	-4,638	-724	-676	-25.6	29.3	-13.0	-56.9	-71.9
1979	-4,425	-25.4	2,860	-1,128	-1,552	113.6	-7.9	-86.5	127.6	29.4
1980	2,668	137.0	3,321	-1,402	-1,311	-98.9	-44.0	-291.0	69.0	245.5
1981	3,452	-21.7	-750	-77	-199	66.6	-54.0	380.6	42.7	303.9
1982	758	-37.2	4,160	1,372	770	-137.5	160.4	328.2	27.0	33.0
1983	~	~	~	499	~	~	~	~	~	~

1. Cf. SALA, 23-2701 to 2720.

a. Data in billions.

SOURCE: IMF-IFS-Y, 1979, 1984, line 79 cd.

Table 2727 (Continued)

IMF TOTAL CHANGE IN RESERVES, 19 LC, 1951–83[a]

(M US)

Year	L. HAITI	M. HONDURAS	N. MEXICO	O. NICARAGUA	P. PANAMA	Q. PARAGUAY	R. PERU	S. URUGUAY	T. VENEZUELA	UNITED STATES[1]
1951	-1.6	-9.7	~	~	~	-6.2	~	~	~	~
1952	-2.8	-2.1	~	~	~	1.9	~	~	~	1.26
1953	5.8	-.6	32	~	~	1.5	~	~	~	.48
1954	-4.5	-1.2	40	~	~	5.8	~	~	~	~
1955	2.7	4.1	-231	~	#	2.3	~	~	-417	.18
1956	1.2	2.0	-72	7.3	-2.3	-21	-15	~	-505	-.87
1957	3.2	4.1	36	-2.4	4.1	4.0	33	~	395	-1.16
1958	2.9	4.3	80	1.9	-4.9	-.3	3	~	~	2.29
1959	1.6	-.8	-62	-4.6	4.7	1.6	-32	2.6	338	1.04
1960	-2.2	-.4	16	.1	-3.4	2.7	-17	-5.9	115	2.14
1961	-2.8	1.8	29	.1	2.5	-3.4	-34	-5.9	29	.61
1962	4.1	.2	-14	-3.9	.1	-.1	-6	6.4	-2	1.53
1963	2.5	-.1	-120	-8.5	-2.6	-1.5	-19	17.0	-163	.38
1964	.3	-4.7	-42	-6.2	2.3	-2.3	-25	-.6	-86	.17
1965	.9	-6.2	61	-18.2	-.6	-5.5	-15	8.0	-11	1.22
1966	1.2	5.0	-2	-2.6	-.2	-.4	17	1.2	67	.57
1967	2.0	-.4	-27	19.4	-.8	-.7	30	8.2	-96	.05
1968	-3.1	-6.5	-94	-4.0	-2.1	.1	18	15.7	-50	-.88
1969	-1.2	.6	53	4.7	-2.6	2.0	-31	-28.4	-11	-1.26
1970	-3.8	9.7	-75	-11.3	-4.0	-7.2	-187	16.7	-82	2.48
1971	-10.7	-2.6	-197	-8.1	-3.5	-3.4	-90	-.4	-469	2.18
1972	-9.8	13.3	-223	-27.5	-22.4	-10.4	-30	-3.1	-208	#
1973	3.5	-6.9	-168	-67.8	1.7	-25.7	-94	-23.8	-637	-.06
1974	11.4	17.4	-43	35.2	11.4	-30.1	-413	40.9	-4,480	-1.51
1975	8.5	-54.1	-112	-41.3	16.4	-27.9	499	57.0	-2,669	-.35
1976	-11.1	-38.0	682	-2.9	-15.5	-42.4	312	-73.8	-72	-2.52
1977	-12.1	-66.2	-384	-9.3	9.8	-112.4	-59	-174.3	114	-.56
1978	-14.3	-9.9	-455	82.8	-78.2	-179.5	-5	-161.2	1,744	1.06
1979	-11.4	-25.0	-439	-3.5	20.6	-165.1	-1,066	-143.6	-1,113	2.76
1980	26.3	73.0	-1,127	187.4	-17.0	-152.9	-607	-175.7	-10	-7.64
1981	56.7	69.0	-1,492	-61.6	66.3	-43.1	512	-20.1	-2,502	-3.21
1982	46.3	52.8	3,470	-76.6	9.3	65.0	57.0	505.1	8,215	-3.86
1983	36.4	~	~	~	3.0	~	~	~	~	.45

1. Cf. SALA, 23-2701 to 2720.

a. Data in billions.

SOURCE: IMF-IFS-Y, 1979, 1984, line 79 cd.

Table 2728

ARGENTINA: ECLA BALANCE OF PAYMENTS, 1977-82[a]
(M US)

Category	1977	1978	1979	1980	1981	1982[b]
Balance on current account	1,127	1,836	-535	-4,774	-4,057	-2,422
Trade balance	1,877	2,520	403	-3,191	-688	2,251
Exports of goods and services	6,588	7,483	9,177	9,891	10,841	9,431
Goods FOB	5,650	6,401	7,810	8,022	9,145	7,600
Real services[1]	935	1,083	1,366	1,870	1,695	1,831
Transport and insurance	439	475	605	810	886	957
Travel	212	278	266	345	413	446
Imports of goods and services	4,711	4,962	8,774	13,081	11,529	7,180
Goods FOB	3,799	3,488	6,027	9,394	8,232	4,670
Real services[1]	912	1,474	2,745	3,688	3,300	2,510
Transport and insurance	459	510	905	1,271	1,160	883
Travel	188	588	1,266	1,792	1,472	1,120
Factor services	-782	-734	-973	-1,607	-3,365	-4,705
Profits	-368	-274	-428	-585	-741	-915
Interest received	128	315	681	1,229	876	525
Interest paid	-499	-720	-1,175	-2,175	-3,435	-4,236
Others	-41	-54	-52	-76	-62	-79
Unrequited private transfer payments	33	48	35	23	-5	32
Balance on capital account	719	302	4,760	2,176	864	1,660
Unrequited official transfer payments	-1	21	22	0	0	0
Long-term capital	476	1,520	3,156	4,492	9,538	2,501
Direct investment	144	273	265	788	917	295
Portfolio investment	0	102	223	153	1,123	1,443
Other long-term capital	332	1,145	2,667	3,550	7,498	763
Official sector[2]	-203	-954	0	478	949	-233
Loans disbursed	99	47	50	510	1,022	490
Amortization payments	-210	-914	-43	-36	-47	-723
Commercial banks[2]	63	101	198	-65	136	529
Loans disbursed	66	124	236	89	171	640
Amortization payments	-3	-22	-37	-155	-36	-111
Other sectors[3]	472	1,997	2,470	3,138	6,413	467
Loans disbursed	1,047	3,745	3,157	4,231	7,993	2,316
Amortization payments	-575	-1,588	-857	-1,229	-886	-1,849
Short-term capital (net)	109	-1,246	1,341	-2,011	-8,434	-4,739
Official sector	-399	335	180	313	299	-211
Commercial banks	20	-27	-286	-365	25	98
Other sectors	488	-1,554	1,447	-1,958	-8,758	-4,626
Errors and omissions	135	9	243	-307	-245	3,898
Global balance[3]	1,846	2,138	4,225	-2,598	-3,193	-762
Total variation in reserves (minus sign indicates an increase)	-1,827	-2,236	-4,424	2,666	3,452	762
Monetary gold	-7	-4	-3	-1	0	0
Special Drawing Rights	1	-121	-116	-1	-76	404
IMF reserve position	0	-169	-34	-133	57	178
Foreign exchange assets	-1,710	-1,522	-4,272	2,801	3,471	180
Other assets	0	0	0	0	0	0
Use made of IMF credit	-111	-419	0	0	0	0

1. Real services also include other official and private transactions, but not factor services.
2. In addition to loans received and amortization payments made, this entry includes net loans granted and other assets and liabilities.
3. The global balance is the sum of the current account balance plus the balance on capital account. The difference between total variation in reserves (of opposite sign) and the global balance represents counterpart items: monetization of gold, allocation of Special Drawing Rights, and variations due to revaluation.

a. Cf. SALA, 21-2625.
b. Preliminary figures.

SOURCE: ECLA-S, 1982, p. 99.

Table 2729

BOLIVIA: ECLA BALANCE OF PAYMENTS, 1977–82[a]

(M US)

Category	1977	1978	1979	1980	1981	1982[b]
Balance on current account	-131	-353	-399	-166	-312	-166
Trade balance	-64	-242	-226	90	17	208
Exports of goods and services	695	703	855	1,043	1,012	913
Goods FOB	634	627	762	942	909	804
Real services[1]	61	76	93	101	103	108
Transport and insurance	12	15	29	32	34	26
Travel	29	35	37	40	36	40
Imports of goods and services	759	946	1,081	953	994	704
Goods FOB	579	724	815	680	680	425
Real services[1]	180	222	266	273	314	279
Transport and insurance	103	140	177	168	196	82
Travel	38	41	45	52	50	40
Factor services	-69	-116	-183	-264	-343	-389
Profits	-1	-18	-28	-19	-29	-26
Interest received	4	1	2	14	15	6
Interest paid	-69	-96	-155	-256	-325	-366
Others	-2	-3	-3	-3	-3	-4
Unrequited private transfer payments	2	5	11	8	13	15
Balance on capital account	198	269	417	19	319	209
Unrequited official transfer payments	13	22	41	48	26	34
Long-term capital	325	293	257	252	473	-11
Direct investment	-1	12	18	41	60	25
Portfolio investment	#	#	#	-3	#	#
Other long-term capital	326	281	240	213	413	-36
Official sector[2]	169	114	89	264	310	-28
Loans disbursed	221	326	149	334	328	187
Amortization payments	-42	-203	-57	-56	-53	-215
Commercial banks[2]	#	#	77	-24	26	-11
Loans disbursed	#	#	87	13	10	24
Amortization payments	#	#	-10	-21	-6	-35
Other sectors[3]	157	167	74	-26	77	3
Loans disbursed	238	275	151	94	96	94
Amortization payments	-81	-108	-77	-90	-55	-91
Short-term capital (net)	-61	40	147	-20	148	-36
Official sector	42	-53	192	-29	200	69
Commercial banks	38	51	-11	-19	6	16
Other sectors	-141	42	-34	28	-58	-121
Errors and omissions	-79	-35	-28	-260	-329	221
Global balance[3]	67	-84	19	-147	6	43
Total variation in reserves (minus sign indicates an increase)	-44	55	-24	136	-23	-43
Monetary gold	-8	-2	-2	-2	-3	-2
Special Drawing Rights	1	-11	18	#	#	#
IMF reserve position	-2	-3	12	#	#	#
Foreign exchange assets	-60	56	-39	72	6	-56
Other assets	24	-4	-14	6	-17	#
Use made of IMF credit	#	20	#	61	-9	15

1. Real services also include other official and private transactions, but not factor services.
2. In addition to loans received and amortization payments made, this entry includes net loans granted and other assets and liabilities.
3. The global balance is the sum of the current account balance plus the balance on capital account. The difference between total variation in reserves of opposite sign and the global balance represents counterpart items: monetization or demonetization of gold, allocation or settlement of Special Drawing Rights, and variations due to revaluation.

a. Cf. SALA, 21-2626.
b. Preliminary figures.

SOURCE: ECLA-S, 1982, p. 132.

Table 2730

BRAZIL: ECLA BALANCE OF PAYMENTS, 1977–82[a]

(M US)

Category	1977	1978	1979	1980	1981	1982[b]
Balance on current account	–5,115	–7,039	–10,482	–12,848	–11,760	–16,279
Trade balance	–1,641	–2,830	–5,019	–5,935	–1,677	–2,794
Exports of goods and services	13,004	13,666	16,707	21,857	25,523	22,013
Goods FOB	11,922	12,473	15,244	20,132	23,275	20,175
Real services[1]	1,082	1,191	1,465	1,726	2,248	1,838
Transport and insurance	546	570	705	843	1,102	1,017
Travel	55	69	74	125	242	65
Imports of goods and services	14,645	16,495	21,725	27,792	27,200	24,807
Goods FOB	12,022	13,632	17,961	22,955	22,091	19,397
Real services[1]	2,621	2,864	3,764	4,838	5,109	5,410
Transport and insurance	1,522	1,580	2.104	2,758	2,786	2,432
Travel	229	254	310	367	407	910
Factor services	–3,472	–4,278	–5,478	–7,041	–10,274	–13,478
Profits	–1,332	–1,535	–1,356	–720	–1,112	–2,121
Interest received	361	644	1,157	1,146	1,144	1,198
Interest paid	–2,464	–3,343	–5,261	–7,456	–10,306	–12,555
Others	–36	–45	–17	–9	–1	0
Unrequited private transfer payments	–5	70	12	128	189	–7
Balance on capital account	5,636	11,666	7,582	9,379	12,381	12,763
Unrequited official transfer payments	4	3	5	42	10	0
Long-term capital	6,041	10,088	6,466	7,104	11,819	8,143
Direct investment	1,688	1,882	2,223	1,544	2,313	2,542
Portfolio investment	0	0	659	354	–2	0
Other long-term capital	4,354	8,205	3,584	5,206	9,508	5,601
Official sector[3]	2,406	3,965	3,370	–14	220	~
Disbursements	4,098	6,240	4,665	1,841	2,008	~
Amortization payments	–1,691	–2,062	–1,278	–1,366	–1,520	~
Commercial banks[3]	450	1,853	486	2,105	4,054	~
Disbursements	1,271	2,898	1,981	4,005	6,409	~
Amortization payments	–819	–1,043	–1,494	–1,917	–2,361	~
Other sectors[2]	1,497	2,387	–272	3,115	5,234	~
Disbursements	3,395	4,979	4,248	6,085	9,633	~
Amortization payments	–1,623	–2,169	–3,781	–3,394	–3,761	~
Net short-term capital	220	1,273	–122	2,572	1,132	3,439
Official sector	–318	499	274	–31	–6	876
Commercial banks	237	897	–422	608	1,039	2,339
Other sectors	300	–123	26	1,996	99	224
Errors and omissions	–628	300	1,233	–343	–578	1,181
Global balance[3]	521	4,627	–2,900	–3,469	621	–3,516
Total variation in reserves (minus sign indicates an increase)	–710	–4,640	2,860	3,322	–747	~
Monetary gold	–7	–4	0	–103	–130	~
Special Drawing Rights	–11	–30	–144	–1	–68	~
IMF reserve position	–6	13	–60	–103	80	~
Foreign exchange assets	–686	–4,619	3,063	3,301	–844	~
Other assets	0	0	0	228	215	~
Use made of IMF credit	0	0	0	0	0	544

1. Real services also include other official and private transactions, but do not include factor services.
2. In addition to loans received and amortization payments made, this entry includes net loans granted and other assets and liabilities.
3. The global balance is the sum of the balance on current account plus the balance on capital account. The difference between the total variation in reserves (of opposite sign) and the global balance represents the value of counterpart items: monetization of gold, allocation of Special Drawing Rights, and variations due to revaluation.

a. Cf. SALA, 21–2627.
b. Preliminary figures.

SOURCE: ECLA-S, 1982, p. 174.

Table 2731

CHILE: ECLA BALANCE OF PAYMENTS, 1976–82[a]

(M US)

Category	1976	1977	1978	1979	1980	1981	1982[b]
Balance on current account	132	−567	−1,111	−1,205	−2,024	−4,869	−2,442
Trade balance	433	−267	−680	−598	−1,056	−3,367	−432
Exports of goods and services	2,413	2,604	2,941	4,619	5,968	5,507	5,027
Goods FOB	2,116	2,186	2,460	3,835	4,705	3,960	3,798
Real services[1]	298	418	482	784	1,262	1,546	1,229
Transport and insurance	120	149	233	348	433	433	409
Travel	87	82	109	150	174	221	200
Imports of goods and services	1,980	2,871	3,621	5,217	7,023	8,873	5,459
Goods FOB	1,473	2,151	2,886	4,190	5,469	6,558	3,580
Real services[1]	507	720	735	1,027	1,554	2,315	1,879
Transport and insurance	284	342	421	584	872	1,049	661
Travel	88	205	130	165	200	259	210
Factor services	−334	−379	−506	−696	−1,028	−1,547	−2,050
Profits	−2	−23	−33	−41	−82	−121	−150
Interest received	10	18	41	127	305	599	474
Interest paid	−333	−358	−497	−761	−1,152	−1,906	−2,374
Others	−8	−14	−16	−21	−99	−119	#
Unrequited private transfer payments	32	81	75	88	60	45	40
Balance on capital account	200	737	1,855	2,261	3,344	5,008	1,277
Unrequited official transfer payments	16	16	23	17	53	55	60
Long-term capital	47	50	1,510	1,786	2,243	3,732	1,233
Direct investment	−1	16	177	233	171	376	365
Portfolio investment	−6	−7	#	50	#	#	#
Other long-term capital	54	41	1,333	1,503	2,072	3,356	868
Official sector[2]	25	−158	167	96	−193	−485	930
Loans disbursed	289	218	587	581	280	152	~
Amortization payments	−259	−357	−421	−485	−472	−637	~
Commercial banks[2]	−18	7	290	525	1,438	2,472	254
Loans disbursed	#	18	295	593	1,617	2,711	~
Amortization payments	−18	−11	−4	−50	−147	−221	~
Other sectors[2]	47	191	876	882	826	1,369	−316
Loans disbursed	448	668	1,439	1,693	1,645	2,334	~
Amortization payments	−401	−478	−562	−810	−819	−965	~
Short-term capital (net)	68	557	449	470	1,000	1,107	71
Official sector	−80	43	14	4	100	70	~
Commercial banks	−36	127	58	39	469	252	71
Other sectors	184	386	378	428	431	785	~
Errors and omissions	69	114	−126	−13	49	114	−87
Global balance[3]	331	169	745	1,056	1,320	139	−1,165
Total variation in reserves[3] (minus sign indicates an increase)	−272	−125	−683	−1,061	−1,331	−162	1,198
Monetary gold	−2	−1	−1	−44	−90	1	~
Special Drawing Rights	−31	−11	39	−2	25	−15	#
IMF reserve position	#	#	−50	1	−33	7	−3
Foreign exchange assets	−318	−11	−654	−848	−1,177	−81	1,402
Other assets	#	#	#	#	#	#	~
Use made of IMF credit	80	−101	−18	−169	−57	−74	−42

1. Real services also include other official and private transactions, but no factor services.
2. In addition to loans received and amortization payments made, this entry includes net loans granted and other assets and liabilities.
3. The global balance is the sum of the current account balance plus the balance on capital account. The difference between total variation in reserves of opposite sign and the global balance represents counterpart items: monetization of gold, allocation of Special Drawing Rights, and variations due to revaluation.

a. Preliminary figures.
b. Cf. SALA, 21-2628.

SOURCE: ECLA-S, 1982, p. 295.

Table 2732

COLOMBIA: ECLA BALANCE OF PAYMENTS, 1977–82[a]

(M US)

Category	1977	1978	1979	1980	1981	1982[b]
Balance on current account	435	294	490	-644	-1,969	-2,291
Trade balance	643	532	606	-482	-1,725	-1,933
Exports of goods and services	3,403	3,959	4,526	5,040	4,204	4,511
Goods FOB	2,713	3,206	3,506	4,092	3,127	3,230
Real services[1]	690	752	1,019	948	1,077	1,281
Transport and insurance	291	305	335	353	393	470
Travel	245	283	358	357	384	420
Imports of goods and services	2,760	3,427	3,920	5,521	5,929	6,444
Goods FOB	1,979	2,564	2,996	4,420	4,789	5,175
Real services[1]	781	863	924	1,101	1,140	1,268
Transport and insurance	383	421	432	551	568	657
Travel	200	229	236	250	270	275
Factor services	-262	-283	-216	-260	-334	-581
Profits	-86	-121	-49	-61	-37	-40
Interest received	65	124	249	470	610	482
Interest paid	-252	-304	-456	-669	-907	-1,022
Others	12	19	40	#	#	#
Unrequited private transfer payments	54	45	99	98	90	223
Balance on capital account	137	154	969	1,702	2,393	1,580
Unrequited official transfer payments	5	28	1	26	26	25
Long-term capital	230	95	725	1,067	1,253	1,534
Direct investment	43	68	105	233	209	268
Portfolio investment	-2	-3	-12	-4	-0	-2
Other long-term capital	189	30	632	838	1,045	1,268
Official sector[2]	12	30	397	661	468	~
Loans received	88	155	601	843	647	~
Amortization payments	-75	-103	-189	-167	-164	~
Other sectors[2]	177	#	235	177	577	~
Loans received	333	208	512	242	659	~
Amortization payments	-155	-208	-276	-65	-83	~
Short-term capital (net)	-257	14	176	405	402	274
Official sector	-4	15	-22	-51	-45	65
Commercial banks	-203	14	376	203	106	67
Other sectors	-50	-15	-178	252	341	142
Errors and omissions	159	19	68	204	711	-253
Global balance[3]	572	448	1,459	1,058	423	-711
Total variation in reserves (minus sign indicates an increase)	-661	-676	-1,552	-1,311	-199	711
Monetary gold	-13	-56	-75	-324	-289	-169
Special Drawing Rights	-4	-18	-45	-14	-31	-40
IMF reserve position	-41	2	-6	-49	-30	-16
Foreign exchange assets	-603	-604	-1,425	-925	151	936
Other assets	~	~	~	~	~	~
Use made of IMF credit	~	~	~	~	~	~

1. Real services also include other official and private transactions, but exclude factor services.
2. In addition to loans received and their amortization, this entry includes net loans granted and other assets and liabilities.
3. The global balance is the sum of the balance on current account plus the balance on capital account. The difference between the total variation of reserves marked with a minus sign and the global balance represents the value of counterpart entries: monetization of gold, allocation of Special Drawing Rights, and variations due to revaluation.

a. Cf. SALA, 21-2629.
b. Preliminary figures.

SOURCE: ECLA-S, 1982, p. 212.

Table 2733

COSTA RICA: ECLA BALANCE OF PAYMENTS, 1977–82[a]

(M US)

Category	1977	1978	1979	1980	1981	1982[b]
Balance on current account	-226	-364	-554	-658	-371	-412
Trade balance	-162	-266	-421	-459	-95	22
Exports of goods and services	959	1,008	1.097	1,198	1,220	1,085
Goods FOB	828	864	942	1,001	1,030	870
Non factor services[1]	131	144	156	197	191	215
Transport and insurance	35	28	33	48	46	56
Travel	62	72	74	85	83	91
Imports of goods and services	1,120	1,274	1,519	1,657	1,316	1,063
Goods FOB	925	1,049	1,257	1,375	1,092	819
Real services[1]	195	225	262	283	225	244
Transport and insurance	115	129	155	177	147	153
Travel	51	62	63	60	36	34
Factor services	-80	-113	-150	--218	-303	-462
Profits	-18	-27	-17	-16	-10	-20
Interest received	9	16	11	16	21	22
Interest paid	-68	-100	-140	-216	--311	-461
Other	-3	-3	-4	-2	-3	--3
Unrequited private transfer payments	15	16	17	20	27	28
Balance on capital account	337	391	436	749	322	547
Unrequited official transfer payments	0	1	-4	-5	0	0
Long-term capital	300	353	353	402	161	235
Direct investment	62	47	42	48	46	~
Portfolio investment	4	21	0	124	1	~
Other long-term capital	234	285	311	230	114	~
Official sector[2]	81	114	221	81	83	~
Loans received	99	241	304	112	143	~
Amortization payments	-18	-120	-79	-25	-53	~
Commercial banks[2]	37	-12	-35	9	-11	~
Loans received	51	12	63	32	9	~
Amortization payments	-14	-23	-28	-23	-20	~
Other sectors[2]	115	182	55	140	43	~
Loans received	236	333	357	267	176	~
Amortization payments	-121	-151	-302	-127	-133	~
Short-term capital	64	88	6	422	65	200
Official sector	4	57	2	287	41	~
Commercial banks	5	2	6	32	5	~
Other sectors	55	29	2	104	18	~
Net errors and omissions	-27	-51	80	-71	96	112
Global balance[3]	111	27	-119	92	-50	135
Total variation in reserves (minus sign indicates an increase)	-110	-22	113	-33	71	~
Monetary gold	0	0	0	0	28	~
Special Drawing Rights	-5	3	-2	6	0	0
IMF reserve position	0	-10	0	10	0	0
Foreign exchange assets	-90	4	77	-43	14	-95
Other assets	-12	-14	12	-5	-17	~
Use made of IMF credit	-2	-4	26	-1	46	-10

1. Real services also include other official and private transactions, but do not include factor services.
2. In addition to loans received and amortization payments made, this entry includes net loans granted and other assets and liabilities.
3. The global balance is the sum of the balance on current account plus the balance on capital account. The difference between the total variation in reserves and the global balance represents the value of counterpart entries: monetization of gold, allocation of Special Drawing Rights and variation due to revaluation.

a. Cf. SALA, 21-2630.
b. Preliminary figures.

SOURCE: ECLA-S, 1982, p. 234.

Table 2734

DOMINICAN REPUBLIC: ECLA BALANCE OF PAYMENTS, 1977-82[a]

(M US)

Category	1977	1978	1979	1980	1981	1982[b]
Balance on current account	-132	-315	-360	-674	-378	-517
Trade balance	-170	-326	-349	-647	-272	-422
Exports of goods and services	927	828	1,135	1,271	1,517	1,101
Goods FOB	780	675	869	962	1,188	768
Real services[1]	147	152	266	309	329	333
Transport and insurance	19	20	22	26	19	21
Travel	92	92	124	173	201	225
Imports of goods and services	1,097	1,154	1,484	1,919	1,789	1,523
Goods FOB	849	862	1,137	1,520	1,439	1,250
Real services[1]	248	292	347	399	350	273
Transport and insurance	103	111	132	175	165	133
Travel	102	126	158	166	126	87
Factor services	-98	-136	-188	-210	-295	--285
Profits	-29	-41	-57	-65	-180	-100
Interest received	12	21	32	42	45	4
Interest paid	-82	-116	-163	-187	-160	-189
Unrequited private transfer payments	136	146	177	183	189	190
Balance on capital account	182	276	358	708	416	373
Unrequited official transfer payments	4	4	29	5	18	15
Long-term capital	199	187	109	423	220	191
Direct investment	71	64	17	93	87	3
Portfolio investment	#	#	#	#	#	#
Other long-term capital	127	123	92	330	133	188
Official sector[2]	83	145	114	268	213	232
Loans disbursed	111	189	322	242	267	223
Amortization payments	-27	-44	-202	-37	-54	-97
Commercial banks[2]	-1	-1	7	#	-7	-1
Loans disbursed	#	#	#	#	#	#
Amortization payments	-1	-1	-1	#	-7	--1
Other sectors[2]	46	-21	-29	62	-73	-43
Loans disbursed	105	56	53	163	14	51
Amortization payments	-60	-77	-82	-101	-87	-95
Short-term capital (net)	-23	40	208	250	204	106
Official sector	-17	40	101	88	12	222
Commercial banks	9	19	-16	92	197	-45
Other sectors	-15	-19	123	71	-5	-71
Errors and omissions	2	46	12	30	-26	62
Global balance[3]	50	-39	-2	33	38	-144
Total variation in reserves (minus sign indicates an increase)	-38	29	-8	-44	-31	162
Monetary gold	-1	#	#	-5	14	15
Special Drawing Rights	1	#	-3	9	-2	1
IMF reserve position	#	#	#	#	#	#
Foreign exchange assets	-57	26	-81	27	-21	95
Other assets	#	#	#	#	#	#
Use made of IMF credit	19	3	77	-76	-29	51

1. Real services also include other official and private transactions, but not factor services.
2. In addition to loans received and amortization payments made, this entry includes net loans granted and other assets and liabilities.
3. The global balance is the sum of the current account balance plus the balance on capital account. The difference between total variation in reserves of opposite sign and the global balance represents counterpart items: monetization or demonetization of gold, allocation or settlement of Special Drawing Rights, and variation due to revaluation.

a. Cf. SALA, 21-2631.
b. Preliminary figures.

SOURCE: ECLA-S, 1982, p. 603.

Table 2735

ECUADOR: ECLA BALANCE OF PAYMENTS, 1977–82[a]

(M US)

Category	1977	1978	1979	1980	1981	1982[b]
Balance on current account	-377	-730	-634	-672	-1,027	-1,070
Trade balance	-182	-463	-299	-147	-304	-297
Exports of goods and services	1,592	1,703	2,411	2,866	2,913	2,662
Goods FOB[1]	1,401	1,529	2,151	2,544	2,544	2,334
Real services[1]	192	174	260	322	369	328
Transport and insurance	93	49	109	113	151	133
Travel	48	65	80	131	131	114
Imports of goods and services	1,774	2,167	2,710	3,014	3,218	2,959
Goods FOB	1,361	1,704	2,097	2,242	2,362	2,181
Real services[1]	414	463	613	772	856	778
Transport and insurance	257	283	295	328	368	342
Travel	82	97	156	228	250	235
Factor services	-196	-279	-356	-525	--722	-773
Profits	-119	-116	-94	-11	-100	-73
Interest received	25	37	68	109	87	80
Interest paid	-76	-176	-329	-523	-709	-780
Others	-27	-24	#	#	#	#
Unrequited private transfer payments	#	12	#	#	#	#
Balance on capital account	489	736	698	942	656	742
Unrequited official transfer payments	36	29	29	30	25	20
Long-term capital	591	782	690	763	1,077	~
Direct investment	34	49	63	70	60	30
Portfolio investment	52	#	#	#	#	~
Other long-term capital	504	733	626	693	1,017	~
Official sector[2]	440	352	344	609	898	~
Loans disbursed	487	498	952	795	1,283	~
Amortization payments	-42	-139	-601	-176	-378	~
Commercial banks[2]	#	63	1	5	2	~
Loans disbursed	#	64	2	8	7	~
Amortization payments	#	-1	-1	-1	-1	~
Other sectors[2]	64	319	281	79	117	~
Loans disbursed	123	469	593	496	462	~
Amortization payments	-58	-88	-374	-416	-345	~
Short-term capital	-88	-120	-24	217	-360	~
Official sector	-101	3	9	-30	1	~
Commercial banks	-26	3	-10	-17	-5	~
Other sectors	39	-126	-22	264	-356	~
Errors and omissions	-50	44	3	-68	-86	~
Global balance[3]	112	5	44	270	--370	-328
Total variation in reserves (minus sign indicates an increase)	-146	-13	-87	-291	381	328
Monetary gold	-1	#	#	#	#	#[c]
Special Drawing Rights	-3	-4	-11	1	-9	34
IMF reserve position	#	-10	-2	-- 15	--1	29
Foreign exchange assets	-143	2	-73	-277	391	266
Other assets	#	#	#	#	#	#
Use made of IMF credit	#	#	#	#	#	#

1. Real services also include other official and private transactions, but not factor services.
2. In addition to loans received and amortization payments made, this entry includes net loans granted and other assets and liabilities.
3. The global balance is the sum of the current account balance plus the balance on capital account. The difference between total variation in reserves of opposite sign and the global balance represents counterpart items: monetization or demonetization of gold, allocation of Special Drawing Rights, and variation due to revaluation.

a. Cf. SALA, 21–2632.
b. Preliminary figures.
c. Does not take account of a US$ 107 million revaluation of gold reserves.

SOURCE: ECLA-S, 1982, p. 323.

Table 2736

EL SALVADOR: ECLA BALANCE OF PAYMENTS, 1977-82[a]

(M US)

Category	1977	1978	1979	1980	1981	1982[b]
Balance on current account	22	-245	123	-117	-281	-240
Trade balance	19	-238	119	-71	-243	-200
Exports of goods and services	1,089	970	1,358	1,109	933	912
Goods FOB	973	849	1,224	969	792	738
Real services[1]	115	121	133	140	141	174
Transport and insurance	19	23	24	25	20	~
Travel	32	37	25	13	16	18
Imports of goods and services	1,070	1,208	1,239	1,180	1,177	1,112
Goods FOB	861	951	939	907	900	822
Real services[1]	209	257	301	273	277	290
Transport and insurance	88	98	107	84	80	69
Travel	58	103	117	106	106	102
Factor services	-28	-52	-40	-63	-54	-91
Profits	-26	-26	-45	-41	-25	~
Interest received	20	15	40	18	9	~
Interest paid	-32	-49	-72	-72	-70	~
Labour and property	10	8	37	31	32	~
Unrequited private transfer payments	30	45	45	17	16	51
Balance on capital account	19	301	-257	44	233	170
Unrequited official transfer payments	9	7	6	31	15	109
Long-term capital	36	175	78	177	270	274
Direct investment	19	23	-10	6	4	~
Portfolio investment	1	4	-6	-1	#	~
Other long-term capital	17	148	94	172	266	~
Official sector[2]	20	115	83	170	253	~
Disbursements	37	127	100	204	339	~
Amortization payments	-16	-10	-16	-29	-86	~
Commercial banks[2]	#	#	#	3	#	~
Disbursements	#	#	#	4	#	~
Amortization payments	#	#	#	-1	#	~
Other sectors[2]	-3	32	11	-2	13	~
Disbursements	51	54	22	36	6	~
Amortization payments	-72	-32	-11	-37	-19	~
Short-term capital (net)	6	195	-127	43	-46	-73
Official sector	-1	24	-15	199	5	~
Commercial banks	20	4	-2	-67	#	~
Other sectors	-14	167	-110	-89	-51	~
Errors and omissions	-32	-76	-214	-208	-6	-140
Global balance[3]	40	55	-134	-74	-48	-70
Total variation in reserves (minus sign indicates an increase)	-41	-57	128	69	43	70
Monetary gold	#	#	#	#	#	~
Special Drawing Rights	-5	#	-7	17	#	~
IMF reserve position	-6	-5	#	11	#	~
Foreign exchange assets	-15	-51	135	34	6	~
Other assets	#	#	#	#	#	~
Use made of IMF credit	-15	#	#	7	37	~

1. Real services also include other official and private transactions, but not factor services.
2. In addition to loans received and amortization payments made, this entry includes net loans granted and other assets and liabilities.
3. The global balance is the sum of the current account balance plus the balance on capital account. The difference between total variation in reserves of opposite sign and the global balance represents counterpart items: monetization of gold, allocation of Special Drawing Rights, and variations due to revaluation.

a. Cf. SALA, 21-2633.
b. Preliminary figures.

SOURCE: ECLA-S, 1982, p. 349.

Table 2737

GUATEMALA: ECLA BALANCE OF PAYMENTS, 1977–82[a]

(M US)

Category	1977	1978	1979	1980	1981	1982[b]
Balance on current account	-37	-271	-209	--165	-567	-315
Trade balance	-98	-354	-320	-228	-570	-275
Exports of goods and services	1,335	1,298	1,473	1,730	1,454	1,276
Goods FOB	1,160	1,092	1,221	1,520	1,299	1,161
Real services[1]	175	205	251	211	155	115
Transport and insurance	28	33	40	43	33	27
Travel	66	67	82	62	30	14
Imports of goods and services	1,433	1,651	1,792	1,958	2,024	1,551
Goods FOB	1,087	1,284	1,402	1,473	5,540	1,234
Real services[1]	346	368	390	486	484	317
Transport and insurance	172	142	161	187	188	135
Travel	100	108	120	164	133	101
Factor services	-33	-32	-13	-45	-86	-105
Profits	-33	-35	-45	-42	-49	-13
Interest received	33	50	78	75	55	24
Interest paid	-32	-47	-46	-92	-109	-96
Others	-1	#	#	14	17	-20
Unrequited private transfer payments	94	115	123	109	89	65
Balance on capital account	216	341	172	-86	262	278
Unrequited official transfer payments	2	1	3	1	1	#
Long-term capital	199	268	258	247	416	354
Direct investment	98	127	117	111	127	82
Portfolio investment	5	12	5	4	#	#
Other long-term capital	96	129	135	132	288	272
Official sector[2]	68	102	112	106	219	277
Loans disbursed	82	117	130	121	246	345
Amortization payments	-14	-15	-18	--18	-27	-68
Commercial banks[2]	#	#	#	#	#	#
Loans disbursed	#	#	#	#	#	#
Amortization payments	#	#	#	#	#	#
Other sectors[2]	28	27	23	26	69	-5
Loans disbursed	43	58	60	25	100	19
Amortization payments	-24	-41	-47	-10	-42	-24
Short-term capital	42	131	-44	-316	-144	-60
Official sector	#	8	2	59	44	-18
Commercial banks	1	3	13	9	-10	#
Other sectors	41	121	-59	-384	-178	-42
Errors and omissions	-27	-59	--44	-18	-11	-17
Global balance[3]	179	70	-37	-251	-304	-37
Total variation in reserves (minus sign indicates an increase)	-180	-71	29	244	300	38
Monetary gold	-1	#	#	#	#	#
Special Drawing Rights	-1	-1	-9	2	20	3
IMF reserve position	-1	-2	-2	-9	18	10
Foreign exchange assets	-176	-70	56	259	257	25
Other assets	-2	2	-15	-7	-106	16
Use made of IMF credit	#	#	#	#	111	-16

1. Real services also include other official and private transactions, but not factor services.
2. In addition to loans received and amortization payments made, this entry includes net loans granted and other assets and liabilities.
3. The global balance is the sum of the current account balance plus the balance on capital account. The difference between total variation in reserves of opposite sign and the global balance represents counterpart items: monetization of gold, allocation of Special Drawing Rights, and variations due to revaluation.

a. Cf. SALA, 21-2634.
b. Preliminary figures.

SOURCE: ECLA-S, 1982, p. 370.

Table 2738

HAITI: ECLA BALANCE OF PAYMENTS, 1977–82[a]

(M US)

Category	1977	1978	1979	1980	1981	1982[b]
Balance on current account	–70	–84	–97	–141	–215	–179
Trade balance	–89	–98	–177	–179	–275	–215
Exports of goods and services	174	211	213	305	250	258
Goods FOB	138	150	138	216	150	157
Real services[1]	37	61	75	89	99	101
Transport and insurance	2	2	3	6	7	3
Travel	30	53	65	77	84	81
Imports of goods and services	263	309	330	484	525	473
Goods FOB	200	207	220	319	356	284
Real services[1]	63	102	110	165	168	189
Transport and insurance	40	49	48	83	89	47
Travel	6	28	33	41	41	42
Factor services	–12	–15	–13	–14	–13	–14
Profits	–8	–9	–7	–8	–6	–8
Interest received	#	#	#	1	1	#
Interest paid	–4	–6	–7	–6	–8	–6
Unrequited private transfer payments	31	29	34	52	73	50
Balance on capital account	83	96	112	112	181	168
Unrequited official transfer payments	33	39	42	37	65	50
Long-term capital	70	50	67	71	82	102
Direct investment	8	10	12	13	18	14
Portfolio investment	#	#	#	#	#	#
Other long-term capital	62	40	55	58	64	88
Official sector[2]	43	29	49	49	45	54
Loans received	45	43	45	49	50	~
Amortization payments	–2	–3	–2	#	–4	~
Commercial banks	#	#	#	#	#	#
Loans received	#	#	#	#	#	#
Amortization payments	#	#	#	#	#	#
Other sectors[2]	20	11	5	9	19	34
Loans received	26	17	10	9	19	~
Amortization payments	–6	–6	–5	#	#	~
Short-term capital	–1	–3	–1	–18	~	17
Official sector	#	#	1	2	~	~
Commercial banks	–1	–3	–2	–20	~	~
Other sectors	#	#	#	#	~	~
Errors and omissions	–19	9	4	23	34	–1
Global balance[3]	13	12	15	–29	–34	–11
Total variation in reserves (minus sign indicates an increase)	–13	–6	–24	26	50	11
Monetary gold	#	#	–5	–4	2	~
Special Drawing Rights	#	–3	–2	4	3	~
IMF reserve position	#	–3	–3	6	#	~
Foreign exchange assets	–8	#	–11	22	15	~
Other assets	#	#	#	#	#	~
Use made of IMF credit	–5	#	–2	–3	30	~

1. Real services also include other official and private transactions, but not factor services.
2. In addition to loans received and amortization payments made, this entry includes net loans granted and other assets and liabilities.
3. The global balance is the sum of the balance on current account and the balance on capital account. The difference between the total variation in reserves (of opposite sign) and the global balance represents the value of counterpart items: monetization of gold, allocation or settlement of Special Drawing.

a. Cf. SALA, 21–2635.
b. Preliminary figures.

SOURCE: ECLA-S, 1982, p. 390.

Table 2739

HONDURAS: ECLA BALANCE OF PAYMENTS, 1977–82[a]

(M US)

Category	1977	1978	1979	1980	1981	1982[b]
Balance on current account	–139	–170	–205	–331	–321	–238
Trade balance	–74	–89	–92	–185	–177	–46
Exports of goods and services	581	687	838	942	884	768
Goods FOB	530	626	750	850	784	678
Real services[1]	51	61	88	92	100	90 ·
Transport and insurance	19	22	30	40	39	34
Travel	14	17	21	25	31	25
Imports of goods and services	655	776	930	1,127	1,061	814
Goods FOB	550	654	783	954	899	681
Real services[1]	105	122	147	173	162	133
Transport and insurance	54	64	79	98	89	71
Travel	22	23	29	31	27	23
Factor payments	–69	–85	–120	–154	–153	–202
Profits	–39	–47	–68	–78	–44	–45
Interest received	12	18	20	24	18	15
Interest paid	–42	–56	–72	–100	–127	–172
Unrequited private transfer payments	4	4	7	8	9	10
Balance on capital account	205	180	225	254	264	149
Unrequited official transfer payments	10	13	14	14	19	20
Long-term capital	149	176	167	268	207	166
Direct investment	9	13	10	6	–4	–2
Portfolio investment	#	#	#	#	#	#
Other long-term capital	140	163	157	262	211	168
Official sector[2]	34	50	60	53	16	~
Loans received	57	73	78	94	71	~
Amortization payments	–17	–20	–19	–31	–40	~
Commercial banks[2]	13	1	1	2	7	~
Loans received	19	17	9	12	18	~
Amortization payments	–6	–17	–24	–11	–11	~
Other sectors[2]	93	112	96	207	188	~
Loans received	134	160	205	279	250	~
Amortization payments	–41	–43	–95	–72	–81	~
Short-term capital	53	–21	68	12	28	–25
Official sector	11	–6	–1	–9	49	~
Commercial banks	10	–17	42	–8	–35	~
Other sectors	32	2	27	29	14	~
Errors and omissions	–7	12	–24	–40	10	–12
Global balance[3]	66	10	20	–77	–57	–89
Total variation in reserves (minus sign indicates an increase)	–66	–10	–25	73	69	89
Monetary gold	#	#	#	#	#	~
Special Drawing Rights	–1	#	–6	10	–2	~
IMF reserve position	#	–8	#	8	#	~
Foreign exchange assets	–48	3	–19	41	51	~
Other assets	–3	#	#	–1	–3	~
Use made of IMF credit	–14	–5	#	15	23	~

1. Real services also include other official and private transactions, but not factor payments.
2. In addition to loans received and amortization payments made, this entry includes net loans granted and other assets and liabilities.
3. The global balance is the sum of the balance on current account and the balance on capital account. The difference between the total variation in reserves (opposite sign) and the global balance represents the value of the counterpart items: monetary gold, allocation of Special Drawing Rights and variation due to revaluation.

a. Cf. SALA, 21–2636.
b. Preliminary figures.

SOURCE: ECLA-S, 1982, p. 411.

Table 2740

MEXICO: ECLA BALANCE OF PAYMENTS, 1977-82[a]

(M US)

Category	1977	1978	1979	1980	1981	1982[b]
Balance on current account	-1,870	-3,259	-5,570	-7,687	-12,997	-2,740
Trade balance	127	-593	-1,629	-1,816	-3,902	7,668
Exports of goods and services	7,792	10,743	15,093	23,531	28,568	28,520
Goods FOB	4,604	6,246	9,302	16,241	19,837	21,270
Real services[1]	3,189	4,497	5,791	7,290	8,731	7,250
Transport and insurance	200	250	318	450	497	420
Travel	2,122	3,208	4,133	5,200	6,242	5,200
Imports of goods and services	7,665	11,336	16,722	25,347	32,471	20,852
Goods FOB	5,625	7,992	12,132	18,551	23,166	14,590
Real services[1]	2,040	3,344	4,590	6,796	9,304	6,262
Transport and insurance	487	779	1,128	1,931	2,379	1,660
Travel	1,183	2,152	2,936	4,178	6,150	4,080
Factor services	-2,151	-2,771	-4,072	-6,002	-9,219	-10,500
Profits	-401	-676	-927	-1,283	-1,827	-700
Interest received	168	405	693	981	1,332	1,250
Interest paid	-1,979	-2,576	-3,739	-5,435	-8,204	-10,500
Work and ownership	61	77	-99	-266	-520	-550
Unrequited private transfer payments	153	104	132	132	125	92
Balance on capital account	2,247	3,690	5,886	8,593	14,082	-180
Unrequited official transfer payments	16	88	94	144	180	133
Long-term capital	4,611	5,121	5,176	7,259	15,199	8,590
Direct investment	556	824	1,337	1,846	2,253	941
Portfolio investment	1,345	737	-392	-71	648	~
Other long-term capital	2,710	3,560	4,231	5,484	12,298	~
Official sector[2]	1,077	362	-180	655	375	~
Loans received	1,143	857	1,753	1,153	1,456	~
Amortization payments	-67	-495	-1,933	-498	-1,080	~
Commercial banks[2]	893	1,006	1,246	1,125	8,551	~
Loans received	2,273	3,338	3,452	2,551	12,847	~
Amortization payments	-1,379	-2,331	-2,206	-1,426	-4,296	~
Other sectors[2]	740	2,192	3,165	3,704	3,372	~
Loans received	1,787	4,246	6,107	5,320	4,689	~
Amortization payments	-982	-2,037	-2,960	-1,627	-930	~
Short-term capital	-2,431	-1,421	-32	3,284	4,063	-3,850
Official sector	-292	-1	33	-51	#	~
Commercial banks	-469	-837	1,076	2,333	2,432	~
Other sectors	-1,669	-583	-1,140	-1,003	1,631	~
Net errors and omissions	49	-98	647	-2,092	-5,360	-5,053
Global balance[3]	377	430	316	906	1,085	-2,920
Total variation in reserves (minus sign indicates an increase)	-384	-455	-399	-1,037	-1,133	2,920
Monetary gold	-6	-6	-4	-3	-8	~
Special Drawing Rights	-56	1	-144	56	-34	~
IMF reserve position	#	#	#	-128	-60	~
Foreign exchange assets	-405	-194	-46	-727	-662	~
Other assets	-55	-46	-42	-100	-370	~
Use made of IMF credit	138	-211	-163	-136	#	~

1. Real services also include other official and private transactions, but exclude factor services.
2. In addition to loans received and amortization payments on these, this entry includes net loans granted and other assets and liabilities.
3. The global balance is the sum of the balance on the capital and current accounts. The difference between the total variation in reserves with the opposite sign and the global balance represents the value of counterpart items: monetization of gold, allocation of Special Drawing Rights and variations due to revaluation.

a. Cf. SALA, 21-2637.
b. Preliminary figures.

SOURCE: ECLA-S, 1982, p. 444.

Table 2741

NICARAGUA: ECLA BALANCE OF PAYMENTS, 1977-82[a]

(M US)

Category	1977	1978	1979	1980	1981	1982[b]
Balance on current account	-192	-34	90	-512	-571	-393
Trade balance	-122	62	162	-427	-478	-240
Exports of goods and services	719	720	672	503	547	476
Goods FOB	636	646	616	451	500	429
Real services[1]	83	74	56	52	47	47
Transport and insurance	29	28	22	7	8	7
Travel	34	25	18	22	23	20
Imports of goods and services	841	658	511	930	1,025	716
Goods FOB	704	553	389	803	897	646
Real services[1]	137	104	122	127	128	70
Transport and insurance	68	56	31	44	53	35
Travel	46	60	48	31	15	14
Factor services	-71	-97	-73	-86	-94	-154
Profits	-28	-35	-13	-10	-8	-3
Interest received	10	8	6	#	#	#
Interest paid	-50	-67	-65	-79	-85	-151
Others	-3	-3	-1	3	-1	#
Unrequited private transfer payments	1	#	1	1	1	1
Balance on capital account	202	-49	-85	400	682[c]	270
Unrequited official transfer payments	11	9	90	80	54	59[c]
Long-term capital	211	135	112	296	575	227
Direct investment	10	7	3	#	#	1
Portfolio investment	#	#	#	#	#	#
Other long-term capital	201	128	109	296	575[c]	226[c]
Official sector[2]	140	123	107	296	575[c]	~
Loans disbursed	172	152	132	371	641[c,d]	319[c,d]
Amortization payments	-27	-24	-22	-75	-66[c]	-93[e]
Commercial banks[2]	#	-7	5	~	~	~
Loans disbursed	#	#	#	~	~	~
Amortization payments	#	#	#	~	~	~
Other sectors[2]	62	12	-2	~	~	~
Loans disbursed	97	58	15	~	~	~
Amortization payments	-35	-46	-17	~	~	~
Short-term capital (net)	-16	-184	-258	~	~	~
Official sector	8	-13	14	~	~	~
Commercial banks	55	55	-20	~	~	~
Other sectors	-80	-227	-252	~	~	~
Errors and omissions	-4	-10	-30	24[e]	53	-16
Global balance[3]	9	-84	5	-112	111	-123
Total variation in reserves (minus sign indicates an increase)	-9	83	-9	107	-115	123[f]
Monetary gold	#	#	-1	#	#	~
Special Drawing Rights	-1	-1	6	-5	-4	~
IMF reserve position	#	#	#	#	#	~
Foreign exchange assets	2	99	-75	120	-86	~
Other assets	1	-15	7	#	#	~
Use made of IMF credit	-8	#	55	-8	-25	~

1. Real services also include other official and private transactions, but not factor services.
2. In addition to loans received and amortization payments made, this entry includes net loans granted and other assets and liabilities.
3. The global balance is the sum of the current account balance plus the balance on capital account. The difference between total variation in reserves of opposite sign and the global balance represents counterpart items: monetization or demonetization of gold, allocation or settlement of Special Drawing Rights, and variations due to revaluation.

a. Cf. SALA, 21-2638.
b. Preliminary figures.
c. Including long-term and short-term capital.
d. Including US$ 223 million for renegotiation of the external debt in 1981 and US $6 million for the same item in 1982.
e. Including short-term capital.
f. Estimates.

SOURCE: ECLA-S, 1982, p. 472.

Table 2742

PANAMA: ECLA BALANCE OF PAYMENTS, 1977-82[a]
(M US)

Category	1977	1978	1979	1980	1981	1982[b]
Balance on current account	-183	-240	-351	-363	-676	-539
Trade balance	-181	-260	-328	-167	-267	-352
Exports of goods and services	795	818	1,013	1,504	1,564	1,511
Goods FOB	288	302	356	375	343	345
Real services[1]	507	516	658	1,129	1,220	1,166
Transport and insurance	133	105	128	507	536	574
Travel	177	201	214	168	171	172
Imports of goods and services	977	1,078	1,341	1,671	1,831	1,863
Goods FOB	790	862	1,070	1,334	1,459	1,459
Real services[1]	186	216	271	337	372	404
Transport and insurance	112	127	159	218	239	243
Travel	35	37	48	56	65	78
Factor services	28	54	17	-143	-360	-133
Profits	-21	-16	-41	-52	-51	~
Interest received	482	795	1,435	2,107	2,705	2,813
Interest paid	-525	-832	-1,496	-2,199	-3,019	-3,027
Others	92	107	119	2	6	~
Unrequited private transfer payments	-30	-34	-39	-54	-49	-54
Balance on capital account	176	327	323	375	595	530
Unrequited official transfer payments	28	31	53	41	49	84
Long-term capital	-113	453	314	295	283	~
Direct investment	11	-1	50	45	45	40
Portfolio investment	13	70	204	16	25	~
Other long-term capital	-137	383	60	234	212	~
Official sector[2]	90	341	114	215	84	~
Loans received	123	685	225	284	217	~
Amortization payments	-32	-344	-111	-66	-131	-324[c]
Commercial banks[2]	-411	-33	43	42	134	~
Loans received	1	#	43	42	135	~
Amortization payments	-412	-33	#	#	#	#
Other sectors[2]	184	76	-97	-23	-6	~
Loans received	246	213	98	113	140	~
Amortization payments	-59	-144	-196	-136	-146	~
Short-term capital	331	-156	391	-429	-151	~
Official sector	3	5	-3	2	2	~
Commercial banks	377	-162	433	-385	-85	~
Other sectors	-50	1	-38	-46	-68	~
Errors and omissions (net)	-70	-2	-435	467	414	~
Global balance[3]	-7	86	-27	11	-81	-9
Total variation in reserves (minus sign indicates an increase)	10	-78	21	-17	66	9
Monetary gold	#	#	#	#	-2	#
Special Drawing Rights	1	#	#	4	-2	-1
IMF reserve position	#	-5	2	-7	10	#
Foreign exchange assets	7	-75	30	5	-11	20
Other assets	#	#	#	#	#	#
Use made of IMF credit	2	1	-11	-18	71	-10

1. Real services also include other official and private transactions, but not factor services.
2. In addition to loans received and amortization payments made, this entry includes net loans granted and other assets and liabilities.
3. The global balance is the sum of the current account balance plus the balance on capital account. The difference between total variation in reserves of opposite sign and the global balance represents counterpart items: monetization of gold, allocation of Special Drawing Rights, and variations due to revaluation.

a. Cf. SALA, 21-2639.
b. Preliminary figures.
c. Includes total amortization payments in respect of long- and short-term debt.

SOURCE: ECLA-S, 1982, p. 490.

Table 2743

PARAGUAY: ECLA BALANCE OF PAYMENTS, 1972–82[a]

(M US)

Category	1972	1973	1974	1975	1976	1977	1978	1979	1980	1981	1982[b]
Balance on current account	-9	-19	-55	-85	-72	-59	-118	-210	-283	-378	-536
Trade balance	0	-10	-36	-60	-52	-42	-93	-218	-276	-412	-508
Exports of goods and services	105	149	207	222	242	390	434	514	566	566	684
Goods FOB	86	128	173	188	202	327	356	384	400	399	394
Real services[1]	20	21	34	34	40	63	78	129	166	168	290
Transport and insurance	1	1	2	2	2	2	2	3	4	5	2
Travel	11	11	12	10	14	35	40	69	91	80	55
Imports of goods and services	105	159	244	282	294	432	528	731	842	978	1,192
Goods FOB	79	127	198	227	236	360	432	577	675	772	810
Real services[1]	26	32	45	55	58	72	96	154	167	206	382
Transport and insurance	10	15	27	32	31	44	64	93	104	118	91
Travel	8	10	10	12	13	16	20	31	35	38	38
Factor services	-12	-12	-20	-26	-20	-18	-25	4	-11	31	-30
Profits	-3	-4	-10	-19	-13	-20	-42	-18	-54	-41	-60
Interest received	1	2	5	6	9	12	18	45	77	102	113
Interest paid	-10	-10	-16	-18	-23	-26	-37	-55	-81	-90	-129
Others	#	#	#	5	7	16	36	33	48	60	46
Unrequited private transfer payments	3	2	2	1	1	1	1	3	3	2	2
Balance on capital account	17	44	85	114	114	171	296	372	434	421	413
Unrequited official transfer payments	4	3	2	13	3	#	5	4	2	3	#
Long-term capital	20	30	53	86	117	85	167	136	192	168	#
Direct investment	3	9	21	24	-3	22	20	50	32	39	#
Portfolio investment	#	#	#	#	#	#	#	#	#	#	#
Other long-term capital	17	20	32	62	120	64	147	85	160	129	#
Official sector[2]	3	5	11	20	36	31	56	10	85	39	#
Loans disbursed	6	7	14	23	40	38	65	21	98	60	#
Amortization payments	-3	-3	-4	-4	-4	-8	-9	-11	-12	-20	#
Commercial banks[2]	#	#	#	7	-2	#	#	3	1	11	#
Loans disbursed	#	#	#	13	3	4	6	9	7	17	#
Amortization payments	#	#	#	-6	-5	-4	-6	-6	-6	-6	#
Other sectors[2]	15	15	22	35	86	33	91	72	74	79	#
Loans disbursed	20	24	32	50	102	55	118	113	135	141	#
Amortization payments	-6	-8	-13	-14	-15	-22	-28	-41	-60	-61	#
Short-term capital (net)	-4	16	33	11	-6	106	108	223	261	263	#
Official sector	1	2	#	-3	-1	3	7	15	3	12	#
Commercial banks	-2	1	-9	-3	-12	4	9	-9	-14	-13	#
Other sectors	-4	13	42	17	7	99	92	218	271	264	#
Errors and omissions	-4	-6	-4	4	#	-20	17	9	-20	-13	#
Global balance[3]	7	24	30	29	42	112	178	162	151	44	-123
Total variation in reserves (minus sign indicates an increase)	-10	-26	-30	-28	-43	-112	-179	-165	-153	-43	123
Monetary gold	#	#	#	#	#	#	#	-4	#	#	#
Special Drawing Rights	-2	-1	#	#	#	-1	-1	-4	-2	-3	-9
IMF reserve position	#	-1	#	#	-1	-1	#	-2	-8	-10	-1
Foreign exchange assets	-8	-24	-30	-28	-42	-109	-180	-154	-143	-30	133
Other assets	#	#	#	#	#	-2	2	-1	#	#	#
Use made of IMF credit	#	#	#	#	#	#	#	#	#	#	#

1. Real services also include other official and private transactions, but not factor services.
2. In addition to loans received and amortization payments made, this entry includes net loans granted and other assets and liabilities.
3. The global balance is the sum of the current account balance plus the balance on capital account. The difference between total variation in reserves of opposite sign and the global balance represents counterpart items: monetization or demonetization of gold, allocation or settlement of Special Drawing Rights, and variations due to revaluation.

a. Cf. SALA, 21-2640.
b. Preliminary figures.

SOURCE: ECLA-S, 1982, p. 529.

Table 2744

PERU: ECLA BALANCE OF PAYMENTS, 1977-82[a]
(M US)

Category	1977	1978	1979	1980	1981	1982[b]
Balance on current account	-976	-244	663	-72	-1,680	-1,675
Trade balance	-557	330	1,599	763	-795	-710
Exports of goods and services	2,131	2,401	4,101	4,650	4,012	4,027
Goods FOB	1,726	1,941	3,519	3,899	3,256	3,198
Real services[1]	406	461	582	751	757	829
Transport and insurance	175	179	255	284	275	289
Travel	112	141	175	292	287	322
Imports of goods and services	2,688	2,071	2,502	3,887	4,806	4,737
Goods FOB	2,164	1,600	1,955	3,062	3,803	3,635
Real services[1]	524	469	547	825	1,004	1,102
Transport and insurance	325	263	319	433	508	532
Travel	36	33	45	107	133	150
Factor services	-422	-579	-936	-835	-885	-965
Profits	-54	-84	-393	-292	-218	-183
Interest received	13	14	56	201	204	135
Interest paid	-381	-509	-601	-743	-873	-917
Unrequited private transfer payments	5	4	#	#	#	#
Balance on capital account	1,042	268	414	725	871	1,762
Unrequited official transfer payments	53	54	122	134	172	~
Long-term capital	955	265	698	273	610	1,264
Direct investment	55	26	70	27	263	59
Portfolio investment	#	#	#	#	#	~
Other long-term capital	901	238	628	246	347	1,205
Official sector[2]	883	225	660	182	213	1,048
Loans disbursed	1,285	1,102	1,684	1,581	1,647	1,919
Amortization payments	-395	-868	-1,008	-1,391	-1,433	-871
Other sectors[2]	18	14	-32	64	134	157
Loans disbursed	118	96	89	181	294	378
Amortization payments	-100	-83	-119	-117	-160	-221
Short-term capital (net)	150	-101	-370	501	277	481
Official sector	109	-37	-300	90	6	~
Commercial banks	39	-66	-53	13	31	~
Other sectors	2	2	-18	398	240	~
Errors and omissions	-113	53	-36	-186	-191	17
Global balance[3]	66	24	1,076	653	-809	87
Total variation in reserves[3]						
(minus sign indicates an increase)	-60	-6	-1,066	-607	649	~
Monetary gold	#	#	-64	-173	#	~
Special Drawing Rights	#	-3	-100	94	1	~
IMF reserve position	#	#	#	#	#	~
Foreign exchange assets	-68	-30	-1,030	-553	769	~
Other assets	-13	-101	-29	43	-35	~
Use made of IMF credit	21	128	158	-17	-87	~

1. Real services also include other official and private transactions, but not factor services.
2. In addition to loans received and amortization payments made, this entry includes net loans granted and other assets and liabilities.
3. The global balance is the sum of the current account balance plus the balance on capital account. The difference between total variation in reserves of opposite sign and the global balance represents counterpart items: monetization of gold, allocation of Special Drawing Rights, and variations due to revaluation.

a. Cf. SALA, 21-2641.
b. Preliminary figures.

SOURCE: ECLA-S, 1982, p. 574.

Table 2745

URUGUAY: ECLA BALANCE OF PAYMENTS, 1977-82[a]

(M US)

Category	1977	1978	1979	1980	1981	1982[b]
Balance on current account	-172	-133	-363	-716	-470	-467
Trade balance	-106	-57	-309	-618	-399	-229
Exports of goods and services	809	913	1,194	1,526	1,681	1,281
Goods FOB	612	686	788	1,059	1,230	1,023
Real services[1]	197	227	406	468	451	258
Transport and insurance	36	44	72	89	92	80
Travel	117	137	268	298	283	106
Imports of goods and services	914	970	1,504	2,144	2,080	1,510
Goods FOB	687	710	1,166	1,668	1,599	1,049
Real services[1]	228	260	337	476	480	460
Transport and insurance	80	95	124	161	174	127
Travel	96	109	136	203	203	304
Factor services	-68	-77	-55	-100	-74	-240
Profits	-2	#	#	#	#	#
Interest received	12	18	50	68	146	133
Interest paid	-77	-95	-108	-168	-220	-373
Others	#	#	3	#	#	#
Unrequited private transfer payments	2	1	2	2	3	2
Balance on capital account	351	262	453	811	496	-332
Unrequited official transfer payments	5	6	6	7	7	8
Long-term capital	101	152	359	404	347	~
Direct investment	66	129	216	289	49	~
Portfolio investment	21	-9	-31	-7	3	~
Other long-term capital	14	32	174	122	295	~
Official sector[2]	#	38	154	108	246	~
Loans received	52	103	163	181	276	~
Amortization payments	-49	-57	-18	-66	-27	~
Commercial banks[2]	#	-2	-3	5	-2	~
Loans received	#	#	#	7	#	-340
Amortization payments	#	-2	-2	-2	-2	~
Other sectors[2]	13	-4	23	9	51	~
Loans received	36	53	41	26	65	~
Amortization payments	-23	-57	-18	-17	-14	~
Short-term capital (net)	203	-54	94	311	325	~
Official sector	16	-9	9	-23	-5	~
Commercial banks	74	-39	128	307	87	~
Other sectors	113	-7	-42	26	244	~
Errors and omissions	42	159	-5	90	-183	~
Global balance[3]	179	129	91	95	27	-799
Total variation in reserves						
(minus sign indicates an increase)	-201	-183	-25	-174	-26	~
Monetary gold	-1	-10	-46	-84	4	~
Special Drawing Rights	-6	-5	-20	1	-10	41
IMF reserve position	#	-22	#	-13	1	33
Foreign exchange assets	-140	-4	49	-50	-37	240
Other assets	-28	-24	-9	-29	16	~
Use made of IMF credit	-26	-119	#	#	#	96

1. Real services also include other official and private transactions, but not factor services.
2. In addition to loans received and amortization payments made, this entry includes net loans granted and other assets and liabilities.
3. The global balance is the sum of the current account balance plus the balance on capital account. The difference between total variation in reserves of opposite sign and the global balance represents counterpart items: monetization of gold, allocation of Special Drawing Rights, and variations due to revaluation.

a. Cf. SALA, 21-2642.
b. Preliminary figures.

SOURCE: ECLA-S, 1982, p. 621.

Table 2746

VENEZUELA: ECLA BALANCE OF PAYMENTS, 1977–82[a]

(M US)

Category	1977	1978	1979	1980	1981	1982[b]
Balance on current account	–3,125	–5,697	371	4,749	4,045	–3,424
Trade balance	–2,985	–5,366	760	4,839	3,611	–931
Exports of goods and services	10,164	9,803	14,959	19,968	20,712	17,259
Goods FOB	9,544	9,085	14,164	19,050	19,859	16,549
Real services[1]	620	720	795	918	853	710
Transport and insurance	326	384	468	513	458	380
Travel	168	205	178	243	251	209
Imports of goods and services	13,150	15,169	14,199	15,129	17,101	18,190
Goods FOB	10,194	11,234	10,004	10,877	12,378	13,166
Real services[1]	2,955	3,935	4,195	4,252	2,724	5,024
Transport and insurance	1,274	1,555	1,454	1,449	1,516	1,612
Travel	1,053	1,635	1,727	1,981	2,349	2,498
Factor services	89	38	–3	328	817	–1,919
Profits	–292	–304	–313	–321	–337	–792
Interest received	782	1,052	1,346	2,263	3,776	2,473
Interest paid	–402	–710	–1,036	–1,613	–2,622	–3,600
Unrequited private transfer payments	–230	–369	–386	–418	–383	–574
Balance on capital account	2,966	3,866	606	–4,797	–1,551	704
Unrequited official transfer payments	–53	–38	–21	–21	–46	–67
Long-term capital	2,131	3,718	1,517	1,230	–25	3,170
Direct investment	–4	68	88	55	160	254
Portfolio investment	–41	124	–74	1,311	–62	0
Other long-term capital	2,175	3,527	1,503	–135	–123	2,916
Official sector[2]	1,282	2,016	1,059	–173	–175	3,062
Loans disbursed	1,719	2,441	1,857	787	779	~
Amortization payments	–393	–412	–776	–855	–945	~
Commercial banks[2]	414	687	–655	220	#	~
Loans disbursed	#	#	#	#	#	~
Amortization payments	#	#	#	#	#	~
Other sectors[2]	479	824	1,098	–182	52	–146
Loans disbursed	1,078	1,752	2,066	1,942	1,292	–28
Amortization payments	–294	–570	–860	–1,007	–1,077	–118
Short-term capital	–1,350	–1,297	–1,373	–4,807	–151	515
Official sector	44	–8	–3	103	11	5,062
Commercial banks	2	–210	–65	–29	39	–4,547
Other sectors	–1,396	–1,079	–1,306	–4,881	–200	~
Errors and omissions (net)	2,238	1,482	485	–1,201	–1,330	–2,914
Global balance[3]	–160	–1,830	977	–48	2,494	–2,720
Total variation in reserves (minus sign indicates an increase)	171	1,833	–1,104	–61	–2,676	–215
Monetary gold	#	#	#	#	#	#
Special Drawing Rights	–19	–52	–135	9	–101	5
IMF reserve position	64	246	229	–87	–14	–113
Foreign exchange assets	344	1,507	–1,379	795	–1,446	1,695
Other assets	–218	133	182	–777	–1,115	–1,802
Use made of IMF credit	#	#	#	#	#	#

1. Real services also include other official and private transactions, but not factor services.
2. In addition to loans received and amortization payments made, this entry includes net loans granted and other assets and liabilities.
3. The global balance is the sum of the current account balance plus the balance on capital account. The difference between total variation in reserves of opposite sign and the global balance represents counterpart items: monetization of gold, allocation of Special Drawing Rights, and variations due to revaluation.

a. Cf. SALA, 21–2643.
b. Preliminary figures.

SOURCE: ECLA-S, 1982, p. 651.

Table 2747

LATIN AMERICA: ECLA BALANCE OF PAYMENTS, 1950-77[a]

(M US)

Item	1950	1951	1952	1953	1954	1955	1956	1957	1958	1959	1960	1961	1962	1963
Current Account														
Exports of Goods and Services	6,608.3	7,815.4	7,223.9	7,846.8	8265.3	8,535.6	9,260.8	9,577.6	8,959.3	9,035.5	9,493.0	9,685.7	10,104.3	10,649.8
Goods FOB	6,037.2	7,085.4	6,412.1	6,973.1	7,367.3	7,517.4	8,083.5	8,282.5	7,724.8	7,659.5	7,952.5	8,163.9	8,621.2	9,061.0
Services	571.1	730.0	811.8	873.7	898.0	1,018.2	1,177.3	1,295.1	1,234.5	1,376.0	1,540.0	1,521.8	1,433.1	1,588.8
Transport	99.8	163.1	225.6	196.6	205.9	226.2	236.7	226.1	185.6	203.1	287.8	319.6	334.4	337.6
Travel	338.2	358.7	364.8	389.2	428.6	476.6	539.3	590.5	613.0	693.3	758.8	804.2	804.7	867.6

Item	1964	1965	1966	1967	1968	1969	1970	1971	1972	1973	1974	1975	1976	1977
Current Account														
Exports of Goods and Services	11,476.0	12152.1	12,945.7	13,125.0	14,128.2	15,852.2	17,206.4	17,896.7	20,768.9	29,206.1	44,010.2	41,449.3	47,724.1	56,354.0
Goods FOB	9,740.1	10,265.3	10,803.6	10,672.4	11,312.6	12,559.2	13,706.6	14,091.4	16,468.4	23,829.2	36,993.6	34,066.3	39,892.0	47,362.4
Services	1,735.9	1,886.8	2,142.1	2,452.7	2,815.6	3,293.0	3,499.8	3,805.2	4,310.6	5,376.8	7,016.7	7,383.1	7,832.1	8,991.6
Transport	357.3	324.9	416.5	490.1	541.3	673.0	782.2	797.5	879.2	1,175.9	1,810.3	1,731.0	1,744.2	2,288.2
Travel	957.5	1,086.9	1,213.3	1,367.5	1,585.7	1,660.8	1,710.0	1,919.7	2,133.5	2,590.7	3,148.4	3,429.8	3,594.8	3,905.0

Continued in SALA, 21-2621.

Table 2748

LAFTA: ECLA BALANCE OF PAYMENTS, 1950-77[a]

(M US)

Item	1950	1951	1952	1953	1954	1955	1956	1957	1958	1959	1960	1961	1962	1963
Current Account														
Exports of Goods and Services	6,068.1	7,177.5	6,559.0	7,169.8	7,533.1	7,786.3	8,457.3	8,722.4	8,138.9	8,237.6	8,640.3	8,824.8	9,096.8	9,529.9
Goods FOB	5,581.2	6,539.6	5,845.5	6,404.8	6,741.8	6,896.9	7,426.8	7,595.1	7,055.1	7,021.8	7,284.2	7,493.3	7,827.4	8,181.5
Services	486.9	637.9	713.5	765.0	791.3	889.4	1,030.5	1,127.3	1,083.8	1,215.8	1,356.1	1,331.5	1,269.4	1,348.4
Transport	90.4	145.5	206.5	175.4	185.9	201.8	210.2	196.8	159.0	176.7	259.4	292.0	301.3	298.6
Travel	299.3	319.8	324.8	349.2	387.2	422.4	478.4	529.3	559.6	635.0	700.3	742.0	735.4	800.0

Item	1964	1965	1966	1967	1968	1969	1970	1971	1972	1973	1974	1975	1976	1977
Current Account														
Exports of Goods and Services	10,247.4	10,849.3	11,527.3	11,619.0	12,460.9	14,089.0	15,216.2	15,794.2	18,208.2	26,103.5	39,900.1	36,713.4	42,347.3	49,746.4
Goods FOB	8,755.8	9,238.3	9,683.5	9,515.4	10,038.1	11,223.4	12,204.0	12,532.7	14,544.7	21,479.7	33,870.9	30,412.2	35,717.7	42,053.7
Services	1,491.6	1,611.0	1,843.8	2,103.6	2,422.8	2,865.6	3,012.2	3,261.5	3,663.5	4,623.8	6,029.2	6,301.2	6,629.6	7,692.8
Transport	315.5	278.4	368.2	434.4	474.9	602.1	694.3	687.4	747.3	1,027.7	1,546.6	1,457.7	1,460.2	1,962.1
Travel	892.1	1,011.8	1,124.1	1,257.0	1,460.0	1,522.4	1,548.8	1,743.1	1,926.8	2,327.8	2,801.1	3,028.7	3,172.8	3,458.1

Continued in SALA, 21-2622.

Table 2749

AG: ECLA BALANCE OF PAYMENTS, 1950-77[a]

(M US)

Item	1950	1951	1952	1953	1954	1955	1956	1957	1958	1959	1960	1961	1962	1963
Current Account														
Exports of Goods and Services														
Goods FOB	2,338.4	2,787.4	3,025.2	3,054.3	3,386.6	3,668.4	4,135.2	4,588.7	4,177.6	4,140.3	4,355.6	4,424.5	4,604.3	4,557.7
Services	2,233.2	2,657.3	2,853.7	2,869.6	3,206.1	3,466.9	3,903.6	4,315.4	3,891.7	3,834.1	4,004.3	4,079.6	4,272.5	4,219.8
Transport	105.2	130.1	171.5	184.7	180.5	201.5	231.6	273.3	285.9	306.2	351.3	344.9	331.8	337.9
Travel	42.7	58.7	65.7	67.6	64.0	78.0	80.8	81.6	75.9	82.5	92.1	110.5	121.9	122.0
	17.2	19.5	26.4	28.2	30.0	32.0	26.7	34.0	47.3	50.3	82.4	87.2	84.0	77.9

Item	1964	1965	1966	1967	1968	1969	1970	1971	1972	1973	1974	1975	1976	1977
Current Account														
Exports of Goods and Services														
Goods FOB	5,038.1	5,182.4	5,413.3	5,643.0	5,984.3	6,361.1	6,777.9	6,967.5	7,366.7	10,367.5	19,762.1	16,748.7	19,035.6	21,074.4
Services	4,655.0	4,746.2	4,906.6	5,035.2	5,301.8	5,592.0	5,973.6	6,146.2	6,453.3	9,245.9	18,131.8	14,913.2	17,109.9	18,637.6
Transport	383.1	436.2	506.7	607.8	682.5	769.1	804.3	821.3	913.4	1,121.6	1,630.3	1,835.5	1,925.7	2,436.8
Travel	135.9	161.4	182.9	241.8	253.3	308.5	329.8	316.7	338.7	428.0	690.0	687.3	584.2	830.1
	105.1	128.2	150.5	182.1	181.9	186.6	217.0	247.7	260.7	335.9	512.4	565.0	677.9	808.0

Continued in SALA, 21-2623.

Table 2750

CACM: ECLA BALANCE OF PAYMENTS, 1950-77[a]

(M US)

Item	1950	1951	1952	1953	1954	1955	1956	1957	1958	1959	1960	1961	1962	1963
Current Account														
Exports of Goods and Services														
Goods FOB	325.4	369.8	394.1	422.1	442.0	467.8	502.2	527.0	523.5	502.2	504.0	524.7	591.1	677.0
Services	300.2	343.5	366.3	392.8	411.3	425.6	450.9	463.3	460.8	436.8	433.8	460.0	523.6	589.5
Transport	25.2	26.3	27.8	29.3	30.7	42.2	51.3	63.7	62.7	65.4	70.2	64.7	67.5	87.5
Travel	3.9	4.7	5.4	6.0	7.5	11.7	14.3	14.2	13.6	14.3	14.4	15.4	17.4	21.6
	6.9	6.9	7.0	6.7	6.4	12.4	14.0	17.7	19.9	22.0	22.3	21.8	22.5	23.5

Item	1964	1965	1966	1967	1968	1969	1970	1971	1972	1973	1974	1975	1976	1977
Current Account														
Exports of Goods and Services														
Goods FOB	776.7	886.2	962.8	987.6	1,098.2	1,130.8	1,298.3	1,327.9	1,630.6	1,993.1	2,538.7	2,777.8	3,603.6	4,661.9
Services	684.9	771.2	844.0	858.9	957.2	982.6	1,120.2	1,133.8	1,377.0	1,689.8	2,165.1	2,349.6	3,079.1	4,114.2
Transport	91.8	115.0	118.8	128.7	141.0	148.2	178.1	194.1	253.6	303.3	373.6	428.2	524.5	547.7
Travel	22.3	26.5	26.4	27.5	31.1	34.7	41.7	48.8	57.7	65.8	85.2	101.6	124.3	141.0
	26.5	30.2	37.2	43.7	48.8	50.0	60.0	65.5	76.6	104.1	153.8	185.3	183.4	187.9

Continued in SALA, 21-2624.

Table 2751

ECLA BALANCE ON CURRENT ACCOUNT,[1] IN DOLLARS OF 1970, 19 LR, 1950-77

(M US)

YEAR	A. ARGENTINA	B. BOLIVIA	C. BRAZIL	D. CHILE	E. COLOMBIA	F. COSTA RICA	H. DOMINICAN REP.	I. ECUADOR	J. EL SALVADOR	K. GUATEMALA
1950	133.8	-.6	150.0	-19.3	-18.9	3.2	27.7	28.1	19.9	0
1951	-393.6	3.7	-586.2	-58.5	5.0	.4	8.0	-.4	11.2	-8.0
1952	-494.2	-8.5	-843.2	19.0	34.9	-7.0	-6.6	24.7	10.4	17.8
1953	352.7	-27.3	18.6	-77.7	17.4	-1.4	3.2	-2.4	10.6	17.8
1954	57.3	-19.8	-281.4	-1.6	-49.6	.1	24.8	-21.1	10.7	1.6
1955	-288.2	-26.7	-43.7	27.0	-145.8	-9.2	-12.4	-27.7	1.7	-8.4
1956	-176.8	-23.4	-2.4	-29.5	-13.7	-20.5	-10.8	-29.9	7.4	-35.5
1957	-347.3	-43.0	-371.2	-131.9	86.7	-20.6	7.4	-7.0	3.1	-57.5
1958	-315.4	-58.5	-339.2	-111.2	68.9	-8.8	-25.8	-13.9	1.5	-72.2
1959	-23.4	-33.9	-443.0	-37.1	71.0	-27.9	-1.8	-4.9	.1	-60.7
1960	-274.8	-37.4	-660.1	-200.5	-99.6	-21.9	50.4	-21.6	-35.9	-34.6
1961	-754.4	-33.6	-328.1	-372.6	-163.1	-19.9	38.8	-30.0	-2.6	-29.5
1962	-358.9	-57.0	-550.2	-267.2	-194.5	-22.2	-18.1	-9.5	0	-31.6
1963	258.0	-52.8	-225.8	-234.3	-157.1	-30.4	-42.6	-8.6	-15.9	-27.1
1964	14.5	-33.1	54.1	-152.2	-156.2	-30.8	-76.4	-31.1	-31.0	-52.5
1965	218.9	-42.4	272.5	-47.2	-21.4	-79.0	-22.1	-28.6	-18.6	-46.0
1966	241.7	-35.7	-69.5	-115.3	-316.8	-52.3	-72.2	-21.4	-50.1	-17.3
1967	155.3	-45.1	-322.2	-68.8	-96.7	-57.8	-73.5	-37.5	-29.9	-67.6
1968	-52.8	-59.7	-569.2	-151.1	-200.1	-49.8	-81.2	-77.8	-19.1	-57.0
1969	-244.0	-56.1	-369.2	-91.3	-218.1	-57.7	-86.7	-106.2	-25.0	-21.2
1970	-156.0	-23.9	-644.0	-95.0	-330.0	-76.6	-126.0	-122.4	6.8	-8.0
1971	-363.7	-42.8	-1,291.9	-193.4	-467.2	-114.3	-119.3	-157.8	14.9	-46.1
1972	-202.3	-48.6	-1,364.2	-430.9	-197.7	-92.9	-44.8	-76.6	8.5	-9.2
1973	565.4	-25.3	-1,387.4	-221.3	-65.0	-88.8	-79.1	-10.9	-36.7	6.4
1974	72.3	70.7	-3,737.3	-112.4	-251.7	-158.9	-153.7	14.7	-79.5	-55.1
1975	-655.3	-96.9	-3,297.1	-320.3	-60.4	-116.4	-35.6	-190.5	-50.6	-31.5
1976	304.4	-71.4	-2,936.9	13.2	-194.5	-104.2	-117.3	-71.6	9.8	-2.1
1977	588.2	-93.0	-1,881.4	-242.0	-225.5	-93.3	-142.0	-201.4	-9.9	-27.5

YEAR	L. HAITI	M. HONDURAS	N. MEXICO	O. NICARAGUA	P. PANAMA	Q. PARAGUAY	R. PERU	S. URUGUAY	T. VENEZUELA	LATIN AMERICA
1950	-2.7	-1.0	61.9	.8	-15.9	12.1	-8.0	56.0	21.7	448.8
1951	.5	-5.0	-250.9	10.2	-22.9	9.9	-49.8	-91.9	90.5	-1,282.8
1952	-2.2	-14.4	-156.2	.5	-29.9	-8.1	-67.6	-38.6	65.6	-1,503.6
1953	-16.0	-8.3	-192.3	-5.5	-19.0	-7.4	-93.2	76.1	-38.7	7.0
1954	6.6	.1	-48.4	-18.4	-23.3	-7.5	-23.2	-46.9	-64.8	-504.8
1955	-21.4	-10.6	140.6	.9	-15.4	-2.3	-55.1	-71.7	15.4	-553.0
1956	-2.9	-9.9	-175.6	-12.1	-30.2	-9.0	-124.0	1.0	-145.2	-843.0
1957	-5.1	-19.5	-457.4	-13.4	-42.7	-11.4	-179.0	-140.4	-167.9	-2,581.2
1958	-9.1	-13.7	-424.0	-17.2	-45.9	-19.8	-134.1	14.4	-167.9	-1,691.8
1959	-8.4	-3.1	-225.4	6.3	-49.4	-7.1	-35.7	-55.6	-234.7	-1,174.7
1960	-6.2	3.4	-455.7	-14.4	-43.9	-15.2	19.2	-94.9	545.2	-1,398.5
1961	-25.4	0	-313.8	-9.0	-38.7	-13.4	-16.5	-29.1	635.8	-1,496.1
1962	-11.3	-4.6	-225.0	-16.7	-32.2	-9.6	-47.7	-90.1	613.5	-1,441.0
1963	-7.5	-23.6	-260.4	-9.7	-37.6	-11.0	-100.6	-4.7	231.3	-378.2
1964	-11.9	-22.7	-504.3	-14.6	-31.2	-12.2	14.4	-6.9	231.3	-852.8
1965	-19.6	-13.0	-448.5	-32.6	-43.3	-14.2	-170.7	75.2	41.5	-439.1
1966	-10.9	-27.6	-430.6	-64.4	-51.6	-24.3	-254.7	53.6	31.7	-1,287.7
1967	-4.8	-38.8	-672.3	-77.4	-38.6	-29.6	-318.3	-16.7	192.7	-1,647.6
1968	-1.7	-32.3	-784.7	-48.4	-22.4	-37.6	-55.1	16.7	-221.6	-2,504.9
1969	-4.6	-37.6	-604.3	-42.6	-36.5	-39.2	-27.9	-28.9	-224.5	-2,139.0
1970	-5.2	-67.5	-1,075.0	-42.6	-71.8	-19.7	146.0	-55.3	-51.0	-2,817.2
1971	-2.3	-25.5	-808.4	-44.2	-78.4	-25.2	-66.1	-69.9	85.7	-3,845.9
1972	-1.4	-14.3	-858.2	17.4	-99.1	-8.4	-58.0	6.6	-21.5	-3,495.6
1973	-8.6	-30.4	-1,168.9	-67.8	-98.0	-16.0	-241.7	14.9	630.6	-2,328.6
1974	-22.1	-77.6	-1,910.4	-169.9	-133.3	-33.1	-491.2	-80.8	3,716.2	-3,593.1
1975	-23.3	-74.3	-2,469.6	-109.7	-86.4	-49.0	-923.1	-105.0	1,240.6	-7,454.3
1976	-24.3	-62.1	-1,978.3	-38.9	-95.5	-51.8	-703.3	-37.6	773.8	-4,999.6
1977	-45.1	-65.4	-983.8	-78.2	-63.3	-69.1	-516.7	-49.5	-275.7	-4,023.6

1. Algebraic sum of net foreign trade (goods and services), net payments on foreign capital (profits and interest), net private transfers, and the effect of the relation of foreign trade prices.

SOURCE: Adapted from ECLA-BPAL.

CHAPTER 28

LOANS, GRANTS, ASSISTANCE, AND PEACE CORPS

Table 2800

TOTAL EXTERNAL PUBLIC AND PRIVATE DEBT,[1] 20 LR, 1977–83
(M US)

Country	1977	1978	1979	1980	1981	1982	1983[‡]
Non-Petroleum Exporters							
A. ARGENTINA[4]	8,210	11,198	17,643	24,409	35,671[a]	38,907	42,000
C. BRAZIL[3]	32,758	43,329	49,689	57,572	65,000	75,000	83,000
D. CHILE[4]	4,899	5,703	7,291	9,513	15,542[a]	17,153	17,600
E. COLOMBIA[4]	3,892	4,444	5,931	7,260	8,160[a]	9,506	10,300
F. COSTA RICA[2]	1,030	1,290	1,742	2,223	2,345[a]	2,603	3,050
G. CUBA	~	~	~	~	~	~	~
H. DOMINICAN REP.[4]	862	951	1,152	1,549	1,837[a]	1,921	2,000
J. EL SALVADOR[3]	539	791	798	847	980	917	1,200
K. GUATEMALA[4]	603	780	983	1,140	1,133	1,053	1,200
L. HAITI[3]	158	185	232	266	326	765	800
M. HONDURAS[2]	726	918	1,150	1,353	1,513	1,409	1,700
O. NICARAGUA[2]	1,300	1,425	1,361	1,687	2,163[a]	2,789	3,400
P. PANAMA[2]	1,501	1,871	2,063	2,248	2,333[a]	2,733	3,100
Q. PARAGUAY[3]	329	503	659	918	1,120	1,195	1,300
S. URUGUAY[4]	973	822	1,032	1,327	3,129[a]	4,255	4,250
TOTAL	58,209	74,701	92,262	112,906	141,939[a]	160,895	175,700
Petroleum Exporters							
B. BOLIVIA[2]	1,633	2,052	2,585	2,439	2,450[a]	2,373	2,700
I. ECUADOR[3]	2,153	3,271	3,865	5,255	5,756	5,788	6,200
N. MEXICO[4]	26,583	29,783	37,450	50,134	72,007[a]	81,350	85,000
R. PERU[3]	6,260	6,802	7,187	7,910	8,227	9,503	10,600
T. VENEZUELA[3]	10,812	16,383	23,071	26,509	28,377	29,934	30,000
TOTAL	47,441	58,291	74,158	92,247	116,777[a]	128,948	134,500
LATIN AMERICA	105,650	132,992	166,420	205,153	258,756[a]	289,843	310,200

1. The end of year debt balance.
2. The public debt.
3. Includes officially guaranteed private and public debt, and non-guaranteed long-term and short-term debts for financial institutions. Based on partial information from Banco de Pagos Internacionales.
4. Includes the private and public debt.

a. Only covers the major external debt.

SOURCE: ECLA-N, May 1984, No. 393–394, p. 4.

Table 2801

RELATIONSHIP BETWEEN TOTAL PUBLIC AND PRIVATE INTEREST PAYMENTS AND THE EXPORTATION OF GOODS AND SERVICES,[1] 20 LC, 1977–83

(%)

Country	1977	1978	1979	1980	1981	1982	1983[‡]
Non-Petroleum Exporters							
A. ARGENTINA	7.6	9.6	12.8	22.0	31.7	54.6	51.0
C. BRAZIL	18.9	24.5	31.5	34.1	40.4	57.0	43.5
D. CHILE	13.7	17.0	16.5	19.3	34.6	47.2	37.5
E. COLOMBIA	7.4	7.7	10.1	13.3	21.6	22.7	21.5
F. COSTA RICA	7.1	9.9	12.8	18.0	25.5	33.4	43.5
G. CUBA	~	~	~	~	~	~	~
H. DOMINICAN REP.	8.8	14.0	14.4	14.7	10.5	22.6	25.0
J. EL SALVADOR	2.9	5.1	5.3	6.5	7.5	11.1	10.5
K. GUATEMALA	2.4	3.6	3.1	5.3	7.5	7.6	7.5
L. HAITI	2.3	2.8	3.3	2.0	3.2	2.3	3.5
M. HONDURAS	7.2	8.2	8.6	10.6	14.5	22.5	16.0
O. NICARAGUA	7.0	9.3	9.7	15.7	15.5	31.7	36.0
P. PANAMA	~	~	~	~	~	~	~
Q. PARAGUAY	6.7	8.5	10.7	14.3	15.9	14.9	15.5
S. URUGUAY	9.8	10.4	9.0	11.0	13.1	22.4	32.5
TOTAL	11.9	15.1	18.8	23.3	31.3	46.2	39.0
Petroleum Exporters							
B. BOLIVIA	9.9	13.7	18.1	24.5	35.5	43.5	35.5
I. ECUADOR	4.8	10.3	13.6	18.2	24.3	29.3	25.5
N. MEXICO	25.4	24.0	24.8	23.1	28.7	37.6	38.0
R. PERU	17.9	21.2	14.7	16.0	21.8	24.7	31.5
T. VENEZUELA	4.0	7.2	6.9	8.1	12.7	21.4	19.0
TOTAL	13.0	16.0	15.7	16.5	22.3	31.3	31.0
LATIN AMERICA	12.4	15.5	17.4	19.9	26.4	38.3	35.0

1. Interest payments include short-term debt interest.

SOURCE: Mexico, NAFINSA-MV, January 1984, No. 4, p. 89.

Figure 28:1
EXTERNAL PUBLIC DEBT,[1] 19 L, 1981–83

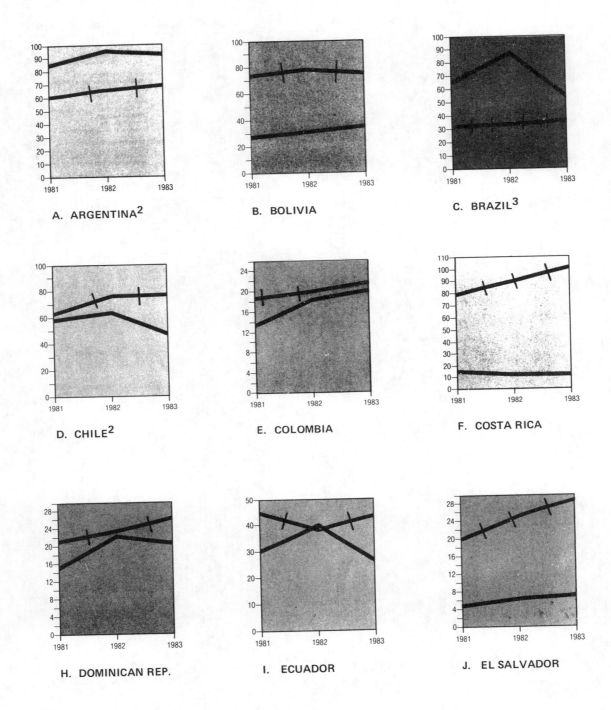

A. ARGENTINA[2]

B. BOLIVIA

C. BRAZIL[3]

D. CHILE[2]

E. COLOMBIA

F. COSTA RICA

H. DOMINICAN REP.

I. ECUADOR

J. EL SALVADOR

Figure 28:1 (Continued)

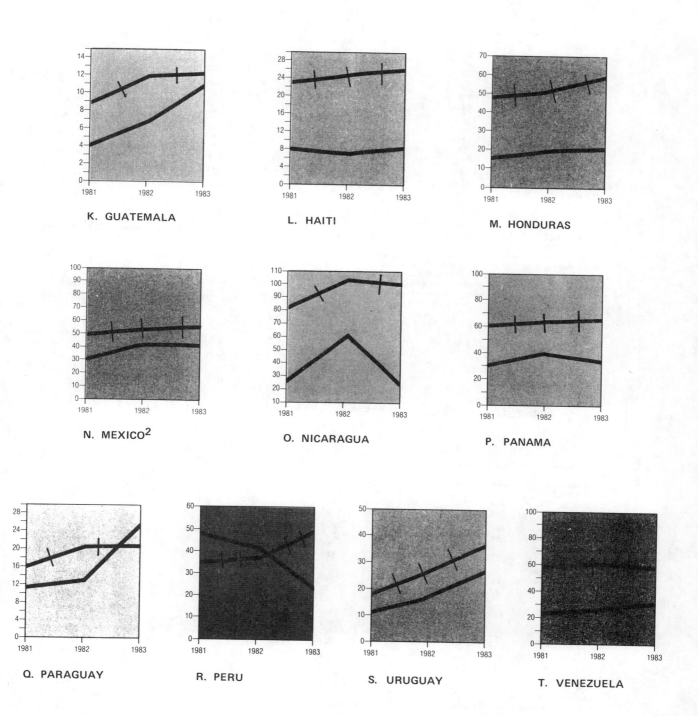

K. GUATEMALA

L. HAITI

M. HONDURAS

N. MEXICO[2]

O. NICARAGUA

P. PANAMA

Q. PARAGUAY

R. PERU

S. URUGUAY

T. VENEZUELA

1. ┼┼ Debt/GDP Ratio

    ── Debt Service/Exports Ratio

SOURCE: IDB-SPTF, 1984, part two.

2. Total External Debt.

3. Total External Debt (including short-term); debt service is for medium- and long-term.

Table 2802

EXTERNAL PUBLIC SECTOR DEBT OUTSTANDING,[1] 19 L, 1960–82

(M US YE)[2]

	Country	1960	1966	1970	1975	1976	1977	1978	1979	1980	1981	1982
A.	ARGENTINA	1,275	1,912	2,455	5,227	6,519	7,531	8,943	10,973	12,524	14,579	18,214
B.	BOLIVIA	179	338	551	1,260	1,641	2,045	2,422	2,836	3,041	3,139	3,158
C.	BRAZIL	2,407	3,202	4,698	17,781	23,307	28,832	38,807	46,045	50,816	57,452	62,676
D.	CHILE	562	1,380	2,534	4,389	4,290	4,643	5,614	5,538	5,160	5,014	5,941
E.	COLOMBIA	377	1,029	1,850	3,032	3,377	3,712	4,337	5,300	6,670	8,031	9,287
F.	COSTA RICA	55	141	227	732	1,002	1,292	1,618	1,934	2,523	3,127	3,395
H.	DOMINICAN REP.	6	183	290	656	784	879	935	1,394	1,843	2,026	2,258
I.	ECUADOR	95	227	353	784	1,073	1,790	2,922	3,498	4,367	5,090	4,913
J.	EL SALVADOR	33	82	126	383	451	451	647	717	927	1,049	1,361
K.	GUATEMALA	51	97	176	268	543	635	745	820	1,050	1,384	1,511
L.	HAITI	38	38	45	106	183	222	278	361	403	488	535
M.	HONDURAS	23	77	144	449	590	810	977	1,269	1,716	1,956	2,044
N.	MEXICO	1,151	2,260	3,792	13,836	18,291	25,149	30,985	36,413	38,938	47,659	54,963
O.	NICARAGUA	41	129	222	823	963	1,108	1,199	1,417	2,145	2,639	3,472
P.	PANAMA	59	108	290	1,124	1,435	1,833	2,368	2,570	2,849	3,137	3,387
Q.	PARAGUAY	22	79	158	430	463	545	747	1,154	1,198	1,527	1,833
R.	PERU	265	901	1,092	4,002	5,559	6,438	6,750	7,997	8,390	8,475	9,951
S.	URUGUAY	132	272	356	1,034	1,153	1,204	1,248	1,415	1,636	1,920	2,287
T.	VENEZUELA	363	461	924	1,393	3,204	4,781	7,384	10,239	11,150	11,535	12,957

1. Includes the undisbursed portion. Does not necessarily include external debt of
   decentralized agencies. For total public and private sector loans, see table 2808, below.
2. Excludes loans under one year. Debts under 90 days normally have been considered
   to involve only "cash flow" management, but in recent years such loans have been
   simply "rolled over" to disguise what are in effect loans for an unspecified term.
   Excludes private sector debt and "purchase" and "repurchase" transactions with IMF.

SOURCE: IDB-SPTF, 1982, p. 387; IDB-SPTF, 1984, p. 456.

Table 2803

DISBURSED PORTION OF THE EXTERNAL PUBLIC SECTOR DEBT OUTSTANDING,[1]
19 L, 1960–82

(M US)[2]

	Country	1960	1966	1970	1975	1976	1977	1978	1979	1980	1981	1982
A.	ARGENTINA	987	1,706	1,878	3,121	4,429	5,033	6,743	8,597	10,177	10,562	15,789
B.	BOLIVIA	168	252	479	813	1,047	1,401	1,692	1,880	2,195	2,509	2,556
C.	BRAZIL	2,202	2,445	3,232	13,831	17,535	21,957	30,040	35,507	39,523	44,513	47,589
D.	CHILE	456	1,058	2,066	3,732	3,592	3,665	4,356	4,812	4,722	4,495	5,239
E.	COLOMBIA	312	713	1,249	2,372	2,472	2,692	2,809	3,374	4,078	5,109	5,789
F.	COSTA RICA	44	103	134	421	536	735	950	1,304	1,687	2,252	2,475
H.	DOMINICAN REP.	6	106	212	411	505	609	735	862	1,185	1,368	1,620
I.	ECUADOR	71	122	213	462	624	1,143	2,250	2,628	3,327	4,218	3,912
J.	EL SALVADOR	23	61	88	196	263	266	334	405	509	663	827
K.	GUATEMALA	26	59	106	143	163	217	304	427	549	809	1,119
L.	HAITI	37	38	40	57	88	138	185	227	278	360	405
M.	HONDURAS	11	37	90	264	344	458	595	763	991	1,234	1,385
N.	MEXICO	827	1,820	3,245	11,537	15,930	20,758	25,615	29,242	33,591	42,736	50,412
O.	NICARAGUA	22	68	155	600	658	867	971	1,113	1,697	2,897	2,810
P.	PANAMA	32	84	194	771	1,093	1,333	1,880	2,078	2,266	2,379	2,820
Q.	PARAGUAY	20	40	112	189	237	336	445	524	633	709	940
R.	PERU	162	524	856	3,021	3,666	4,711	5,402	5,934	6,168	5,980	6,711
S.	URUGUAY	115	227	269	618	694	736	816	952	1,116	1,334	1,829
T.	VENEZUELA	252	290	728	1,262	2,961	4,426	6,893	9,805	10,873	11,352	12,122

1. Included in table 2802, above.
2. Excludes loans under one year. Debts under 90 days normally have been considered
   to involve only "cash flow" management, but in recent years such loans have been
   simply "rolled over" to disguise what are in effect loans for an unspecified term.
   Excludes private sector debt and "purchase" and "repurchase" transactions with
   IMF.

SOURCE: IDB-SPTF, 1982, p. 388; IDB-SPTF, 1984, p. 457.

Table 2804

STRUCTURE OF THE LATIN AMERICAN EXTERNAL PUBLIC SECTOR DEBT,[1]
BY TYPE OF CREDITOR, 1960–82
(%)[2]

Year	Private					Official			Distribution		
	Suppliers	Banks[3]	Bond Issues	National-ization	Total Private	Multilateral	Bilateral	Total Official	Total Debt	Disbursed Portion	Undisbursed Portion
1960	23.9	16.4	8.1	1.2	49.6	12.9	37.5	50.4	100.0	81.0	19.0
1961	25.0	14.2	8.1	.9	48.2	15.3	36.5	51.8	100.0	74.6	25.4
1962	31.6	11.5	8.0	.7	51.8	15.8	32.4	48.2	100.0	79.1	20.9
1963	29.0	11.2	7.7	.5	48.4	18.5	33.1	51.6	100.0	75.2	24.8
1964	25.6	13.1	7.2	.8	46.7	19.8	33.5	53.3	100.0	76.3	23.7
1965	20.2	12.0	7.5	1.0	40.7	22.5	36.8	59.3	100.0	76.8	23.2
1966	19.5	10.5	7.7	1.6	39.3	23.4	37.3	60.7	100.0	75.5	24.5
1967	17.2	11.1	6.1	4.4	38.8	22.1	39.1	61.2	100.0	74.2	25.8
1968	17.4	12.0	6.7	3.4	39.5	22.8	37.7	60.5	100.0	73.2	26.8
1969	16.7	18.3	6.6	2.1	43.7	24.0	32.3	56.3	100.0	75.0	25.0
1970	16.9	19.5	5.9	2.4	44.7	24.4	30.9	55.3	100.0	75.7	24.3
1971	16.4	22.5	5.6	2.3	46.8	24.6	28.6	53.2	100.0	73.8	26.2
1972	14.6	26.2	5.4	1.9	48.0	24.3	27.7	52.0	100.0	74.2	25.8
1973	12.8	32.7	4.6	1.4	51.5	22.6	25.9	48.5	100.0	73.9	26.1
1974	12.0	37.6	4.0	2.0	55.6	19.9	24.5	44.4	100.0	75.1	24.9
1975	10.7	42.4	3.7	1.5	58.3	20.0	21.7	41.7	100.0	76.0	24.0
1976	9.0	46.0	3.6	2.3	60.9	18.8	20.3	39.1	100.0	76.0	24.0
1977	8.1	49.9	5.8	1.4	65.2	17.3	17.5	34.8	100.0	76.2	23.8
1978	7.3	52.6	6.9	.9	67.7	16.4	15.9	32.3	100.0	78.1	21.9
1979	6.9	56.0	6.2	.6	69.7	16.6	13.7	30.3	100.0	77.6	22.4
1980	6.2	56.4	7.1	.3	69.0	17.2	13.8	31.0	100.0	79.8	20.2
1981	5.8	56.8	6.7	.2	69.5	17.6	12.9	30.5	100.0	80.1	19.9
1982	5.0	59.5	5.0	.2	69.7	18.0	12.3	30.3	100.0	81.4	18.6

1. Including the undisbursed portion at year end. Does not necessarily include external debts of decentralized agencies.
2. Excludes debts under one year. Debts under 90 days normally have been considered to involve only "cash flow" management, but in recent years such loans have been simply "rolled over" to disguise what are in effect loans for an unspecified term.
3. Includes also financial institutions other than banks.

SOURCE: IDB-SPTF, 1982, p. 389; IDB-SPTF, 1984, p. 458.

Table 2805

INTEREST PAYMENTS ON THE EXTERNAL PUBLIC SECTOR DEBT,[1]
19 L, 1960–82
(M US)[2]

	Country	1960	1966	1970	1975	1976	1977	1978	1979	1980	1981	1982
A.	ARGENTINA	50	102	121	266	265	318	503	568	841	1,063	1,272
B.	BOLIVIA	3	1	6	24	38	58	86	122	164	167	165
C.	BRAZIL	134	155	133	850	960	1,193	1,846	2,918	4,197	5,166	5,896
D.	CHILE	14	34	78	156	209	201	290	355	484	488	551
E.	COLOMBIA	14	23	44	115	125	139	168	228	278	408	578
F.	COSTA RICA	1	5	7	23	28	36	65	83	130	115	82
H.	DOMINICAN REP.	~	3	4	18	18	24	40	55	92	121	109
I.	ECUADOR	2	4	7	18	25	45	98	208	287	441	561
J.	EL SALVADOR	1	2	3	7	14	16	18	21	24	28	27
K.	GUATEMALA	1	3	6	7	8	9	16	22	30	38	54
L.	HAITI	#	#	#	1	1	4	5	3	6	7	8
M.	HONDURAS	1	1	3	10	16	22	31	46	59	77	97
N.	MEXICO	29	91	218	832	1,086	1,314	1,818	2,855	3,842	4,703	5,892
O.	NICARAGUA	1	2	7	36	41	52	49	41	38	92	120
P.	PANAMA	1	3	6	41	56	73	122	197	251	279	332
Q.	PARAGUAY	1	1	3	8	8	11	16	22	35	32	41
R.	PERU	7	21	43	187	199	248	317	437	544	528	515
S.	URUGUAY	4	9	16	46	57	58	61	70	103	123	156
T.	VENEZUELA	18	11	40	103	122	222	394	658	1,229	1,741	1,557

1. Included in table 2806, below.
2. Does not necessarily include external debts of decentralized agencies. Includes also
financial institutions other than banks. Excludes debts under one year. Debts under
90 days normally have been considered to involve only "cash flow" management,
but in recent years such loans have been simply "rolled over" to disguise what are in
effect loans for an unspecified term.

SOURCE: IDB-SPTF, 1982, p. 390; IDB-SPTF, 1984, p. 459.

Table 2806

AMORTIZATION PAYMENTS ON THE EXTERNAL PUBLIC SECTOR DEBT,[1] 19 L, 1960–82
(M US)[2]

	Country	1960	1970	1971	1975	1976	1977	1978	1979	1980	1981	1982
A.	ARGENTINA	204	341	297	523	604	722	1,613	895	1,146	1,092	1,061
B.	BOLIVIA	13	17	17	51	70	99	290	148	124	104	95
C.	BRAZIL	420	254	325	841	1,085	1,675	2,630	3,596	3,838	3,859	4,007
D.	CHILE	64	163	162	345	546	685	925	903	891	1,176	482
E.	COLOMBIA	68	75	92	123	144	176	219	408	250	256	333
F.	COSTA RICA	4	21	21	41	40	51	173	173	75	80	55
H.	DOMINICAN REP.	~	8	13	31	37	45	47	191	62	109	141
I.	ECUADOR	9	17	25	33	57	73	110	741	270	482	540
J.	EL SALVADOR	2	6	12	47	22	54	12	13	17	14	24
K.	GUATEMALA	1	20	20	7	9	8	10	15	15	22	34
L.	HAITI	2	4	5	7	9	15	14	9	17	18	11
M.	HONDURAS	1	3	4	7	13	20	28	63	39	38	50
N.	MEXICO	181	475	496	761	1,153	2,238	4,406	7,111	4,026	3,778	3,072
O.	NICARAGUA	2	17	24	20	35	50	50	15	39	66	168
P.	PANAMA	1	23	28	31	45	88	443	190	214	214	282
Q.	PARAGUAY	2	7	8	14	12	16	20	31	45	39	39
R.	PERU	45	101	120	254	256	405	432	482	957	1,367	1,021
S.	URUGUAY	6	47	41	182	149	187	366	55	90	58	71
T.	VENEZUELA	93	42	80	436	285	605	356	890	1,735	1,351	1,593

1. Included in table 2807, below.
2. Excludes loans under one year. Debts under 90 days normally have been considered to
involve only "cash flow" management, but in recent years such loans have been simply
"rolled over" to disguise what are in effect loans for an unspecified term.

SOURCE: IDB-SPTF, 1982, p. 391; IDB-SPTF, 1984, p. 460.

Table 2807

SERVICE PAYMENTS ON THE EXTERNAL PUBLIC SECTOR DEBT,[1] 19 L, 1960–82
(M US)[2]

Country	1960	1966	1970	1975	1976	1977	1978	1979	1980	1981	1982
A. ARGENTINA	254	455	462	789	869	1,040	2,116	1,463	1,987	2,155	2,333
B. BOLIVIA	16	7	23	75	108	157	356	270	288	271	260
C. BRAZIL	554	573	387	1,691	2,045	2,868	4,476	6,514	8,035	9,025	9,903
D. CHILE	78	103	241	501	755	886	1,215	1,258	1,375	1,664	1,033
E. COLOMBIA	82	109	119	238	269	315	387	636	528	664	911
F. COSTA RICA	5	20	28	64	68	87	238	256	205	195	137
H. DOMINICAN REP.	~	20	12	49	55	69	87	246	154	230	250
I. ECUADOR	11	13	24	51	82	118	208	949	557	923	1,101
J. EL SALVADOR	3	6	9	54	36	70	30	34	41	45	51
K. GUATEMALA	2	15	26	14	17	17	26	37	45	60	88
L. HAITI	2	~	4	8	10	19	19	12	23	25	19
M. HONDURAS	2	3	6	17	29	42	59	109	98	115	147
N. MEXICO	210	456	693	1,593	2,239	3,552	6,224	9,966	7,868	8,481	8,964
O. NICARAGUA	3	9	24	56	76	102	99	56	77	158	288
P. PANAMA	2	7	29	72	101	162	565	387	465	493	614
Q. PARAGUAY	3	5	10	22	20	27	36	53	80	71	80
R. PERU	52	89	144	441	455	653	749	919	1,501	1,895	1,536
S. URUGUAY	10	31	63	228	206	245	427	125	193	181	227
T. VENEZUELA	111	67	82	539	407	827	750	1,548	2,964	3,092	3,150

1. Service = amortization plus interest on the debt. Does not necessarily include service payments on external debt by decentralized agencies.
2. Excludes loans under one year. Debts under 90 days normally have been considered to involve only "cash flow" management, but in recent years such loans have been simply "rolled over" to disguise what are in effect loans for an unspecified term.

SOURCE: IDB-SPTF, 1982, p. 392; IDB-SPTF, 1984, p. 461.

Table 2808

EXTERNAL PUBLIC SECTOR DEBT SERVICE AS SHARE OF EXPORTS OF GOODS[1]
AND SERVICES, 19 L, 1960–80
(%)[2]

Country	1960	1966	1970	1973	1974	1975	1976	1977	1978	1979	1980
A. ARGENTINA	20.5	25.5	21.8	17.9	17.3	22.4	18.8	15.7	28.2	16.1	19.9
B. BOLIVIA	27.6	4.9	11.0	15.5	11.1	14.6	16.2	21.5	49.8	30.3	26.2
C. BRAZIL	38.7	30.6	12.6	13.9	14.0	17.5	19.3	21.5	31.9	38.5	36.1
D. CHILE	14.2	10.5	19.2	10.9	11.7	28.7	31.5	33.4	40.9	27.1	23.5
E. COLOMBIA	13.9	16.4	11.9	13.4	16.5	11.5	9.9	9.1	10.0	14.5	11.2
F. COSTA RICA	4.8	12.3	10.0	10.3	9.6	10.6	9.5	9.0	23.4	23.0	16.7
H. DOMINICAN REP.	~	12.5	4.7	5.6	4.9	5.0	6.5	7.5	10.8	21.6	12.8
I. ECUADOR	7.1	6.4	9.3	7.5	7.2	4.5	5.8	7.3	12.1	30.0	14.4
J. EL SALVADOR	2.6	2.9	3.5	5.3	4.7	9.1	4.4	6.3	3.0	2.4	3.5
K. GUATEMALA	1.5	5.7	7.4	3.6	3.8	1.7	1.5	1.3	2.2	2.7	3.7
L. HAITI	3.6	~	7.5	7.7	6.5	7.5	7.1	6.9	5.6	3.6	4.5
M. HONDURAS	2.8	1.9	3.0	3.7	3.6	4.9	6.4	7.2	8.7	12.9	10.2
N. MEXICO	15.5	20.9	24.2	24.3	19.2	25.5	31.6	44.3	56.7	65.6	33.2
O. NICARAGUA	3.8	5.2	11.2	22.0	11.6	12.5	12.3	14.1	13.7	8.1	14.6
P. PANAMA	1.6	2.8	7.6	16.9	18.2	8.5	12.3	17.9	60.1	34.6	33.5
Q. PARAGUAY	6.8	7.8	11.2	10.7	8.2	10.5	8.1	6.7	7.6	9.7	12.8
R. PERU	10.5	9.8	11.7	29.7	23.5	26.1	26.1	30.7	31.5	22.7	32.7
S. URUGUAY	5.8	12.5	21.7	22.9	31.0	41.4	29.6	30.3	46.8	10.4	
T. VENEZUELA	4.4	2.7	3.0	6.1	4.4	5.8	4.2	8.1	7.7	10.3	14.8

1. Service = amortization plus interest. Exports of merchandise (f.o.b.). Does not necessarily include external debt service of decentralized agencies.
2. Excludes loans under one year. Debts under 90 days normally have been considered to involve only "cash flow" management, but in recent years such loans have been simply "rolled over" to disguise what are in effect loans for an unspecified term.

SOURCE: IDB-SPTF, 1982, p. 393.

Table 2809

THREE VIEWS OF THE CUMULATIVE FOREIGN LOANS DISBURSED TO MEXICO'S PUBLIC SECTOR,[1] 1970-82

(YE)

| Year | M US[3] | | 1981 = 100.0 | M US of 1981 |
	(A) Nominal Debt One Year or Longer	(B) Nominal Debt 90 Days or Longer[2]	(C) U.S. Export Price Index	(D) Real Debt 90 Days or Longer[2] (B/C)
1970	3,245	4,262	35.2	12,108
1971	3,523	4,546	36.3	12,523
1972	3,962	5,064	37.3	13,576
1973	5,442	7,071	43.5	16,255
1974	8,313	9,975	55.4	18,005
1975	11,533	14,449	61.8	23,380
1976	15,923	19,600	64.2	30,530
1977	20,784	22,912	66.7	34,351
1978	25,638	26,264	71.2	36,888
1979	28,805	29,757	82.8	35,938
1980	~	33,813	91.7	36,873
1981	~	52,961‡	100.0	52,961‡
1982	~	59,000‡,a	102.8b	57,393‡

1. For total public and private sector loans, see table 2808, above.
2. Debts under 90 days normally have been considered to involve only "cash flow" management, but in recent years such loans have been simply "rolled over" to disguise what are in effect loans for an unspecified term.
3. Excludes "purchase" and "repurchase" transactions with IMF. Excludes private sector debt.

a. August.
b. January to May.

SOURCE: SALA, 22-1.

Table 2810

ASSISTANCE FROM INTERNATIONAL ORGANIZATIONS,[1] 20 LRC, 1946-84
(M US)

U.S. Fiscal Year

Country/Organization	1946-48	1949-52	1953-61	1962-TQ[2]	1977	1978	1979	1980	1981	1982	1983	1984	Total
A. ARGENTINA													
Total	0	0	42.1	1,695.9	495.4	548.4	388.7	485.9	479.4	533.4	593.9	210.3	4,915.9
IBRD	0	0	31.0	478.2	320.0	165.0	96.0	237.0	68.0	400.0	100.0	0	1,867.6
IFC	0	0	5.2	40.5	16.0	27.0	6.0	15.0	65.0	10.0	.5	42.7	226.3
IDB	0	0	0	1,140.3	157.2	356.2	280.7	232.2	346.4	119.2	490.5	167.6	2,761.7
UNDP	0	0	5.0	34.4	2.2	.2	6.0	1.7	#	4.2	2.9	0	56.7
Other U.N.	0	0	.9	2.5	0	0	0	0	0	0	0	0	3.6
B. BOLIVIA													
Total	0	#	15.4	482.0	132.0	174.0	149.7	99.3	8.2	99.9	211.3	129.8	1,410.0
IBRD	0	0	0	89.8	108.5	51.0	0	50.0	0	0	0	0	296.0
IFC	0	0	0	1.3	0	2.3	0	0	5.7	0	0	0	9.3
IDA	0	0	0	60.3	0	9.0	10.5	25.0	0	0	0	0	104.8
IDB	0	0	10.0	299.8	22.0	109.7	136.6	22.6	1.0	97.0	211.1	126.8	947.4
UNDP	0	#	4.7	25.9	0	2.0	2.6	1.5	0	2.9	.2	0	40.7
Other U.N.	0	0	.7	4.9	1.5	0	0	.2	1.5	0	0	3.0	11.8
C. BRAZIL													
Total	0	117.6	178.8	4,878.3	844.5	1,180.0	963.3	1,102.8	1,551.1	1,222.8	1,807.0	2,192.8	15,436.0
IBRD	0	117.5	149.5	2,623.9	338.0	705.0	674.0	695.0	844.0	722.1	1,457.5	1,604.3	9,901.4
IFC	0	0	9.9	265.1	46.0	77.9	65.1	74.0	229.2	206.6	77.5	61.2	1,077.2
IDB	0	0	11.2	1,919.7	454.1	394.0	221.3	329.9	477.3	284.6	269.5	524.6	4,348.1
UNDP	0	.1	7.2	54.9	6.4	3.1	2.5	2.6	.6	8.2	2.0	0	87.6
Other U.N.	0	0	1.0	14.7	0	0	.4	1.3	0	1.3	.5	2.7	21.7
D. CHILE													
Total	16.0	1.0	135.3	750.5	68.6	62.3	35.0	43.8	260.1	192.4	573.7	352.2	2,317.3
IBRD	16.0	.9	95.1	187.4	60.0	0	35.0	0	78.0	10.2	128.0	0	600.8
IFC	0	0	5.8	15.4	0	.1	0	0	0	0	44.5	0	69.0
IDA	0	0	19.0	#	0	0	0	0	0	0	0	0	19.0
IDB	0	0	5.7	499.9	8.6	59.5	0	38.0	180.9	182.0	400.5	352.2	1,560.8
UNDP	0	.1	9.0	41.4	#	2.3	#	5.8	.9	.2	.7	0	60.0
Other U.N.	0	0	.7	6.4	0	.4	0	0	.3	0	0	0	7.7
E. COLOMBIA													
Total	0	30.1	191.5	1,850.6	374.4	483.5	523.8	727.4	830.7	512.3	222.4	1,041.3	6,601.5
IBRD	0	30.0	170.6	1,049.5	306.0	354.6	311.5	518.0	550.0	291.3	78.4	464.3	4,116.5
IFC	0	0	2.2	31.7	17.5	0	0	.3	34.8	14.6	28.8	6.8	130.0
IDA	0	0	0	19.5	0	0	0	0	0	0	0	0	19.5
IDB	0	0	10.8	700.9	47.7	127.4	206.0	201.0	244.6	206.1	106.2	570.4	2,248.7
UNDP	0	0	6.9	38.0	1.6	1.5	4.9	1.0	1.3	.3	3.2	0	58.8
Other U.N.	0	.1	1.0	11.0	1.6	0	1.4	7.1	0	0	5.8	0	28.0
F. COSTA RICA													
Total	0	#	18.8	426.9	84.2	131.4	36.4	105.6	120.4	29.8	124.4	35.8	1,048.0
IBRD	0	0	17.3	211.7	18.0	42.1	34.0	30.0	29.0	0	25.2	0	406.4
IFC	0	0	0	0	0	2.5	2.1	0	0	0	1.5	0	6.7
IDA	0	0	0	4.6	0	0	0	0	0	0	0	0	4.6
IDB	0	0	0	199.4	66.1	86.1	.1	74.5	91.3	29.2	97.2	35.8	615.0
UNDP	0	#	1.1	8.0	.1	.7	.2	1.0	.1	.6	.4	0	12.1
Other U.N.	0	0	.4	2.6	0	0	0	.1	0	0	.1	0	3.2

Table 2810 (Continued)

ASSISTANCE FROM INTERNATIONAL ORGANIZATIONS,[1] 20 LRC, 1946-84
(M US)

Country/Organization	1946-48	1949-52	1953-61	1962-TQ[2]	1977	1978	1979	1980	1981	1982	1983	1984	Total
G. CUBA													
Total	0	#	1.7	20.1	6.3	.1	3.0	1.6	#	7.7	1.3	0	41.9
UNDP	0	#	1.5	16.8	6.0	.1	3.0	1.3	#	7.7	1.1	0	37.7
Other U.N.	0	0	.2	3.3	.3	0	0	.3	0	0	.2	0	4.2
H. DOMINICAN REP.													
Total	0	0	.6	311.3	29.7	11.6	176.1	210.5	119.9	91.2	168.4	118.9	1,228.0
IBRD	0	0	0	64.0	3.0	3.0	52.0	120.0	24.0	25.4	7.1	3.8	296.3
IFC	0	0	0	7.4	3.0	3.0	0	2.0	.4	0	10.5	0	26.1
IDA	0	0	0	22.0	0	0	0	0	0	0	0	0	22.0
IDB	0	0	0	199.4	26.7	6.3	120.5	87.5	95.0	61.9	150.0	113.7	850.8
UNDP	0	0	.4	14.9	0	2.1	1.8	1.0	.5	3.9	.8	0	25.7
Other U.N.	0	0	.2	3.6	0	.2	1.8	0	0	0	0	1.4	7.1
I. ECUADOR													
Total	0	.1	52.5	460.3	151.9	106.6	182.1	270.7	94.6	444.0	209.1	117.8	2,004.1
IBRD	0	0	45.0	124.5	70.0	11.0	58.0	106.0	20.0	228.7	40.6	0	702.6
IFC	0	0	0	9.3	.1	13.0	4.3	1.3	10.8	9.3	.1	.1	48.2
IDA	0	0	0	36.9	0	#	0	0	0	0	0	0	36.5
IDB	0	0	0	259.4	81.7	78.5	113.2	161.0	63.5	202.5	167.3	117.7	1,160.7
UNDP	0	.1	6.3	24.1	0	4.1	6.1	.6	.3	3.5	.2	0	45.7
Other U.N.	0	0	1.2	6.1	0	0	.5	1.8	0	0	.9	0	10.4
J. EL SALVADOR													
Total	0	12.6	24.7	318.1	23.6	101.7	60.0	48.9	40.5	112.8	53.3	114.3	877.4
IBRD	0	12.5	22.2	118.5	6.7	32.0	23.5	0	0	0	0	0	215.1
IFC	0	0	.1	.8	6.0	0	0	0	0	0	0	0	1.0
IDA	0	0	0	19.6	6.0	0	0	0	0	0	0	0	25.6
IDB	0	.1	.2	163.1	10.1	69.6	29.5	48.5	40.4	112.4	52.9	114.0	607.7
UNDP	0	0	1.8	11.9	.8	.1	5.6	.4	.1	0	.4	0	21.7
Other U.N.	0	0	.4	4.2	0	0	1.4	0	0	0	0	.3	6.3
K. GUATEMALA													
Total	0	#	21.6	402.5	84.3	108.7	2.2	86.9	26.5	45.9	102.4	134.5	1,136.1
IBRD	0	0	18.2	115.3	55.0	72.0	0	17.0	0	0	18.5	50.0	346.0
IFC	0	0	0	15.0	3.0	0	0	0	0	0	0	0	18.2
IDB	0	0	.1	254.9	25.0	35.7	.3	66.0	25.5	42.5	83.3	84.5	738.3
UNDP	0	#	2.3	10.7	1.3	.8	1.9	2.8	1.0	.9	.6	0	22.3
Other U.N.	0	#	.8	6.6	0	.2	0	1.1	0	2.5	0	0	11.3
L. HAITI													
Total	0	.1	8.4	160.2	26.4	39.1	61.1	9.8	33.9	47.2	89.5	36.5	494.4
IBRD	0	0	2.6	0	0	0	0	0	0	0	0	0	2.6
IFC	0	0	0	0	0	0	0	0	3.2	0	0	0	3.2
IDA	0	0	0	51.9	10.0	31.6	16.5	0	21.2	18.0	56.0	19.1	224.3
IDB	0	0	2.9	88.8	15.7	5.2	38.3	4.1	9.1	17.6	32.6	17.4	214.0
UNDP	0	.1	2.4	13.3	.7	2.3	6.3	3.7	.4	6.5	.9	0	36.6
Other U.N.	0	0	.5	6.2	0	0	0	2.0	0	5.1	0	0	13.7

U.S. Fiscal Year

Table 2810 (Continued)

ASSISTANCE FROM INTERNATIONAL ORGANIZATIONS,[1] 20 LRC, 1946–84

(M US)

Country/Organization	1946–48	1949–52	1953–61	1962–TQ[2]	1977	1978	1979	1980	1981	1982	1983	1984	Total
M. HONDURAS													
Total	0	#	32.5	315.8	155.0	33.8	177.0	224.0	35.5	37.0	89.6	154.3	1,242.4
IBRD	0	0	19.9	110.4	47.0	10.5	65.0	128.0	28.0	30.0	45.0	19.6	503.3
IFC	0	0	0	.4	0	10.0	0	0	0	0	0	0	10.4
IDA	0	0	8.4	39.2	5.0	5.0	0	25.0	0	0	0	0	82.6
IDB	0	0	2.2	150.8	103.0	6.1	106.3	71.0	7.5	0	42.2	134.1	611.4
UNDP	0	#	1.7	11.3	#	1.9	4.2	#	0	7.0	2.4	0	28.4
Other U.N.	0	0	.3	3.7	0	.3	1.5	0	0	0	0	.6	6.3
N. MEXICO													
Total	0	80.4	153.7	3,869.8	305.3	770.4	963.4	971.7	1,439.4	804.5	1,373.2	882.5	11,093.9
IBRD	0	80.3	145.8	2,382.3	162.0	469.5	552.0	300.0	1,081.0	657.3	887.9	576.3	7,198.4
IFC	0	0	1.4	68.0	0	31.0	125.6	275.3	61.2	10.5	179.2	25.2	776.6
IDB	0	0	0	1,374.5	143.0	260.2	280.2	396.2	295.5	134.1	306.0	281.0	3,047.3
UNDP	0	.1	4.3	31.8	0	8.7	5.0	#	.2	2.6	.1	0	52.9
Other U.N.	0	0	2.2	13.2	.3	1.0	.6	0	1.5	0	0	0	18.7
O. NICARAGUA													
Total	0	5.2	33.7	288.8	55.2	66.6	39.0	55.3	117.9	51.3	31.3	.3	732.9
IBRD	0	5.2	30.2	90.9	22.0	13.1	0	20.0	33.7	16.0	0	0	231.1
IFC	0	0	0	9.5	0	0	0	0	0	0	0	0	9.5
IDA	0	0	0	23.0	0	0	0	32.0	5.0	0	0	0	60.0
IDB	0	0	2.0	149.8	33.2	53.5	36.8	3.3	75.0	34.4	30.7	0	403.7
UNDP	0	#	1.0	11.9	0	0	1.7	0	3.5	.9	.6	0	22.9
Other U.N.	0	0	.5	3.7	0	0	.5	0	.7	0	0	.3	5.7
P. PANAMA													
Total	0	#	15.4	305.7	177.0	22.5	68.2	149.9	74.5	126.9	137.7	82.6	1,169.1
IBRD	0	0	14.0	140.2	57.5	12.0	34.0	58.0	45.5	24.4	85.0	74.2	544.8
IFC	0	0	0	1.5	0	3.8	3.0	0	0	0	0	0	8.3
IDB	0	0	0	143.5	119.0	5.4	29.0	91.4	28.5	99.0	52.0	8.4	584.9
UNDP	0	#	1.0	17.1	0.5	1.3	1.7	.5	.5	3.5	.6	0	26.7
Other U.N.	0	0	.4	3.4	0	0	.5	0	.7	0	.1	0	4.4
Q. PARAGUAY													
Total	0	4.6	6.7	288.8	56.7	104.7	97.2	76.6	88.8	176.4	114.7	44.4	1,047.7
IBRD	0	4.5	0	45.9	40.0	39.0	64.0	36.0	58.8	99.4	40.0	30.0	457.6
IFC	0	0	0	5.4	0	0	0	0	1.2	10.4	0	.3	17.2
IDA	0	0	0	41.5	4.0	0	0	0	0	0	0	0	45.5
IDB	0	0	3.2	177.7	11.6	64.2	31.2	39.4	27.5	64.9	72.9	14.1	494.8
UNDP	0	.1	2.8	14.2	.7	1.4	1.4	1.2	1.3	1.0	1.8	0	26.1
Other U.N.	0	0	.7	4.1	.4	.1	.6	0	.7	.7	0	0	6.5
R. PERU													
Total	0	2.5	93.9	813.7	154.8	28.6	191.2	247.5	461.6	443.3	454.1	316.5	3,077.6
IBRD	0	2.4	79.6	348.8	121.6	.1	123.8	111.0	148.0	286.7	302.2	122.5	1,646.4
IFC	0	0	4.4	19.3	0	0	2.5	3.2	8.5	18.2	8.0	9.2	73.3
IDB	0	0	3.9	403.1	32.1	26.7	60.2	132.5	305.0	130.0	142.3	184.8	1,291.1
UNDP	0	.1	5.2	34.5	.8	1.8	2.7	.8	.1	5.4	1.6	0	52.2
Other U.N.	0	0	.8	8.0	.3	.5	2.0	0	0	3.0	0	0	14.6

U.S. Fiscal Year

Table 2810 (Continued)

ASSISTANCE FROM INTERNATIONAL ORGANIZATIONS,[1] 20 LRC, 1946–84
(M US)

Country/Organization	1946-48	1949-52	1953-61	1962-TQ[2]	1977	1978	1979	1980	1981	1982	1983	1984	Total
S. URUGUAY													
Total	0	33.0	39.4	317.2	15.1	43.2	70.3	168.5	108.1	51.3	49.1	167.8	967.5
IBRD	0	33.0	38.0	136.2	0	9.7	26.5	98.0	30.0	40.0	45.0	0	442.2
IFC	0	0	0	3.8	0	0	6.4	10.7	0	0	2.8	0	23.6
IDB	0	0	0	161.5	15.1	32.4	35.7	57.5	78.0	10.0	0	167.8	476.8
UNDP	0	0	1.2	15.1	0	1.1	1.7	2.3	.1	1.3	1.3	0	24.0
Other U.N.	0	0	.2	.6	0	0	0	0	0	0	0	0	.9
T. VENEZUELA													
Total	0	#	15.2	689.9	2.6	17.9	6.2	1.8	.1	2.0	.4	64.3	700.0
IBRD	0	0	0	377.9	0	.1	0	0	0	0	.4	0	348.0
IFC	0	0	3.2	22.2	0	0	0	0	0	0	0	0	25.4
IDB	0	0	9.2	264.4	1.8	17.3	2.3	1.8	0	0	0	64.3	289.2
UNDP	0	#	2.6	23.4	.8	.5	3.9	1.8	.1	2.0	.4	0	35.3
Other U.N.	0	0	.2	2.0	0	0	0	0	0	0	0	0	2.1
LATIN AMERICA REGIONAL[3]													
Total	0	.1	32.8	313.0	2.7	35.0	225.7	1.3	56.3	30.0	4.1	0	767.4
IFC	0	0	0	10.0	0	0	0	0	0	0	0	0	10.0
IDB	0	0	0	104.3	.4	25.7	210.2	0	50.3	24.0	0	0	482.4
UNDP	0	.1	18.2	90.4[a]	1.8	7.7	14.6	.6	4.7	6.0	2.6	0	146.8
Other U.N.	0	0	11.1	27.7	.5	1.6	.9	.7	1.3	0	1.5	0	43.7
EEC	0	0	3.5	80.6	0	0	0	0	0	0	0	0	84.5
LATIN AMERICA (TOTAL)													
Total	16.0	287.5	1,119.7	19,657.4	3,285.6	4,251.1	4,617.6	5,214.9	6,123.1	5,326.3	6,605.5	6,423.9	60,345.1
IBRD	16.0	286.3	880.1	9,006.0	1,747.3	2,054.8	2,232.8	2,595.0	3,119.0	2,962.9	3,396.6	3,003.4	31,083.1
IFC	0	0	32.6	530.0	85.5	171.7	218.2	381.7	422.2	301.1	353.3	146.3	2,591.4
IDA	0	0	27.4	332.0	25.0	55.6	32.0	89.0	34.2	25.0	63.0	24.1	706.9
IDB	0	0	61.3	8,915.6	1,397.5	1,916.2	2,030.0	2,090.6	2,507.9	1,946.6	2,735.6	3,238.1	24,526.1
UNDP	0	1.2	89.7	599.7	25.0	47.6	84.0	40.9	24.0	78.0	32.7	0	1,023.3
Other U.N.	0	0	25.1	145.7	5.3	5.2	12.6	15.2	5.8	12.7	9.3	10.0	244.5
EEC	0	0	3.5	128.4	0	0	8.0	2.5	10.0	0	15.0	2.0	169.8
WORLD REGIONAL[4]													
Total	512.8	835.4	5,071.1	57,518.2	10,277.8	12,730.5	14,401.0	16,856.8	18,468.3	18,873.5	20,804.3	23,016.9	95,765.5
IBRD	512.8	830.8	4,252.8	27,197.0	5,806.0	6,098.8	6,989.0	7,644.2	8,808.9	10,329.6	11,136.3	11,949.2	561.2
IFC	0	0	41.8	1,411.4	209.7	338.4	425.4	680.6	810.7	611.8	844.5	695.6	5,998.1
IDA	0	0	99.3	10,105.0	1,445.8	2,433.2	2,961.5	3,829.5	3,482.1	2,686.5	3,340.7	3,575.0	33,783.1
IDB	0	0	61.3	8,915.6	1,397.5	1,916.2	2,030.0	2,090.6	2,507.9	1,946.6	2,735.6	3,238.1	24,526.1
ADB[5]	0	0	0	3,015.7	732.0	1,001.8	985.8	1,433.4	1,453.0	1,661.2	1,656.1	2,116.5	14,063.7
AFDB[5]	0	0	0	468.4	250.1	204.8	170.9	247.7	250.0	428.3	238.5	910.3	3,158.9
UNDP	0	4.6	329.4	2,667.3	158.9	359.1	471.9	335.4	337.5	567.7	333.0	~	5,495.6
Other U.N.	0	0	98.2	1,114.9	129.4	226.2	186.3	164.5	355.8	206.4	109.4	105.0	2,721.6
ECC	0	0	188.3	2,622.9	148.4	152.0	180.2	430.9	462.4	435.4	410.2	427.2	5,457.2

Table 2810 (Continued)

ASSISTANCE FROM INTERNATIONAL ORGANIZATIONS,[1] 20 LRC, 1946–84

(M US)

1. The data represent assistance from all sources available to the various organizations, including contributions, subscriptions, bond issues, etc. The data do not represent the United States contributions to these organizations. Data are based on United States fiscal years except for "UNDP" and "Other U.N." programs. These are calendar year figures, shown in the fiscal year in which the calendar year ends. As of FY 1982 UNDP data are based on United States fiscal years. Recipient countries have been grouped by region.

WORLD BANK GROUP

International Bank for Reconstruction and Development (IBRD): Data cover loan authorizations of the IBRD made either to governments, government enterprises, or to private firms with government guarantee. No adjustments are made for subsequent sales of loans. Cancellations are deducted from loans authorized in the year originally authorized. Fiscal year activity from FY 1978 onward contains only new loan authorizations.

International Development Association (IDA): Data cover value of agreements with governments for development credits. Cancellations are deducted from credits authorized in the year originally authorized. Fiscal year activity from FY 1978 onward contains only new loan authorizations.

International Finance Corporation (IFC): Data cover the commitments made by the IFC to invest in private enterprises in the various countries. Cancellations are deducted from commitments in the year originally committed.

Starting in FY 1974 reductions are reflected in the cumulative total with no adjustments in annual amounts. Fiscal year activity for FY 1980 onward contains only new loan authorizations; increases in loans authorized in prior years appear only in cumulative data.

OTHER INTERNATIONAL ORGANIZATIONS

Asian Development Bank (ADB): Data cover loan authorizations of the Asian Development Bank which made its first loan in 1968.

African Development Bank (AFDB): Data cover loan authorizations of the African Development Bank which made its first loans in U.S. FY 1968; and the African Development Fund with its first loans in U.S. FY 1974.

Inter-American Development Bank (IDB): Data cover loan authorizations of the IDB made either to governments, government enterprises or to private firms from Ordinary Capital and from the Fund for Special Operations. Cancellations are deducted from authorizations in the year originally authorized. Data exclude original loans from the Social Progress Trust Fund administered by the Bank for the United States; they include, however, any loans purchased from the Bank with SPTF reflows.

United Nations Development Program: Data are shown combining the Special Fund (UNDP-SF) and Technical Assistance (UNDP-TA). Each was previously a separate

program—the Special Fund and the Expanded Program of Technical Assistance (EPTA), respectively. These were combined to form the United Nations Development Programme (UNDP). The Special Fund data cover allocations primarily for costs of preinvestment surveys. In FY 1973 the data represent the value of large-scale and small-scale projects approved and budgeted in the previous calendar year. Starting in FY 1974 the data are project approvals from the UNDP Compendium of Approved Projects.

Other United Nations Programs: Data cover allocations for approved projects and for administrative and operational services financed from government contributions and other sources by the United Nations Childrens' Fund (UNICEF). The data also include the Regular and other programs of technical assistance by U.N. specialized agencies (UNTA). Data for the specialized agencies are not available from FY 1969 onward.

European Economic Community (EEC): Data include obligations from the European Development Funds and from the European Investment Bank (EIB) for developing countries.

2. Transitional quarter.

3. Latin America Regional

AID and Predecessor Agencies. — Excludes Alliance for Progress funds obligated for nonregional programs in FY 1963–71.

Food for Peace (PL 480), Title II—Total Grants, Voluntary Relief Agencies. — Includes programs for French Guiana, Guadeloupe, and Martinique.

Other Economic Assistance, Other. — Represents primarily technical assistance grants for various countries and administrative funds under the Social Progress Trust Fund; Inter-American Foundation, $38.3 million.

Other U.S. Loans, All Other. — Represents OPIC direct loan.

4. World Regional

A.I.D. and Predecessor Agencies, Grants. — Excludes reimbursements by the Department of Defense for grants to Vietnam.

Other Economic Assistance, Contributions to International Financial Institutions (IFI). — Data excludes callable capital.

Other U.S. Loans, All Other. — Represents short-term credits by the Department of Agriculture under the Commodity Credit Corporation Charter Act unless otherwise identified on individual country pages.

5. Data exclude African Development Bank from FY 1979 onward.

a. Includes $825,000 approved in FY 1965 for Paraguay, transferred to Latin America Regional in FY 1971.

SOURCE: USAID-OLG, July 1, 1945-September 30, 1984, pp. 192–193, 201-210.

Table 2811

IMF DEFINITIONS FOR FUND ACCOUNT DATA

Members of the Fund may draw on its financial resources to meet their balance of payments needs through a **reserve tranche** and four additional **credit tranches**. When a member borrows from ("draws on") the Fund, it uses its own currency to *purchase* the currencies of other members or SDRs held by the Fund's General Account. Thus, a drawing results in an increase in the Fund's holdings of a member's currency and in a corresponding decrease in the General Account's holdings of the currencies of other members or of SDRs. As a result, the composition of the Fund's resources changes without affecting the total. Drawings under reserve tranche policies do not cause Fund holdings of a member's currency to exceed its quota; they are unconditional and are referred to as reserve tranche drawings. Drawings in each of four credit tranches are available in amounts equal to 25 percent of a member's quota. The conditionality imposed by the Fund for these drawings is progressively more rigorous after the first tranche. Most credit tranche drawings are made under **stand-by** arrangements, which assure a member that it will be able to draw on the Fund's resources up to a specified amount without a further review of its position and policies. A member is required to repurchase drawings under regular tranche policies in three to five years, or earlier, if its balance of payments position improves.

The Fund's special facilities permit additional use of Fund resources under particular circumstances. The **compensatory financing facility** enables members to draw on the Fund up to 100 percent of quota when they experience payments difficulties as a result of temporary shortfalls in export receipts—or up to 100 percent of quota when they experience payments difficulties as a result of excess cereal import costs—and their payments difficulties are largely beyond their control, as long as total drawings under the facility do not exceed 125 percent of quota. The **buffer stock financing facility** may be used by members in balance of payments difficulty to draw up to 50 percent of quota to finance contributions to international buffer stock arrangements. The **extended facility** assists members suffering from serious balance of payments difficulties resulting from structural imbalances in production, trade, and prices, or having economies characterized by slow growth and inherently weak payments positions, when the Fund is satisfied that its resources are required for longer periods and in larger amounts relative to quota than are available under the regular tranche policies.

Under the Fund's **enlarged access policy**, which replaced the **supplementary financing facility**, the Fund provides supplementary financing in conjunction with the use of the Fund's ordinary resources to all members facing serious payments imbalances that are large in relation to their quotas. It is used only in support of economic programs under stand-by arrangements reaching into the upper credit tranches or under extended arrangements. Such drawings are subject to Fund conditionality, phasing, and performance criteria. The period of such arrangements normally exceeds one year and may extend up to three years in certain cases.

IMF Fund Account Data Abbreviations

Amt. Appr.	Amount Approved	Imp.	Import
Comp. Financ. Pur	Compensatory Financing Facility Purchases	Oil Fac.	Oil Facility
Dist.	Distribution	Ord.	Ordinary
EAR	Enlarged Access to the Fund's Resources	Outstand. Sh-Term Fund Borrow	Outstanding Short-Term Fund Borrowing
Exp.	Expected	Pur.	Purchases
Extend.	Extended	Repurch.	Repurchases
GAB	Guaranteed Arrangements to Borrow	SFF	Supplement Financing Facility
		St-By	Stand-by

Table 2812

ARGENTINA IMF FUND ACCOUNT,[1] 1960–83[a]

Category[1]	1960	1965	1970	1975	1976	1977	1978	1979	1980	1981	1982	1983
General Department					Millions of SDRs: End of Period							
Quota	280.0	280.0	440.0	440.0	440.0	440.0	535.0	535.0	802.5	802.5	803.0	1,113.0
St-By Arrangements: Amount Drawn	#	#	#	#	159.5	#	#	#	#	#	#	601.0
St-By Arrangements: Undrawn Balance	100.0	#	#	#	100.5	159.5	#	#	#	#	#	899.0
Reserve Position in the Fund	#	#	130.2	#	#	#	130.5	154.4	262.8	239.2	91.0	#
Use of Fund Credit	126.0	76.0	#	250.1	455.6	344.5	#	#	#	#	#	1,121.0
Comp. Financ. Purch. Exp. Shortfalls	#	#	#	174.0	220.0	220.0	#	#	#	#	#	520.0
Oil Facility Purchases	#	#	#	76.1	76.1	#	#	#	#	#	#	#
Credit Tranche Pur.: Ord. Resources	126.0	76.0	#	#	159.5	124.5	#	#	#	#	#	337.0
Fund Holdings of Currency: Amount	406.0	356.0	309.8	690.1	895.6	784.5	404.5	380.6	539.7	563.4	712.0	2,234.0
Percent of Quota	145.0	127.1	70.4	156.8	203.5	178.3	75.6	71.1	67.2	70.2	89.0	201.0
					Millions of SDRs: During Period							
Total Purchases[2]	70.0	#	#	311.3	269.5	#	#	#	#	#	137.4	1,289.3
Reserve Tranche	#	#	#	125.3	#	#	#	#	#	#	~	~
Comp. Financ. Export Shortfalls	#	#	#	110.0	110.0	#	#	#	#	#	~	~
Oil Facility	#	#	#	76.1	#	#	#	#	#	#	~	~
Credit Tranche: Ordinary Resources	70.0	#	#	#	159.5	#	#	#	#	#	~	~
Gold Distributions	#	#	#	#	#	6.6	3.3	3.3	#	#	~	~
Total Repurchases	21.5	44.0	#	110.0	64.0	103.1	405.8	#	#	#	~	#
Repurchases of Purchases	21.5	44.0	#	110.0	64.0	103.1	405.8	#	#	#	#	#
Member's Currency Drawn	#	#	#	4.0	#	8.0	48.8	19.2	44.7	#	#	#
Member's Currency Used in Repurch.	#	#	10.1	#	#	#	#	#	4.5	20.5	~	~
SDR Department					Millions of SDRs: End of Period							
Net Cumulative Allocations	#	#	58.8	152.5	152.5	152.5	152.5	208.2	263.8	318.4		
SDR Holdings: Amount	#	#	59.3	34.8	78.2	73.9	161.6	247.9	256.6	347.1	#	#
Percent of Allocations	#	#	100.9	22.8	51.3	48.5	106.0	119.1	97.3	109.0	#	#
Administered Accounts					Millions of SDRs: During Period							
Trust Fund: Dist. of Gold Sale Profits	#	#	#	#	#	#	16.0	16.5	21.9	#	~	~

1. For definitions of terms, see table 2811. For SDR exchange rate, see tables 3102 and 3103.
2. Equals "All Drawings."

a. For data from years 1947–74, see SALA, 23–3100 through 3118.

SOURCE: IMF-IFS-S, No. 3, Supplement on Fund Accounts, 1982; IMF-IFS-Y, 1984.

Table 2813

BOLIVIA IMF FUND ACCOUNT,[1] 1960–83[a]

Category[1]	1960	1965	1970	1975	1976	1977	1978	1979	1980	1981	1982	1983
					Millions of SDRs: End of Period							
General Department												
Quota	22.5	22.5	37.0	37.0	37.0	37.0	45.0	45.0	67.5	67.5	67.5	90.7
St-By Arrangements: Amount Drawn	#	#	#	#	#	#	#	#	534	#	#	#
St-By Arrangements: Undrawn Balance	#	14.0	#	#	#	#	#	#	13.0	#	#	#
Reserve Position in the Fund	#	1.3	#	#	6.4	7.4	9.0	#	#	#	#	#
Use of Fund Credit	3.9	#	6.1	13.9	#	#	15.0	15.0	63.0	61.2	78.1	85.2
Comp. Financ. Purch. Exp. Shortfalls	#	#	#	#	#	#	15.0	15.0	15.0	13.1	5.6	17.9
Buffer Stock Purchases	#	#	#	4.7	#	#	#	#	#	#	24.5	24.5
Credit Tranche Pur.: Ord. Resources	3.7	#	5.8	8.9	#	#	#	#	21.9	22.5	22.5	19.6
Credit Tranche Pur.: SFF	#	#	#	#	#	#	#	#	25.5	25.5	25.5	23.2
Fund Holdings of Currency: Amount	26.4	21.3	43.1	50.9	30.6	29.6	51.0	60.0	130.5	128.7	145.6	176.0
Percent of Quota	117.2	94.4	116.4	137.6	82.6	80.1	173.4	133.3	193.4	190.6	215.7	194.0
					Millions of SDRs: During Period							
Total Purchases	1.0	#	#	4.7	#	#	15.0	8.7	53.4	#	24.5	23.7
Reserve Tranche	#	#	#	#	#	#	#	8.7	#	#	~	~
Comp. Financ. Export Shortfalls	#	#	#	#	#	#	15.0	#	#	#	~	~
Buffer Stock	#	#	#	4.7	#	#	#	#	#	#	~	~
Credit Tranche: Ordinary Resources	1.0	#	#	#	#	#	#	#	27.8	#	~	~
Credit Tranche: SFF	=	=	#	#	#	#	#	#	25.5	#	~	~
Gold Distributions	=	=	#	#	#	.3	.3	.3	.3	#	~	~
Total Repurchases	2.5	1.0	#	5.1	20.4	1.0	1.9	#	#	1.9	7.5	10.8
Repurchases of Purchases	2.5	1.0	#	5.1	20.4	1.0	1.5	#	#	1.9	7.5	10.8
					Millions of SDRs: End of Period							
SDR Department												
Net Cumulative Allocations	=	=	4.9	12.8	12.8	12.8	12.8	17.4	22.1	26.7	#	20.0
SDR Holdings: Amount	#	#	2.7	7.0	6.9	5.7	14.1	#	#	.1	#	.1
Percent of Allocations	#	#	55.9	55.1	54.0	44.7	110.7	#	#	.4	#	.5
					Millions of SDRs: During Period							
Administered Accounts												
Trust Fund: Loans	#	#	#	#	#	#	15.3	#	20.7	.1	36.2	36.2
Trust Fund: Dist. of Gold Sale Profits	#	#	#	#	#	#	1.4	1.4	1.8	#	~	~
SFF Subsidy Payments	#	#	#	#	#	#	#	#	#	.9	~	~

1. For definitions of terms, see table 2811. For SDR exchange rate, see tables 3102 and 3103.

a. For data from years 1947–74, see SALA, 23–3100 through 3118.

SOURCE: IMF-IFS-S, No. 3, Supplement on Fund Accounts, 1982; IMF-IFS-Y, 1984.

Table 2814

BRAZIL IMF FUND ACCOUNT,[1] 1960–83[a]

Category[1]	1960	1965	1970	1975	1976	1977	1978	1979	1980	1981	1982	1983
						Millions of SDRs: End of Period						
General Department												
Quota	280.0	280.0	440.0	440.0	440.0	440.0	665.0	665.0	997.5	997.5	998.0	1,461.0
St-By Arrangements: Amount Drawn	#	75.0	#	#	#	#	#	#	#	#	#	#
St-By Arrangements: Undrawn Balance	#	50.0	50.0	#	#	#	#	#	#	#	#	#
Reserve Position in the Fund	#	#	117.4	116.3	162.2	160.2	138.9	183.2	269.5	226.6	260.0	#
Use of Fund Credit	70.0	89.3	#	#	#	#	#	#	#	#	499.0	2,526.0
Comp. Financ. Purch. Exp. Shortfalls	#	60.0	#	#	#	#	#	#	#	#	499.0	965.0
Credit Tranche Pur.: Ord. Resources	70.0	29.0	#	#	#	#	#	#	#	#	#	249.0
Fund Holdings of Currency: Amount	350.0	369.3	322.6	323.7	277.8	279.8	526.1	481.8	728.0	770.9	1,236.0	3,987.0
Percent of Quota	125.0	131.9	73.3	73.6	63.1	63.6	79.1	72.4	73.0	77.3	124.0	273.0
						Millions of SDRs: During Period						
Total Purchases	47.7	75.0	#	#	#	#	#	#	#	#	498.8	2,402.7
Reserve Tranche	#	#	#	#	#	#	#	#	#	#	~	~
Comp. Financ. Export Shortfalls	#	#	#	#	#	#	#	#	#	#	~	~
Credit Tranche: Ordinary Resources	47.7	75.0	#	#	#	#	#	#	#	#	~	~
Gold Distributions	#	#	#	#	#	6.6	3.3	3.3	#	#	~	~
Total Repurchases	#	55.0	75.2	#	#	#	#	#	#	#	#	#
Repurchases of Purchases	#	55.0	75.2	#	#	#	#	#	#	#	#	#
Member's Currency Drawn	#	#	7.4	#	78.3	15.0	5.0	40.5	33.9	7.0	47.0	#
Member's Currency Used in Repurch.	#	#	#	#	3.5	-1.9	23.0	#	31.3	46.0	13.9	#
						Millions of SDRs: End of Period						
SDR Department												
Net Cumulative Allocations	#	#	58.8	152.5	152.5	152.5	152.5	221.7	290.8	358.7	#	#
SDR Holdings: Amount	#	#	62.3	163.3	171.0	173.2	183.8	290.7	300.7	388.1	#	#
Percent of Allocations	#	#	105.9	107.1	112.1	113.6	120.5	131.1	103.4	108.2	#	#
						Millions of SDRs: During Period						
Administered Accounts												
Trust Fund: Dist. of Gold Sale Profits	#	#	#	#	#	#	16.0	16.5	21.9	#	~	~

1. For definitions of terms, see table 2811. For SDR exchange rate, see tables 3102 and 3103.

a. For data from years 1947–74, see SALA, 23–3100 through 3118.

SOURCE: IMF-IFS-S, No. 3, Supplement on Fund Accounts, 1982; IMF-IFS-Y, 1984.

Table 2815

CHILE IMF FUND ACCOUNT,[1] 1960-83[a]

Category[1]	1960	1965	1970	1975	1976	1977	1978	1979	1980	1981	1982	1983
					Millions of SDRs: End of Period							
General Department												
Quota	100.0	100.0	158.0	158.0	158.0	158.0	217.0	217.0	325.5	325.5	325.5	440.5
St-By Arrangements: Amount Drawn	#	36.0	#	20.0	#	#	#	#	#	#	#	284.0
St-By Arrangements: Undrawn Balance	#	#	#	59.0	#	#	#	#	#	#	#	216.0
Reserve Position in the Fund	#	#	#	#	#	#	38.3	37.1	64.3	64.3	70.5	#
Use of Fund Credit	4.3	100.0	1.5	330.8	402.2	300.6	266.5	135.9	96.3	41.8	5.7	579.0
Comp. Financ. Purch. Exp. Shortfalls	#	#	#	73.0	99.0	79.0	79.0	#	#	#	#	295.0
Oil Facility Purchases	#	#	#	198.3	243.7	241.1	187.5	135.9	96.3	41.8	5.7	#
Credit Tranche Pur.: Ord. Resources	4.4	100.0	1.5	59.5	59.5	#	#	#	#	#	#	155.0
Fund Holdings of Currency: Amount	104.3	200.0	159.5	488.8	560.2	458.6	445.2	315.8	357.6	303.0	260.6	1,019.5
Percent of Quota	104.3	200.0	100.9	309.4	354.6	290.3	205.1	145.5	109.8	93.1	80.1	231.4
					Millions of SDRs: During Period							
Total Purchases	#	36.0	#	176.8	124.4	#	#	#	#	#	#	678.3
Reserve Tranche	#	#	#	#	#	#	#	#	#	#	~	~
Comp. Financ. Export Shortfalls	#	#	#	#	79.0	#	#	#	#	#	~	~
Oil Facility	#	#	#	156.8	45.4	#	#	#	#	#	~	~
Credit Tranche: Ordinary Resources	#	36.0	#	20.0	#	#	#	#	#	#	~	~
Gold Distributions	#	#	#	#	#	2.4	1.2	1.2	#	#	~	~
Total Repurchases	12.4	37.0	47.3	6.0	53.0	101.6	73.6	130.6	39.6	54.5	36.1	5.7
Repurchases of Purchases	12.4	37.0	47.3	6.0	53.0	101.6	73.6	130.6	39.6	54.5	36.1	5.7
					Millions of SDRs: End of Period							
SDR Department												
Net Cumulative Allocations	#	#	21.0	54.7	54.7	54.7	54.7	77.2	99.8	121.9	122.1	123.8
SDR Holdings: Amount	#	#	21.8	20.9	48.3	54.7	20.7	22.0	3.0	16.4	17.7	5.2
Percent of Allocations	#	#	103.9	38.3	88.3	100.0	37.9	28.4	3.0	13.5	14.5	4.2
					Millions of SDRs: During Period							
Administered Accounts												
Trust Fund: Dist. of Gold Sale Profits	#	#	#	#	#	#	5.7	5.9	7.9	#	~	~

1. For definitions of terms, see table 2811. For SDR exchange rate, see tables 3102 and 3103.

a. For data from years 1947–74, see SALA, 23–3100 through 3118.

SOURCE: IMF-IFS-S, No. 3, Supplement on Fund Accounts, 1982; IMF-IFS-Y, 1984.

Table 2816

COLOMBIA IMF FUND ACCOUNT,[1] 1960–83[a]

Category[1]	1960	1965	1970	1975	1976	1977	1978	1979	1980	1981	1982	1983
					Millions of SDRs: End of Period							
General Department												
Quota	100.0	100.0	157.0	157.0	157.0	157.0	193.0	193.0	289.5	289.5	290.0	394.0
St-By Arrangements: Amount Drawn	#	#	23.0	#	#	#	#	#	#	#	#	#
St-By Arrangements: Undrawn Balance	75.0	#	15.5	#	#	#	#	#	#	#	#	#
Reserve Position in the Fund	25.0	#	#	39.3	45.3	76.7	70.1	73.6	114.5	151.7	175.0	262.0
Use of Fund Credit	#	59.5	54.9	#	#	#	#	#	#	#	#	#
Comp. Financ. Purch. Exp. Shortfalls	#	#	#	#	#	#	#	#	#	#	#	#
Credit Tranche Pur.: Ord. Resources	#	59.5	54.9	#	#	#	#	#	#	#	#	#
Fund Holdings of Currency: Amount	75.0	159.5	211.9	117.8	111.8	80.3	123.0	119.4	175.0	137.8	114.0	132.0
Percent of Quota	75.0	159.5	134.9	75.0	71.2	51.1	63.7	61.8	60.4	47.6	39.0	34.0
					Millions of SDRs: During Period							
Total Purchases	#	#	29.3	#	#	#	#	#	#	#	#	#
Reserve Tranche	#	#	#	#	#	#	#	#	#	#	~	~
Comp. Financ. Export Shortfalls	#	#	#	#	#	#	#	#	#	#	~	~
Credit Tranche: Ordinary Resources	#	#	29.3	#	#	#	#	#	#	#	~	~
Gold Distributions	#	#	#	#	#	2.4	#	2.4	#	#	~	~
Total Repurchases	15.0	24.0	72.7	#	#	#	#	#	#	#	~	~
Repurchases of Purchases	15.0	24.0	72.7	#	#	#	#	#	#	#	#	#
Member's Currency Drawn	#	#	#	#	6.0	33.8	2.0	4.0	10.4	40.0	34.1	70.1
Member's Currency Used in Repurch.	#	#	#	#	#	#	5.0	#	#	2.8	9.3	9.4
					Millions of SDRs: End of Period							
SDR Department												
Net Cumulative Allocations	#	#	21.0	54.4	54.4	54.4	54.4	74.5	94.6	114.3	114.1	114.5
SDR Holdings: Amount	#	#	.1	20.3	24.3	25.6	37.8	71.9	85.3	119.4	162.0	189.0
Percent of Allocations	#	#	.3	37.2	44.7	47.0	69.3	96.5	90.2	104.4	142.0	165.0
					Millions of SDRs: During Period							
Administered Accounts												
Trust Fund: Dist. of Gold Sale Profits	#	#	#	#	#	#	5.7	5.9	7.8	#	~	~

1. For definitions of terms, see table 2811. For SDR exchange rate, see tables 3102 and 3103.

a. For data from years 1947–74, see SALA, 23–3100 through 3118.

SOURCE: IMF-IFS-S, No. 3, Supplement on Fund Accounts, 1982; IMF-IFS-Y, 1984.

Table 2817

COSTA RICA IMF FUND ACCOUNT,[1] 1960-83[a]

Category[1]	1960	1965	1970	1975	1976	1977	1978	1979	1980	1981	1982	1983
Millions of SDRs: End of Period												
General Department												
Quota	5.5	20.0	32.0	32.0	32.0	32.0	41.0	41.0	61.5	61.5	61.5	84.1
St-By Arrangements: Amount Drawn	#	10.0	#	#	#	#	#	#	15.4	#	#	#
St-By Arrangements: Undrawn Balance	#	#	#	#	11.6	#	#	#	45.1	#	92.3	#
Extend. Arrangements: Amount Drawn	#	#	#	#	#	#	#	#	#	22.5	#	#
Extend. Arrangements: Undrawn Balance	#	#	#	#	#	#	#	#	#	254.3	#	#
Reserve Position in the Fund	1.4	#	6.0	#	#	#	7.8	7.5	#	#	#	#
Use of Fund Credit	#	15.0	#	30.0	32.3	29.3	24.3	43.8	44.6	88.2	84.2	183.3
Comp. Financ. Purch. Exp. Shortfalls	#	#	#	#	#	#	#	20.5	20.5	50.6	50.6	59.0
Oil Facility Purchases	#	#	#	30.8	37.7	37.3	24.3	23.3	13.9	4.8	.9	#
Credit Tranche Pur.: Ord. Resources	#	15.0	#	#	#	#	#	#	5.1	5.1	5.1	51.5
Credit Tranche Pur.: SFF	#	#	#	#	#	#	#	#	5.1	5.1	5.1	4.5
Extended Facility Pur.: Ord. Resources	#	#	#	#	#	#	#	#	#	11.3	11.3	11.3
Extended Facility Pur.: SFF	#	#	#	#	#	#	#	#	#	11.3	11.3	11.3
Fund Holdings of Currency: Amount	4.1	35.0	26.0	62.0	64.3	61.3	57.5	77.3	106.1	149.7	145.7	267.4
Percent of Quota	74.9	175.0	81.2	193.6	200.9	191.6	140.3	188.5	172.6	243.3	236.9	318.0
Millions of SDRs: During Period												
Total Purchases	#	10.0	1.8	12.0	6.8	#	#	20.5	22.9	52.6	#	116.5
Reserve Tranche	#	#	1.8	#	#	#	#	#	7.5	#	~	~
Comp. Financ. Export Shortfalls	#	#	#	#	#	#	#	20.5	#	30.1	~	~
Oil Facility	#	#	#	12.0	6.8	#	#	#	10.3	#	~	~
Credit Tranche: Ordinary Resources	#	10.0	#	#	#	#	#	#	5.1	#	~	~
Credit Tranche: SFF	#	#	#	#	#	#	#	#	#	11.3	~	~
Extended Facility: Ord. Resources	#	#	#	#	#	#	#	#	#	11.3	~	~
Extended Facility: SFF	#	#	#	#	#	.5	.2	.2	#	#	~	~
Gold Distributions	#	#	#	#	#	#	#	#	#	#	~	~
Total Repurchases	#	1.7	4.0	.9	4.5	3.0	13.0	1.0	9.4	9.1	4.0	11.7
Repurchases of Purchases	#	1.7	4.0	.9	4.5	3.0	13.0	1.0	9.4	9.1	4.0	11.7
Millions of SDRs: End of Period												
SDR Department												
Net Cumulative Allocations	#	#	4.2	11.0	11.0	11.0	11.0	15.3	19.5	23.7	33.3	24.2
SDR Holdings: Amount	#	#	.2	3.8	1.2	5.5	3.0	4.5	#	#	.1	2.9
Percent of Allocations	#	#	4.8	34.6	11.3	50.2	27.2	29.2	#	#	.3	12.0
Millions of SDRs: During Period												
Administered Accounts												
Trust Fund: Dist. of Gold Sale Profits	#	#	#	#	#	#	1.2	1.2	1.6	#	~	~

1. For definitions of terms, see table 2811. For SDR exchange rate, see tables 3102 and 3103.

a. For data from years 1947–74, see SALA, 23–3100 through 3118.

SOURCE: IMF-IFS-S, No. 3, Supplement on Fund Accounts, 1982; IMF-IFS-Y, 1984.

Table 2818

DOMINICAN REPUBLIC IMF FUND ACCOUNT,[1] 1960-83[a]

Category[1]	1960	1965	1970	1975	1976	1977	1978	1979	1980	1981	1982	1983
General Department					Millions of SDRs: End of Period							
Quota	15.0	25.0	43.0	43.0	43.0	43.0	55.0	55.0	82.5	82.5	82.5	112.1
St-By Arrangements: Amount Drawn	#	#	#	#	#	#	#	#	#	#	#	#
St-By Arrangements: Undrawn Balance	#	#	#	#	#	#	#	#	#	#	#	#
Reserve Position in the Fund	#	#	#	#	#	#	#	#	#	#	#	#
Use of Fund Credit	5.3	13.8	6.6	#	21.5	36.5	36.5	94.3	38.0	19.8	64.1	235.2
Comp. Financ. Purch. Exp. Shortfalls	#	#	3.3	#	21.5	21.5	21.5	55.0	16.7	6.0	39.8	79.5
Buffer Stock Purchases	#	#	#	#	#	#	#	11.5	#	#	10.6	23.2
Credit Tranche Pur.: Ord. Resources	5.3	13.8	3.3	#	#	15.0	15.0	27.5	21.3	13.8	13.8	8.7
Fund Holdings of Currency: Amount	20.3	38.8	49.6	43.0	64.5	79.5	91.5	149.3	120.5	102.3	146.6	339.9
Percent of Quota	135.0	155.0	115.2	100.0	150.0	184.9	166.4	271.5	146.1	124.0	177.7	303.2
					Millions of SDRs: During Period							
Total Purchases	9.0	5.0	#	10.8	21.5	15.0	#	68.3	#	#	54.1	179.1
Reserve Tranche	3.8	#	#	10.8	#	#	#	#	#	#	54.1	179.1
Comp. Financ. Export Shortfalls	#	#	#	#	21.5	#	#	#	#	#	~	~
Buffer Stock	#	#	#	#	#	#	#	33.5	#	#	~	~
Credit Tranche: Ordinary Resources	5.3	5.0	#	#	#	15.0	#	11.5	#	#	~	~
Gold Distributions	#	#	#	#	#	.6	#	23.3	#	#	~	~
Total Repurchases	#	#	5.3	10.8	#	#	#	.3	.3	#	~	~
Repurchases of Purchases	#	#	5.3	10.8	#	#	#	10.8	49.8	18.3	9.8	8.1
SDR Department					Millions of SDRs: End of Period							
Net Cumulative Allocations	#	#	5.4	14.5	14.5	14.5	14.5	20.3	26.0	31.6	29.4	28.6
SDR Holdings: Amount	#	#	#	6.5	6.0	5.2	4.7	7.2	#	1.6	.5	.2
Percent of Allocations	#	#	.4	44.9	41.4	35.7	32.5	35.6	#	5.2	1.7	.7
Administered Accounts					Millions of SDRs: During Period							
Trust Fund: Dist. of Gold Sale Profits	#	#	#	#	#	#	1.6	1.6	2.1	#	~	~

1. For definitions of terms, see table 2811. For SDR exchange rate, see tables 3102 and 3103.

a. For data from years 1947-74, see SALA, 23-3100 through 3118.

SOURCE: IMF-IFS-S, No. 3, Supplement on Fund Accounts, 1982; IMF-IFS-Y, 1984.

Table 2819

ECUADOR IMF FUND ACCOUNT,[1] 1960-83[a]

Category[1]	1960	1965	1970	1975	1976	1977	1978	1979	1980	1981	1982	1983
					Millions of SDRs: End of Period							
General Department												
Quota	15.0	20.0	33.0	33.0	33.0	33.0	70.0	70.0	105.0	105.0	105.0	150.7
St-By Arrangements: Amount Drawn	#	8.0	10.0	#	#	#	#	#	#	#	#	118.1
St-By Arrangements: Undrawn Balance	#	4.0	12.0	#	#	#	#	#	#	#	#	39.4
Reserve Position in the Fund	3.8	#	#	13.2	#	#	8.0	9.4	21.8	24.8	#	11.4
Use of Fund Credit	#	6.0	13.8	#	#	#	#	#	#	#	#	203.5
Comp. Financ. Purch. Exp. Shortfalls	#	#	3.3	#	#	#	#	#	#	#	#	85.4
Credit Tranche Pur.: Ord. Resources	#	6.0	10.5	#	#	#	#	#	#	#	#	62.1
Fund Holdings of Currency: Amount	11.3	26.0	46.8	19.8	33.0	33.0	62.0	60.6	83.2	80.2	105.0	342.8
Percent of Quota	75.0	130.0	141.7	59.9	100.0	100.0	88.6	86.6	79.3	76.4	100.0	227.5
					Millions of SDRs: During Period							
Total Purchases	#	11.0	10.0	#	17.6	#	#	#	#	#	24.8	203.5
Reserve Tranche	#	4.0	#	#	17.6	#	#	#	#	#	#	#
Comp. Financ. Export Shortfalls	#	#	#	#	#	#	#	#	#	#	#	#
Credit Tranche: Ordinary Resources	#	7.0	10.0	#	#	#	#	#	#	#	#	#
Gold Distributions	#	#	#	#	#	.5	.3	.3	#	#	#	#
Total Repurchases	#	2.0	6.5	#	#	#	8.3	#	#	#	#	#
Repurchases of Purchases	#	2.0	6.5	#	#	#	8.3	#	#	#	#	#
Member's Currency Drawn	#	#	#	4.0	5.0	#	#	1.5	1.7	3.0	#	#
					Millions of SDRs: End of Period							
SDR Department												
Net Cumulative Allocations	#	#	4.2	11.2	11.2	11.2	11.2	18.5	25.8	32.9	#	33.3
SDR Holdings: Amount	#	#	.1	6.3	6.3	8.2	10.6	19.2	19.0	28.9	#	.1
Percent of Allocations	#	#	2.9	56.0	55.7	73.0	94.5	103.5	73.6	87.6	#	.3
					Millions of SDRs: During Period							
Administered Accounts												
Trust Fund: Dist. of Gold Sale Profits	#	#	#	#	#	#	1.2	1.2	1.6	#	~	~

1. For definitions of terms, see table 2811. For SDR exchange rate, see tables 3102 and 3103.

a. For data from years 1947–74, see SALA, 23–3100 through 3118.

SOURCE: IMF-IFS-S, No. 3, Supplement on Fund Accounts, 1982; IMF-IFS-Y, 1984.

Table 2820

EL SALVADOR IMF FUND ACCOUNT,[1] 1960–83[a]

Category[1]	1960	1965	1970	1975	1976	1977	1978	1979	1980	1981	1982	1983
General Department						Millions of SDRs: End of Period						
Quota	11.3	20.0	35.0	35.0	35.0	35.0	43.0	43.0	64.5	64.5	64.5	89.0
St-By Arrangements: Amount Drawn	11.3	#	#	#	#	#	#	#	#	#	#	#
St-By Arrangements: Undrawn Balance	#	20.0	14.0	#	#	#	#	#	10.8	#	27.5	#
Reserve Position in the Fund	#	5.0	#	#	#	5.1	#	#	#	#	15.5	#
Use of Fund Credit	8.4	#	6.5	17.9	12.8	#	8.8	8.5	#	#	#	#
Comp. Financ. Purch. Exp. Shortfalls	#	#	6.3	#	#	#	#	#	5.4	37.6	97.4	112.9
Oil Facility Purchases	#	#	#	17.9	17.9	#	#	#	#	32.3	64.5	64.5
Credit Tranche Pur.: Ord. Resources	8.4	#	.2	#	#	#	#	#	4.8	5.4	32.9	48.4
Fund Holdings of Currency: Amount	19.7	15.0	41.5	52.9	47.8	29.9	34.3	34.5	69.9	102.1	161.9	201.9
Percent of Quota	175.0	75.0	118.5	151.1	136.6	85.5	79.7	80.3	108.3	158.3	251.0	226.8
						Millions of SDRs: During Period						
Total Purchases	13.3	#	#	#	#	#	#	#	19.0	32.3	59.8	21.6
Reserve Tranche	2.8	#	#	#	#	#	#	#	8.2	~	~	~
Comp. Financ. Export Shortfalls	#	#	#	#	#	#	#	#	#	32.3	~	~
Oil Facility	#	#	#	#	#	#	#	#	#	#	~	~
Credit Tranche: Ordinary Resources	10.4	#	#	#	#	#	#	#	10.8	~	~	~
Gold Distributions	#	#	#	#	#	.5	#	.3	.3	#	~	~
Total Repurchases	7.5	#	5.0	#	5.1	17.9	3.7	#	#	#	~	#
Repurchases of Purchases	7.5	#	5.0	#	5.1	17.9	3.7	#	#	#	#	#
SDR Department						Millions of SDRs: End of Period						
Net Cumulative Allocations	#	#	4.2	11.7	11.7	11.7	11.7	16.1	20.6	25.0	25.4	25.0
SDR Holdings: Amount	#	#	#	3.9	4.0	7.8	7.6	13.2	#	.1	1.7	.1
Percent of Allocations	#	#	.2	33.5	34.6	67.0	65.4	81.9	#	.5	6.7	.4
Administered Accounts						Millions of SDRs: During Period						
Trust Fund: Loans	#	#	#	#	#	#	#	#	19.6	.1	19.7	19.7
Trust Fund: Dist. of Gold Sale Profits	#	#	#	#	#	#	1.3	1.3	1.7	#	~	~

1. For definitions of terms, see table 2811. For SDR exchange rate, see tables 3102 and 3103.

a. For data from years 1947–74, see SALA, 23–3100 through 3118.

SOURCE: IMF-IFS-S, No. 3, Supplement on Fund Accounts, 1982; IMF-IFS-Y, 1984.

Table 2821

GUATEMALA IMF FUND ACCOUNT,[1] 1960–83[a]

Millions of SDRs: End of Period

Category[1]	1960	1965	1970	1975	1976	1977	1978	1979	1980	1981	1982	1983
General Department												
Quota	15.0	20.0	36.0	36.0	36.0	36.0	51.0	51.0	76.5	76.5	76.5	108.0
Outstand. Fund Borrowings: SFF	#	#	#	#	#	#	#	#	#	8.4	#	#
Available: SFF	#	#	#	#	#	#	#	30.0	30.0	21.6	~	~
St-By Arrangements: Amount Drawn	#	#	#	#	#	#	#	#	#	19.1	#	38.3
St-By Arrangements: Undrawn Balance	15.0	#	14.0	#	#	#	#	#	#	#	#	76.5
Reserve Position in the Fund	3.8	#	#	9.0	12.0	12.4	12.9	14.1	21.7	#	~	7.9
Reserve Tranche Position	3.8	#	#	9.0	12.0	12.4	12.9	14.1	21.7	#	~	7.9
Use of Fund Credit	#	#	#	#	#	#	#	#	#	95.6	95.6	133.9
Comp. Financ. Purch. Exp. Shortfalls	#	#	#	#	#	#	#	#	#	76.5	76.5	76.5
Credit Tranche Pur.: Ord. Resources	#	#	#	#	#	#	#	#	#	19.1	19.1	32.2
Fund Holdings of Currency: Amount	11.2	20.0	36.0	27.0	24.0	23.6	38.1	36.9	54.8	172.1	172.1	234.0
Percent of Quota	74.9	100.0	100.0	75.0	66.7	65.7	74.7	72.3	71.6	225.0	225.0	216.6

Millions of SDRs: During Period

Category[1]	1960	1965	1970	1975	1976	1977	1978	1979	1980	1981	1982	1983
Total Purchases	#	5.0	#	#	#	#	#	#	#	116.7	#	38.3
Reserve Tranche	#	5.0	#	#	#	#	#	#	#	21.1	~	~
Comp. Financ. Export Shortfalls	#	#	#	#	#	#	#	#	#	76.5	~	~
Credit Tranche: Ordinary Resources	#	#	#	#	#	.5	.3	.3	#	19.1	~	~
Gold Distributions	#	#	#	#	#	#	#	#	#	#	#	#
Total Repurchases	#	#	8.4	#	#	#	#	#	#	#	#	#
Repurchases of Purchases	#	#	8.4	#	#	#	#	#	#	#	#	#
Member's Currency Drawn	#	#	#	#	3.0	1.5	1.0	1.5	1.6	#	#	#
Member's Currency Used in Repurch.	#	#	#	#	#	#	#	#	1.0	.6	#	#

Millions of SDRs: End of Period

Category[1]	1960	1965	1970	1975	1976	1977	1978	1979	1980	1981	1982	1983
SDR Department												
Net Cumulative Allocations	#	#	4.2	11.9	11.9	11.9	11.9	17.2	22.5	27.7	#	30.0
SDR Holdings: Amount	#	#	2.1	11.5	11.4	11.5	11.6	18.4	17.7	2.2	.1	.6
Percent of Allocations	#	#	48.8	96.5	96.4	96.8	97.7	106.9	78.9	8.0	.1	2.0

Millions of SDRs: During Period

Category[1]	1960	1965	1970	1975	1976	1977	1978	1979	1980	1981	1982	1983
Administered Accounts												
Trust Fund: Dist. of Gold Sale Profits	#	#	#	#	#	#	1.3	1.3	1.8	#	~	~

1. For definitions of terms, see table 2811. For SDR exchange rate, see tables 3102 and 3103.

a. For data from years 1947–74, see SALA, 23–3100 through 3118.

SOURCE: IMF-IFS-S, No. 3, Supplement on Fund Accounts, 1982; IMF-IFS-Y, 1984.

Table 2822

HAITI IMF FUND ACCOUNT,[1] 1960–83[a]

Category[1]	1960	1965	1970	1975	1976	1977	1978	1979	1980	1981	1982	1983
					Millions of SDRs: End of Period							
General Department												
Quota	11.3	11.3	19.0	19.0	19.0	19.0	23.0	23.0	34.5	34.5	34.5	44.1
St-By Arrangements: Amount Drawn	#	1.8	#	.9	#	#	#	#	#	#	22.5	53.0
St-By Arrangements: Undrawn Balance	6.0	2.3	2.2	3.8	6.9	6.9	#	#	#	#	12.0	7.0
Extend. Arrangements: Amount Drawn	#	#	#	#	#	#	#	#	10.8	#	22.5	53.0
Extend. Arrangements: Undrawn Balance	#	#	#	#	#	#	32.2	32.2	21.4	#	#	#
Reserve Position in the Fund	#	#	#	#	#	#	2.4	4.4	#	#	.1	.1
Use of Fund Credit	1.3	6.2	2.2	11.0	12.4	8.4	7.6	5.7	17.2	32.0	43.0	72.2
Comp. Financ. Purch. Exp. Shortfalls	#	#	2.1	#	#	#	#	#	#	17.0	17.0	17.0
Oil Facility Purchases	#	#	#	6.4	9.0	8.9	7.6	5.7	3.5	1.3	.3	#
Credit Tranche Pur.: Ord. Resources	1.3	6.2	#	4.5	3.2	#	#	#	2.4	2.9	9.5	22.9
Extended Facility Pur.: Ord. Resources	#	#	#	#	#	#	#	#	10.8	10.8	10.8	10.8
Fund Holdings of Currency: Amount	12.6	17.4	21.2	30.0	31.4	27.4	28.3	24.3	51.7	66.5	77.4	116.2
Percent of Quota	111.6	154.8	111.5	157.7	165.2	144.4	122.9	105.7	149.7	192.7	224.4	263.5
					Millions of SDRs: During Period							
Total Purchases	#	2.5	#	4.5	4.9	3.0	#	#	20.9	17.0	12.0	31.9
Reserve Tranche	#	#	#	#	#	#	#	#	4.4	#	~	~
Comp. Financ. Export Shortfalls	#	#	#	#	#	#	#	#	#	17.0	~	~
Oil Facility	#	#	#	2.6	2.6	#	#	#	#	#	~	~
Credit Tranche: Ordinary Resources	#	2.5	#	1.9	2.3	3.0	#	#	5.8	#	~	~
Extended Facility: Ord. Resources	#	#	#	#	#	#	#	#	10.8	#	~	~
Gold Distributions	#	#	#	#	#	.3	#	.3	#	#	~	~
Total Repurchases	1.3	2.3	2.8	.2	3.7	6.7	3.2	4.3	2.2	2.2	1.0	.3
Repurchases of Purchases	1.3	2.3	2.8	#	3.7	6.7	3.2	4.3	2.2	2.2	1.0	.3
					Millions of SDRs: End of Period							
SDR Department												
Net Cumulative Allocations	#	#	2.5	6.6	6.6	6.6	6.6	9.0	11.4	13.7	14.5	14.5
SDR Holdings: Amount	#	#	#	2.0	1.2	1.6	3.8	5.5	#	#	1.0	1.0
Percent of Allocations	#	#	#	30.3	18.9	24.4	57.8	61.3	.2	.3	6.9	6.9
					Millions of SDRs: During Period							
Administered Accounts												
Trust Fund: Loans	#	#	#	#	#	2.0	5.8	5.8	4.9	.1	18.5	17.9
Trust Fund: Dist. of Gold Sale Profits	#	#	#	#	#	#	.7	.7	.9	#	~	~
Oil Facility Subsidy Payments	#	#	#	#	.1	.2	.2	.2	.2	.1	~	~

1. For definitions of terms, see table 2811. For SDR exchange rate, see tables 3102 and 3103.

a. For data from years 1947–74, see SALA, 23–3100 through 3118.

SOURCE: IMF-IFS-S, No. 3, Supplement on Fund Accounts, 1982; IMF-IFS-Y, 1984.

Table 2823

HONDURAS IMF FUND ACCOUNT,[1] 1960-83[a]

Category[1]	1960	1965	1970	1975	1976	1977	1978	1979	1980	1981	1982	1983
					Millions of SDRs: End of Period							
General Department												
Quota	11.3	15.0	25.0	25.0	25.0	25.0	34.0	34.0	51.0	51.0	51.0	67.8
St-By Arrangements: Amount Drawn	5.0	#	#	#	#	#	#	#	#	#	15.3	#
St-By Arrangements: Undrawn Balance	2.5	#	#	#	#	#	#	#	#	#	61.2	#
Extend. Arrangements: Amount Drawn	#	#	#	#	#	#	#	#	16.0	23.9	#	#
Extend. Arrangements: Undrawn Balance	#	#	#	#	#	#	#	47.6	31.6	23.7	#	#
Reserve Position in the Fund	#	#	#	#	#	#	6.3	6.1	#	#	#	4.2
Use of Fund Credit	2.2	3.8	#	16.8	16.8	4.3	#	#	11.8	32.4	94.1	140.0
Oil Facility Purchases	#	#	#	16.8	16.8	10.5	#	#	#	#	#	#
Credit Tranche Pur.: Ord. Resources	2.2	3.8	#	#	#	#	#	#	#	12.8	16.8	37.7
Extended Facility Pur.: Ord. Resources	#	#	#	#	#	#	#	#	11.8	19.7	19.7	19.7
Fund Holdings of Currency: Amount	13.4	18.8	25.0	41.8	41.8	29.3	27.8	27.9	62.8	83.4	145.1	203.6
Percent of Quota	119.5	125.0	100.0	167.1	167.1	117.2	81.6	82.2	123.0	163.5	284.5	300.3
					Millions of SDRs: During Period							
Total Purchases	5.0	#	6.3	#	#	#	#	#	21.9	20.7	61.7	45.9
Reserve Tranche	2.8	#	6.3	#	#	#	#	#	5.9	#	~	~
Oil Facility	#	#	#	#	#	#	#	#	#	#	~	~
Credit Tranche: Ordinary Resources	2.2	#	#	#	#	#	#	#	#	12.8	~	~
Extended Facility: Ord. Resources	#	#	#	#	#	#	#	#	16.0	7.9	~	~
Gold Distributions	#	#	#	#	#	#	#	.2	.2	#	~	~
Total Repurchases	3.7	2.5	#	#	#	12.5	10.5	#	#	#	#	#
Repurchases of Purchases	3.7	3.5	#	#	#	12.5	10.5	#	#	#	#	#
					Millions of SDRs: End of Period							
SDR Department												
Net Cumulative Allocations	#	#	3.2	8.5	8.5	8.5	8.5	12.1	15.6	19.1	18.6	18.9
SDR Holdings: Amount	#	#	.2	4.0	2.7	3.6	3.0	7.7	#	1.4	1.6	2.1
Percent of Allocations	#	#	6.0	43.7	31.2	41.7	34.6	63.7	.1	7.3	8.6	11.1
					Millions of SDRs: During Period							
Administered Accounts												
Trust Fund: Loans	#	#	#	#	#	#	#	7.6	6.4	.1	14.7	14.7
Trust Fund: Dist. of Gold Sale Profits	#	#	#	#	#	#	.9	.9	1.3	#	~	~

1. For definitions of terms, see table 2811. For SDR exchange rate, see tables 3102 and 3103.

a. For data from years 1947-74, see SALA, 23-3100 through 3118.

SOURCE: IMF-IFS-S, No. 3, Supplement on Fund Accounts, 1982; IMF-IFS-Y, 1984.

Table 2824

MEXICO IMF FUND ACCOUNT,[1] 1960–83[a]

Category[1]	1960	1965	1970	1975	1976	1977	1978	1979	1980	1981	1982	1983
General Department						Millions of SDRs: End of Period						
Quota	180.0	180.0	370.0	370.0	370.0	370.0	535.0	535.0	802.5	802.5	803.0	1,166.0
St-By Arrangements: Amount Drawn	#	#	#	#	#	#	#	#	#	#	#	#
St-By Arrangements: Undrawn Balance	#	#	#	#	#	#	#	#	#	#	#	#
Extend. Arrangements: Amount Drawn	#	#	#	#	#	100.0	#	#	#	#	#	1,003.0
Extend. Arrangements: Undrawn Balance	#	#	#	#	#	418.0	518.0	#	#	#	#	1,003.0
Reserve Position in the Fund	45.0	54.5	135.3	97.8	#	#	#	#	100.3	161.0	#	2,408.0
Use of Fund Credit	#	#	#	#	319.1	419.1	229.4	103.1	#	#	201.0	91.0
Comp. Financ. Purch. Exp. Shortfalls	#	#	#	#	185.0	185.0	185.0	100.3	#	#	#	1,204.0
Credit Tranche Pur.: Ord. Resources	#	#	#	#	134.1	134.1	41.6	#	#	#	201.0	201.0
Extended Facility Pur.: Ord. Resources	#	#	#	#	#	100.0	#	#	#	#	#	502.0
Fund Holdings of Currency: Amount	135.0	125.5	234.7	272.2	689.1	789.1	764.4	638.1	702.3	641.5	1,003.0	2,279.0
Percent of Quota	75.0	69.7	63.4	73.6	185.2	213.3	142.9	119.3	87.5	79.9	125.0	195.0
						Millions of SDRs: During Period						
Total Purchases	#	#	#	#	416.9	100.0	#	#	#	#	361.7	1,003.1
Reserve Tranche	#	#	#	#	97.8	#	#	#	#	#	~	~
Comp. Financ. Export Shortfalls	#	#	#	#	185.0	#	#	#	#	#	~	~
Credit Tranche: Ordinary Resources	#	#	#	#	134.1	#	#	#	#	#	~	~
Extended Facility: Ord. Resources	#	#	#	#	#	100.0	#	#	#	#	~	~
Gold Distributions	#	#	#	#	#	5.5	2.8	2.8	#	#	~	~
Total Repurchases	#	#	#	#	#	#	192.5	129.0	136.5	59.1	~	~
Repurchases of Purchases	#	#	#	#	#	#	192.5	126.3	133.7	59.1	#	#
Member's Currency Drawn	#	9.5	21.0	#	#	#	#	#	#	6.5	#	#
Member's Currency Used in Repurch.	#	#	15.9	#	#	#	#	#	#	4.9	#	#
SDR Department						Millions of SDRs: End of Period						
Net Cumulative Allocations	#	#	45.4	124.2	124.2	124.2	124.2	179.8	235.5	290.0	250.0	275.0
SDR Holdings: Amount	#	#	47.8	86.3	.9	46.8	42.6	152.4	112.9	152.9	5.0	22.0
Percent of Allocations	#	#	105.4	69.5	.7	37.7	34.3	84.7	48.0	52.7	2.0	8.0
Administered Accounts						Millions of SDRs: During Period						
Trust Fund: Dist. of Gold Sale Profits	#	#	#	#	#	#	13.5	13.9	18.4	#	~	~

1. For definitions of terms, see table 2811. For SDR exchange rate, see tables 3102 and 3103.

a. For data from years 1947–74, see SALA, 23–3100 through 3118.

SOURCE: IMF-IFS-S, No. 3, Supplement on Fund Accounts, 1982; IMF-IFS-Y, 1984.

Table 2825

NICARAGUA IMF FUND ACCOUNT,[1] 1960–83[a]

Category[1]	1960	1965	1970	1975	1976	1977	1978	1979	1980	1981	1982	1983
						Millions of SDRs: End of Period						
General Department												
Quota	11.3	11.3	27.0	27.0	27.0	27.0	34.0	34.0	51.0	51.0	51.0	51.0
St-By Arrangements: Amount Drawn	#	#	10.0	#	#	#	#	#	#	#	#	#
St-By Arrangements: Undrawn Balance	7.5	#	4.0	#	#	#	#	#	#	#	#	#
Reserve Position in the Fund	2.8	#	#	#	#	#	#	#	#	#	#	#
Use of Fund Credit	#	8.4	8.0	15.5	8.7	2.0	2.0	43.5	38.7	21.2	17.5	13.3
Comp. Financ. Purch. Exp. Shortfalls	#	#	#	#	#	#	#	34.0	34.0	17.0	14.9	10.6
Buffer Stock Purchases	#	#	#	#	#	#	#	.6	#	#	#	#
Oil Facility Purchases	#	#	#	15.5	15.5	8.8	2.0	2.0	2.0	1.5	#	#
Credit Tranche Pur.: Ord. Resources	#	8.4	8.0	#	#	#	#	6.5	2.7	2.7	2.7	2.7
Fund Holdings of Currency: Amount	8.4	19.7	35.0	42.5	35.7	29.0	36.0	77.5	89.7	72.2	68.6	64.3
Percent of Quota	75.0	174.9	129.6	157.4	132.4	107.4	105.9	228.0	175.8	141.5	134.4	126.1
						Millions of SDRs: During Period						
Total Purchases	#	#	10.0	12.2	#	#	6.8	43.1	#	#	#	#
Reserve Tranche	#	#	#	#	#	#	6.8	#	#	#	~	~
Comp. Financ. Export Shortfalls	#	#	#	#	#	#	#	34.0	#	#	~	~
Buffer Stock	#	#	#	#	#	#	#	.6	#	#	~	~
Oil Facility	#	#	#	12.2	#	#	#	#	#	#	~	~
Credit Tranche: Ordinary Resources	#	#	10.0	#	#	#	#	8.5	#	#	~	~
Gold Distributions	#	#	#	#	#	.4	#	.4	#	#	~	~
Total Repurchases	#	#	13.3	6.7	6.8	6.8	6.8	2.0	.6	17.5	3.6	4.3
Repurchases of Purchases	#	#	13.3	6.7	6.8	6.8	6.8	2.0	.6	17.5	3.6	4.3
						Millions of SDRs: End of Period						
SDR Department												
Net Cumulative Allocations	#	#	3.2	8.9	8.9	8.9	8.9	12.5	16.0	19.5	20.0	#
SDR Holdings: Amount	#	#	1.0	4.6	3.5	3.8	4.3	#	#	.1	.9	#
Percent of Allocations	#	#	30.1	51.1	38.8	42.2	48.5	.2	#	.3	4.5	#
						Millions of SDRs: During Period						
Administered Accounts												
Trust Fund: Dist. of Gold Sale Profits	#	#	#	#	#	#	1.0	1.0	1.3	#	~	~

1. For definitions of terms, see table 2811. For SDR exchange rate, see tables 3102 and 3103.

a. For data from years 1947–74, see SALA, 23–3100 through 3118.

SOURCE: IMF-IFS-S, No. 3, Supplement on Fund Accounts, 1982; IMF-IFS-Y, 1984.

Table 2826

PANAMA IMF FUND ACCOUNT,[1] 1960–83[a]

Category[1]	1960	1965	1970	1975	1976	1977	1978	1979	1980	1981	1982	1983
					Millions of SDRs: End of Period							
General Department												
Quota	.5	11.3	36.0	36.0	36.0	36.0	45.0	45.0	67.5	67.5	67.5	102.2
St-By Arrangements: Amount Drawn	#	#	#	#	#	#	#	#	#	#	#	50.0
St-By Arrangements: Undrawn Balance	#	7.0	10.0	9.0	#	11.3	25.0	30.0	66.4	#	#	100.0
Reserve Position in the Fund	.1	.1	1.0	#	#	#	3.7	2.5	8.1	#	29.7	8.7
Use of Fund Credit	#	#	#	17.5	42.6	42.2	40.3	31.5	18.1	80.5	76.1	184.1
Comp. Financ. Purch. Exp. Shortfalls	#	#	#	#	18.0	18.0	18.0	14.4	7.2	#	#	58.9
Oil Facility Purchases	#	#	#	17.5	24.6	24.2	22.3	17.1	10.9	#	.9	#
Credit Tranche Pur.: Ord. Resources	#	#	#	#	#	#	#	#	#	5.2	37.8	62.3
Credit Tranche Pur.: SFF	#	#	#	#	#	#	#	#	#	37.8	37.8	37.5
Fund Holdings of Currency: Amount	.4	11.1	35.0	53.5	78.6	78.2	81.6	74.0	77.5	37.5	37.5	37.5
Percent of Quota	74.0	98.8	97.2	148.7	218.4	217.1	181.3	164.4	114.8	148.0	143.6	227.7
										219.2	212.8	271.7
					Millions of SDRs: During Period							
Total Purchases	#	2.7	#	10.2	25.1	#	#	6.0	#	83.3	#	108.9
Reserve Tranche	#	2.7	#	#	#	#	#	6.0	#	#	~	~
Comp. Financ. Export Shortfalls	#	#	#	#	18.0	#	#	#	#	8.1	~	~
Oil Facility	#	#	#	10.2	7.1	#	#	#	#	#	~	~
Credit Tranche: Ordinary Resources	#	#	#	#	#	#	#	#	#	#	~	~
Credit Tranche: SFF	#	#	#	#	#	#	#	#	#	37.8	~	~
Gold Distributions	#	#	#	#	#	.5	.3	.3	#	37.5	~	~
Total Repurchases	#	#	1.7	#	#	.5	5.8	13.8	13.3	#	~	~
Repurchases of Purchases	#	#	1.7	#	#	.5	5.8	13.8	13.3	12.9	4.3	.9
										12.9	4.3	.9
					Millions of SDRs: End of Period							
SDR Department												
Net Cumulative Allocations	#	#	4.7	12.4	12.4	12.4	12.4	17.1	21.7	26.3	26.6	28.6
SDR Holdings: Amount	#	#	3.2	6.4	5.2	4.5	4.0	3.9	1.1	2.8	3.8	.4
Percent of Allocations	#	#	68.9	51.4	42.0	36.4	32.0	23.1	5.0	10.6	14.3	1.4
					Millions of SDRs: During Period							
Administered Accounts												
Trust Fund: Dist. of Gold Sale Profits	#	#	#	#	#	#	1.3	1.3	1.8	#	~	~

1. For definitions of terms, see table 2811. For SDR exchange rate, see tables 3102 and 3103.

a. For data from years 1947–74, see SALA, 23–3100 through 3118.

SOURCE: IMF-IFS-S, No. 3, Supplement on Fund Accounts, 1982; IMF-IFS-Y, 1984.

Table 2827

PARAGUAY IMF FUND ACCOUNT,[1] 1960–83[a]

Category[1]	1960	1965	1970	1975	1976	1977	1978	1979	1980	1981	1982	1983
					Millions of SDRs: End of Period							
General Department												
Quota	10.0	11.3	19.0	19.0	19.0	19.0	23.0	23.0	34.5	34.5	34.5	48.4
St-By Arrangements: Amount Drawn	1.0	#	#	#	#	#	#	#	#	#	#	#
St-By Arrangements: Undrawn Balance	2.5	#	#	#	#	#	#	#	#	#	#	#
Reserve Position in the Fund	#	2.8	4.8	4.8	5.8	6.6	6.5	8.2	14.9	25.2	27.6	32.3
Use of Fund Credit	2.4	#	#	#	#	#	#	#	#	#	#	#
Credit Tranche Pur.: Ord. Resources	2.4	#	#	#	#	#	#	#	#	#	#	#
Fund Holdings of Currency: Amount	12.4	8.4	14.2	14.2	13.2	12.4	16.5	14.8	19.6	9.3	6.9	16.2
Percent of Quota	123.7	75.0	74.9	74.9	69.6	65.2	71.8	64.4	56.9	27.1	19.9	33.4
					Millions of SDRs: During Period							
Total Purchases	1.0	#	#	#	#	#	#	#	#	#	~	~
Reserve Tranche	#	#	#	#	#	#	#	#	#	#	~	~
Credit Tranche: Ordinary Resources	1.0	#	#	#	#	#	#	#	#	#	~	~
Gold Distributions	#	#	#	#	#	.1	.1	.3	#	#	#	#
Total Repurchases	.9	.5	#	#	#	#	#	#	#	#	#	#
Repurchases of Purchases	.9	.5	#	#	#	#	#	#	#	#	#	#
Member's Currency Drawn	#	#	#	#	1.0	1.0	#	2.0	1.4	10.3	3.3	2.1
					Millions of SDRs: End of Period							
SDR Department												
Net Cumulative Allocations	#	#	2.5	6.6	6.6	6.6	6.6	9.0	11.4	13.7	13.7	13.7
SDR Holdings: Amount	#	#	2.5	6.6	6.6	6.6	6.6	9.4	11.1	15.1	23.7	30.4
Percent of Allocations	#	#	100.0	100.0	100.0	100.2	101.1	105.0	97.4	110.1	172.8	222.0
					Millions of SDRs: During Period							
Administered Accounts												
Trust Fund: Dist. of Gold Sale Profits	#	#	#	#	#	#	.7	.7	.9	#	~	~

1. For definitions of terms, see table 2811. For SDR exchange rate, see tables 3102 and 3103.

a. For data from years 1947–74, see SALA, 23–3100 through 3118.

SOURCE: IMF-IFS-S, No. 3, Supplement on Fund Accounts, 1982; IMF-IFS-Y, 1984.

Table 2828

PERU IMF FUND ACCOUNT,[1] 1960-83[a]

Category[1]	1960	1965	1970	1975	1976	1977	1978	1979	1980	1981	1982	1983
General Department					*Millions of SDRs: End of Period*							
Quota	30.0	37.5	123.0	123.0	123.0	123.0	164.0	164.0	246.0	246.0	246.0	246.0
St-By Arrangements: Amount Drawn	#	#	18.0	#	#	10.0	24.0	137.0	#	#	#	#
St-By Arrangements: Undrawn Balance	27.5	30.0	17.0	#	#	80.0	160.0	148.0	#	#	#	#
Reserve Position in the Fund	7.5	9.4	#	30.8	#	#	#	#	#	#	#	#
Use of Fund Credit	#	#	9.9	#	158.8	168.8	256.1	373.1	371.6	332.9	588.8	666.3
Comp. Financ. Purch. Exp. Shortfalls	#	#	#	#	61.5	61.5	123.0	98.3	67.8	53.8	223.0	199.9
Oil Facility Purchases	#	#	#	#	52.7	52.7	52.7	42.8	29.6	16.5	3.3	#
Credit Tranche Pur.: Ord. Resources	#	#	9.8	#	44.6	54.5	78.5	107.0	77.6	67.5	67.5	41.9
Credit Tranche Pur.: SFF	#	#	#	#	#	#	#	122.3	195.1	195.1	195.1	159.5
Fund Holdings of Currency: Amount	22.5	28.1	132.9	92.3	281.8	291.8	420.1	537.1	617.6	578.9	834.8	912.3
Percent of Quota	75.0	75.0	108.0	75.0	229.1	237.2	256.2	327.5	251.0	235.3	339.4	370.9
					Millions of SDRs: During Period							
Total Purchases	#	#	18.0	#	189.5	10.0	85.5	177.0	111.0	#	299.9	165.0
Reserve Tranche	#	#	#	#	30.8	#	#	#	#	#	~	~
Comp. Financ. Export Shortfalls	#	#	#	#	61.5	#	61.5	#	#	#	~	~
Oil Facility	#	#	#	#	52.7	#	#	#	#	#	~	~
Credit Tranche: Ordinary Resources	#	#	18.0	#	44.6	10.0	24.0	54.7	38.2	#	~	~
Credit Tranche: SFF	#	#	#	#	#	#	#	122.3	72.8	#	~	~
Gold Distributions	#	#	#	#	#	.9	1.8	.9	#	#	~	~
Total Repurchases	#	#	26.9	#	#	#	#	60.9	92.1	38.7	43.9	87.5
Repurchases of Purchases	#	#	26.9	#	#	#	#	60.9	91.2	38.7	43.9	87.5
SDR Department					*Millions of SDRs: End of Period*							
Net Cumulative Allocations	#	#	14.3	40.5	40.5	40.5	40.5	57.5	74.6	91.3	91.4	100.0
SDR Holdings: Amount	#	#	14.3	37.1	3.3	2.7	4.8	81.3	9.7	9.8	29.9	.6
Percent of Allocations	#	#	100.0	91.6	8.2	6.7	12.0	141.3	13.0	10.7	32.7	.6
Administered Accounts					*Millions of SDRs: During Period*							
Trust Fund: Dist. of Gold Sale Profits	#	#	#	#	#	#	4.5	4.6	6.1	#	~	~
SFF Subsidy Payments	#	#	#	#	#	#	#	#	#	4.5	~	~

1. For definitions of terms, see table 2811. For SDR exchange rate, see tables 3102 and 3103.

a. For data from years 1947-74, see SALA, 23-3100 through 3118.

SOURCE: IMF-IFS-S, No. 3, Supplement on Fund Accounts, 1982; IMF-IFS-Y, 1984.

Table 2829

URUGUAY IMF FUND ACCOUNT,[1] 1960–83[a]

Category[1]	1960	1965	1970	1975	1976	1977	1978	1979	1980	1981	1982	1983
General Department						*Millions of SDRs: End of Period*						
Quota	15.0	30.0	69.0	69.0	69.0	69.0	84.0	84.0	126.0	126.0	126.0	164.0
St-By Arrangements: Amount Drawn	#	#	27.5	17.3	#	#	#	#	#	#	#	151.0
St-By Arrangements: Undrawn Balance	#	#	#	13.0	25.0	25.0	#	21.0	21.0	31.5	#	227.0
Reserve Position in the Fund	#	#	#	#	#	#	16.7	16.2	26.7	28.0	#	9.0
Use of Fund Credit	#	7.5	18.3	99.7	124.9	98.2	#	#	#	#	87.0	227.0
Comp. Financ. Purch. Exp. Shortfalls	#	#	4.5	13.0	30.3	25.9	#	#	#	#	55.0	44.0
Oil Facility Purchases	#	#	#	82.5	94.7	89.6	#	#	#	#	32.0	#
Credit Tranche Pur.: Ord. Resources	#	7.5	13.7	4.3	#	#	#	#	#	#	#	93.0
Fund Holdings of Currency: Amount	11.3	37.5	87.3	168.7	193.9	167.2	67.3	67.8	99.3	98.0	213.0	381.0
Percent of Quota	75.0	125.0	126.4	244.6	281.0	242.4	80.1	80.7	78.8	77.8	169.0	233.0
						Millions of SDRs: During Period						
Total Purchases	#	#	40.4	53.2	38.0	#	#	#	#	#	114.9	151.2
Reserve Tranche	#	#	9.4	#	#	#	#	#	#	#	~	~
Comp. Financ. Export Shortfalls	#	#	#	#	25.9	#	#	#	#	#	~	~
Oil Facility	#	#	#	35.9	12.1	#	#	#	#	#	~	~
Credit Tranche: Ordinary Resources	#	#	31.0	17.3	#	#	#	#	#	#	~	~
Gold Distributions	#	#	#	#	#	1.0	.5	.5	#	#	~	11.2
Total Repurchases	#	#	28.1	17.3	12.9	21.7	115.5	#	#	#	~	11.2
Repurchases of Purchases	#	#	28.1	17.3	12.9	21.7	115.5	#	#	1.3	#	#
Member's Currency Drawn	#	#	#	#	#	5.0	#	#	#	#	#	#
SDR Department						*Millions of SDRs: End of Period*						
Net Cumulative Allocations	#	#	9.2	23.9	23.9	23.9	23.9	32.7	41.4	50.0	66.7	57.1
SDR Holdings: Amount	#	#	.1	1.6	3.7	8.5	11.4	26.2	26.0	37.2	2.0	4.0
Percent of Allocations	#	#	1.1	6.9	15.5	35.3	47.5	80.1	62.7	74.4	3.0	7.0
Administered Accounts						*Millions of SDRs: During Period*						
Trust Fund: Dist. of Gold Sale Profits	#	#	#	#	#	#	2.5	2.6	3.4	#	~	~

1. For definitions of terms, see table 2811. For SDR exchange rate, see tables 3102 and 3103.

a. For data from years 1947–74, see SALA, 23–3100 through 3118.

SOURCE: IMF-IFS-S, No. 3, Supplement on Fund Accounts, 1982; IMF-IFS-Y, 1984.

Table 2830

VENEZUELA IMF FUND ACCOUNT,[1] 1960–83[a]

Category [1]	1960	1965	1970	1975	1976	1977	1978	1979	1980	1981	1982	1983
General Department												
					Millions of SDRs: End of Period							
Quota	150.0	150.0	330.0	330.0	330.0	330.0	660.0	660.0	990.0	990.0	990.0	1,372.0
Outstand. Fund Borrowings: Oil Fac.	#	#	#	601.6	610.0	559.1	361.3	164.6	110.2	46.8	3.0	#
Outstand. Fund Borrowings: SFF	#	#	#	#	#	#	#	20.0	95.7	229.3	344.0	361.0
Available: SFF	#	#	#	#	#	#	#	480.0	404.3	270.8	~	~
St-By Arrangements: Undrawn Balance	100.0	#	#	#	#	#	#	#	#	#	~	~
Reserve Position in the Fund	37.5	37.5	117.1	804.6	925.6	832.7	588.0	408.1	489.9	548.6	682.0	877.0
Reserve Tranche Position	37.5	37.5	117.1	203.1	315.6	273.6	226.7	223.4	284.0	272.6	~	~
Fund Holdings of Currency: Amount	112.5	112.5	212.9	126.9	14.4	56.5	433.3	436.6	706.0	717.4	656.0	856.0
Percent of Quota	75.0	75.0	64.5	38.5	4.4	17.1	65.6	66.1	71.3	72.5	66.0	62.0
					Millions of SDRs: During Period							
Gold Distributions	#	#	#	#	#	4.9	2.5	2.5	#	#	~	~
Member's Currency Drawn	#	#	8.8	405.6	167.2	10.0	20.0	20.0	75.7	153.5	167.9	129.4
Member's Currency Used In Repurch.	#	#	#	19.7	11.1	34.8	46.0	19.9	32.8	44.7	11.7	18.4
SDR Department												
					Millions of SDRs: End of Period							
Net Cumulative Allocations	#	#	42.0	112.3	112.3	112.3	112.3	180.9	249.6	316.9	316.7	317.9
SDR Holdings: Amount	#	#	47.5	123.6	126.0	136.5	167.0	267.7	269.9	382.1	316.7	317.9
Percent of Allocations	#	#	113.1	110.0	112.2	121.5	148.7	148.0	108.1	120.6	126.0	106.0
Administered Accounts												
					Millions of SDRs: During Period							
Trust Fund: Dist. of Gold Sale Profits	#	#	#	#	#	#	12.0	12.4	16.4	#	~	~

1. For definitions of terms, see table 2811. For SDR exchange rate, see tables 3102 and 3103.

a. For data from years 1947–74, see SALA, 23–3100 through 3118.

SOURCE: IMF-IFS-S, No. 3, Supplement on Fund Accounts, 1982; IMF-IFS-Y, 1984.

Table 2831

INTER-AMERICAN DEVELOPMENT BANK LOANS, YEARLY LENDING, 19 L, 1974-84

(M US)

	Country	1974	1975	1976	1977	1978	1979	1980	1981	1982	1983	1984
A.	ARGENTINA	89.1	201.0	210.9	317.8	57.1	280.5	359.2	292.4	402.4	80.1	458.8
B.	BOLIVIA	46.2	54.1	40.2	83.3	180.7	12.2	42.6	97.0	201.0	58.9	78.0
C.	BRAZIL	187.0	269.5	239.1	361.5	283.2	365.5	424.4	383.1	372.2	441.0	393.7
D.	CHILE	97.3	70.7	70.0	24.5	54.0	~	19.9	161.0	302.5	548.0	293.3
E.	COLOMBIA	#	75.8	109.0	112.7	199.0	151.0	194.6	180.6	191.2	405.9	405.0
F.	COSTA RICA	53.8	41.6	33.0	79.6	90.0	35.9	132.9	35.2	67.4	41.8	92.6
H.	DOMINICAN REP.	36.7	35.5	33.4	#	66.3	195.5	80.5	71.8	155.4	96.2	205.5
I.	ECUADOR	55.5	43.7	73.6	73.1	94.3	210.0	84.5	168.5	101.4	83.3	306.4
J.	EL SALVADOR	33.4	43.0	25.0	109.4	13.2	47.8	63.4	52.4	128.4	25.0	110.2
K.	GUATEMALA	19.4	120.6	70.0	60.5	#	15.0	76.5	112.5	46.0	167.9	13.9
L.	HAITI	#	41.1	5.0	15.7	43.5	4.1	10.1	8.7	33.4	18.8	.4
M.	HONDURAS	35.6	28.7	114.5	32.0	114.0	15.8	67.6	7.5	49.0	130.2	42.0
N.	MEXICO	186.4	167.3	183.2	256.9	238.2	266.4	284.0	279.0	323.2	286.2	229.8
O.	NICARAGUA	10.5	16.5	49.8	20.0	32.0	81.5	70.6	8.0	35.1	30.5	~
P.	PANAMA	14.5	42.2	27.0	122.0	19.0	27.6	77.7	90.2	37.3	112.0	8.4
Q.	PARAGUAY	49.0	3.2	11.6	13.8	60.5	32.4	27.4	32.5	98.3	48.6	37.5
R.	PERU	65.5	16.0	149.0	21.0	29.5	148.6	177.6	226.7	180.1	264.9	195.8
S.	URUGUAY	21.4	35.4	36.4	29.7	#	35.5	57.5	78.0	10.0	50.0	119.8
T.	VENEZUELA	#	#	#	#	#	#	#	#	#	30.0	448.3

SOURCE: *IMF Survey*, April 17, 1978, p. 115; IDB-AR, 1980; IDB-AR, 1982, p. 41; IDB-AR, 1984, p. 53..

Table 2832

WORLD BANK (INTERNATIONAL BANK FOR RECONSTRUCTION AND DEVELOPMENT) ACTUAL LOANS, 20 LR, FY 1949-76

(M US)[1]

Country	1949	1950	1951	1952	1953	1954	1955	1956	1957	1958	1959	1960	1961	1962	1963	1964	1965	1966	1967	1968	1969	1970	1971	1972	1973	1974	1975	1976
A. ARGENTINA	#	#	#	#	#	#	#	#	#	#	#	#	#	5.9	47.5	36.0	17.1	5.2	4.2	7.0	28.5	44.0	31.6	44.9	54.2	50.2	41.4	13.3

Continued in SALA, 22-3108.

Table 2833

AVERAGE FINANCING TERMS OF LOANS TO LATIN AMERICA AUTHORIZED BY THE U.S. GOVERNMENT AND MULTILATERAL INSTITUTIONS, 1961–79

Agency	1961-65	1966-70	1971	1972	1973	1974	1975	1976	1977	1978	1979
Average interest rate	3.63	4.73	5.53	5.84	5.71	5.90	6.75	6.90	7.09	6.41	6.71
AID	1.55	2.43	2.78	2.80	2.76	2.75	2.80	2.75	2.70	2.58	2.64
IDB	3.68	4.38	4.57	5.10	5.17	5.54	5.20	5.29	5.97	5.36	5.80
IBRD	5.60	6.51	7.25	7.25	7.25	7.40	8.37	8.51	8.22	7.49	7.65
Ex-Im Bank	5.63	5.96	6.00	6.01[a]	6.00	6.26	8.09	8.33	8.50	8.19	7.17

Continued in SALA, 23-2633.

Table 2834

U.S. VOTING POWER IN MULTILATERAL AGENCIES
(%)

	United States	Central America
IMF	20.0	.8
IBRD	20.8	.6
IDA	21.4	1.2
IFC	28.4	.6
IDB	34.6	3.1

SOURCE: Tom Berry et al., *Dollars and Dictators* (Albuquerque, N.M.: The Resource Center, 1982), p. 55.

Table 2835

GROSS PROJECTED U.S. ASSISTANCE FOR GRANTS AND LOANS,[1] 19 L, 1970-83[a]

(M US)

Country	Fiscal Year	Total[2] Loans and Grants[3] (A+C)	"Other" Loans A. Total[4]	B. IMF Subtotal[5]	Economic and Military Loans and Grants C. Total[6] (D+E)	D. Military[7]	E. Economics[8]	Some Economic and Military Subtotals F. AID[9]	G. Food[10]	H. Loans[11]	I. Total Loans[12] (A+H)
A. ARGENTINA	1970	23.9	22.3	22.3	1.6	.6	1.0	1.0	#	#	22.3
	1975	94.9	64.7	64.7	30.2	30.1	.1	#	#	30.0	94.7
	1978	27.4	27.4	27.4	#	#	#	#	#	#	27.4
	1979	32.8	32.7	32.7	.1	#	.1	#	#	.1	32.8
	1980	81.0	81.0	81.0	#	#	#	#	#	#	81.0
	1981	82.6	82.6	82.6	#	#	#	#	#	#	82.6
	1982	551.1	551.0	551.0	.1	#	.1	#	#	#	551.0
	1983	#	#	#	#	#	#	#	#	#	#
B. BOLIVIA	1970	9.5	#	#	9.5	1.5	8.0	3.0	3.6	#	#
	1975	33.2	#	#	33.2	7.4	25.8	20.1	5.1	21.2	21.2
	1978	71.5	17.5	5.5	54.0	.8	53.2	34.3	16.5	39.1	56.6
	1979	57.9	#	#	57.9	6.7	51.2	28.9	19.0	38.0	38.0
	1980	30.4	#	#	30.4	.3	30.1	4.5	24.8	17.3	17.3
	1981	12.8	#	#	12.8	#	12.8	2.3	9.5	.2	.2
	1982	19.7	#	#	19.7	#	19.7	2.1	16.4	10.0	10.0
	1983	63.0	#	#	63.0	#	63.0	11.4	49.2	40.4	40.4
C. BRAZIL	1970	218.0	63.2	63.2	154.8	.8	154.0	88.0	62.4	95.0	158.2
	1975	337.2	257.1	256.5	80.1	65.4	14.7	3.1	8.4	60.0	317.1
	1978	106.8	104.7	104.7	2.1	#	2.1	#	.1	#	104.7
	1979	262.0	259.9	212.6	2.1	#	2.1	#	.6	#	259.9
	1980	101.7	99.3	68.8	2.4	#	2.4	#	1.4	#	99.3
	1981	117.0	115.9	115.9	1.1	#	1.1	#	.6	#	115.9
	1982	91.7	91.0	91.0	.7	#	.7	#	.3	.1	91.1
	1983	30.7	30.3	29.3	.4	#	.4	#	.1	#	30.3
D. CHILE	1970	27.1	#	#	27.1	.8	26.3	18.0	7.2	15.0	15.0
	1975	128.6	32.4	23.0	96.2	.7	95.5	31.3	62.4	88.2	120.6
	1978	53.1	46.0	46.0	7.1	#	7.1	.2	5.6	#	46.0
	1979	13.6	#	#	13.6	#	13.6	.3	9.0	#	#
	1980	10.2	#	#	10.2	#	10.2	.1	5.0	#	#
	1981	12.1	#	#	12.1	#	12.1	#	7.7	.1	.1
	1982	6.7	#	#	6.7	#	6.7	#	2.3	#	#
	1983	2.8	#	#	2.8	#	2.8	#	1.0	#	#
E. COLOMBIA	1970	151.8	13.3	13.3	138.5	7.4	131.1	75.8	53.5	84.1	97.4
	1975	32.7	3.5	3.5	29.2	.7	28.5	14.0	11.5	12.2	15.7
	1978	89.5	30.0	30.0	59.5	52.2	7.3	#	2.6	51.0	81.0
	1979	64.5	42.5	42.5	22.0	13.0	9.0	.3	1.6	12.5	55.0
	1980	47.5	24.1	24.1	23.4	.3	23.1	.3	4.6	#	24.1
	1981	51.1	45.1	45.1	6.0	.3	5.7	#	#	#	45.1
	1982	553.5	540.3	540.3	13.5	10.5	3.0	#	#	10.0	550.3
	1983	8.4	3.8	3.8	4.6	.7	3.9	#	#	#	3.8
F. COSTA RICA	1970	20.9	.2	.2	20.7	#	20.7	19.5	.5	17.5	17.7
	1975	9.0	5.3	3.8	3.7	#	3.7	.7	1.0	#	5.3
	1978	13.2	4.1	4.0	9.1	#	9.1	6.9	.8	5.5	9.6
	1979	22.7	4.8	2.7	17.9	#	17.9	16.4	#	15.1	19.9
	1980	22.4	6.4	6.0	16.0	#	16.0	13.6	.4	12.0	18.4
	1981	20.4	5.1	5.1	15.3	#	15.3	11.5	1.8	10.0	15.1
	1982	56.8	3.0	#	53.8	#	51.7	31.5	19.1	42.7	45.7
	1983	218.7	#	#	218.7	4.6	214.1	184.2	28.2	166.2	166.2
H. DOMINICAN REP.	1970	21.9	#	#	21.9	2.1	19.8	5.2	14.0	9.6	9.6
	1975	20.6	7.3	7.3	13.3	1.6	11.7	5.6	5.5	5.3	12.6
	1978	7.0	.2	.2	6.8	.7	6.1	1.3	3.9	#	.2
	1979	75.4	26.0	.7	49.4	1.0	48.4	26.4	20.7	39.2	65.2
	1980	70.1	10.8	3.7	59.3	3.5	55.8	34.6	19.7	36.9	47.7
	1981	43.1	1.2	1.2	41.9	3.4	38.5	17.4	18.6	32.0	33.2
	1982	87.9	#	#	87.9	5.5	82.4	60.0	19.3	76.5	76.5
	1983	69.7	#	#	69.7	6.6	63.1	34.6	25.3	57.4	57.4
I. ECUADOR	1970	31.2	3.0	3.0	28.2	2.4	25.8	23.2	1.6	19.4	22.4
	1975	14.4	6.0	6.0	8.4	.4	8.0	2.1	3.4	#	6.0
	1978	19.9	3.7	.5	16.2	10.7	5.5	.8	2.4	10.0	13.7
	1979	33.1	26.4	26.4	6.7	.4	6.3	.5	2.7	#	26.4
	1980	16.3	1.2	#	15.1	3.3	11.8	8.3	.9	9.0	10.2
	1981	25.5	2.7	#	22.8	4.3	18.5	12.5	2.3	13.6	16.6
	1982	27.9	#	#	27.9	5.0	22.9	17.3	2.4	16.6	16.6
	1983	31.2	#	#	31.2	4.6	26.6	21.5	1.8	6.7	6.7
J. EL SALVADOR	1970	13.2	#	#	13.2	.6	12.6	10.3	1.8	7.8	7.8
	1975	10.0	.6	.6	9.4	5.5	3.9	1.3	1.6	3.0	3.6
	1978	10.9	#	#	10.9	#	10.9	8.0	1.7	5.7	5.7
	1979	11.5	.1	.1	11.4	#	11.4	6.9	2.9	4.2	4.3
	1980	64.3	.1	.1	64.2	5.9	58.3	52.3	5.5	46.1	47.2
	1981	149.5	#	#	149.5	35.5	114.0	78.3	35.3	90.0	90.0
	1982	264.2	#	#	264.2	82.0	182.2	154.6	27.6	80.3	80.3
	1983	326.9	#	#	326.9	81.3	245.6	198.8	46.8	133.1	133.1

Table 2835 (Continued)

GROSS PROJECTED U.S. ASSISTANCE FOR GRANTS AND LOANS,[1] 19 L, 1970-83[a]

(M US)

Country	Fiscal Year	Total[2] Loans and Grants[3] (A+C)	"Other" Loans A. Total[4]	B. IMF Subtotal[5]	Economic and Military Loans and Grants C. Total[6] (D+E)	D. Military[7]	E. Economics[8]	Some Economic and Military Subtotals F. AID[9]	G. Food[10]	H. Loans[11]	I. Total Loans[12] (A+H)
K. GUATEMALA	1970	33.6	#	#	33.6	1.4	32.2	29.1	2.5	25.1	25.1
	1975	17.8	.8	.8	17.0	2.9	14.1	9.4	3.4	9.3	10.1
	1978	10.6	#	#	10.6	#	10.6	4.5	4.6	#	#
	1979	24.7	#	#	24.7	#	24.7	17.4	5.3	14.6	14.6
	1980	13.8	.8	#	13.0	#	13.0	7.8	3.3	5.0	5.8
	1981	19.0	#	#	19.0	#	19.0	9.1	7.5	5.6	5.6
	1982	15.5	#	#	15.5	#	15.5	8.2	5.6	3.0	3.0
	1983	29.7	#	#	19.7	#	29.7	22.3	5.4	17.5	17.5
L. HAITI	1970	3.8	.1	.1	3.7	#	3.7	1.6	2.1	#	.1
	1975	9.3	#	#	9.3	#	9.3	3.6	5.6	2.3	2.3
	1978	29.4	1.2	#	28.2	.7	27.5	8.9	18.5	11.0	12.2
	1979	25.5	.3	#	25.2	.4	24.8	9.1	15.4	8.8	9.1
	1980	27.2	#	#	27.2	.1	27.1	11.1	15.8	8.6	8.6
	1981	35.8	.8	#	35.0	.4	34.6	9.2	24.5	8.9	9.7
	1982	35.6	.8	#	34.8	.5	34.3	12.0	22.2	13.3	14.1
	1983	48.2	1.3	#	46.9	.7	46.2	27.3	18.5	11.3	12.6
M. HONDURAS	1970	8.6	1.0	1.0	7.6	.4	7.2	5.5	.9	2.7	3.7
	1975	41.1	1.3	1.3	39.8	4.2	35.6	25.4	9.0	27.3	28.6
	1978	20.8	.5	.5	20.3	3.2	17.1	13.0	2.4	12.5	13.0
	1979	32.3	.8	.8	31.5	2.3	29.1	22.0	4.8	20.0	20.8
	1980	66.8	13.7	12.5	57.0	3.9	53.1	45.8	5.2	44.1	156.1
	1981	37.3	.9	.9	45.3	8.9	36.4	25.7	8.2	32.2	33.1
	1982	112.6	.6	.3	112.0	31.3	80.7	67.9	10.1	80.5	81.1
	1983	154.3	#	#	154.3	48.3	106.0	87.3	15.5	54.0	54.0
N. MEXICO	1970	36.6	35.5	35.5	1.1	.1	1.0	1.0	#	#	35.5
	1975	196.0	195.7	195.7	.3	.1	.2	#	#	#	195.7
	1978	629.1	608.5	608.5	20.6	.1	20.5	#	#	#	608.5
	1979	170.9	157.2	157.2	13.7	.2	13.5	#	#	#	157.2
	1980	188.3	180.8	180.8	7.5	.1	7.4	#	#	#	180.8
	1981	662.5	652.6	652.6	9.9	.1	9.8	#	#	#	652.6
	1982	302.2	293.4	293.4	8.8	.1	8.7	#	#	#	293.4
	1983	96.5	88.2	37.2	8.3	.1	8.2	#	#	#	88.2
O. NICARAGUA	1970	4.4	.1	#	4.3	1.2	3.1	2.3	.4	#	4.4
	1975	46.8	.3	#	46.5	4.3	42.2	40.1	1.4	42.0	42.3
	1978	14.6	.2	.2	14.4	.4	14.0	12.5	.1	10.5	10.7
	1979	18.5	#	#	18.5	#	18.5	9.7	7.0	2.6	2.6
	1980	38.7	#	#	38.7	#	38.7	19.4	18.0	30.0	30.0
	1981	59.9	#	#	59.9	#	59.9	58.4	1.2	48.0	48.0
	1982	6.3	#	#	6.3	#	6.3	5.8	.4	#	#
	1983	#	#	#	#	#	#	#	#	#	#
P. PANAMA	1970	17.0	2.5	2.5	14.5	1.0	13.5	11.8	1.0	8.5	11.0
	1975	51.9	30.1	30.1	21.8	.6	21.2	8.3	.9	6.7	36.8
	1978	23.6	#	#	23.6	.5	23.1	21.3	1.3	20.0	20.0
	1979	26.3	3.7	3.6	22.6	1.4	21.2	19.9	1.1	17.0	20.7
	1980	2.3	#	#	2.3	.3	2.0	1.0	1.0	#	#
	1981	11.0	#	#	11.0	.4	10.6	8.7	1.9	6.4	6.4
	1982	18.4	#	#	18.4	5.4	13.0	11.7	1.3	13.1	13.1
	1983	12.9	#	#	12.9	5.5	7.4	6.3	1.1	8.8	8.8
Q. PARAGUAY	1970	9.3	#	#	9.3	1.2	8.1	7.1	.5	4.6	4.6
	1975	9.6	#	#	9.6	1.6	8.0	6.7	.4	5.2	5.2
	1978	4.1	#	#	4.1	.6	3.5	1.8	.3	#	#
	1979	10.3	#	#	10.3	#	10.3	7.1	.3	5.0	5.0
	1980	3.6	#	#	3.6	#	3.6	1.3	.4	#	#
	1981	6.2	#	#	6.2	#	6.2	2.0	.7	#	#
	1982	67.7	63.9	63.9	3.8	#	3.8	#	.1	#	63.9
	1983	4.4	1.1	#	3.3	.1	3.2	#	#	#	1.1
R. PERU	1970	17.5	#	#	17.5	.6	16.9	11.3	4.2	#	#
	1975	68.8	31.3	16.3	37.5	21.4	16.1	8.9	6.4	27.5	58.8
	1978	138.5	74.9	.7	63.6	8.9	54.7	22.0	31.9	52.0	126.9
	1979	139.0	62.8	#	76.2	5.5	70.7	34.1	35.3	53.8	116.6
	1980	102.9	46.3	6.2	56.6	3.3	53.3	18.7	33.0	36.0	82.3
	1981	100.5	16.0	13.1	84.5	4.3	80.2	34.5	42.5	51.0	67.0
	1982	59.6	#	#	59.6	5.0	54.6	35.8	16.2	48.7	48.7
	1983	124.4	26.3	26.3	98.1	4.6	93.5	35.5	55.9	52.5	78.8
S. URUGUAY	1970	22.9	#	#	22.9	3.5	19.4	16.9	2.4	17.4	17.4
	1975	22.2	#	#	22.2	9.2	12.9	12.8	#	19.3	19.3
	1978	.2	#	#	2	#	.2	#	#	#	#
	1979	.2	#	#	.2	#	.2	#	#	#	#
	1980	#	#	#	#	#	#	#	#	#	#
	1981	15.0	14.9	14.9	.1	#	.1	#	#	#	14.9
	1982	.8	#	#	.8	#	.8	#	#	#	#
	1983	1.1	#	#	1.1	.1	1.0	#	#	#	#

Table 2835 (Continued)

GROSS PROJECTED U.S. ASSISTANCE FOR GRANTS AND LOANS,[1] 19 L, 1970-83[a]

(M US)

Country	Fiscal Year	Total[2] Loans and Grants[3] (A+C)	"Other" Loans A. Total[4]	B. IMF Subtotal[5]	Economic and Military Loans and Grants C. Total[6] (D+E)	D. Military[7]	E. Economics[8]	Some Economic and Military Subtotals F. AID[9]	G. Food[10]	H. Loans[11]	I. Total Loans[12] (A+H)
T. VENEZUELA	1970	17.0	13.5	13.5	3.5	.8	2.7	1.1	#	#	13.5
	1975	16.4	14.1	14.1	2.3	.7	1.6	#	#	#	14.1
	1978	22.4	22.3	22.3	.1	.1	#	#	#	#	22.3
	1979	18.5	18.5	18.5	#	#	#	#	#	#	18.5
	1980	160.2	160.2	160.2	#	#	#	#	#	#	160.2
	1981	59.6	59.5	59.5	.1	#	.1	#	#	#	59.5
	1982	26.2	26.0	26.0	.2	#	.2	#	#	#	26.0
	1983	12.2	12.0	12.0	.2	.1	.1	#	#	#	12.0

1. The definition of "assistance" is highly debatable and often full of irony as in the case of funding by the Export-Import (Ex-Im) Bank: The U.S. government formerly classified Ex-Im Bank loans as offering "assistance" when interest rates were relatively high in relation to other U.S. aid; since the 1970s when the government accepted criticism of its classification of Ex-Im Bank and took its funding out of figures on "assistance," however, other aid (including U.S. AID) rates and private rates have not compared so favorably and Ex-Im loans perhaps should be classified as offering assistance — indeed, U.S. business firms have complained that Ex-Im Bank loans offer more favorable terms to foreigners than to U.S. companies. Although it can be argued that Ex-Im Bank loans are tied to purchase of U.S. goods and services, it should be remembered that in the end Ex-Im Bank loans must compete in the international finance market or lose borrowers. (Cf. SALA-SNP, part III, for a discussion of supranational policy problems.) Ex-Im loans here are classified as part of U.S. assistance.

2. Total includes all U.S. obligations (i.e., authorizations to expend in contrast to actual expenditures) for assistance administered by (a) the U.S. Agency for International Development (AID or USAID); (b) Peace Corps; (c) other U.S. agencies; and assistance administered through (d) Food for Peace Programs; (e) Social Progress Trust Funds of the Inter-American Development Bank; other selected U.S. programs (e.g., Inter-American Highway) — may include some disbursements; (f) military programs; as well as actual loans held by (h) the U.S. Ex-Im Bank. Does not include AID administrative overhead costs in the host country. Excludes regional obligations to more than one country. Excludes payments made through international agencies (e.g., IDB, IBRD) over which the U.S. has no direct control.

3. Grant and loan data are presented here in *gross* terms which revise previous methodology of reporting obligations in *net* terms; however, Ex-Im Bank data are still reported in net figures, as are AID data prior to FY 1955. Military sums are for deliveries prior to FY 1962, except exclude excess stocks deliveries include in SALA-SNP, XVII-5. Thus, although all data are subject to revisions (as in the case of shortfalls in Food for Peace deliveries), this new historical series will not fluctuate as much as previously.

4. Includes short-term credits by U.S. Department of Agriculture.

5. Before 1973 Ex-Im Bank deobligated sums (except for repayments) for years when originally authorized as it canceled, decreased, terminated, or sold loans to non-U.S. government purchasers. Includes (since 1969 only) loans of less than 5 years maturity. Excludes loans for military assistance (which are included under the military category.)

6. In source, this total is labeled "Total Economic and Military Grants and Loans," but actually economic obligations include funds for social purposes (such as education) as well as administrative functions (such as "Supporting Assistance" to maintain political stability for security objectives).

7. Military data included Ex-Im Bank military loans (but not guarantees) and also represent grant and loan actual assistance prior to FY 1962. Exclude AID obligations for Supporting Assistance (see notes 3 and 9). Excludes excess stock deliveries included in SALA-SNP, XVII-5.

8. Includes AID programs and Food for Peace.

9. AID was established November 4, 1961. Its predecessor agencies were, successively: Economic Cooperation Administration (April 3, 1948 — October 31, 1951); Mutual Security Agency (November 1, 1951 — July 31, 1953); Foreign Operations Administration (August 1, 1953 — June 30, 1955); International Cooperation Administration (July 1, 1955 — November 3, 1961); and the Development Loan Fund (August 14, 1957 — November 3, 1961); see AID/Washington, *U.S. Economic Assistance Programs Administered by the Agency for International Development and Predecessor Agencies*, April 3, 1948 — June 30, 1967. AID data include grant and loan Supporting Assistance for military infrastructure; and includes "402" Mutual Security Aid Program obligations for U.S. agricultural exports.

10. Food for Peace involves (a) sales on credit terms (for dollars and/or local currency) and (b) donations (for emergency relief or for volunteer relief agencies such as CARE) of surplus U.S. agricultural commodities. Former are valued at export market price; latter are valued at cost through FY 1969, subsequently at market value, plus ocean freight. (Donations to volunteer relief agencies do not, however, include ocean freight.) This subtotal does not include any funds generated by such activity as interest on local currency deposits.

11. Included in col. C.

12. Loans include "capitalized interest" (interest for prior years which is due but not paid) added during the year it becomes an accrued liability. Data exclude the export guarantees and insurance which are included in SALA-SNP, XVII-9. Refunding of loans generally is excluded.

a. For prior years, see SALA-SNP, XVII-1.

SOURCE: Adapted from USAID-OLG, July 1, 1945-June 30, 1975; July 1, 1945-September 30, 1983. See pp. 1-3 of these volumes for discussion of concepts and terms as well as coverage.

Table 2836

YEARLY U.S. PROJECTED
ASSISTANCE TO
LATIN AMERICA, 1946–83
(M US)

Fiscal Year	Total Grants and Loans[1]	Loans' Share
1946	104.7	91.7
1947	108.3	86.8
1948	55.9	17.1
1949	70.7	44.5
1950	196.9	169.2
1951	219.1	201.7
1952	103.0	78.7
1953	439.9	388.8
1954	95.0	17.9
1955	357.1	246.2
1956	368.6	217.1
1957	672.4	485.9
1958	398.9	238.6
1959	623.5	488.5
1960	306.1	174.5
1961	923.2	681.3
1962	1,036.0	695.4
1963	984.1	649.9
1964	1,164.2	836.9
1965	961.6	669.6
1966	1,090.6	761.0
1967	1,102.5	886.7
1968	1,080.0	890.2
1969	644.2	493.0
1970	685.1	461.5
1971	647.5	490.0
1972	1,007.3	823.2
1973	896.0	751.8
1974	1,216.2	1,079.1
1975	1,160.3	1,010.0
1976	959.1	809.7
TQ[2]	181.1	136.8
1977	537.0	383.6
1978	1,292.6	1,158.5
1979	1,039.7	866.6
1980	1,051.6	875.8
1981	1,520.9	1,297.4
1982	2,304.4	1,955.4
1983	1,235.1	710.9

1. Excludes amounts and sums allocated to more than one country (e.g., Regional Programs in Central America — ROCAP).
2. Transitional quarter to new fiscal-year basis.

SOURCE: SALA-SNP, p. 360, and calculated from table 2835, above.

Table 2837

U.S. PEACE CORPS BUDGET, 1962–80

Fiscal Year	Appropriated Dollars (T US)	Constant Dollars (T US)	Volunteers and Trainees[1] (N)
1962	30,000	42,523	2,816
1963	59,000	82,414	6,554
1964	95,964	132,896	10,078
1965	104,000	140,070	13,248
1966	114,000	148,645	15,556
1967	110,000	139,205	14,968
1968	107,500	130,193	13,823
1969	102,000	117,620	12,131
1970	98,450	107,760	9,513
1971	90,000	93,730	8,398
1972	72,500	72,500	6,894
1973	81,000	76,473	7,354
1974	77,000	66,276	8,044
1975	77,687	63,584	6,895
1976	81,266	60,755	5,958
1977	80,000	56,493	6,916
1978	86,234	56,714	7,072
1979	99,179	59,927	6,328
1980	99,924	55,268	5,994

1. Volunteers and trainees on-board at the end of the fiscal year (1962–76: June 30; 1977–80: September 30).

SOURCE: U.S. Action, *Annual Report*, 1980, p. 42.

Table 2838

U.S. PEACE CORPS VOLUNTEERS IN FULL-TIME EQUIVALENTS (FTEs), 12 L, 1975–81
(FTEs for Each FY)

	Country	1975	1976	1977	1978	1979	1980	1981
C.	BRAZIL	106	140	120	142	89	32	3.4[a]
D.	CHILE	42	65	88	108	110	94	95.8
E.	COLOMBIA	271	183	167	229	240	136	45.6[a]
F.	COSTA RICA	155	128	136	130	114	105	116.3
H.	DOMINICAN REP.	67	72	94	88	83	88	98.0
I.	ECUADOR	121	211	190	189	187	185	216.8
J.	EL SALVADOR	91	124	119	142	122	19	#
K.	GUATEMALA	140	132	150	154	157	151	118.8
M.	HONDURAS	137	110	163	180	193	186	201.3
O.	NICARAGUA	69	108	110	91	202	- -	#
Q.	PARAGUAY	67	74	67	121	146	144	154.7
T.	VENEZUELA	140	17	- -	- -	- -	- -	- -

a. Partial year.

SOURCE: Data supplied by Peter Lara from Peace Corps/Latin American Regional Management Plans for FYs 1976-79; FYs 1980-81 provided by Wendy Kaufman, Budget Office, Peace Corps.

Table 2839

U.S. PEACE CORPS VOLUNTEER CHARACTERISTICS
(1980)

Peace Corps Volunteers by Human Need Areas	%
Health/Nutrition/Water Supply	.25
Food Production	.18
Knowledge/Skills	.40
Economic Development/Income Generation	.07
Energy/Conservation	.04
Community Services/Housing	.06

Peace Corps Volunteers and Trainees at End of FY 1980	N
Africa	2,464
North Africa, Near East, Asia, and Pacific	1,802
Latin America	1,728
Total	5,994

Sex Ratio of Peace Corps Volunteers	%
Female	.44
Male	.56

Age of Peace Corps Volunteers	%
22 years or younger	.01
23–25 years	.53
26–28 years	.24
29–35 years	.14
36 years or older	.08

SOURCE: U.S. Action, *Annual Report*, 1980, p. 44.

Table 2840

U.S. PEACE CORPS VOLUNTEERS, BY SKILL CLASSIFICATION, 9 L
(N, 1980)

Country	Health	Nutrition	Food	Water	Knowledge/Skills	Economic Development	Housing	Energy Conservation	Community Services	Total
Belize	9	0	8	0	27	7	0	0	7	58
B. BRAZIL	5	0	0	0	17	0	0	2	0	24
D. CHILE	13	3	14	0	38	21	0	4	0	93
E. COLOMBIA	21	11	7	18	13	10	0	0	0	80
F. COSTA RICA	5	13	43	0	15	14	0	6	2	98
H. DOMINICAN REP.	0	22	43	0	0	23	0	3	0	90
Eastern Caribbean	27	0	34	0	44	12	0	1	0	118
I. ECUADOR	21	0	63	0	42	2	0	0	54	182
K. GUATEMALA	18	8	26	2	20	24	0	42	0	140
M. HONDURAS	37	30	18	1	60	1	0	31	34	212
Jamaica	3	0	31	0	64	10	0	5	4	117
Q. PARAGUAY	37	19	0	0	34	28	0	12	0	130
TOTAL	196	106	287	21	374	152	0	106	101	1,342

SOURCE: U.S. Action, *Annual Report*, 1980, p. 53.

Table 2841

GROSS PROJECTED AID ASSISTANCE DURING THREE PERIODS, 20 L, 1949–74

(M US, Descending Order)

Mutual Security Years, 1949–1958		Peak Years of the Alliance for Progress, 1959–1966		Years of Congressional Disillusionment, 1967–1974	
1. BOLIVIA	92.4	1. BRAZIL	842.8	1. COLOMBIA	647.3
2. GUATEMALA	54.5	2. CHILE	499.2	2. BRAZIL	586.9
3. CHILE	24.2	3. COLOMBIA	316.3	3. DOMINICAN REP.	146.3
4. BRAZIL	23.4	4. BOLIVIA	222.8	4. BOLIVIA	145.4
5. PERU	18.4	5. DOMINICAN REP.	202.2	5. PANAMA	127.6
6. HAITI	16.6	6. ARGENTINA	141.0	6. CHILE	126.3
7. HONDURAS	16.1	7. PERU	116.1	7. GUATEMALA	98.2
8. ECUADOR	14.7[a]	8. ECUADOR	107.5	8. PERU	92.2
9. PARAGUAY	14.7[a]	9. MEXICO	70.9	9. NICARAGUA	87.3
10. PANAMA	10.1	10. PANAMA	70.8	10. HONDURAS	68.4
11. COSTA RICA	8.7	11. VENEZUELA	64.2	11. COSTA RICA	59.7
12. COLOMBIA	8.1	12. NICARAGUA	56.3	12. ECUADOR	59.6
13. MEXICO	6.4	13. GUATEMALA	53.7	13. EL SALVADOR	47.9
14. EL SALVADOR	5.5	14. COSTA RICA	47.0[a]	14. PARAGUAY	43.0
15. NICARAGUA	4.9	15. EL SALVADOR	47.0[a]	15. URUGUAY	42.1
16. CUBA	2.6	16. HAITI	42.5	16. HAITI	28.6
17. URUGUAY	1.9	17. HONDURAS	41.4	17. VENEZUELA	6.8
18. DOMINICAN REP.	1.7	18. PARAGUAY	40.7	18. ARGENTINA	5.3
19. VENEZUELA	1.0	19. URUGUAY	27.9	19. MEXICO	1.6
20. ARGENTINA	.2	20. CUBA	.7	20. CUBA	0

a. Tie ranking.

SOURCE: Phillip Paul Boucher, "U.S. Foreign Aid to Latin America: Hypotheses and Patterns in Historical Statistics, 1934-1974," Ph.D. dissertation, University of California, Los Angeles, 1979, p. 98.

Table 2842

AID COMMITMENTS TO INDIVIDUAL LATIN AMERICAN COUNTRIES, 20 L, 1949–74

(M US, Descending Order)

Country	Amount	%
1. BRAZIL	1,453.1	25.3
2. COLOMBIA	971.7	16.9
3. CHILE	649.7	11.3
4. BOLIVIA	460.6	8.0
5. DOMINICAN REP.	350.2	6.1
6. PERU	226.7	4.0
7. PANAMA	208.5	3.6
8. GUATEMALA	206.4	3.6
9. ECUADOR	181.8	3.2
10. NICARAGUA	148.5	2.6
11. ARGENTINA	135.9	2.4
12. HONDURAS	125.9	2.2
13. COSTA RICA	115.4	2.0
14. EL SALVADOR	100.4	1.7
15. PARAGUAY	98.4	1.7
16. HAITI	87.4	1.5
17. MEXICO	78.9	1.4
18. VENEZUELA	72.0	1.2
19. URUGUAY	71.9	1.2
20. CUBA	3.3	.1
LATIN AMERICA	5,746.7	100.0

SOURCE: Calculated by Boucher from table 2841.

Table 2843

AID ACTUAL DISBURSEMENT, 20 LR, 1979–81

(T US)

	Country	FY 1979	1980	1981
A.	ARGENTINA	2	#	#
B.	BOLIVIA	26,526	21,161	16,398
C.	BRAZIL	6,762	92	327
D.	CHILE	9,143	3,097	588
E.	COLOMBIA	11,425	8,061	1,063
F.	COSTA RICA	7,067	4,873	4,026
G.	CUBA	#	#	#
H.	DOMINICAN REP.	11,992	17,620	19,515
I.	ECUADOR	705	1,750	2,493
J.	EL SALVADOR	3,787	12,692	89,868
K.	GUATEMALA	5,760	7,444	11,922
L.	HAITI	10,275	11,397	15,423
M.	HONDURAS	15,598	16,444	22,096
N.	MEXICO	85	107	132
O.	NICARAGUA	11,229	31,003	53,874
P.	PANAMA	12,501	14,398	13,446
Q.	PARAGUAY	4,920	1,713	2,654
R.	PERU	14,841	26,780	22,860
S.	URUGUAY	2,281	4,043	2,835
T.	VENEZUELA	73	67	34
	LATIN AMERICA	154,972	182,742	279,554

a. For data from 1946 to 1972, see SALA-SNP, pp. 369-378, col. 2; for 1973-77 data, see SALA, 22-3202; no data available for 1978.

SOURCE: Unpublished data provided by Ted Panagoss of USAID-OSR; see table 2835, col. 6, above.

Table 2844

EX-IM BANK ACTUAL LOANS, 20 L, 1973–81[a]

(T US)

	Country	1973	1974	1975	FY 1976	1977	1978	1979	1980	1981
A.	ARGENTINA	32,212	5,945	29,142	36,098	19,636	21,000	19,893	11,767	33,552
B.	BOLIVIA	#	#	4,261	107	6,215	8,188	#	96	
C.	BRAZIL	77,243	172,485	283,827	157,057	153,198	90,016	79,734	133,689	132,935
D.	CHILE	#	51,251	3,261	17,614	2,740	#	#	#	#
E.	COLOMBIA	3,859	1,368	8,207	8,451	6,915	192	4,101	11,737	21,747
F.	COSTA RICA	1,649	1,502	2,788	2,018	368	179	3,760	1,150	68,183
G.	CUBA	#	#	#	#	#	#	#	#	#
H.	DOMINICAN REP.	3,087	5,963	22,444	5,940	4,944	1,420	392	12,351	8,827
I.	ECUADOR	1,740	138	2,491	3,339	2,070	368	1,755	11,082	11,966
J.	EL SALVADOR	1,082	31	159	542	4,833	916	653	34,000	#
K.	GUATEMALA	#	#	#	1,329	13,523	5,147	795	243	#
L.	HAITI	#	#	#	#	#	#	#	#	#
M.	HONDURAS	3,650	2,581	4,057	1,769	1,566	1,379	405	1,314	6,337
N.	MEXICO	39,991	96,455	146,054	75,389	127,852	69,764	157,397	198,469	207,363
O.	NICARAGUA	834	620	1,668	1,947	6,161	4,608	159	1,149	1,905
P.	PANAMA	19,737	23,041	9,640	15,952	8,455	4,002	8,039	64	#
Q.	PERU	85	#	26,289	34,200	23,883	8,703	8,319	4,776	2,943
R.	PARAGUAY	368	#	#	#	#	#	#	#	#
S.	URUGUAY	379	#	421	344	#	#	#	#	#
T.	VENEZUELA	19,301	8,031	18,570	12,212	14,187	29,072	22,590	32,723	48,166

a. For prior years, see SALA-SNP, XVII-b.

SOURCE: Unpublished data supplied by Kenneth L. Buschow and Richard Zurn, Reports Division, Export-Import Bank of the United States. For projections, see table 2835, col. 2, above.

Table 2845

EXPOSURE OF U.S. BANK HOLDING COMPANIES, 4 L
(B US, Sept. 30, 1983)[a]

	Country	Citicorp	Bank America	Chase Manhattan	Manufacturers Hanover	J. P. Morgan	Chemical N.Y.	First Interstate	Continental Illinois	Security Pacific	Bankers Trust
A.	ARGENTINA	1.1	.3	.8	1.3	.7	.4	.8	.4[a]	.2[†]	.2[†]
B.	BRAZIL	4.7	2.5	2.6	2.1	1.8	1.3	.5	.5[a]	.5	.7
N.	MEXICO	2.9	2.7	1.5	1.9	1.2	1.4	.7	.7[a]	.5	1.3
S.	VENEZUELA	1.5	1.6	1.2	1.1	.5	.8	#	.4[a]	#	.4
	Total	10.2	7.1	6.1	6.4	4.2	3.8	1.4	2.0[a]	1.3	2.7
	Assets	134.7	121.1	81.9	64.3	58.0	51.2	44.4	42.1	40.4	40.0
	Total Exposure As a Percent of:										
	Assets	7.6	5.9	7.5	10.0	7.2	7.5	3.1	4.7	3.1	6.7
	Primary Capital	154.3	116.7	136.5	200.3	102.9	136.0	53.0	82.7	58.4	119.4

a. Cf. SALA, 23-3135 to 3138.

SOURCE: *Los Angeles Times*, April 15, 1984.

Table 2846

U.S. CLAIMS ON FOREIGN COUNTRIES HELD BY U.S. OFFICES AND FOREIGN BRANCHES OF U.S. — CHARTERED BANKS,[1] 9 L, 1979–84
(B US)

	Country	1979	1980	1981	1982	1983	1984[a]
A.	ARGENTINA	5.0	7.9	9.4	8.9	9.5	8.7
C.	BRAZIL	15.2	16.2	19.1	22.9	23.1	26.3
D.	CHILE	2.5	3.7	5.8	6.3	6.4	7.0
E.	COLOMBIA	2.2	2.6	2.6	3.1	3.2	2.9
I.	ECUADOR	1.7	2.1	2.2	2.2	2.2	2.2
M.	MEXICO	12.0	15.9	21.6	24.5	26.1	25.8
P.	PANAMA[2]	4.3	5.4	7.7	~	~	~
R.	PERU	1.5	1.8	2.0	2.6	2.4	2.2
T.	VENEZUELA	8.7	9.1	9.9	10.5	9.9	9.3

1. The banking offices covered by these data are the U.S. offices and foreign branches of U.S.-owned banks and of U.S. subsidiaries of foreign-owned banks. Offices *not* covered include (1) U.S. agencies and branches of foreign banks, and (2) foreign subsidiaries of U.S. banks. To minimize duplication, the data are adjusted to exclude the claims on foreign branches held by a U.S. office or another foreign branch of the same banking institution.
2. All data for Panama are from USBG-FRB, Sept. 1984, table 3.21; includes Canal Zone.

a. Preliminary data as of Dec. 1984.

SOURCE: USBG-FRB, Sept. 1984, table 3.21; June 1985.

Table 2847

U.S. CLAIMS ON UNAFFILIATED FOREIGNERS[1] AS REPORTED BY NONBANKING BUSINESS ENTERPRISES TO THE FEDERAL RESERVE, 3 L, 1980–84

(M US)

Country	Financial Claims					Commercial Claims				
	1980	1981	1982	1983	1984[a]	1980	1981	1982	1983	1984[a]
C. BRAZIL	96	30	62	53	84	861	668	258	493	219
N. MEXICO	208	313	274	291	232	1,102	1,022	775	884	509
T. VENEZUELA	137	148	139	134	128	410	424	351	272	242

1. The term "foreigners" covers all institutions and individuals domiciled outside the United States (including U.S. citizens domiciled abroad), and the foreign branches, subsidiaries, and offices of U.S. banks and business concerns; the central governments, central banks, and other official institutions of foreign countries, wherever located; and international and regional organizations, wherever located. The term "foreigners" also includes persons in the United States when it is known by reporting institutions that they are acting on behalf of foreigners. (See the *Annual Statistical Digest*, 1970–1979, of the Board of Governors of the Federal Reserve System, pp. 580–582, for an outline of revisions in international statistics.)

a. As of Sept. 1984.

SOURCE: USBG-FRB, June 1985, table 3.23.

Table 2848

U.S. BANKS' OWN CLAIMS ON FOREIGNERS AS REPORTED TO THE FEDERAL RESERVE, 12 L, 1981–85

(M US, YE)

Country	1981[a]	1982	1983	1984	1985[b]
A. ARGENTINA	7,527	10,974	11,749	11,043	11,203
C. BRAZIL	16,926	23,271	24,667	26,307	26,146
D. CHILE	3,690	5,513	6,072	6,839	6,713
E. COLOMBIA	2,018	3,211	3,745	3,499	3,406
G. CUBA	3	3	0	0	1
I. ECUADOR	1,531	2,062	2,307	2,420	2,489
K. GUATEMALA	124	124	129	158	157
N. MEXICO	22,439	29,552	34,802	34,697	33,654
P. PANAMA	6,794	10,210	7,848	7,707	6,200
R. PERU	1,218	2,357	2,536	2,384	2,337
S. URUGUAY	157	686	977	1,088	1,021
T. VENEZUELA	7,069	10,643	11,287	11,017	10,929

a. Liabilities and claims of banks in the United States were increased, beginning in December 1981, by the shift from foreign branches to international banking facilities in the United States of liabilities to, and claims on, foreign residents.
b. Preliminary data as of Feb. 1985.

SOURCE: USBG-FRB, June 1985, table 3.18.

Table 2849

U.S. LIABILITIES DUE TO FOREIGNERS AS REPORTED
TO THE FEDERAL RESERVE, 12 L, 1981–85
(M US)

	Country	1981[a]	1982	1983	1984	1985[b]
A.	ARGENTINA	2,445	3,578	4,038	4,424	4,361
C.	BRAZIL	1,568	2,014	3,168	5,232	6,136
D.	CHILE	664	1,626	1,842	2,001	1,916
E.	COLOMBIA	2,993	2,594	1,689	2,514	2,453
G.	CUBA	9	9	8	10	8
I.	ECUADOR	434	455	1,047	1,092	981
K.	GUATEMALA	479	670	788	896	915
N.	MEXICO	7,235	8,377	10,392	12,695	13,061
P.	PANAMA	4,857	4,805	5,924	6,928	7,156
R.	PERU	694	1,147	1,166	1,247	1,063
S.	URUGUAY	367	759	1,244	1,394	1,413
T.	VENEZUELA	4,245	8,417	8,632	10,545	10,742

a. Liabilities and claims of banks in the United States were increased, beginning in December 1981, by the shift from foreign branches to international banking facilities in the United States of liabilities to, and claims on, foreign residents.

b. Preliminary data as of Feb. 1985.

SOURCE: USBG-FRB, June 1985, table 3.17.

CHAPTER 29

INVESTMENTS AND
CORPORATE BUSINESS ACTIVITY

Table 2900

DIRECT INVESTMENT FLOW,[1] 19 L, 1975-83[a]

(M US; Minus = Debit)

	Country	1975	1976	1977	1978	1979	1980	1981	1982	1983
A.	ARGENTINA	#	#	83	273	265	788	944	257	183
B.	BOLIVIA	53.4	-8.1	-1.2	11.5	18.0	41.5	59.9	36.9	42.1
C.	BRAZIL	1,190	1,372	1,687	1,882	2,223	1,544	2,313	2,534	1,373
D.	CHILE	50	-1	16	177	233	170	362	384	152
E.	COLOMBIA	35	14	43	68	105	48	212	338	285
F.	COSTA RICA	69.0	63.3	62.5	47.0	42.4	48.1	66.2	32.6	49.7
H.	DOMINICAN REP.	63.9	26.7	71.5	63.6	17.1	92.7	79.7	-1.4	~
I.	ECUADOR	95.3	-19.9	34.5	48.6	63.4	70.0	60.0	40.0	50.0
J.	EL SALVADOR	13.1	12.9	18.6	23.4	-10.0	5.9	-5.7	-1.0	~
K.	GUATEMALA	80.0	12.5	97.5	127.2	117.0	110.7	127.1	77.1	45.0
L.	HAITI	2.7	7.8	8.0	10.0	12.0	13.0	8.3	7.1	8.7
M.	HONDURAS	7.0	5.3	8.9	13.2	9.9	5.8	-3.6	13.8	21.0
N.	MEXICO	609	628	556	824	1,337	2,186	2,537	1,399	496
O.	NICARAGUA	10.9	12.9	10.0	7.0	2.8	#	#	#	7.7
P.	PANAMA	7.6	-10.6	10.9	-.7	40.3	-47	#	277	49
Q.	PARAGUAY	24.4	-3.0	21.7	19.6	50.2	31.7	39.0	44.5	4.9
R.	PERU	316	170	54	25	71	27	125	48	38
S.	URUGUAY	#	#	66.0	128.8	215.5	289.5	48.6	-13.7	5.6
T.	VENEZUELA	418	-889	-3	67	88	55	184	253	-62

1. Direct Foreign Investment includes all business enterprises in which foreign investors have a controlling interest or an important voice in management (usually a 25 percent minimum of voting stock). This investment excludes miscellaneous holdings of those stocks and bonds issued by foreign corporations or governments, which ordinarily are termed Portfolio Investments (see table 2907, below). For definitions, see SALA-SNP, p. 252.

a. For 1968-80 data, see SALA, 23-3200.

SOURCE: IMF-IFS, June 1982; IMF-IFS, Oct. 1984, line 77bad.

Table 2901

U.S. DIRECT INVESTMENT IN LATIN AMERICA, 19 LRC, 1950–82
(M US in Book Value)

Country	Year	Total[2]	Mining	Petroleum	Manufacturing[3]	Transport, Communications, and Public Utilities	Trade	Other Industries
A. ARGENTINA	1950	356	~a	~b	161	77	35	16
	1951	360	~a	~a	167	~a	41	~
	1952	382	~a	~a	192	~a	47	~
	1953	391	~a	~a	193	~a	49	~
	1954	405	~a	~a	208	~a	47	~
	1955	418	~a	~a	218	~a	42	~
	1956	429	~a	~a	233	~a	40	~
	1957	333	~a	~a	164	~a	22	~
	1958	330	~a	~a	154	~a	19	~
	1959	366	~a	~a	160	~a	16	~
	1960	473	~a	~a	214	~a	21	~
	1961	560	~a	~a	307	22	29	~
	1962	799	~a	~a	413	23	34	~
	1963	829	~a	~a	454	24	38	~
	1964	882	~a	~a	500	25	40	~
	1965	992	~a	187	618	25	47	327
	1966	758	~a	121	510	9	23	~
	1967	803	~a	125	536	9	31	~
	1968	870	~a	120	589	10	~	50
	1969	973	~a	115	659	8	~	60
	1970	1,022	28	137	669	6	~a	~
	1971	1,089	39	148	712	5	~a	~
	1972	1,128	~a	~a	749	~a	~a	~
	1973	1,144	44	141	768	~a	~a	~
	1974	1,138	50	147	737	11	70	68
	1975	1,154	~	142	764	8	87	60
	1976	1,366	53	174	898	~a	105	~a
	1977	1,490	55	223	921	~	132	~
	1978	1,658	53	259	983	~	157	~
	1979	1,850	~	305	1,184	289	136	~
	1980	2,494	~	395	1,584	409	216	~
	1981	2,735	69	483	1,570	308	202	107
	1982	2,979	71	629	1,718	~e	168	93
B. BOLIVIA	1950	11	6	~	~b	2	2	~b
C. BRAZIL	1950	644	2	112	285	138	73	35
	1951	784	2	131	387	142	88	34
	1952	977	1	167	507	151	112	37
	1953	970	3	197	477	149	106	39
	1954	992	4	165	527	150	114	33
	1955	1,052	4	179	560	156	121	32
	1956	1,143	9	188	612	171	129	35
	1957	835	10	130	378	182	116	19
	1958	795	6	93	398	186	91	20
	1959	828	5	84	432	192	93	21
	1960	953	10	76	515	200	130	23
	1961	1,006	14	92	548	198	129	25
	1962	1,084	26	79	616	191	136	35
	1963	1,132	30	60	664	193	148	38
	1964	997	40	53	668	41	153	41
	1965	1,074	51	57	723	37	162	45
	1966	882	28	70	574	~	92	~
	1967	961	28	76	627	22	88	31
	1968	1,122	27	79	757	17	92	43
	1969	1,290	26	95	899	15	86	52
	1970	1,526	30	114	1,075	15	119	54
	1971	1,745	26	141	1,225	14	150	70
	1972	2,180	45	164	1,561	15	175	80
	1973	2,885	31	198	2,046	16	212	103
	1974	3,760	94	244	2,578	18	363	183
	1975	4,579	130	288	3,106	22	406	269
	1976	5,416	140	336	3,673	26	496	31
	1977	5,930	~	364	3,937	26	495	~
	1978	7,170	268	424	4,684	25	552	521
	1979	7,186	110	301	4,902	548	506	194
	1980	7,703	141	365	5,145	679	571	206
	1981	8,253	152	422	5,420	590	581	216
	1982	9,031	138	448	5,958	633	625	223

Table 2901 (Continued)

U.S. DIRECT INVESTMENT IN LATIN AMERICA, 19 LRC, 1950–82
(M US in Book Value)

Country	Year	Total[2]	Mining	Petroleum	Manufacturing[3]	Transport, Communications, and Public Utilities	Trade	Other Industries
D. CHILE	1950	540	351	~b	29	~b	15	3
	1951	582	382	~a	33	~a	14	~
	1952	626	423	~a	33	~a	11	~
	1953	660	452	~a	34	~a	9	~
	1954	635	418	~a	35	~a	10	~
	1955	643	421	~a	37	~a	11	~
	1956	682	454	~a	39	~a	12	~
	1957	666	483	~a	22	~a	9	~
	1958	687	498	~a	21	~a	8	~
	1959	729	526	~a	21	~a	10	~
	1960	738	517	~a	22	~a	12	~
	1961	735	504	~a	27	171	14	~
	1962	755	504	~a	29	187	14	~
	1963	768	503	~a	27	201	15	~
	1964	769	~a	~a	30	214	20	~
	1965	829	509	~a	39	~a	24	257
	1966	765	439	~a	47	~a	19	~
	1967	820	~	~a	56	~a	21	
	1968	916	566	~a	57	~a	21	12
	1969	817	443	~a	57	~a	20	16
	1970	758	490	~a	57	135	24	20
	1971	739	486	~a	48	133	23	19
	1972	642	~	~a	50	131	25	17
	1973	643	~	~a	47	131	28	16
	1974	287	25	~	44	129	27	23
	1975	174	12	~	49	4	28	~
	1976	179	5	~	49	6	34	~
	1977	193	~	~	56	7	39	~
	1978	230	~	~	71	10	51	26
	1979	250	5	70	~	~	49	~
	1980	536	209	91	~	~	64	~
	1981	834	~	98	112	~	80	~
	1982	854	~d	79	60	~	71	~d
E. COLOMBIA	1950	193	~a	112	25	29	9	~
	1951	221	~	131	27	31	11	~
	1952	261	~a	152	37	31	19	~
	1953	271	~a	159	41	28	22	~
	1954	310	~a	166	51	31	36	~
	1955	336	~a	178	58	33	42	~
	1956	371	~a	193	68	39	44	~
	1957	396	~a	245	61	24	34	~
	1958	383	~a	225	68	26	35	~
	1959	401	~a	225	77	28	41	~
	1960	424	~a	233	92	28	46	~
	1961	425	~a	230	95	29	49	~
	1962	455	~a	257	100	27	52	~
	1963	465	~a	246	120	27	52	~
	1964	508	~a	255	148	30	53	~
	1965	526	~a	269	160	29	49	20
	1966	459	~a	86	193	~	27	15
	1967	482	~a	105	200	~	29	17
	1968	520	~a	130	212	~	25	~
	1969	574	~a	147	240	27	29	~
	1970	584	12	137	250	26	37	~
	1971	650	~a	146	302	25	35	~
	1972	635	~a	129	299	26	37	~
	1973	608	~a	76	326	~a	45	14
	1974	617	18	58	366	14	54	~
	1975	648	17	62	381	13	64	16
	1976	654	11	56	388	~	64	~
	1977	696	9	72	432	~	66	~
	1978	769	9	85	490	~	69	~
	1979	842	~	198	492	~	95	~
	1980	1,012	~	265	548	~	97	~
	1981	1,174	~	318	574	~	98	~
	1982	1,655	~d	569	651	~d	105	~d

Table 2901 (Continued)

U.S. DIRECT INVESTMENT IN LATIN AMERICA, 19 LRC, 1950–82

(M US in Book Value)

Country	Year	Total[2]	Mining	Petroleum	Manufacturing[3]	Transport, Communications, and Public Utilities	Trade	Other Industries
F. COSTA RICA	1950	60	~	4	~	11	1	~b
	1955‡	61	~	6	~	11	~b	~b
G. CUBA	1950	642	~b	20	54	271	21	269c
	1955	736	~b	~b	55	312	30	298
	1960‡	956	~a	147	111	313	44	341
H. DOMINICAN REP.	1950	106	~	~b	9	11	1	81
	1955‡	134	6	~b	13	5	~b	103
	1960	105	~b	~b	~b	~b	~b	~
I. ECUADOR	1950	14	~	~b	1	5	2	4
	1955‡	25	~	~b	~b	6	2	8
	1982	405	#	225	133	5	37	-9
J. EL SALVADOR	1950	19	~b	2	~b	17	1	~b
K. GUATEMALA	1950	106	~b	4	~b	72	3	~b
	1955‡	103	~b	6	~b	73	~b	~b
	1960	131‡	~a	26‡	~a	66‡	5‡	34‡
L. HAITI	1950	13	~	~b	~b	2	~b	8
	1955‡	18	~	~b	~b	3	~b	9
M. HONDURAS	1950	62	~a	~a	~a	9	~b	~a
	1955‡	101	~a	~a	~a	12	~b	~a
	1960	100‡	~a	~a	~a	23‡	1‡	76‡
N. MEXICO	1950	414	121	13	133	107	30	11
	1951	468	126	9	194	87	41	11
	1952	481	128	10	205	89	38	11
	1953	497	138	11	207	89	39	11
	1954	503	135	13	208	88	44	16
	1955	577	143	15	262	87	54	16
	1956	667	158	22	309	88	72	19
	1957	739	139	31	335	134	68	32
	1958	745	139	32	326	120	84	34
	1959	758	137	30	353	118	84	36
	1960	795	130	32	391	119	85	39
	1961	830	129	54	418	29	97	104
	1962	867	121	73	442	26	97	107
	1963	907	116	65	502	25	93	105
	1964	1,034	128	56	606	27	111	106
	1965	1,182	104	48	756	27	138	110
	1966	1,329	95	29	927	20	136	39
	1967	1,426	~a	26	1,016	18	151	~a
	1968	1,566	97	25	1,147	19	165	59
	1969	1,756	117	15	1,277	20	179	94
	1970	1,912	127	10	1,380	23	207	122
	1971	1,980	103	7	1,492	26	224	82
	1972	2,161	98	10	1,631	26	263	82
	1973	2,379	85	10	1,800	31	305	88
	1974	2,854	83	18	2,173	34	400	550
	1975	3,200	80	22	2,443	35	476	87
	1976	2,984	88	17	2,223	47	453	105
	1977	3,230	98	26	2,391	~	502	~
	1978	3,712	97	41	2,752	~	563	~
	1979	4,490	76	145	3,451	508	537	~
	1980	5,989	95	150	4,489	750	727	~
	1981	6,962	77	189	5,140	846	878	~
	1982	5,584	~e	193	4,166	726	626	~e
O. NICARAGUA	1950	9	~b	~b	~b	1	1	~
P. PANAMA	1950	58	- -	6	2	18	11	23
	1951	67	- -	6	2	17	14	28
	1952	69	- -	6	3	18	12	30
	1953	86	- -	7	4	18	14	43
	1954	100	- -	9	4	20	18	49
	1955	109	- -	10	5	21	15	57
	1956	157	1	1	8	24	30	94
	1957	201	5	13	3	19	70	91

Table 2901 (Continued)

U.S. DIRECT INVESTMENT IN LATIN AMERICA, 19 LRC, 1950–82

(M US in Book Value)

Country	Year	Total[2]	Mining	Petroleum	Manufacturing[3]	Transport, Communications, and Public Utilities	Trade	Other Industries
P. PANAMA	1958	268	8	25	6	20	94	115
(Continued)	1959	327	16	29	8	21	118	135
	1960	405	17	56	9	22	145	156
	1961	486	17	62	10	25	195	177
	1962	537	19	81	5	25	224	183
	1963	616	19	94	12	26	273	193
	1964	663	19	107	23	29	281	205
	1965	724	19	130	24	36	293	221
	1966	847	- -	70	18	52	235	151
	1967	872	- -	~a	~a	54	240	155
	1968	971	- -	47	48	60	250	178
	1969	1,055	- -	27	49	62	259	184
	1970	1,190	- -	39	64	60	274	211
	1971	1,380	- -	33	77	63	301	225
	1972	1,352	- -	25	88	51	318	230
	1973	1,549	1	~a	89	42	375	~a
	1974	1,604	−1	55	115	43	456	324
	1975	1,907	1	125	122	39	542	359
	1976	1,957	1	94	139	45	572	381
	1977	2,249	1	106	158	24	654	386
	1978	2,385	1	68	180	26	707	406
	1979	2,874	5	289	214	#	542	242
	1980	3,171	- -	503	262	#	601	~
	1981	3,671	- -	601	302	#	672	377
	1982	4,404	~e	776	327	#	655	~d
R. PERU	1950	145	55	~b	16	~b	13	1
	1951	199	107	~a	21	~a	18	~
	1952	233	129	~a	17	~a	24	~
	1953	274	150	~a	16	~a	29	~
	1954	278	150	~a	18	~a	31	~
	1955	292	154	~a	23	~a	36	~
	1956	332	178	~a	25	~a	38	~
	1957	383	196	86	29	14	42	16
	1958	409	218	86	29	19	38	18
	1959	428	242	79	31	19	36	20
	1960	496	307	79	35	19	42	20
	1961	486	292	71	36	20	45	23
	1962	503	298	66	46	20	48	26
	1963	498	290	56	64	21	41	27
	1964	514	291	60	65	27	46	31
	1965	515	262	60	79	21	54	38
	1966	651	360	~a	128	~a	52	24
	1967	712	416	57	140	~a	45	24
	1968	749	440	62	146	~a	~a	26
	1969	771	~a	66	154	−2	37	26
	1970	744	~a	67	156	−1	35	24
	1971	729	~a	74	156	−1	33	29
	1972	769	442	97	155	−3	32	36
	1973	859	466	149	161	−2	42	32
	1974	900	412	239	155	−2	54	74
	1975	1,221	700	246	166	−1	62	37
	1976	1,367	~	~	168	−1	64	43
	1977	1,397	807	316	159	−1	62	46
	1978	1,429	~a	~a	158	−1	57	47
	1979	1,537	~a	~a	~a	~a	52	24
	1980	1,665	~a	~a	~a	~a	64	19
	1981	1,928	~	~	106	10	76	~
	1982	2,262	~d	~d	106	30	76	23
S. URUGUAY	1950	55	~	3	33	2	4	13
	1955‡	74	~	4	36	2	10	22
	1960	47	~a	~a	20	~a	4	23
T. VENEZUELA	1950	993	~b	857	24	10	24	20
	1951	968	~a	811	29	11	30	~
	1952	1,134	~a	907	36	12	34	~
	1953	1,237	~a	939	41	13	38	~

Table 2901 (Continued)

U.S. DIRECT INVESTMENT IN LATIN AMERICA, 19 LRC, 1950–82
(M US in Book Value)

Country	Year	Total[2]	Mining	Petroleum	Manufacturing[3]	Transport, Communications, and Public Utilities	Trade	Other Industries
T. VENEZUELA	1954	1,271	~a	939	51	14	45	~
(Continued)	1955	1,311	~a	965	67	15	57	~
	1956	1,676	~a	1,278	86	23	83	~
	1957	2,465	~a	1,934	124	24	113	~
	1958	2,658	~a	2,071	151	27	129	~
	1959	2,690	~a	2,046	161	29	166	~
	1960	2,569	~a	1,995	180	32	165	~
	1961	3,007	~a	2,368	195	34	185	~
	1962	2,816	~a	2,197	193	35	175	~
	1963	2,808	~a	2,166	202	36	185	~
	1964	2,780	~a	2,133	220	18	199	~
	1965	2,705	~a	2,024	246	19	223	192
	1966	2,136	~a	1,544	281	18	115	~
	1967	2,081	~a	1,481	288	18	131	~
	1968	2,158	~a	1,480	347	~a	~a	23
	1969	2,196	79	1,474	378	~a	~a	22
	1970	2,241	78	1,440	416	~a	~a	33
	1971	2,199	~a	1,327	461	~a	~a	31
	1972	2,172	~a	1,225	487	28	~a	37
	1973	2,051	~a	~a	517	30	214	70
	1974	1,804	21	659	620	31	244	94
	1975	1,872	~	687	668	32	268	~
	1976	1,571	−21	230	747	~	289	~
	1977	1,896	~	325	932	25	325	~
	1978	2,015	~	290	1,059	26	321	~
	1979	1,797	- -	57	940	22	319	~
	1980	1,908	- -	40	1,032	~	361	~
	1981	2,175	- -	126	1,156	−50	406	~
	1982	2,371	~e	~e	1,278	−39	445	~e
LATIN AMERICA	1977	18,882	1,197	1,873	8,409	~	2,411	~b
	1978	21,467	1,248	2,148	10,961	~	2,644	~b
	1979	22,553	979	2,657	12,048	~	2,385	2,193
	1980	25,964	1,097	3,033	14,044	~	2,806	2,897
	1981	38,883	1,916	4,499	15,762	~	3,933	3,978
	1982	33,039	2,295	6,465	15,625	~	3,799	2,113
WORLD	1977	149,848	~	~	~	~	~	149,848
	1978	167,804	~	~	~	~	~	167,804
	1979	186,760	~	~	~	~	~	186,760
	1980	215,578	~	~	~	~	~	215,578
	1981	227,342	~	~	~	~	~	227,342
	1982	221,343	~	~	~	~	~	221,343

1. The table is updated only insofar as U.S. Department of Commerce data permit. Since post-1950 data for several republics (e.g., El Salvador, Nicaragua) have been included only under the general category of "Other Countries" in Latin America, latest data available for some countries are for 1950.
2. Subtotals do not necessarily add to total; finance and insurance excluded here.
3. Includes food products, chemicals and allied products, primary and fabricated metals, machinery, transportation equipment and other manufacturing.

a. Included in "Other."
b. Included in "Total."
c. Includes $262.7 million in agriculture.
d. Suppressed to avoid disclosure of data of individual companies.
e. Less than $500,000 (±).

SOURCE: U.S. Department of Commerce, *Selected Data on U.S. Direct Investment Abroad, 1966–78*; USDC-SCB, 61:8, Aug. 1981, pp. 31–32; USDC-SCB, 62:8, Aug. 1982, pp. 21–22.

Table 2902

U.S. DIRECT INVESTMENT ABROAD, 1977–83
(M US)

PART I. LATIN AMERICA

Year	Direct Investment Position	Net Capital Outflows (Minus = Inflows)	Equity and Intercompany Account Outflows (Minus = Inflows)	Reinvested Earnings of Incorporated Affiliates	Income	Fees and Royalties
1977	27,514	3,949	2,526	1,423	3,712	299
1978	31,770	4,014	2,096	1,918	4,779	372
1979	35,220	3,362	438	2,924	6,520	422
1980	38,761	2,833	−533	3,366	6,968	581
1981	38,864	−37	−197	3,497	6,143	671
1982	32,546	5,138	−6,500	2,137	2,706	590
1983	29,501	1,541	−3,066	1,712	690	514

PART II. WORLD

Year	Direct Investment Position	Net Capital Outflows (Minus = Inflows)	Equity and Intercompany Account Outflows (Minus = Inflows)	Reinvested Earnings of Incorporated Affiliates	Income	Fees and Royalties
1977	145,990	11,893	5,497	6,396	19,673	3,883
1978	162,727	16,056	4,713	11,343	25,458	4,705
1979	187,858	25,222	6,258	18,964	38,183	4,980
1980	215,375	19,222	2,205	17,017	37,146	5,780
1981	228,348	9,680	−3,803	13,483	32,446	5,813
1982	221,512	4,194	−4,756	6,375	22,888	5,572
1983	226,117	4,760	4,881	9,090	20,757	6,275

SOURCE: USDC-SCB, 59:8 (Aug. 1979); USDC-SCB, 60:8 (Aug. 1980); USDC-SCB, 61:8 (Aug. 1981); USDC-SCB, 62:8 (Aug. 1982); USDC-SCB, 64:8 (Aug. 1984).

Table 2903

ACCUMULATED DIRECT INVESTMENT IN LATIN AMERICA BY ORIGIN, 5 L, 1969–76
(M US and %)

Country of Origin	A. ARGENTINA 1973	C. BRAZIL 1971	C. BRAZIL 1976	E. COLOMBIA[1] 1971	E. COLOMBIA[1] 1975	N. MEXICO 1971	N. MEXICO 1975	P. PANAMA 1969	P. PANAMA 1974
I. TOTAL (M US)	2,274	2,911	9,005	503	632	2,997	4,736	214	534
II. %									
United States	39.5	37.7	32.2	55.9	48.1	80.9	68.7	90.8	86.3
Canada	3.9	10.1	5.3	10.1	10.1	1.7	2.3	~	~
Western Europe									
France	8.5	4.5	3.6	3.4	4.3	1.7	1.0	~	~
Germany	4.5	11.4	12.4	2.4	2.5	2.8	2.3	~	~
Italy	1.1	1.1	.9	~	~	1.6	.5	~	~
Netherlands	6.3	1.2	2.6	3.0	3.5	1.1	2.3	~	~
Spain	.4	#	#	~	~	.8	.1	~	~
Sweden	2.0	2.0	2.4	~	~	1.2	1.1	~	~
Switzerland	9.1	6.6	10.9	2.8	4.6	2.8	3.0	2.5	2.3
United Kingdom	12.0	9.4	4.7	2.0	2.2	3.0	5.6	2.6	3.2
Japan	.3	4.3	11.2	.1	.6	.7	1.3	~	~
Argentina	#	.3	.2	~	~	~	~	~	~
Brazil	.4	#	#	.1	.3	~	~	~	~
Panama	3.5	2.8	3.1	7.2	8.3	#	2.5	#	#
Venezuela	#	.1	.1	2.0	3.0	.2	~	~	~
Other[2]	8.2	8.7	10.4	13.0	12.5	1.7	9.3	4.0	8.1

1. Excluding investment in the petroleum sector.
2. Including developed and developing countries of origin for which no separate data are available.

SOURCE: Adapted from U.N., *Transnational Corporations in World Development: A Re-examination* (New York, 1978). See SALA, 22-3212 and 3213 for inter-regional investment data.

Table 2904

ACCUMULATED FOREIGN DIRECT INVESTMENT BY MAJOR INDUSTRIAL SECTOR,
5 L, 1969–76

Host Country	Year	Total (M US)	Share of Distribution (%)			
			Extraction Sector	Manufacturing	Service	Other
A. ARGENTINA	1973	2,275.2	5.6	65.0	24.5	4.5

Continued in SALA, 23-3211.

Table 2905

ACCUMULATED DIRECT INVESTMENT BY DAC/OECD COUNTRIES,[1] 8 LRC, 1967–78[a]

(M US)

Country	1967		1975	1978	
	DAC/OECD[1]	Other DAC/OECD[2]	DAC/OECD[1]	Other DAC/OECD[2]	DAC/OECD
A. ARGENTINA	1,821	804	2,000	846	3,340
C. BRAZIL	3,728	2,400	9,100	4,521	13,520
D. CHILE	963	84	400	226	1,440
E. COLOMBIA	728	101	1,200	552	1,510
N. MEXICO	1,787	423	4,800	1,600	6,000
P. PANAMA	830	76	2,250	343	3,140[b]
R. PERU	782	122	1,700	479	2,150
T. VENEZUELA	3,495	940	4,000	2,127	3,620
CACM Countries[3]	601	100	960	256	1,090
Other Latin American Countries[4]	515	136	1,340	406	1,710
Other Developing Countries of the American Area	3,199	1,486	9,875	4,168	13,030
Total Developing Countries of the American Area	18,449	6,672	37,625	15,524	50,550

1. Development Assistance Committee — Organization for Economic Cooperation and Development. Includes United Kingdom, Ireland, Federal Republic of Germany, France, Switzerland, Italy, and Belgium.
2. Includes Austria, Denmark, Norway, Finland, Sweden, and the Netherlands.
3. Includes Costa Rica, El Salvador, Guatemala, Honduras, and Nicaragua.
4. Includes Bolivia, Ecuador, Paraguay, Uruguay, Haiti, and the Dominican Republic.

a. For 1967–75 data, see SALA, 21-3011.
b. Off-shore banking center.

SOURCE: DAC/OECD data from *OECD Development Co-operation*, 1977, 1980.

Table 2906

BRITISH DIRECT INVESTMENT FLOWS, 9 L, 1969-75
(M US)[1]

Country	1969	1970	1971	1972	1973	1974	1975
A. ARGENTINA	12.7	−.7	−5.1	19.5	6.4	14.3	19.3

Continued in SALA, 23-3209.

Table 2907

PORTFOLIO INVESTMENT FLOW,[1] 19 L, 1976–83
(M SDR)

	Country	1976	1977	1978	1979	1980	1981	1982	1983
A.	ARGENTINA	−57	−1	81	173	118	957	267	612
B.	BOLIVIA	#	#	#	#	−2	#	#	#
C.	BRAZIL	#	#	#	510	272	−1	−3	−270
D.	CHILE	−5	−6	#	39	#	#	#	#
E.	COLOMBIA	−1	−2	−2	−9	−2	−1	−6	#
F.	COSTA RICA	#	3	16.7	#	95.9	.3	.4	#
H.	DOMINICAN REP.	#	#	#	#	#	#	#	#
I.	ECUADOR	4.9	44.5	#	#	#	#	#	~
J.	EL SALVADOR	15.4	.6	3.2	−4.4	−.8	#	−.9	~
K.	GUATEMALA	.1	4.5	9.4	4.2	3.0	.3	.4	.1
L.	HAITI	#	#	#	#	#	#	#	#
M.	HONDURAS	#	#	−.4	−.1	#	−.2	−.2	.1
N.	MEXICO	373	1,146	603	−306	−57	845	583	−505
O.	NICARAGUA	#	#	#	#	#	#	#	#
P.	PANAMA	.1	10.8	56.2	157.8	−680.3	172.2	318.7	59.6
Q.	PARAGUAY	#	#	#	#	#	#	#	#
R.	PERU	#	#	#	#	#	#	#	#
S.	URUGUAY	28.2	17.8	−6.9	−24.1	−5.2	2.6	−6.2	−14.6
T.	VENEZUELA	626	−35	99	−57	1,007	70	1,433	497
	U.S. Dollars per SDR	1.1545	1.1675	1.2520	1.2920	1.3015	1.1792	1.1040	1.0690

1. Portfolio Investments are miscellaneous holdings of stocks and bonds issued by foreign
   governments or corporations which do not usually exceed 25 percent of voting stock.
   Holdings of more than 25 percent of voting stock are usually considered Direct Foreign
   Investment (see Direct Investment, tables 2900–2906, above). For definitions, see
   SALA-SNP, p. 252.

SOURCE: IMF-BPS-Y, 1984; IMF-BPS, Nov. 1984; IMF-BPS, Jan. 1985.

Table 2908

CAPITAL EXPENDITURES BY U.S. MAJORITY-OWNED FOREIGN AFFILIATES,[1] 9 LR, 1981-84

(M US)

Country	Year	All Industries	Mining	Petroleum	Manufacturing — Total	Food and Kindred Products	Chemicals and Allied Products	Primary and Fabricated Metals	Machinery, Except Electrical	Electric and Electronic Equipment	Transportation Equipment	Other Manufacturing	Trade	Finance[2]	Other Industries
A. ARGENTINA	1981[a]	635	5	130	434	57	80	~[c]	142	4	~[c]	~[c]	57	#	9
	1982[b]	412	4	124	246	35	60	~[c]	54	3	~[c]	~[c]	30	#	7
	1983[b]	425	4	124	263	61	42	7	~[c]	8	66	~[c]	25	#	9
	1984[d]	458	2	132	287	46	63	5	77	7	49	40	20	#	17
C. BRAZIL	1981[a]	1,640	2	86	1,325	108	247	88	250	60	385	188	175	~[c]	~[c]
	1982[b]	1,747	1	100	1,434	100	244	251	258	48	335	199	157	25	30
	1983[b]	1,962	~[c]	~[c]	1,656	119	292	~[c]	262	78	308	~[c]	165	9	27
	1984[d]	1,506	~[c]	125	1,136	62	170	~[c]	246	50	159	~[c]	187	10	17
D. CHILE	1981[a]	287	~[c]	34	12	1	5	2	#	#	#	4	43	~[c]	~[c]
	1982[b]	142	65	27	13	2	3	3	#	1	#	5	21	~[c]	~[c]
	1983[b]	107	49	16	13	3	4	1	#	1	#	4	15	#	14
	1984[d]	144	78	17	19	1	2	~[c]	#	1	#	~[c]	25	#	5
E. COLOMBIA	1981[a]	345	3	235	61	10	32	3	~[c]	1	5	~[c]	40	1	6
	1982[b]	529	2	430	64	13	31	~[c]	#	2	~[c]	9	28	1	5
	1983[b]	602	1	492	73	21	28	3	#	1	~[c]	~[c]	25	~[c]	~[c]
	1984[d]	376	1	254	90	24	43	3	#	4	~[c]	~[c]	25	1	5
I. ECUADOR	1981[a]	62	#	25	21	3	5	1	#	2	#	9	17	#	#
	1982[b]	46	#	22	14	3	5	1	#	2	#	3	10	#	#
	1983[b]	48	#	29	11	2	3	#	#	2	#	3	8	#	#
	1984[d]	57	#	36	14	2	8	#	#	1	#	3	4	2	1
N. MEXICO	1981[a]	1,198	3	12	913	123	100	50	24	103	379	135	212	3	55
	1982[b]	933	2	10	745	56	91	33	20	73	328	144	140	2	34
	1983[b]	775	1	4	619	78	92	21	14	67	243	104	112	1	39
	1984[d]	690	#	#	544	52	100	18	7	68	248	51	120	#	23
P. PANAMA	1981[a]	74	#	3	9	2	2	#	#	#	#	1	7	22	37
	1982[b]	43	#	2	4	2	2	#	#	#	#	1	4	18	15
	1983[b]	32	#	2	5	2	2	#	#	#	#	1	6	15	4
	1984[d]	36	#	6	3	1	1	#	#	#	#	1	10	3	14
R. PERU	1981[a]	455	~[c]	345	9	2	2	3	#	1	#	2	~[c]	~[c]	~[c]
	1982[b]	419	32	340	15	2	7	3	#	1	#	4	30	~[c]	~[c]
	1983[b]	361	11	#	11	4	3	1	#	1	#	2	~[c]	2	2
	1984[d]	260	~[c]	191	10	2	2	2	#	1	#	3	25	#	2
T. VENEZUELA	1981[a]	377	#	66	197	42	58	7	~[c]	9	#	28	93	1	20
	1982[b]	420	#	60	225	41	55	4	7	4	~[c]	~[c]	118	#	17
	1983[b]	380	#	37	188	57	50	5	~[c]	5	~[c]	18	145	#	10
	1984[d]	247	#	24	170	58	37	4	6	2	~[c]	~[c]	42	#	12
LATIN AMERICA	1981[a]	5,072	13	936	3,077	348	531	154	416	180	669	367	644	27	127
	1982[b]	4,691	106	1,115	1,760	154	498	298	339	134	663	364	538	46	108
	1983[b]	4,692	66	704	2,839	347	516	39	276	163	617	132	501	27	105
	1984[d]	4,176	171	956	2,359	269	445	289	337	149	498	372	477	38	176

1. Capital expenditure estimates are for majority-owned nonbank foreign affiliates of nonbank U.S. parents. (An affiliate is majority owned when the combined ownership of all U.S. parents exceeds 50%.) Capital expenditures are those that are made to acquire, add to, or improve property, plant, and equipment, and that are charged to capital accounts. They are on a gross basis; sales and other dispositions of fixed assets are not netted against them. Capital expenditures are in current dollars; they are not adjusted for price changes in host countries or for changes in the value of foreign currencies because the data needed for these adjustments are unavailable.

2. Excludes banking, insurance, and real estate.

a. Based on survey taken in June 1982.

b. Based on survey taken in December 1982.

c. Data suppressed (by source) to avoid disclosure of individual companies.

d. Based on survey taken in December 1983.

SOURCE: USDC-SCB, 63:3 (March 1983); USDC-SCB, 64:3 (March 1984).

Table 2909

GROSS PRODUCT OF U.S. MAJORITY-OWNED FOREIGN AFFILIATES, 1 9 LR

(M US, 1977)

Country	All Industries	Mining	Petroleum	Manufacturing								Trade	Finance	Other Industries
				Total	Food and Kindred Products	Chemicals and Allied Products	Primary and Fabricated Metals	Machinery Except Electrical	Electric and Electronic Equipment	Transportation Equipment	Other Manufacturing			
A. ARGENTINA	1,449	~2	306	945	73	213	35	145	46	179	254	143	3	~2
B. BRAZIL	6,485	12	736	5,169	450	1,003	231	657	535	901	1,392	311	26	231
C. CHILE	162	#	~2	62	6	21	~2	~2	~2	~2	~2	30	6	13
E. COLOMBIA	532	-4	113	320	39	91	~2	1	18	#	~2	84	#	~2
I. ECUADOR	307	#	~2	35	9	10	4	#	5	#	6	~2	#	82
N. MEXICO	2,050	2	21	1,646	232	378	115	79	211	261	369	293	7	75~2
P. PANAMA	289	#~2	89	26	~2	9	#~2	#	13	#~2	~2	73	27	214
R. PERU	404	~2	114	74	14	14	~2	1	13	115	212	49	#	615
T. VENEZUELA	1,370	#	97	745	168	165	36	5	45	115	212	304	10	
LATIN AMERICA	13,048	10	1,476	9,022	1,091	1,904	421	888	873	1,456	2,233	1,287	79	

1. Majority-owned foreign affiliates are those that are owned more than 50% by all U.S. parents combined and that had assets, sales, or net income of more than $3 million in 1977.

2. Data suppressed (by source) to avoid disclosure of individual companies.

SOURCE: USDC-SCB, 63:2 (Feb. 1983), p. 26.

Table 2910

GROSS PRODUCT OF U.S. MAJORITY—OWNED FOREIGN AFFILIATES IN LATIN AMERICA[1]
(M US)

Category	1977
All Industries	16,036
Mining	579
Metal Mining	569
Iron	3
Copper, Lead, Zinc, Gold, and Silver	250
Bauxite, Other Ores, and Services	317
Coal and Other Nonmetallic Minerals	10
Petroleum	3,072
Oil and Gas Extraction	1,194
Crude Petroleum (No Refining) and Gas	1,033
Oil and Gas Field Services	161
Petroleum and Coal Products	~a
Integrated Refining and Extraction	~a
Refining Without Extraction, nie	~a
Petroleum Wholesale Trade	1,149
Other	~
Manufacturing	9,533
Food and Kindred Products	1,156
Grain Mill and Bakery Products	194
Beverages	291
Other	671
Chemicals and Allied Products	1,981
Industrial Chemicals and Synthetics	697
Drugs	511
Soap, Cleaners, and Toilet Goods	457
Agricultural Chemicals	185
Other	130
Primary and Fabricated Metals	587
Primary Metal Industries	278
Ferrous	~a
Nonferrous	~a
Fabricated Metal Products	309
Machinery, Except Electrical	889
Farm and Garden Machinery and Equipment	95
Construction and Related Machinery	254
Office and Computing Machines	~a
Other	~a
Electric and Electronic Equipment	920
Household Appliances	89
Radio, Television, and Communication Equipment	330
Electronic Components and Accessories	151
Other	350
Transportation Equipment	1,506
Motor Vehicles and Equipment	~a
Other	~a
Other Manufacturing	2,494
Tobacco Manufacturers	~a
Textile Products and Apparel	178
Lumber, Wood, Furniture, and Fixtures	19
Paper and Allied Products	476
Printing and Publishing	32
Rubber Products	646
Miscellaneous Plastics	87
Glass Products	114
Stone, Clay, Cement, and Concrete	~a
Instruments and Related Products	~a
Other	~a

Table 2910 (Continued)

GROSS PRODUCT OF U.S.. MAJORITY-OWNED
FOREIGN AFFILIATES IN LATIN AMERICA[1]
(M US)

Category	1977
Trade	1,495
Wholesale Trade	1,195
Durable Goods	867
Nondurable Goods	328
Retail Trade	300
Finance (Except Banking), Insurance and Real Estate	348
Finance, Except Banking	70
Insurance	248
Real Estate	1
Holding Companies	29
Individuals, Estates, and Trusts	#
Other Industries	1,009
Agriculture, Forestry, and Fishing	259
Construction	225
Transportation, Communication and Public Utilities	64
Transportation	22
Communication and Public Utilities	42
Services	461

1. Majority-owned foreign affiliates are those that are owned more than 50% by all
U.S. parents combined and that had assets, sales, or net income of more than
$3 million in 1977.

a. Data suppressed (by source) to avoid disclosure of individual companies.

SOURCE: USDC–SCB, 63:2 (Feb. 1983), p. 27.

Table 2911

ARGENTINA CORPORATE BUSINESS ACTIVITY[1]

(1982, except asterisk indicates 1983)

Sales Rank	Company	Type of Business	M US Sales/ Turnover 1982	1982 Profit or Loss	1982 Employees	M US 1982 Net Assets	Transnational Parent
1	YPF — Yacimentos Petroliferos Fiscales	Petroleum	2,420.7*	7,577.1	31,353	5,357.0	**
2	ENTEL — Emip Nac de Telecomunicaciones	Communications	809.0	−507.3	45,441	10,108.0	**
3	Massalin-Particulares	Tobacco	787.0	29.6	1,800	357.7	Phil mon US
4	Dalmine Siderca	Steel	734.0	124.7	4,925	1,366.3	**
5	Esso SA Petrolera	Petroleum	706.8*	~	2,054	~	Exxon
6	Gas del Estado	Gas	681.4*	~	9,749	5,412.5	**
7	Nidera Argentina	Cereals export	677.4	10.5	130	95.1	**
8	Cargill	Foods	628.0	10.2	799	218.0	US owned
9	Shell Cia Argentina de Petroleo	Petroleum	615.0*	2.8	2,000	340.0	UK-Netherlands
10	Molinos Rio de Plata	Foods	614.4	23.2	3,794	340.6	sub of Bunge y Born
11	Acindar Ind Argentina de Aceros	Steel	528.3*	560.5	7,703	2,574.0	**
12	Segba — Servicios Electricos del Gran Buenos Aires	Electricity	525.8*	464.3	20,301	5,290.0	**
13	Aerolineas Argentinas	Airline	520.3	235.3	9,835	1,308.0	**
14	Renault Argentina	Cars	511.1	43.3	5,476	744.0	France
15	IBM	Information	480.5	80.0	2,319	488.6	US
16	Nobleza-Piccardo	Tobacco	457.8*	24.0	3,164	599.0	sub of Seita (France)
17	Soc Mixta Siderurgica Argentina	Steel	457.6*	30.4	10,847	2,963.4	**
18	Agua y Energia Electrica	Electricity	449.2*	65.3	10,947	10,093.2	**
19	Ford Motor Argentina	Cars	403.2*	~	7,249	835.0	US
20	Mastellone	Foods	365.4	18.0	3,341	176.7	**
21	Aluar Aluminio Argentino	Foods	357.3	34.0	1,234	827.0	**
22	Alpargatas	Textiles	335.4	62.7	~	817.1	**
23	Pirelli	Rubber	334.0	34.3	3,080	348.3	**
24	Sevel Argentina	Cars	325.2	54.3	4,111	555.2	**
25	Equitel	Telecom eqt	315.7	6.2	~	319.0	**
26	Propulsora Siderurgica	Steel	308.4	−19.9	1,453	744.2	sub of Dalmine
27	Techint — Cia Tecnica Intl.	Civil eng.	274.4	−2.0	4,800	239.5	**
28	Emp Lineas Maritimas Argentinas	Shipping	271.0	363.0	5,184	1,807.3	**
29	Alinsa	Food	254.1	24.7	1,152	120.0	**
30	Astra-Cia Argentina de Petroleo	Petroleum	237.4	7.0	250	230.3	**
31	Ducilo	Textiles	232.0	32.2	2,640	205.0	sub of Du Pont (US)
32	Duperial	Chemicals	228.1	12.5	1,692	115.0	sub of ICI (UK)
33	Loma Negra Cia Industrial Argentina	Cement	223.3	25.0	2,767	420.1	**
34	Ferrocarriles Argentinos	Railway	219.2	~	96,095	6,902	**
35	Deba	Electricity	205.0	4.0	1,281	255.6	**
36	Cia Naviera Perez Companc	Forest prod/ship	202.4	19.6	1,560	500.7	**
37	Ledesma — Soc Anon Agricola Industrial	Sugar	196.3	25.7	~	509.7	**
38	Mercedes Benz	Cars	194.0	−93.0	1,929	~	**
39	Obras Sanitarias de la Nacion	Services	181.3	235.0	9,453	4,499.4	**
40	Rio Colorado	Petroleum	179.0	215.0	1,507	240.5	**
41	Alba	Paint	171.4	9.6	1,500	172.2	Sub of Bunge y Born
42	Celulosa Argentina	Paper	158.7	−54.0	5,400	1,777.5	**
43	Lever	Chemicals	157.4	−6.3	1,450	103.2	UK-Netherlands
44	Compania Quimica	Chemicals	155.7	9.2	1,101	114.1	Sub of Bunge y Born
45	Emp Nac de Correos y Telegrafos	Postal service	154.4	−27.4	42,969	338.1	**
46	Bridas Sapic	Petroleum	151.7	17.3	391	702.0	**
47	Volkswagen Argentina	Cars	147.5	117.0	3,149	229.5	**
48	Minetti y Cia	Flour prod	147.0	12.4	1,150	98.0	**
49	Estab. Modelo Terrabusi	Flour prod	144.6	1.6	4,800	172.5	**
50	Arcor	Food & agric	137.0	19.7	1,695	125.7	**

Table 2911 (Continued)

ARGENTINA CORPORATE BUSINESS ACTIVITY[1]

(1982, except asterisk indicates 1983)

| | | | M US | | | M US | |
| | | | Sales/ | 1982 | | | |
Sales Rank	Company	Type of Business	Turnover 1982	Profit or Loss	1982 Employees	1982 Net Assets	Transnational Parent
51	Ciba Geigy	Pharmaceuticals	131.2	11.0	1,200	152.0	Switzerland
52	Bagley SA	Preserves	130	2	3,500	198.4	**
53	Corp Cementera Arg Corcemar	Cement	128.1	−2.4	1,411	240.2	**
54	Bayer Argentina SA	Chemical/pharmac	124	16	1,059	104.6	FRG
55	Canale SA	Food	118.3	4	~	79	**
56	Soc Anon Molinos Felix	Flour prods	110	4.6	631	51	**
57	Soc Anon Azucarera Argentina	Sugar	107.2	−13.3	400	141.4	**
58	Grupo Massuh	Paper	105.7	6	1,770	279.7	**
59	Benito Roggio e Hijos	Construction	104.7	2	1,021	86	**
60	Administracion General de Puertos	Port authority	104.1	−8.0	4,967	2,244	**
61	Laboratorios Bago SA	Pharmaceut.	103.2	2.3	1,025	~	**
62	Desaci — Ingeniería y Obras Industrias	Civil eng	99.1	3.6	3,094	39.3	**
63	Calera Avellaneda	Cement	94.1	11.0	1,068	149.4	**
64	Dragados y Construcciones Arg — Dycasa	Civil eng	93.5	~	140	~	**
65	Productos Roche	Pharmaceut	91.7	~	847	~	Switzerland
66	Atanor — Cia Nac para la Industria Quimica Soc Anon Mixta	Chemicals	90.6	~	1,000	~	**
67	Astilleros Alianza	Shipyard	90.3	~	300	~	**
68	Hierromat	Build mat	90.2	~	~	~	**
69	Hidroelectrica Norpatagonica — Hidronor	Electricity	90.1	~	~	~	**
70	Papel Prensa	Newsprint	87.3	~	~	~	**
71	Tabacal	Cigarettes	83.0	~	~	~	**
72	Kodak Argentina	Photographic eqt	80.6	~	579	~	US
73	Noel y Cia	Confectionery	78	~	1,600	~	**
74	Cia Argentina de Telefonos	Communications	76	~	~	~	**
75	Juan Minetti y Cia	Cement	76	~	1,500	~	**

1. It is almost certain that the Bunge y Born group is, in terms of sales, the largest company in Argentina. The aggregate sales figure of its manufacturing subsidiaries, which employ 20,000, is US$1 billion. Its grain trading operations, though not disclosed, eclipse this. For example, Nidera accounts for half the country's exports of cereals. Bunge apart, Argentina plays host to a number of foreign concerns, mainly in automobiles, chemicals, and petroleum products.

SOURCE: *South*, Jan. 1985, pp. 64–65.

Table 2912

BOLIVIA CORPORATE BUSINESS ACTIVITY[1]

(1982)

| | | | M US |
Sales Rank	Company	Type of Business	Sales/ Turnover
1	YPFB — Yacimentos Petroliferos Fiscales Bolivianos	Petrol sales	380 [a]
2	Comibol — Corporacion Minera de Bolivia	Mining	350 [a]
3	Nacional de Fundiciones[b]	Metals	139.7
4	Lloyd Aerro Boliviano	Airline	37.4[b]
5	Emp. Constructora Bartos y Cia	Construction	35.7[b]
6	Ferrocarriles Bolivianos	Railway	34.9
7	Soc. Comercial e Industrial	Retail	31.6
8	Cerveceria Boliviana Nacional	Brewery	28.7[a]
9	Toyota de Bolivia	Autos and parts	28.5
10	Grupo Comsur — Co. Minera del Sur	Mining	25

1. The list has to be read with a degree of care as much of the information is dated or estimated. Two large groups, Corporación Boliviana de Fomento and Grupo INBO, control 70 companies operating across the economy and including cement, glass, vegetable oils, sugar, and commerce. It is certain that the sales of these groups are as high if not higher than most of the companies listed but as no details are available it has not been possible to include them.

a. Another source gives turnover in M US for YPFB as 257.9, Comibol 203.8, CBN 14.7.
b. 1977 figures.

SOURCE: *South*, Jan. 1985, p. 65.

Table 2913

BRAZIL CORPORATE BUSINESS ACTIVITY[1]
(1982)

Sales Rank	Company	Type of Business	Sales (M US)	Profit or Loss (M US)	Employees 1982	Net Assets (M US)	Transnational Parent
1	Petrobras	Petroleum	8,810	318.98	50,213	4,310	**
2	Petrobras Distribuidora	Petroleum distrib	2,570	40.63	3,907	344.98	**
3	Shell Brasil	Petroleum distrib	1,660	−17.65	3,100	304.91	UK/Netherlands
4	Copersucar	Sugar & alcohol	1,480	0.01	3,000	60.08	**
5	Souza Cruz	Drinks & tobacco	1,340	68.64	16,500	95.66	sub of BAT UK
6	Esso Brasileira de Petroleo	Petroleum distrib	1,300	35.79	1,524	167.54	US
7	Volkswagen do Brasil	Automobiles	966.12	−6.85	35,543	264.52	FRG
8	Cia Vale do Rio Doce	Iron mining	858.91	199.85	19,950	1,910	**
9	General Motors do Brasil	Automobiles	833	−9.2	19,004	160.49	US
10	Pao de Acucar	Supermarkets	823.94	12.2	30,500	160.56	**
11	Texaco Brasil	Petroleum distrib	806.23	16.19	1,637	96.42	US
12	Cia Atlantic de Petroleo	Petroleum distrib	796.41	22.33	1,424	73.01	US
13	Ford Brasil	Automobiles	775.85	−16.77	21,300	102.51	US
14	Eletropaulo	Electricity	651.16	110.5	19,104	383.82	**
15	Casas de Banha	Supermarkets	624.89	12.77	17,664	91.44	**
16	Embratel	Telecom	620.17	138.29	10,216	763.88	**
17	Petroleo Ipiranga	Petroleum distrib	607.05	16.01	1,272	86.39	**
18	Usiminas-Usinas Siderurgicas de Minas Gerais	Steel	563.51	−85.37	15,127	734.14	**
19	Cosipa — Cia Siderurgica Paulista	Steel	547.02	−82.36	14,373	1,170	**
20	Varig	Airline	535.85	8.69	16,799	180.67	**
21	Cobal — Companhia Brasileira de Alimentos	Food Sales	530.42	−1.48	11,907	105.82	**
22	Interbras — Petrobras Comercio Intl.	Wholesale com	525.13	67	1,177	113.42	Sub Petrobras
23	Cia Siderurgica Nac. (CSN)	Steel	520.6	−119.76	22,512	1,690	**
24	RFFSA — Rede Ferroviaria	Railways	479.12	~	84,632	5,950	**
25	Cia Ind. Brasileira Pirelli	Plastics & rubber	479.1	24.12	12,710	250.23	Italy
26	Cia Ind e Com Bras. de Prod. Alimentos Nestle	Food	470.62	45.24	8,876	197.73	Switzerland
27	CESP — Cia Energetica de Sao Paulo	Electricity	447.78	23.87	15,284	2,440	**
28	Copene — Petroquimica do Nordeste	Chemicals & Petrochem	424.73	28.62	1,618	364.84	**
29	Fiat Automoveis	Automobiles	420.78	−49.04	13,000	108.18	Italy
30	Gpo Camargo Correa	Heavy construction	416.14	87.62	21,934	374.02	**
31	Sanbra — Soc Algodoeira do Nordeste Brasileiro	Vegetable oils	399.61	30.21	5,000	119.12	Inv Indus (Panama)
32	Grupo Sadia Concordia	Food processing	380.30	20.5	13,949	~	**
33	Agricola de Cotia	Foods & agroprocurement	369.42	2.9	7,120	31.7	**
34	IBM do Brasil	Information/ computers	365.85	~	~	~	US
35	Rhodia	Petrochemicals	358.48	15.97	10,057	144.19	Rhone Poulenc, France
36	Brastemp	Electrical appliances	354.22	29.49	6,000	144.93	**
37	Construtora Andrade Gutierrez	Construction	338.91	37.69	24,430	250.36	**
38	TELESP — Telecomunicacoes de Sao Paulo	Telecom	338.84	−10.77	24,663	1,380	Sub of. Telebras
39	Mercedes-Benz	Automobiles	327.36	23.16	14,500	421.79	FRG
40	Carrefour	Supermarkets	318.94	~	~	~	**
41	Mesbla	Retail commerce	311.5	3.5	22,276	87.1	**
42	Petroquimica Uniao	Chemicals & Petrochem	301.17	33.81	1,292	106.66	**
43	Light - Servicos de Electricidade	Electricity	297.66	121.1	14,820	937.2	Sub of Brascan (Canada)
44	Goodyear do Brasil	Plastics & rubber	293.27	2.79	5,386	69.62	US
45	Lojas Arapua	Retail commerce	291.64	10.22	4,007	59.38	**
46	Ind Gessy Lever	Detergents	286.08	5.05	5,806	85.6	UK/Netherlands
47	Mendes Junior	Heavy construction	283.77	38.53	20,515	386.64	**
48	Furnas Centrais Eletricas	Power plant	282.28	30.32	9,000	982.81	Sub Eletrobras
49	Fabrica de Tecidos Tatuape	Textiles	278.54	25.18	5,471	169.6	**
50	Ind Textil Cia Hering	Cotton textiles	278	23.4	9,241	~	**
51	Cemig — Centrais Eletricas de Minas Gerais	Power plant	261.54	56.48	12,020	804.22	**
52	Norberto Odebrecht	Heavy construction	246.08	13.48	16,621	118.43	**
53	Sendas	Supermarkets	236.44	6.41	15,797	57.86	**
54	Correios e Telegrafos	Postal service	235.44	0.56	66,785	183.75	**
55	Cervejaria Brahma Cia.	Drinks & tobacco	234.13	12.2	9,000	182.27	**
56	Disco — Distribuidora de Comestiveis	Supermarkets	231.03	4.24	11,000	12.44	**
57	Philips do Brasil	Electronics	225.49	~	1,000	~	Netherlands
58	Cia Uniao dos Refinadores Acucar e Cafe	Coffee/sugar	221.1	13.62	5,266	62.75	Sub Copersucar
59	Philco Radio e Televisao	Electronics	215.24	~	9,535	~	US
60	Copesul	Chemicals & petrochem	214.43	−18.26	~	363.1	**

Table 2913 (Continued)

BRAZIL CORPORATE BUSINESS ACTIVITY[1]

(1982)

Sales Rank	Company	Type of Business	M US Sales	Profit or Loss	Employees 1982	M US Net Assets	Transnational Parent
61	Makro Atacadista	Wholesale commerce	214.36	3.38	2,373	16.59	**
62	Anderson Clayton	Detergents/veg oils	212.85	19.67	3,233	51.78	US
63	Chesf — Cia Hidro Eletrica do Sao Francisco	Hydro-electricity	202.13	87.65	11,449	873.42	**
64	Cargill Agricola	Animal feeds	198.64	60.47	3,000	117.25	US
65	Dist. Petroleo Ipiranga	Petroleum distrib	197.94	7.91	357	50.91	**
66	Alcan Aluminio	Aluminum	194.4	7.13	5,500	103.93	Canada
67	Sao Paulo Alpargatas Gp	Industrial textiles	193.77	14.35	17,510	184.03	**
68	Bompreco SA	Supermarkets	192.45	4.7	9,106	23.76	**
69	Acesita — Cia Acos Especiais Itabira	Steel	188.7	63.84	7,995	412.88	**
70	Hermes Macedo	Retail commerce	188.33	1.61	9,706	80.45	**
71	A Lundgren-Casas Pernambucanas	Retail commerce	188.09	2.23	14,409	118.46	**
72	Ind Pneumaticos Firestone	Plastics & rubber	187.44	39.46	13,000	71.44	US
73	Paes Mendonca	Commerce	186.84	4.48	10,000	41.05	**
74	Dow Quimica	Chemicals & petrochem	186.59	22.83	1,422	115.68	US
75	Verolme Estaleiros Reunidos do Brasil	Shipbuilding	184.03	12.02	7,056	111.06	Netherlands
76	Bordon	Food	173.96	6.44	4,796	28.99	**
77	Cia Siderurgica Belgo-Mineira	Steel	172.77	25.24	8,219	236.46	Sub of Arbed (Lux)
78	Bayer do Brasil	Chemicals & petrochem	171.02	2.99	3,728	69.4	FRG
79	White Martins	Chemicals & petrochem	169.03	24.22	8,169	152.7	US
80	Frigobras	Abattoir/coldstores	168.79	10.25	3,000	42.98	Sub Sadia
81	Ceval Agro Industrial	Cotton	165.91	15.2	1,181	53.12	Sub Hering
82	Vasp — Viacao Aerea Sao Paulo	Airline	164.92	−39.44	9,144	36.07	**
83	Estadual de Energ. Eletrica	Electricity	164.07	−7.95	11,349	396.84	**
84	Paulista de Forca e Luz (CPFL)	Electric supply	163.79	31.45	6,800	179.29	Sub CESP
85	Costigua — Cia Sid. da Guanabara	Steel	163.77	10.34	2,777	102.98	Sub Thyssen, FRG
86	Cotrijui — Cooperative Regional Triticola Serrana	Agroprocurement	163.37	−14.79	2,335	122.22	**
87	Supermercados Eldorado	Supermarkets	162.04	8.81	3,800	45.14	**
88	Sabesp — Cia Saneamento Basico do Estado de Sao Paulo	Water/sewerage	161.06	41.98	21,000	879.69	**
89	Cia de Navegacao Lloyd Brasileiro	Maritime transport	160.35	−73.12	2,659	17.05	**
90	CBA — Cia Brasileira de Aluminio	Aluminum	157.98	23.85	5,000	211.88	**
91	Xerox do Brasil	Information technology	157.27	18.59	4,048	106.33	US
92	Perdigao Alimentos	Cattle	156.84	2.63	978	30.45	**
93	Mannesmann SA	Mechanical engineering	155.62	−10.56	10,825	141.41	FRG
94	Johnson & Johnson	Pharmaceuticals	154.54	13.26	6,349	69.79	US
95	Philip Morris Brasileira	Tobacco	152.1	1.68	1,435	14.17	US
96	Lojas Americanas	Retail commerce	151.18	9.5	12,427	93.4	US
97	Jose Alves/C. Alo Brasil	Wholesale commerce	150.58	1.96	4,850	22.46	**
98	Antarctica Paulista	Drinks	149.95	33.87	4,488	147.75	**
99	Docegeo	Mining	148.75	2.49	~	2.22	**
100	Philip Morris Marketing	Wholesale commerce	148.3	−15.48	~	−14.33	US

1. The powerhouse of the Latin American economy, Brazil now has companies exporting to all parts of the world. Firms have established themselves in a way apparently beyond their obvious means. Copersucar is pioneering the economic extraction of fuel-alcohol from sugarcane; Embraer aircraft are being bought by air forces in Western Europe; local computer companies are, uniquely, challenging the power and influence of IBM. Overseas penetration of the economy is high, noticeable in automobiles, petroleum and chemicals, in parts of the steel industry, and in electronics.

SOURCE: *South*, Jan, 1985, pp. 66–67.

Table 2914

CHILE CORPORATE BUSINESS ACTIVITY[1]

(1981, except some later data are included)

Sales Rank	Company	Type of Business	M US Sales/ Turnover	Profit or Loss	Employees	M US Net Assets	Transnational Parent
1	Codelco Corp. Nac. de Cobres de Chile	Copper mining	1,774.1	~	30,000	500	**
2	ENAP Emp. de Petroleos	Petrol	1,268	35.5	4,200	1,287	**
3	Copec — Compania de Petroleos de Chile	Petroleum prod.	904.9	−70	500	215.7	**
4	ENAMI — Emp. Nac. de Minera	Copper mining	328	3.7	2,300	292.4	**
5	CAP — Comp. de Acero del Pacifico	Steel	311.8	64.6	10,000	1,309.5	**
6	Endesa — Emp. Nac. de Electricidad	Hydroelectricity	309.4	106	4,000	1,670	**
7	Esso Chile Petrolera	Petroleum prod	270.8†	10.2	365	~	US
8	Chilectra — Cia Chilena de Electricidad	Electricity	247.8	24.2	4,100	510.8	**
9	Cia de Manuf Papeles y Cartones	Packaging	233.1	18.5	4,000	575	**
10	Shell Chile	Petroleum prod	225 †	5.6	498	~	UK/Netherlands
11	Cia Industria Indus	Veg oil	215.1	~	412	576.2	Unilever UK/Netherlands
12	Cia de Refineria de Azucar de Vina del Mar	Sugar	202.9	~	629	~	**
13	Soc. El Tattersal	Farm produce	173 †	~	350	~	**
14	Sudamericana Vapores	Shipping	164.2	~	1,000	148.1	**
15	CTC — Cia de Telefonos de Chile	Telephone service	151.2	41.6	6,000	347.5	**
16	Cia Cervecerias Unidas	Beer & soft drinks	128	43	2,000	439.5	**
17	Soquimich — Soc Quimica y Minera de Chile	Nitrates	117	−22.8	6,271	95	**
18	IANSA — Ind. Azuc. Nac. SA	Refined sugar	117	~	349	~	**
19	Indus Lever	Household prod	110.1	~	1,300	~	Unilever UK/Netherlands
20	Chiprodal — Cia Chilena de Productos Alimenticios	Food	105.5	~	1,000	55.6	**
21	General Motors Chile	Motors	103.9	~	653	~	US
22	Emp. Nac. de Comercializacion y Distribuidores	Commerce	101	~	600	~	**
23	Emp. El Mercurio	Publishing	100.7	9.3	1,125	~	**
24	Linea Aerea Nacional	Airline	98.3	~	2,600	~	**
25	Celulosa Arauco y Constitcucine	Cellulose	90.7	0.2	1,106	583.4	**
26	Tabacos — Cia Chilena de Tabacos	Cigarettes	86	7.6	1,200	78.5	BAT (UK)
27	Comp. Chilena de Navegacion Interoceanica	Shipping	84.9	8.7	434	114.2	**
28	Gasco — Cia de Consumidores de Gas de Santiago	Gas	81.5	2.9	1,000	158.3	**
29	Supermercados Almac	Supermarket	79.7	~	620	~	**
30	Cia Tecno Ind	Dom elec appl.	77.1	~	1,200	~	**
31	S.A. Manuf de Cauchos, Tejidos y Cueros	Footwear	73.9	~	1,893	~	**
32	Embotellada Andina	Soft drinks	68.4	3.5	1,000	57.2	**
33	Emp. Minera de Mantos Blancos	Copper mining	68.1	~	2,248	~	**
34	S.A. de Navegacion Petrolera	Shipping	67.7	~	254	~	**
35	Pesquera Colosa	Fish products	66.2	~	1,319	~	**
36	Pesquera Indo-Eperra	Fish products	65.5	~	1,373	~	**
37	Astilleros y Maestranza de la Armada	Shipyard	63.4	~	3,750	~	**
38	Manufacturas de Cobre	Copper products	61.3	4.2	1,500	~	**
39	Peugeot Chile	Motors	60.3	~	104	~	**
40	Emp. Constructorora Delta	Construction	59.6	~	680	~	**
41	Philips Chilena	Radio/television	56.4	~	575	~	Netherlands
42	Molinos y Fideos Lucchetti	Noodles	56.2	~	475	~	**
43	Fiat Chile	Agri. mchy	56.2	~	824	~	Italy
44	Pesquera Guanaye	Fish products	54.8	~	1,200	~	**
45	Molibdenos y Metales	Metal products	53.5	~	165	~	**
46	Petroquimica Dow	Chemicals	51.9	~	300	~	US
47	Salinas y Fabres	Agri. mchy	50.6	~	279	~	**
48	Cemento Cerro Blanco de Polpaico	Cement	50.2	~	512	~	**
49	Cia Frutera Bud Americana	Dried fruit	49	~	1,223	~	US
50	Manufacturas Sumar	Textiles	48.9	~	3,186	~	**

Table 2914 (Continued)

CHILE CORPORATE BUSINESS ACTIVITY[1]

(1981, except some later data are included)

Sales Rank	Company	Type of Business	M US Sales/ Turnover	Profit or Loss	Employees	M US Net Assets	Transnational Parent
51	Bata SA	Shoes	48.6	~	643	~	Canada
52	Cristalerias de Chile	Glassware	46.4	~	927	~	**
53	Gas Licuado — Lipigas	Dom. appl.	46.2	~	228	~	**
54	Television Nac. de Chile	TV services	45.3	~	521	~	**
55	Soc. Agricola y Forestal Colcura	Forest products	44.2	~	354	~	**
56	Ind. Chilenas de Alambre	Metal products	43.2	~	444	~	Belgium
57	Cia General de Electricidad Ind.	Power eqt	43.1	~	700	~	**
58	Enacar — Emp. Nac. del Carbon	Coal	42.6	−7.0	7,699	112	**
59	Inds. de Radio y Television	Elect prods	42.2	~	1,000	~	**
60	Fideos y Alimentos Carozzi	Pasta products	41.8	~	493	~	**
61	Cia. Electrometalurgica	Heavy eng	41.3	~	260	~	**
62	Pesquera Iquique	Fish products	40.5	~	1,383	~	**
63	Industrias Forestales	Forest prods	39.6	~	998	~	**
64	Gildemeister SA	Commerce	39.2	~	582	~	**
65	Ladeco	Milk prods	37.8	~	~	~	**
66	Cantolla y Cia	Engineering	32	~	140	~	**
67	Cemento Cerro Blanco de Polpaico	Cement	30.2	~	512	~	**
68	Vina Concha y Toro	Wine	29.8	~	750	~	**
69	McKay	Confectionery	28.6	~	699	~	**
70	Fab. de Cemento el Melon	Cement	28.6	~	1,050	~	**

1. The level of affiliations to overseas interests portrayed in this list suggests that the level of national ownership is substantially higher than in most other Latin American states. At the same time the proportion of corporate activity linked to extractive and other primary industries is considerable. In turnover terms, 20 percent of the activities listed are in the corporate sector, employing 36,000 people. This is out of a total of primary sector output of around US$3.5-billion.

SOURCE: *South*, Jan. 1985, pp. 69–70.

Table 2915

COLOMBIA CORPORATE BUSINESS ACTIVITY[1]
(1982)

Sales Rank	Company	Type of Business	M US Sales/ Turnover	Profit	Employees	M US Net Assets	Transnational Parent
1	Ecopetrol — Emp Colombiana de Petroleos	Petroleum	1,632.7	~	8,057	1,429	**
2	Federacafe	Coffee exports	1,577	~	3,704	2,802	**
3	Esso Colombiana	Petrol	643.2	.7	1,440	111.9	US
4	Codi-Mobil	Petroleum	410.7	12.2	399	64.5	US
5	Avianca — Aerovias Nac de Colombia	Airline	409.9	~	7,992	425.6	**
6	Texaco — Colombia	Petroleum	349.6	11	694	96.5	US
7	Telecom	Telephone service	316.4	44.2	14,977	484.1	**
8	Bavaria	Brewery	292.2	25.3	4,616	409.6	**
9	Cadenalco — Gran Cadena de Almacenes Colombianos	Supermarkets	288.1	3.8	8,000	115.2	**
10	FMG — Flota Mercante	Shipping	260.9	2.9	2,270	351	**
11	Rafael Espinosa Hnos	Coffee exports	208	~	~	~	**
12	Exito	Commerce	206.9	1.3	2,936	34.1	**
13	Grupo Gonchy	Coffee exports	193.3	~	134	~	**
14	Colpuertos	Port services	192.6	100.1	10,895	~	**
15	Colmotores	Car assembly	183.5	176.9	1,600	~	US, General Motors
16	Carton de Colombia	Packaging	183.5	~	2,340	146	**
17	Coltejez	Textiles	182.3	~	8,193	369.8	**
18	Energia — Bogota	Electricity	173.5	56.6	3,196	789.5	**
19	Idema	Agri products	171	~	3,222	208.6	**
20	Carrajal SA	Office equipment	151.4	15.1	3,782	136.6	**
21	Cerveceria Aguila	Beer	135.8	4.4	834	74.7	**
22	Nacional de Chocolates	Confectionery	135.6	8.3	335	6.9	**
23	Uniban	Banana exports	129.8	.6	645	37	**
24	Fabricato — Fab de Hilados y Tejidos del Hato	Textiles	121.8	~	7,131	173.4	**
25	Industrias Alimenticias Noel	Food	121.3	6.1	2,527	53.8	**
26	Sefasa — Renault	Autos	115	~	2,199	125.4	France
27	Cacharreria — Mandial	Commerce	110.4	1.6	572	34.4	**
28	Carulla	Supermarkets	104.5	.5	2,639	23.9	**
29	Peldar	Textiles	77.9	~	~	~	**
30	Cafetera Mziz	Coffee	77.7	~	~	~	**
31	Cementos Argos	Cement	76.2	~	~	~	**
32	Intl Petroleum Colombia	Petr exploration	73.4	~	700	~	**
33	Acerias Paz del Rio	Steel	65.5	~	7,048	347.2	**
34	Coltabaco — Cia Colombia de Tabaco	Cigarettes	64.1	~	2,483	~	**
35	Manuelita SA	Sugar	60.1	~	2,892	~	**
36	Fabrica de Dulces Colombina	Confectionery	58.5	~	1,350	~	**
37	Fab Materiales de Colombia	Elect eqt	57.1	~	303	~	**
38	Central Castilla	Sugar	57.1	~	4,111	~	**
39	De La Rue Colombia	Security printing	56.4	~	394	~	UK
40	Ingenio Riopaila	Sugar	49.9	~	4,484	~	**
41	Distribuidora Nissan	Motors	49.1	~	340	~	Japan
42	Ing. Providencia	Sugar/cattle	48.7	~	4,257	~	**
43	Finca	Coffee	48.5	~	230	~	**
44	Fab de Cemento Samper	Cement	47.4	~	890	~	**
45	Aceitates SA	Oils	47.2	~	934	~	**
46	Eternit Colombiana	Asbestos	46.6	~	914	~	**
47	Cia Colombiana de Alimentos Lacteos	Milk Products	46	~	850	~	**
48	Cervunion	Brewing	46	~	810	~	**
49	Celanese Colombia	Synth fibres	45.4	~	1,756	~	US
50	Simesa	Steel	44.3	~	~	~	**

1. The 50 companies shown here have a combined output equivalent to approximately 30 percent of national GDP, while the coffee companies account for virtually all the exports of that commodity. Also noticeable is the enormous revenue in petroleum and petroleum products — roughly divided between three U.S. corporations and the national company. Despite the presence of some large manufacturing concerns, the companies listed do show a bias toward the agro-industrial sector and of the total output of the companies shown, agri-related operations account for 30 percent.

SOURCE: *South*, Jan. 1985, pp. 70–71.

Table 2916

COSTA RICA CORPORATE BUSINESS ACTIVITY[1]

(1982)

Sales Rank	Company	Type of Business	M US Sales/ Turnover	Profit	Employees	Net Assets	Transnational Parent
1	Standard Fruit Company	Bananas	90	~	~	~	US, Castle & Cool
2	Federacion de Cooperativos de Caficuetores	Coffee	49.4	~	40,000	~	**
3	Cia Bananera de Costa Rica	Bananas	33	~	~	~	US, United Brands
4	Ticotex	Synth fibres	13	~	~	~	**
5	Scott Paper	Paper products	12.8	~	~	~	US
6	Katiro Chemical	Paints	7.2	~	~	~	**
7	Conducen	Wire cable	6.8	~	~	~	**
8	Vidriera Centroamericana	Glassware	6.5	~	~	~	**
9	Interfashion Industries	Clothing	5.1	~	~	~	**
10	Fertica	Fertilizer	4.5	~	~	~	**

1. The two U.S.-owned banana producers account for all of Costa Rica's banana exports. This is one of the dominant sectors of the economy, which relies on agriculture, both as a direct producer and as a consumer, probably more than any other sector in the region.

SOURCE: *South*, Jan. 1985, p. 71.

Table 2917

DOMINICAN REPUBLIC CORPORATE BUSINESS ACTIVITY[1]

(1982)

Sales Rank	Company	Type of Business	M US Sales/ Turnover	Profit	Employees	Net Assets	Transnational Parent
1	Consejo Estatal de Azucar	Sugar	109.2	~	50,000	~	**
2	Cerveceria Nac Dominicana	Beer	100 †	~	900	~	**
3	Falconbridge Dominicana	Nickel	92.8	~	1,073	~	Canada
4	Soc Industrial Dominicana	Veg. oils & fats	75 †	~	700	~	**
5	Mercantil Antillana	Engineering	74.7	~	~	~	**
6	Cia Dominicana de Telefonos	Telephone serv.	51.3	~	1,902	~	**
7	Delta Comercial	Commerce	38	~	124	~	**
8	Ferreteria Americana	Commerce	35	~	285	~	**
9	Cartonera Hernandez	Cartons	32	~	177	~	**
10	Fertilizantes Quimico Dominicana	Fertilizer	27	~	138	~	**

1. The listing finally arrived at had to account for conflicting information. Seven companies, known to be substantial, provided no information at all. From what is known, however, primary sector companies dominate.

SOURCE: *South*, Jan. 1985, p. 72.

Table 2918

ECUADOR CORPORATE BUSINESS ACTIVITY[1]

(1981)

Sales Rank	Company	Type of Business	M US Sales/ Turnover	1981 Profit	1981 Employees	Net Assets	Transnational Parent
1	C.E.P.E.	Petroleum	1,528.7	124.7	3,652	~	**
2	Texaco Petroleum	Petroleum	340	~	508	~	US
3	Imp. Girola Lodigiani	Commerce	103.4	~	~	~	**
4	Comp. de Cervezas Nacional	Beer	85	~	435	~	Sub of Bavaria (Col)
5	Proveedora Ecuatoriana	Motor parts	79.5	~	65	~	**
6	Tabacalera Andina	Tobacco	71.1	~	~	~	**
7	Empresa Electrica del Ecuador	Electricity	69.9	~	620	~	US, Sub of Boise Cascade
8	Supermercados La Favorita	Supermarket	67.2	~	~	~	**
9	La Cemento Nacional	Cement	64	~	1,150	~	**
10	Emp. Electrica Quito	Electricity	57.6	~	1,000	~	**
11	Exp. Bananera Nobua	Banana exports	56.3	~	~	~	**
12	Electrodomesticos Durex	Dom elec appl	49.4	~	~	~	**
13	Fab. Aceitas La Favorita	Veg oil	48.3	~	400	~	**
14	La Universal Segale Norerv	Food	48	~	~	~	**
15	Automotores y Anexos	Auto parts	45.3	~	~	~	**
16	Cia Ecuatoriana del Caucho	Leather	43.6	~	~	~	**
17	Soc. Agricola e Ind. San Carlos	Sugar	42.5	~	4,800	~	**
18	Ind. Cartonera Ecuador	Boxes	41.5	~	~	~	**
19	Fab. de Tejidos La International	Textiles	41.4	~	2,300	~	**
20	Ind. Molinera	Flour	41	~	~	~	**

1. Ecuadorian business law has changed so that companies are no longer obliged to disclose many of the basic factors associated with analysis. The corporate sector is clearly dominated by CEPE and Texaco. Aside from them the agro-industrial sector is important, especially for employment.

SOURCE: *South*, Jan. 1985, p. 72.

Table 2919

EL SALVADOR CORPORATE BUSINESS ACTIVITY[1]

(1982)

Sales Rank	Company	Type of Business	M US Sales/ Turnover	Profit	Employees	Net Assets	Transnational Parent
1	Instituto Nacional del Cafe	Coffee	420	~	~	~	**
2	Instituto Nacional del Azucar	Sugar	98.5	~	~	~	**
3	Co-op Algodenera Salvadorena	Cotton	78.8	~	~	~	**
4	Laboratorios Vijosa SA	Pharmaceuticals	49	~	~	~	**
5	Empresas Adoc	Stockings, shoes	17	~	3,800	~	**
6	Insinca Ind. Sinteticos de Centroamerica	Textiles	15	~	~	~	**
7	SIGMA	Packaging	14	~	~	~	**
8	Cigarreria Morazan	Tobacco	12.8	~	300	~	Sub of BAT (UK)
9	El Dorado SA	Veg oil, cotton	10.5	~	395	~	**
10	Industrias Unidas	Textiles	10	~	1,700	~	Sub of Toyota (Japan)

1. Agriculture accounts for 25 percent of El Salvador's GDP, so it is not surprising to find agri-related companies dominating the corporate sector. The top three also dominate their own particular sectors while the 10 listed account for approximately one-quarter of the GNP.

SOURCE: *South*, Jan. 1985, p. 73.

Table 2920

GUATEMALA CORPORATE BUSINESS ACTIVITY[1]

(1982)

Sales Rank	Company	Type of Business	M US Sales/ Turnover	Profit	Employees	M US Net Assets	Transnational Parent
1	Empresa Electrica de Guatemala	Electricity	112	~	400	~	**
2	Cia Agro-Comercial SA	Wholesalers	75	~	160	~	**
3	Exploraciones y Explotaciones Mineras Izabal	Nickel mining	60	~	800	~	US, INCO
4	Cia Distribuidora Guatemala Shell	Petrol prods	54	~	~	~	UK/Netherlands
5	Cementos Progreso	Cement	36.9	~	~	87.6	**
6	Texaco Guatemala	Petroleum prods	31.5	~	89	~	US
7	Pantaleon Ingenio Azucarero	Sugar	30	~	~	36.4	**
8	Aceros Prefabricados	Steel prods	30	~	1,200	~	**
9	Intercafe	Coffee	30	~	~	~	**
10	Industrias Centroamericana de Vidrio	Glassware	28.5	~	~	94.6	**
11	Cervecerias Centroamericana	Brewing	26.9	~	440	78.4	**
12	Fabrica Ginsa	Rubber prods	25.4	~	~	20	US
13	Esso Central America	Petro prods	24	~	60	~	US
14	Tabacalera Nacional	Tobacco	23	~	250	20.8	Brown & Willcomson US/UK
15	Ingenio Concepcion	Sugar	23	~	305	~	**

1. This list shows that, apart from the electric utility, companies are more broadly spread across the economy than in many adjacent countries. The other apparent feature is the degree of foreign, particularly U.S. ownership covering some of the major employers. At the same time agriculture is the dominant sector of the national economy. The two sugar companies noted account for around 66 percent of exports.

SOURCE: *South*, Jan. 1985, p. 75.

Table 2921

HAITI CORPORATE BUSINESS ACTIVITY[1]

(1982)

Sales Rank	Company	Type of Business	M US Sales/ Turnover in Gourdes million	Profit	Employees	Net Assets	Transnational Parent
1	Le Ciment d'Haiti	Cement	25	~	400	~	Sub of Lambert Freres (FL)
2	Haytian American Sugar Co	Sugar	22	~	4,000	~	**
3	Flambert Raymond	Commerce	11	~	274	~	**

1. Given that coffee and bauxite are the principal industries of Haiti, it is assumed that companies operating in these sectors would have figures higher than those listed. Yet little is known about these companies. The sugar company listed probably accounts for all exports.

SOURCE: *South*, Jan. 1985, p. 75.

Table 2922

HONDURAS CORPORATE BUSINESS ACTIVITY[1]
(1982)

Sales Rank	Company	Type of Business	M US Sales/ Turnover	Profit	Employees	Net Assets	Transnational Parent
1	Railroad	Bananas	114.3	~	~	~	Sub of United Brands (US)
2	Comercial e Inversiones Galaxia	Commerce	66.8	~	~	~	**
3	Kawas Y Cia	Commerce	40.5	~	~	~	**
4	Cerveceria Hondurena	Brewery	29.4	~	1,200	~	Sub of Castle & Cook (US)
5	Federacion Hondurena de Cooperativas Cafetaleras	Coffee	10	~	325	~	**
6	Cia Azucarera Hondurena	Sugar	5	~	1,148	~	**

1. All of the Honduran principal exports are controlled by three US transnationals, which have large stakes in many other companies. Exports of bananas, coffee, sugar and meat account for over half of the revenue and it is to be expected that corporations in these sectors would dominate. However, in contrast to the domination of banana exports, coffee and sugar exhibit a very low degree of concentration, with the major concerns having around 5 percent of the market. Lack of accurate information has led to an incomplete listing.

SOURCE: *South*, Jan. 1985, p. 75.

Table 2923

MEXICO CORPORATE BUSINESS ACTIVITY[1]

(1982)

Sales Rank	Company	Type of Business	M US Sales/ Turnover	Profit	Employees	M US Net Assets	Transnational Parent
1	Petroleos Mexicanos — Pemex	Petroleum	17,330	~	13,671	3,894	**
2	Conasupo — Cia Nal De Subs Populares	Food	1,200	~	2,920	3,640	**
3	Grupo Industrial Alfa SA	Steel, etc.	1,080	~	31,721	2,850	**
4	Telefonos de Mexico SA	Telephones	804.03	~	41,760	3,020	**
5	Grupo Sidermex de Mexico SA	Steel	716.35	~	51,605	4,040	**
6	Vitro SA	Glass & ceramics	602.13	~	27,156	1,700	**
7	DESC, SA de CV	Chemicals & petrochem	597.35	~	19,768	1,070	**
8	Industrias Penoles, SA de CV	Mining	562.44	~	11,961	725.34	**
9	Aurrera SA	Commerce	555.02	~	20,048	376.55	**
10	General Motors de Mexico, SA de CV	Automobiles	505.39	~	8,451	799.28	US
11	Volkswagen de Mexico, SA de CV	Automobiles	492.6	~	12,416	416.64	FRG
12	Gigante SA	Commerce	486.42	~	9,623	206.89	**
13	Valores Industriales SA	Food/Drink/ services/tourism	480.07	~	33,500	1,320	**
14	Productos Pesqueros Mexicanos, SA de CV	Fish products	434.35	~	15,307	400.19	**
15	Cia Mexicana de Aviacion SA	Airline	425.48	~	12,475	766.46	**
16	Celanese Mexicana SA	Synthetics	412.18	~	9,153	982.51	US
17	Ferrocarriles Nacionales de Mexico	Railways	404.02	~	63,951	4,590	**
18	Ford Motor Company SA	Automobiles	375.81	~	5,891	504.7	US
19	CYDSA, SA	Chemicals	350.79	~	8,022	686.44	**
20	Grupo Industrial Minera Mexico, SA de CV	Metallurgy	349.53	~	13,926	570.75	**
21	Aeronaves de Mexico, SA	Airline	337	~	6,400	266.09	**
22	Grupo Industrial Bimbo SA	Food	300.44	~	20,033	222.77	**
23	Chrysler de Mexico SA	Automobiles	284.24	~	9,000	273.32	US
24	Salinas y Rocha SA	Commerce	255.01	~	6,200	277.77	**
25	Compania Nestle SA	Food	243.48	~	3,476	194.31	Switzerland
26	Grupo Industrias Unidas	Mechanical eng	239.87	~	14,000	621.82	**
27	Grupo Mexicana Hidalgo	Holding Co	226.2	~	1,903	530.49	**
28	Grupo Cementos Mexicanos SA	Cement	212.17	~	5,289	666.97	**
29	Anderson Clayton & Co. SA	Food	204.12	~	4,300	124.11	**
30	Kimberly-Clark de Mexico, SA	Paper	203.12	~	3,780	345.71	US
31	Nissan Mexicana SA de CV	Automobiles	200.79	~	4,518	393.18	Japan
32	Cerveceria Moctezuma SA	Brewery	189.6	~	7,889	378.07	**
33	Grupo Xerox de Mexico SA de CV	Information/office equipment	185.01	~	2,168	271.46	**
34	Grupo Condumex SA	Wire and cable	184.11	~	6,970	294.93	**
35	Transportacion Maritima Mexicana SA	Shipping	182.84	~	1,702	292.19	**
36	Cia Indl. de Sn. Cristobal SA Cias Sub.	Paper	181.77	~	7,128	474.12	**
37	Tubos Acero de Mexico SA	Steel	180.81	~	6,547	1,130	**
38	Mexicana de Cobre SA	Copper mining	175.58	~	4,979	1,200	**
39	Impulsora del Pequeno Comercio SA de CV	Commerce	169.45	~	4,801	64.18	**
40	Grupo Industrial Saltillo	Metal parts/ machinery	161.32	~	11,609	372.26	**
41	Grupo Gamesa SA	Food products	152.18	~	10,460	225.27	**
42	Siderurgica L Cardenas Las Truchas SA	Steel	151.72	~	8,246	1,850	**
43	Fabrica de Jabon La Corona SA de CV	Chemicals	150.24	~	2,689	81.27	**
44	Empresas Tolteca de Mexico SA de CV	Cement	145.9	~	~	671.84	**
45	Industrias Purina SA de CV	Food	142.79	~	~	138.54	US
46	Grupo IMSA SA	Heavy eng.	137.94	~	2,745	131.82	**
47	Cia Hulera Euzkadi SA	Tires	137.87	~	3,413	253.32	US, Goodrich
48	IBM de Mexico SA	Information/ computers	136.11	~	1,685	180.36	US
49	Fabricas de Calzado Canada SA	Footwear	131.2	~	9,630	60.03	**
50	Industrias Nacobre, SA de CV	Metallurgy	130.31	~	4,865	279.13	**

Table 2923 (Continued)

MEXICO CORPORATE BUSINESS ACTIVITY[1]
(1982)

Sales Rank	Company	Type of Business	M US Sales/Turnover	Profit	Employees	M US Net Assets	Transnational Parent
51	El Palacio de Hierro SA	Dept. store	128.73	~	3,052	127.45	**
52	Sabritas SA	Soft drinks	118.22	~	6,000	48.68	US Pepsico
53	Empresas La Moderna SA de CV	Tobacco	114.43	~	3,475	279.1	**
54	Productora y Importadora de Papel SA de CV	Paper	109.95	~	418	85.19	**
55	Organizacion Benavides	Pharmaceuticals	107.37	~	4,600	37.73	**
56	Grupo Rassini Rheem	Motor parts	105.01	~	3,386	169.21	**
57	Copamex SA	Holding Co	97.71	~	2,658	122.95	**
58	Cobre de Mexico SA	Copper production	97.45	~	704	49.74	**
59	Cia Minera Autlan SA de CV	Mining	96.51	~	2,260	296.79	**
60	Ciba-Geigy Mexicana SA de CV	Pharmaceuticals	95.38	~	1,894	104.35	Switzerland
61	Cigarros La Tabacalera, Mex., SA de CV	Cigars	93.64	~	2,029	83.16	**
62	Fibras Quimicas SA	Synthetic fibres	93.11	~	2,285	191.2	Part owned by Cydsa
63	Industrias Luismin SA de CV	Gold/silver mining	92.93	~	3,730	148.53	**
64	Grupo Anahuac	Cement	92.62	~	1,809	205.39	**
65	Ponderosa Ind. SA y Subs	Forest products	92.23	~	400	157.52	**
66	Grupo Continental SA	Holding Co	92.21	~	5,679	125.32	**
67	Transmisiones y Equipos Mec. SA	Transport equip	87.45	~	3,157	171.34	Part owned by Clark Equipment, US
68	Fabricas Monterrey SA	Canning	86.54	~	1,927	151.19	Sub Valores
69	Renault de Mexico SA de CV	Automobiles	86.54	~	2,100	117.29	**
70	Cia Siderurgica de Guadalajara SA	Iron & Steel	85.17	~	1,264	146.09	**
71	Union Carbide Mexicana SA	Ind. gases/chemicals	84.19	~	2,100	254.51	US
72	Industrias EIM SA	Electrical equip	80.67	~	3,062	115.12	**
73	Hoteles Camino Real SA	Hotels	80.22	~	4,442	186.35	**
74	Nylon de Mexico SA	Synthetic fibres	78.82	~	1,669	141.29	**
75	Quimica Hoechst de Mexico SA	Chemicals	77.31	~	953	70.15	FRG
76	El Puerto de Liverpool SA	Dept. store	73.92	~	6,095	321.34	**
77	Bayer de Mexico SA	Pharmaceuticals	69.76	~	1,024	52.46	FRG
78	Grupo Akalli SA de CV	Salt	69.49	~	3,200	104.96	**
79	General Electric de Mexico SA	Elect. appliances	69.03	~	5,871	136.02	US
80	Alumino SA de CV	Aluminum	68.92	~	639	82.11	US, Alcoa
81	Pasteurizadora Laguna SA de CV	Milk products	67.61	~	447	20.28	**
82	Ganaderos y Productores de Leche Pura SA	Milk products	66.29	~	562	15.03	**
83	Bufete Industrial	Construction	66.10	~	4,179	0.88	**
84	Bacardi y Cia SA	Sugar/Rum	64.09	~	635	42.16	Puerto Rico
85	Apasco SA	Cement	62.44	~	1,837	320.06	**
86	Empresas Industria del Hierro SA de CV	Iron	61.93	~	4,674	93.12	**
87	Teleindustria Ericcson SA	Telecom equipment	60.21	~	2,174	96.95	Sweden
88	Conductores Monterrey SA	Wire & cable	59.44	~	1,645	161.04	**
89	Chicle Adams SA de CV	Confectioners	59.15	~	1,502	38.36	US, Warner Lambert
90	General Popo SA	Tires	58.45	~	1,736	87.02	US, General Tire & Rubber
91	Cementos Guadalajara SA	Cement	57.8	~	1,000	175	**
92	Algodonera Comercial, Mexicana, SA	Cotton	56.83	~	138	19.8	**
93	Alcan Mexicana SA de CV	Aluminum prod	55.83	~	1,420	100.81	Canada
94	Uniroyal SA de CV	Tires	55.63	~	1,162	59.51	US
95	Grupo Primex-Lugatom	Construction	52.78	~	790	132.42	**
96	Cia Industrial de Atenquique SA	Paper	51.89	~	1,225	88.54	**
97	Aceros Nacionales SA	Wire	50.63	~	2,114	81.37	US, Armco
98	Frisco SA de CV	Mining	48.71	~	3,300	100.68	**
99	Ind de Telecomunicacion SA de CV	Telephone equip	45.45	~	3,413	55.26	**
100	Grupo Industrial Camesa SA	Wire & cable	45.42	~	1,386	61.47	**

1. After Brazil, Mexico is the dominant economy south of the Rio Grande, the border between the U.S. and its nearest Latin American neighbor. It is host to a large number of affiliates of Western transnationals. This is principally noticeable in the transport sector, led by automobile companies, and also including transport equipment companies. Yet the entire corporate sector is overshadowed by Pemex, the state-owned oil company, with a sales figure greater than the combined total of the 57 companies following it in the list.

SOURCE: *South*, Jan. 1985, pp. 75–77.

Table 2924

NICARAGUA CORPORATE BUSINESS ACTIVITY[1]

(1982)

Sales Rank	Company	Type of Business	M US Sales/ Turnover	Profit	Employees	Net Assets	Transnational Parent
1	Pennwalt-Hercasa	Chemicals	82	~	~	~	US, Hercules
2	Ingenio San Antonio	Sugar	55	~	~	~	**
3	Cia Licorera	Rum	45.5	~	~	~	**
4	Gracsa	Edible oils	31.1	~	~	~	**
5	Fanatex	Textiles	27.3	~	~	~	**
6	Cia Cerveceria Nacional	Beer	24	~	~	~	US, Coca-Cola
7	Milca	Soft drinks	21.6	~	~	~	BAT (UK)
8	Tanic — Tabacallera Nacional	Tobacco	20	~	265	~	**
9	Ingenio Tipitapa — Malacaloya	Beer	17	~	6,000	~	**
10	Ind. Cerveceria Sa — TONA	Beer	6	~	1,108	~	**

1. Of the 10 companies listed, only two, Fanatex and Tipitapa-Malacaloya, are state-owned. This reinforces the Sandinistas' assurance that large-scale expropriation of private assets has not occurred since the revolution. The list, despite some omissions, shows that agro-related companies dominate the corporate sector.

SOURCE: *South*, Jan. 1985, p. 77.

Table 2925

PANAMA CORPORATE BUSINESS ACTIVITY[1]

(1982)

Sales Rank	Company	Type of Business	M US Sales/ Turnover	Profit	Employees	Net Assets	Transnational Parent
1	Canal	Canal Co.	377	~	1,000	~	**
2	Cia Panamena de Alimentos	Canning	51	~	1,000	~	**
3	Melo	Agriculture	45.2	~	~	~	**
4	Cia Azucarera La Estrella	Sugar	25.5	~	200	~	**
5	Cemento Panama	Cement	20	~	~	~	**
6	Central Exportadora Silbros	Commerce	15	~	80	~	**
7	Grupo Ind. Amado	Construction	14.2	~	~	~	**
8	Constructora Frontini	Construction	14	~	~	~	US, Bordon
9	Cia Intl de Ventas	Commerce	13	~	~	~	**
10	Azucarera Nacional	Sugar	9	~	615	~	

1. The export business, dominant in Panama, is only marginally less concentrated in the agro-industrial sector than in other Central American economies. However, one agency's operations totally eclipse those of other companies. What is not represented here is the substantial presence of holding companies and intermediaries that have taken advantage of the 'offshore' provisions of Panamanian business law. While their contribution to the local economy may be minimal, their inclusion would make for a more representative picture, as the firms shown here only account for around 15 percent of GDP.

SOURCE: *South*, Jan. 1985, p. 79.

Table 2926

PARAGUAY CORPORATE BUSINESS ACTIVITY[1]

(1982)

| | | | M US | | | | |
Sales Rank	Company	Type of Business	Sales/ Turnover	Profit	Employees	Net Assets	Transnational Parent
1	CAPSA -- Cia Algodonera Paraguaya	Veg oils & fibres	72.4	~	950	~	**
2	Petropar — Petroleo Paraguayo	Petroleum products	54.3	~	~	~	**
3	ANTELCO — Administracion Nacional de Telecomunicaciones	Telephone services	18.8	~	500	~	**
4	Liebigs Extract of Meat Co	Meat packing	14.8	~	2,000	~	UK, Liebigs
5	Ind. Nac. del Cemento	Cement	12.5	~	776	~	**

1. The paucity of information means that the listing of Paraguayan firms is largely impressionistic. The major enterprise is probably the electricity utility, ANDE. After the petroleum company, a brewery firm, an alcohol and sugar organization, and a soft drinks company are thought to precede the telephone company. This seems likely as Paraguay has one of the lowest levels of telephone penetrations in the world — just over 1 percent. Another factor worthy of note, possibly contributing to the lack of data, is the heavy involvement in the corporate sector of senior members of the government.

SOURCE: *South*, Jan. 1985, p. 79.

Table 2927

URUGUAY CORPORATE BUSINESS ACTIVITY[1]

(1982)

| | | | M US | | | | |
Sales Rank	Company	Type of Business	Sales/ Turnover	Profit	Employees	Net Asset	Transnational Parent
1	ANCAP — Admin Nac de Combustibles, Alcoholes y Portland	Petroleum prods, cement	616.5	~	6,600	~	**
2	Distribuidor ANCAP	Petrol distribution	203.3	~	57	~	**
3	UTE — Admin Nac de Usinas y Transmisiones Electricidad	Electricity	202.8	~	8,543	~	**
4	ANTEL — Adm Nac de Telecomunicaciones	Telephone services	192 †	~	7,900	~	**
5	Conaprole — Co-op Nac de Productos de Leche	Milk prods	139.7	~	2,709	~	**
6	Shell Uruguay	Petroleum	124.8	~	124	~	UK/Netherlands
7	Esso Standard Oil Co Uruguay	Petroleum	111.5	~	40	~	US
8	Texaco Uruguay	Petroleum	87.7	~	84	~	US
9	Montevideo Refrescos	Soft drinks	81.1	~	1,090	~	**
10	Cubalon/Paysandu	Wool, leather products	75	~	1,906	~	**
11	Funsa — Fab Uruguaya de Neumaticos	Tires	63.7	~	2,100	~	**
12	General Motors Uruguay	Motors	63	~	560	~	US
13	Cia Uruguayos de Transportes Colectivos	Public transport	55.5	~	5,800	~	**
14	Sudamtex de Uruguay	Textiles	48.2	~	1,543	~	UMM-US
15	Manzanares	Retail groceries	43.2	~	780	~	**
16	Soc Anon Molinos Arrocera Nac	Rice/agro mchy	38	~	48	~	**
17	Cia Ind de Tabac	Tobacco	35.2	~	230	~	**
18	OSE — Adm de las Obras Sanitarias del Estado	Water/sanitation	33.8	~	5,045	~	**
19	Nirea	Meat prods	33.6	~	879	~	**
20	Pepsi-Cola	Soft drinks	28.6	~	309	~	US

1. The list shows a reasonable balance between economic sectors, other than petroleum, where the combined value of output of the five companies listed is 2.5 times the import value of the raw product. Although not disclosed, profit levels in this area should therefore be interesting. Of the dominant export sectors, Nirea accounts for 13 percent and Cubalon 25 percent of exports.

SOURCE: *South*, Jan. 1985, pp. 79–80.

Table 2928

VENEZUELA CORPORATE BUSINESS ACTIVITY[1]

(1982, except some 1983 figures were included)

Sales Rank	Company	Type of Business	M US Sales/ Turnover	Profit	Employees	M US Net Assets	Transnational Parent
1	Petroleos de Venezuela — Petroven	Petroleum	14,890	2,534	44,414	22,786	**
2	Instituto Nacional de Hipodromos	Lottery	4,650	~	~	~	**
3	Cerveceria Polar	Drinks	1,770	~	3,603	~	**
4	CVG Siderurgica Del Orinoco — Sidor	Iron & Steel	1,060	~	14,119	2,174.4	**
5	Ford Motors de Venezuela	Automobiles	695.58	~	4,058	~	US
6	General Motors CA	Automobiles	683.72	~	3,740	~	US
7	CANTV — C A Nac Telefonos de Venezuela	Telecom	639.5	21	18,450	2,230	**
8	CVG Ferrominera Del Orinoco	Iron Mining	581.4	~	5,300	~	Sub Sidor
9	Cadafe — C A de Administracion y Fomento Electrica	Electricity	514	12	12,010	~	**
10	Cigarrera Bigott Sucs CA	Tobacco products	513.95	~	1,803	20.2	UK
11	CADA — CA Distribuidora de Alimentos	Supermarkets	488.37	~	6,005	177.4	**
12	Sivensa — Siderurgica Venezolana	Steel	443	~	310	250	**
13	Corpomercadeo — Corp. de Mercadeo Agricola	Agri-marketing	417	~	4,755	~	**
14	General Electric de Venezuela SA	Electrical appliances	361.63	~	1,850	~	US
15	Venalum	Aluminum	319	~	2,674	~	Part-owned by 5 Japanese companies
16	CA La Electricidad de Caracas	Electricity	310.47	24.7	3,143	151.5	**
17	Pequiven	Petrochemicals	308.1	~	4,104	100.2	**
18	Venezol. Intl. de Aviacion SA — VIASA	Airline/aviation	277.67	~	4,500	34.8	**
19	Grupo Bulton	Commerce	258.1	~	400	~	**
20	Aluminio Del Caroni — Alcasa	Aluminum	255.81	~	16,011	~	US Reynolds
21	Proctor-Gamble de Venezuela	Detergents	245.58	~	1,030	~	US
22	Maquinarias Venequip	Industrial machinery	244.88	~	~	~	**
23	Catana — CA Tabacalera Nacional	Tobacco	243.26	~	1,803	42	**
24	Corimon	Chemicals	235	816	2,770	200.5	**
25	Refinadora de Maiz Remavenca	Corn products	232.56	~	220	~	**
26	Industrial Yuqueryi	Soft drinks	232	~	4,100	~	**
27	Venezolana de Cementos	Cement	232	~	1,210	~	**
28	Central Madeirense	Supermarkets	209.3	25.1	2,000	101.5	**
29	Tamayo y Cia. SA	Commerce	179.53	~	370	~	**
30	CA Tocars	Machinery	176.7	~	551	~	**
31	Aco SA	Machinery	176.5	~	2,700	~	US, Alcoa
32	Caterpillar	Machinery	176.1	~	1,050	~	US
33	Sears Roebuck	Department store	174.88	~	3,000	~	**
34	CVG Electrificacion Del Caroni — Edelca	Electricity	170.47	~	2,085	~	**
35	Indust. Lacteas Del Perija CA	Milk Products	165.12	~	350	~	**
36	Indust. Lactea Venez. CA — Indulac	Milk Products	163.26	~	1,200	~	**
37	Cerveceria Nacional	Drinks/Brewery	155	~	698	35.5	**
38	Jeep de Venezuela	Automobiles	153.4	~	321	~	US
39	CA Energia Elect. De Venezuela	Electricity	151.16	~	1,507	~	**
40	CA Venez. De Navegacion — CAVN	Shipping	149.07	~	1,350	~	**
41	IBM de Venezuela	Information/ computers	146.5	~	1,100	~	US
42	Intersan SA	Constr equip	144.19	~	400	~	**
43	Casa Paris	Commerce	137.2	~	~	~	**
44	Fiat	Automobiles	137	~	1,030	~	Italy
45	Colgate Palmolive	Detergents	136.74	~	845	~	US
46	La India SA	Confectionery	129.07	~	480	~	US, General Foods
47	Mavesa	Edible fats	127.91	~	626	~	**
48	Venez. de Pulpa y Papel — Venepal	Paper	125.58	~	1,393	6.6	**
49	Enelven	Electricity	123.3	~	~	~	**
50	Goodyear de Venezuela SA	Rubber	123.26	~	1,592	~	US

Table 2928 (Continued)

VENEZUELA CORPORATE BUSINESS ACTIVITY[1]

(1982, except some 1983 figures were included)

Sales Rank	Company	Type of Business	Sales/Turnover (M US)	Profit	Employees	Net Assets (M US)	Transnational Parent
51	Constructora Nacional de Vehiculos CA	Motor parts	118.6	~	1,167	~	**
52	Avensa — Aerovias Venezolanas	Airline	116.28	~	1,850	~	**
53	Molinos Nacionales, CA — Monaca	Flour	116.28	~	1,200	~	Sub Fabrico (Panama)
54	Protinal CA	Animal feeds	116.28	~	1,015	17.3	**
55	Envases Venezolanos SA	Containers	114.65	~	1,500	~	US, American Can Co.
56	Purina de Venezuela	Food	113.2	~	296	~	US
57	Conduven	Steel tubes	110.47	~	1,100	~	Sub Century CA
58	Materiales De Plomeria CA — Maploca	Constr materials	110	~	148	~	**
59	Distribuidora Benedetti CA	Retail commerce	107.67	~	700	~	**
60	Lacteos de Venezuela SA	Milk products	105.12	~	225	~	**
61	Alimentos Kraft de Venezuela CA	Food	104.65	~	680	~	US
62	Productos Mar	Fish products	104.3	~	1,571	~	**
63	Danaven CA	Auto parts	101.16	~	550	~	US
64	Luz Electrica de Venezuela	Electricity	99.5	~	526	~	**
65	Renault	Automobiles	99.2	~	325	~	France
66	Grasas de Valencia	Oils and greases	99.2	~	450	~	**
67	Manpa — Manufacturas de Papel	Paper bags	98.1	~	903	~	**
68	Espalsa SA — Especialidades Alimenticias	Food	97.91	~	600	~	**
69	Dominguez y Cia.	Canning	97	~	300	~	**
70	Ferrum CA	Constr materials machinery	96.98	~	508	~	**
71	Ceramica Carabobo	Ceramics	96.5	~	1,700	~	**
72	Owens Illinois de Venezuela	Glass	93	~	~	~	US
73	Sveça — Soc Venezolana de Electrificacion	Power station construction	92.3	~	1,800	~	Switzerland, Elettrofin
74	Inlaca — Industrias Lara-Carabobo CA	Dairy products/soft drinks	91.1	~	900	~	**
75	Imosa — Industria Mecanica Orion	Civil engineering	90	~	1,400	~	**

1. Although Pemex of Mexico has higher sales than Petroven, the Venezuelan company represents a far greater proportion of total national output: 31 percent in 1980. This is a phenomenal degree of economic power and apparently without parallel in economies on a similar level of development to that of Venezuela. All but 7 percent of Petroven's output appears to be exported. Coincidentally, the country's private external debt is almost equal to the figure showing the net value of Petroven—just over US$22 billion.

SOURCE: *South*, Jan. 1985, pp. 80–81.

Part X: National Accounts, Government Policy and Finance, and Prices

---

CHAPTER 30

GOVERNMENT PLANS, REVENUE AND EXPENDITURE, AND MONEY SUPPLY

General notes:
  Expenditures may be in projected or disbursed terms; deficits may not
    include amortization of the debt and may exclude "off-budget"
    spending; for example, for United States in 1981 such spending
    reached $21.0 billion more than the registered deficit of $72.6 billion
    shown in SALA, 23-2421. (With regard to "off-budget" spending, see
    U.S. News and World Report, Oct. 4, 1982, p. 77.)
  Central government expenditures may include subsidies for decentralized
    agencies.

Note: This volume contains statistics from numerous sources. Alternative
  data on many topics are presented. Variations in statistics can be attributed to differences in definition, parameters, coverage, methodology, as
  well as date gathered, prepared, or adjusted. See also Editor's Note on
  Methodology.

Table 3000

CURRENT DEVELOPMENT PLANS, 17 L

PART I. GOALS

	AAGR					Yearly % Planned Growth Rate								Yearly % Planned Investment[2]			
Country	Population	Domestic Demand for Food	Scope[1]	Duration[3]	GDP	Total Employment	Agricultural Production Total	Agricultural Production Cereals	Fertilizer Consumption	Export Earnings Total	Export Earnings Agricultural	Of GDP	Share of Public Investment in Total Investment	Share of Agriculture in Total Investment	Share of Agriculture in Public Investment	Land and Water Development in Total Investment	External Resources in Total Plan Outlay
A. ARGENTINA	1.3	2.0	PS	1974-77	7.5	2.8	6.5	~	~	19.6	~	9.8[a]	42.0	~	~	~	~
B. BOLIVIA	2.5	5.0	C/AS	1976-80	7.7[b]	2.9	7.4	6.8	9.2	~	17.9	28.0[c]	70.0	9.6	10.1	~	31.0
C. BRAZIL	2.9	4.7	C	1975-79	10.0	3.5	7.0	8.4	14.1	20.0	8.5	25.0[d]	19.0[d]	6.0	3.5	~	~
D. CHILE	1.8	.9	AS	1975-80	6.6[b]	4.0[e]	4.8[f]	7.5	~	~	11.8	13.0[c]	47.0	~	~	~	~
F. COSTA RICA	2.8	4.1	C	1974-78	6.0/6.5[k]	5.3	4.7	~	~	9.6	9.1	27.0[g]	27.9	15.0	~	~	24.8
H. DOMINICAN REP.	2.6	~	AS	1980-82	~	~	5.4	~	~	~	6.9	~	~	~	~	~	~
I. ECUADOR	3.3	4.7	C	1973-77	10.1	6.5	5.3[h]	5.5	~	16.4	3.9	23.0	40.2	18.9	17.3	5.0	16.0
J. EL SALVADOR	3.2	3.2	C/AS	1978-82	7.5	3.6	5.5	4.9	8.4	7.1	5.1	24.0	41.9	~	~	14.0	~
K. GUATEMALA	3.1	~	C	1979-82	5.0	~	3.5	3.8	~	~	~	~	67.0	~	~	~	~
L. HAITI	1.5	2.6	C/AS	1976-81	5.0	6.1[e]	3.0	4.7	~	9.3	8.0	19.9[c]	~	15.0	18.8	29.0	50.0
M. HONDURAS	3.5	3.2	C	1974-78	7.0	1.7	8.1	5.7	~	~	7.9	~	33.6	13.8	11.2	~	25.8
O. NICARAGUA	3.3	3.6	PS	1975-79	6.1		6.5	~	~	~	~	~	~	~	~	~	~
P. PANAMA	2.9	4.1	PS	1976-80	7.0	2.5	5.7	3.7	14.0[i]	7.2	9.5	16.0[a]	54.4	4.9	7.0	~	28.0
Q. PARAGUAY	3.0	~	C	1977-81	7.6	~	6.9	~	~	11.7	~	26.3	26.4	~	10.0	~	24.2
R. PERU	3.0	4.9	C	1975-78	6.5[b]	2.5	4.5[j]	~	~	15.6	~	18.5[c]	50.0	6.4	12.8	7.1	~
S. URUGUAY	1.0	1.1	PS	1973-77	4.0/5.0[k]	1.9[e]	3.8/4.6[k]	~	~	10.0	~	~	~	~	~	~	~
T. VENEZUELA	3.0	2.7	PS	1976-80	8.2	.5	9.6	10.0	18.0	25.4	11.0	25.0	53.0	9.0	7.0	3.0	16.0

1. C = comprehensive; PS = public sector; AS = agricultural sector.
2. Where possible data refer to net investment. In many cases, however, no distinction is made in the plan, and data may refer to gross investment or may include some elements of recurrent expenditure. The agricultural sector includes animal production, fisheries, forestry, irrigation, land reclamation, community development, and agricultural extension.
3. For previous years, see SALA, 18-2304.
a. Share of public investment in GDP.
b. GNP.
c. Share of total investment in GNP.
d. Total investment does not include private investment in agriculture and technology development. Data on investment refer to 1979 only.
e. Employment in agriculture only.
f. Not including fisheries, which is planned to grow at an annual rate of 16.9%.
g. 27% of GDP in 1978.
h. Not including fisheries, which is planned to grow at an annual rate of 9.6%.
i. 1975-76.
k. Low and high hypotheses.

SOURCE: FAO, *The State of Food and Agriculture*, 1977, p. A-47; 1978, p. A-48; 1979, p. A-43; 1980, p. 178. Cf. SALA, 24-208, above.

Table 3000 (Continued)

CURRENT DEVELOPMENT PLANS, 17 L

PART II. ACHIEVEMENTS

(AAGR)

Country	Year	Total GDP		GDP/C		Total Manufacturing[1]	
		Goal	Result	Goal	Result	Goal	Result
A. ARGENTINA	1970-75	7.0	3.2	5.5	1.8	8.6	4.5
C. BRAZIL	1972-74	9.0	9.3	6.0	6.6	11.0	10.2
H. DOMINICAN REP.	1969-74	6.7	10.6	3.7	7.2	7.7	13.3
R. PERU	1970-75	7.2	7.5	4.3	2.2	12.4	7.5
S. URUGUAY	1963-74	4.8	.4[a]	3.5	-.6[a]	6.0[b]	1.4[a,b]
T. VENEZUELA	1970-74	6.3	4.7[a]	2.5	1.7[a]	9.6	8.4[a]

1. AAGR of manufacturing in total GDP.

a. 1970-75.

b. Including mining and quarrying.

SOURCE: ECLA, *Long-Term Trends and Projections of Economic Development of Latin America* (Santiago, 1978).

Table 3001

CENTRAL GOVERNMENT CURRENT REVENUES, 19 L,
1970, 1975, 1980-83

(% of GDP)

	Country	1970	1975	1980	1981	1982	1983[‡]
A.	ARGENTINA	7.8	3.9	12.8	11.5	12.0	10.5
B.	BOLIVIA	8.7	12.0	9.8	8.4	4.5	2.5
C.	BRAZIL	9.1	9.1	9.3	8.6	9.0	8.7
D.	CHILE	19.9	24.7	25.9	26.7	29.1	27.8
E.	COLOMBIA	9.0	9.5	9.6	10.3	10.5	9.8
F.	COSTA RICA	12.9	13.3	12.7	13.1	13.1	17.5
H.	DOMINICAN REP.	16.1	17.7	14.3	13.6	9.5	10.7
I.	ECUADOR	10.6	15.6	12.8	11.3	10.8	11.1
J.	EL SALVADOR	10.9	12.6	11.3	12.4	12.5	13.1
K.	GUATEMALA	8.7	9.0	9.5	8.7	8.4	7.7
L.	HAITI	13.6	10.8	9.5	8.9	9.9	10.0
M.	HONDURAS	12.3	13.6	15.2	14.1	13.7	13.2
N.	MEXICO	9.1	12.0	15.9	16.1	16.4	~
O.	NICARAGUA	10.7	12.2	20.6	21.7	24.5	28.7
P.	PANAMA	15.7	16.1	22.0	21.3	23.4	20.5
Q.	PARAGUAY	11.7	9.4	9.2	8.3	9.3	7.6
R.	PERU	16.1	15.8	20.5	17.9	18.0	13.9
S.	URUGUAY	13.8	12.1	15.9	16.8	14.9	14.1
T.	VENEZUELA	18.2	34.6	24.3	31.7	26.2	27.4

SOURCE: IDB-SPTF, 1984, table 19.

Table 3003

CENTRAL GOVERNMENT DIRECT TAXES, 19 L,
1970-83

(% of Current Revenue)[1]

	Country	1970	1975	1980	1981	1982	1983[‡]
A.	ARGENTINA	33.8	9.2	21.8	7.6	10.4	~
B.	BOLIVIA	17.1	10.8	11.5	18.4	21.9	~
C.	BRAZIL	24.1	25.5	25.2	28.3	29.3	30.8
D.	CHILE	23.5	28.9	23.7	22.5	21.2	~
E.	COLOMBIA	48.3	45.9	31.2	25.9	25.4	34.8
F.	COSTA RICA	23.7	22.1	20.3	20.9	23.7	~
H.	DOMINICAN REP.	22.4	22.3	20.0	19.7	25.0	22.6
I.	ECUADOR	15.8	11.7	9.8	15.0	15.0	~
J.	EL SALVADOR	22.2	25.1	28.3	25.7	26.2	22.5
K.	GUATEMALA	15.0	19.1	13.5	14.7	13.8	13.8
L.	HAITI	10.5	15.6	15.9	19.1	17.9	18.8
M.	HONDURAS	25.0	25.5	31.1	25.0	26.8	25.5
N.	MEXICO	39.7	38.4	37.0	35.4	29.6	~
O.	NICARAGUA	20.9	22.1	17.6	18.4	18.0	19.9
P.	PANAMA	38.8	38.5	32.6	38.1	33.0	~
Q.	PARAGUAY	15.4	18.7	21.9	24.0	30.1	26.1
R.	PERU	33.8	31.9	27.5	20.7	19.5	15.9
S.	URUGUAY	13.8	12.7	21.4	17.1	17.7	18.3
T.	VENEZUELA	48.3	63.9	71.9	79.1	66.6	53.6

1. For definition of current revenue, see table 3002, above.

SOURCE: IDB-SPTF, 1984, table 26.

Table 3002

CENTRAL GOVERNMENT TAX REVENUES, 19 L,
1970-83

(% of Current Revenue)[1]

	Country	1970	1975	1980	1981	1982	1983[‡]
A.	ARGENTINA	88.1	84.3	75.1	76.3	78.5	~
B.	BOLIVIA	92.9	92.9	85.7	98.4	98.6	~
C.	BRAZIL	90.6	88.3	72.0	75.9	73.9	68.6
D.	CHILE	93.9	97.9	92.8	86.3	79.7	~
E.	COLOMBIA	96.4	97.5	98.0	98.1	98.1	~
F.	COSTA RICA	95.6	95.0	89.0	93.0	94.6	~
H.	DOMINICAN REP.	89.7	91.0	77.4	78.5	88.5	85.8
I.	ECUADOR	94.0	96.5	93.7	94.3	94.0	~
J.	EL SALVADOR	93.8	93.5	95.0	89.3	85.7	85.9
K.	GUATEMALA	90.0	91.3	90.8	87.0	84.1	81.6
L.	HAITI[1]	60.1	78.4	92.8	92.1	88.6	93.8
M.	HONDURAS	89.7	81.4	92.8	94.9	92.9	91.4
N.	MEXICO	90.3	94.4	95.5	94.9	94.2	~
O.	NICARAGUA	85.3	86.1	86.2	81.4	79.6	84.9
P.	PANAMA	80.5	76.4	64.8	70.4	61.2	~
Q.	PARAGUAY	89.1	88.7	89.3	88.5	86.9	83.7
R.	PERU	86.2	91.3	92.4	90.7	90.5	89.0
S.	URUGUAY	91.6	95.2	92.1	85.2	84.2	81.6
T.	VENEZUELA	63.6	71.6	81.6	86.7	78.7	76.1

1. Current Revenue: Includes all non-repayable receipts raised by the central government
in the form of tax and non-tax revenue, but excludes social security contributions and
the sale of fixed government capital assets. Current revenue excludes the proceeds from
central government borrowings and from the issuance of government bonds and the
sale of other financial assets. In Haiti donations are included under current revenue and
classified as a form of non-tax revenue.

SOURCE: IDB-SPTF, 1984, table 25.

Table 3004

CENTRAL GOVERNMENT INCOME TAXES, 19 L, 1970-83

(% of Current Revenue)[1]

	Country	1970	1975	1980	1981	1982	1983[‡]
A.	ARGENTINA	17.7	8.9	18.6	6.3	7.7	~
B.	BOLIVIA	15.0	9.5	10.9	18.1	21.5	~
C.	BRAZIL	24.1	25.5	25.2	28.3	29.3	30.8
D.	CHILE	19.4	23.8	23.3	22.4	21.2	~
E.	COLOMBIA	45.4	45.2	31.0	29.9	25.3	~
F.	COSTA RICA	18.2	21.4	19.0	19.0	22.8	~
H.	DOMINICAN REP.	19.1	19.9	19.2	19.0	23.8	21.5
I.	ECUADOR	15.8	11.7	9.8	15.0	15.0	~
J.	EL SALVADOR	14.2	18.9	20.7	19.8	20.3	17.8
K.	GUATEMALA	11.3	16.6	12.7	13.9	13.0	12.8
L.	HAITI	7.0	12.1	12.7	17.5	16.5	17.1
M.	HONDURAS	23.9	24.5	30.3	24.1	25.8	24.6
N.	MEXICO	38.2	37.2	36.2	34.6	28.9	~
O.	NICARAGUA	9.4	13.1	8.3	11.3	11.1	14.2
P.	PANAMA	34.0	34.3	26.2	31.0	27.0	~
Q.	PARAGUAY	9.0	13.1	17.3	18.9	18.4	18.8
R.	PERU	29.8	25.5	21.3	13.4	12.3	9.2
S.	URUGUAY	8.1	9.8	15.8	11.4	10.4	11.7
T.	VENEZUELA	47.9	63.8	71.7	78.9	66.4	53.4

1. For definition of current revenue see table 3002, above.

SOURCE: IDB-SPTF, 1984, table 27.

Table 3005

CENTRAL GOVERNMENT PROPERTY TAXES, 18 L, 1970–83
(% of Current Revenue)[1]

	Country	1970	1975	1980	1981	1982	1983‡
A.	ARGENTINA	15.5	.1	3.2	1.3	2.7	~
B.	BOLIVIA	2.1	1.3	.6	.2	.5	~
C.	BRAZIL	#	#	#	#	#	#
D.	CHILE	4.1	3.4	.3	~	.0	~
E.	COLOMBIA	1.6	.7	.1	.1	.1	~
F.	COSTA RICA	.6	.2	1.3	.9	.9	~
H.	DOMINICAN REP.	3.3	2.3	.7	.7	1.2	1.1
I.	ECUADOR	#	#	#	#	#	#
J.	EL SALVADOR	6.4	4.2	5.9	5.1	4.7	4.1
K.	GUATEMALA	3.1	2.3	.7	.7	.7	.8
L.	HAITI	3.6	1.9	1.5	1.6	1.4	1.7
M.	HONDURAS	1.1	1.0	.8	.9	1.0	.9
N.	MEXICO	#	#	#	#	#	#
O.	NICARAGUA	9.4	6.7	7.4	5.6	4.8	4.6
P.	PANAMA	4.3	4.0	3.9	4.1	3.4	~
Q.	PARAGUAY	6.3	5.6	4.6	5.1	11.7	7.2
R.	PERU	4.0	4.4	3.2	4.0	3.9	3.9
S.	URUGUAY	5.7	2.9	5.6	5.7	7.3	6.0
T.	VENEZUELA	.4	.2	.2	.2	.2	.2

1. For definition of current revenue see table 3002, above.

SOURCE: IDB-SPTF, 1984, table 28.

Table 3007

CENTRAL GOVERNMENT INTERNATIONAL TRADE TAXES, 19 L, 1970–83
(% of Current Revenue)[1]

	Country	1970	1975	1980	1981	1982	1983‡
A.	ARGENTINA	20.9	31.5	11.2	15.8	16.0	~
B.	BOLIVIA	67.5	54.2	56.8	51.2	53.5	~
C.	BRAZIL	7.1	10.0	7.2	6.7	5.1	5.9
D.	CHILE	27.0	21.7	5.4	6.2	3.7	~
E.	COLOMBIA	27.3	23.3	36.1	41.4	43.1	~
F.	COSTA RICA	29.8	30.3	26.3	37.4	38.1	~
H.	DOMINICAN REP.	45.1	52.2	31.1	28.6	24.7	25.5
I.	ECUADOR	56.6	65.5	62.0	57.6	53.2	~
J.	EL SALVADOR	40.5	36.1	37.0	29.6	25.2	26.1
K.	GUATEMALA	28.0	27.7	34.7	22.8	16.3	15.4
L.	HAITI	36.3	47.0	58.4	43.0	38.7	33.5
M.	HONDURAS	28.6	27.7	36.6	42.0	35.2	35.8
N.	MEXICO	18.2	10.1	27.0	28.1	21.5	~
O.	NICARAGUA	28.1	20.2	22.7	16.5	16.9	17.7
P.	PANAMA	23.5	19.6	11.6	12.0	10.5	~
Q.	PARAGUAY	34.2	37.6	33.2	30.2	22.8	17.7
R.	PERU	21.3	22.8	27.6	28.7	23.9	21.2
S.	URUGUAY	20.3	10.2	18.4	15.0	13.6	15.7
T.	VENEZUELA	7.8	5.0	5.4	4.3	6.7	3.2

1. For definition of current revenue see table 3002, above.

SOURCE: IDB-SPTF, 1984, table 31.

Table 3006

CENTRAL GOVERNMENT PRODUCTION AND SALES TAXES, 19 L, 1970–83
(% of Current Revenue)[1]

	Country	1970	1975	1980	1981	1982	1983‡
A.	ARGENTINA	32.8	38.0	39.3	46.9	44.2	~
B.	BOLIVIA	34.5	29.4	27.1	41.8	35.5	~
C.	BRAZIL	59.0	48.4	28.8	28.2	32.7	29.2
D.	CHILE	43.4	47.3	62.6	54.8	52.2	~
E.	COLOMBIA	8.6	18.3	20.1	19.6	19.3	~
F.	COSTA RICA	40.7	41.1	39.6	32.9	31.4	~
H.	DOMINICAN REP.	20.2	14.9	21.5	25.6	36.5	36.3
I.	ECUADOR	16.5	15.0	19.9	21.1	25.0	~
J.	EL SALVADOR	25.6	22.6	20.5	19.9	20.0	22.1
K.	GUATEMALA	43.3	41.1	39.9	47.0	51.3	50.2
L.	HAITI	10.9	12.0	10.1	18.7	20.4	30.4
M.	HONDURAS	36.0	28.2	25.0	27.9	30.8	30.0
N.	MEXICO	27.5	42.0	24.0	24.2	24.5	~
O.	NICARAGUA	36.3	43.7	45.9	46.4	44.7	47.3
P.	PANAMA	14.2	14.6	18.4	18.0	15.6	~
Q.	PARAGUAY	27.1	17.0	16.2	14.7	15.0	19.4
R.	PERU	31.2	36.7	37.2	41.3	47.1	51.9
S.	URUGUAY	40.3	69.9	51.7	52.5	52.3	46.9
T.	VENEZUELA	6.1	2.0	3.2	2.8	3.5	16.8

1. For definition of current revenue see table 3002, above.

SOURCE: IDB-SPTF, 1984, table 30.

Table 3008

CENTRAL GOVERNMENT TOTAL EXPENDITURE, 19 L, 1970, 1975, 1980–83
(% of GDP)

	Country	1970	1975	1980	1981	1982	1983‡
A.	ARGENTINA	9.2	13.1	15.4	16.8	15.9	21.4
B.	BOLIVIA	9.5	13.4	17.0	14.0	12.0	16.7
C.	BRAZIL	9.5	9.0	9.2	8.5	8.8	8.7
D.	CHILE	20.6	24.5	20.9	23.6	27.2	33.8
E.	COLOMBIA	10.0	9.7	10.3	10.8	11.8	12.0
F.	COSTA RICA	12.8	15.6	20.9	16.6	16.1	20.2
H.	DOMINICAN REP.	17.7	18.1	17.5	16.4	12.6	13.5
I.	ECUADOR	13.4	16.2	14.2	16.2	15.3	12.7
J.	EL SALVADOR	12.8	14.9	18.0	20.5	20.2	18.9
K.	GUATEMALA	9.9	10.0	14.2	16.0	12.4	11.6
L.	HAITI	14.3	16.0	17.1	21.2	18.9	17.4
M.	HONDURAS	15.4	18.9	19.9	20.3	21.2	20.3
N.	MEXICO	10.8	17.3	18.8	22.4	26.2	~
O.	NICARAGUA	11.9	18.1	29.6	32.1	44.0	55.5
P.	PANAMA	20.5	23.0	27.5	28.1	34.1	25.7
Q.	PARAGUAY	11.8	9.8	9.5	11.1	10.8	10.9
R.	PERU	17.5	21.3	23.4	22.8	22.0	21.4
S.	URUGUAY	15.1	16.5	15.8	16.9	23.5	15.8
T.	VENEZUELA	19.3	33.8	24.5	29.8	27.8	28.2

SOURCE: IDB-SPTF, 1984, table 20.

Table 3009

TOTAL EXPENDITURE[1] AND DEFICIT OF CENTRAL GOVERNMENTS, 19 L, 1975–81

(M NC)

Country	Code[2]	1975	1976	1977	1978	1979	1980[‡]	1981
A. ARGENTINA[3]	I	212	1,031	1,885	4.5	11.9	25.0	59.7
	II	−155	−608	−497	1.0	2.3	7.8	25.9
B. BOLIVIA	I	6,395	8,240	10,954	11,542	15,035	21,521	24,347
	II	706	−1,399	−3,313	−3,002	−6,651	−9,728	−10,461
C. BRAZIL[3]	I	95.4	165.8	241.9	#	671.4	1,798.9	3,310.1
	II	#	+.4	+1	+4.9	+2.3	+2.0	3.0
D. CHILE[4]	I	7,449	24,102	2,699	2,788	2,846	3,507	4,022
	II	−453	−227	−200	−100	208	75	182
E. COLOMBIA[3]	I	39,351	44.3	57.6	78.2	108.6	163.2	214.9
	II	−909	+4.5	+5.8	+5.9	+6.0	−11.4	−10.0
F. COSTA RICA	I	2,942	3,978	4,654	5,484	6,629	8,279	9,476
	II	−681	−1,285	−1,167	−1,458	−2,390	−3,297	1,780
H. DOMINICAN REP.	I	653	578	631	675	1,005	1,066	1,085
	II	−17	−14	−11	−97	−331	−197	−177
I. ECUADOR	I	11,755	16,813	20,745	26,155	28,189	46,156	58,904
	II	609	−2,160	−4,293	−7,098	−5,109	8,589	−20,804
J. EL SALVADOR	I	600	878	1,032	1,158	1,306	1,514	~
	II	−22	−68	+150	−131	−91	−484	~
K. GUATEMALA	I	395	632	689	799	922	1,256	1,473
	II	−43	−225	−98	−138	−254	−509	−727
L. HAITI	I	495	683	811	911	1,048	1,202	1,460
	II	−270	−398	−453	−370	−442	−511	−803
M. HONDURAS	I	438	524	694	842	912	1,243	1,237
	II	−155	−168	−208	−301	−280	−485	−496
N. MEXICO[3]	I	156	208	267[a]	476	733	1,061	2,100
	II	−54	−74	−75[a]	−174	−321	−381	−1,162
O. NICARAGUA	I	2,106	2,179	3,078	3,287	2,982	6,364	8,412
	II	−783	−652	−1,282	−1,666	−1,090	−1,838	−2,906
P. PANAMA	I	420	443	475	648	933	1,065	1,216
	II	−123	−120	−127	−251	−433	−370	−426
Q. PARAGUAY	I	18,609	22,816	25,799	30,776	40,628	52,976	68,977
	II	−714	−3,569	+579	+3,557	3,024	−1,385	−8,215
R. PERU[3]	I	131.4	175.9	267.1	430.0	728	1,370	2,276
	II	−43.5	−64.5	−113.0	−166	−176	−351	−753
S. URUGUAY	I	1,349	2,048	3,179	4,750	8,300	14,879	21,377
	II	−363	−326	−241	−400	+124	+76	−117
T. VENEZUELA	I	32,345	44,571	50,696	51,213	50,958	72,869	93,962
	II	8,553	−6,461	+10,222	+11,107	−903	−10 172	1,307

1. Current plus capital expenditures.
2. I = Total expenditure; II = Deficit (+ indicates surplus), i.e., current income less total expenditure.
3. BNC.
4. M US of 1976.

a. Excluding treasury certificates issued and redeemed in the same year, since their introduction in 1978.

SOURCE: ECLA-S, 1978, 1979, 1980, 1981

Table 3010

FUNCTIONAL ANALYSIS OF CENTRAL GOVERNMENT EXPENDITURE, 18 LC

(%)

Country	Year	Total Expenditure[1]	General Public Services	Defense	Education	Health	Social Security and Welfare	Housing and Community Amenities	Other Community and Social Services	Subtotal Economic Services[2]	Agriculture, Forestry, Fishing, and Hunting	Roads	Other Transportation and Communication	Other Purposes
A. ARGENTINA	1981	100.00	8.89	11.44	7.32	1.37	33.82	.34	.50	17.95	.82	2.86	4.09	4.82
B. BOLIVIA	1981	100.00	18.52	22.72	24.44	7.21	.92	1.75	.64	17.16	2.06	4.66	6.28	6.65
C. BRAZIL	1981	100.00	16.64	3.43	3.83	7.37	34.62	.20	.10	24.06	7.15	1.69	2.31	9.74
D. CHILE	1981	100.00	11.26	11.97	14.42	6.40	37.95	4.63	.63	11.36	1.36	1.97	.72	1.37
E. COLOMBIA	1979	100.00	~	~	~	~	~	~	~	~	~	~	~	~
F. COSTA RICA	1981	100.00	9.06	2.64	23.66	~	10.27	2.33	1.64	15.20	2.76	10.57	.68	10.53
H. DOMINICAN REP.	1981	100.00	11.98	8.85	13.88	9.67	7.45	6.06	1.72	37.29	17.32	~	10.12	4.17
J. EL SALVADOR	1982	100.00	14.15	11.58	16.41	6.95	3.66	1.17	1.25	23.16	~	~	~	9.64
K. GUATEMALA	1982	100.00	~	~	~	~	~	~	~	~	~	~	~	~
L. HAITI	1982	100.00	~	~	~	~	~	~	~	~	~	~	~	~
M. HONDURAS	1976	100.00	27.72	10.49	20.69	14.69	4.73	2.57	.93	18.76	3.10	12.35	#	#
N. MEXICO	1981	100.00	~	2.48	18.19	1.86	14.70	4.09	1.07	36.41	8.68	1.86	5.62	15.56
O. NICARAGUA	1980	100.00	25.09	10.97	11.58	14.58	4.44	2.92	#	20.58	8.95	5.52	5.93	9.82
P. PANAMA	1981	100.00	20.68	#	12.78	13.24	9.30	3.52	.85	18.39	5.49	3.62	1.28	21.24
Q. PARAGUAY	1981	100.00	19.29	13.15	11.76	4.51	19.03	3.73	.23	19.03	2.62	12.91	.33	9.25
R. PERU	1982	100.00	~	~	~	~	~	~	~	~	~	~	~	~
S. URUGUAY	1982	100.00	8.82	12.54	7.34	3.14	51.73	.03	.75	13.93	1.33	3.72	1.44	3.89
T. VENEZUELA	1982	100.00	5.85	5.82	16.23	7.28	6.20	2.74	2.07	24.42	4.86	2.70	3.20	29.85
UNITED STATES	1982	100.00	5.13	23.08	2.09	10.81	33.54	2.60	.32	8.54	3.32	1.07	1.29	14.13

1. Owing to adjustment items and unallocated transactions, components may not add to totals.
2. Includes other unspecified categories, as well as Agriculture, Roads, and Transportation.

SOURCE: IMF-GFSY, 1983, pp. 27, 29.

Table 3011

DEFENSE AND SOCIAL EXPENDITURES, 20 L, 1972 AND 1981

	Country	Total Expenditure (% of GNP)		Central Government Expenditure[2] Per Capita (1975 dollars)					
				Defense[3]		Education[4]		Health[5]	
		1972	1981	1972	1981	1972	1981	1972	1981
A.	ARGENTINA	16.5	23.6	8.8	11.4	8.8	7.3	2.9	1.4
B.	BOLIVIA	9.2	12.7	16.2	22.7	30.6	24.4	8.6	7.2
C.	BRAZIL	16.6	19.5	8.3	3.4	6.8	3.8	6.4	7.4
D.	CHILE	42.3	31.0	6.1	12.0	14.3	14.4	8.2	6.4
E.	COLOMBIA	~	~	~	~	~	~	~	~
F.	COSTA RICA	18.9	23.7	2.8	2.6	28.3	23.7	3.8	29.7
G.	CUBA	~	~	~	~	~	~	~	~
H.	DOMINICAN REP.	~	44.9	~	8.9	~	13.9	~	9.7
I.	ECUADOR	~	17.1	~	11.8	~	30.1	~	7.9
J.	EL SALVADOR	12.8	18.5	6.6	16.8	21.4	17.9	10.9	8.4
K.	GUATEMALA	9.9	16.2	11.0	~	19.4	~	9.5	~
L.	HAITI	14.5	19.4	~	~	~	~	~	~
M.	HONDURAS	15.4	~	12.4	~	22.3	~	10.2	~
N.	MEXICO	12.1	20.8	4.2	2.5	16.6	18.2	5.1	1.9
O.	NICARAGUA	15.5	30.2	12.3	11.0	16.6	11.6	4.0	14.6
P.	PANAMA	~	36.1	~	~	~	12.8	~	13.2
Q.	PARAGUAY	13.1	10.7	13.8	13.2	12.	11.	3.5	4.5
R.	PERU	17.1	20.2	14.8	13.8	22.7	11.3	6.2	5.3
S.	URUGUAY	25.0	24.4	5.6	12.9	9.5	7.7	1.6	3.8
T.	VENEZUELA	21.3	28.9	10.3	3.9	18.3	18.3	11.7	7.3

1.   Both current and capital (development) expenditures are included. The inadequate statistical coverage of state, provincial, and local governments and the nonavailability of data for these lower levels of government have dictated the use of only central government data. This may seriously understate or distort the statistical portrayal of the allocation of resources for various purposes, especially in large countries where lower levels of government have considerable autonomy and are responsible for many social services. Great caution should therefore be exercised in using the data for cross-economy comparisons.

2.   Central Government Expenditure comprises the expenditure by all government offices, departments, establishments, and other bodies that are agencies or instruments of the central authority of a country. It does not necessarily comprise all public expenditure.

3.   Defense Expenditure comprises all expenditure, whether by defense or other departments, for the maintenance of military forces, including the purchase of military supplies and equipment, construction, recruiting, and training. Also falling in this category is expenditure for strengthening the public services to meet wartime emergencies, for training civil defense personnel, and for foreign military aid and contributions to military organizations and alliances.

4.   Education Expenditure comprises public expenditure for the provision, management, inspection, and support of preprimary, primary, and secondary schools; of universities and colleges; and of vocational, technical, and other training institutions by central governments. Also included is expenditure on the general administration and regulation of the education system; on research into its objectives, organization, administration, and methods; and on such subsidiary services as transportation and medical and dental services in schools.

5.   Health Expenditure covers public expenditure on hospitals, medical and dental centers, and clinics with a major medical component; on national health and medical insurance schemes; and on family planning and preventive care. Also included is expenditure on the general administration and regulation of relevant government departments, hospitals and clinics, health and sanitation, and national health and medical insurance schemes.

a.   1973.
b.   1979.

SOURCE: WB-WDR, 1983, 1984, table 26.

Table 3012

CENTRAL GOVERNMENT EXPENDITURES, LENDING REPAYMENTS, AND DEFICITS, 19 LC

(%)

	Country	Year[1]	Code	(1) Total Expenditure and Lending Repayment (2)+(5)	(2) Total Expenditure (3)+(4)	(3) Current Expenditure	(4) Capital Expenditure	(5) Lending Minus Repayment
A.	ARGENTINA	1981	~	100.00	89.87	72.92	16.95	10.13
B.	BOLIVIA	1981	~	100.00	99.84	92.68	7.16	.16
C.	BRAZIL	1981	D	100.00	74.75	68.25	6.49	25.25
D.	CHILE	1981	A	100.00	95.82	87.44	8.34	4.18
E.	COLOMBIA	1980	C	100.00	98.06	77.47	~	1.94
F.	COSTA RICA	1981	A	100.00	101.32	89.80	16.66	-1.34
H.	DOMINICAN REP.	1981	A	100.00	99.23	68.43	26.53	.77
I.	ECUADOR	1978	~	100.00	100.00	~	~	~
J.	EL SALVADOR	1982	~	100.00	100.22	73.26	14.91	-.22
K.	GUATEMALA	1982	B	100.00	98.41	61.97	33.29	1.59
L.	HAITI	1982	~	100.00	100.00	89.32	10.68	~
M.	HONDURAS	1976	A	100.00	99.47	63.47	36.00	.53
N.	MEXICO	1981	~	100.00	91.85	65.47	26.38	8.15
O.	NICARAGUA	1980	B	100.00	99.01	80.55	18.46	.99
P.	PANAMA	1981	A	100.00	96.90	78.42	18.48	3.10
Q.	PARAGUAY	1981	A	100.00	90.64	68.78	21.85	9.36
R.	PERU	1982	~	100.00	100.00	78.06	21.94	#
S.	URUGUAY	1982	~	100.00	97.56	85.87	11.68	2.44
T.	VENEZUELA	1982	~	100.00	83.93	58.01	26.29	16.07
	UNITED STATES	1982	D	100.00	97.36	92.00	5.58	2.64

1. Letters A-G indicate percent of General Government tax revenue accounted by Central Government, where data are available, as follows: A, 95 and over; B, 90-94.9; C, 80-89.9; D, 70-79.9; E, 60-69.9; F, 50-59.9; G, 20-49.9.

SOURCE: IMF-GFSY, 1979, p. 17; IMF-GFSY, 1982, pp. 26-27; IMF-GFSY, 1983, pp. 28-29.

Table 3013

CENTRAL GOVERNMENT CURRENT SAVINGS, 19 L, 1970, 1975, 1980-83

(% of GDP)

	Country	1970	1975	1980	1981	1982	1983[‡]
A.	ARGENTINA	1.2	-7.9	2.4	.3	1.1	-4.0
B.	BOLIVIA	-.5	1.5	-4.5	-4.4	-6.7	-13.9
C.	BRAZIL	2.7	4.2	3.0	3.5	3.3	3.1
D.	CHILE	4.4	5.0	6.5	4.8	4.2	-2.3
E.	COLOMBIA	3.0	3.0	1.9	2.6	1.9	.8
F.	COSTA RICA	2.0	.7	-3.6	-.8	.5	1.1
H.	DOMINICAN REP.	4.3	9.7	2.6	2.4	-.7	.2
I.	ECUADOR	#	5.2	2.8	-2.1	-.5	.7
J.	EL SALVADOR	.3	2.4	-.7	-1.6	-2.7	-1.8
K.	GUATEMALA	.9	1.7	1.5	.6	.8	.1
L.	HAITI	.5	-1.2	-.2	-2.9	-.8	.3
M.	HONDURAS	1.6	1.3	.7	-1.6	-1.6	-3.2
N.	MEXICO	2.2	.3	1.5	-.2	-3.8	~
O.	NICARAGUA	1.8	2.3	-1.2	-4.2	-8.8	-6.8
P.	PANAMA	.9	.9	.5	-1.3	1.7	-.1
Q.	PARAGUAY	1.9	1.8	2.4	.9	.6	-1.2
R.	PERU	2.8	-.5	2.4	.2	.2	-4.3
S.	URUGUAY	#	-2.7	2.0	1.9	-6.1	-.1
T.	VENEZUELA	4.5	18.2	8.3	13.0	7.9	~

SOURCE: IDB-SPTF, 1984, table 21.

Table 3014

CENTRAL GOVERNMENT OVERALL SURPLUS OR DEFICIT,
19 L, 1970, 1975, 1980–83
(% of GDP)

	Country	1970	1975	1980	1981	1982	1983[‡]
A.	ARGENTINA	-1.4	-9.2	-2.7	-5.3	-3.9	-10.9
B.	BOLIVIA	-.8	-1.4	-7.2	-5.6	-7.5	-14.2
C.	BRAZIL	-.4	.1	.1	.1	.1	#
D.	CHILE	-.7	.2	5.0	3.2	1.9	-6.0
E.	COLOMBIA	-1.0	-.2	-.7	-.5	-1.4	-2.2
F.	COSTA RICA	.1	-2.3	-8.2	-3.6	-3.0	-2.7
H.	DOMINICAN REP.	-1.6	-.4	-3.1	-2.7	-2.9	-2.6
I.	ECUADOR	-2.8	-.6	-1.4	-4.9	-4.6	-1.6
J.	EL SALVADOR	-1.6	-1.8	-6.6	-8.0	-7.7	-5.8
K.	GUATEMALA	-1.3	-.9	-4.7	-7.3	-4.0	-3.9
L.	HAITI	-.7	-5.2	-7.6	-12.2	-9.0	-7.4
M.	HONDURAS	-3.1	-5.3	-4.7	-6.2	-7.4	-7.1
N.	MEXICO	-1.7	-5.3	-2.9	-6.3	-9.8	~
O.	NICARAGUA	-1.2	-5.9	-9.0	-10.4	-19.5	-26.8
P.	PANAMA	-4.8	-6.8	-5.5	-6.8	-10.7	-5.2
Q.	PARAGUAY	-.1	-.4	-.2	-2.8	-.7	-3.3
R.	PERU	-1.4	-5.5	-2.8	-4.9	-4.0	-7.5
S.	URUGUAY	-1.3	-4.4	.1	-.1	-8.6	-1.7
T.	VENEZUELA	-1.2	.7	-.2	1.8	-1.5	-.8

SOURCE: IDB-SPTF, 1984, table 22.

Figure 30:1

GOVERNMENT DEFICIT AS SHARE OF GDP, 19 L, 1981–83

(%)

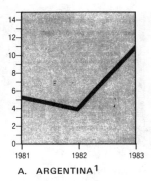

A.   ARGENTINA[1]

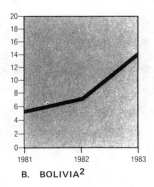

B.   BOLIVIA[2]

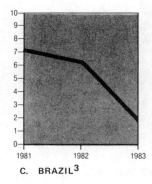

C.   BRAZIL[3]

D.   CHILE[2]

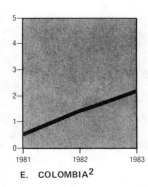

E.   COLOMBIA[2]

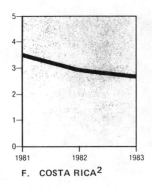

F.   COSTA RICA[2]

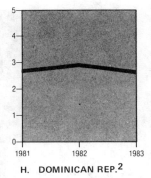

H.   DOMINICAN REP.[2]

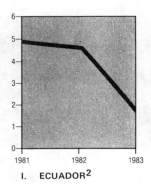

I.   ECUADOR[2]

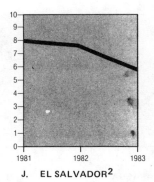

J.   EL SALVADOR[2]

Figure 30:1 (Continued)

GOVERNMENT DEFICIT AS SHARE OF GDP, 19 L, 1981–83

(%)

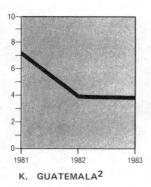

K. GUATEMALA[2]

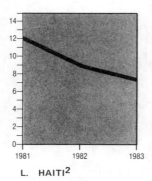

L. HAITI[2]

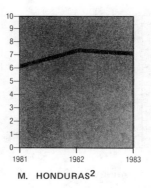

M. HONDURAS[2]

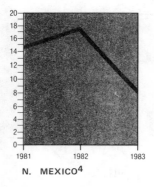

N. MEXICO[4]

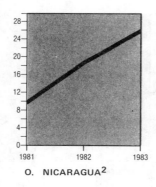

O. NICARAGUA[2]

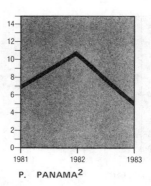

P. PANAMA[2]

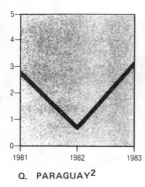

Q. PARAGUAY[2]

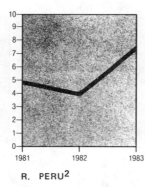

R. PERU[2]

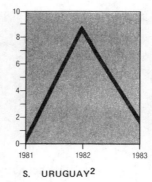

S. URUGUAY[2]

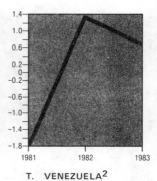

T. VENEZUELA[2]

1.   National administration.
2.   Central government.
3.   Federal public sector.
4.   Public sector.

SOURCE: IDB-SPTF, 1984, Part Two.

Table 3015

CENTRAL GOVERNMENT NET DOMESTIC BORROWING,
19 L, 1970, 1975, 1980-83
(% of GDP)

	Country	1970	1975	1980	1981	1982	1983[‡]
A.	ARGENTINA	1.1	10.7	1.9	5.3	6.6	13.0
B.	BOLIVIA	.9	-.2	3.4	5.5	7.4	13.5
C.	BRAZIL	.4	-.1	-.1	-.1	-.1	#
D.	CHILE	2.3	5.1	-4.0	-2.5	-1.4	2.9
E.	COLOMBIA	-.1	.4	-.3	-.5	.8	1.9
F.	COSTA RICA	-.7	1.6	7.1	2.4	2.0	1.7
H.	DOMINICAN REP.	.7	.6	1.4	1.4	2.3	1.2
I.	ECUADOR	2.8	.4	.9	2.6	1.7	2.3
J.	EL SALVADOR	1.3	1.4	5.2	5.9	5.1	3.9
K.	GUATEMALA	-.1	.6	3.3	6.2	2.9	2.6
L.	HAITI	.3	#	2.8	3.8	2.9	1.1
M.	HONDURAS	.8	1.4	1.7	2.4	2.9	4.1
N.	MEXICO	1.4	4.0	2.3	5.9	7.8	~
O.	NICARAGUA	.1	2.5	4.7	6.9	15.1	18.7
P.	PANAMA	.7	.5	2.0	2.5	1.1	2.9
Q.	PARAGUAY	-.1	-.1	-.2	2.5	5	3.3
R.	PERU	.8	2.5	2.5	3.3	1.5	1.2
S.	URUGUAY	1.2	4.4	-.1	.1	7.9	~
T.	VENEZUELA	.5	-.2	-2.9	-1.7	1.1	.6

SOURCE: IDB-SPTF, 1984, table 23.

Table 3016

CENTRAL GOVERNMENT NET FOREIGN BORROWING,
19 L, 1970, 1975, 1980-83
(% of GDP)

	Country	1970	1975	1980	1981	1982	1983[‡]
A.	ARGENTINA	.3	-1.5	.7	#	-2.7	-2.1
B.	BOLIVIA	#	1.6	3.9	.0	.0	.7
C.	BRAZIL	.0	.0	.0	.0	.0	.0
D.	CHILE	-1.6	-3.5	-1.0	-.6	-.5	3.1
E.	COLOMBIA	1.1	-.1	1.0	1.0	.6	.3
F.	COSTA RICA	.6	.7	1.1	1.2	1.0	1.0
H.	DOMINICAN REP.	1.0	-.1	1.6	1.3	.6	1.5
I.	ECUADOR	#	.2	.5	2.3	2.9	-.7
J.	EL SALVADOR	.3	.4	1.4	2.2	2.7	1.9
K.	GUATEMALA	1.3	.4	1.4	1.1	1.1	1.4
L.	HAITI	.4	5.2	4.8	8.4	6.1	6.3
M.	HONDURAS	2.4	3.9	2.9	3.9	4.5	3.1
N.	MEXICO	.3	1.3	.6	.4	2.0	~
O.	NICARAGUA	1.1	3.4	4.3	3.5	4.4	8.1
P.	PANAMA	3.6	3.8	3.5	4.3	9.6	2.3
Q.	PARAGUAY	.4	.7	.5	.3	#	.2
R.	PERU	.6	3.0	.3	1.6	2.5	6.3
S.	URUGUAY	.2	#	#	#	.7	~
T.	VENEZUELA	.6	-.6	3.1	-.1	.4	.1

SOURCE: IDB-SPTF, 1984, table 24.

Table 3017

CENTRAL GOVERNMENT INTEREST PAYMENTS, 19 L, 1970–83
(% of Total Expenditures)

	Country	1970	1975	1980	1981	1982	1983[‡]
A.	ARGENTINA	3.2	4.9	.3	.6	1.2	~
B.	BOLIVIA	5.3	3.7	10.5	5.0	17.0	~
C.	BRAZIL	4.5	1.8	5.1	3.7	2.5	2.5
D.	CHILE	2.5	7.6	2.4	2.0	1.4	~
E.	COLOMBIA	4.7	6.0	5.1	6.7	6.8	~
F.	COSTA RICA	10.9	7.4	13.6	11.3	11.8	12.7
H.	DOMINICAN REP.	.5	.9	7.3	6.3	5.2	6.3
I.	ECUADOR	12.3	4.4	7.6	9.5	12.7	~
J.	EL SALVADOR	1.2	1.8	2.5	5.4	9.0	10.6
K.	GUATEMALA	4.2	6.0	3.9	4.1	6.7	~
L.	HAITI	4.1	1.7	2.2	2.3	3.5	~
M.	HONDURAS	3.3	5.2	5.6	6.4	7.3	10.7
N.	MEXICO	9.4	7.2	9.6	13.2	20.9	~
O.	NICARAGUA	2.6	7.5	7.6	11.3	11.8	4.6
P.	PANAMA	5.3	9.8	19.2	24.3	25.8	~
Q.	PARAGUAY	2.8	1.9	3.3	2.7	3.0	3.6
R.	PERU	5.2	8.0	18.4	19.7	18.3	21.8
S.	URUGUAY	3.1	5.6	2.2	1.9	2.6	7.7
T.	VENEZUELA	1.6	.8	6.8	6.6	7.5	~

SOURCE: IDB-SPTF, 1984, table 35.

Table 3018

ARGENTINA CENTRAL GOVERNMENT REVENUE, EXPENDITURE, AND FINANCING THE DEFICIT, 1975–81
(B NC)

Category	1975	1976	1977	1978	1979	1980	1981
1. Current Income	57	42.3	1,388	3.5	9.5	17.1	33.9
Tax Revenue	47	370	1,196	2.8	6.8	15.3	29.3
Non-Tax Revenue	9	53	192	.8	2.7	1.9	4.5
2. Current Expenditure	182	849	1,422	3.9	10.3	22.1	48.6
Wages and Salaries	47	196	490	1.5	3.9	9.2	17.7
Non-Personal Goods and Services	~	~	167	.5	1.1	2.4	5.5
Interest	11	117	97	.2	.4	.1	.4
Transfers	114	467	660	1.6	4.8	10.2	24.3
Other Current Expenditure	10	69	8	~	.1	.2	.7
3. Current Savings[1]	-125	-426	-34	-.4	-.8	-4.9	-14.7
4. Capital Expenditure	189	182	463	.6	1.6	2.9	11.1
Real Investment	7	54	184	.4	1.0	1.6	4.8
Loans (Net of Repayments)	23	128	279	.2	.6	1.3	6.3
5. Total Expenditure[2]	212	1,031	1,885	4.5	11.9	25.0	59.7
6. Fiscal Deficit[3]	-155	-608	-497	1.0	2.3	7.8	25.9
7. Financing Deficit							
Central Bank	119	253	312	~	~	9.8	27.8
Unified Official Account Fund	20	111	231	.4	1.0	1.6	1.6
Issue of Securities[4]	27	293	471	1.7	4.3	2.7	16.1
Bond of Amortization Payments	-11	-53	-561	-1.0	-2.9	-5.7	-17.2
Other	#	4	44	.1	-.1	-.5	2.3

1. Current Income minus Current Expenditure.
2. Current Expenditure plus Capital Expenditure.
3. For 1975 and 1976 the National Treasury calculated the deficit by considering
    Amortization of the Public Debt as expenditure and Issues of Securities as income.
4. Less debt amortization payments (1975 and 1976).

SOURCE: ECLA-S, 1978, 1979, 1980, 1981.

Table 3019

BOLIVIA CENTRAL GOVERNMENT REVENUE, EXPENDITURE, AND FINANCING THE DEFICIT, 1975–81

(M NC)

Category	1975	1976	1977	1978	1979	1980	1981[‡]
1. Current Income	5,689	6,841	7.641	8,540	8,384	11.793	13.885
Inland Revenue	1,724	2,332	2,748	3,165	3,621	4,459	5,077
Custom Revenue	1,550	1,456	1,694	1,960	2,064	2,564	3,150
Additional Export Tax	622	589	535	470	807	127	208
Mining Royalties	478	856	1,258	1,545	1,333	1,771	889
Petroleum and Gas Royalties	819	1,270	918	919	80	1,852	3,957
Other Income	496	338	488	481	480	1,999	604
2. Current Expenditure	6,395	8,240	10,954	11,542	15,035	21,521	24,347
Personal Services	2,686	3,389	3,795	4,704	5,948	9,706	11,132
Non-personal Services	~	~	~	513	587	946	1,005
Materials and Supplies	744	808	931	684	692	1,512	2,120
Fixed and Financial Assets	230	241	293	256	317	1,345	1,477
Public Debt	845	1,014	925	1,165	1,831	3,817	4,432
Transfers and Contributions	1,789	2,543	3,153	3,211	3,424	2.552	2,017
Other Expenditure	300	245	1,857	1,009	2,236	1,642	2,162
3. Deficit	-706	-1,399	-3,113	-3,002	-6,651	-9,728	-10,461

SOURCE: ECLA-S, 1978, 1979, 1980, 1981.

Table 3020

BRAZIL CENTRAL GOVERNMENT REVENUE, EXPENDITURE, AND FINANCING THE DEFICIT, 1975–81

(B NC)

Category	1975	1976	1977	1978	1979	1980	1981[‡]
1. Current Income	76.8	116.2	242.9	349.2	509.8	1,219.4	2,262.0
Tax Income	~	~	211.0	309.6	445.1	958.2	1,837.2
Industrialized Products	~	~	67.6	97.5	127.6	263.2	500.9
Income Tax	~	~	60.5	95.5	150.3	307.0	640.4
Imports	~	~	17.1	23.9	34.1	87.7	138.3
Exports	~	~	~	.1	.2	19.3	12.4
Fuels and Lubricants	~	~	30.0	38.7	49.5	51.2	59.3
Financial Operations	~	~	8.8	13.6	23.9	103.1	266.0
Other[1]	~	~	27.0	40.3	59.5	126.7	220.0
Other Income	~	~	31.9	39.6	64.7	261.2	424.7
2. Total Expenditure	72.9	165.8	241.9	~	671.4	1,798.9	3,310.1
Wages and Social Security Expenditure	~	~	~	~	167.6	336.9	719.8
Contribution to Assistance Funds	~	~	~	~	50.5	97.7	222.7
Transfers from the Treasury to Public Enterprises	~	~	~	~	135.2	380.2	916.5
Subsidies Paid Out by the Monetary Authority	~	~	~	~	181.9	896.4	1,303.2
Other Expenditure	~	~	~	~	136.2	87.7	147.9
3. Result	-3.9	-49.6	~	~	-161.6	-579.5	-1,048.1
Treasury Surplus	~	.4	~	4.9	2.3	2.0	3.0
Result of Accounts Administered by the Monetary Authority	~	~	~	~	-163.9	-581.5	-1,051.1
4. Financing of Deficit	~	~	~	~	161.6	579.5	1,048.1
Public Indebtedness	~	~	~	~-78.6	-78.6	-30.4	332.2
Monetary Authority	~	~	~	~	240.2	609.9	715.9

1. Includes taxes on energy, minerals, road transport, and others.

SOURCE: ECLA-S, 1978, 1979, 1980, 1981.

Table 3021

CHILE CENTRAL GOVERNMENT REVENUE, EXPENDITURE, AND FINANCING THE DEFICIT, 1975–81

Category	1975	1976	1977	1978	1979	1980	1981[‡]
A. Income and expenditure in national currency (Millions of current pesos of each year)							
1. Current Income	7,902	25,204	57,601	100,422	160,699	251,023	310,660
Direct Taxes	2,425	6,538	14,746	24,718	48,821	76,396	90,903
Indirect Taxes	5,144	17,947	41,070	69,568	104,419	154,929	198,582
Non-tax Revenue	362	719	1,785	6,136	7,459	19,698	21,175
2. Total Expenditure	7,449	24,102	57,025	94,533	151,242	226,338	291,548
Servicing of Public Debt	88	289	1,055	1,236	7,822	15,849	2,860
Other Expenditure	7,361	23,813	55,970	93,298	143,420	210,489	288,688
3. Deficit (1-2)	453	1,102	576	5,889	9,457	24,685	19,112
4. Deficit/Total Expenditure (Percentage)	6.1	4.6	1.0	6.2	6.3	10.9	6.6
B. Income and expenditure in foreign currency (Millions of dollars at current prices)							
1. Current Income	219	383	374	360	864	1,007	523
Copper	177	352	353	331	840	976	449
Other	42	31	21	29	24	31	74
2. Total Expenditure	556	695	624	675	679	1,178	1,550
Service of Public Debt	388	544	445	507	524	958[a]	1,270[b]
Other Expenditure	168	151	179	168	156	220	280
3. Deficit (1-2)	-337	-312	-250	-315	184	-171	-1,037
4. Deficit/Total Expenditure (Percentage)	-60 6	-44.9	-40.1	-46.7	27.1	-14.5	-66.9
C. Consolidate income and expenditure (Millions of dollars at 1976 prices)							
1. Current Income	1,933	2,126	2,499	2,688	3,104	3,582	3,840
Copper	~	~	314	253	509	519	219
Direct Taxes	~	~	564	604	752	843	914
Indirect Taxes	~	~	1,553	1,681	1,717	1,965	2,290
Non-tax Revenue	~	~	68	150	126	255	417
2. Total Expenditure	2,188	2,362	2,699	2,788	2,846	3,507	4,022
Servicing of Public Debt	~	~	435	418	446	710[c]	651[d]
Other Expenditure	~	~	2,264	2,370	2,450	2,797	3,371
3. Deficit (1-2)	255	236	-200	-100	208	75	-182

a. Includes advance payments of US $42 million.
b. Includes advance payments of US $867 million.
c. Includes advance payments of US $346 million at 1976 prices.
d. Includes advance payments of US $423 million at 1976 prices.

SOURCE: ECLA-S, 1978, 1979 1980, 1981.

Table 3022

COLOMBIA CENTRAL GOVERNMENT REVENUE, EXPENDITURE, AND FINANCING THE DEFICIT, 1975–81
(B NC)

Category	1975	1976	1977	1978	1979	1980	1981[‡]
1. Current Income	38.4	48.8	63.4	84.1	114.6	151.8	204.9
Tax Revenue	37.4	47.7	62.2	82.0	112.6	148.8	201.1
Income and Complementary Taxes	18.0	20.6	23.9	30.4	37.3	47.1	53.0
Sales Taxes	7.7	10.1	12.6	17.5	23.0	30.5	40.3
Customs Duties and Surcharges	5.4	6.8	9.4	13.4	16.6	24.8	29.4
Profits on Exchange Operations	3.6	5.5	8.8	10.9	23.8	30.1	55.5
Gasoline Taxes	1.7	3.2	4.5	5.8	8.0	11.3	18.1
Other	.8	1.4	3.0	4.0	4.3	4.9	4.8
Non-tax Revenue	.9	1.0	1.2	2.1	2.0	3.0	3.8
2. Current Expenditure	26.1	32.0	41.4	57.1	82.6	121.3	153.8
3. Current Savings	12.2	16.8	22.0	26.9	31.9	30.6	51.1
4. Investment	13.1	12.3	16.2	21.0	26.0	42.0	61.1
5. Total Expenditure	39.3	44.3	57.6	78.2	108.6	163.3	214.9
6. Fiscal Deficit (or surplus)	-.9	4.5	5.8	5.9	6.0	-11.4	-10.0
7. Financing of Deficit							
External Credit	-.5	-1.1	-1.6	-2.2	5.2	16.5	19.5
Domestic Credit	1.3	-3.3	-4.2	-3.7	-11.2	-5.9	-9.5

SOURCE: ECLA-S, 1978, 1979, 1980, 1981.

Table 3023

COSTA RICA CENTRAL GOVERNMENT REVENUE, EXPENDITURE, AND FINANCING THE DEFICIT,[1] 1975–81

(M NC)

Category	1975	1976	1977	1978	1979	1980	1981[a]	1981[b‡]
1. Current Income	2,261	2,693	3,487	4,026	4,239	4,982	7,696	7,292
Tax Revenue	2,090	2,520	3,281	3,935	4.126	4,692	7.182	6,933
Direct	447	612	781	1,060	1,066	1,080	1,640	1,555
Indirect	1,643	1,170	1,501	2,875	3,060	3,612	5,542	5,378
On Foreign Trade	678	738	999	~	~	~	~	~
Non-tax Revenue	171	173	206	91	103	290	514	359
2. Current Expenditure	2,210	2,727	3,372	4.276	5,152	6,349	7,704	8,168
Wages and Salaries	1,384	1,667	2,006	~	~	~	~	~
Other Current Expenditures	326	1,060	1,366	~	~	~	~	~
3. Current Saving	51	–34	–115	–250	–913	–1,367	–8	–876
4. Capital Expenditure	732	1,251	1,282	1,208	1,477	1,930	1,772	2,113
Real Investment	370	625	696	~	~	~	~	~
Debt Amortization Payments	210	262	299	~	~	~	~	~
Other Capital Expenditures	152	364	287	~	~	~	~	~
5. Total Expenditures	2,942	3,978	4,654	5,484	6,629	8,279	9,476	10,281
6. Fiscal Deficit	–681	–1,285	–1,167	–1,458	–2,390	–3,297	–1,780	2,989
7. Financing of Deficit								
Domestic Financing	452	1,034	857	646	1,725	2,838	1,530	2,028
Central Bank	24	120	81	~	~	~	~	~
Issue of Securities	161	436	548	~	~	~	~	~
Other	268	478	228	~	~	~	~	~
External Financing	229	251	.310	812	665	459	250	961[c]

1. Includes extra budgetary operations.

a. Budgeted. Includes the changes made during the year.
b. Effective (preliminary figures).
c. Includes arrears of interest.

SOURCE: ECLA-S, 1978, 1979, 1980, 1981.

Table 3024

DOMINICAN REPUBLIC CENTRAL GOVERNMENT REVENUE, EXPENDITURE, AND FINANCING THE DEFICIT, 1975–81

(M NC)

Category	1975	1976	1977	1978	1979	1980	1981[‡]
1. Total Income	657	564	620	578	674	869	908
Current Income	636	564	620	578	674	869	908
Tax Revenue	592	538	589	552	623	714	749
Direct	142	140	126	129	151	204	210
Goods and Services	95	119	140	144	166	189	238
From Taxes on External Trade	332	255	296	251	276	287	272
Others	22	24	27	28	30	34	29
Non-Tax Revenue	45	26	31	26	51	155	159
Extraordinary Income	21	~	~	~	~	~	~
2. Total Expenditure	653	578	631	675	1,005	1,066	1,085
Current Expenditure	353	344	368	443	644	729	776
Capital Expenditure	300	234	263	232	356	337	309
Real Investment	249	166	176	155	97	128	121
Amortization of the Debt	8	17	15	17	25	13	17
Capital Transfers	43	44	65	53	166	193	160
Other Expenditures	~	7	7	7	68	3	11
3. Fiscal Deficit (–) or Surplus	–17	–14	–11	–97	–331	–197	–177

SOURCE: ECLA-S, 1978, 1979, 1980, 1981.

Table 3025

ECUADOR CENTRAL GOVERNMENT REVENUE, EXPENDITURE, AND FINANCING THE DEFICIT, 1975–81

(M NC)

Category	1975	1976	1977	1978	1979	1980	1981
1. Total Income[1]	12,364	14,653	16,453	13,057	23,080	37,567	38,100
Current Income	12,364	14,108	17,282	19,660	23,722	38,512	39,040
Traditional	~	10,278	14,628	17,501	19.372	24,283	25,960
Tax Revenue	10,826	13,314	16,262	16,748	18,445	22,445	24,600
Direct	3,333	4,739	4,722	2,954	3,419	4,179	5,913
Indirect	2,376	3,240	3,923	5,541	6,527	8,616	8,907
On Foreign Trade	5,184	5,335	7,617	8,253	8,499	9,650	9.780
Other Income	1,815	3.036	1,019	753	927	1,838	1,360
From petroleum	2,490	794	2,654	2,159	4,350	14,229	13,080
2. Total Expenditure	11,755	16,813	20,745	26,155	28,189	46,156	58,904
3. Deficit (1–2)	609	2,160	4,293	–7,098	–5,109	–8,589	–20,804
4. Financing	~	613	3,799	6,394	3,890	7,241	22,502
Indebtedness	–237	–312	3,549	6,541	4,260	7,115	23,000
Foreign	–235	386	1,081	1,179	–	3,319	8,872
Domestic	2	–698	2,468	5,362	4,260	3,796	14,128
Cash Balances[2]	–1,176	925	250	–147	–370	132	–498
Difference (3–4)[3]	~	1,547	494	704	1,219	1,342	–1,698

1. Net total income; taxes paid with savings certificates and agrarian reform bonds have been deducted.
2. Use or net accumulation of funds during the financial year, according to whether the balance is positive or negative.
3. Balance of payments deferred until the next year (positive sign) and of payments made to cover expenditure of the previous year (negative sign).

SOURCE: ECLA-S, 1978, 1979, 1980, 1981.

Table 3026

EL SALVADOR CENTRAL GOVERNMENT REVENUE, EXPENDITURE, AND FINANCING THE DEFICIT, 1975–80

(M NC)

Category	1975	1976[‡]	1977	1978	1979	1980[‡]
1. Current Income	578	810	1,182	1,027	1,215	1,030
Tax Revenue (a + b)	541	768	1,131	972	1,162	986
a. Direct	154	187	237	286	277	307
b. Indirect	~	581	894	686	885	679
c. On Foreign Trade	205	355	624	401	571	402
d. Non-Tax Revenue	37	43	51	55	53	44
2. Current Expenditure	445	560	680	783	862	930
Wages and Salaries	229	299	349	411	475	535
Other Current Expenditure	217	261	331	372	387	395
3. Savings on Current Account (1 – 2)	133	250	502	244	353	100
4. Capital Expenditure	154	318	352	375	444	584
Real Investment	62	162	214	219	274	438
Debt Amortization Payments	20	23	29	33	29	21
Other Capital Expenditure	73	133	109	123	141	125
5. Total Expenditure (2 + 4)	600	878	1,032	1,158	1,306	1,514
6. Fiscal Deficit (–) or Surplus (1 – 5)	–22	5	150	–131	–91	–484
7. Financing of Deficit						
Domestic Financing[1]	–62	–83	–199	72	33	393
Central Bank	~	~	~	8	–8	143
Issue of Securities	~	~	~	22	100	300
Other	~	~	~	42	–59	–50
External Financing	83	49	49	59	58	91

1. Includes financing provided by the Central Reserve Bank of El Salvador, sale of securities, changes in treasury position, use of balances remaining from previous financial years, etc. (1975–76).

SOURCE: ECLA-S, 1978, 1979, 1980, 1981.

Table 3027

GUATEMALA CENTRAL GOVERNMENT REVENUE, EXPENDITURE, AND FINANCING THE DEFICIT, 1975–81
(M NC)

Category	1975	1976	1977	1978	1979	1980	1981[‡]
1. Current Income	330	407	591	661	668	747	746
Tax Revenue (a + b)	301	~	557	621	621	678	656
a. Direct	63	~	80	102	97	100	110
b. Indirect	135	~	477	519	524	578	546
c. On Foreign Trade	91	~	249	264	241	259	172
2. Current Expenditure	269	336	405	476	540	678	~
Wages and Salaries	~	~	181	~	~	~	~
Other Current Expenditure	~	~	224	~	~	~	~
3. Saving on Current Account (1 – 2)	61	71	186	185	128	69	26
4. Capital Expenditure	126	296	284	323	382	578	753
Real Investment[2]	85	191	204	216	310	438	591
Debt Amortization Payments	31	57	57	64	72	140	162
Other Capital Expenditure	~	~	23	43	~	~	~
5. Total Expenditure (2 + 4)	395	632	689	799	922	1,256	1,473
6. Fiscal Deficit (1 – 5)	–43	–204	–98	–138	–254	–509	–727
7. Financing of Deficit							
Domestic Financing[1]	52	228	57	37	122	391	646
External Financing	19	22	41	101	132	118	81

1. Includes the floating debt (1975, 1976).
2. Includes other capital expenditure.

SOURCE: ECLA-S, 1978, 1979, 1980, 1981.

Table 3028

HAITI CENTRAL GOVERNMENT REVENUE, EXPENDITURE, AND FINANCING THE DEFICIT,[1] 1975–81
(M NC)

Category	1975	1976[†]	1977	1978	1979	1980[‡]	1981[‡]
1. Current Income	225	285	358	541	606	691	657
Tax Revenue	185	235	299	428	494	629	591
Direct and Indirect	73	87	108	210	250	268	309
On Foreign Trade	112	148	191	218	244	361	282
2. Current Expenditure	204	232	269	325	407	540	719
Wages and Salaries	123	130	147	180	208	293	353
Other Current Expenditure	~	~	122	145	199	247	366
3. Saving on Current Account (1 – 2)	21	53	89	216	199	151	–62
4. Capital Expenditure	291	451	542	586	641	662	741
Real Investment	~	437	535	569	626	642	719
Debt Amortization Payments	~	14	7	17	15	20	22
5. Total Expenditure (2 + 4)	495	683	811	911	1,048	1,202	1,460
6. Fiscal Deficit (1 – 5)	–270	–398	–453	–370	–442	–511	–303
7. Financing of Deficit							
External Financing	153	398	361	~	330	340	434
Grants[2]	95	314	156	~	209	183	328
Loans	58	170	205	~	121	157	106
Domestic Financing	117	84	92	~	112	171	369

1. For 1975 and 1976, Fiscal years Oct. to Sept.
2. Excludes food imports from the U.S. on concessional terms under that country's law on agricultural surpluses (P. L. 480, Title I), and donations by non-governmental organizations.

SOURCE: ECLA-S, 1978, 1979, 1980, 1981.

Table 3029

HONDURAS CENTRAL GOVERNMENT REVENUE, EXPENDITURE, AND FINANCING
THE DEFICIT, 1975–81
(M NC)

Category	1975	1976	1977	1978	1979	1980	1981[‡]
1. Current Income	283	356	486	541	632	758	741
Tax Revenue	252	311	444	503	574	697	695
Direct	78	76	95	128	153	236	186
Indirect	174	235	349	375	421	461	509
2. Current Expenditure	254	327	444	471	527	727	795
Wages and Salaries	160	174	212	258	299	353	430
Other Current Expenditure	94	153	232	213	278	374	365
3. Current Saving (1 – 2)	29	29	42	70	105	31	-54
4. Capital Expenditure	184	197	250	371	385	516	442
Real Investment	76	88	186	172	152	193	134
Debt Amortization Payments	37	41	65	70	88	93	107
Other Capital Expenditure	71	68	79	129	145	231	201
5. Total Expenditure (2 + 4)	438	524	694	842	912	1,243	1,237
6. Fiscal Deficit (1 – 5)	-155	-168	-208	-301	-280	-485	-496
7. Financing							
Domestic	60	88	109	117	123	219	239
External	95	80	99	184	157	266	257

SOURCE: ECLA-S, 1978, 1979, 1980, 1981.

Table 3030

MEXICO CENTRAL GOVERNMENT REVENUE, EXPENDITURE, AND FINANCING
THE DEFICIT, 1975–81
(M NC)

Category	1975	1976	1977	1978	1979	1980	1981[‡]
1. Current Income	102	134	192	302	412	680	938
Tax Revenue (a + b + c)	95	125	181	289	395	651	890
a. Direct	49	67	95	134	173	247	329
b. Indirect	37	45	63	120	158	220	295
c. On Foreign Trade	9	13	23	35	64	184	266
Non-Tax Revenue	7	9	11	13	17	29	48
2. Current Expenditure	92	126	177	286	382	579	884
Wages and Salaries	34	44	64	93	120	159	223
Other Current Expenditure	58	82	113	193	262	420	661
3. Saving on Current Account (1 – 2)	10	8	15	16	30	101	54
4. Capital Expenditure[1]	63	82	90	190	351	482	1,216
Real Investment	37	43	49	57	86	169	329
Debt Amortization Payments[1]	10	10	16	108	232	258	791
Other Capital Expenditure	16	29	25	133	265	313	887
5. Total Expenditure[1] (2 + 4)	156	208	267	476	733	1,061	2,100
6. Fiscal Deficit[1] (1 – 5)	-54	-74	-75	-174	-321	-381	-1,162
7. Financing of Fiscal Deficit							
Domestic Financing[1]	37	46	55	148	296	332	1,091
External Financing	17	28	20	26	25	49	71

1. Excluding treasury certificates issued and redeemed in the same year, since their
introduction in 1978.

SOURCE: ECLA-S, 1978, 1979, 1980, 1981.

Table 3031

NICARAGUA CENTRAL GOVERNMENT REVENUE, EXPENDITURE, AND FINANCING THE DEFICIT, 1975–81

(M NC)

Category	1975	1976	1977	1978	1979	1980	1981[‡]
1. Current Income	1,323	1,527	1,796	1,621	1,892	4,526	5,506
Tax Revenue	1,151	1,352	1,638	1,449	1,487	3,991	4,660
Direct	265	350	392	363	309	934	1,095
Indirect	535	628	752	702	763	1,840	2,684
From Taxes on External Trade	352	374	494	384	415	1,217	881
Non-Tax Revenue	172	175	158	~	~	~	~
2. Current Expenditure	1,121	1,210	1,539	1,875	2,587	5,008	6,986[a]
Wages and Salaries	444	547	588	702	903	1,562	1,954
Other Current Expenditure	677	663	951	1,173	1,684	3,446	5,032
3. Saving on Current Account (1–2)	202	317	257	−254	−695	−482	−1,480
4. Capital Expenditure	985	969	1,539	1,412	395	1,356	1,426
Real Investment	291	370	921	921	314	972	919
Amortization of Debt	144	156	238	384	81	170	274
Other Capital Expenditure	550	443	380	107	~	214	233
5. Total Expenditure (2+4)	2,106	2,179	3,078	3,287	2,982	6,364	8,412
6. Fiscal Deficit (–) or Surplus (1-5)	−783	−652	−1,282	−1,666	−1,090	−1,838	−2,906
7. Financing of Deficit							
Domestic	49	283	130	920	996	450	1,971
External	734	369	1,152	746	94	1,388	935

a. Includes interest in the amount of 888.0 million córdobas.

SOURCE: ECLA-S, 1978, 1979, 1980, 1981.

Table 3032

PANAMA CENTRAL GOVERNMENT REVENUE, EXPENDITURE, AND FINANCING THE DEFICIT, 1975–81

(M NC)

Category	1975	1976	1977	1978	1979	1980	1981[‡]
1. Current Income	297	323	348	397	490	695	790
Tax Revenue	227	224	281	327	406	507	582
Direct	114	109	130	143	193	255	315
Indirect	113	61	96	184	213	252	267
On Foreign Trade	58	54	55	68	80	91	99
Non-Tax Revenue	~	99	67	~	~	~	~
2. Current Expenditure	283	310	342	464	612	766	861
Wages and Salaries	170	178	186	225	264	297	298
Other Current Expenditure	113	132	156	239	348	469	563
3. Current Saving (1 – 2)	14	13	6	−67	−122	−71	−71
4. Capital Expenditure	134	133	133	184	321	299	355
Fixed Investment, Financial Investment, and Transfers	111	105	97	35	53	52	82
Other Capital Expenditure	~	~	~	82	210	162	162
Amortization of the Debt	23	28	36	67	58	85	111
5. Total Expenditure (2 + 4)	420	443	475	648	933	1,065	1,216
6. Fiscal Deficit (1 – 5)	−123	−120	−127	−251	−443	−370	−426
7. Financing of Deficit	~	~	~	113	138	179	178
Domestic	8	25	6	48	52	71	82
External	115	95	121	138	305	191	248

SOURCE: ECLA-S, 1978, 1979, 1980, 1981.

Table 3033

PARAGUAY CENTRAL GOVERNMENT REVENUE, EXPENDITURE, AND FINANCING THE DEFICIT, 1975–81

(M NC)

Category	1975	1976	1977	1978	1979	1980	1981[a]	1981[b]
1. Current Income	17,394	19,432	26,379	34,333	43,629	51,592	60,628	59,107
Tax Revenue	15,877	16,852	23,492	30,334	38,810	46,137	55,092	52,351
Direct Taxes	~	3,644	~	~	8,449	11,323	11,262	14,235
On Personal Income	~	~	~	~	~	~	~	~
On Corporative Earnings	~	~	~	~	6,846	9,395	9,624	11,735
On Real Estate	~	~	~	~	1,603	1,928	1,638	2,500
Indirect Taxes	~	6,710	~	~	30,367	34,814	43,830	38,116
On External Trade	~	6,517	~	~	15,786	17,213	~	17,325
Imports	~	~	~	~	14,645	15,945	~	16,623
Exports	~	~	~	~	1,141	1,268	~	1,202
On Domestic Trade	~	~	~	~	6,945	8,280	~	8,691
Others	~	2,373	~	~	7,636	9,321	~	11,600
Non-Tax Income	2,017	2,392	2,887	3,999	4,819	5,455	5,536	6,756
2. Current Expenditure	14,412	16,157	18,553	21,616	27,193	38,064	46,538	52,998
Consumption	~	12,486	13,977	16,306	20,105	28,278	34,715	40,191
Wages and Salaries	6,126	7,326	~	~	12,205	15,938	17,565	22,474
Goods and Non-Personal Services	~	~	~	~	5,344	7,324	~	9,803
Others	8,286	8,832	~	~	2,556	5,016	~	7,914
Interest Payments	~	~	~	~	1,345	1,766	1,891	2,147
Transfers	~	3,671	4,576	5,310	5,743	7,792	9,932	10,653
Subsidies	~	~	~	~	63	83	83	92
Transfers to the Private Sector	~	~	~	~	3,289	4,725	~	6,233
Transfers to the Public Sector	~	~	~	~	2,151	2,915	~	3,941
Other	~	~	~	~	241	298	~	357
3. Saving	3,482	3,086	7,826	12,717	16,436	13,527	14,224	6,117
4. Capital Expenditure	4,198	6,659	7,246	9,160	13,434	14,912	22,439	25,974
Capital Formation	~	~	~	~	11,379	10,694	18,726	14,743
Financial Investment	3,471	5,872	6,051	7,887	257	2,533	2,121	9,075
Transfers to the Public	~	~	~	~	1,799	1,672	1,422	2,153
Other Capital Expenditure	727	~	~	~	~	~	~	~
5. Total Expenditure	18,609	22,816	25,799	30,776	40,628	52,976	68,977	78,964
6. Global Balance	-714	-3,569	579	3,557	3,024	-1,385	-8,215	-19,857
7. Financing	~	~	~	~	-3,024	1,385	8,215	19,857
Domestic (net)	-649	~	-517	-263	-4,980	-1,153	3,326	17,646
Indebtedness	~	~	~	~	1,052	-1,813	2,913	2,644
Direct Loans	~	~	~	~	1,350	-1,011	3,217	2,801
Central Bank	91	~	340	270	585	236	~	379
Suppliers	~	~	~	~	435	230	~	3,417
Other	-774	~	-667	-125	330	-1,477	~	-995
Bonds	-217	~	-190	-407	-298	-802	-304	-157
Sale	~	~	~	~	~	~	~	~
Amortization	~	~	~	~	-298	-802	-304	-157
Cash Variation (minus sign indicates increase)	~	~	~	~	6,032	660	413	15,002
External (net)	1,363	~	2,526	1,968	1,956	2,538	4,889	2,211
Loans	~	~	~	~	1,923	2,515	4,869	2,167
Disbursements	~	~	~	~	4,226	4,066	7,128	4,639
Amortization	~	~	~	~	-2,303	-1,551	-2,259	2,472
Variations in Reserves	~	~	2,589	5,262	~	~	~	~
Donations	~	~	~	~	33	23	20	45

a. Budgeted amounts.
b. Amounts actually registered (preliminary figures).

SOURCE: ECLA–S, 1978, 1979, 1980, 1981.

Table 3034

PERU CENTRAL GOVERNMENT REVENUE, EXPENDITURE, AND FINANCING THE DEFICIT, 1975–81

(M NC)

Category	1975	1976	1977	1978	1979	1980	1981[‡]
1. Current Income	87.9	111.4	154.1	263	552	1,020	1,523
Tax Revenue	80.6	101	145.6	258	529	1,022	1,480
Income and Property Taxes	24.6	30.2	43.0	65	146	361	414
Export Taxes	5.6	6.0	16.2	31	88	123	116
Import Taxes	18.2	17.9	19.6	39	68	158	321
Production and Consumption Taxes	32.2	46.9	66.8	121	227	379	629
Non-Tax Revenue[1]	9.0	13.4	15	19	58	78	141
Less Refund Certificates[2]	1.7	3.0	−6.5	−13	−36	−80	−98
2. Current Expenditure	90.5	122.7	193.1	291	45	898	1,506
Wages and Salaries	38.8	51.5	70.3	97	122	238	448
Interest	9.4	13.2	29.2	71	138	214	382
Internal Debt	4.5	5.5	13.6	32	62	92	203
External Debt	4.9	7.7	15.6	39	76	122	179
Other Current Expenditure	42.3	58	93.6	121	198	446	676
3. Saving on Current Account (1 − 2)	−2.6	−11.3	−39	−27	93	122	16
4. Capital Expenditure	40.9	53.2	74	139	269	472	770
Gross Capital Formation	15.9	19.8	27.1	42	92	128	352
Other Capital Expenditure[3]	12.1	17.3	13	15	36	84	84
Amortization Payments	12.9	16.1	33.9	81	140	210	334
Internal Debt	6.9	7.8	10.9	14	20	28	60
External Debt	6.0	8.3	23.0	66	120	182	274
5. Total Expenditure (2 + 4)	131.4	175.9	267.1	430	728	1,370	2,276
6. Fiscal Deficit (1 − 5)	−43.5	−64.5	−113	−166	−176	−351	−753
7. Financing of Deficit	43.5	64.5	113	166	176	351	753
Domestic	20.7	40.6	55.2	91	112	154	345
External	22.8	23.9	57.8	74	63	197	408

1. Including wage and salary discounts for pension fund.
2. Mainly tax refund certificates for export promotion and tax capitalization by
   PetroPeru and ElectroPeru.
3. Including financial investment and expenditure of agrarian reform expropriations.

SOURCE: ECLA-S, 1978, 1979, 1980, 1981.

Table 3035

URUGUAY CENTRAL GOVERNMENT REVENUE, EXPENDITURE, AND FINANCING THE DEFICIT, 1975–81

(M NC)

Category	1975	1976	1977	1978	1979	1980	1981[‡]
1. Current Income	986	1,722	2,938	4,350	8,424	14,955	21,260
Internal Taxes	929	1,633	2,771	3,256	5,705	10,695	14,804
On Production, Consumption and Transactions	~	~	~	3,067	5,221	9,287	13,514
Value Added	~	~	~	1,526	2,751	5,677	8,515
Fuels	~	~	~	582	973	1,661	2,117
Tobacco	~	~	~	297	459	912	1,251
Other	~	~	~	662	1,038	1,036	1,631
On Income	~	~	~	569	1,038	2,363	2,427
On Wealth	~	~	~	211	282	724	1,094
Other	57	89	167	59	80	116	116
Less: Documents Received	~	~	~	–527	–717	–1,475	–1,236
Adjustments[1]	~	~	~	–123	–199	–320	–111
Taxes on Foreign Trade	~	~	~	550	1,597	2,753	3,199
Other Income	~	~	~	544	1,123	1,507	3,257
2. Current Expenditure	1,204	1,808	2,796	4,042	7,260	13,080	18,817
Wages and Salaries	871[c]	1,264[c]	1,826[c]	1,948	3,282	5,980	8,800
Contributions and Assistance to Social Security	871[c]	1,264[c]	1,826[c]	665	1,117	3,464	4,866
Purchase of Goods and Services	~	~	~	765	1,397	2,466	3,766
Other Current Expenditure[2]	333	544	970	664	1,464	1,170	1,385
3. Saving on Current Account (1 – 2)	–218	–86	142	308	1,164	1,875	2,443
4. Investments	145[‡]	239	382	708	1,040	1,799	2,560
5. Total Expenditure (2 + 4)	1,349	2,048	3,179	4,750	8,300	14,879	21,377
6. Fiscal Deficit or Surplus (1 – 5)	–363	–326	–241	–400	124	76	–117
7. Financing							
Net Credit Central Bank	95	173	287	159	205	–168	396
Issue of Securities (Net)	263	127	29	90	–363	–313	–49
Other	4	8	–90	151[a]	34	405[b]	–230[b]

1. Discrepancy between treasury information and tax office information.
2. Including transfer payments, interest payments on the public debt and affected income (1978-80).

a. Including external financing of the PALMAR Joint Commission in the amount of 134.4 million pesos.
b. Including variation between treasury position and uncleared checks.
c. Wages and salaries and contributions and assistance to Social Security combined.

SOURCE: ECLA-S, 1978, 1979, 1980, 1981.

Table 3036

VENEZUELA CENTRAL GOVERNMENT REVENUE, EXPENDITURE, AND FINANCING THE DEFICIT, 1975–81

(M NC)

Category	1975	1976	1977	1978	1979	1980	1981[‡]
1. Current Income	40,898	38,130	40,474	40,106	50,055	62,697	92,655
Petroleum	31,655[a]	28,024[a]	29,421	25,127	33,308	45,331	70,887
Direct	3,297	4,722	4,771	6,338	6,347	7,163	10,094
Indirect and Other Income	5,946	5,947	6,282	8,645	10,400	10,203	11,674
2. Current Expenditure	18,244	20,687	24,645	25,107	30,104	35,227	48,303
Wages and Salaries	7,273	8,704	10,180	11,115	12,819	16,485	19,015
Economic Subsidies	1,627	1,159	1,159	813	872	688	3,693
Other Current Expenditure	9,344	10,824	13,306	13,179	16,413	18,054	25,595
3. Saving on Current Account (1 – 2)	22,654	17,423	15,829	14,999	19,951	27,470	44,352
4. Capital Expenditure	12,330	15,956	17,848	18,239	11,707	25,501	33,427
Real Investment	3,487	4,234	5,778	6,481	3,610	4,381	6,775
Financial Investment	3,774	7,569	1,929	1,739	1,766	8,788	14,652
Other Capital Expenditure	7	12	40	31	30	12	14
Transfers	5,062	4,141	10,102	9,987	6,302	12,320	11,986
5. Refinancing Operation	#	4,292	2,902	1,913	~	~	~
6. Servicing of the Public Debt	1,771	3,636	5,301	5,953	9,147	12,141	12,232
7. Total Expenditure (2 + 4 + 5 + 6)	32,345	44,571	50,696	51,213	50,958	72,869	93,962
8. Fiscal Deficit (or Surplus)	8,553	–6,461	10,222	11,107	–903	10,172	1,307
9. Financing of Deficit							
External	77	4,372	8,519	10,038	70	8,792	2,164
Domestic	25	641	2,128	437	#	#	#
Other	–1,123	1,448	–425	632	833	1,380	–857

a. Including royalties.

SOURCE: ECLA-S, 1977, 1980, 1981.

Table 3037

UNITED STATES CENTRAL GOVERNMENT REVENUE, EXPENDITURE, AND FINANCING THE DEFICIT, 1970–83

(B NC)

Category	1970	1972	1974	1975	1976	1977	1978	1979	1980	1981	1982	1983
Deficit (–) or Surplus	–11.38	–17.37	–10.88	–75.40	–56.60	–51.05	–44.18	–27.91	–68.72	–72.62	–130.72	–190.41
Revenue	190.49	221.53	280.29	280.70	317.61	366.11	416.91	480.54	533.04	622.79	608.82	612.93
Expenditure and Lending	201.87	238.88	291.16	356.10	374.21	417.16	461.09	508.45	601.76	695.41	739.54	803.33
Expenditure	201.00	236.57	~	~	~	~	~	~	~	~	~	~
Lending Minus Repayments	.87	2.09	~	~	~	~	~	~	~	~	~	~
Financing												
Net Borrowing	11.86	15.26	11.74	85.49	69.03	56.81	53.69	37.37	79.20	~	~	~
Other Financing	1.06	2.80	–7.52	–6.18	–15.42	–5.39	–7.81	–3.61	–3.80	~	~	~
Use of Cash Balances	–1.52	–.77	6.71	–3.92	2.97	–.36	–1.74	–5.82	–6.68	~	~	~

SOURCE: IMF-IFS-Y, 1983, lines 80-87; IMF-IFS-Y, 1984, lines 80-87.

Table 3038

ARGENTINA MONEY SUPPLY, 1948-83[a]
(B NC YE)

PART I. 1948-58

Year	A. Money[1] (M_1)	B. Quasi-Money[2]	C. Total[3] (M_2)
1948	16.84	7.78	24.62
1949	20.87	9.77	30.64
1950	24.72	10.69	35.41
1961	30.38	11.29	41.67
1952	34.28	12.43	46.71
1953	43.13	14.87	58.00
1954	51.88	17.70	69.58
1955	61.19	20.18	81.37
1956	71.28	25.16	96.44
1957	82.81	29.98	112.79
1958	118.85	41.10	159.95

SOURCE: IMF-IFS-S, 1965-66.

PART II. 1959-68

Year	A. Money[1] (M_1)	B. Quasi-Money[2]	C. Total[3] (M_2)
1959	1.70	.45	2.15
1960	2.18	.60	2.78
1961	2.02	.75	2.77
1962	2.20	.86	3.06
1963	2.83	1.24	4.07
1964	3.96	1.79	5.75
1965	4.97	2.41	7.38
1966	6.71	2.95	9.66
1967	10.91	3.93	14.84
1968	13.6	5.2	18.8

SOURCE: 1959-67 data: IMF-IFS-S, 1973; 1968 data: IMF-IFS-Y, 1979, lines 34 and 35.

PART III. 1970-81

Year	A. Money[1] (M_1)	B. Quasi-Money[2]	C. Total[3] (M_2)
1969	12.5	10	22.1
1970	14.5	12	26.5
1971	19.7	15	34.7
1972	32.9	21	53.9
1973	67	41	108
1974	114	63	177
1975	342	79	421
1976	1,043	531	1,574
1977	2,267	2,916	5,183
1978	588	878	1,466
1979	1,395	2,955	4,350
1980	2,746	5,479	8,225
1981	4,671	12,827	17,498

PART IV. 1982-83

Year	A. Money[1] (M_1)	B. Quasi-Money[2]	C. Total[3] (M_2)
1982	16.234	29.700	45.934
1983	74.960	155.125	230.085

1. Sum of currency outside banks and private sector demand deposits.
2. Time, savings, and foreign currency deposits by residents.
3. Calculated by totaling series A and B.

a. This table has been divided into four series, each presenting data for periods of consistent monetary units.

SOURCE: IMF-IFS-Y, 1984, lines 34 and 35.

Table 3039

BOLIVIA MONEY SUPPLY, 1952-83
(M NC YE)

Year	A. Money[1] (M_1)	B. Quasi-Money[2]	C. Total[3] (M_2)
1952	9	1	10
1953	16	1	17
1954	27	1	28
1955	56	3	59
1956	197	6	203
1957	291	10	301
1958	301	9	310
1959	386	15	401
1960	419	16	435
1961	496	17	513
1962	556	29	585
1963	665	37	702
1964	803	50	853
1965	943	52	995
1966	1,153	100	1,253
1967	1,192	151	1,343
1968	1,287	226	1,513
1969	1,361	306	1,667
1970	1,532	381	1,913
1971	1,766	493	2,259
1972	2,210	634	2,844
1973	2,969	807	3,776
1974	4,257	1,192	5,449
1975	4,759	1,956	6,715
1976	6,497	3,405	9,902
1977	7,855	4,960	12,815
1978	8,831	5,650	14,481
1979	10,304	6,328	16,632
1980	14,694	8,430	23,124
1981	17,587	11,831	29,418
1982	57,827	39,375	97,202
1983	177,500	87,600	265,100

1. Sum of currency outside of banks and private sector demand deposits, source line 34.
2. Time, savings, and foreign currency deposits by residents, source line 35.
3. Calculated by adding columns A and B.

SOURCE: IMF-IFS-Y, 1982; IMF-IFS-Y, 1984; IMF-IFS, March 1985.

Table 3040

BRAZIL MONEY SUPPLY,[1] 1948–83
(B NC YE)

PART I. 1948–59

Year	A. Money[2] (M_1)	B. Quasi-Money[3]	C. Total[4] (M_2)
1948	49	16	65
1949	58	18	76
1950	78	19	97
1951	91	20	111
1952	104	21	125
1953	124	22	146
1954	151	25	176
1955	178	24	202
1956	217	25	242
1957	211	29	240
1958	353	33	386
1959	501	39	540

SOURCE: IMF-IFS-S, 1965–66.

PART II. 1960–83

Year	A. Money[1] (M_1)	B. Quasi-Money[2]	C. Total[3] (M_2)
1960	.7	.1	.8
1961	1.0	.1	1.1
1962	1.7	.1	1.8
1963	2.8	.1	2.9
1964	5.1	.2	5.3
1965	9.1	.3	9.4
1966	10.5	.9	11.4
1967	15.0	1.7	16.7
1968	21.3	2.7	24.0
1969	27.4	4.4	31.8
1970	34.7	6.0	40.7
1971	42.0*	3.3*	45.3*
1972	62.9	6.1	69.5
1973	87.0	7.1	94.1
1974	116.8	8.1	124.9
1975	168.5	12.0	180.5
1976	231.1	19.1	250.2
1977	318.5	44.2	362.7
1978	454.2	94.2	548.4
1979	788.5	154.6	943.1
1980	1,349.1	184.4	1,533.5
1981	2,357.8	506.4	2,864.2
1982	4,036.2	1,293.7	5,329.9
1983	7,671.0	4,390.0	12,061.0

1. Differences between Parts I and II reflect a change in unit of account and not a discontinuity in the series.
2. Sum of currency outside of banks and private sector demand deposits.
3. Time, savings, and foreign currency deposits by residents.
4. Calculated by adding columns A and B.

SOURCE: IMF-IFS-Y, 1984.

Table 3041

CHILE MONEY SUPPLY, 1955–83
(M NC YE)

PART I. 1955–64
(M NC)

Year	A. Money[1] (M_1)	B. Quasi-Money[2]	C. Total[3] (M_2)
1955	93	16	109
1956	130	25	155
1957	165	38	203
1958	222	54	276
1959	294	162	456
1960	384	211	595
1961	432	266	698
1962	557	389	946
1963	747	459	1,206
1964	1,129	720	1,849

SOURCE: IMF-IFS-S, 1965–66.

PART II. 1965–83
(B NC)

Year	A. Money[1] (M_1)	B. Quasi-Money[2]	C. Total[3] (M_2)
1965	.002	.001	.003
1966	.003	.002	.005
1967	.003	.002	.005
1968	.005	.003	.008
1969	.006	.005	.011
1970	.010	.007	.017
1971	.021	.011	.032
1972	.05	.03	.08
1973	.22	.22	.44
1974	.84	1.19	2.03
1975	2.98	4.52	7.5
1976	8.80	11.17	19.97
1977	18.32	27.62	45.94
1978	30.58	57.092	87.670
1979	50.31	96.59	146.90
1980	78.87	152.15	231.02
1981	74.12	237.11	311.23
1982	81.12	311.33	392.45
1983	102.72	308.99	411.71

1. Sum of currency outside banks and private sector demand deposits.
2. Time, savings, and foreign currency deposits by residents.
3. Calculated by adding columns A and B.

SOURCE: IMF-IFS-Y, 1984.

Table 3042

COLOMBIA MONEY SUPPLY, 1952–83

(B NC YE)

Year	A. Money[1] (M_1)	B. Quasi-Money[2]	C. Total[3] (M_2)
1952	1.32	.20	1.52
1953	1.55	.21	1.76
1954	1.84	.38	2.22
1955	1.91	.50	2.41
1956	2.38	.84	3.22
1957	2.70	.65	3.35
1958	3.26	.64	3.90
1959	3.63	.77	4.40
1960	3.99	.76	4.74
1961	4.96	.92	5.88
1962	5.93	1.55	7.48
1963	6.69	1.51	8.20
1964	8.25	1.45	9.70
1965	9.64	2.19	11.83
1966	11.24	1.81	13.05
1967	13.68	2.10	15.78
1968	15.86	2.22	18.08
1969	19.40	2.70	22.10
1970	22.40	3.38	25.78
1971	25.06	4.13	29.19
1972	31.85	5.86	37.71
1973	41.65	9.25	50.90
1974	49.07	14.64	63.71
1975	58.92	19.58	78.50
1976	79.38	25.76	105.14
1977	103.50*	37.19	140.69
1978	132.93	47.08*	180.01
1979	165.89	55.10	220.99
1980	212.40	108.08	320.48
1981	256.57	178.36	434.93
1982	321.43	204.25	525.68
1983	399.55	~	399.55

1. Sum of currency outside of banks and private sector demand deposits, source line 34.
2. Time, savings, and foreign currency deposits by residents, source line 35.
3. Calculated by adding columns A and B.

SOURCE: IMF-IFS-Y, 1982; IMF-IFS, January 1984.

Table 3043

COSTA RICA MONEY SUPPLY, 1952–80

(M NC YE)

Year	A. Money[1] (M_1)	B. Quasi-Money[2]	C. Total[3] (M_2)
1952	265	38	303
1953	291	45	336
1954	325	49	374
1955	340	61	401
1956	342	71	413
1957	370	83	453
1958	399	103	502
1959	427*	120*	547
1960	433	128	561
1961	422	124	546
1962	480	137	617
1963	535	148	683
1964	568	166	734
1965	598	185	783
1966	622	186	808
1967	832	248	1,080
1968	849	219	1,068
1969	959	236	1,195
1970	1,006	270	1,278
1971	1,317	494	1,811
1972	1,501	665	2,166
1973	1,874	767	2,641
1974	2,460	1,300	2,760
1975	2,771	2,133	4,904
1976	3,408	3,182	6,590
1977	4,504	4,160	8,664
1978	5,625	5,442	11,067
1979	6,226	8,642	14,868
1980	7,271	9,965	17,236

1. Sum of currency outside of banks and private sector demand deposits, source line 34.
2. Time, savings, and foreign currency deposits by residents, source line 35.
3. Calculated by adding columns A and B.

SOURCE: IMF-IFS-Y, 1982; IMF-IFS, January 1984; IMF-IFS-Y, 1984.

Table 3044

DOMINICAN REPUBLIC MONEY SUPPLY, 1952–83
(M NC YE)

Year	A. Money[1] (M_1)	B. Quasi- Money[2]	C. Total[3] (M_2)
1952	62.1	13.1	75.2
1953	60.2	12.2	72.4
1954	68.6	26.2	94.8
1955	76.5	32.7	109.2
1956	76.9	37.4	114.3
1957	87.4	43.1	130.5
1958	107.2	36.8	144.0
1959	91.9	36.7	128.6
1960	101.9	27.2	129.1
1961	104.4	22.0	126.4
1962	114.0	26.0	140.0
1963	130.2	27.3	157.5
1964	116.6	30.8	147.4
1965	135.0	60.8	195.8
1966	116.1	49.3	165.4
1967	120.2	53.2	173.4
1968	139.1	72.2	211.3
1969	149.3	93.7	243.0
1970	171.7	118.1	289.8
1971	188.1	144.9	333.0
1972	222.5	188.2	410.7
1973	260.1	244.8	504.9
1974	364.2	361.3	725.5
1975	379.7	467.5	847.2
1976	390.4	484.6	875.0
1977	460.0	545.4	1,005.4
1978	458.0	533.1	991.1
1979	598.4	556.3	1,154.7
1980	579.6	594.9	1,174.5
1981	660.5	677.0	1,337.5
1982	731.5	803.9	1,535.4
1983	781.4	895.1	1,676.5

1. Sum of currency outside of banks and private sector demand deposits, source line 34.
2. Time, savings, and foreign currency deposits by residents, source line 35.
3. Calculated by adding columns A and B.

SOURCE: IMF-IFS-Y, 1982; IMF-IFS, May 1984; IMF-IFS-Y, 1984.

Table 3045

ECUADOR MONEY SUPPLY, 1952–83
(M NC YE)

Year	A. Money[1] (M_1)	B. Quasi- Money[2]	C. Total[3] (M_2)
1952	1,051	182	1,233
1953	1,088	230	1,318
1954	1,273	270	1,543
1955	1,193	352	1,545
1956	1,358	388	1,746
1957	1,412	469	1,881
1958	1,400	391	1,791
1959	1,577	440	2,017
1960	1,732	469	2,201
1961	1,778	598	2,376
1962	2,000	678	2,678
1963	2,241	609	2,850
1964	2,626	569	3,195
1965	2,670	616	3,286
1966	3,016	831	3,847
1967	3,439	1,021	4,460
1968	4,172	1,391	5,563
1969	4,751	1,547	6,298
1970	5,989	1,746	7,735
1971	6,719	2,175	8,894
1972	8,376	2,595	10,971
1973	11,299	3,132	14,431
1974	16,866	4,167	21,033
1975	18,343	4,741	23,084
1976	22,809	6,006	28,815
1977	29,876	6,087	35,963
1978	32,920	6,820	39,740
1979	41,952	10,227	52,179
1980	53,584	12,590	66,174
1981	61,807	13,896	75,703
1982	73,130	20,499	93,629
1983	95,145	22,868	118,013

1. Sum of currency outside of banks and private sector demand deposits, source line 34.
2. Time, savings, and foreign currency deposits by residents, source line 35.
3. Calculated by adding columns A and B.

SOURCE: IMF-IFS-Y, 1982; IMF-IFS, January 1984; IMF-IFS-Y, 1984.

Table 3046

EL SALVADOR MONEY SUPPLY, 1952–82

(M NC YE)

Year	A. Money[1] (M_1)	B. Quasi-Money[2]	C. Total[3] (M_2)
1952	163.7	10.3	174.0
1953	171.8	10.9	182.7
1954	190.4	15.6	206.0
1955	187.4	19.8	207.2
1956	215.0	26.1	241.1
1957	215.2	37.2	252.4
1958	202.3	55.0	257.3
1959	205.7	75.6	281.3
1960	193.0	83.0	276.0
1961	184.2	100.3	284.5
1962	183.4	122.8	306.2
1963	220.9	154.0	374.9
1964	233.5	189.6	423.1
1965	234.2	204.3	437.5
1966	247.0	231.6	478.6
1967	252.7	236.2	488.9
1968	264.7	244.8	509.5
1969	288.1	273.8	561.9
1970	295.3	300.2	595.5
1971	315.4	342.8	658.2
1972	389.6	417.5	807.1
1973	466.0	491.6	957.6
1974	556.6	559.7	1,116.3
1975	648.1	704.6	1,352.7
1976	916.7	853.7	1,770.4
1977	988.3	1,015.3	2,003.6
1978	1,086.9	1,154.4	2,241.3
1979	1,320.9	1,124.8	2,445.7
1980	1,428.6	1,134.7	2,563.3
1981	1,437.2*	1,397.0*	2,834.2*
1982	1,716.6	1,599.5	3,316.1

1. Sum of currency outside of banks and private sector demand deposits, source line 34.
2. Time, savings, and foreign currency deposits by residents, source line 35.
3. Calculated by adding columns A and B.

SOURCE: IMF-IFS-Y, 1982; IMF-IFS, May 1984; IMF-IFS-Y, 1984.

Table 3047

GUATEMALA MONEY SUPPLY, 1952–83

(M NC YE)

Year	A. Money[1] (M_1)	B. Quasi-Money[2]	C. Total[3] (M_2)
1952	63.6	7.0	70.6
1953	76.1	7.2	83.3
1954	77.6	6.7	84.3
1955	86.7	8.6	95.3
1956	103.9	14.6	118.5
1957	116.3	19.0	135.3
1958	106.8	22.7	129.5
1959	108.8	26.4	135.2
1960	105.5	31.3	136.8
1961	106.7	36.4	143.1
1962	108.7	42.5	151.2
1963	121.4	48.4	169.8
1964	129.3	64.8	194.1
1965	135.6	73.8	209.4
1966	143.0	91.5	234.5
1967	148.3	114.5	262.8
1968	151.1	126.2	277.3
1969	160.9	148.3	309.2
1970	172.8	170.9	343.7
1971	178.9	204.4	383.3
1972	214.4	262.5	476.9
1973	264.3	315.5	579.8
1974	305.4	362.9	668.3
1975	353.6	454.9	808.5
1976	493.8	558.0	1,051.8
1977	594.1	655.0	1,249.1
1978	664.0	759.6	1,423.6
1979	734.9	802.3	1,537.2
1980	752.8	939.6	1,692.4
1981	777.8	1,128.9	1,906.7
1982	786.6	1,404.1	2,190.7
1983	833.8	1,321.3	2,155.1

1. Sum of currency outside of banks and private sector demand deposits, source line 34.
2. Time, savings, and foreign currency deposits by residents, source line 35.
3. Calculated by adding columns A and B.

SOURCE: IMF-IFS-Y, 1982; IMF-IFS, May 1984; IMF-IFS-Y, 1984.

Table 3048

HAITI MONEY SUPPLY, 1952–83
(M NC YE)

Year	A. Money[1] (M_1)	B. Quasi-Money[2]	C. Total[3] (M_2)
1952	98.3	21.2	119.5
1953	94.4	21.3	115.7
1954	116.8	27.8	144.6
1955	117.8	29.4	147.2
1956	126.9	34.8	161.7
1957	121.4	34.3	155.7
1958	102.6	32.0	134.6
1959	104.4	32.1	136.5
1960	104.3	34.1	138.4
1961	118.0	37.6	155.6
1962	122.5	37.8	160.3
1963	130.7	38.8	169.5
1964	132.5	38.7	171.2
1965	133.4	37.9	171.3
1966	123.2	38.1	161.3
1967	142.2	36.5	178.7
1968	160.0	40.8	200.8
1969	175.6	48.8	224.4
1970	190.6	58.0	248.6
1971	214.6	75.4	290.0
1972	271.2	110.3	381.5
1973	332.8	154.5	487.3
1974	342.8	241.3	584.1
1975	402.6	332.2	734.8
1976	549.6	465.6	1,015.2
1977	629.1	587.8	1,216.9
1978	717.8	713.7	1,431.5
1979	1,107.8	764.9	1,872.7
1980	924.8	992.9	1,917.7
1981	1,174.6	1,022.9	2,197.5
1982	1,164.3	1,102.9	2,267.2
1983	1,169.3	1,172.9	2,342.2

1. Sum of currency outside of banks and private sector demand deposits, source line 34.
2. Time, savings, and foreign currency deposits by residents, source line 34.
3. Calculated by adding columns A and B.

SOURCE: IMF-IFS-Y, 1982; IMF-IFS, January 1984; IMF-IFS-Y, 1984.

Table 3049

HONDURAS MONEY SUPPLY, 1952–83
(M NC YE)

Year	A. Money[1] (M_1)	B. Quasi-Money[2]	C. Total[3] (M_2)
1952	52.5	7.4	59.9
1953	59.4	8.8	68.2
1954	68.6	10.3	78.9
1955	60.6	11.5	72.1
1956	67.2	15.8	83.0
1957	64.3	12.6	76.9
1958	63.0	11.7	74.7
1959	65.9	14.7	80.6
1960	64.3	20.7	85.0
1961	65.7	23.7	89.4
1962	72.7	29.5	102.2
1963	79.1	34.7	113.8
1964	89.8	39.4	129.2
1965	104.6	46.5	151.1
1966	106.9	58.6	165.5
1967	114.3	68.7	183.0
1968	127.4	.8	128.2
1969	148.1	.2	148.3
1970	158.9	129.5	288.4
1971	169.4	151.7	321.1
1972	192.9	172.8	385.2
1973	238.4	206.6	445.0
1974	242.4	217.8	460.2
1975	262.7	244.5	507.2
1976	361.0	311.0	672.0
1977	411.3	384.5	795.8
1978	480.4	482.0	962.4
1979	545.6	494.8	1,040.4
1980	610.3	517.4	1,127.7
1981	637.4	588.9	1,226.3
1982	716.9	716.2	1,433.1
1983	814.9	918.5	1,733.4

1. Sum of currency outside of banks and private sector demand deposits, source line 34.
2. Time, savings, and foreign currency deposits by residents, source line 35.
3. Calculated by adding columns A and B.

SOURCE: IMF-IFS-Y, 1982; IMF-IFS, January 1984; IMF-IFS-Y, 1984.

Table 3050

MEXICO MONEY SUPPLY, INFLATION, AND GDP, 1952–84

	(A)	(B)	(C)	(D)	(E)	(F)
		B NC YE		M_2 Index	Price Index[4]	Real M_2 Index (D/E)
Year	Money[1] (M_1)	Quasi-Money[2]	Total[3] (M_2)	(1975 = 100.0)		
1952	7.3	1.9	9.2	5.6	32.0	17.5
1953	8.0	2.1	10.1	6.2	31.4	19.7
1954	9.0	3.0	12.0	7.3	34.4	21.2
1955	10.8	3.4	14.2	8.7	39.1	22.3
1956	12.0	3.7	15.7	9.6	40.9	23.5
1957	12.8	4.7	17.5	10.7	42.7	25.1
1958	13.7	5.5	19.2	11.7	44.6	26.2
1959	15.9	5.3	21.2	12.9	45.1	28.6
1960	17.3	5.4	22.7	13.8	47.3	29.2
1961	18.5	6.0	24.5	14.9	47.7	31.2
1962	20.9	6.6	27.5	16.8	48.6	34.6
1963	24.3	8.1	32.4	19.7	48.8	40.4
1964	28.6	9.2	37.8	23.0	50.9	45.2
1965	30.2	10.4	40.6	24.7	51.9	47.6
1966	33.9	11.8	45.7	27.8	52.5	53.0
1967	37.0	13.1	50.1	30.5	54.0	56.5
1968	42.3	14.8	57.1	34.8	55.1	63.2
1969	48.6	16.9	65.5	39.9	56.5	70.6
1970	53.8	18.2	72.0	43.9	59.8	73.4
1971	57.9	19.6	77.5	47.3	62.1	76.2
1972	68.2	22.9	91.1	55.5	63.8	87.0
1973	83.5	31.6	115.1	70.1	73.9	94.9
1974	100.8	38.4	139.2	84.8	90.5	93.7
1975	122.4	41.7	164.1	100.0	100.0	100.0
1976	158.0	85.0	243.0	148.1	122.3	121.1
1977	208.2	324.5	532.7	324.6	172.6	188.1
1978	270.2	434.3	704.5	429.3	199.8	214.9
1979	360.9	597.2	958.1	583.9	236.4	245.0
1980	477.2	832.6	1,309.8	798.2	294.3	271.2
1981	635.0	1,314.6	1,949.6	1,188.1	367.0	323.7
1982[b]	643.3[b]	1,742.3	2,385.6	1,453.7	462.6	314.2
1983	1,466.7	3,936.4	5,398.1	3,290.0	1,184.4	303.4
1984	2,279.8	6,852.2	9,132.0	5,564.9	2,017.6	275.8

1. Sum of currency outside of banks and private sector demand deposits, source line 34.
2. Time, savings, and foreign currency deposits in Mexico by residents, source line 35. According to data calculated from Banco de México, *Indicadores Económicos*, August 1982, p. 6, foreign currency in checking accounts, liquid savings, and in time deposits made up the following % of M_4 (or IMF's M_2): 1968, 5.1%; 1969, 4.3%; 1970, 3.8%; 1971, 2.9%; 1972, 2.2%; 1973, 3.2%; 1974, 2.5%; 1975, 3.1%; 1976, 10.6%; 1977, 14.0%; 1978, 12.5%; 1979, 14.8%; 1980, 18.1%; Mar. 1982, 25.0%. Cf. Leroy O. Laney, "Currency Substitution: The Mexican Case." *Voice* (Federal Reserve Bank of Dallas), January 1981, pp. 1-10.
3. Calculated by adding columns A and B.
4. Bank of Mexico Wholesale Price Index (210 national and import goods), period average, source line 63.

a. Expanded coverage which approximates the Bank of Mexico's concept of M_4.
b. March.

Method: A,B: 1952-74, IFS-Y, 1982; 1974-82, IFS, Aug. 1982, line 34; 1983-84, IFS, May 1985.
            C: Caculated (A + B).
            D: Calculated from column C.
            E: See source A, B, line 63.
            F: Calculated (D/E).

SOURCE: SALA , 22-2.

Figure 30:2
MEXICO MONEY SUPPLY (M$_2$) AND INFLATION INDEXES, 1952–82
(1975 = 100)

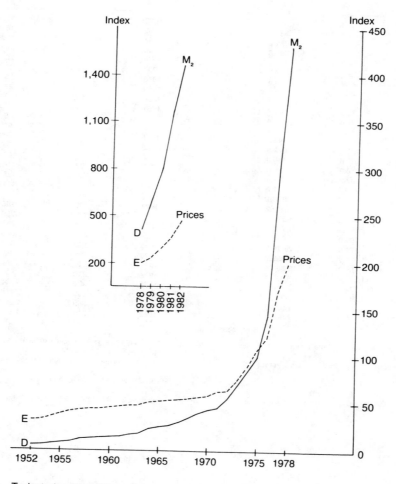

Trajectories D and E are keyed
to columns D and E in table 2

SOURCE: SALA, 22, p. xi.

Table 3051

NICARAGUA MONEY SUPPLY, 1952–83

(M NC YE)

Year	A. Money[1] (M_1)	B. Quasi- Money[2]	C. Total[3] (M_2)
1952	180.2	2.0	182.2
1953	230.2	9.2	239.4
1954	264.4	7.5	271.9
1955	272.5	18.1	290.6
1956	267.0	18.1	285.1
1957	259.6	19.4	279.0
1958	251.6	22.9	274.5
1959	253.2	28.8	282.0
1960	264.0	33.1	297.1
1961	272.7	32.0	304.7
1962	352.9	31.5	384.4
1963	397.4	51.3	448.7
1964	460.3	84.9	545.2
1965	537.3	135.2	672.5
1966	565.1	185.8	750.9
1967	540.7	219.3	760.0
1968	484.8	197.2	682.0
1969	513.1	207.9	721.0
1970	578.2	250.5	828.7
1971	618.9	330.3	949.2
1972	749;8	477.3	1,226.0
1973	1,146.4	587.9	1,734.3
1974	1,313.3	703.0	2,016.3
1975	1,255.8	774.0	2,029.8
1976	1,615.5	1,083.7	2,699.2
1977	1,699.2	1,156.2	2,855.4
1978	1,579.3	1,072.9	2,652.2
1979	2,654.1	772.6	3,426.7
1980	4,102.4	1,644.2	5,746.6
1981	5,206.3	2,720.4	7,926.7
1982	6,545.8	3,349.3	9,895.1
1983	10,937.0	4,151.5	15,088.5

1. Sum of currency outside of banks and private sector demand
   deposits, source line 34.
2. Time, savings, and foreign currency deposits by residents, source
   line 35.
3. Calculated by adding columns A and B.

SOURCE: IMF-IFS-Y, 1982; IMF-IFS, January 1984; IMF-IFS-Y,
1984.

Table 3052

PANAMA MONEY SUPPLY, 1952–83

(M NC YE)

Year	A. Money[1] (M_1)	B. Quasi- Money[2]	C. Total[3] (M_2)
1952	26.6	17.7	44.3
1953	30.2	18.4	48.6
1954	32.6	18.5	41.1
1955	32.7	19.8	52.5
1956	34.2	22.1	56.3
1957	38.0	23.4	61.4
1958	39.9	25.3	65.2
1959	41.6	27.1	68.7
1960	42.1	28.2	70.3
1961	43.9	31.4	75.3
1962	48.8	38.1	86.9
1963	59.7	51.0	110.7
1964	50.8	54.1	104.9
1965	55.5	69.2	124.7
1966	61.9	87.0	148.9
1967	70.3	110.4	180.7
1968	80.9	125.6	206.5
1969	84.8	111.7*	196.5
1970	100.5	155.8	256.3
1971	105.4	196.8	302.2
1972	153.6	239.3	392.9
1973	161.1	283.4	444.5
1974	196.3	333.9	530.2
1975	173.1	374.7	547.8
1976	190.0	388.0	578.0
1977	213.2	459.3	672.5
1978	246.0	586.7	832.7
1979	301.3	742.2	1,043.5
1980	335.3	980.4	1,315.7
1981	359.7	1,201.1	1,560.8
1982	379.3	1,369.8	1,749.1
1983	372.6	1,375.6	1,748.2

1. Sum of currency outside of banks and private sector demand
   deposits, source line 34.
2. Time, savings, and foreign currency deposits by residents, source
   line 35.
3. Calculated by adding columns A and B.

SOURCE: IMF-IFS-Y, 1982; IMF-IFS, May 1984; IMF-IFS-Y, 1983.

Table 3053

PARAGUAY MONEY SUPPLY, 1952–83
(M NC YE)

Year	A. Money[1] (M_1)	B. Quasi-Money[2]	C. Total[3] (M_2)
1952	582	50	632
1953	861	82	943
1954	1,070	102	1,172
1955	1,426	175	1,601
1956	1,941	95	2,036
1957	1,997	180	2,177
1958	2,384	376	2,760
1959	2,609	265	2,874
1960	2,674	357	3,031
1961	3,391	542	3,933
1962	3,311	825	4,136
1963	3,685	1,244	4,929
1964	4,473	1,761	6,234
1965	4,913	2,365	7,278
1966	5,034	2,822	7,856
1967	6,691*	3,648*	10,339*
1968	5,786	4,324	10,110
1969	6,557	5,300	11,857
1970	7,308	6,200	13,508
1971	7,848	7,394	15,242
1972	9,421	9,420	18,841
1973	12,494	11,808	24,302
1974	15,120	14,260	29,380
1975	17,829	19,258	37,087
1976	21,590	24,159	45,749
1977	28,574	31,576	60,150
1978	39,812	38,682	78,494
1979	49,537	47,952	97,489
1980	62,364	68,893	131,257
1981	62,432	94,355	156,787
1982	60,200	105,487	165,687
1983	75,587	117,838	193,425

1. Sum of currency outside of banks and private sector demand deposits, source line 34.
2. Time, savings, and foreign currency deposits by residents, source line 35.
3. Calculated by adding columns A and B.

SOURCE: IMF-IFS-Y, 1982; IMF-IFS, January 1984; IMF-IFS-Y, 1984.

Table 3054

PERU MONEY SUPPLY, 1952–83
(B NC YE)

Year	A. Money[1] (M_1)	B. Quasi-Money[2]	C. Total[3] (M_2)
1952	2.7	1.6	4.3
1953	3.1	1.8	4.9
1954	3.4	2.0	5.4
1955	3.6	2.5	6.1
1956	4.2	3.0	7.2
1957	4.4	3.5	7.9
1958	4.7	3.8	8.5
1959	6.0	4.0	10.0
1960	7.1	4.7	11.8
1961	8.3	5.5	13.8
1962	8.9	6.6	15.5
1963	10.3	7.7	18.0
1964	13.0	9.6	22.6
1965	15.6	12.3	27.9
1966	17.8	13.7	31.5
1967	20.1	14.1	34.2
1968	22.2	14.4	36.6
1969	26.3	14.5	40.8
1970	40.8	14.1	54.9
1971	45.0	15.5	60.5
1972	57.9	16.8	74.7
1973	72.5	19.1	91.6
1974	102.6	21.2	123.8
1975	120.0	23.3	143.3
1976	151.0	26.9	177.9
1977	182.4	39.8	222.2
1978	265.3	91.9	357.2
1979	451.7	234.5	686.2
1980	712.6	546.1	1,258.7
1981	1,044.8	1,077.3	2,122.1
1982	1,408.4	2,191.2	3,599.6
1983	2,763.2	4,560.2	7,323.4

1. Sum of currency outside of banks and private sector demand deposits, source line 34.
2. Time, savings, and foreign currency deposits by residents, source line 35.
3. Calculated by adding columns A and B.

SOURCE: IMF-IFS-Y, 1982; IMF-IFS, May 1984; IMF-IFS-Y, 1984.

Table 3055

URUGUAY MONEY SUPPLY, 1952–83

(M NC YE)

Year	A. Money[1] (M_1)	B. Quasi- Money[2]	C. Total[3] (M_2)
1952	~	~	~
1953	~	~	~
1954	~	~	~
1955	~	~	~
1956	~	~	~
1957	~	~	~
1958	~	~	~
1959	~	~	~
1960	~	2	4
1961	3	2	5
1962	3	2	5
1963	4	4	8
1964	5	6	11
1965	11*	8*	19*
1966	15	9*	24
1967	31	16	47
1968	48	24	72
1969	77	31	108
1970	88	42	130
1971	135	62	197
1972	198	118	316
1973	357	183	540
1974	586	335	921
1975	834	780	1,614
1976	1,380	1,845	3,225
1977	1,938	3,897	5,835
1978	3,588	7,526	11,114
1979	6,160	14,436	20,596
1980	9,082	26,508	35,590
1981	9,838	43,450	53,288
1982	11,790	82,587	94,377
1983	13,094	77,498	87,592

1. Sum of currency outside of banks and private sector demand deposits, source line 34.
2. Time, savings, and foreign currency deposits by residents, source line 35.
3. Calculated by adding columns A and B.

SOURCE: IMF-IFS-Y, 1982; IMF-IFS, January 1984; IMF-IFS-Y, 1984.

Table 3056

VENEZUELA MONEY SUPPLY, 1952–83

(M NC YE)

Year	A. Money[1] (M_1)	B. Quasi- Money[2]	C. Total[3] (M_2)
1952	1,909	273	2,182
1953	2,085	372	2,457
1954	2,169	494	2,663
1955	2,414	669	3,083
1956	2,756	922	3,678
1957	3,649	1,501	5,150
1958	4,017	1,860	5,877
1959	3,823	2,083	5,906
1960	3,574	1,691	5,265
1961	3,684	1,643	5,327
1962	3,604	1,806	5,410
1963	3,840	2,501	6,341
1964	4,399	3,022	7,421
1965	4,489	3,096	7,585
1966	4,620	2,928	7,548
1967	5,237	3,397	8,634
1968	5,699	3,771	9,470
1969	6,186	4,299	10,485
1970	6.732	4,718	11,450
1971	7,868	5,526	13,394
1972	9,467	6,981	16,448
1973	11,318	8,438	19,756
1974	16,006	9,980	25,986
1975	23,312	15,416	38,728
1976	27,105	21,567	48,672
1977	34,027	27,482	61,509
1978	38,987	31,848	70,835
1979	42,460	32,657	75,117
1980	50,209	38,432	88,641
1981	54,954	48,231	103,185
1982	58,015	57,979	115,994
1983	70,049	69,994	140,043

1. Sum of currency outside of banks and private sector demand deposits, source line 34.
2. Time, savings, and foreign currency deposits by residents, source line 35.
3. Calculated by adding columns A and B.

SOURCE: IMF-IFS-Y, 1982; IMF-IFS, May 1984; IMF-IFS-Y, 1984.

Table 3057

MONEY SUPPLY[1] CHANGES, 19 LC, 1955-83

(PC Calculated from Indexes)

Year	A. ARGENTINA	B. BOLIVIA	C. BRAZIL	D. CHILE	E. COLOMBIA	F. COSTA RICA	H. DOMINICAN REP.	I. ECUADOR	J. EL SALVADOR	K. GUATEMALA
1955	~	107.2	~	~	8.9	7.1	15.5	-.3	.1	13.1
1956	~	246.3	~	~	34.2	3.1	5.0	13.1	16.0	24.4
1957	~	48.2	~	~	3.4	9.9	14.2	7.5	3.7	14.2*
1958	~	10.2	~	~	10.5	9.1	5.4	3.3	-1.9	5.3
1959	~	22.3	26.3	~	14.3	10.0*	4.1	7.7	2.2	-1.6
1960	~	13.8	38.3	~	7.3	3.3	-12.7	9.5	6.7	-.9
1961	~	17.4	44.2	~	17.0	-4.2	5.9	8.5	-4.2	3.5
1962	~	15.5	52.5	~	27.9	11.7	-3.2	9.4	10.9	4.6
1963	~	17.1	57.5	~	12.9	10.8	9.7	11.9	14.1	12.5
1964	44.2	23.3	85.6	~	18.8	11.4	11.1	13.4	11.6	19.7
1965	34.4	22.4	83.3	~	19.8	6.8	1.1	.5	5.7	9.0
1966	26.7	22.4	40.7	~	9.6	3.1	5.1	12.3	6.6	13.1
1967	36.8	9.1	36.2	~	21.3	18.9	3.3	16.5	5.9	6.0
1968	31.0	11.5	43.0	~	17.8	17.5	15.0	21.3	.3	12.9
1969	21.5	14.1	32.6	41.6	19.7	11.0	16.3	12.7	5.8	8.4
1970	14.6	12.0	29.4	46.1	20.5	9.5	20.1	20.0	9.9	11.7
1971	16.6	14.9	31.7	76.8	12.0	13.0	12.7	21.0	7.1	5.3
1972	41.2	23.5	34.2	101.6	20.7	31.0	19.1	17.2	15.6	18.3
1973	81.6	33.2	45.6	330.8	31.5	21.2	26.2	29.6	19.9	25.0
1974	86.8	40.6	34.9	435.2	32.7	27.9	34.6	40.1	22.4	18.5
1975	68.4	30.6	34.7	297.8	20.7	37.9	32.6	21.5	16.9	16.9
1976	298.8	33.2	43.3	217.5	27.7	35.5	2.8	11.8	23.6	27.8
1977	257.8	40.2	41.9	147.9	39.3	36.2	10.9	37.0	31.5	22.3
1978	212.7	18.4	49.8	99.5	27.1	26.8	9.1	11.8	2.8	14.1
1979	178.9	11.8	59.1	76.7	23.2	29.4	2.2	22.2	11.0	11.6
1980	127.7	33.1	69.0	56.5	29.1	22.0	14.6	29.8	7.8	8.0
1981	91.1	21.5	67.5	57.0	44.4	~	2.4	18.4	5.3	10.5
1982	141.9	140.9	93.1	27.3	31.6	~	19.8	23.6	12.9	18.1
1983	288.2	~	109.6	3.2	~	~	12.5	20.3	9.4	4.1

Table 3057 (Continued)

MONEY SUPPLY[1] CHANGES, 19 LC, 1955–83
(PC Calculated from Indexes)

Year	L. HAITI	M. HONDURAS	N. MEXICO	O. NICARAGUA	P. PANAMA	Q. PARAGUAY	R. PERU	S. URUGUAY	T. VENEZUELA	UNITED STATES
1955	1.8	1.6	15.4	6.7	2.5	34.9	12.5	?	15.7	4.1
1956	9.8	3.7	10.8	-1.9	7.0	31.8	17.8	?	19.2	1.9
1957	-3.7	2.2	15.6	-2.2	~	4.8	8.3	?	39.8	2.7
1958	1.4	-5.0	12.9	4.8	4.0	14.6	6.2	?	22.3	3.8
1959	-14.4	2.9	9.8	-4.3	19.9	15.7	6.6	?	13.4	4.5
1960	10.3	6.5	5.1	3.6	2.1	5.1	18.0	?	-15.8	1.2
1961	6.2	5.3	6.5	4.6	4.5	20.8	14.9	?	2.0	3.9
1962	3.9	13.1	8.8	19.5	10.9	18.1	12.4	?	#	5.9
1963	4.6	12.4	17.8	21.8	21.0	9.7	12.6	?	10.2	7.1
1964	3.2	14.4	17.4	16.5	.2	21.8	31.2	?	15.2	6.6
1965	-3.1	13.9	11.7	24.2	16.2	21.2	25.4	?	11.4	7.6
1966	.7	11.8	8.8	14.5	18.5	6.0	16.5	40.3	4.7	7.4
1967	3.2	5.5	11.4	4.2	17.7	12.7	7.2	50.7	5.1	8.0
1968	9.3	18.2	11.8	.7	15.2	9.3	10.9	89.3	8.3	8.8
1969	12.0	15.8	13.3	3.1	8.4	3.3	8.4	57.4	9.0	6.1
1970	12.0	18.0	10.1	-1.8	21.4	10.4	25.8	29.9	12.1	4.3
1971	20.8	10.7	7.2	13.5	27.3	18.9	19.0	34.6	11.0	10.3
1972	22.3	10.4	13.5	28.1	18.4	17.7	17.0	60.6	20.9	9.3
1973	27.9	20.3	23.0	42.3	28.4	32.1	24.3	60.2	20.4	7.0
1974	26.3	11.3	26.1	24.1	10.4	21.5	26.1	76.8	27.2	4.7
1975	14.0	3.1	16.3	-5.5	7.8	22.1	26.0	82.2	44.7	8.5
1976	40.9	24.2	47.1	25.3	7.9	25.0	19.3	91.8	33.3	11.2
1977	26.6	28.4	38.5	19.7	10.2	33.9	23.2	85.9	30.0	12.2
1978	20.7	16.2	34.1	-7.2	21.2	29.7	43.6	80.8	17.6	6.1
1979	19.1	18.0	32.7	4.5	24.6	27.0	79.3	102.2	9.4	6.2
1980	8.6	2.4	35.9	81.5	26.6	26.5	95.9	66.0	12.4	8.7
1981	19.9	8.1	46.1	44.6	23.2	24.5	63.7	66.8	13.8	6.7
1982	4.1	9.8	63.1	18.3	15.2	13.2	72.1	36.2	20.8	9.4
1983	7.5	21.9	60.2	~	~	11.2	89.0	33.1	12.7	18.3

1. "Money" equals the sum of currency outside banks and private sector demand deposits.

SOURCE: IMF-IFS-Y, 1983, pp. 64–65; IMF-IFS-Y, 1984, pp. 80–83.

Table 3058

INCOME VELOCITY OF MONEY, 18 L, 1951–82
(1980 = 100)

Country	1951	1952	1953	1954	1955	1956	1957	1958	1959	1960	1961	1962
A. ARGENTINA	~	~	~	~	~	~	~	~	~	~	~	~
B. BOLIVIA	~	137.7	236.1	274.1	317.4	165.6	120.4	122.9	115.6	118.3	108.9	103.9
C. BRAZIL	~	~	~	~	~	~	~	~	~	~	~	~
D. CHILE	~	~	~	~	~	~	~	36.0	38.6	38.6	39.4	41.9
E. COLOMBIA	92.4	85.2	80.6	80.6	80.7	72.8	76.9	76.5	75.3	79.8	78.1	73.2
F. COSTA RICA	104.9	97.1	97.7	94.3	98.6	100.8	101.6	99.1	94.9*	99.3	108.5	104.5
H. DOMINICAN REP.	81.2	74.6	76.5	70.6	65.5	73.0	72.5	65.1	57.4	65.4	54.9	70.8
I. ECUADOR	152.5	139.9	142.7	136.4	153.9	137.9	141.3	140.2	136.2	133.8	134.5	135.6
J. EL SALVADOR	105.9	90.8	92.1	89.6	94.2	85.3	88.5	94.4	101.6	98.2	107.0	118.2
K. GUATEMALA	109.3	104.1	93.2	97.1	90.1	83.3	77.6	78.7	87.7	90.6	95.0	100.1
L. HAITI	~	~	~	~	146.0	143.0	148.3	161.4	167.4	152.8	142.4	142.2
M. HONDURAS	109.4	102.9	98.6	80.8	98.1	92.6	100.3	109.1	108.1	113.0	117.3	115.4
N. MEXICO	70.2	75.4	67.6	74.0	75.6	77.6	83.5	87.2	82.6	83.4	83.6	83.8
O. NICARAGUA	~	~	~	~	~	~	~	~	~	~	~	~
Q. PARAGUAY	58.6	69.5	84.5	87.5	89.1	82.7	95.3	96.8	94.8	158.7	163.1	148.0
R. PERU	89.7	84.4	80.2	86.1	89.8	85.1	89.7	95.6	105.3	107.9	104.8	106.3
S. URUGUAY	~	~	~	~	~	~	~	~	~	~	~	~
T. VENEZUELA	158.1	146.5	142.1	151.1	148.2	148.1	130.7	114.2	110.4	132.8	130.5	144.9
UNITED STATES	41.3	41.4	43.1	41.8	44.5	46.4	49.3	49.2	51.8	53.7	54.6	57.9

Country	1963	1964	1965	1966	1967	1968	1969	1970	1971	1972	1973	1974
A. ARGENTINA	44.4	43.6	46.6	45.1	42.8	37.7	37.6	36.6	50.7	61.2	55.6	40.2
B. BOLIVIA	96.8	88.6	80.3	74.1	79.6	84.2	83.2	85.5	84.4	89.0	99.5	115.9
C. BRAZIL	56.5*	58.7	51.6	53.9	54.1	54.2	54.2	54.4	55.2	55.0	53.5	56.9
D. CHILE	~	~	~	~	~	70.5	75.3	71.3	47.6	43.9	61.2	117.2
E. COLOMBIA	79.6	79.2	78.4	81.8	75.6	73.5	69.9	68.5	72.6	74.3	75.7	79.7
F. COSTA RICA	99.4	94.9	98.9	105.3	95.1	90.0	88.4	93.0	90.5	87.2	87.7	91.9
H. DOMINICAN REP.	74.3	76.5	66.7	76.1	81.3	76.4	82.1	79.3	82.8	85.4	86.2	85.4
I. ECUADOR	131.2	115.6	121.1*	126.7	122.3	111.9	110.3	104.5	99.2	99.5	100.7	104.7
J. EL SALVADOR	116.9	122.1	127.7	131.5	133.1	137.1	134.8	135.2	137.2	120.0	125.4	116.9
K. GUATEMALA	97.4	85.9	85.3	81.6	88.4	91.6	96.5	100.7	106.2	100.2	99.0	97.4
L. HAITI	140.8	149.6	167.5	174.9	168.6	151.0	145.2	138.1	128.8	112.2	99.0	97.1
M. HONDURAS	112.3	109.3	106.8	108.1	120.0	114.1	104.9	99.1	102.4	104.5	123.6	96.6
N. MEXICO	79.7	75.6	80.5	83.0	80.4	79.2	77.8	82.8	84.5	85.9	85.6	93.5
O. NICARAGUA	135.0	141.5	133.2	133.5	145.7	159.9	175.0	170.4	173.4	156.8	128.6	142.3
Q. PARAGUAY	110.0	99.4	93.0	98.6	98.7	99.6	115.3	115.9	112.9	114.5	111.4	122.8
R. PERU	111.1	99.6	94.9	98.2	104.2	105.4	105.5	85.5	74.0	69.1	66.2	62.9
S. URUGUAY	~	~	48.5	66.0	66.3	78.2	62.4	57.4	52.2	58.9	73.8	74.4
T. VENEZUELA	150.5	147.8	140.2	142.8	143.5	150.9*	143.8	147.5	144.8	131.8	128.5	150.0
UNITED STATES	59.3	61.2	63.7	66.6	67.7	68.8	70.7	71.8	72.9	74.7	78.0	80.6

Table 3058 (Continued)

INCOME VELOCITY OF MONEY, 18 L, 1951–82

(1980 = 100)

	Country	1975	1976	1977	1978	1979	1980	1981	1982
A.	ARGENTINA	63.3	80.3	90.9	91.8	106.6	100.0	125.7	~
B.	BOLIVIA	107.3	103.5	90.7	93.7	99.1	100.0	~	~
C.	BRAZIL	59.6	66.9	73.3	76.9	84.0	100.0	124.1	~
D.	CHILE	150.4	165.8	141.4	118.5	117.3	100.0	97.0	98.4
E.	COLOMBIA	91.1	90.5	89.4	89.8	93.5	100.0	102.3	~
F.	COSTA RICA	98.7	98.2	93.7	88.2	91.5	100.0	~	~
H.	DOMINICAN REP.	82.6	93.0	98.6	90.2	96.3	100.0	106.3	~
I.	ECUADOR	98.9	111.6	97.6	98.5	100.3	100.0	97.4	94.2
J.	EL SALVADOR	115.7	117.6	111.0	120.6	120.6	100.0	101.3	103.4
K.	GUATEMALA	104.8	93.8	91.6	90.4	92.6	100.0	108.8	~
L.	HAITI	117.6	110.5	101.5	89.2	78.5	100.0	82.1	80.7
M.	HONDURAS	102.3	94.0	93.8	96.7	94.4	100.0	97.5	100.7
N.	MEXICO	94.0	95.8	102.1	94.1	94.0	100.0	100.5	110.0
O.	NICARAGUA	169.9	162.6	170.4	166.6	125.7	100.0	~	~
Q.	PARAGUAY	119.4	111.3	100.4	91.6	92.4	100.0	108.6	~
R.	PERU	60.7	69.1	77.7	91.9	105.8	100.0	119.6	~
S.	URUGUAY	90.1	85.4	89.2	87.5	82.6	100.0	100.4	~
T.	VENEZUELA	107.0	96.5	88.9	81.8	93.8	100.0	102.0	95.4
	UNITED STATES	83.6	88.1	91.8	96.3	99.7	100.0	106.8	106.1

1. "Money" equals the sum of currency outside banks and private sector demand deposits. "Income Velocity" is defined as "money" divided by "GDP" and then converted to index format. Data "are designed to exhibit variability in the income velocity of money, and not international differences in the ratio of income to money. The ratio is therefore expressed in index number form, rather than in amounts of national currency income per unit of domestic currency" (IMF-IFS-S, no. 5, 1983, p. viii).

SOURCE: IMF-IFS-S, no. 5, 1983, pp. 50-53.

Table 3059

INCOME VELOCITY OF MONEY PLUS QUASI-MONEY,[1] 19 L, 1951–83

(1980 = 100)

Country	1951	1952	1953	1954	1955	1956	1957	1958	1959	1960	1961	1962
A. ARGENTINA	~	~	~	~	~	~	~	~	~	~	~	~
B. BOLIVIA	~	192.1	343.8	417.9	478.9	254.0	184.0	189.6	178.2	181.5	168.2	159.3
C. BRAZIL	~	~	~	~	~	~	~	41.2	44.5	44.5	44.5	48.6
D. CHILE	~	~	~	~	~	~	~	~	~	~	~	~
E. COLOMBIA	109.2	102.1	98.5	92.0	87.7	73.3	84.9	89.2	89.2	94.1	91.4	80.4
F. COSTA RICA	240.6	221.6	221.2	214.2	218.2	218.1	216.5	207.0	193.3*	199.9	213.6	208.0
H. DOMINICAN REP.	141.4	128.6	132.8	105.5	94.8	101.2	100.0	99.9	88.8	107.0	95.8	125.5
I. ECUADOR	165.3	153.5	152.1	145.2	154.0	138.9	137.7	137.2	134.1	133.1	130.8	127.7
J. EL SALVADOR	183.7	159.0	161.1	154.3	159.5	148.8	144.9	147.1	146.2	125.4	131.7	134.4
K. GUATEMALA	219.6	211.9	192.4	202.0	185.2	165.1	150.7*	148.6	160.4	160.0	159.6	162.0
L. HAITI	~	~	~	~	242.1	232.6	239.6	249.1	257.7	235.1	219.5	219.9
M. HONDURAS	189.6	178.4	169.9	139.0	152.9	144.4	156.7	175.7	177.0	179.4	170.7	164.3
N. MEXICO	123.3	122.7	110.4	106.5	112.7	116.0	115.2	113.6	110.8	119.4	119.1	118.8
O. NICARAGUA	~	~	~	~	~	~	~	~	~	184.1	189.4	174.6
P. PANAMA	~	~	~	~	231.1	224.5	227.0	219.4	208.2	211.0	225.3	221.1
Q. PARAGUAY	~	131.9	161.4	166.8	161.5	153.6	187.9	187.0	181.5	202.4	192.8	186.5
R. PERU	104.0	94.9	90.2	94.9	93.4	88.4	89.3	93.9	103.6	103.0	103.0	105.3
S. URUGUAY	~	~	~	~	~	~	~	~	~	~	~	~
T. VENEZUELA	257.9	235.0	221.2	226.0	215.1	205.8	172.1	144.9	132.9	158.5	163.4	178.7
UNITED STATES	74.3	74.1	76.3	73.5	74.7	77.2	79.1	77.3	80.2	82.3	82.0	83.3

Country	1963	1964	1965	1966	1967	1968	1969	1970	1971	1972	1973	1974
A. ARGENTINA	107.3	103.2	108.4	106.7	102.4	90.1	87.5	82.9	102.2	120.1	112.7	82.7
B. BOLIVIA	146.4	133.8	121.4	109.8	113.7	115.8	109.9	109.9	104.7	107.9	122.5	144.8
C. BRAZIL	65.6*	68.4	60.3	62.0	61.5	61.1	61.0	61.4	57.7	56.8	54.7	59.4
D. CHILE	~	~	~	~	~	125.6	129.3	118.8	97.1	85.2	98.9	147.8
E. COLOMBIA	90.7	94.2	89.0	98.3	91.4	90.1	86.6	86.4	90.2	90.9	88.6	88.5
F. COSTA RICA	200.5	190.8	194.4	205.9	187.1	176.1	175.0	184.4	178.5	156.8	160.1	162.7
H. DOMINICAN REP.	130.5	131.0	110.4	118.3	119.6	106.6	107.2	98.6	98.2	98.3	91.9	85.4
I. ECUADOR	123.7	121.4	125.3*	126.5	121.0	107.3	104.8	101.4	95.8	95.7	98.1	104.3
J. EL SALVADOR	125.4	123.8	125.1	123.2	123.2	127.0	124.7	122.5	120.2	110.9	106.9	103.4
K. GUATEMALA	159.0	136.1	128.4	118.7	117.0	114.9	112.9	112.2	111.1	99.4	97.2	100.9
L. HAITI	219.8	235.0	263.5	273.2	265.0	241.7	229.7	215.1	196.1	163.9	173.4	124.6
M. HONDURAS	154.7	150.8	147.2	142.4	146.8	134.9	120.8	109.8	106.4	104.6	97.9	98.1
N. MEXICO	109.3	105.8	110.0	112.9	108.1	107.0	104.4	112.4	115.6	117.4	116.7	120.5
O. NICARAGUA	158.4	158.7	141.1	132.0	137.2	144.3	150.5	159.2	149.2	122.1	107.2	121.4
P. PANAMA	202.5	217.0	205.0	188.6	178.4	166.7	168.7	150.2	133.1	123.5	109.9	113.8
Q. PARAGUAY	181.2	158.3	141.9	140.6	131.9	126.9	132.0	127.8	120.1	118.1	115.8	127.6
R. PERU	100.2	93.9	89.1	91.0	97.3	104.0	107.9	98.8	91.2	86.8	85.2	84.1
S. URUGUAY	~	112.9*	152.1	172.1	168.6	200.6	172.2	157.4	140.5	150.5	193.6	194.4
T. VENEZUELA	176.8	169.9	162.2	161.5	161.9	161.2	152.6	152.3	151.7	134.4	132.9	160.2
UNITED STATES	83.3	82.2	82.3	83.0	84.6	82.8	83.2	94.8	85.4	84.8	84.9	88.0

Table 3059 (Continued)

INCOME VELOCITY OF MONEY PLUS QUASI-MONEY,[1] 19 L, 1951-83

(1980 = 100)

	Country	1975	1976	1977	1978	1979	1980	1981	1982	1983
A.	ARGENTINA	146.1	190.3	146.9	116.8	112.4	100.0	101.2	~	~
B.	BOLIVIA	125.9	108.4	89.4	88.5	95.3	100.0	104.2	105.9	~
C.	BRAZIL	62.8	70.6	76.1	76.9	81.0	100.0	116.2[‡]	119.3	135.6
D.	CHILE	143.1	163.6	147.6	125.3	112.4	100.0	76.4	57.2	~
E.	COLOMBIA	92.2	94.9	91.7	91.6	97.2	100.0	86.9	83.1*	~
F.	COSTA RICA	150.0	136.2	127.3	115.2	101.9	100.0	~	~	~
H.	DOMINICAN REP.	79.1	84.5	88.4	83.5	94.9	100.0	106.5	96.9	~
I.	ECUADOR	99.7	110.0	100.5	103.4	103.5	100.0	100.8	97.1	109.6
J.	EL SALVADOR	100.5	103.6	98.9	103.3	104.1	100.0	92.1	84.1	~
K.	GUATEMALA	99.6	93.2	95.7	92.9	94.6	100.0	98.9	84.9	81.5
L.	HAITI	131.9	120.8	106.4	90.5	83.8	100.0	85.7	83.3	85.7
M.	HONDURAS	100.8	95.2	93.7	92.6	90.1	100.0	98.4	95.2	82.5
N.	MEXICO	126.7	107.4	104.5	98.5	97.4	100.0	94.0	99.4	106.8
O.	NICARAGUA	132.2	121.3	126.1	123.6	120.3	100.0	81.4	79.3	~
P.	PANAMA	117.5	115.8	111.2	108.7	99.6	100.0	88.4	84.9	~
Q.	PARAGUAY	118.5	106.5	98.0	92.5	97.2	100.0	101.6	93.3	~
R.	PERU	82.1	95.6	107.5	118.6	123.1	100.0	104.4	101.0	100.2
S.	URUGUAY	191.6	154.6	131.1	112.6	103.8	100.0	78.5	61.3	~
T.	VENEZUELA	116.5	100.6	88.6	81.8	91.9	100.0	98.6	83.4	~
	UNITED STATES	90.7	90.5	90.2	95.3	99.8	100.0	105.4	100.1	91.2

1. "Money" equals the sum of currency outside banks and private sector demand
   deposits. "Quasi-Money" is time, savings, and foreign currency deposits by residents.
   "Income Velocity" is here defined as "money" plus "quasi-money" divided by "GDP"
   and then converted to index format. Data "are designed to exhibit variability in the
   income velocity of money, and not international differences in the ratio of income to
   money. The ratio is therefore expressed in index number form, rather than in amounts
   of national currency income per unit of domestic currency" (IMF-IFS-S, no. 5, 1983,
   p. viii).

SOURCE: IMF-IFS-S, no. 5, 1983, pp. 54-57; IMF-IFS-Y, 1984.

Table 3060

RATIO OF CURRENCY TO MONEY,[1] 18 LC, 1951–82

(%)

Country	1951	1952	1953	1954	1955	1956	1957	1958	1959	1960	1961	1962
A. ARGENTINA	~	~	~	~	~	~	~	~	~	~	~	~
B. BOLIVIA	~	66.9	70.1	73.2	69.4	74.4	73.6	76.4	81.2	83.2	82.7	82.2
C. BRAZIL	~	~	~	~	~	~	~	27.3	26.6	24.7	24.6	23.9
D. CHILE	~	~	~	~	~	~	~	~	~	~	~	~
E. COLOMBIA	35.8	36.0	34.3	32.2	31.9	30.8	33.9	33.5	31.7	31.5	30.9	26.7
F. COSTA RICA	45.2	44.3	44.4	44.7	42.1	41.3	42.7	43.0	41.0*	41.2	42.5	41.1
H. DOMINICAN REP.	49.5	51.1	54.9	53.8	57.9	59.7	56.3	52.8	50.2	52.1	48.6	54.4
I. ECUADOR	55.1	51.6	52.8	52.7	53.3	52.6	51.9	49.9	47.3	48.2	48.6	48.8
J. EL SALVADOR	56.2	57.5	55.4	54.0	47.3	46.4	44.9	44.6	44.4	47.4	48.6	47.2
K. GUATEMALA	75.5	80.9	79.6	79.3	68.4	64.6	63.3	63.2	65.2	64.2	66.0	65.4
L. HAITI	55.7	53.3	52.9	55.1	50.7	56.2	63.9	65.9	69.4	68.4	63.9	65.2
M. HONDURAS	53.0	54.8	56.4	56.6	55.0	56.2	58.7	57.8	55.1	55.4	52.9	53.1
N. MEXICO	47.5	48.2	46.1	49.3	45.2	45.8	45.6	45.8	44.6	42.9	43.4	43.1
O. NICARAGUA	51.0	48.0	46.1	45.8	43.5	46.8	47.9	47.3	51.0	49.4	48.2	46.2
Q. PARAGUAY	~	60.5	54.7	55.4	56.5	56.3	56.4	57.6	56.6	56.0	56.5	56.8
R. PERU	40.1	40.0	40.7	41.5	41.5	42.3	43.0	45.0	50.1	46.5	45.7	49.4
S. URUGUAY	~	~	~	~	~	~	~	~	~	~	~	~
T. VENEZUELA	54.0	51.0	48.0	49.1	46.5	43.8	38.3	33.9	32.2	42.0	35.4	35.2
UNITED STATES	21.2	21.1	21.5	20.7	20.3	20.4	20.8	20.5	20.2	20.2	20.0	20.3

Country	1963	1964	1965	1966	1967	1968	1969	1970	1971	1972	1973	1974
A. ARGENTINA	49.5	45.4	45.0	44.9	42.5	40.2	40.3	40.0	46.7	43.5	40.7	37.1
B. BOLIVIA	80.0	79.9	80.2	76.8	76.0	73.9	73.8	74.6	73.8	70.9	69.7	65.4
C. BRAZIL	24.5	24.0	20.1	20.9	19.4	18.2	18.6	18.1	16.8	16.9	18.5	18.1
D. CHILE	~	~	~	~	~	38.4	37.8	40.0	41.7	46.6	49.2	40.1
E. COLOMBIA	27.4	27.1	27.4	27.6	25.0	24.9	24.2	24.8	25.1	24.5	22.8	21.1
F. COSTA RICA	39.9	37.4	37.0	38.5	33.8	32.9	32.4	33.6	32.6	31.9	32.4	31.2
H. DOMINICAN REP.	59.8	55.5	53.4	54.9	51.0	45.8	46.3	46.8	45.7	43.7	43.8	42.4
I. ECUADOR	46.7	40.3	43.7	43.6	40.6	37.1	36.7	37.7	35.0	34.7	31.4	29.3
J. EL SALVADOR	45.4	46.0	46.1	44.1	43.4	43.3	43.2	43.6	43.1	43.7	41.4	39.9
K. GUATEMALA	62.5	57.0	50.9	50.2	51.5	49.8	52.4	53.3	54.9	52.5	50.3	50.1
L. HAITI	64.6	63.8	62.3	62.3	60.4	59.4	57.9	58.2	56.2	52.9	49.4	51.1
M. HONDURAS	53.0	53.3	50.5	49.1	49.6	49.0	48.5	49.0	48.4	47.7	48.0	48.9
N. MEXICO	41.7	41.1	40.6	39.9	39.2	39.0	38.5	38.1	37.9	38.6	39.1	41.1
O. NICARAGUA	43.1	40.4	37.3	37.2	38.9	39.0	39.2	41.0	40.0	38.6	34.6	34.0
Q. PARAGUAY	53.7	54.4	55.5	56.4	43.6	46.2	52.5	53.6	52.9	52.9	52.3	51.7
R. PERU	50.7	46.5	44.6	44.2	45.2	45.2	46.3	42.8	41.6	40.6	38.5	35.7
S. URUGUAY	~	~	55.6	61.0	64.9	60.7	63.7	60.7	59.8	56.9	54.1	48.6
T. VENEZUELA	34.0	31.5	31.0	32.5	31.7	29.5	28.9	27.9	26.3	24.6	22.5	21.2
UNITED STATES	20.8	21.2	21.5	21.8	22.0	21.8	22.1	22.7	22.8	22.7	23.1	24.2

1. Currency outside banks divided by money.

SOURCE: IMF-IFS-S, no. 5, 1983, pp. 42-45.

Table 3060 (Continued)

RATIO OF CURRENCY TO MONEY,[1] 18 LC, 1951–82

(%)

	Country	1975	1976	1977	1978	1979	1980	1981	1982
A.	ARGENTINA	40.8	35.7	40.4	45.5	50.7	55.3	60.9	52.9
B.	BOLIVIA	64.2	61.5	59.9	62.2	65.5	66.7	62.8	68.6
C.	BRAZIL	18.0	18.5	18.9	19.4	19.9	19.4	20.5	22.3
D.	CHILE	42.1	46.5	47.6	48.0	48.0	43.5	47.7	52.9
E.	COLOMBIA	24.1	24.5	24.6	26.7	27.6	28.6	29.2	30.8
F.	COSTA RICA	30.4	29.8	29.1	29.5	30.4	30.8	30.9	~
H.	DOMINICAN REP.	37.3	43.8	44.6	45.8	46.2	46.1	47.2	47.4
I.	ECUADOR	28.3	32.8	30.7	29.9	29.4	28.5	28.8	26.0
J.	EL SALVADOR	37.9	38.5	38.2	40.2	44.9	50.7	47.3	47.2
K.	GUATEMALA	50.6	47.1	46.4	48.1	48.0	50.3	51.6	51.8
L.	HAITI	50.2	42.7	40.8	41.6	53.4	44.5	39.2	43.9
M.	HONDURAS	46.2	47.4	48.6	46.6	46.6	49.1	46.2	45.4
N.	MEXICO	42.4	45.6	46.5	39.9	40.4	40.5	41.5	45.7
O.	NICARAGUA	36.4	36.7	37.8	47.0	57.5	46.0	42.4	44.0
Q.	PARAGUAY	49.1	48.0	47.8	44.7	45.9	47.0	47.2	51.1
R.	PERU	34.8	34.8	32.9	33.8	34.9	36.6	40.7	45.4
S.	URUGUAY	50.8	54.8	52.1	51.1	42.7	53.7	58.4	64.6
T.	VENEZUELA	18.7	20.2	20.2	21.3	22.7	23.3	23.6	22.2
	UNITED STATES	25.3	26.4	26.8	27.6	28.0	28.0	28.6	29.3

SOURCE: IMF-IFS-S, No. 5, 1983.

CHAPTER 31

EXCHANGE RATES

Table 3100

IMF DOLLAR YEAR-END EXCHANGE RATES,[1] 20 L, 1948-84[a]

(NC per US)

Year	A. ARGENTINA	B. BOLIVIA	C. BRAZIL	D. CHILE	E. COLOMBIA	F. COSTA RICA	G.[3] CUBA	H. DOMINICAN REP.	I. ECUADOR	J. EL SALVADOR	K. GUATEMALA
1948	.0481	.042	.019	.0066	1.960	6.200	1.00	1.00	13.500	2.500	1.00
1949	.0902	.042	.019	.0099	1.960	6.200	1.00	1.00	13.500	2.500	1.00
1950	.1402	.060	.019	.0073	1.960	5.920	1.00	1.00	15.000	2.500	1.00
1951	.1446	.060	.019	.0093	2.510	5.635	1.00	1.00	15.000	2.500	1.00
1952	.1398	.060	.019	.0013	2.510	5.635	1.00	1.00	15.000	2.500	1.00
1953	.1398	.190	.057	.0011	2.510	5.635	1.00	1.00	15.000	2.500	1.00
1954	.1398	.190	.074	.0011	2.510	5.635	1.00	1.00	15.000	2.500	1.00
1955	.3610	.190	.067	.0011	2.510	5.635	1.00	1.00	15.000	2.500	1.00
1956	.3745	7.760	.066	.0055	2.510	5.635	1.00	1.00	15.000	2.500	1.00
1957	.3745	8.565	.091	.0069	5.425	5.635	1.00	1.00	15.000	2.500	1.00
1958	.7000	11.935	.141	.0099	6.400	5.635	1.00	1.00	15.000	2.500	1.00
1959	.8325	11.880	.184	.0105	6.400	5.635	1.00	1.00	15.000	2.500	1.00
1960	.8270	11.880	.195	.0105	6.700	5.635	1.00	1.00	15.000	2.500	1.00
1961	.8302	11.880	.307	.0105	6.700	6.635	1.00	1.00	18.000	2.500	1.00
1962	1.341	11.880	.475	.0024	9.000	6.635	1.00	1.00	18.000	2.500	1.00
1963	1.325	11.880	.620	.0030	9.000	6.635	1.00	1.00	18.000	2.500	1.00
1964	1.509	11.880	1.850	.0033	9.000	6.635	1.00	1.00	18.000	2.500	1.00
1965	1.885	11.880	2.220	.004	3.500	6.635	1.00	1.00	18.000	2.500	1.00
1966	2.473	11.880	2.220	.044	13.500	6.635	1.00	1.00	18.000	2.500	1.00
1967	3.500	11.880	2.715	.0058	15.760	6.635	1.00	1.00	18.000	2.500	1.00
1968	3.500	11.880	3.830	.008	16.880	6.635	1.00	1.00	18.000	2.500	1.00
1969	4.00	11.880	4.350	.0010	17.850	6.635	1.00	1.00	18.000	2.500	1.00
1970	5.00	11.880	4.950	.0122	19.090	6.635	1.00	1.00	25.000	2.500	1.00
1971	5.00	11.880	5.635	.0158	20.910	6.635	.92	1.00	25.000	2.500	1.00
1972	5.00	20.000	6.215	.025	22.790	6.635	.92	1.00	25.000	2.500	1.00
1973	5.00	20.000	6.220	.360	24.790	6.650	.83	1.00	25.000	2.500	1.00
1974	5.00	20.000	7.435	1.870	28.630	8.570	.83	1.00	25.000	2.500	1.00
1975	60.9	20.000	9.070	8.500	32.960	8.570	.83	1.00	25.000	2.500	1.00
1976	274.5	20.000	12.345	17.420	36.320	8.570	.83	1.00	25.000	2.500	1.00
1977	597.5	20.000	16.050	27.960	37.960	8.570	.83	1.00	25.000	2.500	1.00
1978	.100	20.000	20.920	33.950	41.000	8.570	.740	1.00	25.000	2.500	1.00
1979	.162	24.510	42.530	39.000	44.000	8.570	.720	1.00	25.000	2.500	1.00
1980	.199	24.510	65.500	39.000	50.920	8.570	.710	1.00	25.000	2.500	1.00
1981	.725	24.510	127.80	39.000	59.070	36.090	.830	1.00	25.000	2.500	1.00
1982	4.855	196	252.67	73.430	70.290	40.250	.850	1.00	33.150	2.500	1.00
1983	23.261	500	984	87.530	88.770	43.400	.870	1.00	54.100	2.500	1.00
1984	178.735	9,000	3,184	128.240	113.890	47.750	.900[b]	1.00	67.175	2.500	1.00

Table 3100 (Continued)

IMF DOLLAR YEAR-END EXCHANGE RATES,[1] 20 L, 1948-84[a]

(NC per US)

Year	L. HAITI	M. HONDURAS	N. MEXICO	O. NICARAGUA	P. PANAMA	Q. PARAGUAY	R. PERU[2]	S. URUGUAY[2]	T. VENEZUELA[2]
1948	5.00	2.00	4.855	5.145	1.00	3.12	16.10	.0019	3.220
1949	5.00	2.00	8.650	5.145	1.00	3.12	14.81	.0019	3.220
1950	5.00	2.00	8.650	6.826	1.00	3.12	14.95	.0019	3.220
1951	5.00	2.00	8.650	6.826	1.00	6.00	15.28	.0019	3.220
1952	5.00	2.00	8.650	6.826	1.00	15.00	15.60	.0019	3.220
1953	5.00	2.00	8.650	6.826	1.00	15.00	19.89	.0019	3.220
1954	5.00	2.00	12.500	6.826	1.00	21.00	19.00	.0019	3.220
1955	5.00	2.00	12.500	6.826	1.00	21.00	19.00	.0021	3.220
1956	5.00	2.00	12.500	6.826	1.00	10.00	19.00	.0021	3.220
1957	5.00	2.00	12.500	7.026	1.00	111.30	19.00	.0021	3.220
1958	5.00	2.00	12.500	7.026	1.00	111.30	24.49	.0021	3.220
1959	5.00	2.00	12.500	7.026	1.00	122.00	27.70	.0021	3.220
1960	5.00	2.00	12.500	7.026	1.00	126.00	26.76	.0110	3.220
1961	5.00	2.00	12.500	7.026	1.00	126.00	26.81	.0200	3.220
1962	5.00	2.00	12.500	7.026	1.00	126.00	26.82	.0110	3.220
1963	5.00	2.00	12.500	7.026	1.00	126.00	26.82	.0164	3.220
1964	5.00	2.00	12.500	7.026	1.00	126.00	26.82	.0187	4.450
1965	5.00	2.00	12.500	7.026	1.00	126.00	26.82	.0600	4.450
1966	5.00	2.00	12.500	7.026	1.00	126.00	26.82	.0762	4.450
1967	5.00	2.00	12.500	7.026	1.00	126.00	26.82	.2000	4.450
1968	5.00	2.00	12.500	7.026	1.00	126.00	38.70	.2500	4.450
1969	5.00	2.00	12.500	7.026	1.00	126.00	38.70	.2500	4.450
1970	5.00	2.00	12.500	7.026	1.00	126.00	38.70	.2500	4.450
1971	5.00	2.00	12.500	7.026	1.00	126.00	38.70	.3700	4.350
1972	5.00	2.00	12.500	7.026	1.00	126.00	38.70	.7320	4.350
1973	5.00	2.00	12.500	7.026	1.00	126.00	38.70	.9370	4.285
1974	5.00	2.00	12.500	7.026	1.00	126.00	38.70	1.6660	4.285
1975	5.00	2.00	12.500	7.026	1.00	126.00	45.00	2.7300	4.285
1976	5.00	2.00	19.950	7.026	1.00	126.00	69.37	4.0000	4.293
1977	5.00	2.00	22.736	7.026	1.00	126.00	130.38	5.4100	4.293
1978	5.00	2.00	22.724	7.026	1.00	126.00	196.18	7.0540	4.293
1979	5.00	2.00	22.803	10.050	1.00	126.00	250.12	8.4640	4.293
1980	5.00	2.00	23.256	10.050	1.00	126.00	341.17	10.0250	4.293
1981	5.00	2.00	26.229	10.050	1.00	126.00	506.17	11.5940	4.293
1982	5.00	2.00	96.480	10.050	1.00	126.00	989.67	33.7500	4.293
1983	5.00	2.00	143.80	10.050	1.00	126.00	2,271.2	43.250	4.300
1984	5.00	2.00	192.56	10.050	1.00	240.00	5,696.0	74.750	7.500

1. Line ae, Market Rate/Par Rate (or Central Rate).
2. For multiple exchange rates, see SALA, 17, ch. 24.
3. Beginning 1971, data reflect noncommercial rates applied to tourism and to remittances from outside the ruble area available at the U.N. Statistical Office.

a. For previous years after 1937, see SALA, 17, ch. 24.
b. December.

SOURCE: IMF-IFS-S, no. 1, 1981; IMF-IFS, May 1985; Cuba data from UN-MB, various monthly, 1969-85.

Table 3101

IMF DOLLAR AVERAGE EXCHANGE RATES,[1] 19 L, 1965-84[a]

(NC per US)

Country	1965	1966	1967	1968	1969	1970	1971	1972	1973	1974	1975	1976	1977	1978	1979	1980	1981	1982	1983	1984
A. ARGENTINA	1.7	2.1	3.3	3.5	3.5	3.8	4.6	8.2	9.4	8.9	36.6	140.0	407.6	795.8	1,317.0	1,837.2	4,403	2,592.3	10,530	67,649
B. BOLIVIA	11.88	11.88	11.88	11.88	11.88	11.88	11.88	13.30	20.00	20.00	20.00	20.00	20.00	20.00	20.39	24.51	24.51	64.12	229.78	2,174.21
C. BRAZIL	1.90	2.22	2.66	3.40	4.08	4.59	5.30	5.93	6.13	6.79	8.13	10.67	14.14	18.07	26.95	52.71	93.12	179.51	577.04	1,848.03
D. CHILE	.003	.004	.005	.007	.009	.012	.012	.020	.111	.832	4.911	13.054	21.529	31.656	37.246	39.000	39.000	50.909	78.842	98.656
E. COLOMBIA	10.475	13.500	14.510	16.291	17.320	18.443	19.932	21.886	23.637	26.064	30.929	34.694	36.775	39.095	42.550	47.280	54.491	64.102	78.857	100.817
F. COSTA RICA	6.625	6.625	6.6	6.625	6.625	6.625	6.626	6.635	6.647	7.930	8.570	8.570	8.570	8.570	8.570	8.570	21.763	37.580	41.094	44.533
H. DOMINICAN REP.	1.00	1.00	1.00	1.00	1.00	1.00	1.00	1.00	1.00	1.00	1.00	1.00	1.00	1.00	1.00	1.00	1.00	1.00	1.00	1.00
I. ECUADOR	18.000	18.000	18.000	18.000	18.000	20.917	25.000	25.000	25.000	25.000	25.000	25.000	25.000	25.000	25.000	25.000	25.000	30.026	44.115	62.536
J. EL SALVADOR	2.50	2.50	2.50	2.50	2.50	2.50	2.50	2.50	2.50	2.50	2.50	2.50	2.50	2.50	2.50	2.50	2.50	2.50	2.50	2.50
K. GUATEMALA	1.00	1.00	1.00	1.00	1.00	1.00	1.00	1.00	1.00	1.00	1.00	1.00	1.00	1.00	1.00	1.00	1.00	1.00	1.00	1.00
L. HAITI	5.00	5.00	5.00	5.00	5.00	5.00	5.00	5.00	5.00	5.00	5.00	5.00	5.00	5.00	5.00	5.00	5.00	5.00	5.00	5.00
M. HONDURAS	2.00	2.00	2.00	2.00	2.00	2.00	2.00	2.00	2.00	2.00	2.00	2.00	2.00	2.00	2.00	2.00	2.00	2.00	2.00	2.00
N. MEXICO	12.500	12.500	12.500	12.500	12.500	12.500	12.500	12.500	12.500	12.500	12.500	15.426	22.573	22.767	22.805	22.951	24.515	54.985	120.094	167.83
O. NICARAGUA	7.000	7.000	7.000	7.000	7.000	7.000	7.000	7.000	7.000	7.013	7.026	7.026	7.026	7.026	9.255	10.050	10.050	10.050	10.050	10.050
P. PANAMA	1.00	1.00	1.00	1.00	1.00	1.00	1.00	1.00	1.00	1.00	1.00	1.00	1.00	1.00	1.00	1.00	1.00	1.00	1.00	1.00
Q. PARAGUAY	126.00	126.00	126.00	126.00	126.00	126.00	126.00	126.00	126.00	126.00	126.00	126.00	126.00	126.00	126.00	126.00	126.00	126.00	126.00	201.00
R. PERU	26.82	26.82	30.74	38.70	38.70	38.70	38.70	38.70	38.70	38.70	40.80	57.43*	83.81	156.33	224.55	288.65	422.85	697.57	1,625.1	3,446.9
S. URUGUAY	.0523	.0678	.1158	.2375	.2500	.2500	.2600	.5630	.8746	1.2155	2.2991	3.3950*	4.678	6.060	7.861	9.099	10.820	13.909	34.542	56.135
T. VENEZUELA	4.4997	4.4998	4.5001	4.4999	4.4996	4.4983	4.5007	4.4000	4.3045	4.2845	4.2850	4.2899	4.2925	4.2925	4.2925	4.2925	4.2925	4.2925	4.2975	7.0175

1. Line rf, Implicit Rate/Market Rate.

a. For previous years after 1937, see SALA, 17, ch. 24, and SALA, 22-2501. Rounding by source makes data for Argentina and Chile problematic for all but the last few years.

SOURCE: IMF-IFS-S, no. 1, 1981; IMF-IFS, May 1985.

Table 3102

IMF SDR YEAR-END EXCHANGE RATES,[1] 19 LC, 1970–84

(NC per SDR)[2]

Country	1970	1971	1972	1973	1974	1975	1976	1977	1978	1979	1980	1981	1982	1983	1984
A. ARGENTINA	.004	.0005	.0005	.0006	.0006	.0071	.0319	.0726	.1307	.2132	.2541	.8436	5.3550	24.3531	175.198
B. BOLIVIA	11.88	12.90	21.71	24.13	24.49	23.41	23.24	24.29	26.06	32.29	31.26	28.53	216.21	523.48	8,821.89
C. BRAZIL	4.95	6.12	6.75	7.50	9.10	10.62	14.34	19.50	27.25	56.03	83.54	148.75	278.72	1,030.02	3,120.99
D. CHILE	.01	.02	.03	.43	2.29	9.95	20.24	33.96	44.23	51.38	49.74	45.39	81.00	91.64	125.702
E. COLOMBIA	19.09	22.70	24.74	29.91	35.05	38.59	42.20	46.11	53.41	57.96	64.94	68.76	77.54	92.94	111.636
F. COSTA RICA	6.64	7.20	7.20	8.02	10.49	10.03	9.96	10.41	11.17	11.29	10.93	42.01	44.40	45.44	46.805
H. DOMINICAN REP.	1.00	1.09	1.09	1.21	1.22	1.17	1.16	1.21	1.30	1.32	1.28	1.16	1.10	1.05	.9802
I. ECUADOR	25.00	27.14	27.14	30.16	30.61	29.27	29.05	20.37	32.57	32.93	31.89	29.10	36.57	56.64	65.846
J. EL SALVADOR	2.50	2.71	2.71	3.02	3.06	2.93	2.90	3.04	3.26	3.29	3.19	2.91	2.76	2.62	2.4505
K. GUATEMALA	1.00	1.09	1.09	1.21	1.22	1.17	1.16	1.21	1.30	1.32	1.28	1.16	1.10	1.05	.9802
L. HAITI	5.00	5.43	5.43	6.03	6.12	5.85	5.81	6.07	6.51	6.59	6.38	5.82	5.52	5.23	4.9011
M. HONDURAS	2.00	2.17	2.17	2.41	2.45	2.34	2.32	2.43	2.61	2.63	2.55	2.33	2.21	2.09	1.9604
N. MEXICO	12.50	13.57	13.57	15.08	15.30	14.63	23.18	27.62	29.61	30.04	29.66	30.53	106.43	150.55	188.75
O. NICARAGUA	7.03	7.63	7.63	8.48	8.60	8.23	8.16	8.54	9.15	13.24	12.82	11.70	11.09	10.52	9.851
P. PANAMA	1.00	1.09	1.09	1.21	1.22	1.17	1.16	1.21	1.30	1.32	1.28	1.16	1.10	1.05	.9802
Q. PARAGUAY	126.00	136.80	136.80	152.00	154.27	147.50	146.39	153.05	164.15	165.98	160.70	146.66	138.99	131.92	235.25
R. PERU	42.00	42.00	46.70	47.40	52.70	52.68	80.60	158.40	255.60	329.50	435.10	589.20	1,091.71	2,378.85	5,583.3
S. URUGUAY	.25	.40	.80	1.13	2.03	3.20	4.65	6.57	9.19	11.15	12.79	13.50	37.23	45.28	73.271
T. VENEZUELA	4.45	4.72	4.72	5.17	5.25	5.02	4.99	5.21	5.59	5.65	5.47	5.00	4.74	4.50	7.3516
UNITED STATES	1.00	1.09	1.09	1.21	1.22	1.17	1.16	1.21	1.30	1.32	1.28	1.16	1.10	1.05	.98021

1. Special Drawing Right (SDR) values are based on a market basket of currencies.
2. Line aa, Market Rate.

SOURCE: IMF-IFS-Y, 1983; IMF-IFS, May 1985.

Table 3103
IMF SDR AVERAGE EXCHANGE RATES,[1] 19 LC, 1970-84
(NC per SDR)[2]

Country	1970	1971	1972	1973	1974	1975	1976	1977	1978	1979	1980	1981	1982	1983	1984
A. ARGENTINA	.0004	.0005	.0009	.0011	.0011	.0044	.0162	.0476	.0996	.1702	.2391	.5191	2.8619	11.2565	69.341
B. BOLIVIA	11.88	11.92	14.44	23.84	24.05	24.28	23.09	23.35	25.04	26.35	31.90	28.90	70.79	245.63	2,228.6
C. BRAZIL	4.60	5.30	6.44	7.30	8.17	9.87	12.32	16.51	22.62	34.81	68.61	109.81	198.19	616.86	1,894.2
D. CHILE	.01	.01	.02	.13	1.00	5.96	15.07	25.14	39.63	48.12	50.76	45.99	56.20	*84.28	101.123
E. COLOMBIA	18.44	19.99	23.74	28.18	31.35	37.55	40.06	42.94	48.95	54.98	61.54	64.25	70.77	84.30	103.34
F. COSTA RICA	6.63	6.65	7.20	7.92	9.54	10.41	9.89	10.01	10.73	11.07	11.15	25.66	41.30	43.93	45.646
H. DOMINICAN REP.	1.00	1.00	1.09	1.19	1.20	1.21	1.15	1.17	1.25	1.29	1.30	1.18	1.10	1.07	1.0250
I. ECUADOR	20.92	25.08	27.14	29.80	30.07	30.35	28.86	29.19	31.30	32.30	32.54	29.48	33.15	47.16	64.100
J. EL SALVADOR	2.50	2.51	2.71	2.98	3.01	3.04	2.89	2.92	3.13	3.23	3.25	2.95	2.76	2.67	2.5625
K. GUATEMALA	1.00	1.00	1.09	1.19	1.20	1.21	1.15	1.17	1.25	1.29	1.30	1.18	1.10	1.07	1.0230
L. HAITI	5.00	5.01	5.43	5.96	6.01	6.07	5.77	5.84	6.26	6.46	6.51	5.90	5.52	5.35	3.1251
M. HONDURAS	2.00	2.01	2.17	2.38	2.41	2.43	2.31	2.34	2.50	2.58	2.60	2.36	2.21	2.14	2.0500
N. MEXICO	12.50	12.54	13.57	14.90	15.03	15.17	17.81	26.35	28.51	29.47	29.87	28.91	62.27	128.38	172.02
O. NICARAGUA	7.00	7.02	7.60	8.35	8.43	8.53	8.11	8.20	8.80	11.96	13.08	11.85	11.10	10.74	10.301
P. PANAMA	1.00	1.00	1.09	1.19	1.20	1.21	1.15	1.17	1.25	1.29	1.30	1.18	1.10	1.07	1.0250
Q. PARAGUAY	126.00	126.38	136.80	150.21	151.53	152.98	145.47	147.11	157.75	162.79	163.99	148.57	139.11	134.69	206.03
R. PERU	38.70	38.82	42.02	46.14	46.54	49.54	66.31	97.85	195.73	290.12	375.69	497.93	770.12	1,737.21	3,553.6
S. URUGUAY	.25	.26	.61	1.04	1.46	2.79	3.92	5.55	7.67	10.23	11.92	12.76	15.36	36.93	57.539
T. VENEZUELA	4.50	4.51	4.78	5.13	5.15	5.20	4.95	5.01	5.37	5.55	5.59	5.06	4.74	4.59	7.1930
UNITED STATES	1.00	1.00	1.09	1.19	1.21	1.21	1.15	1.17	1.25	1.29	1.30	1.18	1.10	1.07	1.0250

1. Special Drawing Right (SDR) values are based on a market basket of currencies.
2. Line rb, Market Rate.

SOURCE: IMF-IFS-S, no. 1, 1981; IMF-IFS-S, no. 9, 1985.

Table 3104
IMF DOLLAR VALUE OF SDR, 1969-84a
(YE and YA)

Category	1969	1970	1971	1972	1973	1974	1975	1976	1977	1978	1979	1980	1981	1982	1983	1984
US Dollar/SDR Rate (YE)	1.00000	1.00000	1.08571	1.08571	1.20635	1.22435	1.17066	1.16183	1.21471	1.30279	1.31733	1.27541	1.16396	1.10311	1.04695	.98021
US Dollar/SDR Rate (YA)[1]	1.00000	1.00000	1.00298	1.98571	1.19213	1.20264	1.21415	1.15452	1.16752	1.25200	1.29200	1.30153	1.17916	1.10401	1.06900	1.02501
SDR/US Dollar Rate (YE)	1.00000	1.00000	.92105	.92105	.82895	.81676	.85422	.86071	.82324	.76758	.75911	.78406	.85914	.90653	.95515	1.02019
SDR/US Dollar Rate (YA)[1]	1.00000	1.00000	.99702	.92105	.83883	.83150	.82362	.86616	.85652	.79872	.77399	.76833	.84806	.90579	.93545	.97560

1. Geometric average.
a. Prior to 1970 one dollar equals one SDR (Special Drawing Right).

SOURCE: IMF-IFS-Y, 1983; IMF-IFS, May 1985.

Table 3105

IMF U.S. DOLLAR EFFECTIVE EXCHANGE RATE INDEX (MERM),[1] 1970–85

(1980 = 100, YA)

Year	Index	Year	Index
1970	128.6	1978	102.1
1971	125.4	1979	99.9
1972	116.4	1980	100.0
1973	106.8	1981	112.7
1974	109.5	1982	125.9
1975	106.7	1983	133.2
1976	112.2	1984	143.7
1977	111.7	1985[a]	162.7

1. Combines the exchange rates here between U.S. currency and other major currencies with weights derived from IMF's Multilateral Exchange Rate Model (MERM).

a. March.

SOURCE: IMF-IFS-Y, 1984, p. 593, line amx; IMF-IFS, June 1985.

Table 3106

EXCHANGE RATE AGREEMENTS, 19 L

(As of April 30, 1985)

Currency Pegged to U.S. Dollar	Exchange Rate Adjusted According to a Set of Indicators[1]	Other Managed Floating	Independently Floating
B. BOLIVIA	C. BRAZIL	A. ARGENTINA	H. DOMINICAN REP.
J. EL SALVADOR	D. CHILE	F. COSTA RICA	S. URUGUAY
K. GUATEMALA	E. COLOMBIA	I. ECUADOR	UNITED STATES
L. HAITI	R. PERU	N. MEXICO	
M. HONDURAS			
O. NICARAGUA			
P. PANAMA			
Q. PARAGUAY			
T. VENEZUELA			

1. Includes exchange arrangements under which the exchange rate is adjusted at relatively frequent intervals, on the basis of indicators determined by the respective member countries.

SOURCE: IMF-IFS, June 1985.

Table 3107

PARALLEL OR BLACK MARKET EXCHANGE RATES OF U.S. DOLLARS, 12 L, 1968-82[a]
(NC per US, YE)

Country	1968	1969	1970	1971	1972	1973	1974	1975	1976	1977	1978	1979	1980	1981	1982
A. ARGENTINA	350.0	352.0	4.4[b]	10.1	11.6	11.0	23.2	136.0	280.0	605.0	1,011.0	1,620.0	1,989.0	10,550.0	48,520.0
B. BOLIVIA	13.5	17.0	20.0	19.8	23.0	21.0	21.0	21.0	21.2	21.0	23.0	25.0	~	~	~
C. BRAZIL	4.1	4.9	5.2	6.4	6.9	6.8	8.2	13.6	15.6	20.1	26.5	46.0	65.4	127.7	252.4
D. CHILE	16.3	14.9	28.0	74.7	340.0	790.0	2,010.0	8.9[b]	19.0	28.3	34.8	41.0	~	38.9	72.6
E. COLOMBIA	18.0	19.4	24.5	23.3	25.5	27.0	29.8	34.5	37.7	38.2	41.3	44.8	50.9	50.1	70.3
G. CUBA	5.0	6.0	7.0	9.7	9.9	9.8	9.3	8.6	10.4	11.7	13.6	13.0	~	~	~[c]
H. DOMINICAN REP.	1.2	1.2	1.2	1.2	1.2	1.2	1.3	1.3	1.3	1.4	1.4	1.3	~	~	~
I. ECUADOR	22.4	22.0	28.5	27.8	27.7	25.0	25.2	26.2	27.8	26.0	26.4	27.1	28.0	33.1	64.5
J. EL SALVADOR	2.9	2.9	2.9	2.9	2.9	2.9	2.9	3.0	3.2	3.3	3.0	3.9	~	~	3.75
O. NICARAGUA[1]	8.4	8.3	8.3	8.3	8.5	8.3	8.3	8.4	8.4	8.6	12.0	20.0	~	~[d]	~
R. PERU	44.7	46.0	58.0	70.0	70.0	72.0	59.0	70.0	90.5	145.0	213.0	252.0	341.0	505.9	987.2
S. URUGUAY	251.0	255.0	290.0	640.0	940.0	925.0	2,470.0	2.9[b]	4.1	5.3	7.0	8.4	9.9	11.6	33.5

a.   For prior years, see SALA-SNP, p. 241.

b.   "New peso."

c.   Black market rate in Cuba in 1983 said to be 5 to 1, as told to James W. Wilkie during his visit in June 1983; dollars were accepted at 1 to 1 rate by Cuba's Intourist Agency and its hotels and restaurants.

d.   Black market rate said to be 30 to 1, as told to James W. Wilkie during his visit in July 1981.

SOURCE: 1968-79: adapted from *Pick's Currency Yearbook, 1976-77* and *1977-79*; 1980-82: *Statistische Beihefte Zu den Monatsberichten der Deutschen Bundesbank, Reihe 5 Die Währangen der Welt*, Frankfurt.

Table 3108

DOLLAR EXCHANGE RATES ON THE U.S. MARKET, 18 L, 1977-85
(US per NC)

Country	1977[a]	1978[a]	1979[b]	1980[c]	1981[a]	1982[d]	1983[e]	1984[f]	1985[g]
A. ARGENTINA	.00165	~	~	.000455	~	.0000143	.0322	.0108	~
B. BOLIVIA	.04	.0410	.0450	.0350	.0200	.002	.00085	.00008	~
C. BRAZIL	.05	.0350	.0230	.0140	.0064	.00241	.000784	.000449	~
D. CHILE	~	.0200	.0225	.0235	.0200	.0100	.00900	.00812	~
E. COLOMBIA	.025	.0235	.0220	.0200	.0150	.0120	.0095	.0061	~
F. COSTA RICA	.1025	.1000	.1050	.0700	.0190	.0140	.0195	.008	~
H. DOMINICAN REP.	.75	.70	.80	.76	.74	.62	~	.1624	~
I. ECUADOR	.0325	.0330	.0335	.0325	.0250	.0130	.0105	.00812	~
J. EL SALVADOR	.31	.3500	.29	.24	.22	.16	.19	.1218	~
K. GUATEMALA	.95	.95	.9500	.82	.77	.65	.67	.4872	~
L. HAITI	.1850	.1900	.1800	.17	.10	.1350	.1100	.1218	~
M. HONDURAS	.45	.4600	.4550	.46	.38	.36	.35	.2436	~
N. MEXICO									
Small Peso	.0430	.0425	.0430	.0430	.0380				
Large Peso	.0425	.0420	.0430	.0420	.0370	.00735	.00599	.0049	.0041
O. NICARAGUA	.1225	~	~	.04	.02	~	~	~	~
Q. PARAGUAY	.0060	.00550	.0064	.00600	.00470	.0025	.00185	.0012	~
R. PERU	~	.00380	.00395	.00240	.00165	.00100	.000480	.00024	~
S. URUGUAY	.1650	.1300	.1100	.09	.0750	.0650	.0235	.0081	~
T. VENEZUELA	.2280	.2280	.2300	.2290	.2290	.2270	~	.0920	.0859

a. As of December 1.
b. November and December 1978.
c. December and January.
d. November 5-6, 1982.
e. November 4-7, 1983.
f. As of August 22, 1984.
g. As of June 1985.

SOURCE: Deak-Perera, *Foreign Currency Rate Guide* (New York), "Notes" rate, various monthly, 1977-84.

Table 3109

EXCHANGE RATE HISTORY,[1] 13 L, 1937-74
(U per US; 1937-74 = A; 1948-74 = YE)

A. ARGENTINA

Year	Free	Official	Selling (P)	Selling (B)	Selling (A)	Selling (F)	Selling (C)	Buying (S)	Buying (P)	Buying (B)
1937[a]	3.41	*	3.23	3.23	*	3.33	*	*	3.03	3.03
1938	4.38	*	3.21	36.31	*	3.92	*	*	3.07	3.07
1939	4.40[g]	*	3.83[g]	3.83[g]	*	4.33	*	*	3.27	3.27
1940	*	*	3.73	4.23	*	4.37	*	*	3.36	3.26
1941	*	*	3.73	4.23	4.94	4.24	*	*	4.22	3.36
1942	*	*	3.73	4.23	4.94	4.23	*	*	4.22	3.36
1943	*	*	3.73	4.23	4.94	4.06	*	*	4.04	3.36
1944	*	*	3.73	4.23	4.94	4.02	*	*	3.98	3.36
1945	*	*	3.73	4.23	4.94	4.04	*	*	3.98	3.36
1946	*	*	3.73	4.23	4.94	4.09	*	*	3.98	3.36
1947	*	*	3.73	4.23	4.94	4.08	4.80	*	3.98	3.36
1948[b]	4.81	3.36	3.73	4.23	4.94	4.45	9.25	5.00[h]	3.98	3.36
1949[c]	9.02	3.36	5.37[i]	6.09	10.26	9.02	15.80	7.20[i]	5.73[i]	3.36
1950[d]	14.02	5.00	5.00[j]	5.00	*[k]	14.03	19.50	7.50[j]	7.50[j]	5.00[i]
1951	14.46	5.00	*	*	*	14.46	27.60	7.50	7.50	5.00
1952	13.98	5.00	*	*	*	13.98	23.20	7.50	7.50	5.00
1953	13.98	5.00	*	*	*	*	20.85	7.50	7.50	5.00
1954	13.98	5.00	*	*	*	*	*	*	*	*
1955	36.10	18.00	*	*	*	*	*	*	*	*
1956	37.45	18.00	*	*	*	*	*	*	*	*
1957	37.00	18.00	*	*	*	*	*	*	*	*
1958	70.00	18.00	*	*	*	*	*	*	*	*
1959[e]	*	83.25[l]	*	*	*	*	*	*	*	*
1960	*	82.70	*	*	*	*	*	*	*	*
1961	*	83.02	*	*	*	*	*	*	*	*
1962	*	134.10	*	*	*	*	*	*	*	*
1963	*	132.50	*	*	*	*	*	*	*	*
1964	*	150.90	*	*	*	*	*	*	*	*
1965	*	188.50	*	*	*	*	*	*	*	*
1966	*	247.30	*	*	*	*	*	*	*	*
1967	*	350.00	*	*	*	*	*	*	*	*
1968	*	350.00	*	*	*	*	*	*	*	*
1969	*	4.00[m]	*	*	*	*	*	*	*	*
1970	*	5.00	*	*	*	*	*	*	*	*
1971[f]	8.25[n]	5.00	*	*	*	*	*	*	*	*
1972	9.98	5.00	*	*	*	*	*	*	*	*
1973	9.98	5.00	*	*	*	*	*	*	*	*
1974	9.98[o]	5.00[o]	*	*	*	*	*	*	*	*

1. Code: A, auction; B, basic; C, curb; F, free; P, preferential; S, special

a. Selling rate: subdivided into preferential, basic auction free, and curb (1937-49); buying rate: special, preferential, basic.

b. 1948-72: two categories listed — free and official.

c. October 3, 1949: Argentina readjusted her multiple currency structure, the degree of adjustments varying widely depending upon the particular transactions and commodities to which applied.

d. On August 29, 1950, the number of effective rates was reduced from 9 to 3. The preferential import rates of 3.73 and 5.37 pesos per U.S. dollar and the basic export rate of 3.35 pesos were consolidated into a single rate of 5.00 per U.S. dollar. (Source: IFS, September 1950-country notes.)

e. A new exchange system was made effective January 12, 1959, when the previous official and free market were replaced by a single market for all transactions with a fluctuating exchange rate.

f. On September 20, 1971, a dual exchange rate system was introduced consisting of an official market with a fixed rate of 5.00 pesos per U.S. dollar and a financial market in which the rate is allowed to fluctuate.

g. January/August. Rates quoted for 1940 were established in August 1939. On August 1939 free market discontinued and a system of multiple official rates was established.

h. Beginning June 23.

i. Beginning October 3.

j. Beginning August 29.

k. Auction abolished August 28.

l. Beginning January 12, 1959.

m. A new peso equal to 100 old pesos was introduced on January 1, 1970.

n. On September 20, 1971, a dual exchange rate system was introduced, consisting of an official market with a fixed rate of 5.00 pesos per U.S. dollar and a financial market in which the rate is allowed to fluctuate.

o. August 1974.

Continued in SALA, 17-2401 through 2413.

Table 3110

BOLIVIA OFFICIAL AND PARALLEL MARKET EXCHANGE RATES, 1982–85

(NC)

Year	Month	Official Rate	Parallel Rate
1982	November	200	250
	December	200	290
1983	January	200	390
	February	200	500
	March	200	500
	April	200	420
	May	200	380
	June	200	390
	July	200	600
	August	200	780
	September	200	785
	October	200	1,050
	November	500	1,350
	December	500	1,200
1984	January	500	1,900
	February	500	2,100
	March	500	2,780
	April	2,000	3,560
	May	2,000	3,480
	June	2,000	3,330
	July	2,000	3,500
	August	2,000–5,000	7,190
	September	2,000–5,000	13,515
	October	2,000–5,000	15,160
	November	9,000	18,394
	December	9,000	23,381
1985	January	9,000	64,557
	February	50,000	132,856
	June	75,000	300,000

SOURCE: *Hoy Internacional* (La Paz), March 12, 1985, and June 4, 1985.

Table 3111

CENTRAL AMERICA OFFICIAL, FINANCIAL, AND BLACK MARKET EXCHANGE RATES, 7 L, 1983 and 1985

(NC per US)

PART I. FOURTH QUARTER 1983

Country	Official	Financial or Tourist	Parallel, or Black Market
Belize (dollar)	2.00	~	~
F. COSTA RICA (colón)	20.00	43.15	~
J. EL SALVADOR (colón)	2.50	3.60	4.20
K. GUATEMALA (quetzal)	1.00	~	1.30
M. HONDURAS (lempira)	2.00	~	2.50
O. NICARAGUA (córdoba)	10.00	28.00	70.00
P. PANAMA (balboa)	1.00	~	~

PART II. FIRST QUARTER 1985

Country	Official	Financial or Tourist	Parallel, or Black Market
K. GUATEMALA (quetzal)	1.00	1.50-1.79	1.65
Belize (dollar)	2.00	~	~
J. EL SALVADOR (colón)	2.50	3.75	4.15-5.00
M. HONDURAS (lempira)	2.00	~	2.75
O. NICARAGUA (córdoba)	10.00	28.50	500-600
F. COSTA RICA (colón)	20.00	47.95	53
P. PANAMA (balboa)	1.00	~	~

PART III. SECOND QUARTER 1985

Country	Official	Parallel or Financial[1]	Free or Black Market[2]
K. GUATEMALA (quetzal)	1.00	2.00-2.85	2.90
Belize (dollar)	2.00	~	~
J. EL SALVADOR (colón)	2.50	3.75	4.65-4.90
M. HONDURAS (lempira)	2.00	~	2.75
O. NICARAGUA (córdoba)	10.00	48.00-60.00	500-600
F. COSTA RICA (colón)	20.00	49.50	53
P. PANAMA (balboa)	1.00	~	~

1. An alternative, officially authorized, exchange rate for certain specified transactions. In some countries (such as Guatemala) it fluctuates; in others (such as Nicaragua) it is fixed.
2. Estimated, since in some countries (Honduras, Costa Rica) this market is clandestine, or (as in Nicaragua) the rate fluctuates widely.

SOURCE: *Central America Report* (Guatemala City), first quarter 1984 and second quarter 1985.

Table 3112

OFFICIAL AND REAL MEXICAN PESO VALUES COMPARED TO MEXICO'S REAL TRADE DEFICITS, 1952–82

Year	(A) Official Peso Exchange Rate for Dollars (YA)	(B) Mexico's Wholesale Price Index YA; 1963=100.0	(C) U.S. Wholesale Price Index	(D) Peso 1963 Parity Exchange Rate[1] 12.5 in Col. A Times (B/C)	(E) Peso's Value Index (D/A)[2] 1963=100.0	(F) Merchandise Trade Balance FOB M US	(G) Mexico YE Trade Index 1963 Equals –100.0	(H) Real Merchandise Balance Index[3] 1963 Equals –100 (G/C)
1952	8.650	65.6	93.9	8.7	100.6	~	~	~
1953	8.650	64.3	92.6	8.7	100.6	–169	–84.1	–90.8
1954	12.500	70.5	92.8	9.5	76.0	–92	–45.8	–49.4
1955	12.500	80.1	93.0	10.8	86.4	21	10.5	11.3
1956	12.500	83.8	96.1	10.9	87.2	–174	–86.6	–90.1
1957	12.500	87.5	98.7	11.1	88.8	–362	–180.1	–182.5
1958	12.500	91.4	100.2	11.4	91.2	–338	–168.2	–167.9
1959	12.500	92.4	100.4	11.5	92.0	–220	–109.5	–109.1
1960	12.500	96.9	100.6	12.0	96.0	–354	–176.1	–175.0
1961	12.500	97.7	100.2	12.2	97.6	–260	–129.4	–129.1
1962	12.500	99.6	100.4	12.4	99.2	–167	–83.1	–82.8
1963	12.500	100.0	100.0	12.5	100.0	–201	–100.0	–100.0
1964	12.500	104.3	100.2	13.0	104.0	–370	–184.1	–183.7
1965	12.500	106.4	102.2	13.0	104.0	–352	–175.1	–171.3
1966	12.500	107.6	105.7	12.7	101.6	–337	–167.7	–158.7
1967	12.500	110.7	105.9	13.1	104.8	–608	–302.5	–285.6
1968	12.500	112.9	108.5	13.0	104.0	–634	–315.4	–290.7
1969	12.500	115.8	112.8	12.8	102.4	–529	–263.2	–233.2
1970	12.500	122.5	116.9	13.1	104.8	–888	–441.8	–377.9
1971	12.500	127.3	120.8	13.2	105.6	–749	–372.6	–308.4
1972	12.500	130.7	126.1	13.0	104.0	–894	–444.8	–352.7
1973	12.500	151.4	142.6	13.3	106.4	–1,515	–753.7	–528.5
1974	12.500	185.5	169.4	13.7	109.6	–2,791	–1,388.6	–819.7
1975	12.500	204.9	185.2	13.8	138.0	–3,271	–1,627.4	–878.7
1976	15,426	250.6	193.7	16.2	105.0	–2,296	–1,142.3	–589.7
1977	22.573	353.7	205.6	21.5	95.2	–1,021	–508.0	–247.0
1978	22.767	409.4	221.7	23.1	101.5	–1,746	–868.7	–391.8
1979	22.805	484.4	249.4	24.3	106.6	–2,830	–1,408.0	–564.6
1980	22.951	603.1	284.4	26.5	115.5	–2,310	–1,149.3	–404.1
1981	24.515	752.0	310.2	30.3	123.6	–3,329	–1,656.2	–533.9
1982[a]	46.758	1,010.2	316.1[c]	39.9	85.3	116[b]	57.8[b]	33.9[b]

1. The year 1963 was selected for parity comparison because of the following characteristics: low increase of .4% in Mexican wholesale price index (column B); relatively low deficit of $201 million real dollars in merchandise trade balance (column F); and healthy real GDP gain of 8.0% (see SALA, 22-3).
2. More than 100.0 equals peso "overvaluation" which discourages exports from Mexico and foreign tourism to Mexico; it encourages imports to Mexico, Mexican tourism abroad, and a Mexican shift from pesos into "cheap" dollars. Also in terms of 1963 value, the greater the undervaluation of the peso the greater the chances to reduce Mexico's trade deficit, to increase Mexico's money balance from tourism, and to encourage investment in pesos rather than dollars. Undervalued pesos allow foreigners to buy more goods and services in Mexico than do overvalued pesos.
3. In no years did value of exports equal that of imports (theoretically zero on the index scale). The real merchandise trade deficit of $201 million equals –100.0 on the index scale.

a. May.
b. January–April.
c. January–April = 170.5 U.S. wholesale price index.

Method: A: 1952-74, IFS-Y, 1982; 1975–82, IFS, Aug. 1982, line rf.
B: Bank of Mexico 210-item wholesale price index calculated (base converted) from source A, line 63.
C: Calculated from source A, line 63.
D: Calculated (datum for 1963 in column A times B/C).
E: Calculated (A/D), according to ECLA methodology in ECLA-S2, 1980, p. 394.
F: 1952-74, IFS-Y, 1982, line 77ad; 1975–81, IFS, Aug. 1982, calculated from lines 77aad and 77abd; 1982 calculated from CE, Aug. 1982, p. 904.
G: Calculated from column F.
H: Calculated (G/C).

Source: SALA, 22-4.

Table 3113

ECLA REAL EXCHANGE RATE INDEX, 10 L, 1970–82[a]

(1980 = 100)

Country	1970	1971	1972	1973	1974	1975	1976	1977	1978	1979	1980	1981	1982
A. ARGENTINA	144.6	137.2	155.2	148.5	126.9	194.1	127.9	164.9	148.8	111.7	100.0	125.8	163.2
B. BOLIVIA	93.8	97.2	108.3	146.4	104.9	99.7	105.6	102.8	106.6	106.2	100.0	73.7	128.5
C. BRAZIL	61.6	62.9	65.5	69.0	74.5	76.0	73.7	73.8	77.7	87.6	100.0	84.8	81.6
D. CHILE	133.2	122.4	128.4	142.8	124.5	133.4	116.0	112.4	130.2	116.4	100.0	89.8	105.1
E. COLOMBIA	118.2	120.0	120.9	119.9	113.7	118.9	112.6	102.0	103.3	99.0	100.0	93.5	87.3
F. COSTA RICA	117.3	113.9	115.0	115.8	117.7	113.7	110.5	111.9	114.3	109.1	100.0	160.4	131.4
I. ECUADOR	128.2	128.2	125.4	127.0	118.9	110.3	103.8	98.5	97.6	99.7	100.0	93.4	99.9
N. MEXICO	105.4	105.4	108.8	107.9	104.4	103.2	108.5	120.0	114.4	109.1	100.0	90.8	127.5
R. PERU	73.3	71.6	74.1	79.1	82.1	76.4	81.1	94.4	113.0	107.1	100.0	85.7	85.3
S. URUGUAY	110.5	101.7	125.6	107.5	103.6	119.3	127.1	126.1	122.9	103.9	100.0	95.8	110.8

a. Average of the indexes of real exchange rates of exports and imports. For deflation
   purposes, the national wholesale price index was used, except in the case of Bolivia in
   which the consumer price index was used. For detailed information on methodology
   used, see Part 3 in source.

SOURCE: ECLA-CC, E/CEPAL/G.1280, March 1984, p. 80.

Table 3114

ARGENTINA EVOLUTION OF REAL EXCHANGE RATES AND PRICE INDEXES,[1,2] 1970–82

PART I. EVOLUTION OF PRICES

	Exchange Rate		Index of Prices in Dollars at the Trade Rate of Exchange[5]		Index of Prices in Pesos at the Trade Rate of Exchange[5]		Unit Price Index (Nonagricultural Wholesale)[5]	Relative Prices[5]	
								Of Exported Goods	Of Imported Goods
	Pesos per Commercial Dollar[3,4]	Index	Exports	Imports	Exports (2)x(3)	Imports (2)x(4)		(5)/(7)	(6)/(7)
	(1)	(2)	(3)	(4)	(5)	(6)	(7)	(8)	(9)
1977	410	44	89	80	39	35	30	130	117
1978	799	85	92	99	78	84	75	104	112
1979	1,320	141	116	122	164	172	187	88	92
1980	1,841	196	137	127	269	249	337	80	74
1981	4,411	471	135	121	636	570	724	88	79
1982	21,897	2,337	116	116	2,711	2,711	2,498	109	109

PART II. EVOLUTION OF REAL EXCHANGE RATE INDEXES[6]

(1980 = 100)

Argentine Pesos per:

Annual Averages	US Dollar	Pound Sterling	French Franc	Deutsch Mark	Italian Lira	Dutch Guilder
1970	172.55	119.96	128.20	127.38	137.67	113.34
1971	151.42	113.77	115.13	119.51	122.18	107.90
1972	166.11	131.03	140.66	144.64	142.09	132.96
1973	196.68	106.01	129.27	139.61	125.70	124.26
1974	136.24	94.61	109.55	124.32	127.94	114.28
1975	209.99	156.81	193.69	195.70	195.08	189.52
1976	139.12	93.99	120.76	126.14	120.04	125.19
1977	172.50	123.54	150.25	165.84	154.01	167.63
1978	148.01	116.91	142.02	156.72	138.24	157.72
1979	110.30	97.16	110.41	118.57	107.99	116.91
1980	100.00	100.00	100.00	100.00	100.00	100.00
1981	124.68	111.64	100.95	97.54	107.72	97.15

	Japanese Yen	Spanish Peseta	Brazilian Cruzeiro	Chilean Peso	Uruguayan Peso
1970	128.75	106.71	192.88	140.00	118.46
1971	111.79	98.74	174.29	238.09	116.95
1972	135.78	120.90	193.33	225.00	107.31
1973	132.62	112.27	163.22	182.14	112.14
1974	130.78	105.96	154.39	113.74	116.09
1975	187.04	175.65	232.20	129.39	149.46
1976	124.49	109.90	160.48	103.27	96.52
1977	163.60	140.54	200.98	156.34	121.04
1978	161.93	131.22	172.37	126.84	111.11
1979	110.49	116.19	119.05	97.48	102.65
1980	100.00	100.00	100.00	100.00	100.00
1981	119.60	101.73	132.98	136.92	139.25

Table 3114 (Continued)

ARGENTINA EVOLUTION OF REAL EXCHANGE RATES AND PRICE INDEXES,[1,2] 1970–82

PART III. EVOLUTION OF EFFECTIVE REAL EXCHANGE RATE INDEXES FOR EXPORTS AND IMPORTS[7,8]

(1980 = 100)

Annual Averages	Exports	Imports
1970	140.4	148.8
1971	133.8	140.5
1972	152.1	158.2
1973	142.3	154.7
1974	125.3	128.5
1975	192.3	195.9
1976	126.4	129.3
1977	163.6	166.1
1978	148.3	149.3
1979	112.0	111.4
1980	100.0	100.0
1981[a]	123.5	128.1
I	94.1	95.7
II	116.2	121.5
III	134.2	139.7
IV	147.4	150.9
1982[a]	160.3	166.0
I	132.3	136.7
II	146.6	151.3
III	184.9	191.3
IV	156.4	163.2

1. The base for all indexes is the last quarter of 1978 = 100.
2. Does not include adjustments for taxes, surcharges, reimbursements, or other forms of subsidies.
3. Seller price, average for the period.
4. As of 13 September 1982, this rate represented a combination of the commercial exchange rate (weighted at 85 percent) and the financial exchange rate (15 percent). As of 1 October 1982, the weights used were 80 percent and 20 percent, respectively.
5. Preliminary figures.
6. Corresponds to the quotient of the nominal exchange rate indexes divided by the relative price indexes. For Argentina, the wholesale price index was used.
7. These indexes were obtained by multiplying the weightings of exports or imports by the real exchange rate indexes. The products are added together to give the effective real exchange rate indexes.
8. For trade shares of main trading partners used in computing effective real exchange rate, see ECLA-S, 1981, Statistical Appendix, table 3.

a. The second half of 1981 and 1982, for which the figure used is the 50/50 average of the commercial rate and the financial rate.

SOURCE: ECLA-S, 1981, Statistical Appendix; for Part I and the years 1981–82 of Part III, ECLA-S, vol. 1, 1982, tables 14 and 13 respectively.

Table 3115

BOLIVIA EVOLUTION OF REAL EXCHANGE RATES AND PRICE INDEXES, 1970–81

PART I. EVOLUTION OF REAL EXCHANGE RATE INDEXES[1]

(1980 = 100)

Annual Averages	Bolivian Pesos per:				
	US Dollar	Japanese Yen	French Franc	Deutsch Mark	Dutch Guilder
1970	111.91	83.46	83.10	82.55	73.79
1971	111.08	81.97	84.47	87.69	79,17
1972	121.97	99.67	103.29	106.19	97.63
1973	157.84	147.51	143.75	155.27	138.15
1974	115.51	110.89	92.89	105.41	97.36
1975	116.75	103.99	107.68	108.80	105.37
1976	116.98	104.69	101.55	106.08	105.28
1977	114.77	108.85	99.97	110.34	111.53
1978	112.11	122.65	107.57	118.71	119.46
1979	107.46	107.64	107.56	115.52	113.90
1980	110.00	100.00	100.00	100.00	100.00
1981	82.51	79.15	66.81	64.55	64.29

Annual Averages	Swiss Franc	Pound Sterling	Argentine Peso	Brazilian Cruzeiro	Chilean Peso
1970	65.17	77.77	64.83	125.05	90.76
1971	69.95	83.45	69.57	127.86	174.66
1972	84.51	96.19	73.42	141.94	165.19
1973	126.81	117.88	111.19	181.50	202.53
1974	90.98	80.23	84.70	130.92	96.45
1975	103.68	87.17	55.59	129.09	71.93
1976	104.28	79.04	84.09	134.95	86.84
1977	101.89	82.20	66.53	133.72	104.02
1978	125.10	88.55	75.74	130.56	96.07
1979	118.62	94.65	97.42	115.99	94.97
1980	100.00	100.00	100.00	100.00	100.00
1981	68.76	73.88	66.17	88.00	90.61

Table 3115 (Continued)

BOLIVIA EVOLUTION OF REAL EXCHANGE RATES
AND PRICE INDEXES, 1970–81

PART II. EVOLUTION OF EFFECTIVE REAL EXCHANGE RATE
INDEXES FOR EXPORTS AND IMPORTS[2]

(1980 = 100)

Annual Averages	Exports	Imports
1970	90.8	96.8
1971	95.1	99.2
1972	105.5	111.0
1973	141.9	150.8
1974	101.7	108.1
1975	96.6	102.7
1976	102.8	108.4
1977	99.1	106.4
1978	102.8	110.3
1979	104.8	107.5
1980	100.0	100.0
1981[a]	72.2	75.2
1982[a]	126.1	130.9
January	67.7	70.6
February	101.1	105.0
March	117.9	122.3
April	125.0	129.4
May	122.6	128.3
June	131.5	133.5
July	127.4	134.1
August	135.2	141.6
September	137.3	142.2
October	132.6	136.4
November	114.5	118.7
December	133.6	139.0

1. Corresponds to the quotient of the nominal exchange rate indexes divided by the relative price indexes. For Bolivia, the wholesale price index was used.
2. These indexes were obtained by multiplying the weightings of exports or imports by the real exchange rate indexes. The products are added together to give the effective real exchange rate indexes.

a. These are the indexes of the real official exchange rate for the peso [except during March-October 1982, when a real rate obtained from the average of the official rate (weighted 40 percent) and the open-market exchange rate (weighted 60 percent) was in use] vis-à-vis the currencies of trading partners, the latter, in turn, being weighted according to the relative size of exports or imports, as the case may be, to or from those countries.

SOURCE: ECLA-S, 1981, Statistical Appendix; for years 1981–82 of Part II, ECLA-S, vol. 1, 1982, table 17.

Table 3116

BRAZIL EVOLUTION OF REAL EXCHANGE RATES AND PRICE INDEXES,[1] 1970-82

PART I. EVOLUTION OF PRICES

(1980 = 100)

Annual and Quarterly Averages	(1) Official Exchange Rate Cruzeiros per Dollar	(2) Official Exchange Rate Index	(3) General Wholesale Price Index, Domestic Availability	(4) United States Wholesale Price Index	(5) Real Rate of Exchange (2) / (3)	(6) Adjusted Real Rate of Exchange (5) X (4)
1975	8.13	15.4	11.2	65.1	137.3	89.4
1976	10.67	20.2	15.7	68.1	128.6	87.6
1977	14.14	26.8	22.1	72.3	121.2	87.6
1978	18.07	34.3	30.8	77.9	111.4	86.8
1979	26.95	51.1	47.8	87.7	107.0	93.8
1980	52.71	100.0	100.0	100.0	100.0	100.0
1981	93.13	176.7	213.0	109.0	82.9	90.4
1982	179.51	340.6	413.3	111.4	82.4	91.8
1981						
I	70.80	134.3	163.1	106.7	82.4	87.9
II	83.89	159.2	196.6	109.3	80.9	88.5
III	99.72	189.2	227.9	110.2	83.0	91.4
IV	118.08	224.0	264.6	110.1	84.7	93.2
1982						
I	137.87	261.6	312.9	111.0	83.6	92.8
II	160.18	303.9	377.0	111.1	80.6	89.6
III	189.65	359.8	447.5	111.7	80.4	89.8
IV	230.36	437.0	515.9	111.8	84.7	94.7

Table 3116 (Continued)

BRAZIL EVOLUTION OF REAL EXCHANGE RATES AND PRICE INDEXES,[1] 1970–82

PART II. EVOLUTION OF REAL EXCHANGE RATE INDEXES[2]

(1980 = 100)

Annual Averages	Brazilian Cruzeiros per:					
	US Dollar	Canadian Dollar	Japanese Yen	Deutsch Mark	Spanish Peseta	French Franc
1970	82.15	103.35	61.30	60.62	62.98	60.92
1971	81.13	105.06	59.83	63.87	64.11	61.62
1972	81.28	107.78	66.37	70.67	70.80	103.02
1973	82.58	103.07	77.08	80.99	77.37	74.95
1974	84.52	100.71	81.15	77.11	79.37	67.99
1975	86.46	100.39	76.98	80.42	84.07	79.79
1976	84.08	103.49	75.21	76.20	77.33	72.91
1977	82.89	96.27	78.64	79.56	74.14	72.08
1978	82.34	90.07	90.09	87.07	77.08	78.86
1979	89.76	92.76	89.91	96.18	94.53	89.71
1980	100.00	100.00	100.00	100.00	100.00	100.00
1981	91.79	92.29	88.05	71.69	74.82	74.19

Annual Averages	Italian Lira	Dutch Guilder	Pound Sterling	Swiss Franc	Argentine Peso	Chilean Peso
1970	65.44	54.22	57.13	55.24	46.28	82.61
1971	65.51	57.62	60.93	57.55	50.78	100.04
1972	69.35	64.93	64.06	61.89	48.52	119.92
1973	73.04	72.32	61.61	72.78	57.05	105.04
1974	79.39	70.97	58.74	75.92	62.46	72.15
1975	80.27	78.02	64.63	83.01	41.45	54.83
1976	72.49	75.50	56.86	78.83	60.37	63.82
1977	74.03	80.42	59.42	76.16	48.06	76.86
1978	76.85	87.43	65.16	92.96	55.77	72.22
1979	87.85	95.22	79.06	98.83	81.39	79.33
1980	100.00	100.00	100.00	100.00	100.00	100.00
1981	73.51	71.57	82.16	75.87	73.87	100.75

Annual Averages	Mexican Peso	Paraguayan Guaraní	Venezuelan Bolívar	Saudi Arabian Riyal	Iranian Rial	Iraqui Dinar	Kuwait Dinar
1970	74.60	43.20	74.21	8.10	8.09	7.97	7.10
1971	74.05	46.55	72.49	9.51	9.64	9.72	8.85
1972	72.97	52.88	73.10	10.54	10.21	11.15	9.71
1973	75.94	65.55	71.94	14.55	13.64	14.66	13.45
1974	80.11	73.70	72.74	46.43	43.79	47.16	45.99
1975	82.85	79.47	77.80	47.16	43.97	47.16	43.97
1976	76.34	74.70	78.03	46.75	41.90	46.87	43.06
1977	68.40	74.96	81.43	46.58	42.60	47.82	44.85
1978	72.31	77.90	80.69	45.58	39.32	43.94	42.56
1979	82.74	95.31	86.30	59.56	57.54	62.92	62.05
1980	100.00	100.00	100.00	100.00	100.00	100.00	100.00
1981	98.26	90.36	97.75	93.72	80.38	98.52	95.99

Table 3116 (Continued)

BRAZIL EVOLUTION OF REAL EXCHANGE RATES AND PRICE INDEXES,[1] 1970–82

PART III. EVOLUTION OF EFFECTIVE REAL EXCHANGE RATE INDEXES FOR EXPORTS AND IMPORTS[3]

(1980 = 100)

Annual Averages	Exports	Imports
1970	66.4	50.7
1971	67.7	52.1
1972	73.7	56.2
1973	76.4	59.1
1974	76.6	68.8
1975	80.8	71.2
1976	77.7	69.6
1977	78.2	69.4
1978	83.2	72.2
1979	92.7	82.4
1980	100.0	100.0
1981	82.7	86.9
I	84.5	87.7
II	80.5	84.6
III	80.6	85.6
IV	85.2	88.5
1982	79.6	83.6
I	83.7	87.0
II	79.1	82.5
III	76.5	80.8
IV	80.3	84.7

1. For alternative series 1968–78, see SALA, 21-2406, and for the years 1973–80, see SALA, 23-2507.

2. Corresponds to the quotient of the nominal exchange rate indexes divided by the relative price indexes. For Brazil, the general price index (domestic availability) was used. This is a weighted average of the wholesale price index (60 percent), the Rio de Janeiro cost-of-living index (30 percent), and the index of construction costs for Rio de Janeiro (10 percent).

3. These indexes were obtained by multiplying the weightings of exports or imports (Part III) by the real exchange rate indexes (Part II). The products were added together to give the effective real exchange rate indexes. For the years 1975–79, thirteen countries are included in the estimates for exports, and fifteen in the estimate for imports, which represents 65.2 percent and 82.4 percent of Brazil's foreign trade during this period.

SOURCE: ECLA-S, 1981, Statistical Appendix; for Part I and the years 1975–82 of Part II, ECLA-S, vol. 1, 1982, tables 17 and 16 respectively.

Table 3117

CHILE EVOLUTION OF REAL EXCHANGE RATES
AND PRICE INDEXES, 1970–82

PART I. EVOLUTION OF PRICES

	(1)	(2)	(3)	(4)	(5)	(6)	(7)	(8)	(9)
			Indexes of		Indexes of Real		United		
	Exchange	Indexes	Wholesale		Exchange Rate[1]		States	Indexes of Adjusted	
	Rate	of	Prices of	Consumer			Wholesale	Real Exchange Rate[1]	
	(Pesos	Exchange	Domestic	Price	$\frac{(2)}{(3)}$	$\frac{(2)}{(4)}$	Price		
Period	per US)	Rate[1]	Product[1]	Index[1]			Index[1]	(5) x (7)	(6) x (7)
1974	.83	60	59	62	102	97	94	96	91
1975	4.91	357	348	298	103	121	102	105	123
1976	13.05	948	1,133	990	84	96	107	90	103
1977	21.53	1,564	2,074	2,117	75	74	114	86	84
First quarter	18.43	1,338	1,711	1,653	78	81	111	87	90
Second quarter	19.44	1,412	2,001	1,996	71	71	114	81	81
Third quarter	22.26	1,617	2,209	2,266	73	71	114	83	81
Fourth quarter	25.99	1,877	2,372	2,553	79	74	115	91	85
1978	31.66	2,297	3,007	3,176	76	72	122	93	88
First quarter	29.11	2,112	2,568	2,776	82	76	118	97	90
Second quarter	31.66	2,267	2,872	3,038	79	75	122	96	92
Third quarter	32.69	2,372	3,161	3,335	75	71	123	92	87
Fourth quarter	33.58	2,436	3.428	3.555	71	69	126	89	87
1979	37.25	2,702	4,549	4,254	60	64	137	82	88
First quarter	34.72	2,518	3.648	3,789	69	47	131	90	88
Second quarter	36.26	2,630	4,150	4,011	63	66	135	85	89
Third quarter	39.00	2,829	5,023	4,412	56	64	139	78	89
Fourth quarter	39.00	2,829	5,373	4,805	53	59	144	76	85
1980	39.00	2,829	6.367	5,688	45	50	156	70	78
First quarter	39.00	2,829	5,588	5,120	51	55	151	77	83
Second quarter	39.00	2,829	6,135	5,498	46	51	154	71	79
Third quarter	39.00	2,829	6,670	5,846	42	48	159	67	76
Fourth quarter	39.00	2,829	7,074	6,289	40	45	162	65	73

Table 3117 (Continued)

CHILE EVOLUTION OF REAL EXCHANGE RATES AND PRICE INDEXES, 1970–82

PART II. EVOLUTION OF REAL EXCHANGE RATE INDEXES BASED UPON WHOLESALE PRICES[2]

(1980 = 100)

Annual and Quarterly Averages	Chilean Pesos per:						
	US Dollar	Japanese Yen	Deutsch Mark	Belgian Franc	Spanish Peseta	French Franc	Italian Lira
1970	166.49	110.13	120.47	142.86	126.21	125.00	137.19
1971	146.67	96.67	121.05	128.97	116.36	114.56	123.31
1972	149.13	128.39	128.63	137.55	128.96	125.81	111.13
1973	156.98	147.16	154.51	164.89	148.12	142.71	139.07
1974	136.37	130.96	124.40	140.27	128.21	109.68	128.13
1975	150.04	133.61	139.56	151.44	145.97	138.46	139.27
1976	127.94	114.44	115.94	125.96	117.72	110.94	110.25
1977	122.58	116.28	117.64	125.46	109.69	106.59	109.47
1978	133.92	146.53	141.62	141.90	125.42	128.27	124.98
1979	117.22	117.42	125.61	126.05	123.52	117.16	114.73
I	129.47	139.04	141.66	143.09	130.67	129.65	123.05
II	123.06	123.03	129.00	129.72	129.31	119.34	117.12
III	112.80	113.97	121.13	121.19	122.00	113.16	112.56
IV	109.15	101.91	117.46	117.04	117.40	111.19	110.59
1980	100.00	100.00	100.00	100.00	100.00	100.00	100.00
I	109.79	102.22	114.68	115.57	116.02	110.82	112.84
II	102.09	102.12	104.02	103.76	102.99	102.53	103.12
III	96.94	99.99	98.28	97.42	96.66	99.49	97.86
IV	93.34	97.82	86.79	87.16	88.42	89.85	89.10
1981	99.03	95.00	77.35	77.37	80.76	80.04	79.77
I	95.79	99.32	80.96	81.01	83.84	83.96	83.86
II	98.61	94.25	75.95	76.16	79.97	78.16	78.20
III	99.60	90.90	72.10	73.36	77.02	75.97	75.73
IV	102.27	96.25	81.20	79.59	83.23	82.80	82.16

	Dutch Guilder	Pound Sterling	Argentine Peso	Brazilian Cruzeiro	Ecuadorian Sucre	Iranian Rial	Venezuelan Bolívar
1970	109.09	114.03	94.38	187.21	154.62	20.80	146.31
1971	102.98	111.76	93.04	174.86	119.78	22.60	127.47
1972	116.61	117.45	87.64	172.33	119.03	21.44	127.58
1973	137.69	117.46	108.83	181.46	124.93	25.71	132.03
1974	114.48	94.75	100.90	154.50	114.71	70.64	113.14
1975	135.40	112.16	72.04	165.39	131.59	76.30	130.21
1976	114.87	86.52	91.95	147.11	125.22	63.75	114.51
1977	118.92	87.87	71.14	142.74	122.25	63.00	116.14
1978	142.21	105.98	90.91	155.75	144.65	63.95	126.58
1979	124.36	103.25	106.53	126.67	124.58	75.14	108.71
I	141.99	106.78	103.73	144.80	139.21	60.58	120.57
II	128.25	104.89	105.20	133.96	130.68	71.44	113.12
III	118.99	106.65	109.08	123.66	119.79	78.82	103.51
IV	115.18	99.21	103.74	111.52	114.76	87.17	102.65
1980	100.00	100.00	100.00	100.00	100.00	100.00	100.00
I	112.94	104.29	101.97	96.49	112.51	106.13	108.35
II	103.12	101.87	99.53	95.44	103.13	106.77	101.32
III	99.00	99.74	98.56	99.16	95.45	98.64	97.28
IV	88.24	95.98	99.28	102.86	91.65	90.66	94.67
1981	77.22	88.65	79.89	107.02	98.18	86.72	105.00
I	81.19	94.89	96.81	107.35	94.34	91.39	99.85
II	75.18	90.08	75.04	108.98	96.03	87.36	102.78
III	71.57	81.07	77.12	106.13	97.96	84.07	106.03
IV	82.01	87.50	79.52	106.93	104.62	84.38	111.44

Table 3117 (Continued)

CHILE EVOLUTION OF REAL EXCHANGE RATES AND PRICE INDEXES, 1970–82

PART III. EVOLUTION OF REAL EXCHANGE RATE INDEXES BASED UPON RETAIL PRICES[3]

(1980 = 100)

Annual and Quarterly Averages	Chilean Pesos per:						
	US Dollar	Japanese Yen	Deutsch Mark	Belgian Franc	Spanish Peseta	French Franc	Italian Lira
1970	99.04	66.92	73.21	84.11	76.34	74.37	82.83
1971	80.42	51.79	63.39	69.26	63.62	61.46	67.13
1972	67.59	58.82	58.99	62.29	59.13	57.12	50.81
1973	78.68	73.72	77.07	82.26	73.83	71.28	69.38
1974	117.12	112.53	106.86	120.55	110.18	94.21	110.09
1975	157.69	140.43	146.68	159.16	153.42	145.52	146.37
1976	131.75	117.84	119.39	129.71	121.23	114.24	113.53
1977	107.84	102.31	103.50	110.38	96.50	93.78	96.32
1978	114.00	124.73	120.55	120.80	106.77	109.19	106.39
1979	113.15	113.34	121.24	121.67	119.23	113.09	110.75
I	114.68	123.17	125.49	126.75	115.75	114.84	109.00
II	115.10	115.08	120.66	121.33	120.95	111.62	109.54
III	115.07	116.27	123.57	123.63	124.46	115.44	114.83
IV	109.29	102.04	117.60	117.18	117.55	111.32	110.73
1980	100.00	100.00	100.00	100.00	100.00	100.00	100.00
I	107.15	99.77	111.93	112.80	113.23	108.16	110.13
II	101.80	101.83	103.73	103.47	102.70	102.25	102.83
III	98.81	101.91	100.17	99.30	98.52	101.40	99.74
IV	93.72	98.22	87.15	87.52	88.78	90.22	89.46
1981	91.10	87.40	71.16	71.18	74.30	73.63	73.38
I	92.45	95.86	78.14	78.18	80.92	81.04	80.94
II	92.13	88.05	70.96	71.16	74.71	73.02	73.06
III	90.79	82.85	65.72	66.87	70.20	69.25	69.02
IV	89.27	84.02	70.88	69.48	72.65	72.27	71.72

	Dutch Guilder	Pound Sterling	Argentine Peso	Brazilian Cruzeiro	Ecuadorian Sucre	Iranian Rial	Vene-zuelan Bolívar
1970	65.37	69.21	56.77	111.63	91.89	12.48	87.10
1971	56.54	61.06	50.58	93.20	65.24	12.27	70.05
1972	54.11	53.75	39.82	78.87	54.17	9.74	58.37
1973	68.80	58.65	54.34	90.86	62.36	12.86	66.12
1974	98.35	81.41	86.70	132.72	98.57	60.68	97.23
1975	142.31	117.88	75.71	173.82	138.30	80.19	136.85
1976	118.29	89.10	94.69	151.49	128.94	65.65	117.91
1977	104.62	77.31	62.59	125.59	107.56	55.43	102.18
1978	121.06	90.22	77.37	132.58	123.14	54.44	107.75
1979	120.04	99.66	102.80	122.26	120.25	72.53	104.94
I	125.78	94.59	91.87	128.27	123.31	53.66	106.81
II	119.96	98.11	98.45	125.30	122.23	66.82	105.81
III	121.39	108.80	111.31	126.15	122.21	80.41	105.59
IV	115.33	99.33	103.85	111.66	114.91	87.27	102.77
1980	100.00	100.00	100.00	100.00	100.00	100.00	100.00
I	110.22	101.78	99.56	94.17	109.81	103.58	105.75
II	102.83	101.58	99.23	95.17	102.84	106.46	101.03
III	100.90	101.66	100.45	101.06	97.29	100.54	99.15
IV	88.60	96.37	99.70	103.28	92.02	91.03	95.06
1981	71.04	81.55	73.51	98.45	90.32	79.78	96.60
I	78.36	91.58	93.41	103.61	91.05	88.21	96.37
II	70.24	84.16	70.10	101.82	89.72	81.61	96.02
III	65.24	73.89	70.29	96.75	89.29	76.63	96.64
IV	71.58	76.37	69.36	93.34	91.32	73.66	97.28

Table 3117 (Continued)

CHILE EVOLUTION OF REAL EXCHANGE RATES
AND PRICE INDEXES, 1970–82

PART IV. EVOLUTION OF EFFECTIVE REAL EXCHANGE RATE
INDEXES FOR EXPORTS AND IMPORTS

(1980 = 100)

Annual and Quarterly Averages	Exports		Imports	
	(1)[a]	(2)[b]	(3)[a]	(4)[b]
1970	133.5	80.2	132.9	79.6
1971	124.4	66.9	120.4	65.2
1972	131.3	60.0	125.4	57.2
1973	148.2	74.1	137.4	68.7
1974	126.5	108.7	122.4	105.1
1975	135.7	142.6	131.1	137.8
1976	116.8	120.3	115.2	118.6
1977	113.8	100.2	110.9	97.6
1978	133.3	113.5	127.0	108.1
1979	118.6	114.5	114.2	110.2
I	131.5	116.5	124.4	110.2
II	122.6	114.7	118.1	110.5
III	116.0	118.3	111.6	113.9
IV	109.7	109.8	107.0	107.2
1980	100.0	100.0	100.0	100.0
I	107.5	104.9	107.3	104.7
II	101.5	101.2	101.9	101.5
III	98.5	100.5	98.0	99.9
IV	93.8	94.1	94.2	94.6
1981	87.3	80.5	92.2	84.9
I	92.3	89.0	95.0	91.2
II	87.5	81.6	92.5	86.3
III	83.8	76.6	90.3	82.4
IV	88.6	77.6	94.2	81.8
1982	101.9	90.8	108.2	96.4
I	90.1	75.9	96.0	80.6
II	93.3	78.4	97.8	81.9
III	107.3	96.7	114.4	102.7
IV	111.9	108.5	120.4	116.7

1. Four quarters of 1974 = 100.
2. Corresponds to the quotient of the nominal exchange rate indexes divided by the relative price indexes. The wholesale price index for domestic products was used.
3. Corresponds to the quotient of the nominal exchange rate indexes divided by the relative price indexes. The following price indexes were used: 1971–1973, corrected consumer price index of J. Yáñez; 1974–78, corrected consumer price index of R. Cortázar and J. Marshall; 1979–1981, consumer price index of the National Statistical Institute (INE).

a. These indexes were obtained by multiplying the weightings of exports or imports by the real exchange rate indexes. The products are added together to give the effective real exchange rate indexes. The wholesale price index for domestic products was used.
b. A procedure similar to that described in note a was employed, except that the calculations were based on the following price indexes: 1971–1973, corrected consumer price index of J. Yáñez; 1974–78, corrected consumer price index of R. Cortázar and J. Marshall; 1979–1982, consumer price index of the National Statistical Institute (INE).

SOURCE: For Part I, ECLA-S, 1980; ECLA-S, 1981, Statistical Appendix; for years 1981–82 of Part IV, ECLA-S, vol. 1, 1982, table 16.

Table 3118

COLOMBIA EVOLUTION OF REAL EXCHANGE RATES AND PRICE INDEXES, 1970–82

PART I. EVOLUTION OF PRICES

Period	(1) Exchange Rate (Pesos per US)[1]	(2) Index of Nominal Exchange Rate[2]	(3) Wholesale Price Index for Colombia[2]	(4) Index of Real Exchange Rate $\frac{(2)}{(3)}$	(5) Wholesale Price Index for United States[2]	(6) Index of Adjusted Real Exchange Rate[2] (4)×(5)
1975	30.93	100.0	100.0	100.0	100.0	100.0
1976	34.70	112.1	122.9	91.3	104.6	95.5
1977	36.78	118.9	155.7	76.4	111.0	84.8
1978	39.10	126.4	183.2	69.0	119.7	82.6
1979	42.55	137.6	234.1	59.3	134.7	79.9
1980	47.28	152.9	290.8	52.6	153.5	80.7
First quarter	44.70	144.5	264.2	54.7	148.0	81.0
Second quarter	46.45	150.2	284.7	52.8	151.1	79.7
Third quarter	48.03	155.3	298.0	52.1	155.7	81.1
Fourth quarter	49.91	161.4	316.2	51.0	159.3	81.4

PART II. EVOLUTION OF REAL EXCHANGE RATE INDEXES[4]

(1980 = 100)

Colombian Pesos per:

Annual and Quarterly Averages	US Dollar	Canadian Dollar	Japanese Yen	Deutsch Mark	Spanish Peseta	French Franc	Italian Lira
1970	134.30	168.95	100.20	99.10	103.00	99.59	106.96
1971	134.45	174.13	99.18	105.87	106.31	102.12	108.47
1972	130.20	172.64	106.28	113.19	113.45	109.89	111.12
1973	124.37	155.24	116.10	121.99	116.58	112.89	109.89
1974	119.82	142.78	115.00	109.32	112.70	96.38	112.62
1975	123.85	143.80	110.27	115.20	120.49	114.29	115.07
1976	118.23	145.52	105.78	107.16	108.80	102.53	101.98
1977	104.98	121.92	99.63	100.76	93.93	91.29	93.82
1978	102.28	111.90	111.94	108.16	95.79	97.97	95.54
1979	97.99	101.28	99.19	105.00	103.26	97.94	95.90
1980	100.00	100.00	100.00	100.00	100.00	100.00	100.00
I	100.35	100.27	93.43	104.83	106.05	101.30	103.14
II	98.92	99.02	98.95	100.79	99.80	99.35	100.00
III	100.69	101.44	103.88	102.07	100.38	103.33	101.74
IV	100.68	99.91	105.52	93.61	95.37	96.91	96.16
1981	101.33	101.88	97.21	79.14	82.64	81.90	81.57
I	101.19	100.91	105.97	86.36	89.43	89.57	89.45
II	101.66	100.63	97.17	78.30	82.43	80.58	80.66
III	101.51	101.56	92.65	73.48	78.49	77.42	77.18
IV	100.27	104.58	94.37	79.62	81.60	81.19	80.52

Annual and Quarterly Averages	Dutch Guilder	Swedish Krona	Swiss Franc	Finnish Markka	Pound Sterling	Brazilian Cruzeiro	Venezuelan Bolívar
1970	88.64	102.42	90.30	96.02	93.39	151.88	117.01
1971	95.51	103.96	95.39	97.94	100.99	153.37	115.88
1972	104.00	108.14	99.12	98.96	102.61	150.35	112.94
1973	108.93	109.89	109.61	106.70	92.79	143.83	104.51
1974	100.61	109.84	107.63	108.87	83.26	135.78	99.45
1975	111.77	118.16	118.91	120.03	92.59	136.50	107.48
1976	106.17	112.06	110.85	112.84	79.96	135.95	105.83
1977	101.84	99.49	96.45	99.75	75.26	122.24	99.48
1978	108.62	95.89	115.49	93.09	80.95	118.95	96.68
1979	103.96	96.80	107.90	91.96	86.32	105.89	90.89
1980	100.00	100.00	100.00	100.00	100.00	100.00	100.00
I	103.24	101.25	103.11	96.95	95.33	88.20	99.05
II	99.92	99.51	99.79	99.70	98.70	92.46	98.18
III	102.83	102.23	102.16	103.68	103.60	102.97	101.05
IV	95.17	98.39	95.85	100.22	103.52	110.94	102.12
1981	79.01	86.61	83.73	91.16	90.70	109.47	106.86
I	86.60	94.91	87.55	97.03	101.22	114.52	104.08
II	77.51	88.04	80.40	90.78	92.86	112.34	105.96
III	-72.95	82.48	78.07	86.62	82.62	108.17	109.67
IV	80.41	81.27	90.11	91.09	85.79	104.82	107.89

Table 3118 (Continued)

COLOMBIA EVOLUTION OF REAL EXCHANGE RATES AND PRICE INDEXES, 1970–82

PART III. EVOLUTION OF THE REAL EFFECTIVE EXCHANGE RATE[3]

(1980 = 100)

	Exchange Rate (Pesos per Dollar)	Index of Nominal Exchange Rate	Index of Real Exchange Rate	
			Exports	Imports
1970	~	~	115.3	121.0
1971	~	~	117.6	122.4
1972	~	~	118.8	122.9
1973	~	~	118.9	120.8
1974	~	~	112.3	115.1
1975	30.93	65.4	118.2	119.5
1976	34.70	73.4	112.0	113.1
1977	36.78	77.8	102.0	102.0
1978	39.10	82.7	103.1	103.4
1979	42.55	90.0	99.3	98.6
1980	47.28	100.0	100.0	100.0
1981	54.49	115.2	92.8	94.1
1982	64.08	135.5	86.6	88.0
1981				
I	51.70	109.3	96.3	97.8
II	53.30	112.8	92.6	93.9
III	55.30	116.9	90.4	92.4
IV	57.70	121.8	92.2	93.5
1982				
I	60.24	127.4	89.9	91.2
II	62.66	132.6	87.4	88.4
III	65.13	137.7	85.6	86.5
IV	68.30	144.5	84.7	86.4

1. Average for the period.
2. 1975 = 100.
3. Corresponds to the quotient of the nominal exchange rate indexes divided by the relative price indexes. For Colombia, the wholesale price index was used.
4. These indexes were obtained by multiplying the weightings of exports or imports (Part II) by the real exchange rate indexes (Part I). The products were added together to give the effective real exchange rate indexes.

SOURCE: For Part I, ECLA-S, 1980; ECLA-S, 1981, Statistical Appendix; for years 1981–82 of Part III, ECLA-S, vol. 1, 1982, table 13.

Table 3119

COSTA RICA EVOLUTION OF REAL EXCHANGE RATES AND PRICE INDEXES, 1970–82

PART I. EVOLUTION OF REAL EXCHANGE RATE INDEXES[1]

(1980 = 100)

Annual and Quarterly Averages	Costa Rican Colones per:						
	US Dollar	Japanese Yen	Deutsch Mark	Belgian Franc	Finnish Markka	Dutch Guilder	Pound Sterling
1970	129.91	96.76	95.87	112.01	92.87	85.75	90.33
1971	126.11	93.13	99.28	107.09	91.85	89.57	94.72
1972	124.96	102.10	108.65	116.47	94.98	99.83	98.48
1973	121.80	113.84	119.46	127.42	104.49	106.66	90.87
1974	123.97	118.80	113.10	127.54	112.64	104.10	86.15
1975	119.92	106.85	111.55	121.02	116.22	108.23	89.65
1976	114.77	102.65	104.01	112.99	109.52	103.05	77.61
1977	113.28	107.41	108.72	115.94	107.65	109.90	81.20
1978	113.39	123.98	119.91	120.11	103.18	120.41	89.74
1979	108.63	108.79	116.40	116.80	101.93	115.25	95.68
I	111.88	120.03	122.42	123.66	103.37	122.71	92.27
II	110.27	110.29	115.60	116.22	100.31	114.93	93.99
III	107.77	109.02	115.74	115.77	102.81	113.71	101.90
IV	105.07	98.05	113.06	112.64	101.69	110.88	95.49
1980	100.00	100.00	100.00	100.00	100.00	100.00	100.00
I	102.94	95.87	107.53	108.37	99.45	105.91	97.79
II	100.33	100.27	102.23	101.97	101.12	101.34	100.12
III	100.04	103.07	101.42	100.51	103.01	102.16	102.93
IV	97.12	101.83	90.31	90.68	96.68	91.81	99.86
1981	179.93	172.62	140.53	140.55	161.87	140.31	161.06
I	154.80	160.46	130.83	130.89	146.99	131.20	153.35
II	168.61	161.06	129.79	130.13	150.47	128.48	153.93
III	149.62	136.53	108.31	110.18	127.67	107.52	121.78
IV	231.97	218.32	184.19	180.51	210.73	186.02	198.46

	El Salvador Colón	Guatemalan Quetzal	Honduran Lempira	Mexican Peso	Nicaraguan Córdoba	Panamanian Balboa	Venezuelan Bolívar
1970	110.58	119.61	148.32	117.97	127.17	105.20	113.17
1971	98.29	114.18	142.58	115.12	120.72	104.23	108.67
1972	98.57	108.13	142.44	112.18	118.03	107.14	108.39
1973	102.97	106.44	128.37	112.01	115.80	102.07	102.35
1974	110.47	111.92	124.68	117.50	115.31	113.93	102.90
1975	99.57	111.30	117.40	114.92	109.75	114.98	104.07
1976	122.71	112.53	112.57	104.21	103.23	113.40	102.72
1977	125.75	118.30	113.51	93.49	106.95	113.02	107.34
1978	125.06	113.76	111.83	99.58	103.85	110.62	107.17
1979	120.59	106.81	107.14	100.15	99.40	107.33	100.75
I	111.11	109.11	110.30	102.23	100.15	107.86	104.19
II	119.82	107.67	106.73	101.05	93.34	110.75	101.37
III	128.18	106.55	106.59	99.87	104.57	107.65	98.91
IV	122.26	104.27	105.11	97.63	96.82	103.66	98.81
1980	100.00	100.00	100.00	100.00	100.00	100.00	100.00
I	106.33	101.75	103.91	99.37	96.03	102.51	101.60
II	105.58	100.58	101.41	99.08	102.38	100.78	99.58
III	100.00	100.64	99.26	102.13	101.54	100.17	100.39
IV	89.35	97.49	95.97	99.30	99.80	96.86	98.50
1981	173.29	184.44	182.45	192.62	207.21	181.47	189.65
I	143.51	159.10	155.06	161.83	162.25	156.40	157.68
II	162.99	176.98	169.09	178.02	187.23	168.21	175.63
III	145.16	154.14	152.89	160.13	176.52	150.07	159.28
IV	228.60	229.95	238.66	256.18	293.06	237.02	252.79

Table 3119 (Continued)

COSTA RICA EVOLUTION OF REAL EXCHANGE RATES AND PRICE INDEXES, 1970–82

PART II. EVOLUTION OF REAL EXCHANGE RATE INDEXES[2]

(1980 = 100)

Annual and Quarterly Averages	Costa Rican Colones per:						
	US Dollar	Japanese Yen	Deutsch Mark	Belgian Franc	Finnish Markka	Dutch Guilder	Pound Sterling
1970	88.95	66.27	65.66	76.71	63.61	58.72	61.86
1971	89.21	65.88	70.23	75.75	64.97	63.35	67.00
1972	89.07	72.78	77.45	83.04	67.71	71.15	70.21
1973	87.50	81.79	85.82	91.53	75.07	76.62	65.28
1974	95.71	91.72	87.33	98.47	86.96	80.37	66.51
1975	95.96	85.51	89.26	96.84	93.00	86.60	71.74
1976	96.98	86.75	87.90	95.48	92.55	87.08	65.59
1977	98.81	93.68	94.84	101.13	93.88	95.86	70.84
1978	100.49	109.88	106.28	106.46	91.46	106.72	79.54
1979	103.57	103.73	110.99	111.36	97.19	109.88	91.24
I	102.78	110.27	112.47	113.61	94.97	112.72	84.78
II	104.13	104.16	109.17	109.76	94.73	108.53	88.77
III	104.44	105.64	112.16	112.19	99.62	110.18	98.75
IV	102.86	95.99	110.70	110.27	99.56	108.56	93.51
1980	100.00	100.00	100.00	100.00	100.00	100.00	100.00
I	102.10	95.09	106.66	107.49	98.64	105.03	96.99
II	100.00	99.95	101.89	101.64	100.78	101.00	99.79
III	99.86	102.88	101.24	100.34	102.83	101.99	102.75
IV	98.24	103.01	91.35	91.73	97.80	92.87	101.03
1981	202.06	193.87	157.83	157.85	181.79	157.57	180.89
I	163.78	169.77	138.43	138.48	155.52	138.80	162.25
II	189.01	180.66	145.59	145.96	168.77	144.11	172.68
III	171.78	156.75	124.35	126.50	146.58	123.44	139.81
IV	266.31	250.62	211.46	207.23	241.91	213.54	227.85

Annual and Quarterly Averages	El Salvador Colón	Guatemalan Quetzal	Honduran Lempira	Mexican Peso	Nicaraguan Córdoba	Panamanian Balboa	Venezuelan Bolívar
1970	75.74	81.90	101.59	80.78	87.08	72.05	77.51
1971	69.52	80.76	100.87	81.42	85.39	73.73	76.88
1972	70.27	77.08	101.55	79.96	84.14	76.38	77.27
1973	73.97	76.46	92.22	80.46	83.18	73.32	73.52
1974	84.29	86.40	96.26	80.71	89.02	87.96	79.45
1975	79.68	89.06	93.95	91.95	87.82	92.01	83.29
1976	103.70	95.08	95.13	88.05	87.23	95.83	86.81
1977	109.69	103.19	99.01	81.53	93.28	98.59	93.63
1978	110.84	100.83	99.12	88.24	92.04	98.05	95.00
1979	115.00	101.83	102.15	95.48	94.77	102.34	96.06
I	102.09	100.24	101.34	93.92	92.01	99.10	95.73
II	113.15	101.68	100.79	95.41	88.15	104.59	95.74
III	124.21	103.25	103.30	96.77	101.32	104.32	95.85
IV	119.69	102.09	102.91	95.59	94.78	101.49	96.74
1980	100.00	100.00	100.00	100.00	100.00	100.00	100.00
I	105.45	100.91	103.07	98.56	95.24	101.67	100.78
II	105.23	100.24	101.08	98.74	102.03	100.45	99.25
III	99.82	100.46	99.09	101.93	101.35	99.99	100.22
IV	90.38	98.62	97.09	100.43	100.95	97.99	99.65
1981	194.64	207.13	204.91	216.31	232.69	203.82	213.00
I	151.83	168.33	164.07	171.19	171.65	165.47	166.82
II	182.84	198.51	189.69	199.66	210.03	188.68	197.02
III	166.66	176.95	175.54	183.83	202.65	172.29	182.88
IV	262.45	263.96	273.99	294.09	336.39	272.10	290.21

Table 3119 (Continued)

COSTA RICA EVOLUTION OF REAL EXCHANGE RATES
AND PRICE INDEXES, 1970–82

PART III. EVOLUTION OF EFFECTIVE NOMINAL AND REAL EXCHANGE
RATES INDEXES FOR EXPORTS AND IMPORTS

(1980 = 100)

Annual and Quarterly Averages	Effective Nominal Exchange Rate Index for:		Effective Real Exchange Rate Index for:			
	Exports	Imports	Exports		Imports	
	(1)[a]	(2)[a]	(3)[b]	(4)[c]	(5)[b]	(6)[c]
1970	70.7	74.6	117.4	80.4	117.2	80.3
1971	71.1	75.1	114.3	80.9	113.4	80.2
1972	72.0	76.7	115.7	82.5	114.3	81.5
1973	74.3	78.5	116.5	83.7	115.1	82.6
1974	89.4	93.1	118.0	91.1	117.4	90.6
1975	97.4	100.2	114.8	91.9	112.5	90.0
1976	96.5	98.1	111.6	94.3	109.4	92.5
1977	97.9	97.8	113.1	98.6	110.7	96.5
1978	100.6	102.6	114.5	101.5	114.1	101.2
1979	100.2	100.8	110.1	104.9	108.1	103.1
I	102.5	104.1	112.8	103.6	111.5	102.4
II	98.9	100.2	110.2	104.1	108.7	102.6
III	99.9	100.5	110.4	107.0	108.6	105.2
IV	100.6	99.2	107.2	104.9	104.1	101.9
1980	100.0	100.0	100.0	100.0	100.0	100.0
I	100.5	99.0	103.5	102.6	101.5	100.6
II	100.1	99.6	101.4	101.0	100.8	100.5
III	100.7	100.7	100.6	100.5	101.0	100.8
IV	98.8	101.0	95.2	96.3	97.4	98.5
1981	240.2	249.9	156.8	192.8	163.9	199.9
I	170.8	178.0	143.7	158.7	150.0	163.4
II	206.3	215.3	148.3	179.5	154.9	186.6
III	204.9	213.4	131.4	161.7	137.9	168.0
IV	378.8	391.4	190.8	257.1	198.3	264.9
1982	~	~	130.1	~	132.6	~
I	~	~	157.0	~	161.9	~
II	~	~	137.8	~	140.7	~
III	~	~	120.5	~	121.9	~
IV	~	~	116.0	~	117.7	~

1. Corresponds to the quotient of the nominal exchange rate indexes divided by the relative price indexes. For Costa Rica, the wholesale price index was used.
2. Corresponds to the quotient of the nominal exchange rate indexes divided by the relative price indexes. For Costa Rica, the consumer price index was used.

a. These indexes were obtained by multiplying the weightings of exports or imports by the nominal exchange rate indexes. The products are added together to give the effective nominal exchange rate indexes.
b. These indexes were obtained by multiplying the weightings of exports or imports by the real exchange rate indexes. The products are added together to give the effective real exchange rate indexes. In calculating these indexes for Costa Rica, the wholesale price index was used.
c. A similar procedure to that described in note b was employed, except that the consumer price index were used.

SOURCE: ECLA-S, 1981, Statistical Appendix; for years 1981–82 of Part III, ECLA-S, vol. 1, 1982, table 8.

Table 3120

ECUADOR EVOLUTION OF REAL EXCHANGE RATES AND PRICE INDEXES, 1970–82

PART I. EVOLUTION OF REAL EXCHANGE RATE INDEXES[1]

(1980 = 100)

Ecuadorian Sucres per:

Annual Averages	US Dollar	Canadian Dollar	Japanese Yen	Deutsch Mark	Italian Lira
1970	134.31	178.37	100.16	99.07	107.10
1971	128.09	171.06	94.52	101.12	103.35
1972	124.08	167.40	101.40	108.03	106.13
1973	124.00	158.87	115.89	121.99	109.81
1974	119.67	143.75	114.89	109.21	112.39
1975	113.41	134.53	101.02	105.69	105.35
1976	107.07	131.60	95.82	97.09	92.39
1977	100.55	115.85	95.36	96.67	89.77
1978	97.13	104.50	106.26	102.85	90.72
1979	99.09	104.93	99.26	106.53	97.02
1980	100.00	100.00	100.00	100.00	100.00
1981	93.48	97.11	89.67	73.13	80.76

Annual Averages	Dutch Guilder	Chilean Peso	Colombian Peso	Panamanian Balboa	Peruvian Sol
1970	88.56	108.93	103.73	166.01	178.67
1971	91.29	202.02	97.85	156.49	173.16
1972	99.43	168.06	98.25	152.66	170.56
1973	108.54	159.12	102.71	144.30	161.52
1974	100.41	99.93	97.84	136.74	154.05
1975	102.35	69.88	92.58	125.08	141.32
1976	96.35	79.48	93.24	117.45	115.23
1977	97.71	91.13	99.81	108.62	79.32
1978	103.50	83.24	97.55	101.49	83.05
1979	105.04	87.57	105.26	99.32	100.64
1980	100.00	100.00	100.00	100.00	100.00
1981	72.84	102.65	91.74	92.19	97.17

PART II. EVOLUTION OF EFFECTIVE REAL EXCHANGE RATE INDEXES FOR EXPORTS AND IMPORTS[2]

(1980 = 100)

Annual Averages	Exports	Imports
1970	134.6	121.8
1971	137.3	119.0
1972	132.1	118.6
1973	131.1	122.9
1974	120.7	117.1
1975	111.5	109.0
1976	105.2	102.4
1977	99.0	98.0
1978	96.2	98.9
1979	99.2	100.2
1980	100.0	100.0
1981	93.6	90.6
I	98.4	96.8
II	93.6	90.6
III	92.1	88.0
IV	90.4	87.4
1982	101.5	96.0
I	92.4	89.4
II	113.2	106.9
III	107.0	100.4
IV	97.7	91.7

1. Corresponds to the quotient of the nominal exchange rate indexes divided by the relative price indexes. For Ecuador, the wholesale price index was used.
2. These indexes were obtained by multiplying the weightings of exports or imports (Part II) by the real exchange rate indexes (Part I). The products are added together to give the effective real exchange rate indexes.

SOURCE: ECLA-S, 1981, Statistical Appendix; for years 1981–82 of Part II, ECLA-S, vol. 1, 1982, table 12.

Table 3121

NICARAGUA EVOLUTION OF REAL EXCHANGE RATES AND PRICE INDEXES, 1978–79

Period	(1) Exchange Rate (Córdobas per US)	(2) Exchange Rate Index[1]	(3) Consumer Price Index[1]	(4) Real Exchange Rate Index[1] (2) (3)
1978				
December	7.00	100.0	100.0	100.0
1979				
January	7.00	100.0	103.3	96.8
February	7.00	100.0	103.7	96.4
March	7.00	100.0	104.6	95.6
April[2]	9.40	134.3	108.4	123.9
May	10.00	142.9	112.4	127.1
June	10.00	142.9	123.9	115.3
July	10.00	142.9	133.5	107.0
August	10.00	142.9	137.4	104.0
September	10.00	142.9	141.0	101.3
October	10.00	142.9	143.8	99.4
November	10.00	142.9	143.7	99.4
December	10.00	142.9	148.4	96.3

1. December 1978 = 100.
2. On 7 April 1979 the córdoba was devalued from 7 to 10 per U.S. dollars.

SOURCE: ECLA-S, 1979.

Table 3122

MEXICO EVOLUTION OF REAL EXCHANGE RATES AND PRICE INDEXES, 1970–82

PART I. EVOLUTION OF OFFICIAL AND PARITY EXCHANGE RATES

(1976 = 100)

	(1) Official Exchange Rate[1] (Pesos per Dollar)	(2) Wholesale Price Index (Average for the Period) Mexico	(3) United States	(4) Parity Exchange Rate 19.95 x (2/3)	(5) Relation Between Official and Parity Exchange Rates (1/4) = (5)
1976	19.95	100.0	100.0	19.95	100.00
1977	22.74	141.1	106.1	26.53	85.71
1978	22.72	163.4	114.4	28.50	79.72
1979	22.80	193.3	128.8	29.94	76.15
1980	23.26	240.5	146.9	32.66	71.22
1981	26.23	299.5	160.4	37.25	70.42
1982					
First quarter	45.53	363.2	163.0	44.45	102.43
Second quarter	48.04	419.8	163.2	51.32	93.61
July	48.92	456.2	164.2	55.42	88.27
August	104.00	514.4	164.2	62.50	176.40
September[2]	70.00	528.1	163.6	64.40	108.70
October[2]	70.00	549.4	163.8	66.91	104.62
November[2]	70.00	571.6	164.2	69.45	100.79
December					
Controlled	96.82	640.2	164.2‡	77.78	124.48
Free	148.50	640.2	164.2‡	77.78	190.92
Special	71.96	640.2	164.2‡	77.78	92.52

Table 3122 (Continued)

MEXICO EVOLUTION OF REAL EXCHANGE RATES AND PRICE INDEXES, 1970–82

PART II. EVOLUTION OF REAL EXCHANGE RATE INDEXES[3]

(1980 = 100)

Annual and Quarterly Averages	Mexican Pesos per:					
	US Dollar	Canadian Dollar	Japanese Yen	Deutsch Mark	Spanish Peseta	French Franc
1970	110.11	138.52	82.16	81.26	84.43	81.66
1971	109.56	141.88	80.74	86.26	86.60	83.21
1972	111.38	147.70	90.90	96.85	97.08	94.01
1973	108.73	135.71	101.50	106.64	101.95	98.70
1974	105.50	125.72	101.33	96.26	99.25	84.87
1975	104.35	121.16	92.89	97.07	101.50	96.30
1976	110.14	135.56	98.50	99.82	101.36	95.51
1977	121.19	140.75	115.03	116.31	108.46	105.39
1978	113.87	124.57	124.63	120.41	106.66	109.07
1979	108.48	112.11	108.72	116.24	114.29	108.42
1980	100.00	100.00	100.00	100.00	100.00	100.00
1981	93.41	93.91	89.65	72.96	76.19	75.50
I	95.65	94.46	99.23	80.84	83.71	83.84
II	94.67	93.71	90.49	72.91	76.76	75.03
III	93.44	93.49	85.27	67.64	72.26	71.27
IV	90.55	94.44	85.22	71.90	73.70	73.31
	Italian Lira	Swiss Franc	Pound Sterling	Israeli Shekel	Brazilian Cruzeiro	Venezuelan Bolívar
1970	87.57	74.05	76.57	108.53	124.53	95.94
1971	88.40	77.72	82.29	106.37	124.96	94.42
1972	94.89	84.81	87.79	103.41	128.64	96.62
1973	95.99	95.82	81.13	106.27	125.75	91.38
1974	98.98	94.77	73.32	122.61	119.56	87.57
1975	96.65	100.20	78.01	110.06	115.02	90.56
1976	94.76	103.26	74.49	116.32	126.63	98.58
1977	108.31	111.35	86.88	127.47	141.12	114.83
1978	106.16	128.57	90.12	101.83	132.42	107.63
1979	105.99	119.45	95.55	105.98	117.21	100.61
1980	100.00	100.00	100.00	100.00	100.00	100.00
1981	73.35	77.19	83.61	85.51	100.94	98.51
I	83.88	81.96	94.75	92.48	107.23	97.43
II	74.92	74.87	85.48	86.77	104.61	98.67
III	71.03	71.87	76.05	82.41	99.58	100.95
IV	72.85	81.38	77.47	82.28	94.67	97.41

Table 3122 (Continued)

MEXICO EVOLUTION OF REAL EXCHANGE RATES AND PRICE INDEXES, 1970–82

PART III. EVOLUTION OF EFFECTIVE REAL EXCHANGE RATE INDEXES FOR EXPORTS AND IMPORTS[4]

(1980 = 100)

Annual and Quarterly Averages	Exports	Imports
1970	106.8	103.9
1971	106.5	104.2
1972	109.5	108.0
1973	108.3	107.4
1974	105.4	103.4
1975	103.9	102.5
1976	109.4	107.6
1977	120.7	119.2
1978	114.1	114.8
1979	109.1	109.1
1980	100.0	100.0
1981	91.4	90.2
I	94.7	94.0
II	92.6	91.2
III	90.7	88.9
IV	88.5	87.4

1. End of period.
2. Another preferential exchange rate of 50 pesos per dollar existed during these months, and its relation with the parity rate was 77.64 for September, 74.73 for October, and 71.99 for November.
3. Corresponds to the quotient of the nominal exchange rate indexes divided by the relative price indexes. For Mexico, the wholesale price index was used.
4. These indexes were obtained by multiplying the weightings of exports or imports (Part III) by the real exchange rate indexes (Part II). The products are added together to give the effective real exchange rate indexes.

SOURCE: ECLA-S, 1981, Statistical Appendix; for Part I, ECLA-S, vol. 1, 1982, table 12.

Table 3123

PARAGUAY EVOLUTION OF REAL EXCHANGE RATES AND PRICE INDEXES, 1970–82

PART I. EVOLUTION OF REAL EXCHANGE RATE INDEXES BASED UPON A PEGGED GUARANI[1,2]

(1980 = 100)

Paraguayan Guaranies per:

Annual Averages	US Dollar	Japanese Yen	Deutsch Mark	French Franc	Italian Lira	Dutch Guilder
1970	190.15	141.89	140.33	141.02	151.49	125.51
1971	174.28	128.52	137.20	132.36	140.76	123.77
1972	153.70	125.51	133.64	129.73	131.14	122.78
1973	125.97	117.57	123.55	114.34	111.42	110.32
1974	114.68	110.10	104.63	92.25	107.71	96.29
1975	108.79	96.85	101.19	100.39	101.03	98.18
1976	112.56	100.68	102.00	97.60	97.05	101.06
1977	110.58	104.91	106.13	96.16	98.78	107.28
1978	105.70	115.64	111.78	101.24	98.69	112.24
1979	94.18	94.34	100.91	94.13	92.22	99.91
1980	100.00	100.00	100.00	100.00	100.00	100.00
1981	97.18	93.24	75.91	78.55	77.77	75.78

Annual Averages	Pound Sterling	Swiss Franc	Argentine Peso	Brazilian Cruzeiro	Uruguayan Peso	Algerian Dinar
1970	132.23	127.87	107.11	215.06	130.14	18.07
1971	132.94	123.63	109.06	198.77	134.54	19.10
1972	121.14	117.03	91.73	177.51	99.02	22.26
1973	93.98	111.02	87.00	145.68	99.44	27.52
1974	79.69	103.01	84.72	129.96	97.83	57.29
1975	81.33	104.46	52.14	119.91	77.40	52.27
1976	76.12	105.52	80.80	129.41	78.08	53.75
1977	79.27	101.60	64.09	128.77	77.64	54.80
1978	83.65	119.34	71.57	122.91	79.32	49.94
1979	82.95	103.70	85.40	101.71	87.64	60.50
1980	100.00	100.00	100.00	100.00	100.00	100.00
1981	86.99	80.33	77.86	102.24	91.57	84.11

PART II. EVOLUTION OF REAL EXCHANGE RATE INDEXES BASED UPON A FLOATING GUARANI[1,2]

(1980 = 100)

Paraguayan Guaranies per:

Annual Averages	US Dollar	Japanese Yen	Deutsch Mark	French Franc	Italian Lira	Dutch Guilder
1973	124.11	115.83	121.72	112.65	109.78	108.68
1974	117.23	112.55	106.96	94.30	110.13	98.43
1975	115.24	102.59	107.19	106.34	107.01	103.99
1976	113.40	101.42	102.76	98.33	97.76	101.81
1977	108.95	103.34	104.56	94.74	97.30	105.69
1978	111.18	121.65	117.57	106.49	103.77	118.06
1979	96.27	96.43	103.16	96.22	94.25	102.13
1980	100.00	100.00	100.00	100.00	100.00	100.00
1981	110.15	105.66	86.03	89.02	88.18	85.89

Annual Averages	Pound Sterling	Swiss Franc	Argentine Peso	Brazilian Cruzeiro	Uruguayan Peso	Algerian Dinar
1973	92.59	109.37	85.71	143.52	97.97	27.12
1974	81.46	105.30	86.61	132.85	100.01	58.56
1975	86.15	110.64	55.23	127.01	81.99	55.37
1976	76.68	106.30	81.39	130.37	78.66	54.15
1977	78.10	100.10	63.15	126.87	76.49	53.99
1978	87.99	125.53	75.28	129.29	83.43	52.53
1979	84.80	106.00	87.29	103.97	89.59	61.84
1980	100.00	100.00	100.00	100.00	100.00	100.00
1981	98.59	91.04	88.42	115.88	103.78	95.32

Table 3123 (Continued)

PARAGUAY EVOLUTION OF REAL EXCHANGE RATES
AND PRICE INDEXES, 1970–82

PART III. EVOLUTION OF EFFECTIVE REAL EXCHANGE RATE
INDEXES FOR EXPORTS AND IMPORTS

(1980 = 100)

Annual Averages	Effective Real Exchange Rate Index for:					
	Exports			Imports		
	(1)[a]	(2)[b]	(3)[c]	(1)[a]	(2)[b]	(3)[c]
1970	142.5			141.4		
1971	137.2			134.8		
1972	126.1			121.0		
1973	112.2	120.4	115.2	105.6	126.6	115.6
1974	101.3	112.9	105.5	100.1	119.1	109.3
1975	92.6	110.1	99.0	87.6	108.7	97.6
1976	99.0	107.6	102.2	96.3	115.5	105.5
1977	97.5	105.0	100.2	93.6	109.2	101.1
1978	102.2	112.0	105.8	94.3	115.0	104.2
1979	95.0	97.6	95.9	89.3	98.9	93.9
1980	100.0	100.0	100.0	100.0	100.0	100.0
1981	80.0	97.3	86.3	89.0	105.0	96.6
1982	73.0	124.5	90.8	80.5	136.0	107.0

1. Corresponds to the quotient of the nominal exchange rate indexes divided by the relative price indexes. For Paraguay, the wholesale price index was used.
2. Prepared on the basis of an exchange rate of 126 guaranies per US dollar for the entire period.

a. These indexes were obtained by multiplying the weightings of exports or imports by the real exchange rate indexes. The products are added together to give the effective real exchange rate indexes. These indexes were prepared on the basis of the official exchange rate of 126 guaranies per US dollar.
b. These indexes correspond to a weighted average of the real exchange rate indexes for Paraguay with respect to Argentina, Brazil, the United States, Japan, Italy, France and the Federal Republic of Germany, calculated on the basis of their relative shares in non-registered trade flows with this country. In calculating these indexes, the floating free market exchange rate was used.
c. Corresponds to a weighted average of columns (1) and (2) on the basis of the effective share of the main trading partners of Paraguay in its exports and imports (registered and non-registered).

SOURCE: ECLA-S, 1981, Statistical Appendix; for years 1981–82 of Part III, ECLA-S, vol. 1, 1982, table 19.

Table 3124

PERU EVOLUTION OF REAL EXCHANGE RATES AND PRICE INDEXES, 1970–82

PART I. EVOLUTION OF REAL EXCHANGE RATE

	(1)	(2)	(3)	(4)	(5)	(6)
Period	Exchange Rate (Soles per Dollar)	Index of[1] Exchange Rate	Wholesale[1] Price Index	Index of[1] Real Exchange Rate $\frac{(2)}{(3)}$	Index of[1] Wholesale Prices in United States	Index of[1] Adjusted Real Exchange Rate (4)×(5)
1976	57.4	88.3	112.4	78.6	99.8	78.4
1977	86.9	133.7	164.7	81.1	106.5	86.4
1978	158.9	244.4	289.9	84.3	114.0	96.1
First quarter	130.3	200.4	219.5	91.3	110.3	100.7
Second quarter	145.3	223.5	263.8	84.7	114.0	96.6
Third quarter	169.5	260.7	314.0	83.0	115.0	95.5
Fourth quarter	190.4	292.8	362.1	80.9	117.8	95.3
1979	226.8	349.0	493.9	70.7	128.0	90.5
First quarter	206.4	317.5	411.9	77.1	122.4	94.4
Second quarter	220.8	340.0	458.2	74.2	126.1	93.6
Third quarter	234.1	360.2	522.7	68.9	129.9	89.5
Fourth quarter	246.0	378.4	582.6	65.0	134.6	87.5
1980	292.5	450.0	756.2	59.5	145.8	86.8
First quarter	260.7	401.0	648.7	61.8	141.1	87.2
Second quarter	278.7	428.9	707.7	60.6	143.9	87.2
Third quarter	299.6	460.9	778.4	59.2	148.6	88.0
Fourth quarter	331.0	509.2	889.8	57.2	151.4	86.6

PART II. EVOLUTION OF NOMINAL EXCHANGE RATES

Peruvian Soles per:

Annual Averages	US Dollar	Canadian Dollar	Japanese Yen	Deutsch Mark	Belgian Franc	French Franc	Italian Lira
1970	38.70	37.0619	.1081	10.6129	.7795	7.0005	.0617
1971	38.70	38.3244	.1113	11.1143	.7974	7.0213	.0626
1972	38.70	39.0949	.1277	12.1370	.8792	7.6720	.0664
1973	38.70	38.6961	.1424	14.4803	.9929	8.6888	.0664
1974	38.70	39.5706	.1325	14.9548	.9935	8.0459	.0595
1975	40.80	40.1180	.1375	16.5833	1.1093	9.5185	.0625
1976	57.43	58.2454	.1937	22.8078	1.4876	12.0156	.0690
1977	83.81	78.8058	.3121	36.0908	2.3383	17.0574	.0950
1978	156.34	137.0562	.7429	77.8353	4.9644	34.6437	.1841
1979	224.55	191.6937	1.0247	122.5108	7.6589	52.7794	.2703
1980	288.65	246.8571	1.2730	158.7996	9.8707	68.3034	.3370
1981	426.59	355.8178	1.9244	188.7566	11.4888	78.4952	.3753

	Dutch Guilder	Pound Sterling	Argentine Peso	Brazilian Cruzeiro	Chilean Peso	Ecuadorian Sucre	Venezuelan Bolívar
1970	10.7007	92.7168	10.1842	8.4240	3225.0000	1.8751	8.6033
1971	11.0745	94.5748	8.4130	7.3185	3225.0000	1.5480	8.5987
1972	12.0580	96.6533	4.7195	6.5217	1935.0000	1.5480	8.7947
1973	13.8432	94.8065	4.1170	6.3173	348.6486	1.5480	8.9900
1974	14.3952	90.4628	4.3483	5.6996	46.5144	1.5480	9.0326
1975	16.1329	90.2655	1.1148	5.0203	8.3079	1.6320	9.5216
1976	21.7217	103.1986	.4102	5.3809	4.3994	2.2972	13.3873
1977	34.1482	146.1887	.2056	5.9255	3.8929	3.3524	19.5248
1978	72.2592	299.7891	.1965	8.6519	4.9387	6.2536	36.4217
1979	111.9392	475.5400	.1705	8.3336	6.0288	8.9820	52.3122
1980	145.1889	670.8111	.1571	5.4758	7.4013	11.5460	67.2452
1981	170.9780	865.1186	.0969	4.5808	10.9382	17.0636	99.3803

Table 3124 (Continued)

PERU EVOLUTION OF REAL EXCHANGE RATES
AND PRICE INDEXES, 1970–82

PART III. EVOLUTION OF RELATIVE PRICE INDEXES[2,3]

(1980 = 100)

Peruvian Wholesale Price Index Divided by Price Indexes of:

Annual Averages	US WPI	Canada CPI	Japan WPI[4]	Germany CPI	Belgium WPI[4]	France CPI	Italy WPI
1970	16.142	14.367	13.698	10.902	11.335	16.639	27.672
1971	16.690	14.925	14.751	11.066	11.890	16.848	28.629
1972	16.713	14.887	15.307	10.956	11.951	16.587	28.762
1973	16.170	15.146	14.457	11.212	12.190	16.902	26.856
1974	15.507	15.559	12.539	11.938	11.547	16.938	21.742
1975	17.453	17.282	14.976	13.862	13.635	18.646	24.657
1976	23.207	22.362	19.838	18.487	18.096	23.664	27.702
1977	31.045	29.392	27.635	25.319	24.997	30.706	33.738
1978	48.418	45.369	47.680	41.433	4l.846	47.339	52.352
1979	72.966	70.475	75.367	67.531	68.314	72.517	76.841
1980	100.000	100.000	100.000	100.000	l00.000	l00.000	l00.000
1981	161.463	156.615	173.055	166.262	164.300	155.344	151.982

	Netherlands CPI	United Kingdom CPI	Argentina WPI	Brazil WPI	Chile WPI[4]	Ecuador WPI	Venezuela WPI[4]
1970	13.442	23.932	13855.941	163.674	86682.698	21.826	17.680
1971	13.369	23.368	10652.833	145.732	81032.958	21.499	18.472
1972	12.959	22.788	6274.405	128.520	48428.550	20.859	18.794
1973	13.131	22.848	4576.234	120.406	8936.556	20.190	19.189
1974	13.657	22.445	4333.272	106.244	990.954	18.443	18.717
1975	15.203	22.225	1828.153	102.701	207.943	19.896	20.146
1976	19.436	26.535	424.314	99.702	88.708	23.714	25.946
1977	25.923	32.507	241.499	99.363	68.933	31.129	32.765
1978	41.897	40.481	165.082	121.444	79.871	44.822	51.223
1979	68.165	75.489	112.248	132.114	89.561	68.653	78.677
1980	100.000	100.000	100.000	100.000	100.000	100.000	100.000
1981	164.977	157.406	84.095	84.574	159.887	154.849	151.618

PART IV. EVOLUTION OF REAL EXCHANGE RATE INDEXES[5]

(1980 = 100)

Peruvian Soles per:

Annual Averages	US Dollar	Canadian Dollar	Japanese Yen	Deutsch Mark	Belgian Franc	French Franc	Italian Lira
1970	83.06	104.50	61.99	61.30	69.67	61.59	66.16
1971	80.33	104.02	59.27	63.24	67.94	61.01	64.88
1972	80.22	106.38	65.53	69.76	74.53	67.71	68.50
1973	82.91	103.49	77.37	81.33	82.52	75.26	73.36
1974	86.46	103.02	83.01	78.88	87.16	69.54	81.20
1975	80.99	94.03	72.12	75.33	82.42	74.74	75.22
1976	85.73	105.51	76.70	77.69	83.28	74.34	73.91
1977	93.52	108.61	88.72	89.76	94.77	81.33	83.55
1978	111.86	122.38	122.39	118.30	120.19	107.14	104.41
1979	106.61	110.18	106.80	114.24	113.58	106.56	104.38
1980	100.00	100.00	100.00	100.00	100.00	100.00	100.00
1981	91.53	92.03	87.81	71.49	70.84	73.98	73.27

	Dutch Guilder	Pound Sterling	Argentine Peso	Brazilian Cruzeiro	Chilean Peso	Ecuadorian Sucre	Venezuelan Bolívar
1970	54.83	57.75	46.79	93.99	50.27	74.41	72.36
1971	57.05	60.33	50.27	91.71	53.77	62.36	69.22
1972	64.09	63.23	47.88	92.67	53.98	64.28	69.59
1973	72.61	61.86	57.27	95.81	52.71	66.40	69.67
1974	72.60	60.08	63.87	97.97	63.42	72.69	71.26
1975	73.09	60.54	38.82	89.27	53.98	71.04	70.28
1976	76.98	57.98	61.54	98.56	67.01	83.90	76.73
1977	90.73	67.04	54.19	108.91	76.30	93.27	88.61
1978	118.79	88.53	75.77	130.10	83.54	120.84	105.74
1979	113.11	93.91	96.69	115.20	90.95	113.31	98.88
1980	100.00	100.00	100.00	100.00	100.00	100.00	100.00
1981	71.38	81.93	73.35	98.91	92.43	95.44	97.47

Table 3124 (Continued)

PERU EVOLUTION OF REAL EXCHANGE RATES
AND PRICE INDEXES, 1970–82

PART V. EVOLUTION OF EFFECTIVE REAL EXCHANGE RATE
INDEXES FOR EXPORTS AND IMPORTS[6]

(1980 = 100)

Annual Averages	Exports	Imports
1970	72.7	73.9
1971	71.2	71.9
1972	73.9	74.2
1973	79.2	78.9
1974	82.7	81.5
1975	76.6	76.1
1976	80.7	81.5
1977	90.4	90.3
1978	113.1	112.8
1979	106.9	107.3
1980	100.0	100.0
1981	85.6	85.8
I	89.6	89.5
II	87.6	87.7
III	83.0	83.5
IV	83.3	84.0
1982	84.5	86.1
I	80.4	82.1
II	82.6	83.5
III	84.6	86.0
IV	88.3	91.2

1. June 1976 = 100.
2. Wholesale price index = WPI; consumer price index = CPI.
3. The data on the WPI for Peru were supplied by the National Statistical Institute of that country.
4. WPI for domestic products.
5. Corresponds to the quotient of the nominal exchange rate indexes divided by the relative price indexes.
6. These indexes were obtained by multiplying the weighting of exports or imports by the real exchange rate indexes. The products are added together to give the effective real exchange rate indexes.

SOURCE: For Part I, ECLA-S, 1980; ECLA-S, 1981, Statistical Appendix; for years 1981–82 of Part V, ECLA-S, vol. 1, 1982, table 11.

Table 3125

URUGUAY EVOLUTION OF REAL EXCHANGE RATES
AND PRICE INDEXES, 1970–82

PART I. EVOLUTION OF REAL EXCHANGE RATE

Period	(1) Exchange Rate (Pesos per U.S.)[1]	(2) Index of Exchange Rate[2]	(3) Wholesale Price Index[2]	(4) Index of Real Exchange Rate $\frac{(2)}{(3)}$	(5) United States Wholesale Price Index[2]	(6) Adjusted Real Exchange Rate Index[2] (4)x(5)
1973	.87	100.0	100.0	100.0	100.0	100.0
1974	1.20	137.9	178.7	77.2	118.8	91.7
1975	2.26	259.8	308.0	84.4	129.9	109.6
1976						
Average	3.34	383.9	463.8	82.8	135.8	112.4
December	3.98	457.5	1,563.3	81.2	139.0	112.9
1977						
Average	4.67	536.8	697.2	77.0	144.1	111.0
June	4.62	531.0	674.9	78.7	144.3	113.6
December	5.39	619.5	815.8	75.9	147.1	111.6
1978						
Average	6.06	696.6	1,035.8	67.3	155.5	104.7
June	5.84	671.3	980.8	68.4	155.5	106.4
December	6.98	802.3	1,301.7	61.6	161.4	99.4
1979						
Average	7.86	903.4	1,868.9	48.3	174.9	84.5
June	7.86	903.4	1,811.1	49.9	173.4	86.5
December	8.43	969.0	2,305.0	42.1	185.5	78.1

Table 3125 (Continued)

URUGUAY EVOLUTION OF REAL EXCHANGE RATES
AND PRICE INDEXES, 1970–82

PART II. EVOLUTION OF NOMINAL EXCHANGE RATES[3]

(1980 = 100)

Annual Averages	Uruguayan Pesos per:						
	US Dollars	Japanese Yen	Deutsch Mark	Spanish Peseta	French Franc	Italian Lira	Dutch Guilder
1970	146.11	109.35	107.95	112.41	108.33	116.76	96.41
1971	130.17	89.88	102.56	104.09	98.91	99.98	92.44
1972	155.10	129.61	134.87	135.78	130.94	137.05	123.91
1973	126.76	117.61	124.29	118.70	115.08	112.05	110.99
1974	117.20	113.56	106.94	110.36	94.27	111.86	98.41
1975	140.55	124.38	130.74	136.52	129.71	129.65	126.84
1976	144.15	128.39	130.64	132.47	125.00	124.85	129.43
1977	142.41	135.17	136.68	127.32	123.84	127.53	138.16
1978	133.26	145.78	140.93	124.79	127.64	124.04	141.51
1979	107.45	107.54	115.14	113.22	107.40	104.80	114.00
1980	100.00	100.00	100.00	100.00	100.00	100.00	100.00
1981	105.02	100.76	82.03	85.65	84.88	84.35	81.90

Annual Averages	Pound Sterling	Argentine Peso	Brazilian Cruzeiro	Venezuelan Bolívar	Iraqui Dinar	Kuwaiti Dinar	Nigerian Naira
1970	101.57	82.14	165.29	127.41	14.18	12.62	14.39
1971	97.80	81.27	148.67	112.21	15.60	14.19	17.02
1972	122.25	92.43	179.17	134.48	21.27	18.53	22.57
1973	94.57	87.32	146.47	106.53	22.50	20.65	23.55
1974	81.45	86.42	132.78	97.28	65.39	63.79	54.22
1975	105.07	67.20	154.90	121.96	76.66	71.48	64.16
1976	97.48	103.47	165.68	129.02	80.36	73.82	67.12
1977	102.09	82.69	165.79	134.94	82.16	77.05	68.28
1978	105.46	90.14	154.94	125.96	71.11	68.88	58.15
1979	94.65	96.98	116.09	99.66	75.32	74.28	64.91
1980	100.00	100.00	100.00	100.00	100.00	100.00	100.00
1981	94.01	85.19	113.43	111.84	112.73	109.83	93.03

PART III. EVOLUTION OF EFFECTIVE REAL EXCHANGE RATE
INDEXES FOR EXPORTS AND IMPORTS[4]

(1980 = 100)

Annual Averages	Exports	Imports
1970	125.5	95.5
1971	115.2	88.1
1972	143.2	108.0
1973	122.2	93.0
1974	110.8	96.3
1975	130.2	108.4
1976	136.5	117.6
1977	136.2	115.9
1978	133.8	112.0
1979	109.9	97.9
1980	100.0	100.0
1981	93.8	97.8
I	101.1	107.0
II	97.1	102.5
III	90.0	94.2
IV	92.0	94.0
1982	110.2	111.4
I	96.2	98.4
II	98.8	100.1
III	93.8	94.6
IV	147.2	148.4

1. Annual or monthly average on the commercial market, selling rate; from November 28, 1979, onward, exchange market.
2. 1973 = 100.
3. Corresponds to the quotient of the nominal exchange rate indexes divided by the relative price indexes. For Uruguay, the wholesale price index for domestic product was used.
4. These indexes were obtained by multiplying the weightings of exports or imports by the real exchange rate indexes. The products are added together to give the effective real exchange rate indexes.

SOURCE: For Part I, ECLA-S, 1979; ECLA-S, 1981, Statistical Appendix; for years 1981–82 of Part III, ECLA-S, vol. 1, 1982, table 11.

Table 3126

VENEZUELA EVOLUTION OF REAL EXCHANGE RATES
AND PRICE INDEXES, 1970–81

PART I. EVOLUTION OF REAL EXCHANGE RATE INDEXES[1]

(1980 = 100)

Annual and Quarterly Averages	Venezuelan Bolivares per:				
	US Dollar	Canadian Dollar	Japanese Yen	Deutsch Mark	Spanish Peseta
1970	114.78	144.40	86.04	84.71	87.93
1971	116.06	150.27	85.47	91.36	91.68
1972	115.29	152.87	94.20	100.23	100.47
1973	119.00	148.54	110.96	116.72	111.52
1974	120.48	143.56	116.11	109.93	113.30
1975	115.23	133.79	102.49	107.19	111.97
1976	111.73	137.51	100.33	101.25	102.72
1977	105.54	122.57	100.37	101.30	94.38
1978	105.79	115.74	115.95	111.88	99.05
1979	107.83	111.43	108.25	115.54	113.47
1980	100.00	100.00	100.00	100.00	100.00
1981	94.82	95.35	91.28	74.06	77.29
I	98.18	96.95	102.05	82.98	85.81
II	95.94	94.97	91.79	73.89	77.77
III	92.57	92.61	84.56	67.01	71.51
IV	92.95	96.94	87.59	73.80	75.63

	French Franc	Italian Lira	Pound Sterling	Netherlands Antilles Guilder	Brazilian Cruzeiro
1970	85.12	92.01	79.81	109.59	129.90
1971	88.14	94.21	87.15	110.20	132.44
1972	97.31	98.02	90.85	113.65	133.23
1973	108.01	105.75	88.77	112.12	137.71
1974	96.92	113.65	83.72	114.12	136.63
1975	106.34	107.86	86.14	115.46	127.10
1976	96.88	97.41	75.56	112.71	128.53
1977	91.78	95.18	75.65	105.75	122.99
1978	101.33	99.81	83.72	106.36	123.08
1979	107.76	106.49	94.97	107.24	116.56
1980	100.00	100.00	100.00	100.00	100.00
1981	76.64	77.06	84.88	97.50	102.51
I	86.06	86.42	97.25	100.42	110.07
II	76.05	76.58	87.64	97.74	106.20
III	70.59	69.91	75.33	95.16	98.62
IV	75.25	75.11	79.52	96.93	97.38

PART II. EVOLUTION OF EFFECTIVE REAL EXCHANGE RATE INDEXES FOR EXPORTS AND IMPORTS[2]

(1980 = 100)

Annual and Quarterly Averages	Exports	Imports
1970	116.2	105.0
1971	118.2	107.3
1972	119.4	110.0
1973	120.3	116.9
1974	121.0	117.2
1975	117.1	112.0
1976	114.5	107.6
1977	107.0	103.0
1978	106.7	106.9
1979	107.8	108.8
1980	100.0	100.0
1981	94.9	89.6
I	98.3	95.5
II	95.6	90.3
III	92.2	85.3
IV	93.8	87.6

1. Corresponds to the quotient of the nominal exchange rate indexes divided by the relative price indexes. For Venezuela, the wholesale price index for domestic products was used.
2. These indexes were obtained by multiplying the weightings of exports or imports by the real exchange rate indexes. The products are added together to give the effective real exchange rate indexes.

SOURCE: ECLA-S, 1981, Statistical Appendix.

CHAPTER 32

PRICE CHANGES, COMMODITY PRICES, AND INTEREST RATES

Figure 32:1

**TWELVE-MONTH VARIATIONS IN CONSUMER PRICE INDEXES,
5 LC, 1981–84**

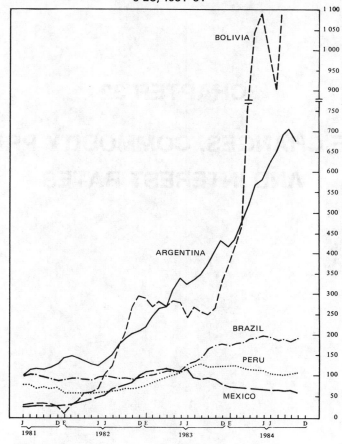

SOURCE: ECLA-N, January 1985.

Figure 32:2

**TWELVE-MONTH VARIATIONS IN CONSUMER PRICE INDEXES,
6 LC, 1981–84**

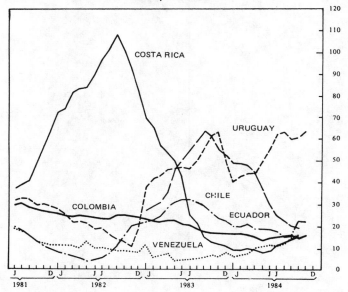

SOURCE: ECLA-N, January 1985.

Table 3200

GUIDE TO TABLES 3201-3221: CONSUMER PRICE CHANGES
(Calculations by Waldo W. Wilkie)

Alternative PC series are presented for each country to illustrate that there is no single measure of price change. The reader must look at the series to interpret trends.

Differences amounting to several percent between alternative series may be due only to rounding in the original data (e.g., between a figure ending in .4 that rounds downward and a figure ending in .5 that rounds upward).

Differences in series may also be due, however, to one or more of the following factors:

1. number of items included in the series
2. weights attached to each item
3. calculations based upon different base years
4. coverage geographically of capital city in contrast to major urban areas, all urban areas, or national scope
5. consumer prices keyed to varying definition of "consumer" as involving:
   a. all households
   b. wage earner households
   c. wage and salary earner households
   d. low income earners
   e. low and middle income earners
   f. middle income earners
   g. "average" working class family with a specified number of dependents
   h. government employees

According to IMF-IFS-S, No. 2, 1981, pp. ii-iii:

The increasing interdependence of national economies, and the increased transmission of inflation between them, has brought with it a need for global measures of price change in order to enable analysts to quantify the magnitude of global inflation and to examine its diffusion and dispersion around the world. The three most commonly used indicators of global price change are consumer prices, GDP deflators, and wholesale prices. GDP deflators have particular relevance in this context since they reflect, in concept, the aggregate price change of all goods and services produced in the domestic economy. As such they have been viewed as broader measures of price change than consumer price indexes, which cover only items of private consumption expenditure. The GDP deflator has several deficiencies, however, as a measure of global inflation. Although its sectoral coverage is wider than that of consumer or wholesale price indexes, the techniques used to obtain constant price data for components of the national accounts other than private consumption expenditure are less than satisfactory in most countries. . . .

[Therefore, the IMF emphasizes] consumer prices. There is a fair degree of similarity in concepts and methodologies between countries for these series. Country coverage is also more comprehensive than that for GDP deflators and wholesale prices.

[In summary,] it should be emphasized [that price] measures are only approximate indicators of overall price trends. In order to summarize into one aggregate measure the large number of transactions whose price movements they purport to reflect, a number of judgements must be made. Depending on the assumptions made concerning such aspects of methodology as the choice of base year, weights, formulae, sample selection, and specification of prices, different results, although perhaps equally appropriate depending on the context in which the measures are to be used, can ensue. In this sense, price index numbers cannot be rigorously defined independent of the methods used in their construction.

Table 3201

ARGENTINA COMPARATIVE PC OF PRICES,[1] 1914–83

(YA)

	PART I.				PART II.						
	Consumer			Consumer[2]						GDP Deflator	
	A.		A.	B.	C.	D.	E.		F.	G.	
Year	Economía Argentina (1914-29)	Year	Economía Argentina (1930-40)	Díaz Alejandro (1936-66)	Martin (1941-73)	IMF (1953-83)	UN-SY[3] (1973-83)		IMF (1961-82)	Díaz Alejandro (1936-65)
1914	0									
1915	7.0	1930	1.5							
1916	7.3	1931	−14.4							
1917	17.6	1932	−10.7							
1918	25.5	1933	6.7							
1919	−5.8	1934	−6.3							
1920	16.9	1935	6.8							
1921	−10.9	1936	9.3	8.5						1.6
1922	−16.0	1937	2.4	2.6						2.4
1923	−2.0	1938	−.9	−.7						3.5
1924	2.0	1939	1.5	1.6						2.2
1925	−2.6	1940	2.4	2.2						1.8
1926	−2.5	1941		2.6	2.6					2.9
1927	−1.4	1942		5.7	5.7					10.4
1928	−1.4	1943		1.1	1.1					5.3
1929	1.4	1944		−.3	−.3					2.1
		1945		19.7	19.8					14.9
		1946		17.7	17.7					20.6
		1947		13.5	13.5					20.0
		1948		13.1	13.1					16.7
		1949		31.1	31.1					26.1
		1950		25.5	14.1					19.5
		1951		36.7	50.4					36.6
		1952		38.7	38.7					28.3
		1953		4.0	4.0	4.0				6.1
		1954		3.8	3.8	3.8				8.7
		1955		12.3	12.3	12.3				10.1
		1956		13.4	13.4	13.4				27.1
		1957		24.7	24.7	24.7				19.0
		1958		31.6	31.6	31.6				32.3
		1959		113.7	114.0	113.7				101.9
		1960		27.3	27.1*	27.3*				19.6
		1961		13.5	13.6	14.0		11.9		11.5
		1962		28.1	28.2	28.1		23.7		27.3
		1963		24.1	24.0	24.0		37.6		26.0
		1964		22.1	22.2	22.1		42.8		24.8
		1965		28.6	28.7	28.5		25.3		28.5
		1966		32.3	32.0	31.7		13.4		
		1967			29.2	29.4		30.2		
		1968			16.2	16.1		11.6		
		1969			7.6	7.7		12.3		
		1970			13.6	13.6		14.1		
		1971			34.7	34.8		28.5		
		1972			58.5	58.4		62.3		
		1973			60.3	61.2	60.6	65.0		
		1974				23.5*	24.3	30.8		
		1975				182.3	182.8	191.8		
		1976				443.2	444.4	430.1		
		1977				176.1	176.0	160.1		
		1978				175.5	175.5	159.7		
		1979				159.5	159.5	155.0		
		1980				100.8	100.8	96.9		
		1981				104.5	104.5	106.7		
		1982				164.8*	164.8	188.8		
		1983				343.8	343.8			

1. See table 3200.
2. Buenos Aires.
3. Greater Buenos Aires since 1981.

SOURCE: Calculations were made from the following:
  A. *Revista de Economía Argentina* 36 (1937), pp. 268-269, and 40 (1941), p. 105.
  B. Carlos F. Díaz Alejandro, *Essays on the Economic History of the Argentine Republic* (New Haven: Yale University Press, 1970), p. 528.
  C. J. L Martin, SALA, 18-1411.
  D. IMF-IFS-Y, 1983, pp. 70; IMF-IFS-Y, 1984, pp. 102-103.
  E. UN-MB, Dec., 1984, p. 220; UN-SY, 1981, p.169.
  F. IMF-IFS-S, No. 2, 1981, pp. 10-11; IMF-IFS-S, No. 8, 1984, pp. 76-77.
  G. See source B, above.

Table 3202

BOLIVIA COMPARATIVE PC OF PRICES,[1] 1932-83
(YA)

Year	Consumer[2] A. Wilkie (1932-66)	B. Martin (1941-75)	C. IMF (1953-83)	D. UN-SY (1973-83)	GDP Deflator E. IMF (1957-82)
1932	26.0				
1933	26.2				
1934	25.8				
1935	26.0				
1936	25.8				
1937	13.9				
1938	28.0				
1939	35.5				
1940	27.6				
1941	26.5	28.1			
1942	31.7	29.9			
1943	17.8	22.2			
1944	7.7	6.6			
1945	8.3	5.5			
1946	11.8	7.5			
1947	15.1	15.9			
1948	10.4	5.3			
1949	7.5	5.0			
1950	22.6	22.9			
1951	33.2	33.3			
1952	24.1	23.8			
1953	101.5	100.0	102.9		
1954	124.4	124.0	123.2		
1955	80.0	80.4	80.0		
1956	178.8	178.7	178.8		
1957	115.1	115.2	115.1		11.0
1958	3.1	3.1	3.1		11.0
1959	19.6	19.6	20.3		15.2
1960	11.9	11.8	11.5		6.8
1961	6.8	6.9	7.6		7.4
1962	5.9	5.9	5.9		6.8
1963	-.7	-.7	-.7*		.8
1964	10.1	10.1	10.2		8.4
1965	2.9	2.9	2.9		5.9
1966	6.9	6.9	7.0		3.3
1967		11.2	11.2		6.2
1968		5.5	5.5		-1.65
1969		2.2	2.2		3.6
1970		3.8	3.8		3.9
1971		3.7	3.7		4.4
1972		6.5	6.5		20.4
1973		31.5	31.5	31.8	41.6
1974		62.9	62.8	62.8	58.1
1975		7.1	8.0	8.1	6.5
1976			4.5	4.7	8.1
1977			8.1	7.9	10.9
1978			10.4	10.4	13.5
1979			19.7	19.8	18.2
1980			47.2	47.2	38.9
1981			32.1	32.2	27.8
1982			123.5	123.5	168.2
1983			275.6	275.6	

1. See table 3200.
2. La Paz.

SOURCE: Calculations were made from the following:
   A. James W. Wilkie, *The Bolivian Revolution and U.S. Aid Since 1952* (Los Angeles: UCLA Latin American Center Publications, 1969), p. 4.
   B. J. L. Martin, SALA, 18-1412.
   C. IMF-IFS-Y, 1983, pp. 70; IMF-IFS-Y, 1984, pp. 102-103.
   D. UN-MB, Dec. 1984, p. 220; UN-SY, 1981, p. 169.
   E. IMF-IFS-S, No. 2, 1981, pp. 10-11; IMF-IFS, No. 8, 1984, pp. 76-77.

Table 3203

BRAZIL COMPARATIVE PC OF PRICES,[1] 1913–83

(YA)

	PART I.			PART II.					
	Consumer[2]			Consumer[2]					GDP Deflator
Year	A. Simonson (1913-29)	Year	A. Simonson (1930-39)	B. Martin (1941-75)	C. IMF (1958-83)	D. ILO (1930-45)	E. UN-SY (1973-83)		F. IMF (1964-80)
1913	2.0	1930	-9.0			-9.8			
1914	.0	1931	-3.7			-2.7			
1915	8.8	1932	.4			0			
1916	7.2	1933	-.9			-1.4			
1917	10.0	1934	7.7			8.5			
1918	12.2	1935	5.6			5.2			
1919	3.4"	1936	14.7			14.8			
1920	9.9	1937	7.6			7.5			
1921	3.0	1938	4.3			4.0			
1922	9.3	1939	2.6			2.9			
1923	10.1	1940				3.7			
1924	16.9	1941		11.7		11.7			
1925	6.6	1942		12.1		12.1			
1926	3.1	1943		10.8		10.8			
1927	2.6	1944		10.4		10.4			
1928	-1.5	1945		15.9		15.9			
1929	-.7	1946		12.7					
		1947		29.6					
		1948		8.7					
		1949		-2.0					
		1950		6.1					
		1951		8.7					
		1952		17.7					
		1953		22.0					
		1954		18.0					
		1955		20.3					
		1956		21.8					
		1957		19.1					
		1958		15.0	16.1				
		1959		37.6	38.9				
		1960		38.0	30.0				
		1961		40.7	32.3				
		1962		52.8	51.2				
		1963		72.3	70.8				
		1964		87.1	91.4				87.9
		1965		61.5	65.9				31.2
		1966		46.7	41.3				39.4
		1967		29.6	30.4				28.9
		1968		24.4	22.0				27.8
		1969		23.1	22.7				20.3
		1970		19.1	22.3				18.2
		1971		21.1	20.2				18.9
		1972		6.8	16.5				18.9
		1973		15.5	12.7		15.0		23.4
		1974		24.9	27.6		25.2		33.5
		1975		28.4	29.0*		30.6		35.3
		1976			42.0		35.1		46.7
		1977			43.7		40.6		44.7
		1978			38.7		38.4		44.1
		1979			52.7		50.2		57.6
		1980			82.8		78.0		94.6*
		1981			105.6		95.6		97.8
		1982			98.0		89.3		96.4
		1983			142.0		135.8		146.0

1. See table 3200.
2. Rio de Janeiro.

SOURCE: Calculations were made from the following:

A. Mario Henrique Simonson, "Brazilian Inflation: Postwar Experience and Outcome of the 1964 Reforms," *Economic Development Issues: Latin America* (New York: Committee for Economic Development, 1967), p. 269.
B. J. L. Martin, SALA, 18-1413.
C. IMF-IFS-Y, 1983, p. 70; IMF-IFS-Y, 1984, pp. 102-103.
D. ILO-YLS, 1945/1946, p. 194.
E. UN-MB, Dec. 1984, p. 220; UN-SY, 1981, p. 169.
F. IMF-IFS-S, No. 8, 1984, pp. 76-77.

Table 3204

CHILE COMPARATIVE PC OF PRICES,[1] 1899–1983
(YA)

PART I.

Year	Consumer[2] — A. Latorre[3] (1899-1928)
1899	22.5
1900	18.4
1901	-16.4
1902	17.5
1903	4.4
1904	4.2
1905	9.7
1906	-3.7
1907	34.4
1908	17.6
1909	-.5
1910	6.3
1911	4.1
1912	-4.8
1913	4.1
1914	8.8
1915	37.4
1916	-18.3
1917	30.8
1918	-8.0
1919	9.9
1920	23.6
1921	-12.2
1922	5.1
1923	4.6
1924	2.1
1925	24.1
1926	-12.9
1927	-9.8
1928	20.3

PART II.

Year	Consumer[2] A. Latorre[3] (1929-57)	B. UN-SY (1931-83)[a]	C. Martin (1941-75)	D. IMF (1964-83)	E. Chile (1930-40)	GDP Deflator F. IMF (1962-82)
1929	1.7					
1930	-24.3					
1931	-19.0	0			-.9	
1932	55.1	6.6			-3.7	
1933	31.3	23.1			8.6	
1934	-4.4	0			23.9	
1935	10.6	2.5			0	
1936	27.4	8.5			0	
1937	25.6	12.4			12.1	
1938	-10.3	4.0			12.1	
1939	-10.2	1.9			4.5	
1940	10.9	12.3			1.6	
1941	21.1	15.1	12.3		12.3	
1942	32.2	26.3	15.1			
1943	6.8	16.2	26.3			
1944	8.9	11.4	16.2			
1945	33.4	8.9	21.4			
1946	6.2	16.0	16.0			
1947	31.3	33.6	34.9			
1948	15.5		17.6			
1949	12.1		19.0			
1950	26.1		15.1			
1951	37.5		21.9			
1952	23.9		22.2			
1953	24.7		25.0			
1954	57.3		72.0			
1955	79.7		75.6			
1956	45.6		56.0			
1957	29.1		33.1			
1958			19.9			
1959			38.7			
1960			9.3			
1961			7.0			
1962			13.1			14.9
1963			44.9			27.1
1964			46.0	46.0		55.2
1965			28.8	28.8*		39.2
1966			22.9	23.1		28.0
1967			18.2	18.8		27.6
1968			26.4	26.3		31.5
1969			30.7	30.6		41.0
1970			32.6	33.0		32.5
1971			20.1	19.2*		32.6
1972			77.5	77.3		79.1
1973		354.0	354.0	353.6		429.5
1974		504.6	504.6	504.7		692.3
1975		374.7	376.6	374.7*		342.5
1976		212.0		211.8		250.7
1977		92.0		91.9		103.6
1978		40.1		40.1		56.6
1979		33.4*		33.4		46.3
1980		35.1		35.1		29.2
1981		19.7		19.7		13.4
1982		9.9		9.9		11.3
1983		27.3		27.3		

1. See table 3200.
2. Santiago.
3. Food only.

a. Selected periods only.

SOURCE: Calculations were made from the following:

A. Adolfo Latorre Subercaseaux, "Relación Entre el Circulante y los Precios en Chile,"
   Memoria para Optar al Título de Ingeniero Comercial, Universidad Católica de Chile, 1958.
B. UN-SY, 1949-50, p. 401; UN-MB, Dec. 1984, p. 220; UN-SY, 1981, p. 170.
C. J. L. Martin, SALA, 18-1414.
D. IMF-IFS-Y, 1984, pp. 102-103.
E. Chile, DGE, Estadística Chilena, Sept. 1933, Jan. 1936, Jan.-Feb., 1940,
   Aug. 1941.
F. IMF-IFS-S, No. 8, 1984, pp. 76-77.

Table 3205

COLOMBIA COMPARATIVE PC OF PRICES,[1] 1929–83

(YA)

Year	Consumer[2]					GDP Deflator
	A. Urrutia (1929-48)	B. IMF (1938-54)	C. Martin (1941-75)	D. IMF (1953-82)	E. UN-SY[3] (1973-83)	F. IMF (1951-83)
1929	-1.8					
1930	-16.6					
1931	-8.8					
1932	-15.9					
1933	2.9					
1934	38.9					
1935	3.6					
1936	5.7					
1937	3.0					
1938	12.6	13.0				
1939	4.3	4.4				
1940	-3.0	-3.4				
1941	-1.4	-1.8	-1.8			
1942	8.7	8.9	8.9			
1943	15.9	15.6	15.6			
1944	20.3	20.6	20.6			
1945	11.4	11.2	11.2			
1946	9.2	9.5	9.5			
1947	18.2	18.4	17.8			
1948	16.4	16.3	16.3			
1949		7.4	7.4			
1950		19.6	20.6			
1951		9.3	8.0			10.1
1952		-2.3	-2.1			1.6
1953		7.4	7.3	8.3		4.8
1954		8.8	9.0	7.7		11.2
1955			0	-.8*		0
1956			6.4	6.5		7.8
1957			14.7	15.2		17.2
1958			15.0	14.6		13.3
1959			9.2	7.2		6.6
1960			3.3	3.8		8.5
1961			8.7	8.7		8.2
1962			2.5	2.5		6.7
1963			31.9	32.0		23.2
1964			17.7	17.6		16.3
1965			3.5	3.5		9.2
1966			19.9	19.9		14.9
1967			8.2	8.1		8.3
1968			5.9	5.8		9.4
1969			10.1	10.1		8.2
1970			6.8	6.8		9.5
1971			9.0	9.0*		10.8
1972			14.3	13.4		13.0
1973			22.7	20.8	22.4	20.2
1974			24.5	24.3	24.2	25.4
1975			29.3	22.9	25.8	22.8
1976				20.2	17.6	25.5
1977				33.1	29.9	29.2
1978				17.8	17.3	17.1
1979				24.7	24.3*	24.0
1980				26.5	28.0	27.6
1981				27.5	29.4	22.8
1982				24.5	24.0	24.6
1983				19.8	19.5	17.1

1. See table 3200.
2. Bogotá.
3. Low income group.

SOURCE: Calculations were made from the following:
 A. Miguel Urrutia Montoya and Mario Arrubla, eds., *Compendio de Estadísticas Históricas de Colombia* (Bogotá, D.E.: Universidad Nacional de Colombia, 1970), pp. 81-82.
 B. IMF-IFS, July 1950 and Jan. 1956.
 C. J. L. Martin, SALA, 18-1415.
 D. IMF-IFS-Y, 1983, p. 70; IMF-IFS-Y, 1984, pp. 102-103.
 E. UN-MB, Dec. 1984, p. 220; UN-SY, 1981, p. 170.
 F. IMF-IFS-S, No. 2, 1981, pp. 10-11; IMF-IFS-S, No. 8, 1984, pp. 76-77.

Table 3206

COSTA RICA COMPARATIVE PC OF PRICES,[1] 1937–83
(YA)

| Year | Consumer[2] | | | | GDP Deflator |
	A. Banco-Central (1937-68)	B. Martin (1941-75)	C. IMF (1953-83)	D. UN-SY[3] (1973-83)	E. IMF (1961-82)
1937	5.3				
1938	-2.8				
1939	2.2				
1940	-4.1				
1941	6.1	3.0			
1942	30.1	20.6			
1943	25.4	28.5			
1944	4.7	5.7			
1945	9.6	6.0			
1946	.1	4.0			
1947	16.1	14.1			
1948	1.6	3.1			
1949	-.9	8.0			
1950	13.0	10.2			
1951	3.2	6.3			
1952	-10.0	-2.0			
1953	-4.4	0	.6		
1954	4.6	3.0	2.5		
1955	1.9	4.4	3.7		
1956	1.1	.9	1.0		
1957	-.5	2.8	2.9		
1958	.7	2.7	2.7		
1959	-.9	.3	.3		
1960	-.4	.9	.8		
1961	2.7	3.4	2.4		3.2
1962	-.5	2.7	2.7		.6
1963	2.7	3.0	3.0		2.0
1964	1.6	3.3	3.2*		1.8
1965	-.8	-.7	-.7		-.9
1966	.4	.2	.2		1.2
1967	3.1	1.1	1.2		2.3
1968	2.2	4.0	4.0		2.0
1969		2.8	2.7		4.6
1970		4.6	4.7		7.3
1971		3.1	3.1		2.4
1972		4.6	4.6		6.4
1973		15.2	15.2	14.8[a]	14.8
1974		30.1	30.1	30.6[a]	23.2
1975		16.3	17.4*	17.3	24.5
1976			3.5	3.2*	16.6
1977			4.2	4.1	16.9
1978			6.0	6.4	7.9
1979			9.2	8.8	9.2
1980			18.1	18.2	18.8
1981			37.1	37.0	44.5
1982			90.1	90.0	82.5
1983			32.6	32.7	

1. See table 3200.
2. San José.
3. Greater San José.

a. Average of less than 12 months.

SOURCE: Calculations were made from the following:
A. Costa Rica, Banco Central, data provided to SALA.
B. J. L. Martin, SALA, 18-1416.
C. IMF-IFS-Y, 1983, p. 70; IMF-IFS-Y, 1984, pp. 102-103.
D. UN-MB, Dec. 1984, p. 220; UN-SY, 1981, p. 70.
E. IMF-IFS-S, No. 2, 1981, pp. 10-11; IMF-IFS-S, No. 8, 1984, pp. 76-77.

Table 3207

CUBA PRICES,[1] 1938–83

Year	A. DGE (1938-62)[a]	B. Havana Related to New York City[2]
1938	-.5	
1939	-5.8	
1940	-1.8	
1941	8.6	
1942	32.5	
1943	13.9	
1944	14.0	
1945	13.0	
1946	9.5	
1947	16.9	
1948	9.1	
1949	-13.2	
1950	-2.7	
1951	10.5	
1952	.3	
1953	-2.4	
1954	-5.5	
1955	-2.3	
1956	-.7	
1957	6.5	
1958	3.1	
1959	~	
1960	~	
1961	~	
1962	5.8[b]	
1963		~
1964		~
1965		~
1966		~
1967		~
1968		~
1969		-3.1[f]
1970		~
1971		~
1972		~
1973		~
1974		2.3[g]
1975		-5.6[h]
1976		0[i]
1977		0[j]
1978		-1.2[k]
1979		13.3
1980		~
1981		~
1982		10.3[d]
1983		-11.5[a]

1. See table 3200.
2. Cost of living for U.N. officials converted to PC.

a. Havana food prices.
b. May 1961 to May 1962.
c. June 1978 to April 1979.
d. December 1981 to March 1982.
e. March 1982 to July 1983.
f. October 1968 to December 1969.
g. March 1973 to April 1974.
h. April 1974 to May 1975.
i. May 1975 to May 1976.
j. May 1976 to May 1977.
k. May 1977 to June 1978.

SOURCE: Calculations were made from the following:
   A. Cuba, DGE, AE, 1957, pp. 409-410, and for 1962, Dudley Seers, ed., *Cuba: The Economic and Social Revolution* (Chapel Hill: University of North Carolina Press, 1964), p. 33.
   B. SALA, 20-2520 and SALA, 24-3222.

Table 3208

DOMINICAN REPUBLIC COMPARATIVE PC OF PRICES,[1] 1942–82

(YA)

| Year | Consumer[2] | | | GDP Deflator |
	A. UN-SY[3] (1942-82)	B. Martin (1942-75)	C. IMF (1953-82)	D. IMF (1951-82)
1942	20.0	20.0		
1943	25.0	25.0		
1944	16.0	16.0		
1945	4.0	4.0		
1946	11.6	11.6		
1947	12.4	12.5		
1948	.9	1.0		
1949	-3.9	-4.0		
1950	-1.1	0		
1951	8.7	7.5		8.7
1952	1.0	1.0		-.4
1953	-1.0	-1.0	-1.6	.6
1954	-2.0	-4.0	-1.8	-.5
1955		0	0	-2.6
1956		1.0	1.3	1.9
1957		5.2	4.8	6.1
1958		-2.0	-1.9	-.8
1959		-.1	-.1	-7.2
1960		3.6	-3.6*	3.9
1961		-3.7	-3.9	-3.0
1962		9.0	9.2	8.3
1963		8.5	8.6	6.7
1964		2.2	2.1	7.0
1965		-1.9	-1.9	-4.7
1966		.3	.3	-.5
1967		1.9	1.2	1.0
1968		1.7	.1	2.0
1969		-1.9	.9*	4.3
1970		5.2	3.8	1.8
1971		3.0	4.3	1.2
1972		7.8	7.8	8.0
1973	14.8	15.1	15.1	4.5
1974	12.9	13.1	13.2	17.9
1975	15.0	13.7	14.5	16.7
1976	7.5		7.8	2.9
1977	13.3		12.8	10.6
1978	3.1		3.5*	1.0
1979	9.4		9.2	11.1
1980	~		16.8	13.7
1981	7.5		7.5	4.6
1982	7.6		7.6	8.0

1. See table 3200.
2. Santo Domingo.
3. Including direct taxes, 1981–82.

SOURCE: Calculations were made from the following:
    A.   UN-SY, 1949-50, p. 41; for 1950–54 data, see UN-SY, 1955, p. 446; UN-MB, Dec. 1984, p. 220; UN-SY, 1981, p. 170. Selected periods only.
    B.   IMF-IFS-Y, 1983, p. 70; IMF-IFS-Y, 1984, pp. 102-103.
    C.   IMF-IFS-S, No. 2, 1981, pp. 10-11; IMF-IFS-S, No. 8, 1984, pp. 76-77.

Table 3209

ECUADOR COMPARATIVE PC OF PRICES,[1] 1922–83
(YA)

PART I.			PART II.					GDP Deflator
Consumer[2]			Consumer[2]					
Year	A. Rodríguez[3] (1922-29)	Year	A. Rodríguez[2] (1930-42)	B. Banco Central[2] (1940-51)	C. Martin (1951-75)	D. IMF (1953-83)	E. UN-SY[4] (1973-83)	F. IMF (1951-83)
1922	13.1	1930	–.7					
1923	9.3	1931	–25.8					
1924	12.9	1932 } 1933	26.4					
1925	4.1	1934	38.0					
1926	25.4	1935	–2.7					
1927	–6.9	1936	22.0					
1928	–18.1	1937	19.9					
1929	3.9	1938	–3.2					
		1939	.5					
		1940	2.1	2.3				
		1941	8.5	3.0				
		1942	30.2	29.2				
		1943		21.8				
		1944		23.0				
		1945		30.0				
		1946		15.2				
		1947		13.7				
		1948		12.1				
		1949		–1.9				
		1950		–1.4				
		1951		14.7	5.4			4.2
		1952			3.0			3.2
		1953			0	.6		2.4
		1954			3.0	3.6		3.4
		1955			2.0	1.4		3.1
		1956			–4.9	–5.0		–1.5
		1957			1.0	1.2		1.2
		1958			1.0	1.3		.6
		1959			0	–.1		.1
		1960			7.0	1.7		1.9
		1961			3.8	4.0		4.9
		1962			2.8	2.9		2.2
		1963			6.3	5.9		4.2
		1964			3.4	4.0		3.3
		1965			3.3	3.1		5.1*
		1966			4.0	5.5*		6.5
		1967			3.8	3.8		4.5
		1968			4.4	4.3		4.4
		1969			6.3	6.3		7.5
		1970			5.3	5.1		9.1
		1971			8.4	8.4		7.6
		1972			7.9	7.9		2.3
		1973			12.9	13.0*	12.8	6.0
		1974			23.4	23.3	23.5	40.0
		1975			15.6	15.4	15.3	10.0
		1976				10.7	10.6	13.0
		1977				13.0	13.0	17.5
		1978				11.7	11.9	7.9
		1979				10.3	10.3	16.1
		1980				13.0*	12.8	19.5
		1981				13.0*	12.0	14.8
		1982				16.3	16.3	17.1
		1983				48.4	48.4	40.4

1. See table 3200.
2. Quito.
3. Food only.
4. Quito.

SOURCE: Calculations were made from the following:
   A.   Linda A. Rodríguez, *The Search for Public Policy: Regional Politics and Govern-
        ment Finances in Ecuador*, 1830–1940 (Berkeley and Los Angeles: University of
        California Press, 1985).
   B.   Ecuador, Banco Central, *Boletín*, July-Aug. 1952, p. 142.
   C.   J. L. Martin, SALA, 18-1418.
   D.   IMF-IFS-Y, 1983, p. 70; IMF-IFS-Y, 1984, pp. 102-103.
   E.   UN-MB, Dec. 1984, p. 220; UN-SY, 1981, p. 170.
   F.   IMF-IFS-S, No. 2, 1981, pp. 10-11; IMF-IFS-S, No. 8, 1984, pp. 76-77.

Table 3210

EL SALVADOR COMPARATIVE PC OF PRICES,[1] 1938-83
(YA)

Year	Consumer[2]			GDP Deflator
	A. UN-SY[3] (1938-83)	B. Martin (1941-75)	C. IMF (1953-83)	D. IMF (1952-83)
1938	−12.5			
1939	−5.7			
1940	3.0			
1941	11.8	11.8		
1942	2.6	2.6		
1943	10.3	10.3		
1944	30.2	30.2		
1945	12.5	12.5		
1946	−1.6	1.6		
1947	6.5	6.5		
1948	1.5	1.5		
1949	4.5	4.5		
1950	17.1	17.1		
1951	15.9	15.9		
1952	−1.1	1.1		−3.1
1953	6.4	6.4	6.6	3.7
1954	4.0	4.0	3.7	4.6
1955		1.0	4.1*	−.8
1956		1.9	1.5	−2.1
1957		−4.7	−4.5	−1.7
1958		4.9	5.7	−1.3
1959		2.8	−.6	−2.8
1960		#	−.1	−5.6
1961		−2.7	−2.8	−2.9
1962		.9	.2	1.1
1963		.9	1.5	2.1
1964		1.8	1.6	.8
1965		#	.7	1.3
1966		−.9	−1.2	−1.2
1967		1.8	1.4	−.4
1968		1.8	2.6	.2
1969		#	−.2	.4
1970		2.6	2.8	4.8
1971		.3	.4	.3
1972		1.7	1.6	1.1
1973	5.9	6.4	6.4	10.0
1974	17.6	16.9	16.9	11.2
1975	18.9	20.8	19.2	7.6
1976	7.3		7.0	22.6
1977	11.7		11.8	18.4
1978	13.3		13.2	.9
1979	~*		14.6	13.9
1980	17.0		17.4	13.4
1981	14.7		14.8	5.7
1982	11.7		11.7	9.9
1983	13.2		13.3	8.0

1. See table 3200.
2. San Salvador.
3. Urban areas since 1983. Selected periods.

SOURCE: Calculations were made from the following:
   A. UN-SY, 1955, p. 446; UN-MB, Dec. 1984, p. 220; UN-SY, 1981, p. 170.
   B. J. L. Martin, SALA, 18-1419.
   C. IMF-IFS-Y, 1983, p. 70; IMF-IFS-Y, 1984, pp. 102-103.
   D. IMF-IFS-S, No. 2, 1981, pp. 10-11; IMF-IFS-S, No. 8, 1984, pp. 76-77.

Table 3211

GUATEMALA COMPARATIVE PC OF PRICES,[1] 1939-83

(YA)

| Year | Consumer[2] | | | | GDP Deflator |
	A. Adler, et. al (1939-49)[a]	B. Martin (1941-75)	C. IMF (1953-82)	D. UN-SY[3] (1973-82)	E. IMF (1951-83)
1939	-3.7				
1940	-2.0				
1941	-6.6	-4.4			
1942	3.2	14.9			
1943	23.6	11.0			
1944	20.8	17.1			
1945	19.3	25.4			
1946	17.8	18.4			
1947	14.0	2.1			
1948	6.9	6.4			
1949	4.3	7.0			
1950		7.5			
1951		4.3			5.0
1952		-2.5			-1.8
1953		3.1	3.0		3.4
1954		3.0	2.7		4.2
1955		1.9	1.7		1.2
1956		1.0	1.0		1.6
1957		-1.9	-1.1		-1.2
1958		1.9	1.1		-.8
1959		-1.0	-.5		1.3
1960		-1.0	-1.2		-1.7
1961		-.5	-.5		-1.1
1962		2.1	2.1		2.6
1963		.1	.1		.8
1964		-.2	-.2		-2.0
1965		-.7	-.8		-1.4
1966		.6	.7		-1.0
1967		.5	.5		.4
1968		1.8	1.9		1.9
1969		2.2	2.1		1.7
1970		2.4	2.4		5.0
1971		-.5	-.5		-1.3
1972		.5	.5		-1.4
1973		14.4	13.8	14.0	14.5
1974		16.0	16.5	16.7	15.7
1975		16.1	13.2*	~*	13.1
1976			10.7	11.0	11.5
1977			12.6	12.6	16.5
1978			7.9	7.2	5.5
1979			11.5	11.9	8.6
1980			10.7	10.7	10.0
1981			11.4	11.4	8.5
1982			.4	#	5.1
1983					#

1. See table 3200.
2. Guatemala City.
3. Urban areas since 1975 (prior to 1975, Guatemala City only).

a. Wholesale prices spliced to consumer price index beginning in 1946.

SOURCE: Calculations were made from the following:
  A. John H. Adler et al., *Las Finanzas Públicas y el Desarrollo de Guatemala*
      (México, D.F.: Fondo de Cultura Económica, 1952), p. 256.
  B. J. L. Martin, SALA, 18-1420.
  C. IMF-IFS-Y, 1983, p. 70; IMF-IFS-Y, 1984, pp. 102-103.
  D. UN-MB, Dec. 1984, p. 222; UN-SY, 1981, p. 171.
  E. IMF-IFS-S, No. 2, 1981, pp. 10-11; IMF-IFS-S, No. 8, 1984, pp. 76-77.

Table 3212

HAITI COMPARATIVE PC OF PRICES,[1]
1949–83
(YA)

| Year | Consumer[2] | | GDP Deflator |
	A. IMF (1949-83)	B. UN-SY (1973-83)	C. IMF (1956-83)
1949			
1950	2.3		
1951			
1952	6.7		
1953	-7.4		
1954	4.3		
1955	1.6		
1956	3.6		-3.0
1957	2.3		5.5
1958	-.3		-2.3
1959	-4.8		-6.8
1960	-5.0		-1.9
1961	3.7		1.6
1962	-.6		-4.0
1963	4.2		7.7
1964	9.3		12.1
1965	2.2		6.3
1966	8.3		2.5
1967	-2.9		2.2
1968	1.3		-3.4
1969	1.4		2.6
1970	1.3		4.2
1971	9.5		3.4
1972	3.2		1.3
1973	22.7	22.8	29.2
1974	15.0	15.7	14.58
1975	16.8	16.0	19.2
1976	7.0	6.4	18.9
1977	6.5	7.0	10.9
1978	-2.7	-2.8	-1.5
1979	13.1	13.0	2.9
1980	17.8*	17.9	21.8
1981	10.9*	11.0	3.6
1982	7.4	7.2	4.3
1983	10.2	10.3	10.0

1. See table 3200.
2. Port-au-Prince.

SOURCE: Calculations were made from the following.
    A. IMF-IFS-Y, 1972, p. 144; for 1954: IMF-IFS-Y, 1983, p. 70; since 1955: IMF-IFS-Y, 1984, pp. 102-103.
    B. UN-MB, Dec. 1984, p. 222; UN-SY, 1981, p. 171.
    C. IMF-IFS-S, No. 2, 1981, pp. 10-11; IMF-IFS-S, No. 8, 1984, pp. 76-77.

Table 3213

HONDURAS COMPARATIVE PC OF PRICES,[1] 1926–83

(YA)

| | PART I. | | PART II. | | | | | GDP Deflator |
| | Consumer[2] | | Consumer[2] | | | | | |
Year	A. Banco Central (1926-29)[a]	Year	A. Banco Central (1930-53)[a]	B. Martin (1949-75)	C. IMF (1953-83)	D. UN-SY[3] (1973-83)		E. IMF (1951-83)
1926	-1.2	1930	-5.2					
1927	2.5	1931	-2.5					
1928	-.3	1932	-7.6					
1929	2.0	1933	-.8					
		1934	1.5					
		1935	1.7					
		1936	-2.6					
		1937	-2.4					
		1938	3.3					
		1939	-1.9					
		1940	7.0					
		1941	4.1					
		1942	11.9					
		1943	1.3					
		1944	9.9					
		1945	7.7					
		1946	3.6					
		1947	1.8					
		1948	1.9					
		1949	4.1	5.0				
		1950	3.8	5.7				
		1951	6.9	10.8				1.6
		1952	-4.8	-2.0				1.8
		1953	6.6	2.0	2.3			2.2
		1954		6.0	5.9			.9
		1955		8.5	8.4			1.2
		1956		-4.3	-4.0			.4
		1957		-1.8	-1.9			-.6
		1958		2.8	2.8			1.0
		1959		.9	1.1			1.3
		1960		-1.8	-1.8			2.1
		1961		1.7	1.7			3.3
		1962		1.1	1.0			3.5
		1963		2.9	3.1			2.5
		1964		4.6	4.5			5.2
		1965		3.2	3.2			.9
		1966		.2	1.7			2.2
		1967		1.2	.8			3.9
		1968		2.6	4.8			1.2
		1969		1.8	2.1			3.4
		1970		2.9	.9			2.5
		1971		3.1	2.1			1.8
		1972		5.4	5.4			4.3
		1973		4.1	5.2	4.7		6.6
		1974		12.6	12.8	12.6		11.7
		1975		5.8	6.3	8.0		9.3
		1976			4.8	5.2		8.5
		1977			8.4	8.5		13.5
		1978			6.1	5.8		6.9
		1979			12.5	8.6		7.5
		1980			15.6	18.6		10.6
		1981			10.2	9.4		5.2
		1982			10.0	9.4		7.4
		1983			9.5	8.9		6.1

1. See table 3200.
2. Tegucigalpa.
3. Honduras.

a. San Pedro Sula.

SOURCE: Calculations were made from the following:
  A. Honduras, Banco Central, *Boletín*, 4 (1954), p. 38.
  B. J. L. Martin, SALA, 18-1421.
  C. IMF-IFS-Y, 1983, p. 70.
  D. UN-MB, Dec. 1984, p. 222; UN-SY, 1981, p. 171.
  E. IMF-IFS-S, No. 2, 1981, pp. 10-11; IMF-IFS-S, No. 8, 1984, pp. 76-77.

Table 3214

MEXICO COMPARATIVE PC OF PRICES,[1] 1901-83

(YA)

PART I.			PART II.					GDP Deflator
	Consumer[2]			Consumer[2]				
Year	A. DGE (1901-29)	Year	A. DGE (1930-75)	B. Martin (1935-75)	C. IMF (1953-83)[a]	D. UN-SY (1973-83)		E. IMF (1949-83)
1901	22.8	1930	.6					
1902	2.5	1931	-10.6					
1903	-.4	1932	-8.8					
1904	-1.8	1933	6.3					
1905	10.7	1934	3.2					
1906	-.6	1935	.7	8.0				
1907	-1.5	1936	6.2	5.6				
1908	3.8	1937	18.6	21.9				
1909	6.3	1938	4.5	10.1				
1910	17.4	1939	2.6	1.8				
1911	-5.2	1940	.5	1.3				
1912	-.7	1941	6.3	3.4				
1913	-1.0	1942	10.6	16.5				
1914	~	1943	19.9	30.7				
1915	~	1944	28.2	25.7				
1916	~	1945	10.0	7.4				
1917	~	1946	17.1	24.7				
1918	~	1947	2.1	11.9				
1919	-20.0	1948	6.2	6.4				
1920	4.8	1949	5.9	5.0				-.1
1921	-8.7	1950	11.1	6.7				3.6
1922	-16.1	1951	20.6	12.5				#
1923	7.1	1952	9.9	14.3				-.4
1924	-4.2	1953	2.0	-2.0	-1.8			-.1
1925	4.9	1954	7.7	5.0	5.2			.6
1926	-1.8	1955	15.4	15.7	16.0			.3
1927	-2.4	1956	6.1	4.9	4.8			-.1
1928	-4.0	1957	6.2	5.5	5.8			#
1929	-.4	1958	4.6	11.5	11.5			.2
		1959	1.5	2.5	2.5			-.1
		1960	5.7	4.9	4.9			-.2
		1961	.9	1.7	1.7			1.3
		1962	1.4	1.2	1.1			3.7
		1963	1.5	.6	.6			.3
		1964	3.6	2.2	2.2			1.7
		1965	3.9	3.6	3.6			9.1
		1966	1.0	4.3	4.3			4.4
		1967	0	3.0	2.9			.3
		1968	1.7	2.4	2.4*			2.4
		1969	1.2	2.8	3.4			4.0
		1970	4.6	5.2	5.2			10.8
		1971		3.2	5.3			5.9
		1972		6.4	5.0			6.2
		1973		16.5	12.0	12.0		12.9
		1974		31.2	23.8	24.1		22.7
		1975		18.3	15.2	17.3		15.8
		1976			15.8	16.6		19.6
		1977			29.0	26.3		30.4
		1978			17.5	16.7		16.8
		1979			18.2	18.2		20.2
		1980			26.4	26.3		28.7
		1981			27.9	28.0		27.2
		1982			58.9	58.9		61.2
		1983			101.9	101.9		94.1

1. See table 3200.
2. Mexico City.

a. Bank of Mexico Series.

SOURCE: Calculations were made from the following:
A.   James W. Wilkie, *The Mexican Revolution: Federal Expenditure and Social Change
     Since 1910* (Berkeley: University of California Press, 1967), p. 23 (and sources
     cited there); and since 1964 Mexico, DGE, *Compendio Estadístico*, 1970, p. 296.
B.   J. L. Martin, SALA 18-1422.
C.   IMF-IFS-Y, 1983, p. 70; IMF-IFS-Y, 1984, pp. 102-103.
D.   UN-MB, Dec. 1984, p. 222; UN-SY, 1981, p. 173.
E.   IMF-IFS-S, No. 2, 1981, pp. 10-11; IMF-IFS-S, No. 8, 1984, pp. 76-77.

Table 3215

NICARAGUA COMPARATIVE PC OF PRICES,[1] 1938-83
(YA)

| Year | Consumer[2] | | | | | GDP Deflator |
	A. UN-SY Food Prices (1938-49)	B. Martin (1941-71)	C. IMF (1956-83)	D. DeFranco and Chamorro (1969-77)	E. UN-SY[3] (1974-80)	F. IMF (1961-83)
1938	51.0					
1939	48.3					
1940	22.3					
1941	-1.8	-1.8				
1942	34.9	34.9				
1943	31.7	31.7				
1944	70.1	70.1				
1945	17.3	17.3				
1946	-19.1	-19.1				
1947	8.0	8.0				
1948	-6.0	-6.0				
1949	-4.5	-4.5				
1950		18.8				
1951		20.2				
1952		.7				
1953		10.9				
1954		8.0				
1955		19.4				
1956		-7.5	-7.6			
1957		-3.3	-3.2			
1958		4.5	4.8			
1959		-2.9	-2.9			
1960		-2.0	-2.0			
1961		.2	.2			.1
1962		-.3	-.3			-.7
1963		.8	.8			-.3
1964		9.6	4.6			4.5
1965		3.9	2.9			.9
1966		3.9	4.0			3.7
1967		1.6	.4			1.3
1968		3.1	3.7			4.5
1969		0	.3	2.0[†]		1.2
1970		5.9	~	5.9		2.4
1971		5.6	~	5.6		1.4
1972			~	3.3		1.5
1973			27.0	16.8[†]		17.5
1974			13.3	20.5[†]	12.4	23.0
1975			7.5	1.8	8.0	3.1
1976			2.8	2.8	2.8	9.3
1977			11.4	11.4	10.8	8.0
1978			4.6		4.9	5.0
1979			48.2		48.1	38.3
1980			35.3*		35.1	37.1
1981			23.9		~	11.8
1982			24.8		~	16.6
1983			31.1		~	14.7

1. See table 3200.
2. Managua.
3. Metropolitan area.

SOURCE: Calculations were made from the following:
    A. UN-SY, 1949-50, p. 401.
    B. J. L. Martin, SALA, 18-1423.
    C. IMF-IFS-Y, 1972, pp. 156-157; IMF-IFS-Y, 1983, p. 71; IMF-IFS-Y, 1984, p. 103.
D. Mario A. De Franco and Carlos F. Chamorro, "Nicaragua: Crecimiento Industrial y Desempleo," in D. Camacho et al., El Fracaso Social de la Integración Centroamericana (San José, Costa Rica: Editorial Universitaria Centroamericano, 1979), cited in John A. Booth, The End and the Beginning: The Nicaraguan Revolution (Boulder, Colorado: Westview Press, 1982), p. 79.
E. UN-SY, 1981, p. 173.
F. IMF-IFS-S, No. 2, 1981, p. 10; IMF-IFS-S, No. 8, 1984, pp. 76-77.

Table 3216

PANAMA COMPARATIVE PC OF PRICES,[1] 1941–83
(YA)

| Year | Consumer[2] | | | GDP Deflator |
	A. Martin (1941-75)	B. IMF (1953-83)	C. UN-SY (1973-83)	D. IMF (1952-83)
1941	28.0			
1942	20.3			
1943	2.0			
1944	1.9			
1945	1.9			
1946	8.0			
1947	11.4			
1948	2.0			
1949	-7.0			
1950	-3.2			
1951	4.4			
1952	1.1			-.7
1953	-1.0	-1.3		-.1
1954	1.0	-.5		1.4
1955	0	-.1		2.0
1956	1.0	-.4		-.4
1957	.3	.1		-.3
1958	-.3	-.3		-1.1
1959	.1	.1		-.6
1960	.1	.1		-2.8
1961	.6	.6		.6
1962	.3	.7*		.6
1963	-.6	.5		2.1
1964	2.4	2.4		2.8
1965	.4	.5		.6
1966	.2	.2		1.3
1967	1.3	1.4		2.6
1968	1.7	1.6		.6
1969	1.8	1.8		1.2
1970	3.1	3.1		3.8
1971	2.0	2.0		2.9
1972	5.3	5.3		5.0
1973	6.9	6.9	7.5	8.5
1974	16.8	16.8	16.5	11.6
1975	5.7	5.5*	5.2	9.4
1976		4.0	4.3	4.5
1977		4.5	4.8	4.7
1978		4.2	3.9	7.9
1979		7.9	8.1	9.3
1980		13.8	13.9	10.4
1981		7.3	7.3	4.6
1982		4.3	4.2	4.6
1983		2.1	2.1	1.9

1. See table 3200.
2. Panama City.

SOURCE: Calculations were made from the following:
  A. J. L. Martin, SALA, 18-1424.
  B. IMF-IFS-Y, 1983, p. 70; IMF-IFS-Y, 1984, pp. 102-103.
  C. UN-MB, Dec. 1984, p. 224; UN-SY, 1981, p. 174.
  D. IMF-IFS-S, No. 2, 1981, p. 10; IMF-IFS-S, No. 8, 1984, pp. 76-77.

Table 3217

PARAGUAY COMPARATIVE PC OF PRICES,[1] 1939–83
(YA)

| Year | Consumer[2] | | | GDP Deflator |
	A. UN-SY (1939-82)	B. Martin (1941-75)	C. IMF (1953-83)	D. IMF (1951-82)
1939	9.0			
1940	3.7			
1941	13.3	9.3		
1942	12.5	12.0		
1943	22.2	9.2		
1944	10.0	14.7		
1945	10.9	11.0		
1946	10.3	10.3		
1947	30.9	30.9		
1948	33.3	25.0		
1949	35.4	35.0		
1950		48.1		
1951		58.0		67.0
1952		117.4		86.4
1953		71.0	62.0	70.7
1954		20.0	28.2	34.1
1955		23.3	24.1	24.2
1956		21.6	20.9	22.4
1957		16.1	16.0	21.0
1958		6.2	6.4	7.0
1959		8.1	10.0	13.5
1960		11.3	8.2	17.7
1961		26.5	18.5	8.6
1962		3.1	1.4	7.9
1963		4.0	2.1	4.5
1964		2.0	1.4*	2.0
1965		3.8	3.8	2.8
1966		3.0	2.9	3.9
1967		1.3	1.4	-.5
1968		.6	.7	1.4
1969		2.3	2.1	3.5
1970		-.9	-.7	2.9
1971		5.0	4.8	6.1
1972		9.2	9.5	8.7
1973	12.2	12.7	12.5	20.8
1974	25.6	25.2	25.2	23.8
1975	6.8	5.0	6.8	6.6
1976	4.0		4.6	5.1
1977	9.4		9.3	9.2
1978	10.7		10.6	10.5
1979	28.4		28.3	20.5
1980	22.5		22.4	16.9
1981	13.0		14.0	16.6
1982	5.1		6.8	6.2
1983			13.4	~

1. See table 3200.
2. Asunción.

SOURCE: Calculations were made from the following:
  A. UN-SY, 1949-50, p. 402; UN-MB, Dec. 1984, p. 224; UN-SY, 1981, p. 174.
  B. J. L. Martin, SALA, 18-1425.
  C. IMF-IFS-Y, 1983, p. 70; IMF-IFS-Y, 1984, pp. 102-103.
  D. IMF-IFS-S, No. 2, 1981, p. 10; IMF-IFS-S, No. 8, 1984, pp. 76-77.

Table 3218

PERU COMPARATIVE PC OF PRICES,[1] 1914–83

(YA)

PART I.

Year	Consumer[2] A. Peru (1914-29)
1914	4.0
1915	7.7
1916	9.8
1917	15.4
1918	15.5
1919	14.6
1920	11.7
1921	-5.2
1922	-4.5
1923	-5.3
1924	3.9
1925	7.0
1926	.5
1927	-3.5
1928	6.7
1929	-2.2

PART II.

Year	Consumer[2] A. Peru (1930-41)	B. UN-SY[3,4] (1931-83)	C. Martin (1941-75)	D. IMF (1938-83)	E. League (1929-38)	GDP Deflator F. IMF (1961-83)
1929					-2.6	
1930	-4.5				-4.2	
1931	-6.5	-6.1			-6.5	
1932	-4.4	-5.4			-4.5	
1933	-2.6	-2.3			-2.6	
1934	2.0	1.2			1.8	
1935	1.3	2.3			1.4	
1936	5.3	5.6			5.0	
1937	6.3	6.4			6.6	
1938	1.2	1.0		1.0	1.4	
1939	-1.2	-1.0		-1.0		
1940	7.6	7.0		7.0		
1941	8.2	8.4	8.4	9.3		
1942		12.9	11.6	12.0		
1943		8.4	10.4	9.2		
1944		14.8	13.8	14.7		
1945		11.7	11.6	11.0		
1946		9.3	9.4	9.3		
1947		29.6	17.2	29.6		
1948		31.0	44.4	30.6		
1949		14.8	14.7	14.8		
1950			12.1	14.0		
1951			10.2	10.2		
1952			7.2	6.3		
1953			9.0	9.5		
1954			5.5	5.1		
1955			4.8	4.8		
1956			5.4	5.5		
1957			7.4	7.4		
1958			8.0	8.1		
1959			12.7	12.7		
1960			7.8	8.6		
1961			7.3	6.1		5.7
1962			6.2	6.6		4.2
1963			6.4	5.9		2.9
1964			10.5	9.9		14.9
1965			16.7	16.2		13.1
1966			9.7	9.0		11.2
1967			9.9	9.9		10.8
1968			19.0	19.0		18.4
1969			5.7	6.3		8.0
1970			5.4	5.0		7.3
1971			6.8	6.8		4.5
1972			7.2	7.2		5.3
1973		9.6*	9.5	9.5		14.8
1974		16.8	16.8	16.9		16.6
1975		24.0	24.0	23.6		20.1
1976		33.7		33.5		34.5
1977		38.0		38.1		38.8
1978		57.8		57.8		61.4
1979		67.7		66.7*		78.3
1980		~*		59.2		55.0
1981		75.4		75.4		65.9
1982		64.5		64.4		65.0
1983		111.2		111.2		112.6

1. See table 3200.
2. Lima.
3. Lima and Callao, 1973–80.
4. Metropolitan area, 1981–83.

SOURCE: Calculations were made from the following:
   A. Peru, Dirección Nacional de Estadística, *Extracto Estadístico*, 1927, p. 103; English
       version, 1931-33, p. 53, 1941, p. 384.
   B. UN-SY, 1949-50, p. 402; UN-MB, Dec. 1984, p. 224; UN-SY, 1981, p. 174.
   C. J. L. Martin, SALA, 18-1426.
   D. IMF-IFS-Y, 1983, p. 70; for 1938–52: IMF-IFS, June 1948 and Nov. 1950;
       IMF-IFS-Y, 1971; IMF-IFS-Y, 1984, pp. 102-103.
   E. League of Nations, *Monthly Bulletin of Statistics*, Jan. 1939, p. 32.
   F. IMF-IFS-S, No. 2, 1981, p. 10; IMF-IFS-S, No. 8, 1984, pp. 76-77.

Table 3219

URUGUAY COMPARATIVE PC OF PRICES,[1] 1930–83
(YA)

	Consumer[2]				GDP Deflator
	A. Instituto de Economía	B. UN-SY	C. Martin	D. IMF	E. IMF
Year	(1930-54)	(1931-83)	(1941-75)	(1953-83)	(1961-83)
1930	0				
1931	0	0			
1932	0	–2.0			
1933	–6.5	–5.0			
1934	1.7	0			
1935	3.2	3.2			
1936	–1.0	–1.0			
1937	2.8	3.1			
1938	–.6	–1.0			
1939	5.6	6.1			
1940	4.5	4.8			
1941	–.7	–.9	–.9		
1942	3.0	2.8	2.8		
1943	6.3	5.4	5.4		
1944	3.3	2.5	2.5		
1945	13.0	14.9	14.9		
1946	10.2	10.1	10.1		
1947	6.0	15.7	15.3		
1948	10.6	1.7	2.0		
1949	5.0	5.0	5.0		
1950	–5.0	–4	–3.8		
1951	14.8	13.0	13.9		
1952	13.9	14.6	13.9		
1953	6.7	6.4	17.0	6.6	
1954	11.8	12.0	1.8	11.6	
1955			.8	8.9	
1956			7.3	6.8	
1957			14.4	14.7	
1958			17.9	17.5	
1959			39.3	39.3	
1960			38.3	38.8	
1961			22.7	22.5	19.0
1962			10.9	10.9	11.2
1963			20.6	21.3	18.5
1964			43.2	42.4	43.0
1965			56.6	56.5	59.2
1966			72.7	73.5	83.4
1967			89.1	89.3	77.3
1968			125.4	125.3*	118.1
1969			20.9	20.3	27.2
1970			16.4	17.0	13.3
1971			23.9	24.0	18.1
1972			76.5	76.5	74.7
1973		96.8*	97.0	97.0	105.5
1974		77.0	77.2	77.2	72.1
1975		81.4	75.3	81.4	69.7
1976		50.7		50.6	48.8
1977		58.1		58.2	55.8
1978		44.6		44.5	47.6
1979		66.8		66.8	75.5
1980		63.5		63.5	51.0
1981		34.1		34.0	28.5
1982		19.0		19.0	17.8
1983		49.2		49.2	52.2

1. See table 3200.
2. Montevideo.

SOURCE: Calculations were made from the following:
- A. Uruguay, Instituto de Economía, *Estadísticas Básicas* (Montevideo: Universidad de Uruguay, 1969), p. 93.
- B. UN-SY, 1949-50, p. 402; and since 1950: UN-SY, 1955, p. 448; UN-MB, Dec. 1984, p. 226; UN-SY, 1981, p. 176.
- C. J. L. Martin, SALA, 18-1427.
- D. IMF-IFS-Y, 1983, p. 70; IMF-IFS-Y, 1984, pp. 102-103.
- E. IMF-IFS-S, No. 2, 1981, p. 10; IMF-IFS-S, No. 8, 1984, pp. 76-77.

Table 3220

VENEZUELA COMPARATIVE PC OF PRICES,[1] 1929-83
(YA)

	Consumer[2]				GDP Deflator
Year	A. DGE (1929-48)	B. Martin (1941-75)	C. IMF (1953-82)	D. UN-SY[3] (1973-83)	E. IMF (1951-83)
1929	-4.9				
1930	-6.0				
1931	-8.7				
1932	-1.7				
1933	-9.4				
1934	-6.2				
1935	-6.2				
1936	6.6				
1937	9.5				
1938	-3.7				
1939	1.7				
1940	-.9				
1941	9.1	-1.0			
1942	3.2	9.9			
1943	1.2	9.9			
1944	17.6	15.6			
1945	8.9	0			
1946	6.1	6.4			
1947	9.6	15.3			
1948	5.9	20.5			
1949		-2.0			
1950		-1.0			
1951		2.1			-1.5
1952		-1.0			.2
1953		-1.0	-1.5		-.2
1954		0	.2		.9
1955		0	-.4		.3
1956		0	.9		3.1
1957		1.0	-2.1		11.0
1958		4.8	4.9		1.8
1959		5.1	5.0		-3.8
1960		3.2	3.4		-3.4
1961		-2.8	-2.6		.2
1962		-.4	-.5*		.2
1963		.4	1.1		1.9
1964		1.0	2.1		1.0
1965		1.7	1.7		.3
1966		1.7	1.8		1.7
1967		0	.1		1.4
1968		1.3	1.2		3.0*
1969		2.4	2.4		-1.2
1970		2.6	2.5		3.6
1971		3.3	3.2		6.6
1972		3.0	2.9		4.3
1973		3.9	4.1	4.7	12.1
1974		8.5	8.3	8.1	44.5
1975		9.8	10.2	10.0	-.8
1976			7.7	7.6	5.2
1977			7.8	7.7	8.0
1978			7.1	7.2	6.3
1979			12.4	12.2	21.3
1980			21.6	23.4	24.9
1981			16.0	16.0	12.5
1982			9.7	9.6	1.4
1983			6.3	6.4	2.9

1. See table 3200.
2. Caracas.
3. Metropolitan area.

SOURCE: Calculations were made from the following:
A. Venezuela, DGE, *Boletín de Estadística*, July 1949, p. 18.
B. J. L. Martin, SALA, 18-1428.
C. IMF-IFS-Y, 1983, p. 68.
D. UN-MB, Dec. 1984, p. 226; UN-SY, 1981, p. 176.
E. IMF-IFS-S, No. 2, 1981, p. 8; IMF-IFS-S, No. 8, 1984, pp. 74-75.

Table 3221

UNITED STATES COMPARATIVE PC OF PRICES,[1] 1901–83

(YA)

	PART I.		PART II.				GDP Deflator
	Consumer[2]		Consumer[2]				
Year	A. USBC (1901-29)	Year	A. USBC (1930-69)	B. Martin (1941-75)	C. IMF (1953-83)	D. UN-SY (1973-83)	E. IMF (1949-83)
1901	0	1930	-2.5				
1902	4.0	1931	-8.8				
1903	3.8	1932	-10.3				
1904	0	1933	-5.1				
1905	0	1934	3.4				
1906	0	1935	2.5				
1907	3.7	1936	1.0				
1908	-3.6	1937	3.6				
1909	0	1938	-1.9				
1910	3.7	1939	-1.4				
1911	0	1940	1.0				
1912	3.6	1941	5.0	0			
1913	2.4*	1942	10.7	2.0			
1914	1.3	1943	6.1	-1.0			
1915	1.0	1944	1.7	3.0			
1916	7.6	1945	2.3	2.9			
1917	17.4	1946	8.5	1.9			
1918	17.5	1947	14.4	2.8			
1919	14.9	1948	7.8	0			
1920	15.8	1949	-1.0	1.8			-.9
1921	-10.7	1950	1.0	8.0			2.1
1922	-6.4	1951	7.9	7.8			6.6
1923	1.8	1952	2.2	2.1			1.5
1924	.2	1953	.8	1.0	.8		1.5
1925	2.5	1954	.5	0	.4		1.2
1926	1.0	1955	-.4	0	-.3		2.2
1927	-1.9	1956	1.5	0	1.5		3.2
1928	-1.3	1957	3.6	1.4	3.5		3.4
1929	0	1958	2.7	3.5	2.8		1.7
		1959	.8	2.8	.8		2.4
		1960	1.6	.8	1.6		1.6
		1961	1.0	1.6	1.1*		.9
		1962	1.1	1.1	1.1		1.8
		1963	1.2	1.2	1.2		1.5
		1964	1.3	1.2	1.3		1.5
		1965	1.7	3.1	1.6		2.2
		1966	2.9	2.8	3.1		3.2
		1967	2.9	2.9	2.8		3.0
		1968	4.2	4.1	4.2		4.4
		1969	5.4	5.4	5.4		5.2
		1970		5.9	5.9		5.4
		1971		4.3	4.3		5.0
		1972		3.3	3.3		4.2
		1973		6.2	6.2	5.6	5.8
		1974		11.0	11.0	11.4	8.8
		1975		8.8	9.1	9.4	9.3
		1976			5.8	5.8	5.2
		1977			6.5	6.1	5.8
		1978			7.6	7.7*	7.4
		1979			11.3	11.3	8.7
		1980			13.5	13.4	9.2
		1981			10.4	10.4	9.6
		1982			6.2	6.1	6.0
		1983			3.2	3.2	3.8

1. See table 3200.
2. National Index.

SOURCE: Calculations were made from the following:
  A. USBC-HS, 1975, vol. I, series E135.
  B. J. L. Martin, SALA 18-1429.
  C. IMF-IFS-Y, 1983, p. 68; IMF-IFS-Y, 1984, pp. 100-101.
  D. UN-MB, Dec. 1984, p. 226; UN-SY, 1981, p. 176.
  E. IMF-IFS-S, No. 2, 1981, p. 8; IMF-IFS-S, No. 8, 1984, pp. 74-75.

Table 3222

RETAIL PRICE INDEX RELATING TO LIVING EXPENDITURES OF U.N. OFFICIALS IN LATIN AMERICAN CAPITALS, 20 L, 1966-83

(New York City = 100, December of Each Year)

Country	1966	1970	1971	1972	1973	1974	1975[l]	1976[l]	1977	1978	1979	1980	1981	1982	1983	1984
A. ARGENTINA	~	75	78[e]	64[l]	78[e]	84[i]	46[h]	47	78	143	143	216	110	81	80	73
B. BOLIVIA	81	78[i]	76[i]	~	73[b]	83[e]	82	85	95	93[e]	109	103	104	62[i]	83	89
C. BRAZIL	108	90	88[f]	86[f]	93	100[i]	101	102[a]	100	104[i]	78	94	84	84	64	61
D. CHILE	76	73	76[c]	61[h]	36[i]	68[i]	75	77	93	97	111	116	132	92	85	73
E. COLOMBIA	63	69	66[g]	65[g]	64[g]	67[i]	67	66[h]	79	84	96	96[i]	107	102[h]	90	66
F. COSTA RICA	84	78	66[f]	75[f]	79[a]	91	95[i]	95[h]	93	86	99	105	49	52	70[i]	70
G. CUBA	~	~	81[b]	~	87[b]	89[c]	84[k]	84[k]	84[k]	83[da]	94[c]	~	87[a]	78[ba]	69	~
H. DOMINICAN REP.	~	90	88	88[k]	94[g]	95[i]	100[g]	98	97	90[g]	88[g]	97	91[e]	95[d]	95[e]	102
I. ECUADOR	~	70	68[e]	75[h]	83[h]	82[i]	80	79	73	86	85	87[i]	80	60[h]	59	51
J. EL SALVADOR	~	82	81[f]	85[f]	83	89[e]	87[g]	87	86	96[f]	99	104[e]	98	87[f]	70[g]	70
K. GUATEMALA	91	82	78[e]	78[k]	77[d]	86[i]	88	88[h]	94	101	100[i]	100[i]	99	86[h]	86[b]	95
L. HAITI	~	76	82[k]	87[k]	86[g]	94[k]	92[g]	90[d]	94	99[g]	98[g]	92	97[d]	104[c]	104[c]	75
M. HONDURAS	~	80	82[d]	90[f]	88[k]	87[f]	90[e]	88	91	89[i]	94[g]	99	93	86[i]	87[i]	87
N. MEXICO	95	85	83[f]	85[k]	89[g]	90[i]	92	90[a]	71	79	86	95	100	71	61	54
O. NICARAGUA	~	82	79[g]	88[k]	88[k]	93[c]	91	95	98	91	87[c]	~	111[f]	1.0[h]	65	65
P. PANAMA	~	81	80	86[k]	86[g]	88[g]	88[g]	88	88	90[g]	90[g]	95[h]	98	73[i]	90[i]	97
Q. PARAGUAY	~	77	76[g]	78[h]	71[g]	75[h]	80[h]	79	84	88[f]	104	110[f]	116[i]	101[h]	104[h]	46
R. PERU	94	76	80[g]	80[g]	82[e]	84[g]	90	93[g]	84	72	80	100	104	101	91	67
S. URUGUAY	66	75	81[c]	52[g]	70[d]	69[i]	72	73	83	81[i]	102[i]	115	123	100	70	55
T. VENEZUELA	103	90	88[e]	89[h]	91	88[g]	87[h]	87	92	123[h]	141[i]	142	141[g]	145[h]	71	68

a. Calculated on the basis of the cost of government or subsidized housing which is normally lower than prevailing rentals.
b. March.
c. April.
d. June.
e. July.
f. August.
g. September.
h. October.
i. November.
j. Prior to devaluation of the peso.
k. May.
l. November unless noted otherwise.

SOURCE: UN-MB, various monthly since 1966.

Table 3223

IMF WHOLESALE PRICE INDEX,[1] 13 LC, 1970-83
(YA, 1980 = 100)

Country	1970	1971	1972	1973	1974	1975	1976	1977	1978	1979	1980	1981	1982	1983
A. ARGENTINA[2]	.05	.07	.12	.18	.21	.62	3.73	9.30	22.87	57.00	100.00	209.58	746.60	3,440.5
C. 1. BRAZIL[3]	4.05	4.86	5.77	6.73	8.69	11.06	15.85	22.58	31.07	48.43	100.00	208.18	399.79	1,072.5
2. BRAZIL[2]	4.11	4.99	5.91	6.79	8.78	11.23	15.75	22.15	30.76	47.80	100.00	213.04	413.31	1,094.8
D. 1. CHILE[2]	.007	.008	.014	.086	.965	5.616	18.032	33.549	47.963	71.654	100.000	109.085	116.927	107.1
2. CHILE[4]	.008	.009	.015	.091*	.932	5.464	17.817	32.545	47.234	71.447	100.000	110.120	117.187	166.2
E. COLOMBIA[2]	11.95	13.32	15.76	20.16	27.42	34.39	42.27	53.56	62.99	80.52	100.00	124.06	155.92	189.8
F. COSTA RICA[5]	24.5	26.0	27.5	31.9	44.7	54.3	59.3	63.8	69.6	80.8	100.0	165.3	344.2	~
I. ECUADOR[6]	~	~	~	~	50.1	57.1	66.6	72.1	84.2	93.2	100.0	109.6	128.1	147.1
J. 1. EL SALVADOR[7]	35.0	33.1	35.0	42.4	53.1	54.1	72.8	107.3	86.0	97.4	100.0	105.8	114.2	121.8
2. EL SALVADOR[8]	32.3	32.6	33.9	40.4	52.7	56.5	62.8	70.2	73.5	84.2	100.0	114.8	121.7	134.1
K. 1. GUATEMALA[9]	37.8	38.6	38.3	43.8	53.8	60.4	66.7	75.4	78.2	86.2	100.0	111.7	105.0	~
2. GUATEMALA[10]	37.8	37.9	37.8	43.6	53.0	59.9	66.1	75.8	78.6	86.4	100.0	111.9	104.1	~
N. MEXICO[11]	20.32	21.10	21.68	25.11	30.75	33.97	41.55	58.64	67.89	80.31	100.00	124.44	194.20	40.27
P. PANAMA[12]	33.3	35.1	38.0	42.0	54.8	62.4	67.3	72.1	76.0	86.7	100.0	110.0	119.1	~
Q. PARAGUAY[13]	21.6	24.4	28.9	39.8	52.0	59.9	60.5	65.1	73.5	92.8	100.0	112.2	116.1	141.6
S. URUGUAY[14]	.77	.92	1.71	3.78	6.74	11.63	17.51	26.32	39.10	70.54	100.00	123.44	139.37	241.77
T. 1. VENEZUELA[15]	39.6	41.0	42.5	45.3	52.8	60.0	64.3	71.0	76.3	83.3	100.0	115.1	123.6	131.6
2. VENEZUELA[16]	37.5	38.4	39.4	42.3	49.4	56.4	61.0	68.5	73.7	81.3	100.0	116.0	124.6	134.4
UNITED STATES	41.1	42.4	44.3	50.1	59.6	65.1	68.1	72.3	77.9	87.7	100.0	109.1	111.4	112.9

1. For data covering period 1952-70 see SALA, 23-2623.
2. Home and import goods.
3. Wholesale prices.
4. Home goods.
5. Wholesale prices in San José. Home and import goods.
6. Index compiled by the Central University of Ecuador.
7. Index of wholesale prices based on a sample of 91 commodities, including coffee.
8. Index of wholesale prices based on a sample of 91 commodities, excluding coffee.
9. Wholesale prices in Guatemala City; compiled by the Dirección General de Estadística from a sample of 65 commodities.
10. Home and export goods series. Refers to national products in K.1. Guatemala.
11. Covers 210 home and import goods in Mexico City.
12. Index for the entire country, covering the agricultural, industrial and import sectors.
13. Data as reported directly by the Central Bank to the IMF; covers Asunción only.
14. Covers home and export goods in agriculture and manufacturing.
15. Covers home and import goods for domestic consumption.
16. Covers home goods for domestic consumption.

SOURCE: IMF-IFS-S, 1983; IMF-IFS, June 1984, line 63.

Table 3224

U.N. WHOLESALE PRICE INDEX, 15 LC, 1971-81

(YA, 1970 = 100)

Country	Index	1971	1972	1973	1974	1975	1976	1977	1978	1979	1980	1981
A. ARGENTINA	General	140	247	370	455	1,301	7,770	19,412	47,729	119,082	209,098	437,826
	Finished goods[2]	136	280	354	441	1,379	8,117	19,860	49,190	122,360	220,324	465,074
	Domestic goods	140	247	369	440	1,270	7,408	18,678	47,086	120,457	213,880	~
	Imported goods	123	247	402	550	1,967	15,549	35,175	61,877	119,561	208,383	536,904
	Farm products	148	289	412	455	1,109	6,906	18,318	44,541	111,110	181,761	351,049
	Textiles	133	234	363	468	1,294	6,698	17,045	43,060	107,895	190,666	~

Continued in SALA, 23-2624.

Table 3225

ECLA IMPORT AND EXPORT PRICE CHANGES, 19 LR, 1976-80

(%)

	Imports					Exports				
Category	1976	1877	1978	1979	1880	1976	1977	1978	1979	1980
Oil-Exporting Countries	6.3	8.5	8.6	8.9	12.8	5.0	5.8	-6.3	35.3	35.6

Continued in SALA, 23-2630.

Table 3226

COMMODITY PRICES, 1970–84[a]

(YA)

Commodity	Code[1]	1970	1975	1976	1977	1978	1979	1980	1981	1982	1983	1984
Aluminum (US cents/pound)												
Canada (United Kingdom)	w	27.90	39.40	40.40	51.90	60.10	70.30	85.51	57.28	44.98	65.25	56.77
Bananas (US cents/pound)												
Latin America (US Ports)	w	7.54	11.11	11.70[†]	12.34	13.00	14.77	17.01	18.20	16.99	19.46	16.76
Bauxite (US $/metric ton)												
Guyana (Baltimore)	w	42.39	105.31	117.28	134.82	138.42	152.60	212.45	216.34	208.35	179.54	~
Beef (US cents/pound)												
All Origins (US Ports)	w	59.16	60.20	72.02	68.42	97.06	131.01	125.19	112.12	108.39	110.67	103.11
Argentina (frozen)	u	33.14	38.87	41.28	52.86	52.54	86.91	93.12	76.87	64.07	66.59	~
Argentina (corned)	u	39.30	74.83	74.19	74.95	75.93	119.19	144.27	135.20	99.99	91.33	~
Butter (US cents/pound)												
New Zealand	w	28.61	50.42	49.33	57.42	68.08	69.35	73.80	96.88	97.16	91.25	76.02
Cacao (US cents/pound)												
Brazil	u	29.42	56.59	77.02	183.53	153.53	140.73	107.06	87.50	68.29	84.25	105.32
Coal (US $/short ton)												
US (Pennsylvania mines)	w	16.60	44.86	46.44	46.13	44.71	45.64	46.18	61.03	68.21	65.83	65.81
Coconut Oil (US cents/pound)												
Philippines	w	12.80	17.00	15.71	26.86	27.01	41.95	28.06	23.27	19.75	24.15	44.83
Coffee (US cents/pound)												
All Coffee (New York)	w	50.53	72.48	141.96	229.09	155.00	169.50	150.71	115.82	125.62	127.94	141.24
Brazil (New York)	w	55.80	82.58	149.48	267.15	165.29	178.47	208.79	186.44	143.68	142.75	149.65
Brazil	u	44.26	49.57	122.37	203.51	142.11	154.72	143.75	83.34	94.88	101.16	113.74
Colombia (New York)	w	56.66	81.71	157.74	240.21	185.20	183.40	178.83	128.09	139.71	131.69	144.25
Colombia	u	54.22	62.38	119.33	216.53	166.86	137.47	161.70	121.77	134.64	126.12	133.31
El Salvador	u	49.37	54.39	113.38	206.24	160.93	154.39	151.41	123.77	128.87	105.64	~
Uganda (New York)	w	41.44	61.05	127.63	223.80	147.50	165.47	147.15	102.91	111.04	124.12	138.18
Copper (US cents/pound)												
Canada	u	62.85	57.30	65.26	62.41	63.21	95.08	99.76	81.96	71.73	72.53	54.66
Copra (US $/metric ton)												
Philippines	u	179.91	226.41	181.99	314.25	356.00	615.27	390.45	310.53	276.66	275.78	~
Cotton (US cents/pound)												
United States (10 markets)	w	25.10	45.10	68.00	61.60	57.60	62.10	81.30	72.02	60.03	68.43	68.15
Mexico	u	26.26	51.15	89.99	63.42	69.91	74.24	83.36	74.82	64.57	77.90	~
Fishmeal (US $/metric ton)												
Peru	u	155.72	202.45	301.38	408.38	387.26	385.60	453.00	505.84	~	~	~
Gold (US $/fine ounce)												
United Kingdom (London)	w	35.94	160.96	124.82	147.72	193.24	306.67	607.87	459.75	375.80	422.47	360.36
Groundnuts (US $/metric ton)												
Nigeria (London)	w	228.17	432.97	422.99	546.86	630.92	562.75	485.57	622.72	383.20	349.44	349.76
Groundnut Cake (US $/metric ton)												
All Origins (Europe)	w	102.00	140.00	176.00	214.00	205.00	211.00	271.41	296.26	208.33	229.00	187.50
Groundnut Oil (US $/metric ton)												
West Africa (Europe)	w	378.50	857.50	740.80	852.80	1,079.20	888.70	858.80	1,042.80	585.20	710.90	1,016.70
Hides (US cents/pound)												
United States (Chicago)	w	12.90	23.30	33.60	37.00	47.20	73.20	45.90	42.98	39.90	46.90	58.87
Australia	u	24.79	43.92	56.63	67.36	73.87	90.57	84.65	60.76	57.72	48.73	30.71
Iron Ore (US $/metric ton)												
Brazil (North Sea Ports)	w	15.22	22.81	22.00	21.59	19.39	23.44	27.24	24.62	26.21	23.97	23.94
Jute (US $/metric ton)												
Bangladesh (Chita-Chaina)	w	270.00	371.00	295.00	319.00	398.00	385.00	313.65	278.38	283.22	298.39	569.80
Lamb (US cents/pound)												
New Zealand	u	24.33	39.77	40.90	48.16	55.62	63.94	72.28	78.46	72.04	62.54	57.29
Lead (US cents/pound)												
United States (New York)	w	15.70	21.60	23.00	30.70	33.80	53.00	43.50	37.46	26.69	22.53	27.00
Linseed Oil (US cents/pound)												
United States (Minneapolis)	w	11.00	41.00	28.33[†]	29.83	21.80	29.10	30.80	37.17	33.13	31.95	36.36
Logs (US $/cubic meter)												
Philippines (Tokyo)	w	43.13	67.51	92.00	89.80	91.78	160.15	187.58	150.07	144.51	135.20	150.98
Maize (US $/bushel)												
United States (US Gulf Pts)	w	1.48	3.03	2.85	2.42	2.56	2.94	3.19	3.32	2.75	3.45	3.45
Manganese (US $/long ton)												
India (US Ports)	w	55.33	140.00	147.33	150.33	144.38	140.00	155.25	167.80	164.12	151.82	143.21
Newsprint (US $/short ton)												
United States (New York)	w	150.50	256.70	276.00	297.60	315.50	345.20	388.50	428.47	440.71	422.41	450.71
Nickel (US cents/pound)												
Canada (Canadian Ports)	w	129.08	205.83	225.58	236.00	209.06	271.52	295.68	270.03	219.43	211.95	215.56
Palm Kernels (US $/metric ton)												
Nigeria (Europe)	w	167.55	206.75	229.92	326.25	363.73	499.50	344.50	317.33	264.83	365.33	524.75
Palm Oil (US $/metric ton)												
Malaysia	u	214.82	471.79	356.76	510.61	532.02	593.86	529.53	490.91	416.78	437.27	~

Table 3226 (Continued)

COMMODITY PRICES, 1970-84[a]

(YA)

Commodity	Code[1]	1970	1975	1976	1977	1978	1979	1980	1981	1982	1983	1984
Pepper, Black (US cents/pound)												
Malaysia (New York)	w	57.30	90.95	89.08	113.62	106.43	96.12	90.43	71.84	70.43	76.63	103.34
Petroleum (US $/Barrel)												
Libya (Es Sidra)	w	2.58	11.59	12.31	13.87	13.71	21.06	35.87	39.83	35.49	30.89	30.15
Saudi Arabia (Ras Tanura)	w	1.30	10.72	11.51	12.40	12.70	16.97	28.67	32.50	33.47	29.31	28.47
Venezuela (Tia Juana)	w	1.73	10.89	11.28	12.42	12.42	16.77	27.60	32.03	32.03	28.05	~
Phosphate Rock (US $/metric ton)												
Morocco (Casablanca)	w	11.00	67.17	35.83	30.67	29.00	33.00	44.96	49.50	41.79	36.92	38.25
Potash (US $/metric ton)												
Canada (Vancouver)	w	31.50	81.33	55.50	51.17	56.38	76.04	115.71	113.67	83.25	75.50	83.71
Plywood (US cents/sheet)												
Philippines (Tokyo)	w	103.10	121.80	147.70	161.50	189.50	262.50	273.80	245.46	234.35	229.87	227.03
Pulp (US $/metric ton)												
Canada	u	154.18	373.04	371.75	347.50	292.62	380.21	470.23	481.36	435.46	368.08	440.34
Rice (US $/metric ton)												
United States (New Orleans)	w	189.60	418.87	308.64	332.89	399.03	381.40	496.04	565.48	366.70	378.46	379.74
Rubber (US cents/pound)												
All Origins (New York)	w	21.10	29.90	39.60	41.60	50.00	64.20	73.50	57.00	45.28	56.18	49.58
Sawnwood (US $/cubic meter)												
Malaysia (French Ports)	w	93.23	166.44	168.13	154.09	203.47	339.08	369.66	314.14	302.11	304.28	306.77
Shrimp (US $/pound)												
United States (N. York Gulf)	w	1.24	2.67	3.79	3.59	3.64	5.43	4.60	4.41	6.21	6.00	5.24
Silver (US cents/troy ounce)												
United States (New York)	w	177.10	441.85	435.35	462.30	540.09	1,109.00	2,057.80	1,052.1	794.9	1,144.1	814.1
Sisal (US $/metric ton)												
Tanzania	u	115.25	410.84	316.90	385.75	358.75	392.81	540.61	587.94	476.13	492.63	~
Sorghum (US $/metric ton)												
United States (Rotterdam)	w	61.45	123.97	116.03	97.96	106.64	130.44	128.86	126.54	108.35	128.42	118.19
Soybeans (US $/metric ton)												
United States (Rotterdam)	w	117.00	220.00	231.00	279.00	268.00	297.00	296.25	288.42	244.50	281.67	282.08
Soybean Meal (US $/metric ton)												
United States (Rotterdam)	w	103.00	155.00	198.00	229.00	214.00	243.00	258.58	252.67	218.00	237.83	197.17
Soybean Oil (US $/metric ton)												
All Origins (Dutch Ports)	w	291.40	563.30	~	574.20	606.70	662.60	597.80	506.93	447.33	526.88	724.00
Sugar (US cents/pound)												
US Import Price (NY)	w	8.07	22.49	13.31	11.07	~	~	30.03	19.73	19.92	22.04	21.74
EEC Import Price	w	5.09	25.79	14.82	12.46	15.11	18.12	22.09	18.93	18.12	17.57	16.04
Caribbean (New York)	w	3.69	20.29	11.57	8.10	7.84	9.65	28.67	16.89	8.41	8.47	5.20
Brazil	u	5.10	29.18	11.52	8.24	7.70	8.79	21.79	16.92	9.42	9.46	9.10
Dominican Republic	u	6.15	26.77	11.88	9.02	8.63	8.73	16.41	27.47	14.45	13.02	~
Australia	u	4.97	19.95	14.35	11.74	12.07	13.30	21.07	19.16	9.99	10.32	7.71
Philippines	u	6.44	26.93	13.24	8.71	8.18	7.61	16.22	20.65	15.09	13.44	12.70
Superphosphate (US $/metric ton)												
United States (US Gulf Ports)	w	42.50	205.00	91.50	97.92	98.04	143.34	178.04	160.87	140.04	134.04	131.25
Tea (US cents/pound)												
Average Auction (London)	w	49.55	62.36	69.85	120.99	99.22	97.88	101.36	91.02	89.87	105.22	156.22
Tin (US cents/pound)												
All Origins (New York)	w	174.40	340.10	349.40	492.50	590.10	713.20	774.60	644.92	583.33	601.42	573.04
Bolivia	u	174.40	312.60	343.90	476.10	566.90	672.40	760.36	633.80	574.63	586.84	~
Tobacco (US cents/pound)												
United States (All Markets)	w	80.61	103.78	105.80	115.07	124.06	134.74	142.59	160.52	182.62[†]	185.52	~
Urea (US $/metric ton)												
Any Origin (Europe)	w	48.25	197.67	111.67	127.42	144.80	172.88	221.88	217.33	159.54	124.46	171.29
Wheat (US $/bushel)												
Australia	u	1.42	4.57	3.92	2.89	3.09	3.93	4.91	5.07	4.41	4.67	3.87
United States (US Gulf Pts)	w	1.50	4.06	3.62	2.81	3.48	4.36	4.70	4.76	4.36	4.28	4.15
Argentina	u	1.48	4.65	3.72	2.61	3.21	3.85	4.94	5.51	4.54	3.90	~
Wool (US cents/kilogram)												
New Zealand (greasy wool)	u	66.10	131.70	180.20	224.90	217.80	265.0	275.33	243.55	212.98	197.79	208.83
Zinc (US cents/pound)												
United States (New York)	w	15.90	38.90	37.50	34.50	31.50	37.80	38.10	45.67	40.01	42.82	49.95
Canada	u	11.94	36.18	34.87	32.14	28.19	32.06	34.51	39.19	36.09	36.30	44.71
Peru	u	6.41	16.73	19.18	16.82	14.05	18.61	21.91	25.25	~	~	~

1. Code: w = wholesale price.
      u = unit price (reported value data divided by reported volume data).

a. For data 1949–70 see SALA, 21-2526.

SOURCE: IMF-IFS-Y, 1979; IMF-IFS-Y, 1980; IMF-IFS-Y, 1981; IMF-IFS-Y, 1982;
    IMF-IFS, May 1985, pp. 74-77.

Table 3227

OPEC CRUDE OIL PRICES, 1973–83
(YA, US per Barrel and PC)

Year	Nominal Dollars	Real Dollars[1]	Real PC[2]
1973	$3.39	3.20	**
1974	11.29	9.80	206.3
1975	11.02	8.80	−10.2
1976	11.77	8.90	1.1
1977	12.88	9.20	3.4
1978	12.93	8.60	−6.5
1979	18.65	11.40	32.6
1980	30.87	17.30	51.8
1981	34.50	17.70	2.3
1982	33.56	16.20	−8.5

1. Dollars of 1972.
2. PC 1982 compared to 1973 = 890.0%; 10-year arithmetic average = 27.2 PC yearly.

SOURCE: *Los Angeles Times*, Aug. 28, 1983, Part I, p. 21.

Table 3228

PRIME RATE OF INTEREST CHARGED
BY U.S. BANKS, 1960–85

PART I. % PER YEAR

Year	%
1960	4.82
1965	4.54
1970	7.91
1971	5.72
1972	5.25
1973	8.03
1974	10.81
1975	7.86
1976	6.84
1977	6.83
1978	9.06
1979	12.67
1980	15.27
1981	18.87
1982	14.86
1983	10.79
1984	12.04

PART II. % PER MONTH

Month	1982	1983	1984	1985
January	15.75	11.16	11.00	10.61
February	16.56	10.98	11.00	10.50
March	16.50	10.50	11.21	~
April	16.50	10.50	11.93	~
May	16.50	10.50	12.39	~
June	16.50	10.50	12.60	~
July	16.26	10.50	13.00	~
August	14.39	10.89	13.00	~
September	13.50	11.00	12.97	~
October	12.52	11.00	12.58	~
November	11.85	11.00	11.77	~
December	11.50	11.00	11.06	~

SOURCE: 1960: USBC-SA, 1978, table 890; USBC-SA, 1981, table 873; USBC-SA, 1983, table 852; since 1982: USDC-SCB, May 1984, March 1985.

Table 3229

INTEREST ON U. S. COMMERCIAL PAPER, 1900–84

(4 to 6 month paper, YA)

Year	%	Year	%
1900	5.71	1944	.73
1901	5.40	1945	.75
1902	5.81	1946	.81
1903	6.16	1947	1.03
1904	5.14	1948	1.44
1905	5.18	1949	1.49
1906	6.25	1950	1.45
1907	6.66	1951	2.16
1908	5.00	1952	2.33
1909	4.67	1953	2.52
1910	5.72	1954	1.58
1911	4.75	1955	2.18
1912	5.41	1956	3.31
1913	6.20	1957	3.81
1914	5.47	1958	2.46
1915	4.01	1959	3.97
1916	3.84	1960	3.85
1917	5.07	1961	2.97
1918	6.02	1962	3.26
1919	5.37	1963	3.55
1920	7.50	1964	3.97
1921	6.62	1965	4.38
1922	4.52	1966	5.55
1923	5.07	1967	5.10
1924	3.98	1968	5.90
1925	4.02	1969	7.83
1926	4.34	1970	7.72
1927	4.11	1971	5.11
1928	4.85	1972	4.69
1929	5.85	1973	8.15
1930	3.59	1974	9.87
1931	2.64	1975	6.33
1932	2.73	1976	5.35
1933	1.73	1977	5.60
1934	1.02	1978	7.99
1935	.75	1979	10.91[a]
1936	.75	1980	12.29[a]
1937	.94	1981	14.76[a]
1938	.81	1982	11.89[a]
1939	.59	1983	8.89
1940	.56	1984	10.16
1941	.53		
1942	.66		
1943	.69		

a. Daily average.

SOURCE: 1900–54: USBC-HS, 1975, series X-445; 1954–78: USBG-FRB, Sept. 1984; since 1979, data are for 6 month paper: USDC-SCB, May 1979–85.

Table 3230

U.S. FEDERAL FUNDS[1] INTEREST RATE, 1955–85

(YA % Per Annum)

Year	%
1955	1.78
1956	2.73
1957	3.11
1958	1.58
1959	3.30
1960	3.22
1961	1.96
1962	2.68
1963	3.18
1964	3.50
1965	4.07
1966	5.12
1967	4.22
1968	5.67
1969	8.21
1970	7.18
1971	4.66
1972	4.43
1973	8.73
1974	10.50
1975	5.82
1976	5.05
1977	5.54
1978	7.93
1979	11.20
1980	13.36
1981	16.38
1982	12.26
1983	9.09
1984	10.23
1985[a]	8.50

1. Short-term borrowings between financial institutions.

a. Feb.

SOURCE: IMF-IFS, April 1985, line 60 b.

Table 3231

NINETY-DAY INTEREST RATES,[1] 11 LC, 1978–82

(% Per Annum)

Period	A. ARGENTINA	B. BOLIVIA	C. BRAZIL	D. CHILE	E. COLOMBIA	I. ECUADOR
Sep. 1978	133.1	~	56.7	82.7	33.7	13.0
Dec. 1978	147.9	20.4	45.8	93.6	32.2	18.0

Period	N. MEXICO	Q. PARAGUAY	R. PERU	S. URUGUAY	T. VENEZUELA	UNITED STATES
Sep. 1978	20.2	22.0	39.3	78.9	10.9	9.75
Dec. 1978	20.5	22.0	45.4	74.5	10.9	11.75

Continued in SALA, 23-2634.

CHAPTER 33

GROSS PRODUCT

DEFINITIONS OF TERMS
I. Market-Country System

National accounting results in a statistical statement of the gross value of goods and services produced by a country's economy in a given period of time, usually one year. Included are primary production (agriculture, forestry, fishing, and mining), whether or not it enters the exchange economy, and all other goods and services produced and exchanged. Nonprimary production performed by producers outside their own trade and consumed by themselves is omitted.

Gross value of output can be calculated either by factor cost or market price:

Gross value of output by *market price* (or purchasers' values) equals market value of output before depreciation provisions for fixed capital consumption.

Gross value of output by *factor cost* equals market value of output less indirect payments (such as excise and sales taxes, depreciation, government subsidies, transfer payments).

Gross domestic product (GDP) and **gross national product (GNP)** differ mainly in treatment of *factor income earned abroad*. Factor income earned abroad (or factor payment abroad) is foreign investment income (rent, interest, dividents, branch profits, undistributed earnings of subsidiaries) and income from working in other countries.

GDP (gross domestic product) equals total value of output accruing *within* a country. Thus, it includes factor income generated by foreign investors or suppliers in the country but excludes factor income invested or supplied abroad by normal residents of the country.

GNP (gross national product) equals total value of output accruing *to* a country. Thus, it excludes factor income earned by foreign investors or suppliers in the country but includes factor income earned in other countries by normal residents of the country.

II. Non-Market-Country System
See SALA, 23-2307)

GSP	(Gross Social Product)
GMP	(Gross Material Product)

Figure 33:1

GDP SHARES OF IMPORTANT ACTIVITIES FOR TOTAL
LATIN AMERICA AND THE UNITED STATES,
TEN-YEAR INTERVALS, 1950–80

(%)

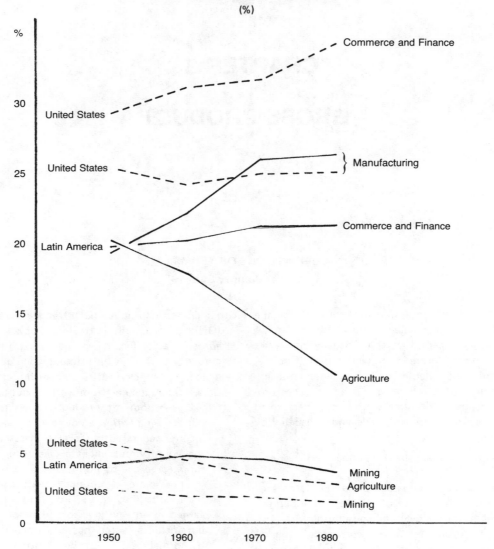

SOURCE: SALA, 23-2324; SALA, 23-2325; SALA, 23-2326; SALA, 23-2330.

Figure 33:2

GROWTH OF GDP, 19 L, 1981–83

(%)

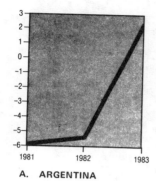

A.   ARGENTINA

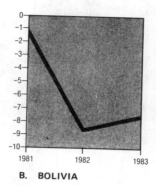

B.   BOLIVIA

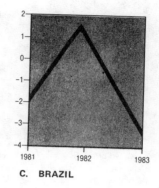

C.   BRAZIL

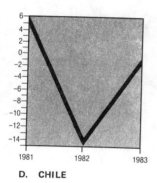

D.   CHILE

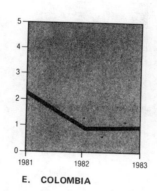

E.   COLOMBIA

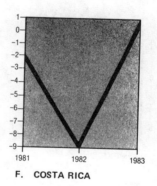

F.   COSTA RICA

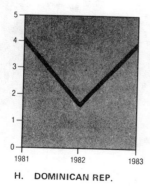

H.   DOMINICAN REP.

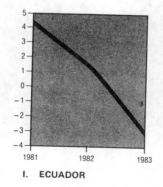

I.   ECUADOR

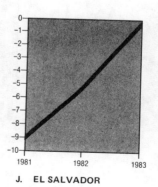

J.   EL SALVADOR

SOURCE: IDB–SPTF, 1984, Part Two.

Figure 33:2 (Continued)

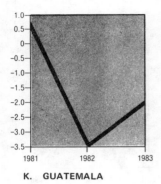

K. GUATEMALA

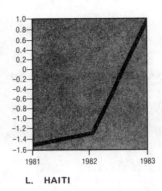

L. HAITI

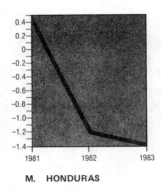

M. HONDURAS

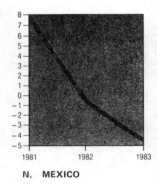

N. MEXICO

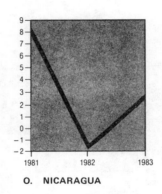

O. NICARAGUA

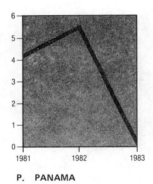

P. PANAMA

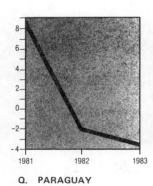

Q. PARAGUAY

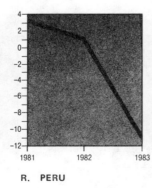

R. PERU

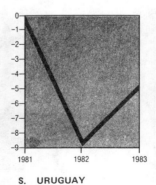

S. URUGUAY

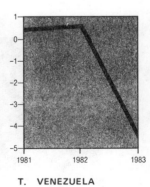

T. VENEZUELA

SOURCE: IDB–SPTF, 1984, Part Two.

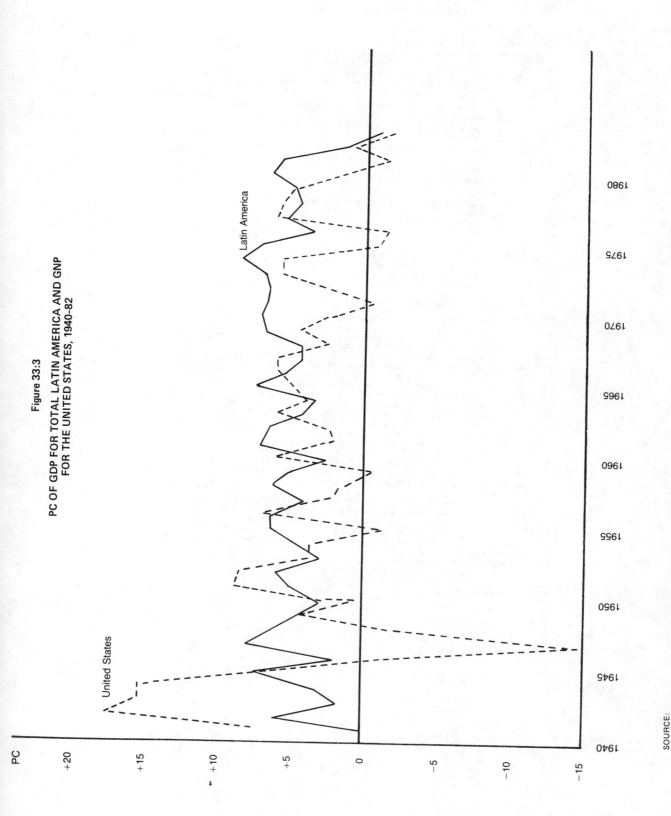

Figure 33:3

PC OF GDP FOR TOTAL LATIN AMERICA AND GNP
FOR THE UNITED STATES, 1940–82

SOURCE:

Latin America: SALA, 23-2331, "ECLA Factor" series through 1974, then "ECLA Market" series; series overlap 1975-79 has an average difference in PC of .4%.

United States: SALA, 23-2322, USDC-SCB series.

Table 3300

GENERAL SOURCES AND METHODS FOR COMPARATIVE
PC OF REAL GDP SERIES PRESENTED IN
TABLES 3301 THROUGH 3322[a,b]

Series	Source[1]
ECLA Factor	At factor cost in 1970 prices: through 1976 from ECLA-SHCAL, pp. 74-195 and 25-88, then also from ECLA-S, 1981, 1980 (table 3 for each country), 1979, 1978, 1977. Data for table 3301 are calculated from 1970 dollars at purchasing power exchange rate for each country. Cf. "ECLA Market" series below.
IMF	In 1975 prices: through 1975 from IMF-IFS-Y, 1982; after 1975 from IMF-IFS-Y, 1984. IMF data are, in general, from UN sources at market prices. Revised with data in 1980 prices (calculated from indexes) in IMF-IFS-Y, 1984.
OECD	Index 1968 = 100 for 1960–70, 1978 = 100 for 1971, and 1980 = 100 for 1972–82; data through 1959 from *National Accounts of Less Developed Areas, 1950-1966*, July 1968, p. 20; after 1960 data are from *Latest Information on National Accounts of Developing Countries, 1960–82*, Nov. 1983, p. 17. Data are in market prices.
SALA	In 1970 dollars at official exchange rates, based upon USAID data synthesized in SALA-SNP, pp. 393-394 and also data and sources given in SALA, 18-2200. Data are, in general, at market prices. For comparison of USAID estimated at three different times, see SALA-SNP, pp. 395-396.
ECLA Market	At market prices in 1970 dollars (compared to factor cost terms in "ECLA Factor" given above). Data are from ECLA-S, 1980, ECLA-N, Jan. 1983, and Mexico-NAFINSA-MV, March 11, 1985. Cf. "ECLA Factor" series above.

1. PC calculations by Waldo W. Wilkie.

a. For Cuba sources, see table 3307; for other Mexico sources, see table 3314; for U.S. sources, see table 3322.

b. For definition of GDP and GNP, see title page to this chapter and tables 3340 through 3360; on GSP and GMP, see table 3307. About GNP (and GDP), the World Bank's *World Development Report*, 1982, includes the following cautions (p. 20): "Gross national product (GNP) measures economic activity—not welfare. But as a measure of aggregate economic output and expenditure, GNP data are often ambiguous or deficient. Ambiguity exists, for example, because public services such as administration and defense are treated as final rather than as intermediate services, and purchases of consumer durables other than residences are regarded as consumption rather than investment. Moreover, GNP does not make allowance for the varying amounts of capital, including mineral and other natural resources, used up during production. These are notoriously difficult to estimate. Gaps exist in basic data, most notably for subsistence production in developing countries and for illegal activities in most countries. Measurement problems also arise because of lack of consistency among countries in calculating changes in real output over time; this is particularly true between the market economies and the centrally planned economies. Moreover, major problems arise in intercountry comparisons of levels of GNP converted to a common currency by using exchange rates.

Welfare could not be fully measured even if it were possible to collect perfect GNP data for each country, based on Standard National Accounting definitions, and make international comparisons. . . . GNP does not measure items that are important to welfare in most societies, such as the distribution of income and wealth, employment status, job security, and opportunities for advancement, availability of health and education services, unpaid services, the quality of the environment, and climatic differences. . . . [Thus economists settle] for partial measures such as GNP—which at least covers most of the goods and services available to meet important consumption needs. GNP data, however, need to be complemented by other indicators, particularly those which relate more directly to the 'quality of life'."

Table 3301

ARGENTINA COMPARATIVE PC OF REAL GDP, 1901–84

I. 1901–39

Year	ECLA Factor (1901-39)
1901	8.5
1902	-2.1
1903	4.3
1904	10.6
1905	13.2
1906	5.0
1907	2.2
1908	9.8
1909	5.0
1910	7.2
1911	1.8
1912	8.2
1913	1.1
1914	-10.4
1915	.5
1916	-2.9
1917	7.2
1918	1.4
1919	3.7
1920	7.3
1921	2.6
1922	8.0
1923	11.0
1924	7.8
1925	-.4
1926	4.8
1927	7.1
1928	6.2
1929	4.6
1930	-14.1
1931	-6.9
1932	-3.3
1933	4.7
1934	7.9
1935	4.4
1936	1.2
1937	8.1
1938	1.3
1939	3.6

II. 1940–84

Year	ECLA Factor (1940-81)	IMF (1953-83)	OECD (1951-82)	SALA (1951-74)	ECLA Market (1975-84)
1940	-2.0				
1941	4.9				
1942	4.6				
1943	.7				
1944	9.7				
1945	-4.8				
1946	8.3				
1947	13.7				
1948	1.2				
1949	-4.6				
1950	1.6				
1951	3.9		4.1	3.4	
1952	-5.1		-6.4	-6.7	
1953	5.4	6.9	7.1	6.8	
1954	4.1	5.0	3.8	3.2	
1955	7.1	15.9	6.9	7.4	
1956	2.8	-5.3	1.6	1.2	
1957	5.1	-3.3	5.5	4.4	
1958	6.1	8.0	7.2	6.7	
1959	-6.4	#	-5.8	-6.1	
1960	7.8	7.4	7.9	8.5	
1961	7.1	6.9	7.1	6.8	
1962	-1.6	-.9	-1.6	-1.5	
1963	-2.4	-3.7*	-2.4	-2.4	
1964	10.3	-2.4	10.3	10.4	
1965	9.1	11.7	9.2	9.3	
1966	.6	10.1	.6	.4	
1967	2.7	.8	2.6	2.5	
1968	4.3	3.4	4.3	4.5	
1969	8.6	4.9	8.5	7.9	
1970	5.4	2.6*	5.4	4.4	
1971	4.8	3.4	4.7	3.0	
1972	3.1	2.2	3.8	4.8	
1973	6.1	3.2	4.7	5.6	
1974	6.1	5.2	6.1	6.1	
1975	-.9	#	-.9		-.9
1976	-1.7	-1.0	-1.7		-.2
1977	4.9	7.0	4.9		6.0
1978	-3.9	-3.7	-3.9*		-3.9
1979	7.1	6.8	6.8		7.1
1980	1.4	.9	1.1		3.7
1981	-6.1‡	-6.3	-6.1*		-6.2
1982		-4.8	-5.8		-5.1
1983		2.0			3.1
1984					2.5†

SOURCE AND METHODS: See table 3300.

Table 3302

BOLIVIA COMPARATIVE PC OF REAL GDP, 1946–84

Year	ECLA Factor (1946–81)	IMF (1953–83)	OECD (1951–82)	SALA (1951–74)	ECLA Market (1975–84)
1946	1.8				
1947	1.7				
1948	2.1				
1949	2.1				
1950	2.1				
1951	7.0		6.4	6.9	
1952	3.0		2.5	1.6	
1953	-9.5	-9.5	-11.4	-10.9	
1954	2.1	2.1	.7	0	
1955	5.3	5.3	7.0	7.1	
1956	-5.9	-5.9	-4.8	-5.0	
1957	-3.3	-3.3	-3.5	-3.4	
1958	2.4	2.4	2.9*	3.9	
1959	-.3	-.3	-.3	-1.3	
1960	4.3	8.6	4.3	6.3	
1961	2.1	1.3	2.1	2.1	
1962	5.6	2.4	5.6	5.8	
1963	6.4	6.8	6.4	6.0	
1964	4.8	4.0	4.8	4.5	
1965	4.9	4.9	6.9	6.9	
1966	7.2	7.2	7.0	6.9	
1967	6.3	6.3	6.3	4.1	
1968	8.5	15.4	7.2	8.3	
1969	4.5	4.6	4.8	4.4	
1970	5.2	7.8	.6	5.8	
1971	4.9	4.9	4.9	6.9	
1972	5.9	5.8	5.7*	6.6	
1973	6.9	6.7	6.8*	6.1	
1974	6.1	5.1	5.1	5.0	
1975	5.3	6.6	6.6		5.1
1976	6.8	6.1	6.1		6.8
1977	4.0	4.2	4.2		3.4
1978	3.1	3.4	3.4		3.1
1979	1.8	1.8	1.8		1.8
1980	.6	.6	.6		1.2
1981	-.6‡	-.9	-.7		-.9
1982		-8.7	-9.1		-8.7
1983		-7.6			-7.6
1984					.5†

SOURCE AND METHODS: See table 3300.

Table 3303

BRAZIL COMPARATIVE PC OF REAL GDP, 1921–84

I. 1921–39

Year	ECLA Factor (1921–39)
1921	.2
1922	5.0
1923	5.8
1924	.2
1925	4.2
1926	.2
1927	5.3
1928	8.2
1929	.7
1930	-3.4
1931	-.6
1932	1.1
1933	5.6
1934	6.8
1935	2.8
1936	9.1
1937	2.6
1938	4.1
1939	2.8

II. 1940–82

Year	ECLA Factor (1940–81)	IMF (1966–83)	OECD (1951–82)	SALA (1952–74)	ECLA Market (1975–84)
1940	1.0				
1941	4.9				
1942	-2.8				
1943	5.8				
1944	4.6				
1945	.9				
1946	7.8				
1947	2.4				
1948	7.4				
1949	6.6				
1950	6.5				
1951	5.9		5.1	5.9	
1952	8.7		5.7	8.9	
1953	2.5		3.2	2.4	
1954	10.1		7.6	10.2	
1955	6.9		6.8	6.8	
1956	3.2		1.9	3.2	
1957	8.1		6.9	8.1	
1958	7.7		6.6	7.7	
1959	3.0		7.3	5.6	
1960	12.5		9.7	9.7	
1961	10.3		10.3	10.3	
1962	5.2		5.2	5.3	
1963	1.6		1.5	1.6	
1964	2.9		2.9	2.8	
1965	2.7		2.7	2.9	
1966	3.8	3.8	3.8	5.1	
1967	4.9	4.9	4.9	4.8	
1968	11.2	11.2	11.2	9.4	
1969	9.9	9.9	9.9	9.0	
1970	8.8	2.4	8.8	9.5	
1971	13.3	12.0	12.0*	11.0	
1972	11.7	11.1	11.2	11.7	
1973	13.9	13.6	14.0	11.3	
1974	9.8	9.7	9.5	10.9	
1975	5.7	5.4	5.6		5.7
1976	9.0	9.7	9.7		9.0
1977	4.7	5.7	5.4		4.7
1978	6.0	5.0	4.8		6.0
1979	6.4	6.4	6.7		6.4
1980	8.0	7.2	7.9		6.8
1981	-1.9‡	-1.6	-3.4*		-1.6
1982		.9	~		.9
1983		-3.2			-3.2
1984					3.5†

SOURCE AND METHODS: See table 3300.

Table 3304

CHILE COMPARATIVE PC OF REAL GDP, 1946–84

Year	ECLA Factor (1940–81)	IMF (1953–83)	OECD (1951–82)	SALA (1951–74)	ECLA Market (1974–84)
1940	5.0				
1941	.1				
1942	5.5				
1943	4.2				
1944	1.4				
1945	9.1				
1946	6.2				
1947	−6.7				
1948	11.5				
1949	−.5				
1950	4.8				
1951	5.2		4.4	4.4	
1952	3.4		5.7	5.9	
1953	7.1	5.1	5.2	5.8	
1954	.7	.5	.3	.4	
1955	2.7	#	−.1	−1.0	
1956	.7	.5	.6	.2	
1957	2.7	10.5	10.5	11.8	
1958	4.8	3.9	2.7	3.9	
1959	6.9	−.6	−.5	−1.1	
1960	5.1	5.7	7.0	6.7	
1961	6.1	6.1	6.1*	6.2	
1962	4.6	4.5	4.6	4.7	
1963	5.1	4.9	5.1	4.9	
1964	4.3	4.7	4.3	4.0	
1965	5.1	5.0	5.1	4.6	
1966	7.0	6.9	7.0	6.1	
1967	2.4	2.5	2.4	1.9	
1968	3.0	2.9	3.0	3.0	
1969	3.5	3.3	3.5	3.2	
1970	3.6	1.4*	3.6	9.2[a]	
1971	7.7	9.0	7.7	9.0	
1972	−.1	−1.2	−1.2	1.8	
1973	−3.6	−5.6	−5.6	−3.6	
1974	5.7	1.0	1.0	3.7	5.7
1975	−11.3	−12.9	−12.9		−12.9
1976	4.1	3.5	3.5		3.5
1977	8.6	9.9	9.9		9.9
1978	7.8	8.2	8.2		8.2
1979	8.3	8.3	8.3		8.3
1980	7.5	7.8	7.8		8.0
1981	5.3‡	5.7	5.7		5.7
1982		−14.3	−14.3		−14.3
1983		−.7			−.8
1984					5.5†

a. USAID calculations in 1973 dollars show PC of 4.5%. Cf. SALA-SNP, p. 416.

SOURCE AND METHODS: See table 3300.

Table 3305

COLOMBIA COMPARATIVE PC OF REAL GDP, 1926–84

I. 1926–39			II. 1940–84					
Year	ECLA Factor (1926–39)		Year	ECLA Factor (1940–81)	IMF (1953–83)	OECD (1951–82)	SALA (1951–74)	ECLA Market (1975–84)
1926	9.5		1940	2.2				
1927	9.0		1941	1.7				
1928	7.3		1942	.2				
1929	3.6		1943	.4				
			1944	6.8				
1930	-.9							
1931	-1.6		1945	4.7				
1932	6.6		1946	9.1				
1933	5.6		1947	3.9				
1934	-2.1		1948	3.1				
			1949	5.5				
1935	11.2		1950	1.8				
1936	5.3		1951	3.1		3.1	3.4	
1937	1.6		1952	6.3		6.4	6.7	
1938	6.5		1953	5.8	6.1	6.0	6.0	
1939	6.1		1954	6.6	6.9	7.0	7.2	
			1955	4.0	3.9	3.9	4.0	
			1956	4.1	4.1	4.0	3.9	
			1957	2.4	2.2	2.2	1.5	
			1958	2.5	2.5	2.5	2.3	
			1959	7.1	7.2	6.9	7.8	
			1960	4.1	4.3	4.3	4.4	
			1961	5.0	5.1	5.1	4.8	
			1962	5.4	5.4	5.4	5.0	
			1963	3.2	3.3	3.3	3.5	
			1964	6.1	6.2	6.2	5.7	
			1965	3.5	3.6	3.6	3.6	
			1966	5.2	5.4	5.4	5.3	
			1967	4.2	4.2	4.2	4.1	
			1968	6.3	6.1	6.1	5.8	
			1969	6.3	6.3	6.4	6.0	
			1970	6.6	9.3	6.7	6.9	
			1971	5.8	6.0	5.8*	6.0	
			1972	7.9	7.7	7.7	6.6	
			1973	7.6	6.7	6.7	8.0	
			1974	6.5	5.7	5.7	6.6	
			1975	4.3	2.3	2.3		3.8
			1976	4.2	4.7	4.7		4.6
			1977	4.7	4.2	4.1		4.9
			1978	8.8	8.5	8.5		8.9
			1979	4.9	5.4	5.4		5.1
			1980	4.2	4.1	4.1		4.7
			1981	2.5‡	2.3	2.3		2.3
			1982		.9	.9		.9
			1983		.8			.8
			1984					3.0†

SOURCE AND METHODS: See table 3300.

Table 3306

COSTA RICA COMPARATIVE PC OF REAL GDP, 1946–84

Year	ECLA Factor (1946–81)	IMF (1961–82)	OECD (1954–82)	SALA (1951–74)	ECLA Market (1975–84)
1946	7.9				
1947	19.0				
1948	5.7				
1949	4.0				
1950	4.1				
1951	2.7			3.6	
1952	12.1			12.6	
1953	15.2			11.5	
1954	.8		4.6	5.3	
1955	11.6		4.5	4.8	
1956	-2.8		1.4	2.3	
1957	8.5		9.2	6.9	
1958	12.4		6.7	6.4	
1959	3.7		3.1	3.9	
1960	8.7		6.1*	3.1	
1961	4.2	-.8	-1.0	2.0	
1962	6.1	8.1	8.1	6.2	
1963	8.6	4.8	4.8	6.4	
1964	4.9	4.1	4.1	-.9	
1965	9.1	9.8	9.8	9.6	
1966	7.8	7.9	7.9	6.6	
1967	6.1	5.7	5.7	8.6	
1968	7.7	8.5	8.5	9.2	
1969	6.7	5.5	5.5	9.5	
1970	6.6	7.5	7.5	5.4	
1971	6.6	6.8	6.8	4.0	
1972	8.2	8.2	8.2	6.7	
1973	7.7	7.7	7.7	7.2	
1974	5.5	5.5	5.5	4.2	
1975	2.1	2.1	2.1		2.1
1976	5.5	5.5	5.5		5.5
1977	8.9	8.9	8.9		8.9
1978	6.3	6.3	6.3		6.3
1979	4.7	4.9	4.9		4.9
1980	.6	.8	.8		2.8
1981	-3.6‡	-4.6	-2.3		-2.3
1982		-6.9	-9.1		-7.3
1983					2.3
1984					3.0†

SOURCE AND METHODS: See table 3300.

Table 3307

CUBA COMPARATIVE PC OF REAL PRODUCT, 1947–81

(Cf. SALA, 24-3300)

PART I. GMP AND GSP[1] DEFINED

(From SALA-Cuba, p. 204)

Category	Example[1] for 1962
(a) Personal Consumption	2,491.1
(b) Collective Consumption	417.1
(c) Gross Capital Formation	607.6
(d) Increase in Stock[2]	277.1
(e) Net Exports	-94.7
(I) Gross Material Product (a + b + c + d + e)	3,698.2
(f) Consumption of Fixed Capital	188.7
(II) Net Material Product (I) – (f)	3,509.5
(III) Expenditures on Non-material Services	2,384.2
(IV) Gross Social Product (I + III)	6,082.4

1. Data refer to the total expenditures (in millions of 1965 pesos) on Gross Social Product (GSP). GSP includes expenditures on Gross Material Product (GMP) which is defined as the total net value of goods and "productive" services (including agriculture, industry, construction, transportation, communication, commerce, and turn-over taxes) produced in the course of the year. In contrast, non-material services cover those economic activities classified as "non-productive" (including public administration, education, health, defense, personal and professional services, and similar activities). Readers should note that calculations of GSP and GMP do not correspond to standard GNP systems. Differences in national accounting practices prevent comparability without adjustment as in the SALA series given in Part II, below, where GNP was computed in source by adding to Cuba's GMP the value added in non-productive services. Cf. CEPAL, *Cuentas Nacionales y Producto Material en América Latina* (Santiago, 1982).
2. Data for "Increase in Stock" not available in original sources and have been approximated by subtracting the sum of available items from GMP.

Table 3307 (Continued)

CUBA COMPARATIVE PC OF REAL PRODUCT, 1947–81

PART II. SERIES, 1947–81

Year	CERP[1] GNP[2] (1947–58)	SALA[3] GNP (1951–75)[a]	Mesa-Lago[4] GMP (1963–80)	ECLA[5] GMP[6] (1971–80)	ECLA[7] GSP (1963–78)	Cuba-CEE[8] GSP (1977–81)
1947	12.1					
1948	-7.5					
1949	-.3					
1950	15.9					
1951	.5	0				
1952	4.3	5.9				
1953	-10.6	-12.0				
1954	1.7	-.1				
1955	2.1	1.0				
1956	9.5	5.1				
1957	6.0	10.7				
1958	-3.9	-3.5				
1959		~				
1960		~				
1961		~				
1962		~				
1963		0	1.0		-1.1	
1964		9.8	9.0		7.3	
1965		2.0	1.5		4.9	
1966		-3.9	-3.7		-.9	
1967		-2.0	2.4		7.5	
1968		6.2	6.7		1.7	
1969		-8.7	-4.0		-1.3	
1970		6.4	.6		15.5	
1971		-3.0	14.6	4.2	6.9	
1972		1.0	25.1	9.7	15.8	
1973		6.1	11.3	13.1	15.1	
1974		1.9	10.5	7.8	12.7	
1975		3.8	19.8	12.3	3.7	
1976			-.1	4.4	1.2	
1977			4.1	1.8	2.6	3.9
1978			9.4	7.7	11.8	4.2
1979			4.3	4.2		3.8
1980			3.0	2.2		4.1
1981				11.7		14.8

1. CERP: *Cuban Economic Research Project: A Study on Cuba* (Coral Gables: University of Miami Press, 1965), p. 605, given in Schroeder, p. 570.
2. Deflated here with U.S. export price index given in SALA, 22-2625.
3. Calculated from index numbers in SALA, 19-200, 201. After 1969, Cuban data converted to GNP by CIA source wherein GMP adjusted to include "non-productive" services such as education and health (see Part I, above).
4. Carmelo Mesa-Lago, *The Economy of Socialist Cuba: A Two-Decade Appraisal* (Albuquerque: University of New Mexico Press, 1982), p. 34.
5. ECLA-S, 1978, 1979, 1980, 1981, p. 296. Cf. SALA, 23-2338.
6. According to ECLA-S, e.g. 1979, p. 183, all data are in constant prices because for Cuba "current" and "constant" prices are equivalent in the case of material product (at producer prices). See also ECLA-S, 1981, p. 303, note 6, for discussion of frozen prices through 1980.
7. ECLA-AE, 1980, pp. 264–265.
8. Cuba-CEE, AE, 1981, p. 67.

a. For 1950s, calculated from index based at 1950; for 1962–75, index based at 1970.

Table 3308

DOMINICAN REPUBLIC COMPARATIVE PC OF REAL GDP, 1946–84

Year	ECLA Factor (1946–81)	IMF (1953–82)	OECD (1951–82)	SALA (1951–74)	ECLA Market (1975–84)
1946	-7.3				
1947	10.2				
1948	10.5				
1949	12.5				
1950	17.9				
1951	11.8		11.8	9.1	
1952	8.1		8.1	11.8	
1953	-1.3	-1.3	-1.3	.8	
1954	5.7	5.8	5.8	5.9	
1955	6.2	6.2	6.2	6.3	
1956	10.0	10.0	9.9	11.2	
1957	6.3	6.3	6.4	5.2	
1958	5.3	5.3	5.3	6.3	
1959	.6	.7	.6	.1	
1960	4.9	1.3	4.9	6.6	
1961	-2.3	-2.2	-2.2	-3.9	
1962	17.0	17.0	17.0	17.3	
1963	6.5	7.5	6.5	8.5	
1964	6.7	4.1	6.7	3.8	
1965	-12.4	-10.9	-12.4	-10.4	
1966	13.4	13.1	13.4	12.2	
1967	3.4	3.4	3.4	3.4	
1968	.2	.5	.2	1.0	
1969	10.9	12.2	11.0	12.0	
1970	10.6	8.4	10.6	11.1	
1971	10.6	10.9	10.9	11.0	
1972	10.4	10.4	10.4	11.7	
1973	12.9	12.9	12.9	8.9	
1974	5.5	6.0	6.0	8.2	
1975	2.1	5.2	5.2		5.2
1976	5.5	6.7	6.7		6.7
1977	8.9	5.0	5.0		5.0
1978	5.7	2.1	2.1		2.2
1979	4.8	4.5	4.5		4.8
1980	5.6	6.1	6.1		5.3
1981	3.4‡	4.1	4.1		4.0
1982		1.6	1.6		1.7
1983					3.9
1984					1.5†

SOURCE AND METHODS: See table 3300.

Table 3309

ECUADOR COMPARATIVE PC OF REAL GDP, 1940–84

Year	ECLA Factor (1940–81)	IMF (1953–83)	OECD (1951–82)	SALA (1951–74)	ECLA Market (1974–84)
1940	6.6				
1941	.5				
1942	4.2				
1943	12.7				
1944	1.3				
1945	.4				
1946	11.9				
1947	11.1				
1948	13.7				
1949	1.8				
1950	8.7				
1951	1.1		2.7	3.4	
1952	12.3		10.4	8.6	
1953	2.1	8.6	3.3	3.6	
1954	8.1	8.1	8.1	8.7	
1955	2.6	2.6	2.6	2.5	
1956	3.7	3.7	3.6	3.0	
1957	4.5	5.1	5.3	5.4	
1958	2.9	2.3	2.3	3.0	
1959	5.4	5.2	5.1	4.6	
1960	6.5	6.6	4.5*	6.8	
1961	2.5	1.5	1.7	1.4	
1962	5.3	4.5	4.5	4.9	
1963	2.6	3.9	3.8	4.8	
1964	7.0	7.8	7.8	7.2	
1965	9.6	12.5	3.2	3.0	
1966	2.6	2.4	8.0	4.6	
1967	5.3	6.9	8.0	6.1	
1968	5.5	4.0	4.5	5.9	
1969	5.5	2.3	4.2	2.7	
1970	7.0	6.5	4.8	8.8	
1971	5.8	6.3	5.0	2.0	
1972	8.0	14.4	7.0*	8.4	
1973	17.9	25.3	25.4	13.0	
1974	4.0	6.4	6.4	4.8	9.0
1975	7.5	5.6	5.6		6.8
1976	8.1	9.2	9.3		9.3
1977	6.4	6.5	6.5		7.5
1978	6.6	6.6	6.5		5.4
1979	5.1	5.3	5.1		5.1
1980	4.8	4.9	4.8		5.1
1981	4.3‡	3.9	4.3		3.9
1982		1.8	1.4		1.8
1983		-3.3			-3.3
1984					2.0†

SOURCE AND METHODS: See table 3300.

Table 3310

EL SALVADOR COMPARATIVE PC OF REAL GDP, 1946–84

Year	ECLA Factor (1946–81)	IMF (1953–83)	OECD (1951–82)	SALA (1951–74)	ECLA Market (1975–84)
1946	1.6				
1947	25.8				
1948	27.4				
1949	-9.2				
1950	2.9				
1951	2.0		-3.6	5.0	
1952	7.5		8.0	7.3	
1953	3.1	2.6	11.5*	4.4	
1954	1.2	3.1	3.6*	2.1	
1955	5.1	4.3	3.6	4.1	
1956	7.9	6.0	4.6	4.0	
1957	5.3	5.6	5.0	5.7	
1958	2.2	1.0	1.0	0	
1959	4.5	4.5	1.9	1.8	
1960	4.1	4.0	4.1	3.0	
1961	3.5	3.5	3.5	3.4	
1962	12.0	12.0	12.0	11.6	
1963	4.3	4.3	4.3	4.3	
1964	9.3	9.3	9.3	9.4	
1965	5.4	5.4	5.4	5.1	
1966	7.2	7.2	7.2	7.3	
1967	5.4	5.4	5.4	5.4	
1968	3.2	3.2	3.2	3.3	
1969	3.5	3.5	3.5	3.4	
1970	3.0	3.0	3.0	3.6	
1971	4.6	4.8	4.8	4.0	
1972	5.7	5.5	5.5	5.8	
1973	5.1	5.1	5.1	5.4	
1974	6.4	6.4	6.4	5.2	
1975	5.6	5.6	5.6		5.6
1976	4.0	4.0	4.0		4.0
1977	5.0	6.1	6.1		5.9
1978	4.4	6.4	6.4		4.4
1979	1.5	-1.7	-1.7		-1.5
1980	-9.6	-8.7	-9.0		-5.3
1981	-9.5‡	-8.3	-9.5		-8.3
1982		-6.0	-5.4		-5.6
1983		-.7			.0
1984					1.5†

SOURCE AND METHODS: See table 3300.

Table 3311

GUATEMALA COMPARATIVE PC OF REAL GDP, 1946–84

Year	ECLA Factor (1946–81)	IMF (1953–83)	OECD (1951–82)	SALA (1951–74)	ECLA Market (1975–84)
1946	7.9				
1947	12.7				
1948	-.8				
1949	-7.9				
1950	.3				
1951	1.4		1.5	1.8	
1952	2.1		2.1	2.1	
1953	3.7	3.6	3.6	2.8	
1954	1.9	1.9	1.9	1.8	
1955	2.5	2.5	2.4	2.8	
1956	9.1	9.1	9.1	9.4	
1957	5.6	5.6	5.7	5.5	
1958	4.7	4.7	4.2	4.6	
1959	4.9	4.9	4.9	4.8	
1960	2.4	2.4	2.4	2.4	
1961	4.3	4.3	4.3	4.2	
1962	3.5	3.5	3.5	3.6	
1963	9.5	9.5	9.5	9.5	
1964	4.6	4.6	4.6	4.5	
1965	4.4	4.4	4.4	4.4	
1966	5.5	5.5	5.5	4.6	
1967	4.1	4.1	4.1	4.0	
1968	8.8	8.8	8.8	8.5	
1969	4.7	4.7	4.7	3.8	
1970	5.7	5.7	5.7	6.8	
1971	5.6	5.6	5.6	5.0	
1972	7.3	7.3	7.3*	8.1	
1973	6.8	6.8	7.3	8.1	
1974	6.4	6.4	6.1	6.6	
1975	1.9	1.9	1.9		1.9
1976	7.4	7.4	7.4		7.4
1977	7.8	7.8	7.8		7.8
1978	5.5	5.0	5.0		5.0
1979	4.7	4.7	4.7		4.7
1980	3.5	3.7	3.7		4.2
1981	1.0‡	.7	.9		.7
1982		-3.5	-3.4		-3.5
1983		#			-2.7
1984					.0†

SOURCE AND METHODS: See table 3300.

Table 3312

HAITI COMPARATIVE PC OF REAL GDP, 1946–84

Year	ECLA Factor (1946–81)	IMF (1953–83)	OECD (1951–82)[a]	SALA (1951–74)[b]	ECLA Market (1975–84)
1945					
1946	.9				
1947	1.7				
1948	1.0				
1949	1.1				
1950	1.6				
1951	1.5		1.4	1.3	
1952	5.7		5.7	5.4	
1953	–3.2	–3.2	–3.3	–2.4	
1954	8.2	8.1	8.1	6.2	
1955	–4.0	–4.0	–4.0	–2.3	
1956	8.7	8.7	8.8	7.5	
1957	–5.9	–5.9	–6.1	–4.7	
1958	7.9	7.9	8.0	7.3	
1959	–4.7	–4.7	–4.8	–4.4	
1960	6.5	2.6	7.3	3.4*	
1961	–4.1	–2.4	–3.0	–2.5	
1962	9.6	8.3	7.9	8.2	
1963	–6.5	–2.9	–1.9	–2.1	
1964	–2.3	–1.6	–1.6	–1.1	
1965	1.1	2.1	2.1	1.1	
1966	–.6	2.0	–.6	0	
1967	–2.0	–2.1	–2.1	–1.1	
1969	3.9	3.2	3.1	4.3	
1969	3.3	3.8	3.9	4.4	
1970	4.7	.7	.6	2.0	
1971	6.5	6.5	6.5	9.0	
1972	3.6	.9	1.0	7.4	
1973	4.5	4.8	4.8	3.3	
1974	4.3	5.8	5.8	4.2	
1975	2.2	1.1	1.1		2.2
1976	5.3	8.4	8.4		5.3
1977	1.3	.5	1.0		1.3
1978	3.9	4.8	4.1		4.4
1979	4.7	7.3	5.4		4.7
1980	5.7	6.4	5.7		7.5
1981	–3.0‡	–.9	.3		–2.8
1982		–1.3	–1.3*		–2.5
1983		–.7			–.6
1984					3.0†

a. Data are at factor cost through 1959.
b. Through 1959 from UN-YNAS, 1970, III, p. 34.

SOURCE AND METHODS: See table 3300.

Table 3313

HONDURAS COMPARATIVE PC OF REAL GDP, 1926–84

I. 1926–39		II. 1940–84					
Year	ECLA Factor (1926–39)	Year	ECLA Factor (1940–81)	IMF (1953–83)	OECD (1951–82)	SALA (1951–74)	ECLA Market (1975–84)
1926	.9	1940	6.9				
1927	9.8	1941	-.3				
1928	12.5	1942	-8.6				
1929	-1.0	1943	.2				
		1944	15.2				
1930	6.5	1945	9.4				
1931	2.2	1946	7.6				
1932	-10.4	1947	6.4				
1933	-6.2	1948	2.1				
1934	-3.1	1949	1.4				
1935	-4.4	1950	3.2				
1936	1.8	1951	5.4		4.6	7.2	
1937	-4.4	1952	3.8		3.0	6.1	
1938	5.8	1953	7.8	6.1	6.0	6.4	
1939	2.8	1954	-5.7	-6.1	-5.1	.9	
		1955	2.6	5.9	2.7	3.0	
		1956	8.1	4.4	9.2	3.8	
		1957	4.6	4.2	6.4	11.1	
		1958	3.2	5.5	2.5	1.3	
		1959	2.5	2.3	4.5	5.2	
		1960	6.2	-.1	1.7	5.4	
		1961	2.6	2.8	2.8	.7	
		1962	5.8	5.1	5.1	3.5	
		1963	3.7	3.3	3.3	3.0	
		1964	5.2	6.0	6.0	1.2	
		1965	8.6	10.3	10.3	7.8	
		1966	5.8	5.9	5.9	8.3	
		1967	5.6	4.6	4.6	4.4	
		1968	5.9	7.3	7.3	8.9	
		1969	.8	.3	.3	2.9	
		1970	2.6	4.7	6.5	5.3	
		1971	3.8	5.4	5.5	4.0	
		1972	4.2	4.0	3.1*	3.8	
		1973	4.2	5.6	3.7*	5.5	
		1974	-.6	-.1	-.1	2.6	
		1975	-1.9	-3.0	-3.0		-1.7
		1976	6.1	8.0	8.0		8.4
		1977	5.8	11.5	11.5		8.7
		1978	7.9	7.4	7.4		7.0
		1979	6.7	6.8	6.8		6.6
		1980	1.6	2.7	2.8		4.7
		1981	-.4‡	1.2	.5		1.2
		1982		-1.8	-1.2		-1.8
		1983		-.7			-.5
		1984					2.0†

SOURCE AND METHODS: See table 3300.

Table 3314

MEXICO COMPARATIVE PC OF REAL GDP, 1896–1984[a]

PART I. 1896–1939   PART II. 1940–84

Year	ECLA Factor (1922–39)	Bank of Mexico[1] (1896–1939)	Year	ECLA Factor (1940–81)	IMF (1953–83)	OECD (1951–82)	Bank of Mexico[2] (1940–80)	Bank of Mexico New System of National Accounts[3] (1971–82)	SALA (1951–74)	ECLA Market (1975–84)
1896		3.1	1940	-.3			1.4			
1897		6.7	1941	14.8			9.7			
1898		5.8	1942	5.6			5.6			
1899		-4.8	1943	3.6			3.7			
1900		.8	1944	7.6			8.2			
1901		8.6	1945	6.3			3.1			
1902		-7.1	1946	7.3			6.6			
1903		11.2	1947	3.7			3.4			
1904		1.8	1948	3.6			4.1			
1905		10.3	1949	7.6			5.4			
1906		-1.0	1950	9.4			9.9			
1907		5.9	1951	7.5		7.8	7.7		9.1	
1908		-.2	1952	3.0		3.9	4.0		3.3	
1909		2.9	1953	5.4	.3	.2	.3		4.6	
1910		.9	1954	5.4	10.0	10.5	10.0		5.4	
1911		~	1955	7.9	8.6	8.8	8.5		7.5	
1912		~	1956	5.3	6.8	6.6	6.8		5.3	
1913		~	1957	7.5	7.5	7.7	7.5		7.5	
1914		~	1958	4.6	5.4	5.4	5.4		4.2	
1915		~	1959	4.3	3.0	2.9	3.0		3.9	
1916		~	1960	7.5	8.1	8.1	8.1		7.6	
1917		~	1961	4.9	4.9	4.9	4.9		4.9	
1918		~	1962	4.7	4.7	4.7	4.7		4.5	
1919		~	1963	8.0	8.0	8.0	8.0		8.0	
1920		~	1964	11.7	11.7	11.7	11.7		11.6	
1921		7.7	1965	6.5	6.5	6.5	6.5		6.3	
1922	2.3	2.3	1966	6.9	6.9	6.9	6.9		6.8	
1923	3.4	3.4	1967	6.3	6.3	6.3	6.3		6.1	
1924	-1.6	-1.6	1968	8.1	8.1	8.1	8.1		8.0	
1925	6.2	6.2	1969	6.3	6.3	6.3	6.3		6.4	
1926	7.7	6.0	1970	6.9	6.9*	6.9	6.9		6.8	
1927	-2.3	-4.4	1971	3.4	4.2	3.4	3.4	4.2	6.0	
1928	1.8	.6	1972	7.3	8.4	7.3*	7.3	8.5	4.7	
1929	-3.3	-3.9	1973	7.6	8.4	7.6*	7.6	8.4	8.1	
1930	-6.8	-6.2	1974	5.9	6.1	6.1	5.9	6.1	5.1	
1931	3.7	3.3	1975	4.1	5.6	5.6	4.1	5.6		5.6
1932	-16.2	-14.9	1976	2.1	4.2	4.2	2.1	4.2		4.2
1933	10.7	11.3	1977	3.3	3.4	3.4	3.3	3.4		3.4
1934	6.6	6.7	1978	7.0	8.3	8.3	7.3	8.2		8.1
1935	5.1	7.4	1979	9.2	9.2	9.2	8.0	9.2		9.2
1936	10.4	8.0	1980	8.3	8.3	8.3	7.4	8.3		8.8
1937	3.4	3.3	1981	8.1[‡]	8.0	7.9		8.0		7.9
1938	1.8	1.6	1982		.6	-.6		-.2	-.2	-.5
1939	5.3	5.4	1983	-4.6						-5.3
			1984							2.5[†]

1. Leopoldo Solís, *La Realidad Económica Mexicana: Retrovisión y Perspectivas,* rev. ed. (México, D.F.: Siglo XXI, 1981), p. 79.

2. Through 1969 data are from NAFINSA-EMC, 1981, pp. 20–21; and since 1970 from Banco Nacional de México, *México en Cifras, 1970–1980,* p. 6. All PC are calculated in 1960 prices.

3. Data are in 1970 prices from NAFINSA-EMC, 1981, p. 51; and Banco Nacional de México, *Informe,* 1982, pp. 30 and 50.

a. SALA recommends that the Bank of Mexico series be used for the period from 1896 through 1970 and the Bank of Mexico New System of National Accounts for the period since 1971—as is also recommended and used by IMF.

SOURCE AND METHODS: See table 3300.

Table 3315

NICARAGUA COMPARATIVE PC
OF REAL GDP, 1946–84

Year	ECLA Factor (1946–81)	IMF (1953–83)	OECD (1951–82)	SALA (1951–74)[a]	ECLA Market (1975–84)
1946	8.6				
1947	.3				
1948	8.7				
1949	–1.8				
1950	16.6				
1951	6.8		6.8	6.8	
1952	16.9		16.9	14.5	
1953	2.4	2.4	2.4	1.5	
1954	9.3	9.3	9.4	12.5	
1955	6.7	6.8	6.7	3.5	
1956	–.1	–.1	–.1	1.8	
1957	8.4	8.5	8.5	9.5	
1958	.3	.3	.3	–.5	
1959	1.5	1.5	1.5	1.9	
1960	1.4	3.6	1.4	1.6	
1961	7.5	7.5	7.5*	7.3	
1962	10.9	10.9	10.9	10.2	
1963	10.9	10.9	10.9	6.7	
1964	11.7	11.7	11.7	11.2	
1965	9.5	9.5	9.5	9.9	
1966	3.3	3.3	3.3	3.0	
1967	7.0	7.0	7.0	6.7	
1968	1.3	1.4	1.3	.3	
1969	6.7	6.2	6.2	5.0	
1970	1.0	1.3	1.4	4.5	
1971	4.9	4.9	4.9	5.0	
1972	3.2	3.2*	3.2	4.8	
1973	5.1	6.4	5.1	1.8	
1974	12.7	14.2	12.7	9.4	
1975	2.2	–.2	2.2		2.2
1976	5.0	5.2	5.0		5.0
1977	6.3	8.4	6.3		6.3
1978	–7.2	–7.8	–7.2		–7.2
1979	–25.5	–26.4	–26.5*		–25.5
1980	10.0	10.0	10.1		–10.0
1981	8.9‡	5.3	8.5		5.3
1982		–1.2	–1.4		–1.2
1983		5.1			4.0
1984					.5†

a. Calculated from SALA, 19-2200.

SOURCE AND METHODS: See table 3300.

Table 3316

PANAMA COMPARATIVE PC
OF REAL GDP, 1946–84

Year	ECLA Factor (1946–81)	IMF (1953–83)	OECD (1951–82)	SALA (1951–74)	ECLA Market (1975–84)
1946	1.6				
1947	4.2				
1948	–5.9				
1949	2.3				
1950	.5				
1951	–.9		–.8	–.7	
1952	5.4		5.4	5.7	
1953	6.1	6.1	6.0	6.4	
1954	3.6	3.6	3.6	1.9	
1955	5.8	5.8	5.8	5.9	
1956	5.2	5.2	5.2	5.2	
1957	10.5	10.5	10.5	10.8	
1958	.8	.8	.8	1.8	
1959	6.4	6.4	6.3	7.6	
1960	6.0	6.0	6.0	7.3	
1961	10.8	10.8	10.8	11.7	
1962	8.4	8.2	8.2	8.8	
1963	9.4	8.5	8.5	8.8	
1964	4.3	4.4	4.4	5.2	
1965	8.8	9.2	9.2	7.4	
1966	7.4	7.6	7.6	7.7	
1967	8.4	8.6	8.6	7.7	
1968	7.3	7.0	7.0	6.9	
1969	7.8	8.4	8.4	8.9	
1970	6.0	4.1	7.0	7.2	
1971	8.1	9.6	8.7	8.0	
1972	5.3	4.6	6.2*	6.5	
1973	6.1	5.4	6.6*	6.1	
1974	.8	2.4	2.4	4.1	
1975	.6	1.7	1.7		.6
1976	–1.1	1.7	1.6		–.3
1977	3.3	1.1	1.1		4.6
1978	3.8	9.8	9.8		6.5
1979	5.7	4.5	4.5		7.0
1980	4.9	15.1	13.1		9.7
1981	3.6‡	4.2	3.8		4.2
1982		5.5	3.7		5.5
1983		.2			.4
1984					.0†

SOURCE AND METHODS: See table 3300.

Table 3317

PARAGUAY COMPARATIVE PC OF REAL GDP, 1939–84

Year	ECLA Factor (1939–81)	IMF (1953–83)	OECD (1951–83)	SALA (1951–74)	ECLA Market (1976–84)
1939	17.5				
1940	-15.1				
1941	13.3				
1942	5.9				
1943	2.1				
1944	2.1				
1945	-3.5				
1946	9.8				
1947	-13.0				
1948	1.1				
1949	16.8				
1950	-1.6				
1951	1.9		-.4	1.1	
1952	-1.7		3.1	-1.0	
1953	2.8	5.2	1.3	5.3	
1954	1.7	2.6	3.8	2.7	
1955	4.6	6.3	7.1	6.2	
1956	4.2	2.4	-1.2	2.5	
1957	4.6	6.0	7.0	10.8	
1958	5.6	6.6	5.3	1.9	
1959	.4	-1.1	-.3	-1.1	
1960	.2	-.4	-.5*	-.5	
1961	4.8	6.0	5.9	5.9	
1962	7.0	5.9	5.5	5.9	
1963	2.7	2.0	2.7	1.7	
1964	4.3	4.3	4.4	4.0	
1965	5.7	5.7	5.7	6.8	
1966	1.1	1.1	1.2	1.3	
1967	6.3	6.3	6.3	5.9	
1968	3.6	3.7	3.5	4.8	
1969	3.9	3.8	3.9	4.0	
1970	6.2	3.8	6.2	5.7	
1971	4.4	5.4	5.4	5.0	
1972	5.1	6.5	6.5	4.8	
1973	7.8	7.2	7.2	7.2	
1974	8.3	8.2	8.2	8.5	
1975	5.0	6.3	6.3		
1976	7.5	7.0	7.0		7.0
1977	11.8	12.8	12.8		12.8
1978	10.3	10.8	10.8		10.9
1979	10.7	10.7	10.7		10.7
1980	11.4	11.4	11.4		11.4
1981	8.5‡	8.5	8.4		8.7
1982		-2.1	1.6*		-1.0
1983		-3.0			-3.0
1984					3.0†

SOURCE AND METHODS: See table 3300.

Table 3318

PERU COMPARATIVE PC OF REAL GDP, 1946–84

Year	ECLA Factor (1946–81)	IMF (1953–83)[a]	OECD (1951–82)[b]	SALA (1951–74)	ECLA Market (1975–84)
1946	4.0				
1947	3.0				
1948	3.4				
1949	7.1				
1950	5.0				
1951	11.3		10.5	10.2	
1952	2.7		2.8	3.0	
1953	2.2	2.5	2.2	2.0	
1954	9.6	8.8	9.6	9.8	
1955	4.9	7.0	4.9	5.0	
1956	5.0	2.5	4.6	4.4	
1957	1.0	1.1	1.1	1.1	
1958	3.2	3.3	3.3	3.3	
1959	4.4	5.4	3.6	3.5	
1960	9.0	9.4	11.4	9.2	
1961	8.2	8.8	7.0	8.0[c]	
1962	8.8	10.3	8.2	9.3[c]	
1963	3.9	4.9	4.1	3.8	
1964	6.8	6.9	7.3	6.9	
1965	4.8	5.1	5.2	4.8	
1966	5.7	7.0	6.4	5.8	
1967	1.8	3.5	3.4	1.6	
1968	.6	#	-.3	.7	
1969	4.4	4.1	3.9	2.4	
1970	9.1	7.3	5.4	9.1	
1971	5.1	5.1	5.0	6.5[c]	
1972	5.8	5.8	1.7	6.1[c]	
1973	6.2	6.2	4.3	6.2	
1974	6.9	6.9	7.5	5.8	
1975	3.3	3.3	4.6		4.5
1976	3.0	3.1	2.0		2.0
1977	-1.2	-1.2	-.1		-.1
1978	-.5	-1.8	-.5		-.5
1979	4.1	3.8	4.1		4.1
1980	3.8	3.0	3.8		4.0
1981	3.9‡	3.1	3.9		3.9
1982		.7	.4		.4
1983		-11.8			-10.8
1984					3.5

a. 1970 prices through 1960.
b. GNP through 1959.
c. Corrects SALA, 18-2200; recalculated from USAID source, in 1973 dollars.

SOURCE AND METHODS: See table 3300.

Table 3319

URUGUAY COMPARATIVE PC OF REAL GDP, 1936–84

Year	ECLA Factor (1936–81)	IMF (1956–83)	OECD (1951–82)	SALA (1951–74)	ECLA Market (1975–84)	Kravis et al.[1] (1951–77)
1936	3.6					
1937	8.7					
1938	-4.9					
1939	-.8					
1940	-2.2					
1941	5.9					
1942	-9.1					
1943	1.5					
1944	12.9					
1945	2.3					
1946	11.1					
1947	6.7					
1948	2.6					
1949	3.7					
1950	3.1					
1951	-8.2		8.2	8.2		12.9
1952	-.4		-.3	-.5		-3.5
1953	6.5		6.4	6.5		4.6
1954	5.7		5.8	5.7		5.5
1955	1.6		1.5*	1.8		1.6
1956	1.7	1.8	1.8	1.8		-.5
1957	1.0	1.2	1.0	.9		13.5
1958	-3.5	-3.5	-3.6	-3.6		-5.7
1959	-2.8	-3.0	-2.8	-2.8		3.6
1960	3.5	3.7	1.1	3.6		2.5
1961	2.9	3.0	2.8	2.8		-.1
1962	-2.3	-2.3	-2.3	-2.3		-2.9
1963	.5	.6	.5	-1.1		-.5
1964	2.0	1.8	2.0	2.8		1.6
1965	1.2	1.2	1.2	1.0		-1.7
1966	3.4	3.4	3.4	3.2		3.5
1967	-4.1	-3.9	-4.1	-5.5		-5.8
1968	1.6	1.1	1.6	1.3		.3
1969	6.1	6.2	6.1	6.2		5.0
1970	4.7	4.8	4.7	5.9		4.1
1971	-1.0	-1.0	.1	-1.0		-1.1
1972	-3.3	-3.6	-1.6	-3.0		-2.1
1973	.8	-2.1	.4	0		1.1
1974	3.1	9.3	3.1	1.0		3.8
1975	4.4	4.5	5.9		4.8	.2
1976	2.6	4.3	4.0		4.2	3.0
1977	3.4	1.8	1.2		1.8	1.9
1978	3.9	6.3	5.3		6.2	
1979	9.6	8.5	6.2		9.6	
1980	3.7	4.7	5.8		6.0	
1981	-.7‡	1.9	-1.3		1.9	
1982		-9.7	-10.0		-9.7	
1983		-4.7			-4.7	
1984					-2,0†	

1. Irving B. Kravis, Alan Heston, and Robert Summers, *World Product and Income: International Comparisons of Real Gross Product* (Baltimore: Published for the World Bank by the Johns Hopkins University Press, 1982), pp. 330–336. Kravis et al. give the results of the International Comparison Project (ICP), supervised by the UN Statistical Office with funding from a consortium organized by the World Bank, which developed international dollars comparable from country to country by applying a common set of prices (representative of the world price structure) to the quantities of the commodities and services entering into each country's final expenditure on GDP. The results theoretically overcome the problem of using nominal exchange rates, as does the "ECLA Factor approach." Data are calculated from 1975 dollars at market prices.

SOURCE AND METHODS: See table 3300.

Table 3320
VENEZUELA COMPARATIVE PC OF REAL GDP, 1937–84

Year	ECLA Factor (1937–81)	IMF (1953–83)	OECD (1951–82)	SALA (1951–74)	ECLA Market (1975–84)
1937	7.3				
1938	3.2				
1939	4.3				
1940	2.8				
1941	7.9				
1942	-4.6				
1943	5.6				
1944	11.3				
1945	9.7				
1946	17.6				
1947	16.4				
1948	12.7				
1949	4.8				
1950	2.4				
1951	11.7		11.6	12.0	
1952	7.3		7.2	7.6	
1953	6.2	6.2	6.2	7.5	
1954	9.6	9.7	9.5	10.1	
1955	8.9	8.9	8.9	7.8	
1956	10.6	10.6	10.5	8.0	
1957	11.6	3.6	11.6	10.3	
1958	1.3	1.3	1.3	7.1	
1959	7.9	8.0	7.9	8.9	
1960	1.4	4.0	4.0*	3.3	
1961	5.0	4.9	5.0	4.5	
1962	9.1	9.1	9.1	8.3	
1963	6.9	7.0	6.9	7.1	
1964	9.7	9.6	9.7	12.9	
1965	5.9	6.0	5.9	5.7	
1966	2.3	2.5	2.3	2.7	
1967	4.0	3.8	4.0	4.6	
1968	5.3	4.9	5.3	5.2	
1969	4.5	4.5	4.5	3.9	
1970	7.1	8.8	8.8	6.2	
1971	3.3	3.0	3.0	0	
1972	3.0	2.7	3.3	5.0	
1973	6.7	6.3	6.1	4.8	
1974	5.8	6.1	6.1	7.3	
1975	5.2	6.1	5.9		5.9
1976	7.8	8.8	8.4		8.4
1977	7.6	6.7	6.8		6.8
1978	4.8	2.1	3.2		3.2
1979	.9	1.3	.8		.9
1980	-1.2	-2.0	-1.5		-3.4
1981	.6‡	-.3	1.0		.3
1982		.7	.6		.7
1983		-5.6			-4.8
1984					-1.5†

SOURCE AND METHODS: See table 3300.

Table 3321
LATIN AMERICA COMPARATIVE PC OF REAL GDP, 1940–84

Year	ECLA Factor[1] (1940–79)	IMF (1953–82)[2]	OECD[3] (1951–82)	SALA[4] (1951–74)	ECLA Market (1975–84)
1940	.2				
1941	6.2				
1942	1.8				
1943	3.1				
1944	7.3				
1945	1.7				
1946	7.8				
1947	6.3				
1948	4.7				
1949	2.7				
1950	4.9				
1951	5.9		5.4	6.2	
1952	3.0		2.3	2.5	
1953	4.5	2.4	3.6	4.6	
1954	6.2	5.2	6.4	5.9	
1955	6.3	4.5	6.3	2.5	
1956	4.1	.7	3.8	3.3	
1957	6.1	2.6	6.4	6.3	
1958	4.9	5.7	4.9	4.5	
1959	2.6	1.7	2.2	1.9	
1960	7.0	6.3	7.4	6.0	
1961	6.6	5.6	6.6	6.6	
1962	4.2	3.6	4.3	4.0	
1963	3.4	3.2	3.2	3.2	
1964	7.5	4.4	6.9	7.6	
1965	5.4	12.0	5.1	5.4	
1966	4.4	6.2	4.4	4.5	
1967	4.3	4.0	4.4	4.1	
1968	6.9	6.9	6.9	6.3	
1969	7.1	6.8	7.1	6.7	
1970	6.9	4.5	6.9	7.0	
1971	6.7	6.8	6.2	7.0	
1972	6.9	7.1	6.2	6.5	
1973	8.5	7.9	8.3	7.9	
1974	7.1	7.2	6.1	7.3	
1975	3.2	4.0	3.3		3.7
1976	4.6	5.8	5.3		5.5
1977	4.6	5.0	4.9		4.8
1978	4.7	4.6	4.4		5.0
1979	6.5	6.9	6.2		6.5
1980		5.6	5.5		6.1
1981		.6	1.0		1.7
1982		-1.5	-1.4		-1.0
1983					-3.1
1984					2.6†

1. Excludes Cuba and through 1944 excludes Bolivia, Costa Rica, Dominican Republic, El Salvador, Guatemala, Haiti, Nicaragua, Panama, and Peru, but the ten countries included generated 88.7% of GDP for the region in 1945.
2. Excludes Cuba and Venezuela. Includes Dominica since 1977, Guyana since 1978, Jamaica since 1961, St. Lucia since 1976, Suriname since 1974. (Reported as Western Hemisphere in Source.)
3. Includes Jamaica, Trinidad and Tobago; includes Netherlands Antilles and Guyana for 1956–59; includes more than ten small republics of the Caribbean through 1959.
4. Excludes Cuba and Haiti.

SOURCE AND METHODS: See table 3300.

Table 3322

UNITED STATES COMPARATIVE
PC OF REAL GNP, 1910–84[a]

PART I. 1910–39

Year	USBC[1] (1910–39)	USDC-SCB[2] (1930–39)
1910	2.8	
1911	2.6	
1912	5.7	
1913	.9	
1914	–4.3	
1915	–.8	
1916	7.9	
1917	.7	
1918	12.3	
1919	–3.5	
1920	–4.3	
1921	–8.6	
1922	15.8	
1923	12.1	
1924	–.2	
1925	8.4	
1926	5.9	
1927	.0	
1928	.6	
1929	6.7	
1930	–9.8	–9.5
1931	–7.6	–7.8
1932	–14.7	–13.8
1933	–1.8	–2.2
1934	9.1	7.6
1935	9.9	8.7
1936	13.9	13.7
1937	5.3	5.0
1938	–5.0	–4.4
1939	8.6	7.8

PART II. 1940–84

Year	USBC[1] (1940–70)	IMF[3] (1953–84)	SALA[4] (1951–74)	USDC-SCB[2] (1940–84)
1940	8.5			7.6
1941	16.1			16.3
1942	12.9			15.3
1943	13.2			15.6
1944	7.2			7.1
1945	–1.7			–1.5
1946	–11.9			–14.7
1947	–.9			–1.7
1948	4.5			4.1
1949	.1			.5
1950	9.6			8.7
1951	7.9		7.9	8.3
1952	3.1		3.1	3.7
1953	4.5	3.8	4.5	3.8
1954	–1.3	–1.2	–1.4	–1.2
1955	7.6	6.7	7.6	6.7
1956	1.9	2.1	1.9	2.1
1957	1.4	1.8	1.4	1.8
1958	–1.1	–.3	–1.1	–.4
1959	6.4	6.0	6.4	6.0
1960	2.5	2.1	2.5	2.2
1961	2.0	2.6	1.9	2.6
1962	6.6	5.7	6.5	5.8
1963	4.0	4.0	4.0	4.0
1964	5.5	5.2	5.5	5.3
1965	6.3	6.0	6.3	6.0
1966	6.5	6.1	6.5	6.0
1967	2.6	2.7	2.6	2.7
1968	4.7	4.6	4.7	4.6
1969	2.6	2.8	2.6	2.8
1970	–.6	–.2	–.7	–.2
1971		3.3	3.0	3.4
1972		5.6	6.8	5.7
1973		5.5	5.5	5.8
1974		–.8	–1.7	–.6
1975		–.9		–1.1
1976		5.3		6.1
1977		5.5		5.9
1978		4.9		5.0
1979		2.4		2.8
1980		–.3		–.3
1981		2.6		2.0
1982		–2.0		–1.9
1983		3.8		3.7
1984		6.8		6.8

1. USBC-HS, Series F-31, in 1958 dollars.
2. USDC-SCB, *The National Income and Product Accounts of the United States, 1929–1976* (Washington, D.C., 1981), revised since 1976 with USDC-SCB, July 1982, and April 1985. All data calculated in 1972 dollars.
3. IMF-IFS-Y, 1984.
4. SALA, 18-2200.

a. At market prices.

SOURCE AND METHODS: See table 3300.

Table 3323

IMF GDP ANNUAL PERCENTAGE CHANGE, 19 LRC, 1955–83
(Constant Market Prices)

	Country	1955	1960	1965	1970	1975	1980	1981	1982	1983
A.	ARGENTINA	15.9	7.4	11.7	2.6	#	.9	-6.3	-4.8	2.0
B.	BOLIVIA	5.3	8.6	4.9	7.8	6.6	.6	-.9	-8.7	-7.6
C.	BRAZIL	~	~	~	2.4	5.4	7.2	-1.6	.9	-3.2
D.	CHILE	#	5.7	5.0	1.4*	-12.9	7.8	5.7	-14.3	-.7
E.	COLOMBIA	3.9	4.3	3.6	9.3	2.3	4.1	2.3	.9	.8
F.	COSTA RICA	~	~	9.8	7.5	2.1	.8	-4.6	-6.9	~
H.	DOMINICAN REP.	6.2	1.3	-10.9	8.4	5.2	6.1	4.1	1.6	~
I.	ECUADOR	2.6	6.6	12.5	6.5	5.6	4.9	3.9	1.8	-3.3
J.	EL SALVADOR	4.3	4.0	5.4	3.0	5.6	-8.7	-8.3	-6.0	-.7
K.	GUATEMALA	2.5	2.4	4.4	5.7	1.9	3.7	.7	-3.5	#
L.	HAITI	-4.0	2.6	2.1	.7	1.1	6.4	-.9	-1.3	-.7
M.	HONDURAS	5.9	-.1	10.3	4.7	-3.0	2.7	1.2	-1.8	-.7
N.	MEXICO	8.6	8.1	6.5	6.9*	5.6	8.3	8.0	.6	-4.6
O.	NICARAGUA	6.8	3.6	9.5	1.3	-.2	10.0	5.3	-1.2	5.1
P.	PANAMA	5.8	6.0	9.2	4.1	1.7	15.1	4.2	5.5	.2
Q.	PARAGUAY	6.3	-.4	5.7	3.8	6.3	11.4	8.5	-2.1	-3.0
R.	PERU	7.0	9.4	5.1	7.3	3.3	3.0	3.1	.7	-11.8
S.	URUGUAY	~	3.7	1.2	4.8	4.5	4.7	1.9	-9.7	-4.7
T.	VENEZUELA	8.9	4.0	6.0	8.8	6.1	-2.0	-.3	.7	-5.6
	LATIN AMERICA	~	6.3	12.0	4.5	4.0	5.6	.6	-1.5	-2.1
	UNITED STATES	6.7	2.1	6.0	-.2	-.9	-.3	2.6	-2.0	3.8

SOURCE: IMF-IFS-Y, 1984; calculated from IMF-IFS, May 1985.

Table 3324

GDP IN CONSTANT DOLLARS OF 1970, 19 LR, 1940–79
(ECLA Factor Series)[1]

PART I. PURCHASING POWER EQUIVALENCES OF LATIN AMERICAN CURRENCY IN RELATION TO THE DOLLAR IN 1970

	Country	1 Dollar U.S. Currency Equals:
A.	ARGENTINA	2.95 pesos argentinos
B.	BOLIVIA	9.03 pesos bolivianos
C.	BRAZIL	4.14 novos cruzeiros
D.	CHILE	.01 pesos chilenos
E.	COLOMBIA	10.68 pesos colombianos
F.	COSTA RICA	5.09 colones costarricenses
H.	DOMINICAN REP.	.87 pesos dominicanos
I.	ECUADOR	14.00 sucres
J.	EL SALVADOR	1.70 colones salvadoreños
K.	GUATEMALA	.81 quetzales
L.	HAITI	3.99 gourdes
M.	HONDURAS	1.75 lempiras
N.	MEXICO	8.88 pesos mexicanos
O.	NICARAGUA	6.41 córdobas
P.	PANAMA	.76 balboas
Q.	PARAGUAY	85.41 guaraníes
R.	PERU	30.72 soles
S.	URUGUAY	.20 pesos uruguayos
T.	VENEZUELA	3.96 bolívares

1. Owing to timing of revisions, the implicit PC since 1970 here may not agree with explicit PC for ECLA factor series in tables 3301 through 3321 above.

SOURCE: ECLA-SHCAL, p. 8.

Table 3324 (Continued)

PART II. SERIES, 1940–80 (M US)[1]

Year	A. ARGENTINA	B. BOLIVIA	C. BRAZIL	D. CHILE	E. COLOMBIA	F. COSTA RICA	H. DOMINICAN REPUBLIC	I. ECUADOR	J. EL SALVADOR	K. GUATEMALA
1940	10,048	~	8,024	2,495	3,013	~	~	424	~	~
1941	10,538	~	8,421	2,498	3,063	~	~	426	~	~
1942	11,028	~	8,183	2,636	3,070	~	~	444	~	~
1943	11,108	~	8,660	2,746	3,082	~	~	500	~	~
1944	12,189	~	9,057	2,785	3,090	~	~	507	~	~
1945	11,602	634	9,137	3,038	3,445	203[a]	356	509	336	795[a]
1946	12,567	645	9,851	3,225	3,757	218	330	570	342	857
1947	14,288	656	10,090	3,010	3,904	260	363	633	430	967
1948	14,464	670	10,841	3,357	4,025	274	402	719	548	959
1949	13,800	684	11,558	3,339	4,248	286	452	732	498	883
1950	14,018	698	12,309	3,499	4,325	298	533	796	512	885
1951	14,562	748	13,037	3,683	4,458	306	596	805	522	897
1952	13,821	770	14,169	3,810	4,739	343	644	904	561	916
1953	14,570	697	14,528	4,078	5,013	395	636	923	601	950
1954	15,164	712	15,996	4,108	5,344	398	673	997	608	967
1955	16,242	749	17,093	4,221	5,559	444	714	1,024	640	991
1956	16,693	705	17,636	4,251	5,788	431	786	1,062	690	1,081
1957	17,550	682	19,058	4,371	5,925	468	835	1,109	727	1,142
1958	18,623	698	20,526	4,582	6,072	526	880	1,142	742	1,196
1959	17,428	696	21,656	4,899	6,501	545	885	1,203	776	1,255
1960	18,789	726	23,774	5,147	6,768	593	929	1,281	807	1,286
1961	20,128	741	26,224	5,461	7,108	617	908	1,313	836	1,340
1962	19,802	782	27,599	5,714	7,490	655	1,062	1,383	935	1,388
1963	19,327	832	28,027	6,004	7,733	711	1,131	1,419	976	1,520
1964	21,327	872	28,848	6,262	8,202	746	1,207	1,518	1,067	1,591
1965	23,275	915	29,634	6,578	8,490	814*	1,057	1,665	1,124	1,660
1966	23,421	981	30,749	7,039	8,935	877	1,199	1,708	1,204	1,752
1967	24,053	1,043	32,250	7,211	9,309	931	1,239	1,799	1,270	1,824
1968	25,078	1,132	35,852	7,427	9,897	1,002	1,242	1,898	1,311	1,984
1969	27,228	1,182	39,412	7,684	10,523	1,069	1,377	2,002	1,357	2,077
1970	28,686	1,269	42,885	7,961	11,217	1,139	1,523	2,190	1,397	2,196
1971	30,065	1,332	48,590	8,574	11,865	1,217	1,689	2,278	1,462	2,319
1972	31,004	1,411	54,294	8,566	12,804	1,316	1,864	2,459	1,544	2,489
1973	32,020	1,485	61,842	8,256	13,781	1,139	2,105	2,855	1,622	2,658
1974	35,039	1,576	67,888	8,724	14,673	1,418	2,231	3,113	1,727	2,827
1975	34,735	1,680	71,748	7,472	15,300	1,496	2,347	3,324	1,823	2,882
1976	34,142	1,782	78,180	7,754	15,939	1,612	2,505	3,632	1,895	3,095
1977	35,828	1,857	81,825	8,506	16,697	1,755	2,630	3,905	2,010	3,337
1978	34,597	1,914	86,757	9,212	18,200	1,865	2,687	4,116	2,131	3,503
1979	37,525	1,955	92,309	9,969	19,088	1,958	2,816	4,339	2,099	3,669
1980	~	1,966.4	99,694	~	19,890	1,969	2,973	~	1,897	3,797

Table 3324 (Continued)

PART II. SERIES, 1940–80 (M US)[1] (Continued)

Year	L. HAITI	M. HONDURAS	N. MEXICO	O. NICARAGUA	P. PANAMA	Q. PARAGUAY	R. PERU	S. URUGUAY	T. VENEZUELA	LATIN AMERICA
1940	~	229	6,632	~	~	342	~	1,273	1,528	38,341[b]
1941	~	229	7,614	~	~	347	~	1,348	1,649	40,736[b]
1942	~	209	8,041	~	~	367	~	1,226	1,572	41,461[b]
1943	~	209	8,333	~	~	375	~	1,244	1,661	42,749[b]
1944	~	241	8,967	~	~	383	~	1,404	1,849	45,854[b]
1945	377	264	9,563	176	363	370	~	1,436	2,029	46,653
1946	380	284	10,227	191	368	406	~	1,595	2,386	50,304
1947	386	302	10,605	192	384	353	~	1,703	2,778	53,470
1948	390	309	10,986	209	361	357	~	1,947	3,132	55,990
1949	394	313	11,819	205	369	417	~	1,811	3,282	57,488
1950	401	323	12,926	239	371	410	~	1,867	3,360	60,286
1951	407	340	13,897	255	368	418	~	2,021	3,752	63,871
1952	430	353	14,314	298	388	411	~	2,013	4,025	65,785
1953	416	381	15,087	305	411	423	~	2,143	4,274	68,772
1954	450	360	15,909	334	426	430	~	2,265	4,686	73,050
1955	432	369	17,167	356	450	450	~	2,301	5,102	77,686
1956	470	399	18,085	356	474	469	~	2,341	5,640	80,909
1957	442	417	19,443	386	524	490	~	2,363	6,296	85,814
1958	477	430	20,335	387	528	518	~	2,280	6,379	90,024
1959	454	441	21,219	393	561	520	~	2,216	6,881	92,393
1960	484	468	22,802	398	595	521	4,882	2,295	6,978	98,857
1961	464	480	23,926	428	659	546	~	2,360	7,329	105,433
1962	508	508	25,044	475	715	584	~	2,307	7,998	109,917
1963	475	527	27,045	526	782	600	~	2,319	8,550	113,663
1964	465	554	30,207	588	816	626	~	2,365	9,380	122,147
1965	470	602	32,166	644	887	662	6,641	2,392	9,935	128,743
1966	467	637	34,396	665	953	669	~	2,474	10,163	134,391
1967	457	673	36,552	712	1,033	712	~	2,371	10,573	140,219
1968	475	713	39,526	721	1,108	737	~	2,409	11,134	149,894
1969	491	719	42,026	769	1,194	766	~	2,556	11,630	160,585
1970	514	733	44,934	777	1,266	813	7,977	2,676	12,457	172,646
1971	547	780	46,480	815	1,369	848	~	2,650	12,873	184,167
1972	567	813	49,858	841	1,441	892	~	2,557	13,261	196,535
1973	592	848	53,495	883	1,529	978	8,882	2,577	14,101	212,649
1974	618	840	56,653	996	1,541	1,059	9,546	2,658	14,962	228,087
1975	632	823	58,964	1,018	1,550	1,126	9,979	2,776	15,848	235,497
1976	665	881	60,218	1,069	1,534	1,205	10,181	2,849	17,179	246,303
1977	674	932	62,182	1,136	1,558	1,358	10,175	2,945	18,352	257,664
1978	703	1,000	66,714	1,055	1,622	1,506	10,124	3,061	18,932	268,772
1979	736	1,067	72,047	786	1,715	1,667	10,542	3,318	19,103	285,566
1980	779	1,084	~	864	1,799	1,857	10,947	~	18,873	~

1. Owing to timing of revisions, the implicit PC since 1970 here may not agree with explicit PC for ECLA factor series in tables 3301 through 3321 above.

a. ECLA estimate to arrive at total for Latin America in 1945.

b. Totals for years from 1940 to 1944 calculated by ECLA on basis of change in countries shown, countries which generated 88.7% of total GDP in 1945.

SOURCE: ECLA-SHCAL, pp. 14-19, except data since 1970 from ECLA-AE, 1979, pp. 128–129, and 1980, pp. 198–199; ECLA-AE, 1981, pp. 206–207.

Table 3325

STRUCTURE AND GROWTH OF GROSS DOMESTIC PRODUCT, BY SECTOR, 1961–83

(%)

Sector	Structure						Growth Rate					
	Average			Annual			Average			Annual Variation		
	1961–70	1971–75	1976–80	1981	1982	1983	1961–70	1971–75	1976–80	1981	1982	1983
Primary	19.1	15.3	13.7	13.6	13.7	14.2	3.5	3.3	3.6	4.6	.1	.4
Agriculture	14.8	12.0	10.9	10.7	10.7	11.2	3.4	3.9	3.3	4.7	-.2	.8
Mining	4.3	3.3	2.8	2.9	3.0	3.0	3.9	1.2	5.0	4.3	1.2	-1.1
Secondary	35.9	38.8	40.5	39.8	39.4	38.7	6.5	7.7	6.3	-1.5	-1.7	-4.8
Manufacturing	22.5	24.3	24.4	23.0	22.7	22.3	6.9	7.1	5.7	-4.2	-2.3	-4.5
Electricity	1.4	2.0	2.4	2.6	2.8	2.8	10.8	10.4	9.7	3.8	4.7	-1.1
Construction	5.4	5.5	5.9	5.9	5.7	5.3	4.9	7.7	6.4	1.0	-4.7	-10.5
Transport	6.5	7.1	7.8	8.2	8.3	8.3	6.0	9.1	7.0	2.9	.0	-2.7
Tertiary	45.0	45.8	45.8	46.6	46.9	47.1	5.9	6.9	5.4	2.8	-.2	-2.6
Commerce	18.1	17.8	17.4	17.6	17.2	16.8	5.6	6.5	5.4	1.6	-3.4	-5.1
Financial Services	10.4	11.0	11.9	11.9	12.2	12.8	6.4	7.1	7.6	-1.4	2.3	1.3
Other Services	9.2	9.4	9.1	9.8	9.9	9.8	6.2	6.2	4.8	9.3	.3	-4.0
Government	7.3	7.6	7.4	7.4	7.6	7.7	5.9	8.3	3.3	4.8	2.5	-1.4
GDP	100.0	100.0	100.0	100.0	100.0	100.0	5.7	6.6	5.5	1.3	-.8	-3.0

SOURCE: IDB-SPTF, 1984, table 6.

Table 3326

AGRICULTURAL SECTOR: VALUE ADDED, DISTRIBUTION, AND GROWTH, 19 LR, 1961–83

(%)

Country	Regional Distribution			Proportion of GDP			Average Annual Growth			Annual Variation		
	1961–70	1971–80	1981–83	1961–70	1971–80	1981–83	1961–70	1971–75	1976–80	1981	1982	1983[‡]
A. ARGENTINA	14.6	13.5	12.5	14.4	13.3	14.8	2.5	2.8	1.3	2.4	7.0	2.1
B. BOLIVIA	1.0	1.0	.9	20.5	17.5	18.2	3.0	5.6	2.2	7.0	-2.2	-22.0
C. BRAZIL	23.3	25.2	27.1	12.5	8.4	8.2	3.2	6.5	4.7	6.8	-2.5	2.2
D. CHILE	3.2	2.6	2.6	9.2	8.6	9.0	2.2	2.3	3.1	5.3	-2.3	-.9
E. COLOMBIA	8.7	9.2	9.6	27.1	23.4	22.7	3.7	4.5	4.3	3.2	-1.3	2.1
F. COSTA RICA	1.0	1.2	1.1	24.4	20.6	20.2	5.2	3.4	1.9	5.1	-4.9	4.4
H. DOMINICAN REP.	1.7	1.7	1.8	26.0	18.5	17.1	1.7	3.1	3.9	5.5	3.8	3.5
I. ECUADOR	2.3	2.3	2.2	26.8	18.6	14.6	4.3	4.1	1.9	5.4	1.1	14.9
J. EL SALVADOR	1.6	1.6	1.3	28.0	24.3	25.9	4.1	4.7	1.6	-9.2	-3.4	.0
K. GUATEMALA	3.2	3.7	3.5	28.7	27.0	25.2	4.5	6.2	3.2	1.2	-2.0	-2.5
L. HAITI	1.1	.9	.8	44.6	38.2	32.1	.8	2.3	.9	-1.5	-4.1	3.1
M. HONDURAS	1.3	1.2	1.2	35.9	31.3	29.9	5.6	-.6	7.1	1.0	.6	-.8
N. MEXICO	21.4	21.0	21.7	14.3	10.4	9.1	3.9	3.0	3.9	6.1	-.6	3.4
O. NICARAGUA	1.2	1.2	1.0	25.1	24.3	24.1	6.9	4.9	-3.7	10.1	2.0	11.7
P. PANAMA	.7	.7	.6	16.7	12.5	10.1	5.5	1.4	2.0	8.3	.3	3.9
Q. PARAGUAY	1.5	1.7	2.0	38.2	33.9	30.0	3.0	7.4	7.3	6.7	-3.0	-4.8
R. PERU	5.2	4.5	4.0	17.8	14.2	13.9	4.3	-.1	.3	10.5	2.8	-11.5
S. URUGUAY	1.7	1.3	1.1	13.9	12.2	11.9	3.8	-1.1	2.8	1.0	-6.8	-2.6
T. VENEZUELA	3.9	4.1	3.9	7.0	6.3	6.3	5.6	3.7	2.4	-1.9	3.6	.0
LATIN AMERICA[1]	100.0	100.0	100.0	14.8	11.5	10.9	3.4	3.9	3.3	4.7	-0.2	.8

1. Includes Bahamas, Barbados, Guyana, Jamaica, Suriname, and Trinidad and Tobago.

SOURCE: IDB-SPTF, 1984, table 7.

Table 3327

MANUFACTURING SECTOR: VALUE ADDED, DISTRIBUTION, AND GROWTH, 19 LR, 1961–83

(%)

Country	Regional Distribution			Proportion of GDP			Average Annual Growth			Annual Variation		
	1961–70	1971–80	1981–83	1961–70	1971–80	1981–83	1961–70	1971–75	1976–80	1981	1982	1983[‡]
A. ARGENTINA	17.4	13.0	9.2	26.1	27.1	22.7	5.5	3.5	.1	−15.9	−4.8	9.0
B. BOLIVIA	.4	.4	.4	13.6	15.3	15.1	6.4	6.8	4.8	−3.8	−15.3	−7.5
C. BRAZIL	31.5	38.6	39.2	25.7	27.4	24.7	7.0	10.8	7.3	−10.1	.1	−6.3
D. CHILE	5.6	3.5	2.8	24.3	23.4	20.0	5.4	−4.0	7.6	2.6	−21.6	3.0
E. COLOMBIA	4.4	4.2	4.2	20.8	22.8	20.8	6.0	7.5	4.6	−2.6	−2.4	−.2
F. COSTA RICA[1]	.5	.6	.5	16.4	21.0	21.2	9.0	8.9	6.0	−.5	−14.9	−1.8
H. DOMINICAN REP.	.7	.8	.9	15.3	18.6	18.3	8.8	9.3	4.4	2.7	5.2	1.7
I. ECUADOR	.8	1.0	1.4	14.9	17.4	19.3	9.4	9.6	9.4	4.8	3.7	−5.6
J. EL SALVADOR	.6	.6	.4	17.1	18.7	17.0	8.2	5.7	.6	−10.4	−8.4	−3.0
K. GUATEMALA	1.1	1.0	1.1	14.5	15.9	15.8	7.7	4.8	7.8	−3.1	−5.2	−2.1
L. HAITI	.2	.2	.2	14.0	15.5	17.1	.7	5.2	11.9	−9.5	1.1	1.1
M. HONDURAS	.3	.3	.3	12.7	15.0	16.4	7.1	2.8	9.5	1.7	−1.8	−4.6
N. MEXICO	21.5	23.2	27.5	21.9	24.4	24.1	9.2	7.1	7.2	7.0	−2.9	−7.3
O. NICARAGUA	.6	.5	.5	19.1	22.2	23.8	10.2	5.9	1.0	2.8	−.2	.3
P. PANAMA	.3	.3	.3	11.7	11.5	9.4	10.9	3.0	4.4	−3.3	2.4	−1.6
Q. PARAGUAY	.4	.4	.5	16.1	16.9	16.2	6.6	5.3	11.1	8.0	−4.5	−4.2
R. PERU	4.3	3.7	3.2	22.7	24.9	23.1	6.2	7.1	.7	.1	−2.7	−15.0
S. URUGUAY[1]	1.8	1.2	1.0	23.3	24.6	22.1	1.6	2.1	5.0	−4.5	−17.1	−7.9
T. VENEZUELA	5.8	5.2	5.3	15.8	16.8	17.7	7.6	5.2	5.0	−1.8	2.1	−2.0
LATIN AMERICA[2]	100.0	100.0	100.0	22.5	24.3	22.7	6.9	7.1	5.7	−4.2	−2.3	−4.5

1. Includes mining.
2. Includes Bahamas, Barbados, Guyana, Jamaica, Suriname, and Trinidad and Tobago.

SOURCE: IDB-SPTF, 1984, p. 200.

Table 3328

SHARES OF AGRICULTURAL GDP IN TOTAL GDP,
19 LR, 1950–75

(%)

Country	Agricultural GDP/Total GDP				Agricultural GDP PI/Nonagricultural GDP PI			
	1950–52	1959–61	1969–71	1973–75	1950–52	1959–61	1969–71	1973–75
A. ARGENTINA	16.5	15.5	12.8	12.0	60.4	73.6	75.1	76.9
B. BOLIVIA	24.1	25.1	17.0	15.9	20.1	21.5	16.3	16.4
C. BRAZIL	20.7	16.5	14.5	12.3	18.2	18.3	20.1	18.4
D. CHILE	10.8	9.7	7.8	7.2	25.4	25.2	27.3	28.1
E. COLOMBIA	37.8	33.4	28.3	26.7	47.2	47.3	64.9	73.1
F. COSTA RICA	39.3	30.1	25.4	23.7	49.9	40.9	46.9	49.1
H. DOMINICAN REP.	33.5	32.5	25.7	20.5	21.3	24.3	22.0	17.8
I. ECUADOR	41.7	38.2	29.5	23.0	53.0	46.0	40.3	31.8
J. EL SALVADOR	39.5	36.2	30.2	28.7	34.9	35.5	33.8	34.2
K. GUATEMALA	34.7	32.3	30.3	30.5	24.6	26.5	27.8	30.8
L. HAITI	52.0	48.4	51.0	46.2	18.7	19.7	31.0	29.0
M. HONDURAS	43.6	34.9	35.1	33.5	31.2	22.7	27.3	27.2
N. MEXICO	17.4	15.9	11.8	10.0	13.7	15.4	16.2	15.6
O. NICARAGUA	32.2	27.3	27.1	27.5	24.9	23.6	38.6	47.2
P. PANAMA	29.9	26.3	29.8	18.7	34.6	34.6	36.9	37.2
Q. PARAGUAY	46.3	39.7	34.0	33.4	67.5	50.7	46.2	49.7
R. PERU	26.3	24.5	19.4	15.9	27.3	29.3	29.7	25.9
S. URUGUAY	15.1	11.6	12.5	11.9	56.8	50.9	79.6	87.7
T. VENEZUELA	7.9	7.1	7.5	7.3	10.6	14.2	23.6	27.3
LATIN AMERICA	20.3	17.9	14.9	13.3	21.6	22.5	24.0	23.4

SOURCE: *25 Años en la Agricultura: Rasgos Principales, 1950–75*
(Santiago: ECLA, 1979), Anexo 1.

Table 3329

AGRICULTURE[1] SHARE IN GDP, 19 LR, 1920-81[a]
(%)[b]

Year	A. ARGENTINA	B. BOLIVIA	C. BRAZIL	D. CHILE	E. COLOMBIA	F. COSTA RICA	H. DOMINICAN REPUBLIC	I. ECUADOR	J. EL SALVADOR	K. GUATEMALA	L. HAITI
1920	30.0	~	22.8	~	~	~	~	~	~	~	~
1930	22.6	~	23.5	~	52.4	~	~	~	~	~	~
1940	23.2	~	21.4	13.0	44.7	~	~	38.3	~	~	~
1950	~	25.4	16.8	11.6	37.7	38.4	34.5	42.1	40.9	35.5	52.2
1960	16.2	24.5	13.4	9.8	32.7	29.4	33.9	39.0	36.0	33.4	49.2
1970	14.9	19.7	10.0	7.9	28.6	25.0	25.8	29.7	30.6	30.1	50.8
1980	12.9	17.1	7.3	7.7	25.4	18.3	18.6	21.1	28.0	28.0	42.0
1981‡	13.7	18.4	8.1	6.9	25.6	19.8	18.3	15.3	29.9	27.7	42.0

Year	M. HONDURAS	N. MEXICO	O. NICARAGUA	P. PANAMA	Q. PARAGUAY	R. PERU	S. URUGUAY	T. VENEZUELA	LATIN AMERICA[2]	UNITED STATES
1920	~	~	~	~	~	~	~	~	~	~
1930	55.2	18.7	~	~	~	~	~	~	~	~
1940	50.5	19.7	~	~	49.2	~	16.3	19.2	~	~
1950	44.8	19.4	36.6	32.6	40.8	25.5	13.5	9.2	25.1	5.5
1960	32.8	16.2	29.5	26.1	39.2	24.4	11.0	7.9	19.7	4.4
1970	32.5	12.7	27.0	20.0	34.3	20.3	12.9	7.6	17.1	3.2
1980	27.0	9.4	26.8	17.0	30.0	13.3	9.8	7.0	13.8	2.7
1981‡	27.5	9.1	28.0	16.3	29.5	12.8	10.1	7.0	11.2[c]	~

1. Includes hunting, fishing, and forestry.
2. For coverage, see table 3321, note 1.

a. For yearly data since 1900, see SALA, 20-2205ff. and 22-2305ff.
b. Calculations based upon constant dollars, factor cost.
c. For 1979 from ECLA-AE, 1980, p. 119.

SOURCE: Latin American data calculated from ECLA-SHCAL, pp. 74ff.; and for 1960 and 1970 from ECLA-S, 1980, table 3, by country, ECLA-S, 1981, table 3, by country. U.S. data calculated from USDC sources given in SALA, 24-3322, note 2.

Table 3330

MINING AND QUARRYING SHARE IN GDP, 19 LR, 1920-81[a]

(%)[b]

Year	A. ARGENTINA	B. BOLIVIA	C. BRAZIL	D. CHILE	E. COLOMBIA	F. COSTA RICA[1]	H. DOMINICAN REPUBLIC	I. ECUADOR	J. EL SALVADOR	K. GUATEMALA
1920	.3	~	.6	~	~	~	~	~	~	~
1930	.3	~	.4	~	3.0	~	~	~	~	~
1940	.9	~	.5	19.4	3.0	~	.3	2.2	1.0	.2
1950	.7	19.8	.4	12.4	2.4	~	1.9	1.2	.2	.2
1960	1.3	12.3	.5	11.1	2.7	~	1.7	1.4	.2	.1
1970	2.2	8.0	.8	11.7	2.1	~	4.9	1.2	.1	.4
1980	2.5	5.5	.9	12.2	1.1	~	5.0	4.7		.4
1981‡	2.6	5.2	.9	10.7	1.2	~		5.0		

Year	L. HAITI	M. HONDURAS	N. MEXICO	O. NICARAGUA	P. PANAMA	Q. PARAGUAY	R. PERU	S. URUGUAY[1]	T. VENEZUELA	LATIN AMERICA[2]	UNITED STATES
1920	~	~	~	~	~	~	~	~	~	~	~
1930	~	2.0	8.5	~	~	~	~	~	20.3	~	~
1940	~	3.1	6.0	~	~	~	~	~	27.3	4.3	2.1
1950	3.3	2.3	4.1	1.5	.2	.2	7.2	~	27.5	4.0	1.8
1960	5.0	1.9	2.4	1.2	.3	.1	11.2	~	22.6	4.6	1.8
1970	1.7	2.3	4.1	.7	.3	.7	7.2	~	8.8	4.3	1.5
1980	.9	1.8	3.1	.2	.3	.7	8.1	~	8.8	3.5[c]	~
1981‡	.5	1.8	3.4	.2	.3	.7	7.3	~	~	~	~

1. Included in table 3331.
2. For coverage, see table 3321, note 1.
a. For yearly data since 1900, see SALA, 20-2205ff. and 22-2305ff.
b. Calculations based upon constant dollars, factor cost.
c. Includes petroleum refining.

SOURCE: See table 3329.

Table 3331

MANUFACTURING SHARE IN GDP, 19 LR, 1920-81[a]
(%)[b]

Year	A. ARGENTINA	B. BOLIVIA	C. BRAZIL	D. CHILE	E. COLOMBIA	F. COSTA RICA[1]	H. DOMINICAN REPUBLIC	I. ECUADOR	J. EL SALVADOR	K. GUATEMALA
1920	17.4	~	12.1	~	~	~	~	~	~	~
1930	20.5	~	12.0	~	5.5	~	~	~	~	~
1940	22.7	~	15.0	11.8			8.3	16.0		~
1950	23.7	12.2	21.2	23.1	14.5	11.5	12.4	16.0	12.9	11.1
1960	26.5	11.6	26.3	24.8	16.7	12.5	14.6	15.7	13.9	11.9
1970	28.0	14.5	28.4	27.2	17.5	15.1	16.7	16.8	17.6	14.6
1980	25.3	15.4	30.2	24.2	18.3	18.1	16.6	20.1	16.3	15.6
1981‡	22.1	15.4	29.0	21.8	17.6	18.4	16.3	23.0	15.2	15.3

Year	L. HAITI	M. HONDURAS	N. MEXICO	O. NICARAGUA	P. PANAMA	Q. PARAGUAY	R. PERU	S. URUGUAY[1]	T. VENEZUELA	LATIN AMERICA[2]	UNITED STATES
1920	~	~	~	~	~	~	~	~	~	~	~
1930	~	4.7	13.8	~	~	~	~	~	~	~	~
1940	~	6.8	16.9	~	~	16.0	~	17.3	13.6	16.6	~
1950	8.1	9.1	18.8	10.8	8.2	15.9	14.2	20.3	11.2	18.7	24.7
1960	8.9	15.3	19.3	13.0	11.8	15.1	17.1	24.3	14.0	21.3	23.5
1970	9.8	13.8	23.4	19.2	15.8	17.3	21.1	23.1	11.2	25.1	24.2
1980	12.5	16.4	23.8	20.6	12.0	15.8	21.2	23.9	14.1	25.4[c]	24.3
1981‡	13.2	16.4	24.0	19.3	11.4	16.1	20.2	23.5	14.8	~	~

1. Includes mining and quarrying.
2. For coverage, see table 3321, note 1.
a. For yearly data since 1900, see SALA, 20-2205ff. and 22-2305ff.
b. Calculations based upon constant dollars, factor cost.
c. For 1979 from ECLA-S, 1980, p. 119.

SOURCE: See table 3329.

Table 3332

CONSTRUCTION SHARE IN GDP, 19 LR, 1920-81[a]
(%)[b]

Year	A. ARGENTINA	B. BOLIVIA	C. BRAZIL	D. CHILE	E. COLOMBIA	F. COSTA RICA	H. DOMINICAN REPUBLIC	I. ECUADOR	J. EL SALVADOR	K. GUATEMALA
1920	1.5	~	~	~	~	~	~	~	~	~
1930	5.5	~	~	~	3.0	~	~	~	~	~
1940	3.7	~	7.5	4.2	4.5	~	~	1.3	~	~
1950	5.3	1.6	9.2	4.4	4.0	4.7	3.8	1.3	2.4	4.2
1960	4.8	3.8	8.3	4.4	4.7	5.0	3.0	2.6	3.3	2.7
1970	6.4	4.4	5.8	4.2	5.5	4.7	5.5	4.4	3.0	2.2
1980	7.6	4.3	6.9	3.3	3.5	6.9	7.7	5.7	4.6	4.0
1981[‡]	7.8	3.9	6.7	4.5	3.9	5.4	7.4	3.4	3.3	4.4

Year	L. HAITI	M. HONDURAS	N. MEXICO	O. NICARAGUA	P. PANAMA	Q. PARAGUAY	R. PERU	S. URUGUAY	T. VENEZUELA	LATIN AMERICA[1]	UNITED STATES
1920	~	~	~	~	~	~	~	~	~	~	~
1930	~	3.5	~	~	~	~	~	~	~	~	~
1940	~	4.5	3.2	~	~	1.3	~	3.8	3.5	4.4	~
1950	~	5.4	4.1	1.2	4.2	1.3	6.7	5.0	6.5	5.6	5.5
1960	~	4.5	4.8	2.2	5.7	2.3	5.3	5.4	5.4	5.5	6.3
1970	2.3	4.8	5.5	3.5	6.3	3.0	3.2	3.9	4.2	5.2	5.0
1980	4.9	4.9	5.7	2.1	6.1	8.4	3.7	7.0	6.8	5.7[c]	3.7
1981[‡]	5.5	4.6	5.9	2.6	5.5	8.7	3.8	6.5	6.1	~	~

1. For coverage, see table 3321, note 1.
a. For yearly data since 1900, see SALA, 20-2205ff. and 22-2305ff.
b. Calculations based upon constant dollars, factor cost.
c. For 1977 from ECLA-ESDER, I, p. 22.

SOURCE: See table 3329.

Table 3333

UTILITIES[1] SHARE IN GDP, 19 LR, 1920-81[a]
(%)[b]

Year	A. ARGENTINA	B. BOLIVIA	C. BRAZIL	D. CHILE	E. COLOMBIA	F. COSTA RICA	H. DOMINICAN REPUBLIC	I. ECUADOR	J. EL SALVADOR	K. GUATEMALA
1920	.5	~	~	~	~	~	~	~	~	~
1930	.5	~	~	~	~	~	~	~	~	~
1940	.7	~	1.4	1.0	~	~	~	.5	~	~
1950	.8	1.3	1.9	.9	.7	1.3	.3	.6	~	.3
1960	1.2	1.3	2.0	1.3	1.1	1.4	.9	1.3	1.0	.5
1970	2.3	1.4	2.4	1.4	1.5	2.0	1.3	1.3	1.6	.9
1980	3.5	1.6	3.3	2.2	1.8	2.4	1.9	1.8	2.7	1.3
1981‡	3.7	1.8	3.5	2.5	1.9	2.7	2.0	1.2	2.8	1.3

Year	L. HAITI	M. HONDURAS	N. MEXICO	O. NICARAGUA	P. PANAMA	Q. PARAGUAY[2]	R. PERU	S. URUGUAY	T. VENEZUELA	LATIN AMERICA[3]	UNITED STATES
1920	~	~	~	~	~	~	~	~	~	~	~
1930	~	~	~	~	~	~	~	~	~	~	~
1940	~	~	.5	~	~	.1	~	.5	.2	.8	~
1950	.3	.2	.4	.4	.8	.3	~	.7	.3	.9	1.3
1960	.8	.7	.8	1.1	1.3	.7	.8	1.1	.9	1.2	2.0
1970	1.3	1.4	1.0	1.7	2.0	1.2	.9	1.5	1.7	1.8	2.4
1980	1.7	1.6	1.3	3.1	3.6	2.5	1.5	1.7	2.8	2.3[c]	2.4
1981‡	2.1	1.6	1.3	3.0	3.8	2.8	1.5	1.9	3.1	~	~

1. Includes electricity, gas, water, and sewerage.
2. Excludes gas before 1970.
3. For coverage, see table 3321, note. 1.

a. For yearly data since 1900, see SALA, 20-2205ff. and 22-2305ff.
b. Calculations based upon constant dollars, factor cost.
c. For 1977 from ECLA-ESDER, I., p. 22.

SOURCE: See table 3329.

Table 3334

TRANSPORT AND COMMUNICATION SHARE IN GDP, 19 LR, 1920-81[a]
(%)[b]

Year	A. ARGENTINA	B. BOLIVIA	C. BRAZIL	D. CHILE	E. COLOMBIA	F. COSTA RICA	H. DOMINICAN REPUBLIC	I. ECUADOR	J. EL SALVADOR	K. GUATEMALA
1920	7.4	~	2.7	~	~	~	~	~	~	~
1930	9.6	~	3.2	~	~	~	~	~	~	~
1940	9.2	~	3.7	~	~	~	~	4.1	~	~
1950	11.3	6.2	4.5	3.4	~	3.1	5.7	5.1	3.7	2.3
1960	10.7	9.6	5.3	3.8	6.5	4.5	6.1	4.7	4.5	3.0
1970	11.3	8.1	5.7	5.7	7.4	4.8	8.6	7.2	5.3	3.5
1980	10.9	11.6	6.6	6.3	9.7	7.5	9.2	7.1	5.9	4.4
1981‡	11.1	12.8	6.6	7.5	9.5	8.0	9.3	9.3	5.4	4.5

Year	L. HAITI	M. HONDURAS	N. MEXICO	O. NICARAGUA	P. PANAMA	Q. PARAGUAY	R. PERU	S. URUGUAY	T. VENEZUELA	LATIN AMERICA[1]	UNITED STATES
1920	~	~	~	~	~	~	~	~	~	~	~
1930	~	~	2.9	~	~	~	~	~	~	~	~
1940	~	~	2.7	~	~	4.0	~	11.1	15.6	~	~
1950	1.6	5.3	2.8	3.5	3.3	4.5	~	10.2	10.8	5.3	6.8
1960	2.1	8.2	2.7	6.0	4.0	3.9	~	9.6	10.9	6.4	5.8
1970	2.4	7.8	5.0	5.8	5.6	4.2	5.8	8.7	12.9	6.1	6.4
1980	3.2	9.6	7.3	5.7	11.4	4.7	7.9	8.7	13.2	6.1	7.3
1981‡	~	9.6	8.0	5.4	12.1	4.6	7.6	9.1	~	6.6c	~

1. For coverage, see table 3321, note. 1.

a. For yearly data since 1900, see SALA, 20-2205ff. and 22-2305ff.

b. Calculations based upon constant dollars, factor cost.

c. For 1977 from ECLA-ESDER, I., p. 22.

SOURCE: See table 3329.

Table 3335

MANUFACTURING REAL RATES OF GROWTH, 18 LC, 1962-83

(PC)

Country	1962	1963	1964	1965	1966	1967	1968	1969	1970	1971	1972	1973	1974	1975	1976	1977	1978	1979	1980	1981	1982[a]	1983[a,b]
A. ARGENTINA	#	#	#	33.3	#	#	#	25.0	#	4.8	4.5	4.3	8.3	-3.8	-4.0	8.3	-11.5	13.0	-3.8	-16.0	-5.1	11.9
B. BOLIVIA	~	~	#	~	#	~	~	~	~	3.6	8.1	5.0	11.3	6.1	8.3	6.9	4.6	2.8	-1.0	-.3[a]	-13.1	-8.2
C. BRAZIL	~	~	~	~	~	~	~	~	~	60.7	11.1	14.0	17.5	7.5	18.1	2.4	6.9	7.5	7.0	-10.1[a]	.1	-4.5
D. CHILE	~	~	~	~	~	~	~	~	~	12.9	2.5	-7.4	-2.7	-26.0	7.4	8.6	7.9	8.8	5.4	2.6	-21.1	3.0
E. COLOMBIA	28.3	2.1	-4.7	-20.6	32.1	10.1	-7.4	19.9	18.8	7.6	11.3	8.9	8.1	1.1	4.3	2.0	10.0	5.5	1.7	-2.6[a]	-2.5	-.2
H. DOMINICAN REP.	~	~	~	~	~	~	~	~	~	13.1	8.0	13.4	4.7	7.3	6.8	5.7	-.2	4.8	5.0	2.6	-2.5	1.7
I. ECUADOR	~	~	~	~	11.1	-1.2	9.5	9.6	9.8	5.0	9.2	9.2	10.4	15.2	13.2	11.9	8.2	8.4	6.4	5.9	5.2	-5.6
J. EL SALVADOR	10.0	8.7	13.0	12.5	11.4	8.4	4.2	.7	3.8	7.1	3.8	7.2	5.7	2.5	11.1	5.2	4.4	-3.9	-16.0	-15.8	3.8	-3.7
K. GUATEMALA	5.6	9.9	6.0	8.5	10.5	8.1	11.8	7.1	3.7	7.1	5.6	8.1	4.6	-1.7	10.4	10.9	6.4	5.6	5.5	-2.3	-8.4	-3.7
L. HAITI	11.2	.4	-8.3	6.3	-3.1	-.2	3.4	.4	-4.6	14.6	7.4	-.6	13.1	-8.3	19.4	11.1	5.4	8.9	12.8	-2.4	-5.3	.1
M. HONDURAS	2.2	5.4	6.1	12.5	7.7	5.6	9.8	8.9	6.9	4.7	3.9	3.8	-1.0	2.6	10.3	9.8	9.7	8.1	7.9	1.7	.1	-4.3
N. MEXICO	6.7	9.4	17.1	9.8	8.9	6.1	11.5	6.9	9.7	4.8	10.0	9.9	6.0	5.0	5.4	3.8	9.3	10.7	7.1	7.1	-1.7	-7.3
O. NICARAGUA	~	~	~	~	~	~	~	~	~	~	~	~	~	~	~	~	~	~	~	2.9[a]	-4.3	#
P. PANAMA	19.0	14.7	4.7	8.9	9.2	12.1	10.0	9.1	6.9	6.3	5.2	5.6	1.3	-3.3	2.7	.7	2.0	11.0	4.1	-2.8	#	-2.3
Q. PARAGUAY	-5.1	3.6	6.0	3.3	3.4	12.5	4.6	4.9	8.0	1.6	11.0	8.4	7.4	-1.8	5.5	20.1	9.8	7.7	12.6	8.0	2.3	-4.3
R. PERU	~	~	~	~	~	-25.0	~	~	~	6.9	1.1	6.4	10.0	4.5	4.3	-5.0	-3.5	4.5	5.2	1.7	-4.3	-14.8
S. URUGUAY	#	#	33.3	#	#	33.3	33.3	#	#	.7	1.4	-.8	~	~	~	~	~	~	~	-4.4[a,c]	-11.1[c]	-7.4[a,c]
T. VENEZUELA	~	~	~	~	~	~	~	~	~	~	~	~	~	~	~	~	~	~	~	-1.5[a]	2.1	-1.9
UNITED STATES	8.3	8.1	7.2	8.9	7.7	-.2	5.1	3.5	-5.3	1.7	9.3	11.4	-4.0	-7.5	9.2	6.5	5.4	3.1	-4.0	3.0	-7.2	~

a. IDB data.

b. Preliminary estimate.

c. Includes mining.

SOURCE: IMF-IFS-S, No. 8, 1984; and IDB-STPF, 1984, table 11, p. 424.

Table 3336

AGRICULTURE, FORESTRY, AND FISHING REAL RATES OF GROWTH, 19 LC, 1962–83

(PC)

Country	1962	1963	1964	1965	1966	1967	1968	1969	1970	1971	1972	1973	1974	1975	1976	1977	1978	1979	1980	1981	1982[a]	1983[a],+
A. ARGENTINA	#	#	#	#	#	#	#	#	#	#	10.0	9.1	#	#	#	8.3	2.1	#	-7.7	8.3	7.0	2.1
B. BOLIVIA	~	~	~	~	~	~	~	~	~	5.9	5.9	4.6	3.7	7.8	5.0	-.6	-3.7	2.9	2.0	7.0[a]	-2.2	-22.1
C. BRAZIL	~	~	~	~	~	~	~	~	~	11.8	5.3	5.0	4.8	4.5	4.3	12.5	-3.6	7.7	3.6	6.8[a]	-2.5	2.2
D. CHILE	~	~	~	~	~	~	~	~	~	#	-8.3	-9.1	25.0	4.0	#	7.7	7.8	7.4	3.4	5.3[a]	-2.3	-.1
E. COLOMBIA	~	~	~	~	~	~	~	10.4	4.1	1.3	7.6	2.4	4.6	6.6	3.1	3.0	6.6	5.4	1.7	3.2[a]	-1.3	2.0
F. COSTA RICA	6.2	-.3	4.4	2.0	9.0	7.8	9.0	~	~	4.6	5.4	5.6	-1.7	3.1	.5	2.2	4.6	.5	-.5	1.2	-4.9	4.4
H. DOMINICAN REP.	~	~	~	~	29.9	12.2	-9.2	6.2	-9.1	5.0	4.0	1.0	#	2.3	7.3	1.9	-3.9	1.1	4.8	5.6	3.8	3.5
I. ECUADOR	~	~	~	~	~	~	~	3.7	6.5	3.8	1.4	1.8	9.0	6.5	2.9	2.4	14.1	3.6	5.2	4.0	1.1	-14.9
J. EL SALVADOR	19.1	-3.5	4.2	-4.3	1.9	5.9	1.8	2.4	5.8	6.9	9.7	5.2	10.3	2.5	2.5	3.6	3.2	3.5	-4.8	-10.1	-3.4	#
K. GUATEMALA	3.4	14.3	.5	1.0	4.9	#	10.8	1.8	.7	3.1	-.3	2.3	6.4	3.8	4.5	3.8	1.8	2.8	1.6	1.4	-2.0	-2.5
L. HAITI	4.1	.1	-.3	-1.1	5.0	-2.1	1.0	-2.8	-1.5	9.1	1.1	4.7	2.4	-9.3	1.0	-6.0	8.0	4.4	-1.4	-2.2	-4.1	3.1
M. HONDURAS	4.3	3.0	8.7	15.7	9.5	3.7	7.9	#	~	5.6	1.8	3.4	-8.7	3.3	9.3	5.6	5.9	7.8	3.1	.9	.1	-.1
N. MEXICO	4.2	8.0	7.4	3.4	3.3	3.2	3.1	5.2	6.1	8.1	5.6	1.3	1.7	3.3	3.3	7.9	~	-1.4	7.0	5.3	-.1	3.4
O. NICARAGUA	~	~	~	~	~	5.0	5.5	2.6	-.6	6.5	-3.7	1.3	-5.7	7.4	~	~	8.0	-4.2	~	10.1[a]	2.0	11.7
P. PANAMA	2.9	4.6	4.4	11.9	5.3	5.0	-.2	~	2.1	~	6.2	6.4	9.8	8.2	5.0	4.8	5.9	6.7	-1.7	2.8	#	3.1
Q. PARAGUAY	19.4	5.0	2.1	5.2	-2.8	5.6	~	~	~	~	-6.8	-1.8	5.6	#	3.7	11.1	#	3.4	9.2	6.7	-3.0	-4.8
R. PERU	~	~	~	~	~	~	~	~	~	-6.3	-10.5	2.6	3.3	5.6	1.9	#	-6.7	-.4	-5.0	10.5	2.8	-11.5
S. URUGUAY	#	50.0	-33.3	50.0	#	-33.3	#	50.0	#	~	~	~	~	~	5.6	3.2	~	~	16.2	1.0	-6.8	-2.6
T. VENEZUELA	~	~	~	~	~	~	~	~	~	~	~	~	~	~	~	~	~	~	~	-1.9[a]	3.6	#
UNITED STATES	-.4	2.4	-2.6	4.1	-4.6	3.7	-1.6	2.4	4.9	4.6	-1.0	1.5	.5	2.6	-4.9	1.9	1.0	5.4	1.5	15.5	-4.4	~

a. IDB data.

SOURCE: IMF-IFS-S, No. 8, 1984, pp. 38–41; IDB-STPF, 1984, table 9, p. 423.

Table 3337

HOUSING, DEFENSE, GOVERNMENT, AND OTHER SERVICES SHARE IN GDP, 1920–79

A. ARGENTINA

Year	Housing	Defense and Government Services	Other Services
1920	2.7	9.8	9.0
1925	2.4	9.2	8.6
1930	2.5	8.4	7.8
1935	2.6	9.2	8.3
1940	2.6	10.0	8.2
1945	2.5	11.8	8.6
1950	2.4	13.8	8.3
1955	2.4	13.4	8.7
1960	2.3	12.4	9.0
1965	2.0	11.2	9.2
1970	1.9	9.3	9.2
1975	1.8	9.2	9.4
1976	4.0	~a	19.7
1977	4.3	~a	18.8
1978	4.9	~a	19.8
1979	4.9	~a	18.7

a. Included in "Other Services."

Continued in SALA 20, 2206-2224.

Table 3338

EXPENDITURE ON GDP,[1] 19 LC, 1960–73
(%)[2]

Country	Year	Government Final Consumption Expenditure	Private Final Consumption Expenditure	Increase in Stocks	Gross Fixed Capital Formation	Goods and Services	
						Exports	Less Imports
A. ARGENTINA	1960	9	71	1	21	10	11
	1963	9	72	1	18	11	9
	1968	9	71	#	19	9	7
	1969	9	70	#	20	9	8
	1970	10	70	#	20	8	8
	1971	10	70	1	19	9	9
	1972	9	69	1	20	9	8

Continued in SALA, 17-2206.

Table 3339

GDP, NATIONAL CURRENCY, AND CURRENT PRICES,[1] 18 LC, 1935–66
(M)

Year	A. ARGENTINA[3]	B. BOLIVIA	C. BRAZIL[4]	D. CHILE[2]	E. COLOMBIA	F. COSTA RICA	H. DOMINICAN REP.	I. ECUADOR	J. EL SALVADOR
1935	9,300.0	~	~	~	~	~	~	~	
1936	9,800.0	~	~	~	~	~	~	~	~
1937	11,300.0	~	~	~	~	~	~	~	~
1938	11,000.0	~	~	~	~	~	~	~	~
1939	11,600.0	~	46.3	~	~	~	~	~	~
1940	12,000.0	~	~	22.1	~	~	~	~	~
1941	12,900.0	~	~	27.2	~	~	~	~	~
1942	14,600.0	~	~	33.9	~	~	~	~	~
1943	15,300.0	~	~	40.4	~	~	~	~	~
1944	17,500.0	~	~	47.0	~	~	~	~	~
1945	19,300.0	~	~	53.6	~	~	~	~	~
1946	26,200.0	~	~	67.6	~	~	~	~	~

Continued in SALA, 17-2205.

Table 3340

ARGENTINA EXPENDITURE ON GDP AND GNP,[1] 1976–82

(M NC)

Category	1976	1977	1978	1979	1980	1981	1982
Exports[2]	93.9	272.9	609.9	1,257.9	1,951.4	5,166.1	19,865
Government Consumption	74.2	198.3	615.2	1,645.0	4,083.0	7,484.5	15,418
Gross Fixed Capital Formation	202.8	569.5	1,311.7	3,348.1	7,072.2	12,391.8	24,737
Increase in Stocks	1.6	#	−27.3	2.1	171.2	−405.1	1,645
Private Consumption	442.7	1,251.0	3,075.6	8,882.0	17.454.6	35,159.3	103,922
Less: Imports[2]	−60.6	−207.6	−405.3	−1,224.5	−2,562.3	−5,296.6	−15,107
Gross Domestic Product	754.6	2,084.0	5,179.8	13,910.6	28,170.0	54,500.0	150,479
Less: Net Factor Payments Abroad	−7.4	−53.0	−54.7	−121.9	−276.2	−2,095.9	−12,938
Gross Nat'l Expenditure = GNP	747.2	2,031.0	5,125.1	13,788.7	27,893.8	52,404.1	137,541

1. Cf. SALA, 18-2208; for historical series comparing GDP to GNP, see SALA, 19-2202.
2. Exports and imports include nonfactor services as well as goods.

SOURCE: IMF-IFS-Y, 1983; IMF-IFS, May 1985.

Table 3341

BOLIVIA EXPENDITURE ON GDP AND GNP, 1976–83

(M NC)

Category	1976	1977	1978	1979	1980	1981	1982	1983
Exports[1]	12,698	14,512	14,236	17,794	26,373	25,788	99,284	287,862
Government Consumption	6,700	8,559	10,781	12,276	18,998	24,374	45,946	140,503
Gross Fixed Capital Formation	10,685	12,414	15,396	15,306	17,328	18,589	41,236	136,383
Increase in Stocks	1,264	1,149	−98	910	−527	1,270	−7,403	−31,697
Private Consumption	39,056	44,940	55,501	68,993	92,292	126,382	309,038	1,425,800
Less: Imports[1]	−13,956	−16,354	−19,342	−23,223	−25,850	−33,593	−89,642	−443,104
Gross Domestic Product	56,447	65,220	76,474	92,056	128,614	162,810	389,459	1,515,800
Less: Net Factor Payments Abroad	−840	−1,684	−2,334	−3,572	−6,645	−8,345	−49,553	~
Gross Nat'l Expenditure = GNP	55,607	63,536	74,140	88,484	121,969	154,465	348,906	~

1. Exports and imports include nonfactor services as well as goods.

SOURCE: IMF-IFS-Y, 1983; IMF-IFS, May 1985.

Table 3342

BRAZIL EXPENDITURE ON GDP AND GNP, 1976–83

(B NC)

Category	1976	1977	1978	1979	1980	1981	1982	1983
Exports[1]	115	181	242	432	1,121	2,311	3,846	~
Government Consumption	170	240	348	585	1,160	2,285	5,057	~
Gross Fixed Capital Formation	391	538	789	1,269	2,769	5,441	10,718	~
Increase in Stocks	22	37	−12	−35	#	#	35,296	~
Private Consumption	1,136	1,725	2,649	4,544	9,458	17,998	−4,182	~
Less: Imports[1]	−154	−197	−285	−556	−1,403	−2,404	50,815	121,055
Gross Domestic Product	1,680	2,523	3,730	6,239	13,104	25,623	−2,590	~
Less: Net Factor Payments Abroad	−25	−40	−84	−163	−404	−1,015	48,225	~
Gross Nat'l Expenditure = GNP	1,655	2,483	3,646	6,077	12,700	24,616	43,123	~

1. Exports and imports include nonfactor services as well as goods.

SOURCE: IMF-IFS-Y, 1983; IMF-IFS, May 1985.

Table 3343

CHILE EXPENDITURE ON GDP AND GNP, 1976–83
(B NC)

Category	1976	1977	1978	1979	1980	1981	1982	1983
Exports[1]	30.55	55.58	100.35	179.74	245.4	209.0	239.9	374.5
Government Consumption	18.93	39.05	66.59	110.40	133.9	167.4	190.1	220.7
Gross Fixed Capital Formation	12.81	28.83	71.59	115.02	178.9	236.8	181.5	186.5
Increase in Stocks	-4.82	0	15.24	22.36	46.7	52.2	-41.6	-33.7
Private Consumption	113.77	257.51	346.63	546.29	760.5	948.3	932.7	1,114.9
Less: Imports[1]	-24.60	-59.78	-112.89	-201.61	-290.1	-340.6	-263.4	-332.1
Gross Domestic Product	146.65	321.19	487.51	772.20	1,075.3	1,273.1	1,239.1	1,557.7
Less: Net Factor Payments Abroad	-4.29	-7.61	-13.34	-25.26	-36.3	-57.1	-95.5	-134.2
Gross Nat'l Expenditure = GNP	142.36	313.58	474.16	746.94	1,037.0	1,216.0	1,143.6	1,423.5

1. Exports and imports include nonfactor services as well as goods.

SOURCE: IMF-IFS-Y, 1983; IMF-IFS, May 1985.

Table 3344

COLOMBIA EXPENDITURE ON GDP AND GNP, 1976–83
(B NC)

Category	1976	1977	1978	1979	1980	1981	1982	1983
Exports[1]	88.1	124.7	155.2	193.1	256.1	235.0	271.1	315.0
Government Consumption	38.7	48.2	65.7	91.1	159.4	206.9	269.5	341.2
Gross Fixed Capital Formation	97.1	134.8	187.7	243.0	264.9	350.1	435.8	~
Increase in Stocks	14.3	34.4	21.2	26.2	36.2	58.9	74.8	~
Private Consumption	373.7	474.9	615.7	805.2	1,108.8	1,437.7	1,818.4	2,109.3
Less: Imports[1]	-77.8	-98.5	-129.0	-163.2	-246.3	-305.7	-376.9	-414.6
Gross Domestic Product	534.0	718.5	916.6	1,195.4	1,579.1	1,982.8	2,492.7	2,943.2
Less: Net Factor Payments Abroad	-10.9	-10.2	-11.8	-10.8	-5.7	-10.5	-36.7	~
Gross Nat'l Expenditure = GNP	523.1	708.3	904.8	1,184.6	1,573.4	1,972.3	2,456.0	~

1. Exports and imports include nonfactor services as well as goods.

SOURCE: IMF-IFS-Y, 1983; IMF-IFS, May 1985.

Table 3345

COSTA RICA EXPENDITURE ON GDP AND GNP, 1976–82
(M NC)

Category	1976	1977	1978	1979	1980	1981	1982
Exports[1]	6,082	8,198	8,589	9,311	10,963	24,963	42,038
Government Consumption	3,306	4,208	5,069	6,243	7,544	8,777	14,485
Gross Fixed Capital Formation	4,846	5,889	6,952	9,050	9,895	13,515	17,822
Increase in Stocks	46	502	132	-295	1,109	2,547	4,900
Private Consumption	13,690	17,143	20,388	23,139	27,140	34,394	55,828
Less: Imports[1]	-7,295	-9,608	-10,936	-12,863	-15,245	-27,018	-38,072
Gross Domestic Product	20.676	26,331	30,194	34,584	41,406	57,176	97,002
Less: Net Factor Payments Abroad	-627	-665	-903	-1,279	-1,988	-6,188	-13,760
Gross Nat'l Expenditure = GNP	20,049	25,676	29,291	33,305	39,418	50.988	83,242

1. Exports and imports include nonfactor services as well as goods.

SOURCE: IMF-IFS, May 1983; IMF-IFS, May 1985.

Table 3346

CUBA GROSS MATERIAL PRODUCT,[1] BY ECONOMIC SECTOR, 1970–81

	1970	1971	1972	1973	1974	1975	1976	1977	1978	1979	1980	1981[‡,5]
M Constant Pesos[2]												
Total Material Product	5,666	5,904	6,478	7,328	7,900	8,142	8,431	10,181	10,962	11,428	11,684	13,051
Agriculture	1,230	1,153	1,216	1,271	1,328	1,607	1,665	1,735	1,842	1,942	2,001	2,183
Industry[3]	4,000	4,177	4,458	4,988	5,393	5,285	5,446	6,996	7,563	7,917	8,115	9,085
Construction	436	574	804	1,069	1,179	1,250	1,320	1,450	1,557	1,569	1,568	1,818
Structure (%)[4]												
Total Material Product	100.0	100.0	100.0	100.0	100.0	100.0	100.0	100.0	100.0	100.0	100.0	100.0
Agriculture	21.7	19.5	18.8	17.3	16.8	19.7	19.7	~	~	~	17.1	16.7
Industry[3]	70.6	70.8	68.8	68.1	68.3	64.9	64.6	~	~	~	69.5	69.5
Construction	7.7	9.7	12.4	14.6	14.9	15.4	15.7	~		~	13.4	13.9
AAGR[4]												
Total Material Product	~	4.2	9.7	13.1	7.8	3.1	3.5	~	7.7	4.2	2.2	11.7
Agriculture	~	-6.3	5.5	4.5	4.5	21.0	3.6	~	6.2	5.4	3.0	9.1
Industry[3]	~	4.4	6.7	11.9	8.1	-2.0	3.0	~	8.1	4.7	2.5	12.0
Construction	~	31.7	40.1	33.0	10.3	6.0	5.6	~	7.4	.8	#	15.9

1. The material product consists of the value of the agricultural, fishery, mining, manufacturing, construction, and electrical energy sectors.
2. The *Anuario Estadístico de Cuba* describes all this information as valued at current prices, whereas according to the National Bank of Cuba, with the exception of trade and transport, the "other sectors"—the material product plus communications—are given at constant 1965 prices. In addition, sources in the State Statistical Committee explained that as of 1965 prices were frozen for inputs and final goods—agricultural, industrial and construction—and only new products were valued at different prices from those fixed then, but at prices frozen from the year in which they were incorporated in the Cuban economic system. Thus the terms current prices and constant prices in the case of the material product (at producer prices) are equivalent, and bearing in mind—according to the National Bank of Cuba— that the group of new products is very small, it is considered that the interpretation stemming from the resulting real growth rates is not affected.
3. Includes mining, manufacturing, and electrical energy; the fishing industry is included in manufacturing.
4. The percentage structure and growth rates correspond to the real and not the rounded figures.
5. Individual activities and total were extrapolated independently on the basis of the variations at constant 1981 prices estimated by the state statistical committee. The sum of the activities does not coincide with the total for 1981.

SOURCE: Adapted from ECLA-S, 1979, p. 183; ECLA-S, 1980, p. 192; ECLA-S, 1981, p. 296.

Table 3347

DOMINICAN REPUBLIC EXPENDITURE ON GDP AND GNP, 1976–82
(M NC)

Category	1976	1977	1978	1979	1980	1981	1982
Exports[1]	840.4	917.9	828.0	1,134.9	1,271.3	1,512.6	1,141.8
Government Consumption	151.9	189.3	271.1	419.6	504.0	693.6	778.4
Gross Fixed Capital Formation	780.3	939.2	1,031.8	1,334.7	1,619.0	1,693.8	1,540.9
Increase in Stocks	101.4	60.3	98.4	59.5	81.8	63.9	104.6
Private Consumption	3,082.5	3,589.3	3,653.1	4,025.8	5,067.8	5,081.3	5,886.4
Less: Imports[1]	-1,005.0	-1,108.9	-1,154.0	-1,484.3	-1,918.7	-1,818.4	-1,534.6
Gross Domestic Product	3,951.5	4,587.1	4,728.4	5,490.2	6,625.2	7,226.5	7,917.5
Less: Net Factor Payments Abroad	-123.8	-123.4	-135.7	-187.7	-210.2	-293.1	-254.1
Gross Nat'l Expenditure = GNP	3,827.7	4,463.7	4,592.7	5,302.5	6,415.0	6,933.4	7,663.4

1. Exports and imports include nonfactor services as well as goods.

SOURCE: IMF-IFS-Y, 1983; IMF-IFS, May 1985.

Table 3348

ECUADOR EXPENDITURE ON GDP AND GNP, 1976–83

(B NC)

Category	1976	1977	1978	1979	1980	1981	1982	1983
Exports[1]	34.17	41.32	40.83	60.62	73.80	75.91	87.78	138.90
Government Consumption	18.63	24.66	26.45	30.08	42.56	49.74	57.51	65.72
Gross Fixed Capital Formation	29.47	39.29	50.09	55.43	69.33	77.63	91.29	91.94
Increase in Stocks	2.11	4.85	4.35	3.86	7.30	3.16	4.48	3.77
Private Consumption	84.52	102.58	121.24	143.29	174.88	214.67	260.20	365.62
Less: Imports[1]	–35.98	–46.31	–51.61	–59.33	–74.53	–71.06	–84.30	–100.35
Gross Domestic Product	132.91	166.38	191.35	233.96	293.34	350.05	416.96	565.80
Less: Net Factor Payments Abroad	–4.06	–4.48	–5.52	–9.95	–14.54	18.31	–30.89	–42.02
Gross Nat'l Expenditure = GNP	128.85	161.90	185.82	224.01	278.80	331.74	386.07	523.79

1. Exports and imports include nonfactor services as well as goods.

SOURCE: IMF-IFS-Y 1983; IMF-IFS, May 1985.

Table 3349

EL SALVADOR EXPENDITURE ON GDP AND GNP, 1976–83

(M NC)

Category	1976	1977	1978	1979	1980	1981	1982	1983
Exports[2]	2,028	2,735	2,328	3,182	3,046	2,307	2,042	2,178
Government Consumption	686	805	969	1,106	1,300	1,369	1,415	1,381
Gross Fixed Capital Formation	1,145	1,521	1,790	1,599	1,109	1,173	1,130	1,143
Increase in Stocks	–26	158	183	45	–27	58	56	67
Private Consumption	4,015	4,607	5,414	6,092	6,665	6,644	6,877	7,648
Less: Imports[2]	–2,101	–2,686	–3,041	–3,197	–2,964	–2,904	–2,553	–2,663
Gross Domestic Product	5,706	7,167	7,692	8,619	8,944	8,647	8,966	9,754
Less: Net Factor Payments Abroad	–17	–72	–130	–60	–128	–149	–229	–286
Gross Nat'l Expenditure = GNP	5,689	7,095	7,562	8,547	8,789	8,498	8,737	9,468

1. Cf. Joseph P. Mooney, "Gross Domestic Product, Gross National Product, and
   Capital Formation in El Salvador, 1945–1965," *Estadística*, Sept. 1968,
   pp. 491–517.
2. Exports and imports include nonfactor services as well as goods.

SOURCE: IMF-IFS, May 1983; IMF-IFS, May 1985.

Table 3350

GUATEMALA EXPENDITURE ON GDP AND GNP, 1976–83

(M NC)

Category	1976	1977	1978	1979	1980	1981	1982	1983
Exports[1]	942	1,340	1,304	1,474	1,748	1,471	1,289	~
Government Consumption	297	354	435	488	627	680	676	~
Gross Fixed Capital Formation	900	1,039	1,218	1,286	1,295	1,442	1,314	~
Increase in Stocks	34	60	95	8	–44	23	–67	~
Private Consumption	3,396	4,127	4,675	5,432	6,217	7,037	7,151	~
Less: Imports[1]	–1,204	–1,439	–1,655	–1,784	–1,963	–2,032	–1,634	~
Gross Domestic Product	4,365	5,481	6,071	6,903	7,879	8,663	8,728	8,724
Less: Net Factor Payments Abroad	–74	–33	–26	–12	–71	–103	–122	~
Gross Nat'l Expenditure = GNP	4,291	5,448	6,045	6,891	7,807	8,505	8,606	~

1. Exports and imports include nonfactor services as well as goods.

SOURCE: IMF-IFS-Y, 1983; IMF-IFS, May 1985.

Table 3351

HAITI EXPENDITURE ON GDP AND GNP, 1976–83

(M NC)

Category	1976	1977	1978	1979	1980	1981	1982	1983
Exports[1]	1,046	1,249	1,495	1,522	2,148	1,944	2,139	2,265
Gross Fixed Capital Formation	678	748	857	938	1,238	1,252	1,230	1,331
Increase in Stocks	26	29	~	~	~	~	~	~
Private Consumption	4,076	4,592	4,687	5,226	6,881	7,550	7,141	7,836
Less: Imports[1]	−1,430	−1,692	−1,982	−2,068	−3,038	−3,334	−3,132	−3,249
Gross Domestic Product	4,395	4,926	5,057	5,618	7,229	7,412	7,378	8,183
Less: Net Factor Payments Abroad	−36	−63	−76	−70	−73	−72	−72	−69
Gross Nat'l Expenditure = GNP	4,359	4,863	4,981	5,548	7,156	7,340	7,306	8,114

1. Exports and imports include nonfactor services as well as goods.

SOURCE: IMF-IFS-Y, 1983; IMF-IFS, May 1985.

Table 3352

HONDURAS EXPENDITURE ON GDP AND GNP, 1976–83

(M NC)

Category	1976	1977	1978	1979	1980	1981	1982	1983
Exports[1]	898	1,149	1,366	1,649	1,860	1,735	1,505	1,547
Government Consumption	348	417	463	544	688	766	805	889
Gross Fixed Capital Formation	550	711	941	1,004	1,235	1,051	968	1,060
Increase in Stocks	−101	109	46	89	68	74	−141	−130
Private Consumption	1,963	2,246	2,560	2,955	3,386	3,793	4,074	4,343
Less: Imports[1]	−1,032	−1,311	−1,562	−1,863	−2,261	−2,126	−1,629	−1,818
Gross Domestic Product	2,626	3,321	3,814	4,378	4,976	5,293	5,582	5,891
Less: Net Factor Payments Abroad	−102	−124	−150	−210	−275	−269	−385	−268
Gross Nat'l Expenditure = GNP	2,524	3,197	3,664	4,168	4,701	5,024	5,197	5,623

1. Exports and imports include nonfactor services as well as goods.

SOURCE: IMF-IFS-Y, 1983; IMF-IFS, May 1985.

Table 3353

MEXICO EXPENDITURE ON GDP AND GNP, 1976–83

(B NC)

Category	1976	1977	1978	1979	1980	1981	1982	1983
Exports[1]	116.4	190.8	244.7	343.3	537.2	701.6	1,635.5	3,340.6
Government Consumption	150.9	199.0	255.2	334.3	462.8	684.5	1,057.6	1,590.3
Gross Fixed Capital Formation	288.4	363.3	492.4	718.5	1,032.9	1,509.4	2,098.8	2,972.3
Increase in Stocks	17.2	59.1	59.2	77.6	169.8	193.2	−98.0	499.9
Private Consumption	933.4	1,226.1	1,543.8	1,975.9	2,651.5	3,583.8	5,776.1	10,356.0
Less: Imports[1]	−135.3	−189.0	−258.0	−382.0	−577.8	−798.1	−1,053.9	−1,617.4
Gross Domestic Product	1,371.0	1,849.3	2,337.4	3,067.5	4,276.5	5,874.4	9,417.1	117,141.7
Less: Net Factor Payments Abroad	~	−42.9	−52.5	−77.1	−117.2	−200.1	−508.9	1,041.7
Gross Nat'l Expenditure = GNP	~	1,806.4	2,284.9	2,990.4	4,159.3	5,674.3	8,908.2	116,099.9

1. Exports and imports include nonfactor services as well as goods.

SOURCE: IMF-IFS-Y, 1983; IMF-IFS, May 1985.

Table 3354

NICARAGUA EXPENDITURE ON GDP AND GNP, 1976–83
(M NC)

Category	1976	1977	1978	1979	1980	1981	1982	1983
Exports[1]	4,268	5,032	5,160	6,100	5,039	5,470	4,530	4,500
Government Consumption	1,208	1,396	1,762	2,591	4,107	5,376	6,649	9,782
Gross Fixed Capital Formation	2,612	3,583	2,180	967	2,882	5,055	4,497	5,384
Increase in Stocks	–372	435	–282	–1,800	482	567	653	787
Private Consumption	9,338	11,101	10,132	10,739	18,381	19,534	21,204	23,607
Less: Imports[1]	–4,119	–5,868	–4,686	–4,083	–8,999	–10,229	–7,837	–8,277
Gross Domestic Product	12,935	15,679	14,266	14,514	21,892	25,773	29,696	35,783
Less: Net Factor Payments Abroad	–491	–604	–602	–801	–922	–1,016	–1,380	–671
Gross Nat'l Expenditure = GNP	12,444	15,075	13,664	13,713	20,970	24,757	28,316	35,112

1. Exports and imports include nonfactor services as well as goods.

SOURCE: IMF-IFS, 1983; IMF-IFS, May 1985.

Table 3355

PANAMA EXPENDITURE ON GDP AND GNP, 1976–83
(M NC)

Category	1976	1977	1978	1979	1980	1981	1982	1983
Exports[1]	840.7	921.1	986.4	1,124.8	1,567.1	1,632.0	1,689.6	1,695.9
Government Consumption	313.4	412.1	482.9	567.2	680.5	812.9	962.6	1,067,8
Gross Fixed Capital Formation	632.9	445.9	606.3	661.2	866.4	1,079.5	1,185.4	925.9
Increase in Stocks	29.0	45.0	45.4	124.5	120.5	87.6	–.8	17.0
Private Consumption	1,175.9	1,242.6	1,431.7	1,693.8	2,009.5	2,107.4	2,311.5	2,370.5
Less: Imports[1]	–987.6	–996.9	–1,100.2	–1,371.3	–1,685.2	–1,841.5	–1,869.4	–1,697.7
Gross Domestic Product	2,004.3	2,069.8	2,452.5	2,800.2	3,558.8	3,878.0	4,278.9	4,379.4
Less: Net Factor Payments Abroad	–53.6	–63.1	–57.4	–102.8	–110.0	–78.6	–138.9	1.7
Gross Nat'l Expenditure = GNP	1,950.7	2,006.7	2,395.1	2,697.4	3,448.8	3,799.4	4,140.0	4,381.1

1. Exports and imports include nonfactor services as well as goods.

SOURCE: IMF-IFS-Y, 1983; IMF-IFS, May 1985.

Table 3356

PARAGUAY EXPENDITURE ON GDP AND GNP, 1976–83
(B NC)

Category	1976	1977	1978	1979	1980	1981	1982	1983
Exports[1]	26.60	39.60	43.28	46.67	53.58	79.11	89.46	70.05
Government Consumption	13.41	16.35	21.50	24.71	34.73	48.63	52.27	53.92
Gross Fixed Capital Formation	48.75	62.92	81.50	116.14	152.65	194.22	176.87	164.51
Increase in Stocks	3.97	2.15	6.46	6.83	8.55	10.06	12.05	9.40
Private Consumption	158.64	195.60	236.52	326.71	414.64	504.07	552.02	642.20
Less: Imports[1]	–37.30	–53.01	–66.48	–90.55	–103.69	–127.40	–145.63	–127.39
Gross Domestic Product	214.07	263.61	322.78	430.51	560.46	708.69	737.04	714.93
Less: Net Factor Payments Abroad	–3.47	–4.57	–7.71	–2.32	–7.71	8.76	8.26	5.00
Gross Nat'l Expenditure = GNP	210.60	259.04	315.07	428.19	552.74	717.45	745.30	823.10

1. Exports and imports include nonfactor services as well as goods.

SOURCE: IMF-IFS-Y, 1983; IMF-IFS, May 1985.

Table 3357

PERU EXPENDITURE ON GDP AND GNP, 1976–83

(B NC)

Category	1976	1977	1978	1979	1980	1981	1982	1983
Exports[1]	100.0	176.4	375.3	942.0	1,335.2	1,676.8	2,861.8	6,140.8
Government Consumption	101.0	157.1	208.9	301.0	627.5	1,095.0	1,908.0	3,482.0
Gross Fixed Capital Formation	127.8	153.5	234.5	441.0	847.2	1,734.4	3,083.2	4,861.6
Increase in Stocks	9.2	5.0	8.7	6.7	33.4	152.1	118.4	266.7
Private Consumption	577.6	776.8	1,165.3	1,947.1	3,239.9	5,887.6	9,545.8	7,824.4
Less: Imports[1]	−146.6	−214.0	−320.4	−553.4	−1,144.6	−2,076.2	−3,382.2	−6,076.4
Gross Domestic Product	769.0	1,054.8	1,672.3	3,084.4	4,938.6	8,489.7	14,134.0	26,479.1
Less: Net Factor Payments Abroad	−10.7	−21.9	−57.0	−143.7	−141.9	−244.6	−405.6	−863.4
Gross Nat'l Expenditure = GNP	758.3	1,032.9	1,615.3	2,940.7	4,796.7	8,245.1	13,728.4	25,635.7

1. Exports and imports include nonfactor services as well as goods.

SOURCE: IMF-IFS-Y, 1983; IMF-IFS, May 1985.

Table 3358

URUGUAY EXPENDITURE ON GDP AND GNP, 1976–83

(M NC)

Category	1976	1977	1978	1979	1980	1981	1982	1983
Exports[1]	2,350	3,774	5,530	9,400	13,861	18,141	18,358	44,308
Government Consumption	1,990	2,451	3,821	6,789	11,482	16,809	20,723	23,672
Gross Fixed Capital Formation	1,683	3,030	4,943	9,312	15,422	18,953	17,544	21,411
Increase in Stocks	−94	−2	8	663	572	−547	−553	−1,763
Private Consumption	9,496	15,018	22,919	43,441	70,479	90,167	94,457	138,735
Less: Imports[1]	−2,398	−4,356	−6,291	−11,980	−19,612	−22,819	−22,126	−40,047
Gross Domestic Product	13,027	19,915	30,930	57,625	92,204	120,704	128,403	186,289
Less: Net Factor Payments Abroad	−244	−317	−465	−454	−912	−797	−2,729	−10,926
Gross Nat'l Expenditure = GNP	12,783	19,598	30,465	57,171	91,292	119,907	125,808	175,363

1. Exports and imports include nonfactor services as well as goods.

SOURCE: IMF-IFS-Y, 1983; IMF-IFS, May 1985.

Table 3359

VENEZUELA EXPENDITURE ON GDP AND GNP, 1976–83

(B NC)

Category	1976	1977	1978	1979	1980	1981	1982	1983
Exports[1]	41.67	43.51	41.96	64.02	85.46	89.62	75.20	74.07
Government Consumption	19.78	22.96	25.29	27.41	33.82	42.64	42.59	41.34
Gross Fixed Capital Formation	42.77	60.48	70.96	65.95	62.83	69.78	70.16	55.35
Increase in Stocks	4.22	4.14	1.46	.90	−.73	−4.37	5.17	−21.20
Private Consumption	66.67	80.34	94.94	111.65	138.63	160.53	182.24	183.44
Less: Imports[1]	−39.79	−55.54	−64.13	−60.03	−64.55	−72.99	−84.09	−42.50
Gross Domestic Product	135.32	155.88	170.48	209.91	255.46	285.21	291.27	290.49
Less: Net Factor Payments Abroad	.18	−.36	−.63	.96	1.18	2.26	−6.60	−9.86
Gross Nat'l Expenditure = GNP	136.50	155.52	169.85	209.26	256.64	287.47	284.67	280.63

1. Exports and imports include nonfactor services as well as goods.

SOURCE: IMF-IFS-Y, 1983; IMF-IFS, May 1985.

Table 3360
UNITED STATES EXPENDITURE ON GDP AND GNP, 1976–83
(B US)

Category	1976	1977	1978	1979	1980	1981	1982	1983
Exports[1]	141.2	149.8	175.7	216.6	264.3	283.4	261.9	252.1
Government Consumption and Investment:	362.1	393.8	431.9	474.4	537.8	596.5	650.5	685.5
Gross Fixed Capital Formation	46.1	47.3	56.8	62.2	67.5	66.1	61.9	~
Private Gross Fixed Capital Formation	246.0	301.0	360.1	408.8	411.7	458.1	441.0	485.1
Increase in Stocks	11.8	23.0	26.5	14.3	-9.8	26.0	-26.1	-13.5
Private Consumption	1,084.3	1,204.0	1,346.5	1,507.2	1,668.1	1,849.1	1,984.9	2,155.9
Less: Imports[1]	-147.9	-177.6	-206.4	-245.9	-285.6	-305.7	-290.8	-308.6
Gross Domestic Product	1,697.5	1,894.9	2,134.3	2,375.2	2,586.4	2,907.5	3,021.3	3,256.5
Net Factor Income from Abroad	20.5	23.4	29.6	42.6	45.3	50.3	48.0	48.3
Gross National Expenditure = GNP	1,718.0	1,918.3	2,163.9	2,417.8	2,631.7	2,957.8	3,069.3	3,304.8

1. Exports and imports include nonfactor services as well as goods.

SOURCE: IMF-IFS-Y, 1983; IMF-IFS, May 1985.

Table 3361
PROVINCIAL LEVEL GDP AND GDP/C IN MEXICO, 1970 AND 1980

PART I. 1970

State (or Territory)	GDP M Pesos	%	Population T	%	GDP/C	Index (Total = 100.0)
Aguascalientes	2,061.0	.5	338.1	.7	6,095.8	69.4
Baja California	11,735.6	2.8	870.4	1.8	13,483.0	153.6
Baja California Sur	1,862.4	.4	128.0	.3	14,550.0	165.7
Campeche	1,667.2	.4	251.6	.5	6,626.4	75.5
Coahuila	15,826.2	3.7	1,115.0	2.3	14,193.9	161.7
Colima	3,077.5	.7	241.2	.5	12,759.1	145.3
Chiapas	5,269.3	1.3	1,569.1	3.3	3,358.1	38.2
Chihuahua	13,061.1	3.1	1,612.5	3.3	8,099.9	92.3
Distrito Federal	142,373.6	33.6	6,874.2	14.3	20,711.3	236.0
Durango	5,101.2	1.2	939.2	1.9	5,431.4	61.9
Guanajuato	11,632.4	2.8	2,270.4	4.7	5,123.5	58.4
Guerrero	8,929.3	2.1	1,597.4	3.3	5,589.9	63.7
Hidalgo	5,272.5	1.3	1,193.8	2.5	4,416.5	50.3
Jalisco	22,148.8	5.2	3,296.6	6.8	6,718.7	76.5
México	28,830.1	6.8	3,833.2	7.9	7,521.1	85.7
Michoacán	9,327.5	2.2	2,324.2	4.8	4,013.2	45.7
Morelos	3,933.5	.9	616.1	1.3	6,384.5	72.7
Nayarit	3,270.6	.8	544.0	1.1	6,012.1	68.5
Nuevo León	25,852.4	6.1	1,694.7	3.5	15,254.8	173.8
Oaxaca	6,263.0	1.5	2,015.4	4.2	3,107.6	35.4
Puebla	12,180.2	2.9	2,508.2	5.2	4,856.1	55.3
Querétaro	2,721.2	.7	485.5	1.0	5,604.9	63.8
Quintana Roo	582.4	.1	88.1	.2	6,611.8	75.3
San Luis Potosí	7,863.5	1.9	1,282.0	2.7	6,133.7	69.9
Sinaloa	8,579.9	2.0	1,266.5	2.6	6,774.5	77.2
Sonora	13,705.7	3.2	1,098.7	2.3	12,474.4	142.1
Tabasco	3,116.6	.7	768.3	1.6	4,056.5	46.2
Tamaulipas	12,849.5	3.0	1,456.9	3.0	8,819.7	100.5
Tlaxcala	1,258.5	.3	420.6	.9	2,992.1	34.1
Veracruz	24,975.6	5.9	3,815.4	7.9	6,546.0	74.6
Yucatán	4,756.4	1.1	758.4	1.6	6,271.6	71.4
Zacatecas	3,217.2	.8	951.5	2.0	3,381.2	38.5
Total	423,302.0	100.0	48,225.2	100.0	8,777.6	100.0

SOURCE: ECLA, *Distribución Regional del Producto Interno Bruto Sectorial en los Países de América Latina* (Santiago, 1981).

PART II. 1980

State (or Territory)	GDP M Pesos	%	GDP/C	Index (Total = 100.0)
Aguascalientes	25,991	.61	51,629	81.3
Baja California	95,860	2.24	78,225	123.3
Baja California Sur	18,003	.42	81,317	128.1
Campeche	22,764	.53	61,149	96.3
Coahuila	126,361	2.96	81,084	127.8
Colima	23,237	.54	68,505	109.9
Chiapas	112,936	2.64	53,861	84.9
Chihuahua	120,439	2.82	62,279	98.1
Distrito Federal	1,075,050	25.14	114,692	180.7
Durango	59,642	1.40	51,407	81.0
Guanajuato	132,481	3.10	43,516	68.6
Guerrero	71,948	1.68	33,092	52.1
Hidalgo	68,836	1.61	45,391	71.5
Jalisco	278,918	6.52	64,962	102.4
México	418,703	9.79	55,489	87.4
Michoacán	105,023	2.46	34,449	54.3
Morelos	52,340	1.22	56,179	88.5
Nayarit	31,490	.74	43,135	68.0
Nuevo León	250,772	5.86	101,803	160.4
Oaxaca	59,723	1.40	23,717	37.4
Puebla	126,567	2.96	38,588	60.8
Querétaro	39,750	.93	54,749	86.3
Quintana Roo	14,228	.33	67,799	106.8
San Luis Potosí	55,822	1.31	33,413	52.6
Sinaloa	103,239	2.41	54,912	86.5
Sonora	104,906	2.45	69,987	110.3
Tabasco	125,413	2.93	109,078	171.9
Tamaulipas	148,860	3.48	77,332	121.8
Tlaxcala	19,312	.45	35,289	55.6
Veracruz	262,764	6.15	49,911	78.6
Yucatán	50,949	1.19	49,243	77.6
Zacatecas	31,796	.74	27,762	43.7
Territorial Waters	42,367	.99	**	**
Total	4,276,490	100.00	63,466	100.0

SOURCE: Mexico, NAFINSA-MV, Feb. 1, 1982.

Table 3362

GDP AND PER CAPITA GDP AT MARKET PRICES, 19 LR, 1960–83
(M 1982 Dollars)

PART I. GDP

	Country	1960	1970	1980	1981	1982	1983[‡]
A.	ARGENTINA	32,679.9	49,037.2	62,589.5	58,910.5	55,721.1	57,113.8
B.	BOLIVIA	1,452.2	2,361.1	3,667.1	3,632.3	3,315.1	3,063.3
C.	BRAZIL	55,018.0	100,037.1	228,985.0	224,634.3	227,779.2	220,262.5
D.	CHILE	10,733.9	16,241.3	20,850.9	22,043.4	18,883.6	18,725.6
E.	COLOMBIA	9,725.8	16,198.9	27,697.3	28,327.9	28,582.7	28,821.3
F.	COSTA RICA	1,263.2	2,249.4	3,893.8	3,805.7	3,460.1	3,486.7
H.	DOMINICAN REP.	2,053.1	3,368.5	6,585.3	6,853.7	6,964.6	7,235.4
I.	ECUADOR	2,577.2	4,145.3	9,/26.8	10,168.9	10,309.6	9,969.4
J.	EL SALVADOR	1,621.9	2,807.7	3,858.4	3,511.1	3,324.2	3,324.2
K.	GUATEMALA	3,299.2	5,637.1	9,769.2	9,834.6	9,487.5	9,298.2
L.	HAITI	972.1	1,053.2	1,662.9	1,638.5	1,616.9	1,632.8
M.	HONDURAS	1,065.5	1,733.9	2,763.4	2,776.7	2,744.6	2,705.9
N.	MEXICO	40,918.0	80,595.3	152,720.8	164,859.0	163,965.4	156,259.0
O.	NICARAGUA	1,211.4	2,361.9	2,574.2	2,793.0	2,753.9	2,832.8
P.	PANAMA	1,078.5	2,315.6	3,958.7	4,124.3	4,351.5	4,391.8
Q.	PARAGUAY	1,200.4	1,852.1	4,230.9	4,588.4	4,494.7	4,328.4
R.	PERU	8,455.9	14,100.6	19,663.6	20,270.4	20,412.5	17,957.4
S.	URUGUAY	4,475.4	5,218.5	7,025.0	7,017.9	6,407.4	6,099.8
T.	VENEZUELA	15,702.2	28,429.0	42,625.9	42,779.5	43,031.3	41,094.9
	LATIN AMERICA[2]	199,954.8	346,931.9	625,733.7	633,628.1	628,650.6	609,576.5

PART II. PER CAPITA GDP

(M 1982 Dollars)

	Country	1960	1970	1980	1983[‡]
A.	ARGENTINA	1,585.6	2,064.9	2,239.6	1,946.2
B.	BOLIVIA	440.9	549.7	654.8	505.2
C.	BRAZIL	760.7	1,078.3	1,924.3	1,717.8
D.	CHILE	1,413.1	1,734.6	1,877.8	1,602.3
E.	COLOMBIA	656.0	764.0	1,059.0	1,033.8
F.	COSTA RICA	956.9	1,313.1	1,765.9	1,466.2
H.	DOMINICAN REP.	596.6	787.8	1,203.4	1,212.7
I.	ECUADOR	581.9	696.6	1,216.5	1,141.1
J.	EL SALVADOR	609.5	784.5	801.7	632.0
K.	GUATEMALA	841.4	1,082.8	1,413.2	1,235.3
L.	HAITI	271.9	248.9	332.0	310.0
M.	HONDURAS	536.0	640.1	746.2	665.3
N.	MEXICO	1,103.7	1,574.9	2,284.7	2,170.7
O.	NICARAGUA	806.0	1,237.9	1,062.9	1,088.7
P.	PANAMA	884.0	1,546.9	2,089.0	2,159.2
Q.	PARAGUAY	612.8	743.5	1,335.5	1,271.2
R.	PERU	814.2	1,051.3	1,135.0	959.9
S.	URUGUAY	1,710.1	1,887.3	2,426.6	2,078.3
T.	VENEZUELA	2,053.6	2,649.2	3,063.7	2,732.4
	LATIN AMERICA[2]	958.8	1,297.4	1,844.3	1,673.6

1. In view of the fact that national series in constant prices have different base years from country to country, their conversion into dollars of a given year—in this instance 1982—was accomplished by multiplying each constant price series by the rate of variation in the implicit deflator of the U.S. gross national product between the year of the constant price series and the year 1982. Each conversion factor is expressed by:

$$\frac{\sum\limits_{k=b-1}^{b+1} GDP_k\, ER_k}{\sum\limits_{k=b-1}^{b+1} GDP_k} \cdot \frac{USD_{1982}}{USD_b}$$

Where "b" represents the base year chosen by the country for the presentation of its constant price national account figures; GDP is the current value of a country's gross domestic product; ER is the reciprocal of the implicit market exchange rate (rf) factor published in the *International Financial Statistics* of the International Monetary Fund; and USD is the U.S. gross national product implicit deflator published in the *Survey of Current Business*.

2. Includes Bahamas, Barbados, Guyana, Jamaica, Suriname, and Trinidad and Tobago.

SOURCE: IDB-SPTF, 1984, p. 420.

Table 3363

GROWTH OF GDP AND OF PER CAPITA GDP, 19 LR, 1961–83

PART I. GROWTH OF GDP

		GDP					
		Average Annual Growth Rate			Annual Variation		
	Country	1961–70	1971–75	1976–80	1981	1982	1983
A.	ARGENTINA	4.2	2.9	2.2	−5.9	−5.4	2.5
B.	BOLIVIA	5.0	5.8	3.2	−.9	−8.7	−7.6
C.	BRAZIL	6.2	10.4	6.9	−1.9	1.4	−3.3
D.	COLOMBIA	5.2	5.7	5.4	2.3	.9	.8
E.	COSTA RICA	6.0	6.1	5.3	−2.3	−9.1	.8
F.	CHILE	4.3	−2.0	7.5	5.7	−14.3	−.8
H.	DOMINICAN REP.	5.4	9.1	4.9	4.1	1.6	3.9
I.	ECUADOR	4.9	11.6	6.5	4.5	1.4	−3.3
J.	EL SALVADOR	5.7	5.5	1.2	−9.0	−5.3	#
K.	GUATEMALA	5.5	5.6	5.7	.7	−3.5	−2.0
L.	HAITI	.9	3.8	5.6	−1.5	−1.3	1.0
M.	HONDURAS	5.0	2.4	7.3	.5	−1.2	−1.4
N.	MEXICO	7.0	6.6	6.7	7.9	−.5	−4.7
O.	NICARAGUA	7.0	5.2	−2.1	8.5	−1.4	2.9
P.	PANAMA	8.0	4.8	6.4	4.2	5.5	.9
Q.	PARAGUAY	4.5	6.7	10.6	8.5	−2.0	−3.7
R.	PERU	5.3	5.5	1.4	3.1	.7	−12.0
S.	URUGUAY	1.6	1.6	4.5	−.1	−8.7	−4.8
T.	VENEZUELA	6.1	4.9	3.5	.4	.6	−4.5
	LATIN AMERICA[1]	5.7	6.6	5.5	1.3	−.8	−3.0

PART II. GROWTH OF PER CAPITA GDP

		GDP Per Capita					
		Average Annual Growth Rate			Annual Variation		
	Country	1961–70	1971–75	1976–80	1981	1982	1983
A.	ARGENTINA	2.8	1.2	.5	−7.4	−6.9	.8
B.	BOLIVIA	2.3	3.1	.5	−3.6	−11.2	−10.1
C.	BRAZIL	3.3	7.7	4.3	−4.3	−1.1	−5.7
D.	COLOMBIA	3.1	3.5	3.2	.1	−.8	−1.7
E.	COSTA RICA	3.3	3.4	2.6	−4.7	−11.4	−1.7
F.	CHILE	2.1	−3.5	5.6	4.1	−15.9	−2.5
H.	DOMINICAN REP.	3.1	6.7	2.0	.8	−2.6	1.8
I.	ECUADOR	1.8	8.4	3.4	1.5	−1.6	−6.1
J.	EL SALVADOR	2.6	2.4	−1.7	−11.7	−8.1	−2.9
K.	GUATEMALA	2.5	2.3	2.4	−2.5	−6.6	−5.1
L.	HAITI	−.8	2.2	3.7	−3.3	−3.1	−.3
M.	HONDURAS	1.8	−.8	4.0	−2.6	−4.5	−4.1
N.	MEXICO	3.6	3.4	3.5	5.2	−3.1	−7.1
O.	NICARAGUA	4.4	2.7	−4.4	6.0	−3.7	.4
P.	PANAMA	5.8	2.3	4.0	1.8	3.1	−1.5
Q.	PARAGUAY	2.0	4.2	7.9	5.1	−4.4	−5.3
R.	PERU	2.5	3.3	−.7	.9	−1.4	−13.9
S.	URUGUAY	1.0	1.1	4.0	−.5	−9.8	−4.5
T.	VENEZUELA	2.6	2.6	.4	−2.4	−2.0	−6.7
	LATIN AMERICA[1]	3.0	4.1	2.9	−1.1	−3.1	−5.3

1. Includes Bahamas, Barbados, Guyana, Jamaica, Suriname, and Trinidad and Tobago.

SOURCE: IDB-SPTF, 1984, p. 184.

Table 3364

TOTAL CONSUMPTION, 19 LR, 1960-83

(M 1982 Dollars)

	Country	1960	1970	1980	1981	1982	1983[‡]
A.	ARGENTINA	26,993.5	38,626.7	50,167.7	48,385.5	43,386.0	45,164.8
B.	BOLIVIA	1,212.6	1,962.0	3,288.6	3,255.7	2,929.7	2,710.8
C.	BRAZIL	44,894.7	77,718.5	179,267.2	175,824.5	175,623.6	172,610.9
D.	CHILE	10,043.3	14,487.2	17,269.4	19,370.3	16,755.1	15,783.3
E.	COLOMBIA	7,518.2	13,372.2	23,129.8	23,827.0	24,257.0	24,340.1
F.	COSTA RICA	1,128.1	1,916.5	3,032.7	2,789.0	2,549.4	2,589.2
H.	DOMINICAN REP.	1,642.4	2,970.1	5,612.7	5,744.4	5,843.3	5,761.9
I.	ECUADOR	2,272.4	3,760.2	8,124.0	8,539.7	8,701.2	8,414.0
J.	EL SALVADOR	1,444.8	2,527.9	3,423.1	3,158.2	2,998.4	2,878.5
K.	GUATEMALA	2,981.6	4,795.6	7,991.6	8,123.4	7,891.7	7,742.9
L.	HAITI	813.1	973.1	1,604.0	1,607.2	1,460.1	1,425.9
M.	HONDURAS	943.8	1,489.3	2,475.9	2,458.5	2,342.2	2,283.4
N.	MEXICO	33,404.3	63,813.7	117,818.6	126,843.3	128,401.3	120,597.8
O.	NICARAGUA	1,042.4	1,948.2	2,644.3	2,546.2	2,447.2	2,406.5
P.	PANAMA	909.3	1,748.5	2,805.4	2,903.9	3,044.9	~
Q.	PARAGUAY	1,141.1	1,641.3	3,203.5	3,426.3	3,442.1	3,380.1
R.	PERU	5,916.8	11,705.8	16,012.1	16,306.6	16,188.4	14,641.6
S.	URUGUAY	4,316.7	5,049.3	6,201.3	6,216.7	5,768.4	5,415.8
T.	VENEZUELA	10,159.7	18,365.1	35,379.2	35,079.4	35,586.4	33,929.8
	LATIN AMERICA[2]	162,328.4	274,425.6	497,749.7	504,920.0	498,367.2	477,138.2

1. Includes change in stocks for years 1980-83.
2. Includes Bahamas, Barbados, Guyana, Jamaica, Suriname, and Trinidad and Tobago.

SOURCE: IDB-SPTF, 1984, p. 421.

Table 3365

GROSS DOMESTIC INVESTMENT,[1] 19 LR, 1960-83

(M 1982 Dollars)

	Country	1960	1970	1980	1981	1982	1983[‡]
A.	ARGENTINA	6,535.9	10,397.6	14,941.1	12,111.1	10,174.0	9,939.7
B.	BOLIVIA	187.2	402.9	450.1	384.0	170.3	127.5
C.	BRAZIL	10,453.4	22,707.2	52,734.4	49,999.8	51,469.2	45,061.3
D.	CHILE	1,570.5	3,793.5	4,980.4	5,264.7	1,820.5	2,099.0
E.	COLOMBIA	2,072.2	3,326.6	5,444.9	6,165.5	6,493.2	6,264.8
F.	COSTA RICA	212.7	455.5	1,111.2	692.0	359.0	379.8
H.	DOMINICAN REP.	203.2	644.7	1,667.8	1,492.5	1,413.4	1,251.7
I.	ECUADOR	508.3	958.6	2,583.9	2,483.1	2,236.0	1,878.2
J.	EL SALVADOR	250.6	337.9	483.3	464.8	398.8	396.4
K.	GUATEMALA	356.0	675.7	1,117.5	1,272.9	1,009.4	968.5
L.	HAITI	61.7	96.1	292.3	294.5	274.5	289.2
M.	HONDURAS	139.0	312.8	596.3	459.9	324.9	343.6
N.	MEXICO	7,714.1	18,314.4	42,808.1	49,485.4	35,281.6	27,140.2
O.	NICARAGUA	176.5	401.8	395.6	591.2	455.9	377.1
P.	PANAMA	184.1	644.7	933.3	1,050.8	1,011.1	~
Q.	PARAGUAY	111.3	242.0	1,292.1	1,442.8	1,274.5	1,212.1
R.	PERU	1,611.6	1,819.2	3,359.5	4,202.9	3,926.0	2,628.3
S.	URUGUAY	573.5	553.0	1,304.0	1,166.5	909.6	638.8
T.	VENEZUELA	3,360.4	7,789.6	17,263.3	17,966.8	18,158.9	17,080.7
	LATIN AMERICA[2]	37,518.7	75,895.0	155,172.1	158,519.5	138,651.4	118,415.7

1. Fixed investment only for years 1980-83.
2. Includes Bahamas, Barbados, Guyana, Jamaica, Suriname, and Trinidad and Tobago.

SOURCE: IDB-SPTF, 1984, p. 421.

Table 3366

GROSS CAPITAL FORMATION AS A PERCENTAGE OF GDP, 18 L, 1962–83

(% of GDP at Market Prices)

	Country	1962	1965	1970	1975	1976	1977	1978	1979	1980	1981	1982	1983
A.	ARGENTINA	21.31	19.20	20.40	26.57	27.18	27.24	23.91	22.62	22.78	18.20	17.53	~
B.	BOLIVIA	16.44	16.96	17.07	24.44	21.17	20.80	20.00	17.62	13.06	12.20	8.49	~
C.	BRAZIL	20.33	21.99	25.50	32.08	27.37	25.87	25.16	22.12	22.53	21.23	21.25	~
D.	CHILE	15.00	17.37	22.22	13.09	12.78	14.42	17.81	17.79	20.98	20.72	9.91	~
E.	COLOMBIA	18.73	17.67	20.23	16.99	17.56	18.75	18.28	18.15	19.07	20.62	20.48	~
F.	COSTA RICA	19.45	19.50	20.54	21.64	23.66	24.27	23.46	25.32	26.58	29.03	23.42	~
H.	DOMINICAN REP.	11.81	8.85	19.14	24.51	22.31	21.79	23.89	25.35	24.86	23.60	20.78	~
I.	ECUADOR	13.91	13.83	18.19	26.73	23.76	26.53	28.45	25.34	26.12	23.08	22.97	16.92
J.	EL SALVADOR	11.45	15.41	13.26	22.12	19.62	23.42	23.85	18.08	13.27	14.24	12.62	13.00
K.	GUATEMALA	8.83	13.29	12.87	16.10	21.40	20.05	21.62	18.75	15.89	17.03	14.28	~
L.	HAITI	~	~	8.42	16.31	16.02	15.87	16.95	16.81	17.13	16.87	16.67	16.27
M.	HONDURAS	14.84	14.55	20.89	17.89	17.10	24.69	25.88	24.97	26.19	21.25	14.82	15.79
N.	MEXICO	15.46	17.19	22.73	23.69	22.29	22.84	23.60	25.95	28.12	28.98	21.25	~
O.	NICARAGUA	17.36	20.93	18.60	21.25	18.75	26.76	13.30	-5.74	15.37	21.81	17.34	17.25
P.	PANAMA	19.59	17.55	27.84	30.82	31.63	23.72	26.57	28.06	27.73	30.10	27.68	21.53
Q.	PARAGUAY	12.55	15.08	14.72	24.10	24.63	24.68	27.25	28.56	28.76	28.83	25.63	~
R.	PERU	22.75	18.62	12.92	19.85	17.92	14.98	14.50	14.35	17.72	22.22	22.65	19.35
S.	URUGUAY	15.96	10.86	11.56	13.49	14.80	15.20	16.01	17.31	17.35	15.25	13.23	10.55

SOURCE: IMF-IFS-S, No. 8, 1984, pp. 60–61.

Table 3367

ESTIMATES OF NATIONAL INCOME,[1] 18 LRC, 1960–80

	Country	Total (M US)							Per Capita (US)						
		1960	1970	1975	1977	1978	1979	1980	1960	1970	1975	1977	1978	1979	1980
A.	ARGENTINA	12,129	23,366	35,227	~	~	~	~	588	984	1388	~	~	~	~
B.	BOLIVIA	339	970	2,334	~	~	~	~	102	226	477	~	~	~	~
C.	BRAZIL	16,357	43,645	116,356	153,258	179,216	198,129	228,884	233	472	1,095	1,365	1,553	1,670	1,860
D.	CHILE	1,732	7,203	4,319	~	~	~	~	228	769	423	~	~	~	~
E.	COLOMBIA	3,461	6,357	11,399	17,537	21,092	25,028	30,214	224	310	503	700	823	949	1,115
F.	COSTA RICA	447	909	1,793	2,838	3,233	3,671	~	357	525	915	1,378	1,525	1,692	~
I.	ECUADOR	885	1,536	3,958	~	~	~	~	204	258	561	~	~	~	~
J.	EL SALVADOR	536	970	1,684	2,730	2,917	3,354	3,187	208	280	420	621	671	755	672
K.	GUATEMALA	984	1,633	3,170	4,823	5,259	6,027	~	248	305	508	749	769	855	~
L.	HAITI[2]	217	319	657	1,318	1,005	1,078	1,370	60	75	143	277	208	219	273
M.	HONDURAS	325	676	1,033	1,338	1,657	1,961	2,314	168	256	334	403	482	551	627
N.	MEXICO	11,166	30,843	71,626	65,486	82,350	106,671	~	307	608	1,191	1,035	1,230	1,537	~
O.	NICARAGUA	320	720	1,462	2,069	1,980	~	~	227	394	677	896	822	~	~
P.	PANAMA[3]	371	924	1,732	1,891	2,177	2,491	2,927	349	646	1,069	1,068	1,244	1,392	1,591
Q.	PARAGUAY	268	549	1,421	1,860	2,243	2,984	3,921	155	239	536	664	776	1,005	1,277
R.	PERU	1,904	6,395	14,264	9,586	10,432	12,833	17,046	190	475	922	586	620	742	959
S.	URUGUAY	1,444	2,292	3,330	3,935	4,667	6,528	9,211	569	833	1,181	1,371	1,632	2,267	3,176
T.	VENEZUELA	6,314	9,987	25,923	33,110	36,756	45,457	56,348	859	972	2,162	2,599	2,802	3,362	4,051
	LATIN AMERICA[4]	64,000	150,100	322,200	392,900	465,600	581,700	~	310	560	1,040	1,210	1,390	1,690	~
	UNITED STATES	454,073	890,823	1,365,737	1,677,346	1,901,006	2,121,889	2,298,000	2,513	4,344	6,324	7,752	8,540	9,429	10,094

1. In market prices; based on 1975 estimates.
2. Twelve months ending September 30 of year stated.
3. Excluding former Canal Zone.
4. Rough estimate, including the Caribbean, Suriname, and Guyana.

SOURCE: UN-SY, 1979/80, table 164A; UN-SY, 1981, table 34A.

Table 3368

ESTIMATES OF NATIONAL DISPOSABLE INCOME,[1] 15 LRC, 1960–80

Country	Total (M US)							Per Capita (US)						
	1960	1970	1975	1977	1978	1979	1980	1960	1970	1975	1977	1978	1979	1980
B. BOLIVIA	346	962	2,311	~	~	~	~	104	224	472	~	~	~	~
D. CHILE	1,752	7,242	4,388	~	~	~	~	231	773	425	~	~	~	~
E. COLOMBIA	~	6,383	11,945	17,581	21,162	25,082	~	~	311	505	702	825	952	~
F. COSTA RICA	452	912	1,803	2,854	3,249	3,683	~	360	527	920	1,385	1,533	1,697	~
I. ECUADOR	893	1,648	3,979	6,322	6,921	8,445	11,052	206	276	564	836	876	1,045	1,324
J. EL SALVADOR	538	984	1,712	2,770	2,968	~	~	209	284	427	630	682	~	~
L. HAITI[2]	225	341	696	1,381	1,073	1,168	~	62	80	152	291	222	237	~
M. HONDURAS	328	683	1,051	~	~	~	~	169	259	340	~	~	~	~
N. MEXICO	11,196	30,899	71,759	65,654	82,546	106,894	~	308	610	1,193	1,037	1,233	1,541	~
O. NICARAGUA	323	727	1,480	2,081	1,991	1,345	~	229	397	685	901	826	510	~
P. PANAMA[3]	370	928	1,727	1,888	2,175	2,508	2,914	349	649	1,066	1,067	1,243	1,401	1,584
Q. PARAGUAY	268	549	1,421	1,860	2,243	2,984	3,922	155	239	536	664	776	1,005	1,278
R. PERU	1,926	6,478	14,307	9,623	10,480	12,940	17,161	192	482	925	588	623	748	965
S. URUGUAY	1,444	2,292	3,329	3,935	4,665	~	~	569	833	1,181	1,371	1,631	~	~
T. VENEZUELA	6,314	9,919	25,772	32,828	36,350	45,051	55,917	859	965	2,149	2,577	2,771	3,332	4,020
LATIN AMERICA	26,375	70,947	147,630	148,777	175,823	210,100	55,917	4,002	6,909	11,540	12,049	13,241	12,468	9,171
UNITED STATES	450,069	884,816	1,359,553	1,672,972	1,896,215	2,116,418	~	2,491	4,315	6,295	7,732	8,519	9,404	~

1. Based on 1975 estimate.
2. Twelve months ending September 30 of year stated.
3. Excluding former Canal Zone.

SOURCE: UN-SY, 1979/80, table 164B; UN-SY, 1981, table 34B.

Part XI: Development of Data

CHAPTER 34

CHANGES IN MEXICO SINCE 1895: CENTRAL GOVERNMENT REVENUE, PUBLIC SECTOR EXPENDITURE, AND NATIONAL ECONOMIC GROWTH

by

James W. Wilkie

James W. Wilkie and Adam Perkal, eds., *Statistical Abstract of Latin America*, vol. 24 (Los Angeles: UCLA Latin American Center Publications, University of California, 1985).

Patterns in Mexico's State Activity Since 1895

A major problem in examining Mexico's history has been the lack of long-term economic statistics that are relatively comparable across time for each series. The purpose of this essay is to develop some basic historical series, dealing specifically with the growth of the Mexican economy, the increase in state expenditures, and patterns in the source of central government revenues.

Of interest here are the presidential periods since the dictatorship of Porfirio Díaz, whose regime was overthrown by the Mexican Revolution of 1910. Out of Mexico's revolutionary upheaval came a periodization that I characterize like this:

1. Two decades (1910–30) of political solutions for Mexico's problems, including violence (to 1920) and a decade of national reconstruction (to 1930)
2. A decade (1930–40) of state emphasis on social reform
3. Two decades (1940–60) of state emphasis on industrialization
4. A decade (1960–70) of attempt to achieve balance between the political, social, and economic approaches to Mexico's problems
5. A period (since 1970) of statism

To place the post-1910 period into some perspective, I trace back data to the year 1900 where possible or feasible.

During the periods outlined above, what began after 1910 as the growth of active state policy intent on balancing private and public needs subsequently grew into statist policy. Under the active state the government sector steadily expanded its attempts to control the economic and social life of Mexico until 1970 when the government began to assert itself as more important than the private sector. This statement is all the more true when the Mexican government's regulatory functions are taken into account along with the nationalization of the private banking system in 1982.

In a significant step to end Mexico's civil war of 1914–17, the contenders for power wrote the country's twentieth-century constitution. Although the Constitution of 1917 has provided for balance between the private and public sectors, the political reality since 1929 of rule by one political party (the Official Party of the Revolution)[1] has led almost inevitably to state domination of affairs.

AUTHOR'S NOTE: In two recent articles (Wilkie 1985a, 1985b) the author has made use of the data defined, organized, and prepared in yearly or periodic form in this chapter of SALA to measure the emergence of the modern Mexican state.

[1] The Official Party has enjoyed three names since 1929: from 1929 to 1938, the Party of National Revolution (PNR); from 1938 through 1945, the Party of the Mexican Revolution (PRM); and since 1946, the Party of Institutional Revolution (PRI).

To understand the extent and pace of the state's emerging role in Mexico, important items on the research agenda include the determination of patterns in types of "revenue" collected by the central government as well as the development of series on the *real* amount of money expended by the government and the *real* value of Mexico's yearly economic production of goods and services (gross domestic product or GDP).

In all epochs people complain with reason that the money of "today" is no longer worth what it was "yesterday." To analyze the economic growth of the state we must convert the value of money which is "current" at different times into amounts according to what that money could really buy as time passes. If we did not adjust for inflation to determine the real value of money, the mere facts of price increases and increasing amounts of money in circulation would prevent us from comparing the situation in one period to that of another.

Therefore, I develop here the following time-series:

1. Composite price index
2. Total and per capita expenditures by the central sector of government as well as the decentralized government (or parastate) sector—which is not dependent upon the Mexican Treasury Department for most of its income as is the central government
3. GDP's value and its relation to national government expenditures
4. Index of GDP and of GDP/C (that is, GDP divided by the size of changing population) in order to know the extent to which GDP is keeping up with or falling behind the size of population which the economy must support
5. Pattern in type of central government revenue collections (including loans received)

Although Mexico's Dirección General de Estadística (DGE) and Banco de México (BDM) have developed data for the above series, the results are not always consistent or presented in meaningful terms.

To prepare data on all but the last series, it is necessary to develop at the outset a single price index that covers all of the years since 1900.

Comparative Price Indexes for Mexico

The Mexican government agency historically in charge of measuring inflation was the DGE. The DGE series covered wholesale prices in Mexico City and extended back into the nineteenth century. Until recently, it stood out as the sole major price index that also covered at least some of the years of Mexico's civil war (except 1914–17). Thus I used the DGE index for my analyses of Mexico's budgets (1967, 1970, 1978), the first to compare planned and actual expenditures and to examine them in terms of real value.

To compete with the DGE wholesale price index, beginning with data for the year 1939 the Banco de México began to develop a wholesale price index that "improved" on the DGE index by including about four times more items in the "basket" of goods measured for change in prices. Unfortunately, the BDM index did not include data prior to 1939.

Apparently realizing the time-depth deficiency in its wholesale price index, the BDM began working seriously on a price index to adjust its historical estimates of real change in Mexico's GDP since 1900. If the BDM did produce a major new index, it did not publicize it as such, and for many years simply let others calculate the "GDP deflator index" by comparing its data on "current GDP" with "real GDP." In short, as a byproduct of its reconstructing the change in real GDP back to 1900, the BDM had created a new price index (without openly publishing its methodology). Known as the implicit deflator of GDP, this BDM index was well refined by 1970 and came to constitute a competing index that could allow knowledgeable observers to assess the amount of yearly inflation in Mexico.

Meanwhile, debate had arisen in Mexico over which *wholesale* price index should be used to adjust time series for the inflation factor (see Wilkie 1974:142). By the early 1970s the DGE wholesale price index was showing inflation to be at an embarrassingly high level compared to the BDM wholesale price index. The issue was resolved in 1975 when the government of President Luis Echeverría Alvarez (1970–76), realizing that it could enjoy better propaganda mileage out of the BDM wholesale price index (and could hold down increases in wage levels if the higher index were dropped), suppressed the DGE wholesale price index.

To resolve the question about which of the three indexes has best measured inflation, table 3400 offers the data for each. The indexes are all based upon the year 1950 as equal to 100 so that not only are data comparable to the same base but also figures for the earliest years show as whole numbers.

Ironically, the DGE's wholesale series and the BDM's GDP deflator are remarkably similar from 1900 to 1965 (except for 1947, 1953, and 1955–57). After 1965, although the deflator and DGE index began to show different amounts of inflation for some years, the two were always closer than the BDM's wholesale price index, which appears to dramatically understate inflation.[2]

[2] It can be argued that theoretically the wholesale price index should yield less inflation than the GDP deflator because, for example, the former involves cost of consumption items (many under government cost control) within the country and the latter includes cost of production and import items that will not directly (if at all) affect most people's lives. But, given the misvaluation of the peso at such a low level over many years, import goods were not necessarily more expensive than goods purchased in Mexico.

It is interesting to see that the DGE index from 1953 through 1964 (except for 1962) shows slightly more inflation than the BDM's GDP deflator index, after which this situation reversed with the BDM deflator showing more inflation. Through 1964 the indexes were essentially similar and if either can be used for the previous 65 years, the DGE price index covered six years (1911–13 and 1918–20) that the GDP deflator index did not include.

The demise of the DGE index of wholesale prices prevents updating my budgetary analysis without using a new index to deflate the Mexican government's planned and actual expenditures. Fortunately, because of the close relationship of the GDP deflator price to the DGE index, the two can be linked at the year 1965 to create what I call the DGE-BDM composite index of prices. The indexes were almost equal in 1963; in 1964 the DGE was higher and in 1965 the GDP deflator became permanently higher. The choice of 1965 as the linkage year means that since 1963, when the indexes were nearly the same, the CPI gives the consistently higher result for the years of overlap up through the 1976 suppression of the DGE index.

The DGE-BDM composite index of prices is given in table 3401. This composite index allows us to link previous, DGE index–based research to present and future research that is based upon the GDP deflator index. In this manner, we maintain a framework for study that yields relatively consistent results over the long term. In any case, it should be clear from the above discussion that there is no one "truth" about the nature of inflation in Mexico, and the composite index of prices is as "realistic" as any we know at present.[3]

To show the use of the DGE-BDM composite index of prices, let me now turn to Mexican public expenditures.

Expenditures of the Mexican National Government

There are not one but two national governments in Mexico. One, the central (or federal) sector, carries out traditional legislative, judicial, and executive functions, including defense, police, mails, transportation, and so on. The other national government, the decentralized (or parastate) sector, administers:

1. The activities of nationalized companies, often formerly owned by foreign interests, such as PEMEX (the national oil company) and Ferrocarriles Nacionales (the national railway system)
2. Companies owned wholly or jointly with minority private shareholders (such as Ferrocarril Chihuahua al Pacífico, S.A. de C.V.)
3. The national trust funds (such as Instituto Mexicano de Seguro Social, the Mexican social security institute)

[3] For research on Mexico's price indexes, see Jeffrey L. Bortz, "Industrial Wages in Mexico City" (Ph.D. dissertation, University of California, Los Angeles, 1984).

4. Trust funds administered jointly with state and local governments (such as the Junta Federal de Mejores Materiales de Acapulco)

5. Other autonomous activities, such as funding programs to stimulate agriculture (e.g., Fideicomiso Relativo a las Siembras de Maíz, Frijol y Cacahuate) and export development (e.g., Impulsora de Empresas Turísticas, S.A. de C.V.)

Several of these parastate agencies and funds are not audited, but their total planned and actual outlays may be included in the total for parastate activity.

Central Government Expenditures

Data on central government planned and actual gross expenditures are given in table 3402. The data include amortization of the debt and transfers to decentralized agencies, states, and local government (discussed in Wilkie 1985*b*), and they are converted to pesos of 1950 with the DGE-BDM composite price index. Essentially these are the figures given in several of my previous studies (1967, 1970, and 1978), except that here I have carried forward since 1976 the data in current pesos and have revised since 1965 the figures in pesos of 1950, utilizing the DGE-BDM price series (which links the DGE series to the BDM series in 1965). I have also revised actual expenditures from 1930 to 1947 to account for "off-budget" spending by presidents Lázaro Cárdenas, Manuel Avila Camacho, and Miguel Alemán. This off-budget activity involved foreign loans for road building and it was considered to be extraordinary until 1947 when all such loans were incorporated into the regular budget process by President Alemán, who included them in a newly created budgetary category entitled *erogaciones adicionales*.

Development of the long-term yearly budgetary series in table 3402 allows us to summarize in table 3403 and figure 34:1 the average number of per capita real pesos of 1950 available during each presidential term. The figures allow us to more clearly assess the differences among the country's political leaders.

The data in table 3403 show startling variation. Under the dictator Díaz, the central government projected expenditure at 31.8 pesos per person and actually spent the amount, 31.9 pesos. (No per capita funds really reach each person, of course, but only show us how much funding is available in relation to population.) Presidents from 1911 through 1924 averaged less than projected; Venustiano Carranza spent less than half that planned owing to civil war. By the early 1940s actual expenditures were in real terms running far ahead of per capita plans, reaching a percentage increase of 60.2 percent under Manuel Avila Camacho, as shown in figure 34:2. The record gain in actual underprojected outlay came under Gustavo Díaz Ordaz, who ran up an increase averaging 82.6 percent. Subsequently, after the results of my budgetary analysis (1967 and 1970) had brought about a reform to limit such increases, the gain in actual underprojected per capita real expenditures was contained at about 20 percent.

Parastate Expenditures

Table 3404 gives the yearly figures on gross decentralized expenditures, including transfers from the central government and parastate transfers to the private and subnational (state and local) units of government as well as amortization of the debt. Although transfers and amortization figures include some double-counting of funds, they are not deducted here because we are interested in knowing the expenditure power of each national sector—that is, the amount of funds each sector controls with respect to kind and amount of allocation.[4] It is important to recall that the parastate agencies mostly have their own funds (either collected for services rendered, as with the national airlines; gained from sales, as with nationally controlled companies; or held in trust funds, as for pensions) and except to cover losses or special expenditures are not dependent (as are agencies of the central government) upon the Treasury Department for allocation of tax revenues.

Actual gross expenditure per capita by the parastate agencies has grown as the decentralized sector has become more important over time and as coverage of the sector has become increasingly complete. The real amount shown in table 3404 came to only about 90 pesos per person in 1940, when fragmentary data are first available. By 1976 when the parastate sector was brought under central government jurisdiction to the extent that projected and actual expenditures must be reported (and an increasing number of agencies audited), the amount per person came to about 625 pesos. As the power of the agencies increased, by 1981 the per capita figure reached 1,178 pesos, before falling during 1982's economic recession to 943 pesos.

Data on expenditures can also be related to GDP, a relationship we are now ready to examine in several ways.

Mexico's National Government Expenditure as Share of GDP

Table 3405 presents yearly data on GDP in current (nondeflated) terms and gives actual central government expenditures also in current terms. These two series allow us to calculate the central government's percentage share in GDP. Under Díaz that share fell from 4.5 percent in 1900 to 3.3 percent in 1910. No GDP figures are available for the years from 1911 through 1920, but by the early 1920s the central government's share in GDP had exceeded by several percentage points the Díaz shares. Not until the Cárdenas era (1935–40) did the share reach more than 7 percent. Under Alemán the share increased to over 10 percent in two of his years in the presidency. During the following years, from 1953 through 1971, central government expenditure as a share of GDP remained in the 10 percent to 12 percent range.

During the 1970s and 1980s, the relative power of central government increased rapidly. From about 14 percent in 1972, the share reached over 20 percent by 1976 when

---

[4] For further discussion, see Wilkie 1985*b*.

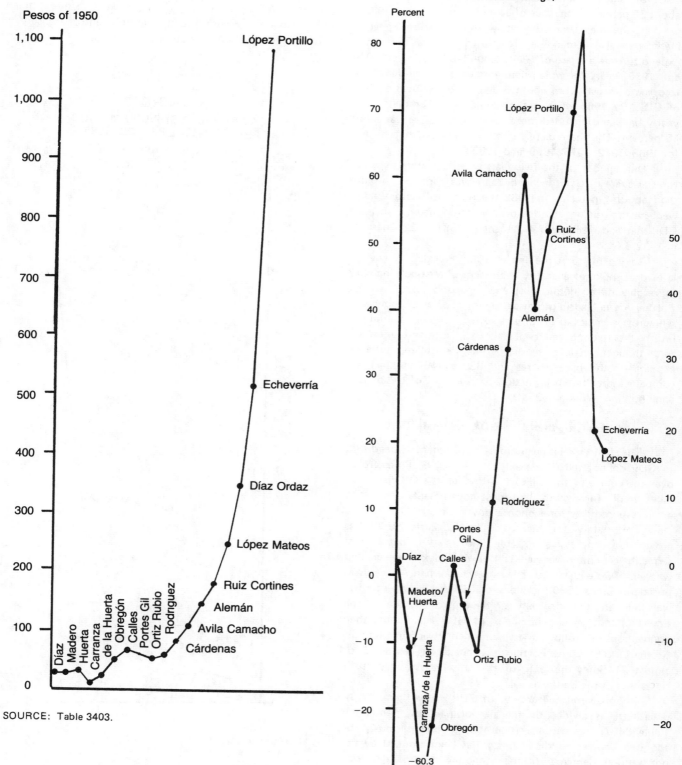

Figure 34:1

MEXICAN CENTRAL GOVERNMENT ACTUAL GROSS
EXPENDITURE PER CAPITA, IN REAL TERMS,
AVERAGE BY PRESIDENT, 1900–82

(Pesos of 1950)

SOURCE: Table 3403.

Figure 34:2

ACTUAL GROSS EXPENDITURE COMPARED TO
PROJECTED GROSS EXPENDITURE IN MEXICO,
BY PRESIDENT, 1900–82

(Percent Change)

SOURCE: Table 3403.

Echeverría left the presidency. During the López Portillo administration and the oil boom of the late 1970s, the stage was set to expand the power of the central government even after the oil boom began to falter in the early 1980s. In 1981 the share reached 42.7 percent, before "declining" to about 36 percent in the face of economic recession in 1982.

In the meantime, the power of the national government was also expanding, illustrated by the parastate's expenditure as a share of GDP (table 3406). Between 1940 and 1958, years for which data are available, the decentralized share ranged from about 5 percent to about 8 percent of GDP. By 1965 when data become more complete on a yearly basis and included more agencies, the share was about 10 percent. The share increased each year after that, except for 1968, 1972, 1976, 1979, and 1982.

During four of the five years when parastate expenditures as share of GDP declined, there was a loss of no more than about 1 percent. In 1982 the parastate sector underwent its first major recorded decline, falling from a share of GDP that had reached 27.4 percent in 1981 to 22.7 percent in 1982.

Taking office at the end of 1982, President Miguel de la Madrid spoke of austerity in the face of Mexico's inability to resolve its economic problems as world oil prices fell. Further, de la Madrid promised to reduce parastate power by selling off agencies to the private sector. Although he did not return the nationalized banks to their former owners (as some thought possible), he did permit them to reacquire 34 percent of the bank shares and 339 of 467 nonbanking companies that had been nationalized as part of the private bank holdings (Wilkie 1985*b*).

Mexico's Growth of Real GDP and Real GDP/C

The figures relating national government expenditure to GDP do not tell us the extent to which GDP has grown over the course of this century. Although the Official Party takes credit for growth, like most governments, it tries to avoid responsibility for economic downturns.

Fortunately for Mexico's Official Party, GDP has grown very impressively. Table 3407 shows that in real terms the economy averaged 31.1 on the index I have created wherein 1950 equals 100, a level reached when Alemán was president. Since 1950 the index of GDP has grown at a tremendous rate, doubling between the time of Alemán and the López Mateos years. The index of GDP again more than doubled in the following two presidential administrations. By the term of López Portillo, the index averaged 641.3, or almost 21 times the GDP of the Díaz years and over 12 times that of the Cárdenas years.

Impressive as the growth of GDP is (see figure 34:3), once GDP is divided by the size of Mexico's population (table 3407), we can see (figure 34:3) how seriously the economic power of the country has been reduced by the population's demands on the economic system. If Mexico had been able to control its population growth earlier, it would be a much richer country today.

Mexico's GDP/C was quite favorable in relation to GDP through the 1940s, as the trends in figure 34:3 reveal, but with the post-World War II improvements in public health, the Mexican population began to overwhelm the ability of the government to maintain social services and provide jobs, especially because Mexico has needed to direct much of its economic wealth into the development of transportation and industrial infrastructures.

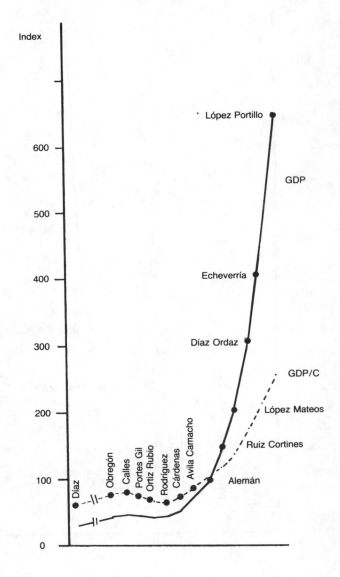

Figure 34:3

REAL GDP AND GDP/C IN MEXICO, BY PRESIDENTIAL PERIOD, 1895–82

(1950 = 100)

SOURCE: Table 3407.

Figure 34:4

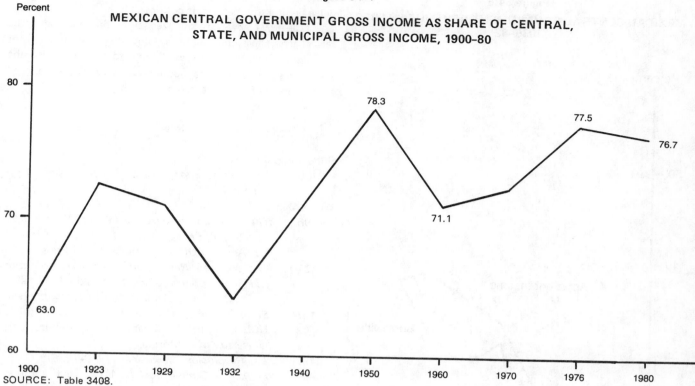

MEXICAN CENTRAL GOVERNMENT GROSS INCOME AS SHARE OF CENTRAL, STATE, AND MUNICIPAL GROSS INCOME, 1900–80

SOURCE: Table 3408.

In the meantime, Mexico's local governments, with differing regional needs, have faced crisis because of a declining share of funds.

Government Based Upon Pooled Finances in Mexico

Table 3408 shows the gross income of Mexico's traditional government which depends upon taxation and borrowing that is pooled for allocation of funds at the federal (or central), state, and local levels. Traditional government contrasts sharply with the parastate agencies which have their own sources of funds, depending upon the central government only to pay for deficits and special programs.

Data in table 3408 reveal that local government (equivalent to county government in the United States) has seen its share of gross income fall from about 13 percent through 1923 to less than 10 percent by the late 1920s and to less than 4 percent by the 1950s.

Meanwhile, state government has seen its share of gross income remain relatively steady over time, the high of 27.1 coming in 1932 and the low of 14.5 in 1923 (table 3408). The high state figure is explained by the central government's retrenchment in the face of world depression. The low can be attributed to the effects of the 1923 military rebellion, which upset state economies.

Although the state income has not greatly varied—at least for the years sampled here—the central government has seen its power in revenue grow at the expense of local government. The central government share is shown in figure 34:4. President de la Madrid has promised to reverse this trend, but so have most presidents—to no avail.

Revenue in Mexico, 1935–82

Central government revenues are clearly the most important source of pooled funds. To understand the components of that revenue, table 3409 shows the major categories of funds, which I have adjusted to develop relative consistency across time. As can be surmised from the complicated generation of data by comparing and adjusting sources, sources of revenue in Mexico have not been clearly understood by the central government officials, who come and go according to administration.

The introduction of the value added tax (VAT), in my view, has not only unnecessarily complicated understanding, but has contributed greatly to inflation in Mexico. The VAT has yet to prove itself of much value at all.

To clarify the meaning of income taxes in relation to borrowing, table 3410 shows that by excluding borrowing in analysis of revenues, the Mexican government has at times made the income tax far more important that it really is. Apparently income taxes were reaching about 40 percent of central government revenues. But when borrowing is considered as revenue (Wilkie 1985a), the "true" importance of the income tax falls to somewhat over 20 percent. Borrowing has become the most important source of regular and recurrent revenue in Mexico, as can be seen in figure 34:5.

Conclusion

In developing the long-term series presented in this chapter, my purpose has been to suggest new approaches for understanding Mexico's increasingly complicated devel-

Figure 34:5

MEXICAN CENTRAL GOVERNMENT REVENUE SHARES,
1935–82

(%)

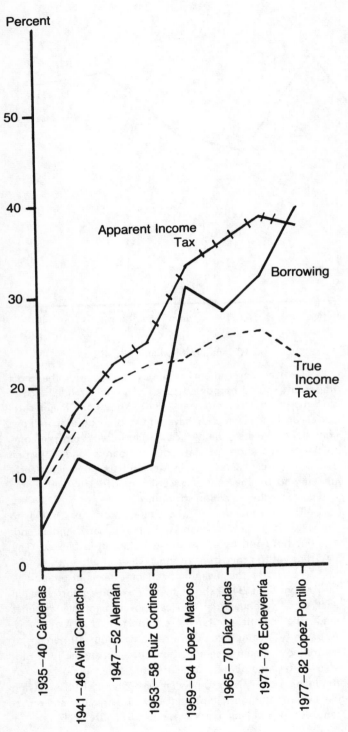

SOURCE: Table 3410.

opment patterns. Historical statistics offer a unique way to delve behind the rhetoric of politics.

Clearly I have not analyzed all of the meaning in the series given here, but in developing the methodology for examining some major series, I hope to have provided the kinds of statistics that can be interpreted by others as well as reorganized for different types of analysis.

References

Solís, Leopoldo
  1981   *La Realidad Económica Mexicana*. México, D.F.: Siglo XXI.

Wilkie, James W.
  1967   *The Mexican Revolution: Federal Expenditure and Social Change Since 1910*. Berkeley and Los Angeles: University of California Press.
  1970   *The Mexican Revolution: Federal Expenditure and Social Change Since 1910*. 2d ed. Berkeley and Los Angeles: University of California Press.
  1974   *Statistics and National Policy*. Los Angeles: UCLA Latin American Center Publications, University of California.
  1978   *La Revolución Mexicana (1910–1976): Gasto Público y Cambio Social*. México, D.F.: Fondo de Cultura Económica.
  1985a   "Borrowing as Revenue, 1935–1982." *The Mexican Forum* 5(2), 3-7.
  1985b   "The Dramatic Growth of Mexico's Economy and the Rise of Statist Government Budgetary Power, 1910–1982." *The Mexican Forum* 5(4) forthcoming.

Table 3400

COMPARATIVE PRICE INDEXES FOR MEXICO, 1900–82
(1950 = 100)

Year	BDM GDP Deflator[1]	DGE Mexico City Wholesale Prices[2]	BDM Mexico City Wholesale Prices[3]
1900	11.3	12.0	**
1901	14.0	14.7	**
1902	14.3	15.0	**
1903	14.3	15.0	**
1904	13.8	14.7	**
1905	15.5	16.3	**
1906	15.3	16.2	**
1907	15.3	15.9	**
1908	15.7	16.6	**
1909	16.8	17.6	**
1910	19.5	20.7	**
1911	**	19.6	**
1912	**	19.4	**
1913	**	19.2	**
1914	**	**	**
1915	**	**	**
1916	**	**	**
1917	**	**	**
1918	**	43.3	**
1919	**	34.6	**
1920	**	36.3	**
1921	31.9	33.1	**
1922	26.2	27.8	**
1923	27.7	29.8	**
1924	26.0	28.5	**
1925	27.7	30.0	**
1926	27.3	29.4	**
1927	26.0	28.7	**
1928	26.0	27.6	**
1929	26.2	27.5	**
1930	26.8	28.0	**
1931	23.5	24.7	**
1932	21.0	22.5	**
1933	22.2	23.9	**
1934	22.9	24.7	**
1935	23.3	24.9	**
1936	25.4	26.4	**
1937	31.2	31.3	**
1938	32.9	32.7	**
1939	33.3	33.6	32.0
1940	34.8	33.8	32.8
1941	35.6	35.9	35.2
1942	39.0	39.7	38.4
1943	45.9	47.5	46.4
1944	61.2	60.9	56.8
1945	65.0	67.0	64.0
1946	82.8	78.5	73.6
1947	88.9	80.1	77.6
1948	91.0	85.0	83.2
1949	95.0	90.0	91.2
1950	100.0	100.0	100.0
1951	119.7	120.6	124.0

Table 3400 (Continued)

COMPARATIVE PRICE INDEXES FOR MEXICO, 1900–82
(1950 = 100)

Year	BDM GDP Deflator[1]	DGE Mexico City Wholesale Prices[2]	BDM Mexico City Wholesale Prices[3]
1952	129.1	132.5	128.0
1953	128.1	135.2	126.6
1954	141.9	145.6	137.6
1955[a]	160.0	168.0	156.0
1956	170.8	178.3	164.0
1957	181.5	189.3	170.4
1958	192.3	198.0	178.4
1959	200.0	200.8	180.0
1960	209.2	212.3	188.8
1961	212.3	214.2	191.2
1962	220.0	217.2	194.4
1963	220.0	221.2[b]	195.2
1964	224.6	228.4	204.0
1965[c]	244.6	237.3	208.0
1966	255.4	239.6	210.4
1967	256.9	239.7	216.0
1968	263.1	243.9	220.8
1969	273.8	246.8	226.4
1970	303.1	258.2	240.0
1971	320.0	265.3	248.8
1972	340.0	276.5	255.2
1973	384.6	332.9	296.0
1974	472.3	418.9	362.4
1975	546.2	475.9	400.0
1976	652.3	550.3	489.6
1977	850.8	**	691.2
1978	993.8	**	800.2
1979	1,195.4	**	946.4
1980	1,538.5	**	1,177.6
1981	1,956.9	**	1,466.4
1982	3,155.4	**	2,288.8

1. Used as part of DGE-BDM Composite Price Index developed in table 3401 for period beginning in 1965.
2. Used as part of DGE-BDM Composite Price Index developed in table 3401 to cover period through 1964.
3. This 210-item wholesale price index for Mexico City should not be confused with BDM's 32-item wholesale price index for Mexico City which was suspended in 1979.

a. Solís (1981) gives 159.3 or .7 difference.
b. Later DGE revision equals 220.5.
c. DGE-BDM linkage point in Composite Index given in table 3401.

SOURCE: BDM's GDP Deflator Index through 1954 is from Solís (1981:92), and since 1955 from IMF-Y, 1984; base converted from both sources.

DGE's Wholesale Price Index through 1963 from Wilkie (1970: 22-23), and 1964–1976 from Wilkie (1978:350).

BDM's Wholesale Price Index is from BDM, *Indicadores Económicos* (Carpeta), "Acervo Histórico" II (1983:II-H-14).

Table 3401

DGE-BDM COMPOSITE INDEX OF PRICES FOR MEXICO, 1900–82

(1950 = 100)

Year	Prices	Year	Prices
1900	12.0	1945	67.0
1901	14.7	1946	78.5
1902	15.0	1947	80.1
1903	15.0	1948	85.0
1904	14.7	1949	90.0
1905	16.3	1950	100.0
1906	16.2	1951	120.6
1907	15.9	1952	132.5
1908	16.6	1953	135.2
1909	17.6	1954	145.6
1910	20.7	1955	168.0
1911	19.6	1956	178.3
1912	19.4	1957	189.3
1913	19.2	1958	198.0
1914	**	1959	200.8
1915	**	1960	212.3
1916	**	1961	214.2
1917	**	1962	217.2
1918	43.3	1963	221.2
1919	34.6	1964	228.4
1920	36.3	1965[a]	244.6
1921	33.1	1966	255.4
1922	27.8	1967	256.9
1923	29.8	1968	263.1
1924	28.5	1969	273.8
1925	30.0	1970	303.1
1926	29.4	1971	320.0
1927	28.7	1972	340.0
1928	27.6	1973	384.6
1929	27.5	1974	472.3
1930	28.0	1975	546.2
1931	24.7	1976	652.3
1932	22.5	1977	850.8
1933	23.9	1978	993.8
1934	24.7	1979	1,195.4
1935	24.9	1980	1,538.5
1936	26.4	1981	1,956.9
1937	31.3	1982	3,155.4
1938	32.7		
1939	33.6		
1940	33.8		
1941	35.9		
1942	39.7		
1943	47.5		
1944	60.9		

a. Linkage point for DGE's wholesale price index and BDM's GDP deflator index to create here what I denominate as the DGE-BDM Composite Index of Prices. For discussion of methodology, see text.

SOURCE: See table 3400.

Table 3402

PROJECTED AND ACTUAL GROSS CENTRAL GOVERNMENT EXPENDITURE IN MEXICO, CURRENT AND DEFLATED TERMS, 1900–82

	A. Thousands of Current Pesos	B.	C. DGE-BDM Composite Price Index (1950 = 100)[2]	D. Thousands of Pesos of 1950	E.	F.
	Projected Budget[1]	Actual Budget		Projected Budget	Actual Budget	Percent Change from Projected (D) to Actual (E)
1900–01	58,941	59,832	14.7	400,959	407,020	1.5
1910–11	102,294	101,237	19.6	521,908	516,515	−1.0
1911–12	105,432	97,293	19.4	543,464	501,510	−7.7
1912–13	111,370	111,272	19.2	580,052	579,542	−.1
1913–14	141,356	~	**	~	~	**
1914–15	140,466	~	**	~	~	**
1917	178,524	73,024	**	~	~	**
1918	187,138	109,717	43.3	432,189	253,388	−41.4
1919	203,482	59,167	34.6	588,098	171,003	−70.9
1920	213,250	131,966	36.3	587,466	363,543	−38.1
1921	250,803	226,353	33.1	757,713	683,846	−9.4
1922	383,659	228,093	27.8	1,380,068	820,478	−40.5
1923	348,487	235,354	29.8	1,169,419	789,779	−32.5
1924	297,982	276,570	28.5	1,045,551	970,421	−7.2
1925	291,864	302,164	30.0	972,880	1,007,213	3.5
1926	304,405	324,938	29.4	1,035,391	1,105,231	6.7
1927	318,721	310,082	28.7	1,110,526	1,080,425	−2.7
1928	291,118	287,946	27.6	1,054,775	1,043,283	−1.1
1929	288,283	275,541	27.5	1,048,302	1,001,967	−4.4
1930	293,774	279,122	28.0	1,049,193	996,864	−5.0
1931	298,489	226,478	24.7	1,208,457	916,915	−24.1
1932	212,987	211,625	22.5	946,609	940,556	−.6
1933	215,015	245,951	23.9	899,644	1,029,084	14.4
1934	243,062	264,740	24.7	984,057	1,071,822	8.9
1935	275,795	300,822	24.9	1,107,610	1,208,120	9.1
1936	286,000	406,098	26.4	1,083,333	1,538,250	42.0
1937	333,226	478,756	31.3	1,064,620	1,529,572	43.7
1938	418,555	536,955	32.7	1,279,985	1,642,064	28.3
1939	445,266	620,291	33.6	1,325,196	1,846,042	39.3
1940	447,800	658,335	33.8	1,324,852	1,947,367	47.0
1941	492,000	777,594	35.9	1,370,474	2,166,003	58.0
1942	554,747	1,005,675	39.7	1,397,348	2,533,186	81.3
1943	707,332	1,195,516	47.5	1,489,120	2,516,876	69.0
1944	1,101,000	1,463,838	60.9	1,807,882	2,403,675	33.0
1945	1,004,250	1,660,149	67.0	1,498,881	2,477,834	65.3
1946	1,200,000	1,920,810	78.5	1,528,662	2,446,892	60.1
1947	1,665,000	2,208,601	80.1	2,078,652	2,757,305	32.6
1948	2,300,000	2,773,365	85.0	2,705,882	3,262,782	20.6
1949	2,550,000	3,740,587	90.0	2,833,333	4,156,208	46.7
1950	2,746,057	3,463,290	100.0	2,746,057	3,463,290	26.1
1951	3,101,713	4,670,088	120.6	2,571,901	3,872,378	50.6
1952	3,995,949	6,464,230	132.5	3,015,811	4,878,664	61.8
1953	4,158,057	5,490,402	135.2	3,075,486	4,060,948	32.0
1954	4,827,681	7,916,807	145.6	3,315,715	5,437,367	64.0
1955	5,681,399	8,883,121	168.0	3,381,785	5,287,572	56.4
1956	6,696,374	10,270,112	178.3	3,755,678	5,760,018	53.4
1957	7,577,874	11,303,248	189.3	4,003,103	5,971,077	49.2
1958	8,402,552	13,287,707	198.0	4,243,713	6,710,963	58.1
1959	9,385,756	14,157,742	200.9	4,674,181	7,050,668	50.8

Table 3402 (Continued)

PROJECTED AND ACTUAL GROSS CENTRAL GOVERNMENT EXPENDITURE IN MEXICO, CURRENT AND DEFLATED TERMS, 1900–82

	A. Thousands of Current Pesos	B.	C. DGE-BDM Composite Price Index (1950 = 100)[2]	D. Thousands of Pesos of 1950	E.	F. Percent Change from Projected (D) to Actual (E)
	Projected Budget[1]	Actual Budget		Projected Budget	Actual Budget	
1960	10,251,341	20,150,330	212.3	4,828,705	9,491,441	96.6
1961	11,041,481	20,362,040	214.2	5,154,753	9,506,088	84.4
1962	12,320,000	20,219,159	217.2	5,672,192	9,309,006	64.1
1963	13,801,440	20,294,906	221.2	6,239,349	9,174,912	47.0
1964	15,953,541	28,285,590	228.4	6,984,913	12,384,234	77.3
1965	17,854,280	36.715,603	244.6	7,299,379	15,010,467	105.6
1966	20,132,252	32,495,967	255.4	7,882,636	12,723,558	61.4
1967	22,108,293	40,852,939	256.9	8,605,797	15,902,273	84.8
1968	24,221,169	41,124,294	263.1	9,206,070	15,630,670	69.8
1969	26,512,844	49,816,139	273.8	9,683,289	18,194,353	87.9
1970	28,133,881	52,679,003	303.1	9,282,046	17,380,074	87.2
1971	30,763,000	55,786,000	320.0	9,613,000	17,433,000	81.3
1972	54,744,000	77,230,000	340.0	16,101,000	22,715,000	41.1
1973	89,381,000	102,241,000	384.6	23,240,000	26,584,000	14.4
1974	114,128,000	135,795,000	472.3	24,164,000	28,752,000	19.0
1975	186,107,000	200,416,000	546.2	34.073,000	36,693,000	7.7
1976	238,043,000	274,963,000	652.3	36,493,000	42,153,000	15.5
1977	349,787,000	355,132,000	850.8	41,113,000	41,741,000	1.5
1978	434,303,000	442,471,000	993.8	43,701,000	44,523,000	1.9
1979	571,401,000	651,432,000	1,195.4	47,800,000	54,495,000	14.0
1980	839,018,000	1,002,013,000	1,538.5	54,535,000	65,129,000	19.4
1981	2,166,369,000	2,506,818,000	1,956.9	110,704,000	128,101,000	15.7
1982	2,216,316,000	3,381,792,000	3,155.4	70,239,000	107,175,000	52.6

1. For distinctions between presidential and congressional budgets, see Wilkie (1970:23).
2. Data can be converted to standard pesos for other years as follows: for example, to shift to pesos of 1970, recalculate index from 1950 = 100 to 1970 = 100 and divide the current pesos by the rebased index to get pesos of 1970.

SOURCE: Projected and actual expenditures:
   1900–63, Wilkie (1970:22-23), except 1938–47 revised here to take into account actual "off-budget" spending by presidents Cárdenas, Avila Camacho, and Alemán. The latter incorporated the off-budget amounts into a new budget category called *erogaciones adicionales*.
   1964–76, Wilkie (1978:350), except data in pesos of 1950 revised here with DGE-BDM Composite Index of Prices.
   1976–82, México, Secretaría de Programación y Presupuesto, *Cuenta Pública*, yearly.
DGE-BDM composite index of prices:
   1900–82, table 3401, above.

Table 3403

AVERAGE PER CAPITA REAL AMOUNT OF MEXICAN CENTRAL GOVERNMENT
GROSS BUDGETARY EXPENDITURE, BY PRESIDENTIAL TERM, 1900–82

(Pesos or 1950)

A.				B.				C.
Projected Expenditure				Actual Expenditure				Percent Change in Actual over Projected Per Capita Expenditure
Years	President	No. of Years in Average	Per Capita[1]	Years	President	No. of Years in Average	Per Capita[1]	
1900–11	Díaz	2[a]	31.8	1900–11	Díaz	2[a]	31.9	.3
1911–13	Madero	2	37.5	1911–12	Madero	1	33.4	–10.9
				1912–13	Huerta	1	38.6	**
1917–20	Carranza	4	38.0	1917–19	Carranza	3	15.1	–60.3
				1920	De la Huerta	1	25.3	**
1921–24	Obregón	4	74.5	1921–24	Obregón	4	55.8	–25.1
1925–29	Calles	4	66.9	1925–28	Calles	4	67.9	1.5
1929–30	Portes Gil	2	63.9	1929	Portes Gil	1	61.5	–3.8
1931–32	Ortiz Rubio	2	63.4	1930–32	Ortiz Rubio	3	56.4	–11.0
1933–34	Rodríguez	2	53.5	1933–34	Rodríguez	2	59.6	11.4
1935–40	Cárdenas	6	63.3	1935–40	Cárdenas	6	85.5	35.1
1941–46	Avila Camacho	6	70.6	1941–46	Avila Camacho	6	113.1	60.2
1947–52	Alemán	6	105.3	1947–52	Alemán	6	147.3	39.9
1953–58	Ruiz Cortines	6	118.6	1953–58	Ruiz Cortines	6	180.8	52.4
1959–64	López Mateos	6	151.0	1959–64	López Mateos	6	256.4	69.8
1965–70	Díaz Ordaz	6	190.5	1965–70	Díaz Ordaz	6	347.8	82.6
1971–76	Echeverría	6	423.5	1971–76	Echeverría	6	516.9	22.1
1977–82	López Portillo	6	907.5	1976–82	López Portillo	6	1,081.7	19.2

1. Total pesos in table 3402 divided by population data in Appendix table 34-A.

a. 1900–01 and 1910–11.

SOURCE: Wilkie (1970:36), except averages beginning in 1964 and revisions for 1935–52 are calculated from table 3402.

Table 3404

PROJECTED AND ACTUAL PARASTATE GROSS EXPENDITURE IN MEXICO,[1]
CURRENT AND DEFLATED TERMS, 1940–82

	A.	B.	C.	D.	E.	F.
	Millions of Pesos		DGE-BDM[2] Composite Price Index (1950 = 100)	Millions of Pesos		Actual Expenditure Per Capita[3]
	Parastate Expenditure			Parastate Expenditure		
Year	Projected	Actual		Projected (A/C)	Actual (B/C)	
1940[a]	~	597	33.8	~	1,766	89.9
1946[a]	~	1,324	78.5	~	1,687	74.1
1952[a]	~	3,675	132.5	~	2,774	101.2
1958[a]	~	9,971	198.0	~	5,036	153.2
1965	19,154	27,304	244.6	7,831	11,163	268.6
1966	32,252	33,558	255.4	12,629	13,139	305.4
1967	33,419	38,599	256.9	13,009	15,025	337.5
1968	37,193	42,298	263.1	14,137	16,077	348.9
1969	39,583	48,185	273.8	14,457	17,599	369.0
1970	44,095	56,582	303.1	14,548	18.668	378.2
1971	48,893	65,545	320.0	15,279	20,483	401.1
1972	68,635	71,538	340.0	20,187	21,041	398.5
1973	84,498	101,792	384.6	21,970	26,467	485.0
1974	116,832	140,688	472.3	24,737	29.788	528.4
1975	160,551	200,234	546.2	29,394	36,659	629.9
1976	201,600	245,065	652.3	30,906	37,569	625.5
1977	327,620	375.461	850.8	38,507	44,130	712.3
1978	478,147	495,363	993.8	48,113	49,845	780.3
1979	552,568	614,778	1,195.4	46,225	51,429	781.3
1980	844,394	1,016,587	1,538.5	54,884	66,077	974.6
1981	1,440,724	1,608,703	1,956.9	73,623	82,207	1,178.3
1982	1,104,253	2,132,974[b]	3,155.4	34,996	67,598	942.6

1. Coverage becomes more complete after 1965, but as of 1985 many
   parastate agencies remain to be incorporated (such as the 1982
   nationalized banking sector).
2. See table 3401, above.
3. Column E divided by population data in Appendix table 34-A.

a. Estimates, often in net terms, exclude dozens of agencies including
   the most important, Petróleos Mexicanos, which is added here
   from Bermúdez (operations + subsidies + capital investments =
   total).
b. Petróleos Mexicanos spent 617,139 million pesos more than projected, or 56% of the entire parastate budget as originally projected.

SOURCE: 1940–58,   Roberto Santillán López and Rosas Figueroa,
           *Teoría General de las Finanzas Públicas y el
           Caso de México* (México, D.F.: Universidad
           Nacional Autónoma de México, 1962),
           Appendix 18; and Antonio J. Bermúdez, *The
           Mexican Petroleum Industry* (Stanford: Insti-
           tute of Hispanic and Luso-Brazilian Studies,
           1963), p. 252.

           1956–82,   México, Secretaría de Programación y Presu-
           puesto, *Cuenta Pública*; México-NAFINSA-
           MV, Feb. and Nov. 1975.

Table 3405
CENTRAL GOVERNMENT GROSS EXPENDITURE AS SHARE OF MEXICO'S GDP, 1900–82

Year[1]	A. Current Pesos — GDP Millions	B. Actual Central Government Expenditure Thousands	C. % (B/A)
1900	1,316.8	59,832[a]	4.5
1901	1,774.1	63,081	3.6
1902	1,672.3	68,223	4.1
1903	1,859.0	76,382	4.1
1904	1,835.7	79,153	4.3
1905	2,272.8	79,470	3.5
1906	2,216.6	85,077	3.8
1907	2,346.0	93,197	4.0
1908	2,407.6	92,967	3.9
1909	2,643.1	95,039	3.6
1910	3,100.5	101,237	3.3
1921	5,455.0	226,353	4.1
1922	4,590.2	228,093	5.0
1923	5,013.6	235.354	4.7
1924	4,632.6	276,570	6.0
1925	5,238.5	302,164	5.8
1926	5,468.8	324,938	5.9
1927	4,987.0	310.082	6.2
1928	5,017.8	287,946	5.7
1929	4,862.9	275,541	5.7
1930	4,667.7	279,122	6.0
1931	4,218.8	226,478	5.4
1932	3,205.5	211,625	6.6
1933	3,781.7	245,951	6.5
1934	4,150.9	264,740	6.4
1935	4,540.3	300,822	6.6
1936	5,345.7	406,098	7.6
1937	6,800.4	478,756	7.0
1938	7,281.1	536,955	7.4
1939	7,785.1	620,291	8.0
1940	8,248.8	658,335	8.0
1941	9,232.4	777,594	8.4
1942	10,680.8	1,005,675	9.4
1943	13,035.3	1,195,516	9.2
1944	18,801.2	1,463,838	7.8
1945	20,565.7	1,660,149	8.1
1946	27,929.6	1,920,810	6.9
1947	31,022.6	2,208,601	7.1
1948	33,101.2	2,773,365	8.4
1949	36,411.8	3,740,587	10.3
1950	42,162.8	3,463,290	8.2
1951	54,374.7	4,670,088	8.6
1952	60,992.6	6,464,230	10.6
1953	60,663.7	5,490,402	9.1
1954	73,935.6	7,916,807	10.7

Table 3405 (Continued)
CENTRAL GOVERNMENT GROSS EXPENDITURE AS SHARE OF MEXICO'S GDP, 1900–82

Year[1]	A. Current Pesos — GDP Millions	B. Actual Central Government Expenditure Thousands	C. % (B/A)
1955	90,053.3	8,883,121	9.9
1956	102,919.9	10,270,112	10.0
1957	118,205.7	11,303,248	9.6
1958	131,376.8	13,287,707	10.1
1959	140,771.5	14,157,742	10.1
1960	159,703.2	20,150,330	12.6
1961	173,236.1	20,362,040	11.8
1962	186,780.7	20,219,159	10.8
1963	207,952.3	20,294,906	9.8
1964	245,500.5	28,285,590	11.5
1965	267,420.2	36,715,603	13.7
1966	297,196.0	32,495,967	10.9
1967	325,024.8	40,852,939	12.6
1968	359,857.7	41,124,294	11.4
1969	397,796.4	49,816,139	12.5
1970	444,271.4	52,679,003	11.9
1971	490,011.0	55,786,000	11.4
1972	564,726.5	77,230,000	13.7
1973	690,891.5	102,241,000	14.8
1974	899,706.8	135,795,000	15.1
1975	1,100,049.8	200,416,000	20.0
1976	1,370,968.3	274,963,000	20.1
1977	1,849,262.7	355,132,000	19.2
1978	2,337,397.9	442,471,000	18.9
1979	3,067,526.4	651,432,000	21.2
1980	4,276,490.4	1,002,013,000	23.4
1981	5,874,385.6	2,506,818,000	42.7
1982	9,417,089.4	3,381,792,000	35.9

1. No data on GDP for the years from 1911 through 1920.

a. Expenditure through 1910 is for fiscal years, e.g., 1900–01.

SOURCE: GDP from BDM, *Indicadores Económicos* (Carpeta), "Acervo Histórico" II (1983, tables II-H-1 and 2); and "Acervo Histórico" III (1984, tables II-H-1 and 2). Expenditure is from table 3402 above, except data for 1901–09 are from [Fernando Rosenzweig], *Fuerza de Trabajo y Actividad Económica por Sectores* (México, D.F.: El Colegio de México, [1965?], p. 251).

Table 3406

PARASTATE ACTUAL EXPENDITURE AS SHARE OF MEXICO'S GDP, 1940-82

A. SELECTED YEARS, 1940-58

Year	%
1940	7.2
1946	4.7
1952	6.0
1958	7.6

B. YEARLY, 1965-82

Year	%	Year	%
1965	10.2	1975	18.2
1966	11.3	1976	17.9
1967	11.9	1977	20.3
1968	11.8	1978	21.2
1969	12.1	1979	20.0
1970	12.7	1980	23.8
1971	13.4	1981	27.4
1972	12.7	1982	22.7
1973	14.7		
1974	15.6		

SOURCE: Calculated from expenditure data in table 3404, Col. B, and GDP data in table 3405, Col. A.

Table 3407

MEXICO'S REAL GDP, AVERAGE BY PRESIDENTIAL PERIOD, 1895-1982

(Pesos of 1970 and Index for 1950)

Year	Total		Per Capita		President
	Pesos of 1970 (Million)	Index (1950 = 100)[1]	Pesos of 1970 GDP/C	Index (1950 = 100)[2]	
1895-1910	38,845.3	31.1	2,763.8	60.6	Díaz
1911-20[a]	~	~	~	~	~[b]
1921-24	52,217.5	41.8	3,527.4	77.4	Obregón
1925-28	57,326.5	45.9	3,633.8	79.7	Calles
1929	54,915.3	44.0	3,344.2	73.4	Portes Gil
1930-32	49,966.3	40.0	2,944.1	65.0	Ortiz Rubio
1933-34	52,058.1	41.7	2,935.3	64.4	Rodríguez
1935-40	64,821.3	51.9	3,407.8	74.8	Cárdenas
1941-46	87,769.5	70.3	3,992.8	87.6	Avila Camacho
1947-52	120,592.4	96.6	4,543.6	99.7	Alemán
1953-58	172,501.9	138.2	5,333.0	117.0	Ruiz Cortines
1959-64	247,367.5	198.2	6,330.5	138.9	López Mateos
1965-70	378,397.2	303.3	7,980.6	175.1	Díaz Ordaz
1971-76	555,428.6	445.1	9,646.1	211.6	Echeverría
1977-82	800,220.7	641.3	11,651.4	255.6	López Portillo

1. GDP Index of 100 for 1950 equals 124,779.4 million pesos of 1970.

2. GDP/C Index of 100 equals 4,558 pesos of 1970.

a. No data for civil-war period.

b. Competing leaders, for whom no GDP data available.

SOURCE: Calculated as follows:

A. 1895-1949, GDP in table 3405, above, deflated by BDM in source B, below, and divided by population data in Appendix table 34-A. Data averaged and index calculated here.

B. 1950-82, Banco de México, *Indicadores Economicos* (Carpeta), "Acervo Histórico," II (1983), tables II-H-1 and 2. Data average and index calculated here.

Table 3408

GROSS INCOME IN MEXICO: CENTRAL, STATE, AND LOCAL GOVERNMENT SHARES IN SELECTED YEARS, 1900–82

Year	Total Pesos Per Capita of 1950	Percent Total	Percent Central	Percent State[1]	Percent Municipio[1]
1900	63	100.0	63.0	24.1	12.9
1923	84	100.0	72.6	14.5	12.9
1929	101	100.0	71.1	21.2	7.7
1932	86	100.0	64.0	27.1	8.9
1940	122	100.0	71.4	23.3	5.3
1950	180	100.0	78.3	18.4	3.3
1960	369	100.0	71.1	26.3	2.6
1970	480	100.0	72.6	24.4	3.0
1976	945	100.0	77.5	20.5	2.0
1981	1,546	100.0	76.7	21.3	2.0

1. Includes subsidies from the central government.

SOURCE: 1900–60, Wilkie (1967, p. 4).
1970–81, México, DGE, AE (1978), pp. 806–812, (1980), p. 176, (1982), p. 499.

Table 3409

ACTUAL MEXICAN CENTRAL GOVERNMENT REVENUE AND SELECTED SHARES, 1935–82

Year	Gross Revenue[1] M Pesos A.	Borrowing M Pesos B.	Borrowing % C.	Income M Pesos D.	Income % E.	Industry[2] M Pesos F.	Industry[2] % G.	Commerce[3] M Pesos H.	Commerce[3] % I.	VAT[4] M Pesos J.	VAT[4] % K.	Foreign Trade[5] M Pesos L.	Foreign Trade[5] % M.	Total Selected Shares[6] % N.
1935	331	18	5.4	31	9.4	67	20.2	24	7.3	(data begin in 1979)		73	22.1	64.4
1936	385	5	1.3	37	9.6	83	21.6	29	7.5			92	23.9	63.9
1937	451	16	3.5	41	9.1	89	19.7	33	7.3			134	29.7	69.3
1938	466	28	6.0	43	9.2	96	20.6	35	7.5			119	25.5	68.8
1939	596	30	5.0	41	6.9	120	20.1	45	7.6			187	31.4	71.0
1940	612	35	5.7	57	9.3	124	20.3	56	9.2			170	27.8	72.3
1941	780	115	14.7	55	7.1	125	16.0	65	8.3			243	31.2	77.3
1942	941	195	20.7	78	8.3	158	16.8	77	8.2			223	23.7	77.7
1943	1,276	182	14.3	218	17.1	198	15.5	94	7.4			314	24.6	78.9
1944	1,313	18	1.4	302	23.0	253	19.3	96	7.3			334	25.4	76.4
1945	1,585	181	11.4	296	18.7	274	17.3	126	7.9			383	24.2	79.5
1946	2,228	216	9.7	371	16.7	356	16.0	232	10.4			486	21.8	74.6
1947	2,245	190	8.5	479	21.3	362	16.1	235	10.5			482	21.5	77.9
1948	2,655	387	14.6	451	17.0	379	14.3	235	8.9			549	20.7	75.5
1949	3,891	840	21.6	586	15.1	466	12.0	319	8.2			882	22.7	79.6
1950	3,641	196	5.4	766	21.0	512	14.1	394	10.8			991	27.2	78.5
1951	4,884	130	2.7	1,196	24.5	580	11.9	489	10.0			1,406	28.8	77.9
1952	6,338	360	5.7	1,441	22.7	741	11.7	482	7.6			1,486	23.4	71.1
1953	5,023	229	4.6	1,137	22.6	789	15.7	472	9.4			1,370	27.3	79.6
1954	7,714	1,297	16.8	1,262	16.5	844	10.9	579	7.5			1,884	24.4	76.1
1955	9,024	1,148	12.7	1,985	22.0	1,066	11.8	719	8.0			2,560	28.4	82.9
1956	10,194	998	9.8	2,565	25.2	1,215	11.9	821	8.1			2,566	25.2	80.2
1957	10,870	1,171	10.8	2,778	25.6	1,224	11.3	880	8.1			2,263	20.8	76.6
1958	13,183	1,352	10.3	2,802	21.3	1,487	11.3	1,003	7.6			2,702	20.5	71.0
1959	14,163	3,814	26.9	3,071	21.7	1,575	11.1	1,155	8.2			2,927	20.7	88.6

Table 3409 (Continued)

Year	A	B	C	D	E	F	G	H	I	J	K	L	M	N
1960	19,458	6,641	34.1	3,648	18.7	1,717	8.8	1,312	6.7			3,087	15.9	84.2
1961	19.941	7,576	38.0	4,073	20.4	1,875	9.4	1,491	7.5			2,954	14.8	90.1
1962	20,398	6,439	31.6	4,725	23.2	2,226	10.9	1,696	8.3			3,041	14.9	88.9
1963	19,704	3,924	19.9	5,475	27.8	2,347	11.9	1,803	9.2			3,278	16.6	85.4
1964	28,976	9,886	34.1	7,262	25.1	2,776	9.6	2,187	7.5			3,813	13.2	89.5
1965	35,781	13,758	38.5	6,008	16.8	3,096	8.7	2,480	6.9			4,627	12.9	83.8
1966	33,255	8,794	26.4	8,631	26.0	3,495	10.5	2,833	8.5			4,844	14.6	86.0
1967	40,517	13,069	32.3	10,235	25.3	3,972	9.8	3,099	7.6			5,980	14.8	89.8
1968	42,894	10,929	25.5	12,084	28.2	5,182	12.1	3,873	9.0			5,761	13.4	88.2
1969	48,861	12,716	26.0	14,020	28.7	5,645	11.6	4,427	9.1			6,335	13.0	88.4
1970	52,092	10,725	20.6	15,478	29.7	6,800	13.1	4,944	9.5			7,386	14.2	87.1
1971	54,874	10,324	18.8	16,858	30.7	8,931	16.3	5,465	10.0			6,783	12.4	88.2
1972	76,624	22,333	29.1	21,010	27.4	11,755	15.3	6,119	8.0			7,472	9.8	89.6
1973	102,927	33,682	32.7	26,094	25.4	12,021	11.7	13,484	13.1			7,512	7.3	90.2
1974	141,137	47,005	33.3	34,409	24.4	18,140	12.9	19,125	13.6			10,354	7.3	91.5
1975	203,049	70,548	34.7	49,203	24.2	30,566	15.1	25,451	12.5			13,386	6.6	93.1
1976	286,814	123,557	43.1	66,046	23.0	31,260	10,9	32,352	11.3			15,002	5.2	93.5
1977	359,722	127,487	35.4	93,411	26.0	47,879	13.3	42,970	11.9			26,240	7.3	93.9
1978	454,330	144,713	31.9	132,184	29.1	56,405	12.4	56,484	12.4			35,439	7.8	93.6
1979	669,848	251.101	37.5	173,015	25.8	a	a	~a	~a	71,606,	10.7	62,964	9.4	83.4
1980	1,039,258	355,478	34:2	246,077	23.7	59,973	5.8	~a	~a	110,379	10.6	184,222	17.7	92.0
1981	1,618,424	686,647	42.4	331,783	20.5	a	a	~a	~a	174,288	10.8	258.146	15.6	89.3
1982	3,527,619	2,007,198	56.9	463,837	13.1	a	a	~a	~a	216,285	6.1	500.003	14.2	90.3

1. Gross revenue includes borrowing and compensating subsidies and virtual income.
2. Prior to 1955 may exclude minor amounts shifted from commerce taxes with reorganization of categories in 1955.
3. Includes mercantile and stamp taxes.
4. Includes industry and commerce, among other categories.
5. Includes export and import taxes.
6. Column N equals total of columns B + D + F + H + J + L.

a. Included in value added tax (VAT).

SOURCE (by column and periods within column):

A, 1935–82: Mexican government's *Cuenta Pública*, yearly, checked against:
A1, 1935–49: México-NAFINSA-EMC (1981, pp. 306-308), corrected here by adding to net income the loans given in source B1, except 1936–37 and 1949 loans are already included in gross totals—data for 1943 corrected with source A.
A2, 1950–78: Source A1, pp. 308-310, deducting parastate sector data.
B, 1935–82: *Cuenta Pública*, yearly, checked against:
B1, 1935–49: Roberto Santillán López and Aniceto Rosas Figueroa, *Teoría General de las Finanzas Públicas y el Caso de México* (México, D.F.: Universidad Nacional Autónoma de México, 1962), anexo 6. (Source A1 includes 1936–37 in "Aprovechamientos," 1949 in "productos," and gives no data on borrowing for other years until 1949.)
B2, 1950–78: Source A1, pp. 308-310.
B3, 1979–82: Source A.
C, 1935–82: Calculated.
D, 1935–70: Source A.
D1, 1970–74: Source A1, p. 310.
D2, 1975–82: Source A.
E, 1935–82: Calculated.
F, 1935–82: Same as D, D1, D2.
G, 1935–82: Calculated.
H, 1935–72: Source A.
H1, 1973–78: Source A1, p. 310.
H2, 1979–82: Source A.
I, 1935–82: Calculated.
J, 1935–82: Source A.
K, 1935–82: Calculated.
L, 1935–78: Source A1, pp. 306-310.
L1, 1979–82: Source A.
M, 1935–82: Calculated.

Table 3410

APPARENT AND TRUE SHARES OF INCOME TAX COMPARED TO BORROWING AS SHARE OF MEXICAN CENTRAL GOVERNMENT REVENUES, 1935–82

(%)

Period	President	A. Apparent Income Tax (In Net Total Revenue[1])	B. True Income Tax	C. Borrowing
			(In Gross Total Revenue[2])	
1935–40	Lázaro Cárdenas	9.3	8.9	4.5
1941–46	Manuel Avila Camacho	16.9	15.2	12.0
1947–52	Miguel Alemán	22.3	20.3	9.8
1953–58	Adolfo Ruiz Cortines	24.8	22.2	10.8
1959–64	Adolfo López Mateos	32.9	22.8	30.8
1965–70	Gustavo Díaz Ordaz	35.7	25.7	28.2
1971–76	Luis Echeverría Alvarez	38.4	25.9	32.0
1977–82	José López Portillo	37.7	23.0	39.7

1. Net excludes borrowing.
2. Gross includes borrowing.

SOURCE: Calculated from table 3409.

Appendix Table 34-A

MEXICO'S ESTIMATED POPULATION, 1895–1982

Year	T	Year	T
1895	12,632	1940	19,654
1896	12,827	1941	20,208
1897	13,022	1942	20,657
1898	13,217	1943	21,165
1899	13,412	1944	21,674
1900	13,607	1945	22,233
1901	13,755	1946	22,779
1902	13,905	1947	23,440
1903	14,056	1948	24,129
1904	14,209	1949	24,825
1905	14,363	1950	25,791
1906	14,519	1951	25,585
1907	14,677	1952	27,403
1908	14,837	1953	28,246
1909	14,998	1954	29.115
1910	15,160	1955	30,011
1911	15,083	1956	30,935
1912	15,007	1957	31,877
1913	14,931	1958	32,868
1914	14,855	1959	33,880
1915	14,780	1960	34,923
1916	14,705	1961	36,075
1917	14,630	1962	37,265
1918	14,556	1963	39,238
1919	14,482	1964	39,781
1920	14,409	1965	41,557
1921	14,335	1966	43,012
1922	14,444	1967	44,517
1923	14,693	1968	46,075
1924	14,945	1969	47,688
1925	15,204	1970	49,357
1926	15,468	1971	51,060
1927	15,738	1972	52,796
1928	16,012	1973	53,565
1929	16,296	1974	56,366
1930	16,553	1975	58,198
1931	16,876	1976	60,060
1932	17,170	1977	61,952
1933	17,470	1978	63,873
1934	17,776	1979	65,821
1935	18,089	1980	67,796
1936	18,410	1981	69,762
1937	18,764	1982	71,715
1938	19,071		
1939	19,413		

SOURCE: 1895–1900, data interpolated from [Moisés González Navarro], *Estadísticas Sociales del Porfiriato, 1877–1910* (México, D.F.: El Colegio de México, 1956), p. 7;

1900–20,   México-NAFINSA-EMC (1981, p. 3);
1921–63,   Wilkie (1967, p. 24);
1964–82,   México-NAFINSA-EMC (1981, p. 3).

INDEX

Accounts, national, **24**-2751, 3300 to 3368; for individual countries, **24**-3301 to 3320, 3322, 3340 to 3360

Adult Education. *See* Education

AG. *See* Andean Group

Age(s) and age groups, **24**-655, 661 to 665, 700, 701, 703, 828, 830, 831, 900 to 905, 1021, 1304, 1313, 1324, 1328, 2839

Agrarian reform. *See* Land reform

Agricultural: labor force, **24**-1304, 1305; landholdings, **24**-302, 303

Agriculture, **24**-200 to 207, 210, 924, 1304 to 1307, 1309 to 1311, 1314, 1315, 1319 to 1321, 1405, 1410, 1515, 1516, 2100 to 2118, 2400 to 2439, 2458 to 2461, 2500 to 2541, 2910, 3000, 3010, 3325, 3326, 3328, 3329, 3336; trade, **24**-2400 to 2439, 2458 to 2461, 2500 to 2541

AID (Agency for International Development), **24**-2833, 2841 to 2843

ALADI (Latin American Integration Association), **24**-1000, 1700, 1712, 2600, 2606, 2607

Aldrin. *See* Pesticide

Aliens. *See* Immigration; Migration

Altitude, **24**-121 to 123

Amebiasis, **24**-710. *See also* Disease

Amerind population, **24**-668, 669

Amortization payments. *See* Public debt

Andean Group, **24**-100, 1000, 2600, 2603, 2604, 2608 to 2610, 2749

Animal oil, **24**-2404, 2605

Antimony, **24**-1800, 1821, 2400 to 2402

Arable land. *See* Land, arable

Archbishops, **24**-100

Area, **24**-100 to 120, 200 to 202, 302, 2300. *See also* Agriculture; Rural; Urbanization

Armed forces, **24**-1200, 1203. *See also* Military

Arms trade, **24**-1201, 1202, 1206, 1207, 1210. *See also* Military; Trade

Arms transfers. *See* Arms trade; Trade

Arrests, **24**-1333, 1334. *See also* Human rights

Assistance. *See* Grants; Loans

Assistance, military. *See* Military assistance

Automobiles. *See* Motor vehicles

Aviation, **24**-400 to 405, 1203

Bagasse, **24**-1924

Balance of payments, **24**-2700 to 2751

Bananas, **24**-2103, 2400 to 2403, 2413, 2414, 2706, 2708, 2712, 2715, 3226

Barley, **24**-2102, 2415, 2416

Bauxite, **24**-1801, 1821, 2400 to 2403, 2711, 2910, 3226

Beans, **24**-2104, 2106, 2420

Beef, **24**-2400 to 2403, 2412, 3226

Beverages, **24**-2500 to 2541, 2605, 2910

Bibles, **24**-1107

BID. *See* IDB

Biomass. *See* Energy, biomass

Birth control, **24**-827 to 832. *See also* Family planning

Births, **24**-701 to 703, 816; crude rates, **24**-702, 703

Bishops, **24**-1100

Bitumen, **24**-1916

Books, **24**-503, 504, 1102, 1107

Building. *See* Construction

Buses. *See* Motor vehicles

Butter, **24**-1702, 2417, 3226

Cacao, **24**-2400 to 2403, 2418, 3226

CACM (Central American Common Market), **24**-100, 1000, 2414,

2457, 2600 to 2604, 2606, 2609 to 2611, 2750

Calories, **24**-820, 821

Cardinals, **24**-1100

Cargo, **24**-415

Cassava, **24**-2105

Catholics, **24**-913, 1100, 1104, 1105, 1108

Cattle, **24**-2200, 2412

Cement, **24**-1628, 1703, 2910

Census, **24**-625 to 645, 649, 650, 658, 665, 670, 1324, 1325, 1511. *See also* Population

Cereals, **24**-2402, 2404, 2521 to 2541, 3000

Charcoal. *See* Coal

Cheese, **24**-1704

Chemicals, **24**-2400, 2401, 2500 to 2520, 2605, 2908 to 2910

Child deaths. *See* Children, deaths; Infant mortality

Children, **24**-706, 816, 817, 829, 1303, 1502, 1503; deaths, **24**-706; health, **24**-816, 817; in the labor force, **24**-1303

Christians, **24**-1104 to 1106

Chromite, **24**-1802

Church: Catholic, **24**-1100, 1104, 1105; Protestant, **24**-1104, 1105

Cigarettes, **24**-1705

Cinema, **24**-513, 514

Cities. *See* Population; Urban; Urbanization

Citrus crops, **24**-2112

Civil aviation. *See* Aviation

Civil divisions. *See* Divisions, civil

Civil rights. *See* Rights

Class: middle, **24**-1330; occupational, **24**-1310 to 1312; upper, **24**-1330

Climate, **24**-128 to 130

Coal, **24**-1900, 1905, 1920 to 1922, 2447, 2910, 3226; anthracite, **24**-1921; bituminous, **24**-1900, 1921, 1922; charcoal, **24**-2447; hard, **24**-1920; lignite, **24**-1922

Cobalt, **24**-2402

Cocoa, **24**-2106, 2403, 2404, 2419, 2521 to 2541

Coconut oil, **24**-3226

Coffee, **24**-2107, 2400 to 2404, 2420, 2421, 2521 to 2541, 2703, 2705, 2706, 2708 to 2712, 2714, 3226

Commerce, **24**-3325, 3409. *See also* Trade

Commodities. *See* Export; Imports; Prices; Trade

Communications, **24**-500 to 514, 800, 801, 1309, 1319, 1320, 1404, 2901, 2910, 3010, 3334. *See also* Media; Newspapers; Roads; Telephones

Communists, **24**-914

Compensation. *See* Wages

Constant dollars. *See* Dollars

Construction, **24**-1309, 1319, 1320, 1403, 1406, 1410, 1600 to 1616, 1628, 1700, 1713, 2910, 3325, 3332; new building authorized and/or new buildings completed, **24**-1600 to 1615

Consumer prices, **24**-3200 to 3221

Consumption, **24**-3364; cement, **24**-1628; energy, **24**-1901, 1906, 1907, 1915, 1917, 1926, 1928; fats, **24**-823; fertilizer, **24**-209, 210; fish, **24**-823, 824; food, **24**-824; newspapers and newsprint, **24**-500; protein, **24**-825

Cooperatives, **24**-1420

Copper, **24**-1803, 1821, 2400 to 2403, 2452, 2704, 2717, 2910, 3226; refined, **24**-1706

Copra, **24**-2108, 3226

Corn. *See* Maize

Corporate business activity, **24**-2911 to 2928

Cost of living, **24**-3200 to 3231

Cotton, **24**-1707, 1708, 2109, 2400 to 2403, 2458, 2461, 2709,

2714, 2716, 3226; lint, 24-2109, 2461; woven, 24-1707; yarn, 24-1708

Cottonseed, 24-2110, 2400, 2401

Cows, milk products, 24-2204, 2205

Creditors, 24-2804. *See also* Loans; Public debt

Crime, 24-1333 to 1335, 1506

Criminals. *See* Crime

Cropland. *See* Land, cropland

Crops: production, 24-1715, 1716, 2102 to 2118; trade, 24-2400 to 2437

Cultivation, 24-202, 203

Currency, 24-3060, 3339. *See also* Money

Dairy products, 24-1702, 2204, 2205, 2404, 2417, 2424, 2521 to 2541, 3226

DDT. *See* Pesticides

Deaths, 24-124, 704 to 709; by earthquakes, 24-124; by principal causes, 24-706, 708; by sex, 24-708

Debts. *See* Loans; Private debt; Public debt

Defense, 24-1203, 1204, 1319, 1320, 3010, 3011

Demography, 24-100, 600 to 670

Density, 24-100, 626 to 645

Dentists, 24-800, 806, 815

Deportations. *See* Migration

Deserts, 24-127

Development, land, 24-208

Development (plans), 24-3000

Development (scientific research), 24-924 to 926

Diet. *See* Calories; Fats; Protein

Diptheria, 24-709. *See also* Disease

Direct foreign investment. *See* Investment

Disease, 24-706, 708 to 710

Distance. *See* Aviation

Distribution of income. *See* Income

Divisions, civil, 24-101 to 120, 626 to 645; political, 24-121

Divorce, 24-712

Doctors. *See* Physicians

Dollars: exchange rate, 24-3100, 3101, 3104 to 3108, 3112; measure of GDP, 24-3362; purchasing power, 24-2550, 3324; value of SDR, 24-3104

Dwellings. *See* Households

Dysentery, 24-706, 708, 709. *See also* Disease

EAP (Economically Active Population), 24-833 to 838, 1307 to 1310, 1313, 1314, 1321, 1415

Earthquakes. *See* Deaths

ECLA (U.N., Economic Commission for Latin America), 24-2546 to 2549, 2606, 2728 to 2751, 3113, 3225, 3300 to 3321, 3324

Economic activity, 24-1323 to 1325, 2839, 2840, 3300 to 3368

Economic characteristics. *See* Economic activity

Economic class. *See* Class

Economic growth, 24-3000 to 3060, 3300 to 3368, 3408 to 3410. *See also* GDP; GNP; Industry; output

Economic indicators, 24-1820, 2700 to 2751

Economic regions. *See* Regions

ECR (Extended Caribbean Region), 24-646, 2611

Education, 24-800, 801, 900 to 924, 1208, 1209, 1319, 1320; adult, 24-916; attainment, 24-904; college, 24-800; compulsory, 24-903; degrees, 24-912; duration, 24-903, 920; enrollment, 24-800, 901, 902, 906 to 909, 915 to 917; entrances ages, 24-903; expenditure, 24-918, 921 to 923, 1209, 3010; field of study, 24-910 to 912; financial period, 24-920; higher, 24-902, 904, 906, 909 to 913, 915, 918, 919, 923, 925; history of enrollment by country, 24-915; immigrants, 24-1514, 1515; intermediate, 24-906; library, 24-918, 919; literacy, 24-800, 900; military, 24-1208, 1209; personnel, 24-905, 906, 907, 918, 922, 1319, 1320; pre-primary, 24-903, 906, 907, 923; primary, 24-800, 902 to 904, 906, 908,

915, 923; private, 24-907; public, 24-919, 921 to 923; research, 24-924 to 926; rural, 24-900, 904; secondary, 24-800, 902 to 904, 915, 923; special, 24-917, 919; specialties, 24-910 to 912; urban, 24-900, 904

Eggs, 24-2404, 2521 to 2541

Elections, 24-1001, 1004 to 1021; absenteeism, 24-1011; by political party, 24-1004, 1005, 1009, 1010, 1012 to 1015, 1017 to 1019; congressional, 24-1004; presidential, 24-1004, 1005, 1008 to 1010, 1016 to 1020. *See also* Politics

Electricity, 24-1309, 1621, 1622, 1700, 1900, 1905, 1925 to 1940, 2908 to 2910, 3325; installed capacity and projections, 24-1929 to 1940

Employees. *See* Employment

Employment, 24-1300 to 1329, 1400, 1820, 2911 to 2928, 3000; by sector, 24-1315, 1820. *See also* EAP; Income; Wages

Energy, 24-1900 to 1941, 2839, 2840; biomass, 24-1900, 1901; commercial, 24-1902 to 1907; geothermal, 24-1900, 1923. *See also* Electricity; Gas; Petroleum

Engineers, 24-805, 924 to 926

Enrollment, student. *See* Education; Students

Enrollment history, 24-915

Exchange rates, 24-3100 to 3126

Ex-Im Bank (Export-Import Bank of the United States), 24-2833, 2844

Expenditure: as share of GDP, 24-3405, 3406; by U.S. majority-owned foreign affiliates, 24-2908; consumer, 24-3200 to 3222; functional analysis of, 24-3010; GDP, 24-3340 to 3360; government, 24-921, 1200, 1204, 3008 to 3012, 3018 to 3037, 3338, 3402 to 3406; housing, 24-3010; military, 24-1200, 1203 to 1205, 1209, 3011; on public education, 24-921 to 923, 3011; on public health, 24-3011; on research and development, 24-926; public sector, 24-3402 to 3406

Exports, 24-1201, 1820, 2400 to 2407, 2409 to 2414, 2416, 2418 to 2421, 2423, 2426, 2428, 2430 to 2433, 2436 to 2445, 2447 to 2461, 2500 to 2541, 2543, 2547, 2548, 2550, 2600, 2602 to 2605, 2609, 2610, 2613 to 2636, 2700 to 2720, 2722, 2728 to 2750, 2808, 3000, 3225, 3338, 3340 to 3360; as share of GDP, 24-2457, 2604; as principal commodities, 24-2400, 2401; intra-regional, 24-2603 to 2605, 2609, 2610; share in value of world, 24-2600; share of public debt, 24-2808

Falkland Islands. *See* Wars

Family planning, 24-827 to 832. *See also* Birth control

FAO (U.N. Food and Agriculture Organization), 24-200, 204, 1000

Fats, 24-823, 2521 to 2541, 2605

Ferroalloy. *See* Iron, ferroalloy

Fertility, 24-701 to 703

Fertilizer, 24-209, 210, 1701, 2459, 2460, 2521 to 2541, 3000; nitrogenous, 24-1701

Fetal mortality, 24-704

Fiberboard, 24-2306

Films. *See* Cinema

Finance, 24-1309, 1319, 1320, 2700 to 2751, 2800 to 2837, 2841 to 2849, 2900 to 2910, 3000 to 3060, 3400 to 3410

Fish, 24-822, 2406, 2407

Fisheries, 24-2000 to 2007

Fishing, 24-1309 to 1311, 2000, 2910, 3010, 3336; in inland waters, 24-2000, 2004 to 2006; in marine waters, 24-2000 to 2003

Fishmeal, 24-2400 to 2403, 3226

Flights, domestic and international. *See* Aviation; Transportation

Fluorspar, 24-1804, 1821

Food, 24-818, 819, 823, 824, 826, 2400 to 2439, 2455, 2500 to 2541, 2605, 2908 to 2910, 3000. *See also* Agriculture, specific food items by name

Food assistance, 24-2835, 2839, 2840

Foreign aid, U.S., 24-2833, 2835, 2836. *See also* AID; Ex-Im Bank; IBRD; IDA; IDB

Foreign exchange, 24-2700 to 2720, 2726, 2728 to 2746
Foreign investment. See Investment
Foreign trade, 24-2400 to 2461, 2500 to 2550, 3409. See also Trade; Trading partners
Forestry, 24-200, 201, 207, 208, 1309 to 1311, 2300 to 2313, 2440, 2910, 3010, 3336
Forests. See Forestry
Freight, 24-405, 409, 414, 415; air, 24-405, 409, 414, 415; railroad, 24-409; seaborne, 24-414
Fuels, 24-1916, 2400, 2401, 2446, 2455, 2500 to 2520, 2605
Fuelwood, 24-1924, 2447

Gas, natural, 24-1309, 1700, 1900, 1905, 1916, 1918, 1919, 2702
GDP (Gross Domestic Product), 24-1205, 1414, 1418, 1419, 1820, 2457, 2604, 3000, 3001, 3050, 3200 to 3221, 3300 to 3334, 3337 to 3363, 3365, 3366, 3405 to 3408; by sector, 24-3325 to 3334. See also Economic activity; GNP
Geography, 24-100 to 130
Geothermal, energy. See Energy, geothermal
Gini coefficient, 24-1415, 1418, 1419
GNP, 24-921, 926, 1200; of U.S. majority-owned foreign affiliates, 24-2909, 2910, 3011, 3322, 3340 to 3361. See also Economic activity; GDP
Gold, 24-1805, 2700 to 2720, 2724, 2728 to 2746, 2910, 3226
Goods and services, 24-2700 to 2720, 2728 to 2750, 2801, 2808, 3338
Government borrowing. See Finance
Government deficits. See Finance
Government employees, 24-1318 to 1320
Government expenditure. See Expenditure
Government taxes. See Taxation
Grants, 24-2835, 2836
Gross product. See GDP; GNP
Gypsum, 24-1806, 1821

Health, 24-800 to 817, 3010. See also Dentists; Hospitals; Physicians; Public health
Health care, 24-801, 803 to 806, 813 to 817
Health establishments. See Health; Health care; Hospitals
Health personnel, 24-800, 803 to 807, 2839, 2840
HEC (Health, Education, Communication) Index, 24-800, 801
Higher education. See Education
Highways. See Roads; Transport
Holdings. See Land
Honey, 24-2404, 2521 to 2541
Horses, 24-2201
Hospitals, 24-808 to 812, 814; hospital beds, 24-800, 810 to 812; short-stay, 24-808, 810; type of ownership, 24-809, 810, 812
Hours worked, 24-1317, 1322
Households, 24-1322 to 1324, 1332, 1333, 1413, 1415, 1418, 1419, 1626, 1627. See also Housing
Household surveys. See Households
Housing, 24-1619 to 1621, 1623 to 1627, 2839, 2840, 3010, 3337; deficit, 24-1623; tenancy, 24-1625; units by number of rooms, 24-1624
Human rights, 24-1002, 1003

IBRD (International Bank for Reconstruction and Development), 24-2702, 2810, 2832 to 2834
IDA (International Development Association), 24-2810, 2834
IDB (Inter-American Development Bank), 24-201, 202, 205, 1000, 2810, 2831, 2833, 2834
Illiteracy, 24-900
IMF (International Monetary Fund), 24-2542 to 2545, 2700 to 2746, 2811 to 2830, 2834, 3100 to 3105, 3223, 3300 to 3323
Immigration, 24-1501 to 1517; by sex, 24-1514; classification, 24-1503; Cuban, 24-1513; educational level of immigrants,

24-1514, 1515; Haitian, 24-1512; Mexican, 24-1505, 1508 to 1511; refugees, 24-1503, 1517; undocumenteds, 24-1510, 1511
Imports, 24-501, 502, 1201, 2404, 2405, 2408, 2415, 2416, 2417, 2422, 2424, 2425, 2427, 2429, 2434, 2435, 2441 to 2450, 2455, 2456, 2459, 2500 to 2542, 2546, 2548, 2550, 2601, 2602, 2606 to 2608, 2612, 2700 to 2721, 2728 to 2746, 3225, 3338, 3340 to 3360; intra-zonal, 24-2606, 2607. See also Trade
Income, 24-1400, 1406, 1413 to 1420, 2700 to 2720, 2839, 2902, 3004, 3058, 3059, 3408, 3409; national, 24-1400, 3367, 3368. See also Wages
Income distribution, 24-1413 to 1420
Index(es): agricultural production, 24-2100, 2101; construction activity, 24-1616; consumption, 24-1907, 1915, 1928; cultivated land, 24-203; energy, 24-1904, 1907, 1915, 1927, 1928; exchange rate, 24-3105, 3113; export unit value, 24-2543, 2547, 2550; Fitzgibbon-Johnson rankings, 24-1003; food production, 24-818, 819; foreign trade, 24-2550; GDP, 24-3324; Health, Education, Communication (HEC), 24-800, 801; import unit value, 24-2542, 2550; industrial production, 24-1700; intra-regional exports, 24-2610; Physical Quality of Life (PQLI), 24-802; political and civil rights, 24-1002, 1003; population, 24-601 to 622; price, 24-3114 to 3126, 3222 to 3224, 3400 to 3402, 3404; production, 24-1904, 1914, 1927; real industrial wage by country, 24-1406 to 1409; retail price, 24-3222; terms of trade, 24-2544, 2545, 2548 to 2550; urbanization, 24-659; wholesale price, 24-3223, 3224
Indians. See Amerind population
Indicators: communication, 24-800, 801; demographic, 24-800 to 803; economic, 24-1820, 2700 to 2751; education, 24-800, 801; employment and income, 24-1300 to 1302, 1406, 1407; health, 24-800, 801; research and development, 24-926; social, 24-800 to 802; urbanization, 24-659
Industry, 24-1700 to 1716, 2302, 2303, 2500 to 2520, 3409; cooperatives, 24-1420; disputes, 24-1412; employment, 24-1304, 1309, 1310, 1316, 1317; energy consumption, 24-1906, 1907; export, 24-2500 to 2520; growth, 24-3325 to 3337; import, 24-2500 to 2520; income, 24-1402 to 1406, 1410; output, 24-1700 to 1716; production index, 24-1700; share in GDP, 24-3228 to 3334; wage index, 24-1408, 1409
Infant mortality, 24-705, 800
Inflation, 24-3050, 3200 to 3221, 3402. See also Prices
Infrastructure. See Communication; Transport
Inhabitants. See Per inhabitant
Institution(s): bilateral and multilateral, 24-2833 to 2836; education, 24-906 to 912; religious, 24-1100, 1104. See also Education; Loans; Religion
Insured population. See Welfare
Inter-American affairs, 24-1206 to 1210, 2831 to 2849, 2901, 2902
Inter-American Development Bank. See IDB
Interest: payments, 24-2801, 2805, 3017; rates, 24-2833, 3228 to 3231
Intermediate education. See Education
Investment: development plans, 24-208, 300; direct, 24-2700 to 2720, 2728 to 2746, 2900 to 2906; direct foreign, 24-2904; gross domestic, 24-3365; land, 24-208, 3000; portfolio, 24-2700 to 2720, 2728 to 2746, 2907. See also Public debt
Iron: ore, 24-1807, 1821, 2400 to 2403, 2703, 2910, 3226; pig and ferroalloy, 24-1710
Irrigation, 24-202, 204, 205, 208

Jehovah's Witnesses, 24-1102
Jews, 24-1103 to 1105

Kerosene, 24-1621, 1916

Labor, 24-1300 to 1329, 1502, 1516; agricultural, 24-1305; by sex, 24-1300 to 1302; by structure, 24-1304; underutilization of, 24-1321

Labor force. *See* Labor
LAFTA (Latin American Free Trade Association), **24**-2748
Lakes, **24**-126
Land, **24**-200 to 211, 3000, 3005; arable, **24**-200 to 202, 205, 206, 210; crop, **24**-206, 208; by soil types, **24**-207. *See also* Agriculture; Land tenure
Land reform, **24**-304
Land tenure, **24**-300 to 304
Lead, **24**-1808, 2400 to 2402, 2451, 2910, 3226
Leftists, **24**-913
Libraries, **24**-918, 919
Life expectancy, **24**-700, 800
Linseed oil, **24**-3226
Liquidity. *See* Money; Reserves, money
Literacy, **24**-800, 801, 900
Livestock, **24**-2200 to 2203
Loans, **24**-2701 to 2720, 2728 to 2746, 2809, 2810, 2831 to 2836, 2844 to 2849
Lodging establishments. *See* Tourism
Longevity. *See* Life expectancy

Machinery, **24**-2400 to 2402, 2455, 2500 to 2541, 2605, 2908 to 2910
Mail, **24**-405, 505
Maize, **24**-2111, 2400 to 2403, 2422, 2423, 3226
Malvinas Islands. *See* Wars
Manganese, **24**-3226; ore, **24**-1809, 1821
Manufacturing, **24**-1309, 1316, 1317, 1319, 1320, 1402, 1410, 1700, 2400 to 2402, 2455, 2456, 2500 to 2520, 2605, 2901, 2904, 2908 to 2910, 3325, 3327, 3335. *See also* Industry, output
Marriage, **24**-711
Maternal mortality, **24**-707
MCCA. *See* CACM
Meat, **24**-1711, 2400 to 2404, 2408 to 2412, 2521 to 2541, 2701, 2718
Media, **24**-500 to 504, 510 to 512. *See also* Books; Cinema; Newspapers
Medical personnel, **24**-800, 803 to 807. *See also* Health; Physicians
Merchant fleets. *See* Vessels
Merchant marine, **24**-413
Merchant vessels. *See* Vessels
Mercury, **24**-1810
Metal(s), **24**-1712, 2400, 2401, 2500 to 2520, 2908 to 2910. *See also* Minerals; Mining
Middle class. *See* class
Midwives, **24**-805
Migration, **24**-1500 to 1517
Military, **24**-1200 to 1211
Military assistance, U.S. **24**-1202, 1206 to 1210, 2835. *See also* Arms trade
Milk, **24**-2204, 2205; dry, **24**-2424
Minerals, **24**-1820, 1821, 2400, 2451 to 2454, 2500 to 2520. *See also* Mining.
Mining, **24**-1309, 1314, 1319, 1320, 1700, 1800 to 1821, 2500 to 2520, 2901, 2908 to 2910, 3325, 3330
Missionaries: Protestant, **24**-1109
Modernization. *See* SMI
Molybdenum, **24**-1811, 1821
Money, **24**-3038 to 3060; income velocity of, **24**-3058, 3059
Mortality. *See* Deaths
Motor vehicles, **24**-411, 412, 800, 1701, 2402, 2500 to 2520, 2910; production, **24**-1701; registration, **24**-411, 412
Mountains, **24**-121 to 123

National accounts. *See* Accounts, national
Natural gas. *See* Gas, natural
Naturalizations, **24**-1504, 1510

Newspapers, **24**-500, 800
Newsprint, **24**-500 to 502, 2313, 3226
Nickel, **24**-1812, 1821, 2402
Nitrates, **24**-2400, 2401
Nitrogenous fertilizer. *See* Fertilizer, nitrogenous
Nurses, **24**-803, 805, 807
Nutrition, **24**-805, 820 to 825, 2839, 2840

Oats, **24**-2425, 2426
Occupational strata. *See* Occupations
Occupations, **24**-1310 to 1312, 1502, 1515, 1516; by sex, **24**-1311. *See also* EAP
Oil: agricultural, **24**-2400, 2401; animal, **24**-2404, 2407, 2520 to 2541, 2605; vegetable, **24**-2404, 2521 to 2541, 3226. *See also* Petroleum
Oranges, **24**-2112
Ore, **24**-1807, 1809, 1821, 2400 to 2403, 2703, 2910, 3226
Outpatient services, **24**-813, 814. *See also* Health care

Paddy rice, **24**-2114
Panels. *See* Wood
Paper, **24**-2311, 2312, 2440, 2444, 2500 to 2520, 2910, 3229
Paperboard. *See* Paper
Particle board, **24**-2307
Passengers: air, **24**-401, 403 to 405, 412; load factor, **24**-404; railroad, **24**-408
Payments, **24**-2700 to 2720. *See also* Loans
Peace Corps, **24**-2837 to 2840
Per capita. *See* Per inhabitant
Per inhabitant, **24**-206, 210, 500, 507, 508, 511 to 513, 658, 706 to 711, 712, 800, 803, 806, 819, 824, 825, 905, 926, 1101, 1303, 1414, 1416, 1906, 1926, 2101, 3362, 3363, 3403, 3404, 3407, 3408
Pesticides, **24**-100, 1000, 2521 to 2541
Petroleum, **24**-1900, 1916, 1917, 2402, 2403, 2450, 2715, 2717, 2901, 2908 to 2910, 3226; crude, **24**-415, 1820, 1905, 1980 to 1910, 1914, 1915, 1918, 2400, 2401, 2448, 2702, 2708, 2910, 3227; derivatives, **24**-1917, 2450; prices, **24**-3226, 3227; products, **24**-415, 1916, 2717, 2910; refined, **24**-1911, 1912, 1916, 2400 to 2402, 2449, 2910; refinery distillation capacity, **24**-1913; reserves, **24**-1918; U.S. investment, **24**-2901, 2908 to 2910
Pharmacists, **24**-805
Phosphate: rock, **24**-1813, 3226
Physical Quality of Life Index (PQLI), **24**-802
Physicians, **24**-800, 803, 804
Pigs. *See* Swine
Planning, **24**-1319, 1320. *See also* Family planning
Plywood, **24**-2308
Political conflict. *See* Politics
Political dependence. *See* Politics
Political divisions. *See* Divisions, civil
Political independence. *See* Politics
Political parties. *See* Politics
Political rights. *See* Rights
Political violence. *See* Politics
Politics, **24**-1000 to 1021
Population, **24**-625 to 646, 658, 661, 662, 664, 665, 668, 1307, 1308, 1324, 1325, 1500, 1617, 1622, 2200 to 2204, 3000; agricultural, **24**-206, 1306, 1307, 1315; Catholic, **24**-1100, 1105; Christians, **24**-1105; economically active population (EAP), **24**-833 to 838, 1307 to 1310, 1313, 1314, 1321, 1324, 1325; economic regions, **24**-100; educated, **24**-904; estimate, **24**-601 to 624, 654, 655, 657, 663, 665, 668, 669, 1103, Chapter 34, Appendix A; growth, **24**-600, 666, 667; Hispanic, **24**-670; illiterate, **24**-900; insured, **24**-834 to 838; Jehovah's Witnesses, **24**-1102; Jewish, **24**-1103, 1105; literate, **24**-900; national, **24**-625; of the largest cities, **24**-647, 648; of the principal cities,

24-649; prison, **24**-1335; projected, **24**-624, 653 to 655, 660, 663, 664, 666, 667, 1335; Protestant, **24**-1105, 1109; rank, **24**-600; rural, **24**-651, 654, 655, 657, 660, 667; urban, **24**-650; 652 to 657, 659, 660, 667, 1314; voting, **24**-1001, 1021; women, **24**-660, 662, 663; world, **24**-600. *See also* Age(s) and age groups; Census; Divisions; Per inhabitant; Regions

Ports. *See* Shipping

Potash, **24**-3226

Potatoes, **24**-2113

Poverty, **24**-1332

Precipitation. *See* Rainfall

Pre-natal deaths, **24**-704

Pre-primary education. *See* Education

Presidents, **24**-1008, 3403, 3407, 3410

Prices, **24**-3114 to 3127, 3339, 3362; commodity, **24**-3226; consumer, **24**-3200 to 3221; export, **24**-3225; import, **24**-3225; Mexico, **24**-3400, 3401; retail, **24**-3222; wholesale, **24**-3223, 3224. *See also* Inflation; Index(es)

Priests, **24**-1100, 1101

Primary education. *See* Education

Prisons, **24**-1335

Private debt, **24**-2800, 2804

Private education. *See* Education

Production, **24**-503, 504, 1310, 1311, 3006; agricultural, **24**-2100 to 2118; book, **24**-503, 504; energy, **24**-1900 to 1905, 1908 to 1912, 1914, 1916, 1918 to 1920, 1925, 1927, 1941; fisheries, **24**-2000 to 2006; food, **24**-818, 826, 1702, 1704, 2102 to 2118; forestry, **24**-2300 to 2312; industrial, **24**-1700 to 1716; mining, **24**-1800 to 1821; ranch, **24**-2200 to 2206. *See also* Crops, production

Professionals, **24**-800, 803 to 807, 1310, 1311, 1502

Projections: land development, **24**-208; population, **24**-624, 653 to 655, 660, 663, 664, 666, 667, 1335

Protein, **24**-825

Protestants, **24**-1104, 1105, 1109. *See* Missionaries

Public debt, **24**-2700 to 2720, 2800 to 2809

Public education. *See* Education

Public health, **24**-800, 805, 813 to 817. *See also* Health

Public utilities, **24**-1319, 1320, 1617 to 1622, 1700, 2901, 2910, 3333

Publishing. *See* Books

Quality of life, **24**-800 to 802

Quarrying. *See* Mining

Quebracho extract, **24**-2400 to 2402

Radio: receivers, **24**-511; transmitters, **24**-510

Railroads, **24**-406 to 409; length, **24**-406

Rainfall, **24**-128 to 130

Ranching, **24**-2200 to 2206

Refugees. *See* Immigration

Regions: civil, **24**-101 to 120; economic, **24**-100, 2600; on land use, **24**-201, 202; political, **24**-121; population, **24**-646

Religion, **24**-913, 1100 to 1109

Religious data history, **24**-1104, 1105

Research, **24**-924, 925

Reserves (money), **24**-2725, 2726, 2727

Reserves (petroleum). *See* Petroleum, reserves

Retail, **24**-1309, 2910, 3222

Retention, educational, **24**-903

Revenue: government, **24**-3001, 3002, 3018 to 3037, 3409, 3410; public, **24**-1820

Rice, **24**-2114, 2427, 3226

Rights: civil and political, **24**-1002, 1003

Rivers, **24**-125

Roads, **24**-410, 3010

Rolling stock, **24**-407. *See also* Railroads

Roundwood, **24**-2301 to 2303, 2440, 2441

Rural: education, **24**-900, 904; health, **24**-814; housing, **24**-1619, 1620, 1625; growth, **24**-667; population, **24**-651, 654, 655, 660, 667; poverty estimates, **24**-1332; sanitation and water supply, **24**-1617, 1619

Salt, **24**-1814

Sanitary facilities. *See* Sewage disposal

Savings: government, **24**-3013

Sawnwood and sleepers, **24**-2304, 2440, 2442, 3226

Schools, **24**-907, 908, 915, 919, 920, 1100; duration, **24**-903, 920; enrollment, **24**-901 to 904, 906, 907, 908, 915; pre-primary, **24**-907; primary, **24**-908. *See also* Education

Science, **24**-924 to 926; by field, **24**-924

Scientists. *See* Science

SDR (Special Drawing Rights), **24**-2700 to 2720, 2728 to 2746, 2811 to 2830, 3102 to 3104

Seaborne goods, **24**-414, 415. *See also* Freight; Shipping

Seaweeds, **24**-2007

Service payments. *See* Public debt

Services: **24**-1304, 1310, 1311, 1502, 1617, 1618, 2807, 2839, 2840, 2910, 3010, 3337; family planning, **24**-827 to 832, 922; health, **24**-813 to 816

Sewage disposal, **24**-1617, 1618, 1620

Sewerage services. *See* Sewage disposal.

Sex, **24**-660, 662, 663, 700, 708, 900, 902, 904, 906 to 911, 916, 917, 1300 to 1302, 1308, 1311, 1328, 1514, 2839

Sheep, **24**-2202, 3226

Shipping, **24**-414. *See also* Freight

Ships. *See* Vessels

Shrimp, **24**-2400 to 2402, 3226

Silver, **24**-1815, 2400 to 2402, 2910, 3226

Sisal, **24**-2401, 2402, 3226

SMI (Social Modernization Index), **24**-1331

Social class. *See* Class

Social conditions. *See* HEC; SMI

Social indicators, **24**-800 to 802, 1331

Socialists, trade with, **24**-2612 to 2636

Social Modernization Index. *See* SMI

Social Security, **24**-833, 1319, 1320, 3010

Social stratification. *See* Class

Soybean, **24**-2403, 2428, 2716, 3226; oil, **24**-2429, 3226; oilcake, **24**-2430

Special Drawing Rights. *See* SDR

Steel, **24**-1714

Storage, **24**-1309, 1404

Stratification. *See* Class

Structure. *See* Age; Class; Labor force

Students, **24**-901, 907 to 914, 916, 917, 922, 1208; enrollment, **24**-901 to 903, 906 to 910, 915 to 917; political orientation, **24**-913

Sugar, **24**-2400 to 2404, 2431, 2432, 2521 to 2541, 2607, 3226; cane, **24**-1924, 2115; Cuban, **24**-1715, 2433; raw, **24**-1715; U.S., **24**-2434

Sulfur, **24**-1816, 1821

Surveys, **24**-1322 to 1324, 1333

Sweet potatoes, **24**-2118

Swine, **24**-2203

Tangerines, **24**-2112

Taxation, government, **24**-3002 to 3007, 3410

Tea, **24**-2404, 2521 to 2541, 3226

Teachers, **24**-905 to 909, 916, 917, 922

Technology, research development, **24**-924 to 926

Telegrams, **24**-506, 508

Telegraph service. *See* Telegrams

Telephones, **24**-507 to 509, 800

Television: sets, **24**-512; transmitters, **24**-510

Temperature, **24**-128, 129
Temporary workers, **24**-1507
Textiles, **24**-2500 to 2541, 2910
Theaters. *See* Cinema
Tin, **24**-1817, 1821, 2400 to 2402, 2453, 3226
Tobacco, **24**-2116, 2400 to 2402, 2500 to 2541, 2910, 3226
Tourism, **24**-1518 to 1523
Tractors, **24**-211
Trade, **24**-1201, 1202, 1206, 1210, 1309, 2400 to 2461, 2500 to 2550, 2600 to 2636, 2700 to 2751, 2901, 2908 to 2910, 3007, 3112; balances, **24**-2723; Cuban, **24**-2506, 2527, 2620 to 2622; purchasing power of, **24**-2550; terms of, **24**-2404, 2545, 2548 to 2550; U.S., **24**-1202, 1206, 1210; value of, **24**-1201, 1206, 2500 to 2541, 2550, 2614 to 2636, 2721, 2722; world, **24**-1202, 1206. *See also* Arms trade; Exports; Imports; Indexes; Prices
Trading partners, **24**-2600, 2614 to 2636. *See also* Trade
Transnational corporations. *See* Corporate business activity
Transport, **24**-400 to 415, 1309 to 1311, 1319, 1320, 1404, 1519, 2400, 2500 to 2520, 2705, 2728 to 2751, 2901, 2908 to 2910, 3325, 3334; air, **24**-400 to 405; expenditure, **24**-3010; railroad, **24**-406 to 409; roads, **24**-410; sea, **24**-413 to 415. *See also* Motor vehicles
Trucks. *See* Motor vehicles
Tungsten, **24**-1818, 1821, 2400, 2401

Underemployment. *See* Employment; Unemployment
Undocumenteds. *See* Immigration
Unemployment, **24**-1314, 1321 to 1323, 1326 to 1329
University education. *See* Education
Upper class. *See* Class
Uranium, **24**-1900, 1941
Urban: concentration, **24**-659, 1625; economically active population (EAP), **24**-1314; education, **24**-900, 904; health, **24**-814; housing, **24**-1619, 1620; growth, **24**-667; income, **24**-1419; minimum wages, **24**-1410; open unemployment, **24**-1329; population, **24**-650, 652 to 657, 660, 667; poverty estimates, **24**-1332; sanitation and water supply, **24**-1617, 1619, 1620

Urbanization, **24**-659
Utilities. *See* Public utilities

Vaccines, **24**-817
Value added, **24**-3326, 3327
Veneer, **24**-2309
Vessels, sea, **24**-413, 414, 1203, 1713
Vital statistics, **24**-700 to 712
Volcanoes, **24**-121, 123
Voting, **24**-1001, 1004, 1007, 1021, 2834. *See also* Elections

Wages, **24**-1400 to 1411; legal minimum, **24**-1410, 1411; real, **24**-1406 to 1409. *See also* Income
Wars, Falkland Islands (1982), **24**-1211
Water, **24**-1309, 1617 to 1619, 1700, 2839, 2840, 3000
Water supply. *See* Water
Weather. *See* Climate
Welfare, **24**-922; social, **24**-800 to 802, 833 to 838, 1309, 3010
Wheat, **24**-2117, 2400, 2401, 2435 to 2437, 3226; flour, **24**-1716
Wholesale, **24**-1309, 2910, 3223, 3224
Women: family planning, **24**-827 to 832; health, **24**-707; immigrants, **24**-1514; labor, **24**-1300 to 1302; life expectancy, **24**-700; marriage and divorce, **24**-711, 712; population, **24**-660, 662, 663
Wood, **24**-2301 to 2310, 2400, 2440 to 2445, 2500 to 2520, 2712, 2910, 3226; panels, **24**-2304, 2440, 2445; pulp, **24**-2310, 2440, 2443, 3226
Wood pulp. *See* Wood
Wool, **24**-2206, 2400, 2401, 2438, 2439, 2718, 3226
Work. *See* Labor
Workers, **24**-1310, 1311, 1502, 1507, 1515
World Bank. *See* IBRD
World Christian Encyclopedia Scheme. *See* Religious data history
World population, **24**-100

Yams, **24**-2118
Yarn. *See* Cotton

Zinc, **24**-1819, 1821, 2400, 2401, 2454, 2910, 3226

planation of Terms (Continued)

PC-PFP	*Population and Family Planning*
PC-RPFP	*Report on Population/Family Planning*
SA	*South American Handbook*
SALA	*Statistical Abstract of Latin America*
SALA, 23:1	Volume 23, figure 1 (sample reference)
SALA, 23-100	Volume 23, table 100 (sample reference)
SALA-Cuba	Supplement 1: *Cuba 1968*
SALA LAPUA	Supplement 8: *Latin American Population and Urbanization Analysis*
SALA-MB	Supplement 9: *Statistical Abstract of the United States—Mexico Borderlands*
SALA-MLR	Supplement 5: *Measuring Land Reform*
SALA-SNP	Supplement 3: *Statistics and National Policy*
SALA-TNG	Supplement forthcoming: *The Narrowing Gap*
Schroeder	Susan Schroeder, *Cuba: A Handbook of Historical Statistics* (Boston: G. K. Hall, 1982)
SIPRI-Y	Stockholm International Peace Research Institute, *Yearbook*
SY	Statistical Yearbook
UN	United Nations (NYC)
UN-CSS	*Compendium of Social Statistics*
UN-DY	*Demographic Yearbook*
UN-MB	*Monthly Bulletin of Statistics*
UN-SP	*Statistical Papers*
UN-SP-A	*Series A, Population and Vital Statistics*
UN-SP-J	*Series J, World Energy Supplies*
UN-SP:T	*Series T, Direction of International Trade*
UN-SY	*Statistical Yearbook*
UN-YCS	*Yearbook of Construction Statistics*
UN-YIS	*Yearbook of Industrial Statistics*
UN-YITS	*Yearbook of International Trade Statistics*
UN-YNAS	*Yearbook of National Account Statistics*
UN-YWES	*Yearbook of World Energy Statistics*
UNESCO	UN Educational and Scientific Organization (NYC)
UNESCO-SY	*Statistical Yearbook*
U.S.	United States (WDC)
USAID	U.S. Agency for International Development

Johns Hopkins
Univeristy Press, 1976, 1980

WCE	*World Christian Encyclopedia*
WHO	World Health Organization
WHO WHSA	*World Health Statistics Annual*
Wilkie	*See* SALA
WTO	World Tourism Organization (Madrid)
WTO-WTS	*World Tourism Statistics*
YC	Yearbook Compendium